WE 175 BRO

WE 175 BRO

SKELETAL TRAUMA

MEDICAL ILLUSTRATORS

The editors would like to recognize the work of the medical illustrators
listed below who created the beautiful art for the first edition,
much of which has been retained for this new edition:

Philip Ashley and Denis Lee

in association with

Leona Allison
Marie Chartrand
Megan Costello
Charles Curro
Glenn Edelmayer
Theodore Huff
Christine Jones
John Klausmeyer
Valerie Loomis
Larry Ward

The editors especially wish to thank Theodore Huff,
who created all of the new artwork for this edition.

Third Edition

SKELETAL TRAUMA

Basic Science, Management, and Reconstruction

VOLUME ONE

BRUCE D. BROWNER, M.D., F.A.C.S.
Gray-Gossling Professor and Chairman
Department of Orthopaedic Surgery
University of Connecticut Health Sciences Center
Farmington, Connecticut
Director, Department of Orthopaedics
Hartford Hospital
Hartford, Connecticut

JESSE B. JUPITER, M.D.
Professor of Orthopaedic Surgery
Harvard Medical School
Director, Orthopaedic Hand Service
Massachusetts General Hospital
Boston, Massachusetts

ALAN M. LEVINE, M.D.
Professor of Orthopaedic Surgery
University of Maryland School of Medicine
Director, Alvin and Lois Lapidus Cancer Institute
Sinai Hospital
Baltimore, Maryland

PETER G. TRAFTON, M.D., F.A.C.S.
Professor and Vice Chairman
Department of Orthopaedic Surgery
Brown University School of Medicine
Surgeon-in-Charge, Orthopaedic Trauma
Rhode Island Hospital
Providence, Rhode Island

SAUNDERS
An Imprint of Elsevier Science

SAUNDERS
An Imprint of Elsevier Science

The Curtis Center
Independence Square West
Philadelphia, Pennsylvania 19106

Volume 1: Part no. 9997621123
Volume 2: Part no. 9997621131
Two volume set ISBN 0-7216-9175-7

SKELETAL TRAUMA

Notice

Orthopaedic medicine is an ever-changing field. Standard safety precautions must be followed, but as new research and clinical experience broaden our knowledge, changes in treatment and drug therapy may become necessary or appropriate. Readers are advised to check the most current product information provided by the manufacturer of each drug to be administered to verify the recommended dose, the method and duration of administration, and the contraindications. It is the responsibility of the treating physician, relying on experience and knowledge of the patient, to determine dosages and the best treatment for each individual patient. Neither the Publisher nor the editor assumes any responsibility for any injury and/or damage to persons or property arising from this publication.

THE PUBLISHER

First Edition 1992. Second Edition 1998.

Library of Congress Cataloging-in-Publication Data

Skeletal trauma: basic science, management, and reconstruction / Bruce D. Browner ... [et al.].—3rd ed.
   p. ; cm.
  Includes bibliographical references and index.
  ISBN 0-7216-9175-7 (set)—ISBN 9997621123 (v. 1)—ISBN 9997621131 (v. 2)
  1. Musculoskeletal system—Wounds and injuries. 2. Fractures. I. Browner, Bruce D.
  [DNLM: 1. Fractures. 2. Bone and Bones—injuries. 3. Dislocations.
  4. Ligaments—injuries. WE 175 S627 2003]
  RD731 .S564 2003
  617.4′71044—dc21

2001042813

Acquisitions Editor: Richard Lampert
Developmental Editor: Faith Voit
Project Manager: Lee Ann Draud

GW/QWK

Printed in the United States of America

Last digit is the print number: 9 8 7 6 5 4 3 2 1

CONTRIBUTORS

Albert J. Aboulafia, M.D., F.A.C.S.
Assistant Clinical Professor, Department of Orthopaedic Surgery, University of Maryland School of Medicine; Co-Director, Sarcoma Service, Alvin and Lois Lapidus Cancer Center, Sinai Hospital, Baltimore, Maryland
Pathologic Fractures

Annunziato Amendola, M.D., F.R.C.S.(C.)
Associate Professor, University of Western Ontario, London, Ontario, Canada
Compartment Syndromes

Paul A. Anderson, M.D.
Associate Professor of Orthopaedic Surgery and Rehabilitation, University of Wisconsin Medical School, Madison, Wisconsin
Injuries of the Lower Cervical Spine

Michael T. Archdeacon, M.D.
Assistant Professor, Department of Orthopaedic Surgery, University of Cincinnati College of Medicine, Cincinnati, Ohio
Patella Fractures and Extensor Mechanism Injuries

Terry S. Axelrod, M.D.
Associate Professor of Surgery,
University of Toronto Faculty of Medicine;
Head, Division of Orthopaedic Surgery,
Sunnybrook and Women's College Health Sciences Centre, Toronto, Ontario, Canada
Fractures and Dislocations of the Hand

Craig S. Bartlett III, M.D.
Assistant Clinical Professor, Orthopaedic Trauma Service, Department of Orthopaedics, University of Vermont College of Medicine, Burlington, Vermont
Fractures of the Tibial Pilon

Michael R. Baumgaertner, M.D.
Associate Professor, Department of Orthopaedics and Rehabilitation, Yale University School of Medicine; Chief, Orthopaedic Trauma Service, Yale-New Haven Hospital, New Haven, Connecticut
Medical Management of the Patient with Hip Fracture; Intertrochanteric Hip Fractures

Fred F. Behrens, M.D.
Professor and Chairman, Department of Orthopaedics, UMDNJ—New Jersey Medical School; Chairman of Orthopaedics, UMDNJ–University Hospital, Newark, New Jersey
Fractures with Soft Tissue Injuries

Mark R. Belsky, M.D.
Associate Clinical Professor of Orthopaedic Surgery, Tufts University School of Medicine, Boston; Chief of Orthopaedic Surgery, Newton-Wellesley Hospital, Newton, Massachusetts
Fractures and Dislocations of the Hand

Stephen K. Benirschke, M.D.
Associate Professor, Department of Orthopaedic Surgery, University of Washington School of Medicine; Orthopaedic Clinic, Harborview Medical Center, Seattle, Washington
Foot Injuries

Daniel R. Benson, M.D.
Professor, Department of Orthopaedics, University of California, Davis, School of Medicine; Orthopaedic Surgeon, University of California, Davis, Medical Center, Sacramento, California
Initial Evaluation and Emergency Treatment of the Spine-Injured Patient

Mohit Bhandari, M.D., M.Sc.
Clinical Research Fellow, St. Michael's Hospital, Toronto, Ontario, Canada
Fractures of the Humeral Shaft

Oren G. Blam, M.D.
Fellow, Spine Institute, Beth Israel Medical Center, New York, New York
Fractures in the Stiff and Osteoporotic Spine

Michael J. Bosse, M.D.
Orthopaedic Trauma Surgeon, Orthopaedic Surgery, Carolinas Medical Center, Charlotte, North Carolina
Orthopaedic Management Decisions in the Multiple-Trauma Patient

Robert T. Brautigam, M.D.
Assistant Professor of Surgery, University of Connecticut School of Medicine, Farmington; Director of Education, Department of Trauma, and Trauma/Critical Care Surgeon, Hartford Hospital, Hartford, Connecticut
Evaluation and Treatment of the Multiple-Trauma Patient

Mark R. Brinker, M.D.
Clinical Professor of Orthopaedic Surgery, Tulane University School of Medicine, New Orleans, Louisiana; Clinical Professor of Orthopaedic Surgery, Texas Tech University Health Sciences Center School of Medicine, Lubbock; Director of Acute and Reconstructive Trauma, Texas Orthopedic Hospital, Fondren Orthopedic Group, LLP, Houston, Texas
Nonunions: Evaluation and Treatment

Bruce D. Browner, M.D., F.A.C.S.

Gray-Gossling Professor and Chairman, Department of Orthopaedic Surgery, University of Connecticut Health Sciences Center, Farmington; Director, Department of Orthopaedics, Hartford Hospital, Hartford, Connecticut

Principles of Internal Fixation; Chronic Osteomyelitis

Richard A. Browning, M.D.

Clinical Professor, Brown University School of Medicine; Anesthesiologist-in-Chief, Rhode Island Hospital, Providence, Rhode Island

Pain Management following Trauma Injury

Frederick W. Burgess, M.D., Ph.D.

Clinical Associate Professor, Brown University School of Medicine; Attending Anesthesiologist, Rhode Island Hospital, Providence, Rhode Island

Pain Management following Traumatic Injury

Andrew E. Caputo, M.D.

Clinical Assistant Professor, Department of Orthopaedic Surgery, University of Connecticut Health Sciences Center, Farmington; Co-Director, Hand Surgery Service, Hartford Hospital and Connecticut Children's Medical Center, Hartford, Connecticut

Principles of Internal Fixation

James B. Carr, M.D.

Clinical Associate, Department of Orthopaedic Surgery, University of South Carolina School of Medicine; Director of Orthopaedic Trauma, Palmetto-Richland Memorial Hospital, Columbia, South Carolina

Malleolar Fractures and Soft Tissue Injuries of the Ankle

Charles Cassidy, M.D.

Assistant Professor of Orthopaedic Surgery, Tufts University School of Medicine; Chief, Hand and Upper Extremity Service, New England Medical Center, Boston, Massachusetts

Fractures and Dislocations of the Carpus

David L. Ciraulo, D.O., M.P.H.

Assistant Professor of Surgery, University of Tennessee College of Medicine—Chattanooga Unit; Trauma/Critical Care Surgeon, Chattanooga, TN

Evaluation and Treatment of the Multiple-Trauma Patient

Mark S. Cohen, M.D.

Associate Professor and Director, Orthopaedic Education, and Director, Hand and Elbow Program, Department of Orthopaedic Surgery, Rush–Presbyterian–St. Luke's Medical Center, Chicago, Illinois

Fractures of the Distal Radius

Christopher L. Colton, M.D., F.R.C.S., F.R.C.S.Ed.

Senior Consultant in Orthopaedic Trauma, Nottingham University Hospital, Nottingham, England

The History of Fracture Treatment

Leo M. Cooney, Jr., M.D.

Humana Foundation Professor of Geriatric Medicine, Yale University School of Medicine; Chief, Section of Geriatrics, and Chief, Section of General Internal Medicine, Yale–New Haven Hospital, New Haven, Connecticut

Medical Management of the Patient with Hip Fracture

Charles N. Cornell, M.D.

Associate Professor, Orthopaedic Surgery, Cornell University Joan and Sanford I. Weill Medical College and Graduate School of Medical Sciences, New York; Chairman, Department of Orthopaedic Surgery, New York Hospital Medical Center of Queens and Flushing Hospital Medical Center, Flushing, New York

Osteoporotic Fragility Fractures

Jerome M. Cotler, M.D.

Professor, Department of Orthopaedic Surgery, Thomas Jefferson University Hospital, Philadelphia, Pennsylvania

Fractures in the Stiff and Osteoporotic Spine

Charles M. Court-Brown, M.D.

Professor of Orthopaedic Trauma, Edinburgh Orthopaedic Trauma Unit, Royal Infirmary of Edinburgh, Edinburgh, Scotland

Femoral Diaphyseal Fractures

Bradford L. Currier, M.D.

Associate Professor and Director, Mayo Clinic Spine Fellowship, Mayo Medical School, Rochester, Minnesota

Christopher W. DiGiovanni, M.D.

Assistant Professor, Department of Orthopaedic Surgery, Brown University School of Medicine; Director, Foot and Ankle Service, Rhode Island Hospital, Providence, Rhode Island

Foot Injuries

Sridhar M. Durbhakula, M.D.

Albany Medical Center, Latham, New York

Reconstructive Total Hip Replacement after Proximal Femoral Injuries

Thomas A. Einhorn, M.D.

Professor and Chairman, Department of Orthopaedic Surgery, Boston University School of Medicine; Chief of Orthopaedic Surgery, Boston Medical Center, Boston, Massachusetts

Enhancement of Skeletal Repair

Frank J. Eismont, M.D.

Vice-Chairman and Professor, Department of Orthopaedic Surgery, University of Miami School of Medicine; Co-director, Acute Spinal Cord Injury Unit, Jackson Memorial Hospital, Miami, Florida

Thoracic and Upper Lumbar Spine Injuries; Gunshot Wounds of the Spine

David V. Feliciano, M.D.
Professor of Surgery, Emory University School of Medicine; Chief of Surgery, Grady Memorial Hospital, Atlanta, Georgia
Evaluation and Treatment of Vascular Injuries

Steven R. Garfin, M.D.
Professor and Chair, Department of Orthopaedics, University of California, San Diego, School of Medicine, La Jolla, California
Thoracic and Upper Lumbar Spine Injuries

Harris Gellman, M.D.
Professor and Co-Director, Hand and Upper Extremity Service, Department of Orthopaedic Surgery, University of Miami, Miami, Florida
Gunshot Wounds to the Musculoskeletal System

Gregory E. Gleis, M.D.
Associate Clinical Professor, Department of Orthopaedic Surgery, University of Louisville School of Medicine, Louisville, Kentucky
Diagnosis and Treatment of Complications

James A. Goulet, M.D.
Professor, Department of Orthopaedic Surgery, University of Michigan Medical School; Director, Orthopaedic Trauma Service, University of Michigan Hospital, Ann Arbor, Michigan
Hip Dislocations

Andrew Green, M.D.
Associate Professor, Department of Orthopaedic Surgery, Brown University School of Medicine, Providence, Rhode Island
Proximal Humeral Fractures and Glenohumeral Dislocations

Stuart A. Green, M.D.
Clinical Professor, Orthopaedic Surgery, University of California, Irvine, School of Medicine, Irvine, California
The Ilizarov Method

Zbigniew Gugala, M.D.
The Joseph Barnhart Department of Orthopaedic Surgery, Houston, Texas
Management Techniques for Spinal Injuries

Munish C. Gupta, M.D.
Associate Professor, Department of Orthopaedics, University of California, Davis, School of Medicine; Orthopaedic Surgeon, University of California, Davis, Medical Center, Sacramento, California
Initial Evaluation and Emergency Treatment of the Spine-Injured Patient

Sigvard T. Hansen, Jr., M.D.
Professor and Chairman Emeritus, Department of Orthopaedic Surgery, University of Washington School of Medicine; Director, Foot and Ankle Institute, Harborview Medical Center, Seattle, Washington
Foot Injuries; Post-traumatic Reconstruction of the Foot and Ankle

Wilson C. Hayes, Ph.D.
Professor of Exercise and Sport Science and Professor of Mechanical Engineering, Oregon State University; President and Chief Executive Officer, Hayes & Associates, Inc., Corvallis, Oregon
Biomechanics of Fractures

Andrew C. Hecht, M.D.
Associate Professor of Orthopaedics, Harvard Medical School; Director of Massachusetts General Hospital Spine Surgery Fellowship; Director of Newton-Wellesley Hospital Spine Center, Boston, Massachusetts
Injuries of the Cervicocranium

David L. Helfet, M.D.
Professor of Orthopaedic Surgery, Cornell University Joan and Sanford I. Weill Medical College and Graduate School of Medical Sciences; Director, Combined Orthopaedic Trauma Service, Hospital for Special Surgery and New York–Presbyterian Hospital, New York, New York
Fractures of the Distal Femur

John A. Hipp, Ph.D.
Assistant Professor, Baylor College of Medicine; Chief Scientific Officer, Medical Metrics, Inc., Houston, Texas
Biomechanics of Fractures

Lenworth M. Jacobs, M.D., M.P.H., F.A.C.S.
Professor of Surgery, University of Connecticut School of Medicine, Farmington; Director, Traumatology, Hartford Hospital, Hartford, Connecticut
Evaluation and Treatment of the Multiple-Trauma Patient

David J. Jacofsky, M.D.
Instructor, Department of Orthopaedic Surgery, Mayo Clinic, Rochester, Minnesota
Complications in the Treatment of Spinal Trauma

Jesse B. Jupiter, M.D.
Professor of Orthopaedic Surgery, Harvard Medical School; Director, Orthopaedic Hand Service, Massachusetts General Hospital, Boston, Massachusetts
Fractures and Dislocations of the Hand; Fractures of the Distal Radius; Diaphyseal Fractures of the Forearm; Trauma to the Adult Elbow and Fractures of the Distal Humerus; Injuries to the Shoulder Girdle

Timothy L. Keenen, M.D.
Clinical Associate Professor of Orthopaedic Surgery, Oregon Health Sciences University School of Medicine, Portland, Oregon
Initial Evaluation and Emergency Treatment of the Spine-Injured Patient

James F. Kellam, M.D., F.R.C.S.(C.)

Director, Orthopedic Trauma Program, and Vice Chairman, Department of Orthopedic Surgery, Carolinas Medical Center, Charlotte, North Carolina; Adjunct Professor of Engineering, Clemson University, Clemson, South Carolina

Orthopaedic Management Decisions in the Multiple-Trauma Patient; Pelvic Ring Disruptions; Diaphyseal Fractures of the Forearm

Choll W. Kim, M.D., Ph.D.

Department of Orthopaedic Surgery, University of California, San Diego, School of Medicine, La Jolla, California

Complications in the Treatment of Spinal Trauma

Christian Krettek, M.D.

Director, Trauma Department, Hannover Medical School, Hannover, Germany

Fractures of the Distal Femur

David Kwon, M.S.

Medical Student, University of California, San Diego, School of Medicine, La Jolla, California

Osteoporotic Fragility Fractures

Joseph M. Lane, M.D.

Professor of Orthopaedic Surgery and Assistant Dean, Cornell University Joan and Sanford I. Weill Medical College and Graduate School of Medical Sciences; Chief, Metabolic Bone Disease, Hospital for Special Surgery, New York, New York

Osteoporotic Fragility Fractures

Loren L. Latta, P.E., Ph.D.

Professor and Director of Research, Department of Orthopaedics and Rehabilitation, University of Miami School of Medicine, Miami; Director of Orthopaedic Biomechanics Laboratory, Mt. Sinai Medical Center/Miami Heart Institute, Miami Beach, Florida

Principles of Nonoperative Fracture Treatment

Sebastian Lattuga, M.D.

Chief Spine Surgeon, Mercy Medical Center, Rockville Center, New York

Gunshot Wounds of the Spine

Paul E. Levin, M.D.

Assistant Clinical Professor, Department of Orthopaedics, State University of New York at Stony Brook, Stony Brook, New York

Hip Dislocations

Alan M. Levine, M.D.

Professor of Orthopaedic Surgery, University of Maryland School of Medicine; Director, Alvin and Lois Lapidus Cancer Institute, Sinai Hospital, Baltimore, Maryland

Pathologic Fractures; Low Lumbar Fractures; Fractures of the Sacrum

Ronald W. Lindsey, M.D.

Professor of Orthopaedic Surgery, The Joseph Barnhart Department of Orthopaedic Surgery, Houston, Texas

Management Techniques for Spinal Injuries

Margaret Lobo, M.D.

Orthopaedic Resident, Thomas Jefferson University Hospital, Philadelphia, Pennsylvania

Osteoporotic Fragility Fractures

Jay D. Mabrey, M.D.

Associate Professor of Orthopaedics, University of Texas Health Science Center of San Antonio; Director, Total Joint Service, University Hospital, San Antonio, Texas

Periprosthetic Fractures of the Lower Extremities

Jeffrey W. Mast, M.D.

Northern Nevada Medical Center, Sparks, Nevada

Principles of Internal Fixation

Joel M. Matta, M.D.

Clinical Professor of Orthopaedic Surgery, University of Southern California School of Medicine; John C. Wilson, Jr., Chair of Orthopaedic Surgery, Good Samaritan Hospital, Los Angeles, California

Surgical Treatment of Acetabular Fractures

Keith Mayo, M.D.

Orthopaedic Center, Tacoma, Washington

Pelvic Ring Disruptions

Augustus D. Mazzocca, M.D.

Assistant Professor, Department of Orthopaedic Surgery, University of Connecticut Health Sciences Center, Farmington, Connecticut

Principles of Internal Fixation

Robert A. McGuire, M.D.

Professor and Chairman, Department of Orthopedics, University of Mississippi Medical Center, Jackson, Mississippi

Thoracic and Upper Lumbar Spine Injuries

Michael D. McKee, M.D., F.R.C.S.(C.)

Associate Professor, Division of Orthopaedics, Department of Surgery, University of Toronto Faculty of Medicine; Staff Surgeon and Assistant Medical Director, Trauma Program, St. Michael's Hospital, Toronto, Ontario, Canada

Trauma to the Adult Elbow and Fractures of the Distal Humerus

Robert Y. McMurtry, M.D.

Professor of Surgery, Division of Orthopaedics, University of Western Ontario Faculty of Medicine and Dentistry; Consultant, Hand and Upper Limb Centre, St. Joseph's Health Centre, London, Ontario, Canada

Fractures of the Distal Radius

Dana C. Mears, M.D., Ph.D.
Attending Orthopaedic Surgeon, University of Pittsburgh Medical Center—Shadyside Hospital, Pittsburgh, Pennsylvania
Reconstructive Total Hip Replacement after Proximal Femoral Injuries

Michael W. Mendes, M.D.
Attending Physician, McLeod Regional Medical Center, Florence, South Carolina
Principles of Internal Fixation

Stuart E. Mirvis, M.D., F.A.C.R.
Professor of Radiology, University of Maryland School of Medicine; Director, Trauma Radiology, University of Maryland R. Adams Cowley Shock-Trauma Center, Baltimore, Maryland
Spinal Imaging

Sohail K. Mirza, M.D.
Assistant Professor, Department of Orthopaedics and Sports Medicine, University of Washington School of Medicine; Harborview Medical Center, Seattle, Washington
Injuries of the Lower Cervical Spine

Todd D. Moldawer, M.D.
Co-Director, Spine Fellowship Program, Southern California Orthopedic Institute, Van Nuys, California
Gunshot Wounds to the Musculoskeletal System

Victor A. Morris, M.D.
Assistant Professor of Medicine, General Medicine, Yale University School of Medicine; Co-Director, Medicine Consult Service, Yale University School of Medicine, New Haven, Connecticut
Medical Management of the Patient with Hip Fracture

Calin S. Moucha, M.D.
Chief Resident, Department of Orthopaedic Surgery, St. Luke's–Roosevelt Hospital Center and Columbia University College of Physicians and Surgeons, New York, New York
Enhancement of Skeletal Repair

Michael L. Nerlich, M.D., Ph.D.
Professor, Trauma Surgery, University of Regensburg Medical School; Chairman, Department of Trauma Surgery, Regensburg University Academic Medical Center, Regensburg, Bavaria, Germany
Biology of Soft Tissue Injuries

Tom R. Norris, M.D.
Department of Orthopaedic Surgery, California Pacific Medical Center, San Francisco, California
Proximal Humeral Fractures and Glenohumeral Dislocations

William T. Obremskey, M.D., M.P.H.
Assistant Professor of Orthopaedics and Rehabilitation, Division of Orthopaedic Trauma, Vanderbilt University Medical Center, Nashville, Tennessee
Evaluation of Outcomes for Musculoskeletal Injury

Dror Paley, M.D.
Professor, University of Maryland School of Medicine; Director, Rubin Institute for Advanced Orthopaedics, Sinai Hospital of Baltimore, Baltimore, Maryland
Principles of Deformity Correction

Ed Pesanti, M.D., F.A.C.P.
Professor, Department of Medicine, University of Connecticut School of Medicine; University of Connecticut Health Center, Farmington, Connecticut
Chronic Osteomyelitis

Michael S. Pinzur, M.D.
Professor of Orthopaedic Surgery and Rehabilitation, Loyola University of Chicago Stritch School of Medicine, Maywood, Illinois
Amputations in Trauma

Spiros G. Pneumaticos, M.D.
Assistant Professor, The Joseph Barnhart Department of Orthopaedic Surgery, Houston, Texas
Management Techniques for Spinal Injuries

Andrew N. Pollak, M.D.
Associate Professor of Orthopaedic Surgery, University of Maryland School of Medicine; Attending Orthopaedic Traumatologist, R. Adams Cowley Shock Trauma Center, Baltimore, Maryland
Principles of External Fixation

Mark A. Prévost, M.D.
Walker Baptist Medical Center, Jasper, Alabama
Thoracic and Upper Lumbar Spine Injuries

David Ring, M.D.
Instructor, Department of Orthopaedics, Harvard Medical School; Department of Orthopaedic Surgery, Massachusetts General Hospital, Boston, Massachusetts
Injuries to the Shoulder Girdle

Craig S. Roberts, M.D.
Associate Professor and Residency Director, Department of Orthopaedic Surgery, University of Louisville School of Medicine, Louisville, Kentucky
Diagnosis and Treatment of Complications

C. M. Robinson, M.D., F.R.C.S.
Consultant Orthopaedic Surgeon, Royal Infirmary of Edinburgh, Edinburgh, Scotland
Femoral Diaphyseal Fractures

Craig M. Rodner, M.D.
Department of Orthopaedic Surgery, University of Connecticut Health System, Farmington, Connecticut
Chronic Osteomyelitis

Leonard K. Ruby, M.D.
Professor of Orthopaedic Surgery, Tufts University School of Medicine; Staff, Hand Surgery, Department of Orthopaedic Surgery, New England Medical Center, Boston, Massachusetts
Fractures and Dislocations of the Carpus

Thomas A. Russell, M.D.
Professor of Orthopaedic Surgery, University of Tennessee, Memphis, College of Medicine, Memphis, Tennessee
Subtrochanteric Fractures of the Femur

Roy W. Sanders, M.D.
Clinical Professor of Orthopaedics, University of South Florida College of Medicine, Tampa, Florida
Patella Fractures and Extensor Mechanism Injuries

Augusto Sarmiento, M.D.
Professor and Chairman Emeritus, University of Miami School of Medicine, Miami; Director, Arthritis and Joint Replacement Institute, Doctors Hospital, Coral Gables, Florida
Principles of Nonoperative Fracture Treatment

Richard A. Saunders, M.D.
Orthopedic Surgeon, The Glen Falls Hospital, Glen Falls, New York
Physical Impairment Ratings for Fractures

Joseph Schatzker, M.D.
Professor, University of Toronto Faculty of Medicine; Orthopaedic Surgeon, Sunnybrook Health Science Center, Toronto, Ontario, Canada
Tibial Plateau Fractures

Emil H. Schemitsch, M.D., F.R.C.S.C.
Professor and Head, Division of Orthopaedic Surgery, St. Michael's Hospital, Toronto, Ontario, Canada
Fractures of the Humeral Shaft

Robert K. Schenk, M.D.
Professor Emeritus of Anatomy, Histology, and Embryology; Head of the Bone Research Laboratory, Department of Oral Surgery, University of Berne, Berne, Switzerland
Biology of Fracture Repair

David Seligson, M.D.
Professor and Vice Chair, Department of Orthopaedic Surgery, University of Louisville School of Medicine; Chief of Orthopaedics, University of Louisville Hospital, Louisville, Kentucky
Diagnosis and Treatment of Complications

Randy Sherman, M.D.
Professor of Plastic, Orthopedic, and Neurologic Surgery, University of Southern California; Chief, Division of Plastic Surgery, Cedars-Sinai Medical Center, Los Angeles, California
Soft Tissue Coverage

D. Hal Silcox III, M.D.
Cervical, Thoracic, and Lumbar Orthopaedic Spine Surgeon, Peachtree Orthopedic Clinic, Atlanta, Georgia
Injuries of the Cervicocranium

John M. Siliski, M.D.
Instructor, Harvard Medical School; Orthopaedic Surgeon, Massachusetts General Hospital, Boston, Massachusetts
Dislocations and Soft Tissue Injuries of the Knee

Michael S. Sirkin, M.D.
Assistant Professor, Department of Orthopaedics, UMDNJ—New Jersey Medical School; Chief, Orthopaedic Trauma Service, UMDNJ–University Hospital, Newark, New Jersey
Fractures with Soft Tissue Injuries

Marc F. Swiontkowski, M.D.
Professor and Chairman, Department of Orthopaedic Surgery, University of Minnesota, Minneapolis; Chief of Orthopaedic Surgery, Regions Hospital, St. Paul; Staff Orthopaedist, Henepin County Medical Center, Minneapolis, Minnesota
Evaluation of Outcomes for Musculoskeletal Injury; Intracapsular Hip Fractures

P. Tornetta, M.D.
Department of Orthopaedic Surgery, Boston Medical Center, Boston, Massachusetts
Femoral Diaphyseal Fractures

Peter G. Trafton, M.D., F.A.C.S.
Professor and Vice Chairman of Orthopaedic Surgery, Brown University School of Medicine; Surgeon-in-Charge, Orthopaedic Trauma, Rhode Island Hospital, Providence, Rhode Island
Tibial Shaft Fractures

Bruce C. Twaddle, M.D., F.R.A.C.S.
Director of Orthopaedic Trauma, Auckland Hospital, Auckland, New Zealand
Compartment Syndromes

John H. Velyvis, M.D.
Albany Medical Center, Albany, New York
Reconstructive Total Hip Replacement after Proximal Femoral Injuries

J. Tracy Watson, M.D.
Professor of Orthopaedic Surgery, Wayne State University School of Medicine; Vice Chief of Orthopaedics, Division of Orthopaedic Traumatology, Detroit Receiving Hospital, Detroit Medical Center, Detroit, Michigan
Tibial Plateau Fractures

Lon S. Weiner, M.D.
Chief of Pediatrics and Trauma, Lenox Hill Hospital, New York, New York
Fractures of the Tibial Pilon

Thomas E. Whitesides, Jr., M.D.

Professor of Orthopaedic Surgery, Emory University School of Medicine; Emory University Hospital, Atlanta, Georgia

Injuries of the Cervicocranium

Sam W. Wiesel, M.D.

Professor and Chair, Department of Orthopedics, Georgetown University, Washington, D.C.

Physical Impairment Ratings for Fractures

Donald A. Wiss, M.D.

Clinical Professor of Orthopedic Surgery, University of Southern California, Los Angeles; Southern California Orthopedic Institute, Van Nuys, California

Gunshot Wounds to the Musculoskeletal System

Michael J. Yaszemski, M.D., Ph.D.

Associate Professor of Orthopaedic Surgery and Biomedical Engineering, Mayo Medical School and Mayo Graduate School; Consultant, Department of Orthopaedic Surgery, Mayo Clinic, Rochester, Minnesota

Complications in the Treatment of Spinal Trauma

Bruce H. Ziran, M.D.

Assistant Professor, Department of Orthopedics, University of Pittsburgh School of Medicine, Pittsburgh, Pennsylvania

Principles of External Fixation

Gregory A. Zych, D.O.

Associate Professor, University of Miami School of Medicine; Chief of Orthopaedic Trauma and Associate Chairman for Clinical Affairs, University of Miami/Jackson Memorial Hospital, Miami, Florida

Principles of Nonoperative Fracture Treatment

FOREWORD

Trauma has always represented—and still represents—a constant threat to all people, young and old. Administering competent treatment to the injured victim at the earliest opportunity has always been the goal, but only in our own time has this goal actually been achievable, being accorded top priority in our concept of modern trauma surgery. Nowadays, trauma surgery is able to treat most injuries successfully, rehabilitate the patients, and return them to their families, occupational positions, and places in society through a wide variety of specific therapeutic procedures administered by committed personnel employing advanced techniques. Such treatment not only represents a humanitarian service, but also produces substantial economic benefits.

It is surprising that these services provided by trauma surgery have long gone unrecognized by the general public. Musculoskeletal injuries and disorders are the commonest causes of serious chronic pain conditions and physical disabilities that affect hundreds of millions across the globe. Since these conditions do not usually prove fatal, they have failed to grab the attention of the public in the same way in which cardiac disease, cancer, or AIDS has done.

Injuries and disorders of the locomotor system lead to a substantial impairment in the health and quality of life of a large part of the world's population and currently account for more than half of all chronic disorders in patients older than 60 years. But musculoskeletal conditions are not just prominent among elderly patients. More than 40% of young adults experience their first contact with a doctor as a result of injuries and disorders of the locomotor system. Moreover, the latter also account for more than 40% of all cases of unfitness for work or early retirement.

Unfitness for work, becoming an invalid, and premature death among those in gainful employment represent a considerable drain on society's resources. In addition, the proportion of the elderly in our society is growing. In just 8 years' time, there will be more older people than young people under 20 in Europe and North America. As time passes, the situation for these developed nations will become even more dramatic: 25% of the population will be older than 65 in 2020 and 35% just 10 years later in 2030. By that time, 6% of the population will be older than 85 years. The group of over 85-year-olds thus forms the fastest growing segment of the population. This has serious implications for trauma surgery. The number of femoral neck fractures worldwide, for example, is expected to rise from 1.7 million in 1990 to 6.3 million by 2050. Traffic accidents—humankind's tribute to the triumph of technology—are assuming epidemic proportions, especially in the developing nations, and they deprive these countries of a substantial percentage of the already limited medical resources available.

Trauma surgery has undergone tremendous changes over the past 50 years. At the same time, the expectations of patients and society as a whole concerning the possibilities and capabilities of trauma surgery have grown disproportionately. Residual damage as the result of chance is no longer tolerated. Nowadays, patients demand restitution to full health, frequently resorting to all available legal means and other resources. Moreover, like the field of medicine as a whole, trauma surgery is affected by conflicting changes in the paradigms of politics, economics, the legal system, science, and the globalization of information and network structures. The trauma surgeon must also be proactive in dealing with this conglomeration of issues and challenges in order to cope with the present and plan for the future.

The pace at which developments appear and change occurs is accelerating all the time. Flexibility and adaptability are becoming increasingly important. The surgeon faces growing pressure from advances in microelectronics and computer technology. In the field of minimally invasive surgery, whole areas of traditional surgical practice are being rendered obsolete through the use of minirobots, percutaneous surgical and microprobe techniques, and radiologically assisted minimally invasive procedures. Trauma surgery must also ensure that it does not lose out to third parties such as medical technicians and radiologists when it comes to deciding on indications and treatment. Advances in genetic engineering and tissue engineering will play a role in the future prevention and treatment of injuries. The effects of the digital revolution on factors such as work flow and disease management cannot be predicted. Finally, the execution of surgical procedures by programmed machines (e.g., Robot Doc), master-slave systems, or autonomous or semiautonomous systems will take us into completely new territory. Surgical training will also enter a new dimension. Simulation and virtual reality will become a perfectly natural part of modular training. As a whole, trauma surgery across the world will require a new generation of motivated surgeons prepared to view the challenges of the future as an opportunity and tackle them with insight and commitment.

Every surgeon concerned with skeletal trauma requires a comprehensive, up-to-date textbook that addresses the problems encountered in daily practice. *Skeletal Trauma* is now recognized worldwide as one of the most important textbooks in the field. With this work, Bruce D. Browner, Jesse B. Jupiter, Alan M. Levine, and Peter G. Trafton have made an important contribution toward maintaining the highest standards of education for orthopaedic trauma surgeons.

The changes in the management of skeletal trauma since the appearance of the second edition are truly phenomenal. The scope of the third edition has been substantially expanded. The original chapters have been thoroughly revised, and all the latest findings are described in detail.

The major new addition is the inclusion of extensive material on post-traumatic reconstruction. In addition to the diagnosis and treatment of acute injuries, the authors of the anatomic chapters were all asked to add detailed information on the following: nonunion, malunion, osteoporosis, bone loss, and osteomyelitis. New chapters have been added on total joint replacement, fusions, osteotomies, and other reconstructive techniques. The chapter on enhancement of skeletal repair covers some of the new biologic and technical advances.

The new edition also addresses the daily needs of the practicing surgeon and provides answers to a number of common difficult problems. The book also contains valuable information on ways to avoid technical difficulties and pitfalls, and to manage complications. The book is extremely well illustrated, and the figures impress with their clarity and the highlighting of important technical details. The style is easy to understand, clear, and unambiguous. Complex problems are clearly presented.

I am confident that the third edition will surpass the first two editions in terms of popularity. The editors can rest assured that they have made available to all those concerned with skeletal trauma a work of outstanding quality.

Professor Harald Tscherne

PREFACE

The first edition of *Skeletal Trauma: Fractures, Dislocations, Ligamentous Injuries* was written between 1988 and 1991. This represented a unique window for the creation of this text, coinciding with the increased recognition of the special needs of trauma victims. By the mid-1980s, more than 500 regional trauma centers had been established throughout the United States and Canada. The volume and acuity of blunt trauma and associated musculoskeletal injuries reached a high-water mark. The editors and contributing authors for *Skeletal Trauma* had been on the front lines working in the major trauma centers throughout this period. They helped to develop a new operative approach to the treatment of these injuries that stressed early skeletal fixation and rapid mobilization. The incomparable firsthand experience that they gained helped shape their contributions to the text. In the early 1990s, many states adopted the child restraint device and seat belt legislation. Successful initiatives to control driving under the influence of alcohol significantly lowered incidence of motor vehicle crashes. Improvements in automotive design, such as airbags and side rails, continued to reduce the incidence and severity of blunt trauma and complex musculoskeletal injuries. Although there was an alarming increase in injuries and deaths from gunshots in our major cities, penetrating trauma does not usually result in the multiplicity and complexity of skeletal injuries that are caused by vehicular crashes. In addition, managed care contracting practices resulted in the dispersion of trauma patients to community hospitals, often reducing the number of injuries seen in trauma centers. In retrospect, the 1980s provided a unique opportunity for the creation of this text.

The excellent manuscripts provided by our contributing authors and the beautiful illustrations created by the artists were assembled into an outstanding text by the W.B. Saunders production department. In the year of its publication, 1992, it won first prize in medical sciences from the Association of American Publishers as the best new medical book. The text has been widely embraced by orthopaedic and trauma surgeons throughout the world for its clarity and its utility. They have consistently expressed their appreciation of our approach, which stresses the discussion of problem-focus clinical judgment and proven surgical techniques. The textbook has been regarded by surgeons in training and practicing physicians to be a practice resource that can help guide them through the management of the musculoskeletal injuries with which they are confronted. We retained and strengthened this basic philosophy and organization in the second edition. We added new chapters to cover important subjects that were not addressed adequately in the first edition.

In the years since the publication of the second edition of *Skeletal Trauma,* major new global epidemiologic trends have been noted that influence the character of musculoskeletal injuries throughout the world. In the developed market economies, decreased birth rates and increasing longevity have resulted in the aging of the population. Osteoporosis and associated fragility fractures have grown in number and significance. Road safety improvements in these countries, such as pediatric restraint devices, seat belts, drunk driving control, airbags, vehicle design improvements, and enhanced law enforcement, have decreased the number and severity of road traffic injuries. In the developing world, however, there is a growing epidemic of road traffic injuries. Vulnerable travelers such as pedestrians, bicyclists, motorcycle riders, and passengers on overcrowded buses and trucks are the main victims. Annually, 1 million people die on the world's roads and an estimated 24 to 33 million are severely injured or disabled.

To raise awareness of the burden of these and other musculoskeletal disorders, empower patients, expand research and improvements for prevention and treatment of these problems, and engender multidisciplinary cooperation, the years 2000–2010 have been declared the "Bone and Joint Decade" by U.N. Secretary General Kofi Annan. The movement has also been endorsed by the World Health Organization, the World Bank, and the governments of forty nations. Although there have been dramatic advances in biology, pharmaceuticals, technology, and fixation to improve the care of patients with musculoskeletal disorders in wealthy countries, a large portion of the world's population lacks basic health care and has very limited orthopaedic services available. The third edition of *Skeletal Trauma* has been written in recognition of the challenges of our era and is dedicated to the improvement of musculoskeletal trauma care throughout the world in keeping with the spirit of the "Bone and Joint Decade."

For many years, the *Skeletal Trauma* editorial group has discussed the possibility of creating a separate volume for skeletal trauma reconstruction. Our contributing authors and others have gained wide experience in post-trauma reconstruction, but there have been no comprehensive texts written on this subject. In conjunction with our publisher, we have made a decision to incorporate this material into the current edition. As we are limited by the established size of the two volumes, some basic science chapters were deleted and other information was condensed to make room for the new reconstructive material. New chapters were added on perioperative pain management, osteoporotic fragility fractures, chronic osteomyelitis, gunshot wounds of the spine, fractures in the stiff and osteoporotic spine, medical management of patients with hip fractures, total hip arthroplasty after failed primary treatment of fractures involving the hip joint, acute foot injuries, foot injury reconstruction, lower extremity alignment, periprosthetic fractures, and amputations for trauma. Some of the authors from previous editions have continued but have made major revisions to revitalize their work. In other cases, new authors have been recruited to add international perspective and broaden the base of expertise. Minimally invasive plating, an important new technique, is covered by one of its major developers in the chapter on the distal femur. New biologic agents are addressed in an expanded chapter on enhancement of fracture healing.

In addition to discussing the treatment of acute injuries, the authors of the anatomic chapters were asked to expand their scholarly writing to include the management of nonunions, malunions, bone loss, osteomyelitis, and fixation in osteoporotic bone. The use of fusion and arthroplasty in post-traumatic arthritis is described in detail.

The editors have been gratified by comments from surgeons from around the world indicating that *Skeletal Trauma* has been adopted by many trauma centers and orthopaedic training programs as the principal fracture text. We have welcomed their constructive criticism as well as their accolades. Many of the changes in the current edition were made in response to comments from these surgeons and our own residents.

We are grateful to our contributing authors, whose high level of scholarship and dedication to their chapter writing makes this such a readable and useful reference. The pressures of modern medical practice have made these surgeons busier than they were during the writing of the second edition. Together we have refashioned our text to better address readers' needs for information concerning basic science, acute injury management, and post-traumatic reconstruction.

Bruce D. Browner, M.D.
Jesse B. Jupiter, M.D.
Alan M. Levine, M.D.
Peter G. Trafton, M.D.

ACKNOWLEDGMENTS

We have had the pleasure of working with another group of people who have carried on the tradition of excellence established in the first and second editions. We particularly wish to acknowledge Richard Lampert, Publishing Director, Surgery, the driving force behind the project, and Faith Voit, our Senior Developmental Editor. Additionally, we acknowledge the work of Lee Ann Draud, our Project Manager, and Natalie Ware, our former Production Manager, as well as Walt Verbitski, our former Illustrations Coordinator. Without their efforts, we could not have hoped to maintain this level of excellence.

No staff was hired by the editors for the production of this text. Again, we relied on the hard work and dedication of our own personal staffs. We recognize that without their help we could not have upheld our commitment to this project.

Bruce Browner gratefully acknowledges the work of Deb Bruno and Sue Ellen Pelletier, Executive Assistants at Hartford Hospital and the University of Connecticut, respectively. Their creative pursuit of manuscripts and communication with authors and the Saunders staff helped keep the project on schedule.

Jesse Jupiter would like to thank his executive secretary, Richard Perotti, for helping him communicate with the authors and illustrators and for keeping him focused on the task at hand. He expresses his gratitude as well to Michel Tresfort, transcriptionist, for proofreading all of the manuscripts in addition to his regular duties.

Alan Levine would like to especially acknowledge the efforts of his office administrator, Joanne Barker, who has kept him organized and focused and assisted him in communicating with the authors, illustrators, and the Saunders staff. Eileen Creeger has spent numerous hours proofreading manuscripts, galleys, and page proofs as well as checking the accuracy of citations. The other members of the office staff have also contributed in myriad ways. Finally, he would like to thank all of the residents, fellows, and staff at both Sinai Hospital and at the Maryland Shock Trauma Unit, without whom he would never have garnered the experience necessary to effectively contribute to the preparation of this book.

Peter Trafton gratefully recognizes his administrative assistant, Robin Morin, for her invaluable help with communications, copying, and logistics. He also appreciates the continuing support of his colleagues and staff at University Orthopedics, the stimulus and helpful critiques of Brown University's Orthopaedic Surgery Residents, and especially the Brown University Orthopaedic Trauma fellows, whose quest for surgical expertise and understanding remains a daily inspiration.

CONTENTS

VOLUME TWO

SECTION I

General Principles

SECTION EDITOR

Bruce D. Browner, M.D., F.A.C.S.

CHAPTER 1

The History of Fracture Treatment

Christopher L. Colton, M.D., F.R.C.S., F.R.C.S.Ed.

EARLY SPLINTING TECHNIQUES

Humans have never been immune from injury, and doubtless the practice of bone setting was not unfamiliar to our most primitive forebears. Indeed, given the known skills of Neolithic humans at trepanning the skull,[49] it would be surprising if techniques of similar sophistication had not been brought to bear in the care of injuries. However, no evidence of this remains.

The earliest examples of the active management of fractures in humans were discovered at Naga-ed-Der (about 100 miles north of Luxor in Egypt) by Professor G. Elliott Smith during the Hearst Egyptian expedition of the University of California in 1903.[74] Two specimens were found of splinted extremities. One was an adolescent femur with a compound, comminuted midshaft fracture that had been splinted with four longitudinal wooden boards, each wrapped in linen bandages. A dressing pad containing blood pigment was also found at approximately the level of the fracture site. The victim is judged to have died shortly after injury, as the bones show no evidence whatsoever of any healing reaction (Fig. 1–1). The second specimen was of open fractures of a forearm, treated by similar splints, but in this case a pad of blood-stained vegetable fiber (probably obtained from the date palm) was found adherent to the upper fragment of the ulna, evidently having been pushed into the wound to stanch bleeding. Again, death appears to have occurred before any bone healing reaction had started. The Egyptians were known to be skilled at the management of fractures, and many healed specimens have been found. The majority of femoral fractures had united with shortening and deformity, but a number of well-healed forearm fractures have been discovered.

Some form of wooden splintage bandaged to the injured limb has been used from antiquity to the present day. Certainly, both Hippocrates and Celsus described in detail the splintage of fractures using wooden appliances,[54] but a fascinating account of external splintage of fractures is to be found in the work of El Zahrawi (AD 936 to 1013). This Arab surgeon, born in Al Zahra, the royal city 5 miles west of Cordova in Spain, was named Abu'l-Quasim Khalas Ibn'Abbas Al-Zahrawi, commonly shortened to Albucasis. In his 30th treatise, "The Surgery," he described in detail the application of two layers of bandages, starting at the fracture site and extending both up and down the limb, after reduction of the fracture. He continued:

> Then put between the bandages enough soft tow or soft rags to correct the curves of the fracture, if any, otherwise put nothing in. Then wind over it another bandage and at once lay over it strong splints if the part be not swollen or effused. But if there be swelling or effusion in the part, apply something to allay the swelling and disperse the effusion. Leave it on for several days and then bind on the splint. The splint should be made of broad halves of cane cut and shaped with skill, or the splints may be made of wood used for sieves, which are made of pine, or of palm branches, or of brier or giant fennel or the like, whatever wood be at hand. Then bind over the splints another bandage just as tightly as you did the first. Then over that tie it up with cords arranged in the way we have said, that is with the pressure greatest over the site of the fracture and lessened as you move away from it. Between the splints there should be a space of not less than a finger's breadth.

It is of interest that the brother of the celebrated French surgeon Bérenger Féraud, an interpreter with the French army in Algeria, wrote in 1868 that all Arab bone setters (tebibs) carried with them "sticks of *kelar*, a sort of fennel, well dried and of extreme lightness, which are used as splints." Albucasis then went on to describe various forms of plaster that may be used as an alternative, particularly for women and children, recommending "mill dust, that is the fine flour that sticks to the walls of a mill as the grindstone moves. Pound it as it is, without sieving, with egg white to a medium consistency, then use." He

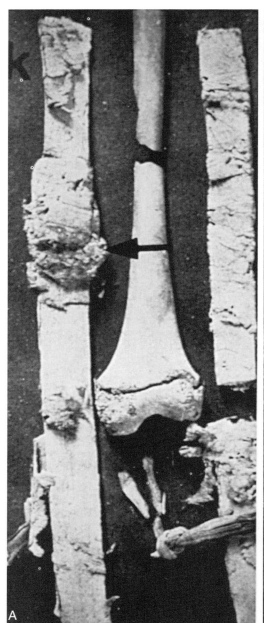

Figure 1–1. *A* and *B,* Specimen of a fracture of an adolescent femur from circa 300 BC, excavated at Naga-ed-Der in 1903. This injury was an open fracture, and the absence of any callus (*arrow* in *A*) indicates early death.

suggested as an alternative plaster a mixture of various gums, including gum mastic, acacia, and the root of *mughath* (*Glossostemon bruguieri*), pounded fine with clay of Armenia or Asia Minor and mixed with water of tamarisk or with egg white.[76]

In 1517, Gersdorf[25] beautifully illustrated a novel method of binding wooden splints, using ligatures around the assembled splint that are tightened by twisting them with cannulated wooden toggles, with a wire then passed down the hollow centers of the toggles to prevent them from untwisting (Fig. 1–2). In this book, he also illustrated the use of an extension apparatus for overcoming overriding of the fractures of the bones, although similar machines had been in use for centuries according to the descriptions of Galen, Celsus, and Paulus Aegineta.[54]

Gersdorf's technique of tightening a circumferential

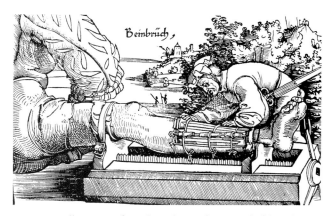

Figure 1–2. Illustration of wooden splintage from Gersdorf (1517). Note the cannulated toggles used to tighten the bindings.

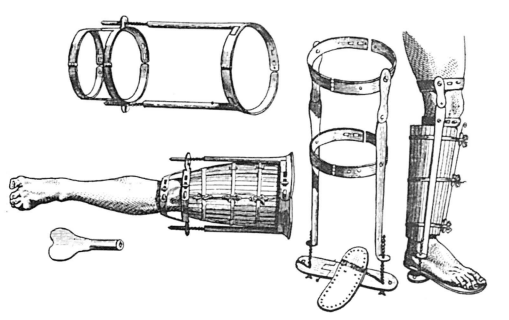

FIGURE 1–3. Benjamin Gooch described the first functional brace in 1767. Note the similarity to Gersdorf's bindings.

splint ligature was plagiarized by Benjamin Gooch,[26] who in 1767 described what must be regarded as the first functional brace (Fig. 1–3), designed as it was to return the worker to labor before the fracture had consolidated. Gooch fashioned shape splints for various anatomic sites; these consisted of longitudinal strips of wood stuck to an underlying sheet of leather that could then be wrapped around the limb and held in place with ligatures and cannulated toggles. I recollect Gooch splintage still being used for temporary immobilization of injured limbs by ambulance crews as late as the 1960s. Gooch's are perhaps the most sophisticated wooden splints ever devised. The 19th century literature abounds with descriptions of many types of wooden fracture apparatus, none of which is as carefully constructed or apparently efficient as those of Gooch.

The use of willow board splints for the treatment of tibial shaft fractures and Colles' fractures in modern times has been described in great detail by Shang T'ien-Yu and colleagues[72] in a fascinating description of the integration of modern and traditional Chinese medicine in the treatment of fractures. Amerasinghe and Veerasingham continued to use shaped bamboo splints, held in place by circumferential rope ligatures, in the functional bracing of tibial fractures in Sri Lanka (Fig. 1–4).[1] They reported 88% of their patients to be weight bearing and freely mobile by

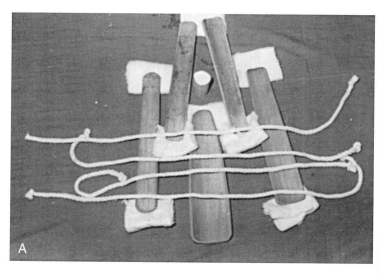

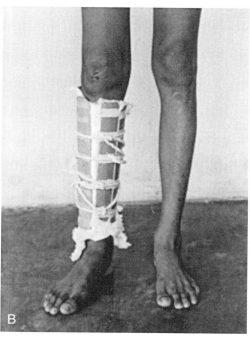

FIGURE 1–4. *A* and *B*, Bamboo functional bracing currently in use in Sri Lanka. (Courtesy of Dr. D.M. Amerasinghe.)

10 weeks, with a 95% union rate, and less than half an inch of shortening in 85% of patients. The Liston wooden board splint for fractures of the femoral shaft is currently in use in one institution in Scotland for the management of this injury in children.

PRECURSORS OF THE PLASTER BANDAGE

As indicated previously, El Zahrawi, probably drawing from the work of Paulus Aegineta, described the use of both clay gum mixtures and flour and egg white for casting materials. In AD 860, the Arab physician Rhazes Athuriscus wrote, "But if thou make thine apparatus with lime and white of egg it will be much handsomer and still more useful. In fact it will become as hard as stone and will not need to be removed until the healing is complete."[3]

William Cheselden (1688 to 1752), the famous English surgeon and anatomist, as a schoolboy sustained an elbow fracture that was treated in this manner. In his book *Anatomy of the Human Body,* he recorded, "I thought of a much better bandage which I had learned from Mr. Cowper, a bone setter at Leicester, who set and cured a fracture of my own cubit when I was a boy at school. His way was, after putting the limb in a proper posture, to wrap it up in rags dipped in the whites of eggs and a little wheat flour mixed. This drying grew stiff and kept the limb in good posture. And I think there is no way better than this in fractures, for it preserves the position of the limb without strict [tight] bandage which is the common cause of mischief in fractures."[55] Cheselden was later reputed to have been able to perform a lithotomy procedure in 68 seconds; it would appear that his functional result was excellent. A more precise use of the technique of Rhazes was introduced into France by Le Dran in the late 18th century; he stiffened his bandage with egg white, vinegar, and powder of Armenian clay or plaster.[80]

The technique of pouring a plaster-of-Paris mixture around an injured limb would appear to have been used in Arabia for many centuries and was brought to the attention of European practitioners by Eaton, a British diplomat in Bassora, Turkey. In 1798 he wrote:

I saw in the eastern parts of the Empire a method of setting bones practised, which appears to me worthy of the attention of surgeons in Europe. It is by inclosing [sic] the broken limb, after the bones are put in their places, in a case of plaster of Paris (or gypsum) which takes exactly the form of the limb without any pressure and in a few minutes the mass is solid and strong [Fig. 1–5]. This substance may be easily cut with a knife and removed and replaced with another. When the swelling subsides, [and] the cavity is too large for the limb, a hole or holes being left, liquid gypsum plaster may be poured in which will perfectly fill up the void and exactly fit the limb. A hole may be made at first by placing oiled cork or a bit of wood against any part where it is required and when the plaster is set it is to be removed. There is nothing in gypsum injurious if it

FIGURE 1–5. *Plâtre coulé* such as Eaton recorded seeing in Turkey in the 18th century.

be free from lime. It will soon become hard and light and the limb may be bathed with spirits which will penetrate through the covering. I saw a case of a most terrible compound fracture of the leg and thigh by the fall of a cannon. The person was seated on the ground and the plaster case extended from below the heel to the upper part of his thigh, where a bandage fastened into the plaster went round his body.[22]

This technique of *plâtre coulé* was enthusiastically embraced in Europe in the early 19th century. Malgaigne[52] recorded in detail the various techniques of its use, stating that he found it first employed by Hendriksz at the Nosocomium Chirurgicum of Groningen in 1814. Shortly afterward Hubenthal,[38] believing himself to be its inventor, described *plâtre coulé* in the *Nouveau Journal de Médecine*. In 1828, Keyl, working with Dieffenbach at the Charity Hospital in Berlin, finally succeeded in calling general attention to it. Although the Berlin surgeons applied the method only to fractures of the leg, Hubenthal had described its use in fractures of the forearm, the hand, and the clavicle, mixing the plaster powder with unsized paper (similar to blotting paper). He encased the limb in a trough made of pasteboard, closed at the top and bottom with toweling, and first poured in the mixture to encase only the posterior half of the limb. After this posterior cast was allowed to set, the edges were smoothed, notched, and then oiled so that a second anterior cast could be created by applying the paste to the front of the limb, thus ending up with two halves of a cast, which could be bandaged together, yet easily separated for wound inspection or to relieve any tension.[51] Malgaigne himself was not keen on *plâtre coulé* and after having problems with swelling within a rigid cast, albeit incomplete over the crest of the tibia, he abandoned the technique in favor of albuminated and starched bandages of the type recommended by Seutin—bandage amidonné.[71]

A great variety of other apparatuses have been devised over the centuries for the management of fractures, notably the copper limb cuirasse described by Heister[32] and what Malgaigne called "the great machine of La Faye." The latter was made of tin and consisted of longitudinal pieces that were hinged together so that it could be laid flat beneath the limb and then wrapped around. It was described as confining "at once the pelvis, thigh, leg and foot, hence it ensured complete immobility." Bonnet of Lyons went one stage further by producing an apparatus for the management of fractures of the femur that enveloped both legs, the pelvis, and the trunk up to the axillae.[10] The great disadvantage of all these extensive and heavy forms of immobilization of the limb was that the patient was largely confined to bed during the whole period of fracture healing. This disadvantage was particularly emphasized by Seutin,[55] who, in recommending his bandage amidonné, or starched bandage, wrote:

> It has not yet been well understood that complete immobility of the body, whilst being recommended by authors as an adjunct to other curative methods, is truly but a last resort which one would be better to avoid than to prescribe. One has not previously dared to say that the consolidation of the bony rupture is certainly more sure and prompt than the injured person's recovery of movements and (ability) to forget thereby his affliction, in order to take up again at least part of his ordinary occupation. Early mobilization causes neither accident nor displacement of the fragments. In permitting the patient to distract himself and take himself out into the fresh air, instead of remaining nailed to his bed, it has the happiest influence on the formation and consolidation of callus.

Again we see the roots of the concept of functional bracing. Seutin showed a man with a light starched bandage on his leg, the limb suspended by a strap around his neck, and walking with crutches.

In the first half of the 19th century, battle lines were drawn between the European surgeons who prescribed total immobilization and those who followed Seutin's *déambulation* regimen, and much intellectual effort was wastefully expended in fruitless argument. Seutin's emphasis on the importance of joint motion was also appreciated by others. In 1875 Sir James Paget wrote, "With rest too long maintained the joint becomes stiff and weak, even though there be no morbid process in it; and this mischief is increased if the joint hath been too long bandaged." A little later, Lucas-Championnière[50] wrote:

> The immobilisation of the members, which was dogma not open for discussion in the treatment of fractures and as well articular lesions, has been practised with such contentment by the authors of the immovable apparatuses, that we threw ourselves with abandon into all forms of immobilisation. It was forbidden even to discuss such immobilisation and to criticise it in the name of healthy physiology. When I attacked, at the Society of Surgery, this forced immobilisation, I was called by Verneuil an *"ankylophobe"* and I remained practically alone in protesting against these practises, which are so contrary to the interests of the injured and the ill. . . . Absolute immobilisation is not a favourable condition for bony repair. . . . [A] certain quantity of movement, regulated movement, is the best condition for this process of repair.

He then described animal experiments that confirm this view and went so far as to recommend massage of the injured limb to produce some degree of movement between the fragments. He was particularly vitriolic in his condemnation of prolonged immobilization of children and became the great champion of early and graduated controlled mobilization, not only to achieve union of the fracture but also to prevent edema, muscle atrophy, and joint stiffness, later to be christened *fracture disease*.

THE PLASTER BANDAGE AND ITS DERIVATIVES

The battle of minds between the mobilizers and the immobilizers was neither won nor lost but rather forgotten with the advent of the plaster-of-Paris bandage. In Holland in 1852, Antonius Mathijsen (1805 to 1878) published a new method for the application of plaster in fractures.[53] As a military surgeon, he had been seeking an immobilizing bandage that would permit the safe transport of patients with gunshot wounds to specialized treatment centers. He sought a bandage that could be used at once, would become hard in minutes, could be applied so as to give the surgeon access to the wound, was adaptable to the form of the extremity, would not be damaged by wound discharge or humidity, and was neither too heavy nor too expensive. His exact technique was described by Van Assen and Meyerding[2] as follows:

> He cut pieces of double folded unbleached cotton or linen to fit the part to be immobilized. Then the pieces were fixed and held in position by woollen thread or pins. The dry plaster which was spread between the layers remained two finger breadths within the edges of the cloth. The extremity was then placed on the bandage, which was moistened with water. Next the edges of the bandage were pulled over so that they overlapped one another and they were held by pins. When an opening in the bandage was necessary, a piece of cotton wool the size of the desired opening was placed between the compresses so that this area remained free of plaster. In cases in which it was found necessary to enlarge the cast, enlargement could be achieved by the application of cotton bandages, four inches wide, rubbed with plaster and moistened.

Mathijsen introduced his plaster bandage in 1876 at the Centennial Exhibition in Philadelphia at the invitation of

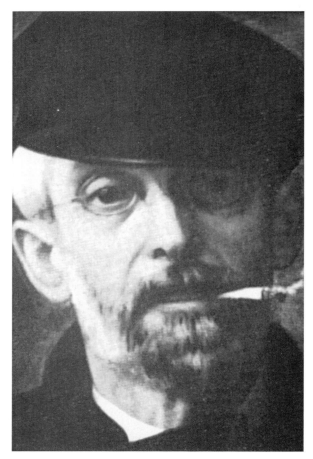

FIGURE 1–6. Hugh Owen Thomas (1834 to 1891), the father of British orthopaedics. (Courtesy of Prof. L. Klenerman, Department of Orthopaedic Surgery, University of Liverpool.)

mobilizers and the immobilizers was reduced to mere embers, it was not extinguished, and the early functional concepts of Gooch, Seutin, Paget, Lucas-Championnière, and many others continued for decades to be regarded by surgical orthodoxy as heretical. In Britain, the great advocate of rest—enforced, prolonged, and uninterrupted—in the management of skeletal disorders, both traumatic and nontraumatic, was Hugh Owen Thomas (Fig. 1–6), who came from a long line of unqualified bone setters residing in the Isle of Anglesey. Hugh Thomas' father, Evan Thomas, left his home and agricultural background to work in a foundry in Liverpool. His native skills as a bone setter rapidly became legendary, and he opened consulting rooms in Liverpool, developing an extensive practice. His eldest son, Hugh Owen, broke with family tradition and qualified in medicine in 1857. His attempt at a partnership with his father failed, and he set himself up as a general practitioner in the slums of Liverpool, where he worked for 32 years, reputedly taking only 6 days of vacation. He died in 1891 at the age of 57.[77]

There cannot be an orthopaedic surgeon in the world who is not familiar with the Thomas splint, still in current use in many centers throughout the world in the management of fractures of the femur, although it was originally designed to assist in the management of tuberculous disease of the knee joint (Fig. 1–7). As discussed later, the use of this splint in World War I saved many lives. Not the least of the contributions of this industrious, single-minded, chain-smoking eccentric was to fire his nephew with enthusiasm for orthopaedic surgery. Robert Jones, later to be knighted, practiced with his uncle Hugh for many years in Liverpool before becoming one of the best known orthopaedic surgeons in the English-speaking world. Hugh Owen Thomas and Robert Jones were the two men to whom Watson Jones dedicated his classical work *Fractures and Joint Injuries*, writing of them, "They whose work cannot die, whose influence lives after them, whose disciples perpetuate and multiply their gifts to humanity, are truly immortal." Watson Jones remained greatly influenced by Hugh Owen Thomas' belief in enforced, uninterrupted, and prolonged

his friend Dr. M. C. Gori. The use of plaster-of-Paris bandages for the formation of fracture casts became widespread after Mathijsen's death and replaced most other forms of splintage.

Although the fire of the intellectual contest between the

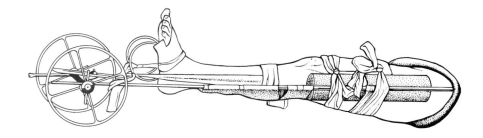

FIGURE 1–7. Early Thomas splint.

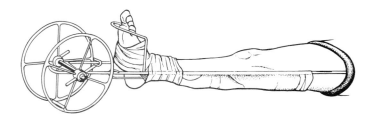

rest, and in the preface to the fourth edition of his book,[81] he described one of its chapters as

> . . . a vigorous attack upon the almost universally accepted belief that contact compression, lag screws, slotted plates, compression clamps, and early weight bearing promote the union of fractures. I do not accept a word of it. Forcible compression of bone is pathological rather than physiological and it avails in the treatment of fractures only insofar as it promotes immobility and protects from shear. In believing this and denying the view that is held so widely, I reiterate the observations of Hugh Owen Thomas. Moreover, I believe that gaps between the fragments of a fractured bone are always filled if immobility is complete. . . . I still believe firmly that, apart from interposition of muscle and periosteum, the sole important cause of nonunion is inadequate immobilisation.

TRACTION

Although longitudinal traction of the limb to overcome the overriding of fracture fragments had been described as early as the writings of Galen (AD 130 to 200), in which he described his own extension apparatus, or *glossocomium* (Fig. 1–8), this traction was immediately discontinued once splintage had been applied. The use of continuous traction in the management of diaphyseal fractures seems to have appeared around the middle of the 19th century, although Guy de Chauliac (1300 to 1367) wrote in *Chirurgia Magna*, "After the application of splints, I attach to the foot a mass of lead as a weight, taking care to pass the cord which supports the weight over a small pulley in such a manner that it shall pull on the leg in a horizontal direction *(Ad pedum ligo pondus plumbi transeundo chordam super parvampolegeam; itaque tenebit tibiam in sua longitudinae)*."[27]

Whereas Sir Astley Cooper in his celebrated treatise on dislocations and fractures of the joints illustrated the method of treating simple fractures of the femur on a double inclined plane with a wooden splint strapped to the side of the thigh, there is no mention in his work of the use of traction.[17] On the other hand, in his book on fractures and dislocations published in 1890, Albert Hoffa of Wurzburg (where Roentgen discovered x-rays) liberally illustrated the use of traction for many types of fractures— not only of the femur in adults and children but also of the humerus.[35] Straight arm traction for supracondylar and intercondylar fractures of the distal humerus recently so in vogue was clearly described and illustrated by Helferich in 1906 (Fig. 1–9).[33]

Certainly one of the earliest accounts of the use of continuous skin traction in the management of fractures must be that of Dr. Josiah Crosby of New Hampshire. He described the application of "two strips of fresh spread English adhesive plaster, one on either side of the leg, wide enough to cover at least half of the diameter of the limb from above the knee to the malleolar processes." Over these he laid a firm spiral bandage before applying weight to the lower ends of the adhesive straps. He recorded the use of this method in a fracture of the femur, an open

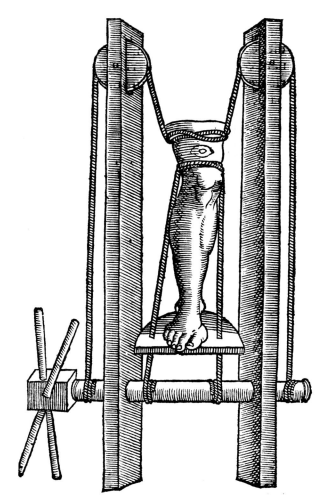

FIGURE 1–8. The glossocomium, here illustrated from the works of Ambroise Paré (1564).

fracture of the tibia, and, surprisingly, two cases of fracture of the clavicle in 2-year-old children. The technique of Dr. Crosby was illustrated in detail by Hamilton in his treatise on military surgery.[29] Billroth, describing his experiences between 1869 and 1870, gave the alternatives of plaster-of-Paris bandages or extension in the management of fractures of the shaft of the femur. He stated, "On the whole, I far prefer extension by means of ordinary strapping. This I apply generally on Volkmann's plan."[7] It is interesting to note that in the early descriptions of traction for the management of fractures of the femoral shaft, when no other form of splintage was used, union was usually said to have been consolidated by 5 or 6 weeks, in comparison with the 10 to 14 weeks that later came to be regarded as the average time to femoral shaft union using traction in association with external splintage.

The rapid consolidation of femoral shaft fractures was, of course, stressed by Professor George Perkins of London in the 1940s and 1950s, when he abandoned external splintage and advocated straight simple traction through an upper tibial pin and immediate mobilization of the knee, using a split bed (so-called Pyrford traction). This was in some ways a development and simplification of the

FIGURE 1–9. Forearm skin traction for the treatment of T fractures of the distal humerus. (From Helferich, H. Frakturen und Luxationen. München, Lehmann Verlag, 1906.)

traction principles outlined by R. H. Russell (who also remarked on rapid consolidation with early movement), describing his mobile traction in 1924.[67] In the same year, Dowden, speaking mainly of upper limb fractures, wrote, "The principle of early active movement in the treatment of practically all injuries and in most inflammations will assuredly be adopted before long."[21] Perkins, like Dowden and the many others before, was a great advocate of movement, both active and passive, of all the joints of the involved limb as being more important than precise skeletal form.

FUNCTIONAL BRACING

Given that Gooch's description in 1767 of the first tibial and femoral functional braces was to remain obscure for more than two centuries, it is surprising that after the intense discussion of the technical minutiae and principles of splintage in the 19th century, there was no real modification of the "standard" plaster-of-Paris cast until the work of Sarmiento,[69] published 200 years after that of Gooch. Following experience with patellar tendon-bearing below-knee limb prostheses, Sarmiento developed a patellar tendon-bearing cast for the treatment of fractures of the tibia, applied after initial standard cast treatment had been used to permit the acute swelling to settle. This heralded the renaissance of functional bracing, and in 1970 Mooney and colleagues[56] described hinged casts for the lower limb in the management of femoral fractures treated initially with some 6 weeks of traction.

Since the mid-1970s, the development of a variety of casting materials and the use of thermoplastics in brace construction have extended the ideas of these pioneers of the 1960s and 1970s to the point where functional bracing, certainly for shaft fractures of the tibia and certain lower femoral fractures, is accepted without question as the natural sequel to early management by plaster casting or traction. The widespread use of functional bracing has liberated countless patients from prolonged hospitalization and permitted early return to function and to gainful employment.

OPEN FRACTURES

Until about 150 years ago, an open fracture was virtually synonymous with death and generally necessitated immediate amputation. Amputation itself carried with it a very high mortality rate, usually with death resulting from hemorrhage or sepsis. Until the 16th century, the traditional method of attempting to control the hemorrhage after amputation was cauterization of the wound, either with hot irons or by the application of boiling pitch. This in itself may well have caused tissue necrosis and encouraged infection and secondary hemorrhage. The famous French surgeon Ambroise Paré (1510 to 1590), who served as surgeon to the Court of Henry II and Catherine de Medici and is rightfully regarded as the father of military surgery, was in 1564 the first to describe the ligation of the bleeding vessels after amputation. He developed an instrument that he called the "crow's beak" (*bec de corbin*) for securing the vessels and pulling them out of the cut surface of the amputation stump in order to ligate them (Fig. 1–10). Notwithstanding this advance, Le Petit, who in 1718 described the use of the tourniquet to control hemorrhage during amputation,[61] is reputed to have claimed that his invention reduced the mortality rate from amputation of the lower limb from 75% to 25%.

In the history of the open fracture, Ambroise Paré[58] features again in documenting for the first time the conservation of a limb after an open fracture. He in fact described his own injury, sustained on May 4, 1561, when, while crossing the Seine on a ferry to attend a patient in another part of Paris, his horse, startled by a sudden lurch

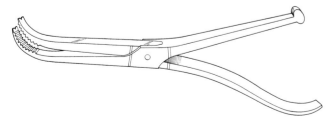

FIGURE 1–10. *Bec de corbin*—crow's beak—devised by Paré for pulling out vessel ends during amputation to facilitate their ligature.

of the vessel, gave him "such a kick that she completely broke the two bones of the leg four fingers above the junction of the foot." Fearing that the horse would kick him again and not appreciating the nature of the injury, he took an instinctive step backward "but sudden falling to the earth, the fractured bones leapt outwards and ruptured the flesh, the stocking and the boot, from which I felt such pain that it was not possible for man (at least in my judgment) to endure any greater without death. My bones thus broken and my foot pointing the other way, I greatly feared that it would be necessary to cut my leg to save my life." He then described how, with a combination of prayer, splintage, and dressing of the open wound with various astringents, coupled with the regular use of soap suppositories, he survived the initial infection and by September, "finally thanks to God, I was entirely healed without limping in any way," returning to his work that month (Fig. 1–11).

Nevertheless, in insisting on conservative management of his open fracture rather than amputation, Paré was flying in the face of orthodox surgical practice, as indeed was the English surgeon Percival Pott, who in 1756 was thrown from his horse while riding in Kent Street, Southwark, and suffered a compound fracture of the lower leg. Aware of the dangers of mishandling such an injury, he would not permit himself to be moved until he had summoned his own chairmen from Westminster to bring their poles, and it is said that while lying in the January cold awaiting them, he bargained for the purchase of a door, to which his servants subsequently nailed their poles and thereby carried him on a litter to Watling Street near St. Paul's cathedral. There he was attended by an Edward Nourse, a prominent contemporary surgeon, who expressed the view that because of the gentle handling of the limb, no air had entered the wound and therefore there was a chance of preserving the leg, which otherwise was destined for amputation. Finally, success attended a long period of immobilization and convalescence.

As late as the 19th century, not all victims of open fracture were so fortunate. Even in circumstances considered ideal at the time, the mortality rate associated with open injuries remained high. Billroth[7] recorded four patients with compound dislocations of the ankle who came under his care in Zurich, with one dying of pyemia, one of septicemia, and a third of overwhelming infection after amputation for suppuration on the 36th day after injury. The fourth patient recovered. Of 93 patients with compound fractures of the lower leg whom he treated in Zurich, 46 died. Recovery from open fracture of the femur was, in Billroth's experience, so unusual that, describing the case of a woman of 23 who recovered from such an injury, he stated, "The following case of recovery is perhaps unique."

Gunshot wounds producing fracture were particularly notorious and generally treated with immediate amputation, certainly until the early part of the 20th century. The results of this policy, however, were in certain instances quite horrifying. Wrench recorded that in the Franco-Prussian War (1870 to 1871), the death rate from open fracture was 41%, and open fractures of the knee joint carried a 77% mortality rate.[82] On the French side, of 13,172 amputees, some 10,006 died. On the other hand, in the American Civil War, the overall mortality rate for nearly 30,000 amputations was on the order of 26%, although for thigh amputations it reached 54% (Fig. 1–12). The difference in the mortality rates for different theaters of war around that time was probably related to the postoperative management, as very often the suppurating amputation stump was sponged daily with a solution from the same "pus bucket" used for all the patients. It has been said of that era that it was probably safer to have your leg blown off by a cannonball than amputated by a surgeon!

During World War I, gunshot wounds of the femur carried a very high mortality rate in the early years. In 1916 the death rate from gunshot wound of the femur was 80% in the British army. Thereafter it became policy to use the Thomas splint, with fixed traction applied via a clove hitch around the booted foot, before transportation to the hospital. Robert Jones reported in 1925 that this simple change of policy resulted in a reduction of the mortality rate to 20% by 1918. With progressive understanding of bacterial contamination and cross-infection after the pioneering work of Pasteur, Koch, Lister, and Semmelweis; the use of early splintage, as learned by the British forces in World War I; and the application of open-wound

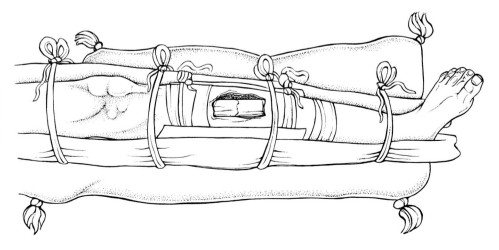

FIGURE 1–11. Illustration from Paré's surgical text of 1564 of his own open tibial fracture treated by splintage and open care of the wound. This is the first well-documented cure of an open limb fracture without amputation.

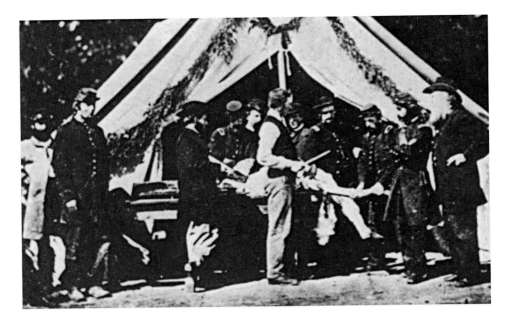

FIGURE **1–12.** Amputation scene at General Hospital during the Civil War. Stereoscopic slide. (Courtesy of the Edward G. Miner Library, Rochester, New York.)

treatment following wound extension and excision as advocated first by Paré and later by Larrey (Napoleon's surgeon and inventor of the *ambulance*),[57, 78] the scourge of the open fracture, even from a femoral gunshot wound, has been greatly reduced.

EARLY FRACTURE SURGERY

Wire Fixation

It is generally believed that the earliest technique of internal fixation of fractures was that of ligature or wire suture and, according to Malgaigne, the first mention of the ligature dates back to the early 1770s. A. M. Icart, surgeon of the Hôtel Dieu at Castres, claimed to have seen it used with success by Lapujode and Sicre, surgeons of Toulouse. This observation came to light when, in 1775, M. Pujol accused Icart of bringing about the death of a young man with an open fracture of the humerus in whom Icart was alleged to have performed bone ligature using brass wire. In his defense, Icart cited the experience of the Toulouse surgeons in the earlier part of the decade, although denying that he himself had personally used this technique in the case in dispute.[39, 63, 64] In a scholarly discussion of Pujol versus Icart, Evans has called into question whether this type of operation was any more than the subject of surgical theory at that time,[24] but Icart's contention was widely accepted by so many French observers in the 19th century that it is highly probable that bone ligature was performed at least by Lapujode (if not Sicre) around 1770.

On July 31, 1827, Dr. Kearny Rodgers of New York is recorded as having performed bone suture.[31] He resected a pseudarthrosis of the humerus and, finding the bone ends to be most unstable, drilled a hole in each and passed a silver wire through to retain coaption of the bone fragments. The ends of the wire were drawn out through a cannula that remained in the wound. Although on the 16th day the cannula fell from the wound with the entire wire loop, the bones remained in their proper position and union was said to have occurred by 69 days after the operation. The patient was not allowed to leave his bed for 2 months after the operation!

In the introduction to his *Traité de l'Immobilisation Directe des Fragments Osseux dans les Fractures* (the first book ever published on internal fixation),[6] Bérenger Féraud recounted that, at the beginning of his medical career when he was an intern at the Hôtel Dieu Saint Esprit at Toulon in 1851, he was involved in the treatment of an unfortunate workman who had sustained a closed, comminuted fracture of the lower leg in falling down a staircase. Initial splintage was followed by a period of infection and suppuration, requiring several drainage procedures; eventually, after many long weeks, amputation was decided on. At the last moment, the poor patient begged to be spared the loss of his leg, so Dr. Long, Bérenger Féraud's chief, exposed the bone ends, freshened them, and held them together with three lead wire ligatures (cerclage) "as one would reunite the ends of a broken stick, and to our great astonishment then guided the patient to perfect cure without limp or shortening of the member, which for so long had appeared to be irrevocably lost." The patient survived, and the lead wires were removed 3 weeks later; the fracture united, and the workman left the hospital 105 days after his accident and resumed work 6 months after the operation. Bérenger Féraud went on to say:

I assisted at the operation and I bandaged with my own hands the injured for many long weeks. Can anyone understand how this extraordinary cure struck me? The strange means of producing and maintaining solid coaptation of the bony fragments by encircling them with a metallic ligature fascinated me as during my childhood I had heard tales of this technique being performed by Arab surgeons and, until then, had considered this to be a mere product of a barbaric empiricism. . . . In my childhood, in 1844 and 1845, I heard an old *tebib**** renowned in the environs of Cherchell, in Algeria, for his erudition and his experience, recount to my father who, a surgeon impassioned with our art, avidly questioned native practitioners of French Africa, in order to sort out, from their experiences and their therapeutic means, the scientific principles, which had been passed down to them from their ancestors, amidst some of the ordinary practices of a more or less coarse empiricism. I tell you, I heard him say that in certain cases of gunshot wounds, or when a fracture had failed to unite, the ancient masters advised opening the fracture site with a cutting instrument, ligating the fragments one to another with lead or iron wire . . . and only to remove the wire once the fracture was consolidated.

It therefore seems that there is some anecdotal evidence to suggest that such techniques had been used in the early part of the 19th century or even before. Bérenger Féraud himself cited the example of Lapujode and Sicre mentioned earlier. Commeiras[15] reported native Tahitian practitioners to be skilled in the open fixation of fractures using lengths of reed.

Screw Fixation

The use of screws in bone probably started around the late 1840s. Certainly in 1850, the French surgeons Cucuel and Rigaud described two cases in which screws were used in the management of fractures.[19] In the first case, a man of 64 sustained a depressed fracture of the superior part of his sternum, into which a screw was then inserted to permit traction to be applied to elevate the depressed sternal fragment into an improved position. In the second case, a distracted fracture of the olecranon, Rigaud inserted a screw into the ulna and into the displaced olecranon, reduced the fragments, and wired the screws together (*vissage de rappel*), thereafter leaving the arm entirely free of splintage and obtaining satisfactory union of the fracture. Rigaud also described a similar procedure for the patella. In his extraordinarily detailed and comprehensive treatise on direct immobilization of bony fragments, Bérenger Féraud made no mention of interfragmentary screw fixation, which was probably first practiced by Lambotte (see following section).

Plate Fixation

The first account of plate fixation of bone was probably the 1886 report by Hansmann of Hamburg entitled "A new method of fixation of the fragments of complicated fractures."[30] He illustrated a malleable plate, applied to the bone to span the fracture site, the end of the plate being bent through a right angle so as to project through the skin. The plate was then attached to each fragment by one

or more special screws, which were constructed with long shanks that projected through the skin for ease of removal (Fig. 1–13). He recorded that the apparatus was removed approximately 4 to 8 weeks after insertion and described its use in 15 fresh fractures, 4 pseudarthroses, and 1 reconstruction of the humerus after removal of an enchondroma.

George Guthrie[28] discussed the current state of direct fixation of fractures in 1903 and quoted Estes as having described a nickel steel plate that he had been using to maintain coaption in compound fractures for many years. This plate, perforated with six holes, was laid across the fracture, and holes were drilled into the bone to correspond to those of the plate. The plate was fixed to the bone by ivory pegs, which protruded from the wound. Removal was accomplished 3 or 4 weeks later by breaking off the pegs and withdrawing the plate through a small incision. Guthrie reported that in a recent letter Dr. Estes had said,

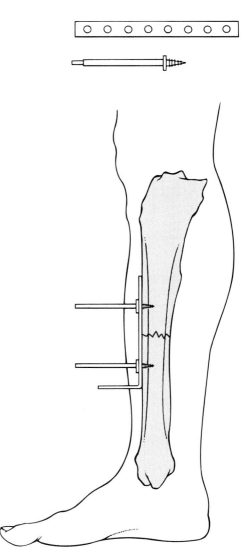

FIGURE 1–13. Redrawn from Hansmann's article of 1886, "A new method of fixation of the fragments of complicated fractures," the first publication on plate fixation of fractures. The bent end of the plate and the long screw shanks were left protruding through the skin to facilitate removal after union.

**Arab medicine man, whence the modern French slang word *toubib*, meaning quack or doctor.

"The little plate has given me great satisfaction and has been quite successful in St. Luke's Hospital." Guthrie also quoted Steinbach as reporting four cases of fractured tibia in which he had used a silver plate by this method and obtained good results. He removed the plate using local anesthesia. Silver was greatly favored at this time as an implant metal, as it was believed to possess antiseptic properties. Interestingly, in this article, Guthrie referred to the use of rubber gloves during surgery, seemingly antedating the reputed first use of gloves by Halstead.

The man who coined the term *osteosynthesis* was Albin Lambotte (1866 to 1955), although Bérenger Féraud referred to the restoration of bone continuity by ligature or bone suture as *synthèsisation*. It is believed, however, that by osteosynthesis Lambotte meant *stable* bone fixation rather than simply suture. Lambotte is generally regarded as the father of modern internal fixation, and in his foreword to a book commemorating the works of Lambotte, Dr. Elst briefly discussed the early attempts in the 19th century at surgical stabilization of bone and then continued, "Thus at the end of the last century, the idea was floating among surgeons. As always in the field of scientific progress, comes the right man in the right place, a genial mind who collects the items spread here and there, melts them into a solid block and forges the whole together. So did Albin Lambotte in Belgium, a pioneer of osteosynthesis."[23]

Lambotte (Fig. 1–14), the son of a professor of comparative anatomy, biology, and chemistry at the University of Brussels, was taught almost exclusively by his brother Elie, a brilliant young surgeon, who sadly died prematurely. Albin had worked under the direction of his brother at the Schaerbeek Hospital in the suburbs of Brussels and then in 1890 became assistant surgeon at the Stuyvenberg Hospital in Antwerp, rapidly progressing to become the head of the surgical department. From 1900, he tackled the surgical treatment of fractures with great enthusiasm and much innovation. He manufactured most of his early instruments and implants in his own workshop, developing not only plates and screws for rigid bone fixation in a variety of materials but also an external fixation device similar in principle to the ones in use today. He met with much intellectual opposition, but his excellent results were persuasive. In 1908, he reported 35 patients who had made a complete recovery after plate fixation of the femur. His classical book on the surgical treatment of fractures was published in 1913.[42] His legendary surgical skill was the product not only of a keen intellect but also of his extraordinary manual dexterity, which was also channeled into his great interest in music. He became a skilled violinist, but this was not enough for him, and he subsequently trained as a lutemaker. He, in fact, made 182 violins and his name is listed in Vanne's *Dictionnaire Universel des Luthiers*. Elst related the following anecdote as an indication of Lambotte's manual skills:

> One day Lambotte was in Paris staying at the Hôtel Louvois, at that time, and even nowadays, the Belgian headquarters in Paris. One morning he was on his way to the Avenue de l'Opéra, accompanied by a young colleague who was the one who told me the story. As he made his way through the old narrow streets, lined with

Figure 1–14. Albin Lambotte (1866 to 1955), the father of osteosynthesis. (Courtesy of la Société Belge de Chirurgie Orthopédique et de Traumatologie.)

windows and workshops belonging to every type of craftsman, Lambotte would enter one or two, admiring each one's dexterity and set of tools and discussing their methods like an expert. All of a sudden he stopped short, gazing with marvel at the instruments of a shoemaker. The idea of a new type of forceps had struck him. Suddenly inspired, he strode quickly towards the famous manufacturer of surgical instruments, the Collin factory, neighbouring the area that he was in. With great gestures and explanations, he tried to describe the instrument he desired. It seemed as if nobody could understand him, and not being able to endure it any longer he took off his jacket and rolled up his sleeves. Before a flabbergasted audience, he began to forge, file, hammer, strike, model and so finish off the piece of iron. They were all stunned with admiration and one of them came up to him and said "I have been here for forty two years sir, and never have I seen anybody work like you." Lambotte went away deeply moved, confiding in his companion "That is the highest prize I have ever received. It moves me as much as all the academic titles."

As if these qualities were not enough, he is also recorded as being an extremely hard-working and kind man, noted for his devotion to his patients; a patron of the arts; and a great surgical teacher. Indeed, before World War I, the brothers Charles and William Mayo would take turns coming and spending several weeks in Antwerp. It is said that as soon as they disembarked, they devoted all their time in Europe to Lambotte and left only when their work in Rochester called them back. As an indication of the esteem in which he was held, among the many international figures attending his jubilee celebration in Antwerp in 1935 were René Leriche, Fred Albee, Ernest Hey Groves, and Vittorio Putti. The Lambotte instrumentarium remained in regular use until the 1950s (Fig. 1–15).

Contemporaneous with the work of Lambotte in Belgium was that of the other great pioneer of internal

FIGURE 1–16. William Arbuthnot Lane (1856 to 1943), seen here shortly after qualifying at Guy's Hospital, London. (From Layton, T.B. Sir William Arbuthnot Lane, Bt. Edinburgh, E. & S. Livingstone, 1956.)

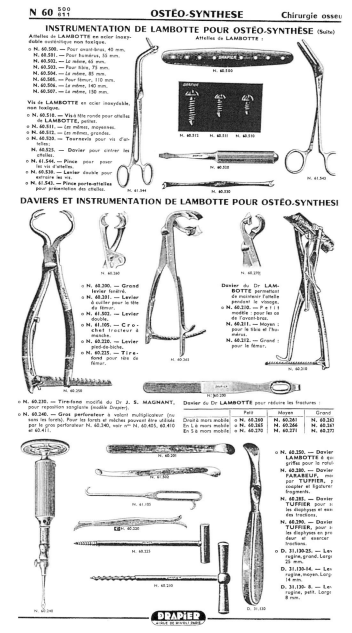

FIGURE 1–15. Instruments and implants designed by Lambotte featured in a surgical catalogue of Drapier (Paris) in the early 1950s.

fixation, William Arbuthnot Lane (Fig. 1–16) of Guy's Hospital, London. The tradition in the late 19th century at this hospital was that fracture patients be admitted under the surgeon of the day and, after discharge, then be reviewed as outpatients by his assistant. Lane, working as the assistant to Clement Lucas, was most unhappy with the results of fracture management. In his biography of Lane, Layton[46] recorded:

Before Lane's time, the criteria of a good result in a fracture were indefinite and vague. They were aesthetic rather than practical. Firm union went without saying, but when a false joint, a nonunion or a weak fibrous one resulted, it was rather the patient's fault than the surgeon's. Given a firm union, the rest was an aesthetic problem, affecting the reputation of the surgeon rather than the way in which the patient could use his limb. "Pay great attention to your fracture cases" was the tradition—"with them alone the grave does not cover your mistakes."

Lane had told Layton of a stevedore, who said:

Mr. Lucas thinks this is a good result. He says there is not much displacement and it looks all right. But I can't work with it. My job is carrying a sack of flour, weighing two hundredweight, up a plank from a barge to the wharfside and I can't do it. The foreman won't have me and I am still out of work.

Lane then went down to the docks and discovered that the stevedore had been telling the truth. Any slip from the plank from the barge to the wharf would have resulted in a fall onto the dock between the barge and the wharfside or between two barges. Lane observed that a man whose foot was in the slightest degree out of alignment could very easily fall. Lane thus became greatly impressed with the need for accuracy and maintenance of good reduction. Initially he started work with wires, and then in 1893 he is recorded as having used screws across a fracture site. Shortly afterward, he devised his first plate. Beginning in 1892, Lane made it his practice, whenever he could, to perform open reduction and fixation in all cases of simple fracture. This practice, however, met opposition from his chief, Mr. Lucas, and it was not until 1894, when Lucas was off work for 6 months after an attack of typhoid, that Lane had his chance to operate on a large series of simple fractures.

Although his attempts at internal fixation of compound fractures were almost universally a failure, Layton recorded that not one case of internal fixation of a simple fracture became infected during this period. During these 6 months of intensive internal fixation, Lane was using Lister's antiseptic techniques, and his dresser, Dr. Beddard, told that Lane and his associates wallowed in carbolic almost from dawn until dusk, with half of them passing black urine from the carbolic absorbed through their skins. At this time Lane insisted on his own variant of the antiseptic technique. Everyone wore long mackintoshes up to the neck, over which they applied gowns wet with carbolic or Lysol solution, and similarly the patients were draped with antiseptic towels introduced by Lane around 1889. The instruments were also soaked in Lysol, but by 1904 dry sterilization of the gowns and the instruments was Lane's routine.

Interestingly, Layton recorded the postmortem exploration of a fracture plated by Lane; the patient subsequently died of an unrelated septicemia. Layton said "I cut down onto the bone and found this firmly joined without the throwing out of any callus around it. The plate was well in place, the screws all firmly fixed without a suspicion of any inflammation of the bone into which they had been put."[46] This surely must have been the first observation of healing without external callus formation in the presence of rigid fixation. In addition, Lane is credited with developing the nontouch technique of bone surgery and devised many instruments to enable him to hold implants without handling them directly. Of operative technique, Lane wrote:

I will now relate the several steps which are involved in an operation for simple fracture. I will do so in some detail as apart from manual dexterity and skill the whole secret of success in these operations depends on the most rigid asepsis. The very moderate degree of cleanliness that is adopted in operations generally will not suffice when a large quantity of metal is left in a wound. To guarantee success in the performance of these operations the surgeon must not touch the interior of the wound even with his gloved hand for gloves are frequently punctured, especially if it be necessary to use a moderate amount of force, and the introduction into the wound of fluid which may have been in contact with the skin for some time may render the wound septic. All swabs introduced into the wound should be held with long forceps and should not be handled in any way. The operator must not let any portion of an instrument which has been in contact with a cutaneous surface or even with his glove enter the wound. After an instrument has been used for any length of time or forcibly it should be resterilised.[45]

He then went on to describe the preparation of the skin with tincture of iodine and the use of skin toweling. By 1900 he had invented a huge variety of different-shaped plates for particular fracture problems, and in 1905 he wrote his classical work on the operative treatment of fractures, in which he illustrated both single and double plating and the use of intramedullary screw fixation for fractures of the neck of the femur.[44] In 1905 and 1906 Lambotte had also performed intramedullary screw fixation in four cases of femoral neck fracture, but this technique was not in fact new. In 1903 Guthrie quoted from Bryant's *Operative Surgery*:

Koenig operated in a case of recent fracture, making a small incision over the outer side of the trochanter major and drilled a hole through it with a metal drill in the direction of the head of the bone, applied extension to the limb to the extent necessary to overcome the deformity and then drove a long steel nail through the canal in the trochanter into the head of the bone and left it there. The limb was then immobilised and extended for six weeks. Good union and free motion of the joint were obtained. Cheyne, in a case of recent fracture, exposed the fragments through a longitudinal incision made over the anterior aspect of the joint, exposed the fracture, made extension and internal rotation of the limb, and with the fingers in the wound, manipulated the fragments into place. Then a small longitudinal incision was made over the outer side of the trochanter major and two canals drilled through the fragments at a distance of half an inch apart. Ivory pegs were then driven through the holes made by the drill and the limb immobilised. Good union and motion were obtained.[28]

It is understood that this procedure was in fact first suggested to Koenig by von Langenbeck, who is reputed to have treated fractures of the neck of the femur by drilling across them with a silvered drill and then leaving the drill bit in place.

Most of the screws used in plating procedures at this time were close derivatives of the traditional wood screw, with its tapered thread, although the later designs of both Lambotte and Lane were of screws with parallel threads, probably inspired by the classical publication of Sherman in 1926.[73] While stressing "the most scrupulous aseptic techniques" along the lines recommended by Lane, Sherman designed his own series of plates and also drew attention to the superior holding power of parallel threaded screws of a self-tapping, fine pitch design (Fig. 1–17). He pointed out that these had something like four times the holding power of a wood or carpenter's screw. He also introduced the use of corrosion-resistant vanadium steel. In addition, he emphasized particularly that the fixation should be firm enough to permit early functional rehabilitation. In describing his postoperative regimen for femoral fracture fixation, he recommended the following:

> Immediately following the operation, the leg is placed in a Thomas' splint, flexed by the use of the Pierson attachment and then swung from a Balkan frame. Plaster is never used. The clips are removed on the fourth day and passive movements of the knee joint begun on the third or fourth day and continued daily. With immobilization of the fracture by transfixion screws, active and passive motion can be freely indulged in without any danger whatsoever of disturbing the position. . . . Early mobilization is the most valuable adjunct in the postoperative treatment and should be instituted within the first few days. Great care should be taken not to permit weight bearing until the union is firm and callus hard.

Sherman reported a series of 78 cases of plating of the femoral shaft with only 1 death (caused by a pulmonary embolism 2 days after operation), no amputations, and no cases of nonunion; in only 2 patients was it necessary to remove the plates and screws because of infection, both nonetheless ending in an excellent functional result after treatment by immediate wound débridement and intermit-

tent irrigation of the cavity with 0.5% sodium hypochlorite. He also cited the reported experience of Hitzrot, who had plated approximately 100 cases of femoral fracture, with 1 death and only 2 infections; in the remainder there were no nonunions, no stiff knees, no plates needed to be removed, and "no appreciable changes in function or anatomy. . . ."[34]

Although now superseded by superior implant design, the Sherman plate is still in current use in hospitals throughout the world. In the 1930s and 1940s, a great variety of plate designs, some bizarre, were reported but with no great conceptual innovations. The so-called slotted plated splint of Egger, designed to hold the fracture fragments in alignment while allowing them to slide toward each other under the influence of weight bearing and muscle force, was neither new nor predictably successful: Lambotte had described, and later abandoned, a slotted plate as early as 1907. It was indeed the work of Danis in the 1940s that heralded the modern era of internal fixation as will be discussed further on.

EXTERNAL FIXATION

Traditionally, the first external fixation device was the *pointe métallique* conceived by Malgaigne in 1840 and subsequently documented in 1843 in the *Journal de Chirurgie*.[5] This apparatus consisted of a hemicircular metal arc that could be strapped around the limb in such a manner that a finger screw, passing through a slot in the arc, could be positioned over any projecting fragment

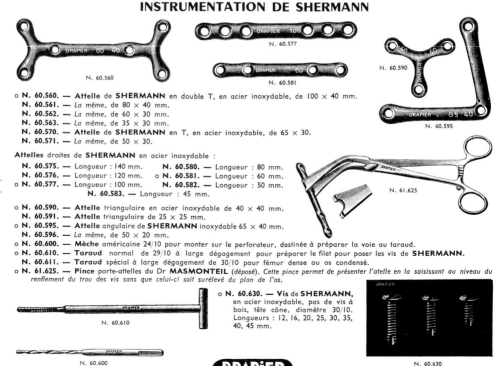

FIGURE 1–17. Sherman instrumentation from the Drapier (Paris) catalogue of the early 1950s.

threatening the overlying skin, the screw then being tightened to press the fragment into a position of reduction. Although this apparatus and modifications of it, such as those of Roux, Ollier, and Valette, gained such a prominent place in contemporary surgery that the chapter on their use in the treatise of Bérenger Féraud occupies 126 pages, it is probably incorrect to regard it as an external fixation device in that it simply pressed one of the fragments into place but did not in itself result in any stability of the fracture.

Nevertheless, Malgaigne still retains the credit for the design of the first external fixator, for in 1843 he also described his *griffe métallique*, or metal claw, which consisted of two pairs of curved points, each pair attached to a metal plate, one plate sliding within grooves on the other and the two components being capable of approximation using a turnbuckle type of screw (Fig. 1–18). This device was designed for use on distracted fractures of the patella, and it was commonly perceived that Malgaigne proposed that the metal points were driven into the bony fragments of the patella in order to approximate them. This, in fact, is incorrect. Malgaigne's concept was that the metal points would engage in the aponeurotic substance of the quadriceps and patellar tendons and thereby obtain purchase in this tough tissue alongside the bone. This concept becomes evident from reading the discussion of Cucuel and Rigaud in which they say, "M. Malgaigne has recommended several years ago a pair of claws to maintain the fragments of the patella, but his claws were only supposed to press upon the fragments. I have gone further. I have driven the claws just inside the substance of the patella and have maintained the fragments, thus hooked, using two *vis de rappel*."[19] The *vis de rappel* was in fact the technique of inserting a screw into each fragment and then binding these screws together with twine as Rigaud described for the olecranon, as mentioned previously. Thus, the metal claw device of Malgaigne became a true external fixator. It is interesting to note in later publications[61] that this device was also used indirectly to approximate fragments of the patella by drawing together molded gutta percha splints (Fig. 1–19).

An ingenious modification of Malgaigne's metal claw was proposed in 1852 by Chassin[13] for use on displaced fractures of the clavicle. It consisted of two pairs of points of claws, smaller than but similar in design to the Malgaigne device, but also incorporating two finger screws that could, in addition, be advanced down on the fragments to correct anteroposterior displacements (Fig. 1–20). These additional pointed screws were admitted by Chassin to be inspired by the other device of Malgaigne, *la*

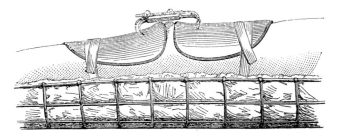

FIGURE 1–19. The Malgaigne claw device (1870), here used to control gutta percha splints for a fractured patella.

pointe métallique. In describing this device in his treatise, Bérenger Féraud gave a glimpse of his vision of the future, saying "Could one not say by varying the form of the claws, surgeons would be able to apply them to a great quantity of bones of the skeleton and I am persuaded that before long we will have observations of fractures of the metacarpus, the metatarsus, the radius or the ulna, the ribs, the apophyses of the scapula treated in this manner. Who knows even if one would not be able to make claws sufficiently powerful, whilst remaining narrow enough, to maintain fragments of the tibia, the femur, or the humerus." Was he not indeed foreseeing the development in the 20th century of the widespread use of external fixation?

Hitherto, these devices had simply punctured the surface of the bone, and it was a British surgeon at the West London Hospital, Mr. Keetley,[40] who first described an external fixation device deliberately implanted into the full diameter of the bone. In 1801, Benjamin Bell wrote that "an effectual method of securing oblique fractures in the bones of the extremities and especially of the thigh bone, is perhaps one of the greatest desiderata of modern surgery. In all ages the difficulty of this has been confessedly great and frequent lameness produced by shortened limbs arising from this cause evidently shows that we are still deficient in our branch of practice."[4]

Inspired by these words, Keetley produced a device to hold the femur out to length in cases of oblique fracture. "A

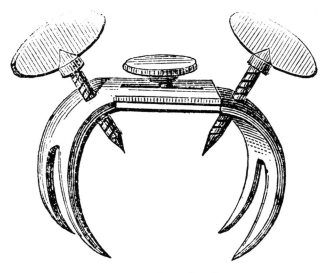

FIGURE 1–20. Chassin's clavicular fixator (1852).

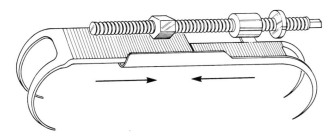

FIGURE 1–18. The *griffe métallique*, or claw, of Malgaigne (1843).

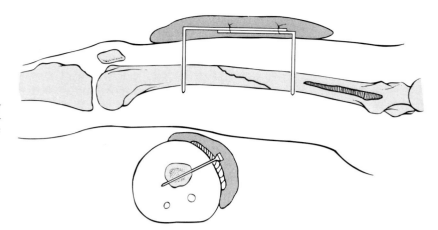

FIGURE 1-21. The external fixation device invented by Keetley of the West London Hospital, England—probably the first to be drilled into the substance of the bone. (Redrawn from Lancet, 1893.)

carefully purified pin of thickly plated steel, made to enter through a puncture in the skin, cleansed with equal care" was passed through drill holes, one in each main fragment, and then the two horizontal arms of each device, suitably notched along the edges, were united by twists of wire, the whole then being dressed with a wrapping of iodoform gauze (Fig. 1–21). This device obviously inspired Chalier, who described his *crampon extensible*, an apparatus very similar in principle but perhaps a little more sophisticated in design.[12] Something approaching the type of external fixation device with which we are today familiar was documented in 1897 by Dr. Clayton Parkhill of Denver, Colorado (Fig. 1–22). He recounted that, in 1894, he devised a new method of immobilization of bones, initially for the treatment of a young man with a pseudarthrosis of the humerus following a gunshot wound 11 months previously. He described the device (Fig. 1–23) as

> . . . a steel clamp made up of separable pieces in order to secure easy and accurate adjustment. It is heavily plated with silver in order to secure the antiseptic action of that metal. Clamps of different sizes are made to correspond with the bone upon which they are used; the largest sizes for the femur, the intermediate sizes for the humerus and tibia, the smallest sizes for radius, ulna, fibula and clavicle. The instrument consists essentially of four screws, or shafts. On these are cut threads at the lower end and also near the upper end. The extreme upper end, however, is made square so that the screw may be governed by a clock key. Two sets of wing plates are attached to these screws, a shorter pair corresponding to the inner screws and a longer pair to the outer. Each is attached to its screws by two nuts, one above the plate and the other below for accuracy of adjustment. When in position, one wing plate overlies the other in each half of the instrument. When ready to be clamped these plates lie side by side. They are fastened together by a steel clamp with a screw at either end.

In 1898, he recorded the use of his device in 14 cases, mainly of pseudarthrosis or malunion of the femur, humerus, forearm, and tibia, although there was one case of a refracture of a previously united patella treated by immediate application of the Parkhill clamp.[60] He claimed that union had been secured in every case in which the clamp had been employed, the clamp was easy to use and prevented motion between the fragments, the screws inserted into the bone stimulated the production of callus, no secondary operation was necessary, and after removal nothing was left in the tissues "that might reduce their vitality or lead to pain and infection."

It was only a few years later, across the Atlantic, on

FIGURE 1-22. Dr. Clayton Parkhill of Denver, Colorado. (Courtesy of Dr. Walter W. Jones and the Denver County Medical Society.)

FIGURE 1–23. The external fixation device of Parkhill (1894). (Redrawn from Annals of Surgery, 1898.)

April 24, 1902, that Albin Lambotte first used his own external fixation device. This device was fairly primitive, consisting of pins screwed into the main fragments of a comminuted fracture of the femur, two above and two below, with the pins then clamped together by sandwiching them between two heavy metal plates bolted together. Subsequently, he devised a more sophisticated type of external fixator in which the protruding ends of the screws were bolted to adjustable clamps linked with a heavy external bar (Fig. 1–24). Lambotte recorded the use of his external fixator in many sites, including the clavicle and the first metacarpal.

Over the next few decades a number of devices were described, two of which were particularly notable for their ingenuity. In 1919, Crile[18] described a method of maintaining the reduction of femoral fragments that consisted of (1) a peg driven into the neck of the femur via the outer face of the greater trochanter, this peg bearing externally a metal sphere; (2) a metallic caliper bearing double points that were driven into the condyles of the distal femur that also bore a metal sphere to form part of a ball joint; and (3) an external linking device with a universal joint at each end capable of being clamped onto the metal spheres and also capable itself of extension via a lengthening screw (Fig. 1–25). He described its use in only one case, that of a gunshot wound of the femur sustained by a young soldier in 1918. This wound had been particularly contaminated and, using his device after a period of initial traction with a Thomas splint, Crile succeeded in gaining control of the soft tissue infection and securing early union of the fracture. The soldier was discharged to England 9 weeks after injury following removal of the apparatus. In 1931, Conn[16] described an articulated external linkage device that consisted of two duralumin slotted plates

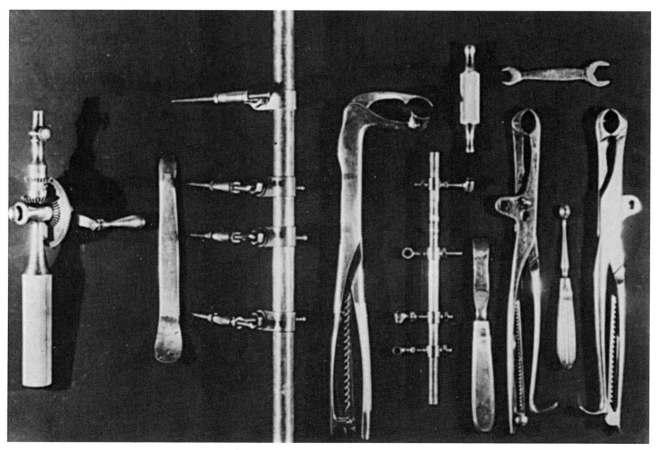

FIGURE 1–24. Some of the instruments of Lambotte in the collection of the University Hospital of Ghent, Belgium, including a Lambotte *fixateur externe.*

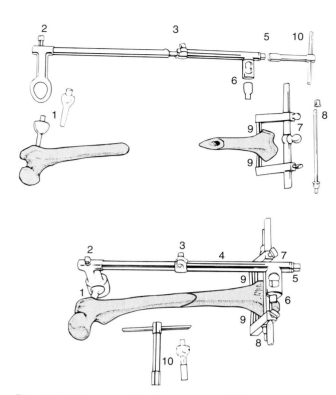

FIGURE 1–25. The external fixation apparatus of Crile.

linked in the center by a lockable ball-and-socket joint. Half pins were then driven into the bone fragments, two above the fracture and two below, with the pins then bolted to the slotted plates and the fracture adjusted at the universal joint before locking it with a steel bolt. He reported 20 cases with no delay in union and emphasized that the early motion of the joints of the limb, permitted by his device, had allowed prompt return to function. Conn also emphasized scrupulous pin tract care, recommending daily removal of dried serum and application of alcohol.

Hitherto, all external fixation devices had relied on half pins and a single external linkage device. The first fracture apparatus using transfixion pins with a bilateral frame was that of Pitkin and Blackfield.[62] In the 1930s and 1940s, Anderson of Seattle experimented with a great variety of external fixation configurations, enclosing the whole of the apparatus in plaster casts. He emphasized the benefits of early weight bearing and joint mobilization, but contrary to the advice of Conn, he recommended that wounds should not be dressed or disturbed "even though there is present some discharge and odour." His ideas were by no means universally accepted, and indeed in World War II, the advice given to American army surgeons working in the European theater was that "the use of Steinmann pins incorporated in plaster of Paris or the use of metallic external fixation splints leads to gross infection or ulceration in a high percentage of cases. This method of treatment is not to be employed in the Third Army."[14]

In Switzerland, Raoul Hoffmann of Geneva was developing his own system of external fixation, the early results of which he published in 1938.[36] Although many devices

had been invented for external fixation and the literature abounded with reports of series of cases treated in this manner, it was not until the 1960s that, building on the groundwork of Hoffman, both Burny and Bourgois[11] and Vidal and co-workers[79] started to outline the biomechanical principles on which external fixation was based. This led the way to the universal acceptance of this method of fracture management. An interesting by-product of improved external fixation has been the opportunity for surgical lengthening of bones, although it has to be pointed out that this was first described in 1921 by Vittorio Putti, who used a transfixion device.[65]

INTRAMEDULLARY FIXATION

As previously discussed, pioneers such as von Langenbeck, Koenig, Cheyne, Lambotte, and Lane had all used intramedullary screw fixation in the management of fractures of the neck of the femur. In addition, there are a number of reported instances of intramedullary devices in the neck of the femur being used for the management of nonunion, including the extensive operation of Gillette, who used the transtrochanteric approach to perform an intracapsular fixation of ununited femoral neck fractures using intramedullary bone pegs.[27] Curtis used a drill bit—as, reputedly, had Langenbeck—in the neck of the femur, and Charles Thompson used silver nails in 1899.[7] Lambotte also recorded the use of a long intramedullary screw in the management of a displaced fracture of the neck of the humerus in 1906.

In the late 19th century, attempts were made to secure fixation of fractures using intramedullary ivory pegs, and Bircher is credited with their first use in 1886.[8] Short intramedullary devices of beef bone and of human bone were also used by Hoglund.[37] Toward the end of the first decade of the century, Ernest Hey Groves, of Bristol, England, was using massive three- and four-flanged intramedullary nails for the fixation of diaphyseal fractures of the femur, the humerus, and the ulna.[66] Hey Groves' early attempts at intramedullary fixations of this type were complicated by infection, earning him the epithet "septic Ernie" among his West Country colleagues. Metallic intramedullary fixation of bone was not at that time generally accepted. In the late 1920s the work of Smith-Peterson,[75] who used a trifin nail for the intramedullary fixation of subcapital fractures of the femur, represented a great step forward in the management of what has since been referred to as the *unsolved fracture*, and that remained the standard management for this type of injury for some 40 years.

The use of stout wires and thin solid rods in the intramedullary cavities of long bones was recommended by Lambrinudi in 1940.[43] This technique was further developed in the United States by the brothers Rush,[68] who subsequently developed a system of flexible nails, still in occasional use.

The concept of a long metallic intramedullary device that gripped the endosteal surface of the bone—so-called elastic nailing—was the brainchild of Gerhardt Küntscher working in collaboration with Professor Fischer and the engineer Ernst Pohl at Kiel University in Germany in the 1930s. Küntscher originally used a V-shaped nail but then changed to a nail with a cloverleaf cross section for greater strength and designed to follow any guide pin more faithfully. Küntscher published his first book on intramedullary nailing at the end of World War II. Although it was written in 1942, the illustrations for it were destroyed in the air raids on Leipzig, so the book was not published until 1945.[41] For reasons that are not entirely clear, this outstanding German surgeon was virtually banished to Lapland from 1943 until the end of the European war. He was dispatched as head of the medical office at the German Military Surgical Hospital in Kemi, northern Finland. It is interesting to note that he departed Kemi in something of a hurry in September 1944 by air and left behind him a huge stock of intramedullary nails that became available for the Finnish surgeons to use.[48]

Küntscher was a brilliant technical surgeon, and his results, being so impressive, caused a somewhat overenthusiastic adoption of intramedullary nailing in Europe in the early years after World War II. According to Lindholm, this was reflected in the comments of the leading European trauma surgeon, Professor Lorenz Böhler of Vienna (Fig. 1–26). In 1944, Böhler[9] said:

> Küntscher in his publication has briefly, thoroughly and with clarity described the techniques and indications for closed marrow nailing of fresh uncomplicated fractures of the thigh, lower leg and upper arm. He has also pointed out how to perform nailing of fresh, complicated, inveterate and nonhealed fractures. It has been an enormous surprise compared with our experiences to see a man with such a serious femoral fracture walk without a plaster cast or any bandage with reasonably moving joints only fourteen days after the accident.

A year later, he wrote in the preface to the next edition of his book,

> Later experience has revealed that the risks with marrow nailing are much greater than first predicted. We therefore use it as a rule only in femoral fractures. . . . Marrow nailing of other long bones which I have also recommended is shown by long term follow ups often to be more deleterious than profitable.

Britain appeared somewhat slow to adopt the teachings of Küntscher, possibly as a result of the influence of Hey Groves' early experiments with metallic intramedullary fixation. The January 3, 1948, issue of *Lancet* contained a somewhat flippant and puerile commentary by a "peripatetic correspondent" on the techniques of Küntscher, in which Lorenz Böhler, by that time advocating caution in relation to intramedullary nailing, was described as the "Moses of the Orthopaedic Sinai"! It is not surprising that the author chose to remain anonymous. In 1950, Le Vay, of London, published an interesting account of a visit to Küntscher's clinic, but in summing up his general impressions of Küntscher's technique, he wrote:

> It was clear that Küntscher disliked extensive open bone operations or any disturbance of the periosteum and he stated that every such intervention delayed healing. He believed that the advantage of closed nailing lay in the avoidance of such disturbance and the fact that surgical intervention could be limited. All his procedures reflected this attitude: refusal to expose a simple fracture for nailing, avoidance of bone grafting operations, dislike of plates and screws and his very limited approach for arthrodesis of the knee joint. One was bound to conclude that such methods were evolved under the pressure of circumstances—the shortage of

Figure 1–26. Professor Lorenz Böhler (in uniform) photographed during World War II, talking to Adolph Lorenz.

FIGURE 1–27. Gerhardt Küntscher (1900 to 1972), the great German pioneer of intramedullary nailing.

skilled nurses, the lack of penicillin, the need for immediate fixation without transfer, and above all the total lack of certainty as to the duration of postoperative stay in hospital determined by the doubtful number of hospital beds that would be available. A virtue was made of necessity.[47]

Sadly, such smug complacency and self-satisfaction were not totally uncharacteristic of the British approach to innovation in fracture surgery at that time. In contrast, Milton Silverman in the *Saturday Evening Post* in 1955 said that Küntscher's invention was the most significant medical advance to come out of Germany since the discovery of sulfonamide. Küntscher developed interlocking femoral and tibial nails, an intramedullary bone saw for endosteal osteotomy, an expanding nail for the distal tibia, the "signal arm" nail for trochanteric fractures, cannulated flexible powered intramedullary reamers, and an intramedullary nail to apply compression across fracture sites. All this was done in collaboration with his engineer, Ernst Pohl, and his lifetime technical assistant, Gerhardt Breske, whom I had the great fortune to visit in his home in 1985. Herr Breske told me that Küntscher was a great lover of life: he swam every day, he enjoyed humor and parties and was a great practical joker, but never married, according to Herr Breske, because "he was far too busy." Gerhardt Küntscher (Fig. 1–27) died in 1972 at his desk, working on yet a further edition of his book on intramedullary nailing. He was found slumped over his final manuscript by Dr. Wolfgang Wolfers, chief of surgery at the St. Franziskus Hospital of Flensberg, where from 1965 onward Küntscher had worked as a guest surgeon.

The pioneering work of Küntscher was taken further by modifications of design and technique made by the AO group (see following section), and the distillation of this

great experience resulted in the work in the 1960s and 1970s of Klemm, Schellmann, Grosse, and Kempf in the development of the current generation of interlocking nailing systems. Aside from this mainstream of development of intramedullary nailing following on the work of Küntscher, there have been a multitude of different designs of intramedullary fixation devices, such as those of Soeur, Westborne, Hansen and Street, Schneider, and Huckstep. The only other device to have achieved anything like widespread acceptance, however, has been that of Zickel, which incorporates at its upper end a trifin nail to secure purchase in the proximal femur in the management of fractures in the high subtrochanteric region.

ROBERT DANIS AND THE DEVELOPMENT OF THE AO GROUP

Robert Danis (1880 to 1962) (Fig. 1–28) must be regarded as the father of modern osteosynthesis. Graduating from the University of Brussels in 1904, he practiced as a general surgeon, his early interests being in thoracic and vascular surgery. He became professor of theoretical and practical surgery at the University of Brussels in 1921 and while there developed a great interest in internal fixation of

FIGURE 1–28. Robert Danis (1880 to 1962), the only known photograph. (Courtesy of his son, Dr. A. Danis.)

fractures. Although there is no direct evidence, one cannot help but feel that he must have been profoundly influenced by the mobilizers—Seutin, Paget, Lucas-Championnière, Lambotte, Lane, and Sherman, to mention but a few—in developing his concepts of immediate stable internal fixation to permit functional rehabilitation. His vast experience in this field was brought together in his monumental publication *Théorie et Pratique de l'Ostéosynthèse*.[20] In the first section of this book on the aims of osteosynthesis, he wrote that an osteosynthesis is not entirely satisfactory unless it attains the three following objectives:

(1) The possibility of immediate and active mobilisation of the muscles of the region and of the neighbouring joints,

(2) Complete restoration of the bone to its original form, and

(3) The *soudure per primam* (primary bone healing) of the bony fragments without the formation of apparent callus.

Danis devised numerous techniques of osteosynthesis based principally on interfragmentary compression, using screws and a device that he called his *coapteur*, which was basically a plate designed to produce axial compression between two main bone fragments (Fig. 1–29). It would appear from his writings that Danis' primary aim was to produce fracture stabilization that was so rigid that he could ignore the broken bone and preserve the function of the other parts of the injured limb. In achieving such sound stabilization of the fracture by anatomic reduction and interfragmentary compression, he also produced, possibly by serendipity, the biomechanical and anatomic environment that permitted the bone to heal by direct remodeling of the cortical bone, without external callus. Having observed this type of healing, which he called *soudure autogène*, or self-welding, he took this as an indication that his osteosynthesis had achieved its primary objective. The other side of this coin, however, was that if callus did appear, it was an indication that he had failed to produce the environment of stability that he had wished. He cannot initially have set out to produce direct bone healing before he had personally observed it, so he seems

finally to have turned an observation of a secondary effect into the third aim of osteosynthesis as outlined previously, later causing some confusion of attitudes to callus. It is interesting to note, however, that Danis was not the first to observe healing of a diaphyseal fracture without external callus, as this was recorded by Layton in one of Arbuthnot Lane's cases.

In the first section of his book, in discussing direct bone healing, Danis made the prophetic statement, "This *soudure autogène* which occurs as discretely as in the case of an incomplete fissure fracture certainly merits experimental study to establish in detail what are the modifications brought about by an ideal osteosynthesis of the phenomena of consolidation." Robert Danis could not have realized how comprehensively this suggestion would be taken up or the profound influence that it would have on the evolution of the surgical management of fractures over the ensuing 40 years.

On March 1, 1950, a young Swiss surgeon, Dr. Maurice Müller, who had read Danis' work, paid the great surgeon a visit in Brussels. This visit left such an impression on young Dr. Müller, to whom Robert Danis presented an autographed copy of his book, that the young Swiss returned to his homeland determined to embrace and develop the principles of the ideal osteosynthesis, as outlined by Danis, and to investigate the scientific basis for his observations. Over the next few years, Müller inspired a number of close colleagues to share his passion for the improvement of techniques for the internal fixation of fractures (Fig. 1–30), gathering around himself particularly Hans Willenegger of Liestal, Robert Schneider of Grosshöchstetten, and subsequently Martin Allgöwer of Chur, who together laid the intellectual and indeed practical groundwork for a momentous gathering in the Kantonsspital of Chur on March 15 to 17, 1958. The other guests at this meeting were Bandi, Baumann, Eckmann, Guggenbühl, Hunziker, Molo, Nicole, Ott, Patry, Schär, and Stähli. Over the 3 days, a number of scientific papers on osteosynthesis were presented, and the assembled surgeons formed a study group to look into all aspects of internal fixation—*Arbeitsgemeinschaft für Osteosynthesefragen*, or AO. This was indeed a very active group that built on Danis' work in an industrious and productive way.

There were basically three channels of activity. First, a laboratory for experimental surgery was set up in Davos, Switzerland, initially under the direction of Martin Allgöwer and subsequently Herbert Fleisch, who was succeeded by the current director, Stefan Perren, in 1967. These workers, in collaboration with Robert Schenk, professor of anatomy at the University of Bern, instituted, and have since continued, an ever-expanding experimental program that early on clearly defined the exact process of direct bone healing and the influence of skeletal stability on the pattern of bone union, laying the foundation for our modern understanding of bone healing in various mechanical environments. Second, the group also set out, in collaboration with metallurgists and engineers in Switzerland, to devise a system of implants and instruments to apply the biomechanical principles emerging from their investigations and so enable them to produce the skeletal stability necessary to achieve the objectives enunciated by

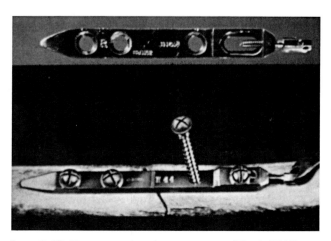

FIGURE 1–29. The compression plate, or *coapteur*, of Danis (1949).

FIGURE 1–30. Hans Willenegger, Maurice Müller, and Martin Allgöwer, three of the founders of Arbeitsgemeinschaft für Osteosynthesefragen (AO), pictured in the late 1950s. (Courtesy of Professor Müller.)

Danis. Third, they decided to document their clinical experience, and a center was set up in Bern, which continues to the present day with the documentation of osteosyntheses from all over the world.

It was not long before the work of this group, and of the other surgeons who over the years became associated with them, bore fruit and laid the foundation for our current practice of osteosynthesis. It became necessary to educate surgeons in both the scientific and the technical aspects of this new system of osteosynthesis, and combined theoretical and practical courses in AO techniques were held from 1960 onward in Davos, Switzerland, continuing annually to the present day (Fig. 1–31). Since 1965, courses have been held in many other institutions, and scholarships have allowed surgeons to visit centers of excellence throughout the world.[70] No other single group of surgeons, coming together to pursue a common scientific and clinical aim, has had such an influence on the management of fractures. It is therefore entirely fitting that this account of the history of the care of fractures should include consideration of this group, which as the AO Foundation, the umbrella under which the clinical, scientific, and educational activities of AO continue, remains at the forefront of the development of scientific thought and technical progress in this field.

■ *Just before Christmas 1999, Hans R. Willenegger passed away. As the head of the Kantonsspital Liestal in 1958, he played a pivotal role in the creation of the AO. Thanks to his initiative, links were forged with Straumann, a metallurgical research institute, which helped to solve problems with the implant material. Out of this collaboration arose the industrial production of Synthes implants and instruments with a scientific background. Parallel with this, Willenegger made contact with R. Schenk, at that time professor at the Institute of Anatomy at Basel, who contributed histologic knowledge to their experimental work in bone healing. Soon Willenegger realized that performing an osteosynthesis in a suboptimal way could create a catastrophic complication. Being willing to help such patients, Liestal became a center for the treatment of post-traumatic osteomyelitis, pseudarthrosis, and malunion.*

This experience led Willenegger to initiate the worldwide teaching of the AO principles. He became the first president of AO International in 1972. This event marked the starting point of many years of global traveling, teaching AO in all five continents. Countless are the slides he gave to future AO teachers, carefully

FIGURE 1–31. Martin Allgöwer instructing the late Professor John Charnley at one of the earliest Arbeitsgemeinschaft für Osteosynthesefragen (AO) instructional courses in Davos, Switzerland, circa 1961.

explaining the basic principles underlying each one. Worldwide, many of us recall a personal souvenir of a direct contact with him and are conscious that we have lost a friend. ∎

GAVRIIL A. ILIZAROV AND THE DISCOVERY OF DISTRACTION OSTEOGENESIS

Stuart A. Green, M.D.

In the 1950s, Gavriil A. Ilizarov, a Soviet surgeon working in the Siberian city of Kurgan, made a serendipitous discovery: slow, steady distraction of a recently cut bone (securely stabilized in an external fixator) leads to the formation of new bone within the widening gap. At the time, Ilizarov was using a circular external skeletal fixator that he had designed in 1951 to distract knee joints that had developed flexion contractures after prolonged plaster cast immobilization (during World War II). The device consisted of two Kirschner wire traction bows connected to each other by threaded rods.

Ilizarov originally developed his fixator to stretch out the soft tissues gradually on the posterior side of a contracted knee joint. One patient, however, had bony, rather than fibrous, ankylosis of his knee in the flexed position. After performing a bone-cutting osteotomy on this patient through the knee, Ilizarov had the patient gradually straighten out the limb by turning nuts on the fixator surrounding his limb. Ilizarov intended to insert a bone graft into the resulting triangular bone defect when the knee was straight. To his surprise, Ilizarov found a wedge-shaped mass of newly regenerated bone at the site of osteotomy when distraction was finished.

Extending his observations, Ilizarov after that time developed an entire system of orthopaedics and traumatology based on his axially stable tensioned wire circular external fixator and the bone's ability to form a "regenerate" of newly formed osseous tissue within a widening distraction gap.

Employing his discovery of distraction osteogenesis, Ilizarov used various modifications of his apparatus to elongate, rotate, angulate, or shift segments of bones gradually with respect to each other. The fixation system's adaptability also permits the reduction and fixation of many unstable fracture patterns.

Until his death in 1992, Professor Ilizarov headed a 1000-bed clinical and research institute staffed by 350 orthopaedic surgeons and 60 scientists with Ph.D. degrees, where patients from Russia and the rest of the world come for the treatment of birth defects, dwarfism, complications of traumatic injuries, and other disorders of the musculoskeletal system.

For many years, Professor Ilizarov and his co-workers have trained surgeons from socialist countries in his techniques. Around 1980, Italian orthopaedists learned of Ilizarov's methods when others from their country returned from Yugoslavia and nearby Eastern European countries with circular fixators on their limbs. Soon thereafter, Italian, other European, and, more recently, North American orthopaedic surgeons have ventured to Siberia for training in the Ilizarov method.

The techniques and applications of the Ilizarov method have continued to improve with time, both in Russia and around the world. One important advance in the technique of fixator application consists of the substitution of titanium half pins for stainless steel wires in many locations, thereby adding to patients' comfort and acceptance of the apparatus.

Nevertheless, much clinical and scientific work investigating the Ilizarov method remains to be done. Biomechanical and histochemical studies are needed. The health care insurance industry has been slow to recognize the magnitude of Ilizarov's discoveries. They must be educated. A generation of orthopaedic surgeons requires training in the method. With time, however, Ilizarov's discoveries will become fully integrated into modern clinical practice.

EMILE LETOURNEL AND THE SURGERY OF PELVIC AND ACETABULAR FRACTURES

Joel M. Matta, M.D.

Emile Letournel (Fig. 1–32) was born on the French island territory of St. Pierre et Miquelon, situated between Newfoundland and Nova Scotia. Thus, he was born in France and also in North America. This small fishing territory is completely under French control, including the economy and language.

As he developed an interest in orthopaedic surgery, it became necessary for him to apply for a postgraduate position to continue his education. The application process required the applicant to visit all the professors who were offering training positions. Being from St. Pierre, Letournel had no letters of support to contend adequately for the available orthopaedic positions. He was very concerned about not being able to acquire an orthopaedic

FIGURE 1–32. Professeur Emile Letournel.

position, when a friend suggested he meet with Professor Robert Judet. He did this out of desperation, without any hope of obtaining a position. The meeting with Judet was very brief. Professor Judet asked Letournel for his letters of recommendation, of which he had none, but Letournel indicated to him his sincere desire to obtain Judet's training position. Judet told him that he had a 6-month opening the following year. The 6-month position lasted 12 months, and Letournel then became Judet's assistant in his private clinic and advanced to associate professor and professor in 1970. He did not leave Judet until Judet's retirement in 1978. Letournel then became head of the Department of Orthopaedic Surgery at the Centre Medico-Chirurgie de la Port de Choisey in southeastern Paris. He remained there until his retirement from academic medicine in October 1993. He subsequently went into private practice at the Villa Medicis, Courbevoie, France, a suburb of Paris.

It was during his time at Choisey that physicians from North America had their greatest contact with Professeur Letournel. The importance of his work, inspired and begun by Robert Judet, was not widely recognized until the 1980s. Despite this long delay in acceptance and recognition, North America was actually one of the first areas to understand and adopt his techniques, which was a fact he certainly recognized and appreciated through his continued contact with us.

An intelligent and creative surgeon is typically able to contribute only a few components of new discoveries during the course of his or her career, but Emile Letournel accomplished much more. He completely revolutionized the way we conceptualize and treat acetabular fractures. Judet recognized problems with nonoperative treatment of acetabular fractures and inspired Letournel to begin the work that would define the surgical anatomy of the acetabulum, the pathologic anatomy of fresh fractures, and the radiographic interpretation to define these injuries. Following this, he developed surgical approaches. First, Judet combined the Kocher and Langenbeck approaches to make the Kocher-Langenbeck. Later Letournel developed the ilioinguinal and finally the iliofemoral approach. Techniques of reduction as well as internal fixation were developed. Finally, the radiographic, clinical, and statistical documentation of immediate and long-term results of the surgical treatment became a lifelong passion of Letournel.

Letournel was committed to the idea of creating a comprehensive instructional course that taught the surgical treatment of fractures of the acetabulum and pelvis. Although he had been received so positively in North America, he felt he remained incompletely recognized in France. Therefore, the first course in 1984 was held in Paris but with faculty from North America and England, and he conducted the course in English. Letournel's Paris course set the standard and educational model for acetabulum and pelvis courses to follow. In all, there were nine courses consisting of lectures with intense study of radiographs. Surgical technique was taught with lectures, plastic bones, and live surgery, and there was always a day at the historic Paris anatomy institute, the Fer à Moulin. Every course included a black-tie banquet, always with the same fine musicians and Letournel singing "La Prune" and, if the spirit was right, the "Marseillaise." His Paris meetings

culminated in the May 1993 first international symposium on the results of the surgical treatment of fractures of the acetabulum. His radiographic description and classification system, which was originally established in 1960 and by this time was a well-established world language, was used throughout the symposium for clear understanding of the statistical results.

Professeur Emile Letournel died relatively suddenly after an illness of only 2 months. Up to this time, he maintained his busy surgical schedule, traveled, and taught. We, his pupils and patients throughout the world, are fortunate to have enjoyed his great persona and contributions.

SUMMARY

Christopher L. Colton, M.D.

As technology advances, so do the severity and frequency of traumatic insult, and the demand for ever-increasing skill on the part of the fracture surgeon grows likewise. It is only by the study of the history of our surgical forebears and by keeping in mind how they have striven, often in the face of fierce criticism, to achieve the apparently unattainable that young surgeons will continue to be inspired to emulate them and so carry forward the progress they have achieved.

Any consideration of the history of 5000 years of endeavor, confined of necessity within the strictures of a publication such as this, is perforce eclectic. Nevertheless, in deciding to highlight the achievements of some, I have not in any way set out to minimize the pioneering work of those whose activities have not been specifically detailed in this overview, and with respect to these necessary omissions I ask the reader's indulgence.

REFERENCES

1. Amerasinghe, D.M.; Veerasingham, P.B. Early weight bearing in tibial shaft fractures protected by wooden splints. Proc Kandy Med Soc 4:(pages unnumbered), 1981.
2. Assen, J. van; Meyerding, H.W. Antonius Mathijsen, the discoverer of the plaster bandage. J Bone Joint Surg Am 30:1018, 1948.
3. Bacon, L.W. On the history of the introduction of plaster of Paris bandages. Bull Soc Med Hist 3:122, 1923.
4. Bell, B. System of Surgery, 7th ed., Vol. 2. Edinburgh, Bell and Bradfute, 1801, p. 21.
5. Bérenger Féraud, L.J.B. De l'emploi de la pointe de Malgaigne dans les fractures. Rev Ther Medicochir 15:228, 256, 1867.
6. Bérenger Féraud, L.J.B. Traité de l'Immobilisation Directe des Fragments Osseux dans les Fractures. Paris, Delahaye, 1870, p. 371.
7. Billroth, W. Clinical Surgery. London, The New Sydenham Society, 1881.
8. Bircher, H. Eine neue Methode unmittelbarer Retention bei Frakturen der Roehrenknochen. Arch Klin Chir 34:91, 1886.
9. Böhler, L. Vorwort zur 1 bis 4 Auflage, Wien, im Januar 1944. Technik der Knochenruchbehandlung im Frieden und in den Kriege, 1944, pp. IV–V.
10. Bonnet: Mémoire sur les fractures du fémur. Gaz Med Paris, 1839.
11. Burny, F.; Bourgois, R. Étude bioméchanique de l'ostéotaxis. In: La Fixation Externe en Chirurgie. Brussels, Imprimerie Médicale et Scientifique, 1965.
12. Chalier, A. Nouvel appareil prothétique pour ostéosynthèse (crampon extensible). Presse Med 25:585, 1907.
13. Chassin. Thèse de Paris, 1852, p. 63.
14. Cleveland, M. Surgery in World War II: Orthopedic Surgery in the European Theater of Operations. Washington, DC, Office of the Surgeon General, Dept. of the Army, 1956, p. 77.

15. Commeiras. J Soc Med Montpellier, 1847.

16. Conn, H.R. The internal fixation of fractures. J Bone Joint Surg 13:261, 1931.

17. Cooper, A. Treatise on Dislocations and on Fractures of the Joints. London, Longman, Hurst, Rees, Orme, Brown and Green, 1822.

18. Crile, D.W. Fracture of the femur: A method of holding the fragments in difficult cases. Br J Surg 4:458, 1919.

19. Cucuel; Rigaud. Des vis métalliques enfoncées dans le tissue des os pour le traitement de certaines fractures. Rev Medicochir Paris 8:113, 1850.

20. Danis, R. Théorie et Pratique de l'Ostéosynthèse. Paris, Masson, 1949.

21. Dowden, J.W. The Principle of Early Active Movement in Treating Fractures of the Upper Extremity. London, Oliver & Boyd, 1924.

22. Eaton W. Survey of the Turkish Empire. London, 1798.

23. Elst, V.E. Les débuts de l'ostéosynthése en Belgique. Private publication for Société Belge de Chirurgie Orthopédique et de Traumatologie. Brussels, Imp des Sciences, 1971.

24. Evans, P.E.L. Cerclage fixation of a fractured humerus in 1775: Fact or fiction? Clin Orthop 174:138, 1983.

25. Gersdorf, H. von. Feldtbuch der Wundartzney. Strasbourg, 1517.

26. Gooch, B. Cases and Practical Remarks in Surgery. Norwich, W. Chase, 1767.

27. Guthrie, D. A History of Medicine. London, T. Nelson, 1945, p. 124.

28. Guthrie, G. Direct fixation of fractures. Am Med March:376, 1903.

29. Hamilton, F.H. Treatise on Military Surgery and Hygiene. New York, Baillière, 1865.

30. Hansmann. Eine neue Methode der Fixirung der Fragmente bei complicirten Fracturen. Verh Dtsch Ges Chir 15:134, 1886.

31. Hartshorne, E. On the causes and treatment of pseudarthrosis and especially that form of it sometimes called supernumerary joint. Am J Med Sci 1:121, 1841.

32. Heister, L. Chirurgie Complète. Paris, 1739.

33. Helferich, H. Atlas and Grundriss der traumatischen Frakturen und Luxationen. München, Lehmann Verlag, 1906, p. 170.

34. Hitzrot. Transactions of New York Surgical Society. Ann Surg 83:301, 1926.

35. Hoffa, A. Lehrbuch der Fracturen und Luxationen für Arzte und Studierende. Wurzburg, 1896.

36. Hoffmann, R. Rotules à os pour la réduction dirigeé, non sanglante, des fractures (ostéotaxis). Helv Med Acta 6:844, 1938.

37. Hoglund, E.J. New intramedullary bone transplant. Surg Gynecol Obstet 24:243, 1917.

38. Hubenthal. Nouveau manière de traiter les fractures. Nouv J Med 5:210, 1817.

39. Icart, J.F. Lettre à réponse au mémoire de M. Pujol. Médicin de Castres et de l'Hôtel-Dieu, sur une amputation naturelle de la jambe avec des réflexions sur quelques autres cas rélatifs a cette operation, 1775.

40. Keetley, C.B. On the prevention of shortening and other forms of malunion after fracture, by the use of metal pins passed into the fragments subcutaneously. Lancet June 10:137, 1893.

41. Küntscher, G. Die Technik der Marknagelung gemeinsam mit B. Maatz. Leipzig, Thieme, 1945.

42. Lambotte, A. Chirurgie Opératoire des Fractures. Paris, Masson, 1913.

43. Lambrinudi, C. Intramedullary Kirschner wires in the treatment of fractures. Proc R Soc Med 33:153, 1940.

44. Lane, W.A. Clinical remarks on the operative treatment of simple fractures. BMJ 2:1325, 1905.

45. Lane, W.A. Operative Treatment of Fractures, 2nd ed. London, 1914, p. 126.

46. Layton, T.B. Sir William Arbuthnot Lane, Bt. C.B., M.S.: An Enquiry into the Mind and Influence of a Surgeon. Edinburgh, Livingstone, 1956.

47. Le Vay, A.D. Intramedullary nailing in the Küntscher clinic. J Bone Joint Surg Br 32:698, 1950.

48. Lindholm, R.V. The bone nailing surgeon: G.B.G. Küntscher and the Finns. Acta Universitatis Ouluensis B10 Historica 5.

49. Lucas-Championnière, J. Trépanation Néolithique, Trépanation Pré-Colombienne des Kabyles, Trépanation Traditionelle. Paris, Steinheil, 1912.

50. Lucas-Championnière, J. Les dangers l'immobilisation des membres—Fragilité des os—Altération de la nutrition du membre—Conclusions pratiques. J Med Chir Prat 78:8187, 1907.

51. Malgaigne, J.F. Traitement des fractures de la jambe par le platre coulé, suivant la méthode de M. Dieffenbach de Berlin. Gaz Med Paris, 1832.

52. Malgaigne, J.F. A Treatise of Fractures. Philadelphia, J.B. Lippincott, 1859.

53. Mathijsen, A. Nieuwe Wijze van Aanwending van het Gipsverband. Eene Bijdrage Tot de Militaire Chirurgie. Haarlem, van Loghen, 1852.

54. Milne, J.S. The apparatus used by the Greeks and the Romans in the setting of fractures and the reduction of dislocations. Interstate Med J 16:3, 1909.

55. Monro, J.K. The history of plaster of Paris in the treatment of fractures. J Bone Joint Surg 23:257, 1935.

56. Mooney, V.; Nickel, V.L.; Harvey, J.P.; Snelson, R. Cast brace treatment for fractures of the distal part of the femur. J Bone Joint Surg Am 52:1563, 1970.

57. Orr, H.W. Wounds and Fractures. A Clinical Guide to Civil and Military Practice. London, Baillière, Tindall & Cox, 1941.

58. Paré, A. Dix Livres de la Chirurgie avec le Magasin des Instruments Necessaires à Icelle, Vol. 7. Paris, Jean le Royer, 1564, Chap. 13.

59. Parkhill, C. A new apparatus for the fixation of bones after resection and in fractures with a tendency to displacement. Trans Am Surg Assoc 15:251, 1897.

60. Parkhill, C. Further observations regarding the use of the boneclamp in ununited fractures, fractures with malunion, and recent fractures with a tendency to displacement. Ann Surg 27:553, 1898.

61. Petit, J Le. D'un nouveau instrument de chirurgie. Mem Acad R Sci 1718, p. 254.

62. Pitkin, H.C.; Blackfield, H.M. Skeletal immobilization in difficult fractures of shafts of long bones: New method of treatment as applied to compound, comminuted and oblique fractures of both bones of the leg. J Bone Joint Surg 3:589, 1931.

63. Pujol, A. Mémoire sur une amputation naturelle de la jambe avec des réflexions sur quelques autre cas rélatifs à l'amputation. J Med Chir Pharm (Paris) 43:160, 1775.

64. Pujol, A. Eclaircissements en réponse à la lettre de M. Icart, chirurgien. J Med Chir Pharm (Paris) 45:167, 1776.

65. Putti, V. The operative lengthening of the femur. JAMA 77:934, 1921.

66. Ratliff, A.H.C. Ernest William Hey Groves and his contributions to orthopaedic surgery. Ann R Coll Surg Engl 65:203, 1983.

67. Russell, R.H. Fracture of the femur. A clinical study. Br J Surg 11:491, 1924.

68. Rush, L.V.; Rush, H.L. Technique for longitudinal pin fixation of certain fractures of the ulna and of the femur. J Bone Joint Surg 21:619, 1939.

69. Sarmiento, A. A functional below the knee cast for tibial fractures. J Bone Joint Surg Am 49:855, 1967.

70. Schneider, R. 25 Jahre AO Schweiz: Arbeitsgemeinschaft für Osteosynthesefragen 1958–1983. Biel, Gassmann AG, 1983.

71. Seutin. Traité de la Méthode Amovo-Inamovible. Brussels, 1849.

72. Shang T'ien-Yu; Fang Hsien-Chih; Ku Yun-Wu; Chow Ying Ch'ing. The integration of modern and traditional Chinese medicine in the treatment of fractures. Chin Med J 83:419, 1964.

73. Sherman, W.O'N. Operative treatment of fractures of the shaft of the femur with maximum fixation. J Bone Joint Surg 8:494, 1926.

74. Smith, G. The most ancient splints. BMJ 28:732, 1903.

75. Smith-Peterson, M.N.; Cave, E.F.; Vangarder, G.H. Intracapsular fractures of the neck of the femur; treatment by internal fixation. Arch Surg 23:715, 1931.

76. Spink, M.S.; Lewis, G.L. Albucasis on Surgery and Instruments. London, Wellcome Institute of the History of Medicine, 1973.

77. Thomas, G. From bonesetter to orthopaedic surgeon. Ann R Coll Surg Engl 55:134, 1974.

78. Trueta, J. An Atlas of Traumatic Surgery: Illustrated Histories of Wounds of the Extremities. Oxford, Blackwell, 1949.

79. Vidal, J.; Rabischong, P.; Bonnel, F. Étude bioméchanique du fixateur externe dans les fractures de jambe. Montpelier Chir 16:43, 1970.

80. Walker, C.A. Treatment of fractures by the immoveable apparatus. Lancet 1:553, 1839.

81. Watson Jones, R. Preface. In: Wilson, J.N., ed. Fractures and Joint Injuries. Edinburgh, Livingstone, 1952, pp. v–vi.

82. Wrench, G.T. Lord Lister: His Life and Work. London, Fisher Unwin, 1914.

CHAPTER 2

Biology of Fracture Repair

Robert K. Schenk, M.D.

In the evolution of supporting tissues, bone occupies the highest rank. It represents the biologic solution to the need for a solid building material for the skeleton of all higher animals. The mechanical properties of bone are based on the structure of its intercellular substance. At the same time, bone is a living tissue, thanks to the osteocytes buried within the intrinsic system of canaliculi and lacunae and the cell population lining the periosteal and endosteal surface as well as the walls of the intracortical canals. The bone cells control and maintain the quality of bone matrix, participate in the regulation of the calcium level in the tissue fluids, and are responsible for the repair of microdamage and fractures. There is no doubt that as the evolutionary precursor of bone, cartilage offers unique properties, especially in view of its avascularity and viscoelasticity. However, the fact that chondrocyte metabolism depends on diffusion limits its usefulness as a scaffold for larger, and especially terrestrial, animals.

Fracture repair is the biologic response to traumatic bone lesions. It is a result of the activation of the processes of cell proliferation and tissue differentiation that contributes to the development and growth of the skeleton. This chapter begins with a discussion of some aspects of the histophysiology of bone that are thought to serve as guidelines for the understanding of bone repair under the many conditions provided by current methods of fracture treatment.

STRUCTURE AND FUNCTION OF BONE

Structural Features of Bone

Bone has two major functions. As a supporting tissue, it provides stability, and metabolically it serves as a calcium bank for calcium homeostasis in the body fluids. These functions determine its structural properties at the macroscopic, microscopic, and ultrastructural levels.

Macroscopically, the mechanical role is reflected in the exterior shape of the bones, the form and size of the marrow cavity, the thickness of the cortex, and the density and architecture of the spongiosa in the metaphyses and epiphyses. They all give proof of the cooperation of various adaptive mechanisms resulting in a maximum of strength achieved by a minimum of material.[43] To a certain extent, adaptation to the functional requirements is genetically controlled, but according to Wolff's law[130] it is further modified by modeling and remodeling activities throughout life.

The specific mechanical properties of mature bone tissue are reflected at the light microscopic level in the structure of the intercellular substance. The most elaborate form of bone tissue is lamellar bone. It consists of 3- to 5-µm-wide layers of parallel collagen fibrils. Their course alternates in consecutive lamellae as in plywood. This arrangement of the collagen fibrils was originally deduced from their birefringence in polarized light and later confirmed in electron micrographs of osteoid and decalcified lamellar bone (Fig. 2–1).

Besides giving evidence of the fibrillar component in the bone matrix, electron microscopy reveals a close association of collagen and the inorganic phase of bone.

This chapter is dedicated to my very good friend and scientific partner, the late Professor Hans Willenegger. I thank him for his everlasting support and untiring enthusiasm in realizing a common effort for better understanding of fracture repair on biologic grounds.

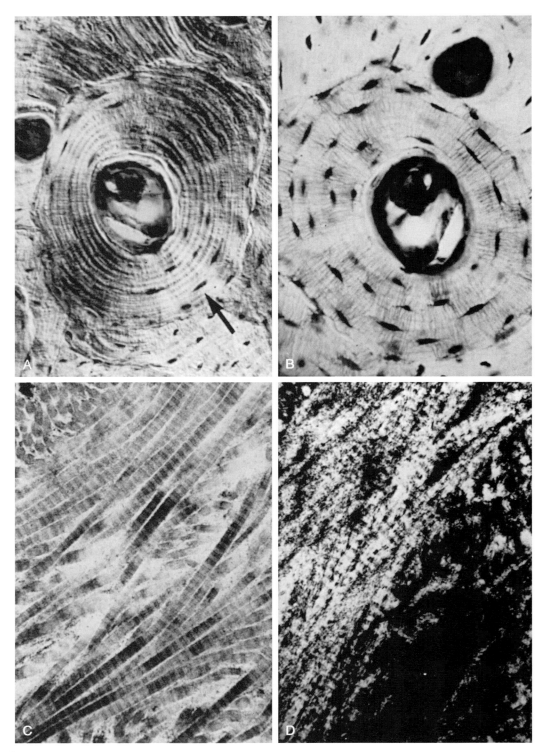

FIGURE 2–1. Structural features of lamellar bone. *A,* Cross section of an osteon. Interference phase contrast to show lamellae and surrounding cement line *(arrow)* in human femur (×380). *B,* Osteons are metabolic units. Staining of osteocytes in the canaliculolacunar system with basic fuchsin (×380). *C,* Electron micrograph of lamellar human osteoid (×38,000). *D,* Electron micrograph of mineralized human lamellar bone (×38,000).

Bone collagen is type I collagen and forms relatively thick fibrils with a distinct periodicity of 64 nm. This repeating pattern results from a quarter-staggered arrangement of the tropocollagen molecules and the presence of holes at their junctions. These holes are preferential sites for deposition of hydroxyapatite crystals.[46, 69] The composite of collagen, with its high tensile strength and apatite as a solid phase, is often compared with ferroconcrete and is ultimately responsible for the outstanding mechanical properties of bone.

Metabolism also has a tremendous influence on the light microscopic structure of bone. Metabolites are supplied to the bone cells via the bone envelopes: the periosteum, the endosteum, and the endocortical envelope within the intracortical canals. The envelopes share two important features: osteogenic potential and abundant vascularization. Thus, the envelopes can participate in modeling and remodeling activities as well as in bone repair. Because the heavily mineralized bone matrix obstructs diffusion of metabolites, the osteocytes are lodged in a system of communicating lacunae and canaliculi (canaliculolacunar system). Osteocyte nutrition and participation in calcium homeostasis depend on this fine network of canaliculi and lacunae surrounding their perikaryon and cytoplasmic processes (see Fig. 2–1). Metabolites are transported either via the cytoplasmic processes and junctions or through the tiny space surrounding them. The transport capacity of this system, however, has its limits. As Ham[49] pointed out in 1952, "the osteocytes receive a meager diet through the tiny canaliculi and must be situated perhaps no more than one tenth of a millimeter from a capillary, if they remain alive." The critical value for the transport distance thus lies around 100 µm and confines the outer diameter of osteons as well as the mean width of plates and trabeculae to about 200 µm.

If analyzed chemically, bone consists of about 65% mineral, mostly in the form of hydroxyapatite, and 35% organic matrix. Collagen forms about 90% (dry weight) of the organic phase, and the remaining 10% comprises proteoglycans of small molecular size and some noncollagenous proteins. Among these, osteocalcin (Gla protein) is of special interest because it is specific for bone tissue. When synthesized by osteoblasts, about half of the production leaks into the extracellular fluid. Its serum concentration, therefore, reflects bone formation.[98] Another specific bone component is osteopontin, a sialoprotein that may be involved in the mediation of cell adherence.[81] The calcium-binding protein 2HS glycoprotein is formed in the liver and is less specific for bone. Osteonectin, a phosphorylated glycoprotein, also seems to come at least partially from sources other than bone. The name *osteonectin* was chosen because it binds the mineral to collagen.[121, 122]

Histophysiology of Bone Cells

OSTEOBLASTS AND BONE FORMATION

In the embryo, bone-forming osteoblasts differentiate from mesenchymal cells originating either from the sclerotomes or, in the head region, from the neural crest (ectomesenchyme). Some mesenchymal stem cells are supposed to persist lifelong,[13, 15, 82] but the main sources of osteoblasts in the adult organism are inducible and determined osteoprogenitor cells located in the bone envelopes and the bone marrow.[36, 37]

Once activated, osteoprecursor cells proliferate rapidly. At this stage, they hardly appear different from fibroblasts, and only after cessation of mitotic division do they acquire the histologic features of osteoblasts. Mature osteoblasts exhibit a cuboidal or ellipsoidal shape, with the nucleus located somewhat eccentrically in a strongly basophilic cytoplasm. A negatively stained juxtanuclear area represents the prominent Golgi field.

Osteoblasts are lined up along the bone formation sites similarly to epithelial cells (Fig. 2–2). In contrast to true

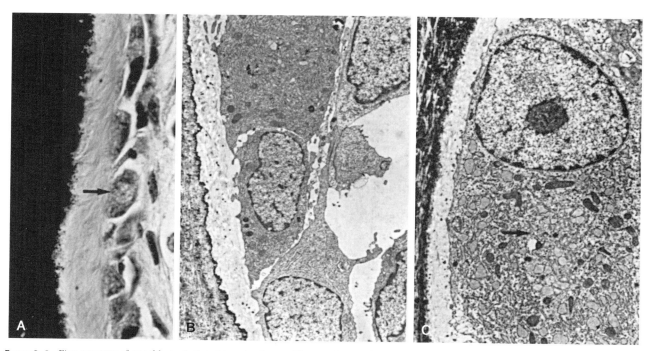

Figure 2–2. Fine structure of osteoblasts. *A*, Osteoblasts in a human iliac crest biopsy. *Arrow* points to Golgi negative (von Kossa–MacNeal tetrachrome, ×800). *B*, Epithelioid arrangement of osteoblasts in the metaphysis of a rat tibia (×2400). *C*, Fine structure of osteoblast cytoplasm. Abundant rough endoplasmic reticulum and an extensive Golgi zone are seen (*arrow*) (×5200).

epithelia, the intercellular space between adjacent cell membranes is not sealed by tight junctions. However, gap junctions, the substrate for intercellular communication, occur between osteoblasts and at the contact sites of the cytoplasmic processes of osteocytes.[52, 53] As in all cells involved in active protein secretion, the rough endoplasmic reticulum is well developed, and abundant Golgi saccules and vesicles occupy the area of the Golgi negative. The high metabolic activity of osteoblasts is also reflected by numerous mitochondria and by a close spatial association with capillaries. Ample vascular supply is essential for all bone-forming metabolic activities.

Formation and Mineralization of Bone Matrix

Bone formation occurs in two stages: first, osteoblasts deposit osteoid, which in a second stage is mineralized along the calcification front. The organic matrix that is interposed between the osteoblasts and the mineralization front forms an osteoid seam. A sharp borderline between the nonmineralized osteoid seam and the mineralized bone represents the mineralization front. Together with apatite, numerous other substances are incorporated in the bone tissue at the level of the mineralization front. Besides metals such as strontium, lead, iron, and aluminum, tetracycline and other fluorochromes are permanently bound to the mineralizing matrix and can be detected in undecalcified sections by fluorescence microscopy (Fig. 2–3C). These labeling techniques have become a conve-

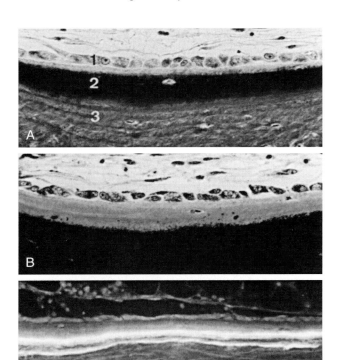

FIGURE 2–3. Bone formation in human iliac crest cancellous bone. *A,* Osteoblasts (1), osteoid (2), and mineralized lamellar bone (3) (Goldner's stain, ×640). *B,* Consecutive section (von Kossa–MacNeal tetrachrome). *C,* Double tetracycline labeling (interval, 1 week) to determine the daily mineralization and bone matrix formation rate (×250).

nient tool for calculating bone formation and bone turnover rates in the growing and adult skeleton. Double labeling with fluorochromes at intervals of 5 to 10 days allows the measurement of the daily mineralization rate, which amounts in human lamellar bone to roughly 1 μm. Osteoid seams, as long as they are lined by mature, active osteoblasts, maintain a remarkably constant width of about 10 μm. This finding indicates that freshly deposited osteoid goes through a maturation period of about 10 days before it reaches the mineralization front. In most mammals these rates are rather constant and show little variation with age. However, the meaning of "maturation" is not clear, given the need for further research on the ability of the osteoblast to elaborate a "calcifiable matrix" and to control mineralization that takes place at a distance of 10 μm.

As far as the mechanism of mineralization is concerned, there is general agreement that it requires a number of conditions, such as (1) an adequate concentration of calcium and phosphate ions, (2) the presence of a calcifiable matrix, (3) a nucleating agent, and finally (4) control by regulators (i.e., promoters and inhibitors). A number of promoters and even more inhibitors are described in the literature. Some inhibitors are of particular interest in prevention of ectopic calcification (e.g., pyrophosphate, bisphosphonates).[32] For example, highly aggregated proteoglycans have been shown to inhibit mineralization in vitro and possibly play a similar role in cartilage.[55, 97] There is much controversy, however, about the definition of a calcifiable matrix and the physiologic role of nucleators.[76]

Two nucleators have been identified and characterized by electron microscopy: matrix vesicles and collagen. Matrix vesicles, as first described in the mineralizing compartments of growth cartilage[1, 7–9] are spherical, membrane-bound bodies with a diameter of 100 to 200 nm. They are pinched off from cytoplasmic processes. The first needle-like calcium phosphate deposits appear in the vicinity of their membrane. Anhydrous embedding techniques (high-pressure freezing and freeze substitution[58, 61]) demonstrate the exact location of the crystals in close contact with the inner leaflet of the membrane. After rupture of the membrane, the crystals are set free and serve as secondary nucleation centers. Numerous matrix vesicles are also seen in the thin osteoid seams of woven bone and occur at the onset of mineralization in parallel-fibered bone.[83] They are found only rarely in lamellar bone.

In *lamellar bone,* the mechanism and outcome of mineralization deviate considerably from this pattern. In mineralized lamellar bone there is a close association between apatite crystals and collagen. In electron micrographs, this accentuates the 64-nm periodicity of the type I collagen fibrils (see Fig. 2–1D). This association is explained by the presence of hole zones in the microfibrils, resulting from the quarter-staggered array of the tropocollagen molecules. It is in these holes that the majority of apatite crystals are deposited. Numerous classical in vitro experiments have shown that collagen with the proper periodicity of 64 nm is able to precipitate apatite crystals in metastable solutions of calcium and phosphate.[44, 46] Highly purified collagen is not able to cause mineral precipitation and it is supposed that nucleation is in fact due to noncollagenous matrix proteins, presumably phosphoproteins, that are bound to collagen.[9, 45]

BONE LINING CELLS AND OSTEOCYTES

Toward the end of the formative period, osteoblasts flatten out and transform into *bone lining cells*. The osteoid underneath the lining cells mineralizes at a lower rate, possibly up to the surface.[10] Others claim that the bone surface underneath the lining cells stays coated by a layer of nonmineralized matrix.[33, 127] In the latter case, the nonmineralized matrix would have to be removed before osteoclasts could get access to the calcified bone.[16] Lining cells still belong to the osteoblastic family and maintain cytoplasmic connection with osteocytes. Whether they act as a barrier for the ion exchange between bone and extracellular fluid is doubtful. Lining cells may participate in the initiation of bone resorption by an active contraction that is thought to expose the bone surface for the attachment of osteoclasts.

Osteocytes are derived from osteoblasts. From time to time, an osteoblast is designated to become an osteocyte, stops matrix extrusion on its bone-facing side, and is subsequently buried by its neighbors. Like all other osteoblasts, the preosteocyte has previously established connections to osteocytes lying deeper in the bone via cytoplasmic processes enclosed within canaliculi. The number of osteocytes per unit volume (numerical density) of lamellar bone matrix is remarkably constant. This constancy suggests that the signal that calls for an osteoblast to become an osteocyte arises from deeper cells when the pathway for the intercellular metabolic communication has reached its critical length. Before and during its burial, the osteocyte establishes connections to osteoblasts lining the osteoid surface above it.

Newly formed osteocytes are contained in relatively large lacunae. For a short period, they continue to produce matrix until the lacunae are narrowed to their final size. This period is a true *osteoblastic phase* in their life cycle. The opposite, enlargement of the lacunae by *osteocytic osteolysis*, was extensively debated in the late 1960s,[6] but there is no doubt that the capacity of this process as a possible alternative to osteoclastic bone resorption has been overestimated. But it cannot be denied that osteocytes participate in calcium homeostasis by actively removing mineral or even organic matrix from the wall of their lacuna.[124] However, this activity is not reflected, or is only poorly reflected, in structural changes because of the enormous extent of the osteocyte-bone interface, once estimated to amount to approximately 220 mm^2 per mm^3 of cortical bone (or a total of 300 m^2 in the human skeleton).[38]

Osteocytes may stay alive for years or even decades provided that nutrition via the caniculolacunar system remains intact. Interruptions of the caniculolacunar system, however, are not infrequent, even under physiologic conditions. Remodeling of the cortical bone and surface remodeling by the envelopes inevitably create cement lines that interrupt the canalicular pathway, and reconnections of the cytoplasmic processes are extremely rare. The osteocytes disintegrate, and the lacunae become empty and are gradually filled with mineral. The surrounding territory, too, achieves a higher mineral density (micropetrosis),[39] and the accumulation of micropetrotic bone compartments ultimately leads to increased brittleness of elderly bone. In view of this mechanism, it seems rather unlikely that the now popular hypothesis of programmed cell death (apoptosis) has to be invoked as an explanation.

OSTEOCLASTS AND BONE RESORPTION

The discovery that osteoclasts stem from bone marrow cells was a breakthrough for the understanding of bone resorption.[3, 47, 72] The concept is now widely accepted, although identification of the precursors is still difficult, and control of the various steps of osteoclast differentiation and stimulation is far from fully understood. Osteoclasts belong to the family of multinucleated giant cells specialized for the breakdown of calcified tissues (bone, dentin, calcified cartilage or fibrocartilage, or calcified fibrous tissue) or the mineral phase alone (calcium phosphate ceramics). To define their localization, it is sometimes appropriate to name them according to the tissue undergoing resorption (e.g., chondroclasts, dentinoclasts), but all these cells are practically identical. They are distinguished from other giant cells by the positive tartrate-resistant acid phosphatase reaction,[18, 77] although this method is only partially specific in demonstrating mononuclear osteoclast precursors.

Light microscopy of osteoclasts was accurately described in 1873 by Kölliker.[68] Their diameter ranges from 10 to 100 μm and the number of nuclei from 3 to 30 or more. Resorbing osteoclasts are attached to the bone surface, and their activity is confined to the contact area, leaving behind traces known as *Howship's lacunae* (Fig. 2–4). The structure of the osteoclast-bone interface was further elucidated by electron microscopy.[54, 110] A marginal rim of relatively dense cytoplasm (clear zone, sealing part) is always found in close contact with the mineralized surface and seems to seal off the space where bone is resorbed. In this resorption chamber, the cell surface is tremendously increased by cytoplasmic folds forming a ruffled border. In their interspaces, the medium is conditioned for bone resorption: the mineral phase is dissolved by hydrochloric acid production and the exposed collagen fibrils are enzymatically digested.[126] Osteoclasts can resorb a layer of 50 μm/day or more. Their activity consumes a significant amount of energy, which is supplied by an extraordinarily high number of cytoplasmic mitochondria that are also involved in acid production.

Enzymes apt to digest the organic bone matrix are stored in numerous lysosomes, and vacuoles of various sizes are distributed throughout the giant cell body,[79] indicating transport of breakdown products from the resorption site to the cell surface facing the body fluid. Inhibition or inactivation of osteoclasts becomes apparent by a numerical reduction of vacuoles, loss of the ruffled border, and detachment from the mineralized surface. However, the lysosomes, and correspondingly the positive tartrate-resistant acid phosphatase reaction, are still pres-

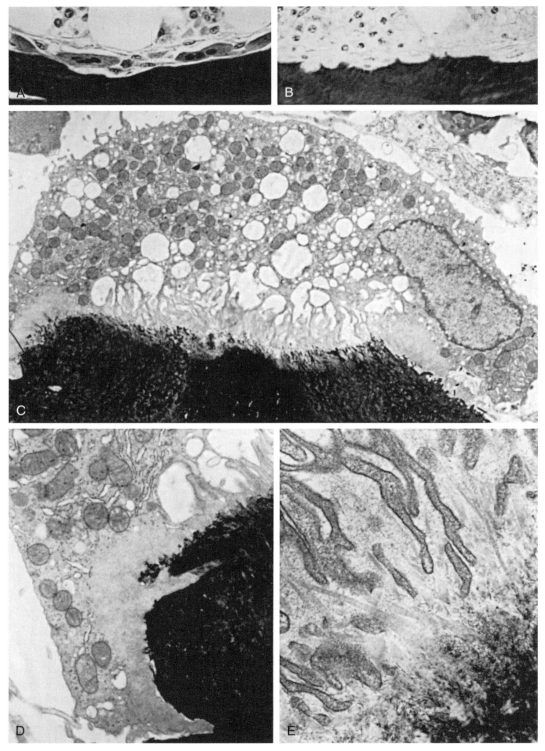

Figure 2–4. Osteoclastic bone resorption. *A* and *B,* Osteoclasts and Howship's lacunae in a human iliac crest cancellous bone (×400). *C,* Osteoclast in a rat's tibial metaphysis. Numerous mitochondria, vesicles, and vacuoles. Clear zone in the marginal cytoplasm, ruffled border in the center (×5400). *D,* Close contact of the cell membrane with mineralized bone matrix in the clear zone (sealing part) (×12,000). *E,* Higher magnification of ruffled border. Dissolution of mineral followed by enzymatic degradation of collagen fibers (×25,000). (*A–E,* From Schenk, R.K. Verh Dtsch Ges Pathol 58:72, 1974.)

ent and therefore do not reflect resorbing activity. This situation is a severe limitation for all quantitative evaluations of bone resorption based on light microscopic osteoclast counts.

Osteogenesis

BASIC CONCEPTS

A simple general rule serves as a key for understanding the structural varieties in bone development, growth, and fracture repair: *bone is deposited only on a solid base.* The obvious reason is twofold. First, the elaboration of highly organized bone matrix, and especially its mineralization, requires mechanical rest. This rest is biologically provided by the formation of a scaffold, similar to the forms used for construction work with concrete. In addition, *bone formation is dependent on an ample blood supply,* and osteoblasts function properly only in the direct vicinity of capillaries. If vascularization is temporarily interrupted or jeopardized by mechanical forces and motion, osteoblasts are likely to change their gene expression and become chondroblasts or fibroblasts.

TYPES OF BONE TISSUE

For the most part, only two types of bone tissue are distinguished: woven bone and lamellar bone. On the basis of Weidenreich's classification of 1930,[129] more than five different bone types can be discerned, some of which occur only in lower vertebrates. For the mammalian skeleton, this number is restricted to three, namely woven bone, lamellar bone, and parallel-fibered, finely bundled bone, or simply parallel-fibered bone. Because the latter forms a remarkably large compartment in the earlier stages of bone regeneration and bone repair, it will be discussed further in this context.

Woven bone is structurally characterized by the random orientation of its rather coarse collagen fibrils; by the numerous large, often irregularly shaped osteocytes; and often by the high mineral density. Under polarized light, the matrix is not birefringent, and uptake of fluorochromes often results in diffuse, ill-defined labels. The most important features, however, are its pattern and dynamics of growth: it forms rapidly growing, branching struts and plates and is able to occupy a relatively large territory within a short space of time. Woven bone is formed predominantly in embryos and during growth. In adults, it reappears when accelerated bone formation is demanded, as in the bony callus during fracture repair, in osseointegration of implants, but also in pathologic conditions such as Paget's disease, renal osteodystrophy, hyperparathyroidism, and fluorosis.

In *parallel-fibered bone*, the collagen fibrils are oriented parallel to the surface but otherwise do not follow a preferential course. Parallel-fibered bone is not, or is only faintly, birefringent. Fluorochrome labels appear as relatively wide bands. The apposition rate is higher than in lamellar bone and amounts to 3 to 5 μm/day. Parallel-fibered bone allows accelerated bone deposition in both intramembranous and endochondral ossification in the growing skeleton as well as in defect repair and fracture healing.

Lamellar bone was characterized earlier in this chapter. It requires a preformed solid scaffold for its deposition, and the newly formed lamellae run strictly parallel to the underlying surface. Deficiencies and irregularities in the surface have to be planed by woven bone prior to lamellar bone deposition. Under such conditions, it is not surprising that the linear apposition rate for lamellar bone amounts to only 1 to 2 μm/day. Fluorochrome labels appear as thin, clearly delineated bands, and the birefringence in polarized light strongly emphasizes the lamellar pattern caused by the arrangement of the collagen fibrils.

TYPES OF OSSIFICATION

As mentioned before, bone formation depends, among other things, on two important prerequisites: ample blood supply and mechanical support. These principles serve as a key for the understanding of the two modes by which bone develops.

In *intramembranous ossification,* connective tissue serves as a mold into which bone is deposited. In embryos it is restricted to the formation of the vault of the skull, the maxilla and other facial bones, the mandible, and part of the clavicle, and mesenchyme acts as its parent tissue. After birth, intramembranous ossification is frequently reactivated in the regeneration of bone defects and fracture repair.

Chondral (indirect) ossification uses mineralized cartilage as a model and solid base that is first covered with and then replaced by bone. Most of the skeleton and presumably all the long bones have a cartilaginous precursor (or anlage). After birth, endochondral ossification plays a key role in fracture healing under unstable conditions, in which the intermediately formed fibrocartilage calcifies and is then replaced by bone.

Development and Growth of Cancellous Bone

CANCELLOUS BONE FORMED BY INTRAMEMBRANOUS OSSIFICATION

In the embryo, intramembranous ossification starts in the mesenchyme, an undifferentiated, pluripotential tissue. Osteogenesis is always coupled with angiogenesis, and, besides its metabolic function, the evolving vascular net has a great influence on the architecture of the outgrowing scaffold, the primary spongiosa. Primary trabeculae consist of woven bone and are later reinforced by parallel-fibered bone. In general, the trabeculae, as well as the blood vessels, are randomly oriented. The volume density of the primary spongiosa is about 40% to 50%, the mean width of the trabeculae around 100 μm, and the diameter of the intertrabecular, vascular spaces about 200 μm. The corresponding values in adult cancellous bone are about 20% to 25% volume density, 150 to 200 μm trabecular width, and 200 to 500 μm for the intertrabecular space.

Whereas intramembranous ossification plays a minor role in embryonic osteogenesis, it gains in importance in postnatal bone repair, both in defect filling and in direct fracture healing. In these conditions the granulation tissue that previously organized the blood clot serves as a matrix for bone ingrowth. The pattern of tissue differentiation in these conditions is almost identical to the formation of the primary spongiosa.

CANCELLOUS BONE FORMED BY ENDOCHONDRAL OSSIFICATION

Endochondral ossification starts in primary and secondary ossification centers. Primary centers arise in short bones such as the vertebral body and in the midshaft of long bones (Fig. 2–5). Secondary ossification centers originate in the epiphyses of long bones and expand by endochondral ossification until the cartilage is restricted to the articular surface and the growth plate. At the junction of articular cartilage and growth plate, both remain connected by a cartilaginous bridge that is still covered by perichondrium (groove of Ranvier). This is the only location where cartilage apposition endures, thereby enlarging the transverse diameter of the epiphyseal plate. During growth, the articular cartilage also participates in endochondral ossification and is responsible for the enlargement and precise shaping of the articular surface,

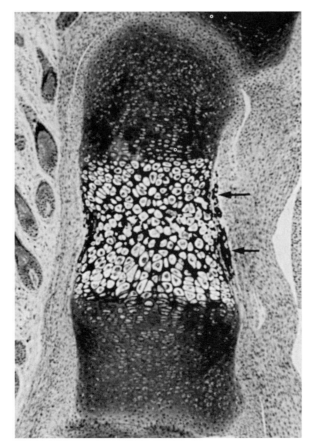

FIGURE 2–5. Perichondrial ossification in a metacarpal bone (2-day-old rat). Mineralized hypertrophic cartilage in the diaphysis forming the solid base for bone deposition by the periosteum (*arrows*).

whereas the growth plates represent the center for longitudinal growth.

HISTOPHYSIOLOGY OF THE GROWTH PLATE

Although all sites of endochondral ossification exhibit the same basic pattern, the growth plates present the histologic events in their most elaborate form.[12, 123] In fully developed growth plates, the chondrocytes are organized in columns that represent functional growth units. Quantitative data given in this chapter are always related to this unit.[59, 60] In the direction from epiphysis to metaphysis, the growth plate is subdivided into three overlapping zones according to the prevailing function of each: (1) interstitial growth, (2) preparation for ossification, and (3) formation of the primary spongiosa (Fig. 2–6).

The nonmineralized part of the growth cartilage, except for the reserve zone, participates in *interstitial growth,* which is based on three cellular activities: proliferation, matrix production, and cell hypertrophy. The proliferation zone comprises relatively flat chondrocytes (see Fig. 2–6B). These cells go through a finite number of mitotic divisions before they stop DNA replication at the borderline with the hypertrophic zone. In rats, the mitotic frequency is about one in 48 hours.[59] During the interphase of the cell cycle, the cells are engaged in *matrix production* by synthesizing predominantly type II collagen and proteoglycans. The matrix volume produced in 24 hours by one proliferating cell again seems to be relatively constant and roughly equals the cell volume.

Cell hypertrophy is probably the most spectacular contribution of the chondrocytes to longitudinal growth. In rats, the chondrocytes increase in volume up to 10 times in becoming hypertrophic. The formerly flat cells become spherical or ovoid, thereby increasing their longitudinal diameter by a factor of 4. The elongation of the column during the process of becoming hypertrophic calls for supplementary matrix production. If hypertrophic chondrocytes are adequately preserved for electron microscopy,[57] they appear well equipped with cytoplasmic organelles required for matrix production (rough endoplasmic reticulum, Golgi apparatus) and mitochondria for production of energy related to osmotic work. The last chondrocyte in the column disintegrates almost instantly at the moment when the last transverse septum is destroyed, either by apoptosis or under the attack of macrophages accompanying the invading capillaries.

Toward the metaphyseal surface, the growth cartilage and its remnants are *prepared for ossification* again by three different but interdependent processes: (1) cartilage mineralization, (2) resorption of nonmineralized cartilage, and (3) resorption of calcified cartilage. All three processes have many things in common with certain types of fracture repair and are therefore discussed more extensively (Fig. 2–7).

Cartilage mineralization is restricted to the interterritorial matrix compartment, which forms the core of the longitudinal septa and is always separated from the chondrocytes by a layer of nonmineralized, territorial matrix.[28, 113] The transverse septa, which consist solely of territorial matrix, remain unmineralized[25] or only occasionally include some isolated, small mineral clusters.

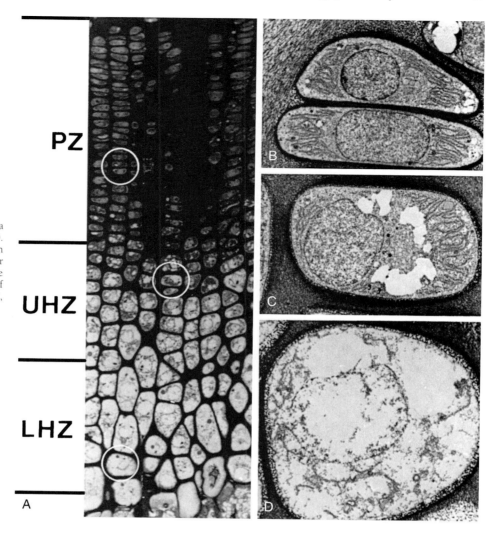

FIGURE 2–6. Cellular organization of a growth plate (proximal tibia of a rat). *A*, Light microscopy (×200). Proliferation zone (PZ) and upper (UHZ) and lower (LHZ) hypertrophic zones. *B* to *D*, The corresponding electron micrographs of the circled areas in PZ, UHZ, and LHZ, respectively (×1800).

Little is known about how this mineralization pattern is controlled. Matrix vesicles accumulate within the interterritorial matrix and are rarely found in transverse septa (see Fig. 2–7). This well-defined pattern of mineralization canalizes the vascular invasion of the cartilage in the longitudinal direction and provides the scaffold and the solid base required for bone deposition in the metaphysis.

Cartilage resorption occurs by two different mechanisms.[107] *Resorption of nonmineralized cartilage* is coupled with vascular invasion and mediated by macrophages accompanying the invading capillary sprouts (see Fig. 2–7). The macrophages not only open up the last lacuna by destroying the last transverse septum, they also remove the nonmineralized coat of the sidewalls of newly opened lacunae, thereby exposing the calcified cartilage for later deposition of bone. *Resorption of calcified cartilage* requires multinucleated giant cells called *chondroclasts*. In rats, these cells remove about half or two thirds of the calcified cartilage septa and thus make room for the ingrowing bone-forming elements, that is, osteoblasts, osteoprogenitor cells, and sinusoidal capillaries.

The *primary spongiosa* formed in the metaphysis differs from the one produced by intramembranous ossification in two respects. First, it is anisotropic; that is, its trabeculae are oriented parallel to the long axis of the bone. Second, the trabeculae are built around a central core of calcified cartilage instead of a core consisting of woven bone.

The primary spongiosa in the metaphyses subsequently undergoes extensive remodeling and is transformed into the secondary spongiosa, which consists solely of bone, mostly of the lamellar type (see Fig. 2–11). At the borderline with the diaphysis, its trabeculae are finally resorbed and replaced by the marrow cavity.

Development and Growth of Cortical Bone

In long bones, the final shape and structure of cortical bone are the result of four different processes: (1) perichondral ossification, (2) periosteal and endosteal bone apposition, (3) corticalization of metaphyseal cancellous bone, and (4) modeling of the external shape by the envelopes.

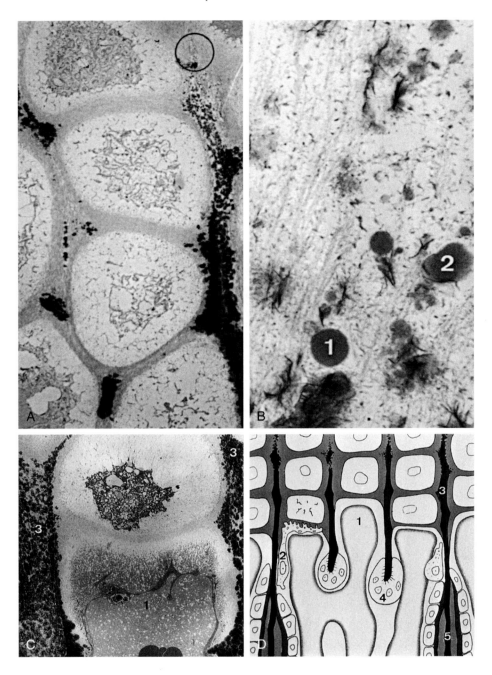

FIGURE 2–7. Fine structural aspects of cartilage mineralization and vascular invasion in the proximal tibial growth plate of rats. *A,* The mineral deposits are concentrated in the longitudinal, intercolumnar septa, whereas the transverse septa remain nonmineralized. The *circle* indicates the position of the field shown in *B* (×1200). *B,* Initial calcification zone with matrix vesicles (1). The first apatite crystal appears in contact with the membrane surrounding the vesicles (2) (×38,000). *C,* A saccular capillary sprout approaches the nonmineralized transverse cartilage septum forming the boundary of the lacuna with the last, disintegrating chondrocyte. Note the heavily calcified longitudinal septa (×2250). *D,* Schematic representation of cartilage resorption and vascular invasion in the growth plate. Thin-walled capillary sprouts (1) invade the last lacunae after the breakdown of the nonmineralized transverse septa by macrophages (2). Calcification of longitudinal septa is confined to the interterritorial compartment (3). After exposure of the calcified core, parts of these septa are resorbed by chondroclasts (4) or serve as a solid base for bone deposition (5).

PERICHONDRAL OSSIFICATION

The onset of perichondral ossification coincides with the formation of the primary ossification center in the midshaft of the cartilaginous precursor (see Fig. 2–5). The original perichondrium converts into a periosteum and deposits a bony cuff around the calcified cartilage that is later resorbed or replaced by endochondral ossification. The initially formed woven bone surrounds longitudinal vascular spaces, which then become narrowed by concentric deposition of parallel-fibered bone. The resulting structural units are primary osteons. Thus, perichondral ossification strictly represents appositional bone formation and not replacement of cartilage by bone. As soon as a cortical layer is present in the diaphysis, further lengthening of the cuff toward the epiphyses occurs by progressive transformation of perichondrium into periosteum.

PERIOSTEAL AND ENDOSTEAL BONE APPOSITION AND RESORPTION

Both the periosteal and endosteal envelopes contribute to the growth and shaping of bones. The basic growth pattern in a diaphyseal cross section attributes bone formation to the periosteal envelope and osteoclastic resorption to the endosteal lining of the marrow cavity. Variation in the local distribution and the dynamics of these activities results in interesting modifications and adaptations of the shape.

The apposition rate can be modulated by changing the type of bone tissue produced. As mentioned earlier, lamellar bone apposition is restricted to 1 to 2 μm/day (Fig. 2–8C). This rate results in a very small gain in areas where circumferential lamellae are formed. Deposition of parallel-fibered bone can increase the apposition rate up to about 5 μm/day (see Fig. 2–8F). Even faster

growing sites show another structural modification, the formation of primary osteons. Thereby, woven bone is deposited as longitudinal ridges in between blood vessels. The ridges fuse above the vessel and enclose it in a vascular canal, which then gives rise to a primary osteon by gradual concentric filling with parallel-fibered bone. Anastomoses located in transverse, Volkmann canals establish connections with the vascular net of the respective envelope.

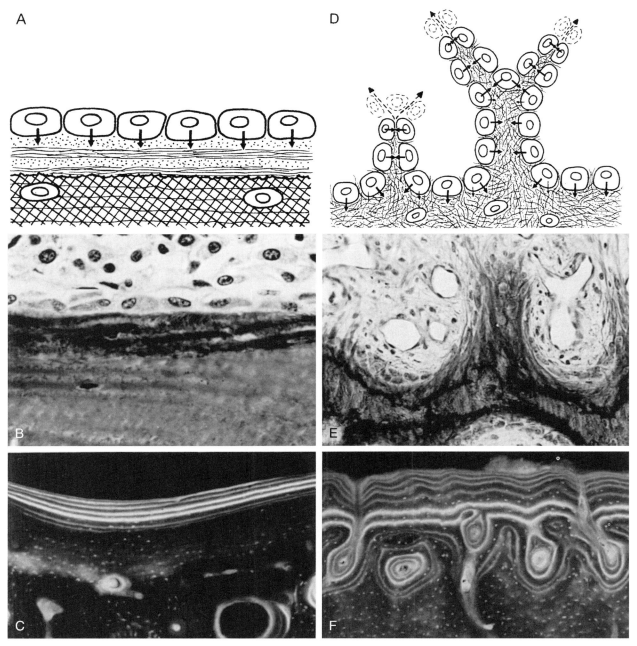

FIGURE 2–8. Appositional growth patterns. *A to C,* Strictly lamellar bone deposition is confined to future layers of circumferential lamellae. Its rate is limited by the daily progress of mineralization (1 to 2 μm), as shown by sequential fluorochrome labeling at weekly intervals in *C. D to F,* Woven bone formation results in ridges and depends on osteoblast recruitment. The resulting canals are concentrically filled by lamellar bone, resulting in primary osteons. *F,* Sequential labeling shows the gain in apposition rate. (*A, B, D, E,* From Schenk, R.K. In: Weber, B.G.; Brunner, C.; Freuler, F., eds. Treatment of Fractures in Children and Adolescents. Berlin, Springer Verlag, 1980, p. 3. *C, F,* From Schenk, R.K. In: Lane, J.M., ed. Fracture Healing. New York, Churchill Livingstone, 1987, p. 23.)

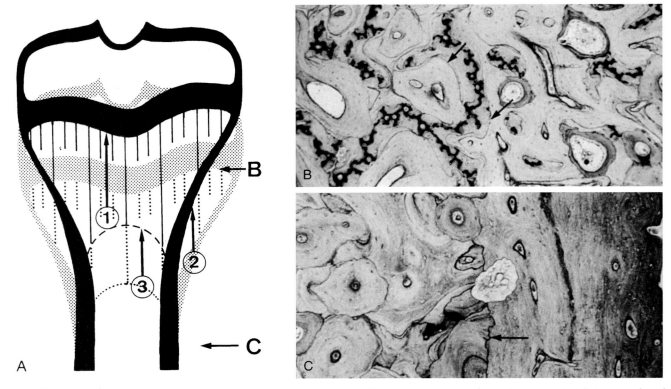

Figure 2–9. Conical modeling and formation of cortical bone in the metaphysis of long bones. *A,* Pattern of osteoclastic resorption during metaphyseal growth. The position of the *dotted* and *black outlines* reflects 1 week of actual growth in the proximal tibia of 35-day-old rats. (1) Chondroclasts remove about two thirds of the calcified cartilage septa. (2) Cortical bone is removed by subperiosteal resorption. (3) The marrow cavity enlarges by resorption of the metaphyseal spongiosa. *B,* Cortical metaphyseal bone, showing concentric lamellar filling of the intertrabecular spaces in the primary spongiosa. Dark inclusions are remnants of calcified cartilage in the former primary trabeculae. These are clearly confined by cement lines of the resting type (*arrows*). (Tibia of a minipig, ×70.) *C,* Further periosteal appositional growth at the level indicated in *A.* A reversal line (*arrow*) indicates the turning point between resorption and formation. To the right, primitive cortical bone with primary osteons; on the left side, secondary osteons delineated by cement lines of the reversal type. There is a newly formed resorption canal in the center. (Tibia of a minipig, ×85.) (*A,* From Schenk, R.; Merz, W.A.; Mühlbauer, R.; et al. Calcif Tissue Res 11:196, 1973.)

CORTICALIZATION (COMPACTION) OF CANCELLOUS BONE

The metaphyses of most long bones exhibit a conical shape. This shape reverses the pattern of apposition and resorption during longitudinal growth: formation prevails now along the endosteal aspect of the cortex, whereas the periosteal surface is subjected to resorption (Fig. 2–9*A*). When the metaphyseal cone advances toward the epiphysis, some peripheral trabeculae are engulfed in the new cortical layer. Corticalization is accomplished by filling the intertrabecular spaces with parallel-fibered or lamellar bone, similar to primary osteons, and finally the compact composite is reconstructed by cortical remodeling (see Fig. 2–9*B* and *C*). In transverse sections of the metaphyseal corticalis, the former trabeculae of the primary spongiosa are identified by inclusions of calcified cartilage.

GROWTH-RELATED MODELING OF CORTICAL BONE

The basic pattern of diaphyseal growth, that is, periosteal apposition and endosteal resorption, is valid for bones with a straight diaphysis but is subjected to manifold alterations in bones with a more complex anatomic shape. Enlow[31] and others have carefully analyzed the principles of shape-deforming modeling in a variety of bones. Instructive examples are the cortical drift in the shaft of long bones and the conical shaping of the metaphysis.

Cortical drift is found in curved bones, such as the femur with its ventral convexity or the ribs that have to displace concentrically in space to reach an outer circumference of the thorax. Thereby, the outer cortical layer undergoes periosteal apposition and endosteal resorption, whereas the inner cortex is subject to endosteal apposition concomitant with periosteal resorption.

Conical shaping of the metaphysis has already been described in the context of corticalization. Again, the basic diaphyseal pattern of formation and resorption is reversed in the conical part of the metaphyseal cortex. At a certain distance from the growth plate, a turning point, or better turning line, between resorption and formation by the same envelope can be expected. There is, however, a reversal phase or quiescent period that brings about spatial separation between the two activities.

Bone Remodeling

It is legitimate to make a distinction between modeling and remodeling activities in the skeleton. *Modeling* is a shape-deforming process exerted by formative and resorptive activities of the envelopes. *Remodeling* results in substitution or replacement of bone moieties and thus means renewal of bone matrix without structural change. Modeling is limited to the growing skeleton and becomes only exceptionally operative in the adult, as after malalignment of fractures. Remodeling occurs throughout life. During growth, it contributes to the maturation of the bone. In the adult, it provides metabolically active bone tissue for calcium homeostasis; eliminates avascular, necrotic bone compartments; and prevents fatigue by local repair of microcracks and microfractures.

REMODELING OF CORTICAL BONE

Primitive compact bone consists to a large extent of primary osteons formed during appositional growth. In many mammals, including humans, this primary bone is replaced during growth by secondary osteons or haversian systems. Microscopically, secondary osteons are delineated from the surrounding interstitial bone by a *cement line* (see Fig. 2–9B and C). Two types of cement lines are distinguished in lamellar bone. *Arresting* (or *resting*) *lines* appear when bone formation is temporarily arrested and then resumes. Arresting lines are smooth and run strictly parallel to the lamellae. The crenated appearance of *reversal lines,* on the other hand, indicates

that bone formation was preceded by osteoclastic resorption. Cement lines forming the outer border of secondary osteons belong to the latter type. They delimit the osteons from the surrounding interstitial lamellae, the latter representing remnants of former osteon generations or circumferential lamellae. It is assumed that reversal lines interrupt the canaliculi and thus prevent communication between osteocytes. Therefore, the interstitial lamellae are often devitalized and become necrotic.

Viewed in transverse sections, formation of secondary osteons starts with a resorption cavity produced by osteoclasts. Shortly thereafter, osteoblasts deposit new concentric lamellae that gradually fill this cavity until the secondary osteon is completed (Fig. 2–10A). Longitudinal sections demonstrate a close coupling of resorption and formation in space and time: the hemispheric tip of a resorption canal contains a group of osteoclasts assembled in a cutter cone (see Fig. 2–10B). Somewhat close behind, the first osteoblasts line up along its wall and start refilling this canal (closing cone).

The coupling of bone resorption and bone formation occurs in discrete remodeling sites called basic multicellular units or bone metabolizing units (BMUs).[40–42] The assembly of osteoclasts in the cutter cone can best be seen in thick ground sections (see Fig. 2–10B). Thin undecalcified microtome sections (see Fig. 2–10C) show further details of the structural organization of BMUs, especially

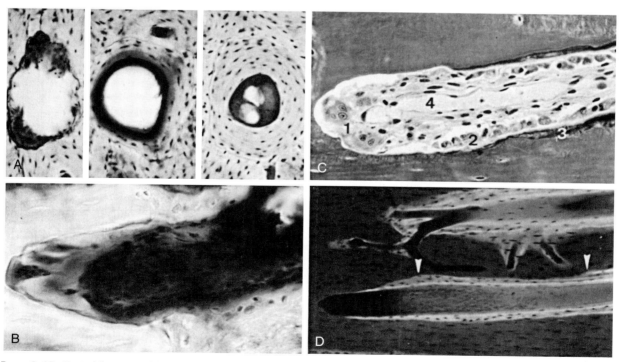

FIGURE 2–10. Cortical bone remodeling (table composed of microphotographs taken from studies of fracture repair in dogs). *A,* Transverse section. From left to right: resorption canal, forming, and completed secondary osteon (×250). *B,* A 90-μm-thick ground section demonstrates particularly well the osteoclastic cutter cone (×220). *C,* Goldner-stained, 5-μm thin microtome section to illustrate osteoclasts (1), osteoblasts (2), osteoid (3), and blood vessel (4), accompanied by perivascular (precursor) cells (×220). *D,* Sequential labeling allows calculation of osteoclastic resorption rates by measurements of the distance between the tips of individual labels (*arrowheads*) (×80). (*A,* From Schenk, R.K. In: Lin, O.C.C.; Chao, E.Y.S., eds. Perspectives on Biomaterials. Amsterdam, Elsevier Science Publishers, 1986, p. 75. *B,* From Schenk, R.K.; Willenegger, H. Experientia 19:593, 1963. *C,* From Schenk, R.K.; Willenegger, H. Langenbecks Arch Klin Chir 308:440, 1964. Copyright 1964, Springer Verlag. *D,* From Schenk, R.K.; Willenegger, H. Symp Biol Hung 7:75, 1967.)

the vascular loop surrounded by perivascular cells (which partially represent osteoblast precursors and possibly preosteoclasts). It is obvious that the osteoclastic cutter cone elongates the resorption canal and at the same time widens it up to the final outer diameter of the new osteon. Resorption is followed by a reversal phase of 1 to 2 days. During this period, inconspicuous mononuclear cells line the wall over a short distance of 100 to 200 μm. Then osteoblasts appear and start lamellar bone formation by depositing an osteoid seam that subsequently mineralizes. Because the whole system advances longitudinally, the concentric filling narrows the canal conically (closing cone).

In appropriate longitudinal sections (see Fig. 2–10D), fluorochrome labeling allows measurements of the daily osteoclastic resorption rate.[63, 106] In experimental studies on healing of osteotomies in the canine radius and tibia, the daily longitudinal advance of the cutting cone (linear rate of osteoclastic bone resorption) was 53 ± 12 μm.[114] In cross sections of completed new osteons, the outer diameter was 158 ± 27 μm and the mean osteonal wall thickness approximately 70 μm. With a daily apposition rate of 1.8 ± 0.4 μm, the completion time for a new osteon (or life span of a BMU) amounts to 5 to 6 weeks in adult dogs. Calculated from these values, the closing cone should be about 2 to 3 mm long. In humans, the outer diameter of osteons is 180 to 220 μm, and the wall thickness is 90 to 100 μm. Because the apposition rate is only 1 μm/day, completion of an osteon takes at least 3 to 4 months.[42]

REMODELING OF CANCELLOUS BONE

The primary trabeculae arising from endochondral ossification are composed of a calcified cartilage core coated with woven or primary parallel-fibered bone. In the growing metaphysis the primary spongiosa is rapidly remodeled and substituted by trabeculae made exclusively of lamellar bone (Fig. 2–11). During this remodeling, the original honeycombed architecture (seen only in transverse sections) is changed into a scaffold made of beams and plates. Later, a great deal of this secondary spongiosa disappears at the expense of the elongating marrow cavity.

At first glance, the trabeculae in the adult spongiosa disclose few structural peculiarities. Their diameter of roughly 200 μm stays within the limits of the canaliculolacunar transport distance and, accordingly, vascular canals or osteon-like structures are extremely rare. Staining of cement lines, however, reveals a surprisingly complex assembly of lamellar bone compartments (lamellar "packets"), deposited at different times and glued together

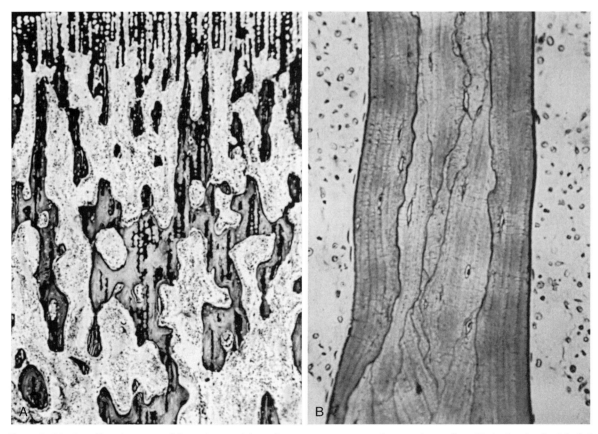

FIGURE 2–11. Cancellous bone remodeling. *A,* Remodeling of primary spongiosa in the metaphysis of a rabbit's tibia (×50). Calcified cartilage remnants (dark inclusions) disappear gradually during the substitution of primary by secondary trabeculae. *B,* Trabeculae in adult human cancellous bone (×250). Staining of cement lines reveals the composite conglomerate of lamellar packets (bone structural units [BSUs]) formed at various times during past remodeling activities.

almost like a wooden conglomerate (see Fig. 2–11B). This finding indicates that cancellous bone, too, is constantly being renewed by a remodeling process that shares many features with that of cortical BMU (Fig. 2–12).

Formation of a new packet begins with the activation of osteoclasts. They form an erosion cavity on the trabecular surface with a diameter of 0.5 to 1 mm and an average depth of 50 µm, seldom more than 70 µm. At the end of this resorption phase the osteoclasts are replaced by inconspicuous mononuclear cells, and after a short intermission or reversal phase, osteoblasts start depositing new bone into the excavation and possibly fill it completely. The completed new lamellar packet represents a bone structural unit, and the cell population involved in its formation is, in analogy to a cortical BMU, called a cancellous BMU. Again, the staining of the cement lines allows a clear demarcation of individual lamellar packets. It is assumed that the dynamics of BMU-mediated cancellous bone remodeling resemble those of cortical BMUs.[84, 85] It is possible that resorption, followed by formation, also moves along the endosteal surface like one half of the cutter cone and closing cone in a cortical BMU, although this is, for geometric reasons, difficult to demonstrate in microscopic sections.[86]

REGULATION OF BONE REMODELING

The physiologic haversian remodeling rate (i.e., the number of BMUs as a percentage of the total number of osteons in cortical cross sections or calculated per unit cross-sectional area) varies from bone to bone and also with age. Turnover values have been established for ribs.[80] Bone biopsy specimens are currently almost exclusively taken from the iliac crest, and considerably more values related to changes in bone structure and turnover are available for cancellous bone. They serve as standard values for studies of metabolic bone disease and therefore are not discussed here.

Bone remodeling is systemically activated by growth, thyroid, and parathyroid hormones and inhibited by calcitonin, cortisone, and possibly calcium. Pharmacologically, bisphosphonates not only are potent inhibitors of osteoclastic resorption but also seem to diminish the overall bone turnover rate.

Locally, bone turnover is greatly stimulated by mechanical lesions such as fractures, surgical defects, and insertion of implants or by any inflammatory process. Temporary interruption of the blood supply (autografts) also triggers revascularization and bone substitution via BMU-mediated remodeling. One common feature of this stimulation is the lag phase of several weeks between activation and onset of the resorptive phase. (These aspects of the local reactions are discussed further in the section "Bone Repair and Fracture Healing.")

The *coupling of resorption and formation,* which is so impressive in microscopic investigations, is still under dispute as far as its regulation is concerned.[79] It has to be recalled that Frost[40] originally defined the BMU as a typical example of intercellular communication. This assumption initiated the search for coupling factors.[26] At present, the idea that a rather complex interaction of multiple factors is involved in the initiation and coordina-

tion of resorptive and formative activities is favored. This interaction includes (1) osteoclast activation, possibly mediated by lining cells; (2) factors released from the bone matrix by osteoclasts to induce osteoblast proliferation and differentiation; and (3) factors produced by other local cells apt to stimulate all these processes.[74]

Lately, not only is the principle of coupling applied to the basic activities of resorption and formation, but it is also suggested that their performances are balanced with respect to each other. That is, the amount of bone resorbed must be replaced by the same volume in the following period of formation.[84, 85] If this is true, cancellous bone remodeling should result in a substitution of bone matrix without any change in trabecular volume and shape. Systemic and persisting negative balance at the BMU level is, according to bone histologists, a plausible mechanism for bone loss and osteoporosis. Localized imbalance or uncoupling (no formation following resorption or formation without preceding resorption) would change not only the dimension but also the shape of the trabeculae and modify the architecture of the spongiosa. If this is a response to changes in magnitude and direction of load, it helps to explain the functional adaptation of bone, as postulated by Julius Wolff in 1882[130] and many others up to recent years.

BONE REPAIR AND FRACTURE HEALING

Basic Pattern of Bone Defect Repair

The healing pattern of bone defects provides an excellent model for the study of the natural course of bone regeneration in mechanically noncompromised sites and under good vascular conditions. This mode of healing is, for obvious reasons, of clinical interest. Open reduction and internal fixation aim to achieve a close adaptation and stable fixation of the fragment ends and result in direct (or primary) fracture healing without any detour via cartilage formation and endochondral ossification. The pattern of defect repair also characterizes the incorporation of bone grafts as well as the osseointegration of orthopaedic and dental implants, where precise fitting and primary stability are essential for success.

Healing of small cortical defects was examined microscopically in bore holes of 0.1 to 1 mm diameter in the cortex of tibias in rabbits.[66] Bone formation within these holes starts within a couple of days without preceding osteoclastic resorption (Fig. 2–13). Woven bone is deposited, first upon the wall of the holes. Holes with a diameter of 200 µm or less are then concentrically filled, like secondary osteons. Larger holes are bridged within the first 2 weeks by a scaffold of woven bone. Then parallel-fibered bone and lamellar bone are deposited upon the newly formed trabeculae until the intertrabecular space is almost completely filled at about 4 to 6 weeks. The threshold value for this rapid bridging is around 1 mm[111] in rabbit cortical bone. Larger holes cannot be covered instantly or, in other words, by one single jump ("osteogenic jumping distance").[50] This does not mean that the holes stay

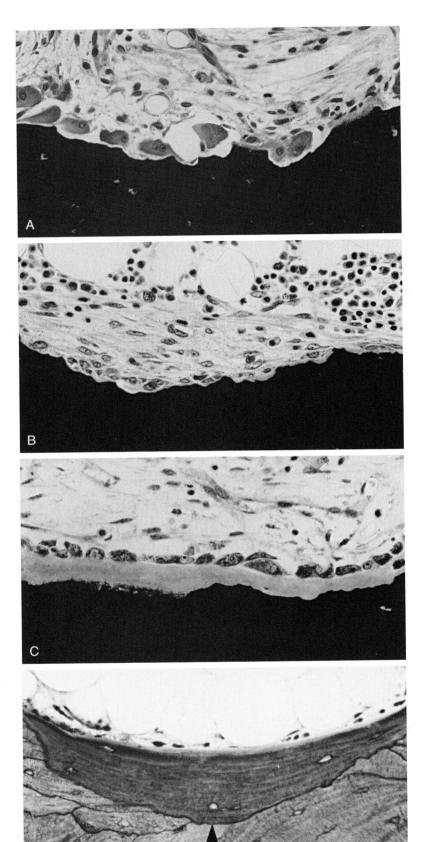

Figure 2–12. Stages of trabecular bone remodeling. Assembly of micrographs collected in human iliac crest biopsies. *A,* Resorptive phase: osteoclasts form a resorption cavity. *B,* Reversal phase: osteoclasts have disappeared, and the cavity is lined by inconspicuous mononucleated cells. *C,* Formative phase: osteoblasts start filling the cavity by deposition of lamellar bone. *D,* Completed new packet (bone structural unit [BSU]), delineated by a reversal line *(arrowhead).* (*A–C,* Undecalcified microtome sections, von Kossa reaction and MacNeal's tetrachrome, ×330; *D,* ground section, surface stained with toluidine blue, ×260.)

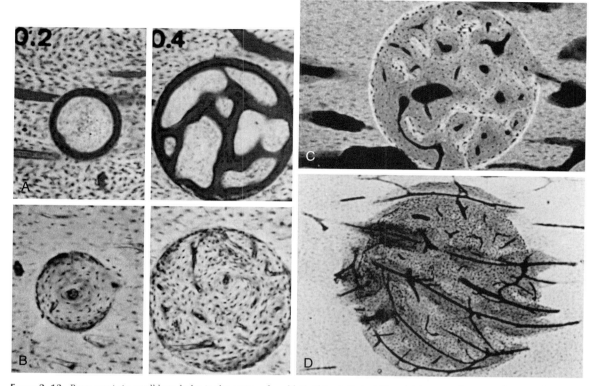

FIGURE 2–13. Bone repair in small bore holes in the cortex of a rabbit's tibia. *A,* Holes 0.2 and 0.4 mm in diameter after 1 week (*A*) and after 4 weeks (*B*). Basic fuchsin stain. Note the size-dependent difference in the healing pattern. *C,* A 0.6-mm hole after 6 weeks. The initially formed woven bone appears brighter in the microradiographs because of its higher mineral density. *D,* After 6 months, most of the originally formed bony filling is replaced by newly formed osteons, thus restoring the original architecture of the cortex (microradiograph, same magnification as *C*). (*A–D,* From Johner, R. Helv Chir Acta 39:409, 1972.)

permanently open, but it takes considerably longer to complete the filling.

The compact bone that fills the holes at 4 to 6 weeks differs markedly from the original cortex. Complete healing in the sense of full restoration of the original structure can be achieved only by haversian remodeling. This remodeling starts in the second and third months and continues for months if not years.

In summary, repair of small cortical defects can be divided into three stages that closely resemble the stages of formation of compact bone during development and growth. First, the defect is bridged with woven bone. The resulting scaffold is then reinforced by parallel-fibered and lamellar bone, and finally the original structure is restored by haversian remodeling.

Promotion of Bone Defect Repair

The healing capacity of bone defects has its limitations. Bore hole experiments have shown that a critical value for the defect size exists. When this value is surpassed, the defect persists, at least partially. The actual dimension of critical size defects varies considerably, depending on species, age, and the anatomic location. Therefore, the critical size of defects has to be specifically defined in animal experiments. Another important aspect is the containment of the defect or, in other words, the condition of the confining walls: bony walls and open communica-

tions with the bone marrow space are more advantageous for a bony filling than contact with connective tissue elements.

Conditions that impede or prevent bone repair include (1) failure of vascular supply, (2) mechanical instability, (3) oversized defects, and (4) competing tissues of high proliferative potential. The problems arising from vascularity and instability are treated in the context of fracture healing. Different procedures are established for promotion of bone repair in oversized defects and for the prevention of fibrous tissue ingrowth. In view of their biologic aspects, the following principles are briefly discussed: osteoconduction, osteogenic transfer, osteoinduction, distraction osteogenesis, and guided bone regeneration.

OSTEOCONDUCTION

Osteoconduction essentially means provision of a temporary or permanent scaffold as a solid base for bone formation. It requires an appropriate structure and dimension for tissue ingrowth and surface properties that favor bone deposition. Adult human cancellous bone offers an almost ideal structure for osteoconduction, namely a bone volume density of 20% to 30% (equal to a porosity of 70% to 80%), a mean trabecular width of about 200 μm, an average intertrabecular pore size of roughly 500 μm, and ample pore interconnections. Most bone substitutes cannot compete with such dimensions. In order to reach sufficient strength, their porosity must stay in the range of 50% at the expense of size and number of the interconnecting pores. Besides these structural features, osteoconduction also depends on the compatibility and the surface properties of the material. It should be bioinert or bioactive, and its surface should be osteophilic, that is, attractive for bone ongrowth and bone matrix apposition.

Osteoconduction is the basis for cancellous bone transplantation, and cancellous autografts set the standard for judging its benefits. Because autografts do not cause any immune reaction, both cells and matrix can be transplanted, and many cells stay alive. As stated over and over again by Burwell[14] and others, cancellous autografts are a composite of bone and bone marrow, and both participate in the mechanism of transplantation in a way that is best characterized as an *osteogenic transfer.*

OSTEOGENIC TRANSFER

In a cancellous autograft, both bone cells and bone matrix are transferred to the recipient site. Transfer of *osteogenic bone cells* includes two different cell populations: bone surface cells and bone marrow stroma cells. As shown by histomorphometry of iliac crest cancellous bone, the endosteal surface is lined to 3% to 5% by osteoblasts, less than 1% osteoclasts, and 90% to 95% inconspicuous bone lining cells. Bone lining cells belong to the osteoblast family and may represent a reserve for the recruitment of osteoblast precursors. Another source for osteoblast precursors is the bone marrow. Bone marrow stroma cells comprise determined and inducible osteoprogenitor cells and possibly mesenchymal stem cells, all considered candidates for osteoblast differentiation. Finally, endothelial cells constitute another important component of the bone marrow. They enable rapid revascularization and angiogenesis in bone formation sites, which is essential for osteogenesis.

Osteogenic bone matrix transfer comprises cytokines, growth factors, morphogens, and other promoters of bone formation, all entombed in the bone matrix. Release of such growth factors has mostly been demonstrated after decalcification of the bone matrix. It is assumed, however, that mechanical lesions at the level of the fracture plane or created by surgical intervention also expose some of these matrix components and make them accessible, at least locally, for cells involved in bone turnover.

OSTEOINDUCTION

The transfer of matrix-bound growth factors is often equated with osteoinduction. It has to be recalled, however, that osteoinduction was originally defined as a process that leads to bone formation in heterotopic sites, that is, in sites where bone normally does not occur. Most of the classical experiments on bone induction focused on heterotopic bone formation. Osteoinduction has attracted numerous investigators, and many substances and tissue components have been tested in different species, including humans. Rats and rabbits are by far the best responders.

Attempts to extract and purify the inductive principle often led to a loss of osteoinductive capacity, and in some older experiments the solvent alone turned out to be effective. Two principles have survived and are currently under intensive investigation: Lacroix's osteogenin and the closely related bone morphogenetic protein (BMP) of Urist and colleagues.[125] BMP becomes effective if bone matrix is demineralized in hydrochloric acid, washed, and lyophilized. The development of new technologies has made it possible to produce recombinant human BMP-2 and made it available for experimental and clinical trials on a larger scale.[133]

Reddi[99] systematically studied the cascade of events that follows the subcutaneous injection of demineralized bone powder in rats. He established a programmed sequence of cell and tissue differentiation that, in fact, mimics endochondral bone formation. During the first 3 to 4 days, mesenchymal cells proliferate. From days 5 to 8, cartilage develops and 1 day later starts calcification, later followed by vascular invasion and bone substitution from day 10 to 11 on. Thus, cartilage seems to be a mandatory intermediate in the evolution of heterotopically formed ossicles originating from inducible osteoprecursor cells.

If the inducing principle acts on determined osteoprecursor cells, their response is direct bone formation without intermediate cartilage differentiation. The lag phase is short, seldom longer than 1 to 3 days, and new bone is laid down on bone surfaces already present. One may argue whether this process is actually osteoinduction or just activation of bone formation.[17] For that reason we prefer to call it simply activation and leave the critical test for true osteoinduction to the capacity of initiating bone formation in heterotopic sites.

CALLUS DISTRACTION (DISTRACTION OSTEOGENESIS)

Although lengthening bones by stretching callus in its early stages of formation goes back to the last century,[87] Ilizarov[64, 65] deserves recognition for the careful and systematic perfection of this principle, which is now applied worldwide for bone lengthening, bridging of diaphyseal defects in long bones by segment transport, or vertical alveolar crest augmentation in dental implantology.

Callus distraction indeed reveals an astonishing plasticity of the initial phase of woven bone formation in bone repair. The concept of the procedure is relatively simple. First, the bone has to be cut in two by osteotomy or corticotomy. After stable fixation in a neutral position, an initial period of about 1 week is allowed for the initiation of bone repair. This time interval allows the invasion of the osteotomy gap by blood vessels and granulation tissue and the activation of woven bone formation along the cut surface of the host cortices. Then the osteotomy gap is stretched at a rate of about 1 mm/day in four or more increments. Distraction is performed with external fixators that exclude any micromovement other than the controlled daily distraction. The importance of stability has been experimentally demonstrated by Ilizarov.[65] Micromotion leads to formation of fibrous tissue or cartilage and inevitably to delayed union or nonunion. Preservation of the vascular supply is another prerequisite for the success of the procedure.

Callus formation in the gradually extended gap can be

followed radiographically (Fig. 2–14). The "fragment ends" serve as the base for formation of new bone that extends from both sides toward a radiolucent interzone. The bony regenerate has a stringy appearance, indicating the formation of parallel columns and plates. They are elongated toward the interzone at a daily rate of up to 500 μm, which is surprisingly high. The fibrous interzone persists as long as distraction continues, and after distraction has ended, it often takes weeks to complete its bridging. In addition, the initial density of the regenerated bone is low and it takes at least months for its compaction and even years until a true cortex is restored by haversian remodeling. Clinical experience, however, has shown that load bearing, especially with the protection of the fixation device, can start earlier and may even accelerate the reinforcement and remodeling.

The *histology of callus distraction* was described in experimental animals[2, 24] and in humans[117, 119] (Fig. 2–15). The fibrous interzone functions as a center for fibroblast proliferation and fibrous tissue formation. Under the tensile forces created by the distraction, the collagen fibers are aligned into longitudinal bundles. The invading blood vessels arise from the periosteal envelope and the bone marrow at both bone ends. Accompanied by perivascular cells, they grow into the longitudinal interfibrillar compartments (see Fig. 2–15B). Bone formation resembles intramembranous ossification and follows the

pattern of woven bone formation described earlier. The bony spicules that climb along the fiber bundles are lengthened by bone deposition on their tips, accomplished by newly recruited osteoblasts (see Fig. 2–15C). The longitudinal growth rate, therefore, depends on proliferation and differentiation of osteoblast precursors, whereas the bone apposition rate determines the daily increase in width of the individual trabeculae. The resulting primary scaffold consists of woven bone, which is later reinforced by parallel-fibered and lamellar bone and finally reorganized by haversian remodeling, strictly according to the rules that characterize bone formation during growth or in small cortical defects.

Side effects and complications of callus distraction result from too rapid distraction. These include local hematoma, caused by rupture of blood vessels, or microfractures in newly formed trabeculae, which usually heal by microcallus formation. Furthermore, extensive limb lengthening may cause complications related to overstretching of soft tissues, such as muscles, tendons, nerves, and blood vessels.

GUIDED BONE REGENERATION (MEMBRANE PROTECTION OF TISSUE DIFFERENTIATION)

The use of barrier membranes is an attempt to promote healing of bone defects of larger than critical size by

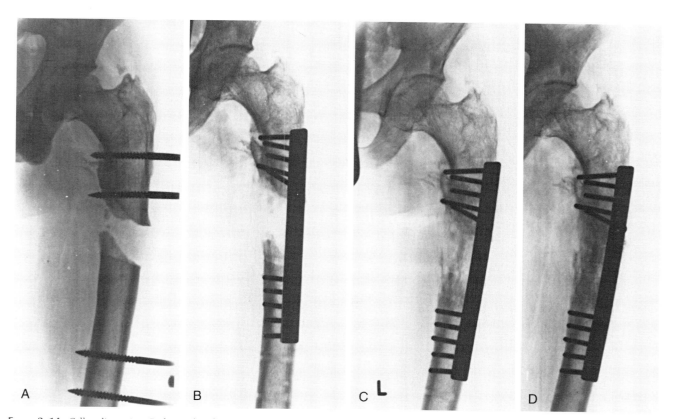

FIGURE 2–14. Callus distraction. Radiographs of a patient who underwent bone lengthening of his left femur. *A,* The corticotomy was distracted with a modified external fixator at a daily rate of 1 mm for 5 weeks, starting in the second week. *B,* At 5 weeks, when a lengthening of about 30 mm was accomplished, the fixator was replaced by a plate that ensured stable fixation of the fragment ends. During this intervention, a superficial biopsy was performed. Note the appearance of calcified areas in the distraction space. *C,* Increased bone density at 3 months. *D,* Dense bony regenerate at 6 months. (From Schenk, R.K.; Gächter, A. In: Brighton, C.T.; Friedlander, G.; Lane, J.M., eds. Bone Formation and Repair. Rosemont, IL, American Academy of Orthopaedic Surgeons, 1994, p. 387.)

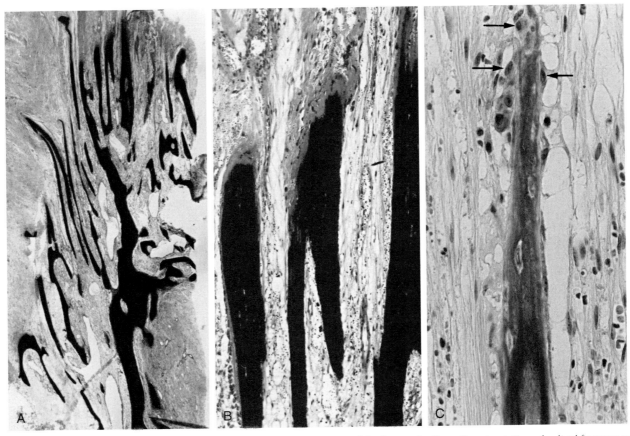

FIGURE 2–15. Longitudinal microtome sections (5 µm) through the distal segment of the distracted callus at 5 weeks. *A*, From the distal fragment end *(below)*, longitudinal bone columns grow proximally into the fibrous interzone (von Kossa and MacNeal's tetrachrome, ×6). *B*, Bone columns, or plates, grow between the stretched collagen fiber bundles and numerous longitudinal blood vessels (von Kossa and MacNeal's tetrachrome, ×30). *C*, Lengthening of a column. Osteoblasts *(arrows)* are continuously added to the proximal end of the bony strut and deposit osteoid (dark) that ultimately forms a mineralized core. (Goldner stain, ×380.) (From Schenk, R.K.; Gächter, A. In: Brighton, C.T.; Friedlander, G.; Lane, J.M., eds. Bone Formation and Repair. Rosemont, IL, American Academy of Orthopaedic Surgeons, 1994, p. 387.)

protection against the ingrowth of competing, nonosteo-genic cells. The method goes back to experimental studies in the late 1950s.[4, 11, 101, 118] Later, it was applied for promotion of periodontal regeneration, in different types of bone defects, and around dental implants.[21, 22] The procedure is now commonly referred to as guided tissue regeneration or, more specifically, guided bone regenera-tion. In view of its importance for the biology of fracture repair, the healing pattern of membrane-protected defects in canine mandibles is discussed in some detail.[115, 116]

After extraction of the premolar teeth and the first molar and an appropriate healing time for the extraction sockets of 3 to 4 months, defects 12 to 15 mm wide and 10 to 12 mm deep were created in the alveolar ridge (Fig. 2–16A). Control defects were simply closed with a mucoperiosteal flap. The test defects were covered with a cell-occlusive, nonresorbable expanded polytetrafluoro-ethylene (Teflon) membrane that was tightly adapted to the margins of the defect and fixed with miniscrews. A homogeneous coagulum was obtained by injection of intravenously aspired blood underneath the membrane. This procedure ensured that ingrowth of cells and vessels was possible only from the opened marrow space in the defect walls. In the control sites, bone formation was restricted at 2 months to the bridging of the surgically created openings (see Fig. 2–16B). At 4 months, there was

no substantial progress, and the cavity in the alveolar crest was filled with gingival mucosa. In the test sites, woven bone had already invaded a considerable part of the space secluded by the membrane at 2 months (see Fig. 2–16C). The newly formed bone resembled a primary spongiosa and was vascularized by an abundance of blood vessels originating from the medullary net.

In the following period, that is, up to 4 months, the filling of the former defect continued and a remarkable development in the new bone compartment took place. The rather uniform primary spongiosa was transformed into a cortical layer, confining a marrow space split up into smaller compartments by the trabeculae of a secondary spongiosa (see Fig. 2–16D and E).

The corticalization of the primary spongiosa closely resembled the formation of cortical bone during intra-membranous ossification and growth (Fig. 2–17). The primary scaffold of woven bone was first reinforced by parallel-fibered bone. Continuing apposition narrowed the intertrabecular spaces and resulted in the formation of primary osteons, still separated by struts and plates of woven bone. Up to this level of differentiation, the maturation process of the cortical layer was clearly dominated by bone formation, and practically no osteo-clasts were seen in the cortical domain. Osteoclasts appeared, however, at 4 months with the onset of bone remodeling, when both the woven bone and the parallel-fibered compartment were replaced by lamellar bone in the form of secondary osteons or haversian systems. At this time, the primary spongiosa in the marrow space had already been replaced by a secondary spongiosa with the typical features of trabeculae composed of lamellar packets formed in earlier cycles of remodeling activity.

The term guided bone regeneration is somewhat misleading. The membrane does not serve as a scaffold for bone apposition but rather protects the bone-forming

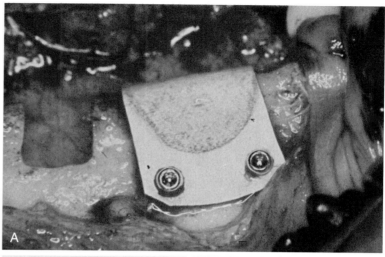

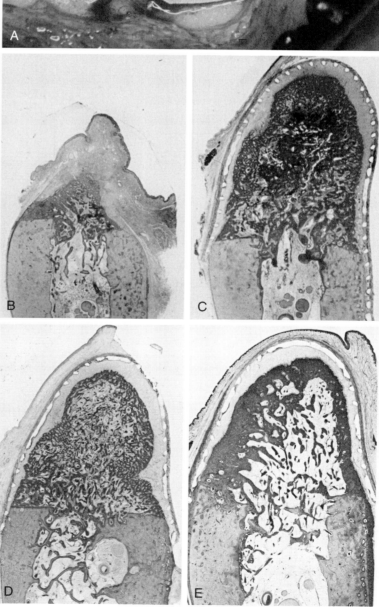

FIGURE 2–16. Guided bone regeneration in experimental defects in the canine mandible. *A,* Critical size defects (10 × 12 × 10 mm) are produced in the edentulous alveolar crest. Control defects are simply covered by the muco-periosteal flap, experimental sites by a nonresorbable barrier membrane. *B,* Control defects at 2 months. New bone formation is restricted to the surgically created opening of the marrow cavity. *C,* Bone formation beneath a barrier membrane at 2 months. The space secluded by the membrane is almost completely filled by newly formed bone. *D,* At 2 months, the newly formed bone resembles a rather dense, primary spongiosa. *E,* At 4 months, a cortical layer, confining a marrow space with differentiation of a secondary spongiosa, has developed. (From Schenk, R.K.; Buser, D.; Hardwick, W.R.; Dahlin, C. Int J Oral Maxillofac Implants 9:1, 1994.)

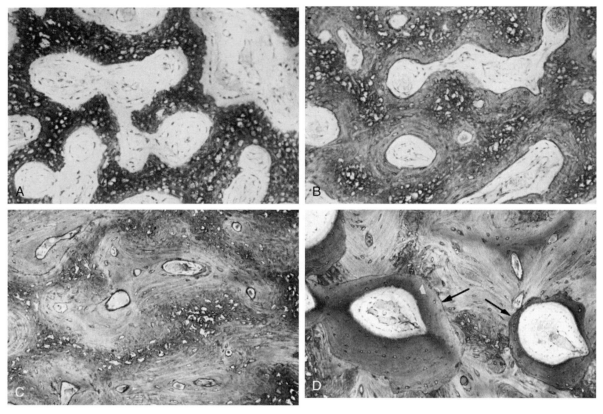

FIGURE 2–17. Differentiation of cortical bone beneath barrier membranes. (Ground sections, surface stained with toluidine blue, ×85.) *A,* At 2 months, a scaffold of woven bone is formed, characterized by the abundance of osteocytes in a heavily stained matrix and numerous, wide vascular spaces. *B,* An increased bone density is achieved by reinforcement of the woven bone by deposition of parallel-fibered bone (less intensely stained). *C,* Continuous deposition of parallel-fibered and lamellar bone narrows the intertrabecular spaces to the vascular canals of primary osteons. *D,* At 4 months, cortical remodeling has started and partially replaces the primary bone by secondary osteons (haversian systems). Note the cement lines *(arrows)* that mark the circumference of secondary osteons. (From Schenk, R.K.; Buser, D.; Hardwick, W.R.; Dahlin, C. Int J Oral Maxillofac Implants 9:1, 1994.)

elements within the defect space against the ingrowth of soft tissues. This concept is in accordance with the observation that a competition exists between the regenerative potentials of lower and higher differentiated tissues. The fact that barrier membranes promote bone regeneration in a defect site is also an argument against the hypothesis that surrounding soft tissues should contribute to the fracture healing by external callus formation.[29, 75]

The histologic observations presented here were made in the mandible of dogs, using a nonresorbable Teflon membrane. The same system is now widely applied for alveolar ridge augmentation in human patients. Healing time differs from the canine data, and a period of 6 to 8 months is recommended before reopening and implant insertion. Further improvement is expected from a shortening of the healing time or even simultaneous performance of implant placement and guided bone regeneration, possibly with newly developed resorbable membranes.

One specific advantage has to be mentioned when callus distraction and guided bone regeneration are compared with osteoconductive procedures: in both situations, the resulting bony regenerate consists exclusively of autogenous, mature and living bone tissue. Even if it is compared with autografts, one has to acknowledge that there are no inclusions of remnants of dead bone in the regenerate, and it can be assumed that, if sufficient

time is allowed for maturation, the recipient site of an implant should offer conditions that are identical to those of original, healthy bone.

Spontaneous Fracture Healing: The Merit of Biologic Stabilization

Fracture of a bone means loss of mechanical integrity and continuity. In addition, the lesion or rupture of blood vessels leads to localized avascularity of the fragment ends, which may become displaced. The natural course of fracture healing (or spontaneous healing) includes (1) interfragmentary stabilization by periosteal and endosteal callus formation and by interfragmentary fibrocartilage differentiation, (2) restoration of continuity and bone union by intramembranous and endochondral ossification, and (3) substitution of avascular and necrotic areas by haversian remodeling. Malalignment of fragments may be corrected to a certain extent by (4) modeling of the fracture site and (5) functional adaptation. In principle, this healing pattern is also effective after external fixation by conservative means and in many instances in which open or closed surgical reduction does not result in rigid fixation. It is often referred to as *secondary* or *indirect healing,* mainly because intermediate connective tissue or fibrocartilage is initially formed within the fracture gap and only secondarily replaced by bone. Radiologic characteristics of secondary healing are more or less abundant callus formation, temporary widening of the fracture gap by osteoclastic resorption, and a relatively slow disappearance of the radiolucent fracture line related to fibrocartilage mineralization and bone formation (Fig. 2–18).

Spontaneous healing of a broken bone is, in fact, an astonishing cellular performance and shares many principles with the development and growth of the skeleton already discussed in previous chapters. They are considered again here in regard to how the mechanical conditions for bone union can be created by means of biologic stabilization, especially by callus production and interfragmentary tissue differentiation (Fig. 2–19).

CALLUS FORMATION

Callus formation is the response of determined osteoprecursor cells in the periosteum and endosteum to activating factors released from freshly injured bone. This response is fast: bone formation starts within a few days, depending mainly on the blood supply in the fracture area. Histologically, callus formation resembles intramembranous bone formation, and the outer and inner surfaces of the fragment ends serve as the solid base on which new bone can be deposited.

At first, woven bone is formed. Its trabeculae surround wide vascular channels that are concentrically narrowed by further woven and lamellar bone apposition. The classical periosteal callus forms a conical cuff around the fragment ends, with its largest diameter facing the fracture plane. To some extent, the amount of periosteal callus reflects the degree of instability or interfragmentary movement, provided vascularization remains intact. The mechanical role of callus formation is obvious: it gradually enlarges the diameter of the fragment ends and thereby the cross section of the fracture area (Fig. 2–20). This effect lengthens the lever arm for the forces generated by the

resistance of the interfragmentary tissue against compression or elongation. This mechanism of biologic stabilization can be understood by considering the gain in bending strength obtained with a wide versus a narrow tube made of equal amounts of an identical material. By increasing the diameter, the callus slowly reduces the mobility of the fragments and the resulting strain on the interfragmentary tissue.

INTERFRAGMENTARY TISSUE RESPONSE

Tissue differentiation in the fracture gap is subject to mechanical influences that act either directly on the cells or indirectly via the blood supply. In general, granulation tissue invades and replaces the initial hematoma and then differentiates into connective tissue and fibrocartilage. There is a wide variation in the time of appearance and local distribution of these tissue types. Differences in width and shape of the fracture gap and in the local blood supply make this understandable. *Granulation tissue* and *loose connective tissue* are well vascularized and rich in fixed and mobile cells. The random orientation of tender collagen fibrils makes for easy deformability. Not only does *dense connective tissue* contain more and thicker collagen fibrils, but these fibrils are also organized in bundles and are often anchored in the bony fragment ends. Their course reflects the main direction of tensile forces created by interfragmentary motion. Cellularity and vascularity, on the other hand, are more prominent in loose connective tissue.

In view of its mechanical and metabolic properties, *fibrocartilage* deserves special attention. It is, in fact, a composite of connective tissue and cartilage. The chondrocytes are surrounded by a cartilaginous matrix distributed as small islands in a meshwork of fibers. In fibrocartilage, the fibrous component consists of unmasked bundles of type I collagen. The cartilaginous portion contains type II collagen, is rich in proteoglycans (aggrecans), and has the capacity of chondrocytes to survive under avascular or anaerobic conditions. Espe-

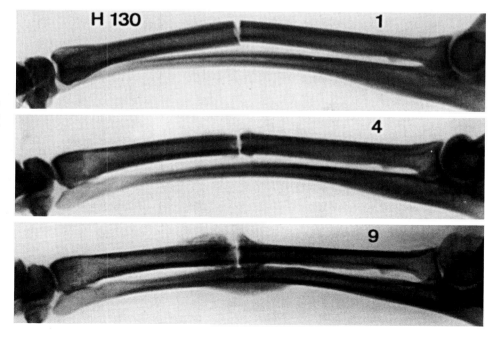

FIGURE 2–18. Spontaneous fracture healing was documented by a series of experimental delayed unions after transverse resection osteotomy in the radii of dogs and unrestricted use of the limbs (Müller et al., 1968). These radiographs elucidate the typical postoperative course: widening of the gap by resorption of the fragment ends and extensive periosteal and endosteal callus formation. Numbers indicate number of weeks from resection.

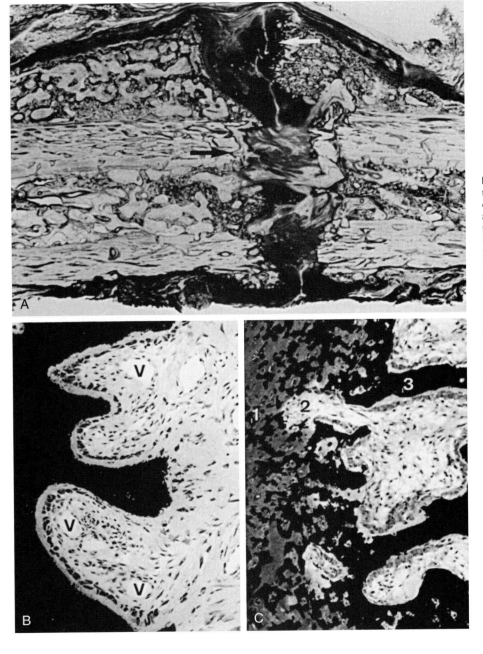

FIGURE 2–19. *A,* Longitudinal section through the fracture site at 14 weeks after operation confirms bony callus formation along the periosteal surface and within the marrow cavity. The central part of the fracture gap contains fibrous tissue, the peripheral fibrocartilage. Bone formation proceeds from both sides toward the fracture plane. Its pattern depends on the type of interfragmentary tissue present. The *black arrow* indicates the area shown in *B;* the *white arrow,* the area in *C. B,* Connective tissue, if sufficiently vascularized, permits intramembranous ossification. The bony fragment ends are lined by osteoblasts and osteoid seams, indicating ongoing bone apposition. V, blood vessels. (von Kossa's and acid fuchsin stains, ×80.) *C,* Fibrocartilage (to the left) has to mineralize (1) before undergoing resorption and vascular invasion (2). As in the growth plate, bone is deposited on persisting calcified cartilage cores (3). (von Kossa's and acid fuchsin stains, ×80.)

cially in the case of delayed healing or in developing hypertrophic nonunions, more and more interfragmentary tissue transforms into fibrocartilage and ultimately occupies the entire fracture gap. In this way, the interfragmentary tissue becomes considerably stiffer and increases the resistance against deformation provoked by motion of the fragment ends.

Cartilage has unique mechanical properties. Its intrinsic swelling pressure makes it viscoelastic and resistant to compression and shear. This capacity depends directly on its *proteoglycan* content. Chemical analysis and isolation of these giant macromolecules have substantially contributed to the understanding of their mechanical role. Proteoglycan aggregates consist of hyaluronic acid, link protein, core protein, and glycosaminoglycan chains, made up mostly of

chondroitin and keratan sulfate. Glycosaminoglycans contain a large number of fixed anionic groups, carboxyls, and sulfate esters, which are negatively charged under physiologic conditions. The high negative charge density causes the proteoglycans to expand and occupy large domains. In cartilage, the network of collagen fibrils confines the interfibrillar space available for proteoglycans to about one fifth of the respective domain in free solution.[51] This confinement creates an intrinsic pressure in the range of 2 to 3 atmospheres. (An alternative explanation is that the negative charges attract and capture positively charged ions, increase the ion concentration, and thus produce osmotic pressure.)

Fibrocartilage occurs preferentially in locations where shape and size of the fracture gap lead to compression of

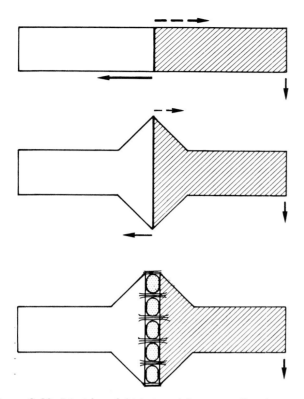

FIGURE 2–20. Principles of biologic stabilization. Callus formation increases the cross section and lever arm against deforming forces. Fibrocartilage differentiation in the fracture gap gradually builds up osmotic pressure and thus further augments stability.

its content.[108, 109, 116] Continuous or intermittent compression is detrimental to the blood supply and favors tissues viable under anaerobic conditions. Because fibrocartilage cells continue to extrude proteoglycans into the surrounding matrix, it can be assumed that this tissue continuously increases its resistance to deformation and thereby reduces instability. The critical question remains, however, whether and when the overall stability reaches a value that allows tissue mineralization, which ultimately provides the solid base indispensable for bone deposition.

BRIDGING OF THE FRACTURE GAP BY BONE (CONSOLIDATION)

A fracture is consolidated as soon as bone union in any site in the fracture gap is achieved. The location of the first bone bridge varies, depending on local anatomic, metabolic, and mechanical conditions. In the interfragmentary region, bone can be formed by direct apposition on the surface of the fragment ends or by substitution of fibrocartilage or fibrous tissue, or both.

Appositional bone formation along the surface lining the fracture gap is restricted to well-vascularized areas that are exposed minimally or not at all to mechanical alterations. For the most part, these are cavities or indentations created by the fracture itself or by osteoclastic resorption. This bone formation follows the pattern of intramembranous (or desmal) ossification. Osteoblasts line up along the fragment ends, intermingled with collagen fibers, which are often incorporated in the newly formed bone (Fig. 2–21*A*; see Fig. 2–19*B*). This type of apposi-

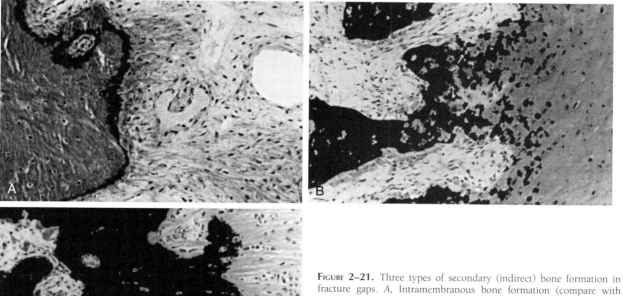

FIGURE 2–21. Three types of secondary (indirect) bone formation in fracture gaps. *A*, Intramembranous bone formation (compare with Fig. 2–19*B*). *B*, Bony substitution of fibrocartilage (compare with Fig. 2–19*C*) (von Kossa's and acid fuchsin stains, ×100). *C*, Bony substitution of dense fibrous tissue. Fibrous tissue undergoes mineralization (1) and is subsequently resorbed and substituted by bone (2) (von Kossa's and acid fuchsin stains, ×100).

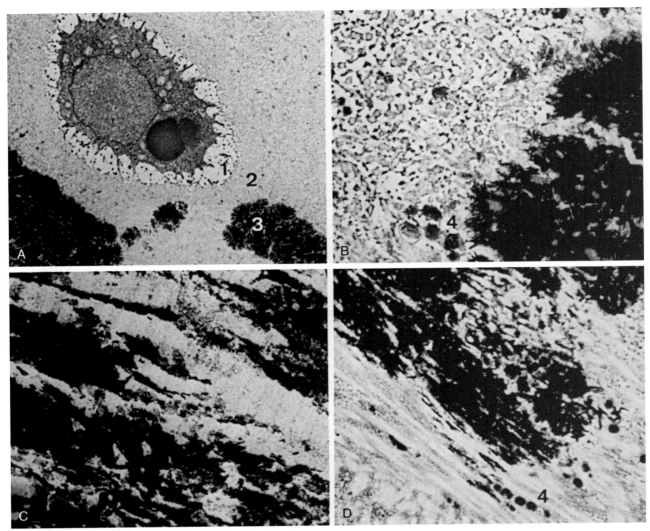

Figure 2–22. Mineralization of fibrocartilage and fibrous tissue. *A,* Fibrochondrocyte, surrounded by proteoglycans (1), cartilaginous matrix (2), and islands of calcification (3). *B,* Matrix vesicles (4) are regularly found along the borderline between mineralized and nonmineralized fibrocartilaginous matrix. *C,* Mineralized fibrous tissue closely resembles bone but lacks the close association of apatite crystals to the cross striation of type I collagen fibrils (×62,000). *D,* Again, matrix vesicles are present along the mineralization front of the connective tissue (×40,000).

tional bone formation, however, helps to decrease the width of the interfragmentary space but is unlikely to contribute substantially to the bridging of the gap.

Fibrocartilage has to undergo mineralization before it can be replaced by bone. Mineral clusters are preferentially located around groups of chondrocytes (see Figs. 2–19C and 2–21B). As in growth cartilage, the mineral deposits are always separated from the cells by a layer of nonmineralized matrix (Fig. 2–22A). The assumption that fibrocartilage mineralization is initiated and controlled by chondrocytes is supported by the presence of matrix vesicles in locations where freshly deposited apatite crystals are found (see Fig. 2–22B).

The further steps of bone substitution closely resemble those of endochondral ossification. Vascular invasion of fibrocartilage is coupled with resorption of mineralized matrix by multinucleated chondroclasts and breakdown of nonmineralized zones by macrophages or endothelial cells. Blood vessels, accompanied by osteoblasts and their precursors, follow the resorbing cells. Calcified fibrocarti-

lage is only partially resorbed, but its remnants are cleaned from adhering nonmineralized parts before osteoblasts start utilizing them as the solid base for new bone deposition. As in the primary spongiosa, newly formed, primary trabeculae are easily recognized by the core of calcified fibrocartilage enclosed. The analogy to the growth plate is further supported by the fact that any disturbance of fibrocartilage mineralization impedes vascular ingrowth and bone substitution of the interfragmentary fibrocartilage, a common finding in delayed unions and nonunions.

Like fibrocartilage, dense connective tissue can mineralize and undergo bone substitution in the fracture gap (see Fig. 2–21C). Seen under light as well as by electron microscopy (see Fig. 2–22C), mineralized fibrous tissue closely resembles bone. It also exhibits rather thick type I collagen fibrils with a 64-nm periodicity. The mineral, however, is not tightly associated with the fibrils but rather occupies the interfibrillar space or is randomly precipitated on the collagen. The cells, originally fibrocytes, are completely surrounded by mineralized matrix and lack cytoplasmic connections via canaliculi. Mineralization seems to be mediated by matrix vesicles (see Fig. 2–22*D*); however, the mineralization front runs perpendicular rather than parallel to the fibrils. Like fibrocartilage, calcified fibrous tissue is replaced by bone. As in cortical bone remodeling, osteoclasts open up resorption canals that are subsequently filled by bone (see Fig. 2–21*C*). The daily progress of this substitution is limited again by the osteoclastic resorption rate of about 50 μm/day, and depending on the size of the fracture gap, it takes weeks to achieve consolidation.

On this histophysiologic background, the classical concept of the *bridging callus* merits reactivation. In older schematic representations of fracture healing, the first bone bridge is often depicted directly underneath the periosteum and unites the most peripheral edges of the periosteal callus cuffs. This picture is somewhat surprising because one expects the largest excursions to occur here when angular deformation is forced on the fracture. A closer look at the microscopic structure of the bone bridge solves the problem (Fig. 2–23). The bridging bone does not contain any remnants of calcified fibrocartilage and therefore must have been formed by apposition by the periosteal envelope. This apposition, however, can be realized only when biologic stabilization by callus formation, stiffening through fibrocartilage differentiation, and finally cartilage mineralization have succeeded in providing the solid base required for bone formation.

TISSUE DIFFERENTIATION IN THE FRACTURE GAPS

At this point it seems appropriate to discuss briefly some of the theories of tissue differentiation in the fracture gap. These can be grouped around three topics:

1. The strain tolerance of interfragmentary tissues
2. Mechanical and metabolic influences on tissue differentiation
3. The influence of bone-inducing substances

The mechanical properties of interfragmentary tissues make possible their survival under the strain exerted by interfragmentary motion. From this standpoint, Perren and colleagues[91–94] have considered earlier data published by Yamada[134] concerning the tolerance of different supporting tissues for elongation (Table 2–1).

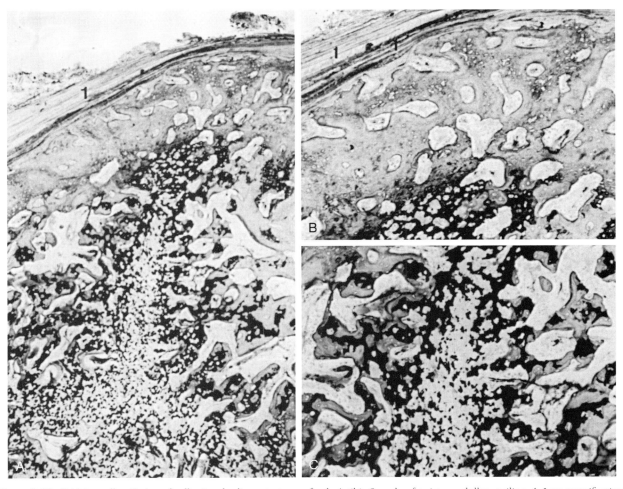

FIGURE 2–23. Bridging callus. Periosteal callus in a healing osteotomy of a dog's tibia 8 weeks after intramedullary nailing. *A,* Low magnification of the callus covered by the periosteum (1) (polished ground section, toluidine blue surface stain, ×50). *B,* The superficial bone bridge lacks any inclusions of calcified cartilage and was therefore formed by direct apposition from its periosteal lining (×85). *C,* In the deeper part, bone is formed by substitution of mineralized fibrocartilage. Accordingly, its trabeculae consist of bone and heavily stained, calcified cartilage cores (×85).

TABLE 2–1 ···

Strain Tolerance of Interfragmentary Tissues

Tissue	Maximal Elongation	Deformation Angle*
Granulation tissue	100%	40°
Connective tissue	5–17%	—
Fibrocartilage	10–13%	5°
Compact bone	2%	0.7°

···

*Bone diameter 30 mm.
Data from Rahn, B.A. In: Sumner-Smith, G., ed. Clinical Orthopedics, Philadelphia, W.B. Saunders, 1982, p. 335; and Yamada, H.; Evans, F.G. Strength of Biological Materials. Baltimore, Williams & Wilkins, 1970.

If these limits are exceeded, the tissue is disrupted. It is worthwhile to remember that strain means deformation (dimension length per length). Therefore, the local strain exerted by a given deformation of the fracture gap causes more strain in narrower and less strain in wider areas. This explains why various tissues, ranging from loose connective tissue to fibrocartilage, may exist simultaneously in gaps of varying sizes. One of the ways to reduce strain and allow a stiffer tissue to exist is to widen the gap by resorption, a common radiologic feature of fracture healing under unstable conditions.

A second assumption of these authors is that only tissue able to survive under a given strain is able to differentiate in a given location. If interfragmentary motion is reduced by increasing callus formation, strain is gradually diminished, and tissue differentiation progresses toward fibrocartilage and ultimately bone. A third assumption is required, however, namely an inherent evolutionary tendency to form bone that is operative in the repair tissue.

Such a tendency might be evoked at the time when determined osteoprogenitor cells in the vicinity of the fragment ends are activated by factors released from injured bone. Mechanical or metabolic conditions, or both, created within the gap could then channel the gene expression of these cells in the direction of connective tissue or cartilage.[103] Lack of oxygen, as a result of compromised capillary circulation, offers another explanation for cartilage formation and is supported by tissue culture experiments from the early 1960s. Other hypotheses are based on the assumption that mechanical forces might directly impinge on the cells and influence tissue differentiation.[5] This possibility was, and still is, discussed, mostly in the German literature, in the context of classical theories about mechanical influences on tissue differentiation. Pauwels[88, 89] thought that unilateral (tensile) forces determine connective tissue formation, whereas uniform hydrostatic pressure would cause the same target cells to become chondrocytes. Minute deformation of a preexisting scaffold of connective or cartilaginous tissue was considered an adequate stimulus for bone formation.

All these assumptions are based on careful biomechanical interpretations of clinical observations with very limited support by experimental data. They thus remain rather hypothetical in nature. It is now well known that a number of alternative local factors, such as streaming potentials, dynamic deformation pattern, static compressive load patterns, ionic conditions, pH variation, and genetic and endocrine factors, may play key roles.[29, 34, 35, 48, 70, 71] Nevertheless, the older, simplified theories still provide a useful concept for a general understanding of some of the tissue reactions in fracture repair.

Propagation of the bone-inducing principles, especially BMP, osteogenin, and derivatives, supports the concept that tissue differentiation in the fracture gap follows the programmed sequence observed in heterotopic bone induction. There is, in fact, a striking conformity in the tissue differentiation in endochondral ossification, heterotopic bone induction, and spontaneous fracture repair. Bone is always formed via a cartilaginous precursor, which has to mineralize before its bony substitution. This apparent analogy seems to support the postulate that fibrocartilage formation gives proof of a BMP-like bone induction taking place in the fracture gap.[56] This assumption, however, neglects the fact that intermediate cartilage formation occurs only in ectopic and not in orthotopic bone induction, in which determined osteoprecursor cells are activated. In addition, cartilage formation is never observed in the repair of bone defects or, as shown later, in cases of primary bone healing under rigid fixation.

REMODELING OF THE FRACTURE SITE

Intramembranous ossification, bone substitution of fibrocartilage and connective tissue, and bridging callus can achieve bone union of the fragments, but the bone that unites the fragments is still rather primitive, and stability can be maintained only with an excess of material. At the same time, avascular and necrotic areas may persist in the fragment ends. The fracture site therefore needs further modeling and remodeling until the ultimate goal—the reconstruction of the original shape and internal architecture of the fractured bone—is accomplished. This reconstruction occurs in all types of fracture repair and becomes especially evident in the course of direct bone healing.

Direct Bone Healing: The Response to Rigid Fixation

Direct or primary bone healing was originally described in radiographs after perfect anatomic reduction and stable fixation. The main criteria were lack of external callus formation and gradual disappearance of the narrow fracture lines. Danis[23] described this as *soudure autogène* (autogenous welding). Although the term *primary healing* is well accepted in the German literature, it has caused some confusion in the Anglo-American scientific community,[132] and *direct healing* therefore seems preferable.

Callus-free direct healing requires what is often called *absolute stability.* A more accurate description of this condition was provided by Steinemann[120]: "Stable fixation by interfragmentary compression results in a solid assembly of bone and implant and avoids any interfragmentary movements." It can be achieved only by exact anatomic reduction of the fracture, and stability of such an assembly can be attained only by compression, as provided by lag screws or compression plates. Microscopically, it is nearly impossible to reduce fragments so perfectly that contact is achieved along their entire interface. There are always some incongruences left, resulting in small gaps separated by contact areas or possibly contact points. Compression must build up enough preload to maintain interfragmentary contact under deforming forces, as created by muscle contraction, physiotherapy, or partial or full weight bearing. A further and decisive requirement for direct bone healing is sufficient blood supply of the fracture area, a condition that depends not only on possible vascular lesions exerted by the fracture itself but also on the handling of soft tissues and bone during the operation.

The histologic equivalent of radiologically defined direct callus-free fracture healing has been verified experimentally in dogs.[104, 105] Transverse osteotomies in the midshaft of canine radii were precisely reduced and rigidly fixed by compression plates with the ulna remaining intact. Postoperatively, full weight bearing was allowed. This experimental procedure was chosen to create reproducible anatomic and mechanical conditions for bone healing and histologic examination.

Radiographs taken at weekly intervals showed uneventful, callus-free direct healing (Fig. 2–24). Histologic examination confirmed this and allowed a further characterization of the tissue reaction in and around the osteotomy. Because relatively thick plates were mounted without any prebending on the dorsal convexity of the radius, compression resulted in interfragmentary contact only in the cortex near the plate. In the far cortex the fragments were regularly separated by 0.2- to 0.5-mm-wide gaps. This approach made it possible to study systematically gap healing and contact healing in identical specimens.

GAP HEALING

In stable (or "quiet") gaps, ingrowth of vessels and mesenchymal cells starts shortly after injury. Osteoblasts differentiate within a few days and start depositing osteoid on the exposed surfaces of the fragment ends, mostly without any preceding osteoclastic resorption (Fig. 2–25). Like periosteal and endosteal callus formation, this appositional bone formation represents the first and most rapid reaction to the release of activating substances from the injured tissue. It shares striking similarities with appositional bone formation during growth and the repair of small cortical defects, especially in view of its size dependence and its pattern and rates. Thus, gaps staying in the range of the outer osteonal diameter (150 to 200 μm) are filled concentrically with lamellar bone, whereas the filling of larger gaps is a composite of initially formed woven bone, completed later on by concentric lamellar bone deposition (see Fig. 2–25C). This rapid filling is restricted to small gaps (i.e., gaps with a width of 1 mm or less) and is usually completed within 4 to 6 weeks. Filling of larger gaps (or better defects) may take considerably longer, and often the defects are first bridged only superficially, mostly underneath the periosteum. This filling may also be observed in the healing of screw holes after implant removal.

If gap healing is successful, bone union is achieved by direct bone formation within a few weeks. However, union is not healing because (1) the newly formed bone within the gaps differs considerably from the original cortex in its morphology and possibly also in its mechanical properties and (2) the fragment ends are at least partially avascular and devitalized or even necrotic (Fig. 2–26A). Both the

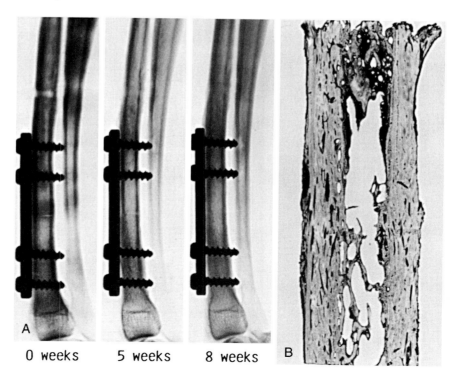

FIGURE 2–24. *A,* Direct bone healing of a transverse osteotomy in the radius of a dog after rigid fixation with a compression plate. In the radiographs, no external callus formation is seen, and the osteotomy line disappears within 5 to 6 weeks. *B,* A longitudinal ground section at 10 weeks confirms minimal callus around the osteotomy but considerable bone deposition around the thread of the screw. (*A, B,* From Schenk, R.K.; Willenegger, H. Experientia 19: 593, 1963.)

0 weeks   5 weeks   8 weeks   B

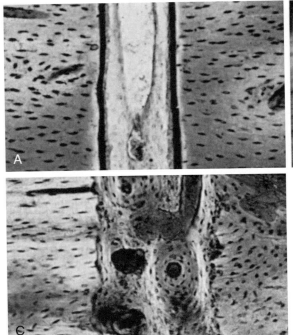

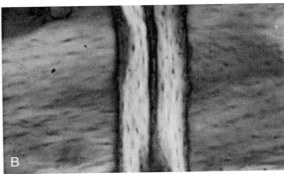

FIGURE 2–25. Direct bone healing in the radii of dogs: gap healing, first stage. Application of straight plates produces small gaps in the cortex opposite to the plate. *A,* A 0.2-mm gap, 1 week after the osteotomy. Blood vessels and mesenchymal cells have invaded the gap, and osteoblasts start bone deposition on the surface of the fragment ends. *B,* After 4 weeks, a 0.2-mm gap is completely filled by lamellar bone. *C,* Six weeks after operation, a 0.4-mm gap is filled directly by bone with a more complicated pattern (compare with repair of cortical bone defects in Fig. 2–15). (*A–C,* From Schenk, R.K. In: Lane, J.M., ed. Fracture Healing. New York, Churchill Livingstone, 1987, p. 23.)

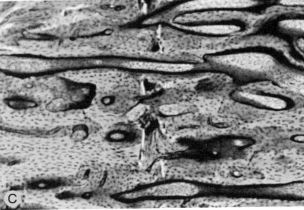

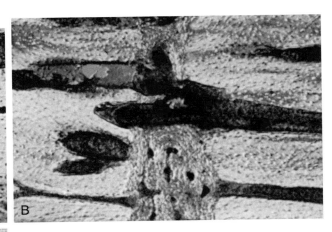

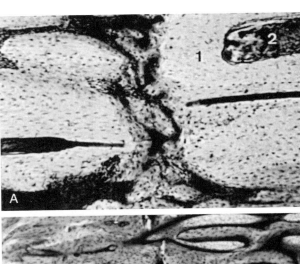

FIGURE 2–26. Direct bone healing in the radii of dogs: gap healing, second stage. *A,* Six weeks after operation, the cortex in the fragment ends shows extensive devitalized areas (1). This bone, as well as the newly formed bone in the gap, is substituted by activation of basic multicellular unit (BMU)–based haversian remodeling (2). *B,* Six weeks after operation the osteoclastic cutter cone in the tip of a BMU has just crossed the former osteotomy gap (compare with Fig. 2–10). *C,* After 10 weeks, a considerable part of the osteotomy site is replaced by newly reconstructed cortical bone.

avascular cortical areas and the repair tissue in the fracture gap have to be substituted by haversian remodeling.

This reconstruction of the cortical bone constitutes the second phase of direct bone healing. Again, we can refer to the principles of cortical bone remodeling already discussed, especially as far as the cellular organization and histodynamics of the BMUs are concerned. Activation of haversian remodeling leads to the appearance of numerous BMUs in the cortical fragment ends. The osteoclastic cutter cones, followed by blood vessels and osteoblasts, advance in the longitudinal direction and also traverse the newly formed bone in the fracture gap. In this way, the avascular cortex as well as the repair bone is substituted by new osteons (see Fig. 2–26B and C).

CONTACT HEALING

The fate of contact zones created in a fracture line by anatomic reduction and compression was seriously questioned in earlier discussions of callus-free diaphyseal bone healing. Such immediate interfragmentary contact was thought to prevent any cellular or vascular ingrowth, considered prerequisite for bone union. This sealing up against cellular invasion is, in fact, effective as long as stability of the fixation is maintained. The discovery that cutter cones of the BMUs are able to cross this contact interface from one fragment into the other (Fig. 2–27) was such an impressive observation that it was and still is often mistakenly considered the main criterion for direct bone healing.

It is well known from histodynamic studies that osteonal remodeling is a slow process. It starts only after a lag phase of several weeks and is further limited by the osteoclastic resorption rate. It was proposed that direct healing should be identical to "osteonal healing"[131, 132] and therefore should represent a rather protracted process of bone repair. This assumption, however, completely ignores the first and most rapid phase: gap healing. In direct bone healing, gap healing plays a dominant role because gaps are far more frequent than contact areas. Contact areas, on the other hand, are indispensable for stabilization by compression and likewise protect the gaps against deformation. Synergism between gap and contact healing is the biologic solution to healing of fractures that are forced together under compression (Fig. 2–28).

ACTIVATION OF HAVERSIAN REMODELING

Internal remodeling of cortical bone is a common feature in later stages of all types of fracture repair. By this mechanism, the internal architecture of compact bone is restored, avascular and necrotic areas are substituted, and perifragmentary and interfragmentary callus is replaced and remodeled. Remodeling is locally activated by any mechanical lesion of bone, by temporary alterations of blood supply, and by inflammation.

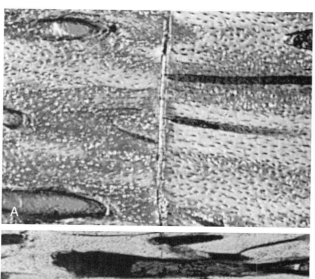

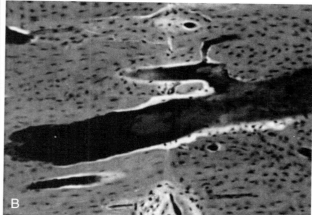

FIGURE 2–27. Direct bone healing in the radii of dogs: contact healing. *A,* Contact interface underneath plate at 1 week after operation (×100). *B,* Tetracycline-labeled BMU crossing the contact interface. Note branching with formation of a Volkmann canal (×100). *C,* Contact healing, 6 weeks after operation. Numerous newly formed osteons have crossed the contact interface. Note the branching osteons (×25).

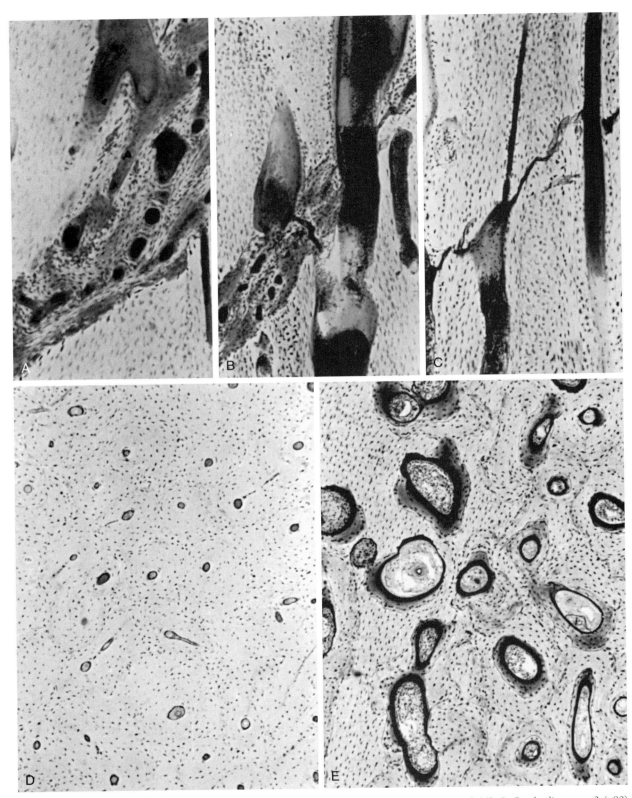

Figure 2–28. Direct bone healing in a human tibia, 12 weeks after operation. *A,* Gap healing stage 1 (×80). *B,* Gap healing stage 2 (×80). *C,* Contact healing (×50). *D,* Transverse section through a cortical area showing the original structure (×100). *E,* Transverse section through a cortical area undergoing haversian remodeling. Activation of numerous BMUs, now presumably in an early formative stage, causes a temporary increase in cortical porosity (×100).

The activation of haversian remodeling has been extensively studied in experiments related to rigid internal fixation. Such experiments offer the unique condition that activation is confined in time and place, as in the case of the insertion of an implant or creation of a defect. This condition also holds true for an osteotomy or fracture with consecutive application of a fixation device. If rigid fixation is achieved, it is unlikely that the bone will be further damaged by interfragmentary movements and that new and overlapping waves of activity will be evoked.

Frost[41] has applied some basic concepts of population statistics to the dynamics of cortical bone remodeling. Thus, the number of BMUs (active basic multicellular or remodeling units) depends on their birth rate (recruitment) and their life span (duration of the resorptive plus formative phase). Because the life span of BMUs is unlikely to change in fracture repair, the obvious increase in number must be due to a sudden increase in birth rate (i.e., the recruitment of new remodeling units). Another useful concept of Frost's is the ARF rule, which simply states that activation is, after a certain lag time, followed by resorption and then by formation. Animal experiments as well as biopsy and autopsy specimens of human fractures confirm these principles. Activation is always followed by a lag phase of 3 or more weeks before resorption starts. The inherent dynamics at the BMU level (osteoclastic resorption rates of 50 μm/day versus a bone apposition rate of only 1 μm/day) are reflected by the presence of numerous resorption cavities in the first period of remodeling (see Fig. 2–28). Full reconstruction of the compact bone depends on the completion time for new osteons and takes at least 3 to 6 months. The relatively large variation in these figures is partially due to species differences.

The course of BMU recruitment can be followed by sequential fluorochrome labeling. An example is given in Figure 2–29, calculated for a canine radius after transverse osteotomy and rigid fixation.[105, 106, 112, 114] In this case, the lag time is 2 to 3 weeks, after which an increasing number of newly activated BMUs appear in the fourth and fifth weeks, and from the sixth week on, the "birth rate" of remodeling units starts declining again. After 8 weeks, about two thirds of the total number of osteons are in the stage of completion or already renewed. One can assume that the remodeling rate slowly returns to normal after about 6 months. This means that devitalized areas, which have escaped the initial wave of remodeling activity, are substituted only at a steadily declining rate and so might persist for years.

Remodeling always depends on intact or reconstructed vascularity in the marrow cavity, periosteum, or adjacent soft tissues. In cases of partial interruption of cortical blood supply, remodeling often starts at the demarcation line between vital and avascular cortical areas.[95] Revascularization is the first step and is realized either by recanalization or by ingrowth of new vessels into preformed haversian and Volkmann canals. This process is often combined with partial or complete substitution of the surrounding osteon. At least a thin coat of newly formed vital bone is deposited upon the inner surface of an otherwise necrotic wall (Fig. 2–30); the rest may be substituted at a later stage.[30]

Anastomoses of the endocortical blood vessels with the periosteal and endosteal envelope are important for the reconstruction of the architecture of compact bone. Osteons are hollow cylinders, but the length of coherent segments rarely exceeds 0.5 to 1 mm. The haversian canals then bifurcate or at least establish transverse connections to neighboring osteons. Such vascular anastomoses are regularly installed during cortical remodeling and complicate the histologic picture with branching BMUs and newly formed Volkmann canals.

Besides these nutritional aspects of remodeling activa-

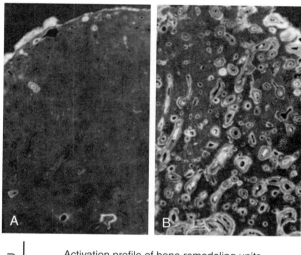

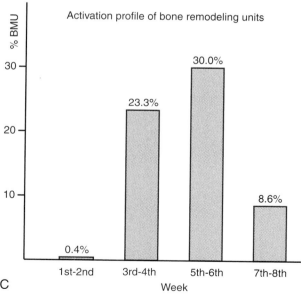

FIGURE 2–29. Activation of cortical remodeling by transverse osteotomies in canine radii. Tetracycline sequential labeling. *A*, Control radius; 2.5% of osteons are in the remodeling stage. *B*, Transverse section near the osteotomy. After 8 weeks, 62.5% of the osteons have been replaced or are in the formative phase of renewal (×25). *C*, Activation profile confirms the lag phase of 2 to 3 weeks between activation and onset of remodeling and the peak of BMU recruitment in the second month (Schenk and Willenegger, 1964). BMU, bone remodeling unit.

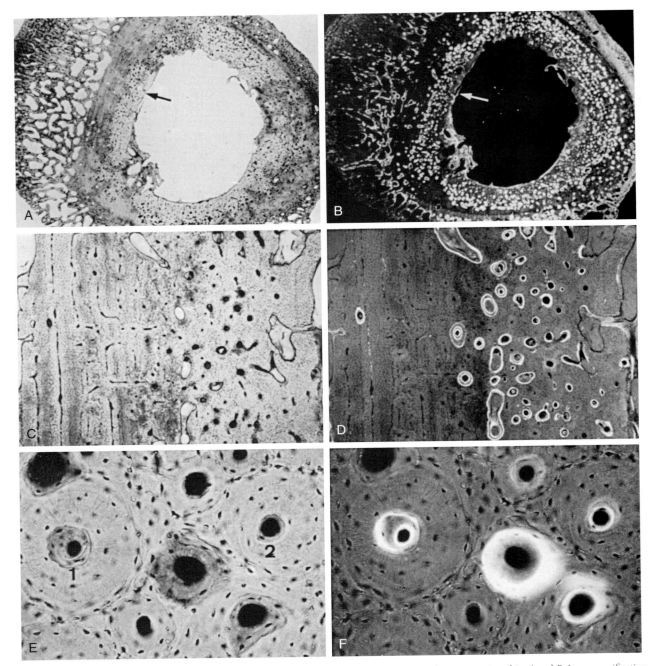

FIGURE 2–30. Revascularization and substitution of cortical bone 8 weeks after intramedullary nailing in a canine tibia. *A* and *B,* Low magnification of a cross section stained with basic fuchsin (*A*) and sequentially labeled with fluorochromes (*B*) (×4). Devascularized areas are less stained by fuchsin (*A*) but undergo intensive remodeling (*B*). *C* (area indicated by *arrow* in *A*) and *D* (area indicated by *arrow* in *B*), The outer half of the lateral cortex still consists of primary osteons connected to periosteal vessels (plexiform bone). Only the inner half was affected by the interruption of the medullary blood supply and became avascular and devitalized (*C*). Activation of remodeling starts at the demarcation line (center) and progresses toward the marrow cavity (*D*). The plexiform layer remains unremodeled (×25). *E* and *F,* Although almost all haversian canals are revascularized, substitution of devitalized bone after 8 weeks is still incomplete (×200). Small osteons in the center have been completely substituted and are viable. Partial substitution (1) or coating of a preformed haversian canal with a thin layer of new bone (2) causes the persistence of large devitalized areas still awaiting substitution.

tion, another often overlooked peculiarity of osteon renewal should be mentioned. Under the lead of their cutter cones, the BMUs advance longitudinally in the cortical bone. The lamellar texture of the preexisting bone seems to serve as a guide structure. Oblique interfaces, such as the border of an incorporated fragment or the wall of a replenished screw hole, may cause deviations. Attempts to change direction by creating mechanical strain

in the preexisting tissue have, to my knowledge, not been successful.

PITFALLS OF DIRECT BONE HEALING

The success of direct bone healing depends on the precision of the reduction and the degree of stabilization obtained at surgery. The limits of tolerance are relatively small, and although it is difficult to give recommendations based on theoretical grounds, three factors should be mentioned: the influence of the gap width, possible damage created by overcompression, and delayed revascularization.

Influence of the Gap Width

As already explained, gaps should not exceed a width of 0.5 to 1.0 mm if one relies on bone filling within 4 to 6 weeks. Bone union in larger gaps is possible but takes considerably longer.[111] The gap width is important not only for direct bone healing (Fig. 2–31) but also for the bone incorporation of prostheses, as convincingly shown in canine experiments where the same critical value was described by the catchword jumping distance.[50] This principle, however, is effective only in perfectly stable gaps. In small unstable gaps, interfragmentary micromovement creates tremendous strain on the tissue and jeopardizes bone tissue formation.

Overload Caused by Compression

Bone is, as a whole, very resistant to compressive forces, and it has been convincingly shown that conditions such as "pressure necrosis" do not exist.[93] Slight incongruences of the fragment ends left after anatomic reduction, however, may result in small contact spots or even pressure points and thus lead to localized overcompression (Fig. 2–32). The load surpasses the elastic limit and leads to irreversible bone deformation. The local collapse is reflected by deviation and deformation of the lamellar structure or, in severe cases, by the appearance of microcracks. Such areas can no longer withstand compression, but the deformation enlarges the contact interface and gradually improves stability if compression is continued. Under stable conditions, the deformed areas are remodeled and heal as well as other contact zones, and shape-deforming resorption occurs only in case of instability.

Failure of Revascularization

Fractures are always associated with alterations of blood supply. Consequences of vascular severance are especially prominent in cortical bone, where they result in more or less extensive necrotic areas. Avascular bone tissue undergoes structural and physiologic changes. Bone seems to die slowly, and depending on how long avascularity persists, the tissue goes through various stages of necrosis. Vascularized autografts demonstrate that osteocytes may survive temporary interruption of vascular supply for a short period of time, whereas most cells in cortical nonvascularized autografts disintegrate. The same seems to be true for cancellous autografts, but the rapid and extensive bone deposition on the trabecular surface makes it less conspicuous. How long osteocytes may survive if nourished only by diffusion is difficult to assess. Histologically, their death is recognized by the empty lacunae that are found 2 to 3 weeks after disintegration of the nuclei.

Cells are the viable components of bone tissue. If the cells lining the outer and inner bone surface and the osteocytes have died, it seems reasonable to call such bone devitalized. This assumes that the matrix still maintains its mechanical and biochemical properties, especially in view of the release of activators for bone apposition (callus formation) or BMU-mediated substitution. If avascularity persists for several months or longer, the matrix undergoes irreversible qualitative changes. These include the degradation of noncollagenous proteins, including cytokines, growth factors, and mediators of cell attachment and mineralization. After this loss, the matrix is no longer able to activate either remodeling or substitution, even if the vascular supply is restored. Such bone is fully necrotic or, in other words, has become a sequestrum.

This distinction of various degrees of bone necrosis is useful for discussion of some aspects of revascularization in fracture repair. An interesting and informative example is cortical revascularization and substitution after intramedullary nailing, especially after reaming of the medullary cavity.[30, 67, 96, 100] This procedure destroys the marrow vessels completely. The pattern and extent of the resulting avascular zones depend on the local participation of periosteal and endosteal vessels in cortical blood supply.

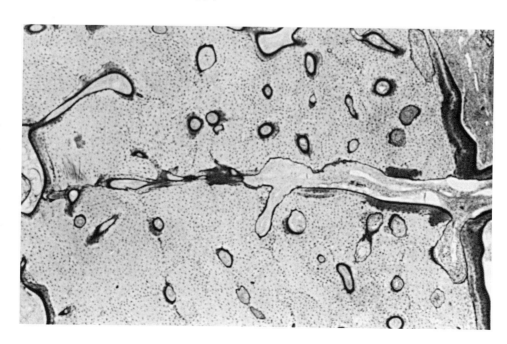

FIGURE 2–31. Influence of gap width on direct gap healing. Transverse section of a human tibia, 12 weeks after stable fixation (×40) (periosteum to the right, marrow cavity on the left side). The small part of the gap is filled by newly formed bone; the wider gap is still open, although bone formation started from both sides shortly after the fracture.

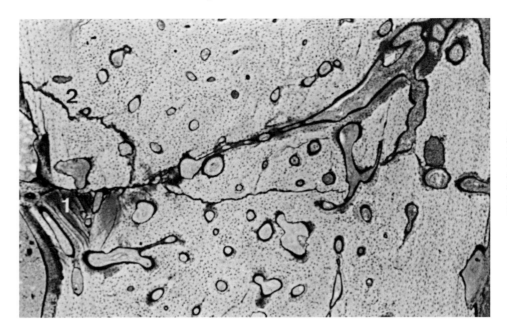

Figure 2–32. Effects of overcompression. Same case and orientation as in Figure 2–31. Toward the endosteal lining, a small incongruence has resulted in an overload during compression. Deformation ("plastification") of the circumferential lamellae (1) and production of a microcrack (2) (×40).

This dependence is shown in a canine tibia examined 8 weeks after intramedullary nailing.[30] In young adult dogs, which are frequently used for such experiments, the diaphyseal cortex of long bones is not completely remodeled and often exhibits a peripheral zone of plexiform bone consisting of several layers of primary osteons.[31] This primary bone is almost exclusively supplied by periosteal vessels. In the sector shown in Figure 2–30C, it makes up the outer half of the cortex and obviously was not at all affected by the destruction of the medullary blood supply. It consists of viable bone that has escaped any haversian remodeling. The inner half, on the contrary, was completely avascular and is in a state of revascularization and intense haversian remodeling. Also in this example, substitution starts at the demarcation line between the vital and the former avascular area and proceeds toward the marrow cavity (see Fig. 2–30D). Higher magnification allows one to distinguish between revascularization of the haversian canals and partial or complete substitution of the surrounding osteons (see Fig. 2–30E and F). In spite of the recruitment of a large number of BMUs, a large fraction of the former avascular cortical area is still "devitalized" and waits to be substituted by the ongoing cortical remodeling. How long this takes and how much of the avascular area becomes necrotic are difficult to predict and definitely depend on species and individual characteristics, such as recovery of the vascular supply, physical activity, metabolic conditions, and age.

Of practical importance is the fate of persisting avascular matrix compartments. As mentioned before, they become necrotic with time and are no longer able to activate and attract substitution by BMUs. The transition from the devitalized to the necrotic stage is gradual and is thought to take place in the 6 to 12 months after the insult. Necrotic fragments are no longer substituted, even when the blood vessels have regained access to them (Fig. 2–33). In spite of satisfactory revascularization, there is almost no substitution and the bulk of the necrotic bone persists. Brittleness, resulting from hypermineralization, causes an accumulation of microcracks, and biologic deficiency leads to the loss of any capacity to stimulate local bone repair. Therefore, it is not surprising that extensive necrotic areas become stress risers and ultimately predispose to refracture. This again underlines the necessity to preserve as much of the local blood supply as possible and, in doubtful situations, to remove loose fragments that are deprived of any blood supply during débridement of the fracture site.

Indirect Bone Healing: The Response to Less Rigid or Flexible Fixation

The characteristics of indirect bone healing, especially callus formation and interfragmentary tissue differentiation, have been considered in the discussion of the biologic course of fracture repair. These principles can also be applied to the modifications of fracture repair under conditions that do not fulfill the requirements of rigid fixation and direct bone repair, such as when rigid fixation by screws and plates was intended but not fully achieved or when methods of internal fixation are used that are neither designed for nor able to provide stable fixation. Cerclage or tension band wires, intramedullary pinning and (noninterlocking) nailing, and external fixators belong to this second category.

As discussed earlier, gap healing requires stable conditions and is possible only in quiet gaps. It is jeopardized by interfragmentary motion (i.e., when not enough preload is built up to compensate for deforming forces). Small gaps are advantageous or even required for direct bone healing but can be dangerous in cases of microinstability. *Microinstability* consists of small, almost invisible displacements of the fragments that suffice to alter or destroy the living tissues in the gap (Fig. 2–34). Widening of a transverse gap under bending may surpass the strain tolerance of supporting tissues. Compression, which is

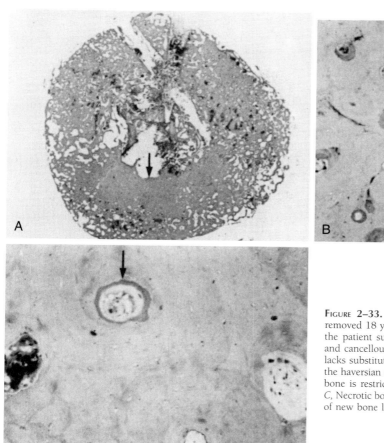

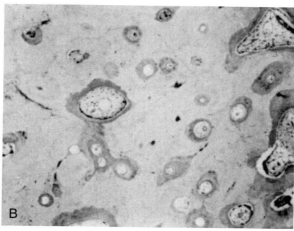

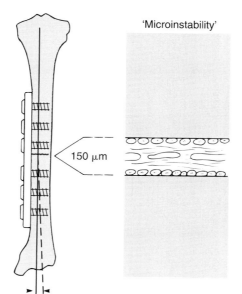

Figure 2–33. Cross section of a surgical specimen of the femur removed 18 years after a comminuted fracture. During this interval, the patient suffered three refractures, treated with internal fixation and cancellous autografts. *A*, A large part of the original cortex still lacks substitution *(arrow)*. *B* (area indicated by *arrow* in *A*), Most of the haversian canals are revascularized, but substitution by vital new bone is restricted to the more intensely stained osteonal segments. *C*, Necrotic bone surrounding revascularized canals. Only a thin layer of new bone lines one of the canals *(arrow)*.

Figure 2–34. Micromovement and microinstability. The drawing is based on the dimensions of a human tibia. A gap of 0.15 mm in the midshaft will be closed completely by a bending of 1 to 2 mm at the end. This will destroy its contents, presumably all the vessels and bone-forming elements.

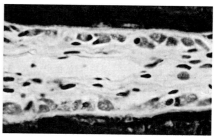

'Microinstability'

150 μm

1-2 mm   Micromovement

even more likely to occur, smashes all invading cells and blood vessels.

The reaction to microinstability is uniform: micromovement induces bone resorption. This statement is based on clinical experience and has been proved by well-controlled animal experiments concerning the tissue reaction around screws.[90] In case of unstable gaps, osteoclasts gather around blood vessels at the periosteal and endosteal entrances to the gap or at the contact interface and start widening it.[62] The resulting wedge-shaped resorption may even be recognizable in radiographs. Widening of the gap reduces the strain on the cells and creates the living conditions necessary for stiffer tissue and ultimately for bone (Fig. 2–35). However, widening of the gap by osteoclastic resorption undoubtedly causes a considerable delay of bone formation and consolidation. Plate-and-screw fixation is particularly detrimental in this respect because both implants act as spacers, keeping the fragments apart and preventing force transmission through the bone. This effect increases the load on the implants and, ultimately, the risk of failure by fatigue or loosening.

Intramedullary devices (and other types of fixation devices mentioned before) are different in this respect because they act as gliding splints and allow self-adaptation of the fragments in case of resorption. This adaptation does not solve the problem within the gap (see Fig. 2–35) but it does improve stability and allows bone to participate in weight bearing, which protects the implant against overload and fatigue. Again, the gap width is enlarged by osteoclastic resorption, and bone or cartilage formation follows. However, in most cases, bone union is first achieved via secondary healing by callus production and endochondral ossification and not primarily by gap healing between the cortices.

Pathogenesis and Healing of Nonunions

CLASSIFICATION OF NONUNIONS

Failure of opposed fracture ends to unite by bone is considered nonunion. As proposed by Weber and Cech,[128] nonunions are first categorized as biologically active or nonactive on the basis of whether or not the fracture site is capable of a biologic reaction. The nonactive type comprises nonunions with dead fragment ends, interposition of partially or completely necrotic fragments, or large defects that prevent any biologic interaction between the fragments. In the scope of this chapter, only viable nonunions, in particular the hypertrophic type, are discussed. Hypertrophic nonunion results from insufficient stabilization and persisting micromotion and is characterized by more or less abundant callus formation, widening of the fracture gap by resorption, and failure of substitution of interfragmentary fibrocartilage by bone.

On the basis of the amount of callus formation in radiographs, biologically active nonunions are subdivided into a hypertrophic form (elephant foot nonunion) and a milder, slightly hypertrophic form (horseshoe callus). In both types, the interfragmentary and perifragmentary tissues are biologically sound, and failure is due to mechanical or technical causes, or both. Both conditions and their subsequent healing after rigid fixation have been studied experimentally in the canine radius.

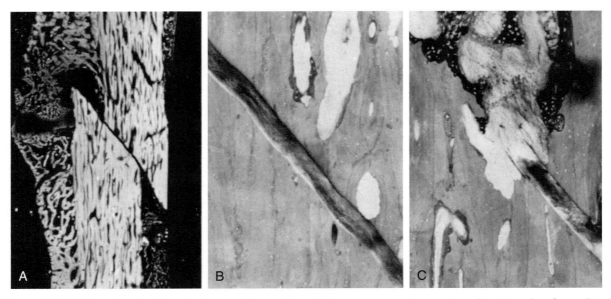

FIGURE 2–35. Indirect bone healing after intramedullary nailing. Oblique osteotomy in a canine tibia, 8 weeks after nailing. *A,* Microradiograph of the lateral cortex showing the osteotomy line and abundant periosteal callus formation. *B,* The 0.1-mm gap underwent intermittent compression and contains only detritus. Activated BMUs in the adjacent cortex are unable to bridge the osteotomy (×60). *C,* At the subperiosteal entrance, osteoclastic resorption starts widening the gap and allows ingrowth of vessels and bone-forming elements (×60). (*A–C,* From Schenk, R.K. In: Lane, J.M., ed. Fracture Healing. New York, Churchill Livingstone, 1987, p. 23.)

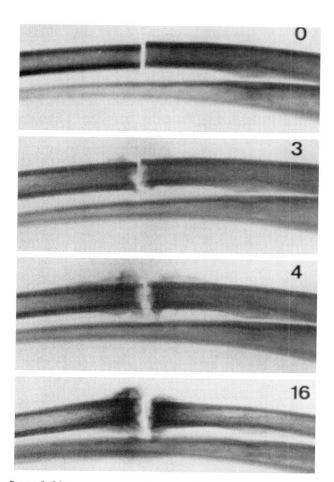

FIGURE 2–36. Experimental production of nonunion in the dog radius after a transverse osteotomy and 3-mm resection in the midshaft. Radiographs show resorption of the fragment ends, callus formation, and persistence of unmineralized interfragmentary tissue. Numbers indicate observation time in weeks. (From Müller, J.; Schenk, R.K.; Willenegger, H. Helv Chir Acta 35:301, 1968.)

EXPERIMENTAL PRODUCTION AND TREAMENT OF VIABLE NONUNIONS

A relatively easy and reliable method consists of a transverse osteotomy of the midshaft of the radius and removal of a 2- to 3-mm-thick disc (Fig. 2–36), followed by full weight bearing without any external fixation.[73, 78, 108, 109] Delayed union and nonunion occur reproducibly in older dogs, but in young adult dogs the defect may heal spontaneously. Another typical complication is fatigue fracture of the ulna related to overload. If this occurs within 4 to 6 weeks, both forearm bones heal spontaneously. The nonunions observed under this condition of persisting instability were of the elephant foot type and could be followed for several months after osteotomy (Fig. 2–37).

In a second type of experiment, less successful because of poor reproducibility, similar defects were treated with unstable plates. This treatment caused delayed healing, radiologically similar to that of the horseshoe type. Loosening of the screws, however, did not allow observa-

tion of the delayed healing over more than 8 weeks, which is too short a time for true nonunions to develop.

Histologically, delayed unions differ only slightly from the pattern described for spontaneous healing. Callus formation is prominent and often abundant, and the interfragmentary tissue consists of fibrous tissue or fibrocartilage, which slowly undergoes bone substitution. Thus, retardation of bone union remains the decisive criterion. Under persistent instability, fibrocartilage expands throughout the whole fracture gap and finally endochondral ossification comes to a standstill. This change is the main characteristic of nonunions, and according to the microscopic aspect, a cessation of fibrocartilage mineralization appears to be the decisive event. The arrest of cartilage mineralization also blocks further vascular invasion and evidently any further substitution of fibrocartilage by bone. The arrest of fibrocartilage mineralization seems to be related to the cyclic loading pattern that stimulates proteoglycan synthesis by chondrocytes.[102] These molecules are indeed capable of inhibiting calcification.[19, 20, 27, 55] The resulting imbalance between proteoglycan production and degradation could explain the lack of mineralization under these circumstances.

In experimental nonunions in canine radii, the transition from delayed union to a nonunion occurred between the 16th and 20th weeks. Further development was followed up to 40 weeks, and even then, bone union had not occurred. Almost classical hypertrophic nonunions are presented on the radiographs. The fragment ends are transformed into "elephant feet" composed of abundant, dense bony callus. A dense bone plate also seals off the marrow cavity. The fragment ends are well vascularized and still undergoing intensive remodeling. The tips of numerous resorption canals line up along the borderline toward the interfragmentary fibrocartilage. However, as long as this tissue does not calcify, it acts as a barrier to any vascular ingrowth. In this respect, the situation resembles the arrest of vascular invasion as caused by rickets in the growth plate.

Even in fully developed hypertrophic nonunions, rigid fixation thoroughly changes the radiographic and histologic appearance. In canine experiments, application of a plate, with or without compression, provided enough stability for bone union to occur within 5 to 7 weeks (Fig. 2–38). The radiolucent fracture gap disappeared, and in later stages excessive callus was gradually resorbed, the remaining bone steadily increased in density, and with time a compact cortical layer was reconstructed in the site of the former nonunion.

Histology gives further information about the sequence of events at the cell and tissue level. Restoration of fibrocartilage mineralization is the first visible change (Fig. 2–39). It spreads out rapidly across the fracture line, and the mineral deposits are again associated with chondrocytes or clusters of these cells. Judged by microradiography, the mineral density of calcified fibrocartilage is high and even surpasses that of adjacent bone. It is possible that the fracture line disappears in the radiographs even before bone union has occurred, but in any case, the recovery of fibrocartilage mineralization sets the pace for renewed vascular invasion, breakdown of mineralized and nonmineralized cartilage, and bone deposition on persisting mineralized cartilage cores, as described before. Fibrocartilage cells, therefore, have preserved all the functional capacities, especially as far as initiation and control of calcification are concerned. This finding supports the now generally accepted recommendation that interfragmentary tissue must be preserved as the main source for resumed endochondral ossification, regardless of what measures are chosen for the surgical treatment of nonunions.

Resorption of callus, remodeling of the primitive interfragmentary bone, and reconstruction of the compact shaft in the diaphysis follow the principles discussed previously (Fig. 2–40). Again, osteon renewal plays a key role. Dynamics at the BMU level, especially the difference in the rates of osteoclastic resorption and bone formation, help to explain transient stages of low bone density or even "cancellization," which are sometimes erroneously taken as a sign of stress protection or stress bypass osteoporosis.

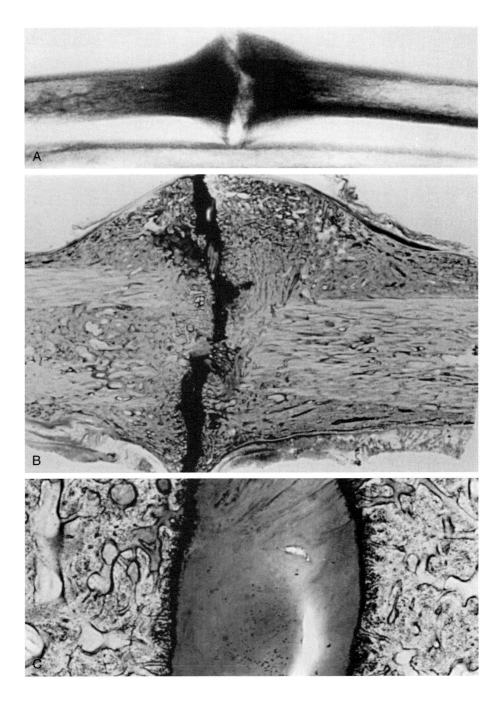

FIGURE 2–37. Same case as in Figure 2–36, 40 weeks after osteotomy. Hypertrophic nonunion (elephant foot type) with sclerotic fragment ends and persistence of fibrocartilage in both the radiograph (A) and the corresponding histologic section (B). A higher magnification (C) demonstrates the intensive remodeling on both sides of the avascular, nonmineralizing interfragmentary tissue. (A–C, From Müller, J.; Schenk, R.; Willenegger, H. Helv Chir Acta 35:301, 1968.)

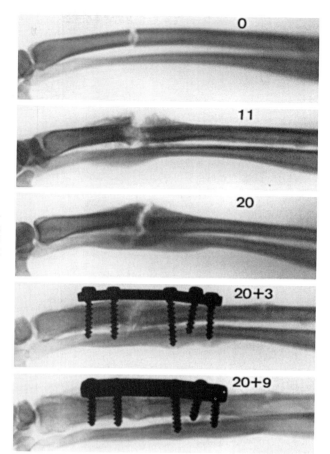

FIGURE 2–38. Healing of experimental hypertrophic nonunions after compression plating in the radii of dogs. Radiographs illustrate development of a nonunion during 20 weeks. The additional weeks after plating (+3 and +9) show the progress of bone union. (A–C, From Müller, J.; Schenk, R.; Willenegger, H. Helv Chir Acta 35:301, 1968.)

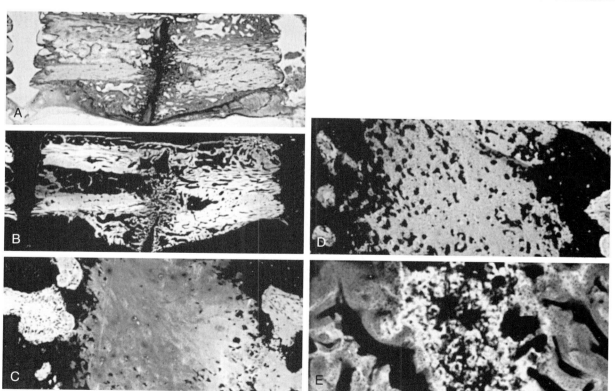

FIGURE 2–39. Histologically, the first and decisive event after stabilization is recommencement of fibrocartilage mineralization. A and B, In this case, bone union starts near the plate and progresses toward the callus, covering the far cortex on the dorsal side. C, Still persisting, nonmineralized fibrocartilage separating the bony callus in the dorsal area. D, Near the diaphyseal cortex, fibrocartilage mineralization has resumed. The dark spots in the von Kossa stain represent mineral clusters in the vicinity of fibrocartilage cells (compare with Fig. 2–22). E, In a corresponding microradiograph, newly mineralized fibrocartilage exhibits a considerably higher mineral density compared with the surrounding bone. Therefore, disappearance of a translucent fracture line in radiographs does not necessarily indicate that bone union has occurred.

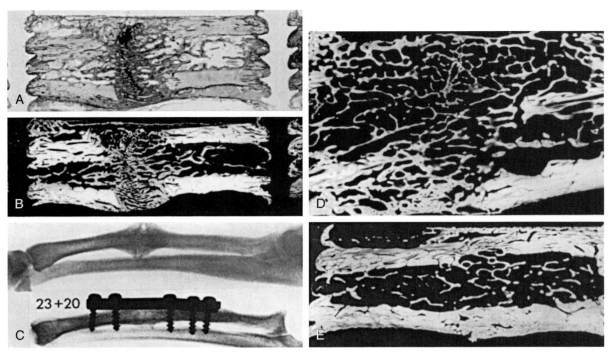

Figure 2–40. Complete healing of nonunions in the dog requires further extensive remodeling of the fracture site. This lasts at least 6 months and goes through several stages. *A* and *B*, Bone union is achieved when mineralized fibrocartilage is substituted by woven bone (fuchsin-stained longitudinal section and microradiograph). *C,* Substitution of woven bone by lamellar bone is often visible in conventional radiographs by the appearance of a radiolucent area in the former fracture site. *D,* Histologically, this is due to the transitory formation of cancellous bone. It is explained by the pronounced difference in the rate of osteoclastic resorption compared with the rate of lamellar bone formation. (This section represents an extreme case.) *E,* Prolonged observation time in the preceding series of experiments has always resulted in the reconstruction of compact diaphyseal bone within 6 months. In all cases, the plate has remained in situ. (*C, D,* From Schenk, R.K.; Willenegger, H.; Müller, J. In: Sumner Smith, G., ed. Bone in Clinical Orthopaedics. A Study in Comparative Osteology. Philadelphia, W.B. Saunders, 1982, p. 415.)

SUMMARY

As stated in the introduction, the aim of this chapter is to analyze some histophysiologic aspects of fracture repair on the basis of general biologic principles. The majority of observations reported here have been elaborated in animal experiments. Experimenters always try to standardize procedures and conditions in order to obtain results that are consistent and reproducible. This purpose is why osteotomies are preferred over the less controllable breaking of bones and why methods of fixation are applied that are rarely used or even may not be indicated for comparable situations in clinical practice. However, clinical recommendations often have to be modified if experiments are to give proof of the hypotheses under consideration.

Thus, the ultimate goal of any experimental design is to provide well-defined and uniform conditions throughout the fracture site. An actual fracture, on the other hand, is characterized by a complexity that makes complete correction by any kind of treatment almost impossible. A considerable local variation in gap width, extent of contact areas, and degree of stability always persists, and differences in preservation or restoration of blood supply, or both, further modify the pattern of tissue differentiation and the time course of bone repair. It can be assumed, however, that the general rules deduced from experimental investigations facilitate the interpretation of radiographs and the understanding of complications arising during healing in individual fracture cases.

A fracture must be considered as a local event from a basic research standpoint. Fracture repair is undoubtedly activated and controlled by local messengers and regulators engaged in cell-to-cell communication and designed for short-range and short-time activity. Progress in this field depends on in vitro studies, and a long and often tedious wait can be anticipated between experimental discoveries and their clinical application.

Acknowledgments

We are indebted to the Swiss National Science Foundation and the AO (ASIF) Foundation for the continuous support of this work. Since 1963, most of the equipment of our bone histology laboratory was purchased or constructed with the aid of these grants. These institutions also sponsored part of the salaries for our technicians. Over more than three decades, we have enjoyed the privilege of collaboration with a remarkably stable staff, whose dedication and technical skill greatly improved the standard of the histologic methods. Our special personal thanks go to Britt Hoffmann, David Reist, Yvonne Litzistorf, and the late Marianne Gaudy and Wolfgang Herrmann.

REFERENCES

1. Anderson, H.C. Matrix vesicles of cartilage and bone. In: Bourne, G.H., ed. The Biochemistry and Physiology of Bone, Vol. 4. New York, Academic Press, 1976, p. 135.
2. Aronson, J.; Harrison, B.H.; Steward, C.L.; Harp, J.H. The histology of distraction osteogenesis using different external fixators. Clin Orthop 241:106, 1989.

3. Baron, R.; Neff, L.; Van, P.T.; et al. Kinetic and cytochemical identification of osteoclast precursors and their differentiation into multinucleated osteoclasts. Am J Pathol 122:363, 1986.

4. Bassett, C.A.L. Contribution of endosteum, cortex, and soft tissues to osteogenesis. Surg Gynecol Obstet 112:145, 1961.

5. Bassett, C.A.L. Current concepts on bone formation. J Bone Joint Surg Am 44:1217, 1962.

6. Bélanger, L.F. Osteocytic osteolysis. Calcif Tissue Res 4:1, 1969.

7. Bonucci, E. Fine structure and histochemistry of "calcifying globules" in epiphyseal cartilage. Z Zellforsch 103:192, 1970.

8. Bonucci, E. The locus of initial calcification in cartilage and bone. Clin Orthop 78:108, 1971.

9. Boskey, A.L. Current concepts of the physiology and biochemistry of calcification. Clin Orthop 157:225, 1981.

10. Boyde, A.; Jones, S.J. Early scanning electron microscopic studies of hard tissue resorption: Their relation to current concepts reviewed. Scanning Microsc 1:369, 1987.

11. Boyne, P.J. Regeneration of alveolar bone beneath cellulose acetate filter implants. J Dent Res 43:827, 1964.

12. Brighton, C.T. Structure and function of the growth plate. Clin Orthop 136:22, 1978.

13. Bruder, S.P.; Fink, D.J.; Caplan, A.I. Mesenchymal stem cells in bone formation, bone repair, and skeletal regeneration therapy. J Cell Biochem 56:283, 1994.

14. Burwell, R.G. The Burwell theory on the importance of bone marrow in bone grafting. In: Urist, M.R.; O'Connor, B.T.; Burwell, R.G., eds. Bone Grafts, Derivatives and Substitutes. Oxford, Butterworth-Heinemann, 1994, p. 103.

15. Caplan, A.I. Mesenchymal stem cells. J Orthop Res 9:641, 1991.

16. Chambers, T.J.; Fuller, K. Bone cells predispose bone surfaces to resorption by exposure of mineral to osteoclastic contact. J Cell Sci 76:155, 1985.

17. Chapman, M.W. Induction of fracture repair: Osteoinduction, osteoconduction, and adjunctive care. In: Lane, J.M., ed. Fracture Healing. New York, Churchill Livingstone, 1987, p. 81.

18. Chappard, D.; Alexandre, C.; Riffat, G. Histochemical identification of osteoclasts. Review of current methods and reappraisal of a simple procedure for routine diagnosis on undecalcified human iliac bone biopsies. Basic Appl Histochem 27:75, 1983.

19. Chen, C.C.; Boskey, A.L. Mechanisms of proteoglycan inhibition of hydroxyapatite growth. Calcif Tissue Int 37:395, 1985.

20. Chen, C.C.; Boskey, A.L.; Rosenberg, L.C. The inhibitory effect of cartilage proteoglycans on hydroxyapatite growth. Calcif Tissue Int 36:285, 1984.

21. Dahlin, C.; Linde, A.; Gottlow, J.; Nyman, S. Healing of bone defects by guided tissue regeneration. Plast Reconstr Surg 81:672, 1988.

22. Dahlin, C.; Gottlow, J.; Linde, A.; Nyman, S. Healing of maxillary and mandibular bone defects using a membrane technique. Scand J Plast Reconstr Hand Surg 24:13, 1990.

23. Danis, R. Théorie et Pratique de l'Ostéosynthèse. Paris, Masson, 1949.

24. Delloye, C.; Delefortrie, G.; Coutelier, L.; Vincent, A. Bone regenerate formation in cortical bone during distraction lengthening: An experimental study. Clin Orthop 250:34, 1989.

25. Dodds, G.S. Osteoclasts and cartilage removal in endochondral ossification of certain mammals. Am J Anat 50:97, 1932.

26. Drivdahl, R.H.; Howard, G.H.; Baylink, D.J. Extracts of bone contain a potent regulator of bone formation. Biochim Biophys Acta 714:26, 1982.

27. Dziewiatkowski, D.D.; Majznerski, L.L. Role of proteoglycans in endochondral ossification: Inhibition of calcification. Calcif Tissue Int 37:560, 1985.

28. Eggli, P.S.; Herrmann, W.; Hunziker, E.B.; Schenk, R.K. Matrix compartments in the growth plate of the proximal tibia of rats. Anat Rec 211:246, 1985.

29. Einhorn, T.A. The cell and molecular biology of fracture healing. Clin Orthop 355S:S7, 1998.

30. Eitel, F.; Schenk, R.K.; Schweiberer, L. Corticale Revitalisierung nach Marknagelung an der Hundetibia. Hefte Unfallheilkd 83:202, 1979.

31. Enlow, D.H. Principles of Bone Remodeling. Springfield, IL, Charles C Thomas, 1963.

32. Fleisch, H. Bisphosphonates in Bone Disease. From the Laboratory to the Patients, 4th ed. San Diego, Academic Press, 2000.

33. Fornasier, V.L. Transmission electron microscopy studies of osteoid maturation. Metab Bone Dis 2(Suppl):103, 1980.

34. Frank, E.H.; Grodzinsky, A.J. Cartilage electromechanics: I. Electrokinetic transduction and the effects of electrolyte pH and ionic strength. J Biomech 20:615, 1987.

35. Frank E.H., Grodzinsky, A.J. Cartilage electromechanics: II. A continuum model of cartilage electrokinetics and correlation with experiments. J Biomech 20:629, 1987.

36. Friedenstein, A.J. Determined and inducible osteogenic precursor cells. Ciba Found Symp 11:169, 1973.

37. Friedenstein, A.J. Precursor or cells of mechanocytes. Int Rev Cytol 47:327, 1976.

38. Frost, H.M. Measurement of osteocytes per unit volume and volume components of osteocytes and canaliculi in man. Henry Ford Hosp Bull 8:208, 1960.

39. Frost, H.M. Micropetrosis. J Bone Joint Surg Am 42:144, 1960.

40. Frost, H.M. Bone Remodeling Dynamics. Springfield, IL, Charles C Thomas, 1963.

41. Frost, H.M. Bone Dynamics in Osteoporosis and Osteomalacia. Springfield, IL, Charles C Thomas, 1966.

42. Frost, H.M. Tetracycline-based histologic analysis of bone remodeling. Tissue Res 3:211, 1969.

43. Frost, H.M. The mechanostat: A proposed pathogenic mechanism of osteoporoses and the bone mass effects of mechanical and nonmechanical agents. Bone Mineral 2:73, 1987.

44. Glimcher, M.J. Molecular biology of mineralized tissues with particular reference to bone. Rev Mod Phys 31:359, 1959.

45. Glimcher M.J. Mechanisms of calcification in bone: Role of collagen fibrils and collagen-phosphoprotein complexes in vitro and in vivo. Anat Rec 224:139, 1989.

46. Glimcher, M.J. The nature of the mineral phase in bone: Biological and clinical implications. In: Avioli, L.V.; Krane, S.M., eds. Metabolic Bone Disease and Clinically Related Disorders, 3rd ed. San Diego, Academic Press, 1998, p. 23.

47. Göthlin, G.; Ericsson, J.L.E. The osteoclast. Review of ultrastructure, origin, and structure-function relationship. Clin Orthop 120:201, 1976.

48. Gray, M.L.; Pizzanelli, A.M.; Lee, R.C. Kinetics of the chondrocyte biosynthetic response to compressive load and release. Biochim Biophys Acta 991:415, 1989.

49. Ham, A.W. Some histophysiological problems peculiar to calcified tissues. J Bone Joint Surg Am 34:701, 1952.

50. Harris, W.J.; White, R.E.; McCarthy, J.C.; et al. Bony ingrowth fixation of the acetabular component in canine hip joint arthroplasty. Clin Orthop 176:7, 1983.

51. Hascall, V.C. Interactions of cartilage proteoglycans with hyaluronic acid. J Supramol Struct 7:101, 1977.

52. Holtrop, M.E.; Weinger, J.M. Ultrastructural evidence of a transport system in bone. In: Talmage, R.V.; Munson, P., eds. Calcium, Parathyroid Hormone and the Calcitonins. Amsterdam, Excerpta Medica, 1970, p. 365.

53. Holtrop, M.E. The ultrastructure of bone. Ann Clin Lab Sci 5:264, 1975.

54. Holtrop, M.E.; King, G.J. The ultrastructure of the osteoclast and its functional implications. Clin Orthop 123:177, 1977.

55. Howell, D.S., Pita, J.C. Calcification of growth plate cartilage with special reference to studies on micropuncture fluids. Clin Orthop 118:208, 1976.

56. Hulth, A.; Johnell, O.; Henricson, A. The implantation of demineralized fracture matrix yields more new bone formation than does intact matrix. Clin Orthop 234:235, 1988.

57. Hunziker, E.B.; Herrmann, W.; Schenk, R.K. Improved cartilage fixation by ruthenium hexamine trichloride (RHT). A prerequisite for morphometry in growth cartilage. J Ultrastruct Res 81:1, 1981.

58. Hunziker, E.B.; Herrmann, W.; Schenk, R.K.; et al. Cartilage ultrastructure after high pressure freezing, freeze substitution and low temperature embedding. II. Chondrocyte ultrastructure implications for the theories of mineralization and vascular invasion. J Cell Biol 98:276, 1984.

59. Hunziker, E.B.; Schenk, R.K.; Cruz-Orive, L.M. Quantitation of chondrocyte performance in growth plate cartilage during longitudinal bone growth. J Bone Joint Surg Am 69:162, 1987.

60. Hunziker, E.B.; Schenk, R.K. Physiological mechanisms adopted by chondrocytes in regulating longitudinal bone growth in rats. J Physiol (Lond) 414:55, 1989.

61. Hunziker, E.B.; Herrmann, W.; Cruz-Orive, L.M.; Arsenault, A.L. Image analysis of electron micrographs relating to mineralization in calcifying cartilage: Theoretical considerations. J Electron Microsc Technol 11:9–15, 1989.

62. Hutzschenreuter, P.; Perren, S.M.; Steinemann, S. Some effects of rigidity of internal fixation on the healing pattern of osteotomies. Injury 1:77, 1969.

63. Jaworski, Z.F.G.; Lok, E. The rate of osteoclastic bone erosion in Haversian remodeling sites of adult dog's rib. Calcif Tissue Res 10:103, 1972.

64. Ilizarov, G.A. The tension-stress effect on the genesis and growth of tissues, part I. The influence of stability on fixation and soft-tissue preservation. Clin Orthop 238:249, 1989.

65. Ilizarov, G.A. The tension-stress effect on the genesis and growth of tissues, part II. The influence of rate and frequency of distraction. Clin Orthop 239:263, 1989.

66. Johner, R. Zur Knochenheilung in Abhängigkeit von der Defektgrösse. Helv Chir Acta 39:409, 1972.

67. Kessler, S.; Rahn, B.A.; Eitel, F.; et al. Die Blutversorgung der Knochencorticalis nach Marknagelung. Vergleichende Untersuchungen an verschiedenen Tierspecies in vivo. Hefte Unfallheilkd 165:7, 1983.

68. Kölliker, A. Die normale Resorption des Knochengewebes und ihre Bedeutung für die Entstehung der typischen Knochenformen. Leipzig, F.C.W. Vogel, 1873.

69. Landis W.J. The strength of a calcified tissue depends in part on the molecular structure and organization of its constituent mineral crystals in their organic matrix. Bone 16:533, 1995.

70. Lavine, L.G.; Grodzinsky, A.J. Electrical stimulation of repair of bone. J Bone Joint Surg Am 69:626, 1987.

71. Mac Ginitie, L.A.; Wu, D.D.; Cochran, G.V.B. Streaming potentials in healing, remodeling, and intact cortical bone. J Bone Miner Res 8:1323, 1993.

72. Marks, S.C., Jr. The origin of osteoclasts: Evidence, clinical implications and investigative challenges on an extraskeletal source. J Oral Pathol 12:226, 1983.

73. Martin, B. Über experimentelle Pseudarthrosenbildung und die Bedeutung von Periost und Mark. Arch Klin Chir 114:664, 1920.

74. Martin, T.J.; Ng, K.W.; Suda, T. Bone cell physiology. Endocrinol Metab Clin North Am 18:833, 1989.

75. McKibbin, B.M. The biology of fracture healing in long bones. J Bone Joint Surg Br 60:150, 1978.

76. Meikle, M.C. The mineralization of condylar cartilage in the rat mandible: An electron microscopic enzyme histochemical study. Arch Oral Biol 21:33, 1976.

77. Minkin, C. Bone acid phosphatase: Tartrate-resistant acid phosphatase as a marker of osteoclast function. Calcif Tissue Int 34:285, 1982.

78. Müller, J.; Schenk, R.; Willenegger, H. Experimentelle Untersuchungen über die Entstehung reaktiver Pseudarthrosen am Hunderadius. Helv Chir Acta 35:301, 1968.

79. Mundy, G.R. Cytokines and local factors which affect osteoclast function. Int J Cell Cloning 10:215, 1992.

80. Olah, A.J.; Schenk, R.K. Veränderungen des Knochenvolumens und des Knochenanbaus in menschlichen Rippen und ihre Abhängigkeit von Alter und Geschlecht. Acta Anat 72:584, 1969.

81. Oldberg, A.; Franzen, A.; Heinegard, D. Cloning and sequence analysis of rat bone sialoprotein (osteopontin). cDNA reveals an Arg-Gly-Asp cell binding sequence. Proc Natl Acad Sci U S A 83:8819, 1986.

82. Owen, M. Marrow stromal stem cells. J Cell Sci Suppl 10:63, 1988.

83. Palumbo, C.; Palazzini, S.; Zaffe, D.; Marotti, G. Osteocyte differentiation in the tibia of newborn rabbit: An ultrastructural study of the formation of cytoplasmic processes. Acta Anat (Basel) 137:350, 1990.

84. Parfitt, A.M. Quantum concept of bone remodeling and turnover: Implications for the pathogenesis of osteoporosis. Calcif Tissue Int 28:1, 1979.

85. Parfitt, A.M. The coupling of bone formation to bone resorption: A critical analysis of the concept and of its relevance to the pathogenesis of osteoporosis. Metab Bone Dis Relat Res 4:1, 1982.

86. Parfitt, A.M. Osteonal and hemi-osteonal remodeling: The spacial and temporal framework for signal traffic in adult human bone. J Cell Biochem 55:273, 1994.

87. Paterson, D. Leg-lengthening procedures: A historical review. Clin Orthop 250:27, 1990.

88. Pauwels, F. Grundriss einer Biomechanik der Frakturheilung. Verh Dtsch Orthop Ges 34:62, 1940.

89. Pauwels, F. Eine neue Theorie über den Einfluss mechanischer Reize auf die Differenzierung der Stützgewebe. Z Anat Entwicklungsgesch 121:478, 1960.

90. Perren, S.M.; Ganz, R.; Rueter, A. Oberflächliche Knochenresorption um Implantate. Med Orthop Technik 95:6, 1975.

91. Perren, S.M.; Cordey, J. Die Gewebsdifferenzierung in der Frakturheilung. Hefte Unfallheilkd 80:161, 1977.

92. Perren, S.M.; Boitzy, A. Cellular differentiation and bone biomechanics during the consolidation of a fracture. Anat Clin 1:13, 1978.

93. Perren, S.M. Physical and biological aspects of fracture healing with special reference to internal fixation. Clin Orthop 138:175, 1979.

94. Perren, S.M.; Cordey, J. The concept of interfragmentary strain. In: Uhthoff, H.K., ed. Current Concepts of Internal Fixation of Fractures. Berlin, Springer Verlag, 1980, p. 63.

95. Perren, S.M.; Cordey, J.C.; Rahn, B.A.; et al. Early temporary porosis of bone induced by internal fixation implants. A reaction to necrosis, not to stress protection? Clin Orthop 232:139, 1988.

96. Pfister, U.; Rahn, B.A.; Perren, S.M.; Weller, S. Vascularität und Knochenumbau nach Marknagelung langer Röhrenknochen. Aktuel Traumatol 9:191, 1979.

97. Pita, J.C.; Muller, F.J.; Morales, S.M.; Alarcon, E.J. Ultracentrifugal characterization of proteoglycans from rat growth cartilage. J Biol Chem 254:10313, 1979.

98. Price, P.; Parthemore, J.; Deftos, J. New biochemical marker for bone metabolism. J Clin Invest 66:878, 1980.

99. Reddi, A.H. Cell biology and biochemistry of endochondral bone development. Collagen Res 1:209, 1981.

100. Rhinelander, F.W. Circulation in bone. In: Bourne, G.H., ed. The Biochemistry and Physiology of Bone, 2nd ed., Vol. 2. New York, Academic Press, 1972, p. 2.

101. Ruedi, T.P.; Bassett, C.A.L. Repair and remodeling in Millipore-isolated defects of cortical bone. Acta Anat 68:509, 1967.

102. Sah, R.I.; Kim, Y.J.; Doong, J.Y. Biosynthetic response of cartilage explants to dynamic compression. J Orthop Res 7:619, 1989.

103. Sandberg, M.M.; Aro, H.T.; Vuorio, E.I. Gene expression during bone repair. Clin Orthop 289:292, 1993.

104. Schenk, R.; Willenegger, H. Zum histologischen Bild der sogenannten Primärheilung der Knochenkompakta nach experimentellen Osteotomien am Hund. Experientia 19:593, 1963.

105. Schenk, R.; Willenegger, H. Histologie der primären Knochenheilung. Langenbecks Arch Klin Chir 308:440, 1964.

106. Schenk, R.; Willenegger, H. Morphological findings in primary fracture healing. Symp Biol Hung 7:75, 1967.

107. Schenk, R.K.; Spiro, D.; Wiener, J. Cartilage resorption in the tibial epiphyseal plate of growing rats. J Cell Biol 34:275, 1967.

108. Schenk, R.K.; Müller, J.; Willenegger, H. Experimentell histologischer Beitrag zur Entstehung und Behandlung von Pseudarthrosen. Hefte Unfallheilkd 94:15, 1968.

109. Schenk, R.; Müller, J. Histologie des Pseudoarthroses. In: Boitzy, A., ed. Ostéogenèse et Compression. Bern, Huber Verlag, 1972, p. 174.

110. Schenk, R. Ultrastruktur des Knochens. Verh Dtsch Ges Pathol 58:72, 1974.

111. Schenk, R.; Willenegger, H. Zur Histologie der primären Knochenheilung. Modifikationen und Grenzen der Spaltheilung in Abhängigkeit von der Defektgrösse. Unfallheilkunde 80:155, 1977.

112. Schenk, R.K. Die Histologie der primären Knochenheilung im Lichte neuer Konzeptionen über den Knochenumbau. Unfallheilkunde 81:219, 1978.

113. Schenk, R.K. Basic histomorphology and physiology of skeletal growth. In: Weber, B.G.; Brunner, C.; Freuler, F., eds. Treatment of Fractures in Children and Adolescents. Berlin, Springer Verlag, 1980, p. 3.

114. Schenk, R.K. Cytodynamics and histodynamics of primary bone repair. In: Lane, J.M., ed. Fracture Healing. New York, Churchill Livingstone, 1987, p. 23.

115. Schenk, R.K.; Buser, D.; Hardwick, W.R.; Dahlin, C. Healing pattern of bone regeneration in membrane-protected defects. A histologic study in the canine mandible. Int J Oral Maxillofac Implants 9:13, 1994.

116. Schenk, R.K.; Hunziker, E.B. Histologic and ultrastructural features of fracture healing. In: Brighton, C.T.; Friedlander, G.; Lane, J.M., eds. Bone Formation and Repair. Rosemont, IL, American Academy of Orthopaedic Surgeons, 1994, p. 117.

117. Schenk, R.K.; Gächter, A. Histology of distraction osteogenesis. In: Brighton, C.T.; Friedlander, G.; Lane, J.M., eds. Bone Formation and Repair. Rosemont, IL, American Academy of Orthopaedic Surgeons, 1994, p. 387.

118. Seibert, J.; Nyman, S. Localized ridge augmentation in dogs: A pilot study using membranes and hydroxyapatite. J Periodontol 61:157, 1990.

119. Shearer, J.R.; Roach, H.I.; Parsons, S.W. Histology of a lengthened human tibia. J Bone Joint Surg Br 74:39, 1992.

120. Steinemann, S.G. Implants for stable fixation of fractures. In: Rubin, L.R., ed. Biomaterials in Reconstructive Surgery. St. Louis, C.V. Mosby, 1983, p. 283.

121. Termine, J.; Kleinman, H.; Whitson, W.; et al. Osteonectin, a bone-specific protein linking mineral to collagen. Cell 26:99, 1981.

122. Termine, J.D.; Belcourt, A.B.; Conn, K.M.; Kleinmann, H.K. Mineral and collagen-binding proteins of fetal calf bone. J Biol Chem 256:10403, 1981.

123. Thyberg, J.; Friberg, U. Ultrastructure of the epiphyseal plate. Z Zellforsch 122:254, 1971.

124. Tonna, E.A. Electron microscopic evidence of alternating osteocytic, osteoclastic and osteoplastic activity in the perilacunar wall of aging mice. Connect Tissue Res 1:221, 1974.

125. Urist, M.R.; Silbermann, B.F.; Büring, K.; et al. The bone induction principle. Clin Orthop 53:243, 1967.

126. Vaes, G. Cellular biology and biochemical mechanism of bone resorption. Clin Orthop 231:239, 1988.

127. Vanderwiel, C.J. An ultrastructural study of the components which make up the resting surface of bone. Metab Bone Dis 2(Suppl):109, 1980.

128. Weber, H.; Cech, O. Pseudarthrosis. Bern, Huber Verlag, 1976.

129. Weidenreich, F. Das Knochengewebe. In: Von Möllendorff, W., ed. Handbuch der Mikroskopipschen Anatomie des Menschen, Vol. 2, Part 2. Berlin, Springer Verlag, 1930, p. 391.

130. Wolff, J. Das Gesetz der Transformation der Knochen. Berlin, Hirschwalk, 1892.

131. Woo, S.L.Y.; Akeson, W.H.; Coutts, R.S. A comparison of cortical bone atrophy secondary to fixation with plates with large differences in bending stiffness. J Bone Joint Surg Am 58:190, 1976.

132. Woo, S.L.Y.; Akeson, W.H. Appropriate design criteria for less rigid plates. In: Lane, J.M., ed. Fracture Healing. New York, Churchill Livingstone, 1987, p. 159.

133. Wozney, J.M.; Rosen, V.; Celeste, A.J.; et al. Novel regulators of bone formation: Molecular clones and activity. Science 242:1528, 1988.

134. Yamada, H.; Evans, F.G. Strength of Biological Materials. Baltimore, Williams & Wilkins, 1970.

CHAPTER 3

Biology of Soft Tissue Injuries

Michael L. Nerlich, M.D., Ph.D.

To assess, classify, and treat a wound properly, a sound understanding of the basic mechanisms of soft tissue injury and the body's response is required. Wounding not only damages morphologic structures but also causes additional loss of cell and organ function. At the time of the trauma, direct external mechanical forces are in contact with the living tissue, transferring energy from the object to the body. The wounding capacity of a moving object is directly proportional to its kinetic energy, and this in turn is proportional to its velocity and mass: $KE = \frac{1}{2}mv^2$. Because kinetic energy increases with the square of the velocity, objects moving with a high speed do substantially greater direct damage to living tissues than low-velocity objects.[62] The magnitude of injury also depends on the type of tissue and the site involved. For example, a blow to the anterior part of the lower leg, the pretibial soft tissues, is much more harmful and associated with much higher morbidity than the same kinetic energy applied to the posterior aspect of the lower leg, the calf. Also important are the size and shape of the damaging object and the direction of the externally applied force in relation to the tissue's biomechanical orientation. A force applied perpendicular to a limb's axis therefore causes much greater injury than an axially applied force.[54]

Besides these effects of direct damage, additional injury results from secondary microcirculatory disturbances. These include vasoreactions related to pain perception, hypovolemia, shock, and the metabolic response to trauma. Therefore, the actual extent of the injury may be much greater than appreciated. For example, in degloving injuries the skin may appear intact, but the vascular network is damaged. This damage is a consequence of the sudden extreme tension caused by shearing strain, which is usually severe enough to cause ischemic necrosis of the skin. In penetrating injuries by high-velocity bullets, a temporary pulsating cavity develops that sucks foreign bodies, bits of clothing, and consequently organisms into a permanent missile track that is surrounded by a zone of damaged tissue.[62] In addition to the more or less hidden extent of injury, the body's response to trauma may be modulated by the load of debris that has to be cleared, resulting in a catabolism that exceeds the initial extent of injury.

THE RESPONSE TO INJURY

General Considerations

The body's response to injury is a fundamental reaction of living organisms to protect tissue integrity. In its broadest sense it includes several different mechanisms, ranging from the "fight or flight" reflex at the moment when danger first occurs to the final stage of repair when the wound has completely healed.

The optimal response to injury would be the full replacement of lost cells and restoration of compound tissues to the preinjury state. Comparing fetal soft tissue injuries, which heal by regeneration, with the adult process of healing by scar formation suggests that progressive differentiation of cells, tissues, and organs for special functional requirements has led to a substantial loss of regenerative capacity.[12] The phenomenon of the autogenous and identical replacement of the tail of a lizard or the completion of a transected earthworm does not exist in humans—it has been replaced by a less complicated and far less valuable process: wound healing.

Wound healing is a highly dynamic integrated series of cellular, physiologic, and biochemical events that is designed to restore local homeostasis. This goal is rapidly achieved by synthesis of fibrous tissue (scar formation), which is the principal process of tissue replacement in most injuries. Fibrous protein synthesis overpowers cellular regeneration in most areas of the body, a phenomenon that is particularly deleterious in peripheral nerve tissue repair. Hepatic cirrhosis, pulmonary fibrosis, esophageal stenosis, and other fibrotic processes such as constricting deformities of cardiac valves are some of the negative side effects of the evolutionary loss of regenerative capacity.

The cells involved in wound healing are mesenchymal cells of a low differentiation grade with some ability for cell specialization, becoming myofibroblasts, chondroblasts, and osteoblasts. These cells produce the surrounding extracellular matrix and the fibrous proteins, collagen, fibronectin, and elastin. Collagen is of greatest importance as it is (together with proteoglycans) the only protein to provide the strength and flexibility needed for human connective tissue function.

Metabolic Response to Trauma

Soft tissue injury profoundly disrupts the normal chemical environment of tissue, and therefore the body's response is aimed at restoring an optimal microenvironment for the cells. According to the fundamental concept of homeostasis, the *milieu intérieur* is kept stable under physiologic conditions.[22] By definition, disturbances of the internal milieu occur in all patients who sustain injury. In a healthy organism with minor injury, the physiologic mechanisms involved in homeostasis are sufficient to maintain stability. More extensive injuries, however, may overwhelm the patient and pathologic processes can develop. Besides the local factors discussed in the following pages, systemic factors such as pain, hypovolemia, and shock act as potent stimuli to the neuroendocrine system.

A significant role for afferent nerve stimulation in mediating the response to injury is seen in studies of cortisol secretion.[10] Pain perception through afferent nerves leads to a neurohumoral response with adrenocorticotropic hormone secretion, followed by cortisol secretion and a sympathetic discharge. Hypovolemia is another strong stimulus to the neuroendocrine system. In major injury, decreased intravascular volume may be secondary to both localized and generalized fluid sequestration as well as to volume loss through hemorrhage.

The metabolic response to trauma is characterized by hypermetabolism and a negative nitrogen balance occurring within days after injury. The consequent catabolism appears to be directed toward supplying energy to the injured tissue and maintaining homeostasis. Therefore, the wound not only is the focus of the reparative process but also participates in initiation of the response.

THE PHASES OF WOUND HEALING

There are different types of wound healing. Proper wound healing requires adequate oxygenation, functioning cellular mechanisms, nutrients and cofactors (e.g., vitamins), normal blood flow, and a clean wound without bacterial contamination.[52] Under these circumstances, primary wound healing with minimal scarring takes place (sanatio per primam intentionem).

In a contaminated wound with necrotic tissue, infection occurs, leading to disruption of the wound. The open, draining wound slowly fills the gap by granulation, and wound closure takes place by wound contraction and epithelialization. Scarring is considerable. This secondary wound healing (sanatio per secundam intentionem) produces a suboptimal result.

If a wound is left open initially and closed after a few days, secondary wound healing (i.e., wound contraction and epithelialization) has already begun. However, delayed surgical closure avoids an extensive gap. Filling by scar is called *delayed primary wound healing* and also results in minimal scarring.

The body's response to injury is a sequence of overlapping reactions that can be divided into four phases. (1) The initial *coagulation phase,* which takes some minutes, is followed by (2) an *inflammatory phase* lasting several hours. After this exudative period, a proliferative period, (3) the *granulation phase,* takes place for days and finally is followed by (4) the *scar formation phase,* a remodeling process that lasts for weeks.

To illustrate this basic pattern of response to injury, we examine the phenomena that occur in ordinary skin wounds such as a clean traumatic wound or an operative incision, a category that encompasses the majority of wounds.

Coagulation Phase

External mechanical forces applied to skin disrupt the normal architecture of tissue, opening up blood vessels and leading to bleeding from the wound. Immediately after injury, the major aim is to reduce blood loss to a minimum by two mechanisms: vasoconstriction and hemostasis. Vasoconstriction is initiated primarily by direct vascular disruption and vascular smooth muscle cell contraction by thromboxane A_2 and secondarily by the neuroendocrine response to pain from the injured area, which causes increased catecholamine levels. Hemostasis is achieved by a platelet plug combined with crosslinked fibrin formed into a clot.

The adherence of platelets to the tissue defect is stimulated by the exposure of subendothelial collagen. Mediators such as thromboxane A_2, an arachidonic acid metabolite, potent vasoconstrictor, and platelet-aggregating agent, are released from the injured endothelial cells. Aggregating platelets release substances from intracellular granules such as adenosine diphosphate, another potent platelet-aggregating agent, thereby recruiting other platelets to the nascent platelet plug (Figs. 3–1 and 3–2).

The damaged tissue releases a phospholipoprotein (tissue thromboplastin) to initiate the clotting mechanism.[47] This extrinsic pathway of coagulation occurs within seconds after injury. Within minutes, the intrinsic pathway of coagulation proceeds as factor XII is activated on exposure to subendothelial collagen. The final common step in both pathways is the conversion of soluble circulating plasma fibrinogen to the insoluble protein fibrin at the site of injury.

The normal physiologic counter-reaction to prevent widespread clot formation and undue thrombosis of uninjured vessels is fibrinolysis. The injured tissue also releases tissue plasminogen activator, which leads to the generation of plasmin. As plasmin degrades the fibrin clot, fibrin split products are formed. These can be found in the circulation during excessive fibrinolysis. Newer data suggest that vascular endothelial growth factor, a multifunctional cytokine, may be involved in modulating levels of the proteins of coagulation and fibrinolysis pathways.

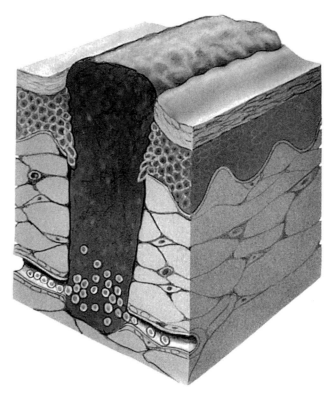

FIGURE 3–1. Coagulation phase of wound healing; wound gap is filled with blood clot.

The coagulation system participates in initiation of the metabolic response to injury not only through the generated primary mediators but also through interaction of the intrinsic system with other mediator systems. The mast cells degranulate and release multiple mediators when exposed to bradykinin.[2] The complement cascade may be initiated by activation of C1r and C1s by kallikrein or through plasmin cleavage of C1s. The generation of the anaphylatoxins C3a and C5a within the complement cascade is started by damaged and nonviable tissue.[20] Chemotactic fragments are released from the kallikrein-kinin system as well as from the complement cascade and from tissue proteases such as alpha$_1$-antitrypsin and alpha$_2$-macroglobulin.

While a large number of different chemical mediators that modulate the microenvironment of the interstitial tissue space are being activated, mitogenic factors for fibroblasts and endothelial cells are released from platelets.[47]

Inflammatory Phase

After the initial vasoconstriction in the coagulation phase, an active vasodilatation of all local small vessels is caused, leading to increased blood flow in the injured area. The vasodilatation is the result of multiple activation of humoral mediators such as arachidonic acid metabolites, the complement cascade, and the kallikrein-kinin system.[6, 51]

On the other hand, these different cascades generate chemotaxins and cytogens that act on migrating elements of the cellular defense mechanism. The chemically attracted cells, primarily polymorphonuclear neutrophils (PMNs), marginate on the endothelial surface of the vessels and adhere, mediated by intercellular cell adhesion molecules. Then the PMNs emigrate through endothelial gaps along with leakage of plasma mediated by the platelet–endothelial cell adhesion molecule.[60]

The consecutive membrane perturbation observed in macrophages, PMNs, platelets, and mast cells appears to stimulate phospholipase A$_2$ activity, which liberates arachidonic acid from membrane phospholipids. Free arachidonic acid is metabolized either to prostanoids by the cyclooxygenase pathway or to leukotrienes by the lipoxygenase pathway. Both of these substance groups act primarily on the surrounding vasculature and on the permeability of cell membranes in the course of inflammatory activation.[21]

The injured tissue suffers an oxygen debt because of the initial underperfusion that leads to anaerobic metabolism of the cells with glycogen breakdown, lactic acid production, acidosis caused by concomitant proton release, and loss of energy-rich phosphates.[46] The degradation of adenosine triphosphate to xanthine and hypoxanthine leads to metabolites that react with oxygen during the vasodilatation phase (reperfusion phase) and form free oxygen radicals.[43] The O$_2^-$ and the products of the Haber-Weiss reaction, OH• and H$_2$O$_2$, are highly reactive cytotoxic substances that interfere with the normal cell membrane to increase cellular permeability. In addition, oxygen radicals deactivate tissue antiproteases such as alpha$_1$-antitrypsin and alpha$_2$-macroglobulin, thereby rendering the tissue susceptible to protease attack and cleavage.

The immigration of PMNs is supported by the anaphylatoxins C3a and C5a, which are liberated from the complement system by contact with nonviable tissue in the wound.[20] The PMNs are thereby activated to produce significant amounts of proteases, mainly elastase and collagenase, to digest and degrade particulate matter, foreign bodies, and bacteria.[39] These enzymes facilitate degradation of necrotic debris by the phagocytes. Further liberation of oxygen free radicals by the respiratory burst of the PMNs enhances cell membrane permeability.[15] Other mediators, such as histamine and serotonin from platelets, may act as well on cell membrane permeability.

As plasma proteins cross the endothelial border more freely, the protein flux is increased, which as well as the increased transvascular fluid and the microvascular injury leads to interstitial edema. This edema is intensified by occlusion of local wound lymphatic channels by fibrin plugs arising from the escaping plasma. The local lymphatolysis prevents drainage of fluid from the injured area, thereby localizing the inflammatory reaction. Although the involvement of PMNs in phagocytosis of foreign substances is limited and mainly directed at the phagocytosis and intracellular killing of bacteria, an increased amount of PMNs significantly accelerates wound healing.[55]

The classic signs of inflammation—dolor (pain), calor (heat), rubor (redness), and tumor (swelling)—can be seen at the wound edges and can be explained by the pathophysiologic events occurring within the wound.[5] Pain is a result of prostaglandin production, heat and redness are due to vasodilatation and the increased local blood flow, and swelling is the consequence of the permeability edema. Concomitant with the tissue influx of PMNs, monocytes, the circulating phagocytes of the reticuloendothelial system, are attracted to the site of injury by the chemotactic substances already mentioned and are transformed into tissue macrophages.[39] They are of utmost importance in the wound-healing sequence because (1) they are the main phagocytes of debris and dead tissue, (2) they form the first channels through the blood clot for capillary re-formation, and (3) they produce angiogenesis and fibroblast-stimulating factors.[25, 32, 33] With increased bacterial contamination, the degree of inflammatory response increases, resulting in pronounced activation of white cells.[55]

Granulation Phase

The granulation phase lasts for days and includes fibroplasia, angiogenesis, epithelialization, and wound contraction. The immigration and activation of fibroblasts result in production of ground substance (e.g., proteoglycans) and structural proteins (e.g., collagen and fibronectin). Simultaneously, angiogenesis takes place by capillary endothelial budding and epithelialization begins from the wound edges.[35] Wound contraction completes this phase of wound healing. In this productive period, the wound gap is finally filled by a well-perfused, infection-resistant granulation tissue (Figs. 3–3 and 3–4).

On the second or third day the number of migratory spindle-shaped fibroblasts, mainly derived from local

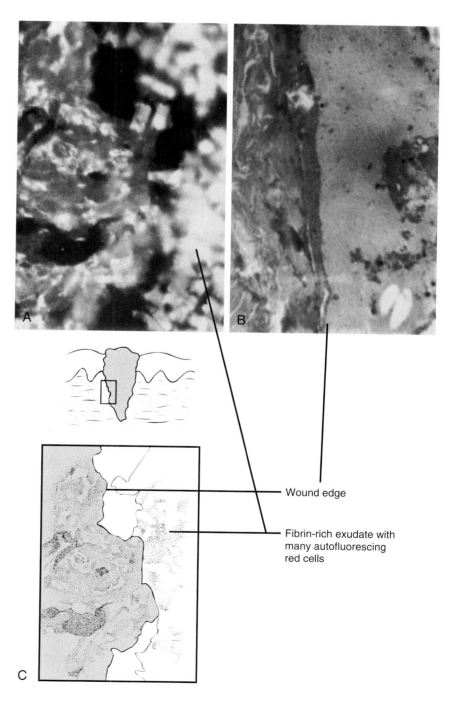

FIGURE 3–2. Wound gap filled with fibrin-rich exudate and red cells (human wound 24 hours after injury). *A,* Type-specific immunohistology of collagen type III, showing normal collagen fiber distribution in subcutaneous tissue. *B,* Hematoxylin and eosin (H&E) stain of the section adjacent to *A,* showing the sharp, nonreactive edge of the wound. *C,* Schematic drawing of *A.* (*A–C,* Courtesy of Andreas G. Nerlich, M.D., Institute of Pathology, University of Munich.)

Wound edge

Fibrin-rich exudate with many autofluorescing red cells

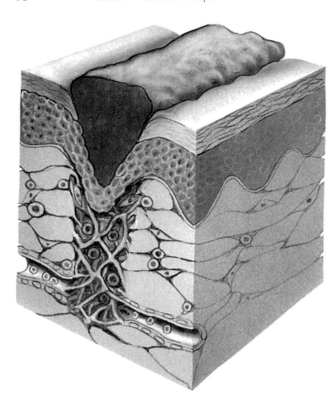

Figure 3–3. Granulation phase: fibroplasia, angiogenesis, epithelialization, and wound contraction.

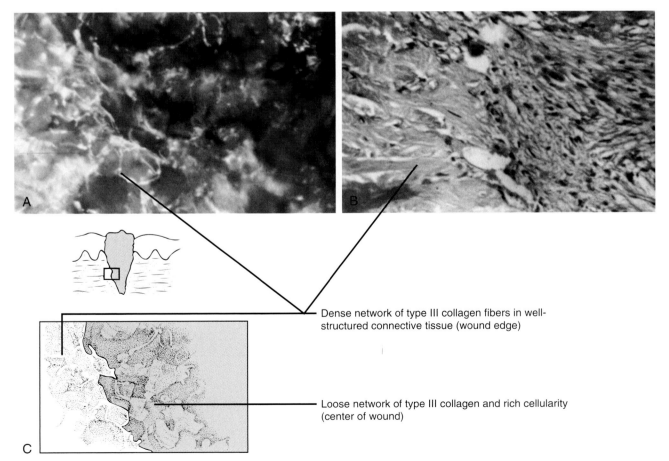

Dense network of type III collagen fibers in well-structured connective tissue (wound edge)

Loose network of type III collagen and rich cellularity (center of wound)

Figure 3–4. Granulation phase, showing dense and loose reticular tissue in the base of the wound (human wound 6 days after injury). *A,* Immunohistology of type III collagen showing widespread reticular collagen type III network and numerous proliferating fibroblasts. *B,* H&E stain of the section adjacent to *A,* showing the cellularity of the newly built tissue in comparison with the wound edge, in which more connective tissue and less cellularity can be demonstrated. *C,* Schematic drawing of *A.*

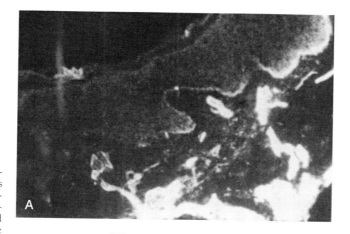

FIGURE 3–5. Basement membrane reconstruction (human wound 8 days after injury). *A,* Type-specific immunohistology with antilaminin antibodies to demonstrate fragmented epithelial basement membrane in the center of the wound and completed epithelial basement membrane along the wound edge. *B,* Schematic drawing of *A.*

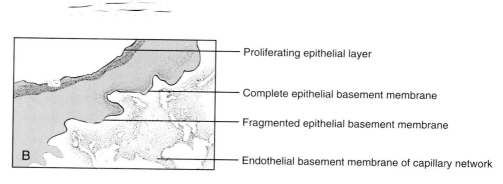

— Proliferating epithelial layer

— Complete epithelial basement membrane

— Fragmented epithelial basement membrane

— Endothelial basement membrane of capillary network

mesenchymal cells, starts to increase, and by the 10th day they are the dominant cells. Shortly after this cellular invasion, an amorphous ground substance can be found and collagen fibers appear in the wound. The mechanism of connective tissue formation is uniform in early lesions of different origin. The fibroblast-capillary system is thought of as an "organ of repair": the fibroblast is the key cell synthesizing both extracellular matrix and structural proteins. The newly formed connective tissue is vascularized by rapid capillary proliferation.[47]

The amorphous ground substance consists mainly of proteoglycans that fill the intercellular space together with the fibrillar structures. Proteoglycans envelop the collagen fibrils with the proteoglycan-to-collagen ratio of mass being 1:60. Nevertheless, the proteoglycans contribute significantly to connective tissue formation and the biologic properties of tissues.[33] Proteoglycans consist of a protein core to which are linked glycosaminoglycans such as chondroitin sulfate, dermatan sulfate, or heparan sulfate that were secreted by fibroblasts.[7] The protein chains aggregate with hyaluronic acid to form very large complexes with molecular masses of about 100,000 kD. Proteoglycans are of increasing interest in research on ligament healing as interactions between proteoglycans and the different types of collagen determine the viscoelastic properties of the tissue concerned.[28, 49, 59]

Fibronectin is an important glycoprotein of the extracellular matrix that can be found in plasma as cold-insoluble globulin. Fibronectin is a multifunctional protein that acts as a cell attachment protein and regulates the distribution of the cells.[59] Regarding connective tissue cells, fibronectin has chemotactic properties.

Laminin is another multifunctional protein of the extracellular matrix, found only in basement membranes.[30] Laminin and fibronectin are important for wound epithelialization, as this process takes place before a complete basement membrane has been reestablished (Fig. 3–5).

Elastin is another noncollagenous glycoprotein that accounts for a major part of the extracellular connective matrix in many tissues. It is distributed in organ systems with high physiologic elasticity, such as major vessels, some ligaments (e.g., nuchal ligament), the lung, and the skin. Its special feature is the presence of two unique amino acids, desmosine and isodesmosine, which are involved in the crosslinking properties of the molecule, rendering it more flexible.[11]

The majority of the structural proteins are collagenous proteins that can be classified into at least 12 different types according to their structure and tissue distribution (Table 3–1).[30] The biomechanical properties of the different connective tissues depend mostly on the predominant type of collagen (e.g., type I collagen in tendons or type II collagen in cartilage) and the degree of interfibrillar crosslinking (Fig. 3–6).[41]

The interstitial collagen molecules are about 300 nm long and have a diameter of 1.4 nm. They consist of three polypeptide chains in a triple-helix configuration of about 1000 amino acids each (Fig. 3–7). At the ends of the

TABLE 3–1 ●

The Collagens

Type	Chains	Localization
I	α1(1), α2(I)	Skin, tendon, bone
II	α1(II)	Cartilage, vitreous humor
III	α1(III)	Skin, tendon, vessels
IV	α1(IV), α2(IV)	All basement membranes
V	α1(V), α2(V), α3(V)	Most interstitial tissues
VI	α1(VI), α2(VI), α3(VI)	Most interstitial tissues
VII	α1(VII), α2(VII), α3(VII)	Anchoring fibrils
VIII	α1(VIII)	Some endothelial cells
IX	α1(IX), α2(IX), α3(IX)	Cartilage
X	α1(X)	Hypertrophic and mineralizing cartilage
XI	α1(XI), α2(XI), α3(XI)	Cartilage
XII	α1(XII), α2(XII)	Interstitial tissues

● ●

Modified from Kühn, K. Rheumatology 10:29, 1986.

molecules are short nonhelical sequences that are important for the crosslinking of the molecules in the extracellular space. The formation of the triple helix is due to an unusual amino acid sequence of the singular chains in which every third amino acid is glycine. In addition, a high percentage of hydroxyproline, proline, and hydroxylysine can be found.[30]

Collagen is synthesized in its precursor form, procollagen, with additional peptides at the amino and the carboxyl terminus. The development from the gene to the functional product includes transcription from DNA to messenger RNA followed by translation of messenger RNA into the amino acid sequence by ribosomes.[41] Characteristic of all collagen molecules is the large number of post-translational modifications, which are enzymatically determined and take place intracellularly and extracellularly. Intracellularly, the hydroxylation of proline and lysine to hydroxyproline and hydroxylysine takes place,

FROM THE GENE TO THE FUNCTIONAL PRODUCT

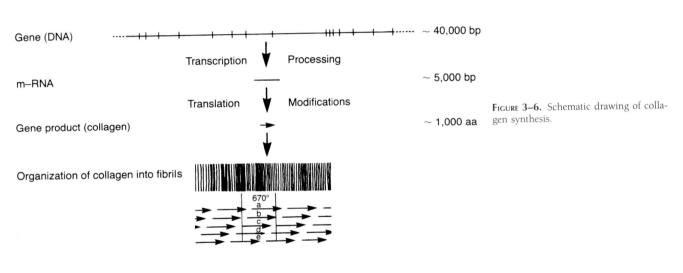

FIGURE 3–6. Schematic drawing of collagen synthesis.

PROCOLLAGEN MOLECULE

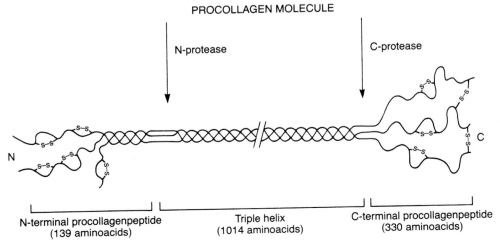

FIGURE 3–7. Structure of the collagen precursor molecule, procollagen.

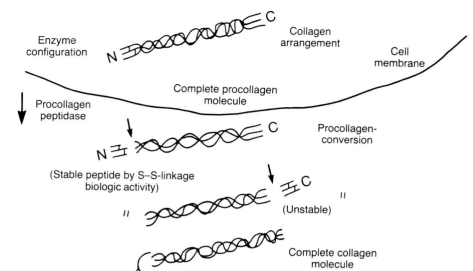

FIGURE 3–8. Intracellular and extracellular collagen synthesis and modification.

followed by the formation of the helix. Extracellularly, the terminal procollagen peptides are cut off and the triple helices are formed into fibrils with a characteristic pattern. Finally, crosslinking takes place, which leads first to labile and then to stable crosslinks, a process that requires complex regulation of fibril production (Fig. 3–8).[30]

The degradation of collagen requires specific collagenases because the triple-helix structure makes collagen molecules resistant to the usual proteolytic enzymes.[53] After a collagenase attack, the fragments are rendered accessible to common tissue proteases.

The contraction of the wound edges is an important feature in open wounds, and epithelialization assumes a more prominent role than in closed wounds. Modified fibroblasts (myofibroblasts) have been identified in contracting tissues.[11]

Scar Formation

The appearance of a scar changes dramatically over many months, a process often termed *scar maturation*. After injury, the delicate balance of synthesis and degradation of collagen is of greatest importance for tissue repair (Fig. 3–9). The reestablishment of tissue integrity and strength produced by normal healing reactions depends mainly on collagen fiber formation, which leads to increased wound strength over time (Fig. 3–10).[26, 38] After an initial rapid increase, the rate of gain in strength remains constant for several months and can continue for over 1 year, depending on the tissue injured.[11] Wound tissue rarely, if ever, regains its full strength, and normal elasticity, so important in tissue function, is lost as well.[45]

The process of scar formation consists mainly of stress-induced orientation of collagen fibers. Quantitatively, the total amount of collagen decreases with time, and qualitatively, the ratio of type III to type I collagen changes in favor of the more rigid type I collagen. Correspondingly, the overhydroxylation of lysine is reduced. Scar tissue contains large amounts of collagenase, indicative of a long period of intensive turnover.[53] The mechanisms controlling remodeling are still poorly understood, but physical forces obviously play an important role.[29] Thus, over the course of many months, initially randomly oriented collagenous tissue is rearranged into structures resembling the conditions before injury.

FIGURE 3–9. Scar formation: remodeling of extracellular matrix and fibril formation, with reduction in cellularity.

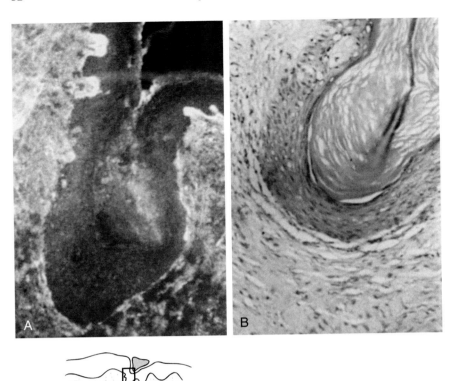

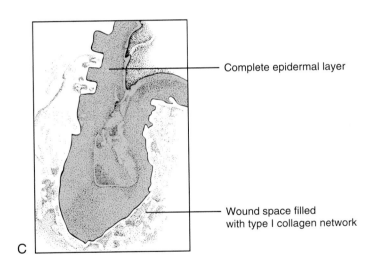

Complete epidermal layer

Wound space filled
with type I collagen network

FIGURE 3–10. Completed epidermal layer (human wound 12 days after injury). *A,* Immunohistology, type specific for collagen type I, showing the complete wound space filled with type I collagen network. *B,* H&E stain of section adjacent to *A,* showing decreased cellularity of the wound ground, indicating maturation of the wound. *C,* Schematic drawing of *A.*

CONDITIONS AFFECTING WOUND HEALING

Various factors can influence the sequence and the result of the wound-healing process. Concerning the general condition of the patient, it is commonly accepted that old age, suboptimal nutritional state, and metabolic disorders such as diabetes mellitus and uremia are unfavorable factors. On the other hand, fetal wounds heal without a scar early in gestation, a process that still remains poorly understood.[36] Certain drugs, such as corticosteroids and cytotoxic agents, have an immunosuppressive effect on macrophage function and reduce collagen synthesis. Radiation produces cell necrosis in the proliferative stage, which slows down the wound-healing process.

A major factor is reduced oxygen tension in the tissues, which may be due to hypovolemia, shock, hypoxia, or other reasons.[23] Tissue perfusion is therefore the most important local factor influencing wound healing. Soft tissue injuries in hypoxic areas heal poorly because the ischemic, desiccated tissue cannot be adequately perfused, rendering the tissue exceedingly susceptible to infection. Lack of oxygen impedes phagocytic activity of white cells as oxygen consumption rises to 15 to 20 times the basal value within seconds after phagocytosis.[55] The microbicidal activity of PMNs and macrophages is markedly reduced by ingestion of too much necrotic tissue.[5] The decisive period of resistance to a bacterial invasion is within the first 3 hours after bacterial contamination of the tissue, when the body's protective mechanisms are maximally involved in keeping bacterial growth and spread under control.[5, 39] If tissue perfusion is not sufficient—for example, because of the localization and the type of the wound (e.g., severe laceration with thrombosis of local blood vessels)—wound infection may occur. The final result of wound infection is increased scar formation and often some loss of function.

INJURY AND REPAIR OF SPECIALIZED TISSUES

Ligament Healing

Ligaments consist of dense and flexible fibrous connective tissue that stabilizes joints and supports them through their full range of motion. Ligamentous injuries therefore negatively affect joint kinematics. Ligaments are composed of cells (mainly fibroblasts); the structural proteins type I and type III collagen, elastin, fibronectin, and other glycoproteins; and the proteoglycans.[13] The specific arrangement of the macromolecular network and the interactions of all the components are responsible for the biomechanical behavior of ligaments. Ligament healing is a complex process similar to wound healing, but there are certain differences even between extra-articular and intra-articular ligaments in regard to the time period needed for healing and the quality of scar tissue.

Ligaments are bradytrophic tissues, and therefore phases of wound healing are modified (Fig. 3–11). In the inflammatory phase, macrophages phagocytose necrotic

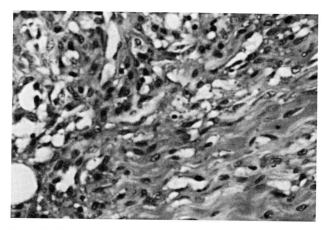

FIGURE 3–12. Histologic appearance of ligament healing at 2 weeks, showing active fibroblastic reaction that accompanies the vascular response (H&E stain, polarized light).

ligament tissue and cellular debris and secrete an angiogenetic factor. This process is followed by an ingrowth of capillary buds into the ligament wound. The predominating fibroblast is actively engaged in both degradation and synthesis of collagen.[53] The majority of newly formed collagen is initially type III, which reinforces the first framework of granulation tissue. Type I collagen appears later in the wound and in a smaller proportion than normal. Glycosaminoglycans are markedly increased within the newly formed extracellular matrix and the fibronectin content is also higher. Fibronectin can be crosslinked to fibrin, to fibrinogen, and to collagen, which enables cell receptors to bind to the fibronectin-collagen complex. This mechanism promotes spreading of fibroblasts into the wound.[27] Because of the poor vascularity of ligaments, this initial inflammatory phase takes longer than in wound healing. After the first week, the process of revascularization forms a diffuse vascular network. Collagen synthesis increases and peaks early in this proliferative phase but remains elevated for a long period. Macrophages are still apparent, but fibroblasts are the predominant cell type (Fig. 3–12).

The newly formed bundles of collagen fibers are initially disorganized (irregularly oriented), and of the immature collagen, the reducible crosslinked dihydroxylysinonorleucine (DHLNL) predominates over normal ligament tissue.[14] During this stage of ligament healing, the glycosaminoglycan concentration remains high and elastin begins to appear in an irregular distribution. The collagenous bundles gradually become arranged along the stress axis of the ligament and the scar tissue becomes less cellular. These changes are responsible for the increasing tensile strength of the matrix.[56] In the scar remodeling phase, a gradual morphologic transition with further decrease in cellularity and in synthetic activity of the fibroblasts can be seen. The extracellular matrix becomes better organized, the bundles of collagen fibers appear more closely packed, and the vascularity of the scar tissue is decreased (Fig. 3–13).

The collagen fibrils increase slightly in diameter, which correlates with increasing tensile strength of the new collagenous tissue. The elevated ratio of type III and type

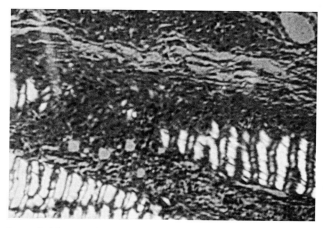

FIGURE 3–11. Granulation tissue between the damaged and the frayed-appearing ligament stumps, 6 days after ligament rupture (anterior cruciate ligament of the sheep, H&E stain, polarized light microscopy). (Courtesy of Ulrich Bosch, M.D., Trauma Department, Hannover Medical School, Hannover.)

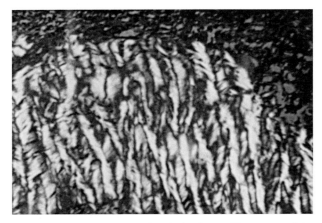

Figure 3–13. Granulation tissue beside the damaged ligament, with loss of the highly organized arrangements of collagen fiber bundles 2 weeks after ligament rupture (H&E stain, polarized light).

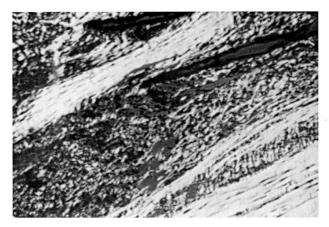

Figure 3–14. Adjacent to normal ligament tissue, immature collagenous tissue with thin, irregularly oriented fiber bundles 10 weeks after trauma (H&E stain, polarized light).

I collagen and the ratio of DHLNL to hydroxylysinonor-leucine (HLNL) reducible crosslinks decline compared with those for normal ligaments. Nevertheless, the proteoglycan content remains slightly elevated for weeks.[8, 38]

The scar matrix in a ligament gradually matures over a period of months to tissue that becomes highly organized and remodeled and closely resembles ligament tissue macroscopically (Fig. 3–14). However, the scar matrix always remains slightly disorganized and hypercellular on microscopic examination. The amount of scar formation depends on local and systemic factors such as mechanical stress, oxygen tension, and pH, all of which differ between extra-articular and intra-articular ligaments.[3, 61] The rehabilitation conditions, such as immobilization or early mobilization, the amount of weight bearing, and functional stress, influence the appearance and the biomechanical properties of ligaments (Fig. 3–15).[4, 14, 38]

Several studies showed that early motion has a beneficial effect on ligament function.[3, 4, 29, 38] The mechanical stress applied by the functional load improves the reorientation of the collagen fiber bundles and increases the fibril size and density. Immobilization, on the contrary, is followed by a protracted state of catabolism within the ligament, and degradation of the structural matrix leads to progressive atrophy and lack of mechanical strength.[4, 61]

Tendon Healing

In comparison with ligaments, tendons have a more mature histologic appearance. They contain fewer fibrocytes or tenocytes, fewer glycosaminoglycans, and more collagen (almost exclusively type I) and have a different, possibly more mature, collagen crosslinking pattern. The collagen includes a higher concentration of HLNL as well as a relatively reduced ratio of DHLNL plus HLNL to histidinohydroxymerodesmosine.[1]

Tendons contain three glycosaminoglycans: hyaluronate, chondroitin sulfate, and dermatan sulfate. During the development and maturation of tendons, there is an increase in fibril diameter, with a change from a unimodal to a more bimodal distribution of fibril diameters.[49] This

change correlates with a decrease in chondroitin sulfate and hyaluronate concentration. Dermatan sulfate is the predominant glycosaminoglycan in mature tendons.[57] Another constituent of tendons is elastic fibers, which are uniformly distributed and arranged in the direction of the collagen fibers.

A partial rupture of a tendon can be repaired by an intrinsic healing process. Near the site of necrotic tissue, resting tenocytes are transformed to active tenoblasts that proliferate after 3 to 4 days.[44] The damaged tendon area is bridged by the new extracellular matrix being produced. Fibronectin, which is bound more to denatured than to native collagen, enables the advance of fibroblasts into the necrotic tissue.[59]

Concerning completely ruptured tendons, the overlying paratenon and surrounding connective tissue play the dominant role in the healing process. On the third to fourth day, the cells of the tendon sheaths start to proliferate and invade the initial blood clot, filling the gap between the damaged tendon stumps.[6] After 1 week, newly formed, irregularly arranged collagen fibers are present in the granulation tissue. The newly synthesized

Figure 3–15. Highly organized scar tissue bridging the ruptured ligament 6 months after trauma (H&E stain, polarized light).

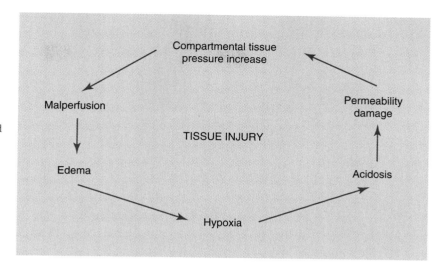

FIGURE 3–16. Vicious circle of pressure increase and permeability edema in tissue injury.

extracellular matrix is rich in type III collagen and glycosaminoglycans.[59]

In the early stage of repair, macrophages are detectable in the granulation tissue. They phagocytose necrotic material and resorb collagen fibers in the regenerating tendon, which are arranged in disorderly fashion in the granulation tissue.[17] In this early period, thin filaments in the fibroblasts, which represent the contractile proteins actin and myosin, are probably responsible for the ameboid movements of the migrating cells.[44] Fibronectin, bound to denatured collagen and fibrin, has a chemoattractant property and promotes migration of fibroblasts into the granulation tissue between the necrotic tendon stumps.[27]

Over a period of weeks to several months, the disorganized and cell-rich fibrous network becomes less cellular and more oriented in the plane of mechanical stress. Type III collagen remains detectable over a prolonged period after injury, although an excess of type I collagen can be observed in the scar matrix. Even in the last stages of tendon healing, the collagen fibrils have a substantially smaller diameter than normal, similar to that observed in the early stages of healing and in the fetal or neonatal tendon.[49] Parallel to the longitudinal arrangement of the collagen fiber bundles, the glycosaminoglycan content decreases. Elastic fibers are formed but remain immature and irregularly distributed between the bundles of collagen fibers, the typical feature of scar tissue.[44] The highly organized and remodeled scar tissue grossly resembles normal tendon tissue but never exhibits its perfect anatomic features.[24, 26] Only a good approximation, similar to that observed in ligament healing, is achieved, and this may well be responsible for the poor biomechanical behavior of ruptured tendons after healing.

Muscle Injury and Repair

Striated muscle reacts to injury just as it does to any other physical disturbance: with contraction. In this way, the well-perfused muscle tissue contributes to coagulation. On the other hand, muscular tissue pressure is, in the state of relaxation, relatively low, which is a rather ineffective counterforce against intramuscular bleeding. The sheath, which includes the muscle, the epimysium, and the overlying fascia, is a rather rigid tissue and gives counterpressure to muscular contraction forces.[34] As a consequence, rather large intracompartmental hematomas can develop within the muscle tissue before the transmural pressure is high enough to prevent further intramuscular fluid expansion.[38]

The special arrangement of muscle tissue within tissue sheaths contributes to the frequent development of compartment syndromes after trauma. Especially in high-energy trauma, the circumscript space within the muscle fascia can be either externally compressed (volume reduction) or disturbed because of internal volume expansion (intramuscular hematoma). The increased tissue pressure leads to reduced perfusion of the capillaries, and the reduction in the microcirculation within the muscle causes a decompensated increase in metabolic needs, leading to neuromuscular deficits.[9, 19] A vicious circle of postischemic edema formation can be established: the increase in tissue pressure reduces perfusion, resulting in interstitial edema, hypoxia, and acidosis. This in turn leads to permeability damage of the capillaries, further increasing tissue pressure (Fig. 3–16).[9, 19]

The peripheral circulation remains intact because the increased tissue pressure has little effect on arterial flow, and because venous outflow pressure distally to the compartment is usually normal, the process is limited to the involved compartment (Fig. 3–17).

The increased tissue pressure impedes microcirculation, which affects the function of neurovascular tissue. The metabolic needs of the tissue cannot be met because of the decreased oxygen supply, leading to anaerobic metabolism. The degradation of intracellular glycogen deposits to glucose and further lactic acid leads to acidosis within the tissues.[40] Increased permeability of the endothelial cell layer causes more fluid exudation, which increases tissue pressure further, thereby worsening the ischemic injury (Figs. 3–18 and 3–19).[42] (Further information on the compartment syndrome may be found in Chapter 12, Compartment Syndromes.)

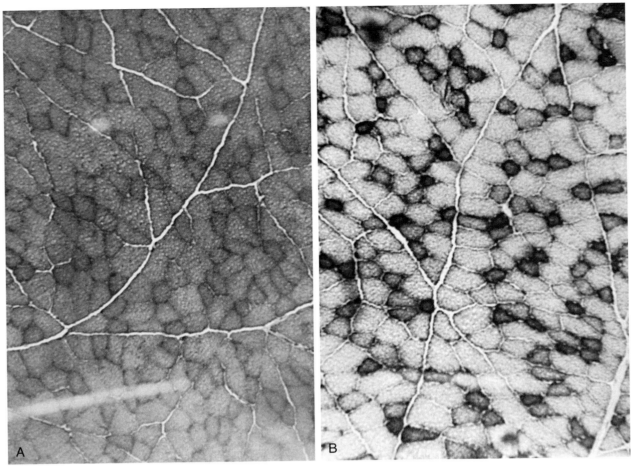

FIGURE **3–17.** Normal muscle, light microscopy (anterior tibial muscle of the rat). *A,* Trichrome stain. *B,* Nicotinamide-adenine dinucleotide (NADH) reductase reaction. (*A, B,* Courtesy of Volker Echtermeyer, M.D., Trauma Department, Klinikum Minden, Minden, Germany.)

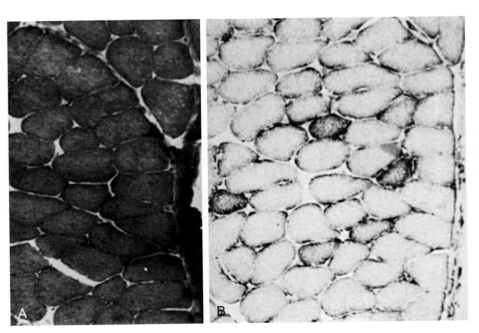

FIGURE **3–18.** Experimental tourniquet trauma to the anterior tibial muscle. Hind limb, 6 hours after a 4-hour tourniquet, shows interstitial widening with interfascicular separation caused by edema formation. *A,* Trichrome stain. *B,* NADH reductase reaction.

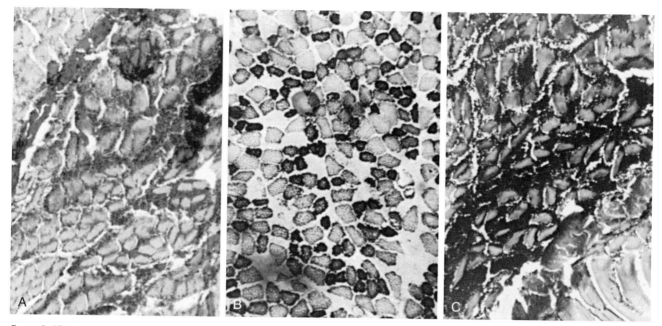

FIGURE 3-19. Experimental standardized contusion of the rat anterior tibial muscle, 6 hours after injury. Massive intracompartmental bleeding with edema formation and focal cell necrosis. *A,* Trichrome stain. *B,* NADH reductase reaction. *C,* Van Gieson's stain.

In addition to the ischemic neuromuscular damage, a mechanism of reperfusion injury can be described. The degradation of such energy-rich nucleotides as adenosine to adenosine monophosphate and to adenosine and inosine results in hypoxanthine, a substrate that in combination with oxygen leads by way of the enzyme xanthine oxidase to xanthine and O_2^-. This superoxide radical production with subsequent tissue destruction has been described in muscle and may further accentuate the ischemic injury.[43]

Healing of skeletal muscle after laceration and repair often leads to extensive scarring and ossification.[16, 48] Muscular necrosis can cause fatty degeneration of the tissue, with replacement of muscular structure by collagenous connective tissue, resulting in considerable or complete loss of function (Fig. 3–20).[9, 37, 58]

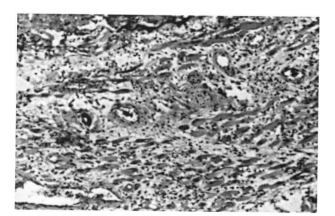

FIGURE 3-20. Late-stage compartment syndrome with complete necrosis of the anterior tibial muscle. Massive fibrosis with interstitial cell infiltration and dissociation of vital muscle fibers by scar tissue (human biopsy 10 months after injury, H&E stain).

Nerve Injury

With soft tissue injuries, nerves can also be affected. The neurotrauma can be classified according to the extent of injury of the neuronal and non-neuronal structures. Seddon[50] divided nerve injuries into the three categories neurapraxia, axonotmesis, and neurotmesis. Sunderland[52] classified them on basis of the degree of damage (degrees 1 to 5).

In nerve injury relatively uniform degenerative and regenerative processes take place. Immediately after injury, the nerve stumps swell. Afterward the whole distal stump begins to degenerate, a step called wallerian degeneration. It is characterized by condensation of axoplasm, the occurrence of macrophages, and proliferation of Schwann cells.

The macrophages and the Schwann cells degrade the remaining axoplasm as well as the myelin sheath in the nerve stump to gain space for a regenerated axon. The regeneration begins at the proximal stump of the nerve, where the wallerian degeneration happens only over a short distance. In this area the axons form sprouts, which are directed distally. If these sprouts do not reach the distal Schwann sheath, a neuroma develops in combination with the proliferating connective tissue. However, if the axon sprouts manage to reach the distal nerve sheath, the axon grows with a maximum growth rate of 1 to 3 mm/day.[31]

CLINICAL CONSIDERATIONS

No wound heals without at least some degree of scarring. Because a scar is always a weak spot in the body's coverage, the guiding therapeutic principle in the treatment of soft tissue injuries is minimal surgical dissection for minimal scar formation. With elective incisions, minimal scar formation is accomplished by following the skin tension lines (Langer's lines), avoiding sharply curved incisions and the danger of skin flap necrosis, protecting the sensory innervation of the skin, and placing the incision for adequate coverage of implants.

Unfortunately, in accidental wounds these principles must be modified or even ignored. One has to deal with tissues with unknown perfusion, especially unstable microcirculation; unknown innervation; an unknown degree of tissue defect; and possible contamination by foreign bodies and bacteria. The amount of kinetic energy absorbed by the tissues can be estimated in cases of concomitant fractures by determining the fracture type according to the Arbeitsgemeinschaft für Osteosynthesefragen (AO/ASIF) classification. The degree of comminution and of dislocation of the fragments correlates with the energy that caused the skeletal injury.

Closed fractures with concomitant soft tissue injury are more difficult to assess because the degree of contusion often remains unclear until some time passes and circumscript areas of skin necrosis develop. Classification systems for open and closed fractures are therefore essential for proper assessment.[18, 54]

The general condition of the patient influences greatly the local situation because the cool and clammy patient in shock has decreased peripheral perfusion that is further reduced in areas of tissue injury. Hypoxia impairs leukocyte functions such as phagocytosis and bacterial killing, thereby rendering the tissue more susceptible to infection. Shock and hypoxia, therefore, have to be treated aggressively by increasing arterial oxygen tension and cardiac output to improve the microcirculation of the injured tissue. The positive effect of improved perfusion of the injured tissue greatly exceeds the disadvantage of possible blood loss into the wound. It is important to undertake these measures quickly to improve tissue perfusion and oxygenation because the decisive period for infection fighting is the first 3 hours after wounding. After this, the body's capacity to combat a bacterial inoculum is lessened.

Infection and necrosis, which lead to prolonged inflammatory reaction, should be aggressively treated because they result in most of the detrimental scarring. Systemic antibiotic therapy may be considered prophylactic, depending on the circumstances and the degree of injury; however, it is mandatory in fractures with severe soft tissue damage.[54] The danger of secondary nosocomial contamination can be minimized by preventing repeated wound inspections under nonsterile conditions. The dressing should be kept intact until the wound is irrigated and débrided in the operating room.

Pressure of bone fragments on vascular structures and compression of the skin caused by fractures and dislocations increase hypoxia and may cause extended areas of soft tissue necrosis. Therefore, proper positioning and splinting of injured extremities and gentle reduction of displaced fragments are essential and should be performed as early as possible. These maneuvers reduce additional tissue swelling, which itself can further compromise the microvascular circulation.

Wound débridement is the essential step in care of the injured limb. This procedure must be well planned to avoid additional damage, to give best access to all injured areas, and to remove completely all necrotic, contaminated tissue. Proper débridement is critical because it reduces the load on the endogenous mechanisms of phagocytosis of dead tissue by macrophages and removes the devitalized tissue that can act as a culture medium for bacteria. The more severely the limb is injured or the more additional injuries the patient has, the more aggressive the débridement should be. All tissues with doubtful perfusion that would be left in place and reassessed at a second-look operation within 48 hours should be removed in a severely injured, polytraumatized patient. Devitalized soft tissue and bone must be débrided aggressively and dead space prevented to decrease the incidence of infection and the amount of scarring.

Decompression of compartment syndromes and evacuation of hematomas are essential to reduce the risk of further soft tissue necrosis, infection, and scarring and to provide a good environment for phagocytic cells. Sufficient drainage of the wound is therefore a prerequisite.

Wound closure should be performed with the smallest needle possible and the smallest suture material. Ischemia and wound edge necrosis can be prevented by tension-free adaptation of the tissues. Open-wound treatment should maintain a physiologic milieu and provide a moist environment to prevent drying of the wound edges. Coverage with synthetic skin (e.g., Epigard) minimizes the risk of swelling-induced tension and skin flap necrosis and allows healing by third intention. Open-wound treatment offers the advantage of secondary assessment, débridement, and closure with less risk of infection and tissue necrosis. Gentle tissue handling without additional operative traumatization should always be the goal.

The general supportive measures for injured soft tissues include transient immobilization of the affected area, which reduces swelling. The immobilization should be followed by early active return to function of the injured limb to restore circulation and lymphatic transport, thereby reducing edema formation and avoiding secondary dystrophic derangements. If these considerations are kept in mind, a satisfactory result is possible, even in extensive soft tissue injuries.

REFERENCES

1. Amiel, D.; Frank, C.; Harwood, F.; et al. Tendons and ligaments: A morphological and biochemical comparison. J Orthop Res 1:257, 1984.
2. Artuc, M.; Hermes, B.; Steckelings, U.M.; et al. Mast cells and their mediators in cutaneous wounds—Active participants or innocent bystanders? Exp Dermatol 8(1):1, 1999.
3. Binkley, J.M.; Peat, M. The effects of immobilization on the ultrastructure and mechanical properties of the medial collateral ligament of rats. Clin Orthop 203:301, 1986.
4. Bosch, U.; Kasperczyk, W.; Decker, B.; et al. The morphological effects of synthetic augmentation in posterior cruciate ligament reconstruction: An experimental study in a sheep model. Arch Orthop Trauma Surg 115(3–4):176, 1996.
5. Burke, J.F.; Miles, A.A. The sequence of vascular events in early infectious inflammation. J Pathol Bacteriol 76:1, 1958.
6. Carlstedt, C.A. Mechanical and chemical factors in tendon healing. Effects of indomethacin and surgery in the rabbit. Acta Orthop Scand Suppl 224:58, 1987.

7. Chen, J.R.; Takahasi, M.; Kushida, K.; et al. Direct detection of crosslinks of collagen and elastin in the hydrolysates of human yellow ligament using single-column high performance liquid chromatography. Anal Biochem 278:99, 2000.

8. Cornelissen, A.M.; Stoop, R.; Von-den-Hoff, H.W.; et al. Myofibroblasts and matrix components in healing palatal wounds in the rat. J Oral Pathol Med 29(1):1, 2000.

9. Echtermeyer, V.; Tscherne, H.; Oestern, H.J.; van der Zypen, E. Compartment syndrome: Etiology, pathophysiology, anatomy, localization, diagnostic and treatment. In: Tscherne, H.; Gotzen, L., eds. Fractures with Soft Tissue Injuries. Berlin, Springer, 1984, p. 98.

10. Fassbender, K.; Kaptur, S.; Becker, P.; et al. Inverse association between endogenous glucocorticoid secretion and L-selectin (CD62L) expression in trauma patients. Life Sci 65:2471, 1999.

11. Forrester, J.C. Collagen morphology in normal and wound tissue. In: Hunt, T.K., ed. Wound Healing and Wound Infection: Theory and Surgical Practice. New York, Appleton-Century-Crofts, 1980, p. 118.

12. Frank, C.; Shrive, N.; Hiraoka, H.; et al. Optimisation of the biology of soft tissue repair. J Sci Med Sport 2(3):190, 1999.

13. Frank, C.; Woo, S.L.Y.; Amiel, D.; et al. Medial collateral ligament healing: A multidisciplinary assessment in rabbits. Am J Sports Med 11:379, 1983.

14. Frank, C.; Amiel, D.; Woo, S.L.Y.; Akeson, W. Normal ligament properties and ligament healing. Clin Orthop 196:15, 1985.

15. Friedman, G.B.; Taylor, C.T.; Parkos, C.A.; Colgan, S.P. Epithelial permeability induced by neutrophil transmigration is potentiated by hypoxia: Role of intracellular cAMP. J Cell Physiol 176:76, 1998.

16. Garret, W.E., Jr.; Seaber, A.V.; Boswick, J.; et al. Recovery of skeletal muscle after laceration and repair. J Hand Surg [Am] 9:683, 1984.

17. Gelberman, R.H. Flexor tendon physiology: Tendon nutrition and cellular activity in injury and repair. Instr Course Lect 34:351, 1985.

18. Gustilo, R.B.; Mendoza, R.M.; Williams, D.H. Problems in the management of type III (severe) open fractures: A new classification of type III open fractures. J Trauma 24:742, 1984.

19. Hargens, A.R.; Romine, J.S.; Sipe, J.C.; et al. Peripheral nerve conduction block by high muscle compartment pressure. J Bone Joint Surg Am 61:192, 1979.

20. Heidemann, M.; Saravis, C.; Clowes, G.H.A., Jr. Effect of nonviable tissues and abscesses on complement depletion and the development of bacteremia. J Trauma 22:527, 1982.

21. Heller, A.; Koch, T.; Schmeck, J.; Van-Ackern, K. Lipid mediators in inflammatory disorders. Drugs 55:487, 1998.

22. Hochachka, P.W.; McClelland, G.B. Cellular metabolic homeostasis during large-scale change in ATP turnover rates in muscles. J Exp Biol 200:381, 1997.

23. Hunt, T.K.; Linsey, M.; Grislis, G.; et al. The effect of different ambient oxygen tensions on wound infections. Ann Surg 181:35, 1975.

24. Hutton, P.A.N. Tendon healing: An histological and electron microscopic study. J Bone Joint Surg Br 63:296, 1981.

25. Jackman, S.H.; Yoak, M.B.; Keerthy, S.; Beaver, B.L. Differential expression of chemokines in a mouse model of wound healing. Ann Clin Lab Sci 30:201, 2000.

26. Jozsa, L.; Réffy, A.; Bálint, J.B. Polarization and electron microscopic studies on the collagen of intact and ruptured human tendons. Acta Histochem 74:209, 1984.

27. Kleinman, H.K. Interactions between connective tissue matrix macromolecules. Connect Tissue Res 10:61, 1982.

28. Kosir, M.A.; Quinn, C.C.; Wang, W.; Tromp, G. Matrix glycosaminoglycans in the growth phase of fibroblasts: More of the story in wound healing. J Surg Res 92:45, 2000.

29. Krippaehne, W.W.; Hunt, T.K.; Jackson, D.S.; Dunphy, J.E. Studies on the effect of stress on transplants of autologous and homologous connective tissue. Am J Surg 104:267, 1962.

30. Kühn, K. The collagen family—Variations in the molecular and supermolecular structure. Rheumatology 10:29, 1986.

31. Lee, S.K.; Wolfe, S.W. Peripheral nerve injury and repair. J Am Acad Orthop Surg 8:243, 2000.

32. Leibovich, S.V.; Ross, R. A macrophage dependent factor that stimulates the proliferation of fibroblasts in vitro. Am J Pathol 84:501, 1976.

33. Letho, M; Järvinen, M. Collagen and glycosaminoglycan synthesis of injured gastrocnemius muscle in rat. Eur Surg Res 17:179, 1985.

34. Letho M.; Alanen, A. Healing of a muscle trauma. Correlation of sonographical and histological findings in an experimental study in rats. J Ultrasound Med 6:425, 1987.

35. Li, W.; Keller, G. VEGF nuclear accumulation correlates with phenotypical changes in endothelial cells. J Cell Sci 113: 1525, 2000.

36. Mackool, R.J.; Gittes, G.K.; Longaker, M.T. Scarless healing. The fetal wound. Clin Plast Surg 25:357, 1998.

37. Matsen, F.A. Compartmental Syndromes. New York, Grune & Stratton, 1980.

38. McGaw, W.T. The effect of tension on collagen remodelling by fibroblasts: A stereological ultrastructural study. Connect Tissue Res 14:229, 1986.

39. Miles, A.A. The inflammatory response in relation to local infections. Surg Clin North Am 60:93, 1980.

40. Morris A.; Henry, W., Jr.; Shearer, J.; Caldwell, M. Macrophage interaction with skeletal muscle: A potential role of macrophages in determining the energy state of healing wounds. J Trauma 25:751, 1985.

41. Nerlich, A.G.; Pöschl, E.; Voss, T.; Müller, P.K. Biosynthesis of collagen and its control. Rheumatology 10:70, 1986.

42. Nikolaou, P.K.; MacDonald, B.L.; Glisson, R.R.; et al. Biomechanical and histological evaluation of muscle after controlled strain injury. Am J Sports Med 15:9, 1987.

43. Parks, D.A.; Bulkley, G.B.; Granger, D.M.; et al. Ischemic injury in the cat small intestine: Role of superoxide radicals. Gastroenterology 82:9, 1982.

44. Postacchini, F.; Accinni, L.; Natali, P.G.; et al. Regeneration of rabbit calcaneal tendon. Cell Tissue Res 195:81, 1978.

45. Reddy, G.K.; Stehno-Bittel, L.; Enwemeka, C.S. Matrix remodeling in healing rabbit Achilles tendon. Wound Repair Regen 7:518, 1999.

46. Richardt, G.; Tolg, R. Cellular sequelae of myocardial ischemia. Z Kardiol 86(Suppl 1):23, 1997.

47. Ross, P. Inflammation, cell proliferation and connective tissue formation in wound repair. In: Hunt, T.K., ed. Wound Healing and Wound Infection. East Norwalk, CT, Appleton-Century-Crofts, 1980, p. 57.

48. Salminen, A.; Kihlström, M. Protective effect of indomethacin against exercise induced injuries in mouse skeletal muscle fibers. Int J Sports Med 8:46, 1987.

49. Scott, J.E.; Hughes, E.W. Proteoglycan collagen relationships in developing chick and bovine tendons. Influence of the physiological environment. Connect Tissue Res 14:267, 1986.

50. Seddon, H. Surgical Disorders of Peripheral Nerves. New York, Churchill Livingstone, 1975.

51. Smith, P.D.; Kuhn, M.A.; Franz, M.G.; et al. Initiating the inflammatory phase of incisional healing prior to tissue injury. J Surg Res 92:11, 2000.

52. Sunderland, S. Nerves and Nerve Injuries, 2nd ed. Edinburgh, Churchill Livingstone, 1978.

53. Ten Cate A.R.; Deporter, D.A. The degradative role of the fibroblast in the remodelling and turnover of collagen in soft connective tissue. Anat Rec 182:1, 1975.

54. Tscherne, H.; Gotzen, L., eds. Fractures with Soft Tissue Injuries. Berlin, Springer, 1984.

55. Ueno, H.; Yamada, H.; Tanaka, I.; et al. Accelerating effects of chitosan for healing at early phase of experimental open wound in dogs. Biomaterials 20:1407, 1999.

56. Vailas, A.C.; Tipton, C.M.; Matthes, R.D.; Gart, M. Physical activity and its influence on the repair process of medial collateral ligaments. Connect Tissue Res 9:25, 1981.

57. Vogel, K.G.; Heinegard, D. Characterization of proteoglycans from adult bovine tendon. J Biol Chem 260:9298, 1985.

58. Walton, M.; Rothwell, A.G. Reactions of thigh tissues of sheep to blunt trauma. Clin Orthop 176:273, 1983.

59. Williams, I.F.; McCullagh, K.G.; Silver, I.A. The distribution of types I and III collagen and fibronectin in the healing equine tendon. Connect Tissue Res 12:211, 1984.

60. Winn, R.K.; Mihelicic, D.; Vedder, N.B.; et al. Monoclonal antibodies to leukocyte and endothelial adhesion molecules attenuate ischemia-reperfusion injury. Behring Inst Mitt 92:229, 1993.

61. Woo, S.L.Y.; Gomez, M.A.; Sites, T.J.; et al. The biomechanical and morphological changes in the medial collateral ligament of the rabbit after immobilization and remobilization. J Bone Joint Surg Am 69:1200, 1987.

62. Yetiser, S.; Kahramanyol, M. High-velocity gunshot wounds to the head and neck: A review of wound ballistics. Mil Med 163:346, 1998.

CHAPTER 4

Biomechanics of Fractures

John A. Hipp, Ph.D.
Wilson C. Hayes, Ph.D.

Bone is a remarkable material with complex mechanical properties and a unique ability for self-repair, making it a fascinating structural material from both a clinical and an engineering perspective. Bone fails when overloaded, initiating a complex series of biologic and biomechanical events directed toward repair and restoration of function. Tremendous progress is being made in understanding, controlling, and enhancing the biologic aspects of fracture healing. The mechanical environment is always a crucial element of fracture healing, with strong interactions between biologic and mechanical factors. Clinical management of fractures must influence both the biologic and the mechanical conditions so that the original load-bearing capacity of the bone is restored as quickly as possible. There are thus three principal aspects of the biomechanics of fractures and their treatment: (1) biomechanical factors that determine when and how a bone fractures, (2) biomechanical factors that influence fracture healing, and (3) control of the biomechanical environment by fracture treatments.

The biomechanical factors that determine whether a bone fractures include the loads applied and the mechanical properties of bone and soft tissue. Humans engage in many activities, resulting in a broad range of loads. For normal bone, the loads that result in fracture are typically extremes; severely osteoporotic or pathologic bone may fracture during normal activities of daily living. In addition, the mechanical properties of bone vary over a wide range, and several pathologic processes can alter bone properties. Therefore, our first objective is to review the mechanical properties of bone, the changes in mechanical properties that accompany aging and certain disease processes, and the fracture risk for normal and diseased bone.

Bone tissue has a unique ability for repair, frequently restoring its original load-bearing capacity in weeks to months. However, this repair process is influenced by the mechanical environment to which the healing bone is subjected, and bone healing fails under adverse conditions. The rate at which the load-bearing capacity is restored is affected by the stability of the fracture site. The second objective of this chapter is to review the biomechanics of fracture healing and the influence of the mechanical environment on the biology of fracture healing.

Successful fracture treatment requires control of both the biologic and the mechanical aspects of fracture healing. Different approaches to fracture treatment control the mechanical environment in different ways and can influence the rate at which load-bearing capacity is restored. The third objective of this chapter, therefore, is to review the biomechanics of fracture treatment, particularly in relation to the stability these approaches provide to healing fractures. Quantitative measurements that can help determine the optimal fracture treatment would be of great clinical benefit. These measurements may help to promote a fracture-healing process that provides the most rapid restoration of load-bearing capacity. Quantitative measurements are being developed that may help determine the stability of a fracture and also the optimal timing for removal of fixation. The optimal treatment plan could be objectively selected by combining these measurements with known mechanical properties of a variety of fracture treatment approaches. The final objective is to review progress toward developing objective clinical tools for selecting and monitoring fracture treatment.

BONE PROPERTIES AND FRACTURE RISK

From a mechanical viewpoint, bone can be examined at two levels. At the first level, bone can be viewed as a material with mechanical properties that can be measured in the laboratory. These properties include the amount of deformation that occurs under load, the mechanism and rate at which damage accumulates in the bone, and the maximal loads that the material can tolerate before catastrophic failure. At a higher level, a bone can be viewed as a structure composed of a tissue organized into a geometry that has evolved for specific mechanical functions. Relevant structural properties include the amount of deformation that occurs during physiologic loading and the loads that cause failure either during a single load event or during cyclical loading. Both the material properties of bone as a tissue and the structural properties of bone as an organ determine the fracture resistance of bone and influence fracture healing. Thus, this section begins by discussing the relevant mechanical properties of bone as a material. This discussion is followed by a review of the structural properties of whole bones. The section closes with a review of several important clinical applications in which the biomechanics of fracture and the risk of fracture have been studied.

Material Properties of Bone

CORTICAL BONE

The mechanical properties of bone tissue are typically determined by measuring the deformation of small, uniform specimens during application of simple, well-defined loads. Figure 4–1 illustrates a typical test that involves subjecting a machined cortical bone specimen to tensile loads. Dumbbell-shaped tensile specimens are typically used, so that failure occurs in a reproducible location. Two parameters are monitored during the tensile test: the applied force and the displacement between two points along the long axis of the specimen. The resulting force-displacement curve provides an indication of the stiffness and failure load of the bone specimen, but the data are useful only for specimens with the same geometry as the one tested. To provide material property data that can be applied to any specimen geometry, the force and displacement data are converted to stress and strain. This conversion is a normalization process that eliminates the

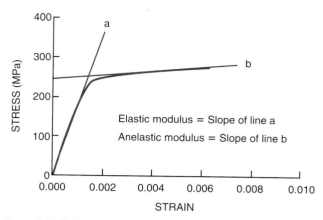

FIGURE 4–2. Typical stress-strain curve for human cortical bone showing the curve regions where the elastic and anelastic moduli are calculated.

influence of specimen geometry. The *stress* in the bone specimen is calculated as the applied force divided by the cross-sectional area, and the *strain* is measured as the percentage change in length of a defined length of the specimen.

A typical stress-strain curve for a tensile test of cortical bone is shown in Figure 4–2. The *elastic modulus* of bone tissue or structural materials such as stainless steel, titanium, or polymethyl methacrylate is determined from the slope of the initial, linear part of the curve. The point at which the slope of the stress-strain curve decreases is the *yield point* of the bone, and the maximal recorded stress is the *ultimate strength* of the tissue. After the bone has yielded, the slope of the stress-strain curve drops to a new value termed the *anelastic modulus*.[120] The area under the stress-strain curve reflects the capacity of bone to absorb energy. The capacity to absorb energy increases with yield strength, but the greatest energy absorption is typically seen for bones with high ultimate strains, where substantial energy is absorbed during postyield deformation. Studies of bone under controlled loading conditions provide data to document the properties of cortical bone in tension, compression, torsion, and bending.[58]

Bone is loaded cyclically during many activities of daily living, and the load required to cause bone to fail is dramatically lower if that load is applied repeatedly. The number of cycles of stress that bone can tolerate decreases as the stress level increases. This property of bone is measured using curves of the stress versus number of cycles to failure. These curves depend on the type of loading (axial, bending, or torsion), the loading rate, and the physical composition of the bone. The internal mechanisms in bone that determine its behavior under cyclical loading are beginning to be understood.[21, 22, 56, 75, 76, 110, 127]

Several factors influence the material properties of cortical bone. For instance, the properties are dependent on the rate at which the bone tissue is loaded. Materials such as bone whose stress-strain characteristics are dependent on the applied strain rate are termed *viscoelastic* or *time-dependent materials*. However, the strain rate dependence of bone is relatively modest, with the elastic modulus and ultimate strength of bone approximately

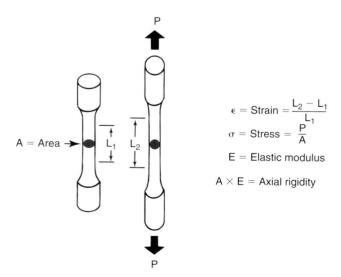

$$\epsilon = \text{Strain} = \frac{L_2 - L_1}{L_1}$$

$$\sigma = \text{Stress} = \frac{P}{A}$$

$$E = \text{Elastic modulus}$$

$$A \times E = \text{Axial rigidity}$$

FIGURE 4–1. Simple uniaxial tensile test with a dumbbell-shaped specimen. P is the applied load and $(L_2 - L_1)/L_1$ is the strain between two points along the specimen's axis.

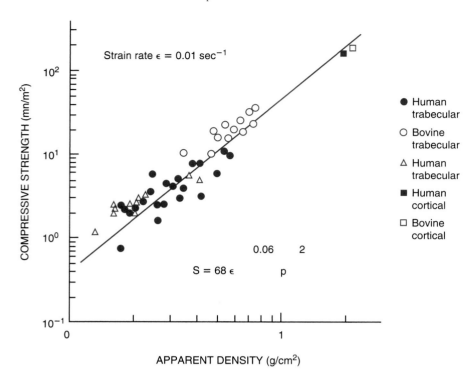

FIGURE **4–3.** Compressive strength as a function of apparent density for human and bovine trabecular and cortical bone. (Data from Carter, D.R.; Hayes, W.C. Science 194:1174–1176, 1976.)

proportional to the strain rate raised to the 0.06 power[20] (Figs. 4–3 and 4–4). Over a wide range of strain rates, the ultimate compressive strength increases by a factor of 3, and the modulus increases by about a factor of 2.[158]

The stress-strain behavior of cortical bone is also strongly dependent on the orientation of bone microstructure with respect to the loading direction.[146] Several investigators have shown that cortical bone is both stronger and stiffer in the longitudinal direction (the predominant orientation of osteons) than in the transverse direction. Materials such as bone whose mechanical properties depend on the loading direction are said to be *anisotropic*. The anisotropy and viscoelasticity of bone distinguish it as a complex material, and both the strain rate and the loading direction must be specified when describing the material properties of bone tissue. Table 4–1

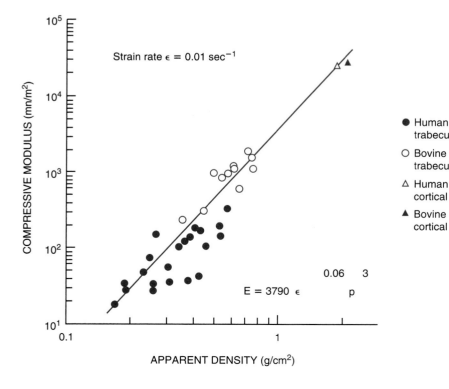

FIGURE **4–4.** Compressive modulus as a function of apparent density for human and bovine trabecular and cortical bone. (Data from Carter, D.R.; Hayes, W.C. J Bone Joint Surg Am 59:954–962, 1977.)

TABLE 4–1

Anisotropic Material Properties for Human Cortical Bone*

Loading Direction	Modulus (GPa)
Longitudinal	17.0
Transverse	11.5
Shear	3.3

*In comparison, moduli for common isotropic materials used in orthopaedic implants are stainless steel, 207 GPa; titanium alloys, 127 GPa; bone cement, 2.8 GPa; ultrahigh-molecular-weight polyethylene, 1.4 GPa.
Source: Data from Journal of Biomechanics, Volume number 8, Reilly, D.T.; Burstein, A.H. The elastic and ultimate properties of compact bone tissue, pp. 393–405, Copyright 1975, with kind permission from Elsevier Science Ltd, The Boulevard, Langford Lane, Kidlington OX5 1GB, UK.

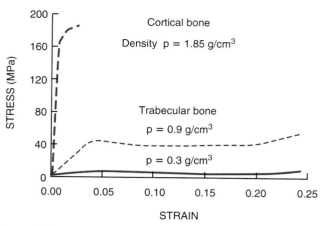

FIGURE 4–5. Compressive stress-strain curves for cortical and trabecular bone of different densities.

provides representative anisotropic material properties for human cortical bone, and ultimate strengths of cortical bone from adult femurs for longitudinal and transverse loads are summarized in Table 4–2.

TRABECULAR BONE

The major physical difference between trabecular bone and cortical bone is the increased porosity exhibited by trabecular bone. This porosity is reflected by measurements of the apparent density (i.e., the mass of bone tissue divided by the bulk volume of the test specimen, including mineralized bone and marrow spaces). In the human skeleton, the apparent density of trabecular bone ranges from approximately 0.1 to 1.0 g/cm³, whereas the apparent density of cortical bone is about 1.8 g/cm³. A trabecular bone specimen with an apparent density of 0.2 g/cm³ has a porosity of about 90%.

The compressive stress-strain properties of trabecular bone are markedly different from those of cortical bone and are similar to the compressive behavior of many porous engineering materials that absorb energy on impact.[51, 145] Stress-strain curves (Fig. 4–5) for trabecular bone in compression exhibit an initial elastic region followed by yield. The slope of the initial elastic region ranges from one to two orders of magnitude less than that of cortical bone. Yield is followed by a long plateau region created as more trabeculae fracture. The fractured trabec-

TABLE 4–2

Ultimate Strength Values for Human Femoral Cortical Bone

Loading Mode	Ultimate Strength (MPa)*
Longitudinal	
Tension	135 (15.6)
Compression	205 (17.3)
Shear	71 (2.6)
Transverse	
Tension	53 (10.7)
Compression	131 (20.7)

*Standard deviations in parentheses.
Source: Data from Journal of Biomechanics, Volume number 8, Reilly, D.T.; Burstein, A.H. The elastic and ultimate properties of compact bone tissue, pp. 393–405, Copyright 1975, with kind permission from Elsevier Science Ltd, The Boulevard, Langford Lane, Kidlington OX5 1GB, UK.

ulae begin to fill the marrow spaces at approximately 50% strain. Further loading of the specimen after the pores are filled is associated with a marked increase in specimen modulus.

Both the compressive strength and the compressive modulus of trabecular bone are markedly influenced by the apparent density of the tissue (see Figs. 4–3 and 4–4). Like cortical bone, trabecular bone is also anisotropic (material properties depend on the direction of loading). The regressions presented in Figures 4–3 and 4–4 include cortical bone with an apparent density of approximately 1.8 g/cm³ as well as trabecular bone specimens from several species representing a wide range of apparent densities. These relationships suggest that the compressive strength of all bone tissue in the skeleton is approximately proportional to the square of the apparent density.[23] The elastic modulus of trabecular bone tissue is approximately proportional to the cube of apparent density.[20] The experimentally observed relationships are consistent with the porous foam analogy for trabecular bone.[51] Although these relationships were initially derived from compression tests, tensile tests of trabecular bone suggest that its tensile modulus and tensile strength are slightly less than its compressive strength.[75] One interesting observation is that even though the stiffness and strength of trabecular bone depend on bone density and the direction of loading, for a range of bone densities, trabecular bone appears to fail at just under 1% strain no matter what the direction of loading.[25]

These relationships between mechanical properties and the apparent density of bone tissue are important. First, they suggest that bone tissue can generate large changes in modulus and strength through small changes in bone density. Conversely, subtle changes in bone density result in large differences in strength and modulus. This consideration is important when we note that bone density changes are usually not radiographically evident until bone density has been reduced by 30% to 50%. The power law relationships of Figures 4–3 and 4–4 indicate that such reductions in bone density result in nearly an order of magnitude reduction in bone stiffness and strength.

Structural Properties of Whole Bones

When the skeleton is exposed to trauma, some regions are subjected to extreme loads. Fracture occurs when the local stresses or strains exceed the ultimate strength or strain of bone in that region. Bone fracture can therefore be viewed as an event that is initiated at the material level and then affects the load-bearing capacity of bone at the structural level. The major difference between behavior at the material level and that at the structural level is related to inclusion of geometric features at the structural level and their exclusion at the material level. Thus, the structural behavior includes the effects of both bone geometry and material properties, whereas material behavior occurs without the effects of complex bone geometries. Any attempt to predict the structural behavior of a skeletal region must therefore reflect both the material properties of different types of bone in that region and the geometric arrangement of the bone.

Several aspects of bone cross-sectional geometry, such as cross-sectional area and moment of inertia, are important in the structural properties. The cross-sectional area is straightforward. When subjected to axial loads and assuming similar bone material properties, a large, thick-walled bone is more resistant to fracture simply because the internal forces are distributed over a larger surface area, resulting in lower stresses. The moment of inertia expresses the shape of the cross section and the particular distribution of tissue or material with respect to applied bending loads. The moment of inertia must be expressed in relation to a particular axis because bending can occur in many different planes. Equations for calculating the moment of inertia of several regular geometric cross sections are shown in Figure 4–6.[123] From these equations, it is apparent that the moment of inertia is highly sensitive to the distribution of area with respect to an axis. Material that is at a greater distance from the axis is more

efficient at resisting bending with respect to that axis. A simple example of this principle is that a yardstick turned on an edge is more resistant to bending than one turned horizontally. An I-beam is a particularly efficient cross-sectional shape for resisting bending in one direction because most of its area is distributed at a great distance from the bending axis.

If bones were subjected to bending in only one direction, their cross-sectional area would probably have evolved to something like an I-beam. Instead, long bones are loaded by axial loads, bending in several planes, and torsion. Under these conditions, a semitubular structure is most efficient. Diaphyseal bone cross-sectional geometries are roughly tubular in some regions but are very irregular elsewhere. The moment of inertia for an irregular bone cross section can be determined from traces of the periosteal and endosteal surfaces, using simple numerical techniques.[103] The moment of inertia partially determines the risk of fracture. For example, small cross-sectional areas and moments of inertia of the femoral and tibial diaphysis predispose military trainees to stress fractures.[12]

Although bones are typically subjected to a variety of complex loads, it is instructive to evaluate the strength of a bone or fracture treatment method for simple, well-defined loads. Three types of loading are typically considered in laboratory experiments: axial loading, bending, and torsion. For each load case, the behavior of the structure is described by a rigidity term that is a combination of both material stiffness (represented by a modulus) and a geometric factor (area or moment of inertia). Structures with high rigidity deform little under a load. For axial loads, the important parameters that govern the mechanical behavior of a structure are the cross-sectional area and the modulus of elasticity (see Fig. 4–1). The product of area and modulus is the axial rigidity. For bending, the applied loads are expressed as a moment with dimensions of force times a distance. The important structural parameters in a bending test are the moment of inertia and the elastic modulus (Fig. 4–7), and their product is the bending (or flexural) rigidity. Torsional loads are also expressed as a force times a distance. The cross-sectional distribution of bone and the shear modulus of bone determine the torsional properties (Fig. 4–8).

Just as the moment of inertia describes the distribution of material about the bending axis for a cylindrical bone, the polar moment of inertia describes the distribution of material about the long axis of the structure being tested. The product of shear modulus and polar moment of inertia gives the torsional rigidity. For noncircular cross sections and for structures with cross sections that vary along the length, a simple polar moment of inertia is not applicable. For these structures, various formulas and simple analytical models can be used to calculate the structural properties under torsional loads.[85, 123] The rigidities already discussed describe how much a bone may deform under a load. Alone, a quantitative estimate of rigidity may be of limited use to a clinician who wants to know whether a bone would break when subjected to physiologic loading. Fortunately, there is evidence that a strong relationship exists between bone stiffness and bone strength.[49]

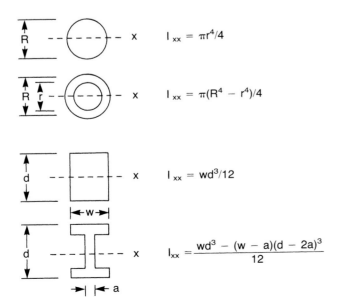

FIGURE 4–6. Some simple geometric cross sections and the corresponding formulas for calculating the moments of inertia with respect to the x-axis.

$$I_{xx} = \pi r^4/4$$

$$I_{xx} = \pi(R^4 - r^4)/4$$

$$I_{xx} = wd^3/12$$

$$I_{xx} = \frac{wd^3 - (w - a)(d - 2a)^3}{12}$$

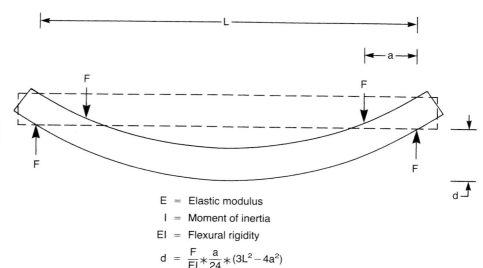

FIGURE **4–7.** Representation of a four-point bending test of a beam. The original shape is shown by the *dashed line,* and the deformed shape is indicated by the *solid lines* (deformations are exaggerated).

E = Elastic modulus

I = Moment of inertia

EI = Flexural rigidity

$$d = \frac{F}{EI} * \frac{a}{24} * (3L^2 - 4a^2)$$

The various loading modes that occur in whole bones can result in characteristic fracture patterns (Fig. 4–9). When loaded in tension, diaphyseal bone normally fractures owing to tensile stresses along a plane that is approximately perpendicular to the direction of loading. When loaded in compression, a bone typically fails along planes that are oblique to the bone's long axis. With compressive loads, high shear stresses develop along oblique planes that are oriented at about 45 degrees from the long axis. These maximal shear stresses are approximately one half the applied compressive stress. However, because the shear strength of cortical bone is much less than the compressive strength (see Table 4–2), fracture occurs along the oblique plane of maximal shear. Thus, compressive failures of bone occur along planes of maximal shear stress, and tensile fractures occur along planes of maximal tensile stress.

When a bone is subjected to bending, high tensile stresses develop on the convex side, whereas high compressive stresses develop on the concave side. The resulting fracture pattern is consistent with that observed during axial compressive and tensile loading of whole bones. A transverse fracture surface occurs on the tensile side, whereas an oblique fracture surface is found on the compressive side. Two fracture surfaces commonly occur on the compressive side, creating a loose wedge of bone that is sometimes referred to as a *butterfly fragment.* The fracture pattern is more complex when a bone is subjected to torsion. Fractures usually begin at a small defect at the bone surface, and then the crack follows a spiral pattern through the bone along planes of high tensile stress. The final fracture surface appears as an oblique spiral that characterizes it as a torsion fracture.

The fracture patterns discussed for idealized loading conditions are consistent with some fractures seen clinically. With many traumatic loading conditions, however, bone is subject to a combination of axial, bending, and torsional loading, and the resulting fracture patterns can be complex combinations of the patterns previously described. In addition, high loading rates often result in additional comminution of the fracture caused by the branching and propagation of numerous fracture planes. Bone may tolerate higher loads if the loads are applied rapidly,[36] although the ability of bone to absorb energy may not change with loading rate. In addition, fractures can be caused by a single load that is greater than the load-bearing capacity of the bone; these loads are commonly called the *ultimate failure load.* Repeated application of loads smaller than the ultimate failure load can fatigue the bone and eventually lead to failure. Fatigue failures of bone are common in military training and in athletes. Few data exist about the loads that cause fatigue fractures. Fatigue fractures are believed to be associated with damage accumulation within the bone. It is difficult to measure the actual fatigue properties of bone because repair of the accumulated damage in the bone occurs in vivo but cannot be reproduced in ex vivo experiments.

Engineering tools that were originally developed to study more traditional engineering problems provide new insights into the structural mechanics of bone, skeletal

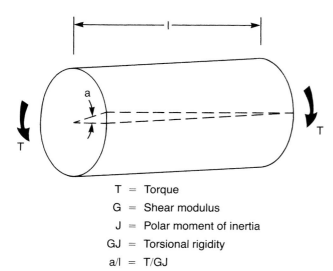

T = Torque

G = Shear modulus

J = Polar moment of inertia

GJ = Torsional rigidity

a/l = T/GJ

FIGURE **4–8.** Simple torsion test of a cylinder. The angular deformation is indicated along with relevant formulas.

LOADING MODE

Tension   Compression   Bending   Torsion

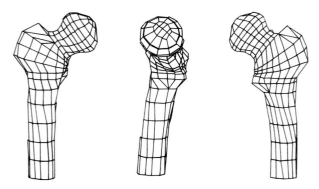

Figure 4–9. Characteristic fractures typically found for bones loaded to failure with "pure" loading modes.

Transverse   Oblique   Butterfly   Spiral

FRACTURE TYPE

fractures, and fracture treatments. Valuable insight into the biomechanics of fractures can be obtained using simple analytical models that can be solved on paper with the help of a calculator.[85, 142] However, the most commonly applied engineering tool is the finite element method.

The finite element method is a powerful engineering modeling tool that is routinely used to investigate complex structures subject to varied loads and supports. The method involves forming a mathematical model of the bone from small elements of simple geometry (such as rectangles or tetrahedrons). Figure 4–10 shows representative views of a finite element mesh used to model the proximal femur. The material properties of each element are specified along with the applied loads and support conditions. The model is then analyzed by a computer to predict the deformations and stresses within the structure.[88] Thus, the behavior of bone at both the material and structural levels can be investigated using the finite element method. The finite element method allows parametric investigation of material properties, geometry, and loading conditions and has been applied in many orthopaedic biomechanical analyses.[69] Several applications of the finite element method in orthopaedic biomechanics are discussed in this chapter. In particular, the finite element method is being developed for understanding and predicting fracture risk and can provide better information about bone strength than conventional bone density measurements.[34]

Age-Related and Pathologic Bone Property Changes

With increasing age, the mechanical properties of bone tissue slowly degrade, and geometric changes provide additional alterations in the structural characteristics of bones. Age-related changes occur in both cortical and trabecular bone, and changes in both regions can result in increased fracture risk. Changes in bone mineral mass, density, mechanical properties, and histology associated with aging have been the subject of intensive investigation. The picture to emerge from this research is a progressive net loss of bone mass with aging, beginning in the fifth decade of life and proceeding more rapidly in women.[122] Concurrent with this general loss of bone mass, bone tissue becomes more brittle and less able to absorb energy. The major clinical consequence of these skeletal changes is an age-related increase in fracture incidence.

At the tissue level, several age-related changes in the material properties of femoral cortical bone have been demonstrated.[19] A small decrease in elastic modulus

Figure 4–10. Different views of a finite element mesh of a proximal femur. (From Lotz, J.C. Ph.D. dissertation, Massachusetts Institute of Technology, 1988.)

occurs with age (1.5% per decade), but the most significant change occurs in the amount of strain that the bone tolerates before fracture. With aging, the ultimate strain decreases by between 5% and 7% per decade. The energy required to fracture a bone is reflected in the area under the stress-strain curve. Because the elastic modulus does not change appreciably, the energy required for failure is predominantly reduced by age-related decreases in ultimate strain. Thus, with aging, the bone behaves more like a brittle material, and the capacity of bone to absorb the energy of a traumatic event decreases.

Studies of skeletal aging often do not consider the overall geometry and distribution of bone tissue. Changes with age in cross-sectional cortical geometry of the lower limb bones were studied at 11 locations along the length of 103 femoral and 99 tibial cadaveric specimens. Results indicate that although both men and women undergo endosteal bone resorption and medullary expansion with aging, only men exhibit concurrent subperiosteal bone apposition and expansion. Consequently, men show little change in cortical area and some increase in second moments of inertia with age. Conversely, both the cortical area and the second moments of inertia decrease with age in women. Thus, only men appear to remodel bone in a way that compensates for loss of bone material strength with aging.[11, 124]

In a study of archaeologic bone specimens from individuals with high activity levels, both men and women exhibited subperiosteal expansion and increases in second moments of area with aging.[125] Together with observed differences in fracture incidence among living populations, these findings suggest that the relatively low activity levels of modern civilization may not stimulate optimal bone remodeling throughout life and thus may contribute to higher fracture risk in aged people. Reductions in the cross-sectional area of the tibia have also been observed in patients after spinal cord injuries.[39]

The preceding discussion examined age-related changes in cortical bone. Trabecular bone plays an important structural role in many bones, and the age-related changes in trabecular bone contribute to the increased fracture risk in elderly people. Quantitative studies of trabecular bone morphology in vertebral bodies demonstrated that the thickness of trabeculae decreases while the spacing between trabeculae increases.[14, 133] These age-related morphologic changes significantly reduce the strength of the vertebral bodies, contributing to the observed increased vertebral fracture incidence in elderly people.[63, 72]

Fracture Risk

A bone fails when the applied loads exceed the load-bearing capacity; hence, both the applied loads and the load-bearing capacity must be known to calculate fracture risk. Most structures, such as a bridge or a building, are designed to withstand loads several times greater than expected. Similarly, the normal human skeleton can support loads much higher than expected during activities of daily living. The ratio of load-bearing capacity to load-bearing requirement is frequently termed the *safety factor*. The inverse of this ratio has been termed the *factor of risk for fracture*.

For loads approximating the midstance phase of gait, the average load-bearing capacity of mature and osteoporotic human femurs ranges from 2000 to 10,000 N (472 to 2250 pounds).[45] Peak loads at the hip joint during the midstance phase of gait have been recorded as three to five times body weight.[13] Therefore, a 600-N (140-pound) individual who applies four times body weight to the femur during walking has a femoral load-bearing capacity that ranges from less than one to more than four times as strong as needed, depending on the properties of that individual's femur. For the tibia, axial loads while walking are estimated to be two to four times body weight,[101] and the greatest bending moment applied during restricted weight bearing is estimated to be about 79 Nm in men.[84] Intact human tibias loaded in three-point bending failed at 57.9 to 294 Nm, so the bending strength of the tibia is also one to four times the maximal applied bending loads. The maximal torque that the tibia can tolerate was estimated to be about 29 Nm. Under torsional loads, tibias failed at 27.5 to 89.2 Nm, which is one to three times the maximal applied torque. These calculations are valid only for particular types of loading. Nevertheless, these estimated factors of risk may help determine when a healing femoral fracture can tolerate moderate weight bearing or when a femur with a bone defect requires prophylactic stabilization.

There are several groups in whom fractures are prevalent and for whom prevention may be possible if fracture mechanisms and the patients at greatest risk can be identified. One group is the growing elderly population, in which age-related fractures are prevalent. Another group is cancer patients with metastatic bone disease, in which prophylactic stabilization of impending fractures may increase patients' quality of life. The next few sections discuss the fracture risk and methods for predicting fracture risk related to aging and metastatic bone lesions.

FRACTURE RISK WITH OSTEOPOROSIS

The epidemiology of age-related fractures suggests a relation between osteoporosis and increased fracture risk[63]; consequently, risk factors associated with hip fractures have been the subject of much research. The effects of age and gender have been documented, but these factors are confounded by an increased propensity for trauma in the elderly population.[63] Fractures related to osteoporosis are commonly associated with falls, and the frequency of falls increases with age. In addition, falls are more common in elderly women than in men, and fracture rates are also greater in women than in men.[6, 54] Common sites for fall-related fractures are the proximal femur and distal forearm. Vertebral fractures are also frequently associated with traumatic loading such as occurs in backward falls, although relatively nontraumatic vertebral fractures may be much more common than nontraumatic femoral fractures.

When age- and sex-specific incidence rates are compared for all major fractures of different skeletal regions, considerable variability is observed. This variability may be due in part to varying proportions of cortical and trabecular bone at different sites and to the difference in pattern of bone loss of these two types.[94] Differences in fracture risk may also be attributed to variations in overall bone geometry. For instance, the relatively short neck and smaller femoral neck angle in Japanese women may explain their lower incidence of hip fracture compared with that in American women.[104] The type and direction of loads during a fall (Fig. 4–11) are very different from those of loads during activities of daily living. Because the femur is adapted to support activities of daily living, it may be particularly sensitive to the abnormal loads during a fall. These factors emphasize both the complex interactions that occur between age-related bone loss and skeletal trauma and the need for improved understanding of the biomechanics of fracture risk in specific skeletal sites. Reduced skeletal resistance to trauma and the increased propensity for falling are cofactors in determining hip fracture risk.[54, 97] These considerations lead to the conclusion that both bone loss and trauma are necessary, but not independently sufficient, causes of age-related hip fractures.

Fractures of the proximal femur are a significant public health problem and a major cause of mortality and morbidity among elderly people,[16, 111, 151] and attempts to reduce the incidence of age-related hip fractures have primarily focused on preventing or inhibiting excessive bone loss associated with osteoporosis. As a result, many noninvasive measures of bone density have been developed in the hope of identifying individuals with the

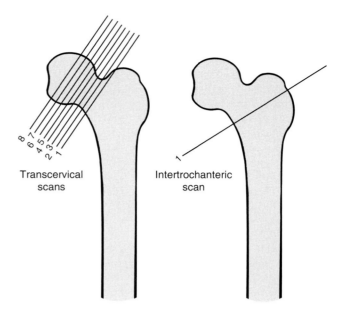

Figure 4–12. Quantitative computed tomography (QCT) scan locations used to compare QCT data with in vitro failure strengths of proximal femurs. (From Lotz, J.C. Ph.D. dissertation, Massachusetts Institute of Technology, 1988.)

greatest fracture risk. Ex vivo studies have shown that the load-bearing capacity of the proximal femur can be predicted from measurements of bone density and femoral geometry.[2, 90] An excellent correlation was found between the ultimate failure load and quantitative computed tomographic (CT) measurements made at intertrochanteric sites[90] (Fig. 4–12). The best correlation was found for the product of the average trabecular CT number and the total bone cross-sectional area. The use of this parameter could result in improved assessment of the degree of osteoporosis and the associated risk of hip fracture.

Lotz and co-workers[89] analytically studied the proximal femur subjected to various load configurations, including one-legged stance and fall. The finite element models (see Fig. 4–10) suggest that the joint load is transferred from the femoral head to the cortex of the calcar region through the primary compressive group of trabeculae during gait. These results contradict the current belief that loads are distributed in proportion to the bone volume fractions. Instead, there is a shift in the distribution of load from mainly trabecular bone near the femoral head to cortical bone at the base of the femoral neck. This result, along with the observation that fractures of the proximal femur usually occur in the subcapital region,[6] supports the hypothesis that fractures in osteoporotic bone result from reduced strength of trabecular bone.[98, 122]

FRACTURE RISK WITH METASTATIC AND BENIGN DEFECTS IN BONE

Metastatic lesions frequently occur in the axial and appendicular skeleton of patients with breast cancer, prostate cancer, and other cancers. Benign bone tumors occur in 33% to 50% of asymptomatic children evaluated by random radiographs of long bones.[129] These lesions can represent a significant fracture risk. As reviewed by

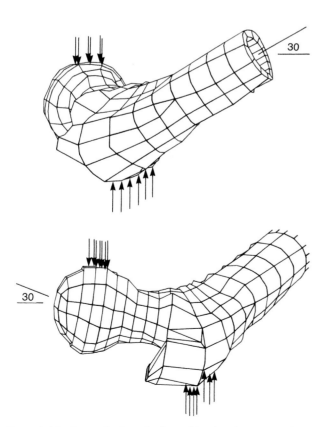

Figure 4–11. Contact loads at the femoral head and greater trochanter representing a fall to the side. (From Lotz, J.C. Ph.D. dissertation, Massachusetts Institute of Technology, 1988.)

Oda and Schurman,[105] 9% to 29% of skeletal metastases seen by orthopaedic surgeons result in pathologic fractures. Prophylactic fixation of an impending fracture has several advantages over treating a pathologic fracture, including relief of pain, decreased hospital stay, reduced operative difficulty, reduced risk of nonunion, and reduced morbidity. On the other hand, operations that do not reduce overall morbidity must be avoided. Clinicians are thus faced with the task of determining whether a defect requires prophylactic stabilization.

Current clinical guidelines can provide contradictory indications for prophylactic stabilization. Beals and colleagues[7] concluded that defects that have a dimension greater than 2.5 cm and that cause pain should be stabilized. Fidler[47] suggested that defects that compromise more than 50% of the cortex should be stabilized. However, many aspects of metastatic defect geometry and material properties determine the structural consequences of the lesion. In common sites of osseous metastases such as the proximal femur, even experienced orthopaedic oncologists cannot predict the strength reduction related to the defect from radiographs or from qualitative observation of CT examinations.[67]

Several ex vivo experiments have been reported that specifically addressed the structural consequences of metastatic defects in long bones:

1. McBroom and associates[95] considered the structural consequences of transcortical holes in long bones subjected to bending loads. They drilled holes of various sizes through one cortex of canine femurs. Defect size was expressed as the hole diameter divided by the bone diameter. The bones were tested to failure using a four-point bending test.
2. Hipp and co-workers[66] created endosteal defects in canine femurs that did not penetrate through the

cortical wall. The size of the endosteal defect was expressed as the average thickness of the cortical wall in the area of the defect divided by the thickness of the intact cortical wall. The femurs were tested to failure using a four-point bending test.
3. In another study, Hipp and colleagues[65] created transcortical defects in sheep femora and tested the bones to failure using a torsion test.

For each of these ex vivo tests, finite element models were developed to complement the experimental data and to investigate parameters that can influence the structural consequences of metastatic lesions in bone. In all experiments, agreement was found between the finite element model predictions and the actual measurements of strength reductions related to the defects.

Existing guidelines for determining when to stabilize prophylactically long bones with metastatic lesions can place a bone at significant risk of fracture. On the basis of our data, the strength of bones with simulated endosteal metastatic defects is proportional to defect size (Fig. 4–13) but is highly dependent on the type of loading. For example, a 65% reduction in bending strength was determined for transcortical lesions destroying 50% of the cortex, whereas the same lesion was found to reduce torsional load-bearing capacity by 85%.

The finite element models show that the material properties of bone along the border of a defect can significantly increase the structural consequences of a metastatic defect. Many metastatic lesions are associated with bone resorption along the border of the lesion that extends beyond the radiographically evident lysis. Thus, for osteolytic metastatic lesions, the structural consequences may be significantly greater than predicted from plain radiographs. The finite element models also demonstrated that for endosteal defects, a critical geometric

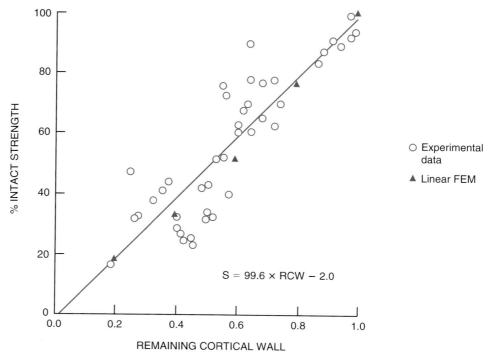

FIGURE 4–13. Percentage of intact bone bending strength (S) as a function of endosteal defect size. Endosteal defect size is expressed as the ratio of reduced wall thickness to intact cortical wall thickness. Both experimental and analytical results are shown. FEM, finite element model; RCW, remaining cortical wall. (Data from Hipp, J.A.; McBroom, R.J.; Cheal, E.J.; Hayes, W.C. J Orthop Res 7:828–837, 1989.)

$$S = 99.6 \times RCW - 2.0$$

○ Experimental data

▲ Linear FEM

% INTACT STRENGTH

REMAINING CORTICAL WALL

parameter is the minimal cortical wall thickness. For example, a bone with an asymmetric defect that compromises 80% of the cortical wall at one point but only 20% of the wall on the opposite side is only 2% stronger in torsion than a bone with a defect that compromises 80% of the cortical wall around the entire circumference.

Even biplanar radiographs fail to detect critical geometric parameters if the critical defect geometry is not aligned with respect to the radiographic planes. In a retrospective study of 516 metastatic breast lesions using anteroposterior radiographs, Keene and associates[77] could not establish a geometric criterion for lesions at risk of fracture, perhaps because critical geometric parameters were missed using plain radiographs. Results of ex vivo experiments with simulated defects suggest that CT scans at small consecutive scan intervals could facilitate evaluation of the fracture risk related to metastatic lesions.

Strength reductions related to vertebral defects can be determined from CT data.[154, 155] These CT-based measurements require placing a phantom under the patient during the examination so that CT attenuation data can be converted to bone density. Known relations between bone density and bone modulus are then used to convert the bone density data to modulus. For each cross section through the vertebrae, the product of area and modulus is summed over the entire cross section, excluding posterior elements. The lowest axial rigidity of all cross sections was linearly related to the measured failure load.[155]

BIOMECHANICS OF FRACTURE HEALING

Fracture healing can be viewed as a staged process that gradually restores the load-bearing capacity of bone, eventually returning it to approximately its original stiffness and strength. The mechanical environment to which a healing fracture is exposed profoundly affects the biology and radiographic appearance of the fracture-healing process. This section addresses in vivo studies in which fracture healing was examined in controlled biomechanical environments. These in vivo animal studies show that the biomechanical environment provided by various fracture treatment devices can alter the biology and the rate of fracture healing.

Two general biologic mechanisms have been identified by which bone can repair itself. Close approximation and rigid immobilization of the fracture fragments result in localized remodeling at the fracture site, a process termed *direct cortical reconstruction*. If a small gap exists between fracture fragments, direct cortical reconstruction is preceded by radial filling of the gap with woven bone, a process termed *gap healing*. This intermediate process is followed by direct cortical reconstruction. It is likely that in most clinical situations using rigid fixation, both gap healing and direct cortical reconstruction are at work.

The conventional, more common mechanism of fracture repair is secondary osseous repair or *natural healing*. With less rigid immobilization, such as in casts or cast braces, fracture repair is characterized by callus formation. The periosteal callus forms from the fracture site hema-

toma with formation of a collar of fibrous tissue, fibrocartilage, and hyaline cartilage around the fracture fragments. Subperiosteal new bone is formed some distance from the fracture site and, through a process similar to endochondral ossification, advances toward the central and peripheral regions of the callus. A similar, less prolific response occurs at the endosteal surface. Over time, the callus is remodeled from randomly oriented woven bone to mature cortical bone. Direct cortical reconstruction and repair by callus formation alter the temporal changes in mechanical properties of the fracture in unique patterns.

Healing by Direct Cortical Reconstruction

Fundamental differences between direct cortical reconstruction and fracture healing by callus formation can be clearly seen in histologic preparations, as reviewed in Chapter 2. With direct cortical reconstruction, there is little evidence of resorption of fracture surfaces. If a small gap exists between bone fragments, a layer of bone forms within the gap. Once any gap has been filled, haversian remodeling directly crosses the fracture. The vascular supply for the osteonal remodeling units is primarily endosteal, although some periosteal contribution is also evident.[118] In contrast, fracture healing by callus formation typically involves resorption of fracture surfaces along with prolific woven bone formation originating primarily from the periosteal surface, although some callus also originates from the endosteal surface. After the fracture has united through the callus, osteonal remodeling occurs across the fracture, and the periosteal callus is remodeled and resorbed to some extent.[112, 115, 118]

Healing by Callus Formation

Formation of callus, especially periosteal callus, offers basic mechanical advantages for a healing fracture. Referring to Figures 4–6 and 4–7, the moment of inertia (and thus the bending rigidity) for a tubular structure depends on the fourth power of the radius. If we represent the femoral shaft as a tubular structure with a normal medullary diameter of 1.5 cm and a normal periosteal diameter of 3 cm, Figure 4–14A shows that the moment of inertia increases by almost 10 times if the periosteal diameter is increased to 5 cm. Figure 4–14B shows that reduction in endosteal diameter offers substantially less improvement. Although bone formed in a callus may not be as strong or stiff as normal bone, the large increase in moment of inertia provides a biomechanical advantage for periosteal callus formation.

Biomechanical Stages of Fracture Healing

For fracture healing involving periosteal callus, the biomechanical stages of fracture healing have been studied in animals. White and co-workers[108, 109, 149, 150] used an

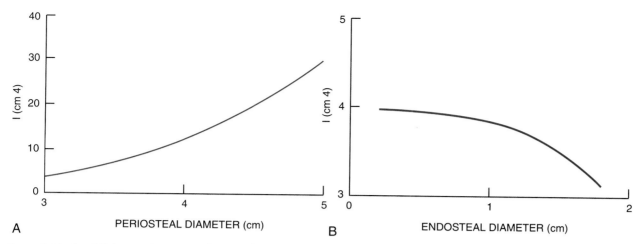

FIGURE 4–14. *A and B,* Increase in moment of inertia afforded by changes in periosteal and endosteal diameters resulting from fracture callus. In both panels a tubular cross section is assumed. A constant 1.5-cm endosteal diameter is assumed in *A* and a constant 3-cm periosteal diameter in *B.*

externally fixed rabbit osteotomy model to correlate radiographic and histologic information with the torsional stiffness and failure strength at several postfracture time periods. They identified four biomechanical stages of fracture healing (Fig. 4–15). The first indication of increasing stiffness occurred after 21 to 24 days. At this stage the fracture exhibits a rubbery type of behavior characterized by large angular deflections for low torques; the bone fails through the fracture site at low loads. This stage corresponds to bridging of the fracture gap by soft tissues. At approximately 27 days, a sharp increase in stiffness identifies the second stage, in which failures occur through the fracture site at low loads. Stiffness approaches that of intact cortical bone. The third biomechanical stage is characterized by failure occurring only partially through the fracture site, with a stiffness similar to that of cortical bone but below normal strength. The final stage is achieved when the site of failure is not related to the

original experimental fracture, and the stiffness and strength are similar to those of intact bone.

In a related study, Panjabi and colleagues[107] compared radiographic evaluation of fracture healing with the failure strength of healing osteotomies. They applied nine different radiographic measures of fracture healing (Fig. 4–16). The best radiographic measure was cortical continuity (4 in Fig. 4–16), for which the correlation coefficient between the radiographic measure and bone strength was $r = .8$. The lowest correlation between radiographic and physical measurements was found for callus area ($r = .17$). The general conclusion of this study was that even under laboratory conditions, radiographic information is not sufficient to decide accurately the biomechanical condition of a healing fracture. This result is important because radiographic diagnosis is commonly applied to assessment of fracture healing, although few studies have objectively tested the predictive capability of this practice. Thus, the

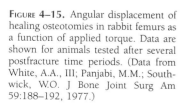

FIGURE 4–15. Angular displacement of healing osteotomies in rabbit femurs as a function of applied torque. Data are shown for animals tested after several postfracture time periods. (Data from White, A.A., III; Panjabi, M.M.; Southwick, W.O. J Bone Joint Surg Am 59:188–192, 1977.)

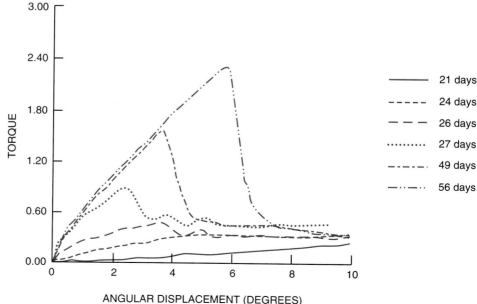

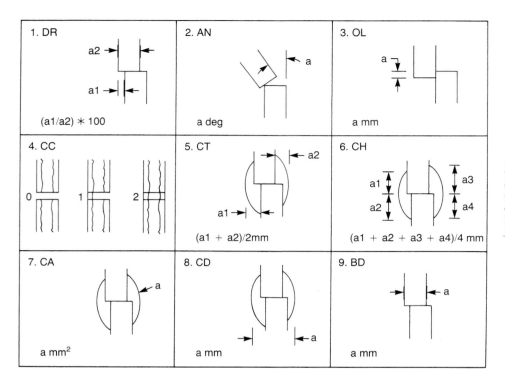

FIGURE **4–16.** Radiographic measures were compared with mechanical tests of partially healed fractures to evaluate the efficacy of radiographic evaluation of fracture healing. (Data from Panjabi, M.M.; Walter, S.D.; Karuda, M.; et al. J Orthop Res 3:212–218, 1985.)

methods for in vivo biomechanical assessment of fracture healing previously discussed have particular clinical significance.

Several other animal experiments have shown similar biomechanical stages of fracture healing,[15, 37, 44] and the time at which each stage of fracture healing is achieved is dependent on several factors. Using a canine model, Davy and Connolly[37] experimentally produced fractures in weight-bearing bones (radii) and presumed non–weight-bearing bones (ribs). Healing bones were tested using four-point bending tests at 2 to 12 weeks. Both weight-bearing and non–weight-bearing bones healed with formation of periosteal callus. For non–weight-bearing bones, bending strength increased more rapidly than stiffness, whereas stiffness increased more rapidly than strength in weight-bearing bones. This result also shows that the stiffness of a healing fracture does not necessarily correlate with bone strength. Davy and Connolly further demonstrated that bone and periosteal callus geometry can theoretically account for observed changes in fracture properties. However, radiographic criteria have not been shown to predict the strength or stiffness of a healing fracture. Under bending loads, the failure mechanism appears to be delamination of repair tissue from the bone fragments, suggesting that the adhesive bond between repair tissue and bone fragments determines the structural properties.[15]

Whereas the mechanical environment clearly influences the morphology of the healing process, the conflicting results of studies that investigated the effect of fixation rigidity on fracture healing leave the question of optimal fixation rigidity unsolved. Perren and co-workers[113, 116] proposed a hypothesis that helps explain how fracture healing is controlled by the local mechanical environment. They postulated that a tissue can be formed in the interfragmentary region of a healing fracture only if the involved tissues can tolerate the local mechanical strain. The tissues that are formed, in turn, contribute to the fracture rigidity, making possible the next step in tissue differentiation. For example, formation of granulation tissue may reduce the strain to a level at which fibrocartilage formation is possible.

Perren and co-workers further hypothesized that the fracture gap is widened by resorption of the bone ends until the local tissue strain falls below a certain limiting value. Resorption of fragment ends may reduce the strain sufficiently to permit completion of a bridging callus. Interfragmentary strain may influence fracture healing in several ways. Local deformations may disrupt vascularization and interrupt the blood supply to developing osteons. Deformation of cells may alter their permeability to macromolecules and increase biologic activity. Strains may also induce changes in the electrical signals within the healing fracture site or elicit a direct cellular response. In all likelihood, a multifactorial relationship exists at various stages of the healing process.

DiGioia and associates[40] examined the interfragmentary strain hypothesis using computer models and compared the model results with the preliminary experimental data of Mansmann and colleagues.[30] Their results show that complex three-dimensional strain fields exist within a fracture gap and that the simple longitudinal strains considered by Perren and co-workers underestimate the strains experienced by the interfragmentary tissues. The analytical models show that the strain in tissue is greatest at the endosteal and periosteal surfaces of the bone fragments (Fig. 4–17). These are also the areas of early bone resorption observed in experimental animals. The models also demonstrate the asymmetric distribution of strains that occur within the tissues at the gap between plated fracture fragments.

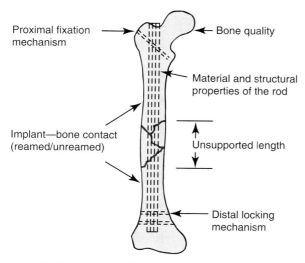

Proximal fixation mechanism

Bone quality

Material and structural properties of the rod

Implant—bone contact (reamed/unreamed)

Unsupported length

Distal locking mechanism

FIGURE 4–17. Representation of the strains experienced by tissues within a uniform osteotomy when the fractured bone is subjected to bending loads. (Data from DiGioia, A.M., III; Cheal, E.J.; Hayes, W.C. J Biomech Eng 108:273–280, 1986.)

BIOMECHANICS OF FRACTURE TREATMENT

Many techniques are currently available for treatment of skeletal fractures, and many factors are important in choosing the best fixation. Many of these clinical factors are discussed in other chapters, but one factor that is crucial to all fractures is the need for sufficient stability to achieve fracture healing. Each method of fixation imparts a specific level of stability to a fracture and thus directly influences fracture-healing biology.

When a fracture treatment method is evaluated, the healing bone and the fracture treatment device should be considered as a mechanical system, with both the tissue and the device contributing to biomechanical behavior.[59] The biomechanical behavior of the system can thus be altered by changes in tissue properties (e.g., resorption at fracture surfaces, osteopenia under plates), changes to the fracture treatment device (e.g., dynamization of external fixation), or changes in the mechanical connection between device and tissue (e.g., pin or bone screw loosening). In addition, bones are subject to diverse loads that can be a combination of axial, bending, and torsional loads. Thus, the axial, bending, and torsional stability of a fracture treatment method should be considered. This section addresses the basic mechanical characteristics of fracture treatment techniques and the effect of each device on fracture healing.

Internal Fixation

INTRAMEDULLARY RODS

Intramedullary rods have several advantages in fracture treatment, including restoration of bone alignment and early recovery of weight bearing. The good clinical results and low rates of nonunion[2] suggest that many current clinical applications of these devices provide a mechanical

environment that facilitates fracture repair for selected fractures. It is therefore useful to consider the stability of this treatment method as an example of a successful mechanical construct.

Intramedullary rods are intended to stabilize a fracture by acting as an internal splint, forming a composite structure in which both the bone and the rod contribute to fracture stability. This load-sharing property of rods is fundamental to their design and should be recognized when they are used for fracture treatment.[137] Consequently, intramedullary rod design must be evaluated with regard to both the structural properties of the rod and the mechanics of the rod-bone interaction. Figure 4–18 illustrates factors that determine the mechanical stability of a femoral fracture stabilized by intramedullary fixation.

Complications that may occur with intramedullary rods include rod migration, permanent deformation of the rod, and fatigue fractures. Delayed union and nonunion after intramedullary nailing are also complications resulting from mechanical factors. Allen and co-workers[2] identified several areas of potential weakness in intramedullary rods, including excessive flexibility, inadequate ability to transmit torsional loads, poor fixation of the rods within the medullary canal, and increased incidence of nonunion and implant failure when proper reaming techniques are not employed.

Several material and structural properties of intramedullary rods alter their axial, bending, and torsional rigidities. These parameters include cross-sectional geometry, rod length, the presence of a longitudinal slot, and the elastic modulus of the material. The cross-sectional geometry can greatly affect all rigidities. Rods with the same nominal outside diameter and similar shape but made by different manufacturers varied in bending rigidity by more than a factor of 2 (Fig. 4–19A and B) and varied in torsional rigidity by more than a factor of 3 (Fig. 4–19C).[138] This variation was attributed to differences in cross-sectional geometry. The data also show that there is not always a simple relationship between rod size and rigidities. The rigidity increases significantly with rod diameter because the moment of inertia is approximately proportional to the fourth power of the rod radius (see Fig. 4–6). However, the magnitude of change varies with different manufacturers, in part because the wall thickness (with hollow rods) may be different for different rod diameters. Reaming increases the rod diameter that can be used but may reduce the strength of the bone and further compromise blood supply.

The unsupported length of intramedullary fixation is the distance between implant–bone contact at the proximal and distal segments of bone. This distance effectively changes as the fracture heals. During the initial stages of

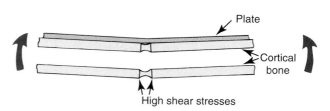

Plate

Cortical bone

High shear stresses

FIGURE 4–18. Factors important in intramedullary fracture fixation.

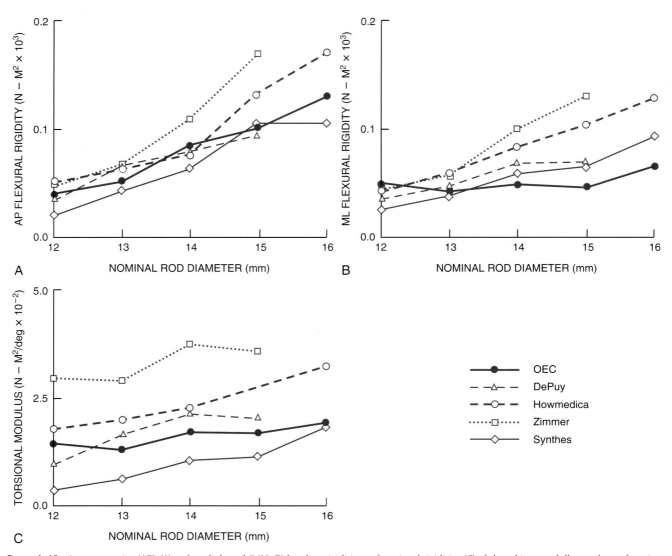

FIGURE 4–19. Anteroposterior (AP) (*A*) and mediolateral (ML) (*B*) bending rigidities and torsional rigidities (*C*) of slotted intramedullary rods as a function of nominal rod diameter for five commercially available rods from different manufacturers. Rods were oriented with the slot in the AP plane. (*A–C,* Data from Tencer, A.F.; Sherman, M.C.; Johnson, K.D. J Biomech Eng 107:104–111, 1985.)

fracture healing, two different unsupported lengths are important with intramedullary rods: the unsupported length in bending and the unsupported length in torsion.

Figure 4–20 illustrates the significance of unsupported length in bending. This length is determined by the points of bone–implant contact on the proximal and distal sides of the fracture and can be different, depending on the direction of bending. For a simple, well-reamed transverse fracture, this distance is small, whereas for a severely comminuted fracture, the unsupported length can be great, resulting in increased deformation at the fracture site.[48] For bending loads, the rod is typically loaded in approximately four-point bending (analogous to Fig. 4–7), and the nominal interfragmentary motion is proportional to the square of the unsupported length. Therefore, a small increase in unsupported length can lead to a considerably larger increase in interfragmentary motion.

With torsional loading, the unsupported length is determined by the points at which sufficient mechanical

interlocking occurs between bone and implant to support torsional loads. Simple rod designs that do not include proximal or distal locking mechanisms have lower resistance to torsion. For rod designs that employ proximal and distal locking mechanisms, the unsupported length is typically determined by the distance between the proximal and distal locking points. Mechanical interlocking may also occur between rod and bone at other places within the medullary canal. Relative motion between fracture fragments during torsional loading is roughly proportional to the unsupported length (calculated according to Fig. 4–8).

Many rod designs have a longitudinal slot either partially or fully along their length. The slot allows the cross section to be compressed like a stiff spring when inserted into a medullary canal. This elastic compression can help promote a tight fit between rod and bone.[10] However, with torsional loads the slot creates an "open section" geometry that is theoretically 400 times less stiff than a closed section.[123] Reduced torsional rigidity can have both positive and negative value. Reduction in rod stiffness allows the rod to conform to minor discrepancies between rod and medullary geometry. Reduced rigidity may also allow twisting of the rod during insertion, easing insertion but compromising the use of external aiming devices used to locate the distal locking points.[78] With a partially slotted rod design, stress concentrations at the end of the slot where the cross section becomes continuous can result in failures at this location.[12] However, the reported incidence of such device failures is small. Despite the potential for intramedullary design variations to result in substantial differences in strength and stiffness, many of the design variations seen in commercially available rods have little effect on the gross mechanical properties.[68]

Intramedullary rod designs that provide mechanisms for locking the rod proximally or distally have increased the indications for intramedullary rod use.[55] Proximal and distal locking mechanisms affect the torsional, axial, and bending properties of a fracture fixed with an intramedullary rod. The use of a locking mechanism on one side of the fracture only (proximal or distal) can increase the forces transmitted between fracture fragments during limb loading. The use of both proximal and distal locking can prevent axial displacement of bone along the rod and provide additional torsional rigidity. Several different types of distal locking mechanisms are currently available, including transverse screws and wings designed to engage cortical or cancellous bone. The strength of these locking mechanisms depends in part on the quality of supporting bone.

Zych and co-workers[160] compared four types of intramedullary rods with distal locking mechanisms designed to engage cortical or cancellous bone. Intramedullary rods were used to fix osteotomies in 100 cadaver femurs. Bone quality was radiographically graded, and

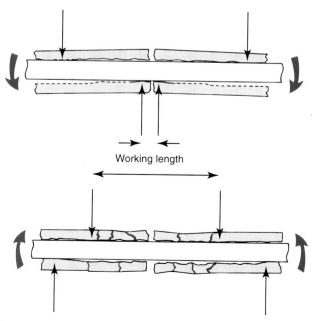

FIGURE 4–20. The unsupported (or working) length of an intramedullary device can be much greater for a comminuted fracture than for a simple transverse fracture.

preparations were tested to failure in torsion with a constant axial load or were subjected to 25 cycles of reversing rotations. The authors concluded that fixation torque was significantly lower in osteoporotic bones. With osteoporotic bone, the amount of loosening is greatest with locking mechanisms that engage cancellous bone as compared with cortical bone, whereas for normal bone, cancellous and cortical locking mechanisms provide similar resistance to loosening.

In combination, the presence of both proximal and distal locking mechanisms helps control the axial stability of a fracture. Without both locking mechanisms, the bone can glide axially along the implant. Thus, the combination of proximal and distal locking can maintain axial separation and bone length or facilitate application of compression between bone fragments. The compression is lost if resorption occurs at the points of contact between fracture fragments.

The mechanical interaction between bone and the implant can also influence the torsional stability of an intramedullary fixed fracture. The mechanical interlock between implant and bone depends on the cross-sectional geometry of the bone and the geometry of the medullary canal. The geometry of the medullary canal is frequently changed by reaming, in which case surgical technique establishes the initial fit of implant in bone. For example, eccentric reaming can compromise mechanical stability with intramedullary rods.[156] Several tests have demonstrated that torsional resistance is a primary shortcoming of some intramedullary rods, with intramedullary rod–fixed femurs achieving only 13% to 16% of the torsional strength of intact femurs.

To improve torsional properties, designs incorporating flutes and ribs to increase contact between rod and bone in torsion and designs that use screws or wings to engage cortical or cancellous bone have been developed. For example, Allen and associates[2] showed that a fluted intramedullary rod can support 30% to 50% greater torque within the medullary canal than simpler cross sections. The use of proximal and distal locking mechanisms also affects the torsional rigidity. Rotation of bone fragments at the fracture site increases significantly as the locking screws are moved farther away from the fracture, consistent with the concept of decreased stability as the working length increases.[50] Surgeons must also recognize that the entry portals used to insert intramedullary rods can significantly reduce the strength of the bone.[136]

FRACTURE HEALING WITH INTRAMEDULLARY RODS

The issue of ideal intramedullary rod flexibility is still debated. Using an osteotomized rabbit femur model, Wang and colleagues[148] compared intramedullary rods with 12% to 100% of the intact femoral bending stiffness. They found that rods with a stiffness equivalent to 20% to 50% of that of an intact femur stimulated abundant external callus and resulted in improved return of structural properties as compared with rods with a stiffness equivalent to 75% of normal. Similarly, Molster and co-workers[100] compared fracture healing in rat femurs stabilized by a stiff stainless steel rod with femurs stabilized by a flexible plastic rod. There was no significant difference in radiographically determined time to union between the groups. The torsional strength was also not statistically different at 8 and 16 weeks, but the femurs fixed with the flexible rod had more callus and significantly greater strength at 24 weeks. These studies support the contention that intramedullary rods should allow some amount of fracture mobility to stimulate callus formation and bone union.

The optimal fixation technique must allow transfer of forces between bone and implant without causing gross failure of either the bone or the implant. For example, failure of bone has been observed with many rigid nail-plate devices used for fractures of the proximal femur. Sliding screws that allow load transmission between bone fragments as well as load transmission between bone and implant reduce, but do not eliminate, penetration of the implant into the femoral head. This penetration is associated with (1) improper placement of the sliding screw in the proximal femur and (2) osteoporotic bone.

Quantitative measurements of bone density in the femoral head can help determine the load-bearing capacity of fractured proximal femurs after fixation with a sliding hip screw or with standard pins and screws[130, 132] and may also help identify when augmentation is required for distal interlocking in osteoporotic bone. The load required to cause penetration of the sliding hip screw superiorly into the femoral head may be insufficient to support activities of daily living in osteoporotic patients. For example, hip screw penetration loads as low as 750 N have been recorded[132] in osteoporotic femurs. Allowing for contact forces of 3.3 times body weight during gait,[31] load-bearing capacities greater than 1300 N would be required in a very lightweight person. Quantitative measurements of bone density may therefore be beneficial to ensure that fixation does not fail because of failure of bone around the fixation system, although sensitive and specific guidelines have yet to be developed.

In combination with bone density measurements, new implant designs can potentially reduce complications from overloading bone around the implant. For example, a sliding hip screw that allows controlled injection of bone cement into surrounding osteoporotic bone can dramatically reduce translation of the hip screw into the femoral head.[32]

BONE PLATES

As with intramedullary devices, several basic biomechanical principles are important in fracture fixation using bone plates. Figure 4–21 illustrates some important parameters. It is crucial to realize that the plate and the bone together form a mechanical construct, with some load supported by the plate and some load passing between bone fragments. Therefore, changes in the plate, the bone, or the interface between plate and bone can dramatically influence the mechanical environment of a fracture. The interaction between plate and bone is also load dependent; the plate may improve stability for one type of loading much more than for other types of loads.

The bending stiffness of a bone plate with a rectangular cross section is related to the third power of the plate

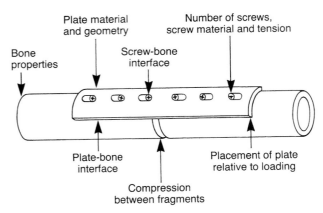

Figure 4–21. Factors affecting the stability of a plated fracture.

thickness, whereas the bending rigidity is directly proportional to the width or elastic modulus of the plate. Therefore, plate rigidity can be changed more by plate thickness than by plate width or modulus, with the limitation that thick plates may not be possible in regions with limited overlying soft tissue thickness.

The mechanical properties of bone also affect the behavior of the plate-bone system. For example, less stiff bone increases the load-sharing contribution of the plate. Also, osteoporosis, osteopetrosis, or other bone diseases may affect bone remodeling at the plate-bone or screw-bone interfaces and thus affect the mechanical performance of the plated bone. However, the role of bone properties in fracture fixation with bone plates has yet to be investigated. Most in vivo animal studies and ex vivo studies of plate fixation have examined the biomechanics of plates applied to osteotomized bones in which reduction and compression of bone fragments could be achieved. In cases of highly comminuted fractures or when bone defects must be stabilized, adequate reduction and stability are more difficult to achieve. In these cases, the mechanical demands on the plate are increased because load transmission between bone fragments may not be possible and all loads must pass through the plate.

Loads can be transmitted between plate and bone through the bone screws and through mechanical interlocking or frictional forces between the plate surface and the bone. Hayes and Perren[61] found frictional forces of about 0.37 (comparable to that of wood sliding on leather) between titanium or stainless steel plates and bone when tested ex vivo. Thus, significant forces may be transmitted between plate and bone under ideal conditions. Perren and associates[114] reviewed studies of coupling between plates and bone that suggest that after 1 year in vivo, the coupling between plate and bone may be limited.

The concept of working length introduced with intramedullary devices is also applicable to bone plates. The working length of the plate, especially in the bending-open configuration, is greater when the inner screws are not placed (Fig. 4–22). Maximal plate deflection is approximately proportional to the square of the working length (see Fig. 4–7), so large decreases in bending rigidity occur when the inner screws are not used.

Cheal and co-workers[29, 40] investigated the biomechanics of plate fixation using a combined experimental and

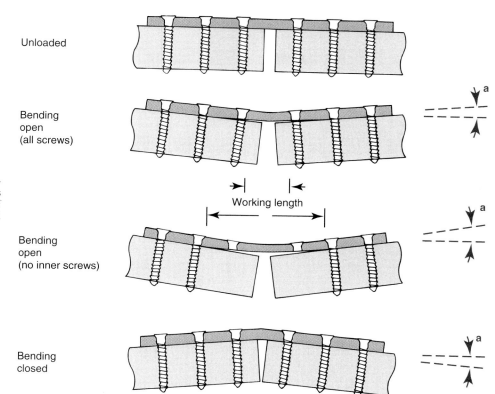

Unloaded

Bending
open
(all screws)

Bending
open
(no inner screws)

Working length

Bending
closed

FIGURE 4–22. Different bending configurations for a plated fracture. This figure also illustrates the concept of working length with bone plates and the value of using all screws.

theoretical approach. The experimental model consisted of an intact Plexiglas tube with an attached six-hole stainless steel compression plate. Several parameters—including friction between plate and bone and screw pretension induced by tightening the bone screws—were investigated using finite element models (Fig. 4–23). Several load cases were considered, including axial loads, off-axis loads, and bending. Excellent agreement was obtained between the theoretical and the experimental models. The analytical models showed that stress shielding of bone should be limited to the central region between the inner screws. This conclusion agrees with radiographic findings from animal studies of bone changes beneath plates.[102, 144]

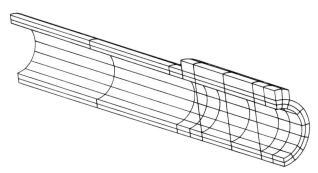

FIGURE 4–23. Three-dimensional finite element mesh of a compression-plated tube used to study analytically the mechanical performance of plate-bone systems. Only one quarter of the plated tube needs to be modeled owing to the symmetry of the problem. (Data from Cheal, E.J.; Hayes, W.C.; White, A.A., III; Perren, S.M. J Biomech 18:141–150, 1985.)

Static preloads, applied by compression plate techniques, can negate any reduction in axial stress levels beneath the plate, but these preloads decay rapidly and have not been shown to affect the long-term fracture-healing process.[93, 131] For fractures fixed with compression plates, experimental studies show the importance of placing the plate on the tensile aspect of the bone because the plated bone is particularly weak under loads that bend open the fracture. Finally, the results show that the outer screws received the highest stresses.

The location of the plate (tension versus compressive side of the bone) is an important factor in the biomechanics of bone plates because application of a bone plate changes the moment of inertia of the plate-bone system compared with an intact bone. With uniform axial loads, the stress throughout a cross section of intact bone is relatively constant. With application of a bone plate, a combination of bending and axial stresses is realized in the same cross section of bone. Subjected to bending loads, a plated bone can be in a bending-open or bending-closed configuration (see Fig. 4–22). The placement of the plate relative to the loading direction determines the proportion of the loads supported by the plate.

Hayes and Perren[60] used osteotomized, plated sheep tibias to test the composite plate-bone system in the bending-open and bending-closed directions, both with and without application of compression between bone fragments (four-point bending). Figure 4–24 shows typical results from these tests, which clearly show that the composite plate-bone system is more stiff in the bending-closed direction and that application of compression also increases the stiffness. Minns and associates[99] also showed

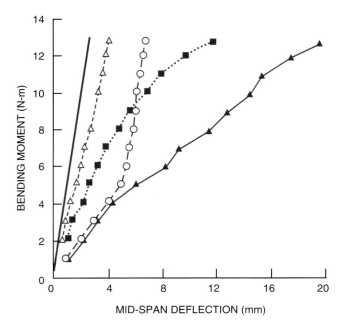

FIGURE 4–24. Maximal deflection versus bending moment for plated sheep tibias. Tibias were plated with or without compression and were tested in both bend-open and bend-closed configurations. (Data from Hayes, W.C. In: Heppenstall, R.B., ed. Fracture Treatment and Healing. Philadelphia, W.B. Saunders, 1980, pp. 124–172.)

that application of a compression plate on the side of the bone normally loaded in tension produces the stiffest fixation. Although experimental efforts have shown that preloading a fracture gap through compression plating can increase fracture stability, Matter and colleagues[93] demonstrated that a static preload does not necessarily affect the pattern of bone remodeling. Slatis and co-workers[131] found that the only difference associated with static preloading was a more rapid appearance of morphologic changes.

The local mechanics within an oblique or comminuted fracture are significantly more complicated than those associated with a transverse osteotomy. Beaupre and associates[8] studied the mechanics of plate fixation where there is insufficient bone to support ideal compression plate fixation. A theoretical model of an idealized plated bone system and strain gauge readings from various animal models showed that the amount of bending is usually not sufficient to place a plated bone in a bending-open configuration when a gap exists between the fracture fragments. The results suggest that if contact between bone fragments cannot be achieved, there are situations in which the risk of plate failure is reduced if the plate is applied to the compression side of the bone. It should be noted, however, that these results have not been substantiated by in vivo studies of fracture healing with insufficient bone support.

FRACTURE HEALING WITH BONE PLATES

The temporal changes in the biomechanics of fractures that heal by direct cortical reconstruction in the presence of rigid internal fixation have been reported by Hayes and Ruff.[62] Compression plate fixation was applied to experimental osteotomies in dogs. Groups of dogs were sacrificed between 8 and 52 weeks. In addition, several groups of dogs were sacrificed 2 to 8 weeks after plate removal at 20 weeks. After sacrifice, the plates were removed, and the

bones were tested to failure in bending. The bending strength of the experimental bone was compared with the bending strength of the contralateral intact bone.

Figure 4–25 shows the change in strength versus time for the plated tibias expressed as percentage of intact bone strength. The results demonstrate a gradual increase in strength from 8 to 20 weeks. At 20 weeks, the plated bones were 80% as strong as the intact bones. From 20 to 30 weeks, plated bone strength declined to approximately 60% of intact strength. The data suggest that for this animal model, 20 weeks would be the optimal time for plate removal. When the plates were removed at 20 weeks, the bending strength fell slightly during the first 4 weeks after plate removal (Fig. 4–26) but then increased. Eight weeks after plate removal, the experimental bones were as strong as or stronger than the contralateral intact bones.

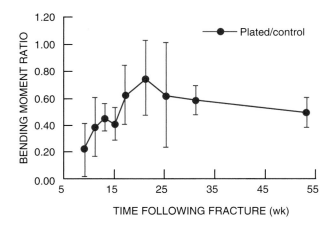

FIGURE 4–25. Bending moment at failure as a function of time after fracture for canine tibial fractures treated with compression plates. Bending moment at failure is expressed as the ratio between the strength of the plated bone and that of the intact control bone. (Data from Hayes, W.C.; Ruff, C.B. In: Uhthoff, H.K.; Jaworski, Z.F.G., eds. Twelfth Annual Applied Basic Sciences Course. Ottawa, University of Ottawa, 1986, pp. 371–377.)

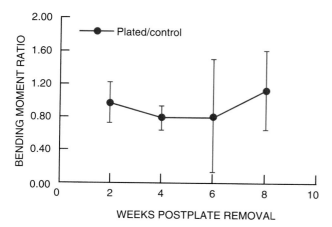

FIGURE 4–26. Bending moment at failure as a function of time following plate removal at 20 weeks for canine tibial fractures treated with compression plates. Bending moment at failure is expressed as the ratio between the strength of the plated bone and that of the intact control bone. (Data from Hayes, W.C.; Ruff, C.B. In: Uhthoff, H.K.; Jaworski, Z.F.G., eds. Twelfth Annual Applied Basic Sciences Course. Ottawa, University of Ottawa, 1986, pp. 371–377.)

The effect of plate stiffness on fracture healing is not clear. Akeson and co-workers[1] compared the failure strength of osteotomies at 4 months treated with stainless steel and less rigid composite internal fixation plates and found no significant difference. In contrast, Bradley and associates[17] found increased structural strength and material strength after treatment of an osteotomy with a less rigid fixation plate compared with treatment of an osteotomy with a more rigid fixation plate. The observation that interfragmentary relative motion influences the fracture-healing pattern of cortical bone has led to several studies examining the healing of fractures treated with plates of varying stiffness.

Woo and colleagues[157] noted that there are several aspects of the structural properties of bone plates. They examined the axial, bending, and torsional stiffness of plates and designed two plates that allowed comparison of plates with high axial stiffness and plates with high bending and torsional stiffness. They found axial stiffness to be the dominant factor that controls stresses in bone. Plates that provide sufficient bending and torsional stiffness to stabilize the bone and low axial stiffness to transfer stress to the bone performed best.

Terjesen and Apalset[139] investigated bone healing of rabbit tibial osteotomies fixed with plates that had 13%, 17%, 61%, or 74% of the bending stiffness of intact bone. After 6 weeks of plate fixation, the amount of periosteal callus was inversely related to plate stiffness. Bones treated with the stiffest plate tended to have lower rigidity and strength than bones treated with less stiff plates. The authors also noted that no relation was found between the amount of periosteal callus and bone strength at 6 weeks.

Rigid internal fixation depends on force transmission between implant and bone and between fractured bone ends. Bone necrosis between implant and bone or between bone fragments compromises fixation stability. To understand better the reaction of living bone to compression plate fixation, Perren and Rahn[116] designed a strain-gauged, four-hole compression plate that enabled them to monitor the compression applied to the bone fragments by the plate. The plates were applied to both intact and osteotomized bones in sheep. The tensile stress in the plate was measured at weekly intervals for 12 weeks after plate application. Plate tension for the intact bone group is shown in Figure 4–27. There was a gradual decrease in plate tension over 12 weeks after a steeper decrease in the first few days following surgery. The general trends found for the osteotomized group were the same as those found for intact bones. These results show that rigid internal fixation can maintain compression between bone fragments for several weeks. This finding suggests that there is no pressure necrosis between bone fragments or at the interface between implant and bone because if a layer of bone 10 to 20 µm thick were resorbed, tensile forces in the plate would drop to zero.

Histologic analysis confirmed the radiographic indication of direct cortical reconstruction. In spite of full weight bearing immediately after plate application, the osteotomies were bridged by direct haversian remodeling. The histologic pattern of bone remodeling suggests a mechanism for the slow decrease in plate tension. It is postulated that bone remodeling at the osteotomy site results in local reductions in bone stiffness, reducing the compressive loads maintained by the plate.

Several studies have concluded that early porosis noted beneath bone plates during the first 6 months is due to the plate's shielding bone from functional stresses.[24, 102, 140, 143, 144, 152] Perren and co-workers[114] suggested that early in fracture healing, the porosis noted beneath bone plates is in fact due to disruption of the blood supply to the bone caused by the contact between bone and plate. Plate-bone contact has been shown to result in porosis by 1 month after surgery. Perren and co-workers presented four arguments in support of vascular disruption as the cause of porosis beneath bone plates[81, 114]:

1. The porosis beneath plates appears to be a temporary, intermediate stage in bone remodeling in response to surgery.

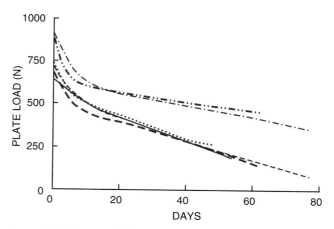

FIGURE 4–27. Force applied by a bone plate to the bone as a function of time after compression plating for plates applied to intact canine tibias in vivo. (Data from Perren, S.M.; Huggler, A.; Russenberger, M.; et al. Acta Orthop Scand Suppl 125:19–28, 1969.)

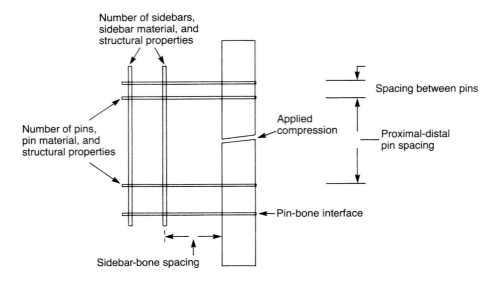

Number of sidebars, sidebar material, and structural properties

Number of pins, pin material, and structural properties

Applied compression

Spacing between pins

Proximal-distal pin spacing

Pin-bone interface

Sidebar-bone spacing

Figure 4–28. Factors affecting the stability of an externally fixed fracture.

2. The bone-remodeling pattern is better explained by the pattern of vascular disruption than by the stress distribution beneath the plate.
3. In a comparative study of plastic plates and steel plates, more porosis was noted beneath the plastic plate, even though the steel plate should provide substantially more stress shielding.
4. Porosis beneath bone plates can be substantially reduced by using plates that provide for improved circulation.

External Fixation

Current external fixation devices provide a wide range of frame configuration and fracture stability options, making external fixation adaptable to many clinical situations. External fixation devices also provide a convenient way to alter fixation rigidity during the course of healing and offer potential for monitoring the biomechanical progression of fracture healing. The stability provided by an external fixation device depends on both the frame configuration

and the interaction between frame and bone fragments. Juan and associates[73] showed that for several types of external fixators, callus formation is essential to a stable fracture. Huiskes and Chao[70] showed that external fixator rigidities can be altered by several orders of magnitude through changes in frame configuration.

As shown in Figures 4–28 and 4–29, several geometric, material, and technical factors, as well as loading directions, can play a role in the biomechanics of externally fixed fractures. The relative contribution of several of these factors has been quantified using computer models.[70] Most biomechanical studies of external fixators examine the effect of various parameters on rigidity under several types of loading. It must be strongly emphasized that if the clamps or other connectors used in an external fixation system become loose, the stability of the fixation is severely compromised.[41] These connections may also actually fail under relatively low loads.

The percutaneous pins are typically the weakest component of an external fixation system. Several studies have shown that high stresses can occur in the pins, possibly resulting in permanent deformation of the pin,

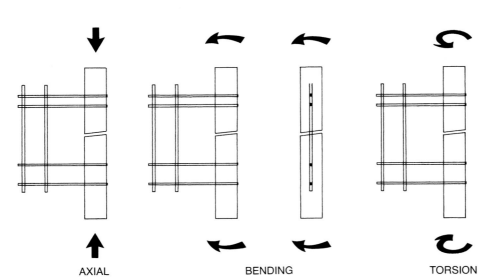

AXIAL   BENDING   TORSION

Figure 4–29. Various loading modes that must be considered when evaluating the mechanical behavior of an externally fixed fracture.

especially when the fracture site is unstable.[71, 74] The bending rigidity of each pin is theoretically proportional to the fourth power of the pin diameter, so increasing the pin diameter from 4 to 6 mm increases the bending stiffness of each pin by five times. Pin diameter has been shown to be one of the most important parameters that determine fixator stiffness.[27] The bending stiffness of each pin is also proportional to the cube of the sidebar-to-bone distance, and small changes in the sidebar-to-bone distance cause large changes in pin rigidity.

The relationship between pin diameter or sidebar-to-bone distance and fixator rigidity is more complicated in most fixators where several fixation pins are used and the fractures are subject to a variety of loads. Figure 4–30 illustrates this point using data from Chao and Hein[26] for a standard Orthofix external fixator tested ex vivo using an artificial fracture model. In this model, a single-plane external fixator is mounted in a plane identified as mediolateral. The axial stiffness data of Figure 4–30A show that, for example, a four-pin Orthofix fixator with a 4-mm sidebar-to-bone span has an axial stiffness of about 3000 N/cm. Thus, a 600-N (61-kg) individual bearing half his or her weight on the fixed limb would cause approximately 1 mm of displacement at the fracture site if a gap existed between the bone fragments. Experimental studies have found gap displacements up to 2 mm for a 600-N load, and these displacements are strongly dependent on the fixation system and the presence of callus.[73] Direct measurements of axial motion in externally fixed tibial diaphyseal fractures showed that displacements reached a maximum of 0.6 mm after 7 to 12 weeks of healing.[80]

Comparing Figure 4–30B and C demonstrates that the mediolateral bending stiffness is more than four times the anteroposterior bending stiffness for the unilateral single-plane Orthofix fixator. The figures also show that the stiffness increases with the number of pins and decreases

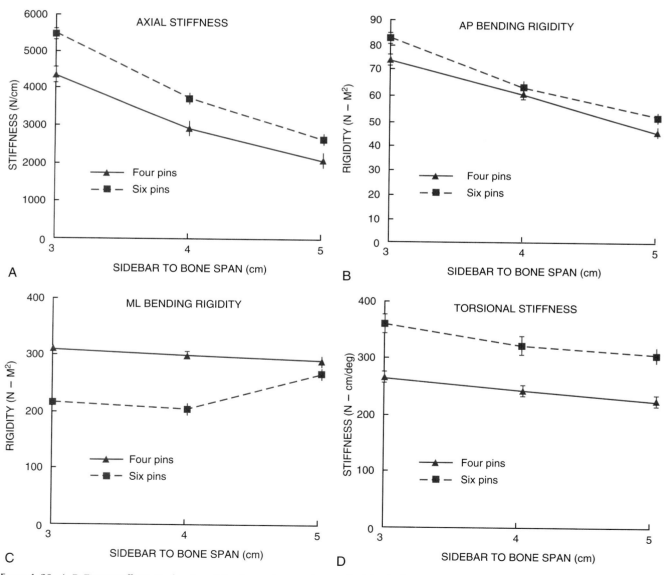

FIGURE 4–30. *A–D,* Fixator stiffness as a function of the distance between bone and sidebar for four different loading configurations. Data for both four-pin and six-pin fixator configurations are shown. The bending stiffness data of Chao and Hein[26] were converted to bending rigidities using the formulas from Figure 4–7. (*A–D,* Data from Chao, E.Y.S.; Hein, T.J. Orthopedics 11:1057–1069, 1988.)

with sidebar-to-bone spacing under all loading configurations. However, the effect of sidebar-to-bone spacing is most pronounced with axial loads. A six-pin fixator is significantly more stiff than a four-pin fixator with axial and torsional loads, whereas the six-pin fixator is less rigid with bending loads applied in the plane of the fixator. Chao and Hein[26] attributed this to uneven clamping pressure on the pins, causing some pins to carry more load than others. If each pin carried the same load, the fixator stiffness should increase by a factor of 6/4 when comparing a six-pin with a four-pin frame.[70] The data of Figure 4–30 show that this is not the case for the Orthofix fixator, reinforcing the hypothesis that some pins must be supporting more load than others and thus may be more susceptible to pin loosening or pin failure.

External fixation is used both in situations where contact between bone fragments can be achieved (fracture reduction) and in cases where a gap remains initially between bone fragments (e.g., limb lengthening, severely comminuted fractures). These two situations provide substantially different biomechanical requirements for external fixation. Bone contact allows load sharing between bone and fixator for compressive, torsional, and certain bending loads. Without bone contact, the external fixator must support the full load, which can have a significant effect on fracture healing. It is also possible to apply compression across a fracture gap using an external fixator. The amount of compression that can be applied depends in part on the rigidity of the external fixator.[96] With transverse fractures, application of compression across the fracture site can greatly increase the stiffness of the frame-bone system.[18]

Fixation pin loosening is a common problem with external fixators. Clinical[128] and analytical[71] studies have demonstrated that the pin-bone interface is potentially a weak link in the stability of an external fixation system. Loose pins can substantially decrease the stability of an externally fixed fracture and lead to soft tissue problems. Commonly cited reasons for pin loosening include pin design, pin placement, pin tract infection, necrosis related to surgical trauma during pin placement, necrosis related to unfavorable bone stress, and contact pressure at the pin-bone interface. Suggested solutions to the pin-loosening problem include changes in surgical technique,[134] changes in pin properties and thread design,[82, 91] and changes in frame rigidity.[28] Rigorous in vivo studies of suggested solutions have yet to be reported, however.

FRACTURE HEALING WITH EXTERNAL FIXATION

Experimental evidence suggesting that fracture fixation rigidity significantly affects the biology of bone healing has prompted several studies that compare bone healing with various external fixation rigidities. Wu and associates[159] used a canine tibial osteotomy model to examine bone healing with a rigid six-pin versus a less rigid four-pin unilateral frame. Union was achieved with all osteotomies, but the clinical characteristics of bone healing depended on fixator rigidity. Bone union was clinically and biomechanically evident earlier with the more rigid frame. There

was greater periosteal callus formation at 90 and 120 days and a higher incidence of pin loosening with less rigid frames. However, at 120 days after osteotomy, the torsional strength and torsional stiffness were not statistically different for the different frame rigidities.

The fracture pattern noted during torsion testing suggested that the more rigidly fixed osteotomies had reached a more mature stage of fracture healing. The increased periosteal callus formation would provide torsional strength and stiffness for the less rigidly fixed tibias. Thus, although the repair tissue formed with less rigidly fixed fractures may be weaker as a material, the geometric distribution of the tissue provides structural stability. Histologic examination suggested that with the rigid frames, fracture healing occurred by direct cortical reconstruction, whereas with less rigid fixation, periosteal callus formation characteristic of secondary bone healing was evident.

The same general conclusions were realized in a study by Williams and co-workers[153] that compared canine tibial osteotomies treated by one or two planes of external fixation. The two-plane fixators were significantly more rigid in bending and torsion than the single-plane fixator, whereas the axial stiffness of the fixators was similar. Bone union was achieved with both fixators. Higher fracture site stiffness early in the fracture-healing process and less callus formation were noted with the more rigid two-plane fixators. After 13 weeks, however, the stiffness and radiographic characteristics of healing fractures were the same for the two external fixation frames. This study supports that of Wu and associates[159] in demonstrating that osteotomy union can be achieved with a range of external fixator rigidities, that stiffer external fixation frames result in more rapid return of fracture site stiffness, and that externally fixed osteotomies converge to similar biomechanical levels during later stages of fracture healing with various fixator rigidities.

Briggs and Chao[18] demonstrated that external fixators that apply compression across the fracture provide more rigid fixation than those without compression. Hart and colleagues[57] created tibial osteotomies bilaterally in dogs. Both sides were treated with external fixators, but compression was applied on only one side. After 90 days, fracture healing was evaluated biochemically, histologically, and biomechanically. All of the osteotomies had healed after 90 days. No significant differences were found in blood flow, histology, or strength between the groups. Hart and colleagues concluded that although compression increases the rigidity of externally fixed transverse osteotomies, it has little effect on the biologic or biomechanical state of fracture healing at the time period studied.[57]

Goodship and Kenwright[52] investigated the influence of induced interfragmentary motion on the healing of tibial osteotomies in sheep. They compared rigid fixation of an osteotomy with a 3-mm gap with a similar situation with the addition of a 1-mm axial deformation applied over 17-minute periods daily. They found significant improvement in healing, as measured radiographically and by fracture stiffness, with the applied micromotion. This improvement was evidently due to greater callus formation with the controlled motion. Kenwright and co-workers[79] extended this study to examine alternate levels of applied micromotion and found that 2-mm deformations were detrimental to healing, whereas 0.5-mm deformations enhanced healing in later stages (8 to 12 weeks). Kenwright and associates[79] used similar regimens of micromotion in a clinical study and found that fracture healing occurred earlier than in patients who received rigid external fixation with no applied micromotion. Goodship and associates[53] also showed that increasing the external fixation frame stiffness by moving the sidebars closer to the bone slowed down fracture healing in an ovine model of tibial fractures.

Although numerous studies have shown that the rigidity of fracture fixation influences bone healing, most of these studies used experimental designs in which fixation rigidity was held constant throughout the study. Consideration of the interfragmentary strain hypothesis of Perren and co-workers leads immediately to the hypothesis that rigid fixation may be desirable early during healing to reduce the strain levels to a point at which bone cells can survive. After osseous union has begun, it might be desirable to increase load transfer across the fracture site in order to stimulate bone remodeling. This concept is in common clinical practice where increased weight bearing is prescribed after a period of reduced weight bearing. External fixators provide a convenient method for altering fixation rigidity during the course of healing. This fact prompted several studies in which fixation rigidity was altered during the course of fracture healing.[4, 5, 42, 80]

Dynamization is a term used to describe mechanisms that decrease the stiffness of a fixation device or mechanisms that allow increased motion between fracture fragments. A few devices specifically allow motion along one axis (axial dynamization). Dynamization is intended to accelerate fracture healing by allowing more load transfer across the fracture site after the initial stages of fracture healing.

To examine the effect of destabilization on unstable osteotomies, Egger and associates[42] externally fixed bilateral oblique osteotomies in adult canine tibias. In this case, a 2-mm gap was left between fracture fragments. After 6 weeks, the rigidity of fixation was reduced on one side. After 12 weeks, the "destabilized" tibia had significantly greater torsional strength, but not stiffness, than the tibia with constant rigid fixation. The difference was attributed to more advanced bone remodeling of the initial bone-healing response. It is also noteworthy that the differences were not radiographically evident.

Egger and co-workers[43] investigated the effect of reducing fixator stability in a canine tibial oblique osteotomy model at various times after osteotomy. Destabilization of fixation stability was accomplished by converting a trilateral external fixation frame to a unilateral frame at 1, 2, 4, or 6 weeks after osteotomy. Reduction in external fixation rigidity at 1, 2, or 4 weeks resulted in increased callus formation with decreased torsional strength as compared with osteotomies treated with continuous rigid fixation. However, destabilization of external fixation after 6 weeks increased torsional strength by 30%, although it had little effect on torsional strength, energy absorption, or pin loosening. The increase in strength was attributed to more rapid maturation of the initial direct cortical reconstruction response. Finally, the

incidence of pin loosening increased when fixation rigidity was reduced, which was attributed to higher stresses at the pin-bone interface.

Dynamization increases the load that is transferred across the fracture and may allow increased micromotion between fragments. The effect of micromotion on fracture healing is not clear. Kershaw and colleagues[80] have shown in a prospective clinical study that imposing micromotion reduced healing time for tibial diaphyseal fractures. In contrast, Aro and associates[5] applied Orthofix unilateral fixators to transverse osteotomies bilaterally in dogs. After 15 days, axial motion was allowed on one side while rigid fixation was maintained contralaterally. After 90 days, the periosteal callus was more uniformly distributed on the side where axial freedom was allowed; however, the torsional stiffness and strength were the same for both bones.

In a sheep model of fracture healing, micromotion at an osteotomy site was controlled by applying rigid or semirigid external fixators. The difference in fracture site micromotion was approximately 25% between the groups. A 25% increase in micromotion resulted in a 400% increase in regional blood flow at the osteotomy site.[147] There was also substantially more callus in the osteotomies treated with semirigid external fixation. Despite the pronounced difference in blood flow and histology, no differences in failure torque or torsional stiffness could be attributed to fixator rigidity or micromotion. Similar results were found by Steen and co-workers[135] in a study in which axial compression was allowed 2 weeks after a 3-week limb-lengthening period. The torsional strength of fixators with and without delayed reduction in external fixator stiffness was statistically equal. Steen and co-workers attributed this result to insufficient differences in the rigidity of the fixators. Dynamization also had no effect in a rabbit model of fracture healing.[117]

Further studies are needed to determine what types of fractures benefit from delayed reduction in fixation rigidity, what magnitude of reduction in rigidity is optimal, what is the optimal time to change rigidity, and how rigidity or other parameters can be noninvasively monitored.

Comparative Studies of Healing with Different Types of Fixation

The preceding discussions have examined the wide range of fracture fixation stability that can be obtained with various treatments and the different types of healing that occur with rigid versus less rigid fixation. However, the relative merits of the different healing patterns are widely debated, and little quantitative evidence is available for comparison on other than clinical grounds. Micromovement between bone fragments facilitates fracture healing, but the acceptable range of micromotion and the optimal range of micromotion have not been determined.

Although nonmechanical clinical aspects of a fracture may dictate the best fracture treatment approach, there are cases in which several options exist, and mechanical considerations are important in selecting a fixation method. Several animal studies have compared fracture healing with different types of fixation (e.g., plates versus rods, internal fixation versus external fixation).

Rand and colleagues[119] compared compression plates and reamed, fluted intramedullary rods using the canine transverse tibial osteotomy model. They evaluated blood flow, fracture site morphology, and bone strength at various times up to 120 days after fracture. Clinical union was evident in all dogs after 42 days. Blood flow to the fracture site reached higher levels and remained high longer in osteotomies treated with reaming and intramedullary rods. There was significantly more new bone formation with intramedullary fixation, with most of the new bone formed in periosteal callus. With compression plating, most of the new bone formed endosteally. Plated bones were significantly stronger and stiffer than rod-fixed bones at 42 and 90 days but not at 120 days. The study demonstrated different healing mechanisms with the two treatments studied, but the time required to establish normal strength and stiffness was not different.

Sarmiento and co-workers[126] compared rigid compression plating with functional braces for closed nondisplaced fractures and found that fractures treated with functional braces produced abundant callus and had greater torsional strength than rigidly fixed fractures. However, Lewallen and associates,[86] using a canine tibial model, radiographically, histologically, and biomechanically compared osteotomies fixed by compression plating with those stabilized by external fixators. Initially, the less rigid, externally fixed osteotomies were significantly less stiff than those fixed by the more rigid compression plating. Dogs applied more load sooner to the compression-plated leg than to the contralateral externally fixed limb. After 120 days, bone union occurred in most animals independent of fixation method. However, compression-plated bones were significantly stronger and stiffer in torsion than those that were externally fixed. Histologically, the total amount of new bone was similar for the two fixation methods, but there was significantly more resorbed bone and intracortical porosity with externally fixed bones and more intracortical new bone on the compression-plated side. Also, there was greater blood flow to externally fixed osteotomy sites, consistent with other results suggesting increased bone remodeling with the less stable fixation.

Terjesen and Svenningsen[141] utilized transverse tibial osteotomies in rabbits to compare fracture healing with metal plates with that with plaster casts and to examine the role of limb loading in fracture healing with different treatments. Four types of fracture treatment were studied: plate fixation, plate fixation with a long plaster cast, a long plaster cast, and a short plaster cast. The long plaster casts were intended to restrict loads on the healing bone. Callus area, bending strength, and bending stiffness were evaluated after 6 weeks. Fractures that were treated with the long plaster cast, both with and without plating, were significantly weaker and less stiff. More periosteal callus developed with both long and short cast treatments than with plated fractures. The authors concluded that weight bearing and muscular activity are more effective than fixation stiffness at promoting bone union.

MONITORING FRACTURE HEALING

Because bones are structural members whose functions are to support the body and permit the skeletal motions necessary for survival, it seems natural that fracture healing should be evaluated by the return of prefracture stiffness and strength. Instead, however, clinical assessments of fracture healing are typically made by imprecise radiographic criteria, by subjective assessments of pain, and by comparison with previous clinical experience. As a result, little is known about the return of stiffness and strength to healing bones. Noninvasive imaging techniques may also allow objective assessment of fracture healing,[92] but the sensitivity and specificity of these techniques are largely unknown.

Several research groups have proposed or implemented noninvasive methods for monitoring the biomechanical progression of fracture healing. The general approach is to apply loads across the fracture gap and measure the resultant deflections. Many of these methods are directed toward externally fixed fractures because the external fixation pins provide a direct mechanical connection to the fractured bone (assuming that the pins have not loosened). As the fracture heals, the slope of the load-versus-displacement curve increases, representing a return to the original stiffness of the bone. The goal is to monitor the load-versus-displacement curve to determine whether the union is proceeding normally. There are two advantages of this information. First, in the case of delayed union, corrective action can be taken earlier than would be possible if using radiographic information alone. Second, the biomechanics of the fracture treatment can be "fine tuned" to provide the optimal mechanical environment for fracture healing.

One clinical objective of fracture treatment is to restore the load-bearing capacity of the bone. In the laboratory, bone from animal models of fracture healing can be removed, and both the stiffness and the load-bearing capacity can be measured. In contrast, only the stiffness of healing bones can be measured in patients. It is therefore important to understand the relationships between stiffness and load-bearing capacity of healing fractures. Henry and co-workers[64] demonstrated that caution is needed when using bone stiffness to determine the strength of a healing fracture. They utilized a rabbit osteotomy model, and fractures were fixed by intramedullary rodding, plating, or no surgical intervention. Bones were tested using four-point bending 5 to 10 weeks after osteotomy. All fracture treatments resulted in similar biomechanical results, so the data were pooled. Figure 4–31 shows the relationship between bone strength and bone stiffness 5 weeks after osteotomy. Both strength and stiffness values are expressed as the ratio of fractured bone to intact bone. The regression line for the data indicates a slope of about 0.5, suggesting that bone strength returns more slowly than bone stiffness.

Proposed methods for monitoring externally fixed

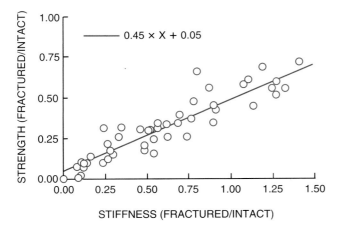

FIGURE 4–31. Bone strength versus fracture stiffness for rabbit tibial osteotomies after 5 weeks of healing with several different fracture treatment methods. (Data from Henry, A.N.; Freeman, M.A.R.; Swanson, S.A.V. Proc R Soc Med 61:902–906, 1968.)

fracture healing can be divided into two groups: methods that involve application of quasistatic loads across the fracture and methods that utilize dynamic or vibration-type loads. Beaupre and associates[9] demonstrated the application of fracture site monitoring using static loads. A Hoffman-Vidal external fixation system was applied to an idealized fracture model ex vivo. The model consisted of Plexiglas cylinders representing a long bone with neoprene discs of various stiffness placed between the ends of the cylinders representing the healing fracture gap. Loads were applied to the fixation pins, and the deflection across the fracture gap was monitored. They also utilized an analytical (finite element) model of the external fixator in which changes in the fracture site stiffness could be

altered. Both the experimental and the analytical results demonstrated that the stiffness of a fracture gap could be evaluated using this method.

The relationships between external fixator pin displacement and the mechanical properties of the fracture site are nonlinear[3, 9, 117] and dependent on the applied load characteristics.[41] Thus, it is important to document the relationship between pin displacement and fracture site stiffness for each external fixator frame configuration before interpreting the data. For most loading configurations, there is a relatively steep decrease in pin displacement with initial increases in fracture site stiffness (0% to 10% of intact bone stiffness). During later stages of fracture healing, the decrease in pin displacement is small, with large increases in fracture site stiffness (Fig. 4–32). It may also be difficult to separate the effect of loosening of connectors in the external fixation system[41] from the effects of fracture healing.

Evans and colleagues[46] developed a displacement transducer that clamps on to the external support of a unilateral fixation system. Axial and bending loads are manually applied to the limb while the reaction force and frame deflection are monitored. Using this system, curves of limb load versus sidebar deflection can be monitored at various times after fracture. Changes in the slope of the load-deflection curve provide an indication of the biomechanical progression of fracture healing. Although the authors did not verify the relationship between fracture site stiffness and transducer signal, they applied the system for monitoring numerous tibial fractures. Utilizing this system, they collected clinical data to determine when an external fixator can be safely removed.

Fracture site monitoring using dynamic tests typically involves applying an oscillating or impulse load across the fracture gap and monitoring the acceleration or displace-

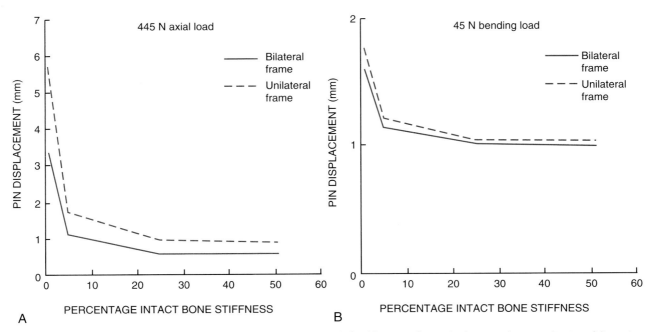

FIGURE 4–32. *A* and *B*, Analytical results for an idealized model of an externally fixed fracture. The pin displacement during application of distraction and bending loads to the bone is shown as a function of fracture site stiffness. (*A* and *B*, Data from An, K.N.; Kasman, R.A.; Chao, E.Y.S. Eng Med 17:11–15, 1988.)

ment of the bone at one or more locations. An example of a dynamic system for monitoring fractures is the bone resonance analysis method, developed and tested by Cornelissen and co-workers[35] for monitoring tibial fractures. This technique is designed to measure the lowest resonant frequency of a fractured tibia. The basis for the method is that the resonant frequency of a tibia decreases significantly with fracture and then increases as the fracture heals. Small, 30- to 300-Hz, cyclical axial loads are applied to the medial malleolus and below the tibial tuberosity, and the acceleration of a point along the anterior surface of the tibia is monitored. The resonant frequency of the limb is determined as the vibration frequency that results in the greatest tibial mobility. In clinical practice, the resonant frequency of the fracture limb is monitored during the course of fracture healing. This technique requires that loads be transmitted across soft tissues. With the presence of joints and variable muscle tension, interpretation of bone resonance analysis test results is complicated. For this reason the absolute values of measured resonant frequencies are not reliable, and the data must be analyzed for temporal changes in resonant frequencies. Comparative measurements using a normal contralateral limb serve as a reference. No significant difference between resonant frequencies of normal left and right limbs were observed in tests of more than 50 normal individuals.

Tibial refractures after external fixation occur in 3% to 11% of patients.[38, 83, 121] Quantitative measurement of structural properties can help determine the optimal time to remove the fixator and may thereby reduce the refracture rate.[121] In a consecutive series of 117 patients with diaphyseal tibial fractures, unilateral external fixation was removed when radiographic and clinical findings suggested that union had occurred. In 8 of these patients (7%), refracture occurred. In the next 95 patients, external fixation was removed when the bending rigidity of the lower leg was greater than 15 Nm/degree, and none of these patients experienced refracture.[121] The sensitivity of the stiffness measurement was 100%, but the specificity was 78% (44 of 160 patients had a stiffness below 15 Nm/degree but did not experience refracture).

Several potential difficulties must be considered. For example, Churches and associates[33] demonstrated that fixation pin loosening significantly alters the stability of an externally fixed fracture. Pin loosening could also lead to misleading results if pin displacements are used to monitor fracture biomechanics. Thus, it is important to monitor pin loosening in studies in which pin displacements are employed to monitor fracture healing. Similarly, none of the connections in the external fixation system can be allowed to loosen because this leads to misleading results.[41] In addition, few studies have adequately characterized the sensitivity of the monitoring techniques to determine the resolution of the in vivo biomechanical measurements and how clinical alterations in frame configurations affect data over the treatment period. Finally, additional clinical data are required for biomechanical characterization of "normal" fracture healing patterns in humans as standard curves are needed to identify abnormal temporal sequences in fracture healing.

SUMMARY

Biomechanical studies of the material and structural properties of bones have provided a basic understanding of bone properties and the alterations that can accompany aging and bone pathologic abnormalities. This information has been applied in several experimental and analytical studies that are enhancing our ability to predict fracture risk associated with aging and metastatic bone disease. This basic understanding of bone biomechanics also facilitates understanding of the fracture treatment biomechanics because the mechanical properties of bone and the mechanical properties of the fracture treatment together determine the biomechanics of a fixation system.

Two basic types of fracture-healing biologies have been identified, and it has been well established that biomechanical factors influence fracture healing. Numerous animal studies have demonstrated that the return of bone stiffness and strength can be altered by fixation rigidity. However, a consensus has not been reached on the optimal fixation rigidity for different types of fractures or on how fixation rigidity should be altered as the fracture heals. The literature, however, does provide information that can facilitate clinical management of orthopaedic fractures.

Selection of the optimal form of fracture management involves balancing sometimes conflicting requirements. Several studies have demonstrated that a wide range of fixation stabilities are available through numerous internal and external fixation device designs and applications. Frequently, several basic mechanical principles can be used to understand the degree of fixation rigidity provided by each treatment method. When specific biomechanical fixation requirements can be identified, sufficient engineering tools are available to choose a treatment method. One application of biomechanical analyses of fracture treatment is in monitoring the biomechanical progression of fracture healing. Methods are being developed that will allow noninvasive biomechanical monitoring. Further research may provide noninvasive and objective measures for selecting treatment methods, altering treatment during the course of healing, and determining the time for removal of the fixation for optimal return of normal weight bearing.

REFERENCES

1. Akeson, W.H.; Woo, S.L.Y.; Rutherford, L.; et al. The effects of rigidity of internal fixation plates on long bone remodeling: A biomechanical and quantitative histiological study. Acta Orthop Scand 47:241–249, 1976.
2. Allen, W.C.; Heiple, K.G.; Burstein, A.H. A fluted femoral intramedullary rod. J Bone Joint Surg Am 60:506–515, 1978.
3. An, K.N.; Kasman, R.A.; Chao, E.Y.S. Theoretical analysis of fracture healing monitoring with external fixators. Eng Med 17:11–15, 1988.
4. Aro, H.; Chao, E. Bone-healing patterns affected by loading, fracture fragment stability, fracture type, and fracture site compression. Clin Orthop 293:8–17, 1993.
5. Aro, H.T.; Kelly, P.J.; Lewallen, D.G.; Chao, E.Y.S. The effects of physiologic dynamic compression on bone healing under external fixation. Clin Orthop 256:260–273, 1990.

6. Backman, S. The proximal end of the femur. Acta Radiol Stockh Suppl 146:1–166, 1957.

7. Beals, R.K.; Lawton, G.D.; Snell, W.E. Prophylactic internal fixation of the femur in metastatic breast cancer. Cancer 28:1350–1354, 1971.

8. Beaupre, G.S.; Carter, D.R.; Dueland, R.T.; et al. A biomechanical assessment of plate fixation, with insufficient bony support. J Orthop Res 6:721–729, 1988.

9. Beaupre, G.S.; Hayes, W.C.; Jofe, M.H.; White, A.A., III. Monitoring fracture site properties with external fixation. J Biomech Eng 105:120–126, 1983.

10. Beaupre, G.S.; Schneider, E.; Perren, S.M. Stress analysis of a partially slotted intramedullary nail. J Orthop Res 2:369–376, 1984.

11. Beck, T.; Ruff, C.; Bissessur, K. Age-related changes in female femoral neck geometry: Implications for bone strength. Calcif Tissue Int 53:S41–S46, 1993.

12. Beck, T.; Ruff, C.; Mourtada, F.; et al. Dual-energy x-ray absorptiometry–derived structural geometry for stress fracture prediction in male U.S. Marine Corps recruits. J Bone Miner Res 11:645–653, 1996.

13. Bergmann, G.; Graichen, F.; Rohlmann, A. Hip joint loading during walking and running, measured in two patients. J Biomech 26:969–990, 1993.

14. Bergot, C.; Laval-Jeantet, A.M.; Preteux, F.; Meunier, A. Measurement of anisotropic vertebral trabecular bone loss during aging by quantitative image analysis. Calcif Tissue Int 43:143–149, 1988.

15. Black, J.; Perdigon, P.; Brown, N.; Pollack, S.R. Stiffness and strength of fracture callus. Relative rates of mechanical maturation as evaluated by a uniaxial tensile test. Clin Orthop 182:278–288, 1984.

16. Boyce, W.J.; Vessey, M.P. Rising incidence of fracture of the proximal femur. Lancet 1:150–151, 1985.

17. Bradley, G.W.; McKenna, G.B.; Dunn, H.K.; et al. Effects of flexural rigidity of plates on bone healing. J Bone Joint Surg Am 61:866–872, 1979.

18. Briggs, B.T.; Chao, E.Y.S. The mechanical performance of the standard Hoffmann-Vidal external fixation apparatus. J Bone Joint Surg Am 64:566–573, 1982.

19. Burstein, A.H.; Reilly, D.T.; Martens, M. Aging of bone tissue: Mechanical properties. J Bone Joint Surg Am 58:82–86, 1976.

20. Carter, D.R.; Hayes, W.C. Bone compressive strength: The influence of density and strain rate. Science 194:1174–1176, 1976.

21. Carter, D.R.; Hayes, W.C. Compact bone fatigue damage. I. Residual strength and stiffness. J Biomech 10:325–327, 1977.

22. Carter, D.R.; Hayes, W.C. Compact bone fatigue damage. II. A microscopic examination. Clin Orthop 127:265–274, 1977.

23. Carter, D.R.; Hayes, W.C. The compressive behavior of bone as a two-phase porous structure. J Bone Joint Surg Am 59:954–962, 1977.

24. Carter, D.R.; Shimaoka, E.E.; Harris, W.H.; et al. Changes in long-bone structural properties during the first 8 weeks of plate implantation. J Orthop Res 2:80–89, 1984.

25. Chang, W.C.; Christensen, T.M.; Pinilla, T.P.; Keaveny, T.M. Uniaxial yield strains for bovine trabecular bone are isotropic and asymmetric. J Orthop Res 17:582–585, 1999.

26. Chao, E.Y.S.; Hein, T.J. Mechanical performance of the standard Orthofix external fixator. Orthopedics 11:1057–1069, 1988.

27. Chao, E.Y.S.; Kasman, R.A.; An, K.N. Rigidity and stress analysis of external fixation devices—A theoretical approach. J Biomech 15:971–983, 1982.

28. Chao, E.Y.S.; An, K.N. Stress and rigidity and external fixation devices. In: Gallagher, R.H.; Simon, B.R.; Johnson, P.C.; Gross, J.F., eds. Finite Elements in Biomechanics. New York, John Wiley & Sons, 1982, pp. 195–222.

29. Cheal, E.J.; Hayes, W.C.; White, A.A., III; Perren, S.M. Stress analysis of compression plate fixation and its effects on long bone remodeling. J Biomech 18:141–150, 1985.

30. Cheal, E.J.; Mansmann, K.A.; DiGioia, A.M., III; et al. Role of interfragmentary strain in fracture healing: Ovine model of a healing osteotomy. J Orthop Res 9:131–142, 1991.

31. Cheal, E.; Spector, M.; Hayes, W. Role of loads and prosthesis material properties on the mechanics of the proximal femur after total hip arthroplasty. J Orthop Res 10:405–422, 1992.

32. Choueka, J.; Koval, K.; Kummer, F.; et al. Biomechanical comparison of the sliding hip screw and the dome plunger. J Bone Joint Surg Br 77:277–283, 1995.

33. Churches, A.E.; Tanner, K.E.; Harris, J.D. The Oxford external fixator: Fixator stiffness and the effects of bone pin loosening. Eng Med 14:3–11, 1985.

34. Cody, D.D.; Gross, G.J.; Hou, F.J.; et al. Femoral strength is better predicted by finite element models than QCT and DXA. J Biomech 32:1013–1020, 1999.

35. Cornelissen, P.; Cornelissen, M.; Van der Perre, G.; et al. Assessment of tibial stiffness by vibration testing in situ. II. Influence of soft tissues, joints and fibula. J Biomech 19:551–561, 1986.

36. Courtney, A.; Wachtel, E.; Myers, E.; Hayes, W. Effects of loading rate on strength of the proximal femur. Calcif Tissue Int 55:53–58, 1994.

37. Davy, D.T.; Connolly, J.F. The biomechanical behavior of healing canine radii and ribs. J Biomech 15:235–247, 1982.

38. de Bastiani, G.; Aldegheri, R.; Brivio, L.R. The treatment of fractures with a dynamic axial fixator. J Bone Joint Surg Br 66:538–545, 1984.

39. de Bruin, E.D.; Herzog, R.; Rozendal, R.H.; et al. Estimation of geometric properties of cortical bone in spinal cord injury. Arch Phys Med Rehabil 81:150–156, 2000.

40. DiGioia, A.M., III; Cheal, E.J.; Hayes, W.C. Three-dimensional strain fields in a uniform osteotomy gap. J Biomech Eng 108:273–280, 1986.

41. Drijber, F.P.; Finlay, J.B.; Dempsey, A. Evaluation of linear finite-element analysis models: Assumptions for external fixation devices. J Biomech 25:849–855, 1992.

42. Egger, E.; Gottsauner-Wolf, F.; Palmer, J.; et al. Effects of axial dynamization on bone healing. J Trauma 34:185–192, 1993.

43. Egger, E.L.; Lewallen, D.G.; Norrdin, R.W.; et al. Effects of destabilizing rigid external fixation on healing of unstable canine osteotomies. Trans Orthop Res Soc 34:302, 1988.

44. Ellsasser, J.C.; Moyer, C.F.; Lesker, P.A.; Simmons, D.J. Improved healing of experimental long bone fractures in rabbits by delayed internal fixation. J Trauma 15:869–876, 1975.

45. Esses, S.I.; Lotz, J.C.; Hayes, W.C. Biomechanical properties of the proximal femur determined in vitro by single-energy quantitative computed tomography. J Bone Miner Res 4:715–722, 1989.

46. Evans, M.; Kenwright, J.; Cunningham, J.L. Design and performance of a fracture monitoring transducer. J Biomed Eng 10:64–69, 1988.

47. Fidler, M. Prophylactic internal fixation of secondary neoplastic deposits in long bones. Br Med J 10:341–343, 1973.

48. Frankle, M.; Cordey, J.; Sanders, R.W.; et al. A biomechanical comparison of the antegrade inserted universal femoral nail with the retrograde inserted universal tibial nail for use in femoral shaft fractures. Injury 30(Suppl 1):A40–A43, 1999.

49. Fyhrie, D.P.; Vashishth, D. Bone stiffness predicts strength similarly for human vertebral cancellous bone in compression and for cortical bone in tension. Bone 26:169–173, 2000.

50. George, C.J.; Lindsey, R.W.; Noble, P.C.; et al. Optimal location of a single distal interlocking screw in intramedullary nailing of distal third femoral shaft fractures. J Orthop Trauma 12:267–272, 1998.

51. Gibson, L.J. Cancellous bone. In: Gibson, L.T.; Ashby, M.F., eds. Cellular Solids. New York, Pergamon Press, 1988, pp. 316–331.

52. Goodship, A.E.; Kenwright, J. The influence of induced micromovement upon the healing of experimental tibial fractures. J Bone Joint Surg Br 67:650–655, 1985.

53. Goodship, A.; Watkins, P.; Rigby, H.; Kenwright, J. The role of fixator frame stiffness in the control of fracture healing: An experimental study. J Biomech 26:1027–1035, 1993.

54. Greenspan, S.; Myers, E.; Maitland, L.; et al. Fall severity and bone mineral density as risk factors for hip fracture in ambulatory elderly. JAMA 271:128–133, 1994.

55. Grosse, A.; Christie, J.; Taglang, G.; et al. Open adult femoral shaft fracture treated by early intramedullary nailing. J Bone Joint Surg Br 75:562–565, 1993.

56. Guo, X.; McMahon, T.; Keaveny, T.; et al. Finite element modeling of damage accumulation in trabecular bone under cyclic loading. J Biomech 27:145–155, 1994.

57. Hart, M.B.; Wu, J.J.; Chao, E.Y.; Kelly, P.J. External skeletal fixation of canine tibial osteotomies. Compression compared with no compression. J Bone Joint Surg Am 67:598–605, 1985.

58. Hayes, W.C. Biomechanical measurements of bone. In: Burstein, A., ed. CRC Handbook of Engineering in Medicine and Biology: Section B. Instruments and Measurements. Cleveland, CRC Press, 1978, pp. 333–372.

59. Hayes, W.C. Biomechanics of fracture healing. In: Heppenstall, R.B., ed. Fracture Treatment and Healing. Philadelphia, W.B. Saunders, 1980, pp. 124–172.

60. Hayes, W.C.; Perren, S.M. Flexural rigidity of compression plate fixation. Med Biol Eng 2:242–244, 1971.

61. Hayes, W.C.; Perren, S.M. Plate-bone friction in the compression fixation of fractures. Clin Orthop 89:236–240, 1972.

62. Hayes, W.C.; Ruff, C.B. Biomechanical compensatory mechanisms for age-related changes in cortical bone. In: Uhthoff, H.K.; Jaworski, Z.F.G., eds. Twelfth Annual Applied Basic Sciences Course. Ottawa, University of Ottawa, 1986, pp. 371–377.

63. Hayes, W.; Myers, E. Biomechanics of fractures. In: Riggs, B.; Melton, L., eds. Osteoporosis: Etiology, Diagnosis, and Management, 2nd ed. New York, Raven Press, 1995, pp. 93–114.

64. Henry, A.N.; Freeman, M.A.R.; Swanson, S.A.V. Studies of the mechanical properties of healing experimental fractures. Proc R Soc Med 61:902–906, 1968.

65. Hipp, J.A.; Edgerton, B.C.; An, K.N.; Hayes, W.C. Structural consequences of transcortical holes in long bones loaded in torsion. J Biomech 23:1261–1268, 1990.

66. Hipp, J.A.; McBroom, R.J.; Cheal, E.J.; Hayes, W.C. Structural consequences of endosteal metastatic lesions in long bones. J Orthop Res 7:828–837, 1989.

67. Hipp, J.A.; Springfield, D.; Hayes, W. Predicting pathologic fracture risk in the management of metastatic bone defects. Clin Orthop 312:120–135, 1995.

68. Hora, N.; Markel, D.C.; Haynes, A.; Grimm, M.J. Biomechanical analysis of supracondylar femoral fractures fixed with modern retrograde intramedullary nails. J Orthop Trauma 13:539–544, 1999.

69. Huiskes, R.; Chao, E.Y.S. A survey of finite element analysis in orthopedic biomechanics: The first decade. J Biomech 16:385–409, 1983.

70. Huiskes, R.; Chao, E.Y.S. Guidelines for external fixation frame rigidity and stresses. J Orthop Res 4:68–75, 1986.

71. Huiskes, R.; Chao, E.Y.S.; Crippen, T.E. Parametric analysis of pin-bone stresses in external fixation. J Orthop Res 3:341–349, 1985.

72. Jacobsen, S.; Cooper, C.; Gottlieb, M.; et al. Hospitalization with vertebral fracture among the aged: A national population-based study, 1986–1989. Epidemiology 3:515–518, 1992.

73. Juan, J.A.; Prat, J.; Vera, P.; et al. Biomechanical consequences of callus development in Hoffmann, Wagner, Orthofix, and Ilizarov external fixators. J Biomech 25:995–1006, 1992.

74. Kasman, R.A.; Chao, E.Y. Fatigue performance of external fixator pins. J Orthop Res 2:377–384, 1984.

75. Keaveny, T.; Guo, X.; Wachtel, E.; et al. Trabecular bone exhibits fully linear elastic behavior and yields at low strains. J Biomech 27:1127–1136, 1994.

76. Keaveny, T.; Wachtel, E.; Guo, X.; Hayes, W. Mechanical behavior of damaged trabecular bone. J Biomech 27:1309–1318, 1994.

77. Keene, J.S.; Sellinger, D.S.; McBeath, A.A.; Engber, W.D. Metastatic breast cancer in the femur: A search for the lesion at risk of fracture. Clin Orthop 203:282–288, 1986.

78. Kempf, I.; Karger, C.; Willinger, R.; et al. Locked intramedullary nailing—Improvement of mechanical properties. In: Perren, S.M.; Schneider, E., eds. Biomechanics: Current Interdisciplinary Research. Boston, Martinus Nijhoff, 1985, pp. 487–492.

79. Kenwright, J.; Richardson, J.B.; Goodship, A.E.; et al. Effect of controlled axial micromovement on healing of tibial fractures. Lancet 2:1185–1187, 1986.

80. Kershaw, C.; Cunningham, J.; Kenwright, J. Tibial external fixation, weight bearing, and fracture movement. Clin Orthop 293:28–36, 1993.

81. Klaue, K.; Fengels, I.; Perren, S.M. Long-term effects of plate osteosynthesis: Comparison of four different plates. Injury 31(Suppl 2):51–62, 2000.

82. Klip, E.; Rosma, R. Investigations into the mechanical behavior of bone-pin connections. Eng Med 7:43–46, 1978.

83. Krettek, C.; Haas, N.; Tscherne, H. The role of supplemental lag-screw fixation for open fractures of the tibial shaft treated with external fixation. J Bone Joint Surg Am 73:893–897, 1991.

84. Laurence, M.; Freeman, M.A.R.; Swanson, S. Engineering considerations in the internal fixation of fractures of the tibial shaft. J Bone Joint Surg Br 51:754–768, 1969.

85. Levensteion, M.; Beaupre, G.; Van der Muelen, M. Improved method for analysis of whole bone torsion tests. J Bone Miner Res 9:1459–1469, 1994.

86. Lewallen, D.G.; Chao, E.Y.S.; Kasman, R.A.; Kelly, P.J. Comparison of the effects of compression plates and external fixators on early bone-healing. J Bone Joint Surg Am 66:1084–1091, 1984.

87. Liew, A.S.; Johnson, J.A.; Patterson, S.D.; et al. Effect of screw placement on fixation in the humeral head. J Shoulder Elbow Surg 9:423–426, 2000.

88. Lotz, J.C.; Cheal, E.J.; Hayes, W.C. Fracture prediction for the proximal femur using finite element models: Part I: Linear models. J Biomech Eng 113:353–360, 1991.

89. Lotz, J.; Cheal, E.; Hayes, W. Stress distributions within the proximal femur during gait and falls: Implications for osteoporotic fracture. Osteoporos Int 5:252–261, 1995.

90. Lotz, J.C.; Hayes, W.C. The use of quantitative computed tomography to estimate risk of fracture of the hip from falls. J Bone Joint Surg Am 72:689–700, 1990.

91. Manley, M.T.; Hurst, L.; Hindes, R.; et al. Effects of low-modulus coatings on pin-bone contact stresses in external fixation. J Orthop Res 2:385–392, 1984.

92. Markel, M.; Chao, E. Noninvasive monitoring techniques for quantitative description of callus mineral content and mechanical properties. Clin Orthop 293:37–45, 1993.

93. Matter, P.; Brenwald, J.; Perren, S.M. The effect of static compression and tension on internal remodeling of cortical bone. Helv Chir Acta 42(Suppl 12):1–57, 1975.

94. Mazess, R.B. On aging bone loss. Clin Orthop 165:239–252, 1982.

95. McBroom, R.J.; Cheal, E.J.; Hayes, W.C. Strength reductions from metastatic cortical defects in long bones. J Orthop Res 6:369–378, 1988.

96. McCoy, M.T.; Chao, E.Y.S.; Kasman, R.A. Comparison of mechanical performance in four types of external fixators. Clin Orthop 180:23–33, 1983.

97. Melton, L.J., III. Epidemiology of hip fractures: Implications of the exponential increase with age. Bone 18:121S–125S, 1996.

98. Melton, L.J., III; Khosla, S.; Atkinson, E.J.; et al. Relationship of bone turnover to bone density and fractures. J Bone Miner Res 12:1083–1091, 1997.

99. Minns, R.J.; Bremble, G.R.; Campbell, J. A biomechanical study of internal fixation of the tibial shaft. J Biomech 10:569–579, 1977.

100. Molster, A.O.; Gjerdet, N.R.; Langeland, N.; et al. Controlled bending instability in the healing of diaphyseal osteotomies in the rat femur. J Orthop Res 5:29–35, 1987.

101. Morrison, J.B. The mechanics of the knee joint in relation to normal walking. J Biomech 3:51–61, 1969.

102. Moyen, B.J.L.; Lahey, P.J.; Weinberg, E.H.; Harris, W.H. Effects on intact femora of dogs of the application and removal of metal plates: A metabolic and structural study comparing stiffer and more flexible plates. J Bone Joint Surg Am 60:940–947, 1978.

103. Nagurka, M.L.; Hayes, W.C. Technical note: An interactive graphics package for calculating cross-sectional properties of complex shapes. J Biomech 13:59–64, 1980.

104. Nakamura, T.; Turner, C.J.; Yoshikawa, T.; et al. Do variations in hip geometry explain differences in hip fracture risk between Japanese and white Americans? J Bone Miner Res 9:1071–1076, 1994.

105. Oda, M.A.S.; Schurman, D.J. Monitoring of pathological fractures. In: Stoll, B.A.; Parbhoo, S., eds. Bone Metastasis. New York, Raven Press, 1983, pp. 271–288.

106. Panagiotopoulos, E.; Fortis, A.P.; Lambiris, E.; Kostopoulos, V. Rigid or sliding plate. A mechanical evaluation of osteotomy fixation in sheep. Clin Orthop 358:244–249, 1999.

107. Panjabi, M.M.; Walter, S.D.; Karuda, M.; et al. Correlations of radiographic analysis of healing fractures with strength: A statistical analysis of experimental osteotomies. J Orthop Res 3:212–218, 1985.

108. Panjabi, M.M.; White, A.A., III; Southwick, W.O. Temporal changes in the physical properties of healing fractures in rabbits. J Biomech 10:689–699, 1977.

109. Panjabi, M.M.; White, A.A., III; Wolf, J.W. A biomechanical comparison of the effects of constant and cyclic compression on fracture healing in rabbit long bones. Acta Orthop Scand 50:653–661, 1979.

110. Parfitt, A. Bone age, mineral density, and fatigue damage. Calcif Tissue Int 53(Suppl):S82–S85, 1993.
111. Parker, M.J.; Pryor, G.A.; Myles, J. 11-year results in 2,846 patients of the Peterborough Hip Fracture Project: Reduced morbidity, mortality and hospital stay. Acta Orthop Scand 71:34–38, 2000.
112. Perren, S.M.; Boitzy, A. Cellular differentiation and bone biomechanics during the consolidation of a fracture. Anat Clin 1:13–28, 1978.
113. Perren, S.M.; Cordey, J. The concept of interfragmentary strain. In: Uhthoff, H.K., ed. Current Concepts of Internal Fixation of Fractures. New York, Springer-Verlag, 1980, pp. 63–77.
114. Perren, S.M.; Cordey, J.; Rahn, B.A.; et al. Early temporary porosis of bone induced by internal fixation implants. Clin Orthop 232:139–151, 1988.
115. Perren, S.M.; Huggler, A.; Russenberger, M.; et al. The reaction of cortical bone to compression. Acta Orthop Scand Suppl 125:19–28, 1969.
116. Perren, S.M.; Rahn, B.A. International symposium on fixation of fractures. Biomechanics of fracture healing. Can J Surg 23:228–232, 1980.
117. Prat, J.; Juan, J.; Vera, P.; et al. Load transmission through the callus site with external fixation systems: Theoretical and experimental analysis. J Biomech 27:469–478, 1994.
118. Rahn, B.A.; Gallinaro, P.; Baltensperger, A.; Perren, S.M. Primary bone healing: An experimental study in the rabbit. J Bone Joint Surg Am 53:783–786, 1971.
119. Rand, J.A.; An, K.N.; Chao, E.Y.S.; Kelly, P.J. A comparison of the effect of open intramedullary nailing and compression-plate fixation on fracture-site blood flow and fracture union. J Bone Joint Surg Am 63:427–442, 1981.
120. Reilly, D.T.; Burstein, A.H. The elastic and ultimate properties of compact bone tissue. J Biomech 8:393–405, 1975.
121. Richardson, J.; Cunningham, J.; Goodship, A.; et al. Measuring stiffness can define healing of tibial fractures. J Bone Joint Surg Br 76:389–394, 1994.
122. Riggs, B.L.; Wahner, H.W.; Seeman, E.; et al. Changes in bone mineral density of the proximal femur and spine with aging. Differences between the postmenopausal and senile osteoporosis syndromes. J Clin Invest 70:716–723, 1982.
123. Roark, R.J.; Young, W.C. Tables of cross-sectional formulae. In: Formulas for Stress and Strain, 5th ed. New York, McGraw-Hill, 1975, pp. 59–72.
124. Ruff, C.B.; Hayes, W.C. Age changes in geometry and mineral content of the lower limb bones. Ann Biomed Eng 12:573–584, 1984.
125. Ruff, C.B.; Hayes, W.C. Bone mineral content in the lower limb: Relationship to cross-sectional geometry. J Bone Joint Surg Br 66:1024–1031, 1984.
126. Sarmiento, A.; Mullis, D.L.; Latta, L.L.; et al. A quantitative comparative analysis of fracture healing under the influence of compression plating vs. closed weight-bearing treatment. Clin Orthop 149:232–239, 1980.
127. Seireg, A.; Kempke, W. Behavior of in vivo bone under cyclic loading. J Biomech 2:455–461, 1969.
128. Seligson, D.; Stanwyck, T. The general technique of external fixation. In: Seligson, D.; Pope, M., eds. Concepts in External Fixation. New York, Grune & Stratton, 1982, pp. 9–108.
129. Silverman, F.N. Essentials of Caffey's pediatric x-ray diagnosis. Pediatr Radiol 1989; 1216.
130. Sjostedt, A.; Zetterberg, C.; Hansson, T.; et al. Bone mineral content and fixation strength of femoral neck fractures. Acta Orthop Scand 65:161–165, 1994.
131. Slatis, P.; Karaharju, E.; Holmstrom, T.; et al. Structural changes in intact tubular bone after application of rigid plates with and without compression. J Bone Joint Surg Am 60:516–522, 1978.
132. Smith, M.D.; Cody, D.D.; Goldstein, S.A.; et al. Proximal femur bone density and its correlation to fracture load and hip-screw penetration load. Clin Orthop 283:244–251, 1992.
133. Snyder, B.D.; Edwards, W.T.; Hayes, W.C. Trabecular changes with vertebral osteoporosis. Letter. N Engl J Med 319:793–794, 1988.
134. Spiegel, P.; Vanderschilden, J. Minimal internal and minimal external fixation in the treatment of open extremity fractures. In: Seligson, D.; Pope, M., eds. Concepts in External Fixation. New York, Grune & Stratton, 1982, pp. 267–278.
135. Steen, H.; Fjeld, T.O.; Bjerkreim, I.; et al. Limb lengthening by diaphyseal corticotomy, callus distraction, and dynamic axial fixation. An experimental study in the ovine femur. J Orthop Res 6:730–735, 1988.
136. Strothman, D.; Templeman, D.C.; Varecka, T.; Bechtold, J. Retrograde nailing of humeral shaft fractures: A biomechanical study of its effects on the strength of the distal humerus. J Orthop Trauma 14:101–104, 2000.
137. Tarr, R.R.; Wiss, D.A. The mechanics and biology of intramedullary fracture fixation. Clin Orthop 212:10–17, 1986.
138. Tencer, A.F.; Sherman, M.C.; Johnson, K.D. Biomechanical factors affecting fracture stability and femoral bursting in closed intramedullary rod fixation of femur fractures. J Biomech Eng 107:104–111, 1985.
139. Terjesen, T.; Apalset, K. The influence of different degrees of stiffness of fixation plates on experimental bone healing. J Orthop Res 6:293–299, 1988.
140. Terjesen, T.; Benum, P. The stress-protecting effect of metal plates on the intact rabbit tibia. Acta Orthop Scand 54:810–818, 1983.
141. Terjesen, T.; Svenningsen, S. The effects of function and fixation stiffness on experimental bone healing. Acta Orthop Scand 59:712–715, 1988.
142. Turner, C.; Burr, D. Basic biomechanical measurements of bone: A tutorial. Bone 14:595–608, 1993.
143. Uhthoff, H.K.; Dubuc, F.L. Bone structure changes in the dog under rigid internal fixation. Clin Orthop 81:165–170, 1971.
144. Uhthoff, H.K.; Finnegan, M. The effects of metal plates on post-traumatic remodelling and bone mass. J Bone Joint Surg Br 65:66–71, 1983.
145. Vajjhala, S.; Kraynik, A.M.; Gibson, L.J. A cellular solid model for modulus reduction due to resorption of trabeculae in bone. J Biomech Eng 122:511–515, 2000.
146. VanBuskirk, W.C.; Ashman, R.B. The elastic moduli of bone. In: Cowin, S.C., ed. Mechanical Properties of Bone. New York, American Society of Mechanical Engineers, 1981, pp. 131–144.
147. Wallace, A.L.; Draper, E.R.C.; Strachan, R.K.; et al. The vascular response to fracture micromovement. Clin Orthop 301:281–290, 1994.
148. Wang, G.J.; Reger, S.I.; Mabie, K.N.; et al. Semirigid rod fixation for long-bone fractures. Clin Orthop 192:291–298, 1985.
149. White, A.A., III; Panjabi, M.M.; Southwick, W.O. Effects of compression and cyclical loading on fracture healing—A quantitative biomechanical study. J Biomech 10:233–239, 1977.
150. White, A.A., III; Panjabi, M.M.; Southwick, W.O. The four biomechanical stages of fracture repair. J Bone Joint Surg Am 59:188–192, 1977.
151. White, B.; Fisher, W.; Laurin, C. Rate of mortality for elderly patients after fracture of the hip in the 1980s. J Bone Joint Surg Am 69:1335–1340, 1987.
152. Williams, D.F.; Gore, L.F.; Clark, G.C.F. Quantitative microradiography of cortical bone in disuse osteoporosis following fracture fixation. Biomaterials 4:285–288, 1983.
153. Williams, E.A.; Rand, J.A.; An, K.N.; et al. The early healing of tibial osteotomies stabilized by one-plane or two-plane external fixation. J Bone Joint Surg Am 69:355–365, 1987.
154. Windhagen, J.; Hipp, J.A.; Hayes, W.C. Postfracture instability of vertebrae with simulated defects can be predicted from computed tomography data. Spine 25:1775–1781, 2000.
155. Windhagen, H.; Hipp, J.A.; Silva, M.J.; et al. Predicting failure of thoracic vertebrae with simulated and actual metastatic defects. Clin Orthop 344:313–319, 1997.
156. Winquist, R.A.; Hansen, S.T.; Clawson, D.K. Closed intramedullary nailing of femoral fractures. J Bone Joint Surg Am 66:529–539, 1984.
157. Woo, S.L.Y.; Lothringer, K.S.; Akeson, W.H.; et al. Less rigid internal fixation plates: Historical perspectives and new concepts. J Orthop Res 1:431–439, 1984.
158. Wright, T.M.; Hayes, W.C. Tensile testing of bone over a wide range of strain rates: Effects of strain rate, microstructure and density. Med Biol Eng Comput 14:671–680, 1976.
159. Wu, J.J.; Shyr, H.S.; Chao, E.Y.S.; Kelly, P.J. Comparison of osteotomy healing under external fixation devices with different stiffness characteristics. J Bone Joint Surg Am 66:1258–1264, 1984.
160. Zych, G.A.; Greenbarg, P.E.; Milne, E.L.; et al. Mechanics of distal locking IM nail fixation in osteopenic and normal femora. Trans Orthop Res Soc 13:406, 1988.

CHAPTER 5

Evaluation and Treatment of the Multiple-Trauma Patient

Robert T. Brautigam, M.D.

David L. Ciraulo, D.O., M.P.H.

Lenworth M. Jacobs, M.D., M.P.H., F.A.C.S.

An estimated 34 million episodes of injuries resulted in 41 million specific injuries in 1997, of which 25% occurred in the home.[34] The injury rates were highest between the ages of 12 and 21 years and older than 65 years.[34] Of those injured, 10 million lost time from work, 33 million lost school time, and 2.5 million were hospitalized.[34] Injuries constitute the leading cause of death between ages 1 to 44.[18] An estimated 400 people die each day from their injures in the United States.[29] The cost of injury overall in 1995 was estimated to be $260 billion.[29]

The trimodal distribution of mortality associated with trauma is categorized as immediate, early, and late.[46] Immediate deaths occur as a result of brain laceration, high spinal cord or brain stem injury, or major vessel or cardiac injury.[46] Given the poor survival with this type of injury, prevention is the best approach in reducing this distribution of fatalities. At the other end of the spectrum, late deaths occur several days to weeks after admission.[46] Eighty percent of these are secondary to head injury, and 20% are attributed to multiple organ failure and sepsis.[6] Early fatalities in the trimodal distribution of trauma deaths occur during the interval between injury and definitive care; this interval is crucial.[46] The America College of Surgeons' Committee on Trauma reported that 62% of all in-hospital deaths occurred in the first 4 hours of admission, which emphasizes the need for expedient and definitive intervention.[3] A trauma system approach to care of this cohort of the injured population reduced morbidity and mortality.

The Committee on Trauma Research in 1985 presented its report entitled *Injury in America*, which documented the significant impact injury has on the general population. This information resulted in the federal government establishing the Center for Injury Control.[35] Funds were allocated to the Department of Transportation's National Highway Traffic Safety Administration and later assigned to the Division of Injury Epidemiology, a division of the Centers for Disease Control and Prevention (CDC).[24] Injury prevention research centers were established and charged with the responsibility to collect data and report to the CDC the results of their research investigation.[24] With government commitment to the investigation of injury, this public health problem could be specifically addressed.

Epidemiologic principles and practice were applied to the investigation of injury. This approach provides information that is generalized to the population, provides quantitative assessment of events, and is based on comparative analysis of observations. The study of injury in epidemiologic terms is divided into two arms: (1) one must identify a phenomenon to be investigated, and (2) one must quantify it on the basis of the number of incidents in reference to severity, time, space, and concentration.[40] This process is described as descriptive epidemiology.[40] Assessment of these descriptive data is termed analytical epidemiology, which strives to identify risk factors and makes inferences concerning the cause of the injury.

William Haddon was at the forefront of epidemiologic investigation for injury.[40] Following the principles of epidemiologic investigation, he devised a strategic plan for the control of injury and identified 10 objectives in the implementation of injury control (Table 5-1).[40] In general terms, these 10 objectives have laid the groundwork from which most epidemiologic investigations of injury originate.[40] This analysis of injuries has assisted with the development of a trauma care system aimed at prevention, resuscitation, treatment, and rehabilitation of the injured patient.

THE TRAUMA SYSTEM

Historical Perspective

Documentation of the effectiveness of a trauma system approach to the care of the injured has been one of the goals of the injury prevention research centers of the CDC

TABLE 5–1 •••••••••••••••••••••••••••••••••

Haddon's Technical Strategies for Injury Control

1. Prevent creation of hazards in the first place.
2. Reduce the amount of hazards brought into being.
3. Prevent the release of the hazards that already exist.
4. Modify the rate or spatial distribution of release of the hazard from its source.
5. Separate, in time or space, the hazard and that which is to be protected.
6. Separate the hazard and that which is to be protected by interposition of a material barrier.
7. Modify basis-relevant qualities of the hazard.
8. Make what is to be protected more resistant to damage from the hazard.
9. Begin to counter the damage already done by the environmental hazard.
10. Stabilize, repair, and rehabilitate the object of the damage.

•••

Adapted from Injury Epidemiology by L. Robertson. Copyright © 1992 by L. Robertson. Used by permission of Oxford University Press, Inc.

and Level I trauma centers accredited by the American College of Surgeons. Jacobs and Jacobs[25] reported on the increased survival of trauma patients who were taken to a trauma center by rapid air transport compared with a cohort of trauma patients taken by ground. This finding was consistent with the improved outcomes of military evacuation in Korea and Vietnam when injured soldiers were immediately transported to mobile army surgical hospitals (MASHs). This concept of providing definitive care as quickly as possible resulted in reduced morbidity and mortality.[19] Guidelines established by the American College of Surgeons' *Resources for Optimal Care of the Injured Patient*[4] and by Shackford and associates[44] and Rauzz[39] demonstrated the improved outcome of injured patients.

The issue of sophisticated trauma care has been challenged by the trends of managed care. In response to this challenge, Demetriades and colleagues[16] demonstrated that the care provided by Level I trauma centers made a difference in improved survival and decreased permanent disability. Miller and Levy[32] demonstrated that states with dedicated trauma systems provide care for patients with major injuries at a reduced cost. The challenge for the future will be to continue outcomes research to demonstrate that trauma systems are cost effective for the injured patient.

Structure

In 1990, the Trauma Care Systems and Development Act created guidelines for the development of an inclusive trauma system integrated with the Emergency Medical Service system to meet the needs of acutely injured patients.[4] The objective of the system is to match the needs of patients to the most appropriate level of care.[4] This process of designation of Level I, II, III, or IV is dependent on the commitment and resources of the medical staff and administration to trauma care at facilities seeking designation. The criteria for each level of designation appear in Table 5–2.

The configuration of the trauma team receiving patients is variable but includes emergency medicine physicians, nurses, allied health personnel, and the trauma surgeon as the team leader.[25] Various subspecialists in surgery, orthopaedics, neurosurgery, cardiothoracic surgery, anesthesia, and pediatrics are readily available at a Level I center.[4] The receiving facility should have a dedicated area for the resuscitation of trauma patients as well as a dedicated operating room available 24 hours a day. A resuscitation room should be well equipped with devices for the warming of fluid, rapid infusers, and appropriate surgical supplies for the performance of lifesaving procedures. Permanently fixed radiographic equipment expedites the evaluation of the injured patient in the resuscitation room. Staffing in the trauma room should be limited to those with experience in trauma resuscitation.

Following the acute phase of resuscitation and operative intervention, a Level I trauma facility maintains a highly trained staff of surgical intensivists. The staff provides 24-hour coverage of the intensive care unit. These patients are susceptible to complications such as sepsis, adult respiratory distress syndrome, and multiple

TABLE 5–2 •••••••••••••••••••••••••••••••••

Criteria for Trauma Designation

LEVEL I

Regional resource trauma center
Provide leadership and total care of the trauma patient
Participate in trauma prevention and rehabilitation
Clinical capabilities:
  • Cardiac, hand, microvascular, and pediatric surgery
  • In-house general surgeon or in-house officer at postgraduate year IV level or greater in surgery
Facility resources:
  • Cardiopulmonary bypass
  • Operating microscope
  • Acute hemodialysis
  • Nuclear scanning
  • Neuroradiology
Provide leadership in education, research, and systems development

LEVEL II

Provide initial definitive trauma care
Clinical capabilities similar to Level I, with exception to the subspecialty areas of surgery
In absence of house staff, general surgeon may be out of house but readily available
Education outreach, research, and prevention programs similar to Level I, but research not essential
System flexibility to transfer complex patients to Level I facilities

LEVEL III

Provide immediate assessment, resuscitation, emergency operations, and stabilization of trauma patients
Have prearranged transfer agreements with Level I facilities
Prompt availability of general surgeon required

LEVEL IV

Provide advanced trauma life support in remote areas prior to transfer to higher level of care

•••

Adapted from American College of Surgeons Committee on Trauma. Resources for Optimal Care of the Injured Patient: 1993. Chicago, American College of Surgeons, 1993.

system organ failure, which require the technical support provided by a Level I center. This support includes jet ventilation, hemodialysis, and cardiac assist devices. Intermediate care units provide intensive supervision of the patient before placement on the trauma floor, which is critical for the recovery of the patient. During this time, patients receive rehabilitation to prepare for dealing with disabilities and limitations related to their injury that may have changed their lives. The patient's physical health and emotional health are evaluated, and treatment is initiated. Patients who have suffered significant injury have special nutritional needs because of their increased caloric demands. The patient's nutritional status is assessed by nutritional services and a recommendation made to the trauma service. As the patient nears discharge, arrangements for home needs and potential placement are made by social services. The availability of and relationships with rehabilitation centers and chronic nursing facilities are essential for injured patients.

ASSESSING SEVERITY OF INJURY

Several scoring systems have been developed for triage and classification of patients both in the field and at the receiving hospital. Champion and co-workers[10] have classified the scoring systems into physiologic and anatomic types. The Glasgow Coma Scale (GCS) for brain injury is perhaps the most widely accepted physiologic scale currently utilized. This scale ranges from 3 to 15, with 15 being normal. The sections, with their weighted scores, are as follows: eye movement (4 points maximum), verbal response (5 points maximum), and motor response (6 points maximum) (Table 5–3). The GCS is a part of the

TABLE 5–3

Glasgow Coma Scale

A. Eye Opening	
Spontaneous	4
To voice	3
To pain	2
None	1
B. Verbal Response	
Oriented	5
Confused	4
Inappropriate words	3
Incomprehensible sounds	2
None	1
C. Motor Response	
Obeys commands	6
Localized pain	5
Withdraw to pain	4
Flexion to pain	3
Extension to pain	2
None	1
Total GCS Points (A + B + C)	3–15

Adapted from Teasdale, G.; Jennett, B. Assessment of coma and impaired consciousness. A practical scale. Lancet 2:81–84, © by The Lancet Ltd, 1974.

TABLE 5–4

Revised Trauma Score

	Variables	Score
A. Respiratory rate (breaths/min)	10–29	4
	>29	3
	6–9	2
	1–5	1
	0	0
B. Systolic blood pressure (mm Hg)	>89	4
	76–89	3
	50–75	2
	1–49	1
	0	0
C. Glasgow Coma Scale score conversion	13–15	4
	9–12	3
	6–8	2
	4–5	1
	3	0

Revised Trauma Score = Total of A + B + C

Adapted from Champion, H.R.; Sacco, W.J.; Copes, W.S.; et al. A revision of the Trauma Score. J Trauma 29:623–629, 1989.

Revised Trauma Score, from which one can make inferences regarding patients' outcomes. The Revised Trauma Score comprises the GCS score, the systolic blood pressure, and the respiratory rate (Table 5–4).[10]

HOSPITAL RESUSCITATION

When the trauma patient has reached the trauma center, resuscitation is continued while following the principles of a primary, secondary, and tertiary survey as established by the American College of Surgeons Committee on Trauma. The primary survey encompasses the "ABCs" (airway, breathing, and circulation), disability, and exposure. The secondary survey involves a head-to-toe evaluation of the patient's injuries and implementation of appropriate interventions. The tertiary survey involves serial reevaluation of the patient's status during his or her hospital course. This section reviews the process of trauma resuscitation and diagnostic modalities and treatment options for specific injuries.

PRIMARY SURVEY

Airway

The first objective is to evaluate, manage, and secure the airway. Inspection of the airway for foreign bodies such as broken teeth, foodstuff, emesis, and clotted blood is essential before placing an artificial airway. In all basic life support courses, the emphasis on chin lift and jaw thrust cannot be overemphasized as the initial treatment.[33] This simple maneuver moves the tongue away from the back of the throat and in many instances reestablishes a patent airway. At this point an oral airway may have to be placed.

It is a semicircular plastic device that is placed into the oral pharynx in such a fashion as to prevent the tongue from occluding the oropharynx. Appropriate size selection is essential to prevent the complication of airway obstruction. The nasopharyngeal airway is a device that is placed through the nasal passage into the back of the oropharynx to prevent the tongue from occluding the airway. It is lubricated before placement to facilitate its passage.

When this maneuver has been performed, the airway may have to be definitively controlled in patients who are unresponsive or have an altered mental status (GCS score < 8), are hemodynamically unstable, or have multiple injuries including the head and neck. Of utmost importance is cervical spine protection while obtaining the optimal airway with in-line stabilization. This maneuver prevents iatrogenic injuries to the spine or spinal cord during the process of definitive airway control.

At the advanced level of training, definitive airway management is accomplished with either endotracheal or nasotracheal intubation. For nasotracheal intubation to be possible, the patient must have spontaneous respirations and be responsive. The tube is advanced while auscultating with one's ear over the opening of the tube. When the tip of the tube is at the vocal cords, the passage of air across the tube provides a characteristic sound. The tube is then advanced into the larynx and trachea. The use of topical anesthetics and sedation may be needed for success. The gold standard of endotracheal intubation can be performed in a breathing patient with the use of sedation. An awake and combative patient may require sedation and paralytic agents. These approaches are the most definitive nonsurgical options for securing an airway.

In the rare instance in which an airway cannot be obtained by the preceding methods, a surgical airway may have to be created.[23] The standard adult surgical airway procedure in the field is cricothyroidotomy (Fig. 5–1). This surgical airway procedure requires a vertical incision to be made in the skin over the cricothyroid membrane, followed by a transverse incision into the trachea through this membrane. An endotracheal or tracheostomy tube is then placed into the trachea and secured to provide ventilation.

A needle cricothyroidotomy may be performed in some instances with positive-pressure ventilation as a bridge to the definitive surgical airway. This procedure involves placing a large angiocatheter (14 gauge) through the cricothyroid membrane and ventilating with pressurized oxygen at 30 to 60 pounds per square inch. The procedure provides oxygenation but is inadequate for the treatment of hypercarbia if used for more than 45 minutes. Needle cricothyroidotomy is appropriate for children, but cricothyroidotomy is not because of anatomic limitations of the trachea.

When the airway is secured, supplemental oxygen must be given to begin the process of providing adequate tissue oxygenation for correction of the metabolic acidosis and normalization of the pH.[22]

Breathing

A wide range of breathing devices are currently available. The use of SteriShields or more sophisticated mouth-to-mask breathing devices has introduced an element of

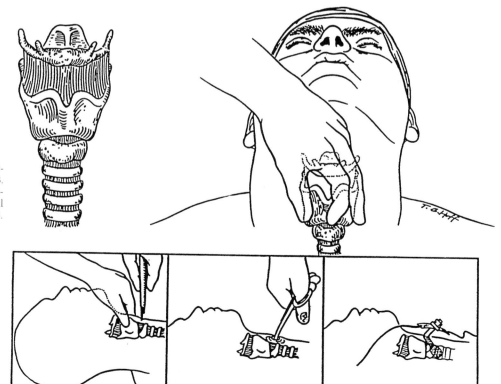

FIGURE 5–1. Technique for cricothyroidotomy. (Adapted from Bone, L.B. In: Browner, B.D.; Jupiter, J.B.; Levine, A.M.; Trafton, P.G., eds. Skeletal Trauma, 1st ed. Philadelphia, W.B. Saunders, 1992.)

safety for the resuscitator. These devices are small and are found in first-responder mobile units as a standard approach to resuscitation. Some of these devices allow supplemental oxygen to be used in the resuscitation. Resuscitation can be accomplished utilizing various ranges of oxygen concentration. Hyperoxygenation is essential for cardiopulmonary stabilization and resuscitation.

At the more advanced level, bag-valve ventilation through an endotracheal tube provides the most effective method of oxygen delivery. Another method of ventilation is the use of portable and stationary ventilators, which have the added benefit of allowing more sophisticated control of ventilatory mechanics.

After the airway has been secured, the patient's chest, neck, and breathing pattern must be assessed. Respiratory rate, depth of respiration, use of accessory muscles, presence of abdominal breathing, chest wall symmetry, and the presence of cyanosis must all be evaluated. Life-threatening injuries causing tension pneumothorax, open pneumothorax, flail chest, and massive hemothorax are identified and treated immediately.

Tension pneumothorax is diagnosed by the identification of jugular vein distention (not always present in the hypovolemic patient), tracheal deviation (toward the unaffected side), decreased breath sounds (on the affected side), hyperresonance to percussion (on the affected side), respiratory distress, hypotension, tachycardia, and cyanosis. In addition, a high level of suspicion must be present to identify this injury. Emergent treatment is lifesaving and consists of a needle thoracostomy (14-gauge needle, 2¼ inches long) at the second intercostal space, midclavicular line on the affected side. This procedure is always followed by placement of a chest tube (No. 40 French) at the fifth intercostal space, anterior to the midaxillary line (Fig. 5–2).

Open pneumothorax is initially treated with a three-sided occlusive dressing, thus preventing a tension pneumothorax, followed by chest tube placement (No. 40 French) as just described. The need for intubation and surgical closure of the defect depends on the severity of the

defect, associated injuries, ability to provide adequate oxygenation, and the patient's overall condition.

Flail chest, described as more than two consecutive rib fractures with multiple fractures in each rib resulting in a loss of chest wall integrity, results in the development of paradoxical chest wall movement and respiratory embarrassment. This condition is usually associated with underlying pulmonary contusion. Both the paradoxical chest wall movement with its resulting ventilation-perfusion mismatch and pulmonary contusion lead to hypoxia. Intubation with mechanical ventilation "splints" the flail segment and recruits alveoli, allowing more effective alveolar ventilation and more efficient oxygenation. Adequate analgesia is essential to provide comfort and facilitate aggressive pulmonary toilet whether or not the patient is intubated. In some cases, placement of chest tubes may be required to prevent development of pneumothorax if high levels of ventilator support are needed or a hemopneumothorax already exists.

Massive hemothorax, described as more than 1500 ml of blood from the affected side or more than 200 ml/hr of blood for 4 consecutive hours, requires surgical intervention.

Injuries to the tracheobronchial tree, indicated by persistent air leaks through the chest tubes, should be considered for evaluation with bronchoscopy as tracheobronchial tree injuries may require surgical intervention.

Circulation

Maintaining adequate circulation and controlling hemorrhage for the prevention or reversal of shock are of utmost importance in the resuscitation of the trauma patient. Shock is defined as a compromise in circulation resulting in inadequate oxygen delivery to meet a given tissue's oxygen demand. The most common cause of shock in the trauma patient is hypovolemia secondary to hemorrhage. The initial management of shock should include establishing two intravenous lines (16 gauge or greater), one in each antecubital fossa vein. Central access in the form of an introducer (8.5-gauge intravenous line) may be necessary for more rapid infusion of crystalloids and blood products in the unstable patient. These lines should be placed in the femoral or subclavian vein, depending on the patient's injuries. Resuscitation with 2 L of lactated Ringer's solution or normal saline solution is recommended, followed by blood if indicated.

If the patient remains unstable after the infusion of 2 L of a balanced salt solution, blood should be given.[45] The type of blood product depends in part on the urgency with which the transfusion must be given. Typed and crossmatched blood is the product of choice, but the crossmatching process may take up to an hour. Type-specific blood is the second choice, but it takes approximately 20 minutes to perform a rapid crossmatch. Universal donor blood, O positive or O negative (for female patients of childbearing years), is usually well tolerated when given to trauma victims in severe shock. Autotransfusion has also been utilized in the trauma setting but requires special equipment. This equipment should be assembled before the initiation of resuscitation.

Figure 5–2. Technique for chest tube thoracotomy. (Adapted from Bone, L.B. In: Browner, B.D.; Jupiter, J.B.; Levine, A.M.; Trafton, P.G., eds. Skeletal Trauma, 1st ed. Philadelphia, W.B. Saunders, 1992.)

There is continuing research in the area of blood substitutes. Early investigations with perfluorocarbon derivatives have failed to show superiority to balanced salt solutions. Preclinical investigations have shown stroma-free hemoglobin derived from outdated red blood cells in either cross-linked or liposome-bound forms produce oxygen dissociation curves similar to those produced by red blood cells.[9]

In the trauma patient, hemorrhage or hypovolemia is the most common cause of shock.[22] Hemorrhagic shock has been classified as follows[2]:

- Class I hemorrhage: loss of 15% of blood volume, or up to 750 ml; clinical symptoms are minimal, and blood volume is restored by various intrinsic mechanisms within 24 hours.
- Class II hemorrhage: loss of 15% to 30% of blood volume, or 750 to 1500 ml; tachycardia; tachypnea; decrease in pulse pressure; mild mental status changes.
- Class III hemorrhage: 30% to 40% blood loss, or 1500 to 2000 ml; significant tachycardia, tachypnea, mental status changes, and decrease in systolic blood pressure.
- Class IV hemorrhage: more than 40% blood loss, or greater than 2000 ml; severe tachycardia; decreased pulse pressure; obtundation; or coma.

Patients who have sustained minimal blood loss (<20%) require a minimal volume of fluid to stabilize their blood pressure. A 20% to 30% blood loss requires at least 2 L of a balanced salt solution, but blood may not be required. Blood loss greater than 30% usually requires blood for stabilization.[47] Patients who become stable initially but then become hemodynamically unstable usually have ongoing bleeding and require further investigation or operative intervention, or both.

Patients who are identified as having ongoing hemorrhage are treated with direct pressure and elevation if applicable. Hemorrhage can be obvious and external or contained in body cavities (chest, abdomen, retroperitoneum, or pelvis) or surrounding a fractured bone. Radiographs of the chest and pelvis can quickly rule out these areas as a source of hemorrhage. Hemothorax is managed as previously described. Blood contained in the pelvis as a result of a fracture is best controlled by stabilization of the pelvis as described in detail in this textbook. This role is perhaps the only remaining one for the use of the pneumatic antishock garment. Operative stabilization in the resuscitation suite utilizing external fixators immediately returns the pelvis to its original size, which decreases the volume of the pelvis and compresses the pelvic hematoma. The resultant rise in intrapelvic pressure compresses the pelvic vasculature and stops the hemorrhage. This method is excellent for controlling pelvic venous hemorrhage but is not as effective for pelvic arterial bleeding. The use of pelvic angiography and embolization provides a method for identifying and treating arterial pelvic bleeding.[1] Other contained areas of significant bleeding occur with long bone fractures. These injuries should be managed by a splint to decrease the potential space into which hemorrhage can occur. Realignment is advantageous for viability of the extremity and

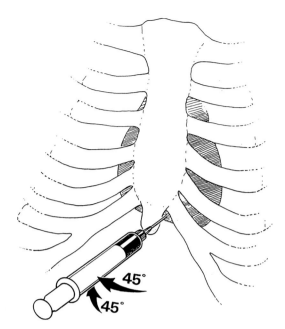

FIGURE 5–3. Pericardiocentesis. (Adapted from Ivatury, R.R. In: Feliciano, D.V.; Moore, E.E.; Mattox, K.L., eds. Trauma, 3rd ed. Stamford, CT, Appleton & Lange, 1996.)

restoring arterial circulation, as evidenced by a return of distal pulses and perfusion. Blood loss associated with intra-abdominal injuries is discussed later in the chapter.

Perhaps the most insidious and lethal of circulatory insults related to trauma is cardiac tamponade. Cardiac tamponade occurs more commonly with penetrating injuries and is rare with blunt injuries.[2] The degree of tamponade depends on the size of the defect, the rate of bleeding, and the chamber involved. As little as 60 to 100 ml of blood in the pericardial space may cause tamponade. Progression from compensated to uncompensated tamponade can be sudden and severe. A pericardial tamponade should be suspected in hypotensive patients when there is evidence of a penetrating injury in the "danger zone," which includes the precordium, epigastrium, and superior mediastinum. Beck's triad, which includes distended neck veins, quiet heart tones, and hypotension, may be present only 10% to 40% of the time. Diagnostic options for a stable patient include a two-dimensional echocardiogram or transesophageal echocardiogram. The type of injury, presence of distended neck veins, distant heart sounds, and hypotension should raise the possibility of the diagnosis of cardiac tamponade. If the patient is in shock, subxiphoid needle decompression of the pericardial space is indicated (Fig. 5–3). Removal of 10 to 50 ml of blood from the pericardial space can significantly improve the patient's survival. Pericardiocentesis may provide a stabilizing option for the unstable patient but is by no means a definitive treatment. Only providers who have received proper training and practice in a laboratory should perform this procedure.

The resuscitation of the patient in full traumatic arrest as a result of blunt trauma typically has a very poor outcome. This case must be differentiated from cases of penetration trauma with short transport to a trauma facility, in which favorable outcomes have been reported.[8]

Disability

An initial brief neurologic evaluation should be performed at the end of the primary survey to ascertain the level of consciousness and whether there is any gross neurologic deficit either centrally or in any of the four extremities. Any progression of a neurologic deficit may require an immediate therapeutic maneuver or operative procedure.[2, 45] A quick way to describe the level of consciousness is using the acronym AVPU (*a*lert, responds to *v*oice commands, responds to *p*ain, *u*nresponsive).[2] The GCS provides a more detailed assessment of the level of consciousness. Patients with a GCS score lower than 8 are considered to be in a coma and require airway control. A score of 9 to 12 signifies a moderate head injury, and a score of 13 to 15 is consistent with a minor head injury.[2]

The cervical spine is protected with the use of a cervical collar, and the thoracic and lumbar spine is protected with long board immobilization. Several devices are available, and preference is often dependent on the cost to the emergency medical units using them. The goal of immobilization can be successfully accomplished with most of the major manufacturers' products. Short backboards or similar devices to protect the thoracic spine during removal of the patient also provide stability to the thoracic spine. When the patient has been successfully extricated, the use of backboard support and restrictive strapping and padding provides stabilization of the entire spine during transportation. Upon arrival in the trauma suite, clinical or radiologic evaluation, or both, of the cervical, thoracic, and lumbar spine for injury must be performed.

Exposure or Environmental Control

A head-to-toe examination of the patient must be performed. All clothing should be removed from the patient to facilitate a complete examination. When this examination has been completed, the patient should be covered with a warm blanket for protection against hypothermia.[2, 27]

Patients exposed to hypothermia or hyperthermia require immediate intervention to return them to normothermia. The patient should be removed from the exposure as quickly as possible. In cold exposure, gradual rewarming is preferred to avoid the potential problem of dysrhythmias. Patients with thermal burns should have any burned clothing removed rapidly to prevent further injury from continued heat transmission. It is essential to determine the type, concentration, and pH of any contaminating agent that has had contact with the patient. The agent should be removed and the area either irrigated with water or saline or neutralized. The skin should be constantly reexamined to be sure that contamination or burning is not continuing. The patient is then covered with sterile dry dressings.

Hazardous materials create a special problem, not only for the victims but also for caregivers, especially in cases of radiation or chemical exposure. The most important step is to develop a plan before caregivers or others are exposed to such materials. Prehospital protocols established in conjunction with receiving facilities capable of handling such emergencies are necessary to protect the staff and other noninvolved patients at that facility. These protocols should be available in the "disaster manual," which should be immediately available in the emergency department. Decontamination protocols are important in the initial phase of any treatment for patients who have been exposed to toxic materials.[25]

After the trauma surgeon completes the primary survey and after life-threatening injuries have been identified and treated, he or she performs a secondary survey. In addition, placing a pulse oximeter, performing electrocardiography, and initiating blood pressure monitoring provide continuous monitoring of vital signs. Placing a nasogastric or orogastric tube, passing a Foley catheter, and obtaining chest and pelvic radiographs are then performed.

SECONDARY SURVEY

The secondary survey begins when the primary care survey is completed. It involves a complete head-to-toe evaluation, combined with definitive diagnosis and treatment of injuries. If indicated, more extensive tests such as ultrasonography, diagnostic peritoneal lavage, computed tomography (CT), angiography, and bone radiography should be performed. The basic evaluation and management of commonly incurred injuries are discussed.

Trauma to the Cranium

Closed head injury is a significant contributor to the morbidity and mortality associated with the multiple-trauma patient. It is estimated that approximately 50% of traffic fatalities involve associated head injuries.[38] The most common mechanism of injury for head trauma in adults is motor vehicle crashes, followed by falls. CT scanning is the diagnostic modality of choice.

Brain injury may be classified in terms of primary and secondary injury. Primary injury is due to the mechanical damage that occurs at the time of insult as a result of the contact between the brain and the interior of the skull or a foreign body. The brain undergoes distortion by shearing forces, which leads to tearing and stretching of axons, causing neuronal injury and destruction with resultant cerebral hemorrhage and edema.

Four categories of primary brain injury have been described.[28] First, a contusion involves injury to the brain parenchyma in the form of a coup injury, in which there is direct brain injury at the point of impact, or a contrecoup injury, in which the injury occurs at a site opposite the point of impact.[28] Clinically, the patient may be asymptomatic or may present with neurologic deficits. Diffuse axon injury is caused by damage to the white matter, resulting in clinical sequelae ranging from confusion to complete coma.[28] A foreign object, such as with a gunshot injury, directly destroys brain parenchyma. Finally, skull fractures occur when a force has been applied to the cranium that resulted in disruption of the continuity of the cranial bones. This disruption may or may not be associated with underlying brain injury or neurologic deficits, or both. Associated periorbital hematoma, or "raccoon eyes," indicates an anterior cranial fossa injury. The presence of cerebrospinal fluid in the external auditory canal (otorrhea) or nasal canal (rhinorrhea) is usually indicative of a basilar skull fracture or middle cranial fossa injury. A mastoid hematoma, or Battle's sign, indicates an injury to the posterior cranial fossa.

Secondary brain injury with continuing neural damage is caused by cerebral hypoxia, hypocapnia and hypercapnia, increased intracerebral pressure, decreased cerebral blood flow, hyperthermia, and electrolyte and acid-base abnormalities.[11] Interventions are geared toward preventing or lessening the neurologic destruction by optimizing cerebral perfusion and oxygenation. Acid-base balance and electrolytes should also be evaluated and corrected. Failure to do so may result in significant morbidity or even death.

Intracranial hematomas also cause secondary brain damage and are classified as epidural, subdural, or intracerebral. Epidural hematomas usually result from injury of the middle meningeal artery and appear on CT scans in a characteristic lentiform or lens shape. Patients may have a classical lucid period followed by an alteration in mental status. Subdural hematomas occur as a result of injury to arteries, veins, or parenchyma of the cerebral cortex. This type of hematoma is more common and may cause greater morbidity than epidural hematomas because of the associated cerebral contusions.[28] Causes of intracerebral hematomas include penetrating injuries, depressed skull fractures, and shearing forces sufficient to tear the brain parenchyma. The hematoma and accompanying cerebral edema can cause a mass that results in a shift of the cerebrum and herniation.

Early evacuation of an intracranial hematoma has been associated with an improved outcome.[28] The extent of the procedure depends on the type and severity of the injury. Subdural hematomas require a large craniotomy to permit adequate evacuation. Epidural hematomas may be evacuated through a more limited craniotomy. Guidelines for the management of severe head injury are outlined more specifically by Chestnut.[12]

Neck Trauma

Penetrating neck injuries account for up to 11% of mortalities. To aid in the diagnosis and treatment of neck injuries, the neck can be divided into three zones, referred to as Monson's divisions (Fig. 5–4). Zone I is inferior to the cricoid cartilage. Zone II extends from the cricoid cartilage to the angle of the jaw. Zone III is located between the angle of the mandible and the base of the skull. These anatomic regions become important in the evaluation and treatment of neck injuries. Vascular injuries in zones I and III pose difficult technical surgical challenges when trying to obtain proximal and distal control. It is essential to delineate the vascular structures by angiogra-

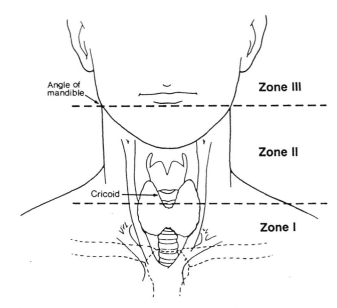

FIGURE 5–4. Monson's anatomic zones for penetrating injury to the neck. (Adapted from Thal, E.R. In: Feliciano, D.V.; Moore, E.E.; Mattox, K.L., eds. Trauma, 3rd ed. Stamford, CT, Appleton & Lange, 1996.)

phy. Zone II vascular structures are more easily accessible and can be evaluated by angiography or by direct surgical exploration.[5]

Blunt injuries to the cervical spine (and thoracic and lumbar spine) resulting in neurologic symptoms should be stabilized and then treated with high-dose steroids.[7] Prompt involvement of neurosurgery and orthopaedics assists with early definitive stabilization. Clearance of the cervical spine after injury is outlined by the Eastern Association for the Surgery of Trauma.[37]

Patients with suspected airway injuries who present with hoarseness, hemoptysis, crepitation, dysphonia, or airway obstruction may have the diagnosis confirmed with laryngoscopy. For patients with suspected esophageal injuries, the combination of esophagography and rigid esophagoscopy in the operating room has proved to be effective in confirming the presence or absence of an injury.[5, 48] An alternative method for evaluation of these injuries has been described by Demetriades and co-workers.[15] In patients with no immediate need for surgery for vascular, respiratory, or digestive tract injuries, the efficacious use of physical examination, color flow Doppler examination, esophagography, and esophagoscopy has been effective.[15]

There are several indications for performing a formal neck exploration in patients with injuries penetrating the platysma. Vascular indications include substantial blood loss; persistent bleeding; and pulsatile, expanding hematoma. Respiratory indications include hemoptysis, crepitus, and dysphonia. Digestive indications include hematemesis, dysphagia, and crepitus, and nervous system indications include neurologic defects.[28]

Vascular injuries may be primarily repaired or may require use of an interposition graft if there is significant vessel wall injury. Injuries to the trachea are usually treated by protecting the airway with an endotracheal tube or may require a surgical airway. Definitive treatment of tracheal injuries may require primary repair or resection, depending on the extent of injury. Esophageal injuries of the neck should be primarily repaired, and adequate closed suction drainage is essential.

Thoracic Trauma

Serious injuries to the thorax result in significant morbidity and mortality.[30] Injuries to the respiratory, vascular, and digestive systems must be ruled out in patients with blunt and penetrating injuries to the thorax. Injuries that require immediate lifesaving therapeutic intervention include tension pneumothorax, open pneumothorax, flail chest, massive hemothorax, and pericardial tamponade as previously described.[2] The use of CT, bronchoscopy, angiography, and esophagoscopy or esophagography further delineates injured structures.

Definitive treatment is performed in the operating room. Known tracheal, cardiac, and great vessel injuries may be managed through a median sternotomy, but this approach does not allow access to the descending aorta and the esophagus. Another incision that can be rapidly performed in an emergency situation is a left anterolateral thoracotomy through the fifth intercostal space (Fig. 5–5). This incision provides access to the heart, left lung, esophagus, and aorta. To gain additional access, the incision may be extended across the sternum. Exposure to the distal esophagus and right lung may be performed through a right lateral thoracotomy.

Injuries to the trachea may be primarily repaired or, if needed, resected and a primary anastomosis performed. Care must be taken not to compromise the vascular supply. Distal pulmonary parenchyma injuries are usually treated effectively with a tube thoracostomy but may require

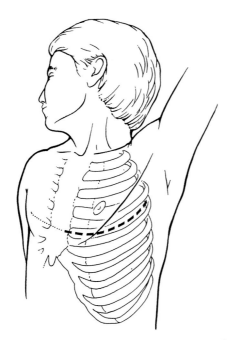

FIGURE 5–5. Anterolateral thoracotomy or emergency room thoracotomy. (Adapted from Ivatury, R.R. In: Feliciano, D.V.; Moore, E.E.; Mattox, K.L., eds. Trauma, 3rd ed. Stamford, CT, Appleton & Lange, 1996.)

primary repair, wedge resection, or, in extreme cases, pneumonectomy. Bronchial injuries may be primarily repaired or, if needed, resected and a primary anastomosis performed.

Great vessel injuries are usually repaired primarily or, if significant vessel wall destruction is present, may require placement of an interposition graft. In the management of these injuries, as with all vascular injuries, it is essential to obtain proximal and distal control of the vessel before starting the repair. Cardiac injuries are repaired primarily with pledgeted sutures. Hemorrhage may be controlled with direct pressure or a Foley catheter using the balloon to tamponade the cardiac wound.

Injuries to the esophagus should be diagnosed as previously described in the section on neck injuries. Trauma to the esophagus should be primarily repaired and covered with pleura, stomach, or an intercostal muscle flap. A drain is placed to limit abscess development. Repair should be performed as soon as possible. If there is a delay in making the diagnosis, surgical débridement, drainage of the injured area with diversion, and esophageal exclusion may be indicated. In either case, broad-spectrum antibiotics should be provided.

Abdominal Trauma

Intra-abdominal injury should be suspected in any victim of a high-speed motor vehicle crash, fall from a significant height, or penetrating injury to the trunk. Up to 20% of patients with hemoperitoneum may not manifest peritoneal signs.[2] The major goal during trauma resuscitation is not to diagnose a specific intra-abdominal injury but to confirm the presence of an injury. The diagnosis of abdominal injury should begin with the physical examination during the secondary survey. This survey should include inspection, auscultation, percussion, and palpation. A rectal examination and examination of the genitalia should also be performed. It is recommended that a nasogastric tube and Foley catheter be placed to aid in diagnosing an esophagogastric or urinary tract injury.

Patients with penetrating injuries to the trunk, especially from gunshot wounds, and trauma patients with obvious peritoneal signs (rebound tenderness, involuntary guarding), presence of a foreign body, hemodynamic instability, and evisceration of omentum or bowel should undergo exploratory laparotomy because of the high likelihood of intra-abdominal injury. Victims of blunt trauma, stable victims with stab wounds, patients with an equivocal abdominal examination because of central nervous system impairment, and multiply injured patients require further diagnostic evaluation. Diagnostic options include abdominal ultrasonography, abdominal or pelvic CT scanning, diagnostic peritoneal lavage (DPL), angiography, and diagnostic laparoscopy. An extensive diagnostic evaluation should be omitted in cases in which there are clear indications for celiotomy.

The focused abdominal sonogram for trauma (FAST) has gained popularity in the United States and has been in use in Europe for many years. It has been demonstrated to have a sensitivity of 93.4%, a specificity of 98.7%, and an accuracy of 97.5% when used by trauma surgeons to detect hemoperitoneum and visceral injury.[41] The FAST ultrasound machine may be kept in the trauma suite to assist with obtaining results rapidly for unstable patients. It is as accurate as DPL and CT in detecting hemoperitoneum but not as helpful as CT in the evaluation of solid organ or retroperitoneal injuries. Four basic areas are evaluated. The Morison's pouch view allows evaluation of the right upper quadrant, liver, and kidney. The subcostal view allows evaluation of the heart and pericardium. The splenorenal view allows evaluation of the left upper quadrant, spleen, and kidney. The pouch of Douglas view allows evaluation of the bladder and pelvis.

CT scanning of the abdomen and pelvis provides the ability to evaluate for intraperitoneal and retroperitoneal injuries as well as injuries associated with the lower thorax, vertebral column, pelvis, and genitourinary system. CT has a sensitivity of 93% to 98%, specificity of 75% to 100%, and accuracy of 95% to 97%. Its major drawback is the low sensitivity for identifying intraperitoneal bowel injuries.[31] A CT scan is indicated for stable patients with no indications for immediate abdominal exploration. The major disadvantage of CT is the need to transport the patient from the trauma suite to the CT scan room; thus, it should be performed only in hemodynamically stable patients.

Diagnostic peritoneal lavage is currently indicated for patients who are hemodynamically unstable or have multiple injuries. The DPL has a sensitivity of 98% to 100%, specificity of 90% to 96%, and accuracy of 98% to 100%.[31] It is also useful in the evaluation of intraperitoneal solid and hollow viscous injury.[17] The procedure may be performed in one of three ways: open, semiopen, or closed. Details of this procedure may be found in the American College of Surgeons' *Advanced Trauma Life Support* manual. Positive DPL results include more than 10 ml of gross blood on initial aspiration, a cell count of more than 100,000 red blood cells or more than 500 white blood cells, or evidence of enteric contents after removal of warmed crystalloid previously instilled for the procedure.

Angiography can be both diagnostic and therapeutic. Diagnostic angiography is useful in detecting injury, defining the precise site of injury, evaluating the patency of the vessel, and assessing collateral flow.[43] There are four categories of vascular insults from trauma that can be treated angiographically. These include therapeutic embolization or stent-graft placement for arterial disruptions, pseudoaneurysms, and arteriovenous fistulas as well as retrieval of embolized foreign objects.[43] Transcatheter embolization has been reported to be successful in 85% to 87% of cases.[26, 36, 42] Indications for angiography in patients with pelvic fractures include transfusion of more than 4 units of packed red blood cells in a 24-hour period, a negative DPL result in an unstable patient, or a large retroperitoneal hematoma.[43] Angiography has also been used to diagnose and embolize active bleeding in the liver[13] and spleen[21] with significant success.

Diagnostic laparoscopy is useful in evaluating the presence of a penetrating injury of the peritoneum and has utility in evaluating the diaphragm for injury.[49] It offers no advantage over DPL or CT for the diagnosis of other intra-abdominal injuries.

Injuries to the spleen may be treated with a wide range of therapeutic interventions ranging from simple direct pressure to extensive resection and removal. Liver injuries are more challenging to manage intraoperatively, and the use of angiography and embolization shows significant benefit in management of high-grade liver injuries. Simple injuries to the bowel may be oversewn. If there are multiple wounds or if they involve more than 50% of the circumference of the bowel, these areas should be resected. Proximal diverting ostomies may be needed to protect the site of repair.

Retroperitoneal Injuries

The duodenum, pancreas, parts of the colon, great vessels, and urinary system are retroperitoneal structures. Injuries to these organs can be missed by physical examination, FAST, and DPL but may be diagnosed with CT scanning of the abdomen and pelvis.

Three fourths of duodenal injuries are due to penetrating injuries, whereas the majority of pancreatic injuries are due to blunt trauma. Injuries to both organs may be diagnosed with a CT scan of the abdomen. DPL with amylase determinations is nonspecific but can contribute to an increased level of suspicion that there may be an injury to one of these organs. In addition, endoscopic retrograde cholangiopancreatography is useful for evaluating the pancreatic duct for disruption.[14] Treatment of duodenal injuries varies depending on the extent and location of the injury. The procedures range from simple primary repair to bypass and pyloric exclusion of the severely injured duodenum. Injuries to the proximal pancreas require wide closed suction drainage, and distal injuries may warrant resection with wide drainage. Significant injury to the duodenum and pancreas may require a pancreaticoduodenectomy.

Management of retroperitoneal hematomas is somewhat controversial, and these hematomas are associated with morbidity and mortality rates of up to 59% and 39%, respectively.[20] The majority of retroperitoneal hematomas are due to blunt trauma, and the most common blunt injury leading to a retroperitoneal hematoma is a pelvic fracture.

When considering management options, one must separate the nature of the injury into blunt and penetrating causes of retroperitoneal hematoma. For retroperitoneal hematomas with blunt causes in hemodynamically stable patients with no other cause for exploratory celiotomy, treatment is conservative. A massive or rapidly expanding hematoma on a CT scan may require an arteriogram of the abdomen and pelvis with concomitant vessel embolization. When exploratory celiotomy is warranted, decision making is centered on anatomic considerations based on zones, of which there are three (Fig. 5–6).

Zone I extends from the diaphragm to the sacral promontory. The aorta, vena cava, proximal renal vessels, portal vein, pancreas, and duodenum are located in this area. In general, a retroperitoneal hematoma in this area should be explored in both blunt and penetrating injuries. Proximal and distal control of the vessels to be explored must always be accomplished before entering the hematoma or attempting to repair an injured vessel.

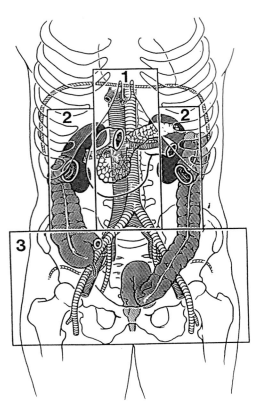

FIGURE 5–6. Anatomic zones for retroperitoneal hematomas. (Adapted from Meyer, A.A.; Kudsk, K.A.; Sheldon, G.F. In: Blaisdell, F.W., Trunkey, D.D., eds. Abdominal Trauma, 2nd ed. New York, Thieme Medical Publishers, 1993.)

Zone II includes the right and left flanks and contains the kidneys and suprapelvic ureters bilaterally and the left colon and mesocolon on the left. Retroperitoneal hematomas in zone II usually do not require exploration when they result from blunt trauma unless there is a colon injury or an expanding hematoma involving Gerota's fascia or a urinoma. Penetrating injuries should be explored.

Zone III is the pelvis and contains the sigmoid colon, rectum, bladder, and distal pelvic segment of the ureters. Hematomas in this area are usually not explored in bluntly injured patients. Those that increase in size warrant angiography and embolization of bleeding vessels. The zone III hematomas associated with pelvic fractures and hemodynamic instability may require reduction and fixation to control the bleeding. Nonexpanding hematomas are observed. Hematomas resulting from penetrating injuries are explored when proximal and distal vascular control has been obtained.

Genitourinary Injuries

Hematuria in the setting of significant blunt abdominal trauma, penetrating trauma, or pelvic fractures should signal that there might be significant injury to the genitourinary tract. Placement of a Foley catheter is important during the initial resuscitation of the trauma patient. Before placing the Foley catheter, a digital rectal examination and quick visual inspection of the urethra meatus, scrotum, or labia should be performed. Blood at the urethra meatus and scrotal or labial hematomas may be indicative of a pelvic fracture or urethra injury, or both. In this case, a retrograde urethrogram must be obtained before Foley catheter placement to rule out a urethra injury.

Further evaluation of significant hematuria may include a cystogram with filling, voiding, and postvoiding radiographs; CT scans of the abdomen and pelvis with intravenous contrast; or an intravenous pyelogram. A penetrating injury to the abdomen may warrant a "one-shot" intravenous pyelogram in the setting of hematuria to help evaluate renal excretory function and investigate the presence of a ureteral injury.

The majority of blunt injuries to the genitourinary tract do not require surgical intervention. If significant disruption of the renal parenchyma, ureter, bladder, or urethra is identified, definitive treatment is warranted. Depending on the extent of the injury, treatment may range from primary repair to resection of the injured area and adequate closed suction drainage.

Musculoskeletal Injuries

Management of specific bone injuries is addressed in detail in this textbook. Fractures with significant displacement may be associated with significant soft tissue injury. For example, patients with rib, scapular, clavicular, or sternal fractures may have great vessel or cardiac injuries that require angiography or echocardiography and possibly operative intervention. Fractures of the axial skeleton may be associated with neurologic, vascular, or visceral injuries that take priority in the management scenario for a patient. Pelvic fractures and long bone fractures may be associated with vascular injuries that result in hemorrhagic shock.

Early reduction and fixation contribute significantly to hemodynamic stabilization of the patient. This stabilization results in significant improvement in the patient's overall pulmonary status, rehabilitation, hospital course, and length of stay. With any fracture of an extremity in a trauma patient, there must be an awareness of the possibility of a compartment syndrome or vascular injury that may result in limb ischemia. Expeditious diagnosis and treatment of concomitant injuries may avert a potentially catastrophic result.

TERTIARY SURVEY

The tertiary survey consists of a repeated head-to-toe evaluation of the trauma patient along with reevaluation of available laboratory data and review of radiographic studies. Any change in the patient's condition must be promptly evaluated and treated. The most expeditious method to accomplish this sometimes overwhelming task is to begin with the ABCs of the primary survey followed by the secondary survey. Any newly discovered physical findings are investigated further. Injuries often missed during earlier assessments include minor fractures, lacerations, and traumatic brain injury. Emphasis on repeated physical examinations and evaluation of newly obtained laboratory and radiology data contributes positively to the patient's outcome.

SUMMARY

Successful resuscitation and treatment of the multiple-injured patient require a carefully systematic, thorough approach. Special priority has to be given to addressing injuries that are life-threatening. When the primary survey has been completed and lifesaving interventions have been initiated, a secondary survey that is designed to identify all injuries has to be performed rapidly. An appropriate management plan can be developed and implemented rapidly so that no injuries are missed. Finally, a tertiary survey should be performed to detect any latent problems that arise hours after the patient has been admitted to the hospital. A comprehensive, careful approach to management results in the best possible outcome for the severely injured patient.

REFERENCES

1. Agolini, S.F.; Shah, K.; Jaffe, J.; et al. Arterial embolization is a rapid and effective technique for controlling pelvic fracture hemorrhage. J Trauma 43:395, 1997.
2. American College of Surgeons Committee on Trauma. Advanced Trauma Life Support. Chicago, American College of Surgeons, 1997.
3. American College of Surgeons Committee on Trauma. Major Outcome Study. Chicago, American College of Surgeons, 1993.
4. American College of Surgeons Committee on Trauma. Resources for Optimal Care of the Injured Patient: 1993. Chicago, American College of Surgeons, 1993.
5. Asensio, J.A. Management of penetrating neck injuries: The controversy surrounding zone II injuries. Surg Clin North Am 71:267, 1991.
6. Baker, C.C.; Oppenheimer, L.; Stephens, B.; et al. Epidemiology of trauma deaths. Am J Surg 140:144, 1980.
7. Bracken, M.B.; Shepard, M.J.; Holford, T.R.; et al. Administration of methylprednisolone for 24 or 48 hours or tirilazad mesylate for 48 hours in the treatment of acute spinal cord injury: Results of the third national acute spinal cord injury randomized controlled trial. JAMA 227:1597, 1997.
8. Branney, S.W.; Moore, E.E.; Feldhaus, K.M.; Wolfe, R.E. Critical analysis of two decades of experience with postinjury emergency department thoracotomy in a regional trauma center. J Trauma 45:87; discussion 45:94, 1998.
9. Carrico, C.J.; Mileski, W.J.; Kaplan, H.S. Transfusion, autotransfusion, and blood substitutes. In: Feliciano, D.V.; Moore, E.E.; Mattox, K.L., eds. Trauma, 3rd ed. Stamford, CT, Appleton & Lange, 1996, p. 181.
10. Champion, H.R.; Sacco, W.J.; Copes, W.S. Trauma scoring. In: Feliciano, D.V.; Moore, E.E.; Mattox, K.L., eds. Trauma, 3rd ed. Stamford, CT, Appleton & Lange, 1996, p. 53.
11. Chestnut, R.M. Secondary brain insults after head injury: Clinical perspectives. New Horiz 3:366, 1995.
12. Chestnut, R.M. Guidelines for the management of severe head injury: What we know and what we think we know. J Trauma 42(5 suppl): S19, 1997.
13. Ciraulo, D.L.; Luk, S.; Palter, M.; et al. Selective hepatic arterial embolization of grade IV and V blunt hepatic injuries: An extension of resuscitation in the non-operative management of traumatic hepatic injuries. J Trauma 42:353, 1998.
14. Clements, R.H.; Reisser, J.F. Urgent endoscopic retrograde pancreatography in the stable trauma patient. Am Surg 62:446, 1996.
15. Demetriades, D.; Theodorou, D.; Cornwell, E.; et al. Evaluation of penetrating injuries of the neck: Prospective study of 223 patients. World J Surg 21:41,1997.
16. Demetriades, D.; Berne, T.V.; Belzberg, H.; et al. The impact of a dedicated trauma program on outcome in severely injured patients. Arch Surg 130:216, 1995.
17. Fabian, T.C.; Croce, M.A. Abdominal trauma, including indications for celiotomy. In: Feliciano, D.V.; Moore, E.E.; Mattox, K.L., eds. Trauma, 3rd ed. Stamford, CT, Appleton & Lange, 1996, p. 441.
18. Fingerhut, L.A.; Warner, M.I. Injury Chartbook. Health, United States, 1996–97. Hyattsville, MD, National Center for Health Statistics, 1997.
19. Franklin, J.; Doelp, A. Shock Trauma. New York, St. Martins Press, 1980.
20. Goins, W.A.; Rodriguez, A.; Lewis, J.; et al. Retroperitoneal hematoma after blunt trauma. Surg Gynecol Obstet 174:281, 1992.
21. Hagiwara, A.; Yukioka, T.; Ohta, S.; et al. Nonsurgical management of patients with blunt splenic injury: Efficacy of transcatheter arterial embolization. AJR 167:159, 1996.
22. Halvorsen, L.; Holcroft, J.W. Resuscitation. In: Blaisdell, F.W., ed. Abdominal Trauma, 2nd ed. New York, Thieme, 1993, p. 13.
23. Isaacs, J.H., Jr.; Pedersen, A.D. Emergency cricothyroidotomy. Am Surg 63:346, 1997.
24. Jacobs, B.B.; Jacobs, L.M. Injury epidemiology. In: Moore, E.E.; Mattox, K.L.; Feliciano, D.V.; et al., eds. Trauma, 2nd ed. Norwalk, CT, Appleton & Lange, 1991, p. 15.
25. Jacobs, B.B.; Jacobs, L.M. Emergency medicine: A comprehensive review. In: Kravis, T.C.; Warner, C.G.; Jacobs, L.M., eds. Prehospital Emergency Medical Services. New York, Raven Press, 1993, p. 1.
26. Jander, H.P.; Russinovich, N.A.E. Transcatheter Gelfoam embolization in abdominal, retroperitoneal, and pelvic hemorrhage. Radiology 136:337, 1980.
27. Krantz, B.E. Initial assessment. In: Feliciano, D.V.; Moore, E.E.; Mattox, K.L., eds. Trauma, 3rd ed. Stamford, CT, Appleton & Lange, 1996, p. 123.
28. Kreiger, A.J. Emergency management of head injuries. Surg Rounds February:57, 1984.
29. MacKenzie, E.J.; Fowler, C.J. Epidemiology. In: Mattox, K.L; Feliciano, D.V.; Moore, E.E., eds. Trauma, 4th Emergency Department. New York, McGraw-Hill, 2000, p. 21.
30. Mattox, K.L.; Wall, M.J.; Pickard, L.R.; et al. Thoracic trauma: General considerations and indications for thoracotomy. In: Feliciano, D.V.; Moore, E.E.; Mattox, K.L., eds. Trauma, 3rd ed. Stamford, CT, Appleton & Lange, 1996, p. 345.
31. Mendez, C.; Jurkovich, G.J. Blunt abdominal trauma. In: Cameron, J.L. Current Surgical Therapy, 6th ed. St. Louis, Mosby, 1998, p. 928.
32. Miller, T.R.; Levy, D.T. The effect of regional trauma care systems on costs. Arch Surg 130:188, 1995.
33. Mulder, D.S. Airway management. In: Feliciano, D.V.; Moore, E.E.; Mattox, K.L., eds. Trauma, 3rd ed. Stamford, CT, Appleton & Lange, 1996, p. 141.
34. National Center for Health Statistics. Injury and Poisoning Episodes and Conditions: National Health Interview Survey. Series 10, No. 202. National Center for Health Statistics, Hyattsville, MD, 1997, p. 46.
35. National Committee for Injury Prevention and Control. Injury Prevention: Meeting the Challenge. Oxford, Oxford University Press, 1989.
36. Panetta, T.; Scalifani, S.J.A.; Goldstein, A.S.; et al. Percutaneous transcatheter embolization for arterial trauma. J Vasc Surg 2:54, 1985.
37. Pasquale, M; Fabian, T.C. Trauma center: Practice management guidelines for trauma from the Eastern Association for the Surgery of Trauma. The EAST Ad Hoc Committee on Practice Management Guideline Development. J Trauma 44:941, 1998.
38. Pitts, L.H.; Martin, N. Head injuries. Surg Clin North Am 62:47, 1982.
39. Rauzz, A.I. The Maryland emergency medical services system. An update. Md Med J 37:517, 1988.
40. Robertson, L. Injury Epidemiology. New York, Oxford University Press, 1992.
41. Rozycki, G.S.; Shackford, S.R. Ultrasound, what every trauma surgeon should know. J Trauma 40:1, 1996.
42. Scalifani, S.J.A.; Cooper, R.; Shaftan, G.W.; et al. Arterial trauma: Diagnostic and therapeutic angiography. Radiology 161:165, 1986.
43. Schwarcz, T.H. Therapeutic angiography in the management of vascular trauma. In: Flanigan, D.P., ed. Civilian Vascular Trauma. Philadelphia, Lea & Febiger, 1992, p. 336.

44. Shackford, S.R.; Mackensie, R.C.; Hoyt, D.B.; et al. Impact of a trauma system on outcome of a severely injured patient. Arch Surg 1221:523, 1987.

45. Shires, G.T., III. Trauma. In: Schwartz, S.I.; Shires, G.T.; Spencer, F.C., eds. Principles of Surgery, 6th ed. New York, McGraw-Hill, 1994, p. 175.

46. Trunkey, D.D.; Blaisdell, F.W. Epidemiology of Trauma, Vol. 4. New York, Scientific American, 1988–1992, p. 1.

47. Weigelt, J.A. Resuscitation and initial management. Crit Care Clin 9:657, 1993.

48. Weigelt, J.A.; Thal, E.R.; Snyder, W.H.; et al. Diagnosis of penetrating cervical esophageal injuries. Am J Surg 154:619, 1987.

49. Zantut, L.F.; Ivatury, R.R.; Smith, R.S.; et al. Diagnostic and therapeutic laparoscopy for penetrating abdominal trauma: A multi-center experience. J Trauma 42:825, 1997.

CHAPTER 6

Orthopaedic Management Decisions in the Multiple-Trauma Patient

Michael J. Bosse, M.D.
James F. Kellam, M.D., F.R.C.S.(C.)

Beginning in 1977, the authors of a series of clinical papers concluded that the aggressive management of long bone fractures had a significant positive effect on the patient, decreasing the overall morbidity and mortality.* The positive clinical reports, mostly retrospective and uncontrolled, had such a strong effect on clinical practice that definitive long bone fixation and pelvic fracture external fixation are now considered part of the initial resuscitative care effort for multiple-injured patients (MIPs).[7, 10, 45, 49] At the same time, the concept of early definitive fixation has been drastically altered from the initial recommendation of "within 2 weeks,"[46] to 48 hours,[4, 10] to the present concept of fixation within 24 hours of injury.[9, 15, 22, 29]

Early definitive fixation of major unstable fractures in MIPs has been credited with resultant reductions in mortality rates, intensive care unit (ICU) and ventilator days, incidence of adult respiratory distress syndrome (ARDS), sepsis, multiple organ dysfunction, fracture complications, length of hospital stay, and overall cost of care. Proponents claim that the stabilization of major fractures decreases the output of inflammatory mediators, reduces catecholamine release and analgesic requirements, facilitates ICU care through earlier mobilization, and is cost-effective.[8] Eleven articles are most often cited to support the claims that early definitive orthopaedic care is beneficial to the trauma patient; 10 are retrospective reviews.† None of the study designs provides adequate mechanisms to control for patient or injury variabilities, and no article credits the parallel advances in prehospital care, trauma resuscitative techniques, closed head injury management, or critical care development with the increased survival and decreased morbidity seen in our current trauma population.

Early and aggressive care of orthopaedic injuries in severely injured and unstable patients affects the patient's systemic physiology both positively and negatively. To treat this complex group of patients, the orthopaedic surgeon who engages in their care must understand the long-term goals of care and the risks and benefits of intervention and must develop a personal philosophy based on a clear understanding of the literature, injury physiology, and clinical experience. In the evaluation and care plan development for the MIP, three questions are routinely asked by the trauma team: "*Do* you need to operate?" "*When* do you need to operate?" and "*How much* surgery is required?" (Fig. 6–1).

RECOGNITION OF THE MULTIPLE-INJURED PATIENT

The orthopaedic surgeon is asked to provide fracture care to patients who fall into three broad categories: patients with isolated extremity injuries, patients with multiple orthopaedic injuries only, and physiologically unstable MIPs with orthopaedic injuries. The orthopaedic injuries are classified as life or limb threatening, emergent, urgent, or elective. On the basis of the presence and severity of other injuries, systemic physiology, and the urgency of the orthopaedic intervention, decisions are made regarding treatment and timing of treatment.

The definition of multiple trauma varies among surgeons, surgical specialties, and hospitals. A patient with bilateral ankle fractures and a both-bone forearm fracture does not meet the usual criteria for multiple-trauma inclusion. The same orthopaedic injuries in a patient with a closed head injury, a pulmonary contusion, or a splenic laceration would meet inclusion criteria.

Classification systems are used to stratify the injury patterns of trauma patients and weight the injuries in an effort to predict patients' survival, functional outcome, and resource utilization. A working knowledge of these scoring systems, the evolution of the systems, and the major weaknesses of the systems is necessary to interact with the trauma team and interpret the trauma-related literature comparing survival rates. The Abbreviated Injury Score

---

*See references 4, 9, 10, 14, 15, 23, 29, 33, 38, 45, 46, 52.
†See references 4, 9, 10, 15, 22, 29, 33, 38, 45, 46, 52.

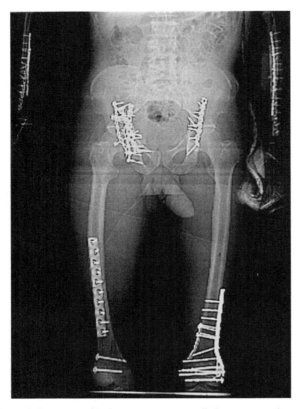

FIGURE 6–1. Victims of high-energy trauma usually have major orthopaedic injuries associated with head, chest, and abdominal trauma. Initial care of the orthopaedic injuries should enhance the patient's physiology. Many injuries are temporized until the patient is in less critical condition and better able to withstand a prolonged reconstructive procedure.

(AIS), the Injury Severity Score (ISS), the Revised Trauma Score (RTS), the Anatomic Profile (AP), and the Glasgow Coma Scale (GCS) score are the scores documented in most trauma registries and are the current "tools" facilitating trauma clinical research. The RTS and GCS score are used routinely to direct admission, triage, and transfer of acute trauma patients. The AIS, ISS, and AP are used to classify the severity of a patient's injury. The severity scores are predictive of survival and resource utilization but have been most useful in grouping patients into similar injury severity ranges to allow treatment and outcome analysis. However, there is no score that assists in decision making during the acute resuscitation phase.

Glasgow Coma Scale

The GCS assesses the patient's level of consciousness.[56] It is the sum of three responses: eye opening, verbal response, and best motor response (see Table 5–3). Patients with a GCS score of 8 or lower are in coma and are considered to have severe head injuries. Patients with GCS scores of 9 to 12 are considered to have moderate head injuries, and those with scores of 13 to 15 have a minor head injury.

Revised Trauma Score

The RTS was developed to provide a methodology to direct triage and evaluate patients' outcomes.[14] The RTS contains measurement scales for systolic blood pressure and respiratory rate separated into five domains. The domains are assigned a point value from 0 to 4. The scores for systolic blood pressure and respiratory rate are added to those allowed for the GCS to yield the RTS (see Table 5–4). The RTS ranges from 0 to 12. American College of Surgeons guidelines direct patients with an RTS of 11 or lower to trauma centers.

Abbreviated Injury Score

The AIS was developed to rate and compare injuries.[2] The AIS divides injuries into nine body sections and stratifies the injuries from minor to fatal on a six-point scale. The scores are based on the injuries' threat to life, expected permanent impairment, treatment period, and energy dissipation. The AIS scores the individual injury (Table 6–1).

Injury Severity Score

The ISS was designed to summarize the severity of multiple injuries. The ISS is the sum of the squares of the highest AIS grades in the three most severely injured ISS body regions.[3, 17] The six body regions of injuries used in ISS are head and neck, face, chest, abdominal or pelvic contents, extremities or pelvic girdle, and external. The score ranges from 1 to 75. A patient with an AIS of 6 in any region is assigned an ISS of 75. Generally, multiple-trauma patients are defined as patients with an ISS of 18 or higher.[9, 10, 29, 40] An ISS less than 30 is usually indicative of a good prognosis unless associated with a severe head injury. An ISS greater than 60 is usually fatal.

The ISS is the most frequently used injury scoring methodology but has major limitations. Because the ISS equally weights injuries in different body regions with the same AIS severity, it can underestimate the injury severity of a patient with multiple injuries in the same body region. When used as a predictor of survival, the ISS tends to overweight combined "nonlethal" injuries. A patient with an isolated severe head injury (AIS = 5, ISS = 25) receives the same score as a patient with a liver laceration (AIS = 4) and a femur fracture (AIS = 3, ISS = 25). The mortality rate, short-term and long-term complication rate, and resource use of the two patients are probably very different despite the ISS equality.

Anatomic Profile

The AP uses a four-value (ABCD) description of injuries.[16] A summary of the scores of all serious injuries to the head and neck region (A) is added to scores obtained for the thorax, abdomen, pelvic contents, and other body regions (BC) and the summary of all nonserious injuries (D). Comparison of the AP and the ISS has identified the AP as better able to discriminate between survivors and nonsurvivors because the AP places a greater weight on the head injury, followed in order by the chest, abdomen, and pelvic contents.

TABLE 6–1

Abbreviated Injury Score

Abbreviated Injury Score Examples	Score
HEAD	
Crush of head or brain	6
Brain stem contusion	5
Epidural hematoma (small)	4
FACE	
Optic nerve laceration	2
External carotid laceration (major)	3
Le Fort III fracture	3
NECK	
Crushed larynx	5
Pharynx hematoma	3
Thyroid gland contusion	1
THORAX	
Open chest wound	4
Aorta, intimal tear	4
Esophageal contusion	2
Myocardial contusion	3
Pulmonary contusion (bilateral)	4
Two or three rib fractures	2
ABDOMEN AND PELVIC CONTENTS	
Bladder perforation	4
Colon transection	4
Liver laceration >20% blood loss	3
Retroperitoneal hematoma	3
Splenic laceration—major	4
SPINE	
Incomplete brachial plexus	2
Complete spinal cord C4 or below	5
Herniated disc with radiculopathy	3
Vertebral body compress >20%	3
UPPER EXTREMITY	
Amputation	3
Elbow crush	3
Shoulder dislocation	2
Open forearm fracture	3
LOWER EXTREMITY	
Amputation	
Below knee	3
Above knee	4
Hip dislocation	2
Knee dislocation	2
Femoral shaft fracture	3
Open pelvic fracture	3
EXTERNAL	
Hypothermia 31°C–30°C	3
Electrical injury with myonecrosis	3
Second-degree to third-degree burns— 20%–29% body surface area	3

CLINICAL OBSERVATIONS: FRACTURE CARE AND THE MULTIPLE-INJURED PATIENT

Conclusions from historical clinical series used as a basis for contemporary clinical decisions must be reassessed on the basis of the outcome definitions at the time of the original research compared with more recent definitions. Definitions of ARDS and multiple organ dysfunction syndrome (MODS) have changed significantly, most importantly in regard to the duration and severity of the symptoms.[5] Sepsis, ARDS, pneumonia, and MODS are currently defined as follows:

Sepsis A diagnosis of generalized sepsis is assigned if the patient has a temperature greater than 38.5°C, a leukocytosis, and a positive bacterial blood culture.

ARDS A diagnosis of ARDS is assigned if the patient has an arterial partial pressure of oxygen/fraction of inspired oxygen (Pao_2/Fio_2) ratio less than 200 for 5 or more consecutive days,[5] bilateral diffuse infiltrates on the chest radiograph in the absence of pneumonia, and absence of cardiogenic pulmonary edema.

Pneumonia A diagnosis of pneumonia is assigned if the patient has a temperature greater than 38°C, a white blood cell count greater than 10,000, a chest radiograph with a persistent infiltrate, and a sputum Gram stain with less than 10 epithelial cells per high-power field, more than 25 white blood cells per high-power field, and organisms present on Gram staining.

MODS Risk factors for MODS (formerly known as *multiple organ failure*) in the trauma patient include multiple injuries, infection, burns, tissue ischemia from hypovolemic shock, transfusion, total parenteral nutrition, and drug reactions. The syndrome usually begins after a profound disruption of systemic homeostasis. MODS is characterized by the involvement of organs or organ systems remote from the site of the original injury. The diagnosis of MODS is assigned to a patient when the patient's condition receives a score of 4 or greater for 3 consecutive days (Table 6–2).[35]

Reports of clinical series with high ARDS, pneumonia, and sepsis rates must be carefully read to determine the criteria used to establish the diagnosis. The definition of mortality, however, has remained unchanged.

Riska and co-workers[46] were among the first authors to note a correlation of systemic outcome with the timing of surgical care. They considered early operative care to be within 2 weeks of injury and attributed the 15% to 0% reduction in the incidence of fat embolism syndrome to the increase in operative intervention on the fractures in their population of patients from 23% to 66%. In a small retrospective series, Goris and associates[23] argued that fixation within 24 hours reduced the morbidity, ARDS, and septic rates. This series included only 58 patients, who were divided into three subgroups.

Building on the "early fracture fixation–reduced mortality" concept, other authors attempted to solidify the relationship between fracture care and outcome for trauma patients. In a small injury- and age-matched retrospective

TABLE 6–2

Recognition and Assessment of Organ System Dysfunctions

Organ System	Indicators of Dysfunction	Degree of Dysfunction				
		*None (0)**	*Minimal (1)**	*Mild (2)**	*Moderate (3)**	*Severe (4)**
Respiratory	Pao$_2$/Fio$_2$ ratio	>300	226–300	151–225	76–150	≤75
		>400	300–400	200–300	100–200	<100
	Duration of mechanical ventilation	—	—	>48 hr	>72 hr	>72 hr (PEEP >10 or Fio$_2$ >0.50)
Renal	Creatinine level	≤100 μmol/L	101–200 μmol/L	201–350 μmol/L	351–500 μmol/L	>500 μmol/L
	Urine output	—	—	—	<500 ml/day	<200 ml/day
	Need for dialysis	—	—	—	—	Dialysis
Neurologic	Glasgow Coma Scale score	Glasgow Coma Scale score, 15	Glasgow Coma Scale score, 13–14	Glasgow Coma Scale score, 10–12	Glasgow Coma Scale score, 7–9	Glasgow Coma Scale score, ≤6
Hepatic	Bilirubin	≤20 μmol/L	21–60 μmol/L	61–120 μmol/L	121–240 μmol/L	>240 μmol/L
	Albumin	<20 μmol/L	20–32 μmol/L	33–101 μmol/L	162–204 μmol/L	>204 μmol/L
	AST	—		<28 mg/dl	<23 mg/dl	<19 mg/dl
			<25 U/L	—	25–50 U/L	>50 U/L
Cardiovascular	Systolic blood pressure	>90 mm Hg	71–90 mm Hg (fluid responsive)	61–70 mm Hg (not fluid responsive)	51–60 mm Hg	≤50 mm Hg
	pH	—	—	—	≤7.3	≤7.2
	Inotropic agent dosages	—	—	Dopamine <5 μg/kg/min *or* Any dose of dobutamine	Dopamine >5 μg/kg/min *or* Epinephrine <0.1 μg/kg/min *or* Norepinephrine <0.1 μg/kg/min	Dopamine >15 μg/kg/min *or* Epinephrine >0.1 μg/kg/min *or* Norepinephrine >0.1 μg/kg/min
	Heart rate (CVP/MAP)	<10.0	10.1–15.0	15.1–20.0	20.1–30.0	>30.0
Hematologic	Platelet count	>120,000/mm³	81,000–120,000/mm³	51,000–80,000/mm³	21,000–50,000/mm³	≤20,000/mm³
	Leukocyte count	—	—	—	>30,000/mm³	>60,000/mm³ *or* <2500/mm³
Gastrointestinal	Enteral nutrition	—	—	Mild intolerance	Moderate intolerance	Severe intolerance
	Stress ulcer bleeding	None	None	None	Stress bleeding	>2 U/day
Metabolic	Insulin requirements	None	None	>1 U/hr	2–4 U/hr	>4 U/hr

*Multiple organ dysfunction syndrome (MODS) score.

Abbreviations: AST, aspartate aminotransferase; CVP, central venous pressure; Fio$_2$, fraction of inspired oxygen; MAP, mean systemic arterial pressure; Pao$_2$, arterial oxygen tension; PEEP, positive end-expiratory pressure.

From Marshall, J.C.; Nathens, A.B. Multiple organ dysfunction syndrome. In: American College of Surgeons: Scientific American Surgery, Vol. 2. New York, Scientific American, 1996, p. 7.

trauma series, Meek and colleagues[38] demonstrated superior outcomes for patients in the early fracture fixation group. Johnson and co-workers[29] retrospectively reviewed 132 patients with an ISS of 18 or greater and with two major fractures, attempting to define a relationship between ARDS and the timing of fracture surgery. A fivefold incidence of ARDS was noted in patients with fracture fixation delayed beyond 24 hours, and severely injured patients had an ARDS rate of 75% when treatment was delayed compared with 17% when it was not. This study, in addition to its retrospective nature, was nonrandomized and probably biased by the fact that the unstable patients experienced surgical delays until optimized for fracture fixation. ARDS was defined as a Pao$_2$ less than 70 with an Fio$_2$ of 40% and ICU admission for 4 days with

intubation. The current definition of ARDS is much more stringent.

The only randomized prospective research on the effect of the timing of fracture fixation on subsequent outcomes was performed by Bone and associates[9]; 178 patients with femoral fractures were entered into an early fixation (<24 hours) or a delayed fixation (>48 hours) group. The incidence of pulmonary complications (ARDS, fat embolism, or pneumonia) was higher, the hospital stay was longer, and ICU requirements increased when femoral fixation was delayed in the MIP. The project, however, had flaws. The randomization process was not clearly defined, and 10 of 37 MIPs in the delayed treatment group had pulmonary parenchymal injuries, compared with only 1 of 46 in the early treatment group. Other authors[15, 44, 58, 63] have found that the pulmonary injury predisposes the patient to the development of both pneumonia and ARDS.

Bone and colleagues[10] later studied the effect of the timing of orthopaedic injuries on patients' outcomes with a retrospective multicenter study design. The outcomes of 676 patients with an ISS greater than 18 and major pelvic or long bone injury, or both, treated under an early fixation (<48 hours) protocol at six major U.S. trauma centers were compared with historical records of 906 patients obtained from the American College of Surgeons' Multiple Trauma Outcome Study (MTOS) database. The patients in the MTOS database were assumed to have been treated by a nonaggressive orthopaedic fracture protocol. The study showed that the mortality rate was significantly reduced in patients who had early fracture stabilization.

Although the findings are perhaps true, the study design significantly biases the MTOS group of patients. As the MTOS patients were historical control subjects treated in a different time frame at potentially dissimilar institutions, their increased mortality rate could be related to the overall clinical expertise of the MTOS hospital and not to the timing of the fracture fixation. In addition, the authors assumed that early fixation of fractures was not a practice in the MTOS pool of patients, essentially stating that long bone fractures in the control group were managed nonoperatively for prolonged periods of time. If this assumption is not true, the authors' conclusion could be reversed: Early fracture care at less experienced clinical centers might result in worse outcomes, possibly secondary to critical care and neurosurgical issues. Parallel advances in associated trauma subspecialty care were not investigated as possible confounders in the study design. Perhaps the effects of the evolution of trauma care—improved prehospital, resuscitative, orthopaedic, and critical care—may have combined to lower the mortality rate at the major trauma centers; the timing of the orthopaedic care might have been a less important variable in the overall care of the patients.

Rogers and co-workers[47] challenged the practice of immediate (within 24 hours) femoral fracture fixation in patients with isolated injury. In a retrospective review of 67 patients with ipsilateral femoral shaft fractures, three groups were identified: immediate fixation (within 24 hours), early fixation (24 to 72 hours), and late fixation (>72 hours). Pulmonary and infectious complications were significantly increased in the late fixation group. Operative time was longer in the immediate fixation group, when all of the cases were performed as "emergencies." When compared with the immediate fixation group, the early fixation group had significantly shorter operating times and a significant reduction in resource utilization (50% of the expense of immediate fixation), with no difference in pulmonary or infectious outcomes.

The practice of early definitive reamed intramedullary nailing for the MIP with a femur fracture and associated chest injuries was challenged by Pape and associates,[40] who found a higher ARDS rate in patients treated acutely as opposed to those whose treatment was delayed. Small numbers in the subgroups of patients (*n* = 25) and exclusion of deaths resulting from hemorrhage and closed head injury weaken the conclusions that surgery should be delayed until the patient is more stable or that alternatives

to reamed intramedullary nails should be considered for patients with femoral fractures and pulmonary injuries if the treatment is to be acute. Pape and associates theorized that embolized marrow products from the reaming initiated an inflammatory cascade in the lung that tipped the injured lung into ARDS.

Pape and associates' study was repeated, with alterations in design, at other centers. Charash and colleagues[15] noted that the overall pulmonary complication rate was 56% in a group of patients with thoracic and femoral fractures treated more than 24 hours after injury, contrasted with 16% if patients with similar injuries were treated acutely. They concluded that delayed surgical fixation was associated with a higher pulmonary complication rate independent of the presence of blunt thoracic trauma.

Ziran and colleagues[63] attempted to clarify the relationship between skeletal injuries, the timing of fracture fixation, and mortality or pulmonary morbidity in patients with and without chest injury. Their analysis of 226 patients concluded that the combination of skeletal and chest injuries does not amplify the pulmonary morbidity or mortality compared with that of patients with isolated chest injuries. The quantity of skeletal injury and the timing of fixation of structures that affected the patient's mobilization (spine, pelvic, and femur fractures), however, were found to have a significant effect on pulmonary morbidity. The authors acknowledged a major weakness in their study, in common with all prior studies on the same topic—the uncontrolled reason for surgical delays of long bone fixation in the MIP. This delay is most commonly associated with unfavorable physiologic parameters.

Bosse and co-workers[11] could not find a difference in ARDS, pneumonia, MODS, or death rates in MIPs with femur fractures and pulmonary injury treated acutely with either reamed nails or plates. The choice of the operative procedure did not appear to potentiate or lessen the risks of ARDS (<3% overall). Turchin and associates[58] examined trauma patients with pulmonary contusion with or without fractures. Outcome appeared to be related more to the presence of the pulmonary contusion than to the fracture. Not all centers subscribe to urgent long bone fixation protocols for MIPs. The timing of the surgical fixation is weighted against ongoing systemic instabilities and the severity of the patient's associated injuries. Nonlifesaving surgical procedures are delayed until the patient's condition is stabilized to a point at which operative exposure involves less risk. The patient is admitted to the surgical ICU, where abnormalities in coagulation, core temperature, hypoxia, and base deficit are corrected.[41, 44, 49]

Reynolds and colleagues[44] believed that fixation of all long bone fractures within the first 24 hours is not the primary determinant of outcome for the severely traumatized patient. In a study to assess the effect of the timing of intramedullary femoral fixation, records of 424 consecutive trauma patients were reviewed. One hundred and five of the patients had an ISS of 18 or higher. A definitive early long bone fixation protocol was not followed at the trauma center. Femur fractures were generally stabilized on the day of admission if the patient was systemically stable. Femoral fixation was typically delayed if the patient required a long resuscitative effort or had a lingering base deficit or an excess serum lactate level indicating under-resuscitation. Surgery was also delayed for patients with hypothermia; coagulopathic conditions; significant intra-pulmonary shunting; or severe head, pulmonary, or pelvic injuries. Fracture fixation was often delayed in MIPs with long bone fractures who had already experienced a significant "lifesaving" operative exposure. Surgery was usually delayed beyond 36 hours to avoid surgical procedures during the period of the patient's anticipated maximal inflammatory response to the initial trauma.

A significant rise in pulmonary complications was noted by Reynolds and colleagues[44] in patients with an ISS lower than 18 with progressive surgical delays. No relationship, however, was found between pulmonary complications and timing of femoral fixation in patients with an ISS of 18 or higher. The data suggest that the severity of the injuries, not the timing of the fracture fixation, determined the MIP's pulmonary outcome. Reynolds and colleagues found no significant difference in pulmonary morbidity related to early versus delayed femoral fixation in the MIP. The incidence of pulmonary complications was found to parallel the frequency of initial thoracic injury.

Reynolds and colleagues[44] argued that the theoretical concerns raised by supporters of immediate long bone fixation involve interpretation of data from an era when fractures were routinely treated with prolonged immobili-zation. There are no data to support fracture fixation immediately or at 12, 24, or 36 hours after injury. Patients with severe closed head injuries or major pulmonary flail segments routinely require prolonged immobilization and ventilatory support. Because of advances in surgical ICUs and the development of critical care subspecialties, these patients, who previously succumbed with multiple co-morbidities, including deep vein thrombosis, pulmonary embolism, decubitus ulcer formation, atelectasis, pneumonia, sepsis, and thrombophlebitis, are currently efficiently managed and preemptively monitored and treated to prevent these conditions. Attention to positioning of the patient, pulmonary toilet, skin care, nutritional support, and sepsis surveillance has significantly reduced the morbidity and mortality of trauma patients since the mid-1980s.

Reynolds and co-workers[44] found that clinical judgment regarding the timing of long bone fixation was the most important determinant of the patient's outcome. Delays in femoral fixation that were made to stabilize the patient or to treat associated injuries did not appear to affect the patient's outcome adversely. Pulmonary complications were found to be related to the severity of the injury, not to the timing of fracture fixation.

Boulanger and co-workers[12] were unable to detect a difference in outcomes when comparing patients with femur fractures, with and without pulmonary injury, treated by either early or late intramedullary fixation. Although the authors concluded that the study did not demonstrate an increased morbidity or mortality associated with early intramedullary nail fixation in the presence of thoracic trauma, the opposite can also be stated—neither did a delay in fracture fixation.

CLINICAL EXPERIENCE: FRACTURE AND THE HEAD-INJURED PATIENT

The trauma surgeon, the orthopaedic surgeon, and the neurosurgeon must communicate and cooperate in planning the care of a patient with brain and orthopaedic injuries. Optimal care for one subspecialty injury may be suboptimal care for the other. Clinical outcome information concerning the optimal care of the patient with a significant closed head injury and major fractures is inconclusive.* Most of the trauma literature regarding fracture and the MIP reports a limited number of variables to assess effectiveness—typically mortality, ARDS, pneumonia, infection, and fracture union rates. Although head injury severity is considered in the frontal analysis—to determine the RTS and the ISS—the outcome of the head injury in the surviving patient is rarely assessed in these studies. When the outcome of the closed head injury is reported, the nonspecific GCS is most commonly employed as the outcome measurement.

In negotiating the care sequence of the MIP with a severe head injury, orthopaedic and trauma surgeons cite the ICU care and mobilization benefits of early surgery to support more aggressive fracture care. Every orthopaedic surgeon, however, has experienced the frustration of observing the emergently stabilized patient who is supine and heavily sedated or pharmacologically comatized to support the intracranial injury. Early mobilization is usually not realized in patients with severe brain or chest injuries. Employment of the mobility benefit argument to justify emergent surgery in this group of patients is difficult to support. Despite attempts by a number of authors employing retrospective techniques,† a major question is still unanswered in care of trauma patients concerning the risk-to-benefit ratio of nonlifesaving emergency surgery in the presence of a severe head injury. There is growing concern regarding the secondary brain injury syndrome.[28, 30, 54] In light of all of these issues, a major question still must be answered: Does emergent or early performance of nonlifesaving fracture surgery affect the final recovery of the brain injury?

A computed tomography scan is taken of a trauma patient to assess the degree of brain injury. An unimpressive initial scan, however, does not correlate with absence of injury, as a delayed brain injury is common in the MIP. Stein and colleagues[54] identified 123 of 253 (48.6%) new or progressive lesions in serial computed tomography scans of head-injured patients. Fifty-five percent of these patients had coagulation abnormalities on admission, compared with 9% with stable or improved follow-up scans. An 85% risk of developing a delayed injury was calculated if the patient had at least one abnormal clotting parameter at the time of admission. Extension of this information suggests to the clinician that therapeutic interventions that affect the coagulation parameters secondary to loss of clotting factors, dilution, or development of hypothermia should be avoided in susceptible patients.

---

*See references 22, 25, 28, 30, 31, 34, 36, 43, 45, 50, 53, 57, 59.
†See references 22, 25, 28, 30, 31, 34, 36, 43, 45, 50, 53, 57, 59.

In an animal model, Schmoker and colleagues[51] showed that hemorrhage after focal brain injury caused a reduction in cerebral oxygen delivery leading to cerebral ischemia. McMahon and co-workers[37] compared patients with brain injury and peripheral injury (n = 378) with patients with peripheral injury alone (n = 2339). When combined with peripheral injury, the risk of death from a brain injury was double that attributable to peripheral injuries. The authors suggested a possible bidirectional interaction between brain injury and peripheral injury— hemorrhagic shock associated with neurotrauma induces a secondary brain injury. The brain injury may affect cardiovascular control mechanisms, further reducing cerebral oxygen delivery and consumption.

Addressing the clinical implications of nonlifesaving trauma care in patients with closed head injuries, Hofman and Goris[25] retrospectively reviewed a consecutive series of 58 patients with major extremity fractures and GCS scores of 7 or less. Fifteen patients underwent fracture fixation on the day of injury. A lower mortality rate was noted in the early fixation group without a deterioration in neurologic outcome, as measured by the GCS score. On the basis of these data, it was concluded that there was no reason for concern about a negative influence of early fracture surgery in patients with severe brain injury.

Poole and co-workers[43] did not find a relationship between pulmonary complications and timing of fracture surgery in a review of records of 114 patients with head injuries and femur or tibia fractures, but they did find a significant correlation with injuries to the head and chest. They also noted that a delay in fracture fixation did not protect the brain, as the outcome appeared to be related to the severity of the initial injury. Because early fracture fixation appeared to simplify the patient's care without a negative neurologic cost, early fracture fixation was advocated.[43]

In reviewing the effect of treatment of unstable pelvic fractures in patients with severe head injuries, Riemer and associates[45] demonstrated a decrease in mortality in patients with pelvic fractures associated with closed head injuries from 43% to 7% after initiation of a protocol involving pelvic external fixation and mobilization.

From the number of recent articles on the topic, it appears that a controversy is brewing surrounding the timing of care in the brain-injured patient. Unfortunately, all of the papers are retrospective and all suffer the same weaknesses identified in the clinical studies attempting to define the appropriate timing of care for long bone fractures in the MIP. What is obvious, however, is the need for a well-designed, multicenter prospective study to shed some evidence-based light on this critical clinical topic.

Jaicks and associates[28] initiated the latest round of rebutting papers by reviewing 33 patients with blunt trauma with significant closed head injuries requiring operative fracture fixation. The early fixation group (n = 19) required significantly more fluids and trended to higher rates of intraoperative hypotension and hypoxia. They concluded that these conditions may contribute to poor neurologic outcomes.

Townsend and co-workers[57] studied 61 patients with femur fractures and severe brain injury. They identified an inversely proportional trend when comparing time until surgery with the percentage of patients who became hypotensive during surgery. Patients in the early femur fixation group were eight times more likely to become hypotensive during the surgery than the patients delayed at least 24 hours (43% overall). The research team concluded that operative delay beyond 24 hours may be necessary to prevent hypoxia, hypotension, and low cerebral perfusion pressure. Kalb and colleagues[30] had similar findings, noting that patients with severe head injury undergoing early fracture fixation had a significant increase in crystalloid and blood infusion and in operative blood loss.

Retrospective clinical studies that conclude in favor of continued early fracture fixation often do so on the basis of reliance on crude outcomes—mortality and final GCS. Unfortunately, the GCS is not a good predictor of long-term cognitive function. McKee and co-workers[36] included cognitive function, matched control groups, and long-term follow-up in their clinical study of the possible effects of timing of femur fracture fixation in patients with severe closed head injuries. They found no difference in outcomes and believed the data supported the continued practice of early intramedullary fixation of femur fractures in patients with closed head injuries.

Velmahos and colleagues[59] found no difference in the rate of intraoperative or postoperative hypoxic or hypotensive episodes in groups of patients with femur fractures and closed head injury treated either early or late. Final GCS scores were similar. Starr and associates[53] found that a delay in stabilization of the femur fracture increased the risk of pulmonary complication but that early fixation did not increase central nervous system complications. The selection bias of the study design was identified by the authors. Lastly, Scalea and colleagues[50] reviewed trauma registry data to determine the timing of fracture care in patients with closed head injuries. No differences were found between the early and late fixation groups as measured by the discharge GCS score or mortality. The authors concluded that they found no evidence to suggest that early fracture fixation negatively influences central nervous system outcomes. As noted before, the contrary is also true.

MULTIPLE-INJURED PATIENTS: BASIC PHYSIOLOGY

To plan and coordinate the acute care of the MIP, the effects of severe trauma on a patient's systemic physiology must be appreciated. The understanding of the impact of the "traumatic wound" on the host physiology allows the care team to optimize wound management and anticipate problems the patient might manifest systemically because of tissue trauma. The impact of the anesthetic and surgical procedure must be considered in the development of care plans to reestablish systemic homeostasis quickly. The orthopaedic surgeon should have a working knowledge of the systemic effects of trauma, coagulation, anesthesia, and the treatment principles of traumatic brain injury to plan the safe orthopaedic recovery of the patient.

Systemic Effects

To understand the systemic effects of trauma, the injury or injuries sustained by the patient can be looked on, in a collective analogy, as a wound. This wound stimulates a variety of responses that must be coped with by the MIP if he or she is to survive. The wound is an inflammatory site that consists of necrotic or devitalized tissue in an ischemic hypoxic region.[6] The larger the inflammatory response, the more critically ill the patient. The host's ability to resolve this inflammatory insult is dependent on both treatment and systemic metabolic response.

The systemic metabolic response to this wounding mechanism is temporal and represented early by the *ebb phase,* which is dominated by cardiovascular instability, alterations in circulating blood volume, impairment in oxygen transport, and heightened autonomic activity. Hypovolemic shock is a typical example of this phase and requires emergent resuscitation. After effective resuscitation and restoration of oxygen transport, a secondary group of responses, the *flow phase,* occurs. Hyperdynamic circulatory changes, fever, glucose intolerance, and muscle wasting are responses of this period.

In response to the ebb phase, the initial need for oxygen delivery is rapidly met by management of the airway and breathing problems through appropriate use of endotracheal intubation and ventilation with appropriate oxygenation. Hypovolemic or traumatic shock is recognized by the clinical manifestations of adrenergic nerve stimulation and increased levels of angiotensin and vasopressin, causing constricture of the vasculature to the skin, fat, skeletal muscle, gastrointestinal tract, and kidneys. This condition is characterized by a usually orderly progression of cutaneous pallor and clamminess with cool extremities, oliguria, tachycardia, hypotension, and finally cerebral and cardiac signs. These clinical manifestations of the compensatory mechanisms occur as the neuroendocrine adrenergic nervous system's vasoactive volume conserving and metabolic hormones cause the peripheral capacitance vessels to constrict and displace residual peripheral blood to the organ systems that require it for the maintenance of life.[26]

Increased heart rate and myocontractility are a second response to the epinephrine released by the neuroendocrine axis. There is also a fluid shift from the interstitial space to the intravascular space, which adds hypo-osmotic fluids. Release of epinephrine, cortisol, and glucagon increases glucose concentration and extracellular osmolarity, thus pulling water out of the cells and into the extracellular space and subsequently forcing it back through the lymphatics and into the vascular space. Without adequate resuscitation, however, these compensatory mechanisms may also have adverse effects. Ongoing ischemia to arterial or smooth muscle may cause dilatation of the arterioles while the postcapillary sphincters are in spasm, resulting in engorgement of the capillaries and extravasation of fluid into the interstitium.[26] Release of endorphins may cause dilatation of the venules and

arterioles, counteracting any positive effect they have by increasing deep spontaneous breathing, which in effect increases cardiac return. In addition, the coagulation and inflammatory responses, both at the site of injury and remotely, are stimulated. The release of cytokines, oxygen radicals, lysozymal enzymes, and leukotrienes leads to vascular endothelial damage and further extravasation of fluid into the interstitium. This disruption of the vascular endothelium becomes a very difficult consequence to handle, as it is likely to lead to pulmonary, renal, and gastrointestinal complications.

In the flow phase, the wound creates an intense metabolic load on the patient. Large arteriovenous shunts, which increase cardiac work, are required to support the profound metabolic changes as the necrotic and contused tissues are broken down and repair processes begin. This process leads to increased metabolic work, elevated energy requirements, and erosion of lean body tissue. Glucose is the main fuel for this wound healing. The glucose is metabolized to lactate, which can then be used by the liver to form more glucose. Gluconeogenesis also occurs, using amino acids, principally alanine, for its substrate. This substrate is obtained from skeletal muscle breakdown. Because of this change in the metabolism of muscles, they no longer serve as a glucose storage site. Glucose is directed to the healing wound. The gut also begins to use glutamine as a principal fuel, converting it to alanine, which is transported through the portal circulation to the liver for gluconeogenesis. The increased portal circulation, along with gastrointestinal mucosal damage, permits entry of bacteria and toxins, which worsen the response.[6] A state of hypermetabolism increases the core body temperature, changing thermal regulation in these patients so that they cannot tolerate cold environments and require a higher ambient temperature.

Significant muscle wasting, nitrogen loss, and accelerated protein breakdown occur. This phenomenon was first described by Cuthbertson,[18] who observed it in patients with long bone fractures. During this time, protein synthesis usually remains normal.

The central nervous system also plays a significant role in the regulation of the hypermetabolic flow phase responses. It appears that an intact central nervous system is required for full expression of the metabolic responses after injury, and it is thought that this occurs through a neuroendocrine reflex arc. The central nervous system is particularly important in the ebb phase for early response to injury, as pain, hypovolemia, acidosis, and hypoxia stimulate the neural afferent signals to the central nervous system. During the flow phase this relationship is not totally understood.[6]

In response to the wound, a number of cells begin to appear soon after the injury. These cells are involved in angiogenesis, production and remodeling of collagen, scavenging of necrotic debris, and lysis of bacteria. The cells tend to release substances that influence the surrounding tissues and the cells that produce them. These factors, known as *cytokines,* are peptide regulatory factors that are synthesized by numerous cells in the body. Two of these cytokines, tumor necrosis factor and interleukin-2, can initiate and propagate metabolic responses after injury and during critical illness. These cytokines have an important role in immunologic homeostasis, particularly with regard to immune cell production and function, and also are important determinants of the cardiovascular and metabolic alterations seen in response to inflammation. These entities are required for an appropriate immunologic response and wound healing, but they can be produced in an exaggerated way and create some significant hemodynamic manifestations, leading to potential problems as well as debilitating tissue loss. These cytokines may also interact with each other to produce other mediators and may have synergistic influences on other mediators as well.[19]

Eicosanoids, metabolites of arachidonic acid, are also produced in response to cytokines as well as other stimuli such as hypoxia and ischemia. Eicosanoids are produced by the activation of phospholipase C, which hydrolyzes a cell membrane constituent and, through a series of chemical reactions, breaks down the cell membrane arachidonic acid into leukotrienes, thromboxanes, prostaglandins, and prostacyclins. Thromboxane is a particularly active substance in vasoconstriction and bronchoconstriction, leading to pulmonary problems. It also increases platelet aggregation, membrane permeability, and neutrophil activation. Prostaglandins control local blood flow by effects on smooth muscle. All of these substances act as mediators of the inflammatory process.[62]

Pain also plays a significant role in the response of the patient. Because neurostimuli are an important part of the stress response, pain relief is important in the modification and modulation of this effect. Relief of pain also improves mobilization and perhaps decreases morbidity through this period.

Understanding the systemic response of the host to an injury or wound is important in the resuscitation and subsequent management of the patient. The orthopaedic surgeon may modulate many of the responses that are occurring. Appropriate recognition of the early manifestations of shock and prompt treatment may alter the decompensation mechanisms and adverse effects of the ongoing inflammatory reaction secondary to necrotic and ischemic tissue. Appropriate and appropriately timed methods of stabilization of fractures decrease pain and provide metabolic and healing responses. Excessive surgery, however, may only add to the already increased metabolic demands of the inflammatory mass of the wounds of the MIP and stimulate decompensation of the homeostatic response to trauma.

Coagulation

Transfusions are often required in the acute resuscitation of the MIP, and the use of additional blood products continues through the emergent surgical procedures. Coagulation defects develop after transfusions and are usually secondary to depletion of host clotting factors and platelets and the development of hypothermia. Transfused blood is deficient in factors V and VIII and platelets. Fresh frozen plasma and platelet replacement therapy must be anticipated if blood requirements are high, and replacement should be initiated as early as possible. Clotting abnormalities can result from intracranial injuries. The etiology of the coagulopathy is thought to be related to the release of tissue thromboplastin from the injured brain tissue.

Hypothermia (<32°C) causes platelet segregation and impairs the release of platelet factor required in the intrinsic clotting pathway. The patient's core temperature begins to drop at the accident scene with the initial administration of intravenous fluids at ambient temperature, and this temperature drop continues in the emergency department and the operating suites as ambient fluid administration continues and as larger body surfaces are exposed to ambient temperature. The coagulation profile should be monitored after major resuscitation or torso surgery, prior to or during the subsequent orthopaedic care. A platelet count less than 100,000/ml³, a fibrinogen level less than 1 g/L, and an abnormal prothrombin time or partial thromboplastin time are associated with a decrease in hemostasis capability and a worsening prognosis.[42]

Anesthesia

Although necessary for the conduct of lifesaving surgical procedures, the anesthetic process and the agents used have systemic effects that are counter to the desired physiology of the acute trauma patient and should be avoided, if possible, in certain patients. Most anesthetic agents are myocardial depressants, and cardiac output diminishes with their use. In elective procedures, crystalloid infusions are used to maintain normal cardiac output. The trauma patient often arrives in the operating room hypovolemic and marginally coagulopathic. Resuscitation with crystalloid solutions and blood products continues throughout the operative procedure. Filling pressure and cardiac output monitoring can help titrate the amount of fluid provided to the patient, but significant amounts are absorbed in the extravascular volume—the "third space" phenomenon. This tissue edema can have negative effects on patients with severe head or pulmonary injuries, or both. Despite the aggressive use of room heaters, warming blankets, and warm infusion fluids, the patient's core temperature often begins to drop. Nonlifesaving surgical procedures increase the blood loss and the demands for additional fluids and blood products and increase the time during which the patient remains anesthetized in the operating room environment.

Transportation of a critically injured or ill patient from the ICU to the operating room poses some risk. Ten percent of such transports have resulted in significant disturbance of cardiovascular or respiratory function.[27, 60] Commonly recognized problems include hypoxemia, hypotension, and arrhythmia.

Treatment of Traumatic Brain Injury

Approximately 50% of all trauma deaths are related to head injury.[21] The general principles employed in the treatment of the brain injured patient are simple: Maintain optimal cerebral perfusion, oxygenation, and glucose delivery. MIPs with suspected brain injury are evaluated by computed tomography scanning, and the nature and severity of the injury are defined. Brain injuries are classified as focal or diffuse and can be associated with open, closed, or depressed skull fractures. Focal injuries consist of brain contusion, hemorrhage, or hematomas. Neurosurgical care is directed toward operative or nonoperative modes on the basis of the presence or absence of open or depressed skull fractures and mass lesions.

Survival of the head-injured patient is dependent on the maintenance of adequate cerebral blood flow. Autoregulated in the normal patient, the blood flow is altered in the trauma patient by a number of factors that include mean arterial pressure (MAP), intracranial pressure (ICP), pH, and the partial pressure of carbon dioxide in arterial blood ($Paco_2$). Cerebral blood flow is indirectly monitored by calculation of the cerebral perfusion pressure (CPP):

$$CPP = MAP - ICP$$

Normal ICP is 10 mm Hg or less. ICP is defined in the Monro-Kellie hypothesis in relation to the volume of the cerebrospinal fluid (CSF), the blood, and the brain matter:

$$K_{ICP} \sim V_{CSF} + V_{Blood} + V_{Brain}$$

CSF production is constant. CSF absorption is regulated by the ICP. Brain volume is a constant unless increased by edema or hemorrhage. Intracranial blood volume is affected by passive venous drainage and arterial blood volume autoregulation. Increased intrathoracic pressure and ICP diminish intracranial venous drainage.

Injury to the brain causes swelling, hemorrhage, or both. CSF and venous blood are removed from the intracranial compartment in an effort to accommodate the increased volume. When this adjustment mechanism is exhausted, additional volume increases the ICP. ICP greater than 20 mm Hg requires monitoring and treatment. Venous drainage is impaired with ICPs in the range 30 to 35 mm Hg, and as with an extremity compartment syndrome, brain edema is exacerbated at this level. Pressures that exceed 40 mm Hg represent severe intracranial hypertension. Cerebral perfusion pressures fall, and ischemia results. Brain death ensues when perfusion is compromised to the point at which oxygen and glucose delivery ceases.

In practical terms, after ruling out or appropriately caring for depressed injuries or mass lesions, the patient's MAP, Pao_2, $Paco_2$, hemoglobin, and ICP and glucose levels are the variables available for manipulation to optimize recovery of the central nervous system. Cerebral oxygen content is dependent on the arterial hemoglobin level and the O_2 saturation. A Pao_2 greater than 80 mm Hg is desired in most brain-injured patients.

ICP is monitored and regulated as necessary. The patient is initially placed in a 30-degree head-up position. The neck is maintained in neutral rotation in an effort not to compress the veins necessary for intracranial drainage. Hyperventilation, fluid restriction, and hyperosmolar agents are used as required to maintain an optimal ICP. If these measures fail to control the ICP, ventriculostomy with CSF withdrawal, sedation, or barbiturate coma—and,

in some institutions, selective lobectomy procedures to decrease the intracranial volume—are used to control elevations in ICP.

ORTHOPAEDIC MANAGEMENT DECISIONS

Survival with normal cognitive function is the primary objective in the initial care of the MIP. Undoubtedly, early stabilization of long bone and pelvic fractures and early mobilization of the patient have been associated with a reduction in mortality, ARDS, and pneumonia rates. This does not mean, however, that early, definitive fracture fixation techniques must be employed in all patients and does not mean that surgery must be accomplished within the first 24 hours. Rigid treatment protocols dictating definitive fracture fixation within 24 hours may not be appropriate in the orthopaedic management plans for the severely injured patient. Understanding the concepts of care for the severely injured patient and attempting to restore physiologic homeostasis as early as possible should be the primary focus of the orthopaedic trauma team.

In the place of rigid "time and implant" protocols, general treatment philosophies should be observed and outcome goals for the patient developed. On the basis of the presence and severity of associated injuries, the resuscitative status of the patient, and the severity of the coagulopathy and pulmonary and head injuries, individualized care plans are tailored for each patient. Investigations have begun to show that the acute monitoring of the by-products of the inflammatory response and shock, such as lactate and base, may help to determine the optimal timing of fracture care. This optimal timing may result in maximal benefit to the patient at minimal complication risk.[20, 39, 61]

In the initial care of the MIP, orthopaedic procedures and eventual musculoskeletal function are of little concern except within the context of the orthopaedic intervention required to enhance the patient's immediate survival potential. The recognition that malunions, nonunions, limb length discrepancies, joint contractures, and chronic infections can be addressed by delayed reconstructive procedures allows the orthopaedic trauma surgeon to focus on the overall immediate needs of the patient and not be distracted by concern about the optimal fixation techniques for the individual orthopaedic injuries.

Isolated orthopaedic injuries in the patient without polytrauma are treated according to the requirements of the injury, the skill and clinical bias of the surgeon, and the characteristics of the patient. The timing and the techniques for treating these injuries are addressed in other sections of this textbook. Orthopaedic surgeons dealing with the multiple-trauma patient must develop a "triage mentality" and learn how to time and titrate interventions to enhance the patient's physiology and recovery. This management philosophy involves the use of rapid temporizing techniques and the maturation of a professional discipline that can avoid the temptation to be overly invasive in the initial care phase.

Goals

The initial goal in the development of the care plan for the MIP is straightforward: Improve the physiology. Care is directed primarily at stabilizing or improving the systemic response to the trauma. Attention to severe extremity injuries is part of this care. The removal of dead tissues and contaminants from associated wounds minimizes the inflammatory response from the wound and decreases sepsis risks and fluid losses. Revascularization of ischemic tissue by fracture reduction or joint relocation, compartment syndrome release, or vascular repair preserves functional tissue and prevents sequelae of systemic ischemic necrosis. Stabilization of major fractures often reduces ongoing blood product requirements and provides the positive benefits previously discussed. Reduction and splinting of closed articular fractures reduce the associated pain and protect the injured area until definitive fixation is possible. Prioritized goals are as follows:

Correct ischemia → Care for wounds →
Stabilize long bones → Reconstruct articular injuries →
Care for lesser fractures

Negotiating Care

The trauma team should clearly establish the severity of the patient's condition and set care parameters before the initiation of surgical procedures.[1] A "captain of the ship" doctrine exists. The trauma surgeon makes the final decision about the timing and complexity of all surgical procedures. The trauma surgeon must clearly communicate desires and intentions and provide an accurate estimate of surgical duration and blood loss. Possibilities for simultaneous surgery (abdominal and extremity or multiple extremity) should be evaluated and planned for, if possible. The immediate long bone stabilization preferences of the orthopaedic surgeon often carries less weight than the neurosurgeon's demand that the patient's surgery be delayed because of a severe closed head injury.

Triage and Timing and Titration of Care

The unstable or deteriorating condition of a patient in the absence of conditions requiring lifesaving surgery may determine against immediate operative intervention for extremity trauma. Such patients are usually admitted to the ICU, and resuscitative and stabilization efforts are continued. Although considered suboptimal by usual standards, provisional care can be given to treat the patient's injuries until more definitive procedures can be used. Wound care, traction, splinting, and application of simple external fixators can be accomplished in most ICUs. With minimal anesthetic and operating room personnel support, fasciotomies can be completed if required emergently. When the patient's condition permits, more formal surgical intervention is planned. This surgery is coordinated to ensure that the right team and the right equipment are available in the operating room before transport of the patient from the ICU.

If the patient requires immediate surgery because of life-threatening conditions, care plans are coordinated between the involved services. Orthopaedic care is often facilitated if the patient is placed on a radiolucent operating table. Hypothermia is anticipated, and the room temperature is raised before the patient's arrival. Warming devices should be available to augment the effort to maintain a normal core temperature.

Regardless of the surgical procedures planned, the patient requires continuous monitoring in the operating room *by the trauma team*. Lifesaving thoracic, abdominal or pelvic, and neurosurgical procedures are accomplished first. Wound care and basic external fixation procedures can often be performed simultaneously with head and torso surgery. At the conclusion of the lifesaving surgeries, the patient's condition is reassessed. If the condition warrants, limb-saving emergent or urgent surgical procedures are started:

Ischemia correction → Wound care →
Long bone stabilization → Articular realignment

Spine fracture surgery is rarely indicated in the critically injured patient. Procedures are sequenced with the expectation that the patient will "crash" momentarily. The critical procedures are accomplished first. Before advancing to the next care sequence, the patient's condition is reassessed, and the trauma surgeon, the neurosurgeon, and the anesthesiologist decide whether to continue to the next surgical step.

Intraoperative decisions are made on the basis of fluctuations in the patient's condition and the expected critical care course. Definitive care of long bone or complex upper extremity and periarticular fractures is often either impractical or impossible, given the patient's overall condition. Optimal fracture care is often suboptimal acute trauma care.

Short, simple, relatively bloodless procedures should be planned. Simple frame half-pin external fixation employing two pins above and below the fracture site provides excellent provisional stability for diaphyseal fractures. External fixation should be considered as an alternative to an intramedullary or a plating procedure for femur fractures and should be encompassed in the wound care delivery plan for major open injuries in the critical patient (Fig. 6–2). Scalea and colleagues[48] demonstrated the efficacy of this philosophy with minimal complications in 43 patients treated with initial external fixation "damage control." Thirty-five were converted to intramedullary nails at an average of 4.8 days. Complex periarticular injuries should not undergo evaluation or definitive treatment on the day of admission of the MIP. If standard compressive dressings and plaster splints are inadequate support for the fracture, bridging external fixation frames can be applied to the extremity to provide fracture stability and reduction through indirect ligamentotaxis techniques. If time and the patient's condition permit, percutaneous pin or lag screw placement can secure and maintain a provisional reduction of the articular surface.

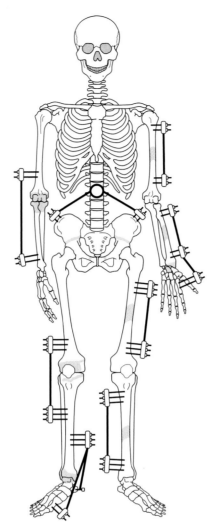

FIGURE 6–2. Simple unilateral external fixation can be rapidly applied to gain provisional control of most upper and lower extremity fractures.

The surgical team needs to know "when to quit." Procedures must be aborted if the patient's condition deteriorates. Falling core temperatures, abnormal clotting studies, unresolved or worsening base deficit, hypoxia, mixed venous desaturation, and increased ICPs are imminent danger signals. Unless the procedures are lifesaving, the patient is better served in the trauma ICU than under additional surgical exposure.

The Mangled Extremity

High-energy open fractures are commonplace in the MIP. The decision concerning limb salvage versus amputation is especially important for the critical patient. Marginal or necrotic tissue cannot be left in the extremity. Follow-up débridements are required in a limb salvage process. Free tissue transfers and other reconstructive surgical procedures usually accompany the decision to salvage an extremity. The metabolic load and expected systemic impact of the salvage process must be weighed before deciding to maintain a mangled extremity. If the mangled extremity is associated with an expected poor functional outcome, coagulopathy, or severe head or spinal cord trauma, early amputation should be considered.

Definitive Care

Windows of opportunity usually develop in the course of the patient's recovery to permit ongoing orthopaedic care. Subsequent visits to the operating room are used to continue the wound débridement and coverage process and to convert long bone traction or external fixation to definitive fixation. Nonurgent reconstruction of other orthopaedic injuries is completed as the patient's general condition allows. In the future, the timing will be determined by the normalization of various inflammatory mediators and metabolic by-products of anoxic metabolism secondary to hypoperfusion.

SUMMARY

Early long bone stabilization is beneficial to the patient and facilitates early mobilization and hospital discharge. Adjustments to definitive femoral fixation techniques and other fracture fixation protocols must be considered, however, when these injuries are present in patients with multiple injuries and associated systemic instability (e.g., profound hypothermia, coagulopathy, head injury with elevated ICP, or pulmonary injury with high shunt).

Adherence to rigid implant and time orthopaedic protocols can be detrimental to the overall recovery of the severely injured patient. The surgical team (trauma surgeon, neurosurgeon, orthopaedic surgeon, and anesthesiologist) must agree on the general concepts of care for the patient and apply these concepts in a planned reconstructive approach tailored to the patient's specific injury constellation and immediate needs. Definitive early long bone stabilization is, of course, the optimal goal for each patient. Pursuit of the goal, however, is counter to the physiologic needs of many trauma patients. In every case, the care team should attempt to improve the patient's physiology before performing nonlifesaving surgery and develop surgical plans that are intentionally simple, quick, and well executed.

REFERENCES

1. American College of Surgeons. Head trauma. In: Advanced Trauma Life Support. Program for Physicians. Chicago, American College of Surgeons, 1993, p. 161.
2. Association for the Advancement of Automotive Medicine. The Abbreviated Injury Scale, 1990 Revision. Des Plaines, IL, Association for the Advancement of Automotive Medicine, 1990.
3. Baker, S.P.; O'Neill, B.; Haddon, W.; Long, W.B. The Injury Severity Score: A method for describing patients with multiple injuries and evaluating emergency care. J Trauma 14:187, 1974.
4. Behrman, S.W.; Fabian, T.C.; Kudsk, K.A.; Taylor, J.C. Improved outcome with femur fractures: Early vs. delayed fixation. J Trauma 30:792, 1990.
5. Bernard, G.R.; Artigas, A.; Brigham, K.L.; and the Consensus Committee. The American-European Consensus Conference on ARDS. Definitions, mechanism, relevant outcomes, and clinical trial coordination. Am J Respir Crit Care Med 149:818, 1994.

6. Bessey, P.Q. Metabolic response to critical illness. In: Wilmore, D.W.; Cheung, L.Y.; Harken, A.H.; et al., eds. American College of Surgeons: Care of the Surgical Patient. New York, Scientific American, 1995, p. 3.

7. Bone, L.; Bucholz, R. Current concepts review. The management of fractures in the patient with multiple trauma. J Bone Joint Surg Am 68:945, 1986.

8. Bone, L.B.; Chapman, M.W. Initial management of the patient with multiple injuries. Instr Course Lect 39:557, 1990.

9. Bone, L.B.; Johnson, K.D.; Weigelt, J.; Scheinberg, R. Early vs. delayed stabilization of femoral fractures. J Bone Joint Surg Am 71:336, 1989.

10. Bone, L.B.; McNamara, K.; Shine, B.; Border, J. Mortality in multiple trauma patients with fractures. J Trauma 37:262, 1994.

11. Bosse, M.J.; MacKenzie, E.J.; Riemer, B.L.; et al. Adult respiratory distress syndrome, pneumonia, ,and pulmonary mortality following thoracic injury and a femoral fracture treated either with intramedullary nailing with reaming or with a plate. J Bone Joint Surg Am 79:799,1997.

12. Boulanger, B.R.; Stephen, D.; Brenneman, F.D. Thoracic trauma and early intramedullary nailing of femur fractures: Are we doing harm? J Trauma 43:24,1997.

13. Buttenschoen, K.; Fleischmann, W.; Haupt, U.; et al. Translocation of endotoxin and acute-phase proteins in malleolar fractures. J Trauma 48:241, 2000.

14. Champion, H.R.; Sacco, W.J.; Copes, W.S.; et al. A revision of the trauma score. J Trauma 29:623, 1989.

15. Charash, W.E.; Fabian, T.C.; Croce, M.A. Delayed surgical fixation of femur fractures is a risk factor for pulmonary failure independent of thoracic trauma. J Trauma 37:667, 1994.

16. Copes, W.S.; Champion, H.R.; Sacco, W.J.; et al. Progress in characterizing anatomic injury. J Trauma 30:1200, 1990.

17. Copes, W.S.; Champion, H.R.; Sacco, W.J.; et al. The Injury Severity Score revisited. J Trauma 28:69, 1988.

18. Cuthbertson, O.P. The disturbance of metabolism produced by bony and from bony injury, with notes on certain abnormal conditions of bone. Biochem J 24:1244, 1930.

19. Fong, Y.; Lowry, S.F. Cytokines and the cellular response to injury and infection. In: Wilmore, D.W.; Cheung, L.Y.; Harken, A.H.; et al., eds. American College of Surgeons: Care of the Surgical Patient. New York, Scientific American, 1995, p. 1.

20. Gebhart, F.; Pfetsch, H.; Steinbach, G.; et al. Is interleukin 6 an early marker of injury severity following major trauma? Arch Surg 135:291, 2000.

21. Gennarelli, T.; Trunkey, D.D.; Blaisdell, F.W. Trauma to the central nervous system. In: Wilmore, D.W.; Cheung, L.Y.; Harken, A.H.; et al., eds. American College of Surgeons: Care of the Surgical Patient. New York, Scientific American, 1995.

22. Glenn, J.N.; Miner, M.E.; Peltier, L.F. The treatment of fractures of the femur in patients with head injuries. J Trauma 13:958, 1973.

23. Goris, R.J.A.; Gimbrere, J.S.F.; van Niekerk, J.L.M.; et al. Early osteosynthesis and prophylactic mechanical ventilation in the multitrauma patient. J Trauma 22:895, 1982.

24. Greene, K.A.; Jacobowitz, R.; Marciano, F.F.; et al. Impact of traumatic subarachnoid hemorrhage on outcome in nonpenetrating head injury. Part II: Relationship to clinical course and outcome variables during acute hospitalization. J Trauma 41:964, 1996.

25. Hofman, P.A.M.; Goris, R.J.A. Timing of osteosynthesis of major fractures in patients with severe brain injury. J Trauma 31:261, 1991.

26. Holcroft, J.W.; Robinson, M.K. Shock. In: Wilmore, D.W.; Cheung, L.Y.; Harken, A.H.; et al., eds. American College of Surgeons: Care of the Surgical Patient. New York, Scientific American, 1995, p. 3.

27. Insel, J.; Weissman, C.; Kemper, M.; et al. Cardiovascular changes during transport of critically ill and postoperative patients. Crit Care Med 14:539, 1986.

28. Jaicks, R.R.; Cohn, S.M.; Moller, B.A. Early fracture fixation may be deleterious after head injury. J Trauma 42:1, 1997.

29. Johnson, K.D.; Cadambi, A.; Seibert, G.B. Incidence of adult respiratory distress syndrome in patients with multiple musculoskeletal injuries: Effect of early operative stabilization of fractures. J Trauma 25:375, 1985.

30. Kalb, D.C.; Ney, A.L.; Rodriguez, J.L.; et al. Assessment of the relationship between timing of fixation of the fracture and secondary brain injury in patients with multiple trauma. Surgery 124:739, 1998.

31. Kotwica, Z.; Balcewicz, L.; Jagodzinski, Z. Head injuries coexistent with pelvic or lower extremity fractures—Early or delayed osteosynthesis. Acta Neurochir (Wien) 102:19, 1990.

32. Kushwaha, V.P.; Garland, D.G. Extremity fractures in the patient with a traumatic brain injury. J Am Acad Orthop Surg 6:298, 1998.

33. LaDuca, J.; Bone, L.; Seibel, R.; et al. Primary open reduction and internal fixation of open fractures. J Trauma 20:580, 1980.

34. Malisano, L.P.; Stevens, D.; Hunter, G.A. The management of long bone fractures in the head-injured polytrauma patient. J Orthop Trauma 8:1, 1994.

35. Marshall, J.C.; Nathens, A.B. Multiple organ dysfunction syndrome. In: Wilmore, D.W.; Cheung, L.Y.; Harken, A.H.; et al., eds. American College of Surgeons: Care of the Surgical Patient. New York, Scientific American, 1995, p. 118.

36. McKee, M.D.; Schemitsch, E.H.; Vincent, L.O.; et al. The effect of a femoral fracture on concomitant closed head injury in patients with multiple injuries. J Trauma 42:1041, 1997.

37. McMahon, C.G.; Yates, D.W.; Campbell, F.M.; et al. Unexpected contribution of moderate traumatic brain injury to death after major trauma. J Trauma 47:891, 1999.

38. Meek, R.N.; Vivoda, E.; Crichton, A. Comparison of mortality in patients with multiple injuries secondary to method of fracture treatment. J Bone Joint Surg Br 63:456, 1981.

39. Nast-Kolb, D.; Waydhas, C.; Gippner-Steppert, C.; et al. Indicators of the posttraumatic inflammatory response correlate with organ failure in patients with multiple injuries. J Trauma 42:446, 1997.

40. Pape, H.C.; Auf'mKolk, M.; Paffrath, T.; et al. Primary intramedullary femur fixation in multiple trauma patients with associated lung contusion—A cause of posttraumatic ARDS? J Trauma 34:540, 1993.

41. Phillips, T.F.; Contreras, D.M. Timing of operative treatment of fractures in patients who have multiple injuries. J Bone Joint Surg Am 72:784, 1990.

42. Phillips, T.F.; Soulier, G.; Wilson, R.F. Outcome of massive transfusion exceeding two blood volumes in trauma and emergency surgery. J Trauma 27:903, 1987.

43. Poole, G.V.; Miller, J.D.; Agnew, S.G.; Griswold, J.A. Lower extremity fracture fixation in head-injured patients. J Trauma 32:654, 1992.

44. Reynolds, M.A.; Richardson, J.D.; Spain, D.A.; et al. Is the timing of fracture fixation important for the patient with multiple trauma? Ann Surg 222:470, 1995.

45. Riemer, B.L.; Butterfield, S.L.; Diamond, D.L.; et al. Acute mortality associated with injuries to the pelvic ring: The role of early patient mobilization and external fixation. J Trauma 35:671, 1993.

46. Riska, E.R.; von Bonsdorff, H.; Hakkinen, S.; et al. Primary operative fixation of long bone fractures in patients with multiple injuries. J Trauma 17:111, 1977.

47. Rogers, F.B.; Shackford, S.R.; Vane, D.W.; et al. Prompt fixation of isolated femur fractures in a rural trauma center: A study examining the timing of fixation and resource allocation. J Trauma 36:774, 1994.

48. Scalea, T.M.; Boswell, S.A.; Scott, J.D.; et al. External fixation as a bridge to intramedullary nailing for patients with multiple injuries and with femur fractures: Damage control orthopaedics. J Trauma 48:613, 2000.

49. Scalea, T.M.; Goldstein, A.; Phillips, T.; et al. An analysis of 161 falls from height: The jumper syndrome. J Trauma 26:706, 1986.

50. Scalea, T.M.; Scott, J.D.; Brumback, R.J.; et al. Early fracture fixation may be "just fine" after head injury: No difference in central nervous system outcomes. J Trauma 45:839, 1999.

51. Schmoker, J.D.; Zhuang, J.; Shackford, S.R. Hemorrhagic hypotension after brain injury causes an early and sustained reduction in cerebral oxygen delivery despite normalization of systemic oxygen delivery. J Trauma 32:714, 1992.

52. Seibel, R.; LaDuca, J.; Hassett, J.M.; et al. Blunt multiple trauma (ISS 36), femur traction, and the pulmonary failure septic state. Ann Surg 202:283, 1985.

53. Starr, A.J.; Hunt, J.L.; Chason, D.P.; et al. Treatment of femur fractures with associated head injury. J Orthop Trauma 12:38, 1998.

54. Stein, S.C.; Young, G.S.; Talucci, R.C.; et al. Delayed brain injury after head trauma: Significance of coagulopathy. Neurosurgery 30:160, 1992.

55. Strecker, W.; Gebhart, F.; Rager, J.; et al. Early biomechanical characteristics of soft-tissue trauma and fractures. J Trauma 47:358, 1999.

56. Teasdale, G.; Jenne, H.B. Assessment of coma and impaired consciousness: A practical scale. Lancet 2:81, 1974.

57. Townsend, R.N.; Lheureau, T.; Protetch, J.; et al. Timing of fracture repair in patients with severe brain injury (Glasgow Coma Scale score < 9). J Trauma 44:977, 1998.

58. Turchin, D.C.; Schemitsch, E.H.; McKee, M.D.; Waddell, J.P. A comparison of the outcome of patients with pulmonary contusion versus pulmonary contusion and musculoskeletal injuries. Paper presented at the 63rd Annual Meeting of the Academy of Orthopaedic Surgeons, Atlanta, Georgia, February 1996.

59. Velmahos, G.C.; Arroyo, H.; Ramicone, E.; et al. Timing of fracture fixation in blunt trauma patients with severe head injuries. Am J Surg 176:324, 1998.

60. Venkataraman, S.T.; Orr, R.A. Intrahospital transport of critically ill patients. Crit Care Clin 8:525, 1992.

61. Waydhas, C.; Nast-Kolb, D.; Trupka, A.; et al. Posttraumatic inflammatory response, secondary operations and late multiple organ failure. J Trauma 40:624, 1996.

62. Weiser, M.R.; Hill, J.; Lindsay, T.; Hechtman, H.B. Eicosanoids in surgery. In: Wilmore, D.W.; Cheung, L.Y.; Harken, A.H.; et al., eds. American College of Surgeons: Care of the Surgical Patient. New York, Scientific American, 1995, p. 1.

63. Ziran, B.H.; Le, T.; Zhou, H.; et al. The impact of the quantity of skeletal injury on mortality and pulmonary morbidity. J Trauma 43:916, 1997.

7

Pain Management following Traumatic Injury

Frederick W. Burgess, M.D., Ph.D.
Richard A. Browning, M.D.

With rare exception, painful sensations are a common experience in life. In the scheme of survival, pain represents the body's early warning system indicating that attention must be paid to the inciting problem. In most cases, the intensity of the pain dictates immediate action, such as immobilization of the injured area. This innate response prevents the likelihood of further injury and potentially improves survival by allowing time for healing. Unfortunately, pain can also adversely affect survival, particularly during the postinjury recovery phase. Persistent pain leading to prolonged immobilization may lead to thrombotic events, muscle wasting, restriction in range of motion, pulmonary infection, and even death.

In addition to these physiologic consequences, there can also be a significant emotional cost to the pain that is associated with traumatic injury. Although of less concern during the immediate evaluation and treatment of the patient with multiple injuries, the emotional impact of pain can be considerable. Most patients do not fully comprehend the extent and nature of their injuries but interpret poorly controlled pain as an indicator of serious injury. The emotional distress and accompanying anxiety that they feel is heightened by inadequate pain control and contributes to an emotionally out-of-control patient. Initial pain treatment may, by necessity, be administered cautiously, but it should not be forgotten. Accompanying family members may also be distressed and tend to focus on the patient's pain complaints rather than the more life-threatening aspects of their injuries. Judicious use of analgesics may facilitate the evaluation process and improve the sense of well-being in the patient and family. This chapter reviews the physiology of pain and attempts to provide a framework for the range of therapeutic options for optimal pain treatment of the trauma victim.

WHY TREAT PAIN?

Pain is by far the major reason for most patient visits to a physician. In most circumstances, the ultimate resolution of the painful condition is dependent on identification and resolution of the underlying inciting factor. In the case of skeletal trauma resulting in a fracture, realignment and splinting of the fracture will reduce the pain but not necessarily eliminate it in the short term. Healing is an inflammatory process that produces a sensitization of the nervous system that contributes to central and peripheral pain generation.[14, 49] Traumatic injury, whether by accident or the surgeon's scalpel, can be accompanied by a more generalized inflammatory or stress response that disturbs the body's normal homeostasis.[41] The extent to which the stress response alters the patient's physiology depends in part on the location(s), severity, and preexisting physiologic impairments. For example, patients with a history of peripheral vascular disease, coronary artery disease, and tobacco use are at high risk for perioperative thrombotic events. Their propensity for clot formation is escalated following surgical trauma, triggered in part by the perioperative stress response, which promotes the formation of various acute phase reactants.[5, 32, 42] One such substance is tissue plasminogen activator inhibitor (t-PAI), which promotes blood clot formation by inhibiting the thrombolytic action of plasmin. Following surgery, t-PAI levels are elevated and may contribute to myocardial infarction, pulmonary embolism, and peripheral arterial revascularization failure.[32] The stress response to surgery can be blunted through the use of regional anesthesia, such as epidural anesthesia, and the aggressive use of postoperative analgesia, which can improve patient outcome.[5, 52]

Recent improvements in our understanding of how painful sensations are conducted and amplified by the nervous system have led to a greater emphasis on early and aggressive perioperative pain control. Pain signals are initiated through the direct stimulation and indirect sensitization of peripheral thermal and mechanical receptors. Local tissue trauma generates a cascade of prostaglandin and kinin substances that promote a lowered threshold for stimulation in the C-type fibers of the surrounding tissues. This process contributes to the hyperalgesia and hyperesthesia associated with tissue trauma and ultimately contributes to the release of several excitatory neurotransmitters within the dorsal horn of the spinal cord, where the peripheral afferent neuron synapses with the second-order neuron.[49]

In the dorsal horn of the spinal cord, peptides, such as substance P, and excitatory amino acids, such as glutamate, are released from the primary afferent neuron onto the second-order sensory neuron. These second-order nociceptive neurons, or wide dynamic range neurons, become sensitized through the action of substance P on the NK-1 receptor–linked sodium channels, and glutamate on the N-desmethyl-D-aspartate receptor linked to a calcium channel, as illustrated in Figure 7–1.[8, 49] Repetitive C-fiber stimulation promotes a central sensitization of the second-order neuron, facilitating the transmission of pain impulses to the thalamus and cortical regions of the brain. This facilitation of central nociceptive transmission is referred to as *wind-up*. Thus, sustained painful stimuli are capable of triggering sensitization of nociceptive signals, both in the periphery and within the central nervous system.

Recent evidence generated from animal models and human clinical trials suggest that early multimodal analgesic interventions improve perioperative pain control and ultimately reduce the duration of postoperative pain.[30, 43, 51] Combined treatment with nonsteroidal anti-inflammatory drugs (NSAIDs), opioids, and local anesthetics provides immediate pain relief, and, when used in combination, reduces analgesic side effects. A review of available drugs and strategies for combined drug therapy follows.

NONSTEROIDAL ANTI-INFLAMMATORY DRUGS

The NSAIDs are an important mainstay of analgesic therapy in orthopaedic medicine. Since the synthesis of acetylsalicylic acid in 1899, the NSAIDs have evolved into the most widely prescribed oral analgesic medication. Unfortunately, the value of this analgesic class is too often forgotten in the management of the acute trauma and postoperative patient. Avoidance of NSAIDs in these settings is directly attributable to concerns over the potential for bleeding complications. These concerns are largely overstated, as demonstrated in the postmarketing surveillance data collected for ketorolac.[40] Their data revealed a minimal risk of perioperative bleeding at the surgical site following perioperative ketorolac administration. Despite this, many physicians and surgeons continue to advise their preoperative patients to discontinue the use of NSAIDs before surgery. As previously indicated, there is a clear rationale for prescribing a NSAID on the day of surgery.[6]

The NSAIDs produce their analgesic action through the inhibition of cyclooxygenase synthetase at the site of injury in the periphery and possibly through actions within the central nervous system. Tissue trauma liberates phospholipids from damaged cellular membranes, which are in turn converted by phospholipase into arachidonic acid. Cyclooxygenase converts the arachidonic acid into prostaglandin precursors that are responsible for the development of regional pain, edema, and vasodilatation. Within the central nervous system, prostaglandins appear to have a role in the transmission of pain signals, independent of their peripheral inflammatory actions. Animal and clinical data have demonstrated a potent central analgesic effect of NSAIDs when delivered intraspinally.[23, 25] The importance of this central mechanism to the analgesic effects of most NSAIDs is uncertain but may provide a useful target for future analgesic development.

There are a large number of different NSAIDs currently on the market. Fortunately, it is not necessary to become familiar with every agent. NSAID selection may be made on the basis of duration of action desired and on the side effect tolerance profile. The most potent anti-inflammatory effect is provided by indomethacin; however, adverse reactions and side effects have led to a decline in the use of this compound. For short-term therapy, ibuprofen remains one of the least expensive and best-tolerated NSAIDs. The one disadvantage of ibuprofen is its short duration of action, which creates a need for multiple daily doses (Table 7–1). Even with pain relievers, compliance can be a problem, often resulting in poor pain control and dissatisfaction with the treatment. Longer acting agents, such as naproxen or piroxicam, offer greater convenience of dosing but appear to carry a greater risk of gastrointestinal bleeding and ulceration.[21] This increased risk of gastric perforation and bleeding may relate to the sustained inhibition of the cyclooxygenase enzyme provided by the

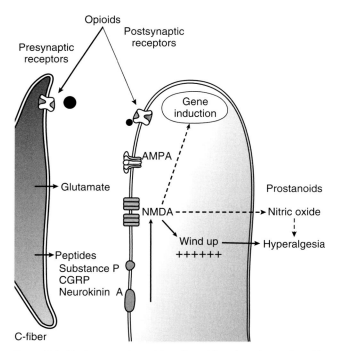

FIGURE 7–1. Excitatory amino acids and peptides released onto the wide dynamic range neuron, located in the dorsal horn of the spinal cord, produce a state of excitation. This excitation process will facilitate the transmission of pain signals to the brain.

TABLE 7–1

Nonsteroidal Anti-inflammatory Agents

Agent	Dose Range (mg)	Dosing Interval (hr)	Maximum Dose (mg)	Half-life (hr)
Acetylsalicylic acid	325–650	4–6	4000–6000	20–30 minutes
Choline magnesium trisalicylate	1000–1500	12	2000–3000	9–17
NONSELECTIVE COX INHIBITORS				
Ibuprofen	200–800	4–8	2400	2–2.5
Naproxen	250–500	6–8	1250	12–15
Naproxen sodium	275–550	6–8	1375	12–15
Ketoprofen	25–50	6–8	300	1.5
Indomethacin	25–50	8–12	100	2
Ketorolac	15–60 i.m.	6	120	6
	10 p.o.			
Diclofenac	50	8	150	1–2
Piroxicam	20–40	24	40	50
Etodolac	200–500	6–12	1000	7
Nabumetone	500–2000	12–24	2000	24
COX-2 SELECTIVE				
Celecoxib	100–200	12	400	11
Rofecoxib	25–50	12–24	50	17
Meloxicam	7.5–15	24	15	20–24

prolonged half-lives of these drugs. Ketorolac deserves mention because it is the only NSAID available for parenteral delivery in the United States, making it convenient for intraoperative and postoperative administration. Unfortunately, ketorolac has received a black box warning by the U.S. Food and Drug Administration to limit parenteral administration to no more than 5 days. This resulted from postmarketing data that revealed an increase in gastrointestinal bleeding when ketorolac was administered parenterally for more than 5 days.[40] Associated risk factors included age older than 70 years and concomitant medical illness.[39]

Selective Inhibition of Cyclooxygenase

Cyclooxygenase exists as two isoenzymes.[38] Cyclooxygenase-1 (COX-1) is a constitutive enzyme, which is continuously expressed in many tissues, including the gastric mucosa, platelets, and kidney. A second isoenzyme, cyclooxygenase-2 (COX-2), is an inducible enzyme usually associated with inflammation and healing.[38] It is now possible to selectively target the COX-2 enzyme for inhibition, which can greatly reduce unwanted effects on platelet function and the mucosal integrity of the gastrointestinal tract.[17] Preliminary data from studies on two new COX-2 selective compounds, celecoxib and rofecoxib, reveal a much lower risk of gastric erosion and ulceration relative to nonselective COX inhibitors such as ibuprofen and naproxen.[22, 34, 35] Furthermore, celecoxib and rofecoxib do not appear to affect platelet function. They are devoid of the antiplatelet effects that are associated with COX-1 inhibition.[17] The COX-2 selective inhibitors may be particularly advantageous during the perioperative period, because they do not need to be discontinued and may be administered on the day of surgery to provide perioperative analgesia. Paracoxib, the prodrug form of valdecoxib, a parenteral COX-2 inhibitor, is currently

under study and may supplant the use of ketorolac during the perioperative period.

Although the COX-2 inhibitors represent a major step forward in safety, several important points must be emphasized. COX-2 inhibitors are safer than the nonselective COX inhibitors, but they do not provide better analgesia or anti-inflammatory effect. Thus, in circumstances in which a less expensive nonselective agent for a short-term course of therapy is acceptable, the nonselective COX inhibitors remain the best choice for the sake of economy. Also, the selective COX-2 inhibitors are not entirely devoid of the potential for gastrointestinal ulceration.[22, 35, 36] Among patients with known peptic ulcerations, the COX-2 inhibitors should be avoided. COX-2 is a component of the healing response and can be identified in healing ulcers. Administration of a COX-2 inhibitor in this setting interferes with the healing process and can contribute to further injury and perforation. The COX-2 inhibitors cannot be used with impunity, particularly in the long-term setting. Finally, the COX-2 inhibitors have the potential to impair renal function.[33] This will be most pronounced in the elderly or the volume-depleted patient. Peripheral edema and renal failure may accompany their use and should be monitored carefully in the high-risk patient.

For the perioperative patient, combining a NSAID with an opioid can result in a 30% to 40% reduction in opioid requirement.[13, 48] Rarely will a NSAID provide adequate analgesia as a solitary analgesic, but as a component of a combined analgesic regimen, it can improve the quality of pain relief and reduce opioid-related side effects.[4, 13, 37, 48] The opioid-sparing effect is most evident in the orthopaedic and dental surgery populations. The advantage of combining a NSAID with an opioid may become evident in a faster return of bowel function, less constipation, less nausea, and improved analgesia.[13, 48] Parenteral ketorolac has been shown to be a useful adjuvant to epidural opioid analgesia.[4, 37] With the availability of the COX-2 inhibitors, more widespread use of NSAIDs during the perioperative period should result in improved analgesia. The lack of platelet interference allows the COX-2 inhibitors to be administered very early in the treatment of the orthopaedic trauma patient, provided careful consideration of renal perfusion and volume resuscitation issues has occurred.

Hazards

As alluded to previously, the NSAIDs carry the potential for numerous side effects and adverse reactions. Most of the adverse effects of the NSAID class can be anticipated and monitored. The relative risk-to-benefit ratio of any medication should be explained to the patient. This approach helps to include the patient in the decision-making process, provides informed consent, and improves early recognition of any developing problems.

GASTROINTESTINAL TOXICITY

There are two forms of gastrointestinal problems associated with the NSAID class. Many patients encounter dyspepsia on starting a course of NSAID therapy. This effect represents a topical irritant effect of the medication and does not herald peptic ulcer formation or gastric perforation. In most cases, this effect fades with continued use and adaptation. It may also be reduced by encouraging the consumption of food along with the NSAID. Often, more serious gastrointestinal damage is not heralded by dyspepsia but instead may manifest as a perforated viscus without prodrome or as a spontaneous hemorrhage.[16] The NSAIDs interfere with the protective generation of mucous and bicarbonate, leading to ulceration of the duodenal region. Concomitant administration of histamine antagonists, proton inhibitors, and misoprostol appears to be somewhat helpful but cannot completely prevent ulcerations.[15] As a general statement, patients with known peptic ulcer disease should not be treated with a NSAID. Patients with a history of peptic ulcer disease, without active ulcers, must be treated cautiously. The combination of a COX-2 selective inhibitor in conjunction with a cytoprotective agent, such as misoprostol, may be a reasonable approach. However, to our knowledge, there are no data that support this assumption.

RENAL TOXICITY

Adverse renal effects of the NSAID class include impaired renal perfusion, sodium retention secondary to reduced glomerular filtration, peripheral edema, congestive heart failure, hyperkalemia, interstitial nephritis, and nephrotic syndrome. Acute renal failure, peripheral edema, and heart failure are all interrelated and can often be anticipated from the patient's medical history. Treating any patient with hypertension, a known history of congestive heart failure, or preexisting renal impairment must be undertaken with caution. Some assessment of renal function should be made before initiating therapy. This is also true with respect to the trauma patient. Hypovolemia produces a reduction in glomerular blood flow, which may be further aggravated by the addition of a NSAID, leading to acute renal failure.

HEPATIC TOXICITY

Although chemically very different, the NSAIDs as a class appear to carry some risk of hepatotoxicity. Two agents in particular have been linked to hepatic injury, necessitating routine monitoring. Bromfenac, which has been withdrawn from the U.S. market, was linked to hepatic failure. Diclofenac has been associated with a hepatitis-type syndrome. Other NSAIDs have been linked to hepatic injury, but as with many drugs undergoing clinical trials, it is not always clear whether there is a direct relationship. Any patient at risk or having a history of liver disease should be evaluated periodically.

BRONCHOSPASM

As a class, the NSAIDs may contribute to the aggravation of asthma. Individuals sensitive to aspirin-induced bronchospasm and those who have nasal polyps should probably avoid the NSAIDs.

HEMATOLOGIC TOXICITY

The well-known potential for aspirin and the NSAIDs to interfere with platelet aggregation has been exploited as a means to prevent perioperative thrombotic complications. However, in the wrong setting this anticoagulant effect may be disastrous. With the availability of the COX-2 selective NSAIDs, the antiplatelet effects have been eliminated. There is still some slight potential for modest prolongation of the prothrombin time in patients receiving warfarin for anticoagulation; however, this effect appears to be small and can be readily compensated for, if necessary.

THE OPIOIDS

When one views the incredible developments that have contributed to modern medicine, it is striking to note how little we have improved with respect to analgesia. The tools of analgesia—local anesthetics such as cocaine, the NSAIDs such as the salicylates, and the opiate alkaloids such as morphine—have been used by various cultures throughout recorded history. Unfortunately, our pharmacologic approaches have not improved over the past thousand years. Refinements in our understanding and improvements in the purity of analgesic compounds have occurred, but in essence we still have the same tools used by the ancient cultures.

Opiate analgesics have been the mainstay of analgesic therapy since before recorded history and continue to be the most important category of analgesic medication. *Opioids,* a term that includes natural opiate compounds derived from the poppy plant and synthetic compounds, produce their analgesic effect by activating one or more opiate receptors. The opiate receptors are the binding sites for an endogenous group of peptides, which includes the endorphins and the enkephalins. Additional peptides and receptors have been discovered, but their contribution to pain and analgesia are still being sorted out. Currently, there are three opioid receptors of clinical importance, mu, kappa, and delta, revealing evidence of selective binding for specific endogenous peptides and to some extent, exogenous compounds. The most important of these receptors appears to be the mu receptor. This is the principle binding site for most of the clinically useful exogenous opioids and mediates the analgesic and respiratory depressant effects of the opioid agonists. Most of the currently available opioids activate multiple receptor types; at present, there are no clinically useful receptor selective compounds available for patient care.

As a general statement, any one of the full agonist opioids can be effective in managing acute pain, provided the opioid is delivered in an effective dose range appropriate to the route of delivery. Obtaining adequate analgesia often depends on striking a balance so that the patient experiences pain relief without suffering from side effects. For patients with severe acute pain, health care providers often must walk a tightrope between patient comfort on the one side and somnolence and respiratory depression on the other. Too often physicians and nurses restrict pain medication for fear of causing unwanted side effects, leaving the patient with an unacceptable level of pain.[26] Another barrier to adequate analgesia may be attributed to the poor understanding or application of opioid pharmacology in the setting of postoperative analgesia. Inappropriate doses, routes of administration, and dosing intervals and the concomitant administration of other sedatives often contribute to inadequate pain relief.[1] Unlike most medications, analgesic administration occurs in a setting in which the patient can actually identify when additional medication is needed. Thus, if a fixed dose schedule is to be applied, some flexibility for supplementation and adjustments for individual variation must be included. Strategies that optimize the delivery of pain medication include using patient-controlled analgesia and allowing for supplemental or breakthrough doses of a rapid-onset analgesic. To be effective, frequent patient assessments must be undertaken. Simply asking a patient whether he or she has pain is not adequate. Directed questions should focus on the location of the pain; the severity of the pain, using a 0 to 10 scale; and activities associated with the pain, such as deep breathing, coughing, and ambulation. Most patients do not experience severe pain while lying still in bed, but once they begin to participate in their rehabilitation activity, pain becomes much more intense.

Opioid Selection

Choosing an opioid is a relatively simple process for the majority of postoperative pain patients. All of the opioids share a common mechanism of action and spectrum of side effects. For any given patient, one opioid may be better tolerated as determined from the medical history and is usually the best choice. Individual differences affecting drug distribution, metabolism, and elimination

may also affect the patient's satisfaction with a given opioid. The following examples of these differences are illustrative.

Morphine continues to be regarded as the gold standard for comparison among the opioids. Morphine has the advantage of being available in a wide range of dose forms, allowing administration via the oral, rectal, parenteral, and intraspinal routes. Unfortunately, morphine suffers from several disadvantages, making it a less than ideal analgesic. Morphine is poorly lipid soluble, which translates into a slow equilibration into the central nervous system. Following intravenous delivery, morphine has a relatively slow onset of action when compared with analgesics such as fentanyl, meperidine, and sufentanil. Administering an opioid as a component of the anesthetic (having anticipated the need for pain medication) and prescribing the drug on a fixed schedule during the postoperative phase can usually overcome this disadvantage. Another disadvantage of morphine is its relatively short duration of action, typically in the range of 2 to 4 hours following a parenteral dose. With repeated doses, an active metabolite, morphine-6-glucuronide, accumulates, providing some increased duration of analgesia. Another important metabolite, morphine-3-glucuronide, may also accumulate particularly in the patient with renal failure. This metabolite may contribute to excitation of the central nervous system, producing myoclonus and possibly seizures. Metabolite accumulation is more pronounced with high doses, oral administration, and renal impairment.

Meperidine continues to be used widely as a parenteral analgesic, despite several disadvantages. Meperidine is a synthetic compound, a phenylpiperidine, in the same structural class as fentanyl. It has the advantage of greater lipid solubility, allowing rapid transit across the blood-brain barrier. This rapid onset of action tends to reinforce its use, particularly among many chronic pain patients. Meperidine is a very effective analgesic; however, it is seldom delivered at an appropriate dosage or interval. Parenteral doses of 75 to 100 mg are often inadequate for many patients.[1] Furthermore, meperidine suffers from a short duration of analgesia, on the order of 3 hours, and is metabolized into a neuroexcitatory metabolite, normeperidine.[19] Normeperidine tends to accumulate rapidly in renal failure or during therapy at high doses. Delivery of meperidine at doses exceeding 1000 mg/24-hour period can lead to seizures even in the absence of renal impairment. Considering the toxicity issues that limit dose escalation, meperidine has become relegated to a second-line drug status. Oral meperidine is a relatively ineffective analgesic. Only one fifth of the oral dose is absorbed into the central circulation. Meperidine is a relatively impotent analgesic, requiring a dose of 500 mg to equal the parenteral dose of 100 mg. There is often a tendency to underdose patients, delivering small doses of 50 to 100 mg, which are equivalent to only 10 to 20 mg of parenteral meperidine.

Hydromorphone is a morphine analogue, which has several decided advantages over morphine and meperidine. The chemical properties of hydromorphone provide for greater lipid solubility and a more rapid onset of action. Hydromorphone is approximately five times more potent than morphine and may be administered via the oral, parenteral, epidural, and rectal routes. It is less predisposed to the accumulation of active metabolites and carries a much lower risk of neuroexcitatory effects. Oral hydromorphone is also poorly absorbed. Equivalent oral doses of hydromorphone are five times the parenteral dose. The duration of action resembles that of most of the other opioids, at about 3 hours, requiring frequent dosing. A sustained release form of hydromorphone is now available, allowing more convenient dosing.

Although there are many other opioids, fentanyl deserves mention as a common perioperative analgesic-anesthetic. Fentanyl is approximately 50 to 100 times as potent as morphine. It is administered in microgram quantities and provides a very rapid onset of action following intravenous delivery. The lipophilic properties of fentanyl are responsible for its rapid onset and relatively short duration of action due to rapid redistribution. The half-life of fentanyl closely resembles that of morphine and meperidine, but in small-to-moderate doses it is rapidly redistributed into peripheral tissues, negating its central effects. Fentanyl has been used as a postoperative analgesic, but its major use has been as a transdermal patch for chronic and cancer pain. The transdermal patch is a useful means of delivery because it only needs to be applied every 72 hours.[9] However, it can be difficult to titrate, is often poorly adherent, and is relatively expensive. The difficulty in adjusting the dose to the individual has led to the recommendation that it not be used for postoperative pain. Fentanyl is not available as an oral tablet, but a transmucosal rapid release system is available and can be used as a rapid-onset medication for breakthrough pain.[31]

Opioid Delivery

As discussed, there are numerous opioids available for clinical use. Similarly, there are many different routes by which to deliver these opioid preparations. Each route or delivery method is available to the trauma patient; however, depending on the patient's overall condition, certain delivery approaches may be more advantageous.

ORAL OPIOIDS

Oral opioid selection can be confusing because of the large and ever-increasing number of opioid combination products. Predominant selections vary by region, but hydrocodone and oxycodone preparations are among the most commonly prescribed. Most of the opioids share a similar spectrum of duration, side effects, and efficacy, when delivered in equipotent doses. Dosing intervals and toxicity are more often related to the nonopioid analgesics, such as acetaminophen, aspirin, and ibuprofen, that are delivered in conjunction with the opioid. Morphine, meperidine, oxycodone, hydromorphone, and codeine all provide a duration of action approaching 3 to 4 hours. For many patients, an every 3-hour dosing interval is appropriate; however, with opioid-nonopioid combination tablets, this short interval could lead to excessive acetaminophen or aspirin delivery. Opioid-only preparations are now available for morphine, oxycodone, meperidine hydromorphone, and codeine. In addition, several sustained-release

opioid preparations are available to allow for more convenient dosing intervals.

INTRAVENOUS PATIENT-CONTROLLED ANALGESIA

Pain is defined by the International Association for the Study of Pain as "a sensory and emotional experience associated with tissue injury or described in terms of tissue damage or injury."[28] Pain is always a subjective experience and can only be accurately assessed by the patient. Nurses and physicians are capable of recognizing many of the signs and symptoms of uncontrolled pain; however, their assessments are frequently inaccurate and tend to underestimate the patient's reported pain score. Objective measures, such as heart rate, blood pressure, posture, and ventilatory pattern are rather insensitive measures and may be distorted by physiologic changes accompanying injury and drug therapy. With this perspective, it becomes obvious that the best person to regulate analgesic therapy is the patient. Patient-controlled analgesia (PCA) allows the patient to titrate small doses of intravenous, epidural, or subcutaneous opioid to regulate pain.[47] The delivery of frequent small doses of analgesic allows the patient to maintain the blood opioid concentration close to his or her own minimum effective analgesic concentration. This approach minimizes wide swings in blood opioid levels, possibly reducing the unwanted side effects by preventing the wide swings associated with oral and parenteral opioid administration. At least theoretically, PCA reduces the potential for overdosage, because the patient will become too sedate to activate the device. In some circumstances, this margin of safety has been impaired by an overzealous spouse who depressed the PCA button to help the patient avoid pain while sleeping or by the rare patient who sought to maintain a state of postoperative oblivion and depressed the button every time he or she was awakened by the low saturation alarm on the pulse oximeter.

Typical starting doses and intervals are listed for commonly used opioids in Tables 7–2 and 7–3. In many patients using PCA, a continuous opioid infusion in addition to the PCA may prove beneficial. However, there is evidence to suggest that a continuous opioid infusion rate does not appear to improve analgesia in postoperative pain patients and that the PCA bolus only may work best. Continuous infusion rates may contribute to opioid-related adverse events, such as respiratory depression, and do not appear to improve global pain scores.[10, 29] Continuous delivery rates may be initiated at a basal level, as indicated in Table 7–3. In patients with a history of extended preoperative opioid use, such as those who have chronic cancer pain or who are on methadone maintenance, a continuous infusion rate should be initiated at a rate to deliver the patient's preoperative opioid dose over a 24-hour period. The PCA mode dose should also be started at a higher dose to account for the patient's opioid tolerance. In all cases, frequent reevaluation is necessary.

Opioid dose requirements and pharmacokinetics vary considerably among patients, depending on age, sex, weight, medical condition, and prior opioid exposure. If set up inappropriately, a patient receiving PCA may spend hours watching the clock until time to administer the next PCA dose, never quite catching up with the pain.

TABLE 7–2

Common Opioid Analgesic Conversions

Agent	Intramuscular	Intramuscular/Oral Ratio	Half-life (hr)	Duration of Analgesia (hr)
Morphine	10	1:3	2–3.5	3–6
Oxycodone	na*	1:2	2–6	2–4
Meperidine	100	1:5	3–4	3–4
Methadone†	10	1:2	15–120	4–8
Fentanyl	0.1	na‡	1–3	1–3
Hydromorphone	1.5	1:5	2–4	2–4

*Oxycodone is not available in an injectable form.

†Methadone is available for intravenous delivery, but subcutaneous and intramuscular injections may cause local tissue injury. Intravenous methadone is roughly equivalent to morphine, except that its half-life is substantially longer and can accumulate with repeated doses.

‡Fentanyl is not available in a tablet form; however, there is a transbuccal form.

Parameters should be included to allow the nursing staff to increase the PCA bolus dose and to provide supplemental opioid doses if necessary. Also, postoperative nausea and vomiting may be more noticeable in patients receiving PCA opioids. Historically, many physicians prescribed a combination of an opioid with promethazine (Phenergan) or hydroxyzine (Vistaril). These agents offer little advantage with respect to pain control but can serve as effective antinausea therapy. Provision for possible nausea and vomiting can be made in the form of an as-needed dose of an antiemetic. This avoids the unnecessary delivery of medications that may provide little benefit to the majority of patients and may reduce side effects such as somnolence.

SPINAL OPIOIDS

It can now be appreciated that opioids have produced analgesia by activating specific receptors found in peripheral nerves, the afferent spinal nerves in the dorsal horn, and at several sites in the brain. Selective targeting of peripheral opioid receptors has been shown to be modestly effective in ameliorating postoperative pain following arthroscopy surgery.[39] A more effective means of selective opioid delivery has been the use of intrathecal and epidural opioids.[20, 24] The potential advantages of targeting the spinal cord opioid receptors include good analgesia and less sedation, fatigue, dry mouth, and dizziness. This is accomplished by delivering the opioid directly into the vicinity of the target receptor, bypassing the systemic circulation. This translates into a sevenfold to 10-fold reduction with epidural administration and a 100-fold reduction in total morphine exposure with

intrathecal delivery, hence the reduction in systemic opioid side effects.

A variety of different opioids have been delivered into the intrathecal and epidural spaces. In contrast to intravenous delivery, lipophilic agents are less attractive as spinal analgesics. The hydrophilic opioids, such as morphine and hydromorphone, appear better suited to epidural delivery because they tend to egress more slowly out of the subarachnoid space and allow for a greater duration and distribution within the central neuraxis. Lipophilic opioids, such as fentanyl, provide a more rapid onset of analgesia, but the duration of effect is relatively short. Continuous epidural infusion of fentanyl allows for more sustained analgesia; however, after the initial 10 to 24 hours, plasma fentanyl levels begin to approach those seen with intravenous fentanyl infusions, minimizing any potential selective spinal advantage.

Spinal opioids are quite useful in managing the pain associated with chest wall trauma, thoracotomy pain, vascular injuries, and upper abdominal surgery pain. In these situations there is evidence to suggest that epidural analgesia may contribute to improved outcome and even improved survival.[52] Combination therapy with an opioid analgesic, primarily morphine and hydromorphone, coupled with a local anesthetic can provide excellent analgesia allowing a further reduction in opioid requirement. Patient-controlled epidural analgesia is also available, which improves the flexibility of delivery and allows for better tailoring of the analgesia to the patient's needs.

Spinal opioid delivery can reduce some opioid side effects, specifically dry mouth, sedation, fatigue, and dizziness.[20] Other opioid side effects, such as nausea, vomiting, constipation, urinary retention, and pruritus, do

TABLE 7–3

Suggested Starting Doses for Intravenous Patient-Controlled Opioid Analgesia

Agent	Concentration (mg/mL)	PCA Dose (mg)	Lockout (min)	Loading Dose (mg/kg)
Morphine	1	1.0	6–8	0.1
Meperidine	10	10	6–8	1.0
Hydromorphone	0.2–0.5	0.2	6–8	0.015
Fentanyl*	50 µg/mL	10–50 µg	6–8	1–3 µg/kg

*Fentanyl is an order of magnitude more potent than the other opioids and the dose is administered in micrograms.

not appear to differ depending on the delivery route. Epidural hematoma formation and nerve compression are unique to spinal opioid delivery and can accompany the placement of an epidural catheter. This is a rare complication, usually associated with an underlying coagulopathy or concomitant administration of warfarin, heparin, or enoxaparin. Epidural or spinal analgesia should not be used in patients at risk for bleeding. Epidural catheter removal should take place only after correction of any coagulopathy or discontinuation of the anticoagulant.

The most feared complication associated with opioid therapy—respiratory depression—initially presented great concern among patients receiving spinal analgesia. This arose from the unexpected finding of respiratory depression developing in patients 6 to 20 hours after receiving a single dose of epidural morphine. The mechanism of this delayed respiratory depression involves the gradual diffusion of morphine through the spinal axis up to the respiratory centers of the medulla. Risk factors for respiratory depression include delivery of opioids in the thoracic or cervical epidural space, opioid naïve individuals, and concomitant systemic opioid delivery. As more experience has developed with the use of spinal opioids, the risk of respiratory depression has diminished and at present is not thought to exceed that seen with other routes of opioid delivery.

Pain Treatment in the Opioid-Tolerant Individual

Preexisting opioid use, in the form of protracted consumption of opioid analgesics following trauma, or a history of substance abuse is not an uncommon finding among orthopaedic trauma patients. Staged surgical procedures to repair multiple injuries will result in the need for and the development of a tolerance to the opioids as indicated by escalating demands. Individuals with a history of opioid abuse are particularly difficult to treat in this setting. Conflicting issues make it very difficult to sort out appropriate demands for pain treatment from "drug-seeking behavior." Unfortunately, there is no simple solution to this problem; however, several generalizations can be made to guide analgesic therapy in these patients.

Patients with a history of prior opiate exposure, illicit or therapeutic, require greater doses of opioid than the opiate naïve population. The degree and duration of the opioid exposure determines the amount of tolerance. Therefore, do not prescribe the usual outpatient opioid regimen because it will not be adequate. Patients with a history of opiate abuse, cancer pain, or chronic pain need higher than usual doses. Failure to provide adequate analgesia will generate appropriate complaining, requests for more medication, and overt pain behavior and hostility. This behavioral pattern has been labeled as *pseudoaddiction*.[46] It can be characterized as a circumstance in which the patient's behavior mimics the drug-seeking behavior commonly attributed to opioid abusers but in fact represents an appropriate response; it typically abates with adequate pain control. A general rule of thumb in treating this population is to provide 50% to 100% more opioid than the patient was taking during the preoperative period. This may be accomplished by converting the patient's usual preoperative opioid dose into morphine or oxycodone equivalents per 24-hour period, add to this preoperative dose an additional 50%, and deliver it as a continuous intravenous infusion or as a long-acting oral dose form. Be careful to factor the route of delivery into the conversion. Remember, only one half to one fifth of the oral dose reaches the central circulation. An additional 50% of the preoperative (24 hour) daily dose should be factored in and be provided in small as-needed doses for breakthrough pain.

One of the greatest challenges in treating the opioid-tolerant population is determining how and when to begin withdrawing opioid therapy. In the majority of patients, withdrawal occurs without specific intervention, because most patients taper themselves off as their pain resolves. This process may be slower in the opioid-tolerant individual or nonexistent in the patient with a history of substance abuse. Issues of chronic pain, protracted disability, and tolerance to the opioids may further complicate the picture. Experience in treating the opioid-naïve population can be used to determine a strategy to wean the tolerant patient off opioids, namely, by doubling the usual recovery phase. Expect the opioid-tolerant patient to require an extended period of analgesic use and to have pain persist for longer than usual. Opioid tapering can begin on a gradual basis. A key point is to avoid becoming frustrated with the resistant patient. Formulation of a treatment plan and adherence to the taper schedule with calm insistence usually achieves the desired goal. Opioid access can also be used as a motivational aide to promote participation in the rehabilitation program. It is also important to use adjuvant medications, such as NSAIDs and tricyclic antidepressants. These agents are often overlooked, but they can provide significant pain relief and offer supplemental benefits that include improved sleep. An evening dose of nortriptyline, amitriptyline, or doxepin can help obviate the need for a hypnotic at bedtime and may offer some supplemental analgesia. The NSAID can be added on a regular dosing interval around the clock for a 5- to 7-day period and then be reevaluated.

ADJUVANT ANALGESICS

Traumatic injuries frequently involve direct injury to neural elements, including the brain, spinal cord, and peripheral nerves. Neuropathic pain often responds poorly to the analgesics used in the treatment of pain arising from bone or tissue trauma (nociceptive pain). Examples of neuropathic pain states include phantom limb pain; neuritis-neuralgia; complex regional pain syndrome, type I (reflex sympathetic dystrophy) and type II (causalgia); and spinal cord injury pain. Opioids may be partially effective in relieving neuropathic pain; however, neuropathic pain states are often refractory to conventional opioid doses. Nonopioid analgesics, often referred to as adjuvant analgesics, include the tricyclic antidepressant, anticonvulsant, and antiarrhythmic drug classes and are often beneficial in treating neuropathic pain.

Tricyclic Antidepressants

Classically, the tricyclic antidepressants, amitriptyline in particular, have been widely used to treat neuropathic pain. These compounds have several possible sites of action in the nervous system. Amitriptyline, nortriptyline, and desipramine block the reuptake of norepinephrine and serotonin into the presynaptic neuron. The norepinephrine pathways are intimately involved with regulating the liberation of enkephalin within the spinal cord. Presumably, the tricyclic antidepressants enhance enkephalin's release, producing analgesia. Other beneficial effects include direct inhibitory effects of the NMDA receptor, reducing the excitatory effects of glutamate on the wide-dynamic range neuron, and anticholinergic effects responsible for producing sedation. When administered for pain treatment, the tricyclic antidepressants need only be administered as a single dose at bedtime. This reduces the impact of the sedative effects during the day, facilitates sleep, and improves patient compliance. As indicated in Table 7–4, these compounds exhibit a long half-life; thus, more frequent delivery is unnecessary. Although amitriptyline has been the most commonly used agent in this class, nortriptyline may be the better choice. Nortriptyline produces fewer anticholinergic effects. This translates into less daytime sedation and better patient tolerance. It is important to start slowly with these drugs, particularly in the elderly, escalating the dose at 1- to 2-week intervals. Side effects common to all of these compounds include weight gain, dry mouth, orthostatic hypotension, urinary retention, and cardiac arrhythmias.

Anticonvulsants

Anticonvulsants are becoming increasingly used in the management of neuropathic pain. The availability of several new compounds that do not appear to share the bone marrow depression and hepatotoxic effects linked to the older anticonvulsants, such as carbamazepine, pheny-

toin, and valproic acid, has resulted in less risk and greater patient acceptance. Gabapentin has become the first choice of many pain treatment specialists.[2, 27, 34] Gabapentin is a novel anticonvulsant that is not metabolized, is relatively devoid of serious toxicity, and can be dramatically helpful in 20% of patients suffering from neuropathic pain. Although relatively nontoxic, gabapentin is not devoid of side effects. Approximately 20% of patients treated with gabapentin experience treatment-limiting side effects such as sedation, fatigue, and dizziness.[2, 34] For many elderly patients, slow escalation, beginning with an evening dose, helps to reduce the impact of these side effects and improves patient acceptance. Most patients realize improvement at doses ranging between 900 and 2400 mg/day. The relatively short half-life requires dosing intervals of 6 to 8 hours.

Topiramate is another compound that has a potential role in treating neuropathic pain. Experience with topiramate is limited to anecdotal reports, but these are encouraging. Unfortunately, topiramate produces considerable sedation in many patients and may contribute to renal stone formation owing to its weak carbonic anhydrase inhibition. Carbamazepine continues to be the gold standard for neuropathic pain treatment. It is the only anticonvulsant approved for this specific indication by the Food and Drug Administration. Unfortunately, carbamazepine has numerous disadvantages that include the need to monitor the results of blood cell counts and liver function tests, frequent gastrointestinal and dermatologic side effects, and the potential for aplastic anemia. Carbamazepine, phenytoin, and valproic acid all carry a similar potential for bone marrow and liver damage. Valproic acid also carries a 1:200 risk of causing pancreatitis. Careful patient counseling and regular monitoring must be undertaken when prescribing these agents. Despite their adverse potential, the anticonvulsants may prove uniquely effective in managing neuropathic pain.

Neural Blockade

Another approach to the management of painful injuries is through the direct blockade of afferent neuronal transmission using local anesthetics. Regional anesthesia may be

TABLE 7–4				
Adjuvant Analgesics				
Agent	**Dose (mg)**	**Target Dose Range (mg)**	**Dosing Interval (hr)**	**Half-life (hr)**
ANTICONVULSANTS				
Gabapentin	100–300	900–2400	6–8	6
Topiramate	25–200	200–400	12	21
Carbamazepine	100–200	600–1200	8	15
Valproate	250	500–1000	8	10–12
Phenytoin	100	300	8	22
ANTIDEPRESSANTS				
Nortriptyline	25–100	50–100	24	31
Amitriptyline	25–100	50–150	24	15
Desipramine	25–100	50–150	24	18

used alone or in combination with general anesthesia to provide perioperative analgesia for patients undergoing surgical repair.[23] Regional anesthesia offers several advantages over general anesthesia that can favorably affect surgical outcome.[23, 42, 52] Beneficial effects include complete pain blockade; prevention of central nervous system sensitization; and a sympathectomy, which may improve circulation.[7, 50] The benefits of regional anesthesia are particularly notable in high-risk patients suffering from advanced medical ailments and in the frail elderly population.[52] Additional benefits of neural blockade can include extended analgesia into the postoperative period, less opioid requirement, and an associated reduction of opioid-related side effects. Neural blockade for postoperative analgesia can be divided into two types: long-acting single injection nerve blocks and continuous techniques using an indwelling catheter.

Long-acting local anesthetics—bupivacaine, etidocaine, tetracaine, and ropivacaine—can be used during the perioperative period to provide prolonged anesthesia-analgesia for 6 to 10 hours from initiation. The addition of epinephrine or clonidine extends the duration of most local anesthetics. Clonidine may be particularly helpful in the pediatric patient because it does not carry as much risk of hypotension or bradycardia as that commonly encountered when it is used in the adult population. Clonidine and other α-agonists may provide supplemental analgesia and prolongation of nerve blocks without introducing the tachycardia and anxiety experienced with epinephrine. Typical settings in which long-acting blocks may be helpful include brachial plexus block for shoulder surgery, femoral nerve block for knee reconstruction, and ankle blocks for foot surgery. The advantages of prolonged neural blockade include faster discharge from the postanesthesia care unit; less pain in the early postoperative period; and lower risk of opioid side effects such as nausea, vomiting, and urinary retention. There is also a body of evidence that indicates early intervention with regional anesthesia, before incision, may reduce the intensity of postoperative pain even 7 to 10 days after surgery. Disadvantages of long-acting anesthesia include limited use of the extremity, potential for nerve or tissue damage secondary to unrecognized nerve compression because of a lack of sensation, and severe pain developing at home when the block resolves on the evening of surgery. The last issue can be a significant problem because the block analgesia may wear off abruptly and the patient may not realize what is happening. The patient or the family may then make many anxious calls to the on-call surgeon, fearing that something is going wrong. It is also difficult to achieve pain control if inadequate analgesics have been prescribed. Successful use of long-acting anesthetic nerve blocks in an outpatient orthopaedic practice is dependent on careful patient education regarding what to expect, emphasis on taking the opioid analgesics in anticipation of the block wearing down, and ensuring that the patient has sufficient analgesic medication available.

Special care must also be taken by the patient to avoid pressure injuries, such as ulnar or common peroneal nerve injuries.[18] These two nerves are particularly susceptible to compression during the postoperative period when brachial plexus or epidural anesthetics are administered. Both the patient and the caretakers should be counseled before surgery about the potential risks and the need for soft padding around the anesthetized region. This counseling should be repeated again before release from the recovery area.

Regional anesthesia of the brachial plexus can be accomplished via several different techniques. The interscalene nerve block is extremely useful in providing anesthesia and analgesia for shoulder and upper arm procedures.[44] Successful anesthesia is usually accomplished by delivering a volume of 20 to 40 mL of local anesthetic into the interscalene groove at the C-6 level. Using an insulated needle with a nerve stimulator can facilitate the identification of the appropriate injection site. Good anesthetic coverage can be obtained over most of the shoulder and upper arm; however, coverage around and below the elbow is often variable. This technique is most useful for shoulder and upper arm procedures. Postoperative analgesia may persist up to 10 to 12 hours following the initial nerve block. Disadvantages of interscalene blocks include the development of Horner's syndrome, hoarseness, risk of a pneumothorax, epidural anesthesia, and accidental spinal injection; in addition, almost every patient experiences diaphragmatic dysfunction.[45] Inhibition of the phrenic nerve commonly accompanies the interscalene nerve block and can lead to a sense of dyspnea, causing anxiety. Rarely does a patient experience significant respiratory embarrassment.

A continuous interscalene block may be performed using several techniques. One method involves the use of a 20- to 16-gauge intravenous catheter to perform the block, which can be sutured or taped into position for repeated injections or a constant infusion. Several commercial systems have become available for continuous nerve blocks. One system uses a modified epidural needle and catheter. The needle is insulated and can be used in conjunction with a neurostimulator and may allow better positioning of the catheter.

Other approaches to the brachial plexus include the supraclavicular, infraclavicular, and axillary techniques. The supraclavicular technique provides access to the plexus at the level of the cords, where the neural structures are the most tightly associated, allowing the delivery of smaller anesthetic volumes. This advantage may be offset by a greater potential for a pneumothorax because the plexus is adjacent to the pleura. The infraclavicular approach may provide a more stable method of securing a continuous catheter. The axillary approach is often the easiest and is very useful in providing anesthesia below the level of the elbow.

Lumbar plexus blocks can be performed using an inguinal approach or paravertebral blocks. These locations provide excellent coverage of the anterior thigh and can be at least partially helpful in providing acute perioperative pain relief for knee reconstruction surgery. As with brachial plexus blocks, a continuous catheter may be inserted for repeated injection or for a continuous infusion. Combined lumbar plexus–sciatic nerve blocks can be used to provide broader coverage of the entire leg. Unfortunately, the amount of anesthetic required to block both regions often approaches the toxic limits for local anesthetics. The advantage of these techniques is that they allow the affected extremity to be isolated, unlike epidural anesthesia, which typically covers both limbs. This allows the patient to ambulate with the assistance of crutches unaided, as the motor function remains intact in the nonoperative limb.

Directed postoperative delivery of local anesthetic can also be accomplished by inserting a continuous catheter, such as an epidural catheter, into the subcutaneous tissue adjacent to a superficial nerve or incision. Continuous or periodic delivery of local anesthetic into sites such as an amputation stump or an iliac crest bone harvest site have been reported to be helpful in controlling postoperative pain and reducing opioid requirement. Several disposable commercial products are now available that include a catheter linked to an auto-infuser device, usually a Silastic or latex balloon reservoir. A flow-regulator provides a near constant delivery of local anesthetic, depending on the reservoir capacity, over hours to days.

EPIDURAL ANALGESIA

Epidural analgesia with local anesthetics gained its initial popularity in the management of labor pain during childbirth. With the discovery of the opioid receptors came the recognition that morphine could be delivered into the intrathecal or epidural spaces to selectively target the spinal opiate receptors to provide excellent analgesia without the large systemic doses needed for intravenous or intramuscular analgesia. In some respects, spinal opioid delivery has not quite lived up to expectations, in part because most opioid side effects are related to the binding of the opioids to receptors located primarily within the central nervous system. Thus, opioid side effects, such as nausea, vomiting, and constipation, have not been reduced with spinal administration. Other side effects, including urinary retention and pruritus, may be more problematic. The one key benefit of intrathecal opioids has been reduced sedation. There may also be some advantages to combining intraspinal opioids with one or more alternative analgesics, such as a local anesthetic, clonidine, and possibly a NSAID, in that these combinations can produce a synergistic effect, reducing individual toxicity and improving analgesia.

Epidural anesthesia and analgesia are most frequently delivered into the lower lumbar region. This is effective for providing anesthetic coverage of the lower extremity and abdomen. If sufficient volume of anesthetic is delivered, anesthetic levels may reach the entire thoracic region and extend to the cervical levels. Coverage of the thoracic region, for example, to provide analgesia for a thoracotomy, can be accomplished easily with lumbar epidural morphine delivery. Morphine tends to distribute rather widely within the intrathecal space and spreads well into the thoracic region. However, when using continuous local anesthetic infusions for postoperative analgesia, the anesthetics do not spread very far within the neuraxis unless driven by sheer volume. Thus, continuous local anesthetic epidural infusions tend to accumulate in the region about the catheter, often creating an area of dense anesthesia, producing a numb and weak limb. For abdominal or

thoracic surgery, this presents little problem if the catheter tip is placed at the appropriate dermatomal level, that is, a thoracic epidural. Most patients rarely notice sensory impairment over the chest or abdomen. However, weakness and the absence of sensation in the nonoperative limb are frequently a source of annoyance to most patients. Diminished sensation may contribute to nerve compression injuries, heel erosion, and bedsores.

The tendency of local anesthetics to show limited spread within the epidural space can at times be exploited to provide focal anesthesia. By directing an epidural catheter laterally within the epidural compartment, it is possible to provide a unilateral anesthetic block. This is occasionally achieved inadvertently during catheter insertion, but the catheter may be positioned intentionally using an angulated paramedian approach. Fluoroscopic guidance is also helpful in steering the catheter into the lateral region adjacent to the targeted nerve roots. By infusing small volumes of local anesthetic through the catheter, a persistent unilateral block may be obtained for days or even weeks. Buchheit and Crews have used cervical epidural infusions in the rehabilitation of complex regional pain syndromes of the upper extremity.[3] Unilateral blockade was attained in their patients without evidence of respiratory embarrassment. Cervical epidural analgesia appears to offer greater catheter stability and may be used for extended periods.

SUMMARY

In summary, multiple medications, routes, and techniques are available for pain control in the patient with multiple injuries. Optimal selection usually involves multimodal therapy. This allows for increased control with minimal side effects. In the same manner a patient's pain control can be optimized even in the face of chronic illness or during the acute physiologic instability of the recently injured patient. Tailoring the analgesic approach to the patient's medical condition, desires, and physical injuries ultimately produces the best outcome.

REFERENCES

1. Austin, K.L.; Stapleton, J.V.; Mather, L.E. Multiple intramuscular injections: A major source of variability in analgesic response to meperidine. Pain 8:47–62, 1980.
2. Backonja, M.; Beydoun, A.; Edwards, K.R.; et al. Gabapentin for the symptomatic treatment of painful neuropathy in patients with diabetes mellitus. JAMA 280:1831–1836, 1998.
3. Buchheit, T.; Crews, J.C. Lateral cervical epidural catheter placement for continuous unilateral upper extremity analgesia and sympathetic block. Reg Anesth Pain Med 25:313–317, 2000.
4. Burgess, F.W.; Anderson, D.M.; Colonna, D.; et al. Ipsilateral shoulder pain following thoracic surgery. Anesthesiology 78:365–368, 1993.
5. Christopherson, R.; Beattie, C.; Frank, S.M.; et al. Perioperative morbidity in patients randomized to epidural or general anesthesia for lower extremity vascular surgery. Anesthesiology 79:422–434, 1993.
6. Dahl, J.B.; Kehlet, H. Nonsteroidal antiinflammatory drugs: Rationale for use in severe postoperative pain. Br J Anaesth 66:703–712, 1991.
7. Devor, M.; Janig, W.; Michaelis, M. Modulation of activity in dorsal root ganglion neurons by sympathetic activation in nerve-injured rats. J Neurophysiol 71:38–47, 1994.

8. Dickenson, A.H. Spinal cord pharmacology. Br J Anaesth 75:193–200, 1995.

9. Donner, B.; Zenz, M.; Tryba, M.; Strumpf, M. Direct conversion from oral morphine to transdermal fentanyl: A multicenter study in patients with cancer pain. Pain 64:527–34, 1996.

10. Fleming, B.M.; Coombs, D.W. A survey of complications documented in a quality-control analysis of patient-controlled analgesia in the postoperative patient. J Pain Symptom Manag 7:463–469, 1992.

11. Galer, B.S.; Butler, S.; Jensen, M.P. Case reports and hypothesis: A neglect-like syndrome may be responsible for the motor disturbance in reflex sympathetic dystrophy. J Pain Symptom Manag 10:385–392, 1995.

12. Gibbons, J.J.; Wilson, P.R.; Lamer, T.J.; Elliott, B.A. Interscalene blocks for chronic upper extremity pain. Clin J Pain 8:264–269, 1992.

13. Gillies, G.W.A.; Kenny, G.N.C.; Bullingham, R.E.S.; McArdle, C.S. The morphine sparing effect of ketorolac tromethamine. Anaesthesia 42:727–731, 1987.

14. Gordon, S.M.; Dionne, R.A.; Brahim, J.; et al. Blockade of peripheral neuronal barrage reduces postoperative pain. Pain 70:209–215, 1997.

15. Graham, D.Y.; White, R.H.; Moreland, L.W.; et al. Duodenal and gastric ulcer prevention with misoprostol in arthritis patients taking NSAIDs. Ann Intern Med 119:257–262, 1992.

16. Griffin, M.R.; Piper, J.M.; Daugherty, J.R; et al. Nonsteroidal antiinflammatory drug use and increased risk for peptic ulcer disease in elderly persons. Ann Intern Med 114:257–263, 1991.

17. Hawkey, C.J. Cox-2 inhibitors. Lancet 353:307–313, 1999.

18. Horlocker, T.T.; Cabanela, M.E.; Wedel, D.J. Does postoperative epidural analgesia increase the risk of peroneal nerve palsy after total knee arthroplasty? Anesth Analg 79:495–500, 1994.

19. Kaiko, R.F.; Foley, K.M.; Grabinski, P.Y.; et al. Central nervous system excitatory effects of meperidine in cancer patients. Ann Neurol 13:180–185, 1983.

20. Kalso, E. Route of opioid administration: Does it make a difference? In: Kelso, E.; McQuay, H.J.; Wiesenfeld-Hallin Z., eds. Opioid Sensitivity of Chronic Noncancer Pain. Progress in Pain Research and Management, Vol. 14. Seattle, IASP Press, 1999, pp. 117–128.

21. Kaufman, D.W.; Kelly, J.P.; Sheehan, J.E.; et al. Nonsteroidal antiinflammatory drug use in relation to major upper gastrointestinal bleeding. Clin Pharmacol Ther 53:485–494, 1993.

22. Lanza, F.L.; Rack, M.F.; Simon, T.J.; et al. Specific inhibition of cyclooxygenase-2 with MK-0966 is associated with less gastroduodenal damage than either aspirin or ibuprofen. Aliment Pharmacol Ther 13:761–767, 1999.

23. Lauretti, G.R.; Reis, M.P.; Mattos, A.L.; et al. Epidural nonsteroidal antiinflammatory drugs for cancer pain. Anesth Analg 86:117–118, 1998.

24. Liu, S.; Carpenter, R.L.; Neal, J.M. Epidural anesthesia and analgesia. Anesthesiology 82:1474–1506, 1995.

25. Malmberg, A.; Yaksh, T.L. Pharmacology of the spinal action of ketorolac, morphine, ST-91, U50488H, and L-PIA on the formalin test and an isobolographic analysis of the NSAID interaction. Anesthesiology 79:270–281, 1993.

26. Marks, R.M.; Sachar, E.J. Undertreatment of medical inpatients with narcotic analgesics. Ann Intern Med 78:173–181, 1973.

27. Mellick, G.A.; Mellick, L.B. Reflex sympathetic dystrophy treated with gabapentin. Arch Phys Med Rehabil 78:98–105, 1997.

28. Merskey, H.; Bogduk, N. Classification of Chronic Pain, 2nd ed. Seattle, IASP Press, 1994.

29. Parker, R.K.; Holtmann, B.; White, P.F. Patient-controlled analgesia: Does a concurrent opioid infusion improve pain management after surgery? JAMA 266:1947–1952, 1991.

30. Perkins, F.M.; Kehlet, H. Chronic pain as an outcome of surgery: A review of predictive factors. Anesthesiology 93:1123–1133, 2000.

31. Portenoy, R.K.; Payne, R.; Coluzzi, P. Oral transmucosal fentanyl citrate (OTFC) for the treatment of breakthrough pain in cancer patients: A controlled dose titration study. Pain 79:303–312, 1999.

32. Rosenfield, B.A.; Beattie, C.; Christopherson, R.; et al. The effects of different anesthetic regimens on fibrinolysis and the development of postoperative arterial thrombosis. Anesthesiology 79:435–443, 1993.

33. Rossat, J.; Maillard, M.; Nussberger, J.; et al. Renal effects of selective cyclooxygenase-2 inhibition in normotensive salt-depleted subjects. Clin Pharmacol Ther 66:76–84, 1999.

34. Rowbotham, M.; Harden, N.; Stacey, B.; et al. Gabapentin for the treatment of postherpetic neuralgia. JAMA 280:1837–1842, 1998.

35. Silverstein, F.E.; Faich, G.; Goldstein, J.L.; et al. Gastrointestinal toxicity with celecoxib vs. nonsteroidal antiinflammatory drugs for osteoarthritis and rheumatoid arthritis. JAMA 284:1247–1255, 2000.

36. Simon, L.S.; Weaver, A.L.; Graham, D.Y.; et al. Antiinflammatory and upper gastrointestinal effects of celecoxib in rheumatoid arthritis. JAMA 282:1921–1928, 1999.

37. Singh, H.; Bossard, R.F.; White, P.F.; Yeatts, R.W. Effects of ketorolac versus bupivacaine coadministration during patient-controlled hydromorphone epidural analgesia after thoracotomy procedures. Anesth Analg 84:564–569, 1997.

38. Smith, W.L.; Dewitt, D.L. Prostaglandin endoperoxide H synthases-1 and -2. Adv Immunol 62:167–215, 1996.

39. Stein, C.; Comisel, K.; Haimerl, E.; et al. Analgesic effect of intraarticular morphine after arthroscopic knee surgery. N Engl J Med 325:1123–1126, 1992.

40. Strom, B.L.; Berlin, J.A.; Kinman, J.L.; et al. Parenteral ketorolac and risk of gastrointestinal and operative site bleeding. A postmarketing surveillance study. JAMA 275:376–382, 1996.

41. Treede, R.D.; Meyer, R.A.; Raja, S.N.; Campbell, J.N. Peripheral and central mechanisms of cutanous hyperalgesia. Prog Neurobiol 38:397–421, 1992.

42. Tuman, K.J.; McCarthy, R.J.; March, R.J.; et al. Effects of epidural anesthesia and analgesia on coagulation and outcome after major vascular surgery. Anesth Analg 73:696–704, 1991.

43. Tverskoy, M.; Cozacov, C.; Ayache, M.; et al. Postoperative pain after inguinal herniorrhaphy with different types of anesthesia. Anesth Analg 70:29–35, 1990.

44. Urban, M.K.; Urquhart, B. Evaluation of brachial plexus anesthesia for upper extremity surgery. Reg Anesth 19:175–182, 1994.

45. Urmey, W.; McDonald, M. Hemidiaphragmatic paresis during interscalene brachial plexus block: Effects on pulmonary function and chest wall mechanics. Anesth Analg 74:352–357, 1992.

46. Weissman, D.E.; Haddox, J.D. Opioid pseudoaddiction—An iatrogenic syndrome. Pain 36:363–366, 1999.

47. White, P.F. Use of patient-controlled analgesia for management of acute pain. JAMA 259:243–247, 1988.

48. Wong, H.Y.; Carpenter, R.L.; Kopacz, D.J.; et al. A randomized double-blind evaluation of ketorolac tromethamine for postoperative analgesia in ambulatory surgery patients. Anesthesiology 78:2–14, 1993.

49. Woolf, C.J. Evidence for a central component of postinjury pain hypersensitivity. Nature 303:686–688, 1983.

50. Woolf, C.J.; Shortland, P.; Coggehsall, R.E. Peripheral nerve injury triggers central sprouting of myelinated afferents. Nature 355:6355, 1992.

51. Woolf, CJ, Wall, PD. Morphine sensitive and morphine insensitive actions of C-fibre input on the rat spinal cord. Neurosci Lett 64:221–225, 1986.

52. Yeager, M.P.; Glass, D.D.; Neff, R.K.; Brinck-Johnsen, T. Epidural anesthesia and analgesia in high-risk surgical patients. Anesthesiology 66:729–736, 1987.

CHAPTER 8

Principles of Nonoperative Fracture Treatment

Loren L. Latta, P.E., Ph.D.
Augusto Sarmiento, M.D.
Gregory A. Zych, D.O.

INTRODUCTION AND RATIONALE

Despite the progress made in the surgical treatment of fractures, many fractures can be managed successfully by nonsurgical means with a lower complication rate and with very acceptable cosmetic and functional outcomes. These nonsurgical treatments are not sufficiently taught during medical training and are seldom mentioned in the many continuing education programs. Publications dealing with nonsurgical treatment of fractures are scarce, and the heavy marketing of surgical appliances by their manufacturers is overwhelming.

Anyone who has witnessed the mechanics and financing of the orthopaedist's education is keenly aware that such education has been skillfully manipulated by the industry to satisfy its marketing needs. Such factors must be seriously considered, as the need for a pragmatic approach to fracture care becomes necessary in light of economic considerations recently introduced by a cost-conscious society.

Costs of Diaphyseal Fracture Treatment

There is no doubt that orthopaedic surgeons find the surgical treatment of fractures more attractive than closed treatment. The immediate aesthetic and emotional gratification offered by the surgical interventions, the prestige associated with surgery, and the greater financial recompense that surgery generates under the current system are major factors contributing to the great popularity of metallic osteosynthesis.

Closed fractures of the tibia treated with functional braces can render a union rate higher than 98%, and more than 90% of those fractures heal with less than 8 degrees of angulation.[98] Even if the remaining 8% of the fractures that heal with more than 8 degrees of angulation needed corrective surgery, the cost of care would still be much lower (and without complications) than if all such fractures had been treated initially by surgical means.

The overall cost of care of closed tibial fractures with intramedullary fixation is higher. We conducted a study comparing intramedullary nailing versus bracing (Tables 8–1 and 8–2).[98] This information does not include the cost of a second hospitalization for the surgically treated patients who frequently required removal of the implant or the cost of the treatment of complications.

Shortening and Angulation

The overwhelming majority of closed diaphyseal tibial fractures ordinarily experience less than 1 cm of shortening.[98] That initial shortening does not increase, even though activity and graduated weight bearing are introduced in the management protocol shortly after the onset of the disability.[94, 99] A close observer of patients who had sustained tibial fractures that healed with 1 cm of shortening readily admits that a limp cannot be detected and that those fractures are not subject to long-term adverse sequelae.

The same applies to angulatory deformities. There is no solid evidence (only anecdotal reports) that angulatory deformities of less than 10 degrees result in late degenerative arthritis of the adjacent joints.[77] On the contrary, reliable information indicates that the absence of osteoarthritis is the pattern. Deformities of 8 degrees are almost always cosmetically acceptable.[58, 77, 96]

The initial shortening of diaphyseal fractures is determined by the degree of soft tissue damage. The more severe the damage, the greater the shortening.[96] In the case of the tibial fracture, the interosseous membrane provides an additional stabilizing mechanism. Casts and braces, therefore, do not play a significant role in providing axial

Table 8–1

Estimated Cost of Treatment with Tibial Intramedullary Nail

Treatment	Cost ($)
Initial emergency room visit	707
Preoperative laboratory examination	250
Operating room cost based on 90-minute operative time	1754
Surgeon's fee	1530
Anesthesiologist's fee	540
Cost of intramedullary nail	250
Follow-up radiographic examination based on five examinations at $68/2-view series	340
Inpatient hospital stay based on 3-day stay at $480/day	1440
Total estimated cost of intramedullary nail	6811

stability. They assist in a very significant way in providing angular and rotary stability.[63, 64, 69, 72, 96, 98, 99, 121]

It is important for the orthopaedic community to reach a clear understanding and an agreement on what constitutes a complication with regard to shortening and angulation at a fracture site. To call a residual shortening of 1 cm a complication following a fracture of a long bone is unreasonable. If such a deviation from the normal does not produce a limp or arthritis and is aesthetically acceptable, the result should be classified as good and without complications. The same should be said about angulatory deformities of a few degrees. As stated previously, those deformities are aesthetically acceptable, and degenerative arthritis is not a late sequela.

Fracture Healing and Stability

Vascularity at the fracture site plays a major role in osteogenesis.[73, 83, 96] The degree of vascularity is determined by the physiologically produced motion at the fracture site. When this motion is present, a rapid capillary invasion is noted. In its absence, such capillaries do not form. At this time, we do not have scientific information to explain this fascinating and most important phenomenon. It cannot be explained by the damage of the periosteum when a plate is used because even on the sides of the bone where no stripping of the tissues takes place the capillary invasion is also prevented. The same is true for fractures that are not surgically treated but simply rigidly immobilized with external fixators. The role of recently discovered

Table 8–2

Estimated Cost of Treatment with Tibial Fracture Brace

Treatment	Cost ($)
Initial emergency room visit	707
Orthopaedic surgeon's fee	650
Cost of prefabricated fracture brace	200
Orthotist fee to observe brace	200
Follow-up office visits based on 8 visits at $60/visit	480
Follow-up radiographic examination based on 8 examinations at $68/two-view series	544
Total estimated cost of closed treatment	2781

bone growth factors has not yet been clearly elucidated. The apparent ability to produce new bone at the site of the fracture when the fragments are rigidly immobilized remains a mystery.

We have speculated that elastic motion at the fracture site becomes osteogenically important as a result of a variety of changes in the limb that have been known for some time. Motion between fragments generates thermal changes that allegedly induce bone formation. That motion may also be responsible for an increase in piezoelectricity at the fracture site with greater formation of callus.[8–10, 13, 37, 75] Probably more important than those two factors is the inflammation produced in the area that brings about the capillary invasion. The perithelial and endothelial cells are capable of undergoing metaplasia.[96, 109, 110] Through a process of differentiation and redifferentiation, those cells become osteoblasts. One readily recognizes the abundance of osteoblasts in fractures that are not immobilized and their scarcity under rigid immobilization.[96] Furthermore, the activity of the osteoblast, measured by the amount of endoplasmic reticulum, is significantly greater in the nonimmobilized fracture.[96]

Return to Function following Fracture Treatment

Many believe that the use of an intramedullary nail to treat a tibial fracture allows a patient to regain full activity sooner than the use of functional nonsurgical methods. The same perception existed when plating of fractures was initially recommended. In those early days, it was believed that patients whose tibias were plated were able to return to athletic activities sooner than patients whose tibias were not plated. No one believes that any longer. Plated tibias require more time for sufficient healing to take place and for a return to strenuous activity. A similar observation can be made about the use of tibial intramedullary nails for closed diaphyseal fractures. Although it is true that, following nailing, some patients are capable of abandoning all types of external support within a few weeks after surgery, not all patients can do this. Many find it difficult to ambulate for long periods without discomfort at the fracture site. Others have significant discomfort at the entrance site of the nail and require the removal of the appliance to get rid of the pain.[27] In some instances, even the removal of the appliance fails to eliminate discomfort.[52]

In general, similar observations can be made about patients whose closed tibial fractures are treated with functional braces. Not all of them graduate to unassisted ambulation within 12 to 14 weeks, because discomfort at the fracture site may still be present. However, once the braces are discontinued, the majority are capable of ambulating with minimal or no symptoms shortly afterward. Obviously, the fact that a second surgical intervention for the removal of the nail and screws is not necessary is an added advantage.

The following text summarizes our knowledge and experimental work related to the nonsurgical treatment of diaphyseal fractures. It should be clearly understood that we readily recognize that the surgical care of fractures is the treatment of choice in many instances. However, we suggest that there is a very large percentage of fractures that can be treated by closed functional means in a rather inexpensive fashion and with a high rate of success.

FRACTURE HEALING

Casts that immobilize the joints adjacent to the fracture site attempt to minimize activity, muscle forces, and motion at the fracture site. This is important in the acute phases of management only. As soon as the patient is comfortable with passive and light active joint motion and load bearing, early functional activities should begin.

The Role of Function

Closed functional casting and bracing treatment of fractures encourages early function of the joints and musculature in the extremity without attempting to immobilize the fracture fragments. Healing in these cases occurs with abundant peripheral callus.[96] Closed functional treatment is based on the proposition that functional activity is conducive to osteogenesis.[96, 98] This type of motion at the fracture site is controlled by the surrounding elastic soft tissues, leading to optimal environmental factors that are conducive to healing with peripheral callus formation.[97]

If a fracture is not rigidly immobilized but simply externally stabilized in a cast or functional brace, the natural feedback mechanism of pain will guide the patient in controlling the level and degree of function in the injured extremity. This proprioceptive feedback seems to be essential not only to protect the tissues from overloading during the acute phases of repair but also to prolong the inflammatory phase of tissue repair in the later stages of callus formation. The soft tissues surrounding the fracture provide an elastic foundation on which motion at the fracture site is controlled.[25, 69, 72, 94, 98] These fractures may not heal with perfect alignment, but they almost inevitably heal even in the absence of any additional treatment. The goal of fracture bracing is to achieve fracture healing while disturbing as little as possible the natural reparative processes.

Natural, undisturbed healing can be observed in fractures of the ribs or clavicle, bones that cannot be immobilized but rapidly heal despite the continued motion required for the maintenance of vital functions. Animals in the wild who do not succumb to predators allow their fractures to heal by simply protecting their injured extremities acutely, then later resuming function to a level that can be tolerated. The control of function is dictated by the degree of comfort. Nonunions in primitive societies as well as in mammals are extremely rare. Researchers who have attempted to create nonunion models in mammals have acknowledged that it is a very difficult task. Nonunion of long bones in humans is for the most part the result of severe open fractures or the sequelae of human attempts to stabilize them internally.

Function and Vascularity

When a diaphyseal fracture occurs, the medullary blood supply as well as the blood supply of the cortical ends is disrupted.[54, 66, 84, 93] A hematoma forms at the fracture site. The disrupted medullary blood supply is slow to reestablish.[93] Metaphyseal blood flow is more abundant than diaphyseal flow and increases when a fracture occurs.[70] However, most of the vascular response to the injury at the fracture site comes from the peripheral soft tissues (Fig. 8–1).[41, 46, 96, 97] The peripheral blood supply is critical to the formation of peripheral callus.[74, 116] The importance of early revascularization from the soft tissue is emphasized by the close association of bone formation and early vascular invasion.[23, 33, 86, 93, 109] When there is motion at the fracture site, the activity level of the osteoblasts and osteoclasts in the area and the number of capillaries are increased.[96]

Function and Symptoms

A very close assessment of clinical signs and symptoms in the early phases of fracture healing in patients treated with closed functional bracing methods correlated with documented studies in animals provides a hypothesis for the interactions of critical environmental factors, which create a milieu to influence early fracture healing (Fig. 8–2). When function of the extremity is introduced early, acute symptoms seem to subside more rapidly and the limb becomes relatively comfortable even though motion at the fracture site is still present. This suggests a potentially important role for function in the early development of callus.

Patients who are reluctant to use the injured extremity early heal more slowly, maintain acute symptoms longer, and seem to have a higher incidence of delayed unions than patients who function aggressively in the early stages of treatment.[98] Whether this reflects the personality of the fracture or the personality of the patient is not known, but the relationship to the time of healing is clear. Fractures that allow shearing motions between the fragments produce a more abundant callus and unite more rapidly and consistently than those that are inherently more stable (i.e., transverse fractures that are anatomically reduced). Although plating also allows motion of the joints and function of the musculature, early motion at the fracture site is prevented and therefore peripheral callus does not form.[63, 68, 94, 97]

When function and weight bearing are introduced in the early stages of healing, motion occurs at the fracture site and is associated with cartilage formation in that area before the revascularization of the center of the callus.[57, 68, 96, 97, 121] Cartilage formation is probably the body's means of dealing with the severe deviatoric strains that prevent early vascular invasion in the tissues in the region of the fracture site. Although there is still much controversy about the ideal type of strain for healing

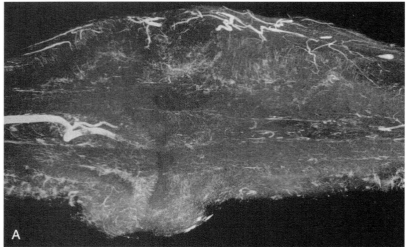

FIGURE 8–1. *A,* Microangiography of a longitudinal section of a dog's radius at 2 weeks postfracture showing the extent of capillary invasion from the soft tissues and disruption of the medullary circulation. *B,* A view of the surface of a peripheral callus after the periosteum has been lifted and the multiple capillary connections have been pulled from the surface. (*A,* From Sarmiento, A.; et al. Clin Orthop 149:232, 1980. *B,* From Sarmiento, A.; Latta, L.L. Closed Functional Treatment of Fractures, Fig. 2.6a, b. New York, Springer-Verlag, 1981.)

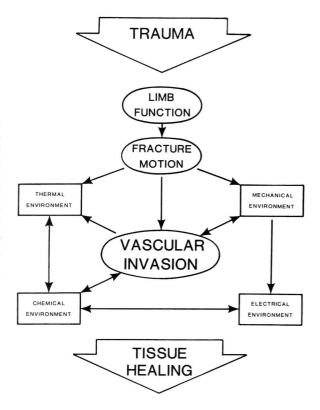

FIGURE 8–2. Interaction of environmental factors that influence tissue healing after trauma of fracture is affected primarily by degree of limb function, fracture site motion, and vascular development. Functional activity provides forces on the bone fragments to produce motion at the fracture site. Motion provokes an irritative inflammatory response, enhancing vascular development and increasing temperature. Motion at the fracture site tends to increase local temperature through friction and also induces localized strains, producing strain-related potentials in the surrounding hard and soft tissues of the developing callus. Strain-related potentials from the mechanical environment also enhance the electrical environment and its influence on the formation and orientation of tissues. The electrical environment may also influence chemical reactions by controlling distribution of ions. Vascular development also provides capillary pressure gradients to the mechanical environment influencing the streaming potentials. Increased vascularity also provides a means of transport for nutrients and waste products of chemical processes. (From Sarmiento, A.; et al. Instr Course Lect 33:83–106, 1984.)

tissues in the callus,[5, 19, 20, 61, 79, 80, 87, 105] only after stability has been achieved from the peripheral callus can the vascular invasion and mineralization of the cartilage occur.

PERIPHERAL CALLUS

New vascularity is very regional when peripheral callus forms and is closely associated with the calcification of the tissues forming in the callus. The location of the tissues in the forming callus has a dramatic effect on its mechanical behavior. Therefore, a structural description of the formation of the callus becomes important for a clear understanding of peripheral callus development and mechanical function.[28, 63, 65, 85, 95, 97]

Radiography versus Symptoms

From a mechanical standpoint, the description of fracture healing must be defined in terms of the macroscopic structural features in callus development. Local biologic and tissue-related events in the individual region of the fracture callus, each with its own temporal and spatial distribution, contribute to the mechanical behavior of the whole callus. The stages for callus development, defined on a structural basis, include a *period of instability* (stage I) caused by the disruption of soft tissues and bone resulting from the initial injury. Motion of the fragments is strictly controlled by the elastic support from the surrounding soft tissues at this stage. Instability is characterized by gross motion of the fracture fragments related to loading and to the degree of soft tissue damage. Displacement of the fragments or external pressure on the surrounding soft tissues can tighten the soft tissue structures that control the fragments and increase bony stability. No bone or organized soft tissue has had time to form in the bridging region, so a hematoma fills the central region and the disrupted soft tissue envelope makes up the peripheral region. Thus, stability can be provided only by the surrounding soft tissues. Pain is probably one of the most important factors in controlling fracture site motion in this stage of healing. If pain is not present to limit the level of activity and tissue strain in the unstable phase, tissue damage may continue and nonunion may develop.[4]

The second event is the *soft callus* (stage II), during which the callus behaves in a rubbery compliant manner controlling the bone fragments. In the soft callus stage, there appears to be a form-function relationship in the early peripheral soft tissue before the bone formation occurs (Fig. 8–3). This may be related to the need for tensile stress resistance in the periphery to provide bending and torsional stability, with the central region providing compressive stress resistance. Because the tension band mechanism in the early phase is provided by relatively compliant soft tissues in the peripheral region, the structure responds in a fairly compliant manner, and this is appropriately termed the stage of soft callus.[115] The soft callus stage provides early stabilization. The adjacent regions have increased in diameter from subperiosteal new bone formation. The

central region has no blood supply; thus, soft tissues and cartilage persist. The fluid-like nature and compressive resistance of these tissues may provide a hydraulic-like resistance mechanism in these tissues (predominantly dilatational tissue strains) confined by the peripheral region. Such a structure could transmit loads such as an intervertebral disk between two rigid vertebral bodies surrounded by a tough, tensile-resistant annulus. Because of the large callus size, the stresses on the tissues are minimal for even heavy loading conditions. Evidence suggests that in the soft callus stage, the ends of the fracture fragments are continually moving as a result of the loading provided by the functional activity. Continued tissue disruption, induction, and inflammation persist because of the deviatoric strains in the tissues. Formation, organization, and maturation of the soft tissues progress in the central region to form at first fibrous and then hyaline cartilage. Thus, a gradient of relatively compliant and rigid tissues exists to resist bending and torsion. A potential form-function relationship develops in the tissues of the central callus region because the most well-organized mature tissue develops peripherally where the compressive stresses should be maximal to resist bending and torsional loads. Peripheral structures supply early vascularization and soft tissue repair (see Fig. 8–1). Peripheral soft tissues provide a compliant strength, which leads to reduction of acute symptoms long before there is radiographic evidence of healing.[63, 97, 98]

The *hard callus* (stage III) is characterized by the initial bony bridge in the peripheral region between the adjacent callus regions. Early in the hard callus stage, a relatively thin rim of bone bridges the proximal and distal adjacent regions (Fig. 8–4). This early hard tissue development is represented by a bony bridge in the periphery that roentgenographically does not appear to be very dense. Thus, the radiographic evidence of healing lags behind the true strength and stiffness of callus as well as the clinical symptoms.[97] The peripheral bone affords an increased mechanical advantage to the callus structure because of its location far from the neutral axis of the original bone. At this time, the callus behaves as a relatively rigid and strong structure, which in many cases has strength that surpasses that of the original cortical bone. In the central callus region, no direct endosteal or extraperiosteal blood supply is available. Vessels invade this region only through the encroachment from the adjacent and peripheral callus regions. Hematoma and cartilage can persist in this region after the peripheral region has begun to calcify and the overall callus structure has become rigid. In the later stages of hard tissue development, endochondral ossification increases the thickness of the peripheral new bone and encroaches on the central region and shrinks this radiolucent zone.

The next stage is termed *fracture line consolidation* (stage IV) and is characterized by shrinkage of the central callus zone and disappearance of the radiolucent fracture line. This stage, although mechanically no stiffer or stronger than the hard callus stage, is significant in that it is commonly referred to in a clinical assessment as the radiographic definition of the healed fracture. It should be noted, however, that the overall callus structure has developed its strength before this stage of fracture healing, as demonstrated by laboratory and clinical experiences

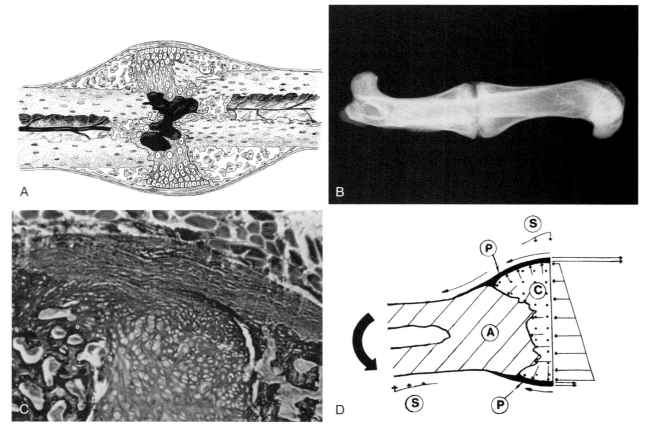

FIGURE 8–3. *A, B,* In the second stage of structural fracture healing (soft callus), subperiosteal bone and medullary callus have formed in the adjacent region, but the central region has filled with cartilage and fibrous tissue, and the peripheral region covers them with dense fibrous tissue, forming a new periosteum (*A*), which is not evident radiographically (*B*). Mechanically, the cartilage and fibrous tissue in the central region can resist compression and possibly shear stresses, but tensile resistance to bending and torsion must be provided by the dense fibrous tissue in the peripheral region. *C,* A low-power histologic section at the junction of the peripheral portion of the adjacent and central regions with the peripheral region shows the fiber bundle alignment in the peripheral region, in the direction of stress, when the callus has formed with function. *D,* This diagram, cut through the central (*C*) and peripheral (*P*) regions, shows how the two combine mechanically (like the nucleus pulposus and annulus fibrosus in the spine) to stabilize the adjacent (*A*) rigid bodies and resist bending. Because bridging zones are completely made up of soft tissues, the callus, as a whole, acts as a relatively compliant structure in this stage of healing. The central region is confined by the peripheral region thus minimizing shear stress on the central tissues, which are weak when subjected to shear, so the surrounding soft tissue (*S*) still provides support to the structure. (*A, B,* From Sarmiento, A.; et al. Instr Course Lect 33:83–106, 1984. *C,* From Sarmiento, A.; Latta, L.L. Functional Fracture Bracing, Fig. 5.14a. New York, Springer-Verlag, 1995. *D,* From Zagorski, J.B.; et al. Instr Course Lect 36:377–401, 1987.)

using closed functional methods of treatment.[96] Simultaneously with fracture line consolidation, local remodeling occurs in the peripheral regions.

The final stage of fracture healing is *structural remodeling* (stage V), which is characterized by callus shrinkage and return toward the original bone geometry. Remodeling is present in all zones. A new medullary canal is established, and the bone begins to approach a normal radiographic appearance.

ALTERATIONS OF THE INFLAMMATORY PROCESS

It has been shown that early function is important to the development of early callus in a qualitative sense by optimizing the environment for healing. To appreciate the importance of function, it is valuable to compare the healing of fractures in a normal functional environment with the healing of fractures in an environment that has been changed by depriving the limb or its parts of normal functional activity or by local or systemic chemical alterations.

Immobilization of the Limb

Immobilization not only causes muscle atrophy and reduced circulation in the limb but also retards the healing process significantly. Radiographic and histologic studies in rats show significantly less cartilage in the callus at any given time during the early stages of healing. Changes in biochemical activity show a retardation of the normal endochondral ossification process.[42, 56, 90] Changes in calcification under reduced stress may be the cause of the increased brittleness of the callus and decreased strength and stiffness measured by refracture. Quantitative changes in mass, metabolism, and strength of healing bones deprived of stress have been measured.[39, 47, 84]

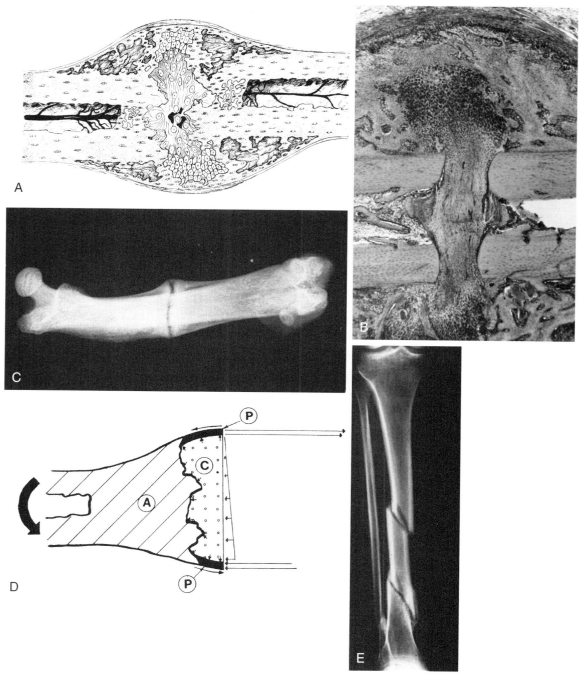

FIGURE 8–4. *A–E,* In the third stage of structural callus formation (hard callus), bone begins to form in the peripheral callus region supplied by vascular invasion from the surrounding soft tissues (*A, B*). This early bone formation may be very thin and not radiographically dense (*C*), and the central region is still the bulk of the bridging tissues. Diagrammatically (*D*), the dense rim of peripheral bone (P) in the periosteal callus that surrounds the old cortical bone can develop both tension and compression stresses to resist bending and torsion. In the rat, this stage III callus even surpassed the strength of the original bone when refractured in bending. This can also hold true for humans. In this patient, stage III healing was reached in the fracture brace (*E*), so the brace was discontinued. The patient resumed his motorcycle activity and refractured in torsion at a new location (*E*), adjacent to the stronger callus (still in stage III healing). (*A, B,* From Sarmiento, A.; et al. Instr Course Lect 33:83–106, 1984. *C,* From Latta, L.L.; Sarmiento, A. In: Symposium on Trauma to the Leg and Its Sequelae, pt. 3. St. Louis, C.V. Mosby, 1981. *D,* From Zagorski, J.B.; et al. Instr Course Lect 36:377–401, 1987. *E,* From Sarmiento, A.; Latta, L.L. Closed Functional Treatment of Fractures, Fig. 2.19b. New York, Springer-Verlag, 1981.)

Immobilization of the Fracture

Immobilization of the fracture fragments provides a different radiologic picture of fracture healing, because peripheral callus is minimal and endosteal and end-to-end bridging callus predominate.[92] The callus is difficult to identify radiologically. No endochondral ossification is evident histologically, and direct bone formation takes place in areas in which there is direct bone contact from one fragment to the other.

Effects of Function

With closed functional bracing treatment, the negative effects on the healing tissues are minimal. Muscle activity and function are introduced as comfort permits and allow elastic motion of the fragments. Progressive irreversible deformation is prevented by elastic support of the soft tissues. Surgical disruption of the healing tissues is prevented. This may account for the differences in mechanical strengths of callus formed with the influences described previously compared with the results from many studies of healing in altered environments.*

Some investigators have attempted to improve or accelerate fracture healing compared with what happens in the natural, undisturbed process. The quantity and quality of callus formed can be altered by limb immobilization,[95] fracture site immobilization,[63, 88] non–weight bearing,[107] imposed loading,[118] imposed fracture site motion,[40, 61, 68] increased venous pressure,[59] applications of bone morphogenic protein,[112] local injection of bone morphogenic protein,[35, 108] altered electrical potentials,[13, 67] vibratory stimulation,[45, 89] prostaglandins,[3, 53, 104, 114] growth hormone,[7, 49] calcium, and vitamin D.[71, 86] However, no one has been able to prove that any substance or phenomenon can produce a stronger callus faster than nature's process of fracture repair.

All of the descriptions of fracture repair discussed in this chapter apply only to diaphyseal fractures. Metaphyseal fracture healing is very different.[21, 111]

MECHANICAL STABILITY

Traction

Traction is applied primarily for acute management to slowly reduce bone fragments that are overriding owing to initial displacement and soft tissue damage at the time of the injury and that have been maintained in their position because of edema and muscle spasm in response to the injury. If tension can be maintained while muscles relax and swelling subsides, length can be restored. One must be careful to monitor muscle compartments during this process, because lengthening a limb segment necessarily lowers the volume of the muscle compartments, which tends to increase compartment pressures. Once limb

---

*See references 14, 20, 32, 36, 39, 47, 53, 55, 65, 78, 80, 83, 91, 95, 100, 107, 118, 120, 121.

length has been restored to an acceptable position, the length must be maintained by some means until soft callus can be achieved before function can be restored without loss of the reduction. A cast or brace can maintain the reduced length *only* if bony stability (i.e.; well-reduced transverse fractures) or soft callus provides limb stability. Traction can be maintained until callus provides stability, but this usually requires several weeks of traction, which is often impractical. Dynamic traction allows controlled activity while maintaining tension on the limb. This method can be modified to remove the traction temporarily to allow patients to get out of bed, engage in limited functional activity for a short time in an upright position, and then return to traction in bed. Of course, the other alternative, after initial traction to obtain the desired reduction, is to use external or internal fixation to maintain the reduction and allow early functional activity.

Joint Immobilization and Mobilization

Numerous studies have demonstrated that fracture stability without the influence of internal fixation is not significantly increased with joint mobility and functional activity compared with that achieved with rest or joint immobilization.[64, 69, 72, 93, 95] Thus, immobilization of joints beyond the acute phases of healing (stage I) is not necessary and is detrimental to the general health of the limb (Fig. 8–5). Joint mobilization can begin within days

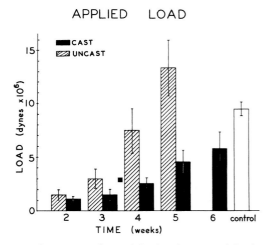

FIGURE 8–5. Comparison of immobilized and nonimmobilized animals showed significant differences in the development of strength, as reflected in the load required to refracture the femurs in bending at corresponding times postfracture. Note that by week 4, the uncast group of animals is nearly healed, and that by week 5, at stage III callus, the healing bones have surpassed the original fracture strength of the normal bones. However, the bone in the immobilized limbs consistently lagged significantly behind that in the uncast animals in strength at all stages of healing. Of clinical significance is the relationship of stiffness and strength in each group. Whereas the nonimmobilized group regained its original stiffness at the same rate that it gained its original strength, the immobilized group regained stiffness much faster than strength. Thus, a manual test of fracture healing in the clinic is *not* a reliable test for strength of healing if the limb has been immobilized, but it *is* a good test for a fracture healing in a functional environment. (From Sarmiento, A.; Latta, L.L. Closed Functional Treatment of Fractures, Figs. 2.26, 2.27. New York, Springer-Verlag, 1981.)

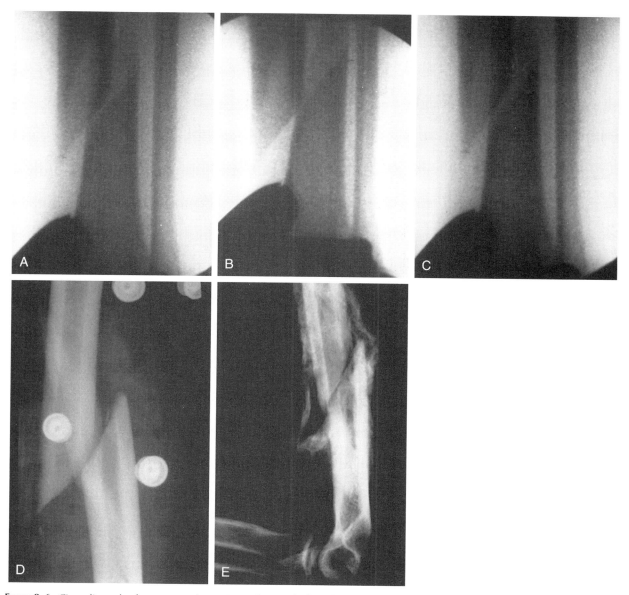

FIGURE 8–6. Cineradiography demonstrates the motion at the site of a fresh fracture that results from application and relaxation of load in vivo. The position of the bone before load is applied (*A*) changes during the application of load (*B*), but the fragments return to their original position once load has been relaxed (*C*). In this example of a humerus fracture at early healing (*D*), the fragments demonstrate overriding, probably due to muscle contraction as a protective mechanism in the acute stage. At final healing (*E*), however, the fragments return to their relaxed position, demonstrating the elastic nature of fracture site motion. (*A–C*, From Sarmiento, A.; et al. Clin Orthop 105:106, 1974. *D, E*, From Zych, G.A.; et al. Instr Course Lect 36:403–425, 1987.)

of most injuries, in weight-bearing bones, without compromising fracture stability in the majority of fractures.

The Mechanical Role of Soft Tissues in Fracture Stability

Because mobilization of adjacent joints and function of the musculature appear to be beneficial for fracture healing, it is important to understand how motion at the fracture site may be controlled to prevent the occurrence of progressive deformities. Laboratory studies on above-the-knee amputations correlate well with in vivo measurements.[62, 64, 69, 72, 94, 96, 99, 103] Such studies have demon-

strated that the motion that takes place at the fracture site is elastic (recoverable when load is relaxed).[64, 72, 94, 99, 122]

SOFT TISSUE COMPRESSION

In a fracture brace that allows joint function and movement of the bone fragments, measurable load is borne by the brace. The soft tissues carry most of these loads while allowing small amounts of motion of the bone fragments. These movements, however, are fully elastic, so that progressive deformity does not occur (Fig. 8–6). The soft tissues control the amount of motion, which is related to the fit of the brace and the extent of soft tissue damage.

The soft tissues have two major mechanisms for load bearing and provision of stiffness to the limb when encompassed in a fracture brace. The first mechanism is related to their incompressibility. The muscle compartments act as a fluid-like structure surrounded by an elastic fascial container. Dynamic load deforms the compartments of fixed volume (incompressible fluid), causing changes in their shape that stretch the fascial boundaries. When these compartments are bound by a relatively rigid container, such as a fracture brace, they can displace under load only until they have filled all the gaps within the container. Once this slack is taken up in the system, the muscle mass becomes rigid because its boundaries (the walls of the brace) do not move. After the load has been relaxed, the elastic, fascial boundaries of each muscle return to their original shape, which brings the fragments to their original positions.

This mechanism of load bearing in the soft tissues is important in the early stages of management when little healing has taken place in the bone or soft tissues. The fragments are loose and must rely heavily on the soft tissues for support until callus forms. The soft tissues must rely heavily on the degree of fit of the fracture brace for this mechanism to be effective. For long-term use, this mechanism cannot be relied on because the dimensions of the soft tissues change with time through loss of edema, atrophy, viscoelastic creep, and fluid flow. The fit of the cast or brace cannot be maintained indefinitely unless it is frequently adjusted.[102] Loss of fit results in increased slack in the system, which increases the displacement of the fragments required to produce mechanical equilibrium between the applied forces and the resistance of the tissues. The hydraulic effect of the tissues is not responsible for the long-term maintenance of the length of the limb. The initial shortening is dictated by the degree of soft tissue damage at the time of injury.[62, 96]

With rapid, dynamic loading, however, the soft tissue compartments act as incompressible fluids, causing the volume of the tissue to be fixed. In this manner, hydraulics can control motion of the fragments and provide support for the intact tissues by increasing the stiffness of the limb and possibly protecting them from further damage. The hydraulic or incompressible fluid-like behavior is responsible for the control of motion of the fragments before callus has developed, and it provides the significant degree of stiffness observed in loaded limbs with fresh fractures fit with fracture braces. Hydraulics controls certain rapid fluctuations in the system but does not control slow, progressive changes.[96]

INTRINSIC SUPPORT

The other soft tissue mechanism for load transfer involves the intrinsic strength of soft tissues in tension as they support the bone fragments at their natural attachments. Their ability to do so is inversely related to the degree of disruption of their attachments to the bone at the initial injury (Fig. 8–7). One factor contributing to intrinsic strength is the degree of soft tissue healing, which is also inversely related to the degree of damage. Through the inherent strength of the tissues, shortening greater than the initial shortening developed at the time of injury is prevented. With the length of the limb controlled by the soft tissues, the brace provides a lever advantage to control angulation by three-point support without creating appreciable pressures in the soft tissues.

The interplay between these soft tissue mechanisms is related to the amount of time after the injury and the degree of soft tissue damage at the time of injury. The incompressible fluid effect, or hydraulics, is most important in the early postinjury period and with extensive soft tissue stripping. Because the snugness of fit of the brace determines the slack in the brace–soft tissue system and the slack determines the amount of motion at the fracture site, the fit of the brace is critical during early healing when the fragments are loose. If the initial shortening is unacceptable at the time of injury and it is corrected by traction, maintenance of that reduction cannot be accomplished through hydraulics. If the fracture geometry naturally provides axial stability, that is, transverse with anatomic reduction, it is possible to maintain a reduced limb length in a cast or brace. But the patient must be observed carefully in case the fragments slip off and the original shortening recurs. This is because the fragments are not supported by the intrinsic strength of the soft tissue until they have returned to the initial shortening experienced at injury (see Fig. 8–6). Because hydraulics cannot be relied on to control such slow progression of shortening if the fracture does not have axial stability (i.e., oblique or comminuted), a loss of the regained length is almost

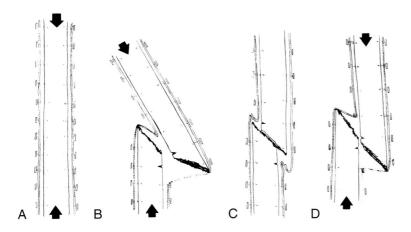

Figure 8–7. *A,* Representation of a bone with attached soft tissues. *B,* Disruption of the soft tissues is associated with a given initial displacement of the fragments at the time of injury. *C,* If the fragments are reduced after the injury, the soft tissues are placed in a relaxed position and cannot support the fragments. *D,* Thus, with the application of load, the fragments are apt to return to the original degree of overriding. Only in this position can the soft tissues be placed in tension and provide a tether to stabilize the fragments. (*A–D,* From Sarmiento, A.; Latta, L.L. Closed Functional Treatment of Fractures, Fig. 2.40a, b, c, d. New York, Springer-Verlag, 1981.)

A   B   C   D

certain to take place with early function. Thus, in such fractures in which the length of the limb must be restored, limb length should be maintained with traction or external or internal fixation until intrinsic strength can be regained in the soft tissues in their new position. Braces do not prevent shortening; the ultimate shortening of a closed fracture takes place at the time of injury!

Even though motion at the fracture site can be readily produced in a fresh fracture with only small amounts of load, that motion will not increase proportionally with higher loads.[64, 69, 72, 96] The reason for this is that the first amount of motion seen at low loads represents the low resistance of the system because of the slack within it. But once this slack is taken up by the tension in the soft tissues or filling of voids in the brace, the system stiffens comparable to an intact limb or an internally fixed limb. The major difference between the stiffness provided by rigid fixation and that of fracture bracing is the initial controlled motion at the fracture site allowed by the fracture brace.

This description of fracture stability applies to diaphyseal fractures surrounded by soft tissue. Because metaphyseal fractures in long bones occur near the joints, where there is minimal surrounding soft tissue and at least one fragment that is very short compared with the one with a diaphyseal segment, the leverage is poor, and direct soft tissue compression is impractical. Thus, joint positioning and motion control by the brace must be used to provide other means of stabilization (i.e., soft tissue tension banding) or direct three-point pressure on the bone fragments if they lie close to the surface. Such methods are described in detail for each specific application, but the description of diaphyseal soft tissue stabilization applies to most situations in which closed, functional treatment is applied to diaphyseal fractures.

APPLICATIONS TO CLINICAL CARE

To apply the concepts developed from laboratory observations to clinical practice, one must look for similar circumstances in a clinical setting and observe the similarities and dissimilarities to the laboratory models. Animals do not behave like humans; their bones do not heal like human bones; and their anatomy and biomechanics of function are not like those of humans. However, many similarities do exist if viewed in the proper context. Humans, like animals, have different demands on each different bone in their bodies; each individual is very different from another individual, and so on. All these factors create variations in the healing and functional requirements.

Implementing Function

The radiographic evidence of healing is very indefinite in the first three stages of fracture healing, but it is precisely within these stages that the most critical events occur in relation to the long-term results. Many clinicians have noted a golden period of about 6 weeks within which

function must begin to have the greatest probability of long-term success. It is unlikely that human diaphyseal bone will reach stage IV healing within the first 6 weeks with closed, functional treatment. Thus, clinical signs and symptoms must guide the surgeon and the patient in introducing function.[96, 98] For the surgeon, this means close communication with the patient to understand these signs and symptoms and to inform the patient of the importance of function and pain as feedback mechanisms. Thus, patient cooperation and understanding are also important.

Identifying Healing Stages

Each bone heals at a different rate, which is modified in varying degrees by the age of the patient, systemic and metabolic conditions, and other factors. For this reason, it is difficult to understand how to use the information provided by laboratory studies directly and how to use radiographs to assess clinical progress.[86] The average patient with a humeral fracture treated by early functional bracing usually requires only about 8 to 10 weeks before healing is complete clinically. On the other hand, a typical tibial fracture that is closed and is the result of a low-energy injury and is treated by similar means usually requires 12 to 16 weeks to reach the same degree of clinical progress. Femoral fractures seem to heal more rapidly than tibial fractures but more slowly than humeral fractures. Most femoral fractures reach stage II healing at 3 to 5 weeks and are radiographically healed (stage IV) by 8 to 10 weeks.

Materials and Devices

The first objective of device design and implementation is to allow as much muscle and joint function near the fracture site as possible without jeopardizing the stability of the fracture. Usually, the joint immediately distal to the fracture has the most important motion that will require activity in the majority of the muscles surrounding the fracture site and thus will provide the best environmental influence to encourage localized revascularization. Stability is best provided by soft tissue molding for diaphyseal fractures and by joint positioning for metaphyseal fractures. Soft tissue molding uses the hydraulic effect of soft tissues to provide stiffness to the limb. Joint positioning provides tension band effects to stabilize the fragments. The tension band can be passive, through the ligamentous and capsular structures, or it can be active, through the orientation of forces from muscles and tendons or the reduction of their mechanical effects.

The degree to which these concepts may be successfully applied relates to the soft tissue damage, the properties and shapes of the materials applied, and the anatomy of the limb segments. Long bones of the upper and lower limbs reside in two types of limb segments based on similarities in anatomy and subsequent inherent stability. The first type of limb segment is that having two bones and an interosseous membrane surrounded by muscular tissues with a lesser amount of fat in the subcutaneous region.

This type of limb segment, in general, is inherently stable and is well controlled with external types of appliances, such as a cast or fracture brace. External cylindrical structures can be molded easily to these soft tissues and can control the position of the soft tissues quite well because of the lack of mobility of the muscle mass underneath the skin and the adherence of the fascial connections of the muscle compartments to the skin. This is partly demonstrated by moving the skin in the forearm or leg back and forth along the long axis of the limb with the fingers, noting that the movement of skin across the adjacent joints is attenuated as in the hand, foot, arm, or thigh.

The bones also seem to be much more superficial in these limb segments, and a bony prominence can be firmly molded to help control the fragments beneath. Most important is the presence of an interosseous membrane that bridges the two bones. In fractures with minor displacement, the interosseous membrane experiences minimal damage and, therefore, does not compromise its ability to stabilize the fracture fragments. The interosseous membrane in both the forearm and the leg is a very dense tissue of collagen fiber bundles, passing primarily in one direction from the periosteal boundary of one bone to the other.[62, 81] If a fracture with angular deformities occurs in both the bones at the same level, the disruption to the interosseous membrane is generally minimal and it can still aid in stabilization of the fragments.

One can take advantage of the strength and stabilizing effect of the interosseous membrane by molding the soft tissues against the interosseous space, thereby providing a certain preload to the membrane. This reduces the amount of motion at the fracture site required before the membrane begins to stabilize the fragments. It is not difficult in a two-bone limb segment to encapsulate the soft tissue mass within a cylindrical container, which still allows full motion of the joints above and below the fracture site. In both the leg and the forearm, the bulky, fluid-like muscle tissues become tendinous by the time they reach the joints above and below the fracture. The tendinous structures as they cross the joints are held down by crural ligamentous and fascial structures that prevent their bowstringing. Therefore, a cast or fracture brace can easily encapsulate the fluid-like tissues without actually spanning the joints above and below the fracture site. Clinical evidence supports the effectiveness of the closed compartment concept because compartment syndromes most frequently occur in two-bone limb segments. The brace is not in danger of causing compartment syndrome because braces are not applied immediately after the initial injury and because soft tissue compression is minimal until loads are placed on the bone. The loading in the limb is dynamic and cyclic, changing with each activity. Therefore, tissue pressures are dynamic and cyclic, changing with each muscle contraction.[43, 44] Even though peak pressures may exceed those of venous return, the peaks are only intermittent, for very short intervals, and only enhance (not retard) circulation.

One-bone limb segments usually have bulky layers of muscular tissue that are surrounded by relatively large layers of adipose tissue. It has been demonstrated, under laboratory conditions, that the subcutaneous fat layer provides an effective lubrication between the skin and the underlying muscle tissue that allows a great deal of mobility of the muscle compartment beneath the skin. This makes it very difficult to control those muscle compartments with a cast or fracture brace and stabilize the fracture fragments. The fact that the single bone in the limb segment has no other bone or interosseous membrane to help provide support and stabilize its fragments leads to a dramatic change in the ability of the fracture brace to control the fracture fragments through the intrinsic strength of the soft tissues. In addition, the proximal joint of a single-bone limb segment always has large masses of muscle crossing the joint, making it impossible to encapsulate the fluid-like muscular tissues with a fracture brace that does not span that proximal joint. Therefore, it is more difficult to take advantage of the incompressible fluid nature of the soft tissues to help control the fracture fragments.

When the functional activity involves weight-bearing and compression loads, as in the case of the fractured femur, the instability is difficult to control and deformities may readily occur. With fractures of the humerus, angular deformities frequently develop early. With the brace applied early, one can take advantage of the inherent instability of the limb segment and allow natural realignment of the fragments. Dependency of the arm causes the compressed fragments to realign angular deformities in stage I or II healing owing to the effects of gravity. Rotational malalignments are corrected by early muscle activity because of the long areas of muscle attachment.

In general, two-bone limb segments are more easily stabilized by braces than are one-bone limb segments. For both types, however, braces assist best in stabilizing against progression of angular deformities. Progressive length deformities are prevented by the intrinsic strength of the soft tissues and are enhanced minimally by the brace. Rotational motions are controlled by the brace.

Many materials are available for application to the limbs for closed functional management of fractures. The properties of these materials are not as important as their proper application. In the laboratory, a model of what has been referred to as the *hot dog principle* demonstrates this concept. A piece of beefsteak by itself is so compliant that it cannot support its own weight as a planar slice. When rolled into a cylinder in the same way as the soft tissues are shaped around a diaphyseal bone, that same meat can support its own weight, but it is still very compliant. If that same meat is tightly wrapped with paper, it becomes much more rigid. This is what soft tissue compression in a brace provides to a limb. In the laboratory, a piece of meat wrapped around a wooden bone model with a joint to simulate a fracture increased its bending stiffness nearly 100 times with simple compression in a compliant sleeve of brown paper (like that from the butcher shop; Fig. 8–8). Use of a much more rigid material (Orthoplast) increased its bending rigidity only twofold. This emphasizes not only the importance of soft tissue compression but also the fact that the material applying that compression need not be rigid to stabilize the limb.

Early function demands stress on the brace soon after its application. Thus, the setting time of the material used for bracing becomes critical. For cylindrical sections that

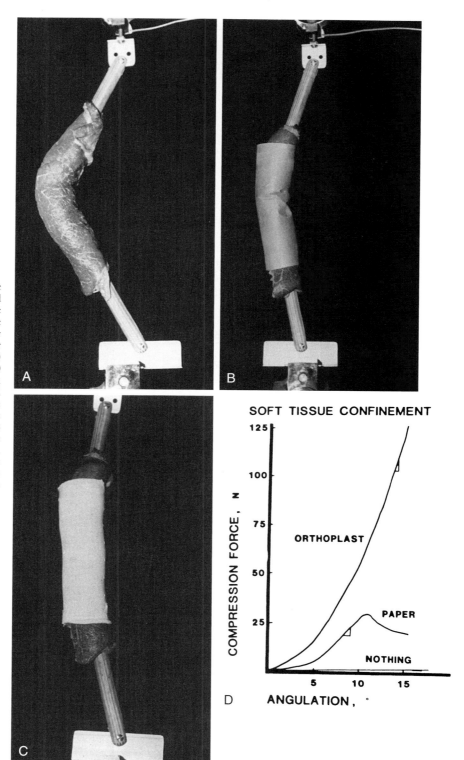

FIGURE 8–8. To illustrate the role of soft-tissue compression, a laboratory simulation provided a measure of the hot dog principle. *A,* A piece of meat was wrapped around a hinge, and the bending rigidity was measured. *B,* Tightly wrapping the meat in a flimsy container (brown paper like that used by a butcher) increased the bending rigidity by nearly 100 times (*D*). *C,* Compressing the soft tissue with much more rigid fracture orthosis material increased the rigidity by only two times more (*D*), demonstrating that the rigidity of the material used for bracing is not as important as the ability of the device to maintain soft tissue compression. (*A–C,* From Zych, G.A.; et al. Instr Course Lect 36:403–425, 1987. *D,* From Sarmiento, A.; Latta, L.L. Functional Fracture Bracing, Fig. 5.37d. New York; Springer-Verlag, 1995.)

compress the soft tissues to provide stability, the strength and stiffness requirements are minimal. For open sections that are cantilevered over a joint to control joint motion or position (e.g., the proximal or distal extensions of the sleeve), the strength and stiffness demands are much greater. In these applications and in any section that crosses a joint to control joint motion, attention should be

paid to the strength and stiffness characteristics of the material being applied. For the most natural function with minimal encumbrance by the brace, the joints should be free to move and the weight of the brace should be minimized. New synthetic casting materials provide much greater strength and rigidity with minimal weight and setting time than does plaster. Prefabricated braces provide the advantage of compliant materials in areas in which strength and stiffness requirements are minimal, thus maximizing comfort. More stiff, strong materials and shapes are provided only where the mechanical demands require them.

INDICATIONS AND CONTRAINDICATIONS FOR CLOSED MANAGEMENT

Nonoperative treatment of diaphyseal fractures implies a noninvasive method of fracture management that uses splints, casts, braces, or traction to provide external support until the fracture has achieved healing. Because many fractures have minimal or no displacement, nonoperative treatment is the choice for these. However, there are many indications for nonoperative treatment in displaced fractures after successful closed reduction technique.[94] Even today, in busy trauma centers, nonoperative treatment still plays an important role in the treatment of the injured patient.

Fractures of the clavicle, scapula, proximal humerus, humeral shaft, and ulnar shaft are those primarily treated nonoperatively in the upper extremity. The majority of pelvic fractures, many spine fractures, and tibial fractures have excellent outcomes when treated nonoperatively as well.[29, 96, 98] It is clear that nonoperative treatment is and will continue to be an important part of the armamentarium of the orthopaedic surgeon.

Nonoperative treatment can be divided into two types based on fracture displacement. Fractures with minimal or no displacement merely require some type of external support or protection to prevent displacement. This usually entails use of splintage, brace, or holding cast as the external support until clinical union is obtained. In general, there is no need for the external support to exert a great deal of force on the fracture. Nondisplaced diaphyseal and metaphyseal fractures are ideally suited for treatment with this technique.

Displaced fractures with initially unacceptable position require some type of reduction to achieve acceptable alignment. This is accomplished with closed reduction by manual manipulation or traction technique. Once reduction has been obtained, the external support becomes the critical factor in maintaining the fracture position. Forces exerted by the external support must be in the correct direction and of sufficient quantity that the fracture is stabilized while natural healing progresses to provide eventual inherent stability. Circumferential casts, some types of splintage, and skeletal traction have the capability for the necessary immobilization of displaced fractures.[122]

Closed Reduction and Immobilization

Fractures that are displaced or unstable require external manipulation to achieve the desired position. A short period of immobilization is necessary until intrinsic stability is present. A basic tenet of nonsurgical fracture care is that clinical healing often precedes complete radiographic healing.[21] If one waits until radiographic consolidation is complete, then immobilization has been excessive, rehabilitation has been delayed unnecessarily, and the functional outcome may be compromised. Rather, this period of immobilization should be determined by the patient's symptoms and type of fracture, not primarily by the radiographic appearance.[97]

Function should be introduced at the earliest opportunity to decrease muscle atrophy, joint stiffness, and distal edema and to enhance maximal recovery. For example, a patient with a distal radius fracture treated in a long arm cast should be encouraged to move the fingers and shoulder actively within the first few days after injury. Patients with foot fractures in a cast or brace should be at least partially able to bear weight, if feasible, to avoid disuse osteopenia and should perform active knee motion with light resistance exercises for the thigh muscles. Joint stiffness, in particular, is commonly seen with distal fractures and is largely preventable. Generally, most patients are willing to participate actively in their treatment and welcome the chance to engage in a dynamic exercise program.

Several treatises have been written on the subject of closed reduction of fractures.[21, 25, 96] The soft tissues assume paramount importance in the maneuvers to reduce the fracture and maintain position. Soft tissues are responsible for the shortening and angulation seen in displaced fractures, and their tension must be overcome to allow proper reduction. However, the majority of closed, oblique, comminuted, and spiral tibial fractures do not require forceful manipulation because the initial shortening is usually acceptable and not likely to increase with ambulation. Severe soft tissue damage, such as might occur in high-energy fractures of the tibia, often preclude optimal anatomic and functional results when treated with nonoperative methods.

Principles of Closed Reduction

ADEQUATE ANALGESIA OR ANESTHESIA

Adequate analgesia or anesthesia is essential to alleviate pain, block proprioceptive neural feedback, and, in certain cases, provide muscle relaxation. The degree required is determined by fracture location, joint proximity, amount of displacement, and patient tolerance. The simplest form of anesthesia is the fracture hematoma block, and this has been most useful in fractures of the ankle and distal radius.[4] Muscle relaxation is not obtained, but pain relief is sufficient to permit most reduction maneuvers. A potential disadvantage of this technique is the theoretical conversion of a closed fracture to an open one, although we have not encountered this in our practices. Intravenous regional, or Bier, block has been effective in severely displaced fractures of the distal extremity.[1, 24, 34, 51] Fractures of the forearm, distal radius, and ankle are particularly suitable for the use of this technique. The entire extremity distal to the tourniquet is anesthetized, and reduction is less hampered by pain and muscle spasm than with fracture hematoma block. Potential complications include cardiac toxicity and seizures with premature release of the tourniquet and consequent injection of a large amount of anesthetic agent into the systemic circulation.[106]

Spinal, epidural, or general anesthesia is reserved for fractures that need total muscle relaxation and complete analgesia. Fractures of the proximal humerus, certain distal radius fractures, and tibial shaft fractures mandate this type of anesthesia. Nonetheless, it should be noted that manipulative reduction is not usually necessary in closed, axially unstable fractures. Spinal or epidural anesthesia should be short acting to avoid prolonged postreduction alteration of neurologic function, making it difficult to detect complications such as compartment syndrome.

Conscious parenteral sedation, which is the administration of narcotic or other agents that affect the central nervous system, has been efficacious in the reduction of some pediatric fractures and adult joint dislocations. This method demands close physiologic monitoring and maintenance of an intravenous line for emergency administration of pharmacologic agents.

TRACTION AND RESTORATION OF LENGTH

Acute displaced fractures are associated with muscle spasm and a tendency to shorten. Angulatory deformity can also contribute to shortening by asymmetric loss of length on the concave side of the angulation. In general, the amount of shortening seen is directly proportional to the degree of soft tissue damage, as classically seen in tibial shaft fractures.[94] If the initial shortening is unacceptable, restoration of length is of primary importance in the initial phase of fracture reduction.

Traction on the affected extremity may be accomplished by manual means or static external devices. Most fractures will be brought out to length, and even distracted, by application of manual force, either in line with the deformity or in the longitudinal axis of the injured bone.[21] If this is not successful or not feasible, then traction to the distal fragment is applied through attachment of finger or toe traps—so-called Chinese traps—with a countertraction force or weight. This has the advantage of exerting gradual traction over time, producing muscle fatigue and viscoelastic soft tissue stretching. Fractures of the forearm, ankle, and foot are ideal indications for this technique. In rare cases, temporary skeletal traction may be used in place of the traps.

REDUCTION MANEUVERS

In many fractures, once length is regained, angulation and rotation are restored simultaneously. This is the basis for the principle of ligamentotaxis, whereby traction on the surrounding soft tissues and ligamentous attachments reduces the fracture.[110] In some instances, a mild corrective manipulation is performed to eliminate the residual angulation or displacement. Fractures of the distal radius are amenable to this form of reduction.

Persistent angulation or displacement after length restoration may necessitate further manipulation in the classic sense. While length is maintained, the fracture deformity is increased to eliminate cortical impingement on the concave side of the deformity. Once this is done, the distal fragment is then brought into alignment with the proximal fragment moving in the opposite direction, while continuing to maintain length. Inability to achieve a satisfactory reduction may indicate soft tissue incarceration in the fracture site and mandate open reduction.

Occasionally, some types of fractures need different maneuvers to obtain reduction. Fractures of the proximal humerus (two part or surgical neck) can be reduced successfully if the proximal fragment is stabilized with a smooth Kirschner wire inserted across the acromion and into the nonarticular portion of the proximal humeral fragment. The distal fragment and shaft can then be brought into proper alignment with the proximal humerus. As another example, proximal extra-articular tibial fractures are best reduced with the knee held in extension to decrease the tendency for the proximal fragment to extend.

APPROPRIATE IMMOBILIZATION

The correct form of immobilization is necessary to maintain fracture position after closed reduction. Functional bracing of humeral shaft fractures does not entail immobilization of either shoulder or elbow, even when used acutely. Tibial shaft fractures, however, require a minimum of 1 week in a long leg cast to control angulation and rotation.[96]

There are two basic types of cast immobilization. A holding cast is used for fractures that are stable or nondisplaced. This type does not require extensive molding, because there is only the need to prevent possible loss of fracture position. The other variety, a molded cast, has specific external molding contours and points to maintain a closed reduction of the fracture. This type of cast must be applied by an expert because precise knowledge of the fracture is necessary to ensure that correct molding has been done to exert the proper external forces. The final reduction is, in essence, perpetuated in the cast molding process, and this is a major determinant of the anatomic outcome. Application of this cast should not be delegated to anyone other than the surgeon responsible for the patient's care. The reader is referred to the classic literature for detailed descriptions of these important aspects of cast techniques.[18, 21, 38]

SKELETAL TRACTION

Skeletal traction is the time-honored method of applying a traction force via a transosseous pin to an extremity or the pelvis. There are numerous ways to accomplish this, but almost all require that the patient remain in bed for some time.[16, 98] All surgeons are familiar with the detrimental effects of prolonged recumbency on the pulmonary, vascular, and musculoskeletal systems. This form of treatment is, therefore, not indicated in the elderly, those with multiple chronic medical conditions, and most patients with multiple traumatic injuries.

Skeletal traction does have a place in modern fracture treatment. In the upper extremity, it has been replaced by state-of-the-art external skeletal fixation devices that allow the patient to be ambulatory. Indications for its use in the pelvis and lower extremity are in patients who are too ill to undergo operative intervention, in those refusing surgical treatment, and in selected cases of various fractures that achieve a satisfactory reduction while in skeletal traction. Patients selected for this method should be treated for the least possible time, consistent with obtaining early fracture stability. Prophylaxis against thromboembolic disease may be instituted. Incentive spirometry is used several times per day to prevent atelectasis. Active exercise of all available extremities and the trunk, while in traction, is necessary in patients who can cooperate. Disuse atrophy of the quadriceps can be eliminated with a specific program, as suggested by Eggers and Mennen.[31] One particular traction method—dynamic roller traction, as advocated by Neufeld and associates—is an effective way to partially mobilize patients in skeletal traction and diminish the complications associated with strict bedrest.[82] Browner and colleagues reported success with this method in a series of patients with femoral fractures, many of whom had polytrauma.[17] This technique has been used in the treatment of selected patients with acetabular fractures.[26]

FAILURE OF NONOPERATIVE TREATMENT

All methods of fracture management have a risk of failure. In most cases, this risk is diminished by proper patient selection, understanding the nature of the fracture, correct treatment technique, and regular follow-up. Certainly, these points are not unique to any one form of treatment. Successful nonoperative treatment with the least possible morbidity incorporates all these considerations.

Factors Associated with Failure

PATIENT

- Noncompliance
- Systemic medical conditions
- Obesity
- Substance abuse

In some respects, nonoperative fracture treatment demands more patient compliance than many operative treatments. For example, intramedullary tibial nailing can be more forgiving of poorly compliant patients than closed reduction and casting. Nonoperative treatment implies maintenance of external support and protected weight bearing for a definite time, and these may be critical factors in the final outcome. Progressive loss of fracture reduction may not be detected unless regular clinical examination follow-up radiographs are obtained.

Patients with diabetes mellitus or peripheral vascular disease or other diseases that affect soft tissues present a host of potential problems. Great care must be exercised with cast molding and avoidance of pressure points to prevent skin damage. Neuropathy alters sensation and makes it difficult to detect cast problems. In these types of patients, it is preferable to use splints or braces rather than circumferential casts.

Obesity is a relative contraindication to nonoperative treatment, because cast or splint immobilization is difficult, uncomfortable, and ineffective.[11] Attempting to control fracture position through a thick, soft tissue layer is biomechanically unsound as well.

Substance abuse, such as of alcohol and cigarettes, has been shown to have an adverse effect on fracture healing in nonoperative management of fractures, notably tibial shaft fractures.[22, 36, 48, 59]

FRACTURE CHARACTERISTICS

- Instability
- Soft tissue damage
- Soft tissue interposition

As stated previously, the major factors determining fracture instability are the fracture pattern and the integrity of the soft tissues. Low-energy fractures, such as those that result from indirect forces, have minimal soft tissue damage and inherent stability. Nonoperative treatment of such fractures, even those with comminution, is frequently associated with excellent outcomes. High-energy trauma, such as pedestrian–motor vehicle or severe open fractures, imparts tremendous forces to the extremity, with fracture comminution and significant soft tissue damage. Because nonoperative treatment is predicated on the status of the soft tissues, these fractures are difficult to reduce closed, or if reduction is accomplished, loss of fracture position is common. Therefore, less than optimal clinical and anatomic outcomes are more frequent than those with low-energy trauma.

Interposition of muscle, tendon, or periosteum between the fracture fragments can occur. In diaphyseal fractures, a persistent gap between the fragments may signal this problem. Another sign is a "rubbery" feel to the fracture during closed reduction maneuvers, associated with continued displacement. A high index of suspicion should be maintained, because open reduction is necessary in these cases to avoid a preventable cause of nonunion.

TREATMENT TECHNIQUE

- Inadequate closed reduction
- Poor casting and molding
- Improper type or duration of immobilization

In our experience, most failures of closed reduction are due to inability to restore length and to lack of recognition of fracture instability. Angulation or translational displacement can be corrected only if length has been restored. Fractures with significant shortening require steady traction, sufficient analgesia, and good muscle relaxation to achieve an acceptable reduction. Acceptance of a marginal reduction seldom leads to improvement and almost always results in progressive loss of position from the action of dynamic muscle forces and normal resorption. Before performing the closed reduction, the surgeon should establish the parameters that will indicate a satisfactory reduction. Bicortical comminution, such as occurs in some Colles' and high-energy distal radial fractures, precludes a stable reduction because there is no intact bone buttress to maintain length, and collapse is the rule. Many successful closed reductions lose fracture position because of poor casting and molding. Excess cast padding dissipates the effects of cast molding and creates more room inside the cast for the fracture fragments to move. Cast material that is too thick produces unnecessary heat and makes it difficult to mold the cast properly. The surgeon faced with a difficult reduction to maintain should use a plaster cast, because the ability to mold plaster is superior to that of other materials.

Much has been written about cast molding and the desired shape of the cast. The concept of three-point fixation, as espoused by Charnley, should be applied to every molded cast.[21] This principle relates to the application of molding forces to produce tension on the side of the fracture with the intact soft tissue hinge, essentially overcorrecting the initial deformity. Thus, three different points are molded into the cast, producing a curved cast for a straight bone.

An incorrect type of immobilization can result in loss of fracture reduction. Fractures with severe rotational instability can be controlled only by inclusion of the proximal joint in the immobilization device. This is the rationale for an initial long arm cast in Colles' fracture treatment. Fortunately, rotational stability is achieved in the fracture healing process and prolonged joint immobilization is unnecessary. Angular instability is controlled by having sufficiently long lever arms to exert adequate force on both fracture fragments. This is demonstrated in the use of long leg casts in the acute phase of nonoperative tibial fracture treatment. As intrinsic fracture stability is gained, the cast can be changed to the short leg variety.

Functional outcome is affected by the duration of immobilization. Stiffness of the joints adjacent to the fracture is related to the duration of joint immobilization and fibrosis of the surrounding muscles. Patients treated in long leg casts for prolonged periods will have permanent loss of motion. Joints of the affected extremity should be freed of immobilization as soon as possible and activation of the muscles permitted.

CLINICAL FOLLOW-UP

- Infrequent
- Inadequate radiograph
- Indecision about change of treatment

The early phases of nonoperative fracture treatment are characterized by lack of inherent fracture stability and dynamic changes in the extremity. Fractures generally begin to lose reduction early, and frequent radiographic evaluation is essential to detect this problem. The surgeon must be aware that often these changes are subtle and may be missed if the radiographic views are not standardized, according to extremity positioning, and high quality. In particular, progressive angulation can remain undetected if successive radiographs are taken with the extremity in differing degrees of rotation. It is also important to obtain repeat radiographs any time there has been a change of immobilization or if the possibility exists that the fracture may have changed. Considerable

objectivity is essential. Perfect restoration of anatomy is rarely necessary for attainment of satisfactory clinical results. In the case of diaphyseal tibial fractures, for example, 1 cm of shortening or angulation less than or equal to 8 degrees is functionally and cosmetically acceptable. Late sequelae such as osteoarthritis are unlikely.[77, 99]

With the resolution of initial fracture swelling, the extremity no longer fits well inside the cast. The forces required to maintain fracture position are diminished, and loss of reduction may ensue. A cast that is too large for the current volume of the extremity needs to be changed to one that fits properly. Ignoring this fact because of a fear that the reduction will be lost if the cast is changed is irrational.

Rarely is a closed reduction of a displaced fracture anatomic. By virtue of nonoperative treatment, some alteration of fracture position from normal anatomy is inevitable. Exactly what constitutes an acceptable reduction varies according to many factors and is the subject of considerable debate in the literature. However, at the outset of nonoperative treatment, the surgeon should decide which parameters of angulation, shortening, and translation will be acceptable for a satisfactory clinical result. It should then be anticipated that some change of reduction is possible in the early treatment, and additional limits need to be determined for any further change of fracture position. If the reduction changes beyond these limits, the surgeon should discontinue nonoperative treatment.

Surgeons should not be reluctant to alter treatment once they have embarked on a certain management plan. It is most probable that the majority of malunited fractures with initially satisfactory reductions are caused by continuation of treatment despite recognition of loss of reduction. One advantage of nonoperative treatment is the relative ease of changing to operative intervention if loss of fracture reduction is diagnosed early, before significant deformity occurs.

Nonoperative treatment requires progressive fracture healing, usually by external callus formation. Ranges for time to clinical union for various fractures have been published, and the surgeon should use these data as a guide to patient follow-up.[94, 98] Of course, not all fractures heal at the same rate, and variation is expected. Ideally, there should be good correlation among the patient's symptoms, functional level, and radiographic healing.

Patients with continued complaints of pain, poor function, and lack of progressive fracture callus formation may have the development of a delayed union. This is especially true in tibial shaft fractures and particularly if weight bearing has not been initiated within the first 6 weeks.[98]

Several noninvasive and invasive methods have been advocated to diagnose a delayed union, but in our experience, clinical evaluation is the most accurate. Diagnosis of delayed union indicates that the treatment plan requires modification in some way. In the upper extremity, it has been found useful to encourage increased active motion and exercises to improve muscle tone. Patients with tibial shaft fractures need to bear weight as dictated by symptoms and practice isometric exercises within the immobilization device. Patients who are functioning maximally could benefit from a trial of noninvasive fracture stimulation with one of the devices specifically approved for this indication.[45] Failure of these methods to increase fracture healing is an indication for operative treatment before such problems such as deformity, disuse osteopenia, and muscle atrophy become established.

SUMMARY

Closed, functional treatment can be applied to a wide variety of fractures with minimal risk to the patient. Healing is consistent with early function. Requirements for rehabilitation are minimal with early function, and many patients can resume independent activities of daily living and often return to work while the limb is healing in a brace or cast. Clinical signs, not radiographic pictures, dictate the level of function.

If a patient with a fracture is not a good candidate for surgery, a nonoperative method can be used even in the most difficult fractures. Thus, it is always important for the surgeon to be aware of the nonsurgical alternatives for fracture care.

If an unacceptable degree of malalignment develops, it usually occurs early, and other means can be used to obtain and maintain acceptable fracture reduction. The advantage of using nonoperative techniques first on properly selected patients is that little has been lost. With most surgical methods, complications are usually more expensive and difficult to correct.

Closed treatment methods can be combined simultaneously or sequentially with certain operative techniques to minimize surgical risk while encouraging early function (e.g.; avoiding prolonged periods of non–weight bearing with small diameter, locked intramedullary nails applied to unstable tibial fractures by applying a cast or brace postoperatively). But the surgeon must fully understand the rationale of each treatment method to avoid biologic and biomechanical conflicts when combining methods (e.g.; a cast or brace provides essentially no mechanical support to a poorly applied rigid fixation with plates or screws).

REFERENCES

1. Abbaszadega, H.; Jonsson, U. Regional anesthesia preferable for Colles' fracture. Controlled comparison with local anesthesia. Acta Orthop Scand 61(4):348, 1990.
2. Alioto, R.J.; Furia, J.P.; Marquardt, J.D. Hematoma block for ankle fractures: A safe and efficacious technique for manipulations. J Orthop Trauma 9(2):113, 1995.
3. Altman, R.D.; Latta, L.L.; Kerr, R.; et al. Effects of nonsteroidal anti-inflammatory agents on fracture healing in the rat. J Bone Joint Surg Orthop Trans 7:332, 1983.
4. Aro, H.T.; Eerola, E.; Aho, A.J. Development of nonunions in the rat fibula after removal of periosteal neural mechanoreceptors. Clin Orthop 199:292, 1985.
5. Aro, H.T.; Wahnert, H.W.; Kelly, P.J.; et al. Comparison of stable transverse and unstable oblique osteotomy healing in the canine tibia under external fixation. Proc 35th Orthop Res Soc 14:121, 1989.
6. Ayyash, S.; Mnaymneh, W.; Ghandur-Mnaymneh, L.; et al. Effect of chemotherapy drugs on musculoskeletal tissues. Orthop Trans 4B3:254, 1980.
7. Bak, B.; Jorgensen, P.H.; Andreassen, T.T. Growth hormone increases the strength of intact bones and healing tibial fractures in the rat. Proc Orthop Res Soc 14:588, 1989.
8. Bassett, C.A.L.; Becker, R.O. Generation of electrical potentials by bone in response to mechanical stress. Science 137:1063, 1962.
9. Bassett, C.A.L. Current concepts of bone formation. J Bone Joint Surg Am 44:1217, 1962.
10. Becker, R.O.; Murray, B.G. The electrical control system regulating fracture healing in amphibians. Clin Orthop 73:169, 1970.
11. Bostman, O.M. Bodyweight related to loss of reduction of fractures of the distal tibia and ankle. J Bone Joint Surg Br 77(1):101, 1995.
12. Bridgman, S.A.; Baird, K. Audit of closed tibial fractures: What is a satisfactory outcome? Injury 24(2):85, 1993.
13. Brighton, C.T.; Friedenberg, Z.B.; Black, J.; et al. Electrically induced osteogenesis: Relationship between charge, current density, and the amount of bone formed: Introduction of a new cathode concept. Clin Orthop 161:122, 1981.
14. Brighton, C.T. Principles of fracture healing. Part I. The biology of fracture repair. Instr Course Lect 33:60, 1984.
15. Brighton, C.T.; Krobs, A.G. Oxygen tension of healing fractures in the rabbit. J Bone Joint Surg Am 54:323, 1972.
16. Brooker, A.; Schmeisser, G. Orthopedic Traction Manual. Baltimore: Williams & Wilkins, 1980.
17. Browner, B.D.; Kenzora, J.E.; Edwards, C.C. The use of modified Neufeld traction in the management of femoral fractures in polytrauma. J Trauma 21(9):779, 1981.
18. Bueck, E.; Duckworth, N.; Hunter, N. Atlas of Plaster Cast Techniques, 2nd ed. Chicago, Year Book, 1974.
19. Carter, D.R. Mechanical stress and vascular influences on fracture healing. Trans 33rd Orthop Res Soc 12:99, 1987.
20. Carter, D.R.; Blenman, P.R.; Beaupre, G.S. Correlations between mechanical stress history and tissue differentiation in initial fracture healing. J Orthop Res 6:736, 1988.
21. Charnley, J. The Closed Treatment of Common Fractures, 3rd ed. Baltimore, Williams & Wilkins, 1968.
22. Cheung, R.C.; Gray, C.; Boyde, A.; et al. Effects of ethanol on bone cells in vitro resulting in increased resorption. Bone 16(1):143, 1995.
23. Chidgey, L.; Chakkalakal, D.; Blotchy, A.; et al. Vascular reorganization and return of rigidity in fracture healing. J Orthop Res 492:173, 1986.
24. Colizza, W.A.; Said, E. Intravenous regional anesthesia in the treatment of forearm and wrist fractures and dislocations in children. Can J Surg 36(3):225, 1993.
25. Connolly, J. Fractures and Dislocations: Closed Management, Vols. 1 and 2. Philadelphia, W.B. Saunders, 1995.
26. Connolly, J.F.; Guse, R.; Tiedeman, J.; et al. Autologous marrow injection for delayed unions of the tibia: A preliminary report. J Orthop Trauma 3(4):276, 1989.
27. Court-Brown, C.M.; Gustilo, T.; Shaw, A.D. Knee pain after intramedullary nailing: Its incidence, etiology and outcome. J Orthop Trauma 11:103–105, 1997.
28. Davy, D.R.; Connolly, J.F. The influence of callus morphology on the biomechanics of healing long bones. Trans 27th Orthop Res Soc 6:45, 1981.
29. De Coster, T.A.; Nepola, J.V.; el-Khoury, G.Y. Cast brace treatment of proximal tibial fractures. A ten year follow-up study. Clin Orthop 231:196, 1988.
30. De Lee, J.C.; Heckman, J.D.; Lewis, A.G. Partial fibulectomy for ununited fractures of the tibia. J Bone Joint Surg Am 63(9):1390, 1981.
31. Eggers, I.M.; Mennen, U. Application of a quadriceps endurance programme to patients with femur fractures immobilised by skeletal traction. S Afr Med J 81(5):258, 1992.
32. Einhorn, T.A.; Bonnarens, F.; Burstein, A.H. The contributions of dietary protein and mineral to the healing of experimental fractures: A biomechanical study. J Bone Joint Surg Am 68:1389, 1986.
33. Erickson, E. Streaming potentials and other water-dependent effects in mineralized tissue. Ann N Y Acad Sci 238:321, 1974.
34. Farrell, R.G.; Swanson, S.L.; Walter, J.R. Safe and effective IV regional anesthesia for use in the emergency department. Ann Emerg Med 14(4):288, 1985.

35. Foster, D.; Tarr, R.R.; Benya, P.; et al. Evaluation in subcutaneous pouches of injectable bone graft using viscous carrier solution. Trans 27th Orthop Res Soc 6:246, 1981.

36. Foulk, D.A.; Szabo, R.M. Diaphyseal humerus fractures: Natural history and occurrence of nonunion. Orthopedics 18(4):333, 1995.

37. Friedenberg, F.B.; Brighton, C.T. Bioelectrical potentials in bone. J Bone Joint Surg Am 98:915, 1966.

38. Freuler, F.; Wiedmer, V.; Bianghini, D. Cast Manual for Adults and Children. New York, Springer-Verlag, 1979.

39. Gillespie, J. The nature of bone changes associated with nerve injuries and disuse. J Bone Joint Surg Br 36:464, 1954.

40. Goodship, A.E.; Kenwright, J. The influence of induced micromovement upon the healing of experimental tibial fractures. J Bone Joint Surg Br 67(4):650, 1985.

41. Gothman, L. Local arterial changes associated with experimental fractures of the rabbit's tibia treated with encircling wires (cerclage). Acta Chir Scand 123:17, 1962.

42. Greenwald, R.A. Proteoglycan and lysozyme content of healing fracture callus. Proc 24th Orthop Res Soc 3:33, 1978.

43. Hardy, A.E. Pressure recordings in patients with femoral fractures in cast braces and suggestions for treatment. J Bone Joint Surg Am 61:365, 1979.

44. Hardy, A.E. Force and pressure recordings from patients with femoral fractures treated by cast brace application. J Med Engl Technol 5:30, 1981.

45. Heckman, J.D.; Ryaby, J.P.; McCabe, J.; et al. Acceleration of tibial fracture healing by noninvasive, low intensity pulsed ultrasound. J Bone Joint Surg Am 76(1):26, 1994.

46. Holden, C.E.A. The role of blood supply to soft tissues in the healing of diaphyseal fractures. J Bone Joint Surg Am 54:993, 1972.

47. Hults, A.; Olerud, S. The healing of fractures in denervated limbs. J Trauma 5:571, 1965.

48. Janicke-Lorenz, J.; Lorenz, R. Alcoholism and fracture healing. A radiological study in the rat. Arch Orthop Trauma Surg 103(4):286, 1984.

49. Jingushi, S.; Nemeth, G.G.; Heydemann, A.; et al. Induction of cartilage proliferation in a rat fracture callus by injections of human recombinant endothelial cell growth factor (ECGF). Proc 85th Orthop Res Soc 14:176, 1989.

50. Johnson, J.; Anderson, C.; Barrett, A.; et al. Roller traction: Mobilizing patients with acetabular fractures. Orthop Nurs 14(1):21, 1995.

51. Julian, P.J.; Mazur, J.M.; Cummings, R.J.; et al. Low dose lidocaine intravenous regional anesthesia for forearm fractures in children. J Pediatr Orthop 12(5):633, 1992.

52. Keating, J.F.; Orfaly, R.; O'Brien, P.J. Knee pain after tibial nailing. J Orthop Trauma 11:10–13, 1997.

53. Keller, J.; Shu-Zheng, H.; Stendler-Hansen, E.; et al. The inflammatory phase of fracture healing: Hemodynamics of rabbit tibial osteotomies during indomethacin or PGE2 treatment. Proc 36th Orthop Res Soc 15:96, 1990.

54. Kellerova, R. Changes in the muscle and skin blood flow following lower leg fracture in man. Acta Orthop Scand 41:240, 1970.

55. Kenwright, J.; Richardson, J.B.; Goodship, A.E.; et al. Effect of controlled axial micromovement on healing of tibial fractures. Lancet 2:1185, 1986.

56. Ketenjian, A.Y.; Charalampos, A. Morphological and biomechanical studies during differentiation and calcification of fracture callus cartilage. Clin Orthop 107:266, 1975.

57. Klug, W. Angiographic demonstration of the medullary space and callus vessels during secondary bone fracture healing: Animal experiments. Z Exp Chir Transplant Kunstiliche Organe 19(1):50, 1986.

58. Kristensen, K.D.; Kiaer, E.; Blicher, J. No arthrosis of the ankle after malaligned tibial shaft fracture. Acta Orthop Scand 60:208, 1989.

59. Kruse, R.L.; Kelly, P.J. Acceleration of fracture healing distal to a venous tourniquet. J Bone Joint Surg Am 56:730, 1974.

60. Kyro, A.; Usenius, J.P.; Aarnio, M.; et al. Are smokers a risk group for delayed healing of tibial shaft fractures? Ann Chir Gynaecol 82(4):254, 1993.

61. Lane, J.M.; Suda, M.; von der Mark, K.; et al. Immunofluorescent localization of structural collagen types in endochondral fracture repair. J Orthop Res 493:318, 1986.

62. Latta, L.L.; Sarmiento, A.; Katz, J. The structure and function of the interosseous membrane. Proceedings of the 24th meeting of the Orthopedics Reseasrch Society, 1978.

63. Latta, L.L.; Sarmiento, A.; Tarr, R.R. The rationale of functional bracing of fractures. Clin Orthop 146:28, 1980.

64. Latta, L.L.; Sarmiento, A. Mechanical behavior of tibial fractures. In: Symposium on Trauma to the Leg and Its Sequelae. St. Louis, C.V. Mosby, 1981.

65. Latta, L.L.; Sarmiento, A. Periosteal fracture callus mechanics. In: Symposium on Trauma to the Leg and Its Sequelae. St. Louis, C.V. Mosby, 1981.

66. Laurnen, E.L.; Kelly, P.J. Blood flow, oxygen consumption, carbon dioxide production, and blood calcium and pH changes in tibial fractures in dogs. J Bone Joint Surg Am 51:298, 1969.

67. Law, H.T.; Annan, I.; McCarthy, I.D.; et al. The effect of induced electric currents on bone after experimental osteotomy in sheep. J Bone Joint Surg Br 67:463, 1985.

68. Lindholm, R.V.; Lindholm, T.S.; Toikkanen, S.; et al. Effect of forced interfragmental movements on healing of tibial fractures in rats. Acta Orthop Scand 40:721, 1970.

69. Lippert, F.G.; Hirsch, C. The three dimensional measurement of tibial fracture motion by photogrammetry. Clin Orthop 105:130, 1974.

70. Lockwood, R.; Latta, L. Bone blood flow changes with diaphyseal fractures. J Bone Joint Surg Orthop Trans 4:253, 1980.

71. McBeath, A.A.; Narechania, R.G. Effects of 1,25(OH)2D3 and calcitonin on fracture healing. Proc 28th Orthop Res Soc 7:341, 1982.

72. McKellop, H.; Hoffmann, R.; Sarmiento, A.; et al. Control of motion of tibial fractures with use of a functional bracing or an external fixator. J Bone Joint Surg Am 75:1019, 1993.

73. McKibben, B. The biology of fracture healing in long bones. J Bone Joint Surg Br 60:150, 1978.

74. Macnab, I. The role of periosteal blood supply in the healing of fractures of the tibia. Clin Orthop 105:27, 1974.

75. Magrassi, B.; Rapuzzi, G.; Riccardi, C. Electrical behaviour of the rat's tibia during growth and fracture healing. Int Orthop 1093:213, 1986.

76. Meister, K.; Segal, D.; Whitelaw, G.P. The role of bone grafting in the treatment of delayed unions and nonunions of the tibia. Orthop Rev 19(3):260, 1990.

77. Merchant, T.C.; Dietz, F.R. Long term follow-up after fractures of the tibial and fibular shafts. J Bone Joint Surg Am 71:599, 1989.

78. Mizuno, K.; Kawai, K.; Sumi, M.; et al. Effect of calcitonin and vitamin D on the process of fracture healing. Proc 31st Orthop Res Soc 10:135, 1985.

79. Molster, A.O.; Gjerdet, N.R.; Alho, A. Effect of rotational instability on the healing of femoral osteotomies in rats. Proc 30th Orthop Res Soc 9:246, 1984.

80. Molster, A.O.; Gjerdet, N.R.; Langeland, N.; et al. Controlled bending instability in the healing of diaphyseal osteotomies in the rat femur. J Orthop Res 5:29, 1987.

81. Moore, T.M.; Lester. D.K.; Sarmiento, A. The stabilizing effect of soft tissue constraints in artificial Galeazzi fractures. Clin Orthop 194:189, 1985.

82. Neufeld, A.J.; Mays, J.D.; Naden, C.J. A dynamic method of treating femoral fractures. Orthop Rev July 1972, pp 19–21.

83. Nilsson, D.E.R.; Smith, R.E. The influence on breaking force of osteoporosis following fracture of the tibial shaft in rats. Acta Orthop Scand 40:72, 1969.

84. Nylander, G.; Semb, H. Veins of the lower part of the leg after tibial fractures. Surg Gynecol Obstet 134:974, 1972.

85. Panjabi, M.M.; Walter, S.D.; Karuda, M.; et al. Correlations of radiographic analysis of healing fractures with strength: A statistical analysis of experimental osteotomies. J Orthop Res 3:212, 1985.

86. Panjabi, M.M.; Lindsey, R.W.; Walter, S.D.; et al. The clinician's ability to evaluate the strength of healing fractures from plain radiographs. J Orthop Trauma 3:29, 1989.

87. Paradis, G.R.; Kelly, P.J. Blood flow and mineral deposition in canine tibial fractures. J Bone Joint Surg Am 57:220, 1975.

88. Perren, S.M.; Rahn, B.A. Biomechanics of fracture healing. Can J Surg 23:228, 1980.

89. Pilla, A.A.; Khan, S.; Nassar, P.; et al. Low intensity pulsed ultrasound accelerates fracture repair in a rabbit model. Proc 35th Orthop Res Soc 14:591, 1989.

90. Pita, J.; Muller, F.; Howell, D.S. Disaggregation of proteoglycan aggregate during endochondral calcification. Physiological role of cartilage lysozyme. In: Burleigh, P.M.C.; Poole, A.R., eds. Dynamics of Connective Tissue Macromolecules. Amsterdam, North Holland, 1973.

91. Pollack, D.; Floman, Y.; Simkin, A.; et al. The effect of protein malnutrition and nutritional support on the mechanical properties of fracture healing in the injured rat. JPEN 10(6):564, 1986.

92. Rahn, B.A. Primary bone healing. J Bone Joint Surg Am 53:783, 1971.

93. Rhinelander, F.W.; Baragry, R. Microangiography in bone healing. Displaced closed fractures. J Bone Joint Surg Am 50:643, 1968.

94. Sarmiento, A.; Latta, L.L.; Zilioli, A.; et al. The role of soft tissues in the stabilization of tibial fractures. Clin Orthop 105:116, 1974.

95. Sarmiento, A.; Schaeffer, J.; Beckerman, L.; et al. Fracture healing in rat femora as affected by functional weightbearing. J Bone Joint Surg Am 59:369, 1977.

96. Sarmiento, A.; Latta, L.L. Functional Bracing of Fractures. New York, Springer-Verlag, 1995.

97. Sarmiento, A.; Latta, L.L.; Tarr, R.R. Principles of fracture healing. Part II. The effects of function on fracture healing and stability. Instr Course Lect 33:83, 1984.

98. Sarmiento, A.; Sharpe, F.E.; Ebramzadeh, E.; et al. Factors influencing the outcome of closed tibial fractures treated with functional bracing. Clin Orthop 315:8, 1995.

99. Sarmiento, A.; McKellop, H.; Llinas, A.; et al. Effect of loading and fracture motions on diaphyseal tibial fractures. J Orthop Res 14:80, 1996.

100. Sato, S.; Kim, T.; Arai, T.; et al. Comparison between the effects of dexamethasone and indomethacin on bone wound healing. Jpn J Pharmacol 42(1):71, 1986.

101. Schmeisser, G. A Clinical Manual of Orthopedic Traction Techniques. Philadelphia, W.B. Saunders, 1963.

102. Schulak, D.J.; Duyar, A.; Schlicke, L.H.; et al. A theoretical analysis of cast wedging with practical applications. Clin Orthop 130:239, 1978.

103. Shannon, F.T.; Unsworth, A. Stability of tibial fractures in plaster cast: A biomechanical study. J Bone Joint Surg Br 60:282, 1978.

104. Shih, M.S.; Norrdin, R.W. Effect of prostaglandin E2 on rib fracture healing in beagles: Histomorphometric study on periosteum adjacent to the fracture site. Am J Vet Res 4797:1561, 1986.

105. Steinberg, M.E.; Lyet, J.P.; Pollack, S.R. Stress generated potentials in fracture callus. Trans 26th Orthop Res Soc 5:115, 1980.

106. Sukhani, R.; Garcia, C.J.; Munhall, R.J.; et al. Lidocaine disposition following intravenous regional anesthesia with different tourniquet deflation techniques. Anesth Analg 68(5):633, 1989.

107. Sweeney, J.; Marshall, G.J.; Gruber, H.; et al. Effects of nonweight bearing on fracture healing. Proc 30th Orthop Res Soc 9:299, 1984.

108. Tiedeman, J.J.; Connolly, J.F.; Strates, B.S.; et al. Treatment of nonunion by percutaneous injection of bone marrow and demineralized bone matrix. Clin Orthop 268:294, 1991.

109. Trueta, J. The role of vessels in osteogenesis. J Bone Joint Surg Br 45:402, 1963.

110. Trueta, J. Blood supply and rate of healing of tibial fractures. Clin Orthop 105:11, 1974.

111. Uhthoff, H.K.; Goto, S.; Cerckel, P.H. Influence of stable fixation on trabecular bone healing: A morphologic assessment in dogs. J Orthop Res 5(1):14, 1987.

112. Urist, M.R.; Lietze, A.; Mizutani, H.; et al. A bovine morphogenetic protein (BMP) fraction. Clin Orthop 162:219, 1982.

113. Vidal, J.; Buscayret, C.; Fischbach, C.; et al. Une methode originale dans le traitement des fractures comminutives de l'extremite inferieure du radius 'le taxis ligamentaire. Acta Orthop Belg 43:781, 1977.

114. Voegeli, T.L.; Chapman, M.W. Utilization of prostaglandins in fracture healing. Proc 31st Orthop Res Soc 10:134, 1985.

115. White, A.A.; Panjabi, M.M.; Southwick, W.O. The four biomechanical stages of fracture repair. J Bone Joint Surg Am 59:188, 1977.

116. Whiteside, L.A. The effects of extraperiosteal and subperiosteal dissection of the rabbit tibia on muscle blood flow. Proceedings of the 23rd Orthopedic Research Society, 1977.

117. Whiteside, L.A.; Lester, P.A.; Sweeney, R.E. The relationship between the biochemical and mechanical characteristics of callus during radiographically determined stages of fracture healing. Trans 24th Orthop Res Soc 3:36, 1978.

118. Wolf, J.W.; White, A.A.; Panjabi, M.M.; et al. Comparison of cyclic loading versus constant compression in the treatment of longbone fractures in rabbits. J Bone Joint Surg Am 63:805, 1981.

119. Wray, J.B. Acute changes in femoral arterial blood flow after closed tibial fractures in dogs. J Bone Joint Surg Am 46:1262, 1964.

120. Yablon, I.G.; Cruess, R.L. The effects of hyperbaric oxygen on fracture healing in rats. J Trauma 8:186, 1968.

121. Yamagishi, M.; Uoshimura, Y. The biomechanics of fracture healing. J Bone Joint Surg Am 37:1035, 1955.

122. Zagorski, J.B.; Latta, L.L.; Finnieston, A.R.; et al. Tibial fracture stability: Analysis of external fracture immobilization in anatomic specimens in casts and braces. Clin Orthop 291:196, 1993.

CHAPTER 9

Principles of External Fixation

Andrew N. Pollak, M.D.
Bruce H. Ziran, M.D.

External fixation has been used to treat fractures for almost 150 years. Its first use was reported in 1853 by Malgaigne,[50] who described using an external claw device to treat patellar fractures. Two other important reports appeared around the turn of the 20th century: in 1897, Parkhill[58] fabricated a modular-type frame fixator, citing its versatility and 100% success rate as reasons to consider its use; and in 1929, Ombredanne[54] described external fixation as a treatment for pediatric forearm and wrist fractures.

Although Parkhill's 100% success rate has not been duplicated, and techniques of internal fixation improved in the 20th century, external fixators remain valuable tools for providing temporary stabilization of acute fractures, dislocations, nonunions, and bony defects. In the management of severe musculoskeletal trauma, they can also be useful for treating difficult periarticular fractures, particularly in the proximal and distal tibia, and for rapidly stabilizing pelvic and extremity fractures in patients with multiple injuries.[18, 20, 36] Fixators with multiplanar adjustability can be used during post-traumatic distraction osteogenesis procedures to provide gradual correction of axial and angular deformities.[41, 42, 57]

External fixators achieve skeletal fixation using threaded pins or smooth wires joined by clamps and rings, respectively, to connecting rods. With the exception of the pins and wires, the fixation, as the name implies, is entirely external to the body. Different types of external fixators have been developed for use in a variety of clinical applications. Although some simple designs may provide maximal bony stability, modular constructs offer ease of rapid application, rings and thin wires provide the capability of controlling small fragments multilaterally, and adjustable connectors allow for dynamization to achieve compression at fracture or nonunion sites.

Only with a thorough understanding of the factors influencing construct mechanics, the stresses at pin-bone interfaces, and how these mechanical factors affect the biology of fracture healing can the orthopaedic surgeon understand the indications for external fixation and use the appropriate type of external fixator in a particular clinical situation.

EXTERNAL FIXATOR COMPONENTS AND CONFIGURATIONS

The first basic component of an external fixator is the pin, because it connects the bone to the rest of the device. Pins vary in size from 2.0 to 6.0 mm and can be terminally threaded, centrally threaded, or smooth. Transfixion pins (usually centrally threaded) enter the extremity on one side (medial or lateral) and exit on the opposite, typically connecting to the rest of the fixator on both ends. In contrast, terminally threaded half pins enter an extremity on one side, pass through the near-cortex of the bone, and gain final purchase in the far cortex (Fig. 9–1). Smooth pins are rarely used because they have a tendency to migrate with time.

Tensioned wires are used to connect segments of bone to the fixator via a ring. Wires vary in diameter from 1.5 to 2.0 mm. They are attached in groups of two or three to rings. Tensioning serves to increase the rigidity of the wire and to prevent migration (Fig. 9–2). An olive wire has a bulbous protuberance that anchors the wire to one cortex of the bone, increasing the purchase of the wire once it is tensioned. Olive wires tensioned on a ring in tandem can also be used to compress split components of fractures (Fig. 9–3).

The second basic component of the external fixator is the device that connects the pin or wire to the rods. Most commercially available external fixators use clamps to connect pins to the rod and specialized clamps to connect wires to a ring that is then secondarily connected to the rods. Simple clamps connect to individual pins. In modular systems, a single clamp attaches to a cluster of two or three parallel pins (Fig. 9–4).

The third basic component of most fixator systems is

the connecting rod. Rods are typically made of stainless steel, aluminum alloy, or, recently, carbon fiber (for improved radiolucency) and are used to connect the rings and clamps to one another. In some modular systems, the clamp and connecting rod form a single component, with the clamp portion being attached to the rod portion by a universal ball joint.

Most manufacturers' frames can be assembled in either a simple or a modular configuration, depending on the components selected and the needs of the patient. A simple configuration implies that each pin is connected to the rod, or rods, independently.[5, 6, 31] The first step in the application of a simple frame for trauma is manual reduction of the fracture. A single pin is then inserted into the proximal or distal fragment at the farthest possible distance from the fracture site. Holding manual reduction, a second pin is then inserted into the second fragment exactly parallel to the first, again as far as possible from the fracture site. Next, clamps are attached to each of these two pins and then joined by a connecting rod. Using additional clamps on the rod as alignment guides, more pins are

placed in the proximal and distal fragments as close as possible to the fracture site to maximize the pin-to-pin distance within each fragment. Throughout the application, the fracture must be held manually reduced in as near an anatomic position as possible. To increase the stability of the construct, compression across the fracture site can be achieved, assuming the fracture pattern permits, and a second bar can be attached to the pins via a second set of clamps placed above the first (Fig. 9–5).[52] Although simple fixators have few articulations and are thus very stable, fracture reduction is required before and must be maintained throughout application of the fixator; therefore, these frames can be technically difficult and time-consuming fixators to apply.

Modular frames allow clusters of pins to be connected to one another before being joined to the remainder of the frame via rods. A major advantage of modular frames is that pins and clamps can be applied before reduction of the fracture and attachment of the connecting rods. In addition, fracture alignment and length can be adjusted easily after all pins and clamps have been placed. Application of a modular frame first involves placement of parallel pins within each fracture fragment. Clusters of two or three pins are connected to a clamp which is then secondarily joined to a connecting rod. Once one cluster of pins has been placed within each fragment and attached to a clamp, the fracture is reduced and the clamps are connected to one another by rods. To increase stability of the construct, a duplicate set of bars can be attached to a duplicate set of clamps attached to the same pins. The modular construct's many articulations make it very adjustable (Fig. 9–6). Several factors, however, make a modular construct less stable than a simple one. First, the frames typically have multiple articulations, each of which is a potential point of instability. Second, the maximal pin-to-pin distance within a given fracture fragment is often limited by the size of the clamps. Finally, the distance between the bar and the bone is often increased because of the orientation of the articulations.

When all pins in an external fixator are coplanar, the fixator is said to be *uniplanar.* Uniplanar frames can be either unilateral or bilateral, depending on whether half pins or full pins are used. Unilateral frames encompass less than a 90° arc of the area around an extremity, whereas bilateral frames encompass more than a 90° arc of area around an extremity. Biplanar frames have pins entering the bone typically at 90° angles to one another to provide increased stability. Like uniplanar frames, biplanar frames can be unilateral or bilateral, depending on whether full pins or half pins are used (Fig. 9–7).[6]

Ring fixators represent a modification of modular fixators to form a semicircular exoskeleton around the limb. Rings are attached to the bone using combinations of tensioned wires and half pins. The rings are subsequently joined to one another with universal joints attached to connecting rods. In spite of the fact that ring fixators are the most cumbersome, the most difficult to apply, and severely limiting in terms of access to the leg for management of soft-tissue injuries, they are clearly the most versatile in terms of their function. They provide excellent mechanical stability and adjustability with the use of rods designed to allow gradual multiplanar

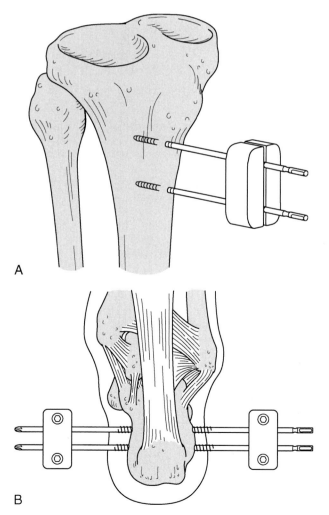

FIGURE 9–1. Fixator pins. *A,* Terminally threaded half pins connect to the fixator frame via clamps attached to the shank, or nonthreaded, portion of the pin. *B,* Centrally threaded transfixion pins attach to the fixator frame via clamps attached to the shank portion on either end.

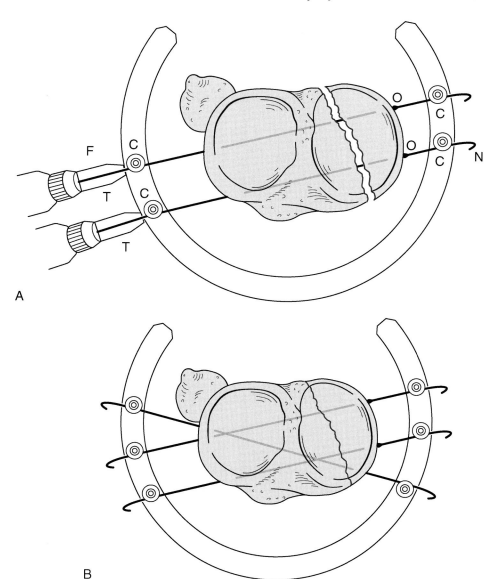

FIGURE 9–2. Olive wires. *A,* Wires with bulbous protuberances (O), that is, olive wires, are used to achieve compression across a split-type fracture. Parallel olive wires are passed through the bone perpendicular to the plane of the fracture until the "olives" engage the near cortex. The tensioning devices (T) are then used to compress the split fragment to the intact segment of bone. The wires are next clamped (C) to the ring on the near-cortical (N) side of the bone and finally tensioned on the far-cortical (F) side. *B,* A third tensioned wire is added to increase the stability of the construct.

correction of deformity. In addition, tensioned wires attached to a ring can provide secure fixation in even very small fragments of fractures, allowing them to be incorporated firmly into the construct while permitting maximal adjustability to ensure fracture healing in the best possible alignment.

One means of combining the advantages of ring fixation with the ease of half-pin modular fixation is to construct a hybrid frame. Hybrid frames use rings to gain purchase of small, typically periarticular fragments and half pins attached to clamps to gain purchase in larger fragments. Many manufacturers make their ring and half-pin modular fixators intercompatible, so that the components can be used together to construct a hybrid fixator.

If an intra-articular fracture has an epiphyseal fragment for which fixation is either technically impossible or not desirable because of soft tissue considerations, bridging fixation with ligamentotaxis can be used to reduce the fracture and provide stability. Bridging external fixation can be combined with limited internal fixation of articular

fragments to optimize articular reductions (Fig. 9–8). This technique has been described most frequently for the management of fractures of the distal radius, but it has also been used for the treatment of articular injuries in the lower extremity.[1, 13, 17, 32, 68, 69]

FACTORS INFLUENCING CONSTRUCT STIFFNESS

Pins are most commonly made from either stainless steel or titanium alloy. Compared with titanium, stainless steel offers a higher modulus of elasticity (stiffer), greater ductility (higher strain to failure), and slightly better fatigue properties.[15, 37, 44, 66] However, although the properties depend on the specific alloy composition of each material, the practical differences are not significant within the physiologic range of forces to which each material is

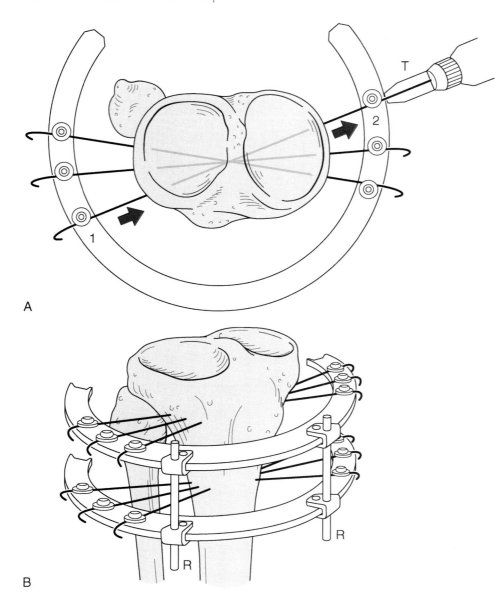

FIGURE 9-3. Tensioned wires. *A*, Tensioned wires attach to external fixators via rings. Converging wires are first drilled into a segment of bone and then anchored at one end (1). A tensioning device (T) is then applied to the opposite end and tightened (typically, 50–130 kg). Selection of the appropriate amount of tension depends on the diameter of the wire, the body weight of the patient, and the density of the bone (arrows show the direction of the force vector). The second clamp (2) is then tightened, securing the wire under tension. Groups of two or three wires are used to secure a single ring to a segment of bone. *B*, Multiple rings placed at different levels on a bone are connected via rods (R) to form a ring fixator.

exposed in clinical practice, except for the fact that titanium is susceptible to early failure when it is excessively bent or deformed before insertion.

Numerous studies have examined the effects of pin characteristics (size, thread, tip design, and material properties) and insertion technique in both clinical and laboratory settings.[37, 44, 66, 72] It is commonly accepted that for pelvic, femoral, and tibial fixation, pin diameter should be at least 5 mm. For the foot and ankle, 3-mm pins are acceptable, depending on the particular location.[62] In the upper extremity, at least 4-, 3-, and 2-mm pins should be used in the humerus, forearm-wrist, and fingers, respectively. When pin diameters are too small, local stresses can lead to micromotion and ultimate pin failure. When pin diameter is too large, the stress riser formed in the bone can lead to fracture even months after removal of the device.

A second consideration is whether to choose pins with a long or a short threaded portion. Pin strength and fatigue resistance are directly proportional to core diameter, which is generally highest in the unthreaded shank portion of the pin. Experimental evidence that shows stresses on the pin are highest at the near-cortical pin-bone interface supports the argument that the junction between the threaded and the shank portions of a pin (where there is a stress riser) should never be placed at the pin-bone interface. Pin design modifications that help move the thread-shank junction away from the pin-bone interface include shorter threads to engage only the far cortex (thus moving the shaft-thread junction of the pin to the far cortical side of the pin-bone interface), tapered pins that gradually alleviate the discrepancy between the threaded and the shank portions of the pin,[48] and pins with longer threaded portions (thus moving the shaft-thread junction of the pin closer to the fixator side of the pin-bone interface) (Fig. 9–9).

Connecting bars are usually made of metal (steel or titanium) or carbon fiber.[46, 66] At low loads, stiffness and ultimate failure strengths are similar for these materials. However, at high physiologic loads, metal rods exhibit

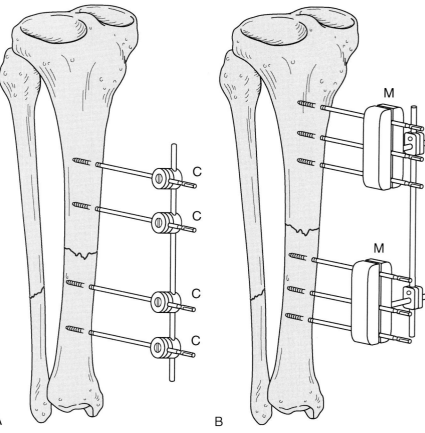

FIGURE 9–4. Frame types. *A,* Simple frame clamps (C) connect single pins individually to the rod(s). *B,* Modular frame clamps (M) connect clusters of two or three pins to the connecting rod(s).

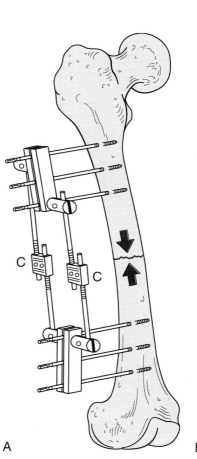

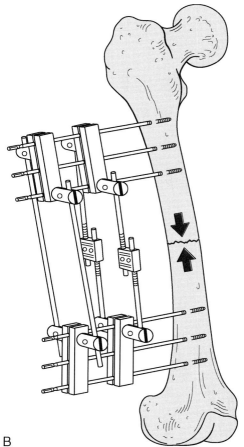

FIGURE 9–5. To increase stability, compression can be achieved across a transverse fracture (*A*) using special devices (*C*), or additional bars can be attached to pins via a second set of clamps (*B*).

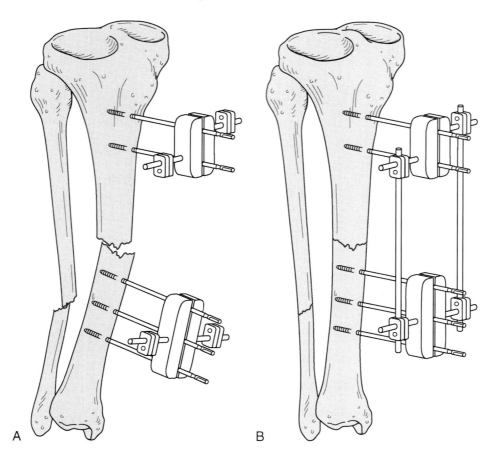

A   B

FIGURE 9–6. *A, B,* In modular constructs, articulations between the clamps and the bars typically allow for great degrees of multiplanar adjustability. The fracture can therefore be reduced after the fixator has been applied.

UNILATERAL FRAMES

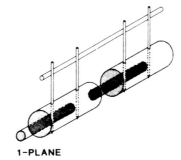

1-PLANE

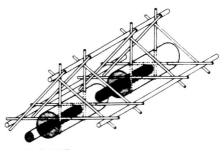

2-PLANE

BILATERAL FRAMES

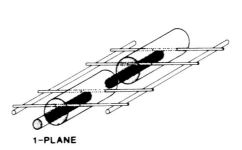

1-PLANE

2-PLANE

FIGURE 9–7. The four basic configurations of external fixation frames. (From Behrens, F.; Searls, K. J Bone Joint Surg Br 68:246–254, 1986.)

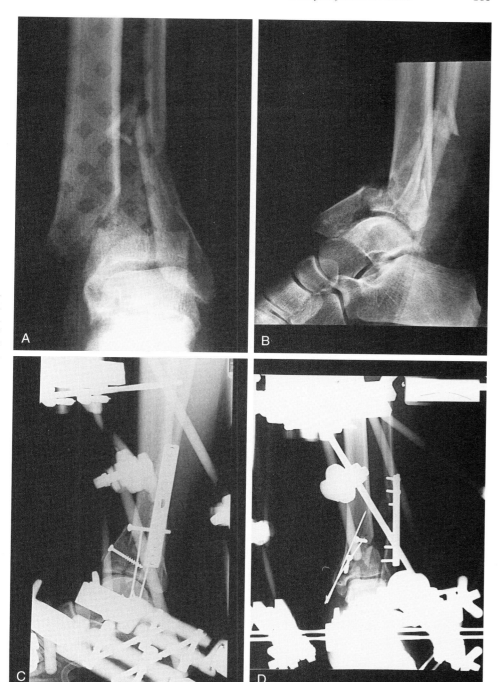

FIGURE 9–8. This 37-year-old equestrienne was thrown by her horse and trampled. She sustained an open pilon fracture with gross displacement of the articular surface (*A, B*). Her injuries were managed with bridging external fixation, combined with limited internal fixation of the articular fragments (*C, D*). Once the fracture had healed, the external fixation was removed and weight bearing was allowed.

greater deformation until failure. Because the overall flexibility of the construct is often more dependent on the structure chosen than on the material properties of the components, subtle differences in material properties become less important.[6–9, 29, 39] Advantages of carbon fiber rods include radiolucency and decreased weight, both very practical considerations.

The stiffness of fixator constructs has been widely studied and depends on many factors. Because each variable has an incremental contribution to overall construct stiffness, an understanding of the relative importance of each is helpful. For example, it has been

demonstrated that pin diameter is the single most important determinant of stiffness in uniplanar-unilateral fixators, yet the addition of multiplanar fixation can easily overcome the effects of small variations in pin size.[6–9, 29, 39] Nonetheless, it is helpful to consider mechanical properties of external fixators in the context of two fundamental features: the number and orientation of fixator frames and the structure of the elements within each frame.

Several studies compare the mechanical performance of uniplanar, multiplanar, and uniplanar-bilateral frames.[6–9, 29, 39] It is obvious that the greater the number

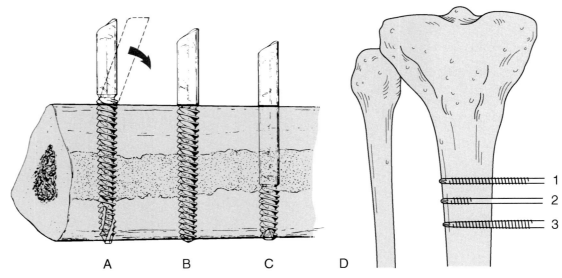

FIGURE 9–9. Pin stress risers. *A–C,* Stress on pins is highest at the pin-bone interface. The threadshank junction of the pin forms a stress riser. When this junction occurs at the same level as the pin-bone interface, fatigue and fracture can result with loading. *D,* Pin modifications designed to prevent breakage include the use of longer threads to move the stress riser away from the near-cortical side of the pin-bone interface (1), shorter threads to move the stress riser to the far-cortical side (2), and a tapered threaded portion to limit the magnitude of the stress riser at any single point (3).

of frames in different planes, the greater the mechanical performance, but practical clinical considerations often limit the number of frames that can be used. In building a frame for a particular injury, it is important to consider that the performance of any construct is highly dependent on the type and direction of transmitted load.[56] For example, in the femur and tibia, physiologic loading usually creates tension on the anterolateral aspect of the femur and the anterior aspect of the tibia.

A fixator provides the greatest mechanical stability when at least one of the frames is in the same plane as the applied load.[6–9, 29] Thus, in the tibia, the performance of a uniplanar-unilateral anterior frame (fixator in sagittal plane) is better than that of a uniplanar-bilateral frame when loaded in the anterior-to-posterior direction. In torsion, the plane of the fixator is a less important consideration than factors such as the pin number and the presence of linkages between frames in perpendicular planes (delta frames). Optimizing factors such as pin diameter, pin spread, and double-stacking bars can increase the rigidity of uniplanar-unilateral constructs to that of multiplanar constructs while retaining the advantages of decreased profile and ease of application.

Several important mechanical considerations relate to ring fixators with tensioned wires. When full or closed ring constructs with multiple longitudinal connecting rods are used, the resulting construct is quite rigid. The most flexible component remains the tensioned wires, whose overall stiffness depends on the number of wires used, the diameter of the ring, the angle between the wires, and the properties of the bone.[60, 66, 71] These constructs exhibit excellent bending and torsional stiffness but are markedly less stiff than half-pin or full-pin frames under axial loading conditions. However, many ring fixators allow the application of controlled compressive loads in the axial direction, which may be more favorable clinically than

constructs that produce greater shear loads at the fracture site. If open ring constructs are used, the torsional stiffness is slightly diminished, creating the potential for deformation created by overtensioned wires. These issues, however, are not frequent problems in the clinical setting.

Research since the mid-1970s has led to a better understanding of the contribution of each component of a fixator frame to overall stiffness. Efforts have focused primarily on improving the performance of uniplanar-unilateral frames. The key features that determine the performance of a frame are pin diameter, pin number, pin spread, number of connecting bars, and distance from the connecting to the loading axis (usually the shaft of the bone). Although no one factor has been clearly demonstrated to be the most important, pin diameter, pin spread, and distance between the connecting bar and the bone have been shown to have significant effects on construct stiffness.[2, 6–9, 14, 24, 39] Pin number is important not only in determining the overall stiffness of the construct but also because increasing the number of pins decreases the stresses at each individual pin-bone interface; such stress is an important contributing factor to radial necrosis and resultant pin loosening. The absolute minimal number of pins for a two-part fracture should be four (two on each side), and the preferred number is six (three on each side).[62] Insertion of more pins is usually limited by soft tissue considerations and has not been shown to add substantially to stiffness. The position of pins within each fracture fragment has been studied both experimentally and theoretically, with the most optimal configuration being one pin close to the fracture site, a second as far from the fracture as possible, and a third halfway between the first two.[56] This configuration maximizes the pin-to-pin spread within each fragment, as described in the section on External Fixator Components and Configurations.

A recent development has been the pinless external

fixator that uses percutaneous clamps attached to connecting bars.[62] A C-shaped clamp grasps the outer cortex of the bone without penetrating the medullary canal. Fixation at the pin-bone interface is substantially weaker than the traditional pin or tensioned wire interface but may offer theoretical advantages. There is less disruption to the blood supply of the bone, less risk of thermal damage, and, thus, possibly less risk of infection, which could limit subsequent conversion to internal fixation. However, the mechanical performance is only 30% to 50% of standard frames in all testing modes. This limits the fixator's use for most fracture patterns but may allow its use as a temporary device in occasional circumstances.[61, 63]

The axial stiffness of several commonly used commercially available fixators has been compared.[47, 66] The EBI-Orthofix frame and the AO uniplanar-unilateral frame with stacked bars were the stiffest (about 50% of the stiffness of an intact tibia), the next stiffest were the Richards unilateral and several bilateral frames (22.7% to 46% of the stiffness of an intact tibia), and the least stiff was the unilateral Hoffmann frame in axial compression (18% of the stiffness of the intact tibia).[66] What is imperative to consider in interpreting these data, however, is that beyond all of the mechanical considerations noted, the quality of reduction and the inherent stability of the fracture pattern play an enormous role in determining the ultimate mechanical performance and therefore the clinical success of the construct. For example, in a study examining the worst case scenario (a fracture model with no bony contact) using an Ilizarov ring fixator, the axial stiffness was only 6% of that of the intact bone.[23, 43, 62, 66, 71] When the model was modified to include cortical contact and compression across the fracture site, the axial stiffness increased to 94% of that of intact bone. This study and numerous clinical reports emphasize that there is no substitute for adequate restoration of bony stability.

FACTORS INFLUENCING LOOSENING AT THE PIN-BONE INTERFACE

Pin loosening is the most frequent complication of external fixation.[12, 35] Factors that influence pin loosening include excess stresses at the pin-bone interface, thermonecrosis and subsequent bony resorption (which can occur as a result of improper pin insertion technique), and osteomyelitis secondary to severe pin tract infection.[4, 7] Clinically, pin loosening can be devastating. It can result in the need to replace a pin operatively, remove a pin, or, in the worst case scenario, remove the fixator entirely and select an alternative means of stabilization. If pin loosening has resulted in substantial infection with osteomyelitis, then alternative forms of fixation (e.g.; internal fixation) may no longer be feasible.

Stress at the pin-bone interface can be either static or dynamic. Static stresses occur in stable fracture patterns fixed in compression. These stresses are unidirectional and constant. Dynamic stresses occur when load is applied across an external fixator in the presence of an unstable fracture pattern. In this situation, stress concentration can alternate between opposite sides of the pin with loading, allowing the pin to toggle and leading to the greatest incidence of pin loosening.[59] Preventing dynamic stresses from occurring clinically involves using the most stable fixator construct possible and limiting weight bearing in all but the most stable fracture patterns.

Mechanical performance of pin clamps and external fixators has been studied carefully. Finite element analysis has demonstrated that high stresses can occur at the clamp-pin interface.[24] When torque resistance is decreased at the clamp-pin interface, increased stress can be transmitted to the pin-bone interface. Using larger diameter pins and placing them symmetrically within the clamp provides the best pin fixation strength. The use of stiff pin clamps or rigid single pin clamps in simple frames also increases stability at the pin-clamp interface.[3]

Initial pin torque resistance is highly correlated with gross pin loosening. Pettine and associates[59] studied loosening of external fixation pins in canine tibias subjected to various loading conditions and found that improving initial pin torque resistance significantly lowered the incidence of gross loosening. Preloading pins by bending them has previously been suggested as a means of augmenting the tightness of the pin within the bone.[64] In a study comparing the effects of bending preload with radial preload in reducing resorption of bone at the pin-bone interface, Hyldahl and colleagues[40] found that radial preloading was superior to bending preloading. However, high degrees of radial preload that exceed the elastic limit of cortical bone may result in microfracture and subsequent resorption.[12] Accurate predrilling of holes before pin insertion is therefore essential.

Although pin loosening can occur after both proper and improper insertion techniques, use of the proper techniques, which limit thermonecrosis and subsequent bone resorption, can dramatically lower the incidence of pin loosening. Matthews and co-workers[51] studied the effects of drill speed, pin point design, and predrilling on thermal conditions and surrounding bone during pin insertion. Although they found that low drill speeds and pin designs that allowed for bone chip storage and extrusion with tip penetration were important techniques for decreasing the possibility of thermonecrosis during insertion, the most important factor was using techniques that involve predrilling of the holes before pin insertion.

The use of appropriate pin insertion techniques is therefore clinically critical in ensuring pin longevity. Holes should be predrilled at low speed with a fresh, sharp drill point. Pins should then be inserted by hand, with care taken not to allow the pin to toggle during insertion, as this may cause microfracture and decrease pin torque resistance. If pins with threads that engage both the near and the far cortices of the bone are chosen, then the drill diameter should match the shank diameter of the pin. If pins with short threads that engage only the far cortex of the bone are selected, then the drill diameter should be 0.2 mm less than the shank diameter of the pin to provide for adequate radial preload at the near cortex without causing microfracture of the surrounding cortical bone.

Pin loosening probably leads to pin tract infection more commonly than the converse. However, severe soft tissue infection secondary to primary bacterial contamination and poor pin site care can lead to osteomyelitis at the pin-bone interface and to secondary loosening. Thus, appropriate pin care is also important in limiting the incidence of pin loosening.

FRACTURE HEALING WITH EXTERNAL FIXATION

One goal of all fracture fixation is to achieve bony union. Multiple factors influence the bone healing process: fixator rigidity, accuracy of restoration of length and alignment, fracture configuration, fracture loading conditions, and the degree to which the blood supply to the bone in the region of the fracture has been disrupted.[30, 34, 45, 49, 55] It is important to consider each of these in determining both the role external fixation plays in the management of a particular injury and the type of fixator to use.

Healing of fractures stabilized by external fixators has been studied using osteotomy models.[30, 34, 49, 55] Stiffer frames that limit micromotion and essentially provide rigid fixation allow fractures to heal by primary bone union. When rigidity of the construct is decreased, more motion occurs at the fracture site and secondary healing results with increased periosteal callus formation. Within the same fracture site, when a unilateral frame provides more stability in one plane than in another, increased periosteal callus formation can be observed along the less stable plane.

The effect of pure variation in healing rates has been studied in ovine tibias. Goodship and associates[34] used a standard osteotomy model and compared healing rates in two groups of animals by both qualitative and quantitative measures. In the first group, a simple unilateral fixator was applied across an osteotomy site. In the second group, the same frame was applied to an identical osteotomy with the sole change being a 10 mm decrease in the offset between the bone and the fixator rod, resulting in a measured 40% increase in frame stiffness. By both radiographic measure and dual-source photon absorption densitometry measure of bone mineral content at the fracture site, the stiffer construct resulted in decreased healing rates for the first 6 weeks after osteotomy, despite decreased weight bearing during the initial postoperative phase in the less rigid group.

Similarly, Wu and colleagues[74] compared periosteal callus formation in canine tibial osteotomies stabilized with unilateral external fixator configurations of varying rigidity. When a four–half pin fixator was chosen, stiffness in all planes was reduced 50% to 70% compared with that using a standard six–half pin frame. Periosteal callus formation was greater in the four–half pin group but so were cortical porosity and the incidence of pin loosening. Subsequently, Williams and co-workers[73] compared unilateral external fixation with two-plane bilateral exter-

nal fixation with similar results. They found that the latter construct resulted in greater rigidity and permitted more direct fracture healing with less periosteal callus formation.

Data from these and other studies confirm that the biomechanical milieu, as determined by both the fracture and the external fixator configuration, determines the type of healing that occurs. Although the less rigid configurations lead to earlier and more prolific periosteal callus formation, there are penalties for decreased rigidity, including increased stress at the pin-bone interface and increased cortical porosity. Techniques such as dynamization that allow load transmission across the fracture site may increase the likelihood of achieving primary fracture healing and decrease the incidence of complications at the pin-bone interface.

ANATOMIC CONSIDERATIONS

When placing pins and wires for external fixation, consideration must be given to the relevant soft tissue anatomy. Improper pin or wire placement can lead to soft tissue irritation, necrosis, or infection; in addition, neurovascular structures and musculotendinous units are at risk for impalement during placement and for secondary injury if pins or wires are placed inappropriately.

Because of their small diameter, wires can generally be placed percutaneously with impunity. Pins, however, should be placed through stab incisions in the skin, with care taken not to injure the underlying soft tissue structures. Protective sleeves should be used when predrilling and placing pins, and blunt dissection should be performed before placing protective sleeves through any soft tissue window onto bone.

When using modular external fixation devices that do not require reduction of the fracture before placement of pins and clamps, consideration must be given to the postreduction position of the fracture fragments with respect to the prereduction position of the soft tissue. Reducing the fracture after inserting the pins and clamps can cause soft tissues to become tight around the pins. Relaxing incisions may be necessary to prevent soft tissue irritation and necrosis.

Care must be taken not to impale muscle-tendon units with pin or wire placement. The resultant scarring around these structures could permanently limit adjacent joint range of motion.

Safe soft tissue zones for pin insertion depend on the cross-sectional anatomy of the limb at the particular level of fixation. Behrens and Searls[10] defined these "safe corridors" in the lower leg (Fig. 9–10). In other areas, optimal insertion sites can be selected by reviewing the cross-sectional anatomy of the limb. Sites that place muscle-tendon units or neurovascular structures at risk should be avoided. Ideal sites are along the subcutaneous border of a bone such as the ulna or the tibia. In other regions, care should be taken to select areas in which the amount of soft tissue between skin and bone is minimized so that the risk of soft tissue infection

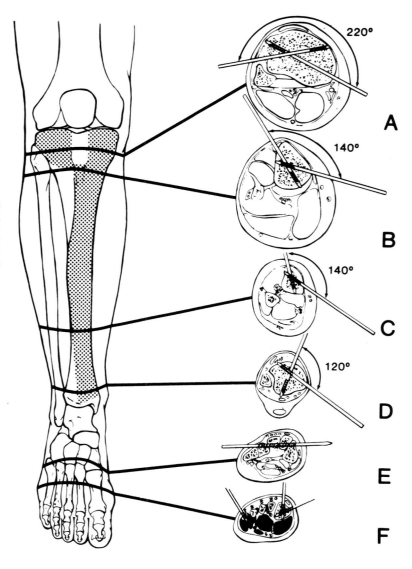

FIGURE 9–10. The safe corridor for pin insertion in the lower leg. At level *A*, proximal to the tibial tubercle, pins can be safely inserted within an arc of 220°. At level *B*, just below the tibial tubercle, the safe arc decreases to 140°. At *C*, in the distal third of the leg, the safe arc remains 140°, but the anterior and tibial vessels and deep peroneal nerves become vulnerable as they cross the lateral tibial cortex. At *D*, above the ankle joint, the safe arc is 120°. At levels *E* and *F*, pins in the tarsal or metatarsal bones may be used to splint the ankle if neurologic or soft tissue injuries prevent the application of an external support. The *dotted area* indicates where the tibia lies subcutaneously and pin insertion is safe. (*A–F*, From Behrens, F.; Searls, K. J Bone Joint Surg Br 68:246–254, 1986.)

secondary to irritation and motion around the pins is decreased.

INDICATIONS FOR THE USE OF EXTERNAL FIXATION

External fixators were formerly considered the treatment of choice for the management of open fractures that required stabilization. This theory was based on the concern that internal fixation in the presence of fresh, open wounds would increase the risk of acute infection and chronic osteomyelitis.[22, 33, 70] However, other findings suggesting that most open fractures can be treated safely with immediate internal fixation have led to a dramatic decrease in the use of external fixation.[16, 25–28, 38, 53] Nevertheless, external fixation devices are very versatile, and many indications for their use remain.

Because the devices can be disassembled easily, allow-

ing for the re-creation of instability and deformity, external fixation is still indicated for the treatment of severe open injuries with massive associated soft tissue injury. The treatment of severe open fractures routinely involves multiple operative débridements.[21, 76, 77] When external fixation is chosen for the stabilization of these injuries, disassembly of the frame at the time of redébridement of the fracture and soft tissue can facilitate thorough circumferential inspection of complex wounds.

Once the surgeon is confident that all devitalized soft tissue has been débrided and that no additional contamination remains, external fixation can be converted to less cumbersome internal fixation at soft tissue coverage. Although some data suggest that late conversion from external fixation to intramedullary fixation, particularly in the tibia, can lead to an increased risk of soft tissue infection and osteomyelitis, the same dangers have not been shown to be present when conversion occurs within the first weeks after injury and in the absence of evidence of pin tract infection.

A second indication for the use of external fixation is

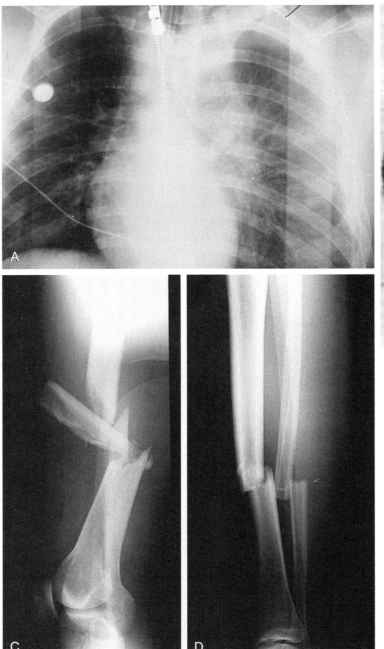

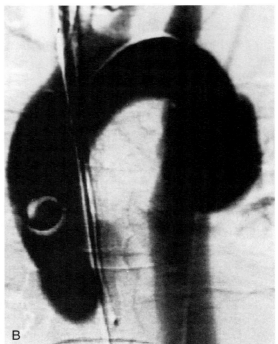

Figure 9–11. This 22-year-old man sustained a transection of his descending thoracic aorta, as seen on the chest radiograph (*A*) and aortogram (*B*). He also sustained open fractures of the left femoral (*C*) and tibial (*D*) shafts.

the management of severe periarticular injury with associated severe soft tissue injury, particularly in the proximal and distal tibia. In these cases, formal open reduction and internal fixation is often associated with devastating soft tissue complications, including full-thickness skin slough and severe infection leading to amputation. Particularly in the distal tibia, external fixation with limited internal fixation has been shown to lead to results comparable with those seen after formal open reduction and internal fixation with a significantly lower complication rate.[65, 75]

A third major indication for the use of external fixation is in the management of the unstable patient with multiple extremity fractures. In these challenging patients, modular external fixation can provide sufficient stability to allow for complete mobilization of the patient. Furthermore, modular external fixators can be applied rapidly in these situations, either in the operating room or in an intensive care setting if necessary (Fig. 9–11). Although the external fixator is not usually used to treat the fracture until it has united in this situation, it can be employed if necessary. When femoral shaft fractures are treated with external fixators because the patient is medically too unstable to undergo primary intramedullary nail fixation, our protocol is to convert the external fixator to an intramedullary nail within the first week after injury. When the patient's medical status delays conversion until after the first month, the external fixator is removed in the operating room and the patient is placed in traction for several days

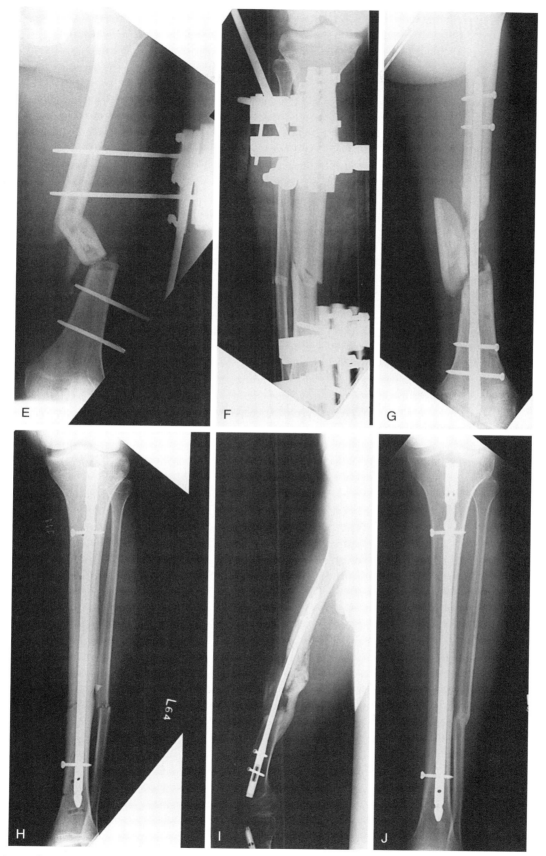

FIGURE 9–11 *Continued.* Hemodynamic instability persisted after aortic repair, necessitating rapid operative treatment of his lower extremity injuries. Irrigation and débridement of his open wounds, fasciotomies for treatment of leg compartment syndrome, and modular external fixation of his femur (*E*) and tibia (*F*) were all performed in less than 45 minutes. Two days later, the external fixators were exchanged for intramedullary nails, which served as definitive fixation (*G, H*). Nine months after injury, the femoral (*I*) and tibial (*J*) fractures have healed without evidence of infection and the patient has regained full function of the injured extremity.

to allow any pin tract contamination to resolve before conversion. Secondary intramedullary nailing is then performed.

Candidates for this type of rapid external fixation include patients with multiple extremity fractures and additional injury, or injuries, that would make early operative intervention hazardous—injuries such as severe head injury with elevated intracranial pressure and severe pulmonary contusion with compromised gas exchange and rapidly deteriorating respiratory function. Patients with severe hypothermia and coagulopathy are also candidates for this type of procedure. Finally, patients with severe pelvic ring injuries and hemodynamic instability can often be stabilized by controlling pelvic volume, and therefore retroperitoneal hemorrhage, with an anterior external fixator.[11, 19, 20, 36]

Many other indications exist for the use of external fixators in the management of nontraumatic conditions and post-traumatic complications and deformity. As described previously, ring fixators with adjustable connectors can allow for the correction of multiplanar deformity. Thus, malunions and malpositioned nonunions can often be treated successfully by external fixation. Osteomyelitis, which results in bony instability, often requires stabilization to achieve infection control and eventual bony union. External fixation is ideally suited in this situation. Finally, external fixation has been used to provide compression across joint surfaces that have been denuded of articular cartilage for the purpose of achieving a formal arthrodesis.[67]

CARE OF THE EXTERNAL FIXATOR

Appropriate care of the external fixator can lower the incidence of pin tract infection dramatically and thereby substantially augment pin longevity. Patients with external fixators should routinely be instructed in pin care before discharge from the hospital and should demonstrate competency in such care under the direct supervision of an experienced professional.

During the first several days after application of an external fixator, sanguineous and serosanguineous drainage from the pin sites can be expected. While this occurs, dry sterile dressings should be applied over the pin sites and changed at least twice daily because saturated dressings provide an excellent bed for bacterial growth. With each dressing change, pin sites should be cleaned with a mixture of 50% normal saline solution and 50% hydrogen peroxide. The purpose of the peroxide is to help clean off any dried blood or serous fluid that has accumulated at the interface between the pin and the skin. It is important to ensure that all dried blood is removed at each dressing change and subsequently while performing routine pin maintenance. Any other wounds underneath the external fixator, such as those associated with limited internal fixation or an open fracture, are managed just as they would be if the fixator were not in place. Dressing changes can be performed either underneath the external fixator or around it, whichever the chosen configuration allows. It is imperative that consideration of the need for

wound care and the type of wound care that is necessary be given while deciding what type of external fixator to use for a given clinical situation.

Once all drainage from around the pins has stopped, dressings are no longer necessary at the pin sites. Routine maintenance at this point consists of twice-daily cleansing of the pin sites with half-strength peroxide solution. If there are no other wounds on the extremity that would prohibit it, showering with the external fixator in place is allowed. Patients are encouraged to scrub the external fixator as well as the leg in the shower and then to rinse the fixator and the extremity thoroughly afterward. Normal soap and water can be used, and often a toothbrush is helpful to clean any dirt or other foreign substances that may have accumulated on the external fixator. The fixator and leg are then patted dry carefully, and final pin site maintenance with half-strength peroxide is performed. Swimming, bathing, and other activities that involve soaking the external fixator in potentially contaminated water are discouraged.

When signs of pin tract infection become evident, early treatment is mandatory to prevent secondary pin loosening. Serous drainage with erythema and pain around the pin site are all signs of superficial pin tract infection. Adequate treatment of the infection involves addressing the underlying cause of the soft tissue reaction. Oral first-generation cephalosporins are used to control any bacterial component of the problem (*Staphylococcus aureus* and other skin-dwelling microbes being the most frequently offending organisms), but rarely is direct bacterial contamination alone responsible for the process. Excessive motion of the soft tissues at the pin site and excessive stress at the pin-bone interface are more commonly the causes of the acute inflammatory process; bacterial contamination of the inflamed or necrotic tissue is a secondary event. Definitive treatment, therefore, involves splinting the joint above and below the area of inflammation to eliminate soft tissue motion around the pins and limiting stresses at the pin-bone interface by preventing weight bearing. If the inflammatory process fails to resolve after a short trial of these measures, radiographs should be obtained to look for signs of bone resorption at the pin-bone interface. Lucency of more than 1 mm around a pin indicates gross loosening.[59] Loose pins must be removed, as they do not provide sufficient fixation to bone, and measures to control infection around them, if they are left in place, will be ineffective. Uncontrolled pin tract infections can lead to frank osteomyelitis and ring sequestration around the pin, which, in turn, can create large stress risers in the bone and secondary fracture.

REMOVAL OF THE EXTERNAL FIXATOR

Elective frame removal is generally performed after the fracture has united or the pathologic process being treated has resolved. Most frames can be disassembled before pin removal to allow for evaluation of stability at the fracture site. This maneuver may help in deciding whether sufficient bony stability is present to warrant fixator removal.

Removal of an external fixator can be performed in the office setting, with or without sedation, or in the operating room, where deeper sedation and anesthesia can be offered. The selection of setting depends mostly on patient-specific factors such as the patient's ability to withstand the discomfort. Although the actual pain associated with pin removal is often tolerable, the sensation of pins being pulled or unscrewed from bone is bothersome to some patients and is better tolerated under sedation. When active pin tract infection with cellulitis is present, simple handling of the frame can cause pain, and deeper sedation than would otherwise be warranted is necessary.

Routine curettage of all pin tracts after fixator removal is probably unnecessary. Infected pin tracts, however, especially those with radiographic evidence of substantial bony necrosis around the pin, should be thoroughly débrided to prevent the development of chronic osteomyelitis.

Pin sites are never closed after pin removal, as doing so prevents drainage and may increase the risk of chronic infection.

FIXATOR SELECTION AND DESIGN

Fixator selection and design should reflect not only the pathologic condition being treated but also the overall clinical scenario. Many commercially available external fixation systems can be assembled in either simple or modular frames and half-pin, ring, or hybrid configurations. Because most hospitals do not keep a large number of external fixation systems in stock, it is important in selecting a system that it have sufficient versatility to allow appropriate management of the breadth of clinical conditions commonly encountered in the facility's patient population.

For example, external fixators used to treat open fractures, either temporarily or until fracture union, must be assembled so as to provide sufficient room between the skin and the clamps to allow for appropriate wound care. Although increasing the bone-clamp distance decreases the rigidity of the construct, it may be necessary to allow for adequate treatment of underlying wounds. Obviously, fixators chosen to correct multiplanar deformity must allow for controlled, gradual adjustment of alignment in multiple planes, and those used to treat periarticular fractures must allow easy fixation of small, thin fragments. Perhaps the most important consideration is that the fixator must be sufficiently versatile to meet the demands of the injury and that the treatment plan should not have to change to be compatible with the capabilities of the hardware.

Choosing a design that maximizes construct stability minimizes stress at the pin-bone interface and decreases the incidence of pin loosening. However, as previously noted, the most important contributing factors to overall construct stability include fracture pattern, degree of anatomic reduction, and fracture configuration, much of which is beyond the influence of the surgeon. In the typical clinical arena, simple, stable fractures are rarely treated with external fixators. Because most fractures that are treated with external fixation are inherently unstable, weight bearing must be prohibited. Preventing weight bearing dramatically reduces stresses at the pin-bone interface, thus limiting the importance of absolute frame rigidity in fixator selection. We do not imply by this that fixator stability is unimportant clinically. Rather, its importance is tempered by the fact that injuries being treated are complex (making fixator versatility crucial), that the most mechanically stable fixators are often the least versatile, and that protection from weight bearing (mandated by the fracture pattern) reduces the stresses on the construct, thereby reducing some of the need for rigidity.

REFERENCES

1. Agee, J.M. External fixation: Technical advances based upon multiplanar ligamentotaxis. Orthop Clin North Am 24:265, 1993.
2. Aro, H.T.; Chao, E.Y. Biomechanics and biology of fracture repair under external fixation. Hand Clin 9:531, 1993.
3. Aro, H.T.; Hein, T.J.; Chao, E.Y. Mechanical performance of pin clamps in external fixators. Clin Orthop 248:246, 1989.
4. Aro, H.T.; Markel, M.D.; Chao, E.Y. Cortical bone reactions at the interface of external fixation half-pins under different loading conditions. J Trauma 35:776, 1993.
5. Behrens, F. A classification of external fixators. In: Uhthoff, H.K., ed. Current Concepts of External Fixation of Fractures. Heidelberg, Springer-Verlag, 1982.
6. Behrens, F. A primer of fixator devices and configurations. Clin Orthop 241:5, 1989.
7. Behrens, F. General theory and principles of external fixation. Clin Orthop 241:15, 1989.
8. Behrens, F.; Johnson, W. Unilateral external fixation. Methods to increase and reduce frame stiffness. Clin Orthop 241:48, 1989.
9. Behrens, F.; Johnson, W.D.; Koch, T.W.; et al. Bending stiffness of unilateral and bilateral fixator frames. Clin Orthop 178:103, 1983.
10. Behrens, F.; Searls, K. External fixation of the tibia. Basic concepts and prospective evaluation. J Bone Joint Surg Br 68:246, 1986.
11. Ben-Menachem, Y.; Coldwell, D.M.; Young, J.W.R.; et al. Hemorrhage associated with pelvic fractures: Causes, diagnosis, and emergent management. AJR Am J Roentgenol 157:1005, 1991.
12. Biliouris, T.L.; Schneider, E.; Rahn, B.A.; et al. The effect of radial preload on the implant-bone interface: A cadaveric study. J Orthop Trauma 3:323, 1989.
13. Bone, L.; Stegemann, P.; McNamara, K.; et al. External fixation of severely comminuted and open tibial pilon fractures. Clin Orthop 292:101, 1993.
14. Briggs, B.T.; Chao, E.Y.S. The mechanical performance of the standard Hoffmann-Vidal external fixation apparatus. J Bone Joint Surg Am 64:566, 1982.
15. Browner, B.D.; Jupiter, J.B.; Levine, A.M.; et al. Skeletal Trauma. Fractures, Dislocations, Ligamentous Injuries. Philadelphia, W.B. Saunders, 1992.
16. Brumback, R.J.; Ellison, P.S., Jr.; Poka, A.; et al. Intramedullary nailing of open fractures of the femoral shaft. J Bone Joint Surg Am 71:1324, 1989.
17. Brumback, R.J.; McGarvey, W.C. Fractures of the tibial plafond. Evolving treatment concepts for the pilon fracture. Orthop Clin North Am 26:273, 1995.
18. Burgess, A.R. External fixation in the multiply injured patient. Instr Course Lect 39:229, 1990.
19. Burgess, A.R. The management of haemorrhage associated with pelvic fractures. Int J Orthop Trauma 2:101, 1992.
20. Burgess, A.R.; Eastridge, B.J.; Young, J.W.R.; et al. Pelvic ring disruptions: Effective classification system and treatment protocols. J Trauma 30:848, 1990.
21. Burgess, A.R.; Poka, A.; Brumback, R.J.; et al. Management of open grade III tibial fractures. Orthop Clin North Am 18:85, 1987.
22. Byrd, H.S.; Cierny, G., III; Tebbetts, J.B. The management of open tibial fractures with associated softtissue loss: External pin fixation with early flap coverage. Plast Reconstr Surg 68:73, 1981.

23. Calhoun, J.H.; Li, F.; Ledbetter, B.R.; et al. Biomechanics of the Ilizarov fixator for fracture fixation. Clin Orthop 280:15, 1992.

24. Chao, E.Y.; Kassman, R.A.; An, K.N. Rigidity and stress analysis of external fracture fixation devices—A theoretical approach. J Biomech 15:971, 1982.

25. Chapman, M.W. The use of immediate internal fixation in open fractures. Orthop Clin North Am 11:579, 1980.

26. Chapman, M.W. Role of bone stability in open fractures. Instr Course Lect 31:75, 1982.

27. Chapman, M.W. The role of intramedullary fixation in open fractures. Clin Orthop 212:26, 1986.

28. Chapman, M.W.; Mahoney, M. The role of early internal fixation in the management of open fractures. Clin Orthop 138:120, 1979.

29. Egan, J.M.; Shearer, J.R. Behavior of an external fixation frame incorporating an angular separation of the fixator pins. A finite element approach. Clin Orthop 223:265, 1987.

30. Egger, E.L.; Gottsauner-Wolf, F.; Palmer, J.; et al. Effects of axial dynamization on bone healing. J Trauma 34:185, 1993.

31. Fernandez Dell'Oca, A.A. External fixation using simple pin fixators. Injury 23:S1, 1992.

32. Frykman, G.K.; Peckham, R.H.; Willard, K.; et al. External fixators for treatment of unstable wrist fractures. A biomechanical, design feature, and cost comparison. Hand Clin 9:555, 1993.

33. Gallinaro, P.; Crova, M.; Denicolai, F. Complications in 64 open fractures of the tibia. Injury 5:157, 1973.

34. Goodship, A.E.; Watkins, P.E.; Rigby, H.S.; et al. The role of fixator frame stiffness in the control of fracture healing. An experimental study. J Biomech 26:1027, 1993.

35. Green, S.A. Complications of external skeletal fixation. Clin Orthop 180:109, 1983.

36. Gylling, S.F.; Ward, R.E.; Holcroft, J.W.; et al. Immediate external fixation of unstable pelvic fractures. Am J Surg 150:721, 1985.

37. Halsey, D.; Fleming, B.; Pope, M.H.; et al. External fixator pin design. Clin Orthop 278:305, 1992.

38. Holbrook, J.L.; Swiontkowski, M.F.; Sanders, R. Treatment of open fractures of the tibial shaft: Ender nailing versus external fixation. A randomized, prospective comparison. J Bone Joint Surg Am 71:1231, 1989.

39. Huiskes, R.; Chao, E.Y. Guidelines for external fixation frame rigidity and stresses. J Orthop Res 4:68, 1986.

40. Hyldahl, C.; Pearson, S.; Tepic, S.; et al. Induction and prevention of pin loosening in external fixation: An in vivo study on sheep tibiae. J Orthop Trauma 5:485, 1991.

41. Ilizarov, G.A. The tension stress effect on the genesis and growth of tissues: Part I. The influence of stability of fixation and soft tissue preservation. Clin Orthop 238:249, 1989.

42. Ilizarov, G.A. The tension stress effect on the genesis and growth of tissues: Part II. The influence of the rate and frequency of distraction. Clin Orthop 239:263, 1989.

43. Juan, J.A.; Prat, J.; Vera, P.; et al. Biomechanical consequences of callus development in Hoffmann, Wagner, Orthofix and Ilizarov external fixators. J Biomech 25:995, 1992.

44. Kasman, R.A.; Chao, E.Y. Fatigue performance of external fixator pins. J Orthop Res 2:377, 1984.

45. Kershaw, C.J.; Cunningham, J.L.; Kenwright, J. Tibial external fixation, weight bearing, and fracture movement. Clin Orthop 293:28, 1993.

46. Kowalski, M.J.; Schemitsch, E.H.; Harrington, R.M.; et al. A comparative biomechanical evaluation of a noncontacting plate and currently used devices for tibial fixation. J Trauma 40:5, 1996.

47. Kristiansen, T.; Fleming, B.; Reinecke, S.; et al. Comparative study of fracture gap motion in external fixation. Clin Biomech 2:191, 1987.

48. Lavini, F.M.; Brivio, L.R.; Leso, P. Biomechanical factors in designing screws for the Orthofix system. Clin Orthop 308:63, 1994.

49. Lewallen, D.G.; Chao, E.Y.S.; Kasman, R.A.; et al. Comparison of the effects of compression plates and external fixators on early bone healing. J Bone Joint Surg Am 66:1084, 1984.

50. Malgaigne, J. Considerations cliniques sur les fractures de la rotule et leur traitement par les griffes. J Conn Med Prat 16:9, 1853.

51. Matthews, L.S.; Green, C.A.; Goldstein, S.A. The thermal effects of skeletal fixation pin insertion in bone. J Bone Joint Surg Am 66:1077, 1984.

52. Muller, M.E.; Allgower, M.; Schneider, R.; et al. Manual of Internal Fixation, 3rd ed. New York, Springer-Verlag, 1991, p. 388.

53. Nowotarski, P.; Brumback, R.J. Immediate interlocking nailing of fractures of the femur caused by low to midvelocity gunshots. J Orthop Trauma 8:134, 1994.

54. Ombredanne, L. L'osteosynthese temporaire chez les enfants. Presse Med 52:845, 1929.

55. O'Sullivan, M.E.; Bronk, J.T.; Chao, E.Y.; et al. Experimental study of the effect of weight bearing on fracture healing in the canine tibia. Clin Orthop 302:273, 1994.

56. Oni, O.O.; Capper, M.; Soutis, C. A finite element analysis of the effect of pin distribution on the rigidity of a unilateral external fixation system. Injury 24:525, 1993.

57. Paley, D.; Chaudray, M.; Pirone, A.M.; et al. Treatment of malunions and malnonunions of the femur and tibia by detailed preoperative planning and the Ilizarov techniques. Orthop Clin North Am 21:667, 1990.

58. Parkhill, C. A new apparatus for the fixation of bones after resection and in fractures with a tendency to displacement: With report of cases. Trans Am Surg Assoc 15:251, 1897.

59. Pettine, K.A.; Chao, E.Y.; Kelly, P.J. Analysis of the external fixator pin-bone interface. Clin Orthop 293:18, 1993.

60. Rapoff, A.J.; Markel, M.D.; Vanderby, R., Jr. Mechanical evaluation of transosseous wire rope configurations in a large animal external fixator. Am J Vet Res 56:694, 1995.

61. Remiger, A.R. Mechanical properties of the pinless external fixator on human tibiae. Injury 23:S28, 1992.

62. Schuind, F.A.; Burny, F.; Chao, E.Y. Biomechanical properties and design considerations in upper extremity external fixation. Hand Clin 9:543, 1993.

63. Stene, G.M.; Frigg, R.; Schlegel, U.; et al. Biomechanical evaluation of the pinless external fixator. Injury 23:S9, 1992.

64. Synthes: The AO/ASIF External Fixation System. Large External Fixator. Paoli, PA, Synthes, 1990.

65. Teeny, S.M.; Wiss, D.A. Open reduction and internal fixation of tibial plafond fractures. Variables contributing to poor results and complications. Clin Orthop 292:108, 1993.

66. Tencer, A.F.; Johnson, K.D., eds. Biomechanics in Orthopedic Trauma: Bone Fracture and Fixation. London, Dunitz, 1994.

67. Thordarson, D.B.; Markolf, K.L.; Cracchiolo, A., III. External fixation in arthrodesis of the ankle. A biomechanical study comparing a unilateral frame with a modified transfixion frame. J Bone Joint Surg Am 76:1541, 1994.

68. Tornetta, P., III; Weiner, L.; Bergman, M.; et al. Pilon fractures: Treatment with combined internal and external fixation. J Orthop Trauma 7:489, 1993.

69. Vaughan, P.A.; Lui, S.M.; Harrington, I.J.; et al. Treatment of unstable fractures of the distal radius by external fixation. J Bone Joint Surg Br 67:385, 1985.

70. Wade, P.A.; Campbell, R.D., Jr. Open versus closed methods in treating fractures of the leg. Am J Surg 95:599, 1958.

71. Weiner, L.S.; Kelley, M.; Yang, E.; et al. The use of combination internal fixation and hybrid external fixation in severe proximal tibia fractures. J Orthop Trauma 9:244, 1995.

72. Wikenheiser, M.A.; Lewallen, D.G.; Markel, M.D. In vitro mechanical, thermal, and microsurgical performance of five external fixation pins. Trans Annu Meet Orthop Res Soc 17:409, 1992.

73. Williams, E.A.; Rand, J.A.; An, K.N.; et al. The early healing of tibial osteotomies stabilized by oneplane or twoplane external fixation. J Bone Joint Surg Am 69:355, 1987.

74. Wu, J.J.; Shyr, H.S.; Chao, E.Y.; et al. Comparison of osteotomy healing under external fixation devices with different stiffness characteristics. J Bone Joint Surg Am 66:1258, 1984.

75. Wyrsch, B.; McFerran, M.A.; McAndrew, M.; et al. Operative treatment of fractures of the tibial plafond. A randomized, prospective study. J Bone Joint Surg Am 78:1646, 1996.

76. Yaremchuk, M.J.; Brumback, R.J.; Manson, P.N.; et al. Acute and definitive management of traumatic osteocutaneous defects of the lower extremity. Plast Reconstr Surg 80:1, 1987.

77. Yaremchuk, M.J.; Burgess, A.R.; Brumback, R.J. Lower Extremity Salvage and Reconstruction: Orthopedic and Plastic Surgical Management. New York, Elsevier, 1989.

CHAPTER 10

Principles of Internal Fixation

Augustus D. Mazzocca, M.D.
Andrew E. Caputo, M.D.
Bruce D. Browner, M.D.
Jeffrey W. Mast, M.D.
Michael W. Mendes, M.D.

A mind that can comprehend the principles will devise its own methods.

—*N. Andry*

Forces that produce fractures cause injury to both the bone and the surrounding soft tissue, which results in an inflammatory reaction in the zone of injury.[5, 19, 39, 92] The release of vasoactive substances mediates a beneficial increase in the flow of blood to the injured part as well as the detrimental effects of edema and pain. Inflammatory substances and neural reflexes cause involuntary contraction of skeletal muscle groups around the fracture to provide splinting, reduce painful motion at the fracture site and neighboring joints, and facilitate fracture healing. Early observations of the pain relief associated with external splinting led to the belief that fractures are best treated by immobilization and prolonged rest of the injured part. Optimal cast immobilization usually included the joints above and below the affected bone.[22] Fractures of the spine, pelvis, and femur were often treated with bedrest and traction for many weeks, followed by months of spica or body cast immobilization. These approaches to treatment focused primarily on achievement of bony union.

Although fractures usually healed with these nonoperative methods, the inability to directly control the position of fracture fragments within the soft tissue envelope led to problems with malunion and nonunion. Long periods of immobilization with restriction of muscle activity, joint function, and weight bearing resulted in muscle atrophy, joint stiffness, disuse osteoporosis, and persistent edema—a complex of problems termed *fracture disease*.[68] In addition, prolonged periods of immobilization sometimes led to psychologic changes, including depression, depen-

dency, and perceived disability.[36] In light of these phenomena, it is clear that fracture treatment methods must be aimed not only at healing of fractures but also at restoration of all preinjury locomotor function. Therefore, the methods must achieve the desired bony alignment and stabilization while permitting early resumption of muscle function, joint mobilization, weight bearing, and functional independence. Treatment methods that impart sufficient skeletal stability to facilitate return to functional activity include functional bracing (nonoperative), the Ilizarov method (a limited operative technique), external fixation devices (used principally in treatment of severe open fractures), and internal fixation.

This chapter is divided into three major sections: metallurgy, hardware, and techniques of internal fixation. Because most of the implants currently used for internal fixation are made of metal, it is important to have a basic understanding of metallurgy.

METALLURGY

Metal implants are used successfully for fracture stabilization because they reproduce the supportive and protective functions of bone without impairing bone healing, remodeling, or growth. In an internal fixation construct, the metal implant is able to withstand tension, unlike the fractured bone, which is best suited to resist compression; the most efficient biomechanical internal fixation takes advantage of this difference by loading the bone in compression and the metal in tension. Because there is no perfect material for use in internal fixation, a variety of issues must be examined when specific metals are considered as surgical implants: (1) biocompatibility—the material must be systemically nontoxic, nonimmunogenic, and noncarcinogenic; (2) strength parameters—tensile, compressive, and torsional strength; stiffness; fatigue resistance; and contourability are all important aspects; (3) resistance to degradation and erosion; (4) ease of integration when appropriate; and (5) minimal adverse effects on imaging.

Basic Metallurgy

Metal atoms form unit cell configurations based on their inherent atomic properties. These unit cells associate in lattices that are crystalline formations. As molten metal cools and solidifies, the crystals line up next to each other and interdigitate; this influences the mechanical and chemical properties of the metal. Microscopic defects or impurities can alter the crystalline structure and possibly the mechanical properties. Some of the differences in the mechanical behavior of metals can be explained by their different atomic structures; for example, crystals of stainless steel are face-centered cubic, and titanium crystals are hexagonal close packed (Fig. 10–1). Further processing with chemical, thermal, or physical means can

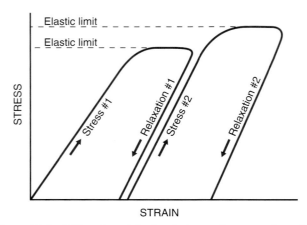

Figure 10–2. Cold working. A load cycle that involves stress above the elastic limit of the metal increases the magnitude of stress necessary to achieve the subsequent elastic limit, producing a material that is harder and stronger. (Redrawn from Olsen, G.A. Elements of Mechanics of Materials, 2nd ed. Upper Saddle River, NJ, Prentice-Hall, 1966, p. 62. Reprinted by permission.)

change the structure of the metal and affect its physical and mechanical properties.

Metal Processing

Iron-based alloys are either cast or wrought. *Casting* is the process of pouring liquid metal into a mold of a specific shape. The problem with this is that the impurities can migrate to the grain boundaries, resulting in areas of mechanical weakness. *Wrought iron* is made by mechanical processing after the metal has been cast, including use of rolling, extruding, or heat force. *Forging* is a process by which a piece of metal is heated and has a force applied through an open or closed die that represents the inverse geometry of the product being manufactured. This process refines the grain structures, increases strength and hardness, and decreases ductility. Vacuum remelting and electroslag remelting are processes that remove impurities and produce a purer grade of metal that is desirable for construction of surgical implants.

Further processing may be accomplished by cold working. This involves repetitive application of stress greater than the elastic limit of the metal. These load cycles increase the hardness and elastic limit of the material through elongation of the grains in the direction of the stress and thinning in other directions. The increased grain boundary area results in a stronger material (Fig. 10–2).

Two practical examples of cold working are shot peening of the surface of intramedullary nails (Zimmer, Warsaw, IN) and cold forging of dynamic hip screw plates (Smith and Nephew Orthopaedics, Memphis, TN). The shot-peening process involves bombardment of the outer surfaces of the metal with a high-velocity stainless steel cut wire. The impact causes residual compressive stress, which reduces surface tensile stress. Shot peening thus minimizes fatigue cracks, which usually begin on the surface and can cause fracture of the metal. The cold-forging process uses substantially more cold working to achieve a higher degree

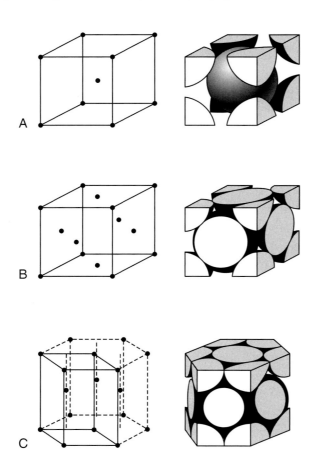

Figure 10–1. Unit cell configuration for three basic crystalline structures. *A,* Body-centered cubic. *B,* Face-centered cubic. *C,* Hexagonal close packed. (*A–C,* Redrawn from Ralls, K.M.; Courtney, T.H.; Wulff, J. Introduction to Materials Science and Engineering. New York, John Wiley & Sons, 1976. Reprinted by permission of John Wiley & Sons, Inc.; redrawn from Simon, S.R., ed. Orthopaedic Basic Science. Rosemont, IL, American Academy of Orthopaedic Surgeons, 1994.)

of deformation. This is coupled with a stress-relieving process to make a cold-forged steel of exceptionally high strength.

Passivation

Passivation is a process that either allows spontaneous oxidation on the surface of the metal or treats the metal with acid or electrolysis to increase the thickness or energy level of the oxidation layer. Commonly, the process involves immersion of the implant in a strong nitric acid solution, which dissolves embedded iron particles and generates a dense oxide film on the surface. This step generally improves the biocompatibility of the implant. Also, passivation enhances the corrosion resistance of the finished implant device (see Fig. 10–8).

Corrosion

Corrosion is the degradation of material by electrochemical attack. All metals used for surgical implantation can undergo this process. The driving force for corrosion is also the basis of the electrical storage battery, which employs materials with two different levels of reactivity. Electrical energy is produced when ions of the more reactive material are released and partial consumption of the material occurs. This electrochemical consumption is termed *corrosion*. Corrosion or galvanic attack can occur if different metals are placed in contact with each other in an internal fixation construct (e.g., inappropriate use of a titanium plate with stainless steel screws).

Corrosion can also occur within a single type of metal or between implants of the same metal. The reactivity level can differ from one area to another within the same metal implant. Differences in local reactivity are seen in areas of higher stress, lower oxygen tension, and crevices. The natural tendency of the base metal to corrode is decreased by the surface oxide coating from the passivation process. Scratches on the surface of the plate can disrupt the protective surface oxide coating and substantially increase corrosion. Crevices can develop from a scratch on the surface or develop macroscopically as the space between a screw and a plate. The metal in this area is subjected to compressive forces, leading to high stress concentration. Oxygenated extracellular fluid cannot circulate in this area, so there is a local decrease in oxygen tension. All these factors can cause differences in local reactivity and subsequent corrosion.

Mechanics

STRESS-STRAIN RELATIONSHIPS

A basic knowledge of mechanical terms is fundamental to understanding comparisons between different materials. Mechanical characteristics are based on the ability of a material to resist external forces, as expressed by stress-strain curves (Fig. 10–3A).

The *ultimate stress* of a material is the force required to

make it fail or break. The *yield point* of a material is the force required to induce the earliest permanent change in shape or deformation.

Elasticity is the material's ability to restore its original shape after a deforming force lower than the yield point is removed. This is quantified by the *modulus of elasticity*, which is the slope of the elastic region of the stress-strain curve. *Stiffness* is defined as the resistance to deformation; it is proportional to the modulus of elasticity.

Plastic deformation is a permanent change in structure of a material after the stress is relieved. Ductility and brittleness are relative characteristics and not numerically quantified. *Ductility* is the ability of a material to further deform beyond the yield point before fracture. A *brittle material* has minimal permanent deformation before failure or fracture. These characteristics are explained by the shape of the plastic (permanent deformation) curve past the yield point; a longer curve implies a more ductile substance.

Toughness is the total energy required to stress a material to the point of fracture (see Fig. 10–3B). It is defined as the area under both the elastic and the plastic parts of the stress-strain curve or as the energy to failure. *Hardness* is the ability to resist plastic deformation at the material surface only. For many materials, the mechanical properties at the surface differ from those found in the bulk of the material.

Metal has a variety of mechanical properties. Some are a function of its chemical composition and do not change with further processing; others are strongly affected by the relative orientation of the crystals and therefore are altered by processing. The elastic moduli in tension and compression do not change with processing, but yield strength, ultimate strength, and fatigue strength can be altered significantly by small changes in chemical composition and processing.[6]

FATIGUE

Fatigue is caused by cyclical (repetitive) stressing of a material. In cyclical loading, the maximal force required to produce failure decreases as the cycle number increases until the endurance limit is reached. The resulting fatigue curve shows the force necessary to cause failure of a material at each specific cycle number (Fig. 10–4). The higher the overall stress, the fewer the cycles required to produce failure (loading to the ultimate stress produces failure in one cycle). The *endurance limit* is the lowest point on the fatigue curve and represents a cyclical applied force below which the material will not have failed after 10 million (1×10^7) cycles. If the material has not failed at this point, it theoretically never will. By choosing different materials and altering implant geometry, manufacturers attempt to design implants that will tolerate cyclical loads without failure.

The *fatigue strength* (point of fatigue failure) of a material is defined as a single stress value on the fatigue curve for a specific number of cycles. In practice, certain points on a metal implant reach the fatigue failure level before others because of localized concentrations of stress (stress risers). Fatigue failure at these points results in the initiation of a crack that can propagate, causing the entire implant to fracture. Based on anatomic location, implants are subject to varying loads and varying frequency of stress cycles. The usual design estimate of cyclical load for orthopaedic implants is 2×10^6 stress cycles per year.[6]

Fatigue fractures of implants result from a high number of cycles of relatively low stress. Single-cycle and low-cycle failures are caused by high stress. Implants that have failed as a result of fatigue can be distinguished from single-cycle failures because they display a series of concentric fatigue striations over the fracture surface (Fig. 10–5). These striations appear to radiate from certain initiation points, which represent areas in which the overall peak tensile stress combined with the presence of stress risers (e.g., cracks, scratches, holes) exceeds the material's local resistance to failure. If the average peak stresses are large, then the striations have more distance between them. When these striations have propagated a sufficient distance to decrease the cross-sectional area of the implant, ultimate strength is reduced, leading to complete failure. This area of final failure is called the *tear zone,* and it can provide clues to the type of failure. High-stress, low-cycle failure produces a larger tear zone than low-stress, high-cycle failure. Implants must be designed to withstand these anticipated loads and cycles. If failure of an implant

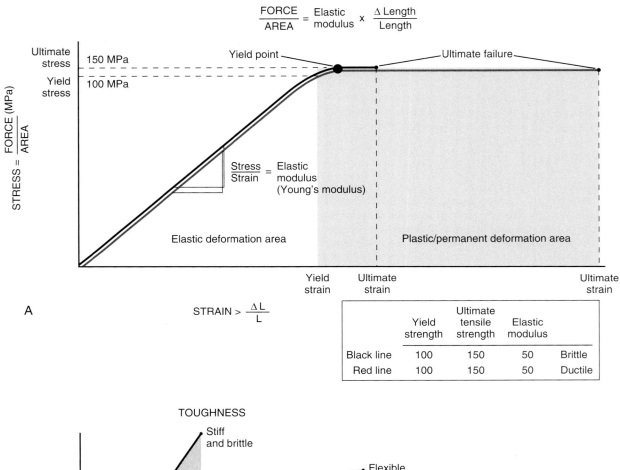

	Yield strength	Ultimate tensile strength	Elastic modulus	
Black line	100	150	50	Brittle
Red line	100	150	50	Ductile

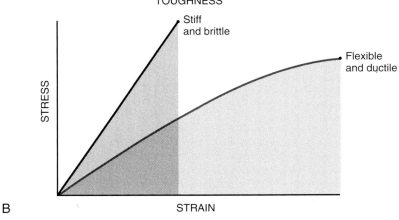

FIGURE 10–3. *A,* Stress-strain curve. The red line is an example of a ductile material; it can be stressed beyond the yield point. If a stress lower than the yield point is applied and released, the object will return to its original shape. The plastic or permanent deformation area is the portion of the curve between the amount of stress needed to reach the yield point and the amount of stress needed to reach the ultimate failure point. *B,* Toughness is defined as the area underneath the stress-strain curve. The two materials illustrated in this diagram have vastly different characteristics; however, they both have the same toughness because of equivalent areas under their respective curves. (*A, B,* Redrawn from Simon, S.R., ed. Orthopaedic Basic Science. Rosemont, IL, American Academy of Orthopaedic Surgeons, 1994.)

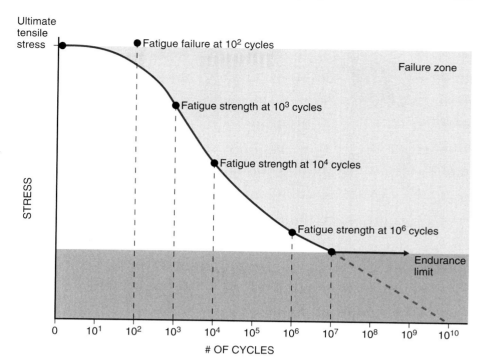

FIGURE 10–4. Fatigue curve. Fatigue curve illustrating the ultimate tensile stress, the failure zone, and the endurance limit. (Redrawn from Perren, S.M. The concept of biological plating using the limited contact-dynamic compression plate [LCDCP]: Scientific background, design, and application. Injury 22[suppl 1]:1–41, 1991; with permission from Elsevier Science Ltd., The Boulevard, Langford Lane, Kidlington OX5 1GB, UK.)

occurs, it should be examined to determine the failure pattern.

The American Society for Testing and Materials (ASTM) and the American Iron and Steel Institute (AISI) are two groups that test and monitor materials. Among other functions, these groups serve as independent sanctioning boards. Materials purchased by implant manufacturers are certified under their specifications. If a company wants to use a material that has not been sanctioned, it must go through rigorous biocompatibility and material testing procedures and submit the results to the U.S. Food and Drug Administration (FDA) for approval.

Types of Metals

The characteristics of various implant materials are shown in Figure 10–6 and Table 10–1.[8]

STAINLESS STEEL

Stainless steel is a combination of iron and chromium. The 316L stainless steel as specified by ASTM F-138 and F-139 is a standard for surgical implants. The number 316 is part of a modern classification system by AISI for metals and represents certain standards that allow the metal to be used for clinical application. The three-digit system separates the iron into four main groups based on composition: series 200 (chromium, nickel, and manganese), series 300 (chromium and nickel), series 400 (chromium), and series 500 (low chromium). The last two digits designate the particular type, and a letter represents a modification of the type (L means low carbon).

Stainless steel is further modified for use in surgical implantation by the addition of a variety of other elements to improve the alloy. The 316L stainless steel contains nickel (13% to 15.5%), which is added to increase corrosion resistance, stabilize crystalline structures, and stabilize the austenitic phase of the iron crystals at room temperature. The terms *austenitic* and *martensitic* describe specific crystallographic arrangements of iron atoms. The austenitic phase is associated with superior corrosion resistance and is favored in biologic implants. The martensitic stainless steels are hard and tough and are favored in the manufacture of osteotomes and scalpel blades. The 316L stainless steel also contains chromium (17% to 19%),

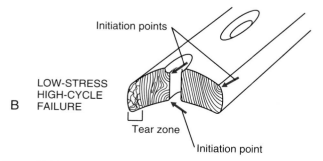

FIGURE 10–5. Types of fatigue failure in fixation plates. *A*, High-stress, low-cycle failure. *B*, Low-stress, high-cycle failure. (*A*, *B*, Redrawn from Black, J. Orthopaedic Biomaterials in Research and Practice. New York, Churchill Livingstone, 1988.)

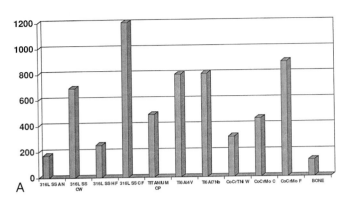

METAL VS YIELD STRENGTH (MPa)

A

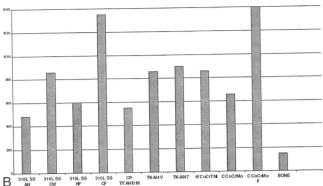

METAL VS ULTIMATE TENSILE STRESS (MPa)

B

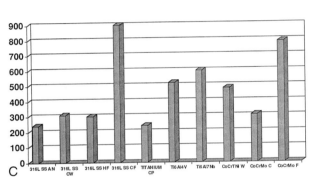

METAL VS FATIGUE STRENGTH (MPA) X 10⁷ CYCLES

C

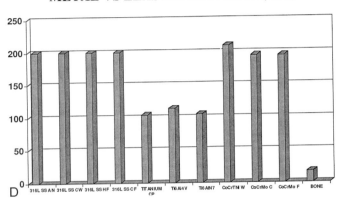

METAL VS ELASTIC MODULUS (GPa)

D

FIGURE 10–6. Compilation of general material characteristics for various implant materials. *A–D,* Graphic representations of various characteristics. *Abbreviations:* AN, annealed; ASTM, American Society for Testing and Materials; C, cast; CF, cold forged; CP, cold processed; CW, cold worked; F, forged; HF, hot forged; SS, stainless steel. (*A–D,* Data from Bronzino, J. The Biomedical Engineering Handbook. Boca Raton, FL, CRC Press, 1995, with permission.)

which is added to form a passive surface oxide, thus contributing to corrosion resistance. Molybdenum (2% to 3%) prevents pitting and crevice corrosion in salt water. Manganese (about 2%) improves crystalline stability. Silicon controls crystalline formation in manufacturing. The 316L stainless steel has a carbon content of 0.03%, whereas 316 stainless steel contains 0.08% carbon. Carbon is added during the smelting process and must be taken out in refining, because the carbon segregates from the major elements of the alloy, taking with it a substantial amount of chromium in the form of chromium carbide precipitate. The corrosion resistance of the final alloy is lessened by the depletion of chromium. Therefore, steel with a lower carbon content has greater corrosion resistance.

TABLE 10–1

Choosing Metals for Internal Fixation

Metal	Yield Strength (MPa)	Ultimate Tensile Stress (MPa)	Fatigue Strength (MPa) (10⁷ cycles)	Elastic Modulus (GPa)
316L SS (AN)	172	485	240	200
316L SS 30% CW	690	860	310	200
316L SS HF	250	600	300	200
316L SS CF	1200	1350	900	200
CP titanium (ASTM F-67)	485	550	240	104
Ti6Al4V (ASTM F-136)	795	860	520	114
Ti6Al7Nb (ASTM F-1295)	800	900	600	105
Wrought CoCrNiMo (F-562)	310	860	485	210
Cast CoCrMo (F-76)	450	655	310	195
Cast CoCrMo (F-75) F	890	1400	793	195
Cortical bone	130	150	—	17

Stainless steel has good mechanical strength with excellent ductility, and it can be worked by rolling, bending, or pounding to increase its strength. Steel is available in different degrees of strength corresponding to the proposed function of the implant.

TITANIUM AND TITANIUM ALLOYS

Titanium is an allotropic material that exists in both alpha and beta phases, which have a hexagonal close-packed crystal structure and a body-centered cubic structure, respectively. It is the least dense of all metals used for surgical implantation. The density of titanium is 4.5 g/cm^3, whereas that of 316 stainless steel is 7.9 g/cm^3 and that of cobalt-chromium alloy is 8.3 g/cm^3.

The four grades of commercially pure titanium that are available for surgical implantation are differentiated by the amount of impurities in each grade. The microstructure of commercially pure titanium is all-alpha titanium with relatively low strength and high ductility. Oxygen has a great influence on the ductility and strength: increasing the oxygen content of a particular grade of titanium makes it stronger and more brittle. Grade 4 titanium contains the most oxygen and is therefore the strongest of the commercially pure titaniums. The material may be cold-worked for additional strength, but it cannot be strengthened by heat treatment because it has only a single phase.

One titanium alloy (Ti6Al4V) is widely used for surgical implantation. The additional elements of the alloy are aluminum (5.5% to 6.5%), which stabilizes the alpha phase, and vanadium (3.5% to 4.5%), which stabilizes the beta phase. The beta phase is stronger because of its crystallographic arrangement, whereas the alpha phase promotes good weldability. For applications in which high strength and fatigue resistance are required, the material is annealed, which corresponds to a universal distribution of alpha and beta phases. The Ti6Al4V alloy can be heat-treated because it is a two-phased alloy and not a single-phase commercially pure titanium. Titanium alloy has greater specific strength per unit density than any other implant material. The most recently developed titanium alloy is Ti6Al7Nb; the niobium produces mechanical characteristics similar to those of the titanium-vanadium alloy but with less toxicity.

COBALT-CHROMIUM ALLOYS

Two cobalt-chromium alloys are currently used for manufacture of surgical implants. The first is CoCrMo (ASTM F-75), which is cast, and the second is CoCrNiMo (ASTM F-562), which is wrought. Cobalt is the main component of both alloys. The cast CoCrMo was originally called Vitallium (Howmedica, Inc., Rutherford, NJ), and this name is sometimes incorrectly used to describe all the cobalt-based alloys. Chromium (7% to 30%) provides good corrosion resistance by forming chromic oxide at the surface. Molybdenum (5% to 7%) increases strength by controlling crystalline size and also increases corrosion resistance. Nickel (1%), manganese (1%), and silicon (1%) are also added to improve ductility and hardness. The most attractive feature of both alloys is their excellent corrosion resistance and biocompatibility. The mechanical

properties (tensile strength and fatigue resistance) of the wrought CoCrNiMo alloy make it desirable for situations in which the implant must withstand a long period of loading without fatigue failure. For this reason, this material has been chosen for the manufacture of stems for hip prostheses.

Comparison of Metals

MECHANICAL PROPERTIES

The mechanical properties of a metal vary depending on whether it is used as a pure base metal or as an alloy with other metals. They also can be altered significantly by processing (e.g., cold working, hot forging, annealing). The mechanical demands that will be placed on the implant determine the appropriate materials and processing methods. Fracture fixation implants have high requirements for yield strength and fatigue resistance. The metals that can best meet these requirements are 316L stainless steel and titanium alloys. The yield stress of Ti6Al4V alloy is greater than that of unprocessed 316L stainless steel, both CoCr alloys, or commercially pure titanium. However, cold working of stainless steel can result in a material of higher yield stress and fatigue resistance than the Ti6Al4V alloy. Stainless steel is an attractive implant material because it has moderate yield and ultimate strengths, is relatively low in cost, is easy to machine, and maintains a high ductility, even with large amounts of cold work. Ti6Al4V is more difficult to machine, more expensive, and sensitive to external stress risers (scratches), which can dramatically shorten its fatigue life. Its lower ductility results in less forewarning of failure when a screw is overtightened (Fig. 10–7A). Stainless steel has favorable fatigue characteristics in the relatively low cycles, but in the higher cycles titanium alloy is more resistant to fatigue (see Fig. 10–7B).

Clinical studies showed that there was no significant advantage in healing time with steel- or titanium-based dynamic compression (DC) plates used for internal fixation of 256 tibial fractures.[62] Both Ti6Al4V and cold-worked 316L stainless steel are used for implants that must withstand unusually high stresses (e.g., intramedullary nails designed for fixation of subtrochanteric fractures). The Russell-Taylor reconstruction nail (Smith and Nephew) and the ZMS reconstruction nail (Zimmer) are made from cold-worked stainless steel; the Uniflex reconstruction nail (Biomet, Warsaw, IN) and the CFX nail (Howmedica) are made from titanium alloy.

The process of casting the CoCrMo (F-75) alloy is expensive and leaves minute defects, which significantly reduce its strength, ductility, and fatigue life. It has superior corrosion resistance. The yield strength of wrought CoCrNiMo (F-562) can range from 600 MPa for fully annealed alloy to 1400 MPa for severely cold-drawn wire. The molybdenum is added to produce finer grains, which results in higher strength after casting and forging. Cobalt-chromium alloys are difficult and expensive to machine because they have high intrinsic hardness. They also have lower ductility (i.e., they are very brittle), and their base alloy costs are significantly higher. For these

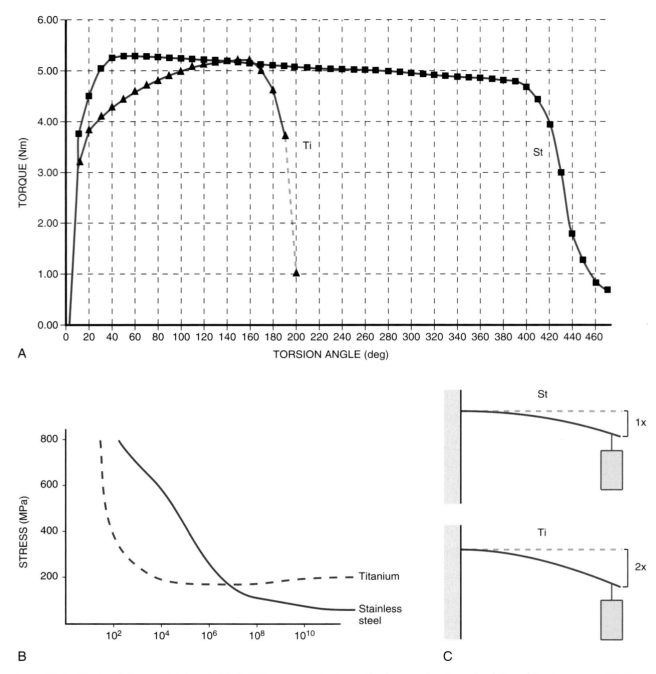

Figure 10–7. Titanium (Ti) versus stainless steel (SS). *A,* Torque versus torsion angle of screws, showing earlier failure of titanium screws. *B,* Fatigue curve showing that SS is stronger in low-cycle stress and Ti is more fatigue resistant in high-cycle stress. *C,* The Ti plate deforms nearly twice as much as the SS plate under similar loading conditions. This is explained by the lower elastic modulus of Ti. (*A–C,* Redrawn from Perren, S.M. The concept of biological plating using the limited contact–dynamic compression plate [LCDCP]: Scientific background, design, and application. Injury 22[Suppl 1]:1–41, 1991; with permission from Elsevier Science Ltd, The Boulevard, Langford Lane, Kidlington OX5 1GB, UK.)

reasons, cobalt-chromium alloys are not generally used to make fracture fixation implants, but because of their superior fatigue resistance, long-term corrosion resistance, and biocompatibility, they are used for stems of hip prostheses.

Although the discussion thus far has emphasized the importance of implant strength and fatigue resistance, it is not possible simply to maximize size and stiffness of implants to meet the mechanical demands of fracture

fixation. Bone is a living tissue that responds to mechanical loads. Both maintenance of bone mineral content and fracture healing require that the bone experience load transmission; if bone is deprived of load by the implant, stress shielding occurs. It is therefore essential that the internal fixation implant be designed to distribute stress to both the implant and the bone, often referred to as *load sharing*. Furthermore, to prevent stress concentrations and stress shielding, the elastic modulus of the implant should be similar to that of bone.[28] The elastic modulus of titanium alloys is 6 times greater than that of cortical bone, but the elastic modulus of stainless steel is 12 times greater, so titanium is the better implant material for prevention of stress shielding (see Fig. 10–7C).

BIOCOMPATIBILITY

Biocompatibility is the ability of a metal and the body to tolerate each other. The goal in choosing a metal for an implant is minimal corrosion and minimal host reactivity to inherent corrosion particles. In 1972, ASTM adopted a biocompatibility standard (F-361) that assesses the effects of all implant metals on the body. Every metal eventually corrodes in every environment; those metals that are deemed acceptable for bioimplantation should demonstrate only a small amount of corrosion over a long period. For optimal biocompatibility, the products of this corrosion should cause minimal inflammatory reaction. Titanium has the greatest corrosion resistance because it rapidly forms titanium oxide on its surface. The oxide layer is tightly adherent and resistant to breakdown; if it is damaged, it reforms in milliseconds. Although implants made of other metals are typically surrounded by a thin fibrous capsule, implants made of titanium and its alloys demonstrate a remarkable ability to form an intimate interface directly with bone. From evaluation of tissue reactivity of implantable materials, Perren[75] found no avascular zone with titanium and a 0.02-mm avascular zone with stainless steel. Titanium promotes bone ingrowth, which can be a problem if late extraction of the implant is necessary.[95]

A small but definite percentage of the population is sensitive to nickel and chromium. These persons cannot tolerate implants made of metals such as stainless steel or chromium cobalt alloy, which contain these elements. Commercially pure titanium can be used in patients who are sensitive to nickel and chromium.

Stainless steel implants have localized areas of corrosion, mostly at microfracture sites, crevices, and abrasion sites (screw-plate interfaces). A capsule forms around stainless steel implants, indicating poor integration at the surface-tissue interface. Stainless steel is compatible but does not promote bone ingrowth at the surface of the implant.[64] This has some advantage in designing devices that eventually will be removed from the body. Cast CoCrMo (F-75) has excellent corrosion resistance compared with stainless steel, and its fatigue strength can be increased by various forging and pressing techniques, making it an excellent material for high-cycle, high-stress environments such as the femoral stem of a hip implant.

Infection is a major concern with internal fixation. Although overt infection is a multifactorial problem, the adherence of bacteria to biomaterials may be an initial step in the process of implant loosening and ultimate implant failure. Minimal clinical research exists comparing bacterial adherence with various biomaterials in humans. The AO (Arbeitsgemeinschaft für Osteosynthesefragen)/ASIF (Association for Study of Internal Fixation) group retrospectively evaluated 1251 titanium DC plates and 25,000 stainless steel plates implanted into humans and did not find significant differences in infection rates. Bacteria have

a natural tendency to adhere to inert surfaces (Fig. 10–8). Bacteria that produce significant amounts of glycocalyx have a greater adherence to biomaterials.[91] Fibronectin is a serum and matrix protein that has been found to bind to various biomaterials. The presence of fibronectin on the surface of these metals is an important determinant of colonization by staphylococci.[26] Chang and Merritt[20] found the in vitro and in vivo adherence of *Staphylococcus epidermidis* was greatest for stainless steel, followed by commercially pure titanium. Stainless steel was also found to inhibit polymorphonuclear cell production of superoxide, thereby decreasing the bactericidal activity of these leukocytes. No effect on superoxide production was found with commercially pure titanium, Ti6Al4V, or cobalt-chromium alloy.[71]

IMAGING

Concerning plain radiographs, titanium alloy produces much less attenuation (scatter of x-rays) than stainless steel or cobalt-chromium and only slightly more than calcium. For computed tomography, titanium alloys have the least amount of scatter and do not lead to skeletal image disruption.[29] Cast CoCrMo (F-75) exhibits the greatest artifact on computed tomography, and stainless steel causes moderate artifact. Concerning magnetic resonance imaging compatibility, commercially pure titanium, titanium alloy, and cobalt-chromium alloy do not have magnetic characteristics and can be imaged with minimal attenuation problems. Surgical manipulations with stainless steel can induce areas of ferromagnetic potential that could either move the implant or cause an electrical current.[28]

A common question is whether orthopaedic implants are perceived by metal detectors. These machines work by detecting eddy currents that depend on a material's conductivity and permeability (ability to temporarily magnetize). Modern orthopaedic implants have both low permeability and poor conductivity and therefore are infrequently detected.[4]

RADIATION THERAPY

Although penetration characteristics are much stronger for external beam irradiation than for diagnostic radiography, implants still cause a significant amount of bulk reflection. Reflected radiation in front of the plate increased the radiation dose by 25% for stainless steel and 15% for titanium; absorption behind the plate reduced the dose by 15% and 10%, respectively.[78] If plates and screws are being placed in an area that will be irradiated, use of the lowest density material (e.g., titanium) and a small, susceptible configuration will maximally reduce the effects of reflection and attenuation.

Summary

The design and manufacture of internal fracture fixation devices are constantly changing as new technology develops. The choice of material depends on its mechanical and biocompatibility properties as well as the cost of processing and machining. There is no single ideal metal for internal

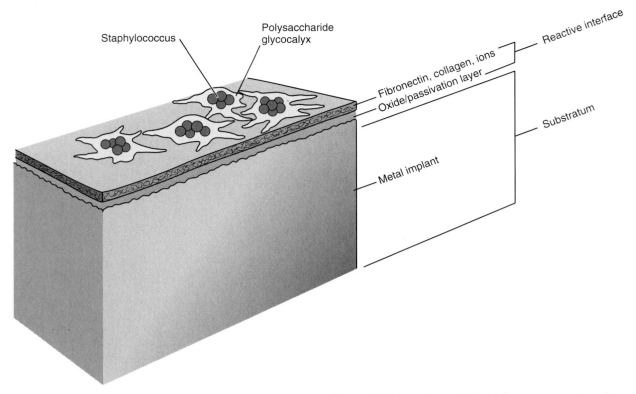

FIGURE 10–8. Biofilm containing bacteria on a metal implant. The biofilm or (slime) is made up of the implant passivation layer, host extracellular macromolecules (fibrogen, fibronectin, collagen), and bacterial extracellular glycocalyx (polysaccharide). Staphylococci are bonded on the implant, which inhibits phagocytosis. Failure of the glycopeptide antibiotics to cure prosthesis-related infection is not caused by poor penetration of drugs into the biofilm but probably by the diminished antimicrobial effect on bacteria in the biofilm environment.

fixation. Although metals are an imperfect implant material, they predominate in current orthopaedic practice. The rigorous requirements imposed by the FDA for premarket demonstration of safety and efficacy of new implant materials and devices may delay or forestall indefinitely the introduction of metal substitutes, such as resin-fiber composites.

HARDWARE

Internal fixation is based on the implantation of various appliances to assist with the body's natural healing process. The following sections describe the basic anatomy, biomechanics, and types of hardware, including screws, drills, taps, plates, intramedullary nails, and reamers.

Screws

Any discussion about different types of screws and their applications should be based on an understanding of basic screw anatomy (Fig. 10–9). The *outer diameter* is defined as the outermost diameter of the threads. *Pitch* is defined as the longitudinal distance between the threads. The bending strength and shear strength of a screw depend on its *root* or *core diameter*. This is the solid section of the screw from which the threads protrude. The core diameter also

determines the size of the drill bit used for the pilot hole. Many screws have a common core diameter. For example, the 4.5-mm cortical, 6.5-mm cancellous, and 4.5-mm malleolar screws all have the same core diameter (3.0 mm). The core diameter of a screw determines its strength in bending because strength is a function of the cross-sectional moment of inertia, which is proportional to the third power of the radius. If the thickness of the core is increased, a significant increase in bending strength is obtained. The core or root diameter is often confused with the *shaft diameter*, which is the unthreaded portion of the screw between the head and the screw threads.

A screw can break in two ways (Fig. 10–10).[88] The first way is through the application of a torque that exceeds the shear strength of the screw. Von Arx[94] determined the range of torque applied by surgeons during insertion to be 2.94 to 5.98 N-m. This force can break a screw with a root diameter of 2.92 mm or less if it jams. The second way is through application of bending forces when a load is applied perpendicularly to the long axis of the screw. If the screws fixing the plate to the bone are not tight enough, the plate can slide between the bone and the screw head. This sliding permits application of an excessive bending force perpendicular to the axis of the screw, which ultimately can result in fatigue failure of the screw.[93] In the clinical setting, the screw must be tight enough to avoid plate sliding but not so tight as to exceed the maximal shear strength of the screw itself. Several factors affect how tight the screw-plate-bone interface can be made, including the maximal torque applied during insertion, thread design, and bone quality. Because of the variation in bone quality among individuals and among different anatomic locations, it is not possible to determine the insertional torque necessary to optimally tighten all screws. For this reason, a torque screwdriver cannot be used, and screw purchase must be assessed empirically. *Purchase* is defined as the perception that the screw is meeting resistance and becoming tight rather than slipping and spinning.

The design of the threads can also influence the strength of the screw and its resistance to breakage. Stress on the core can be increased if the surfaces of adjoining threads intersect with the core at a sharp angle. This sharp notch acts as a stress concentrator, increasing the possibility of screw failure. To minimize this problem, bone screws are designed so that the intersection of the thread surfaces with the core contains curves rather than sharp angles (Fig. 10–11*A*).

Although bending strength and shear strength are important mechanical features, the pullout strength of a screw is of even greater significance in internal fixation.

The ability of a screw to achieve interfragmentary fixation or stable attachment of a plate relates to its ability to hold firmly in bone and resist pullout. The *pullout strength* of a screw is proportional to the surface area of thread that is in contact with bone. There are two methods to increase this surface contact. The first is to increase the difference between the core and the external diameters; this maximizes the amount of screw thread surface that is in contact with bone, resulting in stronger fixation. The second method is to increase the number of threads per unit length—that is, to decrease the point-to-point distance between successive threads (pitch). The smaller the pitch, the greater the number of threads that can engage in the bone, and the more secure the fixation (see Fig. 10–11*B*).

The size, shape, and quality of bone and the physiologic stress on the fracture site determine the number of screws required for adequate fixation. The AO/ASIF group has performed retrospective clinical reviews of large numbers of fracture fixations.[67] These studies have empirically determined the number of screws that should be used to attach a plate to each long bone. Because the diaphysis of

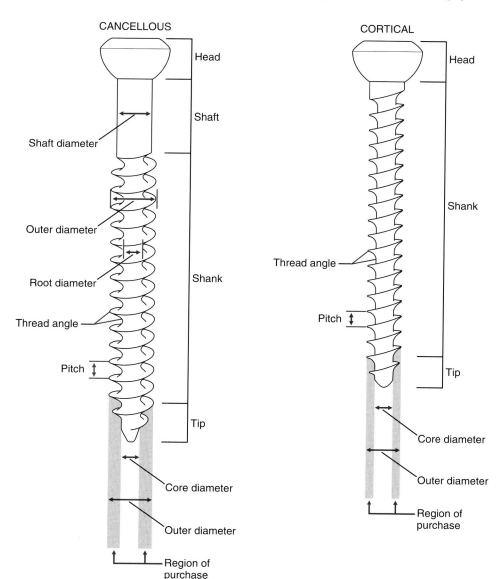

FIGURE 10–9. Anatomy of screws.

long bones is tubular, it is possible to achieve thread purchase in the cortex on one or both sides of the canal. The screw purchase required for stable plate fixation in each long bone is described in the *Manual of Internal Fixation*[68] as a specific number of cortices. The recommended number of cortices on each side of the fracture is seven in the femur, six in the tibia or humerus, and five in the radius or ulna.

Circumstances may dictate the use of a longer plate that has more holes in it than the required number of cortices. The question arises whether all of the holes should be filled. Placement of a screw limits micromotion and reduces stress by increasing the area of surface contact between the plate and the bone. On the other hand, every drill hole in bone represents a site of stress concentration and a point of potential fracture (Fig. 10–12). Brooks and colleagues[9] found that a single hole can reduce overall bone strength by 30%. However, leaving screw holes empty may cause concern about plate failure. Plates can fail because of stress concentration caused by the fracture type or by the screw hole itself. A short defect has an increased stress concentration because the forces are distributed over a smaller area than with a longer, more oblique defect. In addition, the screw hole is the plate's weakest portion because it has the highest stress. Stress equals force divided by area; the presence of a screw hole reduces the area of the plate, so the stress on the plate is greater at the screw hole. Although each hole in the plate acts as a stress concentrator, the load experienced at each hole relates to its location in terms of the fracture site and the shape and stability of the fracture. Empty holes at the

ends of the plate experience less stress than those closer to the fracture. Pawluk and associates[74] reported bending strains for screws proximal to the fracture at 240 $\mu\epsilon$ and for those distal to the fracture at 87 $\mu\epsilon$ under bone-to-bone contact conditions. Filling of these holes is of limited value because the screw does not reinforce the plate and may needlessly increase the risk of fracture at the screw site. When a long plate is used, it is desirable to intersperse screws and open holes at the ends of the plate while concentrating screw placement close to the fracture site.

Empty screw holes in bone, both those drilled but not filled and those left after screw removal, weaken the bone. Burstein and co-workers[18] reported 1.6 times greater stresses around empty holes than in the surrounding bone when in torsion. Within approximately 4 weeks, these holes are filled with woven bone, which eliminates the stress-concentrating effect. This point is important for postoperative management after implant removal.

Drills

Fundamental to screw placement is proper preparation of the bone with drilling. The most important aspect of this process is the design of the drill bit. The anatomy of a drill bit is shown in Figure 10–13 and is relatively simple. The central tip is the first area to bite into the bone. The sharper the tip, the better the bite and the less scive or shift in the proposed drill site. The *cutting edge*, located at the tip of the drill bit, performs the actual cutting and is crucial to efficient penetration. *Flutes* are helical grooves along the

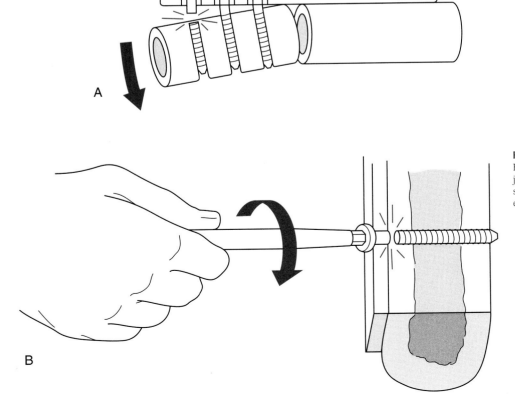

Figure 10–10. Screw failure. *A,* Bending failure secondary to a loose junction between the plate and the screw. *B,* Shear failure secondary to excessive torque.

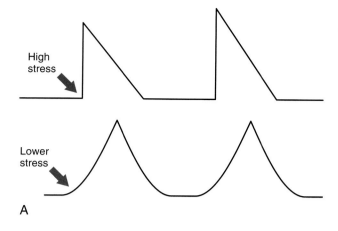

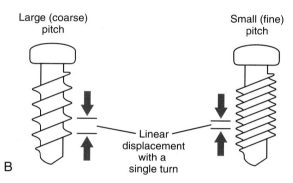

FIGURE 10–11. Effects of thread design. *A,* A sharp intersection between the screw core and the threads acts as an area of stress concentration, increasing the possibility of screw failure. *B,* The effect of thread pitch on the linear advance of a screw for a single turn. (*A, B,* Redrawn from Tencer, A.F.; et al. In: Asnis, S.E.; Kyle, R.F., eds. Cannulated Screw Fixation: Principles and Operative Techniques. New York, Springer Verlag, 1996. Used with permission.)

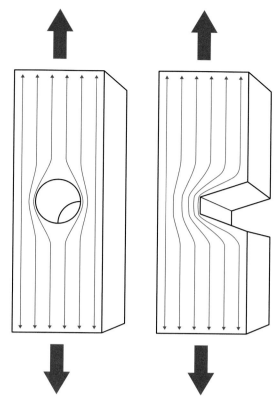

FIGURE 10–12. Stress is concentrated at the equator of the hole and at the bottom of the notch. A sharp notch will concentrate the stress further. (Redrawn from Radin, E.L.; et al. Practical Biomechanics for the Orthopaedic Surgeon. New York, John Wiley & Sons, 1979.)

sides of the bit that direct the bone chips away from the hole. Failure to remove bone debris could cause the drill bit to deviate from its intended path, decreasing drilling accuracy. The *land* is the surface of the bit between adjacent flutes. The *reaming edge* is the sharp edge of the helical flutes that runs along the entire surface, clearing the drill hole of bone debris while performing no cutting function. Disruption of these edges diminishes reaming performance. The *rake* or *helical angle* is the angle made by the leading edge of the land and the center axis of the drill bit. A larger rake angle reduces the cutting forces regardless of the direction in which the bone is cut. This angle can be positive, negative, or neutral. Positive rake angles cut only when rotated clockwise.

Most drill bits are constructed with two flutes; they are used with rotary-powered drills and are provided in standard fracture fixation sets. To limit drilling damage to the soft tissues adjacent to bone, an attachment has been developed that converts a drill's action from rotary to oscillating drive. With the oscillating drive, there is less tendency for the drill bit to wrap up and damage soft tissue. An oscillating drill bit can be placed on skin and will not cut it because of the skin's natural elasticity. A three-fluted drill bit has been developed for use with oscillating drill attachments. To work effectively, a two-

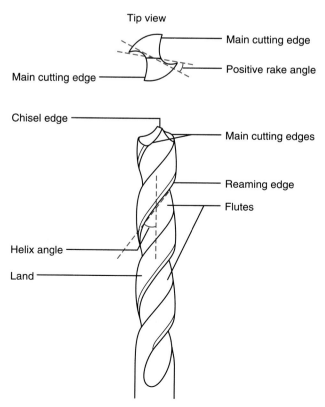

FIGURE 10–13. Anatomy of the drill bit.

fluted drill bit must rotate beyond 180°. Because the excursion of the oscillating device is less than 180°, a three-fluted drill bit must be used to achieve cutting. This drill bit also provides an added advantage when drilling on an oblique angle. Although the oscillating three-fluted drill bit may be safer for soft tissue, the two-fluted rotary drill bit cuts through bone more efficiently and is more commonly used.

Drilling into bone is different from drilling into wood because bone is a living tissue. The process of drilling in bone must minimize physiologic damage. Jacob and Berry[41] determined the optimal drill bit design and method for bone drilling. They found that the cutting forces are higher at lower rotational speeds and suggested a physiologic bone drilling method that includes the following: (1) bone drill bits with positive rake angles between 20° and 35°; (2) a point on the drill to avoid walking (sciving); (3) high torque and relatively low drill speeds (750 to 1250 rpm) to take advantage of a decrease in flow stress of the material; (4) continuous, copious irrigation to reduce friction-induced thermal bone necrosis; (5) reflection of the periosteum to prevent bone chips from being forced under the tissue, clogging the drill flutes; (6) drill flutes that are steep enough to remove chips at any rake angle; (7) sharp and axially true drill bits to decrease the amount of retained bone dust; and (8) drilling of the thread hole exactly in the direction in which the screw is to be inserted for accuracy and strength. These techniques significantly reduce local bone damage.

Most drill bits are constructed with high-carbon stainless steel and are further heat processed for added hardness. Damaged or dull bits decrease drilling efficiency significantly and may cause local trauma to bone. A damaged drill bit can increase drilling time by a factor of 35.[77] Damage is frequently caused by contact with other metal (plate or drill sleeve). The AO/ASIF recommends certain procedures to decrease drill bit damage. The first is to drill only bone. Pohler[77] found that drilling of 110 bone cortices had a negligible effect on the bit itself. The second is to always use the drill guide. This minimizes bending, which is the leading cause of drill failure. The drill guide or sleeve should be of correct size; an excessively large guide results in a larger hole because of wobbling of the drill. The third recommendation is to start the drill only after the drill bit has been inserted into the drill guide. This limits contact with the drill guide and consequent damage to the cutting and reaming edges. These recommendations combined with the defined physiologic bone drilling method limit local damage to bone and result in optimal holes for screw fixation.

Most standard fracture fixation sets provide specific drill bits that are used to drill tap and glide holes appropriate for all screws contained in the set. Drill bits are named by their diameter and, because they should always be used with soft tissue protective sleeves, they have both a total and an effective length, the latter being the portion of the bit that extends past the drill sleeve and is responsible for cutting. The diameters of drill bits correspond to specific screws in the fracture fixation set. Generally, the size of the drill bit used to make the pilot hole for the screw threads is 0.1 to 0.2 mm larger than the core diameter of the corresponding screw. The size of the drill bit used to make glide holes is the same size as the

diameter of the shaft of a shaft screw or the outer diameter of a fully threaded cortical screw. The cutting edge of the bit is at its tip; it should always be protected and should frequently be examined for flaws.

Taps

Taps are designed to cut threads in bone that resemble exactly the profile of the corresponding screw thread. The process of tapping facilitates insertion and enables the screw to bite deeper into the bone. This allows the torque applied to the screw to be used for generating compressive force instead of being dissipated by friction and cutting of threads (Fig. 10–14). Tapping also removes additional material from the hole, thereby enlarging it. The screw pullout strength depends on the material density. The larger hole created by the tap does not decrease pullout strength in cortical bone because of its density; in less dense trabecular or osteopenic bone, the larger hole has a progressively larger effect and can decrease pullout strength by as much as 30%.[88]

Taps are threaded throughout their length and increase gradually in height up to the desired thread depth. A flute extends from the tip through the first 10 threads to facilitate clearing of bone debris, which can collect and jam the tap. Proper technique calls for two clockwise and one counterclockwise turn to facilitate bone chip removal. The entire far cortex should always be tapped, because screw pullout strength increases substantially with full cortical purchase. The tap size, which corresponds to its outer diameter, should be the same as the outer diameter of the screw. For example, a 4.5-mm cortical screw has an outside diameter of 4.5 mm and uses a 4.5-mm tap; a 6.5-mm cancellous screw with an outside diameter of 6.5 mm uses a 6.5-mm tap (Fig. 10–15).

Screw Types

In practice, screws are most commonly referred to by the outer diameter of the threads (3.5, 4.5, 6.5, and 7.3 mm). Screws are also described as self-tapping or non–self-tapping, solid or cannulated, cortical or cancellous, and fully or partially threaded. The final variables are the overall length of the screw and the thread length of a partially threaded screw. The following sections describe self-tapping, non–self-tapping, cortical, shaft, cancellous, cannulated, and malleolar screws.

SELF-TAPPING SCREWS

Self-tapping screws are designed to cut their own thread path during insertion without prior use of a tap (see Fig. 10–14). The feature that differentiates these screws from others is the tip shape and design. Most commonly, the tip has cutting flutes that allow the leading threads to cut a path. Because the flutes are only at the tip and do not extend the full length of the screw, debris cannot be removed completely and is instead impacted into the thread path. These fluted-tipped, self-tapping screws are designed primarily for use in cortical bone. Some screws are designed to drill the pilot hole and tap the threads.

NON–SELF-TAPPING   SELF-TAPPING

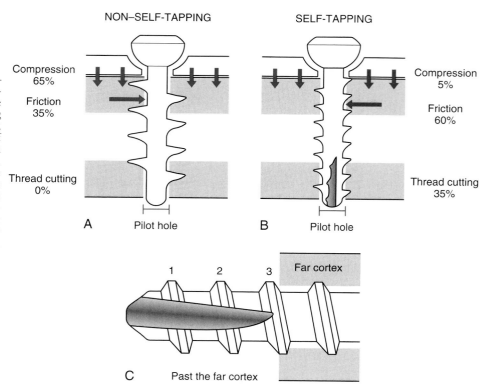

FIGURE **10–14.** Self-tapping versus non–self-tapping screws. *A,* In a non–self-tapping screw, the majority of the torque applied to the screw is used in generating compression. *B,* In a self-tapping screw, the pilot hole is larger and the majority of the torque applied to the screw is used in cutting threads and generating friction, not in generating compression. Also, the threads do not penetrate as deeply into the bone. *C,* To maximize screw thread purchase into the cortical bone, self-tapping screws should be inserted so that the cutting threads extend beyond the far cortex. (*A–C,* Redrawn from Perren, S.M.; et al. Int J Orthop Trauma 2:31–48, 1992; redrawn from Tencer, A.F.; et al. In: Asnis, S.E.; Kyle, R.F., eds. Cannulated Screw Fixation: Principles and Operative Techniques. New York, Springer Verlag, 1996. Used with permission.)

These screws usually have a trochar, diamond-shaped tip as well as flutes. This design is most commonly used in cannulated screw systems.

Although not designated as self-tapping screws, cancellous screws are commonly inserted without tapping of the cancellous bone. The thread tip of these screws has a corkscrew pattern with a gradually increasing thread diameter. The corkscrew shape impacts the bone around the sides of the pilot hole rather than cutting and removing debris. The purchase of the cancellous screw is enhanced by this impaction. Tapping of the entire length of the cancellous threads removes essential bone, reducing pull-out strength.

An advantage of self-tapping screws is that the number of steps necessary for the operation is reduced, decreasing the operative time. An intimate fit of the screw thread in the bone occurs because the screw cuts its own thread and bone is impacted in the thread path. A disadvantage of self-tapping screws is the increased torque required for screw insertion. Ansell and Scales[1] found that three flutes extended over three threads required the least torque for insertion (see Fig. 10–14). However, these flutes weaken the pullout strength of this portion of the screw because the fluted threads have 17% to 30% less thread surface than threads further up the screw. Therefore, the screw should be advanced so that the cutting flutes protrude beyond the far cortex.[2] Because additional axial load and torque are necessary for insertion of self-tapping screws, fracture displacement may occur. This is one reason why self-tapping screws are not recommended for interfragmentary lag screw fixation.[67]

NON–SELF-TAPPING SCREWS

Non–self-tapping screws do not have flutes and are designed with a blunt tip. These screws require a predrilled pilot hole and threads cut with a tap. The most important advantage of non–self-tapping screws is that the axial load and torque applied during tapping and screw insertion are less than that with self-tapping screws (see Fig. 10–14). This allows the screws to be used more effectively for interfragmentary compression, lessening the chance of fracture displacement. In addition, unlike self-tapping screws, these screws can be replaced accurately because they cannot cut their own channel.

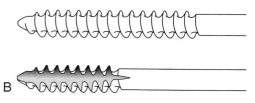

FIGURE **10–15.** Taps and their corresponding screws. *A,* A 4.5-mm cortical screw has an outside diameter of 4.5 mm and uses a 4.5-mm tap. *B,* A 6.5-mm cancellous screw has an outside diameter of 6.5 mm and uses a 6.5-mm tap. (*A, B,* Redrawn from Texhammar, R.; Colton, C. AO/ASIF Instruments and Implants: A Technical Manual. New York, Springer Verlag, 1995.)

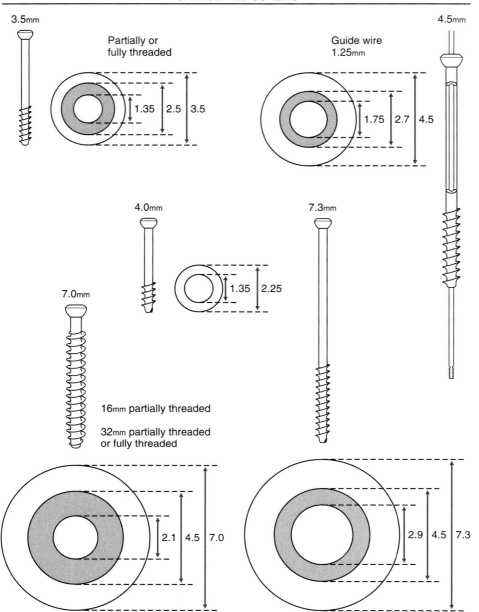

CANNULATED SCREWS

3.5mm

Partially or
fully threaded

Guide wire
1.25mm

4.5mm

1.35 | 2.5 | 3.5

1.75 | 2.7 | 4.5

4.0mm

7.3mm

7.0mm

1.35 | 2.25

16mm partially threaded

32mm partially threaded
or fully threaded

2.1 | 4.5 | 7.0

2.9 | 4.5 | 7.3

FIGURE 10–16. Comparison of the inner and outer diameters of cannulated, cortical, cancellous, shaft, and malleolar screws. (Redrawn from Synthes Equipment Ordering Manual. Paoli, PA, Synthes USA, 1992.)

COMPARISON OF SELF-TAPPING AND NON–SELF-TAPPING SCREWS

Baumgart and colleagues[3] evaluated the insertion torque, pullout force, and temperature on insertion of a self-tapping screw and compared the results with those of non–self-tapping screws with or without the process of proper tapping. They found that 1 to 1.5 N-m of insertion torque was required to insert a 4.5-mm self-tapping screw into human cortical bone. This is slightly more than the torque required to insert a non–self-tapping screw into a pretapped hole. Placement of a non–self-tapping screw into an untapped pilot hole required twice the torque. The pullout force of a self-tapping screw is 450 to 500 N per millimeter of cortex, which is less than but not significantly different from the pullout force of a tapped screw in cortical bone. The heat generated during introduction of

the self-tapping screw causes an increase in temperature at the screw tip, but limited heat is transferred to the surrounding bone. The increase in temperature does not depend on the rate of insertion as long as the insertion is not hindered.

The discussion so far has focused on differentiating screws according to their specific biomechanical function. In the following sections, screws are differentiated based on the type of bone in which they are designed to gain purchase.

CORTICAL SCREWS

Cortical screws are made with a shallow thread, small pitch, and relatively large core diameter (Fig. 10–16). The large core diameter increases the strength of the screw,

CORTICAL SCREWS

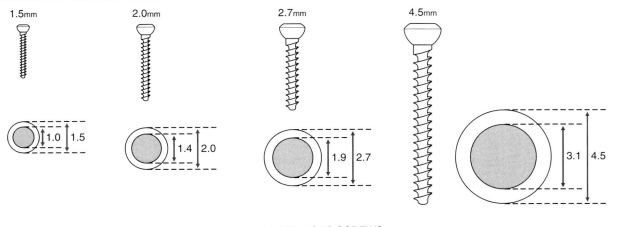

1.5mm 2.0mm 2.7mm 4.5mm

1.0 | 1.5   1.4 | 2.0   1.9 | 2.7   3.1 | 4.5

CANCELLOUS SCREWS

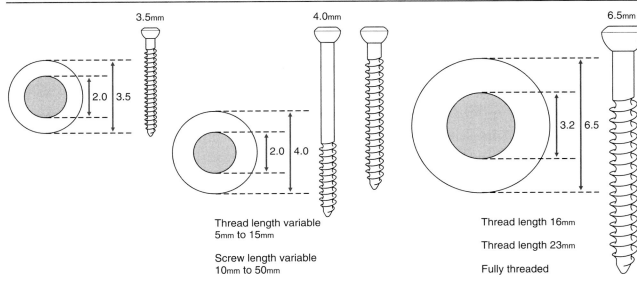

3.5mm 4.0mm 6.5mm

2.0 | 3.5   2.0 | 4.0   3.2 | 6.5

Thread length variable
5mm to 15mm

Screw length variable
10mm to 50mm

Thread length 16mm

Thread length 23mm

Fully threaded

SHAFT SCREWS

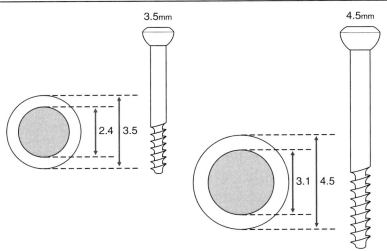

3.5mm 4.5mm

2.4 | 3.5   3.1 | 4.5

MALLEOLAR SCREWS

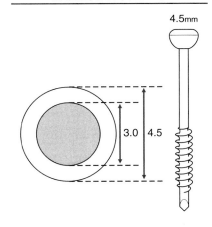

4.5mm

3.0 | 4.5

FIGURE **10–16** *Continued*

which is important for attachment of plates to bone and for resistance to the deforming loads experienced by interfragmentary compression. These screws are fully threaded throughout their length and are commonly non–self-tapping. The thread and the polished surface allow easy removal and replacement if incorrect insertion has been performed.

SHAFT SCREWS

The shaft screw is a partially threaded cortical screw in which the shaft diameter equals the external diameter of the thread (see Fig. 10–16). This screw is used for interfragmentary compression, either in bone alone or positioned through a plate. The nonthreaded shaft presents a smooth surface to sit in the glide hole, eliminating binding. Klaue and associates[52] reported that almost 40% of the compressive effect of a fully threaded cortical lag screw through a plate may be lost because of binding of the screw on the side of the glide hole in the proximal cortex. They termed this binding phenomenon *parasitic force*. The absence of binding removes the parasitic force, resulting in a 60% improvement in lag screw compression (Fig. 10–17).

CANCELLOUS SCREWS

Cancellous screws are characterized by a thin core diameter and wide, deep threads (see Fig. 10–16). The higher ratio of outer to core diameter increases the holding power, which is especially important for cancellous

trabeculae commonly found at the epiphysis and metaphysis. Cancellous screws are available either fully threaded or partially threaded with variable thread lengths. The choice of the specific thread length depends on fracture configuration and bone anatomy. When a cancellous screw is used as a lag screw, the entire length of thread must be contained within the fracture fragment. Allowing the thread to cross the fracture site inhibits compression and may cause distraction. Choosing the correct thread length is critical to ensure maximal purchase while avoiding displacement. Compression of cancellous bone by screw threads does not cause resorption but actually causes hypertrophy and realigns the trabeculae with the force on the side exposed to pressure.[96] The design of a cancellous screw takes into account the fact that cancellous bone is softer than the denser cortical bone. The root diameter is decreased, allowing for increased thread depth. This results in greater holding capacity at the expense of loss of bending and shear strength.

CANNULATED SCREWS

A cannulated screw has a hollow center that allows it to be passed over a guide wire (see Fig. 10–16). The root diameter is increased to account for placement of the screw over the wire. The increased size of the screw is necessary to account for the cannulation wire, which must be of adequate strength to hold steady in bone without bending. The screw cannot be too large, for that would remove too much bone, decreasing the strength of the construct. Guide pins are used to predetermine the

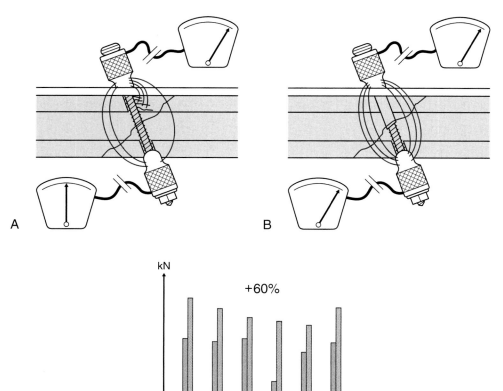

FIGURE 10–17. Loss and recovery of lag screw compression. *A,* With a fully threaded lag screw applied in an inclined position, wedging of the threads within the gliding hole can occur, causing a 40% loss of the compression effect. *B,* The use of a partially threaded shaft screw avoids this wedging problem. *C,* The differences between the measured values of compression for the standard fully threaded lag screw (*black bars*) and the shaft screw (*red bars*). The newer shaft screw is 60% more efficient than the fully threaded inclined lag screw. (*A–C,* Redrawn from Perren, S.M. The concept of biological plating using the limited contact–dynamic compression plate [LCDCP]: Scientific background, design, and application. Injury 22[Suppl 1]:1–41, 1991; with permission from Elsevier Science Ltd., The Boulevard, Langford Lane, Kidlington OX5 1GB, UK.)

optimal screw position and aid in actual fracture reduction. The guide pin makes a relatively small defect in the bone, allowing position changes with little effect on the ability of the screw to compress and hold bone. It is threaded to aid in its fixation into bone and prevents forward or reverse motion when the screw is inserted over it. The guide pin also makes the pilot hole for the cannulated screw. When combined with fluoroscopic imaging, cannulation improves the precision of cancellous screw placement significantly. This is important in areas where inexact placement could result in catastrophic complications. Once the guide pin is in position, the screw is placed over it and advanced through the soft tissues in a counterclockwise fashion to avoid cutting or winding tissue damage. At the proximal cortex, the screw is turned clockwise and self-tapped to the desired level of insertion. Cannulated screw systems are commonly used in areas with abundant cancellous bone; tapping of this type of bone decreases the pullout strength.[2]

The mechanics of a cannulated screw are somewhat different from those of solid screws. The most important factor in maximizing the overall pullout strength of a cannulated screw is the host material density (Fig. 10–18), followed by outer diameter, pitch, and root diameter. Pullout strength depends on two basic parameters, screw fixation and screw design. The patient's variable bone density is the primary factor affecting screw fixation. There are many variables to screw design. The larger the outer diameter, the greater the pullout strength. A 6.4-mm screw has significantly greater holding power than a 4.5-mm screw in bone of comparable density. A smaller pitch also increases holding power. This variable is limited because as the number of threads per inch increases, they become tight and remove too much bone.

COMPARISON OF CORTICAL, CANCELLOUS, AND CANNULATED SCREWS

A cortical screw can handle four times the stress of a cancellous screw of similar size and 1.7 times the stress of a cannulated screw. The thread design and larger root diameter enable it to handle 6.2 and 1.7 times the maximal bending stress of a solid cancellous or cannulated screw, respectively. The increase in strength caused by increased root diameter comes with the disadvantage of decreased thread depth (see Fig. 10–16). However, this decrease in thread depth does not decrease holding power in cortical bone.[2] The resistance of a screw to bending stresses increases with the root diameter.

For screws to have cannulation, the root diameter must be increased. In relation to solid screws of the same external diameter, the thread depth of a cannulated screw is decreased and the root diameter is increased. This is the reason for the decreased pullout strength of cannulated screws. Leggon and coworkers[57] found a 20% decrease in holding power between cannulated and solid screws of similar diameter. To compensate for this difference, a larger diameter cannulated screw is recommended. Hearn and colleagues[40] found no significant difference in pullout strength between solid 6.5-mm cancellous screws and 7.0-mm cannulated cancellous screws.

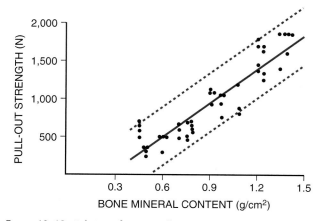

FIGURE 10–18. Relation of screw pull-out strength to bone density in vertebral bodies. Increasing bone density is associated with improved pull-out strength. (From Trader, J.E.; et al. J Bone Joint Surg Am 61:1217–1220, 1979; redrawn from Tencer, A.F.; et al. In: Asnis, S.E.; Kyle, R.F., eds. Cannulated Screw Fixation: Principles and Operative Techniques. New York, Springer Verlag, 1996. Used with permission.)

MALLEOLAR SCREWS

Malleolar screws were originally designed for the fixation of the medial malleolus. They are partially threaded cortical screws with a trephine tip that allows them to cut their own path in cancellous bone. To achieve stable fixation of the malleolar fragment, two points of fixation are necessary. Medial malleolar fractures often have distal fragments that are too small to permit fixation with two of these screws; the large size of the screw often shatters these small fragments. The prominence of the large screw head at the tip of the medial malleolus also causes excessive patient discomfort.

Summary

Proper drilling, tapping, and insertion of screws are critical in internal fixation. Surgeons use different screws based on the design, application, and anatomy of the fracture. This section has attempted to cover basic anatomy, design, and function of screws, drills, and taps to offer a general understanding that can be further applied to specific fractures.

Plates

Plates are a fundamental element of internal fixation. They are principally differentiated by the biomechanical function they perform. Examples of these functions are neutralization, buttressing, prevention of glide, compression, bridging, and formation of a tension band. Also, plates can be categorized according to their specific designs. These include the DC plate; the limited contact-dynamic compression (LCDC) plate; and tubular, reconstruction, angled, and sliding screw plates. Certain specially designed plates can be modified to perform different biomechanical functions based on anatomic need. In addition, some plates have evolved with specific names based on their location (e.g., lateral tibial head plate).

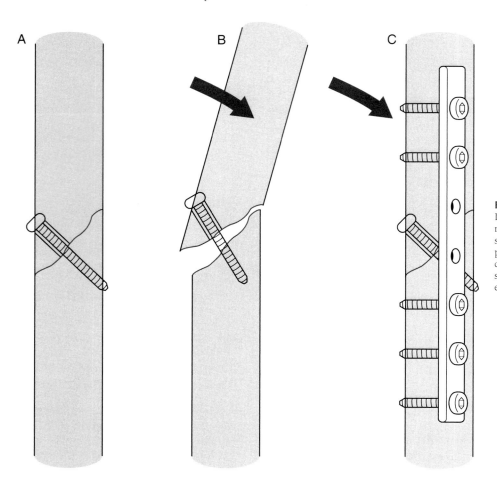

FIGURE **10–19.** Neutralization plate. *A,* Interfragmentary screw fixation without a neutralization plate. *B,* Interfragmentary screw fixation without a neutralization plate in a loaded position, resulting in construct failure. *C,* Interfragmentary screw fixation with a neutralization plate effectively resisting an external load.

Various plates can be used or adapted based on function, design, or anatomic location. This section discusses the basic biomechanical functions of plates and some specific plate designs. The application of particular plates to certain injuries is discussed in other parts of this book.

BIOMECHANICAL FUNCTIONS OF PLATES

Neutralization

A neutralization plate is used to protect lag screw fixations from various external forces. Torsional and bending forces on long bone fractures are too great to be overcome by lag screw stabilization alone. The plate protects the interfragmental compression achieved with the lag screw from torsional, bending, and shear forces exerted on the fracture. This achieves fracture fixation that is sufficiently stable to allow early function. When comparing two plates of the same design, the longer plate provides greater neutralization capability (Fig. 10–19).

Buttressing

The buttress plate is used to counteract bending, compressive, and shearing forces at the fracture site when an axial load is applied. Buttress plates are commonly used to stabilize intra-articular and periarticular fractures at the ends of long bones. Without fixation or with lag screw fixation alone, epiphyseal and metaphyseal fragments can displace when they are subjected to axial compression or bending forces. The buttress plate supports the underlying cortex and effectively resists this displacement, which otherwise could result in an angular deformity of the joint. In this manner, it acts as a buttress or retaining wall (Fig. 10–20A).

To minimize the potential of angular deformity, the screws attaching the plate to the bone must be inserted in such a manner that when a load is applied there will be no shift in the position of the plate in relation to the bone. A screw inserted through an oval hole closest to the fracture is said to be in *buttress mode.* This mode minimizes axial movement at the fracture site. To avoid the possibility of displacing the fracture fragment during application of the plate, the plate should be accurately contoured to match the anatomy of the underlying cortex. Screw placement in a buttress mode does not always imply that the plate is functioning as a buttress plate. A buttress plate applies force to the bone in a direction normal (perpendicular) to the flat surface of the plate, in contrast to a compression plate application, in which the direction of prestress is parallel to the plate. Plates used for this buttressing function are designed to fit in specific anatomic locations (see Fig. 10–20B). If the fracture extends from the metaphysis into the diaphysis, a long plate with a condylar end can be used to combine buttressing with other plate functions. A spring plate is a specialized form of buttress in which the plate is affixed with screws to only one of the two fracture fragments (see Fig. 10–20C).

Plates primarily designed to provide compression (DC or LCDC plates) can be used as buttress plates with proper contouring and fixation in a buttress mode. Other plates are designed specifically to function as buttress plates in particular locations. Some examples of buttress plates by design are the T buttress plate for lateral tibial plateau fractures, the spoon plate for treatment of anterior metaphyseal fractures of the distal tibia, the cloverleaf plate for the medial distal tibia, and the distal femoral condylar buttress plate (see Fig. 10–20B).

Compression

Compression plates can be used to reduce and stabilize transverse or short oblique fractures when lag screw fixation alone is inadequate. The plate can produce static compression in the direction of the long axis of bone in three ways: by overbending of the plate, by application of a tension device, and by a special plate design that generates axial compression by combining screw hole geometry with screw insertion (Fig. 10–21).

Bridging

The purpose of a bridge plate is to maintain length and alignment of severely comminuted and segmental fractures. It is called a *bridge plate* because the fixation is out of the main zone of injury. To avoid additional injury in the comminuted zone, screw fixation is achieved at the ends of the plate. During fracture fixation, the bridge plate can be used as a reduction device to limit the dissection in the zone of injury. This fixation method decreases devitalization of bone fragments by not stripping their tenuous blood supply and thereby allowing for a better healing environment (Fig. 10–22A).

The *wave plate* is similar to a bridge plate; it is primarily used in areas of delayed healing (see Fig. 10–22B). The wave plate is contoured away from the comminuted area or pseudarthrosis to be bridged.[16] This leaves some distance between the cortex of bone and the plate, where autologous bone graft can be placed. In the treatment of nonunions, this space allows for better ingrowth of vessels into the graft beneath the plate. The bending of the plate distributes force over a greater area, decreasing local stress at the comminuted site. The plate also can act as a tension band, creating compression on the opposite comminuted cortex. These factors make the wave plate an efficient tool in the treatment of nonunions.

Tension Band

The tension band principle was adopted by Pauwels from classical mechanics.[72, 73] It is best understood by examining the forces that occur at discontinuity in an I-beam (Fig. 10–23). The stretching and compressing of springs can be used to demonstrate tension and compression forces. As shown in this analogy, applied forces that are coaxial with the central axis of the I-beam produce uniform compression in both springs on either side of the neutral axis and uniform closure of the discontinuity in the beam. In contrast, when the force is applied eccentrically at a distance from the central axis to the beam, a bending moment is created. This bending moment produces

tension on the opposite side of the beam. This is demonstrated by opening of the discontinuity and spring distraction. On the same side of the beam on which the weight is applied, the moment creates compression, evidenced by closing of the discontinuity with spring compression. In anticipation of this eccentrically applied weight, an unyielding band can be applied to the side on which tension will be created by the bending moment. This band is used to create a small amount of compression, evidenced in partial closure of the discontinuity and compression of the spring on the same side as the band. Under these conditions, the application of an asymmetric force to the opposite side of the beam leads to uniform compression on both sides of the discontinuity, evidenced by further closing of the space and compression of the springs. This band, which is placed in tension before the functional application of the eccentric load, is called the *tension band*.

Wires, cables, nonabsorbable sutures, and plates can be used to perform the function of the tension band. Practically speaking, tension band implants can be used to fix fractures in only certain limited locations in the body. Some examples are the greater trochanter of the femur, the olecranon, and the patella. In these situations, the eccentric pull of the muscles forces the joint surface of the fractured bone against the corresponding joint surface of another bone, which acts as a fulcrum. The extensor muscle usually provides the major deforming force causing the bending moment at the discontinuity. A wire or cable is frequently used as a tension band in these situations. It is applied to the surface of the bone, which is subjected to tensile loads during active motion. The wire is tensioned to apply slight compression to the site of the fractures. This creates a small gap on the opposite side. When dynamic forces are applied during subsequent contractions of these antagonistic deforming muscles, the tension band resists the tendency for distraction of the opposite side of the bone, producing uniform compression at the fracture site. Parallel longitudinal Kirschner wires, Steinmann pins, or cancellous lag screws are used as adjunctive fixation to prevent displacement of the fracture site through shearing, translation, or rotation. Because they are placed in parallel orientation, the smooth pins or screw shafts act as rails along which the bone fragment can slide during dynamic compression.

In fractures of the patella and olecranon, dynamic compression is achieved through antagonistic muscle function during active flexion of the knee and elbow. The intercondylar grooves of the distal femur and humeral trochlea act as fulcrums over which these antagonistic muscle groups apply bending forces to the patella and olecranon. Fractures or osteotomies of the greater trochanter of the femur and greater tuberosity of the humerus can also be fixed in a similar fashion using the tension band principle. The antagonistic pull of the gluteals and adductors, using the hip joint as a fulcrum, causes a bending moment at the site of discontinuity between the greater trochanter and the remaining femur. In a similar fashion, the antagonistic pull of the supraspinatus and pectoralis major, using the glenohumeral joint as a fulcrum, causes a bending moment at the site of discontinuity between the greater tuberosity and the remaining

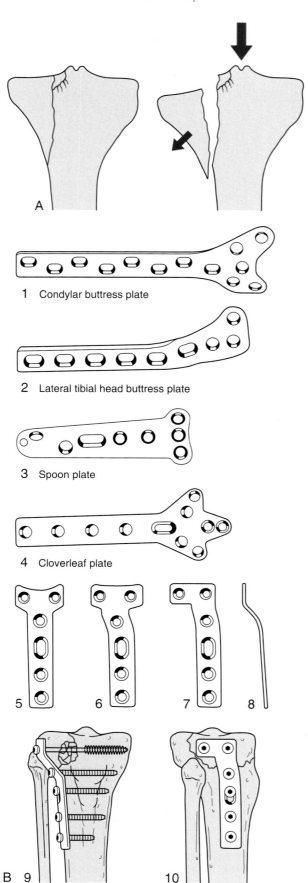

1   Condylar buttress plate

2   Lateral tibial head buttress plate

3   Spoon plate

4   Cloverleaf plate

FIGURE **10–20.** Buttress plates. *A*, Buttress plate supporting the underlying cortex and effectively resisting displacement, which otherwise would result in angular deformity of the joint. The plate acts as a buttress or retaining wall. *B*, Examples of various buttress plates designed for specific anatomic locations. (1) Condylar buttress plate; (2) lateral tibial head buttress plate; (3) spoon plate; (4) cloverleaf plate; (5) medial **T** plate; (6) lateral **T** plate; (7) lateral **L** plate; (8) profile of lateral **L** plate; anteroposterior (9) and lateral (10) views of lateral **L** plate used in conjunction with cancellous bone graft to buttress a lateral tibial plateau fracture.

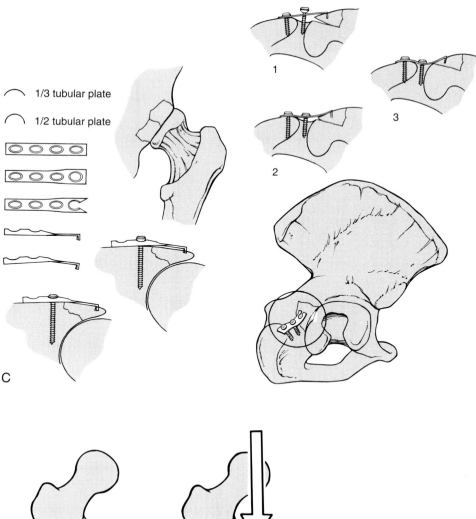

FIGURE 10–20 *Continued. C,* The use of spring plates to buttress small, thin fragments of the acetabular rim. Fork-ended plates are fashioned by cutting into the endhole of a one-third tubular or semitubular plate. The forked prongs, which are bent at 90°, are impaled into the small fragments to improve fixation. By creating a mismatch between the contour of the plate and the bone (1), the plate is pulled down and springs against the bone as the screws are tightened (2, 3). (*B [1–4],* Redrawn from Synthes Equipment Ordering Manual. Paoli, PA, Synthes USA, 1992. *C,* Redrawn from Mast, J.; et al. Planning and Reduction Technique in Fracture Surgery. New York, Springer Verlag, 1989, p. 244.)

1/3 tubular plate

1/2 tubular plate

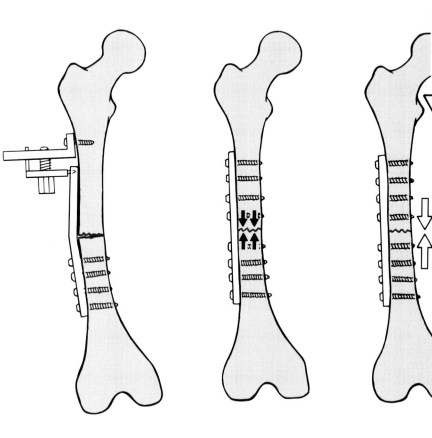

FIGURE 10–21. Application of a compression plate to the lateral aspect of the femur demonstrates the combination of static and dynamic compression. *A,* Immediately after the plate is applied, static compression is achieved at the fracture site. *B,* After functional loading of the curved bone, additional dynamic compression is obtained at the fracture site because of the effect of the laterally placed plate, which acts as a tension band.

A

B

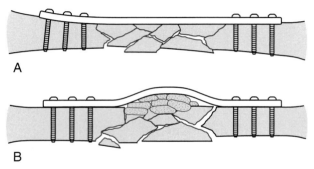

FIGURE **10–22.** Bridging. *A,* The bridge plate maintains length and alignment by fixing to bone away from the comminution and preserving critical blood supply to that area by limiting surgical dissection. *B,* The wave plate is used primarily in areas of delayed healing. The added space created by the bend allows for better ingrowth of vessels into the graft. (*A, B,* Redrawn from Texhammar, R.; Colton, C. AO/ASIF Instruments and Implants: A Technical Manual. New York, Springer Verlag, 1995.)

humerus. Optimal compression is achieved with this method only during functional activity that results in eccentric loading and the production of bending moments.

Prevention of Glide

The antiglide plate is another example of the dynamic compression principle.[15, 82] Although there are many potential applications, the construct is most commonly used for oblique, Weber type B fractures of the distal fibula (Fig. 10–24). A plate applied to the posterior surface of the proximal fragment forms an axilla into which the spike of the distal fragment fits. The axial loads of walking are converted into compression of the surfaces of the two fracture fragments. The plate acts incidentally to prevent external rotation of the distal fragment by a buttress effect.

SPECIFIC PLATE DESIGNS

The discussion thus far has dealt with the biomechanical application of plates. An important concept is that different plates can be used for various biomechanical problems. Some plates are specifically designed for function; others can be functionally modified for the same application. The idea of design versus function versus anatomic location is important for the general understanding of plates. For example, the LCDC plate is designed primarily as a self-compression plate, but it can also be used as a bridging plate or tension band plate or further modified as a medial femoral condylar buttress plate. Therefore, depending on anatomic location and bending modification, it can function in most other biomechanical applications.

To understand the decisions orthopaedic surgeons make in using different plates for different applications, it is important to have a general understanding of the different types of plates manufactured and the mechanics of their designs. This section includes the basic designs such as DC plates, LCDC plates, semitubular and one-third tubular plates, reconstruction plates, point

contact (Schuhli) plates, angle plates, and sliding screw plates.

DC Plate

The special geometry of the DC plate hole allows for two basic functions: independent axial compression and the ability to place screws at different angles of inclination. Perren and colleagues[76] designed a screw housing in which an inclined and a horizontal cylinder meet at an obtuse angle, permitting a downward and horizontal movement of the screw head for axial compression in one direction (Fig. 10–25A). Sideways movement of the screw head is impossible. A screw placed at the inclined plane (i.e., eccentrically in the load position) moves the plate horizontally in relation to the bone until the screw head reaches the intersection of the two circles. *Eccentric position* refers to circles with different centers, whereas *concentric position* refers to circles with the same center. The act of compression is accomplished through the merging of two eccentric circles to become concentric. At this point, the screw has optimal contact with the hole, ensuring maximal stability and producing axial compression of the bone and tension on the plate. There are three areas in which to place a screw in an oval hole, one at each end (eccentrically) and one in the middle (concentrically).

The plate can be placed for neutralization, compression, or buttressing, depending on the insertion of the screw (see Fig. 10–25B). In the neutral mode, the screw is placed in a relatively central position. In actuality, this neutral position is 0.1 mm eccentric, causing horizontal displacement of the plate that results in minimal axial compression.

In the compressive mode, the screw is inserted 1.0 mm eccentrically to its final position in the hole on the side away from the fracture site. When the screw is tightened, its head slides down along the inclined plane, merging the eccentric circles and causing horizontal movement of the plate (1.0 mm). This results in fracture compression, assuming that a plate screw has previously been inserted to affix the plate into the other fracture fragment. This procedure can produce a maximum of 600 N of axial compression if anatomic reduction of the fragments is accomplished.[75] One screw in compression produces 1 mm of displacement, and the horizontal track in the hole still permits a further 1.8 mm of gliding. A second load screw can therefore be inserted into the next hole without being blocked by the first screw, producing another 1.0 mm of horizontal movement.[64] This is sometimes referred to as *double loading* (see Fig. 10–25C).

In buttress mode, the screw is placed eccentrically in the horizontal tract closest to the fracture. This position results in no horizontal movement of the plate when an axial load is placed. Under certain circumstances, the screw position may not be perpendicular to the plate. The design of the DC plate allows for inclined insertion of the screw head up to angles of 25° longitudinally and 7° laterally. The DC plate can be modified for use in most biomechanical applications of fracture fixation, and its use is based on fracture pattern and location.

Certain shortcomings of the DC plate have been discovered through the years. These include a large area of undersurface contact, which can lead to an interference

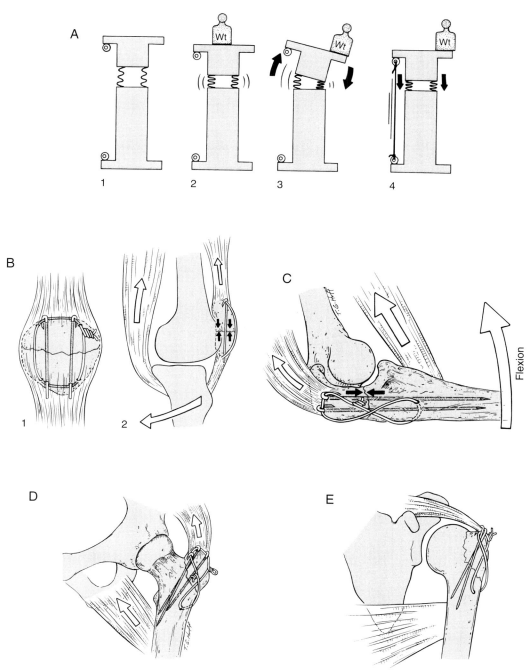

Figure 10–23. Tension band principles. *A,* (1) An interrupted I-beam connected by two springs. (2) The I-beam is loaded with a weight (Wt) placed over the central axis of the beam; there is uniform compression of both springs at the interruption. (3) When the I-beam is loaded eccentrically by placing the weight at a distance from the central axis of the beam, the spring on the same side compresses, whereas the spring on the opposite side is placed in tension and stretches. (4) If a tension band is applied prior to the eccentric loading, it resists the tension that would otherwise stretch the opposite spring and thus causes uniform compression of both springs. *B,* The tension band principle applied to fixation of a transverse patellar fracture. (1) The anteroposterior view shows placement of the parallel Kirschner wires and anterior tension band. (2) The lateral view demonstrates antagonistic pull of the hamstrings and quadriceps, causing a bending moment of the patella over the femoral trochlea. An anterior tension band transforms this eccentric loading into compression at the fracture site. *C,* The tension band principle applied to fixation of a fracture of the ulna. The antagonistic pull of the triceps and brachialis causes a bending moment of the ulna over the humeral trochlea. The dorsal tension band transforms this eccentric load into compression at the fracture site. *D,* The tension band principle applied to fixation of a fracture of the greater trochanter. With the hip as a fulcrum, the antagonistic pull of the adductors and abductors causes a bending moment in the femur. The lateral tension band transforms this eccentric load into compression at the greater trochanteric fracture site. *E,* The tension band principle applied to fixation of a fracture of the greater tuberosity of the humerus. Using the glenoid as a fulcrum, the antagonistic pull of the pectoralis major and supraspinatus causes a bending moment of the humerus. The lateral tension band transforms this eccentric load into compression at the greater tuberosity fracture site.

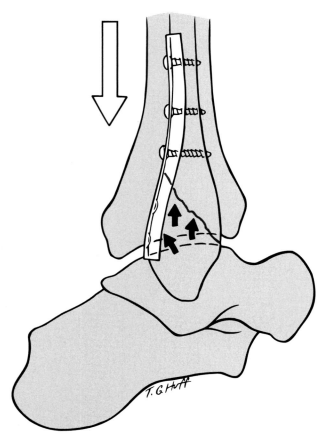

FIGURE 10–24. Dynamic compression—An antiglide plate. Because of the obliquity of the typical Weber type B fracture, a one-third tubular plate, fixed proximally only to the posterior surface of the fibula, acts as an antiglide plate. Dynamic compression is achieved on weight bearing because the distal fragment is trapped between the fracture site and the plate.

with the periosteal blood supply (Fig. 10–26A). This is thought to be the main reason for plate-induced osteoporosis[33] and the possible danger that a sequestrum could form underneath the plate. Also, a soft spot in fracture healing can occur where the periosteal surface of the bone is in contact with the plate. This defect may act as a stress riser because it increases the mechanical stress locally; therefore, the possibility of refracture after plate removal is increased.[75]

Another shortcoming is that the design of the plate limits static compression to one site. This occurs because the orientation of the inclined planes within the screw holes points in one direction on either side of the plate center. The *plate center* is defined as a small area of the plate with no screw hole. These inclines oppose each other, so compression can occur only at a single site.

Because the plate is of uniform width, the holes produce areas of increased stress and decreased stiffness, causing uneven stiffness in the entire plate. With contouring, the plate bends preferentially through the holes rather than with even distribution (see Fig. 10–26B). This further increases stress at the screw holes and the risk of implant failure.

LCDC Plate

The LCDC plate is a modification that attempts to correct some of the design shortcomings found in the DC plate. It

is based primarily on work by Klaue and Perren.[53] Compared with the DC plate, there are three main differences in design. First, the sides of the plate are inclined to form a trapezoidal cross section interrupted by undercuts that form arcs (Fig. 10–27A). This reduces the area of contact between the plate and the periosteal surface of the bone, decreasing the disturbance of the blood supply and reducing bone porosis. The undercuts allow for periosteal callus formation under the plate, decreasing stress concentration at an unhealed fracture gap.[75] Second, the screw hole is made up of two inclined and one horizontal cylinder; they meet at the same angle, permitting compression in both directions (see Fig. 10–27B). As a result, compression can be achieved at multiple sites between screw holes, which is of value in treating certain segmental and comminuted fractures. Third, because of the undercut design, the stiffness between screw holes is relatively similar to that across the screw holes. This allows for more equal distribution of stress, less deformation at the screw holes when contouring, and fewer stress risers within the plate. The more uniform cross-sectional area along the plate decreases the amount of stress concentrated at the screw holes. The undercuts also allow for an increase to 40° of screw horizontal tilt. The biomechanical uses and applications of the LCDC plate are the same as those for the DC plate.

Point Contact (Schuhli) Devices

A Schuhli device consists of a three-pronged nut and a washer (Fig. 10–28). Its function is to lock a cortical screw to a plate if pullout failure due to osteopenic bone is a concern and to elevate the plate from the bone, decreasing periosteal blood flow compromise. It elevates the plate from the periosteal surface further than the LCDC plate does. The nut engages the screw and locks it to the plate at a 90° angle, producing a fixed angle construct. This device has been shown to be effective in withstanding both axial and torsional loads to failure.[56] Matelic and associates[61] reported its use in treatment of femoral nonunions in which the lateral cortex of the femur was deficient.

Semitubular, One-Third Tubular, and Quarter-Tubular Plates

The semitubular plate was the first AO self-compression plate designed in the shape of a half-tube (Fig. 10–29). It provides compression through eccentrically placed oval plate holes. It maintains its rotational stability with edges that dig into the side of the periosteum under tension. The semitubular plate is 1 mm thick and very deformable, so it is prone to fatigue and fracture, especially in areas of high stress. Its main indication is for tension resistance, as in the treatment of open-book injury of the pelvis.[67] The one-third tubular plate is commonly used as a neutralization plate in the treatment of lateral malleolar fractures. The quarter-tubular plates have been used in small bone fixation (e.g., in hand surgery).

Reconstruction Plate

This plate is designed with notches in its side so that it can be contoured in any plane needed (Fig. 10–30). It is mainly used in fractures of the pelvis, where exact contouring may be important in reduction. It can also be used to advantage for fixation of distal humerus and calcaneal fractures. The plate has relatively low strength, which is further diminished with contouring. It offers some self-compression because of its oval screw holes.

Angled Plates

Angled plates were developed in the 1950s for the fixation of proximal and distal femur fractures. They are a one-piece design with a U-shaped profile for the blade portion and a 95° or 130° fixed angle between the blade

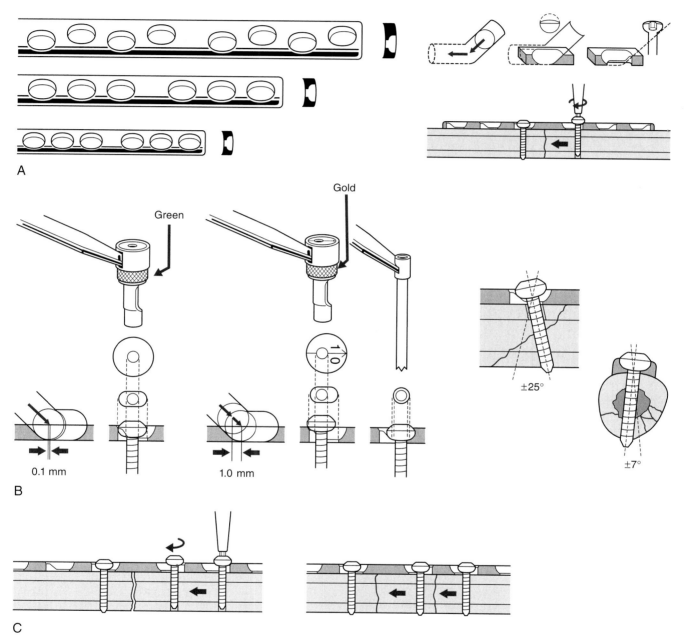

FIGURE 10–25. The dynamic compression (DC) plate. *A,* Perren designed the screw housing in which an inclined and a horizontal cylinder meet at an obtuse angle, permitting a downward and horizontal movement of the screw head for axle compression in one direction. *B,* The plate can be placed in neutral, compression, or buttress modes depending on the placement of the screw in the gliding hole. In a neutral mode, the screw is placed in a relatively central position. In actuality, this neutral position is 0.1 mm eccentric. In the compression mode, the screw is inserted 1.0 mm eccentric to its final position in the hole on the side away from the fracture site. When the screw is tightened, its head slides down along the inclined plane, merging the eccentric circles and causing horizontal movement of the plate (1.0 mm). This results in fracture compression. In buttress mode, the screw is placed eccentrically in the horizontal track close to the fracture. Note that the DC plate allows for incline insertion of the screw head up to angles of 25° longitudinally and 7° laterally. *C,* One screw in compression produces 1 mm of displacement while the horizontal track in the hole still permits a further 1.8 mm of gliding. A second load screw can, therefore, be inserted into the next hole without being blocked by the first screw, producing another 1.0 mm of horizontal movement. This is sometimes referred to as *double loading.* (*A, left,* Redrawn from Synthes Equipment Ordering Manual. Paoli, PA, Synthes USA, 1992, Figs. 2–45, 2–46, 2–65, 2–67, p. 84; *right,* Redrawn from Texhammar, R; Colton, C. AO/ASIF Instruments and Implants: A Technical Manual. New York, Springer Verlag, 1995. *B,* Redrawn from Muller, M.E.; Allgöwer, M.; Schneider, R.; Willenegger, H., eds. Manual of Internal Fixation, 3rd ed. New York, Springer Verlag, 1995. *C,* Redrawn from Texhammar, R; Colton, C. AO/ASIF Instruments and Implants: A Technical Manual. New York, Springer Verlag, 1995.)

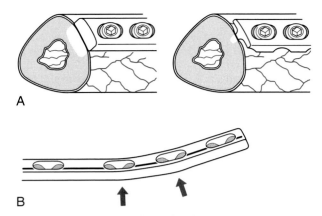

A

B

FIGURE **10–26.** DC plate. *A,* Plate-induced osteoporosis is a temporary stage of intense remodeling and is related to vascular damage produced by both the injury and the presence of the implant. *B,* Since the plate is of uniform width, the holes produce areas of increased stress and decreased stiffness, causing uneven stiffness in the entire plate. With contouring, the plate bends preferentially through the holes rather than with an even distribution. This further increases stress at the screw hole and the risk of implant failure. (*A,* Redrawn from Texhammar, R.; Colton, C. AO/ASIF Instruments and Implants: A Technical Manual. New York, Springer Verlag, 1995. *B,* Reprinted from Perren, S.M. The concept of biological plating using the limited contact-dynamic compression plate [LCDCP]: Scientific background, design, and application. Injury 22[suppl 1]:1–41, 1991; with permission from Elsevier Science Ltd., The Boulevard, Langford Lane, Kidlington OX5 1GB, UK.)

and the plate. The shaft is thicker than the blade and can withstand higher stress. This is important because the subtrochanteric region is the most highly stressed region of the skeleton, a fact that predisposes the region to fixation failure. The forces applied in this area exceed 1200 lb/inch^2, with the medial cortex exposed to compression combined with greater stress and the lateral cortex exposed to tension.[31]

The 130° Blade Plate. The 130° blade plate was originally designed for fixation of proximal femur fractures and has different lengths to accommodate different fracture patterns. The 4- and 6-hole plates are used for fixation of intertrochanteric fractures, and the 9- to 12-hole plates are used for treatment of subtrochanteric fractures. The placement of the blade is critical; improper placement can lead to various healing deformities. In the femoral head, there is a zone where the tension and compression trabeculae intersect. The plate is inserted so it is below this trabecular intersection (6 to 8 mm above the calcar) and in the center of the neck, with no anterior or posterior angulation. The use of this device depends on the specific biomechanics and angulation of the fracture site. It has been replaced for the most part by the dynamic hip screw, which allows for compression of the fragments.

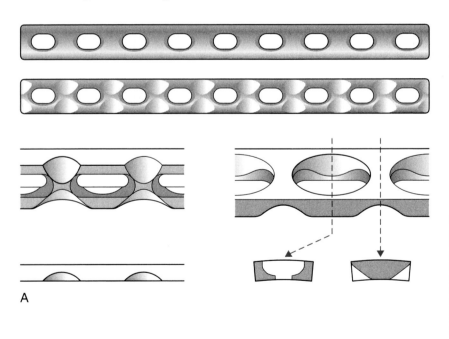

A

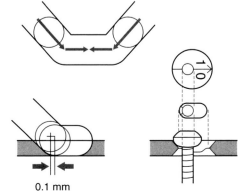

B   0.1 mm

FIGURE **10–27.** The limited contact–dynamic compression (LCDC) plate. *A,* The sides of the plate are inclined to form a trapezoidal cross section interrupted by undercuts that form arcs. *B,* In contrast to the DC plate, the LCDC plate's screw holes are designed with two horizontal cylinders that allow for compression in different directions along a single plate. (*A,B,* Redrawn from Muller, M.E.; Allgöwer, M.; Schneider, R.; Willenegger, H.; eds. Manual of Internal Fixation, 3rd ed. New York, Springer Verlag, 1995.)

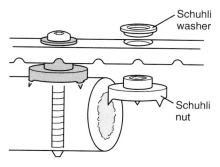

FIGURE 10–28. The Schuhli device is a three-pronged nut and washer that locks in a cortical screw and elevates the plate from the bone. This not only facilitates periosteal blood flow but also creates a fixed angle construct. (Redrawn from Synthes, AO/ASIF Newsletter. Paoli, PA, Synthes USA, November 1996.)

The 95° Condylar Blade Plate. The 95° condylar blade plate was designed for use with supracondylar and bicondylar distal femur fractures, and its length is also based on the fracture pattern (Fig. 10–31). It can also be used for subtrochanteric fractures whose geometry is such that more purchase on the fracture fragment can be gained with a sharper angled plate. With the 130° blade plate, the blade enters the proximal femoral fragment close to the subtrochanteric fracture site, precluding insertion of plate screws into the proximal fragment. In contrast, the blade of the 95° blade plate can be introduced into the proximal fragment just below the tip of the greater trochanter, allowing placement of screws proximal to the fracture site into the calcar for added stability. Although the device is strong and provides stable fixation, its insertion is demanding and unforgiving. The need for precise alignment in all three planes demands careful preoperative planning and intraoperative radiographic control.

Sliding Screw and Compression Plates

Compression/Telescoping Hip Screw. The compression/telescoping or sliding hip screw system is designed for internal fixation of basicervical, intertrochanteric, and selected subtrochanteric fractures.[24, 30, 42, 44, 85] It uses the principle of dynamic compression, which modifies functional physiologic forces into compression of a fracture site. The implant consists of two major parts. A wide-diameter cannulated lag screw is inserted into the femoral head, and a side plate with a barrel at a set angle is attached to the femoral shaft (Fig. 10–32). Weight-bearing and abductor muscle activity cause the screw shaft to slide through the barrel, resulting in impaction of the fracture surfaces and, optimally, a stable load-sharing construct.

Two basic principles must be recognized when using a sliding hip screw. The first is that fracture compression can occur only if the lag screw and barrel are inserted across the fracture site. This occurs when a sliding hip screw is used to fix a fracture at the base of the femoral neck or in the intertrochanteric area. In contrast, when a sliding hip screw is used to fix a high subtrochanteric fracture, the lag screw and barrel are located exclusively in the proximal fragment and do not cross the fracture site. In these circumstances, the lag screw acts only as a fixation device and does not contribute to fracture compression by sliding.

The second principle is that the lag screw must slide far enough through the barrel to allow the fracture gap to close sufficiently for the proximal and distal fragments to impact completely. The desired sliding does not occur if the bending forces (from weight bearing and muscle contraction) on the lag screw cause it to impinge and bind.

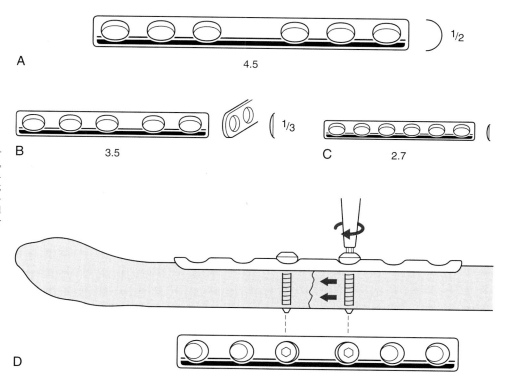

FIGURE 10–29. Examples of semitubular (*A*), one-third tubular (*B*, *C*), and one-quarter tubular (*D*) plates. (*A–D*, Redrawn from Muller, M.E.; Allgöwer, M.; Schneider, R.; Willenegger, H.; eds. Manual of Internal Fixation, 3rd ed. New York, Springer Verlag, 1995.)

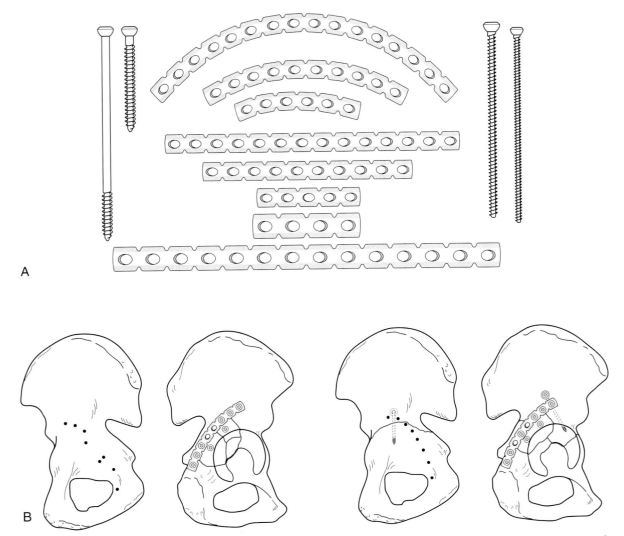

Figure 10–30. A, Examples of reconstruction plates. Note that the notches in the sides are placed there so the plates can be contoured in all dimensions. B, Reconstruction plate for fixation of a posterior wall acetabular fracture. (A, B, Redrawn from Muller, M.E.; Allgöwer, M.; Schneider, R.; Willenegger, H., eds. Manual of Internal Fixation, 3rd ed. New York, Springer Verlag, 1995.)

The lag screw slides more predictably through a longer barrel because it provides more support. Some sliding hip screw systems include two side plates, with one long and one short barrel. Usually, the long barrel is chosen to ensure adequate support and unimpeded lag screw sliding. Lag screws are of varying lengths (60 to 120 mm) to accommodate patient anatomy and fracture configuration. If a lag screw of 80 mm or smaller is used, there may not be enough space between the base of the threads on the screw and the tip of the long barrel to allow full impaction of the fracture. In this small proportion of cases, the short-barrel side plate should be used. Some of these systems provide rotational control, although the fragment still may rotate around the screw itself. Various manufacturers produce systems containing a range of side plate–lag screw angles; the angle used depends on the fracture configuration and the patient's anatomy. The basic principle of these devices is that they collapse and shorten to accommodate comminution, osteopenia, and bone lysis at the fracture site.

Dynamic Condylar Screw. The condylar compression screw system has basically the same design as the 95° condylar blade plate except that the blade is replaced by a cannulated screw (Fig. 10–33). The angle between screw and plate is fixed at 95°, in contrast to the sliding hip screw, which allows different angles to be selected. The compression generated by the large cannulated screw placed across the femoral condyles permits greater impaction of the fracture fragment than can be achieved with the blade plate. The plate itself is contoured to fit the distal end of the femur. It is a two-piece device that can allow for some correction in the lateral and coronal planes after the lag screw is inserted, which is not the case with the blade plates. This system is used for fixation of low, supracondylar and intercondylar T and Y fractures.

Precise positioning of the plate or screw, or both, is critical for fixation and proper alignment. If the screw is inserted in a valgus position (angled away from the midline), a varus deformity will develop on healing. Conversely, if the plate is angled in varus (toward the midline), a valgus deformity will develop. The screw systems allow for some correction of alignment, but the plates do not. This is one reason that screw systems are technically more forgiving.

PLATE FAILURE

Internal fixation is frequently viewed as a race between fracture healing and implant failure. This is particularly true when a fracture is fixed with a plate and there is a cortical gap opposite the plate. When the bone-implant complex is loaded by physiologic muscle forces and weight bearing, repetitive opening and closing of the gap can

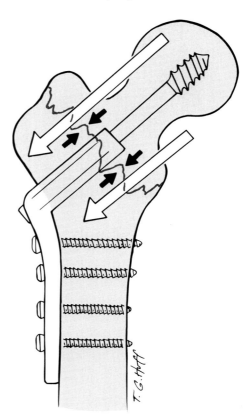

FIGURE 10–32. Dynamic compression–sliding hip screw. Functional loading of a sliding hip screw causes dynamic compression at the fracture site. With functional loading, the screw slides through the barrel of the side plate, allowing the fracture to impact or compress. Note placement of the cannulated screw in the inferior third of the femoral neck.

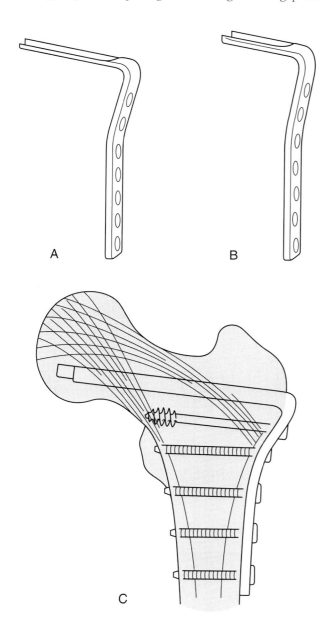

FIGURE 10–31. The 95° blade plate. *A,* **T** profile. *B,* **U** profile. *C,* Use of a blade plate in proximal femoral fixation, as for subtrochanteric fractures. Note placement of the tip of the blade at the intersection of the primary compressive and the primary tensile trabeculae. (*A, B,* Redrawn from Synthes Equipment Ordering Manual. Paoli, PA, Synthes USA, 1992.)

occur, subjecting the plate to cyclical bending stresses. The longer this process continues, the greater the chance that the plate will fail. This cyclical bending of the plate continues until the gap on the opposite cortex is bridged with callus. If the cyclical bending continues long enough, the fatigue limit will be exceeded and the plate will break. Healing of the fracture on the side opposite the plate can be impaired if the bone fragments are devascularized by the injury or by surgical stripping. Fracture healing in the gap can be optimized by protection of remaining periosteal blood supply and addition of bone graft or other inductive substances. Bone grafts speed up the healing in the gap, compared with unassisted callus formation. Biologically, bone graft is osteoconductive and osteoinductive; it both provides support for bone formation and brings potential osteogenic cells and growth factors to the site. Cancellous bone has more osteoblastic cells and loose-knit trabeculae, giving it the potential to have a remodeling rate three times faster than that of cortical grafts,[32] and is generally revascularized within 7 days.[84] Persistent micromotion and cyclical implant loading in the absence of fracture union ultimately lead to failure of any implant regardless of its size and strength.

Summary

The basic biomechanical functions of plates in fracture fixation have been discussed, as well as some of

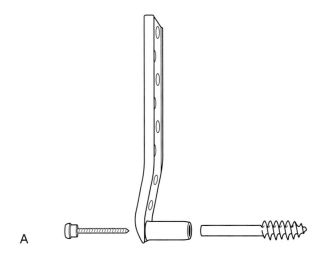

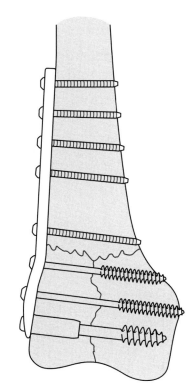

A

B

FIGURE 10–33. Dynamic condylar screw (DCS). *A,* Basic components of the DCS system. *B,* Here the DCS is used to generate compression of a T-type supracondylar fracture of the distal femur. Note the anatomic fit to the lateral femoral cortex. (*A, B,* Redrawn from DHS/DCS Dynamic Hip and Condylar Screw System: Technique Guide. Paoli, PA, Synthes USA, 1990.)

the major plate designs and examples of plates modified for use in particular anatomic areas. It is important to realize that specific design features of plates can be used to fulfill biomechanical needs based on the particularities of the fracture. Research in this area is constantly improving fracture fixation, and continued work is still needed.

Intramedullary Nails

Intramedullary nails are internal fixation devices designed for use in bridging or splinting of fractures of long bones (e.g., femur, tibia, humerus). In contrast to plates and screws, which are placed on the cortical surface, these devices are placed in the medullary canal.

ANATOMY

The basic anatomy of an intramedullary nail is depicted in Figure 10–34. Nails are constructed of various metal alloys. They are described by their outer diameter and their total length. Cannulated nails are by definition hollow to allow them to be placed over guide wires.

BIOMECHANICS OF INTRAMEDULLARY NAILS

Rigidity and strength are the most important characteristics of an intramedullary nailing system. The geometry of an intramedullary nail is responsible for the nail's strength, rigidity, and interaction with the bone. Four main shape characteristics are commonly evaluated, each of which can be divided into two main categories. An understanding of these basic features is necessary when evaluating any intramedullary nailing system.

Longitudinal Curvature. Long bones have variable amounts of anatomic curvature. Early intramedullary nails were all straight. There was a significant mismatch between these straight implants and the normal curve of the femur. Insertion of straight nails was possible only with the use of rigid shaft reamers and small-diameter implants. Also, the single large bow of the intact femur was reduced by breaking it into two or more fragments, thus creating a straighter path for the nail. The introduction of the curved anterior bow on the femoral nails and the associated use of flexible shaft reamers permitted a better fit with the normal anatomy of the femur. These reamers reduced the amount of bone that had to be removed and simplified implant

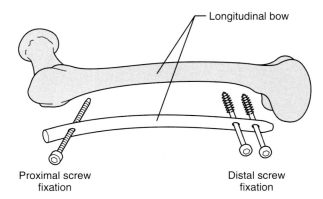

FIGURE 10–34. Basic anatomy of an intramedullary nail. The proximal end has an internally threaded opening for adaptation of driver/extractor instrumentation. It has a longitudinal bow that approximates that of the femur. Proximal and distal screw holes are placed in the nail for interlocking fixation.

CROSS SECTION

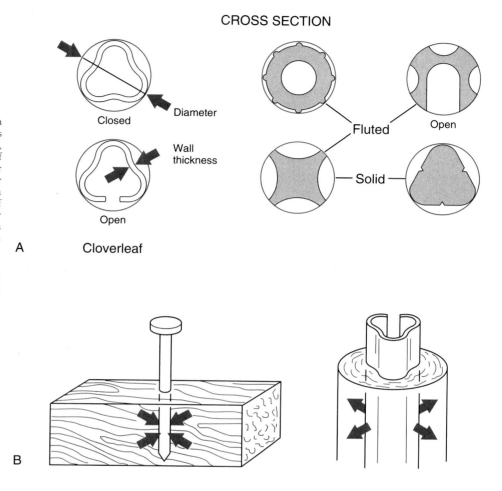

FIGURE 10–35. Geometric features of an intramedullary nail that influence its performance. *A,* Note the cloverleaf, fluted, solid, and open designs. All of these examples have the same diameter but different wall thicknesses. *B,* Similar to the way a nail achieves fixation in wood through elastic compression of the wood, the cloverleaf Küntscher nail achieves fixation in the isthmus through the elastic expansion of the compressed nail. (*A,* Redrawn from Bechtold, J.E.; Kyle, R.F.; Perren, S.M. In: Browner, B.D.; Edwards, C.C.; eds. The Science and Practice of Intramedullary Nailing, 2nd ed. Baltimore, Williams & Wilkins, 1996. *B,* Redrawn from Street, D.M. In: Browner, B.D.; Edwards, C.C., eds. The Science and Practice of Intramedullary Nailing, 2nd ed. Baltimore, Williams & Wilkins, 1996.)

insertion. However, most modern femoral intramedullary nails are designed with a curvature that is less than the curvature of the average femur. This results in a slight bone-nail mismatch, which actually improves frictional fixation. Translation, rotation, and angulation of fracture fragments are partially controlled by frictional contact between bone and nail at a number of locations, including the entry portal, the endosteal surface of the diaphysis, and the cancellous bone at the tip of the nail. Frictional stability is of greater importance in a nonlocked nail than in a locked nail.

Cross-Sectional Shape. The early intramedullary nails developed by Küntscher had a V-shaped cross-sectional design, which allowed the sides of the nail to compress and fit tightly in the canal. The design was modified to a cloverleaf cross-sectional shape with a longitudinal slot running the length of the implant (Fig. 10–35A). This change was made to increase the strength of the nail and permit insertion over a guide wire while retaining the compressibility of the V shape. As with the V shape, the two halves of the cloverleaf are compressed into the slot as the nail is driven into the medullary canal. Because the amount of compression is within the elastic zone of the nail, the nail springs open and presses on the endosteal surface, increasing the frictional contact in the medullary canal (see Fig. 10–35B). Another result of

having a slot running down the nail is that torsional rigidity is decreased.[81] When the nail-bone complex is loaded, the decreased torsional rigidity permits a small amount of motion, which promotes callus formation. The decreased torsional rigidity allows the nail to accommodate itself to the bone and is therefore said to be more forgiving. If the nail does not match the shape of the medullary canal exactly, it is important that it can accommodate, instead of being rigid and thereby increasing the likelihood of iatrogenic fracture. If the nail is too stiff and does not deform on insertion, the bone can be shattered. The cloverleaf shape has been used extensively for decades with great success. The design has been successful because it has adequate torsional rigidity to permit fracture union but sufficient elasticity to adapt to bone anatomy on insertion.

In contrast to the cloverleaf shape with a slot, nails have been designed with no slots and a variety of other cross-sectional shapes. Removal of the slot significantly increases the torsional rigidity of the nail. This is desirable when a small-diameter nail is used. Small nails are used when enlargement of the medullary canal is contraindicated or the medullary canal is small. Closed-section locking nails were designed for the femur to avoid excessive torsional deformation of the nail on insertion, which complicated distal screw fixation. The torsional stiffness of any implant can be increased substantially by the addition of spines that run the entire length of the nail. The curved indentation in the surface of the nail between the spines is called a *flute*. The edges of the spines can be designed to cut into the bone, increasing frictional resistance at the nail-bone interface. However, this can increase the difficulty of implant removal.

The medullary blood supply of a long bone is destroyed by reaming or insertion of a canal-filling implant. The medullary blood supply reconstitutes itself rapidly, provided that some space is allotted between the implant and the endosteal surface. The cloverleaf and fluted designs both provide this space, which is critical for revascularization.

Diameter. The medullary canals of long bones have a narrow central region called the *isthmus*. Before reaming was developed, the diameter of intramedullary nails that could be inserted was limited by the narrowest diameter of the medullary cavity in the isthmus (Fig. 10–36). Reaming permits the introduction of larger implants. Large-diameter nails with the same cross-sectional shape are both stiffer and stronger than small-diameter nails. In practice, the relation between diameter and strength is not linear because manufacturers vary the wall thickness of the nails. The nail stiffness can be kept constant for different diameter nails by changing their wall thickness. For example, wall thickness is 1.2 mm for the 12-mm diameter

nail but is decreased to 1.0 mm for the 14- and 16-mm nails.

Cannulation. The final characteristic is the construction of the core of the nail (hollow or solid). The hollow-core nail allows insertion of the nail over a guide wire. In general, a curved-tip guide wire can be maneuvered across a displaced fracture site more easily than a solid intramedullary nail. The other advantage of the cannulated nail may be a reduction in intramedullary pressure. A disadvantage was reported by Haas and co-workers,[35] who found a 42% increase in compartment pressures with the solid design, compared with 1.6% for the cannulated nail. The clinical significance of this difference has yet to be determined.

Flexural Rigidity

The cross-sectional shape, diameter, and material of the nail all influence its flexural rigidity. Flexural rigidity is defined as the cross-sectional moment of inertia (CSMI) multiplied by the elastic modulus. The CSMI describes the distribution of the cross-sectional area with respect to the central axis. The elastic modulus describes the inherent characteristics of the material. The moment-of-inertia geometry differentiates nails with the same outside diameter and shape. Tencer and colleagues[89] reported that nails can differ in bending rigidity by a factor of two and in torsional rigidity by a factor of three based on different

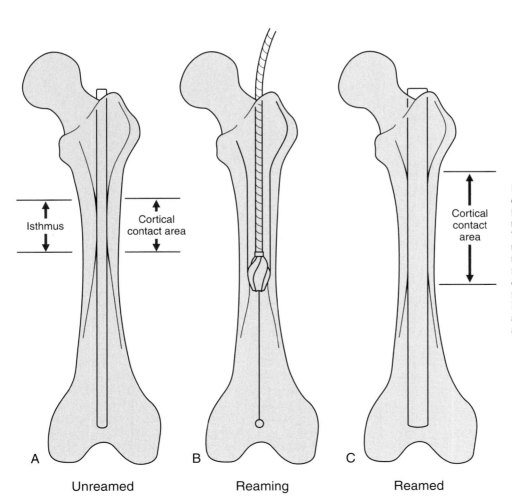

Isthmus

Cortical contact area

Cortical contact area

A — Unreamed

B — Reaming

C — Reamed

Figure 10–36. The effect of reaming on cortical contact area. *A,* The isthmus is the narrowest portion of the intramedullary canal of the femur. Without reaming, the isthmus limits the size of the nail to be placed and the area of cortical contact with the nail. *B,* Reaming widens and lengthens the isthmal portion of the intramedullary canal. *C,* After reaming, a larger diameter nail may be placed and greater cortical contact area is achieved.

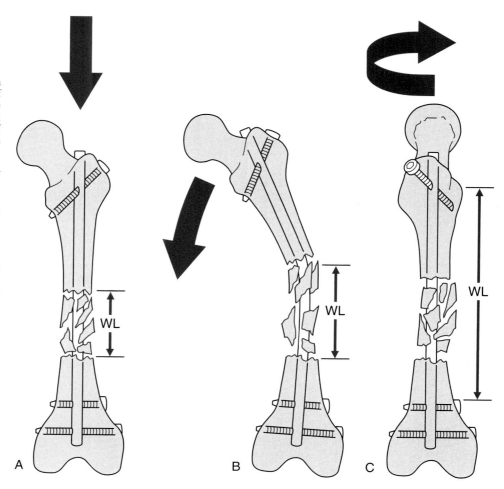

FIGURE 10–37. Working length (WL). *A,* WL describes the length of the nail that is unsupported by bone when loaded. This unsupported length differs based on the mode of testing. *A,* In compression, the WL is the distance between the intact proximal and the intact distal fragments, spanning the comminuted section of the fracture. *B,* In bending, the proximal and distal portions of the main bone fragments come into contact with the nail. Therefore, the WL is the maximal distance between the sites at which the nail is in contact with the bone proximally and distally, which can be equal to the length of the fracture gap. *C,* When comminution exists, the main bone fragments do not resist torsion. In this situation, the WL is the distance between the proximal and the distal locking points. Torsional rigidity is inversely proportional to the WL, whereas rigidity in bending is inversely proportional to the square of the WL. (*A–C,* Redrawn from Browner, B.; Cole, J.D. J Orthop Trauma 1[2]:186, 1987.)

moments of inertia. A basic understanding of the characteristics of intramedullary nails is essential for effective evaluation of different implant systems.

Working Length

Bone healing after intramedullary nailing can occur if the motion at the fracture site falls within an acceptable range. The exact specifications of this motion are not known, but it has been observed that small amounts of motion assist callus formation and excessive motion delays union. If the threshold for the amount of micromotion allowed for callus healing is surpassed, a delay in fracture healing may occur.

Intramedullary nails that are fixed proximally and distally are often used to treat comminuted diaphyseal fractures. Fracture motion results from loading in bending and torsion. The amount of motion that occurs at the fracture site is described in part by the concept of working length. The working length is the portion of the nail that is unsupported by bone under forces of bending or torsion (Fig. 10–37).

The unsupported length of nail differs in bending and in torsion.[21, 87] In bending, the major bone fragments come into contact with the nail, and therefore the unsupported length is the distance between the proximal and the distal fracture fragments. In other words, it is the portion of the fixation that is not

supported by bone, where the nail can bend by itself and not as a bone-nail construct. This distance decreases as the bone heals. In torsion, the major bone fragments do not stabilize the nail. Because these nails are inserted with space between the implant and the endosteal surface, there is limited frictional contact and torsion is resisted primarily by the locking screws. Therefore, the unsupported length in torsion extends the full distance between the two screws. Because the working length in torsion is the distance between the proximal and the distal locking points, it is always greater than the working length in bending, which is the distance of the fracture gap or comminution.

Interfragmentary motion in bending is proportional to the square of the working length. This is derived in part from the four-point bending equation (see Fig. 4–7 in Chapter 4). Increases in bending working length significantly increase interfragmentary motion and increase the likelihood of delayed healing.

With locked nails, *working length* is defined as the distance between the proximal and the distal screws. Motion between the fracture fragments loaded in torsion is directly proportional to working length. This is calculated by the torsional load equation (see Fig. 4–8 in Chapter 4). In an unlocked nail, this becomes an issue of friction and nail-bone interface. Unlocked nails do not significantly resist torsion. This is one reason why unlocked nails are generally not used for comminuted or rotationally unstable fractures.

There are many different designs and types of intramedullary nails. The following sections describe the basic applications of intramedullary nailing.

INTRAMEDULLARY REAMING

Küntscher initially attempted intramedullary fixation of fractures with implants that were designed to fit within the normal medullary canal. The distribution of cortex in long bones results in a narrow area or isthmus of varying length in the midportion of the diaphysis. The canal widens at both ends of the bone, where it merges with the labyrinthine trabecular formations that support the articular surfaces. Küntscher was dissatisfied with the high rates of malunion, nonunion, and implant failure obtained with these small-diameter nails and developed the technique of reaming to enlarge the intramedullary canal.[45] This produced a space of more uniform canal diameter and increased the potential surface area of contact between the endosteum and the implant. This increase in contact facilitated better alignment of the fractured bone fragments on the nail and enhanced the rotational stability of fracture fixation. The enlargement of the canal diameter permitted

insertion of larger nails with greater stiffness and fatigue strength. The successful use of larger diameter intramedullary nails paved the way for the production of nails containing holes through which transfixion screws could be inserted.

A reamer is used to enlarge the medullary canal. Reamers were developed for industry to precisely size and finish an already existing hole and were not intended to remove large amounts of material. They have a larger caliber than drill bits because their main purpose is to enlarge an already existing hole. Reamers are designed to be front cutting or side cutting, or both (Fig. 10–38). The tip design of most reamers is a truncated cone called a *chamfer*. This chamfer, depending on its angle, is responsible for most of the actual cutting. The *chamfer angle* is defined as the angle between the central axis of the reamer and the cutting edge at its end. In front-cutting reamers, the majority of the cutting is accomplished by the chamfer. Additional flutes are added along the sides of the reamer to allow for more cutting surfaces and a more even distribution of force. If additional relief or angle is added to the land (the area between the flutes), it provides for a longitudinal cutting edge. This permits an increase in accuracy but weakens the cutting edge. If cutting is performed primarily by the longitudinal edges, the reamer

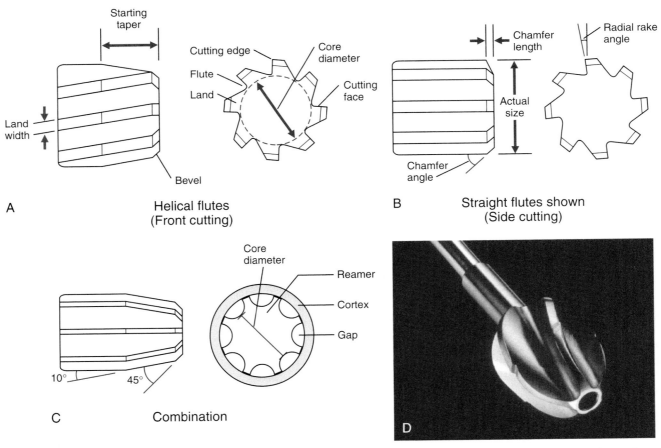

FIGURE 10–38. Reamers. *A*, Note the starting taper of the front-cutting reamer used to initiate a path in bone. *B*, The side-cutting reamers have a sharper chamfer angle and a shorter chamfer length and therefore are used for increasing the size of the path, not for creating a new path. *C*, A combination front- and side-cutting reamer. *D*, A front-cutting reamer tip attached to a flexible shaft. (*A–C*, Redrawn from Donaldson, C.; Le Cain, G.H., eds. Tool Design, 3rd ed. New York, McGraw-Hill, 1973. With permission. *D*, Reproduced with permission from Zimmer, Inc., Warsaw, IN.)

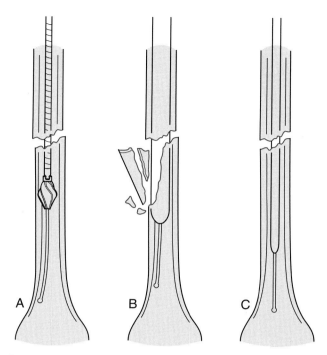

FIGURE 10–39. Example of a front-cutting reamer. *A,* Eccentric reaming of distal fragment resulting from poor guide pin placement. *B,* Splitting of the cortex may follow nail impaction. *C,* Central placement of the guide pin using a small (90 mm) Küntscher nail avoids this problem. (*A–C,* Redrawn from Crenshaw, A.H., ed. Campbell's Operative Orthopaedics, 8th ed. St. Louis, Mosby–Year Book, 1992; redrawn from Rascher, J.J.; Nahigian, S.H.; Macys, J.R.; Brown, J.E. J Bone Joint Surg Am 54:534, 1972.)

is said to be side cutting. Generally, front-cutting reamers are used only for the initial reaming steps. A front-cutting reamer has the potential to cut eccentrically when reaming across displaced fractures because it cuts its own path (Fig. 10–39). Most reamers used for orthopaedic applications are side cutting.

The process of reaming is relatively straightforward. A small-diameter reamer head is selected, and then heads of gradually increasing size are used until the desired medullary canal diameter is reached. The reamer's speed of rotation is usually two thirds of the speed used for drilling. *Chatter* is uneven cutting that causes vibration of the reamer head, which can lead to reamer dullness or damage. Chatter is reduced with slower rotational speeds. Reamers used for orthopaedic applications are of variable design; manufacturers attempt to maximize size and strength of reamers while minimizing physiologic damage.

The process of reaming causes an increase in medullary pressure and an elevation in cortical temperature. The former has been linked to an increase in extruded marrow products and the latter to cortical and medullary vascular damage. Design modifications can decrease the amount of physiologic stress sustained. Three main parts of a reamer apparatus influence the amounts of pressure and temperature generated: the reamer head, which is responsible for the actual cutting; the reamer shaft, which is usually flexible and drives the reamer head; and the bulb tip, which is the diameter inside the reamer head connection to the shaft. These all take up space in the medullary canal and form a gap with the endosteal cortex. The reamer system

acts like a piston and increases pressure in the relatively closed environment of a long bone. The amount of gap or space through which exhaust passes influences the build-up of medullary pressure. This concept has been quantified by a formula modified by Brown and Winquist[10]:

$$?\Delta P = 3\mu \cdot Dm \cdot Vo/h^3$$

ΔP is the change in medullary pressure; μ is the viscosity of the fluid or substance that is being reamed (it usually is highest on the initial reaming pass and thereafter reduced by bleeding in the canal); Dm is the midflute-to-midflute distance, which is influenced by the design of the reamer and the flute depth; Vo is the velocity of advancement, which is influenced by the speed of rotation (faster rotation allows for quicker cutting and faster advancement but causes increased intramedullary pressure; proper reaming procedure is slow advancement of the reamer with frequent pullback to clear debris); and h^3 is the flute depth, which is critical in determining the amount of intramedullary pressure increase. The flute allows for passage or exhaust of pressure and collects and clears bone. The deeper the flute, the lower the pressure generated. This formula can be applied to both the shaft and the bulb tip. If the reamer head has shallow flutes, then the shaft takes on greater importance in increasing intramedullary pressure. Also, a large diameter in the bulb decreases the intramedullary pressure.

Temperature increases during reaming have been reported to occur in stepwise increments with the successive use of larger reamer heads. It was also reported that blunt reamers produce significantly greater temperature increases than sharp reamers.[67] Several factors contribute to the elevation in bone temperature, including the presence or absence of flutes in the reamer head. Deep flutes that clear large amounts of bone attenuate the rise in bone temperature, whereas reamers with shallow or no flutes lead to greater increases in temperature. Sharp reamer cutting edges and slow advancement of the reamer head decrease the rise in temperature. Blood flow to the area also contributes to reducing the overall temperature increase by conductive heat transfer.

Reamer heads are constructed of 455 stainless steel, which is harder than 316L stainless steel, to hold the sharp cutting edge longer. This class of stainless steel has increased corrosive properties, so most reamer heads are coated. The coating actually dulls the edge slightly but prolongs reamer head life. Coatings are made of titanium nitride (gold color), diamond black, and ME-92. The overall clinical significance of reamer design is still being investigated, but a basic understanding of the principles is important in evaluating these tools.

Destruction of the medullary contents by reaming has both local and systemic consequences. Reaming obliterates the medullary blood supply remaining after injury. This vascular system will reconstitute in 2 to 3 weeks.[79] Disruption of the medullary blood supply and intracortical intravasation of medullary fat during reaming result in necrosis of a variable amount of bone in the inner half of the cortical thickness. If the medullary canal becomes infected before the bone is revascularized, the entire area of dead bone can become involved and act as a sequestrum in continuity. The long bones of adults contain primarily fatty marrow, and there is a large reserve of hematopoietic tissue in the marrow cavities of flat bones. Therefore, destruction of marrow during reaming does not produce anemia. During medullary reaming, communication is temporarily created between the marrow cavity and the intravascular space. Use of reamers in the medullary space is somewhat like the insertion of a piston into a rigid cylinder. Exceedingly high canal pressures during medullary broaching before insertion of a femoral total hip component have been found in animals and humans.[69] Unlike the total joint broach, the medullary reamers used to prepare the canal before nail insertion are cannulated. This may offer some decompression of the pressure in the distal canal, but the communication is partially occluded by the guide wire and the pressurized marrow contents. Sampling of femoral vein blood during intramedullary reaming of the femur revealed embolization of fat and tissue thromboplastin. In the early days of reamed intramedullary nailing, there was great concern regarding the danger of death as a result of fat embolization syndrome and shock after this procedure. Although reamed nailing does result in embolization of marrow contents into the pulmonary circulation, this is well tolerated if the patient has had adequate fluid resuscitation and receives appropriate hemodynamic and ventilatory support during surgery.[69]

In addition to obliterating soft tissue in the marrow space, the reaming process shaves cancellous and cortical bone from the inner aspect of the cortex. This mixture of finely morcellized bone and marrow elements has excellent osteoinductive and osteoconductive potential. The rich osseous autograft is delivered by the increased interosseous pressure and by mechanical action of the reamer directly into the fracture site. In the open nailing technique, this material is exuded during reaming, but it can be collected and applied to the surface of the bone at the fracture site after the wound is irrigated, before closure.

TYPES OF INTRAMEDULLARY NAILS

Unlocked Intramedullary Nails

Unlocked or first-generation nails consist of intramedullary implants that are not rigidly stabilized with screw or pin fixation. This type of fixation is termed *splintage* and is defined as a construct that allows sliding of the implant-bone interface. The implant assists fracture healing by supporting bending while allowing axial loads to be transmitted to the surrounding bone. In this mode, the nail cannot control axial or rotational load. It is sometimes referred to as a *flexible gliding implant*. This type of fixation is indicated if the reduced fracture has inherent rotational and longitudinal stability, so that it will not twist or shorten when loaded.

Locking Intramedullary Nails

The first locking intramedullary nail was developed by Modny in 1952.[66] This nail had an **X**-beam design and contained a regularly spaced series of holes that passed through the axilla of the beam on all four sides, allowing screws to be introduced from any direction. Because the holes were placed close together and were larger in diameter than the screws, they could be located with the drill without the use of a target device. This nail was straight and noncannulated and therefore was not suited to the closed nailing technique; it was better inserted after open reduction. Although this design was copied by other developers, locking nails did not gain widespread acceptance until Klemm and Schellman perfected a locking nail based on the cloverleaf Küntscher nail.[55] This implant was cannulated, curved, and had a tapered tip, allowing for insertion with the closed nailing technique. Holes for transfixion screws were placed in the extreme ends of the nail, minimizing the invasion of the fracture zone and increasing the range of fractures that could be stabilized with this device. Subsequent versions of this type of cannulated locking nail contained a cylindrical proximal end with an internally threaded core to allow firmer attachment of the driver, extractor, and proximal target device. Other minor changes were made in the location and orientation of the screw holes. These nailing systems have now been used successfully to stabilize comminuted and rotationally unstable fractures of the femur[12, 43, 47, 48, 54, 90, 99] and tibia.[25, 54, 97, 101]

Second-Generation Locking Nails

Standard first-generation locking nails have been very effective for the stabilization of comminuted fractures of the femoral shaft extending from 1 cm below the lesser trochanter to 10 cm above the articular surface of the knee. Because of the high stresses seen in trochanteric fractures and the proximal location of many pertrochanteric fracture lines, these nails have not provided ideal stabilization for fractures above the lesser trochanter. Most of these nails contain a proximal diagonal screw that is normally inserted in a downward and medial direction. Use of the nail intended for the opposite side allows the screw to be inserted up into the femoral head and neck. The strength of these implants is still not adequate to provide secure, lasting fixation for subtrochanteric fractures, and because the proximal screw is threaded into the nail, no gliding of the screw can occur. This prevents impaction of bone fragments of intertrochanteric and femoral neck fractures. To overcome these problems, a second generation of locking nail has been developed (Fig. 10–40). These nails have an expanded proximal end that contains two tunnels for large-diameter, smooth-shank lag screws. The increase in proximal nail diameter and wall thickness combined with the screw design provides greater fixation and strength for subtrochanteric fractures. The combination of sliding proximal lag screws and distal transfixion screws allows excellent fixation of ipsilateral femoral neck or intertrochanteric fractures and comminuted fractures of the shaft.

TECHNIQUES

To this point, the chapter has dealt with fundamental principles of metallurgy and hardware. The following sections describe the application of metallurgy and hardware to the basic techniques of internal fixation.

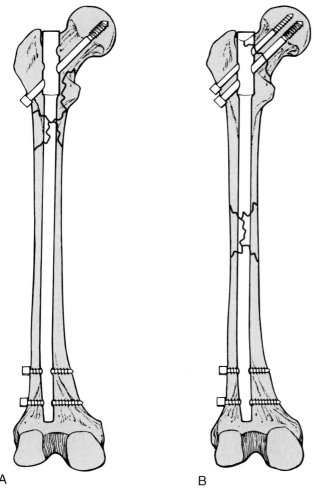

FIGURE 10–40. Schematic representation of second-generation femoral locking nails and their primary indications. *A,* Fixation of a comminuted subtrochanteric fracture. *B,* Fixation of an ipsilateral neck and comminuted shaft fracture.

Basic Modes of Internal Fixation

Internal fixation can be divided into three basic modes: interfragmentary compression, splintage, and bridging. Mechanical characteristics of the bone implant fixation construct vary depending on the consistency of bone, the fracture pattern and location, the specific implant, and the mode of application. The advantages of mechanical stability of the final construct must be balanced against the detrimental surgical trauma associated with fracture reduction and implant insertion. Maintenance of sufficient blood flow to injured soft tissue and bone is essential to avoid infection and facilitate the healing process. Internal fixation must be applied in a way that provides the desired anatomic reconstruction with adequate mobilization to reduce pain and permit fully functional activity while facilitating fracture union and soft tissue healing. The relation between these two major considerations can be expressed in the statement of Tscherne and Gotzen[92]: "Stability is the mechanical basis and vascularity the biologic basis of uncomplicated fracture healing."

The amount of motion at the fracture site in any fixation construct varies according to the mechanical characteristics of the construct and the direction and magnitude of the forces applied. The term *stability* has many definitions and is therefore a source of confusion. The Association for the Study of Internal Fixation (ASIF), also known as AO, considers stable fixation as that achieved in a fixation construct and subjected to loads of functional muscle activity and joint motion without any movement at the fracture site. This is often termed *rigid fixation.* An alternative definition would hold that a fracture construct is stable when it allows pain-free functional activity even though a small amount of motion is present at the fracture site.

Additional clarity is given to the consideration of stability when the level of functional activity (e.g., active motion exercises versus weight bearing) is specified. Under conditions of loading, there is a range of micromotion at the fracture site within which bony union will progress but above which nonunion will occur. Within this safe zone, the histologic pathway to fracture healing varies depending on the relative motion between fracture fragments.[34, 50, 63] If there is motion, the body supplements the immobilization provided by the implant through the development of callus. This small amount of skeletal material laid down at a distance from the central axis of the bone provides a very effective method of bridging and immobilizing the main fracture fragments. The amount of callus is roughly proportional to the amount of motion. If there is complete elimination of motion between fracture fragments, callus formation is not necessary, and healing occurs more directly through intracortical osteogenesis.[83] Small gaps between fragments are filled by woven bone. Where fracture fragments contact directly, new intracortical haversian systems drill across the fracture site, producing direct union. This has been termed *primary union,* which suggests that it is inherently superior to the fracture union that occurs with the production of callus. Although intracortical union does progress more directly to an advanced stage of fracture remodeling, the mechanical strength and therefore the functional capability of this type of bone union are not superior to that of fracture healing through callus formation.

Both types of fracture union are functional, and selection of internal fixation methods should pursue the fixation construct most appropriate for reduction stabilization. This must include consideration of the patient's general state of health, associated injuries, grade of the soft tissue injury, consistency of the bone, location and pattern of the displacement of the fracture, the technical expertise of the surgeon, and the physical and human resources available. We now consider the major fixation techniques that fit within each of the three modes of fixation and discuss their properties, primary indications, basic hardware, and correct technical application.

INTERFRAGMENTARY COMPRESSION

In interfragmentary compression, the fracture fragments are restored to their anatomic position and held together under compression by a metal implant. This compression improves the interference fit and increases friction at the fracture interface, enabling the final bone-implant construct to resist the deforming forces produced by functional activity. The compression of the bone fragments achieved by application of tension to the implant results in a completed construct that is said to have been *prestressed.* This means that the stress that has been applied to the construct during application precedes the stress to which it is exposed when the fixation construct is loaded during functional activity. One result of prestressing is that the bone component of the construct is better able to share functional loading with the implant, thereby partially protecting the metal from cyclical deformation and fatigue failure. Also, load sharing exposes the bone to a mechanical stimulus for fracture healing and maintenance of mineralization. The compression force or prestress on implants must be sufficient to resist the deforming forces to which the fixation construct is exposed during functional activity. If compression is applied incorrectly, excessive micromotion of the fracture fragments occurs, resulting in resorption of the bone ends and formation of small amounts of callus. Even though this is a protective response of the body, in this circumstance it is a warning sign that indicates loosening and fatigue of the implant system. If steps are not taken to reverse this condition, the continued loading will lead to implant failure and nonunion.

The compression applied across the fracture surfaces can be static or dynamic, or both. *Static compression* results from the pretensioning of the implants. *Dynamic compression* is achieved by harnessing forces that act on the skeleton during normal physiologic loading. In addition, implants can be applied in such a way as to combine static and dynamic compression. These concepts are discussed individually and illustrated in the following sections.

Static Compression

The lag screw is a classic example of applied static compression. The screw is tensioned across the fracture line, and the fracture is compressed. The screw has a small length of thread at its tip and a smooth shank between the head and the tip. Tension results when the screw's thread bites into the cortex on one side of the fracture and the screw head blocks its progression into the bone on the other. This is called a lag screw *by design.* These screws are usually employed to achieve interfragmentary compression between two fragments of cancellous bone (as in a metaphysis or epiphysis) (Fig. 10–41). It is critical that threads not cross the fracture site. After the hole is drilled across the fracture, threads in the near cortex must be cut with a tap. The threads of the screw spiral through the cancellous bone, which should be tapped only in the very dense cancellous bone of large, young patients. This type of screw fixation can be used only when the two cancellous surfaces contact or become impacted. Gaps that remain in the cancellous bone after reduction of fragments will be filled by connective tissue, precluding reliable union. Therefore, a cancellous bone graft should be used to fill these gaps when they occur.

Interfragmentary compression can also be applied with simple, fully threaded screws. This technique is usually used in cortical bone. The cortex near the screw head is overdrilled so that the screw thread gains purchase only in the far cortex (Fig. 10–42A). This is called a lag screw *by*

application. The overdrilled hole in the cortex near the screw head is called the *glide hole,* and the hole in the far cortex is called the *thread hole.* Cancellous type lag screws are not used to achieve interfragmentary compression in the cortex, because new cortical bone will fill the space between the drill hole and the smooth screw shank, making screw extraction difficult. Extraction is facilitated in the presence of the continuous thread of the cortical screw. Interfragmentary compression can be accomplished in the cortex with lag screws placed independently or through a plate.

Any cortical lag screw used to affix a plate that crosses a fracture site should be applied with the cortex near the screw head overdrilled as a glide hole. A screw that crosses the fracture line and threads into both cortices prevents compression of the fracture fragments (see Fig. 10–42B). Optimal fixation with a cortical lag screw is achieved by correctly following the steps for screw insertion (Fig. 10–43). The best compression is obtained by aiming the screw into the center of the opposite fragment (Fig. 10–44A–C).

In addition to applying compression across the fracture surface, a screw fixing a simple fracture in a long bone must prevent the shear that would occur in oblique fractures under axial loading. Insertion of the screw perpendicular to the long axis of the bone best prevents this shearing and fracture displacement. Therefore, this is the preferred orientation for screw fixation for most fractures, despite the fact that maximal compression of the fracture surfaces is achieved by lag screws oriented perpendicular to the fracture plane. When butterfly fragments are present, however, equal attention must be given to the need for great interfragmentary compression force at the fracture surfaces. For this reason, screw orientation halfway between perpendicular to the fracture surface and perpendicular to the long axis of the bone is used (Fig. 10–45; see also Fig. 10–44D, E).

Static compression can also be applied with the use of plates. After fracture reduction, the plate is fixed to one fracture fragment. Tension is then applied to the opposite end of the plate, leading to compression at the fracture site. This may be accomplished with the use of an external tension device or plates with specially designed screw holes that, in conjunction with eccentrically placed screws, cause tensioning of the implant (Fig. 10–46). With this technique, it is helpful to initially affix the plate to the fragment that creates an axilla between the plate and the screw (Fig. 10–47A). This facilitates fracture reduction and compression. Plates with specially designed screw holes that permit pretensioning include the Dynamic Compression Plate (DCP; Synthes, Paoli, PA), the Limited Contact Dynamic Compression Plate (LCDCP; Synthes), and the European Compression Technique (ECT; Zimmer, Warsaw, IN). *Dynamic compression plate* is an unfortunate name for an implant designed to provide static compression as defined here and in the AO manual. When a single plate is used, the application of tension to the plate tends to cause eccentric compression, with close apposition of the bone under the plate and slight gapping at the side of the bone away from the plate. This can be prevented by overbending the plate before application (see Fig. 10–47B).

The optimal construct utilizes an interfragmentary lag

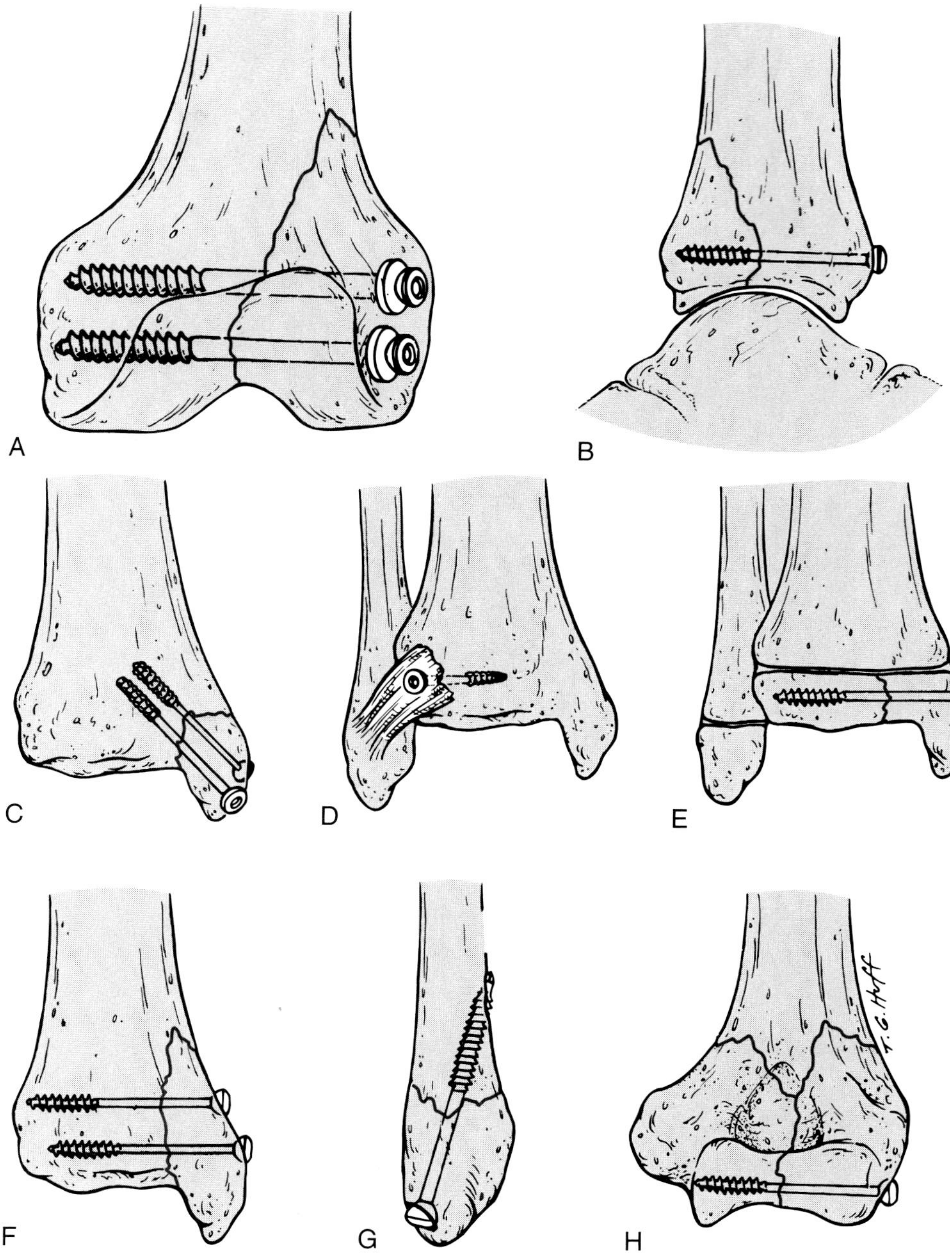

Figure 10–41. Typical indications for cancellous lag screws. *A,* Two 6.5-mm cancellous screws with a 32-mm thread, used with washers to fix a lateral femoral condyle fracture. *B,* A 4.0-mm cancellous screw inserted from front to back to fix the posterior lip fragment of the distal tibia. *C,* Two 4.0-mm cancellous screws used to fix a medial malleolus fracture. *D,* A 4.0-mm cancellous screw used to fix a fragment from the anterior aspect of the distal tibia carrying the syndesmotic ligament. *E,* A 4.0-mm cancellous screw used to fix an epiphyseal fracture of the distal tibia. *F,* Two 4.0-mm cancellous screws used to fix an oblique fracture of the medial malleolus. *G,* A malleolar screw inserted obliquely to fix a short, oblique fracture of the distal fibula. This direction of insertion allows cortical purchase with an increased compression force. *H,* A 4.0-mm cancellous screw used to fix the vertical component of a supracondylar Y fracture of the distal humerus.

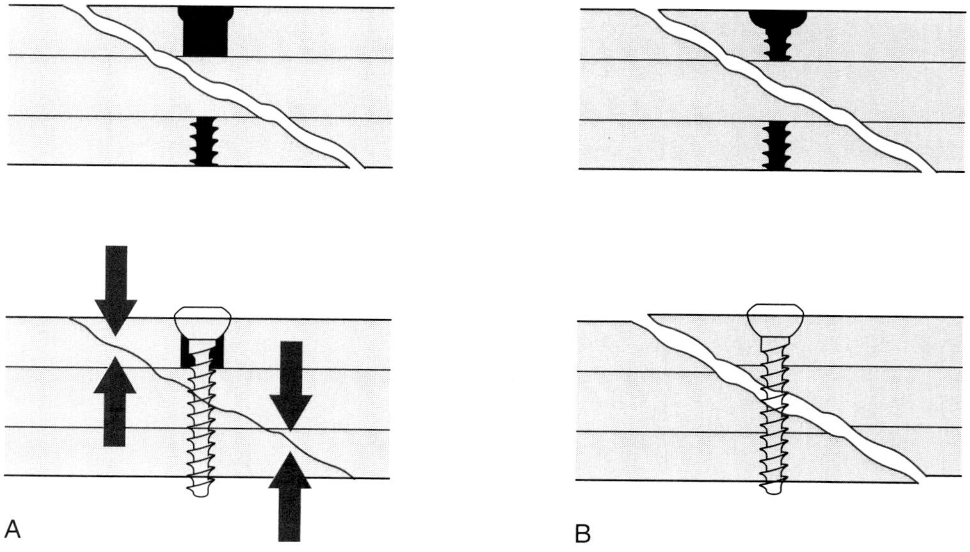

Figure 10–42. Lag screws by application. *A,* Overdrilling the near-cortex to produce a glide hole allows a cortical screw to act as a lag screw. *B,* In the absence of a glide hole, a cortical screw inserted across the fracture site will maintain fracture gapping.

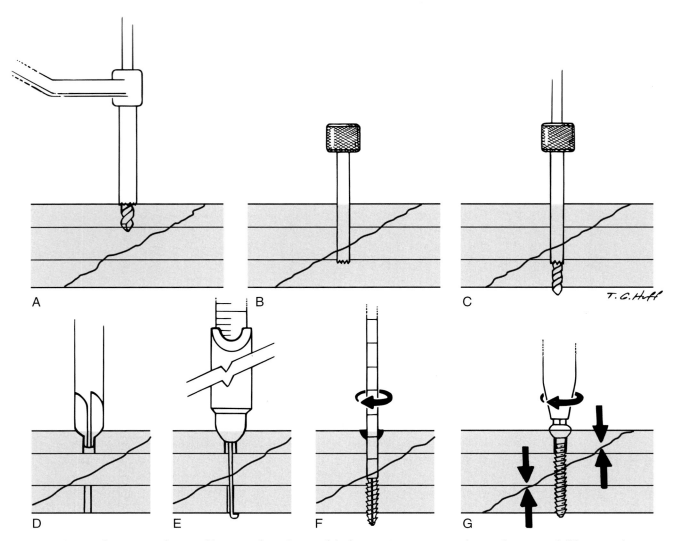

Figure 10–43. Steps for insertion of a cortical lag screw after reduction of the fracture. *A,* A 4.5-mm tap sleeve and a 4.5-mm drill bit are used to create a glide hole in the near-cortex. *B,* The top hat drill sleeve (58-mm long, 4.5-mm outer diameter, and 3.2-mm inner diameter) is inserted into the 4.5-mm glide hole until the serrated teeth abut the cortex. This ensures centering of the drill bit used to make the thread hole, even when the screw hole is drilled at an oblique angle. *C,* A 3.2-mm drill bit is inserted through the top hat guide to make the thread hole in the far cortex. *D,* A countersink with a 4.5-mm tip is inserted and used to produce a recess to accept the screw head. *E,* A depth gauge is used to accurately measure the length of screw needed. *F,* A 4.5-mm tap with a short threaded area is used to tap the thread hole in the far cortex. *G,* The 4.5-mm cortical screw is inserted and tightened lightly to create compression.

screw placed through the plate to achieve greater fracture compression (see Fig. 10–46). Interfragmentary compression created by the screw fixation of the cortex opposite the plate reduces the shearing of this fracture surface that could otherwise occur with torsional forces. This combination of lag screw and plate should be used for most simple, oblique diaphyseal fractures. A pretensioned plate can be applied as the primary mode of compression in a transverse fracture in which lag screws are impractical. If the fracture includes at least one major butterfly fragment, the fracture planes between the butterfly fragment and the major diaphyseal fragments are best fixed with individual interfragmentary screws placed outside of the plate. The strength of this fixation is not great enough to resist all torsional bending and axial loading forces, and it must be supplemented with a plate that spans the fracture site to neutralize the other forces that would disrupt the unprotected compression lag screw fixation. This use of plates is described later.

Dynamic Compression

Stated simply, *dynamic compression* is a phenomenon by which an implant can transform or modify functional physiologic forces into compression of a fracture site. There is little or no prestress or load on the bone when the limb is at rest. Four typical examples of DC constructs are the tension band, the antiglide plate, splintage by noninterlocked intramedullary nails, and the telescoping hip screw.

Combined Static-Dynamic Compression

Plates can be applied as tension bands if applied to the tension or distraction side of a fracture or nonunion. In addition to the anatomic situations noted previously, definite tension and compression sides can be identified at locations where anatomic or pathologic curvature or angulation of the bone or fracture results in loading that is eccentric to the central axis of the bone with weight-bearing and muscle activity. Because of its normal curvature, the femur is under tension antero-laterally and compression posteromedially. When a plate is placed on the lateral surface of the bone, it functions as a tension band. Subsequent weight-bearing and muscle

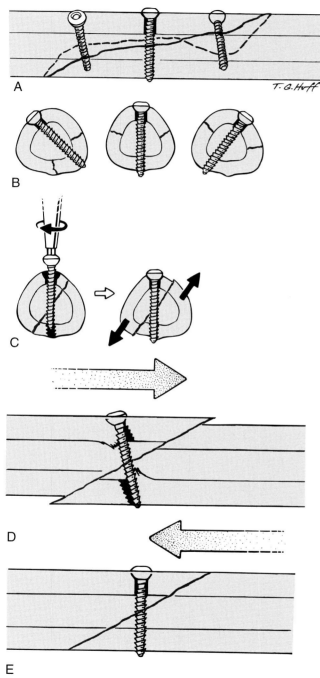

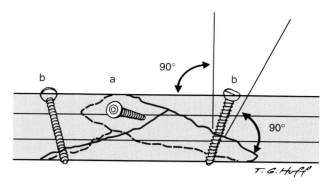

FIGURE 10–45. Screw fixation of a diaphyseal fracture with a single butterfly fragment. The center screw (a) connects the two main fragments. The outer two screws (b) fix the butterfly fragment to the two main fragments. These screws are inserted at an angle that bisects the angle formed between the perpendiculars to the fracture surface and to the long axis of the bone. Final tightening of all three screws should be completed after all are inserted.

FIGURE 10–44. Orientation of screws for fixation of a simple spiral fracture. *A,* Screws are oriented so that the tip passes through the middle of the opposite fragment. *B,* Correct orientation of the screws with their tips passing through the center of the opposite fragment is best seen on cross-sectional views. *C,* On tightening of a screw that is not centered in the middle of the opposite fragment, the fracture fragments displace. *D,* Insertion of the screw at a right angle to the fracture plane results in the best interfragmental compression but offers inadequate resistance to axial loading. *E,* Insertion of a cortical lag screw at right angles to the long axis of the bone provides the best resistance to fracture displacement under axial loading.

activity result in dynamic compression at the fracture site. In varus nonunion of the tibia, the abnormal angulation results in a significant bending moment. By placement of a tensioned plate in the lateral aspect of this bone, it is possible to capitalize on the abnormal eccentric loading to produce dynamic compression with weight-bearing and muscle activity (see Fig. 10–21).

In some situations, fractures and nonunions present conditions that allow their fixation with a combination of static and dynamic compression. This is usually accomplished through the use of plates that are pretensioned to provide static compression. In these situations, conditions permit the identification of a clear tension and compression side of the fracture. By being placed on the tension surface, the plate also acts as a tension band. When functional activity is commenced, weight-bearing and muscle forces cause dynamic compression that supplement the static compression produced by pretensioning the implants.

SPLINTAGE

Intramedullary Nailing

In contrast to the relatively rigid fixation achieved with interfragmentary compression, standard nonlocking intramedullary nails provide fixation through splintage. *Splintage* may be defined as a construct in which sliding can occur between the bone and the implant. Nails extend from entry portals in the bone through the medullary canal over most of its length and allow axial loads to be transmitted to the apposed ends of the fracture fragments. Intramedullary fixation is much less rigid than interfragmentary compression but is no less effective when properly applied. Because a greater amount of motion occurs at the fracture site with functional activity, callus formation is regularly observed.

Closed Nailing

The technique of closed nailing involves the reduction of long bone fractures by closed manipulation with the aid of a specialized traction table and fluoroscopy. The technique avoids the direct surgical exposure of the fracture site that occurs during open reduction. Because the overlying skin

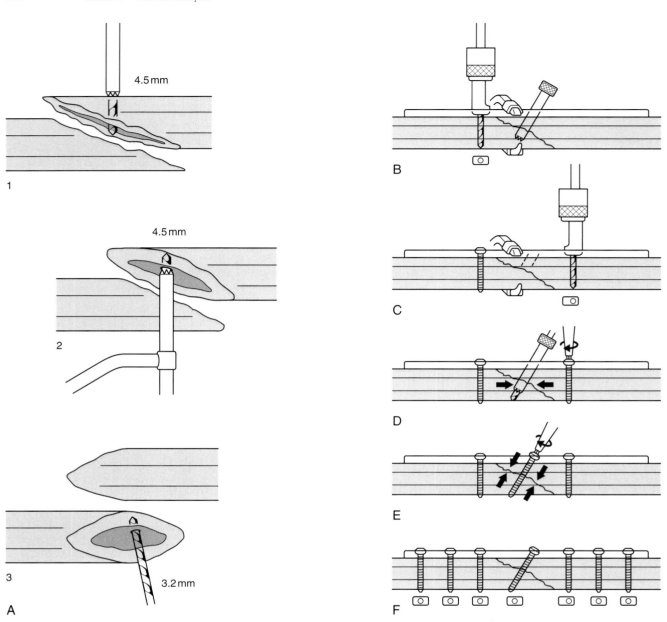

Figure 10–46. The combination of axial compression with a plate and interfragmentary compression with a screw through the plate. *A,* Three methods of drilling the interfragmentary screw hole. (1) The glide hole is drilled first from the outside with a 4.5-mm drill. (2) The glide hole is drilled first from the inside with a 4.5-mm drill. (3) The thread hole is drilled first from the inside with a 3.2-mm drill. *B,* After initial drilling of the glide hole, the plate is applied. Fracture reduction and plate position are held with a clamp. To avoid slipping of the plate while drilling the first plate screw, the 3.2-mm drill guide is inserted through the plate into the hole for the interfragmentary screw. The first plate screw is drilled using the green drill guide. Note that the insertion of the first screw on this side of the fracture creates an axilla between the fracture surface and the plate that will trap the other fragment when it is compressed by placing the plate under tension. *C,* After removal of the drill sleeve, a second screw hole in the plate is drilled, using the yellow load guide. This guide locates the screw hole eccentrically with respect to the hole in the plate. *D,* Tightening of this screw results in tension in the plate and compression at the fracture site. The 3.2-mm drill sleeve is now reinserted in the glide hole and the opposite cortex is drilled. *E,* Insertion of an interfragmentary lag screw through this hole will dramatically increase compression at the fracture site. *F,* The remaining screws are now inserted through the plate, using the neutral green drill guide.

and muscle envelope is left intact, the periosteal vascular supply to the bone at the fracture site is preserved, and the additional surgical trauma to the surrounding soft tissue is minimized. Nails are inserted through entry portals distant from the fracture site at the end of the bone. Reaming is accomplished with the use of flexible reamers, increasing in diameter by 0.5-mm increments. The reamers are inserted over a guide wire that extends across the fracture site. These reamers follow the normal curvature of the

bone. Nails inserted after reaming have a similar curvature and are cannulated to allow insertion over a guide wire. To aid their safe passage into the distal fragment, nails are designed with tapered tips, and a larger guide wire that more completely fills the internal diameter of the nail is used for nail introduction. These two factors help to keep the nail centered in the canal, preventing comminution of the cortex at the fracture site.

In the absence of direct visualization of the fracture,

correct rotational alignment of the bone fragments must be ensured by proper positioning of the distal limb segment on the fracture table. With the pelvis flat in the supine position, the lower leg is positioned so that the patella is pointing directly at the ceiling. In fractures of the mid-diaphysis in which adequate endosteal contact is obtained with the nail on both sides of the fracture site, alignment occurs automatically on nail insertion. Conversely, very proximal or distal fractures that contain the entire diaphysis in one fragment have potential for angulation during nailing. In these cases, lack of endosteal contact in one fragment allows the possibility of angulatory deformity and malunion. In noncomminuted fractures, correct length of the bone is reestablished and maintained through the abutment of the major proximal and distal fragments. If comminution results in reduction of less than 50% of the normal surface contact between the two fragments, loss of abutment and resultant shortening can occur. Standard nonlocked nails serve only as intramedullary splints; they do not provide fixation that can prevent shortening caused by the axial pull of muscles and the forces of weight bearing. When unrestricted by adequate cortical abutment, these forces tend to produce shortening and implant protrusion.

Standard nonlocking, closed intramedullary nailing has been employed with excellent results in the treatment of simple and minimally comminuted midshaft fractures of the femur[23] and tibia.[7, 37, 93] Healing occurs through the callus pathway. Sharing of the load between bone and implant results in a strong union, after which refractures

are almost never encountered. Periosteal cortical osteoporosis is not observed after intramedullary nailing, although it can be seen during plating. After plate removal, the screw holes represent areas of stress concentration until new bone fills in the outer portion of the hole. After nonlocking intramedullary nailing, there are no screw holes through which fractures can propagate.

For appropriately selected fractures, nonlocking intramedullary nailing results in sufficient stability to permit early mobility of adjacent joints and early weight bearing. Avoidance of surgical trauma to the overlying soft tissue through the use of the closed nailing technique promotes early muscle rehabilitation and results in an infection rate of less than 1%, compared with 3.2% for open nailing.[45] Provision of stable fixation through intramedullary nailing precludes the use of skeletal traction and lengthy periods of bedrest, resulting in a substantially shortened hospital stay.

BRIDGING FIXATION

Both interfragmentary compression and splinting through intramedullary nailing require contact between the fracture fragments to achieve stability of fixation. They are best applied to simple fractures and those that contain a small amount of comminution. Achieving apposition of all fragments in a markedly comminuted fracture is mechanically impractical and biologically harmful. These fractures most often result from the rapid dissipation of large amounts of energy into the traumatized skeletal part. The

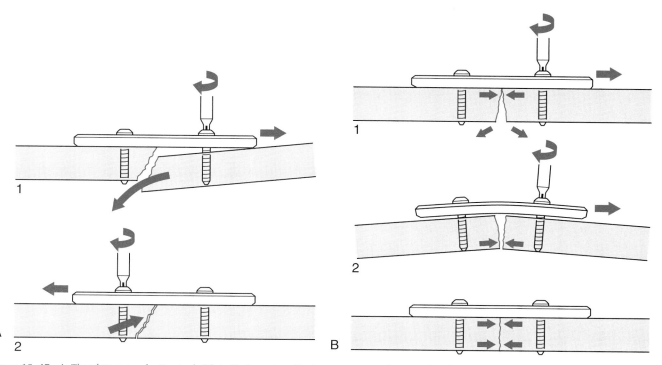

FIGURE 10–47. *A,* The plate as a reduction tool. (1) Axilla formation. During compression, horizontal shifting of the plate on the bone may occur with displacement of the fracture as the nonstationary fragment slides down the oblique fracture plane. (2) The neutral screw should create an axilla between the bone and the plate. This will force the opposite fragment into the side to help ensure adequate compression. Fracture reduction and compression are facilitated when a stable axilla is created between the plate and one of the fracture fragments. *B,* Prebending of the plate. (1) Compression generated across the near-cortices and slight gapping of the far cortices result if the plate is not prebent. (2) Even fracture compression is facilitated with prebending of the plate before fixation.

fracture occurs like an explosion, with great fragmentation of the bone and wide radial displacement of the individual fragments into the surrounding soft tissue. Elastic recoil of the remaining soft tissue envelope causes a reduction in the displacement that occurred at the moment of impact. The injury is considered more severe if it results in an open wound that breaches the soft tissue envelope and communicates directly with the fracture site. If this has not occurred, the presence of a great degree of comminution and marked fragment displacement indicates that there has been significant injury to the soft tissue surrounding the bone.

Because the bone fragments are of variable size and are often rotated and impaled into the surrounding muscle, reduction requires direct surgical exposure and manipulation. Dissection and retraction of the injured soft tissue further compromise its damaged circulation. The use of clamps and reduction forceps to reposition and hold the bone fragments disrupts the tenuous muscle attachments that carry the remaining blood supply to these individual islands of bone. Further devascularization of soft tissue and bone increases the risk of infection and impairs fracture healing. When fracture healing is prevented or delayed, extended cyclical loading of the implants may exceed their fatigue limit and lead to metal failure.

To avoid these consequences, it is necessary to choose a fixation method that achieves the goals of internal fixation without causing severe damage to the vascularity of bone and surrounding soft tissue. This fixation is provided by the technique of bridging. Bridging is accomplished by insertion of implants that extend across the zone of soft tissue injury and fracture but are fixed to the major bone fragments proximal and distal to the fracture site. This can be accomplished with the use of locking intramedullary nails inserted with the closed technique. Bridging fixation can also be achieved with plates by use of the indirect reduction technique.

Although fractures often appear to be held in distraction by bridging fixation with a locking intramedullary rod or plate, healing through periosteal callus rather than nonunion is the usual outcome. This occurs because these methods of fixation protect the viability of bone fragments by sparing their vascular supply and provide a favorable mechanical environment for bone formation. The metals from which most rods and plates are manufactured are somewhat elastic. This material property, combined with the structural geometry of the implants, results in a range of fracture motion consistent with callus formation. The implants allow restoration and preservation of alignment and permit functional activity. The technique of insertion and the method of fixation preserve the viability of bone and soft tissue in the fracture zone. Because these tissues remain viable and a limited amount of motion is permitted at the fracture site during functional activity, a favorable environment for callus formation is present.

Closed Locking Intramedullary Nailing

Fracture reduction and implant insertion follow the same steps outlined previously for standard nonlocking, closed intramedullary nailing. Additional attention must be given to the choice of implant length and final position on insertion, because the transfixion screws must be placed in specific areas of the bone. In the comminuted and extraisthmic fractures in which this bridging technique is used, additional attention must be paid to reduction to establish the correct length, rotation, and alignment.

Lining up the tips of butterfly fragments is an unreliable method for establishing the correct length of the bone. Because the patients are placed in skeletal traction on the fracture table, this method of judging length often results in overlengthening of the bone. Fractures usually heal in spite of this overdistraction, and the added limb length is noticeable and annoying to the patient. In these situations, it is necessary to make a reference length measurement from the opposite intact bone, using obvious landmarks such as the adductor tubercle and the tip of the greater trochanter on the femur. A bead-tip guide wire of known length can then be used as an interoperative measuring device to reestablish the correct length of the fractured bone (Fig. 10–48). In nailing fractures proximal to the isthmus in the diaphysis, correct alignment of the short conical proximal fragment is achieved by accurate placement of the entry portal. Insertion of the nail eccentric to the central axis of the medullary canal will result in angulation of this fragment (Fig. 10–49).

During nailing of fractures distal to the isthmus, a short, conical fragment with a wide medullary canal can easily become angulated because there is insufficient endosteal surface contact to produce automatic alignment. The diameter of the medullary canal at the proximal end of this distal fragment is often larger than the diameter of the medullary nail. Careful reduction of this fragment is necessary to avoid comminution of the fracture on nail insertion or abnormal angulation (Fig. 10–50). Under these circumstances, it is necessary to use two screws to transfix this distal fragment. Failure to do so allows the fragment to toggle or rotate around a single screw, causing unacceptable motion at the fracture site that can lead to nonunion and implant failure (Fig. 10–51).

Biomechanical studies indicate that placement of the proximal distal hole within 5 cm of a femoral fracture produces excessive stress on the nail, resulting in fatigue failure at this hole. The screw hole acts as a stress riser,[17] producing stress in the nail that is greater than its fatigue endurance limit. When proper closed nailing technique is used and the necessary precautions for correct reduction and implant placement are observed, excellent results can be obtained using this bridging technique for treatment of complex diaphyseal fractures of the femur and tibia.*

Proximal Screw Insertion

Developers have attempted to produce locking nail systems that allow predictable, quick, and easy percutaneous insertion of transfixion screws through the holes in both ends of the implants. They have come closer to achieving this goal with the devices for providing proximal screw insertion. Many current nail designs allow drill and screw targeting devices to be firmly bolted onto

---

*See references 12, 25, 43, 47, 48, 54, 90, 97, 99, 101.

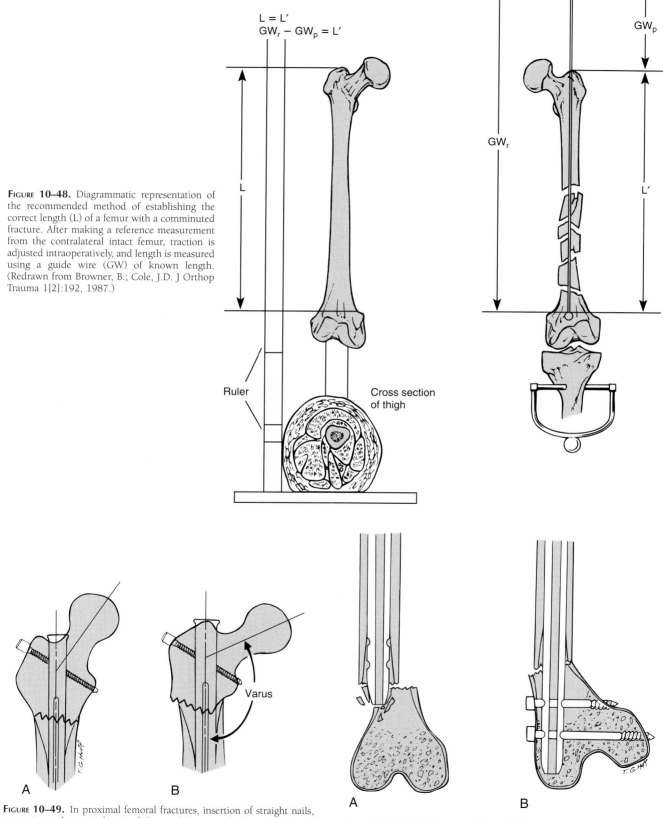

$$L = L'$$
$$GW_r - GW_p = L'$$

FIGURE 10–48. Diagrammatic representation of the recommended method of establishing the correct length (L) of a femur with a comminuted fracture. After making a reference measurement from the contralateral intact femur, traction is adjusted intraoperatively, and length is measured using a guide wire (GW) of known length. (Redrawn from Browner, B.; Cole, J.D. J Orthop Trauma 1[2]:192, 1987.)

Ruler

Cross section of thigh

Varus

A   B

A   B

FIGURE 10–49. In proximal femoral fractures, insertion of straight nails, eccentric to the central axis of the medullary canal, through a lateral trochanteric entry portal, causes varus angulation of the proximal fragment. *A,* Correct entry portal over the medullary axis. *B,* Incorrect entry portal, eccentric to the medullary axis.

FIGURE 10–50. Problems caused by malreduction of a short distal femoral fragment. *A,* Translation resulting in comminution of the distal cortex during nail passage. *B,* Failure to correctly position the distal fragment with a large medullary canal results in fixation in an angulated position.

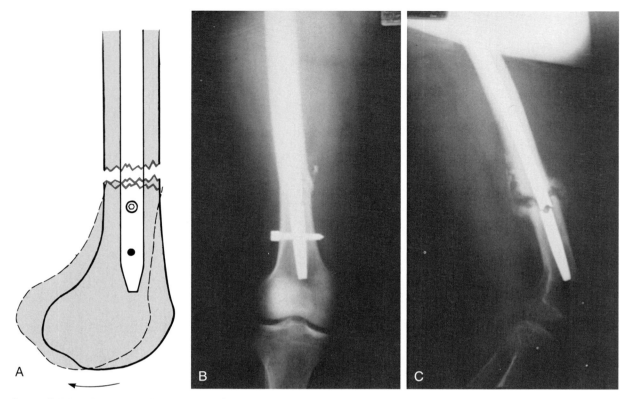

Figure 10–51. Failure to insert both distal transfixional screws in a short, distal femoral fragment in which the medullary canal is larger than the diameter of the nail produces continued toggling of the fragment on the single screw, resulting in nonunion and implant failure. *A,* Diagrammatic representation of fragment motion around the single screw. *B,* Distal femoral fracture fixed with a nail not sunk deeply enough into the femur and with the use of only one screw. *C,* Continued motion of the distal femoral fragment results in nonunion and implant failure.

the top of the nail in a desired position of rotational alignment.

Distal Screw Insertion

Greater difficulty has been encountered in developing satisfactory methods for insertion of distal screws. A number of different methods have been employed with varying success. A target device mounted on the image intensifier has been used by Kempf and colleages.[47] This consists of a guide similar to a gunsight that is inserted into a holder preattached to the image intensifier. After the x-ray beam is aligned coaxially with the tunnel through the nail, as evidenced by a perfectly round hole seen on the monitor of the image intensifier, the guide is folded down in line with the beam and maneuvered against the bone. After the position of the guide is fine-tuned to ensure alignment with the hole, it can be used to guide drilling and screw insertion. This device is used most effectively when it is attached to a rigid, stable Carm assembly. Many surgeons have found it easy to displace this guide if it is attached to the end of the more flexible Carm fluoroscope.

There have been many attempts to design guides for the distal screw holes that attach to the threaded proximal end of the nail. This type of guide requires prealignment with the distal transfixion holes before insertion of the implant. After implant insertion and proximal locking, the distal target device is reattached to the top of the nail, in hopes that the guide will then align with the distal screw holes and facilitate drilling and insertion. However, nails that contain an open section over most of their length frequently undergo torsion on insertion. This changes the relation between the plane of the distal transfixion screw tunnels and the top of the nail and prohibits correct alignment of the proximally mounted target device when it is reattached. Because these guides often extend for a distance of more than 40 cm between their point of proximal attachment and the distal holes, the problem of malalignment is further aggravated by the tendency of the guide to sag toward the floor when used on the femur or tibia with the patient in the supine position.

The most reliable and most frequently used method for distal screw insertion is the freehand method.[13, 59, 65] The tip of an awl, Steinmann pin, or drill is held at an angle and aligned with the center of the hole using the monitor of the image intensifier. With the radiation off, this device is then brought in line with the x-ray beam and driven through the cortex of the femur or tibia (Fig. 10–52). An alternative method uses some form of hand-held guide to aid direct insertion of the drill. After detachment of the Steinmann pin or drill bit from the power drill, passage through the hole in the nail is confirmed radiographically. The opposite cortex is then drilled, the screw length measured with a depth gauge, and the appropriate screw inserted. There has been great concern regarding possible excessive radiation exposure to the surgeon's hands during this portion of the procedure. Measurement of radiation by radiosensitive dosimeter rings worn during locking intramedullary nailing indicates that the surgeon's hands receive very small amounts of radiation, provided that they do not enter the beam and that they show on the Carm monitor.[58, 86] This is now the most widely used technique for distal screw insertion.

Static versus Dynamic Locking

The presence of screw holes at both ends of the nail offers the option to insert screws at only one or at both ends. Insertion of screws at both ends interlocks the nail and the major proximal and distal fragments. This controls both the length of the bone and the rotation of these fragments. Because the screws prevent the sliding together of the two main fragments, this method of fixation is called the *static mode* (Fig. 10–53). It is a true example of the bridging mode of fixation and is used in fractures with marked comminution and bone loss. Although callus formation was regularly observed after this fixation, it was originally feared that the presence of screws at both ends of the nail would prevent axial impaction and impair the ultimate remodeling of the fracture zone. Therefore, it was suggested that the screw or screws at one end of the nail be removed within 8 to 12 weeks after callus was radiographically observed.[11, 46, 49, 90, 100] However, the callus seen on radiographs of some healing fractures is not strong enough to withstand the axial loading that occurs after the transfixion is removed from one end of the nail. Therefore, screw removal can lead to shortening and implant protrusion.[11, 14, 46, 90, 100] Subsequent studies have shown that dynamization by removal of transfixion at one end of the nail is not necessary for satisfactory fracture healing and remodeling.[14]

When screws are inserted at only one end of the nail, the fixation is termed *dynamic*. This type of fixation is used to gain additional rotational control of the short, conical, epiphyseal-metaphyseal fragment that occurs in fractures or nonunions that are proximal or distal to the diaphysis of the femur or tibia. This type of fixation is appropriate only when the area of contact between the two main fragments is at least 50% of the cortical circumference,[98] so that fragment abutment can maintain the length of the bone. The unlocked end of the nail fits into the reamed medullary canal with the long fragment containing the diaphysis and achieves fixation in the splinting mode (Fig. 10–54). Displacement and subsequent instability can occur if dynamic fixation is inappropriately chosen for fractures with insufficient contact between the two main fragments. Axial forces resulting from muscle activity and weight bearing can lead to rotation or displacement of undisplaced butterfly fragments, with resultant loss of abutment and fracture shortening. Because the static or bridging mode of fixation results in predictable fracture healing, it is best to limit the use of dynamic fixation.

INDIRECT REDUCTION AND BRIDGE PLATING

Comminuted fractures involving the articular surface or metaphysis are often inappropriate for locking nail fixation. In these cases, fixation of articular fragments can often be accomplished with the use of interfragmentary lag screws and a plate that is attached to that fragment and that extends across the fracture zone to the diaphysis. After the plate has been fixed to the articular component, it can be used as a handle. An articulating tension device or a lamina spreader and clamp can be used between the plate and an isolated screw in the diaphysis to maneuver the articular fragment to the desired position (Fig. 10–55). This technique, which avoids direct exposure and further muscle stripping of the many small bone fragments in the comminuted fracture zone, is called *indirect reduction*.[51, 60] Because of distraction across the fracture zone, the bone fragments are reduced through generation of tension in their soft tissue attachments. Alternatively, tension can be applied with the AO distractor.

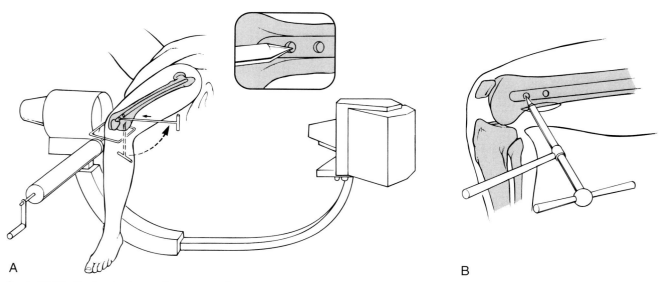

FIGURE 10–52. Freehand technique for insertion of distal transfixion screws with femoral locking nails. *A,* Correct positioning of the image intensifier and use of the awl. Using the image intensifier, the tip of the awl is positioned opposite the hole, as seen on the screen. Fluoroscopy is then stopped, and the awl is brought in line with the beam and perpendicular to the nail. *B,* As an alternative, a drill guide can be aligned with the hole to correctly locate the awl or a drill bit. (*A,* Redrawn from Browner, B.; Edwards, C. The Science and Practice of Intramedullary Nailing. Philadelphia, Lea & Febiger, 1987, p. 248.)

The high-energy forces that produce comminuted fractures result in a major bony discontinuity. Deformities then occur as a result of the original deforming forces in combination with the unopposed pull of muscles attached to the major bone fragments. A highly variable combination of translational, angulatory, and rotatory malalignment is often present, and shortening is almost always a feature. Restoration of bone length with proper consideration for rotational alignment will approximate the reduction in most fracture patterns. As with the indirect reduction technique, the application of longitudinal tension to the soft tissues attached to the bone fragments causes them to come into alignment.

In attempting to align diaphyseal fractures, tension is transmitted through the muscular and fascial attachments to the bone. In similar fashion, periarticular fractures can be partially realigned by generating tension in the ligaments and capsule attached to the articular fragment. Once the correct alignment, rotation, and length

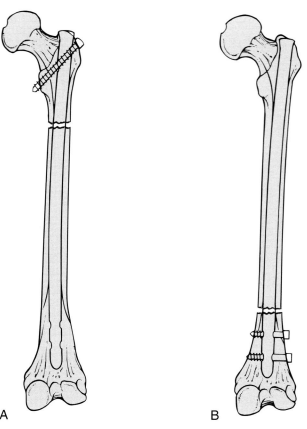

A   B

Figure 10–54. The dynamic mode of fixation. Screws are inserted in only one end of the nail. Abutment of the main fragments prevents shortening. Contact between the endosteum and the nail in the long fragment prevents rotation of that fragment. It allows axial sliding of this fragment with impaction at the fracture site and with loading from muscle forces and weight bearing. *A,* Use of a proximal screw controls only rotation of the short proximal fragment in a closed subtrochanteric fracture. *B,* Two screws are inserted to control the motion of the short distal femoral fragment with the large medullary canal. (*A, B,* Redrawn from Browner, B.; Edwards, C. The Science and Practice of Intramedullary Nailing. Philadelphia, Lea & Febiger, 1987, p. 237.)

Figure 10–53. The static mode of fixation. Screws on both sides of the fracture fix the two main fragments to the nail, preventing them from rotating or sliding together. A small amount of elastic bending and torsion of the nail produces limited motion at the fracture site. This fixation is "static" only with respect to its resistance to shortening and rotation. (Redrawn from Browner, B.; Edwards, C. The Science and Practice of Intramedullary Nailing. Philadelphia, Lea & Febiger, 1987, p. 235.)

of the bone are restored by one of these indirect reduction maneuvers, the smaller bone fragments can be teased into place with a dental pick. If extensive intercalary comminution is present, axial compression cannot be applied, and the resulting bridge plate maintains anatomic length by distraction of the proximal and distal fragments.

Fixation of Osteopenic Bone

The treatment of fractures involving osteopenic bone will become more prevalent as the aging population increases in number. Routine internal fixation techniques may not be adequate to obtain stability. There are three basic concepts that should be considered when dealing with osteopenic bone.

1. **Avoid iatrogenic comminution of the fracture.** Fracture reduction and fixation should proceed with caution to avoid increased comminution of the fragile, fragmented osteopenic bone.

2. **The bone to implant stability and strength should be enhanced in three ways.**
   A. Use longer implants (plate or rod) to avoid failure at the junction of implant and osteopenic bone.[80]
   B. Use additional screws when plating, increase the number of locking screws when using intramedullary rods, and use increased pins when applying external fixators to distribute the force over a greater area, thus unloading the osteopenic bone slightly.
   C. Use fixed angled devices, which prevent pull-out. Bone implant stability can be increased by using fixed angled devices such as blade plates[70] and

Schuhli washers. Prevention of implant to bone failure can be accomplished by attaching a screw to the plate with a threaded hole or by attaching the screw to the plate with a specialized nut.

3. **Augment weakened bone with various substances.** The osteopenic bone itself can be augmented at certain areas with the use of polymethylmethacrylate (PMMA)[38] or biodegradable calcium phosphate bone substitutes.[27]

Screw stability or holding strength is directly related to the cross-sectional area of the screw thread in the material

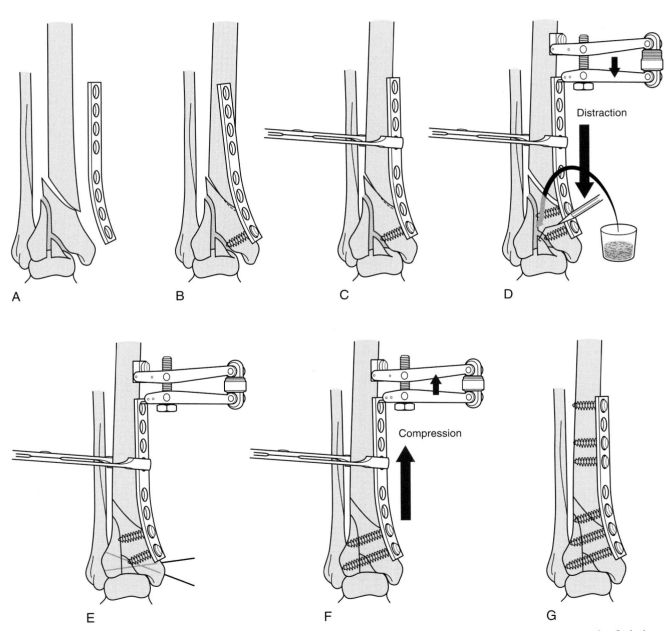

FIGURE 10–55. Indirect reduction technique demonstrated during plating of a pillon fracture of the distal tibia. *A,* The plate is contoured to fit the bone. *B,* The plate is affixed first to the distal articular fragment. *C,* The plate is held against the shaft with the Verbrugge clamp. *D,* An articulating tension device is fixed to the diaphysis above the plate with a single screw. The device is turned so that its jaws open, causing the partially fixed plate to distract the fracture. Bone graft is applied to the impaction defects. *E,* Articular fragments that have been realigned by the pull of the attached soft tissues are now provisionally fixed with Kirschner wires. *F,* Slight compression is applied. *G,* The plate is fixed to the diaphysis above the fracture. (*A–G,* Redrawn from Mast, J.; Jakob, R.; Ganz, R. Planning and Reduction Technique in Fracture Surgery. New York, Springer Verlag, 1989, pp. 73, 74.)

and the density of material that the screw is in. PMMA and calcium phosphate bone substitutes both increase the density for greater screw holding strength and can also improve fracture stability by acting as an intramedullary strut.

Preoperative Planning

The development of a preoperative plan requires decision making on a number of essential issues.

FIXATION

The choice of interfragmentary compression, splinting, or bridging fixation is based on analysis of the fracture pattern and location and the nature and extent of associated injury to the soft tissues and to other bones and organ systems. This decision leads to a specific selection of implants.

When screw and plate fixation is selected for interfragmentary compression or bridging fixation in fractures with multiple fragments, optimal placement of the implants can be facilitated by the creation of a preoperative blueprint. This is a diagram that shows the exact location of the plate and all screws and their relations to the various bone fragments when fixed in their final position of reduction. The shape of each bone fragment is drawn on tracing paper or clear x-ray film from the original injury film. The individual pieces are then assembled like a jigsaw puzzle into a whole bone. This is accomplished by placing them within the outline of the intact whole bone taken from a radiograph of the opposite side. Alternatively, cutouts of these individual fragments can be assembled over line drawings of the anatomic axis of the appropriate bone. A composite tracing is then made of the whole bone, showing all reduced fracture lines. Radiographs used in planning should be taken with the x-ray tube at 1 m from the subject. Under these conditions, images on the radiograph represent a 10% magnification of the real dimensions of the bone. Templates are available carrying an outline of certain plates with the same 10% magnification. These templates can be used with the composite bone drawings to create a blueprint showing the optimal position of the implants. Once completed, this blueprint serves as an important reference during the surgery to guide proper placement of the plate and screws.

REDUCTION

The choice of reduction method also depends on the quality of bone, fracture pattern and location, and extent of associated soft tissue injury. A constant goal in fracture surgery is the preservation of bone viability by minimization of surgical trauma to periosseous muscle and fascial attachments that provide vascular supply to bone. Because these tissues are connected to the bone fragments, the application of longitudinal tension results in alignment of the fragments. The surgeon must decide whether traction will be applied manually by an assistant, by the use of a fracture table or a distractor, or through a plate by the indirect reduction technique. If a fracture table or distractor is used, the exact placement of traction or fixation pins must be chosen. If open reduction is planned, the surgeon should consider which special forceps and clamps will be necessary to achieve and provisionally hold the reduction. The surgeon must also decide whether an image intensifier or serial radiographs will be necessary to guide the reduction and implant insertion.

SURGICAL APPROACH

The fixation and reduction methods chosen, the anatomy of the fractured part, and the condition of the overlying skin and muscle envelope must be considered when deciding the surgical approach. Review of descriptions of standard surgical approaches and practice of these in cadaver dissection improve the surgeon's ability to perform the surgery. The need for special retractors and other instruments must be considered based on the patient's size and the specific surgical approach.

POSITIONING, DRAPING, AND SPECIAL EQUIPMENT

Decisions regarding fixation, reduction, and surgical approach dictate patient positioning and draping. The surgeon should consider whether a pneumatic tourniquet will be used. In contrast, the expectation of large blood loss may indicate the need for a Cell Saver and a specific order of packed cells and other blood components. The surgeon should consider the need for special intraoperative monitoring of such indicators as somatosensory evoked potentials.

PERIOPERATIVE MANAGEMENT

Medical conditions that require intervention before surgery may be disclosed through the patient's history and physical examination. Drugs such as steroids and anticoagulants should be discontinued or adjusted accordingly. A decision must be made regarding use of parenteral antibiotics, including the schedule of administration. The use of an epidural catheter for postoperative pain management should be determined preoperatively to allow patient and family education and consultation with the anesthesiology department.

PRIORITIZATION IN POLYTRAUMA

The presence of multiple injuries to several organ systems and different areas of the skeleton requiring a variety of procedures demands an organized approach to examination, decision making, and implementation. Surgical teams should work simultaneously on different areas of the body to shorten the total anesthesia time. The general surgeon and anesthesiologist should oversee and coordinate the total patient care during resuscitation and initial surgical intervention. The orthopaedic surgeon plays an important role in this early treatment period, and the preoperative plan should be communicated to other specialists with primary responsibility for the patient.

Summary

Collectively, these considerations constitute preoperative planning. By proceeding through these categories sequentially, the necessary decision making can be accomplished in a logical manner. This allows the surgeon to present a more organized explanation to the patient and family, operating room staff, and colleagues. Exact requirements for the operating table, instruments, implants, associated devices, table positioning, draping, and medications can then be transmitted to the operating room staff and anesthesiologists. The blueprints created during the planning phase can be hung on the x-ray view box during the actual procedure to orient the entire surgical team. Effective planning and successful surgery are best accomplished through a clear understanding of the principles of internal fixation.

Acknowledgment

Preparation of this manuscript would have been impossible to complete without the support provided by the residents in the Department of Orthopaedic Surgery, University of Connecticut Health Center. Their experience and encouragement are extremely appreciated. The authors also thank the office staff for their diligence and cooperation.

REFERENCES

1. Ansell, R.; Scales, J. A study of some fractures which affect the strength of screws and their insertion and holding power in bone. J Biomech 1:279–302, 1968.
2. Asnis, S.; Kyle, R., eds. Cannulated Screw Fixation: Principles and Operative Techniques. New York, Springer Verlag, 1996.
3. Baumgart, F.W.; Morikawa, C.K.; Morikawa, S.M.; et al. AO/ASIF Self-Tapping Screws (STS). Davos, Switzerland, AO/ASIF Research Institute, 1993.
4. Beaupre, G.S. Airport detectors of modern orthopaedic implant metal. Comment. Clin Orthop 303:291–292, 1994.
5. Bennett, A.; Harvey, W. Prostaglandins in orthopaedics. Editorial. J Bone Joint Surg Br 63:152, 1981.
6. Black, J. Orthopaedic Biomaterials in Research and Practice. New York, Churchill Livingstone, 1988.
7. Bone, L.B.; Johnson, K.D. Treatment of tibial shaft fractures by reaming and intramedullary nailing. J Bone Joint Surg Am 68:877–887, 1986.
8. Bronzino, J. The Biomedical Engineering Handbook. Hartford, CT, CRC Press, 1995.
9. Brooks, D.B.; Burstein, A.H.; Frankel, V.H. The biomechanics of torsional fractures: The stress concentration effect of a drill hole. J Bone Joint Surg Am 52:507–514, 1970.
10. Brown G.; Winquist, R.A. Personal communication, 1996.
11. Browner, B.D. The Grosse-Kempf locking nail. Contemp Orthop 8:17–25, 1984.
12. Browner, B.D.; Boyle, M.; Morvant, R.; Smith, T.K. Grosse-Kempf nailing of unstable femoral fractures: The initial North American experience. Orthopaedic transactions of American Orthopaedic Association. J Bone Joint Surg Am 8:405, 1984.
13. Browner, B.D.; Wiss, D.A. The Grosse-Kempf locking nail for the femur. In: Browner, B.D.; Edwards, C.C., eds. The Science and Practice of Intramedullary Nailing. Philadelphia, Lea & Febiger, 1987, pp. 233–252.
14. Brumback, R.J.; Uwagie-Ero, S.; Lakatos, R.P.; et al. Intramedullary nailing of femoral shaft fractures, part II: Fracture healing with static interlocking fixation. J Bone Joint Surg Am 70:1453, 1988.
15. Brunner, C.F.; Weber, B.G. Special Techniques in Internal Fixation. New York, Springer Verlag, 1982.
16. Brunner, C.F.; Weber, B.G. Internal fixation plates with a specialized form and function. In: Brunner, C.F.; Weber, B.B.; eds. Special Techniques in Internal Fixation. New York, Springer Verlag, 1982, pp. 151–152.
17. Bucholz, R.W.; Ross, S.E.; Lawrence, K.L. Fatigue fracture of the interlocking nail in the treatment of fractures of the distal part of the femoral shaft. J Bone Joint Surg Am 69:1391, 1987.
18. Burstein, A.H.; Currey, J.; Frankel, V.; et al. Bone strength. J Bone Joint Surg Am 54:1143, 1972.
19. Canalis, E. Effect of growth factors on bone cell replication and differentiation. Clin Orthop 193:246, 1985.
20. Chang, C.C.; Merritt, K. Infection at the site of implanted materials with and without preadhered bacteria. J Orthop Res 12:526–531, 1994.
21. Chapman, M.W. The role of intramedullary nailing in fracture management. In: Browner, B.D.; Edwards, C.C., eds. The Science and Practice of Intramedullary Nailing. Philadelphia, Lea & Febiger, 1987, pp. 17–24.
22. Charnley, J. The Closed Treatment of Common Fractures, 3rd ed. New York, Churchill Livingstone, 1961.
23. Clawson, D.K.; Smith R.F.; Hansen, S.T. Closed intramedullary nailing of the femur. J Bone Joint Surg Am 53:681, 1971.
24. Cobelli, N.J.; Sadler, A.H. Ender rod versus compression screw fixation of hip fractures. Clin Orthop 201:123–129, 1985.
25. Cross, A.; Montgomery, R.J. The treatment of tibial shaft fractures by the locking medullary nail system. J Bone Joint Surg Br 69:489, 1987.
26. Delmi, M.; Vaudaux, P.; Lew, D.P.; Vasey, H. Role of fibronectin in staphylococcal adhesion to metallic surfaces used as models of orthopaedic devices. J Orthop Res 12:432–438, 1994.
27. Elder, S.; Frankenburg, E.; Goulet J.; et al. Biomechanical evaluation of calcium phosphate cement-augmentation fixation of unstable intertrochanteric fractures. J Orthop Trauma 14(6):386–393, 2000.
28. Ellerbe, D.M.K.; Frodel, J.L. Comparison of implant materials used in maxillofacial rigid internal fixation. Otolaryngol Clin North Am 28:2, 1995.
29. Eppley, B.C.; Spartis, C.; Herman, I. Effects of skeletal fixation on craniofacial imaging. J Craniofac Surg 4:67–73, 1993.
30. Esser, M.P.; Kassab, J.V.; Jones, D.H. Trochanteric fractures of the femur: A randomised prospective trial comparing the Jewett nailplate with the dynamic hip screw. J Bone Joint Surg Br 68:557–560, 1986.
31. Frankel, V.H.; Burstein, A.H. Orthopaedic Biomechanics. Philadelphia, Lea & Febiger, 1970.
32. Frost, H.M. Bone Remodeling Dynamics. Springfield, IL, Charles C Thomas, 1963.
33. Gautier, F. Belastungsveran derung des knochens durch platterosteosynthese. Dissertation. Bern, Switzerland, 1988.
34. Goodship, A.E.; Kelly, D.J.; Rigby, H.S.; et al. The effect of different regimes of axial micromovement on the healing of experimental tibial fractures. Trans Orthop 11:285, 1987.
35. Haas, N.; Kretteck, C.; Schandelmaier, P.; et al. A new solid unreamed tibial nail for shaft fractures with severe soft tissue injury. Injury 24:49–54, 1993.
36. Hansen, S.T. The type IIIC tibial fracture. J Bone Joint Surg Am 69:799–800, 1987.
37. Hansen, S.T.; Veith, R.G. Closed Küntscher nailing of the tibia. In: Browner, B.D.; Edwards, C.C., eds. The Science and Practice of Intramedullary Nailing. Philadelphia, Lea & Febiger, 1987, pp. 267–280.
38. Harrington, KD. The use of methylmethacrylate as an adjunct in the internal fixation of unstable comminuted intertrochanteric fractures in osteoporotic patients. J Bone Joint Surg Am 57:744–750, 1975.
39. Hauschka, P.V.; Chen, T.L.; Mavrakos, A.E. Polypeptide growth factors in bone matrix. In: Cell and Molecular Biology of Vertebrate Hard Tissue. CIBA Foundation Symposium 136. New York, John Wiley & Sons, 1988, pp. 207–225.
40. Hearn, T.C.; Schatzker, J.; Wolfson, N. Extraction strength of cannulated cancellous bone screws. J Orthop Trauma 7:138–141, 1993.
41. Jacob, C.H.; Berry, J.T. A study of the bone machining process—Drilling. J Biomech 9:343, 1976.
42. Jacobs, R.R.; Armstrong, J.H.; Whittaker, J.H.; Pazell, J. Treatment of intertrochanteric hip fractures with a compression hip screw and a nail plate. J Trauma 16:599, 1976.
43. Johnson, K.D.; Johnston, D.W.C.; Parker, B. Comminuted femoral shaft fractures: Treatment by roller traction, cerclage wires and an intramedullary nail, or an interlocking intramedullary nail. J Bone Joint Surg Am 66:1222–1235, 1984.

44. Kaufer, H. Mechanics of the injured hip. Clin Orthop 146:53–61, 1980.

45. Küntscher, G. Praxis der Marknagelung. Stuttgart, Germany, Schattauer, 1962.

46. Kellam, J.F. Early results of the Sunnybrook experience with locked intramedullary nailing. Orthopedics 8:1387–1388, 1985.

47. Kempf, I.; Grosse, A.; Beck, G. Closed locked intramedullary nailing: Its application to comminuted fractures of the femur. J Bone Joint Surg Am 67:709, 1985.

48. Kempf, I.; Grosse, A.; Lafforgned, L. L'enclouage avec blocage de la rotation on "clou blogue" principles, technique, indications et premiers resultants. Communication a la journée d'hiver. Sofcot, 1976.

49. Kempf, I.; Grosse, A.; Lafforgue D. L'apport due verrouillage dans l'enclouage centromidullaire, des os longs. Rev Clin Orthop 64:635–651, 1978.

50. Kenwright, J.; Goodship, A.E. Controlled mechanical stimulation in the treatment of tibial fractures. Clin Orthop 241:36, 1989.

51. Kinast, C.; Bolhofner, B.R.; Mast, J.W.; Ganz, R. Subtrochanteric fractures of the femur. Clin Orthop 238:122–130, 1989.

52. Klaue, K.; Perren, S.M.; Kowalski, M. Internal fixation with a self-compressing plate and lag screw: Improvements of the plate hole and screw design. 1. Mechanical investigations. J Orthop Trauma 5:280, 1991. Original work: Klaue, K.; Frigg, R.; Perren, S.M. Die entlastung der osteosyntheseplatte durch interfragmentare plattenzugschraube. Helv Chir Acta 52:19–23, 1985.

53. Klaue, H.; Perren, S.M. Fixation interne des fractures pas lensemble plaque: Vis a compression conjuguée (DVC). Helv Chir Acta 49:77–80, 1982.

54. Klemm, K.W.; Borner, M. Interlocking nailing of complex fractures of the femur and tibia. Clin Orthop 212:89, 1986.

55. Klemm, K.W.; Schellman, W. Dynamische und statische Verriegelung des Marknagels. Unfallheilkunde 75:568, 1972.

56. Kolodziej, P.; Lee, F.S.; Ashish, P.; et al. The Biomechanical Evaluation of the Schuhli Nut. Detroit, Wayne State University, 1992.

57. Leggon, R.; Lindsey, R.W.; Doherty, B.J.; et al. The holding strength of cannulated screws compared with solid core screws in cortical and cancellous bone. J Orthop Trauma 7:450, 1993.

58. Levin, P.E.; Schoen, R.W.; Browner, B.D. Radiation exposure to the surgeon during closed interlocking intramedullary nailing. J Bone Joint Surg Am 69:761, 1987.

59. MacMillan, M.; Gross, R.H. A simplified technique of distal femoral screw insertion for the Grosse-Kempf interlocking nail. Clin Orthop 226:252, 1988.

60. Mast, J.; Jakob, R.; Ganz, R. Planning and Reduction Technique in Fracture Surgery. New York, Springer Verlag, 1989.

61. Matelic, T.M.; Monroe, M.T.; Mast, J.W. The use of endosteal substitution in the treatment of recalcitrant nonunions of the femur: Report of seven cases. J Orthop Trauma 10:1–6, 1996.

62. Matter, P.; Holzach, P. Behandlungsergebnisse von 221 Unterschenkel-Osteosynthesen mit schmalen dynamischen Kompressionsplatten (DCP) aus Stahl oder Titan. Unfallheilkunde 80:195–196, 1977.

63. McKibbin, B. The biology of fracture healing in long bones. J Bone Joint Surg Br 60:150, 1978.

64. Mears, J. Materials and Orthopaedic Surgery. Baltimore, Williams & Wilkins, 1979.

65. Medoff, R.J. Insertion of distal screws in interlocking nail fixation of femoral shaft fractures. J Bone Joint Surg Am 68:1275–1277, 1986.

66. Modny, M.T. The perforated cruciate intramedullary nail: Preliminary report of its use in geriatric patients. J Am Geriatr Soc 1:579, 1953.

67. Muller, M.E.; Allgöwer, M.; Schneider, R.; Willenegger, H. Manual of Internal Fixation: Techniques Recommended by the AOASIF Group. New York, Springer Verlag, 1995. Corrected 3rd printing.

68. Muller, M.E.; Allgöwer, M.; Schneider, R.; Willenegger, H. Manual of Internal Fixation, 2nd ed. New York, Springer Verlag, 1979.

69. Olerud, S. The effect of intramedullary reaming. In: Browner, B.D.; Edwards, C.C., eds. The Science and Practice of Intramedullary Nailing. Philadelphia, Lea & Febiger, 1987, pp. 71–74.

70. Palmer, S.H.; Hanley, R.; Willett, K. The use of interlocked "customized" blade plates in the treatment of metaphyseal fractures in patients with poor bone stock. Injury 31(3): 187–191, 2000.

71. Pascal, A.; Tsukayama, D.T.; Wicklund, B.H.; et al. The effect of stainless steel, cobalt-chromium, titanium alloy, and titanium on the respiratory burst activity of human polymorphonuclear leukocytes. Clin Orthop 280:281–287, 1992.

72. Pauwels, F. Der Schenkelhalsbruch, ein Mechanisches Problem. Stuttgart, Germany, Enke, 1935.

73. Pauwels, F. Gessammelte Abhandlungen zur Funktionellen Anatomie des Bewegungsapparates. Berlin, Springer Verlag, 1965.

74. Pawluk, R.J.; Musso, E.; Tzitzikalakis, G.I. The effects of internal fixation techniques on alternating plate screw strain distributions. Orthop Trans 9:294, 1985.

75. Perren, S.M. The concept of biological plating using the limited contact-dynamic compression plate (LCDCP): Scientific background, design and application. Injury 22(Suppl 1):1–41, 1991.

76. Perren, S.M.; Russenberger, M.; Steinemann, S.; et al. A dynamic compression plate. Acta Orthop Scand Suppl 125:31–41, 1969.

77. Pohler, O. Unpublished study conducted at Strauman Metallurgical Research Institute, Switzerland. In: AO/ASIF Drill Bits. Synthes Update Bulletin No. 87–2. Paoli, PA, Synthes USA, 1987.

78. Postlethwaite, K.R.; Philips, J.G.; Booths, M.D. The effects of small plate osteosynthesis on postoperative radiotherapy. Br J Oral Maxillofac Surg 27:375–378, 1989.

79. Rhinelander, F.W.; Wilson, J.W. Blood supply to developing, mature and healing bone. In: Sumner-Smith, G., ed. Bone in Clinical Orthopedics: A Study in Comparative Osteology. Philadelphia, W.B. Saunders, 1982, pp. 81–158.

80. Ring, D.; Perey, B.H.; Jupiter, J.B. The functional outcome of preoperative treatment of ununited fractures of the humeral diaphysis in older patients. J Bone Joint Surg Am 81:177–190, 1999.

81. Russel, T.A.; Taylor, J.C.; Lavelle, D.G.; et al. Mechanical characterization of femoral interlocking intramedullary nailing systems. J Orthop Trauma 5:332–340, 1991.

82. Schaffer, J.J.; Manoli, A. The antiglide plate for distal fibular fixation. J Bone Joint Surg Am 69:596, 1987.

83. Schenk, R.; Willenegger, H. Zur histologie der primaren knockenheilung. Langenbecks Arch Klin Chir 308:440, 1964.

84. Schweber, L. Experimentelle untersuchungen von knochertransplantation vit unvermdeter und mit denaturierter mochengrandsubstat. Hefte Unfallheilhd 103:1–70, 1976.

85. Sherk, H.H.; Foster, M.D. Hip fractures: Condylocephalic rod versus compression screw. Clin Orthop 192:255–259, 1985.

86. Skjeldal, S.; Backe, S. Interlocking medullary nails: Radiation doses in distal targeting. Arch Orthop Trauma Surg 106:179, 1987.

87. Tarr, R.R.; Wiss, D.A. The mechanics and biology of intramedullary fracture fixation. Clin Orthop 212:10–17, 1986.

88. Tencer, A.F.; Asnis, S.E.; Harrington, R.M.; et al. Biomechanics of cannulated and noncannulated screws. In: Asnis, S.E.; Kyle, R.F., eds. Cannulated Screw Fixation: Principles and Operative Techniques. New York, Springer Verlag, 1997.

89. Tencer, A.F.; Sherman, M.C.; Johnson, K.D. Biomechanical factors affecting fracture stability and femoral bursting in closed intramedullary rod fixation of femur fractures. J Biomech Eng 107:104–111, 1985.

90. Thoresen, B.O.; Alho, A.; Ekeland, A.; et al. Interlocking intramedullary nailing in femoral shaft fractures: A report of forty-eight cases. J Bone Joint Surg Am 67:1313, 1985.

91. Tsai, C.L.; Liu, T.H.; Hung, M.H. Glycocalyx products and adherence of staphylococcus to biomaterials. Acta Med Okayama 46:11–16, 1992.

92. Tscherne, H.; Gotzen, L. Fractures with Soft Tissue Injuries. New York, Springer Verlag, 1984.

93. Velazco, A.; Whitesides, T.E.; Fleming, L.L. Open fractures of the tibia treated with the Lottes nail. J Bone Joint Surg Am 65:879–885, 1983.

94. Von Arx, C. Schubebertragung durch reiburg bei der plattenosteosynthese. Dissertation. Basel, Switzerland, 1973.

95. Vresilovic, E.J.; Spindler, K.P.; Robertson, W.W.; et al. Failures of pin removal after in situ pinning of slipped capital femoral epiphyses: A comparison of different pin types. J Pediatr Orthop 10:764–768, 1990.

96. Wagner, H. Die Einbettung der metallschrauben in Knocher und die Heilungsvorgänge des Knochergewebes unter dem Einfluss der Stabilen Osteosynthese. Langenbecks Arch Klin Chir 305:28–40, 1963.

97. Werry, D.G.; Boyle, M.R.; Meck, R.N.; Loomer, R.L. Intramedullary fixation of tibial shaft fractures with AO and Grosse-Kempf locking nails: A review of 70 consecutive patients. J Bone Joint Surg Br 67:325, 1985.

98. Winquist, R.A.; Hansen, S.T. Segmental fractures of the femur treated by closed intramedullary nailing. J Bone Joint Surg Am 60:934, 1978.

99. Wiss, D.A.; Fleming, C.H.; Matta, J.M.; Clark, D. Comminuted and rotationally unstable fractures of the femur treated with an interlocking nail. Clin Orthop 212:35, 1986.

100. Wolf, J.W.; White, A.A., III; Panjabi, M.M.; Southwick, W.O. Comparison of cyclic loading versus constant compression in the treatment of long bone fracture in rabbits. J Bone Joint Surg Am 63:805–810, 1981.

101. Zinghi, G.F.; Specchia, L.; Montanari, G.; Bruscoli, R. The Grosse-Kempf locked nail in the treatment of diaphyseal and meta diaphyseal fractures of the tibia. Ital J Orthop Traumatol 12:365, 1986.

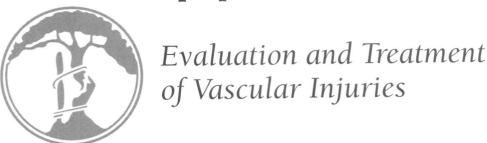

Evaluation and Treatment of Vascular Injuries

David V. Feliciano, M.D.

Recognition of a possible vascular injury is a critical skill for any orthopaedic surgeon. This is true whether the surgeon's primary area of practice is the emergency or urgent procedures associated with orthopaedic trauma or elective reconstruction. When injured patients present with fractures of long bones, the pelvis, or spine; dislocations adjacent to major vessels; or severely contused or crushed extremities, loss of limb or life can occur if recognition of the associated vascular trauma is delayed.[19] In an elective practice, many orthopaedic operative procedures occur in proximity to major vessels, where an iatrogenic injury may result in loss of limb or life.

HISTORY

Although vascular repairs in the extremities were first performed more than 225 years ago, progress in this area was limited until the early part of the 20th century. From 1904 to 1906, Alexis Carrel and Charles C. Guthrie at the Johns Hopkins Hospital and others developed standard vascular operative techniques, including repair of the lateral arterial wall, end-to-end anastomosis, and insertion of venous interposition grafts.[15, 16, 52, 56, 86] Early attempts at operative repair included those by V. Soubbotitch in the Balkan Wars from 1911 to 1913, by British and German surgeons in World War I, and by R. Weglowski during the Polish-Russian War of 1920.[89, 106, 140] Despite the availability of these techniques, it was not until the latter part of World War II that renewed attempts were made to perform peripheral arterial repair rather than ligation.[25] Before that time, the delays in medical care for casualties, the lack of antibiotics, and the significant incidence of late infection in injured soft tissues of the extremities contributed to an operative approach dominated by ligation.

With the more rapid transfer of casualties to field hospitals, the availability of type-specific blood for transfusion, the introduction of antibiotics, and the increased use of the autogenous saphenous vein as a vascular conduit, vascular repairs were performed frequently in the later stages of the Korean War and routinely throughout the Vietnam War.[65, 122] More recently, civilian trauma surgeons have treated large numbers of patients with peripheral vascular injuries, many associated with orthopaedic trauma, and they have been able to build on the techniques for repair of traumatic vascular injuries described originally by military surgeons.[21, 40, 42, 43, 93]

ETIOLOGY

In urban trauma centers, peripheral vascular injuries are most commonly caused by low-velocity missile wounds from handguns. For example, gunshot wounds were a cause of 54.5% and 75.5% of all vascular injuries in the lower extremities in two retrospective reviews from such centers.[42, 92] In contrast, stab wounds account for most of the civilian peripheral vascular injuries in countries in which firearms are more difficult to obtain.[124]

Vascular injuries from blunt orthopaedic trauma, such as fractures, dislocations, contusions, crush injuries, and traction (Fig. 11–1), account for only 5% to 30% of injuries being treated (Table 11–1).* In particular, vascular injuries associated with long bone fractures in otherwise healthy young trauma patients are rare. The reported incidence of injuries to the superficial femoral artery in association with a fracture of the femur has ranged from 0.4% to 1.9% in large series.[79] Injuries to the popliteal artery, tibioperoneal trunk, or trifurcation vessels occur in only 1.5% to 2.8% of all tibial fractures. When open fractures of the tibia are reviewed separately, the incidence of arterial injuries is approximately 10%.[17] With dislocations of the knee joint, the incidence of injuries to the popliteal artery requiring surgical repair has been 16% to 19% in recent large series[77, 101, 152] (Table 11–2). These figures are significantly lower than those reported in the

---

*See references 1, 2, 12, 17, 22, 30, 43, 47, 51, 55, 59, 60, 64, 66, 76, 77, 79, 82, 83, 93, 101, 103, 111, 112, 114, 118, 121, 126, 127, 133, 143–145, 148, 150, 152, 157, 158.

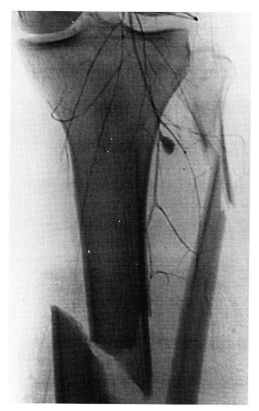

FIGURE 11–1. Pseudoaneurysm of left tibioperoneal trunk in patient with adjacent fracture in the fibula and midshaft fracture of the tibia.

past for posterior dislocations of the knee and presumably reflect, in part, the current nonoperative approach to nonocclusive lesions (i.e., intimal defect, narrowing) of the popliteal artery.[77, 101, 152]

As previously noted, there are also well-documented associations between certain elective and emergency orthopaedic operative procedures and arterial injuries (Table 11–3) (Fig. 11–2).* Some of these may be noted during surgery or in the early postoperative period (e.g., occlusion of the iliac artery during total hip arthroplasty), whereas others may appear weeks or months later (e.g., ruptured pseudoaneurysm of a tibial artery).

LOCATIONS AND TYPES OF VASCULAR INJURIES

The brachial artery and vein in the upper extremity and the superficial femoral artery and vein in the lower extremity are the most commonly injured vessels in both civilian and military reports, in which penetrating wounds predominate.[93, 122] This can be explained by the length of these vessels in the extremities and by the fact that direct compression controls hemorrhage, so that few patients exsanguinate before arrival in the emergency center.

*See references 23, 31, 46, 63, 67, 69, 70, 74, 75, 87, 94, 116, 130, 146, 149, 154.

TABLE 11–1

Arterial Injuries Associated with Fractures and Dislocations

Fracture or Dislocation	Artery Injured
UPPER EXTREMITY	
Fracture of clavicle or first rib	Subclavian artery
Anterior dislocation of shoulder	Axillary artery
Fracture of neck of humerus	Axillary artery
Fracture of shaft or supracondylar area of humerus	Brachial artery
Dislocation of elbow	Brachial artery
LOWER EXTREMITY	
Fracture of shaft of femur	Superficial femoral artery
Fracture of supracondylar area of femur	Popliteal artery
Dislocation of the knee	Popliteal artery
Fracture of proximal tibia or fibula	Popliteal artery, tibioperoneal trunk, tibial artery, or peroneal artery
Fracture of distal tibia or fibula	Tibial or peroneal artery
SKULL, FACE, CERVICAL SPINE	
Basilar skull fracture involving sphenoid or petrous bone	Internal carotid artery
Le Fort II or III fracture	Internal carotid artery
Cervical spine, especially foramen transversarium	Vertebral artery
THORACIC SPINE	Descending thoracic aorta
LUMBAR SPINE	Abdominal aorta
PELVIS	
Anterior-posterior compression	Thoracic aorta
Subtypes of pelvic fractures	Internal iliac, superior gluteal, or inferior gluteal artery
Acetabular fracture	External iliac, superior gluteal, or femoral artery

TABLE 11–2 ....

Popliteal Arterial Injuries Associated with Dislocations of the Knee

Author, Year	Dislocations	+ Arteriogram	Operation Needed
Treiman et al. 1992[152]	115*	27 (23%)	22 (19%)
Kendall et al. 1993[77]	37†	—	6 (16%)
Miranda et al. 2000[101]	35	7 (20%)	6 (17%)

....

*Only patients with an intact pulse or pulse deficit (but not pulseless with cold extremity) are included.
†Arteriograms not performed in all patients with overt symptoms.

Because of the low incidence of injuries to these vessels from blunt trauma, orthopaedic services most commonly encounter occlusions and occasional lacerations of the popliteal, tibioperoneal, tibial, or peroneal arteries from dislocations of the knee or severe fractures of the femur or tibia.[66, 83, 112, 114, 133]

Intimal flaps, disruptions, or subintimal hematomas, spasm, complete wall defects with pseudoaneurysms or hemorrhage, complete transections, and arteriovenous fistulas are five accepted types of vascular injuries. Intimal defects and subintimal hematomas with possible secondary occlusion continue to be most commonly associated with blunt trauma, whereas wall defects, complete transections, and arteriovenous fistulas are usually seen after penetrating wounds. Spasm can occur after either blunt or penetrating trauma to an extremity.

DIAGNOSIS
....

History and Physical Examination

Patients sustaining peripheral arterial injuries usually have hard or soft signs of injury.[139] Examples of hard signs of arterial injury include any of the classic signs of arterial occlusion (pulselessness, pallor, paresthesias, pain, paralysis, poikilothermia), massive bleeding, a rapidly expanding hematoma, and a palpable thrill or audible bruit over a hematoma.[134] In patients with impending limb loss from arterial occlusion or significant external bleeding from an extremity, immediate surgery without preliminary arteriography of the injured extremity is justified. If a hard sign is present but localization of the defect is necessary before the incision is performed, a rapid duplex ultrasound study, formal arteriogram in a radiology suite, or surgeon-performed arteriogram in the emergency center or operating room should be obtained[109, 110] (Fig. 11–3).

Soft signs of an arterial injury include a history of arterial bleeding at the scene or in transit, proximity of a penetrating wound or blunt injury to an artery in the extremity, a small, nonpulsatile hematoma over an artery in an extremity, and a neurologic deficit originating in a nerve adjacent to a named artery. These patients still have an arterial pulse at the wrist or foot on physical examination or with use of the Doppler device. The incidence of arterial injuries in such patients ranges from 3% to 25%, depending on which soft sign or combination of soft signs is present.[28, 110, 120] Most, but not all, of these arterial injuries can be managed without surgery because

TABLE 11–3 ....

Acute or Delayed Arterial Injuries Associated with Orthopaedic Operative Procedures

Orthopaedic Procedure	Artery Injured
UPPER EXTREMITY	
Clavicular compression plate/screw	Subclavian artery
Anterior approach to shoulder	Axillary artery
Closed reduction humeral fracture	Brachial artery
LOWER EXTREMITY	
Total hip arthroplasty	Common or external iliac artery
Nail or nail-plate fixation of intertrochanteric or subtrochanteric hip fracture	Profunda femoris artery
Subtrochanteric osteotomy	Profunda femoris artery
Total knee arthroplasty	Popliteal artery
Anterior or posterior cruciate ligament reconstruction	Popliteal artery
External fixator pin	Superficial femoral, profunda femoris, popliteal, or tibial arteries
SPINE	
Anterior spinal fusion	Abdominal aorta
Lumbar spine fixation device	Abdominal aorta
Resection of nucleus pulposus	Right common iliac artery and vein, inferior vena cava
PELVIS	
Posterior internal fixation of pelvic fracture	Superior gluteal artery
Excision of posterior iliac crest for bone graft	Superior gluteal artery

....

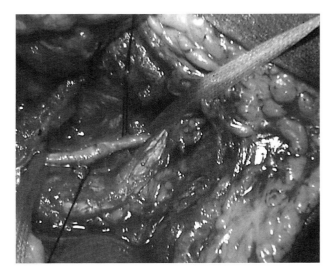

FIGURE 11–2. Occlusion of the left popliteal artery secondary to injury from orthopaedic drill. A below-knee amputation was necessary because of a delay in diagnosis.

they are small and, by definition, allow for continuing distal perfusion. In some centers, serial physical examinations, alone, are used to monitor distal pulses, and no arteriogram is performed to document the magnitude of a possible arterial injury. This approach has been safe

and accurate in asymptomatic patients with penetrating wounds to an extremity in proximity to a major artery.[28] Its accuracy with the higher kinetic energy injuries associated with blunt fractures or dislocations, particularly dislocations of the knee, has been similar.[101] Observation is appropriate only with complete and continuing out-of-hospital follow-up.[28, 34, 101] When there is a concern about a distal pulse deficit, inability to properly examine for distal arterial pulses, or a combination of soft signs of an arterial injury in an extremity, either duplex ultrasound or formal arteriography is indicated (to be discussed).

Beyond the obvious hard or soft signs of vascular injury, physical examination of the injured extremity includes observation of the position in which the extremity is held, the presence of any obvious deformity of a long bone or joint, the presence or absence of an open wound or bony crepitus, the skin color of the distal extremity compared with that of the opposite side (in light-skinned persons), the time required for skin capillary refill in the distal digits, and a complete motor and sensory exam. In the lower extremity, the mobility of the knee joint should be carefully assessed as well. Increased laxity of the supporting ligaments suggests that a dislocation of the knee joint from the original trauma has spontaneously reduced (Fig. 11–4). Because of the previously noted association between posterior and other dislocations of the knee and injury to the popliteal artery, immediate arteriography is indicated if pedal pulses are diminished or absent after reduction.[77, 101, 152] Recent studies suggest that rou-

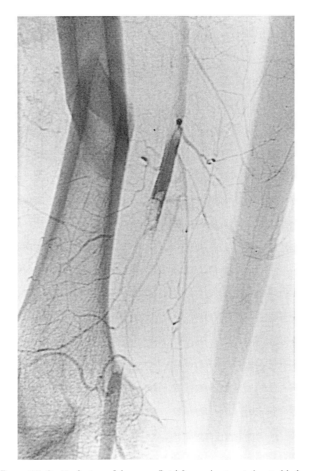

FIGURE 11–3. Occlusion of the superficial femoral artery is located below the site of the oblique fracture of the femur.

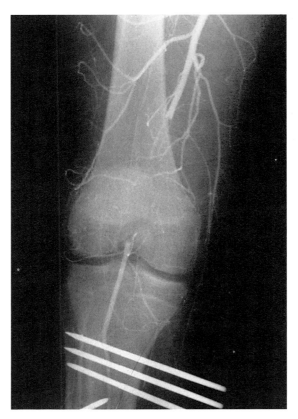

FIGURE 11–4. Occlusion of the right popliteal artery was missed for 48 hours because spontaneous reduction of a knee dislocation occurred before arrival in the emergency center.

tine arteriography is not indicated if normal pulses are present after spontaneous or orthopaedic reduction of a knee dislocation, though not all agree with this approach.[49, 77, 101, 152]

If the exact vascular status of the distal extremity is unclear after restoration of reasonable alignment or reduction of a dislocation, a Doppler flow detector should be applied to the area of absent pulses in the distal extremity for audible assessment of blood flow. The Doppler flow detector also can be used to compare systolic blood pressure measurements in an uninjured upper extremity with those in the injured upper or lower extremity.[4] An arterial pressure index (API) defined as the Doppler systolic pressure in the injured extremity divided by that in the uninjured arm is then calculated.[73, 88] In a study by Lynch and Johansen in which clinical outcome was the standard, an API lower than 0.90 had a sensitivity of 95%, specificity of 97.5%, and accuracy of 97% in predicting an arterial injury.[88]

Radiologic Studies

A noninvasive diagnosis can be made with use of duplex or color duplex ultrasonography in the emergency center, operating room, or surgical intensive care unit (Table 11–4). Duplex ultrasonography, a combination of real-time B-mode ultrasound imaging and pulsed Doppler flow detection, has been used extensively in preoperative screening for acute or chronic occlusive vascular problems.[128] Color duplex imaging adds a color representation of the pulsed Doppler flow detection. In recent years, duplex or color duplex ultrasound has been used to evaluate patients with possible or suspected arterial or venous injuries in the extremities.[10, 50, 78, 81, 98, 131] Accuracy in detection of arterial injuries, using comparison arteriography as the gold standard, has ranged from 96% to 100% in several studies.[10, 78]

Percutaneous arteriography performed in the emergency center or in the operating room by the surgical team is infrequently used in most major trauma centers; several urban trauma centers, however, have extensive experience with the technique.[68, 109, 110] A thin-walled 18-gauge Cournand-style disposable needle is inserted either proximal to the area of suspected injury (e.g., in the common femoral artery for evaluation of the superficial femoral artery) or distal to it (e.g., in retrograde evaluation of the axillary or subclavian arteries above a blood pressure cuff inflated to 300 mm Hg). A rapid hand injection of 35 mL of 60% diatrizoate meglumine dye is administered, and an anteroposterior radiographic view is taken. Extensive experience has suggested that two separate injections and radiographic views may be necessary with this simple technique to allow for clear visualization of injuries to distal vessels such as the tibial and peroneal arteries. The timing for exposure of the x-ray film under the patient's extremity depends on which artery is to be evaluated. Proper evaluation of the tibial and peroneal arteries in the patient with a complex fracture of the tibia mandates that exposure not take place until 4 to 5 seconds after the injection of dye into the common femoral artery. The plane of the film is often changed before the second injection to examine the area in question more thoroughly. False-negative and false-positive results are rare when the technique is performed on a daily basis by experienced practitioners.[110] If a patient presents with severe combined intracranial or truncal trauma and possible peripheral arterial lesions related to orthopaedic injuries, life-threatening injuries should be treated first, followed by percutaneous intraoperative arteriography of the involved extremity.

Percutaneous arteriography performed in a radiology suite by the interventional radiologist is the most commonly used invasive diagnostic technique in patients with suspected vascular injuries. Multiple sequential views of areas of suspected arterial injury can be obtained at differing intervals after injection of the dye.[113] The accuracy of this multiple-view technique has been demonstrated in many studies, although false-negative results have occurred.[113] The disadvantages of the technique are the delays in diagnosis when on-call technicians must return to the hospital and the cost of modern equipment.

Digital subtraction arteriography or aortography is the most common technique used to evaluate patients with possible arterial injuries, as it has an accuracy similar to that of conventional arteriography.[138] Because of its convenience, speed, and economy, compared with conventional arteriography or aortography, the technique has been advocated as the initial imaging procedure for evaluation of patients with possible peripheral vascular injuries.

Venography is rarely performed in major trauma centers, because the sequelae of missed peripheral venous injuries such as venous thromboses or pseudoaneurysms are rare. In recent years, color duplex ultrasonography has been used to evaluate veins of the extremities after penetrating trauma.[50] Some centers choose to explore large peripheral hematomas after penetrating wounds without preliminary venography, even if arteriography results are normal, and to observe small, nonexpanding hematomas.

TABLE 11–4 ....

Diagnostic Techniques for Evaluating Possible
Vascular Injuries

Cerebrovascular

Duplex ultrasound
Color flow ultrasound
Selective carotid arteriography
CT or MRI arteriography

Thoracic Vascular

Spiral CT
Transesophageal echocardiography
Digital subtraction aortography
Standard aortography

Peripheral Vascular

Arterial pressure index
Duplex ultrasound/color flow ultrasound
Emergency center or operating room arteriography by surgeon
Digital subtraction arteriography
Standard arteriography

....

MANAGEMENT OF VASCULAR INJURIES

The Emergency Center

The primary goal of the surgeon in the emergency center is to control hemorrhage in the patient with an extensive injury to the extremity. This is usually accomplished by direct compression with a finger (remembering the aphorism that no vessel outside the human trunk is larger than the human thumb) or by application of a pressure dressing to the area of injury. If neither of these maneuvers controls hemorrhage, a blood pressure cuff is placed proximal to the area of injury and inflated to a pressure greater than the systolic blood pressure. With hemorrhage under temporary control, the patient is transferred to the operating room for definitive vascular repair or ligation.

In a patient with pulses that are questionably palpable or audible by Doppler flow detection distal to a long bone fracture or a dislocation in an extremity, immediate reduction and splinting or application of a traction device should be performed. This relieves compression or kinking, but not spasm, in the adjacent artery. If such a maneuver restores only diminished distal pulses in comparison with the uninjured contralateral extremity, the API should be measured if the bony or ligamentous injury is in the proximal extremity. If an API cannot be obtained because of a distal injury, if the API is lower than 0.90, or if distal pulses are absent after reduction, immediate arteriography is mandatory. In children, because examination of the peripheral vascular system is difficult, arteriography should be used liberally whenever fractures are present and distal arterial pulses are questionably palpable.[47]

Nonoperative Treatment of Arterial Injuries

If an arteriogram shows occlusion of only one major vessel below the elbow or knee when there is not a severely injured or mangled extremity, viability of the distal extremity is rarely compromised, and some centers choose to observe the patient in this situation. Because there can be retrograde flow into an area of arterial injury beyond the proximal occlusion, a repeat arteriogram should be performed within 3 to 7 days to rule out delayed formation of a traumatic false aneurysm.

Several clinical studies have demonstrated that the nonocclusive arterial injuries (e.g., spasm, intimal flap, subintimal or intramural hematoma) that often are detected in patients undergoing arteriography for soft signs of injury heal without operation in 87% to 95% of cases.[27, 48, 141] Careful arteriographic follow-up is necessary in patients who are observed. Even small traumatic false aneurysms have been noted to heal on follow-up arteriograms in some of these patients.[144] Not all centers agree with this approach, and progression of these seemingly benign lesions has been documented in one report.[153]

Therapeutic Embolization

Isolated traumatic aneurysms of branches of the axillary, brachial, superficial femoral, or popliteal arteries, of the profunda femoris artery, or of one of the named arteries in the shank can be treated by therapeutic embolization instead of operation.[9, 32, 96, 142] Although such an approach has been used primarily in patients with penetrating wounds to the extremities, it is appropriate in selected patients with blunt vascular injuries, as well.[32] Patients with injuries to the arteries listed who will especially benefit from therapeutic embolization include those with multisystem injuries, closed fractures, or late diagnosis of a traumatic aneurysm following orthopaedic reconstruction. Contained aneurysms or active hemorrhage from muscular branches is treated with embolization using an absorbable gelatin sponge. When there is a need to occlude a tibial or peroneal artery proximal to a traumatic aneurysm, embolization coils are used.[113]

Endovascular Stents

Balloon-expandable intraluminal arterial stents are now used routinely in patients with atherosclerotic occlusive disease.[155] A limited experience has been reported in patients with penetrating arterial injuries, as well.[91, 159] In patients with orthopaedic injuries, preliminary reports have described the use of endovascular stents in the axillary artery, renal artery, and aortoiliac arterial system.[3, 5, 90, 156] For the treatment of intimal dissection, a angiographic catheter is placed across the area of injury via a sheath in the common femoral artery. This catheter is then exchanged for a separate catheter-mounted balloon inflatable endovascular stent. Finally, the collapsed stent is expanded using a balloon catheter. When a traumatic aneurysm is to be treated, the mesh stent is expanded in place followed by trans-mesh injection of microcoils to induce thrombosis of the blood in the aneurysmal sac.[5] Endovascular stents are most appropriate when arterial flow must be maintained in the same groups as described for therapeutic embolization.

The Operating Room

ARTERIAL REPAIR

If the history, physical examination, and, if needed, duplex ultrasound or arteriogram strongly suggest or document the presence of an arterial injury, the patient is given intravenous antibiotics before being moved to the operating room. During the move, all open wounds are covered with sterile gauze soaked in saline or saline-antibiotic solution. Also, all fractured or dislocated extremities are maintained in a neutral position by splinting or traction.

Skin Preparation and Draping

In the operating room, an operative tourniquet can be applied in place of the blood pressure cuff for control of hemorrhage from injuries in the distal extremity. If the injuries are in the proximal extremity and exsanguinating hemorrhage resumes after removal of finger compression, a compression dressing, or a proximal blood pressure cuff, the surgeon should put on sterile operative gloves immediately. The surgeon then applies direct compression to a large wound with the hands or inserts the fingers into an open fracture site or the entrance and exit sites of a penetrating wound to control hemorrhage as preparation of the skin and draping are performed.

Because of the possibility of an associated vascular lesion in all patients with orthopaedic injuries in an extremity, preparation of the skin and draping should encompass all potential areas of proximal and distal vascular control. Also, one or both lower extremities should be prepared and draped to allow for possible retrieval of the greater saphenous vein in case an interposition graft is required for the vascular repair. It is often helpful to have one entire uninjured lower extremity prepared and draped to the toenails, so that the greater saphenous vein may be retrieved from either the groin or the ankle. It is also helpful to drape the hand or foot of the affected extremity in a sterile plastic bag, so that color changes can be noted in light-skinned patients and distal pulses can be palpated under sterile conditions after arterial repair has been completed. The remainder of the extremity, including the area of the incision, is then covered with an orthopaedic-type stockinette.

Incisions

In patients with peripheral vascular injuries, the skin incision should be generous enough to allow for comfortable proximal and distal vascular control. To this end, it is often best for the inexperienced trauma surgeon to use the most extensive incisions.

There are a number of classic incisions for the management of peripheral vascular injuries. Those used in the upper extremity include the following: (1) supraclavicular incision, with or without resection of the clavicle, for injuries in the second or third portion of the subclavian artery; (2) infraclavicular incision for the first or second portion of the axillary artery; (3) infraclavicular incision curving onto the medial aspect of the upper arm for the third portion of the axillary artery or proximal brachial artery; (4) medial upper arm incision between the biceps and the triceps muscles for the main portion of the brachial artery; and (5) S-shaped incision from medial to lateral across the antecubital crease for the brachial artery proximal to its bifurcation. An injury to the radial or ulnar artery is usually approached by a longitudinal incision directly over the site.

In the lower extremity, the preferred incisions for arterial repair are the following: (1) longitudinal groin incision for injury to the common femoral artery, proximal superficial femoral artery, or profunda femoris artery; (2) anteromedial thigh incision for exposure of the superficial femoral artery throughout the thigh; and (3) medial popliteal incision for exposure of the proximal, middle, or distal portions of the popliteal artery. Injuries to the anterior tibial artery are approached directly over the site of injury in the anterior compartment, whereas the posterior tibial artery is approached through a medial incision that often requires transection of the fibers of the soleus muscle. Finally, the peroneal artery is approached through a lateral incision and requires excision of a portion of the fibula for proper exposure.

Standard Techniques of Arterial Repair

After the skin incision is made proximally and distally to the bleeding site or area of hematoma, dry skin towels are placed to cover all remaining skin edges if a plastic adherent drape has not been applied. If hemorrhage can be controlled by finger or laparotomy pad compression applied by an assistant, proximal and distal vascular control is usually obtained before the area of injury is entered. Not dissecting far enough proximally and distally from an area of injury is a common error. It is frequently necessary for the inexperienced vascular trauma surgeon to move proximal and distal vascular occlusion clamps or loops repeatedly as débridement of the injured artery is extended back to noninjured arterial intima.

In a patient with an extensive hematoma overlying the arterial injury, it can be difficult to obtain proximal and distal vascular control close enough to the injury to prevent backbleeding from collateral vessels. In addition, there are patients in whom external hemorrhage cannot readily be controlled during meticulous dissection. Therefore, if dissection is proceeding extremely slowly through a very large hematoma or the assistant can no longer maintain control of exsanguinating hemorrhage by direct compression, the hematoma or site of hemorrhage should be entered directly. The site of arterial bleeding is visualized and then compressed with a finger or vascular forceps, and a proximal vascular clamp or vessel loop is applied. The dissection is then completed starting from the center rather than waiting for proximal and distal control to be obtained at a distance from the hematoma or bleeding site.

After vascular control is obtained in either classic or rapid fashion, vascular occlusion can be maintained by application of small, angled, vascular clamps (such as those found in an angioaccess tray), bulldog vascular clamps, Silastic vessel loops, or umbilical tapes. Occasionally, with complex arterial injuries at bifurcations, vascular control of major branches can be obtained by passage of an intraluminal Fogarty balloon catheter or a calibrated Garrett dilator.

In general, lateral arteriorrhaphy (or venorrhaphy) with 5-0 or 6-0 polypropylene sutures placed transversely is used for small lacerations or for small puncture, pellet, or missile wounds, especially in the smaller vessels of the extremities. If a transverse repair results in significant narrowing of the injured vessel, patch angioplasty is a useful alternative. Any segment of injured vein that has been resected or a piece of autogenous saphenous vein from the ankle or groin of an uninjured lower extremity can be used to create an oval patch to increase the size of the lumen of an injured vessel. The patch is usually sewn in place with 6-0 polypropylene suture.

Resection of injured peripheral vessels is often required in patients with blunt orthopaedic trauma because of the magnitude of the forces applied to cause both bony and vascular injuries. An increasing number of vascular injuries from penetrating wounds also require resection of the injured segment because of the greater wounding power of firearms now available in the United States.

Resection with an end-to-end anastomosis is performed whenever a segment of a vessel demonstrates extensive destruction of the wall, a long area of disrupted intima (e.g., from blunt traction injury), or through-and-through injury from a penetrating wound. Despite the elasticity of peripheral vessels in the typical young trauma patient, many collateral vessels must be ligated for an end-to-end anastomosis to be performed if more than 2 to 3 cm of the vessel is resected. An end-to-end anastomosis sewn under tension results in an hourglass appearance at the suture line and often leads to thrombosis of the repair in the postoperative period. Although an interrupted suture technique for end-to-end anastomosis is routinely used in growing children, continuous suture techniques can be used by experienced trauma surgeons for small vessels of the extremities (4 to 5 mm diameter) in adults.[36, 38]

If exposure is difficult, as in the axillary artery near the clavicle or the popliteal artery behind the knee joint, it is often helpful to perform the first third of the posterior anastomosis with an open technique (i.e., one in which no knot is tied). This allows for precise suture bites of the posterior walls and prevents leaks after arterial inflow is restored. On completion of the posterior third of the anastomosis, the two ends of the suture are pulled tight, drawing the two ends of the artery together.

Both ends of the artery are then stabilized, and Fogarty embolectomy catheters are passed proximally and distally to remove any thrombotic or embolic material from the arterial tree. The amount of debris distal to an arterial injury can be extensive, especially after a prolonged period of preoperative occlusion. After both ends of the vessel have been cleared, 15 to 20 mL of regional heparin (50 U/mL) is injected into each end and the vascular clamps are reapplied. Injection of a total of 30 to 40 mL of this solution (1500 to 2000 U or 15 to 20 mg heparin) provides significantly less than the 1 to 2 mg/kg of heparin used in many elective vascular procedures. More aggressive systemic heparinization is usually avoided in trauma patients because of the risk of hemorrhage from other injuries.

The end-to-end anastomosis is completed by running the two ends of the suture along the two sides of the approximated artery, leaving the last few loops of suture loose to allow for flushing before final tying. The proximal vascular occlusion clamp is first removed and reapplied after completion of flushing. The distal vascular clamp is then removed to allow for flushing from the distal end of the vessel and to clear any residual air underneath the suture line. As blood from the distal arterial tree fills the area that was between the two clamps or loops, the two suture ends are pulled up tightly and tied. The proximal arterial clamp is not released until the first knot is in place. If small suture hole leaks are present at that time, topical hemostatic agents can be applied temporarily.

If an end-to-end anastomosis cannot be performed with minimal tension, a substitute vascular conduit should be inserted into the defect between the two débrided ends of the injured vessel. An autogenous reversed saphenous vein graft from an uninjured lower extremity remains the conduit of choice for most peripheral vascular injuries.[42, 95, 102] If the vessel to be replaced has a small lumen (4 to 5 mm), the greater saphenous vein at the medial malleolus is a good choice. If the artery or vein to be replaced has a much larger lumen, the greater saphenous vein in the proximal thigh is a better choice. Major advantages of the autogenous saphenous vein include its ready availability, the superiority of natural tissue in maintaining patency, and a long record of success in vascular and cardiac surgery. The patency of the saphenous vein graft can be improved by using gentle dissection, by avoiding overdistention during flushing, and by using only heparinized autologous blood containing papaverine for flushing.

If a saphenous vein graft is to be inserted, it is often helpful to perform the more difficult distal anastomosis first. Because of the floppy nature of a collapsed saphenous vein graft, it is useful to place two 6-0 polypropylene sutures 180° apart at the two corners of the anastomosis. Another option is to use the classic trifurcation technique originally described by Carrel in 1907.[16] After anastomosis of the graft to the distal end of the artery has been completed, a Garrett dilator can be passed through it to ensure adequate luminal size. The proximal anastomosis is then performed. As with simple end-to-end anastomosis, passage of a Fogarty catheter, injection of heparinized saline solution, and flushing should be performed before completion of the second anastomosis (Fig. 11–5).

If the saphenous vein is surgically absent, injured bilaterally, too small, or of an inappropriate size to fit into the injured vessel, or if the patient is critically injured and the speed of repair is important, many trauma centers use polytetrafluoroethylene (PTFE) grafts for interposition.[43, 135] The early complication and infection rates with the use of PTFE prostheses appear to be the same as those with saphenous vein grafts, but long-term patency is less. If a PTFE graft is to be used, it is best to cut it to an appropriate length with a number 11 scalpel blade rather than a pair of scissors. The rigid, open nature of PTFE allows for rapid performance of an arterial anastomosis, and no fixation sutures are needed. The passage of a Fogarty catheter and regional heparinization are performed as previously described. Laboratory and clinical studies have demonstrated that neointimal hyperplasia occurs at PTFE-artery suture lines, and patients in whom such a graft is placed are started on aspirin by rectal suppository every 12 hours while in the intensive care unit.[53, 57] One aspirin orally every 12 hours is continued for the first 3 postoperative months in the absence of a history of gastric or duodenal ulcers.

Bypass grafting can be applied in selected circumstances of extensive vascular injuries. For example, if ligation around an area of injury is required to prevent exsanguinating hemorrhage, a saphenous vein bypass graft can then be inserted in an end-to-side fashion proximally and distally instead of an interposition graft.

Extra-anatomic bypass grafting is used when extensive injury to soft tissues in the antecubital, groin, or below-knee area is accompanied by injuries to the brachial, femoral, popliteal, or tibioperoneal vessels. In such instances, vigorous débridement of the wound is carried out at the first operation, and the extra-anatomic saphenous vein conduit is inserted around the wound underneath healthy soft tissue, with both end-to-end anastomoses also covered by such tissue (Fig. 11–6).[39] Care of the wound is made easier with this approach, and

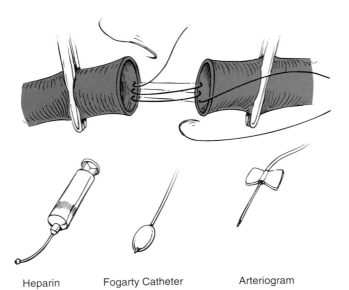

Heparin   Fogarty Catheter   Arteriogram

FIGURE 11–5. Fine points in peripheral arterial repair include use of small vascular clamps or Silastic vessel loops, open anastomosis technique, regional heparinization, passage of a Fogarty catheter proximally and distally, and arteriography on completion. (Courtesy of Baylor College of Medicine, 1981.)

TABLE 11–5
Techniques of Vascular Repair

Lateral arteriorrhaphy or venorrhaphy
Patch angioplasty
Panel or spiral vein graft
Resection of injured segment
   End-to-end anastomosis
   Interposition graft
      Autogenous vein
      Polytetrafluoroethylene
      Dacron
Bypass graft
  In situ
   Extra-anatomic
Ligation

the danger of suture line blowout is decreased by use of the extra-anatomic bypass through noninjured tissue.

Ligation is reserved for injury to the distal profunda femoris artery in the thigh or to main arteries below the elbow or knee when at least one other named vessel to the hand or foot is still patent and there is not a severely injured or mangled extremity. The technique is used in patients with a coagulopathy and in those who are so unstable that the operation must be terminated. See Table 11–5 for a list of all repair techniques.

Completion Arteriography

After arterial inflow has been restored, distal pulses should be present. In the upper extremity, palpation of normal distal pulses is usually acceptable evidence of a satisfactory arterial repair, because distal thrombosis is rare unless a tight arterial tourniquet was in place for several hours preoperatively. Most experienced trauma surgeons, however, use completion arteriography after an end-to-end anastomosis or insertion of an interposition graft of any type in the lower extremity. This is done to rule out technical mishaps at the one or two suture lines and

problems such as distal embolism or in situ thrombosis in the small vessels of the shank. It is helpful to place a small metal tissue clip near any anastomosis, so that it can be localized precisely on the arteriogram. This enables the surgeon to distinguish a narrowed anastomosis from a mark produced by a vascular clamp.

Operative arteriography is easily performed after insertion of a 20-gauge Teflon-over-metal catheter into the artery. Usually, the artery is punctured proximal to the repair, and the Teflon catheter is slipped over the needle into the lumen of the artery. It is particularly useful to stabilize the artery with vascular forceps as the anterior wall of the artery is entered. This maneuver usually prevents posterior perforation of the artery, which commonly occurs when metal or larger arteriography needles or catheters are inserted into an unstable artery. The Teflon catheter is attached by a short piece of intravenous extension tubing to a 50-mL syringe filled with heparinized saline solution. This is injected through the Teflon catheter before arteriography to ensure proper catheter placement in the lumen. Free return of pulsatile blood into the plastic tubing confirms the position of the catheter. The extremity is aligned in an anteroposterior direction over the film cassette. An excellent operative arteriogram can usually be obtained by exposing the film as the last several milliliters of a 35-mL bolus of 60% diatrizoate meglumine dye are injected rapidly (Fig. 11–7).[36] If the lower extremity is allowed to rotate externally during arteriography, the overlying bone may obscure the arterial repair in certain areas around and below the knee joint.

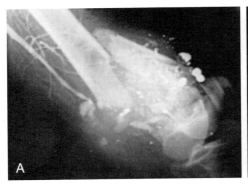

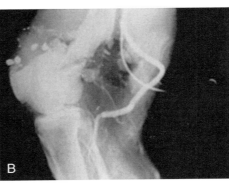

FIGURE 11–6. *A*, The shotgun wound that disrupted the distal femur also avulsed the popliteal artery, as seen on the arteriogram. *B*, An extra-anatomic saphenous vein bypass graft inserted around the posterior aspect of the knee joint is shown on the completion arteriogram. (*B*, From Feliciano, D.V.; Accola, K.D.; Burch, M.J.; et al. Am J Surg 158:506, 1989.)

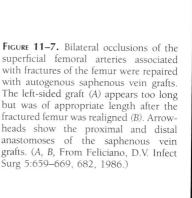

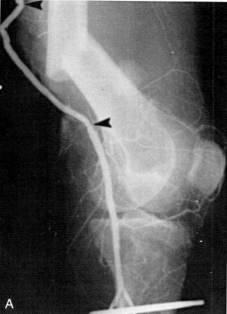

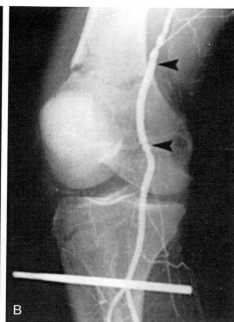

FIGURE 11–7. Bilateral occlusions of the superficial femoral arteries associated with fractures of the femur were repaired with autogenous saphenous vein grafts. The left-sided graft (A) appears too long but was of appropriate length after the fractured femur was realigned (B). Arrowheads show the proximal and distal anastomoses of the saphenous vein grafts. (A, B, From Feliciano, D.V. Infect Surg 5:659–669, 682, 1986.)

After arteriography has been completed, a syringe containing heparinized saline solution is attached to the extension tubing and the artery is flushed with the solution. The Teflon arteriography catheter is not removed until the arteriogram has been returned and is noted to be of satisfactory quality. If the completion arteriogram is satisfactory, a small **U**-stitch of 6-0 polypropylene suture is placed around the Teflon catheter and tied down tightly as the catheter is removed.

If a technical problem such as an intimal flap, a thrombus at the site of anastomosis, or a distal embolus is present on the completion arteriogram, the arterial repair is opened and the problem is corrected. If distal spasm is present but arterial flow to the foot or hand is adequate, no further therapy is required, because spasm usually resolves within 4 to 6 hours. If the spasm is severe and distal flow is compromised, measurement of the below elbow or knee compartment pressures to rule out a compartment syndrome is worthwhile.

VENOUS INJURIES

Venous occlusion or ligation in the groin has a significant adverse effect on femoral arterial inflow.[6, 62] For this reason, and because of the known adverse effect of popliteal venous ligation on viability of the leg, there is more effort to perform venous repair rather than ligation in the modern trauma center.[108, 115, 123, 137] Of interest, follow-up venography after extremity venorrhaphy has documented that more than 20% of simple venous repairs and almost 60% of interposition grafts inserted for venous repair are temporarily occluded in the postoperative period. Fortunately, many of these recanalize over time.[108, 137] And, therefore, the consensus is that venous injuries in the groin or popliteal area should be repaired if the patient is stable and has no life-threatening intraoperative complications such as hypothermia or a transfusion-

induced coagulopathy. If the patient is unstable or has a life-threatening complication that could be aggravated by prolonging general anesthesia, venous ligation should be performed. Although this issue is continually debated, the long-term sequelae of venous ligation in young victims of civilian trauma appear to be less than those originally reported from the Vietnam experience.[11, 104, 151]

Venous injuries are often difficult to manage because of hemorrhage from the large lumen, the fragile nature of the wall, and the many small branches. Excessive manipulation of the injured vein often leads to further hemorrhage. It is helpful to use finger or spongestick compression around the area of perforation for vascular control, rather than to attempt application of vascular clamps to all branches feeding the area of injury. After the area of injury has been isolated, lateral venorrhaphy remains the most common technique of repair for peripheral venous injuries. Occasionally, a more complex repair such as patch venoplasty, resection with end-to-end anastomosis, or resection with insertion of some type of substitute conduit is necessary. The principles of repair for major venous injuries are similar to those for arterial injuries, except that Fogarty catheters are not passed and completion venograms are not obtained.

If resection of an injured segment of a peripheral vein is required, ligation of local collateral vessels is necessary to allow for the performance of an end-to-end anastomosis with only modest tension. If a substitute vascular conduit is required to replace a segmental injury in a critical vein (e.g., popliteal, distal superficial femoral), the surgeon must choose from a variety of less satisfactory alternatives. An autogenous saphenous vein graft from an uninjured lower extremity would appear to be an ideal conduit. The diameter of the greater saphenous vein in the groin, however, is too small to match the size of the proximal superficial femoral or common femoral vein in the lower extremity or the axillary or subclavian vein in the upper extremity. Such a small conduit in a much larger vein would be patent for only a short time.

Two other choices for replacement of an injured vein with autogenous tissue involve the creation of a spiral vein graft or a panel graft. The spiral vein graft is created by opening the harvested autogenous saphenous vein from an uninjured lower extremity over its entire length, wrapping it around a rigid tubular structure such as a thoracostomy tube in a spiral fashion, and sewing the edges together to create a tube of a larger luminal diameter. Construction of a spiral vein graft is time-consuming and cannot be justified for routine use in peripheral venous injuries in light of its 50% patency rate.[115] In extraordinary circumstances, such as impending loss of the distal lower extremity from ligation of the popliteal vein, it must be considered. A panel graft is created by longitudinally opening two separate segments of autogenous saphenous vein from an uninjured lower extremity, placing one on top of the other, and sewing the two edges together to create one tubular structure of a larger luminal diameter. Again, this technique is time-consuming and is rarely justified in the repair of peripheral venous injuries. If the surgeon is willing to insert a temporary venous conduit, an externally supported PTFE graft can be placed into large luminal veins of a proximal extremity. These grafts are available in appropriate sizes, but they remain patent for only 2 to 3 weeks if the type without external support is used.[43] If an externally supported PTFE graft is inserted, there is long-term patency for months and, possibly, years. To encourage dilatation of collateral veins during the period of slow occlusion of an unsupported PTFE graft, it is mandatory to keep the injured extremity elevated and to place elastic wraps around the extremity while the patient is in the hospital.

INDICATIONS FOR FASCIOTOMY

The diagnosis of a compartmental syndrome and techniques of fasciotomy are discussed in Chapter 12.

COMBINED ORTHOPAEDIC-VASCULAR INJURIES

There has been much discussion about the preferred order of repair: orthopaedic stabilization followed by arterial repair or the reverse.[2, 30, 55, 64, 83, 157] A number of authors have emphasized the need for early arterial repair to limit

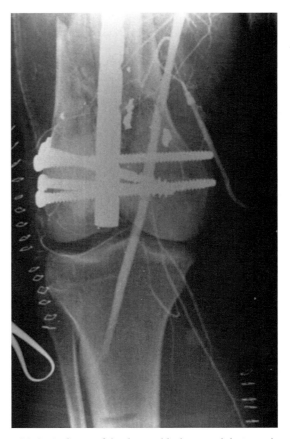

Figure 11–8. Occlusion of distal arterial bed occurred during orthopaedic manipulation *following* graft repair of the right popliteal artery. The patient eventually needed an above-knee amputation.

distal ischemia and lessen the risk of in situ thrombosis.[38, 64] Others have noted that early orthopaedic repair stabilizes the extremity and improves exposure of the vascular injury. This approach also lowers the risk of thrombosis in a recently completed vascular repair during subsequent manipulation to reduce a fracture (Fig. 11–8).[66] With either approach, the ultimate amputation rate is substantial (Table 11–6).

In a patient with neither cold ischemia (pulseless without capillary refill) nor a prolonged period of warm ischemia (capillary refill present), the choice of arterial or orthopaedic repair depends primarily on the stability of

Table 11–6

Amputation Rates with Combined Orthopaedic-Vascular Injuries in an Extremity

Author, Year	Fracture or Dislocation	Amputation Rate
Weaver et al. 1984[157]	Femur, knee, tibia	36%
Gustilo et al. 1984[55]	Humerus, femur, knee, tibia	42%
Lange et al. 1985[83]	Tibia	61%
Howe et al. 1987[64]	Femur, tibia	43%
Caudle et al. 1987[17]	Tibia	78%
Drost et al. 1989[30]	Femur, tibia	36%
Alexander et al. 1991[2]	Femur, tibia	28%
		46% (mean)

the fracture site. If the area of the fracture is reasonably stable and the trauma team is experienced in rapid vascular repair, it is appropriate to perform the arterial repair first. If the fracture is comminuted and the extremity cannot be stabilized for proper exposure of the vascular injury, the orthopaedic repair is performed first. In trauma centers with extensive experience in the management of combined injuries in the extremities, consultation among attending surgeons, fellows, or senior residents is mandatory and allows for proper sequencing of repairs.

In a patient with a cold, pulseless hand or foot and little or no capillary refill or a patient who has undergone a prolonged period of either cold or warm ischemia, restoration of arterial inflow has the highest priority and should be accomplished by formal repair or by the insertion of a temporary intraluminal vascular shunt. Formal arterial repair is preferred if the extremity is reasonably stable despite the presence of a fracture. If an unstable fracture that precludes appropriate exposure of the vascular injury is present, shunts are inserted to allow for continued arterial inflow and venous outflow during the period of orthopaedic stabilization.

TEMPORARY INTRALUMINAL VASCULAR SHUNTS

A shunt is defined as an intraluminal plastic conduit for temporary maintenance of arterial inflow or venous outflow, or both, to or from a body part. First described for use in peripheral arterial injuries in 1971, there has been a significant increase in the use of these devices in trauma centers over the past 20 years.[20, 24, 33, 71, 105, 107] At this time, suggested indications for use of shunts include the following: (1) combined orthopaedic-vascular injuries, including mangled extremities; (2) preservation of an amputated upper extremity at the arm, forearm, or wrist level before replantation; (3) rapid restoration of arterial inflow or venous outflow, or both, as part of a lifesaving peripheral or truncal "damage control" operation.

As described above, insertion of intraluminal shunts in a patient with a combined orthopaedic-vascular injury promptly restores arterial inflow or venous outflow, or both, and allows for appropriate orthopaedic stabilization, reconstruction, or débridement. A properly fixated shunt will withstand vigorous realignment maneuvers. When the orthopaedic operative procedure is completed, the trauma vascular surgeon can then choose one of two options. In the hemodynamically stable patient without intraoperative hypothermia, metabolic acidosis, or a coagulopathy, the shunts are removed and interposition vascular grafts are inserted under the same general anesthetic. When the injured patient is hemodynamically unstable with a body temperature lower than 35°C, a base deficit less than −10 to −15, or a coagulopathy, the original operative procedure is terminated. Removal of the shunts and vascular repairs are then performed at a reoperation in 24 to 48 hours. In patients with mangled extremities, this time delay will allow for combined consultation by orthopaedic and vascular surgeons and discussions with the patient and family.

The value of temporary intraluminal shunts to maintain viability in amputated parts of the upper extremity is obvious. Identification and tagging of nerves and tendons, débridement of crushed tissue, and orthopaedic stabilization can all be completed while the shunts are in place.

With improvements in prehospital emergency medical services in urban environments, more injured patients with near-exsanguination are admitted to the emergency center than in the past. The insertion of temporary intraluminal shunts in the vessels of the arm, antecubital area, groin, thigh, or knee adjacent to a fracture or dislocation will prevent the need for ligation in the injured patient with profound shock. Indications for peripheral (or truncal) "damage control" shunts are as follows: (1) body temperature lower than 34°C to 35°C (on admission or developing during operation), (2) arterial pH less than 7.2 or base deficit less than −15 in patients younger than 55 years of age or less than −6 in patients older than 55 years of age, and (3) intraoperative International Normalized Ratio or partial thromboplastin time greater than 50% of normal. Any trauma operative procedure is terminated whenever one of the listed abnormalities is present. Resuscitation including rewarming, hemodynamic monitoring, transfusion, use of inotropes, and correction of the coagulopathy is then performed in the surgical intensive care unit rather than the operating room. The third stage of damage control is the return to the operating room for definitive repairs when the patient's previous metabolic failure secondary to hypovolemic shock has been corrected.[44]

Intraluminal shunts are readily available in any operating room in which elective surgery on the carotid artery is performed. The range in size from 8-F to 14-F and are held in place with 2-0 silk ties compressing the end of the transected artery or vein onto the shunt. When a large shunt is needed for insertion into the popliteal, superficial femoral, or common femoral veins, standard thoracostomy tubes are used (Fig. 11–9).[45]

THE MANGLED EXTREMITY

A mangled extremity results from high-energy transfer or crushing trauma that causes some combination of injuries to artery, bone, soft tissue, tendon, and nerve. Approximately two thirds of such injuries are caused by motorcycle, motor vehicle, or vehicle-pedestrian accidents, reflecting the significant transfer of energy that occurs during such incidents.[26] Chapman has emphasized that the kinetic energy dissipated in collision with an automobile bumper at 20 mph (100,000 ft-lb) is 50 times greater than that from a high-velocity gunshot (2000 ft-lb).[18]

When a patient with a mangled extremity arrives in the emergency center, the trauma team must work its way through a series of decisions in patient care:

1. If the patient's life is in danger, should the mangled limb be amputated?
2. If the patient is stable, should an attempt be made to salvage the mangled limb?
3. If salvage is to be attempted, what is the sequence of repairs? (See previous section.)
4. If salvage fails, when should amputation be performed?

The most difficult decision is whether to attempt salvage of the limb. Since 1985, at least five separate

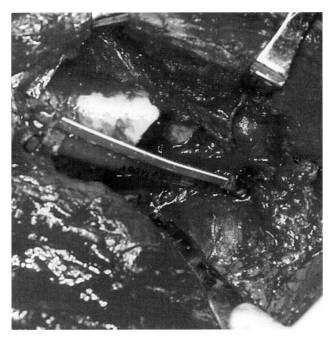

FIGURE 11–9. Patient with open fracture of the left femur from a crush injury had transection of the proximal popliteal artery and vein, also. A 14-F carotid artery shunt was placed into the popliteal artery, while a 24-F thoracostomy tube was placed into the popliteal vein. Because of intraoperative hypothermia, removal of shunts and insertion of interposition grafts was delayed for 18 hours.

scoring systems that describe the magnitude of injuries in a mangled extremity have been published[54, 64, 72, 129, 132] (Table 11–7). All attempt to predict the need for amputation based on a total score derived from the combination of injuries in the extremity and other factors. Only one system, the Mangled Extremity Severity Score developed by Johansen and co-workers,[61, 72] has been studied in a prospective manner. Also, the applicability of any of these systems outside the institutions in which they originated has been questioned.[13, 125]

Two major criteria are used most frequently in clinical decisions regarding immediate amputation versus attempted salvage. If either of the following factors is present, amputation is a better choice than prolonged attempts at salvage[58, 83]:

1. Loss of arterial inflow for longer than 6 hours, particularly in the presence of a crush injury that disrupts collateral vessels[83, 100]
2. Disruption of posterior tibial nerve[72, 82, 83]

Lange and associates[83] and Hansen[58] have described relative indications for immediate amputation in patients with Gustilo IIIC tibial fractures, as well. These include serious associated polytrauma, severe ipsilateral foot trauma, anticipated protracted course to obtain soft tissue coverage, and tibial reconstruction.[83] If two of these are present, immediate amputation is recommended, once again.[58, 83]

SOFT TISSUES

In patients with major peripheral vascular injuries and a transfusion-associated coagulopathy, extensive oozing often occurs in soft tissue as the operation is completed. In such patients, placement of closed or open drains into the blast cavity or area of dissection may be required for several hours postoperatively. The placement of drains prevents formation of a postoperative hematoma that could compress and possibly occlude the vascular repairs.

If a large blast cavity is present in soft tissue near the vascular repairs, some muscle or soft tissue should be sutured in a position that separates the two. A closed or open drain or open packing of the cavity exiting on the opposite side of the extremity from the skin incision and vascular repairs should then be inserted. This allows for drainage of the large blast cavity away from the vascular repairs and helps to avoid the problems of compression by hematoma and of cellulitis and late abscesses near a vascular repair.[37]

Occasionally, primary wound closure is undesirable in patients with extensive muscle hematomas, soft tissue edema, or a severe coagulopathy after a peripheral vascular repair. In such patients, porcine xenografts (pigskin) are placed over the vascular repairs and the wound is packed open with antibiotic-soaked gauze.[84, 85] After 24 hours of elevation of the injured extremity, the patient is returned to the operating room for delayed primary closure or closure with a myocutaneous flap performed by the plastic surgery service.[119]

HEROIC TECHNIQUES TO SAVE A LIMB

If vascular repair is satisfactory on the completion arteriogram but the distal extremity has borderline viability because of vascular spasm, extensive destruction of collateral vessels in soft tissue, or prolonged ischemia, various adjuncts for salvage should be considered. Included among these are sympathetic blocks or sympathectomy of the involved extremity,[160] proximal arterial infusion with a heparin-tolazoline-saline solution (con-

TABLE 11–7 ....

Scoring Systems for Mangled Extremities

Author, Year	Name	Number of Criteria
Gregory et al. 1985[54]	Mangled extremity syndrome index	9
Seiler et al. 1986[132]	—	4
Howe et al. 1987[64]	Predictive salvage index	4
Johansen et al. 1990[72]	Mangled extremity severity score	4
Russell et al. 1991[129]	Limb salvage index	7

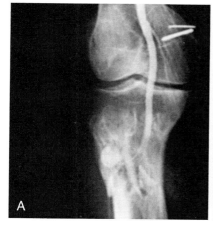
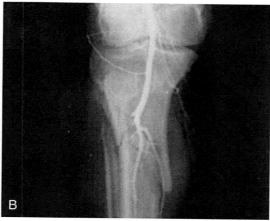

FIGURE 11–10. *A,* Traumatic false aneurysm of the anterior tibial artery related to fractures of the tibia and fibula. *B,* Completion arteriogram after operative ligation of the proximal anterior tibial artery.

taining 1000 U heparin and 500 mg tolazoline in 1000 mL saline) at a rate of 30 mL/hr,[29, 117] and venous infusion with low-molecular-weight dextran at a rate of 500 mL/12 hr.[36]

Postoperative Care

After the patient has been returned to the ward or intensive care unit, the injured extremity should be elevated and wrapped with elastic bandages if venous ligation was performed. Care must be taken to monitor intracompartmental pressure in such a situation as the combination of venous hypertension and external compression may create an early compartment syndrome. Distal arterial pulses are monitored by palpation or with a portable Doppler unit. Transcutaneous oxygen monitoring has also been used to document revascularization in injured limbs.[80] Intravenous antibiotics are continued for 24 hours if a primary repair or end-to-end anastomosis was performed. If a substitute vascular conduit was inserted, intravenous antibiotics are continued for 72 hours in some centers, much as in elective vascular surgery.

Complications

EARLY OCCLUSION OF ARTERIAL REPAIR

In-hospital occlusion of an arterial repair is almost always related to delayed presentation of the patient after injury, delayed diagnosis of the injury by a physician, a technical mishap in the operating room, or occlusion of venous outflow from the area of injury. In a patient with a delay in presentation or diagnosis, in situ distal arterial thrombosis may occur within 6 hours.[100] The passage of a Fogarty embolectomy catheter may not be helpful in such a situation, because it does not remove thrombi from arterial collateral vessels.

Technical mishaps at operation that lead to postoperative thrombosis of a repair include too much tension on an end-to-end anastomosis, failure to remove any thrombi or emboli in the distal arterial tree with a Fogarty embolectomy catheter, narrowing of a circumferential suture line, and failure to flush the proximal and distal arteries before final closure of the repair. Also, ligation or occlusion of a repair in the popliteal vein can lead to occlusion of an arterial repair at the same level.

If distal pulses disappear, the patient is returned immediately to the operating room for thrombectomy or embolectomy and revision of the repair as necessary. If there is not an obvious reason for occlusion of the arterial repair at a reoperation, standard coagulation tests are performed immediately to screen for a thrombotic disorder. Examples include heparin-associated thrombocytopenia, antithrombin III deficiency, deficiency of protein C or S, and the antiphospholipid syndrome.

DELAY IN DIAGNOSIS OF AN ARTERIAL INJURY

Occasionally, a patient presents with a traumatic false aneurysm or an arteriovenous fistula from a previous arterial injury that was not diagnosed.[41] The insertion of an endovascular stent with or without angiographic embolization is possible for many of these lesions, and it can be accomplished readily by an experienced interventional radiologist.[8, 113] If a major artery is involved, operative intervention using the principles described previously may be necessary (Fig. 11–10).

SOFT TISSUE INFECTION OVER AN ARTERIAL REPAIR

A dreaded complication of combined orthopaedic-vascular injuries, particularly in the lower extremity, is infection in the soft tissue overlying the arterial repair. If débridement of the soft tissue infection results in exposure of the arterial repair, one option is to attempt coverage of the arterial repair with a porcine xenograft and hope for the gradual growth of granulation tissue over the healthy artery. If the arterial repair starts to leak or suffers a blowout, the patient is returned to the operating room. The exposed portion of the artery is resected, and an extra-anatomic saphenous vein bypass graft is placed around the area of soft tissue infection, making sure that both end-to-end anastomoses are covered by healthy soft tissue outside the wound as described previously.[35, 39]

Another option is for immediate coverage with a local

muscle or myocutaneous rotation flap or for coverage with a free flap performed by the plastic surgery service.[119, 147]

LATE OCCLUSION OF ARTERIAL REPAIR

Because saphenous vein grafts placed in peripheral arteries undergo the degenerative changes of atherosclerosis over time, late occlusions of some of these grafts can be expected. Management is the same as if the patient had presented with occlusion of a primary artery—that is, arteriography is performed based on symptoms, and bypass grafting is chosen if runoff is adequate to support another graft.

CONCLUSION

Experience with peripheral arterial injuries in the absence of an associated bony injury documents that limb salvage is possible in almost all such patients without shotgun wounds or near amputations who are treated using the principles outlined in this chapter. These principles include early diagnosis by examination, preoperative arteriography or duplex ultrasonography, frequent use of interposition grafting for arterial repair, completion arteriography, repair of venous injuries in stable patients, and liberal use of fasciotomy.[36, 38, 39, 42, 43, 110] If bony injuries accompany arterial injuries, limb salvage is less likely because of delays in diagnosis, a greater magnitude of arterial injury, disruption of vascular collateral vessels in soft tissue, and associated postoperative problems such as infection in adjacent soft tissue or bone.[14, 54, 61, 64, 82, 83, 97, 132] Even so, limb salvage can be accomplished in most properly selected patients in modern trauma centers using the techniques described.[136]

REFERENCES

1. Abbott, W.M.; Darling, R.C. Axillary artery aneurysms secondary to crutch trauma. Am J Surg 125:515–519, 1973.
2. Alexander, J.J.; Piotrowski, J.J.; Graham, D.; et al. Outcome of complex vascular and orthopedic injuries of the lower extremity. Am J Surg 162:111–116, 1991.
3. Althaus, S.J.; Keskey, T.S.; Harker, C.P.; et al. Percutaneous placement of self-expanding stent for acute traumatic arterial injury. J Trauma 41:145–148, 1996.
4. Anderson, R.J.; Hobson, R.W., II; Lee, B.C.; et al. Reduced dependency on arteriography for penetrating extremity trauma: Influence of wound location and noninvasive vascular studies. J Trauma 30:1059–1065, 1990.
5. Babatasi, G.; Massetti, M.; Le Page, O.; et al. Endovascular treatment of a traumatic subclavian artery aneurysm. J Trauma 44:545–547, 1998.
6. Barcia, P.J.; Nelson, T.G.; Whelan, T.J., Jr.; et al. Importance of venous occlusion in arterial repair failure: An experimental study. Ann Surg 175:223–227, 1972.
7. Ben-Menachem, Y. Exploratory angiography and transcatheter embolization for control of arterial hemorrhage in patients with pelvic ring disruption. Tech Orthop 9:271–274, 1994.
8. Ben-Menachem, Y. Vascular injuries of the extremities: Hazards of unnecessary delays in diagnosis. Orthopedics 9:333–338, 1986.
9. Ben-Menachem, Y.; Handel, S.F.; Thaggard, A., III; et al. Therapeutic arterial embolization in trauma. J Trauma 19:944–952, 1979.
10. Bergstein, J.M.; Blair, J.F.; Edwards, J.; et al. Pitfalls in the use of color-flow duplex ultrasound for screening of suspected arterial injuries in penetrated extremities. J Trauma 33:395–402, 1992.
11. Bermudez, K.M.; Knudson, M.M.; Nelken, N.A.; et al. Long-term results of lower-extremity venous injuries. Arch Surg 132:963–968, 1997.
12. Biffl, W.L.; Moore, E.E.; Offner, P.J.; et al. Optimizing screening for blunt cerebrovascular injuries. Am J Surg 178:517–522, 1999.
13. Bonanni, F.; Rhodes, M.; Lucke, J.F. The futility of predictive scoring of mangled lower extremities. J Trauma 34:99–104, 1993.
14. Bondurant, F.J.; Cotler, H.B.; Buckle, R.; et al. The medical and economic impact of severely injured lower extremities. J Trauma 28:1270–1273, 1988.
15. Callow, A.D. Development of vascular surgery and medicine. In: Callow, A.D.; Ernst, C.B., eds. Vascular Surgery: Theory and Practice. Stamford, CT: Appleton & Lange, 1995, pp. xxiii–xxxv.
16. Carrel, A. The surgery of blood vessels. Johns Hopkins Hosp Bull 18:18–28, 1907.
17. Caudle, R.J.; Stern, P.J. Severe open fractures of the tibia. J Bone Joint Surg Am 69:801–807, 1987.
18. Chapman, M.W. Role of bone stability in open fractures. Instr Course Lect 31:75–87, 1982.
19. Cheng, S.L.; Rosati, C.; Waddell, J.P. Fatal hemorrhage caused by vascular injury associated with an acetabular fracture. J Trauma 38:208–209, 1995.
20. Chitwood, W.R., Jr.; Rankin, J.S.; Bollinger, R.R.; et al. Brachial artery reconstruction using the heparin-bonded Sundt shunt. Surgery 3:355–358, 1981.
21. Cooper, C.; Rodriguez, A.; Omert, L. Blunt vascular trauma. Curr Probl Surg 29:281–357, 1996.
22. Crawford, D.L.; Yuschak, J.V.; McCombs, P.R. Pseudoaneurysm of the brachial artery from blunt trauma. J Trauma 42:327–329, 1997.
23. Crowley, J.G.; Masterson, R. Popliteal arteriovenous fistula following meniscectomy. J Trauma 24:164–165, 1984.
24. Dawson, D.L.; Putnam, A.T.; Light, J.T.; et al. Temporary arterial shunts to maintain limb perfusion after arterial injury: An animal study. J Trauma 47:64–71, 1999.
25. DeBakey, M.E.; Simeone, F.C. Battle injuries of the arteries in World War II. An analysis of 2,471 cases. Ann Surg 123:534–579, 1946.
26. Dellinger, E.P.; Miller, S.D.; Wertz, M.J.; et al. Risk of infection after open fracture of the arm or leg. Arch Surg 123:1320–1327, 1987.
27. Dennis, J.W.; Frykberg, E.R.; Crump, J.M.; et al. New perspectives on the management of penetrating trauma in proximity to major limb arteries. J Vasc Surg 11:84–93, 1990.
28. Dennis, J.W.; Frykberg, E.R.; Veldenz, H.C.; et al. Validation of nonoperative management of occult vascular injuries and accuracy of physical examination alone in penetrating extremity trauma: 5- to 10-year follow-up. J Trauma 44:243–253, 1998.
29. Dickerman, R.M.; Gewertz, B.L.; Foley, D.W.; et al. Selective intra-arterial tolazoline infusion in peripheral arterial trauma. Surgery 81:605–609, 1977.
30. Drost, T.F.; Rosemurgy, A.S.; Proctor, D.; et al. Outcome of treatment of combined orthopedic and arterial trauma to the lower extremity. J Trauma 29:1331–1334, 1989.
31. Ebong, W.W. False aneurysm of the profunda femoris artery following internal fixation of an intertrochanteric femoral fracture. Injury 9:249–251, 1978.
32. Edwards, H.; Martin, E.; Nowygrod, R. Nonoperative management of a traumatic peroneal artery false aneurysm. J Trauma 22:323–326, 1982.
33. Eger, M.; Golcman, L.; Goldstein, A. The use of a temporary shunt in the management of arterial vascular injuries. Surg Gynecol Obstet 32:67–70, 1971.
34. Feliciano, D.V. Counterpoint. Editorial. J Trauma 32:553, 1992.
35. Feliciano, D.V. Management of infected grafts and graft blowout in vascular trauma patients. In: Flanigan D.P., ed. Civilian Vascular Trauma. Philadelphia, Lea & Febiger, 1992, pp. 447–455.
36. Feliciano, D.V. Managing peripheral vascular trauma. Infect Surg 5:659–669, 1986.
37. Feliciano, D.V. Vascular injuries. Adv Trauma 2:179–206, 1987.
38. Feliciano, D.V. Vascular trauma. In: Levine, B.A.; Copeland, E.M., III; Howard, R.J.; et al., eds. Current Practice of Surgery. New York, Churchill Livingstone, 1993, pp. 1–18.

39. Feliciano, D.V.; Accola, K.D.; Burch, M.J.; et al. Extra-anatomic bypass for peripheral arterial injuries. Am J Surg 158:506–510, 1989.

40. Feliciano, D.V.; Bitondo, C.G.; Mattox, K.L.; et al. Civilian trauma in the 1980s: A 1-year experience with 456 vascular and cardiac injuries. Ann Surg 199:717–724, 1984.

41. Feliciano, D.V.; Cruse, P.A.; Burch, J.M.; et al. Delayed diagnosis of arterial injuries. Am J Surg 154:579–584, 1987.

42. Feliciano, D.V.; Herskowitz, K.; O'Gorman, R.B.; et al. Management of vascular injuries in the lower extremities. J Trauma 28:319–328, 1988.

43. Feliciano, D.V.; Mattox, K.L.; Graham, J.M.; et al. Five-year experience with PTFE grafts in vascular wounds. J Trauma 25:71–81, 1985.

44. Feliciano, D.V.; Moore, E.E.; Mattox, K.L. Trauma damage control. In: Mattox, K.L.; Feliciano, D.V.; Moore, E.E., eds. Trauma, 4th ed. New York, McGraw-Hill, 2000, pp. 907–931.

45. Feliciano, D.V.; Rozycki, G.S.; Thourani, V.H.; et al. Changing indications for temporary intravascular shunts in peripheral vascular trauma. Publication pending, Am Surg.

46. Freischlag, J.A.; Sise, M.; Quinones-Baldrich, W.J.; et al. Vascular complications associated with orthopaedic procedures. Surg Gynecol Obstet 169:147–152, 1989.

47. Friedman, R.J.; Jupiter, J.B. Vascular injuries and closed extremity fractures in children. Clin Orthop 188:112–119, 1984.

48. Frykberg, E.R.; Vines, F.S.; Alexander, R.H. The natural history of clinically occult arterial injuries: A prospective evaluation. J Trauma 29:577–583, 1989.

49. Gable, D.R.; Allen, J.W.; Richardson, J.D. Blunt popliteal artery injury: Is physical examination alone enough for evaluation? J Trauma 43:541–544, 1997.

50. Gagne, P.J.; Cone, J.B.; McFarland, D.; et al. Proximity penetrating extremity trauma: The role of duplex ultrasound in the detection of occult venous injuries. J Trauma 39:1157–1163, 1995.

51. Gates, J.D.; Knox, J.B. Axillary artery injuries secondary to anterior dislocation of the shoulder. J Trauma 39:581–583, 1995.

52. Goyanes, D.J. Substitution plastica de las arterias por las venas o'arterioplastia venosa, aplicada, como nuevo metodo, al tratamiento de las aneurismas. El Siglo Medico: Sept. 1, 1906, p. 346, Sept. 8, 1906, p. 561.

53. Green, R.M.; Roedersheimer, L.R.; DeWeese, J.A. Effects of aspirin and dipyridamole on expanded polytetrafluoroethylene graft patency. Surgery 92:1016–1026, 1982.

54. Gregory, R.T.; Gould, R.J.; Peclet, M.; et al. The mangled extremity syndrome (M.E.S.): A severity grading system for multisystem injury of the extremity. J Trauma 25:1147–1150, 1985.

55. Gustilo, R.B.; Mendoza, R.M.; Williams, D.N. Problems in the management of type III (severe) open fractures: A new classification of type III open fractures. J Trauma 24:742–746, 1984.

56. Guthrie, C.C. Blood Vessel Surgery. London, Edward Arnold, 1912.

57. Hagen, P.O.; Wang, Z.G.; Mikat, E.M.; et al. Antiplatelet therapy reduces aortic intimal hyperplasia distal to small diameter vascular prostheses (PTFE) in nonhuman primates. Ann Surg 195:328–339, 1982.

58. Hansen, S.I., Jr. The type IIIC tibial fracture: Salvage or amputation? J Bone Joint Surg Am 69:799–800, 1987.

59. Hayes, J.M.; Van Winkle, G.N. Axillary artery injury with minimally displaced fracture of the neck of the humerus. J Trauma 23:431–433, 1983.

60. Helfet, D.J.; Schmeling, G.J. Fractures of the acetabulum. Complications. In: Tile, M., ed. Fractures of the Pelvis and Acetabulum, 2nd ed. Philadelphia, Williams & Wilkins, 1995, pp. 451–467.

61. Helfet, D.L.; Howey, T.; Sanders, R.; et al. Limb salvage versus amputation. Preliminary results of the mangled extremity severity score. Clin Orthop 256:80–86, 1990.

62. Hobson, R.W., II; Howard, E.W.; Wright, C.B.; et al. Hemodynamics of canine femoral venous ligation: Significance in combined arterial and venous injuries. Surgery 74:824–829, 1973.

63. Hoppenfeld, S.; deBoer, P. Surgical exposures in orthopaedics: The anatomic approach. Philadelphia, J.B. Lippincott, 1994, p. 308.

64. Howe, H.R., Jr.; Poole, G.V., Jr.; Hansen, K.J.; et al. Salvage of lower extremities following combined orthopedic and vascular trauma: A predictive salvage index. Am Surg 53:205–208, 1987.

65. Hughes, C.W. Arterial repair during the Korean War. Ann Surg 147:555–561, 1958.

66. Iannacone, W.M.; Taffet, R.; DeLong, W.G., III; et al. Early exchange intramedullary nailing of distal femoral fractures with vascular injury initially stabilized with external fixation. J Trauma 37:446–451, 1994.

67. Iftikhar, T.B.; Kaminski, R.S.; Silva, I., Jr. Neurovascular complications of the modified Bristow procedure: A case report. J Bone Joint Surg Am 66:951–952, 1984.

68. Itani, K.M.F.; Burch, J.M.; Spjut-Patrinely, V.; et al. Emergency center arteriography. J Trauma 32:302–307, 1992.

69. Jarstfer, B.S.; Rich, N.M. The challenge of arteriovenous fistula formation following disc surgery: A collective review. J Trauma 16:726–733, 1976.

70. Jendrisak, M.D. Spontaneous abdominal aortic rupture from erosion by a lumbar spine fixation device: A case report. Surgery. 99:631–633, 1986.

71. Johansen, K.; Bandyk, D.; Thiele, B.; et al. Temporary intraluminal shunts: Resolution of a management dilemma in complex vascular injuries. J Trauma 22:395–402, 1982.

72. Johansen, K.; Daines, M.; Howey, T.; et al. Objective criteria accurately predict amputation following lower extremity trauma. J Trauma 30:568–573, 1990.

73. Johansen, K.; Lynch, K.; Paun, M.; et al. Non-invasive vascular tests reliably exclude occult arterial trauma in injured extremities. J Trauma 31:515–522, 1991.

74. Johnson, B.; Thursby, P. Subclavian artery injury caused by a screw in a clavicular compression plate. Cardiovasc Surg 4:414–416, 1996.

75. Johnson, E.E.; Eckardt, J.J.; Letournel, E. Extrinsic femoral artery occlusion following internal fixation of an acetabular fracture: A case report. Clin Orthop 217:209–213, 1987.

76. Kendall, K.M.; Burton, J.H.; Cushing, B. Fatal subclavian artery transection from isolated clavicle fracture. J Trauma 48:316–318, 2000.

77. Kendall, R.W.; Taylor, D.C.; Salvian, A.J.; et al. The role of arteriography in assessing vascular injuries associated with dislocations of the knee. J Trauma 35:875–878, 1993.

78. Knudson, M.M.; Lewis, F.R.; Atkinson, K.; et al. The role of duplex ultrasound arterial imaging in patients with penetrating extremity trauma. Arch Surg 128:1033–1038, 1993.

79. Kootstra, G.; Schipper, J.J.; Boontje, A.H.; et al. Femoral shaft fracture with injury of the superficial femoral artery in civilian accidents. Surg Gynecol Obstet 142:399–403, 1976.

80. Kram, H.B.; Wright, J.; Shoemaker, W.C.; et al. Perioperative transcutaneous O_2 monitoring in the management of major peripheral arterial trauma. J Trauma 24:443–445, 1984.

81. Kuzniec, S.; Kauffman, P.; Molnár, L.J.; et al. Diagnosis of limbs and neck arterial trauma using duplex ultrasonography. Cardiovasc Surg 6:358–366, 1998.

82. Lange, R.H. Limb reconstruction versus amputation decision making in massive lower extremity trauma. Clin Orthop 243:92–99, 1989.

83. Lange, R.H.; Bach, A.W.; Hansen, S.T., Jr.; et al. Open tibial fractures with associated vascular injuries: Prognosis for limb salvage. J Trauma 25:203–208, 1985.

84. Ledgerwood, A.M.; Lucas, C.E. Biological dressings for exposed vascular grafts: A reasonable alternative. J Trauma 15:567–574, 1975.

85. Ledgerwood, A.M.; Lucas, C.E. Split-thickness porcine graft in the treatment of close-range shotgun wounds to extremities with vascular injury. Am J Surg 125:690–695, 1973.

86. Lexer, E. Die Ideale Operation des Arteriellen und des Arteriellvenosen Aneurysma. Arch Klin Chir 83:459–477, 1907.

87. Lim, E.V.; Lavadia, W.T.; Blebea, J. Vascular impingement by external fixator pins: A case report. J Trauma 38:833–835, 1995.

88. Lynch, K.; Johansen, K. Can Doppler pressure measurement replace "exclusion" arteriography in the diagnosis of occult extremity arterial trauma? Ann Surg 214:737–741, 1991.

89. Makins, G.H. Gunshot Injuries to the Blood Vessels. New York, William Wood, 1919.

90. Maleux, G.; Soula, P.; Otal, P.; et al. Traumatic aortobiiliac dissection treated by kissing-stent placement. J Trauma 43:706–708, 1997.

91. Marin, M.L.; Veith, F.J.; Cynamon, J.; et al. Initial experience with transluminally placed endovascular grafts for the treatment of complex vascular lesions. Ann Surg 222:449–469, 1995.

92. Martin, L.C.; McKenney, M.G.; Sosa, J.L.; et al. Management of lower extremity arterial trauma. J Trauma 37:591–599, 1994.

93. Mattox, K.L.; Feliciano, D.V.; Burch, J.; et al. Five thousand seven hundred sixty cardiovascular injuries in 4459 patients. Epidemiologic evolution 1958–1987. Ann Surg 209:698–707, 1989.

94. McAuley, C.E.; Steed, D.L.; Webster, M.W. Arterial complications of total knee replacement. Arch Surg 199:960–962, 1984.

95. McCready, R.A.; Logan, N.M.; Daugherty, M.E.; et al. Long-term results with autogenous tissue repair of traumatic extremity vascular injuries. Ann Surg 206:804–808, 1987.

96. McNeese, S.; Finck, E.; Yellin, A.E. Definitive treatment of selected vascular injuries and post-traumatic arteriovenous fistulas by arteriographic embolization. Am J Surg 140:252–259, 1980.

97. McNutt, R.; Seabrook, G.R.; Schmitt, D.D. Blunt tibial artery trauma: Predicting the irretrievable extremity. J Trauma 29:1624–1627, 1989.

98. Meissner, M.; Paun, M.; Johansen, K. Duplex scanning for arterial trauma. Am J Surg 161:552–555, 1991.

99. Meyer, J.; Walsh, J.; Schuler, J.; et al. The early fate of venous repair after civilian vascular trauma: A clinical, hemodynamic, and venographic assessment. Ann Surg 206:458–464, 1987.

100. Miller, H.H.; Welch, C.S. Quantitative studies on the time factor in arterial injuries. Ann Surg 130:428–438, 1949.

101. Miranda, F.E.; Dennis, J.W.; Veldenz, H.C.; et al. Confirmation of the safety and accuracy of physical examination in the evaluation of knee dislocation for popliteal artery injury: A prospective study. Publication pending, J Trauma.

102. Mitchell, F.L., III; Thal, E.R. Results of venous interposition grafts in arterial injuries. J Trauma 30:336–339, 1990.

103. Mueller, D.K.; Greenberg, J.J.; Marshall, W.J.; et al. Rupture of the deep femoral artery from blunt trauma. J Trauma 39:1010–1014, 1995.

104. Mullins, R.J.; Lucas, C.E.; Ledgerwood, A.M. The natural history following venous ligation for civilian injuries. J Trauma 20:737–743, 1980.

105. Nicholas, J.G.; Svoboda, J.A.; Parks, S.N. Use of temporary intraluminal shunts in selected peripheral arterial injuries. J Trauma 26:1094–1096, 1986.

106. Noszczyk, W.; Witkowwsk, M. Ramauld Weglowski. Polski Przegl Chir 57:440–445, 1985.

107. Nunley, J.A.; Koman, L.A.; Urbaniak, J.R. Arterial shunting as an adjunct to major limb revascularization. Ann Surg 193:271–273, 1981.

108. Nypaver, T.J.; Schuler, J.J.; McDonnell, P.; et al. Long-term results of venous reconstruction after vascular trauma in civilian practice. J Vasc Surg 16:762–768, 1992.

109. O'Gorman, R.B.; Feliciano, D.V. Arteriography performed in the emergency center. Am J Surg 152:323–325, 1986.

110. O'Gorman, R.B.; Feliciano, D.V.; Bitondo, C.G.; et al. Emergency center arteriography in the evaluation of suspected peripheral vascular injuries. Arch Surg 119:568–573, 1984.

111. Ochsner, M.G., Jr.; Hoffman, A.P.; DiPasquale, D.; et al. Associated aortic rupture-pelvic fracture: An alert for orthopedic and general surgeons. J Trauma 33:429–434, 1992.

112. Odland, M.D.; Gisbert, V.L.; Gustilo, R.B.; et al. Combined orthopedic and vascular injury in the lower extremities: Indications for amputation. Surgery 108:660–666, 1990.

113. Pais, S.O. Assessment of vascular trauma. In: Mirvis, S.E.; Young, J.W.R., eds. Imaging in Trauma and Critical Care. Baltimore, Williams & Wilkins, 1992, pp. 485–515.

114. Palazzo, J.C.; Ristow, A.V.B.; Schwartz, F.; et al. Traumatic vascular lesions associated with fractures and dislocations. J Cardiovasc Surg 27:688–696, 1986.

115. Pappas, P.J.; Haser, P.B.; Teehan, E.P.; et al. Outcome of complex venous reconstructions in patients with trauma. J Vasc Surg 25:398–404, 1997.

116. Paul, M.A.; Patka, P.; van Heuzen, E.P.; et al. Vascular injury from external fixation: Case reports. J Trauma 33:917–920, 1992.

117. Peck, J.J.; Fitzgibbons, T.J.; Gaspar, M.R. Devastating distal arterial trauma and continuous intraarterial infusion of tolazoline. Am J Surg 145:562–566, 1983.

118. Pretre, R.; Bruschweiler, I.; Rossier, J.; et al. Lower limb trauma with injury to the popliteal vessels. J Trauma 40:595–601, 1996.

119. Reath, D.B.; Jeffries, G.E. The mangled lower extremity: Management and long-term results. Adv Trauma Crit Care 6:113–164, 1991.

120. Reid, J.D.S.; Weigelt, J.A.; Thal, E.R.; et al. Assessment of proximity of a wound to major vascular structures as an indication for arteriography. Arch Surg 123:942–946, 1988.

121. Reisman, J.D.; Morgan, A.S. Analysis of 46 intra-abdominal aortic injuries from blunt trauma: Case reports and literature review. J Trauma 30:1294–1297, 1990.

122. Rich, N.M.; Baugh, J.H.; Hughes, C.W. Acute arterial injuries in Vietnam: 1,000 cases. J Trauma 10:359–369, 1970.

123. Rich, N.M.; Collins, G.J., Jr.; Andersen, C.A.; et al. Autogenous venous interposition grafts in repair of major venous injuries. J Trauma 17:512–520, 1977.

124. Robbs, J.V.; Baker, L.W. Cardiovascular trauma. Curr Probl Surg 21:1–87, 1984.

125. Roessler, M.S.; Wisner, D.H.; Holcroft, J.W. The mangled extremity. When to amputate? Arch Surg 126:1243–1249, 1991.

126. Ross, S.E.; Ransom, K.J.; Shatney, C.H. The management of venous injuries in blunt extremity trauma. J Trauma 25:150–153, 1985.

127. Roth, S.M.; Wheeler, J.R.; Gregory, R.T.; et al. Blunt injury of the abdominal aorta: A review. J Trauma 42:748–755, 1997.

128. Rubin, B.G.; McGraw, D.J. The Doppler principle and sonographic imaging: Applications in the noninvasive vascular laboratory. In: Callow, A.D.; Ernst, C.B., eds. Vascular Surgery. Theory and Practice. Stamford, CT: Appleton & Lange, 1995, pp. 309–317.

129. Russell, W.L.; Sailors, D.M.; Whittle, T.B.; et al. Limb salvage versus traumatic amputation. A decision based on a seven-part predictive index. Ann Surg 213:473–481, 1991.

130. Schlosser, V.; Spillner, G.; Breymann, T.H.; et al. Vascular injuries in orthopaedic surgery. J Cardiovasc Surg 23:323–327, 1982.

131. Schwartz, M.; Weaver, F.; Yellin, A.; et al. The utility of color flow Doppler examination in penetrating extremity arterial trauma. Am Surg 59:375–378, 1993.

132. Seiler, J.G., III; Richardson, J.D. Amputation after extremity injury. Am J Surg 152:260–264, 1986.

133. Seligson, D.; Ostermann, P.A.; Henry, S.L.; et al. The management of open fractures associated with arterial injury requiring vascular repair. J Trauma 37:938–940, 1994.

134. Shackford, S.R.; Rich, N.H. Peripheral vascular trauma. In: Mattox, K.L.; Feliciano, D.V.; Moore, E.E., eds. Trauma, 4th ed. New York, McGraw-Hill, 2000, pp. 1011–1046.

135. Shah, D.M.; Leather, R.P.; Corson, J.D.; et al. Polytetrafluoroethylene grafts in the rapid reconstruction of acute contaminated peripheral vascular injuries. Am J Surg 148:229–233, 1984.

136. Shah, P.M.; Ivatury, R.R.; Babu, S.C.; et al. Is limb loss avoidable in civilian vascular injuries? Am J Surg 154:202–205, 1987.

137. Sharma, P.V.P.; Shah, P.M.; Vinzons, A.T.; et al. Meticulously restored lumina of injured veins remain patent. Surgery 112:928–932, 1992.

138. Sibbitt, R.R.; Palmaz, J.C.; Garcia, F.; et al. Trauma of the extremities: Prospective comparison of digital and conventional angiography. Radiology 160:179–182, 1986.

139. Snyder, W.H.; Thal, E.R.; Bridges, R.A.; et al. The validity of normal arteriography in penetrating trauma. Arch Surg 113:424–428, 1978.

140. Soubbotitch, V. Military experiences of traumatic aneurysms. Lancet 2:720–721, 1913.

141. Stain, S.C.; Yellin, A.E.; Weaver, F.A.; et al. Selective management of nonocclusive arterial injuries. Arch Surg 124:1136–1141, 1989.

142. Stanton, P.E., Jr.; Rosenthal, D.; Clark, M.; et al. Percutaneous transcatheter embolization of injuries to the profunda femoris artery. Angiology 36:650–655, 1985.

143. Starnes, B.W.; Bruce, J.M. Popliteal artery trauma in a forward deployed Mobile Army Surgical Hospital: Lessons learned from the war in Kosovo. J Trauma 48:1144–1147, 2000.

144. Stephen, D.J.G. Pseudoaneurysm of the superior gluteal arterial system: An unusual cause of pain after a pelvic fracture. J Trauma 43:146–149, 1997.

145. Stephen, D.J.G.; Kreder, H.J.; Day, A.C.; et al. Early detection of arterial bleeding in acute pelvic trauma. J Trauma 47:638–642, 1999.

146. Storm, R.K.; Sing, A.K.; de Graaf, E.J.R.; et al. Iatrogenic arterial trauma associated with hip fracture treatment. J Trauma 48:957–959, 2000.

147. Strinden, W.D.; Dibbell, D.G., Sr.; Turnipseed, W.D.; et al. Coverage of acute vascular injuries of the axilla and groin with transposition muscle flaps: Case reports. J Trauma 29:512–516, 1989.

148. Tile, M. Disruption of the pelvic ring. Anatomy. In: Tile, M., ed. Fractures of the Pelvis and Acetabulum, 2nd ed. Philadelphia, Williams & Wilkins, 1995, pp. 12–21.

149. Tile, M. Disruption of the pelvic ring. Management. In: Tile, M., ed. Fractures of the Pelvis and Acetabulum, 2nd ed. Philadelphia, Williams & Wilkins, 1995, pp. 102–134.

150. Tile, M. Fractures of the acetabulum. Management. In: Tile, M., ed. Fractures of the Pelvis and Acetabulum, 2nd ed. Philadelphia, Williams & Wilkins, 1995, pp. 321–354.

151. Timberlake, G.A.; O'Connell, R.C.; Kerstein, M.D. Venous injury: To repair or ligate—The dilemma. J Vasc Surg 4:553–558, 1986.

152. Treiman, G.S.; Yellin, A.E.; Weaver, F.A.; et al. Examination of the patient with a knee dislocation. The case for selective arteriography. Arch Surg 127:1056–1063, 1992.

153. Tufaro, A.; Arnold, T.; Rummel, M.; et al. Adverse outcome of nonoperative management of intimal injuries caused by penetrating trauma. J Vasc Surg 20:656–659, 1994.

154. Urban, W.P.; Tornetta, P., III. Vascular compromise after intramed-ullary nailing of the tibia: A case report. J Trauma 36:804–807, 1995.

155. Veith, F.J.; Marin, M.L. The present status of endoluminal stented grafts for the treatment of aneurysms, traumatic injuries and arterial occlusions. Cardiovasc Surg 4:3–7, 1996.

156. Villas, P.A.; Cohen, G.; Putnam, S.G., III; et al. Wallstent placement in a renal artery after blunt abdominal trauma. J Trauma 46:1137–1139, 1999.

157. Weaver, F.A.; Rosenthal, R.E.; Waterhouse, G.; et al. Combined skeletal and vascular injuries of the lower extremities. Am Surg 50:189–197, 1984.

158. Weller, S.J.; Rossitch, E., Jr.; Malek, A.M. Detection of vertebral artery injury after cervical spine trauma using magnetic resonance angiography. J Trauma 46:660–666, 1999.

159. White, R.A.; Donayre, C.E.; Walot, I.; et al. Preliminary clinical outcome and imaging criterion for endovascular prosthesis development in high-risk patients who have aortoiliac and traumatic arterial lesions. J Vasc Surg 24:556–571, 1996.

160. Williams, G.D.; Crumpler, J.B.; Campbell, G.S. Effect of sympathectomy on the severely traumatized artery. Arch Surg 101:704–707, 1970.

CHAPTER 12

Compartment Syndromes

Annunziato Amendola, M.D., F.R.C.S.(C.)
Bruce C. Twaddle, M.D., F.R.A.C.S.

HISTORY

Compartment syndrome is a condition characterized by raised pressure within a closed space with a potential to cause irreversible damage to the contents of the closed space. Clinical awareness of the condition is attributed to the work of Richard von Volkmann. In 1881, he published an article in which he attempted to relate the state of irreversible contractures of flexor muscles of the hand to ischemic processes occurring in the forearm.[127] He believed that the pathophysiology of the contracture is related to massive venous stasis associated with simultaneous occurrence of arterial insufficiency. He thought that the condition may be caused by tight bandages, an observation that proved to be accurate.[127]

Other investigators confirmed Volkmann's conclusion and believed that the cause of the condition is muscle scarring secondary to inflammation.[14, 39, 49, 51, 111] Petersen,[96] in 1888, wrote one of the earliest articles describing surgical treatment of a Volkmann contracture; he was able to demonstrate some return of function after release of contracted scarred tissue, further supporting the observation that the causative factor is related to an ischemic event. Others at that time theorized that neurologic damage secondary to ischemia was causally related to the Volkmann contracture.[89, 126, 128]

It was Hildebrand[49] in 1906 who first used the term *Volkmann's ischemic contracture* to describe the end-point of an untreated compartment syndrome. He was the first to suggest that elevated tissue pressure may be causally related to ischemic contracture. Although he had no scientific proof, he thought that the underlying problem was a result of venous obstruction causing increased pressure in muscle and compromising arterial circulation to the muscle itself.

Thomas,[126] in 1909, attempted to review the data concerning the cause of Volkmann's ischemic contracture published up to that time. In his published review of 112 cases, fractures were found to be a causative factor in most

end-stage Volkmann ischemic contractures. Other predisposing causes of the condition were noted, however, including arterial injury, embolus, and tight bandaging. Of the 112 cases reported up to that time, 107 had occurred in the upper extremity.

Whereas the early investigators into the cause of compartment syndrome concentrated mainly on the development of the contracture, Rowlands,[111] in 1910, was the first to suggest that reperfusion after a prolonged period of ischemia could result in postischemic congestion and edema of muscle and nerve and could lead to the development of acute compartment syndrome. In 1914, Murphy[89] was the first to suggest that fasciotomy, if done before the development of the contracture, may prevent the contracture from occurring. His observations were similar to those of Rowlands in that compartment syndrome after a fracture was probably caused by an effusion of blood and serum into the forearm, sufficient to cause swelling and cyanosis of the hand.[89, 111] Murphy[89] was also the first to suggest the relation among tissue pressure, fasciotomy, and the development of a subsequent contracture.

Brooks and colleagues[15] further investigated the cause of acute compartment syndrome. After a series of extensive investigations, they suggested that the late picture of Volkmann's ischemic paralysis could be explained only on the basis of acute venous obstruction causing diminished perfusion of the extremity. After release of the obstruction (bandage or splint), a period of swelling, heat, and "rapidly developing contracture" is likely to occur. Other investigators concentrated their research efforts elsewhere and suggested that the lesion of ischemic paralysis is primarily related to failures occurring on the venous side of the system.[15, 51]

During and after World War II, many cases of Volkmann's contracture were seen as a complication of high-velocity gunshot wounds causing fractures of the upper or lower extremities.[17] Some believed that the arterial spasms seen at the time of the fracture were related to the subsequent development of a Volkmann ischemic contracture; therefore, treatment was directed more toward the arterial spasm than to the need for a fasciotomy.[39]

Although the existence of arterial trauma complicating a fracture was well known, the concomitant need for fasciotomy at the time of arterial repair was not generally appreciated. Many surgeons of the day thought that treatment of an impending Volkmann ischemia should be directed toward relief of the arterial spasm. Often, direct arterial injury could not be demonstrated at the time of surgery. In spite of that, however, surgical exploration of the "damaged artery" frequently led to reestablishment of flow distally and, in some cases, to reversal of the acute impending compartment syndrome.[93] It is highly likely that, while exposing the artery, the vascular surgeons were actually performing a limited fasciotomy, and this may have been the reason for the improvement in the patient's symptoms.

Patman and Thompson,[93] in 1970, after an extensive review of 164 patients with peripheral vascular disease in whom fasciotomy had been performed after arterial reconstruction, concluded that fasciotomy has much to offer for limb salvage and implied that it should be performed more often after restoration of arterial inflow to an extremity. Similar observations were made in 1967 during the Vietnam War by Chandler and Knapp,[20] who also suggested that, had more fasciotomies been performed after arterial repair to the extremities, the long-term results might have been better.

Many early cases of compartment syndrome seemed to be confined to the upper extremity. Increased attention focused on the lower extremity, however, after the report by Ellis[27] in 1958 of a 2% incidence of ischemic contractures occurring as a complication of tibial fractures. Most early descriptions of compartment syndrome involving the lower extremity were related to the development of the condition in the anterior compartment, but after the reports of Seddon[115] in 1966 and of Kelly and Whitesides[53] in 1967, the existence of four compartments in the leg and hence the need to decompress more than the anterior compartment were pointed out.

Compartment syndrome of the foot has been indirectly alluded to since the description of gangrene as a complication of Lisfranc fracture-dislocations, and increasing reports of this condition have appeared in the literature.[58, 59, 90, 91] Similarly, the involvement of thigh and gluteal compartments is now well recognized, particularly as a complication in the multiply traumatized patient.[17, 113, 114] The anatomy of these various compartments has been documented in the past and has been revisited by several authors in an attempt to define the ideal surgical approaches.[52, 59, 91]

The pathophysiology has been elucidated by a number of researchers, who correlated end-stage muscle contracture with such underlying pathophysiologic factors as raised interstitial pressure and muscle and nerve ischemia. These investigators also noted that a compartment syndrome can occur in any of the compartments of the leg or arm if the prerequisites for its development are present.[60, 85, 92, 94, 100, 108, 109, 116, 129]

PATHOPHYSIOLOGY

The prerequisites for the development of a compartment syndrome include a cause of raised pressure within a confined tissue space. Distortions in the relation between volume and pressure interfere with circulation to the compartment in question, leading to the development of an acute compartment syndrome.[60] Any condition that increases the content or reduces the volume of a compartment could be related to the development of an acute compartment syndrome. Excess tissue pressure secondary to increased volume of a compartment has been shown to occur in various conditions, including hemorrhage, fractures, increased capillary permeability after burns, and a temporary period of ischemia resulting in postischemic swelling.*

Regardless of the underlying cause, raised tissue pressure ultimately leads to some degree of venous obstruction within a closed space. Pressure continues to rise until the low intramuscular arteriolar pressure is exceeded. At that point, no further blood enters the capillary anastomosis, resulting in shunting within a compartment. If the pressure increase is allowed to continue untreated, muscle and nerve ischemia occurs, leading to irreversible damage to the contents of the compartment.[46, 107, 108] Using a canine model, it was demonstrated that the extent of tissue injury depends on pressure and time. Rorabeck and colleagues[107, 108] found that interference with muscle and nerve function becomes progressively more severe according to the duration of applied pressure. They found that a pressure of 30 mm Hg must be maintained in the anterior compartment of a dog's leg for 8 hours before changes in conduction velocity can be demonstrated in the peroneal nerve. However, conduction velocity changes can be shown sooner if higher pressures are introduced and maintained. Others have made similar observations.[36, 49, 65, 72, 83]

A compartment syndrome occurring as a complication of arterial injury is usually observed after restoration of arterial inflow to the compartment. Diminished arterial inflow caused by the injury results in a period of nerve and muscle ischemia within the compartment. The period of hypoxia experienced by the muscle and nerve allows transudation of fluid through capillary basement membranes and the capillaries of striated muscle.[104] It is also thought that the basement membranes may sustain some anoxic damage secondary to impaired arterial inflow. When arterial inflow to the extremity has been reestablished, fluid continues to leak through the basement membrane into the interstitial spaces. This leakage occurs soon after restoration of arterial inflow and, as a result, the pressure within the compartment continues to increase because of the unyielding fascial walls encasing the compartment. The pressure rise continues until the critical closing pressure of the small arterioles is reached. After that point, no further blood enters the striated muscle of the compartment and shunting occurs. The raised compartment pressure further increases the local venous

---

*See references 8, 21, 22, 37, 38, 42, 44, 48, 54, 55, 62, 71, 79, 85, 93, 95, 97, 98, 100, 103, 108, 118, 125.

pressure, thereby reducing the arteriolar-venous gradient. Regardless of the cause of acute compartment syndrome, however, pressure within the compartment never rises sufficiently to obstruct totally the systolic or diastolic pressure in the major vessel traversing the compartment.[104]

Both laboratory and clinical studies have demonstrated that compartment syndrome is not directly comparable to an episode of pure ischemia.[45, 46] Heppenstall and associates demonstrated in an animal model the importance of episodes of hypotension in increasing the extent of irreversible muscle ischemia and confirmed the difference between mean arterial pressure and compartment pressures in determining flow and muscle survival. McQueen and Court-Brown[75] demonstrated this distinction clinically, suggesting that a difference between diastolic pressure and compartment pressure of less than 30 mm Hg has a high clinical correlation with development of a compartment syndrome. This difference between diastolic and compartment pressure was labeled Δp and is probably the most important clinical parameter to identify.

Blood flow studies employing technetium 99m and xenon 133 have demonstrated that skeletal muscle blood flow is reduced during acute compartment syndrome in the experimental animal.[108, 109] Because of the patchy distribution of muscle necrosis found at the time of fasciotomy, however, variations in muscle blood flow probably occur among areas within the same muscle.

Crush syndrome and crush injury have, at times, been grouped with compartment syndrome in pathophysiology and treatment. This grouping is probably conceptually incorrect. These patients present originally with a history of having been trapped or crushed with pressure on a limb or limbs for an extended period of time. They characteristically have a painless flaccid paralysis initially, followed by the rapid development of swelling and rigid compartments in the affected part of the limb. However, it is now clear that the elevation of compartment pressure in crush injury is secondary to intracellular muscle damage rather than being the causative factor and that treatment guidelines are different.[76, 99] In particular, fasciotomy is contraindicated in crush syndrome and is associated with higher morbidity and mortality.

The anesthetized or sedated patient is at particular risk for development of a compartment syndrome, which may go unnoticed. Patients who are intubated very early in their initial care need accurate assessment of their injured extremities while in the intensive care unit. Because unrecognized injuries can lead to compartment syndrome in these patients, remembering to perform a secondary survey of all patients involved in high-velocity accidents resulting in ventilatory support is essential. Prolonged positioning of a limb, particularly with the use of a post or traction, or both, such as with hip fracture fixation or femoral nailing, can place the compartments involved at risk,[73] particularly if there is ongoing bleeding related to injury. Compartment syndrome may, however, also occur in the uninjured leg if positioning restricts venous return. Hyperextension of the hip to improve imaging of a fractured femur or tibia in the lateral position may result in a risk of compartment syndrome in the well leg. A reperfusion phenomenon, as occurs with vascular repair, may also result in compartment syndrome in the well limb if the positioning of this limb affects arterial flow. Therefore, any patient who undergoes prolonged or unexpectedly protracted surgery, particularly to the lower limb, should have careful clinical assessment of the compartments of both the operated and unoperated limbs several times after surgery.

Considering the underlying pathophysiology, the cause of a compartment syndrome may be related more specifically to conditions that decrease the size or increase the content of a compartment.[62] The most common cause of compartment syndrome associated with decrease in the size of the compartment is the application of a tight cast, constrictive dressings, or pneumatic antishock garments.[21, 31, 55, 74, 125]

Closure of fascial defects has been demonstrated to be associated with the development of acute compartment syndrome.[77] This condition most commonly occurs in the anterior compartment of the leg in patients who present with symptomatic muscle hernias and symptoms suggestive of chronic compartment syndrome. Failure to recognize the pitfalls in closing the muscle hernia in this situation can have disastrous consequences for the patient and the surgeon.[77, 94, 116] Attempts to close the anterior compartment after surgery in this region, such as with a tibial plateau fracture, may also increase the risk of compartment problems. Care should be taken when assessing closure of this layer, taking into consideration the extent of swelling, any sign of ongoing bleeding, and the coagulation status of the patient.

A number of conditions have been shown to increase compartment contents and lead to compartment syndrome. These conditions involve hemorrhage within the compartment, which increases the contents of the compartment, or accumulation of fluid (edema) within the compartment. The former is most commonly associated with fractures of the tibia, elbow, forearm, or femur, whereas the latter is most commonly associated with postischemic swelling after arterial injuries or restoration of arterial flow after thrombosis of a major artery.* The compartment syndrome described after arthroscopic treatment of tibial plateau fractures is likely to be related to extravasation of fluid into the compartment through the fracture itself.[9] This event is much more sinister than the fluid extravasation into the superficial soft tissues that can occur during regular arthroscopy because this fluid is generally outside the fascial layer. The use of arthroscopic fluid pumps to increase fluid flow increases the risk of this type of fluid accumulation.

Compartment syndromes have also been reported to occur after other conditions or therapies, including soft tissue injury to an extremity, hereditary bleeding, dialysis, anticoagulant therapy, osteotomy, intraosseous fluid resuscitation in children, and excessive skeletal traction.†

As can be seen, the causes of acute compartment syndrome touch on several medical disciplines, includ-

---

*See references 5, 12, 30, 34, 35, 38, 47, 68, 73, 81, 92, 104, 110, 114, 117, 123, 131, 132.
†See references 19, 25, 29, 33, 37, 38, 62, 68, 81, 83, 92, 101, 131.

ing orthopaedic, general, and vascular surgery and traumatology.*

DIAGNOSIS: CLINICAL ASSESSMENT

The clinical diagnosis of an acute compartment syndrome is sometimes obvious, but usually the findings are not clear-cut. A review of the literature suggests that there is frequently a delay in reaching a diagnosis of compartment syndrome because the symptoms can be masked by those of other injuries.[32, 57, 103, 104, 122]

The presence of an open wound in a compound fracture should not abrogate the possibility of development of a compartment syndrome. Between 6% and 9% of open tibial fractures are complicated by compartment syndrome, with the incidence being directly proportional to the severity of the soft tissue injury.[12, 23]

Assuming the patient is conscious and alert, the most important symptom of an impending compartment syndrome is pain disproportionate to that expected from the known injuries. Frequently, the patient has a relatively pain-free interval (perhaps a few hours) after reduction of the fracture and then pain out of proportion to the problem. The degree of pain can usually be assessed by the need for analgesia. The nursing record may reveal that the patient is requiring more frequent doses of a given drug or a stronger drug. With the advent of prolongation of regional or epidural analgesia in the perioperative period, particular attention should be paid to these patients. Often, junior medical staff from several services become involved in managing pain relief in these patients, and increased vigilance is necessary to ensure that the analgesia requirements of the patients are being monitored. There have been various experiences[87, 119] of such patients having a delayed diagnosis of compartment syndrome, often beyond the time when intervention can prevent permanent muscle necrosis.

The pain felt by the patient is unrelenting and seems to be unrelated to the position of the extremity or to immobilization. It is exacerbated by constricting casts or dressings, and after their release some patients obtain transient but minimal relief of the symptoms. The patient may also complain of feelings of numbness or tingling in the affected extremity. These symptoms are poorly localized and are not to be relied on.

Clinical signs of an impending acute compartment syndrome, irrespective of the underlying cause, include pain on palpation of the swollen compartment, reproduction of symptoms with passive muscle stretch, sensory deficit in the territory of the nerve traversing the compartment, and muscle weakness. The earliest sign of an acute compartment syndrome is a tensely swollen compartment whose palpation reproduces the patient's pain (Fig. 12–1). Because this symptom is frequently associated with a fracture, it can be difficult for the examining physician to be certain how much pain is from the fracture and how much is from the tense, swollen

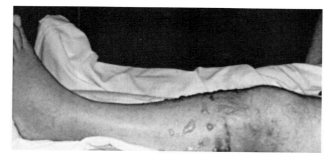

Figure 12–1. Acute compartment syndrome of the leg.

compartment. The compartment feels extremely hard, and the overlying skin can be shiny. Palpation of the compartment at some distance from the level of the fracture is still extremely painful for the patient. Occasionally, the finding of a tense, swollen compartment is not obvious, particularly in the deep flexor compartment of the forearm and the deep posterior compartment of the leg, where the diagnosis can be missed.

Pain referred to a compartment on passive stretching of the digits is a reliable sign of an impending acute compartment syndrome (Fig. 12–2). Stretch pain per se is *not* a specific sign of acute compartment syndrome but is a sign that is usually attributed to muscle swelling or ischemia. Therefore, in patients with a fracture and without a compartment syndrome, some degree of stretch pain can be present.

The symptom of pain and the findings of a tense, swollen compartment with some degree of passively induced stretch pain represent the earliest manifestations of an acute compartment syndrome. By the time sensory deficit is obvious, irreversible changes in nerve or muscle may have occurred. The sensory deficit experienced by the patient is usually in the territory of the nerve traversing the compartment. In acute anterior compartment syndrome, the patient may have hypesthesia in the territory of the first webspace (Fig. 12–3). The appearance of a sensory defect

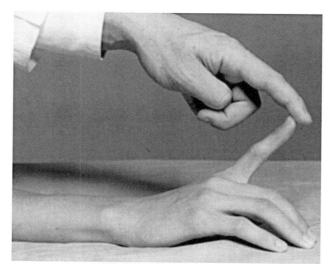

Figure 12–2. Passive extension of the digit causes pain referred to the compartment.

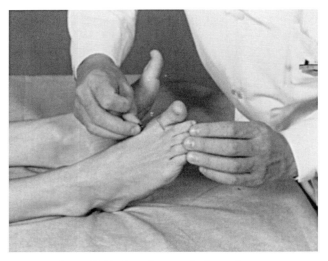

FIGURE 12–3. Hypesthesia in the first webspace.

in acute compartment syndrome is a reliable sign, assuming there is no superimposed injury to the nerve.

To await the development of frank motor weakness in acute compartment syndrome is to invite disaster. Paresis is a late finding and, if present, requires immediate surgical intervention (Fig. 12–4). Many of the other features of an acute compartment syndrome may be altered by the time such weakness has occurred, making the diagnosis more difficult. In particular, pain may become a much less reliable indicator of significant pressure elevation after muscle necrosis has occurred.

Palpable pulses are always present in acute compartment syndrome unless there is an underlying arterial injury. Capillary refill in the digits may be sluggish but is frequently normal and the peripheral pulses are readily palpable, even with the most florid acute compartment syndrome.

Assuming the patient is normotensive, pressure within the compartment can never rise sufficiently to obstruct systolic pressure totally in the major artery traversing the compartment.[33, 56, 108] This finding is explained on the basis of the shunting that occurs within the compartment. The presence of pulses and normal capillary filling does not mean that a compartment syndrome is absent.

The differential diagnosis of an acute compartment syndrome includes arterial occlusion, an injury to a peripheral nerve, or crush injury.

Delay in diagnosis of a major arterial injury may occur if poor or absent pulses are attributed to factors such as blood loss, compression by a fracture hematoma, or malalignment of the fracture. In addition, high-velocity trauma with acute limb ischemia can be obscured by shock. The diagnosis of arterial injury should not be difficult, assuming the surgeon has a high index of clinical awareness.

Johansen and colleagues[50] demonstrated the value of measuring the Doppler-assessed arterial pressure index (the systolic arterial pressure in the injured extremity divided by the arterial pressure in the uninvolved arm). A value less than 0.90 necessitates further arterial investigation; 94% of patients with an index this low have positive arteriographic findings. No major arterial injuries were missed using these criteria.[50] However, in case of doubt, arteriography is *always* indicated (Fig. 12–5). The risk associated with arteriography is small compared with the problems caused by a delayed or missed diagnosis of arterial injury. Doppler ultrasonography is useful in detection of arterial injury and particularly in monitoring minor arterial injuries treated conservatively. It does not, however, provide any useful information regarding the adequacy of blood flow through a compartment. The diagnosis of a concomitant nerve injury is less difficult because pain is rarely a feature of a nerve injury. Usually, however, the diagnosis of a nerve injury is a diagnosis of exclusion with compartment syndrome, arterial injury, or both.

Crush injury is produced by continuous and prolonged pressure. It can occur in persons who are trapped in one position for a prolonged period or who have collapsed or fallen asleep in one position for an excessive period when under the influence of alcohol or drugs. The patient usually suffers no pain initially and may have no physical complaints. Initially there is flaccid paralysis of the injured limb and a patchy sensory loss. Gross edema takes time to develop, and distal pulses are usually present.

The clinical presentation of these patients is the key to making the diagnosis of crush injury as opposed to compartment syndrome. The patients must have had the limb trapped in one position for a prolonged period. Collapse of a building, being trapped beneath a fallen object, lying in an awkward position after collapse from drug overdose, and failed attempted suicide with carbon monoxide are all clinical scenarios in which crush injury may occur. These patients initially have a flaccid paralysis of the limb that is painless. Over the course of hours, swelling rapidly ensues, often far more dramatic than would be seen in compartment syndrome. The swelling is due to rapid release of fluid because of the failure of intracellular mechanisms that allow the cell to retain water. The result is clinical evidence of muscle damage with darkening of the urine related to myoglobinuria and rapid

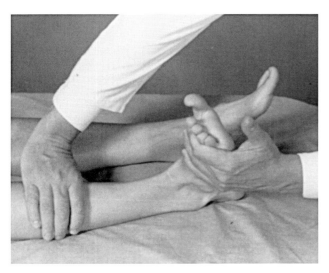

FIGURE 12–4. Weakness of dorsiflexion.

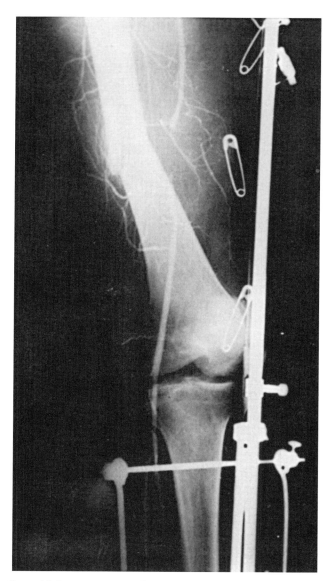

FIGURE 12–5. An arteriogram showing arterial disruption at the site of a fractured femur. (From Seligson, D., ed. Concepts in Intramedullary Nailing. Orlando, FL, Grune & Stratton, 1985, p. 111.)

deterioration of renal function. These features again occur more rapidly than would be expected with compartment syndrome, in a day or two after initial presentation. Because the timing of these changes is important in making the diagnosis, particularly as fasciotomy is contraindicated in this condition, it is often necessary to speak to the ambulance or emergency staff who first found the patient if crush syndrome is considered a possibility.

Crush syndrome refers to the systemic manifestations of this type of injury. The hemodynamic status of the injured person deteriorates and the patient becomes severely hypovolemic as edema develops. Acute renal failure secondary to hypovolemia and muscle breakdown ensues unless appropriate treatment is undertaken. Fasciotomy is not recommended if the diagnosis of crush injury and crush syndrome can clearly be made, even in the presence of dramatically elevated compartment pressures. Active

management of the metabolic complications is the key to treatment.[76, 99]

TISSUE PRESSURE MEASUREMENTS

The earliest pathogenic factor in the production of an acute compartment syndrome complicating musculoskeletal trauma is raised tissue pressure. Without an elevation in the tissue pressure, an acute compartment syndrome would not occur. The clinical manifestations of an acute compartment syndrome were discussed in the previous section, but it should be remembered that elevated tissue pressure, by definition, must *precede* the development of the clinical signs and symptoms. With tissue pressure measurements, the physician should be able to diagnose acute compartment syndrome in the incipient rather than in the fulminant stage. A number of techniques are available for diagnosing an incipient compartment syndrome. It is important to have a thorough understanding of the indications for these techniques and to appreciate their benefits and limitations.

Indications

Ideally, it would be helpful to know the underlying tissue pressure that develops after almost every fracture of the upper or lower extremity. However, this is neither feasible nor cost-effective. The surgeon therefore must decide which patients should be monitored.

If a patient with an acute fracture of the tibia begins to have pain disproportionate to what might be expected, stretch pain referred to the compartment with passive dorsiflexion or plantar flexion of the toes, weakness of the dorsiflexors of the foot, or hypesthesia in the territory of the first webspace, tissue pressure measurement is not required but the patient should be taken immediately to the operating room for four-compartment fasciotomy. Conversely, if the same patient seems to require an unusual amount of analgesia and on examination has a tense, painful compartment in the absence of any other physical signs, pressure monitoring should be considered. The indications discussed in the following paragraphs are only guidelines. There are many other situations that are not so clear-cut, in which the surgeon must decide according to knowledge and experience. If one starts to think about tissue pressure measurements, then one should probably be making them (Fig. 12–6).

POLYTRAUMA PATIENT

The polytrauma patient is at risk for the development of acute compartment syndrome for two reasons. First, associated head injuries, drug and alcohol intoxication, early endotracheal intubation, and the use of paralyzing drugs interfere with history taking and the assessment of physical signs. Second, in patients with low diastolic pressure, compartment syndrome can occur at relatively low threshold pressures. For various reasons, polytrauma patients

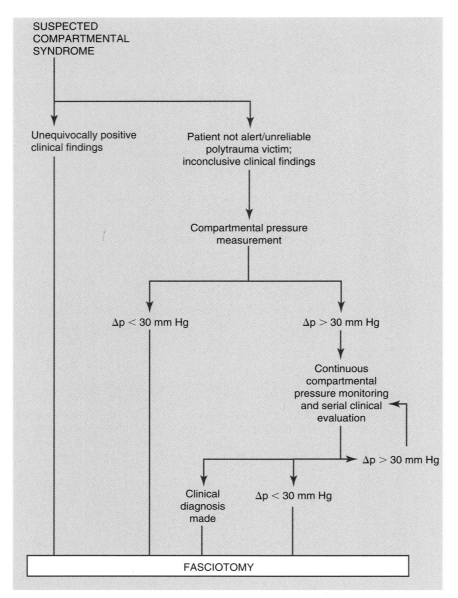

SUSPECTED
COMPARTMENTAL
SYNDROME

Unequivocally positive
clinical findings

Patient not alert/unreliable
polytrauma victim;
inconclusive clinical findings

Compartmental pressure
measurement

$\Delta p < 30$ mm Hg

$\Delta p > 30$ mm Hg

Continuous
compartmental
pressure monitoring
and serial clinical
evaluation

$\Delta p > 30$ mm Hg

Clinical
diagnosis
made

$\Delta p < 30$ mm Hg

FASCIOTOMY

Figure 12–6. An algorithm for management for a patient with suspected compartment syndrome. Δp is defined as the difference between the diastolic pressure and the measured compartment pressure in mm Hg as documented by McQueen and Court-Brown (1996).

may have a lowered diastolic pressure, which again places them at increased risk for acute compartment syndrome.

The approach to this type of patient is to measure pressures in all the compartments at risk and to leave the catheter in place in the compartment with the highest pressure to allow continuous pressure monitoring. This approach can be somewhat cumbersome, and the choice of the compartment may be incorrect. It is extremely important to remain vigilant in the assessment of polytrauma patients and to carry out isolated compartment pressure measurements regularly in the compartments at risk. This monitoring usually involves assessment of the forearm compartments and the compartments of the lower leg. Rarely is continuous pressure monitoring necessary in other compartments, and until more normal baseline data become available, the validity of its use is questionable.

PATIENT WITH CHEMICAL OVERDOSE OR HEAD INJURY AND AN ISOLATED LONG BONE FRACTURE

In these patients it is also difficult to elicit an appropriate history and to assess clinical signs by physical examination. The surgeon must measure compartment pressures in these patients because there is no other way to diagnose the condition.

It is suggested that the pressures in the deep posterior and anterior compartments (for a fracture of the tibia) or in the superficial and deep posterior compartments of the forearm (for a fracture of the forearm) be measured. On the basis of the results, an indwelling catheter is left in the compartment with the highest pressure. Continuous pressure monitoring can be done (see later discussion).

INCONCLUSIVE CLINICAL DIAGNOSIS

Inconclusive diagnosis occurs most commonly with patients in whom, for one reason or another, the symptoms *seem* to be out of proportion to what would be expected given the nature of the injury. Another situation involves the differential diagnosis of a compartment syndrome in a patient with a suspected nerve injury. It is extremely rare to confuse a peripheral nerve injury with an acute compartment syndrome, but occasionally the diagnosis can be confusing. In fact, a nerve injury and a compartment syndrome can coexist, and pressure measurements in this case are valuable adjuncts for interpretation of the physical signs and determination of the timing for fasciotomy.

In other cases, compartment pressure measurements may be of some value but should not be listed as specific indications. For example, with increased reliance on closed intramedullary nailing techniques applied to the tibia (and perhaps the femur), compartment pressure measurements may be required postoperatively. However, in centers experienced in use of intramedullary nails, there has been no evidence to support this concern. Some studies have suggested that the problems of compartment syndrome are less with more rapid and rigid stabilization of the fracture. With any active change in management of an acute long bone fracture, however, signs of compartment syndrome should be sought. If this investigation cannot be done clinically, the patient should be considered for compartment pressure measurements.[73, 115, 125]

Compartment pressure measurements are useful in patients who have undergone successful arterial repair and fasciotomy after a period of limb ischemia. In this situation, if it is difficult to ascertain the efficacy of the fasciotomy, compartment pressure measurement techniques are a valuable adjunct for documenting the adequacy of the decompression.

Measurement Techniques

NEEDLE MANOMETER

The first direct attempt at measurement of interstitial compartment pressure was by Landerer in 1884.[56] Subsequently, French and Price[28] reported on the usefulness of the technique in diagnosis of chronic compartment syndrome. Whitesides and colleagues[129, 130] first applied the needle manometer technique to the diagnosis of acute compartment syndrome. In their original description, an 18-gauge needle was connected to a 20-ml syringe by a column of saline and air, and this column was then connected to a standard mercury manometer. After the needle was injected into the compartment, the air pressure within the syringe was raised until the saline-air meniscus was seen to move. The pressure was then read off the mercury manometer (Fig. 12–7). Details of the technique have been well described.[129, 130]

The needle manometer technique employs standard equipment, available in all hospitals. It has the disadvantage of not being as reproducible as other techniques,[107] and it is not suitable for continuous pressure monitoring.[108]

Matsen and co-workers[63, 66, 68, 69, 79] modified the needle technique by using a continuous infusion of saline into the compartment. Their technique employed three pieces of equipment attached to an 18-gauge needle and high-pressure tubing. A saline-filled syringe was used to inject the saline through a three-way stopcock transducer dome and high-pressure tubing through the needle and into the compartment (Fig. 12–8). The pressure required to infuse the fluid was recorded. The technique measures the tissue resistance to infusion of saline. According to Mubarak,[80] the accuracy of the technique depends on the compliance of the tissue. Because tissue compliance is reduced at pressures greater than 30 mm Hg, the continuous

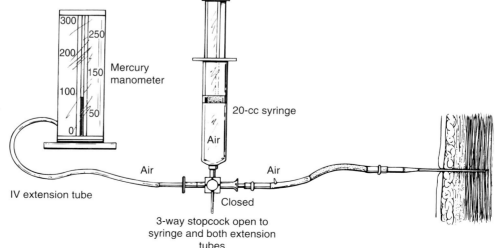

FIGURE 12–7. The needle injection technique measures compartment pressure by looking for movement of the air-saline meniscus. (Redrawn from Whitesides, T.E., Jr.; Haney, T.C.; Morimoto, K.; Hirada, H. Clin Orthop 113:46, 1975.)

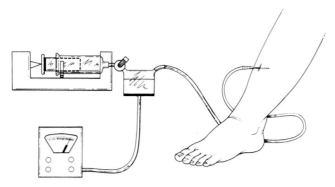

FIGURE 12–8. The continuous infusion technique of compartment pressure measurement. (Redrawn from Matsen, F.A., III; Winquist, R.A.; Krugmire, R.B. J Bone Joint Surg Am 62:286, 1980.)

infusion technique tends to give artificially high readings.[107] Nevertheless, the technique has the advantage of simplicity and allows continuous monitoring of a patient with an acute compartment syndrome. The infusion pump manufacturer recommends an infusion rate of 0.7 mL/day; however, the switch could inappropriately be set to deliver 100 times that amount, with serious implications.[68]

WICK CATHETER

The wick catheter, which consists of a piece of polyglycolic acid suture pulled into the tip of a piece of PE60 polyethylene tubing, was developed by Scholander and colleagues (Fig. 12–9).[112] Originally used to measure tissue pressures in animals, including turtles, snakes, and fish,[104] the technique was subsequently modified for clinical use.[40, 41, 82, 84, 87] It was the first technique for measuring intracompartmental pressure that did not rely on continuous infusion.

The technique requires a catheter placement sleeve and a wick catheter connected to a pressure transducer and recorder. The catheter and tubing are filled by means of a three-way stopcock attached to the transducer. It is imperative to ensure that no air bubbles are present in the system because artificially low readings can result. After the system has been filled, the tip of the catheter must be able to suspend a meniscus of water. It is calibrated and introduced into the tissues through a large trocar (Fig. 12–10). The needle is withdrawn, and the catheter is taped to the skin.

Because of the wick at the end of the catheter, there is a large area of contact and maintenance of catheter patency is not ordinarily a problem. The technique is useful for continuous monitoring of intracompartmental pressure. Its primary disadvantage is that the tip of the catheter may

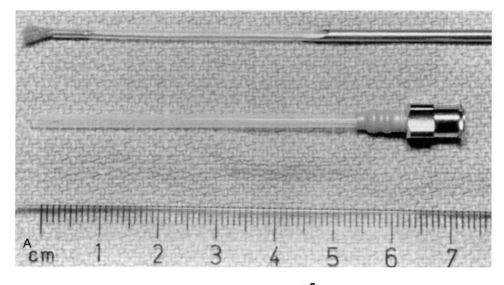

FIGURE 12–9. *A* and *B,* The wick catheter.

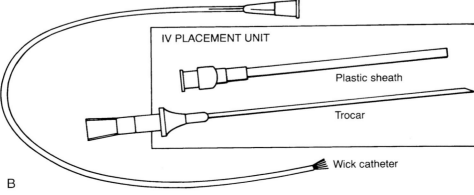

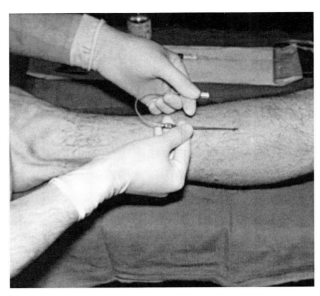

FIGURE 12–10. The catheter should be inserted at an acute angle to the long axis of the extremity.

become blocked by a blood clot. In addition, the polyglycolic acid suture can become hydrolyzed. The wick is pulled into the polyethylene tubing with a very fine suture. Theoretically, if the suture were to become dislodged, the wick would be left in the tissue; according to Mubarak and Hargens,[82] however, this complication did not occur in more than 800 catheterizations.

SLIT CATHETER

The slit catheter technique was originally developed by Rorabeck and associates.[106, 107] The slit catheter consists of a piece of PE60 polyethylene tubing with five 3-mm slits in the end of the tube (Fig. 12–11). This design eliminates the risk of leaving the tip of the catheter in the tissues on removal.

The technique requires a slit catheter, an insertion needle, a pressure transducer connected to a three-way stopcock, and a pressure monitor. The components are connected, and the catheter is filled with sterile saline solution. As with the wick catheter, it is imperative that no air bubbles enter the system. The monitor must be calibrated by placing the tip of the slit catheter level with the transducer dome and adjusting the zero control knob on the monitor until 0.00 appears (Fig. 12–12). The monitor has an alarm; if set, it goes off when the pressure rises above a certain point.

The slit catheter is introduced at an oblique angle to the long axis of the extremity directly into the muscle belly of the compartment to be measured. It is introduced through a 16-gauge needle, which is withdrawn after the catheter has been introduced (Fig. 12–13). The catheter is then taped to the skin. The system can be checked by applying gentle pressure to the skin overlying the catheter. A brisk deflection on the monitor should be noted. Also, if the patient is cooperative, dorsiflexing or plantar flexing of the foot should result in changes on the monitor.

STIC CATHETER SYSTEM

The STIC catheter system manufactured by Stryker is a hand-held device that allows the surgeon to measure acute compartment pressure quickly and simply (Fig. 12–14). The device is easy to use; it can be carried in the pocket and used in the emergency department without having to search for pieces of equipment. It is potentially as accurate as the slit catheter.

The method of use of this device is relatively simple, which has led to its increase in popularity. The device needs to be adequately "charged" for accurate use. A disposable syringe preloaded with fluid is connected to the measuring instrument, and a disposable needle-catheter that comes as part of the set is then added to the other end. After the system is purged with some fluid, the monitor is zeroed at the level of the compartment to be tested and the needle is then inserted through the fascia. The numbers on the monitor screen fall reasonably rapidly, and as the descent levels off a reading of the compartment pressure can be made. In clinical use of this device, the pressure reading on the monitor may continue to drop slowly with time and some individual variation may occur in determining the pressure at which leveling off has occurred.

MICROCAPILLARY INFUSION

The microcapillary infusion technique described by Styf and Korner[120] was developed primarily to aid in the diagnosis of chronic compartment syndrome. It is useful for long-term pressure monitoring and offers excellent dynamic applications.

ARTERIAL TRANSDUCER MEASUREMENT

With advances in technology for arterial pressure monitoring, use of a simple intravenous catheter attached to such pressure transducers has become an alternative for compartment pressure measurement. It is recommended that a catheter of at least 16-gauge diameter be used; the catheter is flushed with saline and connected to the pressure monitor, which is accurately calibrated and set for the level of the compartment being measured. The catheter is placed in the appropriate compartment and the pressure reading taken from an arterial line monitor that is calibrated to the same level as the compartment being measured.

NONINVASIVE TECHNIQUES

Some work has been done on noninvasive techniques of monitoring compartment pressures, mainly in chronic exercise-induced compartment syndrome. These techniques may become more applicable to the investigation of acute compartment syndrome.

Tc 99m–methoxyisobutylisonitrile (Tc 99m–MIBI) scintigraphy was used by Edwards and co-workers[26] to detect regional abnormalities in muscle perfusion with graded treadmill exercise. The method was used as a screening test for invasive pressure monitoring and gave good positive and negative predictive values.

Abraham and colleagues[2] used laser Doppler flow

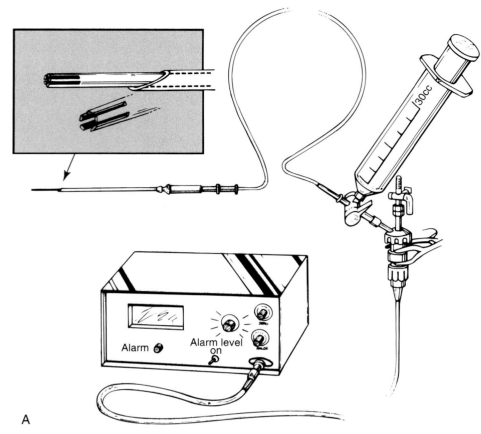

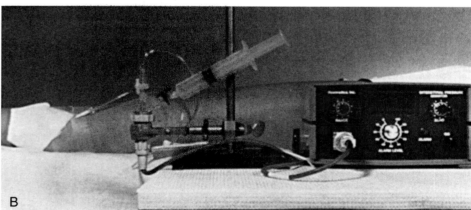

FIGURE 12–11. *A* and *B*, The slit catheter monitoring system. Note that the transducer dome is at the same height as the catheter. (*A*, Redrawn from Mubarek, S.J.; Hargens, A.R. Compartment Syndromes and Volkmann's Contracture. Philadelphia, W.B. Saunders, 1980, p. 13. *B*, Reproduced by permission from AAOS Instructional Course Lectures, Vol. 32. St. Louis, C.V. Mosby, 1983, p. 98.)

measurement in a small number of patients with chronic compartment syndrome and a control group and showed clear differences between the control and compartment syndrome groups.

Near-infrared spectroscopy has similarly been used to measure changes in relative oxygenation in a compartment after exercise and was useful in monitoring the rapid return to normal seen in control patients compared with those with chronic compartment syndrome.[36] Establishing normal values for patients with acute compartment syndrome using this technique has some potential application, although there appears to be a range of preoperative measurements in patients with established compart-

ment syndrome with quite a large variation between individuals.[36]

COMPARISON OF TECHNIQUES

Moed and Thorderson[78] compared the slit catheter, the side-ported needle, and the simple needle techniques in an animal model. Use of an 18-gauge needle produced significantly higher values (18 to 19 mm Hg) than the other two techniques, raising some question about its reliability. Wilson and colleagues[133] showed that use of a simple 16-gauge catheter with or without side ports produced measurements within 4 to 5 mm Hg of the slit catheter or STIC catheter readings.

Pressure Threshold for Fasciotomy

Historically, there has been disagreement about the pressure beyond which fasciotomy can be safely performed. Part of the confusion arises because of failure to appreciate the physiologic differences in the various pressure measurement systems. For example, in the needle manometer techniques, with or without continuous infusion, relatively higher values are acceptable, and values vary according to tissue compliance. With the wick, slit, or STIC catheter systems, continuous infusion is not used, and therefore the published values beyond which fasciotomy should be performed are somewhat lower.[82, 87, 106] Whitesides and colleagues[129] have recommended fasciotomy when compartment pressure rises to within 10 to 30 mm Hg of the patient's diastolic pressure, assuming that the patient has the clinical signs of acute compartment syndrome. Matsen and co-workers[66, 68, 69] have suggested that, with the continuous infusion technique,

fasciotomy should be performed when the pressure rises above 45 mm Hg.

Another important variable, as outlined by Heckman and associates,[43] is the distance from the fracture at which the compartment pressure is recorded. They concluded that failure to measure tissue pressure within a few centimeters of the fracture (the "zone of peak pressure") can result in serious underestimation of the maximal compartment pressure.

As the indications and sites for compartment pressure monitoring increase with improved techniques, the normal values for various compartments need to be clearly documented. Whether the normal pressure in a small compartment of the hand is the same as that in the gluteal compartment is not known. If any doubt exists, it is safest to rely as much on clinical examination as on the measured compartment pressure.

Our experience with slit catheter measurement indicates that a rising pressure greater than 30 mm Hg is a clear indication for fasciotomy. This threshold has been employed successfully at our institution but requires repeated measurements in patients who are at risk or for whom there is clinical concern.

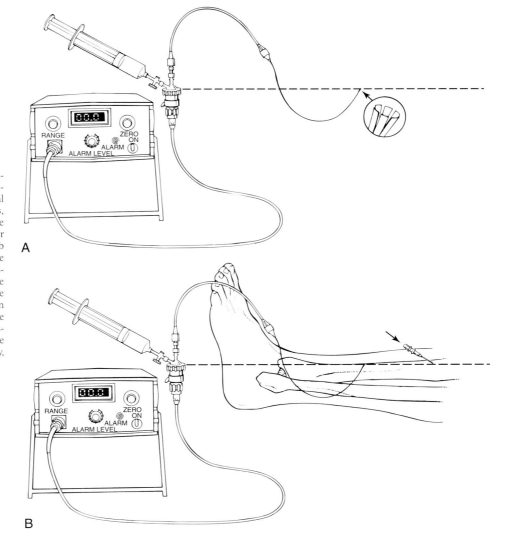

FIGURE 12–12. The slit catheter technique. *A* (Step 1), Assemble the components, fill the system with normal saline solution, remove all air bubbles, and zero the monitor by placing the catheter level with the transducer dome. Adjust the zero control knob until 0.00 appears. Set the alarm at the desired setting. *B* (Step 2), The transducer dome should be level with the insertion site. Prepare the insertion site and insert a 14-gauge catheter at an acute angle to the long axis of the extremity. (*A, B,* Redrawn by permission from AAOS Instructional Course Lectures, Vol. 32. St. Louis, C.V. Mosby, 1983, pp. 99–101.)

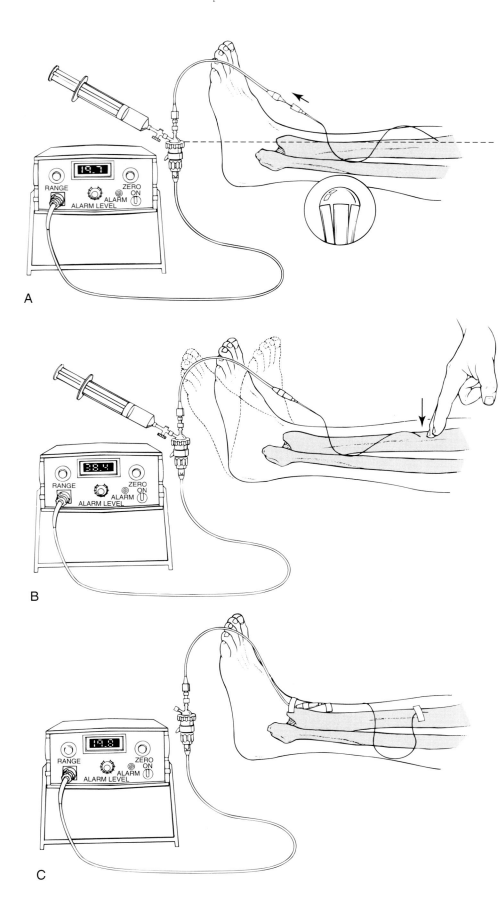

Figure 12–13. *A* (Step 3), Raise a drop of saline solution at the tip of the catheter and insert the catheter through the placement sleeve. Withdraw the sleeve. *B* (Step 4), Check the response by plantar flexion and dorsiflexion of the foot and digital pressure to the compartment. The monitor pressure will show a brisk rise in pressure readings. *C,* Remove the syringe, and record intermittent or continuous pressure as required. (*A–C,* Redrawn by permission from AAOS Instructional Course Lectures, Vol. 32. St. Louis, C.V. Mosby, 1983, pp. 99–101.)

FIGURE 12–14. The STIC catheter. (Courtesy of Stryker Mississauga, Ontario, Canada.)

Others have recommended that decompression be performed when the compartment pressure exceeds 30 to 35 mm Hg.[79, 82, 107] Although it is tempting to use an absolute value as an indication for decompression, the measurement obtained must be considered with regard to the patient's clinical condition and, more important, the patient's diastolic blood pressure. For example, if a patient is in shock, with a low diastolic blood pressure, an acute compartment syndrome can occur at considerably lower pressure.[46, 130] Conversely, when a patient's diastolic pressure is extremely high, an acute compartment syndrome is not likely to occur at the usual pressure threshold. All the compartment pressure measurement techniques are useful, but it is important for the surgeon to understand the pitfalls and limitations of the technique being used.

McQueen and Court-Brown[75] clearly demonstrated that the difference between diastolic pressure and the measured compartment pressure (Δp) is a more reliable clinical indicator of pending compartment syndrome than the absolute compartment pressure. Their recommendation was that a difference of less than 30 mm Hg is surgically significant. Their continued work in this area strongly supports the use of Δp with a threshold of 30 mm or less as the most reliable method of deciding when fasciotomies should be performed. This recommendation is particularly relevant to the monitoring of patients who may have a low diastolic pressure because of blood loss, sedation, or ventilatory support.

Treatment

A major cause of medicolegal problems for surgeons who treat fractures is failure to diagnose and treat a vascular injury or compartment syndrome appropriately. The only effective way to decompress an acute compartment syndrome is by surgical fasciotomy. It cannot be overemphasized how important it is to understand the basic pathophysiology so that the surgeon can recognize the at-risk patient and intervene before the development of irreversible damage to the contents of the compartment.

Incipient Compartment Syndrome

An incipient compartment syndrome is defined as a compartment syndrome that may develop if appropriate steps are not taken to prevent it. An established compartment syndrome obviously must be treated surgically with emergency decompression. With an incipient compartment syndrome, there are some things that the surgeon can do to reduce the chances of the patient's developing a full-blown compartment syndrome.

It is imperative to remove tight dressings and casts in patients complaining of an inordinate amount of pain (Fig. 12–15). Garfin and colleagues,[31] using a canine model, observed that 40% less volume was required to raise compartment pressure to equivalent levels in animals with casts than in those without casts. They also demonstrated that the compartment pressure in the hind limb of an animal could be reduced by up to 30% by changing to a univalve cast. If a bivalve cast was originally used and the sheet wadding underneath was divided, a 55% decrease in compartment pressure occurred. Others have noted that constricting bandages are causative factors in limb ischemia.[9, 11, 61, 72] Implicit in these observations is that removal of casts, tight dressings, or both is an important and simple technique for lowering compartment pressure within the extremity and therefore for maintaining arterial perfusion of muscle and nerve.

Controversy exists about the importance of limb position in a patient with an incipient compartment syndrome. Although it would seem to be a good idea to elevate the swollen extremity, it has been shown experimentally and clinically that limb elevation reduces mean arterial pressure in the arteries of the lower extremity and thereby reduces blood flow to the compartment.[7, 70] Elevation can also reduce the arterial venous gradient within the extremity, which increases the susceptibility of

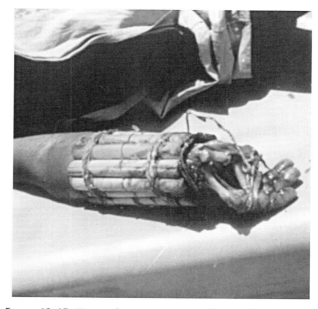

FIGURE 12–15. Untreated compartment syndrome of the forearm, secondary to excessive tightness of an occlusive dressing.

the extremity to a compartment syndrome by reducing oxygen perfusion.[64] Therefore, in a patient with an incipient compartment syndrome, the limb should be placed at the level of the heart to promote arterial inflow.

Established Compartment Syndrome

A patient with an established compartment syndrome has the clinical signs and symptoms of nerve and muscle ischemia in conjunction with elevated compartment pressure. A treatment algorithm (see Fig. 12–6) is a useful guide to management for such patients.

Any surgical decompression for acute compartment syndrome must adequately decompress all compartments that are at risk or likely to become at risk. Skin, fat, and fascial layers must all be widely decompressed and left open. Matsen and co-workers[63, 68] have shown that each layer contributes to the constriction of the muscle compartment, and attempts at closure of part or all of any one of these layers at the time of fasciotomy risk endangering muscle.

COMPARTMENT SYNDROME OF THE HAND

Compartment syndromes of the hand are rare, and the diagnosis can be difficult to make.[97] The diagnostic triad described by Spinner and associates,[117] stretch pain involving intrinsic muscles and intrinsic paralysis, is a hallmark of the condition. It normally occurs as a result of a crush injury but can also occur in association with fractures of the carpal bone.[3, 117] Other causes have been reported.[1, 3, 42, 101]

The most commonly involved compartments of the hand are the interossei. These can usually be decompressed by longitudinal dorsal incisions (Fig. 12–16).

COMPARTMENT SYNDROME OF THE FOREARM

Compartment syndrome of the forearm is again relatively rare. It is usually associated with a fracture with a direct blow or crushing component of the injury. Court-Brown and McQueen's review of their experience showed that forearm compartment syndrome tended to occur with

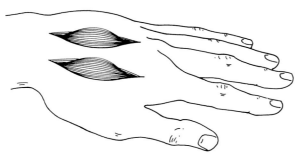

Figure 12–16. Dorsal incisions for decompression of acute compartment syndrome of the hand. (From Mubarak, S.J.; Hargens, A.R. Compartment Syndromes and Volkmann's Contracture. Philadelphia, W.B. Saunders, 1981.)

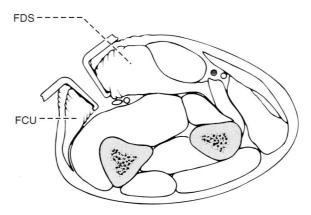

Figure 12–17. The Henry approach to the volar aspects of the forearm. (Modified from Whitesides, T., Jr.; Haney, T.C.; Morimoto, K.; Hirada, H. Clin Orthop 113:46, 1975.)

associated fractures of the distal radius. It has also been seen with inadvertent soft tissue fluid infiltration, grease-gun injuries, and deep infection often associated with intravenous drug abuse. Attempted closure of a tight surgical wound after internal fixation of forearm injuries may also place these compartments at risk.

The forearm consists of three osseofascial compartments—the superficial flexor, the deep flexor, and the extensor compartments.

Fasciotomies of the volar flexor compartments of the forearm are performed through a volar ulnar approach or a volar (Henry) approach. Fasciotomy of the dorsal compartment of the forearm is normally approached through a Thompson exposure. Garber[30] recommended a limited fasciotomy in the forearm, accomplished simply by incising the antecubital aponeurosis, but this did not prove to be effective. Eaton and Green[24] suggested that forearm decompression for an acute compartment syndrome could best be accomplished through a standard Henry approach. Whitesides and colleagues[129] recommended the volar ulnar approach to the forearm. This technique was subsequently adopted by Matsen and co-workers.[67] Gelberman and colleagues[33, 34] found that the standard Henry approach and the volar ulnar approach were equally effective for fasciotomy to decompress an acute compartment syndrome of the volar compartment. Regardless of technique, it is mandatory that both the superficial and deep volar compartments be decompressed.

Volar (Henry) Approach. Decompression of the superficial and deep volar flexor compartments of the forearm can be done through a single incision (Fig. 12–17). The skin incision should begin proximal to the antecubital fossa and extend to the palm across the carpal tunnel. Compartmental pressure measurements can be taken intraoperatively to confirm decompression. No tourniquet should be used. The skin incision begins medial to the biceps tendon, crosses the elbow crease, is carried toward the radial side of the forearm, and extends distally along the medial border of the brachioradialis, continuing across the palm along the thenar crease. The fascia overlying the superficial flexor compartment is readily incised, beginning at a point 1 or 2 cm proximal to the elbow and extending distally across the carpal tunnel

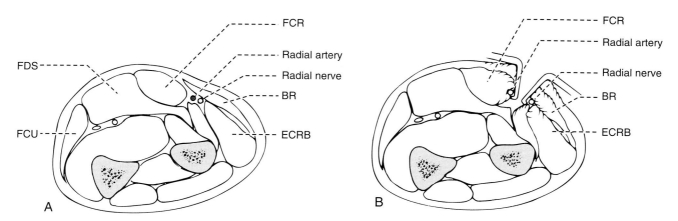

FIGURE 12–18. *A,* A transverse section through the midforearm illustrating relevant anatomy of the volar flexor compartment. BR, brachioradialis; ECRB, extensor carpi radialis brevis; FCR, flexor carpi radialis; FCU, flexor carpi ulnaris; FDS, flexor digitorum sublimis. *B,* The Henry approach to superficial and deep compartments of the forearm. (*A, B,* Modified with permission from AAOS Instructional Course Lectures, Vol. 32. St. Louis, C.V. Mosby, 1983, p. 106.)

into the palm. Anything short of this is viewed as an inadequate decompression (Fig. 12–18).

The superficial radial nerve is identified under the brachioradialis, both are retracted to the radial side of the forearm, and the flexor carpi radialis and radial artery are retracted to the ulnar side. This action exposes the flexor digitorum profundus and flexor pollicis longus in the depths, the pronator quadratus distally, and the pronator teres proximally. Because the effects of forearm compartment syndrome most commonly involve the deep flexor compartment in the forearm, it is imperative to decompress the fascia over each of these muscles to ensure that a thorough and complete decompression has been performed. Eaton and Green[24] recommended epimysiotomy in addition to fasciotomy, but this is not usually necessary in the acute case. Muscle viability is difficult to ascertain intraoperatively. Questionably viable muscle should be excised with caution at the time of fasciotomy. The patient should be brought back to the operating room 24 to 48 hours later for a dressing change and further débridement of muscle. The median nerve should be carefully inspected; if it appears excessively swollen, a neurolysis of the nerve should be performed.

Volar Ulnar Approach. The volar ulnar approach is performed in a similar fashion to the Henry approach. The arm is supinated and the incision is begun proximally medial to the biceps tendon, passes the elbow crease, extends distally along the ulnar border of the forearm, and proceeds across the carpal tunnel along the thenar crease (Fig. 12–19). The superficial fascia overlying the flexor carpi ulnaris is incised along with the elbow aponeurosis proximally and the carpal tunnel distally. The interval

between the flexor carpi ulnaris and flexor digitorum sublimis is identified. Lying deep to the flexor digitorum sublimis and approaching from the radial to the ulnar side are the ulnar nerve and artery, which must be identified and carefully protected (Fig. 12–20). The fascia overlying the deep flexor compartment is now incised. If necessary, the ulnar nerve can be decompressed distally at the level of the wrist and a neurolysis of the median nerve at the level of the carpal tunnel can be performed (Fig. 12–21).

Dorsal Approach. After the superficial and deep flexor compartments of the forearm have been decompressed, it must be decided whether a fasciotomy of the dorsal (extensor) compartment is necessary. The need is best determined by pressure measurements made in the operating room after the flexor compartment fasciotomies have been completed. If the pressure continues to be elevated in the dorsal compartment, fasciotomy should be performed with the arm pronated. A straight incision from the lateral epicondyle to the midline of the wrist is used. The interval between the extensor carpi radialis brevis and the extensor digitorum communis is identified, and fasciotomy is performed (Fig. 12–22).

COMPARTMENT SYNDROME OF THE LEG

For an acute compartment syndrome of the lower extremity, three decompression techniques are available. The technique chosen should allow access to all four compartments. The three techniques for the leg are

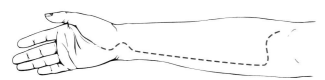

FIGURE 12–19. Ulnar approach to the volar flexor compartment of the forearm. (Modified from Whitesides, T., Jr.; Haney, T.C.; Morimoto, K.; Hirada, H. Clin Orthop 113:46, 1975.)

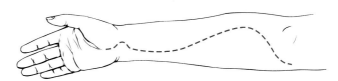

FIGURE 12–20. Ulnar approach to the superficial and deep compartments. Note the ulnar vessels in the depths overlying the deep flexor compartments. FCU, flexor carpi ulnaris; FDS, flexor digitorum sublimis. (Modified with permission from AAOS Instructional Course Lectures, Vol. 32. St. Louis, C.V. Mosby, 1983, p. 105.)

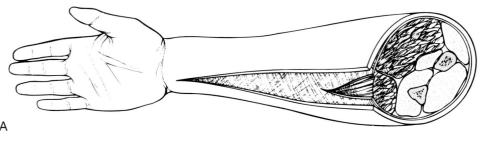

A

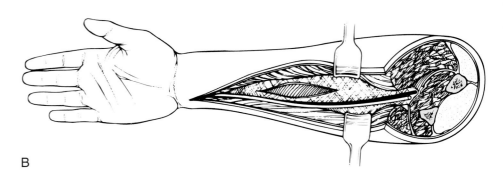

B

FIGURE 12–21. *A* and *B,* Ulnar approach to the forearm between the flexor carpi ulnaris and the flexor digitorum sublimis. (*A, B,* Modified with permission from AAOS Instructional Course Lectures, Vol. 32. St. Louis, C.V. Mosby, 1983, p. 105.)

fibulectomy, perifibular fasciotomy, and double-incision fasciotomy. There is no indication for subcutaneous fasciotomy in acute compartment syndrome of the leg.

Fibulectomy. Although fibulectomy certainly decompresses all four compartments of the leg, this technique, described by Patman and Thompson[93] and popularized by Kelly and Whitesides,[53] is unnecessary and is too radical a procedure to perform. It is now of only historical interest.

Perifibular Fasciotomy. The perifibular fasciotomy, popularized by Matsen and co-workers,[68] allows access to all four compartments of the leg through a single lateral incision that extends proximally from the head of the fibula and distally to the ankle, following the general line of the fibula. The skin incision is made, the skin and subcutaneous tissues are retracted proximally, and the intermuscular septum between the anterior and lateral compartments is identified. Care must be taken to identify and protect the superficial peroneal nerve. A fasciotomy is performed 1 cm in front of the intermuscular septum (anterior compartment) and 1 cm posterior to the intermuscular septum (lateral compartment) (Fig. 12–23*A* and *B*). The superficial posterior compartment is readily identified, and a fasciotomy is performed (see Fig. 12–23*C*). The interval between the peroneal compartment and the superficial posterior compartment is entered by retracting the peroneal compartment anteriorly and the superficial posterior compartment posteriorly to expose the deep posterior compartment. The deep posterior compartment is reached by following the interosseous membrane from the posterior aspect of the fibula and releasing the compartment from this membrane (see Fig. 12–23*D*). Care must be taken proximally because the peroneal nerve can be injured, particularly in compartment syndrome secondary to trauma, in which the anatomy may be badly distorted. It can also be difficult to be sure of having decompressed all compartments in a badly mangled extremity.

Double-Incision Technique. The double-incision fasciotomy employs two vertical skin incisions separated by a bridge of skin at least 8 cm wide (Figs. 12–24 and 12–25).[86, 105] The first skin incision extends from the knee to the ankle and is centered over the interval between the anterior and lateral compartments. The second incision also extends from the knee to the ankle and is centered 1 to 2 cm behind the posteromedial border of the tibia. The skin and subcutaneous tissue are separated from the fascia overlying the anterior and lateral compartments after completion of the vertical anterior incision. Care must be taken to identify and protect the superficial peroneal nerve. A fasciotomy of the anterior compartment 1 cm in front of the intermuscular septum is performed, followed by a fasciotomy of the lateral compartment 1 cm behind the intermuscular septum. It is imperative to extend the fasciotomy distally beyond the musculotendinous junction and proximally as far as the origin of the muscle.

The posteromedial incision is made (described previously), with care taken to protect the saphenous vein and nerve. The fascia overlying the gastrocnemius-soleus complex is incised, exposing the deep posterior compartment of the distal third of the leg. To decompress the deep posterior compartment adequately in the proximal direc-

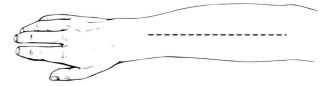

FIGURE 12–22. Dorsal approach to the extensor compartment of the forearm. (Redrawn with permission from AAOS Instructional Course Lectures, Vol. 32. St. Louis, C.V. Mosby, 1983, p. 107.)

tion, it is necessary to detach part of the soleal bridge from the back of the tibia. Doing so exposes the fascia overlying the flexor digitorum longus and the deep posterior compartment, which is then incised, completing the fasciotomy of the deep posterior compartment of the leg.

The double-incision technique is relatively easy to perform. It has the disadvantage of requiring two incisions, which may be inappropriate, particularly in a trauma patient and especially if it results in leaving bone, nerve, or vessel exposed (Fig. 12–26).

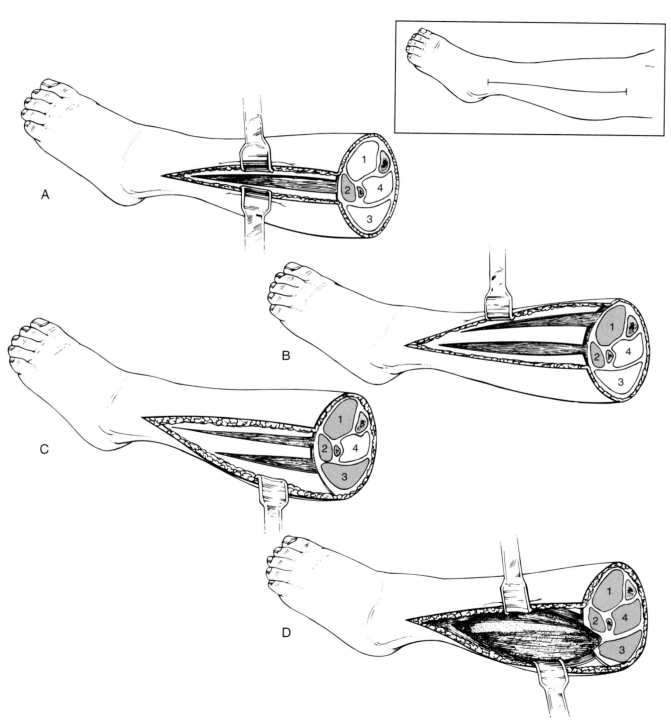

FIGURE 12–23. *A,* A lateral incision is made over the peroneal compartment (2). *B,* A skin incision is retracted anteriorly, exposing the anterior compartment (1). *C,* The posterior skin incision is retracted posteriorly, and the fascia overlying the superficial posterior compartment (3) is incised. *D,* The peroneal and superficial posterior compartments are now retracted, and the fascia overlying the deep posterior compartment (4) is incised. (*A–D,* Redrawn from Seligson, D. Concepts in Intramedullary Nailing. Orlando, FL, Grune & Stratton, 1985, pp. 114–115.)

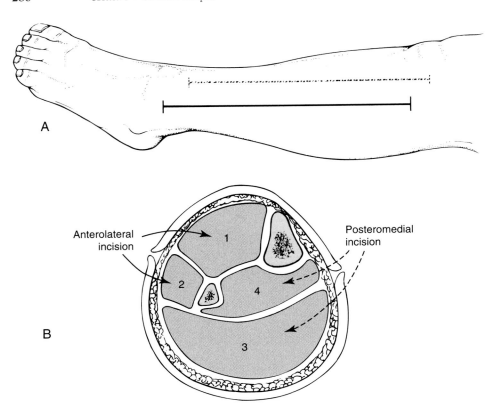

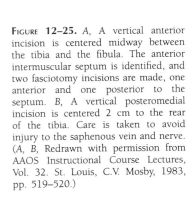

FIGURE **12–24.** *A,* The double-incision technique for performing fasciotomies of all four compartments of the lower extremity. *B,* Cross section of lower extremity showing a position of antero-lateral and posteromedial incisions that allows access to the anterior and lateral compartments (1 and 2) and the superficial and deep posterior compartments (3 and 4). (*A, B,* Modified with permission from AAOS Instructional Course Lectures, Vol. 32. St. Louis, C.V. Mosby, 1983, p. 110.)

Anterolateral incision

Posteromedial incision

FIGURE **12–25.** *A,* A vertical anterior incision is centered midway between the tibia and the fibula. The anterior intermuscular septum is identified, and two fasciotomy incisions are made, one anterior and one posterior to the septum. *B,* A vertical posteromedial incision is centered 2 cm to the rear of the tibia. Care is taken to avoid injury to the saphenous vein and nerve. (*A, B,* Redrawn with permission from AAOS Instructional Course Lectures, Vol. 32. St. Louis, C.V. Mosby, 1983, pp. 519–520.)

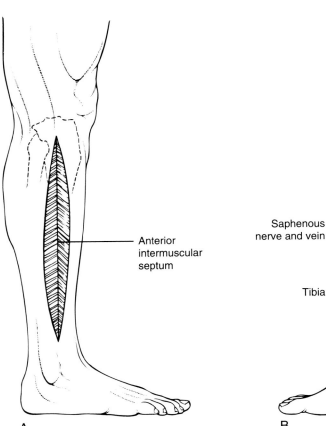

Anterior intermuscular septum

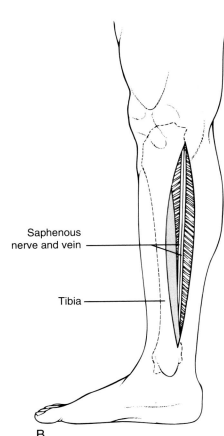

Saphenous nerve and vein

Tibia

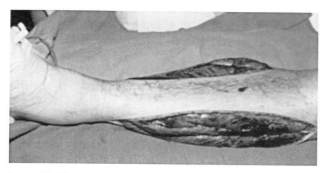

FIGURE 12–26. A double-incision fasciotomy for acute compartment syndrome.

COMPARTMENT SYNDROME OF THE THIGH

Compartment syndromes of the thigh, once thought to be rare, are being reported more frequently.[8, 73, 102, 114] According to Schwartz and associates,[114] compartment syndrome can occur in patients undergoing closed intramedullary nailing of the femur; to some extent, its development depends on the Injury Severity Score and the amount of soft tissue damage to the thigh. There is a concern that overdistraction at the time of closed intramedullary nailing, which in effect decreases the compartment volume, can produce a compartment syndrome.

The thigh consists of three muscle compartments—the quadriceps, hamstrings, and adductors. McLaren and co-workers[73] reported an isolated case of adductor compartment syndrome of the thigh, but compartment syndromes seen as a complication of closed intramedullary nailing usually involve the quadriceps compartment.

The surgical approach recommended depends on the compartment involved, which can be determined by pressure measurements. If the quadriceps compartment is involved, a single anterolateral incision is made along the length of the thigh, splitting the iliotibial band, and the fascia overlying the vastus lateralis is divided along its

length (Fig. 12–27). The hamstring compartment can then be entered by dividing the intermuscular septum, taking care to avoid further injury to perforating vessels. Release of the adductor compartment, if it is necessary, should be performed through a separate longitudinal incision along its length.

COMPARTMENT SYNDROME OF THE FOOT

Like those of the hand, the interosseous muscles of the foot are bound and contained within compartments. Failure to diagnose an acute compartment syndrome of the intrinsic muscles of the foot can result in myoneural necrosis and subsequent claw-toe deformity.[13, 90] It is seen most commonly after calcaneal fractures, Lisfranc injuries, or significant blunt trauma to the foot.

In our experience, the clinical findings for a patient with acute compartment syndrome of the foot are always equivocal. It is difficult to sort out local pain and tenderness to palpation in this area. Also, stretch pain in the foot is not as reliable a sign as it is in the hand. Therefore, the diagnosis must depend on compartment pressure monitoring. However, because no documentation of the normal compartment pressures in the foot is available, clinical suspicion is required to identify patients requiring fasciotomy.

The compartments of the foot are the medial, central, lateral, and interosseous, all of which must be decompressed (Fig. 12–28). A calcaneal compartment that includes the quadratus plantae muscle has also been described.[58, 59] After the diagnosis has been made, decompression of the foot can be carried out by a variety of techniques. Two incisions can be used—a dorsal incision that allows exposure of the interossei and a medial incision that allows exposure of the deep flexor muscles.[90] A single medial incision or two dorsal incisions have also been described, and their use is in part determined by the nature of the injury and other treatment objectives (Fig. 12–29).

FIGURE 12–27. Fasciotomy of the thigh (medial compartment).

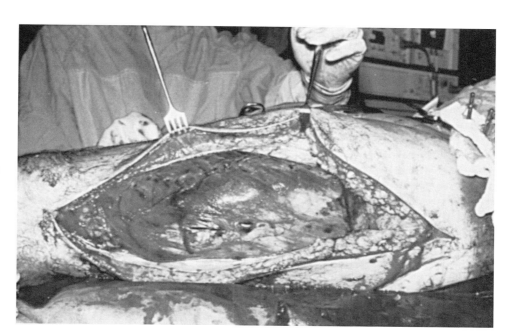

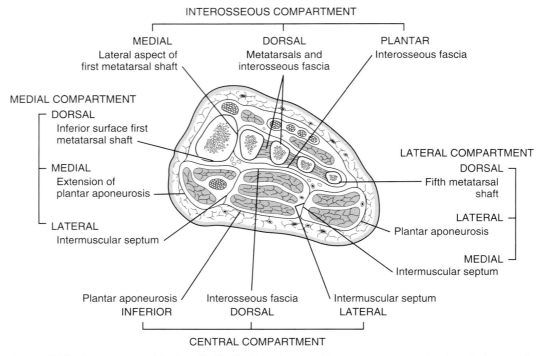

INTEROSSEOUS COMPARTMENT

MEDIAL
Lateral aspect of
first metatarsal shaft

DORSAL
Metatarsals and
interosseous fascia

PLANTAR
Interosseous fascia

MEDIAL COMPARTMENT
DORSAL
Inferior surface first
metatarsal shaft

MEDIAL
Extension of
plantar aponeurosis

LATERAL
Intermuscular septum

LATERAL COMPARTMENT
DORSAL
Fifth metatarsal
shaft

LATERAL
Plantar aponeurosis

MEDIAL
Intermuscular septum

Plantar aponeurosis
INFERIOR

Interosseous fascia
DORSAL

Intermuscular septum
LATERAL

CENTRAL COMPARTMENT

Figure 12–28. Compartments of the foot. Similar detail can be seen with magnetic resonance imaging. (Redrawn with permission from AAOS. Orthopaedic Knowledge Update: Foot and Ankle. Rosemont, IL, American Academy of Orthopaedic Surgeons, 1994, p. 263.)

AFTERCARE OF FASCIOTOMY WOUNDS

Fasciotomy wounds are potentially disfiguring, and much dissatisfaction with the end result can occur. Initial dressing using Sofra-Tulle or rayon is applied to the exposed area along with a bulky dressing. After 48 hours, the wound is inspected and any further necrotic tissue is removed.

It is fundamental to the objectives of the procedure to leave the wounds open; the treating surgeon is then left with the need for delayed skin closure, if possible, or for split-skin grafting.

Various methods of mechanical closure of fasciotomy wounds have been published, and each investigator is an enthusiastic supporter of his or her technique.

The Op-Site roller, designed by Bulstrode and associates,[18] offers a solution for closing larger wounds on the leg or forearm without repeated anesthesia. This technique allows serial tightening of an Op-Site sheet spread over the

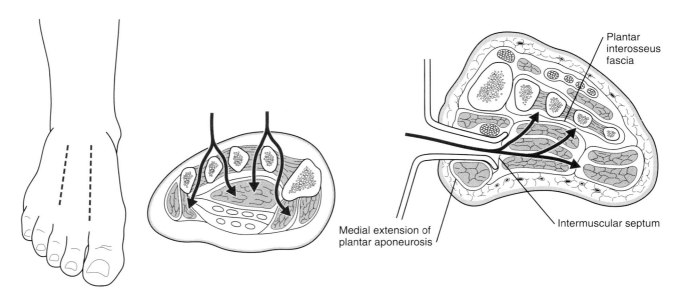

Plantar
interosseus
fascia

Medial extension of
plantar aponeurosis

Intermuscular septum

Figure 12–29. Incisions available for decompression of foot compartment syndromes. (Redrawn with permission from AAOS. Orthopaedic Knowledge Update: Foot and Ankle. Rosemont, IL, American Academy of Orthopaedic Surgeons, 1994, p. 264.)

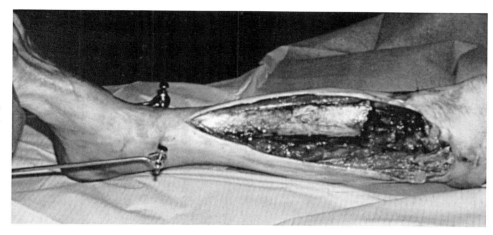

FIGURE 12–30. A closed fracture of the tibia that required a fasciotomy and was subsequently treated in traction.

open wound and can be performed easily by nursing staff or by the patient. A randomized study of this device demonstrated its effectiveness in closing most wounds.[124]

The vessel loop bootlace or shoelace technique is another simple, reliable method of improving wound edge apposition and reducing the need for subsequent skin grafting. Vascular loop cord is zigzagged between the skin edges using staples to attach the rubber loop to the skin and so "bootlace" the skin edges together to maintain some tension.[10] This arrangement can be revised at any dressing change if skin tension has diminished or if part of the wound can be closed and the area left open reduced in size. Asgari and Spinelli[6] used this technique to close all fasciotomy wounds in their series successfully by 3 weeks.

Wire sutures and the STAR (suture tension adjustment reel) mechanical method of fasciotomy closure have also been described.[71, 131]

MANAGEMENT OF SKELETAL INJURIES

Acute compartment syndrome of the upper or lower extremity is seldom an isolated condition and is almost always seen in association with a long bone fracture. Compartment syndrome occurring as a complication of a number of specific lesions, particularly fractures of the tibia and supracondylar fractures of the humerus, forearm, and femur, has been well documented.* The management of a compartment syndrome in association with any of these fractures deserves special emphasis because two problems coexist—an acute compartment syndrome and the fracture of a long bone. Fasciotomy has to be left open, raising the question of what should be done to the fracture (Fig. 12–30).

Whatever the anatomic location of the injury, the need for fasciotomy is an absolute indication for rigid stabilization of the bone. The technique used depends on the location and character of the fracture and the skill of the surgeon and can involve plating, intramedullary nailing, or external fixation. The technique chosen should be one that minimizes operative trauma to a limb that may already have had its circulation compromised. Therefore, if possi-

ble, intramedullary nailing to stabilize the bone (and hence the soft tissues) is recommended. This approach is not always possible, and sometimes the surgeon must resort to a plate or an external fixator. After the osteosynthesis has been completed, soft tissue coverage over the bone should be attempted. Aftercare of the fasciotomy wounds is similar to that described previously (Fig. 12–31).[35]

Gershuni and colleagues[35] have stated that a good functional result is always possible with fasciotomy if the high-risk patient is recognized and the acute compartment syndrome diagnosed early, before the development of irreversible damage to muscle or nerve. On the other hand, if the surgeon procrastinates and fails to recognize the early warning signs and symptoms of an impending compartment syndrome and delays the timing of fasciotomy, irreparable damage can ensue.[35] The most common causes of failure of fasciotomy are delay in the initiation of the operative procedure and an incomplete fasciotomy. Frequently, surgeons do not recognize that adequate decompression for acute compartment syndrome of the leg must involve all four compartments. Similarly, in the arm, both the superficial and deep flexor compartments must be decompressed. The surgeon must have a thorough knowledge of the surgical anatomy of the upper and lower

FIGURE 12–31. If a patient has a fracture of a long bone and requires fasciotomy, the long bone fracture must be stabilized either externally or internally to allow access to fasciotomy wounds. (Reproduced with permission from AAOS Instructional Course Lectures, Vol. 32. St. Louis, C.V. Mosby, 1983, p. 112.)

*See references 4, 5, 12, 26, 30, 34, 35, 81, 92, 104, 110, 116, 121.

extremities to perform an adequate decompression under emergency conditions. If early treatment is better than late treatment, prevention must be better still.

....

Acknowledgment

We would like to acknowledge the work of Dr. C. H. Rorabeck, M.D., F.R.C.S.(C.), in preparing the original text of this chapter in the first edition and his support in allowing us to revise it for this edition.

REFERENCES

1. Abdul-Hamid, A.K. First dorsal interosseous compartment syndrome. J Hand Surg [Br] 12:269, 1987.
2. Abraham, P.; Leftheriotis, G.; Saumet, J.L. Laser Doppler flowmetry in the diagnosis of chronic compartment syndrome. J Bone Joint Surg Br 80:365, 1998.
3. Ali, M.A. Fracture of the body of the hamate bone associated with compartment syndrome and dorsal decompression of the carpal tunnel. J Hand Surg [Br] 11:207, 1986.
4. Allen, M.J.; Steingold, R.F.; Kotecha, M.; Barnes, M. The importance of the deep volar compartment in crush injuries of the forearm. Injury 16:173, 1985.
5. Allen, M.J.; Stirling, A.J.; Crawshaw, C.V.; Barnes, M.R. Intracompartmental pressure monitoring of leg injuries: An aid to management. J Bone Joint Surg Br 67:53, 1985.
6. Asgari, M.M.; Spinelli, H.M. The vessel loop shoelace technique for closure of fasciotomy wounds. Ann Plast Surg 44:225, 2000.
7. Ashton, H. The effect of increased tissue pressure on blood flow. Clin Orthop 113:15, 1975.
8. Bass, R.R.; Allison, E.J., Jr.; Reines, H.D.; et al. Thigh compartment syndrome without lower extremity trauma following application of pneumatic antishock trousers. Ann Emerg Med 12:382, 1983.
9. Belanger, M.; Fadale, P. Compartment syndrome of the leg after arthroscopic examination of a tibial plateau fracture. Case report and review of the literature. Arthroscopy 13:646, 1997.
10. Bermann, S.S.; Schilling, J.D.; McIntyre, K.E.; et al. Shoelace technique for delayed primary closure of fasciotomies. Am J Surg 16:435, 1994.
11. Bingold, A.C. On splitting plasters: A useful analogy. J Bone Joint Surg Br 61:294, 1979.
12. Blick, S.S.; Brumback, R.J.; Poka, A.; et al. Compartment syndrome in open tibial fractures. J Bone Joint Surg Am 68:1348, 1986.
13. Bonutti, P.M.; Bell, G.R. Compartment syndrome of the foot: A case report. J Bone Joint Surg Am 68:1449, 1986.
14. Brooks, B. Pathologic changes in muscle as a result of disturbances of circulation. Arch Surg 5:188, 1922.
15. Brooks, B.; Johnson, J.S.; Kirtley, J.A. Simultaneous vein ligation. Surg Gynecol Obstet 59:496, 1934.
16. Brumback, R.J. Compartment syndrome complicating avulsion of the origin of the triceps muscle: A case report. J Bone Joint Surg Am 69:1445, 1987.
17. Brumback, R.J. Traumatic rupture of the superior gluteal artery, without fracture of the pelvis, causing compartment syndrome of the buttock. J Bone Joint Surg Am 72:134, 1990.
18. Bulstrode, C.K.; King, J.B.; Worpole, R.; Ham, R.J. A simple method for closing fasciotomies. Ann R Coll Surg Engl 67:119, 1985.
19. Bywaters, E.G.L.; Beall, D. Crush injuries with impairment of renal function. Br Med J 1:427, 1941.
20. Chandler, J.G.; Knapp, R.W. Early definitive treatment of vascular injuries in the Viet Nam conflict. JAMA 202:136, 1967.
21. Christensen, K.S. Pneumatic antishock garments (PASG): Do they precipitate lower extremity compartment syndromes? J Trauma 26:1102, 1986.
22. Christensen, K.S.; Klaerke, M. Volkmann's ischemic contracture due to limb compression in drug-induced coma. Injury 16:543, 1985.
23. DeLee, J.C.; Stiehl, J.B. Open tibial fractures with compartment syndrome. Clin Orthop 160:175, 1981.
24. Eaton, R.G.; Green, W.T. Epimysiotomy and fasciotomy in the treatment of Volkmann's ischemic contracture. Orthop Clin North Am 3:175, 1972.
25. Eaton, R.G.; Green, W.T. Volkmann's ischemia: A volar compartment syndrome of the forearm. Clin Orthop 113:58, 1975.
26. Edwards, P.D.; Miles, K.A.; Owens, S.J.; et al. A new non-invasive test for detection of compartment syndromes. Nucl Med Commun 20:215, 1999.
27. Ellis, H. Disabilities after tibial shaft fractures. J Bone Joint Surg Br 40:190, 1958.
28. French, E.B.; Price, W.H. Anterior tibial pain. Br Med J 2:1291, 1962.
29. Galpin, R.D.; Kronick, J.B.; Willis, R.B.; Frewen, T.C. Bilateral lower extremity compartment syndromes secondary to intraosseous fluid resuscitation. J Pediatr Orthop 11:773, 1991.
30. Garber, J.N. Volkmann's contracture of fractures of the forearm and elbow. J Bone Joint Surg 21:154, 1939.
31. Garfin, S.R.; Mubarak, S.J.; Evans, K.L.; et al. Quantification of intracompartmental pressure and volume under plaster casts. J Bone Joint Surg Am 63:449, 1981.
32. Geary, N. Late surgical decompression for compartment syndrome of the forearm. J Bone Joint Surg Br 66:745, 1984.
33. Gelberman, R.H.; Garfin, S.R.; Hergenroeder, P.T.; et al. Compartment syndromes of the forearm: Diagnosis and treatment. Clin Orthop 161:252, 1981.
34. Gelberman, R.H.; Zakaib, G.S.; Mubarak, S.J.; et al. Decompression of forearm compartment syndromes. Clin Orthop 134:225, 1978.
35. Gershuni, D.H.; Mubarak, S.J.; Yaru, N.C.; Lee, Y.F. Fracture of the tibia complicated by acute compartment syndrome. Clin Orthop 217:221, 1987.
36. Giannotti, G.; Cohn, S.M.; Brown, M. et al. Utility of near-infrared spectroscopy in the diagnosis of lower extremity compartment syndrome. J Trauma Injury Infect Crit Care 48:396, 2000.
37. Gibson, M.J.; Barnes, M.R.; Allen, M.J.; Chan, R.N. Weakness of foot dorsiflexion and changes in compartment pressures after tibial osteotomy. J Bone Joint Surg Br 68:471, 1986.
38. Graham, B.; Loomer, R.L. Anterior compartment syndrome in a patient with fracture of the tibial plateau treated by continuous passive motion and anticoagulants: Report of a case. Clin Orthop 195:197, 1985.
39. Griffiths, D. Volkmann's ischemic contracture. Br J Surg 28:239, 1940.
40. Hargens, A.R.; Akeson, W.H.; Mubarak, S.J.; et al. Tissue fluid states in compartment syndromes. Bibl Anat 15(Pt I):108, 1977.
41. Hargens, A.R.; Romine, J.S.; Sipe, J.C.; et al. Peripheral nerve conduction block by high muscle compartment pressure. J Bone Joint Surg Am 61:192, 1979.
42. Hastings, H.; Misamore, G. Compartment syndrome resulting from intravenous regional anesthesia. J Hand Surg [Am] 12:559, 1987.
43. Heckman, M.M.; Whitesides, T.E., Jr.; Grewe, S.R.; et al. Histologic determination of the ischemic threshold in the canine compartment syndrome model. J Orthop Trauma 7:199, 1993.
44. Heim, M.; Martinowitz, U.; Horoszowski, H. The short foot syndrome—An unfortunate consequence of neglected raised intracompartmental pressure in a severe hemophilic child. A case report. Angiology 37:128, 1986.
45. Heppenstall, R.B.; Sapega, A.A.; Izant, T.; et al. Compartment syndrome: A quantitative study of high-energy phosphorus compounds using ^{31}P-magnetic resonance spectroscopy. J Trauma 29:1113, 1989.
46. Heppenstall, R.B.; Scott, R.; Sapiga, A.; et al. A comparative study of the tolerance of skeletal muscle to ischemia. J Bone Joint Surg Am 68:820, 1986.
47. Hernandez, J., Jr.; Peterson, H.A. Fracture of the distal radial physis complicated by compartment syndrome and premature physeal closure. J Pediatr Orthop 6:627, 1986.
48. Hieb, L.D.; Alexander, A.H. Bilateral anterior and lateral compartment syndromes in a patient with sickle cell trait: Case report and review of the literature. Clin Orthop 228:190, 1988.
49. Hildebrand, O. Die Lehre von den ischamische Muskellahmungen und Kontrakturen. Samml Klin Vortr 122:437, 1906.
50. Johansen, K.; Lynch, K.; Paun, M.; Copass, M. Noninvasive vascular tests reliably exclude occult arterial trauma in injured extremities. J Trauma 31:515, 1991.
51. Jepson, P.N. Ischemic contracture—Experimental study. Ann Surg 84:785, 1926.
52. Kamel, R.; Sakla, F.B. Anatomical compartments of the sole of the human foot. Anat Rec 140:57, 1961.
53. Kelly, R.P.; Whitesides, T.E., Jr. Transfibular route for fasciotomy of the leg. J Bone Joint Surg Am 48:1022, 1967.

54. Khalil, I.M. Bilateral compartment syndrome after prolonged surgery in the lithotomy position. J Vasc Surg 5:879, 1987.

55. Kunkel, J.M. Thigh and leg compartment syndrome in the absence of lower extremity trauma following MAST application. Am J Emerg Med 5:118, 1987.

56. Landerer, A.S. Die Gewebspannung in ihrem Einfluss auf die ortliche Blutbewegung und Lymphbewegung. Leipzig, Vogel, 1884.

57. Lee, B.Y.; Brancato, R.F.; Park, I.H.; Shaw, W.W. Management of compartmental syndrome: Diagnosis and surgical considerations. Am J Surg 148:383, 1984.

58. Manoli, A., II. Compartment syndromes of the foot: Current concepts. Foot Ankle 10:340, 1990.

59. Manoli, A., II; Weber, T.G. Fasciotomy of the foot: An anatomical study with special reference to release of the calcaneal compartment. Foot Ankle 10:267, 1990.

60. Matsen, F.A., III. Compartmental syndrome: A unified concept. Clin Orthop 113:8, 1975.

61. Matsen, F.A., III. Compartment Syndromes. New York, Grune & Stratton, 1980.

62. Matsen, F.A., III. A practical approach to compartmental syndromes: Part I, definition, theory and pathogenesis. Instr Course Lect 32:88, 1983.

63. Matsen, F.A., III; Hargens, A.R. Compartment Syndromes and Volkmann's Contracture. Philadelphia, W.B. Saunders, 1981, p. 111.

64. Matsen, F.A., III; Krugmire, R.B., Jr. Compartmental syndromes. Surg Gynecol Obstet 147:943, 1979.

65. Matsen, F.A., III; Mayo, K.A.; Krugmire, R.B., Jr.; et al. A model compartment syndrome in man with particular reference to the quantification of nerve function. J Bone Joint Surg Am 59:648, 1977.

66. Matsen, F.A., III; Mayo, K.A.; Sheridan, G.W.; Krugmire, R.B., Jr. Monitoring of intramuscular pressure. Surgery 79:702, 1976.

67. Matsen, F.A., III; Staheli, L.T. Neurovascular complications following tibial osteotomy in children: A case report. Clin Orthop 110:210, 1975.

68. Matsen, F.A., III; Winquist, R.A.; Krugmire, R.B. Diagnosis and management of compartmental syndromes. J Bone Joint Surg Am 62:286, 1980.

69. Matsen, F.A., III; Wyss, C.R.; King R.V. The continuous infusion technique in the assessment of clinical compartment syndromes. In: Hargens, A.R., ed. Tissue Fluid Pressure and Composition. Baltimore, Williams & Wilkins, 1981, p. 255.

70. Matsen, F.A., III; Wyss, C.R.; Krugmire, R.B., Jr.; et al. The effects of limb elevation and dependency on local arteriovenous gradients in normal human limbs with particular reference to limbs with increased tissue pressure. Clin Orthop 150:187, 1980.

71. McKenney, M.G.; Nir, I.; Fee, T.; et al. A simple device for closure of fasciotomy wounds. Am J Surg 172:275, 1996

72. McLaren, A.; Rorabeck, C.H. The effect of shock on tourniquet-induced nerve injury. Proceedings of the Fifteenth Annual Meeting of the Canadian Orthopaedic Research Society, 1981. Orthop Trans 5:482, 1981.

73. McLaren, A.C.; Ferguson, J.H.; Miniaci, A. Crush syndrome associated with use of the fracture table: A case report. J Bone Joint Surg Am 69:1447, 1987.

74. McLellan, B.A.; Phillips, J.H.; Hunter, G.A.; et al. Bilateral lower extremity amputations after prolonged application of the pneumatic antishock garment: Case report. Can J Surg 30:55, 1987.

75. McQueen, M.M.; Court-Brown, C.M. Compartment monitoring in tibial fractures. J Bone Joint Surg Br 78:99, 1996.

76. Michaelson, M. Crush injury and crush syndrome. World J Surg 16:899, 1992.

77. Miniaci, A.; Rorabeck, C.H. Compartment syndrome: A complication of treatment of muscle hernias. J Bone Joint Surg Am 68:1444, 1968.

78. Moed, B.R.; Thorderson, K. Measurement of intracompartmental pressure: A comparison of the slit catheter, side-ported needle, and simple needle. J Bone Joint Surg Am 75:231, 1993.

79. Mohler, L.R.; Styf, J.R.; Pedowitz, R.A.; et al. Intramuscular deoxygenation during exercise in patients who have chronic anterior compartment syndrome of the leg. J Bone Joint Surg Am 79:844, 1997.

80. Mubarak, S.J. A practical approach to compartmental syndromes: Part II, diagnosis. Instr Course Lect 32:92, 1983.

81. Mubarak, S.J.; Carroll, N.C. Volkmann's contracture in children: Aetiology and prevention. J Bone Joint Surg Br 61:285, 1979.

82. Mubarak, S.J.; Hargens, A.R. Compartment Syndromes and Volkmann's Contracture. Philadelphia, W.B. Saunders, 1981, p. 113.

83. Mubarak, S.J.; Hargens, A.R.; Garfin, S.R.; et al. Loss of nerve function in compartment syndromes: Pressure versus ischemia? Transactions of the Orthopedic Research Society 25th Annual Meeting, San Francisco, February 20, 1979.

84. Mubarak, S.J.; Hargens, A.R.; Owen, C.A.; et al. The wick catheter technique for measurement of intramuscular pressure: A new research and clinical tool. J Bone Joint Surg Am 58:1016, 1976.

85. Mubarak, S.J.; Owen, C.A. Compartment syndrome and its relation to the crush syndrome: A spectrum of disease. Clin Orthop 113:81, 1975.

86. Mubarak, S.J.; Owen, C.A. Double-incision fasciotomy of the leg for decompression in compartment syndromes. J Bone Joint Surg Am 59:184, 1977.

87. Mubarak, S.J.; Owen, C.A.; Hargens, A.R.; et al. Acute compartment syndromes: Diagnosis and treatment with aid of the wick catheter. J Bone Joint Surg Am 60:1091, 1978.

88. Mubarak, S.J.; Wilton, N.C. Compartment syndromes and epidural analgesia. J Pediatr Orthop 17:282, 1997.

89. Murphy, J.B. Myositis. JAMA 63:1249, 1914.

90. Myerson, M. Acute compartment syndromes of the foot. Bull Hosp Jt Dis Orthop Inst 47:251, 1987.

91. Myerson, M.S. Experimental decompression of the fascial compartments of the foot: The basis for fasciotomy in acute compartment syndromes. Foot Ankle 8:308, 1988.

92. Owen, R.; Tsimboukis, B. Ischaemia complicating closed tibial and fibular shaft fractures. J Bone Joint Surg Br 49:268, 1967.

93. Patman, R.D.; Thompson, J.E. Fasciotomy in peripheral vascular surgery. Arch Surg 101:663, 1970.

94. Paton, D.F. The pathogenesis of anterior tibial syndrome. J Bone Joint Surg Br 50:383, 1968.

95. Peck, D.; Nicholls, P.J.; Beard, C.; Allen, J.R. Are there compartment syndromes in some patients with idiopathic back pain? Spine 11:468, 1986.

96. Petersen, F. Uber ischämische Muskellahmungen. Arch Klin Chir 37:675, 1888.

97. Phillips, J.H.; Mackinnon, S.E.; Beatty, S.E.; et al. Vibratory sensory testing in acute compartment syndromes: A clinical and experimental study. Plast Reconstr Surg 79:796, 1987.

98. Reddy, P.K.; Kaye, K.W. Deep posterior compartmental syndrome: A serious complication of the lithotomy position. J Urol 132:144, 1984.

99. Reis, N.D.; Michaelson, M. Crush injury to the lower limbs. J Bone Joint Surg Am 68:414, 1986.

100. Reneman, R.S. The Anterior and the Lateral Compartment Syndrome of the Leg. The Hague, Mouton, 1968.

101. Roberts, R.S.; Csencsitz, T.A.; Heard, C.W., Jr. Upper extremity compartment syndromes following pit viper envenomation. Clin Orthop 193:184, 1985.

102. Rooser, B. Quadriceps contusion with compartment syndrome: Evacuation of hematoma in 2 cases. Acta Orthop Scand 58:170, 1987.

103. Rorabeck, C.H. A practical approach to compartmental syndromes: Part III, management. Instr Course Lect 32:102, 1983.

104. Rorabeck, C.H. The treatment of compartment syndromes of the leg. J Bone Joint Surg Br 66:93, 1984.

105. Rorabeck, C.H.; Bourne, R.B.; Fowler, P.J. The surgical treatment of exertional compartment syndrome in athletes. J Bone Joint Surg Am 65:1245, 1983.

106. Rorabeck, C.H.; Castle, G.S.P.; Hardie, R.; Logan, J. The slit catheter: A new device for measuring intracompartmental pressure. Proceedings of the Canadian Orthopedic Research Society, 14th Annual Meeting, Calgary, Alberta, Canada, June 1980. Surg Forum 31:513, 1980.

107. Rorabeck, C.H.; Castle, G.S.P.; Hardie, R.; Logan, J. Compartmental pressure measurements: An experimental investigation using the slit catheter. J Trauma 21:446, 1981.

108. Rorabeck, C.H.; Clarke, K.M. The pathophysiology of the anterior tibial compartment syndrome: An experimental investigation. J Trauma 18:299, 1978.

109. Rorabeck, C.H.; Macnab, I. The pathophysiology of the anterior tibial compartment syndrome. Clin Orthop 113:52, 1975.
110. Rorabeck, C.H.; Macnab, I. Anterior tibial compartment syndrome complicating fractures of the shaft of the tibia. J Bone Joint Surg Am 58:549, 1976.
111. Rowlands, R.P. Volkmann's contracture. Guys Hosp Gaz 24:87, 1910.
112. Scholander, P.F.; Hargens, A.R.; Miller, S.L. Negative pressure in the interstitial fluid of animals. Science 161:321, 1968.
113. Schwartz, J.T., Jr.; Brumback, R.J.; Lakatos, R., et al. Acute compartment syndrome of the thigh. J Bone Joint Surg Am 71:392, 1989.
114. Schwartz, J.T.; Brumback, R.J.; Poka, A.; et al. Compartment syndrome of the thigh: A review of 13 cases. Proceedings of the 55th Annual Meeting of the American Academy of Orthopaedic Surgeons: Paper 357. Rosemont, IL, American Academy of Orthopaedic Surgeons, 1988, p. 188.
115. Seddon, H.J. Volkmann's ischemia in the lower limb. J Bone Joint Surg Br 48:627, 1966.
116. Sirbu, A.B.; Murphy, M.J.; White, A.S. Soft tissue complications of fractures of the leg. Calif West Med 60:1, 1944.
117. Spinner, M.; Aiache, A.; Silver, L.; Barsky, A. Impending ischemic contracture of the hand. Plast Reconstr Surg 50:341, 1972.
118. Straehley, D.; Jones, W.W. Acute compartment syndrome (anterior, lateral and superficial posterior) following tear of the medial head of the gastrocnemius muscle: A case report. Am J Sports Med 14:96, 1986.
119. Strecker, W.B.; Wood, M.B.; Bieber, E.J. Compartment syndrome masked by epidural anesthesia for postoperative pain. Report of a case. J Bone Joint Surg Am 68:1447, 1986.
120. Styf, J.R.; Korner, L.M. Microcapillary infusion technique for measurement of intramuscular pressure during exercise. Clin Orthop 207:253, 1986.
121. Sundararaj, J.G.D.; Mani, K. Pattern of contracture and recovery following ischaemia of the upper limb. J Hand Surg [Br] 10:155, 1985.
122. Sundararaj, G.D.; Mani, K. Management of Volkmann's ischemic contracture of the upper limb. J Hand Surg [Br] 10:401, 1985.
123. Tarlow, S.D.; Achterman, C.A.; Hayhurst, J.; Ovadia, D.N. Acute compartment syndrome in the thigh complicating fracture of the femur: A report of three cases. J Bone Joint Surg Am 68:1439, 1986.
124. Tasman-Jones, T.C.; Tomlinson, M. Tissue rollers in the closure of fasciotomy wounds. J Bone Joint Surg Br 75:49, 1993.
125. Templeman, D.; Lange, R.; Harms, B. Lower extremity compartment syndromes associated with use of pneumatic antishock garments. J Trauma 27:79, 1987.
126. Thomas, J.J. Nerve involvement in the ischaemic paralysis and contracture of Volkmann. Ann Surg 49:330, 1909.
127. Volkmann, R. Die ischaemischen Muskellahmungen und Kontrakturen. Zentralbl Chir 8:801, 1881.
128. Wallis, F.C. Treatment of paralysis and muscular atrophy after prolonged use of splints or of an Esmarch's cord. Practitioner 67:429, 1901.
129. Whitesides, T.E., Jr.; Haney, T.C.; Morimoto, K.; Hirada, H. Tissue pressure measurements as a determinant for the need of fasciotomy. Clin Orthop 113:43, 1975.
130. Whitesides, T.E., Jr.; Haney, T.C.; Hirada, H.; et al. A simple method for tissue pressure determination. Arch Surg 110:1311, 1975.
131. Wiger, P.; Tkaczuk, P.; Styf, J. Secondary wound closure following fasciotomy for acute compartment syndrome increases intramuscular pressure. J Orthop Trauma 12:117, 1998.
132. Wiggins, H.E. The anterior tibial compartmental syndrome: A complication of the Hauser procedure. Clin Orthop 113:90, 1975.
133. Wilson, S.C.; Vrahas, M.S.; Berson, L; et al. A simple method to measure compartment pressures using an intravenous catheter. Orthopedics 20:403, 1997.

CHAPTER 13

Fractures with Soft Tissue Injuries

Fred F. Behrens, M.D.
Michael S. Sirkin, M.D.

HISTORICAL PERSPECTIVE AND SCOPE

The serious nature of open fractures has been well understood since antiquity.[166] The Hippocratic physicians[95] recognized that wound size, fracture stability, and the proximity of neurovascular structures all influence the ultimate outcome of these severe injuries. They urged speed, removal of protruding fragments, antiseptic wound dressings (compresses soaked in wine), stable reduction without undue pressure at the injury site, dressing changes every 2 days, and free drainage of pus. Even their final advice sounds modern: "One should especially avoid such cases if one has a respectable excuse, for the favorable chances are few and the risks many. Besides, if a man does not reduce the fracture, he will be thought unskillful. If he does reduce it, he will bring the patient nearer to death than to recovery."[95]

Over the ensuing centuries, an open fracture usually meant death from sepsis within a month. To preserve life was the principal treatment goal, and fire seemed the most effective tool. A red-hot iron and boiling oil of elder were meant to clean the wound, destroy devitalized tissue, and prevent wound sepsis. This practice changed abruptly one day in 1538 when Ambroise Paré (1510 to 1590),[117] a French army surgeon, ran out of hot oil during the siege of Turin. He had only "a digestive made of yolke of egge and oyle of Roses and Turpentine" and was baffled the next morning when all patients "dressed with a digestive onely"[166] were alive and nearly pain free.

Despite gentler and speedier care, the use of ligatures and tourniquets, and the practice of delayed stump closure, the surgery of open wounds remained, well into the middle of the 19th century, the surgery of amputations. In 1842, Malgaigne[99, 166] found that the overall mortality rate for amputations was 30%; for major amputations, it was 52%, and for thigh amputations, 60%.

Although primary amputation was recognized as the safest method to treat open fractures, some surgeons were dissatisfied with this mutilating and life-threatening

procedure. This school of thought started with Guy de Chauliac (1546),[39] who first taught the enlargement of open and contaminated wounds to encourage drainage. Paré[166] amputated only when an open fracture was complicated by fever. He advised: "If there bee any strange bodies as peeces of Wood, Irons, Bones, bruised flesh, congealed blood or the like, whether they come from without or from within the body . . . he must take them away for otherwise there is no union to be expected," and "The wound must forthwith be enlarged . . . so there may be free passage for both the pus or matter . . . contained therein."[166] The wounds were held open with a packing of lint or rolls of linen. Just before the beginning of the French Revolution, Pierre Joseph Desault (1738 to 1795)[166] developed the modern concept of débridement, but until World War I the method was used only sporadically because many of the known army surgeons, such as Larrey, continued to favor amputations for combat-related wounds.

Lister's introduction of antisepsis half a century later seemed another major step toward limb salvage; however, when used alone during the Franco-Prussian War (1870 to 1871),[166] it failed. It was left to Carl Reyher,[165] a young German surgeon in the Russian service, to show in a controlled study carried out during the Russo-Turkish War (1877) that a further reduction in mortality rate was possible only when antisepsis was combined with early débridement. Although his observation was soon confirmed experimentally, it was not until the end of World War I that the Interallied Surgical Conference recommended the resection of all contaminated tissues, the removal of all foreign material, and no primary wound closures unless fewer than 8 hours had elapsed since the open injury was inflicted.[51]

The great medical discoveries of the past 150 years,[166] such as anesthesia, antisepsis, asepsis, the germ theory of infections, advances in prehospital care, fluid and cardiorespiratory resuscitation, and early fracture stabilization,[16, 109] brought about a revolution in operative wound care. Although in the past success in treating open fractures was measured in the number of lives lost or limbs amputated, attention is now being focused on reducing wound infections and healing times. Ultimately, we aim to restore our patients with the least delay to as close to their preinjury status as possible. Although the techniques introduced during the past century are important, none was as difficult to learn or as easy to neglect as the art of débridement—and this is still true at the beginning of the 21st century.[166]

Although this chapter emphasizes open fractures and dislocations, it also addresses some closed fractures with associated soft tissue destruction. Pitfalls and complications are common unless these fractures are treated like open lesions.[159, 160] Curiously enough, this was well recognized two millennia ago by the Hippocratic physicians: "The same treatment of the wound applies to cases of fractures which are first without wound but where one occurs during treatment either through too great compression of bandages or the pressure of splint or some other cause. In such cases, the occurrence of ulcerations are recognized while pain is dropping. . . . Treat them for the future in the same manner as cases in which there is a wound from the first. Change the dressing every other day . . . Correctness of position also contributes to a good result. . . ."[95]

ETIOLOGY, MECHANISMS, AND CHARACTERISTICS

The forceful disruption of skin and underlying tissues is the most obvious expression of an open fracture, but it is only one of many manifestations of a violent encounter between the human body and the environment. The potential damage from such a collision is related to the energy dissipated during the event. According to the equation $KE = \frac{1}{2}mv^2$, the kinetic energy involved (KE) is directly proportional to the mass (m) and the square of the speed (v).[57] Traditionally, warfare or natural catastrophes generated most life- and limb-threatening energies. The ingenious harnessing of natural resources during the past 200 years has not only revolutionized industrial productivity and transportation, it has also progressively exposed the human body to forces that exceed the strength and resilience of its organs and tissues[25] (Table 13–1). Today,

TABLE 13–1 ....
Energy Dissipated in Injuries

Injury	Dissipated Energy (foot-pounds)
Fall from a curb	100
Skiing injury	300–500
High-velocity gunshot wound	2000
Automobile bumper collision at 20 miles per hour	100,000

Source: Chapman, M.W. Instr Course Lect 31:75, 1982.

TABLE 13–2 ....
Causes of Open Fractures among Civilians

Cause	%
Motorcycle accident	28
Motor vehicle accident	24
Falls	13
Pedestrian struck by car	12
Crush injuries	8
Firearms	2
Miscellaneous	13

Source: Dellinger, E.P., et al. Arch Surg 123:1320, 1988.

more than two thirds of open fractures seen at trauma centers are caused by objects and mechanisms that emerged during the past century[41] (Table 13–2).

The significance of speed, even when small masses are involved, is vividly apparent in the wounds inflicted in military combat, in urban warfare, and in hunting accidents. Although devastating, these wounds usually involve only a limited, well-circumscribed part of the body. In the modern traffic accident, the driver's or passenger's body becomes a high-mass, high-speed projectile that sustains several impacts and thus many superimposed lesions—a polytraumatized patient with axial and appendicular injuries at multiple levels is the consequential and distressing outcome.[26, 41, 59, 131]

Injuries caused by a direct force are often thought to be the most serious because they disrupt local soft tissue and contaminate the wound. Yet, all too often the effects of indirect forces are gravely underestimated. A high-energy torsional injury can cause a long bone to explode into sharp fragments that swiftly penetrate the centrally located neurovascular structures and the surrounding soft tissue sleeve, a picture typically seen in injuries caused by farm and other equipment driven by power takeoffs.

As typical high-energy injuries, fractures with major soft tissue disruptions differ radically from simple closed lesions. About 40% to 70% are associated with trauma elsewhere,[141] particularly cerebral lesions, cardiothoracic and abdominal disruptions,[79] and fractures or ligamentous injuries involving other extremities.[41] Locally, open fractures usually cause more damage than closed lesions; thus, they are more often associated with soft tissue loss, compartment syndromes,[12, 40] neurovascular injuries,[24, 37, 41, 63, 83, 91, 112] and ligamentous disruptions of adjacent joints. In addition to possible bone loss, the fracture patterns associated with open fractures typically have wider initial displacements[110] and greater comminution than closed lesions.[159]

CLASSIFICATIONS

The treatment and prognosis of fractures and dislocations with soft tissue injuries are influenced by many premorbid, injury, and treatment variables; most act independently, and each is expressed by a different severity scale. To calculate summary indices that take all the known injury components into account is very tempting but often causes further confusion because it is difficult to assign appropriate weight to different variables that can unduly potentiate or negate each other. For these and other reasons, most accepted classifications of fractures with soft tissue injuries have been simple and pragmatic rather than multifactorial and exhaustive.

Open Fractures

Most classifications of open musculoskeletal injuries follow the initial attempt by Cauchoix and associates,[23] who were mainly interested in the size of the skin defect, the degree of contusion and soft tissue crush, and the complexity of the bony lesion. Rittmann and coworkers[131, 132] also maintained three severity groups but focused on direct and indirect injury patterns, amount of dead and foreign material in the wounds, and involvement of neurovascular structures. The classification of Gustilo and Anderson[61] followed the earlier proposals and suggested that gunshot wounds and farm injuries automatically be considered type III in severity.

Although these classifications have some therapeutic and prognostic implications, all lack sensitivity at the upper end of the severity spectrum. In 1982, Tscherne and Oestern[160] presented a multifactorial classification with four severity types. Each type takes into account the extent of the skin injury, soft tissue damage, fracture severity, and degree of contamination. In 1984, Gustilo and colleagues[62] divided their type III lesions into three subgroups. IIIA fractures are characterized by extensive lacerations yet have sufficient soft tissue to provide adequate bone coverage, IIIB fractures are those with extensive soft tissue loss and much devascularized bone, and IIIC lesions are associated with major vascular disruptions (Table 13–3). This revised classification has brought some refinement and enjoys wide popularity. However, as is true for many other classifications,[17, 45, 89, 149, 156] two studies found that interobserver concurrence did not exceed 60%.[21, 73]

Open fractures inflicted by lawn mowers and tornadoes deserve particular consideration. Both generate severe open high-energy injuries either through direct impact (at 3000 revolutions per minute, the blade of a rotary lawn mower generates 2100 foot-pounds of kinetic energy[118]) or through flying debris containing soil and other contaminated material. Post-traumatic infections are common and are usually caused by a mixed flora, mostly gram-negative bacilli.[105] Lawn mower injuries are most common in children younger than 14. They are often complicated by compartment syndromes.[138] Tornado and lawn mower injuries should be treated like farm injuries, with broad-spectrum antibiotics including penicillin or an analogue, repeated wide débridements, and possibly extensive soft tissue and reconstructive procedures.

The Mangled Extremity

With continuous improvements in prehospital rescue and resuscitation, more patients with severe extremity injuries involving vascular compromise[24, 37, 41, 63, 81, 83, 91, 112] or partial amputation[52, 78, 85] are surviving. Traditionally, between 50% and 100% of these injuries resulted in amputation.[91] With the development of free flaps,[53, 171] temporary intraluminal shunts,[77] and microvascular reconstructions, many of these extremities are now replanted, revascularized, or covered with local or free muscle flaps. Unfortunately, many patients may fare better with early amputation followed by vigorous rehabilitation and vocational training.[24, 48, 52, 63]

The difficult choice between sacrificing a potentially useful limb segment and attempting the time-consuming and resource-intensive salvage of a functionally useless extremity has been addressed by several investigators.[57, 74, 78, 91] Johansen and colleagues[78] retrospectively analyzed the charts of 25 patients with severe open lower extremity fractures and found that limb salvage was related to energy dissipation, hemodynamic status, degree of limb ischemia, and age of the patient. They scored each of these four variables according to severity and called the sum of the scores the Mangled Extremity Severity Score (MESS)[78] (Table 13–4). Although based on small numbers, the retrospective and subsequent prospective evaluation[65] showed that a MESS of 7 or higher predicted, with a high degree of confidence, the need for initial or delayed amputation, whereas all limbs with a score of 6 or lower

---

TABLE 13–3

Classification of Open Fractures

Fracture Type	Description
Type I	Skin opening of 1 cm or less, quite clean. Most likely from inside to outside. Minimal muscle contusion. Simple transverse or short oblique fractures.
Type II	Laceration more than 1 cm long, with extensive soft tissue damage, flaps, or avulsion. Minimal to moderate crushing component. Simple transverse or short oblique fractures with minimal comminution.
Type III	Extensive soft tissue damage including muscles, skin, and neurovascular structures. Often a high-velocity injury with severe crushing component.
Type IIIA	Extensive soft tissue laceration, adequate bone coverage. Segmental fractures, gunshot injuries.
Type IIIB	Extensive soft tissue injury with periosteal stripping and bone exposure. Usually associated with massive contamination.
Type IIIC	Vascular injury requiring repair.

Source: Gustilo, R.B., et al. J Trauma 24:742, 1984.

TABLE 13-4 ....

MESS (Mangled Extremity Severity Score) Variables

Component	Points
SKELETAL AND SOFT TISSUE INJURY	
Low energy (stab; simple fracture; "civilian gunshot wound")	1
Medium energy (open or multiplex fractures, dislocation)	2
High energy (close-range shotgun or "military" gunshot wound, crush injury)	3
Very high energy (same as above plus gross contamination, soft tissue avulsion)	4
LIMB ISCHEMIA (SCORE IS DOUBLED FOR ISCHEMIA >6 HR)	
Pulse reduced or absent but perfusion normal	1
Pulseless; paresthesias, diminished capillary refill	2
Cool, paralyzed, insensate, numb	3
SHOCK	
Systolic blood pressure always >90 mm Hg	0
Hypotensive transiently	1
Persistent hypotension	2
AGE (YR)	
<30	0
30–50	1
>50	2

....

Source: Johansen, K., et al. J Trauma 30:568, 1990.

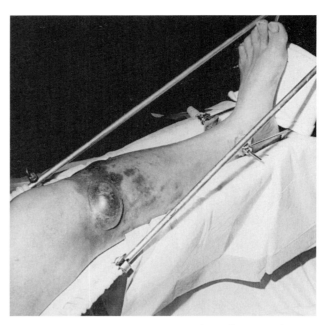

FIGURE 13–1. A closed comminuted tibial plateau fracture with type II soft tissue injury. The injury was held in traction for 10 days until the soft tissues were ready for internal fixation.

remained viable. This scoring system needs further validation in larger field trials. It is also not clear to what extent this classification is applicable to pediatric lesions or fractures other than those affecting the leg.

Although some studies have questioned the sensitivity and reproducibility of the MESS[104] and other similar severity scores that rely on simple, easily obtainable, and quantifiable parameters, such severity scores do facilitate the initial decision-making process because they provide the treating physician with a rational framework to guide an often emotional decision-making process. Possibly the greatest weakness of the MESS is a propensity for false-negative predictions for young patients who present with intact vessels, minimal blood loss, and major muscle or skeletal destruction.[136] Although such injuries can receive a score of less than 7, primary amputation may still be the treatment of choice. None of the current scoring scales helps in making decisions about secondary amputations.

Closed Fractures

Not all fractures and joint disruptions caused by violent forces result in open wounds. In fact, the soft tissue destruction in closed injuries may be more extensive and more severe than that seen in open lesions.[95, 159, 160] Many of these injuries are accompanied by skin contusions, deep abrasions, burns, dermatologic conditions, or frank separation of the cutis from the subcuticular tissues. If hidden under casts or incorporated innocently into a surgical incision, these subtle soft tissue injuries may have

catastrophic consequences, ranging from delayed wound healing to partial or full tissue slough easily leading to a massively infected open wound.

Tscherne and co-workers[159, 160] have classified these closed injuries on a scale from 0 to 3. Although the scale has not been critically validated, it may heighten the physician's awareness of the injury severity and provide some guidance for management (Fig. 13–1 and Table 13–5; see also Fig. 13–25).[142]

TABLE 13-5 ....

Classification of Closed Fractures with Soft Tissue Damage

Fracture Type	Description
Type 0	Minimal soft tissue damage. Indirect violence. Simple fracture patterns. Example: Torsion fracture of the tibia in skiers.
Type I	Superficial abrasion or contusion caused by pressure from within. Mild to moderately severe fracture configuration. Example: Pronation fracture-dislocation of the ankle joint with soft tissue lesion over the medial malleolus.
Type II	Deep, contaminated abrasion associated with localized skin or muscle contusion. Impending compartment syndrome. Severe fracture configuration. Example: Segmental "bumper" fracture of the tibia.
Type III	Extensive skin contusion or crush. Underlying muscle damage may be severe. Subcutaneous avulsion. Decompensated compartment syndrome. Associated major vascular injury. Severe or comminuted fracture configuration.

....

Source: Tscherne, H.; Oestern, H.J. Die Klassifizierung des Weichteilschadens bei offenen und geschlossenen Frakturen. Unfallheilkunde 85:111–115, 1982. Copyright Springer-Verlag.

PATHOPHYSIOLOGY OF MUSCULOSKELETAL INJURIES

Violent injuries to the musculoskeletal system typically result in extensive disruptions of the soft and hard tissues. They may introduce foreign material and bacteria and create ischemic and metabolically deprived soft tissue segments,[76] frank tissue necrosis, and dead space. The ensuing hematoma, contaminated with foreign material, invades the injury zone, dissects along disrupted tissue planes, fills empty spaces, and acts as an ideal culture medium for bacteria. Within the first few hours, neutrophils and macrophages enter the wound, but later, monocytes are more common. Simultaneously, the complement and clotting systems are activated. Serotonin, prostaglandins, and kinins released by platelets and the clotting cascade lead to vascular dilatation and, together with histamine released by basophils and mast cells, increase permeability. Massive exudation of plasma proteins and leukocytes follows. The C3b component of the complement system facilitates opsonization of bacteria and foreign material, whereas the C5a component and histamine are the most powerful chemotactic agents. These events set the stage for the phagocytosis of bacteria and necrotic material by neutrophils and macrophages.[29, 47, 68, 135]

If the injury is minor or if thorough débridement and antibacterial agents have removed most of the necrotic and foreign material, the inflammatory response is controlled and tissue repair ensues. With massive injuries, severe contamination, or timid intervention, however, a different outcome is seen. The macrophages cannot deal with the bacterial load; they die and release lysosomal or other proteolytic enzymes, which cause further necrosis of the surrounding tissues. In concert with increased tissue pressure, this necrotic process propagates a vicious circle leading to progressive inflammation, muscle ischemia, compartment syndromes,[62] tissue loss, and spreading infection (Fig. 13–2).[12, 40] A progressive inflammatory response is seen most often after extensive contamination of an open fracture but may also occur in closed fractures and dislocations and after simple crushes of muscle compartments.

TREATMENT PLAN AND EARLY CARE

Overview

Because fractures with major soft tissue disruption often occur in association with injuries to other parts of the

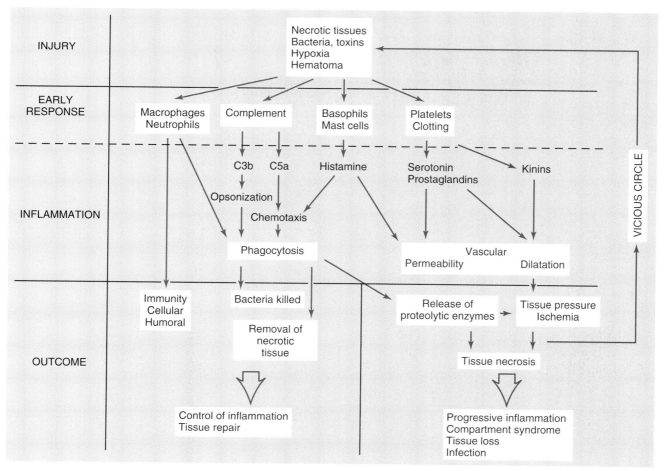

FIGURE 13–2. Results of the necrotic process: cellular, hematologic, and immunologic responses to injury lead to repair or further tissue destruction.

body, they must be considered in the context of polytrauma, recognizing the patient as a whole.[20] Care of these patients progresses from an acute to a reconstructive and then to a rehabilitative phase. The *acute* phase includes (1) initial resuscitation and stabilization at the injury site; (2) complete evaluation of all the patient's injuries, including the open fracture, with primary attention to life-threatening lesions; (3) appropriate antimicrobial therapy; (4) extensive wound débridement followed by wound coverage; (5) fracture stabilization; (6) autogenous bone grafting and other measures that facilitate bone union; and (7) early joint motion and mobilization of the patient.[143] The *reconstructive* phase addresses late injury sequelae, such as nonunions, malalignments, and delayed infections. The *rehabilitative* phase focuses on the patient's psychosocial and vocational rehabilitation.

Traditionally, these three phases have been managed sequentially and with little coordination. Reconstructive problems, such as nonunions, were not addressed until 8 to 12 months after the injury, and vocational rehabilitation was considered only after all soft tissue and bone injuries were healed. Not surprisingly, many patients lost self-esteem, some saw their families disintegrate, and few returned to work before 18 to 24 months, if at all.[52] At present, we are striving to see the patient back at the workplace and in recreational pursuits before the first anniversary of the injury. To achieve these goals, the patient's course of treatment and recovery must be carefully laid out during the initial hospital stay; the three treatment phases are overlapped, and the patient as a whole, rather than a collection of individual injuries, takes center stage.

Prehospital and Emergency Department Care

Open fractures are surgical emergencies. Any delays at the scene of injury, during transport, or in the emergency department, the radiology suite, or the operating room jeopardize limb survival and recovery.[159] After resuscitation and stabilization of vital functions, the rescue workers at the accident scene cover open wounds with sterile dressings and gently align, reduce, and splint the deformed limbs. Profuse bleeding is controlled with local compression. A tourniquet may be indicated for a traumatic amputation or uncontrollable hemorrhage. Inflation time must be clearly marked. Temporary deflation at regular intervals is warranted for long transports. Pneumatic antishock garments are used with caution because they increase rather than decrease mortality for most injury patterns.[101]

On the patient's arrival in the emergency department, vital functions are reassessed and stabilized. Large-bore intravenous access is established. All organ systems are then systematically evaluated. Dressings and splints are partially removed to check soft tissue conditions and neuromuscular function. Bone fragments or dislocations causing undue skin pressure are reduced gently and the extremities resplinted in proper alignment.

All sterile wound dressings are left in place because redressing of wounds in the emergency department raises the ultimate infection rate by a factor of 3 to 4.[159] Before the patient is transferred to the radiography suite or operating room, the history and physical examination are completed and blood is drawn for a complete blood count, serum electrolytes, typing and crossmatching, and possibly arterial blood gases. Tetanus prophylaxis is administered,[150, 167] and intravenous antibiotics are started (Table 13–6). If during the workup a dysvascular limb is suspected, the emergency department stay is curtailed and the patient is quickly transferred to the angiography suite or, preferably, directly to the operating room for further assessment and possible vascular exploration.

WOUND INFECTIONS AND ANTIMICROBIAL AGENTS

Wound Contamination

For practical purposes, all open fractures and closed injuries covered by devitalized skin are contaminated. Severe wound disruption, extensive contamination, associated vascular injuries, advanced age of the patient, and some premorbid conditions (e.g., diabetes mellitus) all predispose to an increased infection rate.

Dellinger and co-workers[41] found that infections were about three times more common in the leg than in the arm. In the same study, 7% of type I, 11% of type II, 18% of type IIIA, and 56% of type IIIB and IIIC fractures became infected. The average infection rate for type I, II, and IIIA fractures was 12%, and the average for all fractures was 16%. These infection rates are typical of modern series, in which systemic antibiotics are used for the initial 1 to 5 days.[42] There has been long-standing concern that a prolonged interval between injury and débridement may increase infection rates. Apparently based on experimental studies carried out by Friedrich in 1898, 6 hours has long

TABLE 13–6		
Schedule of Active Immunization		

Dose	Age and Intervals	Vaccine
Age <7 yr		
Primary 1	Age 6 wk	DPT
Primary 2	4–8 wk after the first dose	DPT
Primary 3	4–8 wk after the second dose	DPT
Primary 4	About 1 yr after third dose	DPT
Booster	Age 4–6 yr	DPT
Additional boosters	Every 10 yr after last dose	Td
Age ≥7 yr		
Primary 1	First visit	Td
Primary 2	4–6 wk after the first dose	Td
Primary 3	6 mo to 1 yr after last dose	Td
Boosters	Every 10 yr after last dose	Td

Abbreviations: DPT, diphtheria and tetanus toxoids and pertussis vaccine absorbed; Td, tetanus and reduced-dose diphtheria toxoids absorbed (for adult use).

Source: Cates, T.R. In: Mandell, G.L.; Douglas, R.G., Jr.; Bennett, J.E., eds. Principles and Practice of Infectious Diseases. New York, Churchill Livingstone, 1990.

been considered the maximal allowable time interval between injury and débridement.[49] The validity of this sacrosanct time interval has rarely been questioned. However, a study by Patzakis and Wilkins[122] documented essentially identical infection rates of 6.8% in open fractures débrided within 12 hours and infection rates of 7.1% in those débrided after 12 hours. These findings have been confirmed by others.[4, 152]

Test results for culture specimens taken in the emergency department are positive in about 60% to 70% of open fractures.[120, 121] Most cultures grow saprophytic organisms such as micrococci, diphtheroids, and saprophytic rods.[159] In one study, 40% to 73% of the fractures from which pathogenic organisms grew on predébridement cultures eventually became infected with one of the pathogens.[159] In another study,[93] 7% of the cases with negative predébridement cultures became infected. For all the cases that did become infected, predébridement cultures included the infective organisms only 22% of the time. Postdébridement cultures were more accurate in predicting infection. Yet, of the cases that did become infected, the infecting organism was present only 22% of the time. On the basis of these conflicting and inconsistent data and considering their substantial cost, both predébridement and postdébridement cultures are at this time deemed to be of little value.

The prevalence of infecting organisms changes over time and with the severity of the injury. Gustillo and colleagues[60, 62] found that the percentage of gram-negative organisms in infected fractures rose from 24% to 77% over a 20-year period. Dellinger and co-workers[41] noted *Staphylococcus aureus* in 43% and aerobic or facultative gram-negative rods in 14% of type I, II, and IIIA fractures that became infected. From most type IIIB and IIIC fractures they recovered a mixed flora; *S. aureus* represented only 7% and aerobic or facultative gram-negative rods accounted for 67% of the recovered organisms.

Clostridial Infections

TETANUS

Tetanus[153, 167] is a rare but often fatal disease caused by *Clostridium tetani*, an anaerobic gram-positive rod that produces a neurotoxin. Tetanus spores are found everywhere in nature, particularly in soil, dust, and animal feces and on the skin of humans. Growth of the bacilli is favored under anaerobic conditions and in the presence of necrotic tissue. Only about 100 to 200 cases occur per year in the United States, mostly in persons older than 50 years. The fatality rate is 20% to 40%.

The effects of the exotoxin tetanospasmin on various receptor sites cause all clinical manifestations of the disease. Tetanospasmin probably travels along motor nerves and affixes to the gangliocytes of skeletal muscle, spinal cord, and brain. Tetanus occurs in a localized and a generalized form. Generalized tetanus is much more common, and such early findings as cramps in muscles surrounding the wounds, hyperreflexia, neck stiffness, and a change in facial expression occur. Later, contractions of

whole muscle groups may follow, causing opisthotonos and acute respiratory failure. Local opisthotonos is rare; it is characterized by muscle rigidity around the site of the injury and usually resolves without sequelae.

Active immunization with tetanus toxoids is the best and most effective method to prevent the disease. For children younger than 7 years of age tetanus toxoid is available as a combination with 7 to 8 limit flocculating (Lf) units of diphtheria, 5 to 12.5 Lf units of tetanus, and fewer than 16 opacity units of pertussis (DTP) or without pertussis (DT). In adults and older children tetanus vaccine (Td) contains fewer than 2 Lf units of diphtheria and 2 to 10 Lf units of tetanus. To obtain long-lasting protective levels of antitoxin, three doses of tetanus toxoid should be given at 2 months, 4 months, and 6 months of age followed by boosters at 12 to 18 months and again at 5 years of age. After this initial series, boosters are given every 10 years for life. Any patient who has not completed a series of toxoid immunization or has not received a booster dose in the 5 years before being wounded should receive tetanus toxoid and, if the wound is tetanus prone, passive immunization with human tetanus immune globulin (HTIG). Any patient wounded more than 10 years after the last booster should receive both HTIG and Td. Generally, 250 to 500 IU HTIG are given intramuscularly and concurrently with toxoid but at a separate site. Protection from HTIG lasts about 3 weeks (see Table 13–6).

Patients with suspected immune deficiencies and patients with tetanus-prone injuries who have not received adequate immunization within the past 5 years should receive passive immunization with HTIG (250 to 500 IU intramuscularly) in addition to active immunization. Wounds that are considered tetanus prone include wounds contaminated with dirt, saliva, or feces; puncture wounds including nonsterile injections; missile injuries; burns; frostbites; avulsions; and crush injuries.[11]

GAS GANGRENE

Gas gangrene remains a constant threat,[46, 54, 70] particularly after primary wound closure, in wounds of type IIIB or IIIC severity, in farm- or soil-related injuries, in wounds contaminated by bowel content, and in patients with diabetes mellitus. *Clostridium* spores are found in soil and in the intestinal tract of humans and animals; *Clostridium perfringens* and *Clostridium septicum* are most prevalent in human disease. Clostridia are anaerobic gram-positive bacteria that produce several exotoxins that can be lethal or act as spreading factors. These toxins induce local edema; necrosis of muscle, fat, and fascia; and thrombosis of local vessels. They also generate hydrogen sulfide and carbon dioxide gases. Because these gases easily spread into the surrounding tissues, the process of tissue swelling, necrosis, and vascular thrombosis becomes self-perpetuating and sets the stage for a fulminant spread of the infection. Hemolysis, with a significant drop in hemoglobin followed by tubular necrosis and renal failure, may occur.[70] The body temperature is often initially subnormal. Locally, the wound may drain foul-smelling, serosanguineous fluid. Edema appears early and is often noted at a distance from the site of trauma. Later, gas can be detected in the tissues by crepitation or radiographically as radiolucent streaks along fascial planes. Most patients are unduly apprehensive and some are fearful of dying.

A patient with suspected or established gangrene should receive intravenous penicillin, 20 to 30 million units daily in divided doses. If the patient is allergic to penicillin, intravenous clindamycin, 1.8 to 2.7 g/day, or metronidazole, 2 to 4 g/day, may be used. A cephalosporin and an aminoglycoside are added to cover other organisms. However, the keys to saving life and limb are extensive fasciotomies and repeated radical débridements at short intervals. Transfer to a major trauma center, possibly one with a hyperbaric chamber, deserves serious consideration. Although major clostridial infections remain a serious threat, all but 8% to 10% of infected patients can be saved with modern management techniques.

Antimicrobials

SYSTEMIC ANTIBIOTICS

Systemic antibiotics to prevent post-traumatic wound infections in open fractures were controversial until 1974, when Patzakis[120, 121] proved their effectiveness in a randomized double-blind trial. Other studies have since confirmed the findings[41, 61, 119, 122] and established the current routine of using intravenous antibiotics for all open fractures during the first 3 to 5 days.

Optimal antibiotic choice depends on the severity of the soft tissue injury, the contaminating agent, and the local nosocomial flora.[115, 146] At present, a first-generation cephalosporin is preferred for type I and II open fractures and closed fractures with soft tissue injuries. These antibiotics are effective against most gram-positive and many gram-negative bacteria except *Pseudomonas*. For example, cefazolin, in an average adult, should be given as a loading dose of 2 g, followed by 1 to 2 g every 8 hours intravenously. In type III open fractures, an aminoglycoside (gentamicin or tobramycin) is added. The historical dosage of 3 to 5 mg/kg of lean body weight per 24 hours given in divided doses has been replaced by a single dose of 5.1 mg/kg once daily.

Experimentally, multiple divided dosing has been associated with a higher incidence of nephrotoxicity because it results in a higher trough concentration; conversely, the higher peak values attained with a single dose are more effective in killing *Escherichia coli* and *Pseudomonas*.[172] In a prospective randomized trial, single-dose gentamycin was shown to be as safe as multiple dosing. There was also a slight decrease in the infection rate.[154] For fractures occurring in a farm environment, vascular compromise, or extensive soft tissue crush, 2 to 4 million units of aqueous penicillin G every 4 hours is added.

Although initial antibiotic coverage is traditionally provided for 1 to 5 days, there is now good evidence that for simple open fractures without major contamination, a first-generation cephalosporin given for 24 hours is as effective as one given for 5 days.[42] More complicated open fractures are usually covered for 48 hours after wound closure.

LOCAL ANTISEPTICS AND ANTIBIOTICS

Although the use of hot liquids and irons by ancient physicians was harmful, soaking wound dressings with vinegar, alcohol, and carbolic acid often had beneficial effects.[166] With the demonstration that many antiseptics have cell-toxic effects, these agents have fallen into disrepute, although the damage they inflict is usually limited to superficial cell layers. Many surgeons[2] soak wound dressings with isotonic saline, iodine-containing solutions with a broad bactericidal and spore-killing spectrum,[13] or such topical antibiotics as neomycin, bacitracin, and polymyxin. There is limited clinical evidence concerning the beneficial or detrimental effects of any of these regimens.

LOCAL ANTIBIOTICS FROM SLOW-RELEASE CARRIERS

In an attempt to increase their local concentration and prolong their action, antibiotics have been mixed with slow-release carriers such as polymethyl methacrylate.[66, 96, 147, 163, 164] Successful in the management of infected arthroplasties, these carriers have also been used in chronic skeletal infections and, more recently, in high-risk open fractures (Figs. 13–3 through 13–7). In the latter application, polymethyl methacrylate is mixed with the desired antibiotics and molded into beads 5 to 15 mm in diameter to facilitate removal; the beads are then lined up on a thin wire.[86] After the beads are transferred to the wound cavity, the wound is sutured water tight or covered with an adhesive drape.[66, 67] The beads are removed or exchanged at intervals from 3 days to 6 weeks. If kept in place longer, they are difficult to separate from ingrown soft tissues.[96] Secondary hematogenous infections of beads that were left permanently have been reported.[94]

Although antibiotic concentrations 10 to 30 times higher than those observed after intravenous use are common,[96] little is known about carrier efficiency, optimal bead size and shape, release characteristics, alteration of the antibiotics during the process of polymerization, or antibiotic effectiveness after release.[163] Many different antibiotics have been tried, but much of the scientific work has been limited to aminoglycosides and vancomycin. Compared with high-dose intravenous antibiotics, this form of local application is cheaper, avoids intravenous lines, eases nursing care, and is nontoxic to sensitive organs such as the liver, inner ear, and kidney. Beads also have an advantage when used with ambulatory and noncompliant patients. A study also indicated that antibiotic beads used alone might be as effective as intravenous antibiotics.[107]

Similar results have been obtained with implantable pumps that deliver antibiotics to the wound at a fixed rate. Although more expensive, this approach appears equally promising.[125]

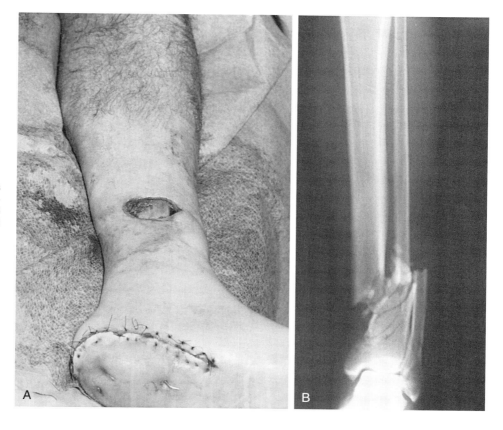

FIGURE 13–3. *A* and *B*, The patient is a middle-aged man with insulin-dependent diabetes and a type IIIB open tibial fracture who was seen 10 hours after the initial injury.

FIGURE 13–4. Same patient as in Figure 13–3. *A,* Irrigation, débridement, and stabilization of the fracture with an external fixator were performed. Antibiotic-impregnated beads were placed under an adhesive drape to fill the dead space and "sterilize" the wound cavity. *B,* Temporary stabilization of fractures.

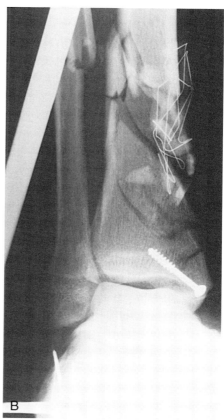

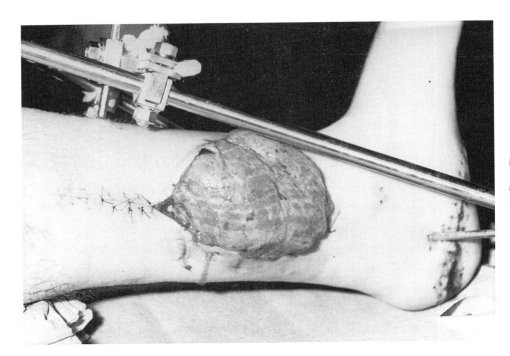

Figure 13–5. Same patient as in Figure 13–3. At 10 days, wound coverage was achieved with a free flap. The beads remain.

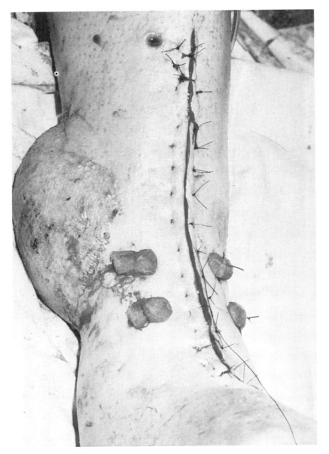

Figure 13–6. Same patient as in Figure 13–3. At 4 weeks, the external fixator and beads were removed. Application of a plate and a bone graft was performed through a standard incision (definitive sterilization).

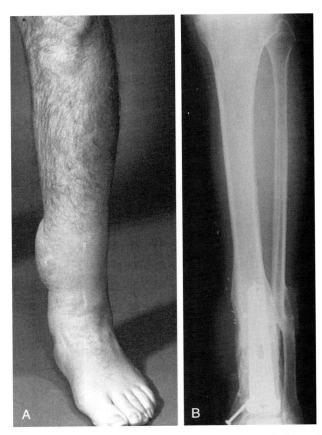

Figure 13–7. Same patient as in Figure 13–3. Clinical (A) and radiographic (B) results at 1 year.

WOUND CARE

Irrigation and Débridement

In the operating room and after induction of anesthesia, all splints and bandages are removed, the skin surrounding the wound is shaved, and the injured body part is prepared and draped. A tourniquet is applied but is inflated only in case of massive bleeding. This approach prevents further ischemic damage and makes it easier to assess soft tissue viability. The wound is then cleansed of all dead and foreign material through a dual process of irrigation and débridement.

IRRIGATION

Irrigation with ample amounts of isotonic solution aids in the removal of coagula, fresh blood, foreign material, necrotic tissue, and bacteria. Pulsating irrigation with a sprinkler head appears to be most effective in removing staphylococcus.[2] Judging from animal studies, adding antibiotics is not more effective than using saline alone. In fact, the most effective additive was benzalkonium chloride.[2, 50, 157] Although it is nontoxic in rats,[157] its use was accompanied by an increased complication rate.[31] However, with sequential irrigation with benzalkonium chloride followed by Castile soap and then saline, these complications were avoided.[30] To what extent these experimental findings can be applied to humans is currently not clear.

Although irrigation is useful for removing blood clots and debris, particularly from deep interstices, it is simply an adjunct to, and by no means a replacement for, thorough débridement.

DÉBRIDEMENT

Débridement means the meticulous removal and resection of all foreign and dead material from a wound.[166] Débridement does not remove all bacteria, but it drastically reduces their number and, by leaving only viable tissue behind, greatly diminishes the opportunity for bacterial proliferation. Casual, uninformed, and incomplete débridement has the gravest consequences: remaining bacteria multiply and the surrounding tissues swell, compromising their own blood supply and causing further necrosis. Frank infection ensues along tissue planes and within necrotic muscle bellies, threatening amputation and reamputation at progressively more proximal levels.

Rather than an aimless clipping of necrotic skin edges and muscle strands protruding from the wounds, débridement can be effective only if it is a carefully planned, systematic process. It starts with a thorough exploration of the wound to determine the real size and extent of the injury, which is always substantially larger than what is apparent from the outside (Fig. 13–8). The real extent of the injury has been delineated when all foreign material and necrotic tissue are sharply resected and only the well-perfused walls of a clean wound cavity are left behind.

ASSESSING THE EXTENT OF INJURY

In assessing the true extent of the injury zone, information from many different sources is assimilated, including the mechanism of injury, events at the accident site (e.g.,

FIGURE 13–8. Same patient as in Figure 13–3. *A,* A simple oblique fracture of the distal tibia and an ankle fracture. Type IIIB anterior and medial ankle wounds with multiple tendon lacerations. *B,* Type IIIB open lesion of the proximal tibia with extensive tissue loss. Note avulsion of the intervening soft tissue sleeve from the anterior tibia and deep fascia.

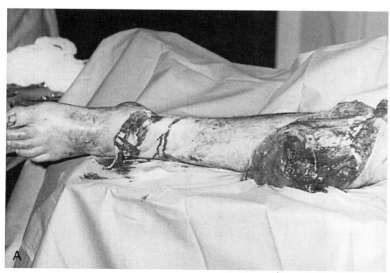

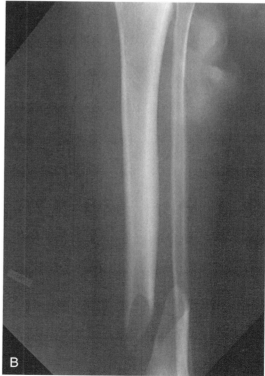

whether a protruding fragment was reduced before splinting), examination of the injured extremity (bruises elsewhere; instability of adjacent joints; vascular and neurologic condition; size, location, and contamination of the wound), laboratory findings, and radiographs. In addition to depicting fracture patterns and location, plain radiographs help delineate the extent of the soft tissue destruction by identifying trapped air in different tissue planes, often at a substantial distance from the apparent injury site. The energy causing the injuries is reflected by the multiplicity of fractures, the severity of comminution, and the distance between displaced fragments. Fractures close to points where arteries or nerves are affixed to bone should alert the physician to possible neural and vascular damage. Unless proved otherwise, multiple soft tissue wounds in the same extremity segment are caused by the same injury mechanism, often a bone fragment. Such wounds usually communicate with the fracture site and each other and are telltale signs of a mangled extremity (Figs. 13–9 through 13–12; see also Fig. 13–8).[78]

The severity of the soft tissue injury is easily misjudged in the proximal extremity segments and in areas in which the bone is covered by a large tissue sleeve, as in the femur or on the posterior aspect of the leg. Because in these areas the external wounds are often small, they easily hide the extent of the underlying muscle disruption, the severity of

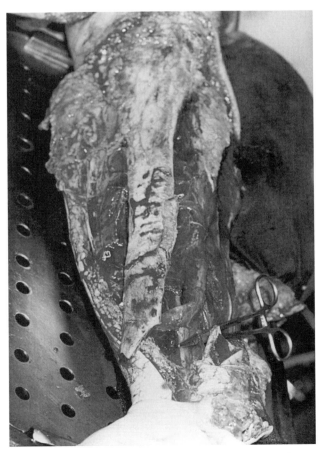

FIGURE 13–9. Same patient as in Figure 13–3. The true extent of injury is revealed at end of débridement.

periosteal stripping, and the degree of contamination at the fracture site.

EXTENDING THE WOUND

Because the cutaneous opening is often just a small peripheral extension of a large underlying injury, the wound must be extended—often by a factor of 3 to 5—until optimal access to all injured tissues is obtained. The enlarging incisions must be extensile, must not create flaps, and must respect neural and vascular territories. They should also facilitate the placement of implants, the transfer of distant soft tissue flaps, and wound closure.

CUTANEOUS TISSUES

Rather than starting with a generous débridement of skin edges, as much of the skin as possible should be preserved during the initial débridement. Obviously, dead and macerated tissues have to be trimmed, but questionable areas become apparent within 24 hours and can easily be removed during a following débridement. Subcutaneous tissue, mainly fat, has a scant blood supply and is freely débrided when contaminated. The skin of amputated parts and large, nonviable, cutaneous flaps can be used as donor sites for the harvest of split-thickness grafts with a dermatome. The resulting skin graft can be used at the end of the procedure or set aside for later needs.

FASCIA

The fascia below the subcutaneous tissue is expendable and can be freely resected if devitalized or contaminated. Contrary to traditional teaching, open fractures do not completely decompress fascial compartments.[62] If constrained spaces remain, the continuing tissue swelling increases the local pressure and interrupts regional blood flow. Further tissue necrosis followed by infection is a common sequela. Prophylactic fasciotomies and epimysiotomies are therefore performed liberally during the initial and subsequent débridements.

MUSCLES AND TENDONS

Because it is a fertile culture medium for bacteria, all muscle of questionable viability should be liberally resected. The "four Cs"—consistency, contractility, color, and capacity to bleed—are not always reliable guides to viability; the capacity to contract after a gentle pinch with a pair of toothed forceps and arterial bleeding are more trustworthy. A contractile muscle response after stimulation with an electrical cautery device is another reliable means of assessing muscle viability.

Each muscle group that passes through the wound must be individually examined and followed beyond the zone of injury toward its origin and insertion. Disruption or resection of a small blood vessel may lead to ischemic necrosis of a whole muscle segment. Occasionally, a whole muscle group is found to be avascular and must be removed in toto. Contaminated tendons should be cleaned carefully but otherwise can be left intact. They are easily accessible and can be further débrided at a later time.

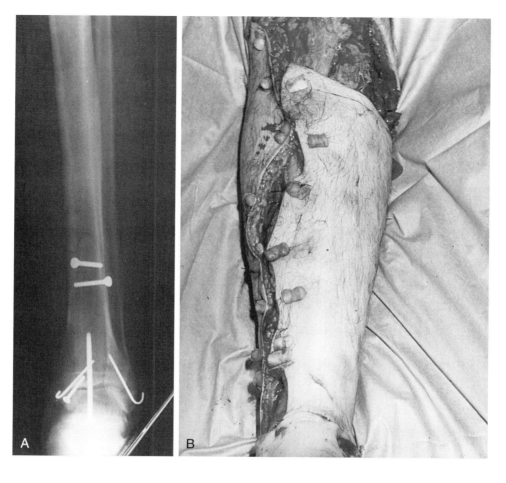

FIGURE 13–10. Same patient as in Figure 13–3. *A,* Internal fixation of the ankle fracture. A transcalcaneal pin was used for additional stabilization. Minimal internal fixation of oblique tibial fracture was achieved with two screws. *B,* Approximation of the incisional wound was accomplished with retention sutures.

BONE

When faced with a small outside wound, the physician is tempted just to trim the wound edges and irrigate blindly through the wound opening. This casual approach easily misses a foreign body or contaminated bone fragments and thus can lead to a major deep infection followed by an amputation. In most open fractures, at least one bone end penetrates through the wound and makes contact with the surrounding environment, which is never sterile. Therefore, the wound opening must be extended so that the free ends of all principal bone fragments can be delivered into the open and carefully débrided.

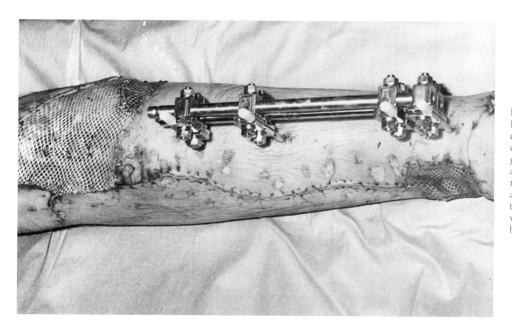

FIGURE 13–11. Same patient as in Figure 13–3. At day 10, after several débridements, the incisional wound is closed. Split-thickness skin has been grafted in the proximal and distal areas where soft tissue was lost. A rigid double-bar anterior external fixator protects the internal fixation of the tibia. At 2 months, the screws were removed and a prophylactic bone graft was applied.

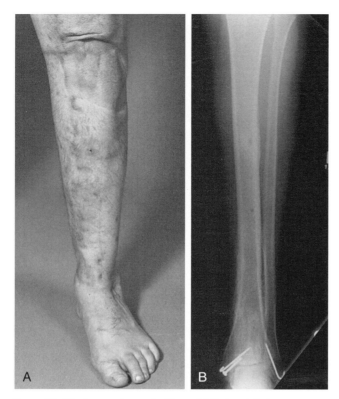

FIGURE 13–12. Same patient as in Figure 13–3. *A* and *B,* Appearance at 14 months.

The intramedullary cavity is cleansed of all dirt and other foreign material. All small, devitalized pieces of cortical bone are removed, but cancellous bone is cleaned and put aside as graft material. Clean large bone fragments, even if avascular, may be retained if they are critical for stable reconstruction of the extremity. Whenever possible, larger articular fragments should be cleaned and used for joint reconstruction. Severely contaminated fragments are discarded, and the defect is later corrected by a bone graft or distraction osteogenesis.

NEUROVASCULAR STRUCTURES

Major arteries and nerves in the injury zone are often serious obstacles to adequate débridement. They must be carefully identified, mobilized, and separated from surrounding nonviable tissue. Major arteries and nerves that are transected must be repaired.

Vascular Injuries and Compartment Syndromes

VASCULAR INJURIES

When an open fracture is associated with a major vascular injury, particularly in the lower extremity, the prognosis for limb survival remains dismal. Lange and colleagues[91] noted that of 23 open tibial fractures requiring vascular repair, 61% were ultimately amputated. Of the patients whose limbs were salvaged by successful vascular repair,

more than 50% developed chronic problems that interfered with routine daily activities. If the warm ischemia time—the crucial survival parameter—exceeded 4 hours, the amputation rate was 50%, and no limbs survived when the warm ischemia time exceeded 6 hours. In another study,[81] the ultimate amputation rate was 58%. Although isolated lesions of the anterior tibial and the peroneal artery had a good prognosis, negative outcomes were more common with transection of the popliteal artery or the posterior tibial artery and with injuries involving all three major arteries distal to the trifurcation.

Extremities with major vascular compromise[24, 37, 41, 63, 83, 91, 112] should be cooled at the site of injury and during transport to the nearest trauma center capable of handling the lesion. After stabilization of vital functions, the injured extremity is carefully assessed by both an extremity surgeon and a vascular surgeon. An expedient treatment plan is then established with the goal of having a fully revascularized extremity in less than 6 hours, a grace period that can be extended somewhat with the use of a temporary silicone elastomer arterial shunt.[79] Considering the serious time constraints, initial internal fixation of the fracture is, under most circumstances, too time consuming, and temporary external fixation or immediate vascular repair is safer. It is well to remember that a study carried out during the Vietnam War showed excellent results when vascular care was followed by skeletal traction.[128] Fasciotomies of all compartments in the affected extremity segment are essential, particularly in the lower limb.[12]

COMPARTMENT SYNDROME

There is a widespread assumption that compartment syndromes[137] rarely, if ever, occur with open fractures. Yet in four series, compartment syndromes were diagnosed in 2% to 16% of cases of open tibial fracture.[20, 33, 72, 75] The incidence of compartment syndromes is directly proportional to the severity of the injury.[62] They occur most often in polytrauma patients, pedestrians stuck by a car, and patients with type III open fractures with major comminution. At risk for a delayed or missed diagnosis are patients under prolonged anesthesia and those who suffer from a compromised sensorium, a cord transection, or a regional nerve lesion. For all patients who are at risk, compartment pressures should be determined before and after the initial operative invention and at regular intervals thereafter. If the pressure in one of the leg compartments is elevated, it is prudent to decompress all four compartments.[12]

Amputations

Primary amputations in cases of open fractures may be indicated if a patient presents with a severely mangled extremity (type IIIB lesion) or with a limb-threatening arterial lesion that is irreparable or has resulted in a failed repair (type IIIC lesion). Whenever possible, the decision to amputate should be made at the time of the initial débridement. Although there are no universally accepted guidelines, information that strongly favors an amputation includes a MESS of 7 or higher,[78] a warm ischemia time exceeding 6 hours,[91] and the presence of a serious secondary bone or soft tissue injury involving the same extremity.

In the past, a loss of protective sensation to the foot[14] was an additional indication to amputate. However, if the lesion is due to a neuropraxia of the posterior tibial nerve, it may recover over time. There are also about 20 reports in the world literature detailing the outcomes of direct repairs and grafting of posterior tibial nerve lesions. Most of the grafts were done on a delayed basis about 6 months after the injury. About 70% to 80% of the patients showed good results with successful sensory recovery and without trophic ulcerations or the need for ambulatory support.[43, 64, 69, 98, 111, 168]

The importance of making the proper decision for a primary amputation is difficult to overestimate because primary amputations lead to better long-term results than either secondary amputations or complex limb reconstructions.[14, 85, 97] Early amputation also enhances patients' survival, reduces pain and disability, and shortens hospital stay.[14, 85, 97]

Considering the massive energy that is involved in most limb-threatening injuries, an open amputation at the time of initial débridement is most appropriate. If an amputation is considered, the process is started with a careful débridement of the local wound. As much as possible of the soft tissue sleeve is preserved and only nonviable tissue is resected. The amputated stump is then dressed open and the definitive decision about amputation level and type of wound closure is made at a later débridement when the size and function of the remaining soft tissue sleeve have become clear. So-called guillotine amputations, which are transverse transection of all soft tissues and bone proximal to the injury level, may have saved lives on the Napoleonic battlefields, but they are not part of modern trauma care (Fig. 13–13). We currently attempt to salvage as much viable soft and bony tissue as possible to attain the most optimal amputation level. As noted, skin and other viable tissues useful for later reconstructions should be harvested before an amputated limb is sent for pathologic evaluation.

Wound Coverage

At the end of the débridement, the wound cavity should be delineated on all sides by viable bleeding tissue. The remaining soft tissue must not be restricted by encasing fascial layers but should be free to expand with the expected tissue edema. Whenever possible, nerves, vessels, tendons, and denuded bone surfaces are covered with local soft tissue. Whereas in children, there is a long-standing and apparently safe tradition to close many open fractures primarily, in adults it appears safest to leave all wounds—or at least the wound that was created by the injury—open. This guideline is based on the rationale that the degree of tissue necrosis and the severity of contamination are easily underestimated during the initial débridement, particularly in fractures with massive tissue destruction.

In a number of studies, primary closures of type I and type II wounds led to significantly higher rates of infection and nonunion.[36, 142] It is also noted that primary wound closure is a principal contributing factor in the development of gas gangrene.[18, 116] Nevertheless, two smaller subsequent studies suggested that low-grade open fracture may be closed primarily without a substantial increase in risk.[44, 148] The wound cavity is dressed with a bandage soaked in isotonic saline to which a topical antibiotic or an antiseptic has been added.[13, 139] Another option is the creation of an antibiotic bead pouch (see Fig. 13–4).[67] To prevent undue soft tissue retraction, the skin edges are placed under a moderate amount of traction with the help of retention sutures (see Fig. 13–10B). This technique facilitates secondary wound closure and precludes unnecessary skin grafts or flaps.

Fractures with severe soft tissue involvement are systematically reexplored and redébrided in the operating room within 48 to 72 hours. All necrotic tissue that has

FIGURE 13–13. Bilateral guillotine amputations after a jackknife trailer accident. Whenever possible, guillotine amputations should be avoided. As much viable soft tissue as possible should be preserved to secure the optimal amputation level.

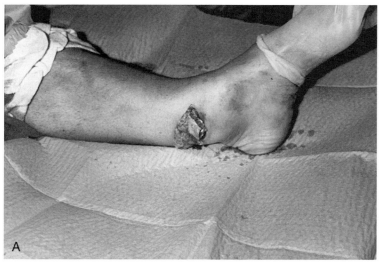
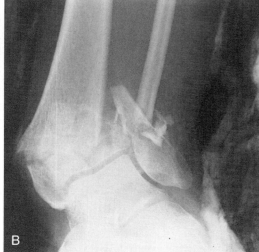

FIGURE 13–14. *A and B*, A type IIIB open pilon (tibial plafond) fracture.

developed since the initial débridement is resected, and more extensive fasciotomies or epimysiotomies are performed if indicated. The process of débridement must be repeated every 2 to 3 days until the wound is clean and can be closed or covered.[108]

Timing and method of wound coverage are carefully assessed when the injury is first seen. An expert in soft tissue and microvascular techniques is consulted if the need for a complex soft tissue technique is anticipated (Figs. 13–14 through 13–17). Whenever possible, open fractures should be covered within a week and before the wound is colonized secondarily.[119]

Delayed primary closure is feasible for most type I, type II, and some type IIIA open wounds as long as retraction of the wound edges is prevented after each débridement with retention sutures under gentle traction (see Fig. 13–10B). Healing by secondary intention is a reasonable option for smaller type I wounds not overlying bone surfaces or articulations. Such wounds are often granulated and epithelialized in less than a week. A dense bed of granulation tissue may also be the best initial goal when dealing with an infected wound needing repeated débridements. If the bacterial counts are low, a local or free flap should follow; otherwise, a split-thickness skin graft should be applied as an intermediary step. Split-thickness skin grafts are ideal for covering large skin defects overlying viable tissue such as muscle. They also provide excellent temporary coverage for granulation tissue covering bone and periarticular structures (see Fig. 13–11).

Myofascial, local, and free muscle flaps have revolutionized the coverage of large, acute, and chronic soft tissue or bone defects.[22, 55, 129, 171] Local flaps are often ideal, but they are limited in size and are not available in the distal segments of an extremity. Their use is also contraindicated if the muscle has been damaged by the initial injury. Free muscle and composite flaps can deal with almost any defect anywhere in the body (see Fig. 13–16). In addition to giving coverage and possibly structural support, muscle flaps can eliminate low type bacterial contamination in the recipient bed and increase

the rate of union in underlying fractures.[129] The placement of a free flap is often the first stage in a complex extremity reconstruction.[55, 171] Flaps are rarely applied during the initial débridement because the real extent of injury is often not obvious and the damage to the donor muscle is difficult to assess.

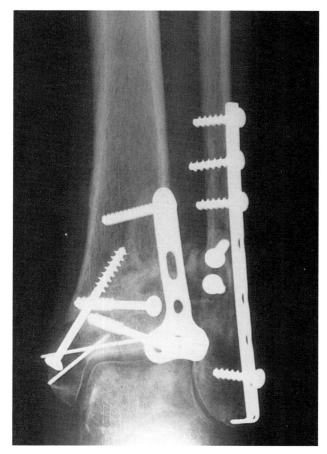

FIGURE 13–15. Same patient as in Figure 13–14 after irrigation and débridement, wound extension, and internal fixation.

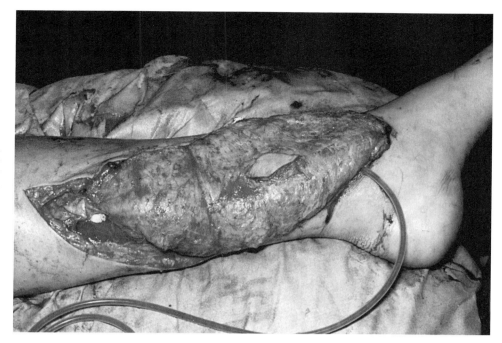

FIGURE 13–16. Same patient as in Figure 13–14. It was not possible to close the anteromedial wound without undue tension. Application of a free flap was performed on day 5.

FRACTURE FIXATION

Immobilization is crucial for the healing of soft tissue and bone.[114, 135] Stabilization of the fracture fragments prevents further injuries to the surrounding soft tissue sleeve, limits the intensity and duration of the inflammatory response, diminishes the spread of bacteria, facilitates tissue perfusion, and encourages early wound repair. Stabilization of the skeletal injury results in decreased pain, greater mobility,[109] fewer respiratory complications such as deaths from adult respiratory distress syndrome,[15, 16, 79] and greater ease in nursing care and the management of injuries elsewhere.

For centuries, skeletal fixation was possible only indirectly, through pressure on the surrounding soft tissues and prolonged immobilization of adjacent extremity segments.[166] Reduced limb function as a result of shortening, malalignment, nonunion, muscle atrophy, joint contractures, osteopenia, and persistent drainage was the expected sequela of this approach. In contrast, the goal of modern fracture care is a stable, clean injury site that proceeds to union with proper alignment and length and finally regains close to normal function.[109] This goal is achievable only if the methods used to stabilize open fractures provide free wound access for repeated débridements and the placement of local or distant flaps and bone grafts. The methods should not interfere with the blood supply of the fracture fragments and should be sufficiently

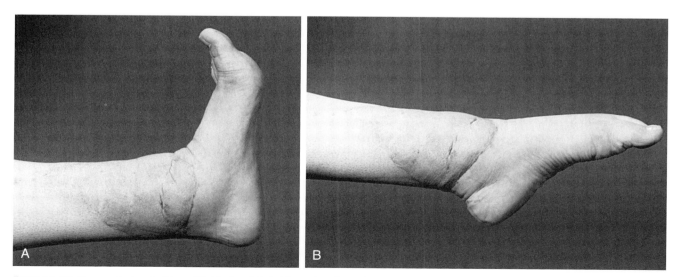

FIGURE 13–17. Same patient as in Figure 13–14. *A* and *B,* Ankle motion, 1 year later.

rigid to allow early joint motion and at least partial weight bearing. Finally, all of this must be achieved without undue risks and complications.

The rigidity of the fixation determines whether a fracture consolidates through primary or secondary bone healing mechanisms,[106, 124] but it does not have a predictable influence on healing times or union rates. Although the literature is replete with reports about the superiority of one method of fracture stabilization over another, most such studies are limited recollections focused on selected populations of patients. They often exclude the most severe injuries, have insufficient follow-up, and are silent about limb length, alignment, and motion in adjacent joints. And rarely do they address functional, occupational, and recreational outcomes.* The optimal fixation method for a particular open fracture depends on numerous variables related to the patient, injury, and treatment, including the surgeon's skill and experience. What constitutes optimal fixation constantly changes with evolving new insights and techniques. Often the best outcome and shortest healing time are achieved when multiple methods are used simultaneously or in sequence (Figs. 13–18 through 13–25; see also Figs. 13–3 through 13–12).

Slings, Splints, Casts, and Traction

For many centuries, only nonrigid methods, including slings, splints, casts, and traction, were used to stabilize open fractures.[166] At present, they are used in the care of some simple, isolated type I and type II injuries and as temporary methods for the care of more complex fractures.

Slings may be indicated for fractures of the humeral neck and shaft and to provide additional support for internally or externally stabilized forearm lesions. Splints, which can be made of a variety of materials, may provide initial stabilization of open fractures until clear decisions can be made about optimal soft tissue coverage or bone fixation.

Circular casts have no place in the early management of open fractures because they cannot accommodate swelling and may prevent the detection of further soft tissue damage, circulatory impairment, or an increase in compartment pressures.[19] They also obstruct the injury site. Casts with openings create window edema and limit the full assessment of the underlying wound. However, casts can be ideal for the subsequent care of stable type I and II open tibial fractures after the soft tissue wounds have been closed and swelling has subsided.[19, 144] Despite their popularity, casts have a dismal record as a secondary method of immobilization after removal of an external fixator from a fracture that is only partially healed. Under these circumstances, they often permit the development of secondary deformities and later a malunion.[71] The technique of pins and plaster should be reserved for situations in which external fixators are not available.

---

*See references 15, 19, 27, 90, 92, 103, 113, 131, 134, 161, 162, 169, 170.

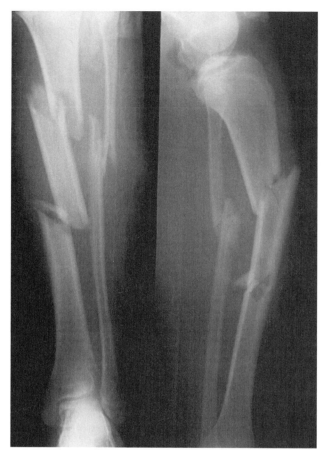

Figure 13–18. A type IIIA open segmental fracture of the tibia.

Skeletal traction is rarely used in the upper extremity but may be indicated for the immobilization of pelvic injuries, acetabular lesions, and type III open femoral fractures. Comminuted fractures of the tibial plafond, particularly those accompanied by severe soft tissue injury, can be managed initially with Böhler's traction.

Internal Fixation

With the development of mechanically and functionally more appropriate implants and safer operating techniques after World War II, internal fixation methods have revolutionized the treatment of many fractures.[109] They provide excellent stabilization of the injury zone, allow early mobilization of the limb and the patient, and facilitate fracture consolidation while preventing malalignment and loss of length.[79] Most of these methods require additional exposure and can cause partial loss of periosteal, cortical, or intramedullary blood supply, which may increase the rate of nonunion and the risk of infection (see Figs. 13–14 through 13–17). Although there is some evidence that rigid fracture fixation promotes the consolidation of infected fractures,[132, 133] metal in contaminated wounds also facilitates the formation of biofilms,[58] which make bacteria inaccessible to antibiotics and host defense mechanisms and thereby promote and maintain a chronic infective process.[126]

FIGURE **13–19.** Same patient as in Figure 13–18. *A*, Irrigation, débridement, and temporary stabilization were accomplished with a two-pin external fixator and Robert Jones dressing. Wound closure at 3 days. *B*, Radiographs: the external fixator maintains length; the Robert Jones dressing prevents bending in the frontal plane.

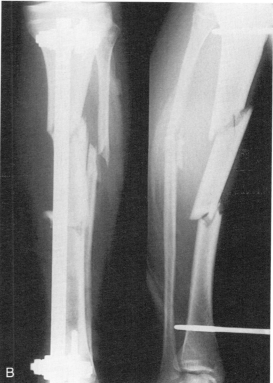

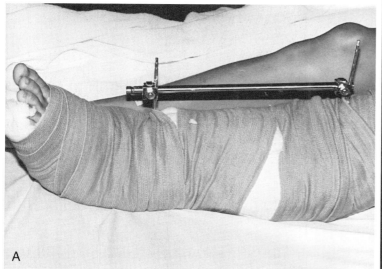

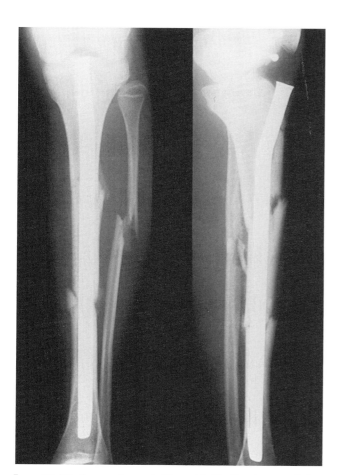

FIGURE **13–20.** Same patient as in Figure 13–18. Closed intramedullary nailing at 10 days.

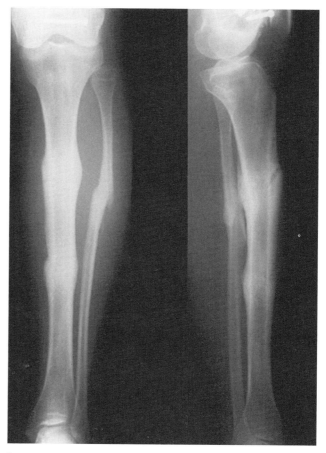

FIGURE **13–21.** Same patient as in Figure 13–18. One year later, after removal of the nail.

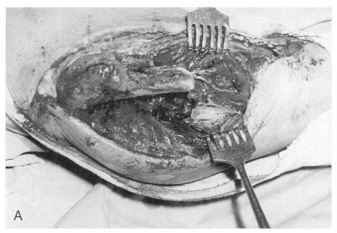

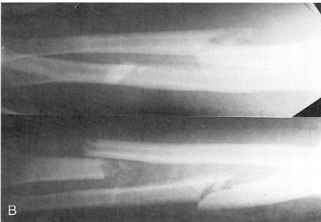

FIGURE **13–22.** *A,* Combination of a type IIIA open ulnar fracture and a type II open radial fracture. *B,* Radiographs before treatment.

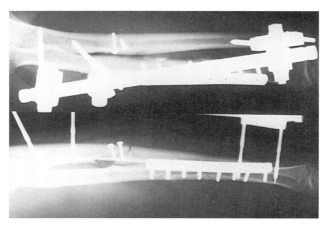

FIGURE **13–23.** Same patient as in Figure 13–22. On the day of admission, irrigation, débridement, and internal fixation of the radial fracture were performed. The combination of minimal internal fixation and external fixation for the fractured ulna allows delayed tissue healing and early rehabilitation.

WIRES AND SCREWS

When used alone to fix diaphyseal fractures, cerclage, wires, and screws rarely result in stable fixation. Screw fixation is most appropriate for the stabilization of intra-articular and periarticular fractures; it is used alone or in combination with a plate or an external fixator (see Figs. 13–10*A* and 13–23).

PLATES

Internal fixation with plates is used with utmost caution in all fractures with severe contamination or type IIIB or IIIC soft tissue lesions.[3, 28, 113] Plates and screws have been particularly successful in the treatment of less severe diaphyseal, periarticular, and intra-articular fractures of the upper extremity.[80, 106, 134, 159] In the lower extremity, these implants are most useful around joints[169] (see Figs. 13–14 through 13–17) but are rarely indicated for fractures of the femoral and tibial diaphyses.[3, 113] Plates are unsuitable for lesions with segmental bone loss.[124]

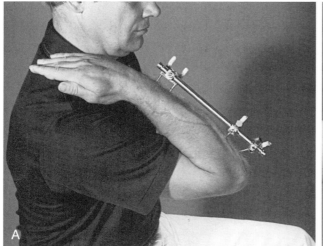

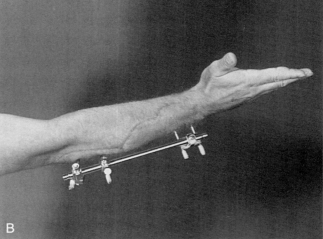

FIGURE **13–24.** Same patient as in Figure 13–22. At 4 weeks, the patient has regained the full range of elbow motion.

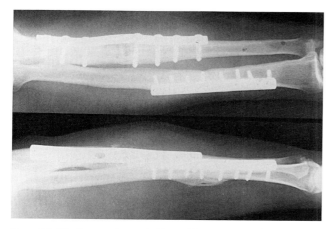

FIGURE 13–25. Same patient as in Figure 13–22. At 10 weeks, removal of the external fixator and plating and bone grafting of the ulna for impending nonunion were performed.

Plates should be applied with minimal additional soft tissue and periosteal stripping and must be covered with well-vascularized soft tissues, preferably muscle.[106] Often, this goal is best achieved if the plate is applied not through the wound but through a separate incision (see Figs. 13–3 through 13–7).[159] Occasionally, application in a nontraditional location, such as the posterior tibial surface, may be indicated.[159] If delayed primary closure within 3 to 5 days is unlikely, a consultant with soft tissue expertise should be involved promptly, and flap coverage of the wound and implant should be obtained before secondary wound colonization occurs (see Figs. 13–14 through 13–17).[171] A primary bone graft is indicated for fractures with extensive soft tissue stripping, comminution, or partial bone loss.

INTRAMEDULLARY NAILS

Because the fragment ends of many diaphyseal fractures are devoid of periosteum, reamed intramedullary nails have been used only cautiously for fear that the additional loss of intramedullary blood supply may increase the chances of infection and nonunion. In fact, animal studies have shown that unreamed nails destroy about 30% of the central cortical blood supply. With the addition of reaming, 70% of the central blood supply is lost.[85, 145] These experimental findings are contrary to the early experience in human tibial fractures, in which reamed nails[31, 32] appeared to be associated with shorter healing times and lower complication rates than unreamed nails.[130] A randomized study found that tibial nailing with and without reaming gave equivalent results.[82]

If the fracture configuration permits, intramedullary nails appear safe for type I to IIIA open diaphyseal fractures.[31, 97] Although they may also be safe for type IIIB lesions,[32, 158] temporary external fixation may represent the more cautious approach.[1, 10, 56, 87, 94, 123]

External Fixation

Although external fixators long appeared ideal for the management of fractures with soft tissue injuries,[6, 7, 92, 162] only the technical and conceptual advances of the past two decades have allowed us to employ these devices effectively and with acceptable risk.[5, 6, 9, 35, 38] Properly applied, external fixators immobilize the fracture at a distance from the injury site without placing foreign material in the wound. They can be applied without additional soft tissue dissection and are easily dismantled if further débridement is necessary. Pin drainage occurs in about 30% of all patients, but pin tract infections that require more than local pin care have become rare.

Compared with other methods of fracture stabilization, external fixators provide great versatility and flexibility because configurations and rigidity can easily be changed to accommodate many different and newly arising circumstances. They are easily removed, replaced by, or combined with other methods of fixation (see Figs. 13–3 through 13–12 and 13–18 through 13–25).

External fixators are indicated for most contaminated IIIB and IIIC open fractures and for many closed fractures with severe soft tissue injury (Figs. 13–26 through 13–28).[9, 35, 38] Transarticular fixators are temporarily applied for some periarticular and intra-articular fractures and joint dislocations[1, 151] (Figs. 13–29 and 13–30). To prevent permanent joint contractures, they are usually removed or replaced by casts, braces, or internal fixation as soon as the soft tissue lesions have healed (see Figs. 13–3 through 13–7 and 13–14 through 13–17). Ring fixators are proving increasingly useful for the stabilization of open periarticular fractures with and without intra-articular extensions.[155]

External fixators seem to do best if they are applied according to principles that have emerged during the past two decades.[6, 8, 9, 38, 100] Most malunions can be avoided if proper fracture reduction has been obtained at the time of fixator application and if the fixator remains applied until the fracture is healed.[9, 38, 100] Fixator replacement with a nail is most successful if done within 8 weeks of fixator application, as long as there have been no fracture site or pin tract infections.[10] However, with suppuration at pin tract and fracture sites, infection rates as high as 70% have been noted with secondary nailing.[102] Although the combination of internal and external fixation can be highly successful in metaphyseal fractures,[155] in diaphyseal fractures this practice leads to an increase in healing times and complication rates.[88]

If a delayed union of a fracture stabilized with an external fixator is noted and secondary nailing is contraindicated, union should be achieved with the help of a bone graft. To guarantee proper alignment, the external fixator should be kept in place until complete union has been achieved. As noted previously, removal of the external fixator and transfer of a delayed union into a cast lead to serious secondary angulatory deformity in up to 30% of cases.[71]

ACHIEVING BONE UNION

Most open diaphyseal fractures have a nonunion rate of 5% to 60%.[20, 32, 110, 140] These nonunion rates are directly proportional to the extent of initial displacement, the

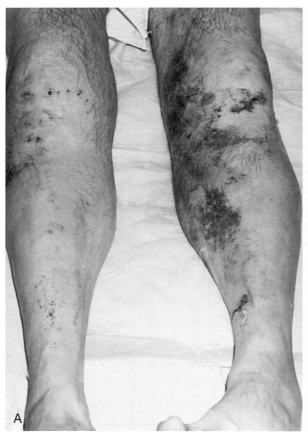
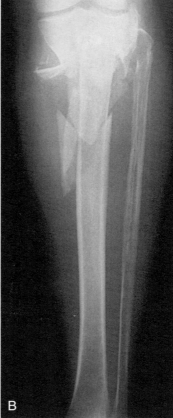

FIGURE 13–26. *A* and *B,* "Bumper" injury caused a comminuted proximal tibial fracture with intra-articular extension. Closed fracture with type II soft tissue compromise.

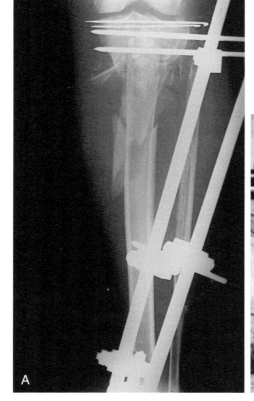
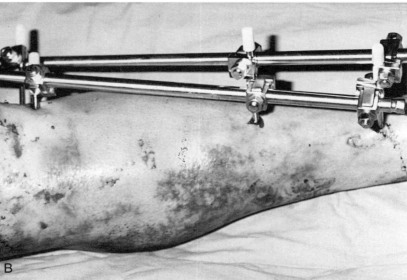

FIGURE 13–27. Same patient as in Figure 13–26. *A* and *B,* On the day of admission, stabilization of the articular surface was performed with percutaneous Kirschner wires (image intensifier). Fracture stability, length, and alignment are maintained with an external fixator. Healing occurred in the external fixator in 4 months.

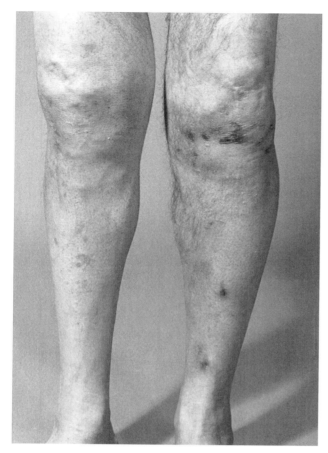

FIGURE 13–28. Same patient as in Figure 13–26. Appearance 15 months later.

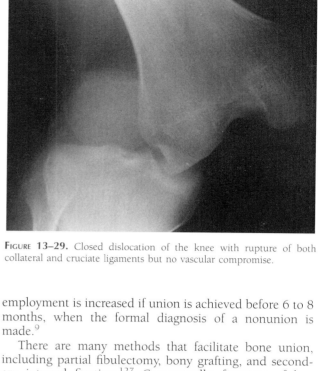

FIGURE 13–29. Closed dislocation of the knee with rupture of both collateral and cruciate ligaments but no vascular compromise.

degree of comminution, the severity of the soft tissue injury, the amount of bone loss, and the presence of an infection.[32, 84, 110, 140] Limb function is improved, healing times are reduced, and the likelihood of return to gainful employment is increased if union is achieved before 6 to 8 months, when the formal diagnosis of a nonunion is made.[9]

There are many methods that facilitate bone union, including partial fibulectomy, bony grafting, and secondary internal fixation.[127] Conceptually, fractures of low severity such as type I and type II open fractures, which are most likely to heal without additional intervention, can be observed for 8 to 12 weeks before a decision to intervene is entertained. As soon as soft tissue coverage without drainage has been established, a secondary intervention such as a bone graft[9] is considered for more severe type III lesions.[32, 56] In the presence of substantial bone loss, free fibular grafts, free composite grafts, or distraction osteogenesis should be

FIGURE 13–30. Same patient as in Figure 13–29. *A–C,* At 3 days, repair and reconstruction of all ligaments were performed. Stabilization of the knee joint with an external fixator for 3 weeks allowed easy assessment of the soft tissue and maintenance of the correct anatomic position.

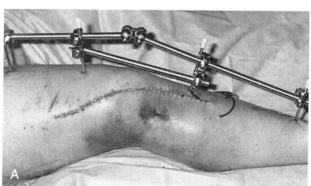

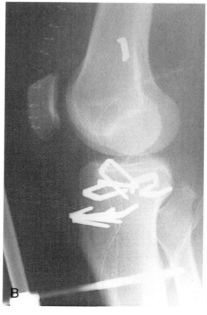

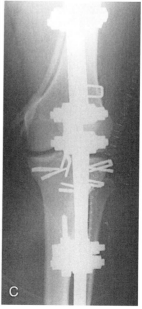

considered as soon as the soft tissue conditions are consolidated.

REGAINING FUNCTION

As soon as the patient has recovered from the initial impact of the injuries, he or she should be made aware of the effects these injuries may have on physical well-being, social circumstances, and recreational and occupational aspirations. The patient is made the most important member of the rehabilitation team and must, in conjunction with family and friends, help set the goals for each stage of the rehabilitation process.

After the fractures are stabilized, the patient is encouraged to get into the upright position, move to a chair, and maintain motion and strength in the uninvolved extremities. As soon as the wounds of the injured extremity are covered, assisted active range-of-motion exercises are started (see Figs. 13–17 and 13–24). If large wounds persist, joint motion can be maintained during daily excursions to the whirlpool. Lower extremity injuries stabilized with plates are protected from weight bearing, but progressive force transmission is allowed across stable injuries held with intramedullary nails or an external fixator.

COORDINATING AND STAGING OF INTERVENTIONS

Fractures with soft tissue injuries present problems of considerable complexity. These injuries not only affect several tissue and organ systems but also require a wide variety of interventions by an often disjointed care team, which ranges from the emergency medical technician applying the initial splint at the scene of an accident to the physical therapist instituting the final work hardening program. The general trauma surgeon usually handles the resuscitative phase of the patient's care, but it is the extremity surgeon's duty to manage and coordinate the care of the local injury and its effects on the patient's overall well-being.

Whereas some of the local treatment interventions must occur simultaneously (e.g., débridement of a contaminated wound under antibiotic coverage), other procedures are best carried out in sequence after a certain stage of the treatment process has been concluded (e.g., placement of a bone graft after an open wound has been fully débrided or covered with a healthy sleeve of soft tissues). Typical situations in which staging should be considered early in the treatment course include the following:

1. *Wound care.* Although one-stage débridement followed by immediate wound closure is almost routine for low-grade open pediatric fractures,[34] a type IIIB open tibial fracture in an adult may involve the following stages: (a) débridement and wound dressing or antibiotic bead pouch; (b) repeated débridement and dress-

ing; (c) staged secondary closure or local and free muscle flap.

2. *Stabilization of a diaphyseal fracture.* Many adult type I and II open tibial shaft fractures are currently treated with a reamed nail and "loose" primary wound closure. Yet a combined open posterior tibial IIIB and IIIC lesion may require (a) arterial shunt, débridement, restoration of functional arterial and venous flow, antibiotic bead pouch, and external fixation; (b) disassembly of fixator frame, redébridement of posterior wound, frame reassembly, and bead pouch; (c) flap coverage of wound with fixator in place; (d) removal of fixator and secondary nailing.

3. *Stabilization of closed intra-articular or periarticular fracture.* For some of these lesions, particularly in the upper extremity, immediate open reduction followed by early range-of-motion exercises provides the best functional results. Yet the same approach can cause major disasters when applied to tibial plateau and pilon fractures, for which the following sequence is often safer: (a) transarticular external fixation (with or without percutaneous articular fixation); (b) removal of transarticular fixator, limited open articular reduction with periarticular fixator or metaphyseal plating; (c) vigorous joint motion exercises and progressive weight bearing.

Although different procedures may be involved in staging the treatment of soft and bony tissues, they are often interdependent and mutually beneficial. Thus, a transarticular fixator is as important in preserving length as it is in resolving soft tissue swelling.

As noted earlier, the proper timing of overlapping interventions is equally important in the reconstructive and rehabilitative phases. In choosing the optimal treatment course for a particular patient's injury, the surgeon is forever torn between a desire to complete the task without delay and thus possibly secure the best outcome and the recognition that a more protracted approach might be safer but not without incurring complexity and possibly a lesser functional result.

REFERENCES

1. Anglen, J.; Aleto, T. Temporary transarticular external fixation of the knee and ankle. J Orthop Trauma 12:431, 1998.
2. Anglen, J.; Apostoles, S.; Christensen, G.; Gainor, B. The efficacy of various irrigation solutions in removing slime-producing *Staphylococcus.* J Orthop Trauma 8:390, 1994.
3. Bach, A.; Hansen, S. Plates versus external fixation in severe open tibial shaft fractures: A randomized trial. Clin Orthop 241:89, 1989.
4. Bednar, D.; Parikh, J. Effect of time delay from injury to primary management on the incidence of deep infection after open fractures of the lower extremities caused by blunt trauma in adults. J Orthop Trauma 7:532, 1993.
5. Behrens, F. External fixation. In: Chapman, M., ed. Operative Orthopaedics, Philadelphia, J.B. Lippincott, 1988, pp. 161–172.
6. Behrens, F. General theory and principles of external fixation. Clin Orthop 241:15, 1989.
7. Behrens, F.; Johnson, J.; Guse, S.; Comfort, T. Early bone grafting for open tibial fractures. Paper presented at the American Academy of Orthopaedic Surgeons, Las Vegas, Nevada, 1989.
8. Behrens, F.; Johnson, W. Unilateral external fixation: Methods to increase and reduce frame stiffness. Clin Orthop 241:48, 1989.
9. Behrens, F.; Searls, K. External fixation of the tibia. J Bone Joint Surg Br 68:246, 1986.

10. Blachut, P.; Meek, R.; O'Brien, P. External fixation and delayed intramedullary nailing of open fractures of the tibial shaft: A sequential protocol. J Bone Joint Surg Am 72:729, 1990.

11. Bleck, T. *Clostridium tetani.* In: Mandell, G.; Douglas,R.; and Bennett, J., eds. Principles and Practice of Infectious Diseases, 4th ed. New York, Churchill Livingstone, 1995, p. 2173.

12. Blick, S.; Brumback, R.; Poka, A.; et al. Compartment syndrome in open tibial fractures. J Bone Joint Surg Am 68:1384, 1986.

13. Bombelli, R.; Giangrande, A.; Malacrida, V.; Puricelli, G. The control of infection in orthopaedic surgery. Orthop Rev 10:65, 1981.

14. Bondurant, F.; Cotler, H.; Buckle, R.; et al. The medical and economic impact of severely injured lower extremities. J Trauma 28:1270, 1988.

15. Bone, L.; Johnson, K. Treatment of tibial fractures by reaming and intramedullary nailing. J Bone Joint Surg Am 68:877, 1986.

16. Bone, L.; Johnson, K.; Weigelt, J.; Scheinberg, R. Early versus delayed stabilization of femoral fractures: A prospective randomized study. J Bone Joint Surg Am 71:336, 1989.

17. Brien, H.; Noftall, F.; MacMaster, S.; et al. Neer's classification system: A critical appraisal. J Trauma 38:257, 1995.

18. Brown, P.; Kinman, P. Gas gangrene in a metropolitan community. J Bone Joint Surg Am 56:1145, 1974.

19. Brown, P.; Urban, J. Early weight-bearing treatment of open fractures of the tibia: an end-result study of 63 cases. J Bone Joint Surg Am 51:59, 1969.

20. Brumback, R. Open tibial fractures: Current orthopaedic management. Instr Course Lect 41:101, 1992.

21. Brumback, R.; Jones, A. Interobserver agreement in the classification of open fractures of the tibia. J Bone Joint Surg Am 76:1162, 1994.

22. Byrd, H.; Spicer, T.; Cierney, G. Management of open tibial fractures. Plast Reconstr Surg 76:719, 1985.

23. Cauchoix, J.; Duparc, J.; Boulez, P. Traitement des fractures ouvertes de jambe. Med Acta Chir 83:811, 1957.

24. Caudle, R.; Stern, P. Severe open fractures of the tibia. J Bone Joint Surg Am 69:801, 1987.

25. Chapman, M. Role of stability in open fractures. Instr Course Lect 31:75, 1982.

26. Chapman, M. Open fractures. In: Chapman, M., ed. Operative Orthopaedics. Philadelphia, J.B. Lippincott, 1988, p. 173.

27. Chapman, M.; Mahoney, M. The role of internal fixation in the management of open fractures. Clin Orthop 138:120, 1979.

28. Clancey, C.; Hansen, S. Open fractures of the tibia. J Bone Joint Surg Am 69:118, 1978.

29. Clowes, G. Stresses, mediators and responses of survival In: Clowes, G., ed. Truma, Sepsis and Shock: The Physiological Bases of Therapy. New York, Marcel Dekker, 1988, p. 1.

30. Conroy, B.; Anglen, J.; Simpson, W.; et al. Comparison of Castile soap, benzalkonium chloride, and bacitracin as irrigation solutions for complex contaminated orthopaedic wounds. J Orthop Trauma 13:332, 1999.

31. Court-Brown, C.; Christie, J.; McQueen, M. Closed intramedullary tibial nailing: Its use in closed and type I open fractures. J Bone Joint Surg Br 72:605, 1990.

32. Court-Brown, C.; McQueen, M.; Quaba, A.; Christie, J. Locked intramedullary nailing of open tibial fractures. J Bone Joint Surg Br 73:959, 1991.

33. Cramer, K.; Limbird, T.; Green, N. Open fractures of the diaphysis of the lower extremity in children. J Bone Joint Surg Am 74:218, 1992.

34. Cullen, M.; Roy, D.; Crawford, A.; et al. Open fracture of the tibia in children. J Bone Joint Surg Am 78:1039, 1996.

35. Dabezies, E.; D'Ambrosia, R.; Shoji, H.; et al. Fractures of the femoral shaft treated by external fixation with the Wagner device. J Bone Joint Surg Am 66:360, 1986.

36. Davis, A. Primary closure of compound fracture wounds. J Bone Joint Surg Am 30:405, 1948.

37. DeBakey, M.; Simeone, F. Battle injuries of the arteries in World War II: An analysis of 2471 cases. Ann Surg 123:534, 1946.

38. DeBastiani, G.; Aldegheri, L.; Brivio, L. The treatment of fractures with a dynamic axial fixator. J Bone Joint Surg Br 66:538, 1984.

39. deChauliac, G. Ars Chirurgica. Venice, 1546.

40. DeLee, J.; Stiehl, J. Open tibia fractures with compartment syndrome. Clin Orthop 160:175, 1981.

41. Dellinger, E.; Miller, S.; Wetz, M.; et al. Risk of infection after open fractures of the arm or leg. Arch Surg 123:1320, 1987.

42. Dellinger, P.; Caplin, E.; Weaver, L.; et al. Duration of preventive antibiotic administration for open extremity fractures. Arch Surg 123:333, 1988.

43. Dellon, A.; McKuinnon, S. Results of posterior tibial nerve grafting at the ankle. J Reconstr Microsurg 7:81, 1991.

44. DeLong, G.; Born, C.; Wei, S.; et al. Progressive treatment of 119 open fracture wounds. J Trauma 46:1049, 1999.

45. Dirschl, D.; Adams, G. A critical assessment of factors influencing reliability in the classification of fractures, using fractures of the tibial plafond as a model. J Orthop Trauma 11:471, 1997.

46. Drake, S.; King, A.; Slack, W. Gas gangrene and related infections: Classification, clinical features and etiology, management and mortality. Br J Surg 64:104, 1977.

47. Farber, J.; Chien, K.; Mittnacht, S. The pathogenesis of irreversible cell injury in ischemia. Am J Pathol 102:271, 1981.

48. Francel, T.; VanderKolk, C.; Hoopes, J.; et al. The pathogenesis of irreversible cell injury in ischemia. Am J Pathol 102:271, 1992.

49. Friedrich, P. Die aseptische Versorgung frischer Wunden. Arch Klin Chir 57:288, 1898.

50. Gainor, B.; Hockman, D.; Anglen, J.; et al. Benzalkonium chloride: A potential disinfecting irrigation solution. J Orthop Trauma 11:121, 1997.

51. General Principles Guiding the Treatment of Wounds of War. Conclusions adopted by the InterAllied Surgical Conference held in Paris, March and May 1917. London, HM Stationery Office, 1917.

52. Georgiadis, G.; Behrens, F.; Joyce, M.; et al. Open tibia fractures with severe soft tissue loss: Limb salvage with microvascular tissue transfer versus below knee amputation. Complications, functional results and quality of life. J Bone Joint Surg Am 75:1431, 1993.

53. Ger, R. The management of open fractures of the tibia with skin loss. J Trauma 10:112, 1970.

54. Gorbach, S. Other *Clostridium* species (including gas gangrene). In: Mandel, G.; Douglas, R.; and Bennett, J. eds. Principles and Practice of Infectious Diseases, 2nd ed. New York, John Wiley & Sons, 1985, p. 1362.

55. Gordon, L.; Chiu, E. Treatment of infected nonunions and segmental defects of the tibia with staged microvascular muscle transplantation and bone grafting. J Bone Joint Surg Am 70:377, 1988.

56. Green, A.; Trafton, P. Early infectious complications in the management of open femur fractures. Paper presented at the American Academy of Orthopaedic Surgeons, Las Vegas, Nevada, 1989.

57. Gregory, G.; Chapman, M.; Hansen, S. Open fractures. In: Rockwood, C.; Green, D., eds. Fractures in Adults. Philadelphia, J.B. Lippincott, 1984, p. 169.

58. Gristina, A.; Costerton, J. Bacterial adherence to biomaterials and tissue: The significance of its role in clinical sepsis. J Bone Joint Surg Am 67:264, 1985.

59. Gustilo, R. Management of open fractures and complications. Instr Course Lect 31:64, 1982.

60. Gustilo, R. Current concepts in the management of open fractures. Instr Course Lect 36:359, 1987.

61. Gustilo, R.; Anderson, J. Prevention of infection in the treatment of one thousand and twenty-five open fractures of long bones. J Bone Joint Surg Am 58:453, 1976.

62. Gustilo, R.; Mendoza, R.; Williams, D. Problems in the management of type III (severe) open fractures: A new classification of type III open fractures. J Trauma 24:742, 1984.

63. Hansen, S. The type IIIC tibial fracture: Salvage or amputation. J Bone Joint Surg Am 69:799, 1988.

64. Hattrup, S.; Wood, M. Delayed neural reconstruction in the lower extremity: Results of interfascicular nerve grafting. Foot Ankle 7:105, 1986.

65. Helfet, D.; Howey, T.; Sanders, R.; Johansen, K. Limb salvage versus amputation: Preliminary results of the Mangled Extremity Severity Score. Clin Orthop 256:80, 1990.

66. Henry, S.; Osterman, P.; Seligson, D. The prophylactic use of antibiotic impregnated beads in open fractures. J Trauma 30:1231, 1990.

67. Henry, S.; Osterman, P.; Seligson, D. The antibiotic bead pouch technique: The management of severe compound fractures. Clin Orthop 295:54, 1993.

68. Heppenstall, R.; Sapega, A.; Scott, R.; et al. The compartment syndrome. An experimental and clinical study of muscular energy metabolism using phosphorus nuclear magnetic resonance spectroscopy. Clin Orthop 226:138, 1988.

69. Higgins, T.; Deluca, P.; Ariyan, S. Salvage of open tibial fracture with segmental loss of tibial nerve: A case report and review of the literature. J Orthop Trauma 13:380, 1999.

70. Hitchcock, C. Gas gangrene in the injured extremity In: Gustilo, R., ed. Management of Open Fractures and Their Complications. Philadelphia, W.B. Saunders, 1982, p. 183.

71. Holbrook, J.; Swiontowski, M.; Sanders, R. Treatment of open fractures of the tibial shaft: Ender nailing versus external fixation. J Bone Joint Surg Am 71:1231, 1989.

72. Hope, P.; Cole, W. Open fractures of the tibia in children. J Bone Joint Surg Am 74:546, 1992.

73. Horn, B.; Rettig, M. Salvage of lower extremities following combined orthopaedic and vascular trauma: A predictive salvage index. Am J Surg 53:205, 1993.

74. Howe, H.; Poole, G.; Hansen, K.; et al. Salvage of lower extremities following combined orthopaedic and vascular trauma. A predictive salvage index. Am Surg 53:205, 1987.

75. Irwin, A.; Gibson, P.; Ashcroft, P. Open fractures of the tibia in children. Injury 26:21, 1995.

76. Jensen, J.; Jensen, T.; Smith, T.; et al. Nutrition in orthopaedic surgery. J Bone Joint Surg Am 64:1263, 1982.

77. Johansen, K.; Bandyk, D.; Thiele, B.; Hansen, S. Temporary intraluminal shunts: Resolution of a management dilemma in complex vascular injuries. J Trauma 22:395, 1982.

78. Johansen, K.; Daines, M.; Howey, T.; et al. Objective criteria accurately predict amputation following lower extremity trauma. J Trauma 30:568, 1990.

79. Johnson, K.; Cadambi, A.; Siebert, G. Incidence of adult respiratory distress syndrome in patients with multiple musculoskeletal injuries: Effect of early operative stabilization of fractures. J Trauma 25:375, 1985.

80. Jupiter, J. Complex fractures of the distal part of the humerus and associated complications. J Bone Joint Surg Am 76:1252, 1994.

81. Katzman, S.; Dickson, K. Determining the prognosis for limb salvage in major vascular injuries with associated open tibial fractures. Orthop Rev 21:195, 1992.

82. Keating, J.; O'Brien, P.; Blachut, P.; et al. Locked intramedullary nailing with and without reaming for open fractures of the tibial shaft. J Bone Joint Surg Am 79:334, 1997.

83. Keeley, S.; Snyder, W.; Weigelt, J. Arterial injury below the knee: Fifty-one patients with 82 injuries. J Trauma 23:285, 1983.

84. Kindsfater, K.; Johassen, E. Osteomyelitis in grade II and III open tibia fractures with late débridement. J Orthop Trauma 9:121, 1995.

85. Klein, M.; Rahn, B.; Frigg, R.; et al. Reaming versus non-reaming in medullary nailing: Interference with cortical circulation of the canine tibia. Arch Orthop Trauma Surg 109:314, 1990.

86. Klemm, K. Antibiotic bead chains. Clin Orthop 295:63, 1993.

87. Klemm, K.; Borner, M. Interlocking nailing of complex fractures of the femur and tibia. Clin Orthop 212:89, 1986.

88. Krettek, C.; Haas, N.; Tscherne, H. The role of supplemental lag screw fixation for open fractures of the tibial shaft treated with external fixation. J Bone Joint Surg Am 73:893 1991.

89. Kristiansen, B.; Andersen, U.; Olsen, C.; Varmarken, J. The Neer classification of fractures of the proximal humerus. An assessment of interobserver variation. Skeletal Radiol 17:420, 1988.

90. LaDuca, J.; Bone, L.; Seibel, R.; Border, J. Primary open reduction and internal fixation of open fractures. J Trauma 20:580, 1980.

91. Lange, R.; Bach, A.; Hansen, S.; Johansen, K. Open tibial fractures with associated vascular injuries: Prognosis for limb salvage. J Trauma 25:203, 1985.

92. Lawyer, R.; Lubbers, L. Use of the Hoffman apparatus in the treatment of unstable tibial fractures. J Bone Joint Surg Am 62:1264, 1980.

93. Lee, J. Efficacy of cultures in the management of open fractures. Clin Orthop 339:71, 1997.

94. Llowe, D.; Hansen, S. Immediate nailing of open fractures of the femoral shaft. J Bone Joint Surg Am 70:812, 1988.

95. LLoyd, G. Hippocratic Writings. New York, Pelican Books, 1978.

96. Lob, G. Lokale antibiotikatherapie bei knochen, gelenk und weichteilinfektionen. Chirurg 56:564, 1985.

97. Lottes, J. Medullary nailing of the tibia with the triflange nail. Clin Orthop 105:253, 1974.

98. Luskin, R.; Battista, A.; Lenzo, S.; Price, A. Surgical management of late post-traumatic and ischemic neuropathies involving the lower extremities: Classification and results of therapy. Foot Ankle 7:95, 1996.

99. Malgaigne, J. Études stastiques sur les résultats des grandes operations dans les hôpitaux de Paris. Arch Gen Med 13:399, 1842.

100. Marsh, J.; Nepola, J.; Wuest, T.; et al. Unilateral external fixation until healing with the dynamic axial fixator for severe open tibial fractures. J Orthop Trauma 5:341, 1991.

101. Mattox, K.; Bickell, W.; Pepe, P.; et al. Prospective MAST study in 911 patients. J Trauma 29:1104, 1989.

102. Maurer, D.; Merkow, R.; Gustilo, R. Infection after intramedullary nailing of severe open tibial fractures initially treated with external fixation. J Bone Joint Surg Am 71:835, 1989.

103. Mayer, L.; Werbie, T.; Schwab, J.; Johnson, R. The use of Ender nails in fractures of the tibial shaft. J Bone Joint Surg Am 67:446, 1985.

104. McNamara, M.; Heckman, J.; Corley, F. Severe open fractures of the lower extremity: A retrospective evaluation of the Mangled Extremity Score System (MESS). J Orthop Trauma 8:81, 1994.

105. Millie, M.; Senkowski, C.; Stuart, L.; et al. Tornado disaster in rural Georgia: Triage response, injury pattern and lessons learned. Am Surg 66:223, 2000.

106. Moed, B.; Kellam, J.; Foster, R.; et al. Immediate internal fixation of open fractures of the diaphysis of the forearm. J Bone Joint Surg Am 68:1008, 1986.

107. Moehring, D.; Gravel, C.; Chapman, M.; Olson, S. Comparison of antibiotic beads and intravenous antibiotics in open fractures. Clin Orthop 372:254, 2000.

108. Moore, T.; Mauney, C.; Barron, J. The use of quantitative bacterial counts in open fractures. Clin Orthop 248:227, 1989.

109. Muller, M.; Allgower, M.; Schneider, R.; Willenegger, H. Manual of Internal Fixation, 3rd ed. New York, Springer-Verlag, 1991.

110. Nicoll, E. Fractures of the tibial shaft: A survey of 705 cases. J Bone Joint Surg Br 46:373, 1964.

111. Nunley, J.; Gabel, G. Tibial nerve grafting for restoration of plantar sensation. Foot Ankle 14:489, 1993.

112. O'Donnel, T.; Brewster, D.; Darling, R.; et al. Arterial injuries associated with fractures and/or dislocations of the knee. J Trauma 17:775, 1977.

113. Olerud, S.; Karlstrom, G. Tibial fractures treated by AO compressions osteosynthesis. Acta Orthop Scand 140(Suppl):3, 1972.

114. Orr, H. The treatment of osteomyelitis by drainage and rest. J Bone Joint Surg 9:733, 1927.

115. Pancoast, S.; Neu, H. Antibiotic levels in human bone and synovial fluid. Orthop Rev 10:49, 1980.

116. Pappas, A.; Filler, R.; Eraklis, A.; Bernhard, W. Clostridial infections (gas gangrene): Diagnosis and early treatment. Clin Orthop 76:177, 1971.

117. Paré, A. The works of that famous chirurgion Ambrose Paré. London, 1634.

118. Park, W.; DeMuth, W. Wounding capacity of rotary lawn mowers. J Trauma 15:36, 1975.

119. Patzakis, F.; Wilkins, J.; Moore, T. Considerations in reducing the infection rate of open tibial fractures. Clin Orthop 178:36, 1983.

120. Patzakis, M. Management of open fractures. Instr Course Lect 31:62, 1982.

121. Patzakis, M.; Harvey, J.; Ivler, D. The role of antibiotics in the management of open fractures. J Bone Joint Surg Am 56:532, 1974.

122. Patzakis, M.; Wilkins, J. Factors influencing infection rate in open fracture wounds. Clin Orthop 243:36, 1989.

123. Patzakis, M.; Wilkins, J.; Wiss, D. Infection following intramedullary nailing of long bones. Clin Orthop 212:182, 1986.

124. Perren, S. The biomechanics and biology of internal fixation using plates and nails. Orthopedics 12:25, 1989.

125. Perry, C.; Rice, S.; Ritterbusch, J.; Burdge, R. Local administration of antibiotics with an implantable osmotic pump. Clin Orthop 192:284, 1985.

126. Petty, W.; Spanier, S.; Shuster, J.; Silverthorne, C. The influence of skeletal implants on incidence of infection: Experiments in a canine model. J Bone Joint Surg Am 67:1236, 1985.

127. Reckling, F.; Waters, C. Treatment of non-unions of fractures of the tibial diaphysis by posterolateral cortical cancellous bone-grafting. J Bone Joint Surg Am 62:936, 1980.

128. Rich, N.; Metz, C.; Hutton, J.; et al. Internal versus external fixation of fractures with concomitant vascular injuries in Vietnam. J Trauma 11:463, 1971.

129. Richards, R.; Orsini, E.; Mahoney, J.; Verschuren, R. The influence of muscle flap coverage on the repair of devascularized tibial cortex: An experimental investigation in the dog. Plast Reconstr Surg 79:946, 1987.

130. Riemer, B.; DiChristina, D.; Cooper, A.; et al. Nonreamed nailing of tibial diaphyseal fractures in blunt polytrauma patients. J Orthop Trauma 9:66, 1995.

131. Rittmann, W.; Matter, P. Die Offene Fraktur. Bern, Hans Huber, 1977.

132. Rittmann, W.; Matter, P.; Allogower, M. Behandlung offener frakturen und infekthaufigkeit. Acta Chir Austriaca 2:18, 1970.

133. Rittmann, W.; Perren, S. Corticale Knochenheilung nach Osteosynthese und Infektion: Biomechanik und Biolgie. Berlin, Springer, 1974.

134. Rittmann, W.; Schibli, M.; Matter, P.; Allgower, M. Open fractures—Long term results in 200 consecutive cases. Clin Orthop 138: 1979.

135. Robbins, S.; Cotran, D.; Kumar, V. Pathologic Basis of Disease, 3rd ed. Philadelphia, W.B. Saunders, 1984, pp. 132–140.

136. Robertson, P. Prediction of amputation after severe lower limb trauma. J Bone Joint Surg Br 73:816, 1991.

137. Rorabeck, C. The treatment of compartment syndromes of the leg. J Bone Joint Surg Br 66:93, 1984.

138. Rosenfield, A.; McQueen, D.; Lucas, G. Orthopedic injuries from the Andover, Kansas, tornado. J Trauma 36:676, 1994.

139. Rosenstein, B.; Wilson, F.; Funderburk, C. The use of bacitracin irrigation to prevent infection in postoperative skeletal wounds. J Bone Joint Surg Am 71:427, 1989.

140. Rosenthal, R.; MacPhail, J.; Ortiz, J. Nonunion in open tibial fractures: Analysis of reasons for failure of treatment. J Bone Joint Surg Am 59:244, 1977.

141. Rothenberger, D.; Velasco, R.; Strate, R.; et al. Open pelvic fracture: A lethal injury. J Trauma 18:184, 1978.

142. Russel, G.; Henderson, R.; Arnett, G. Primary or delayed closure for open tibial fractures. J Bone Joint Surg Br 72:125, 1990.

143. Salter, R.; Simmonds, D.; Malcolm, B.; et al. The biological effect of continuous passive motion on the healing of full-thickness defects in articular cartilage. An experimental investigation in the rabbit. J Bone Joint Surg Am 62:1232, 1980.

144. Sarmiento, A.; Sobol, P.; Hoy, A.S.; et al. Prefabricated functional braces for the treatment of fractures of the tibial diaphysis. J Bone Joint Surg Am 66:1328, 1984.

145. Schemitsch, E.; Kowalski, M.; Swiontkowski, M.; Senft, D. Cortical bone blood flow in reamed and unreamed locked intramedullary nailing: A fractured tibia model in sheep. J Orthop Trauma 8:373, 1994.

146. Schurman, D.; Hirshman, H.; Burton, D. Cephalothin and cefamandole penetration into bone, synovial fluid, and wound drainage fluid. J Bone Joint Surg Am 62:981, 1980.

147. Scott, D.; Rotschafer, J.; Behrens, F. Use of vancomycin and tobramycin polymethylmethacrylate impregnated beads in the management of chronic osteomyelitis. Drug Intell Clin Pharm 22:480, 1988.

148. Shtarker, H.; David, R.; Stolero, J.; et al. Treatment of open tibial fractures with primary suture and Ilizarov fixation. Clin Orthop 335:268, 1997.

149. Sidor, M.; Zuckerman, J.; Lyon, T.; et al. The Neer classification system for proximal humeral fractures. An assessment of interobserver reliability and intraobserver reproducibility. J Bone Joint Surg Am 75:1745, 1993.

150. Simon, B. Treatment of wounds. In: Rosen, P.; Baker, F.J.; Barkin, R.M.; et al., eds. Emergency Medicine: Concept in Clinical Practice. St Louis, C.V. Mosby, 1988, p. 371.

151. Sirkin, M.; Sanders, R.; DiPasquale, T.; Herscovici, D., Jr.. A staged protocol for soft tissue management in the treatment of complex pilon fractures. J Orthop Trauma 13:78, 1999.

152. Skaggs, D.; Kautz, S.; Kay, R.; Tolo, V. Effect of delay of surgical treatment on rate of infection in open fractures in children. J Pediatr Orthop 20:19, 2000.

153. Smith, D.; Cooney, W. External fixation of high energy upper extremity injuries. J Orthop Trauma 4:7, 1990.

154. Sorger, J.; Kirk, P.; Ruhnke, C.; et al. Once daily, high dose versus divided, low dose gentamicin for open fractures. Clin Orthop 366:197, 1999.

155. Stamer, D.; Schenk, R.; Stagger, B.; et al. Bicondylar tibial plateau fractures treated with a hybrid ring external fixator: A preliminary study. J Orthop Trauma 8:455, 1994.

156. Swiontkowski, M.; Sands, A.; Agel, J.; et al. Interobserver variation in the AO/OTA fracture classification system for pilon fractures: Is there a problem? J Orthop Trauma 11:467, 1997.

157. Tarbox, B.; Conroy, D.; Malicky, E.; et al. Benzalkonium chloride. A potential disinfecting irrigation solution for orthopaedic wounds. Clin Orthop 346:255, 1998.

158. Tornetta, P.; Bergman, M.; Watnik, N.; et al. Treatment of grade IIIb open tibial fractures. A prospective randomised comparison of external fixation and non-reamed locked nailing. J Bone Joint Surg Br 76:13, 1994.

159. Tscherne, H.; Gotzen, L. Fractures with Soft Tissue Injuries. Berlin, Springer-Verlag, 1984.

160. Tscherne, H.; Oestern, H. Die klassifizierung des weichteilschadens bei offenen und geschlossenen frakturen. Unfallheilkunde 83:111, 1982.

161. Velazco, A.; Flemin, L. Open fractures of the tibia treated by the Hoffmann external fixator. Clin Orthop 180:125, 1983.

162. Velazco, A.; Whitesides, T.; Fleming, L. Open fractures of the tibia treated with the Lottes nail. J Bone Joint Surg Am 65:879, 1983.

163. VonFraunhofer, J.; Polk, H.; Seligson, D. Leaching of tobramycin from PMMA bone cement beads. J Biomed Mater Res 19:751, 1985.

164. Wahlig, H.; Dingeldein, E.; Bergmann, R.; Reuss, K. The release of gentamicin from polymethylmethacrylate beads. J Bone Joint Surg Br 60:270, 1978.

165. Wangensteen, O.; Wangensteen, S. Carl Reyher (1846–1890), great Russian military surgeon: His demonstration of the role of débridement in gunshot wounds and fractures. Surgery 74:641, 1973.

166. Wangensteen, O.; Wangensteen, S. The Rise of Surgery from Empiric Craft to Scientific Discipline. Minneapolis, University of Minnesota Press, 1978.

167. Wassilak, S.; Brink, E. Tetanus. In: Last, J., ed. Public Health and Preventive Medicine. Norwalk, CT, Appleton-Century-Crofts, 1992, pp. 76–78.

168. Williams, M. Long-term cost comparison of major limb salvage using Ilizarov method versus amputation. Clin Orthop 335:268, 1994.

169. Wiss, D.; Gilbert, P.; Merritt, P.; Sarmiento, A. Immediate internal fixation of open ankle fractures. J Trauma 24:265, 1988.

170. Wiss, D.; Segal, D.; Gumbs, V.; Salter, D. Flexible medullary nailing of tibial shaft fractures. J Trauma 26:1106, 1986.

171. Yaremchuk, M.; Brumback, R.; Manson, P.; et al. Acute and definitive management of traumatic osteocutaneous defects of the lower extremity. Plast Reconstr Surg 30:1, 1987.

172. Yourassowsky, E.; Linden, M.V.d.; Crokaert, F. One shot of high-dose amikacin: A working hypothesis. Chemotherapy 36:1, 1990.

CHAPTER 14

Soft Tissue Coverage

Randy Sherman, M.D.

Open fractures resulting from high-velocity trauma develop a zone of soft tissue injury much larger than the ostensible fracture site itself (Fig. 14–1).[12, 13, 38, 89, 95, 100] As with a burn wound, the traumatic zone of injury includes areas of increasingly severe tissue destruction as the point of impact is approached (Fig. 14–2). A large portion of the soft tissues that are marginally viable at the time of initial injury eventually die or are replaced by scar. The entire area is ultimately characterized by fibrosis, tissue ischemia, lack of normal musculoskeletal architecture, and dead space. Coupled with bone comminution, periosteal stripping, and disruption of the medullary blood supply, these injuries often result in fracture nonunion and post-traumatic chronic osteomyelitis. In open fractures, initial appreciation of the zone of injury is crucial for development of a strategy for fracture stabilization, débridement, and soft tissue coverage, which together determine the success of the patient's orthopaedic outcome.

Aggressive and repeated débridement of not only the fracture site but also the entire zone of injury is paramount to the positive resolution of these complex problems. Neither fracture healing nor soft tissue reconstruction can safely proceed until all necrotic material and foreign bodies have been cleared from the wound. Along with removal of all infected and nonviable tissue, the obliteration of dead space is essential to promote a favorable environment for fracture healing and to avoid development of osteomyelitis.[62] Similarly, radical excision of dead bone, scar, and infected granulation tissue is mandatory in the treatment of established bone infection.

Often, in an attempt to preserve as much bone cortical contact as possible for fracture healing, nonviable bone is left in place, thus promoting the very complications that the surgeon had intended to avoid. There is no evidence that devascularized bone at the site of an open fracture aids in fracture healing. On the contrary, it is well documented that dead bone harbors bacteria, acts as a foreign body, and plays a central role in the development of osteomyelitis.[37] Historically, orthopaedic surgeons have been reluctant to débride wounds radically in the absence of reliable alternatives for bone reconstruction and soft tissue coverage. However, even without the newer plastic surgical techniques for wound management, there is a clear advantage to radical débridement alone, followed by eventual bone grafting by the Papineau technique or by skin grafting over newly developed granulation tissue.

With both musculoskeletal and head and neck neoplasms, the extent of tumor resection is often limited by the surgeon's ability to close the defect. Recurrence of such tumors depends on the extent of free margins. Prevention or cure of post-traumatic musculoskeletal disease (e.g., osteomyelitis) could be compared with adequate oncologic resection of a malignancy for cure. With the ability to transfer vascularized tissue into the traumatic defect, replacing tissue in kind, both the orthopaedic traumatologist and the oncologic surgeon are free to resect for cure. Godina and Lister[34] have shown the clear advantage of this treatment strategy, and our experience, as well that of many centers, corroborates their data.[79, 98]

TIMING

Historically, there has been some controversy about the timing of wound closure, with different centers basing their treatment options on the nature and timing of surgical débridement. Early wound closure with the use of vascularized tissue has long been a prerequisite for optimal rehabilitation of function after complex hand injuries.[6, 20] In several centers across the United States and in Europe, aggressive débridement and early lower extremity wound closure with muscle flaps have decreased the incidence of osteomyelitis, nonunion, and amputation. Godina and Lister's retrospective historical study[34] evaluating more than 534 free tissue transfers in the treatment of extremity trauma clearly revealed the advantages of radical débridement and early (within 72 hours) wound closure with vascularized tissue (Fig. 14–3). When this technique was used for limb salvage, the percentage of cases of nonunion and osteomyelitis decreased. In addition, the number of

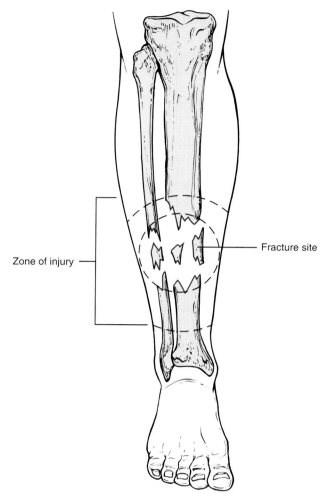

FIGURE **14–1.** Diagrammatic representation of the zone of injury, incorporating an area much greater than the fracture site.

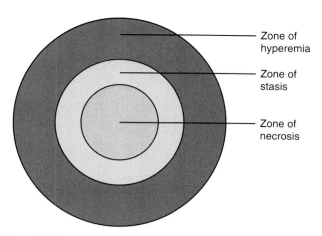

FIGURE **14–2.** Progressive zones of injury in the burn wound are analogous to the soft tissue zone of injury concept.

hospitalizations, use of anesthesia, and time to fracture healing were all substantially reduced.[34]

Byrd and colleagues[12] at the Parkland Medical Center compared on a prospective basis the classical open wound care of type III tibial fractures and the method of early débridement and wound closure with vascularized muscle. Although the numbers were small, there was a distinct advantage in all the parameters mentioned with the latter approach. Both studies[12, 34] found that the number of procedural complications rose markedly if these wounds were not closed in the early phase (defined by Byrd and colleagues as the first 6 days after injury and by Godina and Lister as the first 72 hours after injury). Each study noted that the inflammatory nature of the wound, as it remained open, led to greater chances of continuing infection and an increased rate of thrombosis at the time of delayed flap closure.

FIGURE **14–3.** Graphic compendium of the work of Godina, published by Lister, illustrating the numerous advantages of early wound closure. (Modified from Godina, M.; Lister, G. Plast Reconstr Surg 78:285, 1986.)

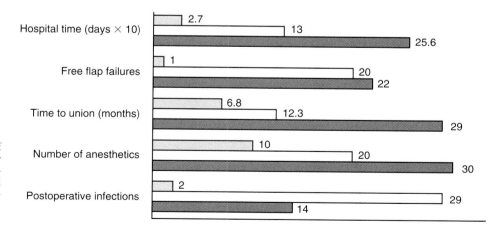

Table 14–1 ....

University of Southern California Protocol for the
Management of Type III Fractures

Stabilization of patient
Tetanus prophylaxis
Broad-spectrum antibiotics
Fracture reduction with external fixation
Radical débridement of all injured tissues
Redébridement at 24–48–72 hours, if necessary
Early muscle flap wound coverage before 5 days, if possible
Bone grafting at 6 weeks

•••

Later, Yaremchuk and colleagues[100] obtained good results despite longer periods between initial injury and ultimate closure, and we have noted similar results. The common denominator in these approaches is the dominant role of radical and repeated débridement as the key to success of any subsequent wound closure techniques (Table 14–1).

WOUND COVERAGE TECHNIQUES

As one approaches the treatment of an open wound in the locomotor system, the fundamental principles of the reconstructive ladder should be kept in mind. For injuries in which little or no soft tissue is lost, direct closure can be attempted when all necrotic tissue has been cleared and a lack of tension can be ensured. For injuries in which skin and its supporting elements have been lost but retention of soft tissue is adequate to ensure joint mobility and coverage of all vital structures (i.e., nerve, tendon, vessels, and bone), free grafts of split-thickness or full-thickness skin can be considered. For complex wounds that do not meet these criteria, pedicle or free transfer of vascularized tissue is necessary to restore blood supply, replace lost or devitalized tissues, and provide stable coverage.

Skin Grafts

Split-thickness skin grafts are defined as those that occupy less than the entire depth of the dermis. They can be subdivided into thin split-thickness skin grafts, which are smaller than 0.016 inch, and thick split-thickness skin grafts. The advantages of these grafts are their ease of acquisition, their reliable take, and the capability of reepithelialization of the donor site, which allows large amounts of split-thickness skin graft to be taken to cover sizable wounds. Their corresponding disadvantages are the need to have sophisticated instrumentation for skin graft harvesting (Brown or Padgett dermatome), scarring of the donor site, and variable contraction of the split-thickness skin graft on the recipient bed.

Full-thickness skin grafts are those that incorporate the entire dermal and epidermal structure. These have the advantages of maintenance of the original texture after transplantation, minimal shrinkage or contraction of the graft, better color match in certain situations, and greater durability. In addition, donor sites can be closed with fine-line scars to minimize unsightly donor site defects. The disadvantages of full-thickness skin grafts are their limitation of size and greater unreliability of take.

Flap Classification

Unlike a graft, which must derive its blood supply from the recipient bed to ensure adequate survival, a flap is by definition vascularized tissue and contains a blood supply that not only serves to keep the flap alive but also aids in rehabilitation of the recipient defect. Two classification systems must be considered when studying the various flaps available.[16, 63]

The flap is classified according to the specific area of skin or muscle from which it is derived (e.g., latissimus dorsi, lateral arm, fibula). The classification should also specify which tissue types are involved in the transfer (e.g., myocutaneous for muscle and skin, osteocutaneous for bone and skin, fasciocutaneous for investing fascia and skin, neural, visceral). In addition, the flap must be classified as to the nature of its blood supply (Fig. 14–4). The major categories include the random skin flap and the axial pattern flap. The latter type can be subclassified into the pedicle flap, the island flap, and the free flap on the basis of how the axial pattern vessels are handled: left attached with surrounding skin, left attached but skeletonized, or detached and revascularized with the use of microsurgical techniques to a distant site, respectively (Fig. 14–5).

The current success in providing alternatives for wound closure and soft tissue reconstruction is based on the work of the physicians who mapped out the anatomic and physiologic territories supplied by individual arteriovenous units, using cadaver dissections, barium latex injection radiography, and animal models for physiologic verification. Our understanding of musculoskeletal anatomy has grown to the point that scores of highly tailored composite tissue flaps are now available (Fig. 14–6).[64, 69]

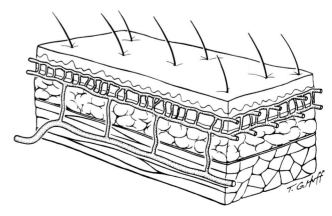

Figure 14–4. Representative cross section of the musculoskeletal system and its arterial blood supply.

RANDOM SKIN FLAPS

Random skin flaps are based on the blood supply that remains at the base of a newly formed pedicle of skin, where no identifiable inflow or outflow vessels can be found. Traditionally, the principle of maintaining a one-to-one ratio of length to width is applied—that is, the length of the proposed flap should be no longer than the width of the flap at its base. Many reports have documented flap designs that incorporate a length-to-width ratio much greater than this, but certainty of survival of the distal portion of these flaps may be less reliable.

In an effort to transfer longer random skin flaps, delay procedures can be undertaken to exclude contributing blood supply sequentially from all sides of the proposed flap except the base. By creating a state of relative tissue hypoxia, these operations, done at 10- to 14-day intervals, can reorient the blood supply into the base of the flap, allowing more tissue to be transferred.[28, 75] This practice, appropriately known as the delay technique, was until lately the standard method for creation of large flaps of tissue for complex wound coverage. With the development of axial pattern flaps, this tactic is now rarely used. Examples of random flaps include local, rotation, transposition, and advancement flaps used to cover small defects on the dorsum of the hand (see later discussion). The flap derives its blood supply from the subdermal plexus, which lies immediately below the dermal subcutaneous junction.

AXIAL PATTERN SKIN FLAPS

Axial pattern skin flaps, best exemplified by the groin flap, are made up of skin and subcutaneous tissue supplied by an identified arteriovenous pedicle lying superficial to the underlying muscle or its invested fascia. This pedicle supplies the entirety of the defined skin territory through an arborization of the dominant pedicle, connecting with the subdermal plexus previously described. These flaps have the advantage of transferring a much larger amount of tissue on a pedicle base that need be only the width of the arteriovenous unit itself. They can be employed as pedicle flaps or as free tissue transfers.

FASCIOCUTANEOUS FLAPS

Certain areas of the cutaneous anatomy derive their blood supply from perforating vessels that run within the investing muscular fascia. These provide a well-vascularized piece of tissue with an anatomically defined boundary that can be raised solely on the pedicle or transferred as free tissue. Such fasciocutaneous flaps, sometimes also known as septocutaneous flaps, have the advantages of lack of bulk, pliability, and improved match of color and texture. Donor site deformities can often be minimized by primary closure, as with the myocutaneous flap. If a cutaneous nerve is present, sensory innervation can occasionally be restored to the transferred tissue.

MYOCUTANEOUS FLAPS

Since the early to middle 1980s, the myocutaneous flap has become the most commonly used of all axial pattern flaps.[62] This flap derives its blood supply from the major pedicle or one of the predominant minor pedicles that

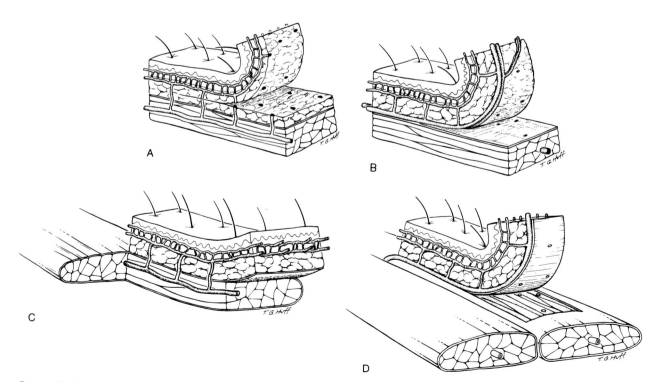

FIGURE 14–5. Flap classification based on the origin of blood supply. *A,* Random pattern. *B,* Axial pattern. *C,* Musculocutaneous. *D,* Fasciocutaneous.

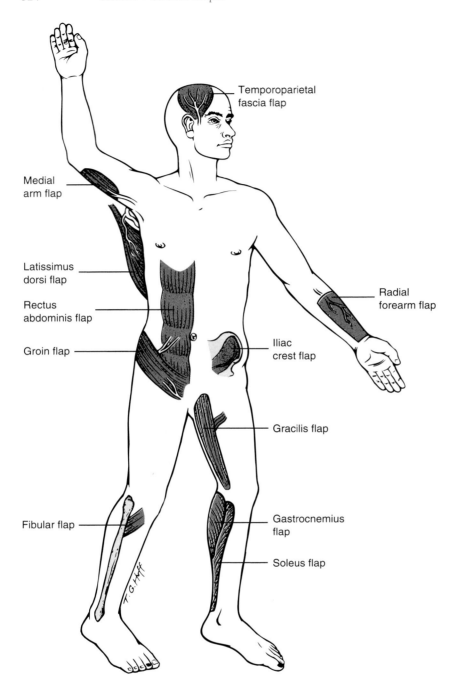

Medial
arm flap

Latissimus
dorsi flap

Rectus
abdominis flap

Groin flap

Fibular flap

Temporoparietal
fascia flap

Radial
forearm flap

Iliac
crest flap

Gracilis flap

Gastrocnemius
flap

Soleus flap

Figure 14–6. Topical atlas of the donor sites most commonly employed for free tissue transfer.

supply the muscle of choice. Through perforating vessels from the muscle, the overlying subcutaneous tissue or skin, or both, can be transferred along with the muscle to provide a flap of sizable bulk and contour.

When taken with the motor nerve in specialized reconstructive situations, these flaps can be used to rehabilitate an otherwise paralyzed or nonfunctional muscle group—for example, the motorized gracilis muscle can be used to restore forearm flexion or to correct facial paralysis.[61] Myocutaneous flaps can be used to cover otherwise nonreconstructible wounds of the extremities because they provide all components necessary for successful healing of the injured tissues.[67] Muscle and myocutaneous flaps also play an increasingly central role in the treatment of upper and lower extremity osteomyelitis.[97]

SOFT TISSUE COVERAGE BY REGION

Upper Extremity

HAND AND FINGERTIPS

Complex injuries to the fingertip can be particularly devastating because of the crucial role this part of the hand plays in human contact. The fingertip pulp is invested with a greater density and specificity of nerve endings than any other region in the body. Examination must assess the integrity not only of the nail but also of its supporting elements, the eponychium and the underlying nail bed. The treatment of pulp injuries varies according to the size of tissue loss and the exposure of underlying structures. For injuries smaller than 1 cm to the fingertip pulp, several authors have shown the advantage of conservative wound management with sterile dressings, granulation, contraction, and eventual epithelialization or split-thickness skin grafting. In circumstances in which patients have lost a larger amount of tissue or the soft tissue loss is combined with an exposed distal phalangeal bone or flexor tendon, soft tissue transposition has its advantages. Because the finger pulp is the ultimate prehensile surface, durability and sensation are of paramount importance to a successfully rehabilitated fingertip. These prerequisites can be met by the use of various local or regional flaps.[51, 82]

Atasoy-Kleinert Flap. This is a proximally based random skin flap that uses the principle of V-Y advancement to move more proximal volar phalangeal tissue distally to cover the tip loss. The advantage of this flap is its transfer of vascularized sensate skin and supporting elements from an adjacent, normal, uninjured area. Its prerequisites are lack of associated injuries to the phalanx proximal to the tip injury and a realistic limitation on the size of the tip defect (Fig. 14–7).

Cutler Flap. Cutler flaps are similar in design and execution to the Atasoy-Kleinert flaps except for their site of origin. These randomly based skin flaps are developed from the lateral soft tissues of the distal phalanx. They can be useful if the geometry of the wound or previous scarring on the volar aspect of the finger mitigates against the use of the Atasoy-Kleinert flap (see Fig. 14–7).[27]

Thenar Flap. This proximally based pedicle flap, well described by Beasley,[6] employs thenar skin and subcutaneous tissue to cover tip losses of the index and long fingers that require more than local distal phalangeal tissue can provide. The advantages of this flap are good color and texture match, excellent durability, and the ability to reconstruct the contour of the fingertip with revisional surgery. When the flap is properly harvested, the donor site should heal without incident. Because of the digital positioning, however, the recipient finger is at major risk for flexion contracture if the flap is tethered longer than 2 weeks. Early division and aggressive postoperative mobilization are mandatory to prevent this complication (Fig. 14–8).[74]

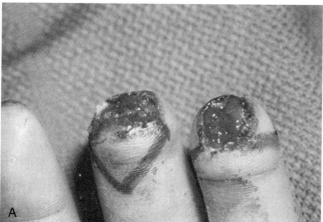

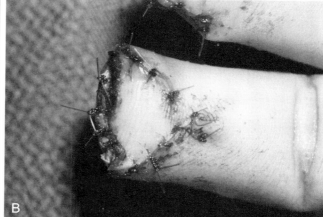

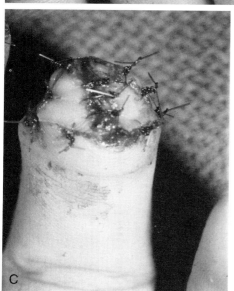

FIGURE **14–7.** *A,* Complex fingertip injuries to the long and ring digits involving distal phalangeal exposure. *B,* The long finger after completion of an Atasoy-Kleinert flap. *C,* The ring finger after completion of Cutler flaps.

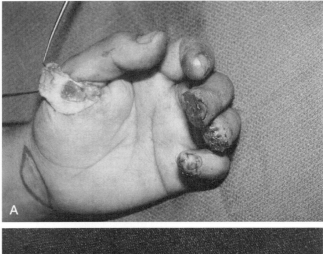

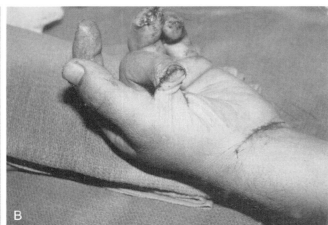

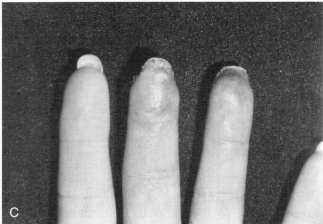

Figure 14–8. *A,* Thenar flap raised for coverage of a middle fingertip injury with loss of volar pulp tissue and an exposed distal phalanx. *B,* The flap in place. *C,* Two months after division.

Volar Advancement Flap. This alternative for fingertip coverage, first described by Moberg in 1964,[3] employs the volar surface of the involved digit proximal to the metacarpal phalangeal joint of the thumb or to a point immediately proximal to the proximal interphalangeal joint of the remaining fingers.[11, 58] The flap is raised by incising along the midaxial line bilaterally and dissecting skin and subcutaneous tissue free along the line of the tendon sheath. The neurovascular bundles are preserved within the flap, and the dorsal branches of these neurovascular bundles are preserved to ensure continued viability of the distal dorsal skin. The finger is slightly flexed at the interphalangeal joint, and the flap is advanced to the distal edge of the tip defect. The flap is then sutured in place and dressed to hold the digit in a position that avoids tension on the advanced tissue. In practice, this procedure is best suited for the thumb and has little clinical value for the remaining digits. Early and aggressive range-of-motion exercises are mandatory to prevent contracture at the interphalangeal joint.

Cross-Finger Flaps. This option for fingertip reconstruction also serves amply for coverage of exposed flexor or extensor surfaces throughout the length of the phalanges. The standard cross-finger flap employs the dorsal skin and subcutaneous tissue down to the epitenon of the extensor surface overlying the middle phalanx. The blood supply to this flap is based on the dorsal branch of the digital neurovascular bundle to the donor digit. The flap is raised from the radial to the ulnar side, or vice versa, and then applied to the fingertip or other defect. The donor defect is simultaneously covered with a full-thickness skin graft for optimal aesthetic result (Fig. 14–9). A period of 10 to 14 days is allowed for revascularization of the flap from the recipient bed before division is attempted.[19, 41, 48, 49, 52, 85, 96]

Neurovascular Island Flap. As a modification of the cross-finger flap, numerous varieties of arterialized island flaps based on the digital neurovascular bundles have been described.[84] They have the advantage of a greater transpositional arc than is available with the flaps previously described for injuries to the middle and proximal portions of the phalanges. They provide vascularized tissue with good color and texture match, excellent durability, and, in the case of the neurovascular island pedicle flap, proper sensibility, which can sometimes approach that of the native tissue. The major drawback with this type of transfer is the need for cortical reeducation. After intensive occupational therapy, the patient may be able to recognize the afferent stimuli from these flaps as coming from the recipient digit. With any period of disuse or immobilization, however, cortical orientation reverts to that of the donor finger.[11, 57, 72]

Other Local Flaps. For small defects about the dorsum of the hand, wrist, or forearm that cannot be closed directly or repaired with skin grafts, flaps created by local transposition, rotation, or advancement can be used.

These are essentially random flaps and consequently are limited by the size of their soft tissue base and their small arc of rotation. Given an understanding of their limitations, however, these flaps can be especially useful to obtain coverage for isolated tendon or bone exposure (Fig. 14–10).[55, 71]

FOREARM

Wounds in the forearm region that require more extensive soft tissue coverage include open fractures with major overlying soft tissue loss, degloving injuries, irreversibly exposed tendons or nerves, and osteomyelitic wounds with draining sinuses. As noted previously, large open wounds caused by degloving injuries are adequately treated after débridement by split-thickness skin grafting provided an adequate bed of granulation tissue is present. Many investigators have noted restoration of reasonable tendon function with a split-thickness skin graft applied directly over the intact epitenon. With loss of vascularized tissues covering the tendon substance, nerve, or bone, the importation of vascularized soft tissue becomes mandatory. Quantitative bacteriology can aid in optimizing the timing of closure in these granulating wounds. Counts of less than 10^3 organisms per gram of tissue ensure a much greater chance of skin graft take.[53]

The groin flap, first described by McGregor and Jackson[73] in 1972, continues to be the mainstay for soft tissue replacement in this region.[72] The flap can be raised quickly and easily, with an extremely high degree of reliability. The area of skin that can be taken without fear of distal tip necrosis extends at least 10 cm beyond the anterior superior iliac spine. This area almost always provides adequate tissue for coverage of composite defects of the dorsum, hand, wrist, or distal forearm. Additional advantages of this flap include ease of donor site closure and the aesthetic superiority of the donor site scar. As with

all pedicle flaps, the main disadvantage is the need for immobilization of the hand in the groin region for 14 to 21 days before division (Fig. 14–11).[56, 73]

The arterial supply of the groin flap arises from the femoral artery, approximately 2.5 cm below the inguinal ligament. This vessel runs parallel to the inguinal ligament and meets it at a point overlying the anterior superior iliac spine. The vessel perforates the sartorius muscle fascia and sends a deep branch below and a superficial branch into the subcutaneous tissue at this point. If the flap is to be elevated medial to the sartorius fascia, the muscle should be included, to protect both branches of the vessel. The venous drainage to the flap is usually supplied by the venae comitantes of the superficial circumflex iliac vein, but it can also drain predominantly into the superficial inferior epigastric vein. This variability in venous drainage need not be taken into account when using the flap as a pedicle transfer. The flap can easily be made 10 cm wide while still closing the donor site primarily.

The deltopectoral flap provides tissue that is similar to that of the groin flap. It is taken from an area on the anterolateral chest wall. This medially based skin flap takes its blood supply from perforating vessels of the internal mammary artery. The flap is transversely oriented and raised from the lateral to the medial side at the level of the pectoralis fascia. This tissue provides an excellent color match with the upper extremity. However, donor sites must be closed with the skin graft, which leaves an unsightly donor defect. With the newer alternatives involving free tissue transfer, this type of flap, like other large thoracoabdominal flaps, is of mainly historical interest.

For more extensive wounds of this region, the axial pattern hypogastric or thoracoepigastric flap (based on the superficial inferior epigastric artery and vein) and the rectus abdominis muscle myocutaneous flap can be of use. These flaps are advantageous because of the large quanti-

FIGURE 14–9. *A,* Gunshot wound to the proximal phalanx of the long finger with exposed, comminuted fracture and tendon loss. Cross-finger flap drawn out. *B,* Flap transferred and full-thickness skin graft applied to the donor site.

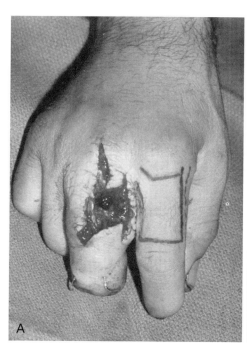

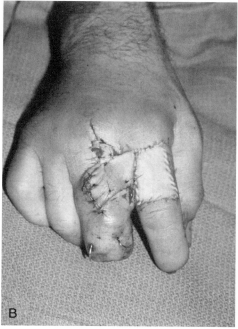

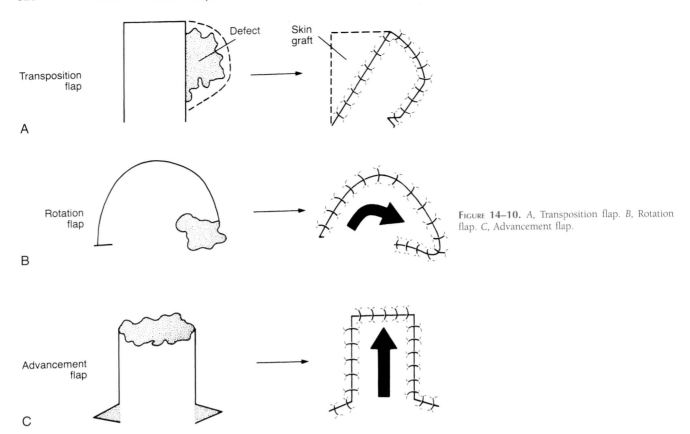

Transposition flap

A

Rotation flap

B

Advancement flap

C

FIGURE **14–10.** *A,* Transposition flap. *B,* Rotation flap. *C,* Advancement flap.

ties of tissue available. As previously described, the disadvantages stem from the need to keep the patient immobilized and relatively dependent for 10 days to 3 weeks. These flaps are in a sense parasitic because they do not bring in new sources of blood supply after division. Rather, they depend exclusively on the wound bed for vascularity and cannot be relied on to enhance the wound environment. In cases of osteomyelitis or other residual infections, additional vascularized tissue is crucial.

A newer flap for the dorsum of the wrist and distal forearm is the pedicle radial artery forearm flap, called the Chinese flap.[26] This fasciocutaneous flap is based on the radial artery and the basilic vein proximally and on the radial artery and cephalic vein distally. The distal flap can be used only if an intact ulnar circulation is ensured by Allen's test and arteriography. The extensive arc of rotation of this flap, given both the proximal and distal pedicles, makes it useful for treatment of wounds of the dorsal and volar surfaces of the forearm, wrist, and hand. However, this soft tissue component cannot be used for complex wounds that involve the flap itself (Fig. 14–12).[23, 26, 76, 92]

The division of pedicle flaps traditionally takes place 14 to 21 days after initial application. This allows time for the skin paddle to become vascularized from the recipient bed. In special circumstances in which the flap has an extremely dominant vascular pedicle or the recipient bed is judged marginal in its ability to revascularize the flap, a delay procedure, with division of only the dominant pedicle on the flap can be done to augment the development of collateral circulation. Along with Meyers and associates,[75] Furnas and colleagues[28] have documented the ability of

intermittent ischemic periods induced by cross-clamping of the flap to augment and speed the formation of collateral circulation from the recipient bed. In a limited clinical study using the progressive intermittent clamping technique, they were able to divide two pedicle flaps only 5 days after initial application.[28] Fluorescein dye studies performed with the clamp applied allow quantification of blood flow from the recipient site before division.

USE OF FREE FLAPS IN THE UPPER EXTREMITY

Although pedicle flaps, such as the groin flap, have worked admirably in many situations for soft tissue coverage, there are increasing indications for the transfer of composite tissues from distant sites using microsurgical techniques, and many such flaps have been developed.[63, 64, 69, 88, 91]

Indications

In many complex extremity wounds, the sheer size and complexity of the injury and the loss of structures obviate the use of a local or pedicle flap for adequate replacement. In this situation, several donor sites to fill specific needs can be chosen. Often, the recipient bed cannot support the vascular requirements of the transferred tissue. However rare it may be, osteomyelitis of the upper extremity with overlying tissue loss is best treated by free muscle transfer after débridement. The addition of this highly vascularized tissue increases oxygen tension and decreases bacterial counts in the experimental model.[15, 62]

Central to the successful rehabilitation of any hand and upper extremity injury is early mobilization. This need is especially acute in the hand and wrist and can be better accomplished in cases of large soft tissue defects with the use of free tissue transfer. This approach frees the patient from immobilization to the donor site and allows early range-of-motion exercise and prevention of stiffness.

Composite transfers can be undertaken to fulfill the needs of the polytraumatized hand. Often, the combina-

tion of tendon and skin or skin and bone is required to complete the reconstruction. With use of the appropriate composite transfer, the reconstruction can frequently be completed in one procedure, allowing more rapid healing and earlier rehabilitation.

Preoperative evaluation requires that the patient be otherwise stable and that more severe injuries be ad-

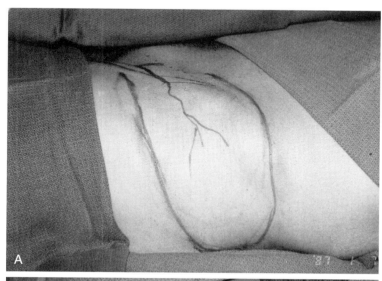

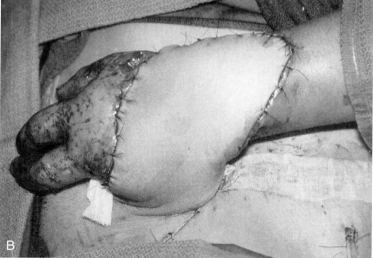

FIGURE **14–11.** *A,* Groin flap donor site with superficial circumflex iliac artery marked. *B,* Flap in place over a composite defect of the hand. *C,* Donor site scar.

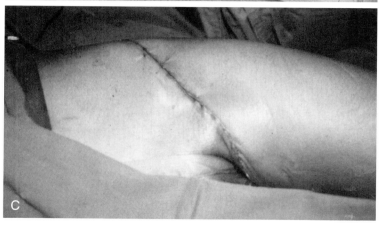

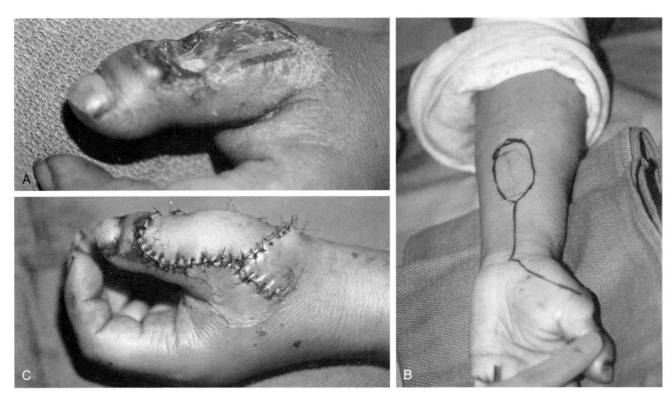

Figure 14–12. *A,* Composite defect of the thumb with exposed extensor pollicis longus and interphalangeal joint. *B,* Distally based radial forearm flap. *C,* Immediate postoperative result.

dressed and resolved. Angiography is often advisable to delineate the vascular anatomy of the injured region.[101] Débridement and skeletal stabilization, preferably with external fixation, should be the first order of business at the time of surgery. These procedures must be carried out with an autonomous set of instruments and irrigating tools; after the wound has been cleaned and all remaining tissues are viable, gowns and gloves should be changed and the transfer accomplished. Repeated débridement may be needed, and several procedures may be required before the transfer is complete. Usually, two teams work simultaneously, one at the harvest site and the other at the recipient site. This arrangement shortens the intraoperative interval; reduces pulmonary, vascular, and neurologic complications related to positioning; and helps avoid physician fatigue.

Various free muscle or myocutaneous flaps are available for soft tissue coverage of complex hand and forearm wounds. In our experience, the rectus abdominis muscle transferred as a pure muscle unit alone has worked admirably (Fig. 14–13). The gracilis myocutaneous flap is frequently transferred as a motorized unit for the treatment of Volkmann's ischemic contracture and of associated conditions in which flexor function is lost (Fig. 14–14).[61] The temporoparietal fascial free flap serves well in situations in which bulk must be kept to a minimum and vascularity is paramount to successful closure of the wound (Fig. 14–15). This is certainly the case in distal forearm osteomyelitis. The latissimus dorsi muscle, the original workhorse of free tissue transfers, always has a place in soft tissue coverage in any

area. Donor site seromas occur more frequently with this muscle than with other donor sites and may necessitate prolonged suction drainage, repeated percutaneous aspiration, or both. The serratus anterior muscle has been used successfully by Buncke and colleagues for coverage of defects over the dorsum and thenar eminence of the hand. The lower three slips are included, and the remainder of the muscle is left to avoid winging of the scapula.

Types of Flaps Available

Free skin and fasciocutaneous flaps useful in the upper extremity include the groin, scapular, lateral arm, dorsalis pedis, and radial forearm flaps (Fig. 14–16).[4, 50, 59, 77, 78]

Groin Flap. This flap has gained increasing popularity as a free tissue transfer because of the amount of skin available and the minimal aesthetic deformity of the donor site defect[1, 5] (Fig. 14–17). This was the first skin flap used as a free tissue transfer by Daniel and Taylor in 1973. It soon fell out of favor because of the variability and brevity of the donor site pedicle. These problems remain, but increased familiarity and greater technical confidence have helped to overcome them. Although not often employed in hand reconstruction, a modification of this flap used commonly in jaw reconstruction incorporates a segment of the iliac crest along with abdominal wall musculature based on the deep circumflex iliac artery and vein.[93] This allows osteomyocutaneous transfer and can be used if a substantial part of the underlying bone architecture has been destroyed along with the overlying soft tissue and skin.[88]

Dorsalis Pedis Flap. This composite flap, based on the dorsalis pedis artery and vein, transfers thin, pliable skin and subcutaneous tissue with a possible addition of vascularized tendon or metatarsal to fit various recipient needs.[59] It is especially useful in the dorsum of the hand, where skin loss and extensor tendon destruction commonly occur together. The main disadvantages of this flap are related to the long and meticulous nature of the dissection and donor site problems. With a successful skin graft take, patients may be bothered by the loss of sensation of the dorsum of the foot and could have problems with durability of the skin graft in holding up to the demands of footwear. The flap is also limited by its size, which can be a problem if the entire dorsum of the hand requires coverage (Fig. 14–18).

Scapular and Parascapular Flaps. These newer types of flap allow the harvest of a large area of tissue on the back, either transversely or longitudinally oriented. The blood supply is based on the circumflex scapular artery and vein that arise from the subscapular vessels. Skin up to 20 cm long can be taken with the scapular flap and up to 30 cm long with the parascapular flap. The vessel diameters are 2.5 to 3.5 mm, and the pedicle length is at least 6 cm. The flap can be taken with the underlying latissimus muscle or lateral border of the scapula, or both, and a composite transfer can be built to address complex defects (Fig. 14–19). The disadvantages of this flap are related mainly to its composition (thick back skin), which may not match the forearm or hand in color or quality. The donor site is usually closed primarily, but this leaves a wide scar along the posterior axillary line or across the upper posterior torso. These flaps work especially well for repair of the large degloving injuries from machinery that require extensive skin resurfacing.[4, 33, 77]

Lateral Arm Flap. This septocutaneous flap is based on the posterior radial collateral artery and vein and carries with it a sensory nerve. The vessels are a branch of the profunda brachii artery and supply a pedicle of 2-mm-diameter vessels with a length of 6 to 7 cm. This flap works well for soft tissue defects alone on the hand and wrist area, which can be covered with 6 to 8 cm of tissue (Fig. 14–20). The flap can be taken with a greater width and length, although the donor site then requires a skin graft for closure. One described advantage of this flap is the ability to use the tissue as an innervated flap.[50]

Osseous and Osteocutaneous Fibula Flap. This is primarily a vascularized bone transfer and is best used to reconstruct long segmental cortical defects of the radius, ulna, or humerus. It can be taken as cortical bone alone or with overlying skin and/or soleus muscle through septocutaneous perforators found concentrated mostly in the distal third of the lower leg. It is based on the peroneal artery coming off the tibioperoneal trunk. There are some variations to collateral blood supply to the foot through the posterior tibial and anterior tibial arteries, raising the question as to whether preoperative angiography is uniformly indicated. With modern, noninvasive duplex ultrasonography, this type of scan performed preoperatively to outline the anatomy is considered prudent. The pedicle can be easily lengthened by clipping the first few branches going from main pedicle to fibula, allowing the surgeon more versatility of inset without compromising

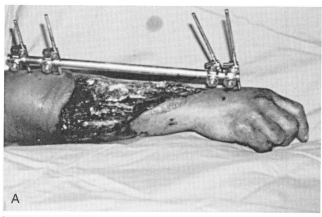

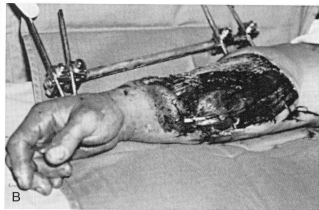

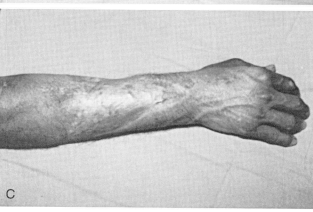

FIGURE 14–13. *A,* Proximal forearm defect involving loss of skin, muscle, and bone. *B,* The injury after radical débridement and transfer of the rectus abdominis muscle. *C,* Postoperative view 4 months after cancellous bone grafting and subsequent removal of the external fixator.

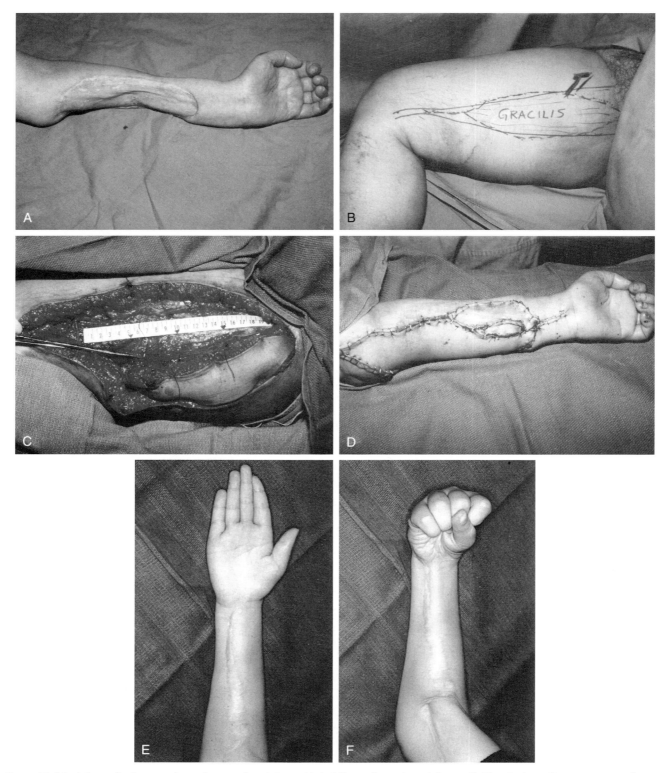

Figure 14–14. *A,* Loss of volar musculature from machete injury with inability to flex wrist and fingers. *B,* Motorized gracilis myocutaneous flap outlined. *C,* Muscle isolated with tracking sutures placed in situ to determine resting muscle fiber length. *D,* Immediately following transfer. *E,* Another patient after gracilis transfer—relaxed. *F,* Fully flexed.

vascularity. (Figure 14–21) gives two examples of various uses of this transfer, one for humeral diaphyseal reconstruction and the other for ulnar segmental reconstruction. The head of the fibula can be taken as well for attempted joint reconstruction but must be studied angiographically

because of vascular supply variations. This type of transfer has met with mixed results at best. Another advantage of the fibula when transferred to the head and neck region for mandible restoration is its ability to accommodate multiple osteotomies.

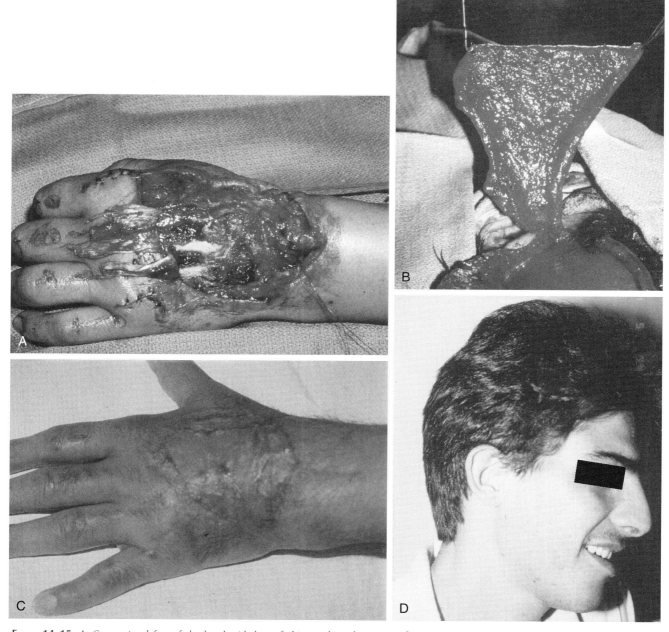

Figure 14–15. *A,* Composite defect of the hand with loss of skin, avulsion laceration of extensor tendons, and exposure of central metacarpals. *B,* Temporoparietal fascia raised and isolated on the superficial temporal artery and vein. *C,* Three months after transfer, with simultaneous tendon grafting and split-thickness skin grafting. *D,* Invisible donor site defect 2 months after surgery.

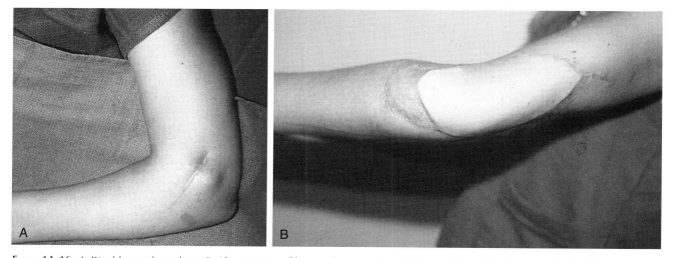

Figure 14–16. *A,* Distal humeral neoplasm. *B,* After resection of bone and surrounding soft tissue with transfer of parascapular free flap.

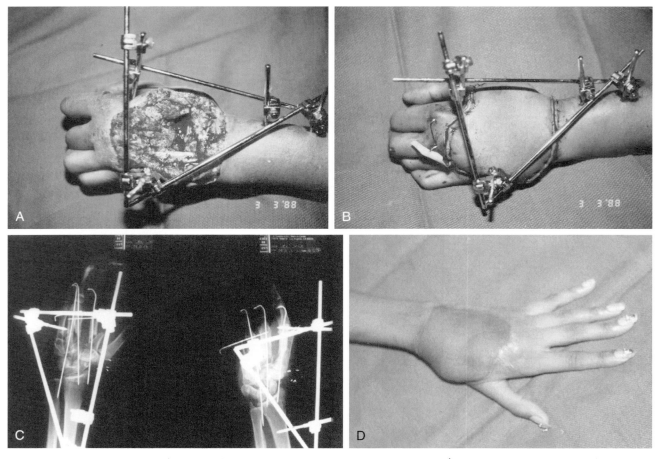

FIGURE 14–17. *A,* Composite wound from exiting high-power gunshot blast involving skin, muscle, tendon, and bone. *B,* One week after free groin flap transfer. Passive range-of-motion exercises were begun shortly after surgery. The patient eventually underwent bone grafting and tendon transfer. *C,* Combination of internal and external fixation for bone stabilization. *D,* Closed wound, healed fracture. The patient is now undergoing occupational therapy.

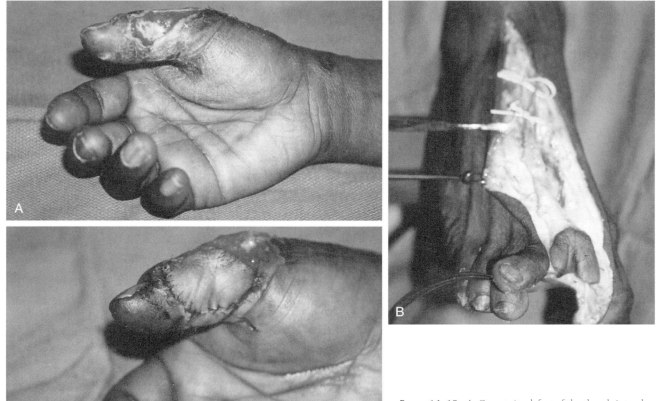

FIGURE 14–18. *A,* Composite defect of the thumb interphalangeal joint with exposed bone. *B,* Harvesting of the dorsalis pedis first webspace flap. *C,* Flap in place.

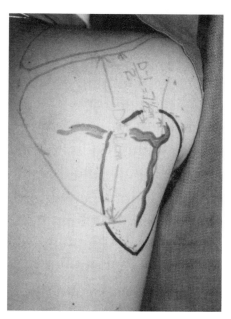

FIGURE **14–19.** Outline of the parascapular flap, noting its relation to the scapula and the cutaneous branches of the circumflex scapular vessels.

Radial Forearm Flap. This is a septocutaneous flap based on the radial artery and on the superficial cephalic vein or the deep venae comitantes. It can be harvested as a pedicle flap or free tissue transfer. Because of perforating branches to the periosteum of the radius, a small wedge of radius can be taken to be transferred as part of an osteocutaneous flap. The advantages of this flap stem from the generous amount of tissue on the forearm and the large caliber of the donor vessels. One must be certain that the proximal ulnar artery inflow is intact and able to supply the entire hand; this can be determined by a clinical Allen's test or arteriographic evaluation. The major disadvantage of this flap is the significant donor site deformity. Many authors have suggested modifications for improving the aesthetic results with the use of full-thickness skin grafts and transposition of native tissue proximally and distally.[76, 86]

ELBOW

Open wounds about the elbow that are short of soft tissue and that include an exposed fracture or joint require special attention because of the elasticity of the tissues normally found here and the wide range of motion required over the joint. Flaps mentioned previously for the forearm are adaptable to this region, with certain provisos.[20] The thoracoepigastric flap is useful for medial-based or ulnar-based defects requiring coverage (Fig. 14–22). Several free tissue transfers described previously can also be used for coverage of the elbow. In modification, the lateral arm flap turned distalward on its axis can be used to close small defects, especially on the posterior and lateral surfaces.

UPPER ARM AND SHOULDER

Compound fractures of the humerus that require vascularized soft tissue coverage are rare but can be reliably ameliorated with a latissimus dorsi muscle or myocutaneous flap brought from the ipsilateral side[94] (Fig. 14–23). With the flap isolated on its pedicle, incorporating the thoracodorsal artery and vein, release of both the origin and the insertion of the muscle allows coverage of the entire volar or dorsal surface of the upper arm, with extension of the muscle into the proximal forearm. The origin and insertion of the muscle can be reattached and used instead of a ruptured or destroyed biceps muscle to restore elbow flexion. In this situation, preservation of the thoracodorsal nerve along with the arteriovenous pedicle is mandatory. The pectoralis major muscle has also been used for these defects, but it does not have as large an arc of rotation as the latissimus. In addition, this donor site is more unsightly than the back.

Lower Extremity

PELVIS

Complex pelvic or acetabular fractures rarely involve marked soft tissue loss. Although many patients with complex pelvic fractures present with contused ecchymotic skin and subcutaneous tissues, most heal without substantial skin and soft tissue defects. For the few patients who require soft tissue coverage in the pelvic region, the flaps used most often include the rectus abdominis muscle or extended myocutaneous flap, tensor fasciae latae flap, and rectus femoris muscle or myocutaneous flap for anterior and lateral lesions. The gluteus maximus myocutaneous flap is most useful for posterior lesions involving the posterior iliac wing or sacroiliac joints.[80] Of these flaps, the rectus abdominis muscle has gained a preeminent position because of its superior arc of rotation, which extends from the subcostal area to the distal femur and laterally to well past the midaxillary line. Its hardy blood supply based on the deep inferior epigastric artery and vein, its long pedicle, and the relative lack of donor site morbidity have made it useful in most hip and pelvic reconstructions.[36] Combinations of these flaps can be used to treat areas massively injured by trauma or chronic osteomyelitis (Fig. 14–24).

THIGH

Because of the ample musculature of the thigh, open fractures of the femur, when reduced, rarely involve enough soft tissue loss to require additional placement of distant tissue for soft tissue coverage. In the few patients in whom such requirements exist, injuries of the proximal two thirds of the thigh in the anterior aspect can be treated by an ipsilateral rotation of the rectus abdominis muscle (described previously). The supracondylar region, both anteriorly and posteriorly, can be treated with the use of one or both gastrocnemius muscles. In cases of massive destruction with marked soft tissue deficits, free tissue transfers remain a reliable alternative for wound coverage over any aspect of the femur.

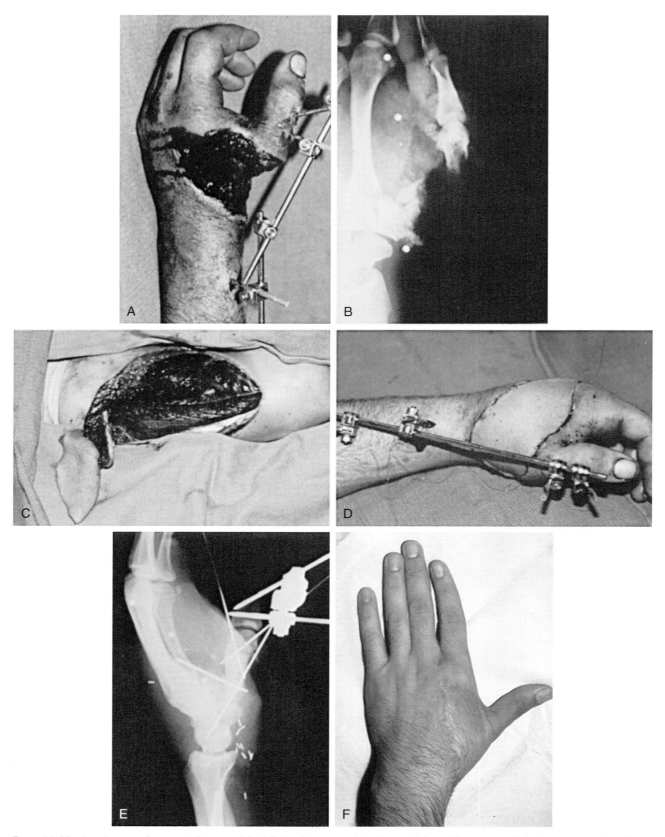

Figure 14–20. Complex open fracture. *A*, Fracture of the left thumb metacarpal. *B*, Osseous defect of the metacarpal. *C*, Osteocutaneous lateral arm flap dissected. *D*, Flap inset. *E*, Bony reconstruction of the metacarpal. *F*, Appearance at 1-year follow-up.

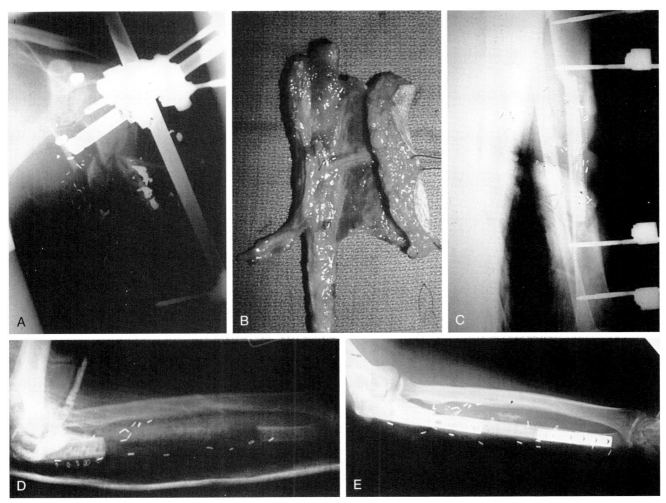

FIGURE **14–21.** *A,* Long humeral diaphyseal defect. *B,* Harvested fibula osteocutaneous flap. *C,* Transfer in place. *D,* Segmental defect of ulna. *E,* Reconstructed with vascularized fibula transfer.

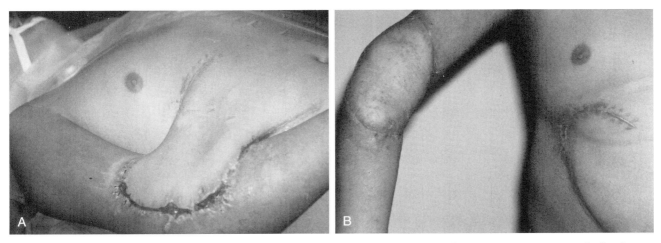

FIGURE **14–22.** *A,* Thoracoepigastric flap in place, covering a large defect of the antecubital region with joint exposure. *B,* One month after division.

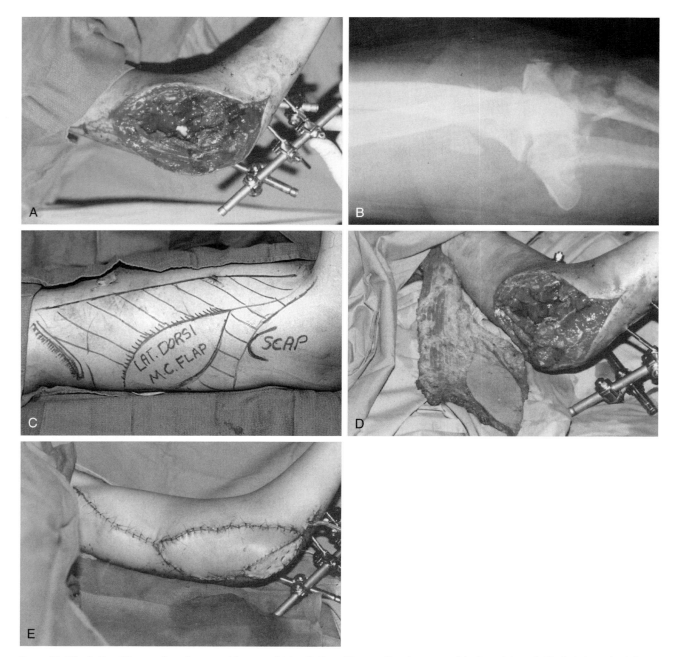

FIGURE 14–23. A, Type III open elbow fracture with exposed joint. B, X-ray film revealing the extent of the bone injury. C, The latissimus dorsi donor site. D, Myocutaneous flap raised and transferred. E, Flap and skin grafts in place.

KNEE AND PROXIMAL TIBIA

The badly displaced tibial plateau fracture with overlying soft tissue loss is a classical example in which internal fixation either alone or coupled with cross-knee external fixation, provides the patient with the best chance of fracture healing and joint congruity. Often in these open injuries, the additional burden of soft tissue stripping and bilateral plate placement converts a tenuous wound into one with no prospect of primary closure. In such cases, as well as in other cases of type III proximal third tibial fractures, the gastrocnemius muscle is unrivaled in its ability to provide wound closure with minimal donor site deficiencies.[2, 24, 29, 31, 32] Based on the sural artery and vein, derived as a direct branch from the popliteal artery in the suprageniculate area, either head of the gastrocnemius muscle can be isolated and transferred to cover the proximal third region (Fig. 14–25).

The muscle can be moved alone, after which it is skin grafted, or it can be transferred with an overlying skin flap, which can measure from 10 to 23 cm. In this situation, the donor site must be skin grafted. To extend its reach, the muscle can be released from its origin on the femoral epicondyle, gaining at least 2 to 3 cm. In addition, serial division of both the posterior and anterior muscular fascia

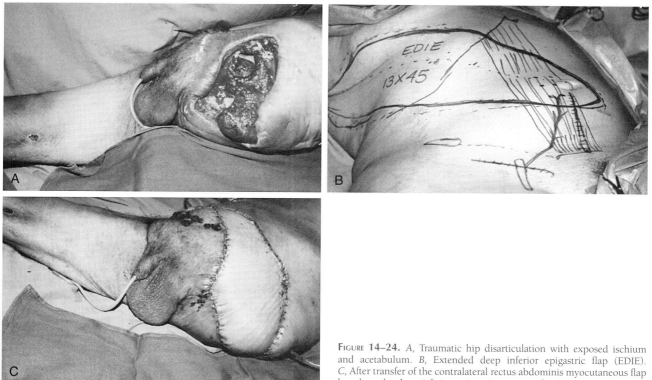

FIGURE **14–24.** *A,* Traumatic hip disarticulation with exposed ischium and acetabulum. *B,* Extended deep inferior epigastric flap (EDIE). *C,* After transfer of the contralateral rectus abdominis myocutaneous flap based on the deep inferior epigastric artery and veins.

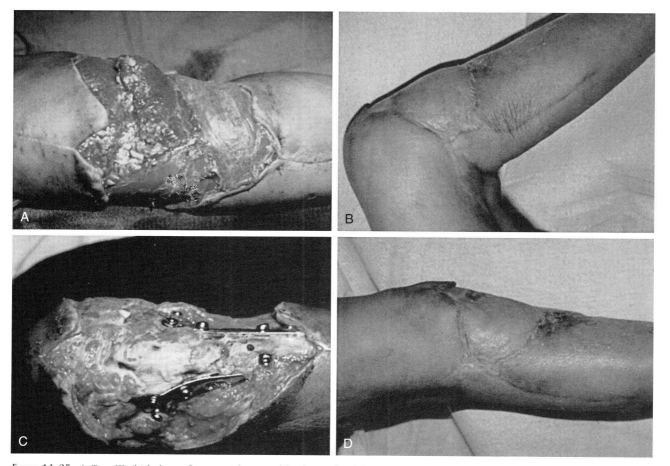

FIGURE **14–25.** *A,* Type III tibial plateau fracture with exposed hardware after débridement of necrotic, infected eschar. *B,* After transfer of bilateral gastrocnemius muscle rotation flaps. *C,* Six months after coverage, full weight bearing in extension. *D,* Full flexion.

allows the muscle to expand further, providing extended coverage for large, open wounds. When harvesting the lateral gastrocnemius muscle, care must be taken to avoid injury to the peroneal nerve, which lies immediately distal to the head of the fibula and anterior to the gastrocnemius as it descends.

MIDDLE THIRD OF THE TIBIA

Type III tibial fractures in this region can often be covered by transposition of the soleus muscle, which lies deep to the gastrocnemius in the posterior compartment. For smaller defects, the soleus can be split longitudinally because it takes its dual blood supply from the posterior tibial artery for the medial aspect of the muscle and from the peroneal artery for the lateral aspect. Because of the nature of its blood supply, its configuration, and the large area of origin, the arc of rotation of the soleus muscle is relatively limited. Dissection should be performed as distally as possible, carefully freeing the muscle from the overlying Achilles tendon and allowing the gastrocnemius Achilles unit to remain intact whenever possible. Because of its variability in the distal third of the lower leg, the muscle must be completely exposed through a long longitudinal incision before the final determination to use this flap is made. The use of a distally based soleus muscle flap has been reported, but is noted here only to be condemned; it should be rejected rapidly because of its extremely variable distal blood supply. Infrequently, the flexor digitorum longus muscle can be used alone or as a supplement to the soleus for small, selected defects in this region.[68]

Both the tibialis anterior and the extensor digitorum longus muscles have been reported to provide options for muscle flap transfers in small, anterior, midthird defects. Again, we have found these two muscles to be of very little use because of their small muscle bellies, segmental-type blood supply, limited arc of rotation, and donor site disability. Furthermore, we have moved away from local muscle transfer in severe, type III, midthird tibial fractures, such as those caused by high-velocity projectiles. Often the soleus muscle is damaged acutely or becomes fibrotic in the more chronic wounds, preventing it from acting as an adequate vascularized transfer flap. Therefore, free tissue transfer, using either the latissimus dorsi or the rectus abdominis muscle for larger defects and the gracilis muscle or groin flap for smaller defects, has become more routine (Fig. 14–26).[10, 54, 65, 67, 90] This change in strategy has led to a decrease in our complication rate. One-stage composite reconstruction, replacing soft tissue, skin, and bone simultaneously, has been practiced successfully but should be reserved for highly selected cases.[86] Still unknown and under study is the potentially deleterious effect on gait stemming from sacrifice of the soleus.

DISTAL THIRD OF THE TIBIA

Donor muscles in the distal third of the tibia are almost nonexistent, so for repair of a plafond fracture in

this area, the free muscle transfer becomes the procedure of choice.[22] Again, the primary options are the latissimus dorsi or rectus abdominis muscle for larger defects and the gracilis muscle for smaller wounds (Fig. 14–27).[10, 35] Fasciocutaneous flaps also play a role in soft tissue coverage of acute type III injuries (Fig. 14–28). In certain cases, the temporoparietal fascia with an overlying skin graft confers the added advantage of a more normal contour, along with a richly vascularized wound cover (Fig. 14–29). Although the larger muscles initially appear extremely bulky and unaesthetic, they rapidly atrophy as a result of surgical denervation and conform to the contour of the recipient extremity (Fig. 14–30). If the traumatic insult has been severe enough to destroy the normal vascular architecture of the lower leg, vein grafts can be brought from the popliteal fossa to allow more distal vascular access of free tissue transfers (Fig. 14–31).

ANKLE AND FOOT

For the purposes of soft tissue reconstruction in the area of the ankle and foot, one must first identify the nature of the injuries, the specific regions of the foot requiring reconstruction, and, most important, the relative and absolute contraindications to foot and ankle reconstruction.[17] Hidalgo and Shaw[43–45] have developed a classification system for foot injuries that takes into account the extent of soft tissue destruction and the associated osseous injuries. Type I injuries are those confined to limited soft tissue defects. Type II injuries include major soft tissue loss, with or without distal amputation. The most severe injuries, type III, are those with major soft tissue loss and accompanying open fracture of the ankle, calcaneus, or distal tibia-fibula complex. According to this classification, the foot is divided into four major reconstructive areas: the dorsum, the distal plantar weight-bearing surface, the weight-bearing heel or hindfoot and midplantar area, and the posterior non–weight-bearing heel and Achilles tendon.[43–45]

Although May and co-workers[66] have shown that cutaneous sensibility is not an absolute prerequisite for adequate weight bearing on the reconstructed foot, complete loss of plantar sensation after avulsion of the posterior tibial nerve in ipsilateral proximal segmental tibial fractures usually serves as a strong contraindication to salvage of the foot in type III injuries.[66] Complete avulsion of the plantar surface of the foot with multiple metatarsal or calcaneal fractures is also best treated with amputation.

After a thorough assessment of the patient's bone, soft tissue, and neurovascular status has been completed and the patient is deemed a candidate for reconstruction, both the size of the defect and the location (as described previously) should be considered in determining the options for coverage. Many limited defects of the dorsum of the foot or the non–weight-bearing plantar surface can be treated adequately with split-thickness skin grafting. The distally based sural fascial or fasciocutaneous flap has become popular for coverage of

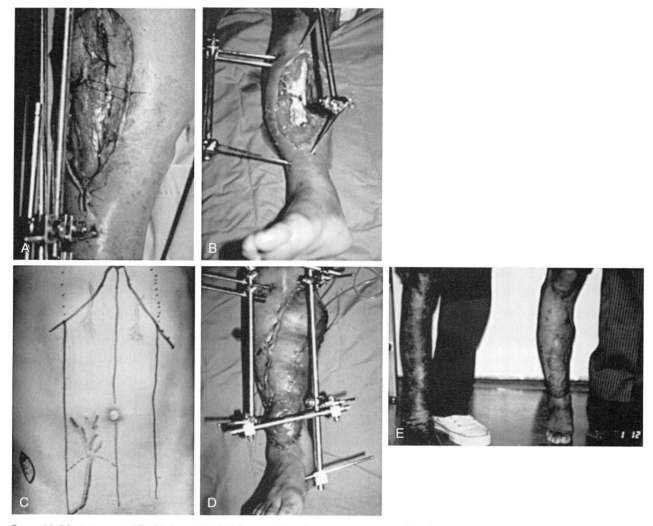

FIGURE 14–26. *A,* Large middle third type III tibial fracture. Note the retention suture pulling the wound edges together under marked tension. *B,* After release of the single retention suture. Note the true extent of the soft tissue loss. *C,* The rectus abdominis donor site diagrammed. *D,* Immediate postoperative view. *E,* Six months after operation, full weight bearing.

composite defects of the malleoli or dorsum of the foot. They require at least 5 to 6 cm of continued contact above the malleoli to ensure sufficient perforators to vascularize the flap adequately. The farther distal one attempts to rotate the flap caudally, the more unreliable it becomes. Figure 14–32 demonstrates one such flap used to close a composite fracture of the lateral ankle. For the limited injuries to the heel and proximal plantar area in which soft tissue padding and retention of sensibility are advantageous, a turnover flexor digitorum brevis muscle flap, dorsalis pedis island flap, or local plantar fascia cutaneous rotation flap based on the proximal plantar subcutaneous plexus may serve well.*

As in the case of the type III distal third tibial fracture, extensive injuries to the plantar surface of the foot are by definition not amenable to coverage by local tissue transfer because of the paucity of donor sites. Numerous

authors have chronicled the advantage of free muscle transfer with overlying split-thickness skin graft for restoration of an appropriately padded weight-bearing plantar surface, and our experience supports this observation (Fig. 14–33). May and co-workers[66] have clearly shown that patients who have such reconstructions maintain closed wounds and regain relatively normal gait and weight-bearing profiles. These conclusions were reached after assessment by force vector analysis and Harris mat studies.

AVULSION INJURIES

The management of avulsion or degloving injuries to the extremities remains problematic. These injuries are usually the result of high-energy shearing forces, which not only separate large areas of skin and subcutaneous tissue from

*See references 7, 14, 18, 21, 39, 40, 46, 70, 81, 99.

their underlying vascular supply but also disrupt the dermal architecture of the elevated flap. On initial evaluation, much of the avulsed skin is obviously necrotic and can be débrided immediately (Fig. 14–34A). Of greater concern are injuries in which the degloved flaps appear viable and even bleed from their free edges. The tendency in management is to maintain all obviously viable tissue or, worse, to redrape it and close the wounds primarily. However, because of the twofold physiologic insult suffered, these flaps almost always die. After reapproximation, tension further compromises vascularity, sealing the fate of this marginally viable tissue.

Although seemingly radical, aggressive débridement of all degloved tissue with subsequent skin grafting is the treatment of choice (see Fig. 14–34). Previous reports have described the successful use of split-thickness or full-thickness skin grafts harvested from the avulsed flap. In our experience, the take of skin grafts harvested from these flaps is variable. If the possibility presents itself, however, this option should be pursued. Thick split-thickness skin grafts taken from uninvolved donor areas serve well in the coverage of these wounds (see Fig. 14–34C).

In certain cases, with widely based flaps in which there is relatively little undermining and no ostensible skin trauma, it may be prudent to leave all wounds open and monitor the flaps for continued viability. Fluorescein, 15 to 25 mg/kg (according to the patient's pigmentation) given intravenously, can serve as a reliable marker of tissue viability. When the tissue is monitored with a Wood lamp or other ultraviolet light source, a deep purple hue is consistent with nonviability, whereas an orange-green speckling denotes vascular inflow. Quantitative assessment can be done with a dermofluorimeter, and blood flow can be expressed as a percentage of normal.[42, 60] Any associated fractures that have a communication with the degloved flaps, even if located well away from the laceration site, must be classified as type II injuries and treated as such. Free tissue transfer can be especially applicable in these situations.[47]

OSTEOMYELITIS: ROLE OF VASCULARIZED MUSCLE FLAP COVERAGE

Stark[87] first reported the efficacy of muscle transposition for coverage of osteomyelitic wounds in 1946. Ger[30] further documented his favorable experience with the use of muscle coverage for the amelioration of tibial osteomyelitis in 1977.

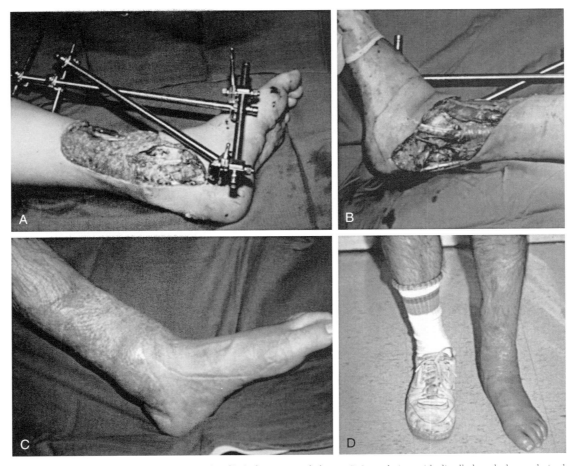

FIGURE 14–27. *A*, Large distal third type III tibia-fibula fracture, medial view. *B*, Lateral view with distally based, devascularized skin flap outlined. *C*, Eight months after transfer of latissimus dorsi and skin grafting. *D*, Full weight bearing.

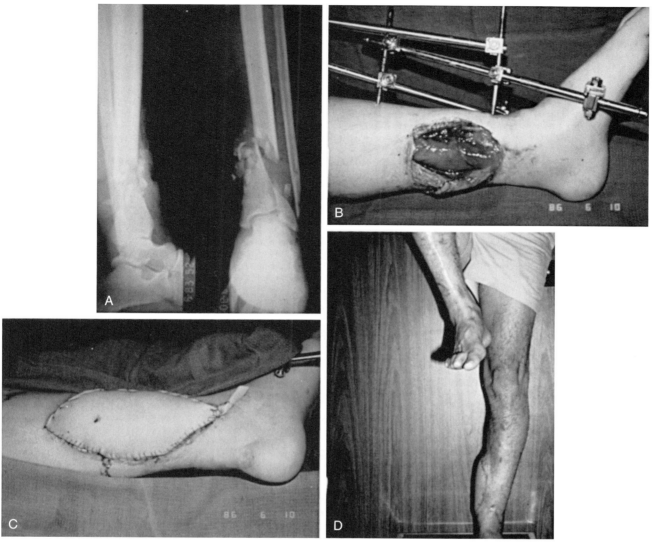

FIGURE 14–28. *A,* Distal third type III tibia-fibula fracture. *B,* Corresponding soft tissue defect. *C,* Placement of parascapular fasciocutaneous flap within 4 days of the injury. *D,* Full weight bearing at 5 months.

Although a number of centers adopted this therapeutic adjunct in the late 1970s, it was not until the reports of Chang and Mathes[15] and later Feng and co-workers[25] on the wound biology of vascularized muscle and skin that some physiologic basis was established for the positive effects of this procedure. In the wound laboratory, muscle flaps were found to be significantly more effective than random flaps in the rat model in reducing the bacterial count in a standardized wound cylinder. Oxygen tension at the flap-cylinder interface was also found to be markedly higher in the muscle.[15, 25] Clearly, aggressive débridement of all necrotic bone, scar, and infected granulation tissue is the cornerstone of the treatment of this most recalcitrant disease. Without this crucial maneuver, no amount of vascularized muscle can resolve the problem.

The classical management of osteomyelitis required multiple 6-week courses of intravenous antibiotics, many of them nephrotoxic, with high rates of failure and recurrence. At best, suppression of the inciting organisms could be expected; because of retained sequestra and persistent dead space, antibiotic delivery to the areas harboring bacteria was unlikely. With our current knowledge of flap physiology, we can now aggressively remove all sequestrum and other nonvascularized tissue, transpose or transplant vascularized muscle to increase blood supply, and more effectively deliver short courses of antibiotics for an increased chance of real cure.[12, 13, 97]

Several advances have been made in regard to flap harvest and transfer, including use of the endoscope to harvest both pedicle and free tissue transfers. Bostwick and associates[8] presented a thorough approach to these procedures in their textbook. Technique and exposure are similar for both pedicled and free latissimus dorsi transfer, by far the most frequently chosen flap. Other tissues amenable to endoscopic harvest are the rectus abdominis and gracilis muscles and nerve, vein, and fascia lata. Although not universally accepted today, endoscopic harvest is sure to play an increasing role in soft tissue coverage.

Text continued on page 348

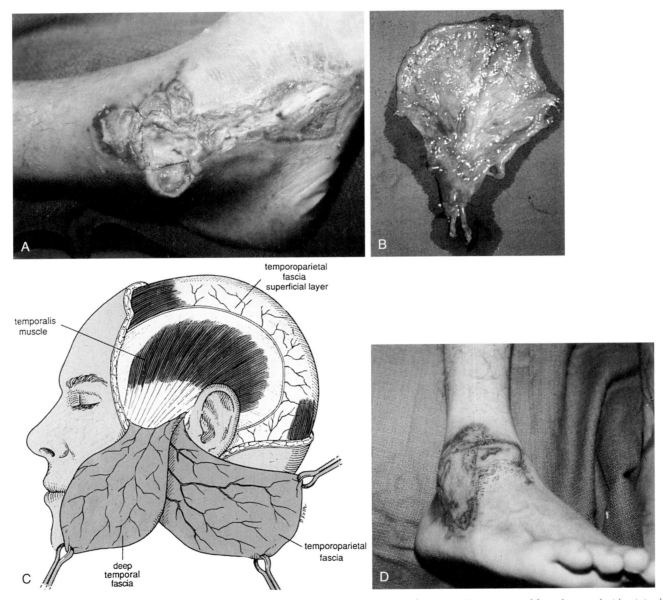

Figure 14–29. *A,* Exposed, infected lateral malleolus. Note retention sutures pulling through soft tissue. *B,* Temporoparietal fascia harvested with minimal bulk. *C,* Flap can be bilaminar. *D,* After wide débridement, transfer of temporoparietal fascia, and split-thickness skin grafting. Normal contour is maintained.

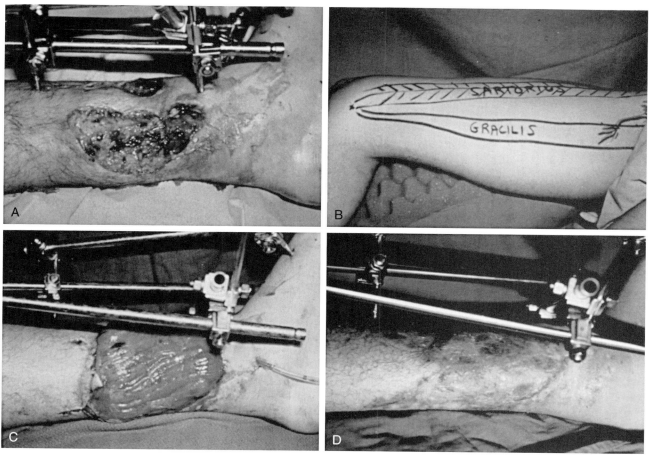

FIGURE 14–30. *A,* Distal third type III tibia-fibula fracture. *B,* Gracilis muscle donor site. *C,* The muscle is in place. Note the excess bulk. *D,* Two months after transfer and skin grafting, the muscle has atrophied to match the surrounding contour. This phenomenon is a frequent occurrence in free muscle transfer.

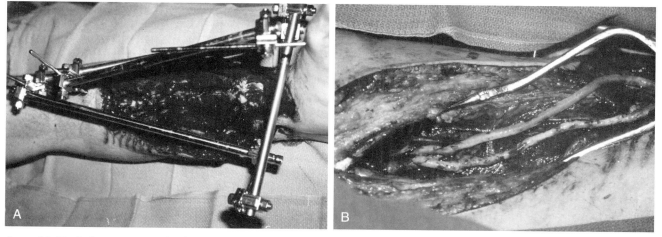

FIGURE 14–31. *A,* Severe type III tibia-fibula fracture with unsuitable recipient vessels below the trifurcation. *B,* Creation of a saphenous vein arteriovenous fistula from the popliteal vessels, which is then used to hook distally into a latissimus dorsi muscle.

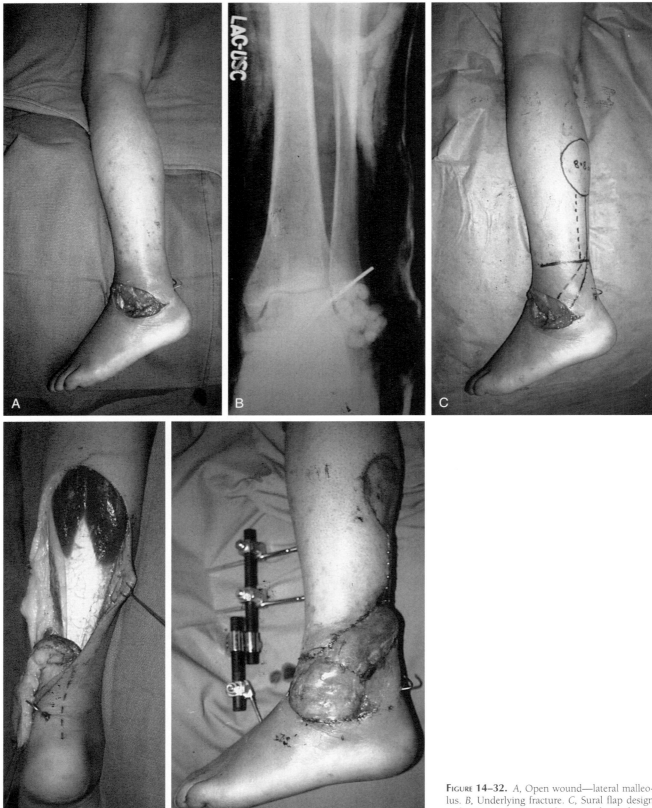

Figure 14–32. *A*, Open wound—lateral malleolus. *B*, Underlying fracture. *C*, Sural flap design and rotation point. *D*, Flap rotated. *E*, Flap in place with skin graft.

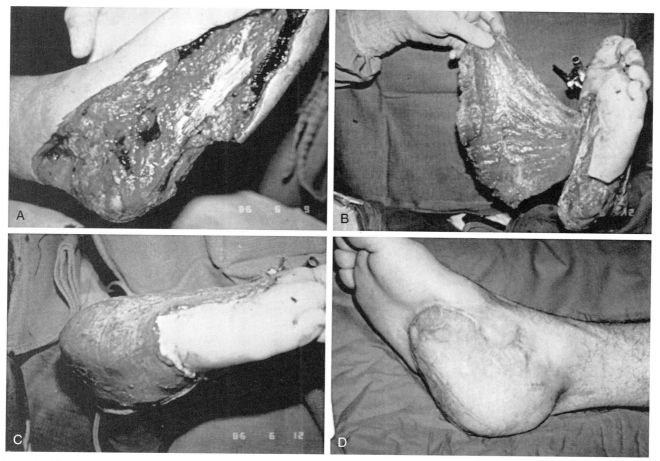

FIGURE 14-33. *A,* Composite heel defect with exposure of the calcaneus. *B,* The latissimus dorsi muscle after transfer. *C,* Immediately after inset. *D,* Six months after surgery, the patient is fully ambulatory without skin graft breakdown.

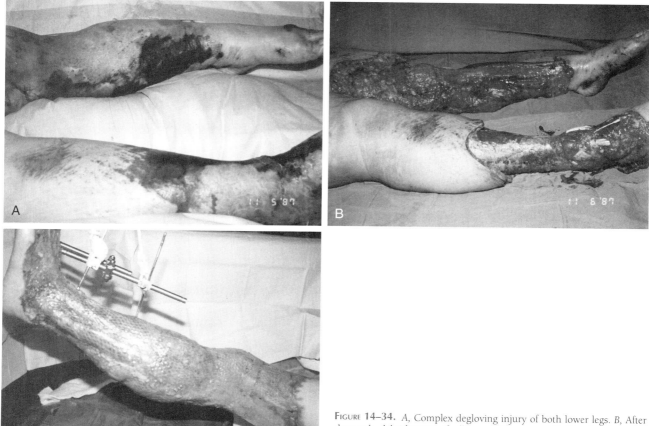

FIGURE 14-34. *A,* Complex degloving injury of both lower legs. *B,* After thorough débridement of all nonviable tissue. *C,* Shortly after skin grafting. Note the placement of an external fixator for wound care purposes alone.

REFERENCES

1. Alpert, B.S.; Parry, S.W.; Buncke, H.; et al. The free groin flap. In: Buncke, H.J.; Furnas, D.W., eds. Symposium on Clinical Frontiers in Reconstructive Microsurgery. St. Louis, C.V. Mosby, 1984, pp. 71–83.
2. Arnold, P.G.A.; Mister, R. Making the most of the gastrocnemius muscles. Plast Reconstr Surg 22:4, 1985.
3. Atasoy, E.; Ioakimidis, E.; Kasdem, M.; et al. Reconstruction of the amputated finger tip with a triangular volar flap. J Bone Joint Surg Am 52:921, 1970.
4. Barwick, W.J.; Goodkind, D.J.; Serafin, D. The free scapular flap. Plast Reconstr Surg 69:779, 1982.
5. Baudet, J.; LeMaire, J.M.; Gumberteau, J.C. Ten free groin flaps. Plast Reconstr Surg 57:577, 1976.
6. Beasley, R.W. Hand Injuries. Philadelphia, W.B. Saunders, 1981.
7. Bostwick, J. Reconstruction of the heel pad by muscle transposition and split thickness skin graft. Surg Gynecol Obstet 143:973, 1976.
8. Bostwick, J.; Eaves, F.; Nahai, F. Endoscopic Plastic Surgery. St. Louis, Quality Medical Publishing, 1995.
9. Brent, B.; Upton, J.; Acland, R.D. Experience with the temporoparietal fascia free flap. Plast Reconstr Surg 76:177, 1985.
10. Brownstein, M.C.; Gordon, L.; Buncke, H.J. The use of microvascular free groin flaps for the closure of difficult lower extremity wounds. Surg Clin North Am 57:977, 1977.
11. Buchau, A.C. The neurovascular island flap in reconstruction of the thumb. Hand 1:19, 1969.
12. Byrd, H.S.; Cierny, G.; Tebbets, J.B. The management of open tibial fractures with associated soft tissue loss: External pin fixation with early flap coverage. Plast Reconstr Surg 68:73, 1981.
13. Byrd, H.S.; Spicer, R.E.; Cierny, G., III. The management of open tibial fractures. Plast Reconstr Surg 76:719, 1985.
14. Caffee, H.H.; Hoefflin, S.M. The extended dorsalis pedis flap. Plast Reconstr Surg 64:807, 1979.
15. Chang, N.; Mathes, S.J. Comparison of the effect of bacterial inoculation in musculocutaneous and random pattern flaps. Plast Reconstr Surg 70:1, 1982.
16. Ciresi, K.; Mathes, S. The classification of flaps. Orthop Clin North Am 24:383, 1993.
17. Clark, N.; Sherman, R. Soft tissue reconstruction of the foot and ankle. Orthop Clin North Am 24:489, 1993.
18. Cohn, L.B.; Buncke, H.J. Neurovascular island flaps from the plantar vessels and nerves for foot reconstruction. Ann Plast Surg 12:327, 1984.
19. Curtis, R.M. Cross-finger pedicle flap in hand surgery. Ann Surg 145:650, 1957.
20. Daniel, R.K.; Weiland, A.J. Free tissue transfers for upper extremity reconstruction. J Hand Surg [Am] 7:66, 1982.
21. Duncan, M.J.; Zuker, R.M.; Manktelow, R.T. Resurfacing weight-bearing areas of the heel. The role of the dorsalis pedis innervated free tissue transfer. J Reconstr Microsurg 1:201, 1985.
22. Ecker, J.; Sherman, R. Soft tissue coverage of the distal third of the leg and ankle. Orthop Clin North Am 24:481, 1993.
23. Fatale, M.F.; Davies, D.M. The radial forearm island flap in upper limb reconstruction. J Hand Surg [Br] 9:234, 1984.
24. Feldman, J.J.; Cohen, B.E.; May, J.W. The medial gastrocnemius myocutaneous flap. Plast Reconstr Surg 61:531, 1978.
25. Feng, L.; Price, D.; Hohu, D.; et al. Blood flow changes and leukocyte mobilization in infections: A comparison between ischemic and well-perfused skin. Surg Forum 34:603, 1983.
26. Foucher, G.; van Genecten, F. A compound radial skin forearm flap in hand surgery: An original modification of the Chinese forearm flap. Br J Plast Surg 37:139, 1984.
27. Freiburg, A.; Manktelow, R. The Cutler repair for fingertip amputations. Plast Reconstr Surg 50:371, 1972.
28. Furnas, D.W.; Lamb, R.C.; Achauer, B.M.; et al. A pair of five-day flaps: Early division of distant pedicles after serial cross-clamping and observation with oximetry and fluorometry. Ann Plast Surg 15:262, 1985.
29. Galumbeck, M; Colen, L. Soft tissue reconstruction. Coverage of the lower leg: Rotational flap. Orthop Clin North Am 24:473, 1993.
30. Ger, R. Muscle transposition for treatment and prevention of chronic posttraumatic osteomyelitis of the tibia. J Bone Joint Surg Am 59:784, 1977.
31. Ger, R. The management of open fractures of the tibia with skin loss. J Trauma 10:112, 1970.
32. Ger, R. The technique of muscle transposition in the operative treatment of traumatic and ulcerative lesions of the leg. J Trauma 11:502, 1971.
33. Gilbert, A.; Teot, L. The free scapular flap. Plast Reconstr Surg 69:601, 1982.
34. Godina, M.; Lister, G. Early microsurgical reconstruction of complex trauma of the extremities. Plast Reconstr Surg 78:285, 1986.
35. Gordon, L.; Buncke, H.J.; Alpert, B.S. Free latissimus dorsi muscle flap with split thickness skin graft cover: A report of 16 cases. Plast Reconstr Surg 70:173, 1982.
36. Gottlieb, M.E.; Chandrasekhar, B.; Terz, J.J.; Sherman, R. Clinical application of the extended deep inferior epigastric flap. Plast Reconstr Surg 78:782, 1986.
37. Gustilo, R.B.; Anderson, J.T. Prevention of infection in the treatment of one thousand and twenty five open fractures of long bones. J Bone Joint Surg Am 58:453, 1976.
38. Gustilo, R.B.; Mendoza, R.M.; Williams, D.N. Problems in the management of type III (severe) open fractures: A new classification of type III open fractures. J Trauma 24:742, 1984.
39. Harrison, D.H.; Morgan, D.G.B. The instep island flap to resurface plantar defects. Br J Plast Surg 34:315, 1981.
40. Hartrampf, C.R.; Scheflan, M.; Bostwick, J. The flexor digitorum brevis muscle island pedicle flap: A new dimension in heel reconstruction. Plast Reconstr Surg 66:264, 1980.
41. Henderson, N.P.; Reid, D.A.C. Long-term follow-up of neurovascular island flaps. Hand 1:21, 1969.
42. Hidalgo, D.A. Lower extremity avulsion injuries. Clin Plast Surg 13:701, 1986.
43. Hidalgo, D.A.; Shaw, W.W. Anatomic basis of plantar flap design. Plast Reconstr Surg 78:627, 1986.
44. Hidalgo, D.A.; Shaw, W.W. Anatomic basis of plantar flap design: Clinical applications. Plast Reconstr Surg 78:637, 1986.
45. Hidalgo, D.A.; Shaw, W.W. Reconstruction of foot injuries. Clin Plast Surg 13:663, 1986.
46. Ikuta, Y.; Murakami, T.; Yoshioka, K.; Tsuge, K. Reconstruction of the heel pad by flexor digitorum brevis musculocutaneous flap transfer. Plast Reconstr Surg 74:86, 1984.
47. Imaya, T.; Harii, K.; Yamada, A. Microvascular free flaps for the treatment of avulsion injuries of the feet in children. J Trauma 22:15, 1982.
48. Iselin, F. The flag flap. Plast Reconstr Surg 52:374, 1973.
49. Johnson, R.K.; Iverson, R.E. Cross finger pedicle flaps in the hand. J Bone Joint Surg Am 53:913, 1971.
50. Katsaros, J.; Schusterman, M.; Beppu, M.; et al. The lateral arm flap: Anatomy and clinical applications. Ann Plast Surg 12:489, 1984.
51. Keitler, W.A. A new method of repair for fingertip amputation. JAMA 133:29, 1947.
52. Kleinert, H.E.; McAlister, C.G.; MacDonald, C.J.; et al. A critical evaluation of cross finger flaps. J Trauma 14:756, 1974.
53. Krizek, T.J.; Robson, M.C. Biology of surgical infection. Surg Clin North Am 55:6, 1975.
54. LaRossa, D.; Mellissinos, E.; Mathews, D.; et al. The use of microvascular free skin-muscle flaps in the management of avulsion injuries of the lower leg. J Trauma 20:545, 1980.
55. Lister, G. Local flaps to the hand. Hand Clin 1:621, 1985.
56. Lister, G.D.; McGregor, I.A.; Jackson, I.T. The groin flap in hand injuries. Injury 4:229, 1973.
57. Littler, J.W. Neurovascular pedicle transfer of tissue in reconstructive surgery of the hand. J Bone Joint Surg Am 38:917, 1956.
58. Macht, S.D.; Watson, H.K. The Moberg volar advancement flap for digital reconstruction. J Hand Surg [Am] 5:372, 1980.
59. Man, D.; Acland, R.D. The microarterial anatomy of the dorsalis pedis flap and its clinical applications. Plast Reconstr Surg 65:419, 1980.
60. Mandel, M.A. The management of lower extremity degloving injuries. Ann Plast Surg 6:1, 1981.
61. Manktelow, R.T.; McKee, N.H. Free muscle transplantation to provide active finger flexion. J Hand Surg [Am] 3:416, 1978.
62. Mathes, S.J.; Alpert, B.S.; Chang, N. Use of the muscle flap in chronic osteomyelitis: Experimental and clinical correlation. Plast Reconstr Surg 69:815, 1982.
63. Mathes, S.J.; Nohai, F. Classification of vascular anatomy of muscles: Experimental and clinical correlation. Plast Reconstr Surg 67:177, 1981.

64. Mathes, S.J.; Nahai, F. Clinical Applications for Muscle and Musculocutaneous Flaps. St. Louis, C.V. Mosby, 1982.

65. Maxwell, G.P.; Manson, P.N.; Hoopes, J.E. Experience with thirteen latissimus dorsi myocutaneous free flaps. Plast Reconstr Surg 64:1, 1979.

66. May, J.W.; Halls, M.J.; Simon, S.R. Free microvascular muscle flaps with skin graft reconstruction of extensive defects of the foot: A clinical and gait analysis study. Plast Reconstr Surg 75:627, 1985.

67. May, J.W., Jr.; Lukash, F.N.; Gallico, G.G., III. Latissimus dorsi free muscle flap in lower extremity reconstruction. Plast Reconstr Surg 68:603, 1981.

68. McCraw, J.B. Selection of alternative local flaps in the leg and foot. Clin Plast Surg 6:227, 1979.

69. McCraw, J.B.; Arnold, P.G. McCraw and Arnold's Atlas of Muscle and Musculocutaneous Flaps. Norfolk, VA, Hampton Press, 1986.

70. McCraw, J.B.; Furlow, L.T. The dorsalis pedis arterialized flap, a clinical study. Plast Reconstr Surg 55:177, 1975.

71. McGregor, I. Flap reconstruction in hand surgery: The evolution of presently used methods. J Hand Surg [Am] 4:1, 1979.

72. McGregor, I.A. Less than satisfactory experiences with neurovascular island flaps. Hand 1:21, 1969.

73. McGregor, L.A.; Jackson, I.T. The groin flap. Br J Plast Surg 25:3, 1972.

74. Melone, C.P.; Beasley, R.W.; Carstens, J.H. The thenar flap. J Hand Surg [Am] 7:291, 1982.

75. Meyers M.B.; Cherry, G.; Milton, S. Tissue gas levels as an index of the adequacy of circulation: The relation between ischemia and the development of collateral circulation (delay phenomenon). Surgery 71:15, 1972.

76. Muhlbauer, W.; Hernall, E.; Stock, W.; et al. The forearm flap. Plast Reconstr Surg 70:336, 1982.

77. Nassif, T.M.; Vidal, L.; Bovet, J.L.; Baudet, J. The parascapular flap: A new cutaneous microsurgical free flap. Plast Reconstr Surg 69:591, 1982.

78. Ohmori, K.; Harii, K. Free dorsalis pedis sensory flap to the hand with microsurgical anastomosis. Plast Reconstr Surg 58:546, 1976.

79. Patzakis, M.J.; Abdollahi, K.; Sherman, R.; et al. Treatment of chronic osteomyelitis with muscle flaps. Orthop Clin North Am 24:505, 1993.

80. Pederson, W.C.; Coverage of hips, pelvis, and femur. Orthop Clin North Am 24:461, 1993.

81. Reading, G. Instep island flaps. Ann Plast Surg 13:488, 1984.

82. Rockwell, W.B.; Lister, G. Coverage of hand injuries. Orthop Clin North Am 24:411, 1993.

83. Russell, R.C.; Zamboni, W.A. Coverage of the elbow and forearm. Orthop Clin North Am 24:425, 1993.

84. Russell, R.C.; Van Beek, A.L.; Warak, P.; et al. Alternative hand flaps for amputations and digital defects. J Hand Surg [Am] 6:399, 1981.

85. Smith, J.R.; Bom, A.F. An evaluation of fingertip reconstruction by cross-finger and palmar pedicle flap. J Plast Reconstr Surg 35:409, 1965.

86. Song, R.; Gao, Y.; Song, Y.; et al. The forearm flap. Clin Plast Surg 9:21, 1982.

87. Stark, W.J. The use of pedicled muscle flaps in the surgical treatment of chronic osteomyelitis resulting from compound fractures. J Bone Joint Surg 28:343, 1946.

88. Swartz, W.M. Immediate reconstruction of the wrist and dorsum of the hand with a free osteocutaneous groin flap. J Hand Surg [Am] 9:18, 1984.

89. Swartz, W.M.; Jones, N.F. Soft tissue coverage of the lower extremity. Curr Probl Surg 22:4, 1985.

90. Swartz, W.M.; Mears, D.C. The role of free tissue transfers in lower extremity reconstruction. Plast Reconstr Surg 76:364, 1985.

91. Takayanagi, S.; Tsukii, T. Free serratus anterior muscle and myocutaneous flaps. Ann Plast Surg 8:277, 1982.

92. Taylor, G.I; Watson, N. One-stage repair of compound leg defects with free vascularized flaps of groin skin and iliac bone. Plast Reconstr Surg 61:494, 1978.

93. Taylor, T.L.; Townsend, P.; Corlett, R. Superiority of the deep circumflex iliac vessels as a supply for the free groin flap: Clinical work. Plast Reconstr Surg 64:745, 1979.

94. Vasconez, H.C.; Oishi, S. Soft tissue coverage of the shoulder and brachium. Orthop Clin North Am 24:435, 1993.

95. Vasconez, L.O.; Bostwick, J., III; McCraw, J. Coverage of exposed bone by muscle transposition and skin grafting. Plast Reconstr Surg 53:526, 1974.

96. Villian, R. Use of the flag flap for coverage of a small area on a finger or the palm. Plast Reconstr Surg 51:397, 1973.

97. Weiland, A.J.; Moore, J.R.; Daniel, R.K. The efficacy of free tissue transfer of osteomyelitis. J Bone Joint Surg Am 66:181, 1984.

98. Wiss, D.; Sherman, R.; Oechsel, M. External skeletal fixation and rectus abdominis free tissue transfer in the management of severe open fractures of the tibia. Orthop Clin North Am 24:549, 1993.

99. Yanai, A.; Park, S.; Iwao, T.; Nakamura, N. Reconstruction of a skin defect of the posterior heel by a lateral calcaneal flap. Plast Reconstr Surg 75:642, 1985.

100. Yaremchuk, M.J.; Brumback, R.J.; Manson, P.N.; et al. Acute and definitive management of traumatic osteocutaneous defects of the lower extremity. Plast Reconstr Surg 80:1, 1987.

101. Yaremchuk, M.J.; Bartlett, A.P.; Sedacca, T.; May, J.W., Jr. The effect of preoperative angiography on experimental free flap survival. Plast Reconstr Surg 68:201, 1981.

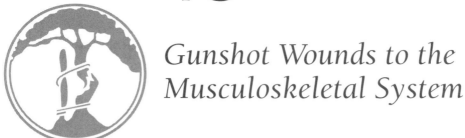

CHAPTER 15

Gunshot Wounds to the Musculoskeletal System

Harris Gellman, M.D.
Donald A. Wiss, M.D.
Todd D. Moldawer, M.D.

The increase in violent crimes in major cities, combined with the easy availability of handguns, has resulted in a significant rise in the number of gunshot wounds seen in many community hospitals.[162, 171] Many injuries include complex soft tissue wounds, comminuted fractures, and nerve, artery, or tendon involvement. The treatment of these injuries varies greatly depending on whether the injury was caused by a low- or high-velocity weapon or by a shotgun. Treatment philosophy has also changed with the development of a better understanding of the differences between civilian (presumably low-velocity) and military (high-velocity) wounds.[162, 230]

BALLISTICS

Knowledge of wound ballistics is basic to an understanding of the damage caused by penetrating missiles.[10, 11, 51, 213] *Low velocity* usually refers to bullets traveling at 1000 ft/sec or less, whereas *high-velocity* bullets travel at 2000 ft/sec or more (Table 15–1). To compensate for barrel friction at high velocities, bullets are coated or jacketed with materials with higher melting points.[1, 54, 59, 89, 98, 102, 104–106, 192] Velocity and missile mass are considered to be the most significant determinants of tissue damage. Velocity is usually thought to be more important than mass; for example, doubling the mass only doubles the kinetic energy, whereas doubling the velocity quadruples the kinetic energy. In reality, it is easier to increase the mass of a bullet than to double its velocity.[130]

Shotgun injuries are very different from gunshot wounds. Although the velocity of a charge of shotgun pellets may be only 1100 to 1350 ft/sec, the weight of the shot in a 12-gauge shotgun shell is high (1⅝ to 2 ounces) (Table 15–2).[52] Therefore, the kinetic energy at the muzzle is great. This energy dissipates quickly as the pellets move farther away from the muzzle. Most injuries

to humans occur at close range, while the shot is still tightly packed, and cause great tissue destruction.[203] At close range, the wadding made of plastic, felt, paper, or cork often becomes embedded in the wound, further complicating management.[172] A wound from a 12-gauge full charge of number .00 buckshot at close range is roughly equivalent to being struck by nine or ten .22 caliber rifle bullets at muzzle velocity.[53]

In gunshot wounds, three primary factors—laceration and crushing, shock waves, and cavitation—determine the tissue damage.[84, 102, 194] As a low-velocity missile penetrates firm tissue such as muscle, the tissue is crushed and forced apart (laceration and crushing). With high-velocity missiles, shock waves occur and can produce injury in areas distant from the direct missile path.[96] Shock waves are not only transmitted but also reflected from tissue interfaces.

Cavitation is the third mechanism of tissue damage. It is seen predominantly with high-velocity weapons.[89] The cavity is at subatmospheric pressure and sucks air and material in from both ends. Secondary missiles are also an important cause of tissue damage. Fragments of bullet or bone resulting from a fracture may tumble around in the tissues, causing injury to blood vessels, nerves, or muscle.[65, 94]

The appearance of entry and exit wounds depends on the type of bullet, its mass, the impact velocity, the presenting area and path of the bullet, the tissue density, and the distance penetrated. Entry wounds vary from small openings to large blowout holes. The presence of a small entrance wound does not necessarily mean minimal interior tissue damage.

PRINCIPLES OF MANAGEMENT

Early treatment protocols for civilian gunshot fractures were based largely on the extensive tissue trauma seen

TABLE 15–1

Kinetic Energy of High- and Low-Velocity Firearms

Weapon	Bullet Weight		Velocity		Kinetic Energy	
	gr	*g*	*ft/sec*	*m/sec*	*ft-lb*	*J*
Civilian (low velocity)						
.22 long rifle	40	2.6	1200	663	128	173
.38 automatic pistol	95	6.2	880	268	163	222
.45 pistol	230	14.9	850	259	369	500
Military (high velocity)						
.22 Savage	70	4.5	2750	838	1175	1593
30/06 Springfield	150	9.7	2750	838	2519	3415
5.56-mm M16	55	3.6	3250	991	1290	1749

Sources: Granberry, W.M. Hand 5:220, 1973; Healy, W.L.; Brooker, A.F. Clin Orthop 174:166, 1983; Shepard, G.H. J Trauma 20:1065, 1980.

with the military experience with high-velocity missiles. Many researchers, however, have shown that extensive débridement is not routinely necessary in low-velocity injuries. Because cavitation effects do not occur or are negligible, tissue damage is usually confined to the missile path. Local wound care with or without antibiotic therapy has virtually eliminated the incidence of deep wound sepsis and osteomyelitis after low-velocity gunshot wounds.*

On arrival at the hospital, the patient should be carefully evaluated for additional injuries from occult gunshot wounds. The entire body should be inspected with the patient undressed, with particular attention to entrance wounds and a detailed search for exit wounds. A careful and thorough evaluation of peripheral circulation and neurosensory status is mandatory. Documentation of wounds and deficits on admission to the hospital is of medicolegal significance. In patients with gunshot wounds to the extremities, diminished or absent pulses, expanding hematomas, or pulsatile masses are absolute indications for emergency angiography or exploration of the vessel. Missile wounds that track in close proximity to a major vessel may be associated with occult vascular injury despite apparently normal peripheral pulses. Careful

*See references 24, 61, 89, 98, 104, 141, 156, 174, 192, 224, 237.

evaluation regarding the need for exploration, Doppler ultrasonography, or angiography is needed. If doubt exists, a duplex ultrasound study is done. If the duplex Doppler study is positive, it should be followed by an angiogram.

Conventional radiographs of the injured part are obtained and should show the joint above and below the injured area in both anteroposterior (AP) and lateral projections. Culture specimens are taken from the missile track, the traumatic wounds are covered with a sterile dressing, and the extremity is splinted. If the femur is fractured, the patient is placed in balanced skeletal traction and intravenous antibiotics (e.g., a cephalosporin) are administered in therapeutic doses for 72 hours.

A gunshot fracture is a unique type of open fracture. It has been demonstrated conclusively that the heat generated in firing a bullet does not render it sterile.[217, 233] Therefore, by definition, gunshot fractures are contaminated. Low-velocity gunshot fractures resemble typical grade II or I open fractures because they involve relatively mild to moderate soft tissue damage. Shotgun and high-velocity missile wounds more closely parallel grade III open fractures because of the magnitude of soft tissue damage and the high incidence of complications such as infection, delayed union, nonunion, and nerve or vessel injury.

The role of early internal fixation of open fractures has been studied by several investigators.[4, 38, 40] Despite

TABLE 15–2

Kinetic Energy of Shotgun Shells

Gauge	Shell Type	Weight of Shot			Muzzle Velocity		Kinetic Energy	
		oz	*gr*	*g*	*ft/sec*	*m/sec*	*ft-lb*	*J*
12	2³/₄ in.	1¹/₄	546	38	1330	405	2145	2912
12	2³/₄ in. mag.	1¹/₂	656	43	1315	401	2519	3416
12	3 in. mag.	1⁵/₈	701	46	1315	401	2726	3700
16	2³/₄ in. mag.	1¹/₄	546	35	1295	395	2033	2761
20	2³/₄ in.	1	437	28	1220	372	1444	1960
20	2³/₄ in. mag.	1¹/₈	492	32	1220	372	1626	2205

Abbreviation: mag., magnum.
Source: Adapted from Shepard, G.H. J Trauma 20:1065, 1980.

improvement in internal fixation devices, increased sophistication of trauma surgeons, and newer and more potent antibiotics, the role of internal fixation in open fractures in general and in gunshot fractures in particular remains controversial. The reluctance of many orthopaedic surgeons to use internal fixation in open fractures comes from a fear that the foreign material in open wounds increases the likelihood of infection. For many years it was believed that implants acted as foreign bodies around which bacteria congregated, thereby producing infection. Gristina and Rovere[86] showed that the presence of metal per se does not promote bacterial growth in vitro. Rather, the level of energy producing the injury, the degree of soft tissue damage, and the amount of wound contamination usually determine whether infection develops.[87] If infection occurs after internal fixation of open fractures, the stabilizing effect of the implant may be advantageous and outweigh the possible deleterious foreign body effect. However, the immediate use of implants to achieve fracture stability is not indicated for all open fractures.

Studies have shown internal fixation in open fractures to be extremely useful in carefully selected cases. The benefits of primary internal fixation should outweigh the risks associated with its use. Immediate internal fixation of compound fractures is particularly useful in patients with multiple injuries, severe injuries that require intensive wound care, complex ipsilateral extremity injuries, open fractures complicated by neurovascular damage, or open displaced intra-articular fractures.[4, 38, 40] The major disadvantage of immediate internal fixation in open fractures is the increased risk of infection caused by further soft tissue dissection with disruption of the local blood supply.

Most low-velocity gunshot fractures can be managed without the use of immediate internal fixation. Except for femur fractures, a splint or cast can be applied to the injured part with a high likelihood of success. Delayed internal fixation can be performed 3 to 10 days later for fractures in which alignment cannot be maintained. For most high-velocity injuries in the extremities, external fixation is the treatment of choice. When used for displaced open joint fractures, limited internal fixation to restore joint congruity may be an important adjunct to external fixation.

A growing body of literature suggests that in low-velocity gunshot fractures, because of minimal soft tissue devitalization, surgical irrigation and débridement may not be necessary.* Local wound care with superficial irrigation, with or without antibiotic coverage, has virtually eliminated significant soft tissue infections and osteomyelitis after low-velocity gunshot wounds.[87, 176] Even the role of intravenous antibiotics in low-velocity gunshot fractures has been called into question. There is a growing body of literature reporting no statistically significant difference between groups of patients treated with or without prophylactic antibiotics.[55, 145, 169, 170, 171] Ordog and colleagues[169] reviewed gunshot wounds in 28,150 patients, 16,891 (60%) of whom were treated as outpatients. Four percent had minor fractures not requiring operative stabilization. All patients were treated with wound dé-

bridement, irrigation, an antibiotic ointment (bacitracin or polymyxin), and a sterile dressing. Although only 5% were treated with prophylactic antibiotics (cephalosporin or dicloxacillin), only 1.8% had wound infections. These infections were generally in patients not already receiving antibiotics, and all responded well to oral antibiotics, without requiring hospital admission.

McCormick and colleagues[145] found an overall infection rate of 5.2% in a series of 229 patients. Infection developed in 6.6% of those receiving antibiotics but in only 2.6% of those not receiving them. In a prospective study of infection after low-velocity gunshot wounds, Dickey and associates[55] found no significant benefit from the use of intravenous antibiotics. Howland and Ritchey,[104] in a study of 111 low-velocity gunshot fractures, concluded that antibiotics were not required in the routine management of these injuries and that débridement should be used only if signs and symptoms of infection develop. However, Patzakis and co-workers,[176] in a review of 78 gunshot fractures, compared treatment without antibiotics with two separate antibiotic protocols. They found that the organism most frequently encountered was *Staphylococcus aureus,* which was best treated by a broad-spectrum cephalosporin. In their study, patients treated with antibiotics had a significant reduction in infection rates compared with patients to whom no antibiotics were given.

If, on the basis of the clinical scenario, antibiotic therapy is believed to be necessary, several studies have compared the efficacy of various drugs. Geissler and associates[73] compared one intramuscular injection of cefonicid (1 g) with 48 hours of intravenous antibiotic treatment in patients with low-velocity gunshot–induced fractures and found no difference in the infection rate. They recommended minimal débridement in the emergency room, copious wound irrigation, intramuscular injection of cefonicid (1 g), and delayed primary wound closure. Hansraj and colleagues[91] showed that there was no difference in the efficacy of two doses of ceftriaxone versus seven doses of cefazolin. The ceftriaxone group was hospitalized for 24 hours, and the cefazolin group was hospitalized for 48 hours. This protocol resulted in savings of $58,700 for 25 patients with no difference in infection rate. In a separate series of 132 gunshot-related fractures, Woloszyn and associates[234] found no statistically significant advantage of intravenous over oral administration of antibiotics.

Brunner and Fallon[30] brought even the time-honored tradition of wound débridement into question. In a series of 163 patients with civilian gunshot wounds, 89 patients had débridement and wound care and 74 patients had local wound care alone. Neither group received antibiotics. All patients were treated as outpatients in the emergency room, and none of the wounds in either group was closed primarily or had a delayed primary closure. No deep infections occurred in either group; four patients in the débridement group and two in the conservatively treated group had superficial infections. From the results of this study, it would appear that most clean, low-velocity gunshot wounds could be treated conservatively on an outpatient basis and without prophylactic antibiotics. One critical point in all of these studies is that no attempt was

*See references 61, 89, 98, 104, 141, 144, 156, 174, 192, 237.

made to close the wounds primarily, thereby allowing natural drainage of the wound.

VASCULAR AND NEUROLOGIC INJURIES

Because of the proximity of nerves and arteries to bone, these structures are frequently injured.[195] Associated arterial or nerve injuries make fracture management significantly more complex. Time becomes a critical factor, and the possibility of a compartment syndrome should always be considered.

Vascular Injuries

Advances in the diagnosis and treatment of vascular injuries have resulted in a considerable decrease in the rate of amputation. Present rates of limb salvage exceed 86%, compared with an amputation rate of almost 50% during World War II.[3, 48, 121, 186, 236] Optimal management of traumatic peripheral arterial injuries is predicated on the prompt restoration of blood flow.[179, 190] Delayed recognition of an arterial injury can result in limb loss or chronic disabling ischemia. If peripheral pulses are present and there is no evident limb ischemia, treatment may be delayed. Occasionally, despite vessel repair, the limb is ultimately lost because of a lack of fasciotomy, leading to compression and occlusion of the vascular supply secondary to tissue swelling.

Arterial damage may result from the missile itself or from cavitation effects or associated fractures (Fig. 15–1).[185–187] Although the association of supracondylar humerus fracture with brachial artery injury and Volkmann's ischemic contracture is well known, in reality arteries of the lower extremity are injured more frequently than those in the upper limb and have a worse prognosis.[134] Although direct collision of a missile with a vessel is highly destructive, with high-energy weapons the missile does not need to strike the artery to cause damage, as the associated shock waves can produce extensive arterial disruption. Although the expanding blast force alone is capable of bursting an artery, laceration and transection are more often caused by bone fragments. Intimal disruption may also occur and cause occlusion of a traumatized segment through thrombosis. Partial lacerations of the arterial wall do not allow constriction, as occurs after complete transection, and massive bleeding and shock may result if the vessel is large. Bleeding into the arm or leg often leads to tamponade by hematoma, resulting in greatly increased tissue pressures that require fasciotomy for decompression.

Evaluation of penetrating injuries should determine whether the site of penetration could involve a major artery. The absence of signs of ischemia with palpable peripheral pulses does not rule out a vascular injury; a small hematoma may plug an arterial wall temporarily, only to dissolve later, allowing hemorrhage to recur.[57, 85] Drapnas and colleagues[57] reported palpable distal pulses

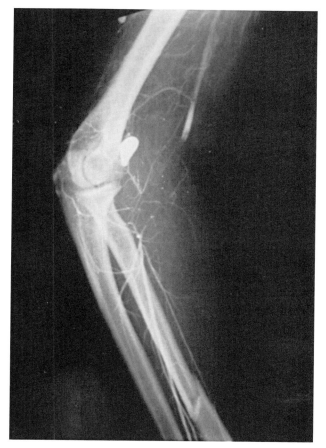

FIGURE 15–1. A low-velocity gunshot wound caused injury to the brachial artery without associated fracture.

in 27.3% of patients with injuries to major arteries in the extremities. Arteriography is essential to evaluate the proximal vascular system, especially the subclavian, axillary, or iliac arteries, which are more difficult to evaluate clinically.[63] Selective arteriography may be misleading, however, if thrombosis prevents extravasation of contrast material.[137]

There are three classes of arterial injury. In the first, the evidence is conclusive and includes absent pulses, unequivocal signs of ischemia, and other evidence of a break in the arterial wall, such as profuse hemorrhage, pulsating hematoma, or unmistakable anatomic proximity of the wound to a critical artery.[204] Urgent surgical intervention is necessary in patients with these injuries. In the second class, the evidence points against immediate exploration: there is no ischemia or only slight ischemia that is not progressive, pulses are equivocal or occasionally absent with a moderate degree of hemorrhage easily controlled spontaneously or by pressure, and the anatomic location is distant from a critical artery. Patients with these injuries are best treated by observation. The third group of patients comprises those in whom evidence of arterial injury is equivocal. There may be absent pulses, but the signs of ischemia are relatively mild, and the significance of the extent of bleeding and of the anatomic relation is doubtful. It is for this group that angiography yields the greatest benefit, particularly in avoiding unnecessary surgery.[204]

For patients with obviously abnormal vascular examination results, angiography is useful before surgical exploration. The diagnostic problem arises in the patient with a normal examination and a proximity injury. Classically, angiography was done to rule out a vascular injury. However, the accuracy of noninvasive studies such as duplex Doppler ultrasonography is now almost as great as that of arteriography in most instances.

Knudson and colleagues[118] reviewed 86 extremity injuries in 77 patients using color-flow duplex imaging. There were four positive studies, confirmed by angiography. No missed arterial injuries were found during follow-up. Gahtan and associates,[72] after their review of angiograms of 453 limbs with gunshot, shotgun, and stab wounds in proximity to a major vessel, recommended the use of arteriography for patients with an abnormal vascular examination and an unclear injury who may require vascular repair. Although arterial injury was demonstrated in 9.4% of limbs with a normal vascular examination, only 2% were deemed to require vascular repair. A detailed physical examination, including Doppler-derived limb blood pressures, is essential. Although the incidence of angiographically demonstrated vascular injury was increased in the presence of an associated long bone fracture, operative intervention was increased only for those with an abnormal vascular examination. Norman and coworkers[165] concluded that the routine use of arteriography is not justified even in gunshot injuries associated with a long bone fracture. Ordog and colleagues[168] recommended screening of patients with asymptomatic injuries by duplex Doppler ultrasonography and performing angiography only if a lesion is found.

Controversy still exists, however, with many investigators recommending that gunshot wounds in the immediate vicinity of the major vessels within an extremity should be studied angiographically or explored surgically. Although negative exploration involves low morbidity (3%) and is often incidental to wound management,[134] the costs associated with unnecessary exploration and hospitalization are high. Anderson and associates[5] recommended arteriography for penetrating injuries to high-risk areas such as the calf, forearm, antecubital and popliteal fossae, and medial and posterior arm and thigh. Snyder and colleagues[206] reviewed 183 penetrating injuries of the extremities in 177 patients. Eighty-six percent were the result of gunshot wounds, and all were surgically explored after angiography. Angiography accurately diagnosed the injury in 92% of the patients. Angiographic findings regarded as significant were obstruction, extravasation of contrast agent, early venous filling, irregularity of the vessel wall, filling defect, and false aneurysm.

If angiography is to be performed for proximity injuries, the entrance and exit wounds of the missile should be clearly marked by radiopaque markers, and the arterial injection site should be several centimeters proximal to the suspected injury. The presence of an intraluminal defect should be assumed to represent an injury unless there is strong evidence for preexisting disease. If there is a significant history of allergy to contrast media, isotope angiography may be an alternative,[158, 191] although the specialized equipment required may make its use impractical in emergency situations. Contrast angiography has an

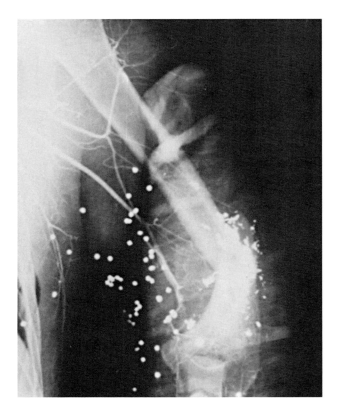

Figure 15–2. A close-range shotgun wound caused concomitant soft tissue, vessel, and bone injuries.

added advantage in that it can also be used intraoperatively.

Shotgun wounds produce a broader spectrum of injuries to blood vessels than do rifle and handgun wounds (Fig. 15–2). Pellet wounds of blood vessels are characterized by pockmark injury associated with shredding and contusion over an extensive length.[140] Because of the wide distribution of pellets, proximity angiography has been found to be more useful in patients with a shotgun injury than in those with individual gunshot wounds.[150] Preoperative angiography helps to reduce the possibility of missed remote injuries to the vessels and provides an accurate estimate of the extent of the vascular injury.[111, 131, 150, 181]

Although periods of severe or absolute ischemia of less than 4 hours' duration are well tolerated in most patients, periods of 6 hours or more almost always result in some permanent muscle damage even after revascularization. Reactive edema caused by increased capillary permeability in the presence of a normal perfusion pressure often leads further to microcirculatory embarrassment as a result of swelling in closed compartments. Although fasciotomy is effective in reducing the pressure in these closed compartments, it fails to prevent muscle necrosis when the muscle has been irreversibly damaged.[142, 159, 175]

Nerve changes secondary to ischemia occur early; initially there is altered sensory function, followed by increasing pain, paresthesias, hypesthesia, and finally anesthesia. The presence or absence of pain in a limb that has been ischemic or avascular for more than 4 hours may be an unreliable sign concerning the need for fasciotomy.

In patients with combined vascular and nerve injuries, prophylactic fasciotomy should be performed at the time of arterial repair unless a method for continuous pressure measurement is available. If pressures reach 40 mm Hg, fasciotomy should be done immediately.[42, 75, 159]

Smith and co-workers,[204] in a review of low-velocity arterial injuries, found that end-to-end anastomosis was possible in 65% of 285 arteries after simple débridement of the damaged arterial ends. Gorman[82] reported on high-velocity injuries to 106 arteries, finding that 37% required vein grafting for successful vascular repair with a limb salvage rate of 90%. Hardin and associates[92] reviewed 99 low-velocity arterial injuries and found primary end-to-end repair possible in 69%, vein graft necessary in 19%, and fasciotomy required in 5% at the time of arterial repair.

Weingarner and colleagues[223] reported a series of 40 patients in whom pulses were present and no vascular injury was suspected. In this group, they found 20 false aneurysms, 12 arteriovenous fistulas, and 6 delayed arterial occlusions. The average delay in diagnosis was 26 days. This series emphasizes the importance of selective angiography in patients in whom vascular injury is suspected but the physical examination result is normal or equivocal.

Nerve Injuries

Nerves are the structure most commonly injured simultaneously with an artery and are the major determinant of long-term disability. The reported incidence of nerve injuries as a result of either low- or high-velocity gunshot injuries in large series ranged from 22% to 100%.* Concomitant nerve injury is likely to result in permanent functional deficit despite successful vascular repair. Visser and colleagues[221] found nerve injury in 71% of patients with arterial injuries caused by gunshots. Thirty-nine percent of patients without nerve injuries achieved a normal extremity after vascular repair, compared with only 7% of those with nerve injury. Forty-four percent had significant functional impairment as a result of their nerve injury.

Hardin and associates[92] reported that nerve deficits associated with upper extremity arterial injuries were severe, with serious limitation of extremity function in 23% and moderate limitation in 23%; only 10% of nerve injuries resolved. Overall complete functional recovery was seen in only 48% of patients. Axillary artery injuries were associated with the highest incidence of severe neurologic impairment because of the anatomic proximity of the brachial plexus. Proximal extremity injuries with nerve involvement tended to have a more negative impact on limb function than did more distal extremity injuries. Multiple nerve involvement impaired functional recovery of the extremity more than isolated nerve injury. Clinical studies of nerve recovery show considerable variation because the return of function depends as much on the total amount of injury to the extremity as on the degree of regeneration of the injured nerve.[21, 49]

The most commonly used classification of traumatic

nerve injuries is the one introduced by Seddon[200] during World War II. Nerve injuries are divided into three basic types: neurapraxia, axonotmesis, and neurotmesis. *Neurapraxia* is a mild injury that produces a physiologic block to conduction rather than an identifiable anatomic lesion. Motor fibers tend to be affected more than sensory fibers, and electrophysiologic responses are normal. The injury may result from localized ischemic demyelinization, and spontaneous recovery usually occurs. *Axonotmesis* results from a greater degree of injury or stretch and involves interruption of the axon and myelin sheath; however, the endoneural tubes remain intact, allowing the regenerating axons to reach their proper peripheral connections. Total loss of neurologic function occurs, but because of the intact endoneural tubes, spontaneous recovery is possible. Because wallerian degeneration occurs distal to the site of injury, the electrical responses are identical to those of denervation. *Neurotmesis* is the most severe form of nerve injury. The nerve is either completely severed or so seriously injured that spontaneous regeneration or recovery is impossible.

Nerve injuries caused by gunshot wounds pose several therapeutic dilemmas. The first important question is whether exploration is necessary and, if so, when. The second question is much more difficult to answer: If a nerve laceration is found as a result of the gunshot, should repair be primary or secondary?

Whether to explore wounds with suspected nerve injuries depends on the mechanism of injury, the percentage of spontaneous nerve recovery expected, and the time required for return of function. The distinguishing feature of gunshot wounds is the pressure disturbance in the tissues, which often results in loss of function without visible disruption of the nerve. As early as 1929, Foerster[68] reported that the improvement in 67% of 2915 patients with motor paralysis who were treated conservatively was sufficient to obviate operative treatment. Sunderland[211] documented spontaneous recovery in 68% of military patients during World War II. Rakolta and Omer[182] noted that a delay in spontaneous regeneration of up to 11 months did not exclude the possibility of complete recovery.

Omer,[167] in his classical paper in 1974, reported the results of a prospective study of 595 gunshot wounds occurring during the Vietnam War. He found that spontaneous recovery occurred in 69% of patients with both low- and high-velocity gunshot wounds. Of the 410 patients with nerve lesions who recovered spontaneously, 90% had clinical recovery from their gunshot injuries within 3 to 9 months. Recovery of function took longer in proximal than in distal injuries. Patients with multiple nerve lesions also required a longer time for return of clinical function than those with isolated nerve injuries. The prognosis for spontaneous recovery of clinical function was the same for both high- and low-velocity injuries. The number of nerves with neurapraxia and axonotmesis was approximately equal, with the time for spontaneous recovery being 1 to 4 months for neurapraxia and 4 to 9 months for axonotmesis. If the nerves were severed, nerve repair was successful, however, in only 25% of patients.

With proximal nerve injury there is often a considerable distance from the level of nerve injury to the first motor

---

*See references 7, 18, 19, 92, 163, 167, 181, 188, 204, 205, 221.

end-point to be reinnervated. The motor end-organs are time sensitive, and the distance from lesion to motor end-plate must be considered when deciding on a course of treatment. It seems appropriate, therefore, to explore complete nerve injuries above the elbow or knee caused by a gunshot at 3 to 4 months after injury. Approximately 50% of explored nerves are found to have a neuroma in continuity, and a decision concerning management of the neuroma is difficult.

Kline and Hacket[116] developed a technique for intraoperative recording of nerve action potentials distal to the neuroma after proximal stimulation of the nerve. They reported spontaneous recovery in approximately 90% of nerves in which a normal nerve action potential was recorded across a neuroma in continuity at 3 months after injury. In a later review, Kline[115] recommended exploration between 3 and 4 months after injury when there is loss confirmed by both clinical and electromyographic examination that persists longer than 2 months or when there is severe noncausalgic pain in incomplete nerve injuries, pseudoaneurysms, or blood clots compressing the plexus. The best outcome was achieved with upper trunk and lateral and posterior cord lesions, but recovery occurred with some C7–to–middle trunk and medial cord–to–median nerve repairs. The results of C8, T1, medial cord, and medial cord–to–ulnar nerve repairs were poor. At exploration, if a nerve action potential was present across the lesion, neurolysis resulted in grade 3 or better function in 92% of cases and grade 4 or 5 in 79%. End-to-end sutures yielded results of grade 3 or better in 69% and grade 4 or 5 in 49%. Nerve graft resulted in grade 3 or better outcome in 55% and grade 4 and 5 in 43% of cases.

One of the most significant complications of nerve injuries is the development of reflex sympathetic dystrophy (RSD).[152] Although an etiologic connection to the sympathetic nervous system is now known, the exact cause is still poorly understood. According to Lankford,[122] three conditions must be present before RSD develops: (1) a persistent painful lesion (traumatic or acquired), (2) diathesis (predisposition, such as increased sympathetic activity), and (3) abnormal sympathetic reflex. The abnormal sympathetic reflex is probably the most important component of the triad. Normally, the sympathetic reflex after injury results in vasoconstriction to prevent excessive blood loss or swelling. Ordinarily, this reflex shuts off after an appropriate period, and gradual vasodilatation occurs as the body begins to repair the damaged tissue. In the patient who develops RSD, the normal sympathetic reflex does not shut off but continues unabated in what appears to be a pathologic positive feedback mechanism. The intense vasoconstriction causes localized ischemia, which in turn causes pain that initiates the "pain reflex" of RSD.[212]

Pain, the most outstanding feature of RSD, is usually accompanied by swelling of the involved extremity. The pain may be localized at first, but in time it may involve the entire extremity. The intense pain produced during attempted motion causes the patient to resist attempts at motion until stiffness ensues. Without treatment, the stiffness becomes progressively worse throughout the course of the disease. Cardinal signs for diagnosis include the presence of pain, swelling, stiffness, and discoloration.

Secondary signs present in most but not all cases are osseous demineralization, sudomotor changes, temperature alterations, trophic changes, vasomotor instability, and palmar fibromatosis. A presumptive diagnosis of RSD is made when all of the cardinal signs and most of the secondary signs are present. Relief of pain after interruption of the sympathetic reflex arc helps confirm the diagnosis. Radiographs usually show periarticular osteoporosis, although this finding is not specific to RSD. Attempts have been made to diagnose RSD using finedetail radiography or bone scintigraphy, but specificity of the test results was low.[77, 119, 120]

MacKinnon and Holder[139] popularized the three-phase bone scan for the diagnosis of RSD. This technique uses intravenous technetium 99m and three phases of exposure: radionuclide angiograph, immediate postinjection blood pool image, and delayed image at 3 or 4 hours. MacKinnon and Holder believed that the third phase of the test verified the diagnosis of RSD on the basis of a diffusely positive delayed image.[139] Radionuclide imaging is more useful in patients whose diagnosis is questionable.

Early diagnosis and prompt treatment are the most important factors in determining the prognosis of RSD. Treatment includes the early institution of aggressive physical or occupational therapy as well as some method of interruption or block of the abnormal sympathetic activity. Stellate ganglion blocks can be helpful by creating a pharmacologic interruption of sympathetic activity. A successful stellate block affects only the sympathetic impulses to the extremity and not the motor or sensory fibers. Peripheral nerve blocks may help establish a diagnosis of RSD, but the effect is usually not as long lasting as with stellate ganglion blockade. Regional intravenous sympathetic blocks can be performed with alphaadrenergic blocking agents such as guanethidine or reserpine.[14, 42, 90]

Oral sympatholytic drugs are sometimes useful, but they may have unwanted systemic side effects. The most commonly used drugs are the alpha-blockers. Phenoxybenzamine is probably the most useful drug with the fewest undesirable side effects.[69] Corticosteroids have not proved helpful in the management of RSD.[41, 80, 209] Acupuncture has been found to be effective in alleviating the symptoms of RSD, and it is gaining widespread popularity among physicians and therapists specializing in the treatment of chronic pain.[100, 126, 183]

UPPER EXTREMITY

Proximal Humerus and Shoulder Joint

VESSEL AND NERVE INJURY

The primary concern after low-velocity gunshot wounds to the proximal humerus and shoulder joint is rapid assessment of the presence or absence of a pneumothorax and vascular or neurologic injuries. A bullet or fracture fragments of the scapula or humerus may puncture the pleura or the major pulmonary vessels, resulting in a pneumothorax or hemopneumothorax. Peripheral pulses must be checked and compared with those on the opposite side. If there is any doubt, angiography should be performed. An algorithm for the evaluation of fractures when associated with vascular injuries is shown in Figure 15–3.

Hardin and associates[92] reviewed 99 low-velocity upper extremity vascular injuries. Eleven (52%) of the 21 patients with axillary artery lesions had concomitant brachial plexus or peripheral nerve injuries, and 27 (63%)

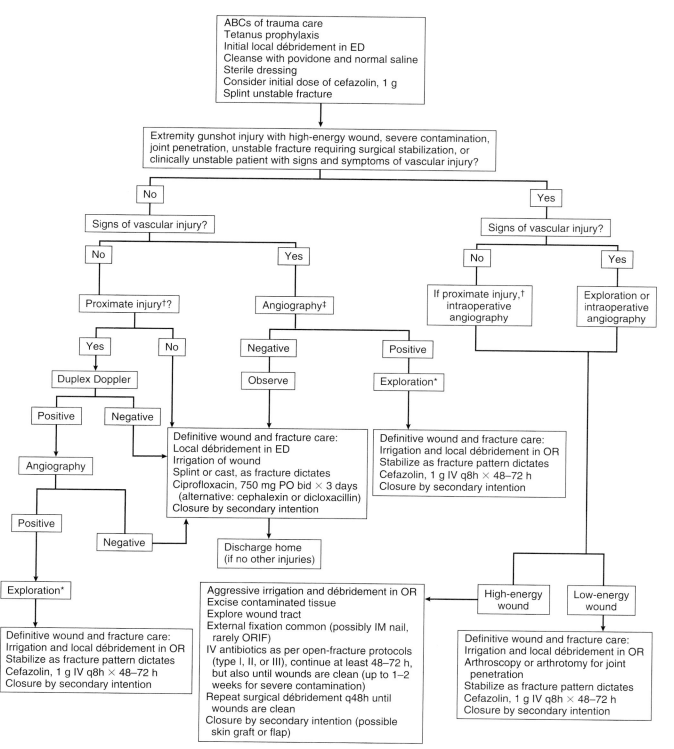

FIGURE 15–3 Suggested treatment of gunshot wounds. *Abbreviations:* bid, twice a day; ED, emergency department; IM, intramuscular; IV, intravenous; OR, operating room; ORIF, open reduction and internal fixation; PO, by mouth; q8h, every 8 hours. *, Guidelines for exploration: exploration is appropriate unless the injury involves only a single vessel below the trifurcation of the popliteal artery or distal to the midforearm (such an injury is not generally explored unless there is a diagnosis of compartment syndrome, arteriovenous fistula, or pseudoaneurysm); †, proximate injuries are defined as those in which the missile track passes within 1 inch of a known anatomic path of a major vessel; ‡, if there are "soft" signs of vascular injury, can consider duplex Doppler first. (From Bartlett, C.S.; Helfet, D.; Hausman M.; Strauss, E. J Am Acad Orthop Surg 8[1]:29, 2000.)

of the 43 limbs with brachial arterial injuries had peripheral nerve injury. At final follow-up, six (54.5%) of the patients with axillary artery lesions still had significant functional deficit, four (36%) had a moderate deficit, and only one patient (9%) had complete return of function. Shotgun injuries produced the most extensive tissue destruction (Fig. 15–4), almost always resulting in permanent functional impairment and often resulting in amputation of all or part of a limb.

Visser and colleagues[221] found four axillary artery injuries in 59 extremities with acute arterial injury, all with associated brachial plexus injury. Borman and co-workers[19] reported the results of 85 arterial injuries after gunshot. These investigators found, as have others, that despite excellent success with arterial reconstruction, functional results were limited by associated nerve injuries.

There is general disagreement about whether and when to explore brachial plexus injuries after a gunshot. Leffert[124] recommended that if no vascular or pulmonary injury is present, initial management should be conservative, with local wound care and physical therapy as needed. Lesions that are complete initially may become partial within the first few weeks after injury.[29, 163] If there is no recovery by 3 months or if the lesion is incomplete with a major area of neurologic deficit, delayed exploration should be considered. Armine and Sugar[6] recommended primary repair of the brachial plexus when there is an associated vascular injury requiring exploration and repair.

In a study of patients with brachial plexus injury during World War II, Brooks[29] found only 4 of 25 who underwent exploration for local complete lesions, entire plexus lesions, or persistent pain in the limb to have divided nerves. In an effort to relate the prognosis to the location of the nerve lesion, Brooks suggested three groups: (1) lesions of the roots and trunk of C5 and C6, (2) lesions of the posterior cord, and (3) lesions of C8–T1 of the medial cord. The recovery in the first group was good; in the second, fair; and in the third, poor. Recovery in the small muscles of the hand did not occur after a

severance in continuity was found. Brooks therefore concluded that routine exploration of open wounds of the plexus was rarely indicated. Millesi,[151] in 1977, stated that missile injuries to the plexus usually result in partial lesions and that chances for recovery are good; he recommended conservative treatment unless spontaneous recovery does not occur or is incomplete.

Mention should be made of foreign body or bullet embolism as a cause of acute arterial occlusion in gunshot injuries. Taylor and associates[216] reported three cases of bullet embolism in a series of 231 patients (83 with chest wounds and 148 with abdominal wounds). Other reported sites of bullet embolism have included the right axillary artery, right innominate artery, and right subclavian artery. Bullet embolism, although one of the rarer causes of acute arterial obstruction, can readily be corrected with embolectomy; results are good if embolism is recognized and treated early. The site of embolization is determined by mechanical factors such as the diameter of the artery and the caliber of the bullet.

FRACTURES

Fractures resulting from gunshots are treated by the same principles and techniques employed in the management of open fractures caused by blunt trauma. Chapman and Mahoney[40] reported that early internal fixation of open fractures may be indicated in displaced intra-articular fractures, in massively traumatized limbs, and in fractures with associated vascular injuries. Reported infection rates of 1.9% and 2.3% after internal fixation of fractures in grade 1 wounds make the risk of infection roughly comparable to that of closed fractures.[39, 87]

In intra-articular fractures with grade 2 and grade 3 wounds, careful judgment is required. Fractures of the proximal humerus with large soft tissue defects are more easily managed with external fixation (Fig. 15–5). Large soft tissue defects around the shoulder can be covered by rotation of a latissimus dorsi musculocutaneous flap on its vascular pedicle. Prosthetic replacement of the humeral head is sometimes necessary in highly comminuted fractures with gross disruption of the joint.

If the gunshot wound involves the glenohumeral joint, the wound should be explored and primary débridement performed, with excision of any foreign bodies[8, 102] by open arthrotomy or arthroscopically. Loose osteochondral fragments in the joint may interfere with active motion, and these fragments should be surgically excised. Intra-articular bullets should be removed as lead may leach out of bullets or fragments of bullets in the joint and may lead to lead deposition within the subsynovial tissues and ultimately periarticular fibrosis. Lead may also have a toxic effect on the articular cartilage.[127]

We have found that most low-velocity gunshot injuries to the shoulder girdle can be treated conservatively. Angiography is performed in all patients with suspected vascular injuries after careful clinical and Doppler examination in the proximity of the subclavian or axillary arteries. If the angiogram is positive, the wound is explored. Nerve injuries are explored acutely only if exploration is necessary because of a vascular injury. Most nerve injuries caused by gunshot wounds are traction

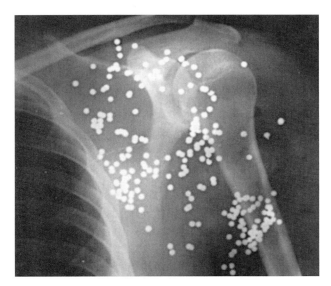

FIGURE 15–4. A close-range shotgun blast to the shoulder injured the brachial plexus.

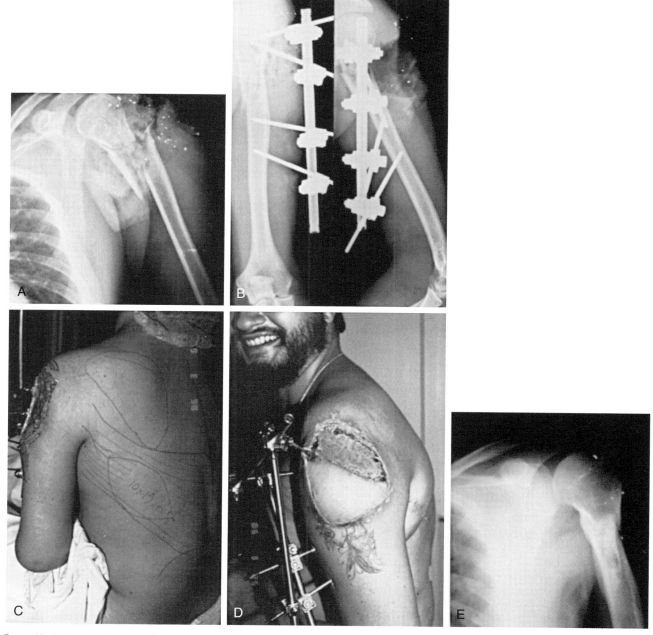

FIGURE 15–5. *A,* A gunshot wound to the proximal humerus resulted in a comminuted fracture with a large soft tissue defect. *B,* After irrigation and débridement, the fracture was reduced and held with an external fixator. *C,* The soft tissue defect was constructed with a latissimus dorsi pedicle flap. *D,* Restoration of the shoulder contour followed flap placement. *E,* At 1 year, the fracture has healed.

injuries and should be treated expectantly. Nerve exploration is done if there is no return of function after 3 months. We have found that the most useful clinical indication of axonal regeneration in nerve injuries is evidence of an advancing Tinel sign. Percussion (tapping) over the site of the nerve injury produces the sensation of radiating "electrical shocks" because of stimulation of the free nerve endings. This procedure is repeated monthly, and if there is no evidence of progression of the Tinel sign during three consecutive examinations, the nerve should be explored.

If a nerve transection is found at exploration for an acute vascular injury, it is probably best to tag the nerve ends and do a delayed nerve repair or graft. A more difficult problem is nerve exploration at 3 to 4 months that reveals a large neuroma in continuity. Various techniques have been recommended to help the surgeon decide whether to resect the neuroma and repair the nerve or simply perform a neurolysis; intraoperative nerve stimulation, sensory evoked potentials, and recording of electrical activity across the neuroma (as described by Kline and Hacket[116]) are probably the most helpful.

Nondisplaced and minimally displaced fractures are best managed as closed fractures on an outpatient basis, with local wound care and either oral antibiotics or one to two doses of a long-acting intramuscular or intravenous cephalosporin antibiotic. Displaced fractures of the humeral head and neck are treated by delayed internal fixation. The indications for surgery are the same as those used for closed proximal humerus fractures: three-part, four-part, and greater tuberosity fractures displaced more than 1 cm or angulated greater than 45° should be fixed if not excessively comminuted. For fractures associated with large soft tissue loss around the shoulder, external fixation should be used to stabilize the fracture and facilitate wound care.

Humeral Shaft and Arm

Fractures of the humeral shaft, when not complicated by vascular injury, are best treated with local wound care and plaster or cast brace immobilization. Humeral fracture bracing may be started as soon as the wound permits. There is no significant difference in the rate of union between closed humeral fractures and uncomplicated humeral fractures caused by a low-velocity gunshot, even if appreciable comminution or displacement is present. In patients with associated brachial artery injury, stabilization of the fracture is desirable after exploration and repair of the vessel. Internal fixation is preferable if the wound is small and clean and the fracture is not excessively comminuted. External fixation is recommended if there is significant contamination or loss of soft tissue or bone. If internal fixation is used, the wound should be left open and then closed on a delayed basis.

McNamara and co-workers[149] found no amputations in 64 patients without humeral fracture who underwent brachial artery repair, but 10% of the 20 patients with humeral fractures had amputations. There was one failure of repair (2.3%) among the 44 patients without fracture, and there were two failures (10%) among those with fracture. Peripheral nerve injuries should be treated expectantly; we favor conservative management with fracture bracing.

Humeral shaft fractures combined with ipsilateral brachial plexus injuries pose special problems in management. Of 26 patients with 30 ipsilateral brachial plexus injuries and long bone fractures treated at the Los Angeles County–University of Southern California Medical Center and Rancho Los Amigos Hospital, 19 had fractures of the humerus. Three were treated by compression plate, 4 by intramedullary nail, 2 with external fixation, and 10 with a cast or brace. All fractures treated by compression plating healed, but 4 of the 6 treated with intramedullary rods or external fixation had malunion or nonunion and 4 of the 10 fractures treated with a cast or cast brace alone had nonunion. All of the fractures with nonunion required open reduction and internal fixation to achieve union. The overall nonunion rate of humeral fractures with nerve injury treated nonoperatively was 40%.[27]

Stabilization of the flail upper extremity becomes particularly important in patients with multiple trauma or traumatic brain injury. In our series of 26 patients, 11 (42%) had traumatic brain injury. It is important to look for peripheral neurologic injuries in these patients and not to attribute the flail extremity solely to the brain injury.

Elbow Injuries

Gunshot around the elbow frequently causes intra-articular, intercondylar, or supracondylar humeral fractures with loss of a significant portion of the articular surface. This loss can make reconstruction difficult or impossible. The elbow has a tendency to become stiff rapidly, and because of the thin cortical bone in the supracondylar region, long periods of immobilization are often required when rigid internal fixation cannot be obtained.[103]

Vascular complication after dislocation or fracture of the elbow takes on special significance. The brachial artery at the elbow is particularly vulnerable because of its location, and displacement of fracture fragments about the elbow can lacerate or completely tear the artery. Compression or occlusion of the brachial artery can result from entrapment between fracture fragments and from the edema that may follow restoration of arterial flow after prolonged ischemia leading to compartment syndrome.[93, 199, 207] If a nerve injury is also present, pain and paresthesia are absent, and the only reliable way to test for increased intracompartmental pressure is by direct monitoring.

Because of the close proximity of nerves to the brachial artery at the elbow, nerve injury frequently accompanies arterial injury, particularly injury to the median nerve. In a review of vascular injuries about the elbow, Ashbell and colleagues[7] reported that 86% of those who sustained arterial injury also had injury to muscle, nerve, or bone in the same area. Concomitant injuries to one or more major nerves in the arm occurred in 69%, with muscle injuries next in frequency (66%). Combined injury to both nerve and muscle was seen in 45%.

When vascular injury is associated with displaced fracture, the fracture should first be stabilized if possible.[7, 19, 136] If the injured artery is repaired first, thrombosis or rupture of the anastomosis may occur during reduction. Because time is critical, the simplest technique of internal or external fixation should be used.

When there is severe soft tissue and muscle damage, we recommend external fixation across the elbow joint. This approach protects arterial repair while allowing soft tissue management. A significant loss of elbow motion often results if the fixator is left on for more than 4 to 6 weeks. Soft tissue coverage around the elbow has always presented a challenge. Evans and Luethke[64] described the use of a combined myo-osseous latissimus-scapula free flap for reconstruction of open elbow joints with soft tissue and bone loss.

The goal of treatment of elbow injuries is to obtain a stable, pain-free arc of motion in the functional range. Morrey and colleagues[157] found that most activities of daily living can be performed within an arc of motion comprising 30° to 130° of flexion with 50° of pronation and supination. Comminuted fractures of the proximal ulna involving up to 75% to 80% of the articular surface can be managed by excision of comminuted fragments and triceps advancement.[43, 138] Fractures with minimal comminution can be treated by tension band as recommended by the AO group. This approach allows early mobilization.[160] More comminuted fractures that extend into the proximal one third of the ulnar diaphysis require more extensive fixation with plates and screws (Fig. 15–6).

For intercondylar and supracondylar fractures with loss of soft tissue or a large bone segment, we recommend external fixation initially. External fixation allows management of the soft tissue injury while maintaining alignment of the fracture fragments and maintenance of the joint space. In fractures with adequate soft tissue cover, stable internal fixation can be done 5 to 7 days after the gunshot injury if there is no sign of infection. We often use the AO 3.5-mm reconstruction plates because they allow excellent contouring to the flare of the distal humerus. After fixation, the extremity is immobilized in a long arm posterior splint with the elbow flexed to 90° until soft tissue healing is complete (usually about 2 weeks). The extremity is then placed into a hinged elbow orthosis, which allows flexion and extension while preventing varus and valgus forces. The brace is continued for 6 to 8 weeks until fracture stability is obtained and healing is evident on the radiograph.

Most investigators agree that the ability to start early motion is the most important factor in obtaining a satisfactory outcome. If stable internal fixation is not possible or if the surgeon is reluctant to attempt fixation in these complex fracture patterns, then skeletal traction applied through the proximal ulnar pin allows early motion and maintenance of alignment of the fracture fragments.[189]

Additional techniques are available for salvage of the severely injured elbow. Hinge distraction can be used to help regain motion after release of contractures or repair of a supracondylar nonunion.[50] Excisional or fascial arthroplasty can be used to obtain motion in stiff elbows and in those with loss of the articular surface of the distal humerus.[34, 35, 71, 117, 201] This technique is particularly helpful in patients who are thought to be too young or too unreliable for total elbow arthroplasty and in those who refuse arthrodesis. Total elbow arthroplasty can be done in the older patient with adequate bone and soft tissue cover who does not place great physical demands on the elbow.

Cadaveric elbow allografts have been used as an alternative to arthrodesis in a final salvage attempt when there is significant stiffness and bone loss. Urbaniak and Black[220] reported satisfactory pain relief, stability, and range of motion in a series of patients with elbow allografts observed for more than 2 years after surgery. Long-term results of this procedure are still unknown, and the procedure is technically demanding. Total or partial elbow allograft may, however, provide enough replacement bone to allow total elbow arthroplasty or arthrodesis to be performed at a later time.

Forearm Injuries

Forearm fractures after gunshots have a high incidence of concomitant peripheral nerve injury and resultant loss of hand function. Initial evaluation should include a careful neurologic examination as well as an accurate assessment of swelling in the forearm. Compartment syndromes are

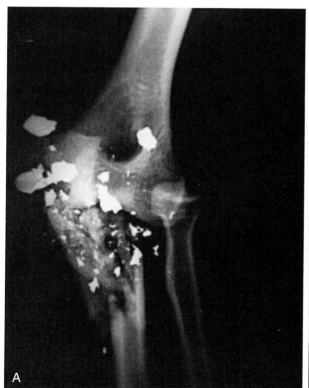
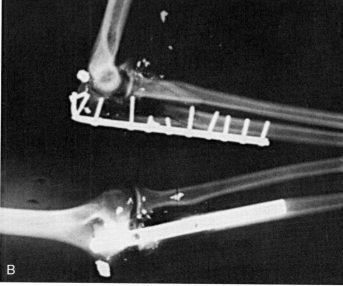

FIGURE 15–6. *A,* A comminuted intra-articular fracture of the proximal ulna had an associated radial head dislocation and a proximal radial shaft fracture (not seen). *B,* Restoration of length and alignment followed use of a contoured, small fragment, dynamic compression plate. Note the large defect remaining in the ulna that will require delayed bone grafting.

common, and a high index of suspicion is essential, especially for fractures in the proximal third of the forearm.

Moed and Fakhouri[154] found a 10% incidence of compartment syndrome in a series of 131 low-velocity gunshot wounds to the forearm (60 with fractures, 71 without bone injury). Fracture location was the only significant risk factor found to be associated with the development of compartment syndrome; displacement, comminution, and metallic foreign bodies in the wound had no effect. If any doubt exists, intracompartmental pressure measurements are indicated. If there is a possibility of vascular injury, an angiogram should be obtained. AP and lateral radiographs of the forearm, including the wrist and elbow, should be taken. Oblique views may be helpful to demonstrate subtle, nondisplaced fractures.

Elstrom and co-workers[61] reviewed 29 extra-articular gunshot fractures of the forearm. Eighty-eight percent of the nondisplaced fractures did well and healed after approximately 7 weeks. Displaced fractures did not do as well, with 77% unsatisfactory results. The results in the six patients treated by delayed primary open reduction and internal fixation were superior to those of patients treated by closed methods (see Fig. 15–6). Twenty-seven percent had long-term disability secondary to the sequelae of nerve injury or problems in obtaining fracture union. When wrist stiffness was included as a criterion for an unsatisfactory result, only 60% of those with adequate follow-up had a satisfactory result.

Lenihan and associates[125] reviewed 32 patients with gunshot fractures of the forearm. Seventeen fractures were nondisplaced, and 10 were displaced. Displaced fractures tended to be comminuted or segmental, whereas the nondisplaced ones were cortical, crease, drill hole, transverse, or oblique. All patients were initially treated with local wound care and intravenous antibiotics for 72 hours. Twenty-three fractures (all 17 nondisplaced fractures and 6 of the displaced fractures) were treated closed. Sixteen (94%) of the 17 nondisplaced fractures healed after an average of 7 weeks. The only patient with significant limitation of range of motion at follow-up had loss of reduction of the fracture resulting in malunion with shortening of the radius. The results of closed treatment of six displaced fractures were unsatisfactory; loss of reduction resulted in malunion or necessitated delayed open reduction and internal fixation. There were no infections, and the only vascular injury was an isolated ulnar artery lesion that was not repaired. Of nine nerve injuries, 55% resolved spontaneously (three of six ulnar, one of two radial, and one of one median nerve injuries). Two patients (7%) underwent fasciotomy for compartment syndrome in the forearm.

Our recommendation for the treatment of uncomplicated, nondisplaced gunshot fractures of the forearm without vascular injury includes local wound care, with or without antibiotics, and cast immobilization. However, displaced fractures of the radius or ulna and injuries involving both bones are best treated by open reduction and internal fixation. Sterile dressings are applied, and the wounds are initially left open. Hartl and Klammer[95] reported on the use of temporary wound coverage with synthetic skin substitutes or silicon foam elastomer.

Wound cultures are taken at the time of initial emergency room débridement, and antibiotics are adjusted as necessary in response to the culture results and sensitivity. The patient must be observed for at least 24 hours for signs of ischemia or impending compartment syndrome. A long arm posterior splint from axilla to palm, followed by a long arm cast, is usually all that is necessary.

Nerve injuries are treated expectantly because more than 50% show some degree of spontaneous recovery. Even if exploration is done acutely, it can be difficult or impossible to determine the extent of damage. If nerve compression is suspected, decompression and removal of the projectile are indicated. While awaiting recovery from nerve injury, paralyzed joints should be splinted appropriately, and passive range-of-motion exercise should be performed regularly to prevent contracture. The most useful splints are the lumbrical bar splint for ulnar nerve palsy (to prevent flexion contracture of the proximal interphalangeal joints of the fourth and fifth fingers) and the thumb opposition splint for median nerve injury (to prevent thumb web contracture). Patients with radial nerve palsy often do not need splinting as contracture can usually be prevented by passive range-of-motion exercise.

Displaced fractures are initially splinted, and delayed primary internal fixation can be done after the initial phase of wound healing. This approach has markedly reduced the incidence of malunion and delayed union in our patients. Displaced radial shaft fractures that heal with shortening can cause wrist pain as a result of disruption of the distal radioulnar joint and also can result in a significant loss of pronation and supination (Fig. 15–7). Fractures with soft tissue loss can be stabilized with external fixation to facilitate wound care.

Cancellous bone grafting is necessary in many patients because comminution frequently leads to gaps. To decrease the time to fracture union and the possibility of mechanical failure or loosening of the implants, an autogenous iliac crest bone graft is recommended. For contaminated segmental forearm fractures of up to 6 cm, the use of an antibiotic-impregnated cement spacer followed by delayed cancellous bone grafting has been reported by Georgiadis and DeSilva.[78]

Wrist and Hand

Because of the proximity and high density of the structures in the hand and wrist, gunshot wounds to the hand frequently result in combined damage to bone, nerves, arteries, and tendons.[2, 214] It has been estimated that up to 80% of missile injuries involve the extremities, with approximately 25% involving the hand.[212] Although hand examination may be difficult because of pain, a detailed and accurate evaluation is imperative. Circulatory, motor, and sensory function; areas of soft tissue loss; and amputated parts should be noted. Radiographic examination should include AP and lateral and oblique views. Photographs can be helpful to document injury and progression.

Fractures are the most common injuries caused by gunshots to the hand, followed by injuries to nerves, tendons, and arteries. Jabaley and Peterson,[108] in a review

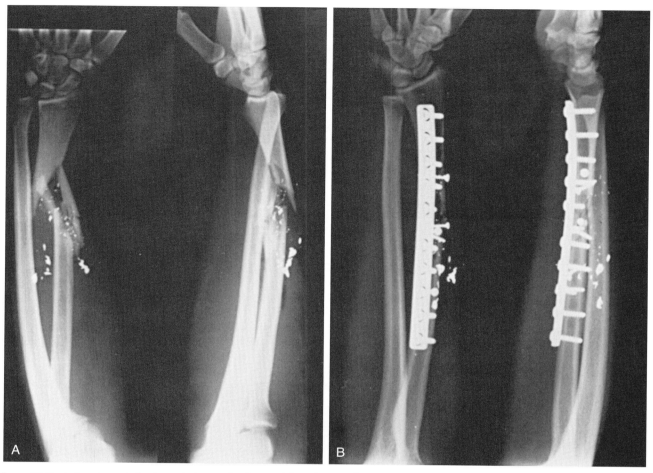

FIGURE 15–7. *A,* An extra-articular, low-velocity gunshot fractured the radius. *B,* After 3 days of intravenous antibiotics, the fracture was stabilized with plates and screws.

of war wounds of the hand and forearm in Vietnam, reported fractures in 63%, nerve injuries in 41%, muscle involvement in 33%, and tendon injuries in 31%; only 10% had an arterial injury. Duncan and Kettelkamp[58] reviewed 32 low-velocity gunshot wounds to the hand (62% with fractures of the metacarpals or phalanges, 31% with nerve injuries). Ninety percent of the nerve injuries resolved spontaneously. These authors reported that primary residual functional impairment in finger function was related to the location and stability of fractures. Fractures involving the proximal interphalangeal joints of the fingers had the greatest impact on motion, followed by fractures of the proximal phalanx. The patients with extra-articular metacarpal fractures had the least residual impairment of function. Open, comminuted, and unstable fractures resulted in a greater loss of motion than did stable fractures. Open fixation of intra-articular fractures should be reserved for single condylar or other fractures in which reconstruction of the articular surface is expected to result in a useful range of motion. Elton and Bouzard,[62] in a review of 26 patients with metacarpal fractures caused by gunshots, reported that 21% also had finger fractures, 13% wrist injuries, 27% nerve injuries, and 22% tendon injuries.

Local wound care, bulky dressing, splinting, and

elevation should manage most uncomplicated civilian gunshot wounds to the hand. Although antibiotic prophylaxis is not necessary, it is associated with low morbidity and is therefore not contraindicated. Splints should be applied with the wrist in slight extension, metacarpal joints flexed 70° to 90°, and proximal and distal interphalangeal joints flexed 10° to 15°.[45] Fingertips should be visible so that circulation can easily be assessed. If there are arterial injuries with ischemia or bleeding, exploration should be done immediately. Displaced fractures with or without tendon and nerve injury can be stabilized immediately if the wound is clean or after 5 to 10 days. Wounds with complex soft tissue loss should be evaluated in the operating room. Débridement of the hand should be approached with considerable caution and thought given to later function, removing only obviously destroyed tissue. Joints should be thoroughly explored and irrigated free of foreign bodies, and the synovial membrane should be closed.[8, 13, 33, 47, 98, 110] Primary closure of the skin is not recommended. Wound closure can usually be safely achieved by delayed primary closure. With larger soft tissue defects, secondary closure, split-thickness skin grafts, or flap coverage may be necessary.

Although most physicians are aware of the role of fasciotomy in the management of trauma to the upper arm, forearm, and leg, the need for fasciotomy in the hand is not always recognized.[31, 88, 108] Because there are no distal sensory or vascular changes associated with this injury, reliance is on paresis of the intrinsic muscles and pain with passive motion of the metacarpophalangeal joint. The sequence of edema, increased intramuscular pressure, and ischemia ultimately leads to muscle necrosis, fibrosis, and joint contracture.[60, 75, 142, 159] To decompress the dorsal interossei muscles, only the fascia over the muscle need be incised to provide space for the swollen intrinsic muscles.[32] If the hand is massively swollen with increased pressure in the carpal canal, release of the transverse carpal ligament can be performed at the time of the initial débridement.

Hand fractures resulting from gunshots frequently have intercalary bone loss. Skeletal stability is necessary to maintain joint mobility before the reconstruction of tendon and nerve injuries. A variety of methods are useful to maintain rotation, alignment, length, and stability in fractures with segmental bone loss before bone grafting.[37, 56, 83] Spacer wires can be made by the surgeon from small Kirschner wires (K-wires) (Fig. 15–8).[31] Alternatively, K-wires can be drilled transversely through the neck or shaft of an injured metacarpal into an adjacent noninjured metacarpal (see Fig. 15–8).[177] The use of two wires is necessary to control rotation and angulation of the distal fragment. However, if several metacarpals have segmental loss, it may be necessary to attach the wires to an external fixator to maintain proper length. If patients are seen late, after soft tissue shortening has occurred, an external fixator can be used to obtain distraction before bone grafting.[3, 113, 177] Longitudinal traction, although not useful in the fingers because of its inability to control rotation, can be used in the thumb to maintain length and mobility before bone grafting.[74] The sooner skeletal stability can be restored, the sooner joint mobilization and other reconstructive procedures can be carried out.

Freeland and colleagues[70] reported the results of 21 delayed primary bone grafts performed within 10 days of wounding in 17 patients. Although there were no infections, there were one malunion and one fibrous union in this group. Gonzalez and co-workers[81] also reported excellent results after early stable fixation and bone grafting within 7 days in 64 metacarpal fractures. There were two superficial infections but no deep infections or chronically draining wounds in their series. This technique can be used if the wound is surgically clean and there is adequate blood supply. For contaminated and potentially

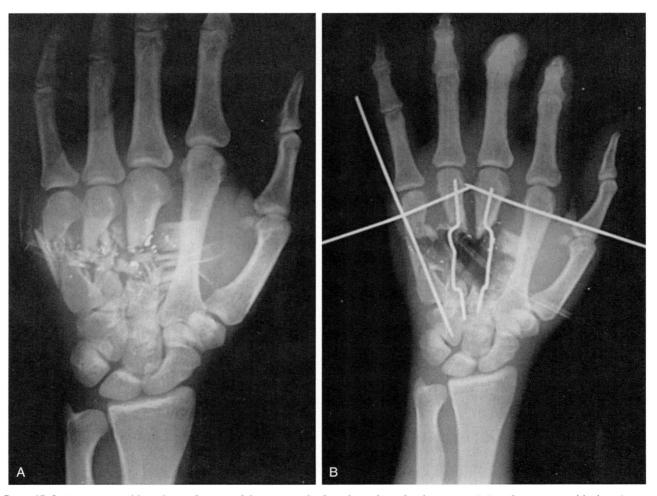

FIGURE 15–8. *A,* Comminuted bone loss in fractures of the metacarpals after a low-velocity handgun injury. *B,* Length is maintained by bent (omega spacers) and transverse Kirschner wires. After soft tissue healing, bone grafting can be done.

infected wounds, Cziffer and colleagues[46] recommended primary application of miniature external fixators and the simultaneous use of antibiotic-loaded bone cement beads, followed by autologous iliac crest bone grafting within 7 to 8 days. In a series of 15 patients, there were no deep infections and no bone grafts were lost. All patients had clinical and radiographic bone union after the first grafting.

Adequate fixation and soft tissue coverage are necessary for early bone grafting to be successful. If early fixation is not stable or soft tissue coverage cannot be achieved, bone grafting should be delayed. Fixation can be accomplished with K-wires or plates and screws. The advantage of plate-and-screw fixation, however, must be weighed against the increased dissection and tissue trauma associated with its use. Bone grafts can be made from corticocancellous dowels of iliac crest or tibial bone.[70, 132]

Disability resulting from loss of the thumb metacarpal is much greater than that from loss of one or more of the other metacarpals. If the metacarpophalangeal joint of the thumb is destroyed, the joint should be fused in flexion at an angle between 20° and 30°. In the fingers, if only the base of the metacarpal remains and the head is destroyed, bone graft can bridge to the proximal phalanx, fusing the metacarpal joint in 30° of flexion.[22, 132]

The greatest difficulty in the reconstruction of a metacarpal after segmental fracture is restoration of appropriate length and correct rotational alignment. We have developed the *metacarpal index angle:* the angle formed by the intersection of a line drawn from the most distal point of the second metacarpal head to the most distal point of the third metacarpal head and a second line drawn from the most distal point of the second metacarpal head to the most distal part of the fifth metacarpal head (see Fig. 15–8). The metacarpal index angle is first measured in the uninjured hand. In a review of 120 AP radiographs, we found this angle to be constant at 26° (±4°), with no statistically significant difference related to handedness, sex, or dominance. The angle obtained from the uninjured hand is drawn on an AP radiograph of the injured hand. Measurement of the distance from the shortened metacarpal to the lines used to form the angle allows calculation of the exact amount of shortening caused by the metacarpal defect.

Many fractures in the fingers are not suitable for fixation with K-wires, plates, or screws because of comminution or bone loss. If other fixation devices cannot be used, external fixation may be necessary. Bilos and Ekestrand[17] used external fixation in 15 phalanx fractures. Thirteen healed in good alignment with preservation of metacarpophalangeal joint motion. Because of extensive damage to the extensor mechanism and soft tissue scarring, motion at the proximal interphalangeal joint was poor. With this technique, care must be taken to avoid overdistraction. If the fracture involves the proximal interphalangeal joint, primary arthrodesis can be obtained with the use of the external fixator or with K-wire or tension band techniques. Useful function of the finger can be retained, however, because of the preservation of metacarpophalangeal joint motion.

Hand wounds with massive soft tissue loss often require local or distant flaps. The classic flap for coverage of the hand has been the groin flap, described by McGreggor and Jackson in 1972.[146] Since that time, the use of osteocutaneous flaps and other free tissue transfers has been described for reconstruction of complex upper extremity wounds with loss of bone and soft tissue.[67, 143, 184, 196, 215]

Many patients with wrist and carpal fractures eventually require limited or total wrist arthrodesis. Midcarpal gunshot injuries can be salvaged by late intercarpal arthrodesis, leaving some useful residual wrist motion.[76]

Most of these wounds can be managed on an outpatient basis with local wound care, splinting in the position of function, and administration of 1 g of a cephalosporin antibiotic with or without the addition of oral antibiotics. Nondisplaced fractures of metacarpals and phalanges are managed by cast immobilization. If a vascular injury results in ischemia, microvascular repair with end-to-end anastomosis or vein graft is done emergently. Isolated nerve injuries without vascular injury are not explored unless there is no evidence of nerve function after 12 to 16 weeks.

Fractures in the hand as a result of a gunshot are commonly displaced, with a portion of bone missing. Most of these are accompanied by soft tissue loss of 2 to 8 cm on the volar or dorsal surface of the hand. Often it is difficult to assess the integrity of the flexor tendons acutely because pain and instability prevent the patient from cooperating with the examination. At the time of the initial exploration, nerve ends are tagged for secondary repair. Vascular injuries to the superficial and deep palmar arches and common digital arteries are common, but repair is usually done only if there is evidence of ischemia.

Fractures are stabilized with K-wires to maintain length and prevent angulation and shortening. Wounds are left open and dressed. Intravenous antibiotics are given for 72 hours. If flexor tendons are found to be divided, the ends are cut back and a primary repair is done unless the wound is grossly contaminated. If the wound is clean at 5 to 14 days with no evidence of infection, a delayed primary bone graft and internal fixation can be done with either small fragment screws and plates or K-wires. At the time of delayed primary fixation and bone grafting, the wound is closed. If the soft tissue defect is too large to allow delayed primary wound closure, coverage is provided either by a groin flap or by a free vascularized tissue flap.[146] Fractures of the phalanges are treated by splinting if they are nondisplaced or by K-wire fixation if they are displaced or unstable. Primary arthrodesis should be considered for comminuted intra-articular fractures of the proximal interphalangeal or distal interphalangeal joint.

LOWER EXTREMITY

Femoral Diaphysis

Historically, these injuries have been managed with local wound care, antibiotics, and skeletal traction. Depending on the location of the fracture, 3 to 6 weeks in traction followed by a spica cast or cast brace was recommended. Deep wound infection and osteomyelitis were rare with this treatment, but there were several drawbacks. Axial

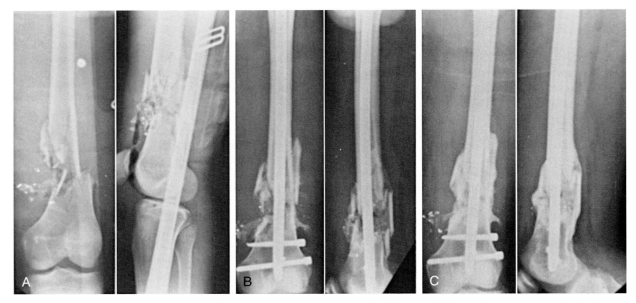

FIGURE 15–9. *A,* A comminuted supracondylar femoral fracture. *B,* Delayed, static locked intramedullary nailing. *C,* At 6 months, the fracture is healed with excellent range of motion of the hip and knee.

alignment was difficult to achieve, particularly in fractures of the proximal and middle thirds of the femur. Skeletal traction led to long periods of recumbency, prolonged convalescence, and residual disability as a result of knee stiffness. Perhaps more important, traction proved difficult in patients with multiple wounds, particularly to the chest and abdomen, for which early mobilization is thought to reduce pulmonary complications.

Brettler and co-workers[24] reviewed 19 cases of femur fractures after gunshot; 11 were displaced or comminuted. All were treated nonoperatively, and all but one united. Ryan and colleagues[193] reported 43 patients treated with skeletal traction after a gunshot to the femur. The average time in traction was 46.8 days, and the average time in spica cast was 97.5 days. The average time from fracture to union was 144.3 days. There were no deep infections or nonunions. The greatest angular deformity was 15° of valgus in a distal third femur fracture. The average angular deformity was 5° or less.

Closed intramedullary interlocking nailing has now become the treatment of choice for virtually all diaphyseal fractures of the femur in adults.[225–227, 229] Nonlocked intramedullary nailing achieves excellent fixation in transverse and short oblique fractures in the middle third of the bone. However, fixation of comminuted fractures or fractures with bone loss with simple nails often leads to excessive shortening or rotation around the implant.[23, 36, 225] The basic concept of locked intramedullary nailing combines the advantages of closed intramedullary nailing with the added stability of transfixing screws. Locking the nail prevents axial sliding and rotation around the nail. In static locked nailing, screws are inserted above and below the fracture site, rigidly maintaining overall length and alignment. With dynamic locking, screws are inserted either proximally or distally alone; this method is used chiefly to control angular or rotational instability. For most gunshot fractures of the femur, static locked nailing

is essential because comminution creates length and rotational instability.*

Interlocked nailing has become the treatment of choice for most low-velocity gunshot fractures located between the lesser trochanter and the femoral condyles (Fig. 15–9). Although the interlocking nail has solved the problems of shortening and malrotation in comminuted fractures, the optimal timing of fixation remains subject to debate. The initial experience with femur fractures caused by gunshot wounds involved locked nailing performed on a delayed basis. In isolated gunshot fractures of the femur or in patients with injuries that are not life-threatening, the injured limb is placed in balanced skeletal traction, intravenous antibiotics are administered, and closed nailing is performed 7 to 10 days later. Using this approach, Wiss and associates[228] as well as Hollmann and Horowitz[101] reported high rates of union with no cases of infection or osteomyelitis.

Increasing experience with intramedullary nailing of open femur fractures resulting from blunt trauma led several investigators to question the concept of delayed nailing in gunshot femur fractures. Immediate stabilization of fractures of the shaft of the femur has significant benefits for the multiply injured victim including a decreased incidence of adult respiratory distress syndrome, decreased duration of ventilator dependence and intensive care unit days, and decreased mortality. Immediate intramedullary nailing of open fractures of the femur secondary to blunt trauma or gunshot has been demonstrated to be safe and effective.

Nowotarski and Brumback[166] reviewed 39 femur fractures caused by low-velocity and midvelocity handgun missiles treated with static interlocking nailing within 18 hours of injury. Thirty-seven fractures healed primarily,

---

*See references 16, 28, 101, 112, 129, 164, 166, 218, 219, 228, 229, 235.

and two nonunions healed after exchange nailing. There was one infection, which was treated by nail removal, reaming of the canal, and reinsertion of a larger nail. These authors concluded that immediate interlocking nailing in this population is an effective and safe treatment resulting in shorter hospital stays and a significant decrease in hospital expenses.

The use of plates and screws for fixation of diaphyseal fractures of the femur caused by gunshot wounds is rarely indicated. Comminution often makes rigid internal fixation difficult or impossible to achieve. In many instances, the plate ends up spanning a gap that requires a supplemental cancellous bone graft. Similarly, routine use of open intramedullary nailing and cerclage wiring, although it provides some control of the fracture, cannot adequately maintain length and alignment in many cases.[109]

Subtrochanteric and Intertrochanteric Fractures of the Femur

As with intertrochanteric fractures, comminution and instability also make stable internal fixation difficult to achieve in these fractures. In many instances, distal extension of the fracture makes treatment with a sliding compression hip screw inadvisable or inadequate. An understanding of the anatomy and biomechanics of the proximal femur is essential if appropriate treatment is to be instituted. The iliopsoas and hip abductors cause deformity in flexion, abduction, and external rotation of the proximal fragment, whereas the strong pull of the adductors produces shortening and varus of the distal fragment. These deformities may be difficult to overcome by nonoperative methods. Despite improved technology and internal fixation devices, delayed union, malunion, infection, and implant failure still occur with disturbing frequency. When comminution or bone loss creates deficiencies in the medial cortex, markedly increased forces occur laterally.[9, 198, 222, 231]

Skeletal traction is still the method of choice for subtrochanteric and intertrochanteric gunshot fractures in children and young adolescents and when fracture comminution is so extreme that internal fixation cannot be achieved. Most authors prefer skeletal traction in the 90°–90° position with placement of a femoral pin. A spica cast or cast brace follows 4 to 8 weeks later. Although this method of treatment eliminates many operative problems such as blood loss, infection, and use of anesthesia, it is not without complications. In adults, prolonged and costly hospitalization is necessary, and acceptable fracture alignment may be difficult to achieve despite frequent adjustment of traction. Knee stiffness and varus malunion remain a common problem after skeletal traction. Furthermore, this method of treatment is not suitable in the multiply injured patient. Surgical treatment enables the surgeon to achieve better alignment of difficult fractures, permits early mobilization of hip and knee joints, and reduces the overall hospital stay. Risks with open fracture reduction include extensive surgical dissection with considerable blood loss. Even under optimal conditions, infection occurs in 5% to 6% of cases.[222]

No single method of treatment is adequate for all intertrochanteric and subtrochanteric gunshot fractures. The AO 95°-angled condylar blade plate is most useful in stable fracture patterns when anatomic reduction can be achieved at the time of surgery[198, 222] (Fig. 15–10). Complication rates up to 20% have been reported after blade plate fixation of complex subtrochanteric fractures, even in experienced trauma centers. The single most important factor related to failure is inability to restore the medial cortex at the time of surgery. Kinast and colleagues[114] reported a dramatic reduction in complications with the blade plate by the use of indirect techniques for reduction of the medial cortex to minimize soft tissue stripping.

The sliding compression hip screw with a long side plate has been advocated by several authors for the treatment of intertrochanteric and subtrochanteric fractures.[9, 198] This method is somewhat more flexible than the blade plate and allows sliding impaction of the fracture surfaces and slight medialization of the shaft in high subtrochanteric fractures with proximal extension into the intertrochanteric region. Secure fixation in the proximal and distal fragments allows controlled collapse with a decrease in the bending moment and resultant forces.

Because of the difficulty with open reduction and internal fixation in this group of fractures, many surgeons have turned to intramedullary nailing.[225–227, 231] The major advantage of the intramedullary nail is that it allows the bone to carry a substantial portion of the load. This significantly reduces the risk of implant failure (Fig. 15–11).

The spectacular success of interlocking nails in the management of comminuted gunshot fractures of the femoral shaft has led to their use in many subtrochanteric gunshot fractures. Locking the nail above and below the fracture site provides immediate fracture stability. Patients can be mobilized shortly after surgery without fear of loss of length or rotation. Wiss and Brien[227] reported the results of treatment in 95 subtrochanteric femoral fractures (69 closed and 26 open) treated with a first-generation interlocking nail. The average time to healing was 25 weeks. There were three delayed unions, one nonunion, and six malunions. The investigators concluded that interlocking nailing, regardless of the fracture pattern or degree of comminution, could stabilize essentially all nonpathologic subtrochanteric femur fractures. Closed interlocking nailing is the preferred treatment for subtrochanteric fractures.[227–229]

The dramatic success of first-generation interlocking nails for complex proximal femur fractures expanded the indications to closed nailing of these difficult injuries. First-generation nails, however, provided inadequate fixation of fractures that extended above the level of the lesser trochanter. These problems led to the development of a new generation of interlocking nails, which provided better fixation by screws directed into the head of the femur and allowed distal interlocking. These implants, called *reconstruction* or *second-generation nails,* have an increased wall thickness proximally, stronger and

FIGURE 15–10. *A,* An oblique subtrochanteric femoral fracture followed handgun injury. *B,* Internal fixation with a 95-degree angled blade plate.

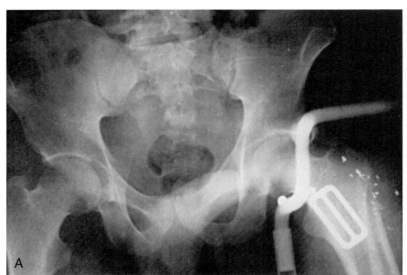

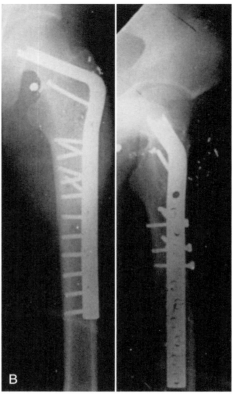

larger proximal screws, and reliable proximal targeting devices.

The best indication for the use of a reconstruction nail is a "high" subtrochanteric fracture, in which the lesser trochanter is fractured but the greater trochanter remains intact (Fig. 15–12). If fracture comminution involves the greater trochanter or the region of the piriformis fossa, reconstruction nailing is associated with an increased incidence of complication, particularly varus deformities and implant cutout.

Supracondylar and Intracondylar Fractures of the Distal Femur

Gunshot fractures to the supracondylar region of the femur are particularly difficult to treat. Severe soft tissue damage, comminution, fracture extension into the knee joint, and injury to the quadriceps mechanism often lead to unsatisfactory results regardless of the method of treatment. Powerful thigh muscles can lead to deformities that may be difficult to overcome by traction or cast-bracing tech-

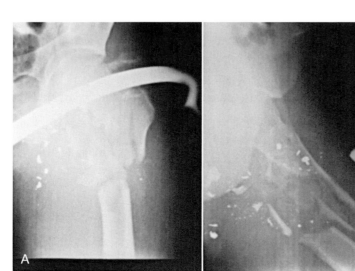

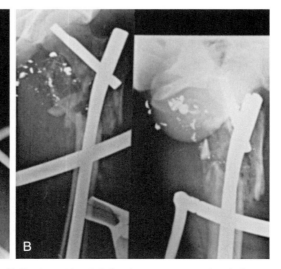

FIGURE 15–11. *A,* Combined intertrochanteric and subtrochanteric femoral fractures. *B,* Fixation with a Zickel nail cannot maintain length despite postoperative traction.

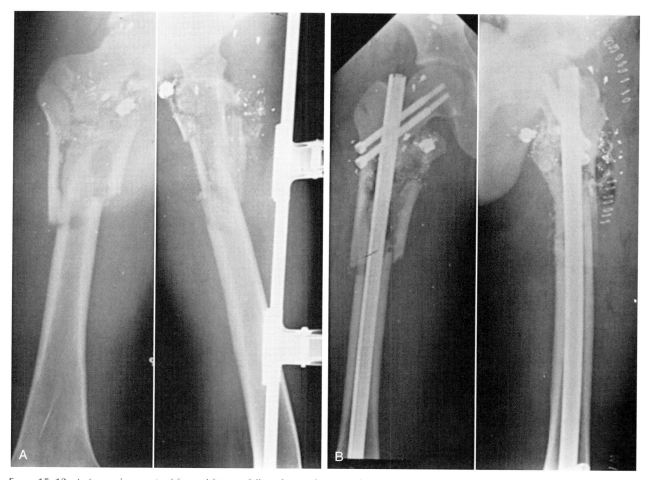

FIGURE 15–12. *A,* A complex proximal femoral fracture followed a gunshot wound. *B,* Fracture stabilization was achieved with a second-generation interlocking nail.

niques. Thin cortices, comminution, osteopenia, and a wide medullary canal make osteosynthesis and secure internal fixation difficult to achieve in these fractures.

Primary use of internal fixation is not indicated for all supracondylar femur fractures, and the associated risks and benefits must be assessed carefully. Advantages include stabilization of the fracture, ease of wound care, pain relief, and mobilization of the patient and injured limb. The major disadvantage of immediate internal fixation in open supracondylar fractures is the increased risk of infection as a consequence of further soft tissue dissection. If infection develops, it may affect not only the fracture site but also the knee joint when there is intra-articular extension.

Most low-velocity gunshot supracondylar fractures can be managed safely by internal fixation within a few days of injury. On the other hand, in high-energy gunshot and shotgun injuries in which extreme comminution exists, hybrid external fixation or retrograde intramedullary nailing becomes the treatment of choice. This treatment is frequently complemented with limited internal fixation to restore joint congruity. Frequently, the external fixator must bridge the knee joint in order to construct a stable frame configuration.[232]

No single method of treatment works for all supra-

condylar femur fractures (Fig. 15–13). A high incidence of malunion, nonunion, and infection has been associated with early attempts at internal fixation of these injuries. Fixation methods used in early studies would not be considered sufficient by today's standards.[155, 161, 202, 210] Skeletal traction requires prolonged bedrest, is time consuming and expensive, and may not be well suited for multiply injured or elderly patients. Although the risks of surgery are avoided, malalignment and knee stiffness are still commonly encountered. Many of the problems of prolonged traction for supracondylar fractures can be avoided by cast brace treatment. This technique results in shorter hospital stays, earlier ambulation and weight bearing, better knee motion, and decreased incidence of nonunion.[155]

Surgical stabilization with early range of motion of the knee and delayed weight bearing can also lead to a satisfactory outcome in many cases. The two major types of internal fixation devices widely used in the management of these injuries are condylar plates and intramedullary nails. Schatzker and co-workers[197] reviewed 68 supracondylar fractures of the femur treated with an AO blade plate. They found a good to excellent result in 75% of the stabilized fractures compared with only 32% of those treated nonoperatively. Mize and colleagues[153] reported

80% excellent or good results in 30 patients with displaced comminuted fractures of the distal femur treated with a blade plate followed for an average of 28.5 months. They stressed that in complex intra-articular fractures, an extensile exposure with osteotomy of the tibial tubercle greatly facilitated reduction and fixation. Healy and Brooker[97] analyzed 98 patients with distal femur fractures and compared open with closed methods of treatment. Thirty-eight (81%) of the 47 surgically treated patients had a good result, compared with only 18 (35%) of 51 with fractures treated by closed methods. These investigators concluded that surgery gave better functional results, returned patients to activity sooner, and decreased the incidence of nonunion.

Several researchers have reported favorable results after treatment of supracondylar femur fractures with a 90°-angled compression screw and side plate. Giles and co-workers[79] used this method in 26 patients and reported no nonunions or deep infections; the average postoperative knee motion was 120°. Pritchett[180] reviewed 19 patients treated in a similar fashion. The results were good or excellent in 74%, fair in 16%, and poor in 10%. There were no nonunions and only one deep infection. The primary advantage of the use of compression screws over blade plates in the distal femur is the decreased risk of displacement of the femoral condyles. The technique is more flexible because the screw and side plate are two separate pieces. The barrel of the side plate can swivel around the screw and consistently line up with the distal shaft of the femur. Regardless of which method is used, the goals of management are anatomic restoration of the knee joint, secure internal fixation, and primary bone grafting to fill defects and protect weight bearing until the fracture has consolidated.

Since the mid-1980s, the role of intramedullary nailing of supracondylar femur fractures has expanded dramatically.[107, 135, 147] These devices are attractive from both a mechanical and a biologic perspective. Closed nailing, done either antegrade or retrograde, eliminates direct exposure of the fracture site. This decreases blood loss, minimizes infection, and increases the rate of union. Locking of the nail into bone above and below the fracture site usually produces immediate fracture stability. Patients can be mobilized soon after surgery, which tends to reduce medical complications, maintain joint motion, and decrease hospital stay.

Reamed antegrade intramedullary nails have a limited role in the management of supracondylar fractures. In infraisthmal fractures of the distal third of the femur, antegrade locked nailing remains the treatment of choice.

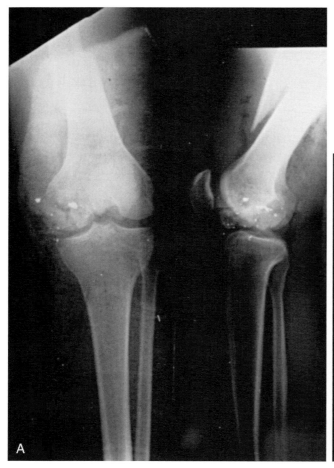

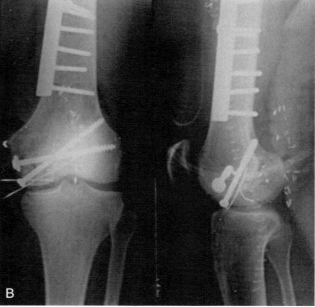

FIGURE 15–13. *A,* A comminuted intra-articular fracture of the medial femoral condyle with an associated arterial injury and femoral shaft fracture. *B,* After popliteal artery repair, the joint surface has been repaired and the femoral fracture has been plated.

However, in true supracondylar fractures, particularly those with intra-articular involvement and displacement, antegrade nailing is technically difficult and may not provide reliable fixation for many fracture patterns. Nevertheless, Leung and colleagues[128] reported 100% healing and no malunions or infections in 37 cases of supracondylar and intracondylar fractures of the distal part of the femur treated by interlocking intramedullary nailing (30 extra-articular and 7 intra-articular). Functional outcomes as assessed by the modified knee rating system of the Hospital for Special Surgery were 35% excellent, 59% good, and 5% fair.

Tornetta and Tiburzi[219] reported the results of antegrade interlocking nailing of distal femoral fractures after gunshot in 38 patients. The distance from the fracture to the distal screws was less than 5 cm in all cases. All fractures healed at an average of 8.6 weeks. No primary or secondary bone grafts were performed. Eight patients had more than 5° of valgus angulation. The authors described the use of two Steinmann pins placed in the distal fragment for better control of alignment during nail insertion.

Several firms have developed and implemented a retrograde intramedullary nail designed specifically for supracondylar and intracondylar femur fractures. The nails can be placed with or without reaming. The nail enters in the intracondylar notch just anterior to the femoral attachment of the posterior cruciate ligament. In patients with intra-articular extension, careful reconstruction of the joint surface is essential before passage of the nail. Intrafragmentary screws must be placed quite anteriorly or posteriorly so as not to impede nail passage. In addition, the nail must be countersunk several millimeters so that it does not interfere with the patellofemoral articulation.

Lucas and associates[135] reported short-term follow-up of 25 supracondylar nailings in 33 patients. All fractures healed with an average arc of knee motion of 100°. Four AO type C fractures required bone graft; there was one bent and broken nail and one late infection with a septic knee. Six patients had open or arthroscopic lysis of adhesions for restricted knee motion. Iannacone and colleagues[107] reported their experience with supracondylar intramedullary nailing in 22 open and 19 closed fractures. There were no infections, four nonunions that required repeated fixation and bone grafting, and two of five delayed unions requiring revision fixation. Thirty-five of the 41 knees achieved at least 90° of knee motion. Four patients experienced fatigue failure of the implant. All of these failures occurred early in the series, when nails of 11 and 12 mm diameter were being used; later, with the use of 12- and 13-mm nails and smaller locking screws, there were no cases of implant breakage.

External fixation is used infrequently in supracondylar femoral fractures. The most common indications for its use are severe open fractures, particularly grade IIIB injuries, high-velocity injuries, and close-range shotgun wounds. With complex fracture patterns, supplemental lag screws are often needed to stabilize intra-articular extension. Depending on the location of the wounds and the degree of fracture comminution, fixation across the knee is often necessary. When soft tissue control is achieved, delayed internal fixation should be considered.

The major advantages of external fixation are rapid application, minimal soft tissue dissection, and ability to maintain length, provide wound access, and allow mobilization of the patient. Problems associated with external fixation include pin tract infection, loss of knee motion secondary to adhesions in the quadriceps mechanism, increased risk of delayed union or nonunion, and loss of reduction after removal of the device.

Gunshot Femur Fractures and Arterial Injuries

Signs and symptoms of arterial injury include absent or diminished pulse, expanding hematoma, bruit, progressive swelling, persistent arterial bleeding, nerve injury, and anatomic proximity of the wound.[44, 148] Even with arterial injury, clot may maintain vascular continuity for several hours, only to lyse or dislodge later, leading to major arterial bleeding.[192] Combined vascular and bone injuries significantly increase morbidity and amputation rates, at least in the military experience.[44, 148] Reports from both Korea and Vietnam showed that when concomitant arterial injuries were present, the amputation rate was double that for fracture alone. McNamara and co-workers[148] reported that combined injury required vein graft more often than arterial injury without fracture; amputation rates were 23.3% and 2.5%, respectively. Arterial repair failed in 33% of patients with associated fracture. Popliteal artery involvement increased the failure rate to 60%.

Before the availability of interlocking nails, external immobilization was felt to be safer and easier to employ than internal fixation. Connolly and associates[44] found that the stability with internal fixation under emergency conditions when associated with arterial repair was frequently less than optimal. They concluded that because the surrounding soft tissues during longitudinal traction protect the arterial suture line, skeletal traction would be the preferred method of treatment.

A patient with a gunshot wound with obvious arterial injury should be taken to the operating room for fracture stabilization and direct exploration of the artery. A temporary shunt allows fracture stabilization in patients with prolonged ischemia or delay in presentation. If vascular repair is done first, temporary stabilization can be accomplished with external fixation. Whenever possible, fixation should be with an intramedullary interlocking nail. Static locked nailing is usually necessary for comminuted fractures. Great care must be taken to ensure correct length, alignment, and rotation of the limb. Postoperatively, the vascular status of the extremity is reassessed. If any doubt exists, direct inspection of the anastomosis or intraoperative angiography should be performed. If ischemia time exceeds 6 to 8 hours, prophylactic fasciotomy may be indicated.

Starr and co-workers[208] reported the results of internal fixation in 19 femur fractures with associated vascular injuries. Ten fractures were fixed before the vascular repair (after placement of a vascular shunt in three) and nine after the vascular repair (seven immediately, one after 2 days, and one after 5 days). Sixteen of the 19 internal fixations were ultimately successful. None of the vascular repairs was adversely affected by subsequent internal fixation.

On rare occasions, comminution is minimal and plating can be done after vascular repair. External fixation is reserved for substantial soft tissue injury or fracture extremely close to the hip or knee joint. If the fracture cannot be stabilized at the time of vascular repair, skeletal traction can be used without fear of vascular disruption. Delayed closed nailing can be carried out in the early postoperative period, provided the fracture is held out to length by traction and alignment is good. The incidence of anastomotic disruptions or vascular thrombosis with delayed nailing is unknown.

Gunshot Fractures of the Tibia

The experience with gunshot fractures of the tibia closely parallels that with open tibia fractures in general. Most low-velocity gunshot extra-articular fractures can be managed by cast immobilization followed by fracture bracing. External fixation or placement of intramedullary nails without reaming better manages extensive comminution or displacement. For unstable fractures in the middle three fifths of the bone, we favor immediate unreamed intramedullary nailing. For complex metaphyseal fractures in the proximal and distal fifth of the bone, hybrid external fixation is the treatment of choice. Length and alignment can be restored with the use of thin wires and a ring in the juxta-articular portion and half pins in the diaphysis. Supplemental lag screws may be used to stabilize articular extensions.[26]

Most patients with gunshot fractures of the tibia or fibula should be admitted to the hospital for observation to rule out vascular injury or evolving compartment syndrome. Injuries in the proximal third of the tibia or fibula are particularly at risk because of the proximity to the arterial trifurcation posteriorly. Innocuous-appearing fractures may have devastating vascular injuries. We favor stabilization of the tibia by external fixation either before or after vascular repair. Four-compartment fasciotomies are carried out to reduce the risk of compartment syndrome. Compartment syndrome may also occur after gunshot fracture without vascular injury. Delayed primary closure or split-thickness skin grafting can usually be performed within 1 week of injury. If a fixator is used, it can usually be removed 6 to 8 weeks after injury and replaced with a weight-bearing cast or fracture brace if sufficient callus is present. In patients with bone loss or extensive comminution, early cancellous bone grafting helps reduce the time to fracture union.

Leffers and Chandler[123] reviewed 41 tibia fractures produced by civilian gunshot wounds. Thirty-two fractures were the result of low-velocity missiles with little soft tissue damage and predictable fracture patterns; most of these were successfully managed by casting and functional bracing. Of the remaining fractures, six were caused by intermediate-energy and three by high-energy missiles. These nine cases were responsible for five of seven vascular injuries, two of three compartment syndromes, four of seven neurologic deficits, and five of the six instances in

which external fixation was required. Furthermore, six of the eight patients who had chronic infection and four of the nine who had soft tissue healing problems were in this group of patients. The investigators concluded that intermediate- and high-energy gunshot fractures of the tibia should be treated with early surgical débridement, external fixation, and appropriate therapy for vascular injury or compartment syndromes.

Ferraro and Zinar[66] reviewed 90 gunshot fractures of the tibia. Patients were divided into two groups according to the degree of fracture comminution. Fifty-two fractures were considered stable, and the remaining 38 were unstable. In the stable group, 50 were managed with casts, 1 was externally fixed, and 1 was nailed; all healed between 12 and 14 weeks without infection. Of the 38 unstable fractures, 8 were managed with a long leg cast, 16 with a fixator, and 14 with nails; healing times were 32, 27, and 18 weeks, respectively. In the unstable fracture group, there were five nonunions, one delayed union, one malunion, and one deep infection with osteomyelitis.

Gunshot Wounds to the Foot

Low-velocity gunshot wounds to the foot often occur accidentally while loading or cleaning a gun (Fig. 15–14).

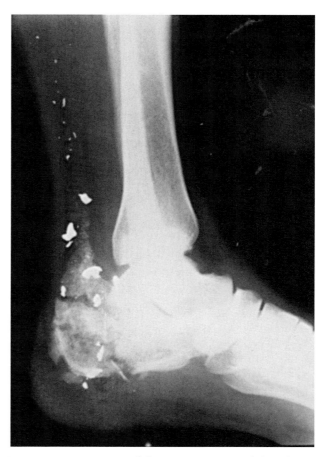

FIGURE 15–14. Destruction of the posterior portion of the calcaneus followed a close-range gunshot wound in the heel.

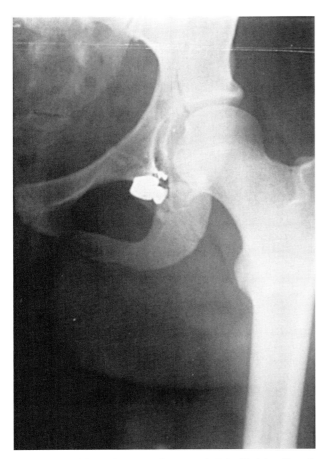

FIGURE 15–15. A low-velocity gunshot wound of the hip joint. Note the nondisplaced acetabular fracture.

Gunshot Wounds to the Hip, Knee, and Ankle Joints

Ultimate functional outcome after low-velocity gunshot wounds involving the major weight-bearing joints of the lower extremity correlates closely with the severity of articular and periarticular involvement. Joint debris may result in significant impairment in joint function. Intra-articular fractures are often not amenable to stable internal fixation, and long periods of immobilization may be necessary, contributing to loss of joint motion.

HIP JOINT

In many instances, intra-articular injury of the hip joint is overlooked because of other life-threatening injuries (Fig. 15–15). Because missile injuries to the proximal thigh, buttock, groin, or abdomen may injure the hip, patients with these injuries should have an AP radiograph of the pelvis (Fig. 15–16).

Decreased range of motion or signs of hip irritability should alert the surgeon to the possibility of a hip injury. The function of the sciatic and femoral nerves should be carefully assessed. Lateral and AP radiographs of the hip usually reveal fractures or joint debris. Occasionally, 45°-oblique (Judet) views of the pelvis better delineate acetabular involvement. In selected cases, computed tomographic scanning yields valuable information despite mild distortion from metallic fragments. All patients with documented bone or joint injury of the hip should be treated with both a cephalosporin and an aminoglycoside antibiotic intravenously for 72 hours to decrease the possibility of infection.

Becker and associates[12] reported 49 patients after gunshot injury to the hip. There were five patients with hip joint involvement associated with abdominal visceral injuries. Four (80%) of these patients had early infection in their hip joint because of a viscerally contaminated projectile and had very poor clinical outcomes. The

Fractures are usually comminuted and minimally displaced and frequently involve one of the many articulations within the foot. The entry wound is usually dorsal and penetrates the footwear. Careful assessment of the neurovascular status is required. Rarely, soft tissue damage necessitates operative débridement or a massively swollen foot requires fasciotomy. More often, however, the wounds are minimally débrided and sterilely covered, the foot is immobilized in a well-molded plaster splint or cast, and the patient is treated with antibiotics. The duration of immobilization varies from 3 to 6 weeks for most fractures. Occasionally, bullet fragments retained on or near the plantar aspect of the foot must be removed to facilitate weight bearing. Fracture healing is rarely a problem, but occasionally joint disruption causes localized traumatic arthritis and may necessitate a limited arthrodesis.

Boucree and colleagues[20] reviewed 101 patients with gunshot wounds to the foot. Eighty-one patients sustained fractures, and 20 had only soft tissue injuries. There were 91 low-velocity, 7 shotgun, and 3 high-velocity wounds. All patients were admitted for intravenous antibiotic therapy, and 22 wounds greater than 2 cm were formally débrided. Infections developed in 12 patients, including all 3 with high-velocity wounds, 3 with shotgun wounds, and 6 with low-velocity wounds.

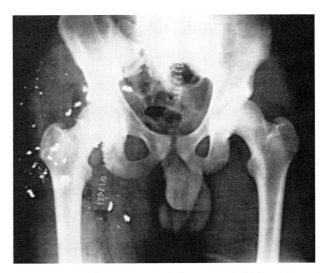

FIGURE 15–16. A shotgun injury of the proximal thigh, groin, and abdomen resulted in injury to the iliac vessels and sciatic nerve.

researchers recommended aggressive management with surgical débridement and a 3-week course of antibiotics in these cases.

Brien and co-workers[25] reported 14 patients treated for gunshot wounds to the hip, including 5 with transabdominal wounds. Diagnosis was established with the use of plain radiographs in three of these patients, arthrogram in one, and gastrointestinal series in one. Three patients had an exploratory laparotomy with diverting colostomy followed by immediate hip arthrotomy within 24 hours, and no joint infections occurred. In the other two patients, hip involvement was identified late, after septic arthritis had occurred. The authors stressed the need for early diagnosis, diverting colostomy, and immediate arthrotomy for gunshot wounds to the hip that involve the alimentary tract.

Long and colleagues[133] reviewed 53 patients who presented to a Los Angeles trauma center with gunshot injuries to the hip. They described a treatment protocol to prevent septic arthritis. Patients were treated with a 3-day course of intravenous antibiotics without arthrotomy if they met the following criteria: (1) the injury was caused by a low-velocity gunshot, (2) the injury was not transabdominal, (3) the bullet was not in communication with synovial fluid, and (4) the fracture was stable and did not require internal fixation. A hip arthrotomy was performed for removal of intra-articular metallic or osteochondral fragments and for all patients with high-velocity gunshot wounds to the hip, transabdominal injury, or fractures that required internal fixation.

We believe that all close-range shotgun wounds, high-velocity injuries, and gunshot wounds to the abdomen with concurrent intestinal violation and hip injury should be débrided urgently. Indications for delayed débridement include low-velocity missiles with residual intra-articular debris and complex fractures requiring fixation. Treatment of intracapsular gunshot wounds to the hip without articular cartilage involvement or mechanical disruption of the femoral neck remains controversial. We prefer to treat these patients with high-dose antibiotics, a brief period of bedrest, and protected ambulation with crutches.

Comminution and bone loss resulting in displaced fractures of the femoral neck make stable internal fixation difficult to achieve. The relatively young age of most of these patients makes primary prosthetic replacement undesirable. For most patients, we attempt internal fixation with multiple cancellous screws with protected weight bearing for up to 3 months. Varus malunion, nonunion, or avascular necrosis can be salvaged with a valgus osteotomy and fixation with an angled blade plate. Late avascular necrosis with segmental collapse and degenerative arthritis is best treated with prosthetic replacement, although in selected patients an arthrodesis may be indicated.

The surgical approach for débridement or fixation is dictated by the location of the injury. Whenever possible, the hip should not be dislocated to lessen the likelihood of avascular necrosis. The use of joint distraction is an invaluable adjunct to joint débridement. As most fractures of the femoral head are not amenable to internal fixation, comminuted displaced osteochondral fracture fragments

within the joint should be excised. Very few acetabular fractures caused by gunshot wounds require internal fixation. The role of arthroscopy in the management of gunshot wounds to the hip is not firmly established.

KNEE AND ANKLE JOINTS

The knee is the lower extremity joint most commonly injured by civilian gunshot wounds. Because of the subcutaneous location of the knee and ankle joints, even very low velocity handgun shots can destroy the joint. Much of what is written about missile injuries to the knee and ankle comes from the military experience. Davis[47] reviewed 77 major joint injuries that occurred during the Vietnam War; 52 involved the knee joint. Treatment consisted of débridement, suction irrigation, delayed closure, and intravenous administration of antibiotics. Despite aggressive treatment, only 26 patients regained useful function of the knee.

Ashby[8] reviewed seven cases of low-velocity gunshot wounds to the knee joint in civilians; retained bullet fragments were the indication for arthrotomy. In several patients, osteochondral fragments were removed that were not apparent on radiographs. Parisien[174] used arthroscopy as a diagnostic and surgical tool to manage gunshot wounds to the knee joint in eight patients. At 1-year follow-up, there were no infections, and seven of the eight patients had normal knee function. Patzakis and co-workers[176] reviewed 44 open knee joint injuries, 90% of which were caused by low-velocity gunshot wounds, and found that arthrotomy with systemic antibiotics prevented infection.

Evaluation of the patient with an isolated gunshot wound to the knee or ankles begins with an assessment of limb viability.[178] Peripheral pulses and function of the posterior tibial and peroneal nerves should be carefully documented. Angiography or duplex Doppler ultrasonography is indicated for absent or diminished pulses. Evidence of compartment syndrome often implies associated vascular injury. All patients are given an intravenous cephalosporin and aminoglycoside antibiotic initially. Plain radiographs of the knee or ankle are obtained, including oblique or special views when indicated.

Missiles that violate the knee or ankle joint without producing intra-articular fracture or joint debris can usually be treated with antibiotics and a brief period of immobilization. Wounds with obvious intra-articular debris or retained bullet fragments are best treated with arthroscopic lavage and débridement.[15] Displaced fractures of the femoral or tibial condyles often require percutaneous pinning or formal open reduction and internal fixation. Significant injury to the cruciate or collateral ligaments of the knee is uncommon with low-velocity bullet wounds; therefore, residual instability is almost always a result of loss of bone or cartilage.

Close-range shotgun wounds and high-velocity missiles usually result in catastrophic damage to the knee or ankle joint. In our opinion, massive injuries to soft tissue, bone, and articular surface are best treated with early definitive amputation (Fig. 15–17). Less severe cases require aggressive and repeated débridement. Bridging the joint with an external fixator provides skeletal stability and wound

FIGURE 15–17. *A,* A close-range shotgun injury of the foot and ankle with massive soft tissue and bone disruption. *B,* Treatment was an immediate below-knee amputation.

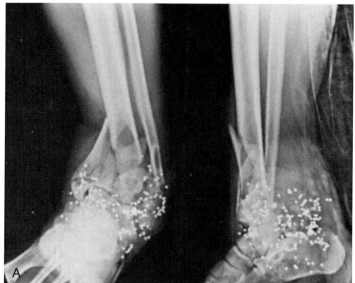

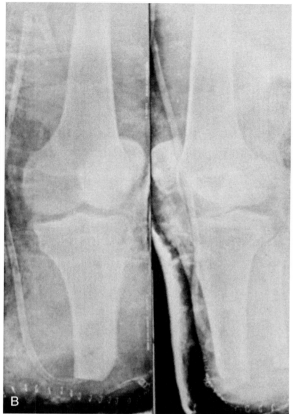

access. Exposed cartilage is poorly tolerated, and tissue cover should be done as soon as possible. Significant loss of knee or ankle motion frequently results. Painful degenerative arthritis is best treated with arthrodesis or, occasionally, arthroplasty.

REFERENCES

1. Adams, D.B. Wound ballistics: A review. Mil Med 147:831, 1982.
2. Adams, R.W. Small caliber blast wounds to the hand: Mechanism and early management. Am J Surg 82:219, 1951.
3. Adinolfi, M.F.; Hardin, W.D.; O'Connell, R.C.; Kerstein, M.D. Amputations after vascular trauma in civilians. South Med J 76:1241, 1983.
4. Anderson, J.T.; Gustilo, R.B. Immediate internal fixation in open fractures. Orthop Clin North Am 11:569, 1980.
5. Anderson, R.J.; Hobson, R.W.; Padberg, F.T.; et al. Penetrating extremity trauma: Identification of patients at high risk requiring arteriography. J Vasc Surg 11:544, 1990.
6. Armine, A.R.C.; Sugar, O. Repair of severed brachial plexus. JAMA 235:1039, 1976.
7. Ashbell, T.S.; Kleinert, H.E.; Kutz, J.E. Vascular injuries about the elbow. Clin Orthop 50:107, 1967.
8. Ashby, M.E. Low velocity gunshot wounds involving the knee joint: Surgical management. J Bone Joint Surg Am 56:1047, 1974.
9. Asher, M.A.; Tippett, J.W.; Rockwood, C.A. Compression fixation of subtrochanteric fractures. Clin Orthop 117:202, 1976.
10. Barach, E.; Tomlanovich, M.; Nowak, R. Ballistics: A pathophysiologic examination of the wounding mechanisms of firearms. Part I. J Trauma 26:225, 1986.
11. Barach, E.; Tomlanovich, M.; Nowak, R. Ballistics: A pathophysiologic examination of the wounding mechanisms of firearms. Part II. J Trauma 26:374, 1986.
12. Becker, V.V., Jr.; Brien, W.W.; Patzakis, M.; Wilkins, J. Gunshot injuries to the hip and abdomen: The association of joint and intra-abdominal visceral injuries. J Trauma 30:1324, 1990.
13. Bennett, J.E.; Hayes, J.E.; Robb, C. Mutilating injuries of the wrist. J Trauma 11:1008, 1971.
14. Benzon, H.T.; Chonka, C.M.; Brunner, E.A. The treatment of reflex sympathetic dystrophy with regional intravenous reserpine. Anesth Analg 59:500, 1980.
15. Berg, E.E.; Ciullo, J.V. Arthroscopic débridement after intra-articular low-velocity gunshot wounds. Arthroscopy 9:576, 1993.
16. Bergman, M.; Tornetta, P.; Kerina, M.; et al. Femur fractures caused by gunshots: Treatment by immediate reamed intramedullary nailing. J Trauma 34:783, 1993.
17. Bilos, Z.J.; Ekestrand, T. External fixator use in comminuted gunshot fractures of the proximal phalanx. J Hand Surg [Am] 4:357, 1979.
18. Bizer, L. Peripheral vascular injuries in the Vietnam War. Arch Surg 98:166, 1969.
19. Borman, K.R.; Snyder, W.H.; Weigeit, J.A. Civilian arterial trauma of the upper extremity: An 11-year experience in 267 patients. Am J Surg 148:796, 1984.
20. Boucree, J.B., Jr.; Gabriel, R.A.; Lezine-Hanna, J.T. Gunshot wounds to the foot. Orthop Clin North Am 26:191, 1995.
21. Bowden, R.E.M. The factors influencing functional recovery of peripheral nerve injuries in man. Ann R Coll Surg Engl 8:366, 1951.
22. Braun, R.M.; Rhoades, C.E. Dynamic compression for small bone arthrodesis. J Hand Surg [Am] 10:340, 1985.
23. Brav, E.A.; Jeffress, V.H. Modified intramedullary nailing in recent gunshot fractures of the femoral shaft. J Bone Joint Surg Am 35:141, 1953.
24. Brettler, D.; Sedlin, E.D.; Mendes, D.G. Conservative treatment of low velocity gunshot wounds. Clin Orthop 140:26, 1979.
25. Brien, E.W.; Brien, W.W.; Long, W.T.; Kuschner, S.H. Concomitant injuries of the hip joint and abdomen resulting from gunshot wounds. Orthopedics 15:1317, 1992.

26. Brien, E.W.; Long, W.T.; Serocki, M.D. Management of gunshot wounds to the tibia. Orthop Clin North Am 26:165, 1995.

27. Brien, W.; Gellman, H.; Becker, V.; et al. Management of upper extremity fractures in patients with brachial plexus injuries. J Bone Joint Surg Am 72:1208, 1990.

28. Brien, W.W.; Kuschner, S.H.; Brien, E.W.; Wiss, D.A. The management of gunshot wounds to the femur. Orthop Clin North Am 26:133, 1995.

29. Brooks, D.M. Open wounds of the brachial plexus. J Bone Joint Surg Br 31:17, 1949.

30. Brunner, R.G.; Fallon, W.F. A prospective, randomized clinical trial of wound débridement versus conservative wound care in soft-tissue injury from civilian gunshot wounds. Am Surg 2:104, 1990.

31. Burkhalter, W.E. Mutilating injuries of the hand. Hand Clin 2:45, 1986.

32. Burkhalter, W.E.; Butler, B.; Metz, W.; Omer, G. Experiences with delayed primary closure of war wounds of the hand in Vietnam. J Bone Joint Surg Am 50:945, 1968.

33. Buxton, S.T. Gunshot wounds of the knee joint. Lancet 1:681, 1944.

34. Buzby, B.F. End results of excision of the elbow. Ann Surg 103:625, 1936.

35. Campbell, W.C. Arthroplasty of the elbow. Ann Surg 76:615, 1922.

36. Carr, C.R.; Turnipseed, D. Experiences with intramedullary fixation of compound femoral fractures in war wounds. J Bone Joint Surg Am 35:153, 1953.

37. Chait, L.A.; Cort, A.; Braun, S. Metacarpal reconstruction in compound contaminated injuries of the hand. Hand 13:152, 1981.

38. Chapman, M.W. The use of immediate internal fixation in open fractures. Orthop Clin North Am 11:579, 1980.

39. Chapman, M.W.; Blackman, R.C. Closed intramedullary nailing of femoral shaft fractures: A comparison of two techniques. J Bone Joint Surg Am 58:732, 1976.

40. Chapman, M.W.; Mahoney, M. The role of internal fixation in open fractures. Clin Orthop 138:120, 1979.

41. Christensen, K.; Jensen, E.M.; Noer, I. The reflex dystrophy syndrome: Response to treatment with systemic corticosteroids. Acta Chir Scand 148:653, 1982.

42. Chuinard, R.G.; Dabezies, E.J.; Gould, J.S.; et al. Intravenous reserpine for the treatment of reflex sympathetic dystrophy. South Med J 74:1481, 1981.

43. Compton, R.; Bucknell, A. Resection arthroplasty for comminuted olecranon fractures. Orthop Rev 18:189, 1989.

44. Connolly, J.F.; Wittaker, D.; Williams, E. Femoral and tibial fractures combined with injuries to the femoral or popliteal artery. J Bone Joint Surg Am 53:56, 1971.

45. Curtis, R.M. Capsulectomy of the interphalangeal joints of the fingers. J Bone Joint Surg Am 36:1219, 1954.

46. Cziffer, E.; Farkas, J.; Turchanyi, B. Management of potentially infected complex hand injuries. J Hand Surg [Am] 16:832, 1991.

47. Davis, G.L. Management of open wounds of joints during the Vietnam War: A preliminary study. Clin Orthop 68:3, 1970.

48. Debakey, M.E.; Simeone, F.A. Battle injuries of the arteries in World War II: An analysis of 2,471 cases. Ann Surg 123:534, 1946.

49. Deitch, E.A.; Grimes, W.R. Experience with 112 shotgun wounds to the extremities. J Trauma 24:600, 1984.

50. Deland, J.T.; Walker, P.S.; Sledge, C.S.; Faberov, A. Treatment of posttraumatic elbows with a new hinge-distractor. Orthopaedics 6:732, 1983.

51. DeMuth, W.E. Bullet velocity and design as determinants of wounding capability: An experimental study. J Trauma 6:222, 1966.

52. DeMuth, W.E. The mechanism of shotgun wounds. J Trauma 11:219, 1971.

53. DeMuth, W.E.; Nicholas, G.G.; Munger, B.L. Buckshot wounds. J Trauma 18:53, 1976.

54. DeMuth, W.E.; Smith, J.M. High velocity bullet wounds of muscle and bone: The basis of rational early treatment. J Trauma 6:744, 1966.

55. Dickey, R.L.; Barnes, B.C.; Kearns, R.J.; Tullos, H.S. Efficacy of antibiotics in low-velocity gunshot fractures. J Orthop Trauma 3:6, 1989.

56. Dickson, R.A. Rigid fixation of unstable metacarpal fractures using transverse K-wires bonded with acrylic resin. Hand 7:284, 1975.

57. Drapnas, T.; Hewitt, R.L.; Weichert, R.F.; et al. Civilian vascular injuries: A critical appraisal of three decades of management. Ann Surg 172:351, 1970.

58. Duncan, J.; Kettelkamp, D.B. Low-velocity gunshot wounds of the hand. Arch Surg 109:395, 1974.

59. Dzieman, A.J.; Medelson, J.A.; Lindsel, D. Comparison of the wound characteristics of some commonly encountered bullets. J Trauma 1:341, 1961.

60. Eaton, R.G.; Green, W.T. Epimysiotomy and fasciotomy in treatment of Volkmann's ischemic contracture. Orthop Clin North Am 3:175, 1972.

61. Elstrom, J.A.; Pankovich, A.M.; Egwele, R. Extra-articular low velocity gunshot fractures of the radius and ulna. J Bone Joint Surg Am 60:335, 1978.

62. Elton, R.C.; Bouzard, W.C. Gunshot and fragment wounds of the metacarpus. South Med J 68:833, 1975.

63. Enge, I.; Aakhus, T.; Evensen, A. Angiography in vascular injuries of the extremities. Acta Radiol Diagn 16:193, 1975.

64. Evans, G.R.D.; Luethke, R.W. A latissimus/scapula myo-osseous free flap based on the subscapular artery used for elbow reconstruction. Ann Plast Surg 30:175, 1993.

65. Fackler, M.L.; Surinchak, J.S.; Malinowski, J.A.; Bowen, R.E. Bullet fragmentation: A major cause of tissue disruption. J Trauma 24:35, 1984.

66. Ferraro, S.P., Jr.; Zinar, D.M. Management of gunshot fractures of the tibia. Orthop Clin North Am 26:181, 1995.

67. Finseth, F.; May, J.W.; Smith, R.J. Composite groin flap with iliac-bone flap for primary thumb reconstruction. J Bone Joint Surg Am 58:130, 1976.

68. Foerster, O. Handbuch der Neurologie, Part 2. Berlin, Springer, 1929.

69. Fowler, F.D.; Moser, M. Use of hexamethonium and Dibenzyline in diagnosis and treatment of causalgia. JAMA 161:1051, 1956.

70. Freeland, A.E.; Jabaley, M.E.; Burkhalter, W.E.; Chaves, A.M.V. Delayed primary bone grafting in the hand and wrist after traumatic bone loss. J Hand Surg [Am] 9:22, 1984.

71. Froimson, A.I.; Silva, J.E.; Richey, D.G. Cutis arthroplasty of the elbow. J Bone Joint Surg Am 58:863, 1976.

72. Gahtan, V.; Bramson, R.T.; Norman, J. The role of emergent arteriography in penetrating limb trauma. Am Surg 60:123, 1994.

73. Geissler, W.B.; Teasedall, R.D.; Tomasin, J.D.; Hughes, J.L. Management of low-velocity gunshot induced fractures. J Orthop Trauma 4:39, 1990.

74. Gelberman, R.H.; Vance, R.M.; Zakib, G.S. Fractures of the base of the thumb: Treatment with oblique traction. J Bone Joint Surg Am 61:260, 1979.

75. Gelberman, R.H.; Zakib, G.S.; Mubarak, S.J.; et al. Decompression of forearm compartment syndromes. Clin Orthop 134:225, 1978.

76. Gellman, H.; Kauffman, D.; Lenihan, M.; et al. An in vitro analysis of wrist motion: The effect of limited intercarpal arthrodesis and the contributions of the radiocarpal and midcarpal joints. J Hand Surg [Am] 13:378, 1988.

77. Genant, H.K.; Kozin, F.; Berkerman, C.; et al. The reflex sympathetic dystrophy syndrome. Radiology 117:21, 1975.

78. Georgiadis, G.M.; DeSilva, S.P. Reconstruction of skeletal defects in the forearm after trauma: Treatment with cement spacer and delayed cancellous bone grafting. J Trauma 38:910, 1995.

79. Giles, J.B.; DeLee, J.C.; Heckman, J.D. Supracondylar-intercondylar fractures of the femur treated with a supracondylar plate and lag screw. J Bone Joint Surg Am 64:864, 1982.

80. Glick, E.N.; Helal, B. Post-traumatic neurodystrophy: Treatment by corticosteroids. Hand 8:45, 1976.

81. Gonzalez, M.H.; McKay, W.; Hall, R.F. Low-velocity gunshot wounds of the metacarpal: Treatment by early stable fixation and bone grafting. J Hand Surg [Am] 18:267, 1993.

82. Gorman, J.F. Combat arterial trauma analysis of 106 limb-threatening injuries. Arch Surg 98:160, 1969.

83. Graham, W.C.; Riordan, D.C. Reconstruction of a metacarpal-phalangeal joint with a metatarsal transplant. J Bone Joint Surg Am 30:848, 1948.

84. Granberry, W.M. Gunshot wounds of the hand. Hand 5:220, 1973.

85. Greenfield, L.J.; Ebert, P.A. Technical considerations in the

management of axillobrachial arterial injuries. J Trauma 7:606, 1967.

86. Gristina, A.G.; Rovere, G.D. An in vitro study of the effects of metals used in internal fixation on bacterial growth and dissemination. J Bone Joint Surg Am 45:1104, 1963.
87. Gustilo, R.B.; Anderson, J.T. Prevention of infection in the treatment of one thousand twenty-five fractures of long bones. J Bone Joint Surg Am 58:453, 1976.
88. Halpern, A.A.; Greene, R.; Nichols, T.; Burton, D.S. Compartment syndrome of the interosseous muscles: Early recognition and treatment. Clin Orthop 140:23, 1979.
89. Hampton, O.P. The indications for débridements of gunshot (bullet) wounds of the extremities in civilian practice. J Trauma 1:368, 1961.
90. Hannington-Kiff, J.G. Relief of Sudeck's atrophy by regional intravenous guanethidine. Lancet 1:1132, 1977.
91. Hansraj, K.K.; Weaver, L.D.; Todd, A.O.; et al. Efficacy of ceftriaxone versus cefazolin in the prophylactic management of extra-articular cortical violation of bone due to low-velocity gunshot wounds. Orthop Clin North Am 26:9, 1995.
92. Hardin, W.D.; O'Connell, R.C.; Adinolfi, M.F.; Kerstein, M.D. Traumatic arterial injuries of the upper extremity: Determinants of disability. Am J Surg 150:266, 1985.
93. Hardy, E.G.; Tibbs, D.J. Acute ischemia in limb injuries. Br Med J 1:1001, 1960.
94. Harrell, B. Hollow-point ammunition injuries: Experience in a police group. J Trauma 19:115, 1979.
95. Hartl, W.H.; Klammer, H.L. Gunshot and blast injuries to the extremities. Acta Chir Scand 154:495, 1988.
96. Harvey, E.N.; McMillen, J.H.; Butler, E.G.; et al. Mechanism of wounding. In: Coates, J.B.; Beyer J.C., eds. Wound Ballistics. Washington, DC, Office of the Surgeon General, Department of the Army, 1962, p. 143.
97. Healy, W.L.; Brooker, A.F. Distal femoral fractures: Comparison of open and closed methods of treatment. Clin Orthop 174:166, 1983.
98. Hennessey, M.J.; Banks, H.H.; Leach, R.B.; Quigley, T.B. Extremity gunshot wounds and gunshot fractures in civilian practice. Clin Orthop 114:296, 1976.
99. Heppenstall, R.B. Fracture Treatment and Healing. Philadelphia, W.B. Saunders, 1980, p. 930.
100. Hill, S.D.; Lin, M.S.; Chandler, P.J. Reflex sympathetic dystrophy and electroacupuncture. Tex Med 87:76, 1991.
101. Hollman, M.W.; Horowitz, M. Femoral fractures secondary to low velocity missiles: Treatment with delayed intramedullary fixation. J Orthop Trauma 4:64, 1990.
102. Hopkinson, D.A.W.; Marshall, T.K. Firearm injuries. Br J Surg 54:344, 1967.
103. Horne, G. Supracondylar fractures of the humerus in adults. J Trauma 20:71, 1980.
104. Howland, W.S.; Ritchey, S.J. Gunshot fractures in civilian practice. J Bone Joint Surg Am 53:47, 1971.
105. Huelke, D.F.; Harger, J.H.; Buege, L.J.; et al. An experimental study in bioballistics: Femoral fractures produced by projectiles. J Biomech 1:97, 1968.
106. Huelke, D.F.; Harger, J.H.; Buege, L.J.; Dingman, H.G. An experimental study in bioballistics: Femoral fractures produced by projectiles. II: Shaft impacts. J Biomech 1:313, 1968.
107. Iannacone, W.M.; Bennett, F.S.; DeLong, W.G., Jr.; et al. Initial experience with the treatment of supracondylar femoral fractures using the supracondylar intramedullary nail: A preliminary report. J Orthop Trauma 8:322, 1994.
108. Jabaley, M.E.; Peterson, H.D. Early treatment of war wounds of the hand and forearm in Vietnam. Ann Surg 177:167, 1973.
109. Johnson, K.D.; Johnston, D.W.C.; Parker, B. Comminuted femoral shaft fractures: Treatment by roller traction, cerclage wires and an intramedullary nail, or an interlocking intramedullary nail. J Bone Joint Surg Am 66:1222, 1984.
110. Keggi, K.J.; Southwick, W.O. Early care of severe extremity wounds: A review of Vietnam experience and its civilian application. Instr Course Lect 19:183, 1970.
111. Kelly, G.L.; Eiseman, B. Civilian vascular injuries. J Trauma 15:507, 1975.
112. Kempf, I.; Grosse, A.; Beck, G. Closed locked intramedullary nailing. J Bone Joint Surg Am 67:709, 1985.

113. Kessler, I.; Hecht, O.; Baruch, A. Distraction-lengthening of digital rays in the management of the injured hand. J Bone Joint Surg Am 61:83, 1979.
114. Kinast, C.; Bulhofner, B.R.; Mast, J.; Ganz, R. Subtrochanteric fractures of the femur: Results of treatment with the 95° condylar blade plate. Clin Orthop 238:122, 1989.
115. Kline, D.G. Civilian gunshot wounds to the brachial plexus. J Neurosurg 70:166, 1989.
116. Kline, D.G.; Hacket, E.R. Reappraisal of timing for exploration of civilian peripheral nerve injuries. Surgery 78:54, 1975.
117. Knight, R.A.; Van Zandt, I.L. Arthroplasty of the elbow. J Bone Joint Surg Am 34:610, 1952.
118. Knudson, M.M.; Lewis, F.R.; Atkinson, K.; Neuhaus, A. The role of duplex ultrasound arterial imaging in patients with penetrating extremity trauma. Arch Surg 128:1033, 1993.
119. Kolmert, L.; Egund, N.; Persson, B.M. Internal fixation of supracondylar and bicondylar femoral fractures using a new semielastic device. Clin Orthop 181:204, 1983.
120. Kozin, F.; Ryan, L.M.; Carrera, G.F.; et al. The reflex sympathetic dystrophy syndrome (RSDS): III. Scintigraphic studies, further evidence for the treatment efficacy of systemic corticosteroids and proposed diagnostic criteria. Am J Med 70:23, 1981.
121. Kurzweg, F.T. Vascular injuries associated with penetrating injuries of the groin. J Trauma 20:214, 1980.
122. Lankford, L.L. Reflex sympathetic dystrophy. In: Omer, G.E., Jr.; Spinner, M., eds. Management of Peripheral Nerve Problems. Philadelphia, W.B. Saunders, 1980.
123. Leffers, D.; Chandler, R.W. Tibial fractures associated with civilian gunshot injuries. J Trauma 25:1059, 1985.
124. Leffert, R.D. Brachial Plexus Injuries. New York, Churchill Livingstone, 1985.
125. Lenihan, M.R.; Brien, W.W.; Gellman, H.; et al. Fractures of the forearm resulting from low-velocity gunshot wounds. J Orthop Trauma 6:32, 1992.
126. Leo, K.C. Use of electrical stimulation at acupuncture points for the treatment of reflex sympathetic dystrophy in a child: A case report. Phys Ther 63:957, 1983.
127. Leonard, M.H. Solution of lead by synovial fluid. Clin Orthop 64:255, 1969.
128. Leung, K.S.; Shen, W.Y.; So, W.S.; et al. Interlocking intramedullary nailing for supracondylar and intercondylar fractures of the distal part of the femur. J Bone Joint Surg Am 73:332, 1991.
129. Levy, A.S.; Wetzler, M.J.; Guttman, G.; et al. Treating gunshot femoral shaft fractures with immediate reamed intramedullary nailing. Orthop Rev 22:805, 1993.
130. Lindsey, D. The idolatry of velocity, or lies, damn lies, and ballistics. J Trauma 20:1068, 1980.
131. Little, J.M.; May, J. Civilian arterial injuries. Med J Aust 1:841, 1972.
132. Littler, J.W. Metacarpal reconstruction. J Bone Joint Surg Am 29:723, 1947.
133. Long, W.T.; Brien, E.W.; Boucree, J.B., Jr.; et al. Management of civilian gunshot injuries to the hip. Orthop Clin North Am 26:123, 1995.
134. Lord, R.S.; Irani, C.N. Assessment of arterial injury in limb trauma. J Trauma 14:1042, 1974.
135. Lucas, S.E.; Seligson, D.; Henry, S.L. Intramedullary supracondylar nailing of femoral fractures. Clin Orthop 296:200, 1993.
136. Luce, E.A.; Griffen, W.O. Shotgun injuries of the upper extremity. J Trauma 18:487, 1978.
137. Lumpkin, M.B.; Logan, W.D.; Couves, C.M.; Howard, J.M. Arteriography as an aid in the diagnosis and localization of acute arterial injuries. Ann Surg 147:353, 1950.
138. MacAusland, W.R.; Wyman, E.T. Fractures of the adult elbow. Instr Course Lect 24:169, 1975.
139. MacKinnon, S.E.; Holder, L.E. The use of the three-phase radionuclide scanning in the diagnosis of RSD. J Hand Surg [Am] 9:556, 1984.
140. Mandal, A.K.; Boitano, M.A. Principles and management of penetrating vascular injuries secondary to shotgun wounds. Am Surg 44:165, 1978.
141. Marcus, N.A.; Blair, W.F.; Shuck, J.M.; Omer, G.E. Low velocity gunshot wounds to extremities. J Trauma 20:1061, 1980.
142. Matsen, F.A. Compartment syndrome: A unified concept. Clin Orthop 113:8, 1975.

143. Maxwell, G.P.; Manson, P.N.; Hoopes, J.E. Reconstruction of traumatic defects utilizing arterial cutaneous, muscle, myocutaneous and free flaps. Am Surg 45:215, 1979.

144. McAndrew, M.P.; Johnson, K.D. Penetrating orthopedic injuries. Surg Clin North Am 71:297, 1991.

145. McCormick, P.; McCarthy, M.; Broadie, T.; et al. Role of antibiotics in the treatment of extremity gunshot wounds. Indiana Med 80:470, 1987.

146. McGreggor, I.A.; Jackson, I.T. The groin flap. Br J Plast Surg 25:3, 1972.

147. McLaren, A.C.; Dupont, J.A.; Schroeber, D.C. Open reduction internal fixation of supracondylar fractures above total knee arthroplasties using the intramedullary supracondylar rod. Clin Orthop 302:194, 1994.

148. McNamara, J.; Brief, D.K.; Beasley, W.; et al. Vascular injury in Vietnam combat casualties: Results of treatment at the 24th evacuation hospital. Ann Surg 178:143, 1973.

149. McNamara, J.; Brief, D.K.; Stremple, J.F.; Wright, J.K. Management of fractures with associated arterial injury in combat casualties. J Trauma 13:17, 1973.

150. Meyer, J.P.; Lim, L.T.; Schuler, J.J.; et al. Peripheral vascular trauma from close-range shotgun injuries. Arch Surg 120:1126, 1985.

151. Millesi, H. Surgical management of brachial plexus injuries. J Hand Surg [Am] 2:367, 1977.

152. Mitchell, S.W.; Morehouse, G.R.; Keen, W.W. Gunshot Wounds and Other Injuries of Nerves. Philadelphia, J.B. Lippincott, 1864, p. 100.

153. Mize, R.D.; Bucholz, R.W.; Grogan, D.P. Surgical treatment of displaced comminuted fractures of the distal end of the femur: An extensile approach. J Bone Joint Surg Am 64:871, 1982.

154. Moed, B.R.; Fakhouri, A.J. Compartment syndrome after low-velocity gunshot wounds to the forearm. J Orthop Trauma 5:134, 1991.

155. Mooney, V.; Nickel, V.L.; Harvey, J.P.; Snelson, R. Cast brace treatment for fractures of the distal part of the femur. J Bone Joint Surg Am 52:1563, 1979.

156. Morgan, M.M.; Spencer, A.D.; Hershey, F.B. Débridement of civilian gunshot wounds of soft tissue. J Trauma 1:354, 1961.

157. Morrey, B.F.; Askew, L.J.; An, K.L.; et al. A biomechanical study of normal functional elbow motion. J Bone Joint Surg Am 63:872, 1981.

158. Moss, C.M.; Veith, F.J.; Jason, R.; et al. Screening isotope angiography in arterial trauma. Surgery 86:881, 1979.

159. Mubarak, S.J.; Owen, C.A. Compartmental syndrome and its relation to the crush syndrome: A spectrum of disease. A review of 11 cases of prolonged forearm compression. Clin Orthop 113:81, 1973.

160. Muller, M.E.; Allgower, M.; Schneider, R.; et al. Manual of Internal Fixation, 2nd ed. New York, Springer-Verlag, 1970.

161. Neer, C.S.; Grantham, S.A.; Shelton, M.L. Supracondylar fractures of the adult femur: A study of 110 cases. J Bone Joint Surg Am 49:591, 1967.

162. Nelson, C.L.; Puskarich, C.L.; Marks, A. Gunshot wounds: Incidence, cost, and concepts of prevention. Clin Orthop 222:114, 1987.

163. Nelson, K.G.; Jolly, P.C.; Thomas, P.A. Brachial plexus injuries associated with missile wounds of the chest. J Trauma 8:268, 1968.

164. Nicholas, R.M.; McCoy, G.F. Immediate intramedullary nailing of femoral shaft fractures due to gunshots. Injury 26:257, 1995.

165. Norman, J.; Gahtan, V.; Franz, M.; Bramson, R. Occult vascular injuries following gunshot wounds resulting in long bone fractures of the extremities. Am Surg 61:146, 1995.

166. Nowotarski, P.; Brumback, R.J. Immediate interlocking nailing of fractures of the femur caused by low- to mid-velocity gunshots. J Orthop Trauma 8:134, 1994.

167. Omer, G.E. Injuries to nerves of the upper extremity. J Bone Joint Surg Am 56:1615, 1974.

168. Ordog, G.J.; Balasubramanium, S.; Wasserberger, J.S.; et al. Extremity gunshot wounds: Part I. Identification and treatment of patients at high risk of vascular injury. J Trauma 36:358, 1994.

169. Ordog, G.J.; Wasserberger, J.S.; Balasubramanium, S.; et al. Civilian gunshot wounds: Outpatient management. J Trauma 36:106, 1994.

170. Ordog, G.J.; Wasserberger, J.; Ackroyd, G. Hospital costs of firearm injuries. J Trauma 38:291, 1995.

171. Ordog, G.J.; Wasserberger, J.; Prakash, A.; Balasubramaniam, S. Civilian gunshot wounds: Determinants of injury. J Trauma 27:943, 1987.

172. Owens, J.C. Causalgia. Am Surg 23:636, 1957.

173. Paradies, L.H.; Gregory, C.F. The early treatment of close-range shotgun wounds to the extremities. J Bone Joint Surg Am 48:425, 1966.

174. Parisien, J.S. The management of gunshot fractures of the extremities. Bull Hosp Jt Dis 41:28, 1981.

175. Patman, R.D.; Thompson, J.E. Fasciotomy in peripheral vascular surgery: Report of 164 patients. Arch Surg 101:663, 1970.

176. Patzakis, M.J.; Harvey, J.P.; Tyler, D. The role of antibiotics in the management of open fractures. J Bone Joint Surg Am 56:532, 1974.

177. Peimer, C.A.; Smith, R.J.; Leffert, R.D. Distraction-fixation in the primary treatment of metacarpal bone loss. J Hand Surg [Am] 6:111, 1981.

178. Perry, D.J.; Sanders, D.P.; Nyirenda, C.D.; Lezine-Hanna, J.T. Gunshot wounds to the knee. Orthop Clin North Am 26:155, 1995.

179. Perry, M.D.; Thal, E.R.; Shires, G.T. Management of arterial injuries. Am Surg 173:403, 1971.

180. Pritchett, J.W. Supracondylar fractures of the femur. Clin Orthop 184:173, 1984.

181. Raju, S. Shotgun arterial injuries of the extremities. Am J Surg 138:421, 1979.

182. Rakolta, G.G.; Omer, G.E. Combat-sustained femoral nerve injuries. Surg Gynecol Obstet 128:813, 1969.

183. Ramamurthy, S. Electroacupuncture's role in the management of reflex sympathetic dystrophy. Tex Med 87:82, 1991.

184. Reinisch, J.F.; Winters, R.; Puckett, C.L. The use of the osteocutaneous groin flap in gunshot wounds of the hand. J Hand Surg [Am] 9:12, 1984.

185. Rich, N.M.; Baugh, J.H.; Hughes, C.W. Popliteal artery injuries in Vietnam. Am J Surg 118:531, 1969.

186. Rich, N.M.; Baugh, J.H.; Hughes, C.W. Acute arterial injuries in Vietnam: 1,000 cases. J Trauma 10:359, 1970.

187. Rich, N.M.; Metz, C.W.; Hutton, J.E.; et al. Internal versus external fixation of fractures with concomitant vascular injuries in Vietnam. J Trauma 11:463, 1971.

188. Rich, N.M.; Spencer, F.C. Vascular Trauma. Philadelphia, W.B. Saunders, 1978, p. 152.

189. Riseborough, E.J.; Radin, E.L. Intercondylar T-fractures of the humerus in the adult: A comparison of operative and nonoperative treatment in 29 cases. J Bone Joint Surg Am 51:130, 1969.

190. Robbs, J.V.; Baker, L.W. Major arterial trauma: Review of experience with 267 injuries. Br J Surg 65:532, 1978.

191. Rudavsky, A.Z. Isotope unmasks arterial injuries in need of repair. Hospital Tribune, December 1978, p. 9.

192. Russotti, G.M.; Sim, F.H. Missile wounds of the extremities: A current concepts review. Orthopaedics 8:1106, 1985.

193. Ryan, J.R.; Hensel, R.T.; Salciccioli, C.G.; Petersen, H.E. Fractures of the femur secondary to low-velocity gunshot wounds. J Trauma 21:160, 1981.

194. Rybeck, B.; Janzon, B. Absorption of missile energy in soft tissue. Acta Chir Scand 142:201, 1976.

195. Saletta, J.D.; Freeark, R.J. Vascular injuries associated with fractures. Orthop Clin North Am 1:93, 1970.

196. Salibian, A.H.; Anzel, S.H.; Mallerich, M.W.; Tesoro, V.E. Microvascular reconstruction for close-range gunshot injuries to the distal forearm. J Hand Surg [Am] 9:799, 1984.

197. Schatzker, J.; Horne, G.; Waddell, J. The Toronto experience with supracondylar fracture of the femur. Injury 6:113, 1974.

198. Schatzker, J.; Waddell, J.P. Subtrochanteric fractures of the femur. Orthop Clin North Am 11:539, 1980.

199. Scully, R.E.; Hughes, C.W. The pathology of ischemia of skeletal muscle in man: A description of early changes in muscles of the extremities following damage to major peripheral arteries on the battlefield. Am J Pathol 32:805, 1956.

200. Seddon, H.J. Three types of nerve injury. Brain 66:237, 1943.

201. Shahriaree, H.; Sajadi, K.; Silver, C.M.; Skeikholeslamzadeh, S. Excisional arthroplasty of the elbow. J Bone Joint Surg Am 61:922, 1979.

202. Shelbourne, K.D.; Brueckman, F.R. Rush pin fixation of supracondylar and intercondylar fractures of the femur. J Bone Joint Surg Am 64:161, 1970.

203. Shepard, G.H. High-energy, low-velocity close range shotgun wounds. J Trauma 20:1065, 1980.

204. Smith, R.F.; Elliott, J.P.; Hageman, J.H.; et al. Acute penetrating arterial injuries of the neck and limbs. Arch Surg 109:198, 1974.

205. Smith, R.F.; Szilagyi, E.; Elliot, J.R. Fractures of the long bones with arterial injury due to blunt trauma. Arch Surg 99:315, 1969.

206. Snyder, W.H.; Thal, E.R.; Bridges, R.; et al. The validity of normal arteriography in penetrating trauma. Arch Surg 113:424, 1978.

207. Staples, O.S. Supracondylar fractures of the humerus in children: Complications and problems associated with traction treatment. JAMA 168:730, 1958.

208. Starr, A.J.; Hunt, J.L.; Reinert, C.M. Treatment of femur fracture with associated vascular injury. J Trauma 40:17, 1996.

209. Steinbrocker, O.; Aroyos, T.G. The shoulder-hand syndrome: Present status as a diagnostic and therapeutic entity. Med Clin North Am 42:1533, 1958.

210. Stewart, M.J.; Sisk, T.D.; Wallace, S.L. Fractures of the distal third of the femur: A comparison of methods of treatment. J Bone Joint Surg Am 48:784, 1966.

211. Sunderland, S. Nerves and Nerve Injury. New York, Churchill Livingstone, 1972.

212. Sunderland, S. Pain mechanism in causalgia. J Neurol Neurosurg Psychiatry 39:471, 1976.

213. Swan, K.G.; Swan, R.C. Principles of ballistics applicable to the treatment of gunshot wounds. Surg Clin North Am 71:221, 1991.

214. Swanson, A.B. The treatment of war wounds of the hand. Clin Plast Surg 2:615, 1975.

215. Swartz, W.M. Immediate reconstruction of the wrist and hand with a free osteocutaneous groin flap. J Hand Surg [Am] 9:18, 1984.

216. Taylor, M.T.; Schlegel, D.M.; Habeggar, E.D. Bullet embolism. Am J Surg 114:457, 1967.

217. Thoresby, F.P.; Darlow, H.M. The mechanics of primary infection of bullets. Br J Surg 54:359, 1967.

218. Thoresen, B.O.; Alho, A.; Ekeland, A.; et al. Interlocking intramedullary nailing in femoral shaft fractures. J Bone Joint Surg Am 67:1313, 1985.

219. Tornetta, P., III; Tiburzi, D. Antegrade interlocked nailing of distal femoral fractures after gunshot wounds. J Orthop Trauma 8:220, 1994.

220. Urbaniak, J.R.; Black, K.E. Cadaveric elbow allografts: A six year experience. Clin Orthop 197:131, 1985.

221. Visser, P.A.; Hemreck, A.S.; Pierce, G.E.; et al. Prognosis of nerve injuries incurred during acute trauma to peripheral arteries. Am J Surg 140:598, 1980.

222. Waddell, J.P. Subtrochanteric fractures of the femur: A review of 130 patients. J Trauma 19:582, 1979.

223. Weingarner, F.G.; Baker, A.G.; Bascom, J.F.; Jackson, G.F. Delayed vascular complications in Vietnam casualties. J Trauma 10:867, 1967.

224. Wilson, C.E. The management of gunshot wounds of the extremities. Nebr Med J 51:132, 1966.

225. Winquist, R.A.; Hansen, S.T. Comminuted fractures of the femur treated by intramedullary nailing. Orthop Clin North Am 11:633, 1980.

226. Winquist, R.A.; Hansen, S.T.; Clawson, D.K. Closed intramedullary nailing of femoral fractures. J Bone Joint Surg Am 66:529, 1984.

227. Wiss, D.A.; Brien, W.W. Subtrochanteric fractures of the femur: Results of treatment by interlocking nailing. Clin Orthop 283:231, 1992.

228. Wiss, D.A.; Brien, W.W.; Becker, V., Jr. Interlocking nailing for the treatment of femoral fractures due to gunshot wounds. J Bone Joint Surg Am 73:598, 1991.

229. Wiss, D.A.; Fleming, C.H.; Matta, J.M.; Clark, D. Comminuted and rotationally unstable fractures of the femur treated with an interlocking nail. Clin Orthop 212:35, 1986.

230. Wiss, D.A.; Gellman, H. Gunshot wounds to the musculoskeletal system. In: Browner, B.D., ed. Skeletal Trauma. Philadelphia, W.B. Saunders, 1992, p. 367.

231. Wiss, D.A.; Matta, J.M.; Sima, W.; Reber, L. Subtrochanteric fractures of the femur. Orthopedics 8:793, 1985.

232. Wiss, D.A.; Missakian, N. Supracondylar fractures of the femur. Orthopedics 8:921, 1985.

233. Wolf, A.W.; Benson, D.R.; Shoji, H.; et al. Autosterilization in low-velocity bullets. J Trauma 18:63, 1978.

234. Woloszyn, J.T.; Uitvlugt, G.M.; Castle, M.E. Management of civilian gunshot fractures of the extremities. Clin Orthop 226:247, 1988.

235. Wright, D.G.; Levin, J.S.; Esterhai, J.L.; Heppenstall, R.B. Immediate internal fixation of low-velocity gunshot–related femoral fractures. J Trauma 35:678, 1993.

236. Zipperman, H.H. Acute arterial injuries in the Korean War: A statistical study. Ann Surg 139:1, 1954.

237. Zipperman, H.H. The management of soft tissue missile wounds in war and peace. J Trauma 1:361, 1961.

CHAPTER 16

Pathologic Fractures

Alan M. Levine, M.D.
Albert J. Aboulafia, M.D., F.A.C.S.

Pathologic fractures occur as a result of an underlying process that weakens the mechanical properties of bone. The causes of pathologic fracture include neoplastic and non-neoplastic conditions. The most common non-neoplastic causes of pathologic fracture are osteoporosis and metabolic bone disease.

Neoplastic causes include metastases as well as primary benign and malignant tumors. Skeletal metastases are the most common neoplastic cause of pathologic fracture. They may be discovered as an incidental finding when a patient is evaluated for an unrelated reason such as trauma; they may cause symptoms such as pain; or they may result in pathologic fracture, prompting medical attention. With the prolonged survival of many patients with solid tumors, the absolute incidence of symptomatic bone metastasis has increased over the last several decades. However, the relative incidence of pathologic fracture secondary to metastatic disease has begun to decrease with the use of bisphosphonates.[17, 47, 145] Fractures that are pathologic and result from the involvement of bone by metastatic tumor are biologically different from fractures that result from non-neoplastic conditions such as trauma. Therefore, the treatment principles for pathologic fractures resulting from neoplastic causes differ from those for fractures resulting from trauma (Table 16–1). The assumption that pathologic fractures resulting from neoplasm can be treated in a similar fashion to nonpathologic fractures often produces a less than satisfactory result for the patient with a neoplastic pathologic fracture (Fig. 16–1). Moreover, the goal of treating a fracture of traumatic origin is to maximize the potential for fracture healing while minimizing the complications. The goal of treating pathologic fractures is to return the patient as rapidly as possible to maximal function, which may or may not result in fracture healing.

The skeleton is the third most common site of involvement by metastatic disease (after the lung and the liver), in terms of both frequency and complications arising from metastatic involvement. Because the incidence of tumors metastatic to bone is far greater than the incidence of primary malignant bone tumors, fractures from metastatic lesions are more common than those from primary tumors. Overall, symptomatic skeletal metastases develop in approximately 20% of patients with metastatic disease from solid tumors,[62] although autopsy series have suggested that the overall incidence of metastases is closer to 70%.[97, 168] Therefore, it is apparent that many patients who die of cancer have skeletal metastases that remain asymptomatic and require no treatment. The incidence of skeletal metastasis varies according to tumor type. The most common tumors that metastasize to the skeleton include tumors of the breast,[49] prostate,[22, 24] thyroid, kidney, and lung. Autopsy series have shown rates of bone metastasis may be as high as 80% in breast cancer, 85% in carcinoma of the prostate, 50% in thyroid carcinoma, 44% in lung carcinoma, and 30% in renal cell carcinoma.[23] Although patients with any type of neoplasm can develop bone metastasis, more than 75% of those seen are from breast, prostate, lung, or kidney tumors.[29] Bone metastases can develop in almost any tumor histology, however, including gastrointestinal and genitourinary carcinomas, melanoma, and even chordoma.[1, 153]

Primary bone tumors, benign and malignant, may manifest initially with pathologic fracture. Benign lesions that may become evident initially with pathologic fracture include solitary bone cysts, aneurysmal bone cysts, nonossifying fibromas, fibrous dysplasia, and giant cell tumor (Fig. 16–2). Pathologic fracture may be the initial manifestation in as many as 10% of patients with malignant bone tumors such as osteogenic sarcoma and chondrosarcoma, although pain is the most common symptom. The treatment of pathologic fractures of long bones resulting from benign tumors depends on the histology and stage of the tumor. In active, nonaggressive lesions (stage 2) fracture healing generally occurs in a fashion similar to that of nonpathologic conditions even before and certainly after local control of the tumor has been achieved. In most bone cyst cases, local tumor control can be accomplished with intralesional procedures such as curettage. Even in aggressive (stage 3) benign

TABLE 16–1 ·
Principles of Management

1. Pathologic fractures differ dramatically from traumatic fractures, and the role of fixation is therefore different.
2. Diagnosis requires two orthogonal radiographic views.
3. Bisphosphonates decrease the rate of pathologic fractures.
4. Nonoperative treatment rarely constitutes acceptable treatment of pelvic and extremity lesions and fractures.
5. In determining therapy, the origin of the patient's pain is important.
6. The method of fixation should allow immediate mobilization and not require fracture healing to achieve stability.
7. For patients with metastases to spine and resultant neurologic deficit, the surgical approach should directly decompress the spinal cord.

· ·

tumors, spontaneous fracture healing may occur. However, because of the amount of bone removed to achieve local control and the use of adjuvant methods to achieve tumor control, healing of large osseous defects usually requires grafting and internal fixation. The treatment of pathologic fractures resulting from primary malignant bone tumors is integrated into the definitive treatment of the tumor, which most commonly requires resection of the bone, so fracture healing is not an issue (Fig. 16–3).

The focus of this chapter is on the management of pathologic fractures resulting primarily from metastatic tumors and not primary tumors other than myeloma. Although myeloma is technically a primary bone tumor, it is a systemic disease, and, as such, the orthopaedic management of pathologic fractures resulting from myeloma is more closely related to the management of metastatic lesions than to that of primary bony tumors. This section emphasizes the differences in biologic behavior of pathologic and traumatic fractures. These biologic differences necessitate a treatment approach intended to maximize benefit and minimize complications for the patient with metastatic bone disease.

The time from initial diagnosis of the primary tumor to the development of the initial osseous metastasis can vary greatly and often has prognostic significance. In some

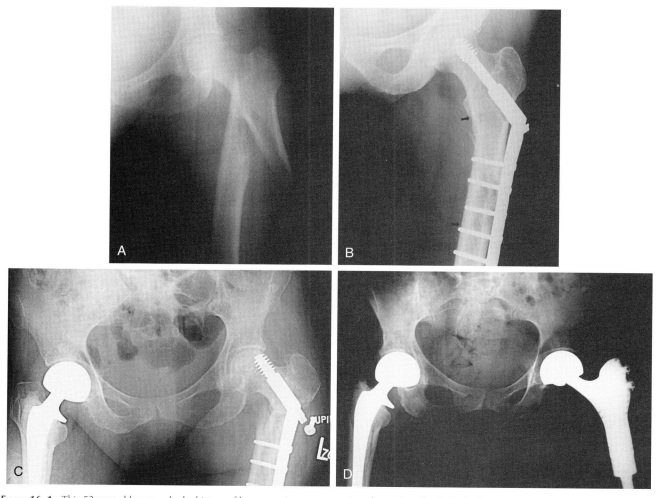

FIGURE 16–1. This 52-year-old woman had a history of breast carcinoma metastatic to bone. Initially, she had a long stem–cemented hemiarthroplasty on the right for a pathologic femoral neck fracture with an ipsilateral midshaft lesion. One year later, she had a pathologic subtrochanteric fracture on the left (*A*) and was treated as if it were a traumatic lesion (*B*), with a sliding hip screw without augmentation in the area of the defect (*arrows*). The patient was allowed partial weight bearing on crutches for 6 months but had failure of the construct with shortening and pain at 9 months (*C*) as a result of delayed healing and poor bone stock. She required a revision by resection of the collapsed segment and reconstruction with a segmental replacement (*D*), which may not have been necessary had the pathologic fracture been treated initially by a method that was rigid enough not to require healing to achieve stability.

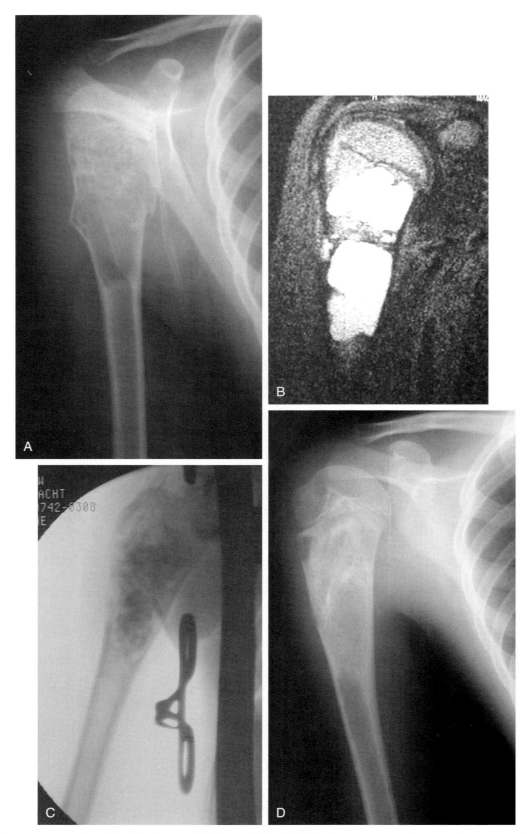

FIGURE 16–2. Anteroposterior radiographs of the humerus of a 12-year-old boy (*A*). He had undergone steroid injection for a unicameral bone cyst and then sustained a pathologic fracture. After the fracture healed, the cyst did not resolve (*B*), as demonstrated on magnetic resonance imaging, and the patient underwent percutaneous filling with calcium sulfate pellets (*C*). Within 3 months, there was a complete resolution of the lesion (*D*).

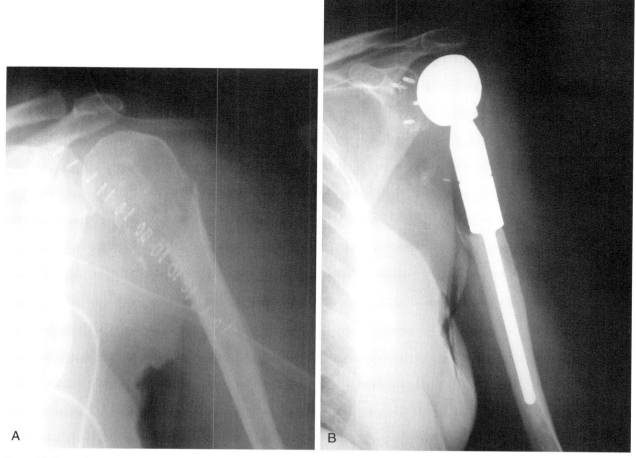

FIGURE 16–3. *A,* This anteroposterior radiograph demonstrates a pathologic fracture of the proximal humerus in a 62-year-old woman. Needle biopsy was nondiagnostic, demonstrating only hematoma, but the open biopsy was interpreted as a leiomyosarcoma. *B,* En bloc resection and prosthetic replacement adequately dealt with the pathologic fracture through this tumor.

patients, bone metastasis may be the first evidence of recurrent disease, even after a prolonged disease-free interval. This is especially true for patients with breast or thyroid cancer, whose first sign of relapse may be a symptomatic bone lesion 10 to 15 years after the diagnosis of the primary tumor. Survival rates for patients with osseous metastatic disease are dependent on several factors, including extent of visceral disease, morbidities, and histology.[24, 49, 152] Median survival for patients with bone metastasis from thyroid carcinoma is 48 months, from prostate carcinoma 40 months, from breast cancer 24 months, and from melanoma and lung cancer 6 months.[31, 129] In patients with breast cancer the mean survival of those with only bone metastases approaches 30 months, but in those who have visceral involvement and osseous metastasis, median survival is only 18 months.[133, 149, 150, 196] The extent of bone metastasis has prognostic importance as well. Patients who present with solitary renal metastasis may survive for many years, especially if they are treated with wide excision.[188] But survival is shortened with presentation of multiple lesions or pathologic fracture.[61]

The spread of cancer is usually by one of two mechanisms: contiguous extension or hematogenous dis-

semination. More than 100 years ago Paget recognized that tumor metastasis involved more than simply the random act of deposition of tumor in a site distant from the primary one.[144] He proposed the "seed and soil" hypothesis, recognizing that properties inherent in the tumor and the host influenced the development of a metastatic focus.

Since then, a variety of factors have been identified that influence the site of bony metastases.[176] Three basic but complex processes are significant in the development of skeletal metastasis.[137] The first process involves the ability of the tumor cells to leave the primary site and travel to a distant site. The initial steps involved in this process include the loss of cell contact inhibition and the production of tumor angiogenesis factor and angiogenin. The modulation of cell contact inhibition is regulated by cell adhesion molecules (CAMs).[130, 142] CAMs regulate the tumor cells' adhesion properties. For tumor cells to separate from the primary site, CAM expression must be down-regulated.[88] Later, CAM expression must take place for tumor cells to accumulate at a distant site.[136] In addition to loss of cell contact inhibition, tumor cells must have a route to gain access into the vascular or lymphatic system to metastasize. Neovascularization takes place with the production of tumor angiogenesis factor and angiogenin by the tumor cells. Tumor cells ultimately cross the vascular basement membrane and gain access to the lymphatic and venous systems.

The second process involves anatomic properties of the host that favor metastatic deposits at selected sites. The most common sites of skeletal metastasis include the spine, pelvis, proximal femur, and humerus. Metastases distant to the elbow or knee are uncommon and are usually associated with a primary lung tumor. These more common sites of skeletal metastasis share the common property of being sites of hematopoietic marrow. These areas are rich in vascular sinuses and allow tumor cells in the circulation access to the marrow.[6] There are regional affinities, especially in the spine, based on primary tumor location (prostate to lumbar, breast to thoracic). Studies attempting to determine the route of dissemination of spinal metastasis (arterial or venous) have not shown differences to suggest a preferred route of metastasis. Batson's plexus[6] probably plays a significant role in the dissemination of tumors to bone (e.g., from prostate or breast).[40] Circulatory distribution alone does not predict metastatic distribution, because the bone receives only about 10% of cardiac output but has a significantly higher metastatic prevalence than other sites that have higher blood flow.[100] Early work demonstrated that injection of malignant cells that have a preference for lung tissue into animals in whom the lung tissue had been transplanted into a subcutaneous location still resulted in metastatic lesions to that tissue. This also has been demonstrated in bone with the Walker carcinosarcoma, which has a propensity to form osseous metastases.

Therefore, it seems that a third factor must be involved in the development of skeletal metastasis, which is the response of the host to the tumor cells. Using Paget's terminology, this is the "soil" portion of the "seed and soil" hypothesis.[144] For tumor cells to survive within bone, they must have a mechanism to leave the vasculature and gain access to the bone. They do so via the production of proteolytic enzymes, type IV collagenase, and metalloproteinases. Osteocalcin produced by bone protein acts on tumor cells as a chemotactic agent. Other chemotactic substances in bone may be derived from resorbing bone or collagen type I peptides.[9, 143] Some investigators suggest that this factor may be related to osteoclasts, because any bone resorption is achieved through stimulation of those cells. However, the relation between the bone resorbing factor and chemotactic activity remains unclear.[112] Without these and other processes taking place, tumor cells lodged in bone cannot survive. Interventions aimed at interrupting these pathways to control skeletal metastasis are under investigation.[17]

Bone metastasis can be lytic, blastic, or mixed.[100] Although some tumor types are typically blastic, lytic, or mixed, there is variability within tumor types and even within the same patient. Two main types of new bone formation occur in response to tumor: stromal and reactive.[66] The formation of stromal new bone, in response to tumor invasion is most likely mediated by humoral factors that stimulate osteoblasts. Reactive new bone formation is somewhat simpler to understand: bone is laid down in response to a stress on weakened bone. Certain tumors (i.e., myelomas, lymphomas, and leukemias) do not seem to stimulate reactive new bone even though they produce obvious osteoclastic bone destruction. Other tumors (e.g., prostate cancers) tend to form a significant amount of stromal new bone as part of the process, independent of osteoclastic activity. The osteolysis of bone metastasis can be mediated by two potential mechanisms: the osteoclast, which has been demonstrated in a number of experimental models,[64] and late-stage bone destruction, with a disappearance of osteoclasts. In the latter case, malignant cells may be responsible for the bone destruction, possibly as a result of their ability to produce lytic enzymes. Human breast cancer has been shown to directly resorb bone.[136] This has also been demonstrated in lung carcinoma, epidermoidomas and adenocarcinomas, and, less commonly, in small-cell anaplastic and large-cell tumors.[36]

Historically, surgical treatment of skeletal metastasis was directed primarily at lesions affecting the femur. This was likely because of the major morbidity and loss of function associated with metastasis in this location. The risk of fracture and the ease of prophylactic treatment are greater in the femur than in other locations. The incidence of pathologic fracture in patients with bone metastases is only 4%, but the incidence in those with breast cancer with lesions in the femur may be as high as 30%, depending on the location within the femur.[61] The distribution of skeletal metastasis within a given bone is not random. Proximal femur lesions are more common than are distal lesions. Lesions distal to the elbow and distal to the knee are relatively rare and are associated most commonly with lung primaries. With improved surgical techniques, interest in the last 15 years has been focused on the treatment of symptomatic metastases affecting not only the femur but also other long bones, the pelvis, and the spine. Vertebral metastases occur most commonly in patients with breast, lung, prostate,[5] and renal cell carcinoma[104]; symptomatic metastases occur in approximately one third of those patients. When symptomatic spine lesions occur, patients most commonly present with back pain. Lumbar and thoracic involvement are nearly equal in frequency, and cervical involvement is less common. Cord compression occurs in about 20% of all patients with symptomatic vertebral metastasis.

Patients with skeletal metastasis are most commonly identified when they seek medical attention because of pain. The mechanism by which skeletal metastasis causes pain is not completely understood. When osteolysis has taken place and has weakened the bone, gross fracture or microscopic fracture is most likely the cause of symptoms. However, in purely blastic lesions, or in lesions without significant lysis leading to mechanical compromise of the bone, this explanation is insufficient to account for the patient's symptoms. Direct tumor invasion with the secretion of humoral factors may play a role in this group of patients. In most cases, once a metastatic focus becomes symptomatic, there is usually some degree of resorption.

Identifying the underlying cause of bone pain in patients with metastatic disease is critical, irrespective of whether the metastases is in the long bones, pelvis, or spine. The pain may be from the tumor volume, from compression of adjacent neural structures, and from compromised structural integrity of the bone. Depending on the tumor type, lesions that have not caused significant cortical destruction may respond well to radiation or chemotherapy. Once significant osseous destruction has taken place, especially in the pelvis and spine, the tumor is less likely to respond to radiation or chemotherapy. In most cases, patients usually have symptoms before pathologic fracture occurs. This is especially true for tumors located in the long bones and pelvis. Pathologic fracture without antecedent symptoms is more common in the spine and ribs. However, development of neurologic compromise generally does not occur without antecedent history of pain. Given the increased morbidity associated with the operative treatment of pathologic fractures compared with that of the prophylactic fixation of an impending fracture, it is preferable to attempt to diagnose the lesions at risk before fracture.

Patients with spinal metastasis may be asymptomatic or may present with pain, neurologic impairment, or both. In the case of neurologic impairment, the cause is usually secondary to epidural metastases but may also be caused by peripheral nerve involvement. These may either be radicular in nature or related to cord compression, resulting in partial or total paralysis. Less frequently, gross instability and vertebral collapse cause neurologic impairment. Overt fracture with metastatic lesions should occur infrequently. The symptomatic patient should be evaluated carefully and appropriate patients selected for prophylactic fixation or vertebroplasty before fracture occurs.

DIAGNOSIS OF BONE METASTASES

Patients who are ultimately diagnosed with skeletal metastasis can be divided into three groups. The first group includes patients with a known history of cancer who seek medical attention because of an occult or obvious painful osseous lesion. The second group includes patients who have a known cancer diagnosis and who have undergone staging studies that identified an asymptomatic skeletal lesion. The third includes patients who seek medical attention because of a symptomatic osseous lesion and are diagnosed as having a skeletal metastasis as the first presentation of an undiagnosed carcinoma. For all three groups, the first step in making the diagnosis includes a careful history. For the first group of patients, it is especially important to have a high degree of suspicion of the possibility of metastatic disease to bone as the cause of the patient's symptoms. Patients commonly seek medical attention because of musculoskeletal pain involving the hip, knee, neck, or back. All too often, the patient's symptoms are evaluated as an isolated problem without obtaining a careful history.

In any patient with a prior cancer diagnosis, the possibility of a skeletal metastasis as the cause of the patient's symptoms should be considered. Commonly, the physician does not obtain and the patient does not offer the history of prior cancer diagnosis. In some cases, the disease-free interval may be so long that the patient, physician, or both, may feel that the patient is "cured" and the possibility of metastasis after so great a time is not possible. Unfortunately, skeletal metastasis after a long disease-free interval is not uncommon, especially for patients with breast and thyroid carcinomas in which skeletal metastasis may develop more than 10 years after the primary cancer diagnosis. The history should include all prior surgeries and the histologic diagnosis Often patients may be uncertain of the final diagnosis. This is especially true for patients who have had "a skin lesion removed" or "breast surgery" and are uncertain as to the final diagnosis. The history is helpful not only in patients with skeletal metastasis and a prior cancer diagnosis but also in many without a cancer diagnosis.

In patients older than 40 years who present with pain and a radiographically destructive bone lesion, the most common diagnosis is still an osseous metastasis. A strong family history or a history of risk factors such as smoking or exposure to carcinogens (i.e., tobacco, asbestos, radiation) may direct the physician to a likely location of a primary tumor. A complete review of systems that focuses on weight loss and respiratory, endocrine, and genitourinary symptoms may strengthen the suspicion. Flank pain and hematuria should raise the possibility of an underlying renal cancer, just as a persistent cough and hemoptysis should suggest an underlying lung carcinoma. Serum and urine studies play only a modest role in evaluating patients with a suspected metastasis without a prior cancer diagnosis. Serum and urine protein electrophoresis will identify most patients with myeloma, and an elevated prostate specific antigen (PSA) may identify some patients with metastatic prostate carcinoma. Tumor markers[10, 43] such as carcinoembryonic antigen (CEA), CA 125, and CA 19-9 lack specificity and are most useful in monitoring response to treatment.

A variety of imaging modalities are now available for evaluating patients with suspected or known metastatic disease. These include plain radiographs, computed tomography (CT), technetium bone scan, single photon emission computed tomography (SPECT), magnetic resonance imaging (MRI), and positron emission tomography (PET).[102, 166, 169] Plain radiographs of the symptomatic area must include good quality films in at least two planes, preferably at right angles to each other (Fig. 16–4). Standard anteroposterior (AP) and lateral views are usually sufficient, although in certain instances these two views may not be completely appropriate. Because destruction of at least 50% of normal cancellous bone is required to show a lytic defect in a long bone, early detection of metastasis by plain roentgenography is not always possible. Lesions in certain areas such as the supra-acetabular region may not be evident on plain radiographs and may require specialized views (e.g., Judet views) (Fig. 16–5). Inadequate plain radiographs may result when the physician does not consider that the patient's symptoms may be secondary to referred pain. A patient with a hip lesion may complain of knee pain, and the lesion may go unrecognized until radiographs of the hip are obtained. This problem can usually be avoided by performing an appropriate physical examination to include the entire extremity.

If plain radiographs do not identify the patient's source of pain and the suspicion of skeletal metastasis remains high, then radioisotope evaluation of the skeleton should be performed. Radiographs are then obtained for follow-up

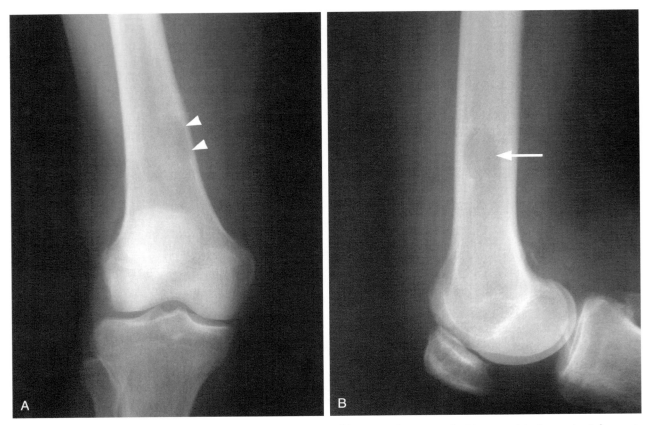

FIGURE 16–4. Anteroposterior (AP) and lateral radiographs of a 70-year-old woman who presented with severe right knee pain. Subsequent positron emission tomography and computed tomography scans demonstrated a large lung mass with a pathologic diagnosis of non–small-cell carcinoma of the lung. These radiographs demonstrate the necessity for obtaining two views of any cylindrical bone to demonstrate a lesion. The patient's AP radiograph (*A*) does not clearly show the lytic lesion in the distal femur (*arrowheads*), but the lateral radiograph (*B*) clearly demonstrates a lytic lesion (*arrow*).

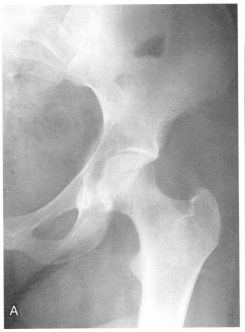
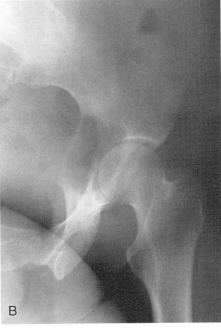

FIGURE 16–5. Radiographs of the hip of a 39-year-old woman with carcinoma of the breast and severe hip pain. The patient initially underwent radiation therapy after a bone scan demonstrated slight activity in the supra-acetabular region and in the proximal femur, but the radiographs were interpreted as negative. *A*, The anteroposterior radiograph of the pelvis suggested the presence of a lytic lesion in the area of the acetabulum. Judet views were necessary to fully demonstrate the extent of the lytic lesion. *B*, As seen on the oblique view of the iliac bone, the lesion occupies the superior aspect and the posterior lip of the acetabulum.

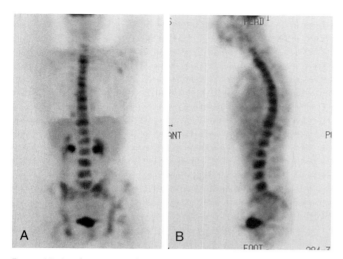

FIGURE 16–6. This 34-year-old woman with a known history of breast cancer had a rising carcinoembryonic antigen level with a negative bone scan and computed tomography scan of the chest and abdomen. *A* and *B,* Positron emission tomography showed diffuse bone metastases involving multiple areas of the body (PET scan).

of areas of increased activity on bone scans. Various imaging modalities have a proven utility for the evaluation of patients with skeletal metastasis. The most appropriate sequence of evaluating patients with suspected skeletal metastasis depends on the presence or absence of a clinical history of cancer. In most patients with a prior cancer diagnosis, the primary imaging study used for screening for potential osseous metastasis is the technetium bone scan. Its timing and application vary depending on the relative risk of skeletal metastasis, the presence or absence of pathologic fracture, interval in the treatment cycle, and the suspected tumor histology. The sensitivity of a technetium 99m bone scan is low with certain histologies such as myeloma and renal cell carcinoma. It may also be misleading in women with osseous metastases from breast carcinoma who have a flare on bone scan after treatment with improving disease status.

Technetium 99m bone scans have a sensitivity of 95% to 97% for the detection of skeletal metastases.[16, 28, 54, 70] Despite their sensitivity for diagnosing bone metastases, they are not without limitations.[95, 101, 105, 175] One limitation of the bone scan is that it lacks specificity and may yield false-positive results in non-neoplastic conditions such as osteoporotic fractures, Paget's disease, or even osteoarthritis. Similarly, some lesions, such as myeloma and extremely aggressive osteolytic tumors, produce extensive destruction without the reparative processes detected on bone scan. In such instances the technetium bone scan may appear normal or even photopenic.[105] Some of these tumors can be better evaluated with a gallium scan.[105] The utility of the bone scan includes its role as a staging study at the time of initial diagnosis for patients with carcinoma who are at high risk for asymptomatic osseous metastases and who may be appropriate candidates for more aggressive systemic therapy.

PET scanning has been shown to be a useful screening tool in patients with skeletal metastasis from lung cancer,

prostate cancer, melanoma, and other primary lesions. It has the advantage over bone scan in potentially identifying nonosseous sites of metastases.[102, 166, 170] PET is also helpful in that a single test can evaluate all sites of metastatic disease with extreme sensitivity (Fig. 16–6).

For lesions of the pelvis, where there is superimposition of structures, plain radiography is often inadequate to assess for the presence of skeletal lesion. A CT scan may be necessary to confirm the presence of a lesion suggested by the bone scan (Fig. 16–7). A Foley catheter should be placed within the bladder before bone scan imaging to avoid obscuring the sacral area by radiopharmaceuticals accumulated in the bladder. MRI is even more sensitive than bone scintigraphy in the detection of bone metastases.[54, 70, 95, 96] Although it is sensitive to bone marrow abnormalities, MRI remains nonspecific and in many cases cannot differentiate benign from malignant lesions.[123] Nonspecific marrow changes secondary to radiation or chemotherapy treatments, or both, may yield false-positive readings. Because of the expense and lack of specificity, its use in evaluation of metastatic lesions of the extremities and pelvis should be restricted to the delineation of difficult lesions or the assessment of soft tissue masses accompanying bone lesions.

The evaluation of metastatic lesions and fractures about the spine can be complicated and requires a progressive and systematic approach. In the patient who presents with symptomatic spinal metastasis, two questions must be answered by the diagnostic tests. The first is the extent of metastatic involvement of the particular spinal level and any resultant instability; the second is the presence or absence of neural compression. Plain radiographs may, in both AP and lateral projections, give some indication of the extent of metastatic involvement but are notoriously inaccurate (Fig. 16–8). If one half of the vertebra is present and the other side is totally absent, the lateral radiograph may appear relatively normal.

The CT scan gives the most accurate assessment of vertebral destruction (Fig. 16–9).[20] Previously, technetium bone scan was used not to evaluate extent of disease at any given level[156] but to assess other potential levels of involvement. MRI has replaced the bone scan in the evaluation of metastatic disease of the spine because it is able to delineate both the number of affected levels and the presence or absence of cord compression. Midsagittal images allow a rapid evaluation of the entire spine; this is also helpful in patients in whom more than one level may be involved (Fig. 16–10).

In the spine, however, MRI has been shown to greatly affect treatment planning for patients with spinal metastasis.[32] This is especially true for patients with spinal cord compression. Cook and co-workers found that in 25% of patients with a sensory level, MRI demonstrated that the site of cord compression was four or more segments distal or three or more segments proximal to the sensory level.[34] With the use of MRI, multiple areas of cord compression were identified in 39% of patients. Other studies have confirmed that MRI of the entire spine is the imaging modality of choice for patients with a history of carcinoma and suspected spinal canal metastases. MRI also has the ability to identify lesions that are extremely destructive, such as myeloma or renal cell carcinoma, that may not be

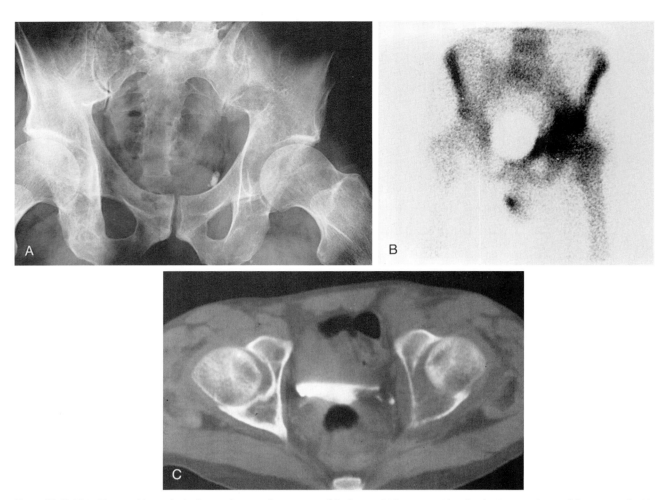

FIGURE 16–7. This 53-year-old man had a known history of carcinoma of the lung, which was considered to be in remission until he presented with left leg pain. The patient's workup for metastatic disease of the spine was negative. *A*, An anteroposterior view of his pelvis was initially interpreted as negative. However, it demonstrates loss of the subchondral plate of the acetabulum and a large but diffuse-appearing lytic lesion in the supra-acetabular and posterior acetabular regions. *B*, A bone scan demonstrated diffuse uptake about the hip on the anterior view. *C*, Computed tomography (CT) was necessary for accurate delineation of the lesion. The CT scan demonstrates significant involvement of the posterior lip of the acetabulum and the supra-acetabular region, with partial loss of the subchondral plate.

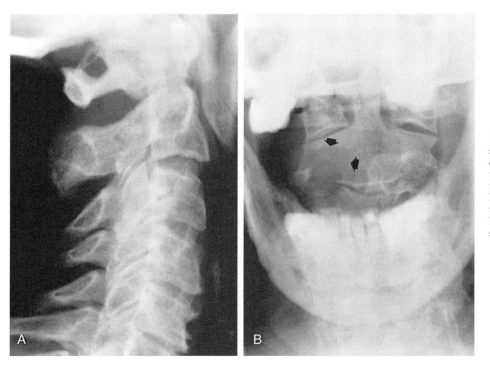

FIGURE 16–8. This 69-year-old man with squamous cell carcinoma of the lung experienced severe neck pain. Antero-posterior radiographs over a 6-month period were repeatedly negative. The large metastatic lesion was not revealed until an open-mouth view (*B*) showed a large lesion (*arrows*) that had not been seen on the lateral radiograph (*A*).

apparent on bone scan. Its shortcomings are that it does not allow accurate delineation of the nature of the metastatic involvement and that it cannot detail the extent of bone destruction (i.e., it does not accurately differentiate a healed metastatic fracture from a nonhealed fracture or an osteoporotic compression fracture).[123]

In patients who have neurologic signs and symptoms and are candidates for surgical intervention, the use of a combination of diagnostic studies is most helpful. Imaging studies are selected to identify the level, extent, nature, and direction of neural compression and to identify additional noncontiguous levels of involvement that may require treatment. Previously, a CT-myelogram was used to determine the nature and extent of the block and to give

accurate definition of the residual vertebral bone.[156] Currently, MRI demonstrates the areas of tumor involvement of marrow, the levels and extent of cord compression, and the direction of compression. The addition of a noncontrast CT scan after MRI further delineates the nature of the compression and clarifies the cortical structure of the level of involvement as well as the levels above and below, which may be used for instrumentation (Fig. 16–11). It also differentiates between cord compression resulting from a bone fragment that has been retropulsed into the canal and soft tissue mass secondary to local tumor extension. The identification of cord compression at two noncontiguous levels by MRI is a poor prognostic indicator.

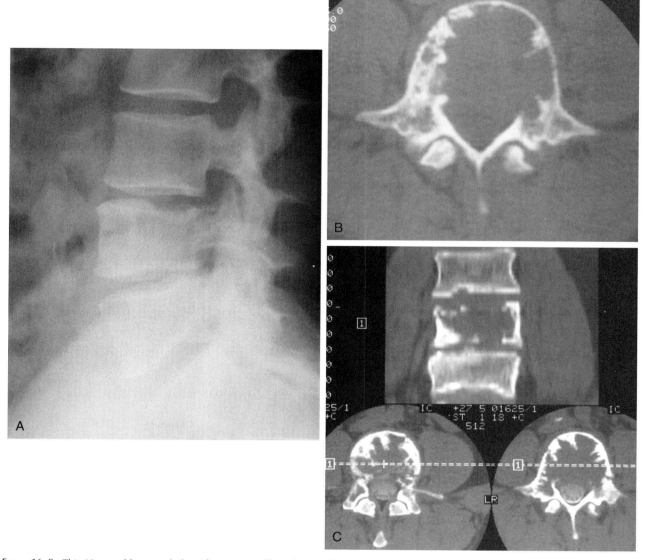

FIGURE 16–9. This 46-year-old man with thyroid carcinoma of long duration began to have back pain. The anteroposterior radiograph was interpreted as normal. *A,* The lateral radiograph was thought to show a minor superior end-plate abnormality. *B,* However, CT demonstrated that the bulk of the body and all of the posterior wall had been destroyed. There was even a minor degree of canal impingement. *C,* Reconstructions showed the extent of destruction. This case demonstrates that a lateral radiograph is a poor tool for screening spinal metastatic disease. The presence of a single cortex, even with complete destruction of the remainder of the body, gives a relatively normal-appearing radiograph.

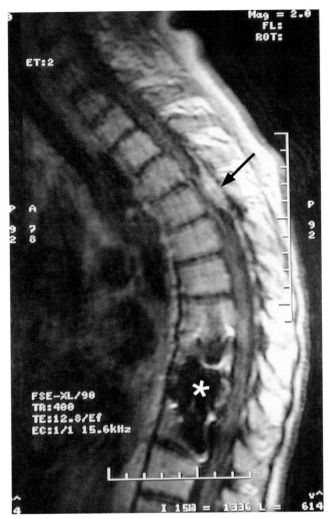

FIGURE 16–10. This midsagittal magnetic resonance image (MRI) of the thoracic spine of a 56-year-old man with metastatic liposarcoma demonstrates the ability to easily visualize areas of vertebral involvement and epidural compression without significant bony involvement. This patient had previous surgery (*asterisk*) in the lower thoracic spine for bony destruction and compression, but 6 months later developed severe midthoracic pain without any change in radiographic appearance. A large epidural plaque with dural compression was found on MRI examination (*arrow*).

TREATMENT

Patients with symptomatic skeletal metastasis who have not sustained a fracture may be treated by operative or nonoperative means. Nonoperative treatments include medical therapy, chemotherapy, hormonal therapy, and radiation.[21, 35] Many, if not most, symptomatic metastatic lesions respond to nonoperative treatments. The use of both hormonal and chemotherapeutic agents can have a significant positive effect on bony metastasis and bone healing.[12] Hormonal manipulation in breast cancer and carcinoma of the prostate can result in marked healing of bony lesions. In carcinoma of the prostate, significant pain relief can occur with estrogen therapy. Hormonal therapy with diethylstilbestrol (1 mg/day)[164] or with leuprolide and flutamide[38] can have a response rate of up to 80%.

Regression is indicated by a reduction in PSA levels. Generally, chemotherapeutic agents are more effective when there is demonstrated asymptomatic progression of the tumor, and they are less effective in patients who have pain. Lesions that remain symptomatic or progress despite systemic therapy usually require surgical stabilization or radiation therapy before the patient can return to chemotherapy.[50, 85, 146, 172]

The efficiency of radiation in treating a metastatic lesion to bone is probably inversely proportional to the degree of structural impairment, but actually most lytic lesions remain problematic.[98] More than 90% of patients who experience pain relief do so within the first 4 weeks of therapy; the average duration of complete relief, however, is only 6 months.[15, 68]

The durability of this treatment method depends on a variety of factors, including size, location, and histology of the lesion. However, radiation may give pain relief without significant bone healing.[103] The repair of metastatic bone lesions after radiation therapy has been described in detail by Matsubayashi and colleagues.[131] They demonstrated that the remineralization of an osteolytic metastatic lesion after radiation therapy is a result of ossification of strands of collagen derived from the proliferative fibrous tissue that has replaced the metastatic cells.

Radiation therapy is useful for the treatment of metastatic lesions before fracture, but once fracture has occurred its role without surgery is limited. The goals of radiation therapy are to relieve pain and to obtain local tumor control. Radiotherapy can be administered by a number of different strategies.[92, 161] The number of fractions and the time over which the treatment is delivered can be varied. Radiopharmaceutical treatment with strontium 89 or phosphorus 32 has shown encouraging results.[27, 38, 45, 140, 165] Most series, however, report major complications including spinal cord compression and long bone fracture during the course of radiation therapy.[68] The incidence of skeletal events varies according to the tumor type, patients with breast cancer having a higher incidence than patients with prostate carcinoma. Similarly, those with lytic lesions have a higher incidence of either cord compression or long bone fracture after radiation therapy than patients with blastic lesions. For patients with a pathologic fracture, radiation is used as an adjuvant following surgical stabilization to help maximize the potential for local tumor control. In the presence of rigid internal fixation, most fractures will go on to union within 6 months after radiation doses of 3000 cGy.

Medical management using bisphosphonates has been shown to decrease the incidence of skeletal complications associated with metastatic disease.[17, 46, 179, 183] Despite these advances in nonoperative treatment of skeletal metastasis, surgery remains an effective and necessary treatment for the prevention and treatment of pathologic fractures.

PELVIC AND EXTREMITY LESIONS

The most common sites of skeletal metastasis include the ribs, humerus, and femur. Pathologic fractures of these bones occur in approximately 4% of all patients with solid tumors.[61] Breast cancer, renal cell carcinoma, myeloma, and lung carcinoma are the most common histologic types of tumors in patients who sustain pathologic fractures. Because most people survive for a considerable period after the occurrence of a pathologic fracture, the treatment of these lesions has become increasingly important. The mean survival after treatment of a pathologic lesion of the humerus is approximately 8 months,[119] and after treatment of a femoral lesion is 14 months. A subgroup of patients with expected longer or shorter predicted survival can be identified depending on the tumor type, extent of visceral disease, and general health of the patient.

Nonoperative management of pathologic fractures involving the pelvis and extremities, either by traction or plaster immobilization has proven to adversely affect patient function, pain control, and fracture healing. Doses of radiation as low as 2000 rads significantly inhibit and prolong bone healing in the absence of rigid fixation.[19] Plaster immobilization diminishes the skin-sparing effect of radiation because electron buildup occurs as the beam traverses the cast. Consequently, radiation through a cast is associated with a higher incidence of skin breakdown than in extremities not covered with a cast. Although it is true

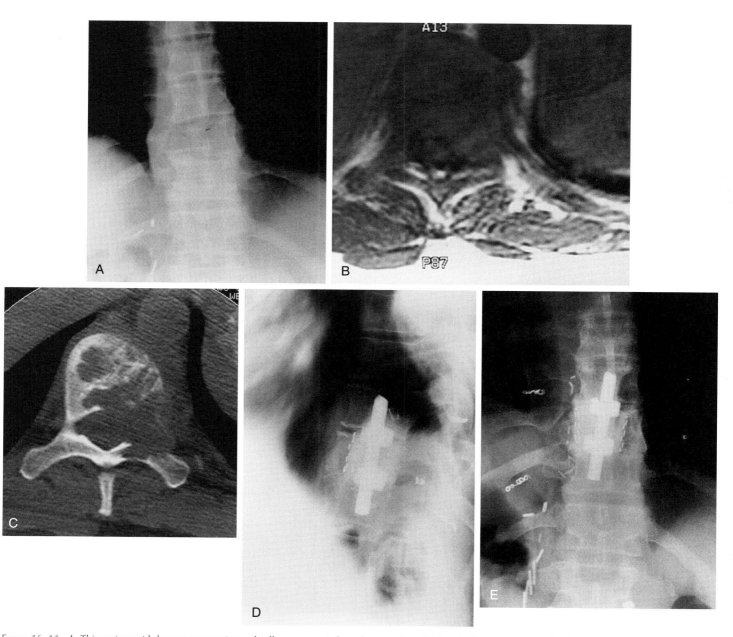

FIGURE 16–11. *A*, This patient with known metastatic renal cell carcinoma to bone began to have back pain that was severe and radicular in nature. He underwent palliative radiation therapy (3500 rads), which did not relieve his pain. *B*, Magnetic resonance imaging demonstrated severe dural compression at the T10 level, with deviation of the dural sac toward the right. *C*, However, a computed tomography scan allowed better differentiation of tumor and remaining bone structure, with clear delineation of the degree of posterior element involvement. This necessitated a left-sided approach after appropriate embolization, with preservation of the right cortical wall of the vertebral body. *D, E*, Frozen section at the time of surgery demonstrated a significant degree of viable tumor despite previous irradiation. The anterior defect was filled with a methyl methacrylate spacer with iodine 125 seeds embedded into the three walls of the cavity not facing the dural sac. The patient remained free of disease in the location 15 months later.

that pathologic fractures can heal without surgical intervention, the decision to treat surgically depends not only on the bone involved but also on the histology of the tumor. Although reports have cited rates of 16% to 35% for spontaneous fracture healing in malignant disease, a more practical indicator of fracture healing must consider the tumor type.[107] The incidence of fracture healing within 6 months following pathologic fracture from multiple myeloma is 67%, 44% for renal cell carcinoma, 37% for breast carcinoma, and less than 10% for lung carcinoma.[64] Anatomic location of the fracture also determines the likelihood of fracture healing with nonoperative intervention. Displaced pathologic fractures of the femoral neck invariably fail to heal even with internal fixation. Nonoperative treatment of long bone fractures in the lower extremities, the pelvis, or both may mandate prolonged bedrest. Such treatment increases the risk of complications such as pulmonary embolus, skin breakdown, osteopenia, and hypercalcemia.[162]

As a result of the unacceptably high complication rate, poor pain control, and low union rate associated with nonoperative treatment of pathologic fractures, surgical treatment has assumed an increasingly important role in their management.[3] For pathologic fractures involving long bones, including those of the humerus, radius, ulna, femur, and tibia, operative treatment has become the preferred treatment method for most patients. Surgical candidacy depends on the patient's expected survival and general health. Indications for surgery include the ability to provide adequate fixation to improve quality of life, be it by providing pain control, improved mobility, and/or general care. The use of radiation therapy immediately after operative stabilization is a significant factor in the successful treatment of pathologic fractures. Before operative treatment can be considered, certain basic criteria should be met:

1. The magnitude of the surgery should be considered with respect to the patient's general medical condition, life expectancy, recovery time, and expected functional outcome. Previously, it had been suggested that surgery should be reserved for patients whose life expectancy was greater than 3 months. This "rule" should not be made without considering the patient's level of pain and functional status. In some cases a relatively short operative procedure (i.e., humeral nailing or plating of the radius) can be performed that provides immediate pain control and restoration of function without prolonged hospitalization.
2. The planned procedure should in some way improve mobility, decrease pain, and facilitate general care of the patient.
3. The quality of bone proximal and distal to the area of the fracture must be sufficient to support fixation across the pathologic lesion.[77, 78] When bone quality is insufficient, more extensive procedures such as resection and prosthesis replacement may be indicated in patients with prolonged survival.

For patients with symptomatic pelvic or extremity lesions, a combination of radiation therapy[26] and surgical stabilization is most commonly employed. However, patients with impending fractures may also benefit from operative treatment alone. The indications for use of either or both of these modalities are reasonably well established. Symptomatic pain relief with radiation therapy can be expected for lesions that do not significantly compromise the integrity of the bone and are radiosensitive, as predicted by histologic type.

Attempts to predict fracture risk in long bones based on radiographic assessment alone have been largely unsuccessful. Harrington used radiographic criteria that included a lesion of 2.5 cm in diameter or greater than 50% cortical involvement as predictive of impending pathologic fracture.[77] These recommendations were, however, based on a series of patients with lesions in the subtrochanteric area of the femur only. Many of the patients studied who went on to subsequent fracture did not receive radiation or chemotherapy.

Some investigators have applied Harrington's criteria to other long bones.[7] However, because of wide variations in the load-bearing capacity of bones, the criteria of a 2.5-cm defect or 50% cortical involvement are not universally applicable.[91] The recommendations were based on lytic osseous lesions.[7, 56] An additional consideration of fracture risk, other than the size and location of the lesion, includes the host bone response to the tumor. Diffuse permeative lesions are harder to assess for their potential for pathologic fractures than purely lytic lesions.[103] Similarly, the assessment of fracture risk for blastic lesions, such as those from metastatic carcinoma of the prostate or breast, is less predictable than that for purely lytic lesions. Experimental data have demonstrated that a hole in the cortex diminishes the ability to resist torsion by 60%.[151] Similar studies have shown that the strength of bone is decreased by 60% to 90% when a diaphyseal defect involving 50% of the cortex is created.[91]

Mirels developed a scoring system to quantify fracture risk in patients with long bone metastases. The scoring system includes factors such as site, pain, radiographic characteristics of the lesion (blastic, mixed, or lytic), and size. These four factors are given a numerical assignment from 1 to 3. The maximum cumulative score is 12 and the minimum is 3. Mirels suggested that a cumulative score of 9 or higher was an indication for prophylactic fixation.[135]

As previously noted, surgical intervention is indicated in most patients with pathologic fractures and in patients with large lytic lesions of long bones or lytic and blastic lesions that have become resistant to other treatment methods.[163] Before proceeding with surgical treatment of a skeletal metastasis, the physician should have a thorough understanding of the anatomic extent of metastatic involvement. In lesions affecting long bones, this includes an understanding of the degree of destruction (i.e., a single area of cortex versus circumferential involvement) that precipitated the fracture as well as areas distal or proximal to the lesion within the same bone. When two or more lesions are located within the same bone, the mode of fixation should allow protection to both areas.

An understanding of the biology and natural history of the tumor is critical to minimize complications related to tumor recurrence, progression, or both. In tumors such as renal cell carcinoma, which are usually relatively resistant to both radiation and chemotherapy, local tumor recurrence is more likely to occur, and more extensive removal

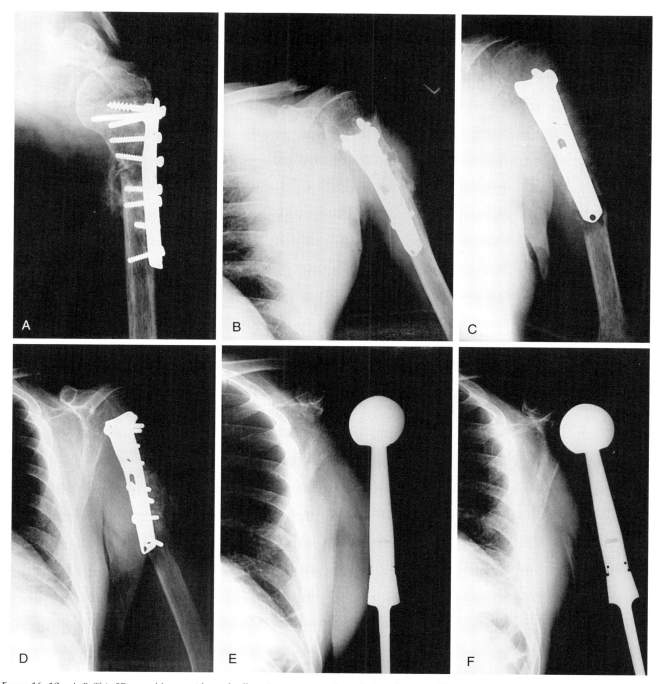

FIGURE 16–12. *A, B,* This 57-year-old man with renal cell carcinoma sustained a pathologic fracture of the proximal humerus and underwent plating and postoperative radiation therapy. *A,* At the time of initial surgery, it was evident that there was tumor involvement of the soft tissue and the distal fragment. Neither intramedullary fixation to bypass the defect nor resection was considered for this tumor, known to be poorly responsive to radiation therapy and most chemotherapy. *C, D,* Within 6 months, complete dissolution of the proximal portion of the humerus had occurred, with gross instability and a soft tissue mass. *E, F,* En bloc resection of the proximal 60% of the humerus was undertaken with reconstruction with a modular prosthesis. One year after resection, the patient continued to function well, having returned to his hobby of fishing.

of the metastatic lesion may be indicated to minimize the risk of local failure (Fig. 16–12). In tumors that typically involve multiple areas in the same bone (e.g., breast carcinoma, myeloma), isolated fixation of a single area may result in fracture in a more distal location within the same bone. Therefore, prophylactic fixation of the entire bone rather than a single area should be considered (Fig. 16–13).

In certain cases when union is unlikely to occur within the life span of the patient, prosthetic replacement is more appropriate than fracture fixation (e.g., displaced subcapital fractures of the hip) to achieve immediate weight bearing. When fracture fixation is indicated, the surgeon cannot rely on the same techniques used for the treatment of nonpathologic fractures. The type of reconstruction and fixation employed must be such that fracture healing is not necessary to achieve full weight bearing to allow mobilization of the patient. Load-sharing devices such as compression hip screws, which are indicated in non-neoplastic conditions are relatively indicated in neoplastic conditions. In non-neoplastic conditions, the internal fixation device maintains fixation until osseous union occurs. In neoplastic conditions, osseous union is usually delayed or may never occur, and the race between osseous union and implant failure is lost. Similarly, large defects in the bone further compromise the stability of the fixation, and areas of deficient bone may need to be restored with the use of methyl methacrylate (see Fig. 16–1). The goals of internal fixation should be directed at achieving immediate rigid rotational and axial stability. If full weight-bearing stability cannot be restored with reconstruction of the remaining bone, then resection and alternative reconstructive techniques such as prosthetic replacement should be considered.

In addition to obtaining immediate rigid internal fixation, the goals of surgery include local tumor control. Curettage followed by fixation and augmentation with methyl methacrylate has been used to decrease tumor burden, thereby possibly improving the effects of radiation and decreasing the risk of local recurrence.[53, 75, 76] This

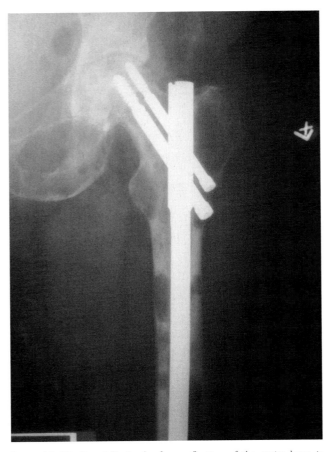

Figure 16–13. Especially in the femur, fixation of the entire bone is critical to prevent subsequent loss of fixation or fracture below or above previous fixation. In this patient with myeloma, the femoral neck intertrochanteric region and distal femur are protected in case the tumor extends proximally or a new lesion arises distally. A standard femoral nail used for this lesion could potentially fail at the proximal end.

does not usually achieve adequate local control, and postoperative radiation therapy is a critical adjunct. With the increased use of the current generation of locked intramedullary nails, more long bone fractures are being treated with closed nailing in lieu of open procedures. Because newer intramedullary nails are stronger and more resistant to failure from repetitive cyclic loading, they can maintain stability for longer times than the previously used intramedullary devices. Careful assessment should be made of the strength of the device before using it, as the reconstruction nail is stronger than others.[109] However, even these devices may need to be augmented with methyl methacrylate when local bone destruction is extensive, fracture healing does not occur, and longer survival is anticipated.

UPPER EXTREMITY LESIONS

Historically, pathologic fractures of the humerus were frequently managed with nonoperative techniques. Although it is true that such fractures, unlike femur fractures, can be managed without hospitalization, they still lead to impaired function, decreased independence, and prolonged pain. There have been few reports showing satisfactory results in patients treated nonoperatively for humeral fractures,[29, 113] whereas most patients treated with operative stabilization achieved excellent pain relief with a low incidence of complications.[110, 113, 122] Following the success of operative treatment of femur fractures, a similar approach to treating pathologic fractures of the humerus has been advocated.[59] The same basic criteria used in the femur regarding fixation of fractures and impending lesions can also be used for decision making in the humerus. If sufficient bone proximal and distal to the lesion remains, fixation of humeral lesions with an intramedullary nail provides immediate and long-lasting pain relief.[117, 122, 148, 172] Fixation of pathologic fractures of the humerus, as well as prophylactic fixation, has been advocated since the 1960s; at that time, antegrade nailing with Rush rods was the method most commonly used. This technique was fraught with a number of complications, including lack of adequate fixation and impingement on the rotator cuff, necessitating removal of the hardware.

Recent advances in instrumentation and surgical technique have allowed surgeons to improve on the methods of treating patients with pathologic or impending fractures of the humerus. The use of locked intramedullary nails has greatly improved the ability of the surgeon to obtain immediate stability and to prevent migration of the implant[95] compared with previous implants.[41, 48, 73, 155]

Techniques for nail insertion include an antegrade[37, 125] or retrograde approach.[127] The functional outcomes using an antegrade technique have been mixed, however. Because the functional expectations for patients with pathologic fractures were minimal, the results were thought to be acceptable.[39, 94, 99, 189] However, in larger series that included patients with both pathologic fractures and nonpathologic fractures treated with an antegrade technique, impaired shoulder function is reported to range from 10% to 37%.[90, 184, 186] Impaired shoulder function resulted from problems associated with the proximal

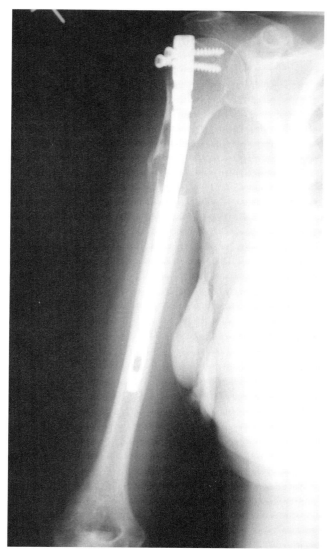

FIGURE 16–14. This patient sustained a pathologic fracture of the proximal humerus and was stabilized using an antegrade nailing technique. The rod was left prominent and resulted in pain and limited shoulder function.

saves blood loss as well as allows range of motion and radiation therapy to begin as early as possible.

Potential advantages to this technique include that the shoulder joint is not violated and therefore problems associated with injury to the rotator cuff are avoided. With this technique, pain relief and stability are achieved in 95% of patients. If insufficient bone stock remains proximally with which to attain satisfactory fixation, prosthetic replacement (with a long stem and polymethyl methacrylate) should be considered (see Fig. 16–12).[25, 63, 173] Functional reconstruction of the rotator cuff is difficult, especially if there is tumor involvement of the deltoid or the rotator cuff muscle. However, the prosthesis gives satisfactory pain relief and restores some function to the extremity. Distal humeral lesions are uncommon but may be difficult to stabilize when they do occur. Augmentation with methyl methacrylate is almost always necessary to

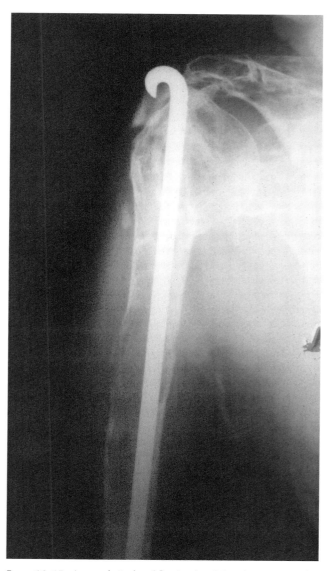

FIGURE 16–15. Antegrade Rush rod fixation that did not have rotational or axial control frequently resulted in rotator cuff impingement. Because the rod was left prominent or because it backed out with shortening of the humerus, the proximal end became symptomatic.

locking screw, impingement from the nail not being adequately seated in bone, and injury to the rotator cuff at the time of surgery (Fig. 16–14).[60, 90, 124]

Retrograde closed humeral nailing had been advocated as a method of achieving fixation while avoiding the complications noted with Rush rods (Fig. 16–15) and antegrade locked nailing.[93, 117, 124, 158, 159] A retrograde locked technique incorporates the advantages of distal entry portal and a more secure fixation in the wide proximal fragment (Fig. 16–16). This technique allows a distal entry portal with proximal fixation extending to just below the subchondral plate of the humeral head (Fig. 16–17). A second surgical incision is made directly over the lesion so that it can be curetted and filled with methyl methacrylate if necessary. However, the proximal fragment may be fixed by a freehand technique for interlocking through a small stab wound in the deltoid muscle. This

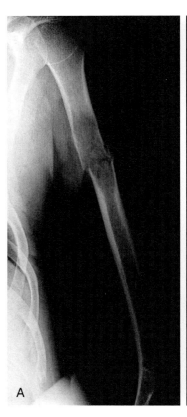
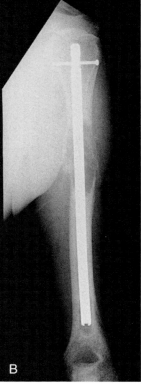
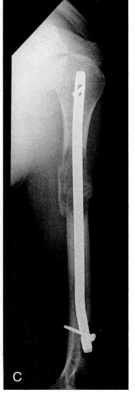

FIGURE 16–16. *A*, This 45-year-old man was swinging a golf club and sustained a sudden pathologic fracture of his nondominant arm. Subsequent evaluation revealed a large renal mass. *B, C*, He underwent closed, locked intramedullary nailing of the humerus, which restored length and stability while bypassing the defect in the shaft. He began radiation therapy and then chemotherapy within several days of surgery.

achieve sufficient stability to allow immediate unrestricted activity (Fig. 16–18).

Whereas 20% of all metastatic lesions occur in the upper extremity, only 0.4% occur in the radius and 0.2% in the ulna.[67, 172] If sufficient bone is present, the most common treatment is plating and augmentation with methyl methacrylate. Occasionally, intramedullary rodding can be employed (Fig. 16–19).

LOWER EXTREMITY LESIONS

Metastatic lesions to the femur account for approximately 25% of all metastatic lesions to bone.[29, 85] However, they can be among the most devastating lesions, when the implications of pathologic fracture are considered.[128] Pathologic fractures of the femur most commonly involve the femoral neck and the intertrochanteric and subtrochanteric regions. Midshaft and distal fractures occur less frequently. The goals of treatment include restoration of immediate and full weight-bearing capability. This often requires techniques that are not used in patients with fractures resulting from non-neoplastic causes. Although the mean survival for patients who sustain a pathologic femur fracture is approximately 14 months, there is a wide range in survival.[118] Therefore, treatment options that allow immediate stability may also need to be durable.

Pathologic fractures of the femoral neck and intertrochanteric region are most commonly treatment with endoprosthetic replacement (Fig. 16–20).[114, 121] This method is preferred to standard fixation techniques for three reasons. First, there is a low probability of healing of pathologic femoral neck fractures.[65] Second, endopros-

thetic replacement alleviates the necessity for prolonged restricted weight bearing in a person with a shortened life span. Significant bone loss often occurs in fractures of the neck and intertrochanteric region, which compromises successful internal fixation.[150] There are several technical considerations, one of which is adequate filling of all defects. When a large area of destruction is present, the region should be filled adequately with methyl methacrylate. When the destruction continues below the lesser trochanter, the defect should be filled with methyl methacrylate, but calcar replacement may be necessary because the methyl methacrylate is not always sufficient to ensure immediate and long-term stability. In patients who have distant metastasis within the femoral shaft, or who are at risk for developing such lesions, a long-stem prosthesis should be chosen to protect those lesions at the same time (Fig. 16–21).[114] It is critical to bypass lesions so that fractures do not occur below the tip of a previously cemented hemiarthroplasty.[106] Before hemiarthroplasty, radiographs of the entire femur in two planes should be obtained to assess the need for prophylactic fixation. In patients undergoing elective surgery for an impending fracture of the proximal femur, the entire femur should be assessed not only with plain radiographs but also with a bone scan and/or MRI. Noncemented arthroplasties, even in young patients, are discouraged in patients with metastatic tumor because of poor bone stock, compromised healing potential, and the risk of prosthetic loosening associated with tumor progression.

There are several methods of treatment available for impending fractures of the femoral neck and intertrochanteric region. The preferred technique depends on the local

Text continued on page 402

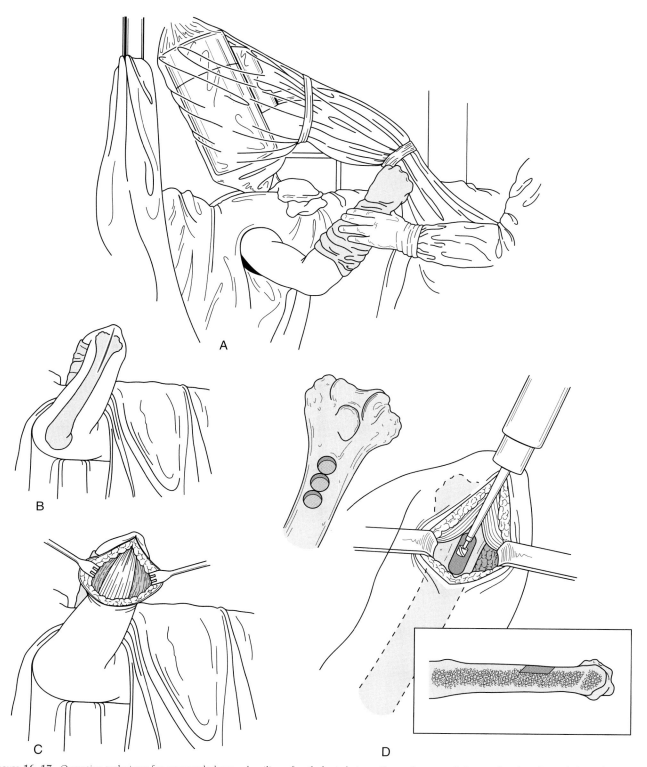

FIGURE 16–17. Operative technique for retrograde humeral nailing of pathologic lesions. Reamed retrograde humeral nailing for pathologic fractures is done with the patient under general or regional anesthesia, such as supraclavicular block. *A,* The patient is placed supine on a regular operating table with the affected extremity extended over the table's edge. If the patient is positioned so that the scapula of the extremity is at the edge of the table, there is sufficient clearance for the use of an image intensifier to adequately visualize the humeral head. The arm is suspended by use of a finger trap, the head is rotated away from the operative side, and the patient is prepared and draped from the shoulder to the wrist, with the arm free in the field. *B,* The arm is placed across the chest and supported on a towel roll, so that the shoulder and elbow are at 90°. The excision line is made from the tip of the olecranon proximally for about 8 cm. *C,* The incision is carried sharply through the skin and subcutaneous tissue until the triceps tendon is identified. The tendon is carefully visualized, and the entry through the tendon is at its midportion. The tendon is split sharply from the proximal tip of the olecranon. The muscle is then opened bluntly throughout the length of the incision by splitting the fibers of the triceps. Subperiosteal dissection of the posterior humerus is completed. *D,* Hayes retractors are then placed, one on each side of the humerus just proximal to the epicondyles beneath the stripped periosteum, to provide retraction of the posterior aspect of the humerus. Beginning 2 cm above the proximal edge of the olecranon fossa, a 14-inch drill hole is made through the posterior cortex of the humerus. This hole must be directly centered between the medial and the lateral cortices. The second and third drill holes are made just proximal to the first. Using a high-speed bur, an oval hole is made and widened out to the medial and lateral cortices. As indicated in the diagram, the bur is used to form a ramp for subsequent reaming of the humerus, and its distal end is beveled to the olecranon fossa; the posterior cortex on the proximal end is undercut. This allows a flexible reamer to slide easily into the humerus. At this point, a 9-mm end-cutting and side-cutting reamer is placed in the trough to ascertain whether it fits easily and will not bind.

Illustration continued on following page

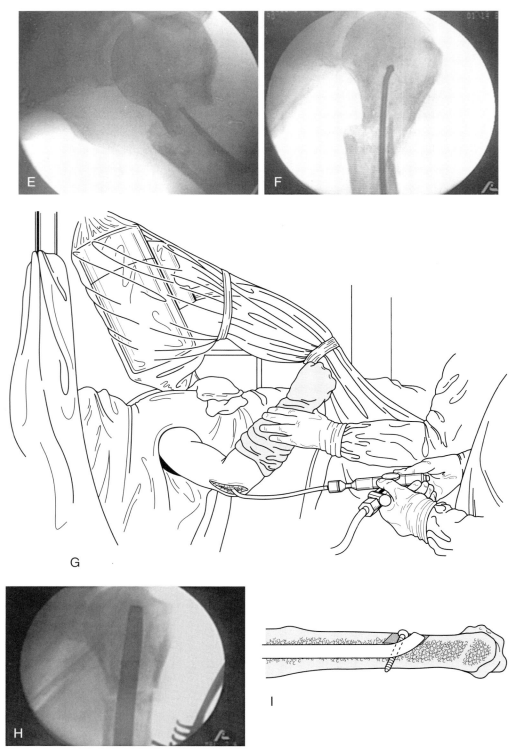

Figure 16–17 *Continued. E,* A guide pin is then passed proximally across the fracture site. *F,* The guide pin is placed just across the fracture site in a closed fashion. The reamer is then advanced up and over the guide pin. Care is taken so that the reamer passes along the canal and does not ream the anterior cortex, *G,* To allow accurate visualization of the humerus with image intensification and to aid in reduction, the arm is positioned at approximately 45° from the side of the table. The humeral shaft is then reamed in 0.5-mm increments. Because most lesions are on the proximal third of the humerus, it is unnecessary to ream this area. All cortical reaming is done at the isthmus, located at the junction of the middle and distal thirds of the humerus. Not reaming the cancellous bone of the proximal third provides more substantial fixation. Care is taken to preserve all cortical bone at the isthmus. Nail sizes are available from 8 mm upward; the smallest possible nail should be used to preserve all cortical bone. Overreaming by 0.5 to 1 mm is necessary to pass the nail. *H,* The length of the nail is measured to ensure that the tip comes within 1 cm of the subchondral plate of the humeral head. The distal end sits within the trough after the correct nail size has been selected. The nail is placed over the guide pin and fully inserted. If curettage of the lesion through a second incision is to be done at this point, the nail is inserted only to the distal end of the lesion. The guide pin is left in place across the fracture side. An incision is made on the anterolateral surface of the proximal humerus, and the lesion is thoroughly curetted. The guide pin is used as a marker. After the lesion has been curetted and the proximal humerus has been filled with methyl methacrylate, the nail is impacted into the fully seated position, and the guide pin is removed. *I,* If a locking nail is selected, the distal lock is placed first by drilling a unicortical screw placed under direct vision through the screw hole in the distal trough.

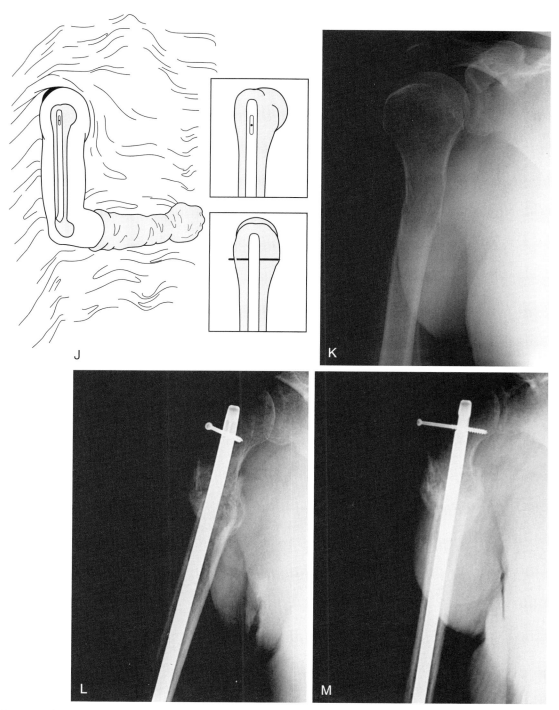

FIGURE 16–17 *Continued. J,* The proximal lock is placed by a freehand technique with the patient in a supine position and the arm in 90° of internal rotation so that the slot in the proximal end of the nail is fully visualized *(top inset)*. Cannulated 3.5-mm screws are used with a 2.0-mm guide pin. A small incision is made in the skin over the slot, and the guide pin is pushed through the deltoid to the bone. Image intensification is used to orient the guide pin so that it is reduced to a dot, indicating that it is parallel to the slot in the nail. It is then pushed or drilled through the humeral head, depending on the density of the bone, through the nail to the opposite cortex. The position is again checked on image intensification, the arm is carefully rotated 90°, and the position is again checked *(bottom inset)*. Care must be taken not to bend the guide wire, and if it needs to be repositioned, the arm must again be internally rotated to fully visualize the slot before changing the position of the guide wire. The final position of the nail and inspection of the joint are accomplished using image intensification. The final position of the nail in the distal humerus is checked to make sure it is in the trough. Drains are placed in both wounds, and the incisions are closed. The arm is postoperatively immobilized in a sling, and motion begins on the third postoperative day, as soon as the drains are removed. For locked nailings, radiation therapy can begin at the site of the lesion on the third postoperative day. *K,* This 70-year-old man sustained a pathologic fracture of the proximal humerus from myeloma. He underwent locked retrograde nailing and was removed from his sling on the third postoperative day, regaining full elbow function by 2 weeks. *L, M,* At 3 months, the fracture demonstrated a solid union.

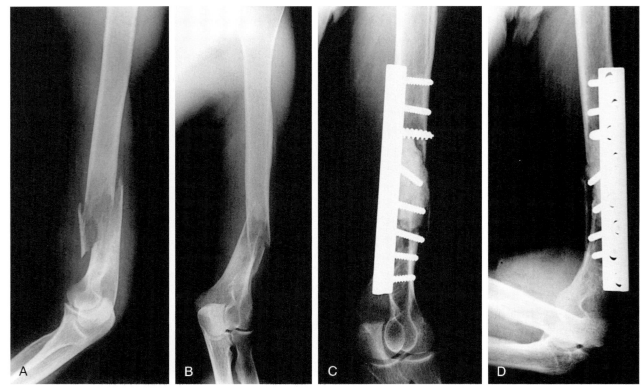

FIGURE 16–18. *A, B,* This patient with multiple myeloma sustained a comminuted fracture of the distal humerus of his dominant arm. *C, D,* Open reduction and internal fixation was done but augmented with methyl methacrylate to enhance fixation and stability. Provisional fixation was obtained by using only three of the screws. The defect was then filled, and the remainder of the screws were placed by drilling and tapping the methacrylate.

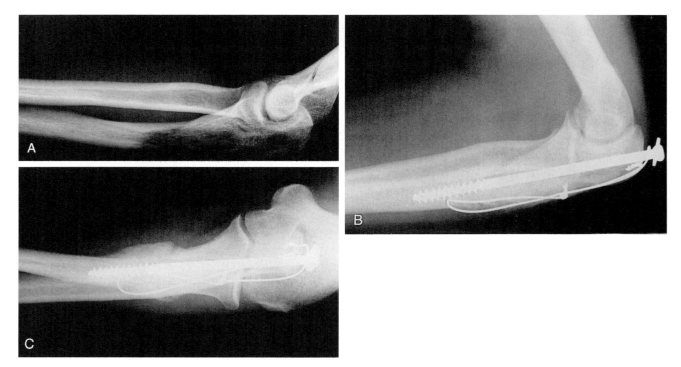

FIGURE 16–19. This 37-year-old man with carcinoma of the breast sustained a pathologic fracture through the proximal third of his ulna. *A,* The lateral radiograph showed a permeative lesion of 3 cm with a pathologic fracture through it. The patient underwent open curettage of the lesion. A 6.5-mm cancellous screw was passed through the lesion and was bound in the normal bone of the distal ulnar canal. *B, C,* The defect was filled with methyl methacrylate, and a tension band wire was used to reinforce the repair. The patient had immediate relief of pain and, within 2 weeks, had regained full range of motion of the elbow.

FIGURE 16–20. This 55-year-old woman had diffusely metastatic carcinoma of the breast. She presented with bilateral hip pain and incomplete paraplegia resulting from a midthoracic lesion. The patient underwent decompression and stabilization of the thoracic lesion and staged, prophylactic fixation of the left femur with a reconstruction nail. *A,* Because of the displaced subcapital fracture, she underwent bipolar cemented arthroplasty on the right side. *B,* One year after surgery, the patient was ambulatory with a cane.

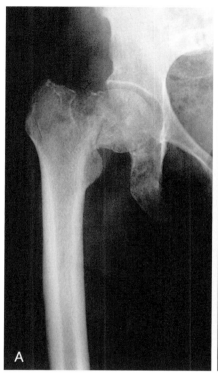

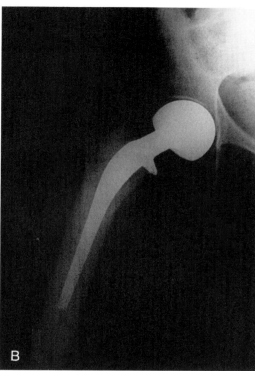

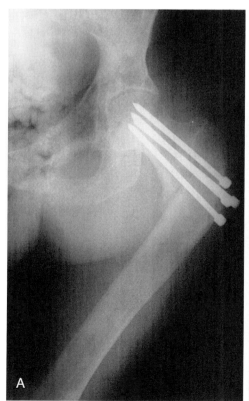

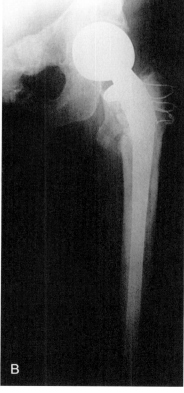

FIGURE 16–21. This 67-year-old woman with diffusely metastatic carcinoma of the breast had significant hip pain with a lytic lesion in the intertrochanteric and subtrochanteric regions. *A,* The patient underwent Knowles pinning at an outside facility and continued to have severe pain despite adjuvant radiation therapy. Follow-up radiographs at 2 months showed a pathologic fracture that was displaced and shortened. The patient had noticed marked shortening of her leg in addition to the severe pain. She also had multiple metastatic lesions throughout the femur on the left side. This fracture was displaced in a varus position and could not be easily moved. It was decided to salvage the proximal femur but to use a cemented arthroplasty with a 305-mm, bowed-leg stem prosthesis to protect the entire femur down to the intercondylar notch. *B,* Eighteen months later, the patient was ambulatory on this long-stem prosthesis. Subsequently, she underwent prophylactic fixation for severe pain after radiation therapy in the contralateral femur.

extent of tumor, the size of the lesion, and the presence or absence of concomitant tumor at a separate site within the femur. In patients in whom the lesion is well-confined within the neck and in whom there is a limited life expectancy (e.g., in those with adenocarcinoma of the lung, squamous cell carcinoma, or other solid tumors), the probability of additional lesions developing within the femur is limited. In such selected cases, curettage of the lesion, and fixation with a compression hip screw may be appropriate but should be augmented with methyl methacrylate.[87] In patients with more than one lesion affecting the femur or with long life expectancy and multiple bone metastases (e.g., those with adenocarcinoma of the breast, multiple myeloma), prophylactic fixation of the entire femur with a single procedure should be considered. This minimizes the chance that a distal lesion in the same bone may become symptomatic or fracture later. The use of locked reconstructive nails, with screws going up into the femoral neck, protect the femoral neck, shaft, and the distal femur and have greatly facilitated the treatment of this patient population.[89, 111]

Subtrochanteric lesions of the femur are potentially the most devastating and most difficult to manage. Early studies reported fixation of subtrochanteric pathologic fractures with the use of the Zickel nail,[72, 132, 197] as opposed to plate and screw combinations, which are generally contraindicated for pathologic subtrochanteric fractures (see Fig. 16–1). The use of this device has been associated with a higher than acceptable failure rate when medial bone loss is present.[82] The results with Zickel nail fixation augmented with methyl methacrylate decreased the failure rate. However, the difficulty in closed insertion because of nail configuration and limited choice of lengths, which resulted in pathologic fractures occurring distal to the tip of the nail (Fig. 16–22), has allowed this device to be supplemented by newer designs.

The current generation of locked nail devices allows fixation of subtrochanteric lesions with protection of the entire femur. Patients with both subtrochanteric and midshaft or distal femoral lesions and patients who have high potential for additional metastatic deposits during their life span (e.g., those with myeloma, breast or prostate cancer) are best treated with a proximal and distal interlocking nail with proximal fixation up into the femoral neck (Fig. 16–23). The use of a transverse or an oblique proximal lock that does not protect the intertrochanteric and femoral neck regions should be discouraged unless patient survival is limited. The nail configuration should have at least one large screw directed up into the neck and two screws for distal locking that can support unaided full weight bearing. The probability of additional lesions proximal to a midshaft or subtrochanteric lesion is significantly high to warrant the use of a device that protects the entire length of the femur in most cases. Augmentation with methyl methacrylate is not necessary unless one or more of the screw entry sites is within or is very close to an area of tumor.[118]

Insertion technique is similar to that used for acute traumatic fractures. Because of bone loss, alignment may have to be adjusted by directing the proximal fragment after screw insertion. In some cases in which extensive bone loss is present, a long stem prosthesis and arthro-

plasty may be preferred. In such cases, the proximal bone segment with the greater trochanter is preserved and the stem passes through the proximal fragment and then across the fracture site.

Metastatic lesions distal to the midshaft femur are less common than those proximal to the midshaft, but the principles of treatment are similar. Protection of the femoral neck and intertrochanteric region with an appropriate second-generation nail is advocated. Very distal femoral lesions (within 6 cm of the joint surface) that are isolated and that occur in patients whose life expectancy is limited can be treated effectively by curettage of the lesion, packing with methyl methacrylate, and stabilization with a distal screw and plate combination. The use of antegrade intramedullary locked fixation is possible when the lesion is in the distal third of the femur and does not penetrate into the femoral condyles. Retrograde intramedullary nail fixation is also useful and may be technically easier to

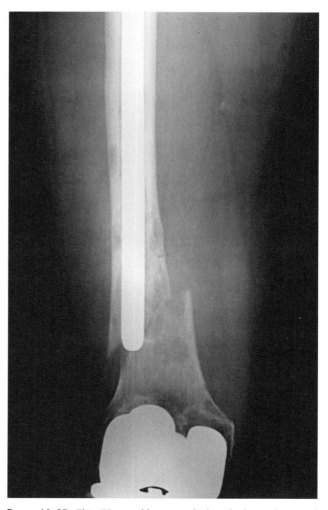

FIGURE 16–22. This 78-year-old woman had multiple myeloma and carcinoma of the breast. She had previously undergone total arthroplasty for degenerative disease of the knee. At 1.5 years before admission, she also underwent a Zickel nail fixation for a subtrochanteric fracture. The patient had subsequent disease below the tip of the Zickel nail and above the total-knee arthroplasty, and she sustained a fracture at the tip of the Zickel nail. This required removal of the Zickel nail and fixation with an interlocking nail system to protect the entire femur.

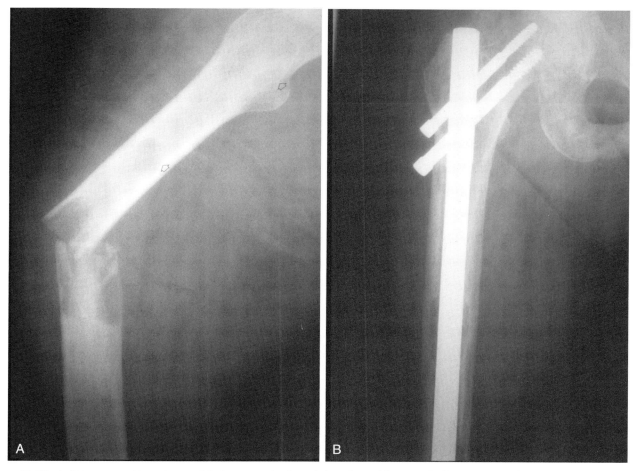

FIGURE 16–23. *A,* This woman with carcinoma of the breast sustained a pathologic femoral fracture. The fracture was stabilized with a reamed, statically locked, intramedullary reconstruction nail. The fracture site was not opened. *B,* Length and rotation of the femur could be maintained with locking screws into the proximal neck and the most distal portion of the femur, despite bone loss. At 12-month follow-up, significant healing of the fracture had occurred, and because of the potentially long survival with this diagnosis, the intertrochanteric region and neck were also protected.

perform with decreased operative time than is antegrade nailing.[89] Pain relief with these techniques is immediate, and full weight bearing can be reinstituted immediately.

It is critical that these femoral lesions are not treated as standard fractures. Because of the significant bone loss, interlocking into good quality proximal and distal bone is necessary, or the fixation should be augmented with methyl methacrylate to restore weight-bearing ability.[4, 16, 134, 178] Methyl methacrylate does not interfere with fracture healing unless it is interposed between fracture fragments.[195] As in the proximal humerus and proximal femur, if insufficient bone stock exists to obtain immediate stability, endoprosthetic replacement may be necessary. In rare cases involving extensive bone destruction, the use of a custom endoprosthesis may be necessary. These prostheses can be assembled in the operating room to accommodate various amounts of bone loss.[25, 173] Lesions in the tibia are rare but may be treated in a fashion similar to that for femoral lesions. Small solitary lesions may be treated with curettage and cementation, with or without internal fixation. Alternatively, as in the femur, a interlocked tibial nail can provide stability and protect the remainder of the bone (Fig. 16–24). Intercalary or segmental replacement may be indicated for solitary renal or thyroid metastasis.

Among the most challenging lesions to evaluate and treat are those involving the pelvis.[182] Because the anterior and posterior portions of the pelvis overlap in plain AP radiographs, acetabular deficiencies are often difficult to recognize and require specialized views. Often, even when a technetium bone scan reveals activity and is correlated with pain, insufficient attention is given to metastatic lesions about the pelvis until extensive destruction occurs. Harrington proposed a radiographic classification to describe various types of bone loss associated with periacetabular metastasis.[79, 80, 85, 87] He described four classes: in class I, all portions of the wall of the acetabulum are present; in class II, the medial wall is deficient; in class III, the lateral and superior portions of the acetabulum are deficient; and in class IV, a resection is necessary for cure. A critical feature for treating patients with metastatic disease to the pelvis is the early recognition of periacetabular disease. Early treatment with radiation or by surgical intervention with curettage of the lesion accompanied by either open or percutaneous methyl methacrylate filling of this lesion yields a highly acceptable result with moderate pain relief and good long-term stability of the acetabulum, preventing acetabular collapse and reconstruction by total hip arthroplasty (Fig. 16–25).

Metastases to the acetabulum occur primarily in two locations. The first is the medial wall (Fig. 16–26). This may be visualized on plain radiographs as destruction of the lateral aspect of the superior pubic ramus. Because the ramus forms a large portion of the medial wall of the acetabulum, destruction of that area appears as destruction of the medial wall of the acetabulum. Early radiation therapy can prevent further destruction and allow the medial wall of the acetabulum to remain intact. Failure to recognize this situation can lead to pathologic fracture and result in protrusion of the femoral head through a defect in the medial wall.

The other common location for metastatic disease is in the supra-acetabular region, extending to the posterior wall of the acetabulum. Again, this is not well seen on plain radiographs and requires Judet views for visualization (see Fig. 16–5). These allow separate visualization of the anterior and posterior columns and bring into perspective large lesions of the superior and posterior aspect that may not be apparent on an AP view of the pelvis. Once a large lytic lesion has come within 1 to 2 mm of the superior dome of the acetabulum, the weight-bearing line of the hip joint is severely disturbed. The use of radiation therapy is infrequently effective in obtaining pain relief for patients with this condition, probably because of the decreased strength of the weight-bearing column and recurrent microfractures, either in the lateral or medial wall, through defects that are not readily apparent. CT scans better define the bony architecture and allow visualization of these areas (Fig. 16–27). Curettage of the lesion through a limited posterior or anterior extra-articular approach and packing with methyl methacrylate lead to long-term relief of pain (Fig. 16–28).[116, 138]

Usually, unless the subchondral plate of the superior dome of the acetabulum has been disrupted, further reconstruction of the hip is not necessary. In a series of 30 patients who underwent surgery for supra-acetabular metastasis 28 had long-term satisfactory results (Fig. 16–29). Even when the lesions are relatively large but the subchondral plate remains intact, a satisfactory result can be obtained with this limited operative approach (Fig. 16–30). For some patients with lytic lesions whose tumor is gelatinous or necrotic, filling the defect percutaneously with methyl methacrylate may be possible. If early destruction of the hip joint is not recognized, the superior weight-bearing dome will fracture, allowing migration of the femoral head proximally into the defect. Such destruction requires a modified total hip arthroplasty to obtain reasonable reconstruction of the hip, using the more proximal iliac bone to buttress the reconstruction of the large defect in the supra-acetabular region (Fig. 16–31). These more complex reconstructions can give satisfactory long-term results,[190] but the operative and perioperative morbidity in patients who undergo them is significantly

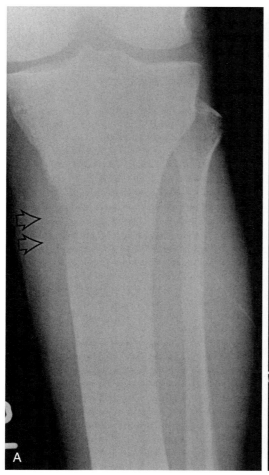
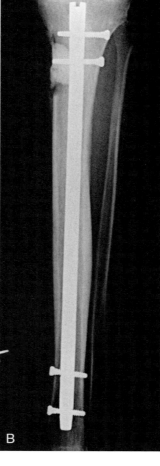

Figure 16–24. This 56-year-old man with carcinoma of the lung had severe pain in his proximal tibia that, after radiation therapy, was unremitting. *A,* Preoperative radiographs demonstrated a 43-cm lytic lesion *(arrows)* in the proximal tibia. *B,* The patient underwent curettage of the subcutaneous and intramedullary lesions and stabilization with a locked intramedullary nail. He achieved immediate pain relief and full weight-bearing status.

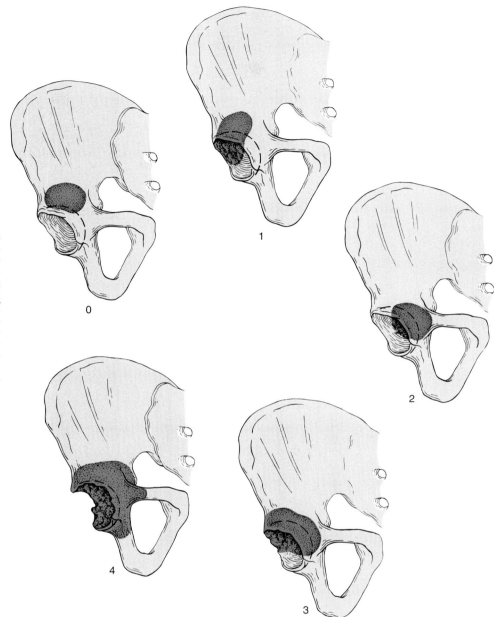

FIGURE 16–25. This diagram shows a modification of the degrees of acetabular insufficiency. Stage 0, a supra-acetabular lesion that does not penetrate the subchondral plate, has been added. In stage 1, there is significant involvement of the superior dome of the acetabulum, but the medial wall is intact. In stage 2, there is significant medial wall involvement. In stage 3, the posterior, superior, and medial walls are involved. In stage 4, total involvement of the acetabulum requires resection for salvage.

higher than in patients who are recognized to have defects and treated primarily with supra-acetabular, extra-articular reconstruction (Fig. 16–32). Occasionally, the destruction of the acetabular bone stock is so great in an otherwise salvageable patient that reconstruction by conventional means is impossible. In those very rare instances, resection and reconstruction with a saddle prosthesis provides a more stable alternative to a resection arthroplasty procedure.[2, 41, 157]

METASTATIC DISEASE OF THE SPINE

Estimates of spinal metastasis for patients who have metastatic disease vary from 36% to 70%.[160, 194] Despite this relatively high incidence, only a small percentage develop symptomatic metastasis and an even smaller percentage go

on to develop neural compression and resulting deficit without pathologic fracture of the vertebrae simply by replacement and contiguous soft tissue mass. Pathologic fractures of the spine do occur, but many resemble osteopenic compression fractures both radiographically and clinically. Rarely, pathologic fractures can result in a fracture dislocation, which usually results in immediate paraplegia. Most patients who become symptomatic from a spinal metastasis do so gradually by one of two mechanisms: replacement by tumor of the vertebra, resulting in mechanical weakening and slow collapse of the vertebral body, or accumulation of a soft tissue mass involving the posterior aspect of the body, the pedicles, or the laminae. The consequences of metastatic disease of the spine are somewhat different from those of the remainder of the skeleton, because the resultant instability and direct neural

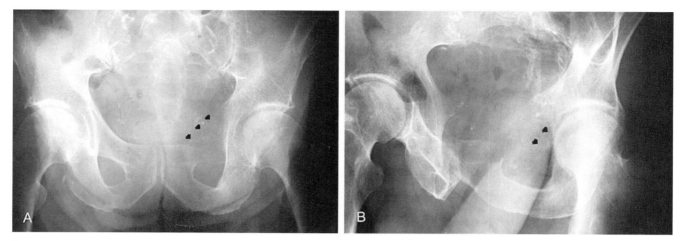

FIGURE 16–26. *A,* This 63-year-old man with metastatic squamous cell carcinoma of the larynx experienced severe hip pain, and an anteroposterior radiograph of the pelvis demonstrated complete loss of the superior pubic ramus *(arrows).* The patient received radiation therapy but continued to have severe hip pain. *B,* Judet views demonstrated that the cause of the hip pain was significant loss of the medial wall of the acetabulum, which is formed by the extension of the superior pubic ramus *(arrows).*

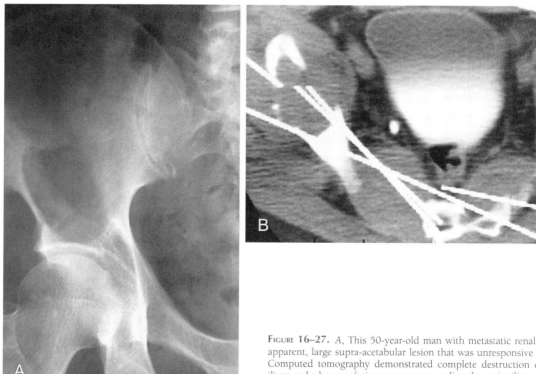

FIGURE 16–27. *A,* This 50-year-old man with metastatic renal cell carcinoma had an apparent, large supra-acetabular lesion that was unresponsive to radiation therapy. *B,* Computed tomography demonstrated complete destruction of both cortices of the ilium and a large, soft tissue mass surrounding the entire iliac crest just above the level of the acetabulum.

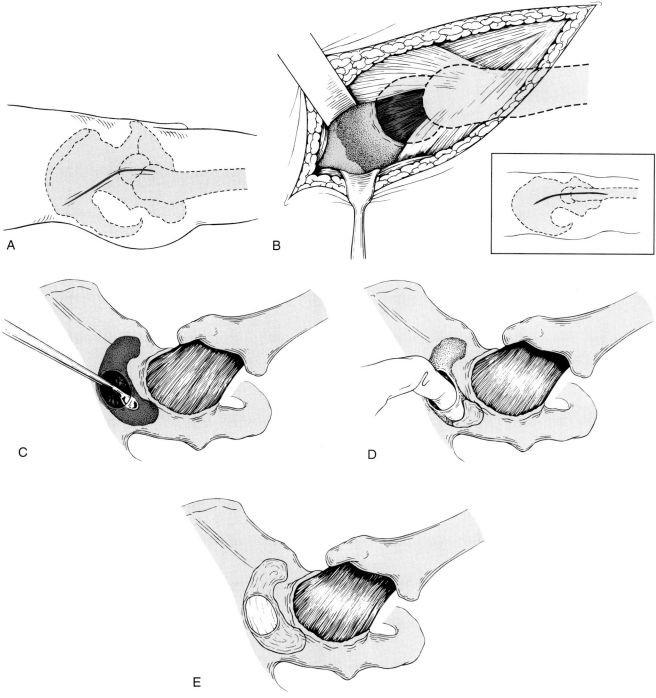

FIGURE 16–28. Surgical technique for supra-acetabular reconstruction. For reconstruction of lesions of the supra-acetabular region, the patient must have an intact subchondral plate with no apparent destruction visible on computed tomography (CT) scan of the acetabulum. *A*, The patient is placed in the lateral decubitus position with the affected hip upward. The patient is prepared and draped in the usual sterile fashion, with the leg free in the field. The posterior approach starts just below the greater trochanter, continues over the trochanter, and then curves posteriorly toward the posterior superior iliac crest. *B*, The subcutaneous tissue is dissected, and the fascia of the gluteus is split. The gluteus is split bluntly, in line with its fibers, from the trochanter to the sciatic notch. At the posterior aspect of the incision, the sciatic notch is exposed subperiosteally, and a blunt cobra retractor is placed in the sciatic notch to protect the nerve and superior gluteal vessels. Additional dissection is carried proximally and superiorly, and a thyroid retractor is placed for visualization of the superior margin of the capsule and posterior lip of the acetabulum. *C*, Frequently, a defect is observed in the cortex, and entry into the lesion is through the defect. Otherwise, depending on whether the site of the lesion is predominantly superior or posterior, the entry hole through the cortical bone is made at the superior end of the acetabulum or slightly posterior, so that better curettage of the posterior lip can be obtained. Generally, the bone is soft, and the area of the lesion is easily entered. Otherwise a 14-inch osteotome is used to remove the cortical window. The lesion is then entered and thoroughly curetted posteriorly, into the lip of the acetabulum, and superiorly with an angled curette. All tumor is removed, and the inferior margin (i.e., subchondral plate of the acetabulum) is checked for defects. If a small defect is seen or has been removed during curettage, a piece of fascia lata is removed and is used to cover the defect. *D*, The window for curettage should be large enough to admit at least the index finger for packing the methyl methacrylate, a single package of which is mixed and, in its doughy stage, finger-packed into the lesion. *E*, Packing continues until the entire space is full. A radiograph is then taken to ascertain that no methyl methacrylate has extruded into the acetabulum and that the lesion is completely packed. Ambulation can begin on the first postoperative day.

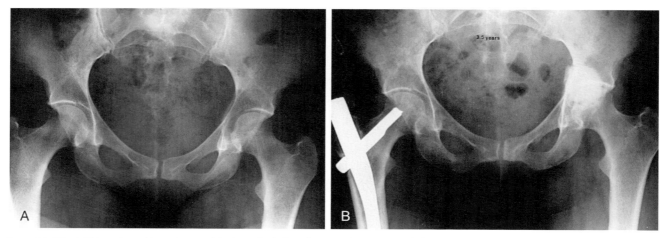

FIGURE 16–29. *A,* This patient with carcinoma of the breast had a large lesion in the supra-acetabular and posterior acetabular regions. Through a posterior approach, the tumor was completely excised from the posterior and superior aspects of the acetabulum. A small defect in the subchondral plate was covered with graft from the fascia lata, and the defect was filled with methyl methacrylate. *B,* At the 3.5-year follow-up, the patient had no degenerative changes about the hip and no hip pain. In the intervening time, a Zickel nail was used for stabilization of a large pathologic lesion in the contralateral femur.

compression may be as likely to cause pain and neurologic compromise as the vertebral fracture. There also may be a significant vascular component to the neural defect.

Patients with metastatic spine disease can be grouped into one of three classes (Fig. 16–33). Class 1 includes patients who are asymptomatic, without neurologic symptoms. The spinal lesion has come to attention because of a finding in an imaging study (bone scan, CT scan, or plain radiograph). Patients with positive bone scan results should have appropriate plain radiographs taken to assess the degree of involvement. The bone scan is more sensitive than the plain radiograph in identifying metastatic disease of the bone.[156] At least 50% of cancellous bone must be destroyed before it can be visualized on a plain radiograph.[18] However, visualization may be possible somewhat earlier in the spine when the pedicle is involved. Because the pedicle is made up predominantly of cortical bone, when erosion in this area takes place it is more easily seen than in areas of cancellous bone. Therefore, the initial clue

radiographically of a metastatic lesion involving the body and the pedicle may be seen only in the pedicle, even when quantitatively more extensive disease is located in the body.

Even if a patient is asymptomatic, if the plain radiographs (AP and lateral) suggest the presence of a destructive process, a CT scan should be obtained to better define the structural integrity of the remaining bone. CT is a more effective study than MRI for defining cortical integrity and thereby structural properties of the remaining bone. Asymptomatic patients with minimal involvement of the vertebral body who are not at risk for instability should continue systemic therapy (i.e., chemotherapy, medical therapy, or hormonal manipulation). However, in patients who have radiosensitive tumors with greater than 50% destruction of the vertebral body, consideration should be given to the use of radiation therapy even in the absence of symptoms or evidence of instability. Most patients with such extensive involvement of the vertebral body, however,

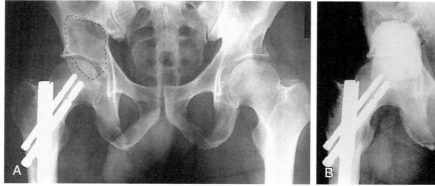
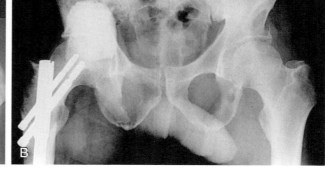

FIGURE 16–30. This patient with renal cell carcinoma metastatic to bone had previously undergone a prophylactic nailing for a painful subtrochanteric lesion. Subsequent hip pain necessitated a course of radiation therapy that did not relieve the pain. *A,* The large supra-acetabular lesion *(dotted area)* did not destroy the subchondral plate despite its size. *B,* The patient underwent curettage and packing of the lesion through a posterior approach with complete relief of pain. Notice the beginning of a similar lesion on the contralateral side.

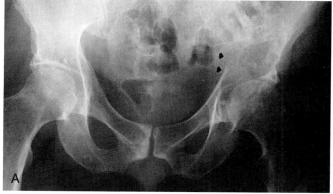

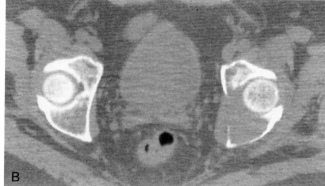

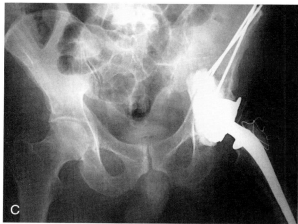

FIGURE 16–31. This patient with multiple myeloma experienced insidious onset of hip pain over an approximately 6-month period. *A*, The patient had significant destruction of the superior and medial walls of the acetabulum (*arrows*) as a result of the myeloma. *B*, Computed tomography showed destruction of the superior and the medial portions of the acetabulum (i.e., a stage 3 lesion). *C*, The patient required a complex reconstruction with Steinmann pins through the intact ilium to support reconstruction of the hip. He has had satisfactory pain relief and excellent functional recovery, and his disease is well controlled with chemotherapy.

are symptomatic. Several studies have attempted to define the risk factors for vertebral collapse. Although they may be helpful, none has proved to be totally accurate (Table 16–2).

The second class of patients consists of those who present with symptoms.[8] Patients in this class may present with local pain, neurologic signs, or both. In the patient who has pain but no neurologic findings, the evaluation must determine whether the pain is related to neural compression or to bone destruction, fracture, and instability. Following a complete history and physical examination, the initial imaging study should be plain radiographs. The documentation of collapse of a vertebra over time answers the question as to whether the pain is related to fracture or neural compression. Any patient with significant collapse should undergo MRI scanning to assess the degree of canal compromise and neural compression of the roots or dural sac. The limitation of MRI is that it does not give an accurate assessment of the cortical bone structure. It is very sensitive to marrow changes but is not specific. Changes within the vertebral body marrow, therefore, may be related to tumor, osteoporosis, radiation changes, or chemotherapeutic effects (especially associated with growth factors)[123] (Fig. 16–34). When compression of the dural sac occurs, MRI may not be able to distinguish bony compression from soft tissue tumor as the cause. CT is the preferred imaging method to distinguish bony compression from soft tissue extension of tumor. The evaluation of

the structural integrity of the vertebrae above and below those to which instrumentation may be attached is best assessed with a CT scan.

The final class of patients are those who present with neurologic deficit and localized symptoms. Before any intervention, the degree of spinal involvement must be adequately discerned. In patients who present with neurologic deficit, the combination of MRI and CT scan is critical to obtain the most information from a limited investigation that will allow appropriate treatment planning.

The patient who is a candidate for surgical intervention must satisfy a number of criteria before surgery is initiated. First, the patient should have only one level or at most two adjacent levels of dural compression. With rare exception, patients with two or more nonadjacent levels of dural compression on the initial MRI have a very limited life expectancy, and their probability for neurologic complications during the procedure is increased. In patients with multiple high-grade lesions, the prognosis for recovery is lower and the overall life span is less than for those with a single lesion.[111] Second, the extent, nature, and direction of the impingement on the dural sac must be delineated. The extent and direction can be demonstrated best by MRI, but the nature of the material causing the dural compression may be difficult to determine. In such cases, the addition of CT is helpful.[156] Third, the patient must be shown to have adequate bone stability for fixation at levels above and below the pathologic lesion, regardless of

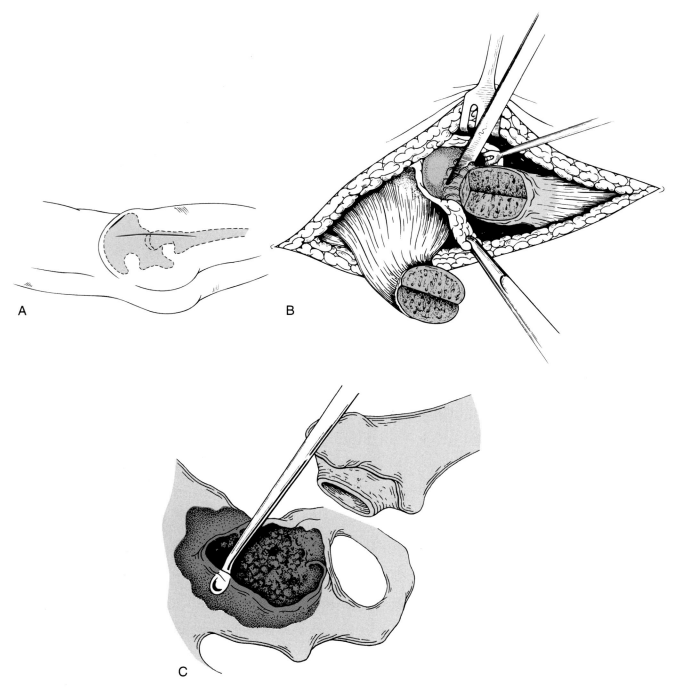

FIGURE 16–32. Surgical technique for reconstruction of a complex acetabular defect. Generally, in patients requiring complex acetabular reconstruction, the superior and medial or the superior and posterior walls of the acetabulum have been destroyed. The patient is placed in a lateral decubitus position and prepared with the leg free in the field. *A,* A straight, lateral incision begins approximately 6 cm above the tip of the greater trochanter and continues down over the midline of the trochanter and femoral shaft. The fascia lata is opened in line with its fibers. A transverse cut is made at the inferior ridge of the greater trochanter, leaving a portion of the fascia of the vastus lateralis for subsequent reattachment. A V-shaped osteotomy in the greater trochanter allows exposure of the superior and posterior portions of the capsule. *B,* The hip is dislocated, and the femoral head and neck are resected in accordance with the configuration of the cemented prosthesis to be used. A large curette is used to remove all tumor from the acetabulum. *C,* Generally, the cartilage remains intact, but with little subchondral bone beneath, it is easily breached to reach the tumor. Curettage is continued until the periosteum is encountered (anteriorly or posteriorly, or both) or a firm cortical margin is encountered on all sides. Because the subchondral plate is totally destroyed, reinforcement must be obtained for the large methyl methacrylate block and acetabular component.

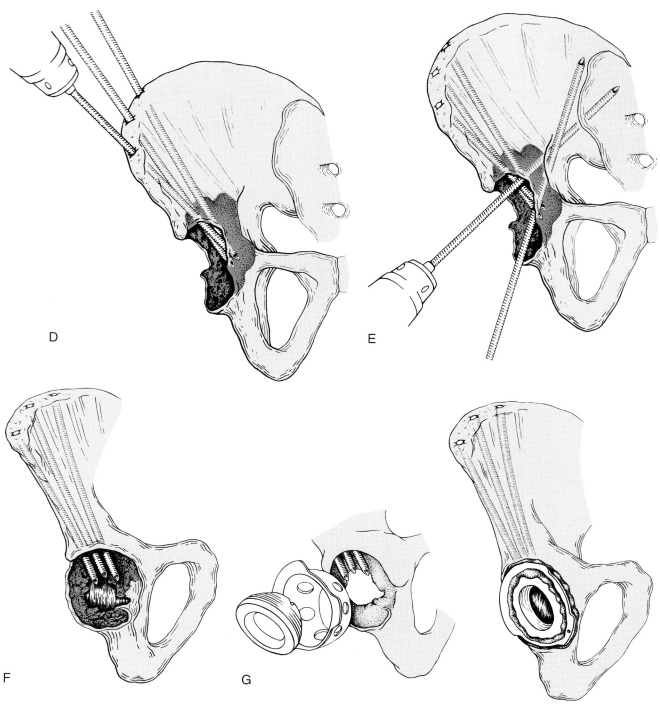

D

E

F

G

FIGURE **16–32** *Continued. D,* Using a separate stab incision made directly over the superior iliac crest approximately 3 to 4 cm posterior to the anterior superior crest, threaded Steinmann pins are inserted. It is suggested that a subperiosteal dissection be done on the inner and the outer tables of the ilium, allowing a finger to be used to ascertain the position of the threaded pin as it transverses the ilium. The threaded pins are aimed into the large defect in the superior dome of the acetabulum. Commonly, three Steinmann pins are placed, fanning out to cover the breadth of the defect for solid attachment of the methyl methacrylate. Care must be taken to ensure that the pins do not protrude so far as to preclude seating of the acetabular component. *E,* If the defect is extensive and encompasses the anterior and the posterior portions of the acetabulum, a second set of Steinmann pins may be placed from the acetabulum and aimed at the posterior superior iliac crest. An additional stab incision is not needed in that location. However, if difficulty is encountered in obtaining adequate pin alignment because of the configuration of the hip, a second stab incision can be made along the posterior superior iliac crest, and the pins can be directed from the crest into the defect. In most cases, the Steinmann pins can be directed from the defect toward the iliac crest. Care should be taken that the pins do not traverse the sciatic notch. This can be ascertained by direct palpation or with interoperative radiographs. Usually, only the pins from the anterior portion of the ilium are necessary. *F,* After complete curettage, the pin length is checked, and the pins are cut off flush with the iliac crest. *G,* A protrusio cup is sized to fill the defect. The cup allows purchase on the superior or the anterior portion of the acetabular rim (if there is any remaining bone) for better fixation. A high-density polyethylene cup or metal-backed polyethylene cup may then be cemented inside the protrusio cup. Two packages of methyl methacrylate are mixed and, in the doughy stage, are packed in and around the Steinmann pins, filling the entire defect. The protrusio cup is pressed into the doughy methyl methacrylate and is filled with the dough. The acetabular component is placed within it and held in correct orientation until the mixture hardens. The femoral component is inserted in routine fashion after wires are placed in the trochanter for repair of the trochanteric osteotomy. Routine closure is accomplished, and the patient is mobilized with toe-touch weight bearing until the trochanteric osteotomy heals, followed by full weight bearing.

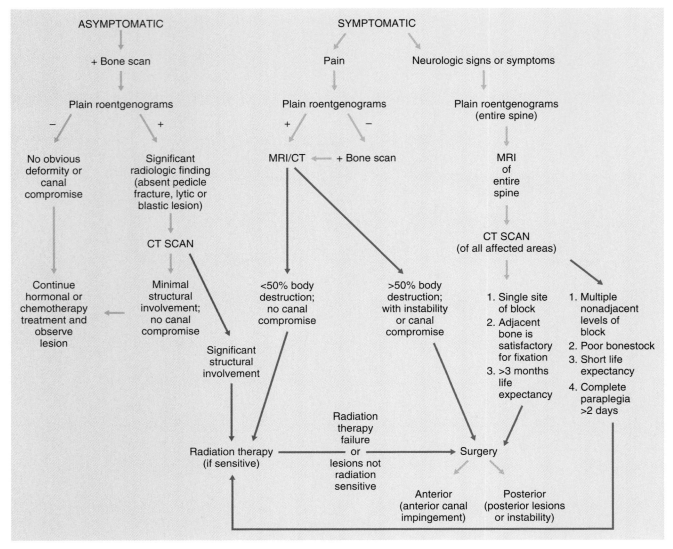

Figure 16–33. An algorithm for the evaluation of patients with metastatic disease of the spine.

Table 16–2

Risk Factors for Collapse with Metastatic Disease of the Thoracic and Lumbar Spine

Thoracic Spine

Risk factors
  Costovertebral joint destruction
  Percent of body involvement
Criteria for impending collapse
  50% to 60% body involvement alone
  25% to 30% of body with costovertebral involvement

Lumbar Spine

Risk factors
  Pedicle destruction
  Percent of body involvement
Criteria for impending collapse
  35% to 40% of body involvement alone
  25% with pedicle and/or posterior element destruction

From Taneichi H, Kaneda K, Takeda N, et al. Spine 22:239–245, 1997.

whether the intervention is anterior or posterior. Although MRI can obtain data on compression, the quality of the cortical bone necessary for fixation at levels above and below the lesion cannot adequately be ascertained. Although it may be suggested by the radiologists that MRI is sufficient to evaluate a pathologic fracture of the spine with neural deficit, additional information significant to planning the surgical intervention can be obtained from a CT scan.

Once the anatomic extent of the lesion has been clearly defined, treatment can be instituted. Treatment considerations include general health of the patient, tumor histology, and presence or absence of instability or neurologic deficit. In an effort to identify prognostic factors preoperatively, for patients with metastatic spine tumors Tokuhashi and co-workers developed a scoring system based on five parameters (Table 16–3). These included general performance, number of extraspinal metastases, number of vertebrae involved, major organ involvement,

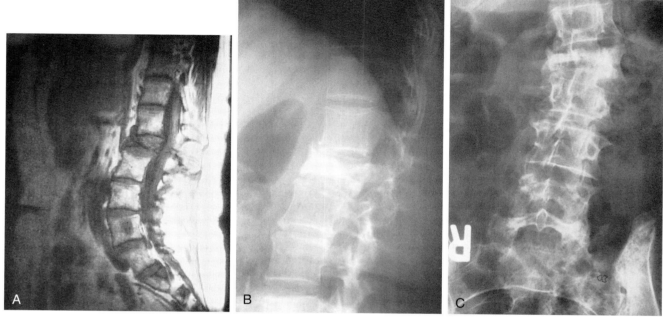

FIGURE 16–34. *A,* A magnetic resonance imaging scan in this patient with metastatic carcinoma of the breast was markedly abnormal, showing dural compression. At that time, the patient was asymptomatic. *B, C,* The radiologists were unable to determine the nature of the block. However, previous radiographs showed this to be an unchanged, healed pathologic fracture of approximately 1.5 years' duration.

TABLE 16–3

Tokuhashi's Evaluation System for Prognosis of Metastatic Spinal Tumors

Symptoms	Score*		
	0	**1**	**2**
General condition (performance status)	Poor (10% to 40%)	Moderate (50% to 70%)	Good (80% to 100%)
No. of extraspinal skeletal metastases	>3	1 to 2	0
Metastases to internal organs	Unremovable	Removable	No metastases
Primary site of tumor	Lung, stomach	Kidney, liver, uterus, unknown	Thyroid, prostate, breast, rectum
Number of metastases to spine	>3	2	1
Spinal cord palsy	Complete	Incomplete	None

*Total score versus survival period:
  9 to 12 points: >12 months survival;
  0 to 5 points: <3 months survival
From Tokuhashi Y, Matsuzaki H, Toriyama S, et al. Spine 15:1110–1113, 1999.

primary site, and spinal cord palsy. For each parameter a score from 0 to 2 is given. The maximum score is 12. They found that patients with a score of 5 or lower survived an average of 3 months or less and patients with a score of 9 or higher survived 12 months or more.[185] In the asymptomatic patient, with a positive bone scan and no indication of gross deformity, major destruction of the vertebral body, or compromise of the canal, appropriate hormonal therapy or chemotherapy can be instituted or continued if previously started. In patients with a tumor who are asymptomatic but have significant destruction of the vertebral body, radiation therapy should be considered. In patients who present with pain but no neurologic deficit, intervention can be based on the results of the information obtained from the imaging studies including plain radiographs, CT scan, and MRI. If the imaging studies fail to demonstrate major destruction of the vertebral body (i.e., less than 50% destruction), cord compression, or instability responsible for the pain, radiation therapy with or without chemotherapy or hormonal therapy can be considered. Vertebroplasty has been shown to be useful for a select group of patients with painful osseous metastasis (Fig. 16–35).[193] This may even be effective in the sacrum.[42] The criteria for patient selection is an intact posterior wall of the vertebra without dural compression. The procedure involves the percutaneous injection of acrylic surgical cement into the vertebral body under fluoroscopic control. The procedure has the advantage of being less invasive than surgery but is associated with complications. These include lack of achieving pain relief and extrusion of cement into the soft tissue with or without associated radiculopathy. In patients who did obtain pain relief, the improvement was stable for greater than 70% of patients at 6 months' follow-up. In patients with pain, secondary to either instability or marked vertebral body destruction (greater than 50%), with or without canal compromise, surgical intervention followed by radiation therapy should be the treatment of choice.[58] Radiation therapy provides a mean of limiting the growth of tumor, but once instability or marked structural impairment has occurred at a given location, it is unlikely that the pain will be relieved by radiation therapy alone. Instability or structural compromise without cord compression in any part of the spine usually responds well to stabilization.

There has been some controversy concerning the relative roles of methyl methacrylate and bone graft in surgical procedures for metastatic disease. Early work[81] suggested that methyl methacrylate could be used in the anterior portion of the spine as a vertebral body replacement, because it forms an effective strut that is strongest in compression. It can be augmented by posterior stabilization and fusion with autologous graft (Fig. 16–36). Its use precludes the use of bone graft anteriorly but allows immediate mobilization. Data indicate that the use of methyl methacrylate posteriorly adds early stability to the construct in extension but little in flexion. If used posteriorly, it should be limited in amount to avoid wound complications, and it should be augmented with an autologous graft laterally in the cervical spine for longer term stability (Fig. 16–37).[30, 51, 52, 167]

With the use of posterior cervical plates, the initial constructs are stiffer than posterior wiring techniques over longer segments. Therefore, the use of methyl methacrylate even to add stiffness initially to a posterior construct is of little value. The combined construct of an anterior methyl methacrylate strut as a vertebral body replacement and a posterior plating with bone graft gives immediate stability and becomes stronger over time if the fusion occurs posteriorly. Use of a methyl methacrylate strut anteriorly plus an anterior plate decreases surgical time and has excellent resultant longevity. In the posterior thoracolumbar spine, the use of methyl methacrylate is contraindicated, because it adds little to rod or screw techniques for stabilization and acts as a space-occupying mass prone to an increased rate of infection. Fixation of the thoracic and lumbar spines should be augmented by segmental fixation to allow early mobilization of the patient when the probability of fusion is limited by the effects of radiation or chemotherapy, the debilitating nature of the disease, and the patient's overall prognosis.

Treatment decisions are most complicated for metastatic lesions to the spine in the patient who has neurologic symptoms as the result of documented cord compression. Many studies have investigated the major treatment procedures for spinal cord compression.[44, 55, 69, 126, 139, 141, 171, 181] Approximately 15% of the metastatic lesions occur in the cervical spine, 50% in the thoracic spine, and 30% in the lumbar spine. One of the most important features is the location of the lesion within the vertebral segment and the direction from which the tumor is compressing the dural sac. Compression occurs anteriorly in 70% of patients, predominantly laterally in 20% of patients, and posteriorly in 10% of patients. It has been well documented, that radiation therapy causes significant improvement in only 50% of patients with neurologic impairment resulting from spinal cord compression caused by metastatic disease of the spine.[14, 15, 71, 147, 187] However, there is a difference in response depending on tumor type. As expected, tumors that are radiosensitive respond better than those that are not sensitive to radiation. Patients who have gross instability as well as collapse of vertebral body with bone impingement have a lower success rate than those who have pure soft tissue involvement in the absence of gross instability. No study has specifically examined these distinctions, so the data can be analyzed only by overall groups.

Laminectomy alone for treatment of metastatic disease is effective in 30% of patients,[74, 174] but it is effective in only approximately 9% of patients with anterior compression.[14] The combination of radiation therapy and laminectomy is no better than laminectomy alone.[33, 177] Anterior corpectomy (i.e., direct anterior decompression for anterior lesions) has a far higher success rate than does laminectomy.[83, 154] In most series, approximately 80% of patients improved with anterior corpectomy,[83, 84, 86, 108, 191] regardless of whether the tumor compression was caused by soft tissue or retropulsed bone. The results were also not affected by the presence of instability, because the procedure requires both direct decompression of the anterior portion of the dural sac and stabilization with a variety of

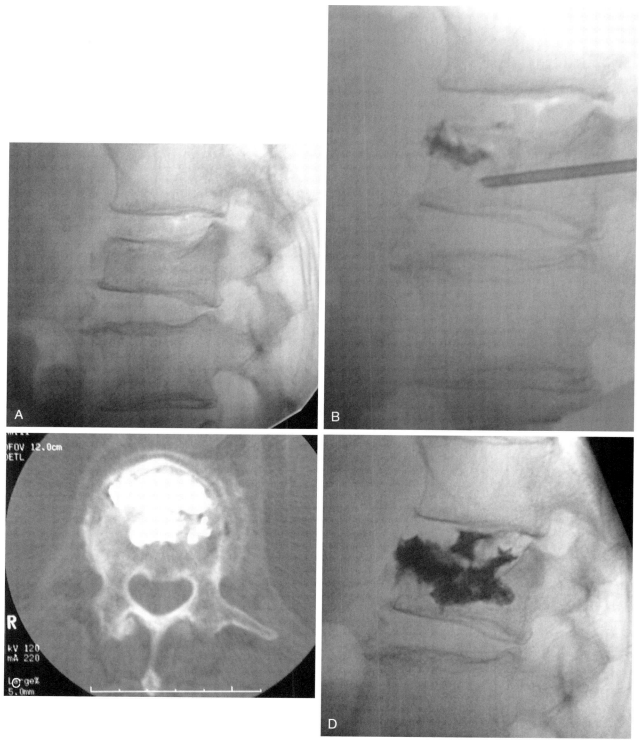

FIGURE 16–35. Vertebroplasty or kyphoplasty are useful for decreasing symptoms in patients with collapse of the vertebral body without cord compression and with an intact posterior wall. This patient with myeloma has a painful 50% compression (A) and underwent percutaneous vertebroplasty (B), filling the anterior two thirds with methyl methacrylate (C). Although the posterior wall was intact, a perforation in the superior end-plate permitted extrusion of methyl methacrylate into the disc space (D), but the patient had excellent pain relief.

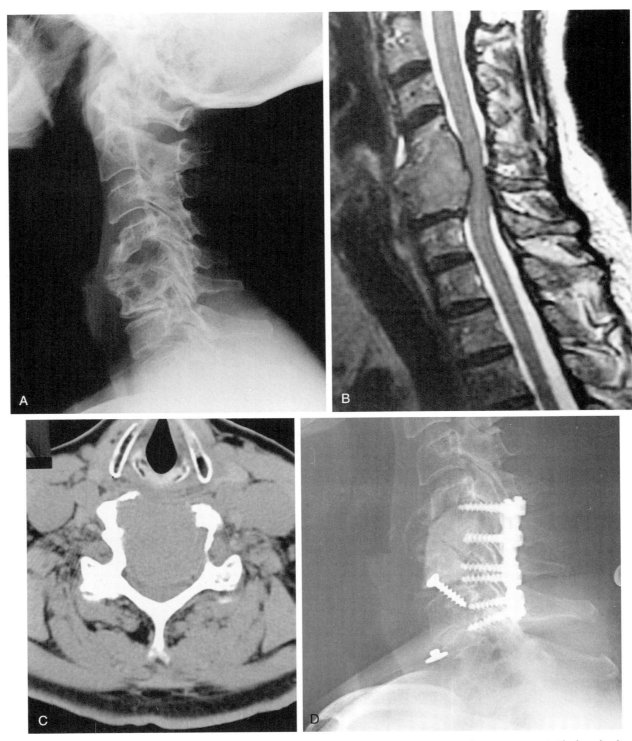

Figure 16–36. This 63-year-old woman presented with pain in her neck of 3 months' duration without neurologic symptoms. *A,* The lateral radiograph showed marked destruction of C4, C5, and C6. *B,* Magnetic resonance imaging showed marked cord compression, but the remainder of the workup showed no source. *C,* The computed tomography scan was helpful in demonstrating the degree of vertebral body destruction. *D,* The patient underwent open biopsy, revealing a solitary plasmacytoma, and as a result of the degree of destruction, a partial C4 and complete C5 and C6 corpectomies were reconstructed with a methyl methacrylate strut, followed by posterior plating and an autologous graft before beginning radiation therapy.

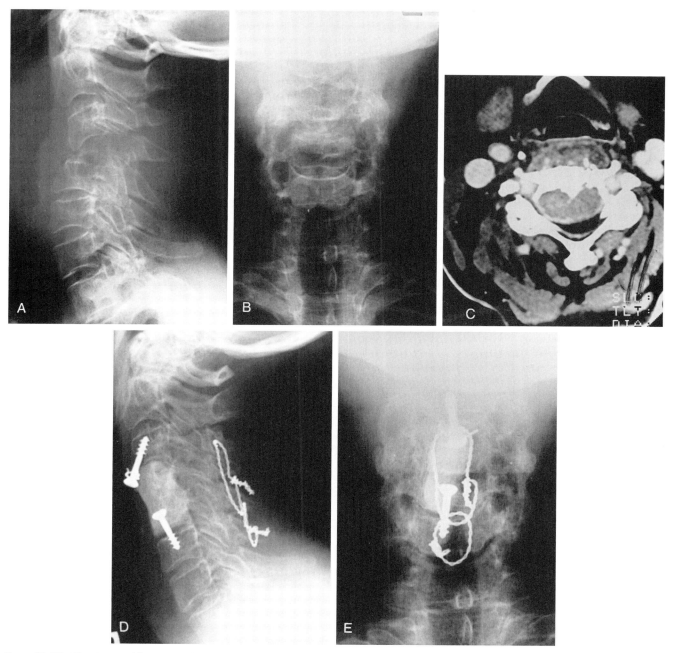

FIGURE 16–37. This 64-year-old woman with carcinoma of the breast began to have progressive neck pain. She was initially treated with anti-inflammatory drugs. *A*, However, a subsequent radiograph demonstrated complete destruction of the C4 body with severe kyphosis and instability. Flexion-extension radiographs did not show significant motion. *B*, An anteroposterior radiograph showed the complete destruction of the C4 body. *C*, The preoperative computed tomography scan demonstrated a large soft tissue mass within the canal, with destruction of the vertebrae. The patient was placed in preoperative traction, and the vertebral height was slowly restored. The patient underwent an anterior corpectomy of C4 and C5, because the latter was partially involved. Cancellous screws were placed in the bodies above and below to stabilize methyl methacrylate, which was then inserted into the space in doughy form to fill the defect. The patient was then turned prone on the Stryker frame and underwent interspinous wiring with iliac graft. *D, E*, At the 10-year follow-up assessment, the patient was asymptomatic, had returned to all activities, and was neurologically normal.

different constructs using methyl methacrylate or bone graft, or both.[51, 75]

Laminectomy alone or in combination with radiation is relatively ineffective for restoration of neurologic function from metastatic disease of the spine. Its only effective role is in the small group of patients with a mass compressing the dural sac emanating from the posterior elements. Current data suggest that anterior corpectomy for patients with pure anterior tumor is the most rational treatment and seems to give the best overall results (Fig. 16–38).[57] The posterolateral transpedicle approach may be appropriate in selected cases.[13] However, it is critical to combine the appropriate surgical procedure with postoperative radiation therapy to improve local tumor control. In tumors that are not radiosensitive, complications related to local recurrence

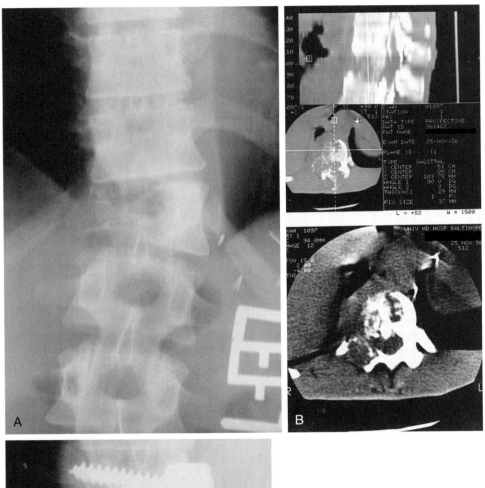

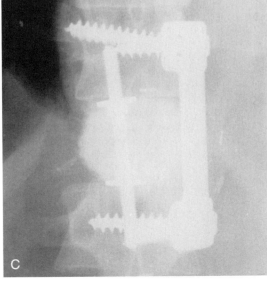

Figure 16–38. *A,* This patient presented with incapacitating pain and a pathologic fracture of the T12 vertebra and a soft tissue tumor anteriorly impinging on a dural sac. *B,* The patient underwent anterior corpectomy and excision of the T12 body, with removal of all soft tissue tumor impinging on the dural sac. *C,* Stabilization with methyl methacrylate and a plate from T11 to L1 was used to replace the vertebral body. The patient had immediate relief of pain and returned to full functional capacity.

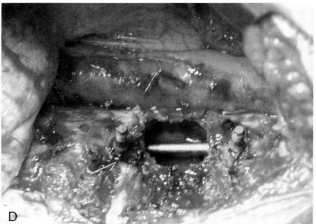 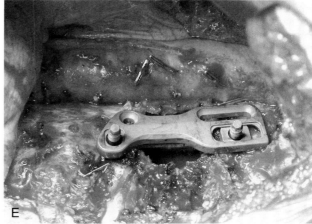

FIGURE 16–38 *Continued. D, E,* Intraoperative photographs demonstrate the technique for insertion of the rod spanning the vertebrectomy and application of a plate.

are not uncommon even after effective decompression and recovery.[104] Adjunctive local techniques can be combined with effective surgery to decrease the recurrence rate (Fig. 16–39). Adjuvant therapies such as embolization and brachytherapy[120] are used in an effort to improve local control. Other adjutants that may lead to improved local control include the use of the slow release chemotherapy from methyl methacrylate.[192] Surgical treatment should be individualized and based on whether the compression is anterior, posterior, or circumferential. In patients with pure anterior disease and anterior dural compression, if there is adequate bone stock and the area of dural compression is isolated (extending no more than to adjacent segments), anterior corpectomy and stabilization give adequate results, with pain relief and recovery from neurologic deficits.[79]

The success of recovery directly correlates with the length of time that the symptoms have been present.[11] The longer the duration of neurologic involvement and the more dense the neurologic involvement, the less likely the patient is to have significant recovery. Early recognition and prompt intervention are critical in preventing permanent neurologic impairment. In patients with primarily posterior involvement, laminectomy with or without stabilization should provide adequate relief of symptoms. In patients with circumferential disease, the involvement of the vertebral body should be assessed. If the compression is predominantly posterior with gross instability anteriorly, laminectomy combined with posterior stabilization is the treatment of choice.[180] If the disease is predominantly anterior with posterior instability or previous laminectomy, anterior corpectomy and a more rigid stabilization construct are indicated (see Fig. 16–39). In some cases, both anterior and posterior surgery is necessary for adequate decompression. The magnitude of the surgery should be considered in relation to the patient's prognosis, overall health, and potential for recovery.[115]

SUMMARY

The treatment of osseous metastatic disease should be based on several firm principles. Assessment of the area of metastatic disease should be complete. The axial and appendicular skeleton should be evaluated for the presence of tumor and the degree of mechanical impairment and instability before any treatment procedures are instituted. If the primary concern is the presence of tumor and there is no significant compromise of the structural stability of that particular body portion, then nonoperative treatment with radiation or chemotherapy, or both, is indicated. If there is significant mechanical weakness with either fracture or impending fracture, surgical stabilization should be considered. Surgical reconstruction after pathologic fracture follows different principles from those used for management of fractures associated with non-neoplastic causes. The impaired healing potential of fractures resulting from metastases indicates that more rigid forms of fixation, combined with use of materials such as methyl methacrylate at times, are needed to regain structural stability. Stabilization of osseous metastases per se may not extend the duration of the patient's life. But among the goals of surgical intervention is an improvement in the quality of life and a decrease in the incidence of complications associated with metastatic bone disease (i.e., loss of mobility, structural instability, pain, and neurologic dysfunction). These goals should be achieved in the immediate postoperative period. Because local tumor control is necessary for long-term success, postoperative irradiation (which further impairs bone healing) is a critical adjunct to the stabilization of pathologic lesions and fractures. If these principles are adhered to, the orthopaedic surgeon can greatly improve the quality of life of patients with metastatic disease.

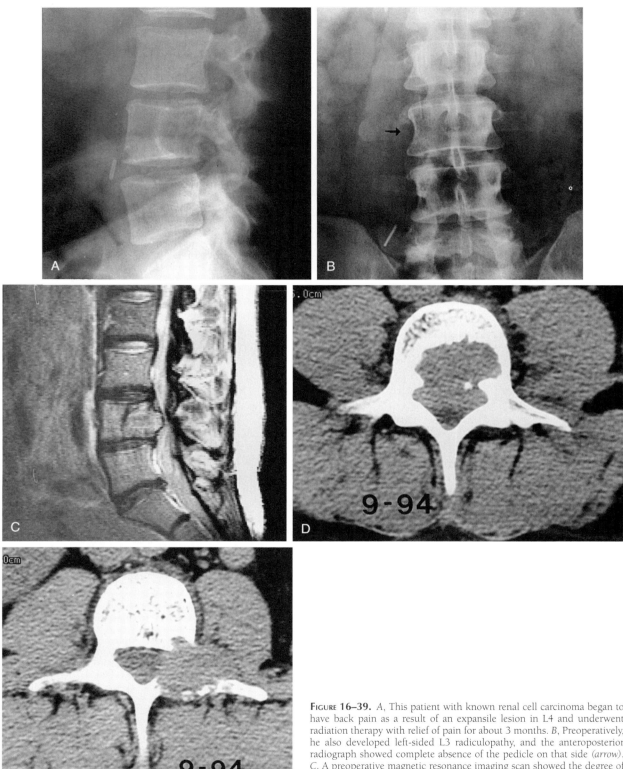

FIGURE 16–39. *A*, This patient with known renal cell carcinoma began to have back pain as a result of an expansile lesion in L4 and underwent radiation therapy with relief of pain for about 3 months. *B*, Preoperatively, he also developed left-sided L3 radiculopathy, and the anteroposterior radiograph showed complete absence of the pedicle on that side *(arrow)*. *C*, A preoperative magnetic resonance imaging scan showed the degree of compression of the dural sac at L4 and the fact that the L3 lesion was completely separate. Preoperative computed tomography scans of L4 *(D)* and L3 *(E)* showed the extent of structural compromise and compression in a previously radiated field.

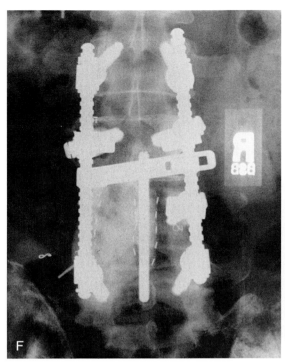

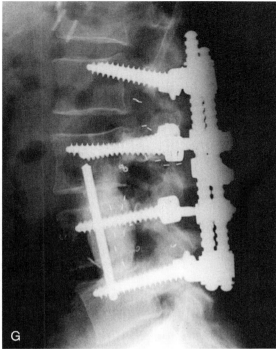

FIGURE 16–39 *Continued. F, G,* The patient underwent an anterior and posterior decompression and stabilization in a single sitting, with implantation of iodine 125 seeds both in the methyl methacrylate block anteriorly and in Gelfoam in the defect in the pedicle posteriorly. He remained stable and disease free in that location 18 months later.

REFERENCES

1. Abdul-Karim, F.W.; Kida, M.; Wentz, W.B.; et al. Bone metastasis from gynecologic carcinomas: A clinicopathologic study. Gynecol Oncol 39:108–114, 1990.
2. Aboulafia, A.J.; Buch, R.; Mathews, J.; et al. Reconstruction using the saddle prosthesis following excision of primary and metastatic periacetabular tumors. Clin Orthop 314:203–213, 1995.
3. Altman, H. Intramedullary nailing for pathological impending and actual fractures of long bones. Bull Hosp Joint Dis 13:239, 1952.
4. Anderson, J.T.; Erickson, J.M.; Thompson, R.C.J.; Chao, E.Y. Pathologic femoral shaft fractures comparing fixation techniques using cement. Clin Orthop 131:273–278, 1978.
5. Barron, K.D.; Harano, A.; Araki, A.; Terry, R.D. Experiences with metastatic neoplasms involving the spinal cord. Neurology 9:91–106, 1959.
6. Batson, O.V. The function of the vertebral veins and their role in the spread of metastases. Ann Surg 112:138–149, 1940.
7. Beals, R.K.; Lawton, G.D.; Snell, W.E. Prophylactic internal fixation of the femur in metastatic breast cancer. Cancer 28:1350–1354, 1971.
8. Bernat, J.L.; Greenberg, E.R.; Barrett, J. Suspected epidural compression of the spinal cord and cauda equina by metastatic carcinoma. Clinical diagnosis and survival. Cancer 51:1953–1957, 1983.
9. Berrettoni, B.A.; Carter, J.R. Mechanisms of cancer metastasis to bone. J Bone Joint Surg Am 68:308–312, 1986.
10. Berruti, A.; Dogliotti, L.; Bitossi, R.; et al. Incidence of skeletal complications in patients with bone metastatic prostate cancer and hormone refractory disease: Predictive role of bone resorption and formation markers evaluated at baseline. J Urol 164:1248–1253, 2000.
11. Bhalla, S.K. Metastatic disease of the spine. Clin Orthop 73:52–60, 1970.
12. Bhardwaj, S.; Holland, J.F. Chemotherapy of metastatic cancer in bone. Review. Clin Orthop 169:28–37, 1982.
13. Bilsky, M.H.; Boland, P.; Lis, E.; et al. Single-stage posterolateral transpedicle approach for spondylectomy, epidural decompression, and circumferential fusion of spinal metastases. Spine 25:2240–2249, 2000.
14. Black, P. Spinal metastasis: Current status and recommended guidelines for management. Review. Neurosurgery 5:726–746, 1979.
15. Blake, D. Radiation treatment of metastatic bone disease. Clin Orthop 73:89–100, 1970.
16. Blari, R.J.; McAfee, J.G. Radiographic detection of skeletal metastases: Radiographs vs scans. J Radiat Oncol 1:1201, 1976.
17. Boissier, S.; Ferreras, M.; Peyruchaud, O.; et al. Bisphosphonates inhibit breast and prostate carcinoma cell invasion, an early event in the formation of bone metastases. Cancer Res 60:2949–2954, 2000.
18. Boland, P.J.; Lane, J.M.; Sundaresan, N. Metastatic disease of the spine. Clin Orthop 169:95–102, 1982.
19. Bonariqo, B.C.; Rubin, P. Nonunion of pathologic fractures after radiation therapy. Radiology 88:889–898, 1967.
20. Braunstein, E.M.; Kuhns, L.R. Computed tomographic demonstration of spinal metastases. Spine 8:912–915, 1983.
21. Bremner, R.A.; Jelliffe, A.M. The management of pathological fractures of the major long bones from metastatic cancer. J Bone Joint Surg 40B:652–659, 1958.
22. Bubendorf, L.; Schopfer, A.; Wagner, U.; et al. Metastatic patterns of prostate cancer: An autopsy study of 1,589 patients. Hum Pathol 31:578–583, 2000.
23. Cadman, E.; Bertino, J.R. Chemotherapy of skeletal metastases. Review. Int J Radiat Oncol Biol Phys 1:1211–1215, 1976.
24. Carlin, B.I.; Andriole, G.L. The natural history, skeletal complications, and management of bone metastases in patients with prostate carcinoma. Review. Cancer 88:2989–2994, 2000.
25. Chan, D.; Carter, S.R.; Grimer, R.J.; Sneath, R.S. Endoprosthetic replacement for bony metastases. Ann R Coll Surg Engl 74:13–18, 1992.
26. Cheng, D.S.; Seitz, C.B.; Eyre, H.J. Nonoperative management of femoral, humeral, and acetabular metastases in patients with breast carcinoma. Cancer 45:1533–1537, 1980.
27. Ciezki, J.; Macklis, R.M. The palliative role of radiotherapy in the management of the cancer patient. Review. Semin Oncol 22:82–90, 1995.
28. Citrin, D.L.; Bessent, R.G.; Greig, W.R. A comparison of the sensitivity and accuracy of the ^{99m}Tc-phosphate bone scan and skeletal radiograph in the diagnosis of bone metastases. Clin Radiol 28:107–117, 1977.

29. Clain, A. Secondary malignant lesions of bone. Br J Cancer 9:15, 1965.
30. Clark, C.R.; Keggi, K.J.; Panjabi, M.M. Methylmethacrylate stabilization of the cervical spine. J Bone Joint Surg Am 66:40–46, 1984.
31. Coleman, R. Skeletal complications of malignancy. Cancer 80: 1588–1594, 1997.
32. Colletti, P.M.; Siegel, H.J.; Woo, M.Y.; et al. The impact on treatment planning of MRI of the spine in patients suspected of vertebral metastasis: An efficacy study. Comput Med Imaging Graph 20:159–162, 1996.
33. Constans, J.P.; de Divitiis, E.; Donzelli, R.; et al. Spinal metastases with neurological manifestations. Review of 600 cases. J Neurosurg 59:111–118, 1983.
34. Cook, A.M.; Lau, T.N.; Tomlinson, M.J.; et al. Magnetic resonance imaging of the whole spine in suspected malignant spinal cord compression: Impact on management. Clin Oncol (R Coll Radiol) 10:39–43, 1998.
35. Coran, A.G.; Banks, H.H.; Aliapoulios, W.A.; Wilson, R.E. The management of pathologic fractures in patients with metastatic carcinoma of the breast. Surg Gynecol Obstet 127:1225–1230, 1968.
36. Cramer S.F.; Fried L.; Carter K.J. The cellular basis of metastatic bone disease in patients with lung cancer. Cancer 48:2649–2660, 1981.
37. Crates, J.; Whittle, A.P. Antegrade interlocking nailing of acute humeral shaft fractures. Clin Orthop 350:40–50, 1998.
38. Crawford, E.D.; Allen, J.A. Treatment of newly diagnosed state D2 prostate cancer with leuprolide and flutamide or leuprolide alone, phase III; intergroup study 0036. J Steroid Biochem Mol Biol 37:961–963, 1990.
39. Crolla, R.M.; de Vries, L.S.; Clevers, G.J. Locked intramedullary nailing of humeral fractures. Injury 24:403–406, 1993.
40. Cumming, J.; Hacking, N.; Fairhurst, J.; et al. Distribution of bony metastases in prostatic carcinoma. Br J Urol 66:411–414, 1990.
41. Damron, T.A.; Sim, F.H. Surgical treatment for metastatic disease of the pelvis and the proximal end of the femur. Review. Instr Course Lect 49:461–470, 2000.
42. Dehdashti, A.R.; Martin, J.B.; Jean, B.; Rufenacht, D.A. PMMA cementoplasty in symptomatic metastatic lesions of the S1 vertebral body. Cardiovasc Intervent Radiol 23:235–237, 2000.
43. Demers, L.M.; Costa, L.; Lipton, A. Biochemical markers and skeletal metastases. Review. Cancer 88:2919–2926, 2000.
44. DeWald, R.L.; Bridwell, K.H.; Prodromas, C.; Rodts, M.F. Reconstructive spinal surgery as palliation for metastatic malignancies of the spine. Spine 10:21–26, 1985.
45. Dickie, G.J.; Macfarlane, D. Strontium and samarium therapy for bone metastases from prostate carcinoma. Australas Radiol 43:476–479, 1999.
46. Diel, I.J.; Solomayer, E.F.; Costa, S.D.; et al. Reduction in new metastases in breast cancer with adjuvant clodronate treatment [see comments]. N Engl J Med 339:357–363, 1998.
47. Diel, I.J.; Solomayer, E.F.; Bastert, G. Bisphosphonates and the prevention of metastasis: First evidences from preclinical and clinical studies. Review. Cancer 88:3080–3088, 2000.
48. Dijkstra, S.; Stapert, J.; Boxma, H.; Wiggers, T. Treatment of pathological fractures of the humeral shaft due to bone metastases: A comparison of intramedullary locking nail and plate osteosynthesis with adjunctive bone cement. Eur J Surg Oncol 22:621–626, 1996.
49. Domchek, S.M.; Younger, J.; Finkelstein, D.M.; Seiden, M.V. Predictors of skeletal complications in patients with metastatic breast carcinoma. Cancer 89:363–368, 2000.
50. Douglass, H.O.J.; Shukla, S.K.; Mindell, E. Treatment of pathological fractures of long bones excluding those due to breast cancer. J Bone Joint Surg Am 58:1055–1061, 1976.
51. Dunn, E. The role of methylmethacrylate in the stabilization and replacement of tumors of the cervical spine: A project of the cervical spine research society. Spine 2:15–24, 1977.
52. Dunn, E.; Anas, P.P. The management of tumors of the upper cervical spine. Orthop Clin North Am 9:1065–1080, 1978.
53. Eftekhar, N.S.; Thurston, C.W. Effect of irradiation on acrylic cement with special reference to fixation of pathological fractures. J Biomech 8:53–56, 1975.
54. Eil, P.J. Skeletal imaging in metastatic disease. Curr Opin Radiol 3(6):791–796, 1991.
55. Fidler, M. Prophylactic internal fixation of secondary neoplastic deposits in long bones. BMJ 1:341–343, 1973.
56. Fidler, M. Anterior decompression and stabilization of metastatic spinal fractures. J Bone Joint Surg 68B:83–90, 1986.
57. Fielding, J.W.; Pyle, R.N.J.; Fietti, V.G., Jr. Anterior cervical vertebral body resection and bone-grafting for benign and malignant tumors. A survey under the auspices of the Cervical Spine Research Society. J Bone Joint Surg Am 61:251–253, 1979.
58. Flatley, T.J.; Anderson, M.H.; Anast, G.T. Spinal instability due to malignant disease. Treatment by segmental spinal stabilization. J Bone Joint Surg Am 66:47–52, 1984.
59. Flemming, J.E.; Beals, R.K. Pathologic fracture of the humerus. Clin Orthop 203:258–260, 1986.
60. Flinkkila, T.; Hyvonen, P.; Lakovaara, M.; et al. Intramedullary nailing of humeral shaft fractures. A retrospective study of 126 cases. Acta Orthop Scand 70:133–136, 1999.
61. Friedl, W. Indication, management and results of surgical therapy for pathological fractures in patients with bone metastases. Eur J Surg Oncol 16:380–396, 1990.
62. Friedlaender, G.E.; Johnson, R.M.; Brand, R.A.; Southwick, W.O. Treatment of pathological fractures. Conn Med 39:765–772, 1975.
63. Fuhrmann, R.A.; Roth, A.; Venbrocks, R.A. Salvage of the upper extremity in cases of tumorous destruction of the proximal humerus. J Cancer Res Clin Oncol 126:337–344, 2000.
64. Gainor, B.J.; Buchert, P. Fracture healing in metastatic bone disease. Clin Orthop 178:297–302, 1983.
65. Galasko, C.S. Pathological fractures secondary to metastatic cancer. J R Coll Surg Edinb 19:351–362, 1974.
66. Galasko, C.S. Mechanisms of bone destruction in the development of skeletal metastases: Mechanisms of lytic and blastic metastatic disease of bone. Nature 263:507–508, 1976.
67. Galasko, C.S.B. Incidence and distribution of skeletal metastases. In: Galasko C.S.B., ed. Skeletal Metastases. London, Butterworths, 1986, pp. 14–21.
68. Gilbert, H.A.; Kagan, A.R.; Nussbaum, H.; et al. Evaluation of radiation therapy for bone metastases: Pain relief and quality of life. AJR Am J Roentgenol 129:1095–1096, 1977.
69. Gilbert, R.W.; Kim, J.H.; Posner, J.B. Epidural spinal cord compression from metastatic tumor: Diagnosis and treatment. Ann Neurol 3:40–51, 1978.
70. Gold, R.I.; Seeger, L.L.; Bassett, L.W.; Steckel, R.J. An integrated approach to the evaluation of metastatic bone disease. Review. Radiol Clin North Am 28:471–483, 1990.
71. Greenberg, H.S.; Kim, J.H.; Posner, J.B. Epidural spinal cord compression from metastatic tumor: Results with a new treatment protocol. Ann Neurol 8:361–366, 1980.
72. Habermann, E.T.; Sachs, R.; Stern, R.E.; et al. The pathology and treatment of metastatic disease of the femur. Clin Orthop 169:70–82, 1982.
73. Habernek, H.; Orthner, E. A locking nail for fractures of the humerus [see comments]. J Bone Joint Surg Br 73:651–653, 1991.
74. Hall, A.J.; Mackay, N.N. The results of laminectomy for compression of the cord or cauda equina by extradural malignant tumour. J Bone Joint Surg Br 55:497–505, 1973.
75. Harrington, K.D. The use of methylmethacrylate as an adjunct in the internal fixation of malignant neoplastic fractures. J Bone Joint Surg Am 54:1665–1676, 1972.
76. Harrington, K.D. Methylmethacrylate as an adjunct in internal fixation of pathological fractures. J Bone Joint Surg Am 58:1047–1054, 1976.
77. Harrington, K.D. The role of surgery in the management of pathologic fractures. Orthop Clin North Am 8:841–859, 1977.
78. Harrington, K.D. The management of malignant pathologic fractures. Instr Course Lect 26:147, 1977.
79. Harrington, K.D. Management of unstable pathologic fracture dislocations of the spine and acetabulum, secondary to metastatic malignancy. Instr Course Lect 29:51–61, 1980.
80. Harrington, K.D. The use of methylmethacrylate for vertebral body replacement and anterior stabilization of pathological fracture dislocations of the spine due to metastatic malignant disease. J Bone Joint Surg Am 63:36–46, 1981.
81. Harrington, K.D. The management of acetabular insufficiency secondary to metastatic malignant disease. J Bone Joint Surg Am 63:653–664, 1981.
82. Harrington, K.D. New trends in the management of lower extremity metastases. Clin Orthop 169:53–61, 1982.

83. Harrington, K.D. Anterior cord decompression and spinal stabilization for patients with metastatic lesions of the spine. J Neurosurg 61(1):107–117, 1984.

84. Harrington, K.D. Metastatic disease of the spine. J Bone Joint Surg Am 68:1110–1115, 1986.

85. Harrington, K.D. Impending pathologic fractures from metastatic malignancy: Evaluation and management. Instr Course Lect 35:357–381, 1986.

86. Harrington, K.D. Anterior decompression and stabilization of the spine as a treatment for vertebral collapse and spinal cord compression from metastatic malignancy. Clin Orthop 233:177–197, 1988.

87. Harrington, K.D. Orthopaedic management of extremity and pelvic lesions. Clin Orthop 312:136–147, 1995.

88. Hashimoto, M.; Hiwa, O.; Niotta, Y.; et al. Unstable expression of E-cadherin adhesion molecules in metastatic ovarian cancer cells. Jpn J Cancer Res 80:459–463, 1989.

89. Healey, J.H.; Lane, J.M. Treatment of pathologic fractures of the distal femur with the Zickel supracondylar nail. Clin Orthop 250:216–220, 1990.

90. Hems, T.E.; Bhullar, T.P. Interlocking nailing of humeral shaft fractures: The Oxford experience 1991 to 1994 [see comments]. Injury 27:485–489, 1996.

91. Hipp, J.A.; Springfield, D.S.; Hayes, W.C. Predicting pathologic fracture risk in the management of metastatic bone defects. Review. Clin Orthop 312:120–135, 1995.

92. Hoskin, P.J. Radiotherapy in the management of bone pain. Review. Clin Orthop 312:105–119, 1995.

93. Hyder, N.; Wray, C.C. Treatment of pathological fractures of the humerus with Ender nails. J R Coll Surg Edinb 38:370–372, 1993.

94. Ikpeme, J.O. Intramedullary interlocking nailing for humeral fractures: Experiences with the Russell-Taylor humeral nail. Injury 25:447–455, 1994.

95. Jacobson, A.F.; Cronin, E.B.; Stomper, P.C.; Kaplan, W.D. Bone scans with one or two new abnormalities in cancer patients with no known metastases: Frequency and serial scintigraphic behavior of benign and malignant lesions. Radiology 175:229–232, 1990.

96. Jacobsson, H.; Goransson, H. Radiological detection of bone and bone marrow metastases. Review. Med Oncol Tumor Pharmacother 8:253–260, 1991.

97. Jaffe, H.L. Palliation of metastatic bone disease. In: Hickey, R.D., ed. Palliative Care of the Cancer Patient. Boston, Little, Brown, 1967, pp 313–340.

98. Janjan, N.A. Radiation for bone metastases: Conventional techniques and the role of systemic radiopharmaceuticals. Review. Cancer 80:1628–1645, 1997.

99. Jensen, C.H.; Hansen, D.; Jorgensen, U. Humeral shaft fractures treated by interlocking nailing: A preliminary report on 16 patients. Injury 23:234–236, 1992.

100. Johnston, A.D. Pathology of metastatic tumors in bone. Review. Clin Orthop 73:8–32, 1970.

101. Kamby, C.; Vejborg, I.; Daugaard, S.; et al. Clinical and radiologic characteristics of bone metastases in breast cancer. Cancer 60:2524–2531, 1987.

102. Kao, C.H.; Hsieh, J.F.; Tsai, S.C.; et al. Comparison and discrepancy of ^{18}F-2-deoxyglucose positron emission tomography and Tc-99m MDP bone scan to detect bone metastases. Anticancer Res 20:2189–2192, 2000.

103. Keene, J.S.; Sellinger, D.S.; McBeath, A.A.; Engber, W.D. Metastatic breast cancer in the femur. A search for the lesion at risk of fracture. Clin Orthop 203:282–288, 1986.

104. King, G.J.; Kostuik, J.P.; McBroom, R.J.; Richardson, W. Surgical management of metastatic renal carcinoma of the spine. Spine 16:265–271, 1991.

105. Kirchner, P.T.; Simon, M.A. Radioisotopic evaluation of skeletal disease. J Bone Joint Surg Am 63:673–681, 1981.

106. Kocialkowski, A.; Wallace, W.A. Reconstruction of the femur with the aid of a combination of a joint replacement and an intramedullary nail. Injury 22:63–65, 1991.

107. Koskinen, E.V.; Nieminen, R.A. Surgical treatment of metastatic pathological fracture of major long bones. Acta Orthop Scand 44:539–549, 1973.

108. Kostuik, J.P. Anterior spinal cord decompression for lesions of the thoracic and lumbar spine, techniques, new methods of internal fixation results. Spine 8:512–531, 1983.

109. Kraemer, W.J.; Hearn, T.C.; Powell, J.N.; Mahomed, N. Fixation of segmental subtrochanteric fractures. A biomechanical study. Clin Orthop 333:71–79, 1996.

110. Kunec, J.R.; Lewis, R.J. Closed intramedullary rodding of pathologic fractures with supplemental cement. Clin Orthop 188:183–186, 1984.

111. Kurdy, N.M.; Kay, P.R.; Paul, A.S.; et al. The Huckstep nail. Stable fixation of mechanically deficient femoral bone. Clin Orthop 316:214–220, 1995.

112. Lam, W.C.; Delikatny, E.J.; Orr, F.W.; et al. The chemotactic response of tumor cells. A model for cancer metastasis. Am J Pathol 104:69–76, 1981.

113. Lancaster, J.M.; Koman, L.A.; Gristina, A.G.; et al. Pathologic fractures of the humerus. South Med J 81:52–55, 1988.

114. Lane, J.M.; Sculco, T.P.; Zolan, S. Treatment of pathological fractures of the hip by endoprosthetic replacement. J Bone Joint Surg Am 62:954–959, 1980.

115. Lee, C.K.; Rosa, R.; Fernand, R. Surgical treatment of tumors of the spine. Spine 11:201–208, 1986.

116. Levine, A.M.; Kenzora, J.E. Management of periacetabular metastatic lesions of bone. Orthop Trans 9:1, 1985.

117. Levine, A.M.; Wouk, V. Retrograde reamed humeral nailing for pathologic lesions of the humerus. Orthop Trans 10:485–486, 1986.

118. Levine, A.M. Locked intramedullary fixation for metastatic disease of the femur. Paper presented at the American Academy of Orthopaedic Surgeons Meeting, Las Vegas, 1989.

119. Levine, A.M. Reamed retrograde intramedullary nailing for metastatic lesions of the humerus. Paper presented at the ENSOS/AMSTS/ISOLS Meeting, Florence, Italy, 1995.

120. Levine, A.M.; Virkus, W.; Amin, P. Brachytherapy in the treatment of spinal neoplasms. Orthop Trans 20:35, 1996.

121. Levy, R.N.; Sherry, H.S.; Siffert, R.S. Surgical management of metastatic disease of bone at the hip. Clin Orthop 169:62–69, 1982.

122. Lewallen, R.P.; Pritchard, D.J.; Sim, F.H. Treatment of pathologic fractures or impending fractures of the humerus with Rush rods and methylmethacrylate. Experience with 55 cases in 54 patients, 1968–1977. Clin Orthop 166:193–198, 1982.

123. Li, J.; Tio, F.O.; Jinkins, J.R. Contrast-enhanced MRI of healed pathologic vertebral compression fracture mimicking active disease in a patient treated for lymphoma. Neuroradiology 35:506–508, 1993.

124. Lin, J.; Hou, S.M.; Hang, Y.S.; Chao, E.Y. Treatment of humeral shaft fractures by retrograde locked nailing. Clin Orthop 342:147–155, 1997.

125. Lin, J.; Hou, S.M. Antegrade locked nailing for humeral shaft fractures. Clin Orthop 365:201–210, 1999.

126. Livingston, K.E.; Perrin, R.G. The neurosurgical management of spinal metastases causing cord and cauda equina compression. J Neurosurg 49:839–843, 1978.

127. Loitz, D.; Konnecker, H.; Illgner, A.; Reilmann, H. [Retrograde intramedullary nailing of humeral fractures with new implants. Analysis of 120 consecutive cases.] In German. Unfallchirurg 101:543–550, 1998.

128. MacAusland, W.R.J.; Wyman, E.T., Jr. Management of metastatic pathological fractures. Clin Orthop 73:39–51, 1970.

129. Marcove, R.C.; Yang, D.J. Survival times after treatment of pathologic fractures. Cancer 20:2154–2158, 1967.

130. Mareel, M.M.; Behrens, J.; Birchmeier, W.; et al. Down-regulation of E-cadherin expression in Madin Darby canine kidney (MDCK) cells inside tumors of nude mice. Int J Cancer 47:922–928, 1991.

131. Matsubayashi, T.; Koga, H.; Nishiyama, Y.; et al. The reparative process of metastatic bone lesions after radiotherapy. Jpn J Clin Oncol 11(suppl):253–264, 1981.

132. Mickelson, M.R.; Bonfiglio, M. Pathological fractures in the proximal part of the femur treated by Zickel-nail fixation. J Bone Joint Surg Am 58:1067–1070, 1976.

133. Miller, F.; Whitehill, R. Carcinoma of the breast metastatic to the skeleton. Clin Orthop 184:121–127, 1984.

134. Miller, G.J.; Vander, G.R.; Blake, W.P.; Springfield, D.S. Performance evaluation of a cement-augmented intramedullary fixation system for pathologic lesions of the femoral shaft. Clin Orthop 221:246–254, 1987.

135. Mirels, H. Metastatic disease in long bones. A proposed scoring system for diagnosing impending pathologic fractures. Clin Orthop 249:256–264, 1989.

136. Mundy, G.R.; Eilon, G.; Altman, A.J.; Dominguez, J.H. Nonbone cell mediated bone resorption. Mechanisms of Localized Bone Loss. pp 229–237, 1978.

137. Mundy, G.R. Mechanisms of bone metastasis. Review. Cancer 80:1546–1556, 1997.

138. Murray, J.A.; Parrish, F.F. Surgical management of secondary neoplastic fractures about the hip. Orthop Clin North Am 5:887–901, 1974.

139. Nather, A.; Bose, K. The results of decompression of cord or cauda equina compression from metastatic extradural tumors. Clin Orthop 150:103–108, 1982.

140. Needham, P.R.; Mithal, N.P.; Hoskin, P.J. Radiotherapy for bone pain. J R Soc Med 87:503–505, 1994.

141. O'Neil, J.; Gardner, V.; Armstrong, G. Treatment of tumors of the thoracic and lumbar spinal column. Clin Orthop 227:103–112, 1988.

142. Oka, J.; Shiozaki, H.; Kobayashi, K.; et al. Expression of E-cadherin cells adhesion molecules in breast cancer tissues and its relationship to metastasis. Jpn J Cancer Res 32:1696, 1993.

143. Orr, W.; Varani, J.; Ward, P.A. Characteristics of the chemotactic response of neoplastic cells to a factor derived from the fifth component of complement. Am J Pathol 93:405–422, 1978.

144. Paget, S. The distribution of secondary growths in cancer of the breast. Cancer Metastasis Rev 8:98–101, 1989.

145. Papapoulos, S.E.; Hamdy, N.A.; van der Pluijm, G. Bisphosphonates in the management of prostate carcinoma metastatic to the skeleton. Review. Cancer 88:3047–3053, 2000.

146. Parrish, F.F.; Murray, J.A. Surgical treatment for secondary neoplastic fractures. A retrospective study of ninety-six patients. J Bone Joint Surg Am 52:665–686, 1970.

147. Patterson, R.H., Jr. Metastatic disease of the spine: Surgical risk versus radiation therapy. Clin Neurosurg 27:641–644, 1980.

148. Perez, C.A.; Bradfield, J.S.; Morgan, H.C. Management of pathologic fractures. Cancer 29:684–693, 1972.

149. Perez, J.E.; Machiavelli, M.; Leone, B.A.; et al. Bone-only versus visceral-only metastatic pattern in breast cancer: Analysis of 150 patients. A GOCS study. Grupo Oncologico Cooperativo del Sur. Am J Clin Oncol 13:294–298, 1990.

150. Poigenfurst, J.; Marcove, R.C.; Miller, T.R. Surgical treatment of fractures through metastases in the proximal femur. J Bone Joint Surg Br 50:743–756, 1968.

151. Pugh, J.; Sherry, H.S.; Futterman, B.; Frankel, V.H. Biomechanics of pathologic fractures. Clin Orthop 169:109–114, 1982.

152. Rana, A.; Chisholm, G.D.; Khan, M.; et al. Patterns of bone metastasis and their prognostic significance in patients with carcinoma of the prostate. Br J Urol 72:933–936, 1993.

153. Ratanatharathorn, V.; Powers, W.E.; Steverson, N.; et al. Bone metastasis from cervical cancer. Cancer 73:2372–2379, 1994.

154. Raycroft, J.F.; Hockman, R.P.; Southwick, W.O. Metastatic tumors involving the cervical vertebrae: Surgical palliation. J Bone Joint Surg Am 60:763–768, 1978.

155. Redmond, B.J.; Biermann, J.S.; Blasier, R.B. Interlocking intramedullary nailing of pathological fractures of the shaft of the humerus. J Bone Joint Surg Am 78:891–896, 1996.

156. Redmond, J.; Spring, D.B.; Munderloh, S.H.; et al. Spinal computed tomography scanning in the evaluation of metastatic disease. Cancer 54:253–258, 1984.

157. Renard, A.J.; Veth, R.P.; Schreuder, H.W.; et al. The saddle prosthesis in pelvic primary and secondary musculoskeletal tumors: Functional results at several postoperative intervals. Arch Orthop Trauma Surg 120:188–194, 2000.

158. Rommens, P.M.; Verbruggen, J.; Broos, P.L. Retrograde locked nailing of humeral shaft fractures. A review of 39 patients [see comments]. J Bone Joint Surg Br 77:84–89, 1995.

159. Rommens, P.M.; Blum, J.; Runkel, M. Retrograde nailing of humeral shaft fractures. Clin Orthop 350:26–39, 1998.

160. Schaberg, J.; Gainor, B.J. A profile of metastatic carcinoma of the spine. Spine 10:19–20, 1985.

161. Schocker, J.D.; Brady, L.W. Radiation therapy for bone metastasis. Clin Orthop 169:38–43, 1982.

162. Scholz, D.A.; Purnell, D.C.; Goldsmith, R.S.; et al. Hypercalcemia and cancer. CA Cancer J Clin 25:27–30, 1975.

163. Schurman, D.J.; Amstutz, H.C. Orthopedic management of patients with metastatic carcinoma of the breast. Surg Gynecol Obstet 137:831–836, 1973.

164. Scott, W.W.; Mennon, M.; Walsh, F.C. Hormone therapy of prostatic cancer. Cancer 45(suppl): 1929–1936, 1980.

165. Serfini, A.N. Current status of systemic intravenous radiopharmaceuticals for the treatment of painful metastatic bone disease. Int J Radiat Oncol Biol Phys 30(5):1187–1194, 1994.

166. Seto, E.; Segall, G.M.; Terris, M.K. Positron emission tomography detection of osseous metastases of renal cell carcinoma not identified on bone scan. Urology 55(2):286, 2000.

167. Sherk, H.H.; Nolan, J.P.J.; Mooar, P.A. Treatment of tumors of the cervical spine. Clin Orthop 233:163–167, 1988.

168. Sherry, H.S.; Levy, R.N.; Siffert, R.S. Metastatic disease of bone in orthopedic surgery. Clin Orthop 169:44–52, 1982.

169. Shreve, P.D.; Grossman, H.B.; Gross, M.D.; Wahl, R.L. Metastatic prostate cancer: Initial findings of PET with 2-deoxy-2-[F-18]fluoro-D-glucose. Radiology 199:751–756, 1996.

170. Shreve, P.D.; Steventon, R.S.; Gross, M.D. Diagnosis of spine metastases by FDG imaging using a gamma camera in the coincidence mode. Clin Nucl Med 23:799–802, 1998.

171. Siegal, T.; Tiqva, P. Vertebral body resection for epidural compression by malignant tumors. Results of forty-seven consecutive operative procedures. J Bone Joint Surg Am 67:375–382, 1985.

172. Sim, F.H.; Pritchard, D.J. Metastatic disease in the upper extremity. Clin Orthop 169:83–94, 1982.

173. Sim, F.H.; Frassica, F.J.; Chao, E.Y. Orthopaedic management using new devices and prostheses. Review. Clin Orthop 160–172, 1995.

174. Smith, R. An evaluation of surgical treatment for spinal cord compression due to metastatic carcinoma. J Neurol Neurosurg Psychiatry 28:152–158, 1965.

175. Soloway, M.S.; Hardeman, S.W.; Hickey, D.; et al. Stratification of patients with metastatic prostate cancer based on extent of disease on initial bone scan. Cancer 61:195–202, 1988.

176. Springfield DS. Mechanisms of metastasis. Clin Orthop 169:15–19, 1982.

177. Stark, R.J.; Henson, R.A.; Evans, S.J. Spinal metastases. A retrospective survey from a general hospital. Brain 105:189–213, 1982.

178. Stubbs, B.E.; Matthews, L.S.; Sonstegard, D.A. Experimental fixation of fractures of the femur with methylmethacrylate. J Bone Joint Surg Am 57:317–321, 1975.

179. Sun, Y.C.; Geldof, A.A.; Newling, D.W.; Rao, B.R. Progression delay of prostate tumor skeletal metastasis effects by bisphosphonates. J Urol 148:1270–1273, 1992.

180. Sundaresan, N.; Galicich, J.H.; Lane, J.M. Harrington rod stabilization for pathological fractures of the spine. J Neurosurg 60:282–286, 1984.

181. Sundaresan, N.; Galicich, J.H.; Lane, J.M.; et al. Treatment of neoplastic epidural cord compression by vertebral body resection and stabilization. J Neurosurg 63:676–684, 1985.

182. Tai, P.; Hammond, A.; Dyk, JV.; et al. Pelvic fractures following irradiation of endometrial and vaginal cancers—A case series and review of literature. Review. Radiother Oncol 56:23–28, 2000.

183. Theriault, R.L.; Lipton, A.; Hortobagyi, G.N.; et al. Pamidronate reduces skeletal morbidity in women with advanced breast cancer and lytic bone lesions: A randomized, placebo-controlled trial. Protocol 18 Aredia Breast Cancer Study Group. J Clin Oncol 17:846–854, 1999.

184. Thomsen, N.O.B.; Mikkelsen, J.B.; Svendsen, R.N.; et al. Interlocking nailing of humeral shaft fractures. J Orthop Sci 3:199–203, 1998.

185. Tokuhashi, Y.; Matsuzaki, H.; Toriyama, S.; et al. Scoring system for the preoperative evaluation of metastatic spine tumor prognosis. Spine 15:1110–1113, 1990.

186. Tome, J.; Carsi, B.; Garcia-Fernandez, C.; et al. Treatment of pathologic fractures of the humerus with Seidel nailing. Clin Orthop 350:51–55, 1998.

187. Tong, D.; Gillick, L.; Hendrickson, F.R. The palliation of symptomatic osseous metastases: Final results of the study by the Radiation Therapy Oncology Group. Cancer 50:893–899, 1982.

188. Tongaonkar, H.B.; Kulkarni, J.N.; Kamat, M.R. Solitary metastases from renal cell carcinoma: A review. J Surg Oncol 49:45–48, 1992.

189. Varley, G.W. The Seidel locking humeral nail: The Nottingham experience. Injury 26:155–157, 1995.

190. Walker, R.H. Pelvic reconstruction/total hip arthroplasty for metastatic acetabular insufficiency. Clin Orthop 294:170–175, 1993.

191. Wang, G.J.; Reger, S.I.; Maffeo, C.; et al. The strength of metal reinforced methylmethacrylate fixation of pathologic fractures. Clin Orthop 135:287–290, 1978.
192. Wang, H.M.; Galasko, C.S.; Crank, S.; et al. Methotrexate loaded acrylic cement in the management of skeletal metastases. Biomechanical, biological, and systemic effect. Clin Orthop 312:173–186, 1995.
193. Weill, A.; Chiras, J.; Simon, J.M.; et al. Spinal metastases: Indications for and results of percutaneous injection of acrylic surgical cement. Radiology 199:241–247, 1996.

194. Wong, D.A.; Fornasier, V.L.; MacNab, I. Spinal metastases: The obvious, the occult, and the impostors. Spine 15:1–4, 1990.
195. Yablon, I.G. The effect of methylmethacrylate on fracture healing. Clin Orthop 114:358–363, 1976.
196. Yamashita, K.; Koyama, H.; Inaji, H. Prognostic significance of bone metastasis from breast cancer. Clin Orthop 312:89–94, 1995.
197. Zickel, R.E.; Mouradian, W.H. Intramedullary fixation of pathological fractures and lesions of the subtrochanteric region of the femur. J Bone Joint Surg Am 58:1061–1066, 1976.

C H A P T E R 17

Osteoporotic Fragility Fractures

Joseph M. Lane, M.D.
Charles N. Cornell, M.D.
Margaret Lobo, M.D.
David Kwon, M.S.

EPIDEMIOLOGY

Osteoporosis is the most prevalent metabolic bone disease, affecting a large portion of the aging, predominantly female, population in the United States.[108] On the basis of World Health Organization criteria, it is estimated that 15% of postmenopausal white women in the United States and 35% of women older than 65 years of age have frank osteoporosis.[110] As many as 50% of women have some degree of low bone density in the hip. An estimated 1.2 million fractures annually are attributable to osteoporosis, including 538,000 vertebral, 227,000 hip, and 172,000 distal forearm (Colles') fractures.[54, 76, 94] Increasing age is significantly correlated with the incidence of fractures.[77] Fractures in the wrist rise in the sixth decade, vertebral fractures in the seventh decade, and hip fractures in the eighth decade.[107] One of every two white women experiences an osteoporotic fracture at some point in life.[66] Among those who live to the age of 90 years, 32% of women and 17% of men sustain a hip fracture.[75] Twenty-four percent of patients with hip fracture die within 1 year as a result; 50% require long-term nursing care, and only 30% ever regain their prefracture ambulatory status.[18, 75, 78, 82] Of patients in nursing homes, 70% do not survive 1 year.[3, 43, 44, 56, 60]

The financial burden of osteoporosis is rapidly escalating as the population ages. Patients with fragility fractures create a significant economic burden. Treating osteoporosis is more costly than 400,000 hospital admissions and 2.5 million physician visits per year.[109] Health care expenditures attributable to osteoporotic fractures were estimated as $13.8 billion, of which $10.3 billion was for the treatment of white women.[90] The cost of acute and long-term care for osteoporotic fractures of the proximal femur alone has been estimated to exceed $10 billion annually in the United States.[84] It is estimated that hip fractures alone may cost the United States $240 billion in the next 50 years.[107] These statistics indicate the need for increased physician awareness and diagnosis and, more important, emphasis on prevention of osteoporosis.

BONE AS A METABOLIC ORGAN

The relation between metabolic bone disease and fracture healing depends on the role of the skeleton as a metabolic resource.[62] Bone consists of a mineral fraction, hydroxyapatite crystals, and an organic fraction, largely (90%) type I collagen.[79] The mineral fraction of bone makes up more than 98% of the body calcium.[64] The bone, therefore, is the principal calcium reservoir of the body, and its specific architecture provides both structural support and an extensive bone surface for easy calcium mobilization. Bone is characterized as a composite material in which the collagen provides the tensile strength and hydroxyapatite the compressive strength.[55]

Bone is constantly renewing itself through a process of formation that is under cellular control.[38] It is a dynamic connective tissue, and its responsiveness to mechanical forces and metabolic regulatory signals that accommodate requirements for maintaining the organ and connective tissue functions of bone are operative throughout life.[68] The half-life of bone varies according to structural and metabolic demands. Bone formation is provided by osteoblast activity (measured by alkaline phosphatase and osteocalcin), and bone resorption is under osteoclast control (measured by N-telopeptides).[79]

The remodeling process and bone turnover appear to be coupled to and influenced by local humoral factors, biophysical considerations (Wolff's law: "form follows function"), and systemic demands.[79] Vitamin D, parathy-

427

roid hormone (PTH), and estrogen are among the hormones that control bone metabolism. Vitamin D, more specifically 1,25-dihydroxyvitamin D, is responsible for facilitating calcium absorption and osteoclastic resorption.[41] Administration of PTH leads to the release of calcium from bone,[53] and bone mass is directly related to the levels of estrogen in both men and women.[98] Bone is primarily cortical (with a large volume and low surface area) or trabecular (with a large surface area and low volume). Because bone is resorbed and formed on surfaces, mainly the endosteal surface, trabecular bone, with its greater surface-to-volume ratio, is metabolically more active.[50, 51, 61]

The material properties of bone are, in large part, related to the microdensity of the material.[9] Because the modulus of bone decreases only minimally with age, its primary strength is determined by its mass and structure.[9, 52] The importance of structural distribution is evidenced by the greater bending and torsional strength of a tube compared with a rod of equal cross-sectional material area. Maximization of the moment of inertia (distribution of the mass away from the epicenter) in nature enhances the structural strength of bone, particularly when the mass is deficient. A 10% shift of bone outward can compensate for a 30% loss in bending and torque.

In the aging human, loss of cortical bone mass is partially compensated by expansion of the diameter of the cortex. However, the increase in the diameter of long bones rarely exceeds 2% of the original diameter per year.[30, 92] Therefore, the actual loss of cortical mass places elderly persons at an increasing risk of fracture. The structural strength is also related to connectivity—the degree of interconnection within bone.[14, 91]

MECHANISM OF OSTEOPENIC FRACTURE

The composite structure of bone allows it to withstand compressive and tensile stresses as well as bending and torsional moments.[97] Trabecular bone is often subjected to large impact stresses, whereas cortical bones often handle torque and bending. The vertebral body is largely protected by its trabecular bone, whereas the femoral neck depends on a mixture of cortical and trabecular bone for protection.[9, 61]

The hallmark of osteoporosis is deficient bone density and lack of connectivity.[37, 73] The decreased bone mass associated with osteoporosis reduces the load-bearing ability of both cortical and trabecular bone, resulting in an increased risk of fracture. Areas of the skeleton rich in trabecular bone sustain the first consequences of osteoporosis; the trabecular bone is thinner in dimension and shows evidence of osteoclastic resorption, leading to disconnectivity of the trabecular elements.[66] Trabecular bone is resorbed at a higher rate (8% per year) than cortical bone (0.5% per year) after menopause. Riggs and Melton[93] recognized this discrepancy and developed the concept of two forms of osteoporosis with separate fracture patterns.

Type I postmenopausal osteoporosis primarily affects women 55 to 65 years of age, is related to estrogen deficiency, results principally in trabecular bone loss, and is manifest in spinal fractures. Type II senile osteoporosis affects both men and women (1:2 ratio) 65 years of age or older, is related to chronic calcium loss throughout life, results in cortical bone loss, and induces long bone fractures.

Although bone mass is clearly related to fracture risk, a true fracture threshold can only be implied. Structure, fall tendency and type, ability of microfractures to heal before they become macrofractures, quality of bone, and such ill-defined factors as aging all play a role in fracture risk.[1] The overlap of mass determination precludes clearly defining persons at absolute risk. Even at the lowest bone mass measurements, a percentage of individuals are free of fracture (Tables 17–1 and 17–2).

For patients with hip fractures, Riggs and Melton[93] demonstrated a fourfold increase in fracture rate with a 50% decrease in bone mass. The exponential increase in fracture rate with loss of bone mass is in agreement with the laboratory structural data of Carter and Hayes.[9] Bone loss places the aging individual at greater risk of fracture, and fracture treatment therefore should include a bone maintenance strategy (see later discussion). Greenspan and co-workers[36] documented etiologic factors for hip fractures in addition to bone density, including falls to the side, lower body mass index, and a higher potential to fall.[39] Courtney and colleagues[16] showed that the femur of an elderly person has half the strength and half the energy absorption capacity of the femur of a younger person. Falls from standing height exceed femoral breaking strength by 50% in elderly people but are below femoral fracture strength by 20% in the young.

Cummings and associates[19] included as hip fracture risks, in addition to low bone mass, aging, history of maternal hip fracture, tallness, lack of weight gain with aging, poor health, previously treated hypothyroidism, use of benzodiazepines, use of anticonvulsant drugs, lack of walking for exercise, lack of unsupported standing for 4 hours a day, a resting pulse rate higher than 80 beats per minute, and a history of any fracture after the age of 50 years. If two of these factors are present, 1 in 1000 individuals sustain a hip fracture in a given year. If five or more hip fracture risk factors are present in a patient who also has a low bone mass, the risk rises to 27 in 1000 individuals per year.[20]

FRACTURE HEALING AND OSTEOPOROSIS

Normal fracture healing is a specialized process in which structural integrity is restored through the regeneration of

TABLE 17–1	
DXA Values in Patients Undergoing Natural Menopause ($P = .001$)	
Spinal fractures ($n = 81$)	0.80 (0.14 g/cm²)
No spinal fractures ($n = 225$)	0.89 (0.16 g/cm²)

Abbreviation: DXA, dual-energy x-ray absorptiometry.

TABLE 17–2 ....

Spinal Fracture Prevalence in Postmenopausal Women as Related to DXA

DXA (g/cm²)	% With Spinal Fractures
0.8–0.9	26
0.7–0.8	33
0.6–0.7	51
0.5–0.6	63

Abbreviation: DXA, dual-energy x-ray absorptiometry.

bone.[48] Fracture healing traditionally proceeds through the six stages of endochondral bone formation: impact, induction, inflammation, soft tissue callus (chondroid), hard tissue callus (osteoblastic), and remodeling.[62] Although the stages from fracture through chondrogenesis are unaltered, the final two stages, hard callus and remodeling, are clearly susceptible to alteration in osteoporotic patients.[84]

The synthesis of bone and its mineralization depend on the calcium environment. Osteoporotic patients have a diminished pool of rapidly soluble calcium, inadequate dietary calcium, and a deficient structural calcium bone reserve.[61] Calcium mineralization is subject to delay, and the stage of remodeling is prolonged because of competition for ionized calcium with the rest of the body. Also, substances that may have been mobilized to maintain systemic calcium homeostasis (PTH and vitamin D) may compromise the latter stages of fracture repair. In addition, up to 40% of elderly patients are mildly to moderately malnourished, and this condition compromises bone collagen synthesis.[81] Bone scans remain positive (indicating continued metabolic remodeling) well into the third year after fracture in elderly persons, and union cannot be fully ascertained until that time.[25] Studies have demonstrated that osteoporotic rats have delayed healing. It is uncertain whether it is the osteoporosis or the estrogen deficiency that compromises fracture repair.[72, 106]

Systemic bone loss occurs in the unaffected skeleton after long bone fractures, even when the patient has adequate calcium intake.[103] Osteoporotic patients, who are typically chronically calcium deficient, may be more affected. Ideally, healing could be stimulated in such patients by physiologic levels of vitamin D (400 to 800 IU/day) and calcium (1500 mg of elemental calcium per day), normal nitrogen balance, and appropriate exercise.[79]

DEFINITION AND DIAGNOSIS

Osteoporosis is defined as a disease of decreased bone mass and changes in the microarchitecture of the skeleton. The disease may be recognized clinically in one of three ways: acute fracture (most commonly of the wrist, ribs, hip, or spine), asymptomatic thoracic wedge or lumbar compression fracture, or generalized osteopenia on a radiograph. More than 65% of individuals presenting with compression fractures are asymptomatic.[35] Critical determinations are the cause and the extent of bone loss. A diagnosis of osteopenia must differentiate among bone marrow disorders, endocrinopathy, osteomalacia, and osteoporosis.[5, 79] The workup for osteopenia involves invasive and noninvasive methods.

Operational definitions of osteopenia and osteoporosis are based on bone mass and density. Noninvasive techniques of determining osteopenia are used to quantitate bone mass and evaluate the efficacy of treatment. The simple radiograph is fraught with technical difficulty and may not identify osteopenia until 30% of the bone mass has been lost.[49] Current methodology centers on dual-photon absorptiometry, quantitative computed tomography (CT), and ultrasonography. Dual-energy x-ray absorptiometry (DEXA) utilizes two energy levels.[33, 58, 98] It permits correction for soft tissue and allows direct measurement of total bone mass (cortical and trabecular) within a specified amount of mineralized tissue of an aerial section of the spine or hip; the measurements are analyzed and expressed as grams per centimeter squared. Radiation is low (5 mrad) and precision (1% in the spine, 3% to 4% in the hip) and accuracy (4% to 6%) are good. Compression fractures, osteophytes, degenerative changes, and vascular calcifications can elevate local readings. A lumbar lateral radiograph is needed to correct for these artifacts.

After the density has been calculated, comparisons can be made with age-matched peers (Z score) and with an adult population with peak bone mass (T score). A bone mass within 1 standard deviation is considered healthy. Osteopenia is defined between 1 and 2.4 standard deviations below peak bone mass. A bone mass 2.5 standard deviations below peak mass is considered frank osteoporosis. Individuals with a bone mass more than 1.5 standard deviations below that of their peers probably have a secondary cause of osteoporosis that must be evaluated.

Alternative methods are also used to determine bone mass. CT is used to measure the midportion of the vertebral body and determine trabecular bone mass against a simultaneous phantom; in this way, it can be used to measure trabecular bone mass directly. It uses 20 times as much radiation and has poorer precision than DEXA.[34] Ultrasonography is used to examine the heel, patella, tibia, and peripheral sites and measure several properties of bone; these measurements have a correlation of 0.75 with central density readings.[100] As discussed previously, these noninvasive methods cannot clearly identify absolute fracture risk, but they can be used as a loose guide for management grouping and as an exacting tool for long-term determination of treatment efficacy.

There are also markers of skeletal metabolic activity. Bone formation markers are bone-specific alkaline phosphatase and osteocalcin. Alkaline phosphatase rises within 5 days after a fracture is sustained. If the level is elevated at the time of fracture, it is due to a high-turnover state until proved otherwise. Hyperparathyroidism and osteomalacia must be considered in the workup. Bone collagen breakdown products can be used to measure bone turnover. Collagen molecules in the bone matrix are staggered to form fibrils that are joined by covalent crosslinks consisting of hydroxylysyl-pyridinoline (pyridinoline, Pyd) and lysyl-pyridinoline (deoxypyridinoline, Dpd). Dpd has greater specificity because Pyd is present in other connective tissues. Dpd and Pyd are linked to collagen where two aminotelopeptides (N-telopeptides [NTX] and C-telopeptides) are linked to a helical site and are released with Dpd and Pyd during osteoclastic bone resorption. These products are released into the circulation, metabolized by the liver and kidney, and excreted in the urine.

Clinical applications of these markers include monitoring effectiveness of therapy,[32] prediction of fracture risk,[31] and selection of patients for antiresorptive therapy.[12] NTX and DEXA provide highly sensitive, commonly used indices of metabolic activity and bone mass in clinical practice.[73] High-turnover states such as hyperparathyroidism are characterized by high NTX levels. Osteoporosis (as determined by DEXA) has been divided into high turnover (high NTX) related to increased osteoclast activity and low turnover (low NTX) related to low osteoclast activity.[73]

No signs, symptoms, or diagnostic tests are specific for osteoporosis. In one study, 31% of osteoporotic women were found to have disorders with possible effects on skeletal health without major risk factors for postmenopausal osteoporosis.[13] An algorithm for the diagnosis of osteopenia has been developed (Table 17–3). When osteopenia has been defined and localized bone disorders have been eliminated, the differential workup commences. First, a hematologic profile, serum protein electrophoresis, and biochemical profile studies are obtained. In common bone marrow disorders, including leukemia and myeloma (which together account for 1% to 2% of cases of osteoporosis), the bone marrow screen is usually abnormal (anemia, low white blood cell count, or low platelet count). A biochemical panel provides information on renal and hepatic function, primary hyperparathyroidism (high serum calcium), and possible malnutrition (anemia, low calcium, low phosphorus, or low albumin).

If the bone marrow screen is negative, the diagnostic testing then centers on endocrinopathies. Premature menopause, iatrogenic Cushing's disease, and type I diabetes mellitus are diagnosed by history. Determinations of PTH and thyroid-stimulating hormone identify hyperparathyroidism and hyperthyroidism. The latter may occur as osteoporosis and severe weight loss or as iatrogenic

hyperthyroidism, caused by overuse of thyroid replacement hormone medication by obese patients to control weight.[80] Malnutrition is common in osteoporotic patients. Osteomalacia occurs in 8% of osteopenic patients in northern areas and may be identified by low levels of 25-hydroxyvitamin D, high secondary PTH, high alkaline phosphatase, low urinary calcium, low serum phosphorus, and low to normal serum calcium values. The mild hyperosteoidosis and lag in mineralization are often indistinguishable from those seen in osteoporosis by laboratory studies. The critical diagnostic study used to differentiate osteomalacia from osteoporosis is the transileal bone biopsy and histomorphometric analysis of the undecalcified bone.[65] These studies permit a definitive diagnosis.

If cost containment were not an issue, bone densitometry would be readily available to almost all postmenopausal women. Medicare now covers DEXA for estrogen-deficient women older than 65 years. A cost-effectiveness analysis supported by the National Osteoporosis Foundation concluded that it is worthwhile to measure bone density in any woman with a vertebral fracture and in all white women older than 60 to 65 years. In healthy postmenopausal women between 50 and 60 years old, indications for DEXA include a history of low-trauma fracture, weight under 127 pounds, smoking, or a family history of an osteoporotic fracture.[24] Most experts also agree that any patients with secondary causes of known bone loss should have their bone density measured.

MEDICAL TREATMENT AND PREVENTION

Osteoporosis is a heterogeneous disease of multifactorial causes. The principles of medical management necessitate decisions about whether bone mass should be maintained or augmented. If the patient has crossed his or her fracture threshold, bone augmentation is required. However, if the

TABLE 17–3

Sequence for the Workup of the Most Common Forms of Osteomalacia

Complete blood count Erythrocyte sedimentation rate Serum protein electrophoresis	Abnormal 1%–2% ⟶ Bone marrow biopsy ↓ Normal		Myeloma Leukemia Benign marrow disorder
Parathyroid hormone Thyroid-stimulating hormone History of type I diabetes History of steroid use	Abnormal 15%–25% ⟶ ↓ Normal		Hyperparathyroidism Hyperthyroidism Diabetes mellitus (type I) Cushing's disease
Normal ↓ Calcium (serum-urine) Phosphorus (serum) Alkaline phosphatase Blood urea nitrogen 25-Hydroxyvitamin D Parathyroid hormone Transileal bone biopsy (?)	Abnormal 8% ⟶ ↓ Normal Osteoporosis		Osteomalacia

trauma level was of sufficient magnitude, maintenance may be all that is needed, even after a fracture. A careful history of the cause of the fracture and a noninvasive measurement of bone mass are essential.

Adequate levels of exercise,[1, 21, 46, 59, 84] calcium,[36, 40] and vitamin D (400 to 800 IU/day) maintain both cortical and trabecular bone mass except in the early postmenopausal spine, when the loss is 2% per year. Physiologic levels of calcium intake, as determined by a National Institutes of Health consensus conference in 1994, are 1200 to 1500 mg/day from age 12 to 24 years, 1000 mg/day from age 25 years until menopause, and 1500 mg/day after menopause.[83] Currently, bisphosphonates (alendronate and risedronate), raloxifene, and calcitonin are approved for treatment and low-dose alendronate and raloxifene are approved for prevention of osteoporosis. The Food and Drug Administration has approved estrogen for prevention and management of osteoporosis. Only alendronate has been labeled specifically for men, and bisphosphonates have not been approved for premenopausal women, particularly because of pregnancy.

A treatment program has been approved by the National Osteoporosis Foundation for patients at risk of fragility fracture.[84] Treatment is recommended for any individual with a T score of −2.5 or a score of −1.5 with four major risk factors, and prevention is recommended for a patient with osteopenia. If an individual has a known vertebral fracture, the use of hormone replacement therapy, alendronate, or calcitonin is recommended. For a patient without fracture and unwilling to consider treatment, physiologic calcium levels, vitamin D (400 to 800 units per day), exercise, and smoking cessation are recommended. Calcium, smoking cessation, and exercise are recommended for postmenopausal patients younger than 65 years without risk factors. These recommendations were made with Food and Drug Administration approval of estrogen for the treatment of osteoporosis; new treatment guidelines need to be established because the new labeled use of estrogen is for the prevention and management of osteoporosis.

Estrogen

Estrogen* has been the most studied and used drug for the prevention of osteoporosis. Epidemiologic studies, cohort and case-control, indicated that estrogen administration to postmenopausal women decreased skeletal turnover (25% to 50%) and the rate of bone loss in women 6 months to 3 years after menopause.[12, 74] A large, longitudinal cohort study of 9704 postmenopausal women 65 years of age and older found that estrogen use was associated with a significant decrease in wrist fracture (relative risk [RR], 0.39) and of all nonspinal fractures (RR, 0.66). It appears to reduce risk of hip fractures by 20% to 60%.[9]

To prevent up to a ninefold increase in the probability of uterine cancer with estrogen alone, estrogen should be cycled with progesterone. Estrogen may not provide cardiac protection, and it increases the risk for breast cancer (by as much as 30%).[2, 6, 42, 86] Currently, estrogen

*See references 6, 10, 28, 29, 44, 45, 57, 70, 71, 104, 105.

is indicated only for prevention and management of osteoporosis, because long-term randomized control studies have not been performed to determine whether estrogen is an effective long-term fracture prevention treatment for osteoporosis.

Raloxifene

A series of synthetic estrogen-like modulators have been developed. These agents can compete with estrogen binding sites and seem to function more like an estrogen at bone and work effectively as antiresorptive agents. They are indicated for prevention of osteoporosis and treatment of vertebral fractures. Tamoxifen was used as an antiestrogen, particularly for patients with breast cancer. Bone cells are also responsive to tamoxifen.[88] Individuals taking tamoxifen have 70% of the benefit of estrogen in terms of maintaining bone mass.[15] It is not used as an antiosteoporotic agent because 70% of women have significant postmenopausal symptoms and a high incidence of uterine cancer. Raloxifene, a newer agent, is not associated with an increased incidence of uterine cancer, and early data suggest that there is a decreased risk of breast cancer in patients using raloxifene compared with control subjects.[22] A trial comparing tamoxifen and raloxifene in preventive action against breast cancer is under way.[18]

Raloxifene is approved for the prevention of osteoporosis. Raloxifene can decrease the risk of vertebral fracture by approximately 40% to 50%, but there is no reported protection for the hip.[28] Adverse effects include an 8% incidence of leg cramps and an increased risk of thrombophlebitis comparable with that associated with estrogen. It is not recommended in the first 5 years of menopause because it enhances postmenopausal symptoms.

Calcitonin

Calcitonin is a peptide hormone secreted by specialized cells in the thyroid. It may play a role in the skeletal development of the embryo and fetus, but its primary action is on bone to reduce osteoclastic bone resorption by diminution of osteoclasts (shrinkage of cells, loss of ruffled border, reduction in resorptive activity, and increased apoptosis).[11] It has been effectively used in patients with hypercalcemia, Paget's disease, and osteoporosis. It is indicated for the treatment of postmenopausal women more than 5 years after menopause with low bone mass compared with healthy premenopausal women. A nasal form of calcitonin at a dosage of 200 units per day appears to increase bone mass in the spine and decrease spinal fractures by 37%. To date, there has been no benefit in hip fracture prevention.[8, 85] Calcitonin does have another benefit of providing some analgesia. It has been used in patients with painful osteoporotic fractures and does not interfere with fracture healing.[89] The only established side effect is rhinitis (23% versus 7% for placebo).[26]

Bisphosphonates

Bisphosphonates are stable, active analgesics of pyrophosphate[68] that inhibit osteoclastic resorption and depress bone turnover[27, 49, 58, 87] by binding to the osteoclast-resorbing surface and acting as a nondegradable shield. When absorbed by the osteoclast, they inhibit osteoclast function. Bisphosphonates have low bioavailability, and less than 1% is absorbed orally. Alendronate is the first bisphosphonate approved for the treatment of osteoporosis. Low-dose alendronate, 5 mg/day or 10 mg three times a week, is approved for prevention of osteoporosis. It has been shown to increase bone mass in the hip and spine. It decreased the risk of all fractures by approximately 50% after 1 year of treatment.[7, 17, 67] Regardless of the degree of bone mass enhancement, all patients treated with alendronate had equal protection against fractures, suggesting an improvement in bone quality.

Alendronate has been associated with esophageal irritation, and as many as 30% of individuals have had esophagitis; in a carefully controlled study, the rate of esophagitis was comparable to that in the placebo group.[67] Currently, a once-weekly dosage of 70 mg is as efficacious and produces significantly less indigestion.

Risedronate, at 5 mg/day, is the second bisphosphonate approved for both prevention and treatment of osteoporosis. It has a profile similar to that of alendronate and may cause less esophageal irritation. It reduced the risk of new vertebral fractures by 49% over 3 years compared with a control group ($P < .001$), and the risk of nonvertebral fractures was reduced by 33% compared with a control group over 3 years ($P = .06$).[96] Risedronate significantly increased bone mineral density at the spine and hip within 6 months. The adverse-event profile of risedronate, including gastrointestinal adverse events, was similar to that of the placebo group.[95] A head-to-head comparison of the two agents has not been performed.

Bisphosphonates have a long-lasting effect on bone. A double-blind, multicenter study of postmenopausal women[101] (at least 2.5 standard deviations below the peak premenopausal mean) compared the efficacy and safety of treatment with oral once-weekly alendronate at 70 mg ($n = 519$), twice-weekly alendronate at 35 mg ($n = 369$), and daily alendronate at 10 mg ($n = 370$) for 1 year. Increases in bone density of the total hip, femoral neck, trochanter, and total body were similar for the three dosing regimens. All three treatment groups similarly showed reduced biochemical markers of bone resorption (urinary N-telopeptides of type I collagen) and bone formation (serum bone-specific alkaline phosphatase) in the middle of the premenopausal reference range. All treatment regimens were well tolerated with a similar incidence of upper gastrointestinal adverse experiences. There were fewer serious upper gastrointestinal adverse experiences and a trend toward a lower incidence of esophageal events in the once-weekly dosing group compared with the daily dosing group. This study suggests that once-weekly dosing of bisphosphonates may provide a more convenient, therapeutically equivalent alternative to daily dosing.

Pamidronate has not been approved for treating osteoporosis but is used for treating patients with metastatic disease, hypercalcemic malignancy, and Paget's disease. At our institution, The Hospital for Special Surgery in New York, intravenous doses of pamidronate have been successful in treating osteoporosis in this population. A combination regimen of alendronate and estrogen has been studied. A randomized controlled trial indicated that a combination of alendronate and estrogen was superior to the single agents in terms of bone density augmentation.[69]

MANAGEMENT OF OSTEOPOROTIC FRACTURES

The impact of skeletal loss becomes most apparent as the skeleton begins to fail in its ability to withstand normal loads. When the skeleton no longer functions structurally, osteoporosis becomes a disease state. The overriding goal of management of fractures in the osteoporotic patient is to achieve early and definitive stabilization of the injured extremity.

At The Hospital for Special Surgery in New York, an osteoporosis treatment center has been established. The experiences derived from management in a large combined population have given rise to the following treatment principles and protocols:

1. Elderly patients are best served by rapid, definitive fracture care that allows early mobilization. In the patient with concurrent illnesses or markedly abnormal laboratory results, medical evaluation and stabilization of reversible medical decompensations should be performed before surgery.[35] In most cases, patients are at their respective homeostatic optimum on the day of injury and should ideally be treated with surgery at that time.

2. Surgical treatment is directed at achieving stable fracture fixation and early return of function. In the lower extremity, this implies early weight bearing. Anatomic restoration is important in intra-articular fractures, whereas stability is the goal in the treatment of metaphyseal and diaphyseal fractures.

3. Surgical procedures are designed with an effort to minimize operative time, blood loss, and physiologic stress.

4. Osteoporotic bone, with its decreased density, lacks the strength to hold screws and plates securely and more often involves comminution.[8] As a result, failure of internal fixation is caused primarily by bone failure rather than by implant failure. Internal fixation devices are chosen that allow impaction of the fracture fragments into stable patterns that minimize the load carried by the implants. In addition, implants that minimize stress shielding are chosen to prevent further skeletal decompensation of the involved bone. For these reasons, sliding nail plate devices and intramedullary devices that are load sharing and allow fracture compression are the devices of choice.

5. Because most of these fractures are related to underlying metabolic bone disease, a full evaluation of the etiologic condition is performed and an appropriate

medical therapeutic program is developed for each patient.

6. An inadequate calcium intake could result in deficits in callus mineralization or remodeling.[25] Because many elderly patients are malnourished, nutritional assessment should be included in the patient's evaluation.

The specific management of fractures about the knee and of Colles', hip, spine, proximal humeral, and pelvic fractures is discussed elsewhere in appropriate chapters. This chapter includes a discussion of the femoral neck fracture because of its strong implications for metabolic bone disease. A series of studies from the fracture service at New York Hospital[99] demonstrated that 8% of patients with femoral neck fracture had frank osteomalacia. Although 40% had marked trabecular bone loss (less than 15% trabecular bone volume, with normal being more than 22%), all patients older than 50 years had some reduction of bone mass when compared with younger persons. Twenty-five percent had increased metabolic turnover indices, including a high osteoclast count.

In the series of Scileppi and colleagues,[101] bone histomorphometry appeared to be a good predictor of outcome after treatment for femoral neck fracture.[61] Patients who had trabecular bone volume that was within 60% of normal (i.e., volume higher than 15%) had an 85% to 95% rate of successful union, whereas for patients who had severe trabecular bone loss (to less than 15% of bone volume) the rate was lower than 33% in women and lower than 50% in men. These combined studies at New York Hospital suggest that significant metabolic bone disease, particularly osteoporosis, leads to a high rate of unsuccessful union after femoral neck fracture. Comparable studies of other fractures commonly associated with osteoporosis are lacking, but presumably osteoporosis per se affects the type, severity, and repair process in these fractures as well.

Application of the outcome studies of femoral neck fractures in relation to osteopenia has resulted in specific protocols at The Hospital for Special Surgery and the New York Presbyterian Hospital. Our current protocol for treatment of a displaced femoral neck fracture in the ambulatory patient who is physiologically younger than 65 years relies on closed reduction and stable internal fixation using the sliding compression screw or cannulated screws as the primary form of treatment. If stability cannot be achieved, the patient is treated with a hemiarthroplasty. The ambulatory patient who is physiologically older than 70 years is treated by hemiarthroplasty. Closed reduction and pinning are the method of choice in caring for the nonambulatory patient. Patients with severe demineralizing bone disease (marked osteoporosis), pathologic fractures secondary to metastasis, or neurologic disorders that require immediate ambulation and patients who cannot comply with physical therapy regimens requiring partial weight bearing are treated with primary hemiarthroplasty.

Traditionally, treatment of vertebral compression fractures consists of medical pain management. In 1984, vertebroplasty, structural reinforcement of the vertebral body with polymethylmethacrylate cement, was first used in the treatment of osteoporotic vertebral fractures. The primary indication for vertebroplasty is pain relief. The procedure is performed under local or general anesthesia and a transpedicle or extrapedicle approach is used to reach the anteroinferior border of the vertebral body. In vertebroplasty, radiodense polymethylmethacrylate cement is injected into the vertebral body under high pressure using Luer-Lok syringes in 2- to 3-ml allotments. Several cohort studies reported a decrease in pain in 80% to 90% of patients, a complication rate of 5% to 6%, and no fracture reduction.[4, 23, 47]

Kyphoplasty is a similar procedure designed to provide significant pain relief, rapid return to activities of daily living, restoration of vertebral body height, and reduction in spinal deformity. In this procedure, a balloon tamp is inserted into the center of the collapsed vertebral body and inflated with radiopaque liquid under fluoroscopic guidance. The patient is continually monitored by sensory evoked potential for neural damage throughout the procedure at The Hospital for Special Surgery. The balloon strikes cancellous bone circumferentially around the tamp and thereby reduces the deformation and restores height to the vertebral body. The balloon is deflated and removed, and the cavity is filled with the surgeon's choice of biomaterial, stabilizing the fracture.

Approximately 1000 fractures in 600 patients have been treated by this technique. A review of 226 kyphoplasties in 121 patients[63] found that 96% of patients had pain relief as determined using a pain analogue scale. There was 45% restoration of height in the anterior plane, 71% at the midline, and 54% posteriorly. In this series, there was one case of epidural bleeding requiring decompression, one incomplete spinal injury, and one report of transient adult respiratory distress syndrome. No episodes of infection, pulmonary emboli, or myocardial infarction have been reported. In this study, the average age was 73.7 years and each patient had on average 3.7 co-morbidities.

A quality-of-life questionnaire (called SF-36) was administered to patients before and after kyphoplasty.[69a] The questionnaire is standardized and validated and is designed to assess functional status and well-being. The questions are used to calculate summary measures of physical and mental health such as bodily pain and physical function. The summary measures are then normalized to a scale of 1 to 100, where 1 is the lowest score and 100 is the highest or best score. In these patients, both bodily pain and physical function scores improved significantly ($P < .004$ for bodily pain, $P < .02$ for physical function) when assessed 1 week after kyphoplasty. These preliminary data suggest that kyphoplasty is an effective, minimally invasive technique for providing pain relief and restoration of vertebral height.

REFERENCES

1. Aloia, J.E.; Cohn, S.H.; Ostuni, J.A.; et al. Prevention of involutional bone loss by exercise. Ann Intern Med 89:356, 1978.
2. American College of Physicians. Guidelines for counseling postmenopausal women about preventive hormone therapy. Ann Intern Med 117:1038, 1992.
3. Avioli, L.V. Postmenopausal osteoporosis: Prevention vs. cure. Fed Proc 40:2418, 1981.
4. Barr, J.D.; Barr, M.S.; Lemley, T.J.; McCann, R.M. Percutaneous vertebroplasty for pain relief and spinal stabilization. Spine 25:923, 2000.

5. Barth, R.W.; Lane, J.M. Osteoporosis. Orthop Clin North Am 19:845, 1988.

6. Belchetz, P.E. Hormonal treatment of postmenopausal women. N Engl J Med 330:1062, 1994.

7. Black, D.M.; Cummings, S.R.; Karph, D.B.; et al. Randomized trial of effect of alendronate on risk of fracture in women with existing vertebral fractures. Lancet 348:1535, 1996.

8. Cardona, J.M.; Pastor, E. Calcitonin versus etidronate for the treatment of postmenopausal osteoporosis: A meta-analysis of published clinical trials. Osteoporos Int 7:165, 1997.

9. Carter, D.R.; Hayes, W.C. The compressive behavior of bone as a two-phase porous structure. J Bone Joint Surg Am 59:954, 1977.

10. Cauley, J.A.; Seeley, D.G.; Ensrud, K.; et al. Estrogen replacement therapy and fractures in older women: Study of Osteoporosis Research Group. Ann Intern Med 122:9, 1995.

11. Chambers, T.J.; Moore, A. The sensitivity of isolated osteoclasts to morphological transformation by calcitonin. J Clin Endocrinol Metab 57:819, 1983.

12. Chesnut, C.H., III; Bell, N.H.; Clark, G.S.; et al. Hormone replacement therapy in postmenopausal women: Urinary N-telopeptide of type I collagen monitors therapeutic effect and predicts response of bone mineral density. Am J Med 102:29, 1997.

13. Clark, J.; Tamenbaum, C.; Posnett, K.; et al. Laboratory testing in healthy, osteopenic women. J Bone Miner Res 12:S141, 1997.

14. Compston, J.E. Connectivity of cancellous bone: Assessment and mechanical implications. Bone 15:63, 1994.

15. Cosman, F.; Lindsay, R. Selective estrogen receptor modulators: Clinical spectrum. Endocr Rev 20:418, 1999.

16. Courtney, A.C.; Washtel, E.F.; Myers, E.R.; Hayes, W.C. Age-related reductions in the strength of the femur tested in a fall-loading configuration. J Bone Joint Surg Am 77:387, 1995.

17. Cummings, S.R.; Black, D.M.; Thompson, D.E.; et al. Effect of alendronate on risk of fracture in women with low bone density by without vertebral fractures. JAMA 280:2077, 1998.

18. Cummings, S.R.; Eckert, S.; Kreuger, K.A.; et al. The effects of raloxifene on the risk of breast cancer in postmenopausal women: Results from the MORE (Multiple Outcome of Raloxifene Evaluation) randomized trial. JAMA 281:2189, 1999.

19. Cummings, S.R.; Kellsey, J.L.; Nevitt, M.C.; O'Dowd, K.J. Epidemiology of osteoporosis and osteoporotic fractures. Epidemiol Rev 7:178, 1985.

20. Cummings, S.R.; Nevitt, M.C.; Browner, W.S.; et al. Risk factors for hip fracture in white women. Study of Osteoporotic Fractures Research Group. N Engl J Med 332:767, 1995.

21. Dalsky, G.P.; Stocke, K.S.; Ehsani, A.A.; et al. Weight-bearing exercise training and lumbar bone mineral content in postmenopausal women. Ann Intern Med 108:824, 1988.

22. Delmas, P.D.; Bjarnason, N.H.; Mitlak, B.H.; et al. Effects of raloxifene on bone mineral density, serum cholesterol concentrations, and uterine endometrium in postmenopausal women. N Engl J Med 337:1641, 1997.

23. Deramond, H.; Darrason, R.; Galibart, P. Percutaneous vertebroplasty with acrylic cement in the treatment of aggressive spinal angiomas. Rachis 1:143, 1989.

24. Eddy, D.M.; Cummings, S.R.; Johnson, C.C.; et al. Osteoporosis: Review of the evidence for prevention, diagnosis, and treatment and cost-effectiveness analysis. Osteoporos Int 8:S1, 1998.

25. Einhorn, T.A.; Bonnarens, F.; Burstein, A.H. The contributions of dietary protein and mineral to the healing of experimental fractures: A biomechanical study. J Bone Joint Surg Am 68:1389, 1986.

26. Ellerington, M.C.; Hillard, T.C.; Whitcroft, S.I.J.; et al. Intranasal salmon calcitonin for the prevention and treatment of postmenopausal osteoporosis. Calcif Tissue Int 59:6, 1996.

27. Endo, Y.; Nakamura, M.; Kikuchi, T.; et al. Aminoalkylbisphosphonates, potent inhibitors of bone resorption, induce a prolonged stimulation of histamine synthesis and increase macrophages, granulocytes, and osteoclasts in vivo. Calcif Tissue Int 52:248, 1993.

28. Ettinger, B; Black, D.M.; Mitlak, B.H.; et al. Reduction of vertebral fracture risk in postmenopausal women with osteoporosis treated with raloxifene. Results from a three year randomized clinical trial. JAMA 282:637, 1999.

29. Ettinger, B.; Genant, H.K.; Cann, C.E. Long-term estrogen replacement therapy prevents bone loss and fractures. Ann Intern Med 102:319, 1985.

30. Frost, H.M. Tetracycline-based histological analysis of bone remodeling. Calcif Tissue Res 3:211, 1969.

31. Garnero, P.; Hauserr, E.; Chapuy, M.C.; et al. Markers of bone resorption predict hip fracture in elderly women: The EPIDOS prospective study. J Bone Miner Res 11:1531, 1996.

32. Garnero, P.; Shih, W.J.; Gineyts, E.; et al. Comparison of new biochemical markers of bone turnover in late postmenopausal osteoporotic women in response to alendronate treatment. J Clin Endocrinol Metab 79:1693, 1994.

33. Genant, H.K.; Boyd, D.P. Quantitative bone mineral analysis using dual energy computed tomography. Invest Radiol 12:545, 1977.

34. Glaser, D.L.; Kaplan, F.S. Osteoporosis: Definition and clinical presentation. Spine 22(Suppl 24):12S, 1997.

35. Glimcher, M.A. On the form and structure of bone from molecules to organs: Wolff's law revisited. In: Veis, A., ed. The Chemistry and Biology of Mineralized Tissues. New York, Elsevier–North Holland, 1982, p. 613.

36. Greenspan, S.L.; Myers, E.R.; Maitland, L.A.; et al. Fall severity and mineral density as risk factors for hip fracture in ambulatory elderly. JAMA 271:128, 1994.

37. Hakkinen, K. Force production characteristics of leg extensor, trunk flexor, and extensor muscles in male and female basketball players. J Sports Med Phys Fitness 31:325, 1991.

38. Hansen, M.A.; Overgaard, K.; Riss, B.J.; Christiansen, C. Role of peak bone mass and bone loss in postmenopausal osteoporosis: 12 year study. BMJ 303:1548, 1991.

39. Hayes, W.C.; Myers, E.R.; Morris, J.N.; et al. Impact near the hip dominates fracture risk in elderly nursing home residents who fall. Calcif Tissue Int 52:192, 1993.

40. Heaney, R.P. Effect of calcium on skeletal development, bone loss, and risk of fractures. Am J Med 91:23S, 1991.

41. Heaney, R.P. Nutrition and Osteoporosis. In: Favus, M.J., ed. Primer on the Metabolic Bone Diseases and Disorders of Mineral Metabolism. Philadelphia, Lippincott Williams & Wilkins, 1999, p. 270.

42. Hemminki, E.; Topo, P.; Malin, M.; Kangas, I. Physician's views on hormone therapy around and after menopause. Maturitas 16:163, 1993.

43. Holbrook, T.; Grazier, K.; Kelsey, J.; et al. The frequency of occurrence, impact and cost of selected musculoskeletal conditions in the United States. Chicago, Ill.: American Academy of Orthopedic Surgeons, 1984.

44. Horseman, A.; Gallagher, J.C.; Simpson, M.; et al. Prospective trial of oestrogen and calcium in postmenopausal women. BMJ 2:789, 1977.

45. Hutchinson, T.A.; Polansky, S.M.; Feinstein, A.R. Postmenopausal oestrogens protect against fractures of hip and distal radius: A case control study. Lancet 2:705, 1979.

46. Jacobsen, P.C.; Beaver, W.; Grubb, S.A.; et al. Bone density in women; college athletes and older athletic women. J Orthop Res 2:328, 1984.

47. Jansen, M.E.; Evans, A.J.; Mathis, J.M.; et al: Percutaneous polymethylmethacrylate vertebroplasty in the treatment of osteoporotic vertebral body compression fractures: Technical aspects. AJNR 18:1897, 1997.

48. Johnson, T.R.; Tomin, E.; Lane, J.M. Perspectives on growth factors, bone graft substitutes and fracture healing. In: Obrant, K., ed. Management of Fractures in Severely Osteoporotic Bone. London, Springer, 2000, p. 111.

49. Johnston, C.C., Jr.; Epstein, S. Clinical, biochemical, epidemiologic, and economic features of osteoporosis. Orthop Clin North Am 12:559, 1981.

50. Jones, B.H.; Bovee, M.W.; Harris, J.M.; et al: Intrinsic risk factors for exercise-related injuries among male and female army trainees. Am J Sports Med 21:705, 1993

51. Jones, B.H.; Cowan, D.N.; Tomlinson, J.P.; et al: Epidemiology of injuries associated with physical training among young men in the army. Med Sci Sports Exerc 25:197, 1993.

52. Jowsey, J. Bone morphology: Bone structure. In: Sledge, C.B., ed. Metabolic Disease of Bone. Philadelphia, W.B. Saunders, 1977, pp. 41–47.

53. Juppner, H.; Brown, E.M.; Kronenberg, H.M. Parathyroid hormone. In: Favus, M.J., ed. Primer on the Metabolic Bone Diseases and Disorders of Mineral Metabolism. Philadelphia, Lippincott Williams & Wilkins, 1999, p. 80.

54. Kelsey, J.F. Osteoporosis: Prevalence and incidence. In: Proceedings of the NIH Consensus Development Conference, April 22, 1984. Bethesda, MD, National Institutes of Health, 1984, p. 25.

55. Kempson, G. The mechanical properties of articular cartilage and bone. In: Owen, R.; Goodfellow, J.; Bullough, P., eds. Scientific Foundations of Orthopaedics and Traumatology. Philadelphia, W.B. Saunders, 1980, p. 49.

56. Kenzora, J.E.; McCarthy, R.E.; Lowell, J.D.; Sledge, C.C. Hip fracture mortality: Relation to age, treatment, preoperative illness, time of surgery, and complications. Clin Orthop 186:45, 1985.

57. Kiel, D.P.; Felson, D.T.; Anderson, J.J.; et al. Hip fracture and the use of estrogens in postmenopausal women. N Engl J Med 317:1169, 1987.

58. Kimmel, P.L. Radiologic methods to evaluate bone mineral content. Ann Intern Med 100:908, 1984.

59. Krolner, B.; Toft, B.; Pors Nielsen, S.; et al. Physical exercise as a prophylaxis against involutional vertebral bone loss: A controlled trial. Clin Sci (Colch) 64:541, 1983.

60. Lane, J.M.; Vigorita, V.J. Osteoporosis. Orthop J 1:22, 1985.

61. Lane, J.M.; Cornell, C.N.; Healey, J.H. Orthopaedic consequences of osteoporosis. In: Riggs, B.L.; Melton, L.J., III, eds. Osteoporosis: Etiology, Diagnosis and Management. New York, Raven Press, 1988, p. 111.

62. Lane, J.M.; Werntz, J.R. Biology of fracture healing. In: Lane, J., ed. Fracture Healing. New York, Churchill Livingstone, 1987, p. 49.

63. Lane, J. M.; Girardi, F.; Parvataneni, H.; et al. Preliminary outcomes of the first 226 consecutive kyphoplasties for the fixation of painful osteoporotic vertebral compression fractures. Paper presented at the World Congress on Osteoporosis 2000, June 2000.

64. Lane, J.M. Metabolic bone disease and fracture healing. In: Heppenstall, R.B., ed. Fracture Treatment and Healing. Philadelphia, W.B. Saunders, 1980, p. 946.

65. Lane, J.M.; Vigorita, V.J.; Falls, M. Osteoporosis: Current diagnosis and treatment. Geriatrics 39:40, 1984.

66. Lane, J.M.; Healey, J.H.; Schwartz, E.; et al. The treatment of osteoporosis with sodium fluoride and calcium: Effects on vertebral fracture incidence and bone histomorphometry. Orthop Clin North Am 15:729, 1984.

67. Lane, J.M.; Russell, L.; Khan, S.N. Osteoporosis. Clin Orthop 372:139, 1999.

68. Leiberman U.A.; Weiss S.R.; Broll J.; et al. Effect of oral alendronate on bone mineral density and the incidence of fracture in postmenopausal osteoporotic women. N Engl J Med 333:1437, 1995.

69. Lian, J.B.; Stein, G.S.; Canalis E.; et al. Bone formation: Osteoblast lineage cells, growth factors, matrix proteins, and the mineralization process. In: Favus, M.J., ed. Primer on the Metabolic Bone Diseases and Disorders of Mineral Metabolism. Philadelphia, Lippincott Williams & Wilkins, 1999, p. 14.

69a. Lieberman, I.; Dudeney, S.; Reinhardt, M-K.; Bell, G. Initial outcome and efficacy of kyphoplasty in the treatment of painful osteoporotic vertebral compression fractures. Spine 26:1631, 2001.

70. Lindsey, R.; Bush, T.L.; Lobo, R.A.; et al. Addition of alendronate to ongoing hormone replacement therapy in the treatment of osteoporosis. A randomized controlled trial. J Clin Endocrinol Metab 84:3078, 1999.

71. Lindsey, R.; Hart, D.M.; Aitken, J.M.; et al. Long-term prevention of postmenopausal osteoporosis by estrogen. Lancet 1:1038, 1976.

72. Lindsey, R.; Hart, D.M.; Aitken, J.M.; et al. Prevention of spinal osteoporosis in oophorectomised women. Lancet 2:1151, 1980.

73. Lindsey, R.; Hart, D.M.; MacLean, A. Bone response to termination of oestrogen treatment. Lancet 1:1325, 1978.

74. Loucks, A.B.; Motorola, J.F.; Girton, L.; et al: Alterations in the hypothalamic-pituitary-ovarian and the hypothalamic-pituitary-adrenal axis in the athletic woman. J Clin Endocrinol Metab 68:402, 1989.

75. Lufkin, E.G.; Wahner, H.W.; O'Fallon, W.M.; et al. Treatment of postmenopausal osteoporosis with transdermal estrogen. Ann Intern Med 117:1, 1992.

76. Melton, L.J., III; Riggs, B.L. Epidemiology of age-related fractures. In: Avioli, L.V., ed. The Osteoporotic Syndrome: Detection, Prevention and Treatment. Orlando, FL, Grune & Stratton, 1983, p. 45.

77. Melton, L.J., III; Riggs, B.L. Epidemiology of age-related fractures. In: Avioli, L.V., ed. The Osteoporotic Syndrome. New York, Grune & Stratton, 1987, pp. 1–30.

78. Melton, L.J.I.; Khosla, S.; Atkinson, E.J.; et al. Relationship of bone turnover to bone density and fractures. J Bone Miner Res 12:1083, 1997.

79. Meunier, P.J. Prevention of hip fractures. Am J Med 95:755, 1993.

80. Mohler, D.G.; Lane, J.M.; Cole, B.J.; Winerman, S.A. Skeletal fracture in osteoporosis. In: Lane, J.M.; Healey, J.H., eds. Diagnosis and Management of Pathological Fractures. New York, Raven Press, 1993, p. 13.

81. Mosekilde, L.; Eriksen, E.F.; Charles, P. Effects of thyroid hormone on bone and mineral metabolism. Endocrinol Med Clin North Am 19:35, 1990.

82. Mullen, J.O.; Mullen, N.L. Hip fracture mortality: A prospective multifactorial study to predict and minimize death risk. Clin Orthop 280:214, 1992.

83. National Institutes of Health Consensus Development Conference Statement on Osteoporosis, Vol. 5, No. 3, 1984. JAMA 252:799, 1985.

84. NIH Consensus Conference. Optimal calcium intake. JAMA 272:1942, 1994.

85. National Osteoporosis Foundation. Osteoporosis: Review of the evidence for the prevention, diagnosis, and treatment and cost-effectiveness analysis. Osteoporos Int 8:1, 1998.

86. Ott, S.M. Clinical effects of bisphosphonates in involutional osteoporosis. J Bone Miner Res 8(Suppl):597, 1993.

87. Overgaard, K.; Hansen, N.A.; Jensen, S.B.; et al. Effect of calcitonin given intranasally on bone mass and fracture rates in established osteoporosis. A dose response study. Bone Miner 305:556, 1992.

88. The Postmenopausal Estrogen/Progestin Interventions (PEPI) Trial. Effects of estrogen on estrogen/progestin regimens on heart disease risk factors in postmenopausal women. JAMA 273:199, 1995.

89. Powels, T.J.; Hicklish, T.; Kanis, J.A.; et al. Effect of tamoxifen on bone mineral density measured by dual energy x-ray absorptiometry in healthy premenopausal and postmenopausal women. J Clin Oncol 18:78, 1995.

90. Pun, K.K.; Chan, L.W. Analgesic effect of intranasal salmon calcitonin in the treatment of osteoporotic vertebral fractures. Clin Endocrinol (Oxf) 30:435, 1989.

91. Ray, N.F.; Chan, J.K.; Thamer, M.; et al. Medical expenditures for the treatment of osteoporotic fractures in the United States in 1995: Report from the National Osteoporosis Foundation. J Bone Miner Res 12:24, 1997.

92. Recker, R.R.; Kimmel, D.B.; Parfitt, A.M.; et al. Static and tetracycline-based bone histomorphometric data from 34 normal postmenopausal females. J Bone Miner Res 3:133, 1988.

93. Riggs, B.L.; Melton, L.J., III. Evidence for two distinct syndromes of involutional osteoporosis. Am J Med 75:899, 1983.

94. Riggs, B.L.; Melton, L.J., III. Involutional osteoporosis. N Engl J Med 314:1676, 1986.

95. Riggs, B.L.; Melton, L.J., III. The prevention and treatment of osteoporosis. N Engl J Med 327:620, 1992.

96. Riginster, J.; Minne, H.W.; Sorsenson, O.H.; et al. Randomized trial of the effects of risedronate on vertebral fractures in women with established postmenopausal osteoporosis. Vertebral Efficacy with Risedronate Therapy (VERT) Study Group. Osteoporos Int 11:83, 2000.

97. Rosen, C.J.; Kiel, D.P. The aging skeleton. In: Favus, M.J., ed. Primer on the Metabolic Bone Diseases and Disorders of Mineral Metabolism. Philadelphia, Lippincott Williams & Wilkins, 1999, p. 57.

98. Rubin, C.T.; Rubin, J. Biomechanics of bone. In: Favus, M.J., ed. Primer on the Metabolic Bone Diseases and Disorders of Mineral Metabolism. Philadelphia, Lippincott Williams & Wilkins, 1999, p. 57.

99. Schneider, R.; Math, K. Bone density analysis: An update. Curr Opin Orthop 5:66, 1994.

100. Schnitzer, T.; Bone, H.G.; Crepaldi, G.; et al. Therapeutic equivalence of alendronate 70 mg once-weekly and alendronate 10 mg daily in the treatment of osteoporosis. Alendronate Once-Weekly Study Group. Aging 12:1, 2000.

101. Scileppi, K.P.; Stulberg, B.; Vigorita, V.J.; et al. Bone histomorphometry in femoral neck fractures. Surg Forum 32:543, 1981.

102. Seeger, L.L. Bone density determination. Spine 22(Suppl 24):49S, 1997.

103. Shinoda, H.; Adamek, G.; Felix, R. Structure-activity relationships of various bisphosphonates. Calcif Tissue Int 35:87, 1983.

104. Silver, J.J.; Einhorn, T.A. Osteoporosis and aging: Current update. Clin Orthop 316:10, 1995.
105. Smith, R.W., Jr.; Walter, R.R. Femoral expansion in aging women: Implications for osteoporosis and fractures. Science 145:156, 1964.
106. Steier, A.; Gegalia, I.; Schwartz, A.; Rodan, A. Effect of vitamin D and fluoride on experimental bone fracture healing in rats. J Dent Res 46:675, 1967.
107. Walsh, W.R.; Sherman, P.; Howlett, C.R.; et al. Fracture healing in a rat osteopenia model. Clin Orthop 342:218, 1997.
108. Wasnich, R.D. Epidemiology of Osteoporosis. In: Favus, M.J., ed. Primer on the Metabolic Bone Diseases and Disorders of Mineral Metabolism. Philadelphia, Lippincott Williams & Wilkins, 1999, p. 257.
109. Weiss, N.S.; Ure, C.L.; Ballard, J.H.; et al. Decreased risk of fractures of the hip and lower forearm with postmenopausal use of estrogen. N Engl J Med 303:1195, 1980.
110. World Health Organization. Assessment of fracture risk and its application to screening for post-menopausal osteoporosis: Report of a World Health Organization Study Group. World Health Organ Tech Rep Ser 843:1, 1994.

CHAPTER 18

Diagnosis and Treatment of Complications

Craig S. Roberts, M.D.
Gregory E. Gleis, M.D.
David Seligson, M.D.

A *complication* is a disease process that occurs in addition to a principal illness. In the lexicon of diagnosis-related groupings, *complications* are co-morbidities. However, a broken bone plate complicating the healing of a radius shaft fracture hardly seems to fit either of these definitions. In orthopaedic trauma language, the term *complication* has come to mean an undesired turn of events specific to the care of a particular injury. Complications can be *local* or *systemic* and are caused by, among other things, physiologic processes, errors in judgment, or fate. A colleague once described a pin tract infection with external fixation as a *problem,* not a complication. Preventing pin tract drainage is indeed a problem that needs a solution, but when it occurs in a patient, it becomes a complication. Additional terminology has been introduced by the Joint Commission on the Accreditation of Healthcare Organizations, such as the "sentinel event," a type of major complication that involves unexpected occurrences such as limb loss, surgery on the wrong body part, and hemolytic transfusion reaction.

This chapter presents current knowledge about three *systemic* complications (fat embolism syndrome, thromboembolic disorders, and multiple system organ failure), five *local* complications of fractures (soft tissue damage, vascular problems, post-traumatic arthrosis, peripheral nerve injury, and reflex sympathetic dystrophy [RSD]).

SYSTEMIC COMPLICATIONS

Fat Embolism Syndrome

Fat embolism syndrome (FES) is the occurrence of hypoxia, confusion, and petechiae a few days after long bone fractures. FES is distinct from post-traumatic pulmonary insufficiency, shock lung, and adult respiratory distress syndrome (ARDS). When known etiologic factors

of post-traumatic pulmonary insufficiency such as pulmonary contusion, inhalation pneumonitis, oxygen toxicity, and transfusion lung are excluded, there remains a group of patients who have FES with unanticipated respiratory compromise several days after long bone fractures.

Fat embolism was first described by Zenker in 1861 in a railroad worker who sustained a thoracoabdominal crush injury.[76] It was initially hypothesized that the fat from the marrow space embolized to the lungs and caused the pulmonary damage.[66] Fenger and Salisbury believed that fat embolized from fractures to the brain, resulting in death.[21] Von Bergmann first clinically diagnosed fat embolism in a patient with a fractured femur in 1873.[73] The incidence of this now recognized complication of long bone fracture was extensively documented by Talucci and co-workers in 1913 and subsequently studied during World Wars I and II and the Korean conflict.[68] Mullins described the findings in patients who died as "lungs that looked like liver."[43] Although the fat in the lungs comes from bone, careful investigation has shown that other processes are required to produce the physiologic damage to lung, brain, and other tissues. Although the term *fat embolism syndrome* does not describe the pathomechanics of this condition as neatly as was originally hypothesized, embolization of active substances and fat from the injured marrow space has traditionally been thought to be the source of embolic fat. However, recent studies suggest otherwise. Mudd and associates did not observe any myeloid tissue in any of the lung fields at autopsy in patients with fat embolism syndrome and suggested that the soft tissue injury, rather than fractures, was the primary cause of fat embolism syndrome.[41] Ten Duis in a current review of the literature stated that "future attempts to unravel this syndrome . . . should pay full attention to differences in the extent of accompanying soft-tissue injuries that surround a long-bone fracture."[71]

The index patient with FES is a young adult with an isolated tibia or femur fracture, transported from a distance with no oxygen therapy and inadequate splinting. Although definitive fracture stabilization is planned, the operative permit is hard to obtain because the patient's behavior is inappropriate and the family notices a change in mood. The pulse rate is increased, the arterial oxygen concentration is decreased, and petechiae are present. Untreated, the patient will shortly be in an intensive care unit, if he or she survives. The chest radiograph shows bilateral fluffy pulmonary infiltrates, and concern shifts from when and how to nail the femur to when to begin life support.[19]

Although there are many unanswered questions about FES, several issues are apparent. It strikes the young and healthy, whereas older patients with significant upper femoral fractures do not seem at risk. It usually occurs after lower, not upper, limb fractures, and is more frequent with closed fractures.[16] Russell and associates reported a case of fat embolism in an isolated humerus fracture.[61] In a prospective study, Chan and associates found an incidence of 8.75% of overt FES in all fracture patients, with a mortality rate of 2.5%.[15] The incidence rose to 35% in patients with multiple fractures. Other investigators reported the incidence of FES between 0.9% and 3.5% in patients with long bone fractures.[37, 57, 72]

Early recognition of the syndrome is crucial to preventing a complex and potentially lethal course.[2] Clinically, FES consists of a triad of hypoxia, confusion, and petechiae appearing in a patient with fractures.[19] The disease characteristically begins 1 to 2 days after fracture, following what has been called the *latent* or *lucid* period.[66] Sixty percent of all cases of FES are seen in the first 24 hours after trauma, and 90% of all cases appear within 72 hours.[7] Gurd and Wilson's criteria for fat embolism syndrome are commonly used, with the clinical manifestations grouped into either major or minor signs of FES.[25] The major signs are respiratory insufficiency, cerebral involvement, and petechial rash. The minor signs are fever, tachycardia, retinal changes, jaundice, and renal changes. Petechiae are caused by embolic fat. They are transient and are distributed on the cheek, neck axillae, palate, and conjunctivae. The fat itself can be visualized on the retina.[1] A fall in hematocrit levels[18] and alterations in blood clotting profile, including a prolongation of the prothrombin time, can be observed. The diagnosis of FES is made when one major and four minor signs are present (Table 18–1), along with the finding of macroglobulinemia.[44] The most productive laboratory test is measurement of arterial oxygenation on room air. When the Po_2 is less than 60 mm Hg, the patient is in the early stages of FES.

Lindeque and colleagues[35] believe that Gurd and Wilson's criteria are too restrictive and should also include the following:

1. A Pco_2 of more than 55 mg Hg or a pH of less than 7.3,
2. A sustained respiratory rate of more than 35 breaths per minute, and
3. Dyspnea, tachycardia, and anxiety.

If any one of these is present, then the diagnosis of FES is made. Other supportive findings include ST segment

TABLE 18–1	
Major and Minor Criteria for the Diagnosis of Fat Embolism Syndrome*	
Major Criteria	**Minor Criteria**
Hypoxemia (Pao_2 < 60 mm Hg)	Tachycardia >110 bpm
Central nervous system depression	Pyrexia >38.3°C
Petechial rash	Retinal emboli on fundoscopy
Pulmonary edema	Fat in urine
	Fat in sputum
	Thrombocytopenia
	Decreased hematocrit

*A positive diagnosis requires at least one major and four minor signs.
Source: Gurd, A.R.; Wilson R.I. J Bone Joint Surg Br 56:408–416, 1974.

changes on electrocardiography and pulmonary infiltrates on chest radiography.[20]

It is important to assess the neurologic status of the patient to differentiate between fat embolization and intracranial mass lesions. Although hypoxia alone can cause confusion, in the FES, petechial hemorrhages, particularly in the reticular system, alter consciousness. These changes persist despite adequate oxygen therapy.[7, 22, 24] Focal neurologic findings should be investigated to rule out lesions caused by associated head trauma. Persistent alteration of consciousness or seizures are bad prognostic signs. Neurologic changes have been noted in up to 80% of patients.[29]

Fat globules are found in blood,[33] sputum, urine, and cerebrospinal fluid. The urine or sputum can be stained for fat using a saturated alcoholic solution of Sudan III. Sudan III stains neutral fat globules yellow or orange. The Gurd test, in which serum is treated with Sudan III and filtered, is also diagnostic.

The specificity of these tests is in question. Fat droplets are normally found in sputum.[46] In addition, Peltier believes that detection of fat droplets in circulating blood and urine is too sensitive a test for the clinical diagnosis of FES.[52] Furthermore, because the embolic phenomena associated with FES are transient and may not be detected on spot testing, these laboratory investigations are of research interest only and are not part of the usual clinical workup.

The experimental study of FES is linked historically to the study of the circulation of blood, the development of intravenous therapy, and transfusion. As early as 1866, Busch experimented with marrow injury in the rabbit tibia and showed that fat in the marrow cavity would embolize to the lungs.[13] Pulmonary symptoms have been produced in the absence of fracture by the intravenous injection of fat from the tibia of one group of rabbits into another.[9] Autopsy studies of accident victims with long bone fracture have identified fat within the pulmonary capillaries in up to 25% of the victims. Uncommonly, massive release of bone marrow fat actually plugs the pulmonary vessels and causes death.

There are several reasons for uncertainty as to the role of bone fat in producing FES. First, researchers have failed to develop an animal model that reproduces the human syndrome. Moreover, injection of human bone marrow fat into the veins of experimental animals has shown that neutral fat is a relatively benign substance, and it is not certain that the bones contain enough fat to cause FES. One hypothesis is that the fat that appears in the lungs originated in soft tissue stores and aggregated in the blood stream during post-traumatic shock.[28] However, chromatographic analysis of pulmonary vasculature fat in dogs after femoral fracture has shown that the fat most closely resembles marrow fat.[31] In contrast, Mudd and colleagues recently reported that there was no evidence of myeloid elements on post-mortem studies of lung tissue in patients with fat embolism syndrome.[41] Furthermore, extraction of marrow fat from human long bones has shown that sufficient fat is present to account for the observed quantities in the lungs and other tissues.[55] The relative lack of triolein in children's bones may explain why they have a significantly reduced incidence of FES compared with that in adults.[24, 26, 32]

ETIOLOGY

Although the precise pathomechanics of FES are unclear, in a literature review, Levy found many nontraumatic and traumatic conditions associated with FES.[34] The simplest hypothesis is that broken bones liberate marrow fat that embolizes to the lungs. These fat globules produce mechanical and metabolic effects culminating in FES. The mechanical theory postulates that fat droplets from the marrow enter the venous circulation via torn veins adjacent to the fracture site.

Peltier[56] coined the term *intravasation* to describe the process whereby fat gains access to the circulation. The conditions in the vascular bed that allow intravasation to take place also permit marrow embolization.[40] Indeed, marrow particles are found when fat is found in the lungs (Fig. 18–1).[70]

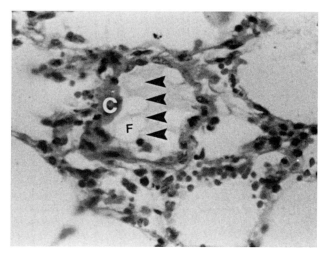

FIGURE 18–1. Histologic appearance of fat from a pulmonary fat embolism in a vessel of the pulmonary alveoli. *Abbreviations:* C, capillary; F, fat globules *(arrowheads).* (From Teng, Q.S.; Li, G.; Zhang, B.X. J Orthop Trauma 9[3]:183–189, 1995.)

Mechanical obstruction of the pulmonary vasculature occurs because of the absolute size of the embolized particles. In a dog model, Teng and co-workers[70] found 80% of fat droplets to be between 20 and 40 µm. Consequently, vessels in the lung smaller than 20 µm in diameter become obstructed. Fat globules of 10 to 40 µm have been found after human trauma.[34] Systemic embolization occurs either through precapillary shunts into pulmonary veins or through a patent foramen ovale.[51]

The biochemical theory suggests that mediators from the fracture site alter lipid solubility causing coalescence, because normal chylomicrons are less than 1 µm in diameter. Many of the emboli have a histologic composition consisting of a fatty center with platelets and fibrin adhered.[75] Large amounts of thromboplastin are liberated with the release of bone marrow, leading to activation of the coagulation cascade. Schlag demonstrated hypercoagulability following hip arthroplasty.[63]

Studies of the physiologic response to the circulatory injection of fats have shown that the unsaponified free fatty acids are much more toxic than the corresponding neutral fats. Peltier hypothesized that elevated serum lipase levels present after the embolization of neutral fat hydrolyzes this neutral fat to free fatty acids and causes local endothelial damage in the lungs and other tissues, resulting in FES.[56] This chemical phase might in part explain the latency period seen between the arrival of embolic fat and more severe lung dysfunction. Elevated serum lipase levels have been reported in association with clinically fatal FES.[59, 65] Alternative explanations are also possible for the toxic effect of fat on the pulmonary capillary bed. The combination of fat, fibrin, and (possibly) marrow may be sufficient to begin a biochemical cascade that damages the lungs without postulating enzymatic hydrolysis of neutral fat.[24, 28, 64] Bleeding into the lungs is associated with a fall in the hematocrit level.[17] The resulting hypoxemia from the mechanical and biochemical changes in the lungs can be severe—even to the point of death of the patient.

Pape and associates[50] demonstrated an increase in neutrophil proteases from central venous blood in a group of patients undergoing reamed femoral nailing. In another study, Pape and colleagues[49] demonstrated the release of platelet-derived thromboxane (a potent vasoconstrictor of pulmonary microvasculature) from the marrow cavity. Peltier[53] demonstrated the release of vasoactive platelet amines. These humoral factors can lead to pulmonary vasospasm and bronchospasm, resulting in vascular endothelial injury and increased pulmonary permeability. Indeed, thrombocytopenia is such a consistent finding that it is used as one of the diagnostic criteria of FES. Barie and co-workers[6] associated pulmonary dysfunction with an alteration in the coagulation cascade and an increase in fibrinolytic activity.

Autopsy findings in patients dying of FES do not, however, show a consistent picture.[66] This may not be caused solely by a lack of clear-cut criteria that define patients included in a given series, but may also be because the manifestations of FES depend on a wide number of patient, accident, and treatment variables.[56]

In light of the incidence of fat emboli and FES in trauma patients, it is likely that other precipitating or predisposing factors such as shock, sepsis, or disseminated intravascular coagulation are needed for the phenomenon of embolized fat to cause FES.[23] Müller and associates[42] summarized that "fat embolism syndrome is likely the pathogenetic reaction of lung tissue to shock, hypercoagulability, and lipid mobilization."

Two questions arise: (1) Is there an association between intramedullary nailing and other injuries? (2) Is there an effect from different nailing methods? Investigations by Pape and associates[47, 48] provided insight into both of these questions. In a study group of patients with multiple trauma and thoracic injury, these researchers found that early operative fracture fixation by nailing was associated with an increased risk of ARDS. These results are in contrast to those of the group without thoracic injury. Thoracic trauma is associated with direct pulmonary injury. The pathogenic mechanisms were examined by Lozman and colleagues.[36] Thus, the timing as well as the associated injuries are crucial in deciding when and how to use a nail.

In a prospective study, Pape and associates[48] showed a significant impairment of oxygenation in multiple trauma patients who underwent reamed nailing. A group of similar patients who had an unreamed nailing did not have the same signs of pulmonary dysfunction. These investigators reasoned that the most likely difference between the two groups was a lower degree of fat embolization in the unreamed group. In sheep, Pape and colleagues[49] demonstrated intravasation of fat associated with reaming of the intramedullary (IM) canal. They concluded that the unreamed procedure caused substantially less severe lung damage than the reamed procedure. However, Heim and associates[27] found that there was a significant increase in IM pressure associated with unreamed nail insertion, and that both reamed and unreamed nailing leads to bone marrow intravasation (Fig. 18–2). Thus, the use of an unreamed nail does not solve the problem of bone marrow embolization and resultant pulmonary dysfunction.

What influences the degree of fat embolization? The answer to this question has not been fully elucidated. High IM pressures have been linked with fat embolization and FES.[30] Wozasek and co-workers[75] looked at the degree of fat intravasation during reaming and IM nailing and correlated this with IM pressure changes and echocardiographic findings. They found peak IM pressures in both the tibial and the femoral nailings in the first two reaming steps. Insertion of the nail caused only minimal pressure rises (but this was after reaming). Echocardiography, however, demonstrated that the maximal infiltration of particles occurred when the nail was inserted. They concluded that the phenomenon of fat intravasation did not depend on the rise in IM pressure. Pinney and associates studied 274 patients with isolated femur fractures and found that waiting more than 10 hours after injury was associated with a 2.5-fold increase in fat embolism syndrome.[58] Bulger and co-workers, in a 10-year review of the literature, state that early intramedullary fixation did not seem to increase the incidence or severity of fat embolism syndrome.[12]

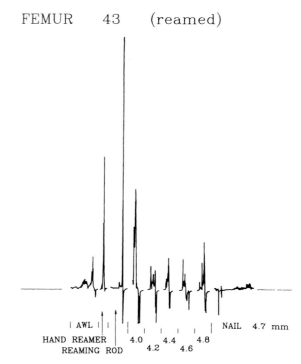

FIGURE 18–2. Intramedullary pressure during reamed nailing of the femur. (From Heim, D.; Regazzori, P.; Tsakiris, D.A.; et al. Intramedullary nailing and pulmonary embolism: Does unreamed nailing prevent embolization? An in vivo study in rabbits. J Trauma 38[6]:899–906, 1995.)

PREVENTION AND TREATMENT

The risk of FES can be decreased by several measures. Proper fracture splinting and expeditious transport, use of oxygen therapy in the postinjury period, and early operative stabilization of long bone fractures of the lower extremities are three important measures that can be taken to reduce the incidence of this complication.[3] Blood pressure, urinary output, blood gas values, and—in the more critically injured—pulmonary wedge pressures should be monitored to evaluate fluid status and tissue perfusion more precisely.[34] Dramatic advances in emergency medical transport have resulted in increasing survival of patients with complex polytrauma and high injury severity scores. This, unfortunately, has led in some instances to a tendency to "scoop and run" without traction splinting. Unsplinted long bone fractures in patients transported over long distances provide the mechanical condition for intravenous fat intravasation. Oxygen therapy by mask or nasal prongs lessens the decrease in arterial oxygenation following fracture and appears to have value in the prevention of FES.

In the hospital, if surgery is delayed, the patient's arterial oxygen on room air is measured daily and supplemental oxygen therapy is continued until the post-traumatic fall in oxygen tension is complete and the Pa_{O_2} on room air returns toward normal. Alternatively, if inspired oxygen tension (Fi_{O_2}) can be measured accurately, the shunt equation can be used to monitor pulmonary performance. Teng and co-workers[70] completed preliminary development of a dog model of FES to establish diagnostic criteria sufficiently sensitive and specific enough for diagnosis of FES in the early stages. They correlated blood gas analysis samples with computer image analysis of oil red O–stained pulmonary artery blood samples. Although fracture fixation and particularly medullary nailing cause a transient decrease in oxygenation, the immediate stabilization of fractures before the development of low arterial saturation may prevent the occurrence of FES.[60]

In a prospective randomized study of 178 patients, Bone and associates[10] confirmed that early fracture stabilization, within the initial 24 hours after injury, decreased the incidence of pulmonary complications. Likewise, Lozman and colleagues,[36] in a prospective randomized study, concluded that patients receiving immediate fixation had less pulmonary dysfunction following multiple trauma and long bone fractures than did those patients receiving conservative treatment. Although current data support primary fracture stabilization over delayed therapy, controversy still exists over the method of stabilization. Böstmann and co-workers found a higher incidence of local infections, delayed bone healing, and decreased stability with plate osteosynthesis compared with a lower incidence of these same complications with IM nailing.[11] In general, IM nailing is the preferred method of stabilization. The timing of nailing, however, is a point of controversy.[12] Among other reasons, this was due to the concern that immediate nailing of long bone fractures early in the post injury period would increase the incidence of pulmonary complications, including FES. The nonoperative method of treating major long bone fractures has been the use of balanced skeletal traction or delayed rigid fixation, or both. External fixation of long bone fractures is another option that can be used as a temporizing alternative to IM nailing. Earlier studies showed no evidence to support the view that the effect of reaming on intravascular fat is additive or that immediate reamed IM fixation causes pulmonary compromise.[5, 68] In fact, the opposite is true, probably because fracture stabilization removes the source of intravascular marrow fat and decreases shunting in the lung, because the patient can be mobilized to an upright position.[38, 39, 72]

In a retrospective study by Talucci and associates,[69] in which 57 patients underwent immediate nailing, no cases of FES were seen. Similarly, Behrman and colleagues[8] reported a lower incidence of pulmonary complications for patients undergoing early fixation among 339 trauma patients who underwent either early or late fixation of femoral fractures. In the study by Lozman and colleagues,[36] patients who had delayed fracture fixation had a higher intrapulmonary shunt fraction throughout the study period compared with that in the early fixation group. However, early IM nailing of long bone fractures is not without complications. Pell and co-workers,[51] using intraoperative transesophageal echocardiography, demonstrated varying degrees of embolic showers during reamed IM nailing. FES developed postoperatively in three patients, and one patient died. Other studies showed an increased number of pulmonary complications associated with reamed IM nailing of femoral shaft fractures.[45, 50, 74]

Specific therapy has been used to try to decrease the incidence of FES. Increased fluid loading and the use of hypertonic glucose, alcohol, heparin, low molecular weight dextran, and aspirin have no clinical effect on the rate of FES. Various studies have looked at the efficacy of steroids in reducing the clinical symptoms of FES. Large doses of steroids immediately after injury do have a beneficial effect.[4, 22, 35, 62, 67, 70] Corticosteroids most likely decrease the incidence of FES by limiting the endothelial damage caused by free fatty acids. Although this is encouraging, routine use of steroids is not without significant risk. Complications, particularly infection and gastrointestinal bleeding, may outweigh the benefits, because many of these patients have significant multiple trauma. Clinical trials in which steroids were effective used a dose of 30 mg/kg body mass of methylprednisolone administered on admission and repeated once at 4 hours[35] or 1 g on admission and two more doses at 8-hour intervals.[67] However, FES is primarily a disease of the respiratory system, and current treatment is therefore mainly with oxygen and meticulous mechanical ventilation.[54] The treatment of FES remains mainly supportive.[12]

Thromboembolic Disorders

PATHOGENESIS

Deep venous thrombosis (DVT) and pulmonary embolism (PE) are the most common causes of morbidity and mortality in orthopaedic patients.[100, 127, 236] In the trauma patient, the presence of DVT may complicate the patient's treatment even more than in the case of elective surgery. If DVT or PE occurs before definitive management of the fracture, the method of treating the fracture may have to be modified because of the use of therapeutic anticoagulants. In contrast, the elective surgery patient can be treated perioperatively with selected prophylactic anticoagulants to reduce the incidence of DVT without altering the operative plan. This is practical for elective surgery patients, because the thrombi most commonly develop at surgery.[107] However, for the trauma patient, it is not known when the patient is at greatest risk for the development of DVT.[92] Certainly DVT can develop preoperatively, as was shown by Heatley and associates,[156] who observed that when patients admitted for gastrointestinal evaluations were hospitalized preoperatively for 4 days or longer, there was a 62% incidence of DVT before operation.

In 1846, Virchow proposed the triad of thrombogenesis: increased coagulability, stasis, and vessel wall damage (Fig. 18–3). These are all factors that are unfavorably affected by trauma. Virchow also linked the presence of DVT with PE and deduced that a clot in the large veins of the thigh embolized to the lungs.[273] Laennec,[191] in 1819, was the first to describe the clinical presentation of an acute pulmonary embolus, and the pathosis of a proximal DVT was first described by Cruveilhier[114] in 1828. Venous thrombi have been shown to develop near the valve pockets on normal venous endothelium and are not necessarily related to inflammation of the vessel wall.[248]

Trauma increases the propensity to develop a hypercoagulable state. Vessel wall injury with endothelial damage exposes blood to tissue factor, collagen, basement mem-

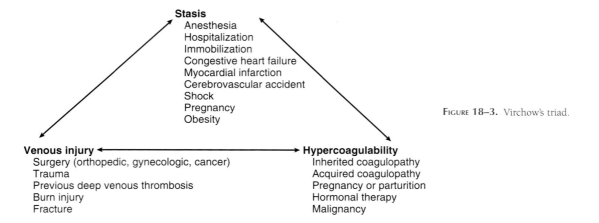

Stasis
  Anesthesia
  Hospitalization
  Immobilization
  Congestive heart failure
  Myocardial infarction
  Cerebrovascular accident
  Shock
  Pregnancy
  Obesity

Venous injury
  Surgery (orthopedic, gynecologic, cancer)
  Trauma
  Previous deep venous thrombosis
  Burn injury
  Fracture

Hypercoagulability
  Inherited coagulopathy
  Acquired coagulopathy
  Pregnancy or parturition
  Hormonal therapy
  Malignancy

FIGURE 18–3. Virchow's triad.

brane, and von Willebrand factor, which induce thrombosis through platelet attraction and the intrinsic and extrinsic coagulation pathway.[184] Antithrombin (AT-III) activity, which decreases the activity of thrombin and factor Xa, was found to be below normal levels in 61% of critically injured trauma patients.[222] Also, fibrinolysis is decreased and appears to be from increased levels of PAI-1, which inhibits tissue plasminogen activator and thus decreases the production of plasmin.[146, 204]

Although DVT is unusual in children, it has been observed in children with previously asymptomatic hypercoagulable disorders and following trauma. The increased risk with age appears to reach a plateau at age 30 years. Any additional increase in risk after age 30 is related to the presence of other risk factors (e.g., trauma, heart disease, infection, and cancer).[107]

The presence of heart disease alone increases the risk of pulmonary embolism by 3.5 times, and this is further increased if atrial fibrillation or congestive heart failure is present.[107, 109] The risk of DVT is increased during pregnancy and is especially great in the postpartum period. Spinal cord injury is associated with a threefold increase in leg DVT and PE.

Many other factors affect the risk of DVT. Obesity has been reported to have a twofold increase in the risk of DVT. Type O blood has a lower incidence of DVT, whereas type A has an increased frequency. The blood type association is related to high concentrations of clotting factor VIII, which is determined mostly by blood group and is related to increased risk of thrombosis.[239] Gram-negative sepsis, myeloproliferative disorders, ulcerative colitis, Cushing's disease, homocystinuria, and Behçet's syndrome have all been reported to have an increased risk of DVT.

Varicose veins are assumed to be an increased risk factor for the development of DVT. However, the presence of venous abnormalities as determined by preoperative plethysmography and Doppler studies alone do not correlate with increased risk.[201] Barnes[85] divided varicose vein patients into two groups: those with primary varicose veins that are usually associated with a strong family history and have no increased risk of DVT, and those with secondary varicose veins that usually occur following a history of DVT. Patients in the latter group do have an increased risk for recurrent thrombophlebitis.

A meta-analysis by Velmahos and co-workers[338] looked at DVT and risk factors in trauma patients. Variables studied that did not have a statistically significant effect for increasing the development of DVT were gender, head injury, long bone fracture, pelvic fracture, and units of blood transfused. The variables, which were statistically significant, were spinal fractures and spinal cord injury, which increased the risk of DVT by twofold and threefold, respectively. The patients with DVT versus those without DVT were significantly older by 8 years and had a significantly higher injury severity score (ISS) by 1.430 ± 0.747, although the ISS difference was of minimal clinical significance. They could not confirm that the widely assumed risk factors of pelvic fractures, long bone fractures, and head injury affected the incidence of DVT but did note that the multiple trauma patients may have already been at the highest risk of DVT.

The incidence of DVT and pulmonary embolism (PE) has always been difficult to establish. Less than 50% of actual DVT incidence can be diagnosed by clinical means. To determine the true incidence for study purposes, the most accurate techniques have been autopsy or venography. In autopsy studies, the incidence of pulmonary embolus as a significant contributor to the cause of death was 7.9%. The incidence of DVT, when determined by complete leg dissections at autopsy, is three to five times greater than that for pulmonary emboli.[107] The risk of DVT is not just in the operated leg. Culver and colleagues[115] found that for hip fractures, the incidence of DVT detected by venography in the fractured limb was 40%, whereas in the uninjured leg it was 50%. Autopsy studies confirm this; thrombosis is generally present bilaterally even when injury is limited to one extremity or when thrombosis is clinically present in just one leg.[249] The nature of the injury has little effect on the incidence of DVT; rather, it is other factors—age, heart disease, and length of immobilization—that determine the incidence.[138, 156]

In immobilized trauma patients with no prophylaxis, the incidence of venography-proven thigh and iliofemoral thrombosis was between 60% and 80%.[135, 190] Even with full prophylaxis, the incidence of DVT is as high as 12%.[187] Some investigators have concluded that "there is no adequate prophylaxis against DVT in the trauma patient."[260]

Trauma to the pelvis and lower extremities greatly increases the risk of DVT and PE.[108, 159, 282] In an autopsy study of 486 trauma fatalities, Sevitt and Gallagher[249] found 95 cases of PE for an incidence of 20%. At autopsy, the rate of PE following hip fracture was 52/114 (46%); for tibia fractures, 6/10 (60%); and for femoral fractures, 9/17 (53%). The rate of DVT for hip fractures increased to 39/47 (83%) and for femur fractures to 6/7 (86%) when supplemental special studies of the venous system were done at autopsy.

PE is significant as a cause of death following lower extremity injury. Two thirds of patients having a fatal pulmonary embolus die within 30 minutes of injury (Fig. 18–4).[120] The incidence of fatal pulmonary embolus without prophylaxis after elective hip surgery is from 0.34% to 3.4%, whereas the incidence following emergency hip surgery is from 7.5% to 10%.[126, 144, 207, 275, 283]

Solheim[258] reported an 0.5% incidence of fatal PE in a series of tibia and fibula fractures. Similarly, Phillips and co-workers[227] reported 1 of 138 patients (0.7%) with severe ankle fractures developed a nonfatal PE. In a study of 15 patients with tibia fractures, Nylander and Semb[219] found that 70% had venographic changes compatible with DVT.

The types of DVT that are at high risk for causing a PE are those that originate at the popliteal fossa or more proximally in the large veins of the thigh or pelvis. Moser and LeMoine[215] found that the risk of pulmonary embolization from distal lower extremity DVT to be relatively low. Of DVTs that are first limited to the calf, about 20% to 30% extend above the knee.[90, 229] Those that extend above the knee carry the same risk as femoral and popliteal thrombi.[243] Kakkar and colleagues[182] speculated that thrombi in the calf are securely attached and resolve rapidly and spontaneously. However, embolization from "calf only" venous thrombi does occur. Calf vein thromboses are responsible for 5% to 35% of symptomatic pulmonary emboli,[200, 226] 15% to 25% of fatal PE,[139, 208, 248] and 33% of "silent" PE.[211, 212]

In addition to PE, complications of DVT include recurrent thrombosis and post-thrombotic syndrome. Symptoms of post-thrombotic syndrome are edema, induration, pain, pigmentation, ulceration, cellulitis, and stasis dermatitis.[174, 176] Symptoms are present in 20% to 40% of those having DVT.

Upper extremity DVT are much less common (2.5%) and can be divided into primary and secondary causes. The primary causes are idiopathic and effort thrombosis (Padget-Schroetter syndrome). Effort thrombosis is most common in athletes and laborers who do repetitive shoulder abduction and extension. Predisposing causes of thoracic outlet obstruction should be investigated. Secondary causes are venous catheters, venous trauma, extrinsic compression or malignancy, and hypercoagulable condition.

DIAGNOSIS

The clinical signs and symptoms of DVT are nonspecific. DVT was clinically silent in two thirds of cases in which thrombosis was found at autopsy or the findings on leg venography were positive.[129, 249] Patients usually present with swelling, calf tenderness, positive Homans' sign, fever, and elevated white blood cell count. Changes in color and temperature, venous distention, edema, and calf tenderness are helpful diagnostic signs when present. Homans' sign—pain in the calf on dorsiflexion of the foot—is nonspecific.

Clinically, the diagnosis of DVT and PE is frequently difficult. With PE, although some patients experience sudden death, many more present with gradual deterioration and symptoms similar to pneumonia, congestive heart failure, or hypotension. Because the clinical diagnosis is difficult, diagnostic studies are necessary so that early treatment can be instituted. Various test are described along with limitations and advantages.

The venogram is the standard against which all other tests are measured. Venography is able to adequately demonstrate the calf veins in 70% of patients with DVT. Only the presence of an intraluminal defect is diagnostic of DVT; chronic venous disease can cause the other findings. Criteria for a diagnosis of DVT should include well-defined defects on at least two radiographs, nonvisualization of the popliteal, superficial femoral, or common femoral veins with good visualization of the proximal and distal veins, and the presence of collateral channels.[145]

The major drawback of venography is that it is usually a one-time test that cannot be done on a serial basis. Venograms can be painful, can cause swelling of the leg, have been reported to cause phlebitis in about 4% to 24% of patients,[91, 243] and may cause thrombosis.[80] As with any contrast agent, anaphylactic reactions are a possibility, as are renal complications.[145] Between 5% and 15% of venograms cannot be interpreted owing to technical considerations.[281] In a study by Huisman and colleagues,[162] 20% of patients either could not undergo venography or had noninterpretable studies.

Radioactive fibrinogen is effective in detecting thrombi in the calf but is less effective in the thigh.[167] Fibrinogen I-125 is incorporated into a forming thrombus and can be detected. DVT in the thigh is poorly detected with this technique, and it is not used as a screening tool for trauma patients.

Impedance plethysmography (IPG) detects the presence

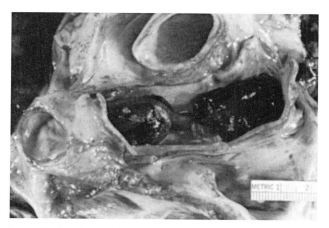

FIGURE 18–4. A large embolus in the pulmonary artery, which was the cause of death. (Courtesy of James E. Parker, M.D., University of Louisville, Louisville, KY.)

of DVT by measuring the increased blood volume in the calf after temporary venous occlusion produced by a thigh tourniquet and the decrease in blood volume within 3 seconds after deflation of the cuff.[169, 278, 279] The IPG is very sensitive in diagnosing proximal DVT but is not sensitive for distal DVT.[97, 155, 164, 280] It is a poor screening tool for the trauma patient.

Continuous-wave Doppler (CWD) or Doppler ultrasound examination is easy to do and can be done at bedside, but it requires experience to reduce the false-positive result rate.[85] The principles of ultrasonic velocity detection have been outlined by Sigel and colleagues.[254] Characteristics of a normal venous system are spontaneity (evidence of a flow signal), phasicity (respiratory variation), and augmentation (increased flow with distal compression of the leg). Venous thrombosis is characterized by the absence of venous flow at an expected site, loss of normal fluctuation in flow associated with respiration, diminished augmentation of flow by distal limb compression, diminished augmentation of flow by release of proximal compression, and lack of change on Valsalva maneuver. Barnes and co-workers[86] found that Doppler ultrasound was 94% accurate, and no errors were made in diagnosis above the level of the knee. However, for isolated calf vein thrombosis, CWD is insensitive. An additional disadvantage is that CWD may fail to detect nonobstructive thrombi even in proximal lesions.[101]

Compression ultrasound is the use of real-time B-mode ultrasonography, with the single criteria of compressibility of the common femoral and popliteal vein needed for the diagnosis of DVT. Normally the lumen of a vein collapses when enough pressure is applied to indent the skin; if a thrombus is present, the vein does not compress.[112] Using this technique to monitor the veins of the thigh and calf and using venography as a control, Froehlich and associates[130] found this test was 97% accurate, 100% sensitive, and 97% specific.

Additionally, real-time B-scan ultrasound is able to visualize the clot and may be able to distinguish acute from chronic thrombus.[265] In a prospective comparison study, Cogo and colleagues[101] concluded that real-time B-mode ultrasonography using the sole criteria of common femoral and popliteal vein compressibility was superior to Doppler ultrasound in the detection of DVT. Likewise, in a prospective randomized trial, Heijboer and co-workers[157] found real-time compression ultrasonography superior to IPG for the serial detection of venous thrombosis because the positive predictive value of an abnormal test was 94% for venous ultrasound versus 83% for IPG. One disadvantage is that B-scan ultrasound does not allow adequate visualization of the calf veins.[97]

A Duplex ultrasound is the combination of real-time ultrasound and pulse-gated Doppler ultrasound. The Doppler scan adds an audible or graphic representation of blood flow.[192, 281] In an extensive literature review, White and associates[282] reported a combined sensitivity of duplex ultrasound for proximal thrombi of 95% and specificity of 99%. An added advantage of duplex scanning is for the diagnosis of nonthrombotic causes of leg swelling such as Baker's cyst, hematoma, and lymphadenopathy.[210]

Color-flow duplex ultrasonography (CFDU) is the most recent advancement in ultrasound technology for the diagnosis of lower extremity DVT. The real-time B-mode component displays stationary tissues in gray scale. The Doppler component is color-enhanced and detects blood flow by the shift in frequency from the backscatter of high-frequency sound. The frequency is shifted by an amount proportional to the flow velocity. Blood flowing away from the transducer appears blue, whereas blood flowing toward the transducer appears red. The newer technology can detect velocities as low as 0.3 cm/sec. The color saturation is proportional to the rate of flow. A black image indicates an absence of flow, flow velocities less than 0.3 cm/sec, or flow vectors at a right angle to the second beam.[205] The addition of color allows for the easier and faster detection of vascular structures. This has provided improved imaging of the iliac region, the femoral vein in the adductor canal, and the calf veins.[234] CFDU is superior to duplex scanning and B-mode imaging in detecting nonocclusive thrombi because the flow characteristics in the vessels are readily detected.[205] Several studies have reported high sensitivity and specificity in symptomatic patients.[89, 96, 206, 238]

For screening of symptomatic trauma patients, ultrasound is an excellent study, but for asymptomatic patients it is less sensitive at detecting DVT, especially in the calf. Serial ultrasound has been used as surveillance screening to detect DVT in trauma patients, but it was thought not to be cost effective.[147, 245] When DVT develops in the calf, about 25% extends to the thigh if left untreated. If the initial ultrasound missed the asymptomatic DVT and no treatment is given, approximately 2% will have an abnormal proximal scan on testing 1 week later.[185]

CONTEMPORARY TECHNIQUES FOR DETECTING DEEP VENOUS THROMBOSIS AND PULMONARY EMBOLISM

Magnetic resonance imaging (MRI) has been recently applied to the detection of deep venous thrombosis. The gradient-recalled echo (GRE) images are obtained in shorter time and are intrinsically sensitive to flow. Flowing blood appears bright, and stationary soft tissues appear dark.[99]

MRI of the lower extremities has been compared with contrast venography for the detection of DVT. Sensitivities are reported to be 90% to 100% with specificities of 75% to 100%.[99, 122, 261] Using the GRE technique, Spritzer and colleagues[262] found that specificity was 100%. MRI is considered to have several advantages over venography and ultrasonography:

- Noninvasive procedure
- Relative lack of operator dependence
- Improved evaluation of the pelvic and deep femoral veins
- Simultaneous imaging of both legs
- Imaging of adjacent soft tissue[98, 128, 270]

The primary disadvantage of MRI is cost, which is typically 2 to 2.5 times the cost of an ultrasound scan and 1.4 times the cost of venography.[99, 193] MRI is rarely used to diagnose DVT.

Multiple modalities exist for the diagnosis of PE. Of interest would be a highly sensitive blood test. Research in this area has been active for many years. A plasma marker for split products of cross-linked fibrin (D-dimer) has been evaluated for the diagnosis of PE and DVT.[93–95, 140, 246] D-dimers are formed when cross-linked fibrin polymers are produced in a stable fibrin clot. When the clot is degraded by plasmin, the D-dimers are released free in the plasma and can be measured by antibody assays.[184] If the D-dimer level is low, the probability of DVT is low. This test has been used in trauma patients, but it has not been accepted as very useful.[246]

PE can be diagnosed with the gold standard pulmonary angiography or more commonly ventilation perfusion (VQ) scan. If the VQ scan results are abnormal but not diagnostic of a PE, then depending on the severity of symptoms, either pulmonary angiography or venous ultrasound can be done. Because PEs are rare in the absence of a DVT, if the venous ultrasound shows a DVT as a possible source of the PE, then anticoagulant therapy is indicated. Positive findings on venous ultrasound are present in 5% to 10% of patients with nondiagnostic lung scans. Of patients who have a negative venous ultrasound result but suspected PE and a nondiagnostic VQ scan, 80% will not have had a PE. The remaining 20% will have had a PE, but the residual leg thrombus is too small or none is present. The risk of recurrent PE and recurrent DVT is highest within 2 weeks and can be monitored with serial venous ultrasounds to determine treatment. With this management approach, there is about 2% incidence of abnormal venous ultrasound on serial testing. The use of serial noninvasive ultrasound scanning has not been evaluated adequately. If there is a high suspicion of PE, then pulmonary angiography should be done.[227]

TREATMENT

There are three major approaches to the treatment of DVT: prevent the thrombus, ignore it if it occurs, or treat the thrombus. Implicit in each of these approaches is a consideration of (1) the risk of the intervention and (2) the risk if no intervention is taken. For prophylaxis of thrombosis, what is the risk of the agent used versus the risk of DVT and its complications? Once DVT develops, if no treatment is undertaken, what is the risk of PE compared with the complications of therapy?

PROPHYLAXIS

Until recently, consideration for prophylaxis in trauma patients was largely based on nonsurgical patients or general surgical and orthopaedic elective surgical patients. DVT prophylaxis in trauma patients is an area of ongoing study. Various methods of DVT prophylaxis are reviewed.

Physical Measures

Prevention of thromboembolism depends on good preoperative conditioning, careful handling of the lower limbs during surgery, and early active postoperative mobilization. These approaches work by limiting venous stasis, one component of Virchow's triad. Muscle tone increased with a preoperative exercise program sets the stage in elective surgery cases for resumption of activity immediately following surgery. The incidence of significant venous

embolic events in the first 3 days after surgery is very small and rises slowly until the fifth postoperative day. Thus, if early mobilization and active use of the limbs can be achieved soon after surgery, many emboli may be prevented. Venous blood flow rate can be increased by muscular exercise and early ambulation.[301, 302] This approach is widely used, and, as noted by Bolhofner and Spiegel,[92] its value has not been proved. Wrapping the limbs with elastic bandages, avoidance of excessive tourniquet times, and good positioning are other factors that are thought to be important. Both the bent knee position and the semisitting position increase the incidence of postoperative thromboembolic complications.

Physical measures can be used to decrease the risk of DVT. Venous stasis can be decreased by elevating the foot of the bed. This has been shown to increase the rate of blood flow and to decrease the incidence of DVT.[154] Coutts[111] reported in preliminary material that continuous passive motion causes venous blood flow rates to be increased and the incidence of DVT to be decreased. Contrary to Coutts' findings, Lynch and colleagues[202] did not find any significant reduction in DVT among total knee arthroplasty patients using a continuous passive motion machine.

External physical measures include graduated and uniform compression stockings, external pneumatic compression device (EPCD), sequential compression device (SCD), and arteriovenous foot pumps (AVFP). External compression decreases the cross-sectional area of the lower limb and increases the venous velocity. Compression improves the emptying of venous vascular cusp and decreases stasis, which can initiate venous thrombosis. Vasodilation can result in internal tears, which predispose to DVT by exposing blood to the thrombogenic subendothelial collagen. An external pressure of 15 mm Hg results in a 20% reduction in venous cross-sectional area.[78]

Graduated compression stockings help to increase venous blood flow velocity by 30% to 40% and therefore help to decrease the rate of DVT.[242, 253] The optimal pressure gradient is 18 mm Hg at the ankle, decreasing to 8 mm Hg at midthigh.[253] Evidence shows that knee-length stockings are as effective as thigh-length stockings and avoid the above-the-knee segment rolling down and acting as a garter-like constriction.[78] Complications from compression stockings can occur by impairing subcutaneous tissue oxygenation, which can be critical if there is peripheral vascular disease. Skin ulcerations and amputations have been reported, so stockings are contraindicated in atrial compromise and peripheral neuropathy. Manufacturers recommend against the use of stockings when the ankle-to-brachial pressure index is less than 0.7. Stockings have been shown in randomized trials to decrease DVT by 57% after total hip replacement compared with that in control subjects.[78] For total knee replacement, below-the-knee stockings decreased DVT by 50% compared with that in control subjects, and above-the-knee stockings were less effective.[161] For hip fractures, evaluations are still pending. No conclusions are available for the trauma patient, but fitting the stockings to patients with lower extremity trauma is difficult.

External pneumatic compression of the legs can decrease the incidence of DVT by 90% in major elective knee surgery.[110, 163, 166, 267] Its beneficial use in elective hip surgery is also established.[220, 257] Fisher and co-workers[126] demonstrated the effectiveness of an EPCD in reducing the incidence of isolated DVT in hip fracture patients. However, in patients with pelvic fracture, these investigators were unable to demonstrate a statistically significant reduction in the incidence of thromboembolism. They postulated that EPCDs were less effective in preventing clots in the pelvic venous system. Cyclic compression prevents stasis, enhances fibrinolysis,[266] and has no associated increased risk of bleeding. With sequential pneumatic compression, venous blood flow velocity can be more than doubled.[110] This technique is more effective than nonsequential devices.[218] Agu reports, "Trauma guidelines currently recommend the use of SCD in high risk trauma patients, although, again, there is a paucity of a good data to support their use."[78] Knudson found no benefit with SCD in multiple trauma patients but did see a decrease in DVT in neurotrauma patients.[188] Dennis also had isolated benefit of DVT reduction in head injuries (16.7% decreased to 1.4%) and spinal cord injuries (27.3% to 10.3%).[119]

An alternative approach to external sequential pneumatic compression of the legs is external intermittent compression of the foot using AVFP. This technique arose out of work by Gardner and Fox,[132] who investigated the physiology of venous return from the foot. Using video phlebography, they identified the presence of a venous pump in the foot. The venous foot pump is not a muscle pump and therefore is not affected by toe and ankle movement. However, it is immediately emptied by weight bearing due to flattening of the plantar arch and the longitudinal stretching of the veins. The AVFP impulse device artificially activates the venous foot pump to maintain pulsatile venous blood flow in patients after surgery or injury.[133] The device consists of an inflation pad that conforms to the plantar arch of the foot. It inflates rapidly, holds a pressure of 50 to 200 mm Hg for 1 to 3 seconds, then deflates for 20 seconds to allow refilling of the venous plexus.

Four studies have been done on high-risk trauma patients using AVFP and SCD. Spain and associates had 184 patients: 64% used SCD and 36% used AVFP with a DVT rate of 7% and 3%, respectively, which was not a significant difference between the two methods.[261] Anglen studied 124 randomized trauma patients with a DVT rate of SCD 0% and AVFP 4%.[82] Purtill had 170 trauma patients: 81 with SCD and 89 with AVFP with a DVT rate of 8.6% and 8.9%, respectively.[233] Knudson compared low molecular weight heparin (LMWH) with AVFP and SCD in trauma patients with a DVT incidence of AVFP 5.7%, SCD 2.5%, and LMWH 0.8%.[187]

Stranks and co-workers found, among patients undergoing surgery for hip fracture, a 23% incidence of proximal DVT in a control group (graduated compression stockings only) versus 0% in the group utilizing AVFP.[265]

Prophylactic Drugs

When significant risk factors are present, active prophylaxis by altering coagulability—the second component of Virchow's triad—becomes increasingly justified. Prophylactic drugs include dextran, aspirin, "mini" heparin (either with or without dihydroergotamine), warfarin, LMWH fractions, and potentially thrombin inhibitors.

Dextran has been shown to be effective in elective and emergency hip procedures[79, 124, 178, 216] and in femur fractures.[83] It has not been studied adequately for knee procedures. It is not being used in the multiple-trauma victim. Dextran is a glucose polymer that is formulated with either a 40,000 or a 70,000 mean molecular weight. The 70,000 formula has a higher rate of allergic reactions associated with it. It is best started preoperatively and limited to less than 500 mL during operations because of increased bleeding associated with larger doses.

Aspirin is an agent that decreases platelet adherence and thereby decreases coagulability. Initially, aspirin was believed to decrease the incidence of DVT. Harris and associates[150–152, 175] and DeLee and Rockwood[118] all reported that aspirin decreased the incidence of DVT. Harris and colleagues[148] in 1982 in a double-blind trial found that aspirin was effective for men but not for women. Evidence then showed that aspirin did not affect the incidence of DVT.[100, 149, 171, 211, 214, 263] The most recent report is that aspirin does decrease the incidence of DVT and PE in hip fracture and arthroplasty patients but it should not be relied on for prophylaxis.[232, 259]

Warfarin has been shown to be effective in preventing DVT in orthopaedic patients.[128, 166, 213, 225] Amstutz and associates[81] reported no deaths from PE while using a prophylactic regimen with warfarin in 3000 total hip replacements. Postoperatively, the prothrombin time (PT) can be lengthened to an International Normalized Ratio (INR) of 2.0 to 3.0 (1.2 to 1.5 times controls).[158, 172] This regimen is effective in decreasing the rate of DVT and has minimal bleeding complications. However, warfarin has a relatively narrow therapeutic window and thus necessitates accurate monitoring of patient response.

Heparin has been tried as a prophylactic agent in an unfractionated (UFH) low dose of 5000 U subcutaneously 2 hours preoperatively and then every 8 hours. Although this is effective for decreasing the rate of DVT in general surgical patients undergoing abdominal procedures, it did not affect the rate of DVT in patients undergoing orthopaedic hip surgery.[165, 211, 213, 243] Once an intravascular clot forms, low dose UFH has no effect on fibrinolysis. Adding low-dose unfractionated heparin to SCD does not provide any further protection over SCD alone.[273] There is no role in trauma for the use of low-dose unfractionated heparin. In a study of adjusted-dose versus fixed-dose heparin, the rate of DVT was 39% when given in a fixed-dose compared with 13% when given in adjusted doses. Doses were adjusted to keep the activated partial thromboplastin time between 31.5 and 36 seconds.[197] A meta-analysis of randomized trials of adjusted-dosage UFH versus LMWH found that LMWH was more effective in preventing DVT and PE in total knee replacements.[160]

Heparin in low doses has also been combined with dihydroergotamine (DHE), an alpha-adrenergic receptor stimulant, and administered to patients undergoing elective hip surgery[181, 183, 240] and to patients with hip fractures.[239] The incidence of DVT was decreased in both groups. The role of this drug combination in trauma has not been studied. Complications include ergotism, which can result from DHE use and can lead to amputation or even death.[134, 270] DHE use has also been associated with myocardial infarction.[116]

Heparin can also lead to multiple complications such as bleeding, allergic reaction, osteoporosis, and thrombocytopenia[196]; in fact, spontaneous venous and arterial thrombosis can occur from a severe form of heparin-induced thrombocytopenia.[84]

One of the newer options for the prevention of DVT is the use of LMWH. Unfractionated heparin has a molecular weight of 6000 to 20,000 daltons, whereas the fractionated products are 4000 to 6000 daltons. Two LMWHs are currently being used; enoxaparin (Lovenox) and dalteparin (Fragmin), and reviparin is in trials.

Like UFH, LMWH has anti–Factor Xa activity, but unlike UFH, LMWH has much less effect on Factor IIa (thrombin).[102] This should have the effect of decreasing thrombosis without inducing a hypocoagulable state. As a result, the rate of bleeding complications should be less with LMWH.[236] LMWH has little effect on platelets and does not affect PT or activated partial thromboplastin time (aPTT) at dosages used. Additional benefits are high bioavailability, longer half-life, and linear dose-dependent anti–Factor Xa activity.[131] Routine blood monitoring of aPTT or anti–Factor Xa level is not recommended. However, in patients who are at risk for accumulating LMWH, such as those with renal insufficiency (eliminated by renal excretion), or in those with active bleeding, then measuring anti–Factor Xa may be a benefit.[121] If excess hemorrhage does occur with LMWH, protamine will partially reverse the effects of LMWH. Repeat protamines dosing is necessary because of its short half-life, compared with that of LMWH.

In a study of 665 patients, Warkentin and co-workers[275] found no cases of heparin-induced thrombocytopenia in 333 patients who received LMWH. Thrombocytopenia can still occur, and platelet counts should be checked at baseline and every 2 to 3 days with discontinuation of LMWH if the platelet count is below 100,000 or to less than half the original value.

Several clinical studies demonstrated the effectiveness of LMWH in reducing the incidence of thromboembolism in elective hip surgery patients.[103, 125, 168, 195] Likewise, LMWH prophylaxis has demonstrated a low incidence of DVT, PE, and bleeding complications in patients with spinal cord injury.[142, 203]

LMWH has also been used as a means of DVT prophylaxis following operative treatment in patients with hip fracture.[87, 137, 180, 228] The incidence of DVT in the patients receiving LMWH was from 7% to 30%. The incidence of bleeding complications was equal to or less than the other treatment groups (placebo or warfarin).

Knudson and associates[187] studied enoxaparin (30 mg subcutaneously every 12 hours) in a controlled high-risk trauma setting. Enrollment required any injury with an abbreviated injury score of 3 or higher; major head injury (Glasgow Coma Scale [GCS] ≤ 8); spine, pelvic, or lower extremity fractures; acute venous injury; or older than 50 years. Exclusion for heparin use were severe neurologic injury, that is, GCS of 8 or lower, or spinal cord injury; lumbar or spleen injuries being treated nonoperatively; or continual bleeding after 24 hours. The no heparin group

all used either SCD or AVFP. In the group that was eligible for heparin, patients were randomized to receive LMWH or bilateral SCD or AVFP. Duplex scan monitoring was performed every 5 to 7 days. The predicted rate of DVT for trauma patients with one risk factor and no prophylaxis was 9.1%.[188] The actual incidence was 0.8% in the LMWH group, 2.5% in the SCD group, and 5.7% in the AVFP group. Of 120 patients on LMWH, only one reoperation for major bleeding complication occurred that was potentially associated with LMWH. In the 199 patients with SCD, 4 had mild skin changes and continued to use SCD. In the 53 patients with AVFP, 8 had blistering and wound problems and 3 of these discontinued the use of AVFP. Only one clinical PE occurred and that was in an SCD patient. Knudson and associates concluded, "the administration of LMWH is a safe and extremely effective method of preventing DVT in high-risk trauma patients. When heparin is contraindicated, aggressive attempts at mechanical compression are warranted." Kelsey and co-workers[184] concur that the literature supports the use of LMWH in trauma for prophylaxis of DVT, but it still must be individualized because of bleeding risk. If there is an increased bleeding risk, then SCD is a "good second-line prophylactic measure."

A meta-analysis[193] comparing LMWH and adjusted low-dose heparin statistically showed that LMWH had relative risk reductions of 53% for symptomatic thromboembolic complications, 68% for clinically significant bleeding, and 47% for mortality. The investigators concluded that LMWH is more effective and safer than UFH for the treatment of venous thrombosis. Their conclusions were based primarily on trials using Fraxiparine (Sanofi, Paris, France) and Logiparin (Novo Nordisk Farmaka, Bagsvaerd, Denmark). The LMWHs each have distinct biologic activity profiles, and each drug needs to be considered as an individual drug. Randomized trials using specific preparations need to be conducted. Nonetheless, LMWHs, because of their ease of administration, predictable response, and apparent effectiveness, are promising tools for the prevention and treatment of venous thromboembolism.

The thrombin inhibitors, melagatran and hirudin, act on the enzymatic properties of thrombin and prevent the fibrin superstructures that support a blood clot. In melagatron clinical trials on total hip and knee replacement prophylaxis, the incidence of proximal DVT was 3% versus about 7% for LMWH. In hirudin (15 mg twice daily) clinical trials on hip replacements, the incidence of proximal DVT was 4.5% versus 7.5% for enoxaparin (40 mg once daily).[123]

The duration of prophylaxis for thromboembolism following orthopaedic procedures is a matter of debate. In a review by Johnson and colleagues,[183] approximately 50% of fatal pulmonary emboli occurred between 7 and 14 days after surgery and 36% between 14 days and 3 months. The duration of prophylaxis should be individualized for a given patient, taking into account known risk factors such as age, type of injury or procedure, prolonged immobilization, estrogen use, and other known risk factors. Prophylaxis using warfarin following total hip arthroplasty can vary from 3 weeks[81] to 12 weeks.[223] Sharrock and co-workers[252] used intravenous fixed-dose

TABLE 18–2 ....

Recommendations for Anticoagulation

Thromboembolism	Recommendations
Suspected	Give heparin 5000 U IV and order diagnostic study
Confirmed	Rebolus heparin 5000–10,000 U IV and start maintenance infusion at 1300 U/hr (heparin 20,000 U in 500 ml D₅W infused at 33 ml/hr)
	Check aPTT at 6 hr to keep aPTT between 1.5 and 2.5 times control
	Check platelet count daily
	Start warfarin therapy on day 1 at 10 mg daily for first 2 days, then administer warfarin daily at estimated daily maintenance dose
	Stop heparin therapy after 5–7 days of joint therapy when INR is 2.0–3.0 off heparin; continue warfarin for 3 months at an INR of 2.0–3.0

....

Abbreviations: aPTT, activated partial thromboplastin time; D₅W, 5% dextrose in water; INR, International Normalized Ratio; IV, intravenous.
Source: Hyers, T.M.; Hull, R.D.; Weg, J.C. Chest 102:408S–421S, 1992.

heparin only during the intraoperative period during total hip arthroplasty, whereas Fauno and associates[125] used heparin for 8 days postoperatively in patients undergoing total knee arthroplasty. In trauma patients, the duration of prophylaxis is even less clear.

TREATMENT OF DEEP VENOUS THROMBOSIS AND PULMONARY EMBOLISM

Once DVT or PE is suspected, the clinical impression should be confirmed with diagnostic testing. Heparin should be started unless contraindicated until diagnostic testing is done (Table 18–2). Contraindications include neurologic, spinal cord, or ocular injuries that could be worsened with bleeding. Heparin is started intravenously to reach therapeutic effect rapidly to prevent clot extension and decrease the risk of PE. Subcutaneous LMWH has also been proven to be effective in initial treatment of DVT. However, further documentation of its role in the trauma setting is needed because controlled trials excluded its use if there had been surgery in the prior 5 to 7 days.[170, 255] Controlled trials of intravenous heparin versus LMWH in the presence of DVT have shown no difference in rates of symptomatic extension, recurrence, pulmonary embolism, or severe bleeding.[170, 189, 194, 198, 231] LMWH has also been used in the treatment of pulmonary embolism.[104, 255]

If DVT is present, the patient is continued on heparin until converting to warfarin and continued for 3 to 6 months (Table 18–3). The dosage of warfarin is not standardized, and in younger patients the dosage is more difficult to predict. Two studies comparing an initial dose of 5 mg or 10 mg suggest that 5 mg is more appropriate.[113, 153] Length of warfarin treatment for DVT and PE is from 3 months to 6 months[98, 184] and depends on the risk of recurrence. The rate of recurrent DVT and PE is higher when the DVT occurred without an identifiable risk factor

TABLE 18–3 ....

Algorithm for Antithromboembolic Prophylaxis in Trauma Patients

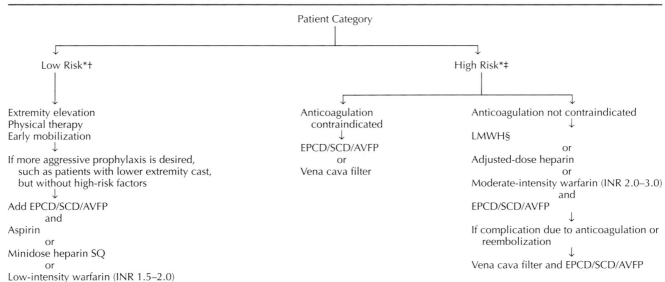

....

Abbreviations: AVFP, arteriovenous foot plexus; EPCD, external sequential pneumatic compression devices; SQ, subcutaneous; INR, International Normalized Ratio; LMWH, low-molecular-weight heparin; GCS, Glasgow Coma Scale; ISS, injury severity score; SCD, sequential compression device.
*Risk factors: Age >40 years; history of venous thromboembolism; complex pelvic fracture; complex lower extremity fracture; greater than 3 days immobilization; coma (GCS <8); spinal cord injury, with or without paralysis; blunt trauma with ISS >15; penetrating injury with repair of major vein; presence of femoral venous catheters.
†A low-risk patient is one without any high-risk factors.
‡A high-risk patient is one with one or more high-risk factors.
§Prospective randomized trials evaluating the safety and efficacy of LMWH in trauma patients are ongoing.

than when there is an identifiable transient risk factor.[230, 235, 247] Longer treatment is indicated for trauma patients with major vein ligation or spinal cord injuries with paralysis. Evidence of reembolization is an indication for permanent anticoagulation and the placement of an inferior vena caval filter.[264]

Thrombolytic drugs are an alternative to heparin, but they are not suitable to the traumatized or postoperative patient for at least 2 weeks because of clot lysis at the surgical site. An advantage of thrombolytic drugs is that the venous system more closely returns to normal when the venous thrombosis is lysed rather than when propagation of the thrombus is arrested with heparin.[105] The Urokinase Pulmonary Embolism Trial (UPET) found a statistically significant lower mortality rate in the patients receiving thrombolytic therapy than in the group receiving heparin anticoagulation.[269] In theory, there should be a lower incidence of post-thrombotic syndrome in patients receiving thrombolytic therapy than in those receiving heparin treatment, but randomized trials are lacking and the beneficial effect of lysis is complicated by increased risk of bleeding.[77, 244]

Vena cava interruption is performed when heparinization is contraindicated, as in patients with a preexisting bleeding disorder; severe hypertension; neurologic injury; or bleeding problems of pulmonary, gastrointestinal, neurologic, or urologic etiology. If anticoagulation fails to stop pulmonary emboli, vena cava interruption is indicated.[179] Also, if patients develop complications with anticoagulation, they can be switched to vena cava interruption. An additional approach is the preoperative use of vena cava interruption in patients who are at extremely high risk for PE. Vaughn and associates[271] preoperatively inserted the Greenfield filter in 42 patients (scheduled for hip or knee arthroplasty) considered to be at extremely high risk for a fatal PE. The principal indication was a history of thromboembolism. None of the patients in this group experienced a PE immediately postoperatively. On follow-up, no filter-related complications were reported.

The prophylactic use of vena cava interruption in trauma patients has also been examined. Rogers and colleagues[237] identified four subsets of trauma patients who were at high risk for PE: (1) those with severe head injury and coma, (2) those with spinal cord injuries with neurologic deficit, (3) those with multiple long bone fracture and pelvic fracture, and (4) elderly patients with isolated long bone fractures. In a prospective evaluation, these investigators prophylactically inserted vena cava filters in 34 patients identified as high risk for PE from among the general trauma population. PE was eliminated in this study group despite an expected incidence of DVT of 17.6%. Filter insertion was without complication. At 1-year follow-up, duplex scan revealed two caval thromboses.

Vena cava filters have associated complications such as venous stasis leading to edema, pain, varicose veins, and skin ulcers in a condition known as the *postphlebitic syndrome*.[277] Other complications include bleeding or thrombus formation at the site of insertion, migration of the filter, and perforation of the vena cava.[141, 143] Martin and co-workers[205] described a case report of phlegmasia cerulea dolens as a complication of an inferior vena cava filter for prophylaxis against PE in a man with a fracture of the acetabulum. In addition, filters are not 100% effective.[117]

Surgical thrombectomy is only indicated for patients with massive thrombosis and those who have absolute contraindications for thrombolytic therapy or do not respond to treatment.[88] Pulmonary embolectomy should be considered when thrombolysis is not effective or not feasible in patients with massive pulmonary embolism and hemodynamic instability.[173]

For elective and traumatic hip and knee surgery, the search for prophylactic measures indicates that modalities can be used to decrease the risk of DVT and PE. Hull and Raskob stated: "The onus is now on the individual orthopedic surgeon to use prophylaxis, particularly in patients over the age of forty years and in the elderly, who are unquestionably at greatest risk."[166]

The trauma patient is in a different category from the elective arthroplasty patient. The incidence of thrombotic complications versus the risk of prophylaxis with anticoagulants is less clear. The first step in solving this problem is identifying the relative degree of risk for the different types of injury or level of severity. The National Institutes of Health Consensus Conference held in 1986 estimated that the incidence of DVT in young multisystem trauma patients is 20%.[106]

Shackford and Moser[251] found an average incidence of venous thromboembolism of 42%, with a range of 18% to 90%, in trauma patients during a literature review. In a study of major trauma patients, Shackford and associates[250] found an incidence of 7% venous thromboembolism among trauma patients with at least one risk factor. Venous thromboembolism occurred within 1 week in 50% of these patients. Of 400 patients admitted into a DVT trauma study by Knudson and colleagues,[188] 251 patients completed the study and 15 (6%) developed lower extremity venous thrombosis. Dennis and co-workers[119] evaluated 395 trauma patients with ISS greater than 9 who survived a minimum of 48 hours. These investigators found an overall incidence of 4.6% lower extremity DVT and 1.0% incidence of PE among patients with and without prophylaxis.

Numerous studies have attempted to identify specific injuries and severity of injury that had a high incidence of DVT and PE. In a study by Myllynen and associates,[217] a 100% incidence of DVT was seen within 25 days in patients with spinal cord injury. In another study, Dennis and co-workers[119] identified the following risk factors for patients at high risk of venous thromboembolism: age older than 39 years; prolonged immobilization; blunt trauma with ISS greater than 9; spinal fractures or subluxations, with or without complete paralysis; severe acute head injuries; and penetrating injury requiring repair of a major vein. They found no basis for routine DVT prophylaxis in injured patients who did not have any recognized risk factors.

Based on historical literature, Shackford and Moser,[251] in a prospective study, placed trauma patients into low- and high-risk groups according to risk factors. They identified the following factors: (1) age older than 45 years and enforced bed rest for more than 3 days, (2) history of venous thromboembolism, (3) spine fracture without neurologic deficit, (4) coma (GCS < 7), (5) quadriplegia or paraplegia, (6) pelvis fracture, (7) lower extremity fracture, (8) repair of a major lower extremity vein, and (9) complex wound of the lower extremity. If none of the factors were present, the patients were placed in the low-risk group. Patients with one or more risk factors were considered high risk for venous thromboembolism. The incidence of venous thromboembolism was 7% in the high-risk group and zero in the low-risk group.

Spain and associates[260] analyzed 2868 consecutive trauma admissions and identified 280 patients (10%) in a high-risk group who survived 48 hours or longer with these risk factors: (1) severe closed head injury with mechanical ventilation 72 hours or longer, (2) closed head injury with lower extremity fractures, (3) spinal column or cord injury, (4) combined pelvic and lower extremity fractures, and (5) major infrarenal venous injury. The remaining nonthermal injury patients were the low-risk group. Of the 280 high-risk patients, 241 patients received some form of prophylaxis, with 213 of these treated with SCD or AVFP. Thromboembolic events were investigated based on clinical suspicion, and routine screening with duplex scans was not done. In the high-risk group, there were 12 DVTs (5%) and 4 nonfatal PEs (1.4%); in the low-risk group, there were 3 DVTs (0.1%) and no PEs. Their conclusion was that aggressive screening and prophylactic IVC filters were not the standard of care. Only in the major venous injury group were they perhaps justified. They thought that compression devices were reasonably effective, low risk, and cost effective for prophylaxis.

Knudson and colleagues[188] also tried to identify which trauma patients were at risk for venous thromboembolism and consequently would benefit from DVT prophylaxis or intense surveillance. Combining the results of their study with the work of other investigators, they developed the following list of risk factors: (1) age older than 30 years, (2) pelvic fractures, (3) spine fractures with paralysis, (4) coma (GCS < 8), (5) immobilization for more than 3 days, (6) lower extremity fractures, (7) direct venous injury, (8) ISS of 16 or greater, (9) large transfusion requirements, and (10) presence of femoral intravenous catheters.

Likewise, Rogers and colleagues[237] identified four groups of injury patterns associated with PE: (1) spinal cord injury with paraplegia or quadriplegia, (2) severe head injury with GCS less than 8, (3) age older than 55 years with isolated long bone fractures, and (4) complex pelvic fractures with associated long bone fractures. In contrast to other studies, two recent reports did not associate isolated long bone fractures with an increased risk for venous thromboembolism.[209, 221]

The current literature clearly indicates that certain subsets of trauma patients are at risk for venous thromboembolism and would benefit from some type of prophylaxis or surveillance. Many experts think that prophylaxis for DVT is safer and more cost effective than surveillance tests.[164, 209, 224, 241] In a study of surveillance venous scans for DVT in prophylactically evaluated multiple trauma patients, Meyer and co-workers[209] performed 261 scans, 92% of which produced normal results. At their institu-

tion, the cost to identify each proximal DVT was $6688. The overall incidence of clinically significant proximal DVT in their patients treated with DVT prophylaxis was 6%. They concluded that the routine use of venous surveillance scans should be limited to high-risk or symptomatic patients.

SUMMARY

The patient with multisystem trauma represents a challenge to provide DVT prophylaxis because of the nature and location of injuries; however, some type of prophylaxis, either pharmacologic or mechanical, is possible in almost every patient and should be instituted when significant risk factors exist. Because orthopaedic injuries and other trauma are unforeseen, "prophylaxis" as stated by Rogers[236] is in effect, "ex post facto." Although current prophylactic regimens in trauma patients significantly reduce the relative risk for DVT and PE, no method provides 100% protection. Further randomized controlled trials of DVT prophylaxis in trauma patients are needed. A suggested algorithm for the management of post-traumatic thromboembolic prophylaxis is given in Table 18–3.

Multiple Organ System Dysfunction and Failure

Multiple organ failure (MOF) can be defined as the sequential failure of two or more organ systems remote from the site of the original insult following injury, operation, or sepsis. The organ failure can be pulmonary, renal, hepatic, gastrointestinal, central nervous system, or hematologic.[306, 329] These systems can be monitored for objective criteria for failure, but criteria vary from series to series (Tables 18–4 and 18–5).[307, 329] The risk of developing MOF and the severity of the MOF can also be graded by measuring the effects on specific organ systems.[312]

MOF is the end result of a transition from the normal metabolic response to injury to persistent hypermetabolism and eventual failure of organs to maintain their physiologic function. A 1991 consensus conference used the term *multiple organ dysfunction syndrome* (MODS) to describe this spectrum of changes.[294] Organ dysfunction is the result of either a direct insult or a systemic inflammatory response, known clinically as the *systemic inflammatory response syndrome* (SIRS),[293] which can be reversible or progress to MODS or MOF. SIRS can be caused by a variety of infectious and noninfectious stimuli[294] (Fig. 18–5). Treatment of the offending source must be undertaken early, because once organ failure has begun, treatment modalities become progressively ineffective.[299] Fry identified the mortality rate for failure of two or more organ systems as about 75%. If two organ systems fail and renal failure occurs, then the mortality is 98%.[307] Today, MOF is the number one cause of death in surgical intensive care units.[303]

The basic theory behind the development of MOF and the closely related ARDS has undergone modification since

TABLE 18–4

Criteria for Organ Dysfunction and Failure

Organ or System	Dysfunction	Advanced Failure
Pulmonary	Hypoxia requiring intubation for 3–5 d	ARDS requiring PEEP >10 cm H_2O and Fio_2 >0.5
Hepatic	Serum total bilirubin ≥2–3 mg/dl or liver function tests ≥ twice normal	Clinical jaundice with total bilirubin ≥8–10 mg/dl
Renal	Oliguria ≤479 ml/d or creatinine ≥2–3 mg/dl	Dialysis
Gastrointestinal	Ileus with intolerance of enteral feeds >5 d	Stress ulcers, acalculous cholecystitis
Hematologic	PT/PTT >125% normal, platelets <50,000–80,000	DIC
Central nervous system	Confusion, mild disorientation	Progressive coma
Cardiovascular	Decreased ejection fraction or capillary leak syndrome	Refractory cardiogenic shock

Abbreviations: ARDS, adult respiratory distress syndrome; PEEP, positive end-expiratory pressure; Fio_2, fraction of inspired air in oxygen; PT, prothrombin time; PTT, partial thromboplastin time; DIC, disseminated intravascular coagulation.
Source: Dietch, E.A.; Goodman, E.R. Surg Clin North Am 79(6), 1999; which was adapted from Deitch, E.A. Ann Surg 216:117–134, 1992, with permission.

the 1970s and mid-1980s. Moore and Moore[326] provided an excellent and concise overview of the evolving concepts of postinjury multiple organ failure. In brief, the earlier models promoted an infectious basis for ARDS/MOF, with two possible scenarios: (1) insult → ARDS → pulmonary sepsis → MOF, or (2) insult → sepsis → ARDS/MOF. The current thinking promotes an inflammatory model of MOF. As previously mentioned, this inflammatory response can arise from a number of infectious and noninfectious stimuli. Again, two patterns exist: the one-hit model (massive insult → severe SIRS → early MOF) and the more common two-hit model (moderate insult → moderate SIRS → second insult → late MOF). In recent years, research into the pathogenesis of MOF has focused on how the inflammatory response is propagated, independent of infection. Moore and Moore have the global hypothesis that postinjury MOF occurs as the result of a dysfunctional inflammatory response.[326] Deitch created an integrated paradigm of the mechanisms of MOF.[303] In general, three broad overlapping hypotheses have been proposed in the pathogenesis of MOF: (1) macrophage cytokine hypothesis, (2) microcirculatory hypothesis, and (3) gut hypothesis. Attempts to understand this highly complex syndrome must extend to the cellular and molecular levels.

TABLE 18–5

Definition of Organ Failure Based on Fry Criteria

Pulmonary	Need of ventilator support at an Fio_2 of 0.4 or greater for 5 consecutive days
Hepatic	Hyperbilirubinemia greater than 2.0 g/dl and an increase of serum glutamic–oxaloacetic transaminase
Gastrointestinal	Hemorrhage from documented or presumed stress-induced acute gastric ulceration. This can be documented by endoscopy; if endoscopy is not performed, then the hemorrhage must be sufficient to require two units of blood transfusion.
Renal	Serum creatinine level greater than 2.0 mg/dl. If a patient has preexisting renal disease with elevated serum creatinine level, then doubling of the admission level is defined as failure.

Research indicates that organ injury in MOF is largely the result of the host's own endogenously produced mediators and less due to exogenous factors like bacteria or endotoxins (Table 18–6).[303] There is increasing evidence that there are biologic markers for the risk of development of MOF that may be more useful than anatomic descriptions of injuries. Nast-Kolb and associates[45] measured various inflammatory markers in a prospective study of 66 patients with multiple injuries (ISS > 18) and found that the degree of inflammatory response corresponded with the development of post-traumatic organ failure.[45] Specifically, lactate, neutrophil elastase, interleukin-6, and interleukin-8 were found to correlate with organ dysfunction. Strecker and co-workers[335] studied 107 patients prospectively and found that the amount of fracture and soft tissue damage can be estimated early by analysis of serum interleukin-6 and creatine kinase and is of great importance with regard to long-term outcome after trauma. Specifically, these investigators found significant correlations between fracture and soft tissue trauma and intensive care unit stay, hospital stay, infections, systemic inflammatory response syndrome, multiple organ failure score, and serum concentrations or activities of serum interleukin-6, interleukin-8, and creatine kinase during the first 24 hours after trauma.

Blood transfusions are a frequent part of polytrauma treatment and an independent risk factor for MOF. Zallen and associates have identified the age of packed red blood cells (PRBCs) to be a risk factor, with the number of units over 14 days and 21 days as independent risk factors for MOF.[339] Old but not outdated PRBCs prime the neutrophils for superoxide production and activate the endothelial cells, which are pathogenic mediators for MOF.

Nonetheless, our knowledge of the pathogenesis of MOF is constantly increasing; the reader is referred to Beal and Cerra,[293] Deitch and Goodman,[304] Baue and associates,[292] Livingston and Deitch,[321] and Moore and Moore.[326] The complexities for evaluating the pathogenesis and treatment of MOF should evolve further because the treatments in the aforementioned articles have continued to fail with therapies aimed at antimediator therapies. This has led to a hypothesis considering "complex nonlinear systems," which Seely has described.[333] Although treatment and recognition of MOF has improved, there has been little impact on the mortality rate in the past

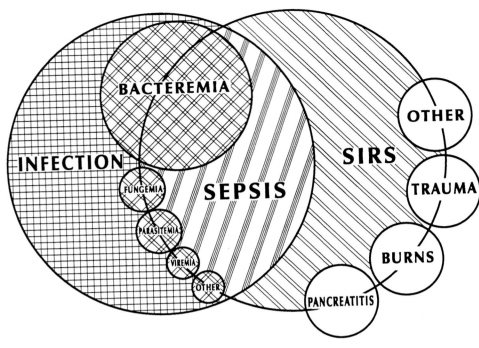

FIGURE 18–5. The interrelationship among systemic inflammatory response syndrome (SIRS), sepsis, and infection. (From Bone, R.C.; Balk, R.A.; Cerra, F.C.; et al. Definitions for sepsis and organ failure and guidelines for the use of innovative therapies in sepsis. Chest 101:1644–1655, 1992.)

 BLOOD BORNE INFECTION

20 years.[304] It has been suggested that future treatment strategies must address multimodality combination therapy aimed at suppressing the inflammatory response while preserving immune competence and antimicrobial defenses.[304]

MOF is a syndrome distinct from respiratory failure, which can complicate airway injury, resuscitation, or anesthesia following an accident. With the development of improved patient categorization, transport, and emergency care, it has become recognized that there is a threshold beyond which the survival from injury is problematic. With simple injuries (e.g., an ankle fracture and laceration from a fall), the physiologic effects are not additive. However, in high-energy blunt trauma, the effects—for example, of a pulmonary contusion, ruptured spleen, and fractured pelvis—become more than additive.

The ISS is one of several scales currently available to quantify the extent of trauma.[288] The ISS was derived from the Abbreviated Injury Score (AIS) of the American Medical Association Committee on Medical Aspects of Automotive Safety,[302] updated in 1985 as AIS-85. Injuries to six body regions (head and neck, face, chest, abdomen and pelvic viscera, extremities and bony pelvis, and integument) are graded as (1) mild, (2) moderate, (3) severe, (4) critical—outcome usually favorable, and (5) critical—outcome usually lethal. The ISS equals the sum of the squares of the three highest AIS grades. The ISS score has a maximal value of 75.

When the ISS is 25 or greater, a patient who is considered polytraumatized and is at risk for MOF will benefit from specialized trauma center care. The median lethal ISS scores have been determined by age group (in years): ages 15 to 44, an ISS of 40; ages 45 to 64, and ISS

TABLE 18–6 . . . .

Potential Mediators Involved in the Pathogenesis of Multiple Organ Failure

HUMORAL MEDIATORS

Complement
Products of arachidonic acid metabolism
    Lipoxygenase products
    Cyclooxygenase products
Tumor necrosis factor
Interleukins (1–13)
Growth factors
Adhesion molecules
Platelet activating factor
Procalcitonin
Procoagulants
Fibronectin and opsonins
Toxic oxygen-free radicals
Endogenous opioids-endorphins
Vasoactive polypeptides and amines
Bradykinin and other kinins
Neuroendocrine factors
Myocardial depressant factor
Coagulation factors and their degradation products

CELLULAR INFLAMMATORY MEDIATORS

Polymorphonuclear leukocytes
Monocytes/macrophages
Platelets
Endothelial cells

EXOGENOUS MEDIATORS

Endotoxin
Exotoxin and other toxins

. . . .

Source: Adapted with permission from Balk, R.A. Crit Care Clin 16(2):1–13, 2000.

TABLE 18–7 ....

Risk Stratification for Postinjury Multiple System
Organ Failure

Category	Risk Factors	MSOF Probability (%)
I	ISS 15–24	4
II	ISS ≥25	14
III	ISS ≥25 plus >6 U RBCs/first 12 hr	54
IV	ISS ≥25 plus >6 U RBCs/first 12 hr plus lactate ≥2.5 mmol at 12–24 hr	75

....

Abbreviations: ISS, injury severity score; MSOF, multiple system organ failure; RBCs, red blood cells.
Source: Moore, F.A.; Moore, E.E. Surg Clin North Am 75:257–277, 1995.

of 29; and ages 65 and older, an ISS of 20.[313] Moore and Moore[326] identified the following variables to be predictive of MOF: age older than 55 years, ISS 25 or greater, more than 6 units of blood in the first 24 hours after admission, high base deficit, and high lactate level. These investigators stratified patients at risk for MOF (Table 18–7).

One of the consequences of MOF is the depletion of body protein reserves. Amino acids are essential components of the energy systems that maintain the body's homeostasis; this deficit cannot be replenished by intravenous glucose or lipids.[295] As the MOF progresses, the peripheral metabolic energy source switches from the conventional energy fuels of glucose, fatty acids, and triglycerides to the catabolism of essential branched-chain amino acids. The multiple-injury patient is like a diesel submarine on the bottom of the ocean with a limited air supply. Once the air supply is exhausted, damage control systems can no longer be maintained. Amino acids are lost as muscles are oxidized for energy, and the supply is not replenished.[315, 322]

Tscherne emphasized the role of necrotic tissue in the pathogenesis of MOF.[337] It is well known that a gangrenous limb, for example, can provoke a systemic catabolic response. Those with military experience have observed the dramatic reversal of alarming symptoms that occurs when an urgent amputation is undertaken for gangrene.

Dead tissue (e.g., muscle, bone, marrow, and skin) provokes an inflammatory autophagocytic response.[310, 328] In this setting, consumption of complement and plasma opsonins has been measured.[287, 316, 327] The complement system is activated in this setting with depletion of factors C3 and C5 with elevated levels of C3a and increased metabolism of C5a. C3a and C5a are anaphylotoxins and may cause the pulmonary edema in ARDS by affecting the smooth muscle contraction and vascular permeability.[316] Plasma opsonin activity is decreased with the consumption of the complement system. The opsonins are critical for antibacterial defense, and their consumption may lead to an increased susceptibility to infection.[287] Several investigators identified serum factors that stimulate muscle destruction.[289, 301] Multiple mediators and effectors have been implicated in the pathogenesis of MOF, but exactly which mediator or combination of mediators is responsible for the hypermetabolic response is not known.[314] This response consumes the individual's energy reserve and

leads to MOF. Once MOF is established, the sequence of organ failure apparently follows a consistent pattern, with involvement first of the lung, then the liver, gastric mucosa, and kidney.[308]

Positive blood culture results have been documented in 75% of patients with MOF, but it is not clear whether infection is the cause or simply accompanies MOF.[308, 323] Most probably, it is a contributing factor. Goris and associates[310] were able to induce MOF in rats by injecting a material that causes an inflammatory response. Sepsis causes tissue destruction and, therefore, like broken bones, releases activators of autophagic systems into the blood stream.

The immune system's response in polytrauma can be measured. Polk and colleagues[329] defined a scoring system for predicting outcome by combining points for ISS and contamination with a measurement of monocyte function (the surface expression of D-related antigen). This method appears promising in predicting survival.[317]

A combined service approach to the multiple-injury patient has proved valuable in preventing the development of MOF (Table 18–8). Avoidance of pulmonary failure, prevention of sepsis, and nutritional support are the keys.[291] Mechanical ventilation is regulated in a special care unit under the supervision of anesthesiologists or traumatologists with experience and training in this area of intensive care. Immediate wound débridement and constant attention to the details of wound management, pulmonary toilet, cleanliness of access lines, and urinary tract sterility are required to prevent sepsis. With open fractures, parenteral or local wound antibiotics are therapeutic. An assessment of nutritional reserve, including measurement of triceps skin fold, a total lymphocyte count, and measurement of serum transferrin, is helpful in determining the need for nutritional support. If possible, the gastrointestinal tract should be used, but in patients with extensive intra-abdominal injury and poor nutritional reserves, early total parenteral nutrition with amino acid supplementation is essential. Nutrition has an important role in preventing the translocation of bacteria and toxins

TABLE 18–8 ....

Prevention of Multiple Organ Failure

RESUSCITATIVE PHASE

Aggressive volume resuscitation in early stages of treatment
Appropriate monitoring of volume resuscitation with measurement of arterial base deficit and serum lactate level, use of pulmonary artery catheters, calculation of oxygen delivery and consumption, use of gastric tonometry

OPERATIVE PHASE

Timely operative management of soft tissue injuries with débridement of nonviable and infected tissue
Early fixation of all possible long bone and pelvic fractures
Vigilance in preventing the missed injury

ICU PHASE

Early nutritional support
Appropriate use of antibiotics
Specific organ support
Timely reoperative surgery for missed injuries and complications of trauma

....

GUT HYPOTHESIS

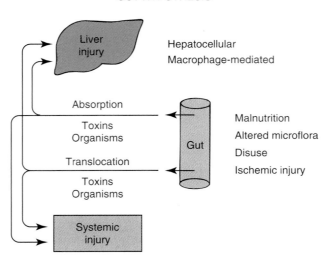

Figure 18–6. Diagrammatic representation of the interrelationship of the gut and liver. Shock, malnutrition, and bacterial overgrowth are hypothesized to potentiate gut absorption and translocation of bacteria or toxins, or both, that can either directly alter liver cell function or indirectly influence it through the Kupffer cell. (Redrawn from Cerra, F.B.; West, M.; Keller, G.; et al. Prog Clin Biol Res 264:27–42, Copyright © 1988. Reprinted by permission of Wiley-Liss, a division of John Wiley and Sons, Inc.)

from the gut into the splanchnic circulation; once bacteria and toxins are in the circulation, they are transported to the liver, altering liver (Kupffer) cell function and causing progressive hepatocyte hypermetabolism and organ failure (Fig. 18–6).[298, 325]

ORTHOPAEDIC MANAGEMENT

Early stabilization of significant pelvic, spinal, and femoral fractures is emerging as a powerful tool in avoiding the cascade of events leading to pulmonary failure, sepsis, and death.[320, 321, 331] Increased understanding of the metabolic consequences of the various techniques of skeletal stabilization, including external fixation, plate osteosynthesis, closed IM nailing, and traction-casting methods in patients with varying injury patterns and metabolic fitness, will be an area of exciting research in the future. Demling[305] stressed control of the inflammatory process to prevent further stimulus to MOF. He recommended early rapid removal of injured tissue and prevention of further tissue damage by early fracture fixation. Necrotic and injured soft tissue in experimental fractures results in a reduction of hepatic blood flow similar to that seen in sepsis.[332] Consequently, early stabilization of fractures may prevent organ dysfunction by improving splanchnic perfusion.

The optimal timing and type of fracture fixation is controversial and unknown. Timing of fracture fixation balances the need to rapidly mobilize the patient versus the deleterious by-products of fracture fixation that can contribute to the inflammatory response. Type of fracture fixation may determine the amount of inflammatory tissue released into the circulation.

Overall, early fixation has been shown to decrease rates of respiratory, renal, and liver failure.[297] Seibel and associates showed that in the blunt multiple-trauma patient with an ISS ranging from 22 to 57, immediate internal fixation followed by ventilatory respiratory support greatly reduces the incidence of respiratory failure, positive blood culture results, complications of fracture treatment, and MOF.[334] When patients were treated with the same ventilatory support but with 10 days of traction before fracture fixation, pulmonary failure lasted twice as long, positive blood culture results increased 10-fold, and fracture complications increased by a factor of 3.5. If no ventilatory support was used and traction was used for 30 days, pulmonary failure lasted three to five times as long, positive blood culture results increased by a factor of 74, and fracture complications increased by a factor of 17. Carlson and co-workers demonstrated that fixation in less than 24 hours after injury versus nonoperative fracture management decreased the late septic mortality from 13.5% to less then 1%.[297] In a series of 56 multiple-injury patients, Goris and colleagues[311] showed that the advantage of controlled ventilation combined with early fracture fixation was greater than that of either ventilation or fracture fixation alone. The greatest advantage was observed in patients with an ISS of more than 50.[311] Meek and co-workers[324] retrospectively studied 71 multiple-trauma patients with similar age and ISS with respect to timing of fracture stabilization. The group with long bone fractures rigidly stabilized within 24 hours had a markedly lower mortality than the group treated with traction and cast methods. In a prospective study, Bone and associates[294] compared the incidence of pulmonary dysfunction in 178 patients with acute femoral fractures who underwent either early (the first 24 hours after injury) or late (more than 48 hours after injury) stabilization. The patients were further divided into those who had multiple injuries and those with isolated fracture of the femur. In none of the patients with isolated femoral fractures, whether treated with early or late stabilization, did respiratory insufficiency, required intubation, or needed placement in the intensive care unit occur. In the patients with multiple injuries, those who had delayed stabilization of fractures had a significantly higher incidence of pulmonary dysfunction.

However, in the aggressively managed surgical intensive care unit, early femoral fixation may not play as critical a role in the outcome. Reynolds and associates studied 424 consecutive patients with femur fractures treated with IM rods and half of these were done in the first 24 hours.[330] Of these 424 patients, 105 had an ISS of 18 or greater; these patients were studied for the relationship of fracture, fixation, timing, and outcomes. IM fixation was done in the first 24 hours in 35 of 105, between 24 and 48 hours in 12 of 105, and more than 48 hours in 58 of 105. Modest delays in fracture fixation did not adversely affect the outcomes, and pulmonary complications were related to the severity of injury rather than to timing of fracture fixation.

The type of fixation may play a role in risk consideration. With IM nailing, there is the risk of additional bone marrow emboli and potential associated lung dysfunction. Pape and associates found ARDS in a higher percentage of patients treated with a reamed IM femoral nail acutely performed (8/24, 33%) versus delayed nailing (2/26, 8%) in patients with femur fractures and severe thoracic injuries.[50] Charash and co-workers repeated the Pape study design and reported contradictory findings with favorable results in acute reamed IM nailing versus delayed nailing; pneumonia (14% vs. 48%), pulmonary complications (16% vs. 56%).[300] Bosse and co-workers studied severe chest injured patients with femur fracture treated within 24 hours with reamed IM nail or plating.[296] The retrospective study was controlled for Group A, femur fracture with thoracic injury; Group B, femur fracture with no thoracic injury; and Group C, thoracic injury with no femur fracture. The overall ARDS rate in patients with femur fracture was 10 of 453 (2%). There was no significant difference in ARDS or pulmonary complications/ MOF whether the femur fracture was treated with rodding or plating. Bosse and associates found no contraindication for reamed femoral nailing in the first 24 hours even if a thoracic injury were present. Pape and associates assessed lung function in two groups of patients undergoing early (≤24 hours) IM femoral nailing.[47] One group had femoral nailing after reaming of the medullary canal (RFN) and the other group had a small-diameter solid nail inserted without reaming (UFN). These investigators found that lung function was stable in UFN patients but deteriorated in RFN patients. They concluded that IM nailing after reaming might potentiate lung dysfunction, particularly in patients with preexisting pulmonary damage such as lung contusion. In contrast, Heim and associates, in a rabbit model, compared reamed versus unreamed nailing of femoral shaft fractures and the effect on pulmonary dysfunction.[27] Their research showed that both techniques resulted in bone marrow intravasation and resulting pulmonary dysfunction. They concluded that the unreamed nailing technique with a solid nail would not prevent pulmonary embolization. These are examples of the controversies—to ream versus not to ream, rod versus plate, early versus late—in which incisive investigation is needed to guide decision making for a complex patient problem.

The preponderance of evidence points to the value of the upright chest position in the prevention of MOF. Immediate fracture fixation in polytrauma, although allowing the patient to sit up, may decrease patient exposure to long periods of stressful nonoperative intervention. Tscherne[337] also drew thoughtful attention to the role of pain in the activation of potentially destructive organism defense responses.

Because many of these patients present with a life-threatening condition, the initial evaluations may overlook minor injuries. These early missed injuries are frequent even in trauma centers and often include small bone fractures and soft tissue injuries. In a series of 206 patients, Janjua and co-workers reported a 39% incidence of missed injuries, which included 12 missed thoracoabdominal injuries, 7 missed hemopneumothoraces, and 2 deaths from missed injury complications.[319] A secondary evaluation of the patient at 24 hours and serial examinations are needed to find these injuries.

In treatment of the patient with overt MOF, the team must recognize that a potentially lethal condition is present and that the usual methods to control specific complications (e.g., pneumonia, renal failure, gastrointestinal bleeding) will be ineffective. The patient must be assessed as a whole, and dramatic intervention is required to turn the situation around. In such conditions, delay in performing operative procedures is deadly. In particular, significant unstable long bone, pelvic, and spinal fractures must be stabilized; any fluid collection should be drained; and all necrotic tissue must be excised. The patient needs blood, calories (preferably enteral when feasible), and effective antibiotics. Controlled ventilation and dialysis is probably necessary. All of these must be continuously monitored in an intensive care setting. In the future, progress will likely be made in the control of mediators of the inflammatory response.[293]

The orthopaedist's role is to assess those fractures that are causing continued recumbency and to locate sources of devitalized tissue and sepsis in the musculoskeletal system. Sacrifice of a crushed but viable limb, loss of fracture reduction, or performance of a quick but not optimal limb stabilization are examples of the difficult choices or procedures that have to be made to save a life. The lower limb fracture in traction has a dual deleterious effect on physiology: the supine position causes shunting with ventilation-perfusion mismatch in the lungs, and continued interfragmental motion of the fractured bone releases necrotic tissue debris into the circulation. Special mechanical beds that allow some tilting of the thorax and prevent pressure sores by alternating contact with the skin are not effective substitutes for skeletal stabilization. External fixation (traveling traction),[318] although not the method of choice for definitive fracture care, is a good option because of its minimal additional tissue trauma.

In summary, in the presence of major thoracic and head injuries, there are potential risks of worsening a brain injury or precipitating ARDS. Carlson[297] and Velmahos and associates[338] have shown no added morbidity of early fixation when chest or head injuries are present. However, Townsend[336] and Pape report increased risk for secondary brain and ARDS associated with early fixation.[47] Reynolds and associates showed modest delay did not affect the outcome.[330] Deitch and Goodman prefer to delay operative fracture fixation for 24 to 48 hours in patients with severe head or thoracic injuries.[304] Deitch and Goodman noted that the best way to treat multiple organ failure is the prevention of MOF in the first place.[304]

LOCAL COMPLICATIONS OF FRACTURES

Local complications, meaning unwanted therapeutic outcomes, are part of the care of broken bones. Local failures of fracture treatment can manifest as immediate, delayed, or long-term adverse outcomes. Delayed complications include complex pain syndromes and disuse atrophy—the "fracture disease." Arthrosis and malunion are examples of the long-term adverse results with permanent impairment and economic importance. Any treatment program, no matter how thoughtfully conceived and carefully performed, has a failure rate that cannot be entirely eliminated. The patient, physician, and system variables inherent in each given clinical situation mean that, in practice, complication rates are usually in excess of those rates published in the literature. With multiple injuries, the rates become more than additive. This is expressed in the ISS by adding the squares of injury components.[342] The purpose of this section is to provide a framework for understanding local complications of fractures.

Soft Tissue and Vascular Problems

An accident, unlike an elective operation, causes the transmission of force of an undetermined magnitude to human tissue. However, through accident reconstruction it is possible to estimate the magnitude of energy transfer. For example, a fall from 30 feet is equivalent to being struck by a car going 30 miles per hour. In the immediate hours, days, and fortnight after injury, it should not be surprising that areas of skin demarcation, skin slough, bruising, or thrombosed vessels appear. These areas, if operative interventions are appropriate, are the consequences of injury and not of its treatment. In addition, after an osteosynthesis, there is additional opportunity for the slow accumulation of hematoma from bleeding from bone surfaces. Today's shortened hospitalization with early mobilization has increased the incidence of postoperative hematoma. Postoperative hematoma manifests as swelling, pain, loss of function, and, not infrequently, serous drainage either from a wound or from the drain tract. Significant hematomas do not resorb but instead continue to increase in size and cause wound separation, skin sloughs, and infection. Collections of blood or fluid can be detected with ultrasonography. It is best to re-explore the wound under an adequate anesthesia, evacuate the hematoma, irrigate the fracture site, and drain the field.

Vascular injuries may manifest acutely with signs of hemorrhage and ischemia, or the presentation may be delayed, as in an arteriovenous fistula or a pseudoaneurysm. In civilian injuries with associated fractures or dislocations, the arterial injury rate is from 2% to 6%. For isolated fractures or dislocations, the arterial injury rate is less than 1%. War-related extremity injuries, a high proportion of which result from high-velocity gunshot wounds, consist of a long bone fracture with associated vascular injury in about one third of cases.[354] Even if a pulse is present, a vascular injury may still have occurred. The most accurate means of diagnosis is an angiogram, which should be performed if there is evidence of an ischemic extremity, a weak or absent pulse, or a bruit, or if the trajectory of the bullet passes in the vicinity of a major artery. Certain injury patterns such as a knee dislocation, especially a posterior one, have a 30% incidence of associated popliteal artery damage. Therefore, with these injuries, an arteriogram is indicated as soon as practical.

When femur fractures are associated with femoral artery injury, the results of vascular repair and limb function are characteristically good, although delayed diagnosis of pseudoaneurysm and claudication can be a problem.[366] Cases requiring amputation because of a delay

in diagnosis can occur. Popliteal artery injury, when diagnosed early, is amenable to vascular reconstruction. However, vascular injuries distal to the popliteal trifurcation carry a much worse prognosis. Revascularization is usually not needed if one vessel is patent on angiogram and the distal pressure is 50% of the brachial artery pressure. When revascularization is required, a good functional result can be expected in only about 25% of cases. In Flint and Richardson's experience, 6 of 16 patients undergoing revascularization required early amputation, and 6 more required late amputation (total, 12/16) for osteomyelitis, nonunion, and persistent neuropathy and its associated complications.[366] Early amputation without revascularization is often appropriate in the patient with loss of vascular inflow, long bone fracture, and extensive soft tissue damage. The high rate of infection and complications can result in a delayed amputation when revascularization is done.[452]

Post-traumatic Arthrosis

Post-traumatic arthrosis is commonly noted to be a complication of fractures (Fig. 18–7). However, there is limited insightful research on the actual pathomechanics of post-traumatic arthrosis. Wright, a retired judge, used a questionnaire to determine a consensus view of the factors

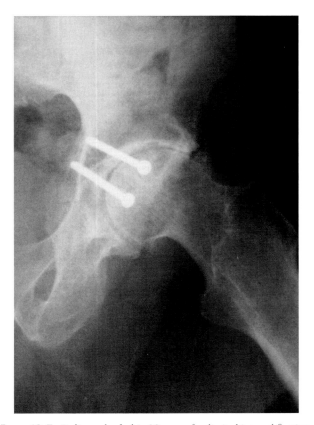

FIGURE 18–7. Radiograph of a hip 18 years after limited internal fixation, an older technique, of a posterior wall acetabular fracture, which demonstrates post-traumatic arthrosis likely secondary to articular cartilage impact and degeneration, and joint incongruity. Total hip replacement is currently being considered.

related to the development of post-traumatic arthrosis after fracture.[475] He found the following: that lower limb joints are more likely to develop arthritis than upper extremity joints, that older patients are at higher risk for the development of post-traumatic arthrosis (although younger patients have a longer time frame to develop post-traumatic arthrosis), and that occupation is a risk factor. Kern and associates also reported the association of osteoarthritis and certain occupations.[389] The potential causes of post-traumatic arthrosis include the following: (1) incongruity of the articular surface, (2) cartilage damage from the load transfer, (3) malalignment, (4) malorientation of the joint, and (5) repetitive loading injury.

JOINT INCONGRUITY

The emphasis on anatomic reduction in fracture surgery focuses on the reestablishment of joint congruity usually at the expense of the soft tissue attachments. Extensive bony comminution of the articular surface, particularly of the knee and the distal tibia, can make a repair of joint congruity a formidable or even an impossible task. Acetabular fractures are a good example of articular fractures that are associated with the development of post-traumatic arthrosis[411] largely because of failure to reestablish joint congruity and the articular cartilage injury itself.[410]

ARTICULAR CARTILAGE DAMAGE

The impact to the articular cartilage at the time of injury in high-energy trauma is a likely contributor to the articular cartilage damage and the subsequent development of post-traumatic arthrosis (Figs. 18–8 and 18–9). However, the clinical data are not clear-cut. Volpin and co-workers reported at an average follow-up of 14 years of intra-articular fractures of the knee joint that there were 77% good-to-excellent results.[467] Repo and associates stated that the impact loads sufficient to fracture a femoral shaft of an automobile occupant are nearly sufficient to cause significant articular cartilage (chondrocyte death and fissuring).[442]

There is an increasing appreciation of cartilage injury from impact. The advent of MRI of knee injuries has enhanced our appreciation of damage to the articular surfaces (bone bruising) (Fig. 18–10). Spindler and associates studied 54 patients with anterior cruciate ligament tears and found a bone bruise present in 80% of cases, of which 68% were in the lateral femoral condyle.[456] Miller and co-workers studied 65 patients who had MRI-detected trabecular microfractures associated with isolated medial collateral ligament injuries.[417] Although these bone bruises were approximately half as common as bone bruises associated with anterior cruciate ligament tears, these investigators stated that medial collateral ligament–associated trabecular microfractures may be a better natural history model.[417] Bone bruises in combination with anterior cruciate ligament tears may be harbingers of future arthritis. Wright and associates noted that isolated bone bruises not associated with ligamentous or

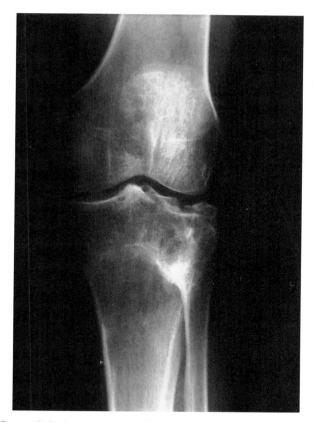

FIGURE 18–8. Anteroposterior radiograph of a knee with post-traumatic arthrosis secondary to joint incongruity and articular cartilage degeneration 5 years after a high-energy tibial plateau fracture.

meniscal injury may have a better prognosis than bone bruises noted in conjunction with ligamentous and meniscal injury.[474]

The biologic basis for the cartilage degradation is being studied: the pathologic process involves degradation of articular cartilage.[417a] It has been theorized that the impact at the time of injury damages the articular

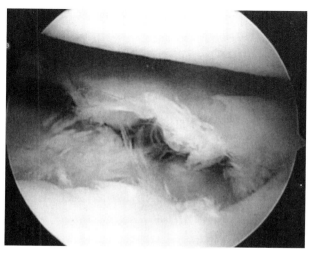

FIGURE 18–9. Correlative arthroscopic view of the lateral compartment of the knee in Figure 18–8, which demonstrates post-traumatic arthrosis secondary to joint incongruity, articular cartilage degradation, and meniscal degeneration 5 years after a high-energy tibial plateau fracture.

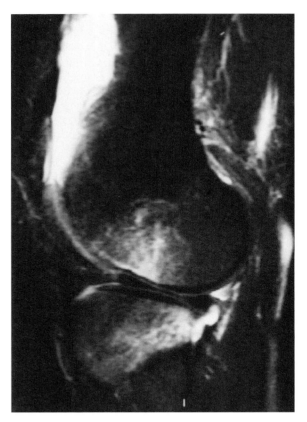

FIGURE 18–10. Sagittal MR image of the lateral compartment of a knee that demonstrates a bone contusion involving the lateral femoral condyle and the lateral tibial plateau in association with a recent anterior cruciate ligament tear. (Courtesy of Theresa M. Corrigan, M.D.)

cartilage or its blood supply irreversibly and initiates a cascade of post-traumatic arthritis.[442] This etiology of impact arthritis has not been well-studied.[442, 465, 468] Attempts to develop a model have been made. Vrahas and co-workers developed a method of impacting quantifying blows to articular cartilage in a rabbit model.[468] Nonetheless, cartilage damage, particularly when it is unassociated with bone changes, may not necessarily progress to arthritis.[438] Radin noted that full-thickness cartilage lesions that are less than 1 cm usually will not progress to arthritis.[438]

MALALIGNMENT

Tetsworth and Paley have focused on the relationship between malalignment and degenerative arthropathy.[464] These investigators focused on degenerative arthritis and changes in the weight-bearing line or mechanical axis (malalignment), changes in the position of each articular surface relative to the axis of the individual segments (malorientation), and changes in joint incongruity. They noted that the joints of the lower extremity are nearly collinear and that any disturbance in this relationship (malalignment) affects the transmission of load across the joint surfaces.[464]

The hip and shoulder joints, because of their sphericity, tolerate malalignment. The ankle joint is also fairly tolerant of deformity because of compensation through the subtalar joint. However, the knee is most vulnerable to changes in the normal coronal plane relationship of the lower extremity.[464] Axial malalignment of the knee, which changes the mechanical axis creates a moment arm, which increases force transmission across either the medial or lateral compartments of the knee joint.[429, 430] This moment arm, termed the *mechanical axis deviation,* is represented by drawing a line from the center of the knee and reflects the magnitude of alteration in stress distribution across the knee.[464] The effect of the deformity on the mechanical axis increases as the apex of the deformity approaches the knee.

Nonetheless, there is conflicting clinical data regarding whether these factors lead to post-traumatic arthrosis. Kettlekamp and associates stated that there are no data to support the position that malalignment always leads to degenerative arthritis.[390] Kristensen and co-workers reported no arthrosis of the ankle 20 years after malaligned tibial fractures.[398] In contrast, Puno and co-workers studied 27 patients with 28 tibial fractures and found that greater degrees of ankle malalignment produced poorer clinical results.[436] Merchant and Dietz stated that they did not find any support in their study for the hypotheses that angulation results in shear rather than compressive forces on articular cartilage and that these forces lead to early arthrosis.[414]

MALORIENTATION

Another postfracture residual deformity that can contribute to post-traumatic arthrosis is malorientation (a change in the orientation of a joint to the mechanical axis). The association of malorientation of the knee and osteoarthritis has been demonstrated.[357, 358] Malorientation can result from translation or rotation. When the orientation of the joint is substantially changed in relation to the mechanical axis, the theory is that abnormal loading of the articular cartilage and subchondral plate will occur, which will accelerate joint deterioration and ultimately lead to osteoarthritis. Malorientation is probably more of a problem with weight-bearing joints such as the knee, which are subject to higher and more frequent loading.

REPETITIVE LOADING INJURY

Articular cartilage damage can occur either by sudden impact loading or by repetitive impulsive loading.[361, 362, 407, 437] As a result, portions of the matrix can be fractured, cause cartilage necrosis, and produce subclinical microfractures in the calcified cartilage layer.[372] The effect on cartilage homeostasis appears to lead to changes that are seen in association with osteoarthritis.[361, 437, 469] Radiographic evidence of knee arthritis after meniscectomy, called Fairbanks' changes,[365] most likely result from repetitive loading to the articular after changes in load distribution of the knee joint. Deterioration of damaged articular cartilage by repetitive loading may be asymptomatic because cartilage is relatively aneural.[372]

Adult canine articular cartilage after indirect blunt trauma demonstrates significant alterations in its histologic, biomechanical, and ultrastructural characteristics without disruption of the articular surface.[362] Thompson and associates found arthritic-like degeneration of the articular cartilage in an animal model within 6 months after transarticular loads.[365] These investigators also noted that degenerative changes that occur in patients who sustained traumatic insult to the joint may represent a phenomenon similar to their animal model.[365]

Damage to articular cartilage often can occur without perceptible alteration in the macroscopic appearance of the tissue.[372] There is limited potential for cartilage self-repair. Yet there is some evidence that some cartilage repair is possible, which has led to the proliferation of procedures such as autologous cartilage transplantation[350] and micro-fracture.[460]

SUMMARY

We have tabulated the incidence of post-traumatic arthrosis associated with some common fractures and dislocations (Table 18–9). In addition, post-traumatic arthrosis is discussed elsewhere in the text.

Post-traumatic arthrosis may be an inevitable consequence of musculoskeletal injury. It appears to be related to the magnitude of the original injury. Fracture surgery techniques cannot fully reverse the articular cartilage injury. Gelber and associates reported that an injury to the knee joint in young adulthood was related to a substantial increased risk for future knee osteoarthritis.[370]

TABLE 18–9

Incidence of Post-traumatic Arthritis

	Upper Extremity		
Shoulder			
	Acromioclavicular joint dislocations		25%–43%
	Scapula fractures	Superior lateral angle	61%
	Anterior shoulder dislocation		7%
Elbow			
	Elbow dislocations—simple	24-yr follow-up	38%
	Elbow dislocations with a radial head fracture		63%
Wrist			
	Colles' fractures		3%–18%
	Colles' fractures	Young adults	57%–65%
	Scapholunate dislocations		58%
	Trans-scaphoid perilunate dislocations; fracture	4.3-yr follow-up	50%

	Lower Extremity		
Acetabular Fractures			6.5%–56%
Hip Dislocations	Anterior		17%
	Posterior	<6 hr time to reduction	30%
	Posterior	>6 hr time to reduction	76%
Supracondylar/Intercondylar Femur Fractures			22% (patellofemoral joint)
			5% (tibiofemoral joint)
Patella Fractures			18%
Tibial Plateau Fractures	Fracture patterns	Bicondylar fractures	42%
		Medial plateau fractures	21%
		Lateral plateau fractures	16%
		valgus	31%
	Association with alignment after plateau fractures	Normal	13%
Ankle Fractures			20–40%
Talar Neck	Ankle Joint	Subtalar Joint	
Fractures			
Hawkins I	15%	24%	
Hawkins II	36%	66%	
Hawkins III	69%	63%	
Subtalar Joint Dislocations			56%
Tarsometatarsal Fracture-Dislocation (Lisfranc Joint Injuries)			78% (15-yr follow-up)

Source: Data from Fagg, P.S.; Foy, M.A. Philadelphia, Churchill-Livingstone, 1995.

Other confounding factors in determining the relationship between fractures and the development of post-traumatic arthrosis are normal age-related changes noted on radiographs. Bonsell and associates reported that age was a significant predictor for degenerative changes observed on radiographs of the shoulder in asymptomatic individuals.[348]

Specific components of the pathomechanics of post-traumatic arthrosis include malalignment, malorientation, joint incongruity, articular cartilage destruction, ligamentous or fibrocartilaginous injury, and repetitive loading injury. Salvage procedures such as joint replacement or osteotomy are less successful for post-traumatic arthrosis than for osteoarthritis.[401] Postinjury counseling and patient education is necessary to convey realistic expectations after fracture surgery. Prospective, long-term studies are needed to better understand the natural history of post-traumatic arthrosis and to be able to decipher it from normal age-related osteoarthrosis.

Peripheral Nerve Injuries

Few entities can overshadow the outcome of the treatment of a fracture as much as a peripheral nerve injury. Whether the nerve palsy is diagnosed before or after surgery, it is certain that the patient and other health care providers will be inordinately focused on the nerve palsy itself. Peripheral nerve injuries in orthopaedic trauma are probably underreported because clinical assessment of peripheral lesions is often impossible or impractical. Electrodiagnostic testing is more sensitive than clinical examination alone and can facilitate the diagnosis of traumatic peripheral nerve injuries. A scientific understanding and approach to peripheral nerve injury is imperative.

HISTORY OF THE TREATMENT OF NERVE INJURY

George Omer traces the history of the treatment of peripheral nerve injuries to William A. Hammond, Surgeon General of the U.S. Army during the American Civil War.[425] Drawing largely on the United States military experience, Omer traces the evolution of understanding and treatment of peripheral nerve injuries from the Civil War through the two World Wars, the Vietnam and Korean conflicts, and the development of "The Sunderland Society."[425] The greatest advances have come from the intraoperative microscope and the ingenuity of the surgeon.[457]

CLASSIFICATION OF NERVE INJURY

Historically, Seddon is credited with the scientific classification of peripheral nerve injury into three categories: neurotmesis, axonotmesis, and neurapraxia (Table 18–10).[451] Seddon, however, noted that these three terms were not his originally and were coined by Professor Henry Cohen in 1941.[451] Understanding peripheral nerve injury is predicated on understanding the anatomy of myelinated nerves (Fig. 18–11).

Neurotmesis implies a cutting or separation of related parts in which all essential structures have been "sun-

TABLE 18–10 ....

Types of Peripheral Nerve Injuries

Injury	Pathophysiology	Prognosis
Neurapraxia	Reversible conduction block characterized by local ischemia and selective demyelination of the axon sheath	Good
Axonotmesis	More severe injury with disruption of the axon and myelin sheath but with an intact epineurium	Fair
Neurotmesis	Complete nerve division with disruption of the endoneurium	Poor

....

Source: Brinker, M.R.; Lou, E.C. General principles of trauma. In: Brinker, M.R., ed. Review of Orthopaedic Trauma. Philadelphia, W.B. Saunders, 2001, p. 8, with permission.

dered."[451] He noted that although there is not necessarily an obvious anatomic gap in the nerve and the epineural sheath may appear to be in continuity, the effect is as if anatomic continuity has been lost.[451]

Axonotmesis involves a lesion to the peripheral nerve of such severity that wallerian degeneration occurs but the epineurium and supporting structures of the nerve have been "so little disturbed that the internal architecture is fairly well-preserved."[451]

Neurapraxia is described as a lesion in which paralysis occurs in the absence of peripheral degeneration. Seddon noted that "neurapraxia" is preferred to "transient block" because the recovery time can be lengthy and is "invariably complete."[451]

Seddon notes that of the three terms neurotmesis is probably the best understood and that in clinical practice the existence of axonotmesis or neurapraxia could only be surmised.[451] The advent of electrodiagnostic testing however has made the distinction between an axonotmesis and a neurotmesis much easier. Seddon noted that the most common variety of neurotmesis was from anatomic division. Wallerian nerve degeneration occurs peripherally, and the clinical picture is that of complete interruption of the nerve.

Axonotmesis is characterized by complete interruption of axons but with preservation of the supporting structures of the nerve (Schwann tubes, endoneurium, and perineurium). On a histologic level, there is complete interruption of the axons, preservation of the Schwann tubes and endoneurium, and wallerian degeneration peripherally. Seddon noted that clinically axonotmesis was indistinguishable from neurotmesis until recovery occurs, which in axonotmesis was spontaneous.[451] When exploration is performed, the finding of an intact nerve suggests that the lesion is an axonotmesis.[451] A fusiform neuroma finding suggests that the injury was a mixed lesion of an axonotmesis and a neurotmesis with the first predominating.[451] A finding of intraneural fibrosis is evidence that the lesion was a neurotmesis.

Seddon noted that with a neurapraxia, there is no axonal degeneration. There is localized degeneration of the myelin sheaths. Blunt injuries and compression were the most common cause of neurapraxias.[451] He noted that

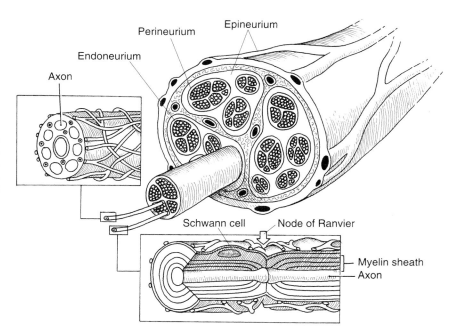

Figure **18–11.** Cross-sectional anatomy of peripheral nerve. Inset at left shows an unmyelinated fiber. Inset at bottom shows a myelinated fiber. (From Lee, S.K.; Wolfe, S.W. Peripheral nerve injury and repair. J Am Acad Orthop Surg 8:243–252, 2000.)

the clinical picture is one of complete motor paralysis and incomplete sensory paralysis.[451] Also, he noted that there was no anatomic "march" to recovery as seen after nerve suture or axonotmesis.[451] Finally, Seddon noted that there were in fact many nerve injuries that were in fact combinations of the three different nerve injuries he described.[451] Of a series of 537 nerve injuries, he noted that there were 96 cases in which a neurotmesis and an axonotmesis were combined.[451]

Sunderland added to the work of Seddon by subdividing peripheral nerve injury into five degrees by basically subdividing the neurotmesis into three types (third, fourth, and fifth degree injuries) while maintaining the concepts of neurapraxia (first-degree injury) and axonotmesis (second-degree injury).[461] He defined five degrees of nerve injury based on changes induced in the normal nerve. Seddon described these injuries in ascending order which affected successively: (1) conduction in the axon; (2) continuity of the axon; (3) the endoneurial tube and its axon; (4) the funiculus and its contents; (5) the entire nerve trunk.[461] The most important part of Sunderland's work is his clarification that injuries previously classified by Seddon as a neurotmesis were not all equal.

Sunderland also added to the knowledge of partial and mixed nerve injuries. He noted that some fibers in a nerve may escape injury while others sustain a variable degree of damage.[461] He noted that in partial severance injuries and fourth-degree injuries, it was unlikely that the remaining fibers would escape some injury. This type of injury should be described as a "mixed lesion."[461] However, fourth- and fifth-degree lesions could not coexist together or in combination with any of the minor types of injuries.[461]

There are problems with the classification of peripheral nerve injury. Many nerve injuries are mixed injuries in which all nerve fibers are affected to varying degrees.[402] In addition, the subtypes of Seddon's classification are usually discernible only on histologic examination of the nerve

and are seldom possible on the basis of clinical or electromyographic data.

INCIDENCE OF NERVE INJURIES ASSOCIATED WITH FRACTURES

There is a fairly high incidence of nerve injury with some common orthopaedic entities (Table 18–11). Conway and Hubbell reported electromyographic abnormalities associated with pelvic fracture and noted that patients with double vertical pelvic fractures (combined injury to the anterior third of the pelvic ring and the sacroiliac area) were most at risk, with a 46% incidence of neurologic injury.[356] Goodall noted that 95% of fractures with an associated nerve injury occur in the upper extremity.[374] Of all fracture types, a humerus fracture is the most likely fracture to have an associated nerve injury.[343] Omer reported, based on a collected series,[424]

TABLE 18–11

Common Orthopaedic Entities Associated with Peripheral Nerve Injuries

Anatomic Location	Type of Injury	Incidence Nerve Injury
Humerus	Midshaft fractures	12%–19% incidence radial nerve palsy[391, 433, 453, 455]
Pelvis	Double vertical pelvic fractures	46% incidence neurologic injury[356]
Tibia	Tibia fractures	19%–30% incidence neurologic findings after intramedullary nailing[396, 472]
Ankle	Ankle eversion injuries	86% incidence of neurologic findings[419]

the following distribution of nerve injuries associated with fractures and fracture-dislocations: radial nerve (60%), ulnar nerve (18%), common peroneal nerve (15%), and median nerve (6%).[374, 377, 403]

EVALUATION OF PERIPHERAL NERVE INJURIES

In the polytrauma patient, the neurologic assessment is incorporated in the initial assessment, which uses the alphabet—ABCD—in which *D* is for disability and neurologic assessment.[463] The GCS, developed by Teasdale and Jennet, specifically assesses eye opening, motor response, and verbal response in a maximum 15-point rating scale.

The assessment of peripheral nerve injury during orthopaedic surgery rounds and emergency department assessments oftentimes is reduced to the terms *neurovascularly intact* or *N/V intact*. In our opinion, such terms, although convenient, should never be used unless a complete neurologic examination (cutaneous sensation including light touch, pain, and temperature; vibratory sensation; motor strength in all muscles with grading; deep tendon reflexes; and special tests for clonus, etc.) and a complete vascular examination (pulses, capillary refill, venous examination, tests for thrombosis, auscultation for bruits, etc.) are performed. Formal assessment of peripheral nerve injury is usually performed using electromyography (EMG).

Electromyography and Electrodiagnostics

In a broad sense, EMG refers to a set of diagnostic tests using neurophysiologic techniques that are performed on muscles and nerves.[462] Strictly speaking, EMG refers to one of these tests, in which a small needle is used to probe selected muscles, recording electrical potentials from the muscle fibers.[462]

Although electrodiagnostic testing has historically been of little interest to the orthopaedic surgeon, there is heightened interest in electrodiagnostics as a result of intraoperative use of sensory-evoked potentials and motor-evoked potentials in spine surgery, brachial plexus surgery, and acetabular surgery.

It has been said that the best times for electrodiagnostic studies are the day before injury and then about 10 to 14 days after injury. The former is, of course, generally impossible but nonetheless underscores the importance of baseline studies and changes over time, particularly when one is looking for evidence of reinnervation (which would

be consistent with an axonotmesis) or denervation (which would be consistent with a neurotmesis). The latter highlights the fact that reinnervation following wallerian degeneration takes at least 10 to 14 days to be able to detect on electrodiagnostic testing.

Basic Science of Electrodiagnostics. To understand EMG, it is necessary to review some basics of nerve structure and function. A motor neuron has a cell body in the spinal cord and extends into the nerve root, an axon that exits the spine, traverses the plexus, travels within a nerve, and then forms many distinct branches.[462] A motor unit consists of one such cell and the several muscle fibers that it innervates.[462] Muscles contain many motor units that are analogous to colored pencils in a bundle.[462] Muscle forces are created by activation of an increasing number of motor units under the command of the brain.[462] When a motor unit fires, a small electrical signal is generated and can be recorded by placing a small needle through the skin and into the muscle near the motor unit fibers acting electronically like an antennae.[462] This signal is amplified, filtered, digitized, and displaced on a computer screen.[462] Single motor unit potentials are sampled first on the oscilloscope. As greater force is generated, there is recruitment of more motor units and an increase in the firing rate.[462] When full muscle force is generated, the oscilloscope screen fills with signals, which has an appearance called the *full interference pattern*.[462] Another important component of EMG interpretation is the sound of the motor potentials, which are amplified and broadcast through a speaker.[462] The experienced electromyographer can recognize characteristic sounds and audible patterns.[462]

The usefulness of EMG for the trauma patient is the ability to localize neurologic lesions anatomically based on a pattern of denervated muscle. EMG is also useful for following nerve recovery over time.

Characteristic Electromyography Patterns. If there is an injury to the axon, as with an axonotmesis or neurotmesis, distal degeneration of the nerve (wallerian degeneration) causes it to be electrically irritable.[462] Needle movement generates denervation potentials called fibrillations and positive waves, which have both characteristic appearances on the oscilloscope and sounds on the loudspeaker.[462] These findings are delayed, occurring at least 10 days even after complete transection.[462] Sprouting and reinnervation that would occur with a recovering axonotmesis creates a high amplitude polyphasic motor unit potential (Table 18–12).[462]

TABLE 18–12

Electromyographic Findings Related to Trauma

Condition	Insertional Activity	Activity at Rest	Minimal Contraction	Interference
Normal study	Normal	Silence	Biphasic and triphasic potential	Complete
Neurapraxia	Normal	Silence	Reduced number of potentials	Reduced
Axonotmesis (after 2 wks)	Increased	Fibrillations and positive sharp waves	None	None
Neurotmesis (after 2 wks)	Increased	Fibrillations and positive sharp waves	None	None

Source: Adapted with permission from Brinker, M.R.; Lou, E.C. General Principles of Trauma. In Brinker, M.R., ed. Review of Orthopaedic Trauma. Philadelphia, WB Saunders, 2001, p. 9, of which the data was adapted with modifications from Jahss, M.H. Disorders of the foot. In Miller, M.D., ed. Review of Orthopaedics, 3rd ed. Philadelphia, WB Saunders, 2000.

TABLE 18–13 ....

Nerve Conduction Study Results Related to Trauma

Condition	Latency	Conduction Velocity	Evoked Response
Normal study	Normal	Upper extremities: >48 m/sec Lower extremities: >40 m/sec	Biphasic
Neurapraxia			
Proximal to lesion	Absent or low voltage (if partial)	Absent or low voltage (if partial)	Absent
Distal to lesion	Normal	Normal	Normal
Axonotmesis			
Proximal to lesion	Absent	Absent	Absent
Distal to lesion (immediate)	Normal	Normal	Normal
Distal to lesion (>7 d)	Absent	Absent	Absent
Neurotmesis			
Proximal to lesion	Absent	Absent	Absent
Distal to lesion (immediate)	Normal	Normal	Normal
Distal to lesion (>7 d)	Absent	Absent	Absent

....

Source: Adapted with permission from Brinker, M.R.; Lou, E.C. General Principles of Trauma. In: Review of Orthopaedic Trauma. Philadelphia, W.B. Saunders, 2001, p. 8, of which the data was from Jahss, M.S. Disorders of the foot. In: Miller, M.D.; Brinker, M.R., eds. Review of Orthopaedics, 3rd ed. Philadelphia, W.B. Saunders, 1982.

Nerve Conduction Studies

Distinct from EMG are nerve conduction studies. Nerve conduction studies can be used to test both sensory and motor nerves and skeletal muscle. These studies test only large myelinated nerve fiber function. Nerve fibers commonly evaluated include the ulnar, medial, radial, and tibial nerves (motor and sensory fibers); the sciatic, femoral, and peroneal fibers (motor fibers only); and the musculocutaneous, superficial peroneal, sural, and saphenous nerves (sensory only). The procedure of nerve conduction testing uses surface electrodes, often silver discs or ring electrodes, to record extracellular electrical activity from muscle or nerve. EMG machines have a nerve stimulator that can apply an electrical shock to the skin surface at accessible points on the nerve.[462] This stimulus depolarizes a segment of the nerve and generates an action potential, which travels in both direction from the point that it was stimulated.[461] When a sensory nerve is tested, the action potential can be recorded from a distal point (surface electrodes or finger electrodes).[462] By measuring the distance from the stimulus point to the recording site and using the oscilloscope values of the time of slight (latency) and action potential amplitude, the examiner can determine the sensory conduction velocity.[462]

Motor nerve conduction velocities (motor NCVs) are recorded from surface electrodes taped over muscles distally in the limb.[461] Normative control values for motor nerve conduction velocities at different ages are used for comparison. This difference is attributable to the degree of myelination, which increases with age over the early developmental years. Although nerve conduction velocities are fairly uniform from age 3 years through adulthood,[462] nerve conduction velocities can vary based on several conditions. Nerve conduction values at birth are about 50% of adult values. As surface temperature decreases below 34° C, there is a progressive increase in latency and a decrease in conduction velocity.[345] Upper extremity conduction velocities are generally about 10% to 15% faster than those of the lower extremity. Conduction velocity in the proximal segments is usually 5% to 10%

faster than in the distal segments,[345] which is a function of nerve root diameter.

To study motor conduction, the nerve is supramaximally stimulated at two or more points along its course where it is most superficial. At a distal muscle that is innervated by the nerve, a motor response is recorded.[345] Various parameters measured include latency, conduction velocity, amplitude, and duration. Characteristic nerve conduction study findings for various nerve injuries are shown in Table 18–13.

Sensory nerve conductions are generally unaffected by lesions proximal to the dorsal root ganglion even though there is sensory loss.[345] Sensory testing is good for localizing a lesion either proximal (root or spinal cord) or distal (plexus or nerve) to the dorsal root ganglia. In addition, sensory nerve potential is lower in amplitude than compound motor action potentials and can be obscured by electrical activity or artifacts. Sensory axons are evaluated in four ways: (1) stimulating and recording from a cutaneous nerve, (2) recording from a cutaneous nerve while stimulating a mixed nerve, (3) recording from a mixed nerve while stimulating a cutaneous nerve, and (4) recording from the spinal column while a cutaneous nerve or mixed nerve is stimulated.[345] Variables measured include onset latency, peak latency, and peak-to-peak amplitude.

Two other parameters, which are measured, are the F-wave and the H-reflex. The F-wave is a late motor response attributed a small percentage of fibers firing after the original stimulus impulse reaches the cell body. These F-waves are particularly useful for the evaluation of the proximal segments of peripheral nerves.[345] However, the F-wave is only useful in the assessment of proximal lesions only in the absence of more distal pathology. There is also variability in the F-wave response because different fibers fire each time, making it less quantitative. The H-reflex is an electrically evoked spinal monosynaptic reflex that activates the Ia afferent fibers (large myelinated fibers with the lowest threshold for activation). The Achilles tendon reflex (S1) is the easiest to record and can differentiate between an S-1 and an L-5 radiculopathy.[345] Again, distal pathology must be ruled out if the latency is prolonged and being used to assess for proximal pathosis.

Somatosensory-Evoked Potentials

Although the use of somatosensory-evoked potentials (SSEPs) was popular[380] for acetabular surgery, SSEPs have been supplanted by spontaneous EMG[379] when monitoring is desired. However, the general use of SSEPs or electromyographic modalities does not seem to be justified.[416]

The method of performing SSEPs involves an afferent pulse of large nerve fiber sensory activity travels proximally and enters the spinal cord and then ascends to the brain via the posterior columns in the brain stem after the nerve is stimulated.[462] This postsynaptic activity ultimately reaches the thalamus and the parietal cortex of the brain.[462] A small brain wave occurs following nerve stimulation at a fixed time following nerve stimulation and is recordable from surface electrodes in the scalp.[462] These SSEPs can be recorded simultaneously from various points such as Erb's point, which overlies the brachial plexus, over the cervical spine, and from the scalp overlying the cortex.[462] SSEPs are useful for monitoring the lower extremity in spinal surgery. Upper extremity SSEPs are useful in brachial plexus surgery.

ASSOCIATION OF PERIPHERAL NERVE INJURY AND CAUSALGIA

There is a potential overlap between peripheral nerve injury and causalgia (type II complex regional pain syndrome). According to Bonica, the incidence of causalgia is 1% to 5% of peripheral nerve injuries.[346] Data from the Vietnam War indicate a lower incidence of causalgia than the data from World War II (1.5% versus 1.8%–13.8%). Rothberg and associates and Bonica[346] suggest that this lower incidence was due to the more rapid transport of the wounded (usually within 1–2 hours and by helicopter) and the high quality of care by an ample number of neurosurgeons in Army hospitals.

PROGNOSIS

Nerve Injuries Associated with Open and Closed Fractures and Dislocations

Omer noted a spontaneous return of nerve function in 83% of nerve injuries associated with fractures.[427] Radial nerve palsy associated with humerus fractures is perhaps a good example in which nerve recovery can be expected in roughly 90% of cases.[391, 433, 453, 455] There are further distinctions in prognosis including lower recovery rates of nerve function with open fractures than with closed fractures (17% vs. 83.5% in one series).[450] Omer also reported that nerve injuries associated with a dislocation were less likely to show spontaneous recovery than nerve injuries associated with a fracture.[426] Omer noted that peripheral neuropathy associated with closed fractures is usually neurapraxia lesions, which have an excellent prognosis for recovery.[426] Peripheral neuropathy associated with open fractures had a prognosis related to the etiology: lacerations are usually neurotmesis

lesions and should be closely examined, explored, and sutured.[426]

Nerve Injuries Associated with Projectile Injuries

Data from Vietnam on 595 gunshot wounds studied by Omer had a 69% spontaneous recovery rate for low-velocity gunshot wounds and a 69% spontaneous recovery rate for high-velocity gunshot wounds.[423] Proximal nerve injuries in extremities take longer to show clinical recovery than more distal extremity injuries.[423] Civilian peripheral nerve injuries from projectiles with associated vascular injury have a poor prognosis. In one series, only 10% of these nerve injuries resolved.[378] Shotgun injuries have a higher incidence of nerve injuries than other types of gunshot injuries, have a worse prognosis (spontaneous recovery rate of about 45%),[405] and have a higher percentage of complete nerve transaction (neurotmesis) than even high-velocity missile wounds. High-velocity missiles often create axonotmesis lesions and have a better prognosis for recovery than low-velocity missile wounds.[423]

SUMMARY

Peripheral nerve injuries associated with fractures and dislocations are probably underappreciated in the acute trauma setting. The orthopaedic surgeon ought to refrain from using the term *neurovascularly intact* unless a complete neurologic and vascular examination has been performed. Instead, documentation should be limited to what was observed and performed (e.g., "toes up and down," "1+ dorsalis pedis pulse"). Heightened surveillance for neurologic injury is protective for the clinician because failure to diagnose nerve injuries may result in patient dissatisfaction, disability, and litigation. The orthopaedic surgeon needs to be facile with the lexicon of nerve injury (neurapraxia, axonotmesis, and neurotmesis) to communicate with neurologic colleagues. From a practical standpoint, evaluation of recovery after a peripheral nerve injury is best performed by serial physical examinations. However, there is a role for electrodiagnostic testing, particularly when there is no sign of recovery of nerve function. Electrodiagnostic studies should be delayed for at least 3 weeks and often need to be repeated serially. Research in nerve regeneration techniques may also hold the key to the treatment of peripheral nerve injuries in the future.

Post-traumatic Reflex Sympathetic Dystrophy

Pain after musculoskeletal injury usually subsides. When patients have peculiar, disagreeable, and persistent painful symptoms several weeks after injury, they may have RSD. RSD, now referred to as type I complex regional pain syndrome (CRPS), is increasingly recognized as a cause of disability after injury.[470] The index of suspicion in general is not high enough, and many patients are not diagnosed until the later stages when the prognosis is less favorable.[470] Advances have been made in the understanding and treatment of RSD. Nevertheless, many treatment methods are empirical, and there is a need for research in this area.[470]

MODERN TERMINOLOGY

More than six dozen different terms have been used over the past two decades to describe RSD in the English, French, and German literature.[470] A complicated lexicon of RSD has evolved from the more general category of "pain dysfunction syndromes,"[341] to the terminology adopted in 1994 by the International Association for the Study of Pain into "complex regional pain syndromes."[459] CRPS is subdivided into type I CRPS (RSD) and type II CRPS (causalgia).[459] The distinction is based on the absence of a documented nerve injury for RSD and a documented nerve injury for causalgia (Table 18–14). The focus here is on RSD associated with traumatic orthopaedic injuries. Because the older terminology is still widely used, we will use the term RSD herein.

ETIOLOGY AND EPIDEMIOLOGY

Trauma secondary to accidental injury has been described as the most common cause of RSD.[346] These injuries include sprains; dislocations; fractures, usually of the hands, feet, or wrists; traumatic finger amputations; crush injuries of the hands, fingers, or wrists; contusions; and lacerations or punctures of the fingers, hands, toes, or feet.[346] It has been reported that RSD develops in 1% to 5% of patients with peripheral nerve injury, 28% of patients with Colles' fracture,[344] and 30% of patients with tibial fracture.[447] In a recent series, the three most common inciting events were a sprain or strain in 29%, postsurgical in 24%, and a fracture in 16%.[340] Interestingly, in this same series, 6% of patients could not remember an inciting event.[340] Saphenous neuralgia has been called a *forme fruste* of sympathetically mediated pain.[432] External fixators appear to be associated with RSD in the upper extremity, although whether it is a result of the fracture immobilization, possible traction injury to the nerves, or direct neural trauma from the pins is unclear. RSD also seems to be associated commonly with arthroscopic surgical procedures[360] and prolonged usage of extremity tourniquets.

Allen and associates[340] reported on the epidemiologic variables of patients with CRPS. They noted in a series of 134 patients evaluated at a tertiary chronic pain clinic that patients presented with a history of having seen on average 4.8 different physicians before referral.[340] The average duration of symptoms of CRPS before presentation was 30 months.[340] In addition 54% of patients had a workmen's compensation claim and 17% of patients had a lawsuit related to the CRPS.[340] Of the 51 of 135 patients who underwent a bone scan, only 53% of the studies were interpreted as consistent with the diagnosis of CRPS.[340]

PATHOPHYSIOLOGY

Breivik noted that, as described by The International Association for the Study of Pain, CRPS is a complex neurologic disease involving the somatosensory, somatomotor, and autonomic nervous system in various combinations, with distorted information processing of afferent sensory signals to the spinal cord.[349, 415] Autonomic nervous system dysregulation occurs only in 25% to 50% of patients with CRPS.[347, 365, 415] The role of the sympathetic system was further clarified by Ide and associates, who used a noninvasive laser Doppler to assess fingertip blood flow and vasoconstrictor response and found that skin blood flow and vasoconstrictor response returned to normal following successful treatment of the condition.[384] These investigators suggested that the sympathetic nervous system function is altered and is different in the various stages of RSD.

Many RSD patients have a combination of sympathetically maintained pain and sympathetically independent pain. Sympathetically maintained pain (SMP) is defined as pain that is maintained by sympathetic efferent nerve activity or by circulating catecholamines.[347, 365, 415] SMP is relieved by sympatholytic procedures.[349] Sympathetically maintained pain follows a nonanatomic distribution.[404] Nonetheless, SMP is not essential in the development of CRPS.[349] In some patients, sympatholytic procedures will not relieve their pain.[349] Breivik notes that more than half of all patients with CRPS have sympathetically independent pain. In one series, symptoms of increased sympathetic activity occurred in 57% of patients, whereas signs of inflammation and muscle dysfunction occurred in 90% of patients.[466]

TABLE 18–14 •

International Association for the Study of Pain: Diagnostic Criteria for Complex Regional Pain Syndrome

COMPLEX REGIONAL PAIN SYNDROME TYPE I (REFLEX SYMPATHETIC DYSTROPHY)

1. The presence of an initiating noxious event or a cause of immobilization.
2. Continuing pain, allodynia or hyperalgesia with which the pain is disproportionate to the inciting event.
3. Evidence at some time of edema, changes in skin blood flow or abnormal sudomotor activity in the painful region.
4. The diagnosis is excluded by the existence of conditions that would otherwise account for the degree of pain and dysfunction.

Note: Criteria 2, 3, and 4 are necessary for a diagnosis of complex regional pain syndrome.

COMPLEX REGIONAL PAIN SYNDROME TYPE II (CAUSALGIA)

1. The presence of continuing pain, allodynia or hyperalgesia after a nerve injury, not necessarily limited to the distribution of the injured nerve.
2. Evidence at some time of edema, changes in skin blood flow or abnormal sudomotor activity in the region of the pain.
3. The diagnosis is excluded by the existence of conditions that would otherwise account for the degree of pain and dysfunction.

Note: All three criteria must be satisfied.

• •

Source: Adapted with permission from Pittman, D.M.; Belgrade, M.J. Am Fam Phys 56(9):2265–2270, 1997; which was adapted with permission from Merskey, H.; Bodguk, N., eds. Classification of Chronic Pain, Descriptions of Chronic Pain Syndromes and Definitions of Pain Terms, 2nd ed. Seattle, IASP Press, pp. 40–43.

Table 18–15 ....

Selected Differential Diagnosis of Reflex
Sympathetic Dystrophy

Musculoskeletal	**Vascular**
Bursitis	Raynaud's disease
Myofascial pain syndrome	Thromboangiitis obliterans
Rotator cuff tear (Buerger's	Thrombosis
disease)	Traumatic vasospasm
Undiagnosed local pathology	
(e.g., fracture or sprain)	**Rheumatic**
	Rheumatoid arthritis
Neurologic	Systemic lupus erythematosus
Poststroke pain syndrome	
Peripheral neuropathy	**Psychiatric**
Postherpetic neuralgia	Factitious disorder
Radiculopathy	Hysterical conversion reaction
Infectious	
Cellulitis	
Infectious arthritis	
Pain of Unexplained Etiology	

....

Source: Adapted with permission from Pittman, D.M.; Belgrade, M.J. Am
Fam Phys 56(9):2265–2270, 1997.

CLINICAL PRESENTATION

Although the differential diagnosis of RSD is extensive (Table 18–15), the diagnosis of florid RSD is not generally difficult.[446] However, recognizing milder cases is challenging because of the changing clinical features of this syndrome over time (that is, vasodilatation first, then vasoconstriction, and finally dystrophic changes), dynamic alterations including diurnal fluctuations, and the subjectivity of some of the complaints.[446] Nonetheless, the importance of early diagnosis is highlighted by the fact that results of treatment are better if treatment is initiated earlier.

Some investigators have prospectively studied whether certain clinical characteristics and laboratory indices correlated with the diagnosis of CRPS type I.[446] They found that both the clinically based CRPS I scoring system, which graded allodynia, vasomotor, and swelling, and the laboratory-based CRPS I grading system, which incorporated a sudomotor index, vasomotor index, and a resting sweat index, were sensitive and reliable tools and could be combined to provide an improved set of diagnostic criteria for CRPS I. Oerlemans and associates found that bedside evaluation of CRPS type I with Veldman's criteria was in good accord with psychometric or laboratory testing of these criteria.[422] Veldman's criteria are defined as follows: (1) the presence of four or five of the following signs and symptoms: unexplained diffuse pain, difference in skin color relative to the other limb, diffuse edema, difference in skin temperature relative to the other limb, or limited active range of motion; (2) the occurrence or increase of the above signs and symptoms after use; and (3) the presence of the above signs and symptoms in an area larger than the area of primary injury or operation and including the area distal to the primary injury.[466] Schurmann and co-workers studied the incidence of specific clinical features in CRPS type I patients and normal post-traumatic patients and assessed the diagnostic value of a bedside test

that measures sympathetic nerve function.[448] Sympathetic reactivity was obliterated or diminished in the affected hands of patients with CRPS type I in contrast to age-matched controls and normal fracture patterns.[448]

STAGING OF REFLEX SYMPATHETIC DYSTROPHY

RSD has been divided into three stages: acute, dystrophic (ischemic), and atrophic.[400, 434, 449] These stages are generally based on chronology, with stage I lasting about 3 months, stage II from 3 to 6 months after the onset of symptoms, and stage III beginning 6 to 9 months after the injury.[359] Stages are also determined based on their symptom complexes, with stage I characterized by swelling, edema, increased temperature in the extremity, and pain aggravated by movement. Stage I is associated with hyperpathia (delayed overreaction and aftersensation to a stimulus, particularly a repetitive one), exaggerated pain response, hyperhidrosis, and allodynia (pain elicited by a normally non-noxious stimuli, particularly if repetitive or prolonged).[359, 440] Sympathetic blocks may be curative during this stage of RSD. After about 3 months, the initial edema becomes brawny, trophic changes of the skin appear, the joint may become cyanotic, and joint motion decreases in the second stage of RSD. In the third stage, the pain may begin to decrease, trophic changes are more pronounced, edema is less prominent, the skin becomes cooler and drier with a thinning and glossy appearance, and joint stiffness occurs.[359]

DIAGNOSTIC TESTING

The diagnosis of RSD is usually based on clinical findings. The new criteria for diagnosing RSD do not include the results of diagnostic testing, and the discerning clinician may disagree on the true presence of RSD. Therefore, diagnostic tests probably have less importance in RSD than they did previously. Selected diagnostic tests are discussed.

Radiography

The early findings of RSD are patchy demineralization of the epiphyses and short bones of the hand and feet.[440] Genant and associates[371] defined five types of bone resorption that may occur in RSD. These are irregular resorption of trabecular bone in the metaphysis, creating the patchy or spotty osteoporosis, subperiosteal bone resorption, intracortical bone resorption, endosteal bone resorption, and surface erosions of subchondral and juxta-articular bone.[371] Other radiographic findings such as subperiosteal resorption, striation, and tunneling of the cortex may occur but are not diagnostic of RSD and may occur with any condition causing disuse.[440] Once patchy osteopenia is present, the patient is usually already in stage II RSD.[364, 473] Osteopenia of the patella is the most common finding of RSD of the knee.[359]

Bone Scanning

Three-phase bone scanning with technetium has long been used as a diagnostic study for RSD, with the pervasive notion that scans will be hot in all three phases. Although this may often be the case in phase I or in acute RSD, the bone scan findings in stage II and stage III RSD are more subtle. There are many false-negative bone scan results in stages II and III RSD.[439] Raj and associates noted that in stage II RSD the first two phases of the bone scan are normal and the delayed images (static phase) of the bone scan demonstrate increased activity.[439] Stage III RSD has decreased activity in phases one and two and normal activity in the third phase (delayed or static phase).[439] Bone scans have been used to assess the response to treatment of RSD and have been found to have no value in monitoring treatment.[476] However, these investigators found that the bone scan had prognostic value: marked hyperfixation of the tracer indicates better final outcome. In contrast, a study of quantitative analysis of three-phase scintigraphy concluded that scintigraphy should not be considered as the definitive technique for the diagnosis of RSD.[477]

Bone Densitometry

Bone density measurements may provide a method of determining a quantitative baseline measurement and be able to assess changes over time in RSD.[439] Otake and associates measured bone mass by microdensitometry in the follow-up of CRPS and for the evaluation of treatment.[428] They found that repeated stellate ganglion blocks did not ameliorate bone atrophy, but the 5-HT2 antagonist sarpogrelate hydrochloride did.

Thermography

Thermography images temperature distribution of the body surface.[440] Gulevich and associates reported on the use of stress infrared telethermography for the diagnosis of CRPS type I and reported that as a diagnostic technique it was both sensitive and specific.[376] Further study of thermography is needed before global usage can be recommended.

PSYCHOLOGIC OR PSYCHIATRIC ASSESSMENT

Psychologic assessment of patients with CRPS have included structured clinical interviews and personality measures such as the Minnesota Multiphasic Personality Inventory (MMPI) and Hopelessness Index.[440] The MMPI profiles of patients with RSD resemble those of patients with chronic pain (increasing elevations on the hypochondriasis, depression, and hysteria scales).[440] Patients in stage I RSD have more pessimism than patients in the second and third stages. More pessimism and depression is seen in younger patients with RSD than in older patients.[439]

Bruehl and Carlson examined the literature for evidence that psychologic factors predispose certain individuals to development of RSD.[351] They found that 15 of 20 studies reported the presence of depression, anxiety, and/or life stress in patients with RSD[351] and hypothesized a theoretical model in which these factors influenced the development of RSD through their effects on alpha-adrenergic activity. These investigators also noted that they could not determine whether depression, anxiety, and life stress preceded the RSD and were etiologically related to it.

CURRENT CONCEPTS IN TREATMENT

Overview

The first line of treatment of RSD includes nonsteroidal anti-inflammatory drugs (NSAIDs), topical capsaicin cream, a low-dose antidepressant, and physical therapy (contrast baths, TENS unit treatments, gentle range of motion to prevent joint contractures, and isometric strengthening exercises to prevent atrophy). Treatment at this time can usually be initiated by the orthopaedic surgeon. However, if the patient fails to respond, then referral to a pain specialist, generally an anesthesiologist with a special interest in pain management, should also be considered. The second line of treatment includes possible sympathetic blocks, anticonvulsants (Neurontin), calcium channel blockers (nifedipine), adrenergic blocking agents (phenoxybenzamine), and antidepressants in higher doses. The third line of treatment includes possible sympathectomy (surgical or chemical), implantable spinal cord stimulators, and corticosteroids. Table 18–16 shows the medications commonly used for RSD.

Nonsteroidal Anti-inflammatory Drugs

The possibility that the inflammatory response is important in the pathophysiology of RSD[466] highlights the role of NSAIDs in treatment. Veldman and associates[466] suggested that the early symptoms of RSD are more suggestive of an exaggerated inflammatory response to

TABLE 18–16 ●

Medications Commonly Used to Treat Reflex Sympathetic Dystrophy

Medication	Initial Dosage*
ADRENERGIC AGENTS	
Beta blocker: propranolol (Inderal)	40 mg bid
Alpha blocker: Phenoxybenzamine (Dibenzyline)	10 mg bid
Alpha and beta blocker: guanethidine (Ismelin)	10 mg/day
Alpha agonist: clonidine (Catapres-TTS)	One 0.1 mg patch/week
CALCIUM CHANNEL BLOCKING AGENT	
Nifedipine (Adalat, Procardia)	30 mg/day
DRUGS FOR NEUROPATHIC PAIN	
Tricyclic antidepressants:	
Amitriptyline (Elavil)	10 to 25 mg/d
Doxepin (Sinequan)	25 mg/d
Serotonin reuptake inhibitors:	
Fluoxetine (Prozac)	20 mg/day
Anticonvulsant: gabapentin (Neurontin)	300 mg on the first day, 300 mg bid on the second day, and 300 mg tid thereafter
Corticosteroid: prednisone	60 mg per day, then rapidly taper over 2–3 wk

*The initial dosage may need to be adjusted based on individual circumstances. Consult a drug therapy manual for further information about specific medications.

Source: Adapted with modifications with permission from Pittman, D.M.; Belgrade, M.J. Am Fam Phys 56(9):2265–2270, 1997.

injury or surgery than a disturbance of the sympathetic nervous system.[466] Nonetheless, Sieweke and associates found no effect of an anti-inflammatory agent and hypothesized a noninflammatory pathogenesis in CRPS that is presumably central in origin.[454]

Antidepressants

Antidepressants are useful in treating RSD primarily by causing sedation, analgesia, and mood elevation. Analgesic action has been attributed to inhibition of serotonin reuptake at nerve terminals of neurons that act to suppress pain transmission, with resulting prolongation of serotonin activity at the receptor.[363]

Narcotic Analgesics

There is a potential for abuse of narcotics in RSD because of the associated chronic pain. These agents do little to relieve sympathetically mediated pain. However, when narcotics are given epidurally in combination with local anesthetic agents, they are very effective. Epidural administration of fentanyl (0.03–0.05 mg/hr) allows maximum effect on the dorsal horn with minimal plasma concentration and minimal side effects.

Anticonvulsants

Mellick reported their results of using gabapentin (Neurontin) in patients with severe and refractory RSD pain.[412] He noted satisfactory pain relief, early evidence of disease reversal, and even one case of a successful treatment of RSD with gabapentin alone. The specific effects noted included reduced hyperpathia, allodynia, hyperalgesia, and early reversal of skin and soft tissue manifestations.

Calcium Channel Blockers (Nifedipine) and Adrenergic Blocking Agents (Phenoxybenzamine)

Nifedipine, a calcium channel blocker, has been used orally to treat RSD. At a dosage of 10 to 30 mg thrice daily, it induces peripheral vasodilatation. Initial treatment is usually at a dosage of 10 mg thrice daily for 1 week, which is increased if there is no effect to 20 mg thrice daily for 1 week, which is increased to 30 mg thrice daily the following week if there is no effect. If partial improvement or relief occurs at any of these doses, then the dosage is continued for 2 weeks and then tapered and discontinued over several days.[435] The most common side effect of nifedipine is headache, which is most likely due to increased cerebral blood flow. Muizelaar and co-workers[418] assessed treatment of both CRPS type I and type II with nifedipine or phenoxybenzamine, or both, in 59 patients. They found a higher success rate using phenoxybenzamine in 11 of 12 patients. A lower success rate was found in treating chronic CRP with a success rate of treatment of 40%. Although long-term oral use of phenoxybenzamine has been reported for the treatment of RSD, there has been a high incidence of orthostatic hypotension (43%).[373] In an attempt to avoid these side effects, intravenous regional phenoxybenzamine has been used to treat RSD with good results in a small series of patients.[406]

Corticosteroids

It has been reported that the patients who respond to corticosteroids had chronic pain of a mean duration of 25 weeks.[397] Although the use of corticosteroids in the treatment of RSD is much less common, Raj and associates note that a trial of steroids might be a reasonable treatment for patients with long-standing pain who have failed to respond to blocks.[440]

Physical Therapy

Physical therapy has long been an integral part of treatment of type I CRPS. Oerlemans and associates prospectively studied whether physical therapy or occupational therapy could reduce the ultimate impairment rating in patients with RSD and found that physical therapy and occupational therapy did not reduce impairment percentages in patients with RSD.[421] Nonetheless, these same investigators have also reported that adjuvant physical therapy in patients with RSD results in a more rapid improvement in an impairment level sum score.[420]

Electroacupuncture

Chan and Chow reported their results with acupuncture with electrical stimulation in 20 patients with features of RSD.[353] They found that 70% had marked improvement in pain relief and an additional 20% had further improvement. In addition, at later follow-up reassessment of these patients showed maintenance or continued improvement of their pain relief 3 to 22 months after their course of electroacupuncture.[353] There has been a resurgence of interest in electroacupuncture.[382, 441]

Regional Intravenous and Arterial Blockade

The use of intravenous or intra-arterial infusions of ganglionic blocking agents is becoming increasingly popular in the treatment of RSD.[440] Guanethidine, bretylium, and reserpine have been used with promising results.[440] Guanethidine has been substituted for reserpine in the intravenous regional block format to lessen side effects.[440]

Sympathetic Blocks

Sympathetic blockade has historically been useful both as a diagnostic test (when placebo injections are included and documented temperature elevation after blockade) and a basic treatment. Increasing recognition of the presence of non-sympathetically mediated pain in RSD has contributed to the decreased use of diagnostic sympathetic blockade.

A series of injections are generally performed on an outpatient basis. Alternatively, continuous epidural infusions can also be performed on an inpatient basis if the patient is unable or unwilling to have a series of outpatient nerve blocks.[360]

For upper extremity RSD, the site of blockade is either the stellate ganglion or the brachial plexus. For lower extremity RSD, the lumbar sympathetic chain or epidural space is the preferred site for sympathetic blockade.

Transcutaneous Electrical Stimulation

Transcutaneous electrical nerve stimulation (TENS) has been useful in the treatment of RSD. It most likely works via the gate theory of pain introduced by Melzack and Wall in 1965 in which stimulation of the larger nerve fibers transcutaneously closes the "gate" and may inhibit the transmission of pain.[413]

Topical Capsaicin

Topical capsaicin cream in concentrations of 0.025% to 0.075%, used previously for postherpetic neuralgia and painful diabetic neuropathy, has been noted to be worth considering for treating localized areas of hyperalgesia.[355, 458] The effectiveness of topical capsaicin cream decreases after 3 weeks of daily usage.

Chemical Sympathectomy

Neurolytic sympathetic block is an alternative for the lower extremity but usually not the upper extremity. The proximity of the cervical sympathetic chain to the brachial plexus makes a cervical neurolytic sympathectomy too hazardous unless placed under fluoroscopic or CT guidance. Neurolytic lumbar sympathetic blockade is considered to be a viable alternative to surgical sympathectomy for lower extremity RSD.[440] However, there are potential complications in such procedures including dermatologic problems and "sympathalgia" in the second or third postoperative weeks, which is characterized by muscle fatigue, deep pain, and tenderness.[381]

Surgical Sympathectomy

Surgical sympathetectomy has been advocated for patients who do not get permanent pain relief from blocks and is somewhat of a last resort or end-of-the-road treatment. Criteria have been suggested that should be met before selecting surgical sympathetectomy: patients should have had pain relief from sympathetic blocks on several occasions, pain relief should last as long as the vascular effects of the blocks, placebo injections should produce no pain relief, and secondary gain and psychopathology should be ruled out.[440] Failure of surgical sympathectomy has been attributed to reinnervation from the contralateral sympathetic chain.[392, 393] Surgical sympathectomy in our opinion is less effective than chemical sympathectomy.

Electrical Spinal Cord Stimulation

Electrical spinal cord stimulation is generally reserved for patients who have severe pain that is unresponsive to conventional treatments. Kemler and associates retrospectively studied the clinical efficacy and possible adverse effects of electrical spinal cord stimulation for the treatment of patients with RSD.[388] About 78% of patients (18 of 23) reported subjective improvement during the test period, and 50% had complications related to the device. Prospective studies are needed to assess the efficacy of spinal cord stimulation.

Nontraditional Therapies

Certain patients are responsive to nontraditional treatment such as art and music therapy, herbal medicines, and massage therapy. These approaches should be viewed with an open mind because evidence-based therapies may not be successful in relieving pain associated with RSD.

PREVENTION OF REFLEX SYMPATHETIC DYSTROPHY

It has been suggested that optimal pain relief after surgery can reduce the incidence of chronic postoperative pain syndromes, such as those that occur in almost 50% of thoracotomies.[387] This hypothesis is based on the concept that an abnormally exaggerated and prolonged hyperalgesia reaction is involved in the development of complex post-traumatic syndromes.[349] Although the potential for dose escalation and dependency has to be considered, perioperative management of pain with appropriate analgesics appears to help prevent RSD.

PROGNOSIS

The prognosis of RSD has historically been grim. The assumption has generally been that stage I RSD will progress in most cases to stage II and then to stage III. In addition, the prognosis has also been linked to the time of diagnosis, with early diagnosis having a better prognosis. Zyluk studied the natural history of post-traumatic RSD without treatment and found that the signs and symptoms of RSD were largely gone in 26 of 27 patients who completed the study at 13 months after diagnosis.[478] Nonetheless, the hands were still functionally impaired, and three patients who withdrew from the study had worsening of the signs and symptoms of RSD.[478] Geertzen and associates studied 65 patients with RSD to analyze the relationship between impairment and disability.[369] They found that RSD patients had impairments and perceived disabilities after a mean interval of 5 years.[369] Furthermore, these investigators found no differences in impairments in patients who were diagnosed within 2 months of the causative event and those diagnosed 2 to 5 months after it. Nonetheless, there is evidence that the effect of treatment for sympathetically mediated pain is better during the first few months after onset.[349] Cooper and DeLee noted that the most favorable prognostic indicator in the management of RSD of the knee was early diagnosis and early institution of treatment (before 6 months of onset).[359]

SUMMARY

Key for the orthopaedic surgeon is to recognize that the fracture patient may have RSD, distinct from either another undetected condition or inadequately treated pain. Tipoffs to the presence of RSD are inordinate requests for narcotic medicine, inappropriate emergency department visits, and aggressive contacts with the office staff. Although RSD takes time to evaluate, it is important to have heightened awareness of it to protect the practitioner if there really is an undetected additional injury (especially in polytrauma patients) and to make the diagnosis of RSD when appropriate to initiate timely treatment and possible referral to a caregiver interested in pain management. RSD should be considered any time that pain is out of proportion to what is expected. In addition, the new International Pain criteria for RSD (type I CRPS) make the diagnosis of RSD easier but less specific. The new terminology appears to make RSD into a constellation of symptoms rather than a distinct disease. New developments in pain management such as the use of intrathecal methylprednisolone for postherpetic neuralgia[395] may expand the armamentarium of treatments for post-traumatic RSD in the future.

MANAGEMENT OF COMPLICATIONS

In this chapter, a complication of fracture treatment has been defined as an *undesired turn of events* in the treatment of a fracture. But because patient, doctor, and insurer each bring a different set of values into the assessment of medical outcomes, the question might be asked, "Undesired by whom?" Patient and doctor, for example, may agree to attempt to salvage a difficult compound tibial fracture with contamination and arterial injury. The insurer, facing charges in excess of a quarter of a million dollars for vascular repair, free flap coverage, fracture fixation, bone grafting, and multiple reoperations if infection develops, combined with a prolonged time of total disability before the patient is able to return to work, may regard the outcome as an undesired event when compared with below-the-knee amputation, prosthesis fitting, and early return to work.

An explicit understanding of the *desired* course of events is therefore crucial to recognizing complications. In this respect, fracture treatment is different from many other areas of orthopaedics and, indeed, medicine in general for two reasons. First, the goal of treatment, although often unstated, is generally obvious: secure complete functional healing of a broken bone with return to full activity. Second, the patient did not anticipate the injury; therefore, patient education begins at the perioperative visit, and the choice of physician is largely determined by institutional lines of case referral. Also, the patient must adjust to pain, inconvenience, and an unexpected loss of productivity. To make matters more difficult, some accident victims have associated psychopathology that makes communication difficult.[486] These patients may be stigmatized as "mentally ill," thereby setting the stage for withholding appropriate care.

Many fractures with good results of treatment yield permanent disability. A difficult supracondylar fracture of the humerus repaired with an open reduction may have a residual loss of 15° of elbow extension. The result is excellent in terms of present state-of-the-art treatment despite the presence of measurable permanent impairment. The chain of causation that led to this impairment began when the patient fell and landed on the elbow. It is crucial to maintain this link. When the physician does not acknowledge the presence of impairment and, even worse, fails to recognize that the patient is bothered, for example, by a prominent screw that has backed out of an olecranon osteotomy, there is a risk that the patient, or the patient's lawyer, will attempt to shorten the chain of causation to the operative event. For many patients, an understanding of the loss sustained in injury and the recognition of the complication by the physician are crucial steps that diffuse a potentially explosive situation and allow the process of controlling and treating complications to put the matter right.

Local complications occurring late in the course of treatment are most often related to disturbances in fracture healing. These may develop insidiously over weeks or months. Often in such cases, the patient is anticipating recovery, and the orthopaedist overlooks a trend toward deformity that, on retrospective viewing of radiographs arranged in sequence, is all too evident.

Each fracture has two complementary problems that must be solved: a biologic and a mechanical one. The biologic problem consists of providing the setting for fracture healing. In most simple closed fractures, adequate biologic factors are present so that healing will occur. In high-grade compound fractures, the biologic issue is an important one. Only a few strategies are available to improve biology; these include autogenous bone grafting, electrical stimulation, and free tissue transfer. New techniques harnessing the power of gene therapy to ensure and accelerate future healing will soon be available. Their safety and cost-effectiveness require incisive evidence-based research. The mechanical problem includes the selection of an operative or nonoperative treatment strategy that anticipates the mechanical behavior of a fractured bone and provides an environment that allows biologic processes to heal the fracture. Work by Goodship and associates[484] and by Rubin and Lanyon[489] have begun to define the mechanical circumstances favorable to fracture healing. Closed reamed IM nailing works well. Although it destroys marrow content, the enveloping soft tissues are not disturbed, and the biomechanics of fracture site loading are favorable. When the vitality of the tissues surrounding a fracture is compromised, the margin of safety is smaller, and adverse outcomes become more prevalent. In this situation, modification of the method (e.g., by eliminating reaming and using a mechanically stronger but thinner improved implant) may reduce the incidence of complications to an acceptable level.

New therapies such as absorbable antibiotic implants, biologic bone "glues," implantable proteins that stimulate fracture healing, absorbable fracture fixation devices, and gene therapy hold promise for improved results.

Database management is at the heart of analyzing complications. Today's information technology explosion provides a tremendous opportunity to improve fracture care information. The data collected must, however, be meaningful. What is put into a database determines what comes out. The standard fracture nomenclature adopted by the Orthopaedic Trauma Association is an attempt to create groupings of similar cases for long-term study.

Because the risk-to-benefit ratio is at the heart of decision making in fracture treatment and in an era of results analysis, new factors will emerge that will have a powerful influence on the expenditure of health care resources for fracture care. The categorization of complications will assume great importance.[492] A model for fracture treatment must be shaped to ensure that equal weight is given to the long-term outcome of a particular treatment pattern and that the focus is shifted from short-term economic monitors (e.g., days in the hospital, readmission within 2 weeks, implant costs), because these factors do not disclose the true socioeconomic morbidity of this disease and the potential lasting impact of local complications of fracture treatment. The insurance industry has a desire to set practice pattern algorithms to predict and control costs. The problem in trying to standardize treatment routines is that algorithms for care of human conditions are based on faulty assumptions.[490] Despite the appearance of systematization in today's microprocessor-produced output, practice patterns are dependent on human variables, and the treatment of broken limbs remains an art as well as a science.

Risk Management

No discussion about complications would be complete without reviewing the risks and medicolegal implications of complications. Many complications result in a degree of permanence, whether it is pain, decreased range of motion, or muscle weakness. The mere existence of a complication potentially fulfills the criterion that there were damages, one of the triad of criteria for medical malpractice. Malpractice is simply defined as an event in violation of the "standard of care" that causes damages. Rogal noted that a theory of fault can be created for any adverse outcome that occurs while a person is under a physician's care.[488] A bad outcome after surgery itself is associated with the risk of a lawsuit.[481]

There are several reasons why orthopaedic surgeons are near the top of the list in the number of malpractice claims.[488] The work of the orthopaedist is often visible on a radiograph.[488] Because of the emphasis on radiographic cosmesis, fracture surgery is particularly susceptible to scrutiny by anyone. These factors, coupled with the fact that fracture surgery can rarely be performed perfectly, makes fracture surgery a target for malpractice allegations. Rogal also notes that many orthopaedic injuries are "irreconcilable" and cites the example of a decimated articular surface, which is coupled with the public perception that modern technology can return any injury back to normal.[488] He also noted that in many situations time is of the essence (e.g., neurovascular compromise, compartment syndrome), and he states that lawsuits are often spawned when care is delayed even if the outcome is minimally adverse. Related to this last scenario, is the unique entity in orthopaedic traumatology of the missed injury.

MISSED INJURIES

Missed injuries are reported in 2% to 9% of patients with multiple injuries.[480, 482, 483, 487, 491] The majority of these injuries are musculoskeletal injuries. In one series, Buduhan and McRitchie reported that 54% of the injuries were musculoskeletal and 14.3% affected the peripheral nerves (14.3%) (Fig. 18–12).[482] They noted that patients with missed injuries tend to be more severely injured and to have initial neurologic compromise. Buduhan and McRitchie reported that in 46 of 567 (8.1%) injuries, 43.8% were unavoidable.[482] Born and associates in 1989 reported a delay in diagnosis of musculoskeletal injuries in 26 of 1006 consecutive blunt trauma patients and a total of 39 fractures with a delay in diagnosis.[480] The most common reason for the delay in diagnosis was a lack of radiographs at admission. Enderson and associates in 1990[483] reported that a tertiary survey was able to find additional injuries in patients who had already undergone primary and secondary trauma surveys and that the use of the tertiary survey found a higher percentage of injuries (9%) then the 2% incidence in their trauma registry. These investigators noted that the most common reason that injuries were missed was altered level of consciousness due to head injury or alcohol. Ward and Nunley in 1991 reported that 6% (24 of 111) of orthopaedic injuries were not initially diagnosed in 111 multitrauma patients.[491] Seventy percent of occult bony injuries were ultimately diagnosed by physical examination and plain radiographs alone. Risk factors for occult orthopaedic injuries were (1) significant multisystem trauma with another more apparent orthopaedic injury within the same extremity, (2) trauma victim too unstable for full initial orthopaedic evaluation, (3) altered sensorium, (4) hastily applied splint obscuring a less apparent injury, (5) poor quality or inadequate initial radiographs, and (6) inadequate significance assigned to minor sign or symptoms in a major trauma victim. These investigators noted that all orthopaedic injuries cannot be diagnosed on initial patient evaluation.

Spine injuries are a subgroup of injuries that are frequently diagnosed late. In 1996 Anderson and co-workers noted that in 43 of 181 patients with major thoracolumbar spine fractures, there was a delay in diagnosis.[479] This delay in diagnosis was associated with an unstable patient condition that necessitates higher-priority procedures than emergency department thoracolumbar spine radiographs. Lumbar transverse process fractures have also been reported to be associated with

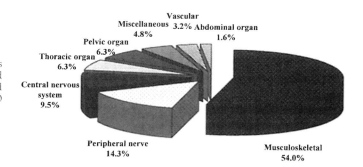

FIGURE 18–12. Pie diagram of the types of missed injuries in patients with multiple trauma, which demonstrates that the majority of missed injuries are musculoskeletal. (From Buduhan, G.; McRitchie, D.I. Missed injuries in patients with multiple trauma. J Trauma 49:600–605, 2000 with permission.)

significant lumbar spine fractures in 11% of cases and can be easily missed if CT scanning is not used in addition to plain radiographs.[485]

DOCUMENTATION OF COMPLICATIONS

Several factors should be considered in documentation. One key point is documenting the precise date that the complication was discussed with the patient. Common sense and tact are critical in these discussions. It may be more difficult to have these discussions in major teaching hospitals, in which the patient and family are seeing the resident physicians daily and the attending physician less frequently. Axiomatic in discussing complications with patients and their families is avoidance of self-blame. In a legal context, statements such as "I wish we had done it differently" have the force of a confession and are known as admissions. The complication needs to be disclosed but not adopted. The mere presence of a complication may place the physician at risk for litigation, because the more disabling the outcome of injury, the higher the chance of an accusation of medical malpractice.[481]

When multiple services are caring for a trauma patient, delineation of responsibility in the medical record is important. It may not be clear to the patient or to the family which service is responsible for what aspect of the patient's care. For example, the patient might assume that the orthopaedic trauma service is responsible for metacarpal fractures when in fact there is a separate hand surgery service. Nevertheless, a team approach that presents a "united front" is important, because there are often multiple services taking care of these patients.

Another significant development is the need to satisfy Health Care Financing Administration compliance issues for billing in the medical record by documenting that the attending physician was present at surgery for the key and critical parts of the operation. The patient, who subsequently acquires a copy of the medical record, will then know for which part of the surgery the attending physician was present. If any complications arose intraoperatively, particularly if the attending physician was not present for that part of the operation, the situation may become a medicolegal nightmare. A clarifying discussion with the patient and family should include the fact that many hands are needed to treat broken bones.

Documenting systems problems is another potential challenge for the orthopaedic traumatologist. Defining such issues in the medical record, for example "that the surgery was delayed an additional 2 days because no operating room time was available," can be risky for the physician. Often, from the patient's and the patient's attorney's perspective, the physician and the institution are inextricably linked, even when the physician is an independent contractor. Furthermore, there is tremendous pressure for physicians to support and not to criticize the institution in which they work. The survival of orthopaedic trauma as a field depends on our skill in negotiating outside of the patient record a good environment for musculoskeletal care.

SUMMARY

This chapter has defined complications of fracture treatment and presented specific information about three important systemic disturbances—fat embolism syndrome, thromboembolic disorders, and multiple system organ dysfunction and failure—that can result from broken bones. In addition, a framework for approaching fracture-specific complications—soft tissue and vascular problems, post-traumatic arthrosis, peripheral nerve injury, and RSD—was presented. Lastly, strategies for realistically managing complications were suggested.

Complications, such as missed injuries, are intrinsic to fracture care and are a part of the natural history of fractures rather than markers that something went wrong. In the final analysis, the management of complications begins with understanding the scientific basis for the treatment of injury, listening to what the patient is telling us, and accepting the fact that we as fracture surgeons cannot avoid adverse circumstances.

REFERENCES

Fat Embolism Syndrome

1. Adams, C.B. The retinal manifestations of fat embolism. Injury 2:221, 1971.
2. Alho, A. Fat embolism syndrome—A variant of post-traumatic pulmonary insufficiency. Ann Chir Gynaecol Suppl 186:31–36, 1982.
3. Allgower, M.; Durig, M.; Wolff, G. Infection and trauma. Surg Clin North Am 60:133–144, 1980.
4. Ashbaugh, D.G.; Petty, T.L. The use of corticosteroids in the treatment of respiratory failure associated with massive fat embolism. Surg Gynecol Obstet 123:493, 1966.
5. Bach, A.W. Physiologic effects of intramedullary nailing: Fat embolism syndrome. In: Seligson, D., ed. Concepts in Intramedullary Nailings. New York, Grune & Stratton, 1985, pp. 91–99.
6. Barie, P.S.; Minnear, F.L.; Malik, A.S. Increased pulmonary vascular permeability after bone marrow injection in sheep. Am Rev Respir Dis 123:648–653, 1981.
7. Beck, J.P.; Collins, J.A. Theoretical and clinical aspects of post-traumatic fat embolism syndrome. Instr Course Lect 23:38–87, 1973.
8. Behrman, S.W.; Fabian, T.C.; Kudsk, K.A.; et al. Improved outcome with femur fractures: Early vs. delayed fixation. J Trauma 30:792–797, 1990.
9. Bisgard, J.D.; Baker, C. Experimental fat embolism. Am J Surg 47:466–478, 1940.
10. Bone, L.B.; Johnson, K.D.; Weigelt, J.; et al. Early versus delayed stabilization of femoral fractures. J Bone Joint Surg Am 71:336–340, 1989.
11. Böstmann, O.; Varjonen, L.; Vainionpaa, S.; et al. Incidence of local complications after intramedullary nailing and after plate fixation of femoral shaft fractures. J Trauma 29:639–645, 1989.
12. Bulger, E.M.; Smith, D.G.; Maier, R.V.; Jurkovich, G. Fat embolism syndrome: A 10-year review. Arch Surg 132(4):435–439, 1997.
13. Busch, F. Über feltembolie. Virchows Arch (A) 35:321, 1866.
14. Carrico, C.J. Early intramedullary nailing of femoral shaft fractures: A cause of fat embolism syndrome. Am J Surg 146:107–110, 1983.
15. Chan, K.; Tham, K.T.; Chiu, H.S.; et al. Post-traumatic fat embolism—Its clinical and subclinical presentations. J Trauma 24:45–49, 1984.
16. Collins, J.A.; Hudson, T.L.; Hamacher, W.R. Systemic fat embolism in four combat casualties. Ann Surg 167:493–499, 1968.
17. Deland, F.H. Bone marrow embolism and associated fat embolism to the lungs. Graduate thesis, University of Minnesota, June 1956.
18. Dunphy, J.E.; Ilfeld, F.W. Fat embolism. Am J Surg 77:737, 1949.

19. Evarts, C.M. The fat embolism syndrome: A review. Surg Clin North Am 50:493–507, 1970.

20. Feldman, F.; Ellis, K.; Green, W.M. The fat embolism syndrome. Radiology 114:535, 1975.

21. Fenger, C.; Salisbury, J.H. Diffuse multiple capillary fat embolism in the lungs and brain is a fatal complication in common fractures: Illustrated by a case. Chicago Mod J Examin 39:587–595, 1879.

22. Fischer, J.F.; Turner, R.H.; Riseborough, E.J. Massive steroid therapy in severe fat embolism. Surg Gynecol Obstet 132:667, 1971.

23. Gong, H., Jr. Fat embolism syndrome: A puzzling phenomenon. Postgrad Med 62:40, 1977.

24. Gossling, H.R.; Pellegrini, V.D., Jr. Fat embolism syndrome: A review of the pathophysiology and physiological basis of treatment. Clin Orthop 165:68–82, 1982.

25. Gurd, A.R.; Wilson, R.I. The fat embolism syndrome. J Bone Joint Surg Br 56:408–416, 1974.

26. Haddad, F.S., ed. Fat embolism. In: Annual Report. Beirut, Lebanon, The Orient Hospital, 1951, p. 25.

27. Heim, D.; Regazzori, P.; Tsakiris, D.A.; et al. Intramedullary nailing and pulmonary embolism: Does unreamed nailing prevent embolization? An in vivo study in rabbits. J Trauma 38:899–906, 1995.

28. Herndon, J.H.; Risenborough, E.J.; Fischer, J.E. Fat embolism: A review of current concepts. J Trauma 11:673, 1971.

29. Jacobson, D.M.; Terrence, C.F.; Reinmuth, O.M. The neurologic manifestations of fat embolism. Neurology 36:847–851, 1986.

30. Kallos, T.; Jerry, E.E.; Golon, F.; et al. Intramedullary pressure and pulmonary embolism of femoral medullary contents in dogs during insertion of bone cement and a prosthesis. J Bone Joint Surg Am 56:1363–1367, 1974.

31. Kerstell, J. Pathogenesis of post-traumatic fat embolism. Am J Surg 121:712, 1971.

32. Kerstell, J.; Hallgren, B.; Rudenstam, C.M.; Svanborg, A. The chemical composition of the fat emboli in the postabsorptive dog. Acta Med Scand 186 (Suppl 499):3, 1969.

33. Kroupa, J. Fat globulemia in early diagnostics of traumatic fat embolism. Czech Med 9:90–108, 1986.

34. Levy, D. The fat embolism syndrome: A review. Clin Orthop 261:281–286, 1990.

35. Lindeque, B.G.P.; Schoeman, H.S.; Dommisse, G.F.; et al. Fat embolism and the fat embolism syndrome: A double-blind therapeutic study. J Bone Joint Surg Br 69:128–131, 1987.

36. Lozman, J.; Deno, D.C.; Feustel, P.J.; et al. Pulmonary and cardiovascular consequences of immediate fixation or conservative management of long bone fractures. Arch Surg 121:992–999, 1986.

37. Magerl, F.; Tscherne H. Diagnose, therapie und prophylaxe der fettembolic. Langenbecks Arch Klin Chir 314:292, 1966.

38. Manning, J.B.; Bach, A.W.; Herman, C.M.; Carrico, C.J. Fat release after femur nailing in the dog. J Trauma 23:322–326, 1983.

39. Meyers, J.R.; Lembeck, L.; O'Kane, H.; Baue, A.E. Changes in functional residual capacity of the lung after operation. Arch Surg 110:576–583, 1975.

40. Morton, K.S.; Kendall, M.J. Fat embolism: Its production and source of fat. Can J Surg 8:214, 1965.

41. Mudd, K.L.; Hunt, A.; Matherly, R.C.; et al. Analysis of pulmonary fat embolism in blunt force fatalities. J Trauma 48(4):711–715, 2000.

42. Müller, C.; Rahn, B.A.; Pfister, U.; et al. The incidence, pathogenesis, diagnosis, and treatment of fat embolism. Orthop Rev 23:107–117, 1994.

43. Mullins, M. Personal communication. December 1988.

44. Murray, D.G.; Racz, G.B. Fat embolism syndrome (respiratory insufficiency syndrome): A rationale for treatment. J Bone Joint Surg Am 56:1338–1349, 1973.

45. Nast-Kolb, D.; Waydhas, C.; Jochum, M.; et al. Günstigster operationszeitpunkt für die versorgung von femurschafttrakturen bei polytrauma? Chirurg 61:259–265, 1990.

46. Nuessle, W.F. The significance of fat in the sputum. Am J Clin Pathol 21:430, 1951.

47. Pape, H.C.; Auf'm Kolk, M.; Paffrath, T.; et al. Primary intramedullary fixation in multiple trauma patients with associated lung contusion: A cause of post-traumatic ARDS. J Trauma 34:540–547, 1993.

48. Pape, H.C.; Dwenger, A.; Grotz, M.; et al. The risk of early intramedullary nailing of long bone fractures in multiple traumatized patients. Contemp Orthop 10:15–23, 1995.

49. Pape, H.C.; Dwenger, A.; Regel, G.; et al. Pulmonary damage after intramedullary femoral nailing in traumatized sheep. Is there an effect from different nailing methods? J Trauma 33:574–581, 1992.

50. Pape, H.C.; Regel, G.; Dwenger, A.; et al. Influences of different methods of intramedullary femoral nailing on lung function in patients with multiple trauma. J Trauma 35:709–716, 1993.

51. Pell, A.C.H.; James, C.; Keating, J.F. The detection of fat embolism by transesophageal echocardiography during reamed intramedullary nailing. J Bone Joint Surg Br 75:921–925, 1993.

52. Peltier, L.F. Fat embolism: A perspective. Clin Orthop 232:263–270, 1988.

53. Peltier, L.F. Fat embolism: A current concept. Clin Orthop 66:241, 1969.

54. Peltier, L.F. Fat embolism: A pulmonary disease. Surgery 62:756–758, 1967.

55. Peltier, L.F. Fat embolism: I: The amount of fat in human long bones. Surgery 40:657, 1956.

56. Peltier, L.F. Fat embolism: An appraisal of the problem. Clin Orthop 187:3–17, 1984.

57. Peltier, L.F.; Collins, J.A.; Evarts, C.M.; Sevitt, S. Fat embolism. Arch Surg 109:12–16, 1974.

58. Pinney, S.J.; Keating, J.F.; Meek, R.N. Fat embolism syndrome in isolated femoral fractures: Does timing of nailing influence incidence? Injury 29(2):131–133, 1998.

59. Riseborough, E.J.; Herndon, J.H. Alterations in pulmonary function coagulation and fat metabolism in patients with fractures of the lower limbs. Clin Orthop 115:248, 1976.

60. Riska, E.B.; Myllynen, P. Fat embolism in patients with multiple injuries. J Trauma 22:891–894, 1982.

61. Russell, G.V.; Kirk, P.G.; Biddinger, P. Fat embolism syndrome from an isolated humerus fracture. J Orthop Trauma 11(2):141–144, 1997.

62. Rokkanen, P.; Alho, A.; Avikainen, V.; et al. The efficacy of corticosteroids in severe trauma. Surg Gynecol Obstet 138:69, 1974.

63. Schlag, G. Experimentelle und Klinische Untersuchungen mit Knochenzementen: Ein Beitrag zur Pathogenese und Prophylaxe der akuten intraoperative Hypotension bei Hüftalloarthroplastik. Wien, Verlag Brüder Hollinek, 1974.

64. Schnaid, E.; Lamprey, J.M.; Volgoen, M.J.; et al. The early biochemical and hormonal profile of patients with long bone fractures at risk of fat embolism syndrome. J Trauma 27:309–311, 1987.

65. Schuttemeyer, W. Klinische auswertungen der lipasebestimmungen zur diagnose der fettembolie. Arch Klin Chir 270:50, 1951.

66. Sevitt, S. Fat Embolism. London, Butterworths, 1962.

67. Stoltenberg, J.J.; Gustilo, R.B. The use of methylprednisolone and hypotonic glucose in the prophylaxis of fat embolism syndrome. Clin Orthop 143:211–221, 1979.

68. Talucci, R.C.; Manning, J.; Lampard, S.; et al. Traumatic lipaemia and fatty embolism. Int Clin 4:171, 1913.

69. Talucci, R.C.; Manning, J.; Lampard, S.; et al. Early intramedullary nailing of femoral shaft fractures: A cause of fat embolism syndrome. Am J Surg 148:107–111, 1983.

70. Teng, Q.S.; Li, G.; Zhang, B.X. Experimental study of early diagnosis and treatment of fat embolism syndrome. J Orthop Trauma 9:183–189, 1995.

71. ten Duis, H.J. The fat embolism syndrome. Injury 28(2):77–85, 1997.

72. ten Duis, H.J.; Nijsten, M.W.N.; Klasen, H.J.; Binnendijk, B. Fat embolism in patients with an isolated fracture of the femoral shaft. J Trauma 28:383–390, 1988.

73. Von Bergmann, E. Ein fall tödlicher Fettembolie. Berl Klin Wochenschr 10:385, 1873.

74. Wenda, K.; Ritter, G.; Degreif, J. Zur genese pulmonaler Komplikationen nach Marknagelosteosynthesen. Unfallchirurg 91:432–435, 1988.

75. Wozasek, G.E.; Simon, P.; Redl, H. Intramedullary pressure changes and fat intravasation during intramedullary nailing: An experimental study in sheep. J Trauma 36:202–207, 1994.

76. Zenker, F.A. Beitrage zur Anatomie und Physiologie de Lunge. Dresden, Germany: J Braunsdorf, 1861.

Thromboembolic Disorders

77. Ageno, W. Treatment of venous thromboembolism. Thromb Res 97:V63–V72, 2000.
78. Agu, O.; Hamilton, G.; Baker, D. Graduated compression stockings in the prevention of venous thromboembolism. Br J Surg 86:992–1004, 1999.
79. Ahlberg, A.; Nylander, G.; Robertson, B.; et al. Dextran in prophylaxis of thrombosis in fractures of the hip. Acta Chir Scand Suppl 387:83–85, 1968.
80. Albrechtsson, U. Thrombotic side effects of lower limb phlebography. Lancet 1:7234, 1976.
81. Amstutz, H.C.; Friscia, D.A.; Dorey, F.; et al. Warfarin prophylaxis to prevent mortality from pulmonary embolism after total hip replacement. J Bone Joint Surg Am 71:321–326, 1989.
82. Anglen, J.O.; Bagby, C.; George, R. A randomized comparison of sequential-graded calf compression with intermittent plantar compression for prevention of venous thrombosis in orthopedic trauma patients; preliminary results. Am J Orthop 27:53–58, 1998.
83. Atik, M.; Harkett, J.W.; Wichman, H. Prevention of fatal pulmonary embolism. Surg Gynecol Obstet 130:403–413, 1970.
84. Barber, F.A.; Burton, W.C.; Guyer, R.C. The heparin-induced thrombocytopenia and thrombosis syndrome. J Bone Joint Surg Am 69:935–937, 1987.
85. Barnes, R.W. Current status of noninvasive tests in the diagnosis of venous disease. Surg Clin North Am 62:489–500, 1982.
86. Barnes, R.W.; Wu, K.K.; Hoak, J.C. Fallibility of the clinical diagnosis of venous thrombosis. JAMA 234:605–607, 1975.
87. Barsotti, J.; Rosset, G.P.; Dabo, F.B.; et al. Comparative double-blind study of two dosage regimens of low-molecular-weight heparin in elderly patients with a fracture of the neck of the femur. J Orthop Trauma 4:371–375, 1990.
88. Bates, S.M.; Hirsh, J. Treatment of venous thromboembolism. Thromb Hemost 82(1):870–877, 1999.
89. Baxter, G.M.; McKechnie, S.; Duffy, P. Colour Doppler ultrasound in deep venous thrombosis: A comparison with venography. Clin Radiol 42:32–36, 1990.
90. Benetar, S.R.; Immelman, E.J.; Jeffery, P. Pulmonary embolism. Br J Dis Chest 80:313–334, 1986.
91. Bettman, M.A.Q.; Paulin, S. Leg phlebography: The incidence, nature and modification of undesirable side effects. Radiology 122:101–104, 1977.
92. Bolhofner, B.R.; Spiegel, P.G. Prevention of medical complications in orthopedic trauma. Clin Orthop 222:105–113, 1987.
93. Bongard, O.; Wicky, J.; Peter, R.; et al. D-dimer plasma measurement in patients undergoing major hip surgery: Use in the prediction and diagnosis of postoperative proximal vein thrombosis. Thromb Res 74(5):487–493, 1994.
94. Bouman, C.S.C.; Ypma, S.T.; Sybesma, J.P.H.B. Comparison of the efficacy of D-dimer, fibrin degradation products and prothrombin fragment 1+2 in clinically suspected deep venous thrombosis. Thromb Res 77(3):225–234, 1995.
95. Bounameaux, H.; Cirafici, P.; de Moerloose, P.; et al. Measurement of D-dimer in plasma as diagnostic aid in suspected pulmonary embolism. Lancet 1:196–200, 1991.
96. Bradley, M.J.; Spencer, P.A.; Alexander, L. Colour flow mapping in the diagnosis of the calf deep vein thrombosis. Clin Radiol 47:399–402, 1993.
97. Büller, H.R.; Lensing, A.W.A.; Hirsh, J.; et al. Deep vein thrombosis: New noninvasive tests. Thromb Haemost 66:133–137, 1991.
98. Carman, T., Jr. Issues and controversies in venous thromboembolism. Clev Clin J Med 66(2):113–123, 1999.
99. Carpenter, J.P.; Holland, G.A.; Baum, R.A.; et al. Magnetic resonance venography for the detection of deep venous thrombosis: Comparison with contrast venography and duplex Doppler ultrasonography. J Vasc Surg 18(5):734–741, 1993.
100. Channon, G.M.; Wiley, A.M. Aspirin prophylaxis of venous thromboembolic disease following fracture of the upper femur. Can J Surg 22:468–472, 1979.
101. Cogo, A.; Lensing, A.W.A.; Prandoni, P.; et al. Comparison of real-time B-mode ultrasonography and Doppler ultrasound with contrast venography in the diagnosis of venous thrombosis in symptomatic outpatients. Thromb Haemost 70(3):404–407, 1993.
102. Colwell, C.W., Jr. Recent advances in the use of low molecular weight heparins as prophylaxis for deep vein thrombosis. Orthop 17(Suppl):5–7, 1994.
103. Colwell, C.W., Jr.; Spiro, T.E.; Trowbridge, A.A., et al. Use of enoxaparin, a LMWH, and UFH for the prevention of deep venous thrombosis after elective hip replacement: A clinical trial comparing the efficacy and safety. J Bone Joint Surg Am 76:3–14, 1994.
104. The Columbus Investigators. Low-molecular-weight heparin in the treatment of patients with venous thromboembolism. N Engl J Med 337:657–662, 1997.
105. Comerota, A.J. Deep vein thrombosis and pulmonary embolism: Clinical presentation and pathophysiologic consequences. Cardiovasc Intervent Radiol 11:9–14, 1988.
106. Consensus Conference. National Institutes of Health: Prevention of venous thrombosis and pulmonary embolism. JAMA 256:744–749, 1986.
107. Coon, W.W. Venous thromboembolism: Prevalence, risk factors, and prevention. Clin Chest Med 5:391–401, 1984.
108. Coon, W.W. Risk factors in pulmonary embolism. Surg Gynecol Obstet 143:385–390, 1976.
109. Coon, W.W.; Coller, F.A. Some epidemiologic considerations of thromboembolism. Surg Gynecol Obstet 109:487–501, 1959.
110. Cotton, L.T.; Roberts, V.C. The prevention of deep venous thrombosis with particular reference to mechanical methods of prevention. Surgery 81:228–235, 1977.
111. Coutts, R. Continuous passive motion. AAOS, Summer Institute, Rosemont, IL, 1988.
112. Cronan, J.J.; Dorfman, G.S.; Scola, F.H.; et al. Deep venous thrombosis: US assessment using vein compression. Radiology 162:191–194, 1987.
113. Crowther, M.A.; Ginsberg, J.S.; Kearon, C.; et al. A randomized trial comparing 5-mg and 10-mg warfarin loading doses. Arch Intern Med 159:46–48, 1999.
114. Cruveilhier, J. Anatomie pathologique du corps humain. Paris, J.B. Bulligère, 1828.
115. Culver, D.; Crawford, J.S.; Gardiner, J.H.; Wiley, A.M. Venous thrombosis after fractures of the upper end of the femur: A study of incidence and site. J Bone Joint Surg Br 52:61–69, 1970.
116. D'Ambrosia, R. Correspondence. J Bone Joint Surg Am 71:311, 1989.
117. Decousus, H.; Leizorovicz, A.; Parent, F.; et al. A clinical trial of vena cava filters in the prevention of pulmonary embolism in patients with proximal deep-vein thrombosis. N Engl J Med 338:409–415, 1998.
118. DeLee, J.C.; Rockwood, C.A., Jr. Current concepts review. The use of aspirin in thromboembolic disease. J Bone Joint Surg Am 62:149–152, 1980.
119. Dennis, J.W.; Menawat, S.; Von Thron, J.; et al. Efficacy of deep venous thrombosis prophylaxis in trauma patients and identification of high-risk groups. J Trauma 35:132–138, 1993.
120. Donaldson, G.A.; Williams, C.; Scannell, J.G.; et al. A reappraisal of the Trendelenburg operation to massive fatal embolism. N Engl J Med 268:171–174, 1963.
121. Dunn, A. Outpatient treatment of deep vein thrombosis: Translating clinical trials into practice. Am J Med 106:660–669, 1999.
122. Erdman, W.A.; Jayson, H.T.; Redman, H.C.; et al. Deep venous thrombosis of the extremities: Role of magnetic resonance imaging in the diagnosis. Radiology 174:425–431, 1990.
123. Eriksson, B.; Kalebo, P.; et al. A comparison of recombinant hirudin with a low-molecular-weight heparin to prevent thromboembolic complications after total hip replacement. N Engl J Med 337(19):1329–1335, 1997.
124. Evarts, C.M.; Feil, E.J. Prevention of thromboembolic disease after elective surgery of the hip. J Bone Joint Surg Am 53:1271–1280, 1971.
125. Fauno, P.; Suomalainen, O.; Rehnberg, V.; et al. Prophylaxis for the prevention of venous thromboembolism after total knee arthroplasty: A comparison between unfractionated and LMWH. J Bone Joint Surg Am 76:1814–1818, 1994.
126. Fisher, C.G.; Blachut, P.A.; Salvian, A.J.; et al. Effectiveness of pneumatic leg compression devices for the prevention of thromboembolic disease in orthopedic trauma patients: A prospective, randomized study of compression alone versus no prophylaxis. J Orthop Trauma 9:1–7, 1995.
127. Fitts, W.T.; Lehr, H.B.; Bitner, R.L.; et al. An analysis of 950 fatal injuries. Surgery 56:663–668, 1964.
128. Francis, C.W.; Marder, V.J.; Evarts, C.M.; Yaukoolbodi, S. Two-step

warfarin therapy: Prevention of postoperative venous thrombosis without excessive bleeding. JAMA 249:374–378, 1983.

129. Freeark, R.J.; Bostwick, J.; Fardin, R. Post-traumatic venous thrombosis. Arch Surg 95:567–575, 1967.

130. Froehlich, J.A.; Dorfman, G.S.; Cronan, J.J.; et al. Compression ultrasonography for the detection of deep venous thrombosis in patients who have a fracture of the hip. J Bone Joint Surg Am 71:249–255, 1989.

131. Frydman, A.M.; Bara, L.; LeRoux, Y.; et al. The antithrombotic activity and pharmacokinetics of enoxaparin, a low molecular weight heparin in humans given single subcutaneous doses of 20 to 80 mg. J Clin Pharmacol 28:609–618, 1988.

132. Gardner, A.M.N.; Fox, R.H. The venous pump of the human foot: Preliminary report. Bristol Med Chir J 98:109–112, 1983.

133. Gardner, A.M.N.; Fox, R.H.; MacEachern, A.G. Reduction of post-traumatic swelling and compartment pressure by impulse compression of the foot. J Bone Joint Surg Br 72:810–815, 1990.

134. Gatterer, R. Ergotism as complication of thromboembolic prophylaxis with heparin and dihydroergotamine. Lancet 1:638–639, 1986.

135. Geerts, W.H.; Code, K.I.; Jay, R.M.; et al. A prospective study of venous thromboembolism after major trauma. New Engl J Med 331:1601–1606, 1994.

136. George, B.D.; Cook, T.A.; Franklin, I.J.; et al. Protocol violation in deep vein thrombosis prophylaxis. Ann R Coll Surg Engl 80:55–57, 1998.

137. Gerhart, T.N.; Yett, H.S.; Robertson, L.K. Low-molecular-weight heparinoid compared with warfarin for prophylaxis of deep vein thrombosis in patients who are operated on for fracture of the hip. J Bone Joint Surg Am 73:494–502, 1991.

138. Giachino, A.A.; Desmarais, R.; Desjardins, D.; Brunet, J.A. Incidence and prevention of deep venous thrombosis. J Bone Joint Surg Br 67:675, 1985.

139. Giachino, A. Relationship between deep-vein thrombosis in the calf and fatal pulmonary embolism. Can J Surg 31:129–130, 1988.

140. Goldhaber, S.Z.; Morpurgo, M. Diagnosis, treatment, and prevention of pulmonary embolism: Report of the WHO/International Society and Federation of Cardiology Task Force. JAMA 268:1727–1733, 1992.

141. Grassi, C.J. Inferior vena caval filters: Analysis of five currently available devices. Am J Roentgenol 156:813–821, 1991.

142. Green, D.; Lee, M.; Lin, A.; et al. Prevention of thromboembolism after spinal cord injury using LMWH. Ann Intern Med 113:571–574, 1991.

143. Greenfield, L.J. Assessment of vena caval filters. J Vasc Interv Radiol 2:425–426, 1991.

144. Haake, D.A.; Berkman, S.A. Venous thromboembolic disease after hip surgery. Risk factors, prophylaxis, and diagnosis. Clin Orthop 242:212–231, 1989.

145. Hamilton, H.W.; Crawford, J.S.; Gardiner, J.H.; Wiley, A.M. Venous thrombosis in patients with fracture of the upper end of the femur: A phlebographic study of the effect of prophylactic anticoagulation. J Bone Joint Surg Br 52:268–289, 1970.

146. Hamsten, A.; Wiman, B.; deFaire, U.; et al. Increased plasma levels of a rapid inhibitor of tissue plasminogen activator in young survivors of myocardial infarction. N Engl J Med 313:1557, 1985.

147. Harris, L.M.; Curl, G.R.; Booth, F.V.; et al. Screening for asymptomatic DVT in SICU patients. J Vasc Surg 26:764–769, 1997.

148. Harris, W.H.; Athanasoulis, C.A.; Waltman, A.C.; Salzman, E.W. High- and low-dose aspirin prophylaxis against thromboembolic disease in total hip replacement. J Bone Joint Surg Am 64:63–66, 1982.

149. Harris, W.H.; Athanasoulis, C.A.; Waltman, A.C.; Salzman, E.W. Prophylaxis of deep-vein thrombosis after total hip replacement: Dextran and external pneumatic compression compared with 1.2 or 0.3 grams of aspirin daily. J Bone Joint Surg Am 67:57–62, 1985.

150. Harris, W.H.; Salzman, E.W.; Athanasoulis, C.; et al. Comparison of warfarin, low-molecular-weight dextran, aspirin, and subcutaneous heparin in prevention of venous thromboembolism following total hip replacement. J Bone Joint Surg Am 56:1552–1562, 1974.

151. Harris, W.H.; Salzman, E.W.; Athanasoulis, C.A.; et al. Aspirin prophylaxis of venous thromboembolism after total hip replacement. N Engl J Med 297:1246–1249, 1977.

152. Harris, W.H.; Salzman, E.W.; DeSanctis, R.W. The prevention of thromboembolic disease by prophylactic anticoagulation: A con-

trolled study in elective hip surgery. J Bone Joint Surg Am 49:81–89, 1967.

153. Harrison, L.; Johnston, M.; Massicotte, P.; et al. Comparison of 5-mg and 10-mg loading doses in initiation of warfarin therapy. Ann Intern Med 126:133–136, 1997.

154. Hartman, J.T.; Altner, P.C.; Freeark, R.J. The effect of limb elevation in preventing venous thrombosis: A venographic study. J Bone Joint Surg Am 52:1618–1622, 1970.

155. Hayt, D.B.; Binkert, B.L. An overview of noninvasive methods of DVT detection. Clin Imaging 14:179–197, 1990.

156. Heatley, R.V.; Hughes, L.E.; Morgan, A.; Okwonga, A. Preoperative or postoperative deep vein thrombosis? Lancet 1:437–439, 1976.

157. Heijboer, H.; Büller, H.R.; Lensing, A.W.A.; et al. A comparison of real-time compression ultrasonography with impedance plethysmography for the diagnosis of deep-vein thrombosis in symptomatic outpatients. N Engl J Med 329:1365–1369, 1993.

158. Hirsh, J.; Dalen, J.E.; Deykin, D.; et al. Oral anticoagulants: Mechanism of action, clinical effectiveness, and optimal therapeutic range. Chest 102(4):312S–323S, 1992.

159. Hjeimsiedt, A.; Bergvali, U. Phlebographic study of the incidence of thrombosis in the injured and uninjured limb in 55 cases of tibial fracture. Acta Chir Scand 134:229–234, 1968.

160. Howard, A.W.; Aaron, S.D. Low molecular weight heparin decreases proximal and distal venous thrombosis following total knee arthroplasty. A meta-analysis of randomized trials. Thromb Hemost 79:902–906, 1998.

161. Hui, A.C.; Heras-Palou, C.; Dunn, I.; et al. Graded compression stockings for the prevention of deep vein thrombosis after hip and knee replacement. J Bone Joint Surg Br 78:550–554, 1996.

162. Huisman, M.V.; Büller, H.R.; ten Cate, J.W.; et al. Serial impedance plethysmography for suspected DVT in outpatients. N Engl J Med 314:823–828, 1986.

163. Hull, R.D.; Delmore, T.J.; Hirsh, J.; et al. Effectiveness of intermittent pulsatile elastic stockings for the prevention of calf and thigh vein thrombosis in patients undergoing elective knee surgery. Thromb Res 16:37–45, 1979.

164. Hull, R.D.; Hirsh, J.; Sackett, D.L.; et al. Replacement of venography in suspected venous thrombosis by impedance plethysmography and 125I fibrinogen leg scanning. Ann Intern Med 94:12–15, 1981.

165. Hull, R.D.; Hirsh, J.; Sackett, D.L.; et al. Cost effectiveness of primary and secondary prevention of fatal pulmonary embolism in high risk surgical patients. Can Med Assoc J 127:990–995, 1982.

166. Hull, R.D.; Raskob, G.E. Current concepts review: Prophylaxis of venous thromboembolic disease following hip and knee surgery. J Bone Joint Surg Am 68:146–150, 1986.

167. Hull, R.D.; Raskob, G.E.; LeClere, J.R.; et al. The diagnosis of clinically suspected venous thrombosis. Clin Chest Med 5(3):439–456, 1984.

168. Hull, R.D.; Raskob, G.E.; Pineo, G. A comparison of subcutaneous LMWH with warfarin sodium for prophylaxis against DVT after hip or knee implantation. N Engl J Med 329:1370–1376, 1993.

169. Hull, R.; Van Aken, W.G.; Hirsh, J.; et al. Impedance plethysmography using the occlusive cuff technique in diagnosis of venous thrombosis. Circulation 53(4):696–700, 1976.

170. Hull, R.D.; Raskob, G.E.; Pineo, G.F.; et al. Subcutaneous low-molecular-weight heparin compared with continuous intravenous heparin in the treatment of proximal-vein thrombosis. N Engl J Med 326:975–982, 1992.

171. Hume, M.; Bierbaum, B.; Kuriakose, T.X.; Surprenant, J. Prevention of postoperative thrombosis by aspirin. Am J Surg 133:420–422, 1977.

172. Hyers, T.M.; Hull, R.D.; Weg, J.C. Antithrombotic therapy for venous thromboembolic disease. Chest 102(4):408S–421S, 1992.

173. Hyers, T.M.; Agnelli, G.; Hull, R.; et al. Antithrombotic therapy for venous thromboembolic disease. Chest 114:561S–578S, 1998.

174. Immelman, E.J.; Jeffery, P.C. The postphlebitic syndrome. Clin Chest Med 5:537–550, 1984.

175. Jennings, J.J.; Harris, W.H.; Sarmiento, A. A clinical evaluation of aspirin prophylaxis of thromboembolic disease after total hip arthroplasty. J Bone Joint Surg Am 58:926–928, 1976.

176. Johnson, B.F.; Manzo, R.A.; Bergelin, R.O.; et al. Relationship between changes in deep venous system and the development of the post-thrombotic syndrome after an acute episode of lower limb

deep vein thrombosis: A one- to six-year follow-up. J Vasc Surg 21:307–313, 1995.

177. Johnson, R.; Green, J.R.; Charnley, J. Pulmonary embolism and its prophylaxis following the Charnley total hip replacement. Clin Orthop 127:123–132, 1977.

178. Johnsson, S.R.; Bygdeman, S.; Eliasson, R. Effect of dextran on postoperative thrombosis. Acta Chir Scand Suppl 42:48–55, 1968.

179. Jones, T.K.; Barnes, R.W.; Greenfield, L.J. Greenfield vena caval filter: Rationale and current indications. Ann Thorac Surg 42(Suppl):48–55, 1986.

180. Jorgensen, P.S.; Knudsen, J.B.; Broeng, L. The thromboprophylactic effect of a low-molecular-weight heparin (Fragmis) in hip fracture surgery. Clin Orthop 278:95–100, 1992.

181. Kakkar, V.V.; Fok, P.J.; Murray, W.J.; et al. Heparin and dihydroergotamine prophylaxis against thromboembolism after hip arthroplasty. J Bone Joint Surg Br 67:538, 1985.

182. Kakkar, V.V.; Howe, C.T.; Flanc, C.; Clark, M.B. Natural history of deep venous thrombosis. Lancet 2:230, 1969.

183. Kakkar, V.V.; Stamatakis, J.D.; Bentley, P.G.; et al. Prophylaxis for postoperative deep vein thrombosis: Synergistic effect of heparin and dihydroergotamine. JAMA 241:39–42, 1979.

184. Kelsey, L.J.; Fry, D.M.; VanderKolk, W.E. Thrombosis risk in the trauma patient. Hematol Oncol Clin North Am 14:417–430, 2000.

185. Kearon, C.; Ginsberg, J.S.; Hirsh, J. The role of venous ultrasonography in the diagnosis of suspected deep venous thrombosis and pulmonary embolism. Ann Intern Med 129:1044–1049, 1998.

186. Knudson, M.; Collins, J.; Goodman, S. Thromboembolism following multiple trauma. J Trauma 32:2, 1992.

187. Knudson, M.M.; Morabito, D.; Paiement, G.D.; et al. Use of low molecular weight heparin in preventing thromboembolism in trauma patients. J Trauma 41:446–459, 1996.

188. Knudson, M.M.; Lewis, F.R.; Clinton, A. Prevention of venous thromboembolism in trauma patients. J Trauma 37:480–487, 1994.

189. Koopman, M.M.; Prandoni, P.; Piovella, F.; et al. Treatment of venous thrombosis with intravenous unfractionated heparin administered in the hospital as compared to subcutaneous low-molecular-weight heparin administered at home. N Engl J Med 334:682–687, 1996.

190. Kudsk, K.A.; Fabian, T.; Baum, S.; et al. Silent deep vein thrombosis in immobilized multiple trauma patients. Am J Surg 158:515–519, 1989.

191. Laennec, R.T.H. De l'auscultation mediate. Paris, Brossen et Shaude, 1819.

192. Lensing, A.W.A.; Prandoni, P.; Brandies, D. Detection of deep venous thrombosis by realtime B-mode ultrasonography. N Engl J Med 320:342–345, 1989.

193. Lensing, A.W.A.; Prins, M.H.; Davidson, B.L. Treatment of deep venous thrombosis with low-molecular-weight heparins. Arch Intern Med 155:601–607, 1995.

194. Levine, M.; Gent, M.; Hirsch, J.; et al. A comparison of low-molecular-weight heparin administered primarily at home with unfractionated heparin administered in the hospital for proximal deep vein thrombosis. N Engl J Med 334:677–681, 1996.

195. Levine, M.N.; Hirsh, J.; Carter, C.J.; et al. A randomized controlled trial of a low-molecular-weight heparin (enoxaparin) to prevent deep-vein thrombosis in patients undergoing elective hip surgery. N Engl J Med 315:925–929, 1986.

196. Levine, M.N.; Raskob, G.; Hirsch, J. Hemorrhagic complications of long-term anticoagulant therapy. American College of Chest Physicians and National Heart, Lung and Blood Institute National Conference on Antithrombotic Therapy. Chest 89:16–25, 1986.

197. Leyvraz, P.F.; Richard, J.; Bachmann, F.; et al. Adjusted versus fixed dose subcutaneous heparin in the prevention of deep-vein thrombosis after total hip replacement. N Engl J Med 309:954–958, 1983.

198. Lindmarker, P.; Holmstrom, M.; Granqvist, S.; et al. Comparison of once-daily subcutaneous Fragmin with continuous intravenous unfractionated heparin in the treatment of deep vein thrombosis. Thromb Haemost 72:186–190, 1994.

199. Litter, J. Thromboembolism: Its prophylaxis and medical treatment. Med Clin North Am 36:1309–1321, 1952.

200. Lohr, J.M.; Kerr, T.M.; Lutter, K.S.; et al. Lower extremity calf thrombosis: To treat or not to treat? J Vasc Surg 14:618–623, 1991.

201. Lotke, P.A.; Ecker, M.L; Alavi, A.; Berkowitz, H. Indications for the treatment of deep venous thrombosis following total knee replacement. J Bone Joint Surg Am 66:202–208, 1984.

202. Lynch, A.F.; Bourne, R.B.; Rorabeck, C.H.; et al. Deep-vein thrombosis and continuous passive motion after total knee arthroplasty. J Bone Joint Surg Am 70:11–14, 1988.

203. MacCouillard, G.; Castagnera, L.; Claverie, J.P.; et al. Prevention of thromboembolism after spinal cord injury using low-molecular-weight heparin. Abstract. J Trauma 35:327, 1993.

204. Mammen, E. Pathogenesis of venous thrombosis. Chest 102:641S, 1992.

205. Martin, J.G.; Marsh, J.L.; Kresowik, T. Phlegmasia cerulea dolens: A complication of use of a filter in the vena cava. J Bone Joint Surg Am 77:452–454, 1995.

206. Mattos, M.A.; Londrey, G.L.; Leutz, D.W.; et al. Color-flow duplex scanning for the surveillance and diagnosis of acute deep venous thrombosis. J Vasc Surg 15:366–375, 1992.

207. McNally, M.A.; Mollan, R.A.B. Venous thromboembolism and orthopedic surgery. J Bone Joint Surg Br 75:517–519, 1993.

208. Meissner, M.H.; Caps, M.T.; Bergelin, R.O.; et al. Propagation rethrombosis, and new thrombus formation after acute deep vein thrombosis. J Vasc Surg 22:558–567, 1995.

209. Meyer, C.S.; Blebea, J.; Davis, K., Jr.; et al. Surveillance venous scars for deep venous thrombosis in multiple trauma patients. Ann Vasc Surg 9:109–114, 1995.

210. Mills, S.R.; Jackson, D.C.; Older, R. The incidence, etiologies, and avoidance of complications of pulmonary angiography in a large series. Radiology 136:295–299, 1980.

211. Mitchell, D.C.; Grasty, M.S.; Stebbings, W.S.C.; et al. Comparison of duplex ultrasonography and venography in the diagnosis of deep venous thrombosis. Br J Surg 78:611–613, 1991.

212. Moreno-Cabral, R.; Kistner, R.L.; Nordyke, R.A. Importance of calf vein thrombophlebitis. Surgery 80:735–742, 1976.

213. Morris, G.K.; Mitchell, J.R.A. Warfarin sodium in prevention of deep venous thrombosis and pulmonary embolism in patients with fractured neck of femur. Lancet 2:869–872, 1976.

214. Morris, G.K.; Mitchell, J.R.A. Preventing venous thromboembolism in elderly patients with hip fractures: Studies of low-dose heparin, dipyridamole, aspirin and flurbiprofen. BMJ 1:535–537, 1977.

215. Moser, K.M.; LeMoine, F.R. Is embolic risk conditioned by location of deep venous thrombosis? Ann Intern Med 94:439–444, 1981.

216. Myhre, H.O.; Holen, A. Tromboseprofylakse: Dextran eller warfarinnatrium? Nord Med 82:1534–1538, 1969.

217. Myllynen, P.; Kammonen, M.; Pokkanen, P.; et al. Deep vein thrombosis and pulmonary embolism in patients with acute spinal cord injury. A comparison with nonparalyzed patients immobilized due to spinal fractures. J Trauma 25:541–543, 1985.

218. Nicolaides, A.N.; Fernandes, E.; Fernandes, J.; Pollock, A.V. Intermittent sequential pneumatic compression of the legs in the prevention of venous stasis and postoperative venous thrombosis. Surgery 87:69, 1980.

219. Nylander, G.; Semb, H. Veins of the lower part of the leg after tibial fracture. Surg Gynecol Obstet 134:974–976, 1972.

220. Ohlund, C.; Fransson, S.G.; Starck, S.A. Calf compression for prevention of thromboembolism following hip surgery. Acta Orthop Scand 54:896–899, 1983.

221. O'Malley, K.F.; Ross, S.E. Pulmonary embolism in major trauma patients. J Trauma 30:748–750, 1990.

222. Owings, J.; Bagley, M.; Gosselin, R.; et al. Effects of critical injury on antithrombin activity: Low antithrombin levels are associated with thromboembolic complications. J Trauma 41:396, 1996.

223. Paiement, G.D. Practice patterns in prophylaxis of deep vein thrombosis among U.S. orthopedic surgeons. Orthopedics 17(Suppl): 11–13, 1994.

224. Paiement, G.D.; Wessinger, S.J.; Harris, W.H. Cost effectiveness of prophylaxis in total hip replacement. Am J Surg 161:519–524, 1991.

225. Paiement, G.D.; Wessinger, S.J.; Hughes, R. Routine use of adjusted low dose warfarin to prevent venous thromboembolism after total hip replacement. J Bone Joint Surg Am 75:893–898, 1993.

226. Passman, M.A.; Moreta, G.L.; Taylor, L.M., Jr. Pulmonary embolism is associated with the combination of isolated calf vein thrombosis and respiratory symptoms. J Vasc Surg 25:39–45, 1997.

227. Phillips, W.A.; Schwartz, H.S.; Keller, C.S.; et al. A prospective, randomized study of the management of severe ankle fractures. J Bone Joint Surg Am 67:67–78, 1985.

228. Platz, A.; Hoffman, R.; Kohler, A.; et al. Thromboembolie prophylaxe bei Hüftfraktur: Unfraktioniertes heparin versus nied-

ermolekulares heparin. Z Unfallchir Vers Med Band 86:184–188, 1993.

229. Powers, L.R. Distal deep vein thrombosis: What's the best treatment? J Gen Intern Med 3:288–293, 1988.
230. Prandoni, P.; Lensing, A.W.A.; Buller, H.R.; et al. Deep vein thrombosis and the incidence of subsequent symptomatic cancer. N Engl J Med 327:1128–1133, 1993.
231. Prandoni, P.; Lensing, A.W.; Buller, H.R.; et al. Comparison of subcutaneous low-molecular-weight heparin with intravenous standard heparin in proximal deep vein thrombosis. Lancet 339:441–445, 1992.
232. Pulmonary Embolism Prevention (PEP) Trial Collaborative Group. Prevention of pulmonary embolism and deep vein thrombosis with low dose aspirin: Pulmonary Embolism Prevention (PEP) trial. Lancet 355:1295–1302, 2000.
233. Purtill, L.; Gens, D.R.; Joseph, L.A.; et al. Randomized prospective comparison of foot pumps versus calf pumps for DVT prophylaxis in trauma patients. Abstract. J Trauma 43:197, 1997.
234. Ramchandani, P.; Soulen, R.L.; Fedullo, L.M.; et al. Deep venous thrombosis: Significant limitations of noninvasive test. Radiology 156:47–49, 1985.
235. Research Committee of the British Thoracic Society. Optimal duration of anticoagulation for deep vein thrombosis and pulmonary embolism. Lancet 340:873–876, 1992.
236. Rogers, F.B. Venous thromboembolism in trauma patients. Surg Clin North Am 75(2):279–291, 1995.
237. Rogers, F.B.; Shackford, S.R.; Wilson, J.; et al. Prophylactic vena cava filter insertion in severely injured trauma patients: Indications and preliminary results. J Trauma 35:637–641, 1993.
238. Rose, S.D.; Zwiebel, W.J.; Nelson, B.D.; et al. Symptomatic lower extremity deep venous thrombosis: Accuracy, limitations, and role of color duplex flow imaging in diagnosis. Radiology 175:639–644, 1990.
239. Rosendaal, F.R. Venous thrombosis: A multicausal disease. Lancet 353:1167–1173, 1999.
240. Sagar, S.; Nairn, D.; Stamatakis, J.D.; et al. Efficacy of low-dose heparin in prevention of extensive deep-vein thrombosis in patients undergoing total hip replacement. Lancet 1:1151–1154, 1976.
241. Salzman, E.W.; Davies, G.C. Prophylaxis of venous thromboembolism: Analysis of cost effectiveness. Ann Surg 191:207–218, 1980.
242. Salzman, E.W. Venous thrombosis made easy. N Engl J Med 314:847–848, 1986.
243. Salzman, E.W.; Harris, W.H. Prevention of venous thromboembolism in orthopaedic patients. J Bone Joint Surg Am 58:903–913, 1976.
244. Sanson, B.J. Is there a role for thrombolytic therapy in venous thromboembolism? Haemostasis 29(Suppl 1):81–83, 1999.
245. Satiani, B.; Falcone, R.; Shook, L.; et al. Screening for major DVT in seriously injured patients: A prospective study. Ann Vasc Surg 11:626–629, 1997.
246. Schmidt, U.; Enderson, B.L.; Chen, J.P.; et al. D-dimer levels correlate with pathologic thrombosis in trauma patients. J Trauma 33:312–320, 1992.
247. Schulman, S.; Rhedin, A.S.; Lindmarker, P.; et al. A comparison of six weeks with six months of oral anticoagulant therapy after a first episode of venous thromboembolism. N Engl J Med 332:1661–1665, 1995.
248. Sevitt, S. Pathology and pathogenesis of deep vein thrombi in venous problems. In: Bergan, J.J.; Yao, J.S.T., eds. Venous Problems. Chicago, Year Book Medical, 1978, pp. 257–279.
249. Sevitt, S.; Gallagher, N. Venous thrombosis and pulmonary embolism: A clinico-pathological study in injured and burned patients. Br J Surg 48:475–489, 1961.
250. Shackford, S.R.; Davis, J.W.; Hollingsworth-Fridlund, P.; et al. Venous thromboembolism in patients with major trauma. Am J Surg 159:365–369, 1990.
251. Shackford, S.R.; Moser, K.M. Deep venous thrombosis and pulmonary embolism in trauma patients. J Intensive Care Med 3:87–98, 1988.
252. Sharrock, N.E.; Brien, W.W.; Salvati, E.A.; et al. The effect of intravenous fixed-dose heparin during total hip arthroplasty on the incidence of deep-vein thrombosis. J Bone Joint Surg Am 72:1456–1461, 1990.
253. Sigel, B.; Edelstein, A.L.; Savitch, L.; et al. Type of compression for reducing venous stasis. Arch Surg 110:171–175, 1975.

254. Sigel, B.; Felix, R.; Popky, G.L.; et al. Diagnosis of lower limb venous thrombosis by Doppler ultrasound technique. Arch Surg 104:174–179, 1972.
255. Simonneau, G.S.; Charbonnier, B.; Page, Y.; et al. A comparison of low-molecular-weight heparin with unfractionated heparin for acute pulmonary embolism. N Engl J Med 337:663–669, 1997.
256. Simonneau, G.; Charbonnier, B.; Decousus, H.; et al. Subcutaneous low-molecular-weight heparin compared with continuous intravenous unfractionated heparin in the treatment of proximal deep vein thrombosis. Arch Intern Med 153:1541–1546, 1993.
257. Smith, F.; Hall, R.; Raskob, G. Effectiveness of intermittent pneumatic compression for preventing deep venous thrombosis after total hip replacement. Presented at the Canadian Orthopedic Association's 44th Annual Meeting, Toronto, Canada, June 1989.
258. Solheim, K. Fractures of the lower leg: Immediate results of treatment in a series of 500 cases of fractures of the shafts of tibia and fibula treated with plaster, traction plaster and internal fixation, with and without exercise therapy. Acta Chir Scand 119:268–279, 1960.
259. Sors, H.; Meyer, G. Place of aspirin in prophylaxis of venous thromboembolism. Lancet 355:1288–1289, 2000.
260. Spain, D.A.; Richardson, J.D.; Polk, H.C., Jr.; et al. Venous thromboembolism in the high-risk trauma patient: Do risks justify aggressive screening and prophylaxis? J Trauma 42:463–469, 1997.
261. Spain, D.A.; Bergamini, T.M.; Hoffman, J.F.; et al. Comparison of sequential compression devices to foot pumps for prophylaxis of DVT in high-risk trauma patients. Am J Surg 64:522–526, 1998.
262. Spritzer, C.E.; Norconk, J.J.; Sostman, H.D.; et al. Detection of deep venous thrombosis by magnetic resonance imaging. Chest 104:54–60, 1993.
263. Stamatakis, J.D.; Kakkar, V.V.; Lawrence, D.; et al. Failure of aspirin to prevent postoperative deep vein thrombosis in patients undergoing total hip replacement. BMJ 1:1031, 1978.
264. Stephen, J.M.; Feied, C.F. Venous thrombosis: Lifting the clouds of misunderstanding. Postgrad Med 97:36–47, 1995.
265. Stranks, G.J.; MacKenzie, N.A.; Grover, M.L. The AV impulse system reduces deep vein thrombosis and swelling after hemiarthroplasty for hip fracture. J Bone Joint Surg Br 74:775–778, 1992.
266. Sullivan, E.D.; Peter, D.J.; Cranley, J.J. Real-time B-mode venous ultrasound. J Vasc Surg 1:465–471, 1984.
267. Tarney, T.J.; Rohr, P.R.; Davidson, A.G.; et al. Pneumatic calf compression, fibrinolysis and the prevention of DVT. Surg 88:489–494, 1980.
268. THRIFT (Thromboembolic Risk Factors Consensus Group). Risk of and prophylaxis for venous thromboembolism in hospital patients. BMJ 305:567–574, 1992.
269. UPET Investigators. The Urokinase Pulmonary Embolism Trial: A national cooperative study. Circulation 47(Suppl 2):1–108, 1973.
270. Van den Berg, E.; Walterbusch, G.; Gotzen, C.; et al. Ergotism leading to threatened limb amputation or to death in two patients given heparin DHE prophylaxis. Lancet 1:955–956, 1982.
271. Vaughn, B.K.; Knezevich, S.; Lombard, A.V., Jr.; et al. Use of the Greenfield filter to prevent fatal pulmonary embolism associated with total hip and knee arthroplasty. J Bone Joint Surg Am 71:1542–1547, 1989.
272. Velmahos, G.C.; Chan, L.S.; Oder, D.; et al. Prevention of venous thromboembolism after injury: An evidence-based report—Part II: Analysis of risk factors and evaluation of the role of vena cava filters. J Trauma 49:140–144, 2000.
273. Velmahos, G.C.; Nigro, J.; Tatevossian, R.; et al. Inability of an aggressive policy of thromboprophylaxis to prevent deep venous thrombosis in critically injured patients: Are current methods of DVT prophylaxis insufficient? J Am Coll Surg 187:529–533, 1998.
274. Virchow, R. Cellular Pathology. Translated by F. Chance. New York, R.M. de Witt, 1860.
275. Warkentin, T.E.; Levine, M.N.; Hirsh, J.; et al. Heparin-induced thrombocytopenia in patients treated with low molecular weight or unfractionated heparin. N Engl J Med 332:1330–1335, 1995.
276. Warwick, D.; Williams, M.H.; Bannister, G.C. Death and thromboembolic disease after total hip replacement: A series of 1162 cases with no routine chemical prophylaxis. J Bone Joint Surg Br 77:6–10, 1995.
277. Webb, L.X.; Rush, P.T.; Fuller, S.B.; Meredith, J.W. Greenfield filter prophylaxis of pulmonary embolism in patients undergoing surgery for acetabular fracture. J Orthop Trauma 6:139–145, 1992.

278. Wells, P.S.; Ginsberg, J.S.; Anderson, D.R.; et al. Use of a clinical model for safe management of patients with suspected pulmonary embolism. Ann Intern Med 129:997–1005, 1998.

279. Wheeler, H.B. Diagnosis of deep venous thrombosis: Review of clinical evaluation and impedance plethysmography. Am J Surg 150(4A):7–13, 1985.

280. Wheeler, H.B.; Anderson, F.A.; Cardullo, P.A.; et al. Suspected deep vein thrombosis. Arch Surg 117:1206–1209, 1982.

281. Wheeler, H.B.; Pearson, D.; O'Connell, D.; et al. Impedance phlebography: Technique, interpretation and results. Arch Surg 104:164–169, 1972.

282. White, R.H.; McGahan, J.P.; Daschbach, M.M.; et al. Diagnosis of deep vein thrombosis using duplex ultrasound. Ann Intern Med 111:297–304, 1989.

283. Wiley, A.M. Venous thrombosis in orthopaedic patients: An overview. Orthop Surg 2:388, 1979.

284. Woolson, S.T.; Watt, M. Intermittent pneumatic compression to prevent proximal deep venous thrombosis during and after total hip replacement. J Bone Joint Surg Am 73:507–512, 1991.

285. Wright, H.P.; Osborn, S.B.; Edmonds, D.G. Effects of postoperative bed rest and early ambulation on the rate of venous blood flow. Lancet 1:22–25, 1951.

286. Wright, H.P.; Osborn, S.B.; Hayden, M. Venous velocity in bedridden medical patients. Lancet 2:699–700, 1952.

Multiple System Organ Failure

287. Alexander, J.W.; McClellan, M.A.; Ogle, C.K.; Ogle, J.D. Consumptive opsoninopathy: Possible pathogenesis in lethal and opportunistic infection. Ann Surg 184:672–678, 1976.

288. Baker, S.P.; O'Neill, B.; Haddon, W., Jr.; Long, W.B. The Injury Severity Score. A method for describing patients with multiple injuries and evaluating emergency care. J Trauma 14:187–196, 1974.

289. Baracos, C.; Rodemann, P.; Dinarello, C.A.; Goldberg, A.L. Stimulation of muscle protein degradation and prostaglandin E_2 release by leukocytic pyrogen (interleukin-1). N Engl J Med 308:553–558, 1983.

290. Baue, A.E. Multiple, progressive, or sequential systems failure. Arch Surg 110:779–781, 1975.

291. Baue, A.E.; Chaudry, I.H. Prevention of multiple systems failure. Surg Clin North Am 6:1167–1178, 1980.

292. Baue, A.E.; Faist, E. Systemic inflammatory response syndrome (SIRS), multiple organ dysfunction syndrome (MODS), multiple organ failure (MOF): Are we winning the battle? Shock 10:79–89, 1998.

293. Beal, A.L.; Cerra, F.B. Multiple organ failure syndrome in the 1990s: Systemic inflammatory response and organ dysfunction. JAMA 271:226–233, 1994.

294. Bone, R.C.; Balk, R.A.; Cerra, F.C.; et al. Definitions for sepsis and organ failure and guidelines for the use of innovative therapies in sepsis. Chest 101:1644–1655, 1992.

295. Border, J.R.; Chenier, R.; McMenamy, R.H.; et al. Multiple systems organ failure: Muscle fuel deficit with visceral protein malnutrition. Surg Clin North Am 56:1147–1167, 1976.

296. Bosse, M.J.; Riemer, B.L.; Brumback, R.J.; et al. Adult respiratory distress syndrome, pneumonia and mortality following thoracic injury and a femoral fracture treated with intramedullary nailing with reaming or with a plate. J Bone Joint Surg Am 79:799–809, 1997.

297. Carlson, D.W.; Kaehr, D.; et al. Femur fractures in chest-injured patients: Is reaming contraindicated? J Orthop Trauma 12:164–168, 1998.

298. Carrico, C.J.; Meakins, J.L.; Marshall, J.C.; et al. Multiple organ failure syndrome. Arch Surg 121:196–208, 1986.

299. Cerra, F.B.; West, M.; Keller, G.; et al. Hypermetabolism/organ failure: The role of the activated macrophage as a metabolic regulator. Clin Biol Res 264:27–42, 1988.

300. Charash, W.E.; Croce, M.A. Delayed surgical fixation of femur fractures is a risk factor for pulmonary failure independent of thoracic trauma. J Trauma 37:667–672, 1994.

301. Clowes, G.H.A., Jr.; George, B.C.; Villee, C.A., Jr.; Saravis, C.A. Muscle proteolysis induced by a circulating peptide in patients with sepsis or trauma. N Engl J Med 308:545–552, 1983.

302. Committee on Medical Aspects of Automotive Safety. Rating the severity of tissue damage. I: The abbreviated scale. JAMA 215:277–280, 1971.

303. Deitch, E.A. Multiple organ failure: Pathophysiology and potential future therapy. Ann Surg 216:117–134, 1992.

304. Deitch, E.A.; Goodman, F.R. Prevention of multiple organ failure. Surg Clin North Am 79:1471–1488, 1998.

305. Demling, R. Wound inflammatory mediators and multisystem organ failure. Prog Clin Biol Res 236A:525–537, 1987.

306. Eisman, B.; Beart, R.; Norton, L. Multiple organ failure. Surg Gynecol Obstet 144:323–326, 1977.

307. Fry, D.E. Multiple system organ failure. Surg Clin North Am 68:107–122, 1988.

308. Fry, D.E.; Pearlstein, L.; Fulton, R.L.; Polk, H.C., Jr. Multiple system organ failure: The role of uncontrolled infection. Arch Surg 115:136–140, 1980.

309. Goris, R.J.A.; Boekholtz, W.F.; van Bebber, I.P.T.; et al. Multiple organ failure and sepsis without bacteria: An experimental model. Arch Surg 121:897–901, 1986.

310. Goris, R.J.A.; Boekholtz, T.P.A.; Nuytinek, J.K.S.; Gimbrere, J.S.F. Multiple organ failure: Generalized autodestructive inflammation? Arch Surg 120:1109–1115, 1985.

311. Goris, R.J.A.; Gimbrere, J.S.F.; van Niekerk, J.L.M.; et al. Early osteosynthesis and prophylactic mechanical ventilation in the multitrauma patient. J Trauma 22:895–903, 1982.

312. Goris, R.J.A.; Nuytinck, H.K.S.; Redl, H. Scoring system and predictors of ARDS and MOF. Prog Biol Res 236B:3–15, 1987.

313. Greenspan, L.; McLellan, B.A.; Greig, H. Abbreviated Injury Scale and Injury Severity Score: A scoring chart. J Trauma 25:60–64, 1985.

314. Hasselgren, P.O.; Pedersen, P.; Sax, H.C.; et al. Current concepts of protein turnover and amino acid transport in liver and skeletal muscle during sepsis. Arch Surg 123:992–999, 1988.

315. Hasselgren, P.O.; Talamini, M.; James, J.H.; Fischer, J.E. Protein metabolism in different types of skeletal muscle during early and late sepsis in rats. Arch Surg 121:918–923, 1986.

316. Heideman, M.; Hugli, T.E. Anaphylatoxin generation in multisystem organ failure. J Trauma 24:1038–1043, 1984.

317. Hershman, M.J.; Cheadle, W.G.; Kuftinec, D.; Polk, H.C., Jr. An outcome predictive score for sepsis and death following injury. Injury 19:263–266, 1988.

318. Hughes, J.L.; Sauer, B.W. Wagner apparatus: A portable traction device. In: Seligson, D.; Pope, M., eds. Concepts in External Fixation. New York, Grune & Stratton, 1982, pp. 203–217.

319. Janjua, K.J.; Sugrue, M.; Deanne, S.A. Prospective evaluation of early missed injuries and the role of tertiary trauma survey. J Trauma 44:1000–1007, 1998.

320. Johnson, K.D.; Cadambi, A.; Seibert, G.B. Incident of adult respiratory distress syndrome in patients with multiple musculoskeletal injuries: Effect of early operative stabilization of fractures. J Trauma 25:384–384, 1985.

321. Livingston, D.H.; Deitch, E.A. Multiple organ failure: A common problem in surgical intensive care unit patients. Ann Med 27:13–20, 1995.

322. McMenamy, R.H.; Birkhahn, R.; Oswald, G.; Reed, R. Multiple systems organ failure: 1. The basal state. J Trauma 21:99–114, 1981.

323. Malangoni, M.A.; Dillon, L.D.; Klamer, T.W.; Condon, R.E. Factors influencing the risk of early and late serious infection in adults after splenectomy for trauma. Surgery 96:775–784, 1984.

324. Meek, R.N.; Vivoda, E.; Crichton, A.; Pirani, S. Comparison of mortality with multiple injuries according to method of fracture treatment. Abstract. J Bone Joint Surg Br 63:456, 1981.

325. Michelsen, G.B.; Askanazi, J. The metabolic response to injury: Mechanisms and clinical implications. J Bone Joint Surg Am 68:782–787, 1986.

326. Moore, F.A.; Moore, E.E. Evolving concepts in the pathogenesis of post injury multiple organ failure. Surg Clin North Am 75:257–277, 1995.

327. Morgan, E.L.; Weigle, W.O.; Hugli, T.E. Anaphylatoxin-mediated regulation of the immune response. J Exp Med 155:1412–1426, 1982.

328. Nuytinek, J.K.S.; Goris, R.J.A.; Heinz, R.; et al. Post-traumatic complications and inflammatory mediators. Arch Surg 121:886–890, 1986.

329. Polk, H.C., Jr.; Shields, C.L. Remote organ failure: A valid sign of occult intra-abdominal infection. Surgery 81:310–313, 1977.
330. Reynolds, M.A.; Spain, D.A.; Seligson, D.; et al. Is the timing of fracture fixation important for the patient with multiple trauma. Ann Surg 222:470–481, 1995.
331. R'duedi, T.; Wolff, G. Vermeidung posttraumatischer Komplikationen durch fr'duhe definitive Versorgung von Polytraumatisierten mit Frakturen des Bewegungsapparats. Helv Chir Acta 42:507–512, 1975.
332. Schirmer, W.J.; Schirmer, J.M.; Townsend, M.C.; et al. Femur fracture with soft tissue injury in the rat is associated with relative hepatic ischemia: Possible role in organ failure. Presented at the Annual Meeting of the Association of VA Surgeons, Portland, Oregon, May 1987.
333. Seely, A.J. Multiple organ dysfunction syndrome: Exploring the paradigm of complex nonlinear systems. Crit Care Med 28:2193–2200, 2000.
334. Seibel, R.; LaDuca, J.; Hassett, J.M.; et al. Blunt multiple trauma (ISS 36), femur traction, and the pulmonary failure septic state. Ann Surg 202:283–293, 1985.
335. Strecker, W.; Gebhard, F.; Rajer, J.; et al. Early biomedical characterization of soft-tissue trauma and fracture trauma. J Trauma 47:358–364, 1999.
336. Townsend, R.H.; Protech, J.; et al. Timing fracture repair in patients with severe brain injury (Glasgow Coma Scale <9). J Trauma 44:977–982, 1998.
337. Tscherne, H.A. Keynote Address. Orthopedic Trauma Association Annual Meeting, Dallas, Texas, October 1988.
338. Velmahos, G.C.; Ramicone, E.; et al. Timing of fracture fixation in blunt trauma patients with severe head injuries. Am J Surg 176:324–329, 1998.
339. Zallen, G.; Offner, P.J.; Moore, E.E.; et al. Age of transfused blood is an independent risk factor for postinjury multiple organ failure. Am J Surg 178:570–572, 1999.

Soft Tissue and Local Complications of Fracture Problems, Post-traumatic Arthrosis, Peripheral Nerve Injuries, and Reflex Sympathetic Dystrophy

340. Allen, G.; Galer, B.S.; Schwartz, L. Epidemiology of complex regional pain syndrome: A retrospective chart review of 134 patients. Pain 80:539–544, 1999.
341. Amadio, P.C. Current concepts review: Pain dysfunction syndromes. J Bone Joint Surg Am 70:944–949, 1988.
342. Baker, S.P.; O'Neill, B.; Haddon, W., Jr.; et al. The injury severity score: A method for describing patients with multiple injuries and evaluating emergency care. J Trauma 14:187–196, 1974.
343. Barton, N.J. Radial nerve lesions. Hand 3:200–208, 1973.
344. Bickerstaff, D.R.; Kanis, J.A. Algodystrophy: An under-recognized complication of minor trauma. Br J Rheumatol 33:240–248, 1994.
345. Bodine, S.C.; Lieber, R.L. Peripheral nerve physiology, anatomy, and pathology In: Simon, S.R., ed. Orthopaedic Basic Science. Rosemont, IL, AAOS, 1994, pp. 325–396.
346. Bonica, J.J. Causalgia and other reflex sympathetic dystrophies. In: Bonica, J.J., ed. The Management of Pain, 2nd ed. Philadelphia, Lea & Febiger, 1990, pp. 221–222.
347. Bonica, J.J. Causalgia and other sympathetic dystrophies. In: Bonica, J.J.; et al., eds. Advances in Pain Research and Therapy. New York, Raven Press 1979, pp. 141–166.
348. Bonsell, S.; Pearsall, A.W., IV; Heitman, R.J.; et al. The relationship of age, gender, and degenerative changes observed on radiographs of the shoulder in asymptomatic individuals. J Bone Joint Surg Br 82:1135–1139, 2000.
349. Breivik, H. Chronic pain and the sympathetic nervous system. Acta Anesthesiologica Scand 1:131–134, 1997.
350. Brittberg, M.; Lindahl, A.; Nilsson, A.; et al. Treatment of deep cartilage defects in the knee with autologous chondrocyte transplantation. N Engl J Med 331:889–895, 1994.
351. Bruehl, S.; Carlson, C.R. Predisposing psychological factors in the development of reflex sympathetic dystrophy: A review of the empirical evidence. Clin J Pain 8:287–299, 1992.
352. Byer, B.F. Management of humeral shaft fractures. Arch Surg 81:914, 1960.

353. Chan, C.S.; Chow, S.P. Electroacupuncture in the treatment of post-traumatic sympathetic dystrophy (Sudeck's atrophy). Br J Anaesth 53:899–901, 1981.
354. Chervu, A.; Quinones-Baldrich, W.J. Vascular complications in orthopaedic surgery. Clin Orthop 235:275–288, 1988.
355. Cheshire W.P.; Snyder C.R. Treatment of reflex sympathetic dystrophy with topical capsaicin: Case report. Pain 42:307–311, 1990.
356. Conway R.R.; Hubbell, S.L. Electromyographic abnormalities in neurologic injury associated with pelvic fracture: Case reports and literature review. Arch Phys Med Rehab 69:539–541, 1988.
357. Cooke, T.D.V.; Pichora, D.; Siu, D.; et al. Surgical contributions of varus deformity of the knee with obliquity of joint surfaces. J Bone Joint Surg Br 71:560–565, 1989.
358. Cooke, T.D.V.; Siu, D.; Fisher, B. The use of standardized radiographs to identify the deformities associated with osteoarthritis. In: Noble, J.; Galasko, C.S.B., eds. Recent Developments in Orthopaedic Surgery. Manchester, Manchester University Press, 1987, pp. 264–273.
359. Cooper, D.E.; DeLee, J.G. Reflex sympathetic dystrophy of the knee. J Am Acad Orthop Surg 2:79–86, 1994.
360. Cooper, D.E.; DeLee, J.C.; Ramamurthy, S. Reflex sympathetic dystrophy of the knee: Treatment using continuous epidural anesthesia. J Bone Joint Surg Am 71:365–369, 1989.
361. Dekel, S.; Weissmann, S.L. Joint changes after overuse and peak overloading of rabbit knees in vivo. Acta Orthop Scand 49:519, 1978.
362. Donohue, J.M.; Buss, D.; Oegema, T.R.; Thompson, C. The effects of indirect blunt trauma on adult canine articular cartilage. J Bone Joint Surg Am 65:948–957, 1983.
363. Elgazzar, A.H.; Abdel-Dayem, H.M.; Clark, J.D. Multimodality imaging of osteomyelitis. Eur J Nucl Med 22:1043–1063, 1995.
364. Fahr, L.M.; Sauser, D.D. Imaging of peripheral nerve lesions. Orthop Clin North Am 19:27–41, 1988.
365. Fairbanks, T.J. Knee joint changes after meniscectomy. J Bone Joint Surg Br 30:665–670, 1948.
366. Flint, L.M.; Richardson, J.D. Arterial injuries with lower extremity fracture. Surgery 93:5–8, 1983.
367. Foy, M.A.; Fagg, P.S. Medicolegal Reporting in Orthopaedic Trauma. New York, Churchill Livingstone, 1996, pp. 2.1-01–4.1-16.
368. Garcia, A; Meach, B.H. Radial nerve injuries in fractures of the shaft of humerus. Am J Surg 99:625, 1960.
369. Geertzen, J.H.B.; Dijkstra, P.U.; Groothoff, J.W.; et al. Reflex sympathetic dystrophy of the upper extremity: A 5.5-year follow-up. Acta Orthop Scand (suppl 279) 69:12–18, 1998.
370. Gelber, A.C.; Hochberg, M.C.; Mead, L.A.; et al. Joint injury in young adults and risk for subsequent knee and hip osteoarthritis. Ann Intern Med 133:321–328, 2000.
371. Genant, H.; Kozin, F; Bekerman, C.; et al. The reflex sympathetic dystrophy syndrome. Radiology 117:21–32, 1975.
372. Ghivizzanni, S.C.; Oligino, T.J.; Robbins, P.D.; Evans, C.H. Cartilage injury and repair. Physical Med Rehab Clin North Am 1:289–307, 2000.
373. Ghostine, S.Y.; Comair, Y.G.; Turner, D.M.; et al. Phenoxybenzamine in the treatment of causalgia: Report of 40 cases. J Neurosurg 60:1263–1268, 1984.
374. Goodall, R.J. Nerve injuries in fresh fractures. Tex Med 52:93–94, 1956.
375. Goodship, A.E.; Lanyon, L.E.; McFie, H. Functional adaptation of bone to increased stress. J Bone Joint Surg Am 61:539–546, 1979.
376. Gulevich, S.J.; Conwell, T.D.; Lane, J.; et al. Stress infrared telethermography is useful in the diagnosis of complex regional pain syndrome, type I (formerly reflex sympathetic dystrophy). Clin J Pain 13:50–59, 1997.
377. Gurdjian, E.S.; Smathers, H.M. Peripheral nerve injury in fractures and dislocations of long bone. J Neurosurg 2:202–211, 1945.
378. Hardin, W.D.; O'Connell, R.C.; Adinolfi, M.F.; Kerstein, M.D. Traumatic arterial injuries of the upper extremity: Determinants of disability. Am J Surg 150:226–270, 1985.
379. Helfet, D.L.; Anand, N.; Malkani, A.L.; et al. Intraoperative monitoring of motor pathways during operative fixation of acute acetabular fractures. J Orthop Trauma 11:2–6, 1997.
380. Helfet, D.L.; Hissa, E.A.; Sergay, S.; Mast, J.W. Somatosensory evoked potential monitoring in the surgical treatment of acute acetabular fractures. J Orthop Trauma 5:161–166, 1991.

381. Hermann, L.G.; Reineke, H.G.; Caldwell, J.A. Post-traumatic painful osteoporosis: A clinical and roentgenological entity. Am J Radiol 47:353–361, 1942.
382. Hill, S.D.; Lin, M.S.; Chandler, P.J. Reflex sympathetic dystrophy and electroacupuncture. Tex Med 87:76–81, 1991.
383. Hollister, L. Tricyclic antidepressants. N Engl J Med 299:1106–1109, 1978.
384. Ide, J.; Yamaga, T.; Kitamura, T.; Takagi, K. Quantitative evaluation of sympathetic nervous system dysfunction in patients with reflex sympathetic dystrophy. J Hand Surg Br 22:102–106, 1997.
385. Janig, W.; Stanton-Hicks, M., eds. Reflex sympathetic dystrophy: A reappraisal. Progress in pain research and management. Seattle, IASP Press, 1996, p. 6.
386. Johansson, O. Complications and failures of surgery in various fractures of the humerus. Acta Chir Scand 120:469, 1961.
387. Kaslo, E.; Perttunen, K.; Kaasinen, S. Pain after thoracic surgery. Acta Anaesthesiol Scand 36:96–100, 1992.
388. Kemler, M.A.; Barendse, G.A.M.; Van Kleef, M.; et al. Electrical spinal cord stimulation in reflex sympathetic dystrophy: Retrospective analysis of 23 patients. J Neurosurg 90:79–83, 1999.
389. Kern, D.; Zlatkin, M.B.; Dalinka, M.K. Occupational and post-traumatic arthritis. Radiol Clin North Am 26:1349–1358, 1998.
390. Kettlekamp, D.B.; Hillberry, B.M.; Murrish, D.E.; Heck, D.A. Degenerative arthritis of the knee secondary to fracture malunion. Clin Orthop Rel Res 234:159–169, 1988.
391. Kettlekamp, D.B.; Alexander, H. Clinical review of radial nerve injury. J Trauma 7:424–432, 1967.
392. Kleiman A. Evidence of the existence of crossed sensory sympathetic fibers. Am J Surg 87:839–841, 1954.
393. Kleinert, H.E.; Cole, N.M.; Wayne, L.; et al. Post-traumatic sympathetic dystrophy. Orthop Clin North Am 4:917–927, 1973.
394. Klenermann, L. Fractures of the shaft of the humerus. J Bone Joint Surg Br 48:105, 1966.
395. Kotani, N.; Kushikata, T.; Hashimoto, H.; et al. Intrathecal methylprednisolone for intractable postherpetic neuralgia. N Engl J Med 343:1514–1519, 2000.
396. Koval, K.J.; Clapper, M.F.; Brumback, R.J.; et al. Complications of reamed intramedullary nailing of the tibia. J Orthop Trauma 5:184–189, 1991.
397. Kozin, F.; Ryan, L.M.; Carrera, G.F.; et al. The reflex sympathetic dystrophy syndrome (RSDS): III. Scintigraphic studies, further evidence for the therapeutic efficacy of systemic corticosteroids, and proposed diagnostic criteria. Am J Med 70:23–30, 1981.
398. Kristensen, K.D.; Kiaer, T.; Blicher, J. No arthrosis of the ankle 20 years after malaligned tibial-shaft fracture. Acta Orthop Scand 60:208–209, 1989.
399. Kuhn, W.F.; Lacefield, P.K. Patient, surgeon, nurse: The psychological impact of fracture treatment. In: Seligson, D., ed. Concepts in Intramedullary Nailing. New York, Grune & Stratton, 1985, pp. 187–197.
400. Lankford, L.L.; Thompson, J.E. Reflex sympathetic dystrophy, upper and lower extremity: Diagnosis and management. Instr Course Lect 26:163–178, 1977.
401. Laskin, R. Rheumatologic and degenerative disorders of the knee. In: Dee, R., ed. Principles of Orthopaedic Practice. New York, McGraw-Hill, 1989, p. 1371.
402. Lee, S.K.; Wolfe, S.W. Peripheral nerve injury and repair. J Am Acad Orthop Surg 8:243–252, 2000.
403. Lewis, D.; Miller, E.M. Peripheral nerve injuries associated with fractures. Ann Surg 76:528–538, 1922.
404. Lindenfeld, T.N.; Bach, B.R.; Wojtys, E.M. Reflex sympathetic dystrophy and pain dysfunction in the lower extremity. J Bone Joint Surg Am 78:1936–1944, 1996.
405. Luce, E.A.; Griffin, W.O. Shotgun injuries of the upper extremity. J Trauma 18:487–492, 1978.
406. Malik, V.K.; Inchiosa, M.A.; Mustafa, K.; et al. Intravenous regional phenoxybenzamine in the treatment of reflex sympathetic dystrophy. Anesthesiology 88:823–827, 1998.
407. Mankin, H.J. The response of articular cartilage to mechanical injury. J Bone Joint Surg Am 64:460, 1982.
408. Mann, R.J.; Neal, E.G. Fractures of the shaft of the humerus in adults. South Med J 58:264, 1965.
409. Mast, J.W.; Spiegel, P.G.; Harvey, J.P., Jr.; Harrison, C. Fractures of the humeral shaft—A retrospective study of 240 adult fractures. Clin Orthop 118:254, 1975.
410. Matta, J.M. Fractures of the acetabulum: Accuracy of reduction and clinical results in patients managed operatively within three weeks after injury. J Bone Joint Surg Am 78:1632–1645, 1996.
411. Mears, D.C.; Velyvius, J.H. Primary total hip arthroplasty after acetabular fracture. J Bone Joint Surg Am 82:1328–1353, 2000.
412. Mellick, G.A.; Mellick, L.B. Reflex sympathetic dystrophy treated with gabapentin. Arch Phys Med Rehabilit 78:98–105, 1997.
413. Melzack, R.; Wall, P.D. Pain mechanisms: A new theory. Science 150:971–978, 1965.
414. Merchant, T.C.; Dietz, F.D. Long-term follow-up after fractures of the tibial and fibular shafts. J Bone Joint Surg Am 71:599–606, 1989.
415. Merskey, H.; Bogduk, N., eds. Classification of chronic pain. Seattle, IASP Press, 1994, pp. 40–44.
416. Middlebrooks, E.S.; Sims, S.H.; Kellam, J.F.; Bosse, M.J. Incidence of sciatic nerve monitoring in operatively treated acetabular fractures without somatosensory evoked potential monitoring. J Orthop Trauma 11:327–329, 1997.
417. Miller, M.D.; Osborne, J.R.; Gordon, W.T.; et al. The natural history of bone brusies. A prospective study of magnetic resonance imaging-detected trabecular microfractures in patients with isolated medial collateral ligament injuries. Am J Sports Med 26:15–19, 1998.
417a. Moskowitz, R.W.; Howell, D.S.; Goldberg, V.M.; Mankin, H.G. Osteoarthritis Diagnosis and Management. Philadelphia, W.B. Saunders, 1984.
418. Muizelaar, J.P.; Kleyer, M.; Hertogs, I.A.M.; DeLange, D.C. Complex regional pain syndrome (reflex sympathetic dystrophy and causalgia): Management with the calcium channel blocker nifedipine and/or the alpha-sympathetic blocker phenoxybenzamine in 59 patients. Clin Neurol Neurosurg 99:26–30, 1997.
419. Nitz, A.L.; Dobner, J.J.; Kensey, D. Nerve injury and grades II and II ankle sprains. Am J Sports Med 13:177–182, 1985.
420. Oerlemans, H.M.; Oostendorp, R.A.B.; de Boo, T.; et al. Adjuvant physical therapy versus occupational therapy in patients with reflex sympathetic dystrophy/complex regional pain syndrome type I. Arch Phys Med Rehabil 81:49–56, 2000.
421. Oerlemans, H.M.; Goris, R.J.A.; de Boo, T.; Oostendorp, R.A.B. Do physical therapy and occupational therapy reduce the impairment percentage in reflex sympathetic dystrophy? Am J Phys Med Rehabil 78:533–539, 1999.
422. Oerlemans, H.M.; Oostendorp, R.A.B.; de Boo, T.; et al. Signs and symptoms in complex regional pain syndrome type I/reflex sympathetic dystrophy: Judgment of the physician versus objective measurement. Clin J Pain 15:224–232, 1999.
423. Omer, G.E., Jr. Peripheral nerve injuries and gunshot wounds. In: Omer, G.E., Jr.; Spinner, M.; Van Beek, A.L., eds. Management of Peripheral Nerve Problems. Philadelphia, W.B. Saunders, 1998, pp. 398–405.
424. Omer, G.E., Jr. The prognosis for untreated traumatic injuries. In: Omer, G.E., Jr.; Spinner, M.; Van Beek, A.L., eds. Management of Peripheral Nerve Problems. Philadelphia, W.B. Saunders, 1998, pp. 365–370.
425. Omer, G.E., Jr. Peripheral nerve injuries: 45-year odyssey . . . and the quest continues. In: Omer, G.E., Jr.; Spinner, M.; Van Beek, A.L.; eds. Management of Peripheral Nerve Problems. Philadelphia, W.B. Saunders, 1998, pp. 3–6.
426. Omer, G.E., Jr. Results of untreated peripheral nerve injuries. Clin Orthop Rel Res. 163:15–19, 1982.
427. Omer, G.E., Jr. Injuries to nerves of the upper extremity. J Bone Joint Surg Am 56:1615–1624, 1974.
428. Otake, T.; Ieshima, H.; Ishida, H.; et al. Bone atrophy in complex regional pain syndrome patients measured by microdensitometry. Can J Anesth 45:831–838, 1998.
429. Paley, D.; Tetsworth, K. Mechanical axis deviation of the lower limbs: Preoperative planning of uniapical angulation deformities of the tibia or femur. Clin Orthop 280:48–64, 1992.
430. Paley, D.; Tetsworth, K. Mechanical axis deviation of the lower limbs: Preoperative planning of uniapical angulation deformities of the tibia or femur. Clin Orthop 280:65–71, 1992.
431. Pennsylvania Orthopedic Society, Scientific Research Committee. Fresh mid-shaft fractures of the humerus in adults: Evaluation of treatment in Pennsylvania during 1951–56. Penn Med J 62:848, 1959.
432. Poehling, G.C.; Pollock, F.E., Jr.; Koman, L.A. Reflex sympathetic

dystrophy of the knee after sensory nerve injury. Arthroscopy 4:31–35, 1988.

433. Pollock, F.H.; Drake, D.; Bovill, E.G.; et al. Treatment of radial neuropathy associated with fractures of the humerus. J Bone Joint Surg Am 63:239–243, 1981.

434. Poplawski, Z.J.; Wiley, A.M.; Murray, J.F. Posttraumatic dystrophy of the extremities. J Bone Joint Surg Am 65:642–655, 1983.

435. Prough D.S.; McLeskey, C.H.; Weeks, D.B.; et al. Efficacy of oral nifedipine in the treatment of reflex sympathetic dystrophy. Anesthesiology 61:3A, 1984.

436. Puno, R.M.; Vaughan, J.J.; Stetten, M.L.; Johnson, J.R. Long-term effects of tibial angular malunion on the knee and ankle joints. J Orthop Trauma 5:247–254, 1991.

437. Radin, E.L.; Ehrlich, M.G.; Chernack, R.; et al. Effect of repetitive impulsive loading on the knee joints of rabbits. Clin Orthop 131:288, 1978.

438. Radin, E.L. Factors influencing the progression of osteoarthrosis. In: Ewing, J., ed. Articular Cartilage and Knee Joint Function: Basic Science and Arthroscopy. New York, Raven Press, 1990, p. 301.

439. Raj, P.P.; Cannella, J.; Kelly, J.; et al. Management protocol of reflex sympathetic dystrophy. In: Stanton-Hicks, M.; Janig, W., eds. Reflex Sympathetic Dystrophy. Boston, Kluwer Academic Publications, 1989.

440. Raj, P.P.; Calodney, A. Complex regional pain syndrome (reflex sympathetic dystrophy) In: Browner, B.; Jupiter, J; Levine, A.; Trafton, P.; eds. Skeletal Trauma, 2nd ed. Philadelphia, W.B. Saunders, 1998, pp. 589–617.

441. Ramamurthy, S. Electroacupuncture's role in the management of reflex sympathetic dystrophy. Tex Med 87:82, 1991.

442. Repo, R.U.; Finlat, J.B. Survival of articular cartilage after controlled impact. J Bone Joint Surg Am 59:1068–1076, 1977.

443. Rothberg, J.M.; Tahmoush, A.J.; Oldakowski, R. The epidemiology of casualgia among soldiers wounded in Vietnam. Milit Med 148:347, 1983.

444. Rubin, C.T.; Lanyon, L.E. Regulation of bone formation by applied dynamic loads. J Bone Joint Surg Am 66:397–402, 1984.

445. Sadler, C. Pitfalls in the use of clinical algorithms. Orthop Clin North Am 17:545–547, 1986.

446. Sandroni, P; Low, P.A.; Ferrer, T.; et al. Complex regional pain syndrome I (CRPS I): Prospective study and laboratory evaluation. Clin J Pain 14:282–289, 1998.

447. Sarangi, P.P.; Ward, A.J.; Smith, E.J.; et al. Algodystrophy and osteoporosis after tibial fractures. J Bone Joint Surg Br 75:450–452, 1993.

448. Schurmann, M.; Gradl, G.; Andress, H.J.; et al. Assessment of peripheral sympathetic nervous function for diagnosing early post-traumatic complex regional pain syndrome type I. Pain 80:149–159, 1999.

449. Schutzer, S.F.; Gossling, H.R. The treatment of reflex sympathetic dystrophy. J Bone Joint Surg Am 66:625–629, 1984.

450. Seddon, H.J. Nerve lesions complicating certain closed bone injuries. JAMA 135:691–694, 1947.

451. Seddon, H.J. Three types of nerve injuries. Brain 66:238–288, 1943.

452. Seiller, J.G.; Richardson, J.D. Amputation after extremity injury. Am J Surg 152:260–264, 1986.

453. Shah, J.J.; Bhatti, N.A. Radial nerve paralysis associated with fractures of the humerus. Clin Orthop Rel Res 172:171–176, 1983.

454. Sieweke, N.; Birklein, F.; Riedl, B.; et al. Patterns of hyperalgesia in complex regional pain syndrome. Pain 80:171–177, 1999.

455. Sonneveld, G.J.; Patka, P.; van Mourik, J.C.; Broere, G. Treatment of fractures of the shaft of the humerus accompanied by paralysis of the radial nerve. Injury 1:404–406, 1987.

456. Spindler, K.P.; Schils, J.P.; Bergfeld, J.A.; et al. Prospective study of osseous, articular, and meniscal lesions in recent anterior cruciate ligament tears by magnetic resonance imaging and arthroscopy. Am J Sports Med 21:551–557, 1993.

457. Spinner, M. Peripheral nerve problems—Past, present, and future. In: Omer, G.E., Jr.; Spinner, M.; Van Beek, A.L., eds. Management of Peripheral Nerve Problems. Philadelphia, W.B. Saunders, 1998, p. 7.

458. Stanton-Hicks, M.; Baron, R.; Boas, R.; et al. Complex regional pain syndrome: Guidelines for therapy. Clin J Pain 14:155–166, 1998.

459. Stanton-Hicks, M.; Janig, W.; Hassenbusch, S.; et al. Reflex sympathetic dystrophy: Changing concepts and taxonomy. Pain 63:127–133, 1995.

460. Steadman, J.R.; Rodkey, W.G.; Singleton, S.B.; Briggs, K.K. Microfracture technique for full-thickness chondral defects: Technique and clinical results. Oper Tech Orthop 7:300–304, 1997.

461. Sunderland, S. A classification of peripheral nerve injuries producing loss of function. Brain 74:491–516, 1951.

462. Swenson, M.R.; Villasana, D.R. Neurologic evaluation of the upper extremity. In: Kasdan, M.L., ed. Occupational Hand and Upper Extremity Injuries and Diseases. Philadelphia, Hanley & Belfus, 1991, pp. 115–130.

463. Swiontkowski, M.F. The multiply injured patient with musculoskeletal injuries. In: Rockwood, C.A., Jr.; Green, D.P.; Bucholz, R.W.; et al., eds. Fractures in Adults, 4th ed. Philadelphia, Lippincott-Raven, 1996, p. 121.

464. Tetsworth, K.; Paley, D. Malalignment and degenerative arthropathy. Orthop Clin North Am 25:367–377, 1994.

465. Thompson, R.C.; Oegema, T.R.; Lewis, J.L.; Wallace, L. Osteoarthrotic changes after acute transarticular load: an animal model. J Bone Joint Surg Am 73:990–1001, 1991.

466. Veldman, P.H.; Reynen, H.M.; Arntz, I.E.; Goris, R.J. Signs and symptoms of reflex sympathetic dystrophy: Prospective study of 829 patients. Lancet 342:1012–1016, 1993.

467. Volpin, G.; Dowd, G.S.E.; Stein, H.; Bentley, G. Degenerative arthritis after intra-articular fractures of the knee. Long-term results. J Bone Joint Surg Br 72:634–638, 1990.

468. Vrahas, M.S.; Smith, G.A.; Rosler, D.M.; Baratta, R.V. Method to impact in vivo femoral rabbit cartilage with blows of quantifiable stress. J Orthop Res 15:314–317, 1997.

469. Walker, J.M. Pathomechanics and classification of cartilage lesions, facilitation of repair. J Orthop Sports Phys Ther 28:216, 1998.

470. Ward, W.W. Posttraumatic reflex sympathetic dystrophy. In: Foy, M.A.; Fagg, P.S., eds. Medicolegal Reporting in Orthopaedic Trauma. New York, Churchill Livingstone, 1995, pp. 5.5-05–5.5-08.

471. Wiesel, S.W.; Michelson, L.D. Monitoring orthopedic patients using computerized algorithms. Orthop Clin North Am 17:541–544, 1986.

472. Williams, J.; Gibbons, M.; Trundle, H.; et al. Complications of nailing in closed tibial fractures. J Orthop Trauma 9:476–481, 1995.

473. Wilson, P. Sympathetically maintained pain. In: Stanton-Hicks, M., ed. Sympathetic Pain. Boston, Kluwer Academic Publishers, 1989.

474. Wright, R.W.; Phaneuf, M.A.; Limbird, T.J.; Spindler, K.P. Clinical outcome of isolated subcortical trabecular fractures (bone bruise) detected on magnetic resonance imaging in knees. Am J Sports Med 28:663–667, 2000.

475. Wright, V. Posttraumatic osteoarthritis—A medico-legal minefield. Br J Rheumatol 29:474–478, 1990.

476. Zyluk, A. The usefulness of quantitative evaluation of three-phase scintigraphy in the diagnosis of post-traumatic reflex sympathetic dystrophy. J Hand Surg [Br] 24:16–21, 1999.

477. Zyluk, A.; Birkenfeld, B. Quantitative evaluation of three-phase scintigraphy before and after treatment of post-traumatic reflex sympathetic dystrophy. Nuc Med Comm 20:327–333, 1999.

478. Zyluk, A. The natural history of post-traumatic reflex sympathetic dystrophy. J Hand Surg [Br] 23:20–23, 1998.

Management of Complications

479. Anderson, S.; Biros, M.H.; Reardon, R.F. Delayed diagnosis of thoracolumbar fractures in multiple-trauma patients. Acad Emerg Med 3:832–839, 1996.

480. Born, C.T.; Ross, S.E.; Iannacone, W.M.; et al. Delayed identification of skeletal injury in multisystem trauma: The "missed" fracture. 29:1643–1646, 1989.

481. Brennan, T.; Sox, C.M.; Burstin, H.R. Relationship between negligent adverse events and the outcome of medical-malpractice litigation. N Engl J Med 335:1963–1967, 1996.

482. Buduhan, G.; McRitchie, D.I. Missed injuries in patients with multiple trauma. J Trauma 49:600–605, 2000.

483. Enderson, B.L.; Reath, D.B.; Meadors, J.; et al. The tertiary trauma survey: A prospective study of missed injury. J Trauma 30:666–669, 1990.

484. Goodship, A.E.; Lanyon, L.E.; McFie, H. Functional adaptation of bone to increased stress. J Bone Joint Surg Am 61:539–546, 1979.

485. Krueger, M.A.; Green, D.A.; Hoyt, D.; Garfin, S.R. Overlooked spine injuries associated with lumbar transverse process fractures. Clin Orthop Rel Res 327:191–195, 1996.

486. Kuhn, W.F.; Lacefield, P.K. Patient, surgeon, nurse: The psychological impact of fracture treatment. In: Seligson, D., ed. Concepts in Intramedullary Nailing. New York, Grune & Stratton, 1985, pp. 187–197.

487. Laaasonen, E.M.; Kivioj, A. Delayed diagnosis of extremity injuries in patients with multiple injuries. J Trauma 31:257–260, 1991.

488. Rogal, M.J. Comment: Orthopaedic malpractice—Identifying and managing the high risk of orthopaedic surgery. Pitt Orthop J 11:242–243, 2000.

489. Rubin, C.T.; Lanyon, L.E. Regulation of bone formation by applied dynamic loads. J Bone Joint Surg Am 66:397–402, 1984.

490. Sadler, C. Pitfalls in the use of clinical algorithms. Orthop Clin North Am 17:545–547, 1986.

491. Ward, W.G.; Nunley, J.A. Occult orthopaedic trauma in the multiply injured patient. J Orthop Trauma 5:308–312, 1991.

492. Wiesel, S.W.; Michelson, L.D. Monitoring orthopedic patients using computerized algorithms. Orthop Clin North Am 17:541–544, 1986.

CHAPTER 19

Chronic Osteomyelitis

Craig M. Rodner, M.D.
Bruce D. Browner, M.D., F.A.C.S.
Ed Pesanti, M.D., F.A.C.P.

In adults, bone infections are most commonly seen after direct skeletal trauma or after operative treatment of bone. These infections, usually referred to as post-traumatic, exogenous, or chronic osteomyelitis, are difficult to treat and usually have a protracted clinical course. Surgical débridement constitutes the cornerstone of management with antibiotic therapy playing only an adjunctive role.

TERMINOLOGY

Before embarking on a review of chronic osteomyelitis, it may be wise to begin with a few basic definitions.

The term *osteomyelitis* simply refers to an infection in bone. Such infections are most often caused by pyogenic bacteria (such as *Staphylococcus aureus*), although other microbes, including mycobacteria and fungi, are sometimes responsible. In *hematogenous osteomyelitis,* which most frequently affects children, blood-borne bacteria seed previously healthy bone. In *post-traumatic* or *exogenous osteomyelitis,* the infection is almost always associated with trauma, whether it be of the unplanned variety (i.e., a motor vehicle accident) or the planned (i.e., a surgical procedure). The term *acute osteomyelitis* is often used interchangeably with the term hematogenous osteomyelitis; in current usage, both terms reflect a form of osteomyelitis in which osteonecrosis has not yet occurred. On the other end of the spectrum, the term *chronic osteomyelitis* is defined as a bone infection predicated on preexisting osteonecrosis. Note that the difference between *acute* and *chronic* osteomyelitis is not based on the duration of infection, as their names might suggest, but rather on the absence or presence of dead bone. It is precisely the presence of dead bone that makes chronic osteomyelitis a primarily surgical disease.

Although theoretically chronic osteomyelitis can result from an untreated or inadequately treated hematogenous infection, it is most frequently traumatic in origin. It is important to recognize that infection occurring in the setting of skeletal trauma, however *acutely* chronologically, is in fact a *chronic* osteomyelitis from the start. In the post-traumatic milieu, opportunistic bacteria can be thought of as "taking advantage" of bone that has been devitalized by injury (quite the opposite from acute osteomyelitis, wherein microbes seed previously healthy bone). Because of the high congruence between osteonecrosis and a history of trauma, the terms *chronic* and *post-traumatic* or *exogenous* osteomyelitis are frequently used interchangeably. This is reasonable as long as one understands the subtle differences among them.

EPIDEMIOLOGY

Bone infection in the adult population is much more likely to be exogenous in origin than hematogenous, in part because of the demographics of high-speed motor vehicle accidents and orthopaedic surgery but also because the predilection for bacterial seeding of bone ceases with closure of the epiphyses. For this reason, hematogenous osteomyelitis is vanishingly rare in people beyond their teens, occurring only in immunocompromised hosts.[31]

Post-traumatic osteomyelitis is one of the few infectious diseases that has become more prevalent in this century, probably because it is one of the few diseases fueled by technology. With the development of bigger and more powerful automobiles, motorcycles, guns, and land mines, the past hundred years have been witness to an ever-increasing potential for devastating soft tissue and skeletal injury. Infection is so closely linked with such injuries for two reasons. First, they provide ubiquitous microbes with an opportunity for breaching host defenses by exposing bone to the contamination of an accident scene. Second, once the microbes have bypassed external defenses, the trauma setting offers an ideal environment for adherence and colonization, namely, devitalized hard and soft tissues. It is not surprising, therefore, that there is a significant incidence of deep infection, of either soft tissue or bone, secondary to open fractures.

A review by Gustilo[54] showed the deep infection rate in the setting of open fractures to be anywhere from 2% to 50%. Naturally, not all open fractures carry the same risk of infection. On the basis of the extent of soft tissue injury, the severity of open fractures has traditionally been classified as type I, II, or III according to criteria put forth by Gustilo and Anderson.[52] Not surprisingly, it has been found that the more severe the open fracture, the greater the likelihood of infection: approximately 2% for type I and II open fractures and 10% to 50% percent in type III open fractures.[25, 52, 54, 114] Gustilo[54] cited several reasons type III fractures have been shown to be more susceptible to infection, such as lack of bone coverage, massive contamination of the wound, compromised perfusion, and instability of the fracture.

The tibia is the most frequent location of open fractures[37] and, accordingly, is also the most frequently infected. One retrospective study of 948 high-energy open tibial fractures reported a 56% post-traumatic infection rate.[130] Although not involved as often as the lower extremity, the upper extremity is also vulnerable to accidental trauma and subsequent infection.[138] In addition to traumatic injury, chronic osteomyelitis can result from surgical implants or, less commonly, from untreated or poorly treated hematogenous infection.

In any discussion of the epidemiology of chronic osteomyelitis, one should not overlook the role of host factors. Patients with vascular insufficiency, from conditions such as diabetes and peripheral vascular disease, have long been known to be at higher risk for post-traumatic or postoperative osteomyelitis.[149] Even subtle injuries in this population, such as a chronic pressure sore, may lead to the development of exposed bone, surrounding cellulitis, and eventual gangrene of the soft tissues.[119] Diabetic ulcers progress quickly in the setting of co-morbid peripheral vascular disease, neuropathy, and repetitive trauma.[58, 87] Additional host factors, such as malnutrition and alcoholism, are also said to contribute to the development of post-traumatic osteomyelitis[77] but have not been rigorously studied. Although there are no studies focusing specifically on the correlation between cigarette smoking and the incidence of post-traumatic osteomyelitis, there is evidence supporting significantly faster healing in nonsmokers with tibial infection compared with smokers.[50] Furthermore, there is a vast literature on the detrimental effects of smoking, and nicotine in particular, on wound healing, the survival of muscle flaps and skin grafts, and the rate of fracture union.

Although it is known that a vascular insult predisposes one to the development of chronic osteomyelitis, this progression should not be viewed solely as an inverse correlation between blood flow and risk of infection. In any acute inflammatory process, the balance between host and microbe is determined in large part by the efficacy of the immune response to the infectious challenge. Patients suffering from a disorder of polymorphonuclear leukocytes, for example, have been shown to be at an increased risk for the development and progression of osteomyelitis. In one series of 42 children with chronic granulomatous disease, the authors identified 13 patients who had osteomyelitis.[129] Other immunocompromised individuals, such as organ transplant recipients,[69, 154] patients with end-stage renal disease, or those receiving chemotherapy,[17] also seem to be at an increased risk. Although human immunodeficiency virus infection has not been identified as an independent risk factor in developing osteomyelitis,[88] skeletal infection in this population is clearly associated with a more severe clinical course that has been associated with elevated morbidity and mortality.[144]

PATHOGENESIS

Although acute osteomyelitis and chronic osteomyelitis both describe infections of bone, they are fundamentally distinguished by the presence of dead bone in the latter. Unlike acute osteomyelitis, which usually occurs in the metaphyseal areas of long bones secondary to hematogenous seeding, chronic osteomyelitis is usually localized to the area of traumatic injury, which can be epiphyseal, metaphyseal, or diaphyseal.

Hematogenous Osteomyelitis

In hematogenous infection, microorganisms infiltrate the metaphyseal end-arteries of long bone and replicate, thereby instigating a vigorous inflammatory response from the host. Because bone is a hard and rigid tissue, this influx of inflammatory cells into its canals has the unintended effect of raising intraosseous pressure and occluding its own blood supply.[153] Unless the infection and subsequent inflammation are rapidly controlled by the early administration of antibiotics, an area of devitalized bone begins to form. This fragment of necrotic bone, which is usually cortical and surrounded by inflammatory exudate and granulation tissue, is called a sequestrum. An involucrum sheath of reactive bone forms around the sequestrum, effectively sealing it off from the blood stream much like a walled-off abscess. With the development of dead bone, the infection can properly be referred to as a chronic osteomyelitis. Because it is possible to interrupt this progression with early antibiotics or drainage, acute hematogenous infection rarely evolves into chronic osteomyelitis.[148]

Chronic Osteomyelitis

The adult immune system normally renders bacterial colonization of bone difficult. In a normal host, there are only a few circumstances in which such infection might occur. These include a large inoculum size ($>10^5$ organisms per gram of tissue),[78, 115] an environment of ischemic bone and surrounding soft tissue, or the presence of a foreign body.[31, 96] Unfortunately for the individual with a contaminated open fracture, virtually all of these conditions are present. In the setting of skeletal trauma and subsequent ischemia, the same bone that is normally quite resistant to bacterial infiltration becomes an ideal target for bacterial adherence and subsequent proliferation.[97]

The first step in the pathogenesis of chronic osteomyelitis is entry of the pathogenic organism through the host's external defenses. Normally a difficult task, breaching the skin and mucous membranes becomes facile in the setting of an open fracture. However, the presence of a foreign microbe at or near bone is not sufficient to produce infection. Indeed, although most open fractures are contaminated by bacteria, only a fraction of these actually progress to osteomyelitis.[139] For osteomyelitis to develop, the microbe must not only penetrate the host's external defenses but actually become adherent to the underlying bone. Whereas the skeleton is normally resistant to bacterial adherence, traumatized tissue is susceptible to attack. This occurs, in part, because pathogenic bacteria have various receptors for host proteins that are laid open by injury to the bone. For example, S. aureus has been shown to have receptors for collagen, which is exposed by skeletal trauma, and fibronectin, which covers injured tissue shortly after the initial insult.[38, 49, 56, 139] Furthermore, external debris (in the case of open fractures) and even the necrotic bone fragments themselves can act as avascular foci for further bacterial adherence. Thus, as the osteonecrotic area expands, the disease is perpetuated by exposure of an increasing number of sites to which opportunistic bacteria can bind. In cases of chronic osteomyelitis secondary to internal fixation, the hardware itself serves as another adherent surface.[29, 34, 38, 49]

After bacteria successfully adhere to bone, they are able to aggregate and replicate in the devitalized tissue. Effectively sealed off from the host immune system, as well as from antibiotics, the organisms at the avascular focus of infection proliferate undeterred in a medium of dead bone, clotted blood, and dead space. Eventually, the bacteria disperse to adjacent areas of bone and soft tissue and the infection expands. The rapid growth of bacteria can lead to abscess and sinus tract formation. As pus accumulates and abscesses form within the soft tissues adjacent to the necrotic tissue, the patient experiences cyclic episodes of pain followed by drainage. A chronic course ensues without aggressive surgical débridement of all avascular tissue.

Bacteriology

Gustilo and Anderson[52] reported that 70% of open fractures had positive wound cultures before the initiation of treatment. Of course, not every contaminated wound leads to frank bone infection. In some circumstances, the combination of host defenses and various treatment modalities is successful in preventing bacteria from reaching some critical threshold necessary for infection. However, as mentioned, there are a few factors that put one at increased risk for skeletal infection, such as a large inoculum size, an environment of ischemia and devitalized tissue, or the presence of a foreign body.[31, 96] Under any of these circumstances, bacteria contaminating an open wound are much more likely to adhere successfully to bone and produce an osteomyelitis.

S. aureus is far and away the most common isolate in all types of bone infection and is implicated in 50% to 75% of cases of chronic osteomyelitis.[22, 26] Although the coagulase-positive staphylococci (S. aureus) are often cultured from the wound at the time of initial inspection, superinfection with multiple other organisms, such as coagulase-negative staphylococci (Staphylococcus epidermidis) and aerobic gram-negatives (Escherichia coli and Pseudomonas species), also commonly occurs.[52] One study suggested that S. epidermidis and various gram-negative bacilli are each involved in approximately one third of cases of chronic osteomyelitis.[8] Other studies implicated gram-negative rods in 50% of cases.[106] Although the exact distribution of microbes may vary from one study to another, a consistent finding has been the much higher incidence of polymicrobial infection in chronic osteomyelitis compared with hematogenous osteomyelitis.[11] This distinction should be recalled when selecting antibiotic coverage for the patient with presumed post-traumatic infection.

Staphylococci are so frequently cultured in open wounds because they are ubiquitous organisms. Both S. aureus and S. epidermidis are elements of normal skin flora, with S. aureus in greater numbers in the nares and anal mucosa and S. epidermidis more prevalent on the skin. Any traumatic event gives these bacteria a conduit to internal tissues. As mentioned, in the presence of wounded tissue, S. aureus has been shown to have an increased affinity for host proteins, a phenomenon ascribed to an interaction between its capsular polysaccharide and the exposed collagen and fibronectin on traumatized bone.[38, 49, 56, 139]

Although S. aureus produces a variety of enzymes, such as coagulase, the role of these in vivo in blunting the impact of host defenses remains unclear. A surface factor that may be important in its pathogenicity is protein A, which has been shown to bind to immunoglobulin G and thereby inhibit host opsonization and phagocytosis. An additional reason S. aureus can lead to such persistent infection may be its ability to alter its structure altogether in surviving without a cell wall. This inactive "L form" allows S. aureus, and a variety of other bacteria, to live dormant for years, even in the presence of bactericidal levels of antibiotic.[33, 42] Antimicrobial agents that exert their bactericidal activity by disrupting cell wall synthesis, as is the case with the beta-lactams (penicillins and cephalosporins), become ineffective when bacteria become cell wall deficient or less metabolically active.[147]

Another way in which staphylococci, in particular S. epidermidis, elude antimicrobial action is by secreting biofilm, a polysaccharide "slime" layer that dramatically increases bacterial adherence to virtually any substrate.[14, 49, 83, 123, 152] First described by Zobell and Anderson in 1936,[158] biofilm is especially significant in the pathogenesis of osteomyelitis because of its adherence to inert substrates, such as osteonecrotic bone, prosthetic devices, and acrylic cement. By establishing tight bonds with the glycoproteins of such substrates, biofilm enables actively dividing staphylococci to form adherent, sessile communities. Like cell wall–deficient strains of S. aureus, these communities of dormant bacteria have demonstrated increased antimicrobial resistance.[47, 91] In a similar fashion, biofilm has been shown to protect *S. epidermidis* from the host immune response itself.[43, 65]

Like staphylococci, *Pseudomonas aeruginosa* is a ubiquitous organism, with soil and fresh water serving as its primary reservoirs. Puncture wounds of the foot involve *P. aeruginosa* in about 95% of cases,[63] probably because of its prevalence in soil and moist, sweaty areas of skin. *Pseudomonas* species are implicated in many opportunistic infections, and thus its presence in the setting of chronic osteomyelitis is not unexpected. However, once *P. aeruginosa* has been introduced into host tissue, its pathogenic properties are less well defined than those of the staphylococci. Because this organism is one of the few obligately aerobic pathogenic bacteria (in contrast to *S. aureus*, a facultative anaerobe), its persistence in areas of hypoxic avascular bone is difficult to understand.

CLASSIFICATION

There are a number of ways to classify a case of osteomyelitis. One way would be to label the osteomyelitis as either *pediatric* or *adult,* distinguishing the infection on the basis of its age of onset. Another possibility is describing it as either *hematogenous* or *exogenous–post-traumatic,* distinguishing the infection on the basis of its pathogenesis. Finally, one could label it either *acute* or *chronic,* distinguishing the infection on the basis of whether it requires preexisting osteonecrosis. All of these classifications are used more frequently than describing the osteomyelitis by its causative organism, which is of course the standard approach for classifying most other infectious diseases, such as labeling a pneumonia "streptococcal" or a meningitis "meningococcal." The reason that the osteomyelitis literature has not used this nomenclature is probably that it is of little prognostic value. For example, it is of much greater therapeutic and prognostic consequence for the clinician to know whether osteonecrosis is present in a skeletal infection than whether *S. aureus* was one of the several microbes cultured.

Whether the infection has been labeled as adult, post-traumatic, or chronic osteomyelitis, it is helpful to classify it further using the staging system developed by Cierny and colleagues in 1985.[21] This system is currently the one most widely used for the classification of osteomyelitis.[59] The Cierny-Mader staging system classifies bone infection on the basis of two independent factors: (1) the anatomic area of bone involved and (2) the immunocompetence of the host. By combining one of the four anatomic types of osteomyelitis (I, medullary; II, superficial; III, localized; or IV, diffuse) with one of the three classes of host immunocompetence (A, B, or C), this system arrives at 12 clinical stages.[21] Probably more important than memorizing each of these stages is understanding the different anatomic sites that can be involved in osteomyelitis (Fig. 19–1).[21]

As described by Cierny and colleagues, the primary lesion in *medullary osteomyelitis* (type I) is endosteal and confined to the intramedullary surfaces of bone (i.e., a hematogenous osteomyelitis or an infection of an intramedullary rod). *Superficial osteomyelitis* (type II) is a true

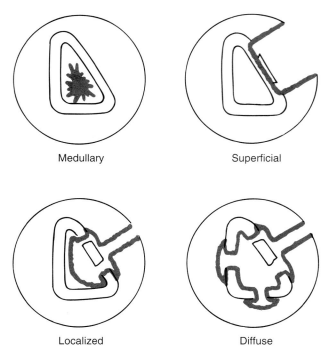

Medullary   Superficial

Localized   Diffuse

FIGURE 19–1. Anatomic types of osteomyelitis as they relate to the osseus compartment. (Redrawn from Cierny, G., III; Mader, J; Penninck, J. Contemp Orthop 10:5, 1985.)

contiguous focus infection in which the outermost layer of bone becomes infected from an adjacent source, such as a decubitus ulcer or a burn. *Localized osteomyelitis* (type III) produces full-thickness cortical cavitation within a segment of stable bone. It is frequently observed in the setting of fractures or when bone becomes infected from an adjacent implant. When the infected fracture does not heal and there is through-and-through disease of the hard and soft tissue, the condition is called *diffuse osteomyelitis* (type IV). Patients with post-traumatic osteomyelitis almost always have type III or type IV disease.

The immunocompetence portion of the Cierny-Mader classification stratifies patients according to their ability to mount an immune response. A patient with a normal physiologic response is labeled an *A host,* a compromised patient a *B host,* and a patient who is so compromised that surgical intervention poses a greater risk than the infection itself is designated a *C host.* A further stratification is made in B hosts on the basis of whether the patient has a local (B^L), systemic (B^S), or combined ($B^{S, L}$) deficiency in wound healing. An example of a local deficit in wound healing would be venous stasis at the site of injury, whereas systemic deficits would include malnutrition, renal failure, diabetes, tobacco or alcohol use, or acquired immunodeficiency syndrome.

Other less frequently used classification systems have also been developed. One of the older classification systems was created by Kelly and co-workers[66, 67] and stratified bone infections on the basis of their etiology: type I described an infection secondary to hematogenous spread, type II referred to an infection with fracture union, type III was an infected nonunion, and type IV meant that there was an exogenous infection without a fracture. A subsequent classification system for post-traumatic tibial osteomyelitis was based on the status of the tibia and fibula after surgical débridement.[82]

Although most of the classification systems developed for osteomyelitis address the extent of the skeletal infection, they do not give a detailed picture of the condition of the bone. Specifically, they do not address issues such as limb length, limb alignment, involvement of adjacent joints, or the presence of bone gaps. Although these are all important, such descriptive features are not necessary in the initial evaluation of osteomyelitis and may only confuse the clinician as he or she tries to determine whether surgical intervention is needed.

In order to make this determination, it is helpful to consult Cierny and Mader's classification system. In their schema, dead space management does not play a large role in any infection deemed to be either a medullary (type I) or superficial (type II) osteomyelitis. However, if an infection is labeled a localized (type III) osteomyelitis, there is usually the need for simple measures to stabilize the bone and dead space management. Any infection classified as diffuse (type IV) osteomyelitis would require extensive skeletal stabilization and extensive dead space management. In this way, the Cierny-Mader classification for osteomyelitis remains the most useful of its kind.

DIAGNOSIS

Initial Assessment

HISTORY

Chronic osteomyelitis is a diagnosis that can potentially be achieved with a thorough history of the patient. It should be suspected in anyone presenting with bone pain who has a past history of trauma or orthopaedic surgery. Complaints include persistent pain, erythema, swelling, and drainage localized to an area of previous trauma, surgery, or wound infection. Walenkamp[150] described a classic history as cyclical pain, increasing to "severe deep tense pain with fever," that often subsides when pus breaks through in a fistula. Although these cyclical episodes are almost pathognomonic for chronic osteomyelitis, they do not occur in everyone with the disease. Most of the time, symptoms are vague and generalized (e.g., "My leg is red and hurts"), making it difficult to differentiate between a cellulitis and a true infection of bone.

EXAMINATION

Classically, the cardinal signs of inflammation are rubor (redness), dolor (tenderness), calor (heat), and tumor (swelling). If these signs are noted on physical examination, it is fair to conclude that an infection is present. However, as with the history, signs of an actual osteomyelitis are often difficult to distinguish from those of an overlying soft tissue infection. One's suspicions of a bone infection may be confirmed by the presence of exposed necrotic bone, surgical hardware, or draining fistulas (Fig. 19–2). However, such physical examination findings are

rare. More commonly, recurrent drainage of small, trivial-appearing sinus tracts is the only sign that infection may be present (Fig. 19–3). The extent of infection and the fact that these tracts communicate with bone are often underappreciated. In addition to determining the presence of infection, the involved limb in general should of course be assessed during the physical examination. This assessment includes a thorough evaluation of its neurovascular status, the condition of its soft tissues, its length, alignment, and the presence of any structural deformities.

CULTURES

Culturing drainage fluid, if any is present, is easy to do in the office. Although potentially helpful in identifying causative bacteria and guiding antibiotic choice, these results must be interpreted with caution, because such specimens often yield opportunistic organisms that have simply colonized the nutrient-rich exudate. As a result, these cultures may provide no evidence of the organisms that are actually infecting the damaged bone.[24] Because the results from cultures of sinus tracts and purulent discharge are dubious, the diagnosis of chronic osteomyelitis can be definitively made only by intraoperative biopsy.[77]

PLAIN FILM

Plain radiographs play an important role in the workup of chronic osteomyelitis, because they provide the clinician with a sense of the overall bony architecture, limb length and alignment and the presence of orthopaedic implants, as well as any fractures, malunions, or nonunions. Radiographic findings of chronic osteomyelitis can be subtle and include osteopenia, thinning of the cortices, and loss of the trabecular architecture in cancellous bone.[110] Once the bone becomes necrotic and separated from normal bone by an involucrum sheath, it becomes easier to identify on plain film. When they are isolated in this way, sequestra appear radiodense relative to normal bone.

It is essential to obtain views of the involved bone that include its adjacent joints so that their integrity may be adequately assessed. Furthermore, it is important to include oblique views so as to detect the presence of subtle malunions that may not be seen in the anteroposterior plane alone. Plain films do not play as large a role in the initial workup of acute osteomyelitis, because they typically do not show changes in the bone characteristic of osteomyelitis until 10 to 14 days after the onset of infection.

LABORATORY STUDIES

White blood cell (WBC) counts, erythrocyte sedimentation rates (ESRs), and C-reactive protein (CRP) levels have traditionally been part of the workup of any patient with suspected musculoskeletal infection. In an immunocompetent individual, elevated levels of these laboratory values are fairly sensitive indicators of some sort of acute infection, particularly when the WBC count has a so-called left shift (i.e., an elevated ratio of polymorphonuclear leukocytes to other white cells). The ESR is a measurement

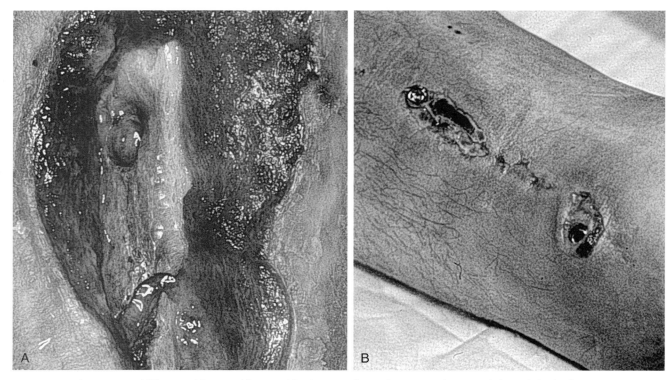

Figure 19-2. The presence of (A) exposed bone or (B) exposed hardware can be an obvious sign that an underlying skeletal infection is present.

of the rate at which red blood cells sink toward the bottom of a test tube and separate from plasma. The ESR is elevated when the erythrocytes clump abnormally well because of an abundance of serum globulins, such as fibrinogen, which are usually produced in response to inflammation. CRP is another acute phase reactant and a similar marker for systemic inflammation.

There is a paucity of studies showing a correlation between laboratory values and the presence of bone infection, although one group of investigators has shown

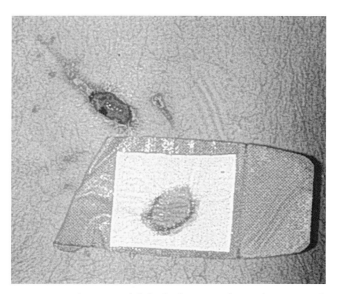

Figure 19-3. The extent of skeletal infection is often underappreciated by physical examination.

CRP to be useful in the early detection of sequelae-prone acute osteomyelitis.[116]

Unfortunately, all of these values are rather nonspecific to skeletal infection and thus add little to the clinician's ability to distinguish a superficial inflammatory process, such as a cellulitis, from a deeper osteomyelitic one. Furthermore, although theoretically helpful in screening for an *acute* infection, the WBC count, ESR, and CRP are frequently normal in the setting of *chronic* osteomyelitis and thus are neither sensitive nor specific for it.[150]

To understand why this may be so, it is helpful to reconsider the pathophysiology underlying acute and chronic osteomyelitis. Because acute osteomyelitis is a disease characterized by a vigorous influx of phagocytes and other inflammatory cells into hematogenously seeded bone, it follows that a laboratory test that indicates systemic inflammation should be a sensitive marker for infection. However, this should not necessarily be the case in chronic osteomyelitis, which is a disease characterized by devitalized tissues and a muted inflammatory response. It makes sense, therefore, that WBC counts and acute phase reactants, such as ESR and CRP, are often normal in cases of chronic osteomyelitis. Although Cierny and Mader[24] recommended following all their patients with monthly WBC counts and ESRs for 6 months, there is reason to believe from the vertebral osteomyelitis literature that these values do not always correlate well with response to treatment and may be of limited value.[16]

Nutritional parameters, such as albumin, prealbumin, and transferrin, are helpful to obtain in the workup of a patient with suspected chronic osteomyelitis so that malnutrition can be identified and reversed before taking the patient to the operating room. It has been shown that

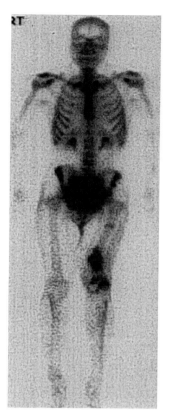

FIGURE 19–4. With its increased localized activity of the tracer 3 to 4 hours after injection, this three-phase bone scan suggests infection of the patient's distal left femur.

orthopaedic surgery patients who are malnourished have significantly higher infection rates than those who have a normal nutritional status.[64] Presumably, it would follow that patients who already have infection present would be more likely to respond to therapy if their nutrition were optimized beforehand.

Advanced Imaging Studies

History, physical examination, plain films, and laboratory work usually establish the diagnosis of infection but do not always define the extent to which the bone is involved and therefore the presence of a true osteomyelitis. Additional imaging modalities, such as a variety of nuclear medicine studies, computed tomography, and magnetic resonance

imaging (MRI), are frequently useful in determining whether skeletal infection is present and, if so, in helping to evaluate the extent of the disease.

NUCLEAR MEDICINE STUDIES

Traditionally, radionuclide scintigraphy has been the initial advanced imaging study ordered. The three-phase bone scan, as it is better known, is regarded as an excellent screening tool for chronic osteomyelitis, with a sensitivity exceeding 90%.[81] Performed in three phases using Tc 99m methylene diphosphonate, the bone scan suggests soft tissue infection when the first two phases (arterial and venous) are positive and the third phase (focal bone uptake) is negative. True skeletal infection should be considered when all three phases are positive, including the delayed (2- to 4-hour) images (Fig. 19–4).[101] However, it is well known that a variety of noninfectious insults to bone, such as the repeated surgeries and hardware implants that are so common in this population of patients, also cause the third phase to be positive. As a result, the three-phase bone scan is a notoriously nonspecific test for chronic osteomyelitis (specificity as low as 10%).[122] With a high sensitivity and a poor specificity, three-phase bone scintigraphy should be regarded as a screening tool for patients with suspected bone infection but may not be relied on for providing a definitive diagnosis.

Another radiopharmaceutical that has been classically used in the diagnosis of osteomyelitis is gallium citrate. Gallium scintigraphy, in conjunction with the three-phase technetium scan, was the first dual-tracer technique available for evaluating chronic osteomyelitis.[74] As a calcium and iron analogue, gallium is thought to bind to transferrin as it leaks from the blood stream to areas of skeletal inflammation. The primary role of gallium scintigraphy currently is in evaluating the patient with suspected vertebral osteomyelitis.[101]

Although gallium provides the best way to detect vertebral osteomyelitis radiographically, labeled leukocyte imaging is the nuclear imaging test of choice for osteomyelitis elsewhere in the body.[101] The principle behind radiolabeled leukocyte imaging, which uses radionuclides such as indium and technetium, is that white blood cells localize around areas of inflammation (Fig. 19–5). What makes this technique so useful in theory is that, unlike the situation in three-phase bone scintigraphy, labeled leukocytes should not accumulate around areas of increased bone mineral turnover unless an infection is present. Results have been variable over the years, with some

FIGURE 19–5. These leukocyte-labeled images suggest multiple areas of bilateral pedal osteomyelitis.

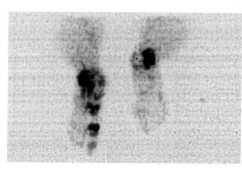
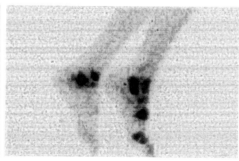

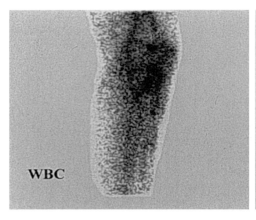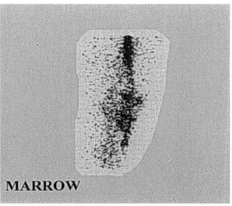

FIGURE 19–6. Sulfur colloid marrow scans can be used in conjunction with other studies to serve as a "control" of normal marrow activity. Congruence between the radionuclide uptake in the leukocyte-labeled image (WBC) and the sulfur colloid marrow scan (Marrow) suggests that there is not an infection present in this patient's proximal tibia. Looking at the leukocyte-labeled image alone might lead one to the incorrect diagnosis.

studies reporting rather poor testing accuracies[156] and others reporting outstanding ones, with sensitivities and specificities exceeding 90% for cases of nonvertebral chronic osteomyelitis.[72, 85]

On the whole, it can be said that most investigators have found leukocyte labeling to be just as sensitive as three-phase bone scintigraphy in detecting chronic osteomyelitis, but with a dramatically increased specificity. A fairly representative study was conducted by Blume and colleagues[10] in 1997 that showed a nearly 60% increase in the specificity of leukocyte labeling (86%) over that of three-phase bone scintigraphy (29%) in the detection of pedal osteomyelitis. Specificity of leukocyte imaging can be increased further when performed in conjunction with a marrow scan. Marrow scans, such as those using sulfur colloid, improve diagnostic accuracy by delineating areas of normal bone marrow activity to compare with the areas of increased radionuclide uptake elsewhere. A congruence between the radionuclide uptake in a leukocyte-labeled image and in a marrow scan suggests that there is not an actual infection present (Fig. 19–6). In contrast, an incongruence between the two is strongly suggestive of infection, with accuracies reported to be as high as 98%.[100, 101]

COMPUTED TOMOGRAPHY AND MAGNETIC RESONANCE IMAGING

Although nuclear medicine studies are frequently the first radiologic tests used to supplement plain film in the evaluation of bone infection, computed tomography and MRI can be useful as well. Computed tomographic scans are known to have excellent resolution of cortical bone and sequestra and may be helpful in the preoperative planning for difficult infections.[126] In the 1990s, MRI began replacing computed tomography at most hospitals for evaluating the extent of osteomyelitis, because it provides the most detailed imaging of the hard and soft tissues (Fig. 19–7). MRI is highly beneficial in surgical planning by providing information regarding the extent of soft tissue edema as well as the location of hidden sinus tracts and abscesses. Initial screening usually consists of T1- and T2-weighted images. On T1-weighted images, there is decreased signal intensity of the marrow in infected areas.

On T2-weighted images, infection is signaled by no change or an increased signal. This bright signal is due to the high water content of granulation tissue.[133]

Although there are false positives caused by tumors or healing fractures,[143] the sensitivity and specificity of MRI in the diagnosis of osteomyelitis remain excellent, ranging from 92% to 100% and 89% to 100%, respectively.[7, 133, 143] Because a negative MRI study effectively rules out the diagnosis of chronic osteomyelitis, it is recommended by some as the most appropriate step after a nondiagnostic radiograph in determining whether to treat.[146] Although MRI has extremely high sensitivity and specificity for chronic osteomyelitis, it is frequently not possible to obtain this study because of the presence of metal at the site of infection, as is

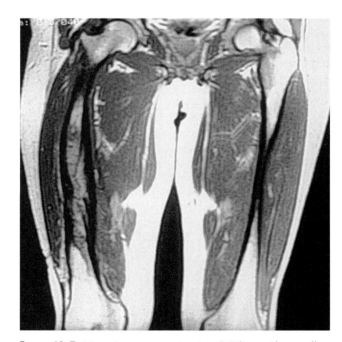

FIGURE 19–7. Magnetic resonance imaging (MRI) provides excellent detail of the hard and soft tissues. This MRI scan demonstrates extensive intramedullary involvement as well as surrounding soft tissue edema in a patient with post-traumatic osteomyelitis of the right femoral diaphysis.

frequently the case in patients with a history of skeletal trauma.

MANAGEMENT

Overview of Decision Making

The definitive treatment of chronic osteomyelitis includes the surgical elimination of all devitalized hard and soft tissues. Only by completely excising all avascular tissue is it possible to arrest this self-perpetuating infection. Filling in the dead space created by débridement, providing adequate soft tissue coverage, stabilizing the fracture or nonunion (if present), and administering antibiotics are important adjuncts in management.

The excision of necrotic tissue represents the key step in arresting infection in patients with chronic osteomyelitis. In certain cases in which the area of osteonecrosis is limited, only a modest excision may be required. In other instances, however, the extent of osteonecrosis may be so great that adequate débridement necessitates a limb amputation. The first question to be asked, then, when dealing with a patient with chronic osteomyelitis is precisely whether the limb can be salvaged. If limb salvage is deemed possible, the second question to ask is whether the patient can tolerate the procedure (or, as is so often the case, multiple procedures) required for complete débridement. The answer to this question depends on the patient's systemic and local capabilities for wound healing. For example, limb salvage procedures that may be feasible for a healthy teenager may be life-threatening for an elderly individual with cancer.

These differences in host immunocompetence hearken back to the Cierny-Mader classification, which introduced the concept of *C hosts* as those in whom the risks of surgery outweigh the risks of infection.[21] In such individuals, an alternative course of action to *arresting* the infection would be to retain the dead bone and *suppress* bacterial activity with long-term antimicrobial therapy. If limb salvage is deemed feasible and the patient is thought to be able tolerate the surgery, a third question to ask is whether the patient wishes to go down a path that frequently involves multiple surgical procedures and months, if not years, of physical and emotional hardship. Answering this question requires a thoughtful dialogue between doctor and patient as well as with the patient's family.

Finally, the patient and his or her family should understand that, despite embarking down the path of limb salvage surgery, the end result may still be an amputation. A study that reviewed 31 patients with long bone chronic osteomyelitis treated with combined débridement, antibiotic bead placement, and bone grafting showed that 4 patients (13%) had received amputations at an average follow-up of 4 years.[20] This figure is not insignificant and suggests that there is a select group of patients who would benefit from early amputation. Because of the tremendous amount of resources allocated to ultimately failed limb salvage procedures, society at large may also benefit from identifying this group.[12]

Although not specifically directed at the population with chronic osteomyelitis, several classification systems have been described over the past few decades that attempt to sort out which post-traumatic injuries would most likely end in amputation. In 1976, Gustilo and Anderson[52] demonstrated that type III open fractures had the worst prognosis for subsequent amputation. A decade later, they created a subclassification for type III fractures (IIIC, defined as those involving arterial injury requiring repair) that predicted even poorer outcomes.[53] Amputation rates for type IIIC fractures have been reported to exceed 50%.[55, 73] The Mangled Extremity Severity Index[46] and Mangled Extremity Severity Score[55] have also traditionally been used as guides for prognosis. Despite all of the classification systems that have been developed, the decision regarding amputation remains a highly subjective one based on the experience of the surgeon and the desires of the patient. Unless obvious criteria for amputation are met, this decision truly remains more of an art than a science.[32]

Amputation

As mentioned, at the beginning of every treatment algorithm for chronic osteomyelitis is the question of whether the limb is, in fact, salvageable. In circumstances in which patients have such extensive infection and osteonecrosis that segmental resection and limb reconstruction are not possible, amputation may be necessary to arrest the disease. Early amputation may give such an individual with extensive infection the best chance to be symptom-free and to return to his or her level of functioning as soon as possible.

Once amputation is selected as a treatment modality, the level of amputation must be chosen. In the 1930s, most amputations for tibial osteomyelitis were done above the level of the knee to ensure that there was enough blood supply for adequate healing. With the experience of large numbers of below-knee amputees in World War II, this approach grew out of favor as it was learned that amputating across the femur put the patient at a disadvantage for future prosthetic use and ambulation.[89]

Although it has been shown that the energy expenditure required for ambulation is much greater in above-knee than below-knee amputees,[41] studies comparing energy expenditure for different levels of transtibial amputees indicate that there is no ideal level at which to perform a below-knee amputation (BKA). A reasonable empirical guideline that adjusts for differences in patients' height is to select the level at which the calf muscle belly flattens out into the aponeurosis. The most proximal level of a BKA that still allows proper knee function is just distal to the tibial tubercle where the extensor mechanism inserts. Using 15 cm below the knee joint line or 3 to 4 fingerbreadths distal to the tibial tubercle as landmarks has been shown to provide safe markers.[5, 13] Although the surgical technique for performing amputations varies among surgeons, most would agree that the key to this operation is identifying and ligating all major neurovascular structures. Unlike amputations done for dry gangrene, amputations in the setting of infection (wet gangrene) are

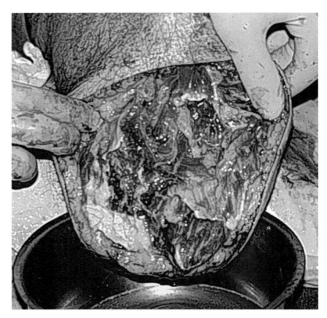

FIGURE 19–8. Below-knee amputations in the setting of osteomyelitis are usually left open and closed in a delayed fashion to minimize the chance of recurrent infection.

usually staged with initial open amputation followed by a delayed closure (Fig. 19–8).

TECHNIQUE

During a BKA, the surgeon should proceed systematically through each compartment of the lower leg, first dissecting the soft tissues of the anterior compartment (anterior to the interosseus membrane) and isolating and clamping the anterior tibial vessels and deep peroneal nerve. Using a periosteal elevator, the periosteum of the tibia should be stripped distally from the level of transection. This process should continue posteriorly, carefully avoiding damage to the tibial vessels of the deep posterior compartment. The fibula is then cleared of soft tissue a few centimeters proximal to the level of the tibial transection. Both the tibia and fibula are transected, usually with an oscillating or Gigli saw. The posterior tibial and peroneal vessels, as well as the tibial nerve, are then isolated and clamped.

The soleus muscle in the superficial posterior compartment is then dissected away from the medial and lateral heads of the gastrocnemius to the level of the tibial stump and transected just distal to the clamped neurovascular structures. The posterior flap, which consists of the remaining gastrocnemius muscle, receives its blood supply from sural arteries coursing off the popliteal artery. The muscles of the lateral compartment are excised and the superficial peroneal nerve is clamped. All vessels are ligated and all nerves are ligated in traction, transected distally, and allowed to withdraw from the stump. To avoid dislodgment of ligatures, pulsatile arteries should be suture-ligated. The end of the tibia, especially the anterior portion that lies subcutaneously, should be beveled and the sharp edges smoothed with a rasp.

After the stump is closed, whether it be in primary or delayed fashion, immediate compressive dressings such as

shrink wraps or Ace bandages become important in protecting the wound, promoting wound healing, and minimizing edema. These dressings are usually kept on for a few days unless signs or symptoms of infection develop.

POSTOPERATIVE CARE

During the first couple of postoperative days, physical therapy should be initiated to aid in transfers and in-bed range-of-motion and strengthening exercises. Non–weight-bearing ambulation with the aid of parallel bars, walkers, or crutches should begin soon thereafter. The patient is ready to be fitted for a temporary prosthesis when the suture line is healed, usually 6 to 8 weeks postoperatively.[5] Some prosthetists favor fitting patients even before the suture line has healed, 10 to 14 days after surgery. Prostheses are of great practical value, because they require a considerably lower energy expenditure than ambulation with crutches.[86]

An important and often overlooked aspect of postoperative care is teaching the patient how to put on his or her prosthesis so that there is total contact between stump and prosthetic socket. Training can take 2 to 3 weeks for unilateral below-knee amputees. After the first several postoperative weeks, physical and occupational therapists should focus their efforts on goals of increasing mobility and functional independence, especially as they relate to activities of daily living. The patient is usually fitted for a permanent prosthesis at about 3 to 6 months, after the greatest amount of stump shrinkage has occurred.

The preceding discussion has focused on BKAs simply because of the prevalence of post-traumatic osteomyelitis of the tibia. Of course, above-knee or through-knee amputations become necessary when the area of osteonecrosis and subsequent infection has expanded more proximally. The principles of these procedures, as well as amputations elsewhere in the body, are basically the same as those outlined for the BKA. Dissection should proceed compartment by compartment, with major neurovascular structures being identified and ligated. At approximately 6 to 8 weeks, the above-knee amputee who is a candidate for a prosthetic limb may be fitted and begin gait training.[5]

Limb Salvage

In circumstances where there is a documented progressive destruction of bone, limb salvage is deemed feasible, and the patient is thought to be able to tolerate surgery, radical débridement should be thought of as the most fundamental intervention. Even if the patient is asymptomatic, symptoms such as fever and pain are likely to return as long as the area of osteonecrosis remains. If the preceding criteria are met and the patient feels that the benefits of limb salvage surgery (surgeries) outweigh its risks and hardships, treatment should be initiated along the following path[21, 23, 24, 54, 134, 150]:

1. Thorough débridement of necrotic tissue and bone
2. Stabilization of bone
3. Obtaining intraoperative tissue cultures
4. Dead space management

5. Soft tissue coverage
6. Limb reconstruction
7. Systemic antibiotic therapy

We discuss each of these treatment principles in turn.

DÉBRIDEMENT

> Make an incision or opening that will thoroughly uncover (saucerize) the infected area. . . . Remove as much foreign material and dead or dying tissue as possible . . . do not remove bony or soft parts that may contribute to repair. . . . Fill entire cavity. . . .[99]

Although this may look like the most recent guidelines for the treatment of chronic osteomyelitis, these excerpts were in fact taken from an article written by H. Winnett Orr in 1930. Although some of his recommendations on the management of bone infection are now outdated, his emphases on thorough débridement and filling in of subsequent dead space are as relevant today as they were 70 years ago. Despite all the advances in medical technology over this time period, the quality of the surgical débridement remains the most critical factor in successfully managing chronic osteomyelitis.[134]

Even with detailed imaging techniques such as MRI, it is often difficult to assess the extent of osteonecrosis and infection preoperatively. Before making an incision, Walenkamp[150] supported the practice of injecting an obvious fistula with methylene blue dye to localize the focus of infection. This, he said, should cause the patient to feel the same or similar pain as during the stowing of pus. Cierny and colleagues[21] have not found the use of dyes to be helpful, however.

Once the area of necrosis is localized, débridement proceeds using a variety of instruments, such as curettes, rongeurs, and high-speed power burrs. Stated simply, the goal of surgery is the complete excision of all dead or ischemic hard and soft tissues (Fig. 19–9). If not removed, they would serve as a nidus for recurrent infection and cure would be impossible. If adequate débridement is the key to treatment, the question arises: how does the surgeon know when all of the necrotic bone has been removed? Classically, punctate haversian bleeding, referred to as the paprika sign,[21] has been used as a sign of healthy bone and helps establish the limits of débridement. However, this sign may not always be relied on, such as during débridements of dense cortical bone or operations in which a tourniquet is used. In such cases where there is less bleeding, the use of a laser Doppler probe may be helpful in establishing skeletal viability.[131] However, in general, this practice can be rather cumbersome and is not currently regarded as the standard of care.[134]

In addition to surgical excision of all necrotic tissues, the infected areas should be copiously irrigated. Authors from Patzakis and colleagues[106] to Gustilo and Anderson[52] have recommended from 10 to 14 L of normal saline to wash out the contaminated material. The efficacy of débridement has been shown to be optimized by high-pressure pulsatile lavage using fluid pressures of 50 to 70 pounds per square inch and 800 pulses per minute.[9] Although adding various antibiotic solutions to the process of irrigation has become common practice for many surgeons, such practices have not been supported by the literature. The work of Anglen and associates[1,2] has, in fact, shown soap solution to be the only mixture more effective than normal saline irrigation in reducing bacterial counts.

Although a thorough débridement is necessary for eliminating all pathogenic bacteria, it is frequently not sufficient. Because of antimicrobial resistance factors, such as bacterial secretion of biofilm, persistent infection is unfortunately a fairly common occurrence. In a study of 53 patients who had positive cultures at the time of their initial débridement for chronic osteomyelitis of the tibia, 26% still did at the time of their second débridement.[105] To arrest this disease, therefore, several trips to the operating room for repeated débridements and a variety of reconstructive procedures are often necessary.

In a study reviewing 189 patients with chronic osteomyelitis, Cierny and colleagues[21] found that the average number of operations for a patient undergoing limb salvage was 3.8. In his approach to chronic osteomyelitis, Cierny's focus during the first operation is on a thorough débridement of all necrotic tissues, fracture stabilization, and the acquisition of tissue biopsies. He then takes patients back to the operating room approximately 5 to 7 days after this initial surgery for a repeated débridement. Cierny uses this second look both to make sure that the wound is viable and to address the issue of dead space management (usually with the placement of antibiotic beads or a cancellous bone graft, or both).

STABILIZATION OF BONE

In 1974, Rittman and Perren[113] conducted a study that showed that rigid stabilization of bone facilitated union in

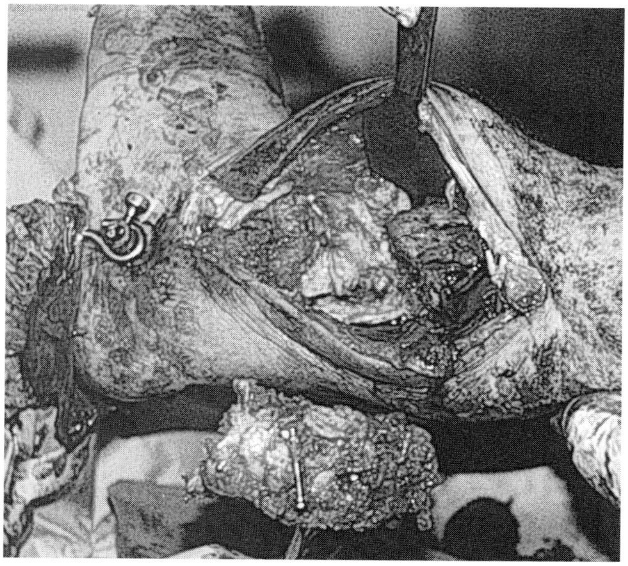

FIGURE 19–9. A thorough excision of all devitalized tissues constitutes the cornerstone of management in chronic osteomyelitis. Although adequate débridement may sometimes require limb amputation, at other times, as shown here, the removal of a solitary mass of necrotic tissue and hardware is sufficient.

the setting of chronic osteomyelitis. In this study, tibial osteotomies were performed on sheep and stabilized by plates of varying rigidities. Pathogenic bacteria were injected into the osteotomy site 1 week after surgery, which produced changes equivalent to those seen in chronic osteomyelitis. After 8 weeks of follow-up, it was shown that bone union of these infected sites was correlated with the degree of skeletal stabilization. One reason for this may be that skeletal stability promotes revascularization, thus enhancing perfusion at the fracture site.[19] This enhanced perfusion may maximize the host's immune response, which allows it to resist infection at the fracture site more effectively.[19]

The method by which fracture stability is obtained is not inconsequential. Although several studies support primary intramedullary nailing of open tibial fractures over external fixation, citing superior postoperative outcomes,[120, 121, 135] this technique is usually not recommended when the trauma is more than 12 hours old, when there is extensive soft tissue damage, or in the presence of osteomyelitis.[109] In such cases, bacteria are more likely to gain access to the intramedullary canal and potentially infect the entire diaphysis.

There are data to support the use of external fixation in the presence of infection. After stabilizing experimental osteotomies with either an external fixator or an intramedullary rod and then contaminating these sites with *S. aureus*, a group of investigators in 1995 found the sites stabilized with external fixators to have fewer and less severe infections than those stabilized internally.[28] Gustilo[54] claimed that primary intramedullary nailing should be avoided altogether in all type III open fractures, arguing that they already have compromised periosteal and extraperiosteal circulations (i.e., from surrounding muscle) secondary to injury. In such cases, he recommended achieving skeletal stabilization through plating or external fixation (Fig. 19–10).[54]

INTRAOPERATIVE CULTURES

The definitive diagnosis of post-traumatic osteomyelitis is made by isolating bacteria from the intraoperative biopsy specimen of the involved bone.[77] Although the best specimens are generally thought to be tissue fragments directly from the center of infection,[150] there is evidence to suggest that copious intraoperative cultures from a variety of sources may be beneficial. Comparing the results of bacterial cultures from various sites in long bone chronic osteomyelitis, Patzakis and co-workers[107] found the culture of bone biopsy specimens to be inadequate for identifying *all* organisms present. As a result, they recommended that intraoperative culture specimens be taken from the sinus tract, samples of purulent material, and samples of soft tissue, in addition, of course, to the involved bone.

To avoid false-negative culture results, patients might be encouraged to stop taking antibiotics at least 1 week before surgery. Unfortunately, doing so may have the unintended effect of instigating a cellulitis in the soft tissues. If this occurs and becomes very uncomfortable for the patient, the clinician may wish to restart antibiotics. If the symptoms of the cellulitis are manageable, it is in the

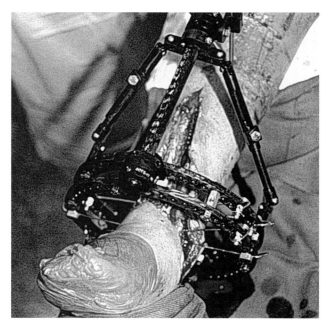

FIGURE 19–10. External fixators are frequently used to achieve fracture stabilization in the presence of infection or massive soft tissue injury.

patient's best interest to remain without antibiotics before surgery. After deep cultures have been obtained in the operating room, broad-spectrum intravenous antibiotics are started if the causative organism is unknown. Coverage is narrowed when culture and sensitivity results return from the laboratory.

DEAD SPACE MANAGEMENT

When the bone and tissues deemed devitalized have been removed, the focus shifts toward managing the dead space that is left behind. Healing with secondary intention is discouraged, because the scar tissue that would fill the defect is avascular and may lead to persistent drainage.[21]

Antibiotic Beads

Since the 1980s, many surgeons have favored filling this space, at least initially, with polymethyl methacrylate beads impregnated with antibiotic, usually an aminoglycoside (such as gentamicin) or vancomycin (Fig. 19–11). Although polymethyl methacrylate is the most widely used drug delivery system, calcium hydroxyapatite implants that become incorporated into host bone have also been shown to be effective.[157] Whatever the material, the antibiotic-laden beads are placed directly in the operative wound, which is then primarily closed. Unless the depot material is biodegradable, almost all antibiotic bead chains are intended for removal at a later date. Generally, they remain in the wound for approximately 4 weeks. Beads placed within the intramedullary canal, however, should be removed sooner (within 2 weeks) before the layer of granulation tissue has formed, which would make removal difficult.[134] The beads should be oriented in layers from deepest to most superficial. Adequate concentrations of

FIGURE **19–11.** Antibiotic beads serve a dual role as a local depot of antibiotic in the débridement site as well as a temporary filler of dead space. Polymethylmethacrylate (PMMA) beads connected together in a chain are the most widely used drug delivery system.

antibiotic can be achieved only when it diffuses from the beads into the postoperative wound hematoma, which serves as a transport medium. Thus, open wound treatment or irrigation-suction drainage is incompatible with this mode of therapy.[70]

Several clinical trials have supported the efficacy of local antibiotic bead implantation.[18, 70, 151] Even though the gentamicin concentration remains at sufficient levels for approximately 30 days after implantation, some skeptics may claim that beads are beneficial only insofar as they are able to fill dead space. This argument is difficult to make in light of animal studies demonstrating the efficacy of antibiotic beads in eradicating osteomyelitis above and beyond placebo beads that have no antibiotic.[92] Thus, it appears that bead chains are helpful not only by serving as a temporary filler of dead space before reconstruction but also as an effective depot for the local administration of antibiotic.

Cancellous Bone Graft

After antibiotic beads are placed, dressings are applied to the wound and changed frequently to promote the growth of a healthy layer of granulation tissue, a process that can take 2 to 4 weeks. After this time period, the wound is usually suitable for the second stage of dead space management, namely, reentry and bone reconstruction. Bone reconstruction is usually achieved with an autogenous cancellous bone graft. Bone chips are typically taken

from the iliac crests, greater trochanter, or proximal tibia. Grafting involves taking small strips of cancellous bone from these areas and packing them down over a fresh granulation bed in the débrided area.

Papineau and colleagues[104] pioneered this technique and recommended taking the grafts in strips 3 to 6 cm long by 3 mm thick by 4 mm wide and placing them in concentric and overlapping layers to fill in the defect completely.[103] Cancellous grafts have the benefit of being able to become rapidly revascularized and incorporated in the final bone structure. Open cancellous grafting has produced some excellent outcomes, with clinical success rates ranging from 89% in 1979[104] to 92% in 1984[118] and 100% in 1995.[36]

SOFT TISSUE COVERAGE

The soft tissues covering the area of skeletal injury must be allowed to heal or the patient will be at a very high risk for persistent or recurrent infection. After the necrotic tissues are excised, the débrided (and possibly bone grafted) area can conceivably be covered in one of three ways: (1) simply by letting the tissues heal by secondary intention, (2) by split-thickness skin grafting, or (3) by muscle transfer (Fig. 19–12). The last two techniques are favored in almost all cases of post-traumatic osteomyelitis and should be performed after a layer of granulation tissue has formed.

Covering the débrided site with a well-vascularized tissue graft offers the healing bone a new blood supply and thus decreases the chance of deep infection.[79, 155] Delayed coverage is associated with a higher chronic infection rate.[60] Local muscle flaps, which have the advantage of keeping vascular supply intact, are almost always used if an adjacent muscle is available. Although local muscle flaps work well for the proximal two thirds of the tibia, the more distal one third requires the use of transplanted flaps in order to provide a sufficient soft tissue envelope for healing. These so-called free flaps were developed in the early 1980s and are usually from such donor muscles as rectus abdominis, latissimus dorsi, gracilis, and tensor fasciae latae.[3]

It is difficult to study the isolated effect that the use of muscle transfers has had on clinical outcome. After all, this technique is almost always used in combination with several other therapeutic modalities, such as bone grafting,

FIGURE **19–12.** The use of muscle transfers, with or without overlying skin grafts, guards against persistent or recurrent infection by filling the dead space created by surgical débridement with well-vascularized tissue.

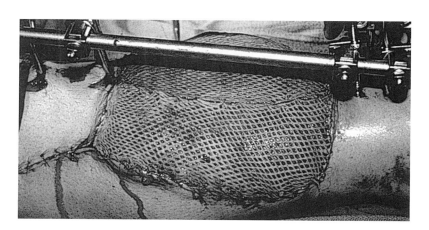

antibiotics, and of course débridement. Nonetheless, there is certainly a large amount of evidence that supports the use of muscle flaps as part of the therapeutic regimen.[3, 4, 39, 84] Fitzgerald and colleagues,[39] using either local or free flaps combined with thorough débridement and antibiotics, reported a 93% success rate in treating a sample of 42 patients with chronic osteomyelitis. These results demonstrated a significant improvement over previous treatment regimens that did not employ the use of muscle flap coverage. In another study, which retrospectively reviewed 34 patients with chronic osteomyelitis of the tibia, it was found that those who had received free muscle flap transfers as part of their surgical treatment were more likely to be drainage-free after more than 7 years of follow-up than patients who had received débridement alone.[84]

Although the primary purpose of local or free muscle transfer is to revascularize the débrided area, it also serves a purpose akin to bone grafting by simply filling in the dead space created by surgery. This notion is supported by studies that have found the recurrence of infection in patients with lower leg osteomyelitis to be significantly reduced when the muscle flaps completely pack the cavity left by surgical débridement.[125, 141]

LIMB RECONSTRUCTION

Sometimes the segmental defects in bone left from débridement or from the injury itself cannot be corrected with antibiotic beads, bone graft, and muscle flaps alone. The technique used for the reconstruction of such defects (and the malunion and angulation deformities so common in the setting of infected open fractures) depends on the patient and the type of deformity that is present.[102] Long-term cast therapy, for instance, is an option for the management of relatively minor nonunions. Other possibilities include open reduction and plate fixation, intramedullary nailing, and electrical stimulation. Electrical stimulation is discussed in "Complementary Therapies" later in the chapter. One of the more recent developments in the management of more severe nonunions and infected nonunions has been the dynamic external fixation technique described by Ilizarov.

In the Ilizarov method,[62] an area of noninfected bone is corticotomized and allowed to begin the healing process with a normal fracture callus. This area of callus is then distracted progressively over small increments using an external fixator device. In this way, Ilizarov external fixation gradually stimulates skeletal regeneration, which can be of obvious value in correcting the segmental, rotational, translational, and angular deformities frequently seen in patients with post-traumatic osteomyelitis. This method of so-called *distraction osteogenesis,* wherein bone is lengthened at one quarter of a millimeter every 6 hours, should be distinguished from *compression osteogenesis,* which can be described as pressing the bone ends together in a fracture or delayed union until they are stable enough to heal by themselves. In both distraction and compression techniques, bone transport may serve as an adjunct to facilitate osteogenesis across segmental defects. Although there are many drawbacks to the Ilizarov method, such as pain from the external fixator, frequent pin infections, and a long period of time spent in the device (almost 9 months on average),[15, 30] it has produced excellent outcomes in several studies.[30, 44, 102, 112, 142] What makes this mode of treatment even more valuable to patients is that it allows them to remain ambulatory throughout its duration.[15, 45, 51, 62]

Although the method of distraction osteogenesis has been shown time and again to aid in limb reconstruction, it should be remembered that it is not a cure-all. As emphasized earlier in the chapter, some extremities are so severely compromised by traumatic injury, infection, or the extent of surgical débridement that amputation may be the inevitable outcome. These patients should be identified early and spared futile reconstructive attempts. However, even in patients who have salvageable limbs, Ilizarov limb relengthening is not a panacea. In part, its success depends on the preoperative planning of the orthopaedic surgeon, who must determine how to employ the principles of distraction osteogenesis during the course of reconstruction.

Generally speaking, the surgeon may wish to proceed down one of two reconstructive paths: (1) acutely shortening the extremity via resection of a diseased or malunited segment of bone with compression at that site, followed by limb relengthening, or (2) holding the extremity out to length and using bone transport to fill in the gap. In patients who have only a short segment of diseased bone (i.e., on the order of 4 cm or less), the first technique is probably the better option. However, if the length of the necrotic bone exceeds 4 cm, this technique becomes less favorable because of both the greater distance through which the limb must be shortened and the potential danger of kinking blood vessels when the excess soft tissue envelope is compressed together. In instances in which a large bone gap exists, it probably makes more sense to hold the limb out to length and transport bone into the defect.

To elucidate the application of these two approaches, we describe how each was used in the care of patients seen in our bone infection clinic at the University of Connecticut Health Center.

Illustrative Cases of Reconstructive Strategies

CASE 1

Acute Shortening and Relengthening

The reconstructive strategy of acute shortening and limb relengthening consists of the following steps: (1) excising the necrotic bone and avascular scar, (2) applying the Ilizarov external fixator, (3) acutely shortening the limb by compression at the excision site, (4) making a corticotomy proximal or distal to the excision site, (5) providing soft tissue coverage if necessary, and finally (6) relengthening through the corticotomy site.

This technique, most effectively employed if the length of the necrotic bone is less than or equal to 4 cm, is illustrated by the case of Mr. J.S., a 27-year-old man who was referred to our clinic with chronic osteomyelitis and nonunion of his right tibia. Three years before, he had sustained a grade IIIB open fracture of his right tibial diaphysis in a motorcycle accident. At the time of the accident, he was initially treated with external fixation, which was later converted to an intramedullary nail. Unfortunately, because Mr. J.S. went on to have a diaphyseal osteomyelitis, this nail had to be removed and a second external fixator was applied (Fig. 19–13). In addition to the massive comminution and displacement of the fracture, his right leg sustained significant soft tissue damage secondary to the accident that required both a gastrocnemius muscle flap and a split-thickness skin graft to cover the exposed bone adequately (Fig. 19–14).

When the patient arrived at our clinic, he had no external fixator in place and the skin grafts were healing quite well (Fig. 19–15). He complained of pain with walking. On physical examination, the patient's right leg was in obvious varus. There was no erythema, fluctuance, or sinus tracts visible on the overlying skin. The gastrocnemius flap was pink, and he was neurovascularly intact with nearly full range of motion at the knee and ankle. Radiographic examination revealed a nonunion of the right tibia with approximately 25 degrees of varus and 30 degrees of dorsal angulation (Fig. 19–16). A bone scan was negative for active infection. At this point, a lengthy conversation was held with the patient and limb salvage was decided on. Mr. J.S. was instructed to stop the oral antibiotics he had previously been prescribed (to optimize the yield of intraoperative cultures), and surgery was scheduled for a few weeks after this visit.

In the operating room, it was first important to determine how much tibial bone was involved in the disease process. To visualize the area in question, an incision was made lateral to the anterior muscle flap and dissection was continued down to the periosteum of the previous fracture site. Using a periosteal elevator to identify its cortices, the bone was found to be very sclerotic about 1.5 cm on either side of the nonunion. There was no evidence of frank pus. At this point, intraoperative biopsy specimens were obtained and sent for culture. Given the fact that the area of necrosis was limited,

the decision was made to pursue a course of acute shortening followed by limb relengthening.

The next aspect of the surgery was thorough débridement of the sclerotic bone at and around the nonunion site. Using an oscillating saw, a 4-cm portion of the tibia that included the nonunion site was resected. The diaphyseal bone both proximal and distal to the débridement area was curetted to bleeding bone. The area was irrigated with several liters of soap and saline by pulsatile lavage. Drill holes were made both proximally and distally to allow adequate purchase of the reduction forceps that would compress the diaphyseal shaft. Before compression, a fibular osteotomy was also done at this level, approximately at the junction of the middle and distal thirds of the fibula. As the two ends of the tibia were compressed together, proper alignment was verified with anteroposterior and lateral fluoroscopic imaging.

After an adequate reduction was achieved, the focus of the operation turned toward application of the Ilizarov external fixator frame. When the fixator was pinned to the proximal and distal portions of the tibia, rotational alignment was verified under fluoroscopy and the frame was secured. The excision site was then placed under forceful compression. The final part of this operation was to make a more distal metaphyseal corticotomy to allow subsequent limb relengthening. Although proximal corticotomies are often employed in this technique, a distal site was chosen in this patient simply because skin graft lay adherent to the bone more proximally. If the corticotomy were performed through the skin graft site, there would not have been the pliability and elasticity in the remaining soft tissue envelope necessary for adequate closure. Thus, the corticotomy that would serve as the regenerate zone for future limb relengthening was made distal to the excision site.

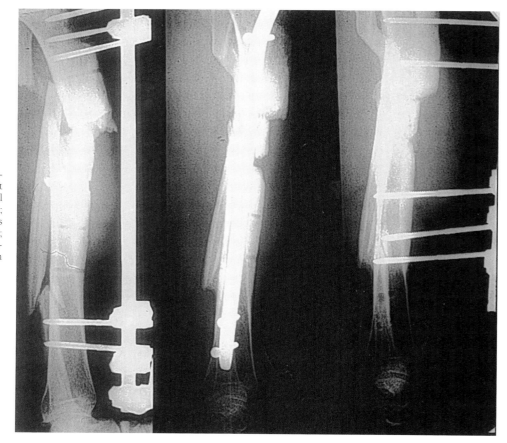

FIGURE 19–13. Sequential radiographs of Mr. J.S. showing, from left to right, his leg after he had his initial injury (with external fixator in place); his leg after the external fixator was replaced with an intramedullary nail; and, lastly, his leg after the nail became infected and was removed in favor of a second external fixator.

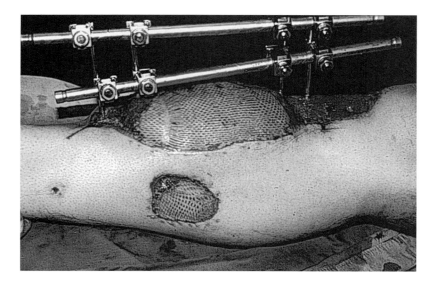

FIGURE 19–14. The massive soft tissue loss Mr. J.S. suffered from his initial injury necessitated a gastrocnemius muscle flap and split-thickness skin graft over the open area.

The immediate postoperative course for Mr. J.S. was unremarkable. He received early mobilization from physical therapy with weight bearing as tolerated on the right lower extremity. Before discharge from the hospital on postoperative day 3, the patient was instructed in how to lengthen the Ilizarov apparatus by approximately one quarter of a millimeter four times a day starting 1 week after the operation. Although he was maintained with intravenous antibiotics during his brief hospital stay, Mr. J.S. was discharged home with oral antibiotics (a first-generation cephalosporin and

rifampin) to which his intraoperative culture (*S. aureus*) would prove to be sensitive.

Radiographs 2 weeks after his operation revealed excellent alignment and distraction at the distal corticotomy but unfortunately some distraction at the more proximal compression site. This area was compressed further in the office by tightening the Ilizarov rings closer together. Three weeks postoperatively, the patient was ambulating on crutches without difficulty. Although the right leg was measured and found to be fully out to length approximately 4 months after the surgery, adequate fusion at the compression site remained problematic and the decision was made to augment the area with multiple half-pins and cancellous bone graft from the posterior iliac crest. After bone grafting, the patient did very well, and follow-up radiographs over the next several months

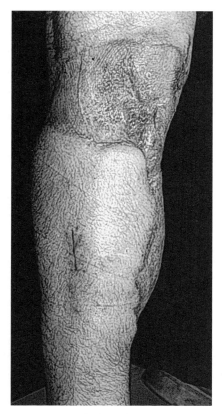

FIGURE 19–15. On our initial physical examination, Mr. J.S. demonstrated well-healed soft tissues of his leg.

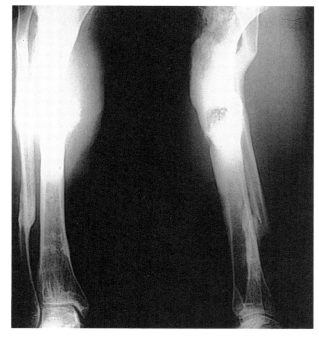

FIGURE 19–16. Initial radiographs of Mr. J.S. at our clinic revealed a nonunion of the right tibia with approximately 25 degrees of varus and 30 degrees of dorsal angulation.

FIGURE 19–17. Sequential radiographs of Mr. J.S.'s leg over several months show, from left to right, increasing incorporation of the bone graft at the more proximal compression site as well as progressive lengthening, though in the more distal regenerate zone.

showed increasing incorporation of the bone graft at the compression site as well as progressive lengthening and bone formation in the regenerate zone (Fig. 19–17).

Because Ilizarov external fixation allows early weight bearing, Mr. J.S. remained active during the course of his treatment and continued to enjoy many of his favorite activities, including bow hunting (Fig. 19–18). Seven months after visiting our clinic, with radiographic evidence of excellent bone formation at both the proximal compression site and the distal regenerate zone, Mr. J.S. was brought back to the operating room to have the external fixator removed. He did extremely well in the months to follow, using only a right leg orthosis for support. One year after the initial operation, Mr. J.S. was found to have no leg length disparity and to be enjoying an extremely active life. Radiographic examination showed excellent leg alignment, with further callus formation at both the proximal and distal sites (Fig. 19–19).

CASE 2

Bone Transport

If the segment of necrotic bone and tissue to be resected is large, employing a strategy of acute shortening and limb relengthening may be difficult. Although it is certainly possible, compressing together two diaphyseal ends over a distance much greater than 4 cm risks buckling the remaining soft tissue envelope and compromising its vascular supply. In such circumstances, a more favorable reconstructive strategy is not to shorten the limb at all but to hold it out to length and subsequently fill in segmental gaps with bone transport. This technique consists of the following steps: (1) excising the necrotic bone and avascular scar, (2) applying the Ilizarov external fixator, (3) holding the limb at length, (4) making a corticotomy proximal or distal to the excision site, (5) providing soft tissue coverage if necessary, (6) lengthening through the corticotomy site, and (7) transporting bone to the excision site.

This strategy can be used to fill large gaps within bone, to fuse diseased joints, or sometimes both, which happened to be the case with Mr. J.L., a 39-year-old man who came to our clinic 15 months after sustaining a grade IIIB open fracture of

his left distal tibia in a motorcycle accident. His past medical history was significant for insulin-dependent diabetes mellitus, intravenous drug abuse, and smoking two packs of cigarettes a day for over 20 years. Previous intraoperative cultures had been positive for methicillin-resistant *S. aureus*, for which Mr. J.L. had been treated with several months of intravenous vancomycin therapy. Surgically, he was initially treated with external fixation, bone grafting, and free flap

FIGURE 19–18. This picture of Mr. J.S. bow hunting with his Ilizarov external fixator frame in place illustrates that patients are able to remain active during their treatment.

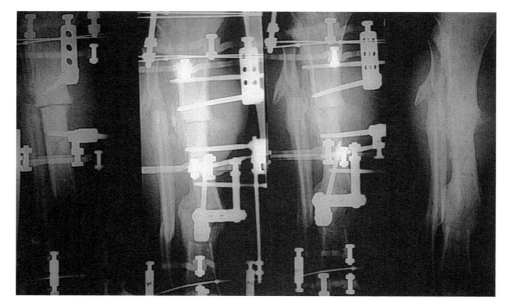

FIGURE 19–19. Sequential radiographs demonstrating, from left to right, progressive bone formation at both the proximal compression site and distal regenerate zone. The last film was taken 1 year after Mr. J.S.'s initial operation, approximately 5 months after his external fixator was removed. It shows abundant callus formation at both the proximal and distal sites.

coverage. He had been doing fairly well until 1 year after his injury, when he suffered a fracture through his bone grafting site. At that point he had a repair of his nonunion, followed by repeated bone grafting. Since that time, from about 12 to 15 months after the initial trauma, he had been complaining of intermittent fevers and persistent drainage from his wounds.

On initial physical examination, the patient's left lower extremity was remarkable for a draining wound on both the medial and lateral aspects of his ankle. He had a free flap over the dorsum of his ankle that appeared to be healthy. He was

neurovascularly intact distally with fair range of motion at the ankle joint. Plain films revealed a nonunion of his left distal tibia and fibula with posterior and medial angulation of the distal fragment (Fig. 19–20A). The presumptive diagnosis of an infected distal tibial metaphysis with articular involvement was made. At this point, a lengthy discussion was conducted with the patient and his family regarding therapeutic options. In particular, given the patient's multiple co-morbidities and his treatment failure over a 15-month period with several previous surgeries and a prolonged vancomycin trial, amputation was given a great deal of consideration.

FIGURE 19–20. *A,* Plain radiograph of Mr. J.L.'s left leg at the time of his initial visit reveals a nonunion of his left distal tibia and fibula with medial angulation of the distal fragment, in which there are five screws. *B,* Plain film 3 months postoperatively shows increasing distraction at the proximal corticotomy site. *C,* Radiograph 10 months after the initial surgery reveals a 9-cm distraction zone at the proximal corticotomy site, allowing the tibia nearly to reach the talus. *D,* At 14 months after the initial placement of the external fixator, plain film demonstrates bone fusion at the tibiotalar docking site and adequate bone growth in the regenerate zone.

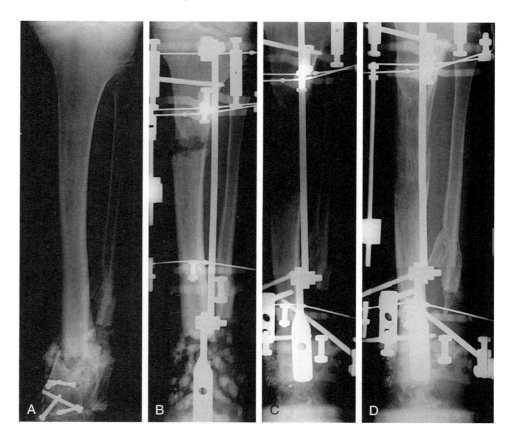

Mr. J.L. understood that amputation would most likely return him to work sooner than if he embarked on a course of limb salvage surgery. Furthermore, he was made aware that proceeding down the path of attempted limb salvage would probably require an additional year in an external fixator. The importance of ceasing all substance and tobacco use was emphasized. Finally, it was discussed that, despite everyone's best efforts, embarking on a course of limb salvage might ultimately result in a below-knee amputation. In the end, Mr. J.L. was firm in his decision to try to save his leg. As a result, all antibiotics were stopped and surgery was scheduled. Because the amount of diseased bone appeared to be extensive (affecting the distal tibia and ankle joint), the planned approach was to resect all of the necrotic areas, hold the limb out to length, and use bone transport to achieve a fusion between the remaining tibia and the talus.

Three weeks after his initial visit, Mr. J.L. was brought to the operating room and underwent a radical excision of approximately 7 cm of necrotic distal tibia. The area was irrigated copiously with pulsatile lavage. In addition, antibiotic beads were placed, an Ilizarov external fixator applied, and a corticotomy performed proximal to the area of resection. Antibiotic beads were used in this case and not in that of Mr. J.S. because the site of disease here was being held out to length rather than being compressed. As a result, a vast potential space was created in which residual bacteria could proliferate. Before filling this dead space with antibiotic beads, intraoperative biopsy specimens were obtained and sent for culture.

In the months that followed his surgery, Mr. J.L. did very well with oral antibiotics (trimethoprim-sulfamethoxazole and metronidazole) to which his intraoperative culture (methicillin-resistant *S. aureus*) was sensitive, remaining afebrile and without drainage. Radiographs showed increasing distraction at the proximal corticotomy site (see Fig. 19–20*B*). The antibiotic beads were exchanged approximately 3 months after their placement and again at 5 months. Exchanging beads is important not only to maintain an adequate depot of local antibiotic but also to adjust to the decreasing size of the resection site. Ten months after the initial surgery, radiographs revealed a 9-cm distraction zone at the proximal corticotomy, allowing the tibia nearly to reach the talus (see Fig. 19–20*C*). Proper alignment continued to be maintained.

Because the limb was determined to be nearly out to length, Mr. J.L. was brought back to the operating room for the bone transport phase of the reconstruction. The antibiotic beads, having fulfilled their role as temporary fillers of dead space, were removed to create room for the graft. The leading edges of the tibia and talus were redébrided to healthy, bleeding bone, and cancellous graft from the posterior iliac crest was transported to augment the fusion site. Although the patient did well immediately after the surgery, he returned 1 month postoperatively complaining of foul-smelling drainage from his medial and lateral ankle wounds. For this, the patient was soon brought back to the operating room for an incision and drainage. Cultures at that time revealed *Xanthomonas* and *Enterococcus* species sensitive to doxycycline. The patient did well with a regimen of doxycycline, trimethoprim-sulfamethoxazole, and metronidazole and his wounds closed secondarily over the next several months.

Approximately 14 months after the initial placement of the external fixator, all of the drainage had cleared. Radiographically, the bone fusion at the tibiotalar docking site and the bone growth in the regenerate zone appeared sufficiently strong (see Fig. 19–20*D*). With the fusion site and regenerate zone no longer needing protection, the decision was made to bring the patient back to the operating room to have the

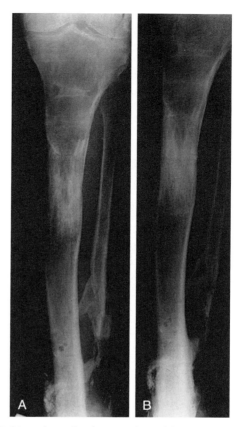

FIGURE 19–21. Radiographs of Mr. J.L.'s leg at (*A*) 2 years and (*B*) 3 years after his initial operation confirm successful tibiotalar fusion and continued cortical re-formation of the regenerate zone.

external fixator removed. This procedure went smoothly, and 6 months later Mr. J.L. was symptom-free and ambulatory. Radiographs at this time and 1 year later confirmed successful tibiotalar fusion and continued cortical re-formation of the regenerate zone (Fig. 19–21).

SYSTEMIC ANTIBIOTIC THERAPY

As mentioned from the outset, systemic antibiotic therapy is the most appropriate therapy for acute osteomyelitis, in which bone is still well vascularized. The treatment of vertebral osteomyelitis is also primarily with antibiotics,[68] although there is a role for surgery in cases of severe vertebral destruction.[80]

In contrast, of course, the role for systemic antibiotics in the management of chronic osteomyelitis is mostly adjunctive, helping to keep the surrounding, viable tissues infection-free after débridement. Much attention has been given in the past to the ability of various antibiotics to penetrate bone and to the role of high blood levels of antibiotics in promoting that penetration. In our view, this is problematic because the site of infection that is of fundamental concern is dead bone, usually surrounded by inflammatory cells or frank pus. The focus of disease therefore is not only avascular but also surrounded by an acidic and hypoxic environment, precisely the conditions that render penicillins and cephalosporins unstable and aminoglycosides inactive.[111, 136, 140, 145] Furthermore, in the necrotic bone, it is likely that the bacteria are not very metabolically active, rendering the action of any antibiotic much less potent.[48, 90] It is clear that, in the setting of chronic osteomyelitis, systemic antibiotics should be thought of as adjuncts in the management of what is a primarily surgical illness.

Antibiotic administration is helpful in this setting only insofar as it allows optimal healing of the operative site and decreases the risk of infection in surrounding and distant sites.[137] After intraoperative tissue culture specimens are taken from the infected bone, the patient should be restarted with broad-spectrum intravenous antibiotics to cover the common offending agents, such as *S. aureus* and *P. aeruginosa*.[52] When culture results are available, the antibiotic choice should be tailored to the patient's specific organisms and their sensitivities. For *S. aureus*, a penicillinase-resistant penicillin or first-generation cephalosporin is usually the best choice. If the *S. aureus* is oxacillin resistant, other agents may be effective, such as trimethoprim-sulfamethoxazole, clindamycin, doxycycline or minocycline, or a quinolone. It is our custom to supplement any agent used in treatment with 1 to 2 months of rifampin on the basis of animal studies[95, 98, 128] as well as clinical data.[93, 94]

The approach is similar for other staphylococci and gram-negative organisms: choose an antibiotic on the basis of in vitro sensitivities and, with laboratory confirmation of rifampin sensitivity, supplement with rifampin. Although commonly used for therapy of tuberculosis and of difficult to treat staphylococcal infections, rifampin is truly a broad-spectrum antibiotic, inhibiting the majority of bacteria of any genus. Although a very active agent, it cannot be used as sole therapy because of a high spontaneous mutation rate in *Staphylococcus*, *Mycobacterium*, and presumably other species of bacteria. Patients treated with rifampin monotherapy for pyogenic infections can be expected to have active infections and rifampin-resistant bacteria within 1 to 2 weeks.

The appropriate duration of systemic antibiotic therapy is not currently known. Interestingly, some of the best results reported in the literature are from a group who used antibiotics only perioperatively, coupled with aggressive débridement.[35] Recalling the pathophysiology of chronic osteomyelitis, this approach seems to be entirely logical but one that requires incredible fortitude on the part of both patient and surgeon. Many of the patients in this study were taken to the operating room several times during the first week. At the University of Connecticut Health Center, we generally have our patients continue antibiotics until the operative site has healed completely (approximately 3 to 4 months).

As long as antibiotics are chosen that have been shown to be active against the infecting microbes in vitro, the route of antibiotic delivery (i.e., oral or intravenous) is probably inconsequential.[132] Although intravenous therapy has long been the norm in the treatment of post-traumatic osteomyelitis, there is evidence to suggest that switching to an oral route of administration earlier in the postoperative course may yield a similar outcome. Swiontkowski and co-workers[132] conducted a study in which they treated 93 patients with chronic osteomyelitis with combined surgical débridement, soft tissue coverage, and an antibiotic regimen of 5 to 7 days of intravenous therapy followed by oral antibiotics for 6 weeks. They compared the outcomes of these patients with those of a group of 22 patients treated previously with the same surgical management but 6 weeks of culture-specific intravenous antibiotics. Interestingly, there were no differences in the outcomes of the two groups. Certainly, if these data are reproduced, an increasing number of centers will adopt this treatment regimen given the inherent advantages of oral therapy: enhanced comfort of the patient, decreased chance of line infection, and improved cost-efficiency.

COMPLEMENTARY THERAPIES

Several so-called *complementary* therapies have been used with some regularity in the treatment of chronic osteomyelitis and deserve mention in this chapter. Such therapies have as their goal either improvement of the host response to infection or promotion of healing of the bone. Hyperbaric oxygen has long been proposed as an adjunctive measure that would improve host defenses at the site of infection. The principle behind this treatment is that low oxygen tensions in infected bone inhibit the normal activity of immune mediators, such as macrophages and polymorphonuclear leukocytes. In in vitro studies, for example, *S. aureus* is not killed by polymorphonuclear leukocytes incubated in either severely hypoxic or anaerobic environments, with intermediate levels of hypoxia causing lesser reductions in killing efficiency. Furthermore, as we have discussed, the activity of many antibiotics is greatest in aerobic environments. Hyperbaric oxygen therapy, which increases oxygen tension above 250 mm Hg, is theorized to augment the host's immune system, create a hostile environment for anaerobes, allow the formation of peroxides that kill bacteria, and promote wound healing.[75, 76] Although the use of hyperbaric oxygenation has shown some promise in several studies,[57, 61, 75, 76] there has not yet been a single controlled study to our knowledge that demonstrates its utility in the treatment of chronic osteomyelitis.

Other complementary modalities are used in an attempt to enhance skeletal healing after the infection has been controlled. One such modality is electrical stimulation. That electrical stimulation may have a role in inducing the healing of delayed unions and nonunions is based on findings that fractures in bone have a negative charge and manipulating that potential can lead to alterations in fracture healing.[6, 40] Three different types of electrical stimulation delivery are commonly described (direct current, inductive coupling, and capacitive coupling),[108] and each of them has data that support its efficacy. One study from 1990 demonstrated healing in 12 of 20 patients with delayed tibial unions treated with inductive coupling compared with 1 of 20 who were in a randomized, blinded placebo group.[127] A 1994 study reported equally impressive results in cases of long bone nonunions: 6 of 10 in the capacitive coupling group were healed versus 0 of 10 who received treatment with placebo.[124] The indication for this mode of therapy is having a nonunion that is in acceptable alignment. Contraindications for electrical stimulation include an unacceptable malalignment, the presence of septic pseudarthrosis, and a gap of greater than half the diameter of the bone.[27]

Another means of stimulating bone healing is ultrasound. In a multicenter, prospective, randomized, double-blind, placebo-controlled study, using low-intensity ultrasound was shown to decrease the amount of time to radiographic union in the treatment of displaced distal radius fractures.[71] Although the reasons behind this finding are currently unclear, it is theorized that ultrasound waves act as a mechanical deforming force that acts as an impetus for accelerated bone formation.[117] The role of ultrasound in treating chronic osteomyelitis is not well defined.

SUMMARY

Chronic osteomyelitis is most often due to trauma and generally has a protracted, indolent clinical course. It should be acknowledged as a *concrete absce*ss and treated with a combined approach of surgical débridement, skeletal stabilization, dead space management, soft tissue coverage, and antibiotic therapy. Although these principles are the cornerstone of management, it is important to recognize the formidable physical and psychologic challenges facing patients with chronic osteomyelitis and foster a multidisciplinary approach in their care. The entire staff of health care professionals, from physicians and nurses to physical therapists and social workers, must work together to communicate effectively and compassionately with the patient and his or her family to establish a dynamic, ongoing dialogue. In so doing, we may be able not only to treat disease but also to educate people about their condition, from the practical importance of dressing changes or quitting smoking to a more global understanding of its frequently unrelenting nature.

REFERENCES

1. Anglen, J.O.; Apostles, P.S.; Christensen, G.; et al. Removal of surface bacteria by irrigation. J Orthop Res 14:251, 1996.
2. Anglen, J.O.; Apostles, P.S.; Christensen, G.; Gainor, B. The efficacy of various irrigation solutions in removing slime-producing *Staphylococcus.* J Orthop Trauma 8:390, 1994.
3. Anthony, J.P.; Mathes, S.J.; Alpert, B.S. The muscle flap in the treatment of chronic lower extremity osteomyelitis: Results in patients over 5 years after treatment. Plast Reconstr Surg 88:311, 1991.
4. Arnold, P.G.; Yugueros, O.; Hanssen, A.D. Muscle flaps in osteomyelitis of the lower extremity: A 20-year account. Plast Reconstr Surg 104:107, 1999.
5. Barnes, R.W. Amputations: An Illustrated Manual. Philadelphia, Hanley & Belfus, 2000.
6. Becker, R.O. The bioelectric factors in amphibian limb regeneration. J Bone Joint Surg Am 43:643, 1961.
7. Beltran, J.; Noto, A.M.; McGhee, R.B.; et al. Infection of the musculoskeletal system: High field strength MR imaging. Radiology 164:449, 1987.
8. Bergman, B.R. Antibiotic prophylaxis in open and closed fractures—A controlled clinical trial. Acta Orthop Scand 53:57, 1982.
9. Bhaskar, S.N.; Cutright, D.; Hunsuck, E.E.; Gross, A. Pulsating water jet devices in the débridement of combat wounds. Mil Med 136:264, 1971.
10. Blume, P.A.; Dey, H.M.; Daley, L.J.; et al. Diagnosis of pedal osteomyelitis with Tc-99m HMPAO labeled leukocytes. J Foot Ankle Surg 36:120, 1997.
11. Bohm, E.; Josten, C. What's new in exogenous osteomyelitis? Pathol Res Pract 1888:254, 1992.
12. Bondurant, F.J.; Cotler, H.B.; Buckle, R.; et al. The medical and economic impact of severely injured lower extremities. J Trauma 28:1270, 1988.
13. Burgess, E.M. The below-knee amputation. Bull Prosthet Res 10:19, 1968.
14. Buxton, T.B.; Horner, J.; Hinton, A.; Rissing, J.P. In vivo glycocalyx expression by *Staphylococcus aureus* phage type 52/52A/80 in *S. aureus* osteomyelitis. Infect Dis 156:942, 1987.
15. Calhoun, J.H.; Anger, D.M.; Mader, J.; Ledbetter, B.R. The Ilizarov technique in the treatment of osteomyelitis. Tex Med 87:56, 1991.
16. Carragee, E.J.; Kim, D.; Van Der Vlugt, T.; Vittum, D. The clinical use of erythrocyte sedimentation rate in pyogenic vertebral osteomyelitis. Spine 22:2089, 1997.
17. Carragee, E.J. Pyogenic vertebral osteomyelitis. J Bone Joint Surg Am 79:874, 1997.
18. Chan, Y.S.; Ueng, S.W.; Wang, C.J.; et al. Management of small infected tibial defects with antibiotic-impregnated autogenic cancellous bone grafting. J Trauma 45:758, 1998.
19. Chapman, M.W. Role of bone stability in open fractures. Instr Course Lect 31:75, 1982.
20. Cho, S.H.; Song, H.R.; Koo, K.H.; et al. Antibiotic-impregnated cement beads in the treatment of chronic osteomyelitis. Bull Hosp Jt Dis 56:140, 1997.
21. Cierny, G., III; Mader, J.; Penninck, J. A clinical staging system for adult osteomyelitis. Contemp Orthop 10:5, 1985.
22. Cierny, G., III. Classification and treatment of adult osteomyelitis. In: Evarts, C.M., ed. Surgery of the Musculoskeletal System, 2nd ed. London, Churchill Livingstone, 1990, p. 4337.
23. Cierny, G., III. Infected tibial nonunions (1981–1995): The evolution of change. Clin Orthop 360:97, 1999.
24. Cierny, G., III; Mader, J.T. Approach to adult osteomyelitis. Orthop Rev 16:259, 1987.
25. Clansey, B.J.; Hansen, S.T. Open fractures of the tibia: A review of 102 cases. J Bone Joint Surg Am 60:118, 1978.
26. Clawson, D.K.; Dunn, A.W. Management of common bacterial infections of bones and joints. J Bone Joint Surg Am 49:165, 1974.
27. Connolly, J.F. Selection, evaluation and indications for electrical stimulation of ununited fractures. Clin Orthop 161:39, 1981.
28. Curtis, M.J.; Brown, P.R.; Dick, J.D.; Jinnah, R.H. Contaminated fractures of the tibia: A comparison of treatment modalities in an animal model. J Orthop Res 13:286, 1995.
29. Hogt, A.; Dankert, J.; Feijen, J. Adhesion of coagulase-negative staphylococci to methacrylate polymers and copolymers. J Biomed Mater Res 20:533, 1986.
30. Dendrinos, G.K.; Kontos, S.; Lyritisis, E. Use of the Ilizarov technique for treatment of non-union of the tibia associated with infection. J Bone Joint Surg Am 77:835, 1995.
31. Dirschl, D.R.; Almekinders, L.C. Osteomyelitis: Common causes and treatment recommendations. Drugs 45:29, 1993.
32. Dirschl, D.R.; Dahners, L.E. The mangled extremity: When should it be amputated? J Am Acad Orthop Surg 4:182, 1996.
33. Domingue, G.J.; Woody, H.B. Bacterial persistence and expression of disease. Clin Microbiol Rev 10:320, 1997.
34. Dougherty, S.L.T; Simmens, R.L. Infections in bionic man: The pathology of infections in prosthetic devices. Curr Probl Surg 19:265, 1982.
35. Eckardt, J.J; Wirganowicz, P.Z.; Mar, T. An aggressive surgical approach to the management of chronic osteomyelitis. Clin Orthop 298:229, 1994.
36. Emami, A.; Mjoberg, B.; Larson, S. Infected tibial nonunion. Good results after open cancellous bone grafting in 37 cases. Acta Orthop Scand 66:447, 1995.
37. Emami, A.; Mjoberg, B.; Ragnarsson, B.; Larson, S. Changing epidemiology of tibial shaft fractures. 513 cases compared between 1971–1975 and 1986–1990. Acta Orthop Scand 67:557, 1996.
38. Fischer, B.; Vaudaux, P.; Magnin, M.; et al. Novel animal model for studying the molecular mechanisms of bacterial adhesion to bone-implanted metallic devices: Role of fibronectin in *Staphylococcus aureus* adhesion. J Orthop Res 14:914, 1996.

39. Fitzgerald, R.H., Jr.; Ruttle, P.E.; Arnold, P.G.; et al. Local muscle flaps in the treatment of chronic osteomyelitis. J Bone Joint Surg Am 67:175, 1985.

40. Friedenberg, Z.B.; Brighton, C.T. Bioelectric potentials in bone. J Bone Joint Surg Am 48:915, 1966.

41. Gonzalez, E.G.; Corcoran, P.J.; Reyes, R.L. Energy expenditure in below-knee amputees: Correlation with stump length. Arch Phys Med Rehabil 55:111, 1974.

42. Gordon, S.L.; Greer, R.B.; Craig, C.P. Report of four cases culturing L-form variants of staphylococci. J Bone Joint Surg Am 53:1150, 1971.

43. Gray, E.D.; Peters, G.; Verstegen, M.; Regelmann, W.E. Effect of extracellular slime substance from Staphylococcus epidermidis on human cellular immune response. Lancet 1:365, 1984.

44. Green, S.A. Skeletal defects. A comparison of bone grafting and bone transport for skeletal defects. Clin Orthop 301:111, 1994.

45. Green, S.A. Osteomyelitis. The Ilizarov perspective. Orthop Clin North Am 22:515, 1991.

46. Gregory, R.T.; Gould, R.J.; Peclet, M.; et al. The mangled extremity syndrome (M.E.S.): A severity grading system for multi-system injury of the extremity. J Trauma 25:1147, 1985.

47. Gristina, A.B.; Jennings, R.A.; Naylor, P.T.; et al. Comparative in vitro antibiotic resistance of surface colonizing coagulase-negative staphylococci. Antimicrob Agents Chemother 33:813, 1989.

48. Gristina, A.G.; Naylor, P.T.; Myrvik, Q.N. Mechanisms of musculoskeletal sepsis. Orthop Clin North Am 22:363, 1991.

49. Gristina, A.G.; Oga, M.; Webb, L.X.; Hobgood, C.D. Adherent bacterial colonization in the pathogenesis of osteomyelitis. Science 228:990, 1985.

50. Gualdrini, G.; Zati, A.; Degli Esposti, S. The effects of cigarette smoke on the progression of septic pseudoarthrosis of the tibia treated by Ilizarov external fixator. Chir Organi Mov 81:395, 1996.

51. Gugenheim, J.J., Jr. The Ilizarov method. Orthopedic and soft tissue applications. Clin Plast Surg 25:567, 1998.

52. Gustilo, R.B.; Anderson, J.T. Prevention of infection in the treatment of one thousand and twenty-five open fractures of long bones. J Bone Joint Surg Am 58:453, 1976.

53. Gustilo, R.B.; Mendoza, R.M.; Williams, D.N. Problems in the management of type III (severe) open fractures. A classification of type III open fractures. J Trauma 24:742, 1984.

54. Gustilo, R.B. Management of infected non-union. In: Evarts, C.M., ed. Surgery of the Musculoskeletal System, 2nd ed. London, Churchill Livingstone, 1990, pp. 4429, 4455.

55. Helfet, D.L.; Howery, T.; Sanders, R.; et al. Limb salvage versus manipulation: Preliminary results of the mangled extremity severity score. Clin Orthop 256:80, 1990.

56. Hermann, M.; Vaudaux, P.E.; Pittet, D.; et al. Fibronectin, fibrinogen and laminin act as mediators of adherence of clinical staphylococcal isolates to foreign material. J Infect Dis 158:693, 1988.

57. Hill, G.B.; Osterhout, S. Experimental effects of hyperbaric oxygen on selected clostridial species. In vitro studies. J Infect Dis 125:17, 1972.

58. Hill, S.L.; Holtzman, G.I.; Buse, R. The effects of peripheral vascular disease with osteomyelitis in the diabetic foot. Am J Surg 177:282, 1999.

59. Holtom, P.D.; Smith, A.M. Introduction to adult posttraumatic osteomyelitis of the tibia. Clin Orthop 360:6, 1999.

60. Hong, S.W.; Seah, C.S.; Kuek, L.B.; Tan, K.C. Soft tissue coverage in compound and complicated tibial fractures using microvascular flaps. Ann Acad Med Singapore 27:182, 1998.

61. Hunt, T.K.; Pai, M.P. The effect of varying ambient oxygen tensions on wound metabolism and collagen synthesis. Surg Gynecol Obstet 135:756, 1972.

62. Ilizarov, G.A. Transosseous Osteosynthesis: Theoretical and Clinical Aspects of the Regeneration and Growth of Tissue. Berlin, Springer-Verlag, 1992.

63. Jacobs, R.F.; McCarthy, R.E.; Elser, J.M. Pseudomonas osteochondritis complicating puncture wounds of the foot in children: A 10-year evaluation. J Infect Dis 160:657, 1989.

64. Jensen, J.E.; Jensen, T.G.; Smith, T.K.; et al. Nutrition in orthopaedic surgery. J Bone Joint Surg Am 64:1263, 1982.

65. Johnson, G.M.; Regelmann, W.E.; Gray, E.D.; et al. Interference with granulocyte function by Staphylococcus epidermidis slime. Infect Immun 54:13, 1986.

66. Kelly, P.J.; William, W.J.; Coventry, M.B. Chronic osteomyelitis: Treatment with closed irrigation and suction. JAMA 213:1843, 1970.

67. Kelly, P.J. Infections of bones and joints in adult patients. Instr Course Lect 26:3, 1977.

68. Khan, I.A.; Vaccaro, A.R.; Zlotolow, D.A. Management of vertebral diskitis and osteomyelitis. Orthopedics 22:758, 1999.

69. Klein, M.B.; Chang, J. Management of hand and upper-extremity infections in heart transplant recipients. Plast Reconstr Surg 106:598, 2000.

70. Klemm, K. Antibiotic bead chains. Clin Orthop 295:63, 1993.

71. Kristiansen, T.K.; Ryaby, J.P.; McCabe, J.; et al. Accelerated healing of distal radial fractures with the use of specific low-intensity ultrasound. J Bone Joint Surg Am 79:961, 1997.

72. Krznaric, E.; DeRoo, M.; Verbruggen, A.; et al. Chronic osteomyelitis: Diagnosis with technetium-99m-D,L-hexamethylpropylene amine oxime labeled leukocytes. Eur J Nucl Med 23:792, 1996.

73. Lange, R.H. Limb reconstruction versus amputation decision making in massive lower extremity trauma. Clin Orthop 243:92, 1989.

74. Lisbona, R.; Rosenthall, L. Observations on the sequential use of 99mTc-phosphate complex and 67Ga imaging in osteomyelitis, cellulitis, and septic arthritis. Radiology 123:123, 1977.

75. Mader, J.T.; Adams, R.K.; Wallace, W.R.; et al. Hyperbaric oxygen as adjunctive therapy for osteomyelitis. Infect Dis Clin North Am 4:433, 1990.

76. Mader, J.T.; Brown, G.L.; Guckian, J.C.; et al. A mechanism for the amelioration by hyperbaric oxygen of experimental staphylococcal osteomyelitis in rabbits. J Infect Dis 142:915, 1980.

77. Mader, J.T.; Cripps, M.W.; Calhoun, J.H. Adult posttraumatic osteomyelitis of the tibia. Clin Orthop 360:14, 1999.

78. Marshall, K.A.; Edgerton, M.T.; Rodeheaver, G.T.; et al. Quantitative microbiology: Its application to hand injuries. Am J Surg 131:730, 1976.

79. Mathes, S.J.; Alpert, B.S.; Chang, N. Use of the muscle flap in chronic osteomyelitis: Experimental and clinical correlation. Plast Reconstr Surg 69:815, 1982.

80. Matsui, H.; Hirano, N.; Sakaguchi, Y. Vertebral osteomyelitis: An analysis of 38 surgically treated cases. Eur Spine J 7:50, 1998.

81. Maurer, A.H.; Chen, D.C.P.; Camargo, E.E. Utility of three-phase scintigraphy in suspected osteomyelitis: Concise communication. J Nucl Med 22:941, 1981.

82. May, J.W.; Jupiter, J.B.; Weiland, A.J.; Byrd, H.S. Clinical classification of post-traumatic tibial osteomyelitis. J Bone Joint Surg Am 71:1422, 1989.

83. Mayberry-Carson, K.J.; Tober-Meyer, B.; Smith, J.K.; et al. Bacterial adherence and glycocalyx formation in osteomyelitis experimentally induced with Staphylococcus aureus. Infect Immun 43:825, 1984.

84. Maynor, M.L.; Moon, R.E.; Camporesi, E.M.; et al. Chronic osteomyelitis of the tibia: Treatment with hyperbaric oxygen and autogenous microsurgical muscle transplantation. J South Orthop Assoc 7:43, 1998.

85. McCarthy, K.; Velchik, M.G.; Alavi, A.; et al. Indium-111–labeled white blood cells in the detection of osteomyelitis complicated by a pre-existing condition. J Nucl Med 29:1015, 1988.

86. Moshirfar, A.; Showers, D.; Logan, P.; Esterhai, J.L. Prosthetic options for below knee amputations and nonunion of the tibia. Clin Orthop 360:110, 1999.

87. Muha, J. Local wound care in diabetic foot complications. Aggressive risk management and ulcer treatment to avoid amputation. Postgrad Med 106:97, 1999.

88. Munoz-Fernandez, S.; Macia, M.A.; Pantoja, L.; et al. Osteoarticular infection in intravenous drug abusers: Influence of HIV infection and differences with non drug abusers. Ann Rheum Dis 52:570, 1993.

89. Murdoch, G. Levels of amputation and limiting factors. Ann R Coll Surg Engl 40:204, 1967.

90. Musher, D.M.; Lamm, N.; Darouiche, R.O.; et al. The current spectrum of Staphylococcus aureus infection in a tertiary care hospital. Medicine (Baltimore) 73:186, 1994.

91. Naylor, P.T.; Myrvik, Q.N.; Gristina, A.B. Antibiotic resistance of biomaterial-adherent coagulase-negative and coagulase-positive staphylococci. Clin Orthop 26:126, 1990.

92. Nelson, C.L.; Hickmon, S.G.; Skinner, R.A. Treatment of experimental osteomyelitis by surgical débridement and the implantation of bioerodable, polyanhydride-gentamicin beads. J Orthop Res 15:249, 1997.

93. Norden, C.W.; Bryant, R.; Palmer, D.; et al. Chronic osteomyelitis caused by *Staphylococcus aureus*: Controlled clinical trial of nafcillin therapy and nafcillin-rifampin therapy. South Med J 79:947, 1986.

94. Norden, C.W.; Fierer, J.; Bryant, R. Chronic staphylococcal osteomyelitis: Treatment with regimens containing rifampin. Rev Infect Dis 5(Suppl 3):S495, 1983.

95. Norden, C.W.; Shaffer, M. Treatment of experimental chronic osteomyelitis due to *Staphylococcus aureus* with vancomycin and rifampin. J Infect Dis 147:352, 1983.

96. Norden, C.W. Experimental osteomyelitis. A description of the model. J Infect Dis 122:410, 1970.

97. Norden, C.W. Lessons learned from animal models of osteomyelitis. Rev Infect Dis 10:103, 1988.

98. O'Reilly, T.; Kunz, S.; Sande, E.; et al. Relationship between antibiotic concentration in bone and efficacy of treatment of staphylococcal osteomyelitis in rats: Azithromycin compared with clindamycin and rifampin. Antimicrob Agents Chemother 36:2693, 1992.

99. Orr, H.W. A New Era of Treatment for Osteomyelitis and Other Infections. St. Paul, MN, Bruce Publishing, 1930, p. 48.

100. Palestro, C.J.; Roumanas, P.; Swyer, A.J.; et al. Diagnosis of musculoskeletal infection using combined In-111 labeled leukocyte and Tc-99m SC marrow imaging. Clin Nucl Med 17:269, 1992.

101. Palestro, C.J.; Torres, M.A. Radionuclide imaging in orthopedic infections. Semin Nucl Med 27:334, 1997.

102. Paley, D.; Catagni, M.A.; Argnani, F.; et al. Ilizarov treatment of tibial nonunions with bone loss. Clin Orthop 241:146, 1989.

103. Panda, M.; Ntungila, N.; Kalunda, M.; Hinsenkamp, M. Treatment of chronic osteomyelitis using the Papineau technique. Int Orthop 22:37, 1998.

104. Papineau, L.J.; Alfageme, A.; Dalcourt, J.P.; et al. Ostéomyélite chronique: Excision et greffe de spongieux a l'air libre après mises a plat extensives. Int Orthop 3:165, 1979.

105. Patzakis, M.J.; Greene, N.; Holtom, P.; et al. Culture results in open wound treatment with muscle transfer for tibial osteomyelitis. Clin Orthop 360:66, 1999.

106. Patzakis, M.J.; Harrey, J.P.; Ivler, D. The role of antibiotics in the management of open fractures. J Bone Joint Surg 56:532, 1974.

107. Patzakis, M.J.; Wilkins, J.; Kumar, J.; et al. Comparison of the results of bacterial cultures from multiple sites in chronic osteomyelitis of long bones. J Bone Joint Surg Am 76:664, 1994.

108. Perry, C.R. Bone repair techniques, bone graft, and bone graft substitutes. Clin Orthop 360:71, 1999.

109. Perry, C.R.; Rames, R.D.; Pearson, R.L. Treatment of septic tibial nonunions with local antibiotics and intramedullary nail. Orthop Trans 12:657, 1989.

110. Peters, K.M.; Adam, G.; Biedermann, M.; et al. Osteomyelitis today: Diagnostic imaging and therapy. Zentralbl Chir 118:637, 1993.

111. Reynolds, A.V.; Hamilton-Miller, J.M.T.; Brumfitt, W. Diminished effect of gentamicin under anaerobic and hypercapnic conditions. Lancet l:447, 1976.

112. Ring, D.; Jupiter, J.B.; Toh, S. Salvage of contaminated fractures of the distal humerus with thin wire external fixation. Clin Orthop 359:203, 1999.

113. Rittman, W.W.; Perren, S.M. Cortical Bone Healing after Internal Fixation and Infection. New York, Springer-Verlag, 1974.

114. Rittmann, W.W.; Schibili, M.; Matter, P.; et al. Open fractures: Long-term results in 200 consecutive cases. Clin Orthop 138:132, 1979.

115. Robson, M.C.; Duke, W.F.; Krizek, T.J. Rapid bacterial screening in the treatment of civilian wounds. J Surg Res 14:426, 1973.

116. Roine, I.; Arguedas, A.; Faingezicht, I.; Rodriguez, F. Early detection of sequelae-prone osteomyelitis in children with use of simple clinical and laboratory criteria. Clin Infect Dis 24:849, 1997.

117. Rubin, J.; McLeod, K.J.; Titus, L.; et al. Formation of osteoclast-like cells is suppressed by low frequency, low intensity electric fields. J Orthop Res 14:7, 1996.

118. Sachs, B.L.; Shaffer, J.W. A staged Papineau protocol for chronic osteomyelitis. Clin Orthop 184:256, 1984.

119. Saltzman, C.L.; Pedowitz, W.J. Diabetic foot infections. Instr Course Lect 48:317, 1999.

120. Santoro, V.; Henley, M.; Benirschke, S.; Mayo, K. Prospective comparison of unreamed interlocking IM nails versus half-pin external fixation in open tibial fractures. J Orthop Trauma 5:238, 1991.

121. Schandelmaier, P.; Krettek, C.; Rudolf, J.; Tscherne, H. Outcome of tibial shaft fractures with severe soft tissue injury treated by unreamed nailing versus external fixation. J Trauma 39:707, 1995.

122. Schauwecker, D.S. The scintigraphic diagnosis of osteomyelitis. AJR 158:9, 1992.

123. Schurman, D.J.; Smith, R.L. Bacterial biofilm and infected biomaterials, prostheses and artificial organs. In: Esterhai, J.L.; Gristina, A.G.; Poss, R., eds. Musculoskeletal Infection. Park Ridge, IL, American Academy of Orthopaedic Surgeons, 1992, p. 133.

124. Scott, G.; King, J.B. A prospective, double-blind trial of electrical capacitative coupling in the treatment of non-union of long bones. J Bone Joint Surg Am 76:820, 1994.

125. Sekiguchi, J.; Haramoto, U.; Kobayashi, S.; Nomura, S. Free flap transfers for the treatment of osteomyelitis of the lower leg. Scand J Plast Reconstr Surg Hand Surg 32:171, 1998.

126. Seltzer, S.E. Value of computed tomography in planning medical and surgical treatment of chronic osteomyelitis. J Comput Assist Tomogr 8:482, 1984.

127. Sharrard, W.J. A double-blind trial of pulsed electromagnetic fields for delayed union of tibial fractures. J Bone Joint Surg Br 72:347, 1990.

128. Shirtliff, M.E.; Mader, J.T.; Calhoun, J. Oral rifampin plus azithromycin or clarithromycin to treat osteomyelitis in rabbits. Clin Orthop 359:229, 1999.

129. Sponseller, P.D.; Malech, H.L.; McCarthy, E.F.; et al. Skeletal involvement in children who have chronic granulomatous disease. J Bone Joint Surg Am 73:37, 1991.

130. Sudekamp, N.; Barbey, N.; Veuskens, A.; et al. The incidence of osteitis in open fractures. An analysis of 948 open fractures. J Orthop Trauma 7:473, 1993.

131. Swiontkowski, M.F. Surgical approaches in osteomyelitis. Use of laser Doppler flowmetry to determine non-viable bone. Infect Dis Clin North Am 4:501, 1990.

132. Swiontowski, M.F.; Hanel, D.P.; Vedder, N.B.; Schwappach, J.R. A comparison of short- and long-term intravenous antibiotic therapy in the postoperative management of adult osteomyelitis. J Bone Joint Surg Br 81:1046, 1999.

133. Tang, J.S.H.; Gold, R.H.; Bassett, L.W.; et al. Musculoskeletal infection of the extremities. Evaluation with MR imaging. Radiology 166:205, 1988.

134. Tetsworth, K.; Cierny, G., III. Osteomyelitis débridement techniques. Clin Orthop 360:87, 1999.

135. Tornetta, P.; Bergman, M.; Watnik, N.; Berkowitz, G. Treatment of grade IIIB open tibial fractures. J Bone Joint Surg Br 76:13, 1994.

136. Tresse, O.; Jouenne, T.; Junter, G.A. The role of oxygen limitation in the resistance of agar-entrapped, sessile-like *Escherichia coli* to aminoglycoside and beta-lactam antibiotics. J Antimicrob Chemother 36:521, 1995.

137. Trueta, J.; Morgan, J.D. Late results in the treatment of one-hundred cases of acute hematogenous osteomyelitis. Br J Surg 41:449, 1954.

138. Tsai, E.; Failla, J.M. Hand infections in the trauma patient. Hand Clin 15:373, 1999.

139. Tsukayama, D.T. Pathophysiology of posttraumatic osteomyelitis. Clin Orthop 360:22, 1999.

140. Tsukayama, D.T.; Guay, D.R.; Gustilo, R.B.; et al. The effect of anaerobiosis on antistaphylococcal antibiotics. Orthopedics 11:1285, 1988.

141. Tvrdek, M.; Nejedly, A.; Kletensky, J.; Kufa, R. Treatment of chronic osteomyelitis of the lower extremity using free flap transfer. Acta Chir Plast 41:46, 1999.

142. Ueng, S.W.; Wei, F.C.; Shih, C.H. Management of femoral diaphyseal infected nonunion with antibiotic beads, local therapy, external skeletal fixation, and staged bone grafting, J Trauma 46:97, 1999.

143. Unger, E.; Moldofsky, P.; Gatenby, R.; et al. Diagnosis of osteomyelitis by MR imaging. AJR 150:605, 1988.

144. Vassilopoulos, D.; Chalasani, P.; Jurado, R.L.; et al. Musculoskeletal infections in patients with human immunodeficiency virus infection. Medicine (Baltimore) 76:284, 1997.

145. Verkin, R.M.; Mandell, G.M. Alteration of effectiveness of antibiotics by anaerobiosis. J Lab Clin Med 89:65, 1977.

146. Vesco, L.; Boulahdour, H.; Hamissa, S.; et al. The value of combined radionuclide and magnetic resonance imaging in the diagnosis and conservative management of minimal or localized osteomyelitis of the foot in diabetic patients. Metabolism 48:922, 1999.

147. von Eiff, C.; Bettin, D.; Proctor, R.A.; et al. Recovery of small colony variants of *Staphylococcus aureus* following gentamicin bead placement for osteomyelitis. Clin Infect Dis 25:1250, 1997.

148. Waldvogel, F.A.; Medoff, G.; Swartz, M.N. Osteomyelitis: A review of clinical features, therapeutic considerations, and unusual aspects (first of three parts). N Engl J Med 282:198, 1970.

149. Waldvogel, F.A.; Medoff, G.; Swartz, M.N. Osteomyelitis: A review of clinical features, therapeutic considerations, and unusual aspects (third of three parts). N Engl J Med 282:316, 1970.

150. Walenkamp, G.H. Chronic osteomyelitis. Acta Orthop Scand 68:497, 1997.

151. Walenkamp, G.H.; Kleijn, L.L.; de Leeuw, M. Osteomyelitis treated with gentamicin-PMMA beads: 100 patients followed for 1–12 years. Acta Orthop Scand 69:518, 1998.

152. Webb, L.X.; Holman, J.; de Araujo, B.; et al. Antibiotic resistance in staphylococci adherent to cortical bone. J Orthop Trauma 8:28, 1994.

153. Weiss, S.J. Tissue destruction by neutrophils. N Engl J Med 320:365, 1989.

154. Williams, R.L.; Fukui, M.B.; Meltzer, C.C.; et al. Fungal spinal osteomyelitis in the immunocompromised patient: MR findings in three cases. AJNR 20:381, 1999.

155. Wood, M.B.; Cooney, W.P.; Irons, G.B. Lower extremity salvage and reconstruction by free-tissue transfer. Clin Orthop 201:151, 1985.

156. Wukich, D.K.; Abreu, S.H.; Callaghan, J.J.; et al. Diagnosis of infection by preoperative scintigraphy with indium-labeled white blood cells. J Bone Joint Surg Am 69:1353, 1987.

157. Yamashita, Y.; Uchida, A.; Yamakawa, T.; et al. Treatment of chronic osteomyelitis using calcium hydroxyapatite ceramic implants impregnated with antibiotic. Int Orthop 22:247, 1998.

158. Zobell, C.E.; Anderson, D.Q. Observations on the multiplication of bacteria in different volumes of stored seawater and the influence of oxygen tension and solid surfaces. Biol Bull 71:324, 1936.

CHAPTER 20

Nonunions: Evaluation and Treatment

Mark R. Brinker, M.D.

Fracture nonunion is a dreadful entity and is often the bane of the orthopaedic surgeon's existence. Although fracture nonunions may represent a very small percentage of the traumatologist's case load, they can account for a high percentage of a surgeon's stress, anxiety, and frustration. Fracture nonunion is often anticipated after a severe traumatic injury, such as an open fracture with segmental bone loss, but it may also make an unanticipated appearance after treatment of a low-energy fracture that seemed destined to heal.

A fracture nonunion represents a chronic medical condition associated with pain and with functional and psychosocial disability.[135] Because of the wide variation in patient responses to various stresses[133] and the impact it may have on a patient's family (e.g., relationships, income), these cases are often difficult to manage.

Between 90% and 95% of all fractures heal without problems.[61, 189] Nonunions comprise the small percentage of cases in which the biologic process of fracture repair is unable to overcome the local biology and mechanics of the bony injury.

DEFINITIONS

A fracture is said to have "gone on to nonunion" when the normal biologic healing processes of bone cease to the extent that solid healing cannot occur without further treatment intervention. The definition is largely subjective and imprecise because it calls for speculation (forecasting) of future events. The criteria are also not specific enough to result in low interobserver variability.

The literature contains myriad definitions of nonunion. For the purposes of clinical investigations, the U.S. Food and Drug Administration defines a nonunion as a fracture that is at least 9 months old and has not shown any signs of progression to healing for 3 consecutive months.[90, 237] Müller's[158] definition of nonunion is failure of a fracture (tibia) to unite after 8 months of nonoperative treatment. Although these two definitions are the most widely used

criteria, their arbitrary use of a temporal limit is flawed.[81] For example, several months of observation should not be required to declare a tibial shaft fracture with 10 cm of segmental bone loss a nonunion. Conversely, how does the orthopaedic surgeon define a slow-healing fracture that continues to consolidate but requires 12 months of observation to heal?

At best, definitions of nonunion and delayed union in the literature are inconsistent, subjective, ambiguous, and arbitrary; therefore, there are no objective criteria. These limitations produce difficulty in synthesizing the literature on series of nonunions. For clarity, I define *nonunion* as a fracture that, in the opinion of the treating physician, has no possibility of healing without further intervention. I define *delayed union* as a fracture that, in the opinion of the treating physician, shows slower progression to healing than was anticipated and is at substantial risk for becoming a nonunion without further intervention.

To fully appreciate the biologic processes and clinical implications of fracture nonunion, an understanding of the normal fracture repair process is required. The following section discusses the local biology of fracture healing, requirements for fracture union, and types of normal fracture repair.

FRACTURE REPAIR

Fracture repair is an astonishing process. The healing response involves spontaneous, structured regeneration of bony tissue that results in a return of mechanical stability to the skeletal system.

At the moment of bony injury, a predetermined response occurs. The response involves proliferation of tissues that ultimately lead to healing at the site of fracture.

The early biologic response at the fracture site is an inflammatory response with bleeding and the formation of a fracture hematoma. In the presence of osteoprogenitor cells from the periosteum and endosteum and hematopoietic cells capable of secreting growth factors, the repair

TABLE 20–1 ....
Type of Fracture Healing Based on Type of Stabilization

Type of Stabilization	Predominant Type of Healing
Cast (closed treatment)	Periosteal bridging callus and interfragmentary enchondral ossification
Compression plate	Primary cortical healing (cutting cone-type remodeling)
Intramedullary nail	Early: periosteal bridging callus Late: medullary callus
External fixator	Depends on extent of rigidity Less rigid: periosteal bridging callus More rigid: primary cortical healing
Inadequate immobilization With adequate blood supply	Hypertrophic nonunion (failed enchondral ossification)
Without adequate blood supply	Atrophic nonunion
Inadequate reduction with displacement at the fracture site	Oligotrophic nonunion

....

response of bone occurs rapidly. After fracture healing, bony remodeling progresses according to Wolff's law.[13, 14, 184, 206, 251]

The process of fracture repair involves intramembranous and enchondral bone formation. The process requires mechanical stability, an adequate blood supply, and good bony contact. The specific biologic response is related to the type and extent of injury and to the type of treatment (Table 20–1).

Healing through Callus

Some fracture treatment methods, such as cast immobilization, lack absolute rigid fixation of the fracture site. In the absence of rigid fixation, stabilization of bony fragments occurs by periosteal and endosteal callus formation. If an adequate blood supply exists at the fracture site, callus formation proceeds and results in a substantial increase in the cross-sectional area at the fracture surface. The increased diameter at the fracture site caused by callus formation enhances fracture stability. Fracture stability is also provided by the formation of fibrocartilage, which replaces granulation tissue at the fracture site. A critical event in the fracture repair process is mineralization of fibrocartilage. Only after calcification of fibrocartilage can enchondral bone formation proceed, in which bone replaces cartilage.

Direct Bone Healing

Direct osteonal healing occurs without the formation of an external callus and is characterized by gradual disappearance of the fracture line. The biologic process requires an adequate blood supply and absolute rigidity at the fracture site, which is most commonly accomplished with a compression plate. In areas of direct bone-to-bone contact, fracture repair resembles cutting-cone–type remodeling.

When small gaps exist between apposing fracture fragments, "gap healing" occurs through appositional bone formation.

Indirect Bone Healing

Indirect bone healing occurs in fractures that have been stabilized with less than absolute rigidity. Examples of fixation resulting in indirect bony healing include intramedullary nail fixation, tension band wire techniques, cerclage wiring, external fixation, and plate-and-screw fixation applied suboptimally. Indirect healing involves coupled bone resorption and formation at the fracture site. Healing occurs by a combination of external callus formation and enchondral ossification.

CAUSES OF NONUNIONS
....

Predisposing Factors: Instability, Inadequate Vascularity, and Poor Bone Contact

The most basic requirements for fracture healing include mechanical stability, an adequate blood supply (i.e., bone vascularity), and bone-to-bone contact. The absence of one or more of these factors predisposes the fracture to development of a nonunion. The basic requirements for healing may be negatively affected by the severity of the injury, suboptimal surgical fixation from a poor plan or a good plan carried out poorly, or a combination of injury severity and the suboptimal performance of the surgical procedure.

INSTABILITY

Mechanical instability can follow internal or external fixation and results in excessive motion at the fracture site. Factors producing mechanical instability include inadequate fixation with hardware (i.e., implants too small or too few), distraction at the fracture site with a gap between the fracture surfaces (recall that orthopaedic hardware is equally capable of holding bone apart as it is holding bone together), bone loss, and poor bone quality (i.e., poor purchase) (Fig. 20–1). If an adequate blood supply exists, excessive motion at the fracture site can result in abundant callus formation, widening of the fracture line, failure of fibrocartilage to mineralize and be replaced by bone, and failure of the fracture to unite.

INADEQUATE VASCULARITY

Loss of blood supply to the fracture surfaces may arise because of the severity of the injury or because of surgical dissection. Open fractures and high-energy closed injuries are associated with soft tissue stripping and damage to the periosteal blood supply. These injuries can also disrupt the nutrient vessels and impair the endosteal blood supply. Several studies have shown a relationship between the extent of soft tissue injury and the rate of the fracture nonunion. Court-Brown and co-workers[45] described 547 tibial shaft fractures treated with intramedullary nail fixation. The rate of nonunion in closed fractures was 3.4%, compared with a nonunion rate of 16.5% for open fractures. Among the group of patients with open fractures, markedly higher rates of nonunion were seen in those with the most severe soft tissue damage. Chatziyiannakis and colleagues[35] reported similar findings for 71 tibial shaft fractures treated with unilateral external fixation.

Vessel injury in certain anatomic areas, such as the posterior tibial artery, may also predispose to development of a nonunion.[24] The vascularity at the fracture site may also be compromised at the time of open reduction with excess stripping of the periosteum and damage to bone and the soft tissues during hardware insertion. Whatever the cause, inadequate vascularity at the fracture site results in necrotic bone at the ends of the fracture fragments, with or without large defects. These necrotic surfaces inhibit the normal biology of fracture healing and often result in fracture nonunion.

POOR BONE CONTACT

Bone-to-bone contact is an important requirement for fracture repair. Poor bone-to-bone contact at the fracture site may result from soft tissue interposition, malposition or malalignment of the fracture fragments, bone loss, or distraction of the fracture fragments. Whatever the cause, poor bone-to-bone contact compromises mechanical stability and creates a defect that the fracture repair process must bridge. As these defects increase in size, the probability of fracture union decreases. The threshold value for rapid bridging of cortical defects through direct osteonal healing, the so-called osteoblastic jumping distance, is approximately 1 mm in rabbits,[221] but the magnitude of this distance varies from species to species. Larger cortical defects may also heal, but they do so at a much slower rate and bridge by means of woven bone. The

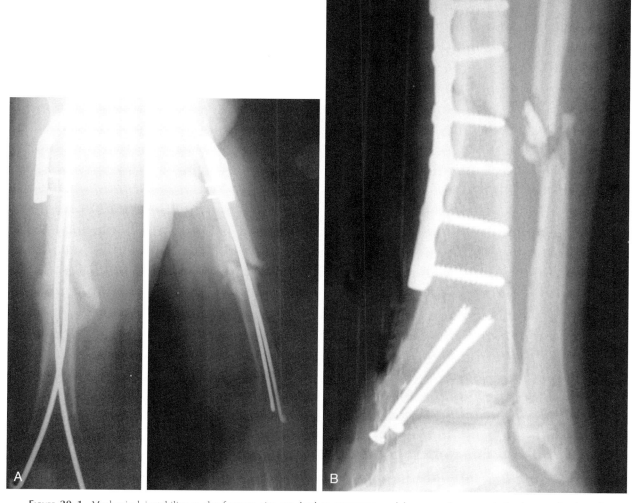

FIGURE 20–1. Mechanical instability at the fracture site can lead to nonunion and has several causes. *A,* Inadequate fixation. A 33-year-old man presented with a femoral shaft nonunion 8 months after inadequate fixation with flexible intramedullary nails. *B,* Distraction. A 19-year-old man with a tibial fracture was treated with plate-and-screw fixation. He is at risk for nonunion because of distraction at the fracture site.

Illustration continued on following page

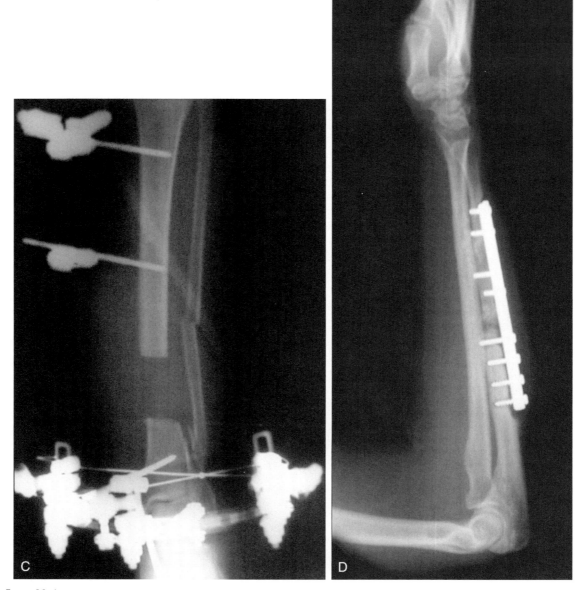

Figure 20–1 *Continued. C,* Bone loss. A 57-year-old man presented with segmental bone loss after débridement of a high-energy, open tibial fracture. *D,* Poor bone quality. A 31-year-old woman presented 2 years after open reduction and internal fixation for an ulnar shaft fracture. Loss of fixation resulted from poor bone caused by chronic osteomyelitis.

critical defect represents the gap distance between fracture surfaces that cannot be bridged by bone without intervention. The magnitude of the critical defect depends on a variety of factors related to the injury and varies considerably among species.

According to the theory of Perren and Cordey,[183] small defects produce high strain at the fracture site. Osteoblasts, which do not tolerate a high-strain environment, are predominated by chondroblasts and fibroblasts, which thrive under high strain. In larger gaps and segmental defects, the strain is too low to promote osteoblastic activity. Perren and Cordey believe that osteoblasts flourish—and thereby give rise to fracture healing—only under specific strain conditions. When fracture-site strain is too high or too low, delayed union or nonunion ensues. The exact amount of strain that promotes fracture repair remains unknown.

Other Contributing Factors

In addition to mechanical instability, inadequate vascularity, and poor bone-to-bone contact, other factors may contribute to the occurrence of a nonunion. These factors, however, should not be considered direct causes of nonunion (Table 20–2).

INFECTION

Infection in the zone of fracture, including bone or the surrounding soft tissues, does not directly cause nonunion. However, an infection may create the same local environment that predisposes noninfected fractures to fail to unite. Infection may result in motion and instability at the fracture site as implants loosen in infected bone (i.e., poor bone quality). Necrotic bone at the fracture site (i.e., sequestrum), a common complication of infection, is avascular and discourages bony union. Infection also produces poor bony contact because osteolysis at the fracture site results from ingrowth of infected granulation tissue.

NICOTINE CONSUMPTION AND CIGARETTE SMOKING

Cigarette smoking adversely affects fracture healing. Experimental evidence suggests that nicotine inhibits vascular ingrowth and early revascularization of bone[47, 195] and diminishes osteoblast function.[54, 70, 191] Animal investigations have shown that cigarette smoking and nicotine impair bone healing in rabbits with fractures,[190] rabbits undergoing spinal fusion,[230, 259] and rabbits undergoing tibial lengthening.[242, 243]

Human studies have reported delayed fracture healing and higher nonunion rates in patients who smoke cigarettes. In a consecutive series of 146 closed and type I open tibial shaft fractures, Schmitz and associates[224]

TABLE 20–2

Causes of Nonunions

PREDISPOSING FACTORS

Mechanical instability
  Inadequate fixation
  Distraction
  Bone loss
  Poor bone quality
Inadequate vascularity
  Severe injury
  Excessive soft tissue stripping
  Vascular injury
Poor bone contact
  Soft tissue interposition
  Malposition or malalignment
  Bone loss
  Distraction

CONTRIBUTING FACTORS

Infection
Nicotine or cigarette smoking
Certain medications
Advanced age
Systemic medical conditions
Poor functional level
Venous stasis
Burns
Radiation
Obesity
Alcohol abuse
Metabolic bone disease
Malnutrition
Vitamin deficiencies

reported a significant delay in clinical and radiographic evidence of fracture healing in smokers treated with external fixation and intramedullary nail fixation. Similarly, Kyrö and co-workers[128] reported an association between the number of cigarettes smoked and delayed union of the tibia. Selznick and colleagues[227] also reported higher rates of delayed union and nonunion in smokers with open tibial fractures treated with external fixation and intramedullary nailing. Hak and associates[87] reported a markedly higher rate of persistent nonunion in smokers compared with nonsmokers who underwent exchange reamed intramedullary nailing for femoral shaft nonunion or delayed union. Cobb and co-workers[41] reported as high as a 16-fold increase in the risk of nonunion of ankle arthrodesis in smokers compared with nonsmokers. The rate of successful spinal fusion has also been reported to be lower in smokers.[25]

Although the exact mechanism remains to be fully elucidated, animal and human investigations show that nicotine consumption and cigarette smoking have a deleterious effect on fracture healing. Adverse effects on local vascularity and cellular function at the fracture site probably constitute part of the mechanism. Cigarette smoking is associated with osteoporosis and generalized bone loss,[188] and mechanical instability due to poor bone quality for purchase may play a role in the production of nonunions in smokers undergoing surgical stabilization with orthopaedic hardware.

CERTAIN MEDICATIONS

Although numerous investigators have studied the effects of nonsteroidal anti-inflammatory drugs (NSAIDs) on fracture healing, the literature does not provide a consensus opinion. Several animal studies have shown that NSAIDs have negative effects on the healing of experimentally induced fractures and osteotomies.[4, 5, 66, 96, 115, 137, 200, 234] Other investigators, however, have reported no significant alterations in the fracture repair process in animals administered NSAIDs.[100, 154] Huo and co-workers[100] were unable to show differences in fracture histology or biomechanics between rats given ibuprofen and controls, but they cautioned against extrapolating their findings to humans.

Three reports have documented delayed long bone fracture healing in human subjects taking oral NSAIDs.[26, 79, 118] Giannoudis and colleagues[79] showed a marked association between delayed fracture healing and NSAID use, as well as between fracture nonunion and NSAID use in fractures of the femoral diaphysis treated by intramedullary nailing. Butcher and Marsh[26] reported similar findings for tibial fractures, as did Khan[118] for clavicle fractures. Although a body of literature exists implicating NSAIDs as a factor in delayed fracture healing, no true consensus exists. Even for those who believe the negative effects exist, the mechanism of action remains obscure (i.e., direct action at the fracture site vs. indirect action through hormonal effect). Whether all NSAIDs display similar effects and the dose-response characteristics of specific NSAIDs to produce delayed union or nonunion remains unknown.

Other medications have been postulated to have an

adverse effect on fracture healing. They include phenytoin,[90] ciprofloxacin,[98] steroids, anticoagulants, and other agents.

OTHER ISSUES

Other issues may retard fracture healing or contribute to fracture nonunion but are not primary causes. These factors include advanced age,[90, 128, 205] systemic medical conditions (e.g., diabetes),[76, 182] poor functional level with an inability to bear weight, venous stasis, burns, irradiation, obesity,[73] alcohol abuse,[73, 76, 182] metabolic bone disease, malnutrition and cachexia, and vitamin deficiencies.[56]

Animal studies (rats) have shown that deficiency of albumin produces a fracture callus that has reduced strength and stiffness,[187] although early fracture healing events proceed normally.[62] Dietary supplementation of protein during fracture repair to achieve and maintain appropriate daily requirements reverses these effects and augments fracture healing,[53, 62] although protein intake in excess of normal daily requirements has not been proven to be beneficial.[84, 187] Inadequate caloric intake, as occurs among the elderly, contributes to failure of fracture union.[233]

EVALUATION OF NONUNIONS

No two patients presenting with a fracture nonunion are identical. The evaluation process is perhaps the most critical step in the patient's treatment pathway. It is here that the surgeon begins to form opinions about how to heal the nonunion. The goal of the evaluation is to discover the cause of the nonunion. Without a clear understanding of the cause, the treatment strategy cannot be based on knowledge of fracture biology. A worksheet for patients with nonunions is an excellent method of assimilating the various data (Fig. 20–2).

Patient History

The evaluation process begins with a thorough history, including the date of injury and mechanism of injury resulting in the initial fracture. Any preexisting medical problems (e.g., diabetes, malnutrition, metabolic bone disease), disabilities, or associated injuries that may have an impact on the treatment plan or expected outcome should be ascertained. The patient should be questioned regarding pain and functional limitations related to the nonunion. An exhaustive review of all prior surgeries to treat the fracture and fracture nonunion, including the specific details of each surgical procedure, must be obtained. These details are collected through discussions with the patient and family, with prior treating surgeons, and by a thorough review of all medical reports and records since the time of the initial fracture.

Knowledge of all prior operative procedures is empowering and critical for designing the right treatment plan for the patient. Conversely, ignorance of any prior surgical procedure can lead to needlessly repeating surgical procedures that have failed to promote bony union in the past. For example, a humeral shaft fracture initially treated with an intramedullary nail and subsequently treated with autologous bone graft on three separate occasions for nonunion is unlikely to heal with a fourth bone graft procedure. Worse, ignorance of prior surgical procedures can lead to the occurrence of avoidable complications. For example, knowledge of the prior use of external fixation is important, particularly when the use of intramedullary nail fixation for nonunion treatment is contemplated. The risk of serious infection after intramedullary nail fixation for a nonunion in a patient whose injury was previously treated with external fixation has been thoroughly described.[16, 108, 140, 144, 149, 196, 260] In general, the risk of infection is greatest when external fixation was in place for a long time (i.e., several months), the time from removal of external fixation to placement of an intramedullary nail was short (i.e., days to weeks), and external fixation wear was complicated by purulent pin-site infections (look for pin-site ring sequestra on current radiographs). A thorough review of all prior surgical procedures is of the utmost importance.

The hospital records and operative reports from the time of the initial fracture may also be a useful source of information regarding the condition of the tissues in the zone of the injury (e.g., description of open wounds, contamination, crush injuries, periosteal stripping, devitalized bone fragments). The history of prior soft tissue coverage procedures can also be readily obtained from these sources.

The history should also include details regarding prior wound infections. Culture reports should be sought in the medical records. Intravenous and oral antibiotic usage should be documented, particularly if the patient remains on antibiotics at the time of presentation. Problems with wound healing and prior episodes of soft tissue breakdown should be documented. Other previous perioperative complications (e.g., venous thrombosis, nerve or vessel injuries) that may affect the treatment plan should also be documented. A history should be sought for the use of adjuvant nonsurgical therapies, such as electromagnetic field and ultrasound therapy.

The patient should be questioned regarding other possible contributing factors for nonunion (see Table 20–2). The pack-year history of cigarette smoking should be documented. Active smokers should be offered a program (i.e., pharmaceutical or counseling or both) to halt the addiction. From a practical standpoint, it is unrealistic to delay treatment of a symptomatic nonunion until the patient stops smoking (you would grow old and gray, and your town would be overrun by oozing, limping hulks of human flesh). A history for NSAID use should be obtained, and their usage should be discontinued.

To summarize, the patient history is an important tool in reconstructing the factors leading to failure of the fracture to heal and is important in planning treatment.

GENERAL INFORMATION

Patient Name: _____   Age: _____ Gender: _____

Referring Physician: _____   Height: _____ Weight: _____

Injury (description): _____

Date of Injury: _____

Mechanism of Injury: _____   Pain (0 to 10 VAS): _____

Occupation: _____   Was Injury Work Related?: Y N

PAST HISTORY

Initial Fracture Treatment (Date): _____

Total # of Surgeries for Nonunion: _____

      Surgery #1 (Date): _____

      Surgery #2 (Date): _____

      Surgery #3 (Date): _____

      Surgery #4 (Date): _____

      Surgery #5 (Date): _____

      Surgery #6 (Date): _____

      (Use backside of this sheet for other prior surgeries)

Use of Electromagnetic or Ultrasound Stimulation? _____

Cigarette Smoking   # of packs per day _____   # of years smoking _____

History of Infection? (include culture results) _____

History of Soft Tissue Problems? _____

Medical Conditions: _____

Medications: _____

NSAID Use? _____

Narcotic Use: _____

Allergies: _____

PHYSICAL EXAMINATION

General: _____

Extremity:

      Nonunion: _____ Stiff _____ Lax

      Adjacent Joints (ROM, compensatory deformities): _____

      Soft Tissues (defects, drainage): _____

      Neurovascular Exam: _____

RADIOLOGIC EXAMINATION

      Comments _____

OTHER PERTINENT INFORMATION _____

_____

_____

NONUNION TYPE

      _____ Hypertrophic

      _____ Oligotrophic

      _____ Atrophic

      _____ Infected

      _____ Synovial Pseudarthrosis

FIGURE 20–2. Worksheet for patients with nonunions.

Physical Examination

After obtaining a thorough history, a physical examination is performed. The general health and nutritional status of the patient should be assessed. Malnutrition and cachexia are factors that contribute to diminished fracture repair.[64, 84, 187, 233] Measurement of arm muscle circumference is the best indicator of nutritional status. Obese patients with nonunions have unique management problems related to achieving mechanical stability in the face of high loads and dealing with large soft tissue envelopes.[112]

The fracture zone should be inspected for the status of the overlying skin and soft tissues. The presence of active drainage and sinus formation should be noted. The presence and description of deformity at the fracture site should be documented.

The nonunion site should undergo manual stress testing to evaluate motion and pain. In general, nonunions that display little or no clinically apparent motion have callus formation to some degree and have good vascularity at the fracture surfaces. Nonunions that display more motion generally have poor callus formation, but they may have vascular or avascular fracture surfaces. Accurate assessment of motion at a nonunion site is difficult in the case of a limb with paired bones when one of the bones is intact.

A neurovascular examination should be performed to rule out or document vascular insufficiency and motor or sensory dysfunction. Active and passive motion of the joints proximal and distal to the nonunion should be performed. Not uncommonly, motion at the nonunion site substitutes for an adjacent joint and thereby diminishes motion at that joint. For example, patients with a long-standing distal tibial nonunion often present with a fixed equinus contracture and a limited arc of ankle motion (Fig. 20–3). Similarly, patients with supracondylar humeral nonunions commonly present with fibrous ankylosis of the elbow joint (Fig. 20–4). Such problems may alter the treatment plan and the expectations for the ultimate functional outcome.

An interesting situation is the case of the stiff nonunion with an angular deformity. These patients may present having already developed a compensatory fixed deformity at an adjacent joint. It is imperative that the fixed deformity at the joint be recognized preoperatively and that the treatment plan include its correction. Realignment of a stiff nonunion with a deformity without addressing an adjacent compensatory joint deformity results in a straight long bone with a deformity at the joint, producing a disabled limb. For example, patients with a stiff distal tibial nonunion with a varus deformity often develop a compensatory valgus deformity at the subtalar joint to achieve a plantigrade foot for gait. On presentation and visual inspection, the distal limb segment paradoxically appears aligned. Radiographs, however, show the distal tibial varus deformity. To determine whether the compensatory valgus deformity through the subtalar joint is fixed or mobile (reducible), the patient is asked to position the subtalar joint in varus (i.e., invert the foot). If the patient cannot achieve inversion through the subtalar joint, and the

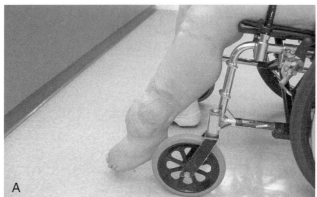

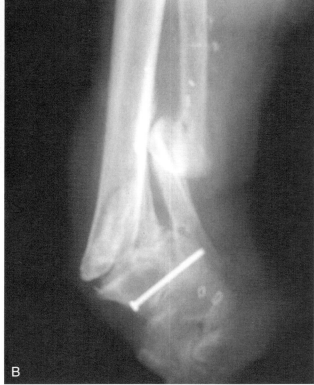

FIGURE 20–3. A 20-year-old woman presented with a distal tibial nonunion 22 months after a high-energy, open fracture. The clinical photograph (*A*) and lateral radiograph (*B*) show apex anterior angulation at the fracture site resulting in the clinical equivalent of a severe equinus contracture.

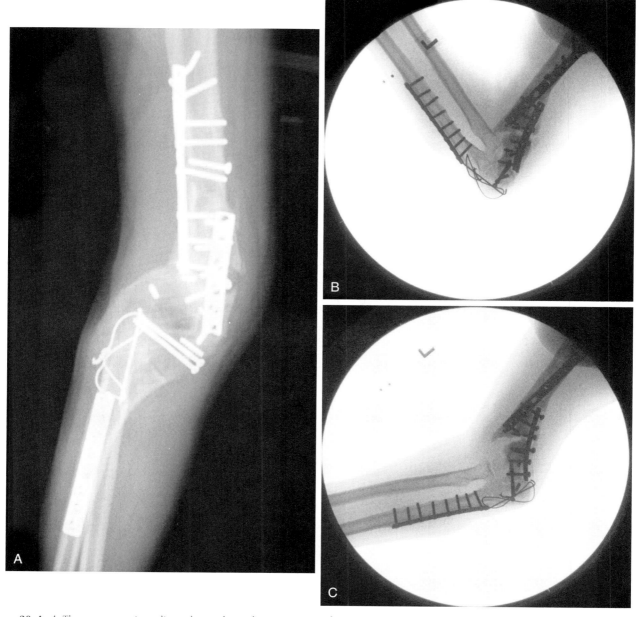

FIGURE 20–4. *A,* The anteroposterior radiograph was obtained at presentation of a 32-year-old man with a supracondylar humeral nonunion. On physical examination, it can be difficult to differentiate motion at the nonunion site and the elbow joint. This patient had very limited range of motion at the elbow but gross motion at the nonunion site. Cineradiography can help evaluate the contribution of the adjacent joint and the nonunion site to the arc of motion. *B, C,* Cineradiography showing flexion and extension of the elbow reveals that most of the motion is occurring through the nonunion site, not the elbow joint. This patient should be counseled preoperatively regarding elbow stiffness after stabilization of the nonunion.

examiner cannot passively invert the subtalar joint, the joint deformity is fixed. Deformity correction is therefore required at the nonunion site and the subtalar joint. If the patient can achieve subtalar inversion, the deformity at the joint will resolve with realignment of the deformity at the nonunion. A patient with a distal tibial nonunion may also present with apex posterior angulation at the nonunion site. This patient may develop a compensatory plantar-flexion deformity at the ankle joint to achieve a plantigrade foot for gait. The physical examination is performed to assess whether the deformity

is fixed. Can the patient position the foot into the apex dorsal angulation of the tibia through ankle dorsiflexion? If the patient cannot place the joint in question into the position that parallels the deformity at the nonunion site, the joint deformity is fixed and requires correction. If the patient can achieve the position, the joint deformity will resolve with realignment of the long bone deformity (Fig. 20–5).

If a bone grafting procedure is contemplated, the anterior and posterior iliac crests should be examined bilaterally for evidence (e.g., incisions) of prior surgical

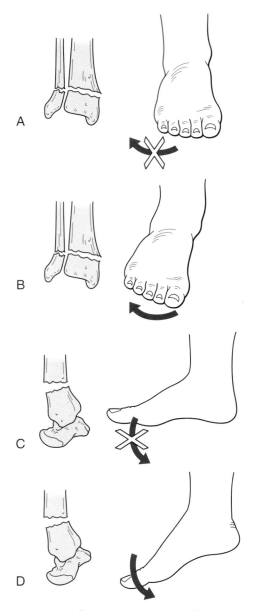

FIGURE 20–5. Angular deformity at a nonunion site that is near a joint can result in a compensatory deformity through a neighboring joint. For example, coronal-plane deformities of the distal tibia can result in a compensatory coronal-plane deformity of the subtalar joint. A deformity of the subtalar joint is fixed if the patient's foot cannot be positioned into the deformity of the distal tibia (*A*) or flexible if it can be positioned into the deformity of the distal tibia (*B*). Sagittal-plane deformities of the distal tibia can result in a sagittal-plane deformity of the ankle joint. A deformity of the ankle joint is fixed if the patient's foot cannot be positioned into the deformity of the distal tibia (*C*) or flexible if it can be positioned into the deformity of the distal tibia (*D*).

harvesting. In the case of a patient who has had prior spinal surgery with bone harvested through a midline posterior incision, it may be difficult to determine which posterior crest has already been harvested. In such a case, the left and right posterior iliac crests can be evaluated for

prior harvesting by plain radiographs or a computed tomography (CT) scan.

Radiologic Examination

Diagnostic radiologic examinations are a critical part of the evaluation process, and the information gathered offers great insight into the causes of poor fracture healing.

PLAIN RADIOGRAPHS

The radiologic examination begins with a review of the original fracture films. This initial step offers tremendous insight into the character and severity of the initial bony injury. It also is instructive in regard to the progress or lack of progress toward healing compared with the most recent plain radiographs.

In addition to the original injury radiographs, radiographs of the salient aspects of the previous treatments rendered should be reviewed. The prior radiographs always tell the story of the nonunion being seen for treatment, although the story may only reveal itself to an astute observer. The prior plain films should be carefully

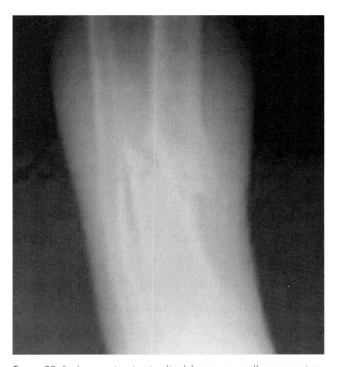

FIGURE 20–6. A nonunion is visualized better on small cassette views than on large cassette views; compare with Figure 20–7.

involved bone (including the adjacent proximal and distal joints); AP, lateral, and two oblique views of the nonunion site itself (on small cassette films that improve magnification and resolution of the nonunion site) (Fig. 20–6); AP and lateral 51-inch alignment radiographs of both limbs for lower extremity nonunions (useful for assessing leg-length discrepancies and deformities) (Fig. 20–7); and flexion-extension lateral radiographs to determine the arc of motion and to assess the relative contributions of the joint and the nonunion site to the overall arc of motion. The current plain films are used to assess several radiographic characteristics of a nonunion: anatomic location, healing effort, bone quality, surface characteristics, status of previously implanted hardware, and deformities.

Anatomic Location

The anatomic location of the nonunion is determined using plain radiographs. Diaphyseal nonunions involve primarily cortical bone, whereas metaphyseal and epiphyseal nonunions mostly involve cancellous bone. The presence or absence of intra-articular extension of the nonunion should also be assessed.

Healing Effort and Bone Quality

The radiographic healing effort and bone quality of a nonunion helps to define the biologic and mechanical causes of the nonunion. The assessment of healing includes evaluating radiolucent lines and gaps and appraising callus formation. Assessment of bone quality includes observing sclerosis, atrophy, osteopenia, and bony defects.

Radiolucent lines seen along fracture surfaces on plain radiographs suggest gaps devoid of bony healing. These gaps can be filled with a variety of tissue types depending on the cause of the nonunion. The simple presence of radiolucent lines on plain radiographs is not synonymous with fracture nonunion. Conversely, the fact that plain radiographs fail to display a clear radiolucent line does not confirm fracture union (Fig. 20–8).

Callus formation occurs only in fractures and nonunions that have an adequate blood supply. The presence of callus, however, does not necessarily imply the bone is solidly uniting. AP, lateral, and oblique radiographs should be reviewed for callus bridging the zone of injury. The radiographs should be carefully checked for the presence of radiolucent lines so that a nonunion with abundant callus is not mistaken for a solidly united fracture.

Weber and Cech[252] classified nonunions based on healing effort and bone quality as seen radiographically into *viable nonunions,* which are capable of biologic activity, and *nonviable nonunions,* which are incapable of biologic activity.

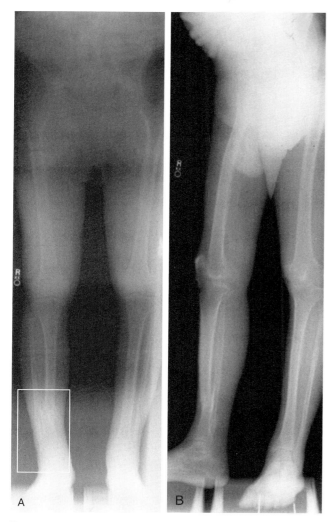

FIGURE 20–7. A 60-year-old man presented with a tibial nonunion and an oblique-plane angular deformity as seen on the 51-inch, anteroposterior view *(A)* and the 51-inch, lateral view *(B).*

examined for the status of any orthopaedic hardware (e.g., loose, broken, or inadequate size or number of implants), including its removal or insertion on subsequent films. The evolution of deformity at the nonunion site over time should be evaluated using the prior radiographs. Has this been a gradual process, or did the deformity occur in a single event? The presence of healed or nonhealed articular fragments, butterfly fragments, and wedge fragments should also be confirmed. The time course of missing or removed bony fragments, added bone graft, and implanted bone stimulators should be reconstructed so that the subsequent fracture repair response can be evaluated.

The next step is to carefully evaluate the nonunion with good-quality radiographs. They should include an anteroposterior (AP) and lateral radiograph of the

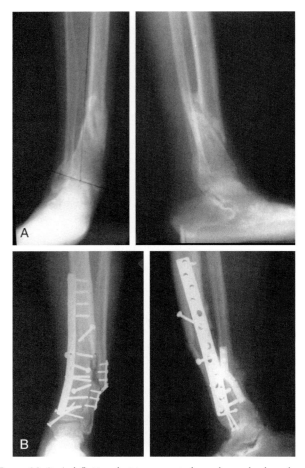

FIGURE **20–8.** A definitive decision cannot always be made about bony union based on plain radiographs. *A,* Anteroposterior (AP) and lateral radiographs show the fracture site of an 88-year-old woman 14 months after a distal tibial fracture that was treated elsewhere with external fixation. Is this fracture healed, or is there a nonunion? Compare with Figure 20–17. *B,* A 49-year-old man presented 13 months after open reduction and internal fixation of a distal tibial fracture. AP and lateral radiographs were obtained. Is this fracture healed, or is there a nonunion? Compare with Figure 20–17.

(i.e., still hypertrophic but with less abundant callus formation).

Oligotrophic nonunions possess an adequate blood supply to mount a healing response but display little or no callus formation. Oligotrophic nonunions arise from inadequate reduction with displacement at the fracture site.

Nonviable nonunions do not display callus formation. Although some of the bony fragments in certain types of nonviable nonunions may possess a blood supply, these nonunions are incapable of biologic activity because their inadequate vascularity precludes the formation of periosteal and endosteal callus. A radiolucent gap is observable on plain radiographs. This gap is bridged with fibrous tissue that has no osteogenic capacity. *Atrophic nonunion* is the most advanced type of nonviable nonunion. The cause of an atrophic nonunion is not completely understood. The ends of the bony surfaces are avascular, perhaps because of the high-energy nature of the initial injury or soft tissue stripping at the time of one or more surgical procedures. Radiographically, the fracture surfaces appear partially absorbed and are usually osteopenic. In severe cases, large sclerotic, avascular bone segments or segmental bone loss may be observed.

Surface Characteristics

The surface characteristics (Fig. 20–10) at the site of nonunion are an important prognostic factor in regard to its resistance to healing with various treatment strategies. Surface characteristics that should be evaluated on plain radiographs include the surface area of adjacent fragments, extent of current bony contact, orientation of the fracture lines (i.e., shape of the bone fragments), and stability to axial compression, which is a function of fracture surface area, orientation, and comminution. The nonunions that are easiest to treat have large, transversely oriented

Viable nonunions include *hypertrophic nonunions* and *oligotrophic nonunions.* Hypertrophic nonunions possess adequate vascularity and display callus formation. They arise because of inadequate mechanical stability with persistent motion at the fracture surfaces. The fracture site is progressively resorbed with accumulation of unmineralized fibrocartilage and displays a progressively widening radiolucent gap with sclerotic edges. The reason persistent motion at the gap of a nonunion inhibits calcification of fibrocartilage remains obscure.[183] Vascular invasion of capillaries and blood vessels occurs on both sides of the nonunion but are unable to penetrate the fibrocartilaginous tissue at the nonunion site (Fig. 20–9).[193] As motion persists or increases at the nonunion site, endosteal callus may accumulate and seal off the medullary canal, resulting in increased production of hypertrophic periosteal callus. Hypertrophic nonunions may be subclassified as *elephant foot type* (i.e., abundant callus formation) or *horse hoof type*

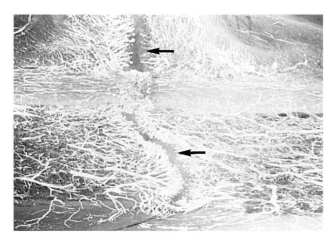

FIGURE **20–9.** Microangiogram of a hypertrophic delayed union of a canine radius. Notice the tremendous increase in local vascularity. The capillaries, however, are unable to penetrate the interposed fibrocartilage *(arrows).* (From Rhinelander, F.W. J Bone Joint Surg Am 50:78, 1968.)

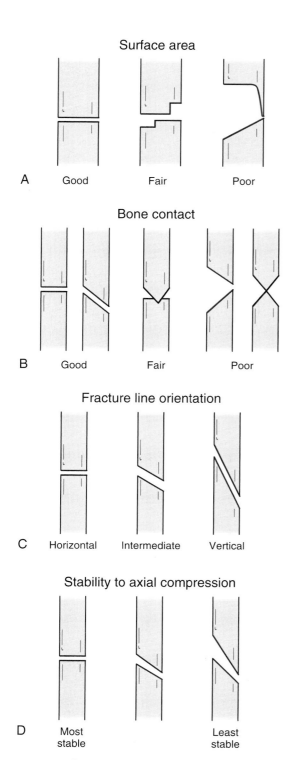

Surface area

A Good Fair Poor

Bone contact

B Good Fair Poor

Fracture line orientation

C Horizontal Intermediate Vertical

Stability to axial compression

D Most stable Least stable

FIGURE 20–10. Surface characteristics at the site of nonunion should be considered. *A,* Surface area. *B,* Bone contact. *C,* Orientation of the fracture line. *D,* Stability to axial compression, which is a function of fracture surface area, orientation, and comminution.

adjacent surfaces with good bony contact that are stable to axial compression.

Status of Previously Implanted Hardware

Plain radiographs are a useful means of evaluating the status of previously implanted hardware and therefore the stability of the mechanical construct used to fixate the bone. Loose or broken implants denote instability at the nonunion site (i.e., the race between bony union and hardware failure has been lost),[158, 174, 201–204, 209] and the injured bone requires further stabilization before union can occur. Radiographs are useful for planning what hardware needs to be removed for the next treatment plan to be carried out.

Deformities

After assessment for clinical deformity with a physical examination, plain radiographs are used to more fully characterize all deformities associated with the fracture nonunion. All deformities are characterized by location (i.e., diaphyseal, metaphyseal, or epiphyseal), magnitude, and direction, including a description of the deformity in terms of length, angulation, rotation, and translation.

Deformities involving length include shortening and overdistraction and are measured in centimeters on plain radiographs compared with the contralateral, normal extremity (an x-ray marker should be used to correct for x-ray magnification). Shortening may result from bone loss (i.e., injury or débridement) or overriding of the fracture fragments (i.e., malreduction). Overdistraction may arise because of a traction injury or improper positioning at the time of internal or external fixation.

Deformities involving angulation are characterized by their magnitude and the direction in which the apex of the angulation points. Pure sagittal- or coronal-plane deformities are easy to characterize. When coronal-plane angulation exists at a nonunion site in the lower extremity, the deformity commonly results in an abnormality to the mechanical axis of the lower extremity (i.e., mechanical axis deviation) (Fig. 20–11). Varus deformities result in medial mechanical axis deviation, and valgus deformities result in lateral mechanical axis deviation.

Oblique-plane angular deformities occur in a single plane that is neither the sagittal nor the coronal plane. The magnitude and direction of an oblique-plane angular deformity can be characterized using the trigonometric method or the graphic method.[23, 95, 167, 168, 170, 171]

Angulation at a diaphyseal nonunion is usually obvious on plain radiographs. The angulation results in divergence of the anatomic axes (i.e., mid-diaphyseal lines) of the proximal and distal fragments (see Fig. 20–11). The magnitude and direction of angulation can be measured on plain radiographs by drawing the anatomic axes of the proximal and distal segments (see Fig. 20–11).

Angular deformities associated with nonunions of the metaphysis and epiphysis (i.e., juxta-articular deformities) may not be as obvious on the initial radiographic review. They are not as simple to evaluate as diaphyseal deformities, and the mid-diaphyseal line method cannot characterize a juxta-articular deformity. Recognition and characterization of a juxta-articular deformity require an analysis using the angle formed by the intersection of a joint orientation line and the anatomic or mechanical axis of the deformed bone (Fig. 20–12). When the angle formed differs markedly from the contralateral normal extremity, a juxta-articular deformity is present. If the contralateral extremity is also abnormal (e.g., in patients with bilateral injuries), the known normal values described for the lower extremity are used[23, 168, 171] (Table 20–3).

The center of rotation of angulation (CORA) is the point at which the axis of the proximal segment intersects the axis of the distal segment (Fig. 20–13). For diaphyseal deformities, the anatomic axes are quite convenient to use. For juxta-articular deformities, the axis line of the short segment is constructed using one of three methods: extension of the segment axis from the adjacent, intact bone if its anatomy is normal; comparing the joint orientation angle of the abnormal side with the opposite side if the latter is normal; or drawing a line that creates the population normal angle formed by the intersection with the joint orientation line.

The bisector is a line that passes through the CORA and bisects the angle formed by the proximal and distal axes (see Fig. 20–13). Angular correction along the bisector results in complete deformity correction without the introduction of a translational deformity.[23, 167, 168, 170, 171]

Rotational deformities associated with a nonunion may be missed on physical and radiologic examinations because attention is focused on the more obvious problems (e.g., ununited bone, pain, infection). When the rotational deformity is recognized, accurate assessment of

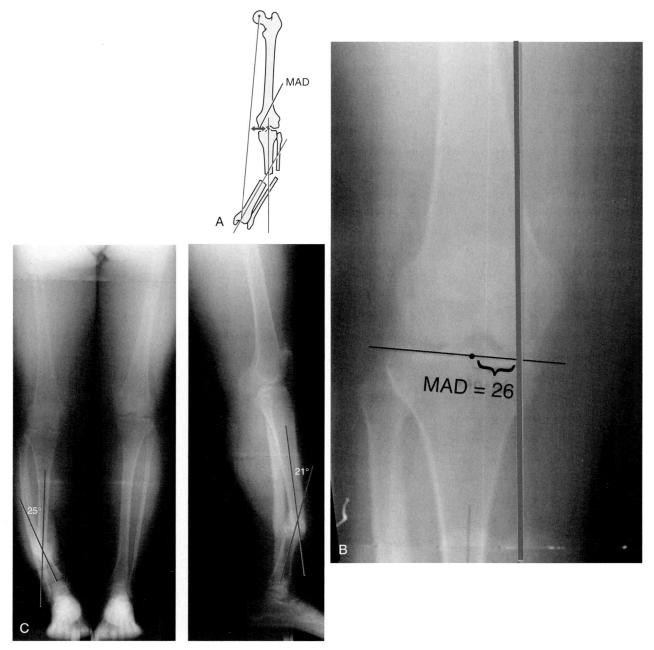

Figure 20–11. *A,* Nonunion of the diaphysis of the tibia with a varus deformity results in medial mechanical axis deviation (MAD). Notice the divergence of the anatomic axis of the proximal and distal fragments of the tibia. *B,* In the close-up view of a section of a 51-inch anteroposterior (AP) radiograph of a 37-year-old woman with an 18-year history of a tibial nonunion, notice the 26-mm medial MAD. *C,* The AP and lateral radiographs show a 25° varus deformity and a 21° apex anterior angulation deformity, respectively.

Trigonometric Method

Magnitude of oblique plane deformity =

$$\tan^{-1} \sqrt{\tan^2 \text{ coronal deformity} + \tan^2 \text{ sagittal deformity}}$$

$$\tan^{-1} \sqrt{\tan^2 \quad 25° \qquad + \tan^2 \quad 21°}$$

Solution = 31°

Orientation of oblique plane deformity =

$$\tan^{-1} \frac{\tan \text{ sagittal deformity}}{\tan \text{ coronal deformity}}$$

$$\tan^{-1} \frac{\tan \quad 21°}{\tan \quad 25°}$$

Solution = 39°

D

Graphic Method

Magnitude of oblique plane deformity =

$$\sqrt{\text{Coronal deformity}^2 + \text{Sagittal deformity}^2}$$

$$\sqrt{\quad 25^2 \quad + \quad 21^2}$$

Solution = 33°

Orientation of oblique plane deformity =

$$\tan^{-1} \frac{\text{Sagittal deformity}}{\text{Coronal deformity}}$$

$$\tan^{-1} \frac{21°}{25°}$$

Solution = 40°

E

FIGURE 20–11 *Continued. D,* The oblique-plane angular deformity is characterized using the trigonometric method. *E,* The oblique-plane angular deformity is characterized using the graphic method.

the magnitude of the deformity can be difficult on clinical examination, and plain radiographs offer little assistance. The best method of radiographic assessment of malrotation is through CT scanning.

Like angular deformities, translational deformities associated with a nonunion are characterized by magnitude and direction. The magnitude of translation is measured as the perpendicular distance from the axis line of the proximal fragment to the axis line of the distal fragment. In instances of combined angulation and translation (in which the fragments are not parallel), translation is measured at the level of the proximal end of the distal fragment (Fig. 20–14).[168]

When angular and translational deformities exist at a nonunion site, the CORA is seen at a different level on the AP and lateral radiographs (Fig. 20–15). When the deformity involves pure angulation (without translation), the CORA is seen at the same level on the AP and lateral radiographs.

In addition to assessing bony deformities related to malpositioned bony fragments, the radiographic evaluation should identify the presence or absence of compensatory deformities of the joints adjacent to the nonunion. In some cases, the compensatory deformities are clinically apparent on initial inspection, but this is not always true. Failure to recognize a compensatory deformity at an adjacent joint results in an incomplete treatment plan. The incomplete treatment plan (i.e., failure to correct the compensatory deformity at an adjacent joint) leads to a paradoxical outcome of apparent successful treatment without clinical benefit: healed nonunion and straight bone but suboptimal functional improvement.

Radiographic analysis should be performed at adjacent joints to identify a compensatory angular deformity when a deformity exists at the site of a nonunion. This is particularly important for a tibial nonunion with a coronal-plane angular deformity, because a compensatory deformity at the subtalar joint is common and commonly missed. Varus deformities of the tibia result in compensatory subtalar joint valgus deformities, and valgus deformities of the tibia result in compensatory subtalar joint varus deformities. Compensatory subtalar joint deformities are evaluated using the extended Harris view (Fig. 20–16). Extended Harris views of bilateral lower extremities allow measurement of the orientation of the calcaneus relative to

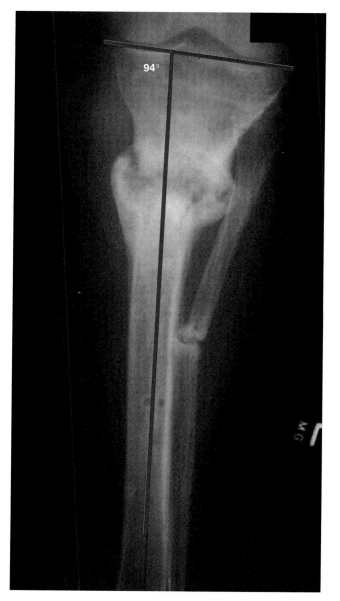

FIGURE 20–12. Nonunion of the proximal tibia with a valgus deformity results in lateral mechanical axis deviation. The proximal medial tibial angle of 94° is abnormally high compared with the contralateral normal extremity and with the population normal values (see Table 20–3).

Table 20-3

Normal Values Used to Assess Lower Extremity Metaphyseal and Epiphyseal Deformities (Juxta-articular Deformities) Associated with Nonunions

Anatomic Site of Deformity	Plane	Angle	Description*	Normal Values
Proximal femur	Coronal	Neck shaft angle	Defines the relationship between the orientation of the femoral neck and the anatomic axis of the femur	130° (range, 124°–136°)
		Anatomic medial proximal femoral angle	Defines the relationship between the anatomic axis of the femur and a line drawn from the tip of the greater trochanter to the center of the femoral head	84° (range, 80°–89°)
		Mechanical lateral proximal femoral angle	Defines the relationship between the mechanical axis of the femur and a line drawn from the tip of the greater trochanter to the center of the femoral head	90° (range, 85°–95°)
Distal femur	Coronal	Anatomic lateral distal femoral angle	Defines the relationship between the distal femoral joint orientation line and the anatomic axis of the femur	81° (range, 79°–83°)
		Mechanical lateral distal femoral angle	Defines the relationship between the distal femoral joint orientation line and the mechanical axis of the femur	88° (range, 85°–90°)
	Sagittal	Anatomic posterior distal femoral angle	Defines the relationship between the sagittal distal femoral joint orientation line and the mid-diaphyseal line of the distal femur	83° (range, 79°–87°)
Proximal tibia	Coronal	Mechanical medial proximal tibial angle	Defines the relationship between the proximal tibial joint orientation line and the mechanical axis of the tibia	87° (range, 85°–90°)
	Sagittal	Anatomic posterior proximal tibial angle	Defines the relationship between the sagittal proximal tibial joint orientation line and the mid-diaphyseal line of the tibia	81° (range, 77°–84°)
Distal tibia	Coronal	Mechanical lateral distal tibial angle	Defines the relationship between the distal tibial joint orientation line and the mechanical axis of the tibia	89° (range, 88°–92°)
	Sagittal	Anatomic anterior distal tibial angle	Defines the relationship between the sagittal distal tibial joint orientation line and the mid-diaphyseal line of the tibia	80° (range, 78°–82°)

*Anatomic axes: femur, mid-diaphyseal line; tibia, mid-diaphyseal line. Mechanical axes: femur, defined by a line from the center of the femoral head to the center of the knee joint; tibia, defined by a line from the center of the knee joint to the center of the ankle joint; lower extremity, defined by a line from the center of the femoral head to the center of the ankle joint.

the tibial shaft in the coronal plane for normal and abnormal extremities (see Fig. 20–16).

COMPUTED AND PLAIN TOMOGRAPHY

Plain radiographs do not always provide definitive information regarding the status of fracture healing. Sclerotic bone and orthopaedic hardware may obscure the fracture site and leave significant doubt about whether the fracture is healed or a nonunion exists. This is particularly a problem in stiff nonunions or those well stabilized by hardware for which there may be little or no pain or evidence of motion at the fracture site. CT scans and plain tomography are useful in further evaluating such cases (Fig. 20–17). CT scans are particularly helpful in estimating the percentage of the cross-sectional area that shows bridging bone (Fig. 20–18). Nonunions typically show bone bridging less than 5% of the cross-sectional area at the fracture surfaces (see Fig. 20–18). Healed or healing fracture nonunions typically show bone bridging greater than 25% of the cross-sectional area at the fracture surfaces. The cross-sectional area of bridging bone may be followed on serial CT scans to evaluate the progression of

fracture consolidation (see Fig. 20–18). CT scans are also useful for assessing articular step-off, joint incongruity, and bony healing in cases of intra-articular nonunions.

Plain tomography is particularly helpful in assessing the extent of bony union when CT images are compromised by hardware artifacts.

Rotational deformities may be accurately quantified using CT. The relative orientations of the proximal and distal segments of the involved bone are compared with that of the contralateral normal bone. Although this technique has been most widely used for assessment of femoral malrotation,[93, 97, 138] it may be used for any long bone.

NUCLEAR IMAGING

Nuclear imaging is a valuable tool for the study of fracture nonunions. A variety of studies are available, and when used in concert, they are useful for assessing for bone vascularity at the nonunion site, the presence of a synovial pseudarthrosis, and infection.

Technetium 99m pyrophosphate complexes reflect increased blood flow and bone metabolism and are absorbed onto hydroxyapatite crystals in areas of trauma, infection, and neoplasia. The technetium bone scan shows increased uptake in viable nonunions because there is a good vascular supply and osteoblastic activity at the fracture surfaces. Uptake may be particularly intense for viable nonunions with hypertrophic callus formation (Fig. 20–19). Decreased tracer uptake is observed in nonviable nonunions in which blood supply and callus formation are poor (see Fig. 20–19).

Synovial pseudarthrosis (i.e., nearthrosis) is distinguished from a nonunion by the presence of a synovium-like fixed pseudocapsule surrounding a fluid-filled cavity. The medullary canals are sealed off, and motion occurs at this "false joint."[207, 252] Synovial pseudarthrosis may arise in sites

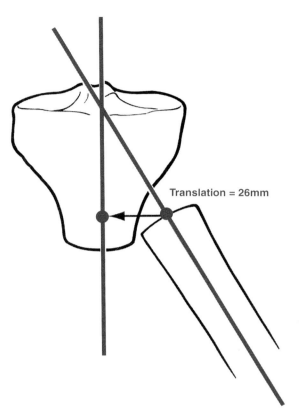

FIGURE 20–14. The magnitude of a translational deformity is measured at the level of the proximal end of the distal fragment.

with hypertrophic vascular callus formation or in sites with poor callus formation and poor vascularity. The diagnosis of synovial pseudarthrosis is made by technetium 99m pyrophosphate bone scanning. Bone scans show a "cold cleft" at the nearthrosis between hot ends of ununited bone (see Fig. 20–19).[20, 67, 68, 207]

Radiolabeled white blood cell scans (e.g., with indium 111 or technetium 99m–hexamethylpropylene amine oxime [HMPAO]) are useful tools for the evaluation of acute infections of bone. Labeled polymorphonuclear leukocytes accumulate in areas of acute infections.

Gallium scans are useful for the evaluation of chronic infections of bone. Gallium 67 citrate is localized in sites of chronic inflammation. The combination of a gallium 67 citrate scan and a technetium 99m–sulfa colloid bone marrow scan can further clarify the diagnosis of chronic infection in cases of nonunion.

OTHER RADIOLOGIC STUDIES

Fluoroscopy and cineradiography (see Fig. 20–4) are a helpful adjunct to plain flexion-extension lateral radiographs for determining the relative contribution of a joint and an adjacent nonunion to the overall arc of motion. Fluoroscopy is also helpful for guided needle aspiration of a nonunion site in the workup for infection.

Ultrasonography is useful for assessing the status of the bony regenerate (i.e., distraction osteogenesis) during bone transport or lengthening. Fluid-filled cysts delay

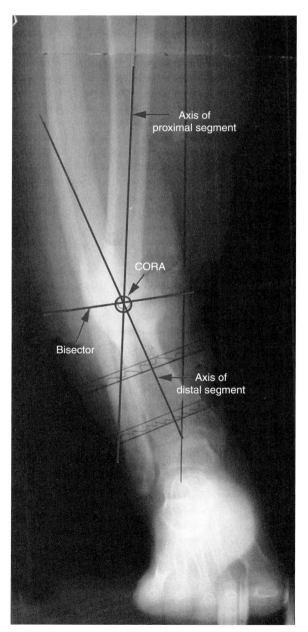

FIGURE 20–13. This is the same case with a diaphyseal nonunion and deformity that is shown in Figure 20–11. The center of rotation of angulation (CORA) and bisector are indicated.

maturation of the regenerate and can be visualized and aspirated using ultrasound technology (Fig. 20–20). Elimination of the cyst by aspiration helps shorten the time of regenerate maturation. Ultrasonography is also useful for confirming the presence of a fluid-filled pseudocapsule in cases of suspected synovial pseudarthrosis by nuclear medicine study.

Magnetic resonance imaging may occasionally be used to evaluate the soft tissues at the nonunion site or the cartilaginous and ligamentous structures of the adjacent joints. Sinograms may be used to image the course of a sinus tract in cases of infected nonunion.

Angiography provides anatomic detail regarding the status of vessels as they course through a scarred and deformed limb. This study is unnecessary for most patients presenting with a fracture nonunion, but it is indicated if there is concern regarding the viability of the limb.

Venous Doppler studies should be performed preoperatively to rule out a deep venous thrombosis in patients with a lower extremity nonunion who have been confined to a wheelchair or bedridden for an extended period. Intraoperative or postoperative recognition of a venous thrombus or an embolus in a patient who has not been screened preoperatively does not make for a happy patient, family, or orthopaedic surgeon.

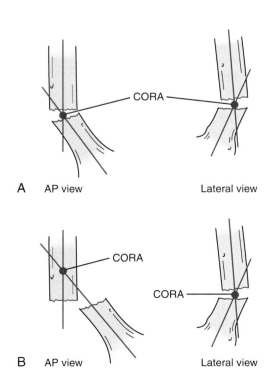

FIGURE **20–15.** *A,* When the deformity at the nonunion site involves angulation without translation, the center of rotation of angulation (CORA) is seen at the same level on the anteroposterior (AP) and lateral radiographs. *B,* When the deformity at the nonunion site involves angulation and translation, the CORA is seen at a different level on the AP and lateral radiographs.

Laboratory Studies

Routine laboratory tests, including electrolyte determinations and a complete blood cell count, are useful for screening general health. The sedimentation rate is a useful measure to follow in regard to the course of infection. If deemed appropriate, the nutritional status of the patient can be assessed by anergy panels, albumin levels, and transferrin levels. If a question exists regarding the patient's wound healing potential, an albumin level ($\geq$3.0 g/dL is preferred), and a total lymphocyte count (>1500 cells/ mm^3 is preferred) can be obtained. In patients with a history of multiple blood transfusions, a hepatitis panel and a human immunodeficiency virus (HIV) test may also be useful.

In cases of suspected infection, the nonunion site may be aspirated or biopsied. This is most easily accomplished using fluoroscopic guidance. The aspirated or biopsied material is sent for a cell count and Gram strain, and cultures are sent for identification of aerobic, anaerobic, fungal, and acid-fast bacillus organisms. To encourage the highest yield possible, all antibiotics should be discontinued at least 1 week before aspiration of the nonunion site.

Consultations

Patients with fracture nonunions rarely present with the isolated problem of an ununited bone. One or more conditions commonly accompany nonunion: soft tissue problems, infection, chronic pain, depression, motor or sensory dysfunction, joint stiffness, and unrelated medical problems.

The complex nature of the problem necessitates the assemblage of a team of subspecialists to assist in the care of the patient with a nonunion. The consultants participate in the initial evaluation of the patient and play a vital role in the care of the patient throughout the course of treatment.

Preoperative consultation with a plastic reconstructive surgeon may be necessary to assess the status of soft tissues, particularly when the need for coverage is anticipated after serial débridements of an infected nonunion. Consultation with a vascular surgeon may be necessary if there is any question regarding the viability (i.e., vascularity) of the limb.

Consultation with an infectious disease specialist is helpful to prescribe the best antibiotic regimen to be used before, during, and after surgery. This is particularly important for the patient with a history of a long-standing infected nonunion.

Many patients with nonunions present with dependency on oral narcotic pain medication. Referral to a pain management specialist is helpful in managing the patient through the course of treatment and ultimately detoxifying the patient so he or she is weaned off all narcotic pain medications.[80, 218, 239]

Depression is a common finding in patients with chronic medical conditions.[58, 113, 114, 127] Patients with nonunions commonly present with signs of clinical

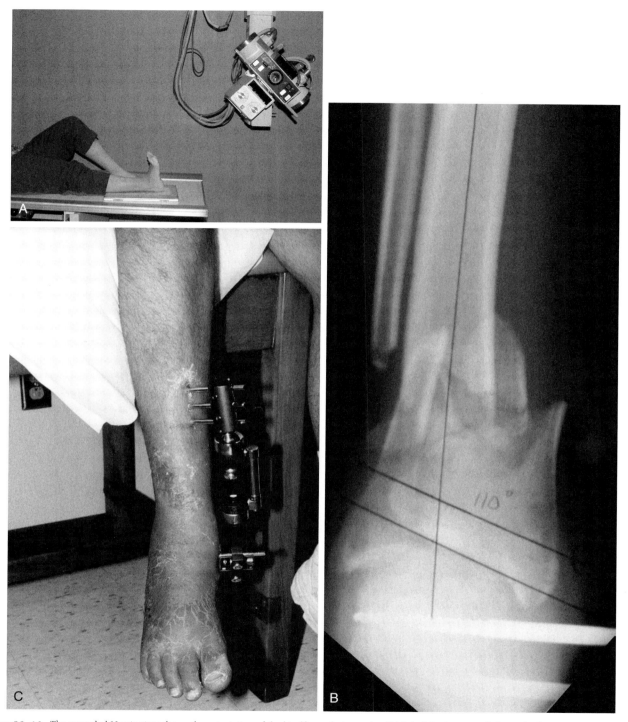

FIGURE 20–16. The extended Harris view shows the orientation of the hindfoot relative to the tibial shaft in the coronal plane. *A,* The patient is positioned lying supine on the x-ray table with the knee in full extension and the foot and ankle in maximal dorsiflexion. The x-ray tube is aimed at the calcaneus at a 45° angle with a tube distance of 60 inches. *B,* An anteroposterior radiograph of the tibia shows a distal tibial nonunion with a valgus deformity. This patient had been treated with an external fixator at an outside facility. In an effort to correct the distal tibial deformity, the hindfoot had been fixed in varus through the subtalar joint. *C,* On clinical inspection, this situation is not always obvious and can be missed.

Illustration continued on following page

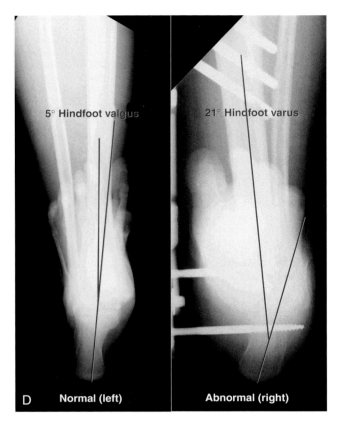

5° Hindfoot valgus   **21° Hindfoot varus**

D   **Normal (left)**   **Abnormal (right)**

FIGURE 20–16   *Continued. D,* The extended Harris view of the normal left side is compared with the abnormal right side. Notice the profound subtalar varus deformity of the right lower extremity. The distal tibial valgus deformity and the subtalar varus deformity must be corrected in this patient.

depression. Referral to a psychiatrist for treatment can be of great benefit.

A neurologist should evaluate patients presenting with motor or sensory dysfunction. Electromyography and nerve conduction studies are used to document the location and extent of neural compromise and to determine the need for nerve exploration and repair.

A physical therapist should be consulted for preoperative and postoperative training. A few preoperative physical therapy visits can be used to educate the patient with respect to postoperative activity expectations and to instruct the patient in the use of expected assistive or adaptive devices. Immediate postoperative (inpatient) rehabilitation includes transfer training, gait training, range of motion exercises, and a simple strengthening program, with the goal of independent transfers and ambulation when possible. Outpatient physical therapy primarily addresses strength and range of motion of the surrounding joints but may include sterile or medicated whirlpool treatments to treat or prevent minor infections (e.g., pin-site irritation in patients treated with external fixation). After the nonunion has united, more aggressive strengthening and return-to-work activities may be indicated, depending on the individual patient's needs. Occupational therapy is also useful for activities of daily living and job-related tasks, particularly those involving

fine motor skills such as grooming, dressing, and use of hand tools. Occupational therapy may also be consulted if adaptive devices are required to complete activities of daily living during nonunion repair. Referral to physical or occupational therapy should be accompanied by a detailed diagnosis, specific precautions or contraindications, and weight-bearing status, if appropriate. The surgeon's goal or purpose for referring a patient to rehabilitation should be made explicit to avoid miscommunication among the therapist, the patient, and the surgeon.

A nutritionist may be consulted for patients who are malnourished or obese. Poor dietary intake of protein (albumin) or vitamins may contribute to delayed fracture union or nonunion.[53, 62–64, 84, 187, 233] A nutritionist may also counsel the severely obese patient about reducing body weight. The technical demands are high in caring for the obese patient with a nonunion, and a higher complication rate should be anticipated.[112]

Anesthesiologists and internists should be consulted early for the elderly patients or those with potentially serious medical conditions. Preoperative planning of special anesthetic and medical needs diminishes the likelihood of intraoperative and postoperative medical complications.

TREATMENT

Objectives

Before embarking on any method of treatment, the orthopaedist should be aware of the objectives in treating nonunions. Although treatment is directed at healing the fracture, this is not the only objective, because a nonfunctional, infected, deformed limb with pain and stiffness of the adjacent joints is an unsatisfactory outcome for most patients even if the nonunion heals solidly. Emphasis must be placed on returning the extremity and the patient to the fullest function possible during and after the treatment process.

Treating a nonunion can be likened to a game of chess. It is difficult to predict the course until the process is under way. Some nonunions heal rapidly with a single intervention. Others require a lengthy treatment involving multiple surgeries. In general, viable nonunions are relatively easy to bring to union, whereas nonviable nonunions can be difficult to heal. Unfortunately, even the most benign-appearing nonunion may mount a terrific battle against healing. Treatment must therefore be planned so that each step anticipates the possibility of failure and allows for additional treatment options without burning any bridges.

The patient's motivation, disability status, social problems, legal involvements, mental status, and desires should be carefully considered before treatment is begun. What does the patient expect from treatment? Are these expectations realistic? Obtaining informed consent is essential before any treatment. The patient must understand the uncertainty of nonunion healing, time course of treatment, and number of surgeries required. No guarantees or warranties should ever be given to the patient by the treating physician. If the patient is unable to tolerate a potentially lengthy treatment course or the uncertainties associated with the treatment and outcome, the option of amputation should be discussed. Although limb ablation has drawbacks, it does resolve the problem rapidly and may therefore be the preferred choice by certain patients.[18, 40, 94, 210, 235] It is unwise to talk a patient into or out of any treatment option; this is particularly true for amputation.

When feasible, eradication of infection and correction of unacceptable deformities are performed at the time of nonunion treatment. This, however, is not always practical or possible, and the treatment plan is then broken into several stages. To maximize function, the priorities of treatment should be as follows:

1. Heal the bone.
2. Eradicate infection.
3. Correct deformities.
4. Maximize joint range of motion and muscle strength.

It should be understood that the priorities of treatment do not necessarily denote the temporal sequencing of surgical procedures. For example, in an infected nonunion with a deformity the first priority is to heal the bone. This does not mean that the treatment cannot begin with a débridement in an effort to eliminate infection; it does mean that the overriding priority is to heal the bone. A residual infection or deformity can be addressed after successful bony union.

Stiff fibrotic joints, associated especially with metaphyseal nonunions, are mobilized by arthrolysis, and contractures inhibiting joint motion are addressed in the treatment plan. Physical therapy is used to maintain or increase motion and muscle strength.

Strategies

After performing an in-depth evaluation using the history and physical examination results, radiologic examinations, laboratory studies, and consulting physicians' opinions, an assessment of the overall situation is required. This assessment culminates in the design of a specific treatment strategy for the patient's particular circumstances.

The choice of treatment strategy is based on accurate assessment and classification of the nonunion (Table

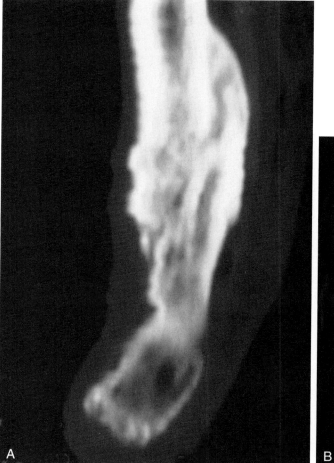
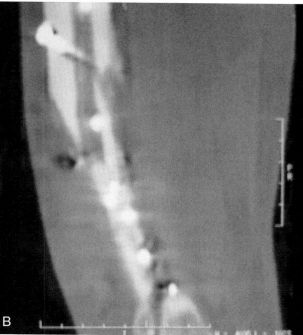

FIGURE 20–17. *A,* The computed tomography (CT) scan of the 88-year-old woman shown in Figure 20–8*A* shows that this fracture is healed. *B,* The CT scan of the 49-year-old man shown in Figure 20–8*B* shows that the fracture has progressed to nonunion.

20–4). Classification is based on one primary consideration and 13 treatment modifiers (Table 20–5).

PRIMARY CONSIDERATION: NONUNION TYPE

The primary consideration for designing the treatment strategy is the nonunion type (Fig. 20–21). The nonunion types include hypertrophic, oligotrophic, atrophic, infected, and synovial pseudarthrosis. By categorizing the nonunion into one of these five types, orthopaedic surgeons are able to understand the mechanical and biologic requirements of fracture healing that have not been met, and they are able to design a strategy to meet the healing requirements.

Hypertrophic Nonunions

Hypertrophic nonunions are viable. They possess an adequate blood supply[193] and display abundant callus formation[156]; they simply lack mechanical stability. The requirement of a hypertrophic nonunion for healing is mechanical stability, and providing mechanical stability leads to a rapid biologic response (Fig. 20–22). Rigid stabilization of a hypertrophic nonunion results in chondrocyte-mediated mineralization of fibrocartilage at

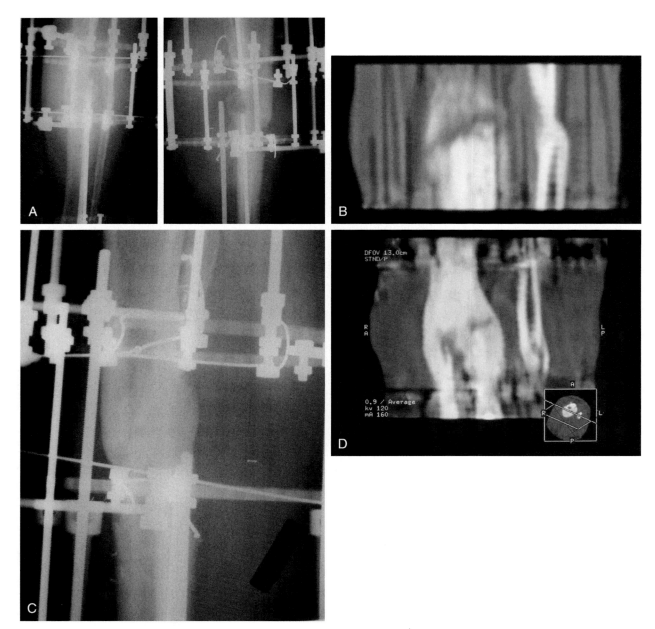

FIGURE 20–18. In addition to helping determine whether a fracture has united or has gone on to nonunion, computed tomography (CT) is useful for estimating the cross-sectional area of healing over time, as in this case of an infected midshaft tibial nonunion. *A,* Using the radiograph of the tibia 4 months after injury, it is difficult to say definitively whether the fracture is healing. *B,* The CT scan shows a clear gap without bony contact or bridging bone (0% cross-sectional area of healing). *C,* The radiograph was obtained 6 months later, after gradual compression across the nonunion site. *D,* The CT scan shows solid bony union (more than 50% cross-sectional area of healing).

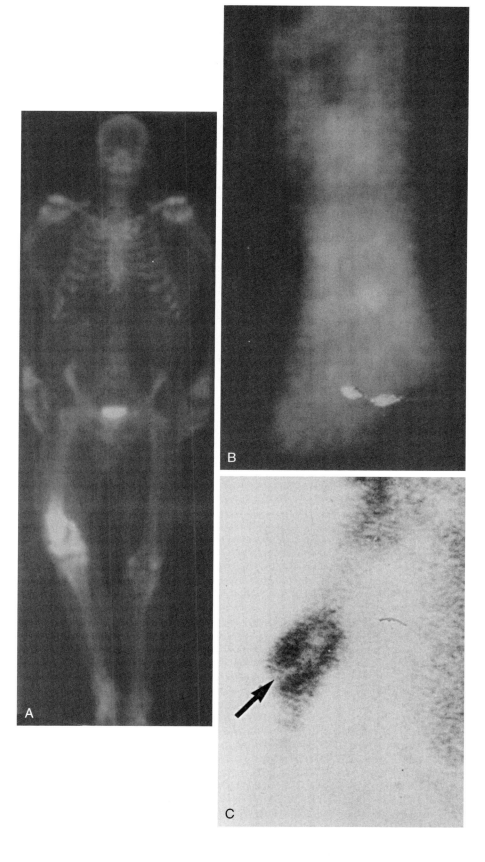

FIGURE 20–19. Technetium bone scanning in three cases shows a viable nonunion (*A*), a nonviable nonunion (*B*), and a synovial pseudarthrosis (*C*); the arrow illustrates the "cold cleft."

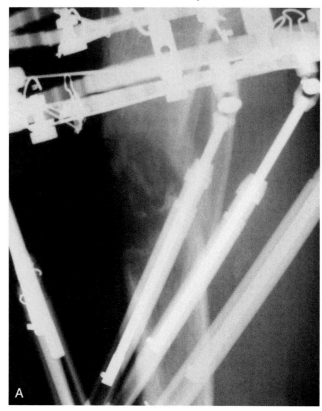

FIGURE 20–20. *A,* Radiograph shows a slowly maturing proximal tibial regenerate. *B,* Ultrasonography shows a fluid-filled cyst *(arrow).*

TABLE 20–4

Nonunion Types and Their Characteristics

Nonunion Type	Physical Examination	Plain Radiographs	Nuclear Imaging	Laboratory Studies
Hypertrophic	Typically does not display gross motion; pain elicited on manual stress testing	Abundant callus formation; radiolucent line (unmineralized fibrocartilage) at the nonunion site	Increased uptake at the nonunion site on technetium bone scan	Unremarkable
Oligotrophic	Variable (depends on the stability of the current hardware)	Little or no callus formation; diastasis at the fracture site	Increased uptake at the bone surfaces at the nonunion site on technetium bone scan	Unremarkable
Atrophic	Variable (depends on the stability of the current hardware)	Bony surfaces partially resorbed; no callus formation; osteopenia; sclerotic avascular bone segments; segmental bone loss	Avascular segments appear cold (decreased uptake) on technetium bone scan.	Unremarkable
Infected	Depends on the specific nature of the infection: Active purulent drainage Active nondraining—no drainage but the area is warm, erythematous, and painful Quiescent—no drainage or local signs or symptoms of infection	Osteolysis; osteopenia; sclerotic avascular bone segments; segmental bone loss	Increased uptake on technetium bone scan; increased uptake on indium scan for acute infections; increased uptake on gallium scan for chronic infections	Elevated erythrocyte sedimentation rate and C-reactive protein; white blood cell count may be elevated in more severe and acute cases; blood cultures should be obtained in febrile patients; aspiration of fluid from the nonunion site may be useful in the workup for infection
Synovial pseudarthrosis	Variable	Variable appearance (hypertrophic, oligotrophic, or atrophic)	Technetium bone scan shows a "cold cleft" at the nonunion site surrounded by increased uptake at the ends of the united bone.	Unremarkable

TABLE 20–5 . . . .

Treatment Strategies for Nonunions Based on Classification

	Treatment Strategy	
Classification	*Biological*	*Mechanical*
PRIMARY CONSIDERATION (NONUNION TYPE)		
Hypertrophic		Augment stability
Oligotrophic	Bone grafting for cases that have poor surface characteristics and no callus formation	Improve reduction (bone contact)
Atrophic	Biological stimulation via bone grafting or bone transport	Augment stability, compression
Infected	Débridement, antibiotic beads, dead space management, systemic antibiotic therapy, biological stimulation for bone healing (bone grafting or bone transport)	Provide mechanical stability, compression
Synovial pseudarthrosis	Resect synovium and pseudarthrosis tissue, open medullary canals with drilling and reaming, bone grafting	Compression
TREATMENT MODIFIERS		
Anatomic location	Treatment modifiers are described in the text.	
Epiphyseal		
Metaphyseal		
Diaphyseal		
Segmental bone defects		
Prior failed treatments		
Deformities		
Length		
Angulation		
Rotation		
Translation		
Surface characteristics		
Pain and function		
Osteopenia		
Mobility of the nonunion		
Stiff		
Lax		
Status of hardware		
Motor/sensory dysfunction		
Patient's health and age		
Problems at adjacent joints		
Soft tissue problems		

. . . .

the interfragmentary gap. Mineralization of fibrocartilage may occur as early as 6 weeks after rigid stabilization and is accompanied by vascular ingrowth into the mineralized fibrocartilage.[156, 222] By 8 weeks after stabilization, there is resorption of calcified fibrocartilage, which is arranged in columns and acts as a template for deposition of woven bone. Woven bone is subsequently remodeled into mature lamellar bone (see Fig. 20–22).[222]

The treatment of a hypertrophic nonunion is simple from a conceptual standpoint: add mechanical stability. No bone grafting is required.[49, 104, 156, 157, 202, 204, 208, 209, 250–252] The nonunion site tissue need not be resected, and it should not be resected. These nonunions want to heal and are relatively easy to bring to union. They simply need a little "push" in the right direction (Fig. 20–23). If the method of rigid stabilization involves exposing the nonunion site (e.g., compression plate stabilization), preparation of the nonunion site with decortication may accelerate the consolidation of bone. If the method of rigid stabilization does not involve exposure of the nonunion site (e.g., intramedullary nail fixation, external fixation), a surgical dissection should

not be undertaken for the purpose of preparing the nonunion site because it is unnecessary.

Oligotrophic Nonunions

Oligotrophic nonunions are also viable. They possess an adequate blood supply but display little or no callus formation. The cause is typically an inadequate reduction that results in little or no contact at the bony surfaces (Fig. 20–24). Treatment methods that result in union of oligotrophic nonunions include reduction of the bony fragments to improve bone contact, bone grafting to promote bridging of the ununited bony gaps, or a combination of reduction of the bony fragments and bone grafting. Reduction of the bony fragments to improve bony contact can be performed with internal or external fixation. This method is particularly indicated for oligotrophic nonunions with friendly surface characteristics (e.g., large surface area without comminution) when compression can be applied at the nonunion site to promote union. Bone grafting can be performed using a variety of techniques (see the Treatment Methods section), including open and percutaneous methods, and serves to stimulate the local biology at the nonunion site.

Atrophic Nonunions

Atrophic nonunions are nonviable. Their blood supply is poor, and they are incapable of purposeful biologic activity (Fig. 20–25). Although the primary problem is biologic, the atrophic nonunion requires a treatment strategy that employs biologic and mechanical techniques. Biologic stimulation is most commonly provided by autogenous cancellous graft laid onto a widely decorticated area at the nonunion site. When stabilized and stimulated, revascu-

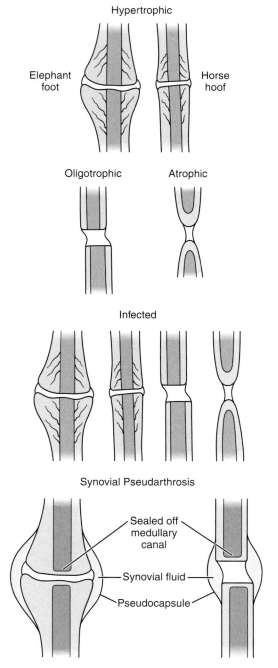

FIGURE 20–21. Classification of nonunions.

larization occurs slowly over the course of several months. Revascularization is visualized radiographically by observing the progression of osteopenia as it moves through sclerotic nonviable fragments.[201, 252] Small, free necrotic fragments are excised, and the resulting defect is bridged with bone graft. Several methods are available to treat larger bony defects and are discussed later in this chapter. Mechanical stability can be achieved using internal or external fixation. Because atrophic nonunions are frequently associated with osteopenic bone, the method of fixation must provide adequate purchase in poor-quality bone (see the Treatment Modifiers section).

Various opinions exist regarding the extent of bone excision that should be performed in uninfected atrophic nonunions. No consensus exists regarding whether large segments of sclerotic bone should be excised at the nonunion site. Those who favor plate-and-screw fixation tend to retain large sclerotic fragments. Rigid plate stabilization, decortication, and bone grafting results in slow revascularization of sclerotic segments over several months and healing of the nonunion. Those who favor other treatment methods tend to excise large sclerotic fragments, resulting in a segmental bony defect that is then reconstructed using one of the several methods available. Both of these treatment strategies result in successful union in a high percentage of cases. My decision about which approach to take largely depends on the treatment modifiers (discussed below).

Infected Nonunions

Infected nonunions pose a dual challenge because they are characterized by two of the most difficult orthopaedic entities to treat: bone infection and ununited fracture. The condition is further complicated by the fact that it is often accompanied by incapacitating pain (often with narcotic dependency), soft tissue problems, deformities, joint problems (e.g., contractures, deformities, limited range of motion), motor and sensory dysfunction, osteopenia, poor general health, depression, and myriad other problems. Of all nonunions, these are the most difficult to treat.

The goals in treating infected nonunions are to obtain solid bony union, eradicate the infection, and maximize function of the extremity and the patient. Before embarking on a course of treatment, the length of time required, the number of operative procedures anticipated, and the intensity of the treatment plan must be discussed with the patient and the family. The course of treatment for nonunions is difficult to predict, especially for infected nonunions. The possibility of persistent infection and nonunion despite adequate treatment should be discussed, and the possibility of future amputation should be considered.

The treatment strategy for infected nonunions depends on the specific nature of the infection (e.g., draining, active nondraining, quiescent)[205] and involves biologic and mechanical approaches.

Active Purulent Drainage. When purulent drainage is ongoing, the nonunion takes longer and is more difficult to heal (Fig. 20–26). The actively draining infection necessitates serial radical débridements to eliminate the infection. The first débridement should include obtaining deep cultures, including specimens of soft tissues and bone. No perioperative antibiotics should be given at least 1 week

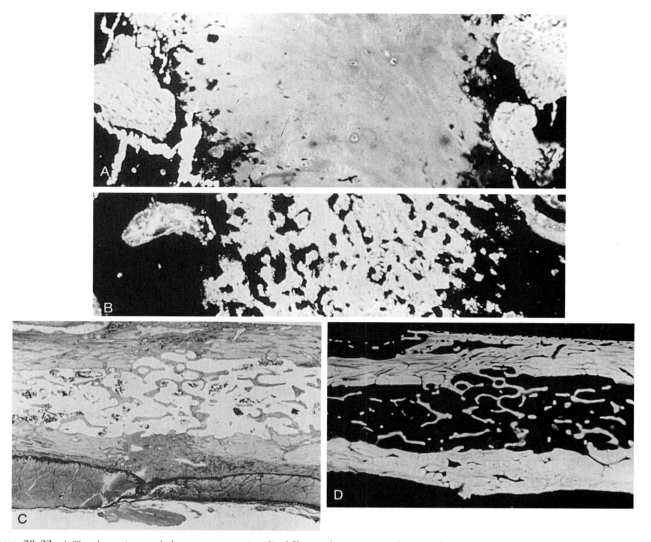

FIGURE 20–22. A, The photomicrograph demonstrates unmineralized fibrocartilage in a canine hypertrophic nonunion (von Kassa stain). B, Six weeks after plate stabilization, chondrocyte-mediated mineralization of fibrocartilage is observed in this hypertrophic nonunion. C, The substance progresses to form woven bone. D, It remodels to compact cortical bone 16 to 24 weeks after stabilization. (From Schenk, R.K. Bull Swiss ASIF October, 1978.)

before obtaining deep intraoperative cultures. Excision of all necrotic soft tissues (e.g., fascia, muscle, abscess cavities, sinus tracts), bone, and foreign bodies (e.g., loose orthopaedic hardware, shrapnel) should be performed. Soft tissues are débrided using a scalpel and electrocautery. The sinus tract specimen should be sent for pathologic evaluation to rule out the possibility of carcinoma. Necrotic bone is débrided using osteotomes, curettes, rongeurs, and gouges. A power bur may be used to saucerize overhanging ledges of necrotic bone. Pulsatile irrigation with an antibiotic solution is an effective means of washing out the open cavity.

After débridement of an actively draining infected nonunion, a dead space is commonly present. The initial treatment typically involves insertion of antibiotic-impregnated polymethyl methacrylate beads, and a bead exchange is performed at the time of each serial débridement. The dead space can subsequently be managed in a number of ways. The most widely used method involves filling the dead space with a rotational vascularized muscle pedicle flap (e.g., gastrocnemius, soleus[184]) or a microvascularized free flap (e.g., latissimus dorsi, rectus, others[254, 255]). Another method of managing the dead space involves open wound care with moist dressings, as in the

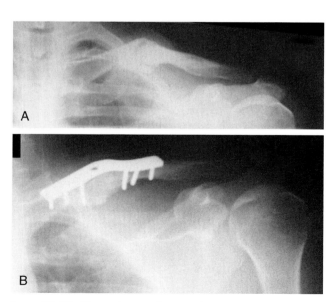

FIGURE 20–23. Plate-and-screw fixation of this hypertrophic clavicle nonunion led to rapid bony union. A, The radiograph shows a hypertrophic nonunion 8 months after injury. B, A radiograph taken 15 weeks after open reduction and internal fixation (without bone grafting) shows complete and solid bony union.

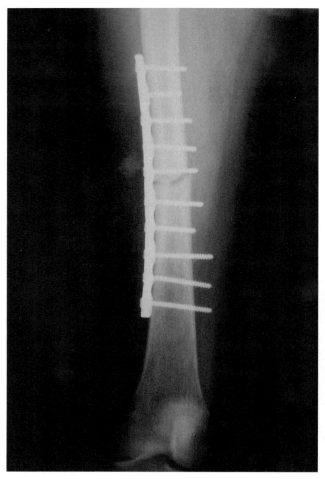

FIGURE 20–24. A patient with an oligotrophic nonunion of the femoral shaft was referred in 21 months following failed treatment of the initial fracture with plate-and-screw fixation. Notice the absence of callus formation and poor contact at the bony surfaces.

Papineau technique,[174] until granulation occurs and skin grafting can be performed.

Bony defects can be reconstructed using a variety of techniques, including bone grafting with cancellous autograft, bulk allograft, and vascularized grafts. These and other techniques are discussed in the section on Segmental Bone Defects. When possible, it is preferable to obtain coverage over bone graft with a vascularized muscle flap. Mechanical stability promotes bony healing in infected nonunions,[78, 199] and a variety of techniques of fixation are available. The Ilizarov method may be used to bridge large bone defects. Assuming that the infection has been eradicated after serial débridements and coverage, the nonunion may be treated as an atrophic nonunion with a bony defect.

The consulting infectious disease specialist generally directs systemic antibiotic therapy. After procurement of deep surgical cultures, the patient is placed on broad-spectrum intravenous antibiotics while the culture results are pending. Antibiotic coverage is later directed at the infecting organisms when the culture results are available.

Active, Nondraining. Infected nonunions that are nondraining but active manifest with swelling, tenderness,

and local erythema (see Fig. 20–26). The history often includes episodes of fever. These nonunions are treated using principles similar to those described for actively draining, infected nonunions: débridement, intraoperative cultures, soft tissue management, mechanical stabilization, bone-healing stimulation, and systemic antibiotic therapy. These cases typically require incision and drainage of an abscess, and only small amounts of bone and soft tissue are excised. Nondraining, infected nonunions are frequently managed with primary closure after incision and drainage, or they may be managed with a closed suction-irrigation drainage system until the infection resolves or becomes quiescent.

Quiescent. Nondraining, quiescent, infected nonunions are those in patients with a history of infection but without drainage or symptoms for 3 months or more[205] or patients without a history of infection but with a positive

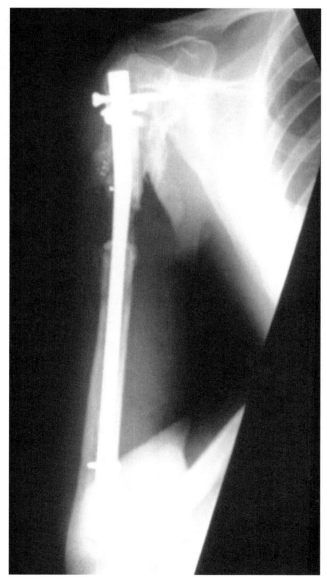

FIGURE 20–25. In this case of an atrophic nonunion of the proximal humerus, notice the lack of callus formation, the bony defect, and the avascular-appearing bony surfaces.

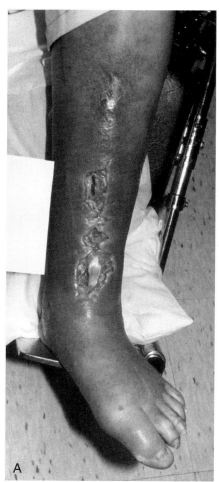
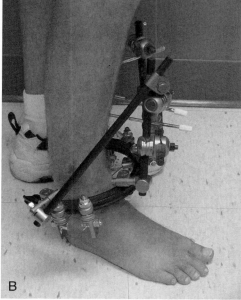
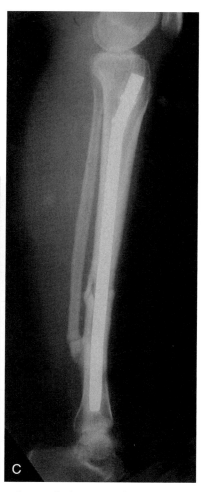

FIGURE 20–26. *A,* The clinical photograph shows an actively draining, infected tibial nonunion. *B,* Another photograph shows a nondraining, infected tibial nonunion. Notice the local swelling (there is also erythema) without purulent drainage. *C,* The radiograph shows a nondraining, quiescent, infected tibial nonunion. This patient had a history of multiple episodes of purulent drainage. Results of the gallium scan confirmed infection.

indium or gallium scan (see Fig. 20–26). These cases may be treated like atrophic nonunions by using internal or external fixation. If the nonunion is to be stabilized with plate-and-screw fixation, the residual necrotic bone may be débrided at the time of surgical exposure. The bone is decorticated and stabilized. Bone grafting may also be performed. If external fixation is the method of choice, the infection and nonunion may be successfully eliminated with compression without open débridement or bone grafting.[225]

Synovial Pseudarthrosis

Synovial pseudarthroses are characterized by fluid bounded by sealed medullary canals and a fixed synovium-like pseudocapsule (Fig. 20–27). Treatment entails biologic stimulation and augmentation of mechanical stability. The synovium and pseudarthrosis tissue are surgically excised, and the medullary canals of the proximal and distal fragments are opened with drilling followed by reaming. Gaps between the major fragments are closed by fashioning the bone ends to allow interfragmentary compression using internal or external fixation.

Bone grafting and decortication at the nonunion site encourages more rapid healing.

Professor Ilizarov described an alternative method of treatment for synovial pseudarthrosis.[105, 225] According to him, slow, gradual compression across a synovial pseudarthrosis results in local necrosis and inflammation, ultimately stimulating the healing process. I have had mixed results with this method and believe that resection at the nonunion followed by monofocal compression or bone transport more reliably achieves good results.

TREATMENT MODIFIERS

The treatment modifiers (see Table 20–5) are important for arriving at a more specific classification of the nonunion. They help to fine tune the treatment plan. Treatment modifiers include the anatomic location, segmental bone defects, prior failed treatments, deformities, surface characteristics, pain and function, osteopenia, mobility of the nonunion, status of hardware, motor or sensory dysfunction, health and age of patients, problems at adjacent joints, and soft tissue problems.

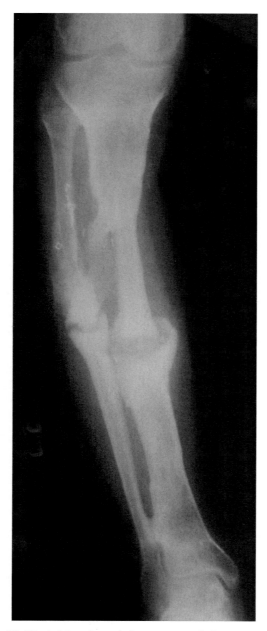

Figure 20–27. A plain radiograph demonstrates a tibial nonunion with a synovial pseudarthrosis.

Anatomic Location

The bone involved and the specific region or regions that the nonunion traverses (e.g., epiphysis, metaphysis, diaphysis) define the anatomic location of a nonunion. Because a discussion on a bone-by-bone basis is beyond the scope of this chapter, I address the influence of anatomic region on the treatment of nonunions in general terms.

Epiphyseal Nonunions. Epiphyseal nonunions are relatively uncommon. When they do occur, the most common cause is inadequate reduction that leaves a gap at the fracture site. These nonunions therefore commonly manifest with oligotrophic characteristics; the other types rarely occur. The important considerations when evaluat-

ing epiphyseal nonunions are reduction of the intra-articular components (e.g., step-off at the articular surface); juxta-articular deformities (e.g., length, angulation, rotation, translation); motion at the joint, which is typically limited by arthrofibrosis; and compensatory deformities at adjacent joints.

Epiphyseal nonunions are typically treated with interfragmentary compression using screw fixation. This is best achieved using a cannulated lag screw technique (i.e., overdrilling a glide hole) with a washer beneath the screw head. Previously placed screws that are holding the nonunion site in a distracted position should be removed. Arthroscopy is a useful adjunctive treatment for epiphyseal nonunions (Fig. 20–28). The articular step-off can be evaluated and usually reduced under arthroscopic visualization, and the lag screws can be placed percutaneously using a cannulated screw system and fluoroscopy. It is possible to freshen the intra-articular component of the nonunion using an arthroscopic bur if deemed necessary, although it is typically unnecessary. Arthroscopy also facilitates lysis of intra-articular adhesions to promote improved range of motion at the joint. Occasionally, an open reduction is required to reduce an intra-articular or juxta-articular deformity. In such cases, the surgical approach may be extended to include an arthrotomy for lysis of adhesions.

Metaphyseal Nonunions. Metaphyseal nonunions are relatively common. In general terms, the nonunion type (i.e., hypertrophic, oligotrophic, atrophic, infected, and synovial pseudarthrosis) determines the treatment strategy.

A variety of methods are available to treat unstable metaphyseal nonunions, including internal and external fixation. Plate-and-screw stabilization provides rigid fixation and is performed in conjunction with bone grafting for all but hypertrophic types (Fig. 20–29). Screw fixation alone (without plating) should never be used for nonunions of the metaphysis.

Intramedullary nail fixation is another fixation option for metaphyseal nonunions (see Fig. 20–29). Because the medullary canal is larger at the metaphysis than at the diaphysis, this method of fixation is predisposed to instability. Special considerations and techniques are therefore required to treat metaphyseal nonunions with nail fixation and include assurance of good bone-to-bone contact at the nonunion site; placement of a minimum of two interlocking screws in the short segment (oblique [nonparallel] interlocking screws add stability; custom-designed nails can provide for multiple interlocking screws); and placement of blocking (Poller) screws[125, 126] to provide added stability (see Fig. 20–29). It is imperative to perform intraoperative manual stress testing under fluoroscopy to ensure stable fixation when treating a metaphyseal nonunion with an intramedullary nail.

External fixation may also be used to treat metaphyseal nonunions. Ilizarov external fixation is the preferred method because it has significant advantages over unilateral, bilateral, and hybrid external fixation. The full-ring Ilizarov system offers enhanced stability (with early weight bearing for lower extremity nonunions), and its dynamic nature allows for gradual compression at the nonunion site (see Fig. 20–29). Metaphyseal nonunions are particularly well suited for treatment with thin-wire external fixation because of the predominance of cancellous bone. However, two specific anatomic sites where internal fixation is generally preferable to external fixation for the treatment of nonunions are the proximal humeral and proximal femoral metaphyses; in these sites, the proximity of the trunk makes frame application technically difficult.

Stable metaphyseal nonunions are most often oligotrophic and typically unite rapidly when stimulated. Conventional cancellous bone grafting or a percutaneous bone marrow injection may provide biologic stimulation of an oligotrophic metaphyseal nonunion. Although both methods have a high rate of success, percutaneous marrow injection provides all the benefits of minimally invasive surgery.

Infected metaphyseal nonunions are treated with the strategy that has been previously outlined: débridement, antibiotic beads, systemic antibiotics, dead space management and wound coverage, bone stabilization, and reconstruction of bony defects.

The special considerations for metaphyseal nonunions

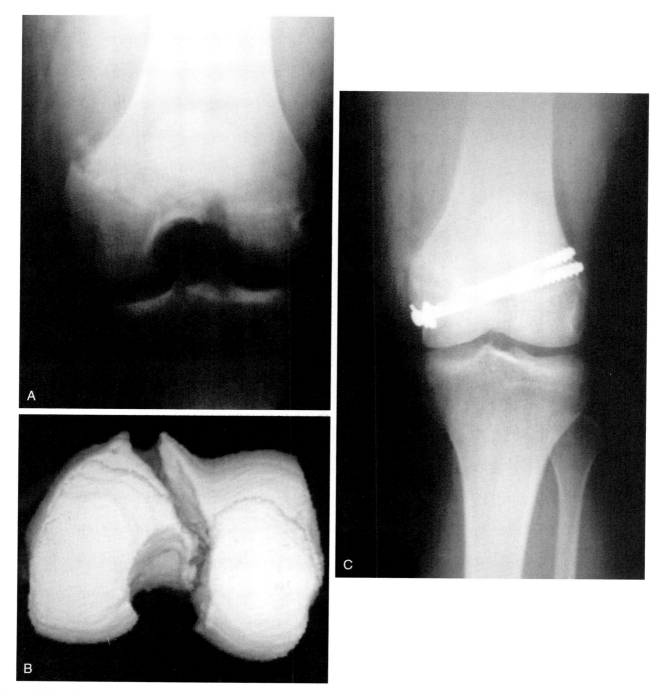

FIGURE 20–28. The preoperative radiograph (A) and preoperative computed tomography scan (B) show an epiphyseal nonunion (oligotrophic) of the distal femur in an 18-year-old patient who was referred in 5 months after the injury. Solid bony union (C) resulted after arthroscopically assisted closed reduction and percutaneous cannulated screw fixation.

are similar to those of epiphyseal nonunions and include juxta-articular deformities, motion at the adjacent joint, and compensatory deformities at the adjacent joints. These issues are addressed in a manner similar to epiphyseal nonunions and are discussed in greater detail later.

Diaphyseal Nonunions. Diaphyseal nonunions traverse cortical bone and therefore may take longer to heal and may be more resistant to union than metaphyseal and epiphyseal nonunions, which traverse primarily cancellous bone. However, by virtue of their more central location, diaphyseal nonunions are friendly to the widest array of fixation methods using orthopaedic hardware (Fig. 20–30). Primarily, the nonunion type determines the treatment strategy, but the other treatment modifiers must also be considered.

Nonunions That Traverse More Than One Anatomic Region. Nonunions that traverse more than one anatomic region are more complex. These nonunions require a strategy plan for each region. In some cases, the treatment can be performed using the same strategy for each region, whereas a combination of strategies must be used in others. For example, a nonunion of the proximal tibial metaphysis with diaphyseal extension could be treated with a single method. In such a case, a reamed intramedullary nail with proximal and distal interlocking screws provides mechanical stability and biologic stimulation (reaming) to both nonunions with a single treatment strategy. In another example, a nonunion of the distal tibial epiphysis with proximal extension into the metaphysis and diaphysis could be treated using a combination of strategies: cannulated screw fixation (compression) of the epiphysis, percutaneous marrow injection of the metaphysis, and Ilizarov external fixation stabilizing all three anatomic regions.

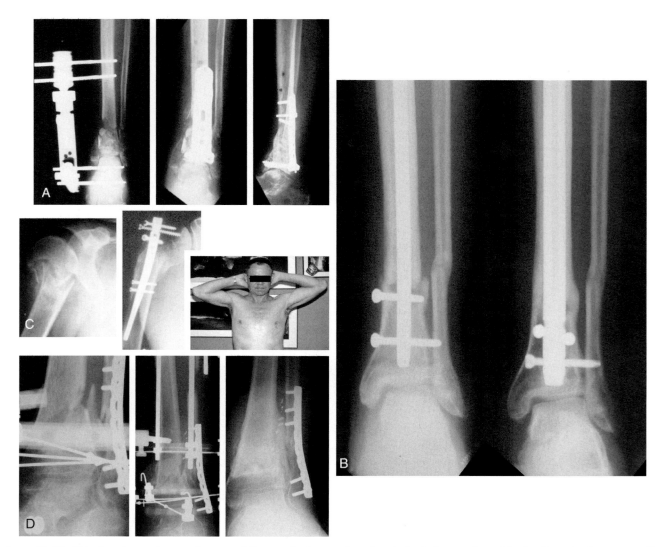

FIGURE 20–29. Metaphyseal nonunions can be successfully treated using a variety of methods. *A,* Preoperative and final radiographs show an atrophic distal tibial nonunion treated with plate-and-screw fixation and autologous cancellous bone grafting. *B,* Preoperative and final radiographs show an oligotrophic distal tibial nonunion treated with exchange nailing. Notice the use of Poller screws in the short distal fragment to enhance stability. *C,* Preoperative and final radiographs and the final clinical photograph show a proximal metaphyseal humeral nonunion treated with intramedullary nail stabilization and autogenous bone grafting. *D,* Radiographs were obtained preoperatively, during treatment, and after treatment of a distal tibial nonunion treated using Ilizarov external fixation.

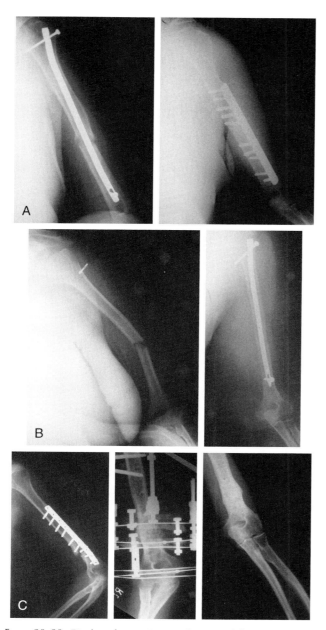

FIGURE 20–30. Diaphyseal nonunions can be successfully treated using a variety of methods. *A,* Preoperative and final radiographs show a left humeral shaft nonunion treated with plate-and-screw fixation and autologous cancellous bone grafting. *B,* Preoperative and final radiographs demonstrate a left humeral shaft nonunion treated with intramedullary nail fixation. *C,* Radiographs were obtained preoperatively, during treatment, and after treatment of an infected humeral shaft nonunion treated using Ilizarov external fixation.

Segmental Bone Defects

Segmental bone defects associated with nonunions result from high-energy open fractures in which bone is left at the scene of the accident; surgical débridement of devitalized bone fragments that are devoid of all soft tissue attachments after a high-energy open fracture; surgical débridement of an infected nonunion; surgical excision of necrotic bone associated with an atrophic nonunion; and surgical trimming at a nonunion site to improve the

surface characteristics (e.g., increased surface area, potential for enhanced bony contact, horizontal orientation of the fracture nonunion line, enhanced stability to axial compression).

Segmental bone defects associated with nonunions may have partial (incomplete) bone loss or circumferential (complete) bone loss (Fig. 20–31). These defects may be managed using a variety of treatments. Treatment fits into three broad categories: static methods, acute compression methods, and gradual compression methods.

Static Treatment Methods. Static treatment methods for bone defects are designed to fill the defect between the bone ends. When using static methods, the proximal and distal ends of the nonunion do not move, but instead remain statically fixed using orthopaedic hardware (i.e., internal or external fixation). When using a static method, it is important to ensure that the bone to be treated is at its appropriate length (i.e., not foreshortened or overdistracted). Static methods for treating bone defects include the use of autogenous cancellous bone graft, autogenous cortical bone graft, vascularized autograft, bulk cortical allograft, strut cortical allograft, mesh cage–bone graft constructs, and synostosis techniques.

Autogenous cancellous bone graft may be used to treat partial or circumferential defects. The other methods are typically used to treat circumferential segmental defects. These methods are discussed in the Treatment Methods section.

Acute Compression Methods. Acute compression methods are designed to obtain immediate bone-to-bone contact at the nonunion site. These methods achieve immediate bone-to-bone contact by acutely shortening the extremity. The extent of acute shortening that is possible is limited by the soft tissues (i.e., soft tissue compliance, surgical or open wounds, and neurovascular structures). Some investigators[82, 106, 225] have suggested that more than 2 to 2.5 cm of acute shortening at the nonunion site may lead to soft tissue problems such as wound closure difficulties or kinking of blood vessels and lymphatic channels. In my experience, up to 4 cm of acute shortening at the nonunion site is well tolerated by the soft tissues in many patients (Fig. 20–32). In a study

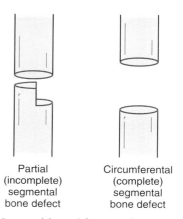

Partial (incomplete) segmental bone defect   Circumferental (complete) segmental bone defect

FIGURE 20–31. Segmental bone defects may be associated with partial (incomplete) bone loss or circumferential (complete) bone loss.

comparing acute shortening with subsequent relengthening versus bone transport for tibial bone defects, Paley and co-workers[169] reported that acute shortening is appropriate for defects up to 7 cm long. Longitudinal incisions tend to bunch up with redundant tissues when acute shortening is performed. An experienced plastic reconstructive surgeon is invaluable for the closure of these wounds. Transverse incisions tend to bunch up less when acute shortening is performed at the nonunion site and therefore are less difficult to close.

In limbs with paired bones, it is necessary to partially excise the unaffected bone to allow for compression across the ununited bone. For example, partial excision of the fibula shaft (when the fibula is intact) is necessary to allow compression and shortening of the tibia.

Acute compression methods offer the advantage of immediate bone-to-bone contact at the nonunion site.

Immediate contact with compression across the segmental defect begins the process of healing as early as possible. The bone ends should be fashioned to create a docking site with bone surfaces that are as parallel as possible. Flat cuts with an oscillating saw improve bone-to-bone contact but probably damage the bony tissues at the docking site. Osteotomes, rasps, and rongeurs create less local damage to the bony tissues but are less effective in creating flat bony cuts. No consensus opinion exists about which method of fashioning the bone ends is best. I prefer to use a wide, flat oscillating saw (using intermittent short bursts of cutting) under constant irrigation to cool the saw blade and bone. Another advantage of acute compression with shortening is the ability to bone graft the docking site immediately. Cancellous bone graft packed around the acute docking site (which has been decorticated) promotes healing of the nonunion.

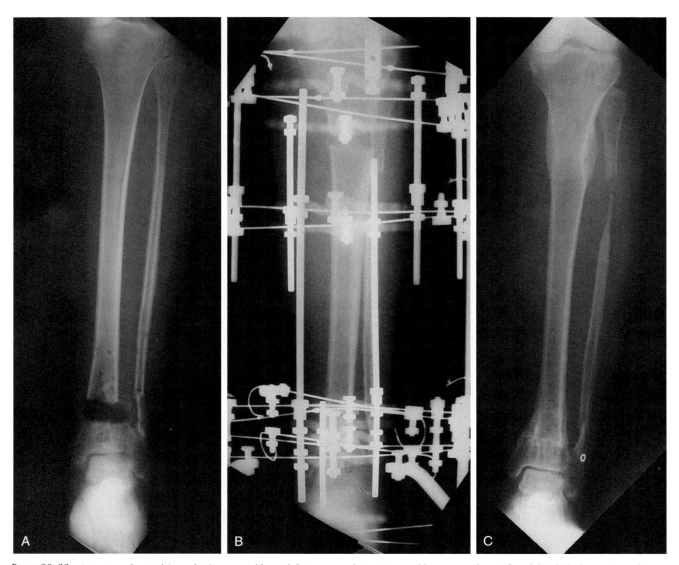

Figure 20–32. A, A circumferential (complete) segmental bone defect was noted in a 66-year-old woman with an infected distal tibial nonunion who was on high-dose steroids for severe rheumatoid arthritis. B, The radiograph was obtained during treatment following acute compression (2.5 cm) using an Ilizarov external fixator and bone grafting at the nonunion site. C, The final radiograph shows a healed distal tibial nonunion and restoration of length from concomitant lengthening at a proximal tibial corticotomy site.

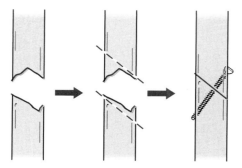

FIGURE 20–33. Oblique, parallel, flat cuts allow enhanced interfragmentary compression through lag screw fixation when a segmental defect is treated with acute compression and plate stabilization.

A disadvantage of acute compression at segmental defects is the resulting functional consequences from foreshortening of the extremity. In the upper extremity, 3 to 4 cm of foreshortening is well tolerated. In the lower extremity, up to 2 cm of foreshortening may be treated with a shoe lift. Many patients poorly tolerate a shoe lift for 2 to 4 cm of shortening, and most do not tolerate more than 4 cm of foreshortening. Many patients undergoing acute shortening with compression across the segmental defect require a lengthening procedure of the ipsilateral extremity or a foreshortening procedure of the contralateral extremity (see Fig. 20–32). These limb-length equalization procedures can be performed concurrently with or sequentially after the acute compression (shortening) procedure to treat the nonunion.

Acute compression across the nonunion site is typically used to treat circumferential segmental defects and can be accomplished using a variety of treatment methods. When using internal fixation devices, acute compression is most effectively applied by the intraoperative use of a femoral distractor or a spanning external fixator. When using plate-and-screw fixation, an articulating tension device may be used to gain further interfragmentary compression. Dynamic compression plates (DCP, Synthes, Paoli, PA) provide rigid fixation and may be used to provide further interfragmentary compression. Oblique, parallel flat cuts allow for enhanced interfragmentary compression through lag screw fixation (Fig. 20–33) and promote bony union when plate-and-screw fixation is used. When using intramedullary nail fixation, acute compression across the segmental defect can also be applied intraoperatively using a femoral distractor or a spanning external fixator (Fig. 20–34). Compression can be applied using these temporary devices before nail insertion or after nail insertion but before static interlocking of the nail. In either case, the medullary canal should be overreamed a minimum of 1.5 mm larger than the diameter of the nail. Overreaming permits nail passage without distraction at the nonunion site when the nail is placed after compression (shortening). Likewise, overreaming allows the proximal and distal fragments to slide over the nail and compress without jamming on the nail when compression with the external device is performed after nail insertion. Before intraoperative removal of the temporary compression device, care must be taken to ensure that the nail is statically locked

proximal and distal to the nonunion site. Some intramedullary devices, such as the Biomet Ankle Arthrodesis Nail (Warsaw, IN), have been designed to allow for the application of acute compression across the fracture or nonunion site during the operative procedure (Fig. 20–35). In my experience, nails that allow for acute compression, when available, are preferable to conventional nails for this specific type of treatment.

Acute compression can also be applied using an external fixator as the definitive mode of treatment. Transverse, parallel flat cuts allow for enhanced axial compression and minimize shear moments at the nonunion site. Because of its biomechanical and biologic advantages, which are discussed later in the chapter, I favor the use of Ilizarov external fixation when using external fixation for acute compression across a segmental defect. The Ilizarov frame can also be used in these cases for restoring length using a corticotomy with lengthening at another site of the bone (i.e., bifocal treatment).

Gradual Compression Methods. Gradual compression methods to treat a nonunion with a circumferential segmental defect include simple monofocal gradual compression (i.e., shortening) or bone transport. Both methods are most commonly accomplished through external fixation; I favor the Ilizarov device. Neither gradual compression nor bone transport is associated with the potentially severe soft tissue and wound problems associated with acute compression. On the other hand, both monofocal compression and bone transport are associated with malalignment at the docking site (the most extreme case being when the proximal and distal fragments completely miss each other), whereas acute compression is not.

When the chosen method of treatment is monofocal, gradual compression, the external fixator frame is constructed to allow for compression in increments of 0.25 mm (Fig. 20–36). Slow compression at a rate of 0.25 to 1.0 mm per day is applied in one or four increments, respectively. When a large defect exists, compression is applied at a rate of 1.0 mm per day; at or near bony touchdown, the rate is slowed to 0.25 to 0.5 mm per day. Compression in limbs with paired bones necessitates partial excision of the intact unaffected bone. When the chosen method is bone transport, the frame is constructed to allow bone transport at a rate ranging from 0.25 mm every other day to 1.5 mm per day (Fig. 20–37). The transport is typically started at the rate of 0.5 mm or 0.75 mm per day in two or three increments, respectively. The rate is often adjusted (increased or decreased) based on the quality of the bony regenerate as viewed on serial plain radiographs (see Fig. 20–37). For both methods, favorable surface characteristics at the nonunion site greatly improve the chances of rapid healing at the docking site.

When poor surface characteristics are present, open trimming of the nonunion site is recommended. When open trimming is performed at the time of the initial procedure, the docking site can be bone grafted if the anticipated time to docking is approximately 2 months or less (e.g., a 6-cm defect treated with gradual shortening or bone transport at a rate of 1.0 mm per day). If the time to docking is significantly greater than 2 months (e.g., for larger defects), two options exist. In the first, gradual

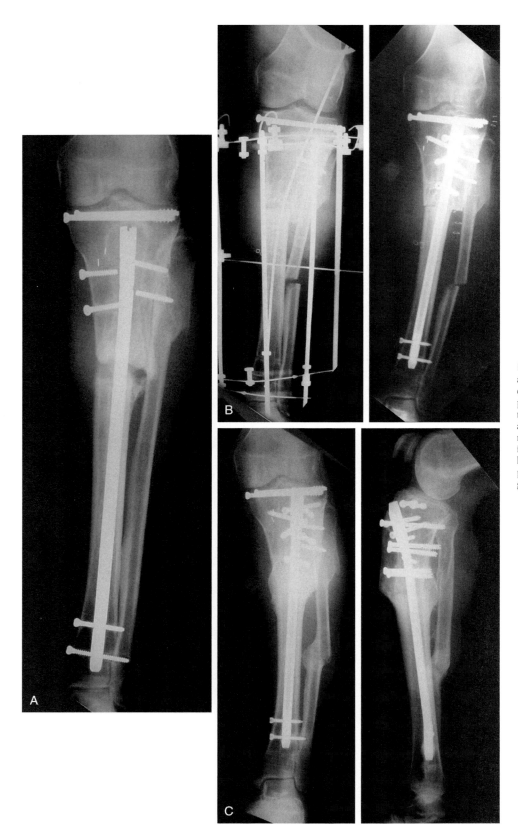

Figure 20–34. Acute compression of a tibial nonunion with a segmental defect was accomplished with a temporary (intraoperative only) external fixator. Definitive fixation was achieved using an intramedullary nail. Notice the use of Poller screws in the proximal fragment for enhanced stability. *A*, Radiograph on presentation. *B*, Intraoperative radiographs. *C*, Final result.

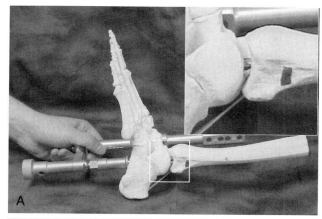

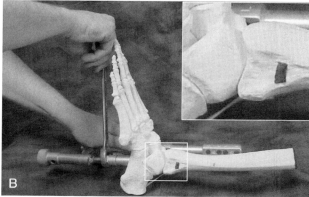

FIGURE 20–35. Some intramedullary nails allow for acute compression across a fracture site or a nonunion site. This example, the Biomet Ankle Arthrodesis Nail (Warsaw, IN) is designed to allow acute compression at the time of the operative procedure. *A,* Before compression. *B,* Acute compression being applied across the ankle joint using the compression device.

compression or transport can be continued even after bony touchdown at the docking site is seen on plain radiographs. Continued compression at a rate ranging from 0.25 mm per week to 0.25 mm per day at the docking site is seen clinically and radiographically as bending of the fixation wires, indicating that the rings are moving more than the proximal and distal bone fragments. In the second option, the docking site can be opened before bone contact (usually when the defect is approximately 1 to 2 cm), the proximal and distal surfaces can be freshened, and the defect can be bone grafted. Gradual compression or transport then proceeds into the graft material.

In my experience, compression at the docking site without open bone grafting and surface freshening leads to successful bony union in many patients. Others believe that bone grafting the docking site significantly decreases the time to healing. The literature is not helpful in clarifying this issue. A useful alternative to open bone grafting is percutaneous marrow injection at the docking site. This technique is minimally invasive and quite effective. I use the technique at the docking site of patients who I believe are at increased risk for persistent nonunion at the docking site; these patients usually have one or more "contributing factors" for nonunion (see Table 20–2). I reserve open bone grafting of the docking site for patients

who fail to demonstrate radiographic evidence of progression to healing despite 4 months of continued compression after bony touch-down, for patients at greatly increased risk of persistent nonunion at the docking site (who have several contributing factors for nonunion), and for those with poor surface contact at the docking site (who require trimming of the bone ends to improve the surface characteristics).

By virtue of their architecture (i.e., point-to-point contact), nonunions with partial segmental defects are not readily amenable to many of the treatment strategies that have been discussed. These defects are most commonly treated with a static method, such as autologous cancellous bone grafting and internal or external fixation. An unusual situation is a nonunion with a large (>6-cm) segment of partial (incomplete) bone loss. As the segment of partial bone loss increases in length, the chances for successful bony union using conventional bone grafting techniques decreases. In these cases, the treatment options are splinter (sliver) bone transport (Fig. 20–38), surgical trimming of the bone ends to enhance surface characteristics followed by an acute or gradual compression method, or strut cortical allogenic bone grafting.

The choice of treatment strategy for nonunions associated with segmental bone defects is complex and depends on a variety of factors. The diverse nature of the patients makes synthesis of the literature quite difficult. The recommendations for treatment of complete segmental bone defects by various surgeons are shown in Table 20–6. My preferred treatment methods for various situations are shown in Table 20–7.

Prior Failed Treatments

The prior failed treatments are always important to consider when evaluating a fracture nonunion. Why did the prior treatments fail? Were the treatment plans appropriate for the patient's condition? Were there problems with the technical aspects of prior treatments? Each of these questions must be answered so that the cycle of treatment failure can be broken.

A careful analysis of prior failed treatments can provide great insight into the character of the nonunion in terms of its response (or lack thereof) to various treatment modalities. Were there any positive biologic responses to any of the prior treatments? Did any treatment improve the patient's condition in terms of pain and function? Did mechanical instability contribute to the prior failures? A prior treatment that has failed to provide any clinical or radiographic evidence of progression to healing should not be repeated. However, if the treating physician believes that improvements in the technical aspects of the treatment may lead to bony union, repeating the procedure may be warranted. Repeating a prior failed procedure may be considered if it demonstrated a measurable clinical or radiographic improvement in the nonunion. For example, repeat exchange nailing of the femur is an effective nonunion strategy in certain groups of patients[87] but relatively ineffective in others.[257] Those who heal after serial exchange nailings tend to show improvement after each successive procedure. Those whose nonunions persist tend to show little or no clinical and radiographic response to each of the nail exchanges,

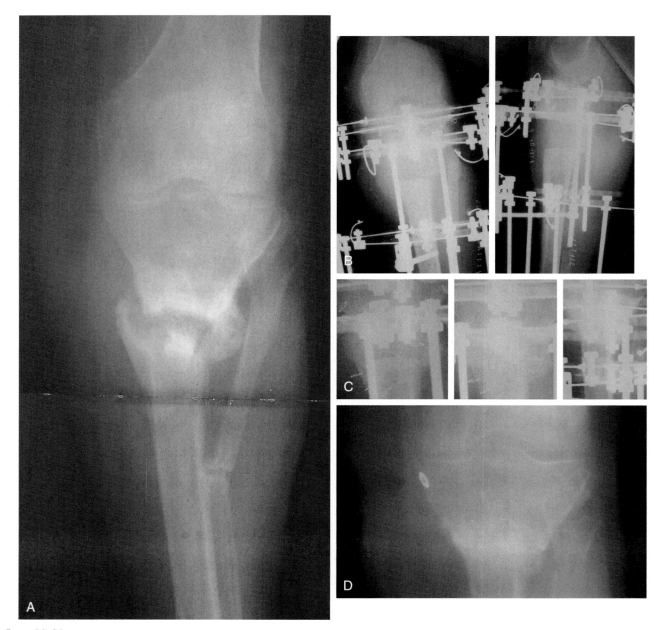

FIGURE 20-36. An example of an infected nonunion treated with gradual, monofocal compression. *A,* The presenting radiograph shows the proximal tibial nonunion in a 79-year-old woman with a history of multiple failed procedures and chronic osteomyelitis. *B,* The intraoperative radiographs after bone excision and Ilizarov application show a segmental defect. *C,* Radiographs show gradual compression at the nonunion site over the course of several weeks. *D,* The radiograph shows the final result with solid bony union.

and it is unlikely that these patients will ever heal with this technique (Fig. 20–39).

The nonunion specialist must be part surgeon, part detective, and part historian. History has a way of repeating itself. Without a clear understanding and appreciation of why the prior treatments have failed, the learning curve becomes a circle.

Deformities

The priority for a patient with a fracture nonunion and a deformity is healing the ununited bone. Although every effort should be made to heal the bone and correct the deformity at the same time, it is not always possible. When planning a treatment strategy for these patients, I ask

whether the effort to correct the deformity at the time of initial treatment will significantly increase the risk of persistent nonunion. If the answer is yes, the treatment is planned to first address the nonunion and later address the deformity in the healed bone (i.e., sequential approach). If the answer is no, both problems are treated concurrently. In my experience, most nonunions with associated deformities benefit from concurrent treatment. Deformity correction most commonly improves bone contact at the nonunion site and therefore promotes bony union. Certain cases, however, are better treated with a sequential approach. Examples include cases in which it is unlikely that the deformity will ultimately limit function after successful bony union, cases in which adequate bony contact is best achieved by leaving the fragments in the deformed position, and cases in which soft tissue restrictions make the concurrent approach more complex than the sequential approach.

Deformity correction at the nonunion site can be performed acutely or gradually. Acute correction is generally easily performed in lax nonunions, particularly when there is a segmental bone defect. In such cases, accurate, acute correction simplifies the overall treatment plan and allows the treating physician to focus on healing the bone, which is without deformity after correction.

Deformity correction of the stiff nonunion is more challenging. Acute correction typically requires surgical takedown of the nonunion site or an osteotomy at the nonunion site. Both approaches are effective in deformity correction but result in local damage at the nonunion site that may impair bony healing. When a large deformity exists, the fate of the surrounding soft tissues and neighboring neurovascular structures must be considered when acute deformity correction is contemplated. Gradual correction of a deformity in a stiff nonunion may be accomplished using Ilizarov external fixation. Correction

of length, angulation, rotation, and translation may be performed in conjunction with compression, distraction, or both at the nonunion site. Introduction of the Taylor Spatial Frame (Smith & Nephew, Inc., Memphis, TN) in 1997 greatly simplified frame construction and expanded the combinations of deformity components that can be solved simultaneously (Figs. 20–40 to 20–43).

The extent of deformity (i.e., length, angulation, rotation, and translation) that can be accepted without correction varies by anatomic location and from patient to patient. Generally, when it is anticipated that the deformity will limit function after successful bony union, correction should be strongly considered.

Surface Characteristics

The surface characteristics at the nonunion site are an important predictor of its resistance to healing with various treatment strategies. Nonunions that have large, transversely oriented adjacent surfaces with good bony contact are generally stable to axial compression and are therefore relatively easy to bring to successful bony union. In contrast, those with small, vertically oriented surfaces

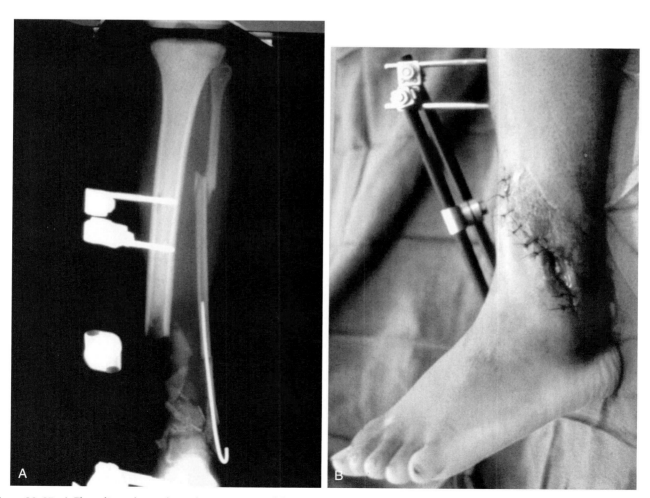

FIGURE 20–37. *A,* The radiograph was obtained at presentation of the patient 8 months after a high-energy, open tibial fracture that was treated elsewhere using an external fixator. *B,* A clinical photograph at presentation shows an open draining sinus tract.

Illustration continued on following page

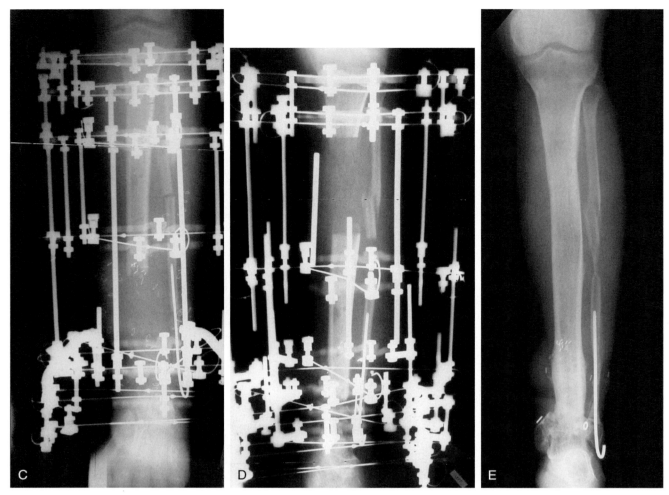

FIGURE 20–37 *Continued. C, D,* Bone transport progresses at a rate of 1.0 mm per day (0.25 mm four times per day). *E,* The final radiograph shows solid union at the docking site, with mature bony regenerate at the proximal corticotomy site. Slow, gradual compression without bone grafting at the docking site resulted in solid bony union.

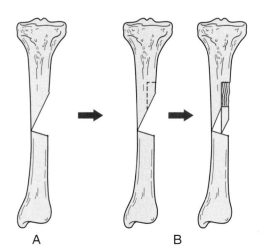

FIGURE 20–38. *A,* The nonunion has a large partial (incomplete) segmental defect. *B,* Splinter (sliver) bone transport can be used to span this defect.

with poor bony contact usually are more difficult to bring to bony union (Fig. 20–44).

Simple compression using internal or external fixation generally leads to bony union in nonunions in which the opposing fragments have a large surface area. When the surface area is small, trimming of the ends of the bone may be necessary to improve the surface area for bony contact (Fig. 20–45). Similarly, transversely oriented nonunions respond well to compression. Oblique or vertically oriented nonunions have some component of shear (with the bones sliding past each other) when subjected to axial compression. These shear moments can be minimized using interfragmentary screws when using plate-and-screw fixation or steerage pins when using external fixation (Fig. 20–46; see also Fig. 20–33).

Pain and Function

Some patients with nonunions may have little or no pain and fairly good function. The "painless" nonunion

TABLE 20–6

Review of the Recent Literature on Segmental Bone Defects

Author	Patient Population	Findings/Conclusions
May et al, 1989	Current Concepts Review based on the authors' experience treating more than 250 patients with post-traumatic osteomyelitis of the tibia.	The authors' recommended treatment options for segmental bone defects are as follows: *Tibial defects 6 cm or less with an intact fibula*—open bone grafting vs. Ilizarov reconstruction *Tibial defects greater than 6 cm with an intact fibula*—tibiofibula synostosis techniques vs. free vascularized bone graft vs. nonvascularized autogenous cortical bone graft vs. cortical allograft vs. Ilizarov reconstruction *Tibial defects greater than 6 cm without a usable intact fibula*—contralateral vascularized fibula vs. Ilizarov reconstruction
Esterhai et al, 1990	42 patients with infected tibial nonunions and segmental defects. The average tibial defect was 2.5 cm (range, 0 – 10 cm); three treatment strategies were employed. All patients underwent débridement and stabilization and received parenteral antibiotics; following this protocol 23 underwent open cancellous bone grafting (Papineau technique), 10 underwent posterolateral bone grafting, and 9 underwent a soft tissue transfer prior to cancellous bone grafting.	Bony union rates for the three groups were as follows: Papineau technique = 49% Posterolateral bone grafting = 78% Soft tissue transfer = 70%
Cierny and Zorn, 1994	44 patients with segmental infected tibial defects; 23 patients were treated with conventional methods (massive cancellous bone grafts, tissue transfers, and combinations of internal and external fixation); 21 patients were treated using the methods of Ilizarov.	The final results in the two treatment groups were similar. The Ilizarov method was faster, safer in B-host (compromised) patients, less expensive, and easier to perform. Conventional therapy is recommended when any one distraction site is anticipated to exceed 6 cm in length in a patient with poor physiologic or support group status. When conditions permit either conventional or Ilizarov treatment methods, the authors recommend Ilizarov reconstruction for defects of 2 to 12 cm.
Green, 1994	32 patients with segmental skeletal defects; 15 were treated with an open bone graft technique; 17 were treated with Ilizarov bone transport	The authors' recommendations are as follows: *Defects up to 5 cm*–cancellous bone grafting vs. bone transport *Defects greater than 5 cm*–bone transport vs. free composite tissue transfer
Marsh et al, 1994	25 infected tibial nonunions with segmental bone loss greater than or equal to 2.5 cm; 15 patients were treated with débridement, external fixation, bone grafting, and soft tissue coverage; 10 were treated with resection and bone transport using a monolateral external fixator	The two treatment groups were equivalent in terms of rate of healing, eradication of infection, treatment time, number of complications, total number of operative procedures, and angular deformities after treatment. Limb-length discrepancy was significantly less in the group treated with bone transport.
Emami et al, 1995	37 cases of infected nonunion of the tibial shaft treated with open cancellous bone grafting (Papineau technique) stabilized via external fixation; 15 nonunions had partial contact at the nonunion site, 22 had a complete segmental defect ranging from 1.5 to 3 cm in length.	All nonunions united at an average of 11 months following bone grafting. The authors recommend cancellous bone grafting for complete segmental defects up to 3 cm in length.
Patzakis et al, 1995	32 patients with infected tibial nonunions with bone defects less than 3 cm; all were stabilized with external fixation and were grafted with autogenous iliac crest bone at a mean of 8 weeks following soft tissue coverage.	Union was reported in 91% of patients (29 of 32) at a mean of 5.5 months following the bone graft procedure; union was achieved in the remaining 3 patients following posterolateral bone grafting.

TABLE 20–7

Author's Recommendations for Treatment Options for Complete Segmental Bone Defects

Bone	Host	Segmental Defect	Recommended Treatment Options
Clavicle	Healthy or compromised	<1.5 cm	Cancellous autograft bone grafting; skeletal stabilization
Clavicle	Healthy or compromised	≥1.5 cm	Tricortical autogenous iliac crest bone grafting; skeletal stabilization
Humerus	Healthy	<3 cm	Cancellous autograft bone grafting vs. shortening; skeletal stabilization
Humerus	Healthy	≥3 cm	Bulk cortical allograft vs. vascularized cortical autograft vs. bone transport; skeletal stabilization
Humerus	Compromised	<3 cm	Cancellous autograft bone grafting vs. shortening; skeletal stabilization
Humerus	Compromised	3–6 cm	Bulk cortical allograft vs. vascularized cortical autograft vs. bone transport; skeletal stabilization
Humerus	Compromised	>6 cm	Bulk cortical allograft vs. vascularized cortical autograft; skeletal stabilization
Radius or ulna	Healthy	<3 cm	Cancellous autograft bone grafting vs. tricortical autogenous iliac crest bone grafting vs. shortening; skeletal stabilization
Radius or ulna	Healthy	≥3 cm	Bulk cortical allograft vs. vascularized cortical autograft vs. bone transport vs. synostosis; skeletal stabilization
Radius or ulna	Compromised	<3 cm	Cancellous autograft bone grafting vs. tricortical autogenous iliac crest bone grafting vs. shortening; skeletal stabilization
Radius or ulna	Compromised	3–6 cm	Bulk cortical allograft vs. vascularized cortical autograft vs. bone transport vs. synostosis; skeletal stabilization
Radius or ulna	Compromised	>6 cm	Bulk cortical allograft vs. vascularized cortical autograft vs. synostosis; skeletal stabilization
Femur	Healthy	<3 cm	Cancellous autograft bone grafting vs. bone transport vs. bifocal shortening and lengthening; skeletal stabilization
Femur	Healthy	3–6 cm	Bone transport vs. bifocal shortening and lengthening; skeletal stabilization
Femur	Healthy	6–15 cm	Bone transport vs. bulk cortical allograft; skeletal stabilization
Femur	Healthy	>15 cm	Bulk cortical allograft; skeletal stabilization
Femur	Compromised	<3 cm	Cancellous autograft bone grafting vs. bone transport vs. bifocal shortening and lengthening; skeletal stabilization
Femur	Compromised	3–6 cm	Bone transport vs. bifocal shortening and lengthening vs. bulk cortical allograft; skeletal stabilization
Femur	Compromised	>6 cm	Bulk cortical allograft with skeletal stabilization vs. bracing vs. amputation
Tibia	Healthy	<3 cm	Cancellous autograft bone grafting vs. bone transport vs. bifocal shortening and lengthening; skeletal stabilization
Tibia	Healthy	3–6 cm	Bone transport vs. bifocal shortening and lengthening; skeletal stabilization
Tibia	Healthy	6–15 cm	Bone transport vs. bulk cortical allograft; skeletal stabilization
Tibia	Healthy	>15 cm	Bone transport vs. bulk cortical allograft vs. synostosis; skeletal stabilization
Tibia	Compromised	<3 cm	Cancellous autograft bone grafting vs. bone transport vs. bifocal shortening and lengthening; skeletal stabilization
Tibia	Compromised	3–6 cm	Bone transport vs. bifocal shortening and lengthening; skeletal stabilization
Tibia	Compromised	6–15 cm	Bone transport vs. bulk cortical allograft vs. synostosis; skeletal stabilization
Tibia	Compromised	>15 cm	Bulk cortical allograft with skeletal stabilization vs. synostosis with skeletal stabilization vs. bracing vs. amputation

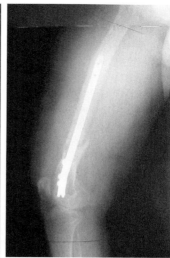

Figure 20–39. This 51-year-old woman has a femoral nonunion and was referred in after failing three prior exchange nailing procedures.

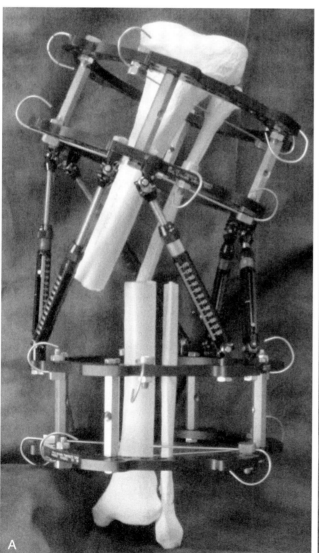
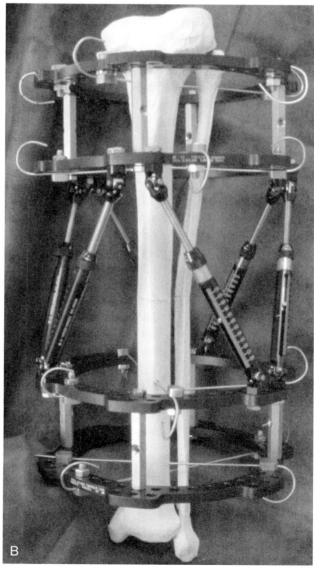

Figure 20–40. The Taylor Spatial Frame (Smith & Nephew, Inc., Memphis, TN) allows simultaneous correction of deformities involving length, angulation, rotation, and translation. *A,* Saw bone demonstration of a tibial nonunion with a profound deformity. Notice how the Taylor Spatial Frame mimics the deformity. *B,* The deformity has been corrected by adjusting the Taylor Spatial Frame struts. The strut lengths are calculated using a computer software program provided by the manufacturer.

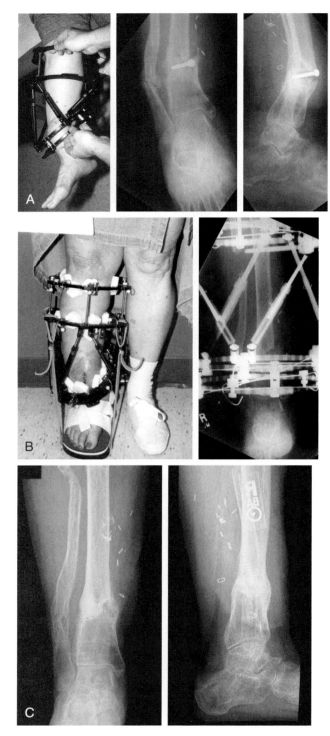

FIGURE 20–41. *A,* The preoperative photograph shows frame fitting in the office. The anteroposterior (AP) and lateral radiographs show a distal tibial nonunion with deformity in a 58-year-old woman referred in 14 months after a high-energy, open fracture. *B,* The clinical photograph and AP radiograph were obtained during correction using the Taylor Spatial Frame (Smith & Nephew, Inc., Memphis, TN). *C,* The radiographs show the final result.

is seen in three cases: patients with hypertrophic nonunions, elderly patients, and patients with Charcot neuropathy.

Some hypertrophic nonunions may have relative stability and may therefore not cause symptoms during normal daily activities. The patient may have some discomfort when the fracture nonunion site is placed under stress, such as running, jumping, lifting, or pushing. These painless hypertrophic nonunions occur most often in the clavicle, humerus, ulna, tibia, and fibula. They are often identified when, after apparent healing seen on a radiograph, an overexposed radiograph reveals a fine line of cartilage at a hypertrophic fracture site. Subsequent tomograms or CT scans confirm the nonunion (Fig. 20–47).

Painless nonunions are also seen in elderly patients. Typically, the nonunion involves the humerus, but it can also occur in the proximal ulna, the femur, and, less frequently, the tibia or lower fibula. Nonsurgical treatment can be acceptable as long as day-to-day function is not affected. In particular, this treatment course should be considered in the elderly patient with multiple medical co-morbidities that increase the risk of perioperative complications. In such cases, immobilization in a brace or cast, possibly including ultrasonic or electrical stimulation of the fracture site, may be warranted (Fig. 20–48). Operative stabilization may be necessary if instability and symptoms at the fracture site impair the patient's routine daily activities or if there is concern that the overlying soft tissues will be compromised over time (Fig. 20–49).

Fracture nonunion in the presence of Charcot neuropathy can produce severely deformed and injured bones and joints that are relatively painless. These cases are usually treated with bracing and avoidance of surgery unless the overlying soft tissues are in jeopardy (see Fig. 20–49).

In all cases of painless fracture nonunion, the medical history, physical examination results, and imaging studies should be carefully considered when determining the treatment strategy. Surgical intervention does not always improve the patient's condition or complaints, and in many cases, it can result in serious problems that reduce the patient's quality of life. Simple, nonsurgical treatment may be all that is needed to control the patient's symptoms and maintain or restore function, leading to a satisfactory outcome.

Osteopenia

Nonunions in patients with osteopenic bone represent an especially challenging management problem. The osteopenia may be isolated to the involved bone, as in an atrophic or infected nonunion, or it may be a preexisting condition that involves many areas of the skeleton, as in cases of osteoporosis or metabolic bone disease. Metabolic bone disease should be suspected in patients with nonunions in locations that do not typically have healing problems (Fig. 20–50), in long-standing cases that have failed to unite

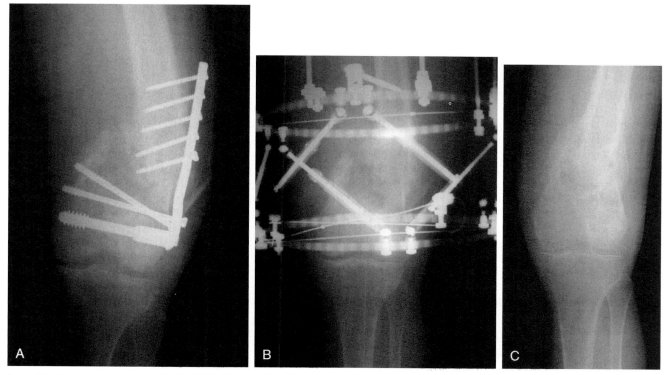

FIGURE 20–42. *A,* The preoperative radiograph demonstrates a distal femoral nonunion with deformity in a 60-year-old man who was referred in 6 months after open reduction and internal fixation. *B,* The radiograph was obtained during correction using the Taylor Spatial Frame (Smith & Nephew, Inc., Memphis, TN). *C,* The radiograph shows the final result.

despite adequate treatment, and in cases with loss of fixation of hardware in the absence of technical deficiencies. A workup for metabolic bone disease should be undertaken in suspected cases.

Intramedullary nail fixation is an exceptionally good technique in patients with osteopenic bone. Intramedullary nails function as internal splints, with contact between the implant and bone along the medullary canal. These devices also benefit by their load-sharing characteristics. Interlocking screws proximal and distal to the fracture site help maintain rotational and axial stability. Specially designed interlocking screws for purchase in poor bone stock are available from several manufacturers. When rigid fixation is desired, an "intramedullary plate" construct can be achieved with a custom-manufactured intramedullary nail with multiple interlocking screw capability (Fig. 20–51).

Plate-and-screw devices depend on fixation at the screw-bone junction and are prone to loosening in patients with osteopenic bone where purchase may be poor. Weber and Cech[252] described a method of reinforcing the screw holes with polymethyl methacrylate (PMMA) bone cement (Fig. 20–52). Using this technique, loose screws are removed, except for those adjacent to or crossing the nonunion and those at the proximal and distal ends of the plate. Slow-setting PMMA is mixed for 1 minute and then poured into a 20-mL syringe. The syringe has an attached nipple, needle, or catheter that is used for injecting PMMA into the screw holes. Each hole is injected with 1 to 2 mL of liquid cement, and the screws are rapidly reinserted into their correct holes. During injection, excess cement may come out through an adjacent empty screw hole. After reinsertion of the screws, all excess cement should be cleaned from around the screws, the plate, and the opposite side of the bone. No cement should enter the nonunion surfaces or gap. After approximately 10 minutes to allow cement hardening, the screws are tightened and checked for stability. If the end screws are essential for fixation and are also loose, they are removed at this point, and another batch of cement is similarly mixed and injected. The end screws are then reinserted by following the same process. The bone cement technique is especially useful for nonunions of an osteopenic metaphysis.

External fixation using the thin-wire Ilizarov technique provides surprisingly good purchase in osteopenic bone. The stability of the construct can be improved by the use of olive wires, which discourage translational moments at the wire–bone interface. The use of a washer at the olive wire–bone interface helps to distribute the load and to prevent erosion of the olive wire into the bone.

Mobility of the Nonunion

Based on the results of manual stress testing, a nonunion may be described as *stiff* or *lax*. These terms are most applicable when the treatment method involves Ilizarov external fixation. A stiff nonunion has an arc of mobility of 7° or less. A lax nonunion has an arc of mobility greater than 7°.[106, 225] Accurate assessment of motion at a nonunion site is difficult in the case of a limb with paired bones where one of the bones is intact.

Stiff hypertrophic nonunions may be treated using compression, distraction, or sequential monofocal compression-distraction. Lax nonunions may be hypertrophic, oligotrophic, infected, or a synovial pseudarthrosis. Lax hypertrophic and oligotrophic nonunions may be treated with gradual compression. Although some surgeons[225] have recommended 2 to 3 weeks of compression followed by gradual distraction, I have not found it necessary to distract in most cases (Fig. 20–53). Other surgeons[166] have recommended sequential monofocal distraction-compression in the treatment of hypertrophic nonunions. Lax, infected nonunions and synovial pseudarthroses are treated in the manner previously described. Further details of the Ilizarov method are given later in this chapter.

Status of Hardware

The status of previously placed hardware directly affects treatment strategy design for a nonunion. One consideration is whether performance of the contemplated plan necessitates removal of the existing hardware. For example, a humeral shaft nonunion that was initially treated with intramedullary nail fixation would likely require removal of the nail if the contemplated plan is plate-and-screw fixation with bone grafting. Alternatively, the patient could be treated with Ilizarov thin-wire external fixation with gradual compression, and the nail could be retained

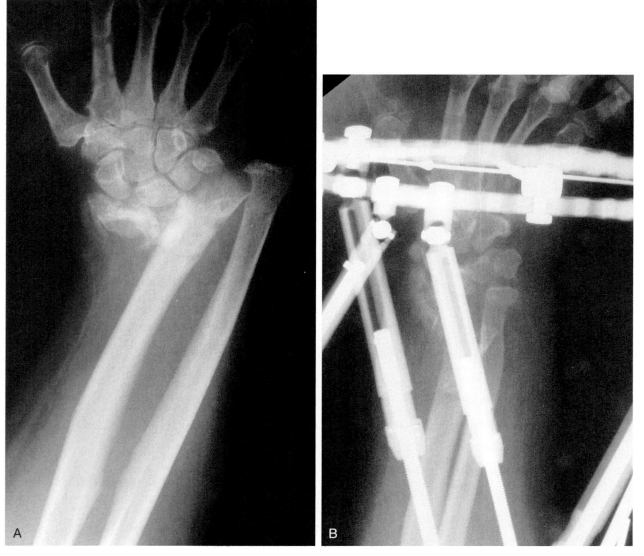

Figure 20–43. *A,* The preoperative anteroposterior (AP) radiograph shows a distal radius nonunion with a fixed (irreducible) deformity in a 73-year-old woman who was referred in 9 months after injury. *B,* This AP radiograph was obtained during deformity correction using the Taylor Spatial Frame (Smith & Nephew, Inc., Memphis, TN).

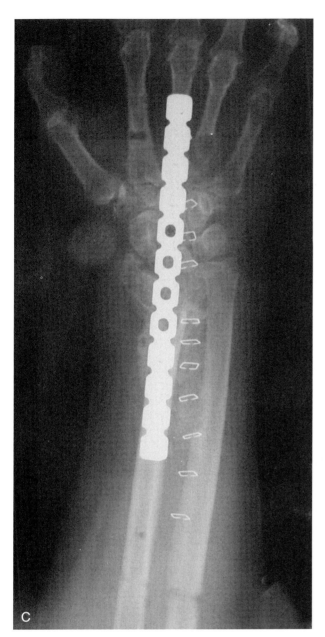

FIGURE 20–43 *Continued. C,* The postoperative radiograph was obtained soon after deformity correction and plate-and-screw fixation with bone grafting for a wrist arthrodesis.

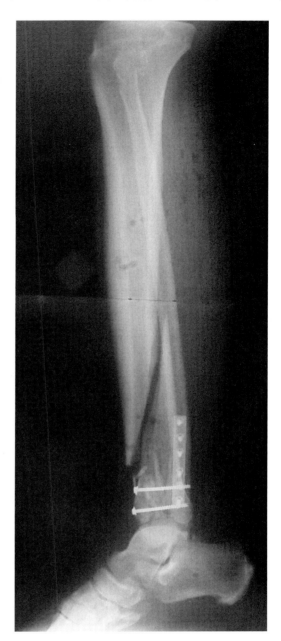

FIGURE 20–44. The lateral radiograph demonstrates a tibial nonunion in a 59-year-old man who was referred in 6 months after the initial fracture. Treating nonunions such as this with vertically oriented surfaces and poor bony contact can be challenging.

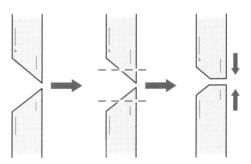

FIGURE 20–45. Trimming the ends of the bone at a nonunion site may be used to improve the surface area for bony contact.

(using slow compression over a nail using external fixation [SCONE], as described in the Treatment Methods section).

Removing previously placed hardware is considered when it is associated with an infected nonunion, when it interferes with the contemplated treatment plan, or when broken or loose hardware causes symptoms. The previously placed hardware may be retained when it augments the contemplated treatment plan (e.g., SCONE). Surgical dissection to remove the hardware may not be desirable in some cases (i.e., obesity, previous infections, or multiple prior soft tissue reconstructions overlying the hardware) and when the hardware does not interfere with the contemplated treatment plan. Removal may be used as the definitive treatment by repositioning the bone fragments,

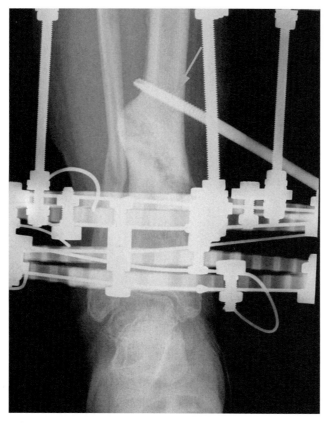

Figure 20–46. Steerage pins (*arrow*) enhance skeletal stabilization.

as in an oligotrophic nonunion with a statically locked nail in which the bone fragments are distracted. In such a case, the interlocking screws may be removed proximally or distally, the nonunion site can be acutely compressed using an externally applied device, and the interlocking screws can be inserted in their new position.

Motor and Sensory Dysfunction

Severe motor or sensory deficits in a limb that has a fracture nonunion present special challenges. Many compensatory and adaptive strategies are available to address substantial motor or sensory deficits associated with a nonunion. Supportive treatments such as bracing, exercise therapy to strengthen the intact muscles in the region, and the use of assistive devices for ambulation or other daily activities may allow preservation or restoration of function and support a plan for retaining the limb. For example, if anterior compartment motor function of the leg is impaired, ambulation can be improved after successful nonunion treatment by applying an ankle-foot orthosis or by performing a tendon transfer.

Some factors to consider when designing a treatment plan for a patient with a nonunion associated with neural dysfunction include the quality and extent of plantar or palmar sensation, which are integral to ambulation and hand function, respectively; the location and extent of other sensory deficits; the magnitude, location, and extent of motor loss (e.g., partial loss of motor function of the extensor hallucis longus versus complete loss of all motor function of the foot and ankle); and the potential for

improvement of sensation or motor function after reconstructive procedures.

If neural reconstruction cannot restore purposeful limb function and other techniques such as tendon transfers or bracing are not thought to be of potential benefit, amputation may be considered. Although ablation of the limb has disadvantages, it is more rapid, less costly, and less traumatizing than prolonged, multiple-staged reconstructions that often do little to improve the status of an insensate or flaccid limb or to increase the patient's quality of life.

Health and Age of Patients

The patient's health and age often influence the design of the treatment plan. Advanced age and chronic illnesses result in diminished biologic activity at the site of fracture nonunion and may make a successful outcome more difficult to achieve. Patients who have multiple or serious medical conditions may be poor candidates for surgical intervention. Although age itself is not a contraindication to surgical treatment of a nonunion, elderly patients are more likely to have concomitant medical conditions that may render surgery inadvisable. Elderly patients who have been nonambulatory for an extended period, who have substantially impaired cognitive status, or who are confined to a long-term care facility often do not benefit from reconstructive surgery for nonunions. The functional status of these patients is not likely to improve with surgery, and lack of compliance with postoperative instructions may become a significant issue that produces further complications. In such cases, conservative treatment such as bracing is appropriate and engenders greater compliance than complicated postoperative care protocols. When the health of the patient is such that survival takes precedence over healing the nonunion, amputation may be considered. On the other hand, elderly patients with a nonunion who have chronic illness need to maintain or increase their functional status as quickly as possible to decrease the likelihood of medical complications such as pneumonia

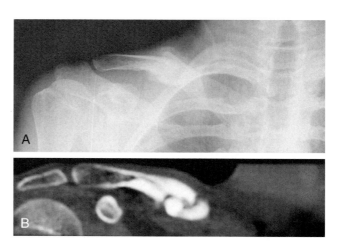

Figure 20–47. *A,* The anteroposterior radiograph shows the clavicle fracture of a 17-year-old boy who presented 6 months after the injury. He had been told by his former physician that his clavicle was solidly healed, and he had no pain. He was brought in by his mother, who was concerned about the bump on his collarbone. *B,* A computed tomography scan confirms the diagnosis of nonunion.

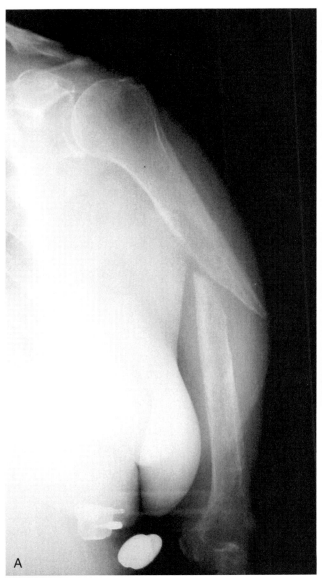

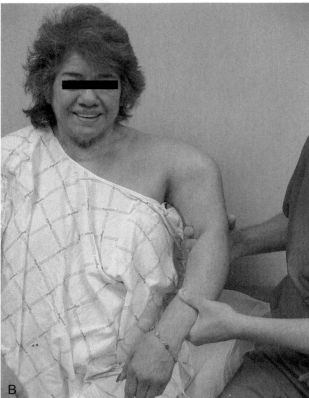

FIGURE 20–48. *A,* The anteroposterior radiograph demonstrates a left humeral shaft nonunion in a 71-year-old, right-hand-dominant woman with multiple medical problems who presented 27 months after the initial injury. *B,* Results of the clinical examination are consistent with a lax (flail) nonunion that is not associated with pain. This patient is an excellent candidate for nonoperative treatment with functional bracing.

and thromboembolism. These patients often benefit from a treatment strategy that allows immediate weight bearing and functional activity (Fig. 20–54).

Problems at Adjacent Joints

Stiffness or deformity of the joints adjacent to the nonunion can limit outcome if they are not identified and addressed. Treatment of the stiff or deformed joints can be operative or nonoperative. Physical therapies, such as joint mobilization and passive range of motion exercises, are commonly prescribed preoperatively to prepare for postoperative activity or postoperatively while restoring general limb function after successful nonunion treatment. Alternatively, joint stiffness or deformity can be treated with arthrotomy or arthroscopy, concomitantly with the procedure for the nonunion to maximize postoperative function quickly or as a subsequent, staged surgical procedure if postoperative physical therapy does not restore joint motion. Compensatory deformities accompanying nonunion constitute a problem that demands careful

consideration. Treatment options for a compensatory deformity adjacent to a nonunion (e.g., subtalar valgus deformity in a patient with a distal tibial nonunion associated with a varus deformity) include joint mobilization through physical therapy, joint mobilization by surgical lysis of adhesions at the time of surgery for the fracture nonunion, joint mobilization by surgical lysis of adhesions after the nonunion has solidly united in a reduced anatomic position, arthrodesis of the involved joint with acute correction of the compensatory deformity at the time of surgery for the fracture nonunion, and arthrodesis of the involved joint with acute correction of the compensatory deformity after the nonunion has solidly united in a reduced anatomic position.

Soft Tissue Problems

Patients with nonunions often present with substantial overlying soft tissue damage from the initial injury, multiple surgical procedures, or both causes. It is advisable to consult a plastic reconstructive surgeon specializing in

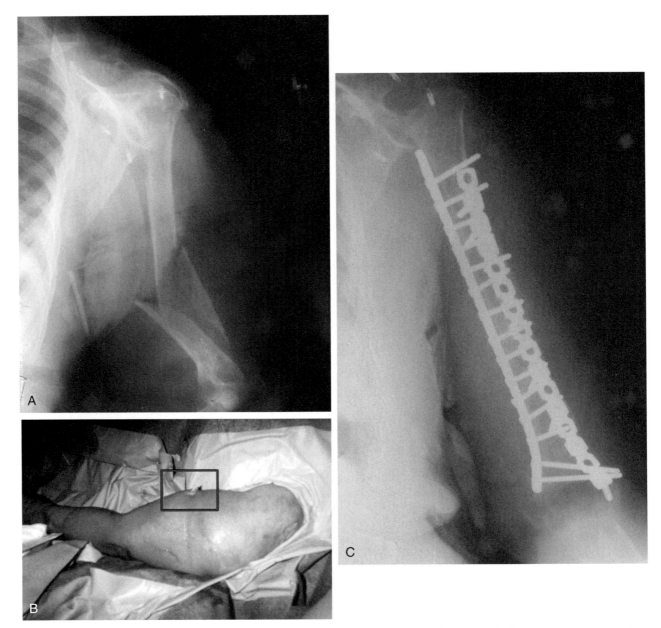

Figure 20–49. *A,* The radiograph shows a humeral shaft nonunion in an asymptomatic 82-year-old woman with Charcot neuropathy (and a Charcot shoulder) of the left upper extremity from a large syrinx. The patient had been managed nonoperatively using a functional brace by the previous physician. *B,* The patient was referred in for skeletal stabilization when a bony spike at the nonunion site eroded through her tenuous soft tissue envelope. *C,* Definitive plate-and-screw stabilization after irrigation and débridement led to bony union.

post-traumatic soft tissue procedures. The decision of whether to approach a nonunion through previous incisions or by elevating a soft tissue flap versus a surgical approach through virgin tissues is difficult and should be handled on a case-by-case basis. Extremities with non-union and extensive soft tissue damage or scarring may benefit from less invasive methods of treatment such as Ilizarov external fixation and percutaneous marrow graft-ing. Nonunions associated with soft tissue defects, open wounds, or infection may require a rotational or free flap coverage procedure as part of the treatment strategy.

Occasionally, local soft tissue advancement with wound

closure is facilitated by creating a deformity at the nonunion site that places the edges of the soft tissue defect in proximity (Fig. 20–55). This technique is particularly useful for elderly patients, immunocompromised patients, those with significant vascular disease, and patients with severe medical problems who are not good candidates for extensive operative soft tissue reconstructions. Between 3 and 4 weeks after wound closure, the deformity at the nonunion site is slowly corrected. In selected patients, this technique obviates the need for rotational or free flap coverage. The technique is best applied using Ilizarov external fixation.

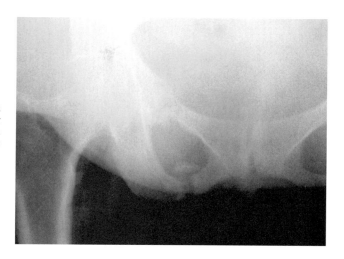

FIGURE 20–50. The anteroposterior radiograph shows the pelvis of a 50-year-old woman who presented 16 months after a superior and inferior pubic rami fracture. The endocrine assessment of this patient with a nonunion in an unusual location revealed an underlying metabolic bone disease.

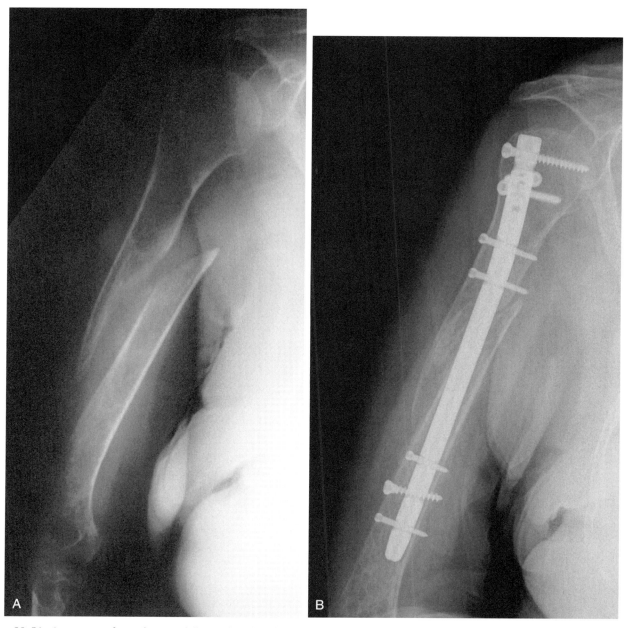

FIGURE 20–51. Custom-manufactured intramedullary nails with multiple interlocking screw capability augment the rigidity of fixation and function as an intramedullary plate. I have used this type of construct with great success in elderly patients with symptomatic humeral shaft nonunions with large medullary canals and osteopenic bone. *A,* The preoperative radiograph was obtained for an 80-year-old woman with a painful humeral nonunion 14 months after fracture. *B,* An early postoperative radiograph was obtained after percutaneously performed "intramedullary plating" using a custom humeral nail.

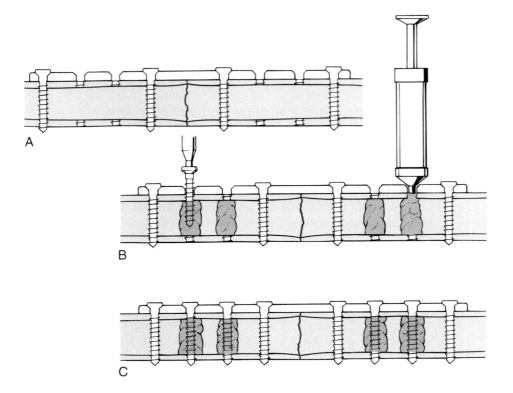

Figure 20–52. Using polymethyl methacrylate cement is an effective, multistep method for obtaining screw purchase in osteoporotic bone. *A,* The loose screws are removed. *B,* Liquid cement is injected into the screw holes using a syringe. *C,* The screws are rapidly reinserted into the cement in the holes. The screws are tightened only after the cement has hardened. The cement should not be allowed to enter the fracture site or go around the bone. (Adapted from Weber, B.G; Cech, O. Pseudarthrosis. Bern, Hans Huber, 1976.)

Treatment Methods

Many treatment methods can be used in the care of patients with fracture nonunions, including those that augment mechanical stability, those that provide biologic stimulation, and those that both augment mechanical stability and provide biologic stimulation. These treatment methods are summarized in Table 20–8. Some nonunions may be successfully treated using a single method. For example, a hypertrophic nonunion of the humeral shaft may be brought to union using a single mechanical method, such as compression plate fixation. Other nonunions may require several methods used in concert. For example, an atrophic nonunion of the humeral shaft may be addressed using plate-and-screw fixation, decortication at the nonunion site, and cancellous autogenous bone grafting.

MECHANICAL METHODS

Mechanical methods promote bony union by providing stability and, in some cases, bone-to-bone contact. These methods may be used alone or in concert with other methods.

Weight Bearing

Weight bearing is a treatment method used for nonunions of the lower extremity, most commonly nonunions involving the tibia. Weight bearing is most commonly used in conjunction with an external supportive device (e.g., casts, braces, cast braces), dynamization, or excision of bone (Fig. 20–56).

External Supportive Devices: Casting, Bracing, and Cast Bracing

Casting, bracing, and cast bracing may be used to augment the mechanical stability at the site of nonunion. In certain instances, especially hypertrophic nonunions, the increased stability from the external supportive device may result in bony union. External supportive devices are most effective when used in conjunction with weight bearing for lower extremity nonunions. Functional cast bracing with weight bearing as a treatment for nonunion has been advocated by Sarmiento,[217] particularly for nonunions of the tibia. Casting, bracing, and cast bracing are advantageous because they are noninvasive and particularly useful for patients with severe medical conditions who are not candidates for operative reconstruction. Disadvantages of these methods are that they do not provide the same degree of stability as operative methods of fixation and are generally less effective treatment methods; do not allow for concurrent deformity correction; may create or worsen deformities; or may result in break down of the soft tissues in lax nonunions (see Fig. 20–49).

Nonunion treatment with an external supportive device is most effective for stiff hypertrophic nonunions of the lower extremity. Oligotrophic nonunions that are not rigidly fixed in a distracted position at the nonunion site may also benefit from casting or bracing and weight bearing. Unless severe medical conditions prohibit surgery, external supportive devices have no role in the treatment of atrophic nonunions, infected nonunions, or synovial pseudarthrosis.

Dynamization

Dynamization entails the creation of a construct that allows axial loading of bone fragments to obtain bony union. When possible, the construct is designed to allow axial loading while discouraging rotational, translational, and shear moments. Dynamization is most commonly used as an adjunctive treatment method in patients with a nonunion of the lower extremity that is being treated with intramedullary nail fixation or external fixation.

Removal of the interlocking screws of a previously statically locked intramedullary nail allows the bone fragments to slide toward one another over the nail during weight bearing. This results in improved bone contact and compression at the nonunion site. In most cases, it is necessary to remove the interlocking screws only on one side of the nonunion (proximal or distal). Generally, the interlocking screws that are at the greatest distance from the nonunion site are removed (Fig. 20–57). When dynamization of an intramedullary nail is contemplated, axial stability and anticipated shortening must be considered. If shortening is anticipated to the extent that the intramedullary nail will penetrate the joint proximal or distal to the nonunion, treatment methods other than dynamization should be employed. Nail dynamization is advantageous because it is minimally invasive and allows for immediate return to weight-bearing activities. Disadvantages include resulting axial instability (which may result in shortening) and rotational instability, although some implant manufacturers have designed intramedullary nails with oblong interlocking screw holes that allow dynamization without the loss of rotational stability (see Fig. 20–57).

The technique may be useful for hypertrophic and oligotrophic nonunions involving the long bones of the

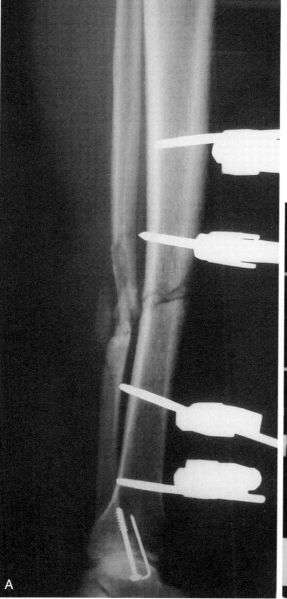

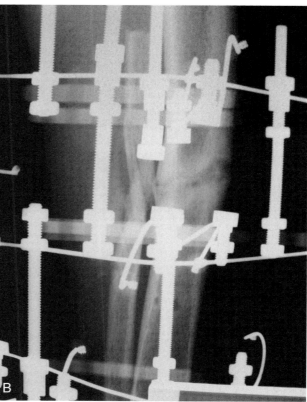

FIGURE 20–53. *A,* The radiograph demonstrates a midshaft oligotrophic (lax) tibial nonunion in a 53-year-old man referred in 10 months after unilateral external fixator stabilization for an open tibial fracture. Because of a history of recurrent pin tract infections and because the external fixator had been removed 3 weeks before presentation, intramedullary nail fixation was not thought to be an entirely safe treatment option for this patient. The patient was treated with gradual compression using an Ilizarov external fixator. *B,* A radiograph obtained during treatment shows gradual dissolution of the nonunion site with gradual compression.

Illustration continued on following page

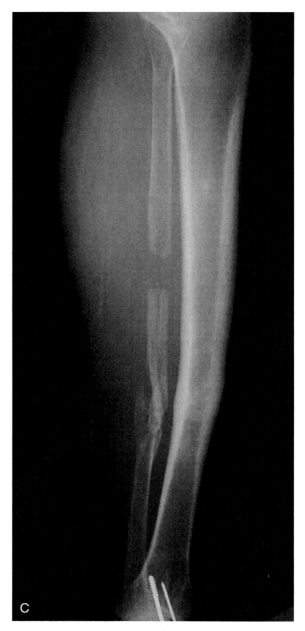

FIGURE 20–53 *Continued. C,* The radiograph shows the final result.

lower extremity. Unfortunately, no literature exists to strongly support or refute the use of nail dynamization in the treatment of nonunions. Atrophic and infected nonunions and synovial pseudarthroses are best treated using other methods.

Dynamization of an external fixator involves removal, loosening, or exchange of the external struts that span the nonunion. The method is most effective for lower extremity cases and is commonly used only after the treating physician believes that bony incorporation at the nonunion site is under way. In its preferred form, dynamization allows axial loading at the nonunion site during weight bearing in the external fixator but discourages rotational, translational, and shear instability.

Dynamizing an external fixator is therapeutic and diagnostic. It is therapeutic to the extent that axial loading at the nonunion site promotes further bony union. Increasing pain at the nonunion site after dynamization is diagnostic of motion and suggests that bony union has not progressed to the extent presumed by the treating physician.

Excision of Bone

Excision of bone as a method of treatment of a nonunion can be used in three distinct ways. Using one method of excision, pain associated with the mechanical rubbing of the bone fragments at the nonunion site can be eliminated by excising one or more of the fragments. The excised bone fragment must be in an anatomic location that does not disrupt function. Anatomic locations in which excision of bone alleviates pain without impairing function include nonunions of the fibula shaft (assuming the syndesmotic soft tissue structures are competent) and the ulna styloid. Partial excision of ununited fragments of the olecranon and patella may also be indicated in certain cases. Partial excision of the clavicle as a treatment for nonunion has been reported by Patel and Adenwalla[176] and by Middleton and associates.[150] Having had excellent results with plate fixation, I am unable to recommend this technique for clavicle nonunions.

In cases of high-energy trauma producing multiple bony injuries, articular injuries, or injury to the surrounding soft tissues, it is not always easy to predict pain relief after simple excision of bone at the nonunion site. Injection of local anesthetic into the nonunion site may help clarify the extent of pain relief anticipated after bone excision (Fig. 20–58).

The second method of bone excision is used in limbs with paired bones when one bone is intact and one has a nonunion. Excision of bone is performed on the intact bone to allow compression across the ununited bone. This technique is most commonly used in the leg in conjunction with external fixation or intramedullary nail fixation. Partial excision of the fibula allows compression across an ununited tibia (Fig. 20–59).

The third method of bone excision is used to improve the surface characteristics at a nonunion site. Trimming and débridement are performed to improve the surface area, bone contact, and bone quality at the nonunion site. This technique of excision is most commonly used for atrophic and infected nonunions and for synovial pseudarthroses.

Screws

Interfragmentary lag screw fixation is an effective method of treatment for epiphyseal nonunions (see Fig. 20–28). Successful healing has also been reported after screw fixation of patella nonunions[122] (Fig. 20–60) and olecranon nonunions.[173] Interfragmentary lag screw fixation may be used in conjunction with other forms of internal or external fixation for metaphyseal nonunions. Screw fixation alone is not recommended for nonunions of the metaphysis or diaphysis.

Cables and Wires

Periprosthetic fracture nonunions are particularly challenging by virtue of their neighboring hardware. A periprosthetic bone fragment that contains an intramedul-

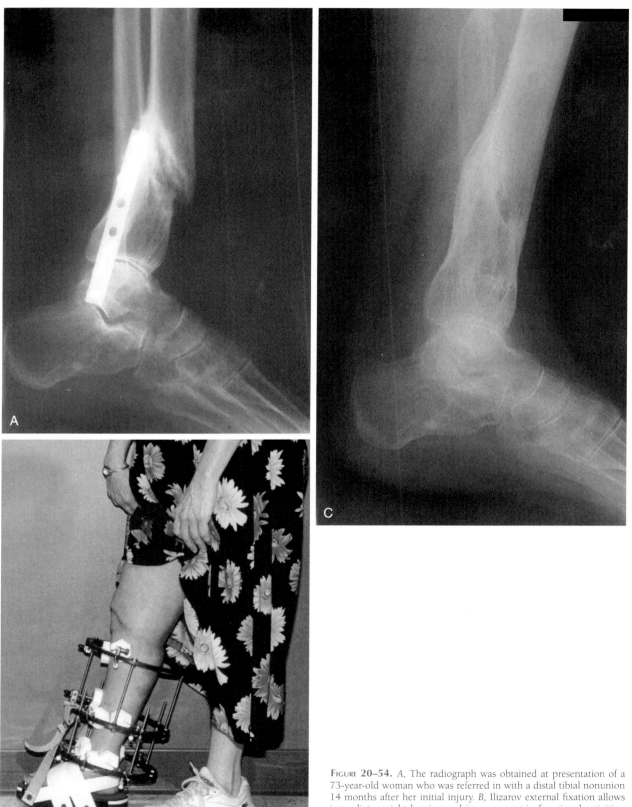

FIGURE 20–54. *A,* The radiograph was obtained at presentation of a 73-year-old woman who was referred in with a distal tibial nonunion 14 months after her initial injury. *B,* Ilizarov external fixation allows immediate weight bearing and improvement in functional activities, which is crucial in elderly patients for decreasing the risk of medical complications. *C,* The radiograph shows the final result.

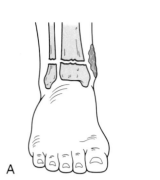

FIGURE 20–55. In certain cases, creating a deformity at the site of a nonunion facilitates wound closure. This is a particularly useful technique in elderly patients, immunocompromised persons, those with significant vascular disease, or patients with severe medical problems who are not good candidates for extensive operative soft tissue reconstructions. *A,* In this example, the distal tibial nonunion with an open medial wound cannot be closed primarily because of retraction of the soft tissues. *B,* Creating a varus deformity at the nonunion site places the soft tissue edges in approximation and allows primary closure. The deformity at the nonunion site may be corrected later after healing of the soft tissues.

lary implant can be stabilized with cables or a cable-plate system, which obviates the need for implants traversing the (occupied) medullary canal. This type of reconstruction is commonly performed in concert with autogenous cancellous bone grafting with or without structural allograft bone struts (Fig. 20–61).

Tension band and cerclage wire techniques may be used to treat nonunions of the olecranon and patella,[122] although I prefer more rigid fixation techniques.

Plate-and-Screw Fixation

The modern era of nonunion management with internal fixation can be traced to the establishment of the Swiss AO (Arbeitsgemeinschaft für Osteosynthesefragen) by Müller, Allgöwer, Willenegger, and Schneider in 1958. Building from the foundation of the pioneers who had preceded them[34, 49, 60, 110, 111, 117, 129, 130, 180] and using the metallurgic skills of the Swiss watch making and instrument industries and a research institute in Davos, the AO Group

developed a system of implants and instruments that remain in use today. The AO Group is responsible for the development of the most widely used modern concepts of nonunion treatment: stable internal fixation under compression, decortication, bone grafting in nonunions associated with gaps or poor vascularity, leaving the nonunion tissue undisturbed for hypertrophic nonunions, and early return to function.

Advantages of plate-and-screw fixation include its rigidity of fixation; versatility for various anatomic locations (Fig. 20–62), especially periarticular and intra-articular nonunions, and situations such as periprosthetic nonunions; facilitation of correction of angular, rotational, and translational deformities (under direct visualization); safety after failed or temporary external fixation. Disadvantages of the method include the requirement for extensive soft tissue dissection and the potential for associated complications; load-bearing nature of the implants that limit early weight bearing for lower extremity applications; and an inability to correct significant foreshortening from bone loss. Stabilization with plate-and-screw fixation is applicable for all types of nonunion. In cases of long bone nonunions with large segmental defects, other methods of skeletal stabilization should be considered.

Published reports by many surgeons have documented success using plate-and-screw fixation for the treatment of nonunions of the intertrochanteric femoral region,[216] femur,[241, 244] proximal tibia,[27, 29, 261] tibia,[92] clavicle,[19, 51, 59, 165, 269] proximal humerus,[91] humeral shaft,[207, 265] distal humerus,[145, 215] olecranon,[50] and distal radius.[71]

A variety of plate types and techniques are available for specific nonunion applications. This information is beyond the scope of this chapter and is provided in each chapter that covers a specific anatomic region.

Intramedullary Nail Fixation

Intramedullary nailing is an excellent method of providing mechanical stability to a fracture nonunion. The method is useful for nonunions of the long bones whose injuries have previously been treated by a method other than an intramedullary nail; if the injury was most recently treated by a nail, placement of a new nail would be classified as an

---

TABLE 20–8 ....

Treatment Methods for Nonunions

Mechanical Methods	Biologic Methods	Methods That Are Both Mechanical and Biologic
Weight-bearing	Nonstructural bone grafts	Structural bone grafts
External supportive devices	Decortication	Exchange nailing
Dynamization	Electromagnetic, ultrasound, and	Synostosis techniques
Excision of bone	shock wave stimulation	Ilizarov method
Screws		Arthroplasty
Cables and wires		Arthrodesis
Plate-and-screw fixation		Amputation
Intramedullary nail fixation		
Osteotomy		
External fixation		

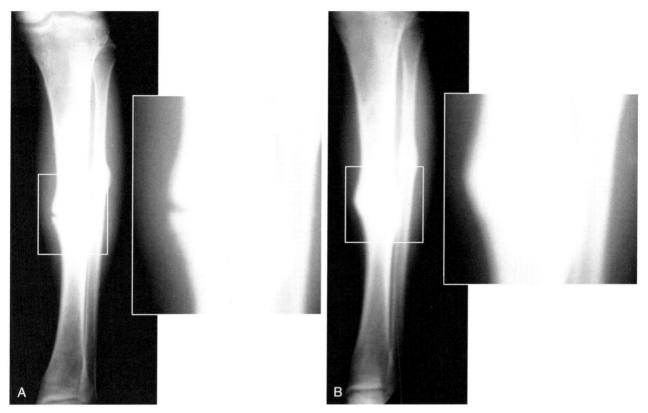

FIGURE 20–56. *A,* The radiograph was obtained for a 44-year-old man 8 months after a tibial shaft fracture. The patient did not want any operative intervention and his painful hypertrophic tibial nonunion was treated with weight bearing in a functional brace. *B,* The radiograph obtained 5 months after presentation shows the resulting solid bony union.

exchange nailing, which is a different technique that is discussed later.

Intramedullary nail fixation is particularly useful for lower extremity nonunions because of the ultimate strength and load-sharing characteristics of intramedullary nails. Intramedullary implants are an excellent treatment option for patients with osteopenic states in whom bone purchase may be poor.

Intramedullary nail fixation as a treatment for nonunion is commonly combined with a biologic method such as open grafting, intramedullary grafting, or intramedullary reaming. These techniques are used to stimulate the local biologic activity at the nonunion site, but the intramedullary nail itself is strictly a mechanical treatment method.

Hypertrophic, oligotrophic, and atrophic nonunions, as well as synovial pseudarthroses, may be treated with intramedullary nail fixation. The use of this method of fixation in cases with active infection has been reported by several investigators,[123, 124, 147, 228] but it remains controversial. Because of the potential risk associated with the technique in patients with infection (i.e., seeding the medullary canal) and because a variety of safer options exist, I and others[142] generally recommend against the use of intramedullary nail fixation in cases of active or prior deep infection. The use of exchange nailing in the face of infection is a different situation entirely because the medullary canal has already been seeded, and it is advocated in selected patients.

Differing opinions exist regarding the use of intramed-

ullary nail fixation in patients previously treated with external fixation.[16, 108, 140, 144, 149, 196, 260] The risk of infection after intramedullary nailing in a patient with prior external fixation is generally accepted to be related to the duration of external fixation, the period from removal of external fixation to intramedullary nailing, and history of pin-site infection.

Other factors affecting the risk of infection are related to the details of the application of the external fixator: implant type (i.e., tensioned wires versus half pins), surgical technique (i.e., intermittent low-speed drilling under constant irrigation decreases thermal necrosis of bone when placing half pins and wires), and implant location (i.e., implants that traverse less soft tissue create less local irritation).

The decision to use intramedullary nail fixation in a patient whose injury has previously been treated with external fixation should be made only after careful deliberation. I proceed with intramedullary nail fixation in a patient who has had an external fixator only when I believe that the benefits outweigh the risks associated with this technique.

A variety of other factors must be considered when treating long bone nonunions with intramedullary nail fixation. First, the alignment (i.e., angulation and translation) of the proximal and distal fragments should be assessed on AP and lateral radiographs to determine if closed passage of a guide wire is possible. Second, plain radiographs and, when necessary, CT scans should be

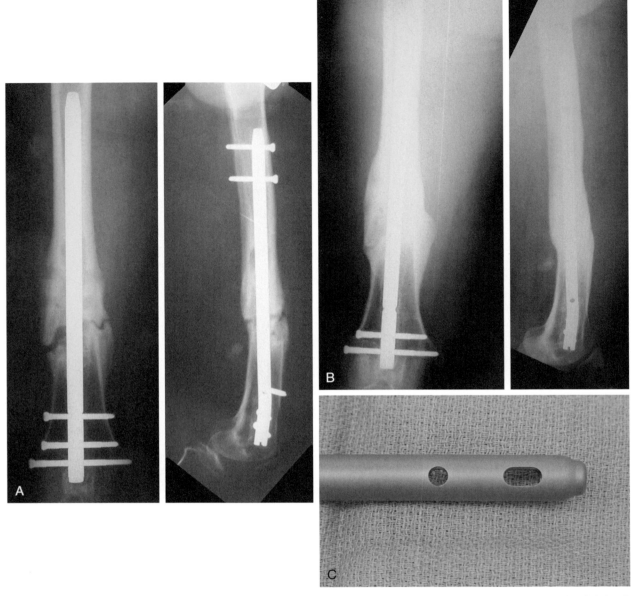

Figure 20–57. *A*, Radiographs were obtained at presentation of a 40-year-old man 31 months after a closed femur fracture. The patient had failed multiple prior procedures, including exchange nailing and open bone grafting. The patient refused to have any type of major surgical reconstruction and was treated with nail dynamization by removing the proximal interlocking screws. *B*, Radiographs show solid bony union 14 months after dynamization. *C*, Intramedullary nails designed with oblong, interlocking screw holes allow dynamization without loss of rotational stability.

studied to determine whether the medullary canal is open or sealed off at the nonunion site and whether it allows passage of a guide wire and reamers. T-handle reamers or a pseudarthrosis chisel (or both) may be useful for closed recanalization, but they are effective only when the proximal and distal fragments are relatively well aligned. If these methods fail, a percutaneously performed osteotomy without a wide exposure of the nonunion site or percutaneous drilling of the medullary canals of the proximal and distal fragments or both (using fluoroscopic imaging) may facilitate passage of the guide wire and nail (Fig. 20–63). After the percutaneously performed osteotomy, deformity correction may be facilitated by the use of a femoral distractor or a temporary external fixator.

Third, the fixation strategy using interlocking screws must be considered. The choices include static interlocking, dynamic interlocking, and no interlocking. This decision is based on a number of factors, including the type of nonunion, the surface characteristics of the nonunion, the location and geometry of the nonunion, and the importance of rotational stability as judged by the treating physician. Fourth, loading and bone contact at the nonunion site can be optimized using a few special techniques. When static locking is to be performed, distant locking followed by "backslapping" the nail (as if to attempt to extract it) may improve contact at the nonunion site; this maneuver is followed by proximate locking. Some intramedullary nails have been designed to allow application of acute compression at the nonunion site during the operative procedure. A femoral distractor or a temporary external fixator may aid in compression, deformity correction, or both at a nonunion site being stabilized with intramedullary nail fixation (see Fig. 20–34). For tibial nonunions, partial excision of the fibula facilitates compression at the nonunion site during nail insertion and later during weight-bearing ambulation. Osteotomy or partial excision of the fibula also facilitates acute correction of tibial deformities associated with a nonunion.

Operative exposure of the nonunion site at the time of intramedullary nail fixation has been recommended[124, 147, 149, 175, 211, 228, 249, 264] for open bone grafting, hardware removal, deformity correction, resection of infected or necrotic bone, recanalization of the medullary canal for an injury that has failed closed technique, and soft tissue release. Some surgeons[175, 228, 263, 264] have advocated routine exposure and open bone grafting for all nonunions being treated with intramedullary nail fixation. Other investigators have recommended open exposure of the nonunion site only in cases requiring hardware removal,[147, 149] deformity correction,[147, 149, 211] "nonunion takedown,"[124] open

recanalization of the medullary canal,[142] or soft tissue release.[147] Still others,[3, 142, 260] as do I, discourage routine open bone grafting of nonunion sites being treated with intramedullary nail fixation. Closed nailing without exposure of the nonunion site is advantageous because it does not damage the periosteal blood supply, the infection rate is lower, and it does not disrupt the tissues that have osteogenic potential at the nonunion site.

In cases requiring a wide exposure of the nonunion site for open bone grafting, resection of bone, deformity correction, or hardware removal, I tend to use alternate methods of fixation such as plate and screws or external fixation. In general, I prefer to avoid treatment methods that impair the endosteal and periosteal blood supply, as do intramedullary nailing and open exposure of the nonunion site, respectively. I may somewhat reluctantly combine these methods for some exceptions:

1. Nonviable nonunions in patients with poor bone quality when bone grafting is needed to stimulate the local biology of the nonunion and nail fixation is mechanically advantageous
2. Segmental nonunions with bone defects when I do not believe reaming will result in union and think nailing is

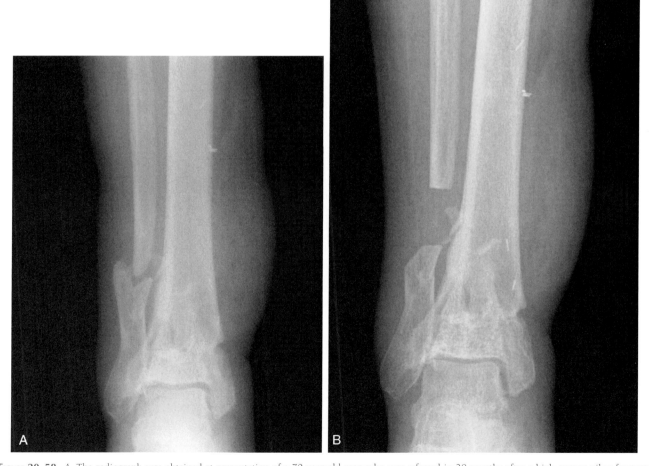

FIGURE 20–58. *A,* The radiograph was obtained at presentation of a 70-year-old man who was referred in 28 months after a high-energy pilon fracture. The patient's primary complaint was pain over the fibular nonunion. Injection in this area with local anesthetic resulted in complete relief of the patient's pain. *B,* The radiograph shows the results after treatment of the fibular nonunion by partial excision. The procedure resulted in complete pain relief.

the best method to stabilize the segmental bone fragments

3. Nonunions associated with deformities in noncompliant or cognitively impaired individuals when the biomechanical advantages of intramedullary nail fixation (over plate fixation) are required and external fixation is a poor option

4. Nonunions with large segmental defects when bulk cortical allograft and intramedullary nail fixation are the chosen treatment (Fig. 20–64)

A technique that may be used in conjunction with nail fixation to treat diaphyseal defects is closed intramedullary bone grafting. This technique was described by Chapman[32] for use in recent fractures of the femoral shaft with segmental bone loss. I have used this technique to treat nonunions of the femur and tibia with excellent results (Fig. 20–65). Grafting by means of intramedullary reaming

is an excellent method of treatment and is discussed in the section on Exchange Nailing.

Intramedullary nail fixation as a treatment for nonunion is most commonly used in the tibia. Reported healing rates for nonunions have been 92% to 100%.[3, 116, 142, 147, 149, 153, 211, 228, 232, 248, 260] With the development of specialized nails and the availability of custom-designed nails, the anatomic zone of the tibia that can be treated with intramedullary nail fixation has expanded from that recommended by Mayo and Benirschke[142] in 1990. I do not favor an algorithmic approach regarding anatomic zones and nailing tibial nonunions. Instead, each tibial nonunion should be evaluated on a case-by-case basis, with templating performed when nail fixation is contemplated for proximal or distal diametaphyseal or metaphyseal nonunions. A situation worth noting is the case of a slow or arrested proximal tibial regenerate (a nonunion of sorts) after an Ilizarov length-

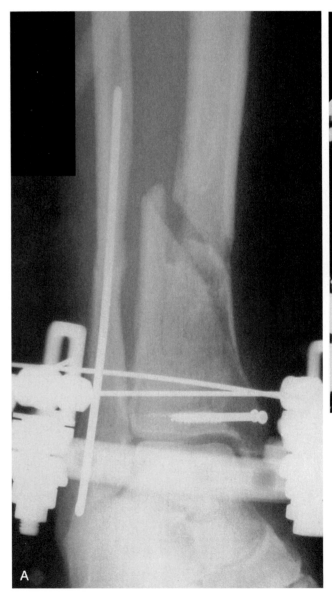

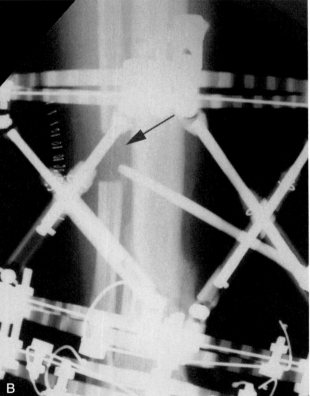

FIGURE 20–59. *A,* The radiograph was obtained at presentation of a 42-year-old man who was referred in 5 months after a distal tibial fracture. *B,* The patient was treated with deformity correction and slow, gradual compression using an Ilizarov external fixator. This approach required partial excision of the fibula *(arrow).*

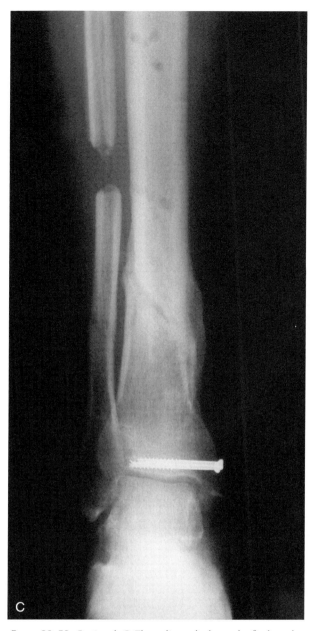

FIGURE 20–59 *Continued. C,* The radiograph shows the final result.

able.[33, 116, 147, 249, 264, 266, 267] Koval and co-workers,[124] however, reported a high rate of failure for distal femoral nonunions treated with retrograde intramedullary nailing. Other sites of nonunion treated by intramedullary nail fixation include the clavicle,[17] proximal humerus,[52, 162] humeral shaft,[263] distal humerus,[175] and fibula.[1]

Osteotomy

The purpose of an osteotomy in the treatment of nonunions is to reorient the plane of the nonunion. Reorientation of the angle of inclination of the nonunion

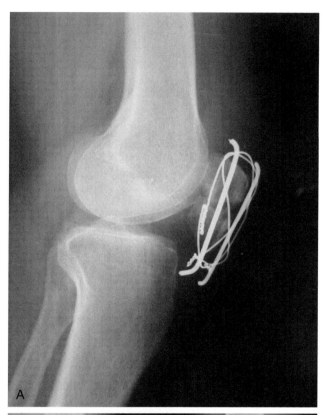

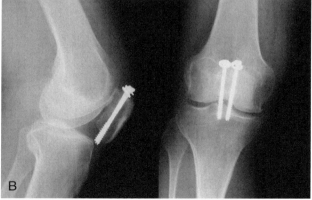

FIGURE 20–60. *A,* The radiograph was obtained at presentation of a 55-year-old woman who was referred in with a patella nonunion after four failed attempts at reconstruction. The patient was treated with open reduction and interfragmentary lag screw fixation. *B,* The final radiographic result shows solid bony union.

ening or bone transport procedure. In a few selected patients, I have treated this problem with the following protocol: external fixator removal, 6 to 8 weeks of casting and bracing (allows complete healing of the pin sites), and reamed, statically locked intramedullary nailing. This technique has been used only in patients who were poor candidates for open techniques (e.g., bone grafting, plate-and-screw fixation) because of soft tissue concerns (e.g., morbid obesity, multiple prior soft tissue reconstructions). All of the regenerates have fully matured 3 to 6 months after reamed nailing, and no patient developed an infection (Fig. 20–66).

Nail fixation for femoral nonunions is not uncommon, and the clinical results have generally been favor-

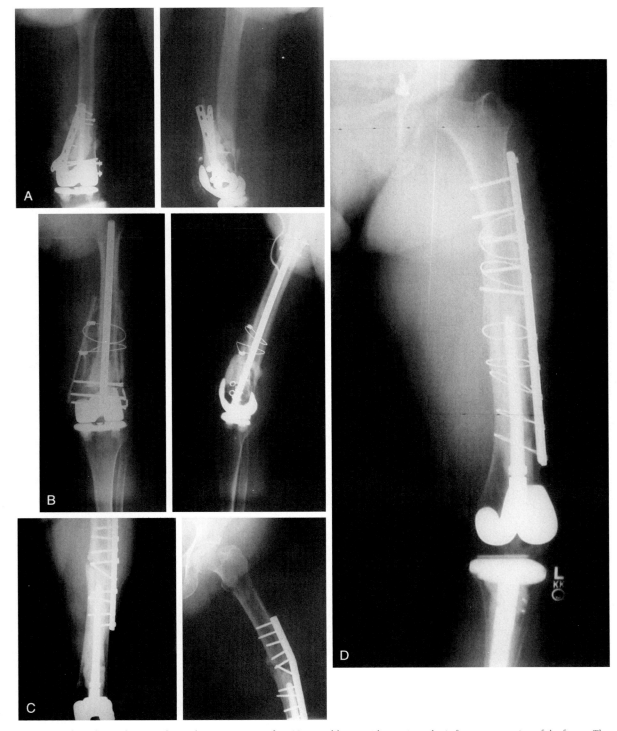

Figure 20–61. *A*, The radiographs were obtained at presentation of an 83-year-old man with a periprosthetic fracture nonunion of the femur. The patient was treated with intramedullary nail stabilization with allograft strut bone graft and with circumferential cable fixation. *B*, The final radiographic result shows solid bony union and incorporation of the allograft struts. *C*, The radiographs were obtained at presentation of an 80-year-old woman who was referred in after failing multiple attempts at surgical reconstruction of a periprosthetic femoral nonunion. The patient was treated with plate stabilization with allograft strut bone graft and with circumferential cable fixation. *D*, The final radiograph shows solid bony union.

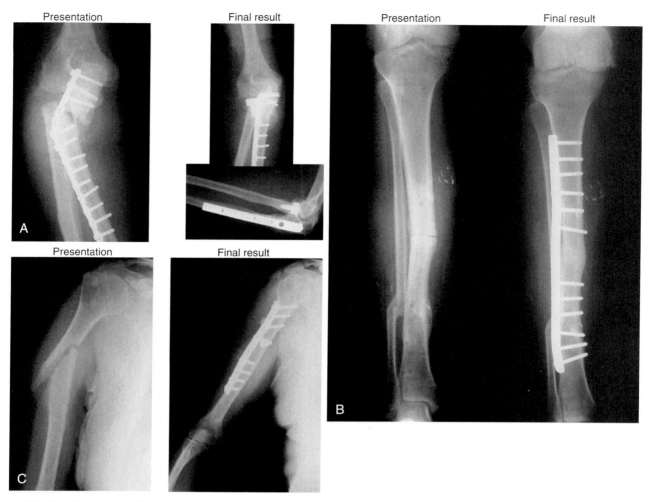

FIGURE 20–62. *A,* Presenting and final radiographs show a proximal ulnar nonunion in a 60-year-old man referred in after failing three prior attempts at reconstruction. Blade plate fixation provided absolute rigid stabilization and, in conjunction with autogenous bone grafting, led to rapid bony union. *B,* Presenting and final radiographs show a tibial shaft nonunion that had failed treatment with an external fixator. Plate-and-screw fixation with autogenous bone grafting led to successful bony union. *C,* Presenting and final radiographs show a humeral shaft fracture that had failed nonoperative treatment and had gone on to nonunion. Plate-and-screw fixation with autogenous bone grafting produced successful bony union.

from a vertical to a more horizontal position encourages healing by promoting compressive forces across the nonunion site. The osteotomy can be performed through the nonunion site, such as to trim the bone ends flat to decrease the inclination of a nonunion of a long bone, or performed adjacent to the nonunion, such as a Pauwels osteotomy for a femoral neck nonunion.[11, 181]

External Fixation

External fixation as a method of bone stabilization has been used primarily in the treatment of infected nonunions. The method is commonly employed in combination with serial débridements, antibiotic beads, soft tissue coverage procedures, and bone grafting. The use of external fixation as a method of skeletal stabilization has been reported for infected nonunions of the femur,[245] tibia,[35, 65, 179] and humerus.[36] The Ilizarov method is discussed in the section on Methods That Are Both Mechanical and Biologic.

BIOLOGIC METHODS

Biologic methods promote bony union by stimulating the local biology at the nonunion site. These methods may be used alone but are more typically used in concert with a mechanical method.

Nonstructural Bone Grafts

Autogenous Cancellous Graft. Autogenous cancellous bone grafting remains an important weapon in the trauma surgeon's armamentarium. Successful treatment of oligotrophic, atrophic, and infected nonunions, as well as synovial pseudarthroses, often depends on copious autologous cancellous bone grafting.

Cancellous autograft is osteogenic, osteoconductive, and osteoinductive. The graft stimulates the local biology at the nonunion site in viable nonunions with poor callus formation and nonviable nonunions. Initially, the graft has poor structural integrity, but this situation improves rapidly during the process of osteointegration.

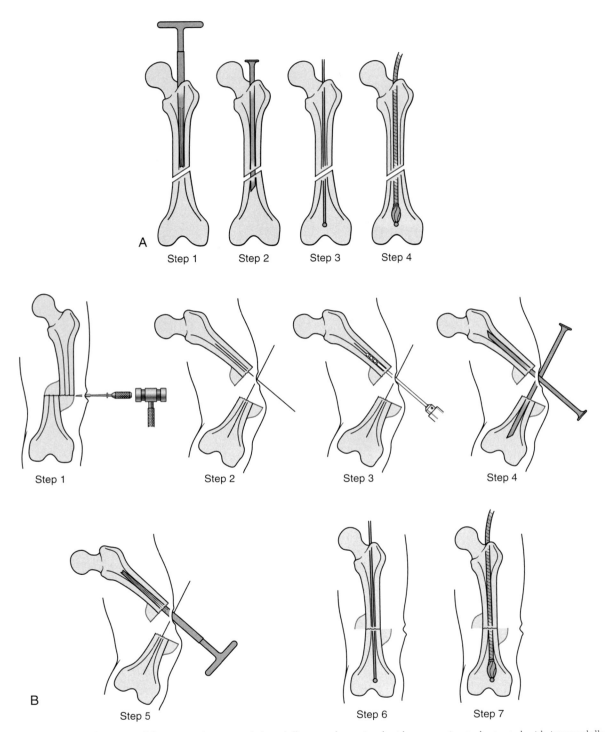

Figure 20–63. This procedure is used for recannulating a sealed medullary canal associated with a nonunion to be treated with intramedullary nail insertion. *A,* The site does not have significant deformity (i.e., proximal and distal canals are aligned): *step 1,* manual T-handle reaming; *step 2,* pseudarthrosis chiseling; *step 3,* passage of a bulb tip guide rod; *step 4,* flexible reaming. *B,* The site may have a significant irreducible deformity (i.e., proximal and distal canals are not aligned): *step 1,* percutaneous osteotomy; *step 2,* percutaneous guide wire placement (fluoroscopically guided) into the proximal and distal canals; *step 3,* cannulated drilling of the proximal and distal canals; *step 4,* pseudarthrosis chiseling; *step 5,* manual T-handle reaming; *step 6,* passage of a bulb-tip guide rod; *step 7,* flexible reaming.

Cancellous autograft is not necessary in the treatment of hypertrophic nonunions. These nonunions are viable and are characterized by motion and often by abundant callus formation. Stabilization results in calcification of unmineralized fibrocartilage and ultimately in bony union. Bone grafting is unnecessary and should not be performed.

Oligotrophic nonunions are viable and typically arise as a result of poor bone-to-bone contact. Cancellous autograft bone promotes bridging of ununited bone gaps. The decision about whether to bone graft an oligotrophic nonunion is determined by the treatment strategy planned. If the strategy involves operative exposure of the nonunion site, such as for plate-and-screw fixation, autogenous bone grafting onto a decorticated bony bed is recommended. If the strategy does not involve exposure of the nonunion site, such as with compression by means of external fixation or dynamization of an intramedullary nail, I do not routinely expose the oligotrophic nonunion for open bone grafting.

Atrophic and infected nonunions are nonviable. Their blood supply is poor, and they are not capable of callus formation. These nonunions are typically associated with segmental bone defects. The many variables in patients with segmental bone defects makes clinical series reported in the literature difficult to interpret. Surgeons' recommendations vary regarding the maximal complete segmental defect that can unite when stimulated with autogenous cancellous bone grafting (see Table 20–6).[39, 65, 69, 83, 139, 141, 179] My treatment recommendations for segmental bone defects are shown in Table 20–7.

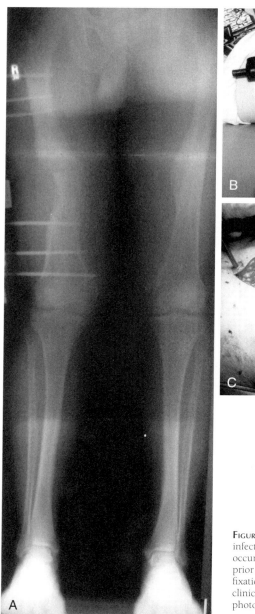

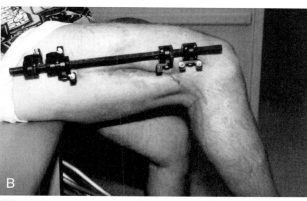

FIGURE 20–64. *A,* The radiograph obtained at presentation shows an infected femoral nonunion resulting from an open femur fracture that occurred 32 years earlier. This 51-year-old man had had more than 20 prior attempts at surgical reconstruction; the most recent was external fixation and bone grafting performed at an outside facility. *B,* The clinical photograph was taken at the time of presentation. *C,* A clinical photograph shows antibiotic beads in situ.

Illustration continued on following page

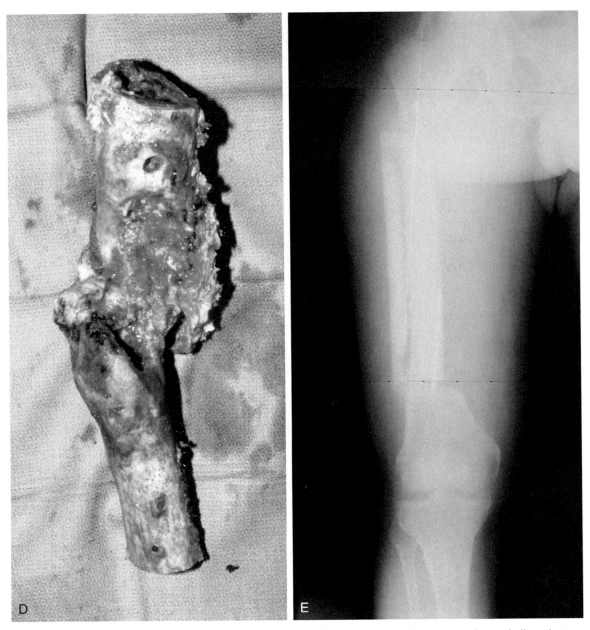

FIGURE 20–64 *Continued. D,* Gross specimen following resection. *E,* A radiograph obtained after radical resection shows a bulk antibiotic spacer that remained in situ for 3 months.

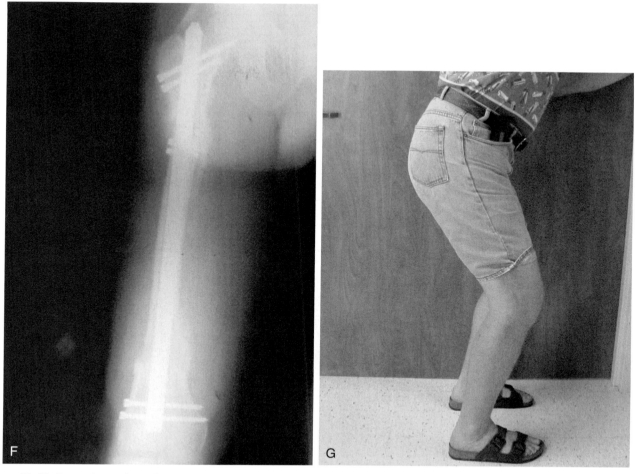

FIGURE 20–64 *Continued. F,* Radiographs were obtained 7 months after reconstruction using a bulk femoral allograft and a custom femoral nail; the proximal portion of the nail is an antegrade reconstruction nail, and the distal portion of the nail is a retrograde supracondylar nail. *G,* The clinical photograph was taken 7 months after reconstruction. The patient is ambulating full weight bearing and is pain free for the first time in 32 years.

Synovial pseudarthrosis is most commonly treated with excision of the pseudarthrosis tissue and opening of the medullary canal. Decortication and autogenous cancellous bone grafting encourage more rapid healing and are recommended.

Cancellous autogenous bone graft may be harvested from the iliac crest, the distal femur, the greater trochanter, the proximal tibia, and the distal radius. More osseous tissue can be harvested from the iliac crest than from any other location. Evidence also exists that bone of intramembraneous origin (e.g., ilium) is more osteoconductive than bone of enchondral origin (e.g., tibia, femur, radius).[186] A dramatically larger quantity of bone can be harvested from the posterior iliac crest compared with the anterior iliac crest.

A variety of techniques have been described for the treatment of nonunions using autogenous cancellous autograft:

Papineau technique (open cancellous bone grafting)[174]
Posterolateral grafting of the tibia

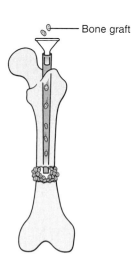

FIGURE 20–65. Closed intramedullary autogenous cancellous bone grafting can be used to treat diaphyseal bony defects. Autogenous cancellous bone harvested from the iliac crest is delivered to the defect through a tube positioned in the medullary canal.

Anterior grafting of the tibia (after soft tissue coverage)
Intramedullary grafting[32]
Intramedullary reaming
Endoscopic bone grafting[121]
Percutaneous bone grafting[15]

Various protocols exist for the timing of bone grafting:

Early bone grafting without prior bony débridement or excision
Early open bone grafting after débridement and skeletal stabilization
Delayed bone grafting after débridement, skeletal stabilization, and soft tissue reconstruction

The major disadvantages of autogenous bone grafting in the treatment of nonunions are the limited quantity of bone available for harvest and donor site morbidity and complications.

Allogenic Cancellous Graft. Allogenic cancellous bone when used in the treatment of nonunions is most commonly mixed with autogenous cancellous bone graft or bone marrow. Because allogenic cancellous bone functions primarily as an osteoconductive graft, mixing it with autograft enhances the graft's osteoinductive and osteogenic capacity. Cancellous allograft may also be added to cancellous autograft bone to increase the volume of graft available to fill a large skeletal defect. Little is known about the efficiency of allograft cancellous bone alone as a treatment for nonunion. I do not recommend the use of allogenic cancellous bone (alone or mixed with cancellous autograft) in patients with any recent or past infection associated with their nonunions.

Allogenic bone can be prepared in three ways: fresh, fresh-frozen, and freeze-dried. Fresh grafts have the highest antigenicity. Fresh-frozen grafts are less immunogenic than fresh grafts and preserve the graft's bone

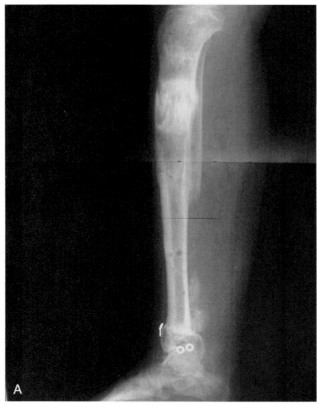

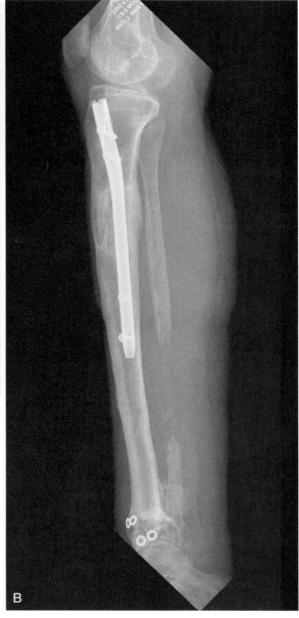

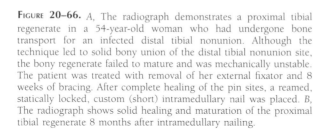

Figure 20–66. *A,* The radiograph demonstrates a proximal tibial regenerate in a 54-year-old woman who had undergone bone transport for an infected distal tibial nonunion. Although the technique led to solid bony union of the distal tibial nonunion site, the bony regenerate failed to mature and was mechanically unstable. The patient was treated with removal of her external fixator and 8 weeks of bracing. After complete healing of the pin sites, a reamed, statically locked, custom (short) intramedullary nail was placed. *B,* The radiograph shows solid healing and maturation of the proximal tibial regenerate 8 months after intramedullary nailing.

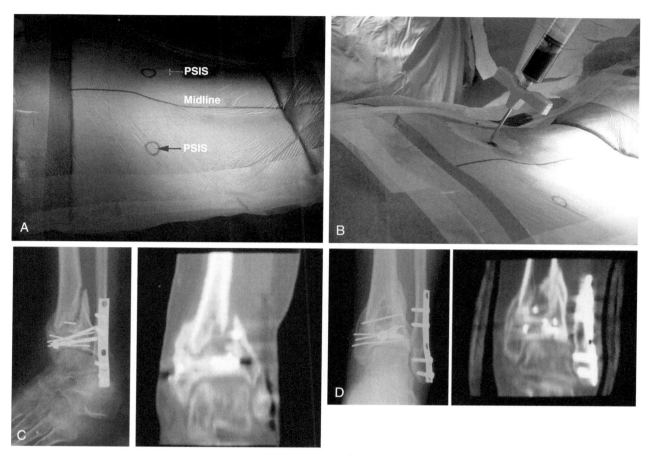

FIGURE 20–67. *A,* The clinical photograph shows the bony landmarks for harvesting bone marrow from the posterior iliac crest. The patient has been positioned prone. *B,* Marrow is harvested in 4-mL aliquots. *C,* The radiograph and computed tomography (CT) scan were obtained at presentation of a 39-year-old woman who was referred in with a stable, oligotrophic, distal tibial nonunion. *D,* The radiograph and CT scan 4 months after percutaneous marrow injection show solid bony union. *Abbreviation:* PSIS, posterior superior iliac spine.

morphogenetic proteins. Freeze-dried grafts are the least immunogenic, have the lowest likelihood of viral transmission, are purely osteoconductive, and have the least mechanical integrity.

Bone Marrow. Bone marrow contains osteoprogenitor cells capable of forming bone at the site of fractures and nonunions. Fracture and nonunion models in animals have shown enhanced healing when stimulated with bone marrow grafting.[172, 240] The healing response in animals has been especially enhanced when demineralized bone matrix is mixed with bone marrow.[240] Animal studies have also shown enhanced bone formation during distraction osteogenesis in a rat femoral model when marrow-derived mesenchymal progenitor cells were injected.[194]

Percutaneous bone marrow injection is a clinical treatment for fracture nonunion that has been reported with favorable results by several surgeons.[43, 44, 226] The technique of percutaneous bone marrow grafting involves harvesting autogenous bone marrow from the anterior or posterior iliac crest using a trocar needle. I prefer to harvest marrow from the posterior iliac crest and use an 11-gauge, 4-inch Lee-Lok needle (Lee Medical Ltd., Minneapolis, MN) and a 20-mL, heparinized syringe (Fig. 20–67). Marrow is harvested in small aliquots to increase the concentration of osteoblast progenitor cells. A study

performed in humans[161] concluded that the preferred volume of bone marrow aspirated from each site is 2 to 4 mL. I harvest marrow in 4-mL aliquots, changing the position of the trocar needle in the posterior iliac crest between aspirations. Depending on the characteristics (e.g., size, location) of the recipient nonunion site, I typically harvest a total of 40 to 80 mL of marrow.

Marrow injection into the nonunion site is performed percutaneously under fluoroscopic image using an 18-gauge spinal needle. The technique is minimally invasive, has low morbidity, and can be performed on an outpatient basis. The technique works well for nonunions with small defects (<5 mm) that have excellent mechanical stability (see Fig. 20–67). Percutaneous marrow injection also enhances healing at the docking site of patients undergoing slow, gradual compression or bone transport.

Bone Graft Substitutes. A variety of bone graft substitutes may have a future role in the treatment of nonunions (Table 20–9). The efficiency and indications for these substitutes in the treatment of nonunions remain unclear.

Growth Factors. Ongoing research in the area of growth factors holds promise for rapid advancement in the treatment of fracture nonunions. This subject is discussed in Chapter 22.

TABLE 20–9 ....

Commercially Available Bone Graft Substitutes

Bone Graft Substitute	Mode of Action	Contents
Collagraft (Zimmer, Inc., Warsaw, IN)	Osteoconduction	Hydroxyapatite, tricalcium phosphate, bovine collagen
Norian SRS (Norian Corporation, Cupertino, CA)	Osteoconduction	Calcium phosphate, calcium carbonate
Osteoset (Wright Medical Technology, Inc., Arlington, TN)	Osteoconduction	Calcium sulfate
ProOsteon (Interpore Cross International Inc., Irvine, CA)	Osteoconduction	Hydroxyapatite converted from marine coral tricalcium phosphate
DynaGraft (Gen Sci Regeneration Sciences, Inc., Mississauga, Ontario)	Osteoconduction and osteoinduction	Demineralized human bone matrix
Grafton DBM (Osteotech, Inc., Eatontown, NJ)	Osteoconduction and osteoinduction	Demineralized human bone matrix
Opteform (Exactech, Inc., Gainsville, FL)	Osteoconduction and osteoinduction	Demineralized human bone matrix, human corticocancellous bone chips
Osteofil (Sofamor Danek Group, Inc., Memphis, TN)	Osteoconduction and osteoinduction	Demineralized human bone matrix, porcine gelatin

....

Decortication

Shingling, as described by Judet and colleagues[110, 111] and Phemister[185] (Fig. 20–68), entails the raising of osteoperiosteal fragments from the outer cortex or callus from both sides of the nonunion using a sharp osteotome or chisel. Using a chisel, 2- to 3-mm fragments of cortex, each approximately 2 cm long, are elevated. The elevated fragments create a decorticated area approximately 3 to 4 cm long on either side of the nonunion and involve approximately two thirds of the bone circumference. The periosteum and muscle, which remain attached and viable, are then carefully retracted with a Hohmann retractor. This approach greatly increases the surface area between the elevated shingles and the decorticated cortex in which cancellous bone graft can be inserted to stimulate bony healing and fill the dead space.

If the bone is very osteoporotic, shingling may substantially weaken the thin cortex and should be used minimally or not at all. Shingling should not be performed over the area of the bone fragments where a plate is to be applied. In these cases, where internal fixation (i.e., a plate) is used, the surfaces of the bone fragments that are not covered by the plate can be petaled or drilled. Petaling,[159] also called fish-scaling (see Fig. 20–68), is performed with a tiny gouge. Once elevated, the osteoperiosteal flakes resemble the petals of a flower or scales of a fish. Alternatively, a small drill bit cooled with irrigation can be used to drill multiple holes. Petaling or drilling is performed over an area 3 to 4 cm on either side of the nonunion. These decortication techniques promote revascularization of the cortex, especially when combined with cancellous bone grafting.

Electromagnetic, Ultrasound, and Shockwave Stimulation

Electrical stimulation of nonunions by invasive and noninvasive methods has gained popularity since the 1970s.[21, 178] Although the exact mechanism by which electricity and electromagnetic fields stimulate osteogenesis remains uncertain, some practitioners claim success in a high percentage of cases; I have been delighted by unexpected successes in a few cases (Fig. 20–69).

The literature, however, does not provide a consensus opinion.

Devices available to treat nonunions through electrical stimulation are of three varieties: constant direct current, time-varying inductive coupling, and capacitive coupling. The usefulness of electrical stimulation is limited to the extent that it does not correct deformities and usually requires a long period of non–weight bearing and cast immobilization, which may give rise to muscle and bone atrophy and joint stiffness. The method is seldom effective for atrophic nonunions (particularly those with bone defects), infected nonunions, synovial pseudarthroses, nonunions with gaps or necrotic ends of more than 1 cm, or lax nonunions. Electrical stimulation may be considered as a treatment method for stiff nonunions when there is no significant deformity or bone defect.

Animal studies[236] and human trials[143] for the treatment of nonunions with ultrasonic stimulation are ongoing. This form of therapy holds promise as an additional adjuvant for nonoperative treatment of nonunions.

High-energy extracorporeal shock wave therapy as a treatment of nonunion has been reported by several

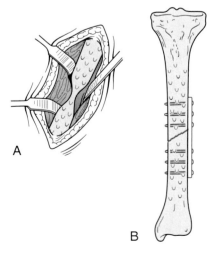

FIGURE 20–68. Decortication techniques. *A,* Shingling. *B,* Fish-scaling (i.e., petaling).

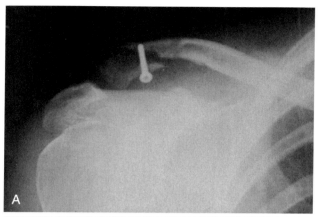

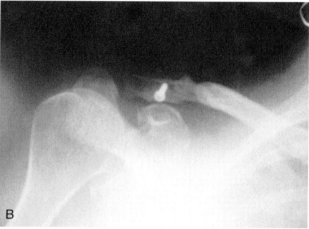

FIGURE 20–69. *A,* The radiograph was obtained at presentation of a 40-year-old woman who was referred in 26 months after open reduction and internal fixation of a distal clavicle fracture. The patient did not want any type of surgical intervention and therefore was treated with external electrical stimulation. *B,* A radiograph after 8 months of electrical stimulation shows solid bony union.

investigators.[220, 223, 246] Valchanou and Michailov[246] reported an 85% union rate in 82 delayed unions and nonunions treated with the technique. Similarly, Schaden and associates[220] reported a 76% healing rate in patients with nonunions. According to Schaden and co-authors,[220] the technique should not be used in patients with a gap at the nonunion site greater than 5 mm; open physes, alveolar tissue, brain or spine, or malignant tumor in the shock wave field; coagulopathy; pregnancy.

METHODS THAT ARE BOTH MECHANICAL AND BIOLOGIC

Treatment methods that may be used to improve both the mechanical and biologic status of an ununited limb include structural bone grafts, exchange nailing, synostosis techniques, the Ilizarov method, arthroplasty, arthrodesis, and amputation.

Structural Bone Grafts

Vascularized Autogenous Cortical Bone Grafts. Vascularized autogenous cortical bone grafts provide structural integrity and living osseous tissue to the site of bony defects. Evidence exists that vascularized grafts respond to functional loading by hypertrophy, in some cases[31, 101] possessing the capacity to increase in strength over time.

Vascularized bone grafts may be obtained from the fibula,[253, 262, 270] iliac crest,[214] or ribs.[253] Because of its shape, strength, size, and versatility, the vascularized fibula has become the preferred graft for most centers using vascularized bone graft techniques. Vascularized fibula techniques include free vascularized fibular transfer, free vascularized "double-barrel" fibula transfer,[109] centralization of the fibula,[99] and reversed-flow vascularized pedicle fibular graft.[212]

Advantages of vascularized grafts include immediate structural integrity, a one-stage procedure (barring problems or complications), potential for graft hypertrophy, and the ability to span massive segmental defects. Disadvantages include the technically demanding nature of the technique; propensity for fatigue fracture, particularly for lower extremity applications; prolonged non–weight bearing for certain lower extremity applications; poorer results in patients with a history of infection[88]; donor site morbidity (e.g., pain, neurovascular injury, knee or ankle joint instability or limited range of motion); and fixation problems when the defect extends to a periarticular region. The procedure is contraindicated for children.

Nonvascularized Autogenous Cortical Bone Grafts. Nonvascularized autogenous cortical bone graft can be harvested from the fibula, tibia, or iliac crest. Whereas these grafts can be used to reconstruct large defects, they suffer from several disadvantages, including a requirement for prolonged non–weight bearing for lower extremity applications, requirement for prolonged support for upper extremity applications, donor-site morbidity (including fracture for cortical grafts harvested from the tibia), and progressive graft weakening during revascularization (years) and a propensity for fatigue fracture.

Bulk Cortical Allografts. Bulk cortical allograft may be used to reconstruct large post-traumatic skeletal defects[37] (Fig. 20–70; see also Fig. 20–64). The technique usually is less technically demanding than vascularized grafting, and there is no associated donor site morbidity; however, the technique is not without significant complications, including infection, graft failure, and nonunion at the host-graft junction. The availability of bone of virtually every shape and size from the bone bank permits reconstruction of massive skeletal defects in virtually any anatomic location.

Graft fixation may be achieved using a variety of methods. Because of the ultimate strength, load-sharing characteristics, and ability to protect the graft, I prefer to use intramedullary fixation in cases of bulk cortical allograft wherever possible. Bulk allografts can be used for intercalary grafts, alloarthrodesis (Fig. 20–71), osteoarticular grafts, and alloprosthesis.

Infected nonunions may be treated with bulk allograft as long as the infected cavity has been adequately débrided and sterilized. When using the technique for infected nonunions with massive defects, I perform serial débridements with antibiotic bead exchanges until the cavity is culture negative. At this point a custom-fabricated, antibiotic-impregnated PMMA spacer is implanted, and the soft tissue envelope is closed or reconstructed. At a minimum of 3 months, the spacer is removed, and the defect is reconstructed using bulk cortical allograft (see Figs. 20–64 and 20–71). Active infection is an absolute contraindication to reconstruction using bulk cortical allograft. The main disadvantages of bulk cortical allograft are its associated complications: infection, fatigue fracture, nonunion of the allograft at the graft-host junctions, and the possibility of disease transmission from donor to recipient.

Strut Cortical Allografts. Strut cortical allografts may be used to reconstruct partial (incomplete) segmental defects, reconstruct complete segmental defects in certain

cases, augment fixation and stability in osteopenic bone, and augment stability in periprosthetic long bone nonunions (see Fig. 20–61).

Intramedullary Cortical Allografts. Intramedullary cortical allografts are most commonly employed for long bone nonunions that are associated with osteopenia for which the chosen method of treatment is plate-and-screw fixation with cancellous autografting. The intramedullary cortical graft is beneficial in that it augments stability by acting as an intramedullary nail, greatly improves the screw purchase of the plate-and-screw construct (i.e., each screw traverses four cortices), and provides the added potential for intramedullary healing between host bone

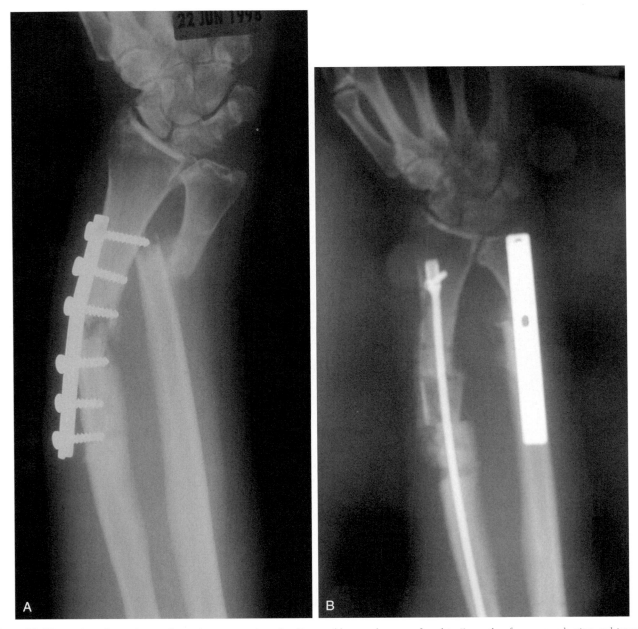

Figure 20–70. *A*, The radiograph was obtained at presentation of a 45-year-old man who was referred in 7 months after open reduction and internal fixation of a both-bone forearm fracture. This patient had an open wound draining purulent material over the radius. The patient was treated with serial débridements and antibiotic beads. After serial débridements, the patient was left with a segmental defect of the radius. *B*, The radiograph shows placement of a bulk cortical allograft over an intramedullary nail and plate-and-screw fixation of the ulna.

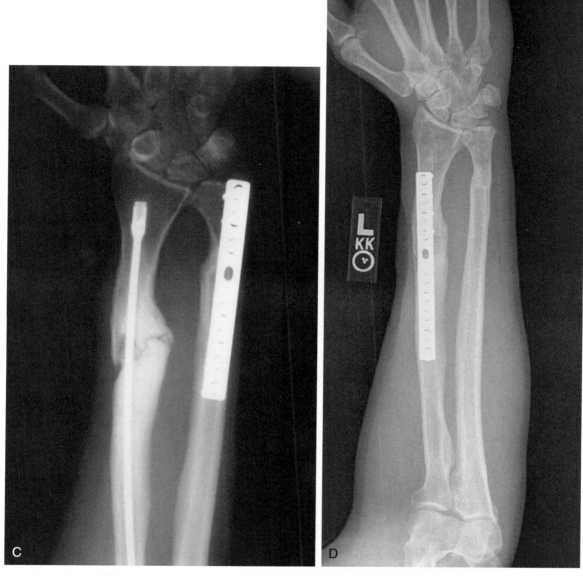

FIGURE 20–70 *Continued. C,* A follow-up radiograph at 11 months after reconstruction shows solid union of the proximal host-graft junction but a hypertrophic nonunion of the distal host-graft junction of the radius. The hypertrophic nonunion was treated with compression plating without bone grafting. *D,* The final radiograph 14 months after compression plating shows solid bony union.

and the allograft. The technique is particularly useful for humeral nonunions in elderly patients with osteopenic bone who have failed multiple prior treatments (Fig. 20–72).

Mesh Cage–Bone Graft Constructs. Cobos and co-workers[42] first described a technique for the treatment of segmental long bone defects using a mesh cage–bone graft construct. The technique involves spanning the segmental defect using a titanium mesh cage (surgical titanium mesh, DuPuy Motech, Warsaw, IN) of slightly larger diameter than the adjacent bone. The cage is packed with allogenic cancellous bone chips and demineralized bone matrix. This construct is reinforced by an intramed-

ullary nail that traverses the mesh cage–bone graft construct.

Exchange Nailing

In a previous section covering mechanical methods of nonunion treatment, intramedullary nail fixation was discussed. That method is distinguished from exchange nailing in that the latter method is both mechanical and biologic.

Technique. Exchange nailing requires the removal of a previously placed intramedullary nail. Because a nail already spans the medullary canal at the nonunion site, the problem of a sealed-off canal, as discussed in an earlier

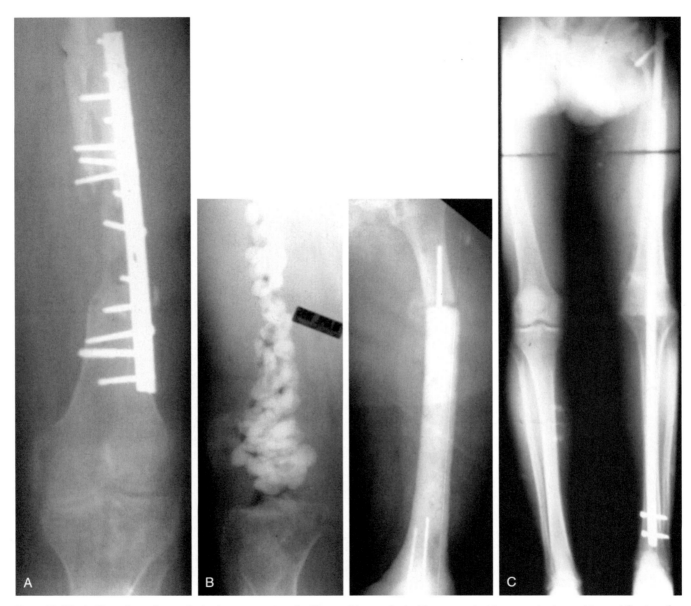

Figure 20–71. *A,* The radiograph was obtained at presentation of a 25-year-old man who had been treated with open reduction and internal fixation of an open femur fracture. The patient was referred in 16 months after the injury. Clinical examination revealed gross purulence and exposed bone at the nonunion site, with global knee joint instability and an arc of knee flexion-extension of approximately 20°. Aspiration of the knee yielded frank pus. *B,* Radiographs show the site after radical débridement with placement of antibiotic beads and later placement of an antibiotic spacer. *C,* A radiograph obtained 6 years after alloarthrodesis using a bulk cortical allograft and a knee fusion nail shows solid bony incorporation. The patient is fully ambulatory and has no pain or evidence of infection.

section, is not an issue. Although a deformity may exist at the nonunion site, the medullary canal is already known to accept passage of an intramedullary nail. A rare exception to this rule is the stiff nonunion with a broken nail in which there has been progressive deformity over time. In such a case, removal of a portion of the nail (and insertion of a new nail) may require extensive bony and soft tissue dissection at the nonunion site, and other treatment options may therefore need to be considered.

After the previous nail has been removed, the medullary canal is reamed. Reaming is performed with progressively larger reamer tips in 0.5-mm increments. Initially, the reamer flutes contain endosteal fibrous tissue. As

reaming continues, bone is observed in the flutes of the reamers. Generally, I try to use an exchange nail that is 2 to 4 mm in diameter larger than the prior nail, and I overream by 1 mm larger than the new nail being implanted. Reaming typically proceeds to a reamer tip size 3 to 5 mm larger than the nail being removed. Occasionally, a custom-manufactured nail with an extra large diameter is necessary for a patient with a very large medullary canal.

After reaming, a larger-diameter nail is inserted. I always perform exchange nailing using a closed technique, because it preserves the periosteal blood supply that is so important for the success of the technique. Closed nailing also lessens the risk of infection at the nonunion site. Provided that good bone contact exists at the nonunion site, I prefer to statically lock all exchange nails to maximize stability; other surgeons do not believe this is always necessary.[45, 87, 238, 257, 267] I do not favor partial excision of the fibula when performing exchange nailing of the tibia, because it diminishes the overall stability of the construct.

Modes of Healing. Exchange nailing stimulates healing of nonunions by improving the local mechanical

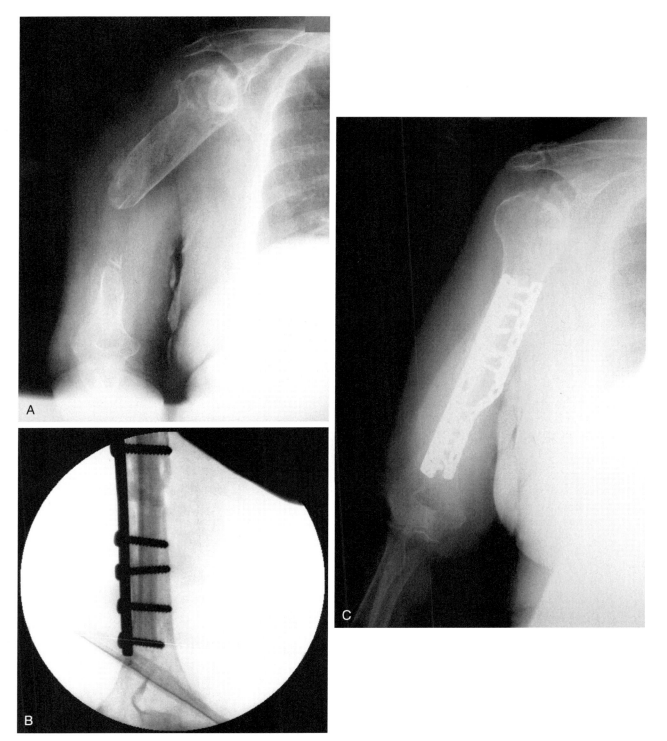

FIGURE 20–72. A, The radiograph was obtained at presentation of an 83-year-old woman who was referred in 15 months after a humeral shaft fracture. The patient found this humeral nonunion very painful and quite debilitating. Because of the patient's profound osteopenia, she was treated with an intramedullary cortical fibular allograft and plate-and-screw fixation. B, The intraoperative fluoroscopic image shows positioning of the intramedullary fibula. C, The final radiograph 7 months after reconstruction shows bony incorporation without evidence of hardware loosening or failure. At follow-up, the patient had no pain and had marked improvement in function.

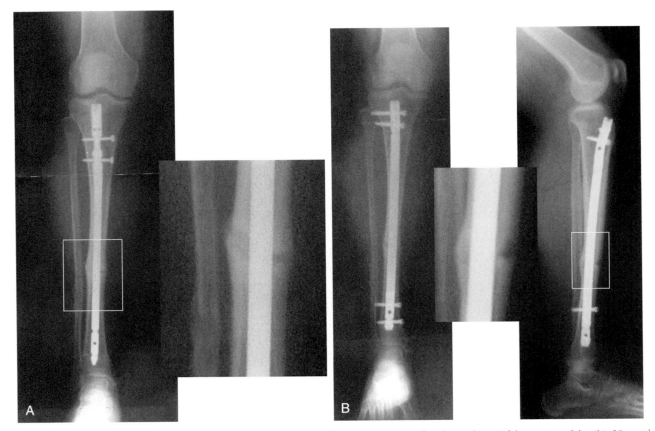

FIGURE 20–73. *A*, The radiograph was obtained at presentation of a 51-year-old woman who was referred in with a painful nonunion of the tibia 29 months after intramedullary nail fixation of an open tibial fracture. *B*, Five months after exchange nailing, the tibia is solidly united.

environment in two ways and by improving the local biologic environment in two ways (Fig. 20–73).

Enlargement of the medullary canal by reaming allows placement of a larger-diameter nail that is stronger and stiffer (provided that the manufacturer does not decrease the wall thickness as the nail diameter increases). The stiffer, stronger nail augments stability at the nonunion site, which promotes bony union. The second mechanical benefit of reaming is the widening and lengthening of the isthmic portion of the medullary canal, which enhances mechanical stability by increasing the endosteal cortical contact area of the nail. This effect is particularly dramatic when exchange nailing is performed on a long bone that was initially treated with a small-diameter nail using an unreamed technique.

Biologically, the products of reaming act as a local bone graft at the nonunion site and stimulate medullary healing. The second biologic benefit of reaming is related to the resulting changes in the endosteal and periosteal circulation. Medullary reaming results in a substantial decrease in endosteal blood flow.[22, 85, 107, 164, 231] The loss is accompanied by a dramatic increase in periosteal flow[192] and periosteal new bone formation.[48]

Other Issues. Because exchange nailing improves mechanical stability and biologically stimulates the nonunion site, it is applicable for viable and nonviable nonunions. Three circumstances worthy of discussion are the use of exchange nailing for nonunions with incomplete bony contact, nonunions associated with deformity, and infected nonunions.

Bone Contact. Exchange nailing is an excellent treatment method when good bone-to-bone contact exists at the nonunion site. The technique is less well suited for cases with large partial or complete segmental bone defects. Because healing of these nonunions depends on many factors (e.g., nonunion type, anatomic location, surface area of bone contact, length of bony defect, soft tissue characteristics, patient health and age), it is unlikely that the dilemma regarding which defects will not unite with exchange nailing will ever be solved. We are therefore left with what drives much of medical care: clinical observation. Templeman and co-authors[238] advocate exchange nailing (in the tibia) when there is 30% or less circumferential bone loss. Court-Brown and colleagues[45] reported failures for exchange nailing only when bone loss (tibia) exceeded a length of 2 cm and involved more than 50% of the circumference of the bone. Although I have used Chapman's[32] method of intramedullary bone grafting with excellent results during exchange nailing of long bones with defects, the indications for this technique for nonunion surgery are still evolving.

Deformity. Deformity is an interesting situation in long bone nonunions that have previously been treated with an intramedullary nail. I am repeatedly astonished by how a straight nail can result in a very crooked bone (Fig. 20–74). Deformities that may ultimately limit the patient's function require correction. Deformity correction can be rapid or gradual and can be performed concurrently with or after (i.e., sequential approach) successful treatment of the nonunion. In the case of a previously nailed long bone, clinically significant deformities may include length, angulation, and rotation. Translational deformities are limited by the nail (if the nail is not broken) and are generally not clinically significant.

When the nonunion is associated with a clinically significant deformity, the first decision to be made is whether to address both problems at the same time or to address healing the bone first, with deformity correction to follow. In the latter case, exchange nailing may be undertaken as described previously. If the decision is to address both problems concurrently, the next decision to be made is whether to correct the deformity gradually or rapidly. If the status of the soft tissues, bone, or both favor gradual correction, exchange nailing is rejected in favor of Ilizarov external fixation. If rapid deformity correction is thought to be safe, exchange nailing with acute deformity correction simplifies the overall treatment strategy and is an excellent technique. Acute deformity correction is relatively simple for lax nonunions. Stiff nonunions may require a percutaneously performed osteotomy and the use of a femoral distractor or a temporary external fixator to perform an acute deformity correction. I do not generally favor direct open exposure of the nonunion site when using intramedullary nail techniques (see section on Intramedullary Nail Fixation).

Infection. Although numerous surgeons have reported cases of intramedullary nail fixation for infected nonunions,[3, 87, 123, 124, 147, 228, 264] the results of exchange nailing as a treatment for these cases has not been well documented in the literature. I do not favor the use of intramedullary nailing as a means of providing mechanical stability in infected nonunions when the injury has been previously treated with a method other than nailing. Placement of an intramedullary nail can result in the conversion of an isolated infection to one that seeds the entire medullary canal. In the case of exchange nailing, the situation is entirely different. Because an intramedullary nail is already in situ, it is likely that the intramedullary canal is already infected to some degree along its entire length. Because medullary contamination is already present, I am not strictly opposed to the use of exchange nailing for infected nonunions (Fig. 20–75).

Exchange nailing for infected nonunions is best suited for the lower extremity in patients who may be poor candidates for plate-and-screw fixation (e.g., osteopenic bone, multiple prior soft tissue reconstructions, segmental nonunions) or external fixation (e.g., poor compliance, cognitive impairment), because the load-sharing characteristics of a nail may be of great benefit. Adequate bone contact and the absence of clinically significant deformity are prerequisites for the use of this technique.

When exchange nailing is used for infected nonunions, the medullary canal should be aggressively reamed as a means of débridement of infected and necrotic bone and endosteal soft tissue. Reaming should continue using progressively larger reamer tips in 0.5-mm increments until the reamer flutes contain what appears to be viable, healthy bone. All reamings should be sent for culture and sensitivity in cases of known or suspected infection. The medullary canal is then irrigated with copious antibiotic solution, and a larger diameter nail is placed, as previously described.

Literature Review. The results reported in the literature for exchange nailing as a treatment for uninfected tibial nonunions have been uniformly excellent. Court-Brown and co-authors[45] reported an 88% rate of union (29 of 33 cases) after exchange nailing of the tibia; the remaining four cases united after a second exchange nailing. Templeman and co-workers[238] reported a 93% rate of union (25 of 27 cases) after an exchange tibial nailing procedure. Wu and colleagues[268] reported a 96%

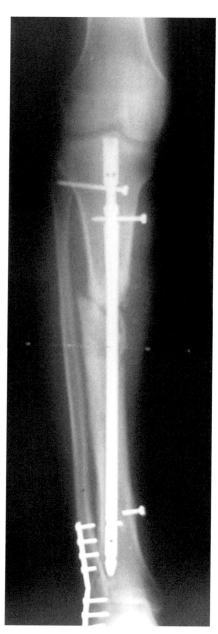

FIGURE 20–74. The radiograph was obtained at presentation of a 22-year-old man who was referred in after multiple failed treatments of a tibial nonunion. Notice that a very crooked bone can result despite the use of a straight nail.

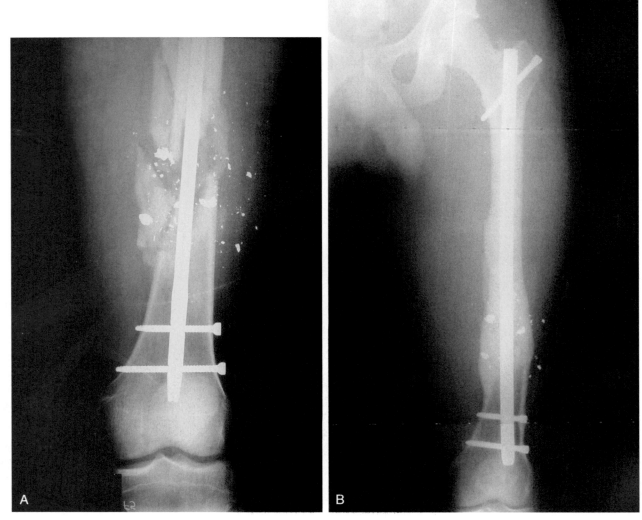

FIGURE 20–75. *A,* The radiograph shows the site of an actively draining infected femoral nonunion resulting from a gunshot blast in a 23-year-old man. This patient was treated with serial débridements followed by exchange nailing (with intramedullary autogenous iliac crest bone grafting) of the femoral nonunion. *B,* The radiograph obtained 13 months after treatment shows solid bony healing. This patient has no clinical evidence of infection.

rate of union (24 of 25 cases) with exchange nailing of the tibia.

The results reported in the literature for exchange nailing of femoral nonunions have been less consistent and generally not as good. Oh and co-workers[163] reported a 100% union rate for 13 femoral nonunions treated with exchange nailing. Christensen[38] also reported a 100% union rate for 11 femoral nonunions treated with exchange nailing. Hak and associates[87] reported a 78% rate of union (18 of 23 cases) after exchange nailing for nonunions of the femoral shaft. The rate of union was 100% (8 of 8 cases) in nonsmokers, compared with only 67% (10 of 15 cases) in smokers. Weresh and associates[257] reported a union rate of only 53% (10 of 19 cases) for exchange nailing of nonunions of the femoral shaft.

The results of exchange nailing for humeral shaft nonunions have also been suboptimal. McKee and co-workers[146] reported a 40% union rate (4 of 10 cases) for

exchange nailing of humeral nonunions. Flinkkilä and co-authors[72] described 13 humeral shaft nonunions treated with antegrade exchange nailing. The rate of union after the first exchange nailing was only 23% (3 of 13 cases). Only three additional nonunions united after a repeat exchange nailing.

Summary of Exchange Nailing. Based on a thorough review of the literature and my own clinical experience with exchange nailing, the following summary comments and recommendations are offered:

1. Exchange nailing achieves healing in 90% to 95% of tibial nonunions.
2. Exchange nailing remains the treatment of choice for nonunions of the femoral shaft, but the rate of success is probably lower than that for tibial nonunions.
3. The supracondylar femur is poorly suited for stabilization of a nonunion with an intramedullary nail

(supracondylar fractures probably require a lesser degree of stability than nonunions). The medullary canal is flared in this region, and there is poor cortical bone contact with the nail. The reamings are probably poorly contained at the site of nonunion when exchange nailing is performed in this region. It is also possible that reaming during exchange nailing for nonunions of the supracondylar region does not produce increased periosteal blood flow and new bone formation. Dismal results have been reported by Koval and co-workers[124] using intramedullary nail fixation for distal femoral nonunions. Exchange nailing is a poor treatment method for supracondylar nonunion of the femur; other treatment methods should be used (Fig. 20–76).

4. Poor results have been reported for exchange nailing of humeral shaft nonunions.[72, 146] Nail removal, plate-and-screw fixation, and autogenous cancellous bone grafting is effective in most cases. Ilizarov methods may be required for more complex cases. In my opinion, there is no clear role for exchange nailing for humeral shaft nonunions.

Synostosis Techniques

The leg and forearm are unique in that structural integrity is provided by paired bones. This anatomic arrangement permits the use of unique methods for the treatment of nonunions that are associated with bone defects.

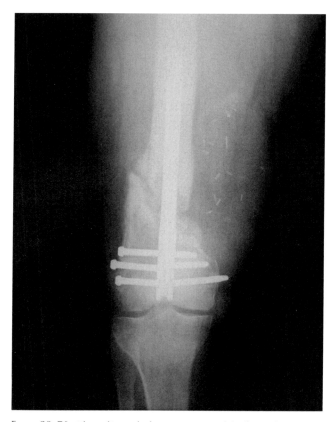

FIGURE 20–76. The radiograph shows a supracondylar femoral nonunion in a 57-year-old man who was referred in after failure of two prior exchange nailing procedures. Exchange nailing is a poor treatment method for nonunions in this region.

The literature regarding these techniques is fraught with inconsistencies and contradictions of terminology. This situation has led to confusion regarding the precise meaning of the following terms: fibula-pro-tibia, fibula transfer, fibula transference, fibula transposition, fibular bypass, fibulazation, medialization of the fibula, medial-ward bone transport of the fibula, posterolateral bone grafting, synostosis, tibialization of the fibula, transtibio-fibular grafting, and vascularized fibula transposition. For clarity and simplicity, all of these various techniques can be distinguished as a synostosis technique or as local grafting from the adjacent bone (Fig. 20–77).

Synostosis techniques for nonunions entail the creation of bone continuity between paired bones above and below the nonunion site. Success of the procedure does not necessarily depend on healing of the fragments of the ununited bone to one another. To qualify as a synostosis technique, the bone neighboring the ununited bone must unite to the proximal and distal fragments of the ununited bone such that the neighboring bone transmits forces across the nonunion site. From a functional standpoint, this becomes a one-bone extremity.

Several techniques have been used to create a tibiofibular synostosis for the treatment of tibial nonunions. Unfortunately, some of the methods described as synostosis techniques are not.

Milch[151, 152] described a tibiofibular synostosis technique for nonunion using a splintered bone created by longitudinally splitting the fibula, which could be augmented with autogenous iliac bone graft. McMaster and Hohl[148] used allograft cortical bone as tibiofibular cross-pegs to create a tibiofibular synostosis for tibial nonunion. Rijnberg and van Linge[197] described a technique to treat tibial shaft nonunions by creating a synostosis with autogenous iliac crest bone graft through a lateral approach anterior to the fibula. Lieberg and Heston[136] described an unusual case report of a distal tibial-fibular fracture, with a bone defect treated by telescoping the proximal fibular fragment into the distal tibial fragment. In the strict definition given earlier, this should not be considered a synostosis technique.

The posterolateral approach to the tibia for bone grafting or fibular transference was described by Harmon[89] in 1945. Posterolateral bone grafting[75, 185] for nonunion can result in bridging of the ununited site directly (which does not create a synostosis or require an intact fibula) or a tibiofibular synostosis above and below the nonunion site (for which the fibula must be intact).

Ilizarov[103] described the technique of medialward (horizontal) bone transport of the fibula to create a tibiofibular synostosis for the treatment of tibial nonunions with massive segmental bone loss (see Fig. 20–77).

Weinberg and colleagues[256] described a two-stage technique for creating proximal and distal tibiofibular synostoses for cases with massive bone loss. In the first stage, a distal tibiofibular synostosis was created; at least 1 month later, a proximal tibiofibular synostosis was created. The surgeons referred to this synostosis technique as a fibular bypass procedure. Doherty and Patterson[57] also described a fibular bypass operation in 14 cases of tibial nonunion. Several different techniques were used, and not all of them involved the creation of a synostosis. Because of

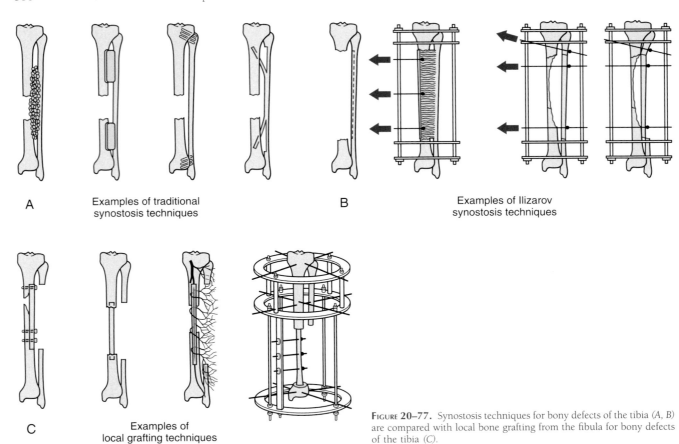

A   Examples of traditional synostosis techniques

B   Examples of Ilizarov synostosis techniques

C   Examples of local grafting techniques

Figure 20–77. Synostosis techniques for bony defects of the tibia (*A, B*) are compared with local bone grafting from the fibula for bony defects of the tibia (*C*).

the inconsistent use of *fibular bypass* in the literature, this term should probably be avoided.

Like fibular bypass, *fibula-pro-tibia* is a term that is used inconsistently in the literature. Campanacci and Zanoli[28] described a technique to create proximal and distal tibiofibular synostoses to treat tibial nonunions without large defects. The surgeons used internal fixation to stabilize the proximal and distal tibiofibular articulations. They referred to this technique as fibula-pro-tibia or double tibiofibular synostosis. Banic and Hertel[12] described a double-vascularized fibula technique for large tibial defects. The lateral graft was the fibula with its intact blood supply, which creates a synostosis proximal and distal to the defect. The authors referred to this lateral graft as a fibula-pro-tibia. Ward and co-authors[247] also described Huntington's fibular transference, which is not a synostosis technique, as a fibula-pro-tibia. May and co-workers[141] described transference of a vascularized fibular graft to fill the defect as a fibula-pro-tibia.

Other terms that are occasionally confused in the literature with tibiofibular synostosis include fibular transference, fibular transfer, fibular transposition, and tibialization. None of these terms refers to procedures that create a synostosis above and below the defect such that the neighboring bone transmits forces across the nonunion.

Huntington[99] was the first to describe a two-stage procedure to transfer a fibular graft (i.e., fibula transference) directly into a tibial defect. Several others have

described various techniques of transferring a vascularized fibular graft into a posterolateral position[2, 31, 229] or directly into the proximal and distal tibial fragments in the line of load bearing.[10, 119, 120] Some also refer to these techniques as tibialization of the fibula[2, 10] or fibula transposition.[229]

The synostosis method may also be used to treat segmental defects or persistent nonunions of the forearm (Fig. 20–78). It results in the creation of a one-bone forearm. In the forearm, this technique is most commonly used for forearm nonunions when there is massive bone loss in the radius and ulna. Successful union of a proximal ulna segment with a distal radial segment leads to restoration of function to the upper extremity with the exception of forearm pronation and supination.

Ilizarov Method

Ilizarov techniques for treatment of nonunions have many advantages, including minimal invasiveness, promotion of bony tissue generation, minimal soft tissue dissection, versatility, use in cases of acute or chronic infection, stabilization of small intra-articular or periarticular bone fragments, simultaneous bony healing and deformity correction, immediate weight bearing, and early joint mobilization.

The Ilizarov construct provides mechanical strength and stability, resisting shear and rotational forces. The technique is unique in that the tensioned wires allow for the "trampoline effect" during weight-bearing activities. The method also allows for augmentation of treatment through frame modification when the nonunion is failing to show progression to healing. Frame modification usually is not associated with pain, does not require anesthesia, and can be performed in the office. The need for frame modification should not be considered treatment failure; rather, it is the need for continued treat-

ment. Modifying the treatment with other methods such as plate-and-screw fixation or intramedullary nail fixation requires repeat surgical intervention and should therefore be considered treatment failure.

The Ilizarov method is applicable for all types of nonunions. The method is particularly useful for non-

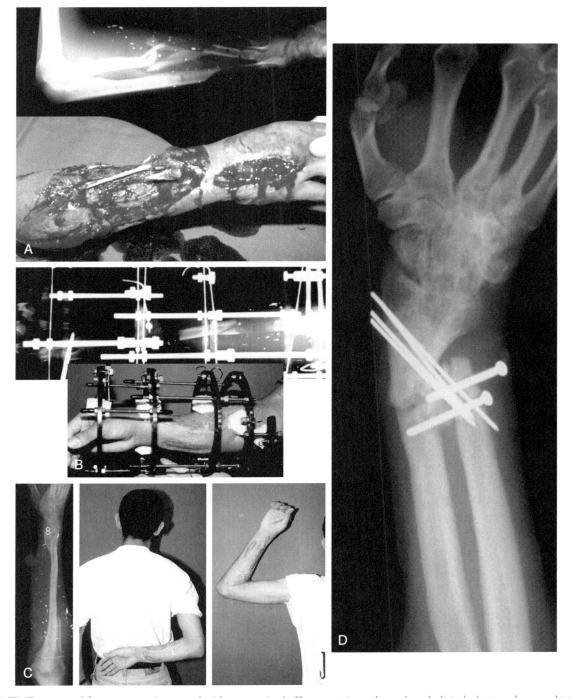

FIGURE 20–78. Two cases of forearm nonunion treated with synostosis. *A,* The presenting radiograph and clinical photograph were obtained for a 32-year-old man who was referred in with segmental bone loss from a gunshot blast to the forearm. *B,* The radiograph and clinical photograph show the forearm during bone transport of the proximal ulna into the distal radius to create a one-bone forearm (i.e., synostosis). *C,* The radiograph and clinical photographs show the final result. *D,* The radiograph was obtained for a 48-year-old man who presented after multiple failed attempts at a synostosis procedure of the forearm.

Illustration continued on following page

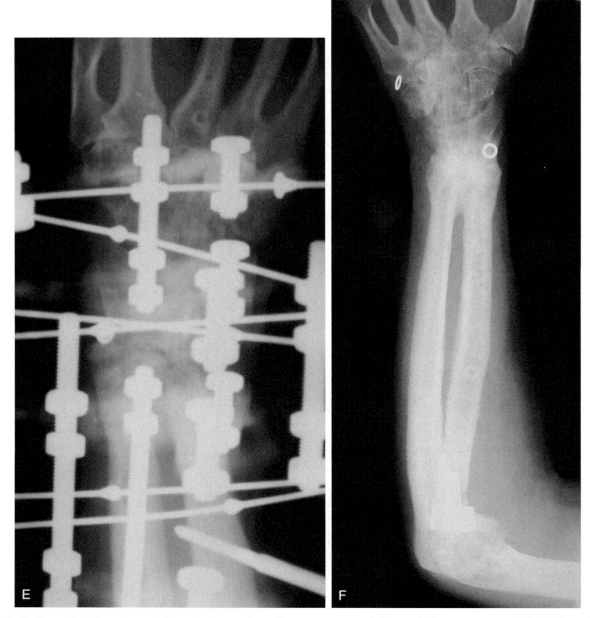

FIGURE 20–78 *Continued. E,* The radiograph shows the forearm during Ilizarov treatment with slow, gradual compression. *F,* The final radiograph shows solid bony union.

TABLE 20–10
....

Ilizarov Treatment Modes

_____

Monofocal
    Compression
    Sequential distraction-compression
    Distraction
    Sequential compression-distraction
Bifocal
    Compression-distraction lengthening
    Distraction-compression transport (bone transport)
Trifocal
    Various combinations

••

unions associated with infection, segmental bone defects, deformities, and multiple prior failed treatments. A variety of modes of treatment can be employed using the Ilizarov external fixator, including compression, distraction, lengthening, and bone transport. Treatment may be monofocal, such as with simple compression or distraction across the nonunion site. Bifocal treatment denotes that two healing sites exist, such as a bone transport where healing must occur at the distraction site (i.e., regenerate bone formation) and the docking (nonunion) site. Trifocal treatment denotes that three healing sites exist, such as in a double-level bone transport (Table 20–10).

Compression (monofocal) osteosynthesis can be used

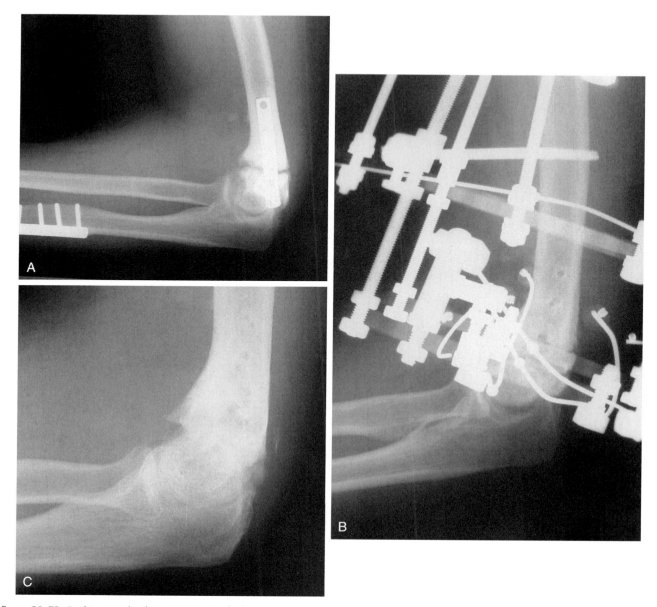

FIGURE 20–79. In this example, Ilizarov treatment of a hypertrophic distal humeral nonunion uses gradual monofocal compression. *A,* The presenting radiograph shows the initial condition. *B,* The radiograph was obtained during treatment using slow compression. Notice the bending of the wires proximal and distal to the nonunion site, indicating good bony contact. *C,* The final radiograph shows solid bony union.

for a variety of nonunion types. The technique allows not only for simple compression, but also for differential compression to enable deformity correction. The technique is applicable for hypertrophic nonunions (although distraction classically is used in these cases) (Fig. 20–79), oligotrophic nonunions (Figs. 20–80 to 20–82), and according to Professor Ilizarov, synovial pseudarthroses.[106, 225] Slow, gradual compression is generally applied at a rate of 0.25 to 0.5 mm per day for a period of 2 to 4 weeks. Because the rings spanning the nonunion site are moving closer together to a greater extent than the bone is moving (because the bone ends are in contact), the wires on either side of the nonunion site are seen to bow (see Figs. 20–79 and 20–80). Compression stimulates healing for most hypertrophic and oligotrophic

nonunions. Compression is usually unsuccessful for infected nonunions with purulent drainage and segments of intervening necrotic bone. There is disagreement regarding the usefulness of simple compression as a treatment for atrophic nonunions.[131, 166]

Slow compression over a nail using external fixation (SCONE) is a useful method for certain patients who have failed treatment using intramedullary nail techniques. I have used this technique with Ilizarov external fixation with great success in two distinct patient populations who have femoral nonunions and retained intramedullary nails: those who have failed multiple exchange femoral nailings (Fig. 20–83) and morbidly obese patients with distal femoral nonunions that failed to unite after primary retrograde nail fracture fixation (Fig. 20–84). The SCONE

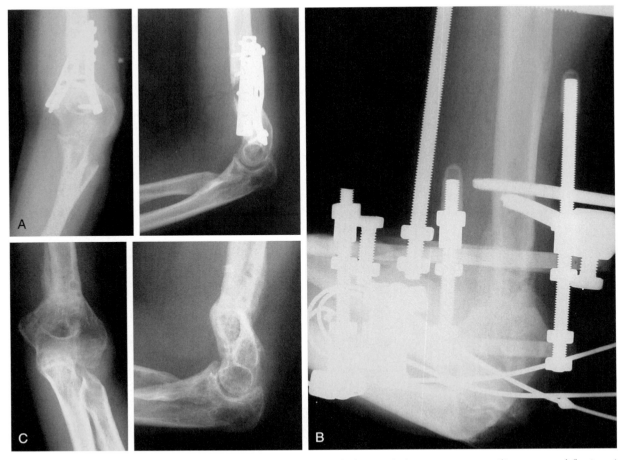

Figure 20–80. An oligotrophic nonunion of the distal humerus was treated with slow, gradual compression using Ilizarov external fixation. *A,* The presenting radiographs show the nonunion. *B,* The radiograph was obtained during treatment using slow, gradual compression. Notice the bending of the wires, indicating good bony contact. *C,* The final radiographs show solid bony union.

method is performed with percutaneous application of the external fixator so that no further disruption of the soft tissues is required at the nonunion site. The method augments stability and allows for monofocal compression at the nonunion site (the nail cannot be left statically locked during compression). The presence of the nail in the medullary canal encourages pure compressive forces and discourages translational and shear moments. Compression over a nail as a treatment for humeral nonunion has been described by Patel and co-workers.[177]

Sequential monofocal distraction-compression has been recommended as a treatment for lax hypertrophic nonunions and atrophic nonunions.[166] According to Paley,[166] "distraction disrupts the tissue at the nonunion site, frequently leading to some poor bone regeneration. This poor bone regeneration is stimulated to consolidate when the two bone ends are brought back together again."

Distraction is the treatment method of choice for stiff hypertrophic nonunions, particularly those associated with deformity (Fig. 20–85). Distraction of the abundant fibrocartilaginous tissue at the nonunion site stimulates new bone formation[30, 103, 166, 213] (although the exact biologic mechanism remains obscure) and results in nonunion healing in a high percentage of cases. Catagni

and co-authors[30] described 21 stiff hypertrophic nonunions (many associated with deformity) treated with distraction using the Ilizarov method. Union was achieved in all cases, with an average Ilizarov treatment time of 6.5 months in the external fixator. Saleh and Royston[213] reported successful treatment of 10 hypertrophic nonunions associated with deformity using distraction.

Sequential monofocal compression-distraction is applicable for stiff hypertrophic and oligotrophic nonunions. The method involves an initial interval of compression followed by gradual distraction for lengthening or deformity correction. This method is not recommended for atrophic, infected, and lax nonunions.[86, 166]

Bifocal compression-distraction lengthening involves acute or gradual compression across the nonunion site with lengthening through an adjacent corticotomy (Fig. 20–86). This method is applicable for nonunions associated with foreshortening. It is also applicable for nonunions with segmental defects. Bone defects may also be treated with bifocal distraction-compression transport (i.e., bone transport) (Fig. 20–87). This method involves the creation of a corticotomy (usually metaphyseal) at a site distant from the nonunion. The bone segment produced by the corticotomy is then transported toward the nonunion site (filling the bony defect) at a gradual rate. As the transported segment arrives at the docking site, compression is successful in many cases in obtaining union. Occasionally, bone grafting with marrow or open bone graft is required as previously described.

In a study of dogs undergoing distraction osteogenesis, Aronson[7] reported that blood flow at the distraction site increased nearly 10-fold relative to the control limb, peaking about 2 weeks after surgery. The distal tibia, remote from the site of distraction, also showed a similar pattern of increased blood flow. Because corticotomy and bone transport result in profound biologic stimulation, similar to bone grafting, many surgeons find bone

transport using the Ilizarov method an attractive alternative for the treatment of atrophic nonunions.

The bone formed at the corticotomy site in lengthening and bone transport is formed under gradual distraction (distraction osteogenesis).[8, 9, 55, 102, 160] The tension-stress effect of distraction causes neovascularity and cellular proliferation. Bone regeneration occurs primarily through intramembranous bone formation.

Distraction osteogenesis depends on a variety of mechanical and biologic requirements being met. The corticotomy or osteotomy must be performed using a low-energy technique. Corticotomy or osteotomy in the metaphyseal or metadiaphyseal region is preferred over

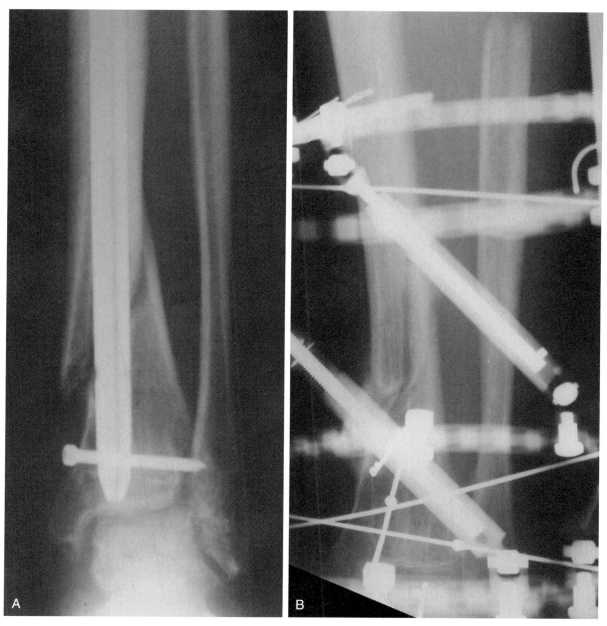

FIGURE 20–81. An oligotrophic nonunion of the distal tibia was treated with gradual deformity correction, followed by slow, gradual compression using Ilizarov external fixation. *A,* The presenting radiograph shows the nonunion. *B,* The radiograph was obtained during treatment.

Illustration continued on following page

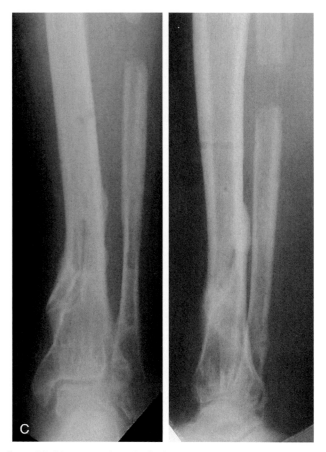

FIGURE 20–81 *Continued. C,* The final radiographs show solid bony union with complete deformity correction.

diaphyseal sites because of the superior regenerate formation. Stable external fixation promotes a good bony regenerate. Depending on patient characteristics, a latency period of 7 to 14 days before distraction is recommended. The distraction phase classically is performed at a rate of 1.0 mm per day in a rhythm of 0.25 mm of distraction performed four times per day. The rate and rhythm is controlled by the treating physician, who carefully monitors the progression of the regenerate as seen on radiographs. Some patients make bony regenerate more slowly and require a rate less than 1.0 mm per day. I typically begin the distraction in most patients at 0.75 mm per day. After distraction, maturation and hypertrophy of the bony regenerate occur during the consolidation phase. The consolidation phase usually is two to three times as long as the number of days of the distraction phase, but this varies widely among patients.

The choice of treatment strategy for infected nonunions and nonunions associated with segmental defects depends on many factors, such as bone, soft tissue, and medical health characteristics, and no clear consensus exists among treating physicians. Treatment options include conventional methods (i.e., resection, soft tissue coverage, massive cancellous bone grafting, and skeletal stabilization), and Ilizarov methods. Using Ilizarov methods, two different strategies can be employed: bifocal compression-distraction (i.e., lengthening) or bifocal distraction-

compression transport (i.e., bone transport). Several published reports have compared these various methods. Green[83] compared bone grafting and bone transport in the treatment of segmental skeletal defects. For defects of 5 cm or less, the author recommended the use of either technique. For larger defects, the author recommended bone transport or free composite tissue transfer. In a similar study, Marsh and co-workers[139] compared the results of resection and bone transport against less extensive débridement, external fixation, bone grafting, and soft tissue coverage. Results for the groups were similar in terms of healing rate, healing and treatment time, eradication of infection, final deformity, complications, and total number of operative procedures. The final limb-length discrepancy was significantly less in the group treated with bone transport. Cierny and Zorn[39] compared the results of treatment of segmental tibial defects using conventional methods (i.e., massive cancellous bone grafts and tissue transfers) with Ilizarov methods. The Ilizarov group averaged 9 fewer hours in the operating room, 23 fewer days of hospitalization, 5 months' less disability, and a savings of nearly $30,000 per case. Ring and co-workers[198] compared autogenous cancellous bone grafting with Ilizarov treatment in 27 patients with infected tibial nonunions. The investigators concluded that the Ilizarov methods may best be used in cases of large limb-length discrepancy and for very proximal or distal metaphyseal nonunions. The results of acute shortening with subsequent relengthening compared with bone transport for tibial defects were reported by Paley and colleagues.[169] Comparing 21 acute shortening with subsequent relengthening cases with 21 bone transport cases, the surgeons concluded that both techniques provided excellent overall results, although acute shortening with subsequent relengthening was associated with a significantly lower complication rate and less time in the external fixator.[169]

Arthroplasty

In certain situations, joint replacement arthroplasty may be the chosen treatment method for a fracture nonunion. This method has the advantages of early return to function with immediate weight bearing and joint mobilization. The main disadvantage of the method is the excision of native anatomic structures (e.g., bone, cartilage, ligaments). Arthroplasty as a treatment of nonunion is indicated in older patients with severe medical problems when a relatively short course of treatment and early ambulation may be required for survival; long-standing, resistant periarticular nonunions; periarticular nonunions associated with small osteopenic fragments if adequate purchase is not obtainable; nonunions associated with painful, post-traumatic or degenerative arthritis; and periprosthetic nonunions that cannot be readily stabilized by conventional methods or that have failed conventional treatment methods (Fig. 20–88). Arthroplasty as a method of treatment for nonunion has been used in the hip,[46] knee,[6, 74, 219, 258] shoulder,[77, 91, 162] and elbow.[155, 173]

Arthrodesis

Arthrodesis as a treatment method for nonunion is indicated for patients with previously failed (ununited) arthrodesis procedures (Fig. 20–89), infected periarticular nonunions, unreconstructable periarticular nonunions in anatomic locations that are not believed to have good long-term result with joint replacement arthroplasty (e.g., ankle), unreconstructable periarticular nonunions in very young patients who are not believed to be good long-term candidates for joint replacement arthroplasty, infected nonunions in which débridement necessitates removal of important articular structures (see Fig. 20–71), and nonunions associated with unreconstructable joint instability, contracture, or pain that are not amenable to joint replacement arthroplasty (see Fig. 20–71).

An alloarthrodesis procedure may be performed when a segmental bone defect extends to include the epiphyseal region in a patient for whom an alloprosthesis is contraindicated (Fig. 20–71).

Amputation

The decision to amputate or reconstruct the severely injured extremity is a difficult one. Lange and associates[132] published absolute and relative indications for amputation in the patient with an acute open fracture of the tibia associated with a vascular injury. Because a delay in amputation of the severely injured limb may lead to serious systemic complications or even death, rapid and resolute decision making in the acute setting is of paramount importance.

The decision to amputate or reconstruct a nonunion is a different matter entirely, and little guidance is found in the literature. These patients do not present in extremis and have typically been living with the problem for a long

Text continued on page 598

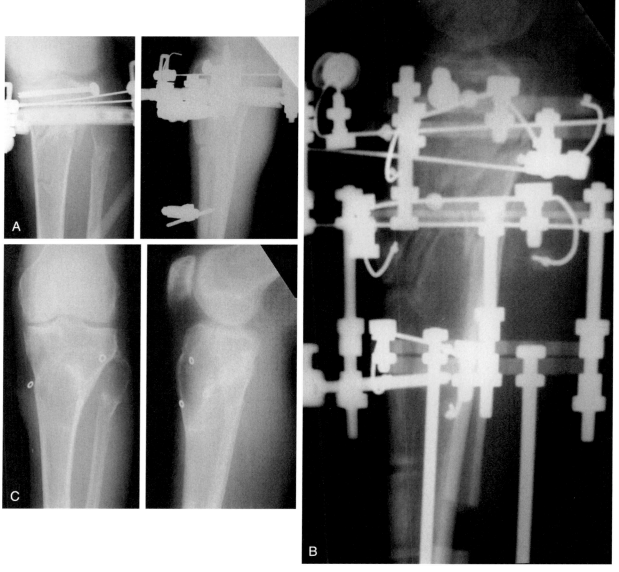

FIGURE 20–82. An oligotrophic nonunion of the proximal tibia was treated with slow, gradual compression using Ilizarov external fixation. *A,* The presenting radiographs show the nonunion. *B,* The radiograph was obtained during treatment using slow, gradual compression. *C,* The final radiographs show solid bony union.

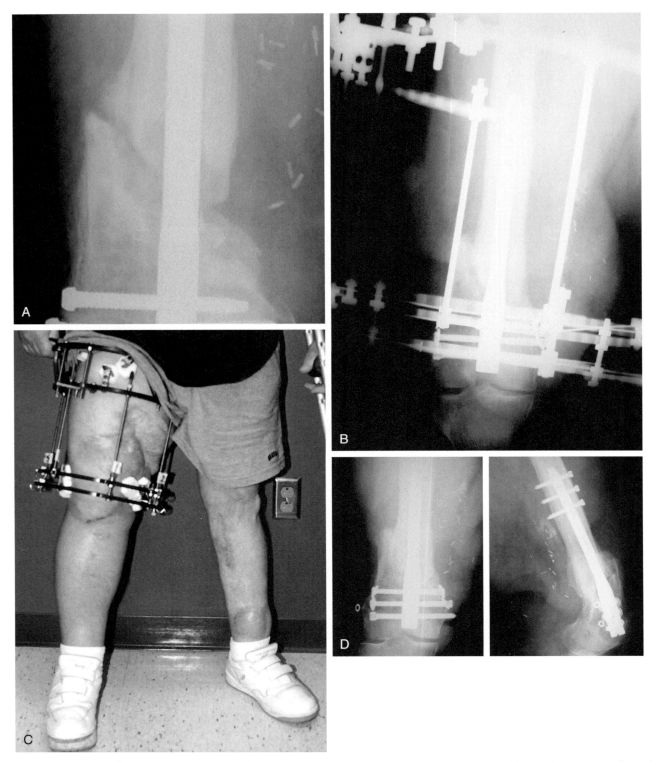

FIGURE 20–83. A resistant femoral nonunion was successfully treated with slow compression over a nail using external fixation (i.e., SCONE technique). *A,* The presenting radiograph shows a femoral nonunion. The patient is a 67-year-old man who was referred in after failure of two exchange nailings and two open bone graft procedures. *B,* The radiograph was obtained during treatment with the SCONE technique. *C,* The clinical photograph was taken during treatment. *D,* The final radiographs show solid bony union.

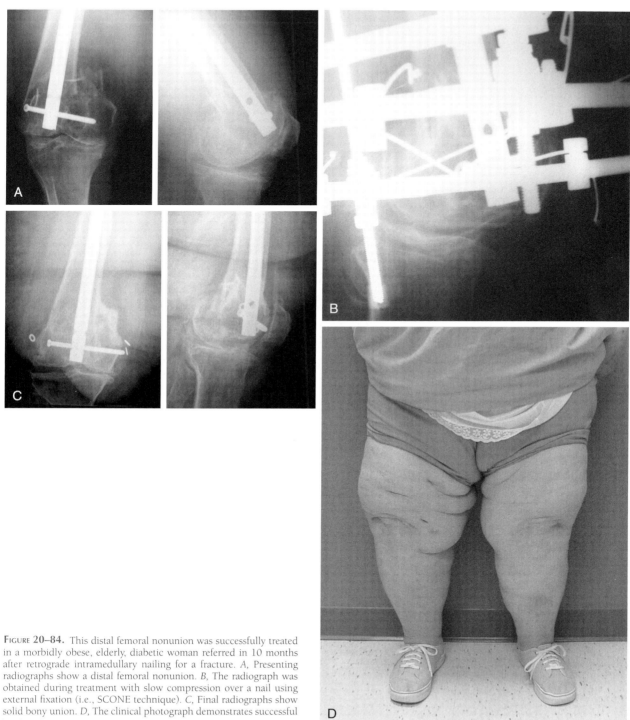

FIGURE 20–84. This distal femoral nonunion was successfully treated in a morbidly obese, elderly, diabetic woman referred in 10 months after retrograde intramedullary nailing for a fracture. *A,* Presenting radiographs show a distal femoral nonunion. *B,* The radiograph was obtained during treatment with slow compression over a nail using external fixation (i.e., SCONE technique). *C,* Final radiographs show solid bony union. *D,* The clinical photograph demonstrates successful treatment.

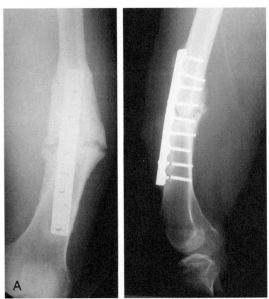

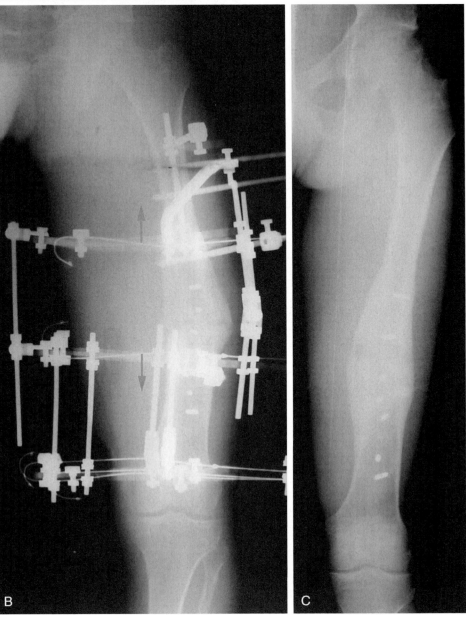

Figure 20–85. A stiff, hypertrophic nonunion of the femoral shaft was treated with distraction. *A,* Presenting radiographs demonstrate the nonunion. *B,* The radiograph was obtained during treatment by distraction using the Ilizarov external fixator. Notice that differential distraction also results in deformity correction. *C,* The final radiograph shows solid bony union and deformity correction.

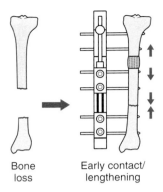

Bone
loss

Early contact/
lengthening

FIGURE 20–86. Compression-distraction lengthening is applicable for nonunions associated with foreshortening or bone defects.

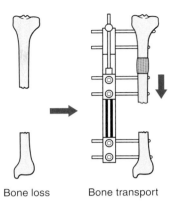

Bone loss

Bone transport

FIGURE 20–87. Distraction-compression transport (i.e., bone transport) can be used to treat bone defects.

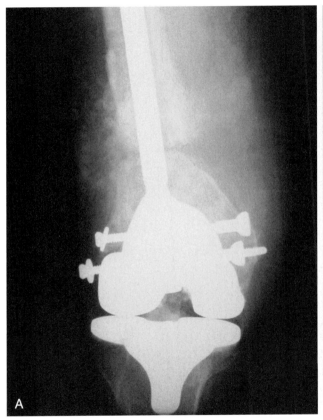

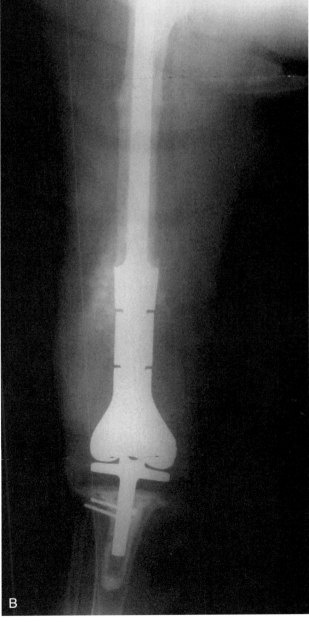

FIGURE 20–88. *A,* The radiograph was obtained at presentation of an 82-year-old woman who was referred in with a distal femoral periprosthetic nonunion. The patient had been wheelchair bound for 2 years and had three prior failed attempts at nonunion treatment. *B,* The radiograph shows the site after resection of the nonunion and revision joint replacement arthroplasty. The patient had excellent pain relief and resumed ambulation without the need for walking aids.

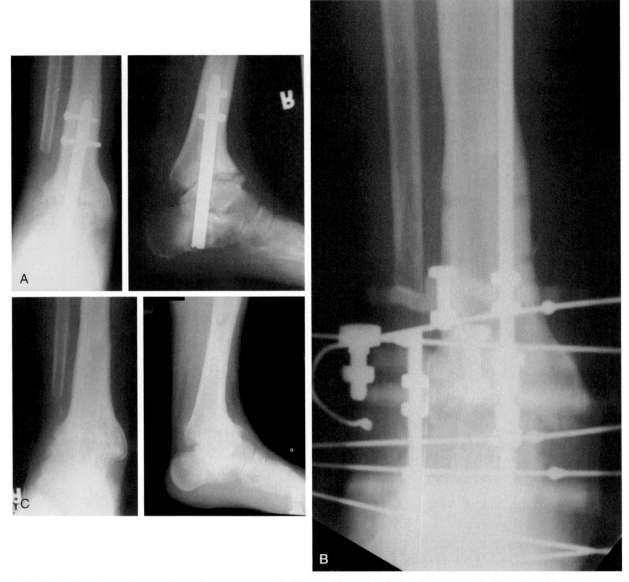

FIGURE 20–89. *A,* The radiographs were obtained at presentation of a 25-year-old man who had undergone a total of 18 prior ankle operations and five failed prior attempts at ankle arthrodesis. *B,* The patient was treated with percutaneous hardware removal and gradual compression using an Ilizarov external fixator. The ankle joint was not operatively approached, and no bone grafting was performed. *C,* The final radiograph after simple, gradual compression shows solid fusion of the ankle.

time. In their study assessing quality of life in 109 patients with post-traumatic sequelae of the long bones, Lerner and co-workers[134] described the choice determinants for patients undergoing amputation:

First choice determinant: cease medical and surgical treatment of the nonunion
Second choice determinant: recommendation by a doctor
Third choice determinant: belief that no cure is possible

There are no absolute indications for amputation of a chronic ununited limb. Because each nonunion case is distinctive and may include multiple complex issues, applying specific treatment algorithms is usually not helpful.

Amputation of an ununited limb should be considered in several situations:

1. Sepsis arises in a frail, elderly, or medically compromised patient with an infected nonunion, and there is concern about the patient's survival.
2. Neurologic function (motor or sensory or both) of the limb is unreconstructable to the extent that it precludes restoration of purposeful limb function.
3. Chronic osteomyelitis associated with the nonunion is in an anatomic area that precludes reconstruction (e.g., diffuse chronic osteomyelitis of the calcaneus).
4. The patient wishes to discontinue medical and surgical treatment of the nonunion and desires to have an amputation.

It is recommended that all patients considering amputation for a nonunion seek a minimum of two opinions from orthopaedic surgeons specializing in reconstructive nonunion techniques. Amputation should not be undertaken simply because the treating physician has run out of ideas, treatment recommendations, or stamina. There is no shame in referring to a colleague the motivated patient who has a recalcitrant nonunion but wishes to retain his or her limb. After the limb has been cut off, it cannot be cut back on.

SUMMARY

The care of the patient who has a nonunion is always challenging and sometimes troubling. These cases are problematic, and the patient often has myriad other health issues. Because of the various nonunion types and the constellation of possible problems related to the bone, soft tissues, prior treatments, patient health, and other factors, no simple treatment algorithms are possible. The care of these patients requires patience with the ultimate goal of bony union and restoration of function, limiting impairment and disability. An approach to the evaluation and treatment of these patients has been provided, but a few simple axioms bear emphasis and are presented as The 10 Commandments of Nonunion Treatment:

1. Examine thy patient, and carefully consider all available information.
2. Thou shall learn about the personality of the nonunion from the prior failed treatments.
3. Thou shall not repeat failed prior procedures that have not yielded any evidence of healing effort.
4. Thou shall base thy treatment plan on the nonunion type and the treatment modifiers, not upon false prophecies.
5. Thou shall forsake the use of the same hammer for every single nail, because the treatment of nonunions requires surgical expertise in a wide variety of internal and external fixation techniques.
6. Honor thy soft tissues, and keep them whole.
7. Thou shall consider minimally invasive techniques (e.g., Ilizarov method, bone marrow injection) when extensive surgical exposures have failed.
8. Thou shall not take the previous treating physician's name or treatment method or results in vain, particularly in the presence of the patient. Honor thy referring physicians, and keep them informed of the patient's progress.
9. Thou shall burn no bridges and shall leave thyself the option of a "next treatment plan."
10. Thou shall covet stability, vascularity, and bone-to-bone contact.

Acknowledgments
The author thanks Daniel P. O'Connor, Joseph J. Gugenheim, M.D., Jeffrey C. London, M.D., Ebrahim Delpassand, M.D., and Michele Clowers for editorial assistance with the manuscript, and Rodney K. Baker for assistance with the figures.

REFERENCES

1. Abhaykumar, S.; Elliott, D.S. Closed interlocking nailing for fibular nonunion. Injury 29:793–797, 1998.
2. Agiza, A.R. Treatment of tibial osteomyelitic defects and infected pseudarthroses by the Huntington fibular transference operation. J Bone Joint Surg Am 63:814–819, 1981.
3. Alho, A.; Ekeland, A.; Stromsoe, K.; Benterud, J.G. Nonunion of tibial shaft fractures treated with locked intramedullary nailing without bone grafting. J Trauma 34:62–67, 1993.
4. Allen, H.L.; Wase, A.; Bear, W.T. Indomethacin and aspirin: Effect of nonsteroidal anti-inflammatory agents on the rate of fracture repair in the rat. Acta Orthop Scand 51:595–600, 1980.
5. Altman, R.D.; Latta, L.L.; Keer, R.; et al. Effect of nonsteroidal antiinflammatory drugs on fracture healing: A laboratory study in rats. J Orthop Trauma 9:392–400, 1995.
6. Anderson, S.P.; Matthews, L.S.; Kaufer, H. Treatment of juxtaarticular nonunion fractures at the knee with long-stem total knee arthroplasty. Clin Orthop 260:104–109, 1990.
7. Aronson, J. Temporal and spatial increases in blood flow during distraction osteogenesis. Clin Orthop 301:124–131, 1994.
8. Aronson, J.; Good, B.; Stewart, C.; et al. Preliminary studies of mineralization during distraction osteogenesis. Clin Orthop 250:43–49, 1990.
9. Aronson, J.; Harrison, B.; Boyd, C.M.; et al. Mechanical induction of osteogenesis. Preliminary studies. Ann Clin Lab Sci 18:195–203, 1988.
10. Atkins, R.M.; Madhavan, P.; Sudhakar, J.; Whitwell, D. Ipsilateral vascularised fibular transport for massive defects of the tibia. J Bone Joint Surg Br 81:1035–1040, 1999.
11. Ballmer, F.T.; Ballmer, P.M.; Baumgaertel, F.; et al. Pauwels osteotomy for nonunions of the femoral neck. Orthop Clin North Am 21:759–767, 1990.
12. Banic, A.; Hertel, R. Double vascularized fibulas for reconstruction of large tibial defects. J Reconstr Microsurg 9:421–428, 1993.
13. Bassett, C.A.L. Current concepts of bone formation. J Bone Joint Surg Am 44:1217–1244, 1962.
14. Bassett, C.A.L.; Pilla, A.A.; Pawluk, R.J. A non-operative salvage of surgically-resistant pseudoarthroses and nonunions by pulsing electromagnetic fields. Clin Orthop 124:128–143, 1977.
15. Bhan, S.; Mehara, A.K. Percutaneous bone grafting for nonunion and delayed union of fractures of the tibial shaft. Int Orthop 17:310–312, 1993.
16. Blachut, P.A.; Meek, R.N.; O'Brien, P.J. External fixation and delayed intramedullary nailing of open fractures of the tibial shaft. A sequential protocol. J Bone Joint Surg Am 72:729–735, 1990.
17. Boehme, D.; Curtis, R.J., Jr.; DeHaan, J.T.; et al. The treatment of nonunion fractures of the midshaft of the clavicle with an intramedullary Hagie pin and autogenous bone graft. Instr Course Lect 42:283–290, 1993.
18. Bondurant, F.J.; Cotler, H.B.; Buckle, R.; et al. The medical and economic impact of severely injured lower extremities. J Trauma 28:1270–1273, 1988.
19. Bradbury, N.; Hutchinson, J.; Hahn, D.; Colton, C.L. Clavicular nonunion: 31/32 healed after plate fixation and bone grafting. Acta Orthop Scand 67:367–370, 1996.
20. Brighton, C.T.; Esterhai, J.L., Jr.; Katz, M.; Schumacher, R. Synovial pseudoarthrosis: A clinical, roentgenographic-scintigraphic, and pathologic study. J Trauma 27:463–470, 1987.
21. Brighton, C.T.; Friedenberg, Z.B.; Mitchell, E.I. Treatment of nonunion with constant direct current. Paper presented at the SICOT XIV World Congress, Kyoto, Japan, 1978.
22. Brinker, M.; Cook, S.; Dunlap, J.; et al. Early changes in nutrient artery blood flow following tibial nailing with and without reaming: A preliminary study. J Orthop Trauma 13:129–133, 1999.
23. Brinker, M.R. Principles of Fractures. In: Brinker, M.R., ed. Review of Orthopaedic Trauma. Philadelphia, W.B. Saunders, 2001.
24. Brinker, M.R.; Bailey, D.E. Fracture healing in tibia fractures with an associated vascular injury. J Trauma 42:11–19, 1997.
25. Brown, C.W.; Orme, T.J.; Richardson, H.D. The rate of pseudoarthrosis (surgical nonunion) in patients who are smokers and patients who are nonsmokers: A comparison study. Spine 11:942–943, 1986.
26. Butcher, C.K.; Marsh, D.R. Non steroidal anti-inflammatory drugs delay tibial fracture union. Abstract. Injury 27:375, 1996.

27. Cameron, H.U.; Welsh, R.P.; Jung, Y.B.; Noftall, F. Repair of nonunion of tibial osteotomy. Clin Orthop 287:167–169, 1993.

28. Campanacci, M.; Zanoli, S. Double tibiofibular synostosis (fibula pro tibia) for non-union and delayed union of the tibia. J Bone Joint Surg Am 48:44–56, 1966.

29. Carpenter, C.A.; Jupiter, J.B. Blade plate reconstruction of metaphyseal nonunion of the tibia. Clin Orthop 332:23–28, 1996.

30. Catagni, M.A.; Guerreschi, F.; Holman, J.A.; Cattaneo, R. Distraction osteogenesis in the treatment of stiff hypertrophic nonunions using the Ilizarov apparatus. Clin Orthop 301:159–163, 1994.

31. Chacha, P.B.; Ahmed, M.; Daruwalla, J.S. Vascular pedicle graft of the ipsilateral fibula for non-union of the tibia with a large defect. An experimental and clinical study. J Bone Joint Surg Br 63:244–253, 1981.

32. Chapman, M.W. Closed intramedullary bone grafting for diaphyseal defects of the femur. Instr Course Lect 32:317–324, 1983.

33. Charnley, G.J.; Ward, A.J. Reconstruction femoral nailing for nonunion of subtrochanteric fracture: A revision technique following dynamic condylar screw failure. Int Orthop 20:55–57, 1996.

34. Charnley, J. Compression Arthrodesis. Edinburgh, London, E&S Livingstone, 1953.

35. Chatziyiannakis, A.A.; Verettas, D.A.; Raptis, V.K.; Charpantitis, S.T. Nonunion of tibial fractures treated with external fixation. Contributing factors studied in 71 fractures. Acta Orthop Scand Suppl 275:77–79, 1997.

36. Chen, C.Y.; Ueng, S.W.; Shih, C.H. Staged management of infected humeral nonunion. J Trauma 43:793–798, 1997.

37. Chmell, M.J.; McAndrew, M.P.; Thomas, R.; Schwartz, H.S. Structural allografts for reconstruction of lower extremity open fractures with 10 centimeters or more of acute segmental defects. J Orthop Trauma 9:222–226, 1995.

38. Christensen, N.O. Küntscher intramedullary reaming and nail fixation for non-union of fracture of the femur and the tibia. J Bone Joint Surg Br 55:312–318, 1973.

39. Cierny, G., III; Zorn, K.E. Segmental tibial defects. Comparing conventional and Ilizarov methodologies. Clin Orthop 301:118–123, 1994.

40. Clarke, P.; Mollan, R.A. The criteria for amputation in severe lower limb injury. Injury 25:139–143, 1994.

41. Cobb, T.K.; Gabrielsen, T.A.; Campbell, D.C., 2nd; et al. Cigarette smoking and nonunion after ankle arthrodesis. Foot Ankle Int 15:64–67, 1994.

42. Cobos, J.A.; Lindsey, R.W.; Gugala, Z. The cylindrical titanium mesh cage for treatment of a long bone segmental defect: Description of a new technique and report of two cases. J Orthop Trauma 14:54–59, 2000.

43. Connolly, J.F. Injectable bone marrow preparations to stimulate osteogenic repair. Clin Orthop 313:8–18, 1995.

44. Connolly, J.F.; Shindell, R. Percutaneous marrow injection for an ununited tibia. Nebr Med J 71:105–107, 1986.

45. Court-Brown, C.M.; Keating, J.F.; Christie, J.; McQueen, M.M. Exchange intramedullary nailing. Its use in aseptic tibial nonunion. J Bone Joint Surg Br 77:407–411, 1995.

46. Crockarell, J.R., Jr.; Berry, D.J.; Lewallen, D.G. Nonunion after periprosthetic femoral fracture associated with total hip arthroplasty. J Bone Joint Surg Am 81:1073–1079, 1999.

47. Daftari, T.K.; Whitesides, T.E., Jr; Heller, J.G.; et al. Nicotine on the revascularization of bone graft. An experimental study in rabbits. Spine 19:904–911, 1994.

48. Danckwardt-Lilliestrom, G. Reaming of the medullary cavity and its effect on diaphyseal bone. A fluorochromic, microangiographic and histologic study on the rabbit tibia and dog femur. Acta Orthop Scand Suppl 128:1–153, 1969.

49. Danis, R. Theorie et Pratique de l'Osteosynthese. Paris, Masson, 1949.

50. Danziger, M.B.; Healy, W.L. Operative treatment of olecranon nonunion. J Orthop Trauma 6:290–293, 1992.

51. Davids, P.H.; Luitse, J.S.; Strating, R.P.; et al. Operative treatment for delayed union and nonunion of midshaft clavicular fractures: AO reconstruction plate fixation and early mobilization. J Trauma 40:985–986, 1996.

52. Davis, B.A.; Rotman, M.B.; Brinker, M.R.; et al. Treatment of proximal humerus nonunions with the Polaris humeral rod: A multicenter study. Abstract. Presented at the American Academy of Orthopaedic Surgeons Annual Meeting, Anaheim, CA, 1999.

53. Day, S.M.; DeHeer, D.H. Reversal of the detrimental effects of chronic protein malnutrition on long bone fracture healing. J Orthop Trauma 15:47–53, 2001.

54. de Vernejoul, M.C.; Bielakoff, J.; Herve, M.; et al. Evidence for defective osteoblastic function: A role for alcohol and tobacco consumption in osteoporosis in middle-aged men. Clin Orthop 179:107–115, 1983.

55. Delloye, C.; Delefortrie, G.; Coutelier, L.; Vincent, A. Bone regenerate formation in cortical bone during distraction lengthening: An experimental study. Clin Orthop 250:34–42, 1990.

56. Dodds, R.A.; Catterall, A.; Bitensky, L.; Chayen, J. Abnormalities in fracture healing induced by vitamin B_6-deficiency in rats. Bone 7:489–495, 1986.

57. Doherty, J.H.; Patterson, R.L., Jr. Fibular by-pass operation in the treatment of non-union of the tibia in adults. J Bone Joint Surg Am 49:1470–1471, 1967.

58. Dworkin, S.F.; Von Korff, M.; LeResche, L. Multiple pains and psychiatric disturbance. An epidemiologic investigation. Arch Gen Psychiatry 47:239–244, 1990.

59. Ebraheim, N.A.; Mekhail, A.O.; Darwich, M. Open reduction and internal fixation with bone grafting of clavicular nonunion. J Trauma 42:701–704, 1997.

60. Eggers, G.W.N. Internal contact splint. J Bone Joint Surg Am 31:40–52, 1949.

61. Einhorn, T.A. Enhancement of fracture healing. Instr Course Lect 45:401–416, 1996.

62. Einhorn, T.A.; Bonnarens, F.; Burstein, A.H. The contributions of dietary protein and mineral to the healing of experimental fractures. A biomechanical study. J Bone Joint Surg Am 68:1389–1395, 1986.

63. Einhorn, T.A.; Gundberg, C.M.; Devlin, V.J.; Warman, J. Fracture healing and osteocalcin metabolism in vitamin K deficiency. Clin Orthop 237:219–225, 1988.

64. Einhorn, T.A.; Levine, B.; Michel, P. Nutrition and bone. Orthop Clin North Am 21:43–50, 1990.

65. Emami, A.; Mjoberg, B.; Larsson, S. Infected tibial nonunion. Good results after open cancellous bone grafting in 37 cases. Acta Orthop Scand 66:447–451, 1995.

66. Engesaeter, L.B.; Sudmann, B.; Sudmann, E. Fracture healing in rats inhibited by locally administered indomethacin. Acta Orthop Scand 63:330–333, 1992.

67. Esterhai, J.L., Jr; Brighton, C.T.; Heppenstall, R.B.; et al. Detection of synovial pseudarthrosis by ^{99m}Tc scintigraphy: Application to treatment of traumatic nonunion with constant direct current. Clin Orthop 161:15–23, 1981.

68. Esterhai, J.L., Jr; Brighton, C.T.; Heppenstall, R.B. Nonunion of the humerus. Clinical, roentgenographic, scintigraphic, and response characteristics to treatment with constant direct current stimulation of osteogenesis. Clin Orthop 211:228–234, 1986.

69. Esterhai, J.L., Jr; Sennett, B.; Gelb, H.; et al. Treatment of chronic osteomyelitis complicating nonunion and segmental defects of the tibia with open cancellous bone graft, posterolateral bone graft, and soft-tissue transfer. J Trauma 30:49–54, 1990.

70. Fang, M.; Frost, P.; Iida-Klein, A.; Hahn, T. Effects of nicotine on cellular function in UMR 106-01 osteoblast-like cells. Bone 12:283–286, 1991.

71. Fernandez, D.L.; Ring, D.; Jupiter, J.B. Surgical management of delayed union and nonunion of distal radius fractures. J Hand Surg Am 26:201–209, 2001.

72. Flinkkilä, T.; Ristiniemi, J.; Hämäläinen, M. Nonunion after intramedullary nailing of humeral shaft fractures. J Trauma 50:540–544, 2001.

73. Foulk, D.A.; Szabo, R.M. Diaphyseal humerus fractures: Natural history and occurrence of nonunion. Orthopedics 18:333–335, 1995.

74. Freedman, E.L.; Hak, D.J.; Johnson, E.E.; Eckardt, J.J. Total knee replacement including a modular distal femoral component in elderly patients with acute fracture or nonunion. J Orthop Trauma 9:231–237, 1995.

75. Freeland, A.E.; Mutz, S.B. Posterior bone grafting for infected ununited fracture of the tibia. J Bone Joint Surg Am 58:653–657, 1976.

76. Frey, C.; Halikus, N.M.; Vu-Rose, T.; Ebramzadeh, E. A review of ankle arthrodesis: Predisposing factors to nonunion. Foot Ankle Int 15:581–584, 1994.

77. Frich, L.H.; Sojbjerg, J.O.; Sneppen, O. Shoulder arthroplasty in

complex acute and chronic proximal humeral fractures. Orthopedics 14:949–954, 1991.

78. Friedrich, B.; Klaue, P. Mechanical stability and post-traumatic osteitis: An experimental evaluation of the relation between infection of bone and internal fixation. Injury 9:23–29, 1977.

79. Giannoudis, P.V.; MacDonald, D.A.; Matthews, S.J.; et al. Nonunion of the femoral diaphysis. The influence of reaming and non-steroidal anti-inflammatory drugs. J Bone Joint Surg Br 82:655–658, 2000.

80. Goldman, B. Use and abuse of opioid analgesics in chronic pain. Can Fam Physician 39:571–576, 1993.

81. Goulet, J.A.; Templeman, D. Delayed union and nonunion of tibial shaft fractures. Instr Course Lect 46:281–291, 1997.

82. Green, S.A. The Ilizarov method. In: Browner, B.D.; Levine, A.M.; Jupiter, J.B., eds. Skeletal Trauma: Fractures, Dislocations, Ligamentous Injuries. Philadelphia, W.B. Saunders, 1998, pp. 661–701.

83. Green, S.A. Skeletal defects. A comparison of bone grafting and bone transport for segmental skeletal defects. Clin Orthop 301: 111–117, 1994.

84. Guarniero, R.; de Barros Filho, T.E.; Tannuri, U.; et al. Study of fracture healing in protein malnutrition. Rev Paul Med 110:63–68, 1992.

85. Gustilo, R.B.; Nelson, G.E.; Hamel, A.; Moe, J.H. The effect of intramedullary nailing on the blood supply of the diaphysis of long bones in mature dogs. J Bone Joint Surg Am 46:1362–1363, 1964.

86. Gyul'nazarova, S.V.; Shtin, V.P. Reparative bone tissue regeneration in treating pseudarthroses with simultaneous lengthening in the area of the pathological focus (an experimental study). Ortop Travmatol Protez 4:10–15, 1983.

87. Hak, D.J.; Lee, S.S.; Goulet, J.A. Success of exchange reamed intramedullary nailing for femoral shaft nonunion or delayed union. J Orthop Trauma 14:178–182, 2000.

88. Han, C.S.; Wood, M.B.; Bishop, A.T.; Cooney, W.P., III. Vascularized bone transfer. J Bone Joint Surg Am 74:1441–1449, 1992.

89. Harmon, P.H. A simplified surgical approach to the posterior tibia for bone-grafting and fibular transference. J Bone Joint Surg Am 27:496–498, 1945.

90. Haverstock, B.D.; Mandracchia, V.J. Cigarette smoking and bone healing: Implications in foot and ankle surgery. J Foot Ankle Surg 37:69–74, 1998.

91. Healy, W.L.; Jupiter, J.B.; Kristiansen, T.K.; White, R.R. Nonunion of the proximal humerus. A review of 25 cases. J Orthop Trauma 4:424–431, 1990.

92. Helfet, D.L.; Jupiter, J.B.; Gasser, S. Indirect reduction and tension-band plating of tibial non-union with deformity. J Bone Joint Surg Am 74:1286–1297, 1992.

93. Hernandez, R.J.; Tachdjian, M.O.; Poznanski, A.K.; Dias, L.S. CT determination of femoral torsion. AJR Am J Roentgenol 137:97–101, 1981.

94. Herve, C.; Gaillard, M.; Rivet, P.; et al. Treatment in serious lower limb injuries: Amputation versus preservation. Injury 18:21–23, 1987.

95. Herzenberg, J.E.; Smith, J.D.; Paley, D. Correcting tibial deformities with Ilizarov's apparatus. Clin Orthop 302:36–41, 1994.

96. Hogevold, H.E.; Grogaard, B.; Reikeras, O. Effects of short-term treatment with corticosteroids and indomethacin on bone healing. A mechanical study of osteotomies in rats. Acta Orthop Scand 63:607–611, 1992.

97. Horstmann, H.; Mahboubi, S. The use of computed tomography scan in unstable hip reconstruction. J Comput Tomogr 11:364–369, 1987.

98. Huddleston, P.M.; Steckelberg, J.M.; Hanssen, A.D.; et al. Ciprofloxacin inhibition of experimental fracture healing. J Bone Joint Surg Am 82:161–173, 2000.

99. Huntington, T.W. Case of bone transference. Use of a segment of fibula to supply a defect in the tibia. Ann Surg 41:249–251, 1905.

100. Huo, M.H.; Troiano, N.W.; Pelker, R.R.; et al. The influence of ibuprofen on fracture repair: Biomechanical, biochemical, histologic, and histomorphometric parameters in rats. J Orthop Res 9:383–390, 1991.

101. Ikeda, K.; Tomita, K.; Hashimoto, F.; Morikawa, S. Long-term follow-up of vascularized bone grafts for the reconstruction of tibial nonunion: Evaluation with computed tomographic scanning. J Trauma 32:693–697, 1992.

102. Ilizarov, G.A. Clinical application of the tension-stress effect for limb lengthening. Clin Orthop 250:8–26, 1990.

103. Ilizarov, G.A. Transosseous Osteosynthesis. Theoretical and Clinical Aspects of the Regeneration and Growth of Tissue. Berlin, Springer-Verlag, 1992.

104. Ilizarov, G.A.; Devyatov, A.A.; Kamerin, V.K. Plastic reconstruction of longitudinal bone defects by means of compression and subsequent distraction. Acta Chir Plast 22:32–41, 1980.

105. Ilizarov, G.A.; Kaplunov, A.G.; Degtiarev, V.E.; Lediaev, V.I. Treatment of pseudarthroses and ununited fractures, complicated by purulent infection, by the method of compression-distraction osteosynthesis. Ortop Travmatol Protez 33:10–14, 1972.

106. Ilizarov, G.A.; Kaplunov, A.G.; Grachova, V.I.; Shpaer, L.I. Close Compression-Distraction Osteosynthesis of the Tibial Pseudoarthroses with Ilizarov Method (Metodicheskoe Posobie). Kurgan, USSR, Kniiekot Institute, 1971.

107. Indrekvam, K.; Lekven, J.; Engesaeter, L.B.; Langeland, N. Effects of intramedullary reaming and nailing on blood flow in rat femora. Acta Orthop Scand 63:61–65, 1992.

108. Johnson, E.E.; Simpson, L.A.; Helfet, D.L. Delayed intramedullary nailing after failed external fixation of the tibia. Clin Orthop 253:251–257, 1990.

109. Jones, N.F.; Swartz, W.M.; Mears, D.C.; et al. The "double barrel" free vascularized fibular bone graft. Plast Reconstr Surg 81:378–385, 1988.

110. Judet, R. La decortication. In: Actualities de Chirurgie Orthopedique. Paris, Masson, 1965.

111. Judet, R.; Judet, J.; Roy-Camille, R. La vascularisation des pseudoarthroses des os longs d'apres une étude clinique et experimentale. Rev Chir Orthop 44:5, 1958.

112. Jupiter, J.B.; Ring, D.; Rosen, H. The complications and difficulties of management of nonunion in the severely obese. J Orthop Trauma 9:363–370, 1995.

113. Katon, W. The impact of major depression on chronic medical illness. Gen Hosp Psychiatry 18:215–219, 1996.

114. Katon, W.; Sullivan, M.D. Depression and chronic medical illness. J Clin Psychiatry 51:3–11, 1990.

115. Keller, J.; Bunger, C.; Bereassen, T.T.; et al. Bone repair inhibited by indomethacin. Acta Orthop Scand 58:379–383, 1987.

116. Kempf, I.; Grosse, A.; Rigaut, P. The treatment of noninfected pseudarthrosis of the femur and tibia with locked intramedullary nailing. Clin Orthop 212:142–154, 1986.

117. Key, J. Positive pressure in arthrodesis for tuberculosis of the knee joint. South Med J 25:909, 1932.

118. Khan, I.M. Fracture healing: Role of NSAID's. Abstract. Am J Orthop 26:413, 1997.

119. Khan, M.Z.; Downing, N.D.; Henry, A.P. Tibial reconstruction by ipsilateral vascularized fibular transfer. Injury 27:651–654, 1996.

120. Kim, H.S.; Jahng, J.S.; Han, D.Y.; et al. Immediate ipsilateral fibular transfer in a large tibial defect using a ring fixator. A case report. Int Orthop 22:321–324, 1998.

121. Kim, S.J.; Yang, K.H.; Moon, S.H.; Lee, S.C. Endoscopic bone graft for delayed union and nonunion. Arthroscopy 15:324–329, 1999.

122. Klassen, J.F.; Trousdale, R.T. Treatment of delayed and nonunion of the patella. J Orthop Trauma 11:188–194, 1997.

123. Klemm, K.W. Treatment of infected pseudarthrosis of the femur and tibia with an interlocking nail. Clin Orthop 212:174–181, 1986.

124. Koval, K.J.; Seligson, D.; Rosen, H.; Fee, K. Distal femoral nonunion: Treatment with a retrograde inserted locked intramedullary nail. J Orthop Trauma 9:285–291, 1995.

125. Krettek, C.; Miclau, T.; Schandelmaier, P.; et al. The mechanical effect of blocking screws ("Poller screws") in stabilizing tibia fractures with short proximal or distal fragments after insertion of small-diameter intramedullary nails. J Orthop Trauma 13:550–553, 1999.

126. Krettek, C.; Stephan, C.; Schandelmaier, P.; et al. The use of Poller screws as blocking screws in stabilising tibial fractures treated with small diameter intramedullary nails. J Bone Joint Surg Br 81:963–968, 1999.

127. Krishnan, K.R.; France, R.D. Chronic pain and depression. South Med J 80:558–561, 1987.

128. Kyrö, A.; Usenius, J.P.; Aarnio, M.; et al. Are smokers a risk group for delayed healing of tibial shaft fractures? Ann Chir Gynaecol 82:254–262, 1993.

129. Lambotte, A. Le Traitement des Fractures. Paris, Masson, 1907.

130. Lambotte, A. L'Intervention Operatoire Dans les Fractures. Paris, A. Maloine, 1907.

131. Lammens, J.; Bauduin, G.; Driesen, R.; et al. Treatment of nonunion of the humerus using the Ilizarov external fixator. Clin Orthop 353:223–230, 1998.

132. Lange, R.H. Limb reconstruction versus amputation decision making in massive lower extremity trauma. Clin Orthop 243:92–99, 1989.

133. Lawlis, G.F.; McCoy, C.E. Psychological evaluation: Patients with chronic pain. Orthop Clin North Am 14:527–538, 1983.

134. Lerner, R.K.; Esterhai, J.L., Jr.; Polomano, R.C.; et al. Quality of life assessment of patients with posttraumatic fracture nonunion, chronic refractory osteomyelitis, and lower-extremity amputation. Clin Orthop 295:28–36, 1993.

135. Lerner, R.K.; Esterhai, J.L., Jr.; Polomono, R.C.; et al. Psychosocial, functional, and quality of life assessment of patients with posttraumatic fracture nonunion, chronic refractory osteomyelitis, and lower-extremity amputation. Arch Phys Med Rehabil 72:122–126, 1991.

136. Lieberg, O.U.; Heston, W.M., III. Primary tibiofibular synostosis in open tibial fracture with segmental bone loss. A report of an unusual case. J Bone Joint Surg Am 55:1521–1524, 1973.

137. Lindholm, T.S.; Tornkvist, H. Inhibitory effect on bone formation and calcification exerted by the anti-inflammatory drug ibuprofen. An experimental study on adult rat with fracture. Scand J Rheumatol 10:38–42, 1981.

138. Mahboubi, S.; Horstmann, H. Femoral torsion: CT measurement. Radiology 160:843–844, 1986.

139. Marsh, J.L.; Prokuski, L.; Biermann, J.S. Chronic infected tibial nonunions with bone loss. Conventional techniques versus bone transport. Clin Orthop 301:139–146, 1994.

140. Maurer, D.J.; Merkow, R.L.; Gustilo, R.B. Infection after intramedullary nailing of severe open tibial fractures initially treated with external fixation. J Bone Joint Surg Am 71:835–838, 1989.

141. May, J.W., Jr.; Jupiter, J.B.; Weiland, A.J.; Byrd, H.S. Clinical classification of post-traumatic tibial osteomyelitis. J Bone Joint Surg Am 71:1422–1428, 1989.

142. Mayo, K.A.; Benirschke, S.K. Treatment of tibial malunions and nonunions with reamed intramedullary nails. Orthop Clin North Am 21:715–724, 1990.

143. Mayr, E.; Frankel, V.; Ruter, A. Ultrasound—an alternative healing method for nonunions? Arch Orthop Trauma Surg 120:1–8, 2000.

144. McGraw, J.M.; Lim, E.V.A. Treatment of open tibial-shaft fractures. External fixation and secondary intramedullary nailing. J Bone Joint Surg Am 70:900–911, 1988.

145. McKee, M.; Jupiter, J.; Toh, C.L.; et al. Reconstruction after malunion and nonunion of intra-articular fractures of the distal humerus. Methods and results in 13 adults. J Bone Joint Surg Br 76:614–621, 1994.

146. McKee, M.D.; Miranda, M.A.; Riemer, B.L.; et al. Management of humeral nonunion after the failure of locking intramedullary nails. J Orthop Trauma 10:492–499, 1996.

147. McLaren, A.C.; Blokker, C.P. Locked intramedullary fixation for metaphyseal malunion and nonunion. Clin Orthop 265:253–260, 1991.

148. McMaster, P.E.; Hohl, M. Tibiofibular crosspeg grafting. A salvage procedure for complicated ununited tibial fractures. J Bone Joint Surg Am 57:720–721, 1975.

149. Megas, P.; Panagiotopoulos, E.; Skriviliotakis, S.; Lambiris, E. Intramedullary nailing in the treatment of aseptic tibial nonunion. Injury 32:233–239, 2001.

150. Middleton, S.B.; Foley, S.J.; Foy, M.A. Partial excision of the clavicle for nonunion in National Hunt jockeys. J Bone Joint Surg Br 77:778–780, 1995.

151. Milch, H. Synostosis operation for persistent non-union of the tibia. A case report. J Bone Joint Surg Am 21:409–413, 1939.

152. Milch, H. Tibiofibular synostosis for non-union of the tibia. Surgery 27:770–779, 1950.

153. Moed, B.R.; Watson, J.T. Intramedullary nailing of aseptic tibial nonunions without the use of the fracture table. J Orthop Trauma 9:128–134, 1995.

154. More, R.C.; Kody, M.H.; Kabo, J.M.; et al. The effects of two nonsteroidal antiinflammatory drugs on limb swelling, joint stiffness, and bone torsional strength following fracture in a rabbit model. Clin Orthop 247:306–312, 1989.

155. Morrey, B.F.; Adams, R.A. Semiconstrained elbow replacement for distal humeral nonunion. J Bone Joint Surg Br 77:67–72, 1995.

156. Müller, J.; Schenk, R.; Willenegger, H. Experimentelle Untersuchungen Über die Entstehung reaktiver Pseudoarthrosen am Hunderadius. Helv Chir Acta 35:301–308, 1968.

157. Müller, M.E. Treatment of nonunions by compression. Clin Orthop 43:83–92, 1965.

158. Müller, M.E.; Allgöwer, M.; Schneider, R. Manual of Internal Fixation: Techniques Recommended by the AO Group. Berlin, Springer-Verlag, 1979.

159. Müller, M.E.; Allgöwer, M.; Willenegger, H. Technique of Internal Fixation of Fractures. New York, Springer-Verlag, 1965.

160. Murray, J.H.; Fitch, R.D. Distraction histogenesis: Principles and indications. J Am Acad Orthop Surg 4:317–327, 1996.

161. Muschler, G.F.; Boehm, C.; Easley, K. Aspiration to obtain osteoblast progenitor cells from human bone marrow: The influence of aspiration volume. J Bone Joint Surg Am 79:1699–1709, 1997.

162. Nayak, N.K.; Schickendantz, M.S.; Regan, W.D.; Hawkins, R.J. Operative treatment of nonunion of surgical neck fractures of the humerus. Clin Orthop 313:200–205, 1995.

163. Oh, I.; Nahigian, S.H.; Rascher, J.J.; Farrall, J.P. Closed intramedullary nailing for ununited femoral shaft fractures. Clin Orthop 106:206–215, 1975.

164. Olerud, S. The effects of intramedullary reaming. In: Browner, B.D.; Edwards, C.C., eds. The Science and Practice of Intramedullary Nailing. Philadelphia, Lea & Febiger, 1987, pp. 61–66.

165. Olsen, B.S.; Vaesel, M.T.; Sojbjerg, J.O. Treatment of midshaft clavicular nonunion with plate fixation and autologous bone grafting. J Shoulder Elbow Surg 4:337–344, 1995.

166. Paley, D. Treatment of tibial nonunion and bone loss with the Ilizarov technique. Instr Course Lect 39:185–197, 1990.

167. Paley, D.; Chaudray, M.; Pirone, A.M.; et al. Treatment of malunions and mal-nonunions of the femur and tibia by detailed preoperative planning and the Ilizarov techniques. Orthop Clin North Am 21:667–691, 1990.

168. Paley, D.; Herzenberg, J.E. Principles of Deformity Correction. New York, Springer-Verlag, 2002.

169. Paley, D.; Sen, C.; Tetsworth, K.; Herzenberg, J.E. Acute shortening with subsequent relengthening versus bone transport in the treatment of tibial bone defects (paper #7). Presented at the 11th Annual Scientific Meeting, Association for the Study and Application of the Methods of Ilizarov—North America: The Limb Lengthening and Reconstruction Society, Berkeley, California, 2001.

170. Paley, D.; Tetsworth, K. Mechanical axis deviation of the lower limbs. Preoperative planning of multiapical frontal plane angular and bowing deformities of the femur and tibia. Clin Orthop 280:65–71, 1992.

171. Paley, D.; Tetsworth, K. Mechanical axis deviation of the lower limbs. Preoperative planning of uniapical angular deformities of the tibia or femur. Clin Orthop 280:48–64, 1992.

172. Paley, D.; Young, M.C.; Wiley, A.M.; et al. Percutaneous bone marrow grafting of fractures and bony defects. An experimental study in rabbits. Clin Orthop 208:300–312, 1986.

173. Papagelopoulos, P.J.; Morrey, B.F. Treatment of nonunion of olecranon fractures. J Bone Joint Surg Br 76:627–635, 1994.

174. Papineau, L.J.; Alfageme, A.; Dalcourt, J.P.; Pilon, L. Osteomyelite chronique: Excision et greffe de spongieux a l'air libre après mises à plat extensives. Int Orthop 3:165–176, 1979.

175. Paramasivan, O.N.; Younge, D.A.; Pant, R. Treatment of nonunion around the olecranon fossa of the humerus by intramedullary locked nailing. J Bone Joint Surg Br 82:332–335, 2000.

176. Patel, C.V.; Adenwalla, H.S. Treatment of fractured clavicle by immediate partial subperiosteal resection. J Postgrad Med 18:32–34, 1972.

177. Patel, V.R.; Menon, D.K.; Pool, R.D.; Simonis, R.B. Nonunion of the humerus after failure of surgical treatment. Management using the Ilizarov circular fixator. J Bone Joint Surg Br 82:977–983, 2000.

178. Paterson, D.C.; Lewis, G.N.; Cass, C.A. Treatment of delayed union and nonunion with an implanted direct current stimulator. Clin Orthop 148:117–128, 1980.

179. Patzakis, M.J.; Scilaris, T.A.; Chon, J.; et al. Results of bone grafting for infected tibial nonunion. Clin Orthop 315:192–198, 1995.

180. Pauwels, F. Grundriss liner biomechanik der Fracturheilung. Verh Dtsch Orthop Ges 34 Kongress, 62–108, 1940.

181. Pauwels, F. Schenkelhalsbruch ein mechanisches Problem: Grundlagen des Heilungsvorganges, Prognose und kausale Therapie. Stuttgart, Ferdinand Enke Verlag, 1935.

182. Perlman, M.H.; Thordarson, D.B. Ankle fusion in a high risk population: An assessment of nonunion risk factors. Foot Ankle Int 20:491–496, 1999.

183. Perren, S.M.; Cordey, J. The concepts of interfragmentary strains. In: Uhthoff, H.K., ed. Current Concepts of Internal Fixation of Fractures. New York, Springer-Verlag, 1980.

184. Pers, M.; Medgyesi, S. Pedicle muscle flaps and their applications in the surgery repair. Br J Plast Surg 26:313–321, 1977.

185. Phemister, D.B. Treatment of ununited fractures by onlay bone grafts without screw or tie fixation and without breaking down of the fibrous union. J Bone Joint Surg Am 29:946–960, 1947.

186. Phillips, J.H.; Rahn, B.A. Fixation effects on membranous and endochondral onlay bone-graft resorption. Plast Reconstr Surg 82:872–877, 1988.

187. Pollak, D.; Floman, Y.; Simkin, A.; et al. The effect of protein malnutrition and nutritional support on the mechanical properties of fracture healing in the injured rat. J Parenter Enteral Nutr 10:564–567, 1986.

188. Porter, S.E.; Hanley, E.N., Jr. The musculoskeletal effects of smoking. J Am Acad Orthop Surg 9:9–17, 2001.

189. Praemer, A.; Furner, S.; Rice, D.P. Musculoskeletal Conditions in the United States. Park Ridge, IL, American Academy of Orthopaedic Surgeons, 1992, pp. 83–124.

190. Raikin, S.M.; Landsman, J.C.; Alexander, V.A.; et al. Effect of nicotine on the rate and strength of long bone fracture healing. Clin Orthop 353:231–237, 1998.

191. Ramp, W.; Lenz, L.; Galvin, R. Nicotine inhibits collagen synthesis and alkaline phosphatase activity but stimulates DNA synthesis in osteoblast-like cells. Exp Biol Med 197:36–43, 1991.

192. Reichert, I.L.H.; McCarthy, I.D.; Hughes, S.P.F. The acute vascular response to intramedullary reaming. Microsphere estimation of blood flow in the intact ovine tibia. J Bone Joint Surg Br 77:490–493, 1995.

193. Rhinelander, F.W. The normal microcirculation of diaphyseal cortex and its response to fracture. J Bone Joint Surg Am 50:784–800, 1968.

194. Richards, M.; Huibregtse, B.A.; Caplan, A.I.; et al. Marrow-derived progenitor cell injections enhance new bone formation during distraction. J Orthop Res 17:900–908, 1999.

195. Riebel, G.D.; Boden, S.D.; Whitesides, T.E.; Hutton, W.C. The effect of nicotine on incorporation of cancellous bone graft in an animal model. Spine 20:2198–2202, 1995.

196. Riemer, B.L.; Butterfield, S.L. Comparison of reamed and nonreamed solid core nailing of the tibial diaphysis after external fixation: A preliminary report. J Orthop Trauma 7:279–285, 1993.

197. Rijnberg, W.J.; van Linge, B. Central grafting for persistent nonunion of the tibia. A lateral approach to the tibia, creating a central compartment. J Bone Joint Surg Br 75:926–931, 1993.

198. Ring, D.; Jupiter, J.B.; Gan, B.S.; et al. Infected nonunion of the tibia. Clin Orthop 369:302–311, 1999.

199. Rittman, W.W.; Perren, S.M. Cortical Bone Healing after Internal Fixation and Infection: Biomechanics and Biology. Berlin, Springer-Verlag, 1974.

200. Ro, J.; Sudmann, E.; Marton, P.F. Effect of indomethacin on fracture healing in rats. Acta Orthop Scand 47:588–599, 1976.

201. Rosen, H. Fracture healing and pseudarthrosis. In: Taveras, J.M., ed. Radiology: Diagnosis–Imaging–Intervention. Philadelphia, J.B. Lippincott, 1986.

202. Rosen, H. Internal fixation of nonunions after previously unsuccessful electromagnetic stimulation. In: Siegel, P.G., ed. Techniques in Orthopedics—Topics in Orthopedic Trauma. Baltimore, University Park Press, 1984.

203. Rosen, H. (Late) reconstructive procedures about the ankle joint. In: Jahss, M.H., ed. Disorders of the Foot and Ankle: Medical and Surgical Management. Philadelphia, W.B. Saunders, 1991.

204. Rosen, H. The management of nonunions and malunions in long bone fractures in the elderly. In: Zuckerman, J.D., ed. Comprehensive Care of Orthopedic Injuries in the Elderly. Baltimore, Urban & Schwarzenberg, 1990.

205. Rosen, H. Nonunion and malunion. In: Browner, B.D.; Levine, A.M.; Jupiter, J.B., eds. Skeletal Trauma: Fractures, Dislocations,

206. Ligamentous Injuries. Philadelphia, W.B. Saunders, 1998, pp. 501–541.

206. Rosen, H. Operative treatment of nonunions of long bone fractures. J Contin Educ Orthop 7:13–39, 1979.

207. Rosen, H. The treatment of nonunions and pseudarthroses of the humeral shaft. Orthop Clin North Am 21:725–742, 1990.

208. Rosen, H. Treatment of nonunions: General principles. In: Chapman, M.W.; Madison, M., eds. Operative Orthopaedics. Philadelphia, J.B. Lippincott, 1988.

209. Rosen, H.; Stempler, E.S. A simplified method of closed suction irrigation for treating orthopedic infections. Orthop Dig 5:21, 1978.

210. Rosenberg, G.A.; Patterson, B.M. Limb salvage versus amputation for severe open fractures of the tibia. Orthopedics 21:343–349, 1998.

211. Rosson, J.W.; Simonis, R.B. Locked nailing for nonunion of the tibia. J Bone Joint Surg Br 74:358–361, 1992.

212. Safoury, Y. Use of a reversed-flow vascularized pedicle fibular graft for treatment of nonunion of the tibia. J Reconstr Microsurg 15:23–28, 1999.

213. Saleh, M.; Royston, S. Management of nonunion of fractures by distraction with correction of angulation and shortening. J Bone Joint Surg Br 78:105–109, 1996.

214. Salibian, A.H.; Anzel, S.H.; Salyer, W.A. Transfer of vascularized grafts of iliac bone to the extremities. J Bone Joint Surg Am 69:1319–1327, 1987.

215. Sanders, R.A.; Sackett, J.R. Open reduction and internal fixation of delayed union and nonunion of the distal humerus. J Orthop Trauma 4:254–259, 1990.

216. Sarathy, M.P.; Madhavan, P.; Ravichandran, K.M. Nonunion of intertrochanteric fractures of the femur. Treatment by modified medial displacement and valgus osteotomy. J Bone Joint Surg Br 77:90–92, 1995.

217. Sarmiento, A. Functional treatment of long bone fractures. Paper presented at the SICOT XIV World Congress, Kyoto, Japan, 1978.

218. Savage, S.R. Opioid use in the management of chronic pain. Med Clin North Am 83:761–786, 1999.

219. Sawant, M.R.; Bendall, S.P.; Kavanagh, T.G.; Citron, N.D. Nonunion of tibial stress fractures in patients with deformed arthritic knees. Treatment using modular total knee arthroplasty. J Bone Joint Surg Br 81:663–666, 1999.

220. Schaden, W.; Fischer, A.; Sailler, A. Extracorporeal shock wave therapy of nonunion or delayed osseous union. Clin Orthop 387:90–94, 2001.

221. Schenk, R.; Willenegger, H. Zur histologie der primären Knochenheilung. Modifikationen und grenzen der spaltheilung in abhängigkeit von der defektgrösse. Unfallheilkunde 81:219–227, 1977.

222. Schenk, R.K. Histology of fracture repair and nonunion. In: Bulletin of the Swiss Association for Study of Internal Fixation. Bern, Swiss Association for Study of Internal Fixation, 1978.

223. Schleberger, R.; Senge, T. Non-invasive treatment of long-bone pseudarthrosis by shock waves (ESWL). Arch Orthop Trauma Surg 111:224–227, 1992.

224. Schmitz, M.A.; Finnegan, M.; Natarajan, R.; Champine, J. Effect of smoking on tibial shaft fracture healing. Clin Orthop 365:184–200, 1999.

225. Schwartsman, V.; Choi, S.H.; Schwartsman, R. Tibial nonunions. Treatment tactics with the Ilizarov method. Orthop Clin North Am 21:639–653, 1990.

226. Seitz, W.H., Jr.; Froimson, A.I.; Leb, R.B. Autogenous bone marrow and allograft replacement of bone defects in the hand and upper extremities. J Orthop Trauma 6:36–42, 1992.

227. Selznick, H.S.; Agel, J.; Chapman, J.R. The effect of cigarette smoking on the healing and treatment of open tibia fractures. Paper presented at the Orthopaedic Trauma Association Annual Meeting, Final Program, New Orleans, LA, 1993.

228. Shahcheraghi, G.H.; Bayatpoor, A. Infected tibial nonunion. Can J Surg 37:209–213, 1994.

229. Shapiro, M.S.; Endrizzi, D.P.; Cannon, R.M.; Dick, H.M. Treatment of tibial defects and nonunions using ipsilateral vascularized fibular transposition. Clin Orthop 296:207–212, 1993.

230. Silcox, D.H., III; Daftari, T.; Boden, S.D.; et al. The effect of nicotine on spinal fusion. Spine 20:1549–1553, 1995.

231. Sitter, T.; Wilson, J.; Browner, B. The effect of reamed versus unreamed nailing on intramedullary blood supply and cortical viability. Abstract. J Orthop Trauma 4:232, 1990.

232. Sledge, S.L.; Johnson, K.D.; Henley, M.B.; Watson, J.T. Intramedullary nailing with reaming to treat non-union of the tibia. J Bone Joint Surg Am 71:1004–1019, 1989.

233. Smith, T.K. Prevention of complications in orthopedic surgery secondary to nutritional depletion. Clin Orthop 222:91–97, 1987.

234. Sudmann, E.; Dregelid, E.; Bessesen, A.; Morland, J. Inhibition of fracture healing by indomethacin in rats. Eur J Clin Invest 9:333–339, 1979.

235. Swartz, W.M.; Mears, D.C. Management of difficult lower extremity fractures and nonunions. Clin Plast Surg 13:633–644, 1986.

236. Takikawa, S.; Matsui, N.; Kokubu, T.; et al. Low-intensity pulsed ultrasound initiates bone healing in rat nonunion fracture model. J Ultrasound Med 20:197–205, 2001.

237. Taylor, J.C. Delayed union and nonunion of fractures. In: Crenshaw, A.H., ed. Campbell's Operative Orthopaedics. St. Louis, Mosby, 1992, pp. 1287–1345.

238. Templeman, D.; Thomas, M.; Varecka, T.; Kyle, R. Exchange reamed intramedullary nailing for delayed union and nonunion of the tibia. Clin Orthop 315:169–175, 1995.

239. Tennant, F.S., Jr.; Rawson, R.A. Outpatient treatment of prescription opioid dependence: Comparison of two methods. Arch Intern Med 142:1845–1847, 1982.

240. Tiedeman, J.J.; Connolly, J.F.; Strates, B.S.; Lippiello, L. Treatment of nonunion by percutaneous injection of bone marrow and demineralized bone matrix. An experimental study in dogs. Clin Orthop 268:294–302, 1991.

241. Ueng, S.W.; Chao, E.K.; Lee, S.S.; Shih, C.H. Augmentative plate fixation for the management of femoral nonunion after intramedullary nailing. J Trauma 43:640–644, 1997.

242. Ueng, S.W.; Lee, M.Y.; Li, A.F.; et al. Effect of intermittent cigarette smoke inhalation on tibial lengthening: Experimental study on rabbits. J Trauma 42:231–238, 1997.

243. Ueng, S.W.; Lee, S.S.; Lin, S et al. Hyperbaric oxygen therapy mitigates the adverse effect of cigarette smoking on the bone healing of tibial lengthening: An experimental study on rabbits. J Trauma 47:752–759, 1999.

244. Ueng, S.W.; Shih, C.H. Augmentative plate fixation for the management of femoral nonunion with broken interlocking nail. J Trauma 45:747–52, 1998.

245. Ueng, S.W.; Wei, F.C.; Shih, C.H. Management of femoral diaphyseal infected nonunion with antibiotic beads local therapy, external skeletal fixation, and staged bone grafting. J Trauma 46:97–103, 1999.

246. Valchanou, V.D.; Michailov, P. High energy shock waves in the treatment of delayed and nonunion of fractures. Int Orthop 15:181–184, 1991.

247. Ward, W.G.; Goldner, R.D.; Nunley, J.A. Reconstruction of tibial bone defects in tibial nonunion. Microsurgery 11:63–73, 1990.

248. Warren, S.B.; Brooker, A.F., Jr. Intramedullary nailing of tibial nonunions. Clin Orthop 285:236–243, 1992.

249. Webb, L.X.; Winquist, R.A.; Hansen, S.T. Intramedullary nailing and reaming for delayed union or nonunion of the femoral shaft. A report of 105 consecutive cases. Clin Orthop 212:133–141, 1986.

250. Weber, B.G. Lengthening osteotomy of the fibula to correct a widened mortice of the ankle after fracture. Int Orthop 4:289–293, 1981.

251. Weber, B.G.; Brunner, C. The treatment of nonunions without electrical stimulation. Clin Orthop 161:24–32, 1981.

252. Weber, B.G.; Cech, O. Pseudarthrosis. Bern, Hans Huber, 1976.

253. Weiland, A.J. Current concepts review: Vascularized free bone transplants. J Bone Joint Surg Am 63:166–169, 1981.

254. Weiland, A.J.; Daniel, R.K. Microvascular anastomoses for bone grafts in the treatment of massive defects in bone. J Bone Joint Surg Am 61:98–104, 1979.

255. Weiland, A.J.; Moore, J.R.; Daniel, R.K. Vascularized bone autografts. Experience with 41 cases. Clin Orthop 174:87–95, 1983.

256. Weinberg, H.; Roth, V.G.; Robin, G.C.; Floman, Y. Early fibular bypass procedures (tibiofibular synostosis) for massive bone loss in war injuries. J Trauma 19:177–181, 1979.

257. Weresh, M.J.; Hakanson, R.; Stover, M.D.; et al. Failure of exchange reamed intramedullary nails for ununited femoral shaft fractures. J Orthop Trauma 14:335–338, 2000.

258. Wilkes, R.A.; Thomas, W.G.; Ruddle, A. Fracture and nonunion of the proximal tibia below an osteoarthritic knee: Treatment by long stemmed total knee replacement. J Trauma 36:356–357, 1994.

259. Wing, K.J.; Fisher, C.G.; O'Connell, J.X.; Wing, P.C. Stopping nicotine exposure before surgery. The effect on spinal fusion in a rabbit model. Spine 25:30–34, 2000.

260. Wiss, D.A.; Stetson, W.B. Nonunion of the tibia treated with a reamed intramedullary nail. J Orthop Trauma 8:189–194, 1994.

261. Wolff, A.M.; Krackow, K.A. The treatment of nonunion of proximal tibial osteotomy with internal fixation. Clin Orthop 250:207–215, 1990.

262. Wood, M.B.; Cooney, W.P., III. Vascularized bone segment transfers for management of chronic osteomyelitis. Orthop Clin North Am 15:461–472, 1984.

263. Wu, C.C. Humeral shaft nonunion treated by a Seidel interlocking nail with a supplementary staple. Clin Orthop 326:203–208, 1996.

264. Wu, C.C.; Shih, C.H. Distal femoral nonunion treated with interlocking nailing. J Trauma 31:1659–1662, 1991.

265. Wu, C.C.; Shih, C.H. Treatment for nonunion of the shaft of the humerus: Comparison of plates and Seidel interlocking nails. Can J Surg 35:661–665, 1992.

266. Wu, C.C.; Shih, C.H. Treatment of 84 cases of femoral nonunion. Acta Orthop Scand 63:57–60, 1992.

267. Wu, C.C.; Shih, C.H.; Chen, W.J. Nonunion and shortening after femoral fracture treated with one-stage lengthening using locked nailing technique. Good results in 48/51 patients. Acta Orthop Scand 70:33–36, 1999.

268. Wu, C.C.; Shih, C.H.; Chen, W.J.; Tai, C.L. High success rate with exchange nailing to treat a tibial shaft aseptic nonunion. J Orthop Trauma 13:33–38, 1999.

269. Wu, C.C.; Shih, C.H.; Chen, et al. Treatment of clavicular aseptic nonunion: Comparison of plating and intramedullary nailing techniques. J Trauma 45:512–516, 1998.

270. Yajima, H.; Tamai, S.; Mizumoto, S.; Inada, Y. Vascularized fibular grafts in the treatment of osteomyelitis and infected nonunion. Clin Orthop 293:256–264, 1993.

C H A P T E R **21**

The Ilizarov Method

Stuart A. Green, M.D.

In 1951, Gavriil A. Ilizarov, a surgeon working in Kurgan, Siberia, developed a circular external skeletal fixator that attached to bone segments with tensioned transfixion wires.[18] His device was a modification of other external fixators, popular at the time in the then Soviet Union, that followed the principle of connecting Kirschner wire (K-wire) bows together with threaded rods. By encircling the limb with solid rings, Ilizarov could attach two or more tensioned wires to limb segments for enhanced fixation. Moreover, his frame proved springy enough to permit axial micromotion, yet stable enough to limit translational movement. Initially, the device was used for fracture management. By adding hinges to the threaded connector rods, Ilizarov could gradually correct deformities in any plane.

When Ilizarov began using his fixator for limb lengthening, he performed the standard Z osteotomy, followed by gradual distraction and bone grafting of the resultant osseous defect. During the course of a lower extremity stump lengthening, Ilizarov observed new bone formation within the distraction gap of an individual who slowly distracted his own frame. Pursuing and extending his observations, Ilizarov developed an entire system of reconstructive orthopaedics and traumatology based on a bone's capacity to form new osseous tissue within a surgically created gap under appropriate conditions of osteotomy, soft tissue preservation, external fixation, and distraction.[23]

GENERAL INDICATIONS

With the Ilizarov method, osseous fixation is achieved with tensioned smooth Kirschner transfixion wires attached to an external fixator frame. The apparatus consists of a small number of components that can be assembled into an unlimited number of different configurations. Ilizarov and his group never use plates and screws, intramedullary nails, or even threaded external fixation pins; nevertheless, they have developed therapeutic strategies that allow a surgeon to achieve the following:

Percutaneous treatment of all closed metaphyseal and diaphyseal fractures, as well as many epiphyseal fractures

Repair of extensive defects of bone, nerve, vessel, and soft tissues without the need for grafting—and in one operative stage

Bone thickening for cosmetic and functional reasons

Percutaneous one-stage treatment of congenital or traumatic pseudarthroses

Limb lengthening or growth retardation by distraction epiphysiolysis or other methods

Correction of long bone and joint deformities, including resistant and relapsed clubfeet

Percutaneous elimination of joint contractures

Treatment of various arthroses by osteotomy and repositioning of the articular surfaces

Percutaneous joint arthrodesis

Elongating arthrodesis, a method of fusing major joints without concomitant limb shortening

Filling in of solitary bone cysts and other such lesions

Treatment of septic nonunion by the favorable effect on infected bone of stimulating bone healing

Filling of osteomyelitic cavities by the gradual collapsing of one cavity wall

Lengthening of amputation stumps

Management of hypoplasia of the mandible and similar conditions

Ability to overcome certain occlusive vascular diseases without bypass grafting

Correction of achondroplastic and other forms of dwarfism

FRACTURE MANAGEMENT

Ilizarov's fixator is first and foremost a system for acute fracture management; most patients treated with the apparatus in Russia have worn the frame for the reduction and fixation of displaced long bone fractures. When used for acute limb trauma, the Ilizarov apparatus allows anatomic repositioning of fracture fragments in a circular external skeletal fixator that is axially dynamic yet minimally invasive. A frame applied to a short, oblique, unstable tibial fracture, for example, might require only eight K-wires for reduction, approximation, and stabilization. Stiffness is imparted to the bone-fixator configuration by tensioning the wires to about 100 to 130 kg at the time the frame is applied.[1] Acute fracture fragments are reduced by a number of strategies, the details of which are beyond the scope of this chapter. In principle, one or two rings are attached perpendicular to each major bone fragment (each with at least one pair of crossed wires). The fracture is reduced and compressed by adjusting the position of the rings with respect to one another.

Ilizarov's method was ideally suited for both the Soviet style of medical care under the Communist regime and the labor-intensive medical care system that, as of this writing, has replaced it, for the following reasons:

1. Implants for internal fixation of unstable fractures are sometimes made of low-quality metals or have limited availability.
2. Periodic shortages of antibiotics—especially the second- and third-generation cephalosporins commonly used for surgical prophylaxis in the Western world—require that such medications be reserved for open fractures and established cases of sepsis, rather than as prophylactic coverage for clean implant surgery.
3. Despite a high initial cost for the apparatus, all parts except the K-wires are reusable, resulting in substantial long-term savings.
4. The labor-intensive application of circular transfixion wire external fixation constitutes no particular problem in a nation with a federalized health care system. Likewise, the high physician-to-population ratio in many areas of Russia permits a "team" of three surgeons to be available for frame application, a measure that greatly speeds up the operation.
5. Russian physicians and surgeons are well trained in topographic anatomy, which reduces the likelihood of complications from inadvertent impalement of neurovascular structures.
6. Full disability insurance, equal to a worker's wages, permits protracted time off work without concern for loss of job or other such problems and allows a more leisurely approach to post-traumatic therapeutics. Also, in a socialized medical system, frequent clinic visits and a prompt return to the operating room for a wire exchange incur no added expense.
7. Image intensification fluoroscopy is not available in general hospitals in Russia, making "closed" intramedullary nailing—the standard of care for many fractures in Western countries—all but impossible.

For orthopaedic traumatology as practiced in Western countries, the rather time-consuming application of circular transfixion wire external fixation will probably never supplant the simpler half-pin frames used to stabilize the types of injuries commonly thought to require external fixation, such as type II and type III open fractures.

Ilizarov's methods of fracture treatment will find a place in the care of displaced articular fractures requiring reduction and stabilization, especially in locations in which extensive internal fixation has proved risky, such as at the lower end of either the tibia or the humerus. After all, the usual method of managing such injuries includes reduction and stabilization with K-wires, followed by the application of more extensive internal fixation components. With the Ilizarov method, the K-wires used for reduction are left in place and attached to an external skeletal fixator, which is secured to intact bone elsewhere on the limb, minimizing the amount of hardware at the site of injury. Closed diaphyseal fractures are treated in circular fixators only if well-controlled studies demonstrate that the Ilizarov apparatus is clearly superior to other methods of care.

Ilizarov's techniques will find their greatest applications in the field of traumatology for post-trauma reconstruction dealing with nonunions, malunions, post-traumatic osteomyelitis, and residual limb shortening.

To understand how the Ilizarov techniques work, it is important to understand the features of his method that encourage bone formation within the distraction gap of a cortical osteotomy.[21, 22, 30] The biologic principles that are required for optimizing neoosteogenesis include the following:

- Maximal preservation of marrow blood supply with a percutaneous "corticotomy-osteoclasis" instead of an open transverse osteotomy.
- External skeletal fixation stable enough to eliminate shear at an osteotomy or fracture site, yet springy enough to allow micromotion in the bone's mechanical axis.
- A delay (latency) after surgery of about 1 week (although this could be more or less, under certain circumstances) before commencement of distraction for limb lengthening or opening a wedge.
- A distraction rate of 1.0 mm/day, modified, if necessary, by the characteristics of regenerate bone formation in the distraction gap.
- Distraction in frequent small steps—at least four times daily (0.25 mm every 6 hours)—instead of in a single step.
- Physiologic use of an elongating limb—a measure that promotes rapid ossification of the newly formed bone. (Obviously, the fixator must be comfortable for the patient and permit an adequate range of joint motion.)
- A period of neutral fixation after distraction to permit the regenerate bone to strengthen, with this period lasting at least as long as the time needed for limb lengthening or correction of a deformity, and possibly longer.

EXPERIMENTAL BACKGROUND

To confirm the importance of these measures, Ilizarov and co-workers performed a series of experiments utilizing a canine tibia model and the Ilizarov transfixion wire-circular external skeletal fixator.[21, 22]

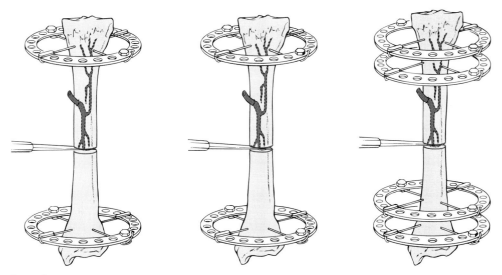

FIGURE 21-1. An experimental design to study the effect of fixator stability on new bone formation during distraction. Open transverse osteotomies were performed in the tibias of dogs that were in external fixators of differing stabilities. The configuration for the first group consisted of two rings loosely affixed to bone with wires. The second group wore more stable fixators of two rings secured to the bone with tensioned wires. The third group of animals were stable in a four-ring frame, each ring of which was affixed to bone with a pair of tension wires. (From Ilizarov, G.A. Clin Orthop 238:250, 1989.)

In the first group of experiments, an open transverse osteotomy of the midtibia was performed, followed by application of a circular external fixator in three configurations of progressively increasing stability. In the first configuration, a two-ring frame was applied with a pair of loosely attached wires at each ring level. In the second configuration, a two-ring frame was also used, but a pair of crossed wires was fixed with tension to each ring. The third (most stable) fixation consisted of a four-ring frame, with each ring affixed to bone with a pair of tensioned crossed wires (Fig. 21–1).

Following a 5-day delay after fixator application, the osteotomy sites were distracted at a rate of 0.125 mm every 6 hours. Ilizarov and co-workers[21] observed that the unstable frame with loosely attached wires led to a fibrous nonunion with, in some cases, full-shaft width displacement at the osteotomy site (Fig. 21–2). The more stable two-ring configuration with tensioned wires led to patchy areas of bone and cartilage formation but ultimately resulted in a pseudarthrosis in most cases (Fig. 21–3). The most stable configuration (four rings) led to direct osteogenesis without intervening cartilage formation (Fig. 21–4).

As part of that study, Ilizarov and co-workers[21] used the same rate of distraction and the four-ring fixator configuration to study a second variable: preservation of blood supply (Fig. 21–5). Three types of osteotomy were performed in this series:

1. Open transverse osteotomy with transection of the bone marrow and nutrient vessels
2. Open transverse osteotomy with transection of only one third of the bone marrow
3. Closed osteoclasis using the apparatus and a curved wire to crack the bone, using the mechanical advantage gained by the apparatus

FIGURE 21-2. The animals maintained in unstable two-ring fixators developed fibrous nonunions with focal areas of hemorrhage and fibrous tissue formation in the distraction gap. (From Ilizarov, G.A. Clin Orthop 238:257, 1989.)

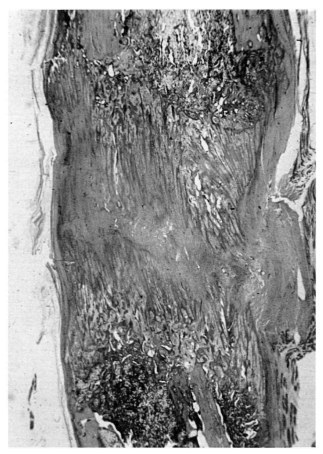

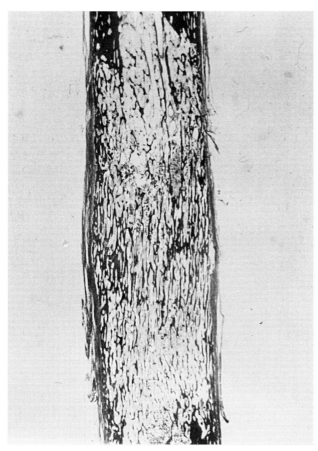

FIGURE 21–3. The animals with two-ring configurations secured to bone with tension wires demonstrated the formation of cones of bone attached to the endosteal canal and areas of cartilage formation in the distraction gap. (From Ilizarov, G.A. Clin Orthop 238:257, 1989.)

FIGURE 21–4. The most stable configuration (four rings) led to direct osteogenesis in the distraction gap without intervening cartilage formation. (From Ilizarov, G.A. Clin Orthop 238:258, 1989.)

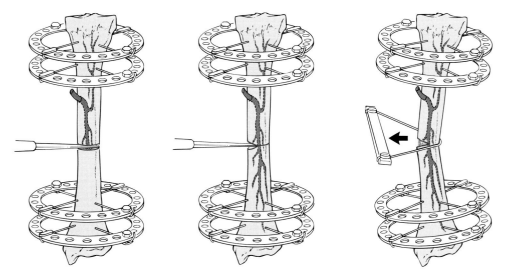

FIGURE 21–5. A study to define the effect of preservation of blood supply. The canine tibia was used in a stable four-ring configuration (each ring was affixed to bone with crossed tension wires). In the first group of dogs, the osteotomy was performed with open technique, transecting the marrow and nutrient artery. In the second group of dogs, an open osteotomy-corticotomy was performed, but only one third of the marrow was transected by the osteotome. In the third group of dogs, the osteotomy was performed by a closed osteoclasis technique using tension developed by the apparatus. The study demonstrated that the best quality of bone formation was associated with the maximal preservation of blood supply. (From Ilizarov, G.A. Clin Orthop 238:250, 1989.)

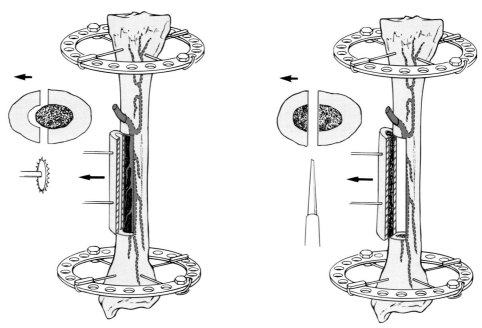

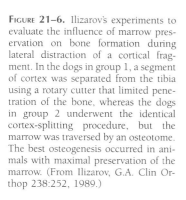

FIGURE 21–6. Ilizarov's experiments to evaluate the influence of marrow preservation on bone formation during lateral distraction of a cortical fragment. In the dogs in group 1, a segment of cortex was separated from the tibia using a rotary cutter that limited penetration of the bone, whereas the dogs in group 2 underwent the identical cortex-splitting procedure, but the marrow was traversed by an osteotome. The best osteogenesis occurred in animals with maximal preservation of the marrow. (From Ilizarov, G.A. Clin Orthop 238:252, 1989.)

The researchers observed that the greater the preservation of bone marrow, the better the quality of new bone formation within the distraction gap.

In the second series of experiments, Ilizarov's group widened canine tibias instead of lengthening them (Fig. 21–6). A split-off segment of tibia, constituting approximately 40% of the bone's length and 30% of the cortical circumference, was moved laterally (after a 3-day delay following osteotomy) by an Ilizarov apparatus modified for lateral traction. In half the animals, the bone was cut with a rotary cutter that limited damage to the marrow, whereas in the other half, the marrow was transected with an osteotome. The new bone that formed was parallel to the lateral distraction vector (i.e., perpendicular to the bone's mechanical axis) (Fig. 21–7).[21] As with longitudinal lengthening, damage to the marrow decreases new bone formation.

In the third experiment, also using the canine tibia, bone was lengthened, after either open osteotomy or closed osteoclasis, at three different rates of distraction (0.5 mm, 1.0 mm, and 2.0 mm) in combination with a second variable: the frequency of distraction (1 step/day, 4 steps/day, or 60 steps/day in an autodistractor). It was learned that a rate of distraction of 0.5 mm/day often led to premature osseous consolidation (Fig. 21–8),[22] whereas a distraction rate of 2.0 mm/day resulted in damage of periosseous soft tissue and suboptimal new bone formation. The best results were achieved with a distraction of 1.0 mm/day. Ilizarov and co-workers[20] also observed that the more highly fractionated the distraction frequency, the better the outcome. Thus, distraction at 60 steps/day resulted in a better quality of bone formation than 4 steps/day which, in turn, produced better neoosteogenesis than distraction at 1 step/day (Fig. 21–9).[22] Likewise, the periosseous soft tissues—including the nerves, fascia, blood vessels, muscles, and skin—responded more favorably to a highly fractionated distraction, which mimicked

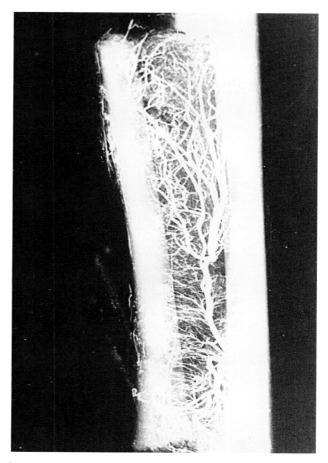

FIGURE 21–7. Neovascularization takes place during lateral distraction of a split-off cortical bone fragment. (From Ilizarov, G.A. Clin Orthop 238:266, 1989.)

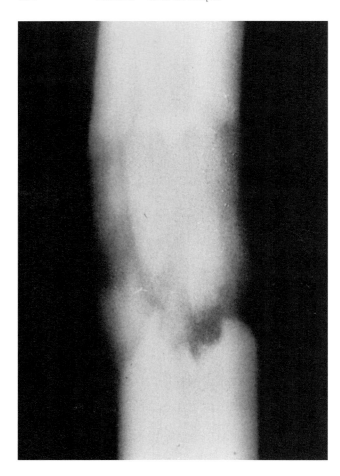

Figure 21–8. A canine experiment to evaluate the effect of the rate of distraction. In this animal, distraction at a rate of 0.5 mm/day in four divided steps led to premature consolidation of the bone in the distraction gap. A secondary fracture occurred at the lower end of the distraction gap between the newly formed bone and the original distal shaft fragment. (From Ilizarov, G.A. Clin Orthop 239:268, 1989.)

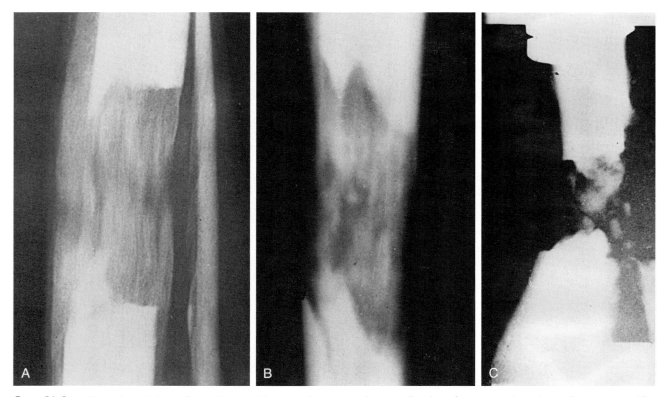

Figure 21–9. *A,* Distraction at 1.0 mm/day in 60 steps with an autodistractor results in excellent bone formation in the widening distraction gap. The growth zone of the distraction regeneration is a dark band that zigzags across the center of the newly formed bone. *B,* Distraction at a rate of 1.0 mm/day in 4 steps results in satisfactory bone formation. *C,* Distraction at a rate of 1.0 mm in 1 step (following open osteotomy) results in poor quality of the newly formed bone. (*A–C,* From Ilizarov, G.A. Clin Orthop 239:268, 1989.)

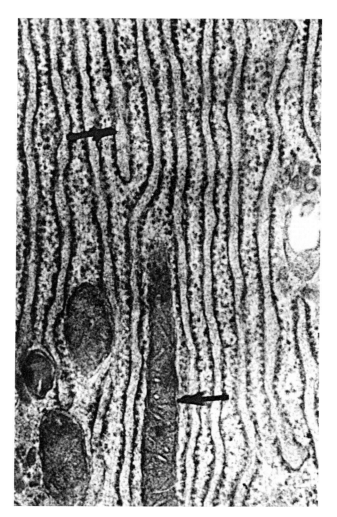

FIGURE 21-10. Under optimal conditions of distraction and stabilization, osteoblasts possess elongated organelles, with stretched-out endoplasmic reticulum forming parallel rows (*upper arrow*) and elongated mitochondria (*lower arrow*). (From Ilizarov, G.A. Clin Orthop 238:270, 1989.)

the natural process of growth (Figs. 21–10 and 21–11).[22] Moreover, with a 60 step/day autodistractor (85 µm every 24 minutes), changes within the elongating tissues took on histologic and electron microscopic features characteristic of cellular growth during embryonic, fetal, and neonatal life (Fig. 21–12).[22]

Clearly, Ilizarov discovered a previously hidden biologic plasticity of osseous tissue. With his techniques, a surgeon can create a sort of growth plate anywhere in bone that ossifies in both the proximal and the distal directions from a central growth zone during distraction (Fig. 21–13).[22] Consolidation of the entire regenerate region takes place during the neutral fixation period that follows distraction.

TRANSFIXION WIRES

Transfixion wire external fixators use smooth K-wires for attachment to bone; therefore, fixation is not secure unless two or more wires are used at each level of fixation. For maximal stability, the two wires should cross each other at a right angle at each plane of fixation.[1] Unfortunately,

anatomic considerations limit the surgeon's ability to insert wires crossing at 90° within the bone. For this reason, transfixion wires usually end up crossing each other at a more acute angle, thereby diminishing fixator stability. To overcome this problem, the surgeon must either use more than two wires at each plane of fixation or insert additional wires away from—or oblique to—the ring's plane of fixation. For added stability, Ilizarov's fixation system also utilizes beaded wires to prevent the bone from sliding along the wire.

INSERTING TRANSFIXION WIRES

When inserting wires, an important technical principle is to avoid necrosis of tissues at the time of insertion. Necrosis of the soft tissues can be caused by either wrapping up of tissues, excessive tension, or thermal injury from heat build-up during drilling.[8, 9, 11, 17]

With transfixion wires, a spinning bayonet point may wrap up soft tissues, causing necrosis (Fig. 21–14). Therefore, the surgeon should push transfixion wires straight through the tissue to the bone before turning on the drill. If the wire misses the bone, the surgeon should withdraw it completely and reinsert it rather than redirecting it within the limb's tissues.

At times, when inserting a transfixion wire with a motorized chuck, wire flexibility may cause the wire to bend, reducing accuracy of placement. For this reason, whenever inserting a wire, manually grasp the wire close to its tip to stabilize it. Because a spinning wire can wrap up surgical gloves, hold the wire with a wet 2 × 2-inch gauze pad (Fig. 21–15).

When inserting transfixion wires into bone with a power drill, the dense cortical bone, by offering substantial resistance to the wire point's progress, may cause heat build-up, which hardens the bone even more, resisting additional progress of the wire point. For this reason, the drill should be stopped every few seconds, using a stop-start action to advance the wire slowly through hard osseous tissue. Furthermore, complete intracortical insertion of a wire—not accompanied by the "feel" of crossing the marrow to encounter a second cortex—is especially prone to excessive heat build-up, thermal damage, and the possibility of wire hole osteomyelitis.

As soon as a transfixion wire's point penetrates a bone's far cortex, the surgeon should not continue drilling, because the spinning wire tip might damage tissues on the limb's opposite side. Instead, the surgeon should grasp the wire with pliers and hit the pliers with a mallet to drive the wire through (Fig. 21–16).

A most important principle when using any transfixion implant: if the tip of a wire (or pin) emerges from the opposite side of a limb either smoking or too hot to be comfortably held between the surgeon's fingertips, then the wire should be withdrawn, cooled, and reinserted elsewhere. With transfixion wires, it is necessary to check the range of motion to make sure that no undue tension occurs during the anticipated range required while the fixator is on the limb. If necessary, a wire should be reinserted if movement of an adjacent joint causes skin tension around a wire.

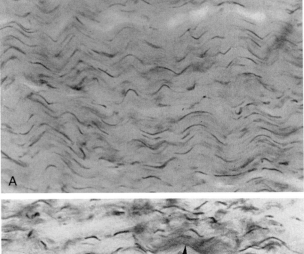

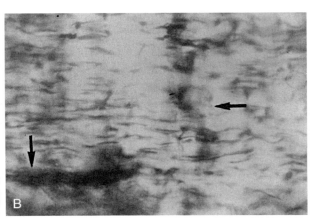

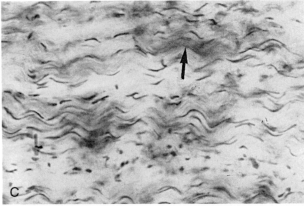

FIGURE 21–11. *A,* Resting fascia has a wavy shape under light microscopy. *B,* Distraction of fascia at a rate of 1.0 mm in one step produces pulled-out collagen fibers and areas of focal homogenization (*arrows*). *C,* Distraction at a rate of 1.0 mm/day in four steps results in retention of the wavy shape of collagen fibers but with a few patches of focal homogenization. Numerous fibroblasts are seen in the lower portion of the field. (*A–C,* From Ilizarov, G.A. Clin Orthop 239:272, 1989.)

Certain important techniques of transfixion wire insertion ensure maximal functional limb use and joint mobility:

• Avoid impalement of tendons.
• Avoid (whenever possible) transfixing synovium.
• Penetrate muscles at their maximal functional length.

This last rule—critically important for a successful long-term application—means that the position of a nearby joint must change as a wire passes through the

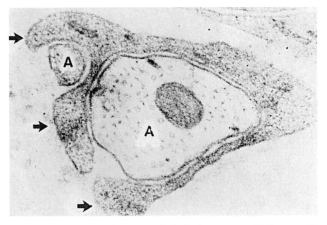

FIGURE 21–12. During elongation of a limb, the nerves and Schwann cells take on the histologic characteristics seen during fetal and embryonic growth. A Schwann cell (*arrows*) is seen in the two developing axons (A). (From Ilizarov, G.A. Clin Orthop 238:272, 1989.)

flexor and extensor muscle groups. For example, when the surgeon is inserting a wire from anterolateral to posteromedial in the distal femoral metaphysis, the knee should be flexed to 90° before the wire is inserted through the quadriceps; the wire is then pushed straight down to the femur before drilling. The wire is driven through the bone with a power drill. As soon as the wire point emerges through the far cortex, the surgeon should stop drilling, extend the knee, and hammer the wire through the limb's opposite side.

When inserting a wire into the lower leg, the surgeon should plantar flex the foot when transfixing the anterior compartment, invert the foot when inserting wires into the peroneal muscles, and dorsiflex the foot during triceps surae impalement.

When a wire is being inserted near a tendon, a simple technique helps the surgeon avoid tendon transfixion. First, palpate the worrisome tendon to determine its exact course and location. Next, holding the transfixion wire in one hand (do not attach the wire to a drill), palpate the position of the tendon with the other hand, and poke the wire through the skin down to, but not quite touching, the bone. Then, wiggle the structure ordinarily moved by the tendon in question. For example, dorsiflex and plantar flex the ankle when a wire is inserted near the tibialis anterior tendon. If the wire tip has impaled the tendon, the wire will move as the involved part is put through a range of motion. If this occurs, withdraw the wire and reinsert it in a slightly different position.

Once wires are in place, after the final frame configu-

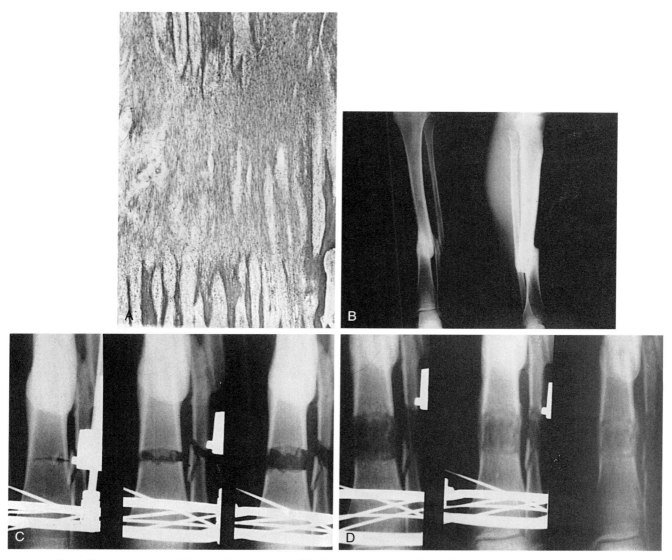

FIGURE 21-13. *A,* Electron micrograph of the central (growth) zone of the distraction regenerated bone. Fibroblast-like cells appear in a relatively avascular central zone, forming collagen fibers that are oriented parallel to the tension-stress vector of elongation. Osteoblasts appear in the vascularized spaces between the collagen fibers and form bone directly on the collagen molecules. The newly formed bone condenses into trabeculae proximally and distally. *B,* Anteroposterior and lateral projection radiographs of a 32-year-old woman with 4 cm of tibial shortening following an injury incurred while skiing. *C,* A distal tibial and fibular corticotomy was performed using the Ilizarov technique. Distraction started on postoperative day 7. The rate was 0.25 mm every 6 hours. *D,* Progressive ossification of the distraction gap occurred during the neutral fixation period that followed elongation. (*A–D,* From Ilizarov, G.A. Clin Orthop 238:262, 1989.)

ration is established, it is important to put the adjacent joints through a range of motion to be sure that the wires do not interfere with joint motion by causing excessive soft tissue tension at the end of either flexion or extension. When transfixion wires are used, bending the wire for ring attachment may cause excessive soft tissue damage, as the wire, being very narrow, concentrates pressures over a small area. For this reason, transfixion wire fixator systems use special strategies to ensure that a wire is not bent during frame attachment. The original Ilizarov equipment uses washers, posts, and other hardware to achieve this goal. Other circular fixators use other techniques. In any case, the principle of not bending a wire when attaching it to a frame is a critical element to successful tensioned wire external fixation (Fig. 21–17).

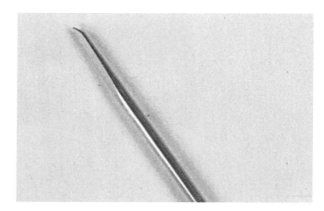

FIGURE 21-14. The bayonet point of an Ilizarov wire can wrap up soft tissues, a possible source of deep sepsis. When inserting a wire, push the implant straight through the tissues down to bone before the wire starts to spin.

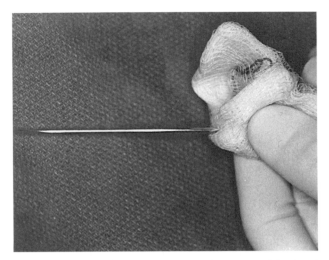

FIGURE 21–15. To stabilize a wire, grasp it with a moistened 2 × 2-inch gauze sponge.

PIN TECHNIQUES

Many circular fixator systems permit supplementary fixation with threaded pins. This technique is especially helpful for proximal femur mountings, because transfixion wires in this region must exit through the buttocks—a situation requiring special beds and chairs for the patient. Also, a high rate of wire sepsis occurs in this region. For these reasons, the Ilizarov method has been modified for the proximal femoral mounting to include half pins for fixation. At Rancho Los Amigos Medical Center, we have had excellent success with configurations that use half pins in many different locations,[9, 10, 12, 15] based on the observation of DeBastiani and associates[5] that good regenerate bone forms in a distraction gap if one follows Ilizarov's biologic principles of marrow preservation, stability, latency, and distraction.

These observations suggest that half pins may be substituted for transfixion wires at one or both ends of an

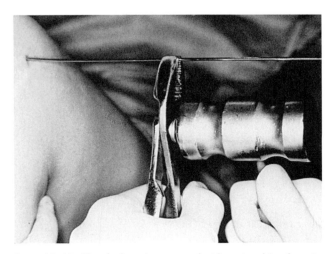

FIGURE 21–16. After the bone is penetrated with a wire, drive the point of the wire through the skin on the opposite side of the limb with pliers and a mallet.

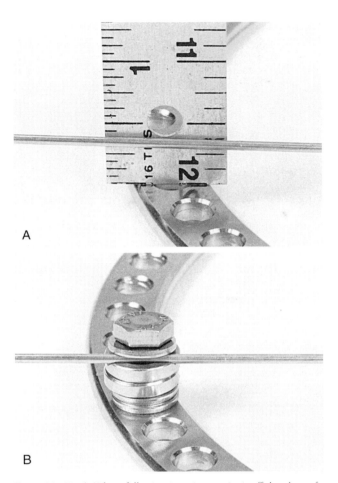

FIGURE 21–17. *A,* When, following insertion, a wire is off the plane of a ring, do not bend the wire to the ring. (This creates undue soft tissue tension.) *B,* Instead, build up hardware to secure the wire where it lies.

external fixator configuration when the frame is used for many, if not all, Ilizarov-type applications. Numerous experienced surgeons have started using half pins in place of wires in many Ilizarov-type fixator configurations (Fig. 21–18).

The use of pins made from a titanium alloy rather than stainless steel has led to a reduction in implant site sepsis at Rancho Los Amigos Medical Center.[10, 15] This observation has been made with respect to other orthopaedic implant systems as well, including total joint implants and intramedullary nails. To elucidate the mechanism of titanium tissue tolerance, Pascual and co-workers added powdered stainless steel, pure titanium, titanium alloy, and cobalt chromium to mixtures of bacteria and viable human polymorphonuclear leukocytes.[29] The investigators then measured respiratory burst activity (a measure of intracellular bacterial killing by white blood cells [WBCs]) at various times after the beginning of incubation. They found that titanium and, to a lesser extent, cobalt chromium, resulted in only a slight inhibition of normal respiratory burst activity when compared with the inoculum that did not contain any metallic powder. Stainless steel, on the other hand, caused a marked reduction in respiratory burst activity, suggesting interference with a critical step in the bactericidal activity of human WBCs.

This inhibition of a vital cellular function probably has the effect of reducing host resistance to implant site sepsis.

The toxic effect of steel on cellular function may be related to the elution of certain metallic ions—perhaps nickel or chromium—from the implant's surface. The use of titanium pins does not completely eliminate pin site sepsis; the effect is to reduce the incidence of pin tract infections by about 50%.[15] Moreover, I have noted that when implant site infections do occur around titanium pins, the problem stays localized to the immediate environment around the implant. Extensive cellulitis that extends for many centimeters around the pin hole (a common phenomenon when stainless steel pins are used) occurs rarely, if at all, with titanium alloy implants.

Despite a substantial reduction in the rate of implant site sepsis during the past two decades, pin and wire site infections remain the principal drawback to the use of external skeletal fixation. Moreover, many additional problems commonly associated with external fixation, such as undue pain and decreased limb usage while in the frame are often secondary consequences of implant-skin interface sepsis.

Two strategies designed to further reduce implant site sepsis have been developed; both involve coating the implants. Because pin site infections are often associated with implant loosening, any technology that reduces the

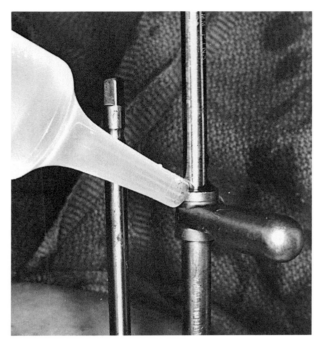

FIGURE 21–19. Irrigate the drill bit with cooled irrigating solution.

possibility of loosening should also decrease the incidence of pin infections. Based on this logic, hydroxyapatite (HA)-coated pins have been developed that reproduce the osseous integration that occurs with HA-coated total joint implants.[3] Clinical studies have confirmed the lower rate of pin site sepsis associated with HA-coated implants.[28] A comparable reduction in pin site sepsis may be associated with the use of titanium pins and wires, rather than those made of stainless steel.

The second technique designed to reduce pin or wire site sepsis involved coating the implants with an antimicrobial substance. So far, silver is the only such substance that has been extensively tested. Proponents of silver-coated pins claim a reduced pin site infection when such implants are used.[31]

A threaded pin—especially a modern one with self-cutting flutes at the tip—can wrap up soft tissues in the thread's grooves. For this reason, surgeons should always use a trochar and sleeve to insert threaded pins into bone.

Surgeons should not use a power drill to insert a threaded pin directly into bone, because heat build-up at the pin's point could cause a thermal injury to the bone. Instead, the bone hole should be predrilled with a sharp fluted drill bit and a drill sleeve and the pin inserted by hand.

When drilling, the surgeon should stop the drill every few seconds to allow the cutting tip to cool down. The heat generated by drilling not only damages the bone but also "work hardens" osseous tissue, which then resists further advancement. A worthwhile practice is to irrigate the exposed portion of the drill bit to cool it and conduct heat away from the tip (Fig. 21–19).

If much resistance is encountered during drilling, check the drill bit tip between the fingertips for excessive temperature. If the tip cannot be comfortably held for 15 or 20 seconds, the implant should not be left in the bone

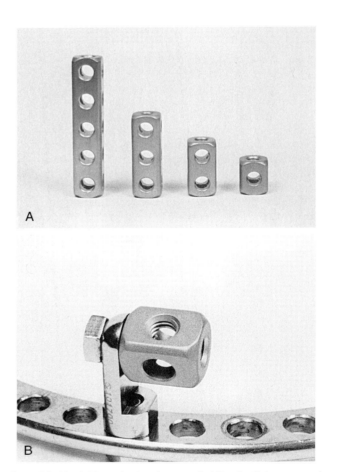

FIGURE 21–18. *A*, Ring-gripping clamps, called Rancho Cubes, are used to secure pins to Ilizarov rings. *B*, A Rancho swivel assembly is used to secure a nonperpendicular pin to a ring.

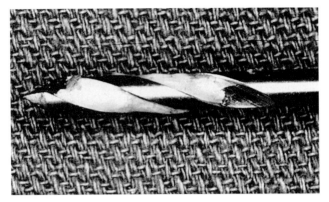

FIGURE 21–20. The bone in the flutes of a drill bit should be white, never black or brown (a sign of thermal injury to bone).

hole, as there will be necrotic (thermally injured) bone in communication with the pin's bacteriologic environment—a setup for chronic osteomyelitis. Instead, the pin (wire) should be inserted elsewhere. Likewise, the bone in the drill bit's flutes should be white, never black or brown, which is a sign of burned bone (Fig. 21–20).

THE IMPLANT-SKIN INTERFACE

After inserting a wire or pin but *before* attaching it to the frame, check the skin interface for evidence of tissue tension while the limb is in its most functional position—that is, with the knee extended and the ankle at neutral. Interface tension creates a ridge of skin on one side of a wire or pin. Incise the ridge to enlarge the skin hole around either a transosseous pin or an olive wire. Close the enlarged hole with a nylon suture on the side of the wire opposite the released ridge.

When the ridge of skin is adjacent to a smooth wire, slowly withdraw the wire (with pliers and a mallet) until its tip drops below the skin surface. Allow the skin to shift to a more neutral location, and advance the wire again

until it passes through the skin in an improved position (Fig. 21–21).

If the interface tension exists on the insertion side of a limb, snap off the wire's blunt end obliquely to create a point, and advance the wire to just below the skin surface by the pliers-mallet method on the limb's far side. Tap the wire back through the skin after making a position adjustment.

MOUNTING STRATEGIES

Juxta-articular Mountings

One might wonder why we should be concerned with the composition of the wire available when the preceding section recommended the use of half pins for external fixation. I have come to the conclusion that in certain anatomic locations, wire mounts are actually superior to pin mountings, regardless of the material from which the implant has been fabricated. In general, wires provide better fixation in the juxta-articular regions of a long bone, whereas half pins are generally superior for diaphyseal locations.

Threaded pins are less than ideal for fixation of cancellous bone near a joint surface for several reasons. First, threads do not hold well in spongiosa, especially if any degree of osteopenia is present. Second, even when a threaded pin achieves initial stability in a juxta-articular fragment, the passage of time frequently leads to loosening, because the loss of a very small volume of bone around the implant diminishes fixation more rapidly than a comparable loss of bone volume around a threaded implant secured in cortical bone. Third, once the fixation of a half pin in a cancellous bone has been decreased by resorption of osseous tissue from around the implant, a substantial hole has been created in the bone fragment that limits the anatomic options for additional or subsequent fixation.

On the other hand, when a wire is used to secure juxta-articular fragments, the bone hole is tiny, and the

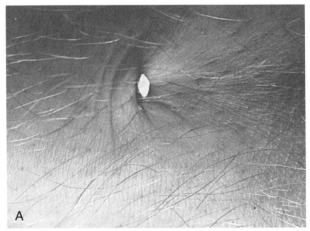
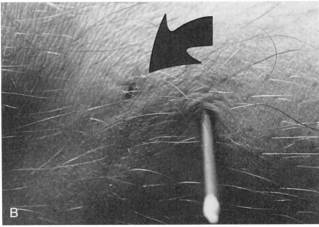

FIGURE 21–21. The wire-skin interface. *A,* Tension on the skin is caused by a transfixion wire. To correct the situation, withdraw the wire to below skin level, allow the skin to shift to a neutral position, and (*B*) drive the wire forward. The *arrow* points to the original wire hole.

loosening that does occur becomes established without creating a very large hole. Furthermore, multiple cross wires can be placed in a fairly small fragment, thereby creating a trampoline effect that supports the bone. Also, in most locations, there are no muscle bellies surrounding juxta-articular bone. For the most part, such fragments are adjacent to either tendons or neurovascular structures that can, with care, be avoided during wire placement. Moreover, most of these neurovascular structures are either anterior or posterior to the articular bone fragments, leaving the mediolateral corridor for safe wire insertion.

The clinical techniques of fracture reduction and deformity correction with circular external fixation by Ilizarov's methods require that the surgeon understand the relationship between the moving bone fragment's initial position and its final position with respect to the stationary bone fragment that serves as the frame of reference for the reduction maneuver. There are four ways that the moving fragment can change position to effect a reduction: angulation, translation, rotation, and axial shortening or lengthening. With the classic Ilizarov fixator configuration, separate assemblies are used to achieve each one of these displacements, although angulation and shortening can often be combined in one maneuver by placing the hinge axis at a distance from the edge of the bone along the line that divides the deformity angle in half, the *bisector line*. In some cases, translation can also be corrected with the same mechanism that realigns angulation and shortening, but only in situations in which the translational offset is in the same plane as the angulation and shortening. In all other cases, separate assemblies must be constructed to eliminate the different deformities.

Taylor realized that regardless of the number of assemblies needed to reduce or align bone fragments, the moving bone makes a single pathway from its displaced position to its reduced position. In some situations, the pathway may be a straight line, and in other cases, the pathway may be spiral or otherwise curved, but the nature of that path can be determined in advance by noting the three-dimensional location of the starting position of the fragment with respect to a frame of reference, and mathematically comparing that position with the final position. Indeed, it is not necessary to consider the entire moving fragment to define the pathway. Instead, a single point on the moving fragment may be used as a substitute for the whole fragment as long as the relationship of the point to the rest of the fragment remains unchanged as the fragment moves through space from its starting position to its final position.

Likewise, if the moving fragment is secured to a ring (or block of rings) and the stationary fragment is secured to another ring or block of rings, then the rings can be considered as part of their respective fragments. Therefore, correction of the deformity or displacement via the rings will correct the osseous deformity as well. Indeed, this is a basic Ilizarov concept. The unique feature of the method that considers the pathway that the moving bone fragment must take as the route to alignment of the fragments is the application of engineering principles to the problem of deformity correction and fracture fragment reduction. Connecting the ring surrounding the moving fragment to the ring of the stationary fragment with six struts allows for complete repositioning of the moving ring by adjusting the lengths of the struts. In this manner, the gradual reduction of a displaced fracture, or the correction of a deformity, or limb elongation or compression in its own axis can be accomplished with ease, provided the exact relationship between the rings and their respective bone fragments are known, as well as the precise position of the rings with respect to each other.

The reduction-repositioning system must be used with a computer program that details the precise amount of lengthening or shortening of each strut required to gradually move a bone fragment into position. With such a program, it is also possible to designate a particular neurovascular bundle as being at risk of stretch injury if the bone fragment is moving too rapidly from its initial to final position. With this information, combined with a parameter that defines the maximum tolerable stretch of the structure at risk, the computer program can tell the clinician how fast the struts can be lengthened without causing injury to that structure.

To use the spatial frame successfully, several parameters must be entered into the computer, including a numerical description of the exact relationship of the fragments to their respective rings in all planes, as well as precise measurements defining both the initial and final position of the moving fragment with respect to the stationary fragment. This particular feature of the system has proved to be most troublesome to surgeons comfortable with the classic Ilizarov reduction techniques, in which errors in measurement are correctable without much difficulty by using the proper correction assemblies, even when they are added to the fixator long after it was applied to the patient. Nevertheless, the system is popular with surgeons who have become familiar with its features.

Hybrid Mountings

For more substantial fragments that include not only the articular end of the bone but also the metaphyseal region, various combinations of pins and wires have proved successful for mount external fixation. The stability of these mounting strategies has been studied by Calhoun and associates.[3] They analyzed a number of different pin and wire combinations to determine the amount of stability available as one converts from an all-wire mounting technique to one that uses only half pins. Using two crossed tension wires as the standard, Calhoun and associates learned that the popular **T** configuration (consisting of a transfixion wire and perpendicular half pin) is not as stable as two tension wires crossed at 90°. Indeed, Calhoun and associates[3] learned that whenever a wire is removed from a circular fixator mounting plan, it should be replaced by two half pins. Thus, stability comparable with that produced by two tensioned wires at 90° to each other requires one wire and two half pins in a reasonable geometric configuration.

At Rancho Los Amigos Medical Center, we are fond of using certain configurations in the periarticular and epiphyseal-metaphyseal regions of bones that, in our clinical experience, have proved to be stable. The first of

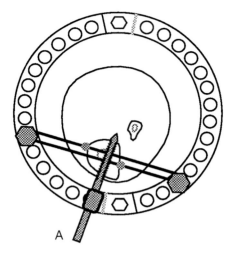 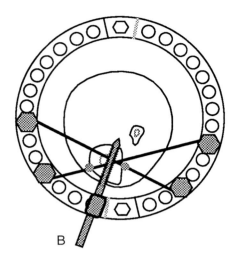

FIGURE 21–22. The **H** mounting. *A,* With parallel counterpulling beaded wires. *B,* With crossed counterpulling beaded wires.

these mountings is what we call the **H** mounting, consisting of two counterpulling olive wires at about the same level and a single half pin, which is either perpendicular to the two wires or at some angle between 60° and 120° to the wires (Fig. 21–22*A*). Alternatively, the wires can be crossed with respect to each other (see Fig. 21–22*B*). Usually, the wires are placed in the coronal plane, so the crossing angle between them cannot be too great. This configuration is especially valuable in the distal radius, calcaneus, and scapula (Fig. 21–23).

The **T** mounting, consisting of a single wire and a perpendicular half pin (Fig. 21–24), is not particularly stable, as noted by Calhoun and associates.[3] The **T** mount, however, can be considered stable if the wire also passes

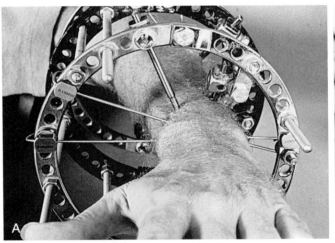 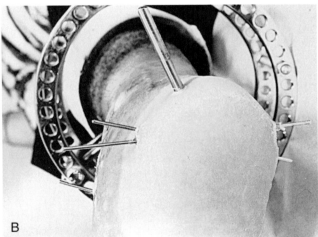

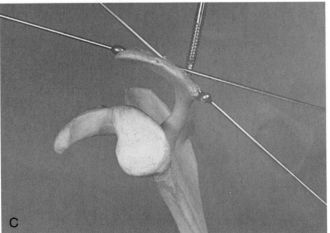

FIGURE 21–23. The **H** mounting of wrist (*A*), calcaneus (*B*), and scapula (*C*).

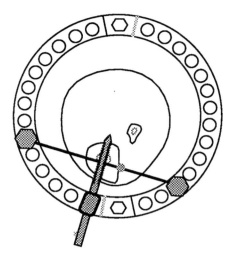

FIGURE 21–24. The T mounting.

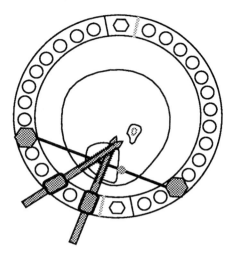

FIGURE 21–26. The A mounting.

through an intact bone. For example, transfixing the distal radius and ulna with a single wire would then require only a single half pin to complete the mounting of the distal radius fragment. Of course, the radius cannot be lengthened when it is fixed to the ulna, but such a configuration is useful in bone transport cases and similar mounting needs (Fig. 21–25).

Another strategy we often use is the **A** mounting, in which two half pins are inserted at the same or nearly the same transverse level in the bone, with the angle between them measuring from 60° to 120°. A single wire (preferably an olive wire) is then inserted perpendicular to the line bisecting the angle between the half pins (Fig. 21–26). (The crossed implants make up the letter **A** within the bone.) This mounting is useful for a proximal tibial fixation (Fig. 21–27).

It is often possible to use titanium half pins in juxta-articular regions, especially if the bone is of good quality. In relatively stable situations, two half pins at right angles will suffice—a **V** configuration (Fig. 21–28). In other cases, more stability can be achieved by employing three half pins in a **W** configuration (Fig. 21–29). We have developed a mounting configuration for the distal femur that secures the condyles without synovial penetration. We first insert K-wires in the coronal plane from distal to proximal, crossing each other 6 mm apart. We next employ a cannulated drill bit to enlarge the K-wire tracts, drilling from proximal to distal. The 6-mm threaded half pins are inserted into the drilled holes from the proximal to the distal direction. A supplementary half pin is added for additional fixation (Fig. 21–30).

TECHNIQUES

Corticotomy

To preserve both the periosseous and the intraosseous soft tissues at the time of osteotomy, Ilizarov developed techniques for percutaneous osteotomy of a bone without transecting the marrow's nutrient vessels. The procedure is called a *corticotomy* if performed in the metaphyseal region of a bone and a *compactotomy* if accomplished in the diaphysis.[26] Through an incision no wider than a narrow osteotome, a small periosteal elevator (or "joker") is used to elevate the periosteum as far around the bone in both directions as possible. Next, a starting notch is made in the bone's near cortex, followed by progressive intracortical advancement of the osteotome, first on one side of the bone and then on the other. Because the osteotome tends to jam as it advances, the surgeon must twist or wiggle the blade within the bone's cortex to make room for further advancement. One should not be overly concerned if the osteotomy crosses the marrow on occasion. Instead, distraction can be delayed 2 to 3 days beyond the planned latency interval.

The opposite cortex is cracked by rotating the os-

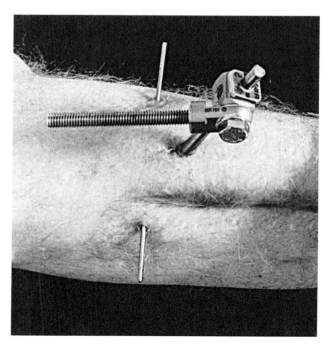

FIGURE 21–25. The T mounting in the ulna for bone transport.

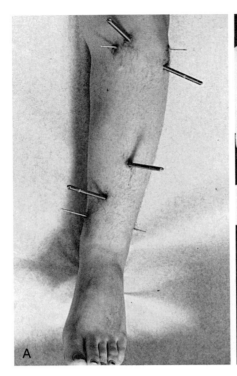
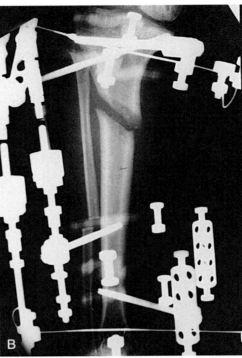

FIGURE 21–27. A mountings in the proximal and distal tibia. *A*, Photograph of the configuration. *B*, Radiograph of the configuration.

teotome 90° within the cortical cuts on both sides of the bone or, alternatively, by performing a closed osteoclasis in torsion by counterrotation of the rings attached to each bone segment. (The distal fragment should always be rotated externally, as internal rotation might unduly stretch the peroneal nerve in the leg or the radial nerve in the arm.)

Because the object of a corticotomy is to create a nondisplaced fracture, it is important to restore the bone to its precorticotomy alignment immediately after completing the procedure. To accomplish this, the external fixator must already be secured to the limb before the bone is osteotomized. Obviously, an intact external fixator would prevent torsional osteoclasis of a bone's far cortex. Therefore, the surgeon must disconnect from the rings all longitudinal rods traversing the corticotomy level. After

corticotomy, the rods must be reattached to their original position—and at their original length—thereby reestablishing the precorticotomy alignment of the bone. To ensure correct alignment, the surgeon should count the holes in the rings, making note of the position of each connecting rod before removing it. Short, threaded sockets can be used between a ring and the threaded rods connected to it, or one-hole posts can serve the same function. The sockets or post can be detached from one ring before corticotomy and reassembled afterward.

Latency

There is a latency (delay) before distraction commences, the purpose of which is to allow the first stage of fracture

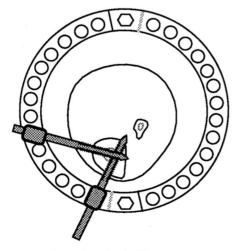

FIGURE 21–28. The **V** mounting.

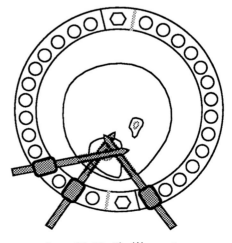

FIGURE 21–29. The **W** mounting.

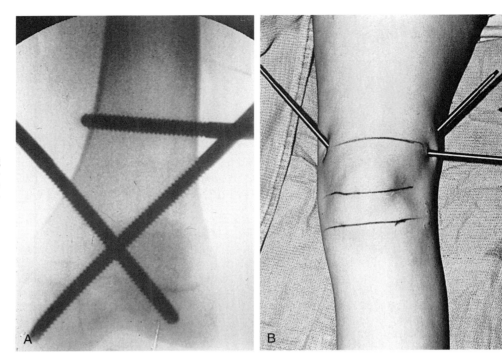

FIGURE 21–30. The **W** mounting for the distal femur avoids trans-synovial pins or wires. *A*, Radiograph of the mounting. *B*, Photograph of the pin configuration.

healing to begin. During distraction, corticotomy site fracture healing tries to "catch up" with the distracting bone ends but under most circumstances does not consolidate the regenerate bone within the distraction gap until the neutral fixation period after elongation.

Generally speaking, the delay is 5 to 7 days, but this can be lengthened or shortened under certain circumstances. When the corticotomy is oblique, the latency should be shortened by 1 to 2 days because oblique corticotomies heal more rapidly than transverse ones. Latency should be prolonged if (1) the osteotome seems to have crossed the marrow canal during corticotomy, (2) there has been considerable comminution at the site of corticotomy (delay should be 3 or 4 days), (3) there has been substantial displacement of the major fragments during corticotomy, and (4) fragments were counterrotated (during torsional osteoclasis of the posterior cortex) more than 30°.

If the bone is of poor quality—either extremely dense or osteopenic—the latency interval should be increased up to 14 days, especially if the soft tissues surrounding the bone are also of suboptimal quality.

Distraction

After latency, the corticotomy gap is usually distracted 0.25 mm every 6 hours. This rate and frequency may be altered, depending on the clinical circumstances. For an adult with dense bone and suboptimal surrounding tissues, a more appropriate rate and frequency would be 0.25 mm every 8 to 12 hours.

Transport Wires

Wires that move a major bone segment through tissues by firmly securing the segment to a movable ring are called transport wires. Usually two crossed wires are used for this purpose; if only one wire is used, the transported segment may twist on that wire's axis. As the transport ring is gradually moved along the fixator frame, the transport wires cut through soft tissues by causing necrosis ahead of the wires; the skin and tissues heal behind the wires. In this manner, transport wires cut through soft tissues as a hot wire cuts through ice. Because the transport wires' movements are gradual, there is little pain associated with the transport process; nevertheless, the area of focal necrosis at the wire's leading surface often becomes infected, as one might expect with any wire causing soft tissue damage by compression. The inflammation surrounding the necrotic area causes patient discomfort. A serous or purulent discharge often accompanies the process. Usually the inflammation stops once bone transport has been completed; nevertheless, I maintain patients on oral antistaphylococcal antibiotics as soon as soft tissue inflammation appears during the course of bone fragment transportation.

When planning to move a bone segment through a limb by way of transport wires, the surgeon must consider both the initial and the final positions of the transport wires, as well as the path the wires will cut through soft tissues. With longitudinal bone segment movement, the transport wires generally move parallel to neurovascular structures and tendons; thus, little likelihood for transection of such structures exists. However, one should recognize the danger of a proximally moving transport wire entering the bifurcation of a nerve or vessel.

Directional Wires

One or more directional wires may be used to pull a bone segment through soft tissues. For this purpose, olive wires, kinked wires, or twisted wires can be used. The technique involves the following: One or two wires are driven obliquely through bone, exiting the soft tissues on the limb's opposite side. The tips of the wires are curved with pliers; by grasping the proximal end of the wire with pliers and striking the pliers with a hammer, the surgeon can back out the wire until the tip is under the skin.

Once the tip is within the soft tissues, the wire is slowly wiggled and advanced (with pliers and a hammer) until the tip moves up the limb. Usually the wire point emerges somewhere in the region of the skeletal defect. Thereafter, the surgeon may have to bend the wire in another direction, withdrawing the wire below the skin line, and advance the wire through the skin farther along the limb. The process of tip protrusion, wire bending, retraction, and advancement may have to be repeated to achieve the optimal final wire position. It may be helpful to rotate the wire 180° so that the curve points away from the limb. The wire's curved end readily passes through the skin without the point's scratching intact skin near the exit hole. As a trick to help determine the direction of the wire's curve, one can bend the proximal end to a right angle, pointing in the same direction as the tip's curve.

In most instances the longitudinal directional wires used for compression-distraction osteosynthesis emerge through the skin adjacent to the target segment. The wires are then secured with nuts into the groove of threaded rods for progressive traction (after the usual latency interval).

Unfortunately, longitudinal directional wires end up at a rather oblique angle to the bone's mechanical axis as the transport process nears completion. For this reason, the directional wires may become progressively less effective in achieving the final stages of interfragmentary compression. When this occurs, the patient must return to the operating room for removal of the directional wires and application of an additional ring and transverse wires as the defect closes.

Problems with treating nonunions and pseudarthroses seem to arise more frequently at the site of original pathology than at the region of elongation. Atrophic nonunions do not magically unite because a transfixion wire external fixator has been applied to a limb. For this reason, Ilizarov's group in Kurgan has developed numerous strategies to encourage bone healing at a site of a likely delayed union, whether due to limited bone contact, atrophic bone ends, or related difficulties.[19, 20, 27]

MANAGEMENT OF NONUNIONS

Although individual nonunion patterns require treatment strategies tailored to the patient, certain general therapeutic strategies can be applied to common nonunion configurations. As a rule, the principles described later apply to cases in which both bone ends are viable—that is, both sides of the nonunion demonstrate proliferative changes on roentgenographic evaluation. If the nonunion has characteristics of a true synovial pseudarthrosis (i.e., formation of a false joint cavity lined with synovium and filled with synovial fluid), then the cavity must be entered surgically and the fibrocartilaginous ends of the bone scraped down to osseous tissue before the treatment plans

outlined later can be put into effect. In some cases it may be sufficient to introduce a curette into a false synovial cavity through a stab incision to débride the bone ends. Ilizarov claims that compression of a synovial pseudarthrosis for 2 weeks—enough time to cause necrosis of fibrocartilage and an inflammatory reaction—may be sufficient to stimulate healing.

If the radiographs demonstrate a pencilin-cup appearance of the pseudarthrosis, in which only one side of the nonunion is showing proliferative changes while the other fragment appears to have the same contour that was present immediately after the injury, the side of the nonunion demonstrating no progress toward healing may be nonviable. In some cases a bone scan will clarify the issue, demonstrating lack of circulation in osseous tissue of questionable viability. If bone scans are to be used in this manner, it is important to obtain a three-phase study, with an initial scan taken shortly after injection of the radionuclide so that the nonviable bone end can be more readily distinguished from any surrounding periosteal tissue reaction. If substantial doubt remains about the viability of the osseous tissue in question, the surgeon should explore the wound. Likewise, if there is persistent or recurrent drainage from the site of the nonunion, débridement of nonviable and marginally viable osseous tissue is necessary, in accordance with the principle described earlier in this chapter. Thereafter, the skeletal defect must be closed by the technique of bone transport. In the absence of nonviable tissue, several strategies can be applied to nonunions. These are discussed in the sections that follow.

Transverse Nonunion without Shortening

Hypertrophic nonunions without shortening and in good axial alignment have long been treated with external skeletal fixation, as well as a variety of other methods. In many cases a percutaneous or open fibular osteotomy or a slice fibular ostectomy may be necessary to promote union. In these situations, the strategy of axial compression usually ensures union, especially if the nonunion is hypertrophic (Fig. 21–31).

A two-ring, three-ring, or four-ring configuration can be applied, depending on the intrinsic stiffness of the fracture configuration. (The more stable the nonunion, the fewer the rings.) If the limb shortening is less than 1.5 cm, no lengthening will be necessary.

Transverse Nonunion with Shortening

In some situations a transverse nonunion with a satisfactory mechanical alignment of the bone may be accompanied by shortening because of traumatic bone loss or a healed fracture elsewhere in the bone. In these situations the surgeon might be inclined to compress the nonunion while performing a lengthening corticotomy elsewhere on the limb. Such a treatment plan is not necessary; instead, the principle of monolocal consecutive compression-distraction osteosynthesis can be applied. By this technique, a nonunion site is first compressed for 2

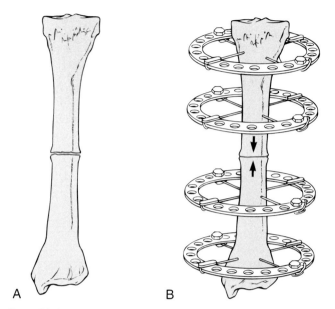

A

B

FIGURE 21–31. *A,* A transverse nonunion of the tibia without shortening or angulation. *B,* Compression of a transverse nonunion of the tibia with a stable four-ring configuration.

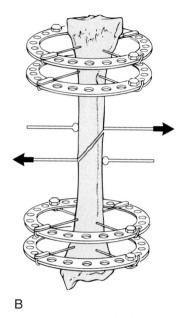

A

B

FIGURE 21–33. *A,* An oblique hypertrophic nonunion of the diaphysis without shortening or angulation. *B,* Treatment with olive wires that provide interfragmentary compression while the fixator acts as a compressor.

weeks and then gradually distracted (Fig. 21–32). The compression stimulates neoosteogenesis, and the distraction stimulates the formation of regenerate bone in the elongating gap. The standard frequency of distraction (0.25 mm every 6 to 12 hours) is used. Bone will fill the distraction gap. If necessary, the hypertrophic nonunion may have to be realigned gradually so that the mechanical axes of both the proximal and the distal fragments are collinear.

Oblique Nonunion without Shortening

In situations in which the fracture line is oblique rather than perpendicular to the bone's mechanical axis, simple

longitudinal compression causes the bone fragments to slide past each other, leading to limb shortening. When there is an oblique nonunion line, it is necessary to achieve side-to-side (transverse) compression combined with compression in the bone's mechanical axis (Figs. 21–33 and 21–34). Such side-to-side compression can be achieved in a number of ways:

1. Olive wires traversing the fracture site from opposite directions, applying interfragmentary compression by way of the apparatus.
2. Rings applied close to the fracture site, achieving transverse compression toward and away from longitudinal plates in the configuration.

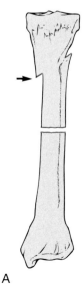

FIGURE 21–32. *A,* A transverse hypertrophic nonunion of the tibial shaft and the concomitant shortening elsewhere in the bone *(arrow). B,* Management was by compression of the hypertrophic nonunion for 2 weeks, followed by distraction to overcome shortening. *C,* Distraction of a hypertrophic nonunion results in new bone formation if the osteogenic process has been stimulated.

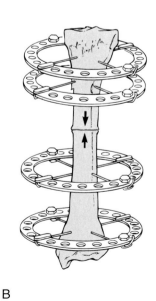

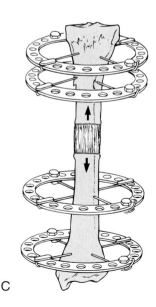

A

B

C

3. "Arched wires," a technique frequently used for fracture reduction whereby transfixion wires are passed through a bone segment and slightly curved in the direction the surgeon wishes to translate the bone segments. The wires are then tightened to straighten them, thereby moving the bone segment toward the concavity of the curve of the wires. Side-to-side interfragmentary compression must be combined with axial compression in the bone's mechanical axis.

Oblique Nonunion with Shortening

This common pattern of nonunion can occur anywhere along the length of the bone. Although the surgeon's inclination might be to attempt side-to-side compression with the bone as it lies, a far more acceptable strategy is to distract the limb to overcome shortening, while at the same time using the rings of the apparatus to simulta-

neously restore the bone's mechanical axis and achieve side-to-side compression (Fig. 21–35). To achieve this goal, it is necessary to construct the frame with the rings closest to the nonunion site sliding along the apparatus during distraction, while at the same time applying transverse traction to the bone ends. To accomplish this, the sliding mechanism that connects the innermost rings to the apparatus can be made with either a buckle (which slides along the plate) (Fig. 21–36) or, alternatively, a bushing that has a nut on either side of it; the bushing will slide along any threaded rod (Fig. 21–37). Because the bushing has a tapped hole in its side, it can be used to connect a ring to the rod while allowing a translation movement in the ring.

Once the distraction has been completed, final adjustment in the ring position should be made to allow restoration of the bone's mechanical axis. Finally, axial compression combined with side-to-side compression should achieve union.

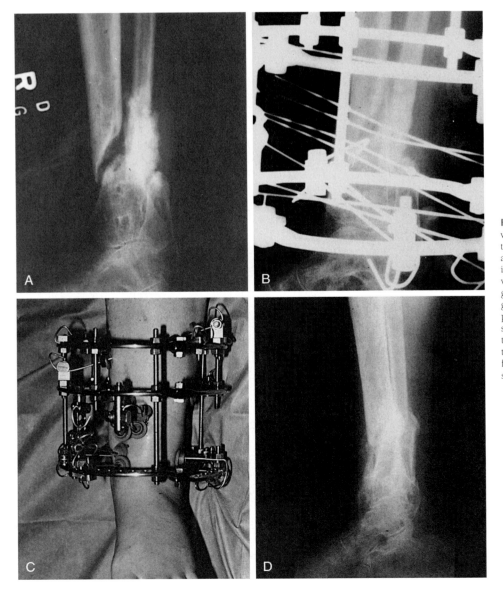

FIGURE 21–34. *A,* A 45-year-old woman with an oblique nonunion of the distal tibia. There had been a previously attempted plating followed by serious infection, with a skin slough. The wound is now closed as a result of skin grafting. *B,* A lateral projection radiograph of the reduction with counterpulling olive wires. *C,* The apparatus seen from the frontal plane. The counterpulling olive wires are attached to the three-hole post, projecting downward from the middle ring. *D,* The final result shows consolidation.

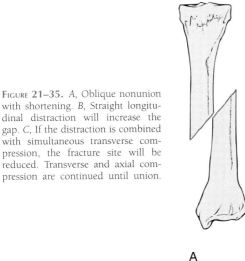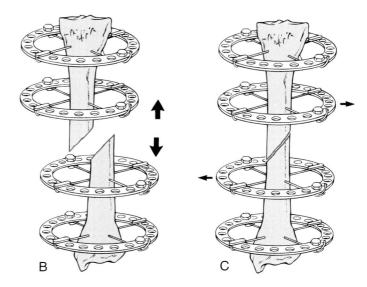

FIGURE 21–35. *A,* Oblique nonunion with shortening. *B,* Straight longitudinal distraction will increase the gap. *C,* If the distraction is combined with simultaneous transverse compression, the fracture site will be reduced. Transverse and axial compression are continued until union.

A   B   C

Angulated Nonunion without Shortening

When a nonunion is angulated, the surgeon should restore the bone's mechanical alignment as nearly perfectly as possible before compression. The technique employed follows the principles of deformity correction. A hinge (or pair of hinges) is placed in the fixator configuration with the axis of the hinge located over the apex of the deformity (Fig. 21–38). (In most cases two hinges are used, with the axis of the hinges forming an imaginary line that passes through the deformity's apex.) Frequently the apex of the deformity is somewhat difficult to ascertain. Standard radiographs in the anteroposterior and lateral projections often demonstrate a deformity in two planes—for example, with the apex posterior on the lateral projection and lateral on the anteroposterior projection. A thoughtful analysis of such a deformity, however, reveals that the deformity, or any deformity for that matter, can exist in only one plane, with the apex posterolateral. To best determine the plane of the deformity, it may be necessary to obtain radiographs of the limb at several oblique projections, with the projection demonstrating the maximal angular deformity being the one that most truly represents the deformity's plane; moreover, the plane of the deformity is perpendicular to the radiographic projection that shows the bone to be straight. Obviously, rotation, translation, or other axial deviations can be included with an angular deformity, but the angular deformity itself can exist in only one plane.

When there is good bone contact and hypertrophic changes on both sides of the nonunion line, the fixator is applied with a pair of rings on the proximal fragment and a pair of rings on the distal fragment; each fragment's rings are perpendicular to that fragment's mechanical axis. Hinges are placed between the proximal and the distal ring clusters, and the nonunion site is compressed for 2 weeks, thereby increasing the deformity slightly. After the preliminary compression, the deformity is gradually corrected, utilizing a threaded distractor on the concave side. Usually, twisted plate and post assemblies are used to accomplish the distraction. If the nonunion is stiff, a "push configura-

tion" can be used, using a plate on the deformity's convex side stabilized to the proximal and distal rings with twisted plates and effecting a pushing action on the rings adjacent to the site of nonunion. With either configuration, it is necessary to calculate the rate of correction at the point

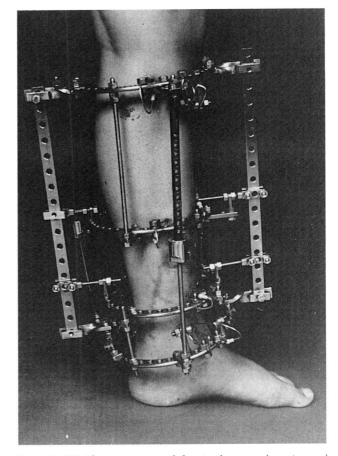

FIGURE 21–36. The apparatus used for simultaneous elongation and side-to-side compression when treating an oblique hypertrophic nonunion with shortening. The 17-hole plates allow sliding of buckle assemblies that push or pull the middle two rings.

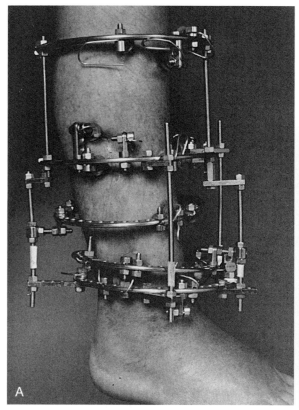

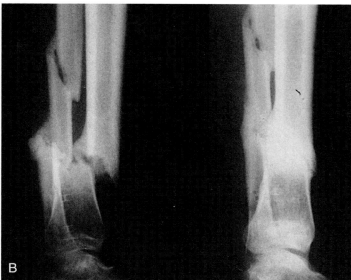

FIGURE 21–37. *A,* Another configuration to provide simultaneous elongation and transverse compression. In this case, bushings slide along threaded rods during lengthening and simultaneously provide a fixation point for transverse compression of the third and fourth rings in the configuration. *B,* Pretreatment and post-treatment radiographs of the same patient (a hypertrophic nonunion of the distal tibia 8 months after an open fracture).

of either distraction or push to correspond to an opening of the base of the deformity at a rate of 1.0 mm/day in divided segments. When the deformity is fully corrected, the nonunion site will have a wedge configuration with triangular regenerate bone filling the gap (see Fig. 21–38*B*).

Angulated Nonunion with Shortening

In many nonunions, shortening without translation may accompany the angulation. In this situation the deformity can be corrected while limb length is simultaneously restored by using a distraction wedge technique. The

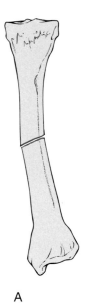

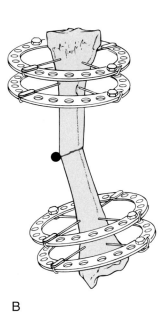

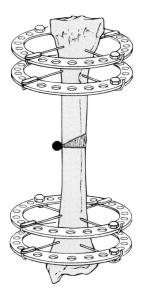

FIGURE 21–38. *A,* Angulated non-union without shortening. *B,* The treatment of an angulated hypertrophic nonunion without shortening involves the placement of a hinge (*black dot*) at the apex of the deformity. The rings of the apparatus are applied perpendicular to the mechanical axis of their associated segments. Gradual distraction (after initial compression) should result in a triangle of regenerated bone in the widening gap.

A   B

regenerate bone within the distraction gap will become trapezoidal, with its length corresponding to the amount of limb elongation (Figs. 21–39 and 21–40). To achieve this goal, the apex of the hinges for deformity correction is placed at a distance away from the bone, which can be determined by making acetate cutouts and rotating the fragments around a thumbtack hinge.

Angulation Nonunion with Translation without Shortening

Many angulated nonunions display some element of translation; if the angular deformity is corrected, the axes of the proximal and distal fragments will not be collinear. Such a residual displacement can often be corrected in a single maneuver based on Ilizarov's concept of a translational hinge. The apex of the hinge must be located at the intersection point of two lines that follow the edge of the bone fragments on the deformity's convex side. A simpler method is to make cutouts of the fracture, placing each cutout on a separate sheet of clear acetate or x-ray film, and to perform the rotation through a thumbtack hinge. It is usually necessary to correct the angulation before correcting the displacement (Fig. 21–41).

Angulated Nonunion with Translation and Shortening

When there is angulation, translation, and shortening, alignment of the bone fragments can be restored utilizing a translational hinge, but the apex of the hinge must be displaced from the convex edge of the deformity by a distance that corresponds to the amount of shortening present. One can use Ilizarov's formula or cutouts for this correction. The shortening must be corrected before the translation, lest one bone fragment block repositioning of the other (Fig. 21–42).

Nonunion with Rotational Malalignment

If there is a rotational deformity combined with angulation, displacement, or shortening, the rotation should be corrected last. A gradual twist distributed over the entire length of the regenerate is more satisfactory than rotation through the corticotomy site that tears at the healing tissue (Fig. 21–43). Another important point: Whenever a rotational correction must be made, it is easier to correct the rotary deformity once the mechanical axis of the bone has been restored to normal, as the surgeon will be dealing with a problem in only one plane. When correcting a rotational malalignment, be sure that the bone segments in question are in the center of the configuration rather than in the more customary eccentric location. If this step is not taken, the bone fragments will rotate around an imaginary axis in the center of the configuration, thereby becoming displaced with respect to each other when the rotation is completed. This principle must be considered whenever a fixator is initially applied to correct the deformity. Obviously, a derotation assembly should be included in the configuration.

Segmental Defects

SEGMENTAL DEFECTS WITHOUT SHORTENING

When a segmental defect is present, angulation, translation, and rotation can be easily corrected at the time the fixator is in place, as the soft tissues in the defect will be sufficiently pliable to allow restoration of the bone's mechanical axis.[13] Thus, the frame configuration for segmental defect management is actually quite a bit simpler than one applied to correct a deformity, because all the rings can be in a straight line. If, after the fixator is applied, an axial displacement, angulation, or rotation is noted, the correction should be done on the operating table while the patient is still anesthetized. Because the

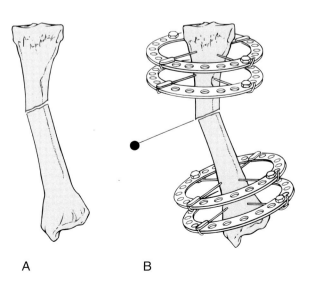
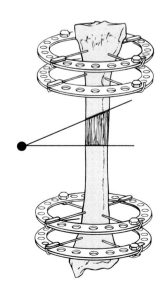

FIGURE 21–39. *A,* Angulated hypertrophic nonunion with shortening. *B,* Correction of the problem with a hinge *(black dot)* in the configuration located at some distance from the apex of the deformity. The rings of the apparatus are applied perpendicular to the mechanical axis of their associated segments. Gradual distraction leads to the formation of a trapezoidal regeneration that simultaneously achieves deformity correction and lengthening.

A   B

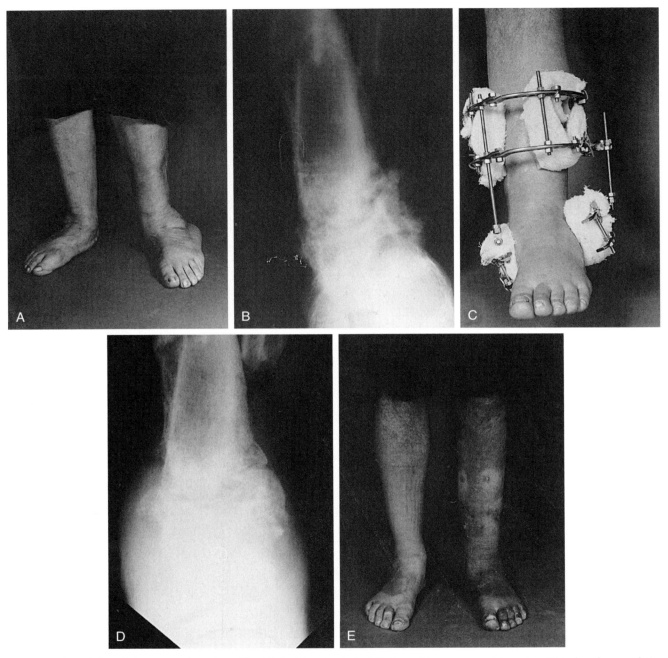

Figure 21–40. *A,* A clinical photograph of a patient with a failed ankle arthrodesis. *B,* Radiographic appearance of the patient. Note the valgus angulation of the failed tibiotalar arthrodesis site. *C,* The apparatus used for correction of the deformity. The distal rings are perpendicular to the hindfoot axis, and the proximal rings are perpendicular to the tibial axis. A lateral distraction assembly is effecting a slow correction. *D,* A gradual realignment of the talus under the tibia has occurred. *E,* A clinical photograph of the patient 1 month after removal of the fixator.

strategy for defect treatment usually involves corticotomy and bone transport, the intercalary transported segment must be in perfect alignment with the target fragment before the corticotomy is performed or the fragments will not be aligned at the completion of bone transport.

When planning the solution to the problem of a segmental defect, the final contact point between the intercalary and the target fragments must be considered before the two bone ends meet. The most stable configuration occurs when one fragment invaginates into the other until firm contact between the exterior surface of the inner

fragment makes circumferential contact with the endosteal surface of the receptacle fragment. As it turns out, however, this process of invagination is at odds with the principle of collinearity between the fragments, because a point carved in the cortex of the intercalary fragment would probably become displaced as it penetrated into the target fragment. Nevertheless, it is surprising how often jagged fragment ends are left after a post-traumatic skeletal deficiency, whether because of an absolute loss of bone at the time of initial injury or as a consequence of débridement.

When the skeletal defect follows a segmental resection of infected osseous tissue, it is advisable to square off the bone ends to create a transverse point of contact (Fig. 21–44). Bear in mind, however, that there is a significant incidence of long delays in bone healing when two seemingly parallel bone surfaces come together. For one thing, the bone "carpentry work" is seldom perfect, so contact is usually made at a high point on one or the other of the cut bone surfaces. Also, it is likely that cutting the bone with an oscillating saw may damage viable bone several cell layers into the tissue. For this reason, it is safer to use an osteotome (or chisel), followed by careful rasping of the cut surfaces and then by roughing up the smooth surface of the cut bone ends with a curette or rongeur after squaring off bone fragments. In any event, if there is delayed union at the point of contact between the intercalary and the target segments, a small cancellous bone graft can be packed around the region to promote healing.

In some situations a surgeon might be tempted to resect abnormal bone, immediately compress the site of pathology, and compensate for the resultant shortening by limb elongation through healthy tissues. Although this proposal is appealing, I have found that immediate compression of a segmental defect larger than 2.5 cm distorts the surrounding soft tissues, making wound closure difficult and leading to edema distal to the area of compression, possibly because of distortion and kinking of lymphatic vessels. For this reason, it is wiser to leave a segmental defect and the surrounding soft tissues at full length and close the defect by the technique of bone transport.

When extensive segmental débridement of nonviable bone is required, one end of the residual osseous tissue can be fashioned into a point while the other side is made trough shaped. After transport of an intercalary bone segment, the point is impaled into the trough, ensuring good bone contact and stability (Figs. 21–45 and 21–46).

PARTIAL SEGMENTAL DEFECT WITHOUT SHORTENING

A method of dealing with a partial segmental defect (i.e., when one cortex is long enough to achieve contact, but there is substantial deficiency of the remaining cortical bone) is to use the method of splinter fragment transport. With this technique, a lengthwise split is created in the

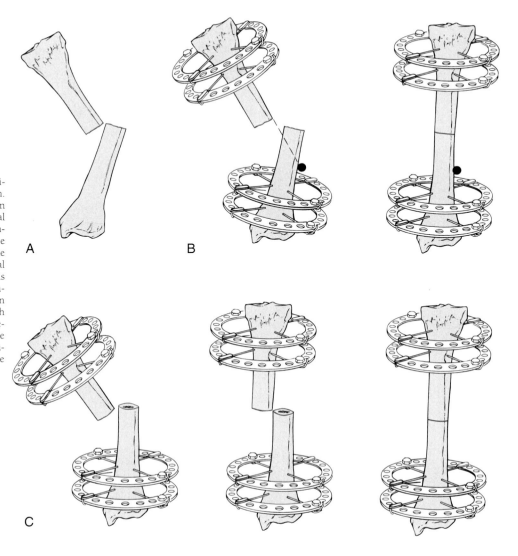

FIGURE **21–41.** *A,* Nonunion associated with angulation and translation. *B,* In some cases, the deformity can be corrected with a distractional hinge *(black dot).* The center of rotation is placed along a line at the intersection of the cortices, along the convex side of the deformity. Gradual correction results in simultaneous correction of the deformity and elimination of the translation. *C,* An alternative strategy for dealing with angulated displaced nonunions. Sequential elimination of, first, the angulation and, second, the translation results in elimination of the deformity.

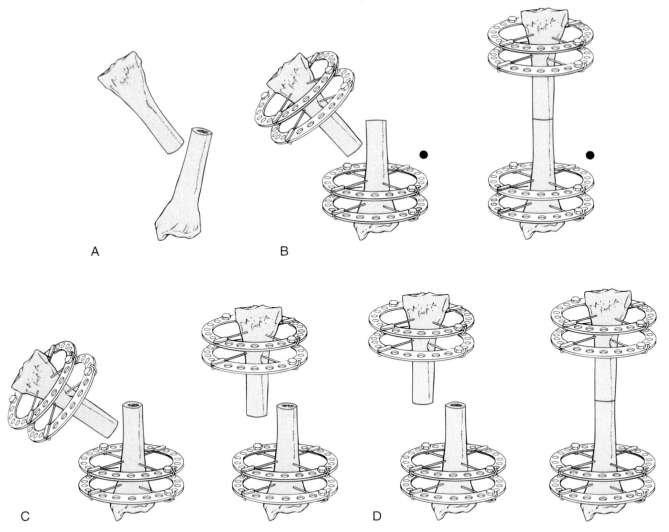

FIGURE 21–42. *A,* A nonunion associated with angulation, translation, and shortening. *B,* In some cases, a translation hinge *(black dot)* placed with its axis at a distance from the point of intersection of the convex edge of the fracture fragments results in correction of angulation, shortening, and translation. *C,* An alternative strategy is sequential correction of the deformity, with angulation corrected first, followed by correction of shortening, and, as the last step, correction of translation *(D).*

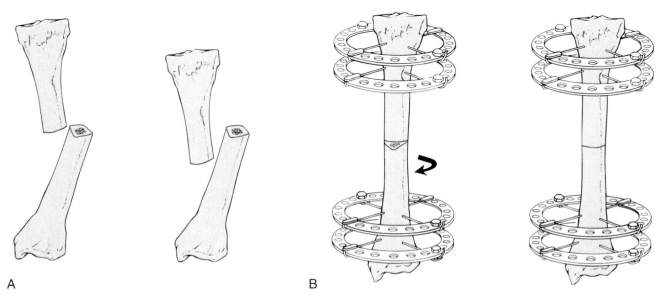

FIGURE 21–43. *A,* Nonunions that combine rotation, angulation, and displacement, with and without shortening. *B,* In both cases, rotation is corrected last; moreover, the axes of the bone fragments must be collinear and in the center of the configuration before malrotation is corrected, lest gradual counterrotation of the fragments result in axial displacement of one with respect to the other.

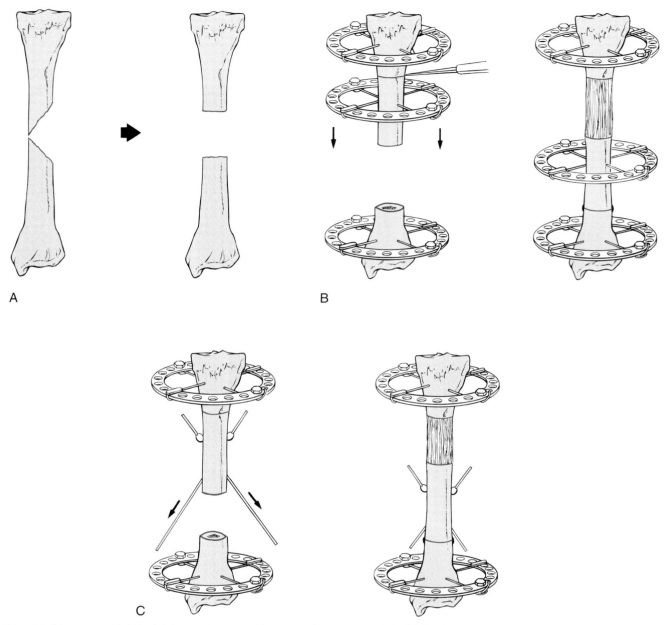

A

B

C

FIGURE 21–44. *A,* A partial skeletal defect can be converted to a complete transverse skeletal defect for reconstruction by the bone transport method. *B,* With a complete transverse defect, a corticotomy through healthy bone is followed by gradual transport of the intercalary segment toward the target segment. New bone forms in the distraction gap. *C,* Crossed directional wires can be used in place of a transport ring to move an intercalary bone segment through a limb.

cortex involving approximately half of the cortical circumference. The split fragment is then drawn longitudinally across the defect, after an appropriate delay, until it makes contact with the target bone on the other side of the gap (Fig. 21–47).

SEGMENTAL DEFECT WITH SHORTENING

When a segmental defect is accompanied by shortening, the problem can be overcome by performing a bone transport procedure identical to the one described in the preceding section. However, after contact and compression between the intercalary and the target fragments, the limb

is lengthened through the corticotomy site, moving the intercalary and target fragments together as a unit away from the corticotomy gap (Figs. 21–48 and 21–49).

In situations requiring lengthening in limb segments with paired bones, both bones will be short (Fig. 21–50*A*). In the lower leg, after completing the bone transport to eliminate a tibial defect, it will be necessary to osteotomize the fibula to restore limb length. If the surgeon performs the bone transport before limb elongation, an osteotomy of the shortened fibula will have already healed before elongation commences (see Fig. 21–50*B*), necessitating a return trip to the operating room for a repeat fibular osteotomy. A wiser strategy is to lengthen the limb,

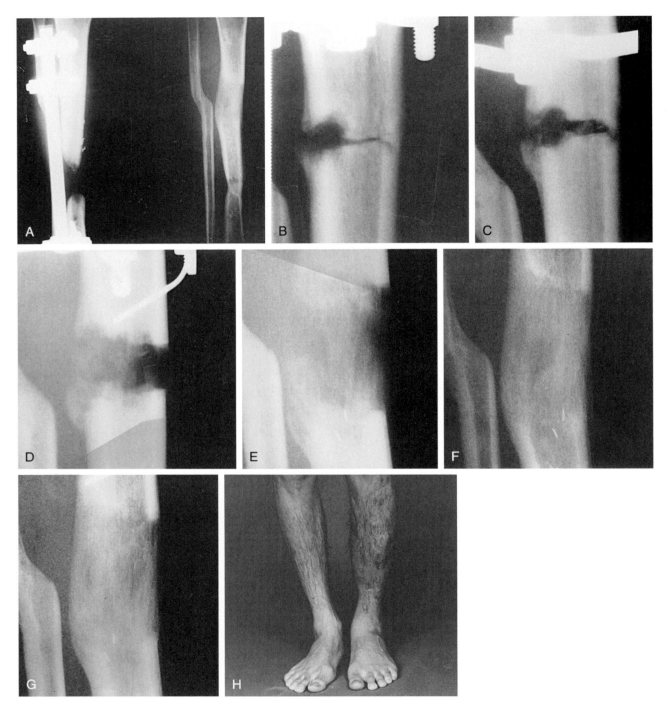

FIGURE 21–45. *A*, Pretreatment and post-treatment radiographs of a 5-cm skeletal defect. There is also a cavitary osteomyelitis around the lower pin in the upper segment (on the left). The radiograph on the right shows the tibia after the fixator has been removed. *B*, A corticotomy performed through the area of cavitary osteomyelitis (which was not draining at the time). *C*, Appearance at the beginning of distraction. *D*, Appearance at approximately 1.5 cm of bone transport. Note the new bone forming in the corticotomy gap. *E*, Appearance at 3.0 cm of bone transport. *F*, Appearance at the completion of bone transport. Note the elimination of the cavity. *G*, Further maturation of the bone in the distraction gap at the end of treatment. *H*, Appearance of the patient at the completion of treatment.

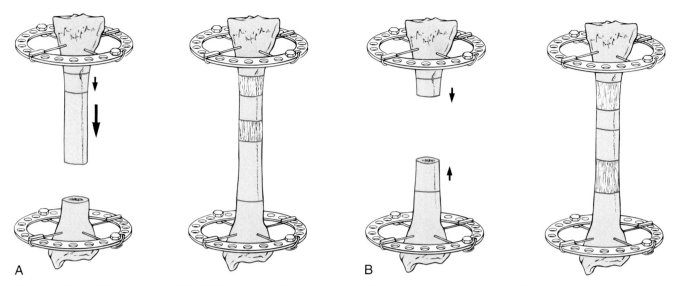

A

B

FIGURE 21–46. *A,* With a substantial skeletal defect, it is possible to create two corticotomies in bone, transporting the first intercalary segment at a rate of 2.0 mm/day and the second at a rate of 1.0 mm/day. Each corticotomy gap widens at a rate of 1.0 mm/day with this strategy. *B,* Another strategy for dealing with a large skeletal defect. Proximal and distal corticotomies are performed, and the two intercalary segments are moved toward each other. The defect closes at the rate of 2.0 mm/day, but each corticotomy site opens at the rate of only 1.0 mm/day.

through a tibial corticotomy and fibular osteotomy, before bone transport to prevent premature union of the fibular osteotomy. Thereafter, the bone transport of the tibia should be continued until the gap is closed (see Fig. 21–50*C*).

Obviously, when paired bones are lengthened, both ends of both bones must be secured to the frame, or one or the other end will subluxate or dislocate from its anatomic position.

Septic Nonunions

External skeletal fixation has long been a weapon in the surgical assault on septic nonunions. The fixator, by virtue of its rigidity, permits control of limb length and alignment without the need for hardware traversing the site of sepsis. A stable biomechanical environment promotes both osseous healing and immune function simultaneously.

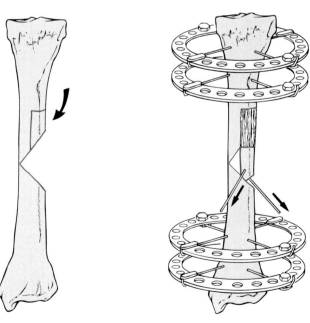

FIGURE 21–47. A method of eliminating a partial skeletal defect using "slivers." A cortical fragment *(curved arrow)* is separated from one bone segment and is gradually drawn across the wound *(straight arrows).*

FIGURE 21–48. A segmental defect accompanied by shortening.

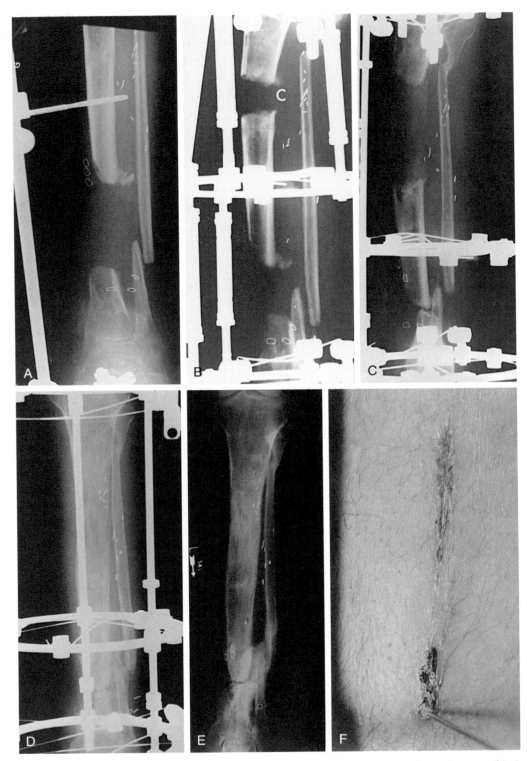

Figure 21–49. A, Roentgenogram of the leg of a 21-year-old man with a 7.5-cm tibial defect and 2.5-cm of limb shortening (note fibular overlap), resulting in a true tibial defect of 10 cm. B, Roentgenographic appearance during bone transport. Note the corticotomy site (C) and the transported intercalary segment. The shortening has not yet been overcome (note fibular overlap). C, Appearance at the completion of bone transport and restoration of limb length. Note that the fibular overlap has been eliminated. New bone is forming in the distraction gap. D, Appearance toward the end of fixation. A small cancellous bone graft has been placed between the distal tibia and the distal fibula because of the atrophy of the bone ends in this region. E, Final radiographic appearance. Note the 10 cm of regenerated bone in the proximal tibia and the small bone graft in the distal interosseous space. F, The clinical appearance of the skin during bone transport. The wires cut through the skin, with necrosis ahead of the wire and healing behind.

DÉBRIDEMENT

Débridement of nonviable tissues remains the hallmark of osteomyelitis surgery. An equally important principle, and one that is often overlooked, is the need for elimination of residual cavities (actually, hard wall abscesses) within infected bone.

In certain septic nonunions, infection may persist in the absence of nonviable bone. In these cases false movement at the septic focus leads to persistent drainage. An infection in which drainage is motion related rather than necrosis related is often called a *fistulous pseudarthrosis* to distinguish it from *post-traumatic osteomyelitis*, in which nonviable bone, usually in the form of sequestered fragments, is present. If osseous healing in such motion-associated infections leads to bone union, the sepsis is usually eradicated. If, however, immobilization of the focus of infection is only temporary—the result of stable external fixation—and not accompanied by osseous union, drainage may reappear shortly after the fixator is removed and false motion starts again. Therefore, as a general principle, an external fixator should not be removed from a patient with an infected nonunion until the fracture is united.[24]

In another common pattern of post-traumatic sepsis, there may be nonviable bone within and surrounded by living osseous tissues. Such a sequestra incontinuity is fairly common in patients with septic nonunions treated at the Problem Fracture Service at Rancho Los Amigos Medical Center. For this reason, I explore every septic nonunion with wound drainage, often to find a sequestra in continuity requiring débridement, even if radiographs fail to demonstrate areas of nonviable bone. Sequestra in continuity is the most difficult to diagnose with standard radiographic, tomographic, scintigraphic, and other non-invasive studies. At times, the lack of callus from one or another side of a fracture site—especially where an experienced eye would ordinarily expect to see callus— may be a tipoff to the presence of sequestra in continuity.

Equally often, however, radiographs do not provide this type of information. Unfortunately, wound exploration may potentially devitalize additional bone as the perios-

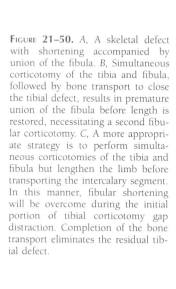

FIGURE 21–50. *A,* A skeletal defect with shortening accompanied by union of the fibula. *B,* Simultaneous corticotomy of the tibia and fibula, followed by bone transport to close the tibial defect, results in premature union of the fibula before length is restored, necessitating a second fibular corticotomy. *C,* A more appropriate strategy is to perform simultaneous corticotomies of the tibia and fibula but lengthen the limb before transporting the intercalary segment. In this manner, fibular shortening will be overcome during the initial portion of tibial corticotomy gap distraction. Completion of the bone transport eliminates the residual tibial defect.

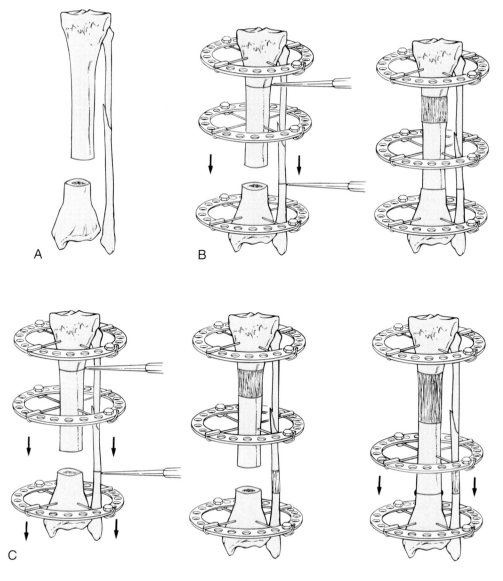

teum is elevated during the course of exposure. For this reason, the surgeon should carefully limit subperiosteal dissection, choosing instead the extraperiosteal route to the bone in question.

An infected nonunion draining to the surface points to a septic focus through an open sinus. Enlarging the sinus opening usually leads to an obvious sequestrum. During débridement, I do not excise the sinus tract, because its epithelialized granulation tissue is a natural response to the infection rather than a source of sepsis. Likewise, healthy granulation tissue, noted for its beefy red color and friability, should be left in place. Grayish-brown granulation, on the other hand, probably represents reactive tissue overwhelmed by microorganisms and calls for débridement.

Densely collagenized fibrous tissue surrounding bone fragments probably has little potential for new bone formation once the limb has been stabilized; indeed, such avascular tissue may inhibit host defenses. For this reason, I resect dense avascular or hypovascular collagenized fibrous tissue. It is often difficult to determine where this reactive tissue ends and normal periosteum, nerves, tendons, or fascia begin. As an aid to the resection, consider the following: First, the dense fibrous tissue represents the end-stage of biologic material that started as granulation tissue. Thus, the pathologic process leading to avascular fibrous tissue formation must be at least several months old. Second, the dense fibrous tissue requiring débridement is usually located within the original periosteal sleeve. Hence, it is often necessary to define the location and extent of the preinjury periosteal envelope before débridement. With this objective in mind, one can find the periosteum where it is adherent to normal bone (i.e., beyond the extent of distorted anatomy) and trace this periosteum toward the center of the infected region. A large curette aids in the separation of periosteum from proliferative tissues lining its inner surface.

Once bone and soft tissue débridement is complete, the surgeon may be left with a sizable segmental defect requiring osseous and soft tissue reconstruction. Since the mid-1980s, numerous strategies have evolved to deal with such post-traumatic tissue deficiencies. These have always included one or another method of bone grafting to compensate for the loss of osseous tissue. Likewise, skin defects are usually eliminated by a cutaneous graft, transposition or musculocutaneous free flaps, or gradual closure by secondary intention. Osseous defects longer than 10 cm seem beyond the limit of cancellous bone grafting; for this reason, microvascular free osseous transfers have gained popularity. For some bones, especially the weight-bearing tubular bones of the lower limb, the transplanted osseous tissue (usually the fibula or iliac crest) may fail to incorporate or may refracture when subjected to unprotected weight bearing.[7]

The techniques already described for reconstructive surgery of uninfected nonunions developed by Ilizarov are ideally suited for eliminating skeletal defects after débridement of infected or nonviable osseous tissues, without the need for bone grafting or free microvascular transfers.[14, 32] After débridement, the mechanical axes of the bone fragments are aligned collinearly, and a corticotomy is performed through healthy tissue after the frame is applied. The defect is closed by bone transport, incorporating the principles outlined previously in the sections dealing with bone transport with and without shortening.

PROBLEMS WITH THE REGENERATE BONE

Ilizarov's method includes the creation of "regenerate" new bone during elongation of the osteotomized segments. Dealing with the regenerate bone is a new experience for most orthopaedic surgeons. The regenerate bone in a distraction gap can ossify too rapidly, limiting distraction, or more commonly, it may mature too slowly, prolonging the period of fixator application.

Ordinarily the distraction gap shows small hazy patches of calcification, often within the first 2 weeks after cortical osteotomy of a long bone. One should not be concerned if no calcification appears within the gap, which is slightly less than 1.0 cm wide by the end of the second postoperative week (5 days predistraction fixation, followed by 9 days of distraction at a rate of 1.0 mm/day). Distraction should continue at a slightly slower rate for 2 more weeks. By the fourth week after surgery, some calcification should be visible within the distraction gap. If not, one should reverse the distraction and begin compressing the gap over 2 to 3 days. Then, after a brief rest of 3 or 4 days, distraction should be commenced once again. Usually bone will form during the second distraction interval.

At any point during elongation, when the quality of neoosteogenesis within the distraction gap causes concern, the distraction can be stopped or reversed briefly in what has been called an *accordion procedure*. Ideally, the regenerate bone should appear on radiographs as longitudinal striations attached to both cortical fragments with a clear "growth zone" in the center.

Once elongation or correction has been completed, the fixator is left in place for at least as long as the time spent during elongation or deformity correction. This period of "neutral fixation" after correction often taxes the patient's—and the surgeon's—tolerance. Ilizarov recommends "training the regenerate" by compressing the frame slightly (0.25 mm twice a week) toward the end of the neutral fixation period. This maneuver is used both for the regenerate bone in a distraction gap and for any areas of tardy bone healing at a fracture or nonunion site.

The fixator can be removed if the site of nonunion is united and the regenerate is mature and demonstrates the following:

1. No defects or "shark bites" along the regenerate bone's edge on three sides of the distraction zone
2. Complete ossification of the radiolucent central growth zone of the regenerate bone
3. Uniform radiographic density of the regenerate bone (in both projections) that appears, to the surgeon's eye, to be halfway between the density of the adjacent normal bone's cortex and that of its marrow canal

Before removal of either a pin or a wire fixator, one should loosen the frame 1 to 2 mm every 1 to 2 days, reversing distraction, and allow it to "float" on the limb to test osseous stability. When a transfixion wire fixator has been used for limb elongation, the wires are usually bent toward the center of the limb segment. If the threaded connecting rods are loosened, the rings above and below the distraction region may not be secure enough for patient comfort. Also, if the frame must be restabilized because the limb is not ready for fixator removal, the wires will be loose. For these reasons, it is often necessary to reapply tension to the wires if ring positions are altered at the end of the neutral fixation period.

COMPLICATIONS

Researchers at Ilizarov's institute summarized the complications associated with 3669 fixator applications during the period from 1970 to 1975.[6] Analyzing wire tract infections, they found an 8.3% rate of purulent soft tissue sepsis and osteolysis. Limb transfixion, whether by smooth wire or threaded pin, violates the body's principal barrier to bacterial invasion: the intact skin.

An important principle designed to prevent pin or wire sepsis is to prohibit tissue motion along the implant. A bulky wrap of gauze filling the space between the skin and the fixator is important for proper fixator management to reduce the incidence of implant sepsis, especially in the first month or so after the frame is applied.[8] Special slotted sponges are available for use with the transfixion wire fixators to accomplish this.[28] In Russia and Italy, medicine bottle stoppers are placed over each transfixion wire to hold gauze sponges against the skin, thereby achieving skin-wire interface stability.

Various pin and wire care protocols have been suggested over the years, but no single technique seems superior. For this reason, I prefer to leave pin or wire sites alone, wrapped up completely in a bulky wrap, not to be touched while the frame is on the patient, unless a problem develops at the site. The patient can shower with the frame on but should rewrap the pin sites afterward with a bulky wrap as described previously.

When pin or wire sepsis does occur, oral antistaphylococcal antibiotics should be started as soon as soft tissue inflammation develops, and the patient's activities should be curtailed. If these measures do not relieve the problem within 48 to 72 hours, the patient may have to be admitted to the hospital for parenteral antibiotic therapy. If necessary, an implant may have to be removed and another inserted elsewhere to control sepsis.

When removing an infected pin or wire, the surgeon should curette the bone hole if there is radiographic evidence of osteolysis or sequestrum formation.

Chronic pin site or wire site osteomyelitis should be treated with a parenteral course of antibiotics, curettage, and perhaps bone grafting or some other technique used to deal with chronic osteomyelitis.[16]

Fixator Problems

A fixator itself may cause problems for the patient, especially if the surgeon has not allowed enough room for limb swelling, as tissues may press up against frame components. Likewise, it is possible for one or another

element of the frame to impede movement of the limb segments. If adjustments are necessary, the fixator should be stabilized with a temporary strut before any important structural elements of the frame are moved.

Pin or wire tips can catch on clothing and bedding, even when they are properly covered or curled into the frame. To avoid this, one can cover the external fixator with a double-thickness stockinette.

The expanded indications for external fixation currently coming from Russia will present remarkable therapeutic opportunities and an entirely new constellation of difficulties as surgeons attempt reconstructions to a degree never before thought possible. With time, surgeons in Western nations will learn of the best use for circular wire external fixators in restorative traumatology.

REFERENCES

1. Aronson, J.; Harp, J.H. Mechanical considerations in using tensioned wires in a transosseous external fixation system. Clin Orthop 280:23–30, 1992.
2. Caja, V.L.; Moroni, A. Hydroxyapatite coated external fixation pins: An experimental study. Clin Orthop 325:269–275, 1996.
3. Calhoun, J.H.; Li, F; Bauford, W.L.; et al. Rigidity of halfpins for the Ilizarov external fixator. Bull Hosp Jt Dis 52:21–26, 1992.
4. Collinge, C.A.; Goll, G.; Seligson, D.; Easley, K.J. Pin tract infections: Silver vs uncoated pins. Orthopedics 17:445–448, 1994.
5. DeBastiani, G.; Aldegheri, R.; Renzi-Brivio, L.; Trivelli, G. Limb lengthening by callus distraction (callotasis). J Pediatr Orthop 7:129–134, 1987.
6. Devyatov, A.; Kaplunov, A.A. Complications of use of the Ilizarov apparatus. In: Ilizarov, G.A., ed. Applications of Compression-Distraction Osteosynthesis in Traumatology and Orthopaedics. Kurgan, USSR, 1978.
7. Gordon, L.; Chiu, E.J. Treatment of infected nonunions and segmental defects of the tibia with staged microvascular muscle transplantation and bone grafting. J Bone Joint Surg Am 70:377–385, 1988.
8. Green, S.A. Complications of External Skeletal Fixation. Springfield, IL, Charles C Thomas, 1981.
9. Green, S.A. The use of wires and pins. Tech Orthop 5:19–25, 1990.
10. Green, S.A. The Ilizarov method: Rancho technique. Orthop Clin North Am 22:677–688, 1991.
11. Green, S.A. Techniques for transfixion wire fixators. In: Chapman, M., ed. Operative Orthopaedics. Philadelphia, J.B. Lippincott, 1991.
12. Green, S.A. The Rancho mounting technique for circular external fixation. Adv Orthop Surg 16:191–200, 1992.
13. Green, S.A. Segmental defects. A comparison of bone grafting and bone transport for segmental skeletal defects. Clin Orthop 300:111–117, 1994.
14. Green, S.A.; Diabal, T. The open bone graft for septic nonunion. Clin Orthop 180:109, 1983.
15. Green, S.A.; Harris, N.L.; Wall, D.M.; et al. The Rancho mounting technique for the Ilizarov method: A preliminary report. Clin Orthop 280:104–116, 1992.
16. Green, S.A.; Ripley, M. Chronic osteomyelitis of pin tracks. J Bone Joint Surg Am 66:1092, 1984.
17. Green, S.A.; Wall, D.M. Ilizarov external fixation—Transfixion wire technique. Mediguide Orthop, January 1989, pp. 1–8.
18. Ilizarov, G.A. A method of uniting bones in fractures and an apparatus to implement this method. USSR Authorship Certificate 98471, 1952.
19. Ilizarov, G.A. Angular deformities with shortening. In: Coombs, R.; Green, S.; Sarmiento, A., eds. External Fixation and Functional Bracing. Frederick, MD, Aspen, 1989.
20. Ilizarov, G.A. Fractures and nonunions. In: Coombs, R.; Green, S.; Sarmiento, A., eds. External Fixation and Functional Bracing. Frederick, MD, Aspen, 1989.
21. Ilizarov, G.A. The tension-stress effect on the genesis and growth of tissues: Part I. The influence of stability of fixation and soft tissue preservation. Clin Orthop 238:249, 1989.

22. Ilizarov, G.A. The tension-stress effect on the genesis and growth of tissues: Part II. The influence of the rate and frequency of distraction. Clin Orthop 239:263, 1989.

23. Ilizarov, G.A. Transosseous Osteosynthesis. Heidelberg, Springer-Verlag, 1991.

24. Morandi, M.; Zembo, M.; Ciotti, M. Infected tibial pseudarthroses: A two year follow up in patients treated by the Ilizarov technique. Orthopedics 12:497–514, 1989.

25. Moroni, A.; Aspenberg, P.; Toksvig-Larsen, S.; et al. Enhanced fixation with hydroxyapatite coated pins. Clin Orthop 346:171–177, 1998.

26. Paley, D. The Ilizarov corticotomy. Tech Orthop 5:41–53, 1990.

27. Paley, D.; Chaudray, M.; Pirone, A.M.; et al. Treatment of malunions and malnonunions of the femur by detailed preoperative planning and the Ilizarov technique. Orthop Clin North Am 21:667–693, 1990.

28. Paley, D.; Jackson, R.W. Surgical scrub sponges as part of the traction apparatus: An alternative to pin site care to reduce pin track infections. Injury 16:605–606, 1985.

29. Pascual, A.; Tsukayama, D.T.; Wicklund, B.H.; et al. The effect of stainless steel, cobalt chromium, titanium alloy, and titanium on the respiratory burst activity of human polymorphonuclear leukocytes. Clin Orthop 280:281–288, 1992.

30. Tajana, G.F.; Morandi, M.; Zembo, M.M. The structure and development of osteogenic repair tissue according to Ilizarov technique in man. Orthopedics 12:515–523, 1989.

31. Wassall, M.A.; Santin, M.; Isalberti, C.; et al. Adhesion of bacteria to stainless steel and silver-coated orthopedic external fixation pins. J Biomed Mater Res 36:325–330, 1997.

32. Weiland, A.J.; Moore, J.R.; Daniel, R.K. Vascularized autografts: Experience with 41 cases. Clin Orthop 174:87, 1983.

CHAPTER 22

Enhancement of Skeletal Repair

Calin S. Moucha, M.D.
Thomas A. Einhorn, M.D.

The process of skeletal repair is considered to be biologically optimal under most clinical conditions. However, of the 6.2 million fractures that occur annually in the United States, 5% to 10% go on to nonunion or delayed union.[210] In many instances, the cause of impaired healing is unknown; however, surgical and nonsurgical interventions can interfere with healing and may cause delayed union or nonunion.[26] Technical errors during surgery,[53] systemic status of the patient,[78, 156, 165, 226, 274] and the nature of the traumatic injury itself[66, 189, 268] are just some of the many factors that may influence fracture healing. Even when some or all of these risk factors are avoided, many fractures fail to heal.[77] Moreover, specific parts of the skeleton are known to be at increased risk for impaired fracture healing. At these sites, there may be problems related to peculiarities of local blood supply or difficulties in controlling the mechanical strain environment. Examples include the neck of the talus, the neck of the femur, and the carpal scaphoid.[32] Therefore, although most fractures heal uneventfully, clinical scenarios exist in which enhancement of fracture healing would be of benefit to ensure rapid restoration of skeletal function. This chapter reviews some of the methods that have been shown to stimulate skeletal repair.

PHYSICAL METHODS OF ENHANCEMENT

A fracture's mechanical environment can play an important role in its healing. For example, unstable fixation causes excessive interfragmentary movement and may retard the repair process. On the other hand, controlled micromotion or controlled, rhythmic distraction of a fracture site can enhance fracture healing.[109, 128, 142, 175] Knowledge of how strategic alteration of the mechanical environment of a fracture influences its healing is based on results obtained from clinical studies using different operative treatments such as rigid internal fixation, external fixation, or intramedullary fixation. To develop new methods for the stimulation of fracture healing by mechanical means, it is necessary to gain a fundamental understanding of the ways by which mechanical forces are transduced into cellular and molecular signals.

Methods for enhancing fracture repair using biophysical techniques include electrical or electromagnetic stimulation of nonunions and ultrasound stimulation of fresh fractures. Each of these techniques has shown substantial efficacy in well-controlled clinical trials and, as we discuss in this chapter, there is abundant cellular and molecular knowledge that exists on which to base hypothetical explanations for the observed effects in fractures. Treatment of a nonunion, however, may differ from that of a fresh fracture, and the successful use of a biophysical modality in one setting may not transfer to another.

Mechanical Enhancement

The quality and the quantity of the callus formed by a healing fracture can be greatly influenced by the operative or nonoperative method used to treat it. Generally, motion at the site of a fracture causes callus formation.[204] The callus functions to decrease the initial interfragmentary motion sufficiently enough to produce an environment suitable for fracture union. This goal is attained by improving the structure of the fracture site (by increasing cross-sectional area) and by recruiting cells that are necessary for bony regeneration. If the motion becomes excessive, however, a hypertrophic nonunion may result.

As early as the 19th century, physicians disagreed as to the implications of weight bearing on a healing bone. Nicholas Andre (1659–1742) and Just Lucas-Championniere (1843–1913) believed that early controlled activity promoted healing of tissues, whereas John Hunter (1728–1793), John Hilton (1807–1878), and Hugh Owen Thomas (1834–1878) did not.[31] In 1892, Julius Wolff[280] suggested that the structure of bone adapts to changes in its stress environment. This concept has come to be known as *Wolff's law.* Several investigators have attempted to delineate the molecular and cellular mechanisms that govern the ability of bone to respond to loading.* The conclusion drawn from these studies is that tissue loading influences cell shape, gene expression, protein synthesis, and proliferation of several cell types found in the fracture callus.

Controlling the weight-bearing status of a limb is one method of clinically altering the stress environment at a fracture site. Reports of the effects of weight bearing, however, have been conflicting. Sarmiento and associates[236] found that weight bearing improved fracture healing in the femurs of normal rats. Kirchen and colleagues[147] suggested that microgravity, such as during space flight, may influence fracture healing. Aro and associates[9] showed no difference in fracture healing, regardless of weight bearing, in paraplegic rats. Similarly, Riggins and co-workers[218] reported that weight bearing had no effect on fracture healing in chickens. Meadows and colleagues[177] evaluated the effect of weight bearing on the healing characteristics of a cortical defect in canine tibias. They demonstrated an increase in the amount of woven bone formed in defects of weight-bearing tibias compared with that in non–weight-bearing tibias. This finding appeared to reflect a disuse response in the underloaded bones as opposed to the formation of more bone in those that bore weight. The investigators concluded that weight bearing was a permissive factor for the formation of woven bone in tibial defects and that it may increase the formation of bone during the process of skeletal repair.

The two factors that have received the most investigative attention with respect to the ways in which mechanical treatment influences fracture healing are blood flow and interfragmentary strain. Smith and associates[251] studied the blood flow to cortical bone in canine tibias that had been subjected to an experimental osteotomy and different modes of fixation. They showed that when no internal fixation was used after the osteotomy, blood flow to the canine tibial diaphysis was reduced. Four hours later, blood flow to the fracture site was further reduced by an additional 50%. Reaming of the tibia and insertion of a tight-fitting intramedullary nail reduced the blood flow even further. On the other hand, fractures that were treated with either internal or external fixation did not experience such dramatic reductions in blood flow.[197] Whereas early stability appears to have a beneficial effect on blood flow, instability and reaming of the endosteal bone have deleterious effects. It is possible, however, that the development of collateral vessels overcomes the latter effect.

The theory of interfragmentary strain suggests that it is the balance that develops between the degree of local interfragmentary strain and the ability of the callus to withstand the strain that determines the type of healing. Granulation tissue can tolerate 100% strain; fibrous tissue and cartilage withstand lower amounts. Therefore, granulation tissue is best able to tolerate the changes in interfragmentary motion that occur during early reparative stages of fracture healing. As the fracture becomes more stable, the presence of cartilage and new bone reduces the strain and allows fracture healing to proceed. Strain is usually proportional to the size of the fracture gap, but a small gap, such as that which is present in a plated femur in which the fracture ends are not actually apposed, has a high strain. As a result, resorption occurs, allowing granulation tissue and callus to form and produce a lower strain environment.

The influences of different mechanical loading conditions on tissue differentiation have been studied in a variety of skeletal settings. These investigations have led to a theory that relates mechanical loading history to tissue differentiation in the process of endochondral bone repair. It identifies tissue vascularity and two key mechanical parameters, cyclic hydrostatic stress (pressure) and cyclic tensile strain, as important determinants of tissue differentiation. Using an osteotomized long bone as the experimental system, Blenman[19] and Carter[40] and their co-workers performed two-dimensional finite element analyses to model idealized fracture callus, including periosteal, endosteal, and fracture gap (interfragmentary) callus regions. The stress and strain histories at each location within the callus were calculated. High levels of compressive hydrostatic stress occurred within the fracture gap. At the middle of the gap, high levels of strain were present in the radial and circumferential directions. In contrast, at the periosteal and endosteal callus regions remote from the interfragmentary gap, low levels of hydrostatic stress and tensile strain were observed. These findings suggest that an association exists among (1) intermittent compressive hydrostatic stress and chondrogenesis, (2) intermittent strain and fibrogenesis, and (3) low levels of mechanical stimulation and osteogenesis (with good vascularity) or chondrogenesis (with poor vascularity). In addition, these studies showed that after cartilage forms within callus, moderate levels of cyclic tensile strain (or distortional strain) accelerate endochondral ossification. Local cyclic hydrostatic stress delays endochondral ossification, however, possibly via an inhibition of revascularization. More recent research by Claes and associates[54] supports similar concepts.

A few investigators have attempted to design systems in which mechanical input would stimulate fracture repair. Goodship and Kenwright[109] studied the influence of controlled micromotion on fracture healing in two groups of sheep in which tibial diaphyseal fractures had been created. The tibial fractures in one group were treated with rigid external fixation, and those in the other group were subjected to a regimen of controlled axial micromotion (500 cycles at 0.5 Hz) for 17 min/day. Enhanced fracture repair was demonstrated by radiographic, histologic, and biomechanical analyses in the group having micromotion. In a subsequent clinical, prospective randomized controlled trial, Kenwright and colleagues[142] compared the effects of controlled axial micromotion on tibial diaphyseal fracture healing in patients who were treated with external fixation and stratified according to fracture severity grade and extent of soft tissue injury. The tibias that were treated with induced micromotion were subjected to controlled longitudinal displacement and loading of the transfixion

---

*See references 36, 47, 113, 114, 116, 129, 138, 145, 172, 198, 227, 264.

pins by means of a pneumatic pump interfaced to a spring module with sliding clamps (Fig. 22–1). Fracture healing was assessed clinically, radiographically, and by biomechanical measurement of the stiffness of the frame. The mean healing time was shortened in the tibias that had undergone micromovement compared with those in the control group. The differences in healing time were independently related to the treatment method, and no statistically significant differences were observed in complication rates between the groups. Other studies by these and other investigators have confirmed these findings, and even suggested that induced micromotion caused by axial loading of tibial fractures produces more rapid healing than rigid fixation.[141, 143, 144, 179, 234, 235]

Electrical Enhancement

The ability of electricity to heal fracture nonunions was first described in several anecdotal reports during the 19th century.[117, 162] Despite these early reports, no further advances were made in this method of fracture healing augmentation until 1953, when Yasuda demonstrated the

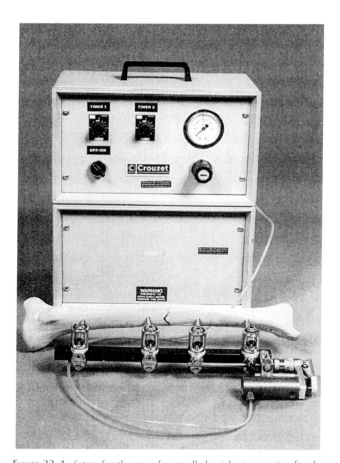

FIGURE 22–1. Setup for the use of controlled axial micromotion for the treatment of tibial fractures. Two sliding clamps are attached to the external fixation column and to a spring assembly. These clamps provide complete control of the longitudinal (axial) displacement and load. A pneumatic pump is attached to the spring module and to the sliding clamps, so that small controlled increments of axial displacement can be applied. (From Kenwright, J.; Richardson, J.B.; Cunningham, J.L.; et al. J Bone Joint Surg Br 73:654–659, 1991.)

appearance of new bone in the vicinity of the cathode (negative electrode) when current in the microampere range was continuously applied for 3 weeks to a dry rabbit femur.[287] This group of investigators also showed that stress-generated potentials develop in bone subjected to a bending load, so that the portion experiencing compressive stresses becomes electronegative and the portion experiencing tensile stresses becomes electropositive.[100] Later, Friedenberg and Brighton[93] described another type of electrical potential in hydrated bone, the bioelectric or steady state potential. This type of potential is electronegative and occurs in nonstressed bone in areas of active growth and repair. Since Yasuda's first report of the piezoelectric properties of bone, there has been an abundance of research on the electric properties of bone, collagen, and other biological tissues.[6, 10, 12, 115, 164, 244] Although the exact mechanism by which electric and electromagnetic fields lead to osteogenesis is still being debated, it has been well documented that electrical stimulation of bone has an effect on several intracellular and extracellular regulatory systems involved in bone formation.[1, 2, 86, 87, 176, 184, 293]

A variety of electrical stimulation devices have been developed, and each of these can be categorized as one of three types: (1) constant direct-current stimulation using percutaneous or implanted electrodes (invasive), (2) time-varying inductive coupling produced by a magnetic field (noninvasive), and (3) capacitive coupling (noninvasive). In direct-current stimulation, stainless steel cathodes are placed into the tissues and electrically induced osteogenesis shows a dose-response curve that relates to the amount of current delivered. Currents lower than a certain threshold result in no bone formation, whereas those higher than that threshold lead to cellular necrosis.[92] In electromagnetic stimulation, an alternating current produced by externally applied coils leads to a time-varying magnetic field, which in turn induces a time-varying electrical field in the bone. In capacitive coupling, an electrical field is induced in bone by an external capacitor; that is, two charged metal plates are placed on either side of a limb and attached to a voltage source.[27]

Most of the studies on the clinical use of electrical stimulation in orthopaedic patients have focused on the treatment of nonunions. Using constant direct current to treat nonunions, Brighton and associates[28] achieve solid bone union in 84% of cases. When this study was expanded to include other clinical centers, an additional 58 out of 89 nonunions achieved solid bone union. The investigators concluded that, with the exception of patients who have synovial pseudarthrosis or an infection, application of constant direct current to nonunions could result in a rate of union that is comparable to that observed after bone grafting procedures and with fewer associated risks. Using the method of pulsing electromagnetic field stimulation in tibial nonunions, another group of investigators showed an 87% success rate for the achievement of union.[11, 13] Scott and King reported the results of a prospective double-blind trial using capacitive coupling in patients with an established nonunion of long bones.[241] Their data, which was statistically significant ($P < 0.004$) showed healing in 60% of the patients who had received electrical stimulation but in none of the patients who had been managed with a placebo unit. More recently, Goodwin and colleagues[110] performed a multicenter randomized double-blind prospective comparison to evaluate the effect of noninvasive capacitively coupled electrical stimulation on the success rate of lumbar spine fusion surgery. For the 179 patients who completed treatment and evaluation, the overall protocol success rate was 84.7% for the active patients and 64.9% for the placebo patients. According to the Yates corrected chi-square test, these results were also statistically significant (P = 0.0043). However, the study had a 12% dropout rate due to noncompliance, the patients had varying degrees of instability of the spine, and the differences among the various surgeons with regard to experience performing internal fixation of the spine were not taken into account in the study.

Although these reports show that electrical stimulation may be successful in the treatment of nonunions and, in a select number of patients, spinal fusion, the application of this technology to the treatment of fresh fractures has not been clearly demonstrated. Two studies have shown that pulsed electromagnetic fields enhance bone regeneration in fresh osteotomies and fracture animal models.[91, 233] In the more recent of these studies, Fredericks and colleagues performed tibial osteotomies stabilized by external fixation in New Zealand white rabbits. One day after surgery, the animals were randomly assigned to receive either no exposure, 30 minutes, or 60 minutes per day of a low-frequency, low-amplitude pulsed electromagnetic field (PEMF). Specimens were examined biomechanically and radiographically, and the results indicated that normal intact torsional strength was achieved by 14 days in the 60-minute PEMF group, by 21 days in the 30-minute PEMF group, and by 28 days in the sham controls. In addition, the 60-minute PEMF-treated osteotomies had significantly higher torsional strength than did sham controls at 14 and 21 days postoperatively. The 30-minute PEMF-treated osteotomies were significantly stronger than those in the sham controls only after 21 days. Lastly, maximum fracture callus area correlated with the time to reach normal torsional strength. Others have failed to reproduce these results.[4, 159] To our knowledge, no published clinical study has shown that electrical stimulation enhances the repair of fresh fractures in humans.

Another potential application of electrical stimulation is in the treatment of fractures that show delayed union. Sharrard[247] conducted a double-blind, multicenter trial of the use of PEMFs in patients who had a delayed union of a tibial fracture. Forty-five tibial fractures that had not united for more than 16 but less than 32 weeks were treated with immobilization in a plaster cast incorporating the coils of an electromagnetic stimulation unit. The unit was activated in 20 of these fractures. The results showed radiographic evidence of union in nine of the fractures that had undergone active electromagnetic stimulation and in only three of the fractures in the control group.

Although there has been an abundance of research on the use of electrical enhancement of fracture healing, numerous questions still abound. More studies are necessary to further understand the use of this modality at both the basic science and clinical levels, especially with regard to its use in fresh fractures.

Ultrasonic Enhancement

Low-intensity pulsed ultrasound has been known for some time to stimulate fresh fracture healing in experimental animals and healing of nonunions in humans.[74, 173, 206, 275, 282] Its use in enhancing the healing of fresh fractures in humans, however, is more controversial. Heckman and co-workers,[123] in a prospective, randomized, double-blind evaluation, examined the use of a new ultrasound stimulating device as an adjunct to conventional treatment with a cast of 67 closed or grade-I open fractures of the tibial shaft. Thirty-three fractures were treated with the active device and 34 with a placebo control device. At the end of the treatment, there was a statistically significant decrease in the time to clinical healing (86 ± 5.8 days in the active-treatment group compared with 114 ± 10.4 days in the control group) (P = 0.01) and a significant decrease in the time to overall (clinical and radiographic) healing (96 ± 4.9 days in the active-treatment group compared with 154 ± 13.7 days in the control group) (P = 0.0001). The patients' compliance with the use of the device was excellent, and no serious complications were reported. This study confirmed earlier studies that demonstrated the efficacy of low-intensity ultrasound stimulation in the acceleration of the normal fracture repair process. Kristiansen showed similar findings in an investigation of patients with fresh distal radius fractures.[152]

Cook and associates[60] investigated the ability of low-intensity ultrasound to accelerate the healing of tibial and distal radius fractures in smokers. The usual healing time for tibial fractures in smokers is 175 ± 27 days, but with ultrasound treatment the healing time was reduced by 41% to 103 ± 8.3 days. Smokers with distal radius fractures had a healing time of 98 ± 30 days, which was reduced by 51% to 48 ± 5.1 days with ultrasound treatment. Treatment with the active ultrasound device also substantially reduced the incidence of delayed unions in tibias in smokers and nonsmokers. These results have optimistic implications because they suggest that ultrasound can mitigate the delayed healing effects of smoking, which is a common risk factor associated with nonunions and delayed unions. Moreover, this study is especially noteworthy because it provides insight into the mechanism that mediates this fracture-healing modality. Although several theories of how ultrasound enhances fracture healing have been proposed,[200, 285] by showing that ultrasound facilitates bony regeneration in a host that has a systemic reduction in generalized healing due to poor oxygen transport,[248] one can hypothesize that ultrasound may elicit its effects, at least in part, by enhancing the delivery of oxygen. This theory is supported by an in vitro study on the effect of ultrasound on human mandibular osteoblasts, gingival fibroblasts, and monocytes.[216] The authors of this study showed that ultrasound stimulates these cells to produce angiogenic factors such as interleukin-8 (IL-8), fibroblast growth factor (FGF), and vascular endothelial growth factor, therefore suggesting that the effects of ultrasound treatment are mediated by stimulation of angiogenesis, which ultimately enhances the healing environment caused by local hypoxia.

Although these studies give credence to the value of ultrasound in enhancing healing of fresh human fractures treated nonoperatively, a study by Emami and co-workers[84] showed no effect of low-intensity ultrasound on healing time of fresh tibial fractures treated with a reamed and statically locked intramedullary rod. Therefore, to date, it appears that the clinical use of ultrasound for enhancing fracture healing has been shown to be beneficial only in delayed unions and nonunions and in fresh fractures in smokers. At least one type of ultrasound device has been approved for marketing in the United States, and it is anticipated that more clinical data will be available on the use of this biophysical signal in the near future.

BIOLOGIC METHODS OF ENHANCEMENT

Knowledge of the cellular and molecular biology of the musculoskeletal system has led to a better understanding of the basic processes that regulate repair of skeletal tissues. To apply this new information to the enhancement of skeletal repair, the specificity of a particular stimulus for its receptor or targeted pathway must first be determined. Local stimulation of skeletal repair involves not only the development of specific molecules to stimulate discrete components of the healing process but also the design of delivery systems to optimize the effect of a stimulating factor. The development of systemic methods for enhancement of skeletal repair is attractive, but the introduction of a systemic agent that targets these processes requires a high degree of specificity, and this approach needs more extensive investigation. Local factors for the stimulation of skeletal healing have been evaluated, and data are available from both clinical and experimental studies.

Local Enhancement

Local methods for the enhancement of skeletal repair can be categorized into osteogenic, osteoconductive, and osteoinductive approaches. Osteogenesis is the process of new bone formation. Osteogenic approaches to fracture healing enhancement include the use of naturally occurring materials that have been shown to induce or support bone formation, such as autologous bone marrow grafts[55, 102, 246] and autologous or allogeneic bone grafts.[33, 35, 96] Experience with bone grafting dates back to the early 1900s,[46] and it has been estimated that there are more than 250,000 bone grafts performed annually in the United States.[182] Osteoconduction is the process by which fibrovascular tissue and osteoprogenitor cells invade a porous structure that acts as a temporary scaffold and replace it with newly formed bone. The most widely studied osteoconductive substances are those composed of hydroxyapatite, calcium phosphate or calcium sulfate composites, and the bioactive glasses.[157] Lastly, the process that promotes mitogenesis of undifferentiated mesenchymal cells, leading to formation of osteoprogenitor cells that have osteogenic capacity, is known as osteoinduction. Urist made the first observation that implantation of demineralized lyophilized segments of bone matrix either subcutaneously or intramuscularly in animals induces bone formation.[270, 272] Follow-up studies of these demineralized allogeneic bone-inductive matrices[21, 79, 107, 137, 181, 269] resulted in identification of a family of compounds known as the bone morphogenetic proteins (BMPs).[281] Several other growth factors have since been shown to play an important role in the development, repair, and induction of bone. These compounds are currently grouped into the transforming growth factor-β (TGF-β) superfamily, which includes the BMPs, the FGFs, the insulin-like growth factors (IGFs), and the platelet-derived growth factors (PDGFs) (Table 22–1).

OSTEOGENIC METHODS

Naturally occurring autogenous and allogeneic bone grafts have been available for more than a century. Although

---

TABLE 22–1

Peptide Signaling Molecules Involved in Skeletal Growth and Repair

Transforming Growth Factor-β Family

Transforming growth factor-β1
Transforming growth factor-β2
Transforming growth factor-β3

Bone Morphogenetic Protein Family

Bone morphogenetic protein-2
Bone morphogenetic protein-3
Bone morphogenetic protein-4
Bone morphogenetic protein-5
Bone morphogenetic protein-6
Bone morphogenetic protein-7 (also known as osteogenic protein-1)
Bone morphogenetic protein-8 (also known as osteogenic protein-2)
Bone morphogenetic protein-9
Bone morphogenetic protein-10
Growth and differentiation factor-1
Growth and differentiation factor-3
Growth and differentiation factor-5
Growth and differentiation factor-6 (also known as bone morphogenetic protein-13)
Growth and differentiation factor-7 (also known as bone morphogenetic protein-12)
Growth and differentiation factor-9
Growth and differentiation factor-10

Inhibin/Activin Family

Inhibin-α
Inhibin-A
Inhibin-B
Inhibin-C
Müllerian inhibiting substance
Growth and differentiation factor-8

Others

Platelet-derived growth factors
Alpha fibroblast growth factor (FGF-1)
Basic fibroblast growth factor (FGF-2)
Insulin-like growth factor I
Insulin-like growth factor II

Properties of Autologous Bone Grafts

Property	Cancellous	Nonvascularized Cortical	Vascularized Cortical
Osteoconduction	++++	+	+
Osteoinduction	++	?	?
Osteoprogenitor cells	+++	−	+
Immediate strength	−	+++	+++
Strength at 6 mo	++	++	+++
Strength at 1 yr	+++	+++	++++

Source: Reprinted from the J Am Acad Orthop Surg Comp Rev 3(1): 2, 1995.

much has been written about the use of bone grafts in skeletal reconstruction, relatively little attention has been devoted to the specific application of bone grafts in the healing of fresh fractures. The scientific principles of autogenous cortical and cancellous bone graft responses suggest that the process begins with the formation of a hematoma around the implanted bone. The hematoma may release bioactive molecules such as growth factors and cytokines from degranulated platelets.[20] Necrosis of the graft follows, and a local inflammatory response is stimulated. Within days, a fibrovascular stroma develops in which host-derived blood vessels and osteogenic precursor cells migrate toward the graft. Eventually the graft is penetrated by osteoclasts, which initiate the resorptive phase of incorporation. Because only a few cells from the graft survive the transplantation, the major contributions of the graft to the process of fracture healing are its osteoconductive properties. The elaboration of any osteoinductive factors from the graft during resorption and the stimulation of an inflammatory response accompanied by cytokines can also contribute to fracture healing.[81] It has been suggested that the host response to cancellous bone grafts differs from the response to cortical bone grafts in terms of the rate and completeness of repair. The more porous nature of the cancellous tissue may permit a more rapid revascularization and lead to a more complete incorporation than that which occurs with cortical bone grafts. Moreover, although the present understanding of the biology of cancellous bone grafts suggests that the process of graft resorption precedes the osteoblastic bone formation response, the reverse may be true with autogenous cortical bone grafts.[124] Although the resorptive phase in the incorporation of cancellous grafts appears to be small, transient, and often difficult to observe radiographically, it leads to a stimulation or triggering of new bone formation, a process involving the elaboration of factors that are specifically mitogenic for osteoprogenitor cells.

Initially, cancellous bone grafts have minimal structural integrity. However, this changes rapidly during the process of osteointegration (new bone formation and incorporation) within preexisting osseous elements. Conversely, Enneking and colleagues[85] demonstrated that cortical grafts initially provide structural strength before the process of osteointegration begins and that while the graft is being remodeled and resorbed by osteoclastic activity it can lose up to one third of its strength over 6 to 18 months.

As reconstructive efforts at limb-sparing surgery have expanded, free vascularized cortical grafts have been used more frequently. The most common grafts involve the fibula, although the ribs, iliac crest, and other bones have also been used. With vascularized grafts, there is no significant cell necrosis, and biomechanical studies have shown that they are superior to cortical grafts for the first 6 months of incorporation. After this initial period, no demonstrable difference exists between cortical and vascularized bone grafts as measured by torque, bending, and tension tests. In addition, when bone grafts are used to bridge gaps greater than 12 cm, vascularized grafts are superior. Vascularized grafts have a reported stress fracture rate of 25% compared with 50% for nonvascularized cortical grafts.[104] Because the procedure is technically demanding, it appears that so far the use of vascularized grafting for fracture healing enhancement has had limited indications such as for nonunions involving irradiated tissue,[75] or those involving the carpal scaphoid[73, 101, 291] (Table 22–2).

Although autogenous bone grafts are effective in enhancing skeletal repair, they are associated with several potential complications. The major disadvantages of autogenous bone grafting include the limited quantity of bone available for harvest and the significant donor site morbidity. Although autogenous bone is widely used and useful, there is morbidity associated with its harvesting. Kurz and associates[154] reviewed the literature for complications of harvesting autogenous iliac bone grafts, with particular attention given to different operative approaches. Younger and Chapman[290] retrospectively studied the medical records of 239 patients with 243 autogenous bone grafts to document donor site morbidity. They found an 8.6% overall major complication rate and a 20.6% minor complication rate.

Considerably less is known about the use of allogeneic bone in the repair of fresh fractures or even nonunions. Because of concerns regarding the transmission of blood-borne diseases through allogeneic tissue transplantation, justification for the use of these materials has become even stricter. Most allografts are either frozen or freeze-dried, although fresh allografts are also available. The latter evoke an intense immune response, and although animal experiments on the use of fresh allografts to enhance fracture healing are beginning,[160] until now they have been used only as osteochondral grafts in cases of joint resurfacing.[51] Frozen allografts are stored at temperatures lower than −60°C, which diminishes degradation by enzymes and allows for decreased immunogenicity without changes in biomechanical properties. Freeze-drying (lyophilization) involves the removal of water and vacuum packing of frozen tissue. Although the freeze-drying of allografts results in a reduction in their immunogenicity,[97] this treatment also affects the mechanical integrity of the graft, resulting in a reduction in its load-bearing capacity.[202] Moreover, because the donor's cells die in the process of allograft preparation and preservation, whatever limited osteogenic contribution could have been provided by cells is lost with allogeneic bone grafts.

Allografts can be used for structural and nonstructural purposes. Morcellation of cancellous and cortical bone has been used to reconstruct defects after curettage of bone cysts and benign neoplasms and to reconstruct periarticular defects during arthroplasty. Some surgeons have mixed allograft bone with autogenous bone graft or bone marrow in an effort to enhance osteogenesis and osteoinduction.

Structurally, allografts can be used to reconstruct diaphyseal defects as intercalary segments or in arthrodeses about the ankle, hip, and spine. In addition, large segments can be conformed to replace acetabular defects. Complications with large structural allografts, however, can be numerous and can include nonunion (10%), fracture (5%–15%), and infection (10%–15%).[249] In addition to local infections, major concerns arise regarding the potential for transmission of hepatitis and the human immunodeficiency virus. The American Association of Tissue Banks has set strict standards that have decreased the risk of disease transmission. Their records indicate that of the 3 million tissue transplantations performed since the identification of the human immunodeficiency virus, only two donors' tissues have been linked with documented transmission. Both cases involved unprocessed, fresh-frozen allografts,[3] and in one of these cases, other samples from the same donor that were lyophilized and irradiated did not transmit the virus. This suggests that lyophilization and irradiation may destroy the human immunodeficiency virus. Although the risk of transmission of an infectious agent is always possible, it is important to realize that owing to strict donor screening practices, procurement techniques, and serologic testing, allografts are used daily in orthopaedic practices without reports of significant associated morbidities.

A number of reports have suggested that autogenous bone marrow alone is an effective osteogenic graft.[55, 102, 242, 246] This concept is based on the fact that autogenous bone marrow contains osteogenic precursors that could contribute to bone formation.[71, 94, 199] Autogenous marrow has been used clinically to augment the osteogenic response to implanted allografts[35] and xenogeneic bone.[208, 229, 230] However, autogenous bone marrow used alone may also be an effective graft for stimulating bone formation and skeletal repair. Connolly and associates[55] investigated the osteogenic capacity of autogenous bone marrow in a controlled study in rabbits. They found that osteogenesis was accelerated in diffusion chambers loaded with centrifuged and concentrated bone marrow cells that had been implanted into the peritoneal cavity (ectopic site) in a delayed union model (orthotopic site). Garg and colleagues[102] treated long bone fractures in patients with plaster cast immobilization and percutaneous injection of autogenous bone marrow. Patients were kept

from weight bearing for 6 weeks after the operation, after which protected weight bearing was allowed until union was achieved. The investigators reported clinical and radiographic healing in 17 of 20 fractures.

The use of autogenous bone marrow preparations for the treatment of fractures may be refined by the development of better methods for the isolation, purification, and cultural expansion of marrow-derived mesenchymal cells.[37, 38] Selective adhesion methods can be used to isolate cells with osteogenic potential from the marrow cell population of hemopoietic origin. Once isolated, these cells may be added to a culture medium containing factors that stimulate cell replication but not differentiation, to ultimately yield a supply of cells that are highly osteogenic. A series of animal studies have already shown that cells prepared in this manner may be combined with a calcium phosphate ceramic delivery system to regenerate bone or enhance the repair of skeletal defects.[29, 111]

OSTEOCONDUCTIVE METHODS

Osteoconductive materials used as bone graft substitutes are designed to provide an optimal setting for ingrowth of sprouting capillaries, perivascular tissues, and osteoprogenitor cells from the recipient host bed.[14, 64, 271] Architectural characteristics of the material (e.g., pore size and pore density), as well as its biologic properties such as cell adherence capabilities, are just several factors that influence its mechanical strength and ability for osteoconduction.[70, 90, 153] The most common osteoconductive bone graft substitutes used to date are porous ceramics composed of hydroxyapatite, calcium phosphate, calcium carbonate, calcium sulfate, bioactive glass, and bovine bone. Ceramics are made by sintering, a process by which mineral salts are heated to temperatures above 1000°C. Sintering has been shown to reduce the amount of carbonated apatite, an unstable and weakly soluble form of hydroxyapatite that allows significant osteoclastic remodeling. Because of this process, many of the ceramics currently in use provide a stable biologic construct for osteoconduction to occur.[83, 273] Chiroff and colleagues[50] were the first to describe the fact that corals made by marine invertebrates have a structure similar to that of cortical and cancellous bone and therefore may have a role as bone graft substitutes. The compounds reviewed below are those that have been the most extensively studied in basic science and clinical investigations.

Collagraft (Zimmer, Inc., Warsaw, IN), a mixture of hydroxyapatite, tricalcium phosphate, and bovine collagen, was designed for use with autogenous bone marrow and acts as a nonstructural bone graft substitute.[63] Two major prospective clinical trials have been reported and both have concluded that Collagraft is both efficacious and safe.[44, 65] The more recent of these two studies, which compared the safety and efficacy of autogenous bone graft obtained from the iliac crest with those of Collagraft, was a prospective, randomized investigation conducted concurrently at 18 medical centers. Two hundred thirteen patients (249 fractures) were followed for a minimum of 24 months to monitor healing and the occurrence of complications. The results showed no significant differences between the two treatment groups with respect to rates of union ($P = 0.94$, power = 88%) and functional measures (use of analgesics, pain with activities of daily living, and impairment in activities of daily living; $P > 0.10$). The prevalence of complications did not differ between the treatment groups except for the rate of infection, which was higher in the patients who were managed with an autogenous graft. Twelve patients who were managed with a synthetic graft had a positive antibody titer to bovine collagen; seven of them agreed to have intradermal challenge with bovine collagen. One patient had a positive skin response to the challenge but had no complications with regard to healing of the fracture. Despite these two optimistic clinical trials, clinicians need to consider (1) the graft's lack of structural support; (2) the need to combine the collagen-mineral composite with the patient's bone marrow, risking complications from another procedure; and (3) the potential immunogenicity and risk of disease transmission with the use of bovine collagen.

Pro Osteon (Interpore Cross International, Inc., Irvine, CA) is produced by harvesting tricalcium phosphate from marine coral exoskeletons and converting it into hydroxyapatite. The coralline material is different from other hydroxyapatite implants in that it is structurally similar to cancellous bone. Owing to this architectural similarity, osteoconduction is optimized. In addition, the material can be cut to fit the area being grafted, and it has been shown to have good strength in compression. Two studies in particular have confirmed the clinical advantages of this bone graft substitute, one in distal radius fractures[279] and another in tibial plateau fractures.[30] Some of the concerns that have been expressed by clinicians with this material include variable quality and strength, undefined resorption rates,[132] and persistent radiopaqueness, making it difficult to estimate fracture healing.[238] Nevertheless, coralline hydroxyapatite is a very popular bone graft substitute with well-documented clinical benefits.

Norian SRS skeletal replacement system (Norian Corp., Cupertino, CA) is a paste consisting of powdered calcium phosphate and calcium carbonate mixed with a solution of calcium phosphate. The material can be injected into a fracture, where within about 10 minutes, it hardens owing to the formation of the mineral dahllite. After 12 hours, the dahllite formation is almost complete, giving the material an ultimate compressive strength of 55 MPa. As a result of these properties, treatment of certain fractures with Norian SRS can augment the fixation that is achieved with a cast or with operative means. Animal studies have shown that Norian SRS is in many cases extensively resorbed and replaced by host bone.[56, 89] Several investigators have confirmed the efficacy of Norian in fractures of the distal radius,[136, 150, 231, 288] the calcaneus,[239] and the hip.[82, 108] This and other calcium phosphate composites will certainly have great potential as bone graft substitutes. As with other types of cement, more research is required concerning resorption rates and long-term consequences of extrusion of the material into the soft tissues.

Osteoset (Wright Medical Technology, Inc., Arlington, TN) is a bone graft substitute composed of calcium sulfate pellets. The preparation is mostly resorbed by as early as 6 to 8 weeks, a property that has been criticized by some. In fact, the manufacturer states that the material does not provide structural support and that it should not be a substitute for internal or external fixation. To our knowledge, no controlled studies have been published to date regarding the clinical efficacy of this product. This is in part because Osteoset was marketed in the United States before the institution of the current Food and Drug Administration approval process. In an effort to introduce a bone graft substitute with osteoconductive and osteoinductive properties, the manufacturer of Osteoset has also introduced Allomatrix Injectable Putty, a combination of AlloGro demineralized bone matrix and Osteoset. To our knowledge, no clinical trials with this product have been reported. Although this and other previously described bone graft substitutes are relatively safe with respect to inducing an immune response or transmitting an infectious disease, there has been a report of three inflammatory reactions associated with the use of Osteoset following resection of bone tumors.[222] Well-designed clinical trials on the use of Osteoset in humans are still needed to better understand the safety and efficacy of this product.

Bioactive glass and bovine bone–derived ceramics are two types of bone graft substitutes that have not yet undergone enough testing to make them clinically useful products. To our knowledge, Novabone and Biogran are the two bioactive glass products that have been developed to act as bone graft substitutes. Neither of these products has been studied extensively, although animal studies have proven bioglass materials to be promising.[195] Although nonphysiologic and offering little structural support, these two products need to be further studied. Endobon, a bovine cancellous bone–derived ceramic, is marketed in Europe as a bone graft substitute. Although anecdotal reports of its success exist, to our knowledge, no clinical trials on this product have been performed.

OSTEOINDUCTIVE METHODS

Demineralized Allograft Bone Matrix

To our knowledge, four commercially available products containing demineralized allograft bone matrix exist. Grafton DBM (Osteotech, Inc., Eatontown, NJ) and DynaGraft (GenSci Regeneration Sciences, Inc., Mississauga, Ontario, Canada) contain only demineralized human bone matrix. Osteofil (Sofamor Danek Group, Inc., Memphis, TN) and Opteform (Exactech, Inc., Gainesville, FL) contain demineralized human bone matrix mixed with either porcine gelatin or compacted corticocancellous human bone chips, respectively. All of these products have osteoinductive effects. The last two have the advantage of hardening at body temperature and the potential for remodeling to normal bone. To date, Grafton DBM and DynaGraft are indicated primarily for nonunions and delayed unions and for patients with potentially poor healing potential such as smokers and diabetics. Although all have the potential for disease transmission, the manufacturers claim that this has not yet occurred. Although Grafton is manufactured with glycerol, which has been suggested to be neurotoxic, no reports of neural toxicity have been made to date. Because of their ability to harden, Osteofil and Opteform have the potential for offering structural integrity to fractures and other bony defects.

Bone Morphogenetic Proteins and Other Growth Factors

The TGF-β superfamily of proteins, which includes the BMPs, FGFs, IGFs, and PDGFs, elicit their actions by binding to transmembrane receptors that are linked to gene sequences in the nucleus of various cells by a cascade of chemical reactions.[171, 265] Because these cascades activate several genes at once, specific growth factors generate multiple effects, both within a single cell type as well as in different cell types.[161, 243] Osteoinduction has been described as occurring in three major phases: chemotaxis, mitosis, and differentiation.[215] The aforementioned growth factors, all polypeptide molecules, provide a mechanism for stimulative and regulative effects on these phases.

Transforming Growth Factor-β. TGF-β, a peptide first identified by its ability to cause phenotypic transformation of rat fibroblasts,[220] has been shown to be a fundamental, multifunctional, regulatory protein that can either stimulate or inhibit several critical processes of cell function.[255] Since then, five different isomers of TGF-β have been identified (three of these are found in humans), as have several other related polypeptide growth factors. These are now all a part of the TGF-β superfamily, which also includes other ubiquitous compounds such as the BMPs, activins, inhibins, and growth and differentiation factors. The largest source of TGF-β in the body is the extracellular matrix of bone, and platelets probably represent the second largest reservoir for this peptide.[42, 251]

All the TGF-βs are disulfide-linked dimers comprising 12- to 18-kD subunits.[146] Most are homodimers (TGF-β1, TGF-β2, and TGF-β3), but some are heterodimers (TGF-β1.2 and TGF-β2.3).[193] TGF-βs are secreted in a latent propeptide form that requires activation by extracellular proteolytic activity. In bone, it is thought that this occurs within the acidic microenvironment formed by the sealing zone directly beneath bone-resorbing osteoclasts.[196] Chondrocytes and osteoblasts have been shown to produce TGF-β,[135, 221] which itself affects protein synthesis in these cell lines.[223]

Joyce and associates[134] were the first to investigate the endogenous expression of TGF-β in organ cultures of fracture callus. Using immunohistochemical and recombinant DNA techniques, they analyzed fresh femur fractures made in male rats at four distinct histologic stages: immediately after the injury, during intramembranous bone formation, during chondrogenesis, and during endochondral ossification. Using immunolocalization, TGF-β was found to persist for up to 10 days after the fracture was created. During intramembranous bone formation, TGF-β was localized both intracellularly in osteoblasts and proliferating mesenchymal cells, as well as extracellularly. TGF-β was localized to mesenchymal cells, immature chondrocytes, and mature chondrocytes during chondrogenesis, as well as to the extracellular matrix surrounding chondrocyte precursors. During endochondral ossification, ossified matrix on the bone side of the ossification front no longer stained for TGF-β, whereas the extracellular matrix surrounding the hypertrophic chondrocytes that bordered the ossification front stained intensely for TGF-β. Gene expression of TGF-β was evaluated by Northern blot analysis from eight pooled fracture calluses, microdissected into soft (fibrous and cartilaginous) and hard (osseous) callus, at 3-day intervals. TGF-β messenger RNA (mRNA) levels peaked in the soft callus 13 days after fracture, corresponding to the histologic progression of chondrogenesis. TGF-β mRNA levels in the hard callus were highest at 5 and 15 days after fracture, corresponding to intramembranous bone formation and endochondral ossification, respectively. Since then, several other investigators have added information to this original report.[7, 224] Some studies have shown that TGF-β decreases rat osteoblast differentiation and mineralization.[260] Overall, however, the in vitro studies indicate that TGF-β increases the expression of osteoblast differentiation markers such as alkaline phosphatase, type I collagen, and osteonectin, and acts in synergy with 1,25-dihydroxyvitamin D3 to increase alkaline phosphatase levels.[130, 277]

To our knowledge, Mustoe and co-workers[183] were the first to show that TGF-β applied exogenously enhances healing of tissues. They applied this peptide directly to linear incisions made through the dorsal skin of rats and demonstrated a 220% increase in maximal wound strength after 5 days and acceleration in the rate of healing by at least 3 days. Numerous investigations on the effect of exogenously introduced TGF-β into injured bone have also been performed.[15, 16, 120, 205] We focus on the three published reports available to date that have evaluated the effect of TGF-β using fracture healing models.[67, 163, 190]

Critchlow and associates studied the effect of TGF-β2 on rat tibial fracture healing. The tibiae were fractured and immobilized with either a six-hole stainless steel dynamic compression plate (stable mechanical conditions) or a plastic plate designed to leave a 0.5-mm gap at the fracture site (unstable mechanical conditions). TGF-β2 was injected into the fracture site as a one-time dose (either 60 or 600 ng) 4 days after the injury was produced. The fractures were examined at 5, 7, 10, and 14 days after the fracture. The callus of fractures healing under stable mechanical conditions consisted almost entirely of bone, whereas those of the fractures healing under unstable mechanical conditions had a large area of cartilage over the fracture site with bone on each side. Under stable mechanical conditions, 60 ng of TGF-β2 had an insignificant effect on callus development, whereas the higher dose of 600 ng led to a larger callus. Under unstable mechanical conditions, the quantity of tissue components changed, but the size of the callus remained unaffected. At the lower dose of 60 ng of TGF-β2, the callus contained more fibrous tissue and less bone and cartilage. The amounts of bone, cartilage, and fibrous tissue in callus treated with 600 ng of TGF-β2 were similar to those in the control group, although the lack of bone between the cartilage and periosteum indicated that the callus is less mature. The investigators concluded that TGF-β2 does not enhance fracture healing.

Lind and colleagues[163] studied the effect of TGF-β administered continuously using an osmotic minipump to unilaterally plated adult rabbit tibial osteotomies. For 6 weeks, the experimental groups received either 1 or 10 µg per day, and the control group received injections without TGF-β. At 6 weeks, fracture healing was evaluated by mechanical tests, histomorphometry, and densitometry. Markedly increased callus volume and statistically significant maximal bending strengths were demonstrated in the groups receiving 1 μg of TGF-β per day. In the group administered 10 μg of TGF-β per day, there was no statistically significant increase in bending strength, although the callus volume persisted to be greater than that in the control group. There was no statistically significant effect in any of the experimental groups on bending stiffness, bone mineral content, cortical thickness, or Haversian canal diameter. The investigators concluded that exogenous administration of TGF-β might enhance fracture healing in rabbits by increasing callus size but that the callus created may be too immature to enhance the mechanical strength of the osteotomy.

Nielson and associates[190] studied the effect of TGF-β administered locally around the fracture line of healing rat tibial fractures stabilized with an intramedullary pin. TGF-β was injected at a dose of either 4 ng or 40 ng every other day for 40 days. The strength, stiffness, energy absorption, and deflection of the fractures were measured. Biomechanical testing showed an increase in load to failure and callus diameter in the group treated with higher (40 ng) dose of TGF-β. The researchers concluded that TGF-β increases callus formation and strength in rat tibial fractures after 40 days of healing.

Comparing these and other studies and making clinically relevant conclusions is difficult owing to differences in models, dose regimens, delivery systems, and isoforms of TGF-β used.[41] Overall, TGF-β appears to have some efficacy in augmenting fracture healing if the fracture is stable. More research using validated and consistent models is needed to further assess the role of TGF-β on enhancement of normal fracture healing.

Bone Morphogenetic Proteins. The BMPs are a subfamily of the TGF-β superfamily of polypeptides. BMPs are distinguished from other members of the superfamily by having, in general, seven rather than nine conserved cysteines in the mature region.[228] Several known members of this family of osteoinductive growth factors can be subdivided into several classes based on structure.[127] BMPs play crucial roles in growth, differentiation, and apoptosis in a variety of cells during development, including chondrocytes and osteoblasts. Compared with TGF-β, however, BMPs have been shown to have more selective and powerful effects on bone healing in animal models.

During fracture repair, endogenously expressed BMPs include BMP-2, BMP-3 (osteogenin), BMP-4, and BMP-7 (osteogenic protein, OP-1). In humans, BMP-2 and BMP-7 have been the most extensively studied, and they have been isolated, sequenced, and manufactured using recombinant DNA technology. The importance of BMPs during bone healing has been demonstrated using numerous in vitro[48, 263, 284] and in vivo models.[23, 119, 131, 186, 194, 289] Several investigators have also studied the ability of exogenously administered BMPs to promote bone regeneration in osseous locations. BMP-2,[106, 148, 149, 240, 286] BMP-7,[58, 59, 61] and BMP-3[257] have all been shown to promote fracture healing of critical-sized defects. A critical-sized defect may be defined as the smallest intraosseous wound that would not heal by bone forma-

tion in the lifetime of the animal. Critical-sized diaphyseal defect models mimic a clinical situation in which so much bone is lost that even normal mechanisms cannot repair it, such as a result of trauma or bone resection for musculoskeletal tumors. Although these defects do not heal without intervention, they are not truly models of normal or impaired bone healing, as it is the inherent size of the defect that leads to failed healing rather than—as in the case of a delayed union or nonunion—the host characteristics or the local fracture environment. Although significant developments in fracture repair enhancement have been achieved using critical-sized diaphyseal defect models, they do not simulate the more common clinical situation in which the cause of a nonunion is a compromised healing environment other than massive bone loss. Therefore, we provide a review of some of the literature that has supported the use of BMPs to enhance the healing of fractures.

Einhorn and co-workers investigated the effects of percutaneously injecting recombinant BMP-2 into standardized, closed mid-diaphyseal femur fractures in rats 6 hours after injury.[80] First, 278 male rats were divided into three groups of 96 animals, each receiving either no injection at all, injection of an aqueous buffer, or injection of the buffer plus 80 μg of rhBMP-2. Animals in each of these groups were then further sub-divided into four groups and were sacrificed at 7, 14, 21, and 28 days after fracture. At the conclusion of the experiment, 18 femora from each subgroup were tested biomechanically and 6 were analyzed histologically. A statistically significant increase in stiffness in the rhBMP-2–treated fractures was observed by day 14 and continued at 21 and 28 days after fracture compared with that in the other two groups. There was also a significant increase in strength in the rhBMP-2–treated fractures at day 28. A robust subperiosteal membranous bone response, greater than that seen in either of the control groups, was demonstrated histologically in the fractures treated with rhBMP-2. In addition, compared with that in controls, there was relative maturation of osteochondrogenic cells in the rhBMP-2 treated fractures. Bridging callus appeared earlier in the rhBMP-2–treated groups, and relatively increased peripheral woven bone was seen in these groups as well. The investigators concluded that local percutaneous injection of rhBMP-2 into fresh fractures might accelerate the rate of normal fracture healing. Bostrom and Camacho[22] and Turek and co-workers[266] studied BMP-2 combined with an absorbable collagen sponge and applied as an onlay graft in a rabbit ulnar osteotomy and confirmed its effects on the healing of fresh fractures described by Einhorn and associates.

Exogenously administered BMP-7 has been evaluated in animal non–critical-sized defect models by three groups of investigators. Using a closed diaphyseal tibial fracture model in the goat, den Boer and colleagues[69] investigated the effect of BMP-7 introduced into a fresh fracture gap and concluded that injections of BMP-7 solution in these fractures accelerates their healing during the first 2 weeks. Cook[57] and Poplich and colleagues[209] created bilateral 3-mm non–critical-sized defects in the midulna of 35 adult male dogs and also showed that BMP-7 enhanced fracture healing as measured by several parameters.

Although the effect of exogenously administered BMP into acute bony defects has been studied for some time, it has not been until recently that investigators have studied the effect of BMPs on the treatment of nonunions. Whereas in acute defects, the species specificity of a BMP does not appear to be important,[292] its effect on the ability of a BMP to enhance healing of a nonunion has been shown in a canine model.[121] Heckman and associates[122] performed standardized nonunions in the midportion of the radial diaphysis in 30 mature mongrel dogs. The nonunion was treated with implantation of a carrier consisting of poly (DL-lactic acid) and polyglycolic acid polymer (50:50 polylactic acid–polyglycolic acid [PLG50]) containing canine-purified BMP or TGF-β1, or both, or the carrier without BMP or TGF-β1. Five groups, consisting of six dogs each, were treated with (1) implantation of the carrier alone, (2) implantation of the carrier with 15 mg of BMP, (3) implantation of the carrier with 1.5 mg of BMP, (4) implantation of the carrier with 15 mg of BMP and 10 ng of TGF-β1, or (5) implantation of the carrier with 10 ng of TGF-β1. The specimens were examined radiographically and histomorphometrically 12 weeks after implantation. The radii treated with either 1.5 mg or 15 mg of BMP showed significantly increased periosteal and endosteal bone formation. No significant radiographic or histomorphometric evidence of healing was observed after implantation of the polylactic acid–polyglycolic acid carrier alone or in combination with 10 ng TGF-β1. The investigators concluded that species-specific BMP incorporated into a polylactic acid–polyglycolic acid carrier implanted at the site of an ununited diaphyseal fracture increases bone formation. In addition, TGF-β1 at the dose used in the study did not have a similar effect and did not potentiate the effect of BMP. The investigators suggested that the biodegradable implant containing BMP that was used in their study was an effective bone-graft substitute. This study confirmed the biocompatibility of polylactic acid–polyglycolic acid composites, the bioavailability of BMP and TGF-β1 released from this implant, and, most important, the capability of BMP to augment bone healing in chronic nonunions.

Clinical experience with exogenously administered BMPs in bony defects or fresh fractures is somewhat limited. To date, only preliminary results exist on the effects of BMP-2 and BMP-7 to enhance bony regeneration in humans. Recently described is an open label safety and feasibility trial using BMP-2 with an absorbable collagen sponge carrier.[217] Twelve patients with Gustillo grade II, IIIA, or IIIB open tibia fractures from four major trauma centers were treated with 3.4 or 6.8 mg of BMP-2. Eight of the 12 patients were treated with a nonreamed tibial rod, and 4 were treated with an external fixator. At the time of definitive wound closure (median, 4 days postoperatively), one or two Helistat (Colla-tec, Plainsboro, NJ) absorbable collagen sponges soaked with 0.43 mg/mL of BMP-2 were applied to the fracture site. Independent radiologists and orthopaedic surgeons reviewed radiographs of the fractures 4 months postoperatively. Nine (75%) of the fractures healed without additional intervention, and three (25%) required a secondary bone graft procedure. Aside from two patients in whom transient serum antibodies against BMP-2 developed, no significant complications

were encountered. Although these results showed that the use of BMP-2 in these types of injuries is safe, feasible, and probably efficacious, the final results of a larger prospective randomized clinical trial are not yet complete.

Friedlaender reported preliminary results of a multicenter clinical trial using NOVOS (Styrker Biotech, Natick, MA), a form of BMP-7 associated with a bovine-derived collagen carrier.[95] In this trial, 124 tibial nonunions in 122 patients were treated in 18 centers. Inclusion criteria were nonunion of at least 9 months and the surgeon's choice of intramedullary fixation with bone graft as the most appropriate method of treatment. None of these nonunions was expected to heal if left untreated. Patients received either autograft or NOVOS. A successful result was defined as a return to full weight bearing, reduction in pain, and radiographic union by 9 months. Preliminary results of this trial indicated that NOVOS was comparable to autogenous grafting in achieving success. The healing rate, however, was not 100% in either group.

Geesink and colleagues investigated the osteogenic potential of BMP-7 in a critically sized human bony defect model.[105] Twenty-four patients undergoing high tibial osteotomy for osteoarthritis of the knee were divided into four groups. In the first group the fibular osteotomy had been left untreated, and in the second group demineralized bone had been used to fill the defect. Radiologic and dual-energy x-ray absorptiometry parameters measured during the first postoperative year showed no evidence of bony changes in the untreated group, whereas matrix formation of new bone was observed from 6 weeks onward in the group treated with demineralized bone. The third group received 2.5 mg of recombinant BMP-7 combined with a collagen type I carrier, and the fourth group received collagen type I carrier only. The results of this part of the study showed that all but one of the patients treated with the BMP-7 exhibited formation of new bone from 6 weeks on as compared with insignificant formation of new bone observed in those who received the collagen carrier alone. The investigators concluded that recombinant human BMP-7 is effective in healing human critical-sized bony defects.

Fibroblast Growth Factors. The FGF family, to our knowledge, currently includes 19 members.[283] The most abundant types in normal adult tissues are acidic fibroblast growth factor (aFGF) and basic fibroblast growth factor (bFGF), also named FGF-1 and FGF-2. Both are heparin-binding polypeptides that have been shown to bind to the same receptor.[188] These molecules are best known for their effects on endothelial cell replication and neovascularization.[34] The expression of FGFs during fracture repair, however, has been well documented,[25, 232] and their role in fracture healing and its enhancement has been investigated in several animal studies.[24]

Although one report[18] has questioned the ability of FGF to enhance fracture healing, the results of most experiments to date have been positive with respect to their effects. Jingushi and associates, using a rat bilateral femoral fracture model, explored the effect of exogenous aFGF on normal fracture healing.[133] Compared with controls, the animals that had received injections of aFGF showed enlarged calluses in the cartilage formation stage of healing, and these calluses remained enlarged until 4 weeks after fracture. Nakamura and associates tested the effects of bFGF on healing tibial fractures in dogs[185] and concluded that bFGF promotes fracture healing in dogs by the stimulation of bone remodeling. Radomsky and co-workers, first in rabbits[212] and more recently in baboons,[211] showed evidence that FGF-2, delivered in a hyaluronan gel, accelerates fracture healing. In the latter study, FGF-2 (4 mg/mL) and hyaluronan (20 mg/mL) were combined into a viscous gel formulation and percutaneously injected as a one-time dose into a 1-mm gap osteotomy that was surgically created in the fibulae of baboons. Radiographically, this combination led to a statistically significant increase in callus area at the treated site. Histologic analysis revealed a significantly greater callus size, periosteal reaction, vascularity, and cellularity in the treated groups compared with those in the untreated controls. Furthermore, specimens treated with 0.1, 0.25, and 0.75 mL of hyaluronan/FGF-2 demonstrated a 48%, 50%, and 34% greater average load at failure and an 82%, 104%, and 66% greater energy to failure than the untreated controls, respectively. Although the aforementioned studies on the effects of exogenously delivered FGF are promising, it does not appear that this class of molecules is as specific or as potent as the BMPs. In addition, only minimal research has been reported on the side effects of high doses of FGF.[174]

Platelet-Derived Growth Factor. PDGF is the major mesenchymal cell mitogen present in serum.[225] PDGF is a dimeric molecule consisting of disulfide-bonded A- and B-polypeptide chains. Both homodimeric (PDGF-AA and PDGF-BB) and heterodimeric (PDGF-AB) forms exist.[125] A PDGF-like peptide has been found in bovine bone,[118] and it has been shown to have in vitro effects on several lines of osteoblastic cells.[43, 112, 261] Early in the course of fracture healing, it has been shown to be released by degranulating platelets in the fracture hematoma, possibly acting as a chemotactic agent.[8] Later in fracture repair, PDGF protein is detectable in both young and mature hypertrophic chondrocytes and osteoblasts.[20]

The effects of exogenously administered PDGF on fracture healing are controversial. Marden and colleagues showed that PDGF inhibits the bone regeneration induced by osteogenin in rat craniotomy defects.[167] Nash and associates tested the effects of exogenously administered PDGF on bone healing using a rabbit tibial osteotomy model.[187] Although histologically the treated groups appeared to have increased callus density and volume, three-point bending to failure testing failed to show an improvement in strength.

Systemic Enhancement

Numerous reports have shown that patients who have sustained traumatic brain injury experience faster fracture healing with more callus than healthy patients,[103, 203, 250, 254] although the mechanism by which this may occur remains unclear. Bidner and colleagues[17] showed that the serum of patients who have sustained a head injury contains a mitogenic activity that is specific for osteoblastic cells. They suggested that there might be a humoral mechanism for the enhanced osteogenesis that accompanies head injury. No conclusive evidence exists for the molecular identification of this factor. A review article insightfully suggested, in fact, that contrary to common belief, fracture healing is not necessarily accelerated in the patient with traumatic brain injury. Hypertrophic callus, myositis ossificans, and heterotopic ossification, however, do occur frequently and are often misperceived as accelerated healing.[155]

IGFs and growth hormone (GH) have been suggested to play a role in skeletal growth and remodeling. IGFs derive their name from observations that they produce insulin-like biochemical effects that are not suppressed by anti-insulin antiserum. IGFs exert biologic activity via both IGF cell surface receptors and insulin-like growth factor–binding proteins.[68, 213] IGF-1 and IGF-2 are the two most important factors of their kind, the former having the higher growth-promoting activity. IGF-1, also known as somatomedin-C, mediates the effect of GH on the skeleton.[62]

Because IGF-1 is known to be GH dependent, it is possible that IGF levels may be increased in vivo by administration of GH. Several studies have been conducted to determine the role of GH in the repair of skeletal tissues. Some showed that GH stimulates skeletal repair,[151] and others failed to show an effect.[192] An investigation of the biomechanics of fracture healing in a rabbit tibial model showed that GH treatment was unsuccessful in the stimulation of fracture healing. However, the animals in this experiment were shown to have a persistent nutritional deficit, so it is possible that the failure of GH to influence skeletal repair resulted from an inability to significantly stimulate circulating levels of IGF-I in this nutritional state.[39] Therefore, the roles of GH and IGF-1 in the systemic enhancement of skeletal repair remain unclear. IGF-2, on the other hand, is one of the most abundant growth factors in bone, circulates at higher concentrations than IGF-1, and binds to the same cell surface receptors but with a lower affinity.[99] The observation that IGF-2 is stimulated in response to externally applied magnetic fields[88] suggests that this molecule may play a role in skeletal repair. The systemic effects of these and other related molecules on the enhancement of skeletal repair may depend not only on their direct effects on the responding cells but also on the concentrations and environmental conditions under which they are permitted to act.

Raschke and co-workers[214] studied the effect of systemic administration of homologous recombinant GH on bone regenerate consolidation in distraction osteogenesis. Tibiae of 30 mature Yucatan micropigs were osteomized at the mid-diaphyseal level. Starting 5 days after surgery, the limbs were distracted using an external fixator at the rate of 2 mm/day for 10 consecutive days. Animals in the treatment group received a daily subcutaneous injection of 100 µg of recombinant porcine GH (rpGH) per kilogram of body weight, and those in the control group received sodium chloride. Nondestructive in vivo torsional stiffness (IVTS) measurements were conducted after surgery and on days 1, 2, 3, 4, 6, 8, and 10 of consolidation. After the animals were euthanized, destructive biomechanical testing was performed. Serum levels of IGF-1 were measured once during the latency period (days 1–5), four times during distraction (days 6–15), and seven times during consolidation (days 16–25) to determine the endocrine response to rpGH. Throughout the consolidation phase, the mean in vivo torsional stiffness of the treatment group was 125% higher than that of the control group on day 16, increased to 207% higher on day 19, and reached 145% on the day after killing. Final regenerate torsional failure load was 131% higher and ultimate torsional stiffness was 231% higher in the treatment group than in the control group. The mean serum level of IGF-1 increased to 440% of preoperative basal level in the treatment group and remained unchanged in the control group. These researchers concluded that systemic administration of growth hormone greatly accelerates ossification of bone regenerate in distraction osteogenesis.

Prostaglandins are another important class of compounds that may be considered for eventual use in the systemic enhancement of skeletal repair. Over the past two decades, almost every skeletal metabolic effect has been described after prostaglandin administration, from increased bone resorption to increased bone formation.[168] The first reports of bone formation after prostaglandin treatment described cortical thickening of the limb bones and ribs of neonatal infants who had been treated systemically with prostaglandin E_1 for the purpose of maintaining a patent ductus arteriosus.[253, 267] Subsequent investigations in which prostaglandin E_2 was administered systemically showed increased cortical and trabecular bone formation in dogs[126, 191] and restoration of normal skeletal mass in ovariectomized rats who had lost cancellous and cortical bone mass.[139, 140] The fact that these effects can be blocked by the administration of indomethacin, an inhibitor of prostaglandin synthesis, supports the contention that prostaglandins directly enhance bone formation.[252] Finally, several studies have shown that normal fracture healing is impaired by administration of prostaglandin inhibitors.[5, 219, 259] Although these reports suggest that prostaglandins may be useful in enhancing fracture healing, the clinical safety and efficacy of systemically administered prostaglandins to enhance skeletal repair in humans have yet to be described.

CLINICAL APPLICATIONS

Although strategies to enhance skeletal repair are the subject of ongoing research, such advances should not be envisioned as substitutes for optimal orthopaedic management. Appropriate internal or external fixation and the attainment of adequate alignment and stability will always be the mainstays of fracture care. Moreover, because of cost-containment and monitoring of practice patterns, physicians will be able to use specific new products only in situations in which their use has been carefully studied, the data scrutinized by peer review, and the indications and labeling approved by a federal regulatory agency. With these considerations in mind, our current recommendations and visions for future possibilities are presented.

Fresh Fractures

Enhancement of fresh fracture healing at the time of initial treatment may be indicated in situations in which the mechanical or physiologic environment predisposes to delayed union or nonunion. In addition, an enhanced healing process could lead to a quicker return of patients to productive work. Although adequate fixation and alignment through traditional orthopaedic principles are sufficient in most cases, even these traditional principles are subject to change. For example, Sarmiento and associates[237] demonstrated successful healing of closed diaphyseal tibial fractures with the use of cast bracing and early weight bearing, but Kenwright and colleagues[142] showed that external fixation augmented by controlled micromotion accelerated the healing process.

For more than 100 years, autogenous cancellous bone grafting has been the standard of care for augmentation of both initial fracture repair and the treatment of a nonunion.[104] As noted previously, it provides osteogenic, osteoinductive, and osteoconductive properties but is limited in its quantity and in its ability to provide immediate structural rigidity. In addition, harvesting of autogenous bone graft is not risk free. Physical methods of enhancing acute fracture healing have varying benefits. Bone graft substitutes have revolutionized fracture treatment and will continue to do so. No single graft substitute, however, is ideal for all injuries, and it is important for the surgeon to be knowledgeable about the advantages and disadvantages of all the available materials.

To summarize, the only physical method that has been shown to enhance the healing of fresh fractures is low-intensity ultrasound. This modality has been shown to be effective clinically only in the treatment of closed tibial and distal radius fractures in smokers. With regard to osteogenic methods of augmenting skeletal repair, it appears that autogenous bone graft is the most beneficial and poses the least risk of infection and complications. Vascularized cortical graft harvesting is highly demanding and has limited indications, perhaps only in the face of infection or for areas that are known to be devoid of adequate blood flow. Allografts have been shown to have up to a 15% rate of infection and therefore should be used with caution. Autogenous bone marrow preparations have not been shown to be efficacious in clinical trials, but these preparations certainly have great theoretical appeal. It is very difficult to form conclusions as to which of the commercially available bone graft substitutes is the most effective. This is in part because clinical experience is limited, and large clinical trials are lacking. The clinical experience of the authors with coralline hydroxyapatite (ProOsteon) for tibial plateau fractures has proven it to be extremely useful. Evaluating healing radiographically, however, is often difficult when using this material. We have also used injectable calcium phosphate cement (Norian SRS) for distal radius fractures with promising results as well. There has been anecdotal evidence that injecting demineralized allograft bone matrices into fresh fractures of patients who have poor healing potential, such as diabetics and smokers, enhances fracture healing in these patients. Statistically significant clinical data supporting these reports are lacking. Early human experiments have shown that injectable BMP has a role in accelerating healing of fresh fractures. Follow-up studies of these and other growth factors are awaited (Table 22–3).

TABLE 22–3 ....

Management of Fresh Fractures: Recommendations and Future Possibilities

Management	Currently Available Techniques	Future Possibilities
Nonoperative	Ultrasound (distal radius, tibia)	
Operative	Autogenous bone grafts	Osteoinductive factor
	Calcium phosphate ceramics	Expanded bone marrow osteo-progenitor cells
	External fixation-induced micro-motion	

....

Delayed Unions

Traditionally, orthopaedists have referred to a delayed union as a fracture that heals more slowly than average.[169] Although this is somewhat of a vague definition, delayed union of fractures, however measured, continues to be a problem. Current nonoperative means of augmenting healing of delayed unions include electromagnetic field stimulation. Bone marrow grafting has been proposed to augment healing in a delayed union setting, but its effectiveness has not been proved in a controlled study. Autogenous iliac grafting has repeatedly been shown to stimulate the healing process in delayed unions.[178] Injection of demineralized bone matrix as well as genetically engineered bone morphogenetic proteins into a fracture that is healing slower than average may greatly enhance the rate of fracture healing; although no detrimental effects of these treatments have been reported to date, more clinical trials are needed to prove their efficacy. Despite the attraction that some of these modalities may hold for augmenting healing, the literature is replete with data demonstrating the efficacy of more standard operative interventions. For example, reamed intramedullary nailing[262] and dynamization of fracture fixation systems[76, 278] remain the mainstays of the management of delayed union (Table 22–4).

Nonunions

Nonunion is the clinical entity that most orthopaedists equate with the need for enhanced bone healing. As with delayed unions of tibial fractures, reamed intramedullary nailing has been shown to stimulate the healing process and to lead to union in more than 90% of cases.[262]

The mainstay of treatment for nonunions remains autogenous cancellous bone grafting.[201] There is currently no evidence to suggest that osteoconductive substances (ceramics or composites) or ultrasound is effective in the healing of nonunions. On the other hand, electrical and electromagnetic stimulation has gained Food and Drug Administration approval for the treatment of certain nonunions (Table 22–5).

Fresh Fractures with Bone Loss and Reconstruction of Segmental Metaphyseal or Diaphyseal Defects

Large bone defects can be created by severe comminution or impaction at the time of initial injury or by operative resection in the treatment of bone tumors or infections. The critical determinants in choosing a material to bridge the gap or fill the defect include the biologic environment in the gap, its location (metaphyseal or diaphyseal), and the size of the defect. Previously infected or irradiated gaps and areas of extensive soft tissue loss create unfavorable biologic milieus. For metaphyseal defects, autogenous cancellous bone grafts have been shown to be successful[180] and can be combined with calcium phosphate ceramics as volume expanders if necessary (Table 22–6). If a defect is not surrounded by bone on all sides, or if its volume is greater than 30 cc, ceramics should not be used alone because they offer no osteoinductive or osteogenic potential.

The reconstruction of diaphyseal defects requires systems that can provide immediate structural rigidity (see Table 22–6). Small defects (1–2 cm) can be managed adequately with rigid fixation and autogenous cancellous bone grafts[201] or possibly with shortening of the involved bone.[52] Larger defects may be treated with autologous cortical grafts, but vascularized autologous grafts are preferable because they enhance local healing by improving blood flow and providing osteogenic cells.[158, 207, 256]

TABLE 22–4 ....

Management of Delayed Unions: Recommendations and Future Possibilities

Management	Currently Available Techniques	Future Possibilities
Nonoperative	Electromagnetic field	Osteoinductive factor
Operative	Autogenous bone grafting	Osteoinductive factor
	Reamed intramedullary nailing/dynamization	

....

TABLE 22–5 ....

Management of Nonunions: Recommendations and Future Possibilities

Management	Currently Available Techniques	Future Possibilities
Nonoperative	Electromagnetic field	Osteoinductive factor
Operative	Autogenous bone grafting	Osteoinductive factor
	Reamed intramedullary nailing	

....

TABLE 22–6 •

Management of Reconstruction of Segmental Metaphyseal or Diaphyseal Defects: Recommendations and Future Possibilities

Finding	Currently Available Techniques	Future Possibilities
Metaphyseal Defects		
<30 cc	Autogenous cancellous graft	Osteoinductive implant
	Calcium phosphate ceramics	
>30 cc	Calcium phosphate ceramic/autogenous composite graft	Osteoinductive implant
Diaphyseal Defects		
<2 cm	Autogenous cancellous graft	Osteoinductive implant
2–6 cm	Nonvascularized cortical autograft	Osteoinductive implant
	Bone transport	
>6 cm	Vascularized cortical autograft	Osteoinductive implant

• •

Vascularized cortical autografts are more appropriate for large diaphyseal defects (>6 cm). The advantages of vascularized grafts are more rapid and complete incorporation, which provides immediate structural support, and the ability of the transplanted bone to form new bone.[276] They also have the ability to hypertrophy (increasing size up to 100%) and to withstand large functional loads.[49] The fibula has been used successfully to bridge large defects in the humerus, tibia, or femur.[245] Allografts can be used in these settings, but their incorporation is markedly slower than that of autografts, and they therefore remain significantly weaker for longer periods after implantation.[98] Delayed fracture healing (up to 3 years after surgery) has been reported to occur in up to 19% of allografted fractures. In addition, complications related to rejection, usually manifest as rapid osteolysis, infection (11%), and nonunion (17%), may occur.[166] Nonvascularized cortical autografts are replaced by creeping substitution, but they eventually become completely replaced at more rapid rates than allografts. Allografts are contraindicated in the setting of a poor local blood supply because they are at increased risk for infection and may become a sequestrum.[45, 258] Bone transport is also an option and has been used successfully in many clinical studies.[72, 170] Limitations of this technique include pain, pintract problems, angulation, docking site nonunion, and poor patient cooperation. Distraction lengths greater than 6 cm are sometimes difficult to achieve.

EXPECTATIONS FOR THE FUTURE
• •

Because not all fractures heal uneventfully, research directed at discovering new methods for fracture healing enhancement will continue to be important. Physical modalities of enhancing fracture healing have been shown to be clinically useful for the treatment of nonunions and delayed unions in all patients and for accelerating fracture healing in smokers. Future investigations on these physical methods need to be directed at their effectiveness in accelerating healing of fresh fractures. Knowledge about biologic methods of fracture healing enhancement has increased tremendously over the past decade. New ceramics and allogeneic bone matrices are being developed and have been found anecdotally to be useful, although large clinical trials evaluating their efficacy and safety are lacking. As our understanding of intracellular and extracellular signaling cascades expands, the use of genetically engineered endogenous compounds such as BMPs to enhance fracture healing will progress as well. It is possible that in the future orthopaedic surgeons will give patients an oral medication that ultimately accelerates fracture healing. Given that fracture care costs societies millions of dollars yearly, such augmentation of fracture healing can be tremendously cost-effective and therefore both clinically and economically beneficial.

REFERENCES

1. Aaron, R.K.; Ciombor, D.; Jolly, G. Stimulation of experimental endochondral ossification by low-energy pulsing electromagnetic fields. J Bone Miner Res 4:227–233, 1989.
2. Aaron, R.K.; Ciombor, D.; Jones, A.R. Bone induction by decalcified bone matrix and mRNA of TGFb and IGF-1 are increased by ELF field stimulation. Trans Orthop Res Soc 22:548, 1997.
3. AATB Information Alert, vol. 3, no. 6. McLean, VA, American Association of Tissue Banks, December 15, 1993.
4. Akai, M.; Yabuki, T.; Tateishi, T.; Shirasaki, Y. Mechanical properties of the electrically stimulated callus: An experiment with constant direct current in rabbit fibulae. Clin Orthop 188:293–302, 1984.
5. Allen, H.L.; Wase, A.; Bear, W.T. Indomethacin and aspirin: Effect of nonsteroidal anti-inflammatory agents on the rate of fracture repair in the rat. Acta Orthop Scand 51:595–600, 1980.
6. Anderson, J.C.; Eriksson, C. Electrical properties of wet collagen. Nature 227:166–168, 1968.
7. Andrew, J.G.; Hoyland, J.; Andrew, S.M.; et al. Demonstration of TGF-beta 1 mRNA by in situ hybridization in normal human fracture healing. Calcif Tissue Int 52:74–78, 1993.
8. Andrew, J.G.; Hoyland, J.; Freemont, A.J.; et al. Platelet-derived growth factor expression in normally healing human fractures. Bone 16:455–460, 1995.
9. Aro, H.; Eerola, E.; Aho, A.J. Fracture healing in paraplegic rats. Acta Orthop Scand 56:228–232, 1985.
10. Bassett, C.A.L.; Becker, R.O. Generation of electric potentials in bone in response to mechanical stress. Science 137:1063–1064, 1962.
11. Bassett, C.A.L.; Mitchell, S.N.; Gaston, S.R. Treatment of ununited tibial diaphyseal fractures with pulsing electromagnetic fields. J Bone Joint Surg Am 63:511–523, 1981.
12. Bassett, C.A.L.; Pawluck, R.J. Electrical behavior of cartilage during loading. Science 814:575–577, 1974.
13. Bassett, C.A.L.; Valdes, M.G.; Hernandez, E. Modification of fracture repair with selected pulsing electromagnetic fields. J Bone Joint Surg Am 64:888–895, 1982.
14. Bauer, T.W.; Muschler, G.F. Bone graft materials. An overview of the basic science. Clin Orthop 371:10–27, 2000.
15. Beck, L.S.; DeGuzman, L.; Lee, W.P.; et al. Bone marrow augments the activity of transforming growth factor beta 1 in critical sized bone defects. Trans Orthop Res Soc 21:626, 1996.
16. Beck, L.S.; DeGuzman, L.; Lee, W.P.; et al. Transforming growth factor beta 1 bound to tricalcium phosphate persists at segmental radial defects and induces bone formation. Trans Orthop Res Soc 20:593, 1995.
17. Bidner, S.M.; Rubins, I.M.; Desjardins, J.V.; et al. Evidence for a humoral mechanism for enhanced osteogenesis after head injury. J Bone Joint Surg Am 72:1144–1149, 1990.
18. Bland, Y.S.; Critchlow, M.A.; Ashhurst, D.E. Exogenous fibroblast

growth factors-1 and -2 do not accelerate fracture healing in the rabbit. Acta Orthop Scand 66:543–548, 1995.

19. Blenman, P.R.; Carter, D.S.; Beaupré, G.S. Role of mechanical loading in the progressive ossification of the fracture callus. J Orthop Res 7:398–407, 1989.

20. Bolander, M.E. Regulation of fracture repair by growth factors. Proc Soc Exp Biol Med 200:165–170, 1992.

21. Bolander, M.E.; Balian, G. The use of demineralized bone matrix in the repair of segmental defects: Augmentation with extracted matrix proteins and a comparison with autologous grafts. J Bone Joint Surg Am 68:1264–1274, 1986.

22. Bostrom, M.P.G.; Camacho, N.P. Potential role of bone morphogenetic proteins in fracture healing. Clin Orthop 355S:274–282, 1998.

23. Bostrom, M.P.; Lane, J.M.; Berberian, W.S.; et al. Immunolocalization and expression of bone morphogenetic proteins 2 and 4 in fracture healing. J Orthop Res 13:357–367, 1995.

24. Bostrom, M.P.; Saleh, K.J.; Einhorn, T.A. Osteoinductive growth factors in preclinical fracture and long bone defects models. Orthop Clin North Am 30:647–658, 1999.

25. Bourque, W.T.; Gross, M.; Hall, B.K. Expression of four growth factors during fracture repair. Int J Dev Biol 37:573–579, 1993.

26. Boyd, H.B.; Lipinski, S.W.; Wiley, J.H. Observations on non-union of the shaft of long bones, with statistical analysis of 842 patients. J Bone Joint Surg Am 43:159–168, 1961.

27. Brighton, C.T. Current concepts review: The treatment of non-unions with electricity. J Bone Joint Surg Am 63:847–851, 1981.

28. Brighton, C.T.; Black, J.; Friedenberg, Z.B.; et al. A multicenter study of the treatment of non-union with constant direct current. J Bone Joint Surg Am 62:2–13, 1981.

29. Bruder, S.P.; Fink, D.J.; Caplan, A.I. Mesenchymal stem cells in bone development: Bone repair and skeletal regeneration. J Cell Biochem 56:283–294, 1994.

30. Bucholz, R.W.; Carlton, A.; Holmes, R. Interporous hydroxyapatite as a bone graft substitute in tibial plateau fractures. Clin Orthop 240:53–62, 1989.

31. Buckwalter, J.A. Activity vs. rest in the treatment of bone, soft tissue and joint injuries. Iowa Orthop J 15:29–42, 1995.

32. Buckwalter, J.A.; Einhorn, T.A.; Bolander, M.E.; Cruess, R.L. Healing of the musculoskeletal tissues. In: Rockwood, C.A., Jr.; Green, D.P.; Bucholz, R.W.; Heckman, J.D., eds. Rockwood and Green's Fractures in Adults. Philadelphia, J.B. Lippincott, 1996, pp. 261–304.

33. Burchardt, H. The biology of bone graft repair. Clin Orthop 174:28–42, 1983.

34. Burgess, W.H.; Maciag, T. The heparin-binding (fibroblast) growth factor family of proteins. Annu Rev Biochem 58:575–606, 1989.

35. Burwell, R.G. Studies in the transplantation of bone: VII. The fresh composite homograft-autograft of cancellous bone: An analysis of factors leading to osteogenesis in marrow transplants and in marrow-containing bone grafts. J Bone Joint Surg Br 46:110–140, 1964.

36. Buschmann, M.D.; Gluzband, Y.A.; Grodzinsky, A.J.; Hunziker, E.B. Mechanical compression modulates matrix biosynthesis in chondrocyte/agarose culture. J Cell Sci 108:1497–1508, 1995.

37. Caplan, A.I. Mesenchymal stem cells. J Orthop Res 9:641–650, 1991.

38. Caplan, A.I. The mesengenic process. Clin Plast Surg 21:429–435, 1994.

39. Carpenter, J.E.; Hipp, J.A.; Gerhart, T.N.; et al. Failure of growth hormone to alter fracture healing biomechanics in a rabbit model. J Bone Joint Surg Am 74:359–367, 1992.

40. Carter, D.R.; Blenman, P.R.; Beaupré, G.S. Correlations between mechanical stress history and tissue differentiation in initial fracture healing. J Orthop Res 6:736–748, 1988.

41. Centrella, M.; Horowitz, M.C.; Wozney, J.M.; McCarthy, T.L. Transforming growth factor-ß gene family members and bone. Endocr Rev 15:27–39, 1994.

42. Centrella, M.; McCarthy, T.L.; Canalis, E. Transforming growth factor-beta and remodeling of bone. J Bone Joint Surg Am 73:1418–1428, 1991.

43. Centrella, M.; McCarthy, T.L.; Kusmik, W.F.; et al. Relative binding and biochemical effects of heterodynamic and homodynamic isoforms of platelet-derived growth factor in osteoblast-enriched cultures from foetal rat bone. J Cell Physiol 146:420–426, 1991.

44. Chapman, M.W.; Bucholz, R.; Cornell, C. Treatment of acute fractures with a collagen-calcium phosphate graft material: A randomized clinical trial. J Bone Joint Surg Am 79:495–502, 1997.

45. Charnell, M.J.; McAndrew, M.P.; Thomas, R.; Schwartz, H.S. Structural allografts for reconstruction of lower extremity open fractures with ten centimeters or more of acute segmental defects. J Orthop Trauma 9:222–226, 1995.

46. Chase, W.S.; Herndon, C.H. The fate of autogenous and homoegeneous bone grafts: A historical review. J Bone Joint Surg Am 37:809–841, 1955.

47. Chen, C.S.; Ingber, D.E. Tensegrity and mechanoregulation. Osteoarthritis Cartilage 7:81–94, 1999.

48. Chen, P.; Carrington, J.L.; Hammonds, R.G.; Reddi, A.H. Stimulation of chondrogenesis in limb bud mesoderm cells by recombinant human bone morphogenetic protein 2B (BMP-2B) and modulation by transforming growth factor-ß1 and ß2. Exp Cell Res 195:509–515, 1991.

49. Chew, W.Y.C.; Low, C.K.; Tan, S.K. Long term results of free vascularized fibular grafts. Clin Orthop Rel Res 311:258–261, 1995.

50. Chiroff, R.; Weber, J.; White, E. Tissue ingrowth of replamineform implants. J Biomed Mater Res 9:29–45, 1975.

51. Chu, C.R.; Convery, F.R.; Akeson, W.H. Articular cartilage transplantation. Clinical results in the knee. Clin Orthop 360:159–168, 1999.

52. Cierny, G.; Zorn, K.E. Segmental tibial defects: Comparing conventional and Ilizarov methodologies. Clin Orthop 301:118–123, 1994.

53. Claes, L.; Augat, P.; Suger, G.; Wilke, H.J. Influence of size and stability of the osteotomy gap on success of fracture healing. J Orthop Res 15:577–584, 1997.

54. Claes, L.E.; Heigele, C.A.; Neidlinger-Wilke, C.; et al. Effects of mechanical factors on the fracture healing process. Clin Orthop 355:S132–S147, 1998.

55. Connolly, J.; Guse, R.; Lippiello, L.; Dehne, R. Development of an osteogenic bone marrow preparation. J Bone Joint Surg Am 71:684–691, 1989.

56. Constantz, B.R.; Ison, I.C.; Fulmer, M.T.; et al. Skeletal repair by in situ formation of the mineral phase of bone. Science 267:1796–1799, 1995.

57. Cook, S.D. Acceleration of bone healing with OP-1 in a canine noncritical size defect model. Abstract. Second International OP-1 Conference, Boston, MA, 1997.

58. Cook, S.D.; Baffes, G.C.; Wolfe, M.W.; et al. The effect of recombinant human osteogenic protein-1 on healing of large segmental bone defects. J Bone Joint Surg Am 76:827–838, 1994.

59. Cook, S.D.; Baffes, G.C.; Wolfe, M.W.; et al. Recombinant human bone morphogenetic protein-7 induces healing in a canine long-bone segmental defect model. Clin Orthop 301:302–312, 1994.

60. Cook, S.D.; Ryaby, J.P.; McCabe, J.; Frey, J.J.; et al. Acceleration of tibia and distal radius fracture healing in patients who smoke. Clin Orthop 337:198–207, 1997.

61. Cook, S.D.; Wolfe, M.W.; Salkeld, S.L.; et al. Effect of recombinant human osteogenic protein-1 on healing of segmental defects in non-human primates. J Bone Joint Surg Am 77:734–750, 1995.

62. Copeland, K.C.; Underwood, L.E.; Van Wyk, J.J. Induction of imunoreactive somatomedin C in human serum by growth hormone: Dose response relationships and effects on chromatographic profiles. J Clin Endocrinol Metab 50:690–697, 1980.

63. Cornell, C.N. Initial clinical experience with use of collagraft as a bone graft substitute. Tech Orthop 7:55–63, 1992.

64. Cornell, C.N.; Lane, J.M. Current understanding of osteoconduction in bone regeneration. Clin Orthop 355:S267–S273, 1998.

65. Cornell, C.N.; Lane, J.M.; Chapman, M.; et al. Multicenter trial of Collagraft as bone graft substitute. J Orthop Trauma 5:1–8, 1991.

66. Court-Brown, C.; McQueen, M. Compartment syndrome delays tibial union. Acta Orthop Scand 58:249–252, 1987.

67. Critchlow, M.A.; Bland, Y.S.; Ashhurst, D.E. The effect of exogenous transforming growth factor-beta 2 on healing fractures in the rabbit. Bone 16:521–527, 1995.

68. Czech, M.P. Signal transmission by the insulin-like growth factors. Cell 59:235–238, 1989.

69. den Boer, F.C.; Bramer, J.A.M.; Blokhius, T.J.; et al. The effect of recombinant human osteogenic protein-1 on the healing of fresh closed diaphyseal fracture. Abstract. Second International OP-1 Conference, Boston, MA, 1997.

70. Dennis, J.E.; Caplan, A.I. Porous ceramic vehicles for rat marrow-derived (*Rattus norvegicus*) osteogenic cell delivery: Effects of pretreatment with fibronectin or laminin. J Oral Implant 19:106–115, 1993.

71. Diduch, D.R.; Coe, M.R.; Joyner, C.; et al. Two cell lines from bone marrow that differ in terms of collagen synthesis, osteogenic characteristics, and matrix mineralization. J Bone Joint Surg Am 75:92–105, 1993.

72. DiPasquale, D.; Ochsner, M.G.; Kelly, A.M.; Maloney, D.M. The Ilizarov method for complex fracture non-unions. J Trauma 37:629–634, 1994.

73. Doi, K.; Oda, T.; Soo-Heong, T.; Nanda, V. Free vascularized bone graft for non-union of the scaphoid. J Hand Surg [Am] 25:507–519, 2000.

74. Duarte, L.R. The stimulation of bone growth by ultrasound. Arch Orthop Trauma Surg 101:153–159, 1983.

75. Duffy, G.P.; Wood, M.B.; Rock, M.G.; Sim, F.H. Vascularized free fibular transfer combined with autografting for the management of fracture non-unions associated with radiation therapy. J Bone Joint Surg Am 82:544–554, 2000.

76. Egger, E.L.; Gottsauner, F.; Palmer, J.; et al. Effects of axial dynamization on bone healing. J Trauma 34:185–192, 1993.

77. Einhorn, T.A. Current concepts review: Enhancement of fracture-healing. J Bone Joint Surg Am 77:940–956, 1995.

78. Einhorn, T.A.; Bonnarens, F.; Burnstein, A.H. The contributions of dietary protein and mineral to the healing of experimental fractures: A biomechanical study. J Bone Joint Surg Am 68:1389–1395, 1986.

79. Einhorn, T.A.; Lane, J.M.; Burstein, A.H.; et al. The healing of segmental bone defects induced by demineralized bone matrix: A radiographic and biomechanical study. J Bone Joint Surg Am 66:274–279, 1984.

80. Einhorn, T.A.; Majeska, R.J.; Oloumi, G.; et al. Enhancement of experimental fracture healing with a local percutaneous injection of rhBMP-2. Abstract. American Academy of Orthopaedic Surgeons Annual Meeting, San Francisco, California, 1997.

81. Einhorn, T.A.; Majeska, R.J.; Rush, E.B.; et al. The expression of cytokine activity by fracture callus. J Bone Miner Res 10:1272–1281, 1995.

82. Elder, S.; Frankenburg, E.; Goulet, J.; et al. Biomechanical evaluation of calcium phosphate cement–augmented fixation of unstable intertrochanteric fractures. J Orthop Trauma 14:386–393, 2000.

83. Ellies, L.G.; Nelson, D.G.; Featherstone, J.D. Crystallographic structure and surface morphology of sintered carbonated apatites. J Biomed Mater Res 22:541–553, 1988.

84. Emami, A.; Petren-Mallmin, M.; Larsson, S. No effect of low-intensity ultrasound on healing time of intramedullary fixed tibial fractures. J Orthop Trauma 13:252–257, 1999.

85. Enneking, W.F.; Burchardt, H.; Puhl, J.J.; Piotrowski, G. Physical and biological aspects of repair in dog cortical bone transplants. J Bone Joint Surg Am 57:237–252, 1975.

86. Fitzsimmons, R.J.; Ryaby, J.T.; Magee, F.P.; Baylink, D.J. IGF-II receptor number is increased in TE-85 cells by low amplitude, low frequency, electromagnetic field exposure. J Bone Miner Res 10:812–819, 1995.

87. Fitzsimmons, R.J.; Ryaby, J.T.; Magee, F.P.; et al. Combined magnetic fields increase IGF-II secretion in osteoblast cultures. Endocrinology 136:3100–3106, 1995.

88. Fitzsimmons, R.J.; Ryaby, J.T.; Mohan, S.; et al. Combined magnetic fields increase insulin-like growth factor II in TE85 human osteosarcoma bone cell cultures. Endocrinology 136:3100–3106, 1995.

89. Frankenburg, E.P.; Goldstein, S.A.; Bauer, T.W; et al. Biomechanical and histological evaluation of a calcium phosphate cement. J Bone Joint Surg Am 80:1112–1124, 1998.

90. Frayssinet, P.; Mathon, D.; Lerch, A.; et al. Osseointegration of composite calcium phosphate bioceramics. J Biomed Mater Res 50:125–130, 2000.

91. Fredericks, D.C.; Nepola, J.V.; Baker, J.T.; et al. Effects of pulsed electromagnetic fields on bone healing in a rabbit tibial osteotomy model. J Orthop Trauma 14:93–100, 2000.

92. Friedenberg, Z.B.; Andrews, E.T.; Smolenski, B.I.; et al. Bone reaction to varying amounts of direct current. Surg Gynecol Obstet 131:894–899, 1970.

93. Friedenberg, Z.B.; Brighton, C.T. Bioelectric potentials in bone. J Bone Joint Surg Am 48:915–923, 1966.

94. Friedenstein, A.J.; Chailakhyan, R.K.; Gerasimov, U.V. Bone marrow osteogenic stem cells in vitro cultivation and transplantation in diffusion chambers. Cell Tissue Kinet 20:263–272, 1987.

95. Friedlaender, G. Treatment of established tibial non-unions using recombinant osteogenic protein-1 (OP-1). Abstract. Second International OP-1 Conference, Boston, MA, 1997.

96. Friedlaender, G.E. Bone grafts: The basic science rationale for clinical applications. J Bone Joint Surg Am 69:786–790, 1987.

97. Friedlaender, G.E. Immune responses to osteochondral allografts: Current knowledge and future directions. Clin Orthop 174:58–68, 1983.

98. Friedlaender, G.E.; Goldberg, V.M., eds. Bone and Cartilage Allografts: Biology and Clinical Applications. Park Ridge, IL, American Academy of Orthopaedic Surgeons, 1991.

99. Frolik, C.A.; Ellis, L.F.; Williams, D.C. Isolation and characterization of insulin-like growth factor II from human bone. Biochem Biophys Res Comm 151:1011–1018, 1988.

100. Fukada, E.; Yasuda, I. On the piezoelectric effect of bone. J Physiol Soc Jpn 12:121–128, 1957.

101. Gabl, M.; Reinhart, C.; Lutz, M.; et al. Vascularized bone graft from the iliac crest for the treatment of non-union of the proximal part of the scaphoid with an avascular fragment. J Bone Joint Surg Am 81:1414–1428, 1999.

102. Garg, N.K.; Gaur, S.; Sharma, S. Percutaneous autogenous bone marrow grafting in 20 cases of ununited fracture. Acta Orthop Scand 64:671–672, 1993.

103. Garland, D.E.; Toder, L. Fractures of the tibial diaphysis in adults with head injuries. Clin Orthop 150:198–202, 1980.

104. Gazdag, A.R.; Lane, J.M.; Glaser, D.; Forster, R.A. Alternatives to autogenous bone graft: Efficacy and indications. J Am Acad Orthop Surg 3:1–8, 1995.

105. Geesink, R.G.T.; Hoefnagels, N.H.M.; Bulstra, S.K. Osteogenic activity of OP-1 bone morphogenetic protein (BMP-7) in a human fibular defect. J Bone Joint Surg Br 81:710–718, 1999.

106. Gerhart, T.N.; Kirker-Head, C.A.; Kriz, M.J. Healing segmental femoral defects in sheep using recombinant human bone morphogenetic protein. Clin Orthop 293:317–326, 1993.

107. Glowacki, J.; Kaban, L.B.; Murray, J.E.; et al. Application of the biological principle of induced osteogenesis for craniofacial defects. Lancet 1:959–963, 1981.

108. Goodman, S.B.; Bauer, T.W.; Carter, D.; et al. Norian SRS cement augmentation in hip fracture treatment. Laboratory and initial clinical results. Clin Orthop 348:42–50, 1998.

109. Goodship, A.E.; Kenwright, J. The influence of induced micromovement upon the healing of experimental fractures. J Bone Joint Surg Br 67:650–655, 1985.

110. Goodwin, C.B.; Brighton, C.T.; Guyer, R.D.; et al. A double-blind study of capacitively coupled electrical stimulation as an adjunct to lumbar spinal fusions. Spine 24:1349–1356, 1999.

111. Goshima, J.; Goldberg, V.M.; Caplan, A.I. The origin of bone formed in composite grafts of porous calcium phosphate ceramic loaded with marrow cells. Clin Orthop 269:274–283, 1991.

112. Graves, D.T.; Antoniades, H.N.; Williams, S.R.; et al. Evidence for functional platelet-derived growth factor receptors on MG-63 human osteosarcoma cells. Cancer Res 44:2966–2970, 1984.

113. Gray, M.L.; Pizzanelli, A.M.; Grodzinsky, A.J.; et al. Mechanical and physicochemical determinants of the chondrocyte biosynthetic response. J Orthop Res 6:777–792, 1988.

114. Grodzinsky, A.J. Electromechanical and physicochemical properties of connective tissue. Crit Rev Biomed Eng 9:133–199, 1983.

115. Grodzinsky, A.J.; Lipshitz, H.; Glimcher, M.J. Electromechanical properties of articular cartilage during compression and stress relaxation. Nature 275:448–450, 1978.

116. Guilak, F. Compression-induced changes in the shape and volume of the chondrocyte nucleus. J Biomech 28:1529–1541, 1995.

117. Hartshorne, E. On the cause of pseudoarthrosis and especially that form of it sometimes called supernumerary joint. Am J Med 1:121–156, 1841.

118. Hauschka, P.V.; Mavrakos, A.E.; Iafrati, M.D.; et al. Growth factors in bone matrix: Isolation of multiple types of affinity chromatography on heparin-sepharose. J Biol Chem 261:12665–12674, 1986.

119. Hayashi, K.; Ishidou, Y.; Yonemori, K.; et al. Expression and localization of bone morphogenetic proteins (BMPs) and BMP receptors in ossification of the ligamentum flavum. Bone 21:23–30, 1997.

120. Heckman, J.D.; Aufdemorte, T.B.; Athanasiou, K.A.; et al. Treatment of acute ostectomy defects in the dog radius with rhTGF-ß1. Trans Orthop Res Soc 20:590, 1995.

121. Heckman, J.D.; Boyan, B.D.; Aufdemorte, T.B.; et al. The use of bone morphogenetic protein in the treatment of non-union in a canine model. J Bone Joint Surg Am 73:750–764, 1991.

122. Heckman, J.D.; Ehler, W.; Brooks, B.P.; et al. Bone morphogenetic protein but not transforming growth factor-ß enhances bone formation in canine diaphyseal non-unions implanted with a biodegradable composite polymer. J Bone Joint Surg Am 81:1717–1729, 1999.

123. Heckman, J.D.; Ryaby, J.P.; McCabe, J.; et al. Acceleration of tibial fracture-healing by noninvasive low-intensity pulsed ultrasound. J Bone Joint Surg Am 76:26–34, 1994.

124. Heiple, K.G.; Chase, S.W.; Herndon, C.H. A comparative study of the healing process following different types of bone transplantation. J Bone Joint Surg Am 45:1593–1616, 1963.

125. Heldin, C.H.; Ostman, A.; Ronnstrand, L. Signal transduction via platelet-derived growth factor receptors. Biochim Biophys Acta 1378:F79–F113, 1998.

126. High, W. Effects of orally administered prostaglandin E1 on cortical bone turnover in adult dogs: A histomorphometric study. Bone 8:363–374, 1987.

127. Hogan, B.L.M. Bone morphogenetic proteins: Multifunctional regulators of vertebrate development. Genes Dev 10:1580–1594, 1996.

128. Ilizarov, G.A. The tension-stress effect on the genesis and growth of tissues: Part I. Clin Orthop 238:249–281, 1989.

129. Ingber, D.E. Tensegrity: The architectural basis of cellular mechanotransduction. Annu Rev Physiol 59:575–599, 1997.

130. Ingram, R.T.; Bonde, S.K.; Riggs, B.L.; et al. Effects of transforming growth factor beta (TGF-ß) and 1,25 dihydroxyvitamin D3 on the function, cytochemistry, and morphology of normal human osteoblast-like cells. Differentiation 55:153–163, 1994.

131. Ishidou, Y.; Kitajima, I.; Obama, H.; et al. Enhanced expression of type I receptors for bone morphogenetic proteins during bone formation. J Bone Miner Res 10:1651–1659, 1995.

132. Jensen, S.S.; Aaboe, M.; Pinholt, E.M.; et al. Tissue reaction and material characteristics of four bone substitutes. Int J Oral Maxillofac Implants 11:55–56, 1996.

133. Jingushi, S.; Heydemann, A.; Kana, S.K.; et al. Acidic fibroblast growth factor (aFGF) injection stimulates cartilage enlargement and inhibits cartilage gene expression in rat fracture healing. J Orthop Res 8:364–371, 1990.

134. Joyce, M.E.; Jingushi, S.; Bolander, M.E. Transforming growth factor-beta in the regulation of fracture repair. Orthop Clin North Am 21:199–209, 1990.

135. Joyce, M.E.; Nemeth, G.G.; Jingushi, S.; et al. Expression and localization of transforming growth factor-ß in a model of fracture healing. Proceedings of the 35th Annual Meeting of the Orthopedic Research Society. Orthop Trans 13:460, 1989.

136. Jupiter, J.B.; Winters, S.; Sigman, S.; et al. Repair of five distal radius fractures with an investigational cancellous bone cement: A preliminary report. J Orthop Trauma 11:110–116, 1997.

137. Kaban, L.B.; Mulliken, J.B.; Glowacki, J. Treatment of jaw defects with demineralized bone implants. J Oral Maxillofac Surg 40:623–626, 1982.

138. Kawata, A.; Mikuni-Takagaki, Y. Mechanotransduction in stretched osteocytes: Temporal expression of immediate early and other genes. Biochem Biophys Res Commun 246:404–408, 1998.

139. Ke, H.Z.; Li, M.; Jee, W.S. Prostaglandin E2 prevents ovariectomy-induced cancellous bone loss in rats. Bone Miner 19:45–62, 1992.

140. Ke, H.Z.; Li, X.J.; Jee, W.S. Partial loss of anabolic effect of prostaglandin E2 on bone after its withdrawal in rats. Bone 12:173–183, 1991.

141. Kenwright, J; Goodship, A.R. Controlled mechanical stimulation in the treatment of tibial fractures. Clin Orthop 241:36–47, 1989.

142. Kenwright, J.; Richardson, J.B.; Cunningham, J.L.; et al. Axial movement and tibial fractures. J Bone Joint Surg Br 73:654–659, 1991.

143. Kenwright, J.; Richardson, J.B.; Goodship, A.E.; et al. Effect of controlled axial microenvironment on healing of tibial fractures. Lancet 2:1185–1187, 1986.

144. Kershaw, C.J.; Cunningham, J.L.; Kenwright, J. Tibial external fixation, weight bearing, and fracture movement. Clin Orthop 293:28–36, 1993.

145. Kim, Y.J.; Grodzinsky, A.J.; Plaas, A.H. Compression of cartilage results in differential effects on biosynthetic pathways for aggrecan, link protein and hyaluronan. Arch Biochem Biophys 328:331–340, 1996.

146. Kingsley, D.M. The transforming growth factor beta superfamily: New members, new receptors, and new genetic tests of function in different organisms. Genes Dev 8:133–146, 1994.

147. Kirchen, M.E.; O'Connor, K.M.; Gruber, H.E.; et al. Effects of microgravity on bone healing in a rat fibular osteotomy model. Clin Orthop 318:231–242, 1995.

148. Kirker-Head, C.A.; Gerhart, T.N.; Armstrong, R.; et al. Healing bone using recombinant human bone morphogenetic protein 2 and copolymer. Clin Orthop 349:205–217, 1998.

149. Kirker-Head, C.A.; Gerhart, T.N.; Schelling, S.H.; et al. Long term healing of bone using recombinant human bone morphogenetic protein 2. Clin Orthop 318:222–230, 1995.

150. Kopylov, P.; Runnqvist, K.; Jonsson, K.; Aspenberg, P. Norian SRS versus external fixation in redisplaced distal radial fractures. A randomized study in 40 patients. Acta Orthop Scand 70:1–5, 1999.

151. Koskinen, E.V.S.; Lindholm, R.V.; Nieminen, R.A.; et al. Human growth hormone in delayed union and non-union of fracture. Int Orthop 1:317–322, 1978.

152. Kristiansen, T.K.; Ryaby, J.P.; McCabe, J; et al. Accelerated healing of distal radial fractures with the use of specific, low-intensity ultrasound. A multicenter, prospective, randomized, double-blind placebo-controlled study. J Bone Joint Surg Am 79:961–973, 1997.

153. Kurioka, K.; Umeda, M.; Teranobu, O.; Komori, T. Effect of various properties of hydroxyapatite ceramics on osteoconduction and stability. Kobe J Med Sci 45:149–163, 1999.

154. Kurz, L.T.; Garfin, S.R.; Booth, R.E. Harvesting autogenous iliac bone grafts: A review of complications and techniques. Spine 14:1324–1331, 1989.

155. Kushwaha, V.P.; Garland, D.G. Extremity fractures in the patient with a traumatic brain injury. J Am Acad Orthop Surg 6:298–307, 1998.

156. Kwiatkowski, T.C.; Hanley, E.N.; Ramp, W.K. Cigarette smoking and its orthopaedic consequences. Am J Orthop 9:590–595, 1996.

157. Ladd, A.L.; Pliam, N.B. Use of bone-graft substitutes in distal radius fractures. J Am Acad Orthop Surg 7:279–290, 1999.

158. Lai-Toh, C.; Jupiter, J.B. The infected non-union of the tibia. Clin Orthop 315:176–191, 1995.

159. Law, H.T.; Annan, I.; McCarthy, I.D.; et al. The effect of induced electric currents on bone after experimental osteotomy in sheep. J Bone Joint Surg Br 67:463–469, 1985.

160. Lee, F.Y.; Hazan, E.J.; Gebhardt, M.C.; Mankin, H.J. Experimental model for allograft incorporation and allograft fracture repair. J Orthop Res 18:303–306, 2000.

161. Lein, P.; Johnson, M.; Guo, X.; et al. Osteogenic protein-1 induces dendritic growth in rat sympathetic neurons. Neuron 15:597–605, 1995.

162. Lente, R.W. Cases of ununited fracture treated by electricity. N Y State J Med 5:317–319, 1850.

163. Lind, M.; Schumacker, B.; Soballe, K.; et al. Transforming growth factor-ß enhances fracture healing in rabbit tibiae. Acta Orthop Scand 64:553–556, 1993.

164. Lotke, P.A.; Black, J.; Richardson S. Electromechanical properties in human articular cartilage. J Bone Joint Surg Am 56:1040–1048, 1974.

165. Macey, L.R.; Kana, S.M.; Jingushi, S.; et al. Defects of early fracture healing in experimental diabetes. J Bone Joint Surg Am 71:722–733, 1989.

166. Mankin, H.J.; Gebhardt, M.C.; Jennings, L.C.; et al. Long-term results of allograft replacement in the management of bone tumors. Clin Orthop 324:86–97, 1996.

167. Marden, L.J.; Fan, R.S.P.; Pierce, G.F.; et al. Platelet derived growth factor inhibits bone regeneration induced by osteogenin, a bone morphogenetic protein, in rat craniotomy defects. J Clin Invest 92:2897–2905, 1993.

168. Marks, S.C., Jr.; Miller, S.C. Effects of prostaglandins on the skeleton. In: Hollinger, J.; Seyfer, A.E., eds. Portland Bone Symposium 1993. Portland, Oregon Health Sciences University, 1993, pp. 39–60.

169. Marsh, J.L.; Buckwalter, J.A.; Evarts, C.M. Non-union, delayed union, malunion and avascular necrosis. In: Epps, C.H., ed. Complications in Orthopaedic Surgery. Philadelphia, J.B. Lippincott, 1994, pp. 183–211.

170. Marsh, J.L.; Prokuski, L.; Biermann, J.S. Chronic infected tibial non-unions with bone loss: Conventional techniques versus bone transport. Clin Orthop 301:139–146, 1994.

171. Massague, J. TGF-B signaling: Receptors, transducers, and mad proteins. Cell 85:947–950, 1996.

172. Matyas, J.R.; Anton, M.G.; Shrive, N.G.; Frank, C.B. Stress governs tissue phenotype at the femoral insertion of the rabbit MCL. J Biomech 28:147–157, 1995.

173. Mayr, E.; Frankel, V.; Ruter, A. Ultrasound—An alternative healing method for non-unions. Arch Orthop Trauma Surg 120:1–8, 2000.

174. Mazue, G.; Bertolero, F.; Garofano, L.; et al. Experience with the preclinical assessment of basic fibroblast growth factor (bFGF). Toxicol Lett 64:329–338, 1992.

175. McKibbin, B. The biology of fracture healing in long bones. J Bone Joint Surg Br 60:150–162, 1978.

176. McLeod, K.J.; Rubin, C.T. The effect of low-frequency electrical fields on osteogenesis. J Bone Joint Surg Am 74:920–929, 1992.

177. Meadows, T.H.; Bronk, J.T.; Chao, E.Y.S.; Kelly, P.J. Effect of weight bearing on healing of cortical defects in the canine tibia. J Bone Joint Surg Am 72:1074–1080, 1990.

178. Meiser, K.; Segal, D.; Whitelaw, G.P. The role of bone grafting in the treatment of delayed unions and non-unions of the tibia. Orthop Rev 19:260–271, 1990.

179. Mooney, V.; Nickel, V.L.; Harvey, J.P., Jr.; et al. Cast-brace treatment for fractures of the distal part of the femur: A prospective controlled study of one hundred and fifty patients. J Bone Joint Surg Am 52:1563–1578, 1970.

180. Moore, T.M.; Patzakis, M.J.; Harvey, J.P. Tibial plateau fractures: Definition, demographics, treatment rationale, and long-term results of closed traction management of operative reduction. J Orthop Trauma 1:97–119, 1987.

181. Mulliken, J.B.; Glowacki, J.; Kaban, L.B.; et al. Use of demineralized allogeneic bone implants for the correction of maxillocraniofacial deformities. Ann Surg 194:366–372, 1981.

182. Muschler, G.F.; Lane, J.M. Orthopaedic surgery. In: Habal, M.B.; Reddi, A.H., eds. Bone Grafts and Bone Substitutes. Philadelphia, W.B. Saunders, 1992, pp. 375–407.

183. Mustoe, T.A.; Glenn, F.P.; Thomason, A.; et al. Accelerated healing of incisional wounds in rats induced by transforming growth factor. Science 237:1333–1336, 1987.

184. Nagai, M.; Ota, M. Pulsating electromagnetic field stimulates mRNA expression of bone morphogenetic protein-2 and-4. J Dent Res 73:1601–1605, 1994.

185. Nakamura, T.; Hara, Y.; Tagawa, M.; et al. Recombinant human fibroblast growth factor accelerates fracture healing by enhancing callus remodeling in experimental dog tibial fracture. J Bone Miner Res 13:942–949, 1988.

186. Nakase, T.; Nomura, S.; Yoshikawa, H.; et al. Transient and localized expression of bone morphogenetic protein 4 messenger RNA during fracture healing. J Bone Miner Res 9:651–659, 1994.

187. Nash, T.J.; Howlett, C.R.; Steele, J.; et al. Effect of platelet-derived growth factor on tibial osteotomies in rabbits. Bone 15:203–208, 1994.

188. Neufeld, G.; Gospodarowicz, D. Basic and acidic fibroblast growth factors interact with the same cell surface receptors. J Biol Chem 261:5631–5637, 1986.

189. Nicoll, E.A. Fractures of the tibial shaft: A survey of 705 cases. J Bone Joint Surg Br 46:373–387, 1964.

190. Nielson, H.M.; Andreassen, T.T.; Ledet, T.; Oxlund, H. Local injection of TGF-beta increases the strength of tibial fractures in the rat. Acta Orthop Scand 65:37–41, 1994.

191. Norrdin, R.W.; Shih, M. Systemic effects of prostaglandin E2 on vertebral trabecular remodeling in beagles used in a healing study. Calcif Tissue Int 42:363–368, 1988.

192. Northmore-Ball, M.D.; Wood, M.R.; Meggitt, B.E. A biomechanical study of the effects of growth hormone in experimental fracture healing. J Bone Joint Surg Br 62:391–396, 1980.

193. Ogawa, Y.; Schmidt, D.K.; Dasch, J.R.; et al. Purification and characterization of transforming growth factor-ß2.3 and ß1.2 heterodimers from bovine bone. J Biol Chem 267:2325–2328, 1992.

194. Onishi, T.; Ishidou, T.; Nagamine, K.; et al. Distinct and overlapping patterns of localization of bone morphogenetic protein (BMP) family members and a BMP type II receptor during fracture healing in rats. Bone 22:605–612, 1998.

195. Oonishi, H.; Kushitani, S.; Yasukawa, E.; et al. Particulate bioglass compared with hydroxyapatite as a bone graft substitute. Clin Orthop 334:316–325, 1997.

196. Oreffo, R.O.; Mundy, G.R.; Seyedin, S.M.; Bonewald, L.F. Activation of the latent bone derived TGF beta complex by isolated osteoclasts. Biochem Biophys Res Commun 158:817–823, 1989.

197. O'Sullivan, M.E.; Chao, E.Y.S.; Kelly, P.J. Current concepts review: The effects of fixation on fracture healing. J Bone Joint Surg Am 71:306–310, 1989.

198. Owan, I.; Burr, D.B.; Turner, C.H.; et al. Mechanotransduction in bone: Osteoblasts are more responsive to fluid forces than mechanical strain. Am J Physiol 273:C810–C815, 1997.

199. Owen, M. Lineage of osteogenic cells and their relationship to the stromal system. In: Peck, W.A., ed. Bone and Mineral Research, 3rd ed. New York, Elsevier, 1985, pp. 1–25.

200. Parvizi, J.; Wu, C.C.; Lewallen, D.G.; et al. Low-intensity ultrasound stimulates proteoglycan synthesis in rat chondrocytes by increasing aggrecan gene expression. J Orthop Res 17:488–494, 1999.

201. Patzakis, M.J.; Scilaris, T.A.; Chon, J.; et al. Results of bone grafting for infected tibial non-union. Clin Orthop Rel Res 315:192–198, 1995.

202. Pelker, R.R; Friedlaender, G.E.; Markham, T.C.; et al. Effects of freezing and freeze drying on the biomechanical properties of rat bone. J Orthop Res 1:405–411, 1984.

203. Perkins, R.; Skirving, A.P. Callus formation and the rate of healing of femoral fractures in patients with head injuries. J Bone Joint Surg Br 69:521–524, 1987.

204. Perren, S.M. Physical and biological aspects of fracture healing with special reference to internal fixation. Clin Orthop 138:138–195, 1979.

205. Peterson, D.R.; Glancy, T.P.; Bacon-Clarke, R.; et al. A study of delivery timing and duration on the transforming growth factor beta 1 induced healing of critical-size long bone defects. Abstract. J Bone Miner Res 12:S304, 1997.

206. Pilla, A.A.; Mont, M.A.; Nasser, P.R.; et al. Noninvasive low-intensity pulsed ultrasound accelerates bone healing in the rabbit. J Orthop Trauma 4:246–253, 1990.

207. Pirela-Cruz, M.A.; DeCoster, T.A. Vascularized bone grafts. Orthopaedics 17:407–412, 1994.

208. Plenk, H.; Hollmann, K.; Wilfert, K.H. Experimental bridging of osseous defects in rats by the implantation of Kiel bone containing fresh autologous marrow. J Bone Joint Surg Br 54:735–743, 1972.

209. Poplich, L.S.; Salfeld, S.L.; Rueger, D.C.; et al. Critical and noncritical size defects healing with osteogenic protein-1. Abstract. Trans Orthop Res Soc 22:600, 1997.

210. Praemer, A.; Furner, S.; Rice, D.P. Musculoskeletal injuries. In: Musculoskeletal Conditions in the United States. Park Ridge, IL, American Academy of Orthopaedic Surgeons, 1992, pp. 85–124.

211. Radomsky, M.L.; Aufdemorte, T.B.; Swain, L.D.; et al. Novel formulation of fibroblast growth factor-2 in a hyaluronan gel accelerates fracture healing in nonhuman primates. J Orthop Res 17:607–614, 1999.

212. Radomsky, M.L.; Thompson, A.Y.; Spiro, R.C.; et al. Potential role of fibroblast growth factor in enhancement of fracture healing. Clin Orthop 355S:283–293, 1998.

213. Rajaram, S.; Baylink, D.J.; Mohan, S. Insulin-like growth factor binding proteins in serum and other biological fluids: Regulation and functions. Endocr Rev 18:801–831, 1997.

214. Raschke, M.J.; Bail, H.; Windhagen, H.J.; et al. Recombinant growth hormone accelerates bone regenerate consolidation in distraction osteogenesis. Bone 24:81–88, 1999.

215. Reddi, A.H. Extracellular matrix and development. In: Piez, K.A.; Reddi, A.H., eds. Extracellular Matrix Biochemistry. New York, Elsevier, 1984, pp. 375–412.

216. Reher, P.; Doan, N.; Bradnock, B.; et al. Effect of ultrasound on the production of IL-8, basic FGF and VEGF. Cytokine 11:416–423, 1999.

217. Riedel, G.E.; Valentin-Opran, A. Clinical evaluation of rhBMP-2/ACS in orthopedic trauma: A progress report. Orthopedics 22:663–665, 1999.

218. Riggins, R.S.; Simanonok, C.; Lewis, D.W.; Smith, A.H. Weight bearing: Its lack of effect on fracture healing. Int Orthop 9:199–203, 1985.

219. Ro, J.; Sudman, E.; Marton, P.F. Effect of indomethacin on fracture healing in rats. Acta Orthop Scand 47:588–599, 1976.

220. Roberts, A.B.; Anzano, M.A.; Lamb, L.C.; et al. New class of transforming growth factors potentiated by epidermal growth factor: Isolation from non-neoplastic tissues. Proc Natl Acad Sci U S A 78:5339–5343, 1981.

221. Robey, P.G.; Young, M.F.; Flanders, K.C.; et al. Osteoblasts synthesize and respond to transforming growth factor-ß in vitro. J Cell Biol 105:457–463, 1987.

222. Robinson, D.; Alk, D.; Sandbank, J.; et al. Inflammatory reactions associated with a calcium sulfate bone substitute. Ann Transplant 4:91–97, 1999.

223. Rosen, D.M.; Stempien, S.A.; Thompson, A.Y.; et al. Transforming growth factor-ß modulates the expression of osteoblasts and chondrocyte phenotypes in vitro. J Cell Physiol 134:337–346, 1988.

224. Rosier, R.N.; O'Keefe, R.J.; Hicks, D.G. The potential role of transforming growth factor beta in fracture healing. Clin Orthop 355:S294–S300, 1998.

225. Ross, R.; Raines, E.W.; Boewn-Pope, D. The biology of platelet derived growth factor. Cell 46:155–169, 1986.

226. Rothman, R.H.; Klemek, J.S.; Toton, J.J. The effect of iron deficiency anemia on fracture healing. Clin Orthop 77:276–283, 1971.

227. Rubin, C.; Gross, T.; Qin, Y.X.; et al. Differentiation of the bone-tissue remodeling response to axial and torsional loading in the turkey ulna. J Bone Joint Surg Am 78:1523–1533, 1996.

228. Sakou, T. Bone morphogenetic proteins: From basic studies to clinical approaches. Bone 22:591–603, 1998.

229. Salama, R.; Burwell, R.G.; Dickson, I.R. Recombined grafts of bone and marrow: The beneficial effect upon osteogenesis of impregnating xenograft (heterograft) bone with autologous red marrow. J Bone Joint Surg Br 55:402–417, 1973.

230. Salama, R.; Weissman, S.L. The clinical use of combined xenografts of bone and autologous red marrow: A preliminary report. J Bone Joint Surg Br 60:111–115, 1978.

231. Sanchez-Sotelo, J.; Munuera, L.; Madero, R. Treatment of fractures of the distal radius with a remodellable bone cement: A prospective, randomized study using Norian SRS. J Bone Joint Surg Br 82:856–863, 2000.

232. Sandberg, M.M.; Aro, H.T.; Vuorio, E.I. Gene expression during bone repair. Clin Orthop 289:292–312, 1993.

233. Sarker, A.B.; Nashimuddin, A.N.; Islam, K.M.; et al. Effect of PEMF on fresh fracture-healing in rat tibia. Bangladesh Med Res Counc Bull 19:103–112, 1993.

234. Sarmiento, A. A functional below-the-knee cast for tibial fractures. J Bone Joint Surg Am 49:855–875, 1967.

235. Sarmineto, A. On the behavior of closed tibial fractures: Clinical/radiological correlations. J Orthop Trauma 14:199–205, 2000.

236. Sarmiento, A.; Schaeffer, J.F.; Beckerman, L.; et al. Fracture healing in rat femora as affected by functional weightbearing. J Bone Joint Surg Am 59:369–375, 1977.

237. Sarmiento, A.; Sharpe, F.E.; Ebramzadeh, E.; et al. Factors influencing outcome of closed tibial fractures treated with functional bracing. Clin Orthop 315:8–24, 1995.

238. Sartoris, D.J.; Gershuni, D.H.; Akeson, W.H.; et al. Coralline hydroxyapatite bone graft substitutes: Preliminary report of radiographic evaluation. Radiology 159:133–137, 1986.

239. Schildhauer, T.A.; Bauer, T.W.; Josten, C.; Muhr, G. Open reduction and augmentation of internal fixation with an injectable skeletal cement for the treatment of complex calcaneal fractures. J Orthop Trauma 14:309–317, 2000.

240. Sciadini, M.F.; Dawson, J.M.; Berman, L.M.; et al. Dose-response characteristics of recombinant human bone morphogenetic protein-2 in a canine segmental defect model. Trans Orthop Res Soc 20:594, 1995.

241. Scott, G.; King, J.B. A prospective, double-blind trial of electrical capacitive coupling in the treatment of non-union of long bones. J Bone Joint Surg Am 76:820–826, 1994.

242. Sebecic, B.; Gabelica, V.; Patrlj, L.; Sosa, T. Percutaneous autologous bone marrow grafting on the site of tibial delayed union. Croat Med J 40:429–432, 1999.

243. Shah, N.M.; Groves, A.K.; Anderson, D.J. Alternative neural crest cell fates are instructively promoted by TGFB superfamily member. Cell 85:331–343, 1996.

244. Shamos, M.H.; Lavine, L.S. Piezoelectricity as a fundamental property of biological tissues. Nature 212:267–268, 1967.

245. Shapiro, M.S.; Endrizzi, D.P.; Cannon, R.M.; Dick, H.M. Treatment of tibial defects and non-unions using ispilateral vascularized fibular transposition. Clin Orthop 296:207–212, 1993.

246. Sharma, S.; Garg, N.K.; Veliath, A.J.; et al. Percutaneous bone-marrow grafting of osteotomies and bony defects in rabbits. Acta Orthop Scand 63:166–169, 1992.

247. Sharrard, W.J.W. A double-blind trial of pulsed electromagnetic fields for delayed union of tibial fractures. J Bone Joint Surg Br 72:347–355, 1990.

248. Silverstein, P. Smoking and wound healing. Am J Med 93(1A):22S–24S, 1992.

249. Sim, F.H.; Frassica, F.J. Use of allografts following resection of tumors of the musculoskeletal system. Instr Course Lect 42:405–413, 1993.

250. Smith, R. Head injury, fracture healing and callus. J Bone Joint Surg Br 69:518–520, 1987.

251. Smith, S.R.; Bronk, J.T.; Kelly, P.J. Effects of fixation on fracture blood flow. Orthop Trans 11:294–295, 1987.

252. Solheim, E.; Pinholt, E.M.; Bang, O.G.; et al. Inhibition of heterotopic osteogenesis in rats by a new bio-erodable system for local delivery of indomethacin. J Bone Joint Surg 74:705–712, 1992.

253. Sone, K.; Tashiro, M.; Fujinaga, R.; et al. Long-term low-dose prostaglandin E1 administration. J Pediatr 97:866–867, 1980.

254. Spencer, R.F. The effect of head injury on fracture healing: A quantitative assessment. J Bone Joint Surg Br 69:525–528, 1987.

255. Sporn, M.B.; Roberts, A.B. Peptide growth factors are multifunctional. Nature 332:217–219, 1988.

256. Springfield, D.S. Autogenous bone grafts: Nonvascular and vascular. Orthopaedics 15:1237–1241, 1992.

257. Stevenson, S.; Cunningham, N.; Toth, J.; et al. The effect of osteogenin (a bone morphogenetic protein) on the formation of bone in orthotopic segmental defects in rats. J Bone Joint Surg Am 76:827–838, 1994.

258. Stoffelen, D.; Lammens, J.; Fabry, G. Resection of a periosteal osteosarcoma and reconstruction using the Ilizarov technique of segmental transport. J Hand Surg [Br] 18:144–146, 1993.

259. Sudman, E.; Bang, G. Indomethacin-induced inhibition of haversian remodelling in rabbits. Acta Orthop Scand 50:621–627, 1979.

260. Talley-Ronsholdt, D.J.; Lajiness, E.; Nagodawithana, K. Transforming growth factor-beta inhibition of mineralization by neonatal rat osteoblasts in monolayer and collagen gel culture. In Vitro Cell Dev Biol Anim 31:274–282, 1995.

261. Tashjian, A.H.; Hohmann, E.L.; Antoniades, H.N.; et al. Platelet-derived growth factor stimulates bone resorption via a prostaglandin mediated mechanism. Endocrinology 111:118–124, 1982.

262. Templeman, D.; Thomas, M.; Vasecka, T.; Kyle, R. Exchange reamed intramedullary nailing for delayed union and non-union of the tibia. Clin Orthop 315:56–63, 1995.

263. Thies, R.S.; Bauduy, M.; Ashton, B.A.; et al. Recombinant human morphogenetic protein-2 induces osteoblastic differentiation in W-20–17 stromal cells. Endocrinology 130:1318–1324, 1992.

264. Toma, C.D.; Ashkar, S.; Gray, M.L.; et al. Signal transduction of mechanical stimuli is dependent on microfilament integrity: Identification of osteopontin as a mechanically induced gene in osteoblasts. J Bone Miner Res 12:1626–1636, 1997.

265. Trippel, S.B. Growth factors as therapeutic agents. Instr Course Lect 46:473–476, 1997.

266. Turek, T.; Bostrom, M.P.G.; Camacho, N.P.; et al. The acceleration of fracture healing in a rabbit ulnar osteotomy model with bone morphogenetic protein 2. Abstract. Trans Orthop Res Soc 22:526, 1997.

267. Ueda, K.; Saito, A.; Nakano, H.; et al. Cortical hyperostosis following long-term administration of prostaglandin E1 in infants with cyanotic congenital heart disease. J Pediatr 97:834–836, 1980.

268. Uhthoff, H.K.; Rahn, B.A. Healing patterns of metaphyseal fractures. Clin Orthop 160:295–303, 1981.

269. Upton, J.; Boyajian, M.; Mulliken, J.B.; Glowacki, J. The use of demineralized xenogeneic bone implants to correct phalangeal defects: A case report. J Hand Surg [Am] 9:388–391, 1984.

270. Urist, M.R. Bone: Formation by autoinduction. Science 150:893–899, 1965.

271. Urist, M.R. Bone transplants and implants. In: Urist, M.R., ed. Fundamental and Clinical Bone Physiology. Philadelphia, J.B. Lippincott, 1980, pp. 331–368.

272. Urist, M.R.; Strates, B.S. Bone morphogenetic protein. J Dent Res 50:1392–1406, 1971.

273. Vaes, G. Cellular biology and biochemical mechanism of bone resorption: A review of recent developments on the formation, activation, and mode of action of osteoclasts. Clin Orthop 231:239–271, 1988.

274. Walsh, W.R.; Sherman, P.; Howlett, C.R.; et al. Fracture healing in the rat osteopenia model. Clin Orthop 342:218–227, 1997.

275. Wang, S.J.; LeWallen, D.G.; Bolander, M.E.; et al. Low intensity ultrasound treatment increases strength in a rat femoral fracture model. J Orthop Res 12:40–47, 1994.

276. Weiland, A.J. Current concepts review: Vascularized free bone transplant. J Bone Joint Surg Am 63:166–169, 1981.

277. Wergedal, J.E.; Matsuyama, T.; Strong, D.D. Differentiation of normal human bone cells by transforming growth factor-beta and 1,25 (OH)2 vitamin D$_3$. Metabolism 41:42–48, 1992.

278. Wiss, D.A.; Stetson, W.B. Unstable fractures of the tibia treated with reamed intramedullary interlocking nail. Clin Orthop 315:56–63, 1995.

279. Wolfe, S.W.; Pike, L.; Slade, J.F.; Katz, L.D. Augmentation of distal radius fracture fixation with coralline hydroxyapatite bone graft substitute. J Hand Surg [Am] 24:816–827, 1999.

280. Wolff, J. Das Gaesetz der Transformation der Knochen. Berlin, A. Hirchwald, 1892.

281. Wozney, J.M.; Rosen, V.; Celeste, A.J.; et al. Novel regulators of bone formation: Molecular clones and activities. Science 242:1528–1534, 1988.

282. Xavier, C.A.M.; Duarte, L.R. Treatment of non-unions by ultrasound stimulation: First clinical applications. Presented at the meeting of the Latin-American Orthopaedic Association and at the annual meeting of the American Academy of Orthopaedic Surgeons, San Francisco, CA, January 25, 1987.

283. Xie, M.H.; Holcomb, I.; Deuel, B.; et al. FGF-19, a novel fibroblast growth factor with unique specificity for FGFR4. Cytokine 11:729–735, 1999.

284. Yamaguchi, A.; Katagiri, T.; Ikeda, T.; et al. Recombinant human bone morphogenetic protein-2 stimulates osteoblastic maturation and inhibits myogenic differentiation in vitro. J Cell Biol 113:681–687, 1991.

285. Yang, K.H.; Parvizi, J.; Wang, S.J.; Lewallen, D.G.; et al. Exposure to low-intensity ultrasound increases aggrecan gene expression in a rat femur fracture model. J Orthop Res 14:802–809, 1996.

286. Yasko, A.W.; Lane, J.M.; Fellinger, E.J.; et al. The healing of segmental bone defects induced by recombinant human morphogenetic protein (rhBMP-2). A radiographic, histological and biomechanical study in rats. J Bone Joint Surg Am 74:659–670, 1992.

287. Yasuda, I. [Fundamental aspects of fracture treatment]. J Kyoto Med Soc 4:395–406, 1953.

288. Yetkinler, D.N.; Ladd, A.L.; Poser, R.D.; et al. Biomechanical evaluation of fixation of intra-articular fractures of the distal part of the radius in cadavers: Kirschner wires compared with calcium-phosphate bone cement. J Bone Joint Surg Am 81:391–399, 1999.

289. Yonemori, K.; Imamura, T.; Ishidou, Y.; et al. Bone morphogenetic protein receptors and activin receptors are highly expressed in ossified ligament tissues of patients with ossification of the posterior longitudinal ligament. Am J Pathol 150:1335–1347, 1997.

290. Younger, E.M.; Chapman, M.W. Morbidity at bone graft donor sites. J Orthop Trauma 3:192–195, 1989.

291. Zaidemberg, C.; Siebert, J.W.; Angrigiani, C. A new vascularized bone graft for scaphoid non-union. J Hand Surg [Am] 16:474–478, 1991.

292. Zegzula, H.D.; Buck D.C.; Brekke J.; et al. Bone formation with use of rhBMP-2 (recombinant human bone morphogenetic protein-2). J Bone Joint Surg Am 79:1778–1790, 1997.

293. Zhuang, H.; Wang, W.; Seldes, R.M.; et al. Electrical stimulation induces the level of TGF-B1 mRNA in osteoblastic cells by a mechanism involving calcium/calmodulin pathway. Biochem Biophys Res Comm 237:225–229, 1997.

CHAPTER 23

Physical Impairment Ratings for Fractures

Richard A. Saunders, M.D.
Sam W. Wiesel, M.D.

Fractures account for only about 10% of all musculoskeletal traumatic injuries, but they cause a disproportionate amount of medical impairment. The costs of fracture care, including lost productivity, medical expenses, and disability payments, make this class of injury a significant burden both to employers and to society in general.

The role of physicians in the medical care of fractures is well established, but their job does not end when union has been achieved and rehabilitation is complete. Physician participation is equally vital in the impairment evaluation process. Many state and federal laws limit physician discretion in assigning permanent impairment ratings, and the physician is often caught between a desire to benefit the patient and the need to comply with these laws. This chapter presents some generic issues of impairment, reviews the epidemiology of fractures in the United States, and comments on commonly used existing impairment guides.

GENERIC ISSUES OF DISABILITY AND IMPAIRMENT

Definitions

There is a certain amount of confusion about the role of the physician in determination of permanent disability and about the difference between impairment and disability. According to *Guides to the Evaluation of Permanent Impairment*, Fifth Edition, published by the American Medical Association (AMA), the following definitions apply.

Impairment is a loss, loss of use, or derangement of any body part, organ system, or organ function. A permanent impairment exists when the patient has reached maximal medical improvement but such a loss or derangement persists. Maximal medical improvement has been achieved when the injury or illness has stabilized and no material improvement or deterioration is expected in the next year, with or without treatment. Many jurisdictions require that

a year elapse after the injury or most recent surgery related to the injury before determining that maximal medical improvement has been attained.

Disability, which is assessed by nonmedical means, is an alteration of an individual's capacity to meet personal, social, or occupational demands because of an impairment. The determination of permanent disability is dependent on a number of nonmedical factors, among them the patients' level of education, their work training and work history, their residual access to the workplace, and their socioeconomic background. Impairment reflects only the patients' limitations with respect to their activities of daily living, excluding work. Physicians, in general, are considered expert only in the determination of impairment.

Role of the Physician

The evaluation of permanent physical impairment is the sole responsibility of the physician. The functions evaluated in determining permanent impairment are self-care, communication, physical activity (including sitting, standing, reclining, walking, and stair climbing), sensory functions, nonspecialized hand activities, travel, sexual function, and sleep. Because musculoskeletal injuries account for the majority of impairment determinations, orthopaedists are frequently involved in this process.

Third-Party Payers

Impairment evaluations are most frequently requested by a third-party payer before settlement of a claim. The largest third-party payers are state workmen's compensation boards, private insurance companies, the Social Security Administration, and Veterans Affairs.[12] Each of these groups has its own requirements for and definitions of impairment. Workmen's compensation laws vary widely from state to state, and federal agency regulations are amended yearly. The agency requesting the disability evaluation should specify which rules apply in the specific case, and the reviewing physician should abide by the specified rules. In some cases, older editions of the AMA guides have been incorporated in state laws, in which case the appropriate edition must be consulted. Tort law (civil litigation or lawsuits) in some states does not specify any particular body of rules; in these cases, the evaluating physician has considerably greater freedom to describe and quantify a given impairment.

Correspondence is between the physician and the third-party payer. Updates should be in the form of letters mailed directly to the representative of the third-party payer. The patient should not act as an intermediary, although the patient's right to review his or her chart in the presence of the attending physician should always be honored.

In general, physicians acting as independent consultants in determination of impairment ratings do not establish a doctor-patient relationship with the patient being examined.

Work Restrictions

In addition to assigning a rating of permanent partial impairment, the physician is often called on to give an estimate of residual work capacity. The physician is responsible for determining the level of physical activity that the patient can safely tolerate. The most widely accepted physical exertion requirement guidelines are those published by the Social Security Administration:

Very heavy work is that which involves lifting objects weighing more than 100 pounds at a time, with frequent lifting or carrying of objects weighing 50 pounds or more.
Heavy work involves lifting of no more than 100 pounds at a time, with frequent lifting or carrying of objects weighing up to 50 pounds.
Medium work involves the lifting of no more than 50 pounds at a time, with frequent lifting or carrying of objects weighing up to 25 pounds.
Light work involves lifting of no more than 20 pounds at a time, with frequent lifting or carrying of objects weighing up to 10 pounds.
Sedentary work involves the lifting of no more than 10 pounds at a time and occasional lifting or carrying of articles such as docket files, ledgers, or small tools.

TEMPORARY TOTAL DISABILITY

In general, a patient is judged temporarily totally disabled if, in the opinion of the treating physician, the patient is incapable of performing any job, for any reasonable period of time, during the course of a workday. Note that, by this definition, a patient's inability to perform his or her own job is not the primary issue. For example, a construction worker in a short arm cast for a Colles fracture may well be incapable of his or her usual work but capable of sedentary or one-handed light work, so the worker is not totally disabled. Temporary total disability is granted for patients whose pain is great enough to warrant regular narcotic use, whose mobility is so severely compromised as to make getting from home to the workplace unreasonably difficult, or who are hospitalized in an inpatient unit.

TEMPORARY PARTIAL DISABILITY— LIGHT DUTY

During the course of recovery from an injury, a patient may be employable in a light duty situation in which the physical requirements of the job do not compromise healing or cause unacceptable discomfort. The physician is responsible for identifying the level of safe activity, which may be limited to sedentary work during the early recovery phase of an injury.

PERMANENT PARTIAL DISABILITY

After maximal medical recovery has been achieved, the physician, possibly in cooperation with other occupational specialists, may be asked to recommend a permanent restricted activity level if the patient is unable to return to his or her original job. There are no widely accepted guidelines for determining the level of job restriction, but, in general, a patient who has any permanent partial impairment secondary to skeletal injury is unable to perform very heavy or heavy work safely.[20, 21] If the permanent partial impairment is greater than 25%, most patients are unlikely to perform successfully in any but part-time or home-based occupations at the sedentary level. Between these two extremes, the physician must decide what is a reasonable expectation for the patient, taking into consideration the type of injury and impairment and the sorts of activities that are likely to exacerbate persistent pain.

As an example, a well-healed 10% compression fracture of the lumbar spine with some chronic back pain may result in a 5% permanent partial impairment. The patient is likely to have exacerbation of pain with bending, twisting, stooping, lifting of more than 20 pounds, or prolonged overhead work. He or she would be qualified for a job involving light work, with the restrictions specified previously.

The physician assigns impairment and specifies work restrictions, but the responsibility for finding an appropriate job lies with the patient or the third-party payer. With more aggressive job retraining and work hardening programs, patients with significant impairment are now returning to the workplace. It is time consuming but often worthwhile for the physician to work with the social worker, nurse, or occupational therapist representing the third-party payer to find an acceptable job for the patient or to encourage occupational retraining when appropriate.

USEFUL GUIDES TO IMPAIRMENT DETERMINATION

Numerous impairment guides are in use in the United States. Most states mandate the use of one particular set of guidelines for workmen's compensation impairment determination. Some states create their own unique guidelines, which are based on a variety of practical, idiosyncratic, or occasionally political considerations. Increasingly, most states and the District of Columbia have adopted the guidelines published by the AMA.[2] Most federal agencies concerned with impairment determination also use the AMA guides. More widespread use of the AMA guides seems to be leading to increasingly uniform and probably fairer impairment determinations across most jurisdictions.

EPIDEMIOLOGY

Little has been published on the epidemiology of fractures or on their economic significance. The United States Public Health Service accumulated records on some aspects of fracture epidemiology between 1957 and the mid-1980s. Unfortunately, data collection has not resumed, and more recent national trends in the incidence of fractures are unknown.

Incidence of Fractures

Data from the National Center for Health Statistics of the Public Health Service indicate that there is little fluctuation in the incidence of fractures and dislocations from year to year (Fig. 23–1). Between 1963 and 1981, fractures and dislocations occurred at the rate of about 3 per 100 persons per year.[16] Men consistently sustain significantly more injuries than women. The type of fracture is not reported by the Public Health Service, and fractures and dislocations are not listed separately.

When fractures are broken down into upper and lower extremity groups, a clear pattern of occurrence with age emerges. Men have a fairly stable rate of fractures of the lower extremities and a decreasing rate of upper extremity fractures with age. In contrast, women show no change in the incidence of upper extremity fractures and have a significant increase in the incidence of lower extremity fractures with increasing age. These changes may be caused by the increased incidence of osteoporosis among older women.

Fractures made up about 10.2% of all orthopaedic injuries during the years 1980 and 1981 (Fig. 23–2),[19] compared with 8.2% between 1957 and 1961.[18] Only injuries resulting in at least 1 day of limited activity were counted in this survey.

Restricted Activity and Bedrest

Fractures and dislocations during the period from 1963 to 1981 resulted in about 60 days of restricted activity per 100 people per year, with men accounting for more restriction than women (Fig. 23–3).[16] The period of restricted activity included about 16 days spent in bedrest.

Older women have a marked increase in the incidence of fracture-related restriction of activity with both upper and lower extremity fractures. Among men, however, the average number of restricted activity days is fairly constant for both upper and lower extremity injuries in all age classes. Despite the large increase in fracture rate among older women, men have a higher average number of restricted activity days when all ages are considered together.[16, 19] The finding of increased musculoskeletal symptoms with age has been noted in other surveys as well.[3–5]

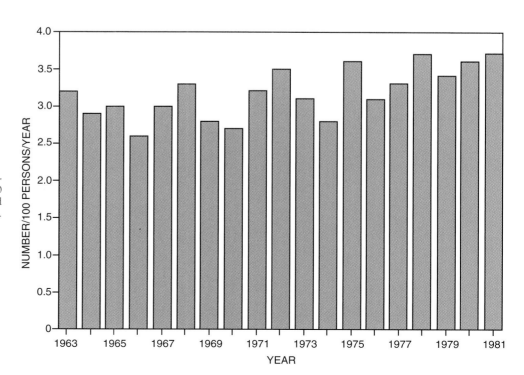

FIGURE 23–1. Incidence of fractures and dislocations per 100 persons per year in the United States from 1963 through 1981.

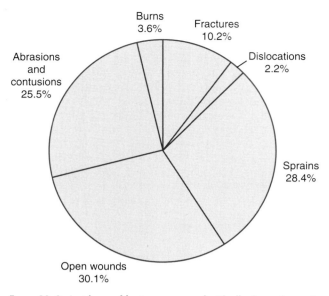

Figure 23–2. Incidence of fractures compared with all other orthopaedic injuries in the United States in 1980 and 1981.

Impairment

Impairment resulting from injury is defined by the National Health Service as any limitation of function lasting longer than 3 months. Orthopaedic injuries, including fractures, were responsible for 64.3% of all impairments between 1980 and 1981, the most recent period for which data are available.[19] Broken down by type of injury, orthopaedic problems of the lower extremity account for 24%, problems of the upper extremity for 13.7%, and those involving the spine for 26.6% of the total impairments noted in this period.

About 44 million of the civilian, noninstitutionalized population reported at least one musculoskeletal disorder during 1980, a prevalence in this population of almost 20%.[13] Musculoskeletal conditions account for 13% of restricted activity days, 8.8% of bed disability days, and 11.2% of work loss days overall. Lost productivity from musculoskeletal conditions totaled about $3.9 billion during 1980, and the medical cost of treating these conditions was more than $12 billion during the same period.[5, 17]

Work Loss Days

Fractures caused 28.6 days of work loss per 100 employed men per year between 1983 and 1986.[17] There was no change in the number of work loss days with increasing age among men (Fig. 23–4). Women older than 45 years lost significantly more days from work because of fractures than their younger peers (25.1 vs. 9.45 days per 100 employed women per year, respectively) (Fig. 23–5). Overall, women miss fewer days of work than men, but in the age group older than 45 the rates become equal.[17]

HISTORICAL PERSPECTIVE

Before the 1930s, in both the United States and Europe, arbitrary disability values were assigned for individual injuries. The entire disability determination process was performed by physicians, despite their lack of special training in social, economic, and occupational evaluation. This practice may have simplified rendering a judgment of disability, but it led to the awarding of the same compensation to individuals with markedly different

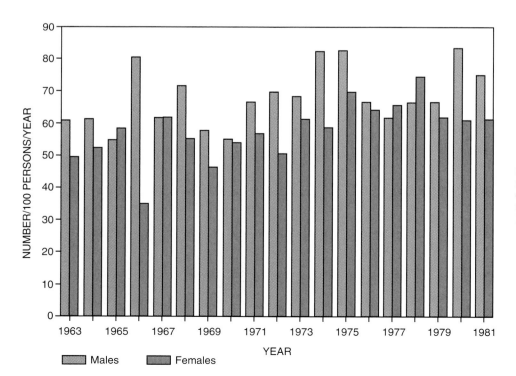

Figure 23–3. Days of restricted activity caused by fractures and dislocations among men and women in the United States from 1963 through 1981.

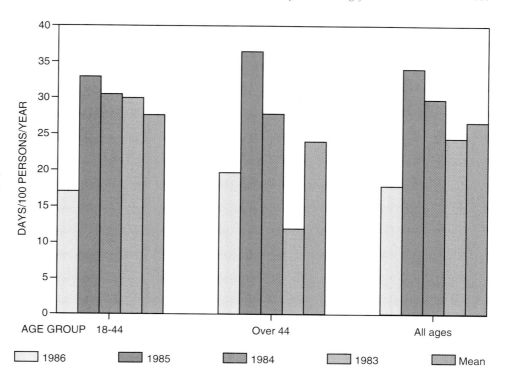

FIGURE 23–4. Days of work loss caused by fractures in men in the United States by age from 1983 through 1986.

degrees of residual disability.[6, 12] Beginning in the 1930s, new systems of classifying residual deficits were introduced in the United States by individual authors in an effort to make the system of disability evaluation more equitable and objective.

Kessler[6–8] described evaluation based on objective criteria such as range of motion in degrees and motor strength measured in foot-pounds. McBride[9, 10] published a 10-point scale based on five anatomic and five functional criteria that, taken together, gave an estimate of overall impairment. In an effort to reduce the influence of subjective and potentially biased data, Thurber[15] published impairment scales based on range of motion alone.

Development of the modern system for rating of permanent partial impairment by physicians began in 1956 with the introduction by the AMA of a series of guides designed to provide objective, reproducible impairment ratings.[1, 2] These guides were intended to standard-

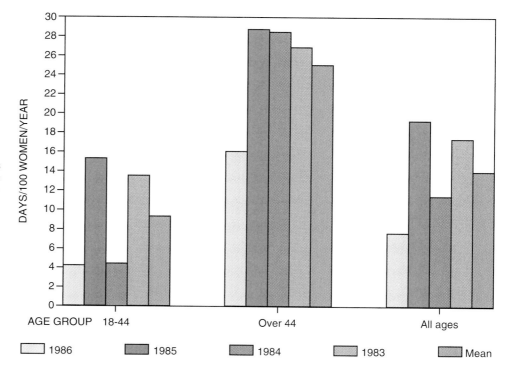

FIGURE 23–5. Days of work loss caused by fractures in women in the United States by age from 1983 through 1986.

ize evaluation of the result of industrial accidents for determining workmen's compensation claims. The AMA series is now complete and is updated regularly. In addition to the guides for the spine and extremities, the AMA provides guides to the evaluation of other organ systems (e.g., neurologic, hematopoietic), but the evaluation of these systems is outside the area of training of orthopaedic surgery.

MODERN IMPAIRMENT SCALES

The AMA guides rate impairment by a "whole person" concept. In this system, each part of the body is assigned a value reflecting the contribution of that part to the patient as a whole. The percentage each part contributes to the whole is based on the notion of function. Loss of function of the extremity is expressed as a percentage of the value of the extremity as a whole, and impairment to the whole person is calculated from this value. The upper extremities are valued at 60% of the whole person, the lower extremities at 40%. As an example, amputation at the wrist results in a 90% loss of function of the arm and a 54% impairment of the whole person.

The AMA guides historically relied solely on range-of-motion measurements for the determination of partial impairments of the spine and extremities, offering no consideration of pain, atrophy, shortening, and other subjective and objective data. The fourth and fifth editions of the guides incorporated a much broader range of evaluation criteria and also introduced the concept of diagnosis-related impairment estimates.

Traditional range of motion–based estimates ignore causal issues and focus solely on measurable outcomes, specifically motion of local joints or spine segments. Diagnosis-related impairment estimates attempt to overcome the inherent limitations of a one-dimensional motion-based estimating tool by focusing on the underlying diagnosis. For example, all patients with multiple operations for a herniated lumbar disc with residual, verifiable neurologic residuals might be grouped together for the purpose of impairment determination, leading to a more uniform and ultimately fairer determination than would be possible using range-of-motion measures alone. Another advantage of diagnosis-based impairment determinations is the reduced dependence on subjective or difficult to measure variables such as range of motion, pain, weakness, or clumsiness.

TEMPORARY IMPAIRMENT

Temporary Total Disability

Patients are temporarily totally disabled from the moment of occurrence of the skeletal injury until they achieve a reasonable degree of mobility and independence, are able to perform their own activities of daily living to a reasonable degree, and are no longer dependent on narcotic analgesics. Obviously, patients who are hospitalized, are inpatients in a rehabilitation facility, or are homebound and require skilled nursing care are temporarily totally disabled. Patients who are dependent on crutches for ambulation are not necessarily totally disabled at all times unless they meet the other definitions of temporary total disability.

Periodic evaluation in the physician's office is necessary during the period of temporary total disability. Most state workmen's compensation laws mandate at least monthly visits during the period of temporary total disability, during which further documentation for ongoing temporary total disability status must be entered in the patient's record.

Temporary Partial Disability

Temporary partial disability begins with the termination of temporary total disability and continues until rehabilitation is complete and the patient is back to full activities with no restrictions or until a permanent impairment is assigned. During the period of temporary partial disability, the patient is allowed to return to the workplace with certain restrictions judged appropriate by the treating physician.

Periodic reevaluations of the patient's clinical status are made, usually at 2- to 6-week intervals. State law varies considerably on the issue of mandatory frequency of reevaluations during a period of temporary partial disability. In general, state laws permit somewhat longer intervals between clinic visits for patients with temporary partial disability, often between 4 and 8 weeks. Again, documentation in the record of the reason for ongoing temporary partial disability is important. Physician records and occasionally physician testimony are required for insurance payments for disability determination. It is worthwhile periodically to record range of motion, functional restrictions, medication use, and degree of autonomy with activities of daily living; these data can be used later to document the patient's degree of disability during any given period.

Once the period of temporary total disability is lifted, appropriate restrictions must be instituted by the physician. Patients recovering from back and neck injuries may benefit from a restriction on bending, twisting, stooping, lifting, and heavy overhead work. Upper extremity injury restrictions often include avoidance of heavy or repetitive use of the involved extremity. Restrictions after lower extremity injuries frequently include prohibitions against excessive walking, climbing, stooping, kneeling, running, and carrying.

Many employers and third-party payers publish and distribute forms with a listing of possible activities for the physician to check off. To the extent that the listed activities are of concern to the physician, these forms may be used, but it is often more useful for the physician to attach a note on letterhead stationery outlining the restrictions rather than to try to make his or her best judgment about appropriate restrictions fit within the confines of existing forms and classifications.

Temporary partial impairment restrictions should be modified as the patient's symptoms warrant. This modification may require instituting greater restrictions and moving the patient back toward more sedentary activities if symptoms become excessive or gradual liberalization of activities as clinical status permits. Occasional periods of temporary total disability may be warranted, particularly after surgical procedures or operative manipulations of fractures.

IMPAIRMENT AND FRACTURES

Fractures cause several kinds of permanent changes, any of which may lead to a degree of partial impairment. Each element of fracture healing must be considered separately in determining the overall level of impairment caused by a given injury. Existing impairment scales address some but not all of these factors. Traditionally, some incremental percentage of increased impairment is assigned for sequelae of fracture healing such as limb length discrepancy, loss of joint motion, or ankylosis. Some complications, including nonunion, infection, and secondary soft tissue injury, are not addressed explicitly in the literature, and the practitioner is left to his or her own discretion in assessing permanent impairment.

Handedness

The AMA does not allow for handedness or side dominance in the determination of impairment, the contention being that activities of daily living, the functional standard by which medical impairment is judged, are not affected by handedness. Therefore, no increased impairment value is allowed for impairments in the dominant upper extremity. Obviously, disability determination must take handedness into consideration. Traditionally, 5% extremity impairment is added for impairments of 1% to 50% of the dominant extremity and 10% for impairments greater than 50% of the dominant upper extremity.

Nonunion

Occasionally, a fracture fails to unite despite optimal medical and surgical intervention, or a patient may legitimately choose not to accept the risks associated with surgical intervention for treatment of a nonunion. Because joint motion above and below the nonunion is compromised, the AMA system recognizes increased impairment in this situation. The impairment resulting from nonunion can be more profound than simple loss of joint motion. Pain, motion at the fracture site, and weakness may complicate nonunion. It is reasonable to add 5% to the limb impairment for an asymptomatic nonunion and 10% for a nonunion that causes significant compromise beyond loss of joint motion.

Limb Length

Limb length discrepancy after fracture is of much greater significance in the leg than in the arm. One convention for dealing with leg length discrepancy is to allow 5% permanent impairment for each half inch of shortening in

excess of the half inch generally considered to be normal.[11] Thus, a leg length discrepancy of 2 inches after fracture would result in a 15% limb impairment on the basis of this factor alone.

Malunion

A fracture healing with angulation may result in loss of motion at the joint above or below it, in which case the AMA guide pertaining to motion deficit provides a correct estimate of impairment.[2] If symptoms other than loss of motion are present, some additional degree of impairment should be allowed. If the malunion causes significant symptoms, such as weakness, skin breakdown, altered gait, or rotational deformity, an additional 10% impairment should be allowed.

Infection

If chronic osteomyelitis occurs, some additional level of impairment should be assigned to compensate for the well-recognized potential complications and daily inconvenience of this disease. If symptomatic osteomyelitis exists at the time permanent impairment is determined, an additional impairment of 10% of the limb value is assigned. If the infection is minimally symptomatic or quiescent at the time of determination, an additional impairment of 5% is assigned.

Intra-articular Involvement

Long-term sequelae of fractures may not be apparent at the time of determination of impairment. Degenerative changes are far more likely to develop in a joint that has sustained an intra-articular fracture, especially in the presence of residual articular displacement. The determination of permanent impairment after a fracture must therefore include an allowance for the occasional development of post-traumatic arthritis. As an example, a well-healed, nonpainful fracture of the medial malleolus with no residual intra-articular displacement warrants a finding of 5% impairment of the limb because of the anticipated future disability such an injury could cause. A similar fracture with intra-articular displacement would merit a 10% impairment of the limb.

Preexisting Conditions and Apportionment

Preexisting medical conditions need to be apportioned before assignment of a scheduled loss-of-use rating. Apportionment is the process of dividing the degree of impairment detected at the time of examination between current and prior injuries or conditions. Apportionment generally implies a preexisting condition that has been made materially or substantially worse by a second injury or illness. Numerous methods can be used to assess apportionment, and no universal standard seems to have been adopted. The AMA guides recommend subtracting the whole person impairment established for the preexisting condition from the current impairment rating. This recommendation clearly assumes that perfect, incontrovertible data exist about the preexisting condition, a circumstance rarely encountered. In most cases, a somewhat more arbitrary division is needed.

A reasonable starting place is a 50%-50% apportionment between preexisting and current causes unless objective new data show a worsening of the condition after onset of the current injury or illness. For example, a patient with a preexisting arthritic knee and a subsequent tibial plateau fracture on the affected side with subjective complaints of worsening symptoms after the fracture warrants an apportionment of 75% to the current injury and 25% to the preexisting condition. A patient with chronic low back pain made subjectively worse after a lifting injury warrants a 50%-50% apportionment in the absence of magnetic resonance imaging, electromyographic, or radiographic evidence of a new condition. If new test findings cannot be reliably assigned to the new or old injury or illness, the 50%-50% apportionment rule should be applied.

Neurologic Injuries

The AMA guides outline appropriate standards for evaluating combined skeletal and neurologic injuries. In general, impairment secondary to joint stiffness after fracture is considered separately from nerve injuries caused by the same injury. Loss of motion related to nerve injury, such as limited shoulder abduction following axillary nerve injury, is not considered separately, as the neurologic injury is solely responsible for the motion deficit. Neurologic loss resulting from spine fractures should be evaluated with the diagnosis-related estimates because of the difficulty of evaluating spine range of motion in the paralyzed patient.

Preexisting Osteoarthritis

Some fractures inevitably occur in individuals already suffering from musculoskeletal disease, most often osteoarthritis. Injuries are slower to heal and residual loss of joint motion may be greater in such patients.[7, 21] Symptoms caused by the osteoarthritis are often perceived to be more disabling after a fracture.

Assuming that radiographs taken at the time of injury show degenerative changes or that late films show changes in excess of what might reasonably be expected to develop in the elapsed time, an allowance for exacerbation of the preexisting disease should be made. To compensate fairly for the contribution of the injury to preexisting arthritis, a 5% additional impairment should be added to the limb impairment for patients who are subjectively worse and a 10% additional impairment to those who are both subjectively and objectively worse after their injury.[21]

SPINE FRACTURES

Individual investigators have offered various schemes for determining impairment related to spinal fracture. Miller,[11] for instance, allowed 5% whole person impairment for lumbar compression fractures up to 25%, 10% impairment for compression of 25% to 50%, and 20% impairment for lumbar compression fractures greater than 50%. He halved these values for fractures of the thoracic spine and allowed no impairment assignment for healed compression fractures of the cervical spine unless some other factor such as nerve injury is present.[11, 14]

In an effort to provide a fair and uniform assignment of impairment for spine injuries, Wiesel and colleagues[20, 21] collected data from 75 members of the International Society for Study of the Lumbar Spine and from 53 American members of the Cervical Spine Research Society. The objective was to establish diagnosis-related impair-

---

TABLE 23–1

Permanent Partial Impairment and Work Restriction after Fractures of the Cervical and Lumbar Spine

Fracture Type	Percent Impairment	Work Allowed
Cervical Spine		
Odontoid, external fixation	10	Medium
Odontoid, surgical fusion	20	Light
Hangman's, external fixation	10	Medium
Hangman's, surgical fusion	15	Light
Burst or compression, lower cervical spine, external fixation, no neurologic deficit	15	Light
Burst or compression, lower cervical spine, surgical fusion, no neurologic deficit		
Lumbar Spine		
Acute spondylolysis or spondylolisthesis, conservative care, complete recovery	0	Heavy
Acute spondylolysis or spondylolisthesis, conservative care, residual discomfort	10	Light
Spondylolysis or spondylolisthesis, laminectomy and/or fusion, complete recovery	10	Light
Spondylolysis or spondylolisthesis, laminectomy and/or fusion, residual discomfort	20	Sedentary
Compression fracture, healed, with		
10% compression	5	Medium
25% compression	10	Light
50% compression	20	Sedentary
75% compression	20	Sedentary
Transverse process fracture, no displacement or malunion	0	Heavy

ment ratings for a variety of common spinal disorders. The results as applied to spinal fractures are presented in Table 23–1.

The AMA offers the most widely used spine impairment guidelines. Again, the AMA guides are used in more than three out of four states and most federal agencies. Starting with the third edition and extending through the fifth, the AMA algorithm has included diagnosis-related impairment estimates, with range of motion–based estimates used only in a few situations where diagnosis-related categories fit the situation poorly. Spine fractures are generally amenable to diagnosis-related grouping, the major exception being multiple fractures within an anatomic region, for example, two compression fractures occurring simultaneously in the lumbar spine. In the case of poor applicability of diagnosis-related categories, the AMA allows impairment determination on the basis of range-of-motion measures.

SUMMARY

Establishing a fair level of permanent partial disability after fracture requires the expertise of many professionals, including the orthopaedist, social worker, and vocational and rehabilitation therapists, as well as input from the patient and third-party payer. The evaluation of permanent partial impairment is the sole responsibility of the physician; this chapter is intended to evaluate some of the factors involved in making impairment determinations. By considering all the factors that contribute to the outcome of fracture care, a level of permanent impairment can be established that is fair to the patient, the third-party payer, and society in general.

REFERENCES

1. American Academy of Orthopaedic Surgeons. Manual for Orthopaedic Surgeons in Evaluating Permanent Physical Impairment. Chicago, American Academy of Orthopaedic Surgeons, 1962.
2. American Medical Association. Guides to the Evaluation of Permanent Impairment, 5th ed. Chicago, American Medical Association, 2001.
3. Cunningham, L.S.; Kelsey, J.S. Epidemiology of musculoskeletal impairments and associated disability. Am J Public Health 74:574, 1984.
4. Kelsey, J.S. Epidemiology of Musculoskeletal Disorders. Monographs in Epidemiology and Biostatistics, Vol. 3. Oxford, Oxford University Press, 1982.
5. Kelsey, J.S.; White, A.A.; Pastides, H. The impact of musculoskeletal disorders on the population of the United States. J Bone Joint Surg Am 61:960, 1979.
6. Kessler, E.D. The determination of physical fitness JAMA 115:1591, 1940.
7. Kessler, H. Low Back Pain in Industry. New York, Commerce and Industry Association of New York, 1955.
8. Kessler, H.H. Disability—Determination and Evaluation. Philadelphia, Lea & Febiger, 1970.
9. McBride, E.D. Disability Evaluation. Philadelphia, J.B. Lippincott, 1942.
10. McBride, E.D. Disability evaluation. J Int Coll Surg 24:341, 1955.
11. Miller, T.R. Evaluating Orthopedic Disability, 2nd ed. Oradell, NJ, Medical Economics Books, 1987.
12. Mooney, V. Impairment, disability, and handicap. Clin Orthop 221:14, 1987.
13. Murt, H.A.; et al. Disability, utilization and costs associated with musculoskeletal conditions, United States, 1980. National Medical Care Utilization and Expenditure Survey. Series C, Analytical Report No. 5. DHHS Publication 8620405. National Center for Health Statistics, Public Health Service. Washington, DC, U.S. Government Printing Office, 1986.
14. Nordby, E.J. Disability evaluation of the neck and back: The McBride system. Clin Orthop 221:131, 1987.
15. Thurber, P. Evaluation of Industrial Disability. New York, Oxford University Press, 1960.
16. Vital and Health Statistics Series 10. Current Estimates from the National Health Interview Survey. Washington, DC, U.S. Government Printing Office, 1962–1981.
17. Vital and Health Statistics Series 10. Current Estimates from the National Health Interview Survey. Washington, DC, U.S. Government Printing Office, 1983–1986.
18. Vital and Health Statistics Series 10. Types of Injuries and Impairments Due to Injuries, 1957–1961. Washington, DC, U.S. Government Printing Office, 1964.
19. Vital and Health Statistics Series 10. Types of Injuries and Impairments Due to Injuries, 1980–1981. Washington, DC, U.S. Government Printing Office, 1986.
20. Wiesel, S.W.; Feffer, H.L.; Rothman, R.H. Industrial Low Back Pain: A Comprehensive Approach. Charlottesville, VA, The Michie Company Law Publishers, 1985.
21. Wiesel, S.W.; Feffer, H.L.; Rothman, R.H. Neck Pain. Charlottesville, VA, The Michie Company Law Publishers, 1986.

CHAPTER 24

Evaluation of Outcomes for Musculoskeletal Injury

William T. Obremskey, M.D., M.P.H.
Marc F. Swiontkowski, M.D.

OUTCOMES ASSESSMENT

Outcomes research has rapidly become the focus of clinical researchers, insurance companies, health care delivery corporations, and hospitals. What is the source of this interest, from what did it evolve, and how does it differ from clinical research that has traditionally taken place in the orthopaedic community?

In a research methodology termed *small-area analysis*, Wennberg and co-workers[147, 148] noted that health care interventions varied widely in terms of population-based rates. In one example, they noted that residents of the New Haven, Connecticut, region were twice as likely to undergo spinal surgery for disc disease as their age- and sex-matched counterparts in Boston, Massachusetts. In contradistinction, the residents of Boston were twice as likely to undergo total hip replacement as their New Haven counterparts.[71, 72] These and other elective conditions have a large (three- to fivefold) variation in incidence in a given population.[2, 74] The incidence of hip fracture surgery and both bone forearm fracture surgery is fairly constant in all regions in the United States.[73, 74] Similar confusing results were noted for medical and other surgical conditions. The explanation for these phenomena is not clear. However, in general, it seems to be due in part to physicians' uncertainty regarding the best way to treat patients and incomplete knowledge of what "works" and how well it works for patients. These uncertainties seem to be founded in the weakness of the clinical literature, poor research design, and difficulties in conducting high-quality clinical research in orthopaedic surgery.[75]

Outcome can be defined as the patient's end result from treatment of a disease. Interestingly, the term *end result* is from Codman,[34, 35] an orthopaedic surgeon in Massachusetts best known for his work in shoulder diseases, who proposed that knowledge of the end result for patients in hospitals be the fundamental yardstick by which medical or surgical treatment be judged worthy to be loosed on the public. Although his concept fell on deaf ears at the time,

it served as a catalyst for further evolution of the concept of assessing the result of treatment. In 1949 Karnofsky and Burchenal[67] first established the survey format to measure outcomes of cancer treatment. The use of surveys has become central to our ability to measure the outcome of treatment. In 1966 Donabedian[45] introduced the framework for conceptualization of medical care by identifying three separate elements: structure, process, and outcomes. He was the first to express Codman's concept of the end result using the term *outcome*.[34, 35]

Other highlights of the history of outcomes measurement include Lembcke[79] using patients' outcomes as an assessment of quality of care (a central concept now widely accepted and imitated); Katz and co-workers[68, 69] measuring the outcomes of elderly patients by activities of daily living scales in 1963; Bradburn[21] measuring psychologic well-being in 1969; Breslow[23] devising scales for measuring physical, mental, and social well-being for the World Health Organization's definition of health; and Bush and associates[27] in 1973 introducing the Health Status Index and the Quality of Well Being scale, the first validated and widely accepted scale of this type.[104] Since that time, many health and well-being assessment instruments have been developed. A partial list includes the Sickness Impact Profile, the Functional Limitations Profile, the McMaster Health Index Questionnaire, the University of North Carolina Health Profile, the Western Ontario and McMaster University Osteoarthritis Index, the Nottingham Health Profile, the Functional Status Questionnaire, and the Medical Outcomes Study Short Form 36 (SF-36) and Short Form 12 (SF-12).*

The types of outcomes that are important for patients include clinical outcomes, functional outcomes, health-related outcomes, and satisfaction with the process of care. Clinical outcomes (e.g., range of motion, radiographic union, implant loosening, and infection) were nearly the singular focus of clinical research in orthopaedic surgery

---

*See references 9, 11–13, 30, 62, 63, 66, 81, 96, 97, 110, 111, 113, 127, 133, 134, 143, 145.

before the 1990s.[51, 57] Functional outcomes primarily involve the patient's function at the most complete level, not in terms of a joint or musculoskeletal condition (or fracture) but as an individual in society.[70–72] These outcomes were typically not evaluated until later. The areas of individual function covered herein include mental health, social function, role function (e.g., worker, spouse, parent), physical function, and activities of daily living.[58, 59, 112] Health-related quality of life involves patients' perception of how they are functioning as affected by their overall health. The paradoxical findings in small-area variation in medical care of Wennberg and co-workers[147, 148] have driven the new interest in discovering how treatments—medical, psychologic, and surgical—affect patients' function at these levels. The interest in outcomes research is founded in these historical roots.

The published clinical literature regarding management of musculoskeletal injury is generally retrospective in design, with rare exception, and is focused on clinical outcomes.[129, 141] These include traditional orthopaedic measures such as range of motion, alignment, stability, healing, and radiographic assessments. The relative lack of controlled trials in the entire field of orthopaedics has made the definition of optimal management strategies impossible. Even in the most highly investigated areas of the field (e.g., joint replacement), deficiencies are severe.[51, 57] Both Gartland[51] and Gross[57] have confirmed that research regarding hip arthroplasty has been process based, meaning that it is focused on elements important to the technical aspects of the procedure (e.g., cement lucency, dislocation rates) or to the delivery of the care and not on the effect of the procedure on patients' function. Examples of process-based elements frequently examined for injured patients include length of intensive care unit stay, ventilator days, wound infection, and knee range of motion. This paucity of patient-oriented functional outcome data is true for injured patients as well.

When these data are assessed, important and interesting findings result.[10, 61] It is the opinion of many researchers that this fundamental lack of end-result information, relevant to patients' function, is responsible for the variations in medical and orthopaedic practice that have become quite apparent.[70, 147] Improvement in the situation requires new emphasis on clinical trial methodology in studying musculoskeletal injury and, when this is not feasible because of low incidences, the use of standardized outcome assessment in multicenter settings whenever possible.[120] Outcome assessment must include relevant clinical outcomes important to the process of care as well as patient-derived health-oriented outcomes generally obtained by questionnaire.[71, 76, 131] In addition, improved training for clinician researchers in the appropriate use of statistics must be undertaken.[141]

The retrospective clinical literature is replete with scales used to divide patients' results into good, fair, or poor. These scales are generally derived from surgeons, are rarely used in more than one retrospective review, and have internal weighting for scoring (e.g., value of pain relative to that of range of motion, alignment) that is determined by the author and not by input from patients.[44, 131] This lack of use of validated scales has further undermined the utility of the literature for the assessment of efficacy of injury treatment strategies. A current example of clinical debate is that of the effect of early stabilization of long bone fractures in the patient with multiple injuries. Although the sense of the literature would push us to a more aggressive clinical protocol, we are limited by the existence of only one published controlled trial on the subject.[16, 17, 49, 64, 98, 121] The lack of adequate numbers of randomized trials for most topics in trauma surgery makes the technique of meta-analysis unavailable for addressing effectiveness issues.[16, 20, 53, 77, 78, 87, 95, 139] All of these factors contribute to current inadequate knowledge on which to base treatment decisions and recommendations.

CLINICAL OUTCOMES: CURRENT UTILIZATION

Trauma Registries

Injury is a major public health problem, being responsible for more death and disability than any other cause in people 1 to 44 years of age.[5, 15, 38–40, 56, 118, 135] Trauma care systems have been definitively shown to improve mortality rates.* Despite the major societal impact of injury, relatively few resources are directed toward studying prevention and optimizing treatment. Data are the key component required to study the major issues that clinicians face in optimizing both prevention and treatment.[26, 117]

As defined by the American College of Surgeons (ACS) Committee on Trauma, the trauma registry forms the backbone for the evaluation of effectiveness and quality for each institution's trauma program.[39, 146] Details regarding the data elements that should be collected are provided in *Resources for the Optimal Care of the Injured Patient.*[39] The critical elements used to monitor the trauma program include timing of prehospital care; mechanism of injury; vital signs in the field and on arrival; and outcome measures such as ventilator days, intensive care unit days, and mortality. In 1934 Codman[34, 35] suggested that all hospitals should have a good grasp of their patients' outcomes so that the effectiveness of care from the physician and institutional aspects could be improved. Much later in the century, cancer registries began to be developed to measure systematically the effectiveness of chemotherapy and radiotherapy protocols.[43]

To deal with the widespread difference of opinion about what trauma registries should monitor,[19] the Centers for Disease Control and Prevention (which has been given the responsibility for studying prevention and treatment of the disease of injury) convened a lengthy workshop on trauma registries in 1988.[114, 115] Participants included organizations with a major interest in the field, such as the ACS Committee on Trauma, the American College of Emergency Physicians, the American Medical Association's Committee on Emergency Medical Services, and the National Highway Traffic Safety Administration. Criteria for inclusion of patients and core data elements were

---

*See references 28, 33, 42, 46, 50, 85, 91, 106, 122, 136–138, 149, 150.

defined by consensus methodology.[110] Further study sponsored by the ACS has led to the development of a standardized preformatted software package available to all institutions for trauma program monitoring.[103] Before this development, many institutions had developed their own registries, and two states (Pennsylvania and Oregon) and several Canadian provinces had successfully implemented statewide or provincewide programs.[140] By 1992, 48% of states had implemented trauma registries.[123] The ACS Tracs system will save important registry development costs for institutions and regional systems in the future.[103]

Systems have been developed to document and record severity of injury. These include critical data elements.[18, 31, 32, 41, 55, 88, 99] The Committee on Medical Aspects of Automotive Safety published the Abbreviated Injury Scale (AIS) in 1971 primarily to characterize blunt trauma.[37] The AIS assigns a score of 1 (minor) to 6 (total) to each of six different body areas (i.e., chest, abdomen, pelvis, extremities). It did not summarize a single score for multiple injuries. The Injury Severity Score (ISS) was developed in 1974 by summing the square of the AIS scores in the three most severely injured areas.[6] For example, a patient with a moderate liver laceration with AIS = 3 and a femur fracture with AIS = 3 as the only injuries, would have an ISS of 18.

Controversy exists regarding the inclusion or exclusion of lower energy trauma cases in comprehensive regional trauma system registries. Many of the patients with ISS less than 10 are elderly patients with limited physiologic reserve and are at risk for significant morbidity and even mortality as a result of these lower energy injuries.[24] Because of this high potential for long-term disability and the fact that populations throughout the world are aging, it is thought to be appropriate to include cases with lower levels of injury in these surveillance registries. This would increase the utility of such registries as injury prevention tools in addition to serving the other key functions of quality assessment and monitoring of outcome for this population.[109, 151]

In many, if not most, hospital systems, discharge databases form a critical source of data elements for the trauma registry. The addition of the E codes (injury mechanism codes) to the universally applied Diagnosis-Related Groups and codes of the International Classification of Diseases, 9th revision, has greatly enhanced the utility of this data source for trauma registries.[108, 126] These data, when combined with ISS,[4, 5, 7] length of stay, mortality, and resource utilization information, make the hospital discharge database a useful tool for monitoring trauma programs.[140] It is anticipated that the use of standardized databases for the monitoring of trauma programs,[103] because of the uniformity of data collection, will allow greater ease of monitoring for regional and statewide systems. These data will be important for monitoring programs that have been established in response to U.S. Public Law 101-590, the Trauma Care Systems and Planning Act of 1990. However, non–mortality-based functional outcomes are widely available and need to be incorporated.[100, 118]

Trauma registries and discharge databases use as their measure of injury severity the ISS, which grew out of the AIS.[4, 37] Although analysis of this data element has proved useful for analysis of mortality risk for a given ISS,[24, 151] the level of detail regarding musculoskeletal injury is insufficient. A criticism of the ISS has been that it underestimates the severity of injury with multiple injuries to a given body area.[22] For example, a patient with extremity fractures of the femur, tibia, and humerus would have an ISS of 9, the same as that of a patient with an isolated femur fracture. Penetrating trauma is also underestimated, as injury is often concentrated in one area (i.e., abdomen), and a patient with a liver, kidney, and mesenteric injury would have an ISS of 16, as would a patient with an isolated significant splenic laceration. The ISS also fails to consider more severe injuries in one body area over less severe injuries in another body area. The New ISS (NISS) was proposed to correct these idiosyncrasies of the ISS by calculating the ISS from the three most severe injuries regardless of body location.[107] The NISS has increased patients' scores in approximately two thirds of cases and was found to predict more accurately patients' mortality risk[107] and risk of multiple organ failure.[8]

Critical components of injury severity (e.g., soft tissue injury detail), fracture classification, details of treatment, and, most critically, non–mortality-based clinical outcomes are totally lacking. This has led the Orthopaedic Trauma Association to develop a software package, available to its members, that allows tracking of more detailed skeletal and soft tissue injury information, details regarding treatment, and a patient-based outcome module inclusive of relevant clinical outcomes (e.g., range of motion, fracture union) and health status (SF-36 and Musculoskeletal Functional Assessment).[47, 93, 127] This type of decentralized data collection tool is critical to developing information on the effectiveness of management strategies for musculoskeletal injury. Regionalization of specialized surgical services has been shown to be an important concept for reducing morbidity and mortality; however, without functional outcome data, this issue cannot be well studied for musculoskeletal injury.[65, 86]

Resources are required to develop and use such registries in a trauma center, proportional to the volume of patients seen. Data forms are most accurately completed by the most senior treating individuals for purposes of injury classification and treatment description. Commitment by the departmental chief and members of the attending staff is required for the registry to be comprehensive for the institution. Data entry clerks are needed to enter data and obtain complete information where forms are lacking. Program updates are available from the Orthopaedic Trauma Association that allow the surgeon to enter data directly, thus bypassing the forms. Generally speaking, one clerk is required for every 1500 orthopaedic injuries per year, more if radiographs are being stored with the injury data. A research coordinator is necessary to develop a program to obtain functional outcome data *systematically* as a routine for injuries under investigation. It is strongly suggested that specific research questions or quality assurance program issues be studied using this approach. Routinely obtaining functional outcome data for all trauma patients is expensive and impractical, resulting in the collection of huge volumes of data that are generally not used in any meaningful analysis.

In essence, because of the broad range of injury (in

terms of bone and soft tissue severity) dealt with in the field of musculoskeletal traumatology, the best way to gather sufficient cases to study outcome is with multicenter study designs. The use of the decentralized database format should become the necessary linking component allowing all centers to collect the same data in the same format, greatly enhancing data management. Internet Web-based databases may further link centers with a common database.

The complexity and range of skeletal injuries have led to a plethora of injury classification systems. The lack of uniformity of fracture classification systems utilized in the published literature has further limited the utility of the literature for assessing effectiveness. Colton[36] has critically analyzed the situation, noting, as an example, 22 different published classification schemes for olecranon fractures. His recommendation of editorial insistence on the use of a broadly accepted classification scheme has been endorsed by the Orthopaedic Trauma Association and incorporated in the software package described earlier.[101] High interobserver and intraobserver variation in applying skeletal and soft tissue injury schemes has become apparent in multiple publications.[25, 52, 124, 125] The explanation for the poor performance in these analyses is that injury is essentially a continuous variable and classification schemes are by definition dichotomous variables. Forcing the infinite variable into these schemes requires judgments that are individual and nonuniform. The solution to this issue is not to create new classification schemes but rather to recognize the problem and have the injury classified by multiple individuals (preferably three) "blinded" to outcomes and, where discrepancies are evident, use consensus methods to reach a final classification. The use of a standard classification scheme in this manner would greatly enhance the utility of the literature for effectiveness analyses.

HEALTH-RELATED QUALITY OF LIFE INSTRUMENTS IN COMMON USE FOR MUSCULOSKELETAL PROBLEMS

Questionnaires should not be derived by aggregating questions that seem important on the basis of a clinician's experience. Questions that are reflective of patients' function cannot simply be developed on the basis of clinical experience, as physicians' perceptions of functional issues are often inaccurate. Guyatt and associates[60] described the following steps in the development of a functional assessment questionnaire:

Item Development   The population of patients to be evaluated must be described, and functional issues of concern to this group must be selected from interviewing patients and clinicians or, alternatively, from a literature and validated questionnaire review.

Item Reduction   Item reduction is determined by the frequency and importance of item endorsement in a sample cohort of patients or by statistical methods such as factor analysis.

Format Selection   Format selection consists of scaled responses or endorsed statements; the former yield better discrimination but are more difficult for patients; the latter format is much easier for patients.

Pretesting   This consists of administration of the questionnaire with an interviewer present to discover poorly worded or confusing items.

Reproducibility and Responsiveness   *Reproducibility* is evaluated by reviewing the variability in responses in relation to the variability in clinical status. This review is addressed by a test-retest exercise in which the same patients complete the questionnaire twice within a short interval during which no clinical change has taken place. *Responsiveness* is the measure of the questionnaire's ability to detect clinically important changes even if they are small. Responsiveness is assessed by administering the questionnaire twice at a minimal 3-month interval after a clinical intervention of known efficacy.

Validity   *Face validity* is assessed by clinician review to ensure intuitive rationale; *construct validity* is assessed by developing hypotheses about how the scores should change between and within subjects and comparing results with already validated instruments. *Criterion validity* is addressed by comparing scores with objective tests (e.g., range of motion, self-selected walking speed) and clinician evaluations of the same group of patients.

Several well-validated general health status instruments have been developed and are available for use in assessing patients' function after musculoskeletal injury (Table 24–1). The four most widely used and evaluated scales that are appropriate for use in musculoskeletal disease or injury are SF-36, the Sickness Impact Profile (SIP), the Nottingham Health Profile, and the Quality of Well-Being Scale (QWB), which forms the backbone of the quality-adjusted life years (QALY) methodology.[151] These scales have the common characteristic of assessing all "domains" of human activity including physical, psychological, social, and role functioning. In addition, they share the characteristic of assessing the patient as a whole (from the patient's perspective) and not as an organ system, disease, or limb. They are internally consistent, reproducible, and discriminate between clinical conditions of different severity. They are also sensitive to change in health status over time.[81] They are not physician administered, which increases their reliability. Brief descriptions of these instruments follow.

The SF-36 was developed by Ware and colleagues[128, 134, 143–145] and the Rand Corporation as a part of the Medical Outcomes Study. It is perhaps the most widely applied general health status instrument and has certain features that make it the most appealing for studying musculoskeletal injury. Its 36 scaled questions relate to eight different functional subscales: bodily pain, role function-physical, role function-emotional, social function, physical function, energy or fatigue, mental health, and general health perceptions. The scales are scored separately with no total score. It has been validated to be a reliable and reproducible questionnaire that has been applied to numerous health conditions. Furthermore, it has been shown to be reliable as administered by the

TABLE 24–1 ....

HR-QOL Instruments and Scoring Resources

Instrument	Method of Administration	Training Time Required	Length of Time to Complete	Populations Designed For	Conditions Used On	Where/How to Get It
SF-36	Self or interviewer	2 hr	5–10 min	All	General health status/ quality of life measures	Medical Outcomes Trust, 20 Park Plaza, Suite 1014, Boston, MA 02116-4313
SIP	Self or interviewer	1 wk	30 min	All	General health status/quality of life measures	Ann Skinner, 624 North Broadway, Room 647, Baltimore, MD 21205
WOMAC	Self	1 wk	10 min	Arthritis patients	Arthritis	Jane Campbell, London Health Science Center, Suite 303, South Campus 375, South Street, London, Ontario N6A 4G5, Canada
Nottingham Health Profile	Self	1 wk	10 min	All	General health status/quality of life measures	Jim McEwan, Department of Public Health, University of Glasgow, Glasgow G128QQ, Scotland, UK
QWB	Trained interviewer	2 wk	12 min	All	General health status/quality of life measures	Holly Teetzel, Department of Family and Preventive Medicine, Box 0622, University of California, San Diego, 9500 Gilman Drive, La Jolla, CA 92093
Separate AAOS Instruments for upper extremity, lower extremity, spine, and pediatrics	Self or interviewer	1 wk	Variable, depending on which modules used; 10–40 min	Patients with specific regions of disease or injury or specific age	Quality of life measure applied to regional (or specific age group) musculo-skeletal populations	Director, Research and Scientific Affairs, American Academy of Orthopaedic Surgeons, 6300 North River Road, Rosemont, IL 60018
MFA	Self or interviewer	2 hr	15 min	Patients with musculo-skeletal disease	Quality of life measure applied to musculo-skeletal disease	www.ortho.umn.edu/research/ clinicaloutcomes.htm

....

Abbreviations: AAOS, American Academy of Orthopaedic Surgeons; MFA, Musculoskeletal Functional Assessment; QWB, Quality of Well-Being Scale; SF-36, Short Form 36; SIP, Sickness Impact Profile; WOMAC, Western Ontario and McMaster University Osteoarthritis Index.

patient or by an interviewer and when administered by telephone or by mail, and it takes only 5 to 7 minutes to complete. These features make its use appealing; it is the most practical for use in a busy office or clinic setting.

This instrument, however, may have a "ceiling effect" (scores are concentrated at best function) for musculoskeletal conditions. This means that clinically important functional problems may not be adequately characterized by this scale because the disability is too minimal to be picked up by the questions in the scale. Patients with mild to moderate dysfunction (repetitive motion disorders, minor sprains and fractures) may score near the highest possible scores and further improvement cannot be measured. This scale is recommended more often than the other scales discussed here to researchers who wish to study musculoskeletal injury. Our experience in administering the SF-36 shows that patients with musculoskeletal disease or injury tend to misinterpret the questions on general health as being exclusive of their musculoskeletal disease.[47, 93] It has particular weakness in assessing upper extremity function.

The SIP, a questionnaire developed by Bergner and associates[11–13] at the University of Washington, is best administered by trained interviewers and takes 25 to 35 minutes to complete. It has 12 different domains that are addressed by 136 endorsable statements (patients simply say "yes" or "no" if the statement of function applies to their current situation). These 12 areas are scored independently and aggregated into a physical and a psychosocial subscale as well as one aggregate score. The scale is 0 to 100 points; the higher the score, the worse the disability. Patients with scores in excess of the mid-30s have seriously diminished quality of life. The SIP has also been used for patients with multiple health conditions and makes comparisons of the impact of disease on health possible. It has been used in musculoskeletal trauma with good success.[89, 90] Because of the difficulty and length of its administration, it may be most useful for well-funded outcome studies or controlled trials. It also suffers from the ceiling effect that lesser degrees of musculoskeletal function are not identified.[94]

The Nottingham Health Profile is interviewer administered and has been used successfully to assess functional outcomes of limb salvage versus early amputation.[54, 96, 97] It has been shown to be valid in trials in Great Britain and Sweden. Part I of the profile measures subjective health status through a series of 38 weighted questions that assess impairments in the categories of sleep, emotional reaction, mobility, energy level, pain, and social isolation. In each category, 100 points represents maximal disability and 0 represents no limitations. Part II consists of seven statements that require a yes or no response. These assess the influence of health problems on job, home, family life, sexual function, recreation, and enjoyment of holidays. The responses to both parts of the profile can be compared with the average scores for the general age- and sex-matched population.

The QWB is interviewer administered. Using data from large populations and multiplying them by years of life expectancy and cost per intervention gives the QALY—cost per year of well life expectancy. QALYs provide a methodology for making difficult decisions regarding resource allocation. When orthopaedic interventions such as hip arthroplasty and hip fracture fixation have been studied using this methodology, they have fared well.[109, 151] The QWB physical function scale also probably suffers from ceiling effects.

In 1993, the American Academy of Orthopaedic Surgeons (AAOS) and members of the Council of Musculoskeletal Specialty Societies began to pool resources to develop a general health questionnaire and disease-specific questionnaires that could be used for musculoskeletal injuries or conditions[130] in an office setting and allow local, regional, and national collection of patient-derived outcome data. The database incorporated the SF-36 and demographic and co-morbidity information and included questionnaires specific for the upper extremity, lower extremity, pediatric patients, and patients with spinal conditions. The database was named the Musculoskeletal Outcomes Data Collection and Management System (MODEMS). The AAOS established a research institute to oversee the MODEMS project. The instruments were validated and take 10 to 30 minutes to complete. The AAOS conducted a trial project to post national data and collected data for more than 30,000 patients in 3 months.[130]

The AAOS sponsored a national database for MODEMS collection but discontinued it in April 2000. The MODEMS questionnaires are still available for use (www.aaos.org). These questionnaires provide health-related quality of life (HR-QOL) data with the SF-36 as well as area- and disease-specific information and thus are a good choice for comprehensive evaluation. If a clinic or practitioner wishes to use only a single instrument for all conditions being studied, the Musculoskeletal Functional Assessment (MFA) and Short Musculoskeletal Functional Assessment (SMFA) questionnaires provide general health- and area-specific information with fewer floor and ceiling effects for musculoskeletal conditions than the SF-36 (see later).[105] The AAOS is also to manage the distribution and utilization of the SMFA.

These examples are general health status instruments that have broad acceptance and have the ability to compare the functional impact of various diseases. Instruments specific to a disease or condition offer increased sensitivity

and limit the floor and ceiling effects.[80] Table 24–1 lists the general health status instruments individually with their attributes and identifies a source for the reader.

All of these HR-QOL scores are significantly affected by a patient's co-morbidities, age, and sex. This has been best described with the SF-36. Xuan and colleagues[153] have shown that co-morbidities of arthritis, back pain, and depression have the greatest effect on altering a QOL score.[142] Understanding this effect is important in the interpretation of HR-QOL scores. The SF-36 has been published with norms of scores for the U.S. population and also for patients with co-morbidities: hypertension, diabetes, congestive heart failure, myocardial infarction, chronic obstructive pulmonary disease, angina, back pain, osteoarthritis, benign prostatic hypertrophy, varicosities, and dermatitis. These co-morbidities affect the mean scores of the SF-36 subscales of physical function, role-physical, bodily pain, general health, and vitality.[142]

Normative values of the SF-36 also vary with age and sex.[142] This variation is most evident in comparing physical function scores across age groups. For example, the mean physical function score for the U.S. population is 84.15 (scale of 0 to 100). The mean for the 18- to 24-year-old age group is 92.13, and the mean for the 75 and older age group is 53.20.[142] Specific subscales of the SF-36 have also been analyzed and stratified for age and sex. Investigators need to be aware of these variances when using an HR-QOL survey to assess a patient's functional recovery, and patients may need to be compared with their appropriate age group to obtain a more accurate assessment of their true functional capacity. The MFA has also been published with reference values to population norms.[48]

DEVELOPMENT OF A MUSCULOSKELETAL OUTCOMES RESEARCH TOOL

In response to the need for a validated instrument that would allow clinicians to determine the functional outcome of patients with musculoskeletal disease or injury (extremity trauma, overuse syndromes, osteoarthritis, or rheumatoid arthritis), the MFA was developed under the sponsorship of the National Institutes of Health, National Institute of Child Health and Human Development.[47, 93] This 100-item instrument allows clinicians to assess their patients' function in 10 distinct domains (self-care, emotional, recreation, household work, employment, sleep and rest, relationships, thinking, activities using arms and legs, and activities using hands). The instrument requires 15 to 17 minutes to complete and can be either self-administered or interviewer administered. When used by members of the orthopaedic and trauma communities who treat the diseases mentioned earlier, it allows analysis of the effectiveness of treatment and comparisons of the functional impact of various diseases and injuries. It is anticipated that incremental improvement will be made in avoiding the ceiling effect evident in other general health status instruments.

The MFA was field tested on patients with extremity trauma (upper and lower), overuse syndromes, osteoarthritis, and rheumatoid arthritis. These specific populations were chosen because they account for significant health care costs both to the patient and to society. Extremity trauma costs range from $75 billion to $150 billion annually.[92, 100, 102] Overuse injuries accounted for 48% of the reported occupational injuries in 1988.[26] Operative procedures related to carpal tunnel syndrome alone cost over $1 billion.[116] Arthritis and related diseases have associated costs, because of resultant morbidity, that are estimated to be as high as $41.6 billion.[116] Numerous evaluation scales are currently in use (e.g., Harris Hip Score, Indiana Knee Scale), but these arbitrarily mix pain, clinical, and functional outcomes. Few have been subjected to rigorous statistical evaluation.

The MFA is a quality of life instrument with applicability to musculoskeletal disease at both the low and high ends of severity. Its domains are functionally designed to give physicians categories with which they can identify and which they can use to help target where individual patients may be having difficulty and thus provide appropriate assistance as indicated. These domains also help physicians to address immediate postinjury concerns or early disease onset concerns of patients about what the future might hold for them. Because it is a single instrument dealing with all musculoskeletal disorders, it alleviates the need for community practice physicians to have many outcome tools available for patients' use and different skills to interpret them.

The MFA was developed using unstructured open-ended interviews with 136 patients and 12 clinicians, resulting in 7800 statements in 35 domains. These items, using the patients' own wording whenever possible, were reduced to a 12-domain, 177-item questionnaire. Three hundred and twenty-seven patients from the Seattle Hand Clinic, Valley Medical Center (Level II trauma center), Northwest Foot and Ankle Clinic, and Harborview Medical Center (Level I trauma center) participated in the first field trial of the MFA.[47, 93] Reliability was between 72.6% and 100% for all items. Internal consistency was .85 on the basis of Cronbach's alpha. Validity was assessed by comparing objective measures (e.g., range of motion, self-selected walking speed, grip dynamometer strength, and isokinetic testing) for 119 patients with relevant domains. Significant relationships ($r > .33$) were found between category scores in mobility, housework, fine motor, self-care, and confinement and objective measure

scores.[90] Physicians' assessments on the basis of review of medical records and radiographs for a sample of 24 patients demonstrated correlation between .04 and .50. Significant relationships were also found on comparing survey scores with the presence of co-morbidities, complications, gender, joint degeneration (arthritis), functional level (overuse), and ISS. The survey was then reduced to its final 100-item format by removing items that were unstable, unclear, unresponsive, significantly intercorrelated, or internally inconsistent using accepted statistical methodology.[47]

The MFA has been given to 557 patients to evaluate its responsiveness, validity, and reliability. It was developed as a tool useful for funded outcome research projects and randomized controlled trials. The MFA may provide the community clinician with more detail and be more demanding for staff and patients than is necessary for routine use or for participation in local, state, and national outcome assessments. Therefore, the Short Musculoskeletal Functional Assessment (SMFA) has been developed[131] and validated.[132]

Clinicians wishing to compare patients' progress over time routinely and quantitatively, as well as against patients from other settings, need a self-administered instrument that requires no lengthy explanations to patients and does not disrupt the daily flow of the office or create huge costs. The SMFA is designed to meet those needs and to be a stand-alone tool for the routine assessment of orthopaedic outcomes, regardless of the disease or injury being evaluated. To formulate the SMFA, investigators selected 46 questions from the longer instrument on the basis of universality, applicability, uniqueness, reliability, and validity as demonstrated by the MFA data. The SMFA has been field tested in academic and community offices with excellent compliance and utility.[1] The SF-36, MODEMS instruments, MFA, and SMFA can be obtained from several web sites (Table 24–2).

RECOMMENDATIONS FOR CLINICAL OUTCOMES RESEARCH AND OUTCOMES ASSESSMENT

Keller and associates[70, 72, 75] made the important differentiation between outcomes research and outcomes assessment for the orthopaedic community. *Outcomes research*

TABLE 24–2	
Useful Web Sites	
Orthopaedic Trauma Association	www.ota.org
American Academy of Orthopaedic Surgeons	www.aaos.org/
Agency for Healthcare Research and Quality (AHRQ)	www.ahcpr.gov
SF-36 Questionnaire	www.sf-36.com/general
MODEMS Questionnaires	www.aaos.org/wordhtm/outcomes/question.htm
MFA/SMFA	www.ortho.umn.edu/research/clinicaloutcomes.htm
Cochrane Collaboration	www.cochrane.org/

Abbreviations: MFA, Musculoskeletal Functional Assessment; MODEMS, Musculoskeletal Outcomes Data Collection and Management System; SF-36, Short Form 36; SMFA, Short MFA.

involves the systematic study of an individual disease process or injury. Such projects generally involve individuals who are trained in research methodology (often health services researchers), are frequently multicenter trials to satisfy targets for accrual of patients, and most often require outside sources of funding to pay individuals responsible for data collection, monitoring of the study, and analysis of data. Results of these studies frequently result in changes in practice informally and through the modification of existing practice guidelines.

The procedure for initiation of such a study involves identifying a condition that has a substantial impact on patients' function or longevity and analyzing retrospective data to identify key elements in the process of treatment that need further study. This is one of the major uses of trauma registry data such as those developed by the Orthopaedic Trauma Association. Once the process issues are identified, a study design based on the data reviewed must be developed and a power calculation performed to determine the number of patients who must be enrolled to detect a clinically important difference in outcome. A trial enrollment period of 1 to 2 months at each potential site gives the investigators a good idea of whether the volume of patients is present to complete the study.

As a part of the study design phase, it is determined which assessment questionnaires are optimal for the study and the intervals at which patients should complete them. It is also determined in this phase which clinical data are to be collected and which physical measurements (e.g., strength, range of motion, self-selected walking speed, and hand-held dynamometer strength) should be collected at follow-up intervals. Data that are not to be used to answer a specific study hypothesis should not be gathered as this overburdens the process. Practicality in terms of staffing for enrollment of patients, tracking and data management, patients' transportation needs, cultural and language issues (which differ from site to site depending on the local population), and institutional cooperation must be considered in the study planning phase for each potential site. Funding of studies allows more rapid accrual of patients, more data collection and analysis, and more clear responsibility lines.

These studies are constructed to address specific hypotheses, and attention must be directed to collecting the data necessary to address the hypotheses. The tendency is often to collect data because "we may find some interesting use for it later." This approach is resource intensive and frustrating for individuals collecting the data and should be avoided.

The current "gold standard" of orthopaedic research is the prospective, randomized, double-blind study.[29] This experimental model was designed for pharmaceutical research, and some of these principles are difficult in surgical, interventional studies. It is difficult to make many studies double blind, especially an operative versus a nonoperative trial. Surgeons tend to have strong opinions or particular skills that make pure randomization of patients difficult or raise ethical questions for the participating surgeons. Rudicel and Esdaile[119] proposed that surgeon randomization is a valid way to limit bias in procedure-based trials. Surgeon randomization has

been done successfully in some well-designed surgical trials.[60, 84, 152]

Much of the earlier published literature in orthopaedics was based on case studies without adequate study design, controls, or statistical analysis.[51, 57] Peer review requirements are improving the quality of the literature to answer hypothesis-driven questions.[3, 8, 14, 60, 83] All studies should enlist a statistician to provide an unbiased assessment of power analysis to avoid a statistical type II or B error (stating that no statistical difference exists when one actually does) because too few patients are enrolled in the study and to ensure that the appropriate statistical analysis is performed.

This process of outcomes research is to be contrasted with *outcomes* assessment, which involves the collection of HR-QOL data for samples of patients to evaluate effectiveness of care. It is often done at the office, group, or health plan level and includes the type of data in which payers are interested. The routine collection of data on patients' satisfaction and HR-QOL is done on a preidentified segment of a practice at predetermined intervals, before and after treatment, forming the basis for outcome assessment. A common approach is to begin such a process by collecting data for all patients in a practice. However, this is to be discouraged. It results in accumulation of data in large volumes, which can be time consuming, if not impossible, to analyze. The collection process quickly leads to frustration of the office staff responsible for form administration and collection. Patients' cooperation and support of these projects are rarely a problem. Patients have been found to be most receptive to completing these types of questionnaires and believe that this process, as well as satisfaction surveys, represents an effort on behalf of the practice to meet their needs. During field testing of the MFA instrument, Harborview Medical Center (a worst-case scenario for patients' compliance) was able to obtain adequate follow-up of more than 95% of patients enrolled.[47]

The best approach in beginning outcomes assessment within a practice or trauma group is to select a musculoskeletal condition or injury that is frequently seen within the practice as a target condition. As a rough indicator, it is best for the staff involved in data collection if an eligible patient is seen 5 to 10 times per week. The patient should be approached before treatment and asked to complete an HR-QOL questionnaire and told that she or he will be notified at predetermined intervals to complete the same survey. The physicians responsible for the project should decide before enrolling patients which clinical data they need to collect to analyze the HR-QOL data properly. Data points involving clinical, demographic, or radiographic assessments should be collected before treatment and at selected intervals. The exact timing of data collection is not standardized, and the appropriate time intervals may be different for different musculoskeletal injuries or conditions. A patient with an isolated ankle fracture returns to normal function more quickly than a patient with a tibial plafond fracture and may require more frequent data collection. Studies are in process and need to be performed that better characterize the rate of functional recovery from a variety of musculoskeletal injuries to answer patients' questions as well as address work-related and legal issues with more accuracy.

A minimalistic approach, in terms of the number of conditions studied, is most fruitful when starting to assess outcomes in clinical practice. Identifying a condition that is common to the practice (and thus important to the success of the practice) and collecting data on patients with this condition lead to a product that is useful for evaluating current practice and planning for changes in the process of care.

Meta-analysis is a technique that has been developed to pool results for randomized controlled trials. It has a rigorous methodology of analysis to grade the rigor of the study design by assigning a quality score and to identify the magnitude of the overall effect of the treatment under study. It was designed to deal with the problem of multiple controlled trials of a given treatment where an overall effect was the desired end-point. Several orthopaedic and traumatic conditions have been studied using these techniques.[82] Because of the invasiveness of surgery and the need for surgeons to follow their own beliefs in recommending treatments to patients in their ethical role as patients' advocates, the classical randomized clinical trial is rarely seen in our field. Surgeon randomization has been suggested as a scientifically sound way around some of these difficult issues,[119] as noted earlier, but has rarely been used.[60, 84] Attempts at meta-analysis have been made for spinal stenosis, hip arthroplasty, tibia fractures, hip fractures, and other conditions.[79, 83, 88, 89, 141] All of these reviews have found serious deficiencies in study design, control subjects, follow-up, and outcome assessment that seriously limited any conclusions concerning treatment or efficacy. Thus, without the available literature on high-quality, controlled, prospective trials, meta-analysis fails as a technique.

The orthopaedic literature is improving with increased awareness of study design and statistical impact and adequate follow-up of clinical and functional outcomes.[3, 14, 20, 61, 77, 84, 85] Regional and statewide organizations such as the Maine Medical Assessment Foundation can be effective in collecting data. The information from pooled orthopaedic data would be instrumental in improving the quality of musculoskeletal care that we are able to provide. It would allow rapid accrual of patients and timely analysis of clinical uncertainties. These data must be collected efficiently at minimal cost in community and academic settings. Cost-benefit analysis of orthopaedic surgery interventions has been shown to be quite favorable[109, 151] and will continue to be to the benefit of orthopaedists and their patients.

Evidence-based medicine has been defined by Sackett and colleagues as "the conscientious, explicit, and judicious use of current best evidence in making decisions about the care of individual patients."[119a] The practice of evidence-based medicine requires integrating individual clinical expertise with the best available evidence from systematic research. As noted earlier, randomized clinical trials are thought to provide the highest quality evidence to influence clinical decision making. Evidence-based medicine has become the new "buzzword" in outcomes literature. The *Journal of Bone and Joint Surgery* introduced a quarterly section on evidence-based orthopaedics in

June 2000 to "assist busy clinicians with real-world questions."[151a]

The Cochrane Collaboration (www.cochrane.org), an international consortium, was developed in 1992 to 1993 to help practitioners and patients make "well informed decisions about health care by a systematic review of the effects of health care interventions." This consortium has multidisciplinary review groups in over 40 areas of health care that systematically collect, review, and electronically publish summaries of randomized clinical trials. The Cochrane Library is maintained on line and includes databases of systematic reviews, randomized control trials (RCTs), and abstracts. There is a Cochrane musculoskeletal injuries group with more than 30 systemic reviews completed and on line. The Cochrane Collaboration is a potentially powerful resource for clinicians and patients who wish to obtain the best available data to help make clinical decisions.

Acknowledgments
The authors appreciate the editorial assistance of Renee Schurtz and Jean Godwin.

REFERENCES

1. Agel, J. The Feasibility of the SMFA. Orthopaedic Trauma Association meeting; Charlotte, NC, 1999.
2. Atlas, S.J.; Deyo, R.A.; Keller, R.B.; et al. The Maine Lumbar Spine Study II. Spine 21:1777, 1996.
3. Aune, A.K.; Ekeland, A.; Odegaard, B.; et al. Gamma nail vs compression screw for trochanteric femoral fractures: 15 reoperations in a prospective, randomized study of 278 patients. Acta Orthop Scand 65:127, 1994.
4. Baker, S.; O'Neill, B.; Haddon, W. The Injury Severity Score: A method for describing patients with multiple injuries and evaluating emergency care. J Trauma 14:187, 1974.
5. Baker, S.P. Injuries: The neglected epidemic. Stone Lecture, 1985 American Trauma Society Meeting. J Trauma 27:343, 1987.
6. Baker, S.P.; O'Neill, B.; Haddon, W.; et al. The Injury Severity Score. J Trauma 14:187, 1974.
7. Baker, S.P.; O'Neill, B. The Injury Severity Score: An update. J Trauma 16:882, 1976.
8. Balogh, Z.; Offner, P.J.; Moore, E.E.; Biff, W.L. NISS predicts post-injury mortality better than the ISS. J Orthop Trauma 48:624, 2000.
9. Bellamy, N.; Buchanan, W.W.; Goldsmith, C.H.; et al. Validation study of WOMAC: A health status instrument for measuring clinically important patient relevant outcomes following total hip or knee arthroplasty in osteoarthritis. J Orthop Rheumatol 1:95, 1988.
10. Benirschke, S.K.; Melder, I.; Henley, M.B.; et al. Closed interlocking nailing of femoral shaft fractures: Assessment of technical complications and functional outcomes by comparison of a prospective database with retrospective review. J Orthop Trauma 7:118, 1993.
11. Bergner, M.; Bobbitt, R.A.; Carter, W.B.; et al. The Sickness Impact Profile: Development and final revision of a health status measure. Med Care 19:787, 1981.
12. Bergner, M.; Bobbitt, R.A.; Kressel, S.; et al. The Sickness Impact Profile: Conceptual formulation and methodological development of a health status index. Int J Health Serv 6:393, 1976.
13. Bergner, M.; Bobbitt, R.A.; Pollaro, W.E.; et al. The Sickness Impact Profile: Validation of a health status measure. Med Care 14:57, 1976.
14. Blanchut, P.A.; O'Brien, P.J.; Meck, R.N.; Brockhuyse, H.M. Interlocking IM nailing with and without reaming of closed fractures of the tibial shaft: A prospective, randomized study. J Bone Joint Surg Am 79:640, 1997.
15. Bondurant, F.; Cotler, H.B.; Buckle, R.; et al. The medical and economic impact of severely injured lower extremities. J Trauma 28:1270, 1988.
16. Bone, L.B.; Johnson, K.D.; Weigelt, J.; Scheinberg, R. Early versus

delayed stabilization of fractures: A prospective randomized study. J Bone Joint Surg Am 71:336, 1989.

17. Bone, L.B.; McNamara, K.; Shine, B.; Border, J. Mortality in multiple trauma patients with fractures. J Trauma 37:262, 1994.

18. Boyd, C.R.; Tolson, M.A.; Copes, W.S. Evaluating trauma care: The TRISS method. J Trauma 27:370, 1987.

19. Boyd, D.R. Trauma registries revisited. Editorial. J Trauma 25:186, 1985.

20. Bracken, M.B.; Shepard, M.J.; Collins, W.F.; et al. A randomized controlled trial of methylprednisolone or naloxone in the treatment of spinal cord injury. N Engl J Med 322:1405, 1990.

21. Bradburn, N.M. The Structure of Psychological Well Being. Chicago, Aldine Publishing, 1969.

22. Brennemen, F.D.; Boulange, B.R.; McLellan, B.A.; et al. Measuring injury severity: Time for a change? J Orthop Trauma 44:580, 1998.

23. Breslow, L. A quantitative approach to the World Health Organization definition of health: Physical, mental and social well-being. Int J Epidemiol 1:347, 1972.

24. Brotman, S.; McMinn, D.L.; Copes, W.S.; et al. Should survivors with an Injury Severity Score less than 10 be entered in a statewide trauma registry? J Trauma 31:1233, 1991.

25. Brumback, R.J.; Jones, A.L. Interobserver agreement in the classification of open fractures of the tibia: The results of a survey of two hundred and forty-five orthopaedic surgeons. J Bone Joint Surg Am 76:1162, 1994.

26. Bureau of Labor Statistics. Occupational injuries and illnesses in the United States by industry in 1988. Bur Labor Stat Bull August: 2368, 1990.

27. Bush, J.W.; Chen, M.M.; Patrick, D.L. Health status index in cost effectiveness and analysis of PKU program. In: Berg, R.L., ed. Health Status Indexes. Chicago, Hospital Research and Educational Trust, 1973, p. 172.

28. Cales, R.; Trunkey, D. Preventable trauma deaths: A review of trauma care systems development. JAMA 254:1059, 1985.

29. Chalmers, I.G.; Collins, R.E.; Dickerson, K. Controlled trials and meta-analysis can help resolve disagreements among orthopedic surgeons. Editorial. J Bone Joint Surg Br 74:7641, 1992.

30. Chambers, L.W. The McMaster Health Index Questionnaire (MHIQ): Methodological Documentation and Report of Second Generation of Investigators. Hamilton, Ontario, Canada, Department of Clinical Epidemiology and Biostatistics, 1982.

31. Champion, H.R.; Copes, W.S.; Sacco, W.J.; et al. The Major Trauma Outcome Study: Establishing national norms for trauma care. J Trauma 30:1356, 1990.

32. Champion, H.R.; Sacco, W.J.; Hannan, D.S.; et al. Assessment of injury severity: The Triage Index. Crit Care Med 8:201, 1980.

33. Champion, H.R.; Teter, H. Trauma care systems—The federal role. J Trauma 28:877, 1988.

34. Codman, E.A. The product of a hospital. Surg Gynecol Obstet 18:491, 1914.

35. Codman, E.A. The Shoulder. Malaber, FL, Krieger Publishing, 1934, p. 1.

36. Colton, C.L. Telling the bones. Editorial. J Bone Joint Surg Br 73:362, 1991.

37. Committee on Medical Aspects of Automotive Safety. Rating the severity of tissue damage. JAMA 215:277, 1971.

38. Committee on Trauma, American College of Surgeons. Advanced Trauma Life Support Manual. Chicago, American College of Surgeons, 1993.

39. Committee on Trauma, American College of Surgeons. Resources for the Optimal Care of the Injured Patient. Chicago, American College of Surgeons, 1990.

40. Committee on Trauma Research. Injury in America: A Continuing Public Health Problem. Washington, DC, National Academy Press, 1985.

41. Copes, W.S.; Champion, H.R.; Sacco, W.J.; et al. The Injury Severity Score revisited. J Trauma 28:69, 1988.

42. Court-Brown, C.M. The treatment of the multiply injured patient in the United Kingdom. J Bone Joint Surg Br 72:345, 1990.

43. Cutler, S.J.; Latourette, H.B. A national cooperative program for the evaluation of end results in cancer. J Natl Cancer Inst 22:633, 1959.

44. Deyo, R.A.; Inui, T.S.; Leninger, J.D.; Overman, S.S. Measuring functional outcomes in chronic disease: A comparison of traditional scales and a self-administered health status questionnaire in patients with rheumatoid arthritis. Med Care 21:180, 1983.

45. Donabedian, A. Evaluating the quality of medical care. Milbank Memorial Fund Quarterly 44(3)(Suppl):166, 1966.

46. Eastman, A.; Lewis, F., Jr.; Champion, H.; Mattox, K. Regional trauma system design: Critical concepts. Am J Surg 154:79, 1987.

47. Engelberg, R.; Martin, D.P.; Agel, J.; et al. The Musculoskeletal Functional Assessment instrument: Criterion and construct validity. J Orthop Res 14:182, 1996.

48. Engelberg, R.; Martin, D.P.; Agel, J.; Swiontkowski, M.F. MFA: Reference values for patient and non-patient samples. J Orthop Res 17:101, 1999.

49. Fakhry, S.M.; Rutledge, R.; Dahners, L.E.; Kessler, D. Incidence, management and outcome of femoral shaft fracture: A statewide population based analysis of 2805 adult patients in a rural state. J Trauma 37:255, 1994.

50. Fortner, G.S.; Oreskovich, M.R.; Copass, M.K.; Carrico, C.J. The effects of prehospital trauma care on survival from a 50 meter fall. J Trauma 23:976, 1983.

51. Gartland, J.J. Orthopaedic clinical research—Deficiencies in experimental design and determination of outcome. J Bone Joint Surg Am 70:1357, 1988.

52. Gehrchen, P.M.; Nielson, J.O.; Olesen, B. Poor reproducibility of Evans classification of the trochanteric fracture: Assessment of four observers in fifty-two cases. Acta Orthop Scand 64:71, 1993.

53. Geisler, F.H.; Dorsey, F.C.; Coleman, W.P. Recovery of motor function after spinal cord injury—A randomized, placebo controlled trial with GM1 ganglioside. N Engl J Med 324:1829, 1991.

54. Georgiadis, G.M.; Behrens, F.F.; Joyce, M.J.; et al. Open tibial fractures with severe soft tissue loss—Limb salvage compared with below knee amputation. J Bone Joint Surg Am 75:1431, 1993.

55. Greenspan, L.; McLellan, B.A.; Greig, H. Abbreviated Injury Scale and Injury Severity Score: A scoring chart. J Trauma 22:60, 1985.

56. Gregory, R.T.; Gould, R.J.; Peclet, M.; et al. The mangled extremity syndrome (MES): A severity grading system for multisystem injury of the extremity. J Trauma 5:1147, 1985.

57. Gross, M. A critique of the methodologies used in clinical studies of hip joint arthroplasty published in the English literature. J Bone Joint Surg Am 70:1364, 1988.

58. Guyatt, G.H.; Feeney, D.H.; Patrick, D.L. Measuring health related quality of life. Basic Sci Rev 118:622, 1993.

59. Guyatt, G.H.; Kirshner, B.; Jaeschke, R. Measuring health status: What are the necessary measurement properties? J Clin Epidemiol 45:1341, 1992.

60. Hardy, D.D.; Descamps, P.Y.; Krallis, P.; et al. Use of an intermedullary hip-screw compared with compression hip-screw with a plate for intertrochanteric femoral fractures. J Bone Joint Surg Am 81:618, 1999.

61. Horne, G.; Iceton, G.; Twist, J.; Malony R. Disability following fractures of the tibial shaft. Orthopedics 13:423, 1990.

62. Hunt, S.M.; McKenna, S.P.; McEwen, J.; et al. The Nottingham Health Profile: Subjective health status and medical consultations. Soc Sci Med 15A:221, 1981.

63. Jette, A.M.; Davies, A.R.; Cleary, P.D.; et al. The Functional Status Questionnaire: Reliability and validity when used in primary care. J Gen Intern Med 1:143, 1986.

64. Johnson, K.D.; Cadambi, A.; Seibert, G.B. Incidence of adult respiratory distress syndrome in patients with multiple musculoskeletal injuries: Effect of early operative stabilization of fractures. J Trauma 25:375, 1985.

65. Jollis, J.G.; Peterson, E.D.; DeLong, E.R.; et al. The relation between the volume of coronary angioplasty procedures at hospitals treating Medicare beneficiaries and short term mortality. N Engl J Med 331:1625, 1994.

66. Kaplan, R.M.; Anderson, J.P.; Wu, A.; et al. The Quality of Well-being Scale: Applications in AIDS, cystic fibrosis and arthritis. Med Care 27(Suppl 3):S27, 1989.

67. Karnofsky, D.A.; Burchenal, J.H. The clinical evaluation of chemotherapeutic drugs. In: MacLeod, C.M., ed. Evaluation of Chemotherapeutic Agents. New York, Columbia University Press, 1949, p. 191.

68. Katz, J.N.; Larson, M.G.; Phillips, C.B.; et al. Comparative measurement sensitivity of short and longer health status instruments. Med Care 30:917, 1992.

69. Katz, S.; Ford, A.B.; Moskowitz, R.W.; et al. Studies of illness in the aged. JAMA 185:914, 1963.

70. Keller, R.; Soule, D.N.; Wennberg, J.E.; Hanley, D.F. Dealing with geographic variations in the use of hospitals: The experience of the Maine Medical Assessment Foundation Orthopaedic Study Group. J Bone Joint Surg Am 72:1286, 1990.

71. Keller, R.B. Outcomes research in orthopaedics. J Am Acad Orthop Surg 1:122, 1993.

72. Keller, R.B.; Rudicel, S.A.; Liang, M.H. Outcomes research in orthopaedics. J Bone Joint Surg Am 75:1562, 1993.

73. Keller, R.B.; Soule, D.N.; Wennberg, J.E.; Hanley, D.F. Dealing with geographic variations in the use of hospitals. J Bone Joint Surg Am 72:1286, 1990.

74. Keller, R.B.; Wennberg, D.E.; Soule, D.N. Changing physician behavior: Maine Medical Assessment Foundation. Qual Manag Health Care 5:1, 1997.

75. Keller, R.B; Rudicel, S.; Liang, M.H. Outcomes research in orthopedics. J Bone Joint Surg Am 75:1562, 1993.

76. Kristianson, T.K.; Ryaby, J.P.; McCabe, J.; et al. Accelerated healing of distal radius fractures with the use of specific, low-intensity ultrasound: A multi-center, prospective, randomized, double-blinded, placebo controlled study. J Bone Joint Surg Am 79:961, 1997.

77. L'Abbe, K.A.; Detsky, A.S.; O'Rourke, K. Meta-analysis in clinical research. Ann Intern Med 107:224, 1987.

78. Labelle, H.; Guibert, R.; Joncas, J.; et al. Lack of scientific evidence for the treatment of lateral epicondylitis of the elbow: An attempted meta-analysis. J Bone Joint Surg Br 74:646, 1992.

79. Lembcke, P.A. Measuring the quality of medical care through vital statistics based on hospital service areas: A comparative study of appendectomy rates. Am J Health 42:276, 1952.

80. Levine, D.W.; Simmons, B.P.; Koris, M.J.; et al. A self-administered questionnaire for the assessment of severity of symptoms and functional status in carpal tunnel syndrome. J Bone Joint Surg Am 75:1585, 1993.

81. Liang, M.H.; Fossel, A.H.; Larson, M.G. Comparisons of five health status instruments for orthopaedic evaluation. Med Care 28:632, 1990.

82. Littenberg, B.; Weinstein, L.P.; McCarren, M.; et al. Closed fractures of the tibial shaft: A meta-analysis of three methods of treatment. J Bone Joint Surg Am 80:174, 1998.

83. Long, G.T.; Richardson, M.; Bosse, M.J.; et al. Efficacy of surgical wound drainage in orthopaedic trauma patients: A randomized, prospective trial. J Orthop Trauma 12:348, 1998.

84. Loucks, C.; Buckley, R. Böhler's angle: Correlation with outcome in displaced intra-articular calcaneal fractures. J Orthop Trauma 13:554, 1999.

85. Lowe, D.K.; Gately, H.L.; Gross, J.R.; et al. Patterns of death, complications and error in management of motor vehicle accident victims: Implications for a regional system of trauma care. J Trauma 23:503, 1983.

86. Luft, H.; Bunker, J.; Enthoven, A. Should operations be regionalized? The empirical relation between surgical volume and mortality. N Engl J Med 301:1364, 1979.

87. LuYao, G.L.; Keller, R.B.; Littenberg, B.; et al. A meta-analysis of 106 published reports. J Bone Joint Surg Am 76:15, 1994.

88. MacKenzie, E.J. Injury severity scales: Overview and directions for future research. Am J Emerg Med 2:537, 1984.

89. MacKenzie, E.J.; Burgess, A.R.; McAndrew, M.P.; et al. Patient-oriented functional outcome after unilateral lower extremity fracture. J Orthop Trauma 7:393, 1993.

90. MacKenzie, E.J.; Cushing, B.M.; Jurkovich, G.J.; et al. Physical impairment and functional outcomes six months after severe lower extremity fractures. J Trauma 34:528, 1993.

91. MacKenzie, E.J.; Morris, J.A.; Smith, G.S.; Fahey, M. Acute hospital costs of trauma in the United States: Implications for regionalized systems of care. J Trauma 30:1096, 1990.

92. MacKenzie, E.J.; Siegel, J.H.; Shapiro, S.; et al. Functional recovery and medical costs of trauma: An analysis by type and severity of injury. J Trauma 28:281, 1988.

93. Mrin, D.; Engelberg, R.; Agel, J.; Snapp, D. Development of the Musculoskeletal Functional Assessment Instrument. J Orthop Res 14:173, 1996.

94. Martin, D.; Engelberg, R.; Agel, J.; Swiontkowski, M.F. Comparison of the Musculoskeletal Function Assessment Questionnaire with the Short Form-36, the Western Ontario and McMaster Universities Osteoarthritis Index, and the Sickness Impact Profile health-status measures. J Bone Joint Surg Am 79:1323, 1997.

95. Mattox, K.L.; Bickell, W.H.; Pepe, P.E.; Mangelsdorff, A.D. Prospective randomized evaluation of antishock MAST in post-traumatic hypotension. J Trauma 26:779, 1986.

96. McDowell, I.; Newell, C.; eds. Measuring Health: A Guide to Rating Scales and Questionnaires. New York, Oxford University Press, 1987, p. 125.

97. McEwen, J. The Nottingham Health Profile: A measure of perceived health. In: Teeling-Smith, G., ed. Measuring the Social Benefits of Medicine. London, Office of Health Economics, 1983, p. 75.

98. Meek, R.; Vivoda, E.; Pirani, S. A comparison of mortality in patients with multiple injuries according to the method of fracture treatment: A retrospective age and injury matched series. Injury 17:2, 1986.

99. Morris, J.A.; Auerbach, P.S.; Marshall, G.A.; et al. The Trauma Score as a triage tool in the prehospital setting. JAMA 256:1319, 1986.

100. Morris, J.A.; Sanchez, A.A.; Bass, S.M.; MacKenzie, E.J. Trauma patients return to productivity. J Trauma 31:827, 1991.

101. Müller, M.E.; Nazarian, S.; Koch, P.; Scatzker, J. The Comprehensive Classification of Fractures of Long Bones. Berlin, Springer-Verlag, 1990.

102. National Safety Council. Accident Facts. Chicago, National Safety Council, 1990.

103. National Trends. Chicago, American College of Surgeons, October 1992.

104. Nelson, E.C.; Wasson, J.; Kirk, A.; et al. Assessment of function in routine clinical practice: Description of the COOP chart method and preliminary findings. J Chronic Dis 40:15S, 1987.

105. Obremskey, W.T.; Brown, O.; Driver, R.; Dirschl, D.R. Comparison of SMFA vs SF-36 in Recovery of Unstable Ankle Fractures. Orthopaedic Trauma Association meeting, San Antonio, TX, October 2000.

106. Ornato, J.; Craren, E.; Nelsonk, N.; Kimball, K. Impact of improved emergency medical services and emergency trauma care on reduction in mortality from trauma. J Trauma 25:575, 1985.

107. Oslen, T.; Baker, S.; Long, W. A modification of the ISS that both improves accuracy and simplifies scoring. J Orthop Trauma 43:922, 1997.

108. Pal, J.; Brown, R.; Fleiszer, D. The value of the Glasgow Coma Scale and ISS: Predicting outcome in multiple trauma patients with head injury. J Trauma 29:746, 1989.

109. Parker, M.J.; Myles, J.W.; Anand, J.K.; Drewett, R. Cost benefit analysis of hip fracture treatment. J Bone Joint Surg Br 74:261, 1992.

110. Parkerson, G.R.; Broadhead, W.E.; Tse, C.K.J. The Duke Health Profile: A 17-item measure of health and dysfunction. Med Care 28:1056, 1990.

111. Parkerson, G.R.; Gehlbach, S.H.; Wagner, E.H.; et al. The Duke-UNC Health Profile: An adult health status instrument for primary care. Med Care 19:806, 1981.

112. Patrick, D.L.; Bergner, M. Measurement of health status in the 1990s. Annu Rev Public Health 11:65, 1990.

113. Patrick, D.L.; Deyo, R.A.; Atlas, S.J.; et al. Assessing health related quality of life in patients with sciatica. Spine 20:1899, 1995.

114. Pollock, D.A.; McClain, P.W. Report from the 1988 trauma registry workshop, including recommendations for hospital based trauma registries. J Trauma 29:827, 1989.

115. Pollock, D.A.; McClain, P.W. Trauma registries—Current status and future prospects. JAMA 262:2280, 1989.

116. Praemer, A.; Furner, S.; Rice, D.P. Musculoskeletal Conditions in the United States. Park Ridge, IL, American Academy of Orthopaedic Surgeons, 1992.

117. Rhodes, M.; Aronsen, J.; Moerkirk, G.; Petrash, E. Quality of life after the trauma center. J Trauma 28:931, 1987.

118. Rice, D.P.; MacKenzie, E.J. Cost of Injury in the United States—A Report to Congress. San Francisco, Institute for Health and Aging; University of California and Injury Prevention Center; Baltimore, The Johns Hopkins University, 1989.

119. Rudicel, S.; Esdaile, J. The randomized clinical trial in orthopaedics: Obligation or option? J Bone Joint Surg Am 67:1284, 1995.

119a. Sackett, D.L.; Rosenberg, W.M.; Gray, J.A.; et al. Evidence-based medicine: What it is and what it isn't. BMJ 312:71, 1996.

120. Schroder, S.A. Outcome assessment 70 years later: Are we ready? N Engl J Med 316:160, 1987.

121. Seibel, R.; LaDuca, J.; Hassett, J.M.; et al. Blunt multiple trauma (ISS 36), femur traction, and the pulmonary failure-septic state. Ann Surg 202:283, 1985.

122. Shakford, S.R.; Hollingsworth Fridlund, P.; Cooper, G.F.; Eastman, A.B. The effect of regionalization upon the quality of trauma care assessed by concurrent audit before and after the institution of a trauma system: A preliminary report. J Trauma 26:812, 1986.

123. Shapiro, M.J.; Cole, K.E., Jr.; Keegan, M.; et al. National survey of state trauma registries—1992. J Trauma 37:835, 1994.

124. Sidor, M.L.; Zuckerman, J.D.; Lyon, T.; et al. The Neer classification for proximal humerus fractures. An assessment of interobserver reliability and intraobserver reproducibility. J Bone Joint Surg Am 75:1745, 1993.

125. Siebenrock, K.A.; Gerber, C. The reproducibility of classification of fractures of the proximal end of the humerus. J Bone Joint Surg Am 75:1751, 1993.

126. Sniezek, J.E.; Finklea, J.F.; Graciter, P.L. Injury coding and hospital discharge data. JAMA 262:2270, 1989.

127. Stewart, A.L.; Hays, R.D.; Ware, J.E. The MOS short form general health survey: Reliability and validity in a patient population. Med Care 26:724, 1988.

128. Stewart, A.L.; Ware, J.E.; Brook, R.H.; Davies Avery, A. Conceptualization and Measurement of Health for Adults in the Health Insurance Study, Vol. II: Physical Health in Terms of Functioning. Publication R1987/3HEW. Santa Monica, CA, The Rand Corporation, 1978.

129. Swiontkowski, M.F. Outcomes measurement in orthopaedic trauma surgery. Injury 26:653, 1995.

130. Swiontkowski, M.F.; Buckwelter, J.A.; Keller, R.B.; Haralson, R. The outcomes movement in orthopaedic surgery: Where we are and where we should go. J Bone Joint Surg Am 81:732, 1999.

131. Swiontkowski, M.F.; Chapman, J.R. Cost and effectiveness issues in care of injured patients. Clin Orthop 318:17, 1995.

132. Swiontkowski, M.F.; Engelberg, R.; Martin, D.P.; Agel, J. SMFA Questionnaire: Validity, reliability and responsiveness. J Bone Joint Surg Am 81:1245, 1999.

133. Tarlov, A.R. Multiple influences propel outcomes field. Med Outcomes Trust Bull 3:5, 1995.

134. Tarlov, A.R.; Ware, J.E.; Greenfield, S.; et al. The Medical Outcomes Study: An application of methods for monitoring the results of medical care. JAMA 262:925, 1989.

135. Trauma Care Systems. Setting the national agenda for injury control in the 1990's. Position paper, Third National Injury Control Conference, Atlanta, U.S. Department of Health and Human Services, Centers for Disease Control and Prevention, 1991.

136. Trunkey, D. Trauma. Sci Am 249(2):28, 1983.

137. Trunkey, D.D. Trauma care systems. Emerg Med Clin North Am 2:913, 1990.

138. Trunkey, D.D.; Lim, R. Analysis of 425 consecutive trauma fatalities: An autopsy study. J Am Coll Emerg Physicians 3:1364, 1974.

139. Turner, J.A.; Ersek, M.; Herron, L.; Deyo, R. Surgery for lumbar spinal stenosis: Attempted meta-analysis of the literature. Spine 17:1, 1992.

140. Vestrup, J.A.; Phang, T.; Vertresi, L.; et al. The utility of a multicenter regional trauma registry. J Trauma 37:375, 1994.

141. Vrbos, L.A.; Lorenz, M.A.; Peabody, E.H.; McGregor, M. Clinical methodologies and incidence of appropriate statistical testing in orthopaedic spine literature: Are statistics misleading? Spine 18:1021, 1993.

142. Ware, J.E. SF-36 Health Survey: Manual and Interpretations Guide. Boston, The Health Institute, New England Medical Center, 1996, pp. 10:6–10:13.

143. Ware, J.E.; Johnston, S.A.; Davies Avery, A.; Brook, R.H. Conceptualization and Measurement of Health for Adults in the Health Insurance Study. Vol. III. Mental Health. Publication R1987/3 HEW. Santa Monica, CA, The Rand Corporation, 1979.

144. Ware, J.E.; Sherbourne, C.D. The MOS 36 item short form health survey (SF36). Med Care 30:473, 1992.

145. Ware, J.E.; Sherbourne, C.D.; Davies, A.R. Developing and testing the MOS 20 item short form health survey: A general population application. In: Stewart, A.L.; Ware, J.E.; eds. Measuring Function and Well Being; The Medical Outcomes Study Approach. Durham, NC, Duke University Press, 1992, p. 277.

146. Weddel, J.M. Registers and registries: A review. Int J Epidemiol 2:221, 1973.

147. Wennberg, J.; Gittelsohn, A. Small area variations in health care delivery. Science 182:1102, 1973.

148. Wennberg, J.E.; Roos, N.; Sola, L.; et al. Use of claims data systems to evaluate health care outcomes: Mortality and reoperation following prostatectomy. JAMA 257:933, 1987.

149. West, J.G.; Cales, R.H.; Gazzinga, A.B. Impact of regionalization: The Orange County experience. Arch Surg 118:740, 1983.

150. West, J.G.; Trunkey, D.D.; Lim, R.C. Systems of trauma care: A study of two counties. Arch Surg 114:455, 1979.

151. Williams, A. Setting priorities in health care: An economist's view. J Bone Joint Surg Br 73:365, 1991.

151a. Wright, J.G.; Swiontkowski, M.F. Introducing a new journal section: Evidence-based orthopaedics. J Bone Joint Surg Am 82:759, 2000.

152. Wyrsch, B.; McFerran, M.A.; McAndrew, M.; et al. Operative treatment of fractures of the tibial plafond: A prospective, randomized study. J Bone Joint Surg Am 78:1646, 1996.

153. Xuan, J.; Kirchdoerter, L.J.; Boyer, J.G.; Norwood, G.J. Effects of co-morbidity on HR-QOL scores: An analysis of clinical trial data. Clin Ther 21:303, 1999.

SECTION II

Spine

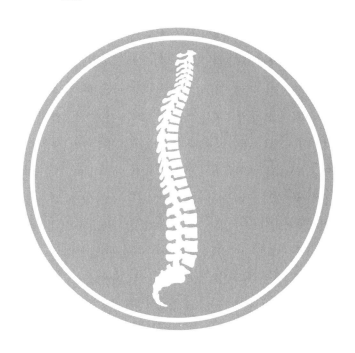

SECTION EDITOR

Alan M. Levine, M.D.

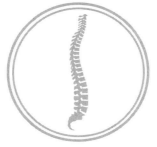

CHAPTER 25

Initial Evaluation and Emergency Treatment of the Spine-Injured Patient

Munish C. Gupta, M.D.
Daniel R. Benson, M.D.
Timothy L. Keenan, M.D.

BASIC CONSIDERATIONS

Incidence, Etiology, and Demographics

Injury to the spinal column can be devastating. Some degree of neurologic deficit occurs in 10% to 25% of patients at all levels of injury,[10, 89] in 40% at cervical spine levels,[10, 12, 89] and in 15% to 20% at thoracolumbar levels.[10, 27] Even with the development of specialized spinal injury centers, the cost to society per patient remains staggering.[28] The ultimate solution rests in prevention of the original injury, but in the meantime, those managing a patient with a spine injury can minimize the risk of further damage by using accepted techniques of initial transportation and treatment. A thorough understanding of the demographics, anatomy, and pathophysiology of spinal cord injury, use of logical algorithms for initial evaluation and treatment, and knowledge of the potential complications seen with specific patient populations are critical for optimal patient management.

The magnitude of the problem and the difficulties with past studies on the incidence rates of spinal injuries prompted the U.S. Centers for Disease Control and Prevention to establish spinal cord injury surveillance systems.[23] The most recent estimates of incidence are generally unchanged from the previous estimates[36, 112] of approximately 4.0 to 5.3 per 100,000 population.[114] This incidence corresponds to 12,000 new spinal cord injuries every year for which treatment is sought and an additional 4800 patients who sustain spinal cord injuries but die before arrival at the hospital.[112]

The causes of spinal column and spinal cord injury are illustrated in Figure 25–1.[10, 12, 13, 27, 89, 112] The most significant cause of spinal column injury is motor vehicle accidents (45%), followed by falls (20%), sports-related accidents (15%), acts of violence (15%), and miscellaneous causes (5%). At the extremes of age, the role of falls increases from 9% in the 0- to 15-year-old group to 60% in those older than 75 years.[112] The male-to-female ratio is

4:1. When a neurologic deficit is associated with spinal column injury, the overall survival rate for all levels of injury is 86% at 10 years.[111] The survival rate drops off for patients injured after age 29 to about 50% at 10 years. In patients older than 55 years, in nonwhites, and in quadriplegics, the leading cause of death is pneumonia. Accidents and suicides are most common in those younger than 55 years of age, in nonwhites, and in paraplegics.[111]

Although improvements in prevention and treatment have been slow in developing, they are clearly represented in the national statistics. The National Spinal Cord Injury Data Base reported fewer complete injuries and a higher percentage of incomplete spinal cord injuries in 1985 than in 1973,[112] an improvement that can be attributed to better initial management. These changes evolved from severe deficiencies in the emergency medical services, which were described in a classic report released by the National Academy of Sciences National Research Council Committee on Shock and the Committee on Trauma in 1966.[22, 49] Progress in prevention was seen in a 14-year report from the National Football Head and Neck Injury Registry,[115] which noted a decrease in the number of football-related cases of permanent quadriplegia and cervical fractures between 1976 (34 and 110 cases, respectively) and 1984 (5 and 42 cases, respectively). This decrease was attributed to tackling rules instituted in 1975 in which deliberate "spearing" and the use of the top of the helmet as the initial point of contact were banned.

The establishment of spinal cord injury centers and the improvement in prehospital management of patients with spinal cord injuries have been of significant benefit in the overall outcome of such patients. The concept of a spinal cord injury center as a separate unit began at the Ministry of Pensions Hospital, Stoke Mandeville, England, under the supervision of Sir Ludwig Guttman in 1943. Founding of this unit was followed by the establishment in 1945 of a unit in Toronto, Canada, and later by the creation of eight units in Veterans Affairs hospitals in the United States. When compared with the outcomes in other centers, such

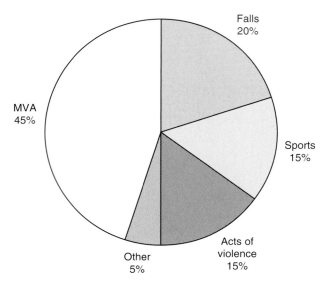

Figure 25–1. Causes of spinal column and spinal cord injury. *Abbreviation:* MVA, motor vehicle accidents.

specialized facilities in the United States are credited with a shorter length of hospitalization, a lower rate of complications (e.g., urinary tract infection, pulmonary complications, decubitus ulcers), and therefore an overall lower cost of patient care. In addition, these centers have greatly lowered the percentage of complete versus incomplete injuries, with a decrease of 65% to 46% in one study[113] and 20% to 9% in another.[79]

Anatomy and Pathophysiology

Understanding the conclusions drawn from the initial physical examination of a spine-injured patient requires a basic knowledge of the osseous and neurologic structures of the spinal column. Details of osseous structures and fracture patterns are presented in Chapters 28 through 31. Knowledge of fracture patterns allows the examining physician to assess the relative stability of the injury, the risk of an associated neurologic deficit, and the indications for treatment.

SPINAL CORD ANATOMY

The spinal cord fills about 35% of the canal at the level of the atlas and then about 50% in the cervical and thoracolumbar segments. The remainder of the canal is filled with cerebrospinal fluid, epidural fat, and dura mater. The cord has a variable diameter, with swellings in the cervical and lumbar regions for the exiting nerve roots of the plexuses. The myelomere, or segment of cord from which a nerve root arises, lies˙ one level above the same-numbered vertebral body in the cervical and high thoracic levels. For example, the T7 myelomere lies at the level of the T6 vertebral body. The lumbar and sacral myelomeres are concentrated between the T11 and L1 vertebral bodies. The end of the spinal cord (i.e., the conus medullaris) is most commonly located at the level of the L1–L2 intervertebral disc. The conus medullaris consists of the myelomeres of the five sacral nerve roots.

The spatial relationships of the gray and white matter structures remain consistent throughout the length of the cord, but their proportions change according to the level. Because the white matter carries the long tract fibers from the sacral, lumbar, thoracic, and cervical levels, it constitutes more of the cervical than the sacral cross-sectional area. The gray matter, with its concentration of lower motor neurons, is predominant in the cervical and lumbar swellings, where the axons exit to the upper and lower extremities. Accurate examination of a patient with a spinal cord injury depends on understanding the reflex arc and the organization of motor and sensory elements.

Figure 25–2 presents a cross-sectional view of the spinal cord in the cervical region. The upper motor neuron, which originates in the cerebral cortex, crosses to the opposite side in the midbrain and then descends in the lateral corticospinal tract to synapse with its respective lower motor neuron in the anterior horn of the gray matter. The sacral fibers of the corticospinal tract are the most peripheral and the cervical fibers the most central (see Fig. 25–2). The lower motor neurons in the gray matter are organized with the extensor neurons anterior to the flexor neurons. Upper motor neurons not crossing in the midbrain descend in the smaller ventral corticospinal tract. The ascending sensory input originates in an axon from a cell body located in the dorsal root ganglion within the vertebral foramen. Sensory input enters the posterior horn of the gray matter and travels beyond, depending on the type of sensation. Pain and temperature sensations cross immediately to the opposite level of the cord and ascend in the lateral spinothalamic tract. Touch sensation also crosses immediately and ascends diffusely but is carried primarily in the ventral spinothalamic tract. Proprioceptive position and vibratory sensation fibers ascend in the posterior column (funiculus cuneatus, funiculus gracilis) and cross higher in the brain stem. The posterior column is structured with the sacral elements more peripheral and posterior relative to the lumbar, thoracic, and cervical levels. The reflex arc (Fig. 25–3; e.g., bulbocavernosus) is a simple sensory motor pathway that can function without using ascending or descending white matter long tract axons. If the level of the reflex arc is both physiologically and anatomically intact, the reflex can function despite disruption of the spinal cord at a higher level.

Below the level of the conus medullaris (L1–L2 interspace), the spinal canal is filled with the cauda equina, with the motor and sensory roots yet to exit their respective intervertebral foramina distally. These roots are less likely to be injured because they have more room within the canal and are not tethered to the same degree as is the spinal cord. Furthermore, the motor nerve root is the lower motor neuron axon (peripheral nerve), which is known to be more resilient to trauma than central nervous tissue.

PATHOPHYSIOLOGY OF SPINAL CORD INJURY

The pathophysiology of spinal cord injury can be divided into two parts—primary and secondary. Primary injury

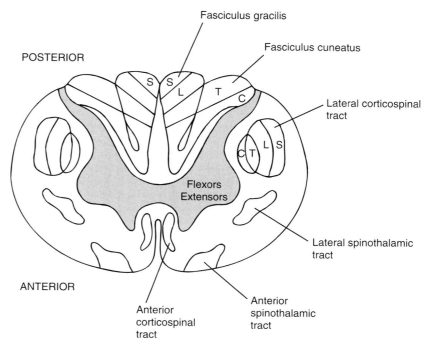

FIGURE 25–2. Transverse view of the spinal cord in the cervical region. Note that the sacral structures (S) are most peripheral in the posterior columns and the lateral corticospinal tracts. The extensors are also more lateral than the flexors in the gray matter. *Abbreviations:* C, cervical structures; L, lumbar structures; T, thoracic structures.

occurs at the moment of impact to the spine. When the energy transmitted to the spinal column musculature, ligaments, and osseous structures exceeds the flexibility of the spinal column, the spinal column and cord become injured. Primary injury to the spinal cord can develop in two ways—direct injury by means of excessive flexion, extension, or rotation of the spinal cord and indirect injury by impaction of displaced bone or disc material. Injury

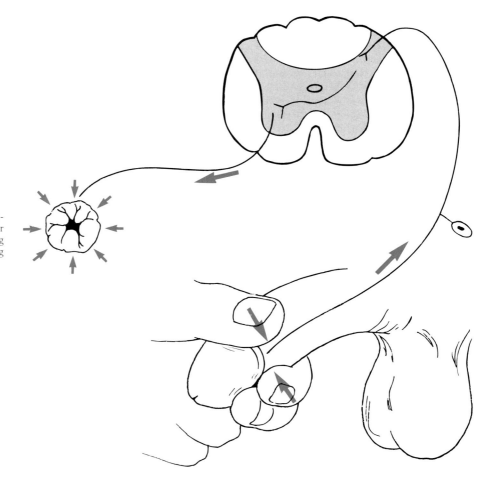

FIGURE 25–3. The bulbocavernosus, a reflex arc that is a simple sensorimotor pathway, can function without using ascending or descending white matter long tract axons.

secondary to contusion and compression is most common and causes physiologic interruption rather than physical transection of the spinal cord.

Secondary injury to the spinal cord occurs after the initial direct injury to neural tissue. The complicated events that take place on a chemical, cellular, and tissue level are not completely understood, however (Fig. 25–4). The cascade is interrelated and eventually leads to cavitation, largely because of cell death (Fig. 25–5). Cell death can occur as a result of necrosis or apoptosis. Necrosis is brought on by cellular swelling and mitochondrial and membrane damage. Apoptosis is programmed cell death that occurs normally but is evident to a greater extent in spinal cord injury. Chromatin aggregation and intact cellular organelles can be seen by electron microscopy, which can differentiate between apoptosis and necrosis.[72]

The three best known factors leading to cell death are exocytosis, inflammatory mediators, and free radicals, but other factors can also be involved. Release of excitotoxins from damaged or hyperactive cells can liberate increased amounts of neurotransmitters, such as glutamate and aspartate. These excessive neurotransmitters can bring about an increase in Ca^{2+} entry into cells and cause an imbalance in the homeostasis of mitochondrial function and swelling, which eventually leads to cell death. Free radicals such as O_2^-, OH^-, and nitric oxide have been found to take part in cell injury through lipid, protein, and nucleic acid damage.

Inflammatory mediators such as prostaglandins and cytotoxins are produced by inflammatory cells that enter the area of spinal cord damage through a break in the blood-brain barrier. Cytokines such as tumor necrosis factor-α can lead to damage to oligodendrocytes. Arachidonic acids break down to prostaglandins, and eicosanoids can lead to an increase in free radicals, vascular permeability, change in blood flow, and cell swelling.

The anatomic and morphologic changes in the spinal cord after injury have been well defined.[3, 30, 31] Within 30 minutes of injury, multiple petechial hemorrhages are seen within the central cord gray matter. Direct disruption of the myelin sheath and axoplasm is also seen. Over the course of 1 hour, these changes extend progressively to the posterior of the cord. Several hours after injury, the hemorrhages tend to coalesce and progressive longitudinal necrosis is seen. Histologic and ultrastructural changes characteristic of edema are seen within 6 hours and are most severe 2 to 3 days after trauma. At 1 week after injury, cystic degeneration of the previously necrotic areas of the cord develops.

Clinically, progressive neurologic deterioration after the initial spinal cord injury is uncommon.[106] It is difficult to define a point in the anatomic injury cascade at which secondary injury factors become important, but the recent success of some pharmacologic agents directed at the agents of secondary injury implies that intervention is possible to some degree.

The initial mechanical injury disrupts neuronal activity in several ways. Microvascular endothelial damage and thrombus formation decrease local blood flow dramatically in the central gray matter without reperfusion. This effect is in contrast to the reperfusion that is frequently seen in the peripheral white matter at about 15 minutes after injury and that is probably induced by vasospasm. Primary injury also leads to altered systemic vascular tone and hypotension, thus worsening this probably reversible white matter hypoperfusion.

Relative cord ischemia can play a major role in the secondary metabolic derangements of nervous tissue. A decrease in membrane-bound sodium potassium adenosine triphosphatase (N^+,K^+-ATPase) causes severe alterations in the product of high-energy phosphorylation and the subsequent lactic acidosis. Abnormalities in electrolyte concentration are believed to be associated with abnormal axonal conduction. Membrane damage and direct damage to intracellular organelles cause severe derangements in calcium homeostasis. Large intracellular shifts of calcium (Ca^{2+}) induce further mitochondrial dysfunction with decreased energy production and eventual cell death. Uncontrolled influx of Ca^{2+} leads to the activation of phospholipases A_2 and C, thereby resulting in accelerated breakdown of cellular membranes and the production of arachidonic acid and free radicals.[59] Many recent advances in the treatment of acute spinal cord injuries have attacked this secondary injury cascade at various levels, with varying degrees of success.

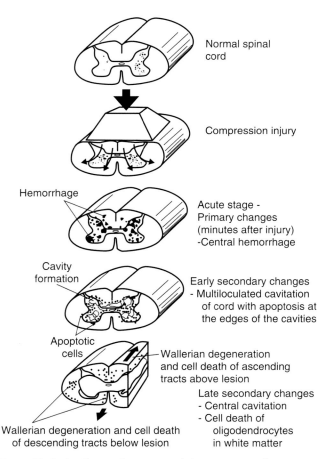

FIGURE 25–4. An illustrated sequence of the progression from acute primary to late secondary injury. (From Lu, J.; Ashwell, K.W.; Waite, P. Advances in secondary spinal cord injury: Role of apoptosis. Spine 25(14):1859–1866, 2000.)

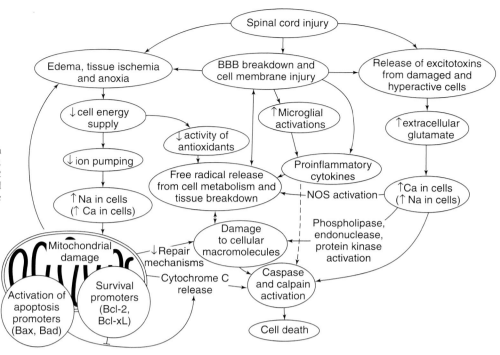

FIGURE **25–5.** Pathways involved in cell death after spinal cord injury. (From Lu, J.; Ashwell, K.W.; Waite, P. Advances in secondary spinal cord injury: Role of apoptosis. Spine 25[14]:1859–1866, 2000.)

SPINAL CORD REGENERATION

The promotion of regeneration of spinal cord axons after injury so that the cord again becomes functional is a monumental challenge that has been approached in many ways. The use of neurotrophic factors such as nerve growth factor, brain-derived neurotrophic factor, neurotrophic factor 3, and ciliary neurotrophic factor has been shown to be helpful in vitro in regenerating axons. Delivery of these factors by cells programmed to secrete them has helped in long-term release directly inside the central nervous system (CNS) so that they do not also have to cross the blood-brain barrier. Growth-inhibiting factors have been identified that may inhibit axonal regeneration in the CNS. Antibodies to these factors increase the regeneration of axons.[97] Electrical stimulation has also been shown to effect axonal growth, but the exact mechanism is not clear.

Peripheral nerve and Schwann cell transplants have shown the ability to lead to regeneration of motor pathways.[24, 51] Fetal spinal cord tissue has been successfully transplanted in neonates. Considerable functional recovery along with growth and regeneration of the cells has been observed.[21, 116] Similar success has not occurred with transplantation in adults. Transplantation of olfactory glial cells, which appear to continue to divide in adulthood, has been reported to regenerate corticospinal tracts in an adult rat.[70]

Classification of Neurologic Injury

An initial responsibility of the examining physician in evaluating a patient with a spinal cord injury is to determine the extent of neurologic deficit. A patient with an incomplete neurologic deficit has a good prognosis for at least some functional motor recovery, whereas functional motor recovery is seen in only 3% of those with complete injuries in the first 24 hours after injury and never after 24 to 48 hours.[12, 108] According to the Standards for Neurological Classification published by the American Spinal Injury Association (ASIA), a complete injury is one in which no "motor and/or sensory function exists more than three segments below the neurological level of injury."[5] Likewise, an incomplete injury is one in which some neurologic function exists more than three segments below the level of injury. Critical to this determination is the definition of level of injury. The ASIA defines it as the most caudal segment that tests intact for motor and sensory functions on both sides of the body. A muscle is considered intact if it has at least antigravity power (grade 3 out of 5) and if the next most cephalic level is graded 4 or 5.[5] These definitions can make determination of completeness of an injury somewhat difficult. At least one study has found the simple presence or absence of sacral nerve root function to be a more stable and reliable indicator of the completeness of an injury.[118]

The concept of sacral sparing in an incomplete spinal cord injury is important because it represents at least partial structural continuity of the white matter long tracts (i.e., corticospinal and spinothalamic tracts). Sacral sparing is demonstrated by perianal sensation, rectal motor function, and great toe flexor activity (Fig. 25–6). Electrical detection of sacral sparing by dermatomal somatosensory potentials has been reported but is not in common use.[99] Comparison of the normal anatomy in Figure 25–2 with that of the injury depicted in Figure 25–7A reveals how preservation of only the sacral white matter is possible. Sacral sparing is defined as continued function of the sacral lower motor neurons in the conus medullaris and their connections through the spinal cord to the cerebral cortex. The presence of sacral sparing therefore indicates an incomplete cord injury and the potential for more function after the resolution of spinal shock. At the time of physical examination in the emergency room, sacral sparing may be the only sign that a lesion is incomplete; documentation of its presence or absence is essential. Waters and coauthors[118] found that the presence of external anal sphincter or toe flexor muscle power or the presence of perineal sensation accurately predicted the completeness of injury in 97% of 445 consecutive patients. In addition, for prognostic purposes, no patients with initial sacral sparing were found to have had complete injuries.

After a severe spinal cord injury, a state of complete spinal areflexia can develop and last for a varying length of time. This state, conventionally termed *spinal shock,* is classically evaluated by testing the bulbocavernosus reflex, a spinal reflex mediated by the S3–S4 region of the conus medullaris (see Fig. 25–3). This reflex is frequently absent for the first 4 to 6 hours after injury but usually returns within 24 hours. If no evidence of spinal cord function is noted below the level of the injury, including sacral sparing, and the bulbocavernosus reflex has not returned, no determination can be made regarding the completeness of the lesion. After 24 hours, 99% of patients emerge from spinal shock, as heralded by the return of sacral reflexes.[107] If no sacral function exists at this point, the injury is termed *complete,* and 99% of patients with complete injuries will have no functional recovery.[107] One

exception to this dictum is an injury to the distal end of the spinal cord itself. A direct injury to the conus medullaris can disrupt the bulbocavernosus reflex arc and thus make its absence an unreliable indicator of spinal shock.

CLASSIFICATION SYSTEMS

After a determination of its completeness, an injury can be further classified according to the severity of the remaining paralysis. Classification systems are useful because they allow patient outcomes to be compared within and between clinical studies. The most commonly used classification system is that of Frankel and colleagues,[39] which divides spinal cord injuries into five groups (Table 25–1). The ASIA has put forth the Motor Index Score, which uses a standard six-grade scale to measure the manual muscle strength of 10 key muscles or functions in the upper and lower extremities (Fig. 25–8). All the individual muscle groups, both right and left, are measured, with a possible maximal score of 100. The disadvantage of the Frankel score is that an infinite continuum of injury severity is divided into five discrete groups. However, because recovery and repair of injured neural tissue must occur through the injury site for an injury to move to a higher grade, improvement by one Frankel grade, especially improvement by two grades, is functionally quite significant. On the other hand, the ASIA Motor Index Score represents injuries along a continuum, but an improvement does not necessarily

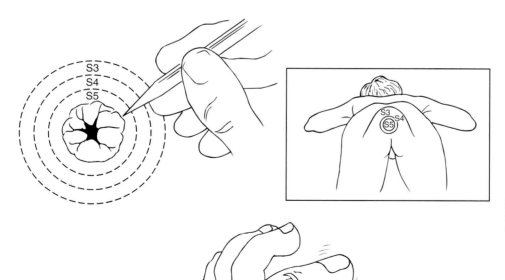

Figure 25–6. Sacral sparing may include perianal sensation, rectal tone, and great toe flexion.

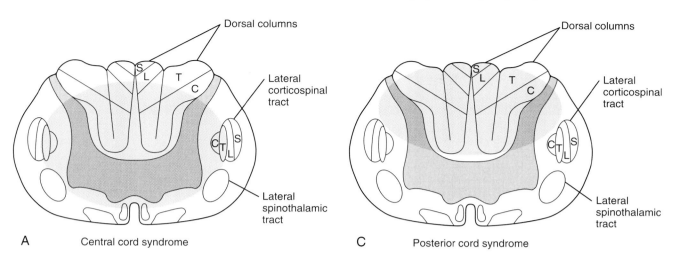

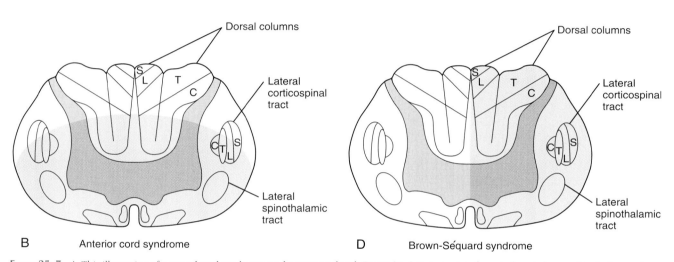

FIGURE 25–7. *A,* This illustration of a central cord syndrome can be compared with Figure 25–2 to appreciate the spinal cord abnormality. An incomplete spinal injury can affect the more central but not the peripheral fibers, thereby preserving the sacral white fibers. *Abbreviations:* C, cervical structures; L, lumbar structures; S, sacral structures; T, thoracic structures. *B,* Anterior cord syndrome. The dorsal columns are spared, so that the patient retains some deep pressure sensation and proprioception over the sacral area and lower extremities. *C,* Posterior cord syndrome, a very rare traumatic lesion with clinical features similar to those of tabes dorsalis. *D,* Brown-Séquard syndrome, also known as hemisection syndrome. Patients have motor paralysis on the ipsilateral side distal to the lesion and sensory hypesthesia on the contralateral side distal to the level of the lesion.

represent recovery in the injured spinal segment. Instead, the improved score may represent recovery in the most caudal level of function in a complete injury or a generalized recovery of motor strength in previously weak but functioning muscles.

TABLE 25–1 ••••••••••••••••••••••••••••••••••

Frankel Classification of Neurologic Deficit

Type	Characteristics
A	Absent motor and sensory function
B	Sensation present, motor function absent
C	Sensation present, motor function active but not useful (grades 2/5 to 3/5)
D	Sensation present, motor function active and useful (grade 4/5)
E	Normal motor and sensory function

••

INCOMPLETE SPINAL CORD INJURY SYNDROMES

If an incomplete spinal cord injury is diagnosed by the protocols discussed, it can usually be described by one of several syndromes (Table 25–2). As a general rule, the greater the function distal to the injury, the faster the recovery and the better the prognosis.[73]

Central Cord Syndrome. Central cord syndrome, the most common pattern of injury, represents central gray matter destruction with preservation of only the peripheral spinal cord structures, the sacral spinothalamic and corticospinal tracts (see Fig. 25–7A). The patient usually presents as a quadriplegic with perianal sensation and has an early return of bowel and bladder control. Any return of motor function usually begins with the sacral elements (toe flexors, then the extensors), followed by the lumbar elements of the ankle, knee, and hip. Upper extremity functional return is generally minimal and is limited by the

STANDARD NEUROLOGICAL CLASSIFICATION OF SPINAL CORD INJURY

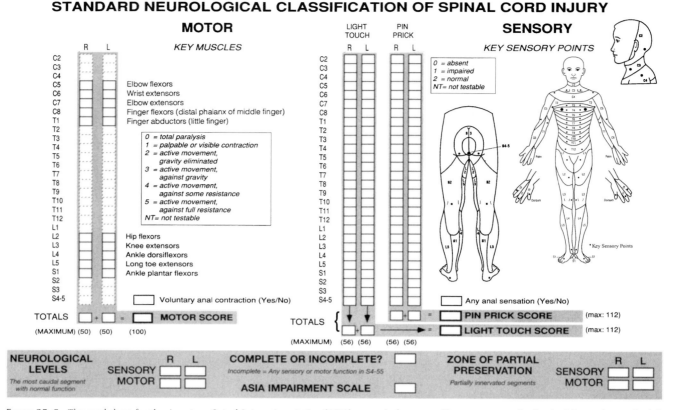

FIGURE 25–8. The worksheet for the American Spinal Injury Association (ASIA) motor index score. The motor strengths for the 10 muscles on the left side of the worksheet are graded on a scale of 0 to 5. All scores are added, for a total maximal score of 100. (Copyright, American Spinal Injury Association, from International Standards for Neurological and Functional Classification, Revised 1996.)

degree of central gray matter destruction. The chance of some functional motor recovery has been reported to be about 75%.[109]

Anterior Cord Syndrome. A patient with anterior cord syndrome has complete motor and sensory loss, with the exception of retained trunk and lower extremity deep pressure sensation and proprioception.[98] This syndrome carries the worst prognosis for return of function, and only a 10% chance of functional motor recovery has been reported (see Fig. 25–7B).[108]

Posterior Cord Syndrome. Posterior cord syndrome is a rare syndrome consisting of loss of the sensations of deep pressure and deep pain and proprioception, with otherwise normal cord function. The patient ambulates with a foot-slapping gait similar to that of someone afflicted with tabes dorsalis (see Fig. 25–7C).

Brown-Séquard Syndrome. Brown-Séquard syndrome is anatomically a unilateral cord injury, such as a missile injury (see Fig. 25–7D). It is clinically characterized by a motor deficit ipsilateral to the spinal cord injury in combination with contralateral pain and temperature hypesthesia. Almost all these patients show partial recovery, and most regain bowel and bladder function and the ability to ambulate.[109]

TABLE 25–2

Incomplete Cord Syndromes

Syndrome	Frequency	Description	Functional Recovery (%)
Central	Most common	Usually quadriplegic, with sacral sparing; upper extremities affected more than lower	75
Anterior	Common	Complete motor deficit; trunk and lower extremity deep pressure and proprioception preserved	10
Posterior	Rare	Loss of deep pressure, deep pain, and proprioception	
Brown-Séquard	Uncommon	Ipsilateral motor deficit; contralateral pain and temperature deficit	>90
Root	Common	Motor and sensory deficit in dermatomal distribution	30–100

Root Injury. The spinal nerve root can be injured along with the spinal cord at that level, or an isolated neurologic deficit of the nerve root can occur. The prognosis for motor recovery is favorable, with approximately 75% of patients with complete spinal cord injuries showing no root deficit at the level of injury or experiencing return of function.[108] Those with higher cervical injuries have a 30% chance of recovery of one nerve root level, those with midcervical injuries have a 60% chance, and almost all patients with low cervical fractures have recovery of at least one nerve root level.[109]

MANAGEMENT

Accident Scene Management

The initial evaluation of any trauma patient begins at the scene of the accident with the time-honored ABCs of resuscitation, such as the advanced trauma life support (ATLS) method described by the American College of Surgeons.[1] The ABC (airway, breathing, and circulation) method can be described more accurately as A (airway), B (breathing), and C (circulation and cervical spine). All patients with potential spine injuries arriving at the emergency department should be on a backboard with the cervical spine immobilized. A spinal column injury should be suspected in all polytrauma patients, especially those who are unconscious or intoxicated and those who have head and neck injuries. Suspicion of a spine injury must begin at the accident scene so that an organized extrication and transport plan can be developed to minimize further injury to neural tissue.

Regardless of the position in which found, the patient should be placed in a neutral spine position with respect to the long axis of the body. This position is achieved by carefully placing one hand behind the neck and the other under the jaw and applying only gentle stabilizing traction.[49] An emergency two-piece cervical collar is then applied before extrication from the accident scene. Any patient wearing a helmet at the time of injury should arrive at the emergency room with it still in place unless a face shield that cannot be removed separately from the helmet is obstructing ventilation, a loose-fitting helmet is preventing adequate cervical spine immobilization, or the paramedic has been trained in helmet removal.[4] A scoop-style stretcher is now recommended for transfer; previously recommended maneuvers such as the four-man lift and the logroll have been shown to cause an excessive amount of motion at thoracolumbar fracture sites.[77] The victim on a scoop stretcher is then placed immediately onto a rigid full-length backboard and secured with sandbags on either side of the head and neck and the forehead taped to the backboard.[86] The method of transportation and initial destination are determined by a multitude of factors, including but not limited to the medical stability of the patient, distance to emergency centers, weather conditions, and the availability of resources. Vale and colleagues[117] have shown that keeping the mean blood pressure above 85 mm Hg results in a better neurologic outcome.

Resuscitation

Patients with spinal injuries are frequently the victims of major trauma and as such are at high risk for multiple injuries. Experience with such patients has documented a clear relationship between head and facial trauma and cervical spine injuries and between specific intrathoracic and abdominal injuries and thoracolumbar fractures. The evaluation and management of hypotension in these multiply injured patients have been the subject of much discussion. Although hemorrhage and hypovolemia are significant causes of hypotension, one must be aware of the syndrome of neurogenic shock in patients with cervical and high thoracic spinal cord injuries. Neurogenic shock is defined as vascular hypotension plus bradycardia occurring as a result of spinal injury. In the first few minutes after spinal cord injury, a systemic pressor response occurs through activation of the adrenal medulla. This state of hypertension, widened pulse pressure, and tachycardia subsequently gives way to a drop in pressure and pulse. Neurogenic shock is attributed to the traumatic disruption of sympathetic outflow (T1–L2) and to unopposed vagal tone, with resultant hypotension and bradycardia.[50, 85]

Hypotension with associated tachycardia is not caused by neurogenic shock, so another cause must be sought. A review of 228 patients with cervical spine injury revealed that 40 (69%) of 58 patients with systolic blood pressure lower than 100 mm Hg had neurogenic shock.[103] The remaining 18 patients had hypotension caused by other associated major injuries. Another study demonstrated that victims of blunt trauma with associated cervical spinal cord injury rarely sustain significant intra-abdominal injuries (2.6%).[2] Nonetheless, hemodynamic instability strongly suggested occult intra-abdominal injuries. The degree of hypotension and bradycardia and the incidence of cardiac arrest are directly related to the Frankel grade. For example, in a study of 45 patients with acute cervical spinal cord injury, 87% of Frankel A patients had a daily average pulse rate lower than 55 beats per minute, 21% had a cardiac arrest, and 39% required the administration of atropine or a vasopressor. Among the Frankel B patients, 62% had average pulses lower than 55 beats per minute, and none had cardiac arrest or needed vasopressors.[85]

A more recent study demonstrated that spinal cord injury secondary to penetrating trauma is distinctly different from that caused by blunt trauma with respect to the origin of hypotension.[119] Penetrating injuries rarely result in neurogenic shock. Of 75 patients with a penetrating spinal cord injury, only 5 (7%) showed classic signs of neurogenic shock, and of the patients in whom hypotension developed, only 22% were found to have a neurogenic origin of their shock. As in all patients with major trauma, hypotension should be assumed to be caused by an injury involving major blood loss, especially in those with penetrating trauma.[119]

No matter what the cause of the hypotension, support

of blood pressure is critical in the early hours after spinal cord injury. As described previously, localized spinal cord ischemia is an important cause of late neurologic disability. As the injured spinal cord loses its ability to autoregulate local blood flow, it is critically dependent on systemic arterial pressure.[32] Hypotension needs to be aggressively treated by blood and volume replacement and, if indicated, by emergency surgery for life-threatening hemorrhage and appropriate management of neurogenic shock. The initial treatment of neurogenic shock is volume replacement, followed by vasopressors if hypotension without tachycardia persists despite volume expansion. The patient's legs should be elevated to counteract venous pooling in the extremities. Fatal pulmonary edema can result from overinfusion of a hypotensive patient with a spinal cord injury.[50] Endotracheal suctioning is a cause of severe bradycardia and can induce cardiac arrest, which is attributed to vagal stimulation. Repeated doses of atropine may be necessary to maintain the heart rate, and vasopressors may be necessary to maintain blood pressure. Use of a gentle sympathomimetic agent (e.g., phenylephrine) may also be helpful.

Assessment

After the patient arrives at the emergency department, rapid assessment of life-threatening conditions and emergency treatment are begun in a logical, sequential manner as dictated by the ATLS protocols.[1] The primary survey includes assessment of airway, breathing, circulation, disability (neurologic status), and exposure (undress the patient) (ABCDE). As resuscitation (described earlier) is initiated, a secondary survey is begun that includes evaluation of spinal column and spinal cord function. The evaluation usually starts with a physical examination, with a more detailed history elicited later. The only part of the initial assessment that absolutely pertains to the spine is the emergency need for a lateral cervical spine radiograph (from the occiput to the superior end-plate of T1) to establish the safest means of maintaining an airway. A patient suspected of having a spine injury should, before intubation, have the airway maintained with a jaw thrust maneuver rather than a head tilt method.

An unconscious or intoxicated patient is difficult to assess in terms of pain and motor sensory function. Careful observation of spontaneous extremity motion may be the only information that can be obtained about spinal cord function, and a detailed examination may have to be delayed until the patient can cooperate. An unconscious patient's response to noxious stimuli and the patient's reflexes and rectal tone can provide some information on the status of the cord. Similarly, spontaneous respirations with elevation and separation of the costal margins on inspiration indicate normal thoracic innervation and intercostal function. Unconscious patients should be rolled onto their side with the cervical spine immobilized while on a full-length backboard, and the entire length of the spine should be inspected for deformity, abrasions, and ecchymosis. The spine should be palpated for a step-off or interspinous widening.

The locations of lacerations and abrasions on the skull are critical for determination of cervical injuries. Occipital lacerations suggest flexion injuries, whereas frontal or superior injuries suggest extension or axial compression, respectively. The presence of a single spinal injury does not preclude inspection of the rest of the spine.

Any associated head and neck trauma should increase the suspicion of cervical spine injury, and any thoracic or abdominal trauma (e.g., shoulder or lap seat belt markings) should raise suspicion of a thoracolumbar spine injury. Clear patterns of associated injuries should be recognized. For example, in addition to the relationship between head trauma and cervical spine injury, the presence of multiple fractured ribs and chest trauma can suggest thoracic spine injury. Massive pelvic injuries are frequently associated with flexion-distraction injuries of the lumbar spine. Finally, falls from heights resulting in calcaneal or tibial plafond fractures are frequently associated with injuries to the lumbar spine.

A responsive patient who is hemodynamically stable can be examined in greater detail. Inspection and palpation of the entire spine should be performed as described for an unconscious patient. The patient should be asked to report the location of any pain and to move the upper and lower extremities to help localize any gross neurologic deficit. If possible, the patient should be questioned about the mechanism of injury, any transient neurologic symptoms or signs, and any preexisting neurologic signs or symptoms. The upper (Fig. 25–9) and lower (Fig. 25–10) extremities are examined for motor function by nerve root level. The motor examination includes a digital rectal examination for voluntary or reflex (bulbocavernosus) anal sphincter contraction.

The sensory examination includes testing of the dermatomal pattern of the proprioceptive and pain temperature pathways, as described previously (Fig. 25–11). The sharp dull sensation of a pin tip is considered to reflect a pain pathway (lateral spinothalamic tract), and this sensation should also be tested in the perianal region. The presence of pinprick sensation around the anus or perineal region may be the only evidence of an incomplete lesion. Proprioception (posterior columns) can be tested easily by having the patient report the position of the toes as up, down, or neutral as the examiner moves them. Temperature sensation (lateral spinothalamic tract) is difficult to establish in the often loud and busy emergency room setting, and testing for this function is usually deferred until a later time. The areas of sensory deficit should be accurately recorded, dated, and timed on the medical record progress note or a spinal injury flow sheet. It is also recommended that the sensory level be marked, dated, and timed in ink on the patient's skin at the affected level. The practice of marking the sensory level on the skin can avoid much uncertainty when a number of examiners are involved.

Figure 25–12 reviews the locations of the upper and lower extremity stretch reflexes and their nerve roots of origin. If spinal shock is present, all reflexes may be absent for up to 24 hours, only to be replaced by hyperreflexia, muscle spasticity, and clonus. If a spine injury patient with a neurologic deficit has a concomitant head injury, it is important to distinguish between the cranial upper motor neuron lesion and a spinal cord lower motor neuron injury.

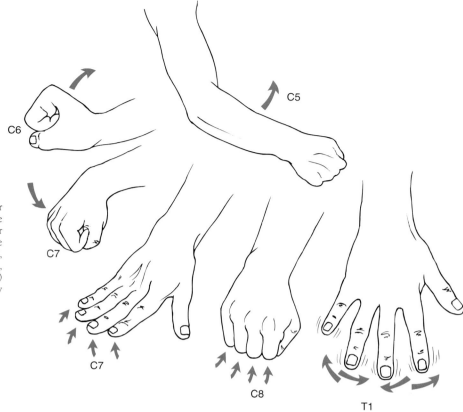

FIGURE 25–9. An examination of the upper extremities must include, at a minimum, the muscle groups that are designated by their respective nerve root innervation. These are C5, elbow flexion; C6, wrist extension; C7, finger extension; C8, finger flexion; and T1, finger abduction. The strength (0 to 5) should be listed on the time-oriented flow sheet.

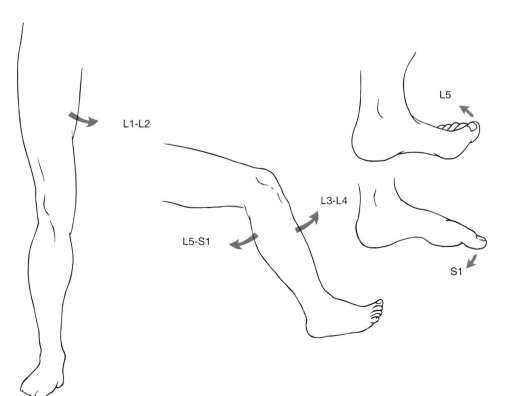

FIGURE 25–10. An examination of the lower extremities needs to include at least these muscle groups, designated by their respective nerve root innervation: L1–L2, hip abductors; L3–L4, knee extension; L5–S1, knee flexion; L5, great toe extension; and S1, great toe flexion.

The presence of extremity stretch reflexes in a patient without spontaneous motion of the extremities or a response to noxious stimuli implies an upper motor neuron lesion. The absence of these reflexes in the same setting implies lower motor neuron injury of the spinal cord.

The plantar reflex in the lower extremity is elicited by stroking the plantar aspect of the foot firmly with a pointed object and watching the direction of motion of the toes. A normal plantar reflex is plantar flexion of the toes. An abnormal plantar reflex (Babinski's sign), in which the great toe extends and the toes splay out, represents an upper motor neuron lesion. Similar information can be obtained by running a finger firmly down the tibial crest;

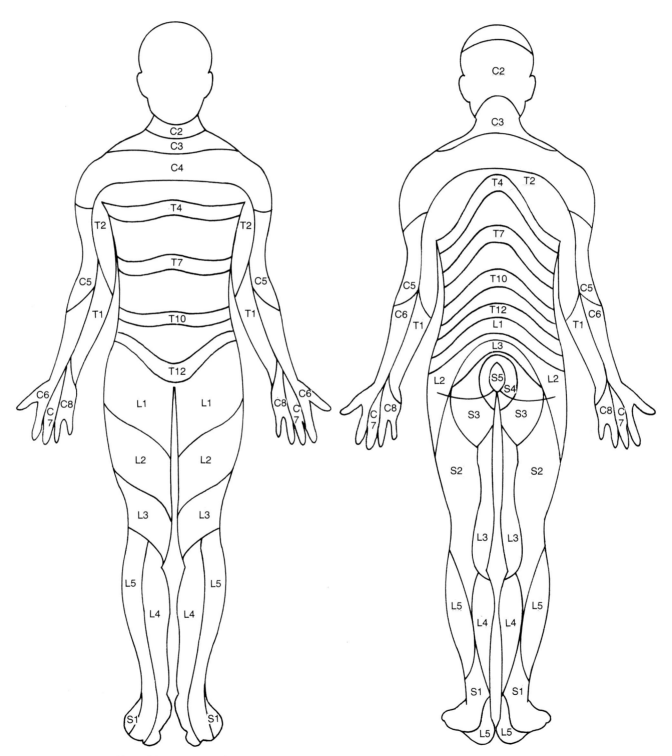

FIGURE 25–11. Sensory dermatome chart. Note that C4 includes the upper chest just superior to T2.

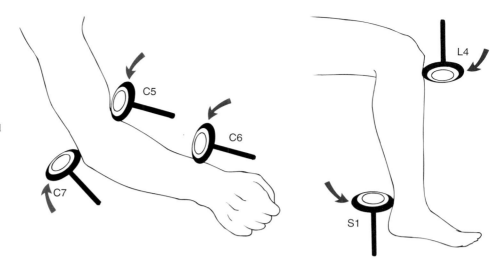

FIGURE 25–12. Stretch reflexes and nerve roots of origin.

abnormal great toe extension with splaying of the toes (Oppenheim's sign) constitutes evidence of an upper motor neuron lesion.

Other significant reflexes include the cremasteric, the anal wink, and the bulbocavernosus reflexes. The cremasteric reflex (T12–L1) is elicited by stroking the proximal aspect of the inner part of the thigh with a pointed instrument and observing the scrotal sac. A normal reflex involves contraction of the cremasteric muscle and an upward motion of the scrotal sac, whereas an abnormal reflex involves no motion of the sac. The anal wink (S2, S3, S4) is elicited by stroking the skin around the anal sphincter and watching it contract normally; an abnormal reflex involves no contraction. The bulbocavernosus (S3, S4) reflex (see Fig. 25–3) is obtained by squeezing the glans penis (in a male) or applying pressure to the clitoris (in a female) and feeling the anal sphincter contract around a gloved finger. This response can usually be elicited more easily by gently pulling the Foley catheter balloon against the bladder wall and feeling the anal sphincter contract. The bulbocavernosus reflex examination in a catheterized female can be misleading; the Foley balloon can be pulled up against the bladder wall and thus be felt by a fingertip that is past the anal sphincter, with this response being misinterpreted as contraction of the anal sphincter.

Not uncommonly, a more detailed history is delayed until the patient is hemodynamically stable and the overall neurologic status can be determined. In addition to a routine review of systems, the patient should be specifically questioned regarding previous spine injury, previous neurologic deficit, and details of the mechanism of injury. If the patient cannot respond, an attempt should be made to interview family members in person or by telephone.

At some time during the physical examination, the initial lateral cervical spine radiograph should be available for review. It should first be examined to ensure that the interval from the occiput to the superior end-plate of T1 can be seen clearly. If the radiographic appearance is normal, the remainder of the cervical spine series is obtained. Interpretation of the film is discussed in Chapter 26. Under no circumstances should spine precautions be removed until the cervical spine and any suspicious areas

of the thoracolumbar spine have been cleared radiographically. In the assessment of a polytraumatized patient, the association between thoracolumbar fractures and other high-energy internal injuries (i.e., aortic and hollow viscus injuries) must be kept in mind. Because these patients' thoracolumbar spines cannot be cleared of injury on clinical grounds, anteroposterior and lateral thoracic and lumbar spine films should be obtained on a routine basis. In addition, the 10% incidence of noncontiguous fractures must be kept in mind in a patient with multiple injuries.[61] For example, the presence of a thoracolumbar burst fracture requires review of a complete plain radiographic series of the cervical, thoracic, and lumbar spine in any patient who is unable to fully cooperate or accurately report pain during the physical examination.

Special Studies

After the initial cross-table lateral cervical spine radiograph, a complete cervical spine series should be obtained. Several studies have reported that a technically adequate radiographic series consisting of a cross-table lateral view, an anteroposterior view, and an open-mouth odontoid view is almost 100% sensitive for detecting cervical injuries.[29] In the trauma situation, it can be difficult to see the atlantoaxial articulation and the cervicothoracic junction, so additional studies may be needed. A limited computed tomographic scan through the C7 to T1 levels can rule out significant cervicothoracic junction injuries; however, most studies have shown such imaging to have very low yield. In addition, computed tomography may be required to clear the C1–C2 levels if plain radiographs are equivocal.[94] In an awake, conversant patient, the physical examination can be used to guide further imaging studies. Numerous studies have demonstrated the occurrence of concomitant spinal fractures.[61] Therefore, if a cervical fracture is identified, especially in a patient with a spinal cord lesion, radiographs of the entire thoracic and lumbar spine are indicated.

Magnetic resonance imaging (MRI) has found an increasing role in the evaluation of patients with spine injuries. In a patient who has a clinical spinal cord injury and minimal or no bony or ligamentous injury on other imaging studies, MRI is useful for the identification of soft tissue (ligamentous or disc) injuries, as well as abnormalities of the spinal cord itself. Findings on MRI have been shown to have some prognostic significance with respect to the severity of spinal cord injury and neurologic recovery.[55, 83] In children, the syndrome of spinal cord injury without radiographic abnormality (SCIWORA) has been described,[8, 56] and more recently, the use of MRI to better define these injuries has proved useful.[48] MRI has found an important role in the evaluation of intervertebral discs in cervical dislocations[35, 91] (see later discussion and ligamentous description[66]).

Transportation of a cervical spine injury patient in skull traction can be done safely with the patient in a hospital bed, on a gurney, or in a Stryker frame, as long as a traction pulley unit is used. The use of a Stryker frame has been associated with loss of reduction after turning and with worsening of neurologic deficits, especially in those with lumbar spine injuries.[102] Traction can be compromised while the patient lies on the radiographic table and the rope hangs over the table edge without the use of a pulley. Disturbance of the magnetic field of MRI by the ferrous elements of traction equipment presents a problem, but solutions are being sought. A traction system has been described in which nonferrous zinc pulleys are bolted to an aluminum ladder with water traction bags attached to the halo ring by nylon traction rope.[76] A patient with a high cervical spine injury and dependence on a ventilator who needs MRI studies must be ventilated by hand or with a nonferrous ventilator.[80] A patient with a thoracolumbar spine injury is easier to manage because plastic construction backboards can now be used during conventional radiographic and MRI studies. Experimental in-board traction sets can allow transport of cervical cord injury patients without the danger of free weights.

Intervention

Once a spine-injured patient is resuscitated adequately, the mainstay of treatment is prevention of further injury to an already compromised cord and protection of uninjured cord tissue. Realignment and immobilization of the spinal column remain critical to this end. Other life-threatening issues in a multiply injured trauma patient may take precedence over time-consuming interventions related to the spine. Perhaps the most rapidly evolving interventions toward limiting the degree of neurologic injury have been pharmacologic.

PHARMACOLOGIC INTERVENTION

The most studied and clinically accepted pharmacologic intervention for a patient with a spinal cord injury has been high-dose intravenous methylprednisolone (MPS). The efficacy of glucocorticoids has been studied since the mid-1960s. In animal studies, high doses of MPS given intravenously after spinal cord injury lessened the degree of post-traumatic lipid peroxidation and ischemia, prevented neuronal degradation, and allowed improved

neurologic recovery.[52] The initial National Acute Spinal Cord Injury Study (NASCIS I) attempted to work out an appropriate dosage for MPS but failed to show a difference in outcome between patients who received a 100-mg bolus per day for 10 days and those who received 1000 mg/day for 10 days. In fact, the high-dose regimen was associated with an increased risk of complications.[16]

A second multicenter randomized trial compared MPS, naloxone, and placebo. The results of the NASCIS II study, completed in 1990, showed that patients who were treated with MPS within 8 hours had improved neurologic recovery at 1 year, regardless of whether their injury was complete or incomplete.[18, 19] Naloxone treatment was no better than the control. When MPS was given at a point longer than 8 hours after injury, patients recovered less function than did placebo controls. A predictable trend toward increased complications was seen in the steroid group, including a twofold higher incidence of wound infection (7.1%); these differences, however, were not statistically significant. Critics of this study question the significance of the improvement in treated patients because the neurologic grading system used did not report a true level of patient function.[34] Nonetheless, this study has made acute treatment with MPS a standard of care for patients with a spinal cord injury. The NASCIS II trial established a dosing schedule of an initial intravenous bolus of 30 mg/kg, followed by a continuous infusion of 5.4 mg/kg/hr for 23 hours. Many centers are now administering a 2-g bolus of MPS in the ambulance or at the accident scene in keeping with the intuition that the earlier the steroid is administered after injury, the better the outcome.

The third multicenter randomized trial, NASCIS III, is completed.[20] One treatment arm in this study is the standard MPS bolus and 23-hour infusion; a second arm extends the infusion another 24 hours. The third treatment arm consists of the initial MPS bolus followed by a 10-mg/kg/day dose of tirilazad mesylate for 48 hours. Tirilazad mesylate is a 21-aminosteroid compound, a group of MPS analogues that lack the hydroxyl function necessary for glucocorticoid receptor binding. Theoretically, these drugs possess no glucocorticoid activity but are potent inhibitors of lipid peroxidation. The negative systemic side effects seen with prolonged use of high-dose MPS should be significantly reduced.[15] The study showed that the high-dose steroid regimen was effective only when given within 8 hours after injury. If the steroid bolus recommendation is administration of the bolus within 1 to 3 hours, the drip should be continued for 24 hours. If the bolus is given between 3 and 8 hours after injury, the drip should continue for 48 hours rather than 24 hours. This difference may increase the risk of complications but at the same time should make the neurologic outcome better. Reanalysis of the data from NASCIS II and III has not demonstrated a statistically solid beneficial effect. Additionally, no other pharmacologic agent has been shown to be effective in modulating secondary damage. The results of these studies have inspired some heated debate in the literature.[82, 101]

Gangliosides are complex acidic glycolipids present in high concentration in the membranes of CNS cells. Experimental evidence has shown that these compounds augment regeneration and sprouting of neurons in vitro and restore neural function after injury in vivo.[45] A prospective, randomized, placebo-controlled trial of GM_1 ganglioside in patients with spinal cord injury showed that GM_1 enhanced motor recovery when compared with placebo controls.[45] However, only 16 patients received GM_1 once a day for 18 to 32 days, with the first dose given within 72 hours. All patients received initial treatment with steroids at a dose much less than the current standard dose. Analysis of the results showed that improved motor scores in both the Frankel and ASIA grading systems were attributable to restoration of power in initially paralyzed muscles rather than improvement in strength in previously weak muscles. The authors postulated that GM_1 allows for enhanced recovery of effectiveness in initiating the motor response of the circumferential white matter. Current trials exploring combination therapy with GM_1 and MPS are under way. The combination of the early antioxidant effects of high-dose bolus MPS and the late neuronal recovery effects of GM_1 may produce greater than additive benefits.[44]

Opiate receptor blockade has been an attractive target for pharmacologic manipulation of the injury process. Theoretically, release of endogenous opiates can cause systemic hypotension and a decrease in spinal cord blood flow. Naloxone and thyrotropin-releasing hormone (TRH) have been studied extensively in animal models and have shown variable success in improving neurologic recovery.[22, 54, 78, 106] The results of the NASCIS do not support the use of naloxone in humans because it performed no better than controls. Clinical trials of a more stable analogue of TRH (longer half-life) are under way.

Various other agents have shown variable promise in the laboratory but remain unproved in clinical trials. The antioxidant effects of vitamin E have been shown to be useful, but the need to give the drug before injury limits its application.[6] Calcium channel blockers have been used in an attempt to minimize the calcium-modulated elements of the secondary injury cascade, but published reports have been variable and clinical use is controversial.[100] An endothelial receptor antagonist has been shown to prevent and delay the degeneration of axons after spinal cord injury in rats. Osmotic diuretics used to reduce edema in head trauma (mannitol, low-molecular-weight dextran) failed to provide evidence of clinical effectiveness with regard to spinal cord injury.[59, 87] Table 25–3 summarizes the most frequently studied drugs used for the treatment of spinal cord injury in humans.

PHYSICAL INTERVENTION

After administration of the standard high-dose steroid NASCIS protocol, an assessment of the overall alignment of the spinal column (and therefore the cord) should be made. Any malalignment or dislocation causing the neural elements to be under a severe degree of tension should be noted. Although treatment of the spinal injury cannot alter the initial trauma, experimental evidence has shown that immediate immobilization protects the spinal cord.[33] In addition, it has been demonstrated experimentally that continued compression causes additive detrimental effects that result in ischemia and electrophysiologic changes in

TABLE 25–3

Pharmacologic Agents for Spinal Cord Injury

Agent	Mechanism of Action
Methylprednisolone (MPS)	Membrane stabilization by decrease in lipid peroxidation, prevention of inflammatory cascade
Tirilazad mesylate	Same as MPS, lacks glucocorticoid activity
GM_1 ganglioside	Augmentation of neuron regeneration
Naloxone	Blocks effects of endogenous opiates that cause local and systemic hypotension and spinal cord ischemia
Thyrotropin-releasing hormone	Same as naloxone

the injured spinal cord.[47] A highly unstable situation may allow an already severely injured cord to undergo repeated injury with the slightest movement. Examination of the dorsal skin may reveal an impending breakdown over a kyphotic deformity, in which case urgent reduction is imperative. If the neurologic injury can be determined to be a complete injury (i.e., the bulbocavernosus reflex is intact), realignment may proceed at a less urgent pace. An exception may be in the cervical spine, where urgent reduction may improve the rate of "root-sparing" recovery. In an incomplete lesion, reduction and stabilization should be performed as quickly as possible to minimize continued neurologic injury. In the cervical spine, such management frequently involves the application of skull traction. In the thoracolumbar spine, traction is less successful, so if positioning does not restore anatomic alignment, emergency surgical reduction is required.

The role of pretraction MRI became a focus of debate after Eismont and colleagues,[35] among others,[74, 93] reported neurologic deterioration in patients with cervical dislocations after they underwent traction and reduction. The high incidence of disc herniations with facet dislocations[91] prompted these authors to advocate that an MRI study be obtained before closed reduction of the cervical spine is attempted. Several large studies have refuted this contention by showing no worsening of neurologic levels with closed traction and reduction in awake, cooperative patients.[25, 65, 105] Nonetheless, expediency is of the utmost importance in the reduction of patients with incomplete injuries. If it can be obtained quickly without putting an unstable patient at risk during transportation, pretraction MRI is reasonable. In many centers, such studies are difficult to obtain within several hours. MRI is required if the patient is otherwise uncooperative, fails closed reduction, or requires reduction under anesthesia for any reason. If MRI demonstrates disc herniation, anterior discectomy plus fusion is performed before other surgery is attempted. If operative reduction of a thoracolumbar dislocation is planned, MRI should be obtained and operative plans modified based on the results.

After adequate alignment and stabilization, further diagnostic studies, such as computed tomography (or MRI, if not obtained previously), can be performed on a less urgent basis. Frequent neurologic examinations, preferably by the same physician, should be documented and recorded, especially when the patient is returned after diagnostic tests. If worsening of a neurologic deficit is documented, emergency surgical decompression is indicated. In a patient with a stable or improving spinal cord injury, the timing of surgical stabilization, if needed, is controversial. In the case of a polytrauma victim, early stabilization, whether in a halo vest or by surgery, has been shown to improve overall outcome and shorten the hospital stay.[37]

An overview of a suggested algorithmic approach to a spine-injured patient is shown in Figure 25–13. Although such an algorithm tends to oversimplify a complicated decision-making process, adherence to a dedicated protocol provides a basic framework from which to manage these often multiply injured, complicated patients.

In patients with isolated injuries, as well as those with complicated multiple injuries, a simple, reliable method of cervical and thoracolumbar immobilization is necessary to safely perform a complete evaluation. The most effective method of initial cervical immobilization is the use of bilateral sandbags and taping of the patient across the forehead to a spine board, along with the use of a Philadelphia collar (which serves to limit extension).[86] In the cervical spine, a soft collar, extrication collar, hard collar, or Philadelphia collar alone is probably not

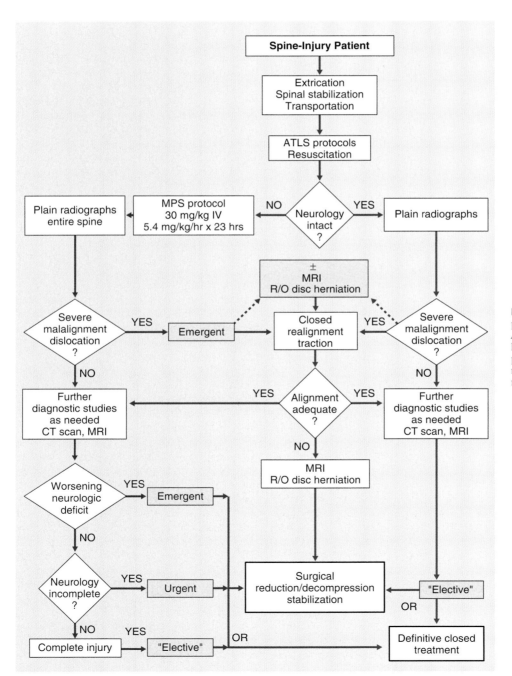

FIGURE 25–13. An algorithmic approach to the spine injury patient. *Abbreviations:* ATLS, advanced trauma life support; CT, computed tomography; MPS, methylprednisolone; MRI, magnetic resonance imaging; R/O, rule out.

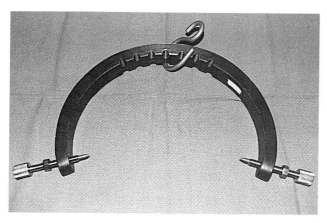

FIGURE 25–14. MRI-compatible graphite Gardner-Wells tongs.

sufficient for immobilization.[60, 86] A poster brace (e.g., four-poster brace) or cervicothoracic brace (SOMI brace) is not practical in the emergency setting. A standard long spine board is adequate for immobilization and turning of the thoracolumbar spine.[77] Immobilization gear is removed only after radiographs have been interpreted as normal.

An unstable or malaligned cervical spine requires either more stable immobilization or axial traction to achieve reduction. Specific indications for skull traction are discussed in Chapters 27 to 29. The concept of skull traction was introduced by Crutchfield in 1933,[26] but the Crutchfield skull tongs for traction have been replaced by the Gardner-Wells[40] and halo immobilization devices. Gardner-Wells tongs are a simple, effective means of applying axial traction for reduction, but they do not significantly limit voluntary rotation, flexion, or extension

in an uncooperative patient. Gardner-Wells tongs can be applied with minimal skin preparation and without assistance. The halo ring allows axial traction for reduction and provides rather stable immobilization with the application of a vest, but in a busy polytrauma setting, its application requires an assistant, and it takes longer to apply than Gardner-Wells tongs.

Gardner-Wells Tongs

The halo should be applied for initial stabilization of cervical spine injuries only if prolonged halo vest or cast immobilization is planned. If short-term traction followed by surgical stabilization and nonhalo external immobilization is planned, the use of Gardner-Wells tongs is preferred. Gardner-Wells tongs are easily applied by one person and without anterior pin sites.

Gardner-Wells tongs (Fig. 25–14) are fast and easy to apply, with no assistance required. Directions for use are generally located on the tongs (Fig. 25–15). The pins should be positioned below the temporal ridges at a point 2 cm above the external auditory canal and above the temporalis muscle (Fig. 25–16). After shaving, the skin is infiltrated with local anesthetic after the application of an antiseptic. The screws must be tightened symmetrically. The tongs are secure when the metal pressure pin protrudes 1 mm (Fig. 25–17). Protrusion of the pressure indicator pin by 1 mm has been demonstrated in cadavers to provide a pull-off strength of 137 ± 34 lb.[64] Pressure indicator pin protrusion of as little as 0.25 mm can support up to 60 lb.[64] It is recommended that the pin be tightened to 1 mm on the next day, but not again thereafter.

Traction should be initiated at 10 lb and increased by 5- to 10-lb increments. Reduction should be performed in awake patients with administration of intravenous mida-

FIGURE 25–15. Directions for use of the Gardner-Wells tongs are usually attached to the traction hook.

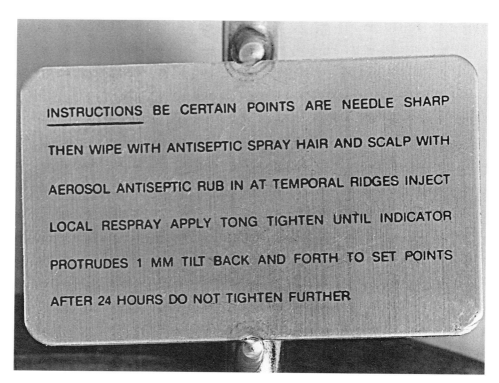

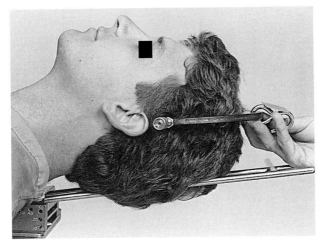

FIGURE 25–16. Correct position for the Gardner-Wells tongs is 1 to 2 cm above the external auditory canal and below the temporal ridge.

zolam if needed. Fluoroscopy or serial radiographs and serial neurologic examinations should be performed to avoid injury. In patients with neurologic symptoms or signs or 1-cm distraction of a disc space, closed reduction should be stopped and further images taken.

Gardner-Wells tongs have been reported to undergo pin and spring wear with repeated use. The pins and the tongs should be inspected and replaced if necessary or the indicator given a lower pin pressure to prevent pull-out.[67] Blumberg and associates[11] have reported that the MRI-compatible titanium alloy Gardner-Well tongs are more predisposed to plastic deformation and slippage than stainless steel Gardner-Wells tongs. They warned against using MRI-compatible tongs for reduction, especially with weights greater than 50 lb. Tongs may be switched after reduction to a lower weight if MRI is needed. A halo ring compatible with MRI would be another option if MRI is needed.

Halo Ring Application

A halo ring can be applied in the emergency department when definitive treatment is anticipated to be in a halo or in cases in which distraction should not be applied through Gardner-Wells tongs. Placing a halo vest underneath the patient during transfer to the bed can help attach the ring to the vest while the patient is in traction after reduction. Open halo rings offer the advantage over previous whole rings of being able to put the ring on without putting the patient's head on a head holder off the stretcher. The correct ring size is selected according to head circumference. The ring is placed around the head, the pin holes in the ring are used to identify the posterolateral pin sites, and the hair is shaved in these areas. The ring can be held in place temporarily with three plastic pod attachments. The skin is prepared, and local anesthetic is infiltrated through the ring holes.

Placement of the halo pins too high on the convexity of the skull can result in slippage of the ring, especially with traction. Placement of the anterior pin, as determined by skull osteology[41] and by supraorbital nerve anatomy, is best at a point in the middle to lateral third of the forehead,

just above the eyebrow (Fig. 25–18). Although not supported by osteologic studies, placement of the anterior pin more laterally and just into the hairline for cosmetic reasons has been reported to give good clinical results.[46] This more lateral pin placement has been used by one of the authors (Benson), with similarly good clinical results. If the more lateral position is to be used, care must be taken to palpate and avoid penetration of the temporal muscle and temporal artery on each side. The posterior pin is placed in the posterolateral position on the halo ring, with care taken to avoid skin contact with the ring because pressure ulceration can result.

All pins are first secured to finger tightness. As the pins are tightened, the patient should be encouraged to keep both eyes tightly closed to avoid stretching the skin, which limits the patient's ability to close the eyes. Once the pins are finger tight, the ring is inspected carefully to ensure a symmetric fit. The pins are then tightened sequentially in a diagonally opposite manner (i.e., right front with left rear and left front with right rear) to 2 inch-lb, then 4 inch-lb, and finally 8 inch-lb in an adult or 4 to 6 inch-lb in a child younger than 5 years. The pins should be retightened within 24 hours (and thereafter) only if they are loose and resistant to tightening. A loose pin without resistance to tightening should be moved to another position on the skull. Traction can then be applied with the traction bar attachment. If a vest is to be applied, the size should be equal to the chest diameter measured in inches at the level of the xiphoid process. MRI-compatible halo vests with graphite rings are used routinely, as shown in Figure 25–19.

Fleming and co-workers[38] devised instrumented halo vest orthoses with gauges that can measure pin force and showed an 83% decrease in compressive force during approximately a 3-month typical halo vest wear period. All patients had some symptoms caused by the degradation in pin force, which signified some loosening. The high stress on the bone may cause resorption and is thus one of the postulated causes of loosening. This potential complication highlights the importance of clinical vigilance during treatment of patients with halo vests. Attention to detail such as pin site care is essential, as well as alertness to

FIGURE 25–17. Pressure indication pins of the Gardner-Wells tongs should protrude 1.0 mm.

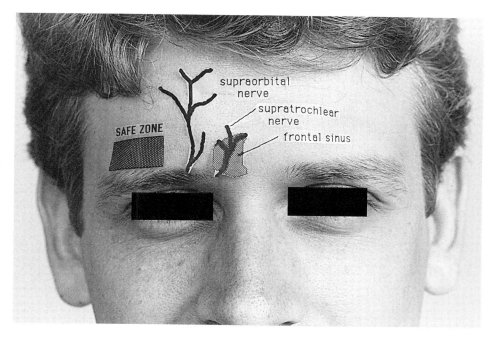

FIGURE 25–18. The anterior pin should be placed above the eyebrow in the medial to lateral third, avoiding the supraorbital nerve.

symptoms of loosening or other complications during treatment.

Reports of complications with use of the halo ring and vest[42, 46] have indicated significant rates of pin loosening (36%), pin site infection (20%), pressure sores under the vest or cast (11%), nerve injury (2%), dural penetration (1%), cosmetically disfiguring scars (9%), and severe pin discomfort (18%). Skull osteomyelitis and subdural abscess have also been described. A lower rate of pin loosening and infection has been reported with an initial torque of 8 inch-lb rather than 6 inch-lb in adults.[14] A prospective randomized study has, however, shown that 6- or 8-lb torque does not lead to any significant difference in pin loosening.[92]

The use of a halo ring in children requires special consideration[43, 63, 81] because of a higher complication rate in this population.[9] The calvaria develops in three significant phases by age: (1) 1 to 2 years, when interdigitation of the cranial sutures ends; (2) 2 to 5 years, a period of rapid growth in diameter; and (3) 5 to 12 years, when skull growth ceases.[43] Overall, the calvaria is thinner in a child 12 years or younger than in an adult, and the middle layer of cancellous bone may well be absent. Computed tomographic studies have demonstrated that the standard adult anterolateral and posterolateral pin positions correspond to the thickest bone in a child, and they are recommended as the site of halo pin placement.[41, 43] In children younger than 3 years, a multiple-

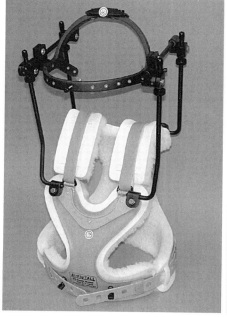
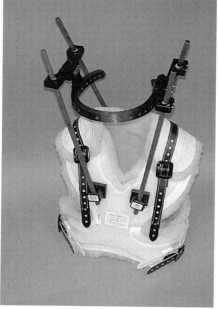

FIGURE 25–19. MRI-compatible halo vests.

pin, low-torque technique is recommended.[81] In this age group, custom fabrication of the halo ring and vest may be required. Ten to 12 standard halo pins can be used. The pins are inserted to a torque tightness of 2 inch-lb circumferentially around the temporal and frontal sinus regions. Halo placement in children younger than 2 years is complicated because of incomplete cranial suture interdigitation and open fontanels.[81]

SPECIAL CONSIDERATIONS

Pediatric Patients

The spine is thought to behave biomechanically as an adult spine by about the age of 8 to 10 years.[8, 56, 57] Until then, spinal column injury is uncommon, usually involves soft tissues, and therefore is not seen on plain radiographs in the emergency room. In patients younger than 10 years, the most common injury occurs in the occiput to C3 region.[57, 110] The entire spectrum of neurologic involvement is associated with these injuries, including cranial nerve lesions and vertebral basilar signs such as vomiting and vertigo. SCIWORA is most common in children younger than 10 years. Flexion, extension, and distraction cervical spine views and MRI scans can be helpful in identifying the level, but they should be used with extreme care to avoid further injury. After the age of 10 years, the pattern of injury is similar to that of adults, except for flexion-distraction injuries in the lumbar spine. As a result of seat belt injuries, pediatric patients can have a lumbar fracture with a more proximal thoracic level of paraplegia.

Initial immobilization of a pediatric patient requires an understanding of the supine kyphosis anterior translation (SKAT) phenomenon.[56] A young child lying supine on a standard backboard can have the head forced into kyphosis because of the normally disproportionate relationship of the larger head and smaller trunk in a child. Cases of forced kyphosis causing anterior translation of an unstable pediatric spine have been reported.[56] In normal development of a child, head diameter grows at a logarithmic rate, with 50% of adult size achieved by the age of 18 months, and chest diameter grows at an arithmetic rate, with 50% of adult size achieved by the age of 8 years. The problem can be avoided by elevating the thorax of a child on a spine board with a folded sheet to bring the shoulders to the level of the external auditory meatus or by the use of a pediatric backboard with a cutout to compensate for the prominent occiput of a young child.

Elderly Patients

Spinal trauma and spinal cord injury have traditionally been thought of as conditions of youth, but as many as 20% of all spinal cord injuries occur in patients older than 65 years.[17] Some particular characteristics and injury patterns are specific to elderly patients. For example, elderly patients with spinal cord injuries are more likely to be female. Whereas spinal injury is commonly associated with high-energy trauma in young adults, simple falls are the most common mechanism in patients older than 65

years.[71, 95, 104] Cervical spine injury predominates in the elderly population and accounts for 80% or more of traumatic spinal injuries. Injury to the C1–C2 complex is significantly more common in elderly people and accounts for a higher percentage of the total number of spinal injuries, with odontoid fractures being the single most common spinal column injury in these patients.[96, 104]

Elderly patients are more likely to have an incomplete injury.[95, 104] The frequent incidence of spondylosis in this population predisposes this patient group to central cord syndromes. Most importantly, the overall mortality rate for the initial hospitalization period has been reported to be 60 times higher in patients older than 65 years than in those younger than 40 years.[104] The causes of death are more commonly related to the stress of the treatment (immobilization, recumbency) than to the injury itself.

Treatment of this patient population is problematic. The overall priority in treatment should be early mobilization of the patient to avoid respiratory and other complications. Although previous reports have suggested that halo vests are poorly tolerated by the elderly population,[84] these patients are frequently poor operative candidates. A high index of suspicion must be maintained when evaluating an elderly patient with neck pain, even after relatively trivial trauma.

Multiply Injured Patients

Several important issues should be raised regarding multiply injured patients with spinal trauma. Delay in diagnosis of a spine injury is a significant problem that can affect a trauma patient's care. The rate of delay in diagnosis in spinal trauma is 23% to 33% in the cervical spine[12, 88] and about 5% in the thoracolumbar spine. As many as 22% of all delays in diagnosis in one series occurred after arrival at a tertiary referral center.[88] The main cause is a low level of suspicion, as represented by the following: (1) failure to obtain a radiograph, (2) missing the fracture on radiography, or less commonly, (3) failure of the patient to seek medical attention. A secondary neurologic deficit developed in 10% of patients with a delayed diagnosis as compared with 1.5% of those in whom spinal injury was diagnosed on initial evaluation,[88] but no progression of an already recognized deficit was observed. Other factors associated with a delay in diagnosis include intoxication, polytrauma, decreased level of consciousness, and non-contiguous spine fractures. Knowledge of the relationships between specific injury patterns and spinal injuries should decrease the incidence of serious missed spinal injuries. Patients with severe head injuries, as evidenced by a decreased level of consciousness or complex scalp lacerations, have a high incidence of cervical spine injuries, which may be difficult to diagnose clinically.[12, 58] The incidence of noncontiguous spine fractures is about 4% to 5% of all spine fractures[10, 61, 62] but is higher in the upper cervical spine.[68] Therefore, diagnosis of a spinal fracture should in itself be an indication for aggressive investigation to rule out other, noncontiguous spinal injuries.

Conversely, the presence of a spinal fracture should heighten the awareness of the possibility of a serious, occult visceral injury. Thoracic fractures resulting in paraplegia have a high incidence of associated multiple rib fractures and pulmonary contusions. Translational shear injuries at these levels have significant associations with aortic injuries.[69] A delay in the diagnosis of a visceral injury can occur in up to 50% of patients with spinal injuries.[90] The relationship between the use of lap-style seat belts and Chance-type flexion-distraction injuries of the thoracolumbar spine is now well appreciated.[7] Almost two thirds of patients with flexion-distraction injuries from lap belts have an associated injury to a hollow viscus. Overall, approximately 50% to 60% of spine-injured patients have an associated nonspinal injury ranging from a simple closed extremity fracture to a life-threatening thoracic or abdominal injury.[10, 62]

REFERENCES

1. Advanced Trauma Life Support Student Manual. Chicago, American College of Surgeons, 1989.
2. Albuquerque, F.; Wolf, A.; Dunham, C.M.; et al. Frequency of intraabdominal injury in cases of blunt trauma to the cervical spinal cord. J Spinal Disord 5:476–480, 1992.
3. Allen, A.R. Remarks on the histopathological changes in the spinal cord due to impact: An experimental study. J Nerv Ment Dis 41:141–147, 1914.
4. American Academy for Orthopedic Surgeons. Emergency Care and Transportation of the Sick and Injured, 4th ed. Menasha, WI, George Banta, 1987.
5. American Spinal Injury Association. Standards for Neurological Classification of Spinal Injury. Chicago, American Spinal Injury Association, 1990.
6. Anderson, D.K.; Waters, T.R.; Means, E.D. Pretreatment with alpha tocopherol enhances neurologic recovery after experimental spinal cord injury. J Neurotrauma 5:61–67, 1988.
7. Anderson, P.A.; Rivara, F.P.; Maier, R.V.; Drake, C. The epidemiology of seatbelt-associated injuries. J Trauma 31:60–67, 1991.
8. Apple, J.S.; Kirks, D.R.; Merten, D.F.; Martinez, S. Cervical spine fracture and dislocations in children. Pediatr Radiol 17:45–49, 1987.
9. Baum, J.A.; Hanley, E.N.; Pullekines, I. Comparison of halo complications in adults and children. Spine 14:251–252, 1989.
10. Benson, D.R.; Keenen, T.L.; Antony, J. Unsuspected associated findings in spinal fractures. J Orthop Trauma 3:160, 1989.
11. Blumberg, K.D.; Catalano, J.B.; Cotler, J.M.; Balderston R.A. The pullout strength of titanium alloy MRI-compatible and stainless steel MRI-incompatible Gardner-Wells tongs. Spine 18:1895–1896, 1993.
12. Bohlman, H.H. Acute fractures and dislocations of the cervical spine. J Bone Joint Surg Am 61:1119–1142, 1979.
13. Bosch, A.; Stauffer, E.S.; Nickel, V.L. Incomplete traumatic quadriplegia: A ten year review. JAMA 216:473–478, 1971.
14. Botte, M.J.; Byrne, T.P.; Garfin, S.R. Application of the halo device for immobilization of the cervical spine utilizing an increased torque pressure. J Bone Joint Surg Am 69:750–752, 1987.
15. Bracken, M.B. Pharmacological treatment of acute spinal cord injury: Current status and future projects. J Emerg Med 11:43–48, 1993.
16. Bracken, M.B.; Collins, W.F.; Freeman, D.; et al. Efficacy of methylprednisolone in acute spinal cord injury. JAMA 251:45–52, 1984.
17. Bracken, M.B.; Freeman, D.H.; Hellenbrand, L. The incidence of acute traumatic spinal cord injury in the U.S., 1970–1977. Am J Epidemiol 113:615–622, 1980.
18. Bracken, M.B.; Shepard, M.J.; Collins, W.F.; et al. A randomized controlled trial of methylprednisolone or naloxone in the treatment of acute spinal cord injury: The results of the National Acute Spinal Cord Injury Study. N Engl J Med 322:1405–1411, 1990.
19. Bracken, M.B.; Shepard, M.J.; Collins, W.F.; et al. Methylprednisolone or naloxone treatment after acute spinal cord injury: 1 year follow-up data. Results of the second National Acute Spinal Cord Injury Study. J Neurosurg 76:23–31, 1992.
20. Bracken, M.B.; Shepard M.J.; Holford, T.R.; et al. Administration of methylprednisolone for 24 and 48 hours or tirilazad mesylate for 48 hours in the treatment of acute spinal cord injury: Results of the third National Acute Spinal Cord Injury Randomized Controlled Trial. JAMA 277:1597–1604, 1997.
21. Bregman, B.S.; Kunkel-Bagden, E.; Reier, P.J.; et al. Recovery of function after spinal cord injury: Mechanisms underlying transplant-mediated recovery of function differ after cord injury in newborn and adult rats. Exp Neurol 11:49–63, 1991.
22. Caring for the injured patient. Bull Am Coll Surg 71:4–10, 1986.
23. Centers for Disease Control. Acute traumatic spinal cord injury surveillance—U.S.: 1987. MMWR CDC Surveill Summ 37:285–286, 1987.
24. Cheng, H.; Cao, Y.; Olson, L. Spinal cord repair in adult paraplegic rats: Partial restoration of hind limb function. Science 273:510–513, 1996.
25. Cotler, J.M.; Herbison, G.J.; Nasuti, J.F.; et al. Closed reduction of traumatic cervical spine dislocations using traction weights up to 140 pounds. Spine 18:386–390, 1993.
26. Crutchfield, W.G. Skeletal traction for dislocation of the cervical spine: Report of a case. South Surg 2:156–159, 1933.
27. Denis, F. The three-column spine and its significance in the classification of acute thoracolumbar spinal injuries. Spine 8:817–831, 1983.
28. Devivo, M.J.; Kartus, P.L.; Stover, S.L.; et al. Benefits of early admission to an organised spinal cord injury care system. Paraplegia 28:545–555, 1990.
29. Dilberti, T.; Lindsey, R.W. Evaluation of the cervical spine in the emergency setting: Who does not need an x-ray? Orthopedics 15:179–180, 1992.
30. Dohrmann, G.J.; Wick, K.M.; Bucy, P.C. Transitory traumatic paraplegia: Electron microscopy of early alterations in myelinated nerve fibers. J Neurosurg 36:425–429, 1972.
31. Ducker, T.B.; Kindt, G.W.; Kempe, L.G. Pathological findings in acute experimental spinal cord trauma. J Neurosurg 35:700–708, 1971.
32. Ducker, T.B.; Saleman, M.; Perot, P.L.; et al. Experimental spinal cord trauma, I: Correlation of blood flow, tissue oxygen and neurologic status in the dog. Surg Neurol 10:60–63, 1978.
33. Ducker, T.B.; Solomon, M.; Daniel, H.B. Experimental spinal cord trauma, III: Therapeutic effect of immobilization and pharmacologic agents. Surg Neurol 10:71–76, 1978.
34. Ducker, T.B.; Zeidman, S.M. Spinal cord injury: Role of steroid therapy. Spine 19:2281–2287, 1994.
35. Eismont, F.G.; Arena, M.J.; Green, B.A. Extrusion of intervertebral disc associated with traumatic subluxation or dislocation of cervical facets. J Bone Joint Surg Am 73:1555–1559, 1991.
36. Ergas, A. Spinal cord injury in the United States: A statistical update. Cent Nerv Sys Trauma 2:19–32, 1985.
37. Fellrath, R.F.; Hanley, E.N. Multitrauma and thoracolumbar fractures. Semin Spine Surg 7:103–108, 1995.
38. Fleming, B.C.; Krag, M.H.; Huston, D.R.; Sugihara, S. Pin loosening in a halo-vest orthosis: A biomechanical study. Spine 25:1325–1331, 2000.
39. Frankel, H.; Hancock, D.O.; Hyslop, G.; et al. The value of postural reduction in the initial management of closed injuries to the spine with paraplegia and tetraplegia. Paraplegia 7:179–192, 1969.
40. Gardner, W. The principle of spring-loaded points for cervical traction. J Neurosurg 39:543–544, 1973.
41. Garfin, S.R.; Botte, M.J.; Centeno, R.S.; Nickel, V.L. Osteology of the skull as it affects halo pin placement. Spine 10:696–698, 1985.
42. Garfin, S.R.; Botte, M.J.; Waters, R.L.; Nickel, V.L. Complications in the use of the halo fixation device. J Bone Joint Surg Am 68:320–325, 1986.
43. Garfin, S.R.; Roux, R.; Botte, M.S.; et al. Skull osteology as it affects halo pin placement in children. J Pediatr Orthop 6:434–436, 1986.
44. Geisler, F.H. GM₁ ganglioside and motor recovery following human spinal cord injury. J Emerg Med 11:49–55, 1993.
45. Geisler, F.H.; Dorsey, F.C.; Coleman, W.P. Recovery of motor function after spinal cord injury: A randomized, placebo-controlled trial with GM₁ ganglioside. N Engl J Med 324:1829–1838, 1991.
46. Glaser, J.A.; Whitehill, R.; Stamp, W.G.; Jane, J.A. Complications associated with the halo vest. J Neurosurg 65:762–769, 1986.
47. Gooding, M.R.; Wilson, C.B.; Hoff, J.T. Experimental cervical myelopathy: Effects of ischemia and compression of the canine spinal cord. J Neurosurg 43:9–17, 1975.

48. Grabb, P.A.; Pang, D. Magnetic resonance imaging in the evaluation of spinal cord imaging without radiographic abnormality in children. Neurosurgery 35:406–414, 1994.

49. Green, B.A.; Eismont, F.J.; O'Heir, J.T. Prehospital management of spinal cord injuries. Paraplegia 25:229–238, 1987.

50. Grundy, D.; Swain, A.; Russell, J. ABC of spinal cord injury: Early management and complications, I. BMJ 292:44–47, 1986.

51. Guest, J.D.; Rao, A.; Olson, L.; et al. The ability of human Schwann cell grafts to promote regeneration in the transected nude rat spinal cord. Exp Neurol 148:502–522, 1997.

52. Hall, E.D. The neuroprotective pharmacology of methyl predniso-lone. J Neurosurg 76:13–22, 1992.

53. Hall, E.D.; Braughler, J.M. Nonsurgical management of spinal cord injuries: A review of studies with the glucocorticoid steroid methylprednisolone. Acta Anaesthesiol Belg 38:405–409, 1987.

54. Hamilton, A.J.; McBlack, P.; Carr, D. Contrasting actions of naloxone in experimental spinal cord trauma and cerebral ischemia: A review. Neurosurgery 17:845–849, 1985.

55. Hayashi, K.; Yone, K.; Ito, H.; et al. MRI findings in patients with a cervical spinal cord injury who do not show radiographic evidence of a fracture or dislocation. Paraplegia 33:212–215, 1995.

56. Herzenberg, J.E.; Hensinger, R.N.; Dedrick, D.K.; Phillips, W.A. Emergency transport and positioning of young children who have injury of the cervical spine: The standard backboard may be hazardous. J Bone Joint Surg Am 71:15–22, 1989.

57. Hill, S.A.; Miller, C.A.; Kosimils, E.J.; et al. Pediatric neck injuries. J Neurosurg 60:700–706, 1984.

58. Irving, M.K.; Irving, P.M. Associated injuries in head trauma patients. J Trauma 7:500–504, 1967.

59. Janssen, C.; Hansebout, R.R. Pathogenesis of spinal cord injury and newer treatments. Spine 14:23–32, 1989.

60. Johnson, R.M.; Hart, D.L.; Simmons, E.F.; et al. Cervical orthoses. J Bone Joint Surg Am 59:332–339, 1977.

61. Keenen, T.L.; Anthony, J.; Benson, D.R. Noncontiguous spinal fractures. J Trauma 30:489–501, 1990.

62. Kewalramani, L.S.; Taylor, R.G. Multiple noncontiguous injuries to the spine. Acta Orthop Scand 47:52–58, 1976.

63. Kopits, S.E.; Steingass, M.H. Experience with the halo cast in small children. Surg Clin North Am 50:934–935, 1970.

64. Krag, M.H.; Byrt, W.; Pope, M. Pulloff strength of Gardner-Wells tongs from cadaveric crania. Spine 14:247–250, 1989.

65. Lee, A.S.; MacLean, J.C.B.; Newton, D.A. Rapid traction for reduction of cervical spine dislocations. J Bone Joint Surg Br 76:352–356, 1994.

66. Lee, H.M.; Kim, H.S.; Kim, D.J.; et al. Reliability of magnetic resonance imaging in detecting posterior ligament complex injury in thoracolumbar spinal fractures. Spine 25:2079–2084, 2000.

67. Lerman, J.A.; Haynes R.J.; Koeneman E.J.; et al. A biomechanical comparison of Gardner-Wells tongs and halo device used for cervical spine traction. Spine 19:2403–2406, 1994.

68. Levine, A.M.; Edwards C.C. Treatment of injuries in the C1-C2 complex. Orthop Clin North Am 17:31–44, 1986.

69. Levine, A.M.; McAfee, P.C.; Anderson, P.A. Evaluation and treat-ment of patients with thoracolumbar trauma. Instr Course Lect 44:33–45, 1995.

70. Li, Y.; Field, P.M.; Raisman, G. Repair of adult rat corticospinal tract by transplants of olfactory ensheathing cells. Science 237:642–645, 1987.

71. Lieberman, I.H.; Webb, J.K. Cervical spine injuries in the elderly. J Bone Joint Surg Br 76:877–881, 1994.

72. Lu, J.; Ashwell, K.W.S.; Waite, P. Advances in secondary spinal cord injury: Role of apoptosis. Spine 25:1859–1866, 2000.

73. Lucas, J.T.; Ducker, T.B. Motor classification of spinal cord injuries with mobility, morbidity and recovery indices. Am Surg 45:151–158, 1979.

74. Mahale, Y.J.; Silver, J.R.; Henderson, N.J. Neurological complica-tions of the reduction of cervical spine dislocations. J Bone Joint Surg Br 75:403–409, 1993.

75. Marshall, L.F.; Knowlton, S.; Garfin, S.R.; et al. Deterioration following spinal cord injury. J Neurosurg 66:400–404, 1987.

76. McArdle, C.B.; Wright, J.W.; Prevost, W.J. MR imaging of the acutely injured patient with cervical traction radiology. Radiology 159:273–274, 1986.

77. McGuire, R.A.; Neville, S.; Green, B.A.; Watts, C. Spinal instability and the log-rolling maneuver. J Trauma 27:525–531, 1987.

78. McIntosh, T.K.; Faden, A.I. Opiate antagonists in traumatic shock. Ann Emerg Med 15:1462–1465, 1986.

79. Midwestern Regional Spinal Cord Injury Care System. Northwest-ern University and Rehabilitation Institute of Chicago Progress Report No. 9. Chicago, Northwestern University, 1980.

80. Mirvis, S.E.; Borg, U.; Belzberg, H. MR imaging of ventilator-dependent patients: Preliminary experience. Am J Radiol 149:845–846, 1987.

81. Mubarak, S.J.; Camp, J.F.; Vuletich, W.; et al. Halo application in the infant. J Pediatr Orthop 9:612–614, 1989.

82. Nesathurai, S. Steroids and spinal cord injury: Revisiting the NASCIS 2 and NASCIS 3 trials. J Trauma 45:1088–1093, 1998.

83. O'Beirne, J.; Cassidy, N.; Raza, K.; et al. Role of magnetic resonance imaging in the assessment of spinal injuries. Injury 24:149–154, 1993.

84. Pepin, J.W.; Bourne, R.B.; Hawkins, R.J. Odontoid fracture, with special reference to the elderly patient. Clin Orthop 193:178–183, 1985.

85. Piepmeier, J.M.; Lehmann, K.B.; Lane, J.G. Cardiovascular instabil-ity following acute cervical spinal cord trauma. Cent Nerv Sys Trauma 2:153–160, 1985.

86. Podolsky, S.; Baraff, L.J.; Simon, R.R. Efficacy of cervical spine immobilization methods. J Trauma 23:461–465, 1983.

87. Reed, J.E.; Allen, W.E.; Dohrmann, G.J. Effect of mannitol on the traumatized spinal cord. Spine 4:391–397, 1979.

88. Reid, D.C.; Henderson, R.; Saboe, L.; Miller, J.D.R. Etiology and clinical course of missed spine fractures. J Trauma 27:980–986, 1987.

89. Riggins, R.S.; Kraus, J.F. The risk of neurologic damage with fractures of the vertebrae. J Trauma 7:126–133, 1977.

90. Ritchie, W.P.; Ersek, R.A.; Bunch, W.L.; et al. Combined visceral and vertebral injuries from lap style seat belts. Surg Gynecol Obstet 131:431–435, 1970.

91. Rizzolo, S.J.; Piazza, M.R.; Cotler, J.M.; et al. Intervertebral disc injury complicating cervical spine trauma. Spine 16(Suppl):187–189, 1991.

92. Rizzolo S.J.; Piazza M.R.; Cotler J.M.; et al. The effect of torque pressure on halo pin complication rates. Spine 18:2163–2166, 1993.

93. Robertson, P.A.; Ryan, M.D. Neurological deterioration after reduction of cervical subluxation: Mechanical compression by disc tissue. J Bone Joint Surg Br 74:224–227, 1992.

94. Ross, S.E.; Schwab, C.W.; David, E.T.; et al. Clearing the cervical spine: Initial radiographic evaluation. J Trauma 27:1055–1060, 1987.

95. Roth, E.J.; Lovell, L.; Heinemann, A.W.; et al. The older adult with a spinal cord injury. Paraplegia 30:520–526, 1992.

96. Ryan, M.D.; Henderson, J.J. The epidemiology of fractures and fracture dislocations of the cervical spine. Injury 23:38–40, 1992.

97. Schell, L.; Schwab, M.E. Sprouting and regeneration of lesioned corticospinal tract fibres in the adult rat spinal cord. Eur J Neurosci 5:1156–1171, 1993.

98. Schneider, R.C. The syndrome of acute anterior cervical spinal cord injury. J Neurosurg 12:95–122, 1955.

99. Schrader, S.C.; Sloan, T.B.; Toleikis, R. Detection of sacral sparing in acute spinal cord injury. Spine 12:533–535, 1987.

100. Shi, R.Y.; Lucas, J.H.; Wolf, A.; et al. Calcium antagonists fail to protect mammalian spinal neurons after physical injury. J Neu-rotrauma 6:261–278, 1989.

101. Short, D.J.; Masry, W.S.; Jones, P.W. High dose methylprednisolone in the management of acute spinal cord injury—a systematic review from a clinical perspective. Spinal Cord 38:273–286, 2000.

102. Slabaugh, P.B.; Nickel, V.L. Complications with the use of the Stryker frame. J Bone Joint Surg Am 60:111–112, 1978.

103. Soderstrom, C.A.; McArdle, D.Q.; Ducker, T.B.; Militello, P.R. The diagnosis of intraabdominal injury in patients with cervical cord trauma. J Trauma 23:1061–1065, 1983.

104. Spivak, J.M.; Weiss, M.A.; Cotler, J.M.; Call, M. Cervical spine injuries in patients 65 and older. Spine 19:2302–2306, 1994.

105. Star, A.M.; Jones, A.A.; Cotler, J.M.; et al. Immediate closed reduction of cervical spine dislocation using traction. Spine 15:1068–1072, 1990.

106. Starr, J.K. The pathophysiology and pharmacological management of acute spinal cord injury. Semin Spine Surg 7:91–97, 1995.

107. Stauffer, E.S. Diagnosis and prognosis of the acute cervical spinal cord injury. Clin Orthop 112:9–15, 1975.
108. Stauffer, E.S. Neurologic recovery following injuries to the cervical spinal cord and nerve roots. Spine 9:532–534, 1984.
109. Stauffer, E.S. A quantitative evaluation of neurologic recovery following cervical spinal cord injuries. Presented at the Third Annual Meeting of the Federation of Spine Associates, Paper 39. Atlanta, Georgia, February 1988.
110. Steel, H.H. Anatomical and mechanical consideration of the atlantoaxial articulation. J Bone Joint Surg Am 50:1481–1482, 1968.
111. Stover, S.L.; Fine, P.R. The epidemiology and economics of spinal cord injury. Paraplegia 25:225–228, 1987.
112. Stover, S.L.; Fine, P.R. Spinal Cord Injury: The Facts and Figures. Birmingham, AL, The University of Alabama, 1986.
113. Tator, C.H.; Duncan, E.G.; Edmonds, V.E.; et al. Demographic analysis of 552 patients with acute spinal cord injury in Ontario, Canada, 1947–1981. Paraplegia 26:112–113, 1988.
114. Thurman, D.J.; Burnett, C.C.; Jeppson, L.; et al. Surveillance of spinal cord injuries in Utah, USA. Paraplegia 32:665–669, 1994.
115. Torg, J.S.; Vegso, J.; Sennett, B.; Das, M. The National Football Head and Neck Injury Registry. JAMA 254:3439–3443, 1985.
116. Uesugi, M.; Kasuya, Y.; Hayashi, K.; Goto, K. SB209670, a potent endothelin receptor antagonist, prevents or delays axonal degeneration after spinal cord injury. Brain Res 786:235–239, 1998.
117. Vale, F.L.; Burns, J.; Jackson, A.B.; Hadley, M.N. Combined medical and surgical treatment after spinal cord injury: Result of a prospective pilot study to assess the merits of aggressive medical resuscitation and blood pressure management. J Neurosurg 87: 129–146, 1997.
118. Waters, R.L.; Adkins, R.H.; Yakura, J.S. Definition of complete spinal cord injury. Paraplegia 29:573–581, 1991.
119. Zipnick, R.I.; Scalea, T.M.; Trooskin, S.Z.; et al. Hemodynamic responses to penetrating spinal cord injuries. J Trauma 35:578–583, 1993.

CHAPTER 26

Spinal Imaging

Stuart E. Mirvis, M.D., F.A.C.R.

Spinal imaging must be considered in the context of the clinical presentation of the entire patient, which dictates management priorities as well as the type and sequence of diagnostic imaging evaluations. For all acutely injured patients with clinical signs of spine or spinal cord injury and all noncommunicative patients in whom the account of the mechanism of injury is consistent with spine or spinal cord injury, at least a frontal (anteroposterior [AP]) and horizontal beam lateral radiographs of the spine must be obtained during the initial evaluation. If the potentially injured segment of the spine, especially the cervical spine, cannot be "cleared" (i.e., declared negative for injury) by this limited examination or if the patient's condition requires immediate surgical intervention or more complex imaging procedures for other organ systems, the spine must be immobilized to protect the cord until the patient has been stabilized sufficiently to complete definitive imaging examinations of the spine.

Spinal imaging refers to evaluation of the spine by any of the various imaging modalities and techniques, or by any combination of such techniques, generally included in radiology. Diagnostic imaging of the spine is the definitive method for determining the presence, location, extent, and nature of injury to the spinal column, including, with the advent of magnetic resonance imaging (MRI), the spinal cord. Diagnostic imaging of the spine is therefore essential to the accurate assessment, evaluation, and management of spinal injury. The efficient and economic application of diagnostic imaging of spinal trauma requires a thorough knowledge of the indications for and limitations of the various imaging techniques available and the sequence in which they should be applied.

The diagnostic imaging of each region of the spine is considered separately because of differences in anatomy and injury patterns. The first section of this chapter considers currently available imaging modalities for evaluating acute cervical spinal injury along with illustrations of normal anatomy and examples of common injuries as they are related to the imaging concepts discussed. The following section describes approaches to the imaging evaluation of potential acute cervical spine trauma and

considers many of the controversies that surround this subject. This section begins with the initial plain film study and includes the types and sequences of recommended imaging techniques, as dictated by the patient's clinical condition, that culminate in a definitive diagnosis as soon as possible. The third section considers imaging of injury involving the noncervical spine. The fourth section reviews the strengths and weaknesses of each major imaging modality potentially used in assessing spinal injury. The final section discusses imaging the traumatized spine of patients with preexisting conditions that may significantly alter the normal appearance of the spine. The diagnostic approach presented reflects experience in the imaging evaluation of acute spinal injuries within the environment of a Level I trauma center, but it is applicable to spinal injuries seen in any setting (Fig. 26–1).

DIAGNOSTIC IMAGING OF THE CERVICAL SPINE

Imaging Modalities: An Overview

The diagnostic imaging modalities useful in the evaluation of spinal trauma include plain film radiography, computed tomography (CT), including two- and three-dimensional data re-formation, CT-myelography (CTM), MRI, and nuclear scintigraphy. Cervical vascular injury, with the potential for devastating neurologic consequences, is not uncommonly associated with cervical spine trauma. These potential vascular injuries may be recognized by CT using intravenous contrast or with routine MRI but are definitively diagnosed by magnetic resonance angiography (MRA), Doppler sonography, CT-angiography, and catheter angiography. The development and increasing availability of ultrafast multirow detector CT will make screening cervical CT-angiography practical for selected trauma patients at high risk for injury to the carotid and vertebral arteries.

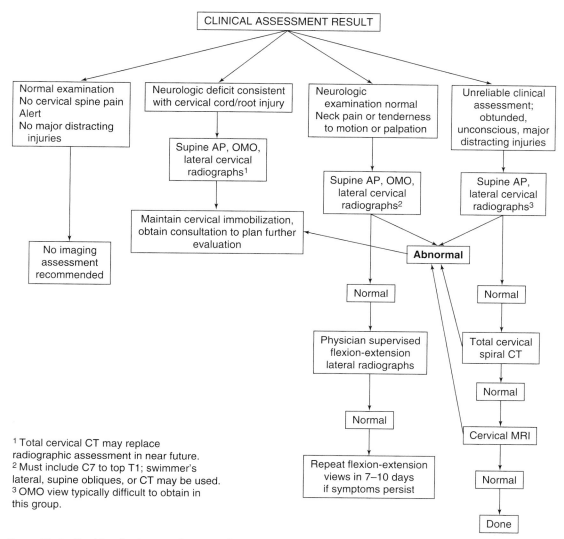

FIGURE 26–1. Algorithm for imaging diagnosis of cervical spine injury. AP, anteroposterior; CT, computed tomography; MRI, magnetic resonance imaging; OMO, open-mouth odontoid.

Plain Film Radiography of the Cervical Spine

All imaging examinations of spinal trauma currently begin with plain radiographic studies. Plain film radiography is readily available in all emergency centers; it is a reliable and quick method for evaluation of patients and can be performed with portable or fixed equipment. Radiography provides an excellent overview of the extent and magnitude of injury and makes a definitive and specific diagnosis possible in certain spinal injuries. The flexibility of the x-ray tube-film geometry provides the positioning latitude necessary for obtaining a comprehensive examination without motion of the patient, which is essential for patients in whom a spinal injury is suspected.

The quality of the plain radiographic study is of paramount importance to the identification of cervical spine injury. A properly exposed radiograph must display both the skeleton and the soft tissues and must be free of motion or grid artifacts that could obscure or mimic fractures. The prevention of artifact is of primary importance in detecting subtle, minimally displaced osseous injuries. A properly collimated plain film study effectively limits patients' exposure to radiation, and the examination is relatively inexpensive.

LATERAL VIEW

Evaluation of the initial screening lateral radiograph should be done methodically. An adequate study must include the cervicothoracic junction (to include the top of T1), and the patient should be positioned without rotation of the head. Every reasonable effort must be made to visualize the cervicothoracic junction on the initial plain radiographic examination. If the C7-T1 level is not adequately visualized on the lateral radiograph, the cervical spine cannot be cleared (i.e., declared negative), and other plain film studies (see later discussion) or CT must be performed.

The cross-table lateral radiograph is at least 74% to 86%

sensitive for detection of cervical spine injuries, depending to a large extent on the expertise and experience of the examiner.[33, 88, 125, 126] Missed injuries may result from (1) overlapping of bone, particularly involving the cervicocranial junction, the articular masses, and the laminae; (2) nondisplaced or minimally displaced fractures, particularly involving the atlas and axis; and (3) ligament injuries that may not be manifest when the radiograph is taken with the patient in a supine position with the neck in extension and stabilized by a cervical collar (i.e., no stress applied). Some cervical spine subluxations or dislocations can reduce spontaneously or be reduced with placement in a cervical collar before imaging evaluation, making their detection more difficult. Obviously, poor imaging technique related to positioning, exposure, or motion can significantly impair diagnostic accuracy.

Review of the lateral cervical radiograph involves assessment of anatomic lines, including the anterior and posterior vertebral margins, alignment of the articular masses, and alignment of the spinolaminar junctions (Fig. 26–2).[57] It is important to recognize minimal degrees of anterior and posterior intervertebral subluxation that occur normally with physiologic motion with cervical flexion and extension (Fig. 26–3). Such physiologic displacement typically occurs at multiple contiguous levels

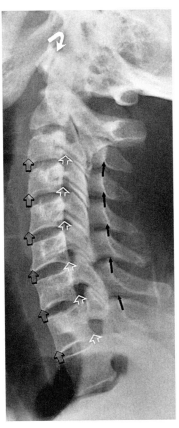

Figure 26–2. Normal lateral cervical spine radiograph. Proper alignment of the cervical spine is seen as smooth continuity of the anterior vertebral margins (*open black arrows*), posterior vertebral margins (*open white arrows*), and spinolaminar junction lines (*solid black arrows*). The anterior atlantodental space (*curved white arrow*) should measure 2.5 to 3 mm or less.

and usually does not exceed 3 mm.[132] The spacing between the laminae, articular facets, and spinous processes should be similar at contiguous levels (see Fig. 26–2). The intervertebral disc spaces should appear nearly uniform in height across the disc space. The orientation of each vertebra should be assessed for any rotational abnormalities. On a true lateral radiograph, the articular masses should be superimposed; abrupt offset of the masses indicates a rotational injury such as a unilateral facet dislocation. Similarly, an abrupt change in the distance from the posterior margin of the articular pillar to the spinolaminar line (the laminar space) also indicates a rotational injury[158] (Fig. 26–4).

Focal prevertebral or retropharyngeal soft tissue edema or hematoma can sometimes indicate an otherwise radiographically occult injury. However, absolute measurements of the prevertebral soft tissues are not particularly accurate indications of injury and can vary with head position, body habitus, and phase of inspiration, among other factors.[65, 146] Herr and colleagues[65] evaluated prevertebral soft tissue measurements at the C3 level in 212 patients with blunt trauma using a 4-mm upper limit of normal. They found that a measurement greater than 4 mm was only 64% sensitive for detecting cervical spine fractures involving the anterior, posterior, upper, or lower cervical spine. Precervical soft tissue prominence from the skull base to the axis is particularly important to recognize, as injuries at the craniocervical junction are often not apparent on the lateral radiograph. Harris[56] has shown that the contour of the cervicocranial prevertebral soft tissues can be particularly useful in detecting subtle upper cervical spine injuries (Fig. 26–5).

Assessment of the axis is aided by identification of the Harris ring,[59] a composite shadow of cortical bone along the margins of the neurocentral synchondrosis (Fig. 26–6). In a true lateral projection, the Harris rings from both sides of C2 are superimposed, whereas two parallel Harris rings result from an oblique (off-lateral) projection. Also in the lateral projection, the ring of cortical bone is interrupted in its posteroinferior aspect by the smaller ring of the foramen transversarium. The Harris ring is particularly helpful in detecting atypical cases of traumatic spondylolisthesis[8] (hangman's fracture) and the classical type III or low odontoid fracture[2] (Fig. 26–7; see also Fig. 26–5).

Radiologic identification of subluxation at the atlanto-occipital articulation can be difficult. Previously, the Powers ratio[60, 61, 117] was emphasized to assess this alignment. However, the anatomic landmarks required for this measurement are often difficult to visualize.[60, 61] Alignment at this articulation can be assessed by reference to three anatomic landmarks in the neutral position. First, the occipital condyle should lie within the condylar fossae of the atlas ring, with no gap between them in the adult patient. Second, a line drawn along the posterior surface of the clivus should intercept the superior aspect of the odontoid process. Third, a line drawn along the C1 spinolaminar line should intercept the posterior margin of the foramen magnum (Fig. 26–8).

A more precise assessment of this anatomic relationship can be determined by direct measurement, regardless of the degree of cervical flexion and extension. The tip of the odontoid process should lie within 12 mm of the basion

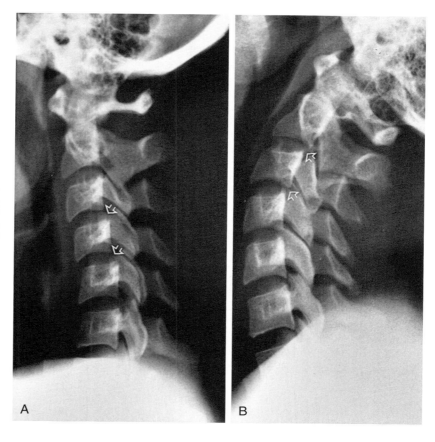

FIGURE 26–3. Physiologic subluxation. Lateral cervical radiograph in flexion (A) shows slight anterolisthesis at several levels (arrows). Relative lack of articular process overlap at C5–C6 is also physiologic. Extension (B) view shows physiologic retrolisthesis at C2–C3 and C3–C4 (arrows).

(inferior tip of the clivus), and a vertical line drawn along the posterior cortex of C2 (posterior axial line) should lie within 12 mm of the basion[60, 61] (Fig. 26–9). Cranial distraction and anterior displacement are indicated by measurements greater than 12 mm. The C1–C2 articulation should be evaluated for the anterior atlantodental interval, normally less than 3 mm in the adult.[21] A larger atlantodental interval associated with a cervicocranial hematoma indicates acute transverse atlantal ligament injury (Fig. 26–10) and instability of the articulation.

ANTEROPOSTERIOR VIEW

The AP radiograph of the cervical spine supplements information provided on the lateral cervical radiograph and can identify additional injuries.[32, 57, 125, 151] On the normal AP view, the spinous processes are vertically aligned, the lateral masses form smoothly undulating margins without abrupt interruption, the disc spaces are uniform in height from anterior to posterior, and the alignment of the vertebral bodies is easily assessed (Fig. 26–11). Typically, the craniocervical junction region and the odontoid process are not visible, being obscured by the face, mandible, and occipital skull. Lateral translation (displacement) of the vertebral bodies is best appreciated in this view. Similarly, lateral flexion injuries compressing a lateral mass or the lateral portion of a vertebral body are also demonstrated to advantage. Rotational injuries are indicated by an abrupt offset of spinous process alignment, as occurs with unilateral facet dislocation.

Fractures of the vertebral body in the sagittal plane are often evident on the AP view. Facet and articular mass fractures can sometimes be visualized as well. Laminopedicular separation (fracture separation of the articular mass), which may occur with hyperflexion-rotation injuries[134] or rarely hyperextension[62] mechanisms, can produce a horizontal orientation of the articular mass, leading to an open-appearing facet joint (Fig. 26–12). Normally, these joints are not seen in tangent on the AP view because of their 35-degree inclination from the horizontal plane. Some studies suggest that the AP view provides no significant diagnostic information in addition to that available from the lateral and open-mouth projection.[67] West and co-workers[155] have shown that a single lateral cervical spine radiograph is as sensitive for injury diagnosis as the standard three-view series for experienced interpreters.

OPEN-MOUTH ODONTOID VIEW

The open-mouth odontoid (OMO) or atlantoaxial view requires cooperation on the part of the patient for optimal studies. Ideally, the skull base (occiput), atlas, and axis are well displayed without overlap from the mandible or dentition (Fig. 26–13). The normal OMO view demonstrates the lateral margins of the C1 ring aligned within 1 or 2 mm of the articular masses of the axis. The articular masses of C2 should appear symmetric, as should the joint spaces between the articular masses of C1 and C2 as long as there is no rotation of the head. The measured distance between the odontoid and the C1 medial border (i.e., the lateral atlantodental space) should be equal, but a discrepancy of 3 mm or greater is often seen for patients without pathology.[69] Finally, a vertical line bisecting the odontoid process should form a 90-degree angle with a line placed horizontally across the superior aspect of the C2 articular masses[147] (Fig. 26–14).

Voluntary rotation, head tilting, or torticollis can be difficult to distinguish from atlantoaxial rotatory subluxation on the basis of radiography alone. Dynamic CT studies can be useful in differentiating a locked atlantoaxial dislocation from subluxation without locking.[105] Injuries that are best seen on the OMO view include the C1 burst fracture (Jefferson fracture) (Fig. 26–15), odontoid fractures (see Fig. 26–14), and lateral flexion fractures of the axis. Lateral spreading of the C1 lateral masses of greater than 6 to 7 mm in the Jefferson burst fracture suggests coexisting disruption of the transverse portion of the cruciate ligament, producing an unstable "atypical" Jefferson fracture.[42] This pattern usually creates two fractures on one side of the C1 ring and probably results from asymmetric axial loading or bending forces (Fig. 26–16).

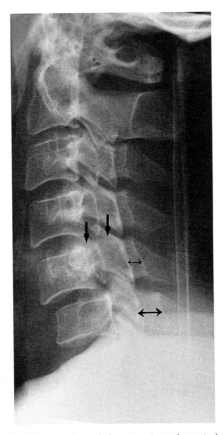

Figure 26–4. Unilateral facet dislocation. Lateral cervical radiograph shows anterior subluxation of C5 on C6. There is offset of the articular masses at C5 (*single-headed arrows*) and superimposition of these at C6, indicating rotation of the articular masses. There is an abrupt alteration in the distance from the back of the articular mass to the spinolaminar line (laminar space), also indicating rotation of the C5 vertebral body relative to C6 (*double-headed arrows*).

SUPINE OBLIQUE (TRAUMA OBLIQUE) VIEW

The supine oblique, or "trauma" oblique, projection is obtained with the patient maintained in collar stabilization in the supine and neutral position. The film-screen cassette is placed next to the patient's neck, and the x-ray tube is angled 45 degrees from the vertical.[57] The normal oblique view shows the neural foramina on one side and the pedicles of the contralateral side. The laminae are normally aligned like shingles on a roof (Fig. 26–17).

This projection can be used to improve visualization of the cervicothoracic junction when the lateral view is insufficient and is often utilized to clear the cervicothoracic junction.[72] Subluxation or dislocation of the articular masses and laminae that may not be seen on other standard views may be shown to advantage in this projection. If the cervicothoracic junction cannot be adequately visualized on the neutral lateral view, most institutions obtain a swimmer's lateral radiograph (89%) as opposed to bilateral supine oblique (11%) as the next imaging study.[71] The supine oblique views are cost-effective compared with CT scanning for selective clearing of the cervicothoracic junction.[72]

SWIMMER'S LATERAL PROJECTION

This view is often acquired to visualize the cervicothoracic junction when it is obscured by the density of shadows produced by the shoulders in the true lateral projection. Optimal positioning requires that one of the patient's arms be abducted 180 degrees and extended above the head—which may be difficult or impossible in patients with arm and shoulder injuries—while the opposite shoulder is extended posteriorly to decrease overlapping of skeletal structures (Fig. 26–18).[57] The projection further requires that the patient be rotated slightly off the true lateral. Positional changes required to obtain the swimmer's view are contraindicated for patients who are unconscious or who have cervical cord injuries.

The swimmer's view results in a somewhat distorted oblique projection of the cervicocranial junction, with the vertebrae obscured by portions of the shoulder girdle or the ribs, or both. Even with its limitations, however, this view is generally suitable to assess alignment and detect gross injuries. A modification of the swimmer's projection[12] is designed to improve the quality of the image by producing a truer lateral projection.

PILLAR VIEW

The pillar view (Fig. 26–19) is specifically designed to visualize the cervical articular masses directly in the frontal projection. Weir[152] contended that the pillar view should be included in all acute cervical injuries. It is generally agreed, however, that this view should be reserved for neurologically intact patients in whom articular mass fractures are suspected on the basis of radiography.

The pillar view is obtained by rotating the patient's head in one direction, off-centering the x-ray tube approximately 2 cm from the midline in the opposite direction, and angling the central x-ray beam approximately 30 degrees caudad, centered at the level of the superior

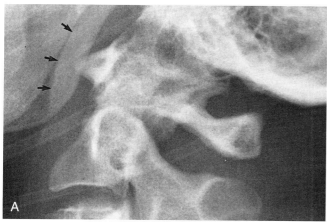

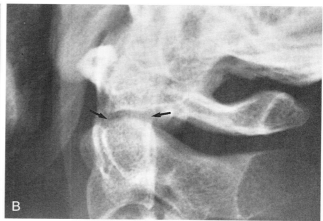

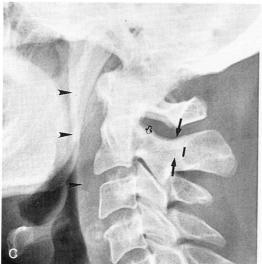

FIGURE 26–5. Subtle soft tissue abnormality indicating fracture. *A,* Coned-down lateral view of the craniocervical junction shows normal prevertebral soft tissue configuration with a slight soft tissue fullness (convex bulge) at the level of the C1 anterior arch and a slight concavity below *(arrows). B,* Coned-down lateral view from another patient with cervical pain shows loss of these contours with uniform prevertebral soft tissue fullness above, at, and below the C1 anterior tubercle. A subtle odontoid fracture *(arrows)* is present. The fracture interrupts the Harris composite ring shadow. *C,* Lateral cervical radiograph from another patient shows prevertebral soft tissue prominence at the cervicocranial junction with loss of normal contours around the C1 anterior tubercle *(arrowheads),* indicating prevertebral hematoma and edema. The spinolaminar line of C2 is also posteriorly displaced *(solid arrows* and *black line).* There is a subtle traumatic spondylolisthesis *(open arrow). (B,* From Mirvis, S.E.; Young, J.W.R. In: Mirvis, S.E.; Young, J.W.R., eds. Imaging in Trauma and Critical Care. Baltimore, Williams & Wilkins, 1992, p. 343.)

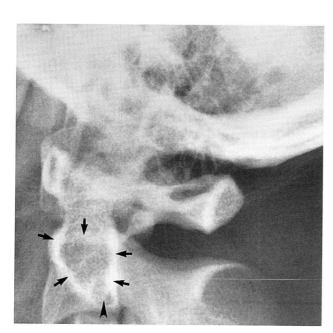

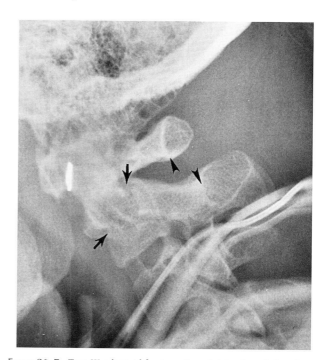

FIGURE 26–6. C2 composite ring shadow. In the lateral projection, portions of the C2 cortex form a composite shadow of bone density *(arrows).* A small circle of the foramen transversarium interrupts the ring in its posterior inferior margin *(arrowhead).* Discontinuity or irregularity of the ring shadow indicates probable type III odontoid fracture or atypical traumatic spondylolisthesis.

FIGURE 26–7. Type III odontoid fracture. Coned-down lateral view shows complete disruption of the Harris composite ring shadow, indicating odontoid fractures *(arrows).* The atlas is anteriorly displaced relative to the axis, as indicated by respective spinolaminar lines *(arrowheads).* (From Mirvis, S.E.; Shanmuganathan, K. J Intensive Care Med 10:15, 1995.)

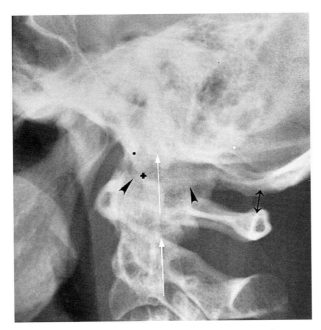

FIGURE 26–8. Normal atlanto-occipital anatomic relationships. In a coned-down lateral view from a normal patient, the spinolaminar line of C1 aligns with the posterior foramen magnum (double-headed black arrow), and the occipital condyle sits within the fossae of the C1 ring without a gap (black arrowheads). The distance between the basion (tip of clivus, asterisk) and the top of the odontoid process (plus sign) is less than 12 mm. The posterior axial line (white arrows) drawn along the posterior margin of the C2 body lies within 12 mm of the basion.

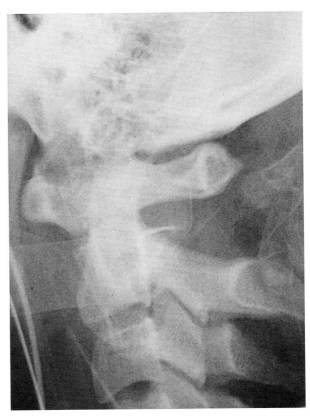

FIGURE 26–10. Atlantoaxial dislocation. Lateral coned-down cervical view shows marked widening of the atlantodental space, indicating disruption of the transverse atlantal ligament. Note the anterior displacement of the C1 spinolaminar junction line relative to that of C2. (From Mirvis, S.E.; Shanmuganathan, K. J Intensive Care Med 10:15, 1995.)

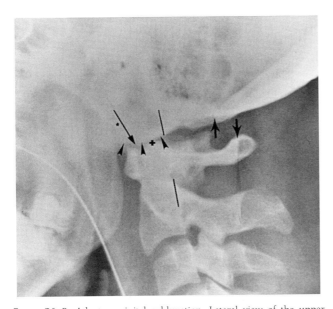

FIGURE 26–9. Atlanto-occipital subluxation. Lateral view of the upper cervical spine shows anterior displacement of the posterior margin of the foramen magnum relative to the C1 spinolaminar line (short arrows), the occipital condyles are displaced from the condylar fossae of the atlas (arrowheads), and a line drawn along the clival posterior margin intercepts the odontoid process along its anterior surface (long arrow). Finally, the distance between the tip of the odontoid (plus sign) and the basion (asterisk) exceeds 12 mm, as does the distance from the posterior axial line (interrupted line) to the basion.

margin of the thyroid cartilage.[57] The caudally angled central beam is tangential to the plane of the facet joints only in the middle and lower cervical spine because of normal cervical lordosis. Rotation of the head is essential to eliminate superimposition of the mandible on the lateral masses. Therefore, the patient must be able to rotate the head on command, and the presence of an upper cervical injury must have been previously excluded in the initial plain radiographic evaluation. Because articular pillar and pedicle fractures often occur with rotational injuries,[135] further rotation is contraindicated when assessing these injuries. If injuries to the lateral cervical pillars are suspected on the basis of the initial plain film screening, they are best assessed further by CT.

FLEXION-EXTENSION STRESS VIEWS

Demonstration of ligament injury may require placing stress on the cervical ligaments. It is imperative that cervical flexion and extension views be obtained only for alert, cooperative, and neurologically intact patients who can describe pain or early onset of any subjective neurologic symptoms. During the evaluation of acute injuries, active flexion-extension radiographs should be supervised by a physician. The use of fluoroscopically

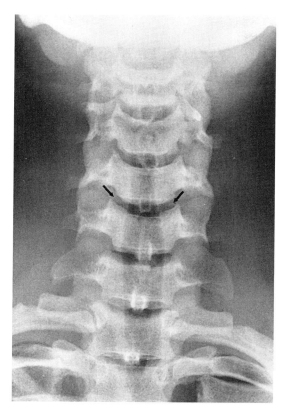

FIGURE 26–11. Normal anteroposterior (AP) cervical radiograph. In the normal AP view, a smoothly undulating lateral border is created by the lateral masses, the spinous processes are vertically aligned, and the spacing of the intervertebral discs and uncovertebral joints (*arrows*) is uniform. The facet joints cannot be visualized because they are inclined about 35 degrees to the horizontal. Enlarged C7 transverse processes (cervical ribs) are seen as a variant. In general, C2 and C1 are poorly seen in this projection. (From Mirvis, S.E.; Young, J.W.R. In: Mirvis, S.E.; Young, J.W.R., eds. Imaging in Trauma and Critical Care. Baltimore, Williams & Wilkins, 1992, p. 298.)

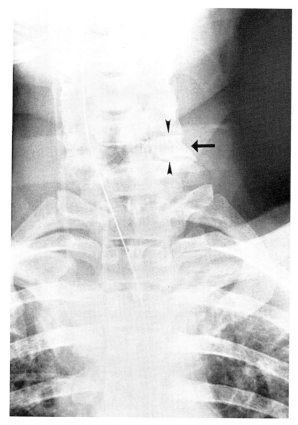

FIGURE 26–12. Isolation of articular pillar. This anteroposterior view shows direct visualization of the facet articulations (*arrowheads*) of C5–C6 and C6–C7 on the left caused by rotation of the articular mass (*arrow*). This finding requires combined fractures of the lamina and ipsilateral pedicle.

guided passive flexion-extension cervical spine assessment is discussed in detail in the following section on imaging approaches. Although for most patients evidence of cervical instability is apparent on the neutral lateral radiograph, some injuries can be effectively reduced to an anatomic position with the patient in a cervical collar and may be completely invisible in the stabilized neutral position.

Normally, flexion and extension produce minimal physiologic motion of adjacent vertebrae and anterior or posterior sliding movement across the articular facets. An abrupt change in facet coverage at one level indicates injury to the ligament support (Fig. 26–20). Finally, degenerative disease (cervical spondylosis) of the facet articulations with loss of the interarticular fibrocartilage may allow excessive anterior translation at one or more levels that can mimic pathologic movement related to acute injury (Fig. 26–21). In degenerative slippage, the shape of the articular facet and width of the facet joint spaces may be normal; however, in most cases the articular facet has become "ground down," the facet joints are narrowed, and the articular processes are thinned. In

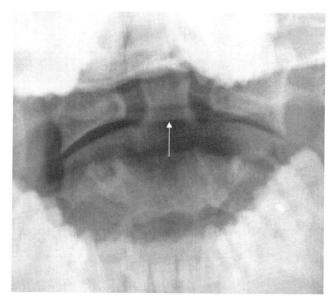

FIGURE 26–13. Normal open-mouth odontoid (OMO) view. The lateral borders of the lateral masses of the atlas are aligned with the lateral borders of the axis. Without rotation of the head, the lateral atlantodental spaces are equivalent. A thin radiolucent Mach line at the base of the odontoid is created by the overlapping inferior surface of the posterior atlas ring (*arrow*).

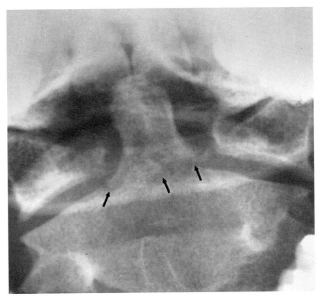

FIGURE 26–14. Odontoid fracture with tilt. The open-mouth odontoid view shows a fracture across the base of the odontoid (*arrows*) and lateral tilting of the odontoid process.

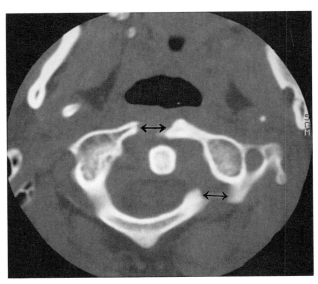

FIGURE 26–16. Unstable Jefferson fracture. Axial computed tomography (CT) scan through the atlas shows wide displacement of parts of the ring (*double-headed arrows*), indicating probable disruption or avulsion of the transverse atlantal ligament, creating both mechanical and neurologic instability.

traumatic subluxation, the articular facets are either normally shaped or fractured and the joint spaces are widened.[82]

In a national survey of 165 trauma centers, Grossman and associates[51] found that flexion-extension views were more likely to be obtained as part of the cervical spine imaging evaluation in Level I as opposed to Level II or lower level centers. Brady and colleagues[15] evaluated use of dynamic flexion-extension views in 451 patients with blunt trauma who manifested neck pain, midline tenderness, or an abnormal spinal contour on static

cervical radiographs. Patients with abnormal cervical static radiographs were statistically more likely to have abnormal active flexion-extension studies than those with normal static studies and more likely to require invasive fixation.

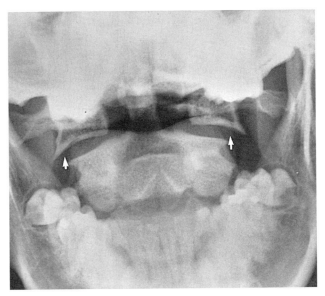

FIGURE 26–15. Jefferson burst fracture. The open-mouth odontoid view shows lateral displacement of the C1 articular masses relative to those of C2 (*arrows*), indicating a C1 burst fracture.

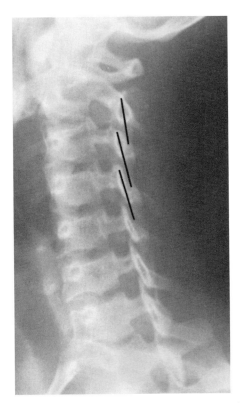

FIGURE 26–17. Normal "shingles-on-the-roof" orientation of laminae seen in an oblique projection of the cervical spine.

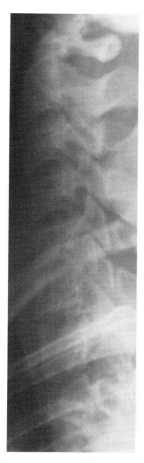

FIGURE 26–18. Swimmer's view of the cervicothoracic junction.

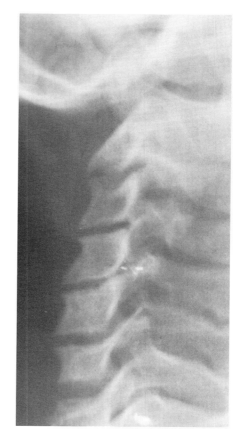

FIGURE 26–19. Pillar view of the right articular masses of the cervical spine.

IMAGING APPROACH TO THE POTENTIALLY INJURED CERVICAL SPINE

Spinal Imaging of the Polytraumatized Patient: An Overview

Acute injuries of the cervical spine range in significance from clinically trivial to permanent paralysis. Therefore, the evaluation of cervical spinal injury must begin with clinical examination of the patient by an experienced physician who can appraise the location, extent, and magnitude of the spinal injury. Unconscious, intoxicated, or elderly patients with a history of trauma must be considered to have a cervical spinal injury until proved otherwise.

The type and extent of imaging evaluation are governed by the patient's neurologic status and overall condition, particularly the hemodynamic status. For all patients with spinal injury, however, the following guidelines should be observed:

1. The spine must remain immobilized to protect it and the cord during the initial examination and until the spine has been declared negative.
2. The radiologic evaluation begins with plain radiographs.

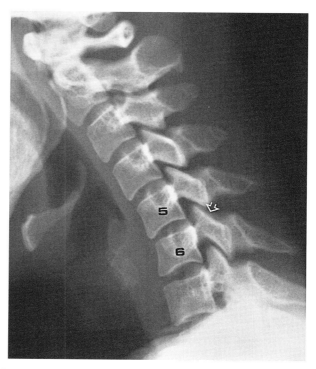

FIGURE 26–20. Flexion subluxation. Flexion lateral radiograph shows a focal decrease in coverage of the articular facets at C5–C6 (*arrow*). There is slight "flaring" of the spinous processes at this level and minimal narrowing of the disc space compared with other levels. All findings indicate hyperflexion subluxation injury.

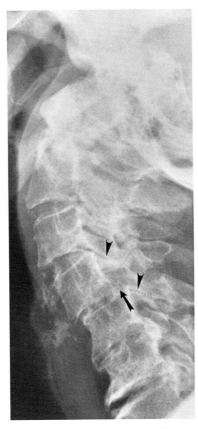

Figure 26–21. Degenerative subluxation. Lateral cervical radiograph shows slight anterolisthesis of C4 on C5 (arrow). There is diffuse degenerative change. Note narrowing of the facet joints and sclerosis of the facet surfaces (arrowheads).

3. The initial examination must be monitored by a radiologist or other qualified physician to establish the radiologic diagnosis as accurately and quickly as possible and to determine whether additional examinations are indicated. If so, the most efficient sequence of studies for optimal care of the patient must be established.

In the absence of neurologic findings and with the spine immobilized, other injuries, if any, can be managed initially. Alternatively, it may be clinically appropriate to clarify the status of the spine before managing a coexistent injury. In any case, the examination of the spine must be personally supervised and sequentially monitored by a radiologist or other qualified physician until either the spine studies have been declared negative or a definitive diagnosis has been established.

Recommended Imaging Approach for Potential Cervical Spine Trauma Based on Clinical Presentation (see Fig. 26–1)

TRAUMA PATIENT WITH A NEUROLOGIC DEFICIT REFERABLE TO THE CERVICAL SPINAL CORD

The optimal radiologic approach to the trauma patient *with spinal injury* and signs of cord damage consists of only frontal and horizontal beam lateral plain radiographs obtained in the emergency center, followed by CT with appropriate image re-formations and MRI of the injured area whenever clinically appropriate. Trauma patients with definite myelopathy but negative plain radiographs are best served by performing MRI or, if MRI is unavailable, myelography and CTM as the next study.

Occasionally, the definitive evaluation of the spinal injury in major trauma patients must be superseded by the evaluation and management of more urgent clinical problems, such as a low Glasgow Coma Scale score, a tension pneumothorax, a suspected aorta injury, or massive or progressive hemoperitoneum. In such instances, and whenever possible, AP and lateral radiographs of the injured region of the spine should be obtained concurrently with initial evaluation of the patient and stabilization procedures. If the spine cannot be declared negative on the basis of this screening examination, it must be immobilized until the patient has been stabilized and the evaluation of the spinal injury can be concluded. If plain radiographs do not reveal the cause of the neurologic deficit, then whenever possible, MRI should be obtained as the next examination.

ALERT TRAUMA PATIENT WITH CERVICAL SPINE PAIN

Radiographic examination of the spine is clearly not indicated for every patient who complains of minimal symptoms after minor trauma. The attending physician, however, must have a high index of suspicion regarding the presence of spinal injury, as failure to recognize and treat a clinically subtle dislocation, fracture, or fracture-dislocation can lead to devastating, irreparable cord injury. Therefore, a history of trauma that could produce spinal injury or the presence of objective physical signs consistent with spinal injury is of particular importance in determining which patients should undergo imaging evaluation.

The appropriate radiologic evaluation of the cervical spine is controversial, particularly with regard to the number of views that constitute an adequate radiologic assessment.* Whereas a single lateral radiograph detects 74% to 86% of cervical spine injuries, sensitivity increases to nearly 100% when an AP and an OMO projection are added.[33] For the neurologically intact alert trauma patient with a complaint of neck pain, physical findings of pain, or point tenderness elicited on palpation of the cervical spine, a minimum of two views, typically a cross-table lateral and an AP view, are obtained. Additional views, including the OMO projection and supine oblique views, can also be obtained and may increase diagnostic yield slightly. If the AP and lateral views obtained with the patient in a rigid collar are negative from the occiput to the C7-T1 level, the collar can be removed to facilitate obtaining the OMO and oblique views.

If all plain radiographs are normal, the possibility of a significant missed skeletal cervical spine injury is minimal. However, ligamentous injuries, including potentially neurologically unstable injuries such as reduced bifacet dislocations or reduced hyperflexion or hyperextension

_____
*See references 33, 62, 63, 68, 97, 125, 126, 133, 142, 150.

subluxations, may still not be demonstrated (Figs. 26–22 and 26–23). It is important to remember that on spinal radiographs obtained only with the patient supine, the patient's body habitus may obscure some spinal injuries.

Initial radiographs obtained with spinal immobilization in place should be examined by a physician skilled in the interpretation of spinal radiographs. At the University of Maryland Shock Trauma Center, clinically stable, alert, cooperative patients with cervical pain and normal initial cervical spine radiographs undergo flexion-extension lateral radiography after the cervical collar is removed in order to assess ligamentous stability. On occasion, in the experience of that center, flexion and extension subluxations may be identified that are not evident on neutral cross-table lateral or AP cervical radiographs obtained in the supine position.[85]

The use of routine flexion and extension lateral cervical radiographs is by no means universal and should not be considered standard practice.[51] This procedure should be *carefully supervised by a physician* and never performed by a radiography technologist alone. The patient should flex and extend the neck to the limit of pain tolerance or onset of subjective neurologic symptoms. Obviously, any suggestion of an onset of neurologic impairment mandates return to the neutral position and reapplication of cervical immobilization. If adequate flexion and extension views are acquired with visualization of the spine through C7-T1, the vast majority of potentially unstable injuries are excluded. Flexion and extension lateral cervical views should not be obtained in uncooperative patients or those with decreased mental acuity and should not be obtained

with passive movement of the patient's cervical spine by a physician.

Alternatively, spiral CT can be used to screen patients with neck pain for subtle fractures that may be difficult or impossible to diagnose from radiographs. Increasingly, spiral CT is being used as a primary screening test in blunt trauma patients with cervical spine symptoms. Patients with neck pain who undergo CT scanning of other body regions may also undergo cervical spine CT to assess the region of neck pain or the entire cervical spine.[106] Although it is well established that CT is more sensitive than plain radiography in detecting cervical spine injury,* a positive cost-benefit ratio has not been determined for CT performed for radiographically negative trauma patients with neck pain. Increasingly, spiral CT and multidetector CT are being used to perform screening studies of the entire cervical spine rather than depending on plain radiographic interpretation for alert patients with cervical spine symptoms. This development is based on the recognized improved accuracy of CT over radiography for osseous pathology, the increased use of CT in general for assessing stable patients with blunt trauma in multiple body regions, the increasing speed of image acquisition and processing, and its general cost-efficacy.[10, 13, 24, 55, 74, 83, 106, 107]

The accuracy of spiral CT in detecting all potentially unstable ligament injuries is not known, although some of these injuries would be suggested by soft tissue swelling or subtle abnormalities of alignment. For this reason, active

*See references 1, 4, 16, 22, 35, 54, 55, 74, 87, 92, 106, 107, 116.

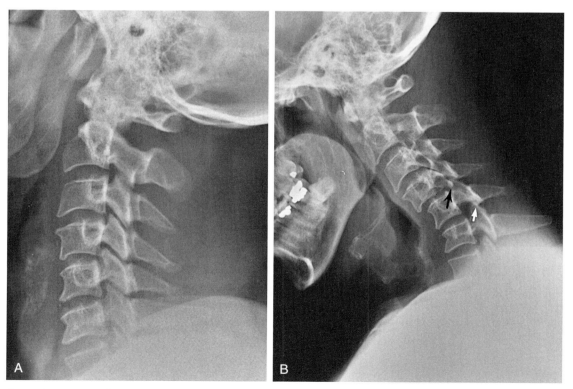

FIGURE 26–22. Hyperflexion ligament injury not apparent on neutral position lateral view radiograph. *A,* Lateral cervical radiograph in a trauma patient with cervical spine pain is unremarkable. *B,* Flexion lateral view (physician supervised) shows hyperflexion subluxation at C5–C6 *(white arrow)* and unilateral facet dislocation at C4–C5 *(black arrow)*. (*A, B,* From Mirvis, S.E.; Shanmuganathan, K. J Intensive Care Med 10:15, 1995.)

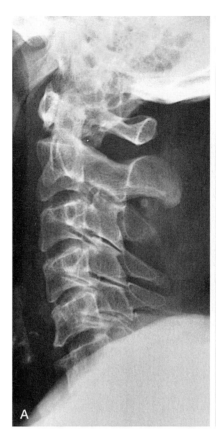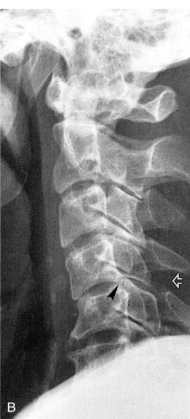

Figure 26–23. Hyperflexion ligament injury not apparent on neutral position lateral cervical radiograph. *A,* Neutral position lateral radiograph of a trauma patient with cervical tenderness is unremarkable. *B,* Repeated view with flexion limited by pain shows hyperflexion sprain at C4–C5 *(arrowhead)* with mild flaring of the spinous processes *(open arrow).*

flexion-extension views are still needed to ensure cervical spine ligament integrity.

TRAUMA PATIENT WITH AN UNRELIABLE PHYSICAL EXAMINATION

Trauma patients presenting without evidence of myelopathy but whose physical examination cannot be considered reliable constitute a major challenge with regard to possible spinal injury. All such patients should be regarded as potentially having unstable spinal injuries until proved otherwise. The radiographic assessment of such patients should include at least lateral and AP cervical spine views. Open-mouth views are often difficult to obtain and suboptimal technically in this population. In addition, supine oblique views of the cervicothoracic junction region can be obtained if needed. Often, CT is used to assess the cervicocranial junction if not well demonstrated by radiography, depending on its availability and indication for CT of other body regions. If injuries are identified, spine immobilization is maintained and further imaging workup performed when clinically feasible. The potential role of spiral CT scanning for screening *the entire* cervical spine for patients with an unreliable clinical examination is currently undergoing study.

If all radiographic evaluations of the spine are negative, the vast majority of injuries are excluded, but again, the potential for a neurologically unstable injury persists. D'Alise and colleagues[26] performed limited cervical spine MRI within 48 hours of trauma in 121 patients who had no obvious injury shown by plain radiography. There were

31 patients (25.6%) who had significant injury to paravertebral ligamentous structures, the intervertebral disc, or bone. Eight of these patients required surgical fixation of the injury.

If MRI is not available, an alternative approach is to obtain an erect AP and lateral cervical radiograph with the patient in collar stabilization to allow limited physiologic stress on the cervical spine. If these films are normal, erect AP and lateral views are repeated out of collar with the cervical spine slightly extended and the head supported by a pillow. If these views are normal, the cervical collar is permanently removed. Although these approaches are considered prudent to avoid missing a cervical spine injury, they are by no means universally followed. In some sites the cervical collar is removed on the basis of negative AP and lateral supine radiography alone, suggesting the rarity with which neurologically unstable cervical spine injuries occur with normal-appearing cervical radiographs.[52]

Some authors have suggested the use of passive flexion and extension imaging under fluoroscopic guidance for patients who cannot have a reliable physical examination.[27, 128, 131] Thus far, no complications of this procedure have been reported. However, almost all the patients studied have been normal, as would be expected from the extremely low pretest probability of an unstable injury. The limited data available do not provide sufficient evidence to support routine use of this technique. A number of cervical spine injuries are not detected by this method, including herniated intervertebral discs and epidural hematomas. These lesions may cause spinal cord compression that creates or worsens a neurologic deficit without evidence of overt subluxation on fluoroscopy.

Cervical disc herniation is a more common cause of central cord syndrome than previously suspected.[25] Benzel and co-workers[9] found 27 acute cervical disc herniations among 174 trauma patients with negative cervical radiographs who underwent cervical MRI. Rizzolo and colleagues[124] observed acute cervical disc herniation in 42% of 55 patients with blunt cervical trauma with cervical fractures or neurologic deficits. In addition, either congenital or acquired spinal stenosis can produce spinal cord lesions in association with blunt trauma when there is no radiographic evidence of injury.[80] Flexion and extension in this population could worsen cord compression and ischemia. To date, only MRI has proven diagnostic accuracy for direct diagnosis of ligament injury from blunt spinal trauma.[9, 26, 76, 79, 102, 110]

ALERT TRAUMA PATIENT WITH NORMAL CERVICAL SPINE EXAMINATION

The need to perform imaging in alert, appropriately oriented trauma victims without evidence of cervical pain, tenderness to palpation of the cervical spine, or major distracting injuries has been highly controversial. Most patients admitted to emergency centers from the scene of a major blunt force trauma are placed in cervical immobilization and are presumed to have a cervical injury until proved otherwise. This scenario places a great deal of pressure on the admitting physician to exclude an injury with an extremely high degree of certainty. There are case reports describing so-called painless cervical spine fractures. A close review of many such articles typically reveals that the patient either had symptoms or was not truly alert.[33, 40, 68, 89, 95, 127]

Many large series published to date indicate that alert trauma patients without major distracting injuries and without subjective complaints of neck pain or positive physical findings invariably have normal imaging evaluations.[33, 49, 67, 159] A prospective series of alert trauma patients without symptoms who underwent cervical spine CT to clear the cervicothoracic junction revealed one nondisplaced C7 transverse process fracture in 146 patients at a cost of more than $58,000.[97] Diliberti and Lindsey[33] recommended omission of radiologic assessment of the cervical spine in any trauma patient with class 1 level of consciousness (i.e., able to follow complex commands, responds immediately) and without evidence of intoxication, neurologic deficit, cervical spine pain, or pain elicited on palpation. Gonzales and associates[48] found that clinical assessment was more sensitive than radiography in detecting cervical spine injury even in intoxicated patients.

CONCOMITANT CERVICAL SPINE AND LIFE-THREATENING INJURIES

As stated throughout this chapter, the imaging evaluation of the spine must be performed in the total context of the trauma patient's management. The radiographic examination of patients with concomitant acute spinal injury and life-threatening injuries should consist of only AP and horizontal beam lateral projections obtained in the emergency center during the clinical evaluation. If a radiologic diagnosis can be made from this limited study (e.g., traumatic spondylolisthesis, bilateral facet dislocation, burst fracture), management of the injury consistent with the patient's clinical condition can be initiated. If results of the initial limited examination are equivocal or if the spinal injury is one that requires additional evaluation by CT or MRI, the spine must be appropriately immobilized until the life-threatening injury has been stabilized and the radiologic evaluation can continue.[139]

IMAGING ASSESSMENT OF POTENTIAL INJURY TO THE NONCERVICAL SPINE

Alert trauma patients with pain in the thoracic, lumbar, or sacral region require lateral and AP radiologic views of the region in question. If these studies are negative but clinical symptoms are impressive, further imaging by CT is indicated. After radiologic identification of a thoracic, lumbar, or sacral fracture, CT is helpful in characterizing complex injuries such as fracture-dislocations and in distinguishing burst fractures from anterior compression fractures.[58] Acute onset of radicular symptoms after acute trauma may also warrant CTM or MRI to exclude acute intervertebral disc herniation. In the patients who are not reliable enough for an accurate physical examination, AP and lateral spine films also provide routine screening.

The improvements in CT technology, introduced with spiral CT and the newer multidetector array systems, create the potential for CT to provide screening of the thoracic and lumbar spine as part of a routine thoracic cavity and abdominal-pelvic CT study in a multiple-trauma patient. Single-slice or multislice spiral CT used in conjunction with scout AP and lateral radiographs of the spine may ultimately provide more accurate identification of thoracic and lumbosacral injuries than is achieved with conventional radiography.

Plain Film Radiography of the Thoracic Spine

Imaging of the thoracic spine is a less complex procedure than that of the cervical spine. The influence of the patient's overall condition on the type and sequence of imaging procedures used to evaluate the thoracic and lumbar areas is identical to that discussed for the cervical spine.

Routine AP and lateral plain radiographs constitute the initial evaluation of the thoracic spine, with the exception of the upper thoracic vertebrae (discussed separately later in this chapter). Unilateral or bilateral focal bulging of the thoracic paraspinous soft tissue shadows (the mediastinal stripe or paraspinal line) is an important marker of subtle thoracic fractures (Fig. 26–24). Alteration in the contour of the paraspinous shadow is not specific for hematoma unless there is an appropriate history and corresponding findings on physical examination. Paraspinous abscess or

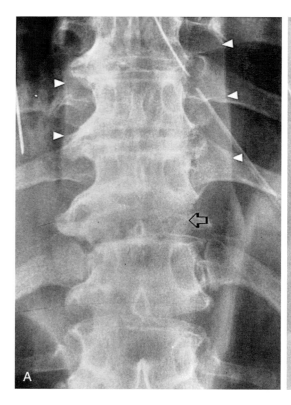
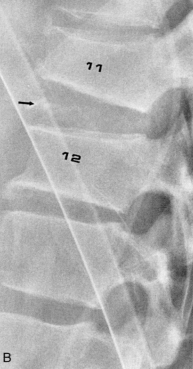

FIGURE 26–24. Paraspinal hematomas indicating thoracic spine fracture. *A,* The anteroposterior coned-down view of the lower thoracic spine shows bulging of the paraspinal stripes (*arrowheads*) accompanied by a widened disc space at T11–T12 (*open arrow*). *B,* The coned-down lateral projection shows hyperextension injury with partial inferior end-plate avulsion from T11 (*arrow*).

neoplasm can produce a soft tissue density similar to that caused by a localized traumatic hematoma.

The great majority of acute thoracic spine injuries are recognizable on the initial plain film examination, and it is not as frequently necessary to use CT to establish the primary diagnosis as it is in the cervical spine. The only segment of the thoracic spine that requires special attention with plain radiography is the cervicothoracic junction. It is essential to be aware that the upper four or five thoracic vertebrae are not routinely visible on lateral radiographs of the thoracic spine because of the density of the superimposed shoulders. It is therefore incumbent on the attending physician *to indicate specifically* to the radiologist when the upper thoracic spine is the area of suspected injury so that additional views can be obtained.

The AP view of both the thoracic and the lumbar spine is also quite helpful in plain film evaluation. Vertebral alignment is assessed using the position of the pedicles, the presence or absence of scoliosis, and alignment of the spinous processes. The architecture of the pedicles at the affected level is important, as the relationship between spinous processes can be helpful in demonstrating ligament disruption. A sudden increase in distance between two adjacent spinous processes, as determined from the AP film, is frequently associated with disruption of the intraspinous and supraspinous ligaments and of the facet capsules. Lateral translation on the AP view, combined with anterior translation on the lateral view, suggests a grossly unstable shearing injury.

When the patient's condition permits, the Fletcher view provides an off-lateral projection of the upper thoracic segments. Positioning for the Fletcher view requires that the patient be rotated slightly from the true lateral, with

one shoulder anterior and the other posterior to the spine. Thus, the upper thoracic segments are projected in slight obliquity between the rotated shoulders. True lateral views of the upper thoracic spine may require CT with sagittal re-formation. Supine oblique views, which can be invaluable in the evaluation of the lower cervical region, are of little value in the upper thoracic spine because of superimposition of the ribs and the complexity of the costovertebral articulations.

Plain Film Radiography of the Lumbar Spine

Radiographic evaluation of the acutely injured lumbar spine, like that of other segments of the spinal column, begins with AP and lateral plain radiographs. When it is clinically inappropriate to place the patient in the true lateral position, the lateral examination should be carried out using a horizontal beam with the patient recumbent. For patients with a history of acute trauma, the lateral "spot" radiograph of the lumbosacral junction is neither indicated nor necessary.

On initial evaluation, the overall alignment of the thoracolumbar junction and lumbar spine is most clearly assessed with a lateral radiograph taken in the supine position. Many fractures demonstrate not only a comminution of the vertebral body but also a local area of kyphosis. The complete loss of lumbar lordosis in the absence of obvious pathology may still be suggestive of injury. As in the cervical spine, subtle rotational injuries are often evident on the lateral projection. In burst fractures of the lumbar spine, the degree of canal compromise can frequently be estimated by observing the posterosuperior corner of the injured vertebral body.

The AP view provides the same information as described previously for the thoracic spine. Oblique projections of the lumbar spine should be obtained only when the AP and lateral radiographs are grossly negative and inconsistent with the clinical evaluation. Also, the patient's condition must allow rotation into the oblique position. The oblique projection provides another perspective of the lumbar vertebral body and excellent visualization of the pars interarticularis and the facet joints.

Plain Radiography of the Sacrum and Coccyx

Acute injuries involving the sacrum are most commonly associated with pelvic ring disruption. However, isolated injuries of the lower sacral segments and coccyx do occur and require special imaging techniques. The sacral and coccygeal concavity makes adequate visualization of all these segments on a single AP projection impossible. Consequently, in addition to the straight AP radiograph, standard plain radiographic examination of the sacrum and coccyx must include rostrally and caudally angulated AP views as well as a true lateral projection. Superimposition of intestinal artifacts, pelvic calcifications, and soft tissue structures can obscure minimally displaced fractures of the sacral and coccygeal segments in the AP projection. In such a case, the fracture is usually evident on the lateral radiograph. CT may be required to detect subtle injuries not evident with radiography. Sacrococcygeal dislocation, even when grossly displaced, is difficult to diagnose radiographically because of the range of normal variation at this level and the effects of pelvic delivery in women. Clinical correlation is particularly important for these patients.

DIAGNOSTIC MODALITIES IN IMAGING SPINAL TRAUMA: ADVANTAGES AND LIMITATIONS

Computed Tomography of the Spine

CT allows images to be obtained in any plane determined by the radiologist to demonstrate the pathology in question to maximal advantage. Multiplanar computed tomography is CT with routinely obtained sagittal and coronal reformatted images. The role of multiplanar CT in the evaluation of injuries of the axial skeleton has been well established.* Simply put, multiplanar CT (including three-dimensional CT) is currently the imaging technique of choice for spinal injury.

The principal value of CT is in the axial image, which demonstrates the neural canal and the relationship of

*See references 1, 3, 7, 35, 36, 54, 58, 87, 92, 115, 116.

fracture fragments to the canal. Axial data obtained in the supine patient are converted electronically into images displayed in the sagittal and coronal planes, without requiring movement of the injured patient. The development of multislice CT technology with 0.5-second gantry rotation allows up to eight axial images to be acquired per second and is expected to continue to expand to more images per second in the near future. The speed of data acquisition decreases the patient's motion and permits thinner section images to be routinely obtained than with single-slice spiral CT. These factors contribute to a major improvement in the quality of reformatted two-dimensional (2-D) and three-dimensional (3-D) images. The volume elements obtained (voxels) with multislice spiral scanning can be made equivalent in size in all three orthogonal axes (isotropic), permitting image quality equivalent to that of axial images in any orientation. Addition of more detector arrays is anticipated to lead to further increases in the speed of image acquisition and improvements in image quality.

Spinal CT imaging is performed without intrathecal contrast to (1) evaluate uncertain radiologic findings, (2) provide details of osseous injury as an aid to surgical planning, (3) assess focal or diffuse spine pain when no radiologic abnormalities are demonstrated, (4) clear the lower cervicothoracic region in symptomatic patients in whom cervical radiography provides inadequate visualization, (5) assess the adequacy of internal fixation and detect postoperative complications, and (6) localize foreign bodies and bone fragments in relation to neural elements.

CT imaging is not indicated for some spinal injuries identified radiographically. These include simple wedge compression, clay-shoveler's fracture, anterior subluxation of the cervical spine, hyperextension teardrop fracture,[38] typical hangman's fractures, and typical odontoid fractures. In the thoracic, lumbar, and sacrococcygeal spine, CT is used primarily to assess the relationship of bone fragments to the neural canal, localize penetrating foreign bodies, record the details of complex fracture patterns, and exclude osseous injury with greater accuracy when plain films are negative in symptomatic patients.[45] Ballock and colleagues[4] showed that CT is more accurate than plain radiography in distinguishing wedge compression fractures from burst fractures in the thoracolumbar spine.

CT often shows additional injuries not suspected on review of plain radiographic views.[74] CT is particularly useful in identifying fractures of the occipital condyles[22] (Fig. 26–25), articular mass and laminae that may occur in association with hyperflexion facet dislocations[134] (Fig. 26–26), hyperextension fracture-dislocations, hyperflexion teardrop fractures (Fig. 26–27), axial loading fractures of C1 (Jefferson fracture) (Fig. 26–28), and vertebral body burst fractures (Fig. 26–29).

Assessment of subluxation and dislocation is aided by two-dimensional multiplanar as well as surface contour 3-D image re-formation (Figs. 26–30 and 26–31). The quality of both two-dimensional re-formations and 3-D surface contour images is improved by the use of thinner axial CT slices and by overlapping axial CT images. Axial CT slice thickness should be no greater than 3 mm in the

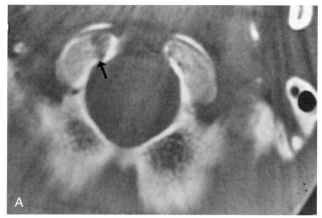

FIGURE 26–25. Computed tomography (CT) scans of occipital condyle fracture. A, Axial CT image through the occipital condyles shows a minimally displaced vertical fracture through the right occipital condyle (arrow) caused by axial loading. B, Coronal plane re-formation shows the fracture crossing vertically through the right condyle (arrow). (A, B, From Mirvis, S.E.; Young, J.W.R. In: Mirvis, S.E.; Young, J.W.R., eds. Imaging in Trauma and Critical Care. Baltimore, Williams & Wilkins, 1992, p. 291.)

cervical spine and 5 mm in the thoracic and lumbar spine and can be routinely made thinner using multislice acquisition scanners. Spiral CT scanners allow reconstruction of images at any slice thickness down to 0.5 mm and therefore generally provide higher-quality reformatted images. Use of such thin-section scans and slice overlap assists in detection of fractures that are oriented in the plane of scanning (axial) such as the type II or low odontoid fracture as well as any minimally displaced fracture.

Potential limitations of axial CT include volume averaging (accentuated by use of thick and nonoverlapping axial images that may simulate or obscure a fracture, particularly those oriented along the axial imaging plane); radiation exposure; and time constraints. Minimally displaced fractures may be difficult to identify on reformatted sagittal and coronal images because of degradation in spatial resolution inherent in these images. CT quality is also adversely affected by motion of the patient. As described earlier, multidetector spiral CT with 0.5-second tube rotation will significantly diminish these current CT limitations.

Computed Tomography with Intrathecal Contrast

CTM is multiplanar CT performed after the intrathecal introduction of nonionic water-soluble contrast medium. Depending on the patient's condition and the level of suspected cord involvement, the contrast medium can be introduced in the usual myelographic fashion or, more often, laterally at the C1-C2 level with the patient supine.[58] Because it is nonviscid, nonionic contrast medium can be introduced through a 22-gauge needle, which can then be removed, and absorbed through the meninges and subarachnoid villi. The water-soluble contrast medium diffuses through the cerebrospinal fluid; as a result, less movement of the patient is required to visualize

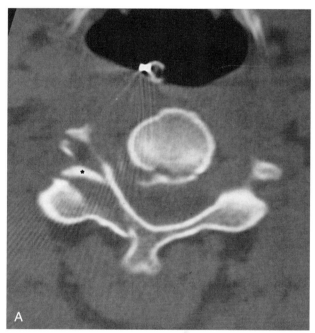

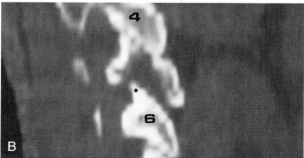

FIGURE 26–26. Computed tomography (CT) scans of unilateral facet fracture-subluxation aided by multiplanar re-formation (MPR). A, Axial CT image shows a complex fracture involving the C5 right articular mass and a posterior avulsion fracture of the C5 vertebral body cortex associated with a rotational injury. B, The two-dimensional (2-D) re-formation in the sagittal plane confirms that the superior articular process of C6 (asterisk) has fractured into and vertically split the C5 right lateral mass, accounting for the complex axial CT image. Vertical splitting fractures of the articular mass are not uncommon in unilateral facet fracture-subluxations. (A, B, From Shanmuganathan, K.; Mirvis, S.E.; Levine, A.L. AJR 163:1165, 1994.)

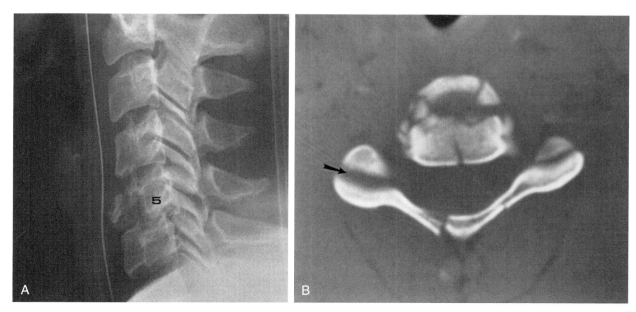

FIGURE 26–27. Computed tomography (CT) of hyperflexion teardrop fracture. *A,* Lateral cervical radiograph shows a triangular, anteriorly displaced fragment at C5 with retrolisthesis of the C5 body. Posterior elements appear intact. *B,* Axial CT image reveals that the fracture has three-column involvement, with two fractures in the laminae. A vertical splitting fracture of C5 is observed in addition to anterior compressions, and there is diastasis of the right facet articulation *(arrow).* In certain complex fracture patterns, CT is far more useful than plain radiography to elucidate the spectrum of injuries.

the clinically indicated areas of the spine.[58] Typically, the area of interest is examined fluoroscopically with spot and overhead radiography. If desired, CTM can be performed immediately after introduction of nonionic contrast medium, as current CT scanners can easily produce good-quality images despite the high density of the contrast material.[16, 23, 77, 84, 157]

CTM provides direct visualization of the spinal cord, cauda equina, and nerve roots, thereby permitting distinction between extramedullary and intramedullary cord or root injury, localization of cord compression by fracture fragments or herniated disc, or identification of root avulsion,[141] partial or complete block of cerebrospinal fluid,[92] dural tear,[104] or post-traumatic syringomyelia.[73] The presence of contrast medium in the cord itself indicates a penetrating injury, such as might be caused by a fracture fragment displaced into the canal.[31]

Many applications of CTM for the evaluation of spinal cord injury have been replaced by MRI. In the institutions in which magnetic field–compatible immobilization, support, and monitoring systems are available, MRI of the spinal cord should be performed as soon as clinically feasible in all patients with myelopathy. If MRI is not available, the traditional indications for CTM remain valid. CTM, however, remains the imaging technique of choice for demonstrating the presence and extent of dural tears, nerve root herniation, and root avulsion[31] (Fig. 26–32).

Computed Tomography with Two-Dimensional Multiplanar and Three-Dimensional Re-formation

3-D CT is the logical extension of the concept of sagittal and coronal re-formation of axial image data. In essence, 3-D CT software programs transform axial CT data into a 3-D optical illusion of the portion of the spinal skeleton being examined. The 3-D images are derived from the data of the axial CT scan.[50, 64, 148] Consequently, 3-D re-formation increases neither examination time nor radiation dose to the patient.

In more contemporary CT systems, the CT data are transferred immediately upon acquisition to independent workstations dedicated to manipulation of large image

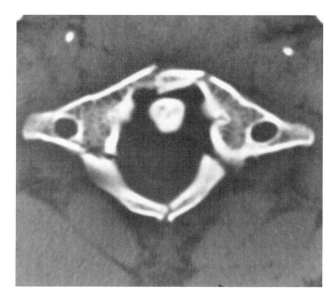

FIGURE 26–28. Computed tomographic scan of a Jefferson burst fracture. Axial image through the C1 level shows a five-part fracture of the C1 ring. Fractures are minimally displaced, making plain radiographic diagnosis more difficult.

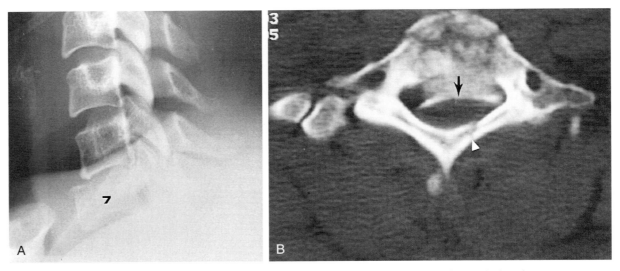

FIGURE 26–29. Imaging of vertebral burst fracture. *A,* Lateral cervical radiograph shows loss of height of the C7 body, indicating compression of the anterior and posterior cortices. *B,* The extent of the injury is better seen by CT, which shows a significant retropulsed fragment *(arrow)* and a left lamina fracture *(arrowhead).*

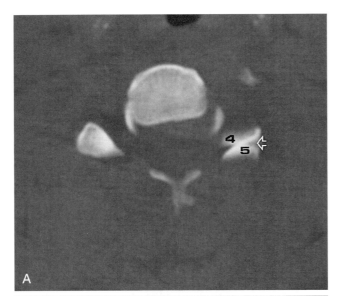

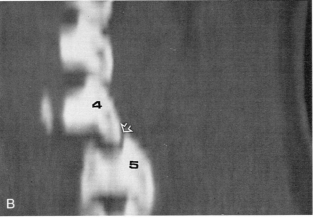

FIGURE 26–30. Computed tomography–multiplanar re-formation. *A,* The axial image shows reversal of the normal alignment of the left articular facets at C4–C5 *(arrow)* and rotation of the vertebral body. *B,* A two-dimensional re-formation of the axial images in the sagittal plane shows the inferior articular process of C4 "locked" anterior to the superior articular process of C5 *(arrow).*

data sets. Some workstations can be programmed to present "instant" preselected 3-D renderings of the spine with or without adding surrounding soft tissues. Tissues of different density are assigned different colors to enhance distinction. The 3-D volume images can then be manipulated in real time to find the preferred angle of viewing or perspective to enhance appreciation of pathology.[37] The spine can be electronically cut along any axis to view the neural canal from within or to delete anatomic structures that might obscure the skeletal pathology. The surface contour–rendered 3-D image clearly defines and reduces or eliminates ambiguity of complex fractures and fracture-dislocations (Fig. 26–33; see also Fig. 26–31).

Magnetic Resonance Imaging of the Spine

Simplistically, MRI scans are derived from the energy released by the hydrogen protons of the body. When placed in a magnetic field, these protons change their orientation and energy state because of an additional radio-frequency current introduced into the static uniform external magnetic field. Only tissues within a specific slice within the body have protons precessing at the correct frequency to absorb the radio-frequency energy. Release of this excess applied radio-frequency energy (relaxation) accompanies reorientation of hydrogen protons with the external magnetic field. A map is created of the location and energy intensity at each point in a slice that reflects the magnetic properties of the particular tissues within the slice. MR images are also influenced by the number of protons within a tissue relative to other tissues, the bulk and microscopic movement of protons, and the chemical state of some tissues such as hemoglobin. Contrast agents such as gadolinium chelates can be used to manipulate tissue relaxation properties and increase or decrease signal and therefore intensity.

The intrinsic advantages of MRI have made it the

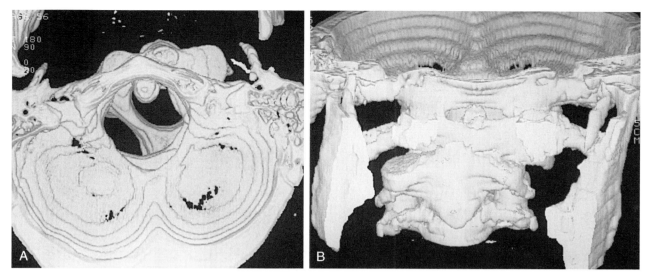

FIGURE 26–31. Three-dimensional (3-D) computed tomographic surface contour rendering of complex injury. 3-D surface contour views from above (*A*) and anterior perspective (*B*) show a complex type II odontoid fracture. The 3-D image improves appreciation of the posterior and lateral translation of the atlas and cranium relative to the C2 body and pronounced compromise of the cervical spinal canal. (*A, B,* From Mirvis, S.E.; Young, J.W.R. In: Mirvis, S.E.; Young, J.W.R., eds. Imaging in Trauma and Critical Care. Baltimore, Williams & Wilkins, 1992, p. 369.)

imaging technique of choice for the central nervous system, including the spinal cord, its meninges, and its roots.[5, 53, 81, 98, 99, 101, 102, 103, 114, 144] These advantages include

1. Direct imaging of the spine in any orientation
2. Superior contrast resolution, when compared with other techniques, in the detection of soft tissue injury, including ligaments, with greater sensitivity
3. Creation of myelography-equivalent images to assess the epidural space for evidence of hematoma, bone fragments, herniated disc material, and osteo-

phytes without use of instilled intrathecal contrast medium
4. Direct imaging of the spinal cord to detect evidence of contusion, hematoma, or laceration
5. Provision of prognostic information regarding the potential for recovery of function based on the MRI appearance of cord injuries
6. Visualization of flowing blood—which appears dark or bright, depending on the imaging sequence used—for assessment of major blood vessels, such as the vertebral arteries, without the necessity for intravascular contrast enhancement

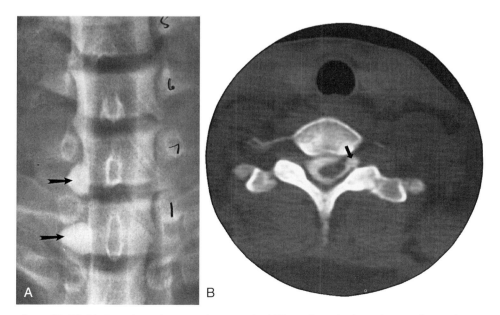

FIGURE 26–32. Myelography and computed tomography (CT)–myelography for evaluation of cervical nerve root avulsion. *A,* Anteroposterior view from the cervical myelogram reveals post-traumatic pseudomeningoceles arising from the torn nerve roots at the C7 and T1 levels (*arrows*). *B,* Axial CT scan through the C7 level after injection of contrast medium shows a small left pseudomeningocele (*arrow*).

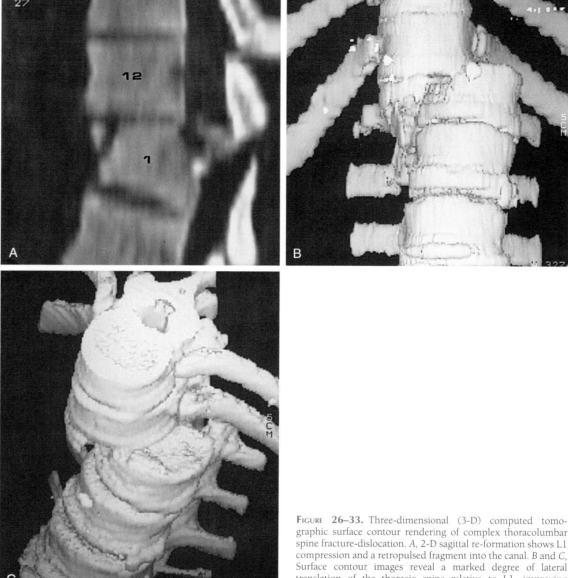

Figure 26–33. Three-dimensional (3-D) computed tomographic surface contour rendering of complex thoracolumbar spine fracture-dislocation. *A,* 2-D sagittal re-formation shows L1 compression and a retropulsed fragment into the canal. *B* and *C,* Surface contour images reveal a marked degree of lateral translation of the thoracic spine relative to L1, improving appreciation of the total injury pattern.

7. No requirement for intravenous contrast material or ionizing radiation

Several imaging sequences are routinely performed to emphasize various aspects of normal and pathologic anatomy. In general, most centers employ the following sequences:

1. Sagittal T1-weighted spin echo to define basic anatomy (Fig. 26–34)
2. Sagittal proton and T2-weighted spin echo sequence to emphasize pathologic processes and ligamentous structures (Fig. 26–35)
3. Sagittal gradient echo sequence to optimize detection of hemorrhage and distinguish osteophytes from disc material (Fig. 26–36)
4. Axial T1-weighted spin echo to assess the epidural space, spinal cord, and neural foramen through areas of interest seen on sagittal sequences (Fig. 26–37)

5. Axial gradient echo sequences to visualize gray-white matter delineation and exiting nerve roots and neural foramen (Fig. 26–38)
6. Optional MRA sequence to assess cervical arteries, depending on the type of spinal injury (Fig. 26–39)

A variety of other sequences are now also available that may improve detection of certain types of spinal pathology. The use of a particular sequence (fluid attenuation inversion recovery [FLAIR]) can improve detection of subtle spinal cord contusions compared with other standard imaging sequences (Fig. 26–40).

The limitations of MRI are few but should be mentioned. Because cortical bone contains essentially no hydrogen atoms, it is not well visualized by MRI. Bone is identified by the proton signal of blood and fat in its medullary portion. Consequently, only major osseous injuries are reliably shown by MRI, and MRI cannot be depended on to diagnose subtle bone injury, particularly that involving the posterior spinal elements.[76, 79] Comprehensive MRI examinations of the spine require more time than comparable CT studies because of the longer data acquisition. New imaging acquisition sequences can potentially make MRI as fast as or faster than CT scanning.

Hemodynamically *unstable* patients should not be studied by MRI, as acute cardiopulmonary resuscitation is not easily or safely performed in the MRI environment. The need for sophisticated physiologic monitoring and support requires MRI-compatible systems that can function reliably with the fringe magnetic field around the MRI device and that do not create radio frequency noise in the image acquisition process. The development of such systems has made the application of MRI to patients with acute spinal injury possible.[75, 93, 94, 96, 99, 136] However, patients with ferromagnetic intracranial aneurysm clips and pacemakers are excluded from the MRI environment. Some aneurysm clips undergo torque when moved through the external magnetic field, and pacemakers can malfunction.[136, 137] Also, patients with metal in close

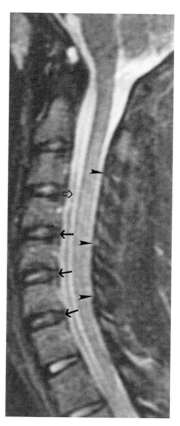

FIGURE 26–35. Magnetic resonance imaging of normal sagittal T2-weighted sequence. The sagittal T2-weighted spin echo image shows the cerebrospinal fluid (CSF) as bright, surrounding an intermediate-signal cord. The vertebral bodies are less dark than on gradient echo sequences and show less contrast with disc material. The posterior longitudinal ligament–anulus fibrosus complex (*closed arrows*) is dark between the disc and the CSF. The ligamentum flavum (*arrowheads*) appears dark, outlined anteriorly by bright CSF. The *open arrow* shows an artifact. (From Mirvis, S.E.; Ness-Aiver, M. In: Harris, J.H., Jr.; Mirvis, S.E., eds. Radiology of Acute Cervical Spine Trauma. Baltimore, Williams & Wilkins, 1995, p. 143.)

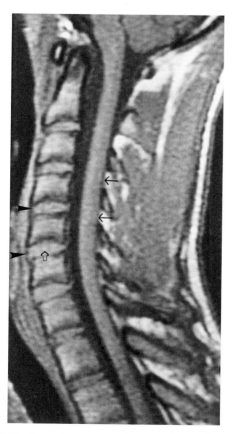

FIGURE 26–34. Magnetic resonance imaging of normal sagittal T1-weighted sequence. On T1 weighting, the cerebrospinal fluid (CSF) appears dark and the cord intermediate in signal. The anterior anulus and anterior longitudinal ligament appear as a low-signal band (*arrowheads*) outlined by brighter signals from the disc material (*open arrow*) and prevertebral fat. The ligamentum flavum appears as a dark signal outlined by brighter signal fat on the posterior aspect (*closed arrows*). The low-signal posterior anulus fibrosus and posterior longitudinal ligament are poorly seen because of the dark CSF. (From Mirvis, S.E.; Ness-Aiver, M. In: Harris, J.H., Jr.; Mirvis, S.E., eds. Radiology of Acute Cervical Spine Trauma. Baltimore, Williams & Wilkins, 1995, p. 140.)

proximity to vital soft tissue structures such as the spinal cord, nerve roots, or orbit are at increased risk for further tissue injury when positioned in the magnet, particularly when metal foreign body penetration is acute. Patients for whom a history regarding possible exposure to metal fragments cannot be obtained (e.g., welders who are unconscious) must be screened radiographically for the presence of metal foreign bodies. Finally, approximately 3% of patients are sufficiently claustrophobic to preclude their being placed inside the magnet bore.[75]

MRI is indicated in the evaluation of all patients with incomplete or progressive neurologic deficit after cervical spinal injury if permitted by the patient's overall clinical status. Patients with complete deficits should also undergo MRI assessment to demonstrate any cord-compressing lesions (e.g., herniated disc material, epidural hematoma, or bone fragments), the removal of which may allow some neurologic improvement. Other patients for whom spinal MRI is indicated include those with myelopathy or radiculopathy after spinal trauma but with radiographic or CT studies that are negative or fail to account for the deficit. Another strong indication is that the level of the

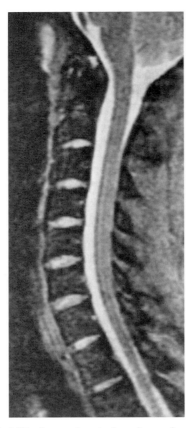

FIGURE 26–36. MRI of normal sagittal gradient echo sequence. The sagittal gradient echo sequence normally shows the vertebral bodies as relatively low in signal (because fat signal decreases). The intervertebral discs and cerebrospinal fluid (CSF) remain bright, allowing demonstration of the combined low signal of the anulus fibrosus and longitudinal ligaments. The intermediate signal intensity of the cord is easily seen, surrounded by bright CSF.

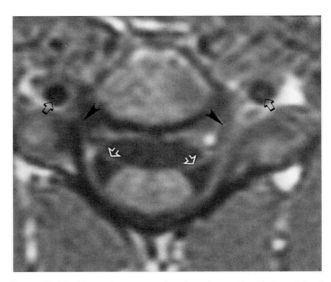

FIGURE 26–37. Magnetic resonance imaging of normal axial T1-weighted sequence. The axial T1-weighted image shows an intermediate signal cord surrounded by dark cerebrospinal fluid. The nerve roots are seen traversing the subarachnoid space (*open white arrows*) and exiting the neural foramen (*arrowheads*). The cortical bone is dark, with brighter signal marrow. The vertebral arteries (*open black arrows*) are dark in this sequence (flow void). No internal anatomy in the cord is discerned. (From Mirvis, S.E.; Ness-Aiver, M. In: Harris, J.H., Jr.; Mirvis, S.E., eds. Radiology of Acute Cervical Spine Trauma. Baltimore, Williams & Wilkins, 1995, p. 144.)

deficit does not correlate with the injury location depicted by radiography or CT.[101, 102, 107, 124]

Finally, MRI can demonstrate the level and extent of ligament disruption and intervertebral disc herniation. This information helps determine the need for and the type of internal fixation required to restore a patent spinal canal and ensure mechanical stability.[28] For thoracic injuries, MRI is useful in defining the extent of posterior

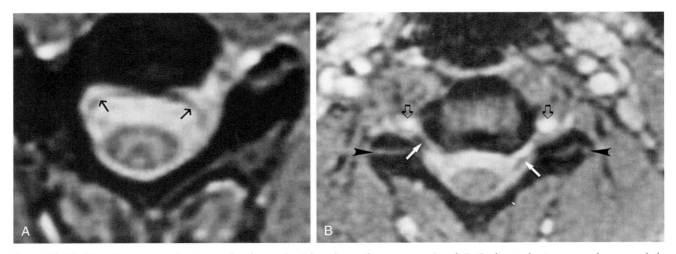

FIGURE 26–38. Magnetic resonance imaging study of normal axial gradient echo sequence. *A* and *B*, Gradient echo images produce very dark bone and bright cerebrospinal fluid (CSF). The dura is outlined by CSF (*arrows in A*). Internal architecture of the cord, with brighter central gray and darker white matter tracts, can be observed (*A*). Vertebral arteries appear bright on this sequence (*open arrows in B*). Nerve roots can be seen within the neural foramen surrounded by high-signal CSF (*white arrows in B*). Facet articular spaces contain high-signal fluid (*arrowheads in B*). (*A, B,* From Mirvis, S.E.; Ness-Aiver, M. In: Harris, J.H., Jr.; Mirvis, S.E., eds. Radiology of Acute Cervical Spine Trauma. Baltimore, Williams & Wilkins, 1995, p. 145.)

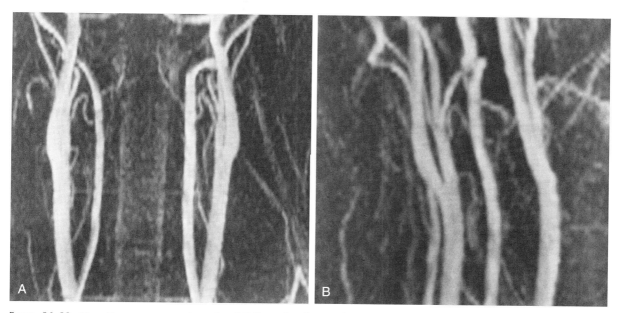

FIGURE 26–39. Magnetic resonance angiography (MRA) study of normal time-of-flight cervical vessels. MRA study demonstrates anteroposterior (AP) (*A*) and oblique (*B*) views of the cervical vasculature. All vessels appear bright on the gradient echo sequence used to acquire images. The venous flow signal is selectively negated. Note the bright signal from moving cerebrospinal fluid in the AP projection. (*A, B,* From Mirvis, S.E.; Ness-Aiver, M. In: Harris, J.H., Jr.; Mirvis, S.E., eds. Radiology of Acute Cervical Spine Trauma. Baltimore, Williams & Wilkins, 1995, p. 146.)

FIGURE 26–40. Increased sensitivity for cord edema with inversion recovery sequence. *A,* Lateral T2-weighted spin echo sequence shows mild spinal stenosis of C4-5 but no cord lesion. *B,* Inversion recovery sequence shows central cord signal increase from C2-3 to mid C6 compatible with neurologic deficit (*arrows*).

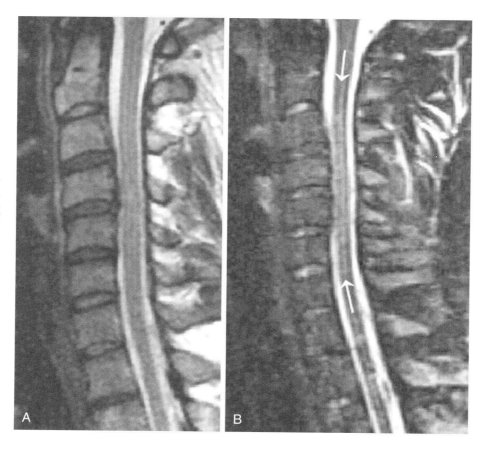

ligament injury, which increases instability when associated with anterior column fractures. MRI is particularly helpful in determining the extent of ligament injury and instability that typically accompany injuries occurring in the fused spine, such as ankylosing spondylitis and diffuse idiopathic skeletal hyperostosis.

MAGNETIC RESONANCE IMAGING OF SPECIFIC ACUTE SPINE INJURY

Parenchymal Lesions

MRI is unique in its ability to detect acute injury to the spinal cord, including edema, hemorrhage, and laceration. Cord edema appears isointense or slightly hypointense in relation to the normal cord on T1-weighted spin echo images but becomes brighter in signal than the normal cord on T2-weighted image sequences (Fig. 26–41). When hemorrhage is present within the cord, its MRI appearance depends on a complex relationship between the chemical state of the blood, the field strength of the magnet, and the imaging sequence used.[14] In the acute to subacute period after injury (1 to 7 days), blood generally appears dark (low-intensity signal) on T2-weighted sequences, whereas edema has a bright signal (Fig. 26–42). After about 7 days, as red cells are lysed, blood acquires a high-intensity signal in both T1- and T2-weighted studies.

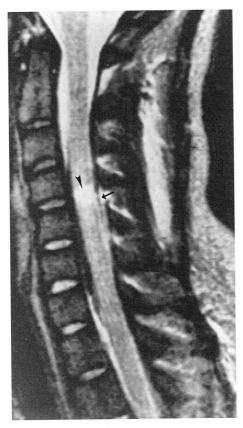

FIGURE 26–41. Magnetic resonance imaging scan of cord edema. Sagittal T2-weighted spin echo study shows area of increased signal in the spinal cord at the C4–C5 level representing focal cord edema (*arrowhead*). There is disruption of the adjacent low-signal ligamentum flavum, indicating disruption from hyperflexion (*arrow*).

Kulkarni and colleagues[81] were the first to describe a relation between the characteristics of the MRI cord signal and the patient's outcome, suggesting that MRI cord signal characteristics reflect the type of cord histopathology— that is, hemorrhage (type 1), edema (type 2), and mixed edema and hemorrhage (type 3). The prognostic information provided by MRI regarding potential recovery of function has been verified by several other studies.[19, 41, 90, 98, 129, 144] The ability of the MRI signals to identify the histopathology of acute cord injury has been confirmed by direct comparison of the MRI signal with histologic findings in experimentally induced spinal cord injuries.[19, 120, 153]

Ligament Injury

Ligament injury sustained in acute spinal trauma is inferred from the mechanism of injury, the ultimate fracture pattern, and the alignment of the spine after injury. However, even significant ligament injury leading to spinal mechanical instability, particularly hyperflexion and hyperextension sprains without concurrent fractures, may not be apparent when the spine is studied radiographically in the neutral position. Furthermore, the spinal alignment demonstrated by plain radiographs may serve to reveal the site of major or principal mechanical instability but may not demonstrate all major ligament injuries and other potential sites of immediate or delayed instability.

MRI depicts normal ligaments as regions of low signal intensity because of lack of mobile hydrogen. Disruption of the ligament is seen on MRI scans as an abrupt interruption of the low signal, ligament attenuation or stretching of the ligament, or association of a torn ligament with an attached avulsed bone fragment (Figs. 26–43 to 26–45; see also Fig. 26–41). Determination of the status of the major support ligaments of the spine as revealed by MRI has a definite bearing on management approaches.[17, 18, 32, 78, 138] MRI can demonstrate unsuspected ligament injury or injury that is greater than anticipated from the results of other available imaging modalities.[151]

Intervertebral Disc Herniation

Acute intervertebral disc herniation may accompany fractures or dislocations or may occur as an isolated lesion. If the disc impinges on the spinal cord or roots, a neurologic injury may result. MRI demonstration of a single-level acute intervertebral disc herniation that impinges on the spinal cord is crucial in surgical management of spinal trauma to optimize neurologic recovery. MRI clearly depicts disc material herniation with essentially all imaging sequences (Fig. 26–46) but best separates disc material from posterior osteophyte with the gradient echo sequence, on which relatively bright disc material is visualized against a dark background of bone.

The advantage of MRI over CTM in detecting acute traumatic disc herniation was shown clearly by Flanders and associates.[41] In their study, 40% of acute disc herniations producing neurologic deficits were demonstrated by MRI but not by CTM. Rizzolo and colleagues[124] found a 42% incidence of herniated nucleus pulposus in 53 patients studied by MRI at 1.5 T within 72 hours of injury. The highest incidence occurred among patients

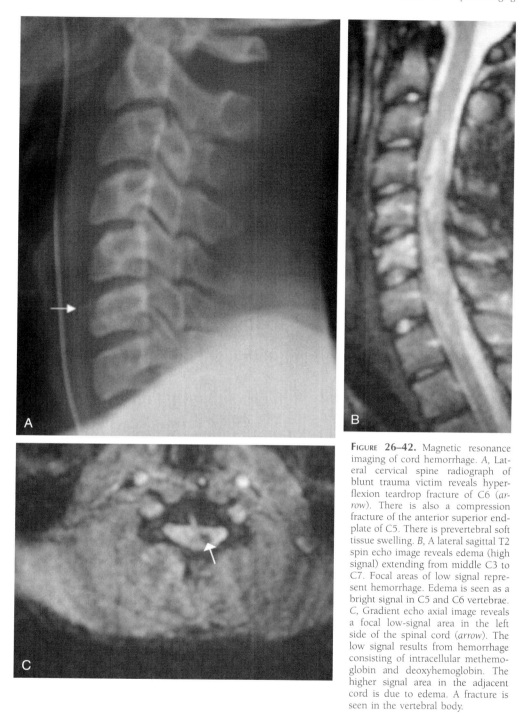

FIGURE 26–42. Magnetic resonance imaging of cord hemorrhage. *A*, Lateral cervical spine radiograph of blunt trauma victim reveals hyperflexion teardrop fracture of C6 (*arrow*). There is also a compression fracture of the anterior superior endplate of C5. There is prevertebral soft tissue swelling. *B*, A lateral sagittal T2 spin echo image reveals edema (high signal) extending from middle C3 to C7. Focal areas of low signal represent hemorrhage. Edema is seen as a bright signal in C5 and C6 vertebrae. *C*, Gradient echo axial image reveals a focal low-signal area in the left side of the spinal cord (*arrow*). The low signal results from hemorrhage consisting of intracellular methemoglobin and deoxyhemoglobin. The higher signal area in the adjacent cord is due to edema. A fracture is seen in the vertebral body.

with bilateral facet dislocations (80%) and anterior cord syndromes (100%). Doran and co-workers[34] described a high incidence of traumatic disc herniation among patients with both unilateral and bilateral facet dislocations. Patients with traumatically herniated intervertebral discs may sustain a neurologic deterioration when the cervical spine is reduced, as the disc may then compress neural tissue.[11, 34, 53, 118] However, this point is controversial, as others find no evidence of neurologic deterioration when closed reduction is performed for patients with disc herniation or disruption.[50]

Epidural Hematoma

Epidural hematomas (EDHs) are an uncommon sequela of spinal trauma and occur in 1% to 2% of cervical spine injuries.[44] The cervical spine is the most common location of EDHs of traumatic origin.[44] EDH most commonly occurs in the dorsal epidural space as a result of close adherence of the ventral dura to the posterior longitudinal ligament.[44] Bleeding most likely arises from sudden increases in pressure in the rich epidural venous plexus, which comprises valveless veins.[44, 109] EDHs may develop acutely after trauma, in a delayed fashion, or after open or closed spinal column reduction. Up to 50% of post-traumatic EDHs may occur among patients without overt cervical spine injuries.[44] For this reason, the presence of myelopathy without an injury demonstrated by radiography or CT without intrathecal contrast should suggest an EDH. Garza-Mercado[44] described an increased likelihood of cervical spine EDH in younger trauma victims owing to increased elasticity of the vertebral column and among patients with fused cervical spines, including those with ankylosing spondylitis and diffuse idiopathic skeletal hyperostosis. The development of progressive, unexplained neurologic deterioration among patients sustaining spinal trauma may herald the onset of cord compression by an expanding EDH.

Again, the MRI appearance of EDH depends on the age of the blood, magnetic field strength, and imaging sequence used. In the acute phase of trauma (1 to 3 days after injury), blood appears isointense (bright) relative to the spinal cord on the T1-weighted sequence (Fig. 26–47) and hypointense (dark) relative to the spinal cord on T2-weighted sequences. At 3 to 7 days after injury, the central portion of the hematoma, which contains intact red blood cells, has low signal intensity on T2-weighted sequences, whereas the periphery, composed of lysed red blood cells, shows increased signal strength on both T1- and T2-weighted sequences.[14]

Congenital or Acquired Spinal Stenosis

Spinal cord injury may be caused by impaction of posteriorly projecting osteophytes or hypertrophied, calcified, or ossified ligaments on the anterior surface of the cord during traumatic deformation of the cervical spine. Posterior spinal cord injury can result from buckling of hypertrophied ligamentum flavum during hyperextension.[122] Patients with congenital spinal stenosis or spinal stenosis acquired from degenerative changes (spondylosis) have an increased likelihood of injury from cervical spine

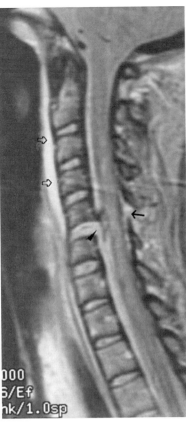

FIGURE 26–44. Magnetic resonance imaging study of ligament injury. Sagittal T2-weighted spin echo scan in a quadriplegic trauma patient reveals interruption of the posterior longitudinal ligament and posterior anulus (arrowhead) and the ligamentum flavum (arrow). Prevertebral edema (open arrows) is observed. The anterior longitudinal ligament appears intact, indicating hyperflexion subluxation mechanism. (From Mirvis, S.E.; Ness-Aiver, M. In: Harris, J.H., Jr.; Mirvis, S.E., eds. Radiology of Acute Cervical Spine Trauma. Baltimore, Williams & Wilkins, 1995, p. 151.)

trauma or even physiologic cervical spine motion. The occurrence of post-traumatic myelopathy without radiologic evidence of acute injury among older patients with posterior spinal osteophytes, ossification of the posterior longitudinal ligament, or congenital spine stenosis suggests that these conditions are etiologic.[80, 145] Cervical spinal cord impaction by posterior cervical osteophytes typically produces a central cord syndrome.[20]

MRI in the sagittal and axial orientation depicts spinal canal compromise produced by degenerative processes (Fig. 26–48). Comparison of T2-weighted spin echo and T2-weighted gradient echo sequences can be helpful in differentiating acutely herniated soft disc material from osteophytes surrounding chronic disc herniations. Both sequences produce a myelographic appearance that demonstrates the relationship of osteophytes and intervertebral discs to the spinal cord. However, gradient echo sequences produce very dark-appearing osteophytes and increased contrast with brighter signal disc material compared with these features on T2-weighted spin echo sequences. MRI is crucial in planning the extent of posterior surgical decompression by showing the points at which the thecal sac and direct spinal cord compression occur. It should be

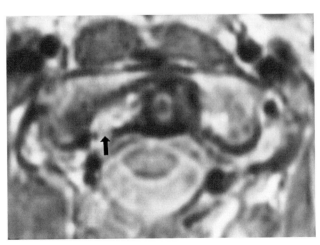

FIGURE 26–43. Magnetic resonance imaging of ligament tear. Axial T2-weighted image through the C2 level in a trauma patient shows interruption of the transverse atlantal ligament (arrow) and displacement of the odontoid process to the left. (From Mirvis, S.E.; Ness-Aiver, M. In: Harris, J.H., Jr.; Mirvis, S.E., eds. Radiology of Acute Cervical Spine Trauma. Baltimore, Williams & Wilkins, 1995, p. 156.)

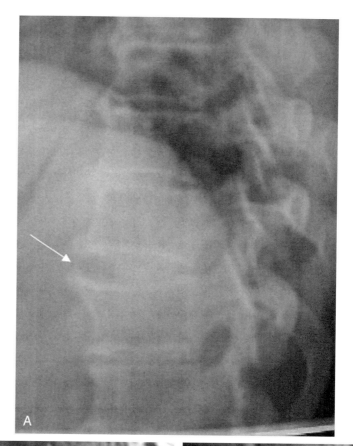

FIGURE 26–45. Magnetic resonance imaging of ligament disruption. *A,* Lateral lower thoracic spine radiograph shows widening anteriorly in the disc space between two thoracic vertebrae *(arrow). B* and *C,* Sagittal T2-weighted spin echo sequence shows minimal bright hemorrhage just above the disc material and complete interruption of the dark (low-signal) anterior anulus fibrosus fibers and longitudinal ligament *(arrow).*

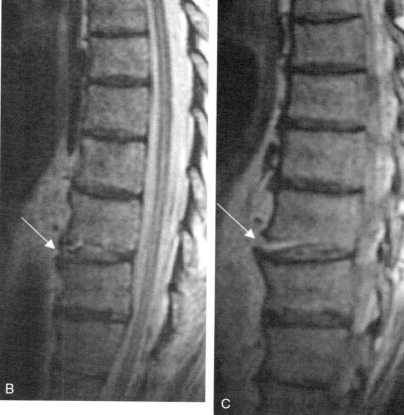

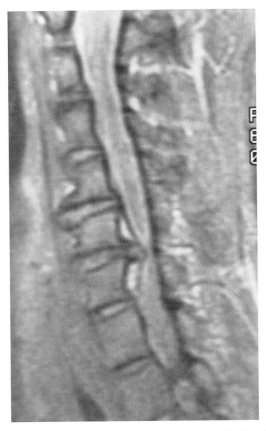

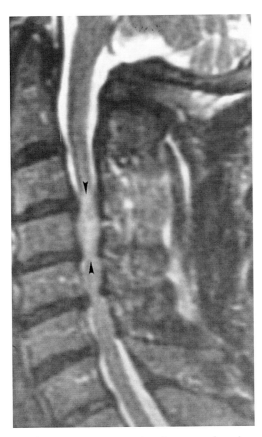

Figure 26–46. Magnetic resonance imaging study of disc herniation. Off-midline sagittal proton density scan shows chronic disc herniation at the C6–C7 level indenting the spinal cord. The presence of low-signal osteophytes around the disc suggests chronicity, possibly with acute exacerbation after trauma.

Figure 26–48. Magnetic resonance imaging scan of cord contusion secondary to spinal stenosis. The sagittal T2-weighted spin echo image in a trauma patient with central cord syndrome shows marked narrowing of the spinal canal at the bottom of C3 to C5–C6 because of bulging discs and hypertrophic ligamentum flavum. A cord contusion at C3 and C4 is evident as increased signal from edema (*arrowheads*).

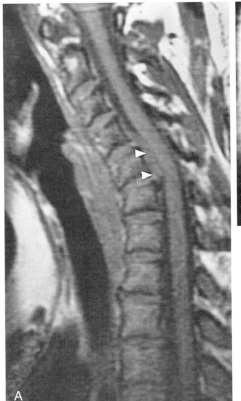

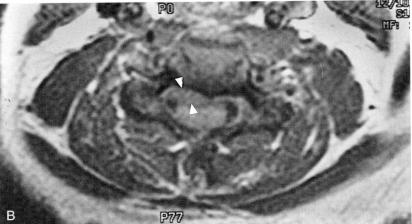

Figure 26–47. Magnetic resonance imaging (MRI) study of epidural hematoma (acute). Lateral (*A*) and axial (*B*) T1-weighted MRI scans of a patient with cervical flexion injury shows an epidural hematoma (*arrowheads*) isointense with the spinal cord, displacing the cord posteriorly. There is C5 on C6 anterior subluxation. (*A, B*, From Mirvis, S.E.; Ness-Aiver, M. In: Harris, J.H., Jr.; Mirvis, S.E., eds. Radiology of Acute Cervical Spine Trauma. Baltimore, Williams & Wilkins, 1995, p. 160.)

noted that the gradient echo pulse sequence tends to make bone appear larger than in actuality (blooming), and this may accentuate the apparent degree of spinal canal encroachment.

MAGNETIC RESONANCE IMAGING OF CHRONIC AND POSTOPERATIVE SPINAL INJURIES

It has been well documented that MRI is superior to myelography, CT, and CTM in evaluation of chronic injuries of the spinal cord, particularly for the differentiation of myelomalacia and post-traumatic spinal cord cyst.[113, 121, 143] Myelomalacia typically appears as a focal low-signal area on T1-weighted sequences and as a high-signal area on T2-weighted sequences in a cord of normal or decreased caliber[18] (Fig. 26–49). Syringomyelia has a similar appearance but is more sharply delineated and typically occurs in an expanded cord. Flow-sensitive imaging sequences may help to demonstrate a syrinx by demonstrating cerebrospinal fluid movement within the cavity.[18] Postoperative MRI studies of patients with internal fixation devices are improved when titanium fixation devices are used.[100] These produce far less magnetic susceptibility artifact than stainless steel fixation

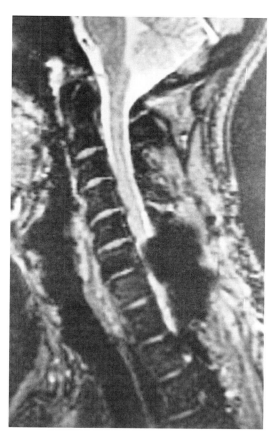

FIGURE 26–50. Magnetic resonance imaging (MRI) study of stainless steel wire internal fixation. Sagittal gradient echo MRI scan after stainless steel wire posterior fixation shows marked artifact surrounding the wire, obscuring the spinal canal and cord. The increased artifact is due to both the increased magnetic susceptibility of steel wire and the gradient echo sequence, which is significantly affected by magnetic susceptibility artifact.

devices and permit visualization of the cord and surrounding epidural space without artifact[36, 100] (Figs. 26–50 and 26–51).

Magnetic Resonance Angiography

MRA is used as a screening assessment of the vertebral arteries. The exact incidence of vertebral artery injury occurring after cervical spine fracture-dislocation is unknown, but the injury is being reported with increasing frequency.* Vertebral artery injuries from cervical spine trauma generally involve the second portion of the artery extending from C6 to C2. Fixation of the artery within the confines of the transverse foramina predisposes this vessel to injury from cervical dislocations. Although a variety of cervical spine injuries have been associated with vertebral artery injury, unilateral and bilateral dislocations are most commonly implicated.[112, 130] Vertebral artery injury can occur from fractures extending across the foramen transversarium and has been reported with lateral cervical dislocations.[112, 149, 154]

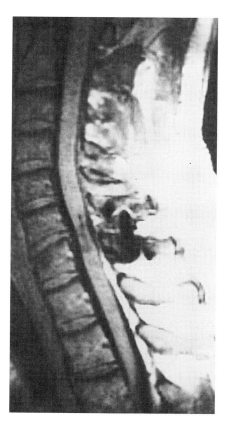

FIGURE 26–49. Magnetic resonance imaging study of chronic spinal cord injury. Sagittal T1-weighted sequence in a patient obtained several months after hyperflexion injury (note loss of C7 anterior height) shows irregular low signal in the cord and focal cord atrophy at C6–C7, representing myelomalacia. Posterior titanium wire fixation produces minimal artifact. (From Mirvis, S.E.; Young, J.W.R. In: Mirvis, S.E.; Young, J.W.R., eds. Imaging in Trauma and Critical Care. Baltimore, Williams & Wilkins, 1992, p. 367.)

*See references 29, 30, 43, 46, 70, 86, 112, 123, 130, 149, 154, 156.

MRA screening of the vertebral arteries should be considered for all patients with blunt cervical spine trauma with significant degrees (>1 cm) of dislocation or subluxation or fracture of the foramen transversarium or with neurologic deficits consistent with vertebral vessel insufficiency.[46, 149, 154, 156] Routine assessment of the cervical spine by MRI should include axial T1-weighted images. On these sequences, flowing blood creates a signal void (dark image). Conversely, on gradient echo sequences, flowing blood creates a bright image. Inspection of the major cervical arteries for the anticipated signal characteristics should be performed as part of overall assessment of the MRI study. Absence or irregularity of the expected flow signal should raise a question of vascular injury (Fig. 26–52). Injuries identifiable by MRA include intimal flaps, intramural dissection or hematoma, pseudoaneurysm, and thrombosis. Care must be taken to distinguish injury from vessel hypoplasia or atherosclerotic disease. Positive MRA findings of vessel injury are confirmed and better characterized by direct contrast angiography, which offers spatial resolution greater than that possible with MRA.

Penetrating injury accounts for the majority of cervical vertebral injuries resulting from trauma. The presence of retained metal fragments from ballistic injury precludes vascular MRA assessment because of artifacts created by close proximity of metal. In addition, because MRA is less sensitive for detection of subtle intimal injuries or mural hematoma, conventional arteriography is in general recommended for evaluation of suspected vertebral artery injury caused by penetrating force. Although the incidence of vertebral artery injury from blunt trauma to the cervical spine appears to be higher than previously suspected, the injury usually results in complete thrombosis without producing a neurologic deterioration.[30, 46, 154, 156] It also appears that thrombosed vessels remain occluded on long-term follow-up without the need to perform endovascular occlusion. Vertebral arteries that are injured but patent can lead to formation of clot and embolization with infarction. These injuries, when identified, require treatment to prevent or minimize the chance of embolization using antiplatelet or anticoagulant treatment as permitted by the patient's condition or open surgical or endovascular treatment.

Catheter Angiography

Conventional angiography is used to detect or confirm vertebral artery injury resulting from cervical spine trauma. Although associated with higher procedure-related morbidity than MRA, the technique offers greater spatial resolution for detection and characterization of vascular injuries (Fig. 26–53). As stated earlier, conventional angiography is the current study of choice for assessment of potential vertebral artery injury resulting from penetrating injury to the cervical spine. In addition, angiography can provide the potential for intravascular thrombolysis and endovascular stent treatment of selected vertebral injuries.[119]

Radionuclide Bone Imaging

Radionuclide bone imaging (RNBI) has been used in the assessment of trauma to the spine primarily to determine whether a radiographic abnormality represents an acute process that is potentially responsible for the patient's pain or to exclude an osseous abnormality as a source of spine pain when radiographs are normal. In the cervical spine, image resolution is improved by placing the patient's neck directly on the collimator surface, decreasing distance from the nuclide activity. Slightly posterior oblique images of the cervical spine can also assist diagnostically.

Reports[91, 140] and anecdotal experience indicate that an acute, nondisplaced cervical fracture cannot be entirely excluded even when the initial RNBI scan is normal. RNBI was assessed in patients with whiplash,[6, 66] and no correlation was found between symptoms and signs of injury and scintigraphic findings. However, one retrospective study of 35 cases[6] found that a negative bone scan excluded a skeletal injury, and in another prospective study of 20 patients[66] with whiplash injuries, no patients had bone scan findings suggestive of fracture and none had a subsequent diagnosis of fracture. Increased activity within the cervical spine on delayed bone imaging includes a differential diagnosis of nonspecific stress response, degenerative arthritis, or healing fracture. Use of single photon emission computed tomography may increase diagnostic accuracy in bone imaging of acute spine trauma.

RNBI in the thoracic and lumbar spine is technically

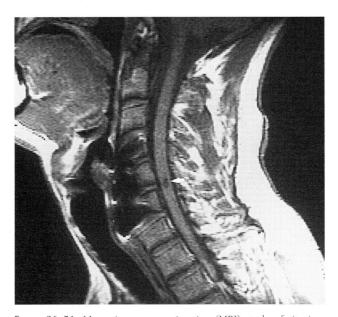

FIGURE 26–51. Magnetic resonance imaging (MRI) study of titanium implant internal fixation. Sagittal T2-weighted MRI scan shows a titanium fixation plate at C4–C6 used to fix a hyperflexion teardrop fracture at C5, producing local magnetic field inhomogeneity and signal dropout. However, the spinal canal and cord are still well seen, with a focal area of post-traumatic cyst formation or myelomalacia visible at the C5 level. There is minimal retrolisthesis of C5.

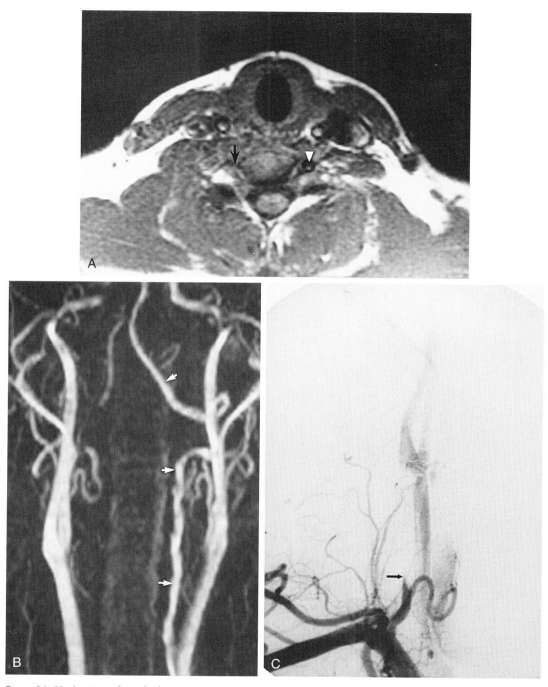

FIGURE 26–52. Imaging of vertebral artery injury. *A,* Axial T1-weighted magnetic resonance imaging scan reveals a lack of expected flow void in the right vertebral artery foramen *(arrow),* whereas left vertebral flow void is observed *(arrowhead). B,* Magnetic resonance angiography scan in anteroposterior view shows absence of the right vertebral artery signal, but the left signal is present *(arrows). C,* Right subclavian angiogram reveals thrombosis *(arrow)* of the vertebral artery that resulted from unilateral facet dislocation. (*A–C,* From Mirvis, S.E.; Ness-Aiver, M. In: Harris, J.H., Jr.; Mirvis, S.E., eds. Radiology of Acute Cervical Spine Trauma. Baltimore, Williams & Wilkins, 1995, p. 175.)

easier than in the cervical spine. Acute fractures can be detected on both blood pool and delayed images (Fig. 26–54). Increased linear activity at the superior end-plate is characteristic of traumatic fracture. RNBI may be particularly helpful in detecting acute compression fractures in patients with severe osteoporosis that may be quite subtle radiographically. Increased lateral activity on the concave side of a scoliotic spine that is not sharply marginated most likely represents stress-related or degenerative change. In patients with nonlocalized lower back pain after trauma and normal lumbar radiographs, large-field-of-view RNBI can screen for small laminar, transverse process or articular process fractures that might otherwise require multilevel CT scanning to detect.

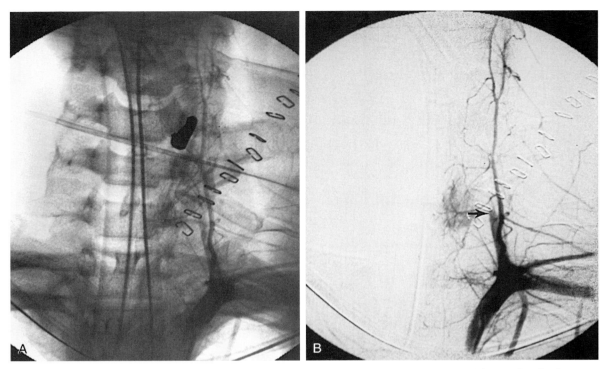

FIGURE 26–53. Angiography of vertebral injury. *A*, Anteroposterior view of the cervical spine obtained from a digital subtraction angiogram shows a deformed bullet overlying the cervical spine at the left C5–C6 articular masses. *B*, Image from a selective left vertebral angiogram shows a thrombosed *(arrow)* left vertebral artery below the level of the bullet (the bullet's density has been subtracted from the image).

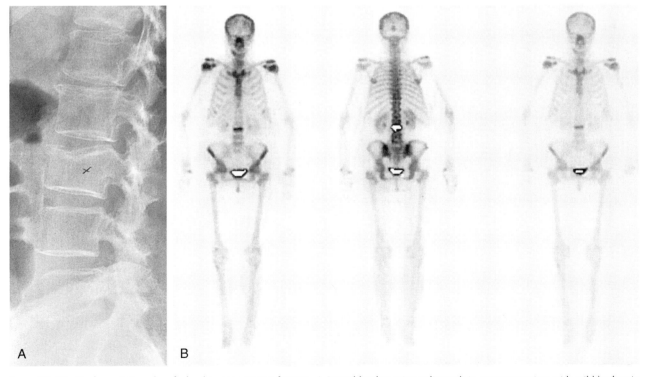

FIGURE 26–54. Nuclear scintigraphy of a lumbar compression fracture. *A*, Lateral lumbar spine radiograph in a trauma patient with mild back pain shows possible L3 compression fracture (X) versus Schmorl's node deforming the superior end-plate. *B*, Static images from bone scintigraphy show end-plate increased tracer activity, indicating acute fracture.

IMAGING SPINAL TRAUMA IN PREEXISTING PATHOLOGIC CONDITIONS

Trauma patients with various conditions that lead to fusion of the spine are at increased risk for spinal injury compared with patients with normal spine mobility. Patients with ankylosing spondylitis can sustain spinal injury from minimal amounts of blunt force impact.[108] Because the spine has undergone bony ankylosis, it is very fragile and fractures equally easily across the bone or disc spaces (Figs. 26–55 and 26–56). Usually, these injuries completely traverse all supporting ossified spinal ligaments, creating marked instability. In my experience, these injuries are typically evident in extension or extension-dislocation patterns. It has been noted that spinal fractures in patients with underlying ankylosing spondylitis are not uncommonly occult radiographically.[39] Fractures and dislocations most typically occur in the lower cervical followed by the thoracic spine. This finding may be due to spontaneous reduction of the fracture, generalized osteoporosis that often occurs in patients with advanced disease, and failure to appreciate second, noncontiguous injuries.[39]

Although patients with ankylosing spondylitis may present with well-established neurologic deficits and obvious imaging abnormalities, about one third have a delayed onset of neurologic deficits as a result of failure to diagnose or properly immobilize the very unstable spine. In general, patients presenting with blunt trauma who have ankylosing spondylitis should be regarded as having unstable injuries until definitely proved otherwise. If radiographs appear normal, further evaluation by thin-section CT is recommended to detect subtle fractures. CT may also assist in differentiating acute fractures from pseudarthrosis related to previous injury.[47] If the patient has cervical pain, further assessment by MRI to detect subtle soft tissue edema or bone marrow edema is also indicated to avoid misdiagnosing a highly unstable injury.

Other preexisting conditions that may be associated with an increased risk of spinal fracture with lower energy blunt trauma include diffuse idiopathic skeletal hyperostosis (DISH) or Forestier's disease, also called ankylosing hyperostosis, spinal spondylosis, and osteoporosis. DISH is similar to ankylosing spondylitis in the sense that the spine contains a segment of bone fusion. DISH may be differentiated from ankylosing spondylitis by the absence of squared vertebral body corners; the larger, coarser, and predominantly anterior syndesmophytes of DISH; and lack of sacroiliac and apophyseal changes that occur in ankylosing spondylitis. Fractures in DISH may occur through the midportion of a fused segment or at the top or bottom through a disc space or odontoid process.[111] The long lever arm created by the fused segment focuses all the energy of the applied force onto a single disc space, increasing the risk of injury. Similarly, spines that are fused because of multiple contiguous levels of degenerative spondylosis are also at increased risk for injury because of inability to distribute straining forces across multiple spinal levels.

Patients with severe osteoporosis are at increased risk for fracture resulting from minor injury or activities of daily living. In the spine, such injuries may appear as minor loss of height of a vertebral body. The age of the injury may not be apparent, and it may be assumed in some cases to be a remote lesion. Compression fractures in patients with structural bone weakness can progress to significant compression with physiologic loading and produce acute or delayed onset of radicular or complete neurologic deficits. The lack of density of demineralized bone associated with suboptimal film technique renders radiographic interpretation of the spine difficult and insensitive to detection of subtle fractures.

If the patient has persistent spinal pain, examination by thin-section CT is recommended initially, as it often demonstrates subtle end-plate fractures and paraspinal hematoma not detected by radiography. If clinical symptoms remain unexplained or CT is not definitive, MRI is suggested. MRI shows paraspinal edema, hematoma, and bone edema with high sensitivity, improving the level of confidence in injury detection or exclusion. Nuclear bone scintigraphy can also play a role in diagnosing fractures in this setting. However, acute fractures may not have abnormal bone turnover activity in the acute phase,

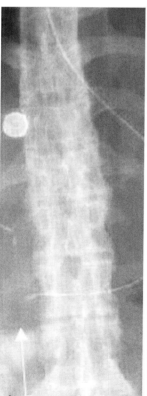
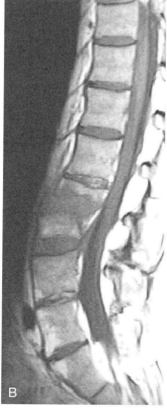

FIGURE 26–55. Hyperextension injury with ankylosing spondylitis. *A,* Anterior thoracolumbar radiograph shows apparent increase in height of L3 compared with superior lumbar levels (*2-headed arrow*). *B,* Sagittal T1-weighted magnetic resonance image shows fracture across mid-L3 body with posterior displacement and angulation of the superior fragment. The anterior and posterior longitudinal ligaments appear striped away from the adjacent vertebral bodies. Low-signal edema replaces high-signal fat in bone marrow.

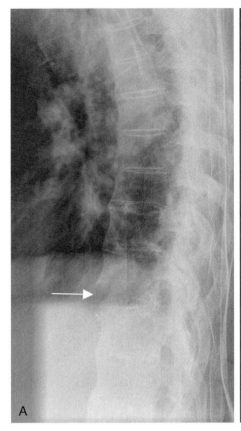

Figure 26-56. Hyperextension injury with ankylosing spondylitis. *A,* Lateral thoracic spine radiograph in blunt trauma patient with ankylosing spondylitis shows widened disc space anteriorly at the T11–T12 (*arrow*) level representing hyperextension injury. *B,* Proton density sagittal image through the injury site indicates that the fracture crosses obliquely through the T11 vertebral body rather than through the disc space. There is focal spinal cord compression in part caused by posterior bony encroachment and cord edema.

particularly in elderly people. Also, foci of increased nuclide deposition in the spine may be due to chronic abnormalities such as seen with spondylosis or subacute injuries as well as acute pathology, making this examination less useful. In general, very careful attention to imaging for these subsets of patients combined with a low threshold to perform additional diagnostic studies in symptomatic patients is warranted.

REFERENCES

1. Acheson, M.B.; Livingston, R.R.; Richardson, M.L.; et al. High-resolution CT scanning in the evaluation of cervical spine fractures. AJR 148:1179, 1987.
2. Anderson, L.D.; D'Alonzo, T.R. Fractures of the odontoid process of the axis. J Bone Joint Surg Am 56:1663, 1974.
3. Angtuaco, E.J.C; Binet, E.F. Radiology of thoracic and lumbar fractures. Clin Orthop 189:43, 1984.
4. Ballock, R.T.; MacKersie, R.; Abitbol, J.; et al. Can burst fractures be predicted from plain radiographs? J Bone Joint Surg Br 74:147, 1992.
5. Banna, M. Clinical Radiology of the Spine and the Spinal Canal. Rockville, MD, Aspen Systems Corporation, 1985, p. 411.
6. Barton, D.; Allen, M.; Findlay, D.; et al. Evaluation of whiplash injuries by technetium 99m isotope scanning. Arch Emerg Med 10:197, 1993.
7. Bauer, R.D.; Errico, T.J.; Waugh, T.R.; Cohen, W. Evaluation and diagnosis of cervical spine injuries: A review of the literature. Cent Nerv Syst Trauma 4:71, 1987.
8. Benzel, E.C.; Hart, B.L.; Ball, P.A.; et al. Fractures of the C2 vertebral body. J Neurosurg 81:206, 1994.
9. Benzel, E.C.; Hart, B.L.; Ball, P.A.; et al. Magnetic resonance imaging for the evaluation of patients with occult cervical spine injury. J Neurosurg 85:824, 1996.
10. Berne, J.D.; Velmahos, G.C.; El-Tawil, Q.; et al. Value of complete cervical helical computed tomographic scanning in the unevaluable blunt patient with multiple injuries: A prospective study. J Trauma 47(5):896, 1999.
11. Berrington, N.R.; Van Staden, J.F.; Willers, J.G.; et al. Cervical intervertebral disc prolapse associated with traumatic facet dislocation. Surg Neurol 40:395, 1993.
12. Bettinger, B.I.; Eisenberg, R.L. Improved swimmers lateral projection of the cervicothoracic region. AJR 164:1303, 1995.
13. Blackmore, C.C.; Ramsey, S.D.; Mann, F.A.; Deyo, R.A. Cervical spine screening with CT in trauma patients: A cost-effectiveness analysis. Radiology 212;117, 1999.
14. Bradley, W.G. MR appearance of hemorrhage in the brain. Radiology 189:15, 1993.
15. Brady, W.J.; Moghtader, J.; Cutcher, D.; et al. ED use of flexion-extension cervical spine radiography in the evaluation of blunt trauma. Am J Emerg Med 17:504, 1999.
16. Brant-Zawadzki, M.; Miller, E.M.; Federle, M.P. CT in the evaluation of spine trauma. AJR 136(2):369, 1981.
17. Brightman, R.P.; Miller, C.A.; Rea, G.L.; et al. Magnetic resonance imaging of trauma to the thoracic and lumbar spine: The importance of the posterior longitudinal ligament. Spine 17:541, 1992.
18. Castillo, M.; Harris, J.H., Jr. MRI of the spine: Recent applications. Mediguide Orthop 10(6):1, 1991.
19. Chakeres, D.W.; Flicking, F.; Bresnahan, J.C.; et al. MR imaging of acute spinal cord trauma. AJNR 8:5, 1987.
20. Chang, C.Y.; Wolf, A.L.; Mirvis, S.E.; et al. Body surfing accident resulting in cervical spine injuries. Spine 17:257, 1992.
21. Christensen, P.C. The radiologic study of the normal spine. Radiol Clin North Am 15:133, 1977.

22. Clayman, D.A.; Sykes, C.H.; Vines, F.S. Occipital condyle fractures: Clinical presentation and radiologic detection. AJNR 15:1309, 1994.

23. Cooper, P.R.; Cohen, W. Evaluation of cervical spinal cord injuries with metrizamide myelography–CT scanning. J Neurosurg 61:281, 1984.

24. Daffner, R.H. Cervical radiography for trauma patients: A time-effective technique? AJR 175:1309, 2000.

25. 25 Dai, L; Jia, L. Central cord injury complicating acute cervical disc herniation in trauma. Spine 25:331, 2000.

26. D'Alise, M.D.; Benzel, E.C.; Hart, B.L. Magnetic resonance imaging evaluation of the cervical spine in the comatose or obtunded patient. J Neurosurg 91:54, 1999.

27. Davis, J.W.; Parks, S.N.; Detlefs, C.L.; et al. Clearing the cervical spine in obtunded patients: The use of dynamic fluoroscopy. J Trauma 39:435, 1995.

28. Davis, S.J.; Teresi, L.M.; Bradley, W.G.; et al. Cervical hyperextension injuries. MR findings. Radiology 180:245, 1991.

29. Deen, H.G.; McGirr, S.J. Vertebral artery injury associated with cervical spine fractures. Spine 17:230, 1992.

30. Demetriades, D.; Theodorou, D.; Asension, J.; et al. Management options in vertebral artery injuries. Br J Surg 83:83, 1996.

31. Denis, F.; Burkus, J.K. Diagnosis and treatment of cauda equina entrapment in the vertical lumbar burst fracture. Spine 16:S433, 1991.

32. Dickman, C.A.; Mamourian, A.; Sonntag, V.K.; et al. Magnetic resonance imaging of the transverse atlantal ligament for the evaluation of atlantoaxial instability. J Neurosurg 75:221, 1991.

33. Diliberti, T.; Lindsey, R.W. Evaluation of the cervical spine in the emergency setting. Who does not need an x-ray? Orthopedics 15:170, 1992.

34. Doran, S.E.; Papadopoulos, M.; Ducker, T.; et al. Magnetic resonance imaging documentation of coexistent traumatic locked facets of the cervical spine and disc herniation. J Neurosurg 79:341, 1993.

35. Dorwar, R.H.; Lamasters, D.L. Applications of computed tomographic scanning of the cervical spine. Orthop Clin North Am 16:381, 1985.

36. Ebrahaim, N.A.; Rupp, R.E.; Savolaine, E.R.; et al. Use of titanium implants in pedicular screw fixation. J Spinal Disord 7:478, 1994.

37. Edeiken-Monroe, B.S.; Wagner, L.K.; Harris, J.H., Jr. Hyperextension dislocation of the cervical spine. AJNR 7:135, 1986.

38. Erb, R.; Schucany, W.G.; Shanmuganathan, K.; et al. Extension corner avulsion fractures of the cervical spine. Emerg Radiol 3:96, 1996.

39. Finkelstein, J.A.; Chapman, J.R.; Mirza, S. Occult vertebral fractures in ankylosing spondylitis. Spinal Cord 37:444, 1999.

40. Fischer, R.P. Cervical radiographic evaluation of alert patients following blunt trauma. Ann Emerg Med 13:905, 1984.

41. Flanders, A.E.; Schaeffer, D.M.; Doan, H.T.; et al. Acute cervical spine trauma: Correlation of MR imaging findings with degree of neurologic deficit. Radiology 177:25, 1990.

42. Flee, C.; Woodring, J.H. Unstable Jefferson variant atlas fracture: An unrecognized cervical injury. AJNR 12:1105, 1992.

43. Gambee, M.J. Vertebral artery thrombosis after spinal injury: Case report. Paraplegia 24:350, 1986.

44. Garza-Mercado, R. Traumatic extradural hematoma of the cervical spine. Neurosurgery 24:410, 1989.

45. Gellad, F.E.; Levine, A.M.; Joslyn, J.N.; et al. Pure thoracolumbar facet dislocation: Clinical features and CT appearance. Radiology 161:505, 1986.

46. Giacobetti, F.B.; Vaccaro, A.R.; Bos-Giacobetti, M.A.; et al. Vertebral artery occlusion associated with cervical spine trauma. A prospective analysis. Spine 22:188, 1997.

47. Goldberg, A.L.; Keaton, N.L.; Rothfus, W.E.; Daffner, R.H. Ankylosing spondylitis complicated by trauma: MR findings correlated with plain radiographs and CT. Skeletal Radiol 22:333, 1996.

48. Gonzales, R.P.; Fried, P.O.; Bukhalo, M.; et al. Role of clinical examination in screening for blunt cervical spine injury. J Am Coll Surg 189:152, 1999.

49. Graber, M.A.; Kathol, M. Cervical spine radiographs in the trauma patient. Am Fam Physician 59:331, 1999.

50. Grant, G.A.; Mirza, S.K.; Chapman, J.R.; et al. Risk of early closed reduction in cervical spine subluxation injuries. J Neurosurg 90:13, 1999.

51. Grossman, M.D.; Reilly, P.M.; Gillet, T.; Gillett, D. National survey of the incidence of cervical spine injury and approach to cervical spine clearance in U.S. trauma centers. J Trauma 47:684, 1999.

52. Gupta, K.J.; Clancy, M. Discontinuation of cervical spine immobilization in unconscious patients with trauma in the intensive care units—Telephone survey of practice in the south and west region. BMJ 314:1652, 1997.

53. Hall, A.J.; Wagle, V.G.; Raycroft, J.; et al. Magnetic resonance imaging in cervical spine trauma. J Trauma 34:21, 1993.

54. Handel, S.F.; Lee, Y.Y. Computed tomography of spinal fractures. Radiol Clin North Am 19:69, 1981.

55. Hanson, J.A.; Blackmore, C.C.; Mann, F.A.; Wilson, A.J. Cervical spine injury: Accuracy of helical CT used as a screening technique. Emerg Radiol 7:31, 2000.

56. Harris, J.H., Jr. Abnormal cervicocranial retropharyngeal soft-tissue contour in the detection of subtle acute cervicocranial injuries. Emerg Radiol 1:15, 1994.

57. Harris, J.H. The normal cervical spine. In: Harris, J.H., Jr.; Mirvis, S.E., eds. Radiology of Acute Cervical Spine Trauma, 3rd ed. Baltimore, Williams & Wilkins, 1995, p. 1.

58. Harris, J.H., Jr. Radiographic evaluation of spinal trauma. Orthop Clin North Am 17:75, 1986.

59. Harris, J.H., Jr.; Burke, J.T.; Ray, R.D.; et al. Low (type III) odontoid fracture: A new radiologic sign. Radiology 153:353, 1984.

60. Harris, J.H., Jr.; Carson, G.C.; Wagner, L.K. Radiologic diagnosis of traumatic occipitovertebral dissociation. 1. Normal occipitovertebral relationships on lateral radiographs of supine subjects. AJR 162:881, 1994.

61. Harris, J.H., Jr.; Carson, G.C.; Wagner, L.K.; Kerr, N. Radiologic diagnosis of traumatic occipitovertebral dissociation. 2. Comparison of three methods of detecting occipitovertebral relationships on lateral radiographs of supine subjects. AJR 162:887, 1994.

62. Harris, J.H. The radiographic examination. In: Harris, J.H.; Mirvis, S.E., eds. Radiology of Acute Cervical Spine Trauma, 3rd ed. Baltimore, Williams & Wilkins, 1995, p. 180.

63. Harris, J.H., Jr.; Harris, W.H.; Novelline, R.A., eds. The Radiology of Emergency Medicine. Spine, Including Soft Tissues of the Pharynx and Neck. Baltimore, Williams & Wilkins, 1993, p. 127.

64. Herman, G.T.; Liu, H.K. Display of three-dimensional information in computed tomography. J Comput Assist Tomogr 1:155, 1977.

65. Herr, C.H.; Ball, P.A.; Sargent, S.K.; Quinton, H.B. Sensitivity of prevertebral soft tissue measurement of C3 for detection of cervical spine fractures and dislocations. Am J Emerg Med 16:346, 1998.

66. Hildingsson, C.; Hietala, S.O.; Tollman, G. Scintigraphic findings in acute whiplash injury of the cervical spine. Injury 20:265, 1989.

67. Hoffman, J.R.; Mower, W.R.; Wolfson, A.B.; et al. Validity of a set of clinical criteria to rule out injury to the cervical spine in patients with blunt trauma. National Emergency X-Radiology Utilization Study Group. N Engl J Med 343:94, 2000.

68. Holliman, C.J.; Mayer, J.S.; Cook, R.T.; et al. Is the anteroposterior cervical radiograph necessary in the initial trauma screening? AJR 9:421, 1991.

69. Iannacone, W.M.; DeLong, W.G.; Born, C.T.; et al. Dynamic computerized tomography of the occiput-atlas-axis complex in trauma patients with odontoid lateral mass asymmetry. J Trauma 3:1501, 1990.

70. Jabre, A. Subintimal dissection of the vertebral artery in subluxation of the cervical spine. Neurosurgery 29:912, 1991.

71. Jenkins, M.G.; Curran, P.; Rocke, L.G. Where do we go after the three standard cervical spine views in the conscious trauma patient? A survey. Eur J Emerg Med 6:215, 1999.

72. Kaneriya, P.P.; Schweitzer, M.E.; Spettell, C.; et al. The cost-effectiveness of oblique radiography in the exclusion of C7-T1 injury in trauma patients. Skeletal Radiol 28:271, 1999.

73. Kassel, E.E.; Cooper, P.W.; Rubenstein, J.D. Radiology of spinal trauma—Practical experience in a trauma unit. J Can Assoc Radiol 34:189, 1983.

74. Katz, M.A.; Beredjiklian, P.K.; Vresilovic, E.J.; et al. Computed tomographic scanning of cervical spine fractures: Does it influence treatment? J Orthop Trauma 13:338, 1999.

75. Katz, R.C.; Wilson, L.; Fraser, N. Anxiety and its determinants in patients undergoing magnetic resonance imaging. J Behav Ther Exp Psychiatry 25:131, 1994.

76. Katzberg, R.W.; Benedetti, P.F.; Drake, C.M.; et al. Acute cervical spine injuries: Prospective MR imaging assessment at a level 1 trauma center. Radiology 213:203, 1999.

77. Kaufman, H.H.; Harris, J.H., Jr.; Spencer, J.A.; et al. Metrizamide-enhanced computed tomography and newer techniques of myelography. In: Bailey, R.W.; Sherk, H.H.; Dunn, E.J.; et al., eds. The Cervical Spine. Philadelphia, J.B. Lippincott, 1983, p. 103.

78. Kerslake, R.W.; Jaspan, T.; Worthington, B.S. Magnetic resonance imaging of spinal trauma. Br J Radiol 64:386, 1991.

79. Klein, G.R.; Vaccaro, A.R.; Albert, T.J.; et al. Efficacy of magnetic resonance imaging in the evaluation of posterior cervical spine fractures. Spine 24:771, 1999.

80. Koyanagi, I.; Iwasaki, Y.; Hida, K.; et al. Acute cervical cord injury without fracture or dislocation of the spinal column. J Neurosurg 93:15, 2000.

81. Kulkarni, M.V.; McArdle, C.B.; Kopanicky, D.; et al. Acute spinal cord injury: MR imaging at 1.5 T. Radiology 164:837, 1987.

82. Lee, C.; Woodring, J.H.; Rogers, L.F.; et al. The radiographic distinction of degenerative (spondylolisthesis and retrolisthesis) from traumatic slippage of the cervical spine. Skeletal Radiol 15:439, 1986.

83. Leidner, B.; Adeils, M.; Aspeln, P.; et al. Standardized CT examination of the multitraumatized patient. Eur Radiol 8:1630, 1998.

84. Leo, J.S.; Bergeron, R.T.; Kricheff, I.I.; et al. Metrizamide myelography for cervical spinal cord injuries. Radiology 129:707, 1978.

85. Lewis, L.M.; Docherty, M.; Ruoff, B.E.; et al. Flexion-extension in the evaluation of cervical spine injuries. Ann Emerg Med 20:117, 1991.

86. Louw, J.A.; Mafoyane, N.A.; Neser, C.P. Occlusion of the vertebral artery in cervical spine dislocations. J Bone Joint Surg Br 72:679, 1990.

87. Lynch, D.; McManus, F.; Ennis, J.T. Computed tomography in spinal trauma. Clin Radiol 37:71, 1986.

88. MacDonald, R.L.; Schwartz, M.L.; Mirich, D.; et al. Diagnosis of cervical spine injury in motor vehicle crash victims. How many x-rays are enough? J Trauma 30:392, 1990.

89. Mace, S.E. Unstable occult cervical spine fracture. Ann Emerg Med 20:1373, 1992.

90. Mascalchi, M.; Pozzo, G.D.; Dini, C.; et al. Acute spinal trauma: Prognostic value of MRI appearances at 0.5T. Clin Radiol 48:100, 1993.

91. Matin, P. The appearance of bone scans following fractures, including immediate and long-term studies. J Nucl Med 20:1227, 1979.

92. McAfee, P.C.; Yuan, H.A.; Fredrickson, B.E.; et al. The value of computed tomography in thoracolumbar fractures. J Bone Joint Surg Am 65:461, 1983.

93. McArdle, C.B.; Nicholas, D.A.; Richardson, C.J.; et al. Monitoring of the neonate undergoing MR imaging: Technical considerations. Radiology 159:223, 1986.

94. McArdle, C.B.; Wright, J.W.; Prevost, W.J.; et al. MR imaging of the acutely injured patient with cervical traction. Radiology 159:273, 1986.

95. McNamara, R.M.; Heine, E.; Esposito, B. Cervical spine injury and radiography in alert, high-risk patients. J Emerg Med 8:177, 1990.

96. Mirvis, S.E.; Borg, U.; Belzberg, H. MRI of ventilator-dependent patients: Preliminary experience. AJR 149:845, 1987.

97. Mirvis, S.E.; Diaconis, J.N.; Chirico, P.A.; et al. Protocol driven radiologic evaluation of suspected cervical spine injury: Efficacy study. Radiology 170:831, 1989.

98. Mirvis, S.E.; Geisler, F.H. Intraoperative sonography of cervical spinal cord injury. Results in 30 patients. AJNR 11:755, 1990.

99. Mirvis, S.E.; Geisler, F.H.; Jelinek, J.J.; et al. Acute cervical spine trauma: Evaluation with 1.5 T MR imaging. Radiology 166:807, 1988.

100. Mirvis, S.E.; Geisler, F.H.; Joslyn, J.N.; et al. Use of titanium wire in cervical spine fixation as a means to reduce MR artifacts. AJNR 9:1229, 1988.

101. Mirvis, S.E.; Ness-Aiver, M. Magnetic resonance imaging of acute cervical spine trauma. In: Harris, J.H., Jr.; Mirvis, S.E., eds. Radiology of Acute Cervical Spine Trauma, 3rd ed. Baltimore, Williams & Wilkins, 1995, p. 114.

102. Mirvis, S.E.; Wolf, A.L. MRI of acute cervical spine trauma. Appl Radiol 21:15, 1992.

103. Modic, M.T.; Masaryk, T.J.; Ross, J.S. Magnetic Resonance Imaging of the Spine. Chicago, Year Book Medical, 1989.

104. Morris, R.E.; Hasso, A.N.; Thompson, J.R.; et al. Traumatic dural tears: CT diagnosis using metrizamide. Radiology 152:443, 1984.

105. Murray, J.B.; Ziervogel, M. The value of computed tomography in the diagnosis of atlantoaxial rotatory fixation. Br J Radiol 63:894, 1990.

106. Nunez, D.B.; Ahmad, A.A.; Coin, C.G.; et al. Clearing the cervical spine in multiple trauma victims: A time-effective protocol using helical computed tomography. Emerg Radiol 1:273, 1994.

107. Nunez, D., Jr. Value of complete helical computed tomography scanning in identifying cervical spine injury in the unevaluable blunt trauma patients with multiple injuries. J Trauma 48;988, 2000.

108. Olerud, C.; Frost, A.; Bring, J. Spinal fractures in patients with ankylosing spondylitis. Eur Spine J 5:51, 1996.

109. Olshaker, J.S.; Barish, R.A. Acute traumatic cervical epidural hematoma. Ann Emerg Med 20:662, 1991.

110. Paleologos, T.S.; Fratzoglou, M.M.; Papadopoulos, S.S.; et al. Posttraumatic spinal cord lesions without skeletal or discal and ligamentous abnormalities: The role of MR imaging. J Spinal Disord 11:346, 1998.

111. Paley, D.; Schwartz, M.; Cooper, P.; et al. Fractures of the spine in diffuse skeletal hyperostosis. Clin Orthop 267:22, 1991.

112. Parent, A.D.; Harkey, H.L.; Touchstone, D.A.; et al. Lateral cervical spine dislocation and vertebral artery injury. Neurosurgery 31:501, 1992.

113. Pathria, M.N.; Petersilge, C.A. Spinal trauma. Radiol Clin North Am 29:847, 1991.

114. Pomeranz, S.J. Craniospinal Magnetic Resonance Imaging. Philadelphia, W.B. Saunders, 1989.

115. Post, M.J.; Green, B.A. The use of computed tomography in spinal trauma. Radiol Clin North Am 21:327, 1983.

116. Post, M.J.; Green, B.A.; Quencer, R.M.; et al. The value of computed tomography in spinal trauma. Spine 7:417, 1982.

117. Powers, B.; Miller, M.D.; Kramer, R.S.; et al. Traumatic anterior occipitoatlantal dislocation. Neurosurgery 4:127, 1979.

118. Pratt, E.S.; Green, D.A.; Spengler, D.M. Herniated intervertebral discs associated with unstable spine injuries. Spine 15:662, 1990.

119. Price, R.F.; Sellar, R.M.; Leung, C.; O'Sullivan, M.J. Traumatic vertebral arterial dissection and vertebrobasilar arterial thrombosis successfully treated with endovascular thrombolysis and stenting. AJNR 19:1677, 1998.

120. Quencer, R.M.; Bunge, R.P.; Egnor, M.; et al. Acute traumatic central cord syndrome: MRI-pathologic correlation. Neuroradiology 34:85, 1992.

121. Quencer, R.M.; Sheldon, J.J.; Post, M.J.D.; et al. MRI of the chronically injured cervical spinal cord. AJR 147:125, 1986.

122. Regenbogen, V.S.; Rogers, L.F.; Atlas, S.W.; et al. Cervical spinal cord injuries in patients with cervical spondylosis. AJR 146:277, 1986.

123. Reid, J.D.S.; Weight, J.A. Forty-three cases of vertebral artery trauma. J Trauma 28:1007, 1988.

124. Rizzolo, S.J.; Piazza, M.R.; Cotler, J.M.; et al. Intervertebral disc complicating cervical spine trauma. Spine 16:187, 1991.

125. Rizzolo, S.J.; Vaccaro, A.R.; Cotler, J.M. Cervical spine trauma. Spine 19:2288, 1994.

126. Ross, S.E.; Schwab, C.W.; Eriberto, T.D.; et al. Clearing the cervical spine. J Trauma 27:1055, 1987.

127. Roth, B.J.; Martin, R.R.; Foley, K.; et al. Roentgenographic evaluation of the cervical spine: A selective approach. Arch Surg 129:643, 1994.

128. Scarrow, A.M.; Levy, E.I.; Resnick, D.K.; et al. Cervical spine evaluation in obtunded or comatose pediatric trauma patients. A pilot study. Pediatr Neurosurg 30:169, 1999.

129. Schaeffer, D.M.; Flanders, A.E.; Osterholm, J.L.; et al. Prognostic significance of magnetic resonance imaging in the acute phase of cervical spine injury. J Neurosurg 76:218, 1992.

130. Schwarz, N.; Buchinger, W.; Gaudernak, T.; et al. Injuries to the cervical spine causing vertebral artery trauma: Case reports. J Trauma 31:127, 1991.

131. Sees, D.W.; Rodriguez Cruz, L.R.; Flaherty, S.F.; Ciceri, D.P. The use of bedside fluoroscopy to evaluate the cervical spine in obtunded trauma patients. J Trauma 45:768, 1998.

132. Seybold, E.A.; Dunn, E.J.; Jenis, L.G.; Sweeney, C.A. Variation on the posterior vertebral contour line at the level of C-2 on lateral cervical roentgenograms: A method for odontoid fracture detection. Am J Orthop 28:696, 1999.

133. Shaffer, M.A.; Doris, P.E. Limitation of the cross table lateral view in detecting cervical spine injuries: A retrospective analysis. Ann Emerg Med 10:508, 1981.

134. Shanmuganathan, K.; Mirvis, S.E.; Levine, A.M. Isolated articular pillar fractures of the cervical spine: Imaging observations in 20 patients. AJR 166:897, 1996.

135. Shanmuganathan, K.; Mirvis, S.E.; Levine, A.M. Rotational injury of the cervical facets: CT analysis of fracture patterns with implications for management and neurologic outcome. AJR 163:1156, 1994.

136. Shellock, F.G.; LipcZak, H.; Kamel, E. Monitoring patients during MR procedures. Appl Radiol 24:11, 1995.

137. Shellock, F.G.; Morisoli, S.; Kamel, E. MR procedures and biomedical implants, material, and devices. 1993 update. Radiology 189:587, 1993.

138. Silberstein, M.; Tress, B.M.; Henessey, O. Prevertebral swelling in cervical spine injury: Identification of ligament injury imaging. Clin Radiol 46:318, 1992.

139. Spain, D.A.; Trooskin, S.Z.; Flancbaum, L.; et al. The adequacy and cost-effectiveness of routine resuscitation area cervical spine radiographs. Ann Emerg Med 19:276, 1990.

140. Spitz, J.; Laer, I.; Tillet, K.; et al. Scintimetric evaluation of remodeling after fractures in man. J Nucl Med 34:1403, 1993.

141. Streiter, M.L.; Chambers, A.A. Metrizamide examination of traumatic lumbar nerve root meningocele. Spine 9:77, 1984.

142. Streitweisser, D.R.; Knopp, R.; Wales, L.R.; et al. Accuracy of standard radiographic views in detecting cervical spine fractures. Ann Emerg Med 12:538, 1983.

143. Takahashi, M.; Yamashita, Y.; Sakamoto, Y.; et al. Chronic cervical cord compression: Clinical significance of increased signal on MRIs. Radiology 173:219, 1989.

144. Tarr, R.W.; Drolshagen, L.F.; Kerner, T.C. MR imaging of recent spinal trauma. J Comput Assist Tomogr 11:412, 1987.

145. Taylor, A.R.; Blackwood, W. Paraplegia in hyperextension cervical injuries with normal radiographic appearance. J Bone Joint Surg Br 30:245, 1948.

146. Templeton, P.A.; Young, J.W.R.; Mirvis, S.E.; et al. The value of retropharyngeal soft tissue measurements in trauma of the adult cervical spine. Skeletal Radiol 16:98, 1987.

147. Thomeir, W.C.; Brown, D.C.; Mirvis, S.E. The "tilted" odontoid: A sign of subtle odontoid fracture. AJNR 11:605, 1990.

148. Vannier, W.; Marsh, J.L.; Warren, J.O. Three-dimensional CT construction images for craniofacial surgical planning and evaluation. Radiology 150:179, 1984.

149. Veras, L.M.; Pedraza-Gutierrez, S.; Castellanos, J.; et al. Vertebral artery occlusion after cervical spine trauma. Spine 25:1171, 2000.

150. Wales, L.R.; Knopp, R.H.; Morishima, M.S. Recommendations for evaluation of the acutely injured cervical spine: A clinical radiologic algorithm. Ann Emerg Med 9:422, 1980.

151. Warner, J.; Shanmuganathan, K.; Mirvis, S.E.; et al. Magnetic resonance imaging of ligamentous injury of the cervical spine. Emerg Radiol 3:9, 1996.

152. Weir, D.C. Roentgenographic signs of cervical injury. Clin Orthop 109:9, 1975.

153. Weirich, S.D.; Cotler, H.B.; Narayana, P.A.; et al. Histopathologic correlation of magnetic resonance image signal patterns in a spinal cord injury model. Spine 15:630, 1990.

154. Weller, S.J.; Rossitch, E., Jr.; Malek, A.M. Detection of vertebral artery injury after cervical spine trauma using magnetic resonance angiography. J Trauma 46:660, 1999.

155. West, O.C.; Anbari, M.M.; Pilgram, T.K.; Wilson, A.J. Acute cervical spine trauma: Diagnostic performance of single-view versus three-view radiographic screening. Radiology 204:819, 1997.

156. Willis, B.K.; Greiner, F.; Orrison, W.W.; et al. The incidence of vertebral artery injury after midcervical spine fracture or subluxation. Neurosurgery 34:435, 1994.

157. Yeakley, J.; Edeiken-Monroe, B.; Harris, J.H., Jr. Computed tomography of spinal trauma and degenerative disease. Instr Course Lect 34:85, 1985.

158. Young, J.W.R.; Resnick, C.S.; DeCandido, P.; et al. The laminar space in the diagnosis of rotational flexion injuries of the cervical spine. AJR 152:103, 1989.

159. Zabel, D.D.; Tinkoff, G.; Wittenborn, W.; et al. Adequacy and efficacy of lateral cervical radiography in alert, high-risk blunt trauma patient. J Trauma 43:952, 1997.

chapter 27

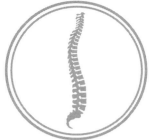

Management Techniques for Spinal Injuries

Ronald W. Lindsey, M.D.
Spiros G. Pneumaticos, M.D.
Zbigniew Gugala, M.D.

Many treatment techniques have been used for managing injuries involving the spine. Initially, most were nonoperative, but over the past century, numerous surgical techniques have also been described. Various types of spinal instrumentation systems have been devised, and the surgical indications for spinal injuries have been better defined to facilitate the success of operative management. However, many types of spinal injuries can still be satisfactorily treated by nonoperative methods without many of the inherent risks of surgery; others can be treated by either operative or nonoperative methods. Therefore, it is imperative that the clinician understand the role of nonoperative treatment and remain facile with techniques such as spinal traction, reduction by manipulation, and orthotic immobilization.

Traditionally, the term *conservative care* has been synonymous with nonoperative treatment. Recent advances in our understanding of the different types of spinal injuries and their risk for complications have allowed the term *conservative care* to be used for either nonoperative or operative treatment. Optimal management must consider early patient mobilization, maintenance of acceptable spinal alignment and stability, the presence of associated injuries, and the risk and severity of potential complications associated with each type of treatment. Being familiar with both surgical and nonsurgical treatment approaches allows the clinician to individualize treatment based on the nature of the injury and the demands of the specific patient.

The objectives of nonoperative management of spinal injuries are similar to those of operative treatment and include the following:

1. Avoiding progression of neurologic deficit and, when deficit is present, enhancing its resolution
2. Reducing unacceptable spinal deformity or malalignment to an acceptable functional range
3. Maintaining spinal alignment within a functional range throughout the course of treatment

4. Healing the spine in a functional alignment sufficient to permit return of physiologic loads through the spine

Nonoperative management should consist of immobilization that is well tolerated, permit timely mobilization, and allow for healing within a reasonable period. Therefore, the ultimate success of nonoperative treatment requires proper patient selection, as well as complete understanding and strict adherence to the principles of nonoperative management.

Detailed descriptions of modern spine biomechanics and pathomechanics, as well as the classification systems used to determine spine stability, are included in the subsequent chapters dealing with each specific injury type. In this chapter, factors determining optimal treatment for spine injuries are presented. Regardless of the treatment method used, the objectives of preserving neurologic function, minimizing post-traumatic deformity, and achieving a stable functional spine remain the standard of care.

CERVICAL TRACTION

Cervical traction is frequently indicated for the treatment of cervical spine injury to achieve the following objectives: (1) reduce cervical spine deformity, (2) indirectly decompress traumatized neural elements, and (3) provide cervical spine stability. Familiarity with the use of cervical traction is essential in the treatment of cervical spine trauma because of its ease of application and low morbidity when applied properly.

The modes by which cervical traction can be applied include a head halter, tongs, or a halo ring. Head halter traction consists of straps that attach to the head at the chin and the occiput, and only small amounts of weight (5 to 10 lb) can be applied safely. In addition to reduced traction weight, limitations of head halter traction

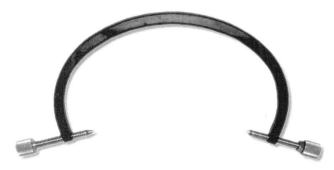

FIGURE 27–1. Gardner-Wells tongs have angulated pins designed to better counteract traction forces. The tongs can be made from magnetic resonance imaging–compatible materials (carbon fiber, titanium), which obviates the need for removal of the tongs and facilitates head and cervical spine imaging.

include poor attachment to the head and the ability to control only axial compression through distraction. Excessive weight over an extended period can cause pressure ulcerations at the chin or occiput. Currently, halter traction is rarely indicated for spine trauma.

Tongs Traction

When applying traction with tongs, in contrast to head halters, fixation into the skull is achieved through the use of special pins with a pointed tip that abruptly flares out. This design allows for pin insertion through the outer cortex of the skull without penetration of the inner cortex. The flared nature of the pin design distributes pin pressure over its entire width on insertion while engaging the outer table.

Several types of tongs presently exist and include the Gardner-Wells or Trippi-Wells models. Tongs, similar to head halters, essentially control motion in a single plane through the application of longitudinal traction. Gardner-Wells tongs (Fig. 27–1) have achieved the widest acceptance because of their ability to withstand high loads and their ease of application. Gardner-Wells tongs can be applied quickly by a single physician. Trippi-Wells tongs consist of the same pins as Gardner-Wells tongs, but they are used in a multipin fashion. Because of the ability of tongs to resist motion in only one plane, they are associated with a high incidence of loosening. Tongs are typically indicated when longitudinal traction is to be temporarily applied or the patient is to remain bedridden.

APPLICATION OF TONGS

In preparation for the application of tongs, the patient is positioned supine with the head resting on the table top and no pillow support. The physician stands at the top (head) of the table above the patient for easy access to either side of the head. Pins should be placed just below the greatest diameter (equator) of the skull in a manner that avoids the temporalis muscle and superficial temporal artery and vein (Fig. 27–2). The standard site for pin insertion is approximately 1 cm posterior to the external auditory meatus and 1 cm superior to the pinna of the ear.

Asymmetric pin placement, either slightly posterior to affect flexion or slightly anterior to affect extension, can either facilitate or inhibit fracture reduction.

The use of Gardner-Wells tongs does not require shaving of the pin site. The skin and hair are prepared with an iodine solution, and the pin can be inserted directly into the skin without an incision. Before pin placement, local anesthetic is injected into the skin with care taken to infiltrate the periosteum down to the galea. The pins, which must be sterile and handled accordingly, are positioned orthogonally on either side of the skull before tightening. Tightening the pins by alternating from side to side will maintain pin symmetry. Gardner-Wells tongs are spring-loaded and thereby prevent perforation of the inner table of the skull. The force of pin insertion is gauged by the spring-loaded force indicator contained in one of the pins, and optimal insertion torque is typically 6 to 8 in-lb. After the tongs are in place, the pins should be cleaned once a day with hydrogen peroxide at the skin–pin interface. After the first 24 hours of tongs application, the spring-loaded pins must be retightened; additional tightening should not be done to avoid the risk of perforating the inner table.

Halo Ring Traction

Cervical traction can be applied more efficiently through a halo ring. The multipin attachment of the halo to the skull reduces the distribution of the pin load, thereby allowing for higher traction loads to be applied for an extended period. Experimentally, the measured pull-out strength for a halo ring is almost twice that of Gardner-Wells tongs (440 versus 233 lb).[72] Furthermore, the circumferential pin fixation to the skull better resists multiplane spine motion and allows for traction in flexion, extension, or simultaneous bivector traction techniques.[110] Finally, a major advantage of halo ring traction is that it can be rapidly converted to a halo vest orthosis once spinal reduction has been achieved.

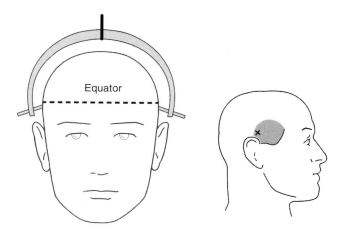

FIGURE 27–2. Pins for traction tongs are placed below the cranial brim or the widest diameter of the skull (equator), anterior and superior to the earlobe. Care must be taken to position the pins posterior to the temporalis muscle. Precalibrated indicator pins are set to protrude at 8 lb of pressure.

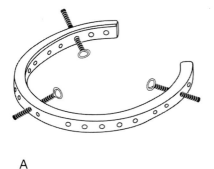

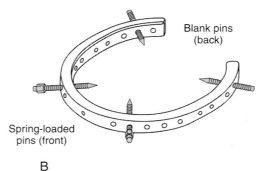

Blank pins
(back)

Spring-loaded
pins (front)

A   B

FIGURE 27–3. The halo ring is held
in a temporary position equidistant
from the patient's head, 1 cm above
the eyebrows and 1 cm above the
tip of the ears, with the use of
blunt positioning pins (A). With the
halo ring held in place, sharp halo
pins are then placed just below the
skull equator. Spring-loaded pins are
placed in front and a blank pin on the
back (B). The pins are inserted and
tightened in a diagonal fashion.

The design of the halo ring has dramatically improved since its advent as a device for stabilization of facial fractures.[19] Currently available halo rings are made of light and radiolucent materials (titanium, carbon composites) that permit computed tomography (CT) and magnetic resonance imaging (MRI). More recently, open-ring and crown-type halo designs that encircle only a part of the head have also been developed. These devices are open posteriorly to avoid the need to pass the head through a ring and thus ease application and improve safety. With some crown designs, the posterior ends of the incomplete ring must be angled inferiorly to ensure posterior pin placement below the equator of the skull. Halo rings are available in a variety of sizes to fit virtually any patient, including young children. A properly fitted halo ring provides 1 to 2 cm of clearance around every aspect of the patient's skull. The appropriate ring size can usually be determined by measuring the circumference of the skull 1 cm above the ears and eyebrows and then referring to the manufacturer's chart for preferred ring sizes.

HALO RING APPLICATION

A halo ring is routinely applied under local anesthesia; occasionally, light pharmacologic sedation may be necessary. The patient is positioned supine, and to permit application of a full-ring halo, the patient's occiput is elevated with a folded towel or the head is gently positioned beyond the edge of the bed. Open-back halo rings can be applied without these maneuvers and are therefore preferred. Before application of a halo ring, all patients should be in a hard collar, including those undergoing conversion of traction tongs to halo immobilization. The halo ring is temporary positioned equidistant from the patient's head, 1 cm above the eyebrows and 1 cm above the tip of the ears. It is extremely important that the ring be positioned just below the greatest circumference of the patient's skull to prevent the halo ring from becoming displaced upward and out of position. The halo ring is provisionally stabilized with three blunt positioning pins, and locations for the sharp head pins are then determined (Fig. 27–3). The optimal location for the anterior pins is 1 cm superior and two thirds lateral to the orbital rim, just below the greatest circumference of the skull (Fig. 27–4A). Along the medial aspect of the safe zone lie the supraorbital and supratrochlear nerves and the underlying frontal sinus. Placement of pins in the temporalis region behind the hairline confers a cosmetic advantage but is, however,

anatomically and biomechanically inferior.[18, 47] Insertion sites for the posterior pins are less critical because neuromuscular structures are lacking and the skull is thicker and more uniform in that area. The posterior sites should be inferior to the widest portion of the skull, yet superior enough to prevent impingement of the ring or crown on the upper helix of the ear (see Fig. 27–4B).

While the halo is held in position, the skin is shaved and prepared with an iodine solution. Local anesthetic, typically a 1% lidocaine solution, is injected with the needle passed through the holes for the sharp pins until the periosteum is elevated. Small stab incisions are made and the pins inserted in a diagonal fashion to maintain equal distance between the halo ring and skull. Pins should be inserted perpendicular to the skull because angulated pin insertion has been reported to be biomechanically inferior.[122] The pins are tightened with a torque screwdriver, and during this maneuver the patient is asked to close the eyes and relax the forehead to prevent eyebrow tenting or tethering. When all sharp pins are in place, the blunt pins are removed and the sharp pins tightened in a diagonal fashion up to a torque of 6 to 8 in-lb.[17] Pin torque should never exceed 10 in-lb because of the risk of penetration of the outer cortex.[17] Breakaway wrenches can be used to prevent the pins from being tightened past the maximal torque; however, torque limits are more reliably measured with a calibrated torque screwdriver. Locknuts are then placed on each pin and gently tightened to secure

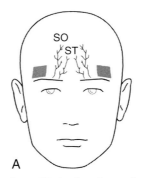

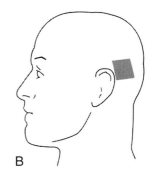

SO
ST

A   B

FIGURE 27–4. The safe zone for the anterior pins is located 1 cm superior and two thirds lateral to the orbital rim, just below the greatest circumference of the skull. On the medial aspect of the safe zone are the supraorbital (SO) and supratrochlear (ST) nerves (A). The zone for the posterior pins is inferior to the widest portion of the skull, yet superior enough to prevent ring or crown impingement on the upper helix of the ear (B).

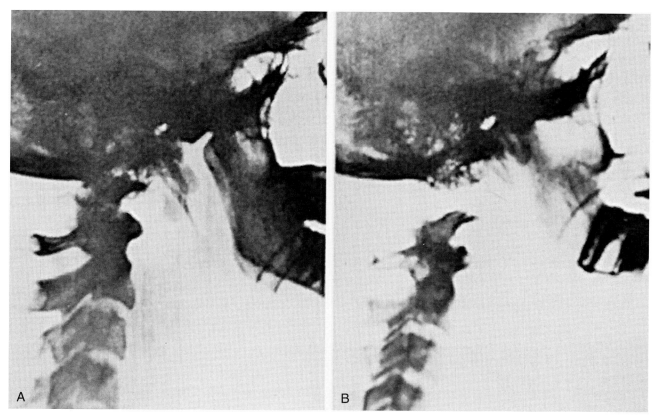

FIGURE 27–5. *A,* Admission lateral radiograph showed no abnormal distraction. *B,* After cervical traction was initiated at 20 lb, it resulted in marked overdistraction. Traction should always be initiated at 10 lb.

the pin to the ring. Once the halo application is complete, a traction bow can be mounted. The traction weight protocol for halo rings can be much more aggressive than that for tongs, and weights can exceed 100 lb when indicated.

Cervical Traction Weight

After tongs or a halo ring has been applied, cervical traction can begin at approximately 10 to 15 lb, with immediate evaluation by lateral radiographs to avoid overdistraction (Fig. 27–5). Traction weight can be increased by 5- to 10-lb increments, depending on the size and weight of the patient. Serial lateral radiographs should be obtained approximately 10 to 15 minutes after each application of weight to allow for soft tissue creep. Fluoroscopy can be used instead of plain radiographs to facilitate this process. The patient must be completely relaxed, and analgesics or muscle relaxants can often assist in minimizing muscle spasm or tension. At higher weights (greater than 40 lb), 30 to 60 minutes should elapse before further load increase. The head of the bed should be slightly elevated to provide body weight resistance to traction.

The maximal amount of weight that can safely be applied for closed traction reduction of the cervical spine remains controversial. It has been suggested that a slow, gradual increase in traction weight will effect spinal reduction at a lower total traction load.[90] Some physicians support a more rapid incremental increase in weight and have applied weights up to 150 lb without any adverse effects.[70] Typically, the maximal weight tolerated will be limited by the skeletal fixation used, and for cranial tongs, the limit is up to 100 lb.

The objective of using cervical traction is to achieve the maximal effect of the weight being applied. The maximal traction weight should be considered to be a function of the patient's size, body weight, or body habitus (or any combination of these attributes) rather than an absolute number (100-lb cervical traction may be well tolerated by a burly 300-lb male weightlifter, but not appropriate for a 115-lb female). The greater the associated ligamentous disruption, the less total weight that is appropriate. The maximal weight should also correspond to the level of the cervical injury; specifically, upper cervical injuries require less weight than do injuries at the cervicothoracic junction. When these parameters are respected and sufficient time is permitted between incremental increases in traction weight, the maximal weight can usually be limited to 70 lb or less for lower cervical injury in an average-sized adult. Regardless of whether spinal reduction has been achieved, it is imperative that the maximal traction weight be decreased to 10 to 15 lb once the monitored reduction process has been terminated.

Most cervical spine injuries can be reduced with only longitudinal traction, but small changes in the vector of traction (i.e., slightly more flexion or more extension) can be helpful in some cases. Spinal manipulation can be hazardous and is therefore controversial.[82] Lee and associates compared cervical traction and manipulation under anesthesia and determined that traction alone was preferable.[70] Cotler and co-workers suggested that gentle manipulation in combination with traction could be of benefit in awake patients.[30] Manual manipulation as a means of achieving cervical spine reduction should never be performed in a patient under general anesthesia or in an unconscious patient. Light sedation in an otherwise alert patient allows the physician to detect neurologic alterations. In general, the authors do not support manual manipulation and prefer that patients who do not respond to traction be treated surgically.

SPINAL BRACING

The Halo-Vest Orthosis

The advent of the halo ring inspired the development of the halo vest apparatus by Perry and Nickel in 1959.[96, 100] The original halo consisted of a complete ring attached to a body cast and was used to immobilize a patient with poliomyelitis. Since then, the halo vest orthosis has undergone dramatic changes in design and currently provides the most effective stabilization available for a cervical orthosis (Fig. 27–6).

The stabilizing property of any halo vest orthosis is most dependent on adequate fitting of the vest to the patient's torso. The appropriate size of vest is determined after measurement of the patient's chest circumference and torso length. The most common body jackets that are attached to the halo ring are adjustable double-shell plastic vests. Occasionally, a plaster body cast can be used for patients who are noncompliant or extremely difficult to fit. The vest is attached to the halo ring with four upright bars. The posterior and anterior shells of the vest can be applied

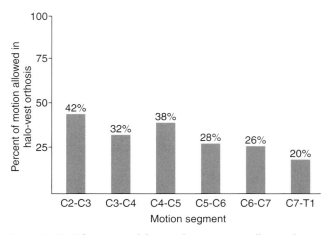

FIGURE 27–7. Halo vest immobilization does not restrict all cervical spine movement. The proportion of normal cervical spine motion allowed in a halo vest at each level averages 31% and ranges from 42% in the upper cervical spine to 20% in the lower cervical spine. (From Koch, R.A.; Nickel, V.L. Spine 3:103–107, 1978.)

before or after halo ring fixation. Care is taken to apply manual traction before the upright bars are completely tightened. The cast or vest must be well fitted to the torso and shoulders to prevent vertical toggle of the apparatus. Although the halo vest is the most stable orthosis for cervical spine immobilization, it does not completely restrict motion across the spine.

Despite adequate fit, the halo vest has been shown to permit up to 31% of normal cervical spine motion, depending on the patient's position, activity, and degree of spinal instability[6, 65] (Fig. 27–7). The most restricted motion was typically below C2, and the least restricted was above C2.[76]

Despite the effectiveness of halo skeletal fixation in achieving cervical spine immobilization, complications are common and include pin loosening, pin site infection, pressure sores, headache, loss of reduction, dural puncture, and dysphagia (Table 27–1). Most of these complications usually result from either improper halo ring application or an ill-fitted vest. In a series of 126 patients treated with halo immobilization, Kostuik reported his experience with halo vest complications.[66] A single case of skull perforation occurred in a patient with severe osteoporosis. Decubitus ulcers, pressure sores, and respiratory compromise were especially prevalent in quadriplegic patients immobilized with a halo cast/vest.

TABLE 27–1

Complications of Halo Ring Immobilization

Complication	% of Patients
Pin loosening	36
Pin site infection	20
Severe pin discomfort	18
Pressure sores	11
Nerve injury	2
Dysphagia	2
Bleeding at pin sites	2
Dural puncture	1

From Garfin, S.R., et al. J Bone Joint Surg Am 68:320–325, 1986.

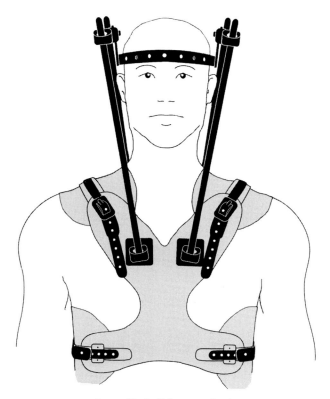

FIGURE 27–6. Halo vest orthosis.

Acute pin infection and subsequent loosening remain the most common problems associated with halo vests and can occur in up to 60% of patients. Pin sites should be cleaned with hydrogen peroxide twice daily, and antibiotic ointments or sterile dressings are not usually necessary. Focal erythema about the pin typically suggests pin loosening, local infection, or both. A loose pin can be gently retightened once; however, multiple attempts at retightening will risk penetration of the internal cortex and should be avoided. In the face of recurrent loosening, a new pin should be placed in an adjacent location and the loose pin removed. Pin site infection can usually be treated with oral and topical antibiotics and retention of the pin. When pin site drainage or abscess formation persists, the pin should be removed only after a new pin is inserted at a different site.

Loss of cervical reduction is a major concern with any halo vest and occurs in about 10% of patients. Poorly fitted vests and patient noncompliance with the orthosis are the major causes of loss of reduction if the original indication for a halo vest is appropriate. Regardless of the reason, an inability to maintain reduction with the halo vest necessitates either longitudinal traction or operative stabilization.

Spinal Orthoses

Spinal orthoses are external devices that can restrict motion of the spine by acting indirectly to reinforce the intervening soft tissue. Because of a lack of standard regulations, spinal orthotic appliances are currently available in a wide diversity of designs and materials. The reported claims touting the stabilizing properties of many spinal braces parallel the paucity of scientific data soundly documenting their clinical efficacy. Additionally, the effectiveness of cervical bracing for the specific injury is difficult to determine because it is entirely dependent on the willingness of the patient to comply with orthotic use.

Despite the heterogeneity of designs, the theoretical functions of all spinal braces are analogous and include restriction of spinal movement, maintenance of spinal alignment, reduction of pain, and support of the trunk musculature. In conjunction with these mechanical functions, spinal braces also function psychologically as kinesthetic reminders for the patient to modify activity. Spinal braces achieve their stabilizing effects indirectly, with their effectiveness being a function of the rigidity of the spine-enveloping tissues, the distance between the spine and the brace (i.e., thickness of the intervening tissue), the length and rigidity of the orthosis, the degree of mobility of the spinal segment to be stabilized, and the presence of potential anatomic fixation points. Although spinal braces are generally applied to stabilize a specific spinal motion segment, their immobilization properties affect the entire spinal region (i.e., cervical, thoracic, and lumbar). The materials used for bracing (rubber, foam, plastics) should be lightweight and elastic and allow for ventilation, improved hygiene, and comfort.

CERVICAL BRACES

Cervical spine bracing is particularly challenging because of the wide range of normal spinal motion in extent,

direction, and variation of movements. As a result of the inability of the vital structures in the neck to withstand prolonged compression, cervical braces use the cranium and thorax as fixation points. The effectiveness of any cervical brace is a function of (1) orthotic design and stabilizing properties, (2) specific injury biomechanics, and (3) the patient's compliance. Cervical orthoses (COs) can be used as definitive therapy for some spinal injuries or as a temporary immobilizer for postinjury transport or during the early hospital diagnostic process. These braces can generally be divided into two basic types: COs and high and low cervicothoracic orthoses (CTOs) (Fig. 27–8).

COs include both soft and rigid cervical collars. The former are basically foam cylinders that encircle the neck (Fig. 27–9A). The mechanical function of soft collars is minimal, and they permit up to 80% of normal cervical motion.[59, 60, 64] Soft collars act principally as proprioceptive "reminders" for the patient to voluntarily restrict neck

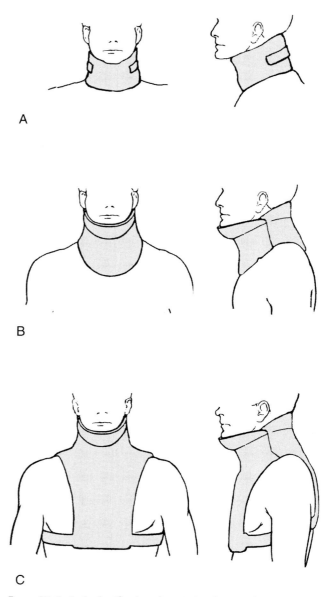

FIGURE 27–8. Basic classification of cervical and cervicothoracic braces: cervical orthoses *(A)*, high CTOs *(B)*, and low CTOs *(C)*. (Redrawn from Sypert, G.W. External spinal orthotics. Neurosurgery 20:642–649, 1987.)

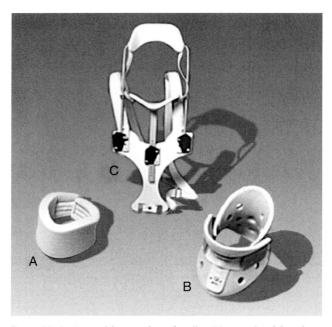

FIGURE 27–9. Cervical braces: the soft collar (A) is made of firm foam held around the neck with Velcro closure; the Philadelphia collar (B), which is made of flexible polymer molded to the mandible and occiput, supports and extends down to the upper part of the thorax; and the SOMI (sternal-occipital-mandibular immobilizer) (C) is an extended cervicothoracic orthosis that consists of a rigid metal frame that rests on the thorax and padded metal strips that pass over the shoulders.

motion and provide some psychologic comfort. Patient compliance with soft collars is usually high because of the comfort and minimally restrictive nature of the brace. Soft collars are indicated for mild cervical sprains or to provide postoperative comfort after stable internal fixation.

High-thoracic CTOs have molded occipital-mandibular supports that extend to the upper part of the thorax, typically not lower than the level of the sternal notch anteriorly and the T3 spinous process posteriorly[22] (see Fig. 27–8B). Rigid collars encompass a very heterogeneous group of cervical brace designs and include the Philadelphia collar, the Miami J brace, the NecLoc collar, the Newport/Aspen collar, the Stifneck collar, the Malibu brace, and the Nebraska collar, among others. High-thoracic CTOs stabilize the cervical spine by maintaining some tension between the occiput/mandible and the upper part of the thorax. They are significantly more effective than soft collars. Biomechanical differences, however, exist even among the various high-thoracic CTO designs. The comparative effectiveness of the various COs and CTOs in restriction of total cervical motion is presented in Table 27–2. The immobilizing properties of selected COs and CTOs for specific cervical motion segments are depicted in Tables 27–3 and 27–4.

The Philadelphia collar (see Fig. 27–9B), the most popular high-thoracic CTO, is a very comfortable orthosis for patients.[60, 86] It can restrict 71% of normal cervical flexion and extension, 34% of lateral bending, and about 54% of normal rotation.[42, 59, 60] Despite its popularity, the Philadelphia collar is less effective than the Miami J, NecLoc, or Stifneck in restricting cervical motion. In addition, its higher skin contact pressure on the occiput may result in scalp ulcerations, especially in supine patients.[101] The Philadelphia collar is optimally indicated for the management of cervical sprains, as a temporary immobilizer during the spine trauma diagnostic process, or to provide postoperative support for an internally stabilized spine.

Among the high-thoracic CTOs, the Miami J collar is the most effective brace in stabilizing all planes of the cervical spine.[52] The Miami J collar generally limits 73% of flexion-extension, 51% of lateral bending, and 65% of rotation.[86] This collar causes less occipital and mandibular skin pressure and is therefore considered an excellent long-term cervical immobilizer for a severely unstable

TABLE 27–2

Comparison of Total Cervical Motion Restricted by Various Cervical Orthoses

Orthosis	Combined Flexion-Extension	Flexion	Extension	Lateral Bending	Axial Rotation
CO					
Soft collar[59, 64]	26	23	20	8	7
High-thoracic CTO					
Philadelphia[59, 64, 109*]	70	74	59	34	56
Miami J[109*]	73	85	75	51	65
NecLoc[64*]	80	86	78	60	73
Newport/Aspen[55*]	62	59	64	31	38
Stifneck[52*]	70	73	63	50	57
Malibu[81]	—	86	82	55	74
Nebraska[2]	87	74	60	75	91
Low-thoracic CTO					
SOMI[59]	72	93	42	34	66
Yale[59]	86	—	—	61	76
Four poster[59]	79	89	82	54	73
Minerva[113]	79	78	78	51	88
LMCO[2]	83	68	66	50	60
Halo vest[59]	96	—	—	99	96

*Askins, V.; et al. Spine 22:1193–1198, 1997.
Abbreviations: CO, cervical orthosis; CTO, cervicothoracic orthosis; LMCO, Lehrman-Minerva CO; SOMI, sternal-occipital-mandibular immobilizer.

TABLE 27–3

Comparison of Flexion Restricted by Various Cervical Orthoses at Each Motion Segment

Orthosis	Normal Flexion Restricted (%)							
	Occ–C1	*C1–C2*	*C2–C3*	*C3–C4*	*C4–C5*	*C5–C6*	*C6–C7*	*C7–T1*
CO								
Soft collar[59]	−86*	33	37	24	18	13	22	14
High-thoracic CTO								
Philadelphia[59]	−29	49	78	68	55	46	50	38
Miami J[†]	27	70	51	62	56	57	62	—
NecLoc[64†]	40	72	71	73	69	58	67	—
Newport/Aspen[55†]	−20	54	27	38	65	15	33	—
Stifneck[52†]	−2	54	38	57	47	49	43	—
Low-thoracic CTO								
SOMI[59]	−300	65	87	84	81	75	77	65
Yale[59]	−100	38	74	83	80	83	80	64
Four poster[59]	−210	43	76	78	82	74	70	69
Minerva[113]	−24	60	62	68	78	67	65	—
Halo vest[59]	−39	77	68	65	80	86	76	—

*Negative values demonstrate a "snaking" effect.
†Askins, V.; et al. Spine 22:1193–1198, 1997.
Abbreviations: CO, cervical orthosis; CTO, cervicothoracic orthosis; SOMI, sternal-occipital-mandibular immobilizer.

cervical injury.[101] Another high-thoracic CTO, the NecLoc collar, is commonly used in the prehospital setting for patient extrication and transport. Its excellent biomechanical properties are further enhanced by its ease of application. The NecLoc collar restricts up to 80% of flexion-extension, 60% of lateral bending, and 73% of axial rotation.[64, 109]

The Newport/Aspen collar provides better spine immobilization than the Philadelphia collar but to a lesser extent than the Miami J or the NecLoc[55, 81]; it limits only 62% of cervical flexion-extension, 31% of lateral bending, and 38% of rotation.[52, 55, 86] The major advantage of the Newport/Aspen collar is its comfort and low risk of skin ulceration. Plaisier and colleagues studied the risk of skin ulceration with various CTOs by measuring their effect on

local capillary closing pressure.[101] Only the Newport/Aspen CTO had contact pressures below capillary closing pressure.

Among high-thoracic CTOs, the Stifneck collar is unique in that it is a one-piece orthosis. The effectiveness of cervical stabilization by the Stifneck is comparable to that of the Philadelphia collar, and its ease of application favors use in the prehospital setting. The Malibu rigid high-thoracic CTO has a design similar to that of an extended Philadelphia collar; however, it is more effective in limiting cervical spine motion. In a study by Lunsford and co-workers, the Malibu brace outperformed the Miami J and Newport/Aspen collars by limiting total cervical motion.[81] The Nebraska collar, which is a variation of the Minerva orthosis, has a high support for the occiput along

TABLE 27–4

Comparison of Extension Restricted by Various Cervical Orthoses at Each Motion Segment

Orthosis	Normal Extension Restricted (%)							
	Occ–C1	*C1–C2*	*C2–C3*	*C3–C4*	*C4–C5*	*C5–C6*	*C6–C7*	*C7–T1*
CO								
Soft collar[59]	24	67	18	26	30	26	9	3
High-thoracic CTO								
Philadelphia[59]	62	25	63	56	41	44	30	51
Miami J*	72	58	64	54	55	55	51	—
NecLoc[64*]	84	51	79	72	65	58	46	—
Newport/Aspen[55*]	57	51	65	56	53	58	37	—
Stifneck[52*]	63	52	39	49	56	55	28	—
Low-thoracic CTO								
SOMI[59]	50	11	8	20	39	43	32	23
Yale[59]	59	42	66	64	58	61	53	63
Four poster[59]	49	47	58	60	65	72	63	64
Minerva[113]	48	49	21	44	41	65	48	—
Halo vest[59]	80	57	85	100	97	84	76	—

*Askins, V.; et al. Spine 22:1193–1198, 1997.
Abbreviations: CO, cervical orthosis; CTO, cervicothoracic orthosis; SOMI, sternal-occipital-mandibular immobilizer.

with a strap placed around the forehead and a short breastplate.[2] The Nebraska collar was found to be even more effective than some low-thoracic CTOs (i.e., SOMI [sternal-occipital-mandibular immobilizer]) in restricting all planes of cervical motion.[2]

Low-thoracic CTOs, similar to high-thoracic CTOs, attach to the cranium at the occiput and mandible, but they extend to the lower part of the thorax below the sternal notch and T3 spinous process[22] (see Fig. 27–8C). Commonly used low-thoracic CTOs include the SOMI, the Yale brace, the four-poster brace, and the Minerva-type orthoses. All these braces provide better fixation to the head and trunk than high-thoracic CTOs and are therefore the most effective of all cervical braces. The major difference between high- and low-thoracic CTOs is the ability of the latter to provide better control of spinal rotation and sagittal motion in the mid and lower cervical spine.

The SOMI (see Fig. 27–9C), the most popular low-thoracic CTO, consists of rigid metal frames with padded shoulder straps, a strap placed around the trunk, and variable sizes of the chest component. The SOMI brace is most effective in stabilizing the C1–C5 region, especially in flexion-extension, and is therefore recommended for upper cervical fractures that are unstable in the sagittal plane (i.e., type II hangman's fracture). SOMI braces are reported to be comfortable and well tolerated by patients, especially in the upright position.

The Yale brace is a modified form of the Philadelphia collar that has a molded plastic shell extending over the front and back of the thorax. The Yale brace restricts 87% of flexion-extension, 61% of lateral bending, and 75% of axial rotation.[60] This brace is more effective than the SOMI in limiting flexion-extension at C2–C3 and C3–T1, but less effective at C1–C2.[58] Similar to other CTOs, the Yale brace does not provide sufficient control of motion at the occiput–C1 level. Patient comfort and compliance are high with the Yale brace, and the lack of bulky posterior components (similar to the SOMI) can further enhance patient comfort while lying prone. Most four-poster braces

are less accepted by patients because of their bulky posterior components.

Minerva-type braces have extended occipital support and are equipped with a forehead strap for better immobilization of the head.[113] These braces provide adequate cervical spine immobilization from C1 to C7. When compared with other CTOs, Minerva-type braces offer better control of flexion-extension at C1–C2 and can limit up to 88% of normal axial rotation.[113] In one analysis of total residual cervical motion, the Minerva orthosis had stabilizing characteristics comparable to those of a halo vest orthosis.[14]

Studies to date have demonstrated that all cervical spine orthoses possess inherent deficiencies. Although both high- and low-thoracic CTOs can significantly restrict upper cervical spine motion, "paradoxical" motion or "snaking" can usually occur in sagittal flexion at the occiput–C1 level. "Snaking," which can also occur with halo vest stabilization,[60] is least pronounced with Minerva-type orthoses.[14] Comparative studies of the biomechanical properties of cervical braces reveal significant variability in all planes of cervical motion measured. Moreover, most clinical studies of cervical bracing typically use healthy volunteers, and it is clear that ultimate orthotic performance may differ significantly in an unstable cervical spine. The altered spinal biomechanics after injury in combination with associated soft tissue spasms may adversely affect the effectiveness of the orthosis in clinical settings. Finally, although general indications have been established for specific cervical brace applications[60] (Table 27–5), no clinical consensus has been reached on the suitability of each CO for a specific spine injury. Therefore, it is imperative that the physician individualize selection of a particular cervical brace on the basis of injury type and patient profile.

The duration that a cervical brace is applied is also controversial and depends on the function that it is serving. Brace use can be limited to protecting the patient during transport or throughout the emergency evaluation process. For confirmed unstable spinal injuries, these orthoses can

---

TABLE 27–5

Recommended Orthosis for Selected Cervical Injuries

Injury	Motion Segment Affected	Plane of Instability	Recommended Orthosis
Ring C1 (Jefferson's fracture)			
Stable	Occ–C1	All	Yale brace
Unstable	Occ–C2	All	Halo vest
Odontoid fracture (types II and III)	C1–C2	All	Halo vest
Atlantoaxial instability	C1–C2	Flexion	SOMI
Hangman's fracture			
Stable	C2–C3	Flexion	SOMI
Unstable	C2–C3	All	Halo vest
Midcervical flexion injuries	C3–C5	Flexion	Yale brace, SOMI
Low-cervical flexion injuries	C5–T1	Flexion	Yale brace, SOMI, Four-poster brace
Midcervical extension injuries	C3–C5	Extension	Halo
Low-cervical extension injuries	C5–T1	Extension	Yale brace, Four-poster brace

Abbreviation: SOMI, sternal-occipital-mandibular immobilizer.

be used in combination with restricted activity until definitive treatment can be implemented. In patients with stable fractures or minor soft tissue injuries, COs can be used for several weeks or months until the patient's symptoms and risk have resolved.

THORACIC AND LUMBAR BRACES

The thoracic spine is unique among spinal regions in terms of its inherent rigidity and location between highly mobile adjacent cervical and lumbar segments. The midspine location of the thoracic segments makes this region particularly amenable to bracing. Furthermore, the rib cage, sternum, and shoulder girdle act as additional stabilizers. However, achieving significant restriction of movement in an unstable thoracic spine can be difficult because of the continuous breathing movements. In addition, rotation, the principal motion of the thoracic spine, is much more difficult to control than flexion and extension. Therefore, thoracic spinal bracing is indicated only for acute spinal trauma or postoperative support, and it is rarely effective for degenerative disorders.

The lumbar spine, particular its lower segments, is difficult to brace because of the limited caudal fixation points and its physiologic hypermobility. Typically, adequate stabilization requires that the brace extend as much as four or five vertebral levels proximal and distal to the unstable segment.[13] Even when the brace includes a hip spica component, hip flexion is not adequately controlled, and this mobility results in inadequate lumbar protection.[8]

The goal of thoracolumbar bracing is to support the spine by limiting overall trunk motion, decreasing muscular activity, increasing intra-abdominal pressure, reducing spinal loads, and limiting spinal motion. Current available orthoses include lumbosacral corsets, Jewett braces, and full-contact custom-molded orthoses. Selection of the appropriate orthotic is dependent on the type of injury, the extent of spinal stability, associated injuries, body habitus, and the patient's age.[7, 119]

Lumbosacral corsets and elastic bands are generally used to diminish pain, decrease lumbar spine mobility, and support the paraspinal muscles. Although these braces reduce overall upper trunk motion, they have little effect on intersegmental spinal motion or loads. Neither soft nor rigid corsets have any stabilizing effect on sagittal, axial, or transverse intervertebral translation.[8] Corsets decrease low back pain primarily because they act as a "reminder" to the patient to avoid excessive forward or lateral bending. Paradoxically, however, increased motion can occur at L5–S1 as a result of long lumbosacral corsets. Corsets should therefore be restricted to patients with stable injury patterns or elderly patients with osteoporosis.[7] Among the potential adverse effects of lumbosacral corsets are disuse muscle atrophy, osteopenia/osteoporosis, psychologic dependency, and concentration of forces at the lumbosacral junction.

One of the oldest and probably the most reliable thoracolumbosacral orthosis (TLSO) is the Jewett hyperextension brace (Fig. 27–10). This brace applies three-point fixation anteriorly at the sternum and pubis and posteriorly at the thoracolumbar junction to maintain the thoracolum-

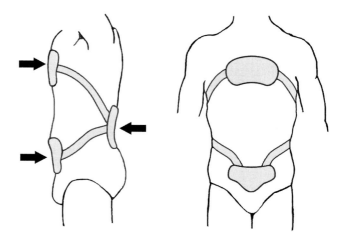

FIGURE 27–10. The Jewett brace is a three-point fixation system (*arrows*) that maintains extension of the thoracolumbar area. The brace has a light adjustable aluminum frame that allows free extension but prevents flexion.

bar spine in extension. The brace allows for hyperextension, prevents flexion, and is lightweight and easily adjustable. The Jewett brace is generally recommended for patients with injuries at the T6–L3 region that are unstable in flexion.[7] Nagel and associates demonstrated that the Jewett brace reduces intersegmental motion and flexion at the thoracolumbar junction whereas lateral bending and axial rotation are not affected because of its lack of pelvic support.[93] In a finite-element model simulating thoracolumbar injuries, the Jewett hyperextension brace restored stiffness to normal values in one- and two-column lumbar fractures, but it was ineffective for three-column injuries.[99]

In a cadaver study, Nagel and colleagues compared the effectiveness of the Taylor-Knight brace, the Jewett brace, and a body cast in immobilizing the L1–L2 segment after progressive ligament injury in the posterior, middle, and anterior columns.[93] The Taylor-Knight brace effectively reduced flexion and lateral bending, but it provided little resistance to axial rotation. The Jewett brace reduced flexion 40%, but it also had minimal effect on lateral bending or rotation. Only the body cast markedly reduced intersegmental spinal motion in all planes.

The full-contact TLSO is currently the most effective orthosis for nonoperative management of patients with thoracolumbar fractures.[99] The advantages of a custom-molded full-contact TLSO (Fig. 27–11) include distribution of force over a large surface area, improved fixation of the pelvis and thorax, better control of lateral bending and axial rotation, consistent patient and nursing acceptance, and improved, nonobscured radiographs.[7] Theoretically, the TLSO allows for correction of deformity by patient positioning during the molding process. In patients with compromised sensation, a total-contact orthosis is always preferable to a cast because it can be removed for skin monitoring and readily adjusted to relieve areas subjected to excessive pressure.

Reid and co-workers reviewed patients with thoracolumbar burst fractures who were treated with a custom-molded TLSO and permitted early ambulation.[102] All patients healed without loss of spinal alignment or progression of neurologic deficit. Studies by Cantor and colleagues and Mumford and co-workers also reported favorable results without complications for patients with thoracolumbar burst fractures treated with custom-molded TLSOs.[25, 92] Studies suggest that custom-molded TLSOs are indicated for patients with instabilities in more than one plane, impaired skin sensation, or multiple osteoporotic compression fractures. A total-contact TLSO may be indicated for very obese or noncompliant patients.[7] Custom-molded TLSOs had a greater immobilizing effect than lumbosacral corsets and chair-back braces; however, overall restriction of trunk rotation was limited in all these braces.[68]

Biomechanically, lumbar braces were found to be most effective at the center and to have increased spinal motion at the ends of the brace.[40] The Baycast jacket limited intersegmental spinal motion to 50% to 60% of normal; extension of the Baycast jacket with a leg spica (Fig. 27–12) additionally reduced spinal motion at the L4–L5 and L5–S1 regions to 12% and 8% of the normal range.[40]

Treatment protocols for application of a thoracolumbar brace vary greatly among physicians. It is preferable that braces be worn at all times, during sleep and all daily activities. Standard total-contact TLSO or other braces do not effectively immobilize segments below L4 and above T8, so a spica TLSO with 15° to 30° of hip flexion is recommended for injuries below L4 and a custom-molded cervical extension for injuries above T8.

SPECIFIC BEDS FOR SPINE-INJURED PATIENTS

Bed selection in the management of patients with spine injuries is critical for optimal reduction and prevention

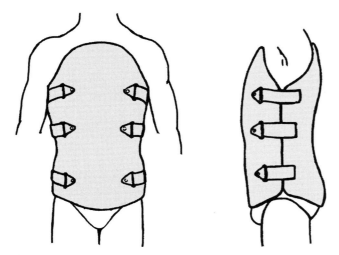

FIGURE 27–11. A custom-molded thoracolumbosacral orthosis must be fabricated by a skilled orthotist. After fitting, the skin should be checked for excessive pressure, and if present, the brace should be modified. Molding for the orthosis should be delayed if the patient has abdominal distention or excessive weight gain from fluid retention. (Redrawn from Sypert, G.W. External spinal orthotics. Neurosurgery 20:642–649, 1987.)

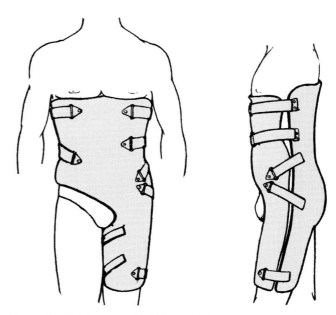

FIGURE 27–12. Custom-molded thoracolumbosacral orthosis extended with a lumbosacral spica. (Redrawn from Sypert, G.W. External spinal orthotics. Neurosurgery 20:642–649, 1987.)

of secondary complications. Standard hospital beds are suitable for most cervical, thoracic, and lumbar injuries in the acute setting but should be modified with an "egg crate" mattress to prevent decubitus ulcers. These beds are preferable for multitrauma patients so that traction can be applied to both the cervical spine and extremities. Patients can be logrolled if the other injuries allow.

Prolonged immobilization can be the principal cause of morbidity in bedridden patients; therefore, early mobilization of spine-disabled patients on special rotating beds was developed for that purpose. The bed is usually maintained in perpetual motion with each patient rotated more than 200 times a day. Bed mobility is generally only interrupted for treatment, feeding, diagnostic tests, and personal hygiene.

Two types of beds with turning frames are currently popular. In the Stryker bed, the patient is turned along the longitudinal axis to allow dorsal skin care and personal hygiene. Traction can be applied in the longitudinal axis, but it is very difficult to achieve traction forces in any other plane. The suitability of this frame for cervical spine immobilization has been criticized.[87, 114] The Rotorest frame is a table that continuously turns the patient equally from side to side in an affixed posture, with a maximal excursion of 124° every 4.5 minutes (Fig. 27–13). Skeletal alignment is achieved by a series of adjustable support packs that create surface compartments. Centrally placed cervical, thoracic, and pelvic hatches permit wound care, personal hygiene, lumbar puncture, chest auscultation, and bowel and bladder hygiene without altering the patient's position. The Rotorest frame allows for traction forces in multiple planes, both to the axial skeleton and to the extremities.

McGuire and colleagues compared the Stryker frame and the Rotorest in unstable cervical and lumbar seg-

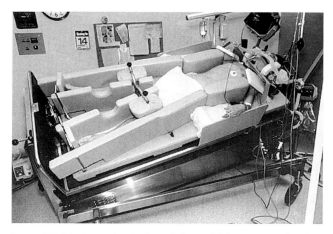

FIGURE 27–13. A rotating bed used for multiple-trauma and spine-injured patients permits access to all areas of the body. Pulmonary and skin problems are reduced by the rotating motion.

ments and demonstrated that the Rotorest bed was more effective.[87] The Stryker frame permitted significant displacement of both unstable lumbar and cervical segments during transition from the supine to the prone position.

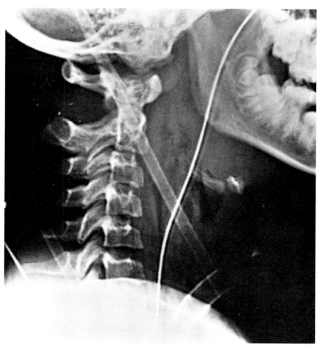

FIGURE 27–14. Fixed occipitocervical subluxation in a 12-year-old boy without a neurologic deficit.

NONOPERATIVE MANAGEMENT OF SPECIFIC SPINAL INJURIES

Occipitocervical Injuries

Occipitocervical injuries (Fig. 27–14) are usually lethal, but when the rare patient is encountered, it is imperative that the physician have a high index of suspicion to properly ensure the patient's survival. Occipitocervical malalignment can be determined by using the Powers ratio to assess the lateral radiograph (Fig. 27–15). Initially, all occipitocervical subluxations or dislocations should be meticulously immobilized on a backboard with sandbags and tape to secure the position of the head. Type I (anterior) and III (posterior) injuries (Fig. 27–16) can be treated with minimal traction (5 lb), but the pins should be placed in a manner that allows slight extension or flexion, respectively, to achieve reduction.[121] In type II (axial distraction) injuries, occiput alignment is generally acceptable, and traction involving any degree of distraction is strictly contraindicated. This injury is extremely unstable, and posterior occipital-cervical fusion with at least 3 months of halo vest immobilization is more appropriate definitive treatment. Lateral flexion-extension stress radiographs are essential to document stability before halo removal.

Occipital condyle fractures occur quite frequently and can usually be managed nonoperatively (Fig. 27–17). Type I (impacted occipital condyle fracture) and type II (occipital condyle fracture in conjunction with a basilar skull fracture) fractures typically require only in situ immobilization with a cervical collar for 8 weeks.[5] The more unstable type III injury (occipital condyle fracture plus an avulsion fracture caused by pull of the alar

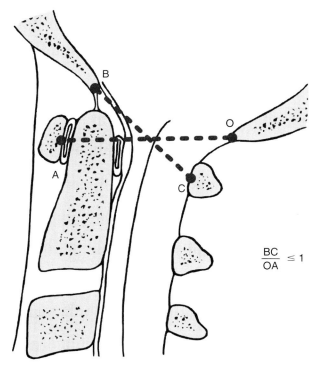

$$\frac{BC}{OA} \leq 1$$

FIGURE 27–15. The Powers ratio is a value of the distance between the basion (B) and the posterior arch of the atlas (C) divided by the distance between the opision (O) and the anterior arch of the atlas (A). Normally, the Powers ratio is 1 or less. A Powers ratio greater than 1 suggests anterior occipitocervical subluxation or dislocation. (Redrawn from Eismont, F.J.; Frazier, D.D. In: Levine A.M.; et al., eds. Spine Trauma. Philadelphia, W.B. Saunders, 1998, p. 198.)

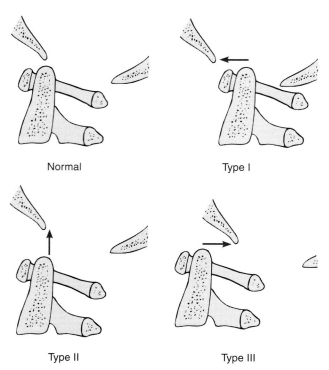

Figure 27–16. Classification of occipitocervical subluxation and dislocation proposed by Traynelis and colleagues. (From Traynelis, V.C.; et al. J Neurosurg 65:863–870, 1986.)

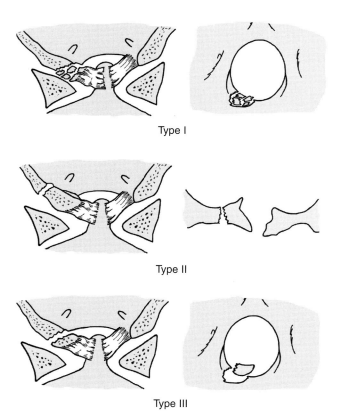

Figure 27–17. Anderson-Montesano classification of occipital condyle fractures. (From Anderson, P.A.; Montesano, P.X. Spine 13:731–736, 1988.)

ligament) requires halo vest immobilization for 12 weeks. Surgery is warranted for occipital condyle fractures only after an attempt at conservative treatment is unsuccessful because of occipitocervical pain.[5]

Fractures of the Atlas

Fractures of the atlas can generally be treated nonoperatively if the fracture is stable and in acceptable alignment. Atlas fractures frequently occur in conjunction with other cervical spine injuries, and these other injuries will often determine the optimal method of treatment. Most isolated atlas fractures are stable because of an intact transverse ligament (Fig. 27–18), are not associated with neurologic deficit, and can usually be treated nonoperatively. Posterior arch fractures are generally stable and nondisplaced and require only a high-thoracic CTO for 2 to 3 months. When the transverse ligament is disrupted, a Jefferson or lateral mass fracture can result in greater than 7 mm of lateral displacement (Fig. 27–19). These fractures will benefit from cervical traction to achieve reduction and eventual halo vest stabilization (Fig. 27–20).

Axial traction should be applied through a halo ring (as opposed to tongs) to facilitate eventual vest application. Weight should begin at about 10 lb and typically be increased gradually up to as much as 40 lb before full reduction of the ring can be appreciated on an open-mouth view. Patients must be maintained in traction for at least 4 weeks for sufficient healing to permit placement in a halo vest. Traction is removed while the patient remains supine, and an open-mouth radiograph is taken after 1 hour. If lateral mass symmetry is maintained, a halo vest is applied. If malalignment recurs, traction is reapplied and healing reevaluated at 2-week intervals. Traction may be necessary for up to 6 to 8 weeks before halo vest support can be

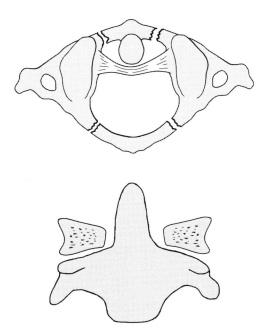

Figure 27–18. A Jefferson fracture of the atlas with a preserved transverse ligament.

applied for an additional 6 weeks. When reduction cannot be achieved or maintained or the patient is unable to tolerate prolonged traction or a halo vest orthosis, surgical reduction and fusion are warranted.

Transverse ligament disruptions without fractures of the atlas are extremely unstable. Additionally, these injuries are inherently at great risk for neurologic compromise and are best managed operatively.

Odontoid Fractures

Type I odontoid fractures (apical ligament and bony avulsion) (Fig. 27–21) are essentially stable and require limited if any external support.[4] Type III fractures (extension extending below the waist of the odontoid into the body of C2) usually heal uneventfully. Reduction is achieved by axial halo traction, and to ensure that dens alignment is maintained, these injuries are optimally immobilized in a halo vest because other COs are associated with up to a 15% incidence of nonunion.[28] Type II odontoid injuries (fracture through the waist of the odontoid) have an extremely high incidence of nonunion and usually warrant operative management. Nonoperative treatment is reasonable if the injury is recognized early, the displacement is minimal and can be reduced, reduction is maintained, and the patient is not elderly.[15, 28]

Nonoperative treatment is initiated with halo ring traction. Traction is usually effective with relatively light weight (10 to 20 lb), and application of bivector traction can assist in correcting translation (if >5 mm) and angula-

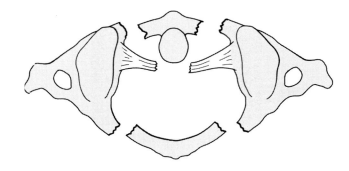

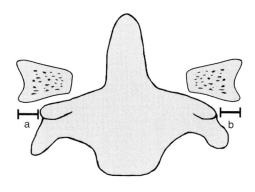

$$a + b > 7\,mm$$

FIGURE 27–19. A Jefferson fracture of the atlas with a disrupted transverse ligament results in laterally displaced masses of C1 more than 7 mm in total (a + b).

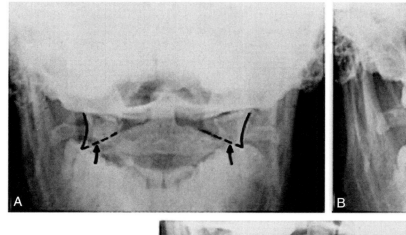

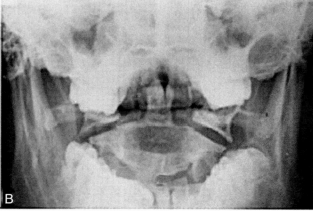

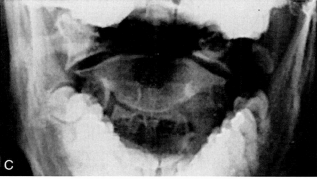

FIGURE 27–20. Open-mouth view of a significantly displaced C1 fracture taken at the time of injury (*A*). Traction (30 lb) reduces the deformity (*B*) and must be maintained for at least 6 weeks before halo vest application. Late follow-up shows maintenance of reduction (*C*).

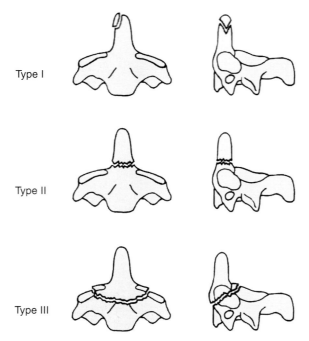

FIGURE 27–21. Anderson and D'Alonzo classification of odontoid fractures.

tion (if >10°). When lateral radiography has confirmed the reduction, a halo vest can be applied. After the patient is upright, serial follow-up radiographs are essential until the fracture has healed. Loss of reduction warrants adjustment of the halo by neck flexion-extension or sagittal-plane translation. When malalignment or instability persists, treatment should be operative.

Traumatic Spondylolisthesis of the Axis (Hangman's Fractures)

Bipedicular or pars interarticularis fractures (hangman's fractures) of the second cervical vertebra have varying degrees of angular or translational stability that determine the appropriate treatment (Fig. 27–22). Type I fractures result from hyperextension and axial loading and have minimal (less than 3 mm) displacement and angulation (less than 11°) (Fig. 27–23).[73] Reduction is not required, and after stable lateral flexion-extension radiographs, a high- or low-thoracic CTO for 2 to 3 months is sufficient immobilization. A similar treatment protocol is appropriate for type IA fractures (less than 3-mm translation, but without angulation). It is critical that the physician accurately distinguish between a stable type I injury and the more unstable type II injury.

Type II hangman's fractures (vertical pars fracture adjacent to the body with significant translation and flexion angulation) are extremely unstable. The patient's supine hyperextended neck position may spontaneously reduce the fracture, and slight flexion stress views may be warranted to confirm the injury pattern. Reduction is achieved by halo ring application and, with the head slightly extended, gentle cervical traction under fluoroscopic control. Angulation may correct easily with exten-

sion, whereas residual translation often requires elevation of the torso by placing a rolled towel at the cervicothoracic junction, which permits the upper cervical spine to translate posteriorly. Postreduction immobilization consists of a halo vest if the reduction can be maintained within 3 to 6 mm of normal alignment. If greater than 6 to 8 mm of translation persists, the patient is preferably maintained in halo traction for 4 to 6 weeks and then secondarily placed in a halo vest. Type II injuries will typically heal at the pars and anteriorly with some degree of C2–C3 ankylosis.

Type IIA hangman's fractures (oblique midpars fractures with severe angulation and no translation) are also extremely unstable injuries that can be reduced with simple extension, but distraction is absolutely contraindicated because of complete disruption of the anterior longitudinal ligament and annulus and the risk of pronounced axial displacement (Fig. 27–24). Once the neck is extended into a reduced position, a halo vest should be applied under fluoroscopic control and worn for 2 to 3 months.

Type III fractures are uncommon and consist of C2 pars fractures associated with unilateral or bilateral C2–C3 facet dislocation. Nonoperative management (i.e., traction, manipulation) is contraindicated in these injuries because of loss of continuity between the C2 body and the posterior elements/facets.

Lower Cervical Spine Injuries

Ligamentous injuries of the lower cervical spine can range from simple sprains without malalignment, to subluxation with partial loss of cervical spine ligamentous stability, to frank dislocation with total ligamentous disruption. Lower cervical spine instability has been described by White and co-workers (Table 27–6) and is based on the extent of segmental angular or translation displacement[129, 130] (Fig. 27–25). Dislocations may spontaneously reduce with supine positioning, and the degree of instability is often not easily appreciated on a static radiograph. Likewise, dislocations may become fixed or locked in a malaligned position and require cervical traction or open manipula-

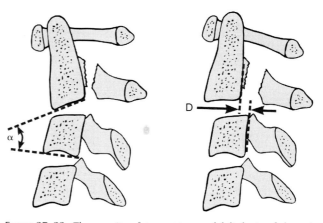

FIGURE 27–22. The severity of traumatic spondylolisthesis of the axis (hangman's fractures) is characterized by angulation (α) and translation (D). (Redrawn from Levine, A.M. In: Levine A.M.; et al., eds. Spine Trauma. Philadelphia, W.B. Saunders, 1998, p. 280.)

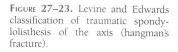

FIGURE 27–23. Levine and Edwards classification of traumatic spondylolisthesis of the axis (hangman's fracture).

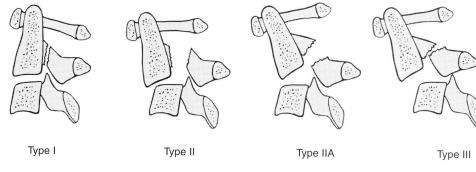

| Type I | Type II | Type IIA | Type III |

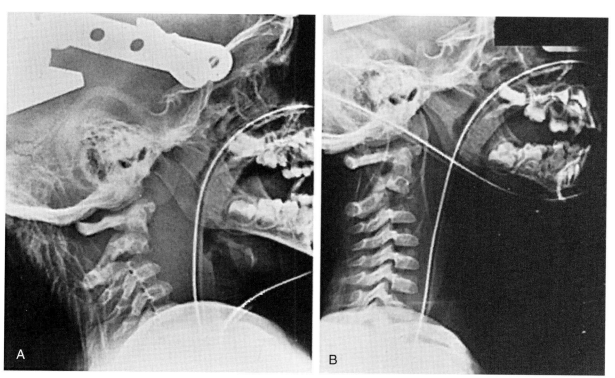

FIGURE 27–24. Type IIA hangman's fracture before traction (A) and after cervical traction has been applied (B). Traction is contraindicated for type IIA hangman's fractures because it leads to significant overdistraction.

tion for reduction. After reduction and depending on the extent of disruption of the posterior ligamentous complex, cervical immobilization in a cervical orthosis for 6 to 8 weeks is sufficient. If reduction cannot be maintained or pain persists after adequate immobilization, operative stabilization is indicated.

Cervical compression fractures involve less than 50% loss of anterior vertebral body height and maintenance of posterior ligamentous integrity. Usually, a CO for symptomatic relief is sufficient treatment for this stable fracture. When compression of the anterior vertebrae exceeds 50% of the vertebral body height, flexion-distraction occurs in conjunction with posterior ligamentous disruption. Flexion–axial compression loading injuries associated with disc disruption plus an anterior vertebral body fracture are more challenging because CO or halo vest immobilization alone is plagued by a high incidence of persistent fracture displacement and loss of alignment.[29] Moreover, when the injury pattern also includes disruption of the facet capsule

TABLE 27–6

Checklist for the Diagnosis of Clinical Instability of the Lower Cervical Spine

Element		Points*
Anterior elements destroyed or unable to function		2
Posterior elements destroyed or unable to function		2
Radiographic criteria		4
Sagittal displacement >3.5 mm	2	
Relative sagittal angulation >11°	2	
Positive stretch test		2
Spinal cord injury		2
Nerve root injury		1
Abnormal disc narrowing		1
Dangerous loading anticipated		1

*A total of 5 or more points represents instability.
Source: White, A.A.; et al. Spine 1:15–27, 1976.

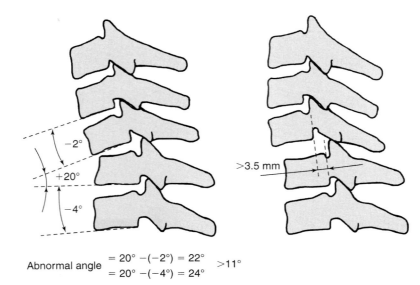

$$\text{Abnormal angle} \quad \begin{aligned} &= 20° - (-2°) = 22° \\ &= 20° - (-4°) = 24° \end{aligned} \quad {>11°}$$

FIGURE 27-25. Angular displacement 11° greater than that at the adjacent vertebral segments suggests instability from posterior ligamentous disruption, just as translation greater than 3.5 mm does. (From White, A.A.; Panjabi, M.M. Clinical Biomechanics of the Spine. Philadelphia, J.B. Lippincott, 1978, pp. 236–251.)

and posterior ligamentous structures, a significant risk for late instability exists.[27, 126]

Although unilateral or bilateral facet subluxations, dislocations, or fractures (or combinations of these injuries) are variations of the same injury patterns, determination of optimal treatment requires that distinctions be made between these specific injuries. As unilateral or bilateral facet injuries progress from subluxation to perched facets and finally to frank dislocation, the extent of cervical spine malalignment reflects the degree of facet capsule or posterior ligament disruption, or both (Fig. 27–26). Facet subluxations or unilateral dislocations may achieve some degree of segmental stability after reduction and nonoperative treatment. However, a facet fracture suggests persis-

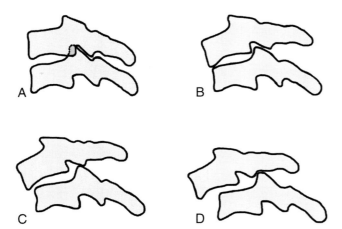

FIGURE 27-26. Normal position (A) of the cervical vertebrae in the lateral projection. A subluxated position (B) is recognized by fanning of the spinous process, increased angulation of the vertebrae, and excessive separation of the facets. Perched facets (C) are recognized by the tip of the inferior facet resting on the tip of the superior facet. Dislocated facets (D) are determined by the displacement of the inferior facet anterior to the superior facet.

tent rotational and flexion instability and is most appropriately managed surgically.

Reduction of Unilateral or Bilateral Facet Injuries

Unilateral and bilateral facet injuries should be reduced by closed means with skeletal traction in patients who are oriented and able to be assessed neurologically. After reduction, unilateral facet dislocations can often be treated in closed fashion with a halo vest, whereas bilateral facet dislocations are best managed with operative stabilization. Gardner-Wells tongs should be applied if operative stabilization is anticipated, whereas a halo ring is used for unilateral facet dislocations that are to be maintained in a halo vest. The patient is placed supine on a bed with approximately 20° of head elevation to offset the skeletal traction to be applied. If sedation is used, only mild doses of analgesics or muscle relaxants (or both) are warranted. Throughout the maneuver, the patient has to remain responsive and neurologically stable.

Initially, a weight of 10 to 15 lb is applied through traction in line with the spine. Serial static radiographs or dynamic fluoroscopy should assess spinal alignment after the initial weight is applied and after each subsequent addition of 5 to 10 lb. Static radiographs are best obtained 15 to 20 minutes after each weight increase to allow for soft tissue distraction. If the facets unlock, the neck should be slightly extended and the traction weight decreased to approximately 10 lb to permit the facets to spontaneously reduce (Fig. 27–27). Changing the direction of the traction vector can facilitate the reduction of unlocked facets and assist in maintaining the reduction (Fig. 27–28). When spinal reduction has been achieved, halo vest application or surgical stabilization should be performed before permitting upright mobilization.

Occasionally, resistant unilateral facet dislocations will benefit from the head and neck being slightly turned away

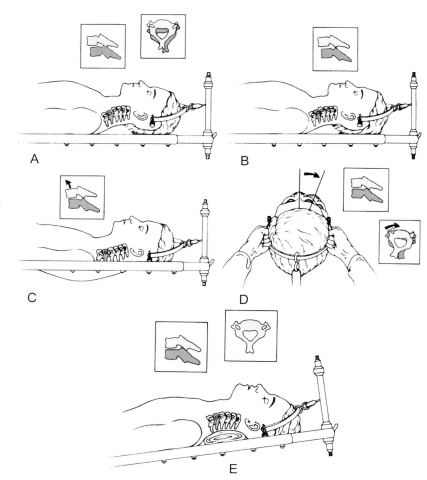

FIGURE 27–27. Initial position of a unilateral facet dislocation in both the sagittal and the axial planes (*A*). Traction permits some distraction but not reduction (*B*). Flexion of the neck increases distraction, but the facet is still dislocated (*C*). Lateral tilt away from the side of dislocation unlocks the dislocation (*D*), and after extending and putting the neck in a neutral position, the reduction is completed (*E*).

from the side of dislocation to facilitate disengagement of the facet. Bilateral facet dislocations are extremely unstable and will generally reduce with low traction weight and slight flexion, followed by neck extension without rotational manipulation. If the patient's neurologic status becomes altered during any of these maneuvers, all traction and manipulation should be terminated and the spine secured in a neutral position. Open surgical reduction is absolutely indicated in these patients, as well as those who simply fail attempts at closed treatment. Reduced unilateral or bilateral facet dislocations can still fail because of persistent instability and pain despite halo vest immobilization and therefore warrant surgical stabilization.

Eismont and coauthors reported the risk of neurologic deficit from an associated disc herniation after closed reduction of cervical spine facet dislocations.[37] Although other authors have reported similar findings,[82, 106] the actual incidence of this catastrophe remains relatively low. Rizzolo and colleagues recommended that immediate closed cervical skeletal traction reduction be performed without a previous MRI scan only in alert, oriented patients who are neurologically intact.[105] MRI is absolutely indicated for patients with neurologic deficit before traction and for patients who require open surgical reduction.

Sears and Fazl reviewed 70 patients with facet injuries treated in a halo vest and found that stability and anatomic reduction could be maintained with a halo in only 44% and 21% of patients, respectively.[111] These results corroborated an earlier study by Koch and Nickel, who demonstrated that maintaining facet reduction requires constant distraction and that halo vest patients typically experience axial compression during standing and walking.[65] Rorabeck and colleagues reviewed a group of patients with facet fractures, 14 of whom were treated operatively without pain or any need for secondary surgery.[108] These patients were compared with a separate injury group that was treated nonoperatively; in this second group, seven patients had pain and five patients required secondary surgical procedures. Therefore, although unilateral facet fractures can respond to nonoperative management, a successful outcome is not guaranteed.

Fracture separation of the lateral articular mass, unlike facet injuries, results from hyperextension or axial loading and lateral bending instead of flexion-rotation. This particular injury is often missed on plain radiography, which depicts segmental translation and rotation without flexion or facet displacement. When the patient is supine, the displaced lateral mass can reduce spontaneously even before the application of traction. Nonoperative treatment

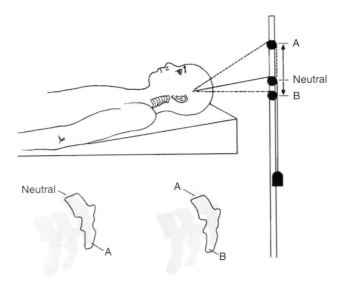

FIGURE 27–28. Reduction of a facet dislocation by traction. Facets treated with traction in the neutral position will unlock and remain perched. Changing the direction of the traction vector above neutral (to point A) permits reduction of the unlocked facets. Changing the traction vector below neutral (to point B) allows maintenance of reduction at lower traction weights.

facet fractures) and injuries associated with significant soft tissue disruption. Soft tissue or ligamentous injuries are extremely difficult to accurately diagnose with static radiographs, and dynamic or stress radiographs are often necessary. Dynamic radiographs are also recommended at the completion of brace treatment. Although nonoperative treatment is quite effective, the medical and economic impact of such treatment has been challenged.[31] Operative treatment results in less time in bed, earlier physical therapy, and an overall decrease in total cost to society. Therefore, the clinician must carefully determine the injuries that are likely to respond favorably to nonoperative treatment without any risk of late instability, pain, or neurologic deficit.

Teardrop fractures are unique flexion/compression injuries in the mid to lower cervical spine (C3–C7) and are extremely dangerous because of the high incidence of associated instability and neurologic deficit. Even when seemingly well aligned, these injuries can progress rapidly to significant deformity as a result of their extensive ligamentous disruption.

Extension teardrop fractures can be stable (no posterior ligamentous disruption), and thus are suitable for cervical brace immobilization for 3 months, with lateral flexion-

consists of a halo vest and is indicated only if the injury is nondisplaced. Unfortunately, even a nondisplaced fracture separation may displace secondarily, so surgical stabilization is preferable for this injury.

Vertebral Body Fractures

Compression fractures of the lower cervical spine are caused by flexion-induced axial compression forces that result in loss of anterior body height and some degree of distraction posteriorly. When flexion is combined with significant rotation or translation, subluxation of the injured vertebra can occur. When the force of injury is predominantly axial, burst fractures are produced along with disruption of the anterior and middle columns and are frequently associated with neurologic injury (Fig. 27–29). Treatment of both these injury patterns should initially consist of halo traction beginning at 15 to 20 lb and increasing in 5-lb increments until normal alignment has been restored. Pronounced instability frequently persists in patients with significant posterior ligamentous disruption or a large anterior teardrop fracture. Nonoperative treatment consisting of a halo vest should be restricted to neurologically intact patients with pure flexion injuries and minimal residual deformity (less than 20° of anterior body compression). Patients with unstable injuries who are not candidates for surgery or a halo vest because of polytrauma require extended bedrest with halo traction until early healing has been achieved.

Most lower cervical spine injuries will heal with sufficient stability if they can be anatomically reduced and the reduction is maintained throughout treatment. Exceptions include torsionally unstable fractures (i.e., lateral mass or

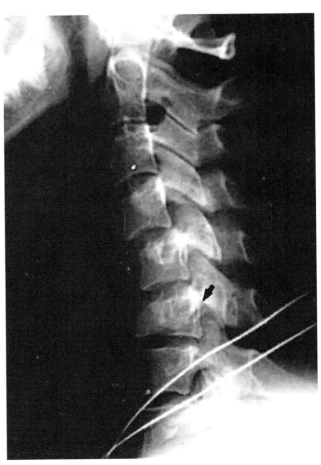

FIGURE 27–29. Burst fracture of the C6 vertebra with partial displacement of the body into the canal (*arrow*).

extension radiographs obtained to document stability. Radiographically, unstable teardrop fractures have greater than 3 mm of retrolisthesis or more than 11° of angulation or give rise to neurologic deficits (or any combination of these findings); such fractures should be placed in tongs traction to restore alignment before surgical stabilization.

Thoracic Spine Injuries

The thoracic spine is inherently stable because of the rigidity created by the structural configuration of the spine, sternum, and rib cage. Injuries in this region usually require a significant component of axial load or flexion (or both), and more severe injuries also involve a component of torsion[130] (Table 27–7).

Associated injuries occur in approximately 75% of thoracic spine injuries and can include rib fractures, pulmonary contusions, pneumothorax, cardiac contusions, and vascular injuries. Profound neurologic deficit occurs more frequently in the thoracic spine than in the cervical or thoracolumbar regions. In a series of 376 thoracic spine fractures, 235 (63%) resulted in complete neurologic injuries.[89] This high incidence of complete neurologic injury is due to the small size of the neural canal, the tenuous arterial blood supply to the thoracic cord, and the high energy required to inflict injury.

TABLE 27–7

Checklist for the Diagnosis of Clinical Instability of the Thoracic and Thoracolumbar Spine

Element		Points*
Anterior elements destroyed or unable to function		2
Posterior elements destroyed or unable to function		2
Radiographic criteria		4
Sagittal displacement >2.5 mm	2	
Relative sagittal angulation >5°	2	
Spinal cord or cauda equina damage		2
Disruption of costovertebral articulations		1
Dangerous loading anticipated		2

*A total of 5 or more points represents instability.
Source: White, A.A.; Panjabi, M.M. Clinical Biomechanics of the Spine. Philadelphia, J.B. Lippincott, 1978, pp. 236–251.

Thoracic spine fractures can usually be managed nonoperatively when the patient is neurologically intact. Even patients with axial load or burst fractures are generally neurologically intact, unless the fracture has a component of significant flexion or angulation, rotation, or translation.

An injured thoracic spine is more inherently stable than its cervical or lumbar counterparts; however, orthotic support is still essential in allowing earlier mobility and maintaining spinal alignment (Fig. 27–30). The standard

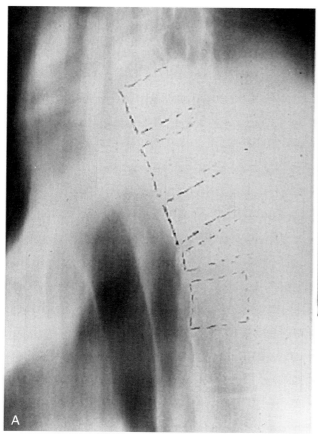

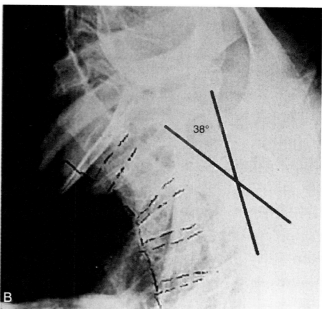

FIGURE 27–30. Fractures of the high thoracic region (T1–T6) are difficult to control. In this typical fracture of T3, no immobilization was used, and at 4 weeks the fracture had collapsed with a kyphotic deformity of 38°.

orthotic device, the TLSO, can include a cervical extension (CTLSO) for a high thoracic injury. Despite appropriate bracing, certain thoracic spine fractures may be complicated by late collapse and deformity. Therefore, these patients must be carefully monitored and occasionally maintained on an initial regimen of strict bedrest before brace application. Surgical intervention is warranted if the fracture is extremely unstable or bracing is poorly tolerated. Fractures secondary to gunshot injury are usually amenable to bracing even in the presence of a complete neurologic deficit.

Thoracolumbar Spine Fractures

Nonoperative measures have traditionally been the standard treatment of most thoracolumbar spine fractures and are most appropriate for stable thoracolumbar fractures. Before the advent of modern surgical techniques, the only treatment available for thoracolumbar fractures was postural reduction with hyperextension and immobilization.[9, 10, 44, 97] Fracture reduction was achieved by gravity, pillows, and manual manipulation in injuries with or without neurologic deficit. Although the risk of early or late neurologic loss was low, the recommended length of bedrest could approach 12 weeks. Union occurred in up to 98% of these patients,[9] and the initial indications for nonoperative treatment have even included irreducible fracture-dislocations, locked facets, and gunshot wounds.

Frankel and coauthors reported on a series of 205 thoracolumbar spine fractures treated with postural reduction, bedrest, and orthotic support.[44] Partial neurologic deficit improved in 72% of patients, whereas neurologic deterioration was noted in only 2% and late instability occurred in only two patients. These authors reserved surgery for patients with significant or progressive neurologic deficit. Currently, nonoperative treatment should be reserved for patients who are neurologically stable or intact and retain spine stability[131] (Table 27–8). Post-traumatic

TABLE 27–8 ....

Checklist for the Diagnosis of Clinical Instability of the Lumbosacral Spine

Element	Points*	
Anterior elements destroyed or unable to function		2
Posterior elements destroyed or unable to function		2
Radiographic criteria		4
Flexion-extension radiographs		
Sagittal translation >4.5 mm or 15%	2	
Sagittal rotation		
>15° at L1–L2, L2–L3, L3–L4	2	
>20° at L4–L5	2	
>25° at L5–S1	2	
Resting radiographs		
Sagittal displacement >4.5 mm or 15%	2	
Relative sagittal angulation >22°	2	
Cauda equina damage		3
Dangerous loading anticipated		1

....

*A total of 5 or more points represents instability.
Source: White, A.A.; Panjabi, M.M. Clinical Biomechanics of the Spine. Philadelphia, J.B. Lippincott, 1978, pp. 236–251.

kyphosis of up to 30° has been deemed acceptable in patients with stable burst fractures and no neurologic deficit.[67]

Weinstein and co-workers reported on the long-term outcome of 42 patients with unstable thoracolumbar burst fractures managed nonoperatively.[127] Neurologically intact patients did not have any worsening of their neurologic deficit. Spinal kyphosis was 26° in flexion and 17° in extension, and although some back pain was present in 90% of patients, only three required late operations. Interestingly, canal patency improved by 22% at follow-up as a result of resorption of bone fragments and canal remodeling. No correlation was found between the initial radiographic severity of the injury and residual deformity or symptoms at follow-up. These authors recommended nonoperative treatment of thoracolumbar fractures in patients with a nonpathologic single-level burst fracture and no neurologic deficit.

Denis reviewed 52 burst fractures without neurologic deficit that were treated nonoperatively and compared these patients with 13 who were stabilized with Harrington rods.[34] The large sagittal diameter of the spinal canal at the thoracolumbar junction appeared to also favor nonoperative treatment of selected burst fractures. However, 25% of the nonoperative patients were unable to return to work full-time, and late neurologic deterioration developed in 18%. Finn and Stauffer determined that the extent of thoracolumbar spinal canal encroachment did not directly correlate with the degree of neurologic deficit.[41]

Nonoperative treatment of thoracolumbar fractures typically begins with a period of recumbency ranging from 3 to 8 weeks. During this time, acceptable alignment of the spine should be achieved and maintained. Afterward, the patient is maintained in a TLSO for 3 to 4 months and permitted to ambulate as tolerated. Nonoperative treatment is preferred for stable burst fractures in patients without neurologic deficit or significant canal compromise (<50%) and with an initial kyphosis of less than 30°. All nonoperative patients required serial clinical and radiographic assessment to detect potential deformity or progression of neurologic deficit.

Factors associated with a successful outcome in the nonoperative treatment of burst fractures of the thoracolumbar spine have been identified by several authors and include the degree of initial kyphosis, the extent of anterior and posterior body height collapse, the number of columns injured, and the degree of initial canal compromise.[20, 25, 49, 67, 104] James and associates suggested that an intact posterior column was the best predictor of success in treating a stable burst fracture nonoperatively.[56] Reconstitution of canal size over time with conservative treatment was found to be age dependent, with greater canal reconstitution occurring in younger patients. Other predictors have been reported to be residual motion at the fracture site and the extent of the initial kyphosis.[25, 67, 92, 131]

Fredrickson and colleagues recommended that nonoperative treatment be reserved for patients without significant neurologic involvement (single nerve root or less), significant posterior ligamentous disruption, and translation injuries and with less than 25° of initial kyphosis.[45] Immobilization in a standard hospital bed and special turning frames (i.e., Rotorest bed) were reserved for polytraumatized patients restricted to prolonged bedrest.

Nonoperative patients are initially treated with a period of bedrest that can range from several days to 8 weeks, depending on the degree of fracture instability. Before ambulation, the patient is fitted for a molded body cast or custom TLSO. Injuries treated in this manner must be able to withstand normal weight bearing, but more strenuous activities (excessive bending, exercising, or lifting) are prohibited. Serial radiographs are taken throughout the treatment course to ensure that the kyphosis is less than 30° and canal compromise is less than 50%. Clinically, pain should progressively decrease and the patient should remain intact neurologically; otherwise, surgery is indicated.

SURGICAL MANAGEMENT OF CERVICAL AND THORACOLUMBAR INJURIES

Goals of Surgical Management

Most spine fractures can be treated nonoperatively. Only a small select group of unstable spine injuries with or without neurologic involvement warrant surgical treatment. Objectives of surgery include (1) restoration of spinal alignment, (2) restoration and maintenance of spinal stability, and (3) decompression of compromised neural elements.

The first goal of surgery is to reduce significant spine deformity to functionally acceptable alignment. The ability of any spinal instrumentation system to achieve this goal is based on its ability to effectively oppose the deforming forces and counteract the existing instability. Selection of appropriate instrumentation should therefore be determined by the mechanism of the fracture and its subsequent deforming forces. For example, the use of distraction instrumentation for a flexion-distraction type of fracture will further destabilize the spine. By contrast, the application of extension and compression type of instrumentation posteriorly would correct this deformity. In cases with associated facet dislocations, care must be taken when performing the reduction maneuver to avoid extruding disc material into the spinal canal.[74]

The second goal of surgery is to restore and maintain spinal stability in an unstable spine. The appropriate selection of instrumentation is again crucial in preventing recurrence of the deformity. Modern fixation devices for both anterior and posterior surgical procedures permit better stabilization while compromising a minimal number of motion segments. Advocates of anterior surgical stabilization contend that posterior fixation provides insufficient support for either axial or compressive loads on a compromised anterior spinal column.[35] The disadvantage of anterior surgery is the increased risk of morbidity because of the proximity of great vessels, chest and abdominal viscera, and the spinal cord. Furthermore, deformity reduction and stabilization seem to be less reliable with anterior techniques than with posterior procedures despite the recent improvements in anterior instrumentation.[3, 46, 62]

Posterior fixation, particularly with the evolution of pedicle screws, has achieved excellent correction of deformity through indirect reduction techniques. Aebi and colleagues used limited segmental fixation in one clinical series and reported correction of kyphosis from 15.8° to 3.5°.[1] Lindsey and co-workers demonstrated similar short-term results with these techniques, although the initial kyphotic deformity had recurred by the 2-year follow-up.[78, 79]

A principal goal of surgical management is adequate decompression of the neural elements to allow for maximal restoration of neurologic function. Decompression can be performed anteriorly, posteriorly, posterolaterally, transpedicularly, indirectly, or any combination of these approaches. Usually, the type of injury and timing of surgical intervention will determine the most appropriate type of decompression (i.e., posterior versus anterior).

Indirect decompression secondary to posterior restoration of spinal alignment has been shown to be very effective in patients undergoing surgery within 48 to 72 hours.[50] By applying distraction and correcting angulation with posterior instrumentation, indirect reduction is achieved through ligamentotaxis. The posterior longitudinal ligament becomes taut and can reduce retropulsed bony fragments away from the spinal canal (Fig. 27–31).

The literature suggests that the results of anterior direct versus posterior indirect spinal canal decompression are similar in patients with incomplete neurologic deficits.[26, 54, 71, 92] Gertzbein and colleagues reviewed the outcomes of patients with thoracolumbar fractures and incomplete neurologic deficits treated by anterior (direct) versus posterior (indirect) decompression.[48] In patients treated posteriorly versus anteriorly, neurologic status improved in 83% and 88%, respectively. Neurologic improvement in both groups was significantly better than the 60% to 70% recovery rate with nonoperative treatment cited in the literature. In a separate multicenter study[49] of 1019 patients with thoracolumbar spine fractures who were monitored for 2 years, the neurologic outcome of anterior and posterior surgery was similar.

Currently, the posterior indirect reduction technique is the standard method of treatment of most thoracolumbar spine fractures. Absolute indications for anterior decompression include a neurologically incomplete patient with greater than 50% canal compromise and one or more of the following: (1) more than 72 hours postinjury, (2) failed attempt at posterior reduction, and (3) significant loss of anterior and middle column (vertebral body) support despite posterior reduction.

Timing of Surgery

The optimal timing of surgery after spinal injury remains controversial. Some clinicians contend that surgery is urgent and should be performed as soon as possible, whereas others support a delay in surgery to allow for resolution of post-traumatic swelling. The only absolute indication for immediate or emergency surgery is progressive neurologic deterioration in patients with spinal fracture-dislocations and incomplete or no neurologic deficit.[16]

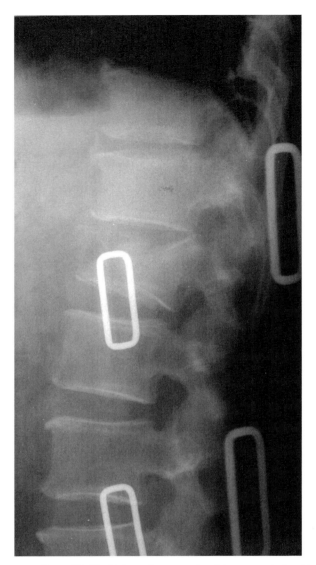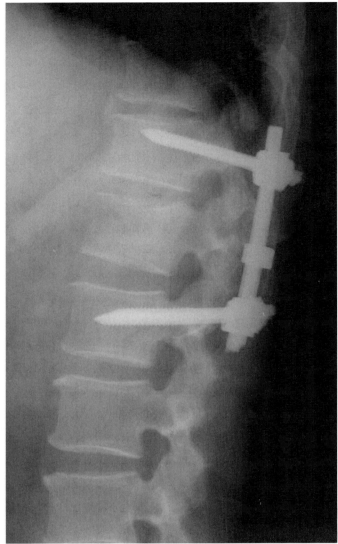

FIGURE 27–31. L1 burst fracture reduced intraoperatively with ligamentotaxis and stabilized with posterior segmental instrumentation.

Acute spinal deformity in a traumatized patient always warrants immediate spinal realignment to restore spinal canal diameter, effect some degree of neural decompression,[16] and theoretically maximize the potential for neurologic recovery. Currently, no clear scientific evidence has demonstrated that immediate surgical intervention will improve neurologic recovery in patients with acute spinal cord injury. One retrospective study suggests that surgery within 72 hours of injury might improve neurologic recovery and decrease hospitalization time in those with cervical spinal cord injuries.[91] In a prospective study, however, Vaccaro and associates found no significant neurologic benefit associated with post-traumatic surgical decompression performed less than 72 hours after injury versus waiting more than 5 days.[124] Furthermore, comparison of the two groups demonstrated no significant difference in the length of postoperative intensive care stay or the length of inpatient rehabilitation.

Early stabilization and mobilization of patients with long bone fractures have proved advantageous in avoiding complications such as adult respiratory distress syndrome and deep venous thrombosis.[51, 57] Such treatment appears to also be advantageous for spinal injury patients.[21, 39] Surgical intervention should be performed expediently to avoid these complications, as well as to allow for early mobilization, proper skin care, and upright patient positioning. In the absence of neurologic deficit, it is reasonable to delay surgery to facilitate surgical planning and decrease spinal cord and nerve root edema. Furthermore, hematoma organization occurs at about 48 hours after injury and decreases intraoperative blood loss.[44] An excessive delay in surgery, however, may have adverse effects on the surgeon's ability to reduce the fracture and achieve canal clearance. Other reports have shown that optimal canal clearance is realized when spine surgery is performed within 4 days and no later than 7 to 10 days after injury.[36, 49, 131]

Management of a polytrauma patient with an associated spinal injury presents a particularly difficult problem, depending on the severity of the other injuries, the degree of spinal instability, and the patient's neurologic status.

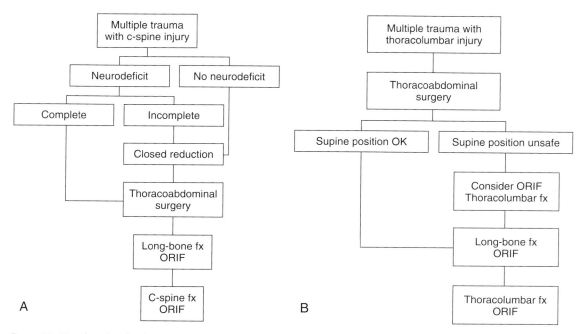

FIGURE 27–32. Algorithm for the surgical management of polytrauma patients with cervical (A) and thoracolumbar fractures (B). *Abbreviation:* ORIF, Open reduction internal fixation.

Surgical planning in these patients can be facilitated with the use of a simple algorithm (Fig. 27–32). The effects of early versus late stabilization of spinal fractures in polytrauma patients have been the focus in several recent clinical studies.[24, 88, 112] These studies consistently demonstrated that surgery performed within 72 hours in patients with an Injury Severity Score greater than 18 significantly decreased overall patient morbidity and hospital stay (Table 27–9). No significant difference in the rate of perioperative complications was associated with early surgery in polytrauma patients, but blood loss was noted to be significantly higher in those requiring early anterior spinal approaches.

In most institutions, stabilization of spinal fractures is performed in a semiurgent fashion once medical optimization of the patient has been accomplished, preferably within 3 days of the injury. Within this time frame, the surgical approach/technique should be predicated only on the nature of the injury. When a prolonged delay is anticipated, every effort should be made to maintain spinal alignment within an acceptable range. Late surgical intervention may require more extensive surgery (i.e., both anterior and posterior approaches or more extensive decompression) to achieve adequate spinal alignment, decompression, and stability.

Anesthesia

Induction of anesthesia can be very challenging in patients with spinal trauma, particularly those with unstable cervical spine fractures and incomplete neurologic deficit. Maintaining alignment of the cervical spine during intubation is vital in preventing neurologic deterioration. Awake fiberscopic intubation is the safest method to achieve airway control, especially in a medically stable patient who does not require urgent intubation. Fiberscopic intubation can be performed through either the nasotracheal or orotracheal route. Nasotracheal intubation is preferred in patients with associated maxillofacial fractures, but it is absolutely contraindicated in those with basilar skull fractures.

Multiple reports have shown the beneficial effects of hypotensive anesthesia in the intraoperative reduction of estimated blood loss.[43, 69, 83, 116] Similar findings were reported by Ullrich and co-workers in a retrospective study comparing normotensive anesthesia with hypotensive anesthesia in patients stabilized with Harrington rod instrumentation for thoracolumbar fractures.[123] Blood loss was significantly reduced with hypotensive anesthesia, and no neurologic deterioration was noted intraoperatively with either the Stagnara wake-up test or somatosensory evoked potentials (SEPs). Theoretically, low oxygen ten-

TABLE 27–9

Effect of Surgical Timing for Patients with Spine Fractures and an ISS Greater Than 18

	Timing of Stabilization	
	Early (<48 hr)	**Late (>48 hr)**
Patients (*n*)	16	46
GCS	14	13
AISS—head	1	3
AISS—chest	2	2
Ventilator days	1.0	11.0
ICU days	3.9	14.0
Hospital days	11.0	26.0
Average cost	$26,250	$54,130

Abbreviations: AISS, Abbreviated Injury Severity Score; GCS, Glasgow Coma Scale; ICU, intensive care unit; ISS, Injury Severity Score.

sion can potentially inflict further ischemic injury to the already traumatized cord, and it is recommended that mean arterial pressure be kept between 80 and 90 mm Hg during hypotensive anesthesia.[77, 118]

Selection of the anesthetic agent is also of critical importance and may influence the surgical procedure. It has been well documented that some inhalation agents have an effect on evoked potentials. Sloan maintains that the most effective anesthetic regimen used in conjunction with SEPs is low-dose inhalation agents in combination with intravenous infusion of sedatives, preferably propofol with an analgesic.[115] This regimen not only allows for reliable recording of SEPs but is also readily reversible and thus facilitates the use of a wake-up test. In patients with spinal cord injury, succinylcholine, a depolarizing agent, should not be used because it can lead to the rapid release of potassium and thereby increase the risk for ventricular arrhythmias and cardiac arrest.

Operative Positioning

The surgical positioning of patients with spinal trauma is a delicate endeavor. Care must be taken to avoid any neurologic deterioration, yet positioning should not compromise the exposure for the planned surgical approach. Care must be taken to avoid pressure around the eyes and prevent injury to the globe or retinal artery thrombosis. Padding of all bony prominences and protection of superficial neural structures are important. Proper positioning of the upper extremities when the patient is prone is crucial to avoid brachial plexus injury. For that purpose, the shoulder should not be overextended and not abducted beyond 90°. Similarly, the ulnar nerve must be protected with the arm either secured at the patient's side or flexed 90° on a padded arm board. Compression stockings on the lower extremities are useful in preventing venous congestion. Finally, after positioning, it is important to check for the presence of distal pulses, especially when the patient is in the prone position.

CERVICAL SPINE—ANTERIOR APPROACH

The patient can be placed on a regular bed or Stryker frame in the supine position. During positioning, care is taken to maintain spinal alignment. The occiput is padded with a circular foam pillow with a center cutout or placed in a Mayfield horseshoe cushion. In that position, axial traction may be applied in the form of head halter traction or skull tongs traction (Gardner-Wells tongs). The elbows are carefully padded to protect the ulnar nerve, and the arms are tucked at the patient's side. The shoulders may be retracted distally, and longitudinal tape strips can be applied to allow better intraoperative radiographic evaluation of the cervical spine. Care must be taken to avoid excessive constriction of the arms with the tape and taping directly over the nipples. A roll is placed longitudinally between the scapulae to allow for shoulder retraction and extension of the cervical spine for better exposure of the operative field. Extreme cervical extension should be carefully avoided to prevent increased spinal cord compression under anesthesia.

The head is turned away from the incision site. A left- or right-sided approach can be carried out, depending on the surgeon's preference. Advocates of the left-sided approach claim that it is preferable because of the recurrent laryngeal nerve's more consistent course on the left side; proponents of the right-sided approach maintain that it is more convenient for a right-handed surgeon.

For anterior cervical spine surgery we prefer the use of a regular operating table with the occiput placed on a well-padded circular foam pillow with a center cutout. Gardner-Wells tongs are used to maintain alignment and apply traction intraoperatively. Exposure of the fracture site is carried out through a left-sided surgical approach.

CERVICAL SPINE—POSTERIOR APPROACH

After general anesthesia has been induced, the patient is turned in the prone position on a regular operative table with longitudinal chest rolls to allow decompression of the abdominal and chest cavities. Turning of the patient can also be facilitated with the Stryker frame. The principal surgeon must maintain control of the head and neck of the patient during all turns. The head can be placed in a Mayfield horseshoe head cushion. Positioning must avoid circumferential pressure around the eye, which could result in retinal artery thrombosis or globe injuries. The Mayfield headrest attaches to the outer layer of the skull and rigidly fixes the head and the neck in the prone position without any pressure on the face or the eyes. This frame can be adjusted to exert longitudinal traction and flexion or extension as needed through the universal joints and finally fix the entire head and neck rigidly before surgery.

Alternatively, the Mayfield skull clamp can be used to securely fix the head and neck in the desired position. Furthermore, in situations in which a halo vest is in place, the halo ring can be secured to the three-pin Mayfield skull clamp (Fig. 27–33), as described by Rhea and coauthors.[103]

Figure 27–33. In cases in which a halo ring has previously been applied, the three-pin Mayfield skull clamp can be used to secure the halo ring.

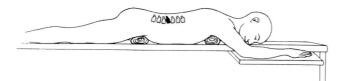

FIGURE **27–34.** Kyphotic deformity occurs in most thoracolumbar spine fractures. Sagging the spine between two rolls both decompresses the abdomen and permits postural reduction.

The operating table should be placed in a slight reverse Trendelenburg position to prevent sliding of the patient and provide the surgeon with comfortable access to the operative field. The presence of distal pulses must be documented. The arms are tucked along the side of the patient, and care is taken to protect the ulnar nerves at the elbows. The shoulders are retracted distally and secured in that position with longitudinal tape to facilitate radiographic access.

For posterior cervical spine surgery, it is our preference to position the patient prone on chest rolls on a regular operating table, using a Mayfield skull clamp to secure the patient's head and neck.

THORACOLUMBAR SPINE

Operative positioning for the posterior approach to the thoracolumbar spine can be accomplished with the use of a regular or radiolucent operating table and well-padded chest rolls. The rolls are positioned transversely at the level of the sternum and the iliac crests. Most thoracolumbar spine fractures have some degree of kyphosis, and the position of the rolls will allow the thoracolumbar junction to sag, thereby both decompressing the abdomen and allowing for postural reduction (Fig. 27–34). The arms should not be overly extended nor abducted past 90° to prevent brachial plexus injuries. The elbows are padded to protect the ulnar nerves, and the arms are rested on well-padded arm boards. The knees are flexed with care taken to avoid pressure on the patellas and feet, and the presence of distal pulses must be documented. Alternatively, the Stryker frame can be used for the posterior approach and will facilitate rotational positioning of the patient. We prefer the use of a four-poster frame on a regular operating table for patient positioning in the posterior approach to the thoracolumbar spine. This frame will allow postural reduction of the spine and will also facilitate access for intraoperative radiographs.

Anterior thoracolumbar spinal surgery is recommended for patients who require direct decompression of the dural sac. This technique is accomplished by making a left anterolateral incision with the patient in the right decubitus position on a regular operating table, although in some instances a right-sided approach may be used. The patient is positioned so that the fracture is located at the flexion break of the table. It is critical that the patient be in the true lateral position, especially if instrumentation is to be used. Hip supports are used to maintain the relative position of the patient on the operating table. The arm on the side of the operative approach is placed on a Mayo stand, and the other is allowed to rest on an arm board.

Padding is applied, particularly over the bony prominences. The hips and knees are slightly flexed with a pillow placed between the knees to prevent pressure injury. An axillary roll is placed under the axilla on the down side, approximately 6 inches from its apex to prevent injury to the brachial plexus. When a thoracotomy is planned, intubation should be done with a double-lumen tube so that the lung on the side of the approach can be selectively deflated.

Intraoperative Monitoring

Prevention of neurologic deterioration is one of the major objectives of spinal surgery after trauma. Intraoperative monitoring, though not beneficial in patients with complete spinal cord injuries, may be helpful in a neurologically intact or incomplete patient.[125] Spinal monitoring techniques, traditionally used in spinal deformity surgery, are also becoming popular for treatment of spine fractures.[11, 12] The most commonly used intraoperative spinal monitoring measures are SEPs and the Stagnara wake-up test.

STAGNARA WAKE-UP TEST

The concept of waking the patient during the surgery to determine the integrity of the spinal cord was introduced in 1973 by Vauzelle and colleagues.[125] The wake-up test, named after one of its originators, is a simple, cost-effective, and very reliable test for assessing gross motor function when administered appropriately. The patient, after having been informed preoperatively about the details of the test, is awakened intraoperatively and asked to perform specific voluntary movements to demonstrate gross motor function. If the patient demonstrates symmetric motor function on command, the test is negative, the patient is reanesthetized, and the surgical procedure resumes. If the test is positive, a motor deficit has been detected, immediate corrective measures (i.e., removal of spinal instrumentation, more extensive decompression) must be undertaken, and the examination is then repeated. The results are usually very reliable, provided that the patient is adequately awakened and able to cooperate. The Stagnara wake-up test has two major weaknesses: it is a test of gross motor function that provides no information regarding specific nerve root integrity, and it does not evaluate sensory function. Medical considerations include hypertension, which could potentially precipitate a cardiac insult in patients with preexisting cardiovascular disease, and the greater risk of air embolism from increased intrathoracic pressure—hence the recommendation to flood the operative field with irrigation fluid before the test. Thus far, however, no reports have evaluated the efficacy of the wake-up test for spinal trauma surgery.

SOMATOSENSORY EVOKED POTENTIALS

SEPs are widely used for spinal monitoring during surgery.[38, 94, 95, 120] They are elicited by stimulating a mixed peripheral nerve, preferably the tibial or peroneal nerve in the lower extremities and the median and ulnar nerves in the upper extremities, to record responses from levels caudal and cephalad to the level of the surgery. The data are recorded and the amplitude and latency are compared with baseline values. Monitoring of the tibial and peroneal nerves predominantly reflects the function of the L5 and S1 roots, respectively. Robinson and colleagues demonstrated the efficacy of femoral SEPs for monitoring the midlumbar roots during surgical treatment of thoracolumbar fractures, particularly those involving the T12–L4 levels.[107] Interestingly, SEPs are used to monitor the motor function of the spinal cord. Such monitoring is based on the close proximity of the sensory tracts to the motor tracts and the assumption that trauma to the motor tracts will affect the sensory responses. This reasoning is generally valid when the mechanism of injury is trauma, but it is not always the case when a vascular insult has occurred.[61] A decrease in amplitude of greater than 50% or prolongation of latency by 10% in comparison to baseline values (or both) is significant.[32, 98] Muscle relaxation, core temperature, and mean arterial pressure of 60 mm Hg and higher seem to have no significant effect on SEPs. In contrast, anesthetic agents have a dose-related effect.[115]

SEPs are typically elicited by stimulating a peripheral mixed nerve and recording a response at sites caudal and cephalad to the level of the surgery. Delays in conduction or depression of the spinal response may indicate cord damage or a physiologic block of function. On the other hand, absence of conduction is associated with severe and usually irreversible cord damage.[33, 53, 75] The mean SEP was shown to have the strongest individual relationship to the outcome of improvement in the Motor Index Score at 6 months.[75] In contrast to this study, Katz and associates reviewed 57 patients who were studied with SEPs and dermatomal evoked potentials and monitored for more than 1 year.[63] The study examined the ability of these tests to predict motor recovery after acute spinal cord injury. Evoked potentials added little or no useful prognostic information to the initial physical examination in patients with either complete or incomplete spinal cord injury. The beneficial role of SEP monitoring in spine injury surgery is limited and yet to be determined.

Postoperative Care

Patients whose spine injuries are treated surgically also require special postoperative management. In the immediate postsurgical period, vital functions are meticulously monitored. Observation of upper airway function is especially important after anterior cervical spine surgery. Airway obstruction can be due to local edema, wound hematoma, postoperative dryness, or gland hypersecretion. The patient's neurologic function should clearly be monitored in the immediate postoperative period, and monitoring should include both motor and sensory examinations. Progressive deterioration of the patient's neurologic status is suggestive of an epidural hematoma and is an indication for immediate decompressive surgery.

The postoperative use of orthotic devices, despite internal spine fixation, further restricts excessive spine motion, allows for soft tissue healing, and decreases postoperative pain. Spinal bracing also has a psychologic effect in assisting the patient's postoperative pain tolerance. Furthermore, postoperative bracing results in a lower incidence of hardware failure, surgical loss of correction, and pseudarthrosis. Indications for postoperative bracing depend on the severity of injury, the degree of spinal instability, the presence of neurologic deficit, the type and quality of internal fixation, bone quality, and the patient's individual profile. The specific characteristics and indications for spinal braces have been presented earlier in this chapter.

Rigid internal fixation of the cervical spine usually obviates the need for a halo vest. A halo vest is still recommended when instability persists after internal fixation or when the risk of loosening after operative reduction is high. Cervical braces, such as high- or low-thoracic CTOs, usually provide sufficient additional postsurgical external stabilization. The duration of bracing can vary from 2 to 6 weeks and has to be individualized to the specific patient.

A total-contact thoracolumbar orthosis (TLO) is recommended for the postoperative management of thoracolumbar injury. The TLO should be applied during the immediate postoperative period. A TLSO is used for fractures extending between T8 and L4. A hip spica TLSO can be used for injuries to the lumbosacral junction, whereas a sternal pad can be fitted for injuries above T8 to counteract kyphotic forces.

After uneventful spine surgery, patients are routinely discharged from the hospital on the second or third postoperative day. Return to sedentary occupational activity can be expected within 2 weeks, and full functional recovery can range from 6 weeks to 3 months, depending on the specific injury. Postoperative follow-up visits are usually scheduled at 7 to 10 days, 6 weeks, and 3 months. At the completion of spine healing, dynamic stress radiographic should be taken to document recovery of the spine injury.

Postoperative management of a neurologically impaired spinal injury patient requires special attention. Bedridden patients must be frequently turned to avoid skin breakdown over pressure areas. Custom-molded braces are provided as soon as possible to facilitate early mobilization. Occasionally, orthoses are fitted on the upper and lower extremities to prevent contractures and maintain joint flexibility. Physical therapy is a crucial component of the overall care and must be instituted as soon as possible. Depending on the level of spinal injury, patients must become proficient with transfers, self-catheterization, and maintenance of a bowel routine. Emotional and psychologic support should be readily available to both the patient and family. Unfortunately, these injuries usually involve young adults and are an enormous individual tragedy; they also incur considerable socioeconomic cost and require a short- and long-term multidisciplinary approach.

Complications

Complications of surgical treatment of spinal trauma have been reported frequently. Most complications are the result of failure to understand the patient's altered spinal mechanics, poor surgical technique, or poor choice of instrumentation. Failure to achieve and maintain adequate reduction can be related to the severity of the fracture, the quality of the patient's bone, and technical difficulties with the surgery.

McAfee and co-workers reviewed the complications of 40 patients with thoracolumbar fractures treated with Harrington distraction rods.[85] Twenty-six of the 30 patients who were monitored for more than 2 years required additional spine surgery. Deep wound infection occurred in 15% of patients and wound dehiscence in 7%; five patients experienced neurologic deterioration. In approximately 30% of patients, dislodgement or disengagement of the instrumentation occurred along with loss of fixation. Loss of fixation was more likely in translational injuries because Harrington distraction instrumentation relies on intact ligamentous structures for stability. The use of a claw-type configuration of hooks placed segmentally cephalad and caudal to the lamina appears to decrease this complication.

The development of pedicle screws for spinal segmental instrumentation has provided more rigid and reliable posterior fixation; however, complications have accompanied the use of pedicle screws. Lonstein and coauthors reported their experience with 4790 pedicle screws inserted in 915 operative procedures.[80] Penetration of the cortex of the pedicle occurred in 2.2%, and penetration of the anterior cortex of the vertebral body, the most common type of perforation, occurred in 2.8%. Late-onset discomfort or pain caused by pseudarthrosis or the instrumentation and requiring removal of the instrumentation occurred with 23% of the screws. Nerve root irritation was caused by 0.2% of the screws, and 0.5% of the screws had broken.

Failure of instrumentation can be attributed to improper implant selection or implant construct for a specific spinal injury. The choice of an implant and its mode of application is always determined by the biomechanical stability of the segment to be instrumented. Poor bone quality or poor fixation technique can result in hardware dislodgement and cause the construct to fail. Finally, all hardware will eventually fail in the presence of pseudarthrosis, regardless of the design, strength, or the manner in which the instrumentation is applied.

Postoperative wound infections are also a common complication after spine surgery. The risk of infection ranges between 1% and 6% and is highly dependent on expedient surgery, meticulous surgical technique, and the use of perioperative prophylactic antibiotics. The most frequent offending organism, *Staphylococcus aureus*, is responsible for about 50% of cases. Aggressive treatment is the mainstay of management of postoperative spinal wound infection. Irrigation and débridement of the wound must be performed as soon as possible, cultures obtained, and empirical antibiotic administration started until culture results are available. The implants, along with viable bone graft, must be retained if they are well tolerated and provide stability to the spine. Repeat débridement is performed as needed. Wounds can be closed over drains or can be packed open. Some recommend the use of inflow-outflow systems for deep infections. Most reports concur that a satisfactory outcome can be achieved after this form of treatment.[84, 117, 128, 132]

The most devastating complication in spinal trauma surgery is neurologic deterioration. Most situations of neurologic decompensation result from inadequate decompression of neural structures. When an incomplete deficit persists, repeat imaging (i.e., myelography, CT, and other techniques) is indicated to determine whether the patient would benefit from additional surgery. Postoperative neurologic deterioration may be caused by several factors, including direct neural injury from manipulation, instrumentation, or correction of a deformity during the surgery. Rapid postoperative deterioration when the patient is initially improved may be the result of an expanding epidural hematoma. The treating physician must be alert for this potentially catastrophic complication and evacuate the hematoma emergently to minimize residual long-term neurologic deficit.

Finally, leakage of cerebrospinal fluid may complicate spinal trauma surgery. The leakage can be a result of an iatrogenic laceration or may be caused by the initial injury. When cerebrospinal fluid leakage is recognized intraoperatively, an attempt should be made to repair the injury. Leakage of cerebrospinal fluid because of a dural tear at the injury level is a special concern in spinal trauma. Cammisa and colleagues reviewed 30 patients with a laminar fracture in association with a burst fracture of the thoracic or the lumbar spine.[23] Eleven of the 30, all with preoperative neurologic deficits, had evidence of a dural laceration at surgery; 4 of the 11 had neural elements entrapped in the laminar fracture site. Therefore, a high index of suspicion is warranted in any patient with a neurologic deficit and a burst fracture in association with a laminar fracture. If leakage of cerebrospinal fluid is recognized postoperatively, treatment may include reoperation and repair of the leak in the lumbar spine or antibiotics, recumbency, and lumbar subarachnoid drains for both the cervical and lumbar spine.

REFERENCES

1. Aebi, M.; Etter, C.; Kehl, T.; et al. Stabilization of the lower thoracic spine with the internal spinal skeletal fixation system. Indications, techniques, and first results of treatment. Spine 12:544–551, 1987.
2. Alberts, L.R.; Mahoney, C.R.; Neff, J.R. Comparison of the Nebraska collar, a new prototype cervical immobilization collar, with three standard models. J Orthop Trauma 12:425–430, 1998.
3. An, H.S.; Lim, T.H.; You, J.W.; et al. Biomechanical evaluation of anterior thoracolumbar spinal instrumentation. Spine 15:1979–1983, 1995.
4. Anderson, L.D.; D'Alonzo, R.T. Fractures of the odontoid process of the axis. J Bone Joint Surg Am 56:1663–1674, 1974.
5. Anderson, P.A.; Montesano, P.X. Morphology and treatment of occipital condyle fractures. Spine 13:731–736, 1988.
6. Anderson, P.A.; Budorick, T.E.; Easton, K.B.; et al. Failure of halo vest to prevent in vivo motion in patients with injured cervical spines. Spine 16(Suppl):501–505, 1991.
7. Anderson, P.A. Nonsurgical treatment of patients with thoracolumbar fractures. Instr Course Lect 44:57–65, 1995.
8. Axelsson, P.; Johnsson, R.; Strömqvist, B. Lumbar orthosis with unilateral hip immobilization. Spine 18:876–879, 1993.
9. Bedbrook, G.M.; Hon, O.B.E. Treatment of thoracolumbar dislocation and fractures with paraplegia. Clin Orthop 112:27–43, 1975.
10. Bedbrook, G.M. Spinal injuries with tetraplegia and paraplegia. J Bone Joint Surg Br 61:267–284, 1979.
11. Ben-David, B.; Taylor, P.D.; Haller, G.S. Posterior spinal fusion complicated by posterior column injury: A case report of a false negative wake-up test. Spine 12:540–543, 1987.
12. Ben-David, B. Spinal cord monitoring. Orthop Clin North Am 19:427–448, 1988.
13. Benzel, E.C. Spinal orthosis. In: Benzel, E.C., ed. Biomechanics of Spinal Stabilization. New York, McGraw-Hill, 1995, pp. 247–258.

14. Benzel, E.C.; Hadden, T.A.; Saulsbery, C.M. A comparison of the Minerva and halo jackets for stabilization of the cervical spine. J Neurosurg 70:411–414, 1989.

15. Blockey, N.J.; Purser, D.W. Fractures of the odontoid process of the axis. J Bone Joint Surg Br 38:794–817, 1956.

16. Bohlman, H.H. Surgical management of cervical spine fractures and dislocations. Instr Course Lect 34:163–187, 1985.

17. Botte, M.J.; Byrne, T.P.; Garfin, S.R. Application of the halo device for immobilization of the cervical spine utilizing an increased torque pressure. J Bone Joint Surg Am 69:750–752, 1987.

18. Botte, M.J.; Garfin, S.R.; Byrne, T.P.; et al. The halo skeletal fixator: Principles of application and maintenance. Clin Orthop 239:12–18, 1989.

19. Botte, M.J.; Byrne, T.P; Abrams, R.A.; Garfin, S.R. Halo skeletal fixation: Techniques of application and prevention of complications. J Am Acad Orthop Surg 4:44–53, 1996.

20. Bravo, P.; Labarta, C.; Alcaraz, M.; et al. Outcome after vertebral fractures with neurological lesion treated either surgically or conservatively in Spain. Paraplegia 31:358–366, 1993.

21. Brazinski, M.; Yoo, J.U. Review of pulmonary complications associated with early versus late stabilization of thoracic and lumbar fractures. Paper presented at the 12th Annual Meeting of the Orthopaedic Trauma Association, Boston, 1996.

22. Brown, C.W.; Chow, G.H. Orthoses for spinal trauma and postoperative care. In: Goldberg, B.; Hsu, J.D., eds. AAOS Atlas of Orthoses and Assistive Devices, 3rd ed. St. Louis, Mosby–Year Book, 1997.

23. Cammisa, F.P., Jr.; Eismont, F.J.; Green, B.A. Dural laceration occurring with burst fractures and associated laminar fractures. J Bone Joint Surg Am 71:1044–1052, 1989.

24. Campagnolo, D.I.; Esquieres, R.E.; Kopacz, K.J. Effect of stabilization on length of stay and medical complications following spinal cord injury. J Spinal Cord Med 20:331–334, 1997.

25. Cantor, J.B.; Lebwohl, N.H.; Garvey, T.; et al. Nonoperative management of stable thoracolumbar burst fractures with early ambulation and bracing. Spine 18:971–976, 1993.

26. Chapman, J.R.; Anderson, P.A. Thoracolumbar spine fractures with neurologic deficit. Orthop Clin North Am 25:595–612, 1994.

27. Cheshire, D.J.E. The stability of the cervical spine following the conservative treatment of fractures and fracture-dislocations. Paraplegia 7:193–203, 1969.

28. Clark, C.R.; White, A.A. Fractures of the dens. J Bone Joint Surg Am 67:1340–1348, 1985.

29. Cooper, P.R.; Maravilla, K.R.; Sklar, F.H.; et al. Halo immobilization of cervical spine fractures. J Neurosurg 50:603–610, 1979.

30. Cotler, H.B.; Miller, L.S.; DeLucia, F.A.; et al. Closed reduction of cervical spine dislocations. Clin Orthop 214:185–199, 1987.

31. Cotler, H.B.; Cotler, J.M.; Alden, M.E.; et al. The medical and economic impact of closed cervical spine dislocations. Spine 15:448–452, 1990.

32. Dawson, E.G.; Sherman, J.E.; Kanim, L.E.; Nuwer, M.R. Spinal cord monitoring. Results of the Scoliosis Research Society and the European Spinal Deformity Society survey. Spine 16(Suppl):361–364, 1991.

33. Delamarter, R.B.; Bohlman, H.H.; Dodge, L.D.; Biro, C. Experimental lumbar spinal stenosis. Analysis of the cortical evoked potentials, microvasculature, and histopathology. J Bone Joint Surg Am 72:110–120, 1990.

34. Denis, F. Spinal instability as defined by the three-column spine concept in acute spinal trauma. Clin Orthop 189:65–76, 1984.

35. Dunn, H.K. Anterior spine stabilization and decompression for thoracolumbar injuries. Orthop Clin North Am 17:113–119, 1986.

36. Edwards, C.C.; Levine, A.M. Early rodsleeve stabilization of the injured thoracic and lumbar spine. Orthop Clin North Am 17:121–145, 1986.

37. Eismont, F.J.; Arena, M.J.; Green, B.A. Extrusion of an intervertebral disc associated with traumatic subluxation or dislocation of cervical facets. J Bone Joint Surg Am 73:1555–1560, 1991.

38. Engler, G.L.; Spielholz, N.J.; Bernhard, W.N.; et al. Somatosensory evoked potentials during Harrington instrumentation for scoliosis. J Bone Joint Surg Am 60:528–532, 1978.

39. Fellrath, R.F.; Hanley, E.N. Multitrauma and thoracolumbar fractures. Semin Spine Surg 7:103–108, 1995.

40. Fidler, M.W.; Plasmans, C.M. The effect of four types of support on the segmental mobility of the lumbosacral spine. J Bone Joint Surg Am 65:943–947, 1983.

41. Finn, C.A.; Stauffer, E.S. Burst fracture of the fifth lumbar vertebra. J Bone Joint Surg Am 74:398–403, 1992.

42. Fisher, S.V.; Bowar, J.F.; Awad, E.A.; et al. Cervical orthoses effect on cervical spine motion: Roentgenographic and goniometric method of study. Arch Phys Med Rehabil 58:109–115, 1977.

43. Fox, H.J.; Thomas, C.H.; Thompson, A.G. Spinal instrumentation for Duchenne's muscular dystrophy: Experience of hypotensive anaesthesia to minimize blood loss. J Pediatr Orthop 17:750–753, 1997.

44. Frankel, H,L,; Hancock, D.O.; Hyslop, G.; et al. The value of postural reduction in the initial management of closed injuries of the spine with paraplegia and tetraplegia. Paraplegia 7:179–192, 1969.

45. Fredrickson, B.E.; Yuan, H.; Miller, H.M. Burst fractures of the fifth lumbar vertebra. J Bone Joint Surg Am 64:1088–1094, 1982.

46. Gardner, V.O.; Thalgott, J.S.; White, J.I.; et al. The contoured anterior spinal plate system (CASP). Indications, techniques, and results. Spine 19:550–555, 1994.

47. Garfin, S.R.; Botte, M.J.; Centeno, R.S.; et al. Osteology of the skull as it affects halo pin placement. Spine 10:696–698, 1985.

48. Gertzbein, S.D.; Court-Brown, C.M.; Marks, P. The neurological outcome following surgery for spinal fractures. Spine 13:641–644, 1988.

49. Gertzbein, S.D. Scoliosis Research Society multicenter spine fracture study. Spine 17:528–540, 1992.

50. Gertzbein, S.D.; Crowe, P.J.; Fazl, M.; et al. Canal clearance in burst fractures using the AO internal fixator. Spine 17:558–560, 1992.

51. Goto, G.; Crosby, G. Anesthesia and the spinal cord. Anesth Clin North Am 10:493–519, 1992.

52. Graziano, A.F.; Scheidel, E.A.; Cline, J.R.; Baer, L.J. A radiographic comparison of prehospital cervical immobilization methods. Ann Emerg Med 16:1127–1131, 1987.

53. Grundy, B.L.; Friedman, W. Electrophysiological evaluation of the patient with acute spinal cord injury. Crit Care Clin 3:519–548, 1997.

54. Hu, S.S.; Capen, D.A.; Rimoldi, R.L.; et al. The effect of surgical decompression on neurologic outcome after lumbar fracture. Clin Orthop 288:166–173, 1993.

55. Hughes, S.J. How effective is the Newport/Aspen collar? A prospective radiographic evaluation in healthy adult volunteers. J Trauma 45:374–378, 1998.

56. James, K.S.; Wenger, K.H.; Schlegel, J.D.; et al. Biomechanical evaluation of the stability of thoracolumbar burst fractures. Spine 19:1731–1740, 1994.

57. Johnson, K.D.; Cadambi, A.; Seibert, G.B. Incidence of adult respiratory distress syndrome in patients with multiple musculoskeletal injuries: Effect of early operative stabilization of fractures. J Trauma 25:375–377, 1985.

58. Johnson, R.M.; Hart, D.L.; Owen, J.R.; et al. The Yale cervical orthosis: An evaluation of its effectiveness in restricting cervical motion in normal subjects and a comparison with other cervical orthoses. Phys Ther 58:865–871, 1978.

59. Johnson, R.M.; Hart, D.L.; Simmons, B.F.; et al. Cervical orthoses: A study comparing their effectiveness in restricting cervical motion in normal subjects. J Bone Joint Surg Am 59:332–339, 1977.

60. Johnson, R.M.; Owen, J.R.; Hart, D.L.; et al. Cervical orthoses: A guide for their selection and use. Clin Orthop 154:34–45, 1981.

61. Kai, Y.; Owen, J.H.; Lenke, L.G., et al. Use of sciatic neurogenic motor evoked potentials versus spinal potentials to predict early-onset neurologic deficits when intervention is still possible during overdistraction. Spine 18:1134–1139, 1993.

62. Kaneda, K.; Abumi, K.; Fujiya, M. Burst fractures with neurologic deficit of the thoracolumbar-lumbar spine. Results of anterior decompression and stabilization with anterior instrumentation. Spine 9:788–795, 1984.

63. Katz, R.T.; Toleikis, R.J.; Knuth, A.E. Somatosensory-evoked and dermatomal-evoked potentials are not clinically useful in the prognostication of acute spinal cord injury. Spine 16:730–735, 1991.

64. Kaufman, W.A.; Lunsford, T.R.; Lunsford, B.R.; Lance, L.L. Comparison of three prefabricated cervical collars. Orthot Prosthet 39:21–29, 1986.

65. Koch, R.A.; Nickel, V.L. The halo vest: An evaluation of motion and forces across the neck. Spine 3:103–107, 1978.

66. Kostuik, J.P. Indications for use of the halo immobilizations. Clin Orthop 154:46–56, 1981.

67. Krompinger, W.J.; Fredrickson, B.E.; Mino, D.E.; et al. Conservative treatment of fractures of the thoracic and lumbar spine. Orthop Clin North Am 17:161–170, 1986.

68. Lantz, S.A.; Schultz, A.B. Lumbar spine orthosis wearing. Spine 11:834–842, 1986.

69. Lawhon, S.M.; Kahn, A.; Crawford, A.H.; Brinker, M.S. Controlled hypotensive anesthesia during spinal surgery. A retrospective study. Spine 9:450–453, 1984.

70. Lee, A.S.; MacLean, J.C.B.; Newton, D.A. Rapid traction for reduction of cervical spine dislocations. J Bone Joint Surg Br 76:352–356, 1994.

71. Lemons, V.R.; Wagner, F.C.; Montesano, P.X. Management of thoracolumbar fractures with accompanying neurological injury. Neurosurgery 30:667–671, 1992.

72. Lerman, J.A.; Haynes, R.J.; Koeneman, E.J.; et al. A biomechanical comparison of Gardner-Wells tongs and halo device used for cervical spine traction. Spine 19:2403–2406, 1994.

73. Levine, A.M.; Edwards, C.C. The management of traumatic spondylolisthesis of the axis. J Bone Joint Surg Am 67:217–226, 1985.

74. Levine, A.; Bosse, M.; Edwards, C.C. Bilateral facet dislocations in the thoracolumbar spine. Spine 13:630–640, 1988.

75. Li, C.; Houlden, D.A.; Rowed, D.W. Somatosensory evoked potentials and neurological grades as predictors of outcomes in acute spinal cord injury. J Neurosurg 72:600–609, 1990.

76. Lind, B.; Sihlbom, H.; Nordwall, A. Forces and motions across the neck in patients treated with halo-vest. Spine 13:162–167, 1988.

77. Lindop, M.J. Complications and morbidity of controlled hypotension. Br J Anaesth 47:799–803, 1975.

78. Lindsey, R.W.; Dick, W. The Fixateur Interne in the reduction and stabilization of thoracolumbar spine fractures in patients with neurologic deficit. Spine 16(Suppl):140–145, 1991.

79. Lindsey, R.W.; Dick, W.; Nuchuck, S.; et al. Residual intersegmental spinal mobility following limited pedicle fixation of thoracolumbar spine fractures with the Fixateur Interne. Spine 18:474–478, 1993.

80. Lonstein, J.E.; Denis, F.; Perra, J.H.; et al. Complications associated with pedicle screws. J Bone Joint Surg Am 81:1519–1528, 1999.

81. Lunsford, T.R.; Davidson, M.; Lunsford, B.R. The effectiveness of four contemporary cervical orthoses in restricting cervical motion. J Orthot Prosthet 6:93–99, 1994.

82. Mahale, Y.J.; Silver, J.R.; Henderson, N.J. Neurological complications of the reduction of cervical spine dislocations. J Bone Joint Surg Br 75:403–409, 1993.

83. Malcolm-Smith, N.A.; McMaster, M.J. The use of induced hypotension to control bleeding during posterior fusion for scoliosis. J Bone Joint Surg Am 65:225–228, 1983.

84. Massie, J.B.; Heller, J.G.; Abitbol, J.J.; et al. Postoperative posterior spinal wound infections. Clin Orthop 284:99–108, 1992.

85. McAfee, P.C.; Bohlman, H.H.; Yuan, H.A. Anterior decompression of traumatic thoracolumbar fractures with incomplete neurological deficit using a retroperitoneal approach. J Bone Joint Surg Am 67:89–104, 1985.

86. McGuire, R.A.; Degnan, G.; Amundson, G.M. Evaluation of current extrication orthoses in immobilization of the unstable cervical spine. Spine 15:1064–1067, 1990.

87. McGuire, R.A.; Green, B.A.; Eismont, F.J.; et al. Comparison of stability provided to the unstable spine by the kinetic therapy table and the Stryker frame. Neurosurgery 22:842–845, 1988.

88. McLain, R.F.; Benson, D.R. Urgent surgical stabilization of spinal fractures in polytrauma patients. Spine 24:1646–1654, 1999.

89. Meyer, P.R. Fractures of the thoracic spine. In: Meyer, P.R., ed. Surgery of Spine Trauma. New York, Churchill Livingstone, 1989, pp. 525–624, 717–820.

90. Miller, L.S.; Cotler, H.B.; De Lucia, F.A.; et al. Biomechanical analysis of cervical distraction. Spine 12:831–837, 1987.

91. Mirza, S.K.; Krengel, W.F.; Chapman, J.R.; et al. Early versus delayed surgery for acute cervical spinal cord injury. Clin Orthop 359:104–114, 1999.

92. Mumford, J.; Weinstein, J.N.; Spratt, K.F.; et al. Thoracolumbar burst fractures: The clinical efficacy and outcome of nonoperative management. Spine 18:955–970, 1993.

93. Nagel, D.A.; Koogle, T.A.; Piziali, R.L.; et al. Stability of the upper lumbar spine following progressive disruptions and the application of individual internal and external fixation devices. J Bone Joint Surg Am 63:62–70, 1981.

94. Nash, C.L.; Lorig, R.A.; Schatzinger, L.A.; et al. Spinal cord monitoring during operative treatment of the spine. Clin Orthop 126:100–105, 1977.

95. Nash, C.L.; Brown, R.H. Spinal cord monitoring. J Bone Joint Surg Am 71:627–630, 1989.

96. Nickel, V.L.; Perry, J.; Garret, A.; Heppenstall, M. The halo. J Bone Joint Surg Am 50:1400–1409, 1968.

97. Nicoll, E.A. Fractures of the dorso-lumbar spine. J Bone Joint Surg Br 31:376–393, 1949.

98. Nuwer, M.R.; Dawson, E.G.; Carlson, L.G.; et al. Somatosensory evoked potential spinal cord monitoring reduces neurologic deficits after scoliosis surgery: Results of a large multicenter survey. Electroencephalogr Clin Neurophysiol 96:6–11, 1995.

99. Patwardhan, A.G.; Li, S.P.; Gavin, T.; et al. Orthotic stabilization of thoracolumbar injuries: A biomechanical analysis of the Jewett hyperextension orthosis. Spine 15:654–661, 1990.

100. Perry, J.; Nickel, V.L. Total cervical-spine fusion for neck paralysis. J Bone Joint Surg Am 41:37–60, 1959.

101. Plaisier, B.; Gabram, S.G.; Schwartz, R.J.; Jacobs, L.M. Prospective evaluation of craniofacial pressure in four different cervical orthoses. J Trauma 37:714–720, 1994.

102. Reid, D.C.; Hu, R.; Davis, L.A.; et al. The nonoperative treatment of burst fractures of the thoracolumbar junction. J Trauma 28:1188–1194, 1988.

103. Rhea, A.H.; Tranmer, B.I.; Gross, C.E. Intraoperative cervical spine stabilization using the halo ring and the Mayfield three-pin skull clamp. J Neurosurg 64:157–158, 1986.

104. Rimoldi, R.; Zigler, J.; Capen, D.; Hu, S. The effect of surgical intervention on rehabilitation time in patients with thoracolumbar and lumbar spinal cord injuries. Spine 17:1443–1449, 1992.

105. Rizzolo, S.J.; Vaccaro, A.R.; Cotler, J.M. Cervical spine trauma. Spine 19:2288–2298, 1994.

106. Robertson, P.A.; Ryan, M.D. Neurological deterioration after reduction of cervical subluxation: Mechanical compression by disc tissue. J Bone Joint Surg Br 74:224–227, 1992.

107. Robinson, L.R.; Slimp, J.C.; Anderson, P.A.; Stolov, W.C. The efficacy of femoral nerve intraoperative somatosensory evoked potentials during surgical treatment of thoracolumbar fractures. Spine 18:1793–1797, 1993.

108. Rorabeck, C.H.; Rock, M.G.; Hawkins, R.J.; et al. Unilateral facet dislocation of the cervical spine. An analysis of the results of treatment in 26 patients. Spine 12:23–27, 1987.

109. Rosen, P.B.; McSwain, N.E.; Arata, M.; et al. Comparison of two new immobilization collars. Ann Emerg Med 21:1189–1195, 1992.

110. Rushton, S.A.; Vaccaro, A.R.; Levine, M.J.; et al. Bivector traction for unstable cervical spine fractures: A description of its application and preliminary results. J Spinal Disord 10:436–440, 1997.

111. Sears, W.; Fazl, M. Prediction of stability of cervical spine fracture managed in the halo vest and indications for surgical intervention. J Neurosurg 72:426–432, 1990.

112. Schiegel, J.; Bayley, J.; Yuan, H.; et al. Timing of surgical decompression and fixation of acute spinal fractures. J Orthop Trauma 10:323–330, 1996.

113. Sharpe, K.P.; Rao, S.; Ziogas, A. Evaluation of the effectiveness of the Minerva cervicothoracic orthosis. Spine 20:1475–1479, 1995.

114. Slabaugh, P.B.; Nickel, V.L. Complications with use of the Stryker frame. J Bone Joint Surg Am 60:2222–2223, 1978.

115. Sloan, T.B. Anesthesia during spinal surgery with electrophysiological monitoring. Semin Spine Surg 9:302–308, 1997.

116. Sollevi, A. Hypotensive anesthesia and blood loss. Acta Anaesthesiol Scand Suppl 89:39–43, 1988.

117. Stambough, J.L.; Beringer, D. Postoperative wound infections complicating adult spine surgery. J Spinal Disord 5:277–285, 1992.

118. Strunin, L. Organ perfusion during controlled hypotension. Br J Anaesth 47:793–798, 1975.

119. Sypert, G.W. External spinal orthotics. Neurosurgery 20:642–649, 1987.

120. Tamaki, T.; Nogushi, T.; Takano, H.; et al. Spinal cord monitoring as a clinical utilization of the spinal evoked potential. Clin Orthop 184:58–64, 1984.

121. Traynelis, V.C.; Marano, G.D.; Dunker, R.O.; et al. Traumatic atlantooccipital dislocation. J Neurosurg 65:863–870, 1986.

122. Triggs, K.J.; Ballock, R.T.; Lee, T.Q.; et al. The effect of angled insertion on halo pin fixation. Spine 14:781–783, 1989.

123. Ullrich, P.F.; Keene, J.S.; Hogan, K.J.; et al. Results of hypotensive anesthesia in operative treatment of thoracolumbar fractures. J Spinal Disord 3:329–333, 1990.

124. Vaccaro, A.R.; Daugherty, R.J.; Sheehan, T.P.; et al. Neurologic outcome of early versus late surgery for cervical spinal cord injury. Spine 22:2609–2613, 1997.

125. Vauzelle, C.; Stagnara, P.; Jouvinroux, P. Functional monitoring of spinal cord activity during spinal surgery. Clin Orthop 93:173–178, 1973.

126. Waters, R.L.; Adkins, R.H.; Nelson, R.; Garland, D. Cervical spinal cord trauma: Evaluation and nonoperative treatment with halo-vest immobilization. Contemp Orthop 14:35–45, 1987.

127. Weinstein, J.N.; Collalto, P.; Lehmann, T.R. Thoracolumbar "burst" fractures treated conservatively: A long-term follow-up. Spine 13:33–38, 1988.

128. Weinstein, M.A.; McCabe, J.P.; Cammisa, F.P. Postoperative spinal wound infection: A review of 22,391 consecutive index procedures. J Spinal Disord 12:422–426, 2000.

129. White, A.A.; Southwick, W.O.; Panjabi, M.M. Clinical instability of the lower cervical spine. Spine 1:85–96, 1976.

130. White, A.A.; Panjabi, M.M. Clinical Biomechanics of the Spine. Philadephia, J.B. Lippincott, 1978, pp. 236–251.

131. Willen, J.; Lindahl, S.; Irstam, L.; Nordwall, A. Unstable thoracolumbar fractures: A study by CT and conventional roentgenology of the reduction effect of Harrington instrumentation. Spine 9:215–219, 1984.

132. Wimmer, C.; Gluch, H. Management of postoperative wound infection in posterior spinal fusion with instrumentation. J Spinal Disord 9:505–508, 1996.

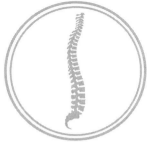

Injuries of the Cervicocranium

Andrew C. Hecht, M.D.

D. Hal Silcox III, M.D.

Thomas E. Whitesides, Jr., M.D.

Fractures and dislocations from the occiput to the axis, the cervicocranium, are a treacherous yet interesting and important group of injuries that are relatively uncommon in clinical practice. They include occipital condyle fractures, occipitoatlantal dislocations, dislocations and subluxations of the atlantoaxial joint, fractures of the ring of the atlas, odontoid fractures, fractures of the arch of the axis, and lateral mass fractures. All are similar in that the basic mechanisms of these injuries have been relatively well delineated and many share a common mechanism of injury. They are vastly different, however, in both their potential for causing neurologic injury and their optimal method of treatment.

The true incidence of these injuries is difficult to determine and is obscured by their often devastating nature. Most cervicocranial injuries are the result of automobile accidents or falls.[1–6] The predominant mechanism of injury is usually forced flexion or extension secondary to unrestrained deceleration forces, causing anterior displacement of the occiput and upper two cervical segments in relation to the more caudal segments.

The prognosis for patients who sustain these injuries has been highlighted by Alker and colleagues.[1] In their analysis of 312 victims of fatal traffic accidents, 24.4% had evidence of injury to the cervical spine. Of this group, 93% involved injuries from the occiput to the C2 vertebra. The work of Bohlman further underscores the perilous nature of these injuries.[2] In his analysis of 300 patients who sustained acute cervical spine injuries, it was noted that the correct diagnosis was missed in one third of the patients. Of these, 30% involved the occiput, atlas, and axis. In those who survived, occipitoatlantal dislocations occurred in only 0.67%, and atlantoaxial injuries were sustained by only 23%. The main factor responsible for missed diagnoses was related mainly to error or lack of suspicion on the part of the physician because of associated problems, including the presence of a head injury, decreased level of consciousness,

alcohol intoxication, multiple injuries, and inadequate radiographs.

ANATOMY

As a result of the complex anatomic and kinematic relationships of the occipitoatlantoaxial complex, knowledge of regional anatomy is essential to those dealing with patients who have injuries in this region (Figs. 28–1 through 28–3). The skull and atlas are bound together by the paired occipitoatlantal joints laterally and by the anterior and posterior occipitoatlantal membrane. Each occipitoatlantal joint is formed by the caudally convex occipital condyle, along with the reciprocally concave superior articular facet of the atlas. The articular capsules are thin, loose ligaments that blend laterally with ligaments that connect the transverse processes of the atlas with the jugular processes of the skull; these capsular ligaments provide very little stability. The anterior occipitoatlantal membrane is a structural extension of the anterior longitudinal ligament that connects the forward rim of the foramen magnum to the arch of C1, homologous to the ligamentum flavum, and unites the posterior rim of the foramen magnum to the posterior arch of C1. The tectorial membrane, a continuation of the posterior longitudinal ligament, runs from the dorsal surface of the odontoid process to the ventral surface of the foramen magnum. It is thought to be the prime ligament responsible for stability of the occipitoatlantal articulation.[42]

The atlas is a bony ring consisting of two lateral masses connected by an anterior and a posterior arch. The superior articular surfaces face upward and medially to receive the occipital condyles of the skull. The inferior articulating surfaces face downward and slightly medially and rotate on the convex slope of the shouldering facets of the axis. In addition, they are cup shaped to accommodate

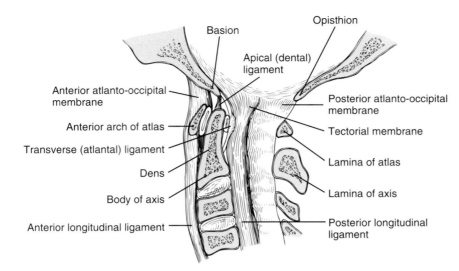

FIGURE 28-1. Sagittal anatomy of the cervicocranium.

the convex surfaces of the occipital condyles. The posterior arch consists of a modified lamina that is more round than flat in cross section and a posterior tubercle that gives rise to the suboccipital muscles. The anterior arch forms a short bar between the lateral masses and has a tubercle on which the longus colli muscles insert.

The atlantoaxial articulation comprises three joints: the paired lateral atlantoaxial facet joints and the central atlantoaxial joint. The lateral atlantoaxial facet joints are formed by the corresponding superior and inferior facet joints, facets of the C1 and C2 vertebrae. They are covered by thin, loose capsular ligaments that accommodate the large amount of rotation at this level. The central atlantoaxial joint is the articulation of the odontoid process with the atlas and is stabilized by the transverse atlantal ligament (cruciform ligament). This ligament takes origin from two internal tubercles on the posterior aspect of the anterior arch of C1 (see Fig. 28-3). Its function is to hold the dens against the anterior arch of the atlas and allow rotation. The paired alar ligaments are alar expansions of the transverse ligament that attach to tubercles on the lateral rim of the foramen magnum; they provide important, additional rotational and translational stability to the occipitoatlantal articulation. The

apical dental ligament runs from the tip of the odontoid process to the ventral surface of the foramen magnum and is only a minor stabilizer of the craniocervical junction.[28, 32]

The axis provides a bearing surface on which the atlas may rotate. It possesses a vertically projecting odontoid process that, together with the transverse atlantal ligaments, serves as a pivotal restraint against horizontal displacement of the atlas. The apex of the odontoid is slightly pointed and serves as the origin for the paired alar ligaments and solitary apical dental ligament. The superior articulating surfaces of the axis are convex and directed slightly laterally to receive the direct thrust of the lateral masses of the atlas. The inferior articulating surfaces are typical of those of the more caudal cervical vertebrae. The pedicles of the axis project 20° superiorly and 33° medially when tracing the course of the pedicle in a posterior-to-anterior direction.[273] The pedicles' dimensions average 7 to 8 mm in height and width, with slight variations between males and females.[273] The vertebral artery begins to angulate laterally at the base of the C2 pedicle and then courses through the foramen transversarium of C2 and C1 only to then move medially and superiorly into the foramen magnum.

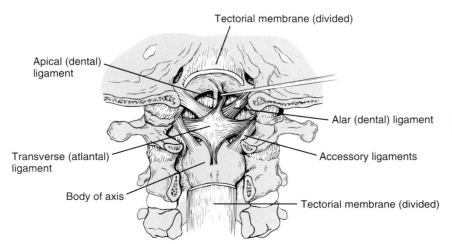

FIGURE 28-2. Coronal anatomy of the cervicocranium.

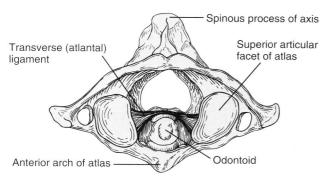

Spinous process of axis

Transverse (atlantal) ligament

Superior articular facet of atlas

Anterior arch of atlas

Odontoid

FIGURE 28–3. The atlantoaxial articulation.

OCCIPITAL CONDYLE FRACTURES

Fractures of the occipital condyle are rarely reported and usually occur in conjunction with other fractures of the cervical spine, most commonly C1 fractures. As with all upper cervical spine fractures, injuries in this region are associated with a high rate of mortality. In patients who manage to survive these injuries, the incidence of these fractures remains unknown because such fractures go undiagnosed in many patients secondary to vague complaints of neck pain. Evaluation of the craniovertebral junction by computed tomography (CT) has enabled more subtle detection. Bloom and colleagues reported that 9 of 55 patients (16.4%) had occipital condyle fractures detected on CT scans but had nondiagnostic plain cervical radiographs.[8] Important physical findings suggestive of an occult injury are paravertebral swelling, impaired skull mobility, torticollis, and cranial nerve symptoms (nerves IX to XII).[9–13, 15, 17] These nerve injuries can occur acutely or in a delayed fashion.

Occipital condyle fractures can be divided into three injury patterns, depending on whether the injury was produced by axial compression, a direct blow, or shear or lateral bending (or both). These fractures are commonly associated with cranial nerve injuries.[7, 14] The Anderson and Montesano classification of occipital condyle fractures is based on the mechanism of injury. Type I injuries are impaction fractures of the condyle secondary to an axial load (Fig. 28–4). Type II injuries are basilar skull fractures that extend through the condyle and communicate with the foramen magnum. These injuries are due to a direct blow to the occipital region. Type III injuries are avulsion fractures of the condyle caused by tension placed on the alar ligaments secondary to shear, lateral bending, rotational forces, or a combination of these mechanisms.

The key to treating these injuries is to maintain a high degree of suspicion because of the subtlety of their signs and symptoms. Treatment of these injuries is based on the degree of associated occipitoatlantal instability. Type I and type II fractures are stable injuries and are therefore best treated with a rigid cervical orthosis or halo vest for 3 months. Type III injuries represent a potentially unstable injury that at the very least requires 3 months of halo vest immobilization, but because of the rarity of this fracture, surgical indications are not well defined. After 3 months of immobilization for all three fracture types, flexion-

extension views should be performed to rule out any residual instability. Only three cases of surgical intervention have been reported. The indications included brain stem compression, vertebral artery injury, and concomitant suboccipital injury.[8, 18] Any findings of instability of the occipitoatlantal joint will require definitive treatment with occiput–C1 arthrodesis.

OCCIPITOATLANTAL DISLOCATIONS

Occipitoatlantal dislocations are extremely rare injuries because of the strength of the supporting ligaments, and reports of survival are even more unusual.[27, 30] Although first reported by Blackwood in 1908, the true incidence is unknown and obscured by the devastating, usually fatal nature of these injuries when they occur.[20] Moreover, the diagnosis is often subtle and may easily be overlooked on routine radiographs. The dislocations are thought to represent approximately 0.67% to 1.0% of all acute cervical spine injuries, and Bucholz and Burkhead noted this injury in 8% of victims of fatal motor vehicle accidents.[21, 22, 39]

Craniocervical dislocations have been classified into three types, depending on which direction the occiput is displaced in relation to the atlas.[19, 26, 35] Although anterior, posterior, and longitudinal dislocations have been reported, by far the most common is anterior dislocation, which occurs in nearly all reported cases in the literature.[33, 39] Because of anatomic variations, this injury is thought to be roughly twice as common in children as in adults.[22, 28] This difference in incidence may be a result of the fact that the occipital condyles in children are smaller and the plane of the occipitoatlantal joint is relatively horizontal in an immature skeleton when compared with the steep inclination that develops with aging.[22, 23, 27, 28]

Anterior occipitoatlantal dislocations, which were first described in postmortem specimens by Kissinger[36] and Malgaigne,[37] are probably the result of a hyperextension and distraction mechanism such as that frequently seen in traffic accidents. This mechanism is confirmed by their frequent association with submental lacerations, mandibular fractures, and posterior pharyngeal wall laceration.[22, 23, 25, 28, 30, 32, 38, 45] Also supporting this theory is Werne's classic description of the anatomy of this region.[42] His work demonstrated that occipitoatlantal flexion is limited by skeletal contact between the foramen magnum and the apex of the odontoid process. Similarly, hyperextension is limited by the tectorial membrane and by contact between the posterior arch of the atlas and the occiput. Lateral tilting is controlled by the alar ligaments. By carefully dividing the tectorial membrane and the alar ligaments, Werne was able to show that these two structures are the primary stabilizers of this inherently unstable joint and that division of these structures allows for forward dislocation of the occiput on the axis.[42] Although frequently overlooked, radiographic diagnosis of the injury is usually made from lateral cervical spine radiographs taken in neutral, flexion, and extension. Soft tissue planes may be enlarged (often >7 mm at the occipital-cervical junction). Any soft tissue swelling in this area is a significant finding and warrants further evaluation.

Alterations in the normal cervicocranial prevertebral soft tissue contour because of hemorrhage into the retropharyngeal fascial space from subtle fractures or ligamentous injuries should prompt further assessment of the cervicocranium by CT. Cervicocranial CT performed to evaluate an abnormal cervicocranial prevertebral soft tissue contour has yielded a 16% positive injury rate, approximately three times the rate of acute cervical spine injuries reported in the literature.

The dens-basion relationship and the Powers ratio are useful in making the diagnosis. In a normal cervical spine with the head in neutral, the tip of the odontoid is in vertical alignment with the basion.[16, 46, 118, 143, 175] The normal distance between these two points in adults is 4 to 5 mm, and any increase in this distance is considered significant.[43, 44] In children, however, this distance may approach 10 mm.[43] The maximal amount of horizontal translation between the odontoid tip and the basion on

flexion and extension radiographs is 1 mm.[40, 42, 44] Anything greater than 1 mm is thought to represent instability.

Because these relationships are somewhat dependent on the position of the skull, Powers and co-workers in 1979 described a method suitable for pure discrimination of anterior occipitoatlantal dislocations.[39] In their technique, two distances are measured between four points: the distance between the basion and the posterior arch of C1 is measured in relation to the distance between the opisthion and the anterior arch of C1. This distance is expressed as a ratio that, if greater than 1, establishes the radiographic diagnosis of anterior occipitoatlantal dislocation (Fig. 28–5). Ratios less than 1 are normal except in posterior occipitoatlantal dislocations, associated fractures of the odontoid process or ring of C1, and congenital abnormalities of the foramen magnum.[23, 39] The ratio does not vary with skull flexion or extension and is not affected by magnification. If difficulties are encountered in interpreting the relationships on a lateral radiograph, these

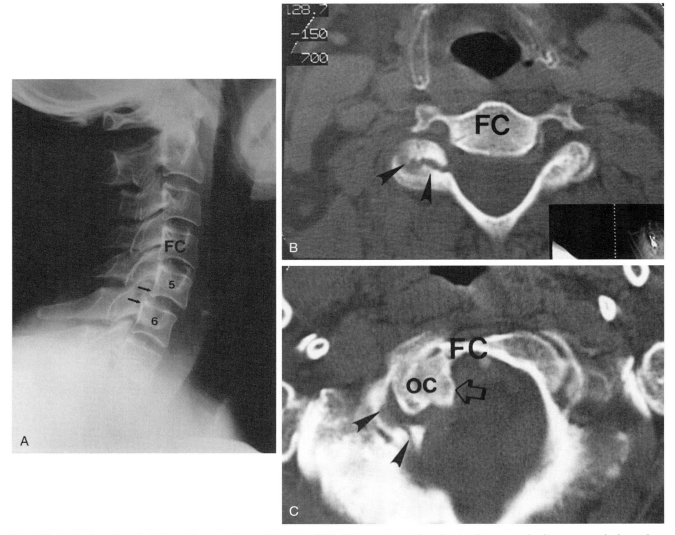

FIGURE 28–4. *A,* A lateral cervical spine radiograph shows subluxation of C5–C6 in a patient with neck pain who was involved in a motor vehicle accident. *B,* An axial computed tomographic (CT) scan shows a lateral mass fracture of C5. The patient's inability to speak normally was initially mistaken as a tongue bite injury. *C,* In reality, he had a hypoglossal nerve palsy caused by the displaced occipital condyle fracture (OC) as seen on the axial CT scan.

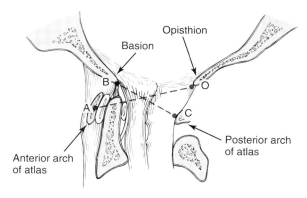

FIGURE 28–5. Powers ratio. If BC/OA is greater than 1, an anterior occipitoatlantal dislocation exists. Ratios less than 1 are normal except in posterior dislocations, associated fractures of the odontoid process or ring of the atlas, and congenital anomalies of the foramen magnum. *Abbreviations:* B, basion; C, posterior arch of C1; O, opisthion; A, anterior arch of C1.

relationships may be established easily on a lateral tomogram or sagittal reconstruction obtained by a CT scan of the area (Fig. 28–6).

Associated injuries are noted frequently in survivors. The most susceptible areas of neurologic injury are the 10

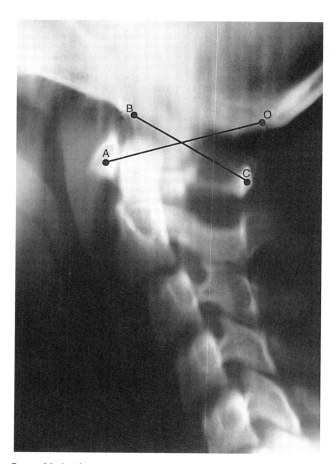

FIGURE 28–6. The Powers ratio shows a normal relationship with the basion (B), opisthion (O), anterior arch of C1 (A), and posterior arch of C1 (C). The BC/OA ratio should be approximately 0.77 in the normal population. A value greater than 1.15 indicates anterior dislocation. (From Levine, A.M; Edwards, C.C. Clin Orthop 239:53–68, 1989.)

caudal pairs of cranial nerves (with the abducens nerve being most frequently injured), the brain stem, the proximal portion of the spinal cord, and the upper three cervical nerves.[25, 28, 30, 32, 38, 39] Fatalities are usually caused by transection of the medulla oblongata or the spinomedullary junction and are due to respiratory compromise secondary to compression or injury to the respiratory centers in the lower brain stem. The clinical manifestations may vary from mild to catastrophic, depending on the nature and degree of injury. Peripheral motor defects are relatively common and may often demonstrate improvement. Neurologic lesions secondary to central cranial nerve lesions are frequent as well, and most appear to be permanent.[32] In addition, injuries to the vertebral artery are occasionally seen.[29, 31, 45] Lesions include vasospasm, intimal tears, thrombosis, dissection, and pseudoaneurysmal dilatation. Vertebral artery injuries can result in a neurologic deficit that is acute or delayed from minutes to days. They can appear even with normal-appearing radiographs. Carotid artery injuries have also been reported secondary to compression by the malrotated lateral mass of C1. Typical clinical features of a vertebral artery injury include altered consciousness, nystagmus, ataxia, diplopia, and dysarthria. The diagnosis is made by magnetic resonance angiograms or conventional arteriography.[24]

Initial management of patients with these injuries should focus on respiratory support and stabilization of the cervical spine, with early halo trunk immobilization or 1 to 2 kg of skeletal traction to avoid distraction of the occipitoatlantal joint and further neurologic injury. Definitive treatment is not universally agreed on. Most authors would advocate surgical stabilization[28, 31, 32, 38, 39, 45] in preference to prolonged immobilization.[39, 45] Because of the potential dangers of persistent instability at the occipitoatlantal junction secondary to severe ligamentous disruption, cervical stabilization by posterior spinal fusion from the occiput to the upper cervical spine should be accomplished with the use of internal fixation (i.e., occipitocervical plates) as soon after the injury as the patient's overall medical and neurologic condition permits. Important determinants of the type of fixation include the presence or absence of posterior arch fractures, which may preclude the use of these structures for fusion. Vieweg and Schultheiss performed a retrospective review of upper cervical spine injuries treated with halo vest immobilization. They identified 2 patients out of 682 with atlantooccipital ligament injuries, and both injuries failed to unite or heal.[41] As with most ligamentous injuries in the cervical spine, nonoperative treatment rarely results in stability.

ATLAS FRACTURES

First described by Cooper in 1823, atlantal fractures are usually the result of falls or automobile accidents.[47, 53, 68] Jefferson subsequently described their mechanism of injury, reviewed the world literature at the time, and proposed a classification system.[56] Fractures of the ring of the atlas, unlike most other fractures of the cervical spine,

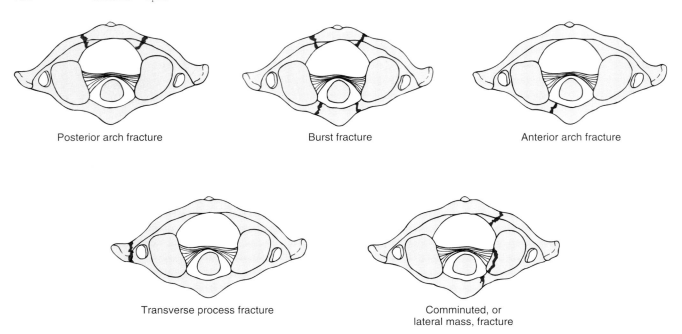

Posterior arch fracture   Burst fracture   Anterior arch fracture

Transverse process fracture   Comminuted, or lateral mass, fracture

FIGURE 28–7. Classification of fractures of the atlas.

are rarely associated with neurologic deficit unless they are seen in association with an odontoid fracture or rupture of the transverse atlantal ligament.[48] As a group, they account for 2% to 13% of all cervical spine fractures and approximately 1.3% of all spine fractures.[48, 52, 69]

Jefferson, whose name is usually associated with the bursting type of atlantal fracture, actually proposed an anatomic classification system in 1920 that included burst fractures, posterior arch fractures, anterior arch fractures, and lateral mass and transverse process fractures (Fig. 28-7).[56] Before the advent of CT, the exact incidence of these injuries could only be estimated, and it was thought that posterior arch fractures made up the largest group.[60, 69] Since the introduction of CT scanning for the routine evaluation of most cervical spine injuries, concepts of fracture classification and incidence have changed. Segal and associates in 1987 expanded Jefferson's original

fracture classification to include six subtypes useful in predicting patient outcome.[68] Most recently, a seventh subtype has been added by Levine and Edwards[14]:

1. Burst fractures (33%) are usually the result of an axial loading force transmitted through the occipital condyles to the superior articulations of C1; these structures are radically forced apart, and either three- or four-part fractures are produced.[65, 67] They are the most common and least likely to cause neurologic injury (Fig. 28–8).
2. Posterior arch fractures (28%) are generally the result of hyperextension injuries and are often associated with odontoid fractures or traumatic spondylolisthesis of the axis[60, 68] (Fig. 28–9z).
3. Comminuted fractures (22%) are usually the result of combined axial compression and lateral flexion forces.

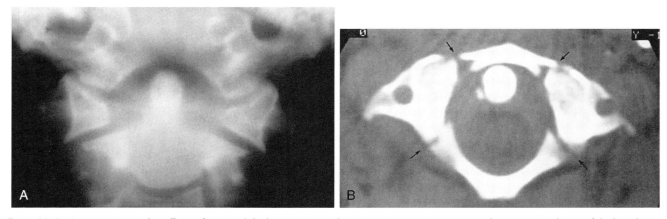

FIGURE 28–8. A patient sustained a Jefferson fracture while diving into a pool. *A,* An anteroposterior tomogram demonstrates splaying of the lateral mass of C1. *B,* A computed tomographic scan in the plane of C1 demonstrates the four fractures of the ring, two anterior and two posterior *(arrows). (A, B,* From Levine, A.M.; Edwards, C.C. Orthop Clin North Am 17:31–44, 1986.)

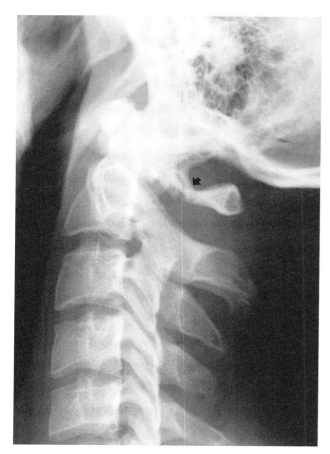

FIGURE 28–9. Lateral cervical spine radiograph demonstrating an isolated posterior arch fracture (*arrow*). (From Levine, A.M.; Edwards, C.C. Orthop Clin North Am 17:31–44, 1986.)

They generally include an avulsion fracture of the transverse ligament in addition to ipsilateral anterior and posterior arch fractures. These fractures are the most likely to result in nonunion and a poor functional outcome.

4. Anterior arch fractures are thought to be caused by hyperextension with the atlantoaxial facet fixed and the anterior arch of C1 abutting the dens[57, 72] (Fig. 28–10), with subsequent avulsion of the fragment.
5. Lateral mass fractures are generally the result of combined axial loading and lateral compression (Fig. 28–11).
6. Transverse process fractures may be unilateral or bilateral as a result of avulsion or lateral bending.
7. Inferior tubercle avulsion fractures are thought to be an avulsion injury of the longus colli muscle caused by hyperextension of the neck.

Levine and Edwards[59] classified atlas fractures according to the mechanism of injury and head position at the time of injury: bilateral fractures of the posterior arch caused by hyperextension with an axial load, unilateral lateral mass fracture caused by lateral bending and an axial load, and a Jefferson (burst) fracture caused by a straight axial load. Posterior arch fractures have a greater than 50% chance of concomitant fracture, usually type II or type III

fractures of the odontoid process, traumatic spondylolisthesis of C2, or an occipital condyle fracture.[48, 61]

Bursting atlantal fractures have been subdivided by Spence and colleagues into stable and unstable types based on radiographic assessment of the integrity of the transverse ligament.[72] In their classic study, the atlantoaxial offset was measured in experimentally produced burst fractures. Burst fractures in which the transverse ligament remained intact produced an atlantoaxial offset of less than 5.7 mm, whereas those associated with rupture of the transverse ligament produced an atlantoaxial offset greater than 6.9 mm (Figs. 28–12 and 28–13). The latter injuries are somewhat less common, and the usual case is that of a stable burst fracture with an intact transverse ligament. It should be appreciated that simple rotation and lateral bending of the normal cervical spine may produce up to 4 mm of lateral offset on the open-mouth odontoid view at the C1–C2 articulation.[53, 69] Congenital anomalies should also be considered because they may produce 1 to 2 mm of lateral offset.[51]

The radiographic diagnosis of these injuries has been greatly enhanced in recent years with the advent of CT scanning. Plain radiographs are also helpful in their evaluation. Aside from routine plain film evaluation, flexion-extension lateral and open-mouth odontoid views

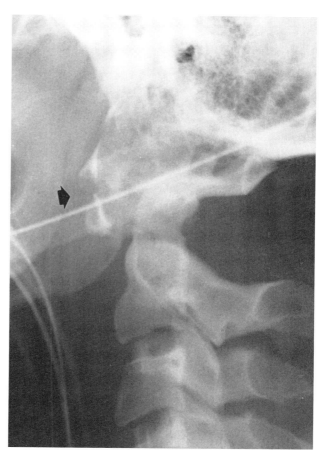

FIGURE 28–10. Lateral radiograph showing a horizontal fracture of the anterior arch of C1 (*arrow*). (From Levine, A.M; Edwards, C.C. Clin Orthop 239:53–68, 1989.)

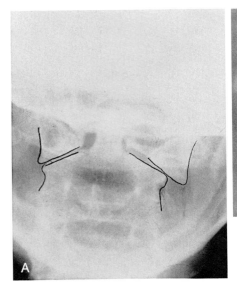

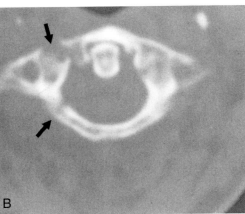

FIGURE **28–11.** Lateral mass fracture of the atlas. *A,* An open-mouth view shows no displacement of one lateral mass and marked displacement of the opposite side. *B,* A computed tomographic scan through the ring of the atlas shows the fractures (*arrows*) anterior and posterior to the lateral mass on one side, with no fractures in the posterior arch on the second side. (*A, B,* From Levine, A.M; Edwards, C.C. Clin Orthop 239:53–68, 1989.)

should be regularly obtained. Other cervical spine injuries, particularly odontoid fractures and traumatic spondylolisthesis of the axis, should be carefully sought during plain film evaluation because they are frequently associated injuries. As noted previously, the open-mouth odontoid view should be reviewed for atlantoaxial overhang to aid in assessing the integrity of the transverse ligament. Lateral flexion and extension radiographs should be reviewed for specific evaluation of the atlantodental interval, which is normally less than 3 mm in adults and less than 5 mm in children[49, 52, 73] (Fig. 28–14).

Injuries associated with atlas fractures most commonly include neurapraxia of the suboccipital and greater occipital nerves as they course around the posterior arch of C1, cranial nerve palsies of the lower six pairs of cranial nerves, and injuries to the vertebral artery or vein as they cross the posterior atlantal arch.[50, 51, 54–57] Occipital nerve injuries may cause neurologic symptoms in the suboccipital region, such as scalp dysesthesias. However, vertebral artery injuries may cause symptoms of basilar artery insufficiency, including vertigo, dizziness, blurred vision, and nystagmus.

These fractures tend to decompress the spinal canal, and thus rarely produce neurologic symptoms. Most isolated injuries will heal with conservative nonoperative treatment.[62] Inferior tubercle avulsion fractures will heal with simple orthotic immobilization. Simple, uncomplicated arch fractures, minimally displaced burst and lateral mass fractures (combined atlantoaxial offset <5.7 mm), and transverse process fractures can be reliably managed with halo or semirigid collar immobilization until union occurs.[60] Lee and co-workers performed a retrospective review to evaluate the use of a rigid cervical collar alone as treatment of stable Jefferson fractures. All patients in their series healed and showed no signs of instability at 12 weeks.[58]

According to Levine and Edwards,[59] atlas fractures that show 2 to 7 mm of combined lateral mass offset on the open-mouth anteroposterior view can be treated with a halo and vest for 3 months. Fractures with an offset greater than 7 mm should first be treated with 4 to 6 weeks of axial traction to maintain reduction and allow preliminary bone healing, followed by 1 to 2 months of halo vest wear.

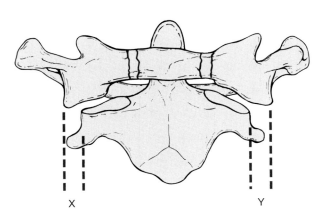

FIGURE **28–12.** Atlantoaxial offset. If X + Y is greater than 6.9 mm, transverse atlantal ligament rupture is implied. (Redrawn from White, A.A.; et al. Clin Orthop 109:85, 1975.)

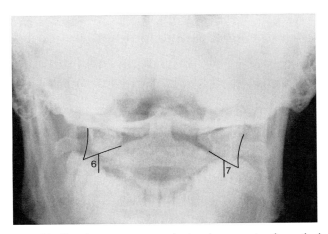

FIGURE **28–13.** Admission open-mouth view demonstrating the method for determining total lateral translation. (From Levine, A.M.; Edwards, C.C. Orthop Clin North Am 17:31–44, 1986.)

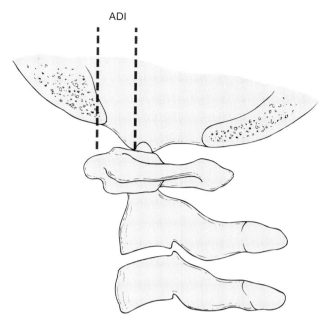

FIGURE 28–14. Atlantodental interval (ADI). If the ADI is greater than 3 mm on flexion and extension radiographs, rupture of the transverse ligament is implied. If the ADI is larger than 5 mm, the accessory ligaments are also functionally incompetent.

After 3 months of immobilization, stability of the atlanto-axial articulation should be verified with lateral flexion-extension films, and any significant instability (atlanto-dental interval >5 mm in adults, >4 mm in children) should then be treated with posterior C1–C2 fusion. Levine and Edwards did not find any instability in their patient group with the use of this treatment algorithm; furthermore, other authors who have treated these injuries nonoperatively have noted an extraordinarily low incidence of problems associated with late C1–C2 instability.[41, 57, 60, 64, 68, 70, 72] This low incidence is most likely a result of the fact that portions of facet capsules and alar ligaments may remain intact.[60, 64] Previous cadaveric studies found that the atlantodental interval increases to approximately 5 mm when the transverse ligament is transected alone and the alar ligaments, apical ligament, and facet capsules are left intact.[82] The transverse ligament tear that occurs with atlas fractures is due to spreading of the lateral masses secondary to axial compression and is different from a tear of the ligament secondary to a hyperflexion injury, which is more unstable because it includes tears in the accessory supporting structures (alar and apical ligaments, facet capsule).

An alternative to treatment of massively unstable atlas fractures (lateral mass offset >7 mm) is that of internal fixation/fusion of C1–C2 after the fracture is reduced in traction. Transarticular screws can be used to secure the C1–C2 articulation in the appropriate position without requiring an intact ring of C1 as is necessary with older posterior wiring techniques.[63, 241, 245] Furthermore, trans-articular screws can aid in the treatment of patients with concomitant odontoid fractures or traumatic spondylolis-thesis of C2.[241] This technique, though technically demanding, is attractive because it can negate the need for

prolonged bedrest and traction, as well as the need for halo vest immobilization. The downside to C1–C2 fusion is the sacrifice of 50% of normal cervical rotation.

Occipitocervical fusion is also an option for the treatment of massively unstable atlas fractures with concomitant fractures of the upper cervical spine. However, this type of treatment requires sacrifice of occiput–C1 motion, which constitutes 50% of cervical flexion-extension, as well as sacrifice of C1–C2 motion, which is responsible for 50% of normal cervical rotation.[66, 74] We would strongly recommend traction or transarticular screw fixation followed by immobilization, as outlined previously, before sacrificing occiput–C2 motion.

Regardless of treatment, many patients with fractures of the atlas have long-term clinical complaints of scalp dysesthesias, neck pain, and decreased range of motion.[59, 68] The incidence of these long-term complications increases with involvement of the lateral masses, as well as with other injuries to the occiput or C1–C2 articulation.[71] Other reported complications include nonunion.[68]

ATLANTOAXIAL INSTABILITY

Although atlantoaxial dislocations and subluxations are relatively common in the cervical spines of patients with rheumatoid arthritis,[77, 78] traumatic atlantoaxial sublux-ations and dislocations secondary to rupture of the transverse ligament are relatively rare.[79] Even rarer are dislocations without evidence of spinal cord injury because these injuries are usually fatal.[81, 88, 89, 99] They differ from other injuries of the upper cervical spine in that they most frequently occur in an older age group than do more traumatic cervical spine injuries.[91, 92] Post-traumatic C1–C2 instability is generally seen in the fifth decade of life and beyond, whereas most other injuries are seen during the third decade. As with other injuries of the upper cervical spine, these injuries usually result from automobile accidents or falls, and the mechanism of injury is most frequently forced flexion of the neck.[79, 91, 92]

The stability of the atlantoaxial articulation depends on the ligamentous integrity of this area. Anterior stability of the atlantoaxial joint is maintained primarily by the transverse ligament, with the paired alar ligaments acting as secondary stabilizers (see Fig. 28–2). Other ligaments that act to a much lesser degree as tertiary stabilizers are the apical ligament of the odontoid, the cruciate and accessory atlantoaxial ligaments, and the capsular ligaments of the facet joints.[82] Posterior stability depends on mechanical abutment of the anterior arch of the ring of the atlas against the odontoid process. Fielding and associates noted that after rupture of the transverse ligament, the secondary and tertiary stabilizers are usually inadequate to prevent further significant displacement of the atlantoaxial complex when a subsequent force similar to the one that resulted in rupture of the transverse ligament is applied.[82]

Although this injury is usually fatal, patients occasionally survive and may have a clinical picture ranging from a dense, mixed neurologic deficit to only severe upper neck pain.[80, 85, 91, 92] Radiographic diagnosis of patients with suspected C1–C2 instability may be difficult and misleading because of the unfamiliar anatomy of this region and also because if the radiograph is made with the neck in slight extension, the spatial relationships of the C1–C2 articulation may appear relatively normal.[79] Routine radiographic evaluation should consist of open-mouth odontoid, anteroposterior, lateral, and oblique views of the cervical spine. In an awake, neurologically intact patient with neck pain, carefully supervised flexion-extension radiographs with constant neurologic monitoring are indicated to assess the atlantodental interval. A lack of apparent instability may be caused by protective paraspinous muscle spasm, and repeat radiographs should be obtained after resolution of the muscle spasm. In patients with neurologic deficits, a myelogram and CT scan are usually helpful. Flexion-extension radiographs in a patient with a swollen cord and neurologic deficit are contraindicated because of the potential for further neurologic injury. Fielding and others noted that up to 3 mm of anterior displacement of C1 on C2, as measured by the atlantodental interval, implies that the transverse ligament is intact. If the displacement is 3 to 5 mm, the transverse ligament is ruptured, and if the displacement is greater than 5 mm, the transverse ligament and accessory ligaments are probably ruptured and deficient[82, 86, 90, 93, 94, 97, 98] (Fig. 28–15; see also Fig. 28–14).

Traumatic overdistraction between C1 and C2 may occur when all the ligaments connecting C2 to the skull are ruptured and may be manifested when an attempt is made to reduce C1–C2 subluxation by traction. A recent case report discussed a patient with traumatic anterior atlantoaxial dislocation in whom atlantoaxial vertical dissociation developed after Gardner-halo skull traction with 4.02 lb (1.5 kg). Five pounds of skeletal traction was associated with marked neurologic deterioration from unanticipated longitudinal instability. Identification of patients who are susceptible to this complication is difficult. In this case, avoiding spinal traction might have prevented it. Several reports have suggested that vertical dissociation may occur in C1–C2 anterior dislocation treated by spinal traction and that other forms of reduction must be used to treat these pathologies and avoid this potentially fatal complication.[75, 95]

Atlantoaxial instability can be the result of a purely ligamentous injury or an avulsion fracture, but in either case, no effective nonoperative method is available to reliably reestablish the stability of the atlantoaxial articulation. Most authors agree that nonoperative management is not indicated and that reduction followed by posterior fusion is the treatment of choice.[79, 82, 83, 91, 92] The timing of surgery is somewhat controversial, however. Delaying fusion for several days seems reasonable to allow cord edema to subside and enable the patient's neurologic condition to stabilize without greatly enhancing the risk of prolonged recumbency. Because axial rotation is the major motion that occurs at the C1–C2 articulation, a fusion that resists this type of motion is most appropriate. Biomechanical studies have compared the Brooks-type fusion[76] with that of Gallie wiring, Halifax clamps, and Magerl's transarticular screw technique.[87, 240] One study found that rotational stability was greatest with the transarticular screw and Brooks fusion techniques and that the strongest overall fixation was achieved with the transarticular screw.[240] Other authors, however, believe that because the purpose of the surgical construct should be to reduce and prevent further anterior translation of C1 on C2, transarticular screws (see Fig. 28–30) or a Gallie wiring technique should be considered for the reason that anterior translation is best prevented with these two techniques.[84, 87, 91, 92, 240] If a patient has a concurrent injury to the upper cervical spine that is adequately treated by immobilization (e.g., a ring fracture of C1 or traumatic spondylolisthesis of the axis), nonoperative treatment until healing has occurred, followed by posterior C1–C2 fusion, is a reasonable alternative. However, transarticular screw technique allows for immediate surgical stabilization and eliminates the time necessary to heal the posterior element fractures of C1 or C2. However, the screw fixation without supplemental wire fixation needs to be augmented with rigid cervical immobilization, potentially halo fixation.

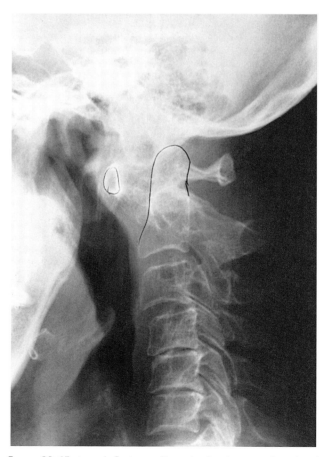

FIGURE 28–15. Lateral flexion radiograph showing an atlantodental interval of 12 mm, which is diagnostic of complete rupture of the transverse ligament and the alar and apical ligaments as well as disruption of some fibers of the C1–C2 joint capsule. (From Levine, A.M; Edwards, C.C. Clin Orthop 239:53–68, 1989.)

ATLANTOAXIAL ROTATORY SUBLUXATIONS AND DISLOCATIONS

Rotatory injuries of the atlantoaxial joint, first described by Corner in 1907, include a rare spectrum of lesions ranging from rotatory fixation within the normal range of C1–C2

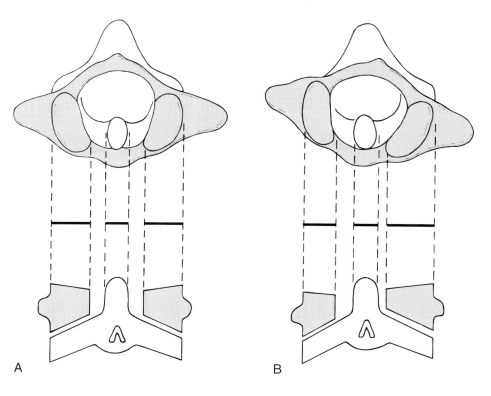

Figure 28–16. The atlantoaxial joint in neutral position (*A*) and on rotation to the right (*B*). With rotation, the antero-posterior view demonstrates (1) an apparent approximation of the left atlantal articular mass to the odontoid, (2) an increase in width of the left atlantal articular mass with decreased width of the right atlantal articular mass, and (3) a widened left and a narrowed right atlantoaxial joint because of the slope of these joints, as is evident on a lateral view. (*A, B,* Redrawn from Wortzman, G. Radiology 90:479–487, 1960.)

A   B

motion to frank rotatory atlantoaxial dislocation.[100] The significance of these injuries lies in the fact that with an intact transverse ligament, complete bilateral dislocation of the articular processes can occur at approximately 65° of atlantoaxial rotation with significant narrowing of the neural canal and subsequent potential damage to the spinal cord.[101] With deficiency of the transverse ligament, complete unilateral dislocation can occur at approximately 45° with similar consequences. In addition, the vertebral arteries can be compromised by excessive rotation with resultant brain stem or cerebellar infarction and death.[112, 114] Levine and Edwards pointed out that rotatory dislocations at the C1–C2 articulation rarely occur in adults and are significantly different from those in children.[103, 104, 111] Subluxations in children usually are related to a viral illness, are almost always self-limited, and generally resolve with conservative treatment. The injury seen in adults is a more severe form of subluxation or dislocation and usually is related to vehicular trauma. Additionally, the adult form is frequently associated with a fracture of a portion of one or both lateral masses and is due to an injury mechanism of flexion and rotation.

Because of the rarity of the injury, the infrequency of neurologic involvement, and the difficulty in obtaining adequate radiographs, the diagnosis may be difficult to make and is usually delayed. With minimal amounts of subluxation, patients may complain of only neck pain. With more severe degrees of subluxation or dislocation, torticollis may be noted and the patient may present with the typical "cock robin" posture with the head tilted toward one side and rotated toward the other and in slight flexion. The anterior arch of the atlas and the step-off at C1–C2 may be palpable orally. Plagiocephaly is commonly seen in younger patients with late symptoms.[103] Neuro-

logic involvement is rare but may be catastrophic as a result of compromise of the neural canal at the medullo-cervical junction.[103, 110] The diagnosis, therefore, requires a certain degree of clinical suspicion based on the patient's history, symptoms, and physical examination. It should always be considered in the evaluation of patients with cervical spine trauma and secondary angulatory deformities of the neck. The mechanism of injury is thought to be a flexion-extension type of injury or a relatively minor blow to the head.[116]

Jacobson and Adler in 1956 and Fiorani-Gallotta and Luzzatti in 1957 were the first to describe the radiologic manifestations of these injuries, which were also seen in cases of torticollis.[105, 108] Wortzman and Dewar suggested a dynamic method of differentiating rotatory fixation from torticollis by using plain radiographs, and Fielding and co-workers suggested cineradiography and CT as additional tools for evaluation of these injuries.[103, 104, 116] On an open-mouth odontoid radiograph with the atlantoaxial joint in neutral rotation, the articular masses of the atlas and axis are symmetrically located with the odontoid midway between the lateral masses of the atlas (Fig. 28–16). With rotation to the right, the left lateral mass of C1 travels forward and to the right with an apparent approximation of the left atlantal articular mass to the odontoid process. Associated with forward movement of the left articular mass and posterior movement of the right articular mass, the leftward lateral mass increases in width because of a larger radiographic shadow, whereas the right lateral mass demonstrates a diminished width because of a narrower radiographic shadow. The facet joint on the left appears widened, and the right facet joint appears narrowed because of the corresponding slope of these joints. This abnormality produces the so-called wink

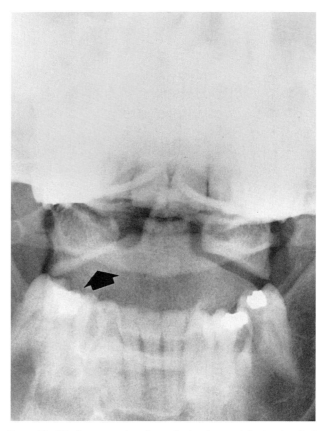

FIGURE 28–17. Open-mouth radiograph showing a wink sign in which the lateral mass of C1 overlaps the lateral mass of C2 on the affected side (*arrow*). (From Levine, A.M.; Edwards, C.C. Clin Orthop 239:53–68, 1969.)

sign[110] (Fig. 28–17). When plain cervical spine radiographs demonstrate evidence of a rotational anomaly at the atlantoaxial joint, additional radiographic investigation is indicated and should consist of open-mouth odontoid views with the patient's head rotated 15° to each side to determine whether true atlantoaxial fixation is present. Persistent asymmetry of the odontoid and its relationship to the articular masses of the atlas, with the asymmetry not being correctable by rotation, forms the basic radiologic criteria for the diagnosis of atlantoaxial rotatory fixation.[116] Additionally, cineradiography in the lateral projection may

be considered if it is available. Alternatively, a CT scan through the C1–C2 articulation with the patient's head rotated to the right and to the left approximately 15° will confirm or disprove the presence or absence of rotatory fixation at the atlantoaxial joint. Most commonly, acute or chronic traumatic injuries are in a fixed position. Currently, CT with two- or three-dimensional reconstruction gives the most accurate delineation of the injury. Flexion-extension lateral radiographs are also essential to inspect the integrity of the transverse atlantal ligament.

Fielding and associates in 1977 first coined the term *rotatory fixation* to describe this injury because rotatory fixation of the atlas on the axis may occur with subluxation or dislocation or when the relative positions of the atlas and axis are still within the normal range of atlantoaxial rotation.[102, 103] Fielding and associates' classification, which does not include frank dislocations, divides these injuries into four types based on their radiographic appearance (Fig. 28–18). Levine and Edwards added to this classification by describing the extreme injury pattern of rotatory dislocation.[110]

Type I rotatory fixation, the most common, was seen in 47% of Fielding and associates' series. Rotatory fixation without anterior displacement at the atlas was noted, and the atlantodental interval was less than 3 mm because the transverse ligament was intact and acting as a pivot. This type of fixation is thought to occur within the normal range of motion at the C1–C2 articulation (Fig. 28–19).

Type II rotatory fixation occurred with 3- to 5-mm anterior displacement of the atlas. It was the second most common injury (30%) and was associated with deficiency of the transverse ligament and unilateral anterior displacement of one lateral mass of the atlas when the opposite intact joint acted as a pivot. The amount of abnormal anterior displacement of the atlas from the axis and the amount of fixed rotation were in excess of the normal maximal rotation of the atlantoaxial joint.

Type III rotatory fixation was seen with greater than 5-mm anterior displacement of the atlas on the axis. It was observed in patients with associated deficiency of the transverse ligament and the secondary stabilizers. Both lateral masses of the atlas were subluxated anteriorly, one more than the other, thus producing the rotated position.

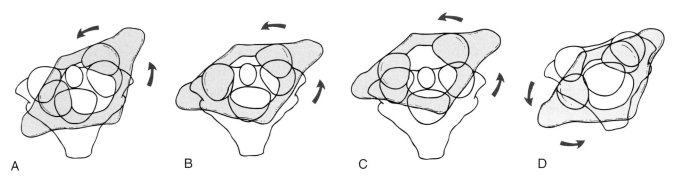

A   B   C   D

FIGURE 28–18. Drawings showing the four types of rotatory fixation. *A,* Type I: rotatory fixation with no anterior displacement and the odontoid acting as the pivot. *B,* Type II: rotatory fixation with anterior displacement of 3 to 5 mm and one lateral articular process acting as the pivot. *C,* Type III: rotatory fixation with anterior displacement of more than 5 mm. *D,* Type IV: rotatory fixation with posterior displacement.

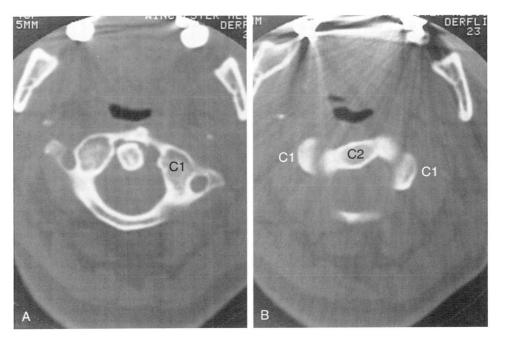

FIGURE 28–19. Computed tomographic scan slices showing rotatory fixation with the transverse ligament intact. *A,* The ring of C1 is shown, with the left lateral mass rotated anteriorly in comparison to the C2 lateral mass. *B,* The C2 ring shows that the right lateral mass is rotated posteriorly. (*A, B,* From Levine, A.M; Edwards, C.C. Clin Orthop 239:53–68, 1989.)

Type IV rotatory fixation was the most uncommon, with posterior displacement of the atlas noted on the axis. It was seen in association with a deficient dens (Fig. 28–20).

Type V, frank rotatory dislocation, may also be seen, although it is extremely uncommon.[109, 110]

The cause of this injury in adults is almost universally associated with trauma involving a flexion-rotation mechanism of injury; however, the cause of the nontraumatic form of this condition is unknown, and many different theories have been proposed. Wittek suggested that effusion of the synovial joint produced stretching of the ligaments.[115] Coutts indicated that synovial fringes, when inflamed or adherent, may block atlantoaxial reduction.[101] Fiorani-Gallotta and Luzzatti postulated rupture of one or both of the alar ligaments and transverse ligament, whereas Watson-Jones proposed hyperemic decalcification with loosening of the ligaments.[105, 113] Grisel related the condition to muscle contraction that might follow a combination of factors, including muscle spasm that prevents reduction in the early stages.[106, 107] More recently, Fielding and colleagues noted that this injury is occasionally associated with lateral mass articular fractures, and they consider most swollen capsular and synovial tissues to be associated with muscle spasm.[104] They believe that if the abnormal position persists because of failure to achieve reduction, ligament and capsular contractures may develop secondarily and cause fixation.

ODONTOID FRACTURES

As a result of their significant potential for neurologic injury and nonunion, no other injury of the upper cervical

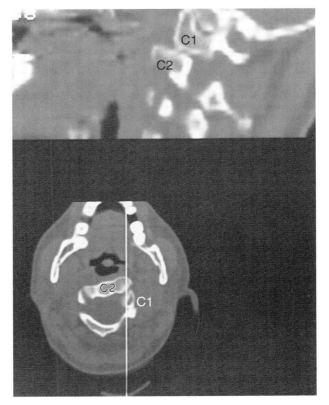

FIGURE 28–20. Computed tomographic scan showing traumatic, posteriorly displaced rotatory fixation after an automobile accident. Posterior displacement of the right lateral mass of C1 in reference to the right lateral mass of C2 is causing a neurologic deficit. This abnormality is well demonstrated on the sagittal reconstruction of that side. The opposite side is nondisplaced. (From Levine, A.M; Edwards, C.C. Clin Orthop 239:53–68, 1989.)

spine has generated as much controversy as fractures of the odontoid process. In the early 1900s, odontoid fractures were thought to be almost uniformly fatal. Later evaluations dropped the estimated mortality to approximately 50%, and more recent figures indicate that the mortality rate is approximately 4% to 11%.[117, 121, 122, 140, 146] These figures may be misleading in that some patients with this injury may never reach the hospital because of rapidly fatal brain stem or spinal cord injury. This scenario is probably more a possibility than a reality inasmuch as Bohler in an autopsy series reported only one case of fatal quadriplegia from an odontoid fracture.[124] The overall incidence of odontoid fractures ranges from 7% to 14% of all cervical fractures,[122, 124, 132, 161, 166] and as with most other injuries to the upper cervical spine, they are usually the result of falls or motor vehicle accidents.[121, 122, 130, 146, 159, 174]

The odontoid, in conjunction with the transverse atlantal ligament, is the prime stabilizer of the atlantoaxial articulation and acts to prevent anterior and posterior dislocation of the atlas on the axis. The apophyseal joints of the atlantoaxial complex confer little stability at this level because they lie in a horizontal plane; thus, with fractures of the dens, stability is lost and anterior and posterior subluxation and dislocation may occur.[169] Despite a large number of autopsy and biomechanical studies, the exact mechanism of injury remains unknown but probably includes a combination of flexion, extension, and rotation.[120, 126, 159, 172]

An understanding of the ligamentous and vascular anatomy of this region is important to appreciate the potential for problems with healing of these controversial injuries, particularly those occurring at the odontoid base. The dens is connected to the occiput and C1 by a number of small, but important ligamentous structures (see Fig. 28–2). From the cephalic aspect of the dens, the single apical and paired alar ligaments fan out in a rostral direction to their attachments on the anterior lip of the foramen magnum and occipital condyles, respectively.

More caudally, the transverse ligament arises from the anteromedial aspect of the lateral masses of the atlas, curves posteriorly around the dens, and is separated from the dens by a small synovial joint (see Fig. 28–3). Additionally, ligamentous bands called the *accessory ligaments* arise in conjunction with the transverse ligament and pass directly into their attachment on the lateral aspect of the dens immediately above the base. This complex ligamentous arrangement attached to the dens allows for movement of the dens separate from the body of C2 in most fractures and explains in part why displacement and associated problems with union are frequent with these injuries.

The vascular anatomy of the odontoid has also been said to contribute to the problem of nonunion in these injuries. The paired right and left posterior and anterior ascending arteries of the axis form the principal blood supply to the dens and are branches of the vertebral arteries. A third source of supply is the paired cleft perforating arteries from each carotid artery that anastomose with the anterior ascending arteries. The ascending arteries penetrate the axis at the base of the dens and also continue outside the dens in a cephalic direction to form the apical arcade over the tip of the dens. Because of this complex vascular anatomy, fractures of the base of the dens probably cause damage to the vessels in this area and create problems with healing[170] (Fig. 28–21). The concept of end-vessel supply does not exist; therefore, the high nonunion rates of many odontoid fractures may result from other factors such as the degree of displacement, distraction, motion, and soft tissue interposition.[174] However, autopsy retrieval studies of odontoid nonunion have not shown evidence of osteonecrosis, so this notion has for the most part been discarded. Many authors espouse the view that the odontoid actually has a rich blood supply.[117] Govender and colleagues performed selective vertebral angiography on 18 patients, 10 with acute fractures and 8 with nonunion, and revealed that the blood supply to the odontoid process was not disrupted.[143]

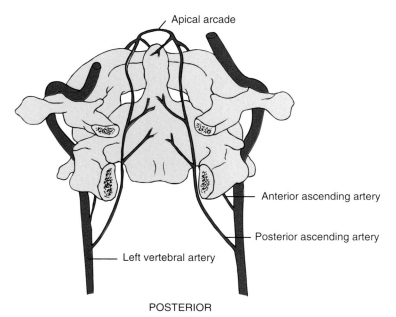

Apical arcade

Anterior ascending artery

Posterior ascending artery

Left vertebral artery

POSTERIOR

FIGURE 28–21. Vascular anatomy of the odontoid process.

Another factor that may contribute to the potential for nonunion is that the dens is almost completely surrounded by synovial cavities, thus making it almost entirely an intra-articular structure.[126] The tip of the dens is also tethered by ligaments as noted previously, which would tend to distract a fracture of the base of the dens because the injury is below its attachments to the alar and apical ligaments. Therefore, an injury to the dens at or above the accessory ligaments would leave the tip of the dens fragment floating entirely within a synovial cavity. With almost no soft tissue to provide periosteal blood supply, healing must rely on new bone formation from an intact endosteal blood supply. One last cause of odontoid fracture nonunion is the potential for soft tissue interposition between the fracture fragments. Crockard and co-workers reported several cases in which the transverse ligament was caught between the fracture fragment of the odontoid process and the body of C2.[133] Govender and associates performed postmortem studies on 10 adult axis vertebrae and showed that the difference in surface area between type II and type III fractures was statistically significant and may represent another factor contributing to the increased nonunion rates seen with this fracture pattern.[143]

The frequent association of head trauma, drug and alcohol abuse, and the occurrence of concomitant cervical spine fractures may cause these injuries to be overlooked on initial evaluation.[146, 158, 174] In addition, some of these injuries will not be evident initially on plain radiographs but will be visualized on subsequent follow-up films as early callus formation is seen. In the evaluation of a patient with a suspected odontoid fracture, it is important to rule out associated cervical spine injuries by appropriate plain radiographs, tomography, and CT.[136] Widening of the prevertebral soft tissue space, as is occasionally found in lower cervical spine injuries, is relatively less frequent with injuries to C1 and C2.[160] However, an increase in the prevertebral soft tissue shadow greater than 10 mm anterior to the ring of C1 suggests an anterior fracture. As with other injuries to the craniocervical junction, most of these injuries result from motor vehicle accidents or falls, and a high percentage of patients with this injury also have injuries to the skull, mandible, other cervical vertebrae, long bones, and trunk.[126, 171] Thus, a complete and thorough physical examination is essential. Neurologic injury, which is seen in approximately 25% of patients, may range from high tetraplegia with respiratory center involvement to minimal motor and sensory weakness involving a portion of an upper limb secondary to minor loss of one or several cervical nerve roots.[117, 174]

Anderson and D'Alonzo classified these injuries into three anatomic types based on the level of injury[117] (Fig. 28–22). Type I fractures account for approximately 5% of these injuries and are the least common. They are characterized by oblique fractures through the upper end of the odontoid process and probably represent avulsion fractures in which the alar ligaments attach to the tip of the odontoid. However, type I fractures may be accompanied by gross instability because of traction injury to the alar or apical ligaments. Type II fractures, which account for approximately 60% in most series, are fractures occurring at the junction of the odontoid process and the body of the

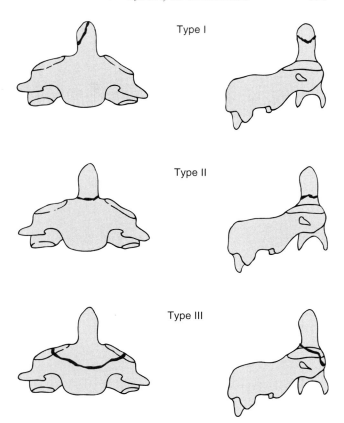

FIGURE 28–22. Three types of odontoid fractures as seen in the anteroposterior *(left)* and lateral *(right)* planes. Type I is an oblique fracture through the upper part of the odontoid process itself. Type II is a fracture at the junction of the odontoid process and the vertebral body of the second cervical vertebra. Type III is really a fracture through the body of the atlas. (Redrawn from Anderson, L.D.; D'Alonzo, R.T. J Bone Joint Surg Am 56:1663–1674, 1974.)

axis. These injuries are the most controversial with regard to management because of their significant potential for nonunion[135, 141, 146, 160, 171] (Fig. 28–23). Type III fractures account for approximately 30% of odontoid fractures. In these injuries, the fracture line extends down into the cancellous portion of the body and is really a fracture through the body of the axis. In addition, the fracture line may extend laterally into the articular facet. Problems associated with obtaining union are thought to be relatively infrequent with this injury.[174] Not included in the classification is a fracture pattern described as that of a vertical fracture through the odontoid process with the fracture continuing inferiorly through the body of C2.[123] This fracture, although it involves the odontoid, behaves more like a variant of traumatic spondylolisthesis of C2.

The issue of treatment of these injuries is a complex one, and the optimal treatment remains to be resolved. Because all methods of treatment are associated with problems, no single method has been universally accepted; however, certain principles do apply. Type I fractures represent an avulsion fracture of the alar or apical ligaments. These injuries do not compromise the integrity of the C1–C2 articulation and are not of great clinical significance. However, after muscle spasm from the injury has resolved, subtle injury to the occipitoatlantal region must be ruled out with flexion-extension lateral radiographs. These injuries will heal quite well with a brief period of simple collar immobilization.[117] Type II injuries in particular and type III injuries to a certain degree are the fractures for which answers are less clear. Both surgical* and nonsurgical† management have strong advocates. However, if the surgeon understands the risk factors for nonunion and appropriately selects patients for surgical treatment, nonoperative techniques in low-risk patients have yielded fracture union rates of 90%.

Several factors have been pointed out that predispose to problems with nonunion or malunion of type II fractures, including displacement of greater than 4 to 5 mm,[121, 130, 143] the type of immobilization, and angulation greater than 10°.[130] Type II fractures with anterior or posterior displacement of greater than 5 mm have been associated with nonunion rates approximating 40% regardless of the treatment method, and some reports suggest that posterior displacement is a worse prognostic indicator. The effect of increased age of the patient on union rate and tolerance to halo immobilization has been increasingly stressed as an important factor and will be discussed in detail later in the chapter.[143, 148] When angulation is greater than 10°, the nonunion rate approximates 22%.[130] The two most critical factors influencing union are obtaining and holding a reduced fracture. Union rates with halo immobilization for type II and type III fractures have been reported to be 66% and 93%, respectively.[121, 130] Vieweg and Schultheiss performed a meta-analysis of 35 studies to determine the outcome of immobilization in a halo vest for various injuries to the upper cervical spine. This study reviewed the results of

---

*See references 117, 124, 125, 129, 130, 135, 138, 141, 167, 174, 233.
†See references 118, 121, 128, 131, 149, 156, 161, 162, 164, 165, 175, 179.

312 patients with odontoid fractures. Of the fractures studied, only two were type I odontoid fractures and both were treated with halo vests. Treatment outcomes were reviewed for 189 patients with type II fractures (177 isolated fractures and 12 combined C1/C2 injuries). Complete healing took place in 150 cases (85% union rate). A 67% healing rate was noted in the 12 patients with combined injuries. In 123 type III odontoid fractures, the authors observed a 96% union rate.[41] Information in the literature regarding successful healing of type II odontoid fractures varies to a great extent. Union rates of injuries managed by internal fixation of the dens have been reported to be 92% to 100%,[129, 138, 167, 233] and stabilization rates associated with posterior spinal fusion have been reported to be on the order of 96% to 100%.[121, 130, 243, 245, 262]

No randomized or controlled studies on this subject can be found in the literature. Seybold and Bayley evaluated the functional outcome of surgically and conservatively managed odontoid fractures (37 type II and 20 type III) over a 10-year period at a single institution.[189] Pain scores were higher in patients with type II fractures and in patients treated conservatively with halo immobilization, especially those older than 60 years. No statistical differences in these parameters were found. Older patients treated surgically did not have a better functional outcome score than did those treated nonoperatively. The rate of union for halo immobilization, regardless of fracture type, was 80.9%. The healing rate for type II fractures was 65.3%. Patients with displaced fractures were treated with reduction and placement into a halo. They found no differences in the nonunion and union groups with regard to age, fracture type, delay in diagnosis, displacement, and direction of displacement or mechanism of injury. However, more nonunions were noted in the type II group. Older patients treated by halo fixation had more compli-

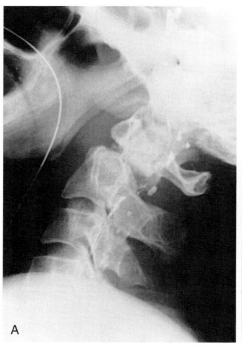
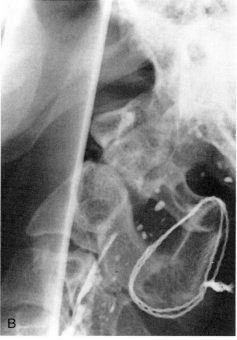

FIGURE 28–23. *A,* A posteriorly displaced type II dens fracture. *B,* Reduction of the fracture by using a bone block construct with a sublaminar wire beneath the arch of C1 and the lamina of C2. (*A, B,* From Levine, A.M.; Edwards, C.C. Orthop Clin North Am 17:31–44, 1986.)

cations: increased rates of pin loosening, decreased range of motion and shoulder discomfort, and dysphagia. Some trends toward improved outcome scores were observed in elderly patients treated operatively, but the trends were not statistically significant.

A recent case-control study by Lennarson and colleagues studied 33 patients with isolated type II fractures treated with halo vest immobilization. Cases were defined as those with nonunion after halo immobilization, whereas control subjects represented those with successful bony union attained with halo immobilization. The groups had similar concomitant medical conditions, sex ratios, amount of fracture displacement, direction of fracture displacement, length of hospital stay, and length of follow-up. Age older than 50 years was found to be a highly significant risk factor for failure of halo immobilization. The odds ratio indicated that the risk of failure of halo immobilization is 21 times higher in patients 50 years or older.[155]

Julien and associates performed an evidence-based analysis of odontoid fracture management by reviewing 95 articles based on the American Medical Association data classification schema. Only 35 articles met the selection criteria of at least class III evidence (based on retrospectively collected data—clinical series, database reviews, case reviews). No class I or class II papers (which are prospective studies or retrospective studies using reliable data) were included. The remainder of the studies were class IV data. This study used fusion as the only outcome criterion. They grouped the studies by treatment: no treatment, halo/Minerva, traction, posterior surgery, or anterior surgery. They concluded that for type I and type III fractures, immobilization yields satisfactory results in 84% to 100% of cases. Anterior fixation for type III fractures improves the union rate to nearly 100%. For type II fractures, halo vest application and posterior fusion have similar fusion rates of 65% to 84%, respectively. Anterior fixation produces a fusion rate of 90%, whereas traction alone is less successful at 57%. These observations were based on review of class III data that "are inadequate to establish a treatment standard or guideline. Therefore all management modalities described remain treatment options."[152] However, the generally accepted standards will be reviewed.

The reported incidence of nonunion in the literature for type II injuries ranges from 10% to 60%.[169, 176] Because of the potential catastrophic pitfalls with surgery, including the risk of infection and paralysis, it would seem reasonable to initially manage type II injuries with attempted reduction and halo immobilization for 12 weeks for displaced fractures. Before the introduction of odontoid screw fixation methods, surgical alternatives for type II fractures consisted of posterior C1–C2 fusion by several techniques, with predictably good fusion results. Most studies reported success rates of 90% to 100%. However, the expense to the patient was not the only potential pitfall of surgery; 50% of normal cervical rotation is also sacrificed. The attractiveness of odontoid screw fixation lies in preservation of atlantoaxial motion, as well as negation of the need for halo immobilization or posterior fusion.[151] Unfortunately, odontoid screw fixation is technically demanding. Furthermore, studies of external and

internal dens morphology have found that not all odontoid processes are created equal; close attention must be paid when evaluating preoperative CT scans because some odontoid processes and C1–C2 articulations cannot accommodate screws.* Patients with type II injuries that demonstrate inadequate reduction and those initially seen more than 2 weeks after injury[166] should be considered candidates for surgical stabilization. Also, patients with fractures that are treated with halo thoracic immobilization for a period of 12 to 16 weeks and afterward demonstrate residual instability on lateral flexion and extension radiographs should also be considered for surgery. Odontoid screw fixation for nonunion has been shown to give reasonable results.[119, 129, 233] Apfelbaum and co-workers found that anterior screws produce union rates of 88% if done before 6 months but that the rate drops to 25% after 18 months.[119] Late instability may be found in patients who had transverse ligament injuries in addition to their odontoid fracture.[145] As previously stated, posterior wiring or C1–C2 transarticular screws and fusion produce good results in stabilization of C1–C2.[147, 154]

As demonstrated by Clark and White, type III injuries are more problematic than previously thought.[130] With significant fracture displacement or angulation, the incidence of malunion and possibly nonunion increases. Cervical orthoses are therefore probably not adequate management for type III injuries. Displaced, angulated fractures should be reduced in halo traction and held in halo thoracic immobilization until united.[108] Alternatively, "shallow" type III fractures have been found to heal well with the odontoid screw technique.[129, 137, 138, 233] Malunion of odontoid fractures can lead to potential problems of cervical myelopathy[133] and post-traumatic C1–C2 arthrosis.

FRACTURES IN OLDER PATIENTS

Upper cervical spine fractures in older patients are encountered with relative frequency and account for up to 23% of all cervical fractures.[193] Ryan and Henderson, in a review of 17 cervical spine fractures, found that the incidence of C1–C2 fractures progressively rises with age because of the preponderance of odontoid fractures in this patient group.[188] Mortality rates have approached 25% to 30%.[124, 193] Many series have reported a high incidence of combination fractures of C1 and C2, with most of the C2 fractures being odontoid.[182, 193] Management of cervical spine fractures in older patients is often complicated by preexisting medical conditions, poor ability to tolerate halo immobilization, and poor healing potential. The decision to treat with immobilization or surgery remains controversial. Most studies are retrospective reviews with low patient numbers that vary in their decision making, so conclusions cannot be drawn.[124, 156, 183, 185–187, 191–193] However, many important trends have started to emerge. Olerud and colleagues retrospectively examined whether cervical spine fractures carried an increased risk of death in patients older than 65 years and tried to define risk factors

---

*See references 139, 142, 150, 153, 157, 162, 163, 168, 173

influencing survival. Five years after the injury, 25 of 65 patients had died. Severe co-morbidity (ASA physical status classification >2), neurologic injury (Frankel grades A to C), age, and ankylosing spondylitis proved to be significant risk factors for death.[186] This study did not address differences in outcome between surgical and nonsurgical treatment. Finelli and colleagues found that trauma in the elderly population results in increased mortality for a given level of injury severity in comparison to younger persons.[181]

Proponents of halo immobilization as the treatment of choice for most C1 and C2 fractures in elderly patients stress that it obviates the need for surgery and allows for reduction and prompt mobilization, a positive effect because prolonged periods of bedrest are poorly tolerated.[124, 183] Hannigan and coauthors reported that one third of patients with odontoid fractures treated by bedrest suffered respiratory complications, as opposed to no patients who ambulated early after treatment. They attributed two deaths to bedrest.[148]

Many investigators have stressed that halos are well tolerated in this patient subset.[124, 183, 193] Several studies also maintain that halos are associated with a high complication rate in this patient population[189] and that the risk of nonunion is increased with halo treatment in older patients.[155] Age older than 50 years was found to be a highly significant risk factor for failure of halo immobilization. The odds ratio for these data indicates that the risk of failure of halo immobilization is 21 times higher in patients 50 years or older. Surgical intervention should be considered in patients 50 years or older who have a type II dens fracture, if it can be performed with acceptable risk of morbidity and death.[155]

Taitsman and Hecht recently examined the rate of complications associated with halo immobilization in the elderly population.[192] Seventy-five patients older than 65 years were treated over a 10-year period at two Level I trauma centers. Patients were excluded if they were multitrauma patients, if they died of obvious complications of their other injuries or within the first week of hospitalization, or if they were in respiratory arrest on admission. Finally, patients were excluded if they underwent surgery within 1 month of admission. Isolated odontoid fractures were most common and were found in 32 of the 75 patients (43%). Five patients (7%) had C1 fractures. Fourteen patients (19%) had combination C1/C2 fractures; 10 (13%) of this group had a C1/odontoid fracture. Nine people (12%) had other C2 fractures. Two patients (3%) had three or more cervical vertebrae involved. Thirteen (17%) had other cervical injuries. Most elderly patients who are placed in halos are unable to return home immediately after leaving the acute care hospital. Only 11 of the 75 patients (15%) were discharged directly to home. Two of the 11 were readmitted and then placed in a rehabilitation center or nursing home. Forty-one patients (55%) experienced at least one complication. Twenty-two patients (29%) had pin problems—primarily loose or infected pins. Aspiration pneumonia is a significant risk for elderly patients in halos. Pneumonia developed in 17 patients (23%) either during their initial hospitalization or during readmission. All 17 were treated with intravenous antibiotics. Thirteen pa-

tients experienced significant respiratory compromise or arrest necessitating intubation or tracheostomy and intensive care management. All deaths were related to respiratory compromise. Because of the risk of aspiration, eight patients (11%) had gastric (7) or jejunal (1) feeding tubes placed. Six patients (8%) died while in the hospital. Five expired during their initial hospitalization and one on readmission. All these patients sustained isolated cervical spine fractures except for one, who had a head injury as well. His mental status was much improved and he was discharged to rehabilitation. He returned to the hospital 1 month later with aspiration pneumonia, became septic, and expired shortly thereafter. This number does not include several multitrauma patients who died of other causes (i.e., bleeding diathesis after acetabular surgery) or five patients who had cervical spinal fractures and were immediately intubated in the field or the emergency room. The literature is unclear regarding the union rates of these types of fractures managed operatively versus nonoperatively. Many authors continue to advocate treatment with halo vests. Several reports indicate that the older age group has increased morbidity and mortality when managed with halo vests; however, most studies are limited by the number of patients and the details of the complications.

Andersson and colleagues conducted a retrospective analysis of 29 consecutive patients older than 65 years (mean age, 78) with odontoid fractures. Eleven patients were treated with anterior screw fixation according to the technique of Bohler, 7 with posterior C1–C2 fusion. Ten patients with either minimally displaced fractures or with complicating medical conditions were treated conservatively. At follow-up, 7 of 7 patients who underwent posterior fusion had healed without any problems, whereas 8 of 11 patients treated with anterior screw fixation and 7 of 10 conservatively treated patients either failed treatment or had healed, but after a complicated course of events. Anterior screw fixation is associated with an unacceptably high rate of problems in the elderly population. Probable causes may be osteoporosis with comminution at the fracture site or stiffness of the cervical spine preventing ideal positioning of the screws. They also maintained that nonoperative treatment often fails. They advocated posterior C1–C2 fusion.[118, 180] Other studies have also confirmed that posterior instrumentation with C1–C2 transarticular screws may permit early mobilization, with complications related to halo immobilization. Campanelli and co-workers revealed that this procedure can be performed safely in elderly patients with good results and few complications.[127] Hannigan and colleagues reached similar conclusions in their retrospective review of 19 patients 80 years or older with odontoid fractures. Eight patients with posterior displacement of 5 mm or less were treated with cervical immobilization, three of whom had stable nonunion of the fracture site at follow-up review. One patient with 10 mm of displacement refused operative treatment. Three of the patients without surgical treatment subsequently died of unrelated causes; all remaining patients resumed their routine activity. Five patients with displacement of 5 mm or greater and instability at the fracture site were treated with posterior C1–C2 fusion using wire and autologous iliac bone grafts. In this group, no operative morbidity or mortality was noted, and stable constructs developed in all patients. One patient died of an unrelated cause during the follow-up period, and the other patients resumed their normal activity. Prolonged bedrest caused respiratory complications in two of six patients who survived the initial hospitalization; complications requiring alternative treatment developed in two of three patients treated with rigid immobilization.[148]

C2 LATERAL MASS FRACTURES

Lateral mass fractures of the C2 vertebra are rarely reported injuries and have a mechanism of injury similar to that causing lateral mass fractures of the atlas. Axial compression and lateral bending forces combine to compress the C1–C2 articulation and result in a depressed fracture of the articular surface of C2 (Fig. 28–24). Patients generally have a history of pain without neurologic deficit. Plain radiographs may be unremarkable, although anteroposterior and open-mouth views will sometimes demonstrate lateral tilting of the arch of C1 and asymmetry of the height of the C2 lateral mass. If suspected, CT scanning of the area is helpful to more clearly delineate the injury. A search for additional fractures in the cervical spine should also be made because these injuries are frequently combined with other C1–C2 fractures.[184, 190]

Treatment is based on the degree of articular involvement. In patients in whom depression of the articular surface is slight and incongruity is minimal, simple collar immobilization is sufficient. More extensive involvement of the lateral mass may require cervical traction to realign the lateral mass, followed by halo vest immobilization until healing has occurred. In those in whom articular incongruity remains, degenerative changes may

occur after injury and necessitate C1–C2 stabilization at a later date.

TRAUMATIC SPONDYLOLISTHESIS OF THE AXIS

The term *hangman's fracture* has been used extensively in the literature to describe both the injury produced by judicial hanging and axis pedicle fractures after motor vehicle accidents and falls.[195, 196, 198] The historical description of these injuries has led to confusion in nomenclature. In 1866 Haughton was the first to describe fracture-dislocations of the axis secondary to hanging.[208] Wood-Jones, in the early 1900s, clarified the injuries produced by varying positions of the hanging knot and recommended a submental position to produce a consistently fatal result.[223] These studies were later confirmed by Vermooten.[220] Grogono, in 1954, first published radiographs of a fracture of the posterior arch sustained in a motor vehicle accident.[205] Garber proposed the term *traumatic spondylolisthesis* for this injury because he thought that the primary distraction force seen with hanging was absent in these cases.[203] Schneider and co-workers in 1965 actually coined the phrase *hangman's fracture* for these injuries because of their radiographic similarity to the injuries produced by judicial hanging.[214] The choice of this phrase is unfortunate because these two separate lesions differ markedly in their mechanism of injury, associated soft tissue disruption, clinical features, and prognosis.[222] Although this fracture appears to be radiographically similar to that incurred in a hanging injury, it is different in that a hanging injury produces bilateral axis pedicle fractures with complete disruption of the disc and ligaments between C2 and C3 by hyperex-

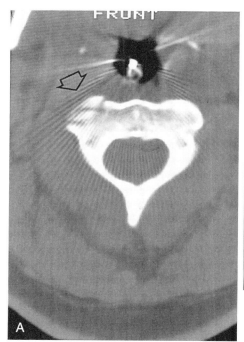
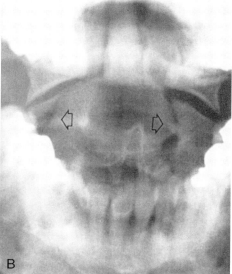

FIGURE 28–24. Lateral mass fracture of C2. *A,* Computed tomographic scan showing minimal impaction of the joint surface of C2 *(arrow)*. *B,* Open-mouth view showing bilateral, lateral mass fractures of C2 *(arrows)* from a severe vehicular accident with axial loading of the spine. *(A, B,* From Levine, A.M; Edwards, C.C. Clin Orthop 239:53–68, 1989.)

tension and distraction.[216, 220, 223] This mechanism is in contradistinction to the injury produced by falls and motor vehicle accidents, which results from various combinations of extension, axial compression, and flexion, along with associated varying degrees of disc disruption.[198, 203, 205, 214, 218, 222] The exact incidence of these injuries is unknown; however, in individuals involved in fatal motor vehicle accidents, only occipitoatlantal dislocations are more common.[196] Traumatic spondylolisthesis of the axis is also noted to be approximately half as common (a reported incidence of 27%) as odontoid fractures in patients who have sustained cervical trauma in motor vehicle accidents.[207]

The unusual anatomy of the axis accounts for its injury pattern. The axis is thought to be a transitional vertebra between the ringlike atlas above and the more typical cervical vertebra below. The narrow elongated isthmus between the superior and inferior articular processes of the axis functions as a fulcrum in flexion and extension between the cervicocranium (skull, atlas, dens, and body of the axis) and the relatively fixed lower cervical spine, to which the neural arch of the axis is anchored by its inferior articular facets, stout bifid spinous process, and strong nuchal muscles. The elongated pedicles are the thinnest portion of the bony ring of the axis and are additionally weakened by the foramen transversarium on either side, which further enhances the susceptibility of this area to injury.[195, 222]

Because traumatic spondylolisthesis tends to produce acute decompression of the neural canal by fracture of the pedicles, neurologic involvement is relatively uncommon in survivors (seen in 6% to 10%).[195, 196, 198, 201, 202, 214] Most investigators have noted a high incidence of craniofacial injuries associated with this fracture.[202, 212] Vertebral artery and cranial nerve injuries have also been reported.[211] As regards other injuries in the spine, Francis and co-workers noted that approximately 31% of patients sustaining this injury have associated injuries of the cervical spine, 94% of which are in the upper three vertebrae.[201, 202] In addition, 7% of patients had other spinal fractures below the neck.

Bucholz was the first to divide these injuries into stable and unstable configurations based on the integrity of the C2–C3 disc.[196] Effendi and associates further subdivided these injuries according to radiographic evidence of displacement and stability.[200] The most recent and most useful classification is that proposed by Levine and Edwards, which is essentially a modification of Effendi and associates' radiographic system.[200, 209] The classification system is based on pretreatment lateral cervical spine radiographs and is useful in predicting the mechanism of injury and planning treatment:

Type I fractures are nondisplaced fractures and all fractures showing no angulation and less than 3 mm of displacement (Fig. 28–25A).
Type II fractures have significant angulation and translation (see Fig. 28–25B).
Type IIA fractures show slight or no translation but very severe angulation of the fracture fragments (see Fig. 30–25C).
Type III fractures have severe angulation and displacement,

as well as concomitant unilateral or bilateral facet dislocations at the level of C2 and C3 (see Fig. 28–25D).

Type I fractures are stable with an intact C2–C3 disc; types II, IIA, and III are unstable fractures because of disruption at the C2–C3 interspace. Type II fractures are the most common and are seen in 55.8% of patients, followed by type I injuries, which account for 28.8%. Types IIA and III are relatively uncommon and are found in 5.8% and 9.6% of patients, respectively.

Although most hangman's fractures do not compromise the spinal canal, reports of atypical hangman's fractures have shown the potential for spinal canal compromise.[217] These fractures extend into the posterior vertebral body, with a fragment of the posterior vertebral body being displaced dorsally into the spinal canal. It is important to recognize this injury because it has significant potential to cause neurologic injury.

Although "hangman's" fractures are relatively benign injuries because of the large diameter of the vertebral canal at this level of injury, optimal management of these injuries is very controversial.[195, 210, 214] Despite the fact that the vast majority of these injuries do well with conservative treatment[195, 200, 202, 206, 209, 210, 212, 215, 218] and that the reported nonunion rate with external immobilization is approximately 5%,[195, 201, 221] some authors have continued to advocate primary surgical treatment.[194, 198, 210, 213, 218, 222] Given the usually good prognosis in survivors of these injuries, a conservative approach seems justified in most cases. Gross and Benzel reviewed 533 reported cases of nonoperatively managed hangman's fractures of any classification available for follow-up and noted that only 8 patients did not achieve bony union. The cases of nonunion were complicated by complex additional cervical injuries and completely disrupted C2–C3 intervertebral discs.[204, 206] Their meta-analysis found a 98.5% union rate and suggested that nonoperative treatment should be the primary method except in cases of failure of this therapy, compressive lesions, or extreme contraindications to bracing. They stress that the ability to achieve osseous union despite incomplete or nonanatomic closed fracture reduction is well recognized.[197]

According to Levine and Edwards, type I fractures are stable, as determined by physician-supervised flexion-extension radiographs.[209] Varying degrees of reduction are noted with extension. Cord damage is extremely rare with these injuries because of their inherent stability. The mechanism of injury is probably the result of a hyperextension and axial loading force that fractures the neural arch posteriorly but is not strong enough to disrupt the integrity of the disc or seriously compromise the integrity of the anterior or posterior ligaments. Because the restraining ligaments have little laxity, anterior displacement is minimal and the fracture is stable. A high association is seen with other hyperextension and axial loading injuries, such as fractures of the posterior arch of the atlas, fractures of the lateral mass of the atlas, and odontoid fractures. Because these injuries are stable, treatment with the Philadelphia collar or a halo until healing of the fracture is satisfactory, and no further displacement is expected with healing.

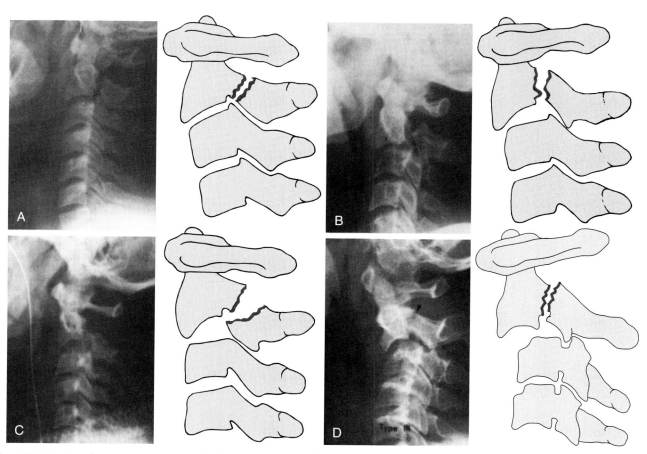

FIGURE 28–25. Classification of traumatic spondylolisthesis of the axis. *A,* Type I injuries have a fracture through the neural arch with no angulation and as much as 3 mm of displacement. *B,* Type II fractures have both significant angulation and displacement. *C,* Type IIA fractures show minimal displacement, but severe angulation is present. *D,* Type III axial fractures combine bilateral facet dislocation between C2 and C3 with a fracture of the neural arch of the axis. *(A–C,* From Levine, A.M.; Edwards, C.C. J Bone Joint Surg Am 67:217–226, 1985. *D,* From Levine, A.M. Orthop Clin North Am 17:42, 1986.)

Type II fractures are noted to be unstable on physician-supervised flexion and extension radiographs. They are frequently associated with other cervical spine fractures, especially wedge compression fractures of the anterosuperior portion of the body of C3. The mechanism of injury, as with type I fractures, is initially hyperextension plus axial loading, which fractures the neural arch or lamina but causes no more than slight injury to the anterior longitudinal ligament, disc, or posterior capsular structures. The second force in this injury is anterior flexion and compression, which when coupled with the initial fracture through the neural arch, allows the entire cervicocranium to be displaced anteriorly and caudally. This displacement causes rupture of the posterior longitudinal ligament and disc in a posterior-to-anterior direction and frequently results in a compression fracture of the anterosuperior portion of the body of C3. Treatment of these injuries is usually conservative, with halo or tongs traction in extension and a weight of 6.8 to 9.1 kg for 5 to 7 days. If the reduction is adequate and demonstrates less than 4 to 5 mm of displacement or less than 10° to 15° of angulation, a halo vest may be applied. If the reduction is inadequate, continued traction in extension for 4 to 6 weeks is recommended, followed by further halo treatment for an additional 6 weeks. The presence of C2–C3 disc herniation is a contraindication to traction.

An alternative to conservative treatment or failure of bony union after adequate immobilization of type II fractures is the use of a C2 transpedicular screw or anterior cervical plate. The fracture must first be reduced with halo traction, and then fixation can be achieved with a pedicle lag screw. Originally described by Roy-Camille and colleagues,[260] the transpedicular technique, though technically demanding, can replace the need for long-term immobilization and give very satisfactory results.[246] Anterior cervical plating for unstable, inadequately reduced Effendi type II fractures has been reported and has yielded good results with no complications.[219] Anterior plating allows the reconstitution of two columns of vertebral stability; it can address the level of pathology with only a single motion segment and allows for decompression of the disrupted C2–C3 disc.

Type IIA fractures are also unstable to flexion and extension. The predominant mechanism of injury with this fracture is flexion with distraction, which causes a distraction type of injury through the pedicles with the injury extending anteriorly. These injuries are not usually recognized before obtaining radiographs in traction, and such radiographs will demonstrate opening of the posterior disc space between C2 and C3. Reduction is therefore obtained by applying mild compression and extension in a halo vest under fluoroscopic control until the reduction is adequate. Treatment is continued until fracture healing has occurred. As with type II fractures, it has been found that type IIA fractures can be treated with C2 transpedicular screws[246] or anterior C2–C3 plating,[219] although experience in treating this fracture with these techniques is limited (Fig. 28–26).

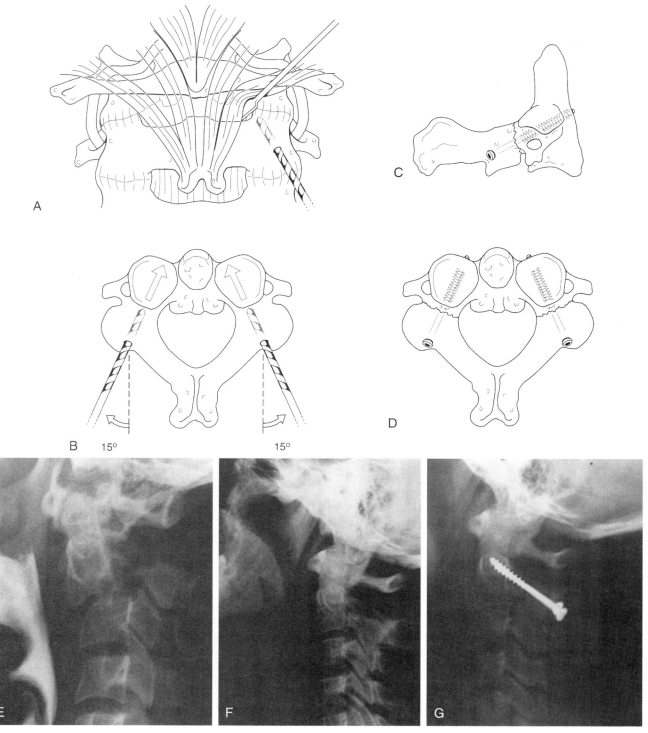

Figure 28–26. Technique for screw fixation of a type II hangman's fracture. Fluoroscopy should be used, preferably biplanar, to visualize reduction of the fracture, as well as screw trajectory. *A,* The medial wall of the C2 pedicle should be visualized. Dissection performed in a posterior-to-anterior direction will usually expose the fracture of the pedicle. *B,* The trajectory of the screws should be along the line of the pedicle just lateral to the medial wall of the pedicle and slightly convergent. *C,* The screw should be oriented to capture the distal fragment with the screw threads. A lag screw can be used. The C1–C2 facet joint should be avoided. *D,* The final axial view. *E,* The patient has a markedly displaced type II traumatic spondylolisthesis of the axis, which can be totally reduced with traction (*F*). *G,* Rather than prolonged traction, the patient elected operative treatment with lag screw fixation. (From Levine, A.M.; et al. In: Spine Trauma. Philadelphia. W.B. Saunders, 1998, p. 293.)

Type III fractures occur with concomitant unilateral or bilateral facet dislocations and are also unstable. They are unique in that patients with dislocated facets and fracture of the neural arch of the axis have a higher mortality rate (33% versus 5%), a higher incidence of permanent neurologic injury (11% versus 1%), and a higher incidence of cerebral concussion (55% versus 21%) than do patients with intact facets.[199] The mechanism of these injuries is primarily flexion-compression, which produces failure through the pedicles in an injury pattern that extends anteriorly.

Virtually all type III injuries require surgery for one of two indications. First, if the fracture line of the neural arch is anterior to either a unilateral or bilateral facet dislocation, the facet dislocation is irreducible with traction because of loss of integrity of the neural arch. Therefore, the facet dislocation should be reduced surgically and stabilized with interspinous wiring or lateral mass plates. The fracture of the neural arch is then treated conservatively in traction or a halo, or at the time of surgery, a transpedicular C2 screw can potentially be used to secure the neural arch. Second, if the fracture of the neural arch is at the level of the facet dislocation or just posterior to it, surgical stabilization by bilateral oblique wiring or lateral mass plating is necessary after reduction of the dislocation in traction because the reduction of the facet dislocation is usually unstable.

Transpedicular screws can be placed in C2 and lateral mass screws in C3 along with the application of lateral mass plates; this technique affords very stable fixation and can negate the need for postoperative halo immobilization. If satisfactory reduction can be maintained in a halo vest, however, immobilization may be a reasonable option.

Teardrop fractures involving the axis are unusual and deserve mention because these injuries differ greatly from those of the lower cervical spine. Lower cervical spine teardrop fractures are due to a flexion injury, are unstable, and are associated with neurologic injury 75% of the time. C2 teardrop fractures are caused by an extension injury, are stable, and are not associated with neurologic injury. Radiographically, flexion- and extension-type teardrop fractures are distinguishable by the fact that in an extension-type injury, the teardrop fragment is rotated 35° anteriorly. Conversely, a flexion-type teardrop fracture remains aligned with the anterior margin of the spine. A C2 extension-type teardrop fracture is associated with traumatic spondylolisthesis of C2. Fortunately, an extension-type fracture is stable and can be successfully treated with a rigid cervical orthosis unless precluded by a concomitant unstable fracture.

SURGICAL TECHNIQUES

Bracing

A variety of braces were discussed in Chapter 27. Methods of immobilization range from soft collars to cervical thoracic orthoses to halo vests. These devices immobilize the spine to varying degrees, and specific devices are best for certain regions of the cervical spine (see Table 27–2).

Increasing rigidity and length of the orthosis correlate with improved ability to restrict motion. The braces recommended for some of the injuries discussed in this chapter are presented in Table 27–5. This chapter does not discuss applications of the halo ring or its complications.

Skeletal Traction

Skeletal traction with either tongs or a halo is frequently indicated in the initial stabilization and ultimate management of patients with upper cervical spine injuries. Considerations should include the nature of the injury, the presence or absence of other injuries, and the estimated duration of treatment. Indications for the use of skeletal traction, as well as halo vest immobilization, were discussed earlier in this chapter.

Occipitocervical Arthrodesis

Occipitocervical arthrodesis can be accomplished with one of several posterior techniques and can be performed more safely with spinal cord monitoring. All techniques involve placing the patient in a halo or tongs traction apparatus and radiographically assessing the reduction preoperatively. A cross-table lateral radiograph should specifically confirm that the occiput is not distracted from the atlas. After standard skin preparation and draping, a longitudinal midline skin incision is fashioned from the inion to the midcervical spine. With meticulous hemostasis and careful subperiosteal dissection, the base of the occiput, from the inion to the foramen magnum, and the upper cervical spine are exposed. During dissection of the upper cervical spine, it should be appreciated that the vertebral vessels lie on the superior aspect of the arch of C1 approximately 1.5 to 2.0 cm lateral to the midline. One should also be wary of frequently encountered congenital anomalies, particularly defects in the posterior arch, which are seen in approximately 1.4% of atlases and in approximately 60% of those associated with congenital occipitoatlantal fusion.[268]

The simplest method for obtaining fusion involves careful decortication of the posterior elements of C1, C2, and the suboccipital area with a bur, followed by the application of a copious amount of freshly obtained iliac crest bone graft. After routine closure over drains, the patient is immobilized in a halo vest or cast for 12 weeks or until serial radiographs demonstrate healing of the fusion mass. The limitations of this technique are that early fixation is not obtained and the risk of nonunion is considerable.[231, 253]

More involved methods of performing occipitocervical arthrodesis incorporate different types of metal fixation devices intended to add stability to the fusion construct.[228, 241, 242, 250, 256, 257, 270, 271] These devices vary from simply occipital and cervical sublaminar wires, which require additional halo immobilization, to posterior occipitocervical plates, which require only soft or semirigid cervical collars postoperatively. Oda and colleagues performed a biomechanical evaluation of five different occipitoatlantoaxial fixation techniques. They found that the addition of C2 transpedicular or C1–C2 transarticular screws significantly increased the stabilizing effect when compared with sublaminar wiring and laminar hooks.[255]

Occipital and cervical sublaminar wires are used to secure bone graft plates, either iliac corticocancellous grafts or rib grafts, from the occiput to the upper cervical spine.[229, 248, 258, 259, 272] This technique allows for early stabilization and is thought to diminish the chance of nonunion. The technique of Robinson and Southwick, which involves the use of iliac crest grafts, has been most popular and is summarized here[258] (Fig. 28–27). After exposure of the base of the occiput and upper cervical spine, two 1-cm bur holes are fashioned through both tables of the skull approximately 0.5 cm lateral to the midline and 0.5 mm from the edge of the foramen magnum. Great care must be taken to avoid damage to the dura. The underlying dura and periosteum adherent to the posterior arches of C1, C2, and the foramen magnum are then carefully separated from the bone with small, angled curettes and a dural dissector. Two 24-gauge twisted wires are then passed under each of these bony structures,

looped through or around a previously harvested iliac crest graft, and gently secured into place by gradually twisting the wires tight. Strips of cancellous graft can then be added to fill any remaining gaps. After closure of the wound in routine fashion, the patient is immobilized in a halo until healing has occurred.

The use of posterior occipitocervical plating affords rigid internal fixation and is growing in popularity (Fig. 28–28). Three different groups reported fusion rates varying from 94% to 100% when posterior occipitocervical plates were used.[241, 242, 261, 262] In all three studies, postoperative immobilization involved the use of a soft or semirigid cervical collar; halo immobilization was not used. Other than degeneration of adjacent segments, no significant complications occurred with the use of posterior occipitocervical plates.[242]

Application of posterior occipitocervical plates requires the same surgical dissection as described previously. Screws are placed in the occiput as close to the midsagittal line as possible, at or below the level of the inion. One advantage of this type of fixation is that screws can be

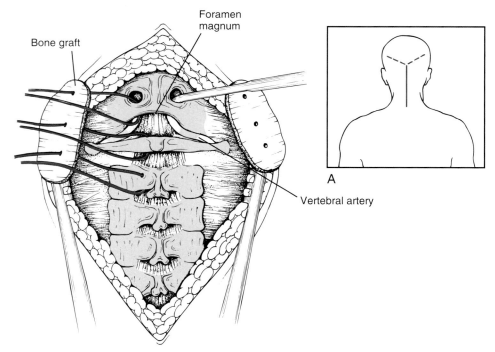

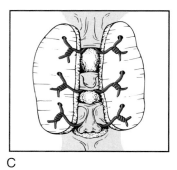

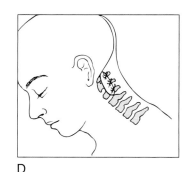

FIGURE 28–27. *A–D,* Method of occipitocervical fusion. This method is particularly useful if the posterior arch of C1 has to be partly removed to relieve dural and cord compression.

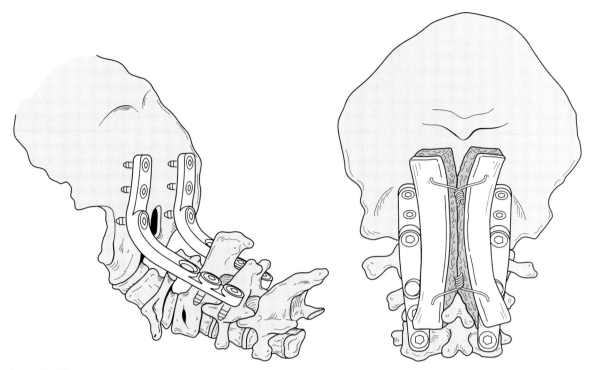

FIGURE 28–28. Method of posterior occipitocervical plating and fusion. This type of rigid internal fixation allows for postoperative cervical immobilization with a soft collar. (Redrawn from Frymoyer, J.W., ed. The Adult Spine: Principles and Practice, 2nd ed. Philadelphia, Lippincott-Raven, 1997, p. 1428.)

placed in the pedicles of C2, which give excellent bony purchase, but C1–C2 transarticular screws can also be used to anchor the plate and augment stability at the C1–C2 articulation when no posterior bony purchase of C1 can be obtained. The plate is contoured to restore the normal curvature of the occipital cervical region (105°). Dual plates or a Y plate has been used. At the C2 level, the pedicle is used for screw fixation. The entry point is at the upper and inner quadrant, and the drill is angled 10° to 15° medially and 35° superiorly to avoid injury to the vertebral artery. Alternatively, a transarticular C1–C2 screw can be used. Holes are drilled in the occiput through the plate holes after the plate has been screwed to the cervical spine, and two or three screws are inserted into the occiput (Y plate). The second plate is secured with the same technique. Corticocancellous and cancellous bone grafts can be packed into the area between the plates.[239, 241, 260]

Several other techniques that allow rigid fixation of the occipitocervical spine use rod-wire constructs such as contoured Wisconsin or Loquat rods with occipital wires or stainless steel or titanium cables[230] or occipital bolts. These techniques have likewise been highly successful, with fusion rates ranging from 89% to 93%.[252] Halo immobilization has also not been necessary with these methods.

Atlantoaxial Arthrodesis

Several different techniques are available for posterior fusion of the atlantoaxial joint. Gallie in 1939 popularized a technique involving midline posterior wiring with bone grafting and facet joint arthrodesis.[237] Unfortunately, reported failure rates with this technique have ranged from 60% to 80%.[235, 251] Other techniques, however, including a posterior bone block between the posterior arches of the atlas and axis and wiring to achieve a wedge compression arthrodesis, are associated with consistently successful fusion rates of 92% to 100%.[96, 226, 267, 269]

These techniques include the modified Gallie fusion as described separately by Fielding and co-workers (Fig. 28–29) and by McGraw and Rusch, as well as the Brooks or modified Brooks technique.[226, 234, 238] A C1–C2 transarticular screw technique was first described by Magerl,[251] and fusion rates ranging from 95% to 100% have subsequently been reported.[243, 245, 263] Biomechanical testing has found the transarticular screw technique to be superior to Gallie wiring, Brooks-Jenkins wiring, and Halifax clamp fixation in flexion-extension, rotation, and lateral bending.[240]

The Brooks technique has been the most popular because of the theoretical mechanical considerations previously noted and because it is less technically demanding than transarticular screws[226] (Fig. 28–30). Once a satisfactory level of general anesthesia has been obtained and reduction radiographically confirmed, a standard posterior exposure of the upper cervical spine is carried out. A No. 2 Mersilene suture is passed on either side of the midline in a cranial-to-caudal direction under the arch of the atlas and then the axis. Two doubled 20-gauge stainless steel wires or titanium cables[230] are then passed into place by using the previously placed suture as a guide. Two full-thickness bone grafts measuring 1.25 × 3.5 cm are then harvested from the posterior iliac

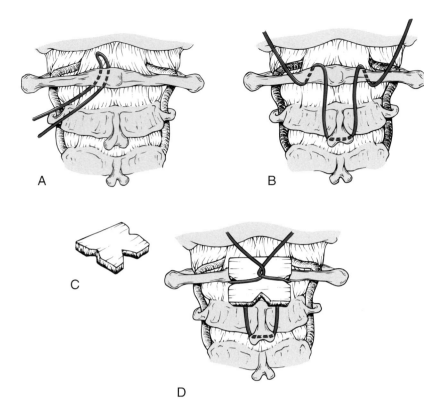

A

B

C

D

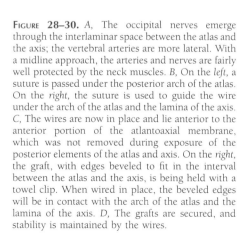

A

B

C

D

FIGURE 28–29. Surgical technique. *A,* Exposure, with the wire loop being passed under the arch of the atlas. Note the proximity of the vertebral vessels. *B,* Wire passed below the spine of the axis. Note the decortication of the atlas and axis. *C,* The graft configuration. *D,* The graft and wire in place, with the wire being tightened over the graft.

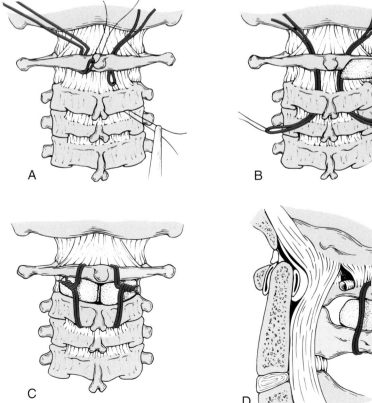

A

B

C

D

FIGURE 28–30. *A,* The occipital nerves emerge through the interlaminar space between the atlas and the axis; the vertebral arteries are more lateral. With a midline approach, the arteries and nerves are fairly well protected by the neck muscles. *B,* On the *left,* a suture is passed under the posterior arch of the atlas. On the *right,* the suture is used to guide the wire under the arch of the atlas and the lamina of the axis. *C,* The wires are now in place and lie anterior to the anterior portion of the atlantoaxial membrane, which was not removed during exposure of the posterior elements of the atlas and axis. On the *right,* the graft, with edges beveled to fit in the interval between the atlas and the axis, is being held with a towel clip. When wired in place, the beveled edges will be in contact with the arch of the atlas and the lamina of the axis. *D,* The grafts are secured, and stability is maintained by the wires.

crest. These grafts are beveled to fit between the posterior arches of the atlas and the axis on either side of the midline, and the wires are tightened while held in place to maintain the width of the interlaminar space. If the atlantoaxial membrane has been left intact, it will help prevent displacement of the grafts into the neural canal. Postoperatively, the patient can then be mobilized in a sternal-occipital-mandibular immobilizer (SOMI) or four-poster brace until the arthrodesis is solidly united. Griswold and colleagues described a modification of the original Brooks technique that incorporates the use of four doubled 24-gauge wires to hold trapezoidal grafts measuring 1.55 × 1.2 to 1.5 × 1.0 cm in place.[238]

Transarticular screw stabilization of C1 and C2 is growing in popularity, especially given its superior biomechanics.[240] Although consecutive cases have been reported without significant complications, Jeanneret and Magerl cautioned that this procedure is exacting.[245] The surgeon must become familiar with the local neurovascular anatomy and bone morphology of the

atlantoaxial interval as determined best by CT evaluation.[139, 142, 153, 157, 162, 163, 173] CT will help discern anatomic variations, the size and location of vertebral artery, and the isthmus diameter of C2.[249] Contraindications to this procedure include incomplete reduction of C1–C2 subluxation, pathologic destruction or collapse of C2, aberrant vertebral artery anatomy or a large vertebral artery groove with a secondarily narrow C2 isthmus (20% of cases), previous transoral resection of the odontoid, or cranial assimilation of C1.[157, 173, 227]

The entrance point and trajectory of the screws are critical and difficult to achieve (Fig. 28–31). Visualization of the C2 pedicle allows the surgeon to aim just lateral to the pedicle's medial wall to avoid penetration of the spinal canal. Because lateral deviation may threaten the vertebral artery, intraoperative fluoroscopy is essential in this procedure. Failure to angle the screws sufficiently cephalad will compromise purchase in the C1 articular mass; too steep an angle risks injury to the occipitoatlantal joints.[243] Depending on the patient's size and the amount of thoracic

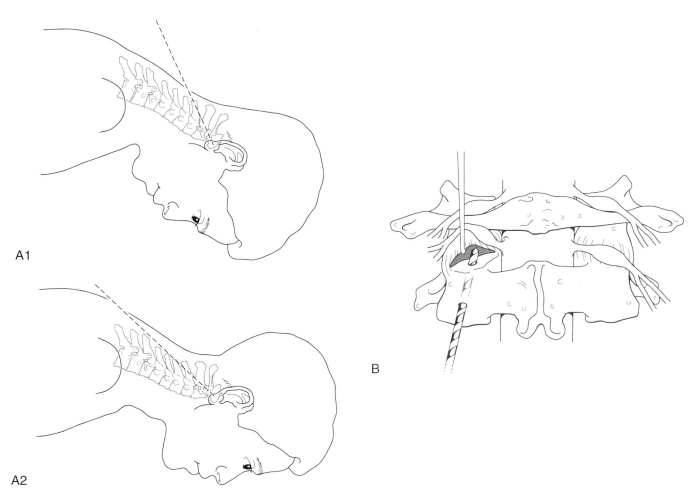

FIGURE 28–31. Method of Magerl for fixation with transarticular C1–C2 screws. The patient is placed prone and the head immobilized with Mayfield skull tongs. The position of the neck needed for reduction of the deformity will influence the exposure. *A1,* If the head can be flexed forward, the transarticular screws can be placed through the same posterior incision; however, if extension is needed to maintain the reduction of C1 (*A2*), a shorter incision is needed for exposure of the posterior elements of C1–C2, and the drill bit and instrumentation are passed into the wound through percutaneous incisions. *B,* The medial wall of the C2 pedicle should be exposed to aid in orienting the direction of the drill. The starting point for drilling is just medial to the edge of the facet joint and the inferior margin of the lamina of C2. Progress of the drill bit across the C1–C2 facet should be monitored using image intensification.

Illustration continued on following page

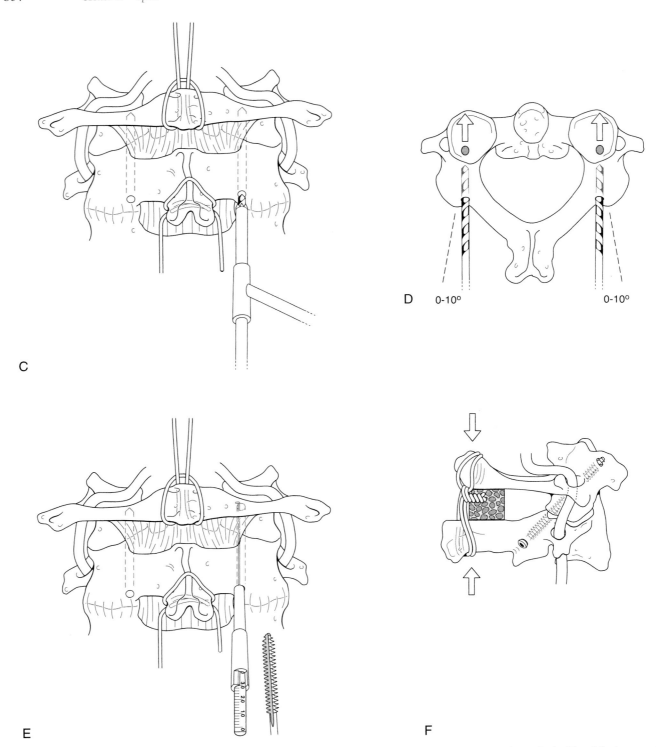

FIGURE **28–31** *Continued. C,* A wire or suture can be passed around the arch of C1 to assist in reduction or manipulation (or both) and for later use in securing a bone graft to the posterior elements of C1–C2. *D,* The drill bit should be directed anteriorly and cephalad under lateral fluoroscopic visualization and exit the posterior aspect of the C2 lateral mass. *E,* The holes are tapped, and 3.5-mm fully threaded screws between 40 and 50 mm long are inserted. *F,* A tricortical bone graft is harvested and secured between the posterior arches of C1 and C2. The final lateral view is shown. (From Levine, A.M., et al. Spine Trauma. Philadelphia, W.B. Saunders, 1998, pp. 274, 275.)

kyphosis, obtaining the correct trajectory for screw placement may be difficult. It is not unusual to carry the posterior incision down to T2 to obtain the correct trajectory, or alternatively, special instruments must be used to make percutaneous approaches to the C2 pedicles. Furthermore, examination of a large number of C2

specimens has demonstrated that the size and location of the vertebral arteries within the lateral masses of C2 are quite variable.[266, 273] On occasion, a vertebral artery and its associated venous plexus may fill an entire lateral mass. In view of these potential problems, it is important that preoperative CT scans be thoroughly scrutinized to identify these variants. Sagittal reconstructions of the axis are extremely helpful in deciding whether the vertebral artery will interfere with the placement of screws. Jeanneret and Magerl[245] described the use of screws in this technique to augment Gallie wiring and posterior fusion, and under these circumstances, they did not recommend postoperative immobilization; however, in the event that wiring is not used in addition to screw placement and posterior fusion, immobilization with a semirigid collar brace is recommended.[263]

Anterior Stabilization of the Dens

Direct internal fixation of fractures of the dens was introduced in 1980 by Nakanishi.[254] Several authors have since reported on the utility of this approach for type II and type III odontoid fractures and fracture nonunions, and fracture union rates of 92% to 100% were achieved.[129, 137, 225, 231, 233, 236] The reported advantage of this technique is preservation of atlantoaxial motion and the requirement for minimal postoperative immobilization.[225, 236, 254] The disadvantage is that the procedure is technically difficult with the potential for catastrophic neurologic complications, as well as injury to the adjacent segment (C2–C3).[178] Physical characteristics that have been found to hinder fracture reduction or adequate surgical clearance of the chest include short-necked patients, cervical spines with limited motion, extreme thoracic kyphosis, barrel-chested habitus, and fracture configurations that can be held reduced only while in flexion.[138]

Bohler recommended standard anteromedial exposure of the upper cervical spine after reduction of the fracture.[225] The anterior longitudinal ligament is split longitudinally over the body of the axis. Then, under biplanar image intensification, one or two holes are drilled, starting at the anteroinferior border of C2 and progressing through the body of C2 and into the dens. After gauging depth and tapping the hole, a small-fragment cancellous lag screw is inserted (Fig. 28–32). Great debate exists over the use of one or two interfragmentary screws for fixation.[137, 144, 233] Biomechanical studies suggest that there is no significant biomechanical difference between the use of one or two screws and that screw fixation restores the dens to half its prefracture strength.[134, 144, 167] Double-threaded compression screws have been used with good results.[129, 246] Postoperatively, rigid collar immobilization is recommended until union is solid.

Transoral Approach to C1–C2

The direct transoral approach to the upper cervical spine, first described by Southwick and Robinson and later popularized by Fang and Ong, allows relatively easy access to the occipitoatlantoaxial complex for arthrodesis and decompression.[232, 264] With lateral approaches, the mandible, parotid gland, branches of the external carotid artery, and the 7th, 9th, 10th, 11th, and 12th cranial nerves may interfere with exposure.[232] With a more direct anterior exposure, the front of the spine is separated from the pharynx by only the pharyngeal mucosa, the constrictor muscles, the buccopharyngeal fascia, and the prevertebral

muscle. The limitations of this technique lie in its significant potential for morbidity and mortality. The major catastrophic complication associated with this approach was wound infection, which was initially reported to occur in 33% to 50% of cases.[232, 271] More recent series have addressed the issue of wound closure in detail, and subsequently, wound infection rates have dropped tremendously.[224, 247] In addition, whereas initial studies reported a 25% perioperative death rate, more recent series have not found perioperative mortality to be a problem.[224, 247] Initially, the procedure involved a tracheostomy, which was fraught with complications,[232] but the procedure is now performed with oral endotracheal intubation.[224]

The primary indication for this approach is the need for anterior decompression of the atlantoaxial region because of fracture nonunion, malunion, or infection.[224, 265] Fusion of C1 and C2 can be performed from this approach with predictable success, but from the authors' viewpoint, more accessible ways are available to fuse C1 and C2.

After establishing the endotracheal airway, the skin and hypopharynx are prepared and draped. A self-retaining oral retractor is inserted. This retractor depresses the tongue as well as the soft palate. A separate arm of the retractor holds the endotracheal and nasogastric tubes to the side. An operating microscope is necessary for the procedure. After infiltrating the posterior pharyngeal wall with a dilute epinephrine solution, a longitudinal midline incision measuring approximately 5 to 6 cm is made at the center of the anterior tubercle of the atlas. The anterior arch of the atlas and the body of the axis, as well as the atlantoaxial joints on either side, are then exposed. After the conclusion of the procedure, wound cultures are obtained in the event that the patient shows any signs of infection postoperatively. The wound is closed in layers, and antibiotic use is discontinued at 72 hours.

Lateral Retropharyngeal Approach to the Upper Cervical Spine

In the vast majority of patients, problems requiring surgery in the upper cervical spine can be handled through a standard posterior exposure. Infrequently, an anterior approach may be necessary. The problems with direct transoral approaches have already been mentioned. Therefore, a safe, extensile exposure based on Henry's approach to the vertebral artery has been developed that allows anterior exposure from the atlas caudally to the upper thoracic spine[244, 269, 270] (Fig. 28–33). Because instability is usually present, patients are placed in a halo preoperatively, and in the absence of contraindications, the neck is extended and rotated to the opposite side.

After induction of anesthesia and sterile preparation, a hockey stick incision is begun transversely across the tip of the mastoid process and carried distally along the anterior border of the sternocleidomastoid muscle. The greater auricular nerve is identified and retracted cephalad; if it is in the way, it may be resected with a negligible sensory deficit. In most cases, the sternocleidomastoid muscle is detached from the mastoid process. The spinal accessory nerve is then identified at its entrance into the sternocleidomastoid muscle approximately 3 cm from the mastoid tip. If only the C1–C2 area needs to be approached, it is retracted anteriorly with the contents of the carotid sheath. If a more extensive approach is necessary, the nerve is dissected from the jugular vein up to an area near the jugular foramen and retracted laterally with the sternocleidomastoid muscle.

After eversion of the sternocleidomastoid muscle, the transverse processes of the cervical vertebrae are easily palpable. The transverse process of C1 extends more

laterally than the rest and is thus especially prominent. By proceeding anteriorly along the front border of these processes and posterior to the carotid sheath and after identifying the internal jugular vein and delineating it with certainty, the vertebral artery can be avoided with safety. With further medial dissection, Sharpey's fibers can be divided and the retropharyngeal space entered.

Exposure of the appropriate vertebral bodies is then possible with subperiosteal stripping and, if necessary,

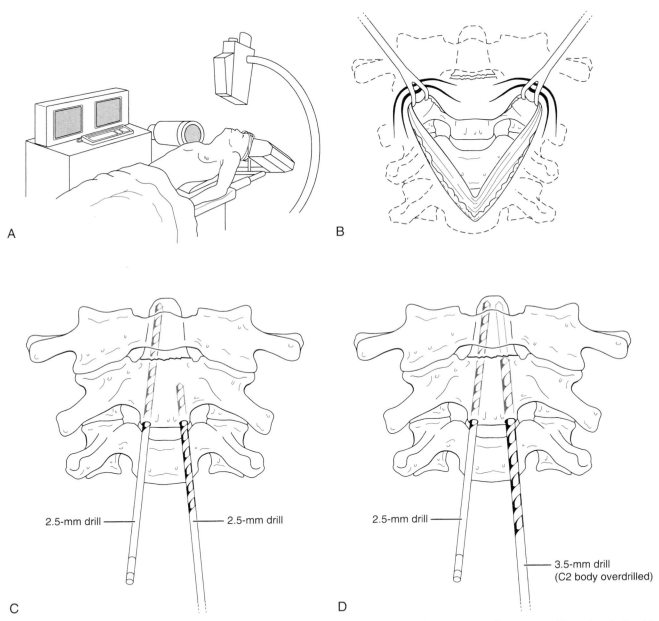

FIGURE 28–32. Anterior stabilization of the dens. Positioning of the patient for anterior dens stabilization is critically important. The patient is placed in the supine position with the neck extended so that exposure of the inferior edge of C2 is possible. If fracture reduction is lost (as may happen with posteriorly displaced dens fractures), less extension should be obtained until provisional fixation has been achieved. *A,* Biplanar image intensification is essential. *B,* A standard transverse incision is made on either the left or right side. A retropharyngeal approach as described by Smith-Robinson is performed at the C5–C6 disc space level and the dissection carried up to the C2–C3 disc space. An incision is made in the anterior longitudinal ligament at the level of the inferior portion of the C2 body. A one- or two-screw technique can then be used. *C,* Starting points are either side of the midline and on the caudal edge of the body, and a 1.5-mm K-wire is initially placed to ascertain the trajectory and stabilize the fragment. Two K-wires can be placed and a cannulated system used, but inadvertent advancement of the wire is a serious complication; preferably, one wire is removed and replaced at a time, with a solid 2.5-mm drill bit advancing to the tip of the dens. *D,* Because interfragmentary compression is desired, either a partially threaded screw can be used or one drill bit can be removed and the near fragment overdrilled with a 3.5-mm drill bit. The near cortex only is tapped.

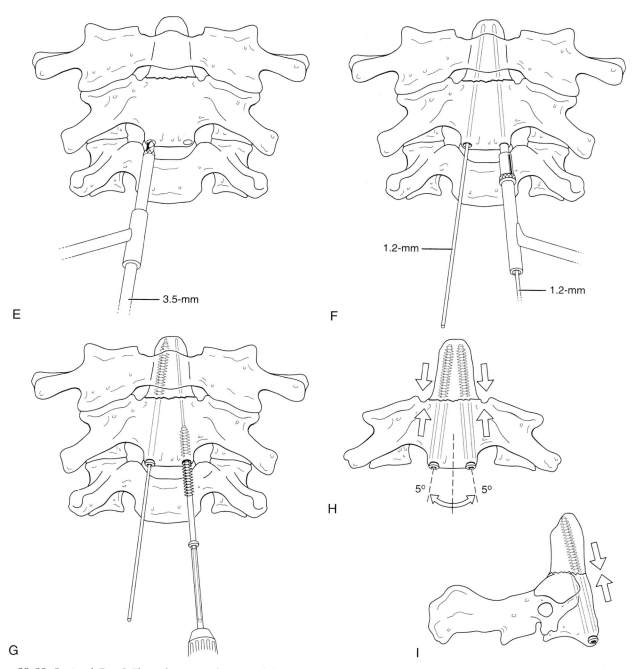

FIGURE 28–32 *Continued. E to G,* This technique can be accomplished with a cannulated set as well. *H* and *I,* Final screw fixation should have the screw slightly oblique toward the midline and may optionally perforate the cortex of the tip of the dens. Care should be taken to begin the screw on the undersurface and not the anterior surface of the C2 body to achieve the proper trajectory (*I*). (From Levine, A.M., et al. Spine Trauma. Philadelphia, W.B. Saunders, 1998, pp. 243, 244.)

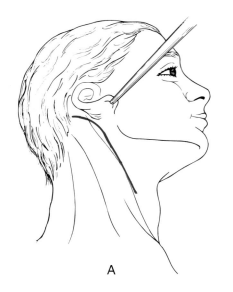

A

FIGURE **28–33.** *A* and *B,* Lateral retropharyngeal approach to the upper cervical spine. (*A, B,* Redrawn from Whitesides, T.E.; Kelly, R.P. South Med J 59:879–883, 1966.)

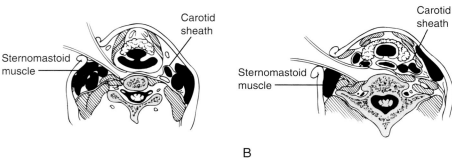

B

removal of the anterior cervical muscles down to the upper thoracic region. Localization is easy because of the prominent, transversely oriented anterior arch of C1 and the prominent vertical midline ridge of the base of the odontoid and body of C2. At the conclusion of the procedure, the sternocleidomastoid is sewn back into place over suction drains. The platysma and skin are closed in layers. Because of the potential for significant retropharyngeal edema, postoperative intubation or prophylactic tracheostomy should be considered.

REFERENCES

Introduction and Anatomy

1. Alker, G.; Oh, Y.S.; Leslie, E.V. High cervical spine and craniocervical junction injuries in fatal traffic accidents: A radiologic study. Orthop Clin North Am 9:1003–1010, 1978.
2. Bohlman, H.H. Acute fractures and dislocations of the cervical spine—an analysis of 300 hospitalized patients and review of the literature. J Bone Joint Surg Am 61:1119–1142, 1979.
3. Bundens, D.A.; Rechtines, G.R.; Bohlman, H.H. Upper cervical spine injuries. Orthop Rev 13:556–563, 1984.
4. Davis, D.; Bohlman, H.H.; Walker, A.E.; et al. The pathological findings in fatal craniospinal injuries. J Neurosurg 34:603–623, 1971.
5. Horlyck, E.; Rahbek, M. Cervical spine injuries. A clinical and radiological follow-up study, in particular with a view to local complaints and radiological sequelae. Acta Orthop Scand 45:845–853, 1974.
6. Levine, A.M.; Edwards, C.C. Treatment of injuries in the C1–C2 complex. Orthop Clin North 17:31–44, 1986.

Occipital Condyle Fractures

7. Anderson, P.A.; Montesano, P.X. Morphology and treatment of occipital condyle fractures. Spine 13:731–736, 1988.
8. Bloom, A.I.; Neeman, Z.; Slasky, B.S.; et al. Fracture of the occipital condyles and associated craniocervical ligament injury: Incidence, CT imaging and implications. Clin Radiol 52:198–202, 1997.
9. Bozboga, M.; Unal, F.; Hepgul, K.; et al. Fracture of the occipital condyle. Case report. Spine 17:1119–1121, 1992.
10. Cartmill, M.; Khazim, R.; Firth, J.L. Occipital condyle fracture with peripheral neurological deficit. Br J Neurosurg 13:611–613, 1999.
11. Cirak, B.; Akpinar, G.; Palaoglu, S. Traumatic occipital condyle fractures. Neurosurg Rev 23:161–164, 2000.
12. Devi, B.I.; Dubey, S.; Shetty, S.; et al. Fractured occipital condyle with isolated 12th nerve paresis. Neurol India 48:93–94, 2000.
13. Legros, B.; Fournier, P.; Chiaroni, P.; et al. Basal fracture of the skull and lower (IX, X, XI, XII) cranial nerves palsy: Four case reports including two fractures of the occipital condyle—a literature review. J Trauma 48:342–348, 2000.
14. Levine, A.M.; Edwards, C.C. Traumatic lesions of the occipitoatlantoaxial complex. Clin Orthop 239:53–68, 1989.
15. Miyazaki, C.; Katsume, M.; Yamazaki, T.; et al. Unusual occipital condyle fracture with multiple nerve palsies and Wallenberg syndrome. Clin Neurol Neurosurg 102:255–258, 2001.
16. Sharma, B.S.; Mahajan, R.K.; Bhatia, S.; Khosla, V.K. Collet-Sicard syndrome after closed head injury. Clin Neurol Neurosurg 96:197–198, 1994.

17. Urculo, E.; Arrazola, M.; Riu, I.; Moyua, A. Delayed glossopharyngeal and vagus nerve paralysis following occipital condyle fracture. Case report. J Neurosurg 84:522–525, 1996.

Occipitoatlantal Dislocations

18. Bailey, D.K. The normal cervical spine in infants and children. Radiology 59:712–719, 1952.
19. Banna, M.; Stevenson, G.W.; Tumiel, H.; Tumiel, A. Unilateral atlantooccipital dislocations complicating an anomaly of the atlas. J Bone Joint Surg Am 65:685–687, 1983.
20. Blackwood, N.J. Atlantoccipital dislocations. Ann Surg 47:654–658, 1908.
21. Bohlman, H.H. Acute fractures and dislocations of the cervical spine—an analysis of 300 hospitalized patients and review of the literature. J Bone Joint Surg Am 61:1119–1142, 1979.
22. Bucholz, R.W.; Burkhead, W.Z. The pathological anatomy of fatal atlantooccipital dislocations. J Bone Joint Surg Am 61:248–250, 1979.
23. Collato, P.M.; De Muth, W.W.; Schwentker, E.P.; Boal, D.K. Traumatic atlantooccipital dislocations. J Bone Joint Surg Am 67:1106–1109, 1986.
24. Dickman, C.A.; Papadopoulos, S.M.; Sonntag, V.K.; et al. Traumatic occipitoatlantal dislocations. J Spinal Disord 6:300–313, 1993.
25. Dublin, A.; Marks, W.M.; Weinstock, D.; Newton, T.H. Traumatic dislocation of the atlantooccipital articulation. J Neurosurg 52:541–546, 1980.
26. Eismont, F.J.; Bohlman, H.H. Posterior atlantooccipital dislocation with fracture of the atlas and odontoid process. Report of a case with survival. J Bone Joint Surg Am 60:397–399, 1978.
27. Englander, O. Nontraumatic occipitoatlantoaxial dislocation. A contribution to the radiology of the atlas. Br J Radiol 15:341–345, 1942.
28. Evarts, C.M. Traumatic occipitoatlantal dislocations. Report of a case with survival. J Bone Joint Surg Am 52:1653–1660, 1970.
29. Finney, H.C.; Roberts, T.S. Atlantooccipital instability. Case report. J Neurosurg 48:636–638, 1978.
30. Furin, A.H.; Pirotte, T.P. Occipital dislocation. Case report. J Neurosurg 46:663–666, 1977.
31. Gabrielson, T.O.; Maxwell, J.A. Traumatic atlantooccipital dislocations with case report of a patient who survived. AJR Am J Roentgenol 97:624–639, 1966.
32. Georgopoulos, G.; Pizzutillo, P.D.; Lee, M. Occipitoatlantal instability in children. A report of five cases and review of the literature. J Bone Joint Surg Am 69:429–436, 1987.
33. Gehweiler, J.A.; Osborne, R.L., Jr.; Becker, R.F. The Radiology of Vertebral Trauma. Philadelphia, W.B. Saunders, 1980, pp. 132–133.
34. Harris, J.H. The cervicocranium: Its radiographic assessment. Radiology 218:337–351, 2000.
35. Kauffman, R.A.; Dunbar, J.A.; McLaurin, R.L. Traumatic longitudinal atlantooccipital distraction injuries in children. Am J Neuroradiol 3:415–419, 1982.
36. Kissinger, P. Lexations Fraktur im Atlantooccipitagelenke. Zentralbl Chir 27:933–934, 1900.
37. Malgaigne, J.F. Traite des Fractures et des Luxations. Paris, J.B. Bailliere, 1850, pp. 320–322.
38. Page, C.P.; Story, J.L.; Wissinger, J.P.; Branch, C.L. Traumatic atlantooccipital dislocation. Case report. J Neurosurg 39:394–397, 1973.
39. Powers, B.; Miller, M.D.; Kramer, R.S.; et al. Traumatic atlantooccipital dislocation with survival. Neurosurgery 4:12–17, 1979.
40. Shapiro, R.; Youngberg, A.S.; Rothman, S.L.G. The differential diagnosis of traumatic lesions of the occipitalatlantoaxial segment. Radiol Clin North Am 11:505–526, 1973.
41. Vieweg, U.; Schultheiss, R. A review of halo vest treatment of upper cervical spine injuries. Arch Orthop Trauma Surg 121:50–55, 2001.
42. Werne, S. Studies in spontaneous atlas dislocation. Acta Orthop Scand Suppl 23:1–150, 1957.
43. Wholey, M.H.; Browner, A.J.; Baker, H.L., Jr. The lateral roentgenogram of the neck (with comments on the atlantoodontoid-basion relationship). Radiology 71:350–356, 1958.
44. Wiesel, S.W.; Rothman, R.H. Occipitoatlantal hypermobility. Spine 4:187, 1979.
45. Woodring, J.H.; Selke, A.C.; Duff, D.E. Traumatic atlantooccipital dislocation with survival. AJR Am J Roentgenol 137:21–44, 1981.

Atlas Fractures

46. Botelho, R.V.; de Souza Palma, A.M.; Abgussen, C.M.; Fontoura, E.A. Traumatic vertical atlantoaxial instability: The risk associated with skull traction. Case report and literature review. Eur Spine J 9:430–433, 2000.
47. Cooper, A. A Treatise on Dislocations and Fractures of the Joints. London, Longman, Hurst Rees, Orme Browne, E. Cox & Son, 1823, p. 542.
48. Esses, S. Fracture of the atlas associated with fracture of the odontoid process. Injury 12:310–312, 1981.
49. Fielding, J.W.; Cochran, G.V.B.; Lawsing, J.F.; Hohl, M. Tears of the transverse ligament of the atlas. A clinical and biomechanical study. J Bone Joint Surg Am 56:1683–1691, 1974.
50. Gaudagni, A.P. Fracture of the first cervical vertebra, complicated by a cervical rib. JAMA 130:276–277, 1946.
51. Gehweiler, J.A.; Daffner, R.H.; Roberts, L. Malformations of the atlas vertebra simulating the Jefferson fracture. AJR Am J Roentgenol 140:1083–1086, 1983.
52. Grogano, B.J.S. Injury of the atlas and axis. J Bone Joint Surg Br 33:397–410, 1954.
53. Han, S.Y.; Witten, D.M.; Musselman, J.P. Jefferson fracture of the atlas. Report of six cases. J Neurosurg 44:368–371, 1976.
54. Hinchey, J.J.; Bickel, W.H. Fracture of the atlas, review and presentation of data on eight cases. Ann Surg 121:826–832, 1945.
55. Hohl, M.; Baker, H.R. The atlantoaxial joint. Roentgenographic and anatomical study of normal and abnormal motion. J Bone Joint Surg Am 46:1739–1752, 1964.
56. Jefferson, G. Fracture of the atlas vertebra. Report of four cases and a review of those previously recorded. Br J Surg 7:407–422, 1920.
57. Landels, C.D.; Petegher, K.V. Fractures of the atlas: Classification, treatment and morbidity. Spine 13:450–452, 1988.
58. Lee, T.T.; Green, B.A.; Petrin, D.R. Treatment of stable burst fracture of the atlas (Jefferson fracture) with rigid cervical collar. Spine 23:1963–1967, 1998.
59. Levine, A.M.; Edwards, C.C. Fractures of the atlas. J Bone Joint Surg Am 73:680–691, 1991.
60. Levine, A.M.; Edwards, C. Treatment of injuries in the C1–C2 complex. Orthop Clin North Am 17:31–44, 1986.
61. Lipson, S.J. Fractures of the atlas associated with fractures of the odontoid process and transverse ligament ruptures. J Bone Joint Surg Am 59:940–942, 1977.
62. Marlin, A.E.; Williams, G.R.; Lee, J.F. Jefferson fractures in children. J Neurosurg 58:277–279, 1983.
63. McGuire, R.A., Jr.; Harkey, H.L. Trauma update: Unstable Jefferson's fracture treated with transarticular screws. Orthopedics 18:207–209, 1995.
64. O'Brien, J.J.; Butterfield, W.L.; Gossling, J.R. Jefferson fracture with disruption of the transverse ligament. A case report. Clin Orthop 126:135–138, 1977.
65. Pierce, D.S.; Ojemann, R.G. Injuries of the spine, neurologic considerations. Fractures and dislocations. In: Cave, E.G.; Burke, J.F.; Boyd, R.J., eds. Trauma Management. Chicago, Year Book, 1974, pp. 343–397.
66. Rogers, W.A. Fractures and dislocations of the cervical spine. An end-result study. J Bone Joint Surg Am 39:341–376, 1957.
67. Ruge, D. Spinal Disorders: Diagnosis and Treatment. Philadelphia, Lea & Febiger, 1977, p. 358.
68. Segal, L.S.; Grimm, J.O.; Stauffer, E.S. Nonunion of fractures of the atlas. J Bone Joint Surg Am 69:1423–1434, 1987.
69. Sherk, H.H. Lesions of the atlas and axis. Clin Orthop 109:33–41, 1976.
70. Shilke, L.H.; Calahan, R.A. A rational approach to burst fractures of the atlas. Clin Orthop 154:18–21, 1981.
71. Silveri, C.P.; Nelson, M.C.; Vaccaro, A.; Cotler, J.M. Traumatic injuries of the adult upper cervical spine. In: Cotler, J.M.; Simpson, J.M.; An, H.S.; Silveri, J.M., eds. Surgery of Spinal Trauma. Philadelphia, Lippincott Williams & Wilkins, 2000, pp. 179–217.
72. Spence, K.F.; Decker, S.; Sell, K.W. Bursting atlantal fracture associated with rupture of the transverse ligament. J Bone Joint Surg Am 52:543–549, 1970.

73. Steel, H.H. Anatomical and mechanical considerations of the atlantoaxial articulations. Proceedings of the American Orthopedic Association. J Bone Joint Surg Am 50:1481–1482, 1968.

74. White, A.A., III; Panjabi, M.M. Clinical Biomechanics of the Spine. Philadelphia, J.B. Lippincott, 1978, pp. 92–97.

75. Zimmerman, E.; Grank, J.; Vise, W.M.; et al. Treatment of Jefferson fracture with a halo apparatus. J Neurosurg 44:372–375, 1976.

Atlantoaxial Instability

76. Brooks, A.L.; Jenkins, E.W. Atlantoaxial arthrodesis by the wedge compression method. J Bone Joint Surg Am 60:279–284, 1978.

77. Cabot, A.; Becker, A. The cervical spine in rheumatoid arthritis. Clin Orthop 121:130–140, 1978.

78. Conlon, P.W.; Isdale, I.C.; Rose, B.S. Rheumatoid arthritis of the cervical spine: An analysis of 333 cases. J Am Rheum Dis 25:120–126, 1966.

79. De Beer, J.D.; Thomas, M.; Walter, J.; Anderson, P. Traumatic atlantoaxial subluxation. J Bone Joint Surg Br 70:652–655, 1988.

80. Dunbar, H.S.; Ray, B.S. Chronic atlantoaxial dislocations with late neurologic manifestation. Surg Gynecol Obstet 113:757–762, 1961.

81. Evarts, C.M. Traumatic occipitoatlantal dislocation. Report of a case with survival. J Bone Joint Surg Am 52:1653–1660, 1970.

82. Fielding, J.W.; Cochran, G.V.B.; Lawsing, J.F.; Hall, M. Tears of the transverse ligament of the atlas: A clinical and biomechanical study. J Bone Joint Surg Am 56:1681–1691, 1974.

83. Fielding, J.W.; Hawkins, R.J.; Ratzan, S.A. Spine fusion for atlantoaxial instability. J Bone Joint Surg Am 58:400–407, 1976.

84. Gallie, W.E. Fractures and dislocations of the cervical spine. Am J Surg 46:495–499, 1939.

85. Goel, A.; Muzumdar, D.; Dindorkar, K.; Desai, K. Atlantoaxial dislocation associated with stenosis of canal at atlas. J Postgrad Med 43:75–77, 1997.

86. Grogono, B.J.S. Injuries of the atlas and axis. J Bone Joint Surg Br 36:397–410, 1954.

87. Hanson, P.B.; Montesano, P.X.; Sharkey, N.A.; Rauschning, W. Anatomic and biomechanical assessment of transarticular screw fixation for atlantoaxial instability. Spine 16:1141–1145, 1991.

88. Hensinger, R.N.; MacEwen, G.D. Congenital anomalies of the spine. In: Rothman, R.H.; Simeone, F.A., eds. The Spine. Philadelphia, W.B. Saunders, 1982, pp. 194–201.

89. Hentzer, L.; Schalimtzek, M. Fractures and subluxations of the atlas and axis. Acta Orthop Scand 42:251–258, 1971.

90. Hinck, V.C.; Hopkins, C.E.; Savara, B.S. Sagittal diameter of the cervical spinal canal in children. Radiology 79:97–108, 1962.

91. Jackson, H. The diagnosis of minimal atlantoaxial subluxations. Br J Radiol 23:672–674, 1950.

92. Levine, A.M.; Edwards, C.C. Traumatic lesions of the occipitoatlantoaxial complex. Clin Orthop 239:53–68, 1989.

93. Levine, A.M.; Edwards, C.C. Treatment of injuries in the C1–C2 complex. Orthop Clin North Am 17:31–44, 1986.

94. Martel, W. The occipitoatlantoaxial joints in rheumatoid arthritis and ankylosing spondylitis. AJR Am J Roentgenol 86:223–240, 1960.

95. Przybylski, G.J.; Welch, W.C. Longitudinal atlantoaxial dislocation with type III odontoid fracture. Case report and review of the literature. J Neurosurg 84:666–670, 1996.

96. Rodrigues, F.A.C.; Hodgson, B.F.; Craig, J.B. Posterior atlantoaxial arthrodesis: A simplified method. Spine 16:878–880, 1991.

97. Steel, H.H. Anatomical and mechanical considerations of the atlantoaxial articulations. Proceedings of the American Orthopaedic Association. J Bone Joint Surg Am 50:1481–1482, 1968.

98. von Torklus, D.; Gehle, W. The Upper Cervical Spine. New York, Grune & Stratton, 1972.

99. Wigren, A. Traumatic atlantoaxial dislocation without neurological disorder. A case report. J Bone Joint Surg Am 55:642–644, 1973.

Atlantoaxial Rotatory Subluxations and Dislocations

100. Corner, E.S. Rotary dislocations of the atlas. Ann Surg 45:9–26, 1907.

101. Coutts, M.B. Rotary dislocations of the atlas. Ann Surg 29:297–311, 1934.

102. Fielding, W.J.; Hawkins, R.J. Atlantoaxial rotatory fixation (fixed rotatory subluxation of the atlantoaxial joint). J Bone Joint Surg Am 59:37–44, 1977.

103. Fielding, W.J.; Stillwell, W.T; Chynn, K.Y.; Spyropoulos, E.C. Use of computed tomography for the diagnosis of atlantoaxial rotatory fixation. J Bone Joint Surg Am 60:1102–1104, 1978.

104. Fielding, W.J.; Hawkins, R.J.; Hensinger, R.N.; Francis, W.R. Atlantoaxial rotary deformities. Orthop Clin North Am 9:955–967, 1978.

105. Fiorani-Gallotta, G.; Luzzatti, G. Sublussazione lateral e sublessazione rotatoria dell'ante. Arch Ortop 70:467–484, 1957.

106. Grisel, P. Enucleation de l'atlas et torticollis nasopharyngien. Presse Med 38:50–53, 1930.

107. Hess, J.H.; Bronstein, I.P.; Abelson, S.M. Atlantoaxial dislocations. Unassociated with trauma and secondary to inflammatory foci in the neck. Am J Dis Child 49:1137–1147, 1935.

108. Jacobson, G.; Adler, D.C. Examination of the atlantoaxial joint following injury: With particular emphasis on rotational subluxation. AJR Am J Roentgenol 76:1081–1094, 1956.

109. Jones, R.N. Rotatory dislocation of both atlantoaxial joints. J Bone Joint Surg Br 66:6–7, 1984.

110. Levine, A.M.; Edwards, C.C. Treatment of injuries in the C1–C2 complex. Orthop Clin North Am 17:31–44, 1986.

111. Levine, A.M.; Edwards, C.C. Traumatic lesions of the occipitoatlantoaxial complex. Clin Orthop 239:530–568, 1989.

112. Schnieder, R.C.; Schemm, G.W. Vertebral artery insufficiency in acute and chronic spinal trauma. With special reference to the syndrome of acute central cervical spinal cord injury. J Neurosurg 18:348–360, 1961.

113. Watson-Jones, R. Spontaneous hyperaemic dislocation of the atlas. Proc Soc Med 25:586–590, 1932.

114. Werne, S. Studies on spontaneous atlas dislocation. Acta Orthop Scand 23:1–150, 1957.

115. Wittek, A. Ein Fall von Distensionsluxation im Atlantoepistrophealgelenke. Muench Med Wochenschr 55:1836–1837, 1908.

116. Wortzman, G.; Dewar, F.P. Rotatory fixation of the atlantoaxial joint: Rotational atlantoaxial subluxation. Radiology 90:479–487, 1968.

Odontoid Fractures

117. Anderson, L.D.; D'Alonzo, R.T. Fractures of the odontoid process of the axis. J Bone Joint Surg Am 56:663–674, 1974.

118. Andersson, S.; Rodrigues, M.; Olerud, C. Odontoid fractures: High complication rate associated with anterior screw fixation in the elderly. Eur Spine J 9:56–59, 2000.

119. Apfelbaum, R.I.; Lonser, R.R.; Veres, R.; Casey, A. Direct anterior screw fixation for recent and remote odontoid fractures. J Neurosurg 93:227–236, 2000.

120. Alker, G.J., Jr.; Oh, Y.S.; Leslie, E.V. High cervical spine and craniocervical injuries in fatal traffic accidents. Orthop Clin North Am 9:1003–1010, 1978.

121. Apuzzo, M.L.J.; Heiden, J.S.; Weiss, M.H.; et al. Acute fractures of the odontoid process. An analysis of 45 cases. J Neurosurg 48:85–91, 1978.

122. Aymes, E.W.; Anderson, E.M. Fracture of the odontoid process. Arch Surg 72:377–393, 1956.

123. Bergenheim, A.T.; Forssel, Å. Vertical odontoid fracture: Case report. J Neurosurg 74:665–667, 1991.

124. Bohler, J. Fractures of the odontoid process. J Trauma 5:386–390, 1965.

125. Bohlman, H.H. Acute fractures and dislocations of the cervical spine. An analysis of three hundred hospitalized patients and review of the literature. J Bone Joint Surg Am 61:1119–1142, 1979.

126. Bucholz, R.W.; Burkhead, W.Z. The pathological anatomy of fatal atlantooccipital dislocations. J Bone Joint Surg Am 61:248–250, 1979.

127. Campanelli, M.; Kattner, K.A.; Stroink, A.; et al. Posterior C1–C2 transarticular screw fixation in the treatment of displaced type II odontoid fractures in the geriatric population—review of seven cases. Surg Neurol 51:596–600, 1999.

128. Chan, D.D.K.; Morwessel, R.M.; Leung, K.Y.K. Treatment of odontoid fractures with halo cast immobilization. Orthop Trans 5:118–119, 1981.

129. Chang, K.W.; Liu, Y.W.; Cheng, P.G.; et al. One Herbert double-threaded compression screw fixation of displaced type II odontoid fractures. J Spinal Disord 7:62–69, 1994.

130. Clark, C.R.; White, A.A. Fractures of the dens. A multicenter study. J Bone Joint Surg Am 67:1340–1348, 1985.

131. Cooper, P.R.; Maravilla, K.R.; Sklar, F.H.; et al. Halo immobilization of cervical spine fractures. Indications and results. J Neurosurg 50:603–610, 1979.

132. Crooks, F.; Birkett, A.N. Fractures and dislocations of the cervical spine. Br J Surg 31:252–265, 1944.

133. Crockard, H.A.; Heilman, A.E.; Stevens, J.M. Progressive myelopathy secondary to odontoid fractures: Clinical, radiological, and surgical features. J Neurosurg 78:579–586, 1993.

134. Doherty, B.J.; Heggeness, M.H.; Esses, S.I. A biomechanical study of odontoid fractures and fracture fixation. Spine 18:178–184, 1993.

135. Donovan, M.M. Efficacy of rigid fixation of fractures of the odontoid process. Retrospective analysis of fifty-four cases. Orthop Trans 4:46, 1980.

136. Ehara, S.; el-Khoury, G.Y.; Clark, C.R. Radiologic evaluation of dens fracture: Role of plain radiography and tomography. Spine 17:475–479, 1992.

137. Esses, S.I.; Bednar, D.A. Screw fixation of odontoid fractures and nonunions. Spine 16(Suppl):483–485, 1991.

138. Etter, C.; Coscia, M.; Jaberg, H.; Aebi, M. Direct anterior fixation of dens fractures with a cannulated screw system. Spine 16(Suppl): 25–32, 1991.

139. Farey, I.D.; Nadkarni, S.; Smith, N. Modified Gallie technique versus transarticular screw fixation in C1–C2 fusion. Clin Orthop 359:126–135, 1999.

140. Fielding, J.W.; Hensinger, R.N.; Hawkins, R.J. Os odontoideum. J Bone Joint Surg Am 62:376–383, 1980.

141. Fielding, J.W.; Hawkins, R.R.; Ratzan, S.A. Spine fusion for atlantoaxial instability. J Bone Joint Surg Am 58:400–407, 1976.

142. Fuji, T.; Oda, T.; Kato, Y.; et al. Accuracy of atlantoaxial transarticular screw insertion. Spine 25:1760–1764, 2000.

143. Govender, S.; Maharaj, J.F.; Haffajee, M.R. Fractures of the odontoid process. J Bone Joint Surg Br 82:1143–1147, 2000.

144. Graziano, G.; Jaggers, C.; Lee, M.; Lynch, W. A comparative study of fixation techniques for type II fractures of the odontoid process. Spine 18:2383–2387, 1993.

145. Greene, K.A.; Dickman, C.A.; Marciano, C.F.; et al. Transverse atlantal ligament disruption associated with odontoid fractures. Spine 19:2307–2314, 1994.

146. Griswold, D.M.; Albright, J.A.; Schiffman, E.; et al. Atlantoaxial fusion for instability. J Bone Joint Surg Am 60:285–292, 1978.

147. Hacker, R.J. Screw fixation for odontoid fracture; a comparison of the anterior and posterior technique. Nebr Med J 81:275–278, 1996.

148. Hanigan, W.C.; Powell, F.C.; Elwood, P.W.; Henderson, J.P. Odontoid fractures in elderly patients. J Neurosurg 78:32–35, 1993.

149. Hart, R.; Saterbak, A.; Rapp, T.; Clark, C. Non-operative management of dens fracture nonunion in elderly patients without myelopathy. Spine 25:1339–1343, 2000.

150. Heller, J.G.; Alson, M.D.; Schaffler, M.B.; Garfin, S.R. Quantitative internal dens morphology. Spine 17:861–866, 1992.

151. Henry, A.D.; Bohly, J.; Grosse, A. Fixation of odontoid fractures by an anterior screw. J Bone Joint Surg Br 81:472–477, 1999.

152. Julien, T.D.; Frankel, B.; Traynelis, V.C.; Ryken, T.C. Evidence-based analysis of odontoid fracture management. Neurosurg Focus 8:1–6, 2000.

153. Jun, B.Y. Anatomic study for ideal and safe posterior C1–C2 transarticular screw fixation. Spine 23:1703–1707, 1998.

154. Jun, B.Y. Complete reduction of retro-odontoid soft tissue mass in os odontoideum following the posterior C1–C2 transarticular screw fixation. Spine 24:1961–1964, 1999.

155. Lennarson, P.J.; Mostafavi, H.; Traynelis, V.C.; Walters, B.C. Management of type II dens fractures: A case-control study. Spine 25:1234–1237, 2000.

156. Lind, B.; Nordwall, A.; Sihlbom, H. Odontoid fractures treated with halo-vest. Spine 12:173–177, 1987.

157. Madawi, A.A.; Casey, A.T.; Solanki, G.A.; et al. Radiological and anatomical evaluation of the atlantoaxial transarticular screw fixation technique. J Neurosurg 86:961–968, 1997.

158. Marar, B.C.; Tay, C.K. Fracture of the odontoid process. Aust N Z J Surg 46:231–236, 1976.

159. Mouradian, W.H.; Fietti, V.G., Jr.; Cochran, G.V.B.; et al. Fracture of the odontoid: A laboratory and clinical study of mechanisms. Orthop Clin North Am 9:985–1001, 1978.

160. Murphy, M.J.; Wu, J.C.; Southwick, W.O. Complications of halo fixation. Orthop Trans 3:126, 1979.

161. Nachemson, A. Fracture of the odontoid process of the axis: A clinical study based on 26 cases. Acta Orthop Scand 29:185–217, 1959.

162. Nadim, Y.; Sabry, F.; Xu, R.; Ebraheim, N. Computed tomography in the determination of transarticular C1–C2 screw length. Orthopedics 23:373–375, 2000.

163. Paramore, C.G.; Dickman, C.A.; Sonntag, V.K. The anatomical suitability of the C1-2 complex for transarticular screw fixation. J Neurosurg 85:221–224, 1996.

164. Pepin, J.W.; Bourne, R.B.; Hawkins R.J. Odontoid fractures of the axis with special reference to the elderly patient. Orthop Trans 5:119, 1981.

165. Polin, R.S.; Szabo, T.; Bogaev, C.A.; et al. Non-operative management of types II and III odontoid fractures: The Philadelphia collar versus the halo vest. Neurosurgery 38:450–456, 1996.

166. Ryan, M.D.; Taylor, T.K.F. Odontoid fractures. A rational approach to treatment. J Bone Joint Surg Br 64:416–421, 1982.

167. Sasso, R.; Doherty, B.J.; Crawford, M.J.; Heggeness, M.H. Biomechanics of odontoid fracture fixation: Comparison of the one- and two-screw technique. Spine 18:1950–1953, 1993.

168. Schaffler, M.B.; Alson, M.D.; Heller, J.G.; Garfin, S.R. Morphology of the dens: A quantitative study. Spine 17:738–743, 1992.

169. Schatzker, J.; Rorabeck, C.H.; Waddell, J.P. Fractures of the dens. Analysis of thirty-seven cases. J Bone Joint Surg Br 53:392–405, 1971.

170. Schiff, D.C.M.; Parke, W.W. The arterial supply of the odontoid process. J Bone Joint Surg Am 55:1450–1456, 1973.

171. Sherk, H.H. Fractures of the atlas and odontoid process. Orthop Clin North Am 9:973–984, 1978.

172. Skold, G. Fractures of the neural arch and odontoid process of the axis. A study of their causation. Z Rechtsmed 82:89–103, 1978.

173. Solanki, G.A.; Crockard, H.A. Preoperative determination of safe superior transarticular screw trajectory through the lateral mass. Spine 24:1477–1482, 1999.

174. Southwick, W.O. Current concepts review. Management of fractures of the dens (odontoid process). J Bone Joint Surg Am 62:482–486, 1980.

175. Stoney, J.; O'Brien, J.; Wilde, P. Treatment of type-two odontoid fractures in halothoracic vests. J Bone Joint Surg Br 80:452–455, 1998.

176. Sweigel, J.G. Halothoracic brace in the management of odontoid fractures. Orthop Trans 3:126, 1979.

177. Vaccaro, A.R.; Cook, C.M.; McCullen, G.; Garfin, S.R. Cervical trauma: Rationale for selecting the appropriate fusion technique. Orthop Clin North Am 29:745–754, 1998.

178. Verheggen, R.; Jansen, J. Fractures of the odontoid process: Analysis of the functional results after surgery. Eur Spine J 3:146–150, 1994.

179. Ziai, W.C.; Hurlbert, R.J. A six-year review of odontoid fractures: The emerging role of surgical intervention. Can J Neurol Sci 27:297–301, 2000.

C2 Lateral Mass Fractures

180. Blauth, M.; Lange, U.F.; Knop, C.; Bastian, L. [Spinal fractures in the elderly and their treatment.] Orthopade 29:302–317, 2000.

181. Finelli, F.C.; Jonsson, J.; Champion, H.R.; et al. A case control study for major trauma in geriatric patients. J Trauma 29:541–548, 1989.

182. Hadley, M.N.; Dickman, C.A.; Browner, C.M.; Sonntag, V.K. Acute traumatic atlas fractures: Management and long term outcome. Neurosurgery 23:31–35, 1988.

183. Johnston, R.A. Management of old people with neck trauma. BMJ 299:633–634, 1989.

184. Levine, A.M.; Edwards, C.C. Traumatic lesions of the occipitoatlantoaxial complex. Clin Orthop 239:53–68, 1989.

185. Lind, B.; Bake, B.; Lundqvist, C.; Nordwall, A. Influence of halo vest treatment on vital capacity. Spine 12:449–452, 1987.

186. Olerud, C.; Andersson, S.; Svensson, B.; Bring, J. Cervical spine fractures in the elderly: Factors influencing survival in 65 cases. Acta Orthop Scand 70:509–513, 1999.
187. Pepin, J.W.; Bourne, R.B.; Hawkins, R.J. Odontoid fractures, with special reference to the elderly patient. Clin Orthop 193:178–183, 1985.
188. Ryan, M.D.; Henderson, J.J. The epidemiology of fractures and fracture-dislocations of the cervical spine. Injury 23:38–40, 1992.
189. Seybold, E.A.; Bayley, J.C. Functional outcome of surgically and conservatively managed dens fractures. Spine 23:1837–1845, 1998.
190. Signoret, F.; Feron, J.M.; Bunfait, H.; Patel, A. Fractured odontoid with fractured superior articular process of the axis: Repair of three cases. J Bone Joint Surg Am 68:182–184, 1985.
191. Sonntag, V.K.; Hadley, M.N. Nonoperative management of cervical spine injuries. Clin Neurosurg 34:630–649, 1988.
192. Taitsman, L.; Hecht, A.C.; Pedlow, F.X. Complications of halo treatment in elderly patients with cervical spine fractures. Submitted for publication.
193. Weller, S.J.; Malek, A.M.; Rossitch, E. Cervical spine fractures in the elderly. Surg Neurol 47:274–280, 1997.

Traumatic Spondylolisthesis of the Axis

194. Borne, G.M.; Bedou, G.L.; Pinaudeau, M. Treatment of pedicular fractures of the axis. A clinical study and screw fixation technique. J Neurosurg 60:88–93, 1984.
195. Brashear, H.R.; Venters, G.C.; Preston, E.T. Fractures of the neural arch of the axis. A report of twenty-nine cases. J Bone Joint Surg Am 57:879–887, 1975.
196. Bucholz, R.W. Unstable hangman's fractures. Clin Orthop 154:119–124, 1981.
197. Coric, D.; Wilson, J.A.; Kelly, D.L., Jr. Treatment of traumatic spondylolisthesis of the axis with nonrigid immobilization: A review of 64 cases. J Neurosurg 85:550–554, 1996.
198. Cornish, B.L. Traumatic spondylolisthesis of the axis. J Bone Joint Surg Br 50:31–43, 1968.
199. Dussault, R.G.; Effendi, B.; Roy, D.; et al. Locked facets with fracture of the neural arch of the axis. Spine 8:365–367, 1983.
200. Effendi, B.; Roy, D.; Cornish, B.; et al. Fractures of the ring of the axis. A classification based on the analysis of 131 cases. J Bone Joint Surg Br 63:319–327, 1981.
201. Francis, W.R.; Fielding, J.W. Traumatic spondylolisthesis of the axis. Orthop Clin North Am 9:1011–1027, 1978.
202. Francis, W.R.; Fielding, J.W.; Hawkins, R.J.; et al. Traumatic spondylolisthesis of the axis. J Bone Joint Surg Br 63:313–318, 1981.
203. Garber, J.N. Abnormalities of the atlas and axis vertebra: Congenital and traumatic. J Bone Joint Surg Am 46:1782–1791, 1964.
204. Greene, K.A.; Dickman, C.A.; Marciano, F.F.; et al. Acute axis fractures. Analysis of management and outcome in 340 consecutive cases. Spine 22:1843–1852, 1997.
205. Grogono, B.J.S. Injuries of the atlas and axis. J Bone Joint Surg Br 36:397–410, 1954.
206. Gross, J.D.; Benzel, E.C. Non-operative treatment of hangman's fracture. In: Zdeblick, T.A.; Benzel, E.C.; Anderson, P.A.; Stillerman, C.B., eds. Controversies in Spine Surgery. St Louis, Quality Medical Publishing, 1999, pp. 51–71.
207. Hadley, M.N.; Sonntag, V.K.; Graham, T.W.; et al. Axis fractures resulting from motor vehicle accidents. The need for occupant restraints. Spine 11:861–864, 1986.
208. Haughton, S. On hanging, considered from a mechanical and physiological point of view. Lond Edinb Dublin Philos Mag J Sci 32:23–34, 1886.
209. Levine, A.M.; Edwards, C.C. The management of traumatic spondylolisthesis of the axis. J Bone Joint Surg Am 67:217–226, 1985.
210. Marar, B.C. Fracture of the axis arch. Clin Orthop 106:155–165, 1975.
211. Pelker, R.R.; Dorfman, G.S. Fracture of the axis associated with vertebral artery injury. A case report. Spine 11:621–623, 1986.
212. Pepin, J.W.; Hawkins, R.J. Traumatic spondylolisthesis of the axis: Hangman's fracture. Clin Orthop 157:133–138, 1981.

213. Roy-Camille, R. Recent Advances in Orthopaedics, Vol. 3. Edinburgh, Churchill Livingstone, 1979.
214. Schneider, K.C.; Livingston, D.; Cave, A.; Hamilton, G. Hangman's fracture of the cervical spine. J Neurosurg 22:141, 1965.
215. Seljeskog, E.L. Nonoperative management of acute upper cervical injuries. Acta Neurochir (Wien) 41:87–100, 1978.
216. Sherk, H.H.; Howard, T. Clinical and pathologic correlations in traumatic spondylolisthesis of the axis. Clin Orthop 174:122–126, 1983.
217. Starr, J.K.; Eismont, F.J. Atypical hangman's fractures. Spine 18:1954–1957, 1993.
218. Termansen, N.B. Hangman's fracture. Acta Orthop Scand 445:529–539, 1974.
219. Tuite, G.F.; Papadoupoulos, S.M.; Sonntag, V.K.H. Caspar plate fixation for the treatment of complex hangman's fractures. Neurosurgery 30:761–765, 1992.
220. Vermooten, V. A study of the fracture of the epistropheus due to hanging with a note of the possible causes of death. Anat Rec 20:305–311, 1921.
221. White, A.A. Hangman's fracture with nonunion and late cord compression. A case report. J Bone Joint Surg Am 60:839–840, 1978.
222. Williams, T.G. Hangman's fracture. J Bone Joint Surg Br 57:82–88, 1975.
223. Wood-Jones, F. The ideal lesion produced by judicial hanging. Lancet 1:53, 1913.

Surgical Techniques

224. Ashraf, J.; Crockard, H.A. Transoral fusion for high cervical fractures. J Bone Joint Surg Br 72:76–79, 1990.
225. Bohler, J. Anterior stabilization for acute fractures and nonunions of the dens. J Bone Joint Surg Am 64:18–27, 1982.
226. Brooks, A.L.; Jenkins, E.B. Atlantoaxial arthrodesis by the wedge compression method. J Bone Joint Surg Am 60:279–284, 1978.
227. Casey, A.T.; Madawi, A.A.; Veres, R.; Crockard, H.A. Is the technique of posterior transarticular screw fixation suitable for rheumatoid atlanto-axial subluxation? Br J Neurosurg 11:508–519, 1997
228. Cantore, G.; Ciappetta, P.; Delfine, R. New steel device of occipitocervical fixation. J Neurosurg 60:1104–1106, 1984.
229. Cone, W.; Turner, W.G. The treatment of the fracture-dislocation of the cervical vertebrae by skeletal traction and fusion. J Bone Joint Surg Am 19:584–602, 1937.
230. Crockard, A. Evaluation of spinal laminar fixation by a new, flexible stainless steel cable (Sof'wire): Early results. Neurosurgery 35:892–898, 1994.
231. Elia, M.; Mazzara, J.T.; Fielding, J.W. Onlay technique for occipitocervical fusion. Clin Orthop 280:170–178, 1992.
232. Fang, H.S.Y.; Ong, G.B. Direct anterior approach to the upper cervical spine. J Bone Joint Surg Am 44:1588–1604, 1962.
233. Fehlings, M.G.; Errico, T.; Cooper, P.; et al. Occipitocervical fusion with a five-millimeter malleable rod and segmental fixation. Neurosurgery 32:198–207, 1993.
234. Fielding, J.W.; Hawkins, R.J.; Ratzan, S.A. Spine fusion for atlantoaxial instability. J Bone Joint Surg Am 58:400–407, 1976.
235. Fried, L.C. Atlantoaxial fractures. Failure of posterior C1 to C2 fusion. J Bone Joint Surg Br 55:490–496, 1973.
236. Fujii, E.; Kobayashi, K.; Hirabayashi, K. Treatment in fractures of the odontoid process. Spine 13:604–609, 1988.
237. Gallie, W.E. Fractures and dislocation of the cervical spine. Am J Surg 46:495–499, 1939.
238. Griswold, D.M.; Albright, J.A.; Schiffman, E.; et al. Atlanto-axial fusion for instability. J Bone Joint Surg Am 60:285–292, 1978.
239. Grob, D.; An, H.S. Posterior occiput and C-1 and C-2 instrumentation. In: An, H.S.; Cotler, J.M., eds. Spinal Instrumentation. Philadelphia, Lippincott Williams & Wilkins, 2000, pp. 191–201.
240. Grob, D.; Crisco, J.J., III; Panjabi, M.M.; et al. Biomechanical evaluation of four different posterior atlantoaxial fixation techniques. Spine 17:480–490, 1992.

241. Grob, D.; Dvorak, J.; Panjabi, M.; et al. Posterior occipitocervical fusion: A preliminary report of a new technique. Spine 16(Suppl): 17–24, 1991.

242. Grob, D.; Dvorak, J.; Panjabi, M.; Antinnes, J.A. The role of plate and screw fixation in occipitocervical fusion in rheumatoid arthritis. Spine 19:2545–2551, 1994.

243. Grob, D.; Jeanneret, B.; Aebi, M. Atlantoaxial fusion with transarticular screw fixation. J Bone Joint Surg Br 73:972–976, 1991.

244. Henry, A.K. Extensile Exposure, 2nd ed. Edinburgh, E. & S. Livingstone, 1957, pp. 53–80.

245. Jeanneret, B.; Magerl, F. Primary posterior fusion C1/2 in odontoid fractures: Indications, technique, and results of transarticular screw fixation. J Spinal Disord 5:464–475, 1992.

246. Knoringer, P. Osteosynthesis of injuries and rheumatic or congenital instabilities of the upper cervical spine using double-threaded screws. Neurosurg Rev 15:275–283, 1992.

247. Levine, A.M.; Lutz, B. Extension teardrop injuries of the cervical spine. Paper presented at the 21st Annual Meeting of the Cervical Spine Research Society, New York, December 1993.

248. Louis, R. Anterior surgery of the upper cervical spine. Chir Organi Mov 77:75–80, 1992.

249. Mandel, I.M.; Kambach, B.J.; Petersilge, C.A.; et al. Morphologic considerations of C2 isthmus dimensions for the placement of transarticular screws. Spine 25:1542–1547, 2000.

250. McAfee, P.C.; Cassidy, J.R.; Davis, R.F.; et al. Fusion of the occiput to the upper cervical spine: A review of 37 cases. Spine 16(Suppl):490–494, 1991.

251. McGraw, R.W.; Rusch, R.M. Atlantoaxial arthrodesis. J Bone Joint Surg Br 55:482–489, 1973.

252. Montesano, P.X.; Anderson, P.A.; Schlehr, F.; et al. Odontoid fractures treated by anterior odontoid screw fixation. Spine 16(Suppl):33–37, 1991.

253. Murphy, M.J.; Southwick, W.O. Posterior approaches and fusions. In: Editorial Committee of Cervical Spine Research Society. The Cervical Spine. Philadelphia, J.B. Lippincott, 1989, pp. 775–791.

254. Nakanishi, T. [Internal fixation of odontoid fracture] [Japanese]. Orthop Traumat Surg 23:399–406, 1980.

255. Oda, I.; Abumi, K.; Sell, L.C.; et al. Biomechanical evaluation of five different occipito-atlanto-axial fixation techniques. Spine 24:2377–2382, 1999.

256. Perry, J.; Nickel, V. Total cervical fusion of neck paralysis. J Bone Joint Surg Am 41:37–60, 1959.

257. Ransford, A.O.; Crockard, H.A.; Pozo, J.L.; et al. Craniocervical instability treated by contoured loop fixation. J Bone Joint Surg Br 68:173–177, 1986.

258. Robinson, R.A.; Southwick, W.O. Surgical approaches to the cervical spine. Instr Course Lect, Vol. 17, 1960.

259. Rogers, W.A. Treatment of fracture-dislocation of the cervical spine. J Bone Joint Surg 24:245–258, 1942.

260. Roy-Camille, R.; Saillant, G.; Mazel, C. Internal fixation of the unstable cervical spine by a posterior osteosynthesis with plates and screws. In: Sherk, H.H.; Dunn, H.J.; Eismont, J.J.; et al., eds. The Cervical Spine, 2nd ed. Philadelphia, J.B. Lippincott, 1989, pp. 390–403.

261. Sasso, R.C.; Jeanneret, B.; Fischer, K.; Magerl, F. Occipitocervical fusion with posterior plate and screw instrumentation: A long-term follow-up study. Spine 19:2364–2368, 1994.

262. Smith, M.D.; Anderson, P.; Grady, M.S. Occipitocervical arthrodesis using contoured plate fixation. Spine 18:1984–1990, 1993.

263. Stillerman, C.B.; Wilson, J.A. Atlantoaxial stabilization with posterior transarticular screw fixation: Technical description and report of 22 cases. Neurosurgery 32:948–955, 1993.

264. Southwick, W.O.; Robinson, R.A. Surgical approaches to the vertebral bodies in the cervical and lumbar regions. J Bone Joint Surg Am 39:631–644, 1957.

265. Subin, B.; Liu, J.F.; Marshall, G.J. Transoral anterior decompression and fusion of chronic irreducible atlantoaxial dislocation with spinal cord compression. Spine 20:1233–1240, 1995.

266. Tominaga, T.; Dickman, C.A.; Sonntag, V.K.H.; Coons, S. Comparative anatomy of the baboon and the human cervical spine. Spine 20:131–137, 1995.

267. Weiland, D.J.; McAfee, P.C. Posterior cervical fusion with triple-wire strut graft technique: One hundred consecutive patients. J Spinal Disord 4:15–21, 1991.

268. Wheeler, T. Variability in the spinal column as regards defective neural arches (rudimentary spina bifida). Contrib Embryol 9:97–107, 1920.

269. White, A.A., III; Panjabi, M.M. Biomechanics of the occipitoatlantoaxial complex. Orthop Clin North Am 9:867–883, 1966.

270. Whitesides, T.E.G., Jr.; Kelly, R.P. Lateral approach to the upper cervical spine for anterior fusion. South Med J 59:879–883, 1966.

271. Whitesides, T.E.G., Jr.; McDonald, A.P. Lateral retropharyngeal approach to the upper cervical spine. Orthop Clin North Am 9:1115–1127, 1978.

272. Willard, D.; Nicholson, J.T. Dislocation of the first cervical vertebra. Ann Surg 113:464–475, 1941.

273. Xu, R.; Nadaud, M.C.; Ebraheim, N.A.; Teasting, R.A. Morphology of the second cervical vertebra and the posterior projection of the C2 pedicle. Spine 20:259–263, 1995.

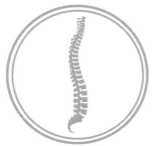

CHAPTER 29

Injuries of the Lower Cervical Spine

Sohail K. Mirza, M.D.
Paul A. Anderson, M.D.

Patients with blunt trauma injuries have a 2% to 6% prevalence of cervical spine injury. Victims of motor vehicle crashes, a subgroup of blunt trauma, have a higher rate of cervical injury (12%). The risk of cervical injury in specific settings can be further estimated by patient age, circumstances of the injury, and findings at initial evaluation[24] (Table 29–1). The clinical findings in the initial evaluation define the relative risk of a cervical spine injury, and combining these factors further identifies the population at risk for such injury. These risk estimates can serve as a guide for the initial management of high-risk patients, as well as for prioritization of the subsequent clinical and radiographic evaluation.

INJURY PATTERNS

Categorization of lower cervical spine injuries is variable, inconsistent, and problematic. Difficulties are partly due to the inherent structural complexity of this region of the spine. With intertwined neural and vascular elements, load-bearing articular joints, and highly mobile articulations, the lower cervical spine is indeed complex. Variation in the interpretation of imaging studies adds to this complexity. Because injuries with distinct clinical implications require recognition first and foremost, injury classification schemes that attempt comprehensive inclusion of all possible injury patterns have generally been too elaborate to be clinically useful. Simpler schemes fail to capture the essential defining characteristics of individual injuries. For simplicity and clarity in discussing important characteristics, we have divided the presentation of injury patterns in the lower cervical spine into separate anatomic, mechanistic, and morphologic considerations. However, it is important to keep in mind that evaluation of each injury involves a component of all three general categories of assessment.

Anatomic Considerations Specific to the Lower Cervical Spine

The vertebrae and articulations of the subaxial cervical spine (C3–C7) and the first thoracic vertebrae have similar morphologic and kinematic characteristics (Fig. 29–1). Injuries and disease processes usually behave similarly in this region. However, important differences in lateral mass anatomy and in the course of the vertebral artery exist between the mid and lower cervical spine. Surgical techniques place special emphasis on detailed knowledge of cervical anatomy to avoid neurovascular complications.

NEURAL ELEMENTS

The size and configuration of the spinal canal vary among humans and are important factors in determining the severity of spinal cord injuries.[81, 120] Spinal cord dimensions, however, have remarkably little variation in humans. The midsagittal diameter of the spinal canal is measured from the base of the spinous process to the posterior margin of the vertebral body. In the subaxial spine, the spinal cord has an average midsagittal diameter of 8 to 9 mm. Cervical spinal canal stenosis exists when the midsagittal diameter is less than 10 mm. The Pavlov ratio may be used to estimate the size of the spinal canal[229] and is defined as the ratio of the midsagittal diameter to the anteroposterior (AP) diameter of the vertebral body. If this ratio is less than 0.8, cervical stenosis is present. Cervical stenosis correlates with neurologic injury in patients with cervical fractures.[81]

The spinal nerves form from the ventral and dorsal roots and pass through the neural foramina. The boundaries of the neural foramina are the pedicles above and below the facet joint and the capsules posteriorly. Anteriorly, the foramina are above and below the disc annulus, the posterior vertebral body, and the uncinate process. The size of the neural foramina can be affected by displaced bone and disc fragments, by malalignment, or by loss of disc height. Patients with spinal cord injuries should be

814

TABLE 29-1 •••••••••••••••••••••••••••••••••

Frequency of Cervical Spine Fracture in Patients Admitted to the Emergency Room of a Regional Trauma Center

Clinical Characteristics	Prevalence of Cervical Spine Fracture (%)
Trauma patient with focal deficit	19.7
Trauma patient with severe head injury	7.2
Trauma patient, no focal deficit, no severe head injury, moderate-energy cause, age >50	2.2
Trauma patient, no focal deficit, high-energy cause	1.9
Trauma patient, no focal deficit, high-energy cause, age <50	1.1
Trauma patient, no focal deficit, no severe head injury, low-energy cause, age >50	0.5
Trauma patient, no focal deficit, no severe head injury, moderate-energy cause, age <50	0.4
Trauma patient, no focal deficit, no severe head injury, low-energy cause, age <50	0.04

•••

Data from Blackmore, C.C., et al. Radiology 211:759–765, 1999.

carefully evaluated for foraminal encroachment because such encroachment could account for isolated root radiculopathies. After exiting the neural foramina, the spinal nerve lies on the transverse process before it forms the brachial plexus. When compared with the lumbar spine, the nerve roots of the cervical spine have a more horizontal course; they exit from the spinal cord and lie directly above the pedicle.

SKELETAL STRUCTURES

Like all vertebrae, the subaxial cervical spine is characterized by a vertebral body connected to the neural arch by

pedicles. The vertebral body is small in comparison to the lower segment and is usually slightly concave along its superior surface (Fig. 29–2). The posterolateral projections of the superior end-plate are called the uncinate processes. The concavity of the ventral body is matched by slight convexity on the inferior surface, which allows the cranial vertebrae to sit in a shallow saddle. The transverse processes are complex amalgamations of the rudimentary rib anteriorly and the true transverse process posteriorly. These structures form a cuplike process that supports the exiting nerve root. The foramen transversarium exists within the transverse process, and the vertebral artery above C7 passes through this structure.[212] The pedicles are short bony canals that connect the vertebral bodies to the lateral masses (Fig. 29–3). They are oriented 15° to 40° medially and slightly upward.[169] The relatively large lateral masses or pillars are cuboid structures with facets on the superior and inferior surfaces. These facets form diarthrodial articulations typical of synovial joints and are oriented 30° to 45° upward from the horizontal. The lamina are thin, bony structures that extend from the lateral masses to the base of the spinous process. At the junction of the lamina and lateral mass is a valley that is an important landmark in lateral mass fixation. The spinous process projects posteriorly and is bifid at C3–C5 and often at C6 as well. The first easily palpable spinous process is usually C7, which makes it such an important surface landmark.

Because of the lack of intrinsic bony stability, integrity of the ligamentous anatomy is essential to maintain stability. The ligamentous anatomy can be divided into that involving the articulation between the vertebral bodies and that involving the articulation between the neural arches and the facet joints.

The anterior and posterior longitudinal ligaments extend the length of the spinal column and lie on the

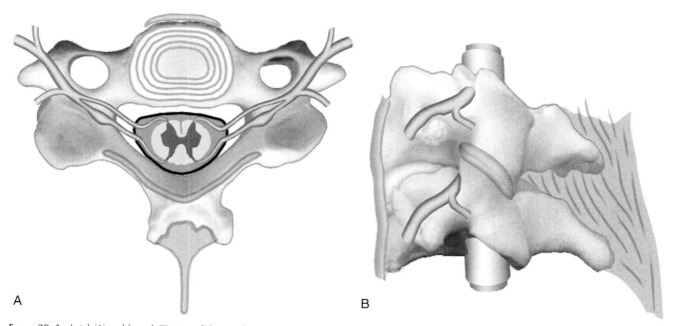

A   B

FIGURE 29–1. Axial (*A*) and lateral (*B*) view of the vertebra representative of the lower cervical spine. (From Mirza, S.K.; Chapman, J.R.; White, A.A. The Spine Manual. New York, Thieme, 2003.)

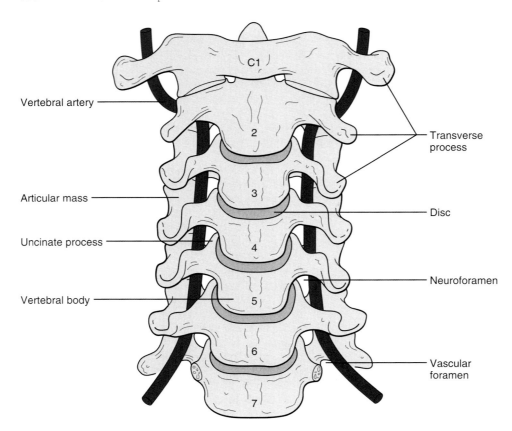

Vertebral artery

Articular mass

Uncinate process

Vertebral body

C1

2

3

4

5

6

7

Transverse process

Disc

Neuroforamen

Vascular foramen

Figure 29–2. This anterior view of the cervical spine demonstrates a number of pertinent features. All segments below C1–C2 have a posterolateral projection of the superior end-plate known as the *uncinate process.* The end-plates are firmly fixed to the anulus fibrosus. The vertebral foramina are anterolateral to the neural canal.

respective surfaces of the vertebral bodies (Fig. 29–4). The intervertebral disc is composed of a cartilaginous end-plate on either surface, a central nucleus, and a tough outer covering called the anulus fibrosus. The anulus is a strong stabilizing structure that is often overlooked as a source of pain. It is also often ignored in the evaluation of instability in patients sustaining cervical trauma. Laterally, the disc is buttressed by the uncus, which forms pseudojoints, or false joints, with the next cranial vertebrae, called the joints of Luschka.

The articulations of the neural arch are maintained by the nuchal ligaments, the ligamentum flavum, and the joint capsules. The nuchal ligaments are the ligamentum nuchae and the supraspinous and interspinous ligaments. The nuchal ligament is a strong, broad structure that

extends from the external occipital protuberance and attaches to the tips of the spinous processes. The supraspinous and interspinous ligaments lie on and between adjacent spinous processes, respectively. The ligamentum flavum is an elastic structure that attaches between adjacent lamina. The facet joint capsules are redundant to allow motion between vertebrae.

Anatomic Considerations Relevant to Surgery

Understanding injury patterns and planning surgical treatment require accurate and intricate knowledge of spinal anatomy. Surgical techniques are not without

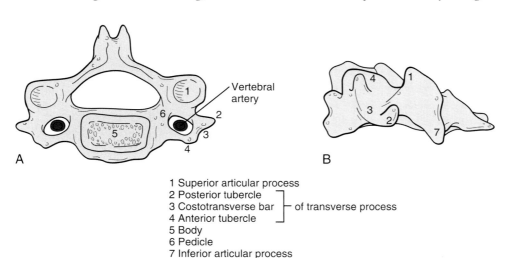

A

Vertebral artery

1

6

2

3

4

5

B

4   1

3

2

7

1 Superior articular process
2 Posterior tubercle
3 Costotransverse bar ⎫ of transverse process
4 Anterior tubercle ⎭
5 Body
6 Pedicle
7 Inferior articular process

Figure 29–3. This demonstrates a typical fifth cervical vertebra seen from above (*A*) and from the left side (*B*). A number of important structures are delineated. The superior articular process is seen to be oblique and posterolateral to the neural canal (1). The transverse process is composed of three portions: the posterior tubercle (2), costotransverse bar (3), and anterior tubercle (4). The vertebral body (5) has posterolateral lips on the superior surface (6), the pedicle is extremely short. The inferior articular facet (7) parallels the superior articular facet.

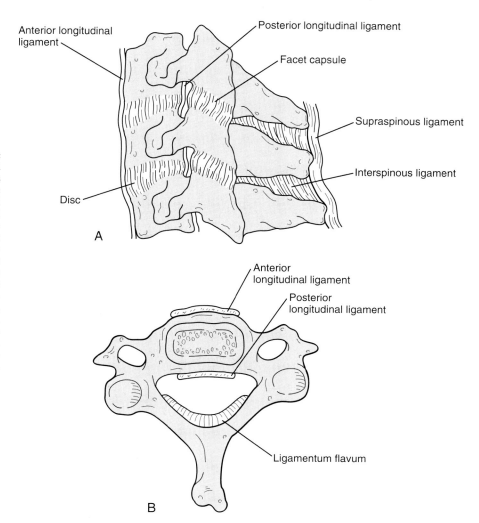

Anterior longitudinal ligament

Posterior longitudinal ligament

Facet capsule

Supraspinous ligament

Interspinous ligament

Disc

A

Anterior longitudinal ligament

Posterior longitudinal ligament

Ligamentum flavum

B

FIGURE 29–4. Ligamentous anatomy of the cervical spine. *A,* Lateral view. *B,* Axial view. Anteriorly, the ligamentous structures include the intervertebral disc with the annulus fibrosis, the anterior longitudinal ligament, and the posterior longitudinal ligament. Posteriorly, anchored to the spinous processes, are the nuchal ligaments including the ligamentum nuchae, the supraspinous ligament, and the interspinous ligament. The ligamentum flavum spans the laminae, and the joint capsules enclose the facet articulations. (*A,* Redrawn from Anderson, P.A. In: Hansen, S.T.; Swiontkowski, M.F., eds. Orthopaedic Trauma Protocols. New York, Raven, 1993. *B,* Redrawn from White, A.A., III; Panjabi, M.M. In: White, A.A., III; Panjabi, M.M., eds. Clinical Biomechanics of the Spine, 2nd ed. Philadelphia, J.B. Lippincott, 1990.)

hazard, and risks include iatrogenic injury to the vertebral artery, nerve roots, and the spinal cord. Below, we review three primary areas of surgical interest: the anatomy of the lateral mass, pedicle, and vertebral artery.

LATERAL MASS ANATOMY

The use of plates and screws for cervical fixation has increased in popularity.[11, 60, 102, 199] Theoretical advantages of plates and screws over wire fixation include improved maintenance of reduction, increased stability, decreased necessity for postoperative bracing, the ability to stabilize the segment even if the spinous process is fractured or missing, the potential to decrease the number of levels subjected to permanent arthrodesis, early mobilization of the patient, and the ability to extend the fixation to the occipitocervical and cervicothoracic junctions. Disadvantages include an increased risk of neurovascular complications and higher cost. Emphasizing the potential for complications, Heller and co-workers reported a 7% incidence of nerve root injuries in lateral mass platings.[111]

Safe screw placement requires meticulous surgical technique, including knowledge of the individual patient's anatomy, correct selection of the starting point and screw

direction, and accurate drilling depth and selection of screw length. When viewed dorsally, the lateral mass is square or rectangular (Fig. 29–5). To aid in proper screw insertion, the borders of the lateral masses must be correctly identified. The medial border lies at the junction of the lamina, and the lateral mass is located at an easily perceptible valley. The lateral border is at the far edge of the lateral mass. The cranial and caudal borders are the superior and inferior facet joints, respectively. When viewed from a lateral projection, the lateral mass slopes upward 30° to 40° and is shaped like a parallelogram. The lateral mass is as thick anteriorly as posteriorly, except at C7, where it is thinner anteriorly.[6] Frequently at C7, the lateral mass cannot be identified because the lamina sweeps laterally to form a short transverse process. This anatomic relationship accounts for the increased incidence of neurologic deficits caused by screw fixation at C7.[111] If the anatomy is abnormal, screw insertion into the lateral masses should be avoided or screws with shorter lengths should be used. Alternatively, some authors recommend insertion of pedicle screws in C7 or T1.[2, 126]

Lying directly anterior to the medial border or valley is the foramen transversarium and the vertebral artery. The AP distance from this valley to the foramen transversarium averages 14.6 mm, with a standard deviation of 1.98

mm.[168] However, findings on computed tomography (CT) or magnetic resonance imaging (MRI) must be scrutinized preoperatively because anomalies in the course of the vertebral artery frequently exist. The exiting nerve root passes dorsally to the vertebral artery at the medial border of the lateral mass. From there, it courses obliquely downward, outward, and anteriorly. From a dorsal projection, the nerve root passes through the lower half of the lateral mass (under the inferior facet). To avoid neurovascular complications, Pait and associates divided the lateral mass into four equal quadrants.[168] They recommended that screws be directed to the upper outer, or "safe," quadrant. Too much angulation can threaten the nerve root above, whereas too little upward angulation threatens the nerve root below.

CERVICAL PEDICLE ANATOMY

Pedicle fixation of the cervical spine has been described in detail.[2] Between C3 and C6 the course of the vertebral artery makes this technique precarious, so fixation in this region should be avoided except in unusual circumstances. Because of the increased risk of neurologic injury and the variable anatomy at C7 and T1, pedicle fixation may be preferable to lateral mass fixation. At the C7 and T1 levels, the lateral masses are often poorly identifiable, and insertion of screws at these levels increases the risk of neurologic injury.[111] Pedicle fixation is also more feasible because of absence of the vertebral artery.

Abumi and associates reported 13 patients with cervical fractures and dislocations treated with Steffee vertebral plates and 5.5-mm pedicle screws.[2] Postoperative CT scans revealed three perforations of the pedicles without consequence. Kotani and co-workers confirmed the biomechanical superiority of this fixation over posterior interspinous wires, lateral mass plates, and anterior plate fixation.[126] The AO group described pedicle fixation of the upper thoracic spine.[155] The starting point for screw insertion is just below the center of the facet joint. Screws are directed 7° to 10° medially and 10° to 20° downward.

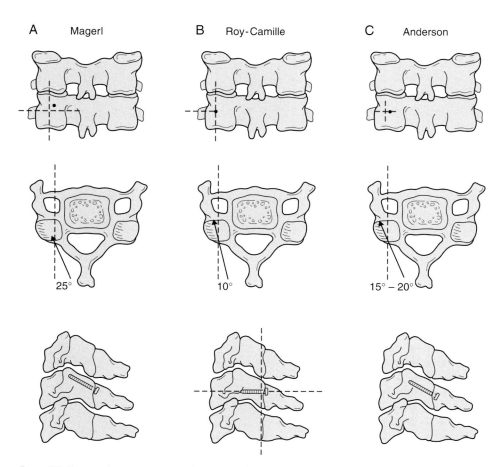

FIGURE 29–5. Lateral mass anatomy and technique for screw placement. When viewed dorsally, the lateral mass is rectangular. The borders of the rectangle must be identified for accurate screw placement. The medial border is the valley at the junction of the lamina and the lateral mass. The vertebral artery lies anterior to this valley and, therefore, screws must be placed laterally and angled outward. The lateral border is the far edge of the lateral mass. The superior and inferior borders are the respective facet joints. *A*, The Magerl technique. Screws are started 1 to 2 mm medial and cranial to the center of the lateral mass and angled 25° outward and 30° upward, parallel to the facet joint. *B*, The Roy-Camille technique. The starting point is the center of the lateral mass, and screws are directed straight forward and 10° outward. *C*, The Anderson technique. Screws are placed 1 to 2 mm medial to the center of the lateral mass and are angled 15° to 20° outward and 20° to 30° upward. (*A–C*, Redrawn from Abdu, W.A.; Bohlman, H.H. Orthopedics 15:293, 1992.)

These landmarks can be similarly used at C7 and T1, as described by Chapman and associates.[56]

Several anatomic studies of cervical pedicle morphology have been performed. Panjabi and colleagues found that the cervical pedicles are elliptical in cross section, with the minimal diameter ranging from 5.4 to 7.5 mm.[169] The pedicles were directed 41° to 44° medially at C3 and C4 and only 30° at C6. In the transverse plane, the pedicle angled upward 5° to 10° from C3 to C5 and downward 6° to 11° at C6 and C7. Xu and associates identified the projection of the C7 pedicle axis on its posterior aspect.[255] They determined the starting point for screw insertion to be 0 to 2 mm inferior to the midpoint of the transverse process and 2 to 3 mm medial to the outer margin of the lateral mass. The C7 pedicle axis angle averaged 17° medially and 14° cephalad. An and co-workers and Chapman and associates found that the C7 pedicle angled 34° and 41° medially.[6, 56]

VASCULAR ANATOMY

The vertebral arteries are a major source of blood supply to the vertebrae and spinal cord. They originate from the first branch of the subclavian arteries and enter the spine at C6, where they pass craniad through the foramen transversarium to the atlas. Although clinical consequences are rare, fractures and fracture-dislocations of the transverse process are associated with a significant incidence of occlusion of the vertebral artery.[252] Clinical consequences of vertebral artery injury are more likely in the upper cervical spine.

The cervical spinal cord is perfused by the anterior spinal artery, the paired posterior spinal arteries, and two to three segmental arteries in the cervical spine. The anterior and posterior spinal arteries originate intracranially from the vertebral arteries. The segmental vessels arise from the vertebral artery, pass through the neural foramina with the spinal nerve root, and enter the spinal cord with the anterior root. The segmental vessels may be compromised by displaced bone or disc fragments, thereby exacerbating cord ischemia.[31]

Precise knowledge of the location of the vertebral artery is essential as surgeons have become more aggressive in removing the anterior vertebral body and achieving stabilization with vertebral screws. Although vertebral artery injuries have been associated with fracture of the transverse processes, facet dislocation, and burst-type fractures, clinical consequences are usually rare. However, iatrogenic injury may be associated with significant morbidity and mortality. Smith and co-workers reviewed 10 patients with vertebral artery injury during anterior decompression, 5 of whom had major neurologic deficits.[212] The three most common causes of iatrogenic injury were that the surgeon lost the orientation of the midline, decompression was excessive laterally, and the lateral aspect of the vertebral body was pathologically soft. To avoid the first of these most common causes of injury, the surgeon can use the origin of the longus colli muscles and the uncus as a standard aid in determining the midline. If still in doubt, an AP radiograph will help.

The vertebral artery originates from the subclavian or innominate artery and enters the spine through the foramen transversarium at C6. At C7, it lies anterior and lateral to the transverse process and is generally out of harm's way as far as spinal surgery is concerned. Throughout its course in the foramen transversarium from C6 to C2, the vertebral artery is at risk during anterior decompression. At the axis base it turns posteriorly and laterally to pass within the foramen transversarium of the atlas. It then turns medially and anteriorly and perforates the atlanto-occipital membranes passing through foramen magnum. There, the two vertebral arteries join to form the basilar artery. The course of the vertebral artery at C2 can be variable and frequently places the artery at risk during Magerl C1–C2 transarticular screw fixation.[171]

Rizzolo and colleagues studied 97 CT scans to evaluate the position of the foramen transversarium.[187] The distance between the medial walls of the foramen transversarium ranged from 25.9 to 29.3 mm. The AP location was only 0.28 mm anterior to the posterior vertebral wall at C2 and increased to 3.5 mm at C6. In general, the foramen transversarium gradually moves anteriorly from C6 to C2. The AP diameter of the body increased from 15.3 mm at C3 to 16.8 mm at C6, which corresponded to an increasing distance between the medial borders of the foramen transversarium from C3 to C6. Thus, the vertebral artery appeared to be more at risk at the cephalad levels. However, individual variations exist, so it is critical that in each case the patient's anatomy be assessed preoperatively.

Mechanisms of Cervical Injury

Understanding the mechanism of injury is essential to deliver thoughtful and timely care to spine injury patients. The mechanism of injury determines the severity and pattern of neural tissue disruption,[243] and the severity of the neurologic injury determines the functional outcome.[236] The mechanism of injury in large part determines the potential for ultimate neurologic recovery.[115] For clarity, the following discussion of mechanisms of injury separates neural injury from skeletal injury. Of course in real life, these two types of injuries occur concurrently in patients.

MECHANISMS OF SPINAL CORD INJURY

Structural failure of the spinal column displaces bone and ligaments into the spinal canal and neural foramina. These displaced and disrupted structures may apply force to neural tissue, resulting in either functional or anatomic disruption. Loss of structural integrity of the vertebral column may also expose the neural structures to deformations exceeding the physiologic range.[23] Most spinal cord injuries are crushing injuries, resulting in acute tissue contusion from the externally applied mechanical force.[122] Laceration and transection of the cord is rare, however, even in dislocations.

Experimental models of spinal cord injury have identified the rate, depth, and duration of compression as important determinants of the severity of neurologic injury.[121] The risk of tissue injury is proportional to the energy absorbed by these tissues.[14] For a direct impact on neural tissue, contact velocity and maximal compression are better predictors of injury severity than either force or acceleration. The viscoelastic properties of soft tissues provide the principal resistance to deformation in the early stages of the impact.[23, 235] Spinal cord tolerance for compression decreases as the velocity of maximal compression increases.[121] Minimal deformations at high contact velocity may produce severe anatomic and functional spinal cord injury. With injuries causing more than 50% cord compression, functional recovery is unlikely regardless of the contact velocity. Although this threshold effect denotes an upper limit of compression in the injury model, it is not a limiting factor in patients with an extremely slow onset of cord compression, as observed in chronic degenerative conditions such as spondylotic myelopathy.

The size of the spinal canal is a critical determinant of neurologic damage in cervical spine trauma.[81] The preinjury spinal canal diameter and cross-sectional area are also important in determining the severity of neural cord injury.[141] A narrow spinal canal is associated with a greater likelihood of neurologic injury and a higher probability of complete cord injury. The spinal cord can withstand considerable axial displacement without structural damage and neurologic deficit.[40] The cord does not slide up and down with physiologic flexion and extension but deforms as an accordion might.[179] The average stretch is 10%, with the greatest change being 17.6%. Maximal stretching occurs between C2 and T1. Cord deformation may be more severe in patients with cervical spondylosis and contributes to cord injury in these patients even in the absence of disruption of the skeletal spinal column.

Spinal cord injury can occur without obvious radiographic abnormalities,[206, 227] and hyperextension may be a mechanism in these injuries.[206] Patients with such injuries are generally older and have cervical spondylosis and a congenitally narrow spinal canal. Forced hyperextension causes the ligamentum flavum to buckle, further narrowing the spinal canal. In patients with bulging discs and anterior osteophytes, the spinal cord may be significantly compressed from the AP direction. A theoretical model indicates that these forces may generate high AP compressive forces in the central gray matter, in the anterior spinothalamic tract, and medially in the lateral corticospinal tract.[206] Because of the lamination of axonal fibers in these tracts, combined with the respective cervical segment placed anteriorly and medially in the anterior spinothalamic and lateral corticospinal tracts, the upper extremities are more affected than the lower extremities or the sacrum. This greater involvement of the upper extremities correlates with the high incidence of central cord syndrome observed in such patients. The prognosis for return of sacral and lower extremity function is good, but return of hand function is less certain.[139] Because of the generally good prognosis, however, most authors have recommended that patients be treated nonoperatively initially.[91, 158, 206]

The kinetic energy of the injury causes immediate depolarization of axonal membranes that is clinically manifested as spinal shock.[119] This immediate depolarization involves the entire cord. The functional neurologic deficit associated with spinal shock exceeds the deficit from actual irreversible neural injury. The clinical examination reflects actual neural injury when the spinal shock resolves as uninjured neural structures repolarize.

Blunt trauma to the spinal cord causes a contusion of neural tissue and the subsequent evolution of a cavity.[176] The primary injury displaces neural tissue within the cord, with the most severe injury occurring in the innermost regions of the spinal cord. Post-traumatic central cord syndrome can result from such compressive demyelination without hemorrhage.[45, 177] The primary neural injury causes wallerian degeneration in the ascending dorsal columns, as well as the descending motor tracts. This process is independent of any secondary injury or vascular insult. These changes result in a gap largely devoid of neural parenchymal matrix.

After a blunt trauma injury, erythrocytes leak out of the broken blood vessels and macerated tissue (hematomyelia). Fragments of cord tissue are displaced away from the primary injury site, and tissue breakdown expands the zone of injury within the first few hours after injury. The size of the injury zone is well-defined by 1 week. Macrophages remove damaged tissue and form a fluid-filled cavity, and the cavity expands to fill the entire area of tissue damage. Cysts form at the injury region. This process reaches a steady state if the surface of the cord remains intact and the pia, arachnoid, and dura do not form adhesions. Expanding intramedullary cysts are associated with scarring and adhesion of the pia to the dura, and these cysts contain an outer border of astrocytes. Nonexpanding cysts show cavitation with loose borders and no astrocyte boundary. Progressive noncystic myelomalacia is associated with tethering of the cord to the dura and apparent expansion of the cord. Patients with neurologic worsening from expanding post-traumatic cord cysts may improve with duraplasty and untethering.

Cellular Changes

An optimal experimental design with which to model spinal cord injury does not exist, and investigators have used various methods in attempting to mimic human spinal cord injury. The variability in the method of injury used and the animal species tested has resulted in diverse characterizations of the injury response. Additionally, experimental constraints in these injury models limit the potential to generalize the findings to human spinal cord injury.

The physiologic response to spinal cord injury is rapid and complex[207] (Table 29–2). The initial mechanical tissue disruption (primary injury) triggers a domino effect of interrelated processes. After tissue disruption, local tissue elements undergo structural and chemical changes. In

TABLE 29–2

Timing of Pathologic Responses in Spinal Cord Injury

Pathologic Process	Time from Injury
Hemorrhage	First few minutes
Rapid necrosis and apoptosis	First few hours
Inflammatory cell infiltration	6 to 48 hr
Reactive microglia formation	2 days to 2 wk
Reactive astrocyte formation	3 days to 2 wk
Second peak of apoptosis	7 days
Cavity and scar formation	After 2 wk
Wallerian degeneration	After 2 wk

turn, these changes initiate systemic responses. Within minutes of injury, hemorrhage from mechanical disruption of blood vessels occurs in the gray matter and expands radially to involve the white matter and lateral columns. Endothelial cell disruption increases fluid extravasation and swelling. The most extensive neuronal cell death occurs within the first few hours after injury.[207] Reactive cellular changes in gray matter are evident within 1 hour of injury, whereas white matter begins necrosis within 4 hours of injury. However, loss of neural tissue is not purely a response to local excitoxic processes.[136] Apoptosis, or programmed cell death that is dependent on active protein synthesis, contributes to neuronal and glial cell death as early as 4 hours after injury; it peaks initially at 24 hours and recurs 7 days after injury.

Axonal injury is a gradual process.[175] Disruption of cytoskeletal protein in the axonal membrane causes separation of the axon and wallerian degeneration. Above the wound, sterile end-bulbs form at failed regeneration sites in the descending tracts. Axons die back at 1 mm per month. Below the lesion, abortive sprouting by dorsal root ganglion cells results in schwannosis.

Changes in local blood flow, tissue edema, metabolite concentrations, and levels of chemical mediators propagate interdependent reactions. This pathophysiologic response to the primary mechanical injury can propagate tissue destruction and functional loss (secondary injury). Ischemia and inflammation are prominent mechanisms in these secondary events.[48, 49] Ischemia contributes to delayed secondary injury.[87, 225] The severity of neurologic injury is proportional to the duration of cord deformation, and structural neural damage is associated with irreversible injury.[167] What began as a reversible injury may become irreversible as a result of local ischemia. Irreversible axon injury also leads to cell death beyond the injury site.[161] The inflammatory response consists of infiltration of polymorphonuclear cells within 6 hours of injury. Macrophages appear at 24 hours and subsequently increase in concentration.[50]

The mechanism of cellular injury differs between white and gray matter.[178] Spinal cord axons contain voltage-gated sodium channels (Na) that exchange hydrogen (H) and calcium (Ca) ions.[180] Traumatic axonal injury is associated with a rise in intracellular sodium.[3] The reduction in extracellular sodium is neuroprotective, whereas increasing intracellular sodium exacerbates traumatic axonal injury. Pharmacologic blockade of voltage-gated Na channels is neuroprotective, as is inhibition of the Na-H exchanger. Reverse operation of the Na-Ca exchanger does not explain the effects of sodium in white matter injury. Axons in spinal cord white matter lack receptor-coupled and voltage-sensitive calcium channels. The mechanism of sodium ion–induced cell injury in traumatic white matter injury does not involve reverse operation of the Na-Ca exchanger as observed in anoxic cell injury.[220]

Intracellular influx of sodium and calcium is a key event in the pathogenesis of hypoxic-ischemic injury to neurons.[85, 92] As Janssen and Hansebout proved, influx of these ions disrupts mitochondria and uncouples oxidative phosphorylation.[118] Incomplete conversion of oxygen to carbon dioxide and water results in free radical formation, lipid peroxidation, and membrane breakdown.[107, 260, 261]

The excitatory amino acid glutamate activates the *N*-methyl-D-aspartate (NMDA)-Ca channels. Blocking these NMDA channels with choline, ketamine, and MK-801 prevents glutamate-induced neuronal swelling. Meanwhile, methylprednisolone and the 21-aminosteroid tirilazad mesylate inhibit membrane peroxidation.[105, 106]

Regeneration

When dealing with regeneration in the lower cervical spine, the primary injury frequently spares a peripheral rim of white matter.[261] Very few axons need to traverse the injury zone to support functional recovery. The ability to regain ambulation correlates with the amount of white matter remaining after injury.[16, 261] Most patients with spinal cord injury show some neurologic recovery,[224] but it is not clear whether this recovery is related to resolution of the acute physiologic responses to injury or related to active injury repair mechanisms.

The spontaneous regenerative capacity of the central nervous system is different from that of the peripheral nervous system.[207] Fish and various amphibians show successful regeneration of axons in the central nervous system. Higher vertebrates demonstrate this capacity in the embryonic and perinatal periods,[116] but adult mammals show some regeneration only under controlled circumstances. These particular circumstances of regeneration involve an absence of myelin and neurite growth inhibitory proteins.

Injured spinal axons can invade and grow in peripheral nerves outside the injured spinal cord microenvironment.[69] Proteins that inhibit axonal growth limit regeneration in the spinal cord.[207] Bregman and associates have shown that blocking these proteins enhances regeneration.[39] Using experimental findings related to the potential for regeneration, Cheng and colleagues reported a promising new surgical treatment.[57] They bridged surgically created complete transection gaps of 5 mm in the spinal cord of the adult rat by using white matter–to–gray matter grafts of peripheral nerves. Up to 18 fine nerve implants bridged one gap. This procedure produced measurable structural and functional recovery, including the regeneration of pyramidal tract axons, hind limb movement, and weight support.

Neurons in the adult brain and spinal cord can survive after traumatic lesions but usually regress into an atrophic inactive state.[207] Transplants of embryonic cells or cells cultured from peripheral nerves or olfactory tracts can enhance the growth of transected spinal axons.[134] In these experiments, grafts of cells harvested from the olfactory nerve induced functionally useful regeneration in the surgically transected corticospinal tracts of rats. Administration of agents that block scar formation at the injury site may also produce functional regeneration.[237] A polysaccharide derived from group B streptococci, CM101, inhibited angiogenesis, as well as infiltration of inflammatory cells and scar formation. Intravenous administration of this agent dramatically improved walking ability and survival in mice paralyzed by a surgical crush lesion.

However, it is important to understand that human spinal injury differs from the experimental conditions in these regeneration experiments. A crushing neural injury in patients with spinal cord injury disrupts different structures than surgical transection does. For example,

TABLE 29–3 ....

Results of Randomized Controlled Clinical Trials for Treating Spinal Cord Injury with Pharmacologic Agents[33, 34, 36, 93, 172–174]

Year	Intervention	Number of Patients	Treatment Groups	Neurologic Improvement	Functional Improvement
1984	Methylprednisolone	306	High dose Low dose	No	Not measured
1990	**Methylprednisolone**	487	**Methylprednisolone** Naloxone Placebo	**Yes**	Not measured
1991	**GM₁ ganglioside**	34	**GM₁** Placebo	**Yes**	Not measured
1995	Thyrotropin-releasing hormone (TRH)	20	TRH Placebo	No	Not measured
1997	Tirilazad	499	Methylprednisolone for 24 hr **Methylprednisolone for 48 hr** Methylprednisolone + tirilazad	**Yes**	**No**
1998	Calcium channel blocking agent (nimodipine)	166	Nimodipine Methylprednisolone Both	No	Not measured
1998	Potassium channel blocking agent (fampridine SR)	26	Fampridine SR Placebo	Yes	No

traversing axons are frequently preserved in crush injuries. In addition, the local biologic responses may be different. Surgical interventions to promote healing must be tempered by concern for further iatrogenic injury.

Effects of Pharmacologic Treatment

The complexity of the chain of interdependent secondary events that follow a spinal cord injury makes it difficult to determine the optimal interruption point for preserving neurologic function.[207] The secondary responses to spinal injury are reparative and, conversely, contributory to additional injury. Interrupting the cascade of events has the potential to change either aspect of the physiologic response. Experimental treatments have investigated agents that block specific pathophysiologic events occurring after the injury, but only a few of these treatment interventions have shown sufficient promise in laboratory studies to prompt clinical trials[33, 35, 36, 93, 173, 174] (Table 29–3). A critical component missing from these trials is measurement of clinically meaningful functional changes. The National Acute Spinal Cord Injury Study (NASCIS) found evidence of sufficient neurologic improvement with the early administration of high-dose methylprednisolone. They hoped to establish this intervention as the standard for acute care of spinal cord injury patients[33, 35–37, 156, 193–195] (Table 29–4). The NASCIS trials demonstrated that large-scale, high-quality randomized clinical trials are methodologically feasible, even when addressing difficult problems such as the emergency management of spinal cord injury. This achievement is as significant for future work in this area as the clinical impact of the study findings.

Administering high doses of methylprednisolone produced a protective dose-response curve against neurologic injury in animal experiments.[38] The most benefit is seen in the first 8 hours, with additional effect occurring within the first 24 hours.[105] Three large-scale randomized clinical trials investigated methylprednisolone in the treatment of spinal cord injury. The first trial compared low-dose with high-dose methylprednisolone administered within 48

hours of injury.[33] The results showed no difference in outcome but an increased infection rate in the high-dose group. The second trial compared methylprednisolone (30 mg/kg loading dose given intravenously over 1 hour, followed by 5.4 mg/kg/hr intravenously for 23 hours) with naloxone and placebo.[35] Statistically significant improvement in motor and sensory scores in both complete and incomplete injuries occurred in the group given methylprednisolone.[32, 34] However, careful reassessment of the data from that trial and others seems to suggest that there were no useful differences in function achieved and that the differences seen were not statistically significant.

Lazaroids are 21-aminosteroid free radical scavengers.[7] The lazaroid 21-aminosteroid U7-4006F also inhibits membrane peroxidation.[107] Gangliosides are large glycolipid molecules found on the outer surface of most cell membranes.[93] They are highly concentrated in neural tissue and involved in immunologic processes, binding, transport, and nerve cytogenesis. Gangliosides have a trophic effect on nerve cells and stimulate dendritic outgrowth and neuronal recovery.

MECHANISMS OF CERVICAL SKELETAL INJURY

Injuries to the lower cervical spine or the spinal cord usually occur indirectly as the result of a blow to the cranium or from rapid head deceleration. Mechanisms of

TABLE 29–4 ....

Summary Recommendations of the Three National Acute Spinal Cord Injury Studies for Methylprednisolone Administration in Treatment of Acute Spinal Cord Injury

Methylprednisolone bolus, 30 mg/kg, then infusion at 5.4 mg/kg/hr
Infusion for 24 hr if bolus given within 3 hr of injury
Infusion for 48 hr if bolus given within 3 to 8 hr after injury
No benefit if methylprednisolone started more than 8 hr after injury
No benefit with naloxone
No benefit with tirilazad

injury include flexion, axial loading, rotation, and extension. Fracture patterns depend on vertebral alignment at the time of injury, the force vector, and the physical characteristics of the patient. Muscle contraction, either voluntary or reflexive, requires a much longer time interval than available between impact and spinal injury.

A description of the mechanism of injury is based on the magnitude and direction of forces applied to the head and neck complex. These forces include both direct force from impaction onto the cranium or neck and indirect force from rapid deceleration of the thorax or head and neck. An important concept is the major injury vector, which describes the type of injury and aids in the specific fracture classification.[249] Common injury vectors are flexion, compression, rotation, and extension. In reality, many injuries occur in combination. The patterns of injury are related not only to the magnitude and direction of the applied force but also to the position or attitude of the head and neck at the time of injury.

The dynamics of cervical spine injury are extraordinarily complex.[160, 181] In different situations and different victims, the same injury mechanism can result in different cervical spine injury patterns.[159] For impact injuries, vertebral column failure precedes any measurable head motion (see Fig. 29–5). The local vertebral alignment at the level of injury and the magnitude of impact force determine the pattern of cervical injury. Head deflection occurs secondarily. In general, cervical fractures and fracture-dislocations occur without head contact in restrained front seat occupants of motor vehicle crashes.[114] These observations explain a fundamental problem of spinal injury classification when based on presumed injury mechanisms: the same injury mechanism may result in morphologically different injuries, and patterns of head deflection do not predict spinal injury patterns.

Attempts to determine the specific forces applied to the spine as based on radiographs taken after injury have significant limitations. These limitations can lead to incorrect conclusions.

Events occurring at the time of injury are not necessarily reflected in subsequent static anatomic assessment of the injured tissues.[51] As Carter and co-workers observed, the transient canal occlusion occurring during a burst fracture of the vertebral body greatly exceeds the canal occlusion observed radiographically in postinjury measurements. This observation provides one explanation for the lack of correlation in clinical studies between radiographic assessment of canal occlusion and loss of neurologic function. Postinjury positioning of the cervical spine also influences spinal canal geometry. Axial compression and extension diminish canal volume.[58] Applying cervical traction and preventing neck extension in injured patients may decrease further cord compression and additional mechanical injury.

At low loading rates, spinal column structures fail through the soft tissues.[145] Rotation contributes to disc injury.[188] In both flexion and extension, the posterior longitudinal ligament and facet capsules provide the greatest resistance to disruption (Fig. 29–6). Panjabi and colleagues discovered that the functional spinal unit is stable if all anterior plus one posterior structure is intact or if all posterior plus one anterior structure is intact.[170] Bilateral facet dislocation requires rupture of the inter-

spinous ligament, rupture of both capsules, rupture of the posterior longitudinal ligament, rupture of the anulus fibrosus, or any combination of these injuries.[17] Although damage to the anterior elements can also occur with unilateral facet dislocation, the disc and contralateral facet capsule are usually intact in these injuries. That these structures remain intact can make closed reduction difficult.[192]

Impact Compression Injuries

Compression injuries appear to result from axial loading forces combined with resultant comminution of the vertebral bodies or posterior elements.[209] Although wedge compression fractures can result from hyperflexion mechanisms, they are grouped with impact compression injuries because of their involvement with the vertebral body. Compression injuries are commonly observed after accidents during diving, football games, and vehicular crashes and after accidents involving trampolines. The injury pattern observed depends on the initial head position at impact. If the head and neck were flexed during the accident, anterior dislocation may be seen. If the head was in a neutral position, wedge, compression, or burst fractures generally occur.[209] Buckling plus shortening of the spinal column in impact injuries causes a relative loss of volume of the spinal canal because of infolding of the soft tissue structures. This shortening can lead to a greater degree of spinal cord injury than explained by the original cervical fractures.[159, 160, 260]

In burst fractures, compressive loading increases intradiscal pressure until failure of the superior end-plate results. End-plate failure causes displacement of the disc into the vertebral body and creates a vertebral compression fracture.[188] The large force created in the vertebral body by the displaced disc causes the vertebral body to explode and results in a burst fracture. Bone fragments are displaced in all directions, including into the spinal canal.

Flexion Acceleration Injuries

Hyperflexion injuries occur when the head is rotated over the trunk beyond the physiologic limits of the bone and ligament components of the cervical spine. These injuries occur most commonly in victims of vehicular crashes. During hyperflexion, the distraction or tensile forces created in the posterior ligamentous structures cause rupture to occur in a posterior-to-anterior direction. During injuries involving rapid deceleration of the head, distractive flexion forces result in facet dislocation and longitudinal ligament disruption. Hyperflexion can also result in compression failure of the vertebral body in association with disruption of the posterior ligament.[209]

Extension Acceleration Injuries

Hyperextension injuries associated with whiplash are by far the most common injury in victims of vehicular crashes. Car crashes result in many vertebral and soft tissue injuries, including muscular avulsion and hemorrhage in the deep muscles of the anterior aspect of the neck, occult fractures, facet joint injuries, and injuries to the intervertebral disc. Extension injuries also occur in falls in which the victim strikes the front area of the head

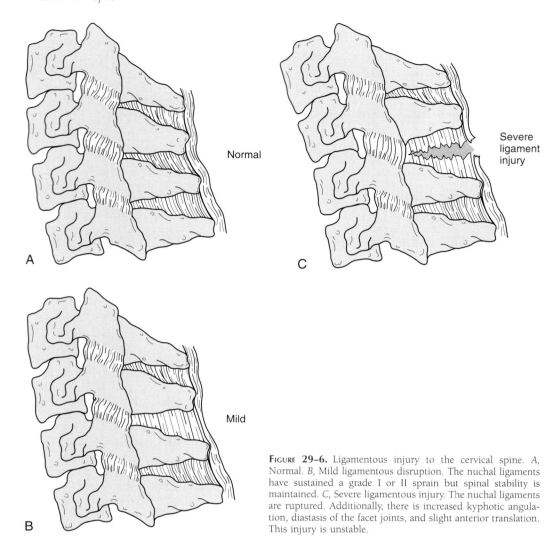

Normal

Mild

Severe
ligament
injury

FIGURE 29–6. Ligamentous injury to the cervical spine. *A,* Normal. *B,* Mild ligamentous disruption. The nuchal ligaments have sustained a grade I or II sprain but spinal stability is maintained. *C,* Severe ligamentous injury. The nuchal ligaments are ruptured. Additionally, there is increased kyphotic angulation, diastasis of the facet joints, and slight anterior translation. This injury is unstable.

or face. Therefore, extension acceleration injuries are highly associated with maxillofacial injuries. Because of the transient narrowing of the spinal canal that occurs with hyperextension, significant spinal cord injuries can occur even with a minimal amount of obvious skeletal injury.[206]

During forced hyperextension, compression of the posterior elements can cause isolated fractures of the lamina, the spinous processes, the articular pillars, and the pedicles (Fig. 29–7).[249] These fractures are generally

stable as long as vertebral body displacement is not present. If the buttressing effect to resist anterior translation of the lateral mass is lost, the extension moment can continue anteriorly across the disc and result in forward translation of the vertebral bodies.[5, 110] This injury may appear similar to a bilateral facet dislocation, but it has instead occurred from an extension moment. Such an injury is highly unstable and should be treated similar to a hyperflexion bilateral facet dislocation. However, the surgeon must note that extension injuries can produce

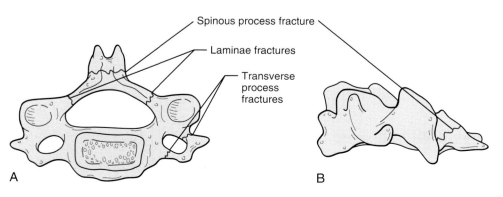

Spinous process fracture

Laminae fractures

Transverse process fractures

FIGURE 29–7. Isolated fractures of the posterior element. *A,* Axial view. *B,* Lateral view.

significant comminution of the posterior column, thus making posterior fixation more difficult.

With more significant force, the extension moment can cause posterior displacement of the vertebral body into the spinal canal. This injury is commonly referred to as a hyperextension dislocation or traumatic retrolisthesis. When this condition occurs, the spinal cord is pinched between the posterior of the body above and the lamina below. Because the longitudinal ligaments are injured, this injury is difficult to reduce and the reduction is difficult to maintain. Hyperextension injury associated with central cord syndrome was classically described as occurring in patients with stable, stenotic, or spondylotic spines[206, 227] (Fig. 29–8). Closer observations have identified that many patients with hyperextension dislocation or traumatic retrolisthesis have small amounts of posterior translation (2 to 3 mm of retrolisthesis) that are reducible with traction.[31, 139] MRI has demonstrated disc and posterior ligamentous disruption at the site of spinal cord injury, which is indicative of a more significant amount of instability. Although initially thought to cause a central cord syndrome, a variety of spinal cord injury syndromes can result from this mechanism.[139] Despite minimal

findings on radiographs, each patient should be treated initially with traction.

Combined Mechanisms

Real-world injuries are more complex than the injury mechanisms modeled in laboratories. Certainly, the laboratory concepts of impact, flexion, and extension forces help us understand the potential deformation that may have occurred locally at the injured vertebral levels during the injury event. However, most real-life injuries are a result of complex, combined forces. These specific combinations of forces are responsible for the inordinately wide variety of injury patterns. Combined forces are also a factor in real-life injuries and remain difficult to simulate in laboratory circumstances. For example, flexion combined with rotation is the probable mechanism of unilateral facet dislocation.[188] Flexion combined with axial loading forces results in flexion teardrop fractures.[205] Flexion teardrop fractures are common in tackling injuries in football players and occur when the neck is flexed. When flexed, the neck creates a straight spinal column, which is then forcibly loaded in compression. Flexion teardrop injuries are high-energy injuries that result in

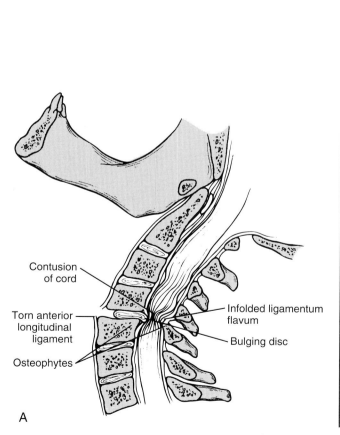 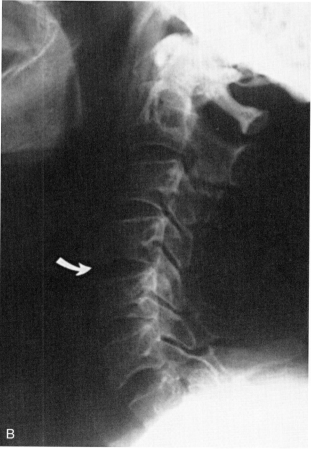

Contusion of cord
Torn anterior longitudinal ligament
Osteophytes
Infolded ligamentum flavum
Bulging disc

A

B

FIGURE 29–8. Hyperextension injuries to the lower cervical spine are somewhat less frequent than other injuries and occur in a different population than the majority of acute cervical spine injuries. Generally the elderly patient falls and strikes the front of the head, hyperextending the spine. *A,* The cervical cord may be pinched between an infolded and buckled ligamentum flavum and lamina posteriorly and cervical osteophytes anteriorly. *B,* The only apparent findings on a post-injury radiograph, such as this from a 65-year-old woman with Brown-Séquard syndrome, are small avulsion fractures of the anteroinferior portion of the vertebral body *(arrow).*

bony and ligamentous disruption both anteriorly and posteriorly.

When distraction is combined with hyperextension, the anterior longitudinal ligament is initially loaded and may fail. When viewed radiographically, subtle widening of the intervertebral disc may be observed. Such widening is usually associated with soft tissue swelling. More commonly, a small avulsion fracture of the anteroinferior corner of the vertebral body occurs.[90, 129] This injury is an extension teardrop fracture and must be distinguished from a flexion–axial loading teardrop fracture. In contrast to flexion teardrop injuries, an extension teardrop fracture is a stable injury that requires minimal external bracing for treatment. Extension teardrop fractures occur most commonly at C2.

Clinical Patterns of Lower Cervical Spine Injury

Classification systems are useful in facilitating communication between physicians and researchers, determining the prognosis, and directing treatment. Several systems have been developed for use in classifying injuries to the cervical spine, although none has been uniformly accepted.

NEURAL INJURY PATTERNS

Spinal Cord Injury

Neural injuries are classified by both their anatomic location and the severity of the injury. Generally, isolated nerve root injuries do not change the treatment algorithm. This condition is different from the classification of spinal cord injuries. When the spinal cord is injured, the damage itself is the primary determinant of treatment and, often, the entire course of trauma treatment for the patient as a whole. The classification terms for spinal cord injury have been well defined[142] (Table 29–5). Similarly, other general terminology is widely used in the spinal cord injury literature, most of which is without consistent definition. To understand discussions of spinal cord injury, it is important to differentiate between the two etiologic components of the injury. The first is the primary injury that results from the mechanical forces causing tissue disruption. The second component is the secondary injury that results from pathophysiologic responses triggered by mechanical tissue disruption. The gross pathologic changes at the cord tissue level are sometimes described by the extent of tissue disruption. Such disruption includes changes caused by concussion (physiologic disruption without structural anatomic changes), tissue contusion (hemorrhage or edema), or laceration (physical discontinuity of cord tissue). The physiologic response to injury and the clinical course of injured patients are often described in temporal terms, such as acute (first few hours), subacute (hours to days), and chronic (weeks to months). Finally, the functional severity of the neurologic injury is defined by designations of clinical syndromes of spinal cord injury (complete, incomplete, or transient) or by the clinical pattern of neurologic dysfunction in incomplete cord injuries (central, anterior, posterior, and Brown-Séquard cord syndromes or cruciate paralysis).[238]

Transient Tetraplegia

Patients with a narrow cervical canal may experience transient spinal cord dysfunction after impact injuries. The occurrence of these symptoms correlates with the presence of a narrow spinal canal, measured as a ratio of the space available for the spinal cord divided by the diameter of the corresponding vertebral body (Pavlov's ratio). A ratio less than 0.8 designates a congenitally narrow spinal canal. Individuals with such narrow canals typically report an inability to sense or move the extremities for a short period lasting from a few seconds to as long as 10 to 15 minutes. This interval is usually followed by full neurologic recovery. These patients frequently have a history of "stingers" or "burners," which are transient episodes of dysesthesia in the extremities after impact collisions of the head and neck.

TABLE 29–5		

Clinical Patterns of Incomplete Spinal Cord Injury

Syndrome	Lesion	Clinical Findings
Bell's cruciate paralysis	Long tract injury at the level of decussation in the brain stem	Variable cranial nerve involvement, greater upper extremity weakness than lower, greater proximal weakness than distal
Anterior cord	Anterior gray matter, descending corticospinal motor tract, and spinothalamic tract injury with preservation of the dorsal columns	Variable motor and pain and temperature sensory loss with preservation of proprioception and deep pressure sensation
Central cord	Incomplete cervical white matter injury	Sacral sparing and greater weakness in the upper limbs than the lower limbs
Brown-Séquard	Injury to one lateral half of the cord and preservation of the contralateral half	Ipsilateral motor and proprioception loss and contralateral pain and temperature sensory loss
Conus medullaris	Injury to the sacral cord (conus) and lumbar nerve roots within the spinal canal	Areflexic bladder, bowel, and lower limbs. May have preserved bulbocavernosus and micturition reflexes
Cauda equina	Injury to the lumbosacral nerve roots within the spinal canal	Areflexic bladder, bowel, and lower limbs
Root injury	Avulsion or compression injury to single or multiple nerve roots (brachial plexus avulsion)	Dermatomal sensory loss, myotomal motor loss, and absent deep tendon reflexes

Radiculopathy

Isolated nerve root deficits are associated with unilateral facet injuries and disc herniations. Symptoms are confined to a dermatomal distribution of one or several cervical nerve roots and consist of numbness, weakness, and decreased deep tendon reflexes. Fortunately, the prognosis for neurologic recovery is good in isolated root deficit situations. Involvement of several or all the roots on one side may signify avulsion injuries of the brachial plexus. This injury is more complex than an isolated root deficit and usually has a worse prognosis that may result in little or no neurologic recovery.

SKELETAL INJURY PATTERNS

The anatomic characteristics of the lower cervical vertebrae predispose them to certain patterns of structural disruption that are specific to this region. Although these patterns are generally recognized by spine surgeons, the classification systems described in the literature on lower cervical spine injuries are quite variable. The classifications are commonly based on injury groups and then further divided by the presumed mechanism of injury. However, classification systems also include descriptions based on damaged anatomic structures. None of the commonly cited classification schemes has been validated and standardized for reproducibility or for their ability to predict the most effective treatment or the treatment results. Despite this serious limitation, a classification system remains necessary to establish a common ground for discussing evaluation and treatment.

The most important classification is based on the concept of stability. Stability is best defined according to White and Panjabi as "loss of ability of the spine under physiologic loads to maintain relationships in such a way that there is neither damage nor subsequent irritation of the spinal cord or nerve roots and . . . no incapacitating deformity or pain".[250] Nicoll correlated fracture patterns with outcome and recognized that stable fractures heal and allow patients to return to work.[158] He recognized that fractures with disruptions of the posterior osteoligamentous structures were generally unstable. Holdsworth confirmed Nicoll's observations.[113] He furthered the understanding of fracture mechanics by dividing the spine into two columns. According to his classification, the anterior column includes the vertebral body, disc, and longitudinal ligaments, whereas the posterior column is the neural arch and associated posterior ligamentous structures. Stable injuries involve only one column, and unstable injuries involve damage to both columns. The two-column framework is very appropriate when considering the subaxial cervical spine.

White and Panjabi[250] performed cadaveric testing of human cervical spines and confirmed Holdsworth's two-column theory. Additionally, they defined parameters that can be used to determine clinical instability. Experimentally, they serially sectioned ligamentous structures in a posterior-to-anterior and in an anterior-to-posterior direction. The specimens had flexion and extension moments applied after each ligament division, and then kyphotic and angular displacements were measured. Significant increases in translation or vertebral angulation occurred

when all posterior ligamentous structures and a single anterior structure were sectioned, as well as when all anterior structures and a single posterior structure were sectioned. When the spine became unstable, 3.5 mm of anterior translation and 11° of increased kyphotic angulation were observed (Fig. 29–9). On the basis of these experiments and other clinical observations, they developed a checklist to quantitatively assess cervical stability (Table 29–6). To use the checklist, each element is assessed and assigned a value of either 1 or 2 if present or 0 if absent. If the sum of all values is 5 or greater, the spine is probably unstable, but such instability does not indicate that the patient should have surgical treatment. However, in acute situations, a score of 5 or more probably means that the patient should be treated with at least a halo brace. This checklist is not uniformly accepted, nor is it clinically validated, but it does provide a useful framework to quantify the degree of stability. Injuries are placed into three divisions based on the location of the most significant point of injury. The three divisions are the posterior column, the facet articulations, and the anterior column. In general, stable injuries are isolated to one region of the spine, whereas unstable injuries involve two or all three divisions.

At our trauma institution, we use a general classification scheme for injuries to the lower cervical spine that is modeled on three broad treatment categories. Our categories include minimal external immobilization (soft or hard collar), maximal external immobilization (halo device), or surgical treatment (Table 29–8). Injury patterns characteristic of the lower cervical vertebrae also apply to the first thoracic vertebra. The American Spinal Injury Association (ASIA) impairment scale should be mentioned as well (Table 29–9).

Soft Tissue Injury

Rapid hyperflexion of the head and neck creates large tensile forces on the posterior ligamentous structures and causes a variable amount of sprain of the nuchal ligaments (see Fig. 29–8). Large forces are usually needed to create these injuries, except in elderly patients, who because of age-related degeneration, may have more brittle ligaments. Once injured, the vertebra is free to rotate in flexion over the next caudal segment, thereby resulting in kyphotic angulation. Additionally, anterior translation can occur if the tensile forces have injured the anterior structures, such as the posterior longitudinal ligament or the disc annulus.

The severity of the posterior ligamentous disruption can be graded as mild or severe. In mild injuries, the forces have resulted in partial ligament disruption, and stability is still maintained. Clinically, patients have focal tenderness but no neurologic signs or symptoms. Radiographically, slight widening may be seen between the spinous processes, but no kyphosis or anterior translation is apparent. Neither hemorrhage nor increased signal intensity is noted with MRI technology. Objectively, patients have fewer than 5 points on the White and Panjabi checklist, and therefore their condition is considered clinically stable.

With increased hyperflexion, complete disruption of the posterior osteoligamentous complex may occur. Again, patients have focal tenderness. A gap is often present in

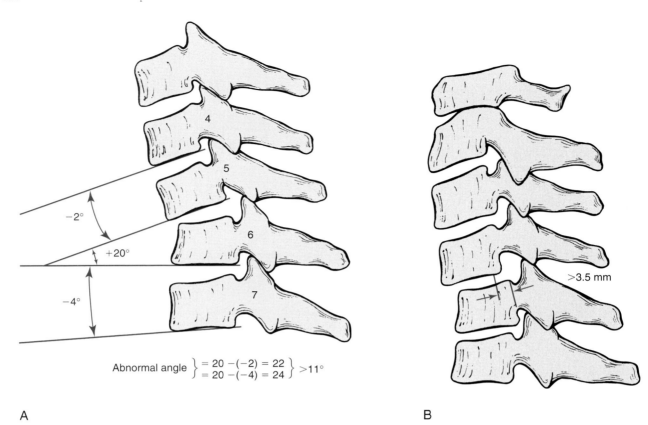

$$\text{Abnormal angle} \left. \begin{array}{c} = 20 - (-2) = 22 \\ = 20 - (-4) = 24 \end{array} \right\} > 11°$$

A   B

Figure 29–9. *A,* White and co-workers demonstrated that angular displacements of 11° greater than those at the adjacent vertebral segments suggest instability secondary to posterior ligamentous disruption. *B,* In addition, vertebral body translation greater than 3.5 mm similarly suggests ligamentous instability even in the absence of fracture. (*A* and *B,* Redrawn from White, A.; et al. Spine 3:12, 1978.)

such injuries to the thoracolumbar junction, but it is less easily palpable in cases involving the cervical spine. Radiographs may show only subtle abnormalities. Local kyphosis, facet joint diastasis, malrotation of the facet joints, or interspinous widening may be present. If patients are positioned in extension for cervical radiographs, the

Table 29–6

Instability Checklist Proposed by White and Panjabi

Point Value	Criterion
2	Anterior elements destroyed or unable to function
2	Anterior elements destroyed or unable to function
2	Positive stretch test
	Flexion-extension radiographs
2	Sagittal plane translation > 3.5 mm or 20%
2	Sagittal plane rotation > 11°
	Resting radiographs
2	Sagittal plane displacement 3.5 mm or 20%
2	Relative sagittal plane angulation > 20°
1	Abnormal disc narrowing
1	Developmentally narrow spinal canal (sagittal diameter < 13 mm or Pavlov's ratio < 0.8)
2	Spinal cord damage
1	Nerve root damage
1	Dangerous anticipated loading

Point total of 5 or more = UNSTABLE INJURY → treat with prolonged immobilization or surgery.

kyphotic angulation may be reduced, thereby obscuring the presence of this injury. Interspinous widening is one of the most consistent findings in this sort of injury, but it is often overlooked. The widening may be better visualized on AP radiographs. The use of flexion-extension radiographs to assess stability and potential ligamentous injuries is a controversial subject. We personally recommend MRI with fat suppression technique to evaluate the posterior ligaments (Fig. 29–10). If these images demonstrate high-intensity signals between the spinous processes, our patients are treated as they would be for a severe ligamentous injury. Again, patients are evaluated with the White and Panjabi criteria; when the point value is greater than 5, they are considered to have an unstable severe ligamentous injury.

Nonspecific Soft Tissue Injury (Whiplash). Posterior ligamentous injuries most often result from hyperflexion and distractive forces, and more severe injuries occur when small degrees of rotation are added. Posterior ligamentous injuries proceed in a dorsal-to-ventral direction. The nuchal ligaments are injured first, followed by injury to the facet joint capsules, the ligamentum flavum, and the intervertebral disc. Clinically, a variable amount of ligamentous disruption may be observed and, therefore, varying degrees of instability.

No formal, clinically useful classification of these injury patterns has been universally accepted. Mild injuries are partial ligament injuries with focal tenderness but normal alignment and structural integrity. Moderate injuries have

TABLE 29–7

White and Panjabi's Guidelines for Applying Interpreting the Instability Checklist

GENERAL CONSIDERATIONS

The checklist is not validated in an applied clinical setting.
Checklist functions as a safety factor, like a pilot's checklist.
Checklist is helpful in determining which patients need surgery or prolonged immobilization.
Instability threshold is arbitrarily set at 5 to balance unnecessary surgery versus irreversible catastrophe.
If any criterion has a borderline decision, add 1/2 the value to the sum.
Checklist is not applicable to children < 7 years.

ANATOMIC CONSIDERATIONS

All anterior or all posterior elements destroyed → potentially unstable
Anterior elements destroyed → more unstable in flexion
Posterior elements destroyed → more unstable in extension
Developmentally narrow canal → lower threshold for neurologic problems with spinal injury

RADIOGRAPHIC CONSIDERATIONS

Translation measurement is based on a x-ray tube to film distance of 72 inches.
Sagittal plane translation: 3.5 mm on a static film or F/E views (3.5 mm = 2.7 mm lab value + 30% magnification) or ratio of (translation distance) / (vertebral body diameter) > 20%
Sagittal plane rotation: > 20° on F/E views or at least 11° more than FSU above or FSU below the level on a static view
Stretch test: more than 1.7 mm difference in interspace separation pre- and post-test or more than 7.5° angulation
Disc space height: disc narrowing may suggest annulus disruption and instability; disc space widening may also indicate annulus disruption and instability.
Canal width: canal AP diameter < 15 mm or Pavlov ratio < 0.80 (Pavlov ratio = (midlevel posterior vertebral body to nearest point on spinolaminar line) / (midlevel vertebral body AP diameter); normal ≥ 1)

NEUROLOGIC CONSIDERATIONS

If the trauma is severe enough to cause initial neurologic damage, the support structures have *probably* been altered sufficiently to allow subsequent neurologic damage, and the injury is clinically unstable.
Root involvement is a weaker indicator for clinical instability (one point) vs. cord injury (two points).

PHYSIOLOGIC CONSIDERATIONS

Anticipated dangerous loads are in occupations such as heavy laborer, contact sport athlete, or motorcyclist.
Intractable pain also indicates instability.

associated pain with some displacement. Radiographs show isolated kyphosis and spreading of the spinous processes. However, the displacements do not meet the criteria of White and Panjabi and produce a score of less than 5 on the clinical instability checklist. Severe cases are associated with pain and instability and complete ligament disruption. Radiographs demonstrate widening of the spinous processes, increased local kyphosis when compared with adjacent levels, small amounts of anterior subluxation, and facet subluxation or even facet perching. Severe posterior ligamentous injuries score greater than 5 on the clinical instability checklist. Posterior ligamentous injuries associated with vertebral body compression fracture are

highly unstable and, according to Webb and colleagues, frequently overlooked.[246]

Disruption of the Anterior Longitudinal Ligament. Hyperextension creates tensile forces in the anterior longitudinal ligament, occasionally resulting in failure (Fig. 29–11). This injury leads to failure of the anterior longitudinal ligaments and disc annulus. In cases involving more severe extension (50% or greater), retrolisthesis can occur. When retrolisthesis does develop, increased widening or excessive lordosis of the intervertebral disc will be visible radiographically. MRI will show high signal intensity in the disc and retropharyngeal spaces on T2-weighted images.

Traumatic Disc Disruption. Forced hyperextension with injury to the disc and longitudinal ligaments can result in traumatic retrolisthesis (see Fig. 29–11). Usually, only a subtle degree (2 to 3 mm) is present, and it is easily overlooked or else thought to be secondary to preexisting spondylosis. In patients with congenitally narrow spinal canals, even these small amounts of retrolisthesis can cause a significant amount of cord compression. Rarely, 50% or greater retrolisthesis develops. These injuries are highly unstable and difficult to reduce, and any reduction is difficult to maintain.

Extension injuries are frequently associated with 2 to 4 mm of posterior vertebral subluxation (Fig. 29–12). This injury has commonly been called traumatic retrolisthesis. Extension injuries are of intermediate instability. This degree of traumatic retrolisthesis may be difficult to differentiate from the retrolisthesis caused by degenerative changes. MRI with fat suppression can clearly identify traumatic discoligamentous injuries in questionable cases. Treatment of traumatic retrolisthesis is based on neurologic involvement. Patients who are neurologically intact may be

TABLE 29–8

General Categories of Spinal Column Disruption in the Lower Cervical Spine

Injury	General Treatment Category
Soft tissue injury	
Nonspecific soft tissue injury	*Soft collar*
Avulsion of the anterior longitudinal ligament	*Hard collar*
Traumatic disc disruption	*Surgery*
Isolated fractures	
Spinous process fracture	*Hard collar*
Transverse process fracture	*Hard collar*
Lamina fracture	*Hard collar*
Vertebral body injuries	
Extension teardrop fracture	*Hard collar*
Compression fracture	*Hard collar or halo device*
Burst fracture	*Halo device or surgery*
Flexion teardrop fracture	*Surgery*
Facet injuries	
Unilateral facet fracture	*Hard collar or surgery*
Lateral mass fracture-separation	*Hard collar or surgery*
Unilateral facet dislocation	*Surgery*
Bilateral facet dislocation	*Surgery*
Fracture-dislocations	
Shear fractures with displacement	*Surgery*
Distraction-dissociation injury	*Surgery*

TABLE 29–9 ....

ASIA Impairment Scale

Scale	Type of SCI	Description of SCI Pattern
A	Complete	No motor or sensory function in the lowest sacral segment (S4–S5)
B	Incomplete	Sensory function below neurologic level, and in S4–S5 no motor function below neurologic level
C	Incomplete	Motor function is preserved below neurologic level *and* more than half of the key muscle groups below neurologic level have a muscle grade < 3
D	Incomplete	Motor function is preserved below neurologic level *and* at least half of the key muscle groups below neurologic level have a muscle grade 3 or better
E	Normal	Sensory and motor functions are normal

Abbreviation: SCI, spinal cord injury.

treated in a collar or cervicothoracic brace, as outlined earlier. The height of the collar should be carefully assessed to avoid extension. Patients with a transient or persistent neurologic deficit should be placed in tongs traction and undergo MRI. If the neural deficits do not resolve, anterior discectomy and fusion with plate fixation are warranted.

Isolated Fractures

Isolated fractures of the spinous processes, lamina, and transverse processes occur frequently and are most often the result of major injury vectors (see Fig. 29–7). They are stable as long as the facet articulations are competent and no vertebral body translation is involved. Rarely, lamina fractures can be displaced into the spinal cord; when such displacement occurs, extraction is required. Isolated fractures of the pedicles are rare because the neural arch is usually broken in two places (Fig. 29–13).

Vertebral Body Injuries

Extension Teardrop Injury. Hyperextension can also result in an avulsion fracture of the anteroinferior vertebral body (see Chapter 28). This fracture is associated with discoligamentous disruption and occurs most commonly at the C2–C3 interspace. Such fractures have been termed extension teardrop fractures, and they must be differentiated from the flexion–axial loading teardrop fracture described by Lee, Schneider, and their co-workers.[129, 204] A frequent source of confusion is osteophyte formation. The osteophytes may be fractured or incompletely ossified and therefore called a fracture. MRI has been useful in identifying acute extension injuries that result in disc annular disruption.

Compression Fractures. Vertebral body compression fracture can occur from hyperflexion or axial loading (Fig. 29–14). When viewed radiographically, the body is wedge shaped, but the posterior vertebral body wall is intact. In isolated compression fractures the posterior osteoligamentous complex is also intact. These isolated fractures are stable. However, compression fractures frequently occur in association with disruption of the posterior ligaments; the disrupted ligaments are notoriously unstable and usually fail if treated nonoperatively.

Burst Fractures. Burst fractures are characterized by vertebral body comminution with retropulsion of the

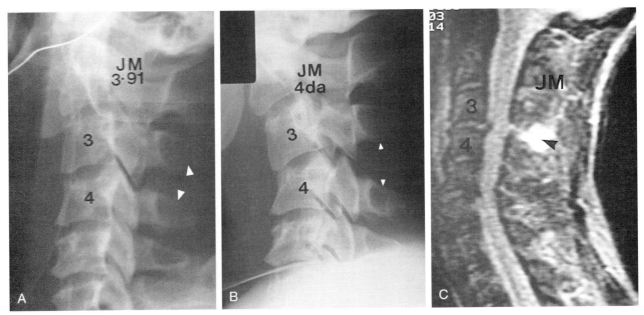

FIGURE 29–10. *A,* Initial radiograph shows minimal separation of the C3–C4 spinous processes *(arrowheads). B,* Upright radiograph 3 days later shows near-dislocation *(arrowheads)* despite immobilization in a collar. *C,* Magnetic resonance imaging (MRI) T2-weighted image demonstrates a high-intensity signal in the nuchal ligaments *(arrowhead)* due to edema and hemorrhage. A small traumatic disc herniation is seen ventral to the cord.

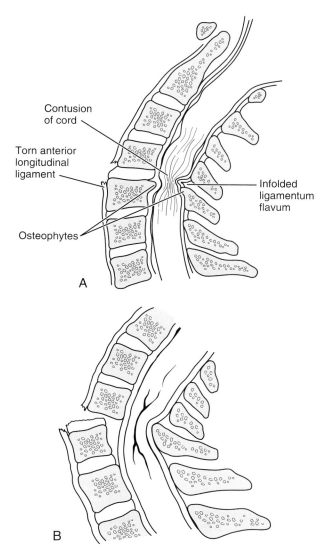

Contusion of cord

Torn anterior longitudinal ligament

Osteophytes

Infolded ligamentum flavum

A

B

FIGURE 29–11. Traumatic retrolisthesis is associated with disruption of the arterial longitudinal ligament and disc annulus, allowing varying degrees of posterior translation. *A,* In less-severe cases, 2 to 3 mm is present. *B,* In more severe cases, up to 50% retrolisthesis can occur. This causes compression of the spinal cord between the posterior body of the cranial vertebrae and the lamina of the caudal vertebrae. (*B,* Redrawn from Harris, J.H.; Yeakley, J.W. J Bone Joint Surg 74B:567–570, 1992; from Forsyth, H.F. J Bone Joint Surg Am 46:1792, 1964.)

fracture fragments into the spinal cord (Fig. 29–15). Viewed radiographically, both the anterior and posterior vertebral body height is shortened, and the interpedicular distance is widened. Burst fractures are associated with a variable amount of posterior ligamentous disruption, depending on the degree of flexion or distraction present during injury. If intraspinous widening is observed or if facet disruptions are present, the lesion should be considered unstable and treated surgically.

Flexion Teardrop Injury. A flexion teardrop fracture is a complex injury often associated with spinal cord injury.[204, 230] The teardrop is a small bony fragment located off the anteroinferior corner of the body that is rotated anteriorly (Fig. 29–16). More importantly, the vertebral body is fractured coronally and has undergone

posterior retrolisthesis into the spinal canal. Posteriorly, interspinous widening or comminution of the lamina and spinous processes is observed. Teardrop fractures are often seen in trauma from diving accidents and football injuries, and they are usually associated with significant spinal cord injury. The classic neurologic syndrome is anterior spinal cord injury with loss of all motor and sensory functions except proprioception. Teardrop fractures differ significantly from burst fractures in that the neural injury is due to the posteroinferior corner of the body rotating into the canal and not from retropulsion of the posterior body wall. In general, a teardrop fracture is more unstable than a burst fracture. Similar to burst fractures, varying degrees of instability of flexion teardrop injuries exist. Mild cases have less than 3 mm of vertebral body displacement and minimal disruption of the posterior ligaments. In more severe cases, the spine is unstable because of the combination of vertebral body displacement and disruption of the posterior ligaments.

Facet Injuries

Isolated Facet Fracture. Isolated fractures of the facet or lateral masses must be examined and observed with extraordinary care because they may represent a more unstable injury than first appreciated. These fractures are often missed on initial radiographs. They are best recognized from the lateral radiograph or sagittal CT reconstructed image. Isolated fractures not associated with any AP subluxation are stable. This may be deceiving as both the radiograph and the CT scan are done in the supine position and displacement may occur when the patient is upright. Missed facet fractures are the cause of chronic neck pain after trauma.

Lateral Mass Fracture-Separation. Fracture-separation of the lateral mass occurs from lateral extension and rotation forces[132, 198] (Fig. 29–17). Compressive forces on the lateral masses create fracturing of the pedicle and the lamina at its junction with the lateral mass. When a fracture occurs, the lateral mass is separated from the vertebral body and lamina and thus becomes free floating. The side becomes rotationally unstable and allows forward rotation of the vertebral bodies. All the facets of the lateral mass work to stabilize both at a cranial and caudal level, and when a fracture-separation takes place, two motion segments may be affected. Initially, minimal translation may be present, although progressive deformity can occur despite bracing. Radiographically, malrotation of the entire facet is visible from lateral views. The AP view demonstrates facet joints rotated into view in the articular pillars. Though easily visible, fracture of the lamina at the junction of the lateral mass is often overlooked.

Unilateral Facet Dislocation. Unilateral facet dislocations and unilateral facet fractures with subluxation have varying mechanisms of injury and prognosis (Fig. 29–18). Typically, unilateral facet fractures and dislocations result from exacerbated kinematics of the normal cervical spine.[209] In lateral bending and rotation, coupled motion enables one facet to move upward and the contralateral facet to move downward. The spinous process moves laterally toward the convexity of the curve. With excessive

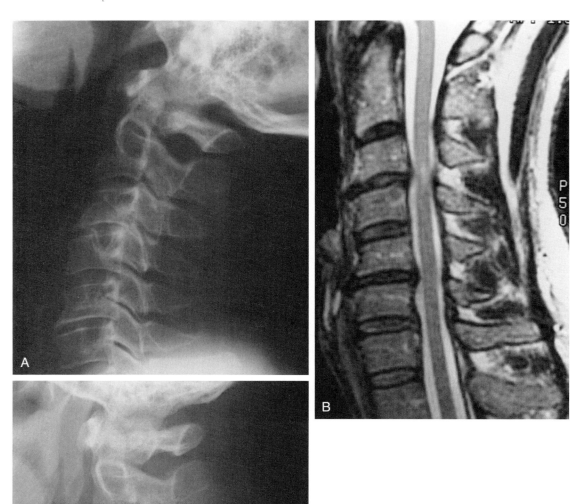

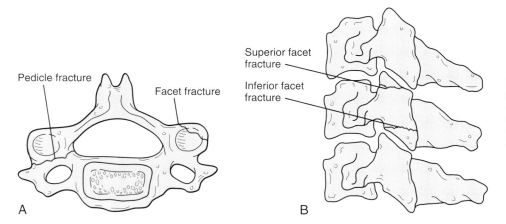

FIGURE 29–12. A 30-year-old patient sustained a central cord injury from hyperextension during a fall while skiing. *A*, Plain radiographs show 2-mm retrolisthesis with a congenitally small canal at C4–C5. *B*, Increased signal intensity in the spinal cord is seen on the MRI scan. *C*, Because of persistent neurologic deficits, an anterior decompression, fusion, and anterior plate fixation with cervical spine locking plate (CSLP) was performed.

Pedicle fracture

Facet fracture

Superior facet fracture

Inferior facet fracture

FIGURE 29–13. *A* and *B*, Isolated fractures of the pedicle and facet. These are usually stable. If pedicle fractures are associated with other posterior element injuries, the injury may prove to be unstable.

A

B

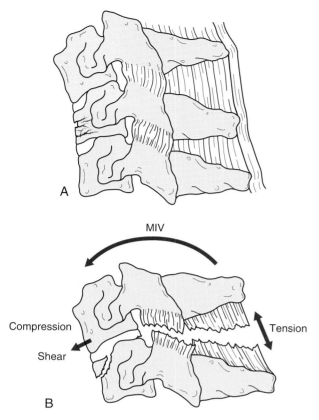

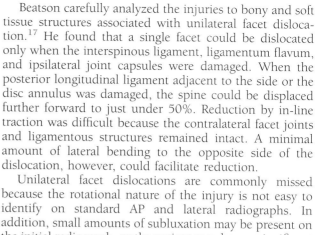

FIGURE 29–14. *A,* Stable vertebral body compression without involvement of the posterior osteoligamentous structures. *B,* Disruption of the posterior ligament creates a highly unstable fracture that usually will fail nonoperative treatment. *Abbreviation:* MIV, major injury vector. *(A,* Redrawn from Holdsworth, F. J Bone Joint Surg 45:6–20, 1963. *B,* Redrawn from White, A.A., III; Panjabi, M.M. In: White, A.A., III; Panjabi, M.M., eds. Clinical Biomechanics of the Spine, 2nd ed. Philadelphia, J.B. Lippincott, 1990, p. 225.)

force, one side of the neck will move too far inferiorly while the other moves too far craniad, thereby resulting in facet dislocation. Fractures of the facet articulation and occasionally the entire lateral mass are often present. These fractures result from the addition of shear or compressive forces, which cause excessive loading on the joint surfaces. Common causes of unilateral facet dislocation are trauma sustained in vehicular crashes and in athletics.

Beatson carefully analyzed the injuries to bony and soft tissue structures associated with unilateral facet dislocation.[17] He found that a single facet could be dislocated only when the interspinous ligament, ligamentum flavum, and ipsilateral joint capsules were damaged. When the posterior longitudinal ligament adjacent to the side or the disc annulus was damaged, the spine could be displaced further forward to just under 50%. Reduction by in-line traction was difficult because the contralateral facet joints and ligamentous structures remained intact. A minimal amount of lateral bending to the opposite side of the dislocation, however, could facilitate reduction.

Unilateral facet dislocations are commonly missed because the rotational nature of the injury is not easy to identify on standard AP and lateral radiographs. In addition, small amounts of subluxation may be present on the initial radiograph, or the patient may have a significant degree of spontaneous reduction. Unilateral facet dislocation occurs most commonly at C5–C6 and C6–C7, where visualization may be obscured by the overlying shoulders. In many cases, the injury is stable in the dislocated position, thereby minimizing pain.

Radiographic features include vertebral body displacement of about 25% (Fig. 29–19). Rarely, a minimal compression fracture of the caudal vertebral body is present. Interspinous widening is variable and depends on the amount of distraction, as well as the initial head and neck position. An important finding in diagnosing a unilateral facet dislocation is noticing asymmetry of the facets above and below the injury on the lateral view. Normally, the right and left facets are overlapping and viewed as a single unit on the lateral view. When a unilateral facet dislocation is present, the symmetry of the left and right facets is lost and both are visualized. Most commonly, two cranial facets are seen while the caudal facets are still overlapping and can be seen as a single facet. This arrangement creates the "bow tie" sign, which is pathognomonic for unilateral facet dislocation. The AP radiograph requires careful scrutiny because fractures of the pedicle or the laminar mass may be present. In this situation, the spinous processes are rotated to the side of the dislocation. If the facet is rotated into a flexed position, the joint surface is visualized in the articular pillar. Trauma oblique radiographs are useful in determining facet alignment and foraminal encroachment, but they must be performed without turning the patient's head. CT demon-

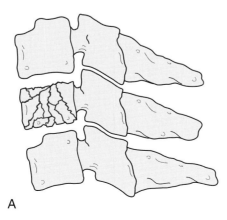

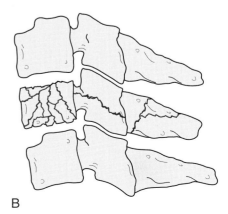

FIGURE 29–15. Cervical burst fractures are associated with comminution of the vertebral body with retropulsion into the spinal canal. *A,* In stable burst fractures, there is minimal involvement of the posterior osteoligamentous structures. *B,* In unstable burst fractures, there is fracturing or disruption of the posterior ligaments due to distractive forces.

A   B

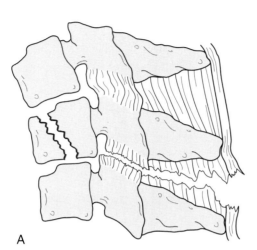

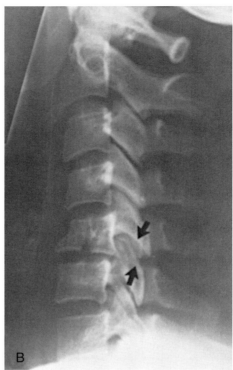

FIGURE 29–16. Axial loading injuries to the cervical spine have several variants. *A*, One common variant is a teardrop fracture. The injury is predominantly a flexion-axial loading injury resulting in an oblique fracture of the anterior portion of the body with the line of injury propagating through the vertebral body. It exits out through the posterior aspect of the disc at the injured level with disruption of the facet capsules and interspinous ligaments. *B*, Notice the spreading of the facets indicating disruption of the capsules (*arrows*).

strates fractures in more than 75% of cases. CT reformations in the sagittal and oblique planes show detailed alignment of the facets. MRI is useful in some cases to show foraminal encroachment, as well as the status of the intervertebral disc, which can be herniated into the spinal canal in up to 15% of cases.

Clinically, patients with a unilateral facet dislocation have pain, radiculopathy, a spinal cord injury, or any combination of these manifestations. Radiculopathies are easily overlooked and require careful upper extremity muscle and sensory testing. Palpation of gaps between spinous processes or malrotation of a spinous process is difficult in the cervical spine.

The variability in injury mechanisms, bony injuries, and their prognoses led Levine to the following tripart classification of unilateral facet dislocations. The first category is unilateral facet dislocation, the second is unilateral facet fracture with subluxation, and the third is fracture-separation of the lateral mass.[130] Each category is characterized by subluxation with 10% to 25% displacement of the vertebral body and rotation of the spinous process to the side of the facet subluxation.

Unilateral facet dislocations (see Fig. 29–18A) occur less frequently than fractures. Twenty-five percent of vertebral body translation is present in dislocations, and spinal cord injury occurs in up to 25% of cases. These dislocations may be difficult to reduce with cranial traction, but fortunately, they may be stable after reduction.

Unilateral facet fractures with subluxation occur in up to 80% of cases[130] (see Fig. 29–18C). They are associated more commonly with fractures of the superior facet and less frequently with fractures of the inferior facet (see Fig. 29–19). Although these two fractures result from different

mechanisms, both are unstable because the inadequate facet makes the spine unable to prevent anterior shear or rotation to the ipsilateral side. Unlike unilateral facet dislocations, these two fracture types do not usually involve any juxtaposition of the relationship of the anterior and posterior portions of the joint. Instead, rotational deformity carries the fragment forward. Both fracture types generally reduce anatomically with axial traction.

Bilateral Facet Dislocation. Bilateral facet dislocations (Fig. 29–20) result from several mechanisms, most often hyperflexion in combination with some rotation.[250] Allen and associates described these injuries as distraction flexion stage III and distraction flexion stage IV lesions.[5] Roaf created various spinal injuries in cadaveric models and found that pure hyperflexion resulted in compression fractures of the vertebral body.[188] He also discovered that small amounts of rotation pretensed the ligaments, thereby allowing bilateral facet dislocations to occur with much lower force. Others have created bilateral facet dislocations by compressive loading onto the skull with the neck placed in slight flexion.[209] This mechanism occurs frequently in young athletes. Regardless of the mechanism of injury, bilateral facet dislocations are highly unstable injuries and are associated with neurologic deficit in most cases. Dissection of cadavers demonstrates a significant injury to all posterior ligamentous structures and the posterior longitudinal ligament and disc annulus. The anterior longitudinal ligament is often the only structure that remains intact.

Injuries to the disc annulus are of special importance. When injured, the annulus is avulsed from its vertebral attachments, and the nucleus pulposus and portions of the annulus and end-plate can then retropulse into the spinal canal and further compress neural tissues (Fig. 29–21).

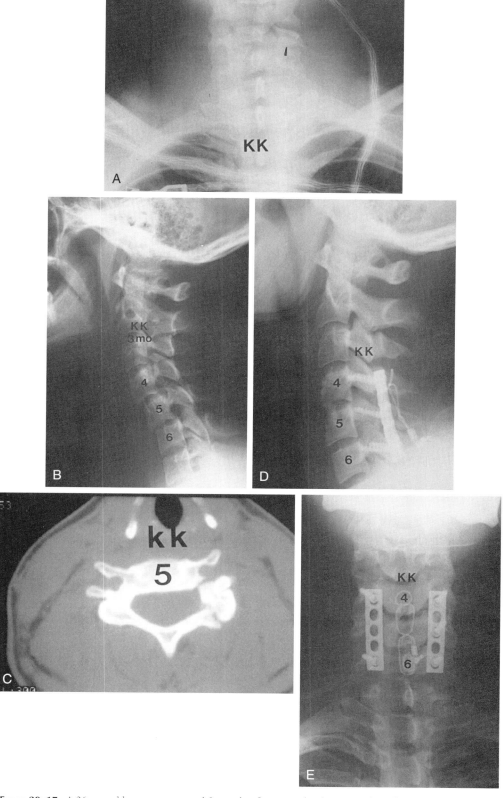

FIGURE 29–17. A 26-year-old woman presented 3 months after severe head injury with neck pain and bilateral C6 radiculopathy. *A,* On the initial chest radiograph, the C5 lateral mass is rotated into the plane of the x-ray beam because fractures of the pedicle and lamina create a fracture-separation of the lateral mass. *B,* The lateral radiograph 3 months later shows subluxation of C4–C5 and C5–C6. *C,* The axial computed tomography (CT) scan demonstrates the pedicle and lateral mass fractures. *D, E,* After reduction, she was treated by a lateral mass fixation using AO reconstruction plates. Her neurologic deficits completely resolved after the stabilization procedure.

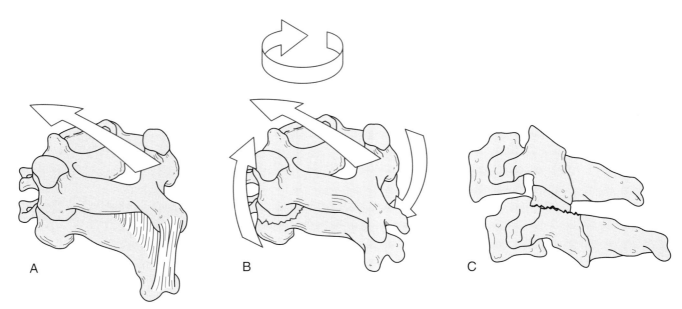

FIGURE 29–18. *A,* Facet fractures and dislocations in the cervical spine are a result of a combination of flexion and rotational forces. Depending on the relative relationship of the amount of flexion and rotation, either a facet fracture or a dislocation may occur. When the forces are predominantly rotational, without a significant flexion force, a unilateral facet fracture can occur. *B,* However, when the rotation is preceded by flexion, so that the facets are at least partially disengaged before the rotational force is applied, a unilateral facet dislocation results. *C,* Unilateral facet fracture-dislocation. Fracture of the superior articular facet with subluxation. (*B, C,* Redrawn from White, A.A., III; Panjabi, M.M. In: White, A.A., III; Panjabi, M.M. eds. Clinical Biomechanics of the Spine, 2nd ed. Philadelphia, J.B. Lippincott, 1990.)

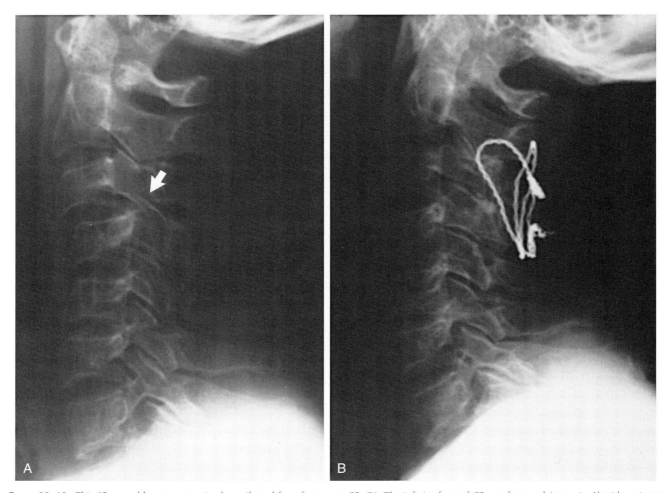

FIGURE 29–19. This 63-year-old woman sustained a unilateral facet fracture at C3–C4. The inferior facet of C3 was fractured (*arrow* in *A*) with an intact superior facet of C4. This is a less common pattern. A single level of oblique wiring cannot be done, as the wire needs to be passed through the inferior facet of the level above, which in this case is fractured. *A,* The oblique wire construct was extended to the inferior facet of C2, and an interspinous wire was used to augment the stability of the construct in flexion. *B,* Follow-up radiograph at 1 year demonstrates a solid arthrodesis with anatomic alignment.

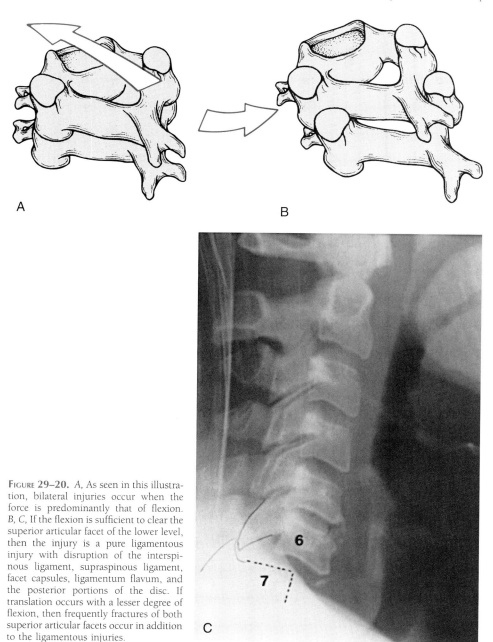

FIGURE 29–20. *A,* As seen in this illustration, bilateral injuries occur when the force is predominantly that of flexion. *B, C,* If the flexion is sufficient to clear the superior articular facet of the lower level, then the injury is a pure ligamentous injury with disruption of the interspinous ligament, supraspinous ligament, facet capsules, ligamentum flavum, and the posterior portions of the disc. If translation occurs with a lesser degree of flexion, then frequently fractures of both superior articular facets occur in addition to the ligamentous injuries.

MRI has documented that 10% to 40% of patients with bilateral facet dislocations have associated disc herniations.[75, 80, 186] However, significant disc herniations with cord compression occur much less frequently. Usually, the disc material and cartilaginous end-plate are behind the body and located under the posterior longitudinal ligament. Patients with disc herniations may deteriorate after closed reduction.

Bilateral facet dislocations have 50% vertebral body translation on lateral radiographs. Fracturing of the posterior elements occurs in more than 80% of cases. Abnormal disc space narrowing is an ominous sign and often associated with disc herniation.[250] The spine is kyphotic, and widening between the spinous processes is usually present. Bilateral laminar fractures or fractures in the spinous processes are frequent and complicate posterior fixation. Fracturing of the facets is common and often results in the combination of a facet dislocation on one side and fracture of the facet with displacement on the other. Rarely, bilateral pedicle fractures are present and create a spondylolisthetic condition that is difficult to reduce.[146]

With more severe distraction forces, the dislocation can increase to 100% or result in vertical separation between vertebral bodies. These lesions are dangerous because skull tongs traction will not be useful and can in fact result in further neurovascular injury. These injuries also appear to be associated with an increased likelihood of neuro-

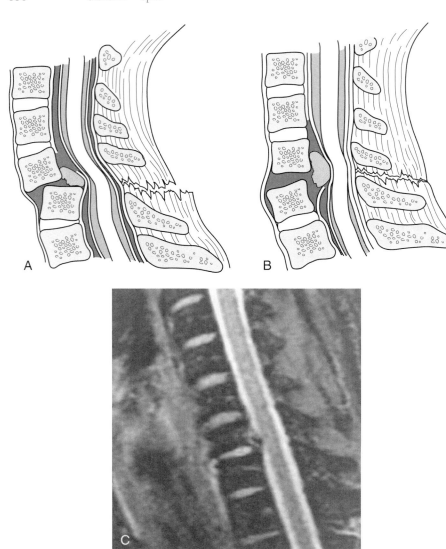

FIGURE **29–21.** *A,* A bilateral disc facet dislocation with the intervertebral disc displaced into the spinal canal. *B,* After reduction, the disc is causing spinal cord compression. *C,* This midsagittal MRI scan demonstrates postreduction disc herniation into the spinal canal. The patient sustained a bilateral facet dislocation in the lower cervical spine and was neurologically intact on presentation. Closed reduction was done, but complete anatomic restoration of alignment was not possible. However, the patient remained neurologically intact. Therefore, before surgical stabilization, an MRI scan was obtained to determine the cause of incomplete reduction. This image demonstrates disruption of the posterior longitudinal ligament and disc herniation sufficient to minimally compress the anterior surface of the cord. Note also the stripping of the anterior longitudinal ligament from the surface of the bodies. (*A, B,* Redrawn by permission of the publisher from Cervical intervertebral disc prolapse associated with traumatic facet dislocations by Berrington, N.R.; van Staden, J.F.; Willers, J.G.; vander Westhuizen, J., Surg Neurol 40:395–399, Copyright 1993 by Elsevier Science Inc.; modified from Eismont, F.J.; et al. J Bone Joint Surg Am 73:1555–1560, 1991.)

logic deterioration, a higher level of neural than skeletal injury, and vertebral artery injury leading to subsequent death.

Fracture-Dislocations

Fractures with Dislocation. Injury patterns associated with translation displacement across the injury site imply a severe injury with complete disruption and marked instability. These injury patterns are designated fracture-dislocations, and the particular type of complete disruption may result from several different high-energy mechanisms, including compression, bending, and distraction. In severe injuries, the injury patterns acquire a common appearance of gross structural disruption, loss of stability, and damage to all components of the spinal column, including bone, ligaments, cord, nerve roots, and associated structures such as blood vessels and paraspinal muscles. The disconnected cephalad and caudad segments of the spine show translational displacement in the coronal and sagittal planes, consistent with dislocation.

Distraction-Dissociation Injury. Complete disruption of the longitudinal ligaments in the lower cervical spine results in severe instability equivalent to the instability in fracture-dislocation patterns. This injury is characterized by complete loss of structural continuity of the spinal column, and it is frequently accompanied by severe spinal cord injury. Often in distraction-dissociation injuries, the large blood vessels of the neck, the carotid and vertebral arteries, sustain a stretch injury that may result in cerebral ischemia, stroke, and death.

Distraction may be associated with an extension-type injury, which is seen more often in patients with stiff spines caused by severe spondylosis, DISH, or ankylosing spondylitis. These injuries may in some cases be highly unstable fracture dislocations. If not accompanied by immediate neurologic deficit, they have the potential for causing neural deterioration. Therefore, patients with these injuries should have provisional stabilization with a halo vest. Cervical traction is contraindicated, as distraction or change in position may cause further neural deterioration. Forsyth, Harris and Yeakley, and Allen and associates have identified extension fractures that result in 50% posterior vertebral body translation, as well as bilateral facet dislocations that occur from hyperextension mechanisms.[5, 90, 109] Severe comminution of the posterior elements is often present in these fractures. Because of loss of all spine stability, the posterior dislocation can reduce spontaneously. With further head flexion, the posterior dislocation can continue forward and simulate a bilateral facet dislocation. Merianos and associates documented similar cases associated with bilateral pedicular fractures.[146] These injuries are difficult to reduce, and any reduction achieved is hard to maintain because of separation of the anterior and posterior spinal columns.

Patients with severe traumatic retrolisthesis are difficult to manage in terms of both treatment and pain. Attempts at traction should be made, and if such attempts are successful, anterior decompression and interbody fusion with a plate should be performed. If reduction cannot be achieved or maintained, open reduction through an anterior approach is warranted. These patients may also require posterior fixation with lateral mass plates to achieve alignment and spinal stability. In patients with displaced laminar fractures in whom neurologic deficit is present, a laminectomy procedure is indicated in combination with stabilization.

CERVICAL IMAGING

Standard Views

The three standard views of the cervical spine are the AP, the lateral, and the open-mouth views. Some medical centers, including ours, add right and left oblique views to the standard set. If the lateral view does not show the cervicothoracic junction, it is supplemented by a swimmer's lateral view (see Chapter 26). This projection separates the shoulder overlap to allow better visualization of the lower cervical and upper thoracic vertebrae (Table 29–7).

Dynamic Studies

UPRIGHT RADIOGRAPHS

Upright radiographs are a useful tool for diagnosing spine injuries, but they allow only one level of dynamic assessment. Upright radiographs show the cervical spine under physiologic load, and although this view is limited, it is helpful because ligament injuries not apparent on supine radiographs may become apparent with loading. Examining the cervical spine under a physiologic load results in focal kyphosis or translation at the injured segment. Minor bone injuries such as compression fractures may also show more deformation with load bearing.

Upright radiographs are also useful in evaluating the success of spinal stabilization with external bracing or surgical fixation. An upright radiograph allows surgeons to view change in position as it relates to the supine view, which may necessitate a change in treatment. As for other assessment tools, flexion-extension radiographs and the stretch test provide other dynamic measurements.

FLEXION-EXTENSION RADIOGRAPHS

Flexion-extension radiographs are often recommended to evaluate the stability of the cervical spine after injury. They must be used with caution because significant displacement can occur even in patients who are awake, and such displacement can cause additional spinal cord injury.[44] Furthermore, their usefulness is limited by muscle spasms that decrease overall neck excursion. Although such stress radiographs can demonstrate instability, the clinical evaluation of stability, as per White's discussion, does not require dynamic radiographs. Recently, Harris and colleagues recommended a rigid protocol of flexion-extension cinefluoroscopy obtained from obtunded patients under anesthesia who were otherwise undergoing surgery.[110] In 187 of the patients evaluated, no adverse effects occurred from this protocol. Three patients in this study were identified with unstable spines. Despite these promising initial results, further evaluation of this protocol must be performed before it is routinely accepted.

Our current recommendation is to refrain from attempts to obtain flexion-extension radiographs in the acute trauma setting. Instead, patients with questionable injuries are immobilized in their extraction collars and then reevaluated as outpatients, where subacute flexion-extension radiographs can be obtained. MRI is a helpful alternative and an excellent tool for identifying ligamentous injuries. Because ligamentous injuries are the most dangerous occult injuries, MRI is an excellent resource.

STRETCH TEST

The stretch test is a diagnostic procedure used to evaluate occult cervical instability. The test is based on the assumption that an occult, but unstable ligament injury can be demonstrated by the application of a controlled distraction force. Patients with an apparently minor cervical fracture but one that could have a more severe associated ligamentous injury are placed in a cervical traction apparatus. The traction apparatus may be a head halter harness or cervical traction tongs. With the patient in a supine position, incremental weights are applied, typically in 5-lb increments, up to 25 lb total weight. Alignment of the cervical spine is assessed radiographically, and the patient is examined between each weight increment. If the cervical spine shows distraction (a 50% increase in disc height) or if the patient has neurologic symptoms, instability is indicated. If none of these signs are present, the patient is deemed to have a stable cervical spine.

Computed Tomography and Magnetic Resonance Imaging

CT shows bone in exquisite detail. It is routinely performed on all patients with cervical spinal injuries to identify facet fractures and malalignment. CT is indicated for most patients with bony injuries, such as vertebral body fractures or fractures of the lamina or facets. Before surgery, patients should undergo CT scanning to determine the extent of the osseous injury and to help plan surgical treatment, especially when using newer methods of screw fixation. If a fracture has been identified, CT or MRI is always recommended. In patients with neurologic injury or facet fracture-dislocation, MRI is preferred because it visualizes the cause of the cord damage and the status of the intervertebral disc.[62, 201] However, MRI does not define bony pathoanatomy as well as CT does. MRI or myelography is warranted in patients with progressive or unexplained neural deficits. To assess disc pathology, foraminal patency, and possible epidural hematoma formation, these diagnostic imaging procedures should be performed before any surgical treatment is attempted.

According to Eismont, Rizzolo, and their co-workers, disc herniation is associated with bilateral facet fracture-dislocation in 10% to 15% of patients.[80, 186] Patients with hyperflexion-type injuries may have increased signal intensity in the posterior nuchal ligaments on MRI, which is indicative of ligamentous disruption. Fat suppression techniques such as T2-weighted or short T1 inversion recovery (STIR) sequences can be particularly helpful.

TREATMENT

Errors in the initial care of spinal injury patients can have catastrophic, even fatal results.[70] Minimizing these errors requires management of spinal injury patients at highly specialized centers with experienced personnel.[191] It has been shown that patients with spinal cord injury benefit from early transfer to a trauma center.[162] For patients with spinal cord injury, early referral to a spinal cord injury center improves patient survival and neurologic recovery.[123]

Management of spinal injury patients requires the concerted energy and action of a talented trauma team. Experienced field personnel, emergency room physicians, orthopaedic surgeons, neurosurgeons, rehabilitation physicians, radiologists, and general surgeons are integral members of the team. The physicians who will ultimately assume the long-term management of trauma patients are critical in directing optimal initial care.[98] Definitive treatment of the spinal injury may be nonoperative or surgical.[253]

The surgeon must protect and immobilize the spine until injury is definitively excluded or treated, which means that all trauma patients should be in a supine position at strict bedrest on a flat bed, with spine board transfers. Logrolling must be used for decubitus ulcer prophylaxis. Patients may alternatively be placed in a rotating frame for improved pulmonary mechanics and skin care.

The objective in treating any spinal cord injury includes protecting the spinal cord from further damage and providing an optimal environment for neurologic recovery. This goal requires reducing and stabilizing fractures and dislocations, decompressing the neurologic tissue, and providing the most stable, painless spine possible.[55, 99, 191] An environment for maximal neurologic recovery should be created within the first several hours after injury.[72, 78, 185] The basic elements of treatment are resuscitation of the patient with advanced trauma life support

principles, identification of the fracture pattern, classification and assessment of fracture stability, early closed reduction if possible, pharmacologic treatment (if indicated), and finally, definitive treatment.

Definitive treatment is aimed at achieving complete decompression of the neural tissues in patients with neurologic deficits and providing sufficient stabilization to allow patient mobilization. This goal can be achieved by either operative or nonoperative methods. Patients with persistent neural compression who are neurologically intact do not usually require decompression. Surgical stabilization, if selected, should include as few motion segments as possible. In neurologically impaired patients, stabilization should allow mobilization of the patient without the use of a halo brace. Although experimental treatments have shown that neurologic recovery can be improved by decompressive surgery in animal models, only the use of corticosteroids and correction of adverse mechanical factors have been demonstrated to be effective in minimizing neurologic deficits in humans.

The timing of surgery for a cervical injury remains a controversial topic. No definitive data have demonstrated that early treatment in humans has any influence on neurologic recovery.[118] Opponents of early surgical intervention insist that the stress of an operation adds to the rapidly changing biochemical, vascular, and cellular events that invariably follow spinal cord injury and that these events will ultimately be harmful to the patient.[33, 140] This scenario may occur in patients with bilateral facet dislocations and is discussed later.[80, 186] Marshall and co-workers performed a prospective study of neurologic deterioration in 283 spinal cord–injured patients.[140] They found that four patients who had undergone surgery within 5 days of injury experienced deterioration. No patient who had surgery after 5 days had deterioration. However, five patients had evidence of deterioration during nonoperative treatment while awaiting surgery, including two cases of deterioration from halo vest placement, two from rotation of a Stryker frame, and one from loss of reduction. Conversely, other researchers insist that early operative stabilization enhances neurologic recovery and decreases the morbidity associated with long periods of immobilization. Studies by Schlegel and associates[203] and by Anderson and Krengel[8] showed no difference in complications, but better patient outcome in patients treated early. The protocols for spinal cord injury at our particular institution call for early fracture reduction, stabilization, and decompression of neural tissues.

Animal studies have consistently shown a strong inverse relationship between the timing of decompression and neurologic recovery. Shorter time to decompression has been shown to lead to greater recovery.[15, 29, 72, 74, 77, 185] Delamarter and colleagues placed constricting bands in beagles that narrowed the spinal cord to 50%.[72] The animals had decompression (removal of the constricting bands) at time 0, 1 hour, 6 hours, and 24 hours. Animals that had early removal (0 and 1 hours) made full clinical neurologic recovery, whereas those decompressed later (6 and 24 hours) did not. This outcome correlates well with histopathologic findings demonstrating that the axonal tracts in the white matter are intact immediately after experimental trauma.[15, 77] However, these results were followed by progressive destruction over a period of 24 to 48 hours because of secondary injury from adverse mechanical, biochemical, and vascular factors.[115, 117, 209, 257, 260]

A short "window of opportunity" may exist in which reduction of the deformity combined with reestablishment of spinal cord perfusion can completely reverse the spinal cord injury.[72, 128] We have observed six such cases in patients who underwent reduction of a bilateral facet dislocation within 2 hours of trauma. All experienced immediate reversal of their quadriplegia. From these observations and studies, it appears that neurologically injured patients should indeed have fracture reduction performed in a timely fashion.[31, 40, 72, 128]

Another concern in managing patients with cervical spinal injuries is the effect of prolonged traction on their general medical condition. Cranial tongs traction requires recumbency, which can lead to pulmonary, gastrointestinal, and skin complications. Schlegel and associates[203] and Anderson and Krengel[8] reported decreased morbidity and length of hospitalization in patients with multiple injuries if treated surgically within 72 hours of injury when compared with those treated in delayed fashion.

Provisional Care

The initial treatment of cervical spinal cord injuries consists of reduction with cranial tongs traction. Because flaccid patients, elderly patients, and those with ligament injuries can easily be overdistracted by traction, traction weight should be applied judiciously. In many cases, reduction can be facilitated by adjusting the relative position of the head to the thorax instead of simply adding more traction weight. Special care must be taken in positioning children, whose heads are relatively larger than their chests, and also in positioning elderly patients with preexisting thoracic kyphosis. Generally, an initial traction weight of 2.5 kg is used for injuries in the upper cervical spine and 5.0 kg is used for injuries in the lower cervical spine. Traction weight is increased in increments of 2.5 to 5.0 kg at 15-minute intervals to allow for soft tissue relaxation. A neurologic examination should be performed and a lateral radiograph obtained after the addition of each increment of weight. Weight is increased until the fracture or dislocation is reduced.

During reduction, radiographs should be scrutinized for signs of overdistraction, such as widening of the intervertebral disc or the facet joints. To facilitate unlocking a facet dislocation, the head can be gently flexed by placing towels under the occiput. Burst fractures may require substantial traction weight—we have used up to 70% of the body's weight without incurring complications. However, manual manipulation is not recommended to achieve reduction.

Gardner-Wells tongs are applied in the emergency department to patients with unstable cervical injuries (see Fig. 29–4). In so doing, the skin is prepared with a povidone-iodine (Betadine) solution and infiltrated to the level of the periosteum with a local anesthetic. Shaving the scalp is not necessary. The pins are inserted into the skull 1 cm above the tips of the ears and in line with the external auditory meatus. The pins are tightened symmetrically until the spring-loaded plunger protrudes 1 mm from the pin surface. The locking nuts are tightened and weight applied with a rope and pulley. The pins are retightened after 24 hours and are not disturbed again. This protocol requires thinking ahead, for if an MRI study is anticipated, MRI-compatible tongs must be used from the start of treatment. The use of MRI-compatible tongs can facilitate postreduction imaging, although these tongs do not hold as much traction weight as stainless steel tongs do.[25]

Weights of 5 to 10 lb are then applied, a repeat neurologic examination is performed, and a lateral radiograph is obtained. If reduction has not occurred, the weight is increased by 5 to 10 lb and the process is repeated. Interval radiographs are scrutinized carefully for signs of overdistraction, such as increasing disc height or facet joint diastasis. Traction of up to 70% of body weight can be applied safely by this meticulous protocol.[65] The use of C-arm fluoroscopy can also facilitate reduction. Once reduction has been achieved, the traction weight can be decreased, except in some patients with burst or flexion teardrop fractures. Cranial tongs traction is contraindicated in patients with skull fractures or large cranial defects. Traction should also be used judiciously in patients with complete ligamentous injury.

After reduction, patients should be imaged by MRI. Those with persistent cord compression are considered candidates for surgical decompression and stabilization. In most patients who achieve indirect decompression by fracture reduction, the choice of treatment is based on the clinical course and fracture type, as described later. Indications for immediate surgery include neurologic deterioration and ongoing compressive lesions or malalignment. Patients with failure of reduction by closed technique should also be considered candidates for early surgery within the first 24 hours.[31, 211]

Cervical injuries almost always require skull traction. The only exception to this rule is the case of a distraction injury. Distraction at the skull-spine junction or between any vertebrae indicates complete ligament disruption. These injuries are the most unstable spine injuries, and skull traction in these patients will lead to catastrophic iatrogenic neurologic and vascular injury. Patients with these injuries are better immobilized with sandbags and tape or a halo apparatus. Even when immobilized in the halo apparatus, patients should be kept in strict bedrest with full spine precautions until definitive surgical stabilization.

Hemodynamic instability is commonly seen after spinal cord injury because interruption of the descending sympathetic fibers results in vasodilatation and hypotension. Vagal predominance causes bradycardia, further lowering cardiac output. A low pulse rate can distinguish hypotension associated with spinal cord injury from hypovolemic shock. Neurogenic shock should be treated with vasopressors or agents to increase peripheral vascular resistance rather than fluid resuscitation. The bradycardia may require atropine or, rarely, a pacemaker. Because of loss of autoregulation, spinal cord blood flow to the injured region is determined solely by blood pressure. Therefore, when hypotension is present, rapid correction is essential to patient survival.

Minor spinal injuries include laminar fractures, spinous process fractures, lateral mass fractures without vertebral body displacement, and avulsion fractures of the anterior longitudinal ligament. These injuries are usually stable and occur with hyperextension; they are not associated with neurologic deficits. Flexion injuries include vertebral compression fractures without posterior wall involvement and grade I or II ligament injuries. Patients suffering these more minor injuries, if the injuries are stable, are immobilized with a cervical collar. Tongs traction is applied only to patients who are to undergo concurrent procedures such as femoral intramedullary nailing or pelvic fixation.

Anterior vertebral translation is normally prevented by the orientation of the facets, the posterior ligamentous structure, and the disc annulus. Translation of 25% occurs under three particular conditions: unilateral facet dislocations, bilateral perched facet fractures, and facet fracture-dislocations. In unilateral dislocations, the spinous process is rotated to the side of the facet dislocations on AP radiographs. Bilateral facet dislocations result in at least 50% vertebral body translation. Widening of the interspinous process is an important indicator of posterior ligament injury. In these instances, CT has been useful in identifying facet fractures and malalignment. MRI has been used successfully to identify intervertebral disc herniation in 35% of bilateral dislocations and 15% of unilateral cases.[81]

Methylprednisolone is given to patients with spinal cord injuries according to the protocols outlined earlier. Rapid closed reduction is accomplished by tongs traction and weights. In the case of spinal injury, because all the major surrounding ligaments are potentially damaged, overdistraction is always a potential and painstaking effort must be taken to avoid this peril. If reduction cannot be achieved by closed methods, open reduction and internal fixation are indicated. Closed manual manipulation is not recommended.

Axial loading can fracture the vertebral body and retropulse bony fragments into the spinal canal. When this mechanism is combined with flexion, as it often is in the case of diving injuries, a teardrop fracture is produced.[120] In this injury, the fractured anterior-inferior corner of the vertebral body forms a teardrop shape and the remaining vertebral body is rotated posteriorly into the canal. In addition, rupture of the posterior ligament structures produces kyphosis and a highly unstable fracture (see Fig. 29–20). Under these conditions, spinal cord damage is often severe.

In treating a teardrop fracture, spinal realignment and reduction of the retropulsed fragments can be achieved by axial traction. Up to 70% of body weight can be used without incurring complications in burst fractures. After reduction, the amount of traction weight can be reduced, but the fracture must be monitored radiographically to ensure maintenance of reduction.

Schneider and Knighton described a syndrome involving damage to the cervical spinal cord in patients without any obvious spinal fractures.[206] This syndrome is due to hyperextension in patients with narrow spinal canals and results in compression of the spinal cord between the bulging disc and the infolded ligamentum flavum. Neurologically, this injury produces a central cord syndrome in which patients retain better lower extremity than upper extremity function. The prognosis for recovery in the lower extremities is good, although many patients suffering from this syndrome experience residual loss of hand

function. Patients who have sustained an extension injury concurrently with a central cord syndrome should be placed in traction even when radiography reveals no evidence of an acute injury. This precaution protects the cord from further injury and reduces small malalignments, such as 1 to 2 mm of retrolisthesis. Traction can be used to open the canal by applying tension to the ligamentum flavum and pulling it out of the spinal cord.

Closed Reduction

Closed reduction in cervical spine injuries has proved safe and effective.[124] It is possible that successful reduction may require weights higher than 140 lb. Sabiston and colleagues provided evidence that traction weight totaling up to 70% of body weight is safe.[200] However, weight heavier than 80 lb should not be applied to most carbon fiber MRI-compatible tongs. The traditional steel Gardner-Wells tongs are less likely to slip with larger weights. Traction should not be applied to patients with injuries involving distraction of the spinal column.

Decompression of spinal cord injury should proceed immediately.[71] Emergency attempted closed reduction is the treatment of choice for alert cooperative patients with acute cervical spine dislocations.[216] In these patients, imaging is not necessary before reduction and should be avoided so that reduction is not delayed.[128] Open or closed reduction under general anesthesia in an uncooperative or unconscious patient can be preceded by an MRI scan. In this situation, a herniated disc may be treated by surgical decompression before reduction.[187] Patients with highly unstable injuries, such as craniocervical dissociation, can undergo reduction and be provisionally immobilized with a halo device.[151]

Closed reduction decreases the need for more complicated surgical procedures.[221] Reduction also improves stability by preventing neurologic deterioration in the interval preceding definitive treatment.[137] Closed reduction can improve neurologic status.[210] Spinal cord–injured patients may have an excellent capacity for spinal cord recovery regardless of the initial findings.[42] Reduction within the first few hours of injury may lead to dramatic improvement in neurologic status. Reduction within 2 hours of injury may reverse tetraplegia.[95] Although case reports have described neurologic deterioration during reduction,[163] larger series have not noted neurologic deterioration with closed reduction.[65]

Definitive Care

CLOSED TREATMENT

Closed treatment remains the standard of care for most spinal injuries. Clinical observation reports, biomechanical investigations of stability, and radiographic measurements of stability have not produced definitive recommendations applicable to specific cases in terms of certain decisions regarding closed or operative treatment. The only consistent indication for surgical treatment may be skeletal disruption in the presence of a neurologic deficit. One consistent contraindication to closed treatment is a purely ligamentous and unstable spinal column injury in a skeletally mature patient. Although these injuries may heal adequately in pediatric patients who still have significant growth remaining, in adult patients, the healing response does not restore sufficient strength to provide spinal column stability, regardless of the length of bedrest or external immobilization. Unstable ligamentous injuries always require fusion. Osseous injuries will heal adequately but require treatment to control deformity.

Closed treatment options are bedrest, a halo apparatus, an external orthosis, or a cast.[83] Bedrest as definitive treatment may be indicated in rare patients unable or unwilling to undergo bracing or surgery. Such patients may include those with a severe preexisting deformity, morbid obesity, or medical co-morbidity, or it may simply be their personal preference. Bedrest for the initial few weeks preceding bracing is an option for severely unstable injuries. The level of injury serves as a guide for the category of external orthosis (see Table 29–6). Most commercially available braces within each category are equally effective.[149] Custom-molded trunk orthoses provide added rotational control, and casts can be applied in hyperextension to improve kyphosis. Bracing is continued until bone healing is sufficient for load bearing. The guideline for load bearing is 8 weeks for cervical injuries and 12 weeks for thoracolumbar injuries.

Mild Soft Tissue Injury

Neck pain or tenderness without associated imaging abnormalities is generally treated with initial immobilization in a collar. Flexion-extension radiographs are obtained when the tenderness resolves, typically 2 to 6 weeks after injury. Instability on flexion-extension views requires surgical treatment. If dynamic studies do not show instability and the patient remains symptomatic, a short course of physical therapy for strengthening plus the addition of mobility exercises is usually helpful. Patients with chronic symptoms require specialized pain management.

Isolated Minor Fractures

Isolated pedicle or facet fractures without vertebral subluxation are usually stable and can be treated in a cervical orthosis for 6 to 8 weeks. Careful follow-up is required because of the potential for late subluxation. Patients with chronic neck pain after trauma may have occult fractures of the facet that are not easily discernible on plain radiographs. These injuries can be identified by bone scanning or CT and can be treated with late posterior fusion.

Vertebral Body Injuries

Extension Teardrop Injury. Patients with extension injuries but without a fracture can be mobilized in a cervical collar after 5 to 7 days in traction. Because the prognosis for nonoperative management of these injuries is generally good, no initial surgical treatment is required. If a patient fails to make a satisfactory recovery and cord compression is documented by myelography or MRI, late anterior decompression should be considered.

Stable extension injuries of the anterior column include rupture of the anterior longitudinal ligament, rupture of the disc annulus, and an extension teardrop fracture without vertebral body subluxation. In all cases, spinal alignment should always be evaluated because small degrees of retrolisthesis are easily overlooked. Patients with anterior longitudinal ruptures can be identified radiographically by the notable increase in disc space. Occasionally, these patients will also have increased lordotic angulation. These injuries reduce easily with upright positioning. The most effective treatment of an anterior longitudinal ligament injury is the use of an orthosis for 6 to 8 weeks, as outlined previously for the treatment of stable injuries.

Compression Fractures. Compression fractures are best treated with external bracing. A hard cervical collar or a Minerva-type brace for 6 to 8 weeks is usually adequate. Flexion-extension views should be obtained at the end of bracing to exclude any residual ligamentous instability.

Patients with vertebral body compression fractures should be carefully examined for disruption of the posterior osseous ligament. Symptoms of this condition include tenderness along the spinous processes, gaps between the spinous processes, interspinous widening on plain radiographs, an abnormal signal in the nuchal ligaments on MRI, or any combination of these signs and symptoms. Compression fractures associated with ligamentous injuries are treated surgically by posterior interspinous fusion. Webb and colleagues identified hidden flexion injuries that initially appeared to be simple wedge compression fractures.[246] These injuries are caused by hyperflexion forces and consist of an anterior vertebral fracture with posterior osteoligamentous disruption. They are unstable, and when carefully analyzed, they will exceed 5 points on the White and Panjabi scale. This injury is sinister and notorious for slow progression of increasing deformity until dislocation or facet perching occurs.

Burst Fractures without Associated Neurologic Injury. Burst fractures of the cervical spine have an appearance similar to fractures of the thoracolumbar junction. Their stability and treatment depend on the stability of the posterior elements. These injuries often occur at C6 and C7 and can be missed easily if radiographs are inadequate. CT and MRI should be performed to fully evaluate the posterior osseous ligamentous structures. The initial treatment of all burst fractures is reduction with cranial tongs traction. In most cases, the posterior longitudinal and anterior longitudinal ligaments are spared, and therefore large traction weights can be safely used. Initially, 10 to 15 lb is applied and then progressed up to 70% of body weight to obtain the most complete reduction.[66]

Definitive treatment is based on fracture stability and neurologic function. Patients with stable fractures that do not involve the posterior elements can be treated with halo immobilization for 12 weeks. The halo vest cannot maintain axial distraction, and therefore some loss of reduction will necessarily occur, including retropulsion of bone into the canal.

Patients with unstable fractures and injury to the posterior osseous and ligamentous structures are best treated with surgical stabilization. Before the development of effective and safe anterior cervical plates, these injuries were successfully treated by posterior wire fixation with or without a postoperative halo vest. However, modern-day surgery has proved that plate fixation of the lateral masses is biomechanically more effective than interspinous wire fixation in controlling the axial forces. Anderson and associates reported successful outcomes in 12 patients with unstable burst fractures and flexion teardrop fractures treated with AO reconstruction plates applied to the lateral masses.[13] However, the anterior approach with the use of rigidly locked plates is our particular recommended treatment. This technique allows removal of the fractured vertebral body and displaced discs, as well as reconstruction with a strut graft and plate spanning the two injured motion segments. Others have recommended combined anterior and posterior surgeries performed sequentially for these highly unstable fractures. We have found that this approach is rarely warranted because of the effectiveness of anterior cervical plate stabilization.[41]

Cervical burst fractures in patients with neurologic injury should be treated by anterior decompression and fusion with anterior cervical plates. Anterior decompression is the most viable method because it removes displaced bone and disc fragments and may allow viable, but nonfunctional neural tissue to recover. Patients with stable burst fractures but no associated neurologic injuries are treated in a halo vest for 12 weeks. Anterior decompression and strut fusion are performed in patients who have sustained stable burst fractures with associated neurologic injuries. Late anterior decompression is indicated in patients who fail to improve neurologically and for those with persistent cord compression.

The technique of posterior cervical fusion for burst fractures or facet fracture-dislocations requires communication and careful coordination between the anesthesiologist and the surgeon. Nasotracheal intubation is performed with a fiberoptic light system on an alert patient. The patient is transferred to a Stryker frame and placed in a prone position. After a neurologic examination is repeated and a lateral radiograph is obtained to confirm adequate alignment, general anesthesia is administered. Spinal cord monitoring is performed when intraoperative reduction is anticipated. A modified Rogers wiring technique provides adequate fixation for ligament injuries with intact bony structures.[61] Posterior cervical plate fixation is indicated for fractures with associated posterior ligament instability and for burst fracture patterns.[102] In this technique, the fracture is reduced by traction weight and fixed internally with 2.7- or 3.5-mm reconstruction plates affixed to the lateral masses with screws (see Fig. 29–21). Autogenous iliac cancellous bone graft is placed in the decorticated facet joint and along the lamina and spinous processes.

Extension Injuries

Anterior Longitudinal Ligament Avulsion and Extension Teardrop Injury. An extension teardrop fracture is a small, triangular bone fragment displaced from the anterior inferior corner of the vertebral body. In some cases, the fracture may be an osteophyte or it may be confused with incomplete ossification of an osteophyte. This injury is stable but must be differentiated from a flexion teardrop fracture with associated comminution of the vertebral body, nor should it be confused with retropulsion of the spinal canal with interspinous disruption. Treatment of these injuries involves the use of a collar or cervicothoracic brace for 6 to 8 weeks—the same treatment outlined earlier for stable injuries.

SURGICAL TREATMENT

Surgical management of patients with spinal cord injury is based on reports of experience and observation as opposed to rigorous clinical trials. Surgical stabilization of the spinal column is an essential technique because it can prevent further mechanical injury to the damaged cord tissue. Removing any residual compressive mass effect, as when reducing a vertebral dislocation or removing bone fragments pressing on the spinal cord, may also allow better neurologic recovery. Closed treatment of unreduced injuries may lead to chronic pain requiring surgical treatment.[21]

According to recent studies, time plays a potentially pivotal role in neurologic recovery. Early intervention in this setting is not defined in terms of days after injury, but rather in terms of minutes and hours. Animal studies have suggested that a potential window of opportunity occurs in the first 3 to 6 hours after injury. It is during this time that significant neurologic recovery may be possible[48, 72] (see Table 29–4 and Figs. 29–6 and 29–8).

Patients suffering multiple injuries with burns should be managed with early surgical treatment of fractures.[76] Mortality rates in trauma patients are determined more by severe head injury than by injury to any other organ system.[62] A prognosis based on the Injury Severity Score or Glasgow Coma Scale should not deter the surgical team from optimal management of orthopaedic injuries.

Surgery for spinal injuries always involves fusion except in the two rare exceptions of odontoid fractures and C2 arch fractures. Under specific circumstances, these two injuries may be treated with internal fixation osteosynthesis.[26] Some researchers believe that open reduction and instrumentation may be just as effective as fusion for spinal fractures.[165] Early surgery reduces time in the hospital.[166] Spinal cord blood flow may be adversely affected by an anterior cervical approach.[63] Anterior interbody grafts are prone to displacement in patients with posterior instability or gross deformity of the vertebral body unless supplemented by fixation.[234]

Anterior plating and posterior plating are equally successful in treating cervical trauma.[86, 96] Earlier studies reported high complication rates with anterior cervical surgery.[217] However, anterior plating provides immediate stabilization, even with posterior ligamentous injury.[52] The strength of the fixated spine is relatively unchanged by corpectomy and anterior grafting. Anterior grafting has also been shown to improve alignment,[138, 196] and fixation maintains the alignment.[150] Anterior fusion has likewise proved to be an excellent choice of procedure because it allows early mobilization, a shorter hospital stay, and less financial burden.[223]

A general approach to the treatment of patients with stable fractures resulting from any mechanism is discussed separately in this section. These types of injuries are usually isolated to one side of the spinal column and are not associated with vertebral body translation or neurologic deficit. To determine treatment options, these injuries are assessed with the White and Panjabi criteria. Stable injuries are those determined to have a value of 4 or less. Common types of these stable injuries are vertebral body compression fractures, avulsion of the anterior longitudi-

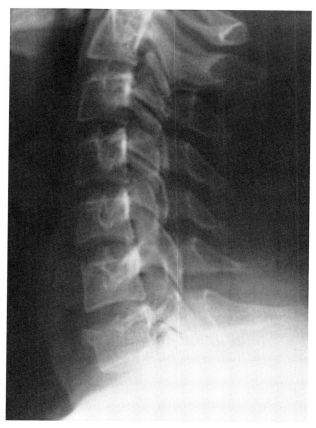

FIGURE 29–22. This 29-year-old man sustained a minor flexion injury of C7 without neurologic deficit. The patient was treated in a cervicothoracic orthosis for 12 weeks and healed without subsequent instability on flexion-extension radiographs.

nal ligament, extension teardrop fractures, mild posterior longitudinal ligament injuries, and isolated fractures of the posterior elements (Fig. 29–22).

When suffering a stable fracture injury, patients are treated in a hard collar or cervicothoracic brace for 6 to 8 weeks. After orthotic placement, an upright radiograph and flexion-extension radiographs are obtained to check alignment. These radiographs are repeated biweekly until healing, which usually takes another 6 to 8 weeks to be completed. During the period of immobilization, patients should perform isometric neck exercises and low-impact aerobics. Physicians must be mindful that their assessment of stability may be incorrect. Only careful follow-up with frequent radiographs can determine whether adequate alignment of the spine is maintained. Increasing pain or new neurologic deficits may indicate motion of the fracture site or loss of position. What was once determined to be a stable fracture could indeed be unstable.

Nonunion may develop in displaced spinous process fractures, but it is rarely symptomatic. Simple wedge compression fractures may occur from axial loading with fracture of the superior end-plate and vertebral body wedging. Minimal kyphosis and no canal compromise are present. These injuries are stable and can be treated successfully with a cervicothoracic brace, as outlined previously.

Traumatic Disc Disruption and Cord Contusion

Taylor and Blackwood first reported traumatic disc disruption and cord contusion as a particular type of spinal cord injury, and they did so in the absence of radiographic changes.[227] These authors correctly postulated that the spinal cord was pinched between the disc anteriorly and the infolded ligamentum flavum posteriorly. Schneider and Knighton clarified the neuroanatomic basis for the development of central cord syndrome, which so often results in these extension injuries.[206] They believed that the condition had a good prognosis and thus surgery was rarely warranted. To solidify these particular findings, Marar carefully reviewed 45 spinal cord injuries caused by extension mechanisms.[139] He found that the neurologic injury was more variable than Schneider and Knighton initially reported and that it did not conform to the typical central cord syndrome. Only 10 of the patients had normal radiographs. Eleven patients had retrolisthesis and 24 had extension teardrop fractures. Of the four patients who died during treatment, all had transverse fractures through the vertebral body that were not apparent on plain radiographs. Clinical outcome in the Schneider and Knighton study was correlated with initial hand strength. Thirty-one of 32 patients could ambulate at long-term follow-up. However, only those with at least grade 3 hand strength at the time of admission had recovered significant hand function. Merriam and associates also correlated outcome with initial hand strength, as well as outcome with the presence of perineal pinprick sensation.[147]

The standard initial treatment of extension spinal cord injuries is the application of tongs traction. Such management may reduce any malalignment and help lengthen the spinal column, thereby indirectly decompressing the spinal cord and stabilizing the spine to prevent further injury. Definitive treatment is determined by imaging studies and the progress of neurologic recovery. Patients who are improving neurologically are mobilized in a collar for 5 to 7 days, and upright radiographs are obtained to ensure alignment. Patients whose condition is not improving or who have reached a neurologic plateau are candidates for surgical decompression. The approach for surgical decompression is dependent on the site of cord compression and the extent to which the cord is compressed. Anterior decompression is indicated in patients with one to three levels of anterior or AP cord compression or if the spine is kyphotic. Posterior decompression is indicated in rare cases when compression is localized posteriorly or when more than three levels of AP compression are present. For maximal effectiveness, posterior decompression is best performed in spines with neutral or lordotic postures. After either anterior or posterior decompression, plate fixation is added in patients with traumatic cord injuries.

Vertebral Body Injuries

Burst Fractures with Associated Neurologic Injury. Neurologic injury in burst fractures typically occurs from posterior displacement of fracture fragments of the vertebral body. Disruption of neural structures primarily takes place during the injury event. However, persistent cord compression from displaced bone fragments can cause further neurologic deterioration. The most immediate goal in patients with these injuries is to indirectly decompress the spinal cord by cranial traction. Because these injuries are compressive, ligaments at the fracture site are usually intact and traction can be applied safely. Closed reduction of burst fractures can require traction weights up to and over 100 lb. If closed reduction is successful and postreduction MRI confirms that the spinal cord is no longer compressed, surgical treatment can be performed on a somewhat elective schedule. Surgery usually consists of an anterior approach, corpectomy of the fractured vertebra, interbody fusion with a structural graft, and anterior plate fixation with locking screws. Although severe burst fractures are associated with concurrent posterior facet joint injury, anterior fixation with a rigid plate and external brace provides fixation. In rare circumstances, such as patients with osteoporosis or an injury at the cervicothoracic junction involving the C7 vertebral body, posterior fixation may be the preferred treatment or could be necessary to supplement anterior fixation.

Decompression of an injured spinal cord is the primary objective in treating patients with a burst fracture and an associated spinal cord injury. If closed reduction is unsuccessful in this setting, direct decompression should be performed urgently through an anterior cervical approach. Reconstruction with an anterior structural graft and plate is usually adequate if supplemented with external bracing in a Minerva brace. Occasionally, additional fixation may be necessary through a posterior approach.

Flexion Teardrop Injury. Unfortunately, flexion teardrop fractures are associated with significant spinal cord injury and generally occur in younger patients. Similar to burst fractures, the stability and long-term healing potential of flexion teardrop injuries are dependent on the degree of disruption of the posterior osteoligamentous structures. The initial treatment of patients with this injury is skeletal tongs traction. Patients with deformities should be imaged acutely to ensure adequate indirect decompression. In patients with a mild degree of instability (noted by lack of separation of the spinous process and less than 3 mm of displacement of the vertebral body into the canal), halo vest treatment for 12 to 16 weeks can be used. At the end of immobilization, flexion-extension radiographs are obtained to ensure stability. Patients with unstable flexion teardrop fractures who have achieved reduction are best treated surgically with stabilization over two motion segments. Patients must have documented indirect decompression of the spinal canal before any attempt at posterior fixation. In most cases, the best approach is an anterior one involving the use of an autogenous iliac crest graft and plate fixation (Fig. 29–23). Alternatively, lateral mass fixation has been used successfully in a large series of patients.[13]

Patients with neurologic deficits or those with residual cord compression are treated by anterior decompression and reconstruction with an iliac crest strut graft and plate fixation. Although some authors have recommended combined anterior/posterior approaches, we have found that a cervical locking plate is usually successful.[41]

Facet Injuries

Posterior cervical fusion is performed on all patients with bilateral facet dislocations. In the past, surgery was generally delayed until 5 to 7 days after injury to avoid neurologic deterioration. Neurologic deterioration occasionally occurs in quadriplegic patients treated within 5 days of trauma,[212] and the previous policy of delay in surgery was intended to circumvent such deterioration. However, earlier surgery may be beneficial for reducing patient complications but not for enhancing neurologic recovery. Before attempting surgical treatment, the status of the intervertebral disc is determined by CT, myelography, or MRI. If the disc is retropulsed into the spinal canal, it should be removed before posterior cervical fusion. If the facet cannot be reduced preoperatively, reduction can be accomplished easily during surgery by applying traction to the spinous process or by levering the dislocated facet joint with an elevator. Rarely, a small portion of the facet must be removed to aid in reduction.

Treatment of unilateral facet dislocations remains controversial. Closed treatment in a halo vest is frequently ineffective because reduction is not successful in 50% of cases or else the reduction is not maintained.[169] Better results are achieved when anatomic alignment has been maintained. Therefore, posterior cervical fusion is recommended for patients with unilateral facet dislocations and those with facet fracture-dislocations.[11]

Lateral Mass Fracture-Separation. Levine identified a particular fracture type characterized by two vertical fracture lines in the pedicle and lamina that create a separation of the lateral mass.[130] In this fracture, the lateral mass rotates to a horizontal position, which allows subluxation of both the cranial and caudal levels. This injury is highly unstable and is best treated surgically. Because of the high degree of instability, lateral mass fixation of two motion segments is recommended (see Fig. 29–17).

Unilateral Facet Dislocation. Unilateral facet dislocations may still remain stable even if reduction can be achieved, and therefore nonoperative treatment with a halo vest is a viable option. Extension and slight contralateral rotation may decrease the likelihood of redisplacement. Patients with this type of injury should be evaluated frequently to ensure maintenance of reduction. After 12 weeks, the halo vest can be removed, and flexion-extension radiographs should then be obtained. If instability is still present, late posterior fusion is indicated. Most patients with pure unilateral facet dislocations that require posterior fusion can be treated by the Rogers or Bohlman interspinous wire technique.[30, 191]

Spines that have sustained unilateral facet fracture-dislocations have lost their mechanical resistance to rotation and anterior translation. Reductions are usually easily performed with pure axial traction, although redisplacement occurs frequently during nonoperative treatment. Therefore, operative treatment is recommended for these injuries, and most patients respond well to posterior fusion. To increase rigidity and to resist rotatory moments, the oblique wire technique or lateral mass plate fixation can be used in association with the interspinous technique[13, 79] (Fig. 29–24). Patients with neurologic deficits should undergo MRI before surgery. If a disc herniation is present, anterior cervical discectomy plus fusion is indicated. In a small percentage of patients, foraminal stenosis is present secondary to displaced bone fragments. In these cases, posterior foraminotomy

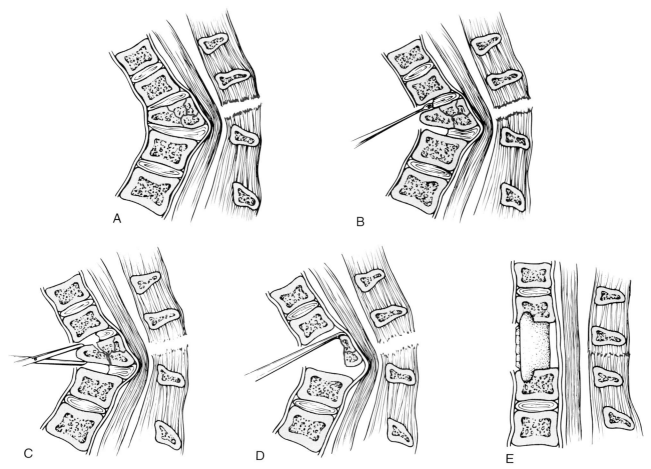

FIGURE 29–23. *A,* Anterior corpectomy is frequently necessary to decompress the dural sac after a cervical burst fracture. It is usually performed with the patient in the supine position with light traction applied. If more than three levels need to be exposed, then a vertical incision is used, as it is extended more easily than a transverse excision. *B,* Following exposure of the appropriate level and a localizing radiograph, the disc material is removed on either side of the fractured vertebrae. *C,* After removing a majority of the disc material, the vertebral body is excised using Leksell rongeurs. This is continued until approximately two thirds to three fourths of the body is removed. *D,* The remaining fragments are dissected off the posterior longitudinal ligament. The ligament is generally not disrupted and should not be removed. The central portion of the body is removed. Generally it is not necessary to remove the lateral portion unless it significantly impinges on the dural sac. The use of a laminar spreader to open up the injured space is sometimes helpful in completing the débridement of the bony fragments. The upper and lower vertebral end-plates of the adjacent segments are burred with a high-speed bur to allow seating of a tricortical strut graft. The strut graft is fashioned and impacted into place. *E,* If difficulty is encountered in seating the graft, then an L-shaped trough can be fashioned in the upper end-plate of the lower body to facilitate seating of the graft.

in conjunction with posterior fusion should be performed.

As is the case with so many other fracture treatment methods, management of unilateral facet dislocations is controversial. Important factors in the treatment decision process include an assessment of stability, ease of reduction, presence of facet fractures, adequacy of reduction, and neurologic deficits. Pathologically significant soft tissue injuries to the joint capsule, ligamentum flavum, nuchal ligaments, and posterior longitudinal ligament have occurred and are responsible for the displacements observed.[17] Closed reduction can be achieved in a high percentage of patients with facet fractures. Unilateral facet dislocations may be difficult to reduce because of locking up by the contralateral ligamentous structures that were spared, or difficulties may be due to fracturing and malrotation of the lateral masses. Hadley and co-workers used tongs traction but were successful in reducing only 70% of cases.[104] Others have used larger weights and

gentle manipulative maneuvers and reported over 90% success rates.[66, 216]

Several studies have documented that a successful long-term outcome correlates with anatomic alignment regardless of treatment.[21, 192] Rorabeck and colleagues analyzed 26 patients with unilateral facet dislocations and found that 7 of the 10 patients who healed in the displaced position had chronic neck and arm pain whereas none of the other 16 patients with anatomic positioning had pain. Beyer and co-workers found that closed reduction could be achieved in only 75% of patients. In patients with residual subluxation, they found a higher incidence of instability, neck pain, and stiffness. They recommended open reduction and fusion if closed reduction fails.

Controversy has arisen regarding the benefits of surgery over the use of a halo vest. In general, purely ligamentous injuries respond poorly to a halo vest. In unilateral facet dislocations without fractures, the contralateral ligaments may be spared, and with proper mobilization, recurrent

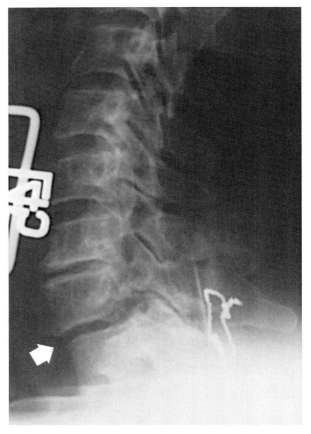

FIGURE 29–24. This 48-year-old man with a unilateral facet fracture at C7–T1 underwent interspinous wiring, which was ineffective for the rotational instability of this injury. Rotational malalignment has already occurred even with the patient immobilized postoperatively in the orthosis (arrow).

dislocation may be prevented. If a facet is fractured, the buttress preventing rotation and anterolisthesis is lost. This complication frequently results in loss of position. Therefore, in all cases of unilateral facet dislocation, an attempt at closed reduction should be made (see Chapter 27). If this treatment fails, open reduction plus posterior fusion is recommended. As in most instances, before any surgical procedure is undertaken, the patient should be imaged to fully evaluate the intervertebral disc and the neural foramina. If a disc herniation is compressing the spinal cord, the patient should be treated with anterior cervical discectomy, fusion, and anterior plating. We recommend that patients with foraminal encroachment despite closed reduction have posterior foraminotomies performed in conjunction with posterior fusion.

Patients with spinal cord injuries and unilateral facet dislocations are best treated by posterior fusion after emergency closed reduction. In patients with spinal cord injury, halo vest use should be avoided because it will slow the rehabilitation process, interfere with nursing care, and possibly restrict pulmonary function, thereby increasing the risk of pulmonary complications.

Bilateral Facet Dislocation. Bilateral facet dislocations are often the most dramatic of the cervical injuries. They are usually associated with significant spinal cord injury, and unfortunately, many patients suffering this sort of dislocation will first be reported to be intact, but then experience deterioration of their injury after reaching a medical facility.[29] Beatson and others have shown that in a bilateral facet dislocation, complete rupture of all ligamentous structures is present with the exception of the anterior longitudinal ligament, which is often stripped periosteally from the vertebral bodies.[17, 250] Although prolonged treatment with recumbency or halo vest immobilization has been advocated, because of the high degree of instability and the ligamentous nature of the injury, most patients would benefit by surgical treatment.

Several important factors must be considered in the treatment of patients with bilateral facet dislocations, including the status of the intervertebral disc, associated fractures of the posterior elements, the timing and method of reduction, the possibility of vertebral artery injury, and the timing and type of surgical approach. Rarely will patients be neurologically intact, and if they are, it is usually due to the presence of a capacious canal, to an increased spinal diameter as a result of pedicular fractures, or to slow onset of the dislocation.

The flexion-distraction forces responsible for a bilateral facet dislocation often cause tearing of the disc annulus and possible extrusion of the intervertebral disc into the spinal canal. These complications can mean further spinal cord compression and prevention of neurologic recovery even after reduction of the dislocation.[54] In the worst cases, patients who are neurologically intact may have increased cord compression after reduction because of persistent disc herniation, along with the development of progressive neurologic deficits.[80, 232] Rizzolo and associates identified acute disc disruptions in 42% of patients with cervical trauma.[186] Fifty-six percent of the patients with facet trauma had a disc disruption, although the presence of a disruption was not correlated with neurologic outcome. Disc disruption should always be differentiated from disc herniation.[100]

Posterior ligamentous injuries are best assessed by using the criteria of White and Panjabi. According to these standardized criteria, patients with mild ligamentous injuries or with spinous process fractures caused by hyperflexion are stable, and their injuries have a value of less than 4. Clinically, patients in this category have reproducible focal neck tenderness but minimal kyphotic angulation, minimal interspinous widening, and limited vertebral body translation. These injuries can be successfully treated with 6 to 8 weeks of immobilization in a hard collar or brace, as described earlier.

Posterior ligamentous injuries associated with mild compression fractures generally have a poor prognosis and are often undertreated. Webb and colleagues described six patients who had minor wedge compression fractures with hidden flexion injuries that became progressively unstable.[246] Mazur and Stauffer similarly reported on five patients who suffered progressively increasing kyphosis and failure of nonoperative treatment.[143] Based on these two studies, patients with this injury pattern should be treated either in a halo brace or by posterior fusion. Patients treated nonsurgically should be advised of the poor prognosis and that they may require delayed posterior fusion in the future.

Patients with severe ligamentous injuries have interspinous widening and kyphotic angulation, but usually less than 3 mm of anterior translation (see Fig. 29–10). The facets may be in the perched position almost to the point of dislocation. Extension may reduce this deformity to a variable degree. Definitive treatment of a severe hyperflexion injury requires posterior cervical fusion with an interspinous wire technique.[30, 191] To restore alignment in these injuries, the surgeon should tighten the interspinous wire. The fixation is stable enough to allow early mobilization in an orthosis. If the spinous processes or laminae are fractured, posterior fusion with lateral mass plates or anterior plate fixation should be performed.

Doran and co-workers identified nine patients with a herniated nucleus pulposus and bilateral facet dislocations.[75] They recommended obtaining an MRI scan before any attempt at reduction. Others have disagreed with this recommendation and instead proposed immediate closed reduction to indirectly decompress the spinal cord and maximize the chance for neurologic recovery.[186, 232] Several case reports have noted reversal of complete spinal cord injury when reduction was performed in the first 2 to 3 hours after injury.[128] This outcome correlates with the benefits observed after early decompression in animal studies as presented by Delamarter and colleagues.[71] Delays in performing MRI can push patients beyond this window of opportunity and decrease their chance for neurologic recovery.

Reduction of bilateral facet dislocations has resulted in neurologic deterioration in rare cases. Eismont and associates identified six patients treated surgically who had concomitant herniated discs.[80] Two patients experienced deterioration after open reduction through a posterior approach while under anesthesia, whereas only one had neurologic worsening during closed reduction attempted while the patient was awake. Robertson and Ryan had three patients who worsened, one 3 days after closed reduction, one after open reduction performed from a posterior approach, and one who deteriorated during transport to the hospital.[189] Berrington and co-workers similarly reported two patients who experienced deterioration secondary to displaced intervertebral discs, one after open reduction and one after spontaneous reduction.[20] From these studies, certain observations can be made regarding neurologic deterioration associated with reduction of bilateral facet dislocation. To begin, neurologic worsening was associated with open reduction after failure of attempted closed reduction in patients in whom paresthesias or worsening radiculopathies were developing during closed reduction. Neurologic worsening was also an increased possibility when abnormal disc space narrowing was present. It was also associated with patients who were initially neurologically intact.

Regarding options for immobilizing the cervical spine, a halo vest provides the most secure degree of external immobilization. However, although this method of immobilization is often successful in the upper cervical spine, results in patients with facet dislocations in the mid to lower cervical spine are poor. Whitehill and co-workers reported six cases of loss of reduction in patients treated with a halo vest.[251] Bucholz and Cheung treated 125 patients with cervical trauma by a halo vest.[43] Nine of 20

patients with bilateral facet dislocations or perched facets failed treatment and required surgery. Sears and Fazl reported that only 44% of their patients achieved stability and over 50% had residual malalignment.[208] Anderson and colleagues evaluated fracture site motion during a change in position from supine to upright in 47 patients treated with the halo vest.[11] They found that translation increased by 1.7 mm and angulation by 11°. Clearly, the halo vest is poorly suited for unstable lower cervical injuries because of its inability to control intersegmental motion. In patients who are not otherwise surgical candidates, a halo vest provides temporary or even definitive immobilization.[149]

We recommend a specific management protocol for patients with bilateral facet dislocations. To begin, patients who are neurologically intact should have strict cervical immobilization and be evaluated by MRI or CT myelography before any attempt is made at reduction. If these imaging modalities are not available, closed reduction performed by strict protocol should be attempted. If an extruded disc is identified on MRI, anterior discectomy should be performed before reduction. After discectomy, reduction can be obtained by traction while the patient is under general anesthesia or by the use of a Caspar cervical distractor. The spinal cord should be monitored during this attempt at reduction. If reduction occurs, anterior cervical plating and interbody fusion should be performed. If reduction is not obtained, open reduction plus posterior fusion is performed. Before closing the anterior wound, a Smith-Robinson graft can be placed between the vertebrae. However, this graft may become displaced with reduction and necessitate a third procedure to replace the interbody graft.

Patients with significant cord deficits and bilateral facet dislocation should have immediate closed reduction with tongs traction (Fig. 29–25). The patient should be carefully monitored, and any neurologic symptoms such as paresthesias or increased sensory or motor loss will dictate discontinuation of traction and immediate MRI. If reduction is achieved, the patient should undergo MRI immediately to evaluate the status of the disc. If a disc herniation is compressing the spinal cord, anterior cervical discectomy and fusion with a plate should be performed. If the intervertebral disc is normal, posterior fusion can be performed. Interspinous wire techniques appear to be adequate if the bone structures are not fractured. In cases of facet, laminar, or spinous process fractures, posterior lateral mass fixation or anterior cervical plate fixation can be performed.[41]

Severe bilateral facet dislocations with 100% translocation or those manifested as intervertebral distraction require careful analysis. We have observed dangerous vertebral artery injuries and higher levels of paralysis in such cases. Traction is potentially perilous because all ligamentous structures are torn. These patients are best treated by early open reduction with anterior or posterior plates.

Bilateral facet dislocations are infrequently associated with bilateral pedicular fractures. This combination creates an increase in the spinal canal and thus decreases the chance of neurologic injury.[110, 146] The proposed mechanism of injury has been hyperextension. These fractures

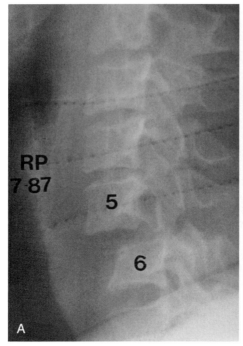
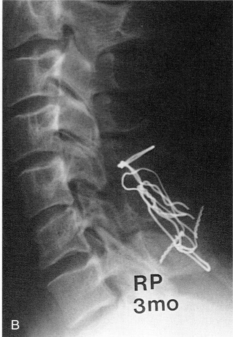

Figure 29–25. *A*, A 34-year-old construction worker was struck from behind, causing a C5–C6 bilateral facet dislocation with C6 complete quadriplegia. *B*, Ninety minutes after the injury, the dislocation was reduced with tong traction in the emergency department with immediate return of sensation and then motor function in all extremities. Within 36 hours, the patient was neurologically intact.

are difficult to reduce, and reduction by traction is hard to maintain because of the pedicle fracture. For best results, an anterior surgical approach with plate fixation is recommended.[146]

Fracture-Dislocations

Fracture-dislocations of the cervical spine are highly unstable injuries that are usually associated with a spinal cord injury. This injury pattern is the common end-point for high-energy burst fractures, facet dislocations, and combined injury mechanisms. Cranial traction should be used with caution in these patients because it may cause overdistraction. These injuries are usually treated with multilevel posterior fixation. Anterior decompression may also be necessary if residual cord compression is present after realignment of the spine through a closed or, more often, an open posterior procedure.

Distraction-Dissociation Injury

Distraction-dislocations are an extreme form of fracture-dislocation. In these injuries, all ligaments between the distracted vertebrae are completely torn. Distraction–extension dislocations are common in older patients with severe spondylosis. These injuries can easily result in catastrophic distraction, disruption of the cerebral blood supply, stroke, and death. Patients with distraction injuries require careful maintenance of head and neck alignment with sandbags or a provisional halo device until surgical stabilization is performed. Even with halo immobilization, these patients require meticulous care during transfers to avoid excessive distraction.

Surgical treatment is performed through a posterior approach with fixation of two to three vertebrae above and below the injury level. Supplemental anterior fixation may

be necessary in patients who have a persistent anterior gap after posterior surgery.

Surgical Technique

ANTERIOR DECOMPRESSION AND FUSION

Near or cephalad to the site of spinal cord injury may be found neuronal tissue that though intact, is impaired by displaced bone or disc fragments that prevent the return of function. Anterior decompression can remove these bone fragments. Once removed, any existing anterior horn cell function will improve, as will the existing function of the nerve root and the axonal tracts in the white matter (Fig. 29–26). Because most patients have compression from the ventral side of the cord, anterior decompression offers patients the best chance for full recovery. Other advantages of anterior decompression include the simplicity of the approach and positioning, limited soft tissue stripping of the paraspinal muscles, and the potential to restore anterior column height.

An anterior approach may minimize the number of levels fused if the posterior elements are extensively comminuted. Bohlman and Anderson reviewed 57 cases of incomplete motor quadriplegia treated by anterior decompression and fusion at least 1 month after injury.[31] Twenty-nine patients became ambulatory after the procedure and another 6 significantly improved their ambulatory status. Thirty-nine patients had objective improvement in upper extremity function. Fifty-two patients with complete motor quadriplegia were similarly treated with late anterior decompression.[10] The goal of surgery was to restore upper extremity function. Sixty percent of patients experienced functional improvement in their upper extremities after decompression, and one patient became ambulatory. In both groups, only one patient experienced neurologic deterioration after the procedure. The results in both groups were significantly better if decompression occurred within 1 year of the injury. Unfortunately, the efficacy of decompression in the first few days after the injury is unknown.

The primary disadvantage of anterior decompression is loss of stability, which is caused by removal of the anterior longitudinal ligament and residual disc annulus. Several authors have noted recurrent neurologic deficits after anterior decompression secondary to progressive instability.[89, 217] Such deficits are more likely to take place in patients with posterior osteoligamentous injuries. Additionally, in quadriplegic patients with impaired ventilation, respiratory compromise may develop because of an inability to overcome the retropharyngeal soft tissue swelling that often occurs after decompression. In Anderson and colleagues' series,[11] respiratory compromise occurred in 10% of patients. To avoid respiratory complications, they recommended that patients be intubated and mechanically ventilated for 2 to 3 days after surgery.

Anterior decompression plus fusion is indicated in patients with persistent neurologic deficits and residual anterior cord or root compression. Preoperatively, the patient should be evaluated by MRI. The timing of anterior decompression is controversial, and no published studies are available to support either aggressive early treatment or delayed treatment. Prophylactic decompression to prevent neurologic injury in a patient with spinal compromise is rarely warranted. In most centers, anterior plate fixation is performed in conjunction with anterior decompression and fusion.

In this procedure, after awake nasotracheal intubation, the patient is positioned supine with a small roll behind the shoulders to promote slight neck extension. A roll is placed behind the left buttock to shift the pelvis forward to facilitate bone grafting. In a patient with an extension injury and central cord syndrome, excessive neck extension must be avoided. Ideally, the patient is in tongs traction and has achieved maximal reduction before surgery. A lateral radiograph to confirm satisfactory alignment is taken before the surgical incision. The skin of the anterior aspect of the neck and the left iliac crest is prepared. We recommend a left-sided Smith-Robinson approach to decrease the likelihood of recurrent laryngeal nerve injury. At this point, the skin is incised transversely at the appropriate level from the midline to the anterior border of the sternocleidomastoid muscle. The platysma and superficial layer of the deep cervical fascia are divided transversely with Metzenbaum scissors. The middle layers of the deep cervical fascia are released from the sternocleidomastoid. The dissection is deepened bluntly between the trachea and strap muscles medially and the carotid sheath laterally. The alar and prevertebral fasciae are identified and divided vertically to expose the anterior vertebral bodies, the intervertebral discs, and the longus colli muscles. A bent spinal needle is placed into the most cranial disc for radiographic localization. If a discectomy is required, the anterior longitudinal ligament and annulus are incised and the disc and end-plates are removed with small curettes back to the posterior longitudinal ligament. In facet dislocations, the disc and end-plate may be herniated behind the vertebral body; this situation requires partial vertebrectomy for safe disc removal. In all instances, an operating microscope or loop magnification can facilitate lighting and minimize trauma. In trauma cases, the posterior longitudinal ligament is either ruptured or should be removed to ensure complete decompression of the neural tissue. The neural foramina are palpated with small nerve hooks. If required, an anterior

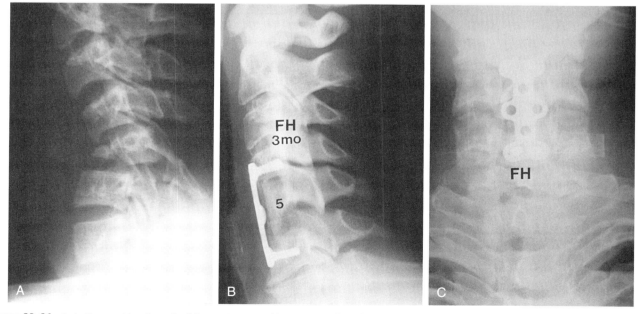

FIGURE 29-26. *A,* A 43-year-old male roofer fell, sustaining a mild anterior cord syndrome secondary to a C5 flexion teardrop fracture. He was initially treated by a halo vest but had recurrence of the deformity and neurologically plateaued. *B, C,* An anterior decompression fusion with iliac strut and CSLP fixation was performed. He made a full neurologic recovery and was able to return to work.

foraminotomy can be performed with 1-mm Kerrison rongeurs or high-speed burs.

If a corpectomy is necessary, the discs above and below the vertebral body must be completely removed. The vertebral body is extracted piecemeal with rongeurs and burs. Bony decompression with a diamond bur proceeds posteriorly until only a thin shell of bone remains. This shell is then removed with small curettes to expose the posterior longitudinal ligament. The decompression is extended laterally until the dura or the posterior longitudinal ligament bulges into the defect, usually requiring a 12- to 14-mm wide trough. Care is needed to maintain the orientation of the midline to avoid iatrogenic vertebral artery injury. Intervertebral distraction with the Caspar disc spreader facilitates exposure and can correct shortening of the anterior column. In trauma cases, however, distraction should be used with extreme caution to avoid overdistraction.

After distraction, the cartilaginous end-plates are completely removed and squared with a bur. The cortical bony end-plate is preserved as much as possible. Holes are punched into the end-plates with small, angled curettes to encourage revascularization of the graft. After measuring the depth and length of the grafting area, an appropriately sized full-thickness autogenous iliac crest bone graft is harvested with a saw. In discectomy cases, the disc-shaped graft is gently tapped into place while maintaining traction with the disc spreader. The graft is countersunk 1 to 2 mm. In corpectomy reconstruction, the graft's ends are squared and the graft is similarly tapped into place. A lateral radiograph is obtained before wound closure. An anterior cervical plate is then applied, which requires the platysma and skin to be closed in two layers. A small Penrose drain is placed in the deep tissue and brought out through the same skin incision. It should be removed the next day. Patients with spinal cord injuries are routinely monitored in the intensive care unit for 1 to 2 days after anterior decompression. Patients may be allowed out of bed immediately. Postoperatively, patients are immobilized in a cervicothoracic brace for 8 to 12 weeks.

In cases in which anterior fixation is not used, the bone graft reconstruction is modified. Mortises are created in the end-plates with burs or curettes. The iliac crest graft is machined into a T shape, with tenons created on its end. One graft tenon is made to fit into the mortise in the end-plate, and under traction the opposite end of the graft is tapped downward until the tenon clears the margin of the vertebral body. The tenon then locks into place to prevent dislodgment. Postoperatively, these patients are maintained in a cervicothoracic brace for 12 weeks.

The anterior cervical plate was developed to stabilize the injured spine segment after anterior decompression and to increase the success of fusion. The first generation of these implants were thin stainless steel plates with round or oblique holes.[27, 52, 164, 182] Screws 3.5 mm in diameter were placed through holes into the vertebral body. To prevent screw loosening from toggling, many authors recommended screw engagement of the posterior cortex.[52] This practice increased the risk of neurologic damage, required C-arm fluoroscopy, and generally increased the surgeon's anxiety. Second-generation plates with a rigid locking screw to the plate interface were developed to avoid screw loosening[154] (Fig. 29–27). The

benefit of this second generation of plates was that they did not require engagement of the posterior vertebral cortex. Traynelis and colleagues compared unicortical and bicortical screw purchase in anterior cervical plate constructs.[231] They found that unicortical cervical locking plates had stiffness equal to that of nonrigid plates with bicortical screw purchase. Biomechanically, the anterior cervical plates performed poorly in flexion-distraction models when compared with posterior fixation techniques. However, the clinical results of both rigid and nonrigid plate-screw constructs have been excellent.[27, 154, 157] In extension, the anterior cervical plate has proved to be a significantly better surgical option than posterior cervical devices. Newell and associates reported on 37 patients with combined AP instability from fractures and dislocations treated with the AO cervical spine locking plate.[157] In 34 patients, the fusions healed. Asymptomatic nonunion developed in one patient, one patient had a plate fracture with a symptomatic nonunion, and one patient experienced acute failure from the screws pulling out of the vertebral body. This study supports the use of anterior cervical plates in the management of most patients with cervical trauma, despite the adverse biomechanical results.

ANTERIOR FIXATION

Anterior cervical fixation devices are usually thin and are available in a wide variety of lengths (see Fig. 29–23). Anterior fixation in general is not as strong biomechanically as posterior fixation. In traumatic conditions, the damaged structures may involve the entire substance of the cervical ligaments and the intervertebral disc at a particular level, in contrast to the limited resection of these structures in surgical decompression for degenerative disease. Therefore, the strength of surgical fixation in injuries to the cervical spine is a more important consideration than surgical fixation of degenerative disorders, even when the surgical approach and surgical decompression may be similar. Most currently available rigid fixation devices meet the minimal strength requirement for fixation in trauma. New devices that attempt to allow dynamic fixation, such as settling and greater graft loading, may not provide adequate stiffness for stabilization in cervical injuries.

In anterior plate fixation, screws 3.5 mm in diameter are placed through the round holes, two at each level. Anterior decompression and grafting are performed as described in the previous sections. Next, the vertebral bodies to be instrumented are subperiosteally exposed. Osteophytes or bony prominences are removed to allow proper plate seating. The correct length of plate is selected and the plate contoured if required. Before screw placement, the plate is placed on the vertebra and a lateral radiograph is obtained to check plate position. It is important that the vertebral body screws do not cross into any nonfused disc spaces and that the plate does not overlie an adjacent disc. Ideally, the plate holes are positioned directly over the midpoint of the vertebral body. The initial drilling depth is selected by measuring the AP diameter of the disc space, and when correctly determined by C-arm fluoroscopy, a 2-mm drill bit with a stopped drill guide is advanced slightly medially and upward in a posterior direction. The posterior cortex is carefully monitored on fluoroscopy to check for perforation. If

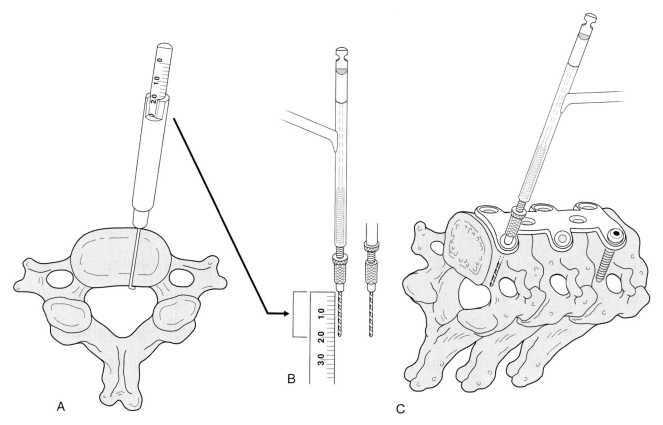

FIGURE 29–27. Technique of plate fixation with bicortical screws. *A,* The screw depth is initially estimated using a depth gauge or calipers placed along exposed end-plates. *B,* An adjustable drill guide is set 1 to 2 mm short of this depth and then drilled. *C,* The posterior wall is checked for perforation, and the drilling is repeated until the posterior wall is engaged. C-arm fluoroscopy facilitates this potentially dangerous step. The hole is tapped, and the appropriate length screw is inserted. No screws are placed into the strut graft. (*A–C,* Redrawn from Müller, M.E.; et al. Manual of Internal Fixation: Techniques Recommended by the AO-ASIF Group, 3rd ed. Berlin, Springer-Verlag, 1991.)

required, the drill guide is adjusted to allow 1 more mm of advancement, and the process is repeated until the posterior cortex has been perforated. The drilling depth is noted to help gauge screw selection. The near cortex is tapped and 3.5-mm screws are inserted. Two screws are placed in each vertebral body, but no screws are inserted in the vertebral bone graft. After all screws have been initially placed, final tightening is performed. After tightening, a lateral radiograph is obtained to ensure proper screw placement. The platysma and skin are closed in layers and a small Penrose drain is brought out through the same skin incision. After the procedure, patients are immobilized in a cervicothoracic brace for 8 to 12 weeks.

There are now a number of plates that enhance unicortical fixation by predetermining the angle of screw insertion and/or by locking the screw to the plate. These devices allow rigid locking of the screws to the plate[154] (Fig. 29–28). In one system, the screw head was hollow and slotted to allow expansion against the plate hole when a small setscrew is inserted into the hollow-headed screw. This technique creates a rigid interlock between the screw and plate. Screws 4.0 and 4.35 mm in diameter are available in 14- and 16-mm lengths. Standard plates are available in lengths of 14 to 55 mm. Longer plates for multiple-level decompression are available but have been shown to have a significantly higher failure rate because of

caudal loosening of the screws. If a longer plate is required, adjunctive treatment with posterior fusion or a halo vest should be considered.

When affixing the plate, anterior decompression/fusion is performed as previously described. The anterior surface of the vertebral bodies is exposed subperiosteally. Osteophytes and bony prominences are removed to allow proper plate seating. The plate is positioned and checked radiographically, and the plate holes should lie over the midpoint of the vertebral bodies. Laying the plate over unfused discs or placing the screws into disc spaces should be avoided. While maintaining plate position, a hole is made with a stopped drill guide. The drill guide should theoretically direct proper screw angulation, although in vivo we have discovered that precise angulation is rarely achieved with the drill guide. In the cranial holes, the drill is directed 12° craniad and 15° medially. Caudad, the drill is directed orthogonally to the plate and 15° medially. The near cortices are tapped and then the 14- or 16-mm screws are inserted. After all screws are inserted, the final tightening process takes place. The screws are locked to the plate, and the construct is checked radiographically. The wound is closed in layers, as described earlier, for an anterior decompression process. Postoperatively, the patient is immobilized in a cervicothoracic brace for 8 to 12 weeks.

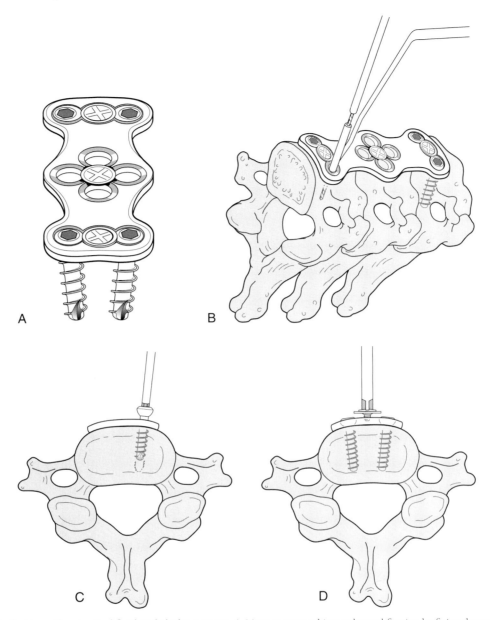

FIGURE 29–28. Plate fixation with unicortical fixed angle locking screws. *A,* Many systems achieve enhanced fixation by fixing the angle of the screw and locking the screws to the plate. *B,* Once the plate is properly positioned on the vertebra, a drill hole is made through the plate, using a drill guide that orients the hole and limits the drilling depth. *C,* A self-tapping screw is inserted. *D,* The locking mechanism fixes the screwheads to the plate.

POSTERIOR DECOMPRESSION BY LAMINECTOMY

After the laminectomy procedure was first introduced (Fig. 29–29), it became a routinely performed operation that offered hope to unfortunate patients with spinal cord injury. Rarely, however, did the laminectomy result in any patient improvement. Morgan and many of his colleagues have, in separate studies, assailed the laminectomy procedure, and these attacks have led to a much more conservative approach in the care of spinal cord–injured patients.[29, 103, 153, 218] Biomechanical studies indicate that laminectomy has little mechanical effect on neural tissues compressed by an anterior lesion.[228] Deformity and residual kyphotic deformity frequently recur after laminectomy, thus making it an additionally risky surgery. If

laminectomy must be performed in trauma cases, fusion should accompany the procedure.

Laminectomy is indicated in patients with neurologic deficits who have residual posterior compressive lesions. These lesions are rare, but they can be caused by displaced laminar fractures or hyperlordotic deformities after extension injuries. Laminectomy or laminoplasty may also be indicated in patients who have central cord syndromes with multilevel AP compressive lesions and a lordotic posture. Epstein and Epstein showed that the spinal cord will become displaced posteriorly, away from the anterior ventral lesions, only if the initial alignment is neutral or lordotic.[82] Kyphosis prevents the natural displacement of the cord and therefore lessens the extent of neurologic recovery.

To prepare for a laminectomy, patients are positioned prone on a turning frame in Gardner-Wells traction. The sitting position should not be used in trauma cases. The best possible alignment is achieved, with care taken to avoid hyperextension. Exposure is carried out to the lateral edge of the facets, and the levels to be decompressed are localized radiographically. Two different techniques of laminectomy are described, the first for the presence of

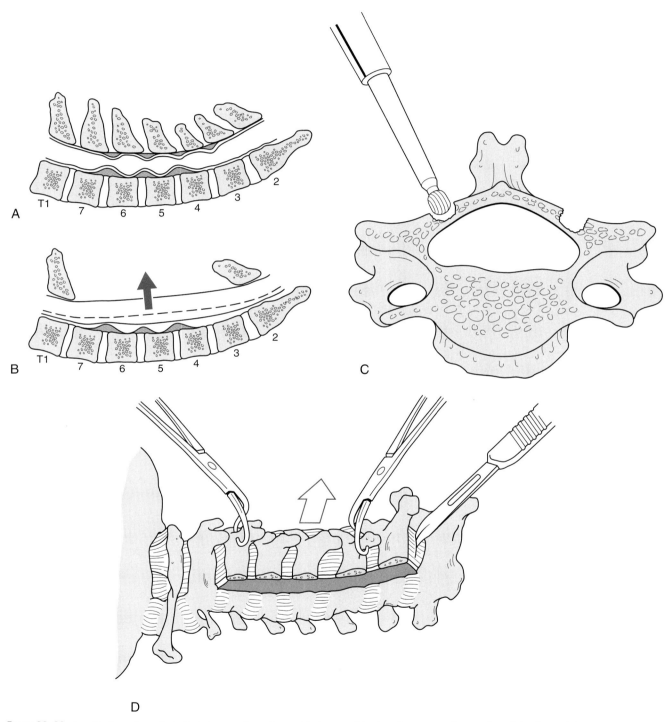

FIGURE 29–29. Laminectomy is rarely indicated except in patients with depressed laminar fractures or those with multilevel spondolytic myelopathy. To achieve decompression over multiple levels, the spine must be in lordotic or neural alignment. *A, B,* Laminectomy or laminoplasty will then allow the spinal cord to drift posteriorly, thus decompressing the ventral surface of the cord. *C,* The technique requires division of the laminae at their attachment to the lateral mass with an air-driven bur. As the anterior laminal cortex is approached, a diamond bur is used. *D,* Once all the laminae are freed, they can be lifted upward and removed by division of the ligamentum flavum. In trauma cases, after decompression, lateral mass fixation is performed. (*A, B,* Redrawn from Epstein, J.A.; Epstein, M.E. In: The Cervical Spine Research Society Staff, eds. The Cervical Spine, 2nd ed. Philadelphia, J.B. Lippincott, 1989; from Epstein, J.A. Contemp Neurosurg 7[18]:3, 1985. *C, D,* Redrawn from Dante, S.J.; et al. Oper Tech Orthop 6:30–37, 1996.)

displaced laminar fractures and the second for multilevel decompression of spondylitic spines with central cord syndrome.

Depressed Laminar Fractures

Depressed laminar fractures may be associated with torn or entrapped dural and neural tissue.[147] Great care is therefore needed to avoid further dural damage during decompression. After initial surgical inspection, the exposed fracture edges can be removed with small burs or rongeurs. If possible, the ligamentum flavum should be dissected free to allow mobilization of the depressed fragment. Most surgeons gravitate toward burring into the defect, but such treatment may injure any trapped nerve tissue. If possible, the lamina should be divided vertically away from the fracture with a bur, and while drilling, an assistant should be positioned to maintain upward pressure on the laminar fracture. Once freed, the laminar fracture can be gently elevated and removed. If necessary, further drilling can be performed. The dura is then carefully inspected during this process and may require release from the lamina. If dural tears are present, they should be repaired with fine suture if technically possible. After laminectomy, a posterior lateral mass fusion is performed, as described later.

Multilevel Laminectomy for Central Cord Syndrome

In this procedure, the patient is positioned as described in the previous section regarding depressed laminar fractures. Neck extension is always scrupulously avoided. In general, one to two levels above and below the compressed lesions should be removed to allow posterior displacement of the cord as needed to indirectly decompress the ventral surface.[82] The interspinous ligaments and ligamentum flavum are divided craniad and caudad to the level to be decompressed. A 2- to 3-mm air-driven bur is used to create bilateral vertical troughs in all lamina to be decompressed (see Fig. 29–29). The trough should be located at the junction of the lamina and lateral mass. During drilling, it is safest to position the bur along the caudal half of the lamina, where the ligamentum flavum can protect the dura. As the anterior cortex of the lamina is approached, the bur is changed to a diamond tip. This bur can usually safely complete the laminotomy. If needed, a 1-mm Kerrison rongeur may be used. Once all the individual laminotomies have been performed, beginning caudad, the spinous processes are grasped and lifted upward. Residual ligaments can be divided with scissors until the lamina and spinous processes have been removed, and any residual lateral compression can subsequently be removed with 1- to 2-mm Kerrison rongeurs. A posterior fusion is then performed with lateral mass fixation. The most craniad or caudad lateral masses may be drilled and tapped before laminectomy. This procedure is facilitated in the presence of normal bony landmarks. The proper plate is chosen, contoured, and fixed at both ends with screws. The intervening lateral masses are then drilled, tapped, and affixed with screws. An autogenous bone graft is packed into the decorticated facet joints lateral to the facets. Postoperatively, patients are managed in a cervicothoracic brace for 12 weeks.

POSTERIOR FIXATION

Interspinous wire fixation is a utilitarian process and remains the most common procedure for promoting long-term cervical stability. It is highly effective and proven to be safe. Two common methods of interspinous wire fixation are the Rogers interspinous wire and the Bohlman triple wire.[30, 191] The most appropriate type of wire fixation depends on the nature of the injury. Posterior wire fixation is most effective in the stabilization of one to two motion segments with intact posterior elements. If facet fractures are present, the buttress to rotation and forward vertebral body translation may be lost, which could allow recurrent deformity after wire fixation. Although the Bohlman triple-wire technique increases rigidity, it may be insufficient to control rotational forces. In this case, Rogers' technique may be preferable. It requires a single steel wire or braided wire looped around the spinous process to restore the tension band to the posterior column. In Rogers' study, 35 of 37 patients had healing of their fusion and only 1 patient had loss of reduction. This technique is indicated for patients with hyperflexion injuries without posterior element comminution or rotational instability.

Rogers' Interspinous Wire Technique

When implementing Rogers' method, the patient is positioned prone as described in Chapter 27. Before skin preparation and draping, a radiograph is taken to ensure adequate alignment. The patient's head may be held in a Mayfield headrest. Alternatively, the patient may be positioned prone on a Stryker turning frame while maintaining tongs traction (Fig. 29–30).

A posterior midline exposure is used, with dissection carried out to the lateral masses. When operating, it is important to expose only the levels that are to undergo arthrodesis and to maintain a midline cuff of soft tissue. This technique will prevent extension of the fusion, as well as iatrogenic instability of adjacent levels. The level is confirmed radiographically.

If needed, open reduction of the facet dislocation can be performed. Spinal cord monitoring should be used in patients with distal cord function. Several techniques are helpful in performing the open reduction, and the surgeon must choose the most appropriate one. The spinous processes can be manipulated as levers with Kocher clamps or towel clips. A small elevator such as a Freer can be inserted into the dislocated facet joint and levered in an attempt to unlock the joint. If necessary, the cranial aspect of the superior facet can be removed with a bur to unlock the facet. In unilateral facet dislocations, lateral bending to the opposite side can facilitate unlocking of the facet.[17]

After exposure, the bony structures are carefully inspected to identify any occult fractures that may preclude interspinous wire fixation. Rogers' interspinous fixation is performed by bilaterally drilling 3-mm holes in the base of the spinous process of the superior vertebra (Fig. 29–31). The holes are enlarged with a Lewin clamp or towel clip to enable them to accept several passes of wire. Careful hole selection is required to avoid intracanal placement and to ensure adequate fixation. In the caudal vertebrae, fixation may be similarly achieved with holes in

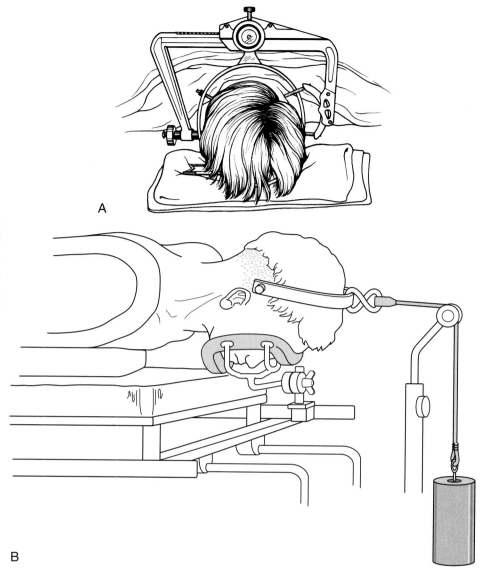

A

B

FIGURE 29–30. Techniques for Rogers wiring. This patient is prepared for posterior cervical fusion by use of Gardner-Wells tongs (A) or a halo (B). The halo can be attached directly to a Mayfield headrest, or the Mayfield can be used independently. The patient is then logrolled, with the surgeon controlling the head, into the prone position on the table and appropriately positioned with the neck slightly extended and the chin flexed in a military position.

the base of the spinous process or by passing the wire under the caudal edge of the spinous process. Twenty-gauge stainless steel wire, braided 24-gauge stainless steel wire, or titanium cables may be used. Titanium cables offer the advantage of MRI compatibility, and their crimping mechanism theoretically increases strength. However, long-term results of cable use in cervical fusion are not available.[67, 214]

Threading of the wire takes a particular course. First, it is passed through the superior spinous process; then it is looped back over the top of the spinous process and again through the spinous process. The wire is next passed through the caudal spinous process, then under the inferior edge of the spinous process, and then back through the hole so that both free ends are on the same side. Alternatively, the wire is looped under the inferior edge of the caudal spinous process. To facilitate tightening, the wire is gently snugged on the opposite side. To secure the wire, the wire ends are twisted together with needle drivers. If a kink develops during wire handling, the wire

should be changed to prevent early fatigue failure. After tightening, lateral radiographs are obtained to ensure adequate alignment. Careful attention should be paid postoperatively because posterior interspinous wiring can result in retrolisthesis with possible neural compromise, especially in patients with injuries to the intervertebral disc.

After the wiring process, the lamina are decorticated with a 3-mm bur, and an autogenous iliac crest graft is placed along the spinous processes and lamina. Rogers recommends the placement of small cortical cancellous struts under the wire. The paraspinal muscles and nuchal ligament are closed in two layers. After skin closure and dressing, the neck is immobilized in a hard collar or cervical thoracic brace. Patients are rapidly mobilized within 24 hours. The orthosis is worn continuously for 8 to 12 weeks, and fusion is assessed with flexion-extension radiographs at 2 to 3 months. During immobilization, the patient is placed on a regimen of cervical isometric neck exercises and aerobic conditioning.

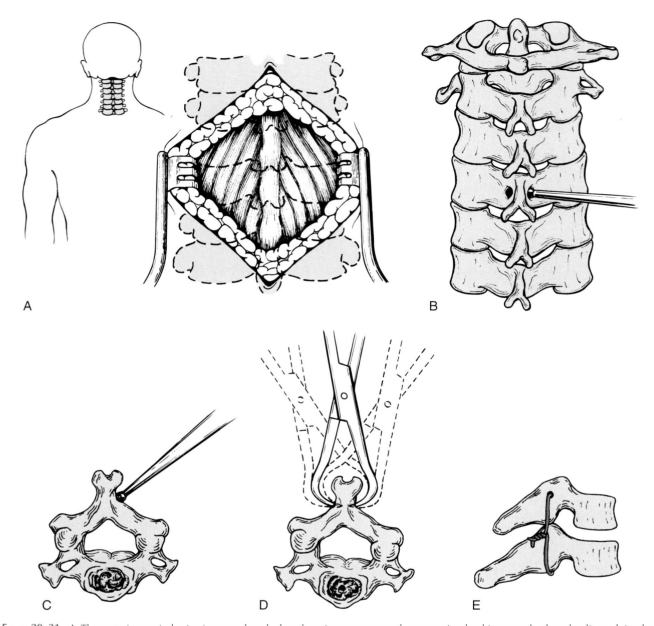

FIGURE 29–31. *A,* The posterior cervical spine is exposed, and when the spinous process at the appropriate level is exposed, a lateral radiograph is taken to ascertain position. Once the position is verified, the exposure is completed out to the lateral aspect of the facet joints at only the two levels to be fused. A high-speed bur *(B, C,)* is used to open the cortex on either side of the spinous process at the level of the base of the spinous process but not in the lamina. *D,* The holes are then communicated using a towel clip. *E,* The wiring can be done in a number of ways, including through holes in both spinous processes or through a hole at the junction of the middle and upper thirds of the spinous process of the superior level, with the wire passed beneath the interspinous ligament and around the inferior edge of the spinous process at the lower level.

Bohlman Triple-Wire Technique

The Bohlman triple-wire technique is indicated for traumatic posterior instability of the cervical spine. To increase the rigidity of the injured spine, especially when operating on spines with rotational deformities, Bohlman developed the triple-wire technique (Fig. 29–32). Mechanically, this technique has been shown to increase both flexional and rotational stiffness to a higher degree than in either an intact spine or the Rogers' wire fixation technique.[59, 222] Weiland and McAfee documented that all 100 patients treated with the Bohlman triple-wire technique had healing of their fusions.[247] Despite its increase in rotational

rigidity, we have found that recurrent dislocations can occur if the facet articulations are incompetent.

In the Bohlman technique, an interspinous wire is placed similarly to the Rogers' method. A 3-mm hole is drilled at the base of the spinous processes bilaterally and enlarged to allow easy wire passage of a Lewin clamp or towel clip. Care is taken to select the correct hole position to avoid intraspinal wire passage and ensure adequate fixation. Twenty-gauge stainless steel wire or 24-gauge braided stainless steel wire is used. The wire is passed through the hole in the cranial vertebra superior to the spinous process and then drawn back through the hole.

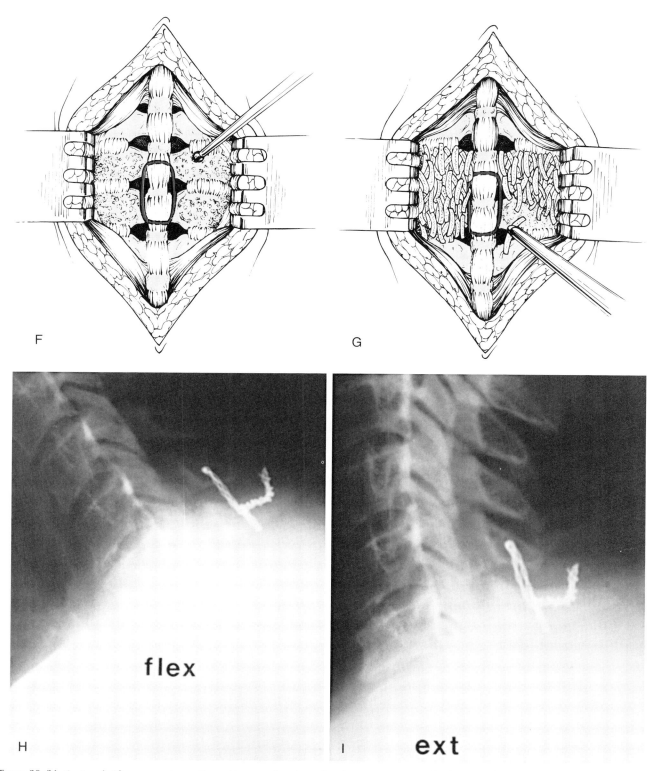

FIGURE 29–31 *Continued.* After appropriate radiographic control to determine the correct amount of tightening of the wire, the two affected levels are decorticated using a high-speed bur (*F*), and cancellous bone from the iliac crest is then placed over the decorticated lamina (*G*). The attempt to reconstruct the paraspinous musculature to the spinous process is made so that gaping of the posterior spinous musculature does not occur postoperatively. The flexion (*H*) and extension (*I*) radiographs following an interspinous wiring for C5–C6 instability show a solid arthrodesis 2 years postoperatively. Motion has been preserved at the adjacent motion segments.

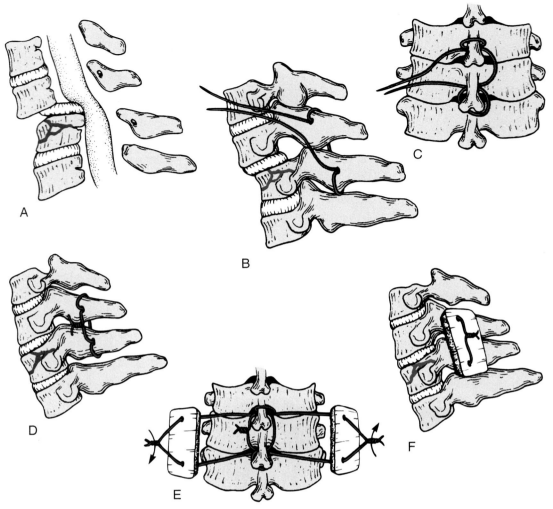

FIGURE 29–32. Triple-wire technique: The triple-wire technique may be used to stabilize cervical injuries. *A,* Two holes are placed through the adjacent spinous processes and a wire passed through the holes as indicated in *B* and *C.* The first wire is then tightened to stabilize the injury. *D,* An additional two wires are passed through the holes and used to compress two large corticocancellous iliac struts against the laminae (*E* and *F*).

One end of the wire is double-looped caudad around the spinous process. The free ends of the wires are tightened to create a tension band. The second and third wires are 22-gauge wires passed through each spinous process. Though not necessarily required, light decortication of the lamina is performed before graft placement. After decortication, autogenous cortical cancellous plates of iliac crest bone graft are harvested, each one measuring 1.75 mm wide, 1 cm thick, and 3 to 4 cm long. The grafts are machined with a rongeur to fit snugly along the spinous processes and lamina. Two 3-mm holes are drilled at the ends of each graft to accept the second and third wires. The 22-gauge wires are passed through the bone grafts. When the wires are twisted over the grafts, the grafts will be secured down on the spinous process and lamina. Care is needed to avoid notching or breaking the wire during handling and tightening. Patients are mobilized the next day in a cervical thoracic brace or a hard collar. The orthosis is worn for 6 to 8 weeks. Flexion-extension radiographs are checked at 12 weeks.

Oblique Wire

Facet wire fixation was initially described by Robinson and Southwick as a process suited to treat the kyphotic and swan neck deformities associated with cervical laminectomies[190] (Fig. 29–33). In this process, multiple wires are passed through the facet holes and tightened over the long struts of the cortical cancellous grafts or over the rib grafts.[47] The oblique wire obtains purchase by a wire passed through the facet and looped around the next caudal spinous process. This wire is combined with an interspinous wire and an autogenous bone graft. Edwards and associates documented successful outcomes of facet wire fixation in 26 of 27 patients treated with the oblique wire.[79]

In facet wire fixation, the patient is positioned and a midline approach is performed. Dissection is carried out to the far edge of the lateral mass to facilitate the easiest wire placement. Reduction of the dislocated facet, if not initially achieved by closed means, can be performed at this point by following the method described previously. The involved facet joint is opened and the joint cartilage is gently curetted with 3–0 curettes. After curettage, an elevator can be placed into the joint to allow for distraction. At this point, an air-driven bur is used to make a 3-mm hole directed into the midpoint or the summit of

the lateral mass and pointing downward toward the facet joint. A Penfield elevator is placed in the joint to act as a skid. A 20-gauge wire (or preferably a cable) is passed through the hole and into the joint. A small hemostat or needle driver is used to grasp the wire end and pull it out

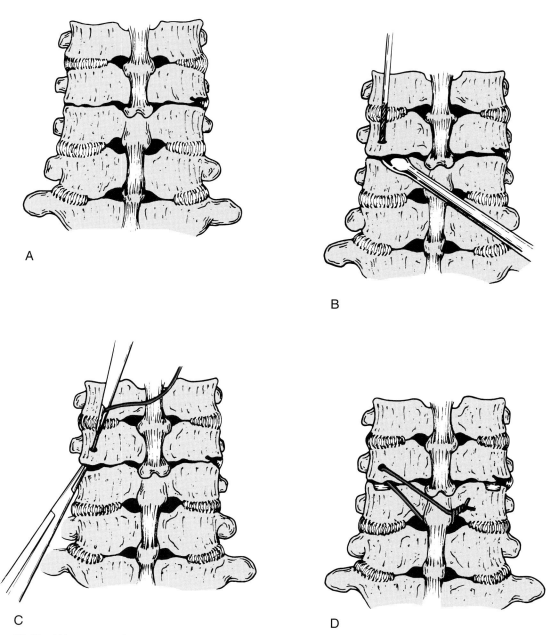

A

B

C

D

FIGURE 29–33. Oblique wire technique. Oblique wiring is most frequently utilized for a unilateral facet fracture when the superior facet of the inferior level is fractured. Most unilateral facet dislocations can be appropriately stabilized by an interspinous wire once the facet dislocation is reduced. Should reduction of the dislocation require compromise of the superior facet of the inferior level, then an oblique wire may be appropriately used. The surgical approach is similar to that for interspinous wiring, with the patient placed prone in traction, most commonly with Gardner-Wells tongs on a Stryker frame. A midline exposure is accomplished and the level checked using a marker and a radiographic control. The exposure is carried out to the tips of the facets, and care is taken to expose only the facet at the injured level. The facet capsules generally will be totally disrupted on the fractured side and intact on the uninjured side. In addition, the interspinous ligament will usually be present but somewhat attenuated. *A,* After removing all soft tissue at the appropriate level, a Penfield elevator is placed within the joint after removing all cartilage from the joint surfaces with a small curette. Using a hand drill and ³⁄₃₂-inch drill bit, a hole is made in the center of the facet directed perpendicular to the facet joint and slightly inferior and medially. *B,* A 20-gauge wire or a braided 22-gauge wire is passed through the facet joint from superior to inferior and grasped using a needle holder. *C,* The small cancellous plugs are placed into the facet joints to preserve height and promote fusion, and the wire is placed around the spinous process of the lower level. It is progressively tightened, and radiographs are taken until anatomic reduction has been achieved. *D,* Generally, 1 mm of overreduction is desired so that the reduction will be anatomic when the patient is mobilized.

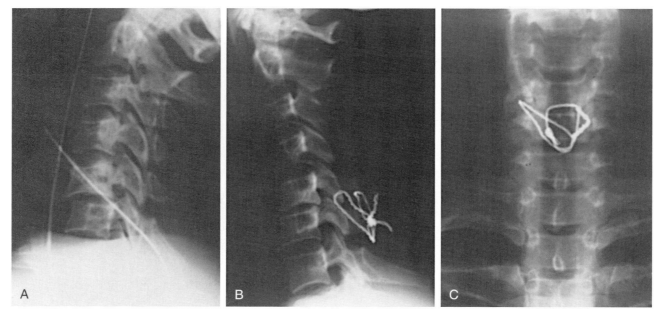

FIGURE 29–34. This 44-year-old woman sustained multiple injuries, including a unilateral facet fracture at C5–C6. *A,* On admission, she had a step-off between C5 and C6 with loss of height at the disc space and radicular findings in the C6 root distribution on the right. The patient underwent reduction and traction with 25 lb, which was followed by improvement in neurologic findings. She then underwent an oblique wiring of C5–C6. This was augmented with an interspinous wire because of complete destruction of the interspinous ligament between C5 and C6 as well as fracture of the superior facet of C6 on the right. *B,* At follow-up, the patient is shown to have reduction of the rotational deformity but complete loss of the C5–C6 disc height, which is a common finding. *C,* A follow-up radiograph shows the wire construct as well as the complete restoration of alignment.

of the joint. Distraction of the spinous processes or small elevators placed into the joint can facilitate passage of the wire. The wire is looped around the base of the next caudal spinous process and twisted until full reduction is achieved. At this point, a lateral radiograph is taken to assess the quality of the reduction. After the radiograph, a Rogers interspinous wire is inserted. The lamina, spinous processes, and facet joints are decorticated with a bur, and an autologous cancellous bone graft is placed in the decorticated bed. Postoperatively, the patient is immobilized in a cervicothoracic brace for 8 to 12 weeks (Fig. 29–34).

Lateral Mass Fixation

Lateral mass fixation of the cervical spine was first introduced in Paris by Roy-Camille and co-workers, who used Vitallium plates with 14-mm screws.[199] The technique was modified by Grob and Magerl to provide fixation for the AO hook plate.[102] These techniques gained popularity because of their increased rigidity, reduced incidence of loss of reduction, and decreased postoperative brace requirements.[13, 61] Other advantages to lateral mass fixation include its effectiveness when the lamina or spinous processes are missing or fractured, its capability for multilevel fixation, and its ability to control rotational deformities. Lateral mass fixation can also be used in conjunction with fixation across the occipitocervical or cervicothoracic junction.

Several techniques for screw placement have been described (see Fig. 29–5). Roy-Camille and co-workers recommended that the screw be positioned at the summit or the center of the lateral mass and be directed forward

and outward 10°.[199] Grob and Magerl recommended a screw starting point 1 to 2 mm medial to the center and craniad to the center of the lateral mass and directed 30° upward and 30° outward.[102] Anderson and associates modified this technique by placing the screw 1 mm from the center of the lateral mass and angling upward 30° and outward 15° to 20°.[13] An and colleagues performed a cadaveric analysis and found that the nerve root exits the neural foramen at the anterolateral aspect of the superior articular face.[6] They documented a higher frequency of risk as upward angulation and lateral angulation increased. However, it is important to note that less upward and outward angulation puts the vertebral artery at more risk. They recommended 30° of lateral and 15° of upward angulation.

Heller and co-workers performed an analysis of cadaveric specimens after inserting screws according to the Roy-Camille and Magerl techniques.[111] Their most striking finding involved the effect of screw placement. With experienced surgeons, they discovered that the Magerl technique was associated with a 7% incidence of nerve root injury as compared with 5.4% with the Roy-Camille method.

Biomechanical studies by various teams of surgeons have confirmed the superiority of lateral mass fixation over posterior wire fixation or anterior plate fixation.[1, 59, 152, 199, 233] However, complications including nerve root injury and loosening have also been reported. Heller and co-workers documented a 6% incidence of iatrogenic nerve injury and a 0.2% incidence of facet joint violation in 654 lateral mass screw procedures.[112] Loosening was observed in over 1% of cases and hardware fracture occurred in 0.5% of cases. Biomechanical studies show that longer screws can be inserted with the Magerl technique, which correlates with increased pull-out strength.[152]

Clinically, lateral mass fixation has been shown to be highly effective.[13, 61] Anderson and Grady reported a study of 102 patients with unstable cervical spines treated by lateral mass fixation with AO reconstruction plates. Based on flexion-extension radiographs taken at a 14-month follow-up, all patients had healing of their fusion.[12] Reduction was well maintained with an average of only 1.5° increased kyphosis and 0.1 mm of increased translation. Two patients had iatrogenic C7 radiculopathies from the drilling and screwing process. Heller and co-workers noted that the C7 roots were most at risk because of screw placement in the C7 lateral mass.[112] This increased risk is due to the thinner lamina and less defined lateral mass of the C7 vertebra.[6] If the lateral mass borders of C7 are not easily identified, it is best to avoid screw placement in this vertebra. Alternatives are to use C7 pedicles, T1 fixation, or wire fixation alone.

To prepare for lateral mass fixation, patients are positioned prone on a turning frame with the neck in the neutral position. A lateral radiograph confirms a reduced position before a skin incision is made. The midline is incised to expose the spinous process, lamina, and lateral masses out to their far edge. A midline cuff of tissue is maintained to prevent iatrogenic instability or extension of the fusion.

Proper screw placement requires accurate identification of the borders of the lateral mass. When viewed dorsally, the lateral masses appear to be square or rectangular. The medial border is an easily perceptible valley at the junction of the lamina and the lateral mass, the lateral border is the far edge of the lateral mass, the superior border is marked by the cranial-most facet joint, and the caudal border is marked by the inferior-most facet joint. The vertebral artery is located directly anterior to the valley or medial border. With these borders delineated, all screws must start lateral to this valley and angle outward.

Several screw insertion techniques have been described and are discussed in the section on lateral mass anatomy[102, 171, 199] (see Fig. 29–5). A modification of the Magerl technique is recommended because of its biomechanical strength, its technical ease with the plates currently available, and its safety when performed by experienced surgeons[12, 13, 102, 171, 199] (Fig. 29–35). The starting point for screw insertion is 1 to 2 mm medial to the center of the lateral mass. The screws are oriented in an upward direction, parallel to the facet joints at approximately 30° and outward 10° to 20°. Drilling is performed with a drill guide and a 2-mm Kirschner wire rather than a drill. The initial length of the Kirschner wire is set to 14 mm. The wire is advanced in an upward and outward direction. The hole is checked for perforation of the far cortex, and if perforation has not occurred, the drill guide is adjusted to allow advancement in 1- to 2-mm steps. This process continues until the far cortex has been perforated or until 18 mm of drilling depth has been achieved. The drilling depth is noted to gauge selection of the appropriate screw length. The hole is then tapped with a 3.5-mm cancellous bone tap.

Several lateral mass fixation devices are currently available. Rod-screw devices allow more flexibility in lateral mass screw placement than plates. The lateral masses are initially drilled freehand rather than drilling through the plate. This technique facilitates safe screw placement. Once the holes have been made, a template is used to guide implant selection. The proper rod is chosen and may be bent into lordosis if required. The posterior third of the facet is decorticated with a bur, and an autogenous iliac crest bone graft is packed into the facet. The plates are then placed over the lateral masses and affixed with the properly chosen length of 3.5-mm screws. The screws are tightened in a sequential fashion. During screw tightening, orientation of the screw should be observed carefully. If the screw begins to move laterally, it is an indication that the screw is beginning to cut out. A Rogers interspinous wire procedure may be added to ameliorate such lateral movement. In cases of multilevel fixation, the cranial and caudal lateral masses are initially drilled to provide perfect screw position at both ends. Postoperatively, patients may be rapidly mobilized in a hard collar or cervicothoracic brace. The brace should be worn for 8 to 10 weeks (see Fig. 29–17).

Common Pitfalls

1. Inadequate-quality radiographs are accepted for definitive decision making, and "no injury" is the diagnosis (suspect injury until clearly proved otherwise).
2. The necessary radiographs are not obtained.
3. An inexperienced team member performs a definitive review of radiographs for final decisions.
4. The steroid protocol for spinal cord injury is not implemented (missed opportunity).
5. Patients with isolated nerve root injuries are given steroids (no benefit).
6. Patients are given steroids more than 8 hours after injury (no benefit).
7. Observations of neurologic function at the scene and en route are not solicited from the paramedic team (potentially critical information).
8. Outside evaluation is deemed complete and accurate without directly reviewing the studies (potentially erroneous assumption).
9. Outside studies are not reviewed (may identify injury or facilitate evaluation).
10. Diagnostic tests are repeated when acceptable outside studies are available for review (unnecessary workup).
11. The initial lateral radiograph is not adequately reviewed (oversight or inexperience).
12. An initial lateral radiograph "clear to C5" is interpreted as "no cervical injury" (assume injury until proved otherwise).
13. An opportunity is missed to perform a neurologic examination before intubation or pharmacologic paralysis (recognizing a deficit may alter treatment priorities).
14. A neurologic deficit is assumed to be due to head injury (spine evaluation should not be delayed on the basis of assumptions).

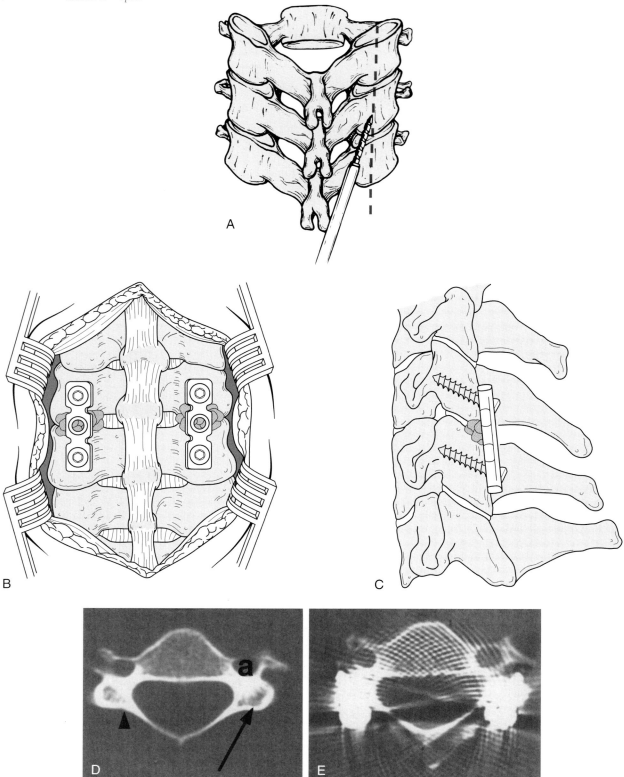

FIGURE 29–35. Cervical plate technique. *A–E,* Cervical plating can be utilized for a variety of lower cervical injuries, including teardrop fractures, facet fractures, and facet dislocations. The approach is similar to other posterior techniques with the exception that exposure of the facets must extend out to and around the lateral edge of the articular mass. For facet dislocations, if reduction has not been achieved with traction, a manual reduction is done first. For a unilateral or bilateral facet dislocation, a single-level plating is sufficient. *A,* The starting point for screw insertion is 1 to 2 mm medial to the center of the lateral mass. Angling 15° to 20° outward and 20° to 30° upward, a 2-mm Kirschner wire (K-wire) is advanced. An adjustable drill guide is set at 15 mm and prevents plunging. After drilling, the hole is checked for perforation with a smaller K-wire. If the far cortex has not been perforated, the drill guide is adjusted to allow 1 to 2 mm more of K-wire advancement. The process is repeated until the far cortex has been perforated or until a depth of 20 mm has been reached. The hole is tapped with a 3.5-mm tap, and the process is repeated at the other lateral masses. Using templates, the best plate is chosen, bent to restore lordosis, and fixed to the spine with 3.5-mm screws. Screw lengths should be chosen so that they do not extend out anteriorly. Before plate placement, autogenous iliac crest bone graft is packed into decorticated facet joints. After fixation, the laminae and spinous processes are decorticated and covered with bone graft. An interspinous wire, using the Rogers technique, can be added. (*B, C,* Redrawn from Anderson, P.C.; et al. Spine 16 [3 Suppl]: S73–S74, 1991. *D, E,* From Anderson, P.C.; et al. Spine [3 Suppl]: S73–S74, 1991.)

15. A neurologic deficit is attributed to intoxication or drug effect (perform a complete examination and workup).
16. A neurologic deficit is attributed to a medical diagnosis, medical debilitation, or aging in patients "found down" (assume potential cord injury until proved otherwise).
17. Lower extremity neurologic function is not evaluated in patients admitted for nontrauma diagnoses (perform a complete evaluation and document clearly).
18. Neurogenic shock is misdiagnosed and treated as hypovolemic shock with resulting volume overload (inexperience).
19. The neurologic examination is not adequate (perform a complete evaluation and document clearly).
20. The motor examination consists of "squeeze my hand" and "wiggle your toes" (perform a complete evaluation and document clearly).
21. Pinprick sensation is not diligently checked or documented (perform a complete evaluation and document clearly).
22. Sacral sparing is not checked (perform a complete evaluation and document clearly).
23. Proprioception is not checked (perform a complete evaluation and document clearly).
24. Deep tendon reflexes are not checked (perform a complete evaluation and document clearly).
25. Inhibition of patient effort by pain on strength testing is interpreted as a deficit (inexperience).
26. Unusual neurologic deficits are dismissed as not real (dangerous assumption).
27. The neurologic examination is not adequately documented (e.g., "MAE," or moving all extremities) (perform a complete evaluation and document clearly).
28. Injured extremities are not evaluated for neurologic function (dangerous compassion for the patient or unfounded fear of causing injury).
29. A compartment syndrome is missed because of the neurologic deficit (inexperience).
30. The patient is not rolled to examine the back (dangerous compassion for the patient or unfounded fear of causing injury).
31. Pseudosubluxation is diagnosed as an injury in pediatric patients (inexperience).
32. Pediatric spine radiographs are reviewed by a physician with insufficient training or experience (inexperience).
33. A discrepancy between the neurologic level on examination and the radiographic level of injury is not fully investigated (inexperience).
34. A neurologic deficit in a patient with normal radiographs is not evaluated with an MRI study (inexperience).
35. An extremely unstable injury (atlanto-occipital dislocation or vertebral distraction) is not adequately immobilized during resuscitation and transfers (inexperience).
36. A distraction injury is placed in cervical traction (inexperience).
37. Traction pins are applied in the wrong location, with a subsequent risk of slippage (inexperience).
38. Traction pins are placed in a dangerous location, with a subsequent risk of iatrogenic injury to the supra-

orbital nerve, supratrochlear nerve, frontal sinus, or temporalis muscle (inexperience).
39. Traction pins are placed in a patient with a skull fracture without consulting a neurosurgeon (inexperience).
40. Traction tongs or pins are not MRI compatible (inexperience).
41. The examination is not repeated after incrementally increasing traction (perform a complete evaluation and document clearly).
42. Traction is applied and necessary subsequent immediate radiographic confirmation of alignment deferred (lack of precise execution).
43. Traction is not applied for an appropriate injury type of cervical injury (inadequate mobilization).
44. Time is wasted in shaving the area for traction pins in critically ill patients, thereby delaying subsequent evaluation and treatment (inexperience).
45. Closed reduction is delayed to obtain diagnostic tests not essential before reduction (inexperience).
46. The backboard is not removed within 2 hours, causing sacral decubitis (inexperience).
47. Removal of the backboard is unnecessarily delayed until all imaging is completed; spine precautions can be observed without a backboard (inexperience).
48. Traction is not applied because the patient is anticipated to require surgery "soon" for definitive treatment (inadequate mobilization).
49. Flexion-extension radiographs are obtained without first adequately reviewing the static studies (inexperience).
50. Flexion-extension radiographs are obtained acutely without physician supervision (inexperience).
51. The patient is passively flexed and extended for dynamic flexion-extension radiographs (may cause injury).
52. A patient with subjective symptoms is discharged without a complete evaluation to exclude injury (perform a complete evaluation and document clearly).
53. A patient with a recognized potential for an undiagnosed injury is discharged without specific follow-up instructions (perform a complete evaluation and document clearly).
54. An additional level of spinal injury is missed after diagnosing injury at one level (inexperience).
55. A repeat examination is not performed to clear the spine in patients unresponsive during the initial evaluation (perform a complete evaluation and document clearly).
56. The level of concern regarding potential spine injury is not communicated to the surgical team in charge of the patient.
57. Significant findings diagnosing injury or excluding injury are not expeditiously communicated to other physicians caring for the patient (perform a complete evaluation and document clearly).

Complications

The complications that could follow all types of cervical spine operations are many and dangerous. Complications during initial hospitalization add approximately $1.5

Table 29–10 ....

Frequency of Complications in Patients with a Spinal Cord Injury and Patients without a Spinal Cord Injury

Complication	Cord Injury (%)	No Cord Injury (%)
Overall	52.9	20.6
Urinary tract infection	24.0	8.6
Respiratory	23.1	56.0
Cardiac	11.5	3.2
Decubitus ulcer	7.7	1.0
Pneumonia	13.5	7.3
Mortality	9.6	4.8

....

billion annually to the cost of caring for patients with vertebral fractures in the United States.[88] Complications in lower cervical spine injuries are usually related to the sequelae of quadriplegia. Patients selected for nonoperative treatment must be monitored by serial radiography to document maintenance of spinal alignment. Patients with seemingly benign injuries sometimes sustain occult ligament instability and displacement during treatment. Patients with anterior vertebral body compression and concurrent posterior ligament damage are especially prone to failure of closed treatment methods. Careful observation is the best preemptive measure a surgical team can take to prevent the onset and advancement of severe complications.

Complications associated with spinal cord injuries frequently result in significant morbidity and mortality (Table 29–10). Hemodynamic complications, including bradycardia and hypotension, can be treated with vasopressors, atropine, or rarely, a temporary pacemaker. Stress ulceration is common after quadriplegia and may be aggravated by the use of corticosteroids. All patients with spinal cord injuries are placed on a regimen of antacid medication to maintain pH levels over 7, and they should also be maintained on H_2 blocking agents. An indwelling Foley catheter is inserted into the urinary tract until fluids are stabilized, at which time the patient is placed on an intermittent self-catheterization program.

Complications of lower cervical injuries are primarily associated with medical problems relating to spinal cord injury and to loss of reduction of the fracture. Medical problems are especially common in patients with associated quadriparesis or quadriplegia and include gastrointestinal hemorrhage, pulmonary insufficiency, deep venous thrombosis, urinary tract infection, and decubitus ulcers. Occult intra-abdominal injuries occur in approximately 4% of patients with traumatic quadriplegia, and therefore routine peritoneal lavage is indicated if abdominal injury is at all suspected.[213] The multidisciplinary management of these multiple problems is best performed in a center for the management of spinal cord injuries.[18, 28] Gastrointestinal hemorrhage occurs in up to 6% of patients with spinal cord injury who are given corticosteroids.[35] Such hemorrhage can be mitigated by monitoring and correcting gastric acidity with antacids and the administration of H_2 blockers. Pulmonary insufficiency may be caused by pulmonary edema, atelectasis, or pneumonia, all secondary to poor respiratory excursion and prolonged recumbency.[19]

Early death from spinal cord injury is usually secondary to a pulmonary complication. Deep venous thrombosis occurs in approximately 25% of quadriplegic patients after their acute injury, but rapid mobilization of the patient after stabilization of the spine will minimize its incidence.[131] Anticoagulants are indicated after the initial treatment. Urinary tract infections are very common and are often secondary to the use of indwelling catheters. Intermittent catheterization is preferred during the immediate postinjury period. Decubitus ulcers are less frequent with early stabilization of the injury and mobilization of the patient. Excellent nursing care at a spinal cord injury center minimizes this complication.

Prolonged traction increases the risk of atelectasis or adult respiratory distress syndrome, but early spinal stabilization and mobilization appear to help relieve these pulmonary complications. Skin breakdown in insensate areas can be prevented by logrolling the patient to a different position every 2 hours. Patients with neurologic deficits are at high risk for deep vein thrombosis and pulmonary embolism and often require prophylactic measures to prevent these complications.

Neurologic deterioration occurs in 1% to 5% of patients after spinal injury.[9, 60, 84] In approximately 50% of cases, the causes of deterioration are preventable or attributed to physician actions. Common causes are fractures occurring in patients with ankylosed spines, missed diagnoses, loss of reduction during turning, or placement of a halo device. Other causes such as timing of surgery and intervertebral disc extrusion have been discussed previously. To minimize the chance of neurologic deterioration, all patients should undergo cervical spine stabilization until the spine has been "cleared," including three radiographic views. Early reduction and stabilization are advisable except in patients with minimal neurologic injury and bilateral facet dislocations. Stabilization with rigid fixation is especially important in patients with ankylosing spondylitis. Patients with deterioration should undergo immediate imaging with radiographs and MRI, and those with an operative lesion should have immediate surgery aimed at decompressing the cord and stabilizing the spinal column. All patients should wear sequential pneumatic stockings and receive appropriate DUT prophylaxis. The incidence of these complications can also be decreased by early physical therapy intervention that includes mobilization and range-of-motion exercises for all joints.

OUTCOME
....

The prognosis for neurologic recovery and functional rehabilitation after spinal cord injury has improved. In a recent study of 55 patients with incomplete quadriplegia, the average American Spinal Injury Association (ASIA) motor score increased from 22 to 49 in the first year after injury. Lower extremity and upper extremity recovery occurred simultaneously, thus indicating that recovery was not based on upper motor neuron regeneration. Forty-seven percent of these patients had regained the ability to ambulate with aids. In patients with complete motor quadriplegia at 1 month, the ASIA motor score increased by only 9 points at 1 year. No patients regained the ability to ambulate. Important determinants of recovery were completeness of the cord injury, the presence of perianal pinprick sensation, and the type of cord syndrome. Patients with Brown-Séquard or central cord syndrome had a better prognosis than did those with anterior cord syndrome.[245] Patients can also be evaluated for functional outcome by using functional independence measures. Improvement in these outcomes is strongly correlated with improvement in motor recovery.

The outcome of spinal cord injury is predominantly determined by patient age and the severity of the neurologic injury. The most common causes of death after surgery are renal failure and respiratory disease.[133] Older patients with complete tetraplegia have nearly 100% acute mortality[248] (Table 29–11). In contrast, over 90% of patients with central cord injury survive the initial hospitalization.

The prognosis for neurologic recovery is determined by the nature and magnitude of the initial injury (Table 29–12). The pattern of spinal cord injury does not correlate with the pattern of skeletal injury on plain radiographs.[68, 202] Unfortunately, cord hemorrhaging is associated with less neurologic recovery. When controlling for the level (paraplegia versus tetraplegia) and completeness of spinal cord injury, motor recovery does not differ for the type of injury (penetrating versus nonpenetrating), the type of fracture, or the bullet location in gunshot injuries.[243] Complete cord injuries are more likely in flexion-rotation patterns of injury, bilateral facet dislocation, and gunshot injuries in which the bullet traverses the canal. Incomplete cord injuries are associated with preexisting spondylosis and gunshot injuries in which the bullet does not traverse the canal. The initial motor index score correlates with overall function at the time of discharge from rehabilitation in tetraplegia and complete injuries, but in paraplegia and incomplete injuries, the initial motor score may not correlate with overall function.[127] Levels that have some voluntary motor function 1 week after injury are likely to achieve 60% of the previous strength.[73] Pediatric patients with incomplete injuries generally have a good prognosis because of their youth and ongoing body development. Neurologic deficit improved in 74% and resolved in 59% of the pediatric patients reported by Hamilton and Myles[108]; however, complete injuries improved in only 10% and resolved in none of these pediatric patients.

Encouraging levels of recovery have been achieved in

TABLE 29–11

Relationship between Age at Injury and Expected Survival after a Spinal Cord Injury (Median)

Age at Injury (yr)	Survival (yr)
<30	43
30–50	24
>50	11

TABLE 29–12

Ability to Ambulate as Predicted by Neurologic Deficit 4 Weeks after Injury

Incomplete tetraplegia → 47% community ambulators
Incomplete paraplegia → 76% community ambulators
Most with LE motor score >10 achieved community ambulation at 1 yr
LE motor score correlates with physiologic energy expenditure and gait performance
LE motor score >30: all had reciprocal gait
LE motor score <30: increased energy expenditure, preferred w/c ambulation
LE motor score <20: none were community ambulators

Abbreviations: LE, lower extremity; w/c, wheelchair.

some complete lesions.[91] Waters and colleagues have shown that late conversion of complete to incomplete spinal cord injury can occur.[244] In their study, 4% of injuries labeled as complete at 21 days would later convert to incomplete, and half of these patients regained bladder and bowel control. A full third gained the ability to ambulate. However, no patients with complete paraplegia at or above the T9 level 1 month after injury regained any lower extremity motor function. Of the patients with complete paraplegia below the T9 level, 38% regained sufficient lower extremity motor function to ambulate with orthoses. Patients regaining ambulation all had a level of injury below T12.

Preservation of bilateral sacral pin sensation in patients with no lower extremity motor function is associated with an average gain of 12 motor score points at 1 year.[241] Forty-six percent of these patients are able to ambulate with a reciprocal gait. However, adding the intraoperative spinal sonographic injury grade to the initial ASIA motor score does not improve the predictive ability of the follow-up ASIA motor score.[148] Fortunately, it has been shown that patients with complete injuries can also improve in neurologic status. According to a study performed by Yablon and co-workers, 32% of patients descend one level and 18% descend two levels.[256]

A direct relationship exists between the ASIA motor score and walking ability.[242] The average increase in motor score after complete tetraplegia is 9 points at 1 year.[239] A Brown-Séquard injury has a similarly promising prognosis.[197] Seventy-five percent of patients in this category ambulate independently at discharge, and all regain bladder and bowel control. Incomplete paraplegia is associated with a 12-point increase in motor score at 1 year.[240] This rate of recovery is the same for injuries at the T12 level, as well as all injuries above and below the T12 level.

SPECIAL CONSIDERATIONS

Spinal Cord Contusion

Significant spinal cord injury can result from trauma without any fractures or ligamentous ruptures necessarily being present.[97] Spinal cord injury without radiographic abnormality (SCIWORA) commonly occurs in children younger than 10 years. The mechanism of these injuries is likely to be physical failure through a fracture in the hypertrophic zone of the end-plate, which in turn leads to distraction of the cord and ischemic injury. Spinal cord damage can also occur without instability as a result of bulging of the ligamentum flavum.[226] Two thirds of patients who suffer this sort of damage are older than 50 years.[22] Unfortunately, this diagnosis is often missed, and patients with SCIWORA are sent home as normal, deemed hysterical, or go undiagnosed during stupor or coma.

Cervical spine injury is a common occurrence after relatively minor trauma in patients 65 years or older. C2 injuries, especially odontoid fractures, must be ruled out in older patients with neck pain after even a minor injury.[215] The mortality rate for these patients is 26% with associated spinal cord injury. Complete cervical cord injuries in patients older than 50 years have a 60% mortality rate.[4] Predictably, the severity of the injury decreases the chance of survival, particularly in older patients.[101] Bedrest and traction are not tolerated well by older people.[135] However, age does not influence the outcome after halo vest treatment.[43]

Gunshot Injuries

Gunshot injuries rarely cause spine instability. Studies show that decompression does not improve recovery if the bullet traverses the canal without any residual mass effect on neural elements.[219] Surgery for this type of injury risks neurologic deterioration.[258] However, surgery may be necessary for dural repair in patients with a cerebrospinal fluid leak or fistula. Débridement plus removal of the bullet is an option if laparotomy for abdominal injury reveals that the area around the spinal injury is without added surgical morbidity. If the projectile traverses the oropharynx or colon, intravenous antibiotics should be administered for 3 days for infection prophylaxis.

Pediatric Patients

Pediatric spine injuries represent 2% of all spine trauma cases in the United States. The prevalence of pediatric spine injuries is 7 per 100,000 population annually.[144] The fatality rate in children's cervical trauma is twice that in adults, in part because radiographs appear normal in 10% to 20% of pediatric cases of spinal injury. When injured, children are also more likely to have a neurologic deficit. Pediatric spine injury usually involves the upper three segments.[94, 125] Age-related differences include the fact that children have more lax ligaments, more horizontal cervical facets, and greater range of flexion and extension.[53] The age-related differences in pediatric injury patterns may also be associated with larger head size, delay in muscular control, or lack of protective reflexes. In children, ligamentous injuries are more frequent than bone injury. These pediatric injury patterns transition to adult types at 11 years of age.

Birth trauma can result from rotation in hyperextension. Lower cervical or thoracic traction injury can be caused by breech presentation and upper cervical injury by a cephalic presentation. Shaking injuries can occur in instances of child abuse. Pediatric spine injury is common in trampoline injuries.

Factors that contribute to the difficulty of evaluating a child's spine include incomplete ossification of the vertebrae, the presence of multiple growth centers, and the physiologic hypermobility of the spine. Most pediatric cervical injuries occur in the upper cervical spine between the occiput and C3 because the ratio of mass between the head and the body is disproportionate at this location. In addition, at this particular point the muscles and ligaments supporting the cervical spine are weak. Ligament injuries are common, particularly atlanto-occipital dislocations.

Spinal cord injuries may be present in children who exhibit no radiographic abnormalities. This phenomenon occurs in cord traction injuries and is due to greater elasticity in the immature spinal column than in the spinal cord. Moreover, injuries at the junction of cartilaginous and bony end-plates are not easily identified on radiographs. Children with spinal tenderness or questionable radiographic findings should be treated by immobilization until their symptoms resolve or until experienced physicians can review the radiographs.

Injuries in the lower cervical spine are rare in children. When they occur, they are best treated according to the same principles and protocols as for identical fractures in adults.

Elderly Patients

Elderly patients with cervical spine injuries present additional challenges. Spondylosis results in a higher prevalence of associated spinal cord injury. Spondylosis also makes identification of fractures difficult on plain radiographs. What would otherwise be a minor, low-energy injury mechanism can result in markedly unstable injuries in an older patient. Treatment of elderly patients is similarly complicated because they poorly tolerate external bracing. Surgical treatment often carries an additional risk of complications because of the presence of coexisting age-related medical conditions. Osteoporosis compromises surgical fixation.

INJURY PREVENTION

Injury prevention offers the best-value return for interventions aimed at decreasing the medical and social burdens of cervical spine injuries.[183, 184] Strategies to prevent or minimize functional loss include changing modifiable risk factors, altering the mechanics of the injury event, altering the mechanisms of the initial injury, interrupting the ensuing deleterious biologic responses, or any combination of these strategies. Implementing injury prevention measures can be a slow process because it requires a high initial investment of resources. Success in these efforts is difficult to achieve and difficult to measure.[254]

SUMMARY

Clinically, the hope of neural regeneration and functional recovery for those suffering injuries to the lower cervical spine thus far has remained unrealized. Progress in recent years has renewed hopes of marked functional recovery for patients with spinal cord injury. New pharmacologic interventions in conjunction with novel surgical approaches promise to bring us closer to our goal of decreasing or even reversing the functional loss from spinal cord damage. The challenge facing physicians now is to transfer the success in the laboratories to successful clinical practice.

Lower cervical spine injuries are associated with significant morbidity and mortality. Improvements in prehospital, emergency, and rehabilitative care have resulted in a better prognosis for many patients. Proper initial care is essential for successful healing, and all trauma patients must be meticulously screened for spinal injury. Once a lower cervical spine injury is identified, the fracture type should be determined with the use of CT or MRI. Patients with stable fractures may be treated in an orthosis and must be carefully monitored until healing is ensured. Patients with unstable patterns and those with spinal cord injuries are placed in traction and must have immediate fracture reduction. An exception is a neurologically intact patient with a bilateral facet dislocation. These patients should undergo MRI evaluation before reduction. Spinal cord–injured patients treated within 8 hours of injury are currently given high doses of methylprednisolone according to the NASCIS II protocol. Definitive treatment is based on fracture patterns, residual neurologic compression, and the level of neurologic function. The timing of surgery remains controversial. Early surgery appears to decrease the morbidity and mortality of recumbency but may increase the chance of neurologic deterioration.

Newer surgical techniques are available that provide rigid fixation from either an anterior or a posterior approach. These new techniques allow rapid patient mobilization. Successful use of these techniques requires correlation of the fracture pathomechanics with the biomechanical properties of the given implant, a complete understanding of the individual patient's anatomy and the surgical technique, adjunctive bone grafting, and postoperative use of an orthosis.

REFERENCES

1. Abitbol, J.; Zdeblick, T.; Kuntz, D: A biomechanical analysis of modern anterior and posterior cervical stabilization techniques. Paper presented at the 20th Annual Meeting of the Cervical Spine Research Society, Palm Springs, California, 1992.
2. Abumi, K.; Itoh, H.; Taneichi, H.; Kaneda, K. Transpedicular screw fixation for traumatic lesions of the middle and lower cervical spine: Description of the techniques and preliminary report. J Spinal Disord 7:19–28, 1994.
3. Agrawal, S.K.; Fehlings, M.G. Mechanisms of secondary injury to spinal cord axons in vitro: Role of Na+, Na(+)-K(+)-ATPase, the Na(+)-H+ exchanger, and the Na(+)-Ca²⁺ exchanger. J Neurosci 16:545–552, 1996.
4. Alander, D.H.; Andreychik, D.A.; Stauffer, E.S. Early outcome in cervical spinal cord injured patients older than 50 years of age. Spine 19:2299–2301, 1994.
5. Allen, B.L., Jr.; Ferguson, R.L.; Lehmann, T.R.; O'Brien, R.P. A mechanistic classification of closed, indirect fractures and dislocations of the lower cervical spine. Spine 7:1–27, 1982.
6. An, H.S.; Gordin, R.; Renner, K. Anatomic considerations for plate-screw fixation of the cervical spine. Spine 16(10 Suppl):548–551, 1991.
7. Anderson, D.K.; Braughler, J.M.; Hall, E.D.; et al. Effects of treatment with U-74006F on neurological outcome following experimental spinal cord injury. J Neurosurg 69:562–567, 1988.
8. Anderson, P.; Krengel, W. Early versus delayed stabilization after cervical spinal cord injury. Paper presented at the 6th Annual Specialty Day of the Federation of Spine Associations, San Francisco, 1993.
9. Anderson, P.; Henley, M.B. Progressive neurologic deficit in spinal injured patients at a level I trauma center. Orthop Trans 14:603, 1991.
10. Anderson, P.A.; Bohlman, H.H. Anterior decompression and arthrodesis of the cervical spine: Long-term motor improvement. Part II—improvement in complete traumatic quadriplegia. J Bone Joint Surg Am 74:683–692, 1992.
11. Anderson, P.A.; Budorick, T.E.; Easton, K.B.; et al. Failure of halo vest to prevent in vivo motion in patients with injured cervical spines. Spine 16(10 Suppl):501–505, 1991.
12. Anderson, P.A.; Grady, M.S. Posterior stabilization of the lower cervical spine with lateral mass plates and screws. In: Albert, T.J., ed. Operative Techniques in Orthopaedics. Philadelphia, W.B. Saunders, 1995.
13. Anderson, P.A.; Henley, M.B.; Grady, M.S.; et al. Posterior cervical arthrodesis with AO reconstruction plates and bone graft. Spine 16(3 Suppl):72–79, 1991.
14. Anderson, T.E. Spinal cord contusion injury: Experimental dissociation of hemorrhagic necrosis and subacute loss of axonal conduction. J Neurosurg 62:115–119, 1985.
15. Assenmacher, D.R.; Ducker, T.B: Experimental traumatic paraplegia. The vascular and pathological changes seen in reversible and irreversible spinal-cord lesions. J Bone Joint Surg Am 53:671–680, 1971.
16. Basso, D.M.; Beattie, M.S.; Bresnahan, J.C.; et al. MASCIS evaluation of open field locomotor scores: Effects of experience and teamwork on reliability. Multicenter Animal Spinal Cord Injury Study. J Neurotrauma 13:343–359, 1996.
17. Beatson, T.R. Fractures and dislocations of the cervical spine. J Bone Joint Surg Br 45:21–35, 1963.
18. Bedbrook, G. The Care and Management of Spinal Cord Injuries. New York, Springer-Verlag, 1981.
19. Bellamy, R.; Pitts, F.W.; Stauffer, E.S. Respiratory complications in traumatic quadriplegia. Analysis of 20 years' experience. J Neurosurg 39:596–600, 1973.
20. Berrington, N.R.; van Staden, J.F.; Willers, J.G.; van der Westhuizen, J. Cervical intervertebral disc prolapse associated with traumatic facet dislocations. Surg Neurol 40:395–399, 1993.
21. Beyer, C.A.; Cabanela, M.E.; Berquist, T.H. Unilateral facet dislocations and fracture-dislocations of the cervical spine. J Bone Joint Surg Br 73:977–981, 1991.
22. Bilston, L.E.; Thibault, L.E. The mechanical properties of the human cervical spinal cord in vitro. Ann Biomed Eng 24:67–74, 1996.
23. Bicknell, J.M.; Fielder, K. Unrecognized incomplete cervical spinal cord injury: Review of nine new and 28 previously reported cases. Am J Emerg Med 10:336–343, 1992.
24. Blackmore, C.C.; Emerson, S.S.; Mann, F.A.; Koepsell, T.D. Cervical spine imaging in patients with trauma: Determination of fracture risk to optimize use. Radiology 211:759–765, 1999.
25. Blumberg, K.D.; Catalano, J.B.; Cotler, J.M.; Balderston, R.A. The pullout strength of titanium alloy MRI-compatible and stainless steel MRI-incompatible Gardner-Wells tongs. Spine 18:1895–1896, 1993.
26. Bohler, J. [Screw-osteosynthesis of fractures of the dens axis.] Unfallheilkunde 84:221–223, 1981.
27. Bohler, J.; Gaudernak, T. Anterior plate stabilization for fracture-dislocations of the lower cervical spine. J Trauma 20:203–205, 1980.

28. Bohlman, H. Complications in the treatment of fractures and dislocation of the cervical spine. In: Epps, C., ed. Complications in Orthopedic Surgery. Philadelphia, J.B. Lippincott, 1978.

29. Bohlman, H.H. Acute fractures and dislocations of the cervical spine. An analysis of three hundred hospitalized patients and review of the literature. J Bone Joint Surg Am 61:1119–1142, 1979.

30. Bohlman, H.H. The triple-wire technique for posterior stabilization of fractures and dislocations of the lower cervical spine. In: Cervical Spine Research Society, ed. An Atlas of Surgical Procedures, Vol. 9. Philadelphia, J.B. Lippincott, 1994, pp. 145–150.

31. Bohlman, H.H.; Anderson, P.A. Anterior decompression and arthrodesis of the cervical spine: Long-term motor improvement. Part I—improvement in incomplete traumatic quadriparesis. J Bone Joint Surg Am 74:671–682, 1992.

32. Bracken, M.B. Treatment of acute spinal cord injury with methylprednisolone: Results of a multicenter, randomized clinical trial. J Neurotrauma 8(Suppl):47–50, 1991.

33. Bracken, M.B.; Collins, W.F.; Freeman, D.F.; et al. Efficacy of methylprednisolone in acute spinal cord injury. JAMA 251:45–52, 1984.

34. Bracken, M.B.; Shepard, M.J.; Collins, W.F.; et al. A randomized, controlled trial of methylprednisolone or naloxone in the treatment of acute spinal-cord injury. Results of the Second National Acute Spinal Cord Injury Study. N Engl J Med 322:1405–1411, 1990.

35. Bracken, M.B.; Shepard, M.J.; Collins, W.F., Jr.; et al. Methylprednisolone or naloxone treatment after acute spinal cord injury: 1-year follow-up data. Results of the second National Acute Spinal Cord Injury Study. J Neurosurg 76:23–31, 1992.

36. Bracken, M.B.; Shepard, M.J.; Holford, T.R.; et al. Administration of methylprednisolone for 24 or 48 hours or tirilazad mesylate for 48 hours in the treatment of acute spinal cord injury. Results of the Third National Acute Spinal Cord Injury Randomized Controlled Trial. National Acute Spinal Cord Injury Study. JAMA 277:1597–1604, 1997.

37. Bracken, M.B.; Shepard, M.J.; Holford, T.R.; et al. Methylprednisolone or tirilazad mesylate administration after acute spinal cord injury: 1-year follow up. Results of the third National Acute Spinal Cord Injury randomized controlled trial. J Neurosurg 89:699–706, 1998.

38. Braughler, J.M.; Hall, E.D. Pharmacokinetics of methylprednisolone in cat plasma and spinal cord following a single intravenous dose of the sodium succinate ester. Drug Metab Dispos 10:551–552, 1982.

39. Bregman, B.S.; Kunkel-Bagden, E.; Schnell, L.; et al. Recovery from spinal cord injury mediated by antibodies to neurite growth inhibitors. Nature 378:498–501, 1995.

40. Breig, A. The therapeutic possibilities of surgical bio-engineering in incomplete spinal cord lesions. Paraplegia 9:173–182, 1972.

41. Brodke, D.; Anderson, P; Newell, D. Anterior versus posterior stabilization of cervical spine fractures in spinal cord injured patients. Paper presented at a meeting of the Cervical Spine Research Society, Sante Fe, New Mexico, 1995.

42. Brunette, D.D.; Rockswold, G.L. Neurologic recovery following rapid spinal realignment for complete cervical spinal cord injury. J Trauma 27:445–447, 1987.

43. Bucholz, R.D.; Cheung, K.C. Halo vest versus spinal fusion for cervical injury: Evidence from an outcome study. J Neurosurg 70:884–892, 1989.

44. Budorick, T.E.; Anderson, P.A.; Rivara, F.P.; Cohen, W. Flexion-distraction fracture of the cervical spine. A case report. J Bone Joint Surg Am 73:1097–1100, 1991.

45. Bunge, R.P.; Puckett, W.R.; Becerra, J.L.; et al. Observations on the pathology of human spinal cord injury. A review and classification of 22 new cases with details from a case of chronic cord compression with extensive focal demyelination. Adv Neurol 59:75–89, 1993.

46. Callahan, R.A.; Johnson, R.M.; Margolis, R.N.; et al. Cervical facet fusion for control of instability following laminectomy. J Bone Joint Surg Am 59:991–1002, 1977.

47. Cammisa, F.P., Jr.; Eismont, F.J.; Green, B.A. Dural laceration occurring with burst fractures and associated laminar fractures. J Bone Joint Surg Am 71:1044–1052, 1989.

48. Carlson, G.D.; Minato, Y.; Okada, A.; et al. Early time-dependent decompression for spinal cord injury: Vascular mechanisms of recovery. J Neurotrauma 14:951–962, 1997.

49. Carlson, G.D.; Warden, K.E.; Barbeau, J.M.; et al. Viscoelastic relaxation and regional blood flow response to spinal cord compression and decompression. Spine 22:1285–1291, 1997.

50. Carlson, S.L.; Parrish, M.E.; Springer, J.E.; et al. Acute inflammatory response in spinal cord following impact injury. Exp Neurol 151:77–88, 1998.

51. Carter, J.W.; Mirza, S.K.; Tencer, A.F.; Ching, R.P. Canal geometry changes associated with axial compressive cervical spine fracture. Spine 25:46–54, 2000.

52. Caspar, W.; Barbier, D.D.; Klara, P.M. Anterior cervical fusion and Caspar plate stabilization for cervical trauma. Neurosurgery 25:491–502, 1989.

53. Cattell, H.S.; Filtzer, D.L. Pseudosubluxation and other normal variations in the cervical spine in children. A study of one hundred and sixty children. J Bone Joint Surg Am 47:1295–1309, 1965.

54. Chang, D.G.; Tencer, A.F.; Ching, R.P.; et al. Geometric changes in the cervical spinal canal during impact. Spine 19:973–980, 1994.

55. Chapman, J.R.; Anderson, P.A. Internal fixation techniques for the treatment of lower cervical spine injuries. J Int Orthop Trauma 1:205–219, 1991.

56. Chapman, J.R.; Anderson, P.A.; Pepin, C.; et al. Posterior instrumentation of the unstable cervicothoracic spine. J Neurosurg 84:552–558, 1996.

57. Cheng, H.; Cao, Y.; Olson, L. Spinal cord repair in adult paraplegic rats: Partial restoration of hind limb function. Science 273:510–513, 1996.

58. Ching, R.P.; Watson, N.A.; Carter, J.W.; Tencer, A.F. The effect of post-injury spinal position on canal occlusion in a cervical spine burst fracture model. Spine 22:1710–1715, 1997.

59. Coe, J.D.; Warden, K.E.; Sutterlin, C.E., 3rd; McAfee, P.C. Biomechanical evaluation of cervical spinal stabilization methods in a human cadaveric model. Spine 14:1122–1131, 1989.

60. Colterjohn, N.R.; Bednar, D.A. Identifiable risk factors for secondary neurologic deterioration in the cervical spine–injured patient. Spine 20:2293–2297, 1995.

61. Cooper, P.R.; Cohen, A.; Rosiello, A.; Koslow, M. Posterior stabilization of cervical spine fractures and subluxations using plates and screws. Neurosurgery 23:300–306, 1988.

62. Copes, W.S.; Champion, H.R.; Sacco, W.J.; et al. Progress in characterizing anatomic injury. J Trauma 30:1200–1207, 1990.

63. Cornish, B. Early definitive control of unstable cervical injuries. J Bone Joint Surg Br 47:597, 1965.

64. Cotler, H.B; Kulkarni, M.V.; Bondurant, F.J. Magnetic resonance imaging of acute spinal cord trauma: Preliminary report. J Orthop Trauma 2:1–4, 1988.

65. Cotler, H.B.; Miller, L.S.; DeLucia, F.A.; et al. Closed reduction of cervical spine dislocations. Clin Orthop 214:185–199, 1987.

66. Cotler, J.M.; Herbison, G.J.; Nasuti, J.F.; et al. Closed reduction of traumatic cervical spine dislocation using traction weights up to 140 pounds. Spine 18:386–390, 1993.

67. Crockard, A. Evaluation of spinal laminar fixation by a new, flexible stainless steel cable (Sof'wire): Early results. Neurosurgery 35:892–898, 1994.

68. Dall, D. Does the type of bony injury affect spinal cord injury. S Afr Med J 46:1048, 1972.

69. David, S.; Aguayo, A. Axonal elongation into peripheral nervous system "bridges" after central nervous system injury in adult rats. Science 214:931–933, 1981.

70. Davis, J.W.; Phreaner, D.L.; Hoyt, D.B.; Mackersie, R.C. The etiology of missed cervical spine injuries. J Trauma 34:342–346, 1993.

71. Delamarter, R.; Sherman, J.; Carr, J. Spinal cord injury: The pathophysiology of spinal cord damage and subsequent recovery following immediate or delayed decompression. Paper presented at the 21st Annual Meeting of the Cervical Spine Research Society, New York, 1993.

72. Delamarter, R.B.; Sherman, J.; Carr, J.B. Pathophysiology of spinal cord injury. Recovery after immediate and delayed decompression. J Bone Joint Surg Am 77:1042–1049, 1995.

73. Ditunno, J.F., Jr.; Stover, S.L.; Freed, M.M.; Ahn, J.H. Motor recovery of the upper extremities in traumatic quadriplegia: A multicenter study. Arch Phys Med Rehabil 73:431–436, 1992.

74. Dolan, E.J.; Tator, C.H.; Endrenyi, L. The value of decompression for acute experimental spinal cord compression injury. J Neurosurg 53:749–755, 1980.

75. Doran, S.E.; Papadopoulos, S.M.; Ducker, T.B.; Lillehei, K.O. Magnetic resonance imaging documentation of coexistent traumatic locked facets of the cervical spine and disc herniation. J Neurosurg 79:341–345, 1993.

76. Dossett, A.B.; Hunt, J.L.; Purdue, G.F.; Schlegel, J.D. Early orthopedic intervention in burn patients with major fractures. J Trauma 31:888–892, 1991.

77. Ducker, T.B.; Kindt, G.W.; Kempf, L.G. Pathological findings in acute experimental spinal cord trauma. J Neurosurg 35:700–708, 1971.

78. Ducker, T.B.; Saleman, M.; Daniell, H.B. Experimental spinal cord trauma: III. Therapeutic effect of immobilization and pharmacologic agents. Surg Neurol 10:71–76, 1978.

79. Edwards, C.C.; Maltz, S.O.; Levine, A.M. The oblique wiring technique for rotational injuries of the cervical spine. Orthop Trans 10:455, 1986.

80. Eismont, F.J.; Arena, M.J.; Green, B.A. Extrusion of an intervertebral disc associated with traumatic subluxation or dislocation of cervical facets. Case report. J Bone Joint Surg Am 73:1555–1560, 1991.

81. Eismont, F.J.; Clifford, S.; Goldberg, M.; Green, B. Cervical sagittal spinal canal size in spine injury. Spine 9:663–666, 1984.

82. Epstein, J.A.; Epstein, M.E. The surgical management of cervical spine stenosis, spondylosis and myeloradiculopathy by means of the posterior approach. In: Cervical Spine Research Society, ed. The Cervical Spine. Philadelphia, J.B. Lippincott, 1989, pp. 625–643.

83. Ersmark, H.; Dalen, N.; Kalen, R. Cervical spine injuries: A follow-up of 332 patients. Paraplegia 28:25–40, 1990.

84. Farmer, J.; Vaccaro, A.; Albert, T.J. Neurologic progression following cervical spinal cord injury. Orthop Trans 19:308, 1995.

85. Fehlings, M.G.; Agrawal, S. Role of sodium in the pathophysiology of secondary spinal cord injury. Spine 20:2187–2191, 1995.

86. Fehlings, M.G.; Cooper, P.R.; Errico, T.J. Posterior plates in the management of cervical instability: Long-term results in 44 patients. J Neurosurg 81:341–349, 1994.

87. Fehlings, M.G.; Tator, C.H.; Linden, R.D. The relationships among the severity of spinal cord injury, motor and somatosensory evoked potentials and spinal cord blood flow. Electroencephalogr Clin Neurophysiol 74:241–259, 1989.

88. Fletcher, D.J.; Taddonio, R.F.; Byrne, D.W.; et al. Incidence of acute care complications in vertebral column fracture patients with and without spinal cord injury. Spine 20:1136–1146, 1995.

89. Flynn, T.B. Neurologic complications of anterior cervical interbody fusion. Spine 7:536–539, 1982.

90. Forsyth, H.F. Extension injuries of the cervical spine. J Bone Joint Surg Am 46:1792–1797, 1964.

91. Frankel, H.L.; Hancock, D.O.; Hyslop, G.; et al. The value of postural reduction in the initial management of closed injuries of the spine with paraplegia and tetraplegia. I. Paraplegia 7:179–192, 1969.

92. Friedman, J.E.; Haddad, G.G. Removal of extracellular sodium prevents anoxia-induced injury in freshly dissociated rat CA1 hippocampal neurons. Brain Res 641:57–64, 1994.

93. Geisler, F.H.; Dorsey, F.C.; Coleman, W.P. Recovery of motor function after spinal-cord injury—a randomized, placebo-controlled trial with GM-1 ganglioside [published erratum appears in N Engl J Med 1991 Dec 5;325(23):1659–60]. N Engl J Med 324:1829–1838, 1991.

94. Georgopoulos, G.; Pizzutillo, P.D.; Lee, M.S. Occipito-atlantal instability in children. A report of five cases and review of the literature. J Bone Joint Surg Am 69:429–436, 1987.

95. Gillingham, J. Letter. J Neurosurg 44:766–767, 1976.

96. Goffin, J.; Plets, C.; Van den Bergh, R. Anterior cervical fusion and osteosynthetic stabilization according to Caspar: A prospective study of 41 patients with fractures and/or dislocations of the cervical spine. Neurosurgery 25:865–871, 1989.

97. Gosch, H.H.; Gooding, E.; Schneider, R.C. An experimental study of cervical spine and cord injuries. J Trauma 12:570–576, 1972.

98. Grace, T.G. The orthopaedist as traumatologist. Editorial. J Bone Joint Surg Am 73:319, 1991.

99. Grady, M.S. Cervical spine injuries: Management. Contemp Neurosurg 13:1–6, 1991.

100. Grant, G.A.; Mirza, S.K.; Chapman, J.R.; et al. Risk of early closed reduction in cervical spine subluxation injuries. J Neurosurg 90(1 Suppl):13–18, 1999.

101. Greenspan, L.; McLellan, B.A.; Greig, H. Abbreviated Injury Scale and Injury Severity Score: A scoring chart. J Trauma 25:60–64, 1985.

102. Grob, D.; Magerl, F. [Dorsal spondylodesis of the cervical spine using a hooked plate.] Orthopade 16:55–61, 1987.

103. Guttmann, L. Spinal Cord Injuries: Comprehensive Management and Research. Philadelphia, J.B. Lippincott, 1976.

104. Hadley, M.N.; Fitzpatrick, B.C.; Sonntag, V.K.; Browner, C.M. Facet fracture-dislocation injuries of the cervical spine. Neurosurgery 30:661–666, 1992.

105. Hall, E.D.; Braughler, J.M. Effects of intravenous methylprednisolone on spinal cord lipid peroxidation and Na$^+$ + K$^+$-ATPase activity. Dose-response analysis during 1st hour after contusion injury in the cat. J Neurosurg 57:247–253, 1982.

106. Hall, E.D.; Braughler, J.M. Glucocorticoid mechanisms in acute spinal cord injury: A review and therapeutic rationale. Surg Neurol 18:320–327, 1982.

107. Hall, E.D.; Braughler, J.M. Role of lipid peroxidation in post-traumatic spinal cord degeneration: A review. Cent Nerv Syst Trauma 3:281–294, 1986.

108. Hamilton, M.G.; Myles, S.T. Pediatric spinal injury: Review of 174 hospital admissions. J Neurosurg 77:700–774, 1992.

109. Harris, J.H.; Yeakley, J.W. Hyperextension-dislocation of the cervical spine. Ligament injuries demonstrated by magnetic resonance imaging. J Bone Joint Surg Br 74:567–570, 1992.

110. Harris, M.B.; Kronlage, S.C.; Carboni, P.A.; et al. Evaluation of the cervical spine in the polytrauma patient. Spine 25:2884–2892, 2000.

111. Heller, J.G.; Carlson, G.D.; Abitbol, J.J.; Garfin, S.R. Anatomic comparison of the Roy-Camille and Magerl techniques for screw placement in the lower cervical spine. Spine 16(10 Suppl):552–557, 1991.

112. Heller, J.G.; Silcox, D.H., 3rd; Sutterlin, C.E., 3rd. Complications of posterior cervical plating. Spine 20:2442–2448, 1995.

113. Holdsworth, F. Fractures, dislocations, and fracture-dislocations of the spine. J Bone Joint Surg Am 52:1534–1551, 1970.

114. Huelke, D.F.; Mackay, G.M.; Morris, A.; Bradford, M. A review of cervical fractures and fracture-dislocations without head impacts sustained by restrained occupants. Accid Anal Prev 25:731–743, 1993.

115. Ikata, T.; Iwasa, K.; Morimoto, K.; et al. Clinical considerations and biochemical basis of prognosis of cervical spinal cord injury. Spine 14:1096–1101, 1989.

116. Iwashita, Y.; Kawaguchi, S.; Murata, M. Restoration of function by replacement of spinal cord segments in the rat. Nature 367:167–170, 1994.

117. Jacobs, R.R.; Asher, M.A.; Snider, R.K. Thoracolumbar spinal injuries. A comparative study of recumbent and operative treatment in 100 patients. Spine 5:463–477, 1980.

118. Janssen, L.; Hansebout, R.R. Pathogenesis of spinal cord injury and newer treatments. A review. Spine 14:23–32, 1989.

119. Kakulas, B.A. Pathology of spinal injuries. Cent Nerv Syst Trauma 1:117–129, 1984.

120. Kang, J.D.; Figgie, M.P.; Bohlman, H.H. Sagittal measurements of the cervical spine in subaxial fractures and dislocations. An analysis of two hundred and eighty-eight patients with and without neurological deficits. J Bone Joint Surg Am 76:1617–1628, 1994.

121. Kearney, P.A.; Ridella, S.A.; Viano, D.C.; Anderson, T.E. Interaction of contact velocity and cord compression in determining the severity of spinal cord injury. J Neurotrauma 5:187–208, 1988.

122. Kerslake, R.W.; Jaspan, T.; Worthington, B.S. Magnetic resonance imaging of spinal trauma. Br J Radiol 64:386–402, 1991.

123. Kiwerski, J. The results of early conservative and surgical treatment of cervical spinal cord injured patients. Int J Rehabil Res 9:149–154, 1986.

124. Kleyn, P.J. Dislocations of the cervical spine: Closed reduction under anaesthesia. Paraplegia 22:271–281, 1984.

125. Koop, S.E.; Winter, R.B.; Lonstein, J.E. The surgical treatment of instability of the upper part of the cervical spine in children and adolescents. J Bone Joint Surg Am 66:403–411, 1984.

126. Kotani, Y.; Cunningham, B.W; Abumi, K.; McAfee, P.C. Biomechanical analysis of cervical stabilization systems. An assessment of transpedicular screw fixation in the cervical spine. Spine 19:2529–2539, 1994.

127. Lazar, R.B.; Yarkony, G.M.; Ortolano, D.; et al. Prediction of functional outcome by motor capability after spinal cord injury. Arch Phys Med Rehabil 70:819–822, 1989.

128. Lee, A.S.; MacLean, J.C.; Newton, D.A. Rapid traction for reduction of cervical spine dislocations. J Bone Joint Surg Br 76:352–356, 1994.

129. Lee, C.; Kim, D.S.; Rogers, L.F. Triangular cervical vertebral body fractures: Diagnostic significance. AJR Am J Roentgenol 138:1123–1132, 1982.

130. Levine, A.M. Facet injuries in the cervical spine. In: O'Leary, P.F.; Camins, M.B., eds. Disorders of the Cervical Spine. Baltimore, Williams & Wilkins, 1992, pp. 293–302.

131. Levine, A.M.; Edwards, C.C. Complications in the treatment of acute spinal injury. Orthop Clin North Am 17:183–203, 1986.

132. Levine, A.M.; Mazel, C.; Roy-Camille, R. Management of fracture separations of the articular mass using posterior cervical plating. Spine 17(10 Suppl):447–454, 1992.

133. Levine, A.M.; Waters, R.L.; Yoshida, G.M. Prognosis of spinal cord injuries. pp. 303–310.

134. Li, Y.; Field, P.M.; Raisman, G. Repair of adult rat corticospinal tract by transplants of olfactory ensheathing cells. Science 277:2000–2002, 1997.

135. Lieberman, I.H.; Webb, J.K. Cervical spine injuries in the elderly. J Bone Joint Surg Br 76:877–881, 1994.

136. Liu, X.Z.; Xu, X.M.; Hu, R.; et al. Neuronal and glial apoptosis after traumatic spinal cord injury. J Neurosci 17:5395–5406, 1997.

137. Mahale, Y.J.; Silver, J.R. Progressive paralysis after bilateral facet dislocation of the cervical spine. J Bone Joint Surg Br 74:219–223, 1992.

138. Maiman, D.J.; Pintar, F.; Yoganandan, N.; Reinartz, J. Effects of anterior vertebral grafting on the traumatized lumbar spine after pedicle screw-plate fixation. Spine 18:2423–2430, 1993.

139. Marar, B.C. Hyperextension injuries of the cervical spine. The pathogenesis of damage to the spinal cord. J Bone Joint Surg Am 56:1655–1662, 1974.

140. Marshall, L.F.; Knowlton, S.; Garfin, S.R.; et al. Deterioration following spinal cord injury. A multicenter study. J Neurosurg 66:400–404, 1987.

141. Matsuura, P.; Waters, R.L.; Adkins, R.H.; et al. Comparison of computerized tomography parameters of the cervical spine in normal control subjects and spinal cord–injured patients. J Bone Joint Surg Am 71:183–188, 1989.

142. Maynard, F.M., Jr.; Bracken, M.B.; Creasey, G.; et al. International standards for neurological and functional classification of spinal cord injury. American Spinal Injury Association. Spinal Cord 35:266–274, 1997.

143. Mazur, J.M.; Stauffer, E.S. Unrecognized spinal instability associated with seemingly "simple" cervical compression fractures. Spine 8:687–692, 1983.

144. McGrory, B.J.; Klassen, R.A.; Chao, E.Y.; et al. Acute fractures and dislocations of the cervical spine in children and adolescents. J Bone Joint Surg Am 75:988–995, 1993.

145. McLain, R.F.; Aretakis, A.; Moseley, T.A.; et al. Sub-axial cervical dissociation. Anatomic and biomechanical principles of stabilization. Spine 19:653–659, 1994.

146. Merianos, P.; Manousidis, D.; Samsonas, P.; et al. Injuries of the lower cervical spine associated with widening of the spinal canal. Injury 25:645–648, 1994.

147. Merriam, W.F.; Taylor, T.K.; Ruff, S.J.; McPhail, M.J. A reappraisal of acute traumatic central cord syndrome. J Bone Joint Surg Br 68:708–713, 1986.

148. Mirvis, S.E.; Geisler, F.H. Intraoperative sonography of cervical spinal cord injury: Results in 30 patients. AJNR Am J Neuroradiol 11:755–761, 1990.

149. Mirza, S.K.; Moquin, R.R.; Anderson, P.A.; et al. Stabilizing properties of the halo apparatus. Spine 22:727–733, 1997.

150. Moerman, J.; Harth, A.; Van Trimpont, I.; et al. Treatment of unstable fractures, dislocations and fracture-dislocations of the cervical spine with Senegas plate fixation. Acta Orthop Belg 60:30–35, 1994.

151. Montane, I.; Eismont, F.J.; Green, B.A. Traumatic occipitoatlantal dislocation. Spine 16:112–116, 1991.

152. Montesano, P.X.; Juach, E.C.; Anderson, P.A.; et al. Biomechanics of cervical spine internal fixation. Spine 16(3 Suppl):10–16, 1991.

153. Morgan, T.H.; Wharton, G.W.; Austin, G.N. The results of laminectomy in patients with incomplete spinal cord injuries. Paraplegia 9:14–23, 1971.

154. Morscher, E.; Sutter, F.; Jenny, H; Olerud, S: [Anterior plating of the cervical spine with the hollow screw-plate system of titanium.] Chirurg 57:702–707, 1986.

155. Müller, M.E.; Allgöwer, M.; Schneider, R.; Willenegger, H. Manual of Internal Fixation: Techniques Recommended by the AO-ASIF Group. Berlin, Springer-Verlag, 1991, pp. 644–669.

156. Nesathurai, S. Steroids and spinal cord injury: Revisiting the NASCIS 2 and NASCIS 3 trials. J Trauma 45:1088–1093, 1998.

157. Newell, D.; Anderson, P.; Armengaro, M. Stabilization of combined anterior and posterior instability with the cervical locking plate. Orthop Trans 191:195–196, 1995.

158. Nicoll, E.A. Fractures of the dorsolumbar spine. J Bone Joint Surg Br 31:376–394, 1949.

159. Nightingale, R.W.; McElhaney, J.H.; Richardson, W.J.; et al. Experimental impact injury to the cervical spine: Relating motion of the head and the mechanism of injury. J Bone Joint Surg Am 78:412–421, 1996.

160. Nightingale, R.W.; McElhaney, J.H.; Richardson, W.J.; Myers, B.S. Dynamic responses of the head and cervical spine to axial impact loading. J Biomech 29:307–318, 1996.

161. Nockels, R.; Young, W. Pharmacologic strategies in the treatment of experimental spinal cord injury. J Neurotrauma 9(Suppl):211–217, 1992.

162. Oakes, D.D.; Wilmot, C.B.; Hall, K.M.; Sherck, J.P. Benefits of early admission to a comprehensive trauma center for patients with spinal cord injury. Arch Phys Med Rehabil 71:637–643, 1990.

163. Olerud, C.; Jonsson, H., Jr. Compression of the cervical spine cord after reduction of fracture dislocations. Report of 2 cases. Acta Orthop Scand 62:599–601, 1991.

164. Orozco, D.; Llovet-Tapies, J. Osteosintesis en las fractures de raquis cervical. Rev Ortop Traumatol 14:285–288, 1970.

165. Osti, O.L.; Fraser, R.D.; Cornish, B.L. Fractures and fractures-dislocations of the lumbar spine. A retrospective study of 70 patients. Int Orthop 11:323–329, 1987.

166. Ostl, O.L.; Fraser, R.D.; Griffiths, E.R. Reduction and stabilisation of cervical dislocations. An analysis of 167 cases. J Bone Joint Surg Br 71:275–282, 1989.

167. Owen, J.H.; Naito, M.; Bridwell, K.H.; Oakley, D.M. Relationship between duration of spinal cord ischemia and postoperative neurologic deficits in animals. Spine 15:846–851, 1990.

168. Pait, T.G.; McAllister, P.V.; Kaufman, H.H. Quadrant anatomy of the articular pillars (lateral cervical mass) of the cervical spine. J Neurosurg 82:1011–1014, 1995.

169. Panjabi, M.M.; Duranceau, J.; Goel, V.; et al. Cervical human vertebrae. Quantitative three-dimensional anatomy of the middle and lower regions. Spine 16:861–869, 1991.

170. Panjabi, M.M.; White, A.A., 3rd; Johnson, R.M. Cervical spine mechanics as a function of transection of components. J Biomech 8:327–336, 1975.

171. Paramore, C.G.; Dickman, C.A.; Sonntag, V.K. The anatomical suitability of the C1–2 complex for transarticular screw fixation. J Neurosurg 85:221–224, 1996.

172. Petitjean, M.E.; Pointillart, V.; Dixmerias, F.; et al. [Medical treatment of spinal cord injury in the acute stage.] Ann Fr Anesth Reanim 17:114–122, 1998.

173. Pitts, L.H.; Ross, A.; Chase, G.A.; Faden, A.I. Treatment with thyrotropin-releasing hormone (TRH) in patients with traumatic spinal cord injuries. J Neurotrauma 12:235–243, 1995.

174. Potter, P.J.; Hayes, K.C.; Segal, J.L.; et al. Randomized double-blind crossover trial of fampridine-SR (sustained release 4-aminopyridine) in patients with incomplete spinal cord injury. J Neurotrauma 15:837–849, 1998.

175. Povlishock, J.T. Traumatically induced axonal injury: Pathogenesis and pathobiological implications. Brain Pathol 2:1–12, 1992.

176. Quencer, R.M.; Bunge, R.P. The injured spinal cord: Imaging, histopathologic clinical correlates, and basic science approaches to enhancing neural function after spinal cord injury. Spine 21:2064–2066, 1996.

177. Quencer, R.M.; Bunge, R.P.; Egnor, M.; et al. Acute traumatic central cord syndrome: MRI-pathological correlations. Neuroradiology 34:85–94, 1992.

178. Regan, R.F.; Choi, D.W. Glutamate neurotoxicity in spinal cord cell culture. Neuroscience 43:585–591, 1991.

179. Reid, J.D. Effects of flexion-extension movements of the head and spine upon the spinal cord and nerve roots. J Neurol Neurosurg Psychiatr 23:214, 1960.

180. Reithmeier, R.A. Mammalian exchangers and co-transporters. Curr Opin Cell Biol 6:583–594, 1994.

181. Reynen, P.D.; Clancy, W.G., Jr. Cervical spine injury, hockey helmets, and face masks. Am J Sports Med 22:167–170, 1994.

182. Ripa, D.R.; Kowall, M.G.; Meyer, P.R., Jr.; Rusin, J.J. Series of ninety-two traumatic cervical spine injuries stabilized with anterior ASIF plate fusion technique. Spine 16(3 Suppl):46–55, 1991.

183. Rivara, F.P.; Grossman, D.C.; Cummings, P. Injury prevention. First of two parts. N Engl J Med 337:543–548, 1997.

184. Rivara, F.P.; Grossman, D.C.; Cummings, P. Injury prevention. Second of two parts. N Engl J Med 337:613–618, 1997.

185. Rivlin, A.S.; Tator, C.H. Effect of duration of acute spinal cord compression in a new acute cord injury model in the rat. Surg Neurol 10:38–43, 1978.

186. Rizzolo, S.J.; Piazza, M.R.; Cotler, J.M.; et al. Intervertebral disc injury complicating cervical spine trauma. Spine 16(6 Suppl):187–189, 1991.

187. Rizzolo, S.J.; Vaccaro, A.R.; Cotler, J.M. Cervical spine trauma. Spine 19:2288–2298, 1994.

188. Roaf, R. A study of the mechanics of spinal injury. J Bone Joint Surg Br 42:810–823, 1960.

189. Robertson, P.A.; Ryan, M.D. Neurological deterioration after reduction of cervical subluxation. Mechanical compression by disc tissue. J Bone Joint Surg Br 74:224–227, 1992.

190. Robinson, R.A.; Southwick, W.O. Indications and techniques for early stabilization of the neck in some fracture dislocations of the cervical spine. South Med J 53:565–579, 1960.

191. Rogers, W.A. Fracture and dislocations of the cervical spine: An end result study. J Bone Joint Surg Am 39:341–376, 1957.

192. Rorabeck, C.H.; Rock, M.G.; Hawkins, R.J.; Bourne, R.B. Unilateral facet dislocation of the cervical spine. An analysis of the results of treatment in 26 patients. Spine 12:23–27, 1987.

193. Rosner, M.J. Methylprednisolone for spinal cord injury. Letter. J Neurosurg 77:324–325, 1992.

194. Rosner, M.J. National Acute Spinal Cord Injury Study of methyl-prednisolone or naloxone. Letter. Neurosurgery 28:628–629, 1991.

195. Rosner, M.J. Treatment of spinal cord injury. Letter. J Neurosurg 80:954–955, 1994.

196. Rossier, A.B.; Hussey, R.W.; Kenzora, J.E. Anterior fibular interbody fusion in the treatment of cervical spinal cord injuries. Surg Neurol 7:55–60, 1977.

197. Roth, E.J.; Park, T.; Pang, T.; et al. Traumatic cervical Brown-Séquard and Brown-Séquard-plus syndromes: The spectrum of presentations and outcomes. Paraplegia 29:582–589, 1991.

198. Roy-Camille, R.; Saillant, G.; Laville, C.; Benazet, J.P. Treatment of lower cervical spinal injuries—C3 to C7. Spine 17(10 Suppl):442–446, 1992.

199. Roy-Camille, R.; Saillant, G.; Mazel, C. Internal fixations of the unstable cervical spine by a posterior osteosynthesis with plates and screws. In: Cervical Spine Research Society, ed. The Cervical Spine. Philadelphia, J.B. Lippincott, 1989, pp. 390–403.

200. Sabiston, C.P.; Wing, P.C.; Schweigel, J.F.; et al. Closed reduction of dislocations of the lower cervical spine. J Trauma 28:832–835, 1988.

201. Schaefer, D.M.; Flanders, A.; Northrup, B.E.; et al. Magnetic resonance imaging of acute cervical spine trauma. Correlation with severity of neurologic injury. Spine 14:1090–1095, 1989.

202. Scher, A.T. Is the pattern of neurological damage of diagnostic value in the radiological assessment of acute cervical spine injury? Paraplegia 19:248–252, 1981.

203. Schlegel, J.; Bayley, J.; Yuan, H.; Fredricksen, B. Timing of surgical decompression and fixation of acute spinal fractures. J Orthop Trauma 10:323–330, 1996.

204. Schneider, R.C.; Crosby, E.C.; Russo, R.H.; Gosch, H.H. Chapter 32. Traumatic spinal cord syndromes and their management. Clin Neurosurg 20:424–429, 1973.

205. Schneider, R.C.; Kahn, R. Chronic neurologic sequelae of acute trauma to the spine and spinal cord. Part I. The significance of the acute flexion or "teardrop" fracture-dislocation of the cervical spine. J Bone Joint Surg Am 38:985–991, 1956.

206. Schneider, R.C.; Knighton, R. Chronic neurological sequelae of acute trauma to the spine and spinal cord: The syndrome of chronic injury to the cervical spinal cord in the region of the central canal. J Bone Joint Surg Am 41:905–919, 1959.

207. Schwab, M.E.; Bartholdi, D. Degeneration and regeneration of axons in the lesioned spinal cord. Physiol Rev 76:319–370, 1996.

208. Sears, W.; Fazl, M. Prediction of stability of cervical spine fracture managed in the halo vest and indications for surgical intervention. J Neurosurg 72:426–432, 1990.

209. Shono, Y.; McAfee, P.C.; Cunningham, B.W. The pathomechanics of compression injuries in the cervical spine. Nondestructive and destructive investigative methods. Spine 18:2009–2019, 1993.

210. Shrosbree, R.D. Neurological sequelae of reduction of fracture dislocations of the cervical spine. Paraplegia 17:212–221, 1979.

211. Slucky, A.V.; Eismont, F.J. Treatment of acute injury of the cervical spine. Instr Course Lect 44:67–80, 1995.

212. Smith, M.D.; Emery, S.E.; Dudley, A.; et al. Vertebral artery injury during anterior decompression of the cervical spine. A retrospective review of ten patients. J Bone Joint Surg Br 75:410–415, 1993.

213. Soderstrom, C.A.; McArdle, D.Q.; Ducker, T.B.; Militello, P.R. The diagnosis of intra-abdominal injury in patients with cervical cord trauma. J Trauma 23:1061–1065, 1983.

214. Songer, M.N.; Spencer, D.L.; Meyer, P.R., Jr.; Jayaraman, G. The use of sublaminar cables to replace Luque wires. Spine 16(8 Suppl):418–421, 1991.

215. Spivak, J.M.; Weiss, M.A.; Cotler, J.M.; Call, M. Cervical spine injuries in patients 65 and older. Spine 19:2302–2306, 1994.

216. Star, A.M.; Jones, A.A.; Cotler, J.M.; et al. Immediate closed reduction of cervical spine dislocations using traction. Spine 15:1068–1072, 1990.

217. Stauffer, E.S.; Kelly, E.G. Fracture-dislocations of the cervical spine. Instability and recurrent deformity following treatment by anterior interbody fusion. J Bone Joint Surg Am 59:45–48, 1977.

218. Stauffer, E.S.; Rhoades, M.E. Surgical stabilization of the cervical spine after trauma. Arch Surg 111:652–657, 1976.

219. Stauffer, E.S.; Wood, R.W.; Kelly, E.G. Gunshot wounds of the spine: The effects of laminectomy. J Bone Joint Surg Am 61:389–392, 1979.

220. Stys, P.K.; Waxman, S.G.; Ransom, B.R. Ionic mechanisms of anoxic injury in mammalian CNS white matter: Role of Na+ channels and Na(+)-Ca2+ exchanger. J Neurosci 12:430–439, 1992.

221. Subin, B.; Liu, J.F.; Marshall, G.J.; et al. Transoral anterior decompression and fusion of chronic irreducible atlantoaxial dislocation with spinal cord compression. Spine 20:1233–1240, 1995.

222. Sutterlin, C.E., 3rd; McAfee, P.C.; Warden, K.E.; et al. A biomechanical evaluation of cervical spinal stabilization methods in a bovine model. Static and cyclical loading. Spine 13:795–802, 1988.

223. Svendgaard, N.A.; Cronqvist, S.; Delgado, T.; Salford, L.G. Treatment of severe cervical spine injuries by anterior interbody fusion with early mobilization. Acta Neurochir 60:91–105, 1982.

224. Tator, C.H. Biology of neurological recovery and functional restoration after spinal cord injury. Neurosurgery 42:696–707, 1998.

225. Tator, C.H.; Fehlings, M.G. Review of the secondary injury theory of acute spinal cord trauma with emphasis on vascular mechanisms. J Neurosurg 75:15–26, 1991.

226. Taylor, A.R. The mechanism of injury to the spinal cord in the neck without damage to the vertebral column. J Bone Joint Surg Br 33:543, 1951.

227. Taylor, A.R.; Blackwood, W. Paraplegia in hyperextension cervical injuries with normal radiographic appearances. J Bone Joint Surg Br 30:245–248, 1948.

228. Tencer, A.F.; Allen, B.L., Jr.; Ferguson, R.L. A biomechanical study of thoracolumbar spine fractures with bone in the canal. Part III. Mechanical properties of the dura and its tethering ligaments. Spine 10:741–747, 1985.

229. Torg, J.S.; Pavlov, H.; Genuario, S.E.; et al. Neurapraxia of the cervical spinal cord with transient quadriplegia. J Bone Joint Surg Am 68:1354–1370, 1986.

230. Torg, J.S.; Sennett, B.; Vegso, J.J.; Pavlov, H. Axial loading injuries to the middle cervical spine segment. An analysis and classification of twenty-five cases. Am J Sports Med 19:6–20, 1991.

231. Traynelis, V.C.; Donaher, P.A.; Roach, R.M.; et al. Biomechanical comparison of anterior Caspar plate and three-level posterior fixation techniques in a human cadaveric model. J Neurosurg 79:96–103, 1993.

232. Tribus, C.B. Cervical disk herniation in association with traumatic facet dislocation. Tech Orthop 9:5–7, 1994.

233. Ulrich, C.; Worsdorfer, O; Claes, L.; Magerl, F. Comparative study of the stability of anterior and posterior cervical spine fixation procedures. Arch Orthop Trauma Surg 106:226–231, 1987.

234. Van Peteghem, P.K.; Schweigel, J.F. The fractured cervical spine rendered unstable by anterior cervical fusion. J Trauma 19:110–114, 1979.

235. Viano, D.C.; Lau, I.V. A viscous tolerance criterion for soft tissue injury assessment. J Biomech 21:387–399, 1988.

236. Wagner, F.C., Jr.; Chehrazi, B. Early decompression and neurological outcome in acute cervical spinal cord injuries. J Neurosurg 56:699–705, 1982.

237. Wamil, A.W.; Wamil, B.D.; Hellerqvist, C.G. CM101-mediated recovery of walking ability in adult mice paralyzed by spinal cord injury. Proc Natl Acad Sci U S A 95:13188–13193, 1998.

238. Waters, R.L.; Adkins, R.H.; Yakura, J.S. Definition of complete spinal cord injury. Paraplegia 29:573–581, 1991.

239. Waters, R.L.; Adkins, R.H.; Yakura, J.S.; Sie, I. Motor and sensory recovery following complete tetraplegia. Arch Phys Med Rehabil 74:242–247, 1993.

240. Waters, R.L.; Adkins, R.H.; Yakura, J.S.; Sie, I. Motor and sensory recovery following incomplete paraplegia. Arch Phys Med Rehabil 75:67–72, 1994.

241. Waters, R.L.; Adkins, R.H.; Yakura, J.S.; Sie, I. Motor and sensory recovery following incomplete tetraplegia. Arch Phys Med Rehabil 75:306–311, 1994.

242. Waters, R.L.; Adkins, R.; Yakura, J.; Vigil, D. Prediction of ambulatory performance based on motor scores derived from standards of the American Spinal Injury Association. Arch Phys Med Rehabil 75:756–760, 1994.

243. Waters, R.L.; Sie, I.; Adkins, R.H.; Yakura, J.S. Injury pattern effect on motor recovery after traumatic spinal cord injury. Arch Phys Med Rehabil 76:440–443, 1995.

244. Waters, R.L.; Yakura, J.S.; Adkins, R.H.; Sie, I. Recovery following complete paraplegia. Arch Phys Med Rehabil 73:784–789, 1992.

245. Waters, R.L.; Yoshida, G.M. Prognosis of spinal cord injuries. In: Levine, A.M., ed. Orthopaedic Knowledge Update: Trauma. American Academy of Orthopaedic Surgery, Rosemont, IL, 1996, pp. 303–310.

246. Webb, J.K.; Broughton, R.B.; McSweeney, T.; Park, W.M. Hidden flexion injury of the cervical spine. J Bone Joint Surg Br 58:322–327, 1976.

247. Weiland, D.J.; McAfee, P.C. Posterior cervical fusion with triple-wire strut graft technique: One hundred consecutive patients. J Spinal Disord 4:15–21, 1991.

248. Weingarden, S.I.; Graham, P.M. Falls resulting in spinal cord injury: Patterns and outcomes in an older population. Paraplegia 27:423–427, 1989.

249. White, A.A., III; Panjabi, M.M. Clinical Biomechanics of the Spine. Philadelphia, J.B. Lippincott, 1978.

250. White, A.A., III; Panjabi, M.M. The problem of clinical instability in the human spine: A systematic approach. In: White, A.A., III; Panjabi, M.M., eds. Clinical Biomechanics of the Spine. Philadelphia, J.B. Lippincott, 1990, pp. 277–378.

251. Whitehill, R.; Richman, J.A.; Glaser, J.A. Failure of immobilization of the cervical spine by the halo vest. A report of five cases. J Bone Joint Surg Am 68:326–332, 1986.

252. Willis, B.K.; Greiner, F.; Orrison, W.W.; Benzel, E.C. The incidence of vertebral artery injury after midcervical spine fracture or subluxation. Neurosurgery 34:435–441, 1994.

253. Wilmot, C.B.; Hall, K.M. Evaluation of the acute management of tetraplegia: Conservative versus surgical treatment. Paraplegia 24:148–153, 1986.

254. Wright, M.; Rivara, F.P.; Ferse, D. Evaluation of the Think First head and spinal cord injury prevention program. Inj Prev 1:81–85, 1995.

255. Xu, R.; Ebraheim, N.A.; Yeasting, R.; et al. Anatomy of C7 lateral mass and projection of pedicle axis on its posterior aspect. J Spinal Disord 8:116–120, 1995.

256. Yablon, I.G.; Palumbo, M.; Spatz, E.; et al. Nerve root recovery in complete injuries of the cervical spine. Spine 16(10 Suppl):518–521, 1991.

257. Yashon, D. Pathogenesis of spinal cord injury. Orthop Clin North Am 9:247–261, 1978.

258. Yashon, D.; Jane, J.A.; White, R.J. Prognosis and management of spinal cord and cauda equina bullet injuries in sixty-five civilians. J Neurosurg 32:163–170, 1970.

259. Yoganandan, N.; Sances, A., Jr.; Maiman, D.J.; et al. Experimental spinal injuries with vertical impact. Spine 11:855–860, 1986.

260. Young, W. Secondary injury mechanisms in acute spinal cord injury. J Emerg Med 11(Suppl):13–22, 1993.

261. Young, W. Spinal cord regeneration. Science 273:451, 1996.

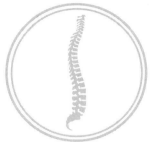

CHAPTER 30

Thoracic and Upper Lumbar Spine Injuries

Mark A. Prévost, M.D.
Robert A. McGuire, M.D.
Steven R. Garfin, M.D.
Frank J. Eismont, M.D.

The primary goals in providing care for patients who have sustained thoracolumbar spinal trauma must include preservation of life and protection of neurologic function, in addition to restoration and maintenance of alignment and stability of the spine. Upholding these goals while managing thoracolumbar fractures is both challenging and controversial to the spinal surgeon. Many times the bottom line is whether the spine can function as a load-bearing column. If it can, is an orthosis necessary? If not, can stability and alignment be restored with surgical intervention? Each of these objectives is best accomplished when the treating physician understands the anatomy of the spinal column, appreciates the biomechanics of the injury and instability, and has an awareness of the expanding treatment options available for the care of a spine-injured patient.[104, 105]

HISTORICAL BACKGROUND

For physicians taking care of patients with spinal injuries, it is helpful to gain perspective regarding diagnosis and treatment of these injuries as they have evolved through time.

The earliest written record of spinal cord injury is found in the Edwin Smith Papyrus (3000 BC).[35] Later, Egyptian physicians noted that patients with vertebral trauma often had paralysis of the arms and legs and urinary incontinence, thus suggesting an association among vertebral injuries, spinal cord damage, and loss of function.

Celsus made the next important contribution to the description of spinal cord trauma when he distinguished cervical from thoracolumbar spinal cord injuries. He reported that fractures of the cervical spine produced respiratory embarrassment and vomiting whereas trauma to the lower portion of the spinal column produced

paralysis of the lower extremities and urinary incontinence. He also expanded on Hippocrates' concept of manual extension for reduction of spinal deformities.[35]

In the 16th century, Ambroise Paré readdressed the problem of spinal injury.[25, 118] He accurately described the symptoms of cord compression as follows:

> Amongst the symptoms are the stupidity, or numbness or palsy of the arms, legs, fundament and bladder, which take away their sense and motion, so that their urine and excrements come from them against their wills and knowledge, or else are wholly suppressed. Which when they happen saith Hippocrates, you may foretell that death is at hand, by reason that the spinal marrow is hurt. . . . Having made such a prognostication, you may make an incision so to take forth the splinters of the broken vertebrae, which driven in press the spinal marrow in the nerves thereof.

Modern management of vertebral column trauma arrived with the development of anesthesia and radiography. In the 1920s, based heavily on principles advocated by Guttman, emphasis in the treatment of vertebral trauma was placed on closed reduction of fractures.[117] Davis proposed a method of reduction in which the patient was anesthetized and placed in the prone position. An overhead pulley suspension raised the lower limbs and produced marked hyperextension. The physician then made a manual thrust over the fractured vertebra in an attempt to realign the fracture. When reduction was achieved, the patient was immobilized in a plaster jacket. In 1931, Watson-Jones modified this technique by using tables of different height to hyperextend the spine and obtain reduction.[269]

Internal fixation of thoracic and lumbar spinal fractures began after the Second World War with the development of spinous process plating for unstable fractures.[133, 135]

Later, Harrington revolutionized spinal care and rehabilitation with the introduction of his posterior spinal instrumentation devices.[66] Since then, surgical techniques and instruments have proliferated and have continued to improve the ability to anatomically reduce and internally stabilize the injured spinal column.* Neurologic recovery, however, has remained unchanged or only slightly improved over the results obtained with postural reduction and nonoperative care.[18, 32, 49, 66, 95, 139, 151, 192] At this time, the major predictable benefits of internal fixation of spinal fractures are decreased hospital stay, early rehabilitation, and prevention of deformity.[49] However, root function and, in properly selected patients, spinal cord function can be dramatically altered and improved with appropriate surgery and stabilization.

ANATOMY

The thoracolumbar spine is characterized by a dynamic and complex interaction between the bony vertebral elements, discs, and interconnecting ligaments. It would be impossible to make sound diagnostic and therapeutic decisions regarding thoracolumbar trauma without a solid understanding of this anatomy.

The human spine has 12 thoracic and 5 lumbar vertebrae with interspaced intervertebral discs. Stagnara and associates studied spinal alignment in healthy persons aged 20 to 29 years without back complaints.[259] Wide variation was noted in this healthy population, the range of thoracic kyphosis being 7° to 63°, with 91% between 18° and 51° (Fig. 30–1A). In the thoracic spine, this configuration is maintained by the wedge-shaped vertebral bodies and discs, which are larger posteriorly than anteriorly. Across the thoracolumbar junction (T10–L2), where most injuries occur, the normal range is reported to be 0° to 10° kyphosis. In the lumbar spine, the average lordosis in this same group of normal people was 50°, with a range of 32° to 84°; 92% of these individuals had between 42° and 74° of lordosis[259] (see Fig. 32–1B). In the lumbar spine, the discs have an increased height anteriorly, which helps create this lordosis.

White and Panjabi investigated the types of motion present throughout the spine[273] (Fig. 30–2). The thoracic spine has significantly less flexion-extension motion than the cervical or lumbar spines. In the cervical spine from the occiput to C7, the average motion between flexion and extension is 13° per level, with a range of 8° to 17°. At C7–T1 this motion decreases to 9°, and in the thoracic spine from T1 to T6, each level has only 4° of total flexion-extension motion. From the T6–T7 to the T12–L1 levels, flexion-extension motion gradually increases from 5° to 12°, in contrast to the average 15° flexion-extension motion at each lumbar level (range of 12° to 20°).

The thoracic spine is less capable of bending laterally than the cervical spine. Lateral bending in the cervical spine from occiput to C7 averages 8° per level, whereas it is only about 6° per level from T1 to T10. At the area of the T10–L1 thoracolumbar junction, lateral bending increases to an average of 8° per level. In the lumbar spine, this motion decreases to about 6° per level. Much of the thoracic-level rigidity is related to the presence of the rib cage and the costovertebral articulations.[216]

Axial rotation in the thoracic spine averages 8° from T1 to T8 but decreases to approximately 2° per level below T10. Axial rotation is greater in the thoracic spine than in the lumbar spine because the facets are aligned in the coronal plane, as opposed to the more sagittal alignment that occurs in the lumbar spine (Fig. 30–3). The transition region for facet orientation is the area from T10 to T12. Because of this alteration in facet orientation, the motion characteristics of the lower thoracic spine more closely resemble those of the lumbar spine. In the lumbar spine, the facet joints gradually attain an almost true sagittal orientation at the L4–L5 level. Such alignment provides significant restriction to rotation and side bending.

The thoracolumbar junction is more susceptible to injury than are other adjacent portions of the spine. Approximately 50% of all vertebral body fractures and 40% of all spinal cord injuries occur from T11 to L2. This greater susceptibility to injury can be explained by the decrease in rib restraint, changes in stiffness for flexion-extension and rotation, and changes in disc size and shape, which occur relatively acutely in the transitional area between the upper thoracic and the midlumbar spine.

The conus medullaris usually begins at T11 and, in most males, ends at the L1–L2 disc space. The conus in females frequently stops slightly more proximally. The conus medullaris can occasionally extend much lower into the lumbar spine and is often associated with a hypertrophic filum terminale. The neural elements of the lumbar spine below the L1–L2 disc are usually purely spinal nerve rootlets (cauda equina). In addition, an extensive collateral circulation is located distal to the nerve roots and proximal to the spinal cord, thus making this region less prone to vascular compromise and more likely to recover from a spinal cord injury.[218] The thoracic spinal cord has relatively poor vascularity and limited collateral circulation when compared with the cervical spinal cord and the conus medullaris. Adamkiewicz in 1882 described the blood supply of the spinal cord, including a relatively constant medullary artery known as the great medullary artery or the artery of Adamkiewicz. This artery may be injured as a result of trauma or thoracic disc herniation or from one of the lateral or posterolateral extracavitary approaches. Injury to this artery may cause serious ischemic insult to the cord and lead to paralysis. In most people, the artery of Adamkiewicz originates from the intercostal artery on the left side between T10 and T12, where it joins the nerve root sleeve and becomes intradural. The artery then crosses one to three disc spaces, at which point it anastomoses with the anterior spinal artery. Knowledge of this artery and its course is important during certain approaches and may explain certain neurologic deficits that may not recover despite adequate anterior decompression.[184]

The spinal canal in the midthoracic region is considerably narrower than in the cervical or lumbar region.[86, 237] At the T6 level, the spinal canal has a circular configura-

---

*See references 8, 22, 23, 27, 51, 63, 64, 76, 80, 87, 93, 107, 131, 140, 149, 160, 181–183, 185, 186, 197, 207, 212, 243–245, 262, 264, 276, 284.

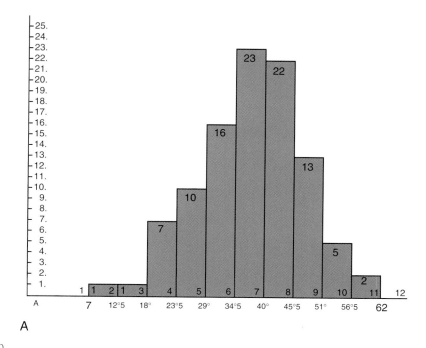

A

FIGURE 30–1. *A,* Distribution of thoracic kyphosis in 100 French people, 43 women and 57 men. *B,* Distribution of lumbar lordosis in the same group of 100 French people. (*A, B,* Data from Stagnara, P.; et al. Spine 7:335–342, 1982.)

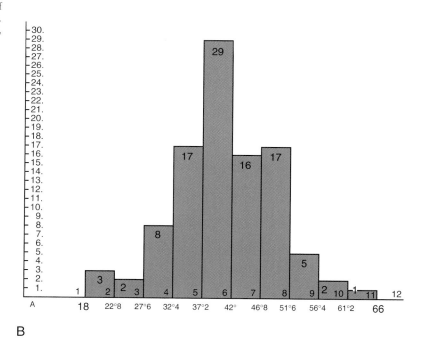

B

tion with a 16-mm diameter. In the middle to lower cervical spine, the canal is 23 × 14 mm, and in the lumbosacral region, it is 26 × 17 mm.[183] The small size of the thoracic spinal canal must be appreciated for two reasons. First, because less space is available, even minor spinal column displacement may produce significant spinal cord compression. Second, when considering reconstruction of the spine, many systems use sublaminar fixation within this already narrowed region of the spinal canal. Therefore, the patient's specific injuries, the availability of fixation devices, and spinal anatomy must be

taken into account when selecting instrument shape and size.

As Dommisse and others have shown, in the thoracic spine the free space between the spinal cord and the borders of the spinal canal is relatively minimal.[69] Although the thoracic cord tends to be smaller than the cervical and lumbar enlargements, the free space also narrows. In addition and of significance with regard to spinal trauma, the blood supply in the middle and lower thoracic spine is less abundant than elsewhere in the spinal cord. Adding to the variability is the location of the conus

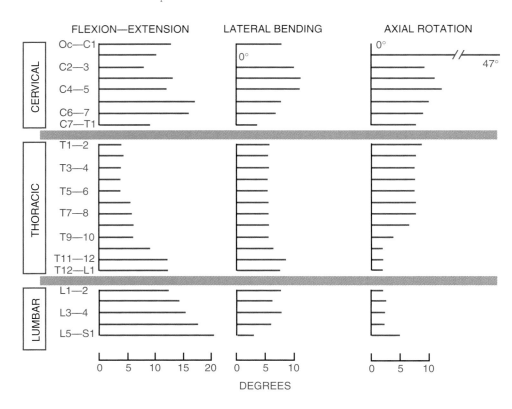

FIGURE 30–2. The motion present at each level of the spine. (Data from multiple reviews and from the experimental work of White, A.; Panjabi, M. Spine 3:12–20, 1978.)

FIGURE 30–3. Rotation in the midthoracic spine and at the thoracolumbar junction. *A,* The rotation at T5–T6 is represented by the *arrow* between the spinous processes. The *inset* shows how the lamina of T5 glides over the posterior elements of T6 with no resistance to rotation. *B,* After facetectomy, the motion present between T5 and T6 (*arrow*) is unchanged from *A. C,* The rotation present between T12 and L1 is represented by the *arrow* between the spinous processes. Because of the sagittal orientation of the facets (*inset*), rotation is markedly restricted. *D,* After bilateral facetectomy, motion between T12 and L1 (*arrow*) is markedly increased. The restriction from the sagittally oriented facets has been eliminated.

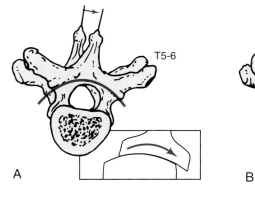

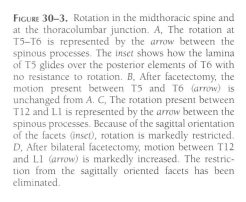

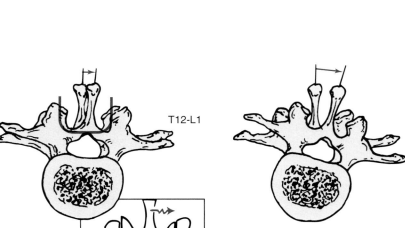

medullaris, with terminations in the general population following almost a bell-shaped curve from the T12 to the L3 level.[69]

The cord is usually wider in the lateral plane than in the anterior-to-posterior direction. Elliott demonstrated that the largest diameter of the cervical enlargement, which is at approximately C5–C6, was 13.2 mm in the lateral plane and 7.7 mm from anterior to posterior. In the thoracic region, the smallest measurements were 8 mm laterally and 6.5 mm from anterior to posterior, and the lumbosacral enlargement was 9.6 and 8.0 mm, respectively.[86] These dimensions can be correlated with the space available within the spinal canal. Aebi and Thalgott demonstrated that the largest area (i.e., the space available in the cervical canal) was 24.5 mm laterally and 14.7 mm from anterior to posterior in the thoracic region, thus correlating with the small size of the spinal cord at this location.[4] The largest space available was 17.2 mm in the lateral plane and 16.8 mm anterior to posterior. At the level of the lumbar enlargement, it was 23.4 mm laterally and 17.4 mm from anterior to posterior. In general, the cord occupies approximately half the space available in each direction. In the thoracic spine, according to Dommisse, the anterior-to-posterior diameter of the spinal canal changes minimally; it averages approximately 13 mm throughout but increases to 15 mm in the lower thoracic spine.[69] His measurements of interpedicular distance (lateral measurement) averaged about 15 mm at the smallest point (approximately T6) and increased to 17 mm at T10–T11.

The morphometry of the pedicles of the thoracic and lumbar spines varies considerably from level to level, as well as from patient to patient.[24, 166, 246, 267, 285] Zindrick and colleagues,[286] in an evaluation of 2900 pedicles, determined pedicle isthmus widths and pedicle angles in the sagittal and transverse planes. In general, pedicle isthmus widths were significantly smaller in the thoracic spine than in the lumbar spine (Fig. 30–4A and B). The pedicle angles in the transverse plane varied from 27° medial inclination (in a posterior-to-anterior direction) in the proximal thoracic spine to approximately 1° at T11 and −4° at T12. At L1, the angle again inclines medially at 11° and gradually increases to approximately 30° at L5 (see Fig. 32–4C). In an anatomic study investigating the internal architecture of thoracic pedicles, Kothe and associates showed that the medial wall is two to three times thicker than the lateral wall. This difference in thickness could explain the fact that most pedicle fractures related to pedicle screw insertion occur laterally.[162] An understanding of these dimensions and angles is important when considering the use of pedicle screw fixation systems to stabilize thoracic and thoracolumbar spinal injuries.

The flexion axis of the normal thoracic spine and the thoracolumbar junction occurs at the middle to posterior third junction of the vertebral body.[235, 275] This location of the axis results in an anterior compressive force moment arm that is approximately one fourth the length of the posterior tensile force.[257] Brown and colleagues in 1957 demonstrated that posterior elements fail under tension at approximately 400 lb.[37] This amount of posterior force corresponds to a resultant anterior compressive force of approximately 1200 to 1600 lb. Comprehension of this biomechanical principle is essential to gain an

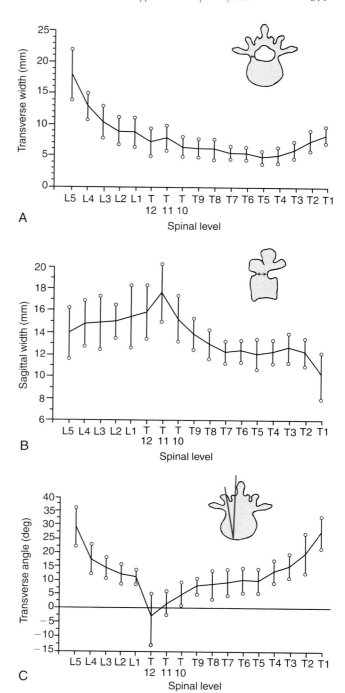

FIGURE 30–4. Analysis of the morphometric characteristics of the thoracic and lumbar pedicles. *A,* The transverse width of the pedicle at each level of the thoracic and lumbar spine is shown. The average pedicle width of the lumbar spine ranges from 9 to 18 mm. In the thoracic spine, all pedicles are smaller than 9 mm. *B,* The longitudinal pedicle width of each level in the thoracic and lumbar spine is represented. It peaks at 17 mm at the T11 vertebra and decreases to 10 mm at T1 and to 14 mm at L5. *C,* The transverse angle of the pedicles for each level of the thoracic and lumbar spine is shown. The angle is −4° at the T12 vertebra and increases to 30° at L5 and to 27° at T1. (*A–C,* Redrawn from Zindrick, M.R.; et al. Spine 12:160–166, 1987.)

understanding of spinal stability (described later). In the thoracic spine, the human body's center of gravity is anterior to the spine. As a result, the resting condition in the thoracic spine and at the thoracolumbar junction is one of vertebral body compression and posterior ligamentous complex tension. In the thoracic spine, the ribs anterior to the spinal column and the thick ligaments posteriorly, acting in tension, restrict any further forward flexion in the normal situation.[234] In the lumbar spine, particularly in the more lordotic lower lumbar spine, the center of gravity is located more posteriorly, and the posterior elements provide approximately 30% of the weight-bearing support. These considerations are important for realignment or for maintenance of alignment after spinal injury.[216, 252, 273]

One of the important components of thoracolumbar spinal anatomy is the soft tissue that interconnects the bony elements. The complex interaction of ligaments, disc, and musculature allows for both controlled motion and stability of the spine. Trauma to the soft tissues of the thoracolumbar spine can have profound effects on function and stability.

The anterior longitudinal ligament is a strong, broad-based ligament that runs on the anterior aspect of the vertebral body from the atlas to the sacrum. It is firmly attached to both the ventral aspect of the disc and the periosteum of the vertebral body. It is a major contributor to spinal stability and limits hyperextension of the vertebral column. The posterior longitudinal ligament also runs the length of the spinal column, but it is narrower and weaker than its anterior counterpart. Its primary function is to limit hyperflexion. The intervertebral disc is composed of the anulus fibrosus and the nucleus pulposus. The anulus is formed by concentric bands of fibrocartilage that run obliquely from one vertebral body to another. This arrangement allows for some motion, yet is one of the strongest connections between vertebral segments. The nucleus, which is encased in the anulus, acts as a shock absorber for axial forces. Of importance in thoracolumbar trauma is that the disc is essentially an avascular structure that relies on passive diffusion through the end-plates and peripheral aspect of the anulus for nutrition. When this structure is disrupted, the potential for healing is limited.

Posteriorly, the lamina are joined by the ligamentum flavum, a broad band of elastic fiber. The spinous processes are joined by a weak interspinous ligament and a strong supraspinous ligament. The intrinsic muscles of the back include the erector spinae group of muscles (spinalis, longissimus, iliocostalis) and the transversospinalis group (rotatores, multifidus, semispinalis). The intrinsic muscles maintain posture and provide movement of the vertebral column. Any deformity resulting from trauma can alter the function of these muscles. In addition, it is important to have an understanding of these muscle groups when considering the various anatomic approaches to the spine described later in this chapter.

MECHANISMS OF INJURY

Frequently, many complex forces occur at the time of injury, each of which has the potential to produce structural damage to the spine.[119] Most often, however, one or two forces account for most of the bone or ligamentous injuries encountered. The forces most commonly associated with thoracic, thoracolumbar, and lumbar spine injuries are axial compression, flexion, lateral compression, flexion-rotation, shear, flexion-distraction, and extension. Each is discussed from a mechanical viewpoint, and their effect on the bone-disc-ligament complex of the spine is described.

Axial Compression

Because of the normal thoracic kyphosis, axial loading in this area usually results in an anterior flexion load on the vertebral body. The resultant spine injuries are discussed under Flexion.

An axial load in the straight thoracolumbar region (Fig. 30–5) often results in pure compressive loading of the vertebral body.[156] As described by Roaf, this mechanism

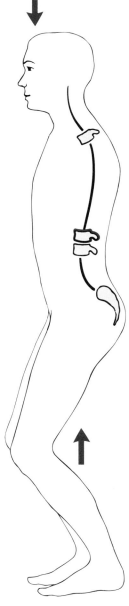

FIGURE 30–5. Axial compression across the straight thoracolumbar region results in pure compressive loading of the vertebral body and most often causes a thoracolumbar burst fracture.

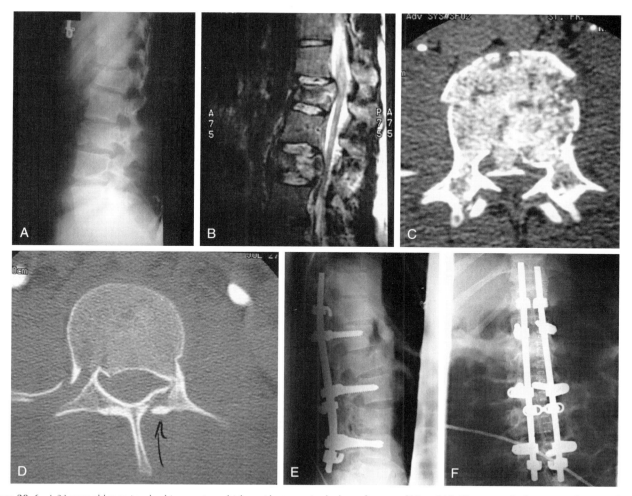

FIGURE 30–6. A 21-year-old man involved in a motor vehicle accident sustained a burst fracture of L1 and L3. The patient had an incomplete spinal cord injury. *A,* A preoperative lateral view shows loss of height predominately at L1. *B,* A sagittal-cut magnetic resonance image shows compression at both L1 and L3. *C,* An axial-cut computed tomographic (CT) scan at L3 shows a retropulsed fragment filling half the canal. *D,* An axial CT scan at L1 shows a fracture of the lamina and retropulsion of a fragment into canal. *E,* This injury was stabilized with ISOLA instrumentation combining both pedicle screws and laminar hooks. Sagittal alignment was maintained. Note the use of a lamina hook at L4 to protect the pedicle screw at that level. *F,* Postoperative anteroposterior radiograph showing a cross-connection added for additional stability.

produces end-plate failure, followed by vertebral body compression.[235] With sufficient force, vertical fractures develop through the vertebral body and produce a burst fracture[21, 62, 157, 209] (Fig. 30–6). Frederickson and co-workers observed that this fracture then propagates through the midportion of the posterior cortex of the vertebral body through the vascular foramina.[99] With further loading, centripetal displacement of the bone occurs, frequently with disc fragmentation and posterior disruption. This centripetal force can produce fractures at the pedicle-body junction and result in widening of the interpedicular distance and, particularly if a flexion component is present, a greenstick fracture of the lamina (see Fig. 30–6). With severe compression, significant disruption of the posterior element may occur.

Heggeness and Doherty studied the trabecular anatomy of the thoracolumbar vertebrae and documented a trabecular framework that originates from the medial corner of the base of the pedicle and extends in a radial fashion throughout the vertebral body, with thinning of the vertebral cortex near the base of the pedicle at the site of origin of this trabecular array. Such anatomy may produce a site of stress concentration and may explain the trapezoidal shape of the bony fragments that are frequently retropulsed into the spinal canal in burst-type fractures caused by an axial load[130] (Fig. 30–7).

Flexion

Flexion forces (Fig. 30–8) cause compression anteriorly along the vertebral bodies and discs, with tensile forces developed posteriorly. The posterior ligaments may not tear, particularly with rapid loading rates, but posterior avulsion fractures may develop.[235] Anteriorly, as the bone fractures and angulation increase, the force is dissipated. With intact posterior ligaments, a stable fracture pattern most often results. Frequently, the middle column remains intact with no subluxation or retropulsion of bone or disc fragments (Fig. 30–9). However, with disrupted posterior ligaments and facet capsules, instability may occur.[58, 133, 150, 195, 196, 211] If the anterior wedging exceeds 40% to 50%, posterior ligamentous and facet joint failure can be assumed, and late instability with progressive deformity may occur.[271] Flexion-compression injuries with concomitant middle element failure have a higher potential for causing mechanical instability, progressive deformity, and neurologic deficit.[146]

Lateral Compression

Lateral compression forces produce an injury similar to the anterior wedge compression injuries previously described, except that the force is applied laterally (Fig. 30–10). Lesions may be limited to vertebral body fractures, or associated posterior ligamentous injury may occur[92, 93] (Fig. 30–11). The former are usually stable injuries, whereas the latter may be chronically unstable and lead to progressive pain and deformity.

Flexion-Rotation

A flexion-rotation injury pattern includes a combination of flexion and rotation forces (Fig. 30–12). As described previously for pure flexion, the predominant injury pattern may be anterior bone disruption. However, as rotational forces increase, the ligaments[127, 128, 215] and facet capsules tend to fail, with subsequent disruption of both the anterior and posterior columns. A highly unstable injury pattern frequently develops, with the posterior ligaments and joint capsules ruptured and the anterior disc and vertebral body disrupted obliquely. This mechanism can result in the classic slice fracture originally described by Holdsworth.[133]

In contrast to the cervical spine, pure dislocations are uncommon in the thoracic or lumbar spine[174] because of the size and orientation of the facets, which require

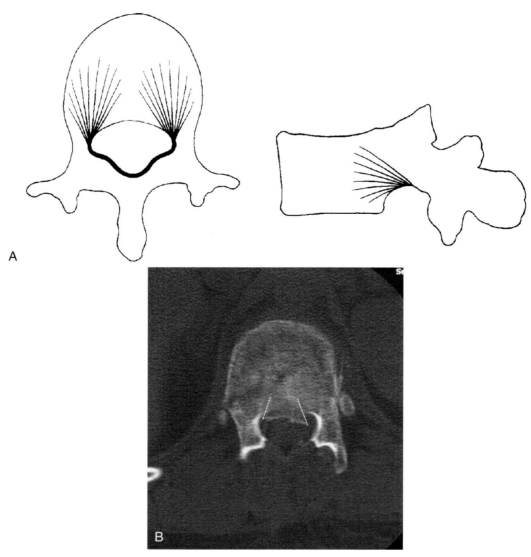

A

B

FIGURE 30–7. *A,* Line drawing of a coronal and sagittal section from a vertebral body illustrating the trabecular array. *B,* Computed tomographic image of a burst injury with a typical trapezoidal-shaped fragment taking origin from the point in the posterior cortex where it thins abruptly. Also note that the trapezoidal shape of the fragment roughly parallels the direction of the trabecular arrays. (Line drawing from Heggeness, M.H.; Doherty, B.J. J Anat 191:309–312, 1997.)

axis of flexion is moved anteriorly (usually toward the anterior abdominal wall), and the entire vertebral column is subjected to large tensile forces. The bony vertebral elements, discs, and ligaments are torn or avulsed, not crushed as typically occurs in most spinal injuries. These forces can produce a pure osseous lesion, a mixed osteoligamentous lesion, or a pure soft tissue (ligamentous or disc) injury.[118] The pure osseous lesion, described by Chance, involves a horizontal fracture beginning in the spinous process, progressing through the lamina, transverse processes, and pedicles, and extending into the vertebral body (Fig. 30–15). This pure osseous lesion usually occurs in the region of L1–L3, and even though it is acutely unstable, it has excellent potential for healing with good long-term stability if alignment can be obtained. Combined osteoligamentous or pure soft tissue injuries most commonly occur from T12 to L2 and should be considered unstable with low spontaneous healing potential (Figs. 30–16 and 30–17).

Flexion-distraction can cause a bilateral facet dislocation in the thoracic or thoracolumbar spine[173] (see Fig. 30–17). The ligaments, capsules, and disc are disrupted, but the anterior longitudinal ligament usually remains intact; however, it is sometimes stripped off the anterior aspect of the caudal vertebra. If the axis of flexion is far enough anterior and the energy is sufficient, rupture of the anterior longitudinal ligament may occur and result in a severely unstable injury.[150, 256] Generally, this injury is a pure distraction rather than a flexion-distraction injury. If the axis of rotation is at the anterior border of the vertebral bodies, compression may occur. The locus of the axis of rotation changes the nature of the injury.

Shear

A pure shear force (Fig. 30–18) was found by Roaf to produce severe ligamentous disruption, similar to the combination of flexion and rotation described previously.[235] This force can result in anterior, posterior, or lateral spondylolisthesis of the superior vertebral segments on those inferior. Traumatic anterior spondylolisthesis is most common and usually results in a complete spinal cord injury. Occasionally, concomitant fractures through the pars interarticularis may occur and result in an autolaminectomy with neural sparing.[128] Shear is frequently combined with other mechanisms to cause complex injuries.

Extension

Extension forces (Fig. 30–19) are created when the head or upper part of the trunk is thrust posteriorly; these forces produce an injury pattern that is the reverse of that seen with pure flexion. Tension is applied anteriorly to the strong anterior longitudinal ligaments and the anterior portion of the anulus fibrosus, whereas compression forces are transmitted to the posterior elements (Fig. 30–20). This mechanism may result in facet, lamina, and spinous process fractures.[96] Avulsion fractures of the anteroinferior portion of the vertebral bodies may occur, but they are not

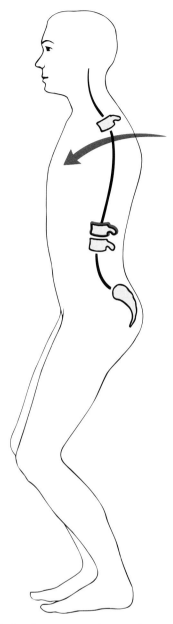

FIGURE 30–8. Flexion forces are causing anterior compression of the vertebral bodies and discs and tension in the posterior elements. This mechanism of injury usually results in a stable compression fracture of the vertebral body anteriorly, but as the force continues, posterior ligamentous disruption may occur.

distraction in addition to flexion and rotation for dislocation to occur. With only a flexion-rotation mechanism of injury, fracture of the facets or other posterior elements will occur more commonly and allow the spine to dislocate[139, 177, 261] (Fig. 30–13).

Flexion-Distraction

Flexion-distraction lesions were first demonstrated radiographically by Chance in 1948,[44] but the mechanism of this so-called seat belt injury was not fully elucidated until later.[136, 150, 229, 239] In this injury pattern (Fig. 30–14), the pathognomonic of extension injuries, as previously thought. Most of these injuries are stable unless significant retrolisthesis of the upper vertebral body on the lower vertebral body has occurred or they are combined with shear forces.[38, 273] Denis and Burkus reported on a hyperextension injury pattern that they termed a *lumber-jack fracture-dislocation.*[60] The mechanism of this injury is a falling mass, often timber, striking the midportion of the patient's back. The injury involves complete disruption of the anterior ligaments and is an extremely unstable injury pattern.

SPINAL STABILITY

The concept of thoracic, thoracolumbar, and lumbar stability after trauma continues to evolve.[161] Work by Nicoll[211] and Holdsworth[133] suggested that the posterior ligamentous complex was the major determinant of spinal stability. They considered fracture-dislocations and severe shear injuries with complete disruption of the posterior ligamentous complex to be highly unstable injuries and most other injuries to be stable. Roaf biomechanically confirmed that gross instability was produced by flexion-rotation forces and shear stress.[235]

Bedbrook disagreed with the importance given to the posterior ligamentous complex and believed that the anterior disc and vertebral body were the prime determinants of stability.[18] He cited the lack of instability after laminectomy as an example of the relative importance of the anterior spinal elements, as opposed to the posterior structures, in providing stability.

These two concepts gradually merged into a two-column concept of spinal stability: an anterior weight-bearing column of vertebral bodies and discs and a posterior column of neural arches and ligaments resisting tension.[153] It was believed that destruction of either of these columns was enough to produce instability. This model helped explain the chronic instability often seen after spinal injuries, especially those that result in a kyphotic deformity. However, it was unable to fully explain all cases of acute instability. Experiments had shown that complete section of the posterior elements alone does not result in acute instability with flexion, extension, rotation, or shear.[216, 225, 230, 236] It was necessary to also section the posterior portion of the anterior column to produce acute instability, at least in flexion.

Further progress was made when Denis proposed his three-column model of the spine (Fig. 30–21) to better reconcile these clinical and biomechanical observations.[58] In his classification system, the posterior column is composed of the posterior bony arch (including the spinous process, the lamina, the facets, and the pedicles) and the interconnecting posterior ligamentous structures (including the supraspinous ligament, interspinous ligament, ligamentum flavum, and facet joint capsules). The middle column is composed of the posterior aspects of the vertebral body, the posterior portion of the anulus fibrosus, and the posterior longitudinal ligament. The anterior column includes the anterior longitudinal ligament, the anterior portion of the anulus fibrosus, and the anterior vertebral body. Though useful in helping define vertebral column instability, this basic anatomic description of the support columns of the spine does not include the spinal cord and spinal nerves. The neural elements, although they do not directly contribute to spinal stability, cannot be forgotten or ignored in stability considerations.[138, 139]

Denis reviewed his fracture classification system and proposed four categories based on the presence and type of instability.[58] These categories were stable injuries, mechanical instability, neurologic instability, and mechanical and neurologic instability.

Stable injuries include minimal and moderate compression fractures with an intact posterior column, which prevents abnormal forward flexion. By definition, the

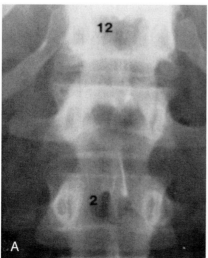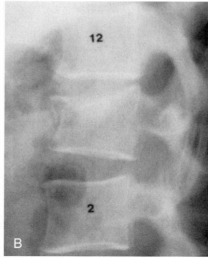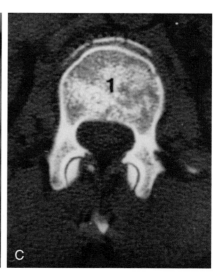

FIGURE 30–9. Radiographs and computed tomographic (CT) scans of a compression fracture in a 48-year-old woman involved in a motor vehicle accident. *A,* An anteroposterior radiograph of the thoracolumbar junction shows a slight irregularity of the superior end-plate of the body of L1 with minimal interspinous widening between T12 and L1. *B,* A lateral radiograph shows loss of height anteriorly and preservation posteriorly at L1. *C,* A CT scan through the body of L1 shows disruption of the cortex anteriorly *(black dots)* with an intact posterior cortex.

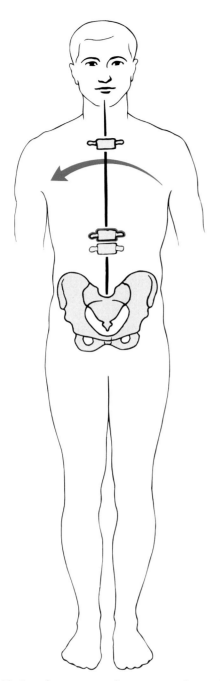

FIGURE **30–10.** Lateral compression forces may produce stable lateral wedge compression injuries. They are most often not associated with posterior ligamentous injury.

middle column is intact; it prevents any extrusion of bone or disc into the spinal canal and protects against significant subluxation. A compression fracture without posterior column involvement is an example of a stable injury.[154]

Mechanical instability includes injuries in which two of the three columns are injured, thereby allowing abnormal motion. An example is a severe compression fracture with disruption of the anterior and posterior columns, which allows abnormal flexion across an intact middle column. This instability is often associated with pain, but not necessarily with a neurologic deficit. It is important to closely evaluate the status of the posterior elements when evaluating this type of injury. The position of these elements in relation to each other in the horizontal and vertical planes can give clues regarding flexion and rotatory deformity and possible instability. A second example is a flexion-distraction injury with disruption of the posterior and middle columns; this mechanism causes abnormal flexion with a fulcrum at the intact anterior column, which functions as a hinge. Chronic instability and pain may result, but again, the injury does not necessarily jeopardize neurologic function. Panjabi and colleagues performed a biomechanical study on a high-speed trauma model and measured multidirectional flexibility. The results of this study supported the three-column theory of Denis and also showed that the middle column appears to be the primary determinant of mechanical stability in the thoracolumbar spine.[217]

Neurologic instability refers specifically to a burst fracture. Denis believed that most of these lesions heal and that they often become mechanically stable. However, he found that a neurologic deficit developed in 20% of his patients with a burst fracture after mobilization as a result of middle column failure and protrusion of bone into the spinal canal. Neurologic compromise is a strong indication for surgical stabilization and decompression. The decompression may be accomplished either directly or indirectly by reduction of deformity and rigid internal immobilization of the segment. It is generally assumed that injuries severe enough to cause neurologic deficits are unstable. One's index of suspicion should remain high when evaluating these patients.

The typical example of *mechanical and neurologic instability* is a fracture-dislocation with disruption of all three columns and either a neurologic deficit or "impending neurologic deterioration" with the neural elements either being compressed or "threatened."[58]

As with the use of any classification system, treatment failure may result from rigid adherence to definitions without individualizing treatment for each patient.[70] To keep the use of these definitions in proper perspective, White and Panjabi defined generic clinical instability as "the loss of the ability of the spine under physiologic conditions to maintain relationships between vertebrae in such a way that there is neither damage nor subsequent irritation to the spinal cord or nerve root and, in addition, there is no development of incapacitating deformity or pain from structural changes."[273]

White and Panjabi[273] defined *physiologic loads* as loads incurred during normal activity, *incapacitating deformity* as gross deformity unacceptable to the patient, and *incapacitating pain* as discomfort uncontrolled by non-narcotic analgesics. This definition addresses both the acute and the late stages of vertebral column trauma. It also draws attention to the neural elements as a major structure of the spinal column and requires the physician to consider these structures, in addition to bones, ligaments, discs, and other soft tissues, as determinants of stability.[232] Though less specific than Denis' classification, it requires a basic understanding of spinal anatomy, the mechanism of injury, and modes of failure when undertaking treatment.

The preceding discussion should be supplemented with a reminder that instability does not always require surgical treatment. In some cases, prolonged bedrest may be able to achieve the same long-term degree of spinal stability as surgery, and it may be appropriate for the particular circumstances of an individual patient.

Denis' Classification of Spinal Injuries

Many classification systems have been designed to describe thoracic and thoracolumbar injuries. They may be based on the mechanism of injury, radiologic/descriptive characteristics, or stability. Denis' three-column concept is frequently used because it includes each of the injury patterns most commonly seen and relates them to a specific mechanism of injury.[58]

Denis developed his classification system after a review of 412 patients with thoracic and lumbar spinal injuries. He divided them into minor and major injuries. Minor injuries included isolated articular process fractures (0.7%), transverse process fractures (13.6%), spinous process fractures (1.7%), and pars interarticularis fractures (1.0%). The four major injury types were compression fractures (47.8%), burst fractures (14.3%), flexion-distraction (seat belt) injuries (4.6%), and fracture-dislocations (16.3%). Each of these major injuries was further subdivided, depending on the specific radiographic findings.

COMPRESSION FRACTURES

By definition, compression fracture injuries are associated with fracture of the anterior portion of the vertebral body, but the middle column of the spine is intact (Fig. 30–22). In some cases, the posterior column may be disrupted in tension as the upper segments hinge forward on the intact middle column. The mechanism of the injury is either anterior or lateral flexion.

Compression fractures may be anterior or lateral, with the former accounting for 89% of this group (see Figs. 30–9 and 30–11). Fractures may involve both end-plates (type A, 16%), the superior end-plate only (type B, 63%), the inferior end-plate only (type C, 6%), or a buckling of the anterior cortex but with both end-plates intact (type D, 15%).

None of the 197 patients with compression fractures reported by Denis had a neurologic deficit related to the spinal fracture. Compression fractures with less than 40% to 50% compression and without posterior ligamentous disruption tend to be stable, low-energy injuries. However, it is still important to assess the patient for noncontiguous spinal fractures.[7] A 40% to 50% anterior body compression fracture with the posterior body intact in a physiologically young individual (with no osteoporosis) strongly suggests that the posterior ligaments were disrupted.

BURST FRACTURES

Burst fractures are characterized by disruption of the posterior wall of the vertebral body (middle column of the spine), which differentiates them from compression fractures (Figs. 30–23 through 30–28). Spreading of the posterior elements may occur and can be seen as a widening of the interpedicular distance on a plain anteroposterior (AP) radiograph of the spine.[12]

Lamina fractures may also occur (see Fig. 30–6). Cammisa and associates[40] found that lamina fractures were present on computed tomographic (CT) scans in 50% of patients with severe burst fractures, especially in the lower lumbar spine. In this surgical series, 11 of 30 patients with burst fractures and lamina fractures also had posterior dural tears located at the site of the posterior lamina fracture (Fig. 30–29). The incidence was almost 70% in those with burst fractures, retropulsed bone in the canal, and neurologic injury. The possibility of a dural tear

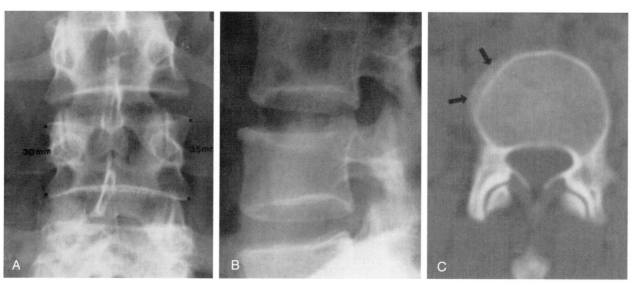

FIGURE 30–11. Example of a lateral compression fracture. *A,* An anteroposterior radiograph demonstrates lateral compression with asymmetric loss of height. No interspinous process widening is present. *B,* A lateral radiograph confirms a wedge compression injury with maintenance of height of the posterior portion of the vertebral body. *C,* A computed tomographic scan through the injured vertebra shows that the injury is limited to the right anterolateral aspect *(arrows),* with the remaining cortex intact.

with a burst fracture, which are accompanied by horizontal fractures not only in the posterior but also in the middle column. This fracture pattern seems to be more unstable than burst fractures with no horizontal splitting and may require surgical stabilization to prevent progression of kyphosis.[2]

The mechanism of injury for burst fractures is primarily axial loading. Axial loading is combined with other forces such as flexion (either anterior or lateral) or rotation to account for the different fracture patterns seen.

Denis noted that burst injuries can be divided into five frequently observed subgroups (Fig. 30–30). One involves fractures of both end-plates (type A, 24%) and is usually seen in the lower lumbar spine. Another involves fracture of only the superior end-plate (type B, 49%) and usually occurs at the thoracolumbar junction. Fracture of only the inferior end-plate is much less common (type C, 7%). A fourth pattern is diagnosed by the presence of a burst fracture of the middle column in combination with a rotational injury leading to some degree of lateral subluxation or tilt (type D, 15%); this pattern is best seen on a plain AP radiograph. The final subgroup is a burst fracture of the middle column associated with asymmetric compression of the anterior column, as seen in a lateral compression fracture (type E, 5%).

Willen and co-workers verified these injury types anatomically in autopsy specimens.[278] Neurologic deficits were seen in 47% of the 59 patients studied with burst fractures. There did not appear to be a simple, direct relationship between the extent of spinal canal compromise and the severity of neurologic deficit. Willen and colleagues found increased neurologic damage with type D fractures, whereas Gertzbein[111] found only a weak correlation between canal compromise and neurologic deficit in a study of more than 1000 patients with thoracolumbar spine injuries. Gertzbein thought that most trauma to the neural elements probably occurred at the instant of injury. A relationship was, however, found between the location of injury and subsequent neurologic deficit, with the incidence of complete neurologic injury being significantly lower below the thoracolumbar junction (T12–L1).

Burst fractures may be unstable because they represent at least a minimum of a two-column injury,[154] but additionally, they may also be accompanied by extensive disc injury at the levels directly adjacent to the fracture. This possibility has to be considered when deciding on treatment options.[99, 278]

FLEXION-DISTRACTION INJURIES

The flexion and distraction mechanism of injury, which most commonly occurs in a motor vehicle accident when the passenger is using a lap seat belt with no shoulder harness, results in failure of the posterior and middle columns in tension with the anterior column serving as the fulcrum (see Figs. 30–15 to 30–17).

Denis divided these injuries into one-level and two-level lesions (Fig. 30–31). A one-level lesion can occur through bone, as described by Chance (type A, 47%), or it may be primarily ligamentous (type B, 11%). Two-level injuries involve the middle column by disruption through

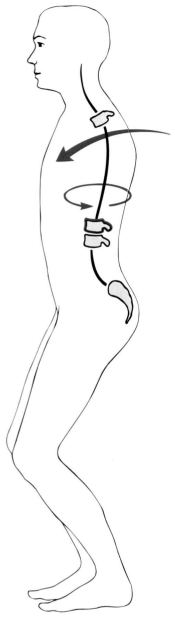

FIGURE 30–12. Flexion-rotation forces are much more likely to produce serious spinal injuries than is flexion alone. The combination frequently disrupts the posterior ligaments and joint capsules and obliquely disrupts the anterior disc and vertebral body.

should be taken into consideration if posterior decompression and stabilization procedures are planned. It should not, however, mandate treatment to routinely repair the dural laceration. Some burst fractures are accompanied by horizontal fractures of the posterior column. In a retrospective study by Abe and colleagues, nine patients with a thoracolumbar burst fracture and an associated horizontal fracture of the posterior column were studied. They found that this type of fracture pattern is not rare; it represented 21% of the burst fractures treated by them over an 8-year period. It is best visualized on plain radiographs because it is not easily seen on CT axial cuts. This type of burst fracture differs from flexion-distraction injuries combined bone (type C, 26%) or through the ligaments and disc with no middle column fractures (type D, 16%).

One weakness of this classification system is that it does not include a category for patients who have distraction failure of the posterior column with axial load failure of the middle and anterior columns resulting in a compression or burst fracture. This shortcoming has been noted by several authors, who have added additional categories for seat belt injury.[112, 120]

In none of the 19 patients with a seat belt injury in Denis' series did a neurologic deficit related to the spinal fracture develop. In other series, the incidence is also low, usually less than 10%.[111] Injuries with ligamentous involvement should be considered acutely and chronically unstable, whereas those with significant bone involvement are acutely unstable but may heal well.

FRACTURE-DISLOCATIONS (SHEAR)

Fracture-dislocations are caused by failure of all three columns of the spine as a result of compression, tension, rotation, or shear forces (Figs. 30–32 through 30–34).

Three different mechanisms (i.e., three types of fracture-dislocation) can occur (see Fig. 30–34). One pattern (type A) is a flexion-rotation injury, which was originally described by Holdsworth in victims of mining

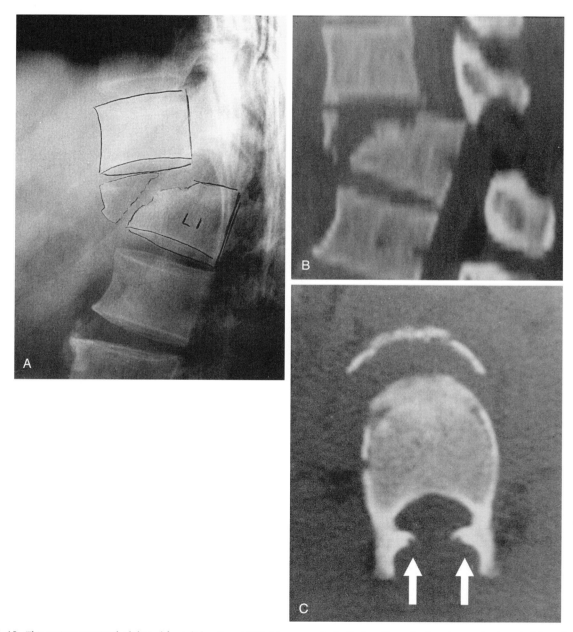

FIGURE 30–13. This patient sustained a bilateral facet dislocation at T12–L1 as a result of a flexion-distraction/rotation mechanism. A, A lateral radiograph shows significant translation of T12 over L1 with maintenance of the integrity (height) of the posterior wall of L1 but some slight comminution of the anterosuperior portion of the body. B, This relationship is well demonstrated on a midsagittal reconstruction of the computed tomographic (CT) scan. C, The characteristic findings on axial images of the CT scan are the double-body image and the empty facet sign (arrows).

failure of either the anterior intervertebral disc or the anterior vertebral body. The anterior longitudinal ligament is usually stripped off the inferior vertebral body, thereby allowing significant subluxation to occur.

Denis described 67 patients with fracture-dislocations. Of these patients, 56 had flexion-rotation injuries, 7 had shear injuries, and 4 had bilateral facet dislocations resulting from flexion-distraction injuries. All these injuries involve significant destruction of each of the three columns. This group of injuries was associated with the highest incidence of neurologic deficit. Of the patients with flexion-rotation injuries, only 25% were neurologically normal, and 39% had complete spinal cord injuries. All seven patients with shear injuries had complete neurologic deficits. Of the four patients with flexion-distraction injuries, three had incomplete neurologic deficits, and one was neurologically normal. Other investigators have also reported a significantly higher incidence of neurologic deficit in patients with fracture-dislocations than in those with other injury patterns.[111] These injuries are acutely highly unstable.

"Comprehensive" Classification

Various attempts have been made to develop a universal classification of spinal injuries. In reality, to be effective, such a classification must include structural injury to both bone and soft tissue, as well as consideration of the patient's neurologic status. Gertzbein and colleagues[103, 110] formulated a classification system dealing with the structural components of spinal injury, similar to the AO fracture classification used for the extremities. The lesions are differentiated on the basis of not only the mechanism and radiographic appearance of the injury but also the associated soft tissue disruption. The classification consists of well-defined categories based on common morphologic characteristics, as well as common primary forces producing the particular injury pattern (Fig. 30–36).

Three main injury types are recognized. Type A injuries are vertebral body compression fractures (Fig. 30–37). They are caused by axial loading with or without additional flexion forces and are associated with loss of vertebral height. Type B injuries involve both the anterior and the posterior elements and are caused by distractive forces (Fig. 30–38). The hallmark of these injuries is elongation of the distance between portions of the adjacent vertebrae. In type C injuries, anterior and posterior disruption is present along with associated evidence of rotational instability, such as offset vertebral bodies, unilateral facet fracture-dislocations, or fractured transverse processes (Fig. 30–39).

The three major patterns and their associated subtypes represent a continuum of injury severity, from type A lesions, which are axially unstable, to type B lesions, which have additional sagittal-plane instability, to type C, with instability in all three planes. Because the classification progresses according to the severity of bony and soft tissue disruption, as well as stability, it may be used as a guide for treatment, with injuries more advanced on the classification being more likely to benefit from surgical treatment. However, it has not been validated as a reproducible

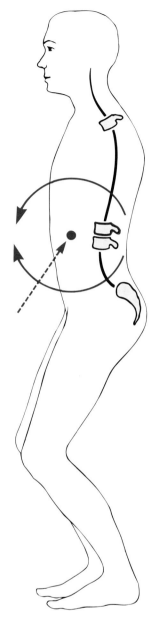

FIGURE 30–14. Flexion-distraction forces across the thoracolumbar spine frequently produce the typical seat belt injury. The axis of rotation is anterior to the spine, with all the elements of the spine in tension. If this axis of rotation is moved posteriorly into the vertebral body, it is possible to have compressive forces across the anterior vertebral body and distraction forces across the posterior elements and middle column of the spine.

accidents.[133] This type may also occur after ejection from a motor vehicle or a fall from a height (Fig. 30–35A). A shear fracture-dislocation (type B) can be caused by a violent force directed across the long axis of the trunk. One such example, as described by Denis and Burkus, occurs when a lumberjack is struck across the midportion of his back by a falling tree (see Fig. 30–35B).[60] Denis' third type (type C) is a bilateral facet dislocation (see Fig. 30–35C) caused by a flexion-distraction injury. It resembles the seat belt injury previously described, but with failure of the anterior column. This injury most commonly occurs with

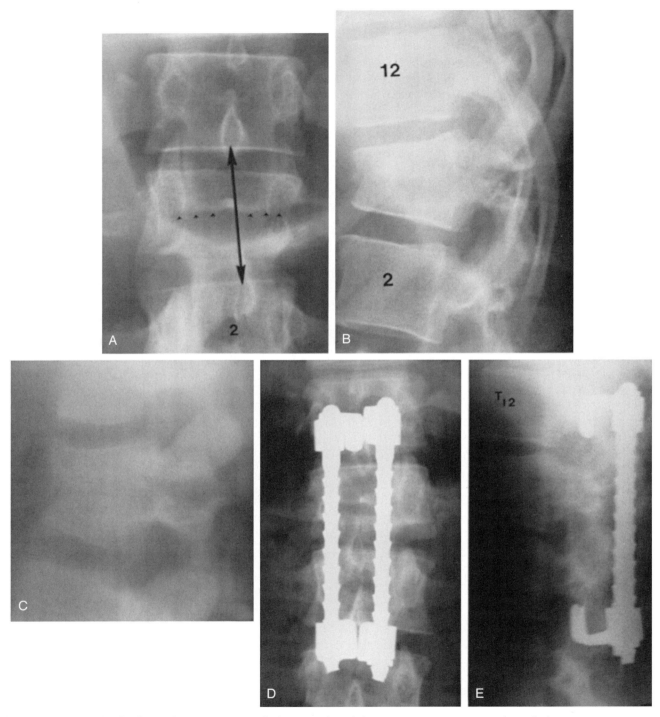

FIGURE 30–15. Example of a flexion-distraction injury with disruption through bone. *A,* An anteroposterior radiograph demonstrates interspinous widening *(arrow)* with a fracture line through the lamina of L1 *(arrowheads). B,* A lateral radiograph confirms the pure osseous lesion, with the fracture line coursing posteriorly through the upper portion of the lamina anteriorly into the vertebral body. *C,* The injury is better seen on this lateral tomogram, with the fracture line extending through the pedicle. *D,* The patient was treated operatively with Edwards compression rods from T12 to L2. In this instance, the L1 lamina could not be used for anchoring hooks because of the injury to the lamina at this level. *E,* A lateral radiograph shows reduction of the fracture and restoration of anterior height.

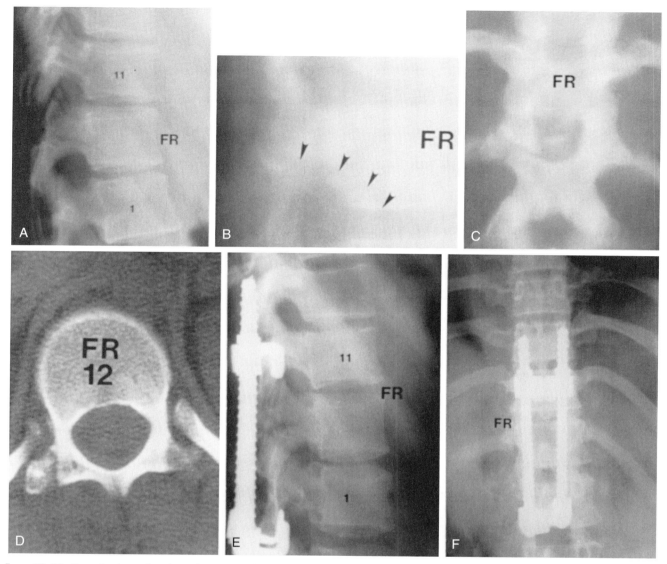

FIGURE 30–16. Example of a combined osseoligamentous flexion-distraction injury at T12. *A,* A lateral radiograph demonstrates the fracture line coursing through the pedicle and traversing the posteroinferior aspect of the body to the T12–L1 disc space. *B,* A lateral tomogram highlights the path of the fracture *(arrowheads). C,* An anteroposterior (AP) tomogram clearly demonstrates the fracture through the pars interarticularis. Note the distinctive interspinous widening with this injury. *D,* A computed tomographic scan through the upper portion of T12 demonstrates absent inferior T11 facets as a result of the distraction component. *E,* This injury was corrected with Edwards compression rodding from T11 to L1, with reduction of the fracture and realignment of the spine. *F,* A postoperative AP radiograph confirms reduction of the interspinous widening.

classification and is unlikely to be validated because of its extreme complexity.

Other useful classification systems are those described by Ferguson and Allen[92] and by McAfee and co-workers.[191, 195, 196] These classification systems focus primarily on the mechanical forces involved and describe the type of bone or ligamentous injuries associated with these forces. The American Spinal Injury Association (ASIA) classification system for neurologic injury is the most commonly used objective system currently available.

Because the primary goal of this chapter is to provide clinical guidelines for diagnosing and treating specific injuries, the more pragmatic classification system of Denis is preferred. For purposes of consistency in this book, a nomenclature and classification system consisting of a

combination of mechanistic and descriptive features is used; it is the same for thoracic, thoracolumbar, and lumbar injuries. The first group of injuries consists of minor injuries, such as avulsion and minor fractures. The second group includes compression fractures, or injuries generated by a combination of flexion and bending that can be either stable or unstable, depending on the degree of anterior compression and ligamentous disruption. The third major group represents burst fractures caused by a combination of flexion and axial loading in varying proportion, and they are easily subdivided by Denis' classification. The fourth group is flexion-distraction injuries, which are subdivided according to the injured tissues: the pure bony form is a Chance fracture, the purely ligamentous form is a bilateral facet dislocation, and the combination form is either an anterior bony injury with posterior ligamentous disruption or a posterior bony injury with anterior discal disruption. The fifth group of injuries results from an extension force. The final type is caused by shear. Clearly, no comprehensive or truly universal system exists because the optimal classification system would have to combine the fracture pattern with instability and neural status.

OPERATIVE VERSUS NONOPERATIVE TREATMENT

Nonoperative treatment of thoracic and thoracolumbar spine injuries can be extremely effective. The data presented by Frankel and associates in 1969 remain the standard against which most treatments and final outcomes are measured.[98] Similar excellent results were published by Davies and colleagues.[56, 139] Postural reduction, as described by Frankel, is still used in some European centers, reportedly with good results.[34, 268]

A comparison of the results of surgical and nonsurgical treatment in the literature is difficult because of the variations in injury type and differences in severity in the two groups, with the surgically treated groups often containing patients with more severe injuries.[111] Some series show a slight trend toward better neurologic improvement with surgical treatment, but the statistical significance is not high.[159] Most investigators describing better neurologic improvement with surgery have directed their attention at neural decompression through either an anterior or a posterior approach.[3, 4, 73, 111, 113, 135, 160, 233, 284] Edwards and Levine described better neurologic recovery than would be expected with nonoperative treatment by using the Edwards instrumentation system posteriorly while depending on indirect decompression based on improved fracture reduction.[80, 81] Gertzbein, in a study of 1019 spine fractures, found no significant improvement in neurologic function with operative treatment.[111] In addition, Bravo and co-workers did not find a significant difference in neurologic improvement in patients treated with surgery versus those treated by postural reduction and immobilization.[34]

Neurologic deterioration can occur during nonoperative treatment and was documented in 6 of 33 patients with burst fractures of the thoracic or thoracolumbar spine.[59] Denis and co-workers concluded that surgical treatment was a safer treatment option for this specific injury.[59] However, Frankel and associates,[98] in their review of 371 patients with thoracic or thoracolumbar fractures, found that only 0.5% had neurologic deterioration when treated by postural reduction and recumbency. Mumford and co-workers reported a 2.4% incidence of neurologic deterioration in patients with burst fractures treated nonoperatively.[206] If patients do experience neurologic deterioration during nonoperative treatment, surgical treatment, including decompression by an anterior ap-

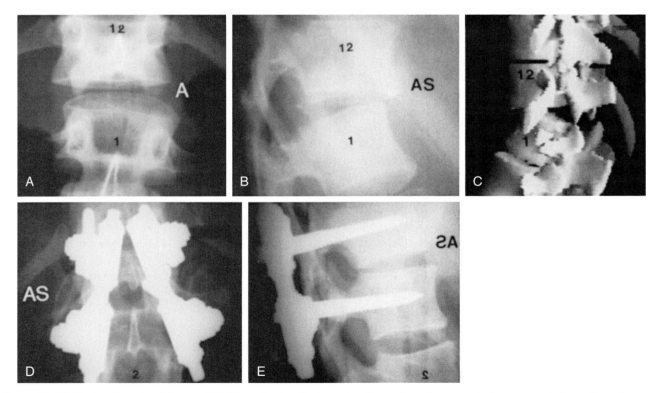

FIGURE 30–17. Flexion-distraction injury at T12–L1 predominantly disrupting ligamentous structures. *A,* An anteroposterior radiograph shows interspinous widening between T12 and L1. *B,* A lateral radiograph demonstrates the predominantly ligamentous involvement, with the anterior bodies remaining intact. Note the subluxation of T12 on L1 as a result of the dislocated facets. *C,* A three-dimensional computed tomographic reconstruction of the injured level shows the dislocated, locked facets. Note the fractured transverse process at L1. *D,* This patient was operatively managed with an AO internal fixator from T12 to L1. *E,* A postoperative lateral radiograph demonstrates reduction and realignment of the injured level.

that kyphosis of more than 30° was associated with a significantly increased amount of back pain at 2-year follow-up.[111] Edwards and Levine's data also suggest that anatomic restoration is important in obtaining good long-term results.[79–81, 83]

Some authors believe that chronic back pain is diminished in operatively treated patients when compared with those treated nonoperatively.[111] This improvement in relief of pain may be a result of better correction and maintenance of alignment with operative treatment. In addition, operative treatment includes fusion of motion segments with significantly damaged soft tissue elements. These injured tissues often have poor healing potential,

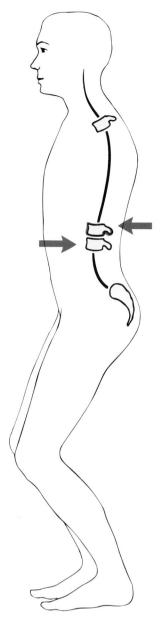

FIGURE 30–18. Shearing requires forces from opposing directions to pass through the spine at slightly different levels. This mechanism tends to produce extremely unstable injuries with disruption of all columns of the spine and may produce severe spondylolisthesis with the cephalic spine positioned anteriorly, posteriorly, or laterally in relation to the caudal portion of the spine.

proach, is recommended.[111] Finally, whether surgical treatment or nonoperative treatment is safer depends to some degree on the experience and preference of the treating physician and the medical team.

Deformity can be corrected with surgery, but it is unclear whether it is clinically relevant.[34, 56, 215] Nicoll[211] noted no correlation between deformity and symptoms, whereas Soreff and colleagues[258] found a significant correlation. McAfee and associates,[193] in their review of late anterior decompression and fusion for thoracolumbar and lumbar injuries, found that residual kyphosis did not inhibit neural improvement. Gertzbein, however, reported

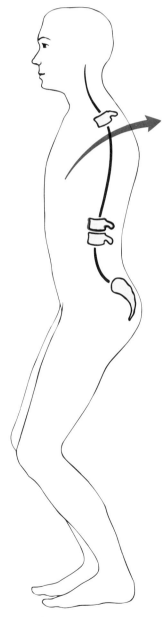

FIGURE 30–19. Extension forces occur when the upper part of the trunk is thrust posteriorly, with the application of anterior tension and posterior compression. Most of these injuries are stable unless retrolisthesis of the upper on the lower vertebral body has occurred.

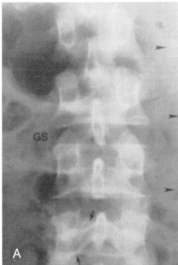

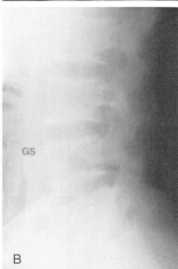

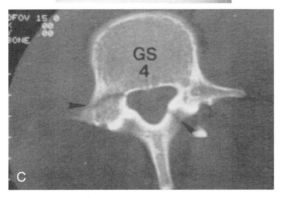

FIGURE 30–20. This 26-year-old man was involved in a motor vehicle accident and sustained an extension injury to the lower part of the spine. *A,* An anteroposterior radiograph shows a fracture line coursing through the lamina of L4 (*arrows*). *Arrowheads* point to transverse process fractures. *B,* A lateral radiograph was unremarkable. *C,* Computed tomographic scan through the injured body of L4 with multiple fracture lines noted in the posterior column (*arrowheads*).

ysis.[49, 66, 95, 139, 233] Mobilization and rehabilitation can be facilitated by rigid surgical stabilization, which decreases the associated morbidity of prolonged immobilization. However, Gertzbein, in a multicenter spinal fracture study, found the complication rate in surgical patients to be more than 25%, whereas patients treated nonoperatively had a complication rate of only 1%.[111] The patients treated surgically tended to have more severe injuries and a higher incidence of neurologic deficit, both of which increase the likelihood of complications regardless of treatment type. Place and colleagues compared operative and nonoperative treatment of patients who sustained spinal fractures with resultant complete spinal cord injuries. The length of inpatient hospital and rehabilitation stay was 19% less for the surgically treated group, even though their rate of complications was almost twice as high as that in the nonoperative group.[223] At this time, early mobilization remains the primary predictable advantage of instrumentation.

TREATMENT OF SPECIFIC INJURIES

Minor Fractures

Fractures of the transverse processes usually occur either from direct trauma or as a result of violent muscular contraction (avulsion injuries) in response to injury. Isolated fractures of the spinous processes may result from a direct blow over the posterior aspect of the spine. Similarly, fracture of the articular process may occur as a result of direct trauma. In each of these cases, even though the injury may appear benign, further evaluation is necessary to be certain that no other associated spinal injuries are present. Such evaluation is most easily accomplished by obtaining a CT scan through the vertebra in question and the adjacent vertebrae. If the CT scan is negative (no other injuries detected), lateral flexion and extension radiographs should be considered if dynamic instability is a concern. Once other major injuries to the spine have been excluded, these patients can be mobilized with no special brace or activity restrictions, except as needed for painful symptoms. Transverse process fractures are painful, and orthotics may be helpful.

Another minor injury is an isolated fracture of the pars interarticularis at one level, either unilaterally or bilaterally. In Denis' series, four individuals had this type of fracture,[58] with all four being the result of a sports injury. If the patient has this injury along with a negative previous history of local spine pain (particularly in a young adult or teenager), it can be assumed that this fracture is an acute injury that is best treated with immobilization. In the thoracolumbar and upper lumbar regions of the spine, a total-contact thoracolumbosacral orthosis (TLSO) is appropriate. At the L5 level of the spine, it may be necessary to include one thigh to provide adequate immobilization.

Fractures of the pars interarticularis in the thoracolumbar or upper lumbar spine in combination with a history of more severe trauma suggest a major spine injury (e.g., seat belt injury). This injury can be discerned on thin-cut CT scans with reconstructions of the spine and may also be well visualized on flexion-extension radiographs if the

and the patient is left with an abnormal motion segment even after adequate healing of bone.

Most authors agree that hospitalization time can be shortened by surgical stabilization in patients with paral-

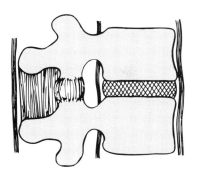

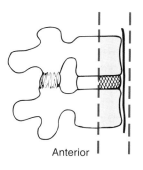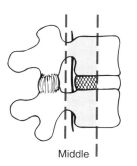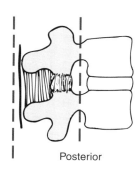

Anterior | Middle | Posterior

Figure 30–21. Denis' three-column model of the spine. The middle column is made up of the posterior longitudinal ligament, the posterior portion of the anulus fibrosus, and the posterior aspect of the vertebral body and disc.

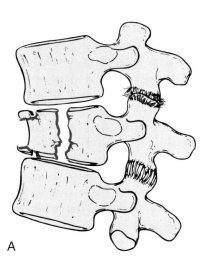

A

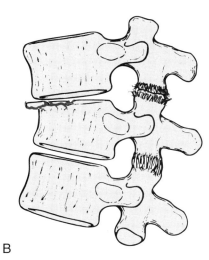

B

Figure 30–22. Denis' classification of compression fractures. These fractures may involve both end-plates (*A*, type A), the superior end-plate only (*B*, type B), the inferior end-plate only (*C*, type C), or a buckling of the anterior cortex with both end-plates intact (*D*, type D).

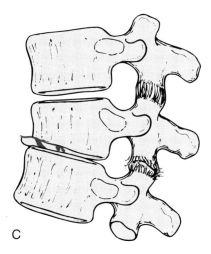

C

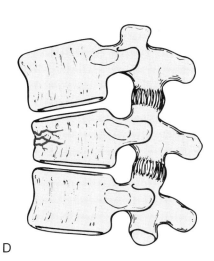

D

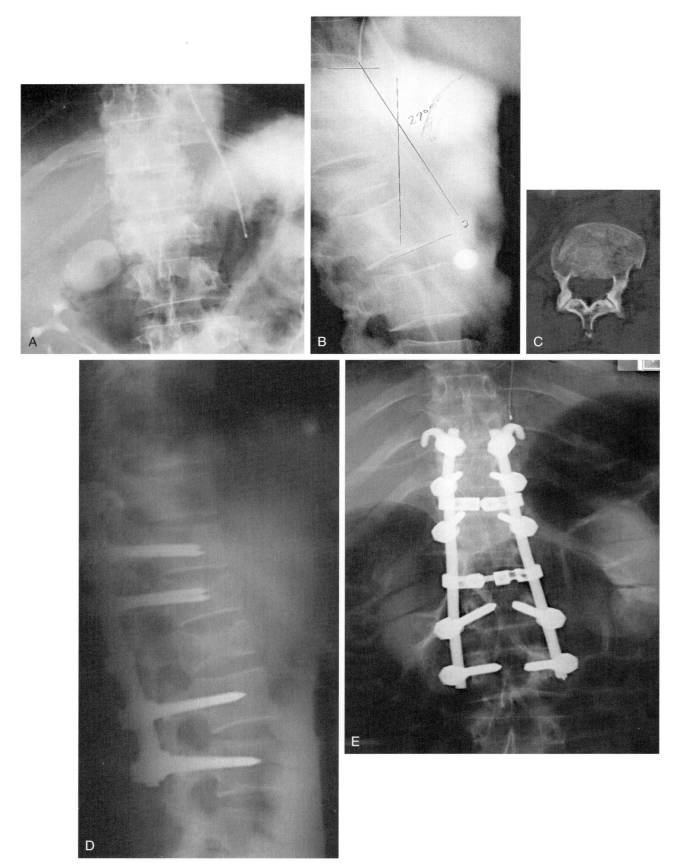

FIGURE 30–23. A 43-year-old man sustained a T12 and L1 burst fracture when a mobile home roof fell on him during a storm. The patient was neurologically intact. *A,* A preoperative anteroposterior (AP) radiograph shows approximately 50% loss of height at T12 and L1. *B,* A preoperative lateral view shows local kyphosis measuring 27°. *C,* An axial computed tomographic scan shows a minimal burst component at L1. *D,* This injury was stabilized with Synthes USS instrumentation. A pedicle screw was placed in the burst-fractured vertebra of T12 (the pedicles were intact) to act as a fulcrum in the reduction of his 27° of kyphosis. *E,* Postoperative AP radiograph showing two cross-connectors used for additional stability.

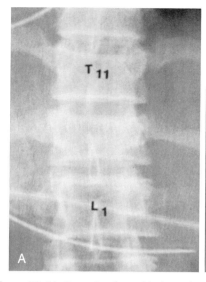
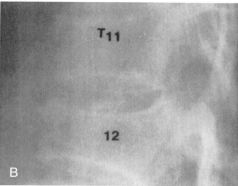
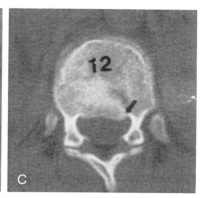

FIGURE 30–24. Example of a stable burst fracture (Denis type B) in a 52-year-old man who was neurologically intact. The fracture was treated nonoperatively. *A,* An anteroposterior radiograph demonstrates loss of height of the body of T12, with minimal interpedicular widening and no interspinous separation noted. *B,* A lateral radiograph confirms involvement of the anterior and middle columns with loss of height at both sites. *C,* A computed tomographic scan through T12 demonstrates disruption of the posterior vertebral cortex *(arrow)* but only minimal displacement of the fragment. The posterior ring remains intact.

patient can tolerate the motion. A CT scan, unless the cuts are fine, may not be helpful in determining whether the pars fracture is isolated or a component of a seat belt injury because the fracture lines often lie in the transverse plane of the spine and are difficult to visualize with standard CT scanning.[33]

Compression Fractures

By definition, compression fractures include disruption of the anterior column with an intact middle column. Differentiation between a compression fracture and a minimally displaced burst fracture with associated middle column involvement may be subtle. McGrory and colleagues[200] described the use of the posterior vertebral body angle (PVBA) measured on a lateral plain radiograph. The PVBA is the angle formed by either the superior or the inferior end-plate and the posterior vertebral body wall. An angle greater than 100° for either the superior or the inferior PVBA is considered diagnostic of a burst fracture. A slight decrease in height of the posterior wall in comparison to the vertebra above and below and loss of the biconcave contour may also suggest the presence of a burst rather than a compression fracture. Even with careful scrutiny, 20% or more of subtle burst fractures can be misdiagnosed on plain radiographs. Therefore, the routine use of CT scanning for patients with probable compression fractures is a better method to evaluate the middle column.[17] Treatment of these injuries depends on the status of the posterior elements, which may or may not be disrupted. If the anterior column is compressed 40% or more or if the kyphosis exceeds 25° to 30°, it can be inferred that the ligaments of the posterior column have been attenuated to the point that they can no longer function normally. Magnetic resonance imaging (MRI) has been shown to be a useful adjunct for identifying the

presence of posterior ligament injury.[155] In addition, MRI may be useful in helping differentiate benign from pathologic compression fractures.[9]

Nonoperative treatment is adequate in most compression fractures with less than 40% anterior compression and less than 25° to 30° kyphosis. These patients can usually be managed in a restrictive orthosis, such as a total-contact TLSO or, occasionally, a Jewett brace. They can be allowed to participate in most of their normal activities while wearing the brace (see Fig. 30–9). These patients should be encouraged to lie in the prone position, which tends to minimize the deformity. They should be discouraged from lying supine on a soft mattress with multiple pillows because this position can accentuate the deformity. Hazel and associates reviewed the long-term outcome of neurologically intact patients with compression fractures treated nonoperatively. Of the 25 patients monitored, 8 had no symptoms, 11 had occasional back pain, 5 needed treatment or modification of activity because of frequent pain, and only 1 patient had chronic disabling back pain.[129]

The brace should be worn for 3 months or longer. Standing lateral flexion and extension radiographs out of the brace should then be obtained. If no abnormal motion is seen through the fractured vertebra or the disc above and if significant progression of the deformity has not occurred, use of the orthosis can be discontinued. Muscle weakness may be significant, and gradual cessation of bracing over a few weeks may be beneficial, along with a muscle-strengthening program to help support the spine. In those with abnormal motion at the level of injury, continued pain, or progression of deformity to a degree unacceptable to the patient, surgery may be indicated. Some authors believe that stable fractures in the upper and middle thoracic spine do not require brace treatment at all because of the inherent stability of the rib cage. Most authors tend to be more cautious and usually recommend external immobilization at the thoracolumbar junction or in the lumbar spine. Schlickewei and associates[249] compared a group of patients with stable thoracolumbar injuries treated by early mobilization with or without a brace. After an average of 2.5-years' follow-up, they found good or excellent results in both groups, without clinically significant differences in progression of deformity between groups.

Initial surgical treatment should be recommended if the anterior column is compressed more than 40% or if the kyphosis exceeds 25° to 30°. For those with borderline indications, surgery could be considered as an option in a young patient with a high-energy injury, but it would

probably not be recommended in an elderly patient with marked osteoporosis and low-energy trauma. In the former case, the posterior ligaments are much more likely to be disrupted than in the latter.

Because the posterior elements are disrupted, a posterior surgical approach is indicated, and any dual-rod technique would be adequate. A distraction system can be used with three-point fixation (e.g., hook-rod system or segmental fixation systems). If the middle column is definitely intact, a compression system can be used (e.g., a segmental fixation system with hooks or screws). The surgeon should be aware that a compression system may cause posterior protrusion of an already disrupted disc at

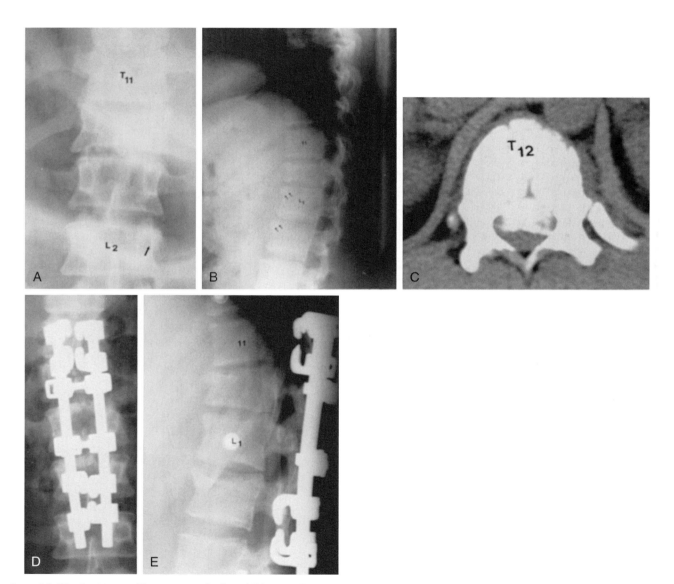

Figure 30–25. This 19-year-old man was involved in a fall from an all-terrain vehicle and sustained a burst injury at T12 that resulted in a complete spinal cord injury. *A,* An anteroposterior (AP) radiograph demonstrates significant loss of height at T12 with interpedicular widening, classically seen with burst fractures. A compression fracture of the superior corner of L2 is also noted (*arrow*). *B,* A lateral radiograph shows significant loss of height of both the anterior and middle columns of T12. Small compression injuries at L1 and L2 (*arrows*) are also seen. *C,* A computed tomographic scan through T12 confirms the presence of a burst fracture with a large retropulsed fragment compromising 80% of the canal and resulting in injury to the conus. *D,* A postoperative AP radiograph shows placement of Cotrel-Dubousset instrumentation. A laminar claw configuration was used above and below T12. Two Texas Scottish Rite Hospital cross-links were used to reinforce the construction. The patient was postoperatively mobilized without a brace. *E,* Lateral postoperative radiograph. It would have been better had the upper claw been placed around the T10 lamina to increase the superior lever arm and minimize "metal stenosis" at the site of the retropulsed bone fragment.

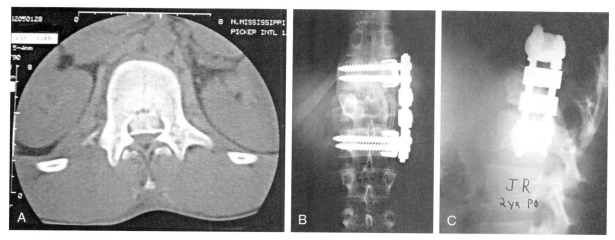

FIGURE 30–26. This 30-year-old man was an unrestrained passenger involved in a motor vehicle accident and was ejected from his car. He sustained an L1 burst fracture with an incomplete spinal cord injury. *A,* An axial computed tomographic scan through the body of L1 shows a large retropulsed fragment occupying most of the spinal canal. *B,* The patient was treated by anterior corpectomy and decompression at L1. Stability was achieved with the Kaneda system. *C,* A 2-year postoperative lateral view shows continued restoration of height and reestablishment of sagittal alignment.

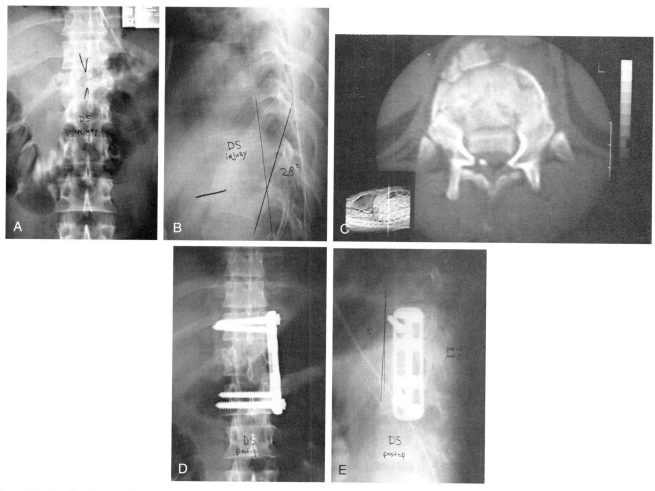

FIGURE 30–27. This 38-year-old man was involved in a motor vehicle accident and sustained a burst fracture of T12. The patient had decreased motor function in both lower extremities as well as bladder dysfunction. *A,* An anteroposterior (AP) radiograph shows collapse of the body and interpedicular widening. *B,* A lateral radiograph shows loss of height and segmental kyphosis measuring 28°. *C,* An axial-cut computed tomographic scan through T12 shows a large retropulsed fragment compromising most of the canal. *D,* A postoperative AP radiograph shows stabilization after corpectomy with a tibia allograft strut and instrumentation consisting of the University Plate (Acromed). *E,* A lateral postoperative radiograph shows restoration of height and sagittal alignment with 3° of kyphosis.

the level of injury and that this protrusion may be large enough to cause neurologic deterioration. If a compression construct is being considered, the use of intraoperative evoked potentials is important because it may provide early documentation of protrusion and allow the surgeon to change the technique or perform a posterolateral decompression to remove the disc fragment.

The use of anterior surgery is not required for neural decompression with these fractures because the middle column remains intact. However, supplemental anterior surgery may occasionally be necessary for patients with marked anterior destruction to restore bone stock. This situation is usually seen in patients with severe osteopenia who are involved in high-energy injuries. These same patients may also undergo late collapse with progressive kyphosis and subsequent neurologic deficit. They are best treated by an anterior approach, although the use of vertebroplasty has obviated this approach in most cases.[146]

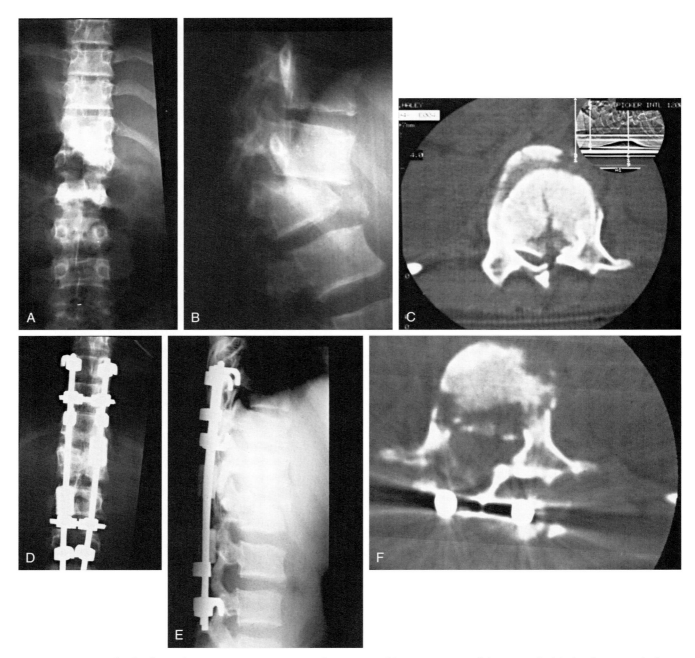

FIGURE 30–28. Example of a flexion-distraction injury at T12–L1 with an associated burst component of the L1 vertebral body. This patient had an incomplete cord injury. *A,* Anteroposterior radiograph showing interpedicular widening and increased distance between the posterior spinous processes at T12–L1. *B,* A lateral radiograph shows the local kyphosis and burst injury at L1. *C,* A preoperative computed tomographic (CT) scan shows severe canal encroachment from the burst component. *D,* The patient was treated with ISOLA instrumentation and Edwards sleeves. *E,* A postoperative lateral radiograph shows good sagittal alignment and reduction of the vertebral body height. *F,* A postoperative axial CT scan shows partial restoration of the canal.

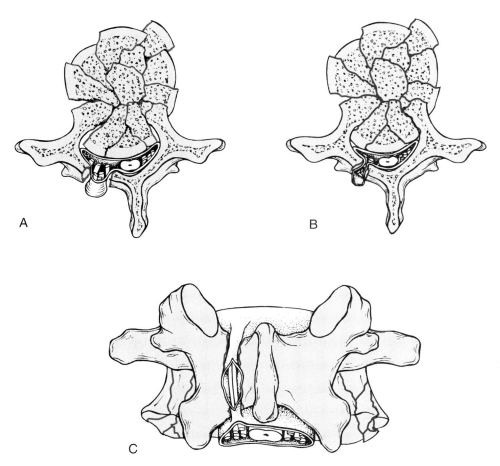

FIGURE 30–29. Illustration of the proposed mechanism of injury in patients with burst fractures along with associated laminar fractures and posterior dural tears. *A,* With axial loading and spreading of the pedicles, a laminar fracture is produced and bone is retropulsed from the vertebral body into the spinal canal. This mechanism of injury may result in protrusion of the dura between the laminar fracture fragments. *B,* As the axial load is dissipated, the laminar fracture fragments recoil and may entrap the dura and nerve rootlets. *C,* If approached posteriorly, the laminar fracture is difficult to visualize, and if not carefully sought, the dura and nerve rootlets may be further injured. (*A–C,* Redrawn from Eismont, F.J.; Green, B.A. J Bone Joint Surg Am 71:1044–1052, 1989.)

Burst Fractures

By definition, every burst fracture includes disruption of the anterior and middle columns, with or without disruption of the posterior column. The type of treatment depends on the severity of the injury.[150] The three most important factors to be considered are the percentage of spinal canal compromise, the degree of angulation present at the site of injury, and the presence or absence of a neurologic deficit.

No strong clinical basis is available to develop a consensus regarding the best treatment of patients with burst fractures. James and co-workers,[141] using a human cadaver L1 burst fracture model, showed that the condition of the posterior column was the most important factor in determining the acute stability of a burst fracture and, therefore, the suitability for nonoperative treatment. They went on to review a series of patients with intact posterior columns, but varying degrees of anterior and middle column disruption, and noted that they healed without deformity. Willen and colleagues[277] reported on 54 patients with thoracolumbar burst fractures treated nonoperatively, including patients with neurologic deficit. Most of the deformity occurred on initial mobilization, with little progression of deformity noted at follow-up. Patients with more than 50% loss of height or more than 50% canal compromise were found to have significantly increased complaints of pain at follow-up. Cantor and

co-workers[41] also recommended operative treatment for patients with evidence of posterior column disruption. Treatment of burst fractures can be logically defined with regard to the goals of surgery. Three parameters determine these goals: neurologic status, instability, and deformity. In patients with neurologic compromise accompanied by instability, cord compression, marked deformity, or any combination of these conditions, surgical intervention is the most appropriate treatment. Nonoperative treatment of a patient with a neural deficit can be considered in the rare instance of a stable burst fracture without deformity or residual cord compression. If the patient is neurologically intact and has less than 50% canal compromise and less than 30° kyphosis (see Fig. 30–24), nonoperative treatment is indicated. Patients with minimal angulation and a two-column or stable burst pattern should be placed in a total-contact orthosis with early ambulation as tolerated.[41] If the canal compromise is greater than 40% or a three-column injury is present, recumbency for several weeks should be considered if surgery is not performed; ambulation can then begin in a total-contact TLSO. Surgery is the preferred treatment in patients with more than 50% canal compromise or more than 30° kyphosis at the level of injury, even if they do not have any neurologic deficit.

It should be emphasized that a neurologic deficit includes not only lower extremity motor and sensory dysfunction but also perineal sensory loss and bowel or bladder dysfunction. A rectal examination should be performed to determine whether anal tone is normal with voluntary contracture. Postvoid residual urine should also be checked to be certain that the volume of retained urine is less than 50 mL. Any abnormality in bowel or bladder function should be considered a neurologic deficit.

Controversies in the nonoperative treatment of burst fractures include the appropriateness of bedrest and the duration and types of orthosis. However, the duration of using a total-contact orthosis should be at least 3 months. During that time, once ambulation is initiated and no change in alignment is observed on standing lateral radiographs, an increase in activities can be allowed. Some progressive loss of height of the involved disc space is to be expected; however, if posterior spinous process widening is noted or angulation increases to more than 30°, surgical treatment is recommended.[141] Mumford and co-workers[206] studied 41 patients with thoracolumbar fractures and no neurologic deficit who were treated nonoperatively. The average collapse at follow-up was only

8%, with significant resorption of protruding bone and diminution in canal compromise (22%). Almost 90% of patients had satisfactory work status at last follow-up. The authors were unable to correlate residual deformity with symptoms. Cantor and associates[41] reported their results on 18 neurologically intact patients with burst fractures treated nonoperatively. They found no prolonged hospital stay, no significantly increased kyphosis, and little or no restriction of function at follow-up.

If nonoperative treatment is used, prolonged riding in automobiles and participation in impact activities should be discouraged for 3 to 6 months. The patient should also be instructed to avoid marked flexion at the level of injury while lying in bed and to avoid lying supine with multiple pillows because this position could increase the deformity. Patients should be encouraged to sleep in the prone position. If they are unable to understand or follow these instructions, either a cast or surgery should be considered. Patients should be instructed to notify the physician immediately if any paresthesias, cramping in their lower

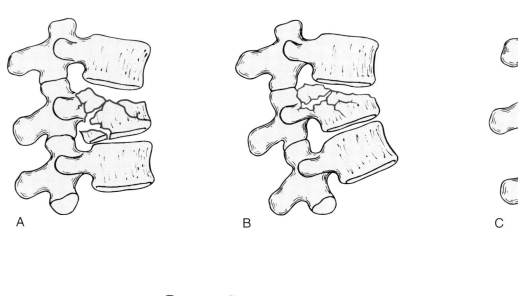

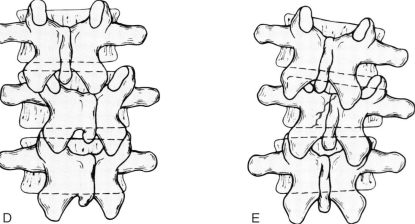

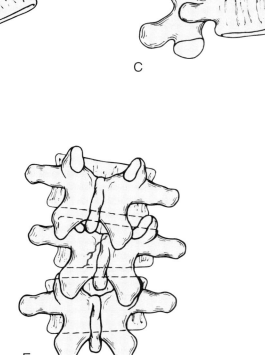

FIGURE 30–30. Denis' classification of burst fractures. *A–C,* Types A, B, and C represent fractures of both end-plates, the superior end-plate, and the inferior end-plate, respectively. *D,* Type D is a combination of a type A burst fracture with rotation, which is best appreciated on an anteroposterior (AP) radiograph. *E,* A type E burst fracture is caused by a laterally directed force and hence appears asymmetric on an AP radiograph. The superior or inferior end-plate, or both, may be involved in this fracture.

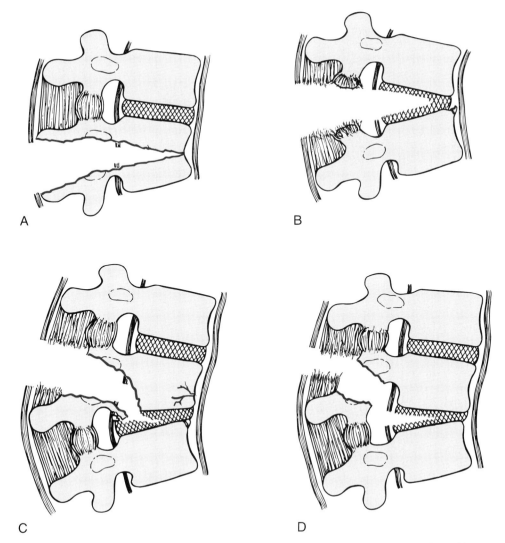

A

B

C

D

FIGURE 30–31. Denis' classification of flexion-distraction injuries. These injuries may occur at one level through bone *(A)*, at one level through the ligaments and disc *(B)*, at two levels with the middle column injured through bone *(C)*, or at two levels with the middle column injured through ligament and disc *(D)*.

extremities, weakness in their legs, or a change in bowel or bladder control develops. Patients should be evaluated frequently (1 week, 1 month, 2 months, and 3 months after injury) with standing lateral radiographs to be certain that the angulation at the level of injury has not increased. After healing appears to be adequate, flexion-extension radiographs are taken with the patient out of the brace to make sure that no excessive motion has occurred at the fracture level. If nonoperative treatment fails and either progressive deformity or a neurologic deficit develops, surgical intervention should be initiated. The type of surgery is dependent on the method of failure of nonoperative treatment. If a neurologic deficit develops, anterior decompression should be considered because posterior instrumentation performed more than 2 to 3 weeks after injury will not adequately reduce the canal compromise. Similarly, posterolateral decompression may be difficult as the fragment begins to heal into position. However, if the patient fails nonoperative treatment because of persistent pain or increasing deformity, poster-

ior surgery is usually adequate. If the deformity is partially corrected on flexion-extension views, satisfactory reduction of kyphosis can be achieved with posterior instrumentation and fusion.

Burst fractures that require operative treatment can be appropriately reduced and stabilized with any system that allows distraction and three- or four-point fixation. By means of force vectors placed by posterior instrumentation, the ligaments of the middle column can be tightened, thereby reducing the intracanal fragment. Indirect reduction was originally thought to be caused by tensing of the posterior longitudinal ligament, but more recent studies point to the annular attachments as being responsible for indirect reduction.[39, 99, 127] The most commonly used posterior systems are currently those that allow segmental fixation with varying combinations of hooks and screws. Such systems allow variation in the length of the construct, as well as in methods of attachment to the vertebra, depending on the location of the fracture within the spine and the fracture pattern.

Zou and colleagues[287] studied the use of various posterior fixation devices for the treatment of burst fractures in a cadaver model. They noted that devices capable of providing distraction and restoration of sagittal alignment resulted in significantly better canal decompression than did systems that used only distraction. Mann and associates[188] compared the Syracuse I-Plate (applied anteriorly) with the AO Fixateur Interne pedicle screw system for the treatment of burst fractures. They found that both systems provided adequate stability in patients without posterior column disruption. In the presence of posterior disruption, posterior instrumentation provided significantly increased stability. Gurwitz and colleagues[122] compared the use of the Kaneda device for anterior fixation with pedicle screws and a variable spinal plate (VSP) posteriorly for fixation of a corpectomy model used to simulate a burst fracture. They found that short-segment posterior instrumentation did not adequately restore spinal stability. Farcey and co-workers[91] reported that posterior fixation does not adequately prevent late collapse if significant anterior destruction with concomitant kyphosis has occurred. They recommended the addition of an anterior strut graft for mechanical reasons, in addition to posterior instrumentation.

With posterior distraction systems, intraoperative evoked potentials, posterolateral decompression, and spinal sonography may all be used to document and treat any residual neural compression that remains after alignment and stabilization of the fracture. An alternative is to obtain postoperative CT scans to determine the extent of residual neural compression and decide whether additional anterior decompression and fusion may be necessary (see Fig. 30–47). This decision should be predicated on the patient's postoperative neurologic status with a plateau at a less desired or expected level of function. Surgeons who perform posterior stabilization procedures should be aware that patients who have burst fractures with concomitant lamina fractures and a neurologic deficit have a 50% to 70% chance that a posterior dural laceration secondary to the injury is also present.[40] Should this complication be encountered, the surgical team should be prepared to make appropriate repairs.

Burst fractures that require surgery should not be treated with a compression construct, which may increase the extent of bone retropulsion into the spinal canal. This injury should also not be treated with Luque rods because the spine is not protected from axial loading with this type of fixation and increased retropulsion of bone into the spinal canal is possible.

A neutralization system such as one using plates and screws may be adequate for the treatment of midlumbar and lower lumbar injuries, if realignment (distraction lordosis) can be obtained. If reduction is achievable, pedicle screw systems allow the surgeon to minimize the length of the fusion and still provide stability. Although these systems have also been advocated for thoracolumbar junction injuries, they fail more often in such applications, with resultant recurrent deformity and neural compression, particularly if the normal spinal contour is not achieved. If a pedicle screw–based construct with

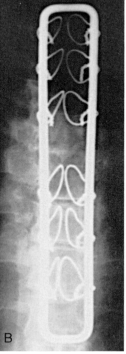
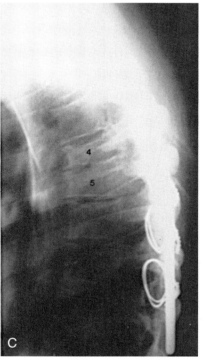

FIGURE 30–32. A T4–T5 fracture-dislocation resulted in a complete spinal cord injury in a 30-year-old man. *A,* A computed tomographic scan through the injured level demonstrates marked displacement and comminution at T4–T5, with multiple bone fragments within the canal. *B,* A postoperative anteroposterior radiograph shows stabilization with a Luque rectangle and sublaminar wires. This instrumentation provided rigid fixation and allowed early mobilization with minimal external support. The strength of fixation could have been improved with the use of double wires around the lamina bilaterally. *C,* Postoperative lateral radiograph.

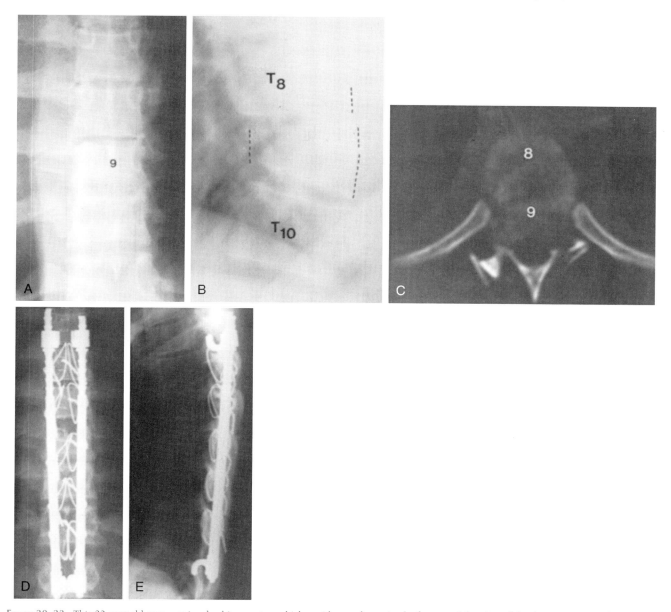

FIGURE 30-33. This 32-year-old man was involved in a motor vehicle accident and sustained a fracture-dislocation of the thoracic spine and a complete spinal cord injury. *A*, An anteroposterior radiograph demonstrates loss of height at T9, with a minimal rotatory component. *B*, A lateral radiograph confirms fracture of the body of T9 with forward subluxation of the body of T8 on T9. Involvement of the posterior wall of T9 appears minimal. *C*, A computed tomographic scan through the injured level reveals the offset of the T8 vertebra in comparison to T9. The canal compromise is predominantly related to the malalignment. *D*, The patient was treated operatively, with instrumentation applied by using the Harrington-Luque technique. Segmental sublaminar wires are used to enhance fixation and allow mobilization with minimal external support. *E*, A lateral radiograph demonstrates restoration of height and realignment at the injury level.

only two-point fixation extending one level above and one level below the injury is used at the thoracolumbar junction, it may be necessary to combine this procedure with anterior fusion to provide axial support through the injured vertebra. Such fusion is often not necessary in the lower and midlumbar spine, in which more weight is carried through the posterior elements. Insertion of screws into the fractured vertebra (if the pedicles are intact) to create three-point fixation and re-create the normal lordosis may obviate the need for concurrent anterior stabilization.

Anterior decompression and fusion (with instrumenta-

tion) may be performed to treat burst injuries. This procedure is best for patients with significant neural compression and neurologic deficit, particularly those with minimal kyphotic deformity. Anterior decompression and fusion should be routinely considered if the injury occurred 3 or more weeks previously. The use of this approach best ensures adequate neural decompression, and although more residual deformity may remain than with most posterior instrumentation systems, it is tolerated by the patient if the anterior fusion is solid. With the use of anterior instrumentation it is possible to obtain adequate correction of deformity, as well as decompression and rigid stabilization in the thoracolumbar, midlumbar, and low lumbar spine.

Laminectomy *by itself* is never indicated for the treatment of burst fractures. It cannot relieve the anterior neural compression, further destabilizes the spine, and is often associated with an increase in neurologic deficit.[16, 28, 30]

Flexion-Distraction Injuries

Flexion-distraction injuries are characterized by disruption of the posterior and middle columns of the spine in tension, whereas the anterior column usually remains intact and acts as a hinge. The decision to perform nonoperative rather than operative treatment depends primarily on whether this injury is through bone, as originally described by Chance[44] (Denis type A), or whether it also involves significant ligamentous injuries, as seen in atypical Chance fractures (Denis types B, C, and D). A Chance fracture extending only through bone has an excellent prognosis for healing, although it may be unstable early and difficult to hold in anatomic reduction without surgery. Injuries with significant ligamentous disruption tend to heal in a less predictable fashion and should be considered unstable both acutely and chronically.

Nonoperative care of a patient with a seat belt injury through bone may consist of bedrest for 2 weeks or longer, followed by mobilization in a total-contact TLSO molded in hyperextension. This orthosis is best molded with the patient in the prone position or supine on an extension frame. The patient should be instructed to wear the TLSO and participate in activities as tolerated while wearing the brace. Frequent evaluation with radiographs taken in the standing position should be made to ensure that the

deformity has not progressed. After 3 to 4 months, the level of injury should be assessed for excess motion with flexion-extension radiographs obtained out of the brace. If nonoperative treatment has failed to produce a stable spine with minimal deformity, surgical treatment consisting of posterior fusion with a compression system is indicated. Even if treatment is performed late after the injury, the chance of obtaining successful fusion and satisfactory alignment of the spine is good. Alternatively, early fixation with compression instrumentation can be considered if fracture-ligament stability or patient compliance is a concern.

If a seat belt injury is to be treated operatively, a posterior compression system is generally used. The system often needs to extend only one level above and one level below the disruption if the laminae are intact. Hook-and-rod or pedicle screw systems can be used. Positioning the patient in the prone position with support under the chest and pelvis can often anatomically reduce the fracture. The Luque rod system with segmental wires is not indicated because it is less able to resist forward flexion unless many levels above and below the injury are included in the construct. Anterior decompression is not usually appropriate or necessary (unless a large disc herniation is present at the level) because it removes the last intact column and further destabilizes the spine.

Fracture-Dislocations

In fracture-dislocations, all three columns of the spine are disrupted. These injuries have the highest incidence of neurologic deficit, and most patients should be treated surgically. If a fracture-dislocation is present and the patient is neurologically normal, surgery is performed to

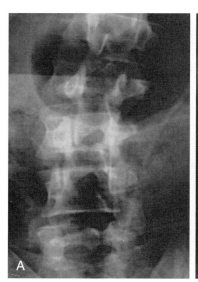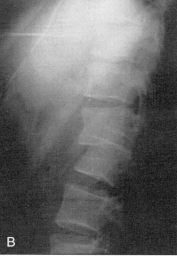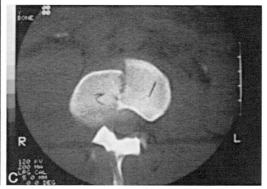

FIGURE 30–34. This 24-year-old man was a victim of a fall from a height that resulted in a fracture-dislocation at L1–L2 and a complete spinal cord injury. *A,* An anteroposterior radiograph highlights the malalignment at L1–L2 with a significant rotatory component and lateral slip at this level. *B,* A lateral radiograph confirms the displacement with forward subluxation and overlap at L1–L2. *C,* A computed tomographic scan through L1–L2 highlights the displacement and malalignment resulting in significant canal compromise and spinal cord injury.

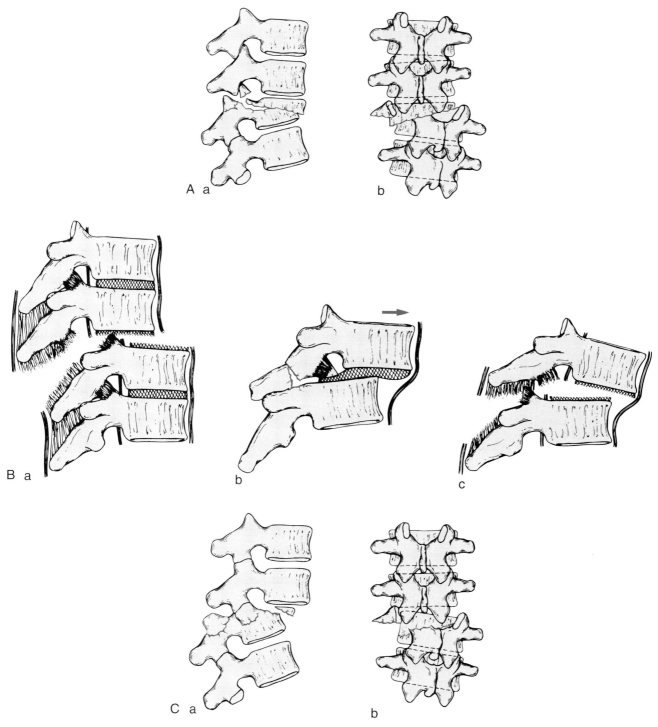

FIGURE 30–35. Denis' classification of fracture-dislocation of the spine. *A,* Type A is a flexion-rotation injury occurring either through bone or through the disc. All three columns of the spine are completely disrupted, usually with the anterior longitudinal ligament being the only intact structure. Commonly, this ligament is stripped off the anterior portion of the vertebral body below. These injuries are usually associated with fractures of the superior facet of the more caudal vertebra. *B,* Type B is a shear injury. The type that produces anterior spondylolisthesis of the more cephalad vertebra usually fractures a facet, and that causing posterior spondylolisthesis of the more cephalad vertebra normally does not cause a fracture of the facet joint. *C,* Type C is bilateral facet dislocation. This injury is a flexion-distraction injury but with disruption of the anterior column in addition to the posterior and middle columns. This disruption through the anterior column may occur through either the anterior intervertebral disc or the anterior vertebral body.

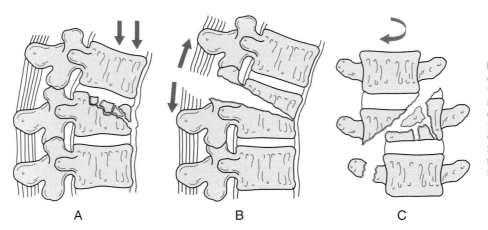

FIGURE 30–36. Comprehensive classification of spine injuries. Type A (A) is vertebral body compression. Type B (B) is anterior and posterior element injury with distraction. Type C (C) is anterior and posterior element injury with rotation. (Redrawn by permission from Gertzbein, S.D. In: Gertzbein, S.D., ed. Fractures of the Thoracic and Lumbar Spine. Baltimore, Williams & Wilkins, 1992.)

A   B   C

FIGURE 30–37. Comprehensive classification of type A spinal injuries. The three categories of type A fractures include impaction injuries (A1), of which wedge fractures are most commonly seen; split fractures (A2), of which a pincer fracture is the typical injury; and burst fractures (A3). (Redrawn by permission from Gertzbein, S.D. In: Gertzbein, S.D., ed. Fractures of the Thoracic and Lumbar Spine. Baltimore, Williams & Wilkins, 1992.)

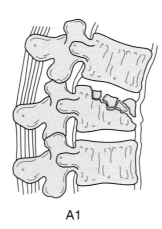
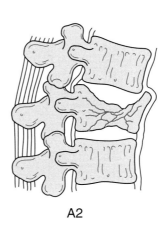
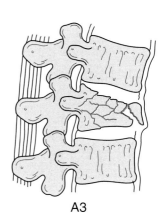

A1   A2   A3

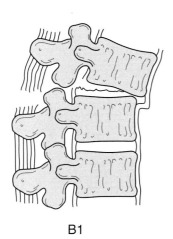
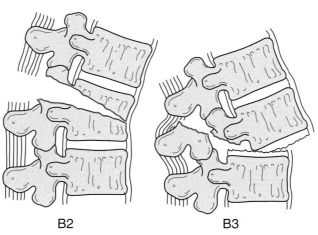

B1   B2   B3

FIGURE 30–38. Comprehensive classification of type B spinal injuries. Flexion-distraction injuries can result in disruption of soft tissues posteriorly through the capsule of the facet joints (B1) or through the bony arch (B2). If distraction and extension occur, anterior disruption through the disc may often be seen (B3), with or without associated fractures or soft tissue injuries of the posterior elements. (Redrawn by permission from Gertzbein, S.D. In: Gertzbein, S.D., ed. Fractures of the Thoracic and Lumbar Spine. Baltimore, Williams & Wilkins, 1992.)

stabilize the spine and prevent the occurrence of a neurologic deficit while allowing the patient to be mobilized. If a fracture-dislocation is present and the patient has an incomplete neurologic deficit, surgery should be performed to stabilize the spine and decompress the neural elements. If a fracture-dislocation is present and the patient has a complete neurologic deficit, surgery should be performed to stabilize the spine, shorten the hospital stay, minimize the need for rigid external immobilization, and maximize the patient's potential for rehabilitation.

The surgical management of fracture-dislocations varies according to the type of injury. If the patient is neurologically normal or has an incomplete neurologic deficit, it is best to intubate and turn the patient to the prone position while still awake. The patient's muscle tone helps stabilize the spine during turning, and the patient can be quickly monitored after turning to make certain that neurologic function is unchanged. Most patients do not find this maneuver particularly distressful, provided that they are informed of it in advance. It makes the turning and positioning maneuvers safer than logrolling an anesthetized patient with a spinal column injury and no inherent ability to protect the cord. After positioning has been completed and neurologic assessment has been performed, the patient may be anesthetized.

In both flexion-rotation and flexion-distraction injuries, the anterior longitudinal ligament most often remains intact. These injuries can be reduced with the use of any of the previously described distraction systems. If overdistraction occurs, a shorter central compression system acting as a tension band can be used between the two distraction rods, with the system spanning one level above to one level below the fracture-dislocation. In many cases, a double-looped 1.20-mm wire passed around the spinous processes can prevent overdistraction. In the case of flexion-rotation injury, a compression system by itself cannot usually provide anatomic realignment. However, with a flexion-distraction injury, it allows excellent fixation and stabilization of the injury. Conversely, in flexion-rotation or flexion-distraction injuries with jumped facets, distraction may be applied to reduce the dislocation. After reduction has been achieved with the distraction system, a neutralization system with a plate and screws can be used

to hold the reduction while the distraction component is removed. The Luque instrumentation system is secure enough to maintain reduction in a flexion-rotation injury, but it may be difficult to achieve anatomic reduction with this technique because the system does not allow application or maintenance of distraction. The use of rigid segmental fixation systems allows better stabilization in this type of injury.

Shear injuries are the most unstable of the injuries because all three columns are disrupted and all supporting ligaments are completely torn.[60] Overdistraction is a common occurrence. The combination of long distraction with short compression should be considered. An alternative is to reduce these injuries with long distraction and short local compression, followed by fixation with a plate-and-screw system extending two levels above and two levels below the injury. The distraction and compression instrumentation can then be removed. A segmental claw with transverse fixation devices or pedicle screws is also useful. Another possibility is to achieve reduction, again with distraction and compression systems, and then fix the reduction in situ with Luque rods and segmental wires. All these approaches provide excellent stability and allow postoperative mobilization of the patient, usually with a TLSO.

Primary acute anterior decompression rarely has a role in fracture-dislocations because the main problem in these injuries is usually stability and malalignment. Realignment by itself frequently decompresses the compromised neural elements. Anterior decompression may be used in conjunction with posterior instrumentation if adequate decompression cannot be achieved. This option is particularly important in a patient with a partial neurologic deficit.[253]

Soft Tissue Injuries

Soft tissue injuries (grades 1 and 2 sprains) involving the thoracic and lumbar spine without complete ligamentous disruption are diagnosed by exclusion after obtaining a detailed history, performing a thorough physical examination, and ordering appropriate tests. Treatment is symptomatic, as for soft tissue injuries that occur elsewhere in

FIGURE 30–39. Comprehensive classification of type C spinal injuries. The common feature of these injuries is rotation associated with compression (*C1*), distraction (*C2*), or rotational shear (*C3*). (Redrawn by permission from Gertzbein, S.D. In: Gertzbein, S.D. ed. Fractures of the Thoracic and Lumbar Spine. Baltimore, Williams & Wilkins, 1992.)

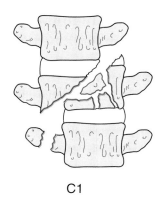

C1

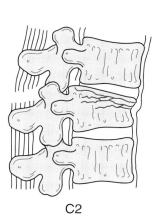

C2

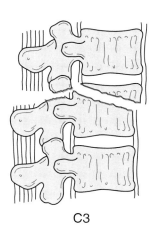

C3

the body. Standard physical therapy measures coupled with short-term bedrest may prove helpful, if necessary, to relieve symptoms. Provided that structural integrity is present, gradual mobilization of the patient should be encouraged. The use of analgesics is appropriate, and the use of nonsteroidal anti-inflammatory drugs may also shorten the course of disability and decrease symptoms. Two treatment options to be avoided are prolonged rigid immobilization and chronic use of narcotic analgesics.

If symptoms of the soft tissue injury persist, the patient should be reevaluated with the use of plain radiographs with flexion and extension lateral views. If results are negative, a bone scan or MRI may be performed to rule out an occult spinal fracture or ligamentous injury. If any area is abnormal in the bone scan or MRI, a thin-section CT scan with reconstructions should be obtained. Additionally, if the symptoms warrant, MRI can be performed to rule out disc herniation or other soft tissue injury.

Disc Injuries

High-energy injuries of the intervertebral discs in the thoracic and thoracolumbar spine are uncommon, but they can be a significant source of morbidity and cause pain or even paralysis. Disc herniations down to the T12–L1 and sometimes the L1–L2 interspaces can involve spinal cord compression, whereas in disc herniations below these levels, compression is limited to the cauda equina. As stated previously, the spinal cord is more susceptible to injury and less likely to recover once injured. This discussion is limited to disc herniations in the thoracic and thoracolumbar regions.

The classification of disc herniations in the thoracic spine is the same as for herniations in the low lumbar spine. Disc abnormalities are defined as bulging, protruded, extruded, or sequestered. A *bulging* or *protruded* disc is defined as an injury in which the nucleus pulposus migrates posteriorly but remains confined within the anulus fibrosus. With an *extruded* disc, the nucleus pulposus ruptures through the anulus fibrosus but is still confined anterior to the posterior longitudinal ligament. When a disc is *sequestered,* the nucleus pulposus has ruptured through the anulus fibrosus, as well as the posterior longitudinal ligament, and lies within the spinal canal. The thoracic and thoracolumbar regions of the spine are less tolerant than the lumbar spine of any of these disc abnormalities. Even a protruded intervertebral disc may be symptomatic because the spinal canal is narrower than in the cervical and low lumbar regions and the thoracic cord is more susceptible to pressure because of the limited vascular supply and small space.

Though significantly less common, limbus fractures of the lumbar vertebrae must be considered in the differential diagnosis of any adolescent or young adult thought to have a traumatic herniated nucleus pulposus. Fracture of the lumbar vertebral limbus consists of a fracture of the peripheral apophyseal ring from either the posterosuperior or the posteroinferior aspect of the vertebra, and the symptoms are similar to those seen with a herniated nucleus pulposus. Although they were originally thought to occur exclusively in the pediatric population, a number

of studies have shown the existence of fragmented, unfused apophyseal rings in adults. Epstein and Epstein[88] reported on 27 patients who sustained limbus vertebral fractures at an average age of 32 years and a range extending to 44 years of age. Treatment of these lesions is by surgical excision.

Symptoms of thoracic and thoracolumbar disc herniation include pain, paresthesias, and neurologic deficits. The pain may be local and axial at the level of injury, or it may be radicular in nature, with radiation to the flank, along a rib, or down toward the groin if the disc herniation is at the thoracolumbar junction. Less commonly, pain may involve all areas distal to the spinal cord compression. When this type of dysesthetic pain occurs, significant neural compression and weakness are usually present.

Neurologic findings can include a wide-based, ataxic gait. Sensation may be decreased either in a radicular distribution or in a distribution involving all regions distal to the level of spinal cord compression. Weakness may be present and may follow any of the patterns of spinal cord syndromes, from a central cord or Brown-Séquard syndrome to an anterior cord syndrome. On occasion, complete paralysis may also be associated with thoracic or thoracolumbar disc herniation. In addition, abnormal findings related to rectal tone, perineal sensation, and bladder function may be observed. Subtle changes may be detected with cystometric evaluation. The reflexes may range from normal in patients with minimal spinal cord compression to marked hyperreflexia with a positive Babinski sign in patients with significant spinal cord compression.

Thoracic disc herniation can be detected by MRI (see Fig. 30–52), myelography, or myelography followed by CT scanning (which has the added advantage of demonstrating spinal cord deformity at the level of the disc herniation). A CT scan alone is not usually adequate to demonstrate thoracic disc herniation or accurately assess the extent of spinal cord compression. Plain radiographs are seldom diagnostic. Plain films can, however, be helpful if the patient has Scheuermann's disease because thoracic disc herniation is more likely to develop in these patients.

Appropriate treatment of thoracic and thoracolumbar disc herniation is surgical, provided that the herniation is associated with incapacitating pain or abnormal neurologic findings. Surgical approaches to treatment of disc herniation in this region include anterior transthoracic discectomy (see Fig. 30–52) with or without fusion, posterolateral decompression from a transpedicular approach, and a costotransversectomy approach. Standard laminectomy should not be used to remove a thoracic or thoracolumbar herniated disc. Because spinal cord manipulation is required to remove a disc through a standard posterior laminectomy, worsening of the neurologic condition can occur and has been reported in up to 45% of patients treated with this approach. The results reported for the anterior transthoracic, costotransversectomy, and posterolateral transpedicle approaches all show that 80% to 90% of patients improve after surgery, with the remainder being without change or deterioration.[83, 170, 187, 216, 219] Because the condition is traumatically induced, internal fixation and fusion should be considered, concurrent with the discectomy.

Bohlman and Zdelblick[31] reviewed 19 patients treated surgically for thoracic disc herniation; 8 were treated with a transthoracic approach, and the remaining 11 were treated with a costotransversectomy approach. They concluded that the transthoracic approach was preferable because it greatly improved visualization of the pertinent anatomic structures, including the disc and the neural elements. All seven patients with paralysis improved after anterior transthoracic decompression.

Thoracoscopy has been used as a diagnostic tool for many years. It has been successfully used in complex surgical procedures, including thoracic discectomy. The potential benefits of video-assisted thoracoscopic surgery include reduced postoperative pain, improved early shoulder girdle function, and a shorter hospital stay.[171] Regan and associates reported on video-assisted thoracoscopic surgery performed on 12 thoracic spinal patients, including 5 discectomies.[227] Postoperative CT scans showed adequate spinal cord decompression, and pain was relieved in all patients. Huntington and associates undertook a randomized comparison of 30 thoracoscopic and 30 open thoracic discectomies for anterior spinal fusion in a live sheep model.[137] Their data showed no significant difference in the amount of disc end-plate resected between the two techniques.

OPERATIVE TREATMENT

Selection of the instrumentation and type of construct is not random, nor should it be based entirely on the preference of the surgeon. All systems have relative strengths and weaknesses that can be used to advantage. The optimal system and construct for a given fracture should counteract the deforming forces and maximally diminish the degree of instability. For example, burst fractures are caused by flexion and axial loading forces, so correction of deformity and restoration of stability are best achieved by a system that can impart extension and distraction. Therefore, neither a Harrington rod nor Luque segmental instrumentation is optimal for these fractures; the use of segmental fixation with multiple hook or screw fixation is preferable.

Hook-Rod Systems

The Harrington rod system was one of the first rod-hook systems to treat fractures in the thoracic and the lumbar segments of the spine.[1, 28, 95, 127, 177, 225, 279] Although it has allowed fracture reduction and spine stabilization, as well as early rehabilitation, it has little intrinsic stability and is mentioned here primarily for historical purposes.*

Reduction of anterior vertebral body fractures is dependent on both distraction and extension (lordotic) forces created by the rods and hooks (see Figs. 30–22 and 30–32). With contouring, the rods must achieve three- or four-point fixation to provide force vectors that pull

posteriorly at the hook sites cephalad and caudad to the injury while constantly pushing anteriorly toward the fractured vertebra through the lamina and pedicles, either at or above and below the level of injury. These vectors are achieved at the expense of increased force at the hook-laminar junction with the use of square-ended Moe rods.[61] This three- or four-point fixation translates to vector forces that reduce the vertebral body fracture deformity anteriorly and close the disruption posteriorly. The distraction rod can be used successfully to stabilize and reduce burst fractures, fracture-dislocations, and compression fractures with associated posterior element disruption. They may also be appropriate in flexion-distraction injuries that have a burst component associated with the vertebral body injury. In the latter case, placement of a tension band (spinous process wires or laminar compression rod) may be necessary posteriorly before application of the distraction force.[96]

Compression rods fixed to hooks around the lamina have been shown to provide a stronger construct than possible with distraction systems when tested against flexion loading,[263] although some authors disagree.[222, 242] Rod-hook distraction systems tend to fail by dislodgment at the rod-hook junction, at the hook-lamina junction, or at the ratchet-rod junction. Compression rods, perhaps because they better resist flexion and rotation forces, contribute to failure by fracturing the lamina to which the hooks are attached.[82, 170]

Many varied recommendations have been made regarding the number of spinal segments to instrument, the number of spinal segments to fuse,[45] and whether the instrumentation should be removed after the spinal injury has healed. Early recommendations were to apply instrumentation from three levels above the injury to two levels below the injury, fuse all the intervening segments, and not remove the instrumentation unless specific problems occur.[66] The optimal length should be determined by the length of the lever arm necessary to achieve the reduction.[14]

Rod Sleeve Distraction Instrumentation

The Edwards instrumentation system, which was initially designed for treating spinal trauma, used ratcheted universal rods with an outer diameter similar to that of the Harrington distraction rods but with a large core diameter; the system could be used for either distraction or compression. It is combined with polyethylene rod sleeves and an improved anatomic hook in three sizes rather than the standard curved Harrington hooks.[79–81, 83, 176]

Most burst fractures result from varying degrees of axial compression and flexion, and the two components of the Edwards system allowed individual adjustment of distraction and extension forces to correct the deformity. The rod provided distraction across the fracture site, which in most cases restored vertebral and disc height. The rod sleeves (in three sizes) were used to generate the central, anteriorly directed force vector to allow for sagittal plane reduction (Fig. 30–40). Sagittal-plane correction was better than with other posterior instrumentation systems because the rod sleeves allowed some continued postoperative increase in reduction by gradual accommodation to the spine's

---

*See references 1, 51, 67, 71, 72, 96, 101, 142, 143, 145, 152, 200, 225, 231, 242, 251, 263.

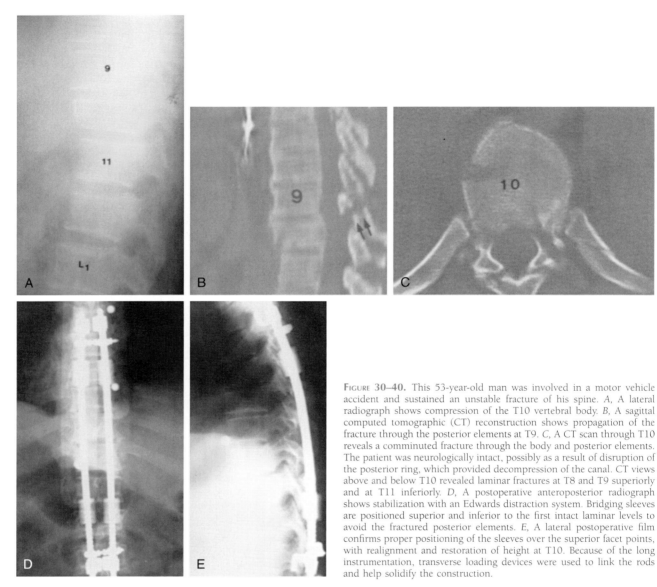

FIGURE 30–40. This 53-year-old man was involved in a motor vehicle accident and sustained an unstable fracture of his spine. *A,* A lateral radiograph shows compression of the T10 vertebral body. *B,* A sagittal computed tomographic (CT) reconstruction shows propagation of the fracture through the posterior elements at T9. *C,* A CT scan through T10 reveals a comminuted fracture through the body and posterior elements. The patient was neurologically intact, possibly as a result of disruption of the posterior ring, which provided decompression of the canal. CT views above and below T10 revealed laminar fractures at T8 and T9 superiorly and at T11 inferiorly. *D,* A postoperative anteroposterior radiograph shows stabilization with an Edwards distraction system. Bridging sleeves are positioned superior and inferior to the first intact laminar levels to avoid the fractured posterior elements. *E,* A lateral postoperative film confirms proper positioning of the sleeves over the superior facet points, with realignment and restoration of height at T10. Because of the long instrumentation, transverse loading devices were used to link the rods and help solidify the construction.

normal viscoelastic creep and by constant tensioning of the anterior longitudinal ligament through interoperative bowing of the rods within their elastic range.[47] In addition, the sleeves produced increased rotational stability by securely wedging between the spinous process and the facet joints. Such wedging improved the overall rotational rigidity of the system in comparison to other rod-hook systems.

The results of use of the Edwards system for fracture management in 135 patients treated at a single center were reported by Edwards and Levine.[81] Postoperative follow-up results at 1 to 4 years and at 6 to 10 years were reported in 122 of these patients. After partial reduction with the use of transverse rolls on a Stryker frame, preoperative deformity averaged 14° of kyphosis, 8 mm of displacement, and 68% loss of vertebral body and disc height. The initial study included 61 patients with incomplete paralysis, 41 with complete paralysis, and 33 who were neurologically normal. The immediate postoperative kyphosis was reduced from 14° to −1° (±4°). At late follow-up, the kyphosis had increased to 0.5° (±5°).

Vertebral height was restored from 68% preoperatively to 96% in the immediate postoperative period and was 90% (±8%) at late follow-up. Translation was similarly reduced from 8 mm preoperatively to 0.8 mm (±1.5 mm) immediately after surgery and at late follow-up. For the last 32 cases in this series, preoperative and postoperative CT scans of the spinal canal area were performed at the level of injury, and findings were compared with those for the adjacent normal levels. For injuries treated within 2 days, rod sleeve reduction increased the canal area from 55% to 87% of normal. If surgery was performed between 3 and 14 days after injury, the canal area was increased from 53% to 76% of normal.[81]

Segmental Instrumentation Systems

The use of segmental fixation instrumentation systems has improved the treatment of spinal deformities such as kyphosis and scoliosis.[51] The primary advantage of these systems is that multiple hooks and pedicle screws can be used in both distraction and compression modes, thereby allowing correction of complex deformities and providing stability while maintaining normal sagittal contours. This system is further strengthened with the use of transverse traction devices to convert the system to a rigid rectangle[46] (see Figs. 30–25, 30–44, and 30–47). With these systems, increased stability is obtained without the apparent increased risk of neurologic damage reported with the Luque sublaminar wiring technique.

The role of segmental fixation in the treatment of spinal trauma continues to evolve. One disadvantage is that the surgical time required to insert the instrumentation may be slightly greater than with distraction rod systems, especially early in the surgeon's experience. A second disadvantage is that a moderate amount of manipulation is required when connecting multiple hooks to rods while simultaneously reducing the unstable spinal injury. One advantage of segmental fixation is that under certain circumstances postoperative bracing may be eliminated (especially in the thoracic spine) without jeopardizing the stability and eventual healing of the fusion. Another potential advantage is that these techniques may allow shorter instrumentation length, thus immobilizing fewer segments.[222, 272, 280–283]

The pattern of hook placement varies from author to author, but a few general principles for the constructs may be used in most cases (Fig. 30–41). Cephalad, a claw configuration either at a single level or at adjacent levels is the mainstay of most constructs (Fig. 30–42). Many different recommendations have been made regarding the length of instrumentation and configuration of the hooks and pedicle screws. Shufflebarger (personal communication) recommended that the lever arms be of equal length above and below the fracture and stressed the use of a double lamina claw at both the rostral and caudal extremes of instrumentation. Although in the thoracic spine he would not hesitate to extend fixation to three levels above and two levels below the injury, at the thoracolumbar junction, he recommended instrumentation two levels above and one level below the fracture. However, a short construct should not be used unless the comminution of the anterior column is minimal or anterior stability is restored with a strut graft.

A minimum of three hooks must be used on each rod proximal to the fracture, whether in the thoracic area or at the thoracolumbar junction. The construct may consist of at least one single-level claw plus an additional pedicle hook below it (augmented claw) or two single-level claws spaced one segment apart. A bilaminar claw must be placed distal to the fracture because distal single-level claws fail 20% of the time as a result of laminar fractures caused by the huge force placed on that single level.[203] If a single-level distal claw is used, it must be augmented with an anterior strut.

The claw provides significantly increased holding power over a single upgoing hook, thereby allowing greater potential for correction of deformity while decreasing the rate of instrumentation failure. Another advantage of segmental fixation over single hook-rod systems is the ability to provide both distractive and compressive forces over the same construct and thus allow maintenance of

normal sagittal contours. In general, compression maintains lumbar lordosis, and distraction is used to maintain thoracic kyphosis.[197]

Pedicle screws placed either above or below a vertebral body fracture can be used like the rod sleeves of the Edwards system to generate a central, anteriorly directed force vector to assist in maintaining or creating sagittal-plane reduction (Fig. 30–43).

In fractures at the thoracolumbar junction, where the pedicles are relatively large, a construct of all pedicle screws may be considered. In fractures occurring in the lower thoracic spine, a combination of hooks cephalad to the fracture and pedicle screws below the fracture may be used. In fractures occurring in the middle and upper thoracic spine, hook constructs are most commonly used. Pedicle screws used in this manner, with adequate fixation above and below with either a claw configuration or additional pedicle screws, can improve the overall rigidity of the system and maintain the reduction until fusion occurs. When treating significant burst fractures with posterior instrumentation, it is important to look at the biomechanical implications. In a mechanical study by Duffield and colleagues, it was concluded that single-level posterior instrumentation adjacent to a comminuted segment will have a finite fatigue life and that anterior column support equivalent to a healthy motion segment can reduce the internal bending moments within an implant to levels that have a low probability of causing fatigue of the implant. They also showed that instrumentation of two levels adjacent to a comminuted vertebra as opposed to a single level will reduce the flexion bending moment in the implant. These results illustrate the clinical need to create load sharing when possible and to select implants capable of maintaining reduction and supporting the spine until fusion has occurred.[72] Other studies have shown the importance of transfixing these constructs with cross-connectors. In a mechanical study of transpedicular spine instrumentation, Carson and associates showed that transfixing bilevel constructs stabilizes them to all modes of loading and will reduce the excessive increase in internal components of force and moment associated with linkage instability.[43]

Akbarnia and colleagues[5] reviewed 67 patients with thoracic and lumbar spine injuries treated at two different centers; the range of follow-up was 3 to 26 months. Thirty-nine of these patients had injuries between T11 and L2. Most had instrumentation extending over five to eight vertebral levels, with an average of 10 hooks or screws per patient. The degree of preoperative and postoperative kyphosis and canal compromise was not detailed in this report. The authors stated that alignment was maintained in 65 patients throughout the duration of follow-up. Fusion was definitely achieved in 31 patients, and two pseudarthroses were performed. It was too early to assess fusion status in the remaining 34 patients. No patient was neurologically worse after surgery. Complications included two deep wound infections. Hook dislodgment or screw pull-out occurred in five patients, although all five had fusion at follow-up. In the thoracic spine, these authors recommended instrumentation three levels above and three levels below the injured segment, with claws at the extremes of instrumentation and segmental fixation at the

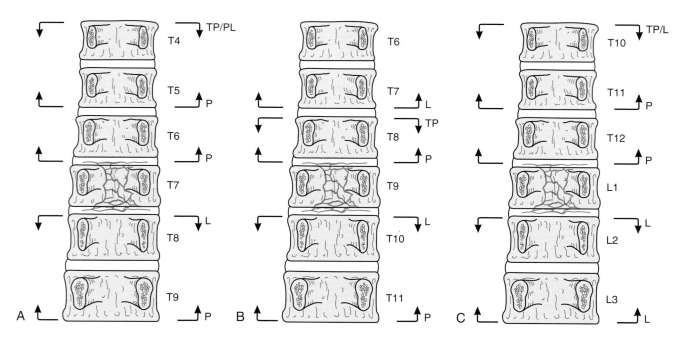

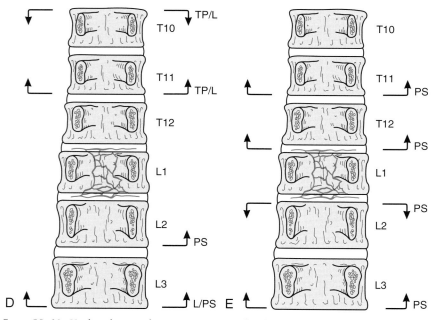

FIGURE 30–41. Hook and screw placement patterns used with rigid segmental instrumentation systems for the treatment of thoracic and thoracolumbar spine injuries. *A,* T7 fracture. The instrumentation used is a claw configuration above and below the injury. For a very unstable injury pattern, pedicle hooks may be added one level above the injury. *B,* T9 fracture. An alternative hook pattern can be used in low thoracic fractures. A unilaminar claw is formed with hooks over the top of the transverse process and a pedicle hook at the same level to create a single-level claw, which is then reinforced with a single upgoing hook at the adjacent level to place the upper portion of the construct in two levels rather than three. *C,* L1 burst fracture. A construct similar to that in *A* may be used. Note that below T10, pedicle hooks are replaced by cephalad-facing lamina hooks. *D,* In the lumbar spine, where the pedicles are large enough, screws may be substituted for hooks, with the addition of cephalad lamina hooks placed at the distal end of the construct for additional stability in highly unstable injury patterns. *E,* Another construct consisting of pedicle screws two levels above and below the fracture to provide stability in all planes. *Abbreviations:* L, lamina hook; P, pedicle hook; PS, pedicle screw; TP, transverse process hook.

intervening levels. In the thoracolumbar spine they recommended that fusion extend three levels above and two levels below the fracture. In the lumbar spine they suggested extending the fixation two levels above and one level below the injured segment. For both thoracolumbar

and lumbar hook arrangements they recommended that double claws be used superiorly but had varied recommendations for the caudal spinal fixation.

Stambough[260] reported on 55 patients treated with Cotrel-Dubousset instrumentation by a single surgeon,

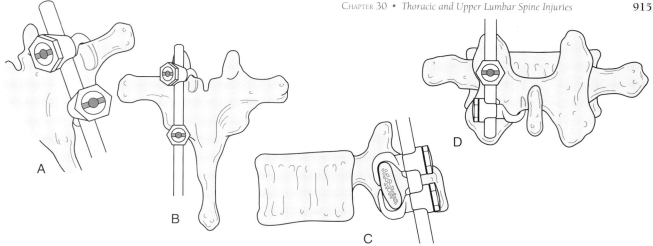

Figure 30–42. Claw configurations used for proximal and distal fixation in rigid segmental instrumentation systems. All these constructs may be used at single levels or two adjacent levels. *A,* Transverse process hook with a pedicle hook claw. *B,* Superior lamina hook with a pedicle hook claw. *C,* Supralaminar and infralaminar hook claw, useful below T10 where application of pedicle hooks is not recommended. *D,* Pedicle screw with an infralaminar hook; this is useful in the lumbar spine, where pedicles are large enough to accept pedicle screws. (*A–D,* Redrawn from Bridwell, K.H.; DeWald, R.L., eds. The Textbook of Spinal Surgery. Philadelphia, J.B. Lippincott, 1991.)

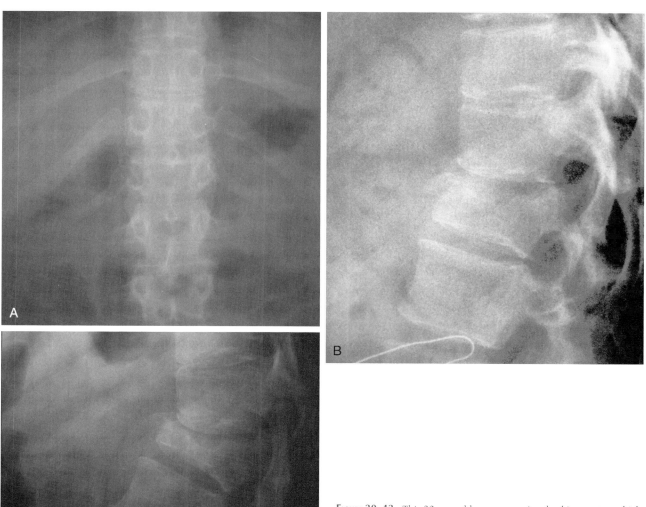

Figure 30–43. This 30-year-old woman was involved in a motor vehicle accident and sustained a T12 burst fracture without neurologic deficit. *A,* An anteroposterior radiograph shows minimal loss of height with widening of the pedicles. *B,* A lateral radiograph shows approximately 30% loss of height and local kyphosis of 8°. The patient was treated initially with bedrest and a thoracolumbosacral orthosis. *C,* Two weeks after the injury, a repeat lateral radiograph shows greater than 50% loss of height and local kyphosis of 25°.

Illustration continued on following page

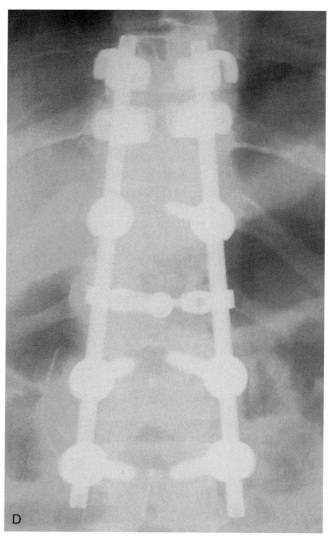

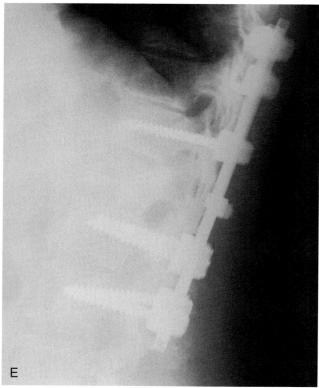

FIGURE 30–43. *Continued. D,* The patient was treated operatively with posterior segmental instrumentation with a claw at T9 and pedicle screws at T11 and at L1 and L2. *E,* A lateral radiograph shows restoration of height and sagittal alignment at the injury level.

with an average of 48 months' follow-up. No instances of failure of instrumentation or pseudarthrosis formation were reported in his series. At final follow-up, deterioration in alignment was minimal in comparison to the immediate postoperative period.

Argenson and co-workers reported their results in 65 patients treated for thoracic or lumbar spine fractures with a follow-up of 6 months or longer.[13] They recommended that instrumentation extend three levels above and two levels below the injured segment in the thoracic spine and the use of pedicular or double laminar hooks (claws) at the extremes of instrumentation with varied intermediate connections. Forty-nine patients had fractures from T11 to L2. Argenson and co-workers initially extended the instrumentation two levels above and two levels below the fracture with the use of hooks only and obtained satisfactory early results. With shortening of the instrumentation, they noted considerable problems (e.g., loss of fixation in two patients and loss of reduction in four others). Their current recommendations are to use pedicle screws one level above and one level below the level of fracture, accompanied by pedicle or laminar hooks two levels cephalad to the fractured vertebra and at the same

level as the caudal pedicle screws. In 12 patients treated in this fashion, 1 had considerable loss of reduction as a result of sepsis, whereas the others averaged only 4.3° loss of reduction at follow-up. The earlier results of this group with the use of only hooks or only screws resulted in an average loss of reduction of 8.6°.

Graziano[118] reported his results in 14 patients for whom he used lumbar pedicle screws and thoracic pedicle–transverse process hook claws in a hybrid Cotrel-Dubousset construct. The pedicle screw fixation was used one level below the injured segment. Graziano reported breakage of only one screw, and increased kyphosis developed in one patient after surgery. This construct offers the advantages of short-segment fixation in the lumbar spine, where motion preservation is important, while providing a longer fixation span above the level of injury, which helps add rigidity to the construct.

In the lumbar spine, Argenson and co-workers[13] recommended the use of short instrumentation and pedicle screw fusion one level above and one level below the injury, combined with a sublaminar hook at the inferior extent of the instrumentation. Twenty patients were treated in this fashion, and the average loss of correction in the first 15 patients was 9°. Even though this loss of reduction seems significant, the final lordosis at the level of injury was −4°, which is very close to normal physiologic alignment. Complications in this series included partial fixation loosening in three, broken screws in four, and postoperative infection in eight patients. The authors attributed this high infection rate to the increased duration of surgery associated with the learning curve of the surgeon.

Suk and associates[265] reviewed their treatment of 18 lumbar fractures, including 5 fractures of L1, 2 fractures of L2, and 1 fracture of L3. They used pedicle screws for fixation, and their average instrumentation extended over two segments. This technique contrasts with their previous experience of using segmental wiring in combination with Harrington distraction rods that spanned almost six segments. They found a postoperative kyphosis angle of 3.2° with the use of Cotrel-Dubousset instrumentation as compared with 4.3° for segmentally wired Harrington rods. Because the follow-up period was longer than 4 months in only 11 patients, these results must be categorized as preliminary. McBride recommended that when instrumentation is to be extended to L5, the fusion should be stopped short (at L4) and the hardware removed 9 to 12 months later, as with the "rod long, fuse short" technique with Harrington rods.[197]

The appropriate length of instrumentation was addressed by McKinley and colleagues[202] in a review of only seven patients monitored for more than 24 months after Cotrel-Dubousset pedicle instrumentation with screws one level above and one level below the fractured vertebra. They observed an average loss of 18° of correction (range of 8° to 26°) and a significant incidence of screw breakage requiring reoperation. They concluded that patients with significant injury to the anterior and middle columns of the spine require anterior corpectomy and fusion to prevent this type of late deterioration if short-segment Cotrel-Dubousset instrumentation with screw fixation is used posteriorly. However, the data supporting this conclusion were limited, but a similar conclusion was also reached by Gereesan.[109]

Fabris and co-workers reported their results with Cotrel-Dubousset instrumentation on nine cases of seat belt–type injuries of the thoracolumbar spine.[90] They used a short compression construct spanning only a single motion segment and reported excellent maintenance of correction of deformity and no instrumentation failure. Benzel also described the use of short-segment compression instrumentation for the treatment of burst fractures after first reconstructing the vertebral body with a strut graft.[23] The construct consisted of a claw above and a claw below the injured segment. It spanned significantly fewer motion segments than typical of traditional constructs while still maintaining excellent correction of deformity (<2° loss of correction at last follow-up). They noted that short constructs functioned best in compression and warned that short distraction constructs tended to fail over time.

In these studies, the recommendations concerning postoperative use of a TLSO are variable. Akbarnia and colleagues[6] recommended the use of a brace if the patient had osteoporotic bone or at surgery received less than a double laminar claw, or its equivalent, both proximally and distally. Thirty-six of their patients had no immobilization, and 31 used a TLSO or other brace for an average of 4 months. Argenson and co-workers[13] did not recommend the use of a postoperative brace for any of their patients, whereas Suk and associates[265] treated all their patients with a postoperative TLSO. In general, the shorter the fixation and the less secure the spine-implant interface, the more likely the authors were to recommend postoperative TLSO immobilization.

SURGICAL TECHNIQUE

With the patient in the prone position, a midline incision is made and extended one level further both proximally and distally than the expected length of instrumentation. The most frequently recommended scheme for instrumentation includes fixation two levels above and one level below the injury. Shorter instrumentation is desirable in the lumbar spine if possible, but it is not as physiologically important to limit the levels of instrumentation in the thoracic spine.

The construct described is based on a claw configuration on the lamina two levels above and one below the level of injury (see Figs. 30–41 and 30–43). For the hooks facing caudad, a laminotomy is performed just cephalad to the lamina so that the hooks may be placed around the lamina under direct vision. For the hooks directed cephalad, a ligamentum flavum stripper should be inserted beneath the lamina to prepare the site for hook placement. In the thoracic spine, thoracic hooks should be used, and in the lumbar spine, lumbar hooks should be used to obtain maximal purchase on the lamina without increasing the chance of neural compression by canal intrusion. The superior portion of the rod should be bent appropriately to conform to the slanting of the lamina in the sagittal plane and thereby minimize the chance of fracture of the lamina and failure of the system. The same attention should be paid to contouring of the rod at the caudal lamina.

Additional fixation can be obtained with the use of a hook facing cephalad under the lamina one level above the level of injury (see Fig. 30–42A). An alternative to this system would be the use of instrumentation extending three levels above and two levels below the injury, along with cephalic and caudal claws. Hooks are directed cephalad two levels above the level of injury and caudad one level below the injury. This construct is relatively safe and extremely rigid. To improve fixation in the thoracic area, the hooks directed cephalad may be pedicle hooks rather than standard lamina hooks (Fig. 30–44). Additionally, the top hook may be placed on the transverse process, provided that it is of adequate size.

Two transverse traction devices should be applied to connect the rods if space allows. No medial or lateral force should be applied to the rods at the time of insertion of the transverse traction device. The fusion technique should include decortication of the transverse processes, laminae, and spinous processes within the instrumentation, with care taken to not weaken any laminae that are directly supporting hooks.

Sequential application of segmental instrumentation can also be used for reduction of dislocations, as well as definitive stabilization (Fig. 30–45). A single-rod construct is placed in distraction, and distractive forces are applied until reduction of the dislocation occurs. After the reduction is achieved, the appropriate construct is placed on the contralateral side to stabilize the spine. Finally, the distraction rod is removed and replaced with a symmetric construct on the opposite side. Others have described the use of rotational maneuvers, similar to those used for correction of scoliosis, to reduce fracture-dislocations.[87]

For patients treated with instrumentation three levels above and two levels below the injury, a circumferential rigid postoperative brace is necessary. Similarly, when instrumentation two levels above and one level below the injury is used in the lower lumbar spine, where more of the weight-bearing forces are carried through the posterior elements, use of the brace can be eliminated or reduced. The use of a TSLO for mobilization of patients instrumented two levels above and one level below an injury at the level of the thoracolumbar junction is advised. In patients with severe anterior comminution and short posterior instrumentation, anterior corpectomy and strut fusion will decrease the chance of instrumentation failure.[23, 121, 191, 193]

Segmental Sublaminar Wires

The Luque technique was originally used to treat patients with scoliosis, with the presumed advantage of not requiring postoperative bracing. It entailed the use of two smooth, L-shaped stainless steel rods (either ¼ or ³/₁₆ inch in diameter) combined with segmental wires. The wires were made of 16-gauge malleable stainless steel, passed sublaminarly, and twisted around the rods at each level to provide segmental fixation (see Fig. 30–32). As originally described, no hooks or pedicle screws were used.

This system had two major disadvantages. Many surgeons noted an increased incidence of neurologic deficits after passage of the sublaminar wires. The frequency of new neurologic deficits decreased as each surgeon became more familiar with the technique (the learning curve).[21, 144] This incidence of neurologic deficit also varied greatly from series to series, from 0% in some to as high as 10% in others.[144] Because this increase was associated with segmental wiring at the level of the fracture in both cases, these authors recommended against insertion of segmental wires in the immediate area of the fracture. The risk of dural impingement may be even greater during wire removal.[116, 210] In 27% of cases, Nicastro and associates[210] demonstrated more than 25% canal narrowing with removal of a single wire.

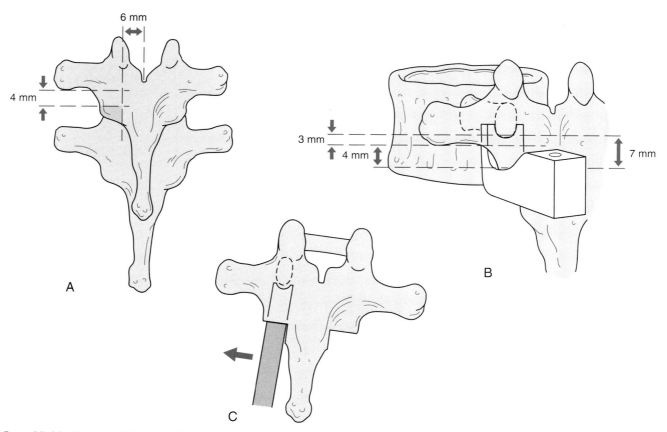

FIGURE 30–44. Placement of thoracic pedicle hooks. *A,* Appropriate landmarks to remove a piece of inferior articular facet to permit adequate positioning of a pedicle hook. *B,* A pedicle elevator is inserted into the facet joint, and after engaging the pedicle, placement is checked by moving the vertebra laterally by lateral translation of the elevator tip. *C,* The distance between the inferior part of the pedicle and the inferior part of the remaining inferior articular facet must be equal to the depth of the hook plate from its base to the notch. (*A–C,* Redrawn from Bridwell, K.H.; DeWald, R.L., eds. The Textbook of Spinal Surgery. Philadelphia, J.B. Lippincott, 1991.)

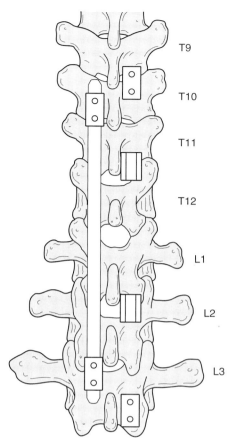

FIGURE **30–45.** Use of a unilateral distraction rod for reduction of a T12–L1 fracture-dislocation. Note the placement of the hooks for definitive rigid segmental instrumentation on the opposite side of the distraction instrumentation before application of the distraction. Once distraction is achieved, a rod is placed on the opposite side and secured, and then the distraction instrumentation is removed and replaced with rigid segmental instrumentation. If the injury involves disruption of the anterior longitudinal ligament, consideration should be given to placement of spinous process wiring at the level of injury before reduction to prevent overdistraction. (Redrawn from Garfin, S.; Northrup, B.E., eds. Surgery for Spinal Cord Injuries. New York, Raven, 1993.)

The second major problem with this system was that it was not able to provide significant axial support to the spine. As originally designed, the L-shaped rods had no means to resist sliding axially. Modifications included use of the Harrington outrigger to achieve intraoperative distraction and, later, modified rods to resist axial collapse by fixation to the lamina and the spinous processes.[8, 71, 92, 93] However, collapse still remains one of the major weaknesses of this system because the spinous processes are the weakest part of the posterior elements. After their prospective study, Ferguson and Allen recommended that this system not be used for treating any injury in which the middle column is disrupted, such as a thoracolumbar burst injury, because of the danger of spinal canal narrowing with axial collapse.[92, 93]

This inability to provide axial support has been verified in laboratory testing. Nasca and co-workers[208] instrumented thoracolumbar swine spines and then subjected them to cyclical axial compression loading. The segmentally wired L rods allowed three times greater axial

shortening than did Harrington distraction rods (1.5 versus 0.5 cm).

To combine the advantages of both systems, a hybrid system consisting of segmentally wired Harrington distraction rods was developed.[100] This system offered the obvious advantage of increased control of translation and rotation and maintained an axial distractive force while minimizing the effect of ligament relaxation and resultant hook cutout (see Fig. 30–32).

Pedicle Screw Fixation Systems

Each of the various pedicle screw fixation systems currently in use has different types and sizes of screws, different mechanisms for linking the screws, and different options concerning the ability to compress, distract, or stabilize in situ.*

One of the major advantages of these systems is that shorter fixation is often possible, frequently with instrumentation only one level above and one level below the injured segment (see Fig. 30–18). As discussed previously, the advantages of this short fixation are greatest in the lumbar spine. Fortunately, the larger pedicles allow for safer placement of pedicle screws in the lower lumbar spine than possible at more proximal levels. Conversely, the benefits of short-segment fixation in the thoracic spine are minimal; one additional level of motion does not affect the long-term functional results. Proper screw placement in the pedicle is more difficult in the thoracic spine and upper lumbar spine because pedicle size decreases from caudad to cephalad.[166, 266, 286] In addition, the risk of serious neurologic deterioration from errant screws is greater in the thoracic and thoracolumbar spine because of the presence of the spinal cord rather than only nerve roots and rootlets. Vaccaro and co-workers studied 90 screws placed in the pedicles of cadaver spines from T4 to T12 by five experienced spine surgeons.[266, 267] They found a 41% incidence of cortical perforation of the pedicle, with 23% of the screws entering the spinal canal. In view of these potential risks and benefits, we believe pedicle screw systems to be most appropriate in the lumbar spine, although they can be used successfully in the thoracic spine when appropriate and when good operative technique is used (Fig. 30–46).

Laboratory data are available for several of these systems. Gurr and colleagues[121] used a calf spine corpectomy model to evaluate different posterior instrumentation systems in combination with an anterior bone graft. Of the systems tested, they found that the Cotrel-Dubousset pedicle screw system and the VSP system of Steffee could be applied one level above and one level below the defect with restoration of the spine to original strength in terms of axial loading, forward flexion, and rotation. These systems were significantly superior to the Harrington distraction system and the Luque segmentally wired L-rod system. The limitations of this research, as stated by the authors, are that the animals were young with uniformly

---

*See references 3, 4, 6, 22, 52, 54, 55, 57, 64, 65, 67, 79, 108, 109, 148, 157, 166, 180, 187, 215, 244, 245, 249, 252, 265, 275, 277, 287, 289.

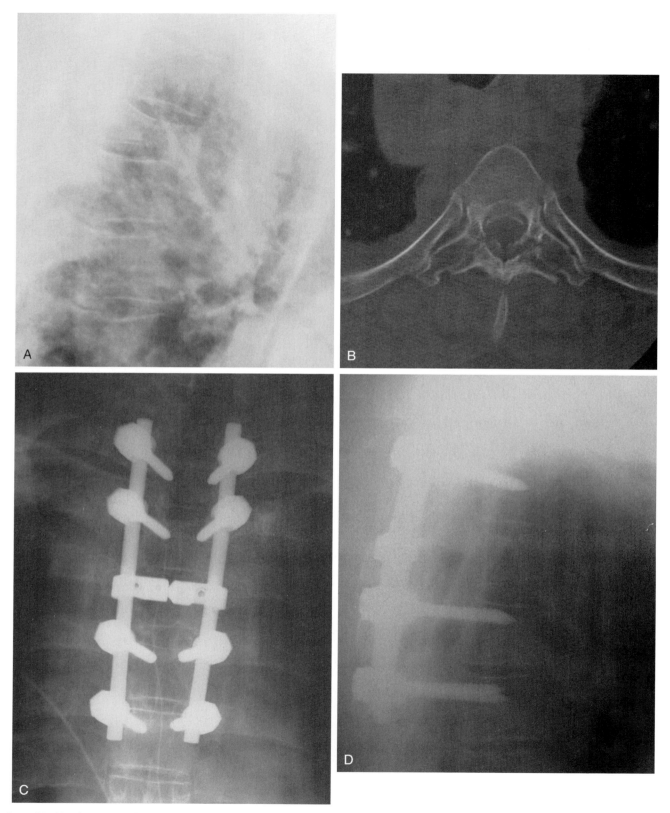

FIGURE **30–46.** This 50-year-old man fell at work from a height of approximately 16 ft and sustained a T4 burst fracture and multiple posterior element fractures from C7 to T5. He was neurologically intact. *A*, A lateral radiograph shows greater than 50% loss of height and local kyphosis. *B*, A preoperative computed tomographic (CT) scan shows approximately 30% canal compromise and disruption of the posterior elements. *C*, The patient was treated operatively with segmental instrumentation involving pedicle screws from T2 to T6. *D*, A lateral radiograph shows restoration of height and sagittal alignment.

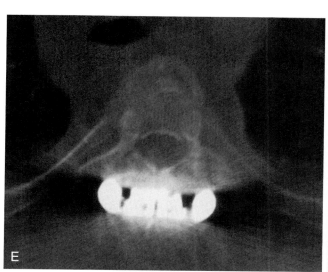

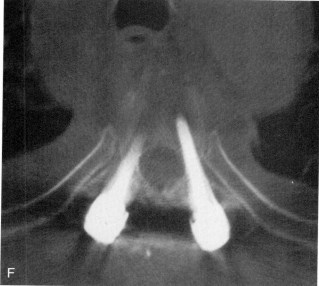

FIGURE 30–46. *Continued. E,* A postoperative CT scan shows partial restoration of the canal by ligamentotaxis and correct placement of the pedicle screws (F).

good-quality bone and the tests were performed immediately after instrumentation, thus allowing no chance to show the effect of time on loosening or fatigue failure. In addition, an anterior bone graft was implanted in each animal to provide anterior axial support.

The effect of the rigidity of this instrumentation was also investigated in an in vivo animal model.[121, 193] The spine beneath the instrumentation became significantly osteoporotic, and this effect increased with time. However, the rate and quality of the fusion increased with increased rigidity of the instrumentation.

The proper length of screw penetration was investigated by Krag and co-workers.[164] Although most of the resistance to pull-out is achieved within the pedicle, increasing the penetration into the vertebral body from 80% to 100% (up to the anterior vertebral cortex) increased resistance to flexion by 54% and to torsion by 24%. However, this increased penetration markedly increases the risk of injury to the vessels immediately adjacent to the vertebral bodies. Pull-out strength also varies significantly with screw design.[165, 286] In general, the larger the outer diameter of the screw body, the greater the resistance to bending, and larger thread depth results in greater pull-out strength. The pitch of the thread was less significant.

Crowe and Gertzbein[53] evaluated the AO Fixateur Interne in a prospective study involving pedicle fixation one level above and one level below the injury. They analyzed the ability of this system to reduce burst fractures of the thoracic and lumbar segments of the spine. The average spinal canal cross-sectional area in 25 patients, which had been compromised 54% preoperatively, improved to 40% compromise after surgery. This benefit was most marked in patients who initially had moderate spinal canal encroachment (34% to 64%); canal compromise in this group improved on average from 54% to 31%. The improvement was less marked in patients with mild or severe spinal canal compromise and in those treated more

than 4 days after injury. In view of this modest change of 14% over all their patients, it must be questioned whether this improvement is significant. It was the authors' conclusion that when canal clearance is essential, anterior decompression is the treatment of choice. However, Doerr and co-workers[68] noted that the Fixateur Interne provided canal decompression equal to that achieved with Harrington rod systems.

Esses and colleagues conducted a prospective, multicenter study on the effectiveness of the Fixateur Interne for the treatment of thoracolumbar spine trauma.[89] They reported a mean improvement of 30% in canal compromise and a mean correction of 14° in kyphotic deformity. Complications included screw misplacement in seven cases and three cases of broken hardware noted incidentally on follow-up radiographs. In no patient did a pseudarthrosis develop.

Akbarnia and associates reviewed 61 cases of thoracolumbar and lumbar spine fractures treated with the VSP system.[6] Most of their patients were instrumented one level above and one level below the injury. Ninety percent maintained their reduction, but pseudarthrosis developed in 15%, and 15% had screw breakage or dislodgment. Follow-up was short, averaging only 1 year with a range of 2 to 36 months.

Liu and colleagues treated 42 patients by short segmental posterior fixation with the AO Fixateur Interne. After an average follow-up of 66.1 months, they showed an average postoperative improvement of 14.2° in their kyphotic angle with an average loss of 3.3° of correction at follow-up. Complications were seen in seven patients. Implant failure occurred in six, but no complaints were noted from these patients. One patient experienced a nonunion with screw breakage, which was revised by repairing the posterior fusion and replacing the instrumentation.[180]

Sasso and Cotler compared Harrington instrumentation, Luque sublaminar wire instrumentation, and pedicle screw instrumentation in 70 patients with thoracolumbar spine fractures.[247] The mean number of levels instrumented was 6.0, 6.3, and 3.3, respectively. No patient sustained postoperative neurologic injury or deterioration, and complication rates were similar in all three groups. At last follow-up, the pedicle screw group had the best maintenance of sagittal contours. Markel and Graziano, in comparing Cotrel-Dubousset instrumentation with pedicle screw instrumentation, found a significantly fewer number of levels fused in patients treated with the latter systems.[189]

In another study, Cresswell and colleagues compared the stability of the AO internal fixation system with the Hartshill rectangle and sublaminar wiring in the treatment of thoracolumbar burst fractures. They reported that both systems allowed good initial restoration of anterior and posterior vertebral body height. However, at a 2-year follow-up, loss of body height occurred in the Hartshill group, whereas body height was significantly better maintained in the AO group. They thought that transpedicle body grafting, which was performed as part of the treatment with the AO system, contributed in some measure to their success with this system.[52]

Although most studies have shown excellent initial reduction of deformity with pedicle screw instrumentation, the ability of this instrumentation to maintain that correction has been questioned.[107, 248] However, loss of correction is not necessarily associated with a poor clinical result or late neurologic deterioration. For example, Carl and co-workers[42] reported an average correction of deformity of 7.4° with pedicle screws, and at last follow-up the average loss of correction was 6°, which left a final correction of just over 1°. Nevertheless, 97% of their patients were satisfied with their result, and 85% of them went back to work.

Although instrumentation failure would appear to be the most likely reason for late collapse, such is not usually the case. Rather, damage to the discs adjacent to the level of injury and to supporting soft tissues may be responsible. Because the pedicle screw instrumentation spans fewer segments than the traditional (Harrington, Luque, or Cotrel-Dubousset) systems do, it may fail to include all the damaged motion segments in the fusion, thus allowing for the occurrence of late deformity.

The initial series describing the use of short-segment pedicle screw systems had an unacceptable high early failure rate. McLain and associates[203] reported on 19 patients in whom thoracolumbar fractures were managed with short-segment pedicle screw instrumentation. Although no neurologic or vascular complications occurred in this small group, the rate of early fixation failure was disturbingly high (10 of 19 patients), with resultant progressive deformity and pain. They noted three main modes of screw failure: bending, breaking, and pull-out. A significant number of screw failures were associated with in situ rod bending, which possibly weakened the screws by prestressing them. Others have reported similarly high rates of early failure of short-segment pedicle screw instrumentation. However, such failure does not appear to be a problem when pedicle screw systems are used for degenerative conditions, possibly because the anterior and middle columns are intact and, therefore, the instrumentation is load sharing. With significant disruption of the anterior and middle columns (i.e., in traumatic injury), most of the load must be borne by the instrumentation, a situation that can lead to failure. Kostuik and colleagues[161] performed a biomechanical study on short-segment pedicle screw instrumentation systems and noted that the bending moment of the screws increased 300% after disruption of the anterior and middle columns. McCormack and associates[198] were able to clinically predict patients who were at higher risk for instrumentation failure by classifying the amount of anterior and middle column disruption.

A number of alternatives can be used for the prevention of such failures, including reconstruction of the anterior and middle columns by strut grafting. Ebelke and co-workers[76] performed a survivorship analysis of pedicle screw instrumentation in patients with burst fractures treated with or without additional anterior decompression and strut grafting. Patients treated by anterior reconstruction had a 100% implant survivorship rate at 22 months, whereas those treated with posterior pedicle screws alone had an implant survival rate of 68% at 9 months, which dropped to 50% at 19 months. Other suggestions include the use of a hybrid hook-claw construct two to three segments above the level of injury with pedicle screws below.[42] This construct is particularly useful at the thoracolumbar junction, where fusion of an increased number of motion segments does not result in increased morbidity from loss of motion. In a prospective study treating thoracolumbar injuries with Cotrel-Dubousset segmental transpedicular fixation two levels above and one level below, Katonis and colleagues showed decreased instrument failure and sagittal collapse.[149] Mermelstein and associates performed a biomechanical study to analyze the stability of burst fractures when reinforced with hydroxyapatite cement through a transpedicular approach and stabilized with short-segment pedicle screw instrumentation. Their results showed that reconstruction with hydroxyapatite cement reduced pedicle screw bending moments by 59% in flexion and 38% in extension. They concluded that this technique may improve outcomes in burst fracture patients without the need for an anterior approach.[204] Finally, the addition of supplemental hooks at the same levels as the pedicle screws, either cephalad, caudad, or both, may significantly decrease failure rates.[46, 132] Also, the addition of pedicle screws at the level of the fracture gives three-point fixation and may prevent collapse, as with the Edwards hook-rod-sleeve construct. If this technique is used, the screws need to be angled away from the fractured end-plates.

It should also be remembered that most screw-plate systems cannot easily provide distraction or anteriorly directed forces to achieve maximal reduction and preserve anatomic sagittal alignment. Systems that use hooks or screws (or both) attached to rods are better able to achieve these goals.[288]

SURGICAL TECHNIQUE

Because many different pedicle screw fixation devices are currently available and more are in the process of

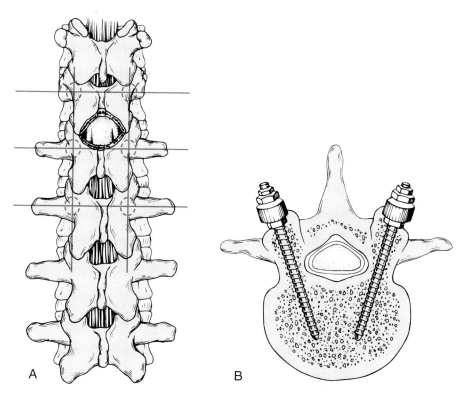

FIGURE 30–47. Proper positioning of pedicle screw instrumentation. *A,* The central portion of the pedicle can be identified by the intersection of two lines. The transverse line bisects the transverse process of each level, and the longitudinal line runs in a cephalad-to-caudal direction and bisects the facet joints. *B,* A transverse section shows the ideal location for the pedicle screws. It also indicates the proximity of the neural elements to these screws, both within and outside the spinal canal. The medial-to-lateral inclination of each of these pedicles and screws will vary, depending on the level of the spine (as outlined in the section of this chapter on anatomy). (*A* Redrawn from Leona Allison.)

development, this surgical description is general, with emphasis on proper positioning of the pedicle screws. As stated in the previous section, fixation of one pedicle above and one pedicle below the level of injury may be adequate, provided that the anterior fragmentation is minimal. If the anterior comminution is more significant, the alternatives are to extend the instrumentation to two levels above and two levels below the injury or plan to perform anterior corpectomy and fusion of the fractured vertebra at a later date to provide anterior axial support.

The patient is placed in the prone position, and a midline incision is made to expose the spinous processes, laminae, facet joints, and transverse processes of each level to be instrumented. The orientation of the pedicles is approximately −4° from sagittal at T12 and 11° from sagittal at L1, slowly increasing to 30° from sagittal at the L5 level.[285] Pedicle diameter similarly varies and is approximately 8 mm at T12, L1, L2, and L3. It increases to approximately 1 cm at L4 and almost 1.3 cm at L5. A helpful way to assess angulation from the sagittal plane is to measure it on the patient's CT scan. Pedicle diameter can also be determined from the CT scan.

The central portion of the pedicle in a cranial-to-caudal direction can be approximated by passing a line through the center of the transverse processes of the vertebral body bilaterally. This line bisects the midpoint of the pedicles. The midportion crosses the transverse process line in a medial-to-lateral direction at a point defined by a line

drawn through the facet joints[244] (Fig. 30–47A). In the lumbar spine, the mammillary process, just lateral to the facets, is useful to guide entry into the pedicle.

Once the soft tissues have been completely removed and the bone in the area exposed, a high-speed bur can be used to remove the outer cortex over the chosen entry point. An awl or 000 curette can then be used to penetrate the pedicle and the vertebral body while maintaining the appropriate inclination from the sagittal plane. Craniocaudal tilt is best discerned from a lateral scout radiograph. Intraoperative radiography or fluoroscopy can be used to assess the position. If insertion of these screws is based only on anatomic landmarks and the experience of the spinal surgeon, the chance of having a screw outside the desired boundaries of the pedicle may be as high as 30%.[270] The use of intraoperative radiographs and fluoroscopy helps decrease this risk. Each hole can be probed with an angled instrument, such as a nerve hook or depth gauge, in all four quadrants from its anterior to its posterior extent to be certain that the pedicle has been entered and the cortex has not been violated. The hole can be tapped, if necessary, for the instrumentation to be used. The pedicle screws are then inserted.

Regardless of the type of instrumentation, care should be taken to insert the screws with only two to three fingertips on the wrench or screwdriver to avoid stripping the threads within the pedicle and vertebral body. Because of the high risk of vascular and visceral injury, the anterior cortex of the vertebra should not be violated from the midthoracic region to L5, unless it is essential to increase fixation strength, as in an osteoporotic spine. Over the sacrum, it is often necessary to advance one or two threads through the anterior cortex because fixation strength increases with bicortical purchase.[164]

An additional consideration during placement of these screws is whether the plate, rod, or pedicle screw itself will violate an adjacent normal joint. The potential for this complication is determined by the basic design of the pedicle screw fixation device and cannot usually be altered by the surgeon, so it must be considered when initially selecting the pedicle screw instrumentation system.

As with all other instrumentation systems used to treat spinal fractures, achievement of reduction and normal sagittal alignment is one of the primary goals of surgical treatment. Both lordosis forces and distracting forces can be applied through short-segment pedicle screw constructs to achieve these desired outcomes (Fig. 30–48). Radiographs in both the AP and the lateral planes should be obtained with the final instrumentation system in place to be certain that the fracture is adequately reduced, sagittal spinal alignment is satisfactory, and each of the pedicle screws is in the desired position (see Fig. 30–47B).

A useful method for re-creating lordosis is placement of a screw at the level of injury. When used in conjunction with contouring of the rod, excellent three-point fixation may be achieved. Another method of restoring lordosis is to leave the caudal aspect of the rod angled at approximately 15° up from the cephalad screw (best performed with screw heads that allow angulation), with the cephalad aspect fixed to the spine. The rod is then forced down to engage the caudal screws. This technique provides distraction and lordosis of the proximal segments.

As with all other instrumentation systems, solid fusion is one of the primary goals of surgery. Adequate care should be taken to decorticate the transverse processes and the lateral aspects of the superior facets to increase the

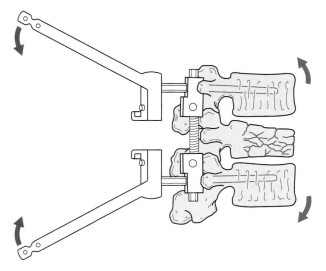

FIGURE 30–48. Application of both distraction and lordosis forces through short pedicle screw constructs is necessary to achieve normal sagittal alignment. (Redrawn from Müller, M.E.; Allgöwer, M., eds. Manual of Internal Fixation, 2nd ed. Heidelberg, Springer-Verlag, 1991.)

chance of achieving fusion. If the pedicle screw fixation system uses plates, it is important that the bone graft be inserted before application of the plates because the procedure becomes more difficult after the plates have been secured in position. Finally, a number of newer instrumentation systems are made of titanium, which allows for better postoperative imaging, particularly MRI.[77]

Posterolateral Decompression

Surgical decompression frequently equates to surgical reduction when discussing treatment of thoracic and thoracolumbar spine injuries. If complete reduction can be achieved, no other decompression is needed. Edwards and Levine showed that surgical reduction performed within 2 days of injury restores the spinal canal area by an additional 32% whereas surgery performed between 3 and 14 days after injury restores only 23%.[80, 83] They also found that little or no improvement occurs when posterior instrumentation is delayed for more than 2 weeks. Crutcher and co-workers[54] reported similar results with the use of a simple Harrington construct and achieved an approximately 50% reduction in canal clearance. The fracture pattern influences the adequacy of decompression, with Denis type A fractures having significantly better canal clearance by indirect means than Denis type B fractures. Therefore, with early surgery and better surgical reduction, the chance of needing any formal neural decompression is lessened.

The adequacy of reduction cannot be easily assessed by plain radiography. A postoperative myelo-CT scan is an effective way to assess for residual neural compression.[33, 105] If a significant abnormality is found, anterior decompression can be performed at a later date.

In addition, if anatomic realignment has been achieved, some resorption of bone from within the spinal canal will occur over the course of the next year, thereby lessening the extent of neural compression.[53] Krompinger and colleagues[168] reviewed 29 patients with injuries of the thoracic or lumbar spine treated nonoperatively; 14 had canal compromise greater than 25% on initial evaluation. Bone remodeling of the compromised canal was noted in 11 of these 14 patients, and canal compromise of less than 25% resolved completely in 4 of 8 cases. Similar results during nonoperative treatment of burst fractures have been reported by others.[41] Edwards and associates[82] noted comparable canal fragment resorption in patients treated with rod sleeve reduction and fusion, and Sjostrom and colleagues[256] noted resorption of intracanal fragments after the application of pedicle screw constructs and fusion. Willen and co-workers,[279] however, reported that patients with more than 50% canal compromise rarely had significant resorption. With these factors kept in mind, some patients in whom significant neural compression remains and is not improved by posterior instrumentation and reduction may still require late operative treatment of fractures of the thoracic or thoracolumbar spine. Posterolateral decompression has also been used at the time of posterior instrumentation.

The advantage of the posterolateral technique is that it allows stabilization of severe spine injuries, including fracture-dislocations, and at the same time allows some degree of neural decompression without requiring a second surgical procedure.[74] One disadvantage of this technique is that it necessarily requires removal of posterior and posterolateral bone and may thus further jeopardize spinal stability and eventual fusion.[16] The second major disadvantage is that it is a relatively blind procedure because the dura and neural elements lie between the surgeon and the anterior compressive tissue.

The posterolateral technique has been evaluated by Garfin and colleagues.[106] In that series, nine patients with burst fractures of the thoracic or lumbar spine were treated by posterolateral decompression and evaluated with postoperative CT scans. Postoperative CT scanning showed only one patient with bone remaining in the canal. Hardaker and co-workers[126] reported the use of bilateral transpedicular decompression with posterior instrumentation and fusion for severe burst fractures with an average canal compromise of more than 65%. Although anterior decompression would normally be required for such extreme amounts of canal compromise, only one patient in the study underwent an additional anterior procedure. Seventy-seven percent of the patients with a neurologic deficit had significant improvement, and significant kyphotic deformity had not developed in any patient at follow-up. Hu and associates[135] compared anterior decompression with transpedicular decompression in patients with incomplete neurologic deficits and found no additional benefit for anterior vertebrectomy over simple transpedicular decompression. Both treatments resulted in significant neurologic improvement when compared with a similar group of patients treated by indirect reduction maneuvers alone. Others have reported comparable results with the use of transpedicular decompression.[268] In contrast, Lemons and colleagues[172] compared direct decompression by a posterolateral route with indirect reduction and found no significant differences in improvement in canal clearance or neurologic function. They concluded that the posterolateral transpedicular approach is of questionable value for the treatment of burst fractures.

SURGICAL TECHNIQUE

Posterolateral decompression is performed as part of a posterior stabilizing operation in patients with thoracic, thoracolumbar, or lumbar spine injuries. Before the instrumentation system is applied and before any posterolateral decompression, the CT transverse sections at the level of the injury should be studied to determine which side of the spinal canal has the more severe neural compression. The instrumentation should be inserted first on the side with the smaller amount of neural compression and corrective forces then applied to reduce the spine injury. In most cases, these forces include a combination of distraction and lordosis with three- or four-point fixation and the force vector directed anteriorly at the level of injury.

Attention is then directed to the side of the spine that is free of instrumentation (Fig. 30–49A). A laminotomy is performed at the level of maximal neural compression, which is most commonly the area between the pedicles of the fractured vertebra. At this level, the adjacent spinous processes are each trimmed and the intervening ligamentum flavum is excised. Five millimeters of adjacent bone is removed, including portions of the cephalic and caudal laminae, as well as the medial portion of the facet joint at that level.

The posterior edge of the fracture (anterior to the dura) can be palpated with an angled dural elevator (e.g., Frazier elevator) to assess the degree of residual canal compromise. The laminotomy should be extended distally at least to the inferior edge of the pedicle. Once the medial border of the pedicle is identified, a power bur is used to drill into the central portion of the pedicle with all cortices left intact (see Fig. 30–49B). A thin rongeur or curette is then used to remove the medial cortex of the pedicle, with care taken to preserve the nerve root exiting below it (see Fig. 30–49C). A trough is cut 1 cm into the vertebral body anterior to the medial portion of the pedicle that has been thinned. Reverse-angle curettes can be inserted through this opening, and any bone fragments compressing the anterior neural elements can be impacted into the vertebral body or brought out through the lateral trough previously made (see Fig. 30–45D). Mimatsu and co-workers[205] have designed a variety of impactors specifically for use in the transpedicular approach. It is possible to extend this decompression slightly past midline through this unilateral exposure (see Fig. 30–49E).

If the decompression is adequate on both sides of the canal, no further decompression is needed. If further decompression is needed on the side that has already been instrumented, a second rod is inserted on the side already decompressed, the instrumentation is removed, transpedicular decompression is performed on the first side, and the instrumentation is reinserted.

Anterior Transthoracic Decompression and Fusion

Anterior transthoracic decompression and fusion may be used for the treatment of thoracic and thoracolumbar spine fractures (T2 to L1), either as a single operative procedure or in conjunction with a posterior stabilization procedure. It is most indicated in patients with maximal anterior neural compression, patients with an incomplete spinal cord injury, and those with minimal instability, as well as for the delayed treatment of injuries, including late post-traumatic deformities[123–125, 131] (see Fig. 30–26).

This transthoracic approach for trauma was first described by Paul and colleagues,[220] and detailed techniques along with long-term results of this treatment have been published by Bohlman and associates.[29, 30] In a review of acute injuries of the upper thoracic spine with paralysis, eight patients were treated by anterior decompression and fusion for residual neural compression. All had reached a plateau in terms of neurologic recovery at the time of anterior decompression. Postoperatively, five patients were able to walk without aid, two recovered partially and were able to walk with crutches and braces, and one patient improved but remained unable to ambulate. No patient lost neurologic function as a result of this procedure, and solid fusion developed in all patients, even though three had previously undergone laminectomy.

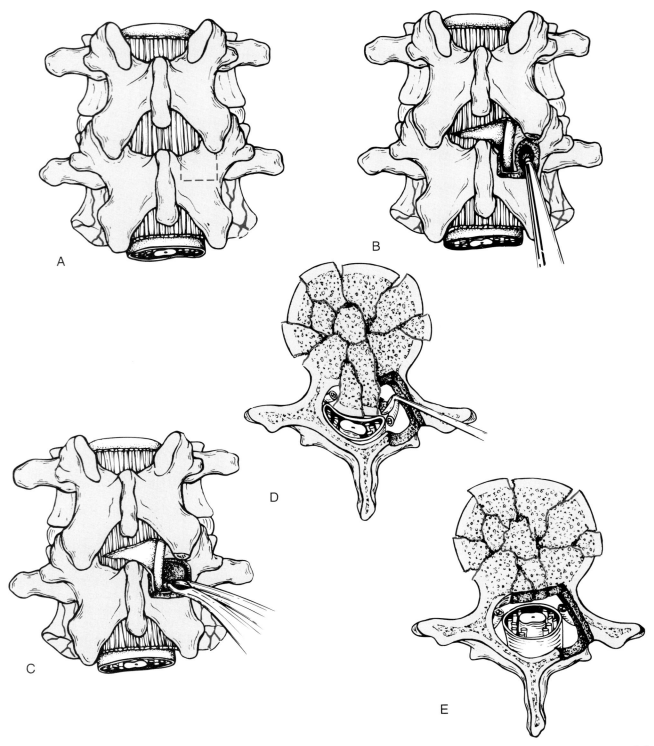

Figure 30–49. Technique of posterolateral decompression of the spinal canal. *A,* A posterior view of the spine shows the region of exposure and the amount of pedicle resection required to achieve posterolateral decompression. Care should be taken to not cut inferolaterally across the pars interarticularis. *B,* The ligamentum flavum has been resected at the level of injury, and the dura has been exposed. Bone is resected laterally up to the medial extent of the pedicle and caudally to the inferior extent of the pedicle. A bur is used to make a hole in the central portion of the pedicle, with the hole proceeding anteriorly toward the vertebral body. A circumferential rim of cortical bone is left in place. The nerve root is shown medial to the pedicle and exiting below the pedicle. Care should be taken to not injure this nerve root. *C,* The medial wall of the pedicle is removed with a rongeur such as a pituitary rongeur. *D,* A transverse section shows the hole burred down through the pedicle and into the vertebral body. A reverse-angle curette is used to tap bone out of the spinal canal and into the trough that has been drilled out of the vertebral body. Large bone fragments may also be pulled out through this lateral trough. Care must be taken to not hook the anterior aspect of the dura. *E,* A transverse section shows the final result after decompression. By performing unilateral posterolateral transpedicle decompression, it is usually possible to adequately decompress slightly past the midline.

None was augmented with any type of instrumentation either anteriorly or posteriorly. No data were given concerning residual angulation at the site of injury.[30]

Most published series of transthoracic decompression for treatment of spinal trauma review either patients with minimal to moderate levels of instability or those who are no longer in the acute stage after their injury. In the latter group, some healing with partial stabilization may already have occurred. Gurr and colleagues[121] showed in an animal corpectomy model that the strength of the spine is markedly reduced after corpectomy in comparison to the strength of an intact spine. This reduction in strength is true for axial loading, flexion loading, and rotation testing. The addition of an iliac graft still allows three times the displacement with axial compression, as well as displacement with flexion testing, and torsional stiffness is less than one third that of an intact spine. In trauma patients with significant posterior disruption and an anterior corpectomy, additional instability is probably present. For this reason, uninstrumented anterior transthoracic decompression plus fusion is rarely indicated and should be reserved for patients with significant neural compression and minimal instability. As the degree of instability increases, it becomes necessary to supplement the anterior decompression and fusion with either anterior instrumentation or posterior stabilization. In severe injuries associated with three-column disruption, some authors recommend supplementation of anterior instrumentation with posterior instrumentation and spinal fusion.[19, 20] Almost all patients should have postoperative immobilization in a TLSO, except perhaps for those stabilized with rigid posterior segmental fixation devices.

Beginning in the late 1980s, the development of more sophisticated anterior plate systems has improved the quality of anterior fixation in the thoracic and thoracolumbar spine.[15, 158, 167] However, anterior plate fixation to L4, L5, and S1 remains problematic. Most of the current systems are based on the principle of two screws per level, with one screw placed posteriorly, parallel to the posterior cortical wall of the vertebral body, and the second angled obliquely from anterior in the body to posterior. This triangular arrangement improves pull-out strength. In addition, in most systems an element of compression or distraction can be applied between the upper and the lower segments of fixation before fixing the bolt or screw to the plate. This technique may improve incorporation of the graft anteriorly, as well as the stability of the construct.

Kaneda and associates reported their results in treating 150 consecutive patients with thoracolumbar burst fractures by anterior decompression and stabilization with the Kaneda device (see Fig. 30–26). After a mean follow-up of 8 years, radiographs showed a successful fusion rate of 93%. Ten patients with a pseudoarthrosis were successfully managed by posterior spinal instrumentation and fusion. They believe that all their pseudoarthroses occurred in patients who had poor placement of the anterior strut graft. Kaneda thought that the success of his device relied directly on load transmission through a strong tricortical iliac crest graft, with placement of the tricortical portion beyond the contralateral pedicle. The mean percent canal obstruction preoperatively was 47% and, postoperatively, 2%. Neurologic function improved by at least one grade in 95% of patients. Breakage of the implant occurred in nine patients, with no iatrogenically induced neurologic deficits. Of the patients who were employed before the injury, 96% returned to work. The average kyphosis was 19° preoperatively, 7° immediately postoperatively, and 8° at follow-up.[147] In a separate report,[146] Kaneda and co-workers used the Kaneda device after anterior decompression in patients with neurologic deficits caused by post-traumatic kyphosis. All patients reported excellent results. Gardner and associates[102] used the contoured anterior spinal plate (CASP) system for a variety of conditions, including acute burst fractures, and had a fusion rate of 100%. McGuire reported 14 unstable three-column injuries treated by anterior decompression and stabilization with the University Plate (Acromed Corp.). Radiographically, vertebral height was maintained, and no measurable graft subsidence or kyphosis developed. He reported no hardware failures and one nonunion treated successfully with a posterior compression construct.[201] Okuyama and associates reviewed 45 patients with unstable burst fractures treated by anterior decompression and stabilization. They reported 84% with no or minimal pain, a 74% return-to-work rate, and minimal loss of the kyphotic angle until fusion.[213] Other recently published studies have also shown similar results with anterior decompression and stabilization for thoracolumbar burst fractures.[115, 190]

Most recent studies reporting the results of anterior decompression and stabilization have used rib or iliac crest bone grafts (or both) for their fusions. Finkelstein and associates reported the results of a prospective cohort study to evaluate the use of cortical allograft bone for anterior spine reconstruction in thoracolumbar fractures. They packed the medullary canal of tibial allografts with autogenous bone from the corpectomy. Twenty-two patients underwent anterior surgery alone, and 14 patients had both anterior and posterior surgery. In the latter group, posterior instrumentation was combined with autogenous bone grafting. They reported an overall fusion rate of 81%, with a trend suggesting that patients undergoing anterior surgery alone had a higher rate of nonunion, 5 of 22, than did those undergoing anterior and posterior instrumentation, 2 of 14. In addition, of eight patients who had loss of correction or loss of stability after anterior fixation alone, three required revision surgery with the addition of posterior instrumentation.[94]

Other authors have noted high complication rates with anterior fixation (30%), as well as significant loss of the initial deformity correction over time (50%).[121] Yuan and co-workers,[284] reporting on their results with the Syracuse I-Plate, cautioned that osteoporosis and significant posterior column disruption are relative contraindications to anterior fixation.[15]

SURGICAL TECHNIQUE

The patient should be intubated with a double-lumen tube for approaches above T10 so that the left and right main stem bronchi may be ventilated separately; this tube allows for later collapse of one lung to provide adequate exposure of the spine. From T10 distally, a single-lumen tube is adequate. For exposure of T10 and above, the patient is usually turned to the left lateral decubitus position. The right side of the chest is chosen as the side for surgery, assuming that the patient does not have any contraindications or exposure-related considerations. This position avoids any encroachment on the heart and great vessels, as would be encountered in a left-sided approach, especially in the middle and upper thoracic spine regions. A left-sided approach can be chosen if necessary, but prominent internal fixation should not be used from this side.

Special care should be taken to place a pad just distal to the patient's downside axilla to prevent a stretch palsy of the brachial plexus. Also, an arm support should be used to hold the upper part of the arm in a neutral position: 90° forward flexion at the shoulder, neutral abduction adduction, and almost straight at the elbow. Both arms should be adequately protected and padded, especially in the region of the radial nerve in the posterior aspect of the upper part of the arm and near the ulnar nerve at the elbow. Forward flexion of more than 90° at the shoulder should be avoided to minimize the risk of brachial plexus palsy. Tape can be securely placed across the patient, both at the level of the greater trochanter and across the shoulder, and then affixed to the table. A beanbag placed under the patient is also useful to help maintain this position.

The patient's entire right flank, anterior part of the chest, and posterior portion of the torso should be prepared from just inferior to the level of the axilla to inferior to the lateral aspect of the iliac crest. Care should be taken to prepare the skin to the midline anteriorly and beyond the midline posteriorly. Such preparation minimizes the chance of disorientation during the operation and also makes it possible to perform anterior transthoracic decompression and fusion and posterior instrumentation and fusion simultaneously, if necessary.

From T6 through T10, the incision should be made directly over the rib of the same number as the fractured vertebra (Fig. 30–50A) or one level proximal to it. It is technically easier to work distally than proximally. Removal of a rib one level higher works well, especially if the corpectomy involves more than one level. For fractures above T6, the skin incision should extend over the T6 rib anteriorly and laterally. Posteriorly, it should extend to the inferior tip of the scapula and then curve gently more cephalad, halfway between the medial border of the scapula and the midline spinous processes (see Fig. 30–50B). For exposure of T11, T12, or L1, the incision should be made over the T10 rib to simplify wound closure.

The incision should be made through skin and subcutaneous tissue down to the deep fascia. From T6 through T10, the deep fascia and underlying muscles are incised in line with the skin incision down to the rib, which is stripped subperiosteally on both its outer and inner surfaces. The surgeon should be cautious in the use of electrocautery near the neurovascular bundle. A rib cutter is used to cut the rib at the costovertebral angle posteriorly and at the costochondral junction anteriorly. The remaining inner periosteum is then incised over the length of the rib bed. For T2–T5, it is important to note that the long thoracic nerve courses in the midaxillary line from the region of the axilla to its innervation of the serratus anterior muscle. Rather than cut this nerve and lose innervation to the more caudal portion of the muscle, it is preferable to detach the serratus anterior muscle from

the anterior chest wall and reflect it cephalad. This technique can be performed to provide exposure up to the T3 rib, with additional exposure achieved by mobilization of the scapula. Division of the dorsal scapular muscles, rhomboids, and trapezius allows the scapula to be elevated and displaced laterally from the midline. This maneuver offers a simple method of gaining a more extensive thoracotomy through the bed of the third rib.

After the chest has been opened, the surgeon should place a hand in the chest in the midlateral line and count the cephalic and caudal ribs because that is more accurate than counting the ribs outside the chest wall. The surgeon should make certain that the rib removed is the rib that was planned for removal. It should also be verified that the total number of ribs corresponds to that seen on a good-quality AP radiograph of the thoracic spine.

A self-retaining thoracotomy retractor is then inserted over moistened sponges in such a manner that the neurovascular bundle of the cephalic rib and the neurovascular bundle from the removed rib are not compressed by the retractor. The chest retractor is opened slowly to minimize the chance of fracture of adjacent ribs. At this point, the lung can be deflated on the ipsilateral side to provide adequate exposure to the spine.

The spine can be seen and palpated within the chest cavity. It is covered by the relatively thin and translucent parietal pleura. The rib base of the previously resected rib is traced down to its costovertebral junction, and with the knowledge that each rib inserts at the cephalic quarter of its own vertebra, the levels of each of the vertebral bodies and discs can be determined. At this point, a spinal needle should be placed in a disc and a radiograph obtained to definitively identify the levels.

The parietal pleura is incised halfway between the vertebral neural foramina posteriorly and the anteriorly located azygos vein and inferior vena cava. After division of the parietal pleura one level above and one level below the vertebral body of interest, the segmental vessels are identified in the midportion of the vertebral body at each of these three levels. These segmental vessels should be isolated and either tied or ligated with vascular clips. The vessels should be cut over the anterior third of the vertebral bodies so that they do not interfere with any collateral flow to the spinal cord, which enters the segmental vessels near the neuroforamen. With a small sponge on a clamp or a periosteal elevator, the segmental vessels and parietal pleura can be swept anteriorly and posteriorly to expose the vertebral bodies and discs in an extraperiosteal fashion. Blunt dissection can then be carried out in this same plane, with a sponge on the surgeon's finger used to expose the opposite side of the vertebral body at the site of primary interest. At this time, a malleable or cobra retractor can be inserted between the exposed spine and the parietal pleura that has been dissected anteriorly (see Fig. 30–50C). The retractor protects the esophagus and great vessels during excision of the vertebral body.

Because the rib extends anteriorly over the lateral aspect of the vertebral body, it is necessary to cut it just anterior to the neural foramina. The discs above and below the vertebra to be resected can be removed with a scalpel and rongeurs (see Fig. 30–50D). The vertebral body may then be removed with a rongeur, as well as gouges, osteotomes, and power burs (see Fig. 30–50E). Loupe magnification and a headlamp should be used for this procedure. In the case of an acute fracture with many loose pieces of bone, a large curette can be used to remove the bulk of the vertebral body. As the posterior margin of the vertebral body is approached, red cancellous bone begins to be replaced by white cortical bone, which represents the posterior cortex of the vertebral body. A high-speed bur may then be used to perforate the posterior cortex at the point of minimal neural compression (see Fig. 30–50F). Another technique to gain access to the spinal canal is to use a small Kerrison rongeur to enter through the adjacent disc space. Alternatively, one can begin by removing the pedicle and following the nerve root to the spinal cord. Once a point of entry into the spinal canal has been made, the remainder of the

posterior cortex of the vertebral body can be removed with appropriately shaped rongeurs and curettes (see Fig. 30–50G and H). Removal is often facilitated with the use of fine-angled curettes to allow the surgeon to push or pull the posterior cortex away from the spinal canal. This decompression should be performed from pedicle to pedicle to ensure that no spinal cord compression remains (see Fig. 30–50I). If the bone has been removed and the posterior longitudinal ligament does not bulge anteriorly, the ligament should be removed while at the same time looking for other disc or bone fragments that may be causing continued compression of the dura. At the end of the decompression, the ligament or dura, or both, should be bulging anteriorly.

A trough can be cut into the vertebral bodies through the end-plates above and below the area of decompression

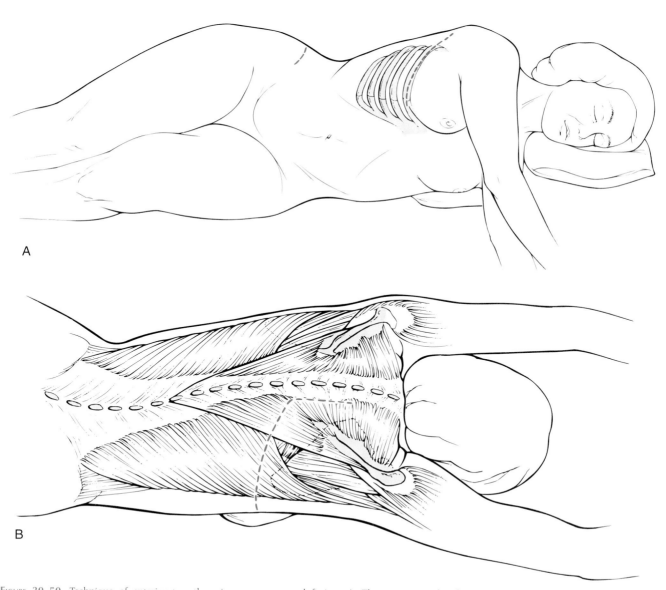

FIGURE 30–50. Technique of anterior transthoracic corpectomy and fusion. *A,* The patient is placed in a straight decubitus position with the shoulders extended forward 90°, neutral in terms of abduction and adduction, and with the elbows straight. Care is taken to protect the downside brachial plexus by using a pad just distal to the axilla. The *dotted line* over the rib represents the incision placed one level above that of the spinal fracture. *B,* If the incision is used to expose the region above the T6 rib, the posterior limb of the incision is extended cephalad halfway between the medial border of the scapula and the spinous processes. All the intervening muscles down to the chest wall are divided and tagged for later repair.

Illustration continued on following page

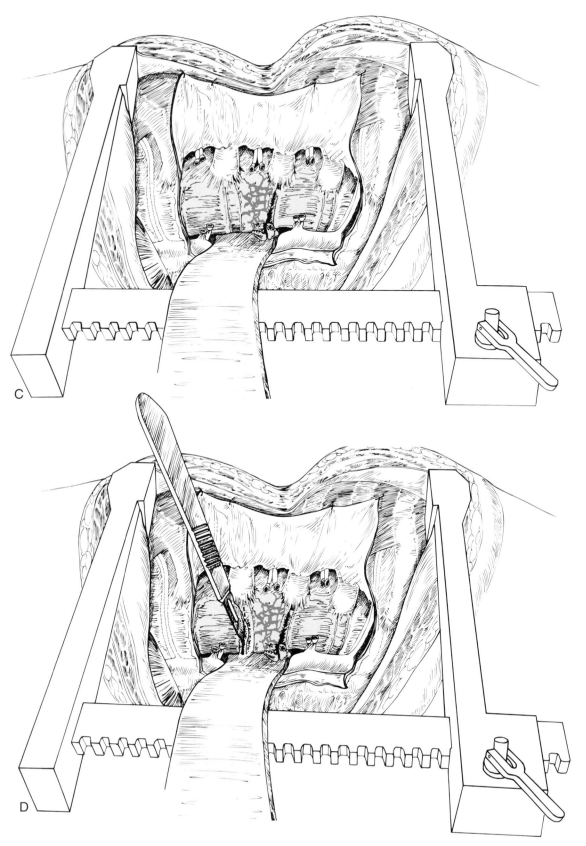

FIGURE 30–50. *Continued.* *C,* After the thoracic cavity has been entered, a self-retaining chest retractor is inserted. The parietal pleura is incised halfway between the anterior great vessels and the posterior neural foramina, and the segmental vessels are ligated at this same level. The vertebra to be excised, as well as one vertebra above and one vertebra below, is exposed. Extraperiosteal dissection provides the best plane. A malleable retractor is placed on the opposite side of the spine and connected to the self-retaining chest retractor with a clamp. This malleable retractor serves to protect the great vessels during the vertebral corpectomy. *D,* A scalpel and rongeur are used to remove the discs above and below the level of the vertebral fracture.

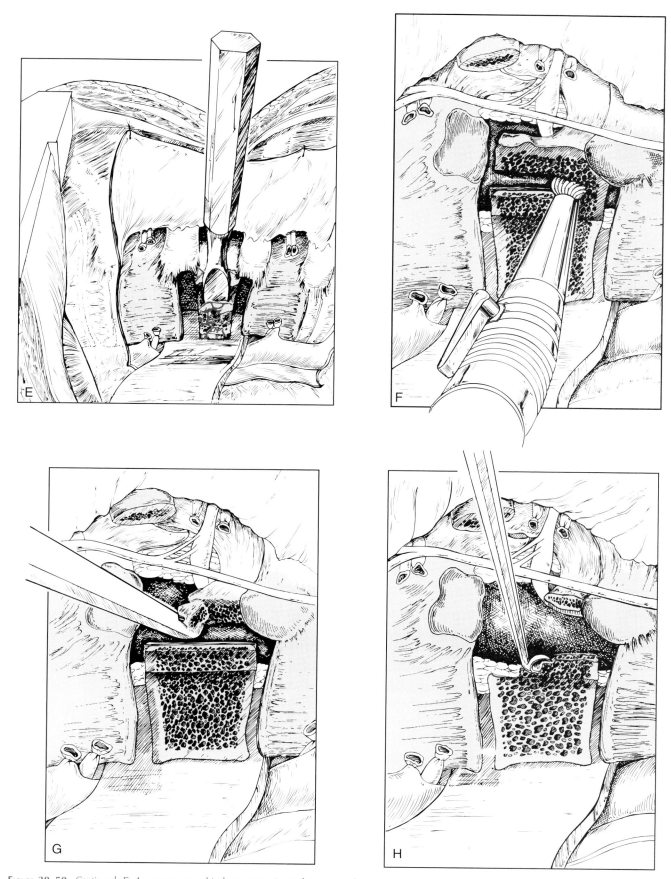

FIGURE 30–50. *Continued. E,* An osteotome, chisel, or gouge is used to excise the vertebral body back to its posterior cortex. Special care is taken to originally position the patient exactly in the straight decubitus position. During resection of the vertebral body with these instruments, each of the cuts is made perpendicular to the floor. These instruments can be used as long as red cancellous bone is encountered. As soon as white cortical bone is observed, these instruments should no longer be used. *F,* A high-speed bur can be used to perforate the posterior vertebral body cortex and gain access to the spinal canal. When the neural compression is significant, a diamond-tipped bur can be used to minimize the chance of dural or neural injury. *G,* Downbiting 90° Kerrison rongeurs are used to remove bone on the most superficial portion of the vertebral body. *H,* The bone from the spinal canal on the far side of the vertebral body is carefully impacted with reverse-angle curettes.

Illustration continued on following page

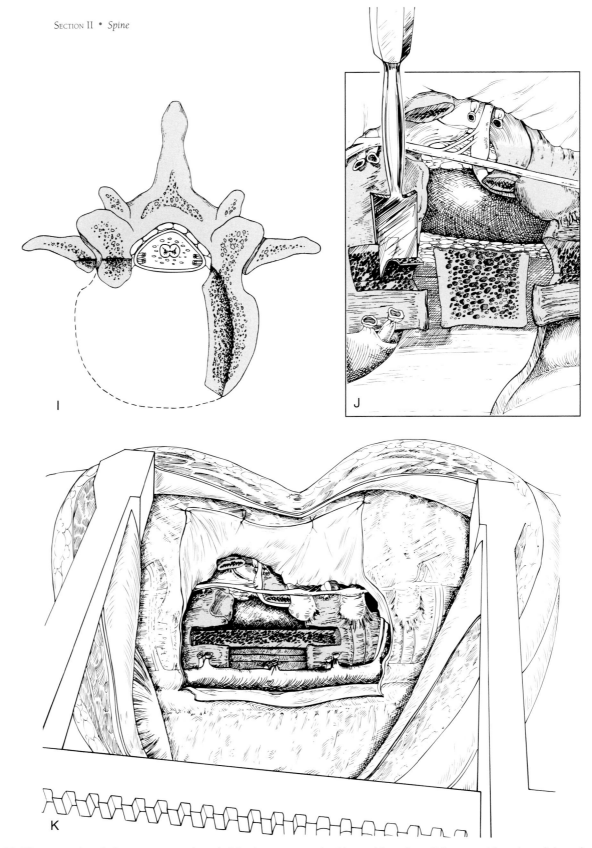

FIGURE 30–50. *Continued. I,* The bone resection at the end of the decompression should extend from the pedicle on one side to the pedicle on the opposite side. It is easy to underestimate the extent of bone removal necessary to achieve this goal. At the end of the neural decompression, the dura should bulge anteriorly in a uniform fashion from the end-plate of the vertebra above to the end-plate of the vertebra below and from pedicle to pedicle. If the dura does not bulge out concentrically, the surgeon should check for residual neural compression. *J,* After the corpectomy and resection of the disc above and below the level of fracture have been accomplished, a trough is cut into the vertebral body above and below the corpectomy. If any degree of osteoporosis is present, the trough should be cut through the cancellous bone up to the next intact end-plate at the superior end of the cephalad vertebra and the inferior aspect of the caudal vertebra. A ridge of bone should be preserved at the posterior aspect of these adjacent vertebrae to prevent migration of the bone graft into the spinal canal. *K,* At the end of the neural decompression and fusion, the space between the bone graft and the dura and neural elements should be adequate to minimize the chance of producing any iatrogenic neural compression. This illustration shows three strips of rib being used as bone graft, but a single, large piece of iliac crest can also be used and may actually provide a stronger anterior strut.

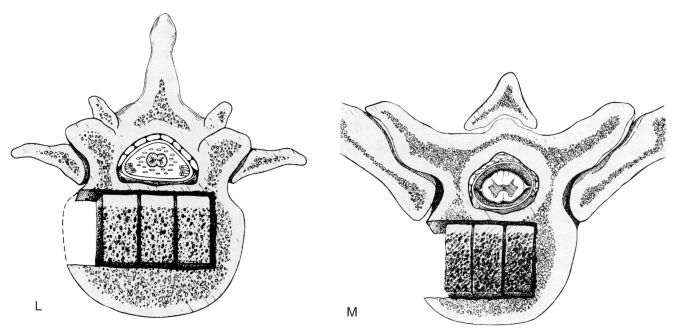

FIGURE 30–50. *Continued.* A transverse section at the vertebrae above (L) and below (M) the level of the corpectomy should reveal an adequate posterior rim of cortical bone to prevent migration of the bone graft into the spinal canal and an anterior cortical and cancellous rim of bone to prevent dislodgment of the bone graft.

(see Fig. 30–50*J*), but creation of a trough can weaken stabilization with the graft and is not routinely recommended. Alternatively, all the cartilage can be removed from the end-plates, but care must be taken to maintain cortical integrity of the end-plates. Appropriate bone graft is then obtained for insertion across this level of decompression. The patient's own iliac crest may be harvested; a tricortical bone graft provides maximal support. Another option, particularly if the injury is associated with minimal instability and the patient's rib is of adequate strength, is to impact three tiers of rib graft into this trough while an assistant pushes on the patient's gibbus to minimize the deformity (see Fig. 30–50*K*). Alternatively, fresh frozen corticocancellous allograft (iliac crest or distal end of the femur) can be used with good fusion success anteriorly; the use of metal or composite cages filled with autograft is also another good option. At the end of the decompression and bone grafting, adequate space should be left between the neural elements and the bone graft (see Fig. 30–50*K*), and a posterior ridge should be present on the vertebra both cephalad and caudad to the decompression to prevent migration of the bone graft toward the neural elements (see Fig. 30–50*L* and *M*).

After the corpectomy is completed, an appropriately sized plate is selected to center the two screws at the level above and below the corpectomy as closely as possible on the adjacent bodies. A template (if supplied) is used to place the drill holes parallel to the posterior cortex of the vertebral body so that they accept screws or bolts in that location; the screws or bolts are commonly used to provide compression or distraction. Care must be taken to precisely understand the orientation of the patient on the operating table and the resulting direction of drilling. A bicortical hole is drilled. It is then depth-gauged to accept the proper length screw or bolt. The bolts are screwed tightly into position and may then be used to apply distraction to the interspace, thereby achieving restoration of body height at the injured level. An appropriately sized tricortical iliac bone graft can be fashioned to fit into the interspace. Placement of the graft should be slightly biased anteriorly in the corpectomy defect. The distraction can then be released and a plate of proper size selected so that it does not impinge on the open disc spaces above and below the stabilized levels. The plate is placed over the bolts and the nuts provisionally placed on the bolts. Slight compressive force is applied across the reconstructed level, and the nuts are tightened down to maintain position. Finally, the two anterior screw holes are drilled and the screws placed into position to complete the construct.

The malleable retractor is removed, and hemostasis is obtained before closure. The parietal pleura is reapproximated with the use of absorbable suture material. One or two large chest tubes are inserted. The thoracotomy is closed with sutures placed above the cephalic rib and below the caudal rib, with care taken to avoid the neurovascular bundle immediately beneath the caudal rib. A rib approximator is used to close the chest wall defect, and the pericostal sutures are tied. All the muscles are sutured back to their original positions, including the serratus anterior if it was detached from the chest wall.

If the spine injury was relatively stable and is at a level of the spine that can be adequately braced with an orthosis, the patient may be mobilized while wearing the brace. The brace is worn until solid union is demonstrated radiographically. If the spinal fracture was judged to be moderately or severely unstable, the anterior procedure should be combined with posterior instrumentation (usually in compression) and fusion to allow early mobilization. As an alternative, anterior instrumentation can be used to supplement the anterior decompression and fusion, provided that the instability is only moderate (Fig. 30–51).

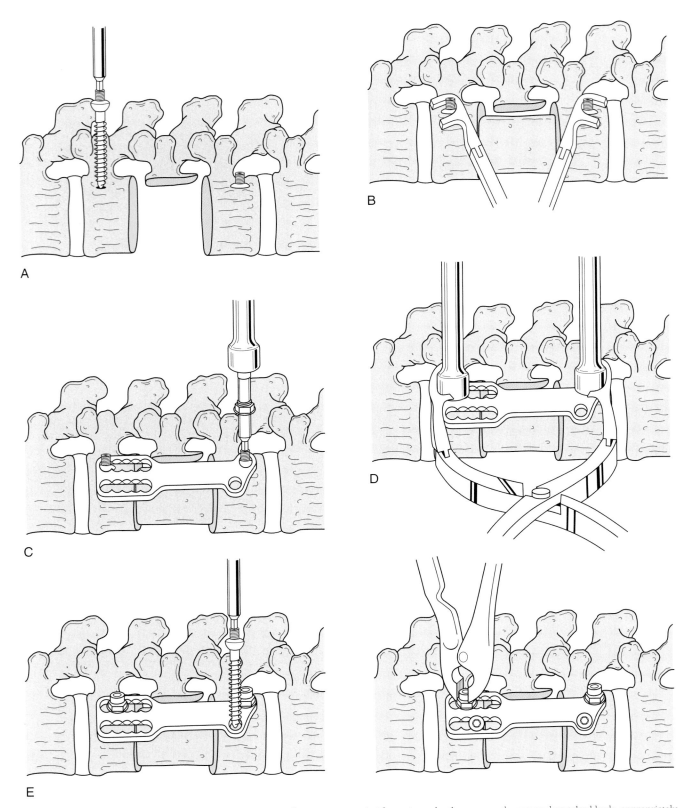

A

B

C

D

E

Figure 30–51. Technique for anterior spinal instrumentation after corpectomy. *A,* After using a depth gauge on the exposed vertebral body, appropriately sized screw lengths are selected to engage the opposite cortex of the vertebral body. The bolts are placed parallel to the adjacent end-plate to avoid intrusion into the disc space above or below the corpectomy site. *B,* Distraction is applied against the bolts to allow easy insertion of the strut graft into the corpectomy site. *C,* Determination of the proper length of plate with a template is important to avoid impingement of the superior or inferior disc space. Locking nuts are applied and provisionally tightened. *D,* Compressive force is applied and the locking nuts tightened down firmly. *E,* Finally, two anterior screws are placed and the nuts are crimped down to prevent possible backing out or loosening. (*A–E,* Redrawn with permission from Zdeblick, T.A. Z-Plate–ATL Anterior Fixation System: Surgical Technique. Sofamor Danek Group, Inc. All rights reserved.)

COMPLICATIONS

With the correct application of currently available spinal instrumentation, it is possible to stabilize and anatomically correct most disrupted spinal columns. However, these procedures are not risk free and may be associated with major complications. This section does not address all complications related to spinal surgery, but focuses on those associated with the treatments described in this chapter. Certain complications such as death, deep vein thrombosis, and pulmonary embolism, though intimately related to surgery, are not peculiar to spine surgery and are therefore not discussed here. Other complications such as iliac crest bone graft donor site morbidity are common to all spinal surgeries.[134, 169] It cannot be emphasized strongly enough that many potential intraoperative complications may be avoided, or their severity reduced, by careful preoperative planning. Accurate identification of the mechanism of injury and selection of the appropriate instrumentation and levels constitute the first critical step. However, despite detailed planning, surgical complications may still occur.

Neurologic Deterioration

Neurologic deterioration can occur before initiation of definitive treatment. Gertzbein[111] reported a 3.4% incidence of new or increased neurologic deficit after patients were admitted to trauma centers. He noted, however, that this group of patients had a significantly increased return of neurologic function after initiation of treatment in comparison to those who initially had a neurologic deficit. For patients whose neurologic function deteriorates after the initial evaluation, surgical treatment is recommended. In addition, progressive deformity with associated late neurologic deterioration may develop in fractures managed nonoperatively, even if initially stable.[114] Neurologic deficit occurring during or after treatment is one of the most serious complications associated with the surgical treatment of spinal injuries. The reported incidence is approximately 1%.[175] Neurologic deterioration may be associated with overdistraction, overcompression, direct injury resulting from the introduction of instrumentation into the spinal canal, or loss of position or reduction.

Overdistraction can be reduced to a minimum, or its possibility anticipated, by careful preoperative assessment of the mechanism of injury and prediction of the presence of an intact anterior longitudinal ligament. With this ligament intact and with proper contouring of the posterior instrumentation system to place the spine in some degree of lordosis and the anterior longitudinal ligament under tension, overdistraction can usually be avoided. MRI may provide useful information concerning the status of the anterior longitudinal ligament before any reduction requiring distraction.[36, 155] Neurologic injury related to compression instrumentation can generally be avoided if this construct is used primarily when the posterior cortex of the involved vertebral bodies is intact and the mechanism of injury does not strongly suggest an accompanying discal injury, which may frequently occur with flexion-distraction injuries (Fig. 30–52).

Segmental wires, sublaminar hooks, and pedicle screws can all provide significant intrusion into the spinal canal and transiently or permanently injure or compress the spinal cord or nerve roots. Proper positioning of the instrumentation and awareness of this complication may reduce the incidence of occurrence but cannot completely eliminate it.

During instrumentation, if evoked potentials deteriorate, if an intraoperative wake-up test is not achieved successfully, or if radiographs show overdistraction or overcompression, the instrumentation system should be altered. The alteration may be as simple as relieving some degree of the distraction or compression or removing one or two segmental wires. Alternatively, it may be necessary to remove the entire implanted system, insert a different instrumentation system, or leave it out altogether. The injury pattern, the preceding portion of the procedure, and co-morbid conditions may affect this decision.

Neurologic deterioration observed in the postoperative period may be related to disc herniation, loss of reduction, spinal cord edema, hematoma, or some combination of these complications. Immediate study with myelography, CT scanning, or MRI should be considered, and the patient should be returned to the operating room as necessary to relieve any neural compression.

INJURY RESULTING FROM INSERTION OF PEDICLE SCREWS

The spinal nerves are particularly susceptible to injury if the pedicle is violated medially or inferiorly. In addition, a screw that is too long can transgress the anterior cortex of the vertebral body and injure a major vascular structure.

The risk of neural damage can be minimized if the surgeon is aware of the spinal anatomy and familiar with the process of localizing and entering the pedicle. Careful identification of the pedicle and proper screw placement under radiographic control help minimize potential injuries. In earlier studies, some authors reported a 10% to 20% rate of inaccurate pedicle screw placement, even in well-controlled environments. This rate reportedly increased to as high as 41% in the thoracic spine.[254] It may also be increased with deformity and instability. Fortunately, not all errant screws lead to clinical consequences.

Neural damage can result from direct contact by a screw or by a drill, curette, or tap. Late screw cutout through the pedicle may also result in nerve damage.[26] If a postoperative radiculopathy is noted, CT evaluation of the screw and bone should be performed, with consideration of screw removal if the results are positive. However, stability issues must also be considered when making these decisions. Rose and associates described a technique involving persistently electrified pedicle stimulation instruments, which can be used to detect whether the pedicle screws have fractured or broached the cortical bone during placement. This technique may help confirm intraosseous placement of pedicle screws and prevent neurologic injury.[240]

Kothe and colleagues simulated pedicle fractures in an in vitro model to determine the effect on multidirectional stability when pedicle instrumentation is used. After simulation of an intraoperative pedicle fracture, the results of three-dimensional flexibility testing showed a significant

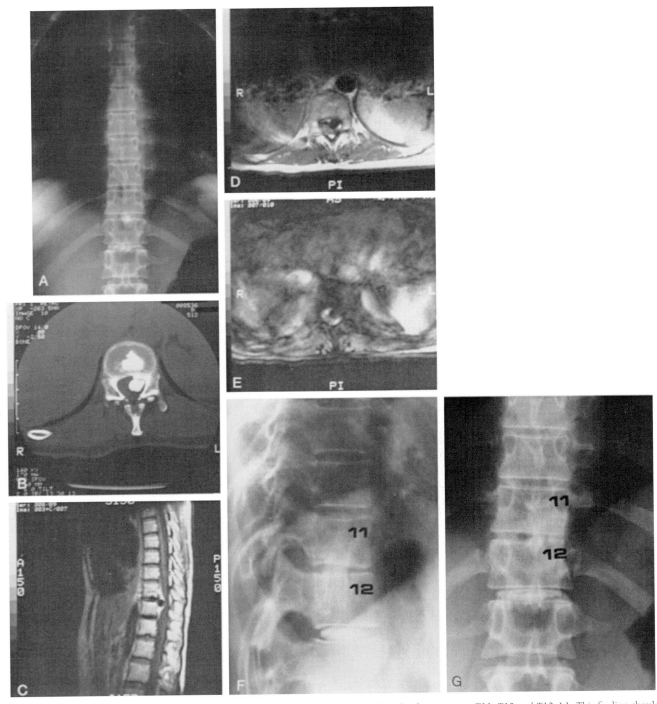

FIGURE 30–52. *A,* An anteroposterior (AP) radiograph shows abnormal calcification within the disc spaces at T11–T12 and T12–L1. This finding should arouse expectations of detecting a herniated thoracic disc in this symptomatic patient. *B,* A computed tomographic (CT) scan at T11–T12 documents a large herniation of a calcified disc fragment with significant compromise of the spinal canal. *C,* Midsagittal, T1-weighted magnetic resonance imaging (MRI) confirms the significant extent of extrusion of the T11–T12 disc. *D,* T1-weighted transverse MRI correlates well with the CT scan and again shows the severe extent of spinal canal compromise. *E,* T2-weighted transverse MRI best shows the extent of spinal cord compression and actual spinal cord deformation secondary to herniation of the disc. *F,* This patient was treated by transthoracic T11–T12 discectomy and fusion. *G,* A follow-up AP radiograph confirms satisfactory alignment of the spine.

decrease in axial rotation and lateral bending stability provided by the instrumentation.[163]

If screw loosening occurs, loss of correction may develop before the fusion heals. Loss of fixation can result from errant placement of a screw, fracture of the pedicle, inadequate purchase of the screw into bone, poor bone quality, or inadequate screw size.[194] Pedicle fracture may occur if too large a screw is placed into the pedicle or the screw is driven out of the pedicular cortex. Sjostrom and associates[255] used CT scans to study the pedicles of patients after removal of pedicle screw instrumentation following successful fusion for burst fractures. They found that 65% of instrumented pedicles increased in width, as did 85% of those in which the screw diameter was greater than 65% of the diameter of the pedicle. This result, however, may not have clinical consequences. The authors emphasized the importance of correct screw size to avoid injury to the pedicle and subsequent loosening of the implant.

Occasionally, with severe deformity, maximal bone–screw interface strength is required and necessitates placement of the screw deep within the vertebral body or through the anterior cortex. This situation is more common in a patient with an osteoporotic spine than in one with normal bone density. The need for anterior cortical fixation must be balanced against the risk of injury to the anterior vascular structures. This problem may be handled by adding screws at other levels or by augmenting the fixation with polymethyl methacrylate (rarely used in trauma). However, in fractures, alternatives are usually available, including noninstrumented fusion, bedrest, and alteration of the instrumentation to a system with laminar fixation.

INJURY RESULTING FROM PLACEMENT OF LAMINAR HOOKS

Dislodgment of laminar hooks occurs most commonly in the lower lumbar segments. However, proximal dislodgment also occurs, particularly when the reduction is inadequate and viscoelastic properties are not taken into consideration after the initial distraction. If hooks are not properly seated or are placed into laminar bone rather than deep to the anterior lamina or if the rod is not properly contoured, the hooks may cut out, fracture the lamina, or angulate into the underlying neural tissue. The incidence of neurologic complications after placement of hooks and rods is reportedly about 1%. The use of anatomic hooks helps limit some of these problems. Hook dislodgment may be associated with excessive force, weak bone, or technical errors (e.g., faulty surgical technique, improper implant selection, improper contouring). Edwards and Levine[80] found that dislodgment of distal hooks placed proximal to L4 occurred in only 4% of their large series of patients, but that percentage almost doubled at L4 and tripled at L5.

To avoid these complications, the proper instrumentation should be selected, particularly one with a more anatomic design. Adequate rod contouring or the addition of a rod sleeve is useful to minimize late failure. Excessive bone resection at the laminotomy site should be avoided, particularly at the upper lamina. It is often necessary to remove only a small portion of the superior lamina to square the edge before inserting the hook. Excessive notching leads to the formation of a stress riser and increases the risk of subsequent fracture. The lateral joint ligaments should also be protected, as much as possible, because they help resist lateral hook cutout. Inferiorly, the laminotomy should not be extended too far laterally because the pars interarticularis may be weakened. Many of the problems with hook dislodgment from the lamina or dislodgment of the rod from the hook have now been eliminated with the newest generation of segmental fixation hook-rod systems.

Dural Tears

A dural laceration and concomitant leak of cerebrospinal fluid may result from the injury or from surgery (see Fig. 30–24). Intraoperatively, laceration can occur during exposure, instrumentation, or decortication. Regardless of the cause, the site of the injury, once identified, should be adequately visualized (with bone removed as necessary) and the dura repaired.[83, 84] If primary repair is not possible, muscle or fascia grafting should be performed to close the defect. In addition, if the seal is less than adequate, a lumbar transdural drain can be placed to reduce cerebrospinal fluid pressure and permit dural healing.

Infections

Infections can occur after spine surgery, but they are relatively less common than after instrumentation and fusion for degenerative conditions. Infections superficial to the fascia can be treated with early and aggressive débridement and either open packing of the wound or closure over a drainage tube.

Deep infections should also be treated by aggressive irrigation and débridement as soon as the infection is noted. If this complication occurs, we attempt to leave the bone graft and the metal instrumentation system in place. After thorough irrigation, outflow tubes are placed deep to the fascia and all layers are tightly closed. The outflow drainage system is maintained for at least 4 days until cultures from the effluent are clear. Inflow-outflow systems can also be used. They usually require early high flow (up to 500 mL/hr) of saline solution through the system to keep the tubes patent and functioning. Because superinfections have been noted to occur after 7 to 10 days, the tubes should be removed after this length of time, even if culture results are still positive. If the infection persists, the procedure can be repeated once, again trying to salvage the bone graft, the instrumentation, and the reduction. Occasionally, this treatment fails and it is necessary to remove the metal, the bone graft, or both to help eradicate the infection. An alternative is to pack the wound open, deep to the fascia, and change the dressing at least daily.

Associated Medical Conditions

Improved medical management has reduced the complications associated with spinal cord injury and is responsible for a marked increase in life expectancy. However, head injury, musculoskeletal trauma, and visceral damage, which occur concomitantly in up to 60% of patients with spinal cord injury, often complicate treatment. If the patient is unconscious at initial evaluation, the diagnosis of spinal cord injury may be difficult to make. Screening radiographs of the spine and all long bones below the level of injury should be performed in all patients with head or spinal cord injury. Additionally, after blunt trauma, a significant number of spinal cord–injured patients have an associated abdominal injury and may be unable to feel or communicate the underlying problem. Reid and co-workers[228] reported a 50% incidence of intra-abdominal injury associated with Chance fractures in children and adolescents. Anderson and colleagues[10] reported a 66% incidence of hollow viscus lesions associated with seat belt–type injuries, which climbed to 86% in a pediatric subset. A perforated viscus with associated peritonitis may go undetected. Because this complication is responsible for significant morbidity and death, peritoneal lavage should be a routine part of the initial evaluation of all patients with spinal cord injury.

Renal failure is a frequent occurrence in patients with spinal cord injury. A gradual decline in the incidence of this problem, particularly as a cause of death, has occurred as a result of advances in bladder drainage techniques (e.g., intermittent catheterization). Once the fluid status (inflow and outflow) is normalized in the acute injury state, intermittent bladder catheterization should be used in the management of a neurogenic bladder. After further urologic evaluation, individualized treatment may be instituted. Pulmonary complications, already increased in neurologically injured patients, are further worsened if the anterior transthoracic approach is used.[11]

Late complications in a spinal cord–injured patient can relate to painful nonunion of the spine, limited neurologic recovery of spinal cord or root function (particularly because limited recovery leads to persistent nerve compromise and pain), and medical complications associated with prolonged bedrest, many of which can be avoided by early, rigid immobilization, as discussed earlier in this chapter. In particular, disuse osteoporosis is a common problem in paraplegic patients immobilized for even short periods, and it increases their susceptibility to recurrent injuries.[85] Finally, individuals with spinal cord injuries may experience intractable spasticity. For this condition, studies have shown the efficacy of implantable intrathecal baclofen pumps.[65]

CONCLUSION

The major objective of any treatment is to construct the most stable environment for the spinal cord, nerve roots, and spinal column to allow neurologic improvement. Although the emphasis in this chapter has been on rigid spinal stabilization, it should be stressed that such stabilization is only one means of achieving this goal. Its major advantage at this time, in addition to stabilizing and protecting the spinal cord, is that it allows the patient to rapidly initiate rehabilitation. Reversibility of spinal cord injury remains an unsolved medical and surgical problem. However, rehabilitation has greatly improved the quality of life of patients with spinal injuries.

Intensive rehabilitation should begin as early as possible, with the major objective being attainment of functional independence. The final functional level depends primarily on the level and severity of the neurologic deficit. Surgical instrumentation of the spine and effective spinal orthoses permit earlier mobilization of the patient in the acute phase and may allow patients to reach their functional level sooner. The best selection of treatment depends on understanding the anatomy, the mechanics of the injury and the forces involved, and the options that are available to stabilize and protect the spinal column and cord.

Avoidance of complications associated with the surgical treatment of spine injuries requires a thorough knowledge of the anatomy, an accurate diagnosis, and an understanding and experience with the implants chosen.[238] However, although complications can be minimized, they cannot be eliminated.

REFERENCES

1. Aaro, S.; Ohlen, G. The effect of Harrington instrumentation on the sagittal configuration and mobility of the spine in scoliosis. Spine 8:570–575, 1983.
2. Abe, E.; Sato, K.; Shimada, Y.; et al. Thoracolumbar burst fracture with horizontal fracture of the posterior column. Spine 22:83–87, 1997.
3. Aebi, M.; Etter, C.H.R.; Kehl, T.H.; Thalgott, J. The internal skeletal fixation system. Clin Orthop 227:30–43, 1988.
4. Aebi, M.; Thalgott, J.S. Fractures and dislocations of the thoracolumbar spine treated by the internal spinal skeletal fixation system. Proc North Am Spine Soc 68, 1987.
5. Akbarnia, B.A.; Crandall, D.G.; Burkus, K.; et al. Use of long rods and short arthrodesis for burst fractures of the thoracolumbar spine. J Bone Joint Surg Am 76:1629–1635, 1994.
6. Akbarnia, B.A.; Fogarty, J.P.; Tayob, A.A. Contoured Harrington instrumentation in the treatment of unstable spinal fractures. Clin Orthop 189:186–194, 1984.
7. Albert, T.J.; Levine, M.J.; An, H.S.; et al. Concomitant noncontiguous thoracolumbar and sacral fractures. Spine 18:1285–1291, 1993.
8. Allen, B.L., Jr.; Ferguson, R.L. The Galveston technique for L-rod instrumentation of the scoliotic spine. Spine 7:276–284, 1982.
9. An, H.S.; Andreshak, T.G.; Nguyen, C.; et al. Can we distinguish between benign versus malignant compression fractures of the spine by magnetic resonance imaging? Spine 20:1776–1782, 1995.
10. Anderson, P.A.; Rivara, F.P.; Maier, R.V.; et al. The epidemiology of seatbelt-associated injuries. J Trauma 31:60–67, 1991.
11. Anderson, T.M.; Mansour, K.A.; Miller J.I. Thoracic approaches to anterior spinal operations: Anterior thoracic approaches. Ann Thorac Surg 55:1447–1452, 1993.
12. Angtuaco, E.J.C.; Binet, E.F. Radiology of thoracic and lumbar fractures. Clin Orthop 189:43–57, 1984.
13. Argenson, C.; Lovitt, J.; Camba, P.M.; et al. Osteosynthesis of thoracolumbar spine fractures with CD instrumentation. Paper presented at the Fifth International Congress on CD Instrumentation, Paris, June 1988, pp. 75–82.
14. Ashman, R.B.; Birch, J.G.; Bone, L.B.; et al. Mechanical testing of spinal instrumentation. Clin Orthop 227:113–125, 1988.
15. Bailey, J.C.; Yuan, H.A.; Fredrickson, B.E. The Syracuse I-Plate. Spine 16(Suppl):120–124, 1991.
16. Balasubramanian, K.; Ranu, H.S.; King, A.I. Vertebral response to laminectomy. J Biomech 21:813–823, 1978.
17. Ballock, R.T.; Mackersie, R.; Abitbol, J.; et al. Can burst fractures be predicted from plain radiographs? J Bone Joint Surg Br 74:147–150, 1992.
18. Bedbrook, G.M. Recovery of spinal cord function. Paraplegia 18:315–323, 1980.
19. Been, H.D. Anterior decompression and stabilization of thoracolumbar burst fractures by the use of the Slot-Zielke device. Spine 16:70–77, 1991.
20. Been, H.D. Anterior decompression and stabilization of thoracolumbar burst fractures using the Slot-Zielke device. Acta Orthop Belg 57:144–161, 1991.
21. Benson, D.R. Unstable thoracolumbar fractures, with emphasis on the burst fracture. Clin Orthop 280:14–29, 1988.
22. Benson, D.R.; Burkus, J.K.; Montesano, P.X.; et al. Unstable thoracolumbar and lumbar burst fractures treated with the AO Fixateur Interne. J Spinal Disord 5:335–343, 1992.
23. Benzel, E.C. Short-segment compression instrumentation for selected thoracic and lumbar spine fractures: The short-rod/two-claw technique. J Neurosurg 79:335–340, 1993.
24. Berry, J.L.; Moran, J.M.; Berg, W.S.; et al. A morphometric study of human lumbar and selected thoracic vertebrae. Spine 12:362–367, 1987.
25. Bishop, W.J. The Early History of Surgery. London, Robert Hale, 1960.

26. Blumenthal, S.; Gill, K. Complications of the Wiltse pedicle screw system. Spine 18:1867–1871, 1993.

27. Bohler, J. Operative treatment of fractures of the dorsal and lumbar spine. J Trauma 10:1119–1122, 1970.

28. Bohlman, H.H. Current concepts review: Treatment of fractures and dislocations of the thoracic and lumbar spine. J Bone Joint Surg Am 76:165–169, 1985.

29. Bohlman, H.H.; Eismont, F.J. Surgical techniques of anterior decompression and fusion for spinal cord injuries. Clin Orthop 154:57–67, 1981.

30. Bohlman, H.H.; Freehafer, A.; Dejak, J. The results of treatment of acute injuries of the upper thoracic spine with paralysis. J Bone Joint Surg Am 67:360–369, 1984.

31. Bohlman, H.H.; Zdelblick, T.A. Anterior excision of thoracic discs. J Bone Joint Surg Am 70:1038–1047, 1988.

32. Bradford, D.S.; McBride, G.G. Surgical management of thoracolumbar spine fractures with incomplete neurologic deficits. Clin Orthop 218:201–216, 1987.

33. Brant-Zawadski, M.; Jeffrey, R.B.; Minagi, H.; et al. High resolution CT of thoracolumbar fractures. AJNR Am J Neuroradiol 3:69–74, 1982.

34. Bravo, P.; Labarta, C.; Alcaraz, M.A.; et al. Outcome after vertebral fractures with neurological lesion treated either surgically or conservatively in Spain. Paraplegia 31:358–366, 1993.

35. Breasted, J.H., ed. The Edwin Smith Papyrus. Chicago, University of Chicago Press, 1930.

36. Brightman, R.P.; Miller, C.A.; Rea, G.L.; et al. Magnetic resonance imaging of trauma to the thoracic and lumbar spine. Spine 17:541–550, 1992.

37. Brown, T.; Hansen, R.T.; Yorra, A.J. Some mechanical tests on the lumbosacral spine with particular reference to the intervertebral discs. J Bone Joint Surg Am 39:1135–1164, 1957.

38. Burke, D.C. Hyperextension injuries of the spine. J Bone Joint Surg Br 153:3–12, 1971.

39. Cain, J.E.; DeJong, J.T.; Dinenberg, A.S.; et al. Pathomechanical analysis of thoracolumbar burst fracture reduction: A calf spine model. Spine 18:1647–1654, 1993.

40. Cammisa, F.P.; Eismont, F.J.; Green, A.B. Dural laceration occurring with burst fractures and associated laminar fractures. J Bone Joint Surg Am 71:1044–1052, 1989.

41. Cantor, J.B.; Lebwohl, N.H.; Garvey, T.; et al. Nonoperative management of stable thoracolumbar burst fractures with early ambulation and bracing. Spine 18:971–976, 1993.

42. Carl, A.L.; Tromanhauser, S.G.; Roger, D.J. Pedicle screw instrumentation for thoracolumbar burst fractures and fracture-dislocations. Spine 17(Suppl):317–324, 1992.

43. Carson W.L.; Duffield R.C.; Arent, M.; et al. Internal forces and moments in transpedicular spine instrumentation. The effect of pedicle screw angle and transfixation—The 4R-4bar linkage concept. Spine 15:893–901, 1990.

44. Chance, G.Q. Note on a type of flexion fracture of the spine. Br J Radiol 21:452–453, 1948.

45. Chen W.J.; Niu C.C.; Chen, L.H.; et al. Back pain after thoracolumbar fracture treated with long instrumentation and short fusion. J Spinal Disord 8:474–478, 1995.

46. Chiba, M.; McLain, R.F.; Yerby, S.A.; et al. Short-segment pedicle instrumentation: Biomechanical analysis of supplemental hook fixation. Spine 21:288–294, 1996.

47. Clark, J.A.; Hsu, L.C.; Yau, A.C.M.C. Viscoelastic behavior of deformed spines under correction with halo pelvic distraction. Clin Orthop 110:90–111, 1975.

48. Clohisy, J.C.; Akbarnia, B.A.; Bucholz, R.D. Neurologic recovery associated with anterior decompression of spine fractures at the thoracolumbar junction (T12-L1). Spine 17(Suppl):325–328, 1992.

49. Convery, F.R.; Minteer, M.A.; Smith, R.N. Fracture dislocation of the dorsal lumbar spine: Acute operative stabilization by Harrington instrumentation. Spine 3:160–166, 1978.

50. Cotler, J.M.; Vernace, J.V.; Michalski, J.A. The use of Harrington rods in thoracolumbar fractures. Orthop Clin North Am 17:87–103, 1986.

51. Cotrel, Y.; Dubousset, J.; Guillaumat, M. New universal instrumentation in spinal surgery. Clin Orthop 227:10–23, 1988.

52. Cresswell, T.R.; Marshall, P.D.; Smith, R.B. Mechanical stability of the AO internal spinal fixation system compared with that of the Hartshill rectangle and sublaminar wiring in the management of unstable burst fractures of the thoracic and lumbar spine. Spine 23:111–115, 1998.

53. Crowe, P.; Gertzbein, S.D. Spinal canal clearance in burst fractures using the AO internal fixator. Paper presented at the Combined Meeting of the Scoliosis Research Society and the European Spinal Deformity Society, Amsterdam, September 1989, pp. 590–591.

54. Crutcher, J.P.; Anderson, P.A.; King, H.A.; et al. Indirect spinal canal decompression in patients with thoracolumbar burst fractures treated by posterior distraction rods. J Spinal Disord 4:39–48, 1991.

55. Daniaux, H.; Seykora, P.; Genelin, A.; et al. Application of posterior plating and modifications in thoracolumbar spine injuries: Indications, techniques, and results. Spine 16(Suppl):125–133, 1991.

56. Davies, W.E.; Morris, J.H.; Hill, V. An analysis of conservative (nonsurgical) management of thoracolumbar fractures and fracture-dislocations with neural damage. J Bone Joint Surg Am 62:1324–1328, 1980.

57. Dekutoski, M.B.; Conlan, E.S.; Salciccioli, G.G. Spinal mobility and deformity after Harrington rod stabilization and limited arthrodesis of thoracolumbar fractures. J Bone Joint Surg Am 75:168–176, 1993.

58. Denis, F. The three column spine and its significance in the classification of acute thoracolumbar spinal injuries. Spine 8:817–831, 1983.

59. Denis, F.; Armstrong, G.W.D.; Searls, K.; et al. Acute thoracolumbar burst fractures in the absence of neurologic deficit. Clin Orthop 189:142–149, 1984.

60. Denis, F.; Burkus, J.K. Shear fracture-dislocations of the thoracic and lumbar spine associated with forceful hyperextension (lumberjack paraplegia). Spine 17:156–161, 1992.

61. Denis, F.; Ruiz, H.; Searls, K. Comparison between square-ended distraction rods and standard round-ended distraction rods in the treatment of thoracolumbar spinal injuries: A statistical analysis. Clin Orthop 189:162–167, 1984.

62. Dewald, R.L. Burst fractures of the thoracic and lumbar spine. Clin Orthop 189:150–161, 1984.

63. Dick, W. The "Fixateur Interne" as a versatile implant for spine surgery. Spine 12:882–900, 1987.

64. Dick, W.; Kluger, P.; Magerl, F.; et al. A new device for internal fixation of thoracolumbar and lumbar spine fractures: The "Fixateur Interne." Paraplegia 23:225–232, 1985.

65. Dickman, C.A.; Yahiro, M.A.; Lu, H.T.C.; et al. Surgical treatment alternatives for fixation of unstable fractures of the thoracic and lumbar spine: A meta-analysis. Spine 19(Suppl):2266–2273, 1994.

66. Dickson, J.H.; Harrington, P.R.; Erwin, W.D. Results of reduction and stabilization of the severely fractured thoracic and lumbar spine. J Bone Joint Surg Am 60:799–805, 1978.

67. Dodd, C.A.F.; Fergusson, C.M.; Pearcy, M.J.; et al. Vertebral motion measured using biplanar radiography before and after Harrington rod removal for unstable thoracolumbar fractures of the spine. Spine 11:452–455, 1986.

68. Doerr, T.E.; Montesano, P.X.; Burkus, J.K.; et al. Spinal canal decompression in traumatic thoracolumbar burst fractures: Posterior distraction rods versus transpedicular screw fixation. J Orthop Trauma 4:403–411, 1991.

69. Dommisse, G.F. The arteries, arterioles, and capillaries of the spinal cord. Surgical guidelines in the prevention of postoperative paraplegia. Ann R Coll Surg 62:369–376, 1980.

70. Dorr, L.D.; Harvey, J.P.; Nickel, V.L. Clinical review of the early stability of spine injuries. Spine 7:545–550, 1982.

71. Dove, J. Internal fixation of the lumbar spine: The Hartshill rectangle. Clin Orthop 203:136–140, 1986.

72. Duffield R.C.; Carson W.L.; Chen L.; Voth B. Longitudinal element size effect on load sharing, internal loads, and fatigue life of tri-level spinal implant constructs. Spine 18:1695–1703.

73. Dunham, W.K.; Langford, K.H.; Ostrowsky, D.M. The management of unstable fractures and dislocations of the thoracic and lumbar spine. Ala J Med Sci 21:194–204, 1984.

74. Durward, Q.J.; Schweigel, J.F.; Harrison, P. Management of fractures of the thoracolumbar and lumbar spine. Neurosurgery 8:555–561, 1981.

75. Dwyer, A.F. Experience of anterior correction of scoliosis. Clin Orthop 93:191, 1973.

76. Ebelke, D.K.; Asher, M.A.; Neff, J.R.; et al. Survivorship analysis of VSP spinal instrumentation in the treatment of thoracolumbar and lumbar burst fractures. Spine 16(Suppl):428–432, 1991.

77. Ebraheim, N.A.; Rupp, R.E.; Savolaine, E.R.; et al. Use of titanium implants in pedicular screw fixation. J Spinal Disord 7:478–486, 1994.

78. Edwards, C.C. Sacral fixation device design and preliminary results. Paper presented at a meeting of the Scoliosis Research Society, 1984.

79. Edwards, C.C.; Levine, A.M. Complications associated with posterior instrumentation in the treatment of thoracic and lumbar injuries. In: Garfin, S., ed. Complications of Spine Surgery. Baltimore, Williams & Wilkins, 1989, pp. 164–199.

80. Edwards, C.C.; Levine, A.M. Early rod-sleeve stabilization of the injured thoracic and lumbar spine. Orthop Clin North Am 17:121–145, 1986.

81. Edwards, C.C.; Levine, A.M. Fractures of the lumbar spine. In: Evarts, C.M., ed. Surgery of the Musculoskeletal System. New York, Churchill Livingstone, 1990, pp. 2237–2275.

82. Edwards, C.C.; Levine, A.M.; Weigel, M.C. Determinants of neurologic recovery following posttraumatic incomplete paraplegia. Orthop Trans 11:453, 1987.

83. Edwards, C.C.; Rosenthal, M.S.; Gellard, F.; et al. The fate of retropulsed bone following vertebral body fractures. Orthop Trans 13:19, 1989.

84. Eismont, F.J.; Wiesel, S.W.; Rothman, R.H. Treatment of dural tears associated with spinal surgery. J Bone Joint Surg Am 63:1123–1136, 1982.

85. Elias, A.N.; Gwinup, G. Immobilization osteoporosis in paraplegia. J Am Paraplegia Soc 15:163–170, 1993.

86. Elliott, H.C. Cross-sectional diameters and areas of the human spinal cord. Anat Rec 93:287–293, 1945.

87. Engler, G.L. Cotrel-Dubousset instrumentation for the reduction of fracture dislocations of the spine. J Spinal Disord 3:62–66, 1990.

88. Epstein, N.E.; Epstein, J.A. Limbus lumbar vertebral fractures in 27 adolescents and adults. Spine 16:962–966, 1991.

89. Esses, S.I.; Botsford, D.J.; Wright, T.; et al. Operative treatment of spinal fractures with the AO internal fixator. Spine 16(Suppl):146–150, 1991.

90. Fabris, D.; Costantini, S.; Nena, U. Cotrel-Dubousset instrumentation in thoracolumbar seat belt–type and flexion-distraction injuries. J Spinal Disord 7:146–152, 1994.

91. Farcy, J.C.; Weidenbaum, M.; Glassman, S. Sagittal index in management of thoracolumbar burst fractures. Spine 15:958–965, 1990.

92. Ferguson, R.L.; Allen, B.L. A mechanistic classification of thoracolumbar spine fractures. Clin Orthop 189:77–88, 1984.

93. Ferguson, R.L.; Allen, B.L. An algorithm for the treatment of unstable thoracolumbar fractures. Orthop Clin North Am 17:105–112, 1986.

94. Finkelstein, J.A.; Chapman, J.R.; Mirza, S. Anterior cortical allograft in thoracolumbar fractures. J Spinal Disord 12:424–429, 1999.

95. Flesch, J.R.; Leider, L.L.; Erickson, D.L.; et al. Harrington instrumentation and spine fusion for unstable fractures and fracture-dislocations of the thoracic and lumbar spine. J Bone Joint Surg Am 59:143–153, 1977.

96. Floman, Y.; Fast, A.; Pollack, D.; et al. The simultaneous applications of an interspinous compressive wire and Harrington distraction rods in the treatment of fracture-dislocation of the thoracic and lumbar spine. Clin Orthop 205:207–215, 1988.

97. Forsyth, H.F. Extension injuries of the cervical spine. J Bone Joint Surg Am 46:1792–1797, 1984.

98. Frankel, H.L.; Hancock, D.O.; Hyslop, G.; et al. The value of postural reduction in the initial management of closed injuries of the spine with paraplegia and tetraplegia. I. Paraplegia 7:179–192, 1969.

99. Fredrickson, B.E.; Edwards, W.T.; Rauschning, W.; et al. Vertebral burst fractures: An experimental, morphologic, and radiographic study. Spine 17:1012–1021, 1992.

100. Gaines, R.W.; Breedlove, R.F.; Munson, G. Stabilization of thoracic and thoracolumbar fracture-dislocations with Harrington rods and sublaminar wires. Clin Orthop 189:195–203, 1984.

101. Gardner, V.O.; Armstrong, G.W.D. Long-term lumbar facet joint changes in spinal fracture patients treated with Harrington rods. Spine 15:479–484, 1990.

102. Gardner, V.O.; Thalgott, J.S.; White, J.I.; et al. The contoured anterior spinal plate system (CASP). Spine 19:550–555, 1994.

103. Garfin, S.R.; Gertzbein, S.D.; Eismont, F. Fractures of the lumbar spine: Evaluation, classification, and treatment. In: Wiesel, S., ed. The Lumbar Spine. Philadelphia, W.B. Saunders, 1996, pp. 822–873.

104. Garfin, S.R.; Katz, M.M. The vertebral column: Clinical aspects. In: Nahum, A.M.; Melvin, J., eds. The Biomechanics of Trauma. Norwalk, CT, Appleton-Century-Crofts, 1985, pp. 301–340.

105. Garfin, S.R.; Katz, N.M.; Marshall, L.F. Spinal cord. In: Cales, R.H.; Heelig, R.W., Jr., eds. Trauma Care Systems. Rockville, MD, Aspen, 1986.

106. Garfin, S.R.; Mowery, C.A.; Guerra, J.; et al. Confirmation of the posterolateral technique to decompress and fuse thoracolumbar spine burst fractures. Spine 10:218–228, 1985.

107. Garin, D.M.; Leal, C.V.; Granell, J.B. Stabilization of the lower thoracic and lumbar spine with the internal skeletal fixation system and a cross-linkage system: First results of treatment. Acta Orthop Belg 58:36–42, 1992.

108. Georgis, T.; Rydevik, B.; Weinstein, J.N.; Garfin, S.R. Complications of pedicle screw fixation. In: Garfin, S., ed. Complications of Spine Surgery. Baltimore, Williams & Wilkins, 1989, pp. 200–210.

109. Gereesan, G. Cotrel-Dubousset pedicle fixation in fractures of thoracic and lumbar spine. Abstract. Paper presented at the Sixth International Congress on CD Instrumentation, Monte Carlo, September 1989.

110. Gertzbein, S.D. Classification of thoracic and lumbar fractures. In: Gertzbein, S.D., ed. Fractures of the Thoracic and Lumbar Spine. Baltimore, Williams & Wilkins, 1993.

111. Gertzbein, S.D. Scoliosis Research Society: Multicenter spine fracture study. Spine 17:528–540, 1992.

112. Gertzbein, S.D.; Court-Brown, C.M. Flexion-distraction injuries of the lumbar spine: Mechanisms of injury and classification. Clin Orthop 227:52–60, 1988.

113. Gertzbein, S.D.; Court-Brown, C.M.; Marks, P.; et al. The neurologic outcome following surgery for spinal fractures. Spine 13:641–644, 1988.

114. Gertzbein, S.D.; Harris, M.B. Wedge osteotomy for the correction of posttraumatic kyphosis. Spine 17:374–379, 1992.

115. Ghanayem, A.J.; Zdeblick, T.A. Anterior instrumentation in the management of thoracolumbar burst fractures. Clin Orthop 335:89–100, 1997.

116. Goll, S.R.; Balderston, R.A.; Stambough, J.L.; et al. Depth of intraspinal wire penetration during passage of sublaminar wires. Spine 13:503–509, 1988.

117. Grantham, S.A.; Malberg, M.I.; Smith, D.M. Thoracolumbar spine flexion-distraction injury. Spine 1:172, 1976.

118. Graziano, G.P. Cotrel-Dubousset hook and screw combinations for spine fractures. J Spinal Disord 6:380–385, 1993.

119. Griffith, H.B.; Gleave, J.R.; Taylor, R.G. Changing patterns of fractures of the dorsal and lumbar spine. BMJ 1:891, 1966.

120. Gumley, G.; Taylor, T.K.F. Distraction fractures of the lumbar spine. J Bone Joint Surg Br 64:520–525, 1982.

121. Gurr, K.R.; McAfee, P.C.; Shih, C.M. Biomechanical analysis of anterior and posterior instrumentation systems after corpectomy: A calf spine model. J Bone Joint Surg Am 70:1182–1191, 1988.

122. Gurwitz, G.S.; Dawson, J.M.; McNamara, M.J.; et al. Biomechanical analysis of three surgical approaches for lumbar burst fractures using short-segment instrumentation. Spine 19:977–982, 1993.

123. Guttman, L. History of the National Spinal Injuries Centre, Stoke Mandeville Hospital, Aylesbury. Paraplegia 5:115–126, 1967.

124. Guttman, L. Spinal Cord Injuries: Comprehensive Management and Research. Oxford, Blackwell, 1973.

125. Haas, N.; Blauth, M.; Tscherne, H. Anterior plating in thoracolumbar spine injuries. Spine 16(Suppl):100–111, 1991.

126. Hardaker, W.T.; Cook, W.A.; Friedman, A.H.; et al. Bilateral transpedicular decompression and Harrington rod stabilization of severe thoracolumbar burst fractures. Spine 17:162–171, 1992.

127. Harrington, R.M.; Budorick, T.; Hoyt, J.; et al. Biomechanics of indirect reduction of bone retropulsed into the spinal canal in vertebral fracture. Spine 18:692–699, 1993.

128. Harryman, D.T. Complete fracture-dislocation of the thoracic spine associated with spontaneous neurologic decompression: A case report. Clin Orthop 207:64–69, 1986.

129. Hazel, W.A.; Jones, R.A.; Morrey, B.F.; Stauffer, R.N. Vertebral fractures without neurological deficit. A long-term follow-up study. J Bone Joint Surg Am 70:1318–1321, 1988.

130. Heggeness, M.H.; Doherty, B.J. Trabecular anatomy of thoracolumbar vertebrae: Implications for burst fractures. J Anat 191:309–312, 1997.

131. Herring, J.A.; Wenger, D.R. Segmental spinal instrumentation: A preliminary report of 40 consecutive cases. Spine 7:285–298, 1982.

132. Hilibrand, A.S.; Moore, D.C.; Graziano, G.P. The role of pediculolaminar fixation in compromised pedicle bone. Spine 21:445–451, 1996.

133. Holdsworth, F.W. Fractures, dislocations, and fracture-dislocations of the spine. J Bone Joint Surg Am 52:1534–1551, 1970.

134. Hu, R.W.; Bohlman, H.H. Fracture at the iliac bone graft harvest site after fusion of the spine. Clin Orthop 309:208–213, 1994.

135. Hu, S.; Capen, D.A.; Rimoldi, R.L.; et al. The effect of surgical decompression on neurologic outcome after lumbar fractures. Clin Orthop 288:166–173, 1993.

136. Huelke, D.F.; Kaufer, H. Vertebral column injuries and seat belts. J Trauma 15:304–318, 1975.

137. Huntington, C.F.; Murrell, W.D.; et al. Comparison of thoracoscopic and open thoracic discectomy in a live ovine model for anterior spinal fusion. Spine 23:1699–1702, 1998.

138. Jackson, R.H.; Quisling, R.G.; Day, A.I. Fracture and complete dislocation of the thoracic or lumbosacral spine: Report of three cases. Neurosurgery 5:250–253, 1979.

139. Jacobs, R.R.; Asher, M.A.; Snider, R.K. Thoracolumbar spinal injuries: A comparative study of recumbent and operative treatment in 100 patients. Spine 5:463–477, 1980.

140. Jacobs, R.R.; Schlaepfer, F.; Mathys, R.R.; et al. A locking hook spinal rod system for stabilization of fracture-dislocations and correction of deformities of the dorsolumbar spine: A biomechanics evaluation. Clin Orthop 189:168–177, 1984.

141. James, K.S.; Wenger, K.H.; Schlegel, J.D.; et al. Biomechanical evaluation of the stability of thoracolumbar burst fractures. Spine 19:1731–1740, 1994.

142. Jelsma, R.K.; Kirsch, P.T.; Jelsma, L.F.; et al. Surgical treatment of thoracolumbar fractures. Surg Neurol 18:156–166, 1982.

143. Jodoin, A.; DuPuis, P.; Fraser, M.; et al. Unstable fractures of the thoracolumbar spine: A 10-year experience at Sacre Coeur Hospital. J Trauma 25:197–202, 1985.

144. Johnston, C.E.; Happel, L.T.; Norris, R.; et al. Delayed paraplegia complicating sublaminar segmental spinal instrumentation. J Bone Joint Surg Am 68:556–563, 1986.

145. Kahanovitz, N.; Bullough, P.; Jacobs, R.R. The effect of internal fixation without arthrodesis on human facet joint cartilage. Clin Orthop 189:204, 1984.

146. Kaneda, K.; Asano, S.; Hashimoto, T.; et al. The treatment of osteoporotic-posttraumatic vertebral collapse using the Kaneda device and a bioactive ceramic vertebral prosthesis. Spine 17(Suppl):295–303, 1992.

147. Kaneda, K.; Taneichi, H.; Abumi, K.; et al. Anterior decompression and stabilization with the Kaneda device for thoracolumbar burst fractures associated with neurological deficits. J Bone Joint Surg Am 79:69–83, 1997.

148. Karlstron, G.; Olerud, S.; Sjostrom, L. Transpedicular segmental fixation: Description of a new procedure. Orthopedics 11:689–700, 1988.

149. Katonis, P.G.; Katonis, G.M.; Loupasis, G.A.; et al. Treatment of unstable thoracolumbar and lumbar spine injuries using Cotrel-Dubousset instrumentation. Spine 24:2352–2357, 1999.

150. Kaufer, H.; Hayes, J.T. Lumbar fracture-dislocation. J Bone Joint Surg Am 48:712–730, 1966.

151. Keene, J.S.; Goletz, T.H.; Lilleas, F.; et al. Diagnosis of vertebral fractures. J Bone Joint Surg Am 64:586–595, 1982.

152. Keene, J.S.; Wackwitz, D.L.; Drummond, D.S.; et al. Compression-distraction instrumentation of unstable thoracolumbar fractures: Anatomic results obtained with each type of injury and method of instrumentation. Spine 11:898–902, 1986.

153. Kelly, R.P.; Whitesides, T.E. Treatment of lumbodorsal fracture-dislocations. Ann Surg 167:705–717, 1968.

154. Kifune, M.; Panjabi, M.M.; Liu, W. Fracture pattern and instability of thoracolumbar injuries. Eur Spine J 4:98–103, 1995.

155. Kerslake, R.W.; Jaspan, T.; Worthington, B.S. Magnetic resonance imaging of spine trauma. Br J Radiol 64:386–402, 1991.

156. King, A.G. Burst compression fractures of the thoracolumbar spine: Pathologic anatomy and surgical management. Orthopedics 10:1711–1719, 1987.

157. Kinnard, P.; Ghibely, A.; Gordon, D.; et al. Roy-Camille plates in unstable spinal conditions: A preliminary report. Spine 11:131–135, 1986.

158. Kirkpatrick, J.S.; Wilber, R.G.; Likavec, M.; et al. Anterior

159. Klose, K.J.; Goldberg, M.L.; Smith, R.S.; et al. Neurological change following spinal cord injury: An assessment technique and preliminary results. Model Sys Sci Digest 3:35–42, 1980.

160. Kostuik, J.P. Anterior fixation for fractures of the thoracic and lumbar spine with or without neurologic involvement. Clin Orthop 189:103–115, 1984.

161. Kostuik, J.P.; Munting, E.; Valdevit, A. Biomechanical analysis of screw load sharing. J Spinal Disord 7:394–401, 1994.

162. Kothe R.; O'Holleran J.D.; Liu, W.; Panjabi, M.M. Internal architecture of the thoracic pedicle. An anatomic study. Spine 21:264–270, 1996.

163. Kothe, R.; Panjabi, M.M.; Liu, W. Multidirectional instability of the thoracic spine due to iatrogenic pedicle injuries during transpedicular fixation. A biomechanical investigation. Spine 22:1836–1842, 1997.

164. Krag, M.H.; Beynnon, B.D.; Pope, M.H. Depth of insertion of transpedicular vertebral screws into human vertebrae: Effect upon screw-vertebra interface strength. J Spinal Disord 1:287–294, 1988.

165. Krag, M.H.; Beynnon, B.D.; Pope, M.H.; et al. An internal fixator for posterior application to short segments of the thoracic, lumbar or lumbosacral spine. Clin Orthop 203:75–78, 1986.

166. Krag, M.H.; Weaver, D.L.; Beynnon, B.D.; et al. Morphometry of the thoracic and lumbar spine related to transpedicular screw placement for surgical spine fixation. Spine 13:27–32, 1988.

167. Krengel, W.F.; Anderson, P.A.; Henley, M.B. Early stabilization and decompression for incomplete paraplegia due to a thoracic-level spinal cord injury. Spine 18:2080–2087, 1993.

168. Krompinger, W.J.; Fredrickson, B.E.; Mino, D.E.; et al. Conservative treatment of fractures of the thoracic and lumbar spine. Orthop Clin North Am 17:161–170, 1986.

169. Kurz, L.T.; Garfin, S.R.; Booth, R.E. Harvesting autogenous iliac bone grafts: A review of complications and techniques. Spine 14:1324–1331, 1989.

170. Laborde, J.M.; Bahniuk, E.; Bohlman, H.H.; et al. Comparison of fixation of spinal fractures. Clin Orthop 152:303–310, 1980.

171. Landreneau, R.J.; Hazelrigg, S.R.; Mack, M.J.; et al. Postoperative pain related morbidity: Video assisted thoracoscopy vs. thoracotomy. Ann Thorac Surg 56:1285–1289. 1993.

172. Lemons, V.R.; Wagner, F.C.; Montesano, P.X. Management of thoracolumbar fractures with accompanying neurological injury. Neurosurgery 30:667–671, 1992.

173. Lesoin, F.; Leys, D.; Rousseaux, M.; et al. Thoracic disc herniation and Scheuermann's disease. Eur Neurol 26:145–152, 1987.

174. Levine, A.; Bosse, M.; Edwards, C.C. Bilateral facet dislocations in the thoracolumbar spine. Spine 13:630–640, 1988.

175. Levine, A.M.; Edwards, C.C. Complications in the treatment of acute spinal injury. Orthop Clin North Am 17:183–203, 1986.

176. Levine, A.M.; Edwards, C.C. Lumbar spine trauma. In: Camins, M.; O'Learly, P., eds. The Lumbar Spine. New York, Raven, 1987, pp. 183–212.

177. Lewis, J.; McKibbin, B. The treatment of unstable fracture-dislocations of the thoracolumbar spine accompanied by paraplegia. J Bone Joint Surg Br 56:603–612, 1974.

178. Lindahl, S.; Willen, J.; Irstam, L. Unstable thoracolumbar fractures: A comparative radiologic study of conservative treatment and Harrington instrumentation. Acta Radiol 26:67–77, 1985.

179. Lindsey, R.W.; Dick, W. The Fixateur Interne in the reduction and stabilization of thoracolumbar fractures in patients with neurologic deficits. Spine 16(Suppl):140–145, 1991.

180. Liu, C.L.; Wang, S.; Lin, H.J.; et al. AO Fixateur Interne in treating burst fractures of the thoracolumbar spine. Zhonghua Yi Xue Za Zhi (Taipei) 62:619–625, 1999.

181. Logue, V. Thoracic intervertebral disc prolapse with spinal cord compression. J Neurol Neurosurg Psychiatry 15:227–241, 1952.

182. Louis, R. Fusion of the lumbar and sacral spine by internal fixation with screw plates. Clin Orthop 203:18–33, 1986.

183. Louis, R. Surgery of the Spine. New York, Springer-Verlag, 1983, p. 78.

184. Lu J.; Ebraheim, N.A.; Biyani, A.; et al. Vulnerability of great medullary artery. Spine 21:1852–1855, 1996.

185. Luque, E.R.; Cassis, N.; Ramirez-Wiella, G. Segmental spinal instrumentation in the treatment of fractures of the thoracolumbar spine. Spine 7:312–317, 1982.

stabilization of thoracolumbar burst fractures using the Kaneda device: A preliminary report. Orthopedics 18:673–678, 1995.

186. Magerl, F.P. Stabilization of the lower thoracic and lumbar spine with external skeletal fixation. Clin Orthop 189:125–141, 1984.

187. Maiman, D.J.; Larson, S.J.; Luck, E.; et al. Lateral extracavitary approach to the spine for thoracic disc herniations: Report of 23 cases. Neurosurgery 14:178–182, 1984.

188. Mann, K.A.; McGowan, D.P.; Fredrickson, B.E. A biomechanical investigation of short segment spinal fixation for burst fractures with varying degrees of posterior disruption. Spine 15:470–478, 1990.

189. Markel, D.C.; Graziano, G.P. A comparison study of treatment of thoracolumbar fractures using the ACE posterior segmental fixator and Cotrel-Dubousset instrumentation. Orthopedics 18:679–686, 1995.

190. Matsuzaki, H.; Tokuhashi, Y.; Wakabayashi, K.; et al. Rigix plate system for anterior fixation of thoracolumbar vertebrae. J Spinal Disord 10:339–347, 1997.

191. McAfee, P.C. Biomechanical approach to instrumentation of thoracolumbar spine: A review article. Adv Orthop Surg 313–327, 1985.

192. McAfee, P.C.; Bohlman, H.H.; Yuan, H.A. Anterior decompression of traumatic thoracolumbar fractures with incomplete neurological deficit using a retroperitoneal approach. J Bone Joint Surg Am 67:89–104, 1985.

193. McAfee, P.C.; Farey, I.D.; Sutterlin, C.E.; et al. Device-related osteoporosis with spinal instrumentation: A canine model. Abstract. Paper presented at a meeting of the International Society for the Study of the Lumbar Spine, Kyoto, Japan, 1989, p. 20.

194. McAfee, P.C.; Weiland, D.J.; Carlow, J.J. Survivorship analysis of pedicle spinal instrumentation. Spine 16(Suppl):422–427, 1991.

195. McAfee, P.C.; Yuan, H.A.; Frederickson, B.A.; Lubicky, J.P. The value of computed tomography in thoracolumbar fractures. An analysis of one hundred consecutive cases and a new classification. J Bone Joint Surg Am 65:461–473, 1983.

196. McAfee, P.C.; Yuan, H.A.; Lasda, N.A. The unstable burst fracture. Spine 7:365–378, 1982.

197. McBride, G.G. Cotrel-Dubousset rods in surgical stabilization of spine fractures. Spine 18:466–473, 1993.

198. McCormack, T.; Karaikovic, E.; Gaines, R.W. The load sharing classification of spine fractures. Spine 19:1741–1744, 1994.

199. McEvoy, R.D.; Bradford, D.S. The management of burst fractures of the thoracic and lumbar spine: Experience in 53 patients. Spine 10:631–637, 1983.

200. McGrory, B.J.; VanderWilde, R.S.; Currier, B.L. Diagnosis of subtle thoracolumbar burst fractures: A new radiographic sign. Spine 18:2282–2285, 1993.

201. McGuire RA; The role of anterior surgery in the treatment of thoracolumbar fractures. Orthopedics 20:959–962, 1997.

202. McKinley, L.M.; Obernchain, T.G.; Roth, K.R. Loss of correction and late kyphosis as the result of short segment pedicle fixation with posterior transpedicular decompression. Abstract. Paper presented at the Sixth International Congress on CD Instrumentation, Monte Carlo, September, 1989.

203. McLain, R.F.; Sparling, E.; Benson, D.R. Early failure of short-segment pedicle instrumentation for thoracolumbar fractures: A preliminary report. J Bone Joint Surg Am 75:162–167, 1993.

204. Mermelstein, L.E.; McLain, R.F.; Yerby, S.A. Reinforcement of thoracolumbar burst fractures with calcium phosphate cement. A biomechanical study. Spine 23:664–671, 1998.

205. Mimatsu, K.; Katoh, F.; Kawakami, N. New vertebral body impactors for posterolateral decompression of burst fracture. Spine 18:1366–1368, 1993.

206. Mumford, J.; Weinstein, J.N.; Spratt, K.F.; et al. Thoracolumbar burst fractures: The clinical efficacy and outcome of nonoperative management. Spine 18:955–970, 1993.

207. Nagel, D.A.; Koogle, T.A.; Piziali, R.L.; et al. Stability of the upper lumbar spine following progressive disruptions and the application of individual internal and external fixation devices. J Bone Joint Surg Am 63:62–70, 1981.

208. Nasca, R.J.; Hollis, J.M.; Lemons, J.E.; et al. Cyclic axial loading of spinal implants. Spine 10:792–793, 1985.

209. Nash, C.L.; Schatzinger, L.H.; Browno, R.H.; et al. The unstable stable thoracic compression fracture. Spine 2:261, 1977.

210. Nicastro, J.F.; Hartjen, C.A.; Traian, J.; et al. Intraspinal pathways taken by sublaminar wires during removal. J Bone Joint Surg Am 68:1206–1209, 1986.

211. Nicoll, E.A. Fractures of the dorsolumbar spine. J Bone Joint Surg Br 31:376–394, 1949.

212. O'Brien, J.P.; Stephens, M.M.; Prickett, C.F.; et al. Nylon sublaminar straps in segmental instrumentation for spinal disorders. Clin Orthop 203:168–171, 1986.

213. Okuyama, K.; Abe, E.; Chiba, M.; et al. Outcome of anterior decompression and stabilization for thoracolumbar unstable burst fractures in the absence of neurologic deficits. Spine 21:620–625, 1996.

214. Olerud, S.; Karltrom, G.; Sjostrom, L. Transpedicular fixation of thoracolumbar vertebral fractures. Clin Orthop 227:44–51, 1988.

215. Osebold, W.R.; Weinstein, S.L.; Sprague, B.L. Thoracolumbar spine fractures: Results of treatments. Spine 6:13–34, 1981.

216. Panjabi, M.M.; Brand, R.A., Jr.; White, A.A, 3rd. Three-dimensional flexibility and stiffness properties of the human thoracic spine. J Biomech 9:185–192, 1975.

217. Panjabi, M.M.; Oxland, T.R.; Kifune, M.; et al. Validity of the three-column theory of thoracolumbar fractures. A biomechanical investigation. Spine 20:1122–1127, 1995.

218. Parke, W.W.; Gammall, K.; Rothman, R.H. Arterial vascularization of the cauda equina. J Bone Joint Surg Am 63:53–62, 1981.

219. Patterson, R.H.; Arbit, E. A surgical approach through the pedicle for protruded thoracic discs. J Neurosurg 48:768–772, 1978.

220. Paul, R.L.; Michael, R.H.; Dunn, J.E.; Williams, J.P. Anterior transthoracic surgical decompression of acute spinal cord injuries. J Neurosurg 43:299–307, 1975.

221. Perot, P.H.; Munro, D.D. Transthoracic removal of midline thoracic disc protrusions causing spinal cord compression. J Neurosurg 31:452–458, 1969.

222. Pinzur, M.S.; Meyer, P.R., Jr.; Lautenschlager, E.P.; et al. Measurement of internal fixation device support in experimentally produced fractures of the dorsolumbar spine. Orthopedics 2:28, 1979.

223. Place, H.M.; Donaldson, D.H.; Brown, C.W.; et al. Stabilization of thoracic spine fractures resulting in complete paraplegia: A long-term retrospective analysis. Spine 19:1726–1730, 1994.

224. Post, P.L.; Green, B.A.; Quencer, R.M.; et al. The value of computed tomography in spinal trauma. Spine 7:417–431, 1982.

225. Purcell, G.A.; Markolf, K.L.; Dawson, E.G. Twelfth thoracic–first lumbar vertebral mechanical stability of fractures after Harrington-rod instrumentation. J Bone Joint Surg Am 63:71–78, 1981.

226. Purnell, M.; Drummond, D.S.; Keene, J.S.; et al. Hex-nut loosening following compression instrumentation of the spine. Clin Orthop 203:172–178, 1986.

227. Regan, J.J.; Mack, M.J.; Picetti, G.G., 3rd; et al. A technical report on video-assisted thoracoscopy in thoracic spinal surgery. Preliminary description. Spine 20:831–837, 1995.

228. Reid, A.B.; Letts, R.M.; Black, G.B. Pediatric chance fractures: Association with intra-abdominal injuries and seatbelt use. J Trauma 30:384–391, 1990.

229. Rennie, W.; Mitchell, N. Flexion dislocation fractures of the lumbar spine. J Bone Joint Surg Am 55:386–390, 1973.

230. Reuben, M.; Schultz, A.; Denis, F.; et al. Bulging of lumbar intervertebral discs. J Biomech 104:187–192, 1982.

231. Riebel, G.D.; Yoo, J.U.; Fredrickson, B.E.; et al. Review of Harrington rod treatment of spinal trauma. Spine 18:479–491, 1993.

232. Riggins, R.S.; Kraus, J.F. The risk of neurological damage with fractures of the vertebrae. J Trauma 17:126–133, 1977.

233. Rimoldi, R.L.; Zigler, J.E.; Capen, D.A.; et al. The effect of surgical intervention on rehabilitation time in patients with thoracolumbar and lumbar spinal cord injuries. Spine 17:1443–1449, 1992.

234. Rissanen, P.M. The surgical anatomy and pathology of the supraspinous and interspinous ligaments of the lumbar spine with special reference to ligament ruptures. Acta Orthop Scand 46(Suppl):1, 1960.

235. Roaf, R. A study of the mechanics of spinal injuries. J Bone Joint Surg Br 42:810, 1960.

236. Roberts, J.B.; Curtiss, P.H., Jr. Stability of the thoracic and lumbar spine in traumatic paraplegia following fracture or fracture-dislocation. J Bone Joint Surg Am 52:1115–1130, 1970.

237. Rockwell, H.; Evans, F.G.; Pheasant, H.C. The comparative morphology of the vertebral spinal column: Its form as related to function. J Morphol 63:87, 1938.

238. Roffi, R.P.; Waters, R.L.; Adkins, R.H. Gunshot wounds to the spine associated with a perforated viscus. Spine 14:808–811, 1989.

239. Rogers, L.F. The roentgenographic appearance of transverse or Chance fractures of the spine: The seat belt fracture. AJR Am J Roentgenol 111:844–849, 1971.

240. Rose, R.D.; Welch, W.C.; Balzer, J.R.; Jacobs, G.B. Persistently electrified pedicle stimulation instruments in spinal instrumentation. Technique and protocol development. Spine 22:334–343, 1997.

241. Rosenthal, R.E.; Lowery, E.R. Unstable fracture-dislocations of the thoracolumbar spine: Results of surgical treatment. J Trauma 20:485–490, 1980.

242. Rossier, A.B.; Cochran, R.P. The treatment of spinal fractures with Harrington compression rods and segmental sublaminar wiring: A dangerous combination. Spine 9:796–799, 1984.

243. Roy-Camille, R.; Saillant, G.; Berteaux, D.; et al. Osteosynthesis of thoracolumbar spine fractures with metal plates screwed through the vertebral pedicles. Reconstr Surg Traumatol 15:2–15, 1976.

244. Roy-Camille, R.; Saillant, G.; Mazel, C. Plating of thoracic, thoracolumbar, and lumbar injuries with pedicle screw plates. Orthop Clin North Am 17:147–159, 1986.

245. Ryan, M.D.; Taylor, T.K.F.; Sherwood, A.A. Bolt-plate fixation for anterior spinal fusion. Clin Orthop 203:196–202, 1986.

246. Saillant, G. Anatomical study of vertebral pedicles: Surgical application. (In French.) Rev Chir Orthop Reparatrice Appar Mot 62:151–160, 1976.

247. Sasso, R.C.; Cotler, H.B. Posterior instrumentation and fusion for unstable fractures and fracture-dislocations of the thoracic and lumbar spine. Spine 18:450–460, 1993.

248. Sasso, R.C.; Cotler, H.B.; Reuben, J.D. Posterior fixation of thoracic and lumbar spine fractures using DC plates and pedicle screws. Spine 16(Suppl):134–139, 1991.

249. Schlickewei, W.; Schutzhoff, G.; Kuner, E.H. Fruhfunktionelle Behandlung von Frakturen der unteren Brust und Lendenwirbelsaule mit dem Dreipunktekorsett. Unfallchirurg 94:40–44, 1991.

250. Schmidek, H.H.; Gomes, F.B.; Seligson, D.; et al. Management of acute unstable thoracolumbar (T11-L1) fractures with and without neurological deficit. Neurosurgery 7:30–35, 1980.

251. Shiba, K.; Katsuki, M.; Ueta, T.; et al. Transpedicular fixation with Zielke instrumentation in the treatment of thoracolumbar and lumbar injuries. Spine 19:1940–1949, 1994.

252. Shultz, A.; Benson, D.; Hirsch, C. Force deformation properties of human costosternal and costovertebral articulations. J Biomech 7:311, 1974.

253. Shuman, W.P.; Rogers, J.V.; Sickler, M.E.; et al. Thoracolumbar burst fractures: CT dimensions of the spinal canal relative to postsurgical improvement. AJNR Am J Neuroradiol 6:337–341, 1985.

254. Sim, E. Location of transpedicular screws for fixation of the lower thoracic and lumbar spine. Acta Orthop Scand 64:28–32, 1993.

255. Sjostrom, L.; Jacobsson, O.; Karlstrom, G.; et al. CT analysis of pedicles and screw tracts after implant removal in thoracolumbar fractures. J Spinal Disord 6:225–231, 1993.

256. Sjostrom, L.; Jacobsson, O.; Karlstrom, G.; et al. Spinal canal remodelling after stabilization of thoracolumbar burst fractures. Eur Spine J 3:312–317, 1994.

257. Smith, W.S.; Kaufer, A. Patterns and mechanisms of lumbar injuries associated with lap seat belts. J Bone Joint Surg Am 51:239–254, 1969.

258. Soreff, J.; Axdorph, G.; Bylund, P.; et al. Treatment of patients with unstable fractures of the thoracic and lumbar spine. Acta Orthop Scand 53:369–381, 1982.

259. Stagnara, P.; Demauroy, J.V.; Dran, G.; et al. Reciprocal angulation of vertebral bodies in a sagittal plane: Approach to references for the evaluation of kyphosis and lordosis. Spine 7:335–342, 1982.

260. Stambough, J.L. Cotrel-Dubousset instrumentation and thoracolumbar spine trauma: A review of 55 cases. J Spinal Disord 7:461–469, 1994.

261. Stanger, K.J. Fracture-dislocation of the thoracolumbar spine. J Bone Joint Surg Am 29:107, 1947.

262. Stauffer, E.S. Current concepts review: Internal fixation of fractures of the thoracolumbar spine. J Bone Joint Surg Am 66:1136–1138, 1984.

263. Stauffer, E.S.; Neil, J.L. Biomechanical analysis of structural stability of internal fixation in fractures of the thoracolumbar spine. Clin Orthop 112:159–164, 1975.

264. Steffee, A.D.; Biscup, R.S.; Sitkowski, D.J. Segmental spine plates with pedicle screw fixation: A new internal fixation device for disorders of the lumbar and thoracolumbar spine. Clin Orthop 203:45–53, 1986.

265. Suk, S.I.; Shin, B.O.; Lee, C.S.; et al. CD pedicle screws in the treatment of unstable lumbar fractures. Paper presented at the Fifth International Congress on CD Instrumentation, Paris, June 1988, pp. 93–102.

266. Vaccaro, A.R.; Rizzolo, S.J.; Allardyce, T.J.; et al. Placement of pedicle screws in the thoracic spine: Part I. Morphometric analysis of the thoracic vertebrae. J Bone Joint Surg Am 77:1193–1199, 1995.

267. Vaccaro, A.R.; Rizzolo, S.J.; Balderston, R.A.; et al. Placement of pedicle screws in the thoracic spine: Part II. An anatomical and radiographic assessment. J Bone Joint Surg Am 77:1200–1206, 1995.

268. Viale, G.L.; Silvestro, C.; Francaviglia, N.; et al. Transpedicular decompression and stabilization of burst fractures of the lumbar spine. Surg Neurol 40:104–111, 1993.

269. Watson-Jones, R. Fractures and Joint Injuries, 4th ed. Baltimore, Williams & Wilkins, 1960.

270. Weinstein, J.N.; Spratt, K.F.; Spengler, D.; et al. Spinal pedicle fixation: Reliability and validity of roentgenogram-based assessment and surgical factors on successful screw placement. Spine 13:1012, 1988.

271. Weitzman, G. Treatment of stable thoracolumbar spine compression fractures by early ambulation. Clin Orthop 76:116–122, 1971.

272. Wenger, D.R.; Carollo, J.J.; Wilkerson, J.A., Jr.; et al. Laboratory testing of segmental spinal instrumentation versus traditional Harrington instrumentation for scoliosis treatment. Spine 7:265–269, 1982.

273. White, A.A.; Panjabi, M.M. The basic kinematics of the human spine: A review of past and current knowledge. Spine 3:12–20, 1978.

274. Whitecloud, T.S.; Butler, J.C.; Cohen, J.L.; et al. Complications with the variable spine plating system. Spine 14:472–476, 1989.

275. Whitesides, T.E. Traumatic kyphosis of the thoracolumbar spine. Clin Orthop 128:78–92, 1977.

276. Wildburger, R.; Mahring, M.; Paszicsnyek, T.; et al. Dorsal stabilization of thoracolumbar spinal instability: Comparison of three different implantation systems. Arch Orthop Trauma Surg 113:244–247, 1994.

277. Willen, J.; Anderson, J.; Toomoka, K.; et al. The natural history of burst fractures at the thoracolumbar junction. J Spinal Disord 3:39–46, 1990.

278. Willen, J.A.G.; Gaekwad, U.H.; Kakulas, B.A. Acute burst fractures: A comparative analysis of a modern fracture classification and pathologic findings. Clin Orthop 276:169–175, 1992.

279. Willen, J.; Lindahl, S.; Irstam, L.; et al. Unstable thoracolumbar fractures: A study by CT and conventional roentgenology of the reduction effect of Harrington instrumentation. Spine 9:214–219, 1984.

280. Williams, E.W.M. Traumatic paraplegia. In: Mathews, D.N., ed. Recent Advances in the Surgery of Trauma. London, Churchill Livingstone, 1963, p. 171.

281. Wilson, P.D.; Straub, L.R. Lumbosacral fusion with metallic plate fixation. Instr Course Lect 9:53–57, 1952.

282. Yosipovitch, Z.; Robin, G.C.; Makin, M. Open reduction of unstable thoracolumbar spinal injuries and fixation with Harrington rods. J Bone Joint Surg Am 59:1003–1013, 1977.

283. Yuan, H.A.; Garfin, S.R.; Dickman, C.A.; et al. A historical cohort study of pedicle screw fixation in thoracic, lumbar, and sacral spinal fusions. Spine 19(Suppl):2279–2296, 1994.

284. Yuan, H.A.; Mann, K.A.; Found, E.M.; et al. Early clinical experience with the Syracuse I-Plate: An anterior spinal fixation device. Spine 13:278–285, 1988.

285. Zindrick, M.R.; Wiltse, L.L.; Doornik, A.; et al. Analysis of the morphometric characteristics of the thoracic and lumbar pedicles. Spine 12:160–166, 1987.

286. Zindrick, M.R.; Wiltse, L.L.; Wiidell, E.H.; et al. A biomechanical study of intrapedicular screw fixation in the lumbosacral spine. Clin Orthop 203:99–112, 1986.

287. Zou, D.; Yoo, J.U.; Edwards, T.; et al. Mechanics of anatomic reduction of thoracolumbar burst fractures: Comparison of distraction plus lordosis. Spine 18:195–203, 1993.

288. Zu, Z.; Maohua, C.; Tianhua, D. Unstable fractures of thoracolumbar spine treated with pedicle screw plating. Chin Med J (Engl) 107:281–285, 1994.

CHAPTER 31

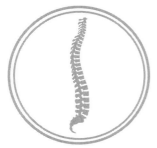

Low Lumbar Fractures

Alan M. Levine, M.D.

Treatment of injuries to the low lumbar spine requires consideration of a number of additional factors beyond those relevant to injuries of the thoracic and thoracolumbar spine. These factors are related to the anatomic complexity of the lower lumbar spine, as well as the lordotic sagittal alignment and increased normal mobility of the lumbosacral junction. During the 1970s and 1980s, the lack of satisfactory instrumentation and techniques for reduction and stabilization of injuries in the low lumbar spine while preserving motion and alignment frequently resulted in less than optimal treatment results and led most authors to espouse nonoperative techniques as a better alternative.[26, 49] Occasional reports, however, suggested that an operative approach yielded better anatomic results and perhaps even better functional outcomes.[84, 133] Even with the more widely accepted use of pedicle screw fixation for the lumbar spine in the late 1980s and early 1990s combined with more effective methods of sacral fixation, some early, poorly conceptualized operative approaches to fractures in this region also led to early failure.[4, 5, 62, 129] Although anterior approaches to these fractures have been advocated, rigid fixation to the sacrum from an anterior approach has been problematic and requires a combined approach if anterior decompression is used.[119] This problem caused some surgeons to accept chronic pain and the failure to return to preinjury occupation as the norm in this very young group of patients. Additionally, the relatively high complication rate associated with operative treatment of low lumbar fractures[132] has caused some to advocate nonoperative over operative treatment for these patients. A number of studies in the last 10 years have suggested that nonoperative treatment yields satisfactory results in this group of patients, all of whom are relatively young at the time of injury (average age in most series, 27 years). However, many problems still exist with regard to interpreting data on these fractures inasmuch as most series report short to intermediate follow-up (<4 years) in a group of predominantly young male patients (27 years old) more often than not employed in manual labor tasks.[21, 46, 107] Additionally, these conclusions are based on analysis of retrospective series with many discrep-

ancies and inconsistencies, such as marked variation in the elements of "nonoperative care." In some series, recumbency for up to 6 weeks is included as part of treatment,[4, 5, 8, 21, 124, 132, 133] whereas in others, it is not used. The type and duration of immobilization have also varied. Finally, the severity of injury has likewise not been uniform in comparisons of types of treatment[4, 5, 132] in that patients with less structural instability and those without neurologic deficit are most commonly treated nonoperatively whereas those with gross instability and neural deficit are treated with surgical decompression and stabilization. All these factors, in addition to studies suggesting comparable complication rates[124] for the two types of treatment, make selection of optimal therapy for an individual patient difficult.

In the lumbar spine, anatomic and motion considerations have made instrumentation more difficult than in other regions of the spine. Injuries to the lumbar spine and upper part of the sacrum disrupt the normal lordotic alignment of the spine, and restoration of that lordotic alignment is critical to overall vertebral mechanics and spinal alignment in the sagittal plane. Failure to maintain or restore normal sagittal alignment in the lower lumbar spine after either elective fusion or fracture has led to the occurrence of late symptoms and even degenerative changes in long-term follow-up. The lumbosacral junction in particular must resist a number of large forces, but it must also permit a significant amount of motion. It has therefore been difficult to achieve anatomic reduction and reconstruction of the lumbar spine and sacrum until the most recent advances in instrumentation. This difficulty has led many authors to suggest either limited procedures and goals or "benign neglect" as the method of treatment of low lumbar and sacral injuries. Fixation to the bone of the sacrum has been even more problematic. These numerous features and problems distinguish fractures of the lower lumbar spine from the more numerous and common fractures at the thoracolumbar junction.

More accurate diagnostic imaging studies, as well as advances in instrumentation techniques, should now allow us to treat injuries of the lumbar spine with the same degree of accuracy and competence as more proximal spinal injuries. To do so, however, we must have a clear understanding of the anatomic and functional differences that distinguish the lumbar spine from the remainder of the more proximal areas of the spine. As described in Chapter 30, a specific set of technical considerations and fixation methods are applicable to the treatment of spinal trauma in the thoracic region (T2–T10), and similarly, a set is applicable to the thoracolumbar junction (T10–L1). Fractures of the second lumbar vertebra form a transitional group, both functionally and technically, between those of the thoracolumbar junction (T10–L1) and those of the lumbar region (L3–S1). The major differences in anatomic considerations and techniques apply predominantly to L3–S1, whereas L2 should be considered the transitional level because treatment at this level involves borrowing techniques from above and below.

The treatment goals for spine trauma in general are (1) anatomic reduction of the injury, (2) rigid fixation of the fracture, and when necessary, (3) decompression of the neural elements. For treatment of low lumbar fractures, we must add the considerations of (4) maintenance of sagittal alignment, (5) conservation of motion segments, and (6) prevention of frequent complications (e.g., recurrence of kyphosis, loss of sacral fixation, pseudarthrosis). As the characteristics of the lumbar spine are reviewed, it will become evident that techniques discussed previously for the treatment of cervical, thoracic, and thoracolumbar spine injuries are not applicable to the treatment of lumbar spine injuries.

ANATOMIC FEATURES

The first critical anatomic consideration is the sagittal alignment of the lumbar spine. Normal kyphosis of the thoracic spine falls within a range of 15° to 49°,[155] whereas normal lumbar lordosis is generally thought to be less than 60°. This curvature is in part determined by the slope of the sacral base, which averages approximately 45° from the horizontal. This angle is critical in determining the amount of shear force[139] to which the lumbosacral junction is subjected (Fig. 31–1). Anatomic differences in the structure of the lumbar vertebrae and sacrum influence therapeutic decisions and affect the attachment of fixation devices differently than for proximal levels in the thoracic and lumbar spine.

With caudal descent in the lumbar spine, the overall dimensions of the canal enlarge and the area occupied by the neural elements decreases. The cord in the thoracic region measures approximately 86.5 mm² and is housed within a canal that averages about 17.2 × 16.8 mm². Thus, in the thoracic region, the cord occupies about 50% of the canal area. In the thoracolumbar region, the conus broadens, as does the canal. The spinal cord usually terminates at approximately L1. In the lumbar region, the canal is typically large (23.4 × 17.4 mm²).[41, 123] Here, the roots of the cauda equina are the only contents. In the sacrum, however, the diameter of the canal again begins to narrow and flatten. In addition, with the normal, slightly kyphotic angle at the midpoint of the sacrum

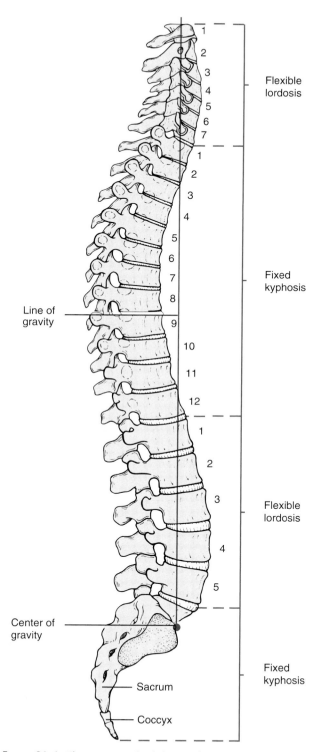

FIGURE 31–1. The spine is divided into four segments, two with relatively fixed kyphosis (the sacral and thoracic spine) and two with relatively flexible lordosis (the cervical and lumbar spine). The weight-bearing axis is anterior to the thoracic spine and thoracolumbar junction. Because it falls posterior to the vertebral bodies of the lumbar spine, the pattern of fracture with axial loading injuries is significantly different in the lumbar spine than in the thoracic and thoracolumbar spine.

(S2–S3), the roots are tethered in a relatively fixed location. This anatomic arrangement allows less flexibility in placing fixation devices within the canal in the sacrum. In addition, the size and shape of the laminae change configuration at the various levels of the spine. The laminae in the thoracic and thoracolumbar region are rectangular, somewhat longer than wide. In the midlumbar spine, the width and length of the laminae equalize. At L5, the laminae are considerably wider than long (Fig. 31–2). The sacral laminae are extremely thin and might be absent in some areas. Similarly, it has been shown that in the lumbar spine, the minimal and maximal pedicle diameters increase to reach a mean minimal diameter of approximately 10 mm at L5 and 8.5 mm at L3.[131]

With the increasing emphasis on innovative methods of fixation for injuries in the low lumbar spine,[13, 92, 119] an understanding of the pertinent anatomic dimensions takes on new significance. Previously, with hook fixation or sublaminar wiring to the posterior elements, the only important consideration was posterior topographic anatomy. However, the dimensions, position, and orientation of the pedicles, as well as the shape of the vertebral body, are likewise critical. The initial anatomic description of pedicle morphology referable to pedicle screw fixation was made by Saillant[129] in 1976 and confirmed by two later studies from North America.[77, 157] The critical features are sagittal and transverse width of the pedicles, pedicle length, pedicle angle, and chord length (depth to the anterior cortex along a fixed orientation). These dimensions vary widely within regions of the spine (thoracic versus lumbar), but they also vary within the lumbar spine, with progression from L1 to L5. The mean transverse diameter measured on either computed tomography (CT) or an anatomic specimen was approximately 9 mm at L1 and increased to as much as 18 mm at L5 (Fig. 31–3). The sagittal width in the lumbar spine is relatively constant, with a mean of between 14 and 15 mm at all levels (see Fig. 31–3B). The angle of the pedicle axis generally increases in the lumbar spine, with a mean of about 11° at L1, 15° at L3, and over 20° at L5 (see Fig. 31–3A). Finally, the angle of insertion of the screw is critically important inasmuch as the shape of the lumbar vertebrae changes dramatically from L1 to L5 (see Fig. 31–3C and D). Because the distance between the pedicles is greater at L5 and the anteroposterior (AP) diameter of the vertebral body is effectively less at that location, the chord length or distance from the posterior cortex to the anterior cortex can vary dramatically with the angle of insertion. If screws are inserted perpendicular to the posterior cortex along a 0° axis, as originally described by Roy-Camille, the mean depth at L1 is about 45 mm, whereas at L5 it is only 35 mm. Increasing the angle of insertion to 10° or 15° or to the angle of the axis of the pedicle can increase the cortex-to-cortex distance by as much as 5 mm at L1 (to 50 mm) and 15 mm at L5 (to about 50 mm).

For fractures of L5 or even very unstable shear injuries involving L4, fixation to the sacrum is a necessary component. Understanding the three-dimensional anatomy of the various sacral levels, as well as the position of the neurovascular structures applied to the anterior surface of the sacrum, is critical for the conceptualization of

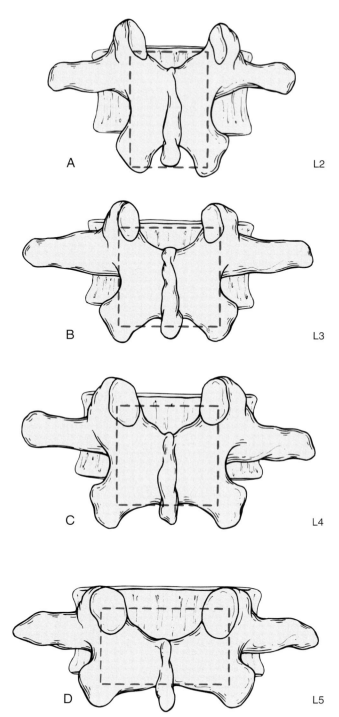

FIGURE 31–2. *A–D,* The shape of the lumbar laminae and the relative size of the pedicles dramatically influence the ability to position hardware. From L2 to L5, the length of the laminae becomes less and the width becomes greater. Therefore, hook placement is easier proximally in the spine but may cause impingement when placed over the lamina of L5 because of its relatively short length. However, pedicle fixation is easier distally with the larger pedicle size.

adequate and safe fixation to the sacrum. The anatomic structures that may be encountered at the level of the S1 body are the internal iliac vein, the lumbosacral plexus, and the sacroiliac joint. A safe zone bordered by the sacral promontory medially and the iliac vein laterally can, however, be used for fixation; it is about 2 cm wide and is invariably entered by orientation of a screw along the S1 pedicle.[109] Screws placed laterally at either 30° or 45° are aimed at a smaller lateral safe zone. The more lateral orientation provides for a longer screw length of 44 mm.[109] At the S2 level, the only vulnerable structure is the sigmoid colon on the left side. Penetration through the cortex by more than 1 cm is usually necessary for injury. At the S2 level, the thickness of the sacral bone is significantly decreased from that of the S1 level, and thus, the holding power of the bone in an axis parallel to the placement of S1 would be significantly less. To compensate for these deficiencies, orientation of fixation devices both proximally and laterally will significantly increase the length of screw purchase and thus pull-out strength. Variations in the amount of cancellous and cortical bone mass in different regions of the sacrum significantly affect fixation possibilities and the risk of fixation. Sacrum fixation is more secure in the sacral ala because of its increased bone mass or in the sacral vertebral bodies, as opposed to fixation in the very thin posterior laminar structures. Entry points for lateral and medial screw orientation at S1 are sufficiently separate to make it

technically feasible to obtain both medial and lateral fixation into S1, thus increasing stability and resistance to pull-out.

The next significant anatomic feature is the extreme flexion-extension mobility of the lumbar spine in comparison with other areas. The thoracic spine is relatively stiff as a result of the orientation of the facet joints. Flexion-extension in the thoracic spine is limited, and in fact, rotation exceeds flexion-extension at each level. At the thoracolumbar junction, flexion-extension increases, whereas lateral bending and rotation decrease. The orientation of the facet joints in the lumbar spine becomes sagittal, and the facet joints become quite large.[151] Therefore, the degree of freedom of motion progressively increases in flexion-extension from L1 to L5 and decreases in rotation. Flexion-extension increases from approximately 12° at the L1–L2 level to 20° at the L5–S1 level, with lateral bending remaining similar at about 6°.[150] This extreme flexion-extension mobility needs to be taken into account when considering injuries to the lumbar spine and sacrum because the relative position and orientation of one vertebra to another can change according to the position of the victim at

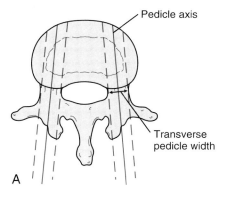

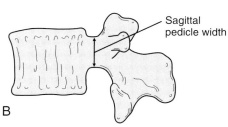

A

B

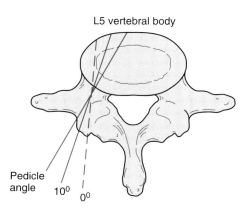

C

D

FIGURE 31-3. *A,* This axial view of a lumbar vertebral body shows the transverse pedicle width, which increases from L1 to L5. It also demonstrates the pedicle axis, which likewise increases from L1 to L5. *B,* A sagittal view of the vertebral body shows the sagittal pedicle width, which is relatively constant in the lumbar spine. *C,* This diagram shows an L1 axial view with the axis of the pedicle demonstrating the larger cortex-to-cortex distance. *D,* An axial view of L5 demonstrates how the anteroposterior length can increase with increasing angle.

impact. The extreme lumbar lordosis and lumbosacral angle can be flattened dramatically by sitting and the spine oriented in a vertical rather than lordotic position. This change in angle and orientation contributes to differences in the relative incidence of specific types of injuries in the lumbar spine in comparison with those in more proximal regions.

LUMBAR SPINE INJURY PATTERNS

Most operatively treated fractures of the thoracic, thoracolumbar, and lumbar spine occur at the thoracolumbar junction. As a result of the anatomic differences previously discussed, the relative incidence of patterns of injuries is different in the lumbar spine than in the thoracic or thoracolumbar spine. The thoracic spine is additionally stabilized by the rib cage, whereas the thoracolumbar junction is a transitional zone at the end of a relatively stiffer segment. The lumbar spine is protected by only the abdominal and paraspinous musculature and is more subject to forces such as distraction and shear. In addition, factors extrinsic to the spine, such as the type of accident (motor vehicle accident versus fall) and the use of restraints such as lap belts versus shoulder harnesses, also influence the number and types of injuries. For instance, the use of a lap belt alone by a passenger in a motor vehicle accident predisposes to flexion-distraction injuries of the lumbar spine.[7, 114] Because the lower lumbar spine and lumbosacral junction are normally quite lordotic, severe flexion injuries are less common than in the thoracic or thoracolumbar spine. The extreme flexion-extension range of motion frequently tends to negate the flexion moment of an injury. Therefore, more low lumbar injuries are axial loading injuries as the spine is brought to a straight neutral position at the moment of impact and is then axially loaded. Some flexion-distraction injuries occur as the pelvis or low lumbar spine becomes fixed in a given position and the remainder of the body is flexed and distracted over it.

A variety of different injury patterns can occur in the lumbar spine. The purpose of dividing them into subgroups and classifying the injuries is to be able to predict their natural history and behavior. Easy recognition of these subgroups is important for determining optimal treatment. In addition, such classification should help the treating physician understand the nature of the instability[16, 35] and thus construct a treatment regimen based on counteracting that instability. Although many classification systems exist, none has been totally successful in achieving those goals. Therefore, as in the other sections describing spinal injuries, these injuries are grouped and described by both radiologic criteria and their major deforming forces. The major forces contributing to the injuries are flexion, extension, compression, lateral bending, rotation, distraction, and shear. Most injuries are caused not by a single force but by a major force with minor components from other, different types of forces.

Soft Tissue Injuries, Avulsion Fractures, and Ligamentous Injuries

Although this group of injuries may conceptually appear to be quite simple to understand and treat, it may be the most challenging because the injuries encompass a large and highly variable group. Until the early 1990s, these injuries were very poorly imaged because we relied on plain radiographic and CT scan findings that were merely indirect evidence of the soft tissue and ligamentous injury. In some cases, these findings poorly reflect the force imparted to the spine or the subsequent severity of the injury. The improved use of magnetic resonance imaging (MRI) has at least allowed the physician to directly visualize the location of the injury; however, direct correlation between the visualized soft tissue or ligamentous injury and its effect on spinal stability has still not been clarified. The significant force needed to overcome the muscular and ligamentous restraints of the lumbar spine should be considered when evaluating these problems. For example, fractures of the transverse processes of the lumbar spine may represent several different injuries, depending on the mechanism. The significance of an L5 transverse process fracture associated with a vertical shearing injury to the pelvis is different from that of multiple transverse process fractures. A more severe injury would normally be expected from a direct blow, such as when a pedestrian is struck by a motor vehicle, and a less severe injury from indirect muscular tension. The significant force produced by the paraspinous musculature at the time of impact can result in an avulsion fracture of the transverse process (Fig. 31–4). More severe injuries can be accompanied by nerve root avulsion at the same level. Before any treatment and especially in combination with other significant bony injuries, avulsion fractures should be thoroughly investigated to ascertain that the nerve root exiting at the level of the transverse process is intact. Preoperatively, myelography often does not demonstrate dye leakage at the level of the avulsion, but preoperative MRI or intraoperative exploration at the time of surgery for an associated injury might confirm the diagnosis (see Fig. 31–4).

End-plate avulsion[106] is a recognized phenomenon in adolescent patients. Disc herniation can occur in an adult who sustains significant trauma, whereas in a child, the ligamentous attachments are somewhat stronger than the bony attachment of the end-plate (Fig. 31–5). Therefore, end-plate avulsion with displacement and neurologic findings might be present. This pattern of injury can be visualized by a combination of CT and MRI and should be treated by excision of the end-plate fragment, which usually resolves the neurologic symptoms completely. End-plate avulsion is most frequently seen in adolescents and young adults at the L4–L5 and L5–S1 levels.[42] In a younger child, it might occur only with avulsion of the cartilaginous ring apophysis. In adolescents and young adults, an isolated portion of the limbus or the entire bony end-plate can fracture off.[42] Neural impingement is the result of both the bony fragment and disc herniation.[42, 61, 145]

Disruption of the posterior ligamentous complex (i.e.,

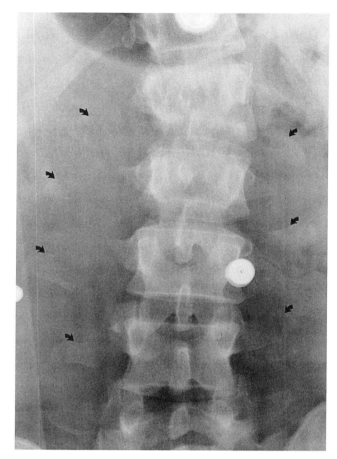

FIGURE 31–4. Anteroposterior radiograph of the lumbar spine of a 24-year-old man involved in a motorcycle accident. The patient had a burst fracture of L1 and multiple avulsion fractures of the transverse processes at L1, L2, L3, and L4 (*arrows*).

supraspinous ligament, intraspinous ligament, facet capsules, ligamentum flavum, and annulus of the disc) constitutes a continuum of injuries usually occurring in concert with other bony flexion injuries.[55, 58] If a significant ligamentous injury occurs alone or in combination with a very innocent-appearing bony injury, such as insignificant anterior compression of the vertebral body (Fig. 31–6), it may be easily overlooked initially. If the patient has considerable spasm from the soft tissue injury, the full significance of the ligamentous instability might be masked. CT scanning does not help demonstrate the extent of the ligamentous injury. Some evidence has indicated that MRI might be able to define the degree of ligamentous destruction, but not the instability. Clinical correlation of these findings is yet to be proved. Most of these patients do not have any neurologic deficit.[138] If a lap belt has been used without a shoulder harness, the patient might have significant abdominal injuries. A high level of suspicion for lumbar ligament disruption should be present in any patient with L3, L4, or L5 anterior compression who has sustained a high-impact injury. To achieve compression of the anterior portions of the low lumbar vertebrae, the entire lumbar lordosis needs to be overcome and the patient placed in significant

flexion, which should lengthen the posterior ligamentous structures beyond their elastic limit. Supervised flexion-extension radiographs after resolution of the initial spasm can make the diagnosis evident. Indications for surgical intervention and techniques are discussed in Chapter 27.

Wedge Compression Fractures

Wedge compression fractures (less than 50% anterior compression) result from a predominantly flexion injury. They can vary from mild anterior compression with little or no instability to gross instability with significant posterior ligamentous disruption. In all cases, the middle column is spared. By definition, the bony architecture of the posterior wall of the vertebral body must remain intact, and that is the critical defining difference between a compression fracture and a burst fracture. The degree of compression differs and results in the various fracture

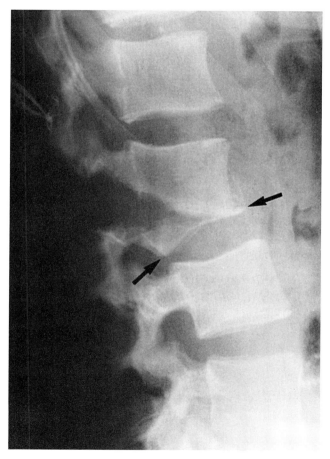

FIGURE 31–5. Lateral radiograph of the lumbar spine of a 16-year-old girl demonstrating an end-plate avulsion. She was involved in a motor vehicle accident and sustained complete paraplegia from the flexion-distraction injury several levels above the area of bone injury. Note the avulsion of the end-plate of the vertebral body (*arrows*) with translation of the end-plate anteriorly, in addition to the flexion and distraction of the posterior portion of the end-plate.

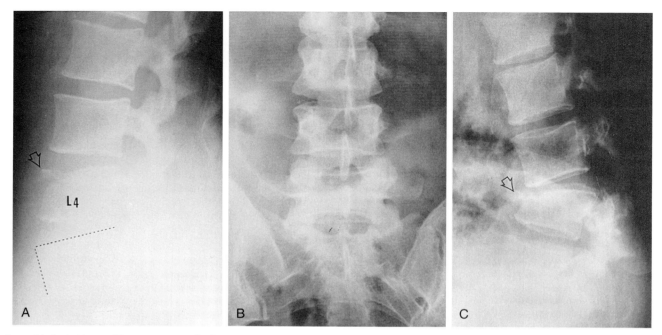

FIGURE 31–6. A 44-year-old woman was involved in a motor vehicle accident and sustained bilateral tibia fractures in addition to a fracture of L4. *A,* Lateral admission radiograph demonstrating alignment of her low lumbar spine at the time of acute evaluation. She underwent anterior compression *(arrow)* with satisfactory alignment in the sagittal plane. *B,* The anteroposterior radiograph does not show any apparent disruption of the posterior elements. She was therefore placed in an orthosis. *C,* Five months after the injury, the patient had significant back pain after being out of the orthosis for 2 months. A lateral radiograph shows not only the anterior compression *(arrow)* but also disruption of the ligamentous restraints posteriorly with subluxation of the facets and apparent disruption of the interspinous ligament.

patterns. The flexion load applied to the spine causes it to rotate about its axis of rotation and produces a fracture of the superior subchondral plate of the vertebral body (Fig. 31–7). Such fractures can occur at multiple adjacent levels in the lumbar spine. Care must be taken to differentiate this injury from one with a distractive force; in the latter case, severe ligamentous disruption can occur and the patient has significant kyphosis and ligamentous instability.

Compression fractures of the lumbar spine are a frequent consequence of severe osteopenia in older men and women. Although fractures of the lumbar spine occur less frequently than fractures of the thoracic region, once a single fracture has occurred, the risk of another fracture in either location is increased.[115] Approximately 10% of white women older than 50 years have at least one fracture[105]; the proportion increases to almost 50% of women older than 80 years who have at least one fracture.[100] These fractures may be associated with trivial trauma or may have no apparent trauma associated with them. They differ from compression fractures observed with trauma in younger individuals in that they may have a progressive course. When initially diagnosed at the time of onset of pain, these fractures may exhibit as little as 10% anterior compression with preservation of the posterior wall. However, over a period of 2 to 3 months, they can progress to almost 100% anterior compression with involvement of the posterior wall, canal compromise, and neurologic deficit. Intervention by vertebroplasty may be appropriate in patients with increasing compression and persistent pain.

Burst Fractures

The fractures of most patients who ultimately require operative treatment of injuries to the low lumbar spine fall into this category. The injury patterns can differ markedly, depending on the level of the injury, as well as the predominant forces responsible for causing the injury. All burst fractures are produced by a combination of forces that always include flexion and axial loading, with the pattern of the injury related to the relative proportions of the forces applied. These variations in pattern have been well described by Denis[34] (see Chapter 30). In the upper portion of the lumbar spine (L2 and L3), either a predominant axial loading injury (Denis type A) or a predominant flexion injury with some axial compression (Denis B) is possible. The former generally has little kyphosis but significant axial compression of the body with comminution of both the superior and inferior end-plates. The body-pedicle junction is disrupted, and posterior element fractures also frequently occur. The latter consist of a fracture of the superior end-plate and a portion of the body, with retropulsion of bone into the canal. The critical features on CT are that the lower portion of the pedicle remains intact and in continuity with the body. The retropulsed fragment is the posterosuperior portion of the vertebral body. These injuries usually involve significant anterior compression of the vertebral body, a variable amount of posterior ligament disruption, and sparing of the posterior elements (Fig. 31–8). A variant of this fracture type is the most common pattern that occurs in the low lumbar spine at the L4 and L5 levels. Fractures at L4 and

L5 demonstrate little kyphosis but can nevertheless cause significant canal impingement.

Reports by Levine and Edwards[82, 84] indicate that most of these injuries occur in younger patients, with slightly more than 50% younger than 20 years.[82, 84, 86] The fractures were equally divided between the L4 and the L5 levels and equally divided between patients with and those without neurologic deficit. The mean canal compromise was only 47%, but in 5 of 22 patients, the retropulsed bone was so severe that it was in contact with the undersurface of the lamina. In 18 of 22 patients, the vertebral comminution involved approximately the upper half of the vertebral body, and the inferior halves of the pedicles were not comminuted and remained connected to the lower portion of the body (Fig. 31–9). The inferior section of the vertebral body was split into two halves in the sagittal plane, as described by Lindahl and co-workers.[90] The mean loss of vertebral height was approximately 25% and was not as dramatic as in injuries to the thoracic and thoracolumbar spine. In addition, the measured kyphosis across the fracture level was only 8°. This figure is less than the average traumatic kyphosis of approximately 21° at the thoracolumbar junction, but it

must be placed in context with the normal lordotic posture of the low lumbar spine. If a normal value of approximately 15° of lordosis is accepted for each level (L4–L5 and L5–S1), the total relative kyphosis is approximately 23° (although the absolute kyphosis is only 8°). These figures are compatible with the amount of deformity seen in comparable injuries at other levels.

A smaller number of patients with L4 and L5 fractures have a classic burst fracture pattern (Denis A) (Fig. 31–10). This pattern also occurs more commonly in the upper portion of the lumbar spine at L2 and L3 and is characterized by marked widening of the pedicles on the AP radiograph, along with comminution of the pedicles and disruption of the body-pedicle junction. A large retropulsed fragment of bone and severe comminution of the anterior portion of the body are frequently seen. This scenario represents one extreme of the spectrum of flexion-compression injuries, with the dominant force being axial loading. Such a force complex yields more impressive comminution of the vertebral body, with less kyphosis. If the force is applied asymmetrically or if the patient twists during impact, a rotational or lateral bending component of the injury can be involved and induce scoliosis or lateral wedging (Denis E) (Fig. 31–11).

More recent studies have emphasized an additional feature of these fractures that is clinically significant. A small proportion of patients have a longitudinal laminar fracture that seems to be associated with traumatic dural lacerations.[25, 36] In patients with lumbar burst fractures, a sagittal split can occur in the spinous process. This split should be differentiated from a fracture or comminution of the lamina. An incomplete sagittal split of the spinous process is frequently recognized on CT. When combined with a burst fracture and neurologic deficit, a dural tear is usually indicated[87] (Fig. 31–12). Nerve roots can be outside the dural sac and might in fact be trapped in the split in the lamina. When evaluating these fractures, care should be taken to distinguish this feature so that appropriate surgical intervention can be undertaken.

Flexion-Distraction Injuries

Although most flexion-distraction fractures occur in the upper lumbar spine, less than 10% of all major fractures of the lumbar spine result from flexion-distraction forces. They are usually a result of the pelvis and lower part of the spine being anchored in a fixed position (e.g., by an automobile lap belt).[7] On impact, the upper portion of the spine accelerates and is thus distracted and flexed away from the fixed lower portion. Three major types of injuries occur. The first is a completely bony injury (Chance fracture), the second is a completely ligamentous injury (facet dislocation), and the third is part ligamentous and part bony. The implications for stability and treatment differ tremendously.

The Chance fracture, described by Chance in 1948,[22] is a pure bony injury with a fracture line extending in a posterior-to-anterior direction through the spinous process, pedicles, and body. It is frequently associated with seat belt wear.[60] The injury generally hinges off the

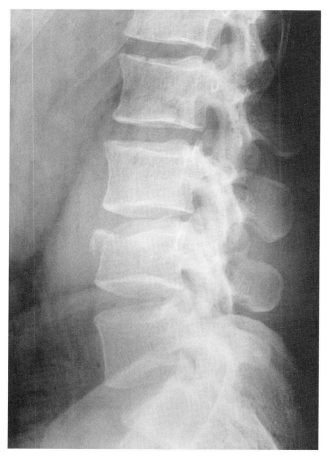

FIGURE 31–7. Lateral radiograph of the lumbar spine demonstrating an L4 compression fracture sustained during a motor vehicle accident. Note the compression of the anterior portion of the vertebral body. However, the posterior wall of the L4 body importantly remains intact with its normal biconcave appearance. The interspinous distance is not widened, and overall alignment of the lumbar spine remains within physiologic norms.

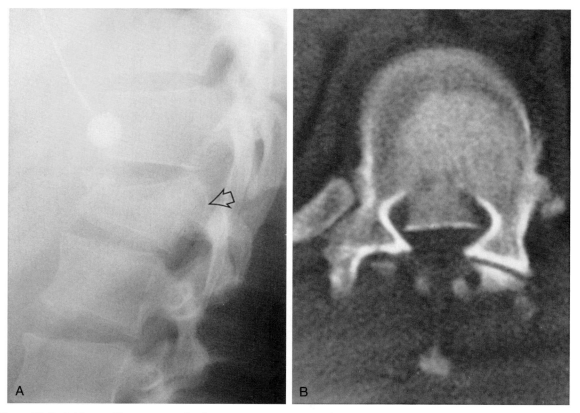

FIGURE 31–8. A 19-year-old man sustained a flexion-compression variant of a burst fracture when thrown from a motorcycle. *A*, A lateral radiograph demonstrates kyphosis at the level of the fracture with compression of the anterior portion of the vertebral body. The posterior wall is likewise disrupted, but its height is diminished to a lesser extent. The posterosuperior corner of the vertebral body is retropulsed into the canal (*arrow*) and is causing significant compression of the dural sac. Some widening of the interspinous distance has occurred, along with disruption of the interspinous ligament from the extent of flexion. *B*, A computed tomography (CT) scan at the level of the injury demonstrates two important features. First, a large central fragment of bone has been retropulsed back into the canal and is causing high-grade neural compression. This fragment, at the level of the pedicles, is seen on the lateral view. Importantly, the pedicles are intact. No break is noted in the lateral wall of the pedicle, nor is the pedicle comminuted. The pedicle remains connected to the vertebral body, so any lordotic pressure applied to the pedicles will be translated to the vertebral body. The posterior neural arch is also intact, although it is not seen on this cut of the CT scan.

anterior longitudinal ligament. In its common form, it has no significant shear component, nor is associated displacement present. It is infrequently associated with neurologic deficit. The diagnosis can be made from lateral and AP radiographs. The lateral radiograph demonstrates a split in the spinous process, whereas the AP radiograph demonstrates a coronal split through the pedicles on both sides (Fig. 31–13). Although a Chance fracture involves disruption of the posterior and anterior portions of the vertebral body, it is considered to be a stable injury and does not tend to angulate further into kyphosis.

Two reviews of flexion-distraction injuries[55, 58] showed that this injury occurred only between T12 and L4, and that approximately 50% of the injuries were at L2, L3, or L4. This injury has an extremely high incidence of associated intra-abdominal injuries (50%), including bowel rupture and liver or spleen lacerations.* These injuries were originally classified by Gumley and associates,[58] but the classification system was modified by Gertzbein and Court-Brown, who added anterior body

fractures.[55] Although the system is somewhat complex, the principle of differentiating the ligamentous from the bony component of the injury is critical. Injuries with a fracture line traversing the spinous process, pedicles, and body are likely to achieve satisfactory union and stability if acceptable sagittal alignment can be maintained (see Fig. 31–13). If the line of injury goes through the interspinous ligament and facets into the pedicle and body (Fig. 31–14), satisfactory union of the body can occur, but residual instability can result from the posterior ligament disruption.

Facet injuries of the lumbar spine occur infrequently. Levine and colleagues noted that bilateral facet dislocations below L1–L2 represent only 10% of the total cases.[85] The important feature of this type of flexion-distraction injury is that it is mainly a soft tissue injury that results in complete disruption of the posterior ligamentous complex as well as the intravertebral disc. The bony architecture of the facets remains intact but totally dislocated. The minor compression of the anterior portion of the inferior body is merely a result of the severe ligamentous injury and does not contribute to the overall instability of the injury. The posterior walls of both vertebral bodies remain intact, and

---

*See references 22, 31, 47, 53, 57, 60, 67, 70, 90, 99, 125–127.

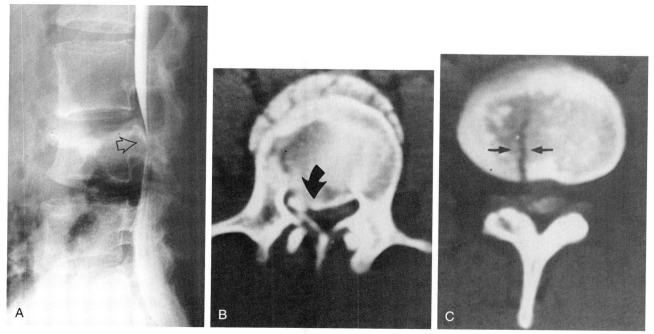

FIGURE 31–9. The flexion-compression variant (Denis type B) of a burst fracture is the most commonly seen pattern in L4 and L5 fractures. An 18-year-old man involved in a motor vehicle accident has rather typical findings. *A*, A lateral radiograph of the metrizamide myelogram shows kyphosis of 8° across the L4 vertebral level. Minimal to moderate compression of the superior portion of the vertebral body can be noted. The degree of compression seen at this level is frequently less than that at more rostral levels. In spite of the minimal compression of the vertebra, a large retropulsed fragment can create significant compression on the dural sac *(arrow)*; the dural sac compression may be asymmetric, in which case it frequently traps a specific nerve root or roots and causes radicular symptoms. *B*, This patient had compression of his right-sided roots as a result of a retropulsed fragment *(arrow)* and a laminar fracture posteriorly on the same side with depression of the laminar fracture. The displaced posterior wall fragment and the depressed laminar fragment were in continuity on the right side and causing right-sided radicular symptoms. The pedicles remain intact in most patients with L4 and L5 burst fractures. The superior portion of the pedicle may be comminuted, but the lower portion remains attached to the vertebral body. *C*, In addition, the lower half of the vertebral body is most commonly split in half in the sagittal plane *(arrows)*, with one pedicle remaining attached to each of the lower halves of the body.

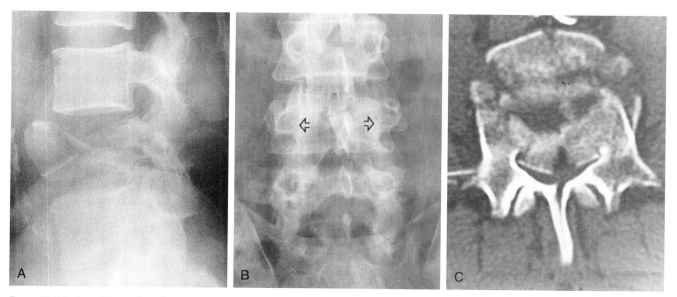

FIGURE 31–10. A smaller number of patients with L4 and L5 burst fractures have a classic burst pattern with comminution of the vertebral body and the pedicles. This 46-year-old man represents a typical example after a fall. *A*, A lateral radiograph demonstrates complete destruction of the L4 body with comminution of the pedicles and vertebral body. Little kyphosis is present, but there is a moderate degree of loss of height. The overall sagittal configuration of the spine remains relatively normal. *B*, An anteroposterior (AP) radiograph demonstrates splaying of the pedicles *(arrows)*. Loss of height at the vertebral body can be noted on the AP radiograph as well. *C*, Computed tomography demonstrates severe comminution of the vertebral body with marked retropulsion of bone into the neural canal. There is a disruption of the body at the pedicle junction and, in fact, comminution of the pedicles. This patient has a sagittal split of the spinous process at L4 as well.

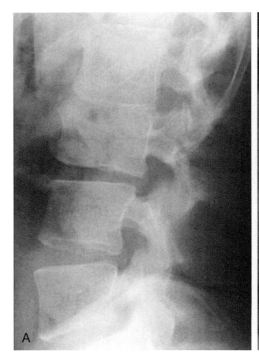

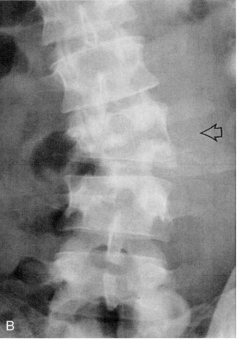

FIGURE 31–11. A 17-year-old boy sustained a burst fracture of the L3 level with severe lateral compression. *A*, A lateral radiograph demonstrates loss of height of the disc space at L2–L3 and slight kyphosis between L2 and L3. Comminution of the posterior elements (the spinous processes) is also noted. *B*, An anteroposterior radiograph demonstrates the major deformity: severe lateral wedging to the left side with severe compression of the left lateral side of the vertebral body. In addition, the transverse process and lamina of L3 on the right side are split *(arrow)*.

canal compromise results from the translation of one intact vertebral ring in reference to the adjacent ring. This injury must be differentiated from a facet fracture, which is mechanically a different injury with comminution of the facets and sometimes also the laminae, pars interarticularis, and vertebral body.

The severe translation seen in bilateral facet dislocations frequently results in significant neurologic injury (80%)[29, 54, 85] when the injury occurs at the thoracolumbar junction, but complete neurologic injury does not usually occur with these injuries in the low lumbar spine. Although severe translation resulting from disruption of the posterior ligaments occurs in association with severe disc disruption, the canal area is large enough that the nerve roots may be at least partially spared. Denis[34] suggested that complete posterior disruption is insufficient to account for the degree of flexion instability seen in this injury. Only incompetence of the posterior longitudinal ligament, anulus fibrosus, and disc could produce such a degree of translational instability. The anterior longitudinal ligament is often stripped from the anterior portion of the inferior body but remains intact. A number of authors[66, 89, 101, 152] have suggested that this injury is a flexion-distraction injury with the axis of rotation posterior to the anterior longitudinal ligament.

Radiographs of bilateral facet dislocations are usually diagnostic.[54, 85, 117] They demonstrate intact posterior walls of the vertebral bodies with significant translation (36%) and lesser degrees of anterior compression and loss of disc height (Fig. 31–15). AP radiographs of the lumbar spine often reveal the dislocation of the facets. CT scans confirm the pathology and demonstrate an empty facet sign,[117] as well as the severity of canal compromise on sagittal reconstructions.[54] The neurologic injury in patients with bilateral facet dislocations in the lumbar spine is less severe than in those with dislocations in the thoracic and thoracolumbar spine, 80% of whom are complete paraplegics. This decreased severity is clearly a result of the larger canal area and the resilience of the cauda equina. Unilateral and bilateral facet dislocations and fractures at the lumbosacral junction may be associated with sacral fractures and are therefore addressed in the chapter on injuries to the sacrum (Chapter 35).

Shear Injuries and Mixed Instabilities

Only about 3% of all major lumbar spine injuries are complex combinations of deformities or significant shear injuries. The addition of a shear force in combination with any other injury type markedly complicates the instability and treatment (Fig. 31–16). For example, the combination of shear force with a bilateral facet fracture-dislocation or Chance fracture can cause complete rupture of the anterior longitudinal ligament and marked translation. "Stiff spines," especially those affected by diffuse idiopathic skeletal hyperostosis or ankylosing spondylitis, are extremely susceptible to shear-type injuries, and dramatic deformity is noted on admission (Fig. 31–17). Although not all shear injuries demonstrate tremendous deformity initially, a more subtle indicator of this extremely unstable injury is bidirectional translation (anterior as well as lateral) (Fig. 31–18) on initial radiography.

These injuries are most significant in that they are grossly unstable and compromise the surgeon's ability to achieve anatomically stable reduction. Recognition of disruption of the anterior longitudinal ligament and the circumferential nature of the injury is important. Most posterior fixation techniques rely in part for their stability on an intact anterior longitudinal ligament. Care must be taken to recognize this phenomenon and to be certain that the constructs used to reduce and stabilize the injury counteract the instability.

NEUROLOGIC DEFICIT

The anatomic relationship of the conus and cauda equina to the lumbar spine largely determines the pattern of

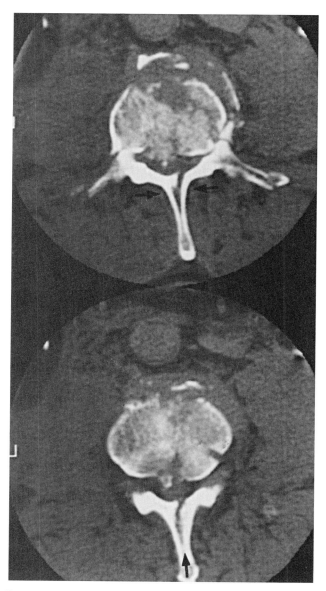

FIGURE 31–12. A 62-year-old man sustained a severe burst fracture of L3 with an incomplete neurologic deficit from L3 distally. Computed tomography demonstrates a burst fracture of L3 with severe comminution of the vertebral body and pedicles. In addition, the spinous process of L3 is split in a sagittal plane within the spinous process (*arrow*). On dissection of the posterior of the spine, this sagittal split is not evident. However, the combination of a sagittal split with a burst fracture of the lower lumbar spine and neurologic deficit is pathognomonic of a posterior dural tear. On exploration, the patient was found to have a 3-cm laceration of the posterior aspect of the dural sac with herniation of nerve roots through the sac and entrapment of the roots within the sagittal split of the spinous process.

neurologic deficit. At the upper end of the lumbar spine, the conus broadens and can occupy as much as 50% of the canal diameter.[123] In the distal portion of the canal, however, the cauda equina occupies less than a third of the cross-sectional area. Generally, spinal trauma from L2 down results in cauda equina (root-type) injuries, and thus recovery is different from that of injuries in the proximal portion of the canal. The relative position of the nerve roots within the dural sac is also important. The most posterior roots are usually those that exit more distally, because the more proximal roots are already anterior and lateral and somewhat more tethered by the bony foramen. This relationship is especially important for fractures of the lamina of L4 or L5, where roots may become entrapped after a traumatic dural laceration. These roots are generally the distal sacral roots, so injury to them may be evident only as changes in perineal sensation or subtle changes in bowel or bladder function.

Neurologic injuries related to lumbar spine injuries are usually of two types. The first is a complete cauda equina syndrome, which is often seen in severe burst fractures with canal retropulsion and large amounts of bone within the neural canal. The second type of injury is an isolated root injury or combinations of root injuries. These injuries may be nonrecoverable root avulsions and can occur in combination with avulsion of the transverse processes. Lesser degrees of root injury occur with canal impingement. Isolated root injury is common and is caused by a retropulsed fragment of bone catching the exiting root between it and the undersurface of the lamina. Root deficits are also frequent in patients with low lumbar fractures that have sagittal splits in the lamina associated with dural tears. Posterior dural tears allow herniation of the roots outside the dural sac or entrapment within the spinous process or laminar fracture.[25, 36, 87] Canal narrowing by translational deformity, such as in bilateral facet dislocation, is less likely to cause severe neurologic deficit in the low lumbar spine than at the thoracolumbar junction. Burst fractures of the lumbar spine are associated with neurologic deficit in about 50% of patients.

MANAGEMENT

Indications

Various systems have been devised in an attempt to classify spinal injuries according to both mechanism and degree of instability. In addition, a number of definitions have been proposed—for example, stable versus unstable. A generic definition of spinal stability includes fracture patterns that are not likely to change position with physiologic loads and will therefore not cause additional neurologic deficit or increasing deformity. Although many systems have been proposed that are applicable to lumbar spine injuries, no pragmatic system has been devised that clearly groups the injuries so that treatment approaches can be differentiated. Most classifications of thoracolumbar trauma have either an anatomic reference[14, 65] or a mechanistic reference,[44] but all clearly fail to achieve the desired goal of classifying injuries according to subsequent treatment categories.

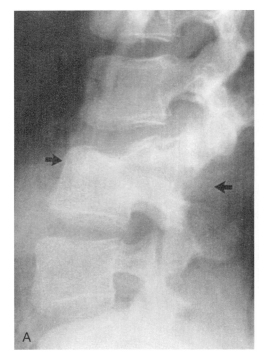

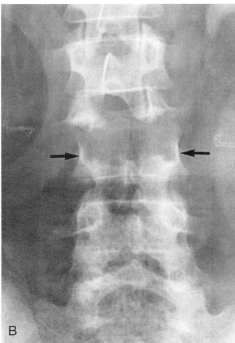

Figure 31–13. An 11-year-old boy was a passenger restrained by only a seat belt (without a shoulder harness) in a motor vehicle accident. He sustained a flexion-distraction injury with paraplegia at the T12 level. *A*, A lateral radiograph demonstrates a Chance fracture with the fracture line proceeding through the pedicles and the vertebral body in a line between the *arrows*. *B*, An anteroposterior radiograph shows both the transverse processes and the pedicle to be split in a coronal plane as marked by the *arrows*. Because this injury is strictly a bony injury, adequate bone-bone contact can be maintained and healing achieved without ligamentous instability.

Therefore, other criteria must be used to aid in making decisions about the treatment of lumbar and sacral fractures.

In general terms, the indications for surgery in patients with lumbar and sacral injuries are the following: (1) the presence of detectable motion at the fracture site that cannot be controlled by nonoperative methods (instability), (2) neurologic deficit, and (3) severe disruption of axial or sagittal spinal alignment. In lumbar and sacral fractures, the presence of neurologic deficit can indicate gross instability. With a large canal–neural element ratio, significant translation or angulation must take place to have neural injury. This rule is not universal, however, because transverse process fractures and avulsions can have accompanying nerve root avulsions. Additionally, in children, neurologic injury can occur at a level above that of the actual bony injury because of the differential elasticity of the cord and spinal elements.

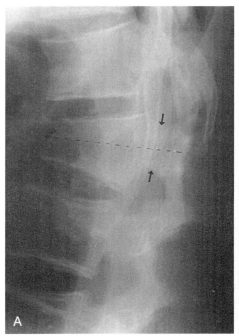

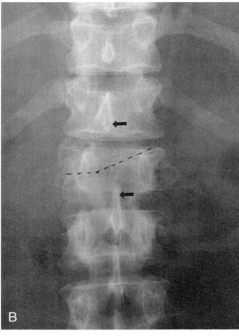

Figure 31–14. A 26-year-old man who had a car fall on him off a jack stand and cause severe flexion sustained a variant of a Chance fracture. *A*, On a lateral radiograph, kyphosis is centered at L1. The fracture line goes through the interspinous ligament and into the pedicle on one side and the pars on the other side and into the vertebral body. Both end-plates are intact, and the fracture line is seen in the vertebral body (*dotted line*). Note the widening of the pedicles (*arrows*). *B*, Widening of the interspinous ligament is evident (*arrows*) on an anteroposterior radiograph, and the fracture line is seen obliquely traversing the pedicle on one side and the pars on the other (*dotted line*). Because the interspinous ligament is disrupted, residual posterior ligamentous instability occurs after healing of the bone injury.

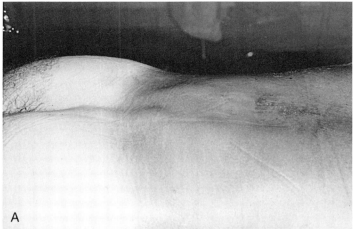

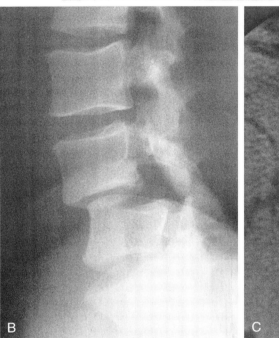

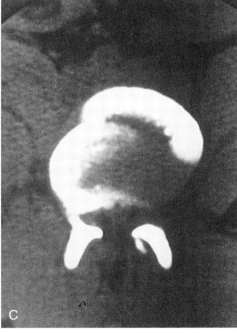

FIGURE 31–15. A patient sustained a bilateral facet dislocation at L4–L5. *A,* He presented with severe back pain, diffuse weakness below L4, and severe kyphosis, as seen in this preoperative photograph. *B,* A lateral radiograph shows severe translation of L4 over L5 with maintenance of height of the vertebral bodies. No fractures of the posterior wall were evident, although slight comminution of the anterosuperior portion of L5 occurred. *C,* A computed tomographic (CT) scan shows an empty facet sign. In addition, the translational and slight rotational deformities are apparent on this cut of the CT scan.

INSTABILITY

In lumbar fractures, certain patterns of injury can be defined as unstable, even in the absence of neurologic deficit. Patients with severe disruption of the posterior ligamentous complex from a flexion or flexion-distraction injury are considered to have unstable injuries. Treatment is clearly indicated, and there is little controversy regarding the appropriate treatment. Most authors believe that nonoperative treatment of ligamentous injuries does not restore stability and prefer limited operative stabilization. Similarly, flexion-distraction injuries, such as bilateral facet dislocations with complete disruption of the posterior ligamentous complex and the disc, are considered to have gross ligamentous instability that will result in continued loss of sagittal alignment. In addition, shear injuries with circumferential disruption are known to be grossly unstable and in fact require operative stabilization. Burst fractures present a much more complex problem because they represent a spectrum of injuries. Patients who are

neurologically intact with minimal deformity require less aggressive treatment than do those with more severe injuries. The problem is predicting behavior of the injury based on static radiographic studies. Burst injuries that demonstrate significant canal compromise, disruption of the anterior and posterior portions of the vertebral body, and laminar fractures are commonly considered unstable and require aggressive treatment. Mixed instabilities with gross displacement and shear injuries demonstrate markedly unstable clinical behavior.

NEUROLOGIC DEFICIT

The second criterion that constitutes an indication for treatment is neurologic deficit. The benefits of operative treatment of spinal injury have stimulated considerable controversy with regard to neurologic recovery of cord-level injuries,[23, 24, 27, 62, 81, 111, 136] but it is generally agreed that surgery is needed in the lumbar spine for the reason that most injuries involve the nerve roots.[25, 68, 87] Because the canal–neural element ratio is very large, a small degree of canal compromise (30%) in the absence of severe deformity (kyphosis) tends to not be significant with regard to neural recovery. A larger degree of canal compromise (50%) accompanied by high-grade neurologic compromise (cauda equina syndrome) can often be treated successfully by direct neural decompression.[84, 103] In addition, specific root involvement with localized compression of the root can be improved by direct exploration of the root and decompression. Finally, patients with sagittal spinous process fractures, neurologic deficit, and dural tears with roots outside the dural sac also benefit from direct decompression and dural repair.[25, 36, 87]

DISRUPTION OF AXIAL OR SAGITTAL SPINAL ALIGNMENT

The next indication for treatment is severe sagittal- or coronal-plane deformity. Most fractures of the lumbar spine result in kyphotic deformities and may be accompanied by translational and rotational deformities. Because normal lumbar sagittal alignment (i.e., lordosis) is critical to establishment of the normal weight-bearing axis of the body and to optimal function of the paraspinous musculature, restoration of sagittal alignment to normal is a critical element of treatment. It may be an important parameter in obtaining long-term pain-free functional results. However, the validity of this statement has not been fully verified because most of these injuries occur in

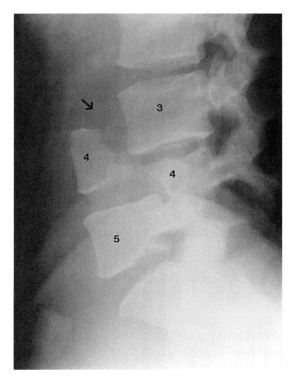

FIGURE 31–16. This lateral lumbar radiograph demonstrates a severe shear injury in a 26-year-old man ejected from a motor vehicle. The spinal column is totally disrupted, and a fracture line (*arrow*) is traversing obliquely in an anterosuperior-to-posteroinferior direction through the body of L4.

relatively young individuals and the follow-up in most operative and nonoperative series is still relatively short.[4, 5, 21, 46, 72, 74, 107, 142] Clinically stable fractures that do not have significant associated kyphosis or scoliosis can be optimally treated with external immobilization. However, fractures that have significant kyphosis or other deformities that cannot be reduced and maintained with external immobilization need operative intervention for reestablishment of normal spinal alignment. Less emphasis was previously given to operative intervention because of the lack of appropriate methods to restore spinal alignment in a predictable manner. In fact, the use of spinal instrumentation for fractures of the lumbar spine resulted not in restoration of spinal alignment but in iatrogenically induced flat back and other significant alignment deformities with secondary symptoms. If the aim of treatment is accurate restoration of alignment, the surgeon must be certain that the method selected can achieve that goal.

Treatment Options

A number of treatment measures can be used for the management of lumbar fractures, and, in general, consist of nonoperative and operative treatment. Nonoperative treatment may include varying combinations of immobilization by cast or orthosis, postural reduction, recumbency, or immediate mobilization. For low lumbar injury, as with thoracolumbar injury, treatment regimens have not been very consistent from series to series. Operative intervention can involve various procedures, including (1) reduction, stabilization, and fusion of spinal fractures from a posterior approach; (2) indirect or direct decompression of neural elements from a posterior or posterolateral (transpedicular) approach; and (3) decompression or reduction, stabilization, fusion, and fixation from an anterior approach.

NONOPERATIVE TREATMENT

Nonoperative treatment can be used for both stable and unstable injuries in the lumbar region. It is most often indicated for minor fractures such as spinous process fractures, transverse process fractures, compression fractures with less than 50% anterior compression, and Chance fractures. In addition, some burst fractures[21, 65] can be regarded as stable and therefore appropriate for nonoperative treatment. The trend in the last 5 to 10 years has been an overwhelming transition toward nonoperative treatment for burst fractures of the low lumbar spine. This shift in approach has been the result of a number of factors, such as the relatively high complication rate with operative treatment of these fractures, loss of correction after operative treatment, and finally, failure to demonstrate improved functional results in short- to intermediate-term follow-up with operative treatment. However, no randomized, prospective studies have directly compared the two approaches. Currently, therefore, a major consideration in making the decision should be the degree of disruption of the posterior wall of the vertebral body and the extent of disruption in sagittal and axial alignment. Optimal nonoperative treatment of lum-

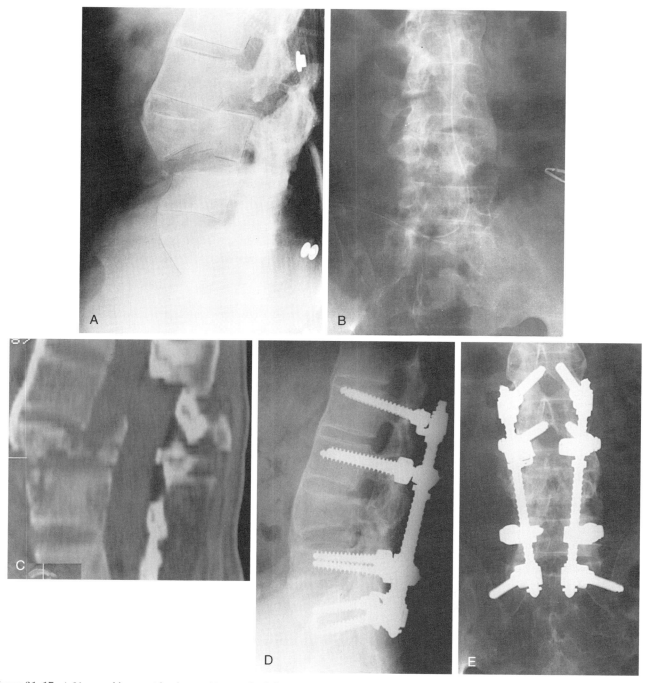

FIGURE 31–17. A 31-year-old man with a known history of ankylosing spondylitis fell from a roof, landed on the upper part of his back, and sustained this shear injury. *A,* The lateral radiograph is the most dramatic, with the fracture line going through the ankylosed spine at the level of L4. There was 50% translation but relatively minimal angulation. *B,* The anteroposterior (AP) view shows little or no angulation or translation in this plane. *C,* Most likely as a result of the uniplanar translation and the significant comminution of the spinal canal without retropulsion seen on this computed tomographic reconstruction, the patient had minimal neural deficit. Anatomic reduction was achieved with multiple points of fixation on the two rigid segments, and reduction was maintained in both the lateral (*D*) and the AP (*E*) planes at 1-year follow-up.

bar burst fractures should involve prolonged bedrest (3 to 6 weeks) before mobilization in an appropriate orthotic device. Failure to provide sufficient protection from axial loading forces by the use of bedrest can result in further deformity. At present, patients without neural deficit or with only minor isolated root deficit are optimal candidates for nonoperative treatment. Those with more dense neural deficits or severe deformity are better treated operatively. Even advocates of postural reduction have indicated that certain fracture patterns, such as bilateral facet dislocations, are not amenable to postural reduction and must be treated surgically regardless of the patient's neurologic status.[66]

Optimal orthotic use for most fractures of the low

lumbar spine requires immobilization of the pelvis by a single leg spica cast or a thoracolumbosacral orthosis to fix the relationship of the low lumbar spine. Immobilization by standard lumbar orthoses could actually accentuate motion at L4–L5 and L5–S1.[45, 116] For upper lumbar fractures, a molded total-contact orthosis provides optimal immobilization. Care should be taken to not use an orthosis with a thoracolumbar extension (e.g., a Jewett brace) in the lumbar spine because it might increase motion at the index level by rigidly immobilizing more proximal levels. Thus, pain and deformity might increase in the low lumbar spine.

Some authors have advocated the use of nonoperative treatment for unstable injuries. Treatment consisted mainly of using bedrest to reduce gross malalignment and allow the fracture to begin to consolidate in the supine position before mobilization. Although such management was once an accepted method of treatment,[11, 48] the current demands to reduce the length and cost of hospitalization, combined with the effectiveness of operative methods, render nonoperative treatment less desirable for unstable fractures.

OPERATIVE TREATMENT GOALS AND INSTRUMENTATION

Once the decision has been made to consider surgery for a patient with a spinal injury, the goals must be clearly

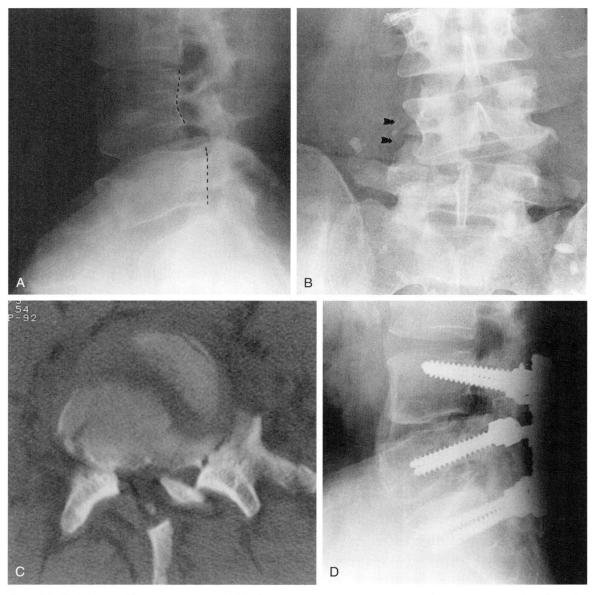

FIGURE 31–18. A 44-year-old man was sitting in the bleachers as a spectator at a sporting event when a runaway van plowed into the stands. He sustained this L4–L5 shear injury with complete three-column disruption. A, The anteroposterior radiograph shows both angulation and translation, whereas the lateral film (B) shows predominantly translation (arrows). C, An axial cut of a computed tomographic scan through the disc space gives the best visualization of the severity of the injury, which consists of total disruption of the entire spinal column. D, Reduction and stabilization were achieved through the use of segmental fixation, including reapproximation of the fractured pedicles to the vertebral body with central screws.

defined to aid in selecting the appropriate procedure to achieve optimal results. With specific reference to the lumbar spine, the goals of operative treatment are reviewed here, and the various surgical methods by which those goals can be achieved are discussed. Details of the operative methods for specific injuries and their treatment plans are described subsequently.

The major goals in the treatment of lumbar spine injuries are anatomic reduction of the fracture, maintenance of correction, decompression of neural elements (when indicated), maintenance of sagittal alignment, minimization of fixation length, and minimization of the complication rate. The time from injury must also be considered because the efficacy of various methods changes with the time course.

The controversy concerning the relative benefits and risks of operative versus nonoperative treatment of fractures of the lumber spine continues to rage. Since the early 1990s, with the advent of patient satisfaction scales, measurement of the outcome of treatment has become more objective and is now considered to be as important as objective neurologic and radiologic criteria. A major problem still exists when attempting to decide on the optimal treatment for lumbar burst fractures. The average age of patients sustaining these injuries is around 27 years, and many are employed in manual labor at the time of injury. Although short-term studies have suggested that the fractures heal relatively reliably, the long-term outcome has not been clearly delineated. If we are technically able to restore anatomic alignment of the spine, do these patients do better with less pain and return to previous employment in both short- and long-term evaluation? Part of the problem in decision making is that some surgical techniques were used that either did not restore or did not maintain anatomic alignment.[4, 142] Thus, the appropriate comparison is restoration of alignment with nonoperative treatment. With relatively short follow-up (<4 years), the trends in current studies suggest that patients with neurologic deficit appear to recover more quickly and more completely with surgical intervention.[68, 107] Some authors believe that nonoperative treatment of low lumbar burst fractures will provide satisfactory short-term results, but when the data are critically analyzed, most patients have a significant degree of residual back pain and disability, even in the short term.[4, 5, 21, 46] More accurate reduction and longer-term follow-up will yield different conclusions. In a series of 30 patients with a range of follow-up of 5 to 11 years (mean, 8.2 years) and with anatomic restoration of alignment in most patients, the incidence of back pain was less than 20% and the norm was return to preinjury employment.[88] Thus, the current trend is nonoperative treatment for patients who are neurologically intact and have minimal to moderate deformity. For those with significant deformity, neurologic deficit, or both, operative treatment should give better long-term results.

Anatomic Reduction of the Fracture

The first goal of operative intervention is anatomic reduction of the fracture. A general principle of achieving anatomic reduction is that the deforming forces that caused the injury must be directly counteracted by the instrumentation system used to achieve the reduction. In addition, in the lumbar spine, the deforming influence of normal physiologic forces must also be counteracted, specifically, the shear force acting at the lumbosacral junction. For the lumbar spine, selection of an instrumentation system should be determined by the ability of that system to achieve reduction of the deformity and by the relative length of the instrumentation required. If a shorter construct can achieve the same degree of reduction and rigid fixation, it should be used preferentially to maintain as many mobile levels as possible in the lumbar spine. Flexion and axial loading contribute in varying degrees to most deformities in the lumbar spine, and counteracting these forces should be carefully considered. The fixation procedure should have an element of distraction and lordosis to restore normal alignment. Experimental data have demonstrated that devices offering variable and independent application of distraction and lordosis are more able to achieve anatomic reduction.[17, 158]

Not all instrumentation systems can achieve optimal results in all portions of the spine. In the following sections, some general types of instrumentation and their feasibility for use with different types of injury in the lumbar spine are considered. Over the last decade, a rapid transition has occurred in the types of instrumentation used for both elective fusion and fixation of fractures in the lumbar spine. Although Harrington distraction rods were initially used for stabilization of spinal fractures, even in the lumbar spine, they proved inadequate because of the loss of lumbar lordosis imparted by the distraction. They failed either by hook dislodgement or by creating a lumbar flat back. Even the rod-sleeve method, which allowed anatomic reduction with distraction while maintaining some lordosis, had a higher complication rate when used in the lumbar spine.[40] Contoured rod systems with segmental fixation by either wires or hooks (e.g., Moe rods, Harri-Luque, Cotrel-Dubousset, Synthes, TSRH [Texas Scottish Rite Hospital]) allowed correction of deformity and restoration of sagittal alignment for many patients, but with the disadvantage of requiring a longer length of instrumentation. The advent of pedicle screw systems allowed reduction and fixation of lumbar injuries while immobilizing fewer levels, thus more easily maintaining lordosis with less hardware dislodgement. Whereas the early systems such as the Olerud device and the Fixateur Interne were bulky and complicated, more current systems have technical advantages over the early pedicle screw systems. Although no appreciable improvement in outcome was noted in the treatment of thoracolumbar fractures,[156] the differences are more pronounced in the low lumbar spine. In addition, most pedicle screw systems can achieve rigid fixation and maintenance of sagittal contours. Additionally, the length of instrumentation does not need to be increased when removing portions of the posterior elements for repair of dural lacerations or for direct root decompression.

Pedicle screw systems are of two basic types: plate-based systems and rod-based systems. Most plate-based systems have no significant capability of achieving reduction other than by postural reduction on the operating table.[39, 93, 128, 141] Rod-based pedicle fixation devices[37, 76, 94, 95, 118] allow progressive reduction of deformities after screw fixation, with maintenance of correction.

Anterior Procedures. Anterior procedures for decompression, reduction of deformity, and stabilization have been used in the acute setting. In the absence of instrumentation, the long-term results of anterior correction of deformity with the use of a strut graft have been poor in terms of maintenance of anatomic alignment.[103] A tricortical bone graft cannot provide progressive correction, but when augmented by the use of a plate, it may be a satisfactory alternative in certain L3 and L4 fractures. Fixation to the sacrum is not truly feasible from an anterior approach, and fixation to L5 can even be difficult because of the relationship of the hardware to the iliac vessels. The ability to slightly compress and distract is now built into the slotted holes and instrumentation of several different plate designs.[69] This addition is an improvement over previous plates that simply functioned as neutralization devices. These plate systems now allow decompression and reasonable stabilization to be accomplished from an anterior approach for upper lumbar spine fractures.

For the correction of deformity from spinal fractures that are more than 6 weeks old, the mechanics of correction are different because secondary changes have occurred that complicate the fracture deformity. Primary healing of the cancellous fractures has begun, along with scarring of the soft tissues. At this stage, an anterior procedure for release of tissues becomes important in achieving and maintaining correction as the complexity and stiffness of the deformity increase. When reduction is attempted with posterior instrumentation alone more than 6 weeks after injury, it is difficult to overcome the kyphosis that has resulted from the shortening of anterior structures and the formation of anterior bony bridges. Some preliminary evidence is now available that anatomic reduction can be achieved and maintained from a posterior approach with appropriate application of forces if no synostosis has formed anteriorly. Total reduction from an anterior approach alone can be difficult in these late cases because posterior scarring or healing of posterior element fractures may have occurred. In addition, most anterior spinal devices lack sufficient lever arms and rigidity of fixation points to be able to apply forces adequate for achieving total reduction.

Maintenance of Correction

The second goal of surgical treatment, maintenance of correction, is related to the rigidity of fixation and to the ability of the selected instrumentation to counteract both the deforming forces and the normal physiologic forces of the lumbar spine. Long-term results with regard to the rigidity of fixation have been poor for devices that do not counteract all the deforming forces, such as straight distraction rods and segmental spinal instrumentation. In addition, in the lumbar spine, where construct length is important, shorter constructs impart more load bearing to the hardware and may therefore have a higher failure rate. The concept of load sharing either with intact posterior elements or with supplemental anterior graft should be considered. Experimental data on short constructs for the lumbar spine often lead to the conclusion that restoration of the anterior column with a strut graft is important,[39, 59, 75, 96, 137] although in practice, load sharing with

the intact posterior elements, if properly applied, seems to be sufficient. In addition, in areas of the spine where stability of the construct is compromised by inadequate terminal fixation (e.g., the sacrum), maintenance of long-term anatomic restoration of alignment has been unsatisfactory. Posterior devices that achieve rigid fixation and counteract deforming forces can produce satisfactory results with hook or pedicle screw fixation. The use of anterior grafts as the sole stabilizer after anterior decompression and correction of deformity has had disappointing results. More rigid anterior devices have improved the outcome in maintaining satisfactory long-term results.[97] The combination of anterior surgery to restore stability of the anterior column plus posterior pedicle screw fixation can allow optimal stability, but it requires more extensive surgery with higher risk and is probably not indicated except when anterior decompression is necessary. Even when the anterior portion is performed thoracoscopically, the operative time and relative risks are still high.[119]

Decompression of Neural Elements

The third goal, decompression of neural elements, is not always a critical one for surgical treatment of lumbar burst fractures. Although it was originally thought that a patient who was neurologically intact but had significant canal compromise might benefit from neural decompression, it has been shown that this assumption is false. Late spinal stenosis does not occur in either operated or nonoperated patients in whom reasonably normal anatomic reduction is achieved. It has been well demonstrated that resorption of residual bone within the canal predictably occurs both with and without surgery.[19, 28, 32, 79, 136, 143] Thus, the sole indication for neural decompression is neural deficit. Neural decompression can be achieved in several different ways, both directly and indirectly, and the most favorable method depends on the specific clinical situation. Laminectomy alone rarely plays a role in decompression of retropulsed bone that has been retropulsed against the anterior portion of the dural sac. It is effective in removing pressure from a posterior fragment of lamina driven into the canal or in decompression of an isolated root. Significant experimental[50, 63] and clinical evidence[27, 38, 83, 135, 147, 154] has indicated that immediate indirect decompression by ligamentotaxis and complete correction of the deformity can provide adequate decompression of the neural elements. This technique has been shown to be most effective in the first 48 hours after injury. Transpedicular decompression is a direct posterior technique,[62, 146] but one with limited visibility of the anterior portion of the dural sac and with results that do not differ from those of indirect decompression. In the low lumbar spine and sacrum, however, indirect decompression is not as successful because the technique depends on distraction and tensioning of the posterior longitudinal ligament. It is therefore less effective in an area of extreme lordosis or kyphosis. Thus, at L4 and L5, direct decompression by laminectomy or laminotomy can be effective in revealing the area of compression and allowing decompression by removal of the bone fragments that are compressing the dural sac or nerve roots. This technique can be done because limited retraction of the dural sac to achieve exposure is possible at this level. It is recommended only for areas of the spine involving the cauda equina. Direct decompression is most easily performed when the compression is one sided and bilateral exposure is not necessary. It is technically easier when carried out within the first 2 weeks after injury because the fragments are more mobile and more easily removed. In the upper lumbar spine, a transpedicular posterolateral approach to direct decompression might be indicated. In this case, removal of a portion of the lamina and the pedicle exposes the dural sac adequately on one side and allows direct decompression.

For patients who have had inadequate indirect decompression with posterior instrumentation or who are initially seen late (more than 2 weeks after injury) and require decompression of the dural sac, anterior corpectomy and direct decompression are the most effective procedures. Some authors have advocated direct anterior decompression and stabilization in the immediate acute setting for the treatment of lumbar trauma, but the increased morbidity and potential for decreased stabilization noted with the anterior approach make it a somewhat less attractive alternative. In addition, the use of pedicle fixation for the stabilization of especially low lumbar fractures allows laminectomy and posterior decompression along with a very short construct length, without compromising the quality of the reduction and stabilization.

Maintenance of Sagittal Alignment

The next important goal in the treatment of low lumbar fractures is maintenance of sagittal alignment. Any instrumentation system used for these fractures should be able to impart and maintain the lordosis of the lumbar spine and lumbosacral junction. When crossing the lumbosacral junction, as is the case with many low lumbar fractures, fixation to the pelvis needs to be accomplished to maintain lordosis. Hook fixation to the sacrum is inadequate.[13] Several systems have used rods driven into either the sacral ala or the ilium; the latter has the disadvantage of crossing the sacroiliac joint. Most fixation constructs crossing the lumbosacral junction require screw fixation. Such fixation is especially critical in maintaining the lumbosacral angle, lumbosacral lordosis, and overall sagittal alignment of the spine.

Minimization of Fixation Length

Minimizing fixation length to maintain the maximal number of mobile lumbar segments is the next important treatment goal and consideration in instrumentation of fractures of the lumbar spine. However, satisfactory balance must be maintained between the number of levels requiring instrumentation to achieve satisfactory reduction plus stabilization and preservation of important lumbar motion segments. Fixation rigidity should not be compromised to shorten levels, such as with the use of Luque rectangles in fractures of the lumbar spine. Similarly, plate fixation requires an adequate number of screws above and below the fracture. Even the Cotrel-Dubousset system has been found to be inadequate in maintaining alignment with the use of short constructs[1, 9, 10] (less than four levels) and requires augmentation with an anterior strut graft to achieve anatomic reduction. Parker and colleagues[122] attempted to quantify the degree of disruption of the anterior column to understand which fractures had

sufficient residual integrity to allow short-segment posterior instrumentation. Although this concept is helpful, in reality, the most stable fracture patterns that would maintain alignment with short-segment fixation would also most probably maintain alignment with nonoperative treatment. Even anteriorly, attempts have been made to shorten the construct to only the injured segment.[110] Thus, when selecting a construct, the surgeon should keep in mind both the rigidity of fixation and the length of the construct to avoid compromising other treatment goals.

Minimization of the Complication Rate

The final treatment goal of lumbar and sacral fractures is to minimize the extremely high complication rate associated with instrumentation of these injuries. The major complications are pseudarthrosis, failure of sacral fixation, and iatrogenic flat back.[80] Care must be taken when achieving the other treatment goals so that the instrumentation system does not jeopardize the results with an unacceptably high complication rate.

Standard Techniques for Specific Types of Injuries

MINOR BONY, DISCAL, AND LIGAMENTOUS INJURIES

Most minor bony injuries, such as avulsion fractures, spinous process fractures, and ligamentous strains, are satisfactorily treated by external immobilization for symptomatic relief. Patients with posterior ligamentous instability but no significant fracture might not be initially recognized, but once the spasm of the acute injury has subsided, flexion-extension radiographs can usually demonstrate the instability. With a minor degree of disruption (sprain), external immobilization for 6 weeks to 2 months can allow sufficient healing to achieve symptomatic relief and stability. If the disruption is complete, with tearing of the ligamentum flavum and annulus and anterior wedging of the disc space on flexion-extension radiographs, arthrodesis may be necessary to restore sagittal alignment and control the ligamentous instability (Fig. 31–19). Avulsion fractures of the transverse processes can be treated symptomatically by external immobilization to support the severe muscular trauma associated with the more minor bony injury. Transverse process fractures associated with more severe bony injury can be secondarily treated by immobilization of the primary injury. End-plate avulsions in children simulating disc herniation in the acute injury setting require surgical intervention for direct decompression after appropriate diagnostic studies.[40, 42, 145] A laminotomy, as used for discectomy, is generally sufficient to allow excision of the protruding portion of the end-plate. The remaining portion of the end-plate generally heals without further intervention.

ANTERIOR WEDGE COMPRESSION FRACTURES

Compression fractures of the lumbar spine are relatively frequent as either single or multiple injuries. Their outcome is usually favorable, except in an osteopenic

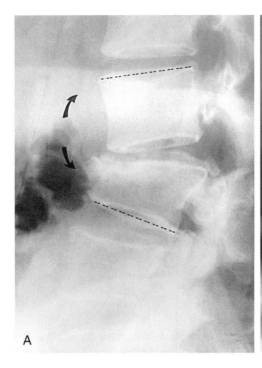

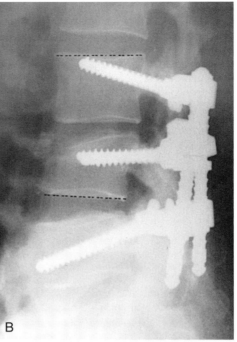

A   B

FIGURE 31–19. A 44-year-old woman whose initial radiographs are shown in Figure 31–6 presented 5 months after injury with severe kyphosis and ligamentous instability. *A*, Unfortunately, her maximal hyperextension radiograph shows only minimal correction of kyphosis (*arrow*). The patient underwent posterior correction, stabilization, and fusion of her kyphosis. *B*, She eventually achieved solid arthrodesis and is pain free with no evidence of instability.

patient. The two most common diagnostic problems are failure to recognize accompanying severe ligamentous disruption and the incorrect identification of a burst fracture as merely a compression fracture. In evaluating these injuries, care must be taken to prove that the posterior wall of the vertebral body remains intact.

Another common pitfall in the treatment of these injuries is failure to recognize the extent of the injury. Although the degree of sagittal-plane deformity might not be severe, CT scanning is indicated to confirm the integrity of the posterior wall of the vertebral body. Careful examination of centered AP and lateral plain radiographs will differentiate the two injuries in most cases. Often, the lateral radiograph shows displacement of the posterosuperior corner (Fig. 31–20). Comminution of the posterior wall converts the injury to the more significant burst pattern, which alters the prognosis and the treatment program. In addition, the surgeon must be certain that the compression fracture is not accompanied by ligament disruption (see Fig. 31–19).

For wedge compression fractures with loss of less than 50% of the height of the vertebral body, no ligamentous instability generally exists. The goal of treatment is to prevent further anterior compression and residual kyphosis.[78] Nonoperative treatment, even in hyperextension, cannot restore vertebral height, but affected patients are still best treated nonoperatively. Careful attention needs to be paid to the ability of the orthosis chosen to immobilize that segment of the spine. Compression fractures of L2–L4 are not hyperextended by a Jewett brace and might in fact be made worse. These fractures require a lumbar orthosis, such as a chair-back orthosis, Norton-Brown brace, or total-contact orthosis. Compression fractures of L5 are not well immobilized by the standard lumbar orthoses, and in fact, motion at the L5 level is accentuated by the use of a lumbar orthosis, which blocks movement at the other levels.[45, 116] Immobilization of L5 fractures requires a

single leg included in the orthosis to immobilize the lumbosacral junction. Immobilization needs to be extended for a period of 3 months, until the vertebral body has consolidated. After immobilization, the patient should be checked with flexion-extension radiographs to determine whether any residual instability is present. Increasing compression during the course of treatment that interferes with the normal lordotic sagittal alignment of the spine might require a change in treatment, surgical restoration of alignment, and single-level arthrodesis.

Compression fractures secondary to osteoporosis require two critical elements in their treatment. First, compression fractures in the lumbar spine can result in a significant retroperitoneal hematoma, which in an elderly patient may result in an ileus. Additionally, establishment of a pain medication level that is tolerated by an elderly patient may be difficult. Therefore, it is recommended that the patient be admitted to the hospital for a period of 24 hours after the diagnosis is made to ascertain that an ileus that could potentially result in life-threatening dehydration does not develop. Second, the pain medication needs to be regulated so that the patient is functional but sufficiently comfortable. Next, if the patient is not already taking a bisphosphonate, a basic workup should be done to establish the level of osteopenia, and a treatment program should be initiated. Finally, immobilization should be applied to help relieve the pain. A semirigid corset is sufficient for lumbar fractures, and it is usually well tolerated and helps relieve pain. After discharge, follow-up should be scheduled in 1 week for repeat radiographs and to ascertain that the pain relief is acceptable. Follow-up should again be performed at 1 month for careful evaluation of healing of the fracture and for measurement to determine whether the vertebral body is continuing to collapse. If severe pain and continued collapse are still present at 4 weeks, consideration of vertebroplasty or kyphoplasty should be made at that time.

BURST FRACTURES OF THE LUMBAR SPINE

Most patients who sustain injuries to the lumbar spine that require operative stabilization have burst fractures. The key to selecting the most appropriate treatment for these patients is recognition of the components of the fracture pattern. As previously described, all burst injuries involve comminution of the anterior portion of the body and significant involvement of the posterior wall (middle column), along with retropulsion of bone into the canal. The types of burst fractures that occur most commonly in the lumbar spine are Denis A (comminution of the entire body and the body-pedicle junction with or without involvement of the posterior elements) and Denis B (comminution of only the upper end-plate with an intact body-pedicle junction and usually sparing of the posterior elements). These two fracture types have reasonably equal distribution at L2 and L3, but the Denis B fracture predominates at L4 and L5. Lateral burst fractures (Denis E) are also occasionally seen. Review of the care of these injuries illustrates most of the techniques required for the surgical treatment of lumbar injuries. Differentiation between the types of treatment appropriate for fractures occurring in the upper and the lower lumbar spine is necessary for optimal results. However, with the adoption of pedicle screw fixation as the standard for the lumbar spine, constructs used in the upper and lower lumbar spine are not dissimilar, with the exception of length.

Flexion-compression (Denis B) injuries, a subset of burst fractures, are characterized by fracture of the posterior wall of the vertebral body with retropulsion of the posterosuperior corner into the spinal canal causing compression. The critical feature on AP radiographs and CT scans is that the pedicles are not splayed. On CT scans, it is evident that they are still attached to the lateral sides of the vertebral body, although a large central fragment is present and can cause canal compression. This finding is usually accompanied by a significant degree of kyphosis. The instrumentation construct used for this area needs to

be able to correct the kyphosis in the upper lumbar spine and restore lordosis in the lower lumbar spine. This ability is related to the length of fixation and thus the length of the lever arm applying the forces, as well as the rigidity of the system and the types of forces applied to the screws.[121]

Previously, hook and rod constructs such as the Edwards rod-sleeve method or multiple-hook systems such as the TSRH, Cotrel-Dubousset, and Isola were appropriate for the treatment of upper lumbar fractures because the length of the instrumentation was not thought to be as critical in this region. However, certain systems were associated with a significant rate of loss of correction, nonunion, and hook dislodgment, especially related to the upper level, and all were dependent on intact posterior elements. With more common use, pedicle fixation constructs have slowly replaced most of these other systems in the lumbar spine, and they clearly maintain their effectiveness and use for thoracolumbar and thoracic fractures. The application of these systems has been thoroughly discussed in Chapter 30. Before discussing the use of surgical techniques for lumbar fractures, it must be reemphasized that the role of surgical treatment of these injuries is still being defined. The most common current surgical indications are traumatic dural lacerations, neurologic deficit (other than isolated root deficit), and significant deformity (greater than 25° of relative kyphosis with or without deficit). Although most of the reports to date have relatively short (<5 years) follow-up,[4, 5, 107] data on intermediate-length (5 to 10 years) follow-up are now becoming available.[132]

Pedicle screw fixation for upper lumbar injuries can be used over more levels to achieve rigid fixation, especially for fractures with more disruption of the anterior column. Thus, for an L2 fracture, the type of construct applied can vary considerably. If it is a Denis B fracture, it may require only one screw above and below (L1 and L3) (Fig. 31–21A), or it may also accommodate a screw directed into the lower portion of the fractured body for a three-screw construct (two screws above and one below

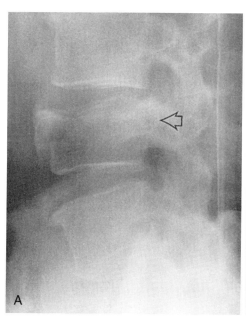 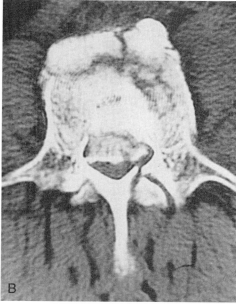

FIGURE 31–20. *A,* An L4 burst fracture might be mistaken for a simple compression fracture of L4 on this lateral radiograph. The key to the diagnosis is the posterosuperior corner *(arrow)* of the affected vertebral body (L4). *B,* The posterosuperior corner is retropulsed into the canal as confirmed on computed tomographic (CT) scans. Although the comminution of the vertebral body and the loss of height are unimpressive, the degree of canal occlusion and the overall structural disruption of the vertebral body are not fully appreciated except on the CT scan.

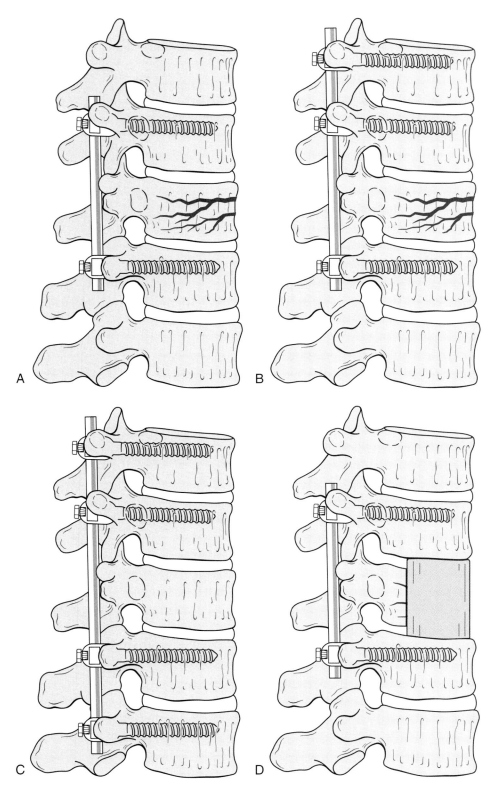

FIGURE 31–21. *A,* The use of pedicle screw constructs or hybrid screw-hook constructs allows correction of both the flexion component and the compression component of a deformity. A number of options exist, and the length of the construct and the number of screws used depend on the stability of the fracture, as well as the level of the fracture. For relatively stable Denis B burst fractures, one screw above and below the fractured level is adequate at the L2 or L3 level. *B,* For Denis B fractures requiring a longer lever arm for reduction or those that are less stable (more disruption of the anterior column), two screws above and one below can be used. *C,* For Denis A fractures with severe comminution, two screws above and two below increase the stability of the construct and also increase the lever arms to achieve reduction. *D,* Alternatively, some authors suggest an anterior graft to restore the stability of the anterior column; however, this procedure increases the duration of surgery and risk and is harder to justify unless the patient requires anterior decompression for a neurologic deficit.

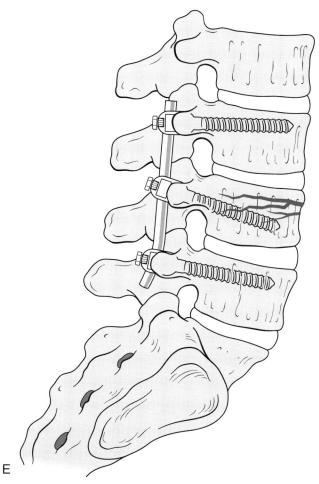

E

FIGURE 31–21 *Continued. E,* In certain fractures increased stability can be achieved by angling a screw into the noncomminuted portion of the fractured vertebral body.

the fracture) to achieve greater reduction force (Figs. 31–21B and E and 31–22). For Denis A fractures (Fig. 31–23) with complete anterior disruption, the same two screws above (T12 and L1) and either one below (L2) or two below (L2 and L3) can be used (see Fig. 31–21B and C). Some authors advocate restoration of the anterior column with a cage or graft and an adjunctive one above and one below the posterior construct (see Fig. 31–21D). For fractures of the upper lumbar spine, the length of fixation is not as critical in terms of incorporating distal segments and maintaining motion. Stability and maintenance of correction are important. For the lower lumbar spine, the length of fixation becomes more critical. Pedicle fixation has the advantage of allowing fixation across short levels (three segments, two interspaces). For an L4 burst fracture, instrumentation extends from L3 to L5 (see Fig. 31–21E), and for an L5 burst fracture, instrumentation extends from L4 to S1. Various pedicle fixation systems that can achieve these goals are currently available.*

Technically, the existing fixation systems have three

———————————
*See references 12, 18, 26, 38, 39, 43, 56, 91, 98, 104, 130, 134, 143, 153.

major differences. The first involves the number of points of fixation on the spinal column. Most spinal fixators allow only two points of fixation, generally above and below the fracture site (Fig. 31–24A). Most plate systems (Steffe, Roy-Camille) and rod-screw systems (Cotrel-Dubousset, TSRH, Synthes, Modular) have fixation at each instrumented level (at least three points), including the apical or fractured level (Fig. 31–24B). Second, the direction of sacral fixation is down the pedicle of S1 into the body (see Fig. 31–24C) or laterally into the sacral ala (see Fig. 31–24D). Bidirectional or two-point fixation into the sacrum can be achieved with some systems to enhance the fixation of L5 fractures. Third, pedicle screw systems can be static and simply become rigidly fixed in the position attained by postural reduction (plate system), or they can allow progressive reduction of the fracture after the insertion of screw fixation and attachment of the device by the application of progressive force. The following discussion of pedicle fixation illustrates the basic principles of the technique.

Initial evaluation with appropriate AP and lateral plain radiographs and CT scans to determine pedicle and vertebral size and location is critical. Patients are positioned on a standard operating room table in a neutral position on longitudinal rolls or a radiolucent spinal frame. A radiolucent operating table allows for easier radiographic control of screw placement. In either case, AP and lateral imaging or radiographic control for positioning of the pedicle screws is mandatory.

A midline posterior incision is used. Dissection is done carefully with a cautery to avoid excess motion of the injured spine. Frequently, spinous process and posterior element fractures are encountered when exposing L4 and L5 fractures. If the spinous processes and the interspinous ligament are intact, the ligament should not be removed but instead preserved during the dissection. The integrity of the interspinous ligament should be maintained at the levels just proximal and distal to the construct to prevent hypermobility postoperatively. The ligament can also be used during closure to restore the integrity of the lumbodorsal fascia. Care is also taken while stripping soft tissue from the spine at the proximal level that the capsule of the adjacent facet joint that remains unfused not be disturbed when exposing the transverse process (see Fig. 31–25A). Specifically, the L2–L3 facet joint (adjacent to the L3 transverse process) for an L4 burst fracture and the L3–L4 facet joint for an L5 burst fracture should remain unfused, and their capsules must be competent to resist the increased stress on adjacent instrumented levels. The pedicle screw can be placed inferior and lateral to that facet joint so that it does not impinge on the unfused facet and cause secondary changes. Exposure of the transverse processes of the appropriate levels can reveal fractures and landmarks helpful in screw placement. The facet capsules are removed only at the two or more levels to be fused. When fusion is extended to the sacrum, the L5–S1 facet is cleared of all soft tissue and the sacrum is stripped back to the first dorsal foramen. Complete exposure of all landmarks is critical for accurate screw placement.

For positioning of screws in L3, L4, and L5, a line is drawn across the transverse processes and through the

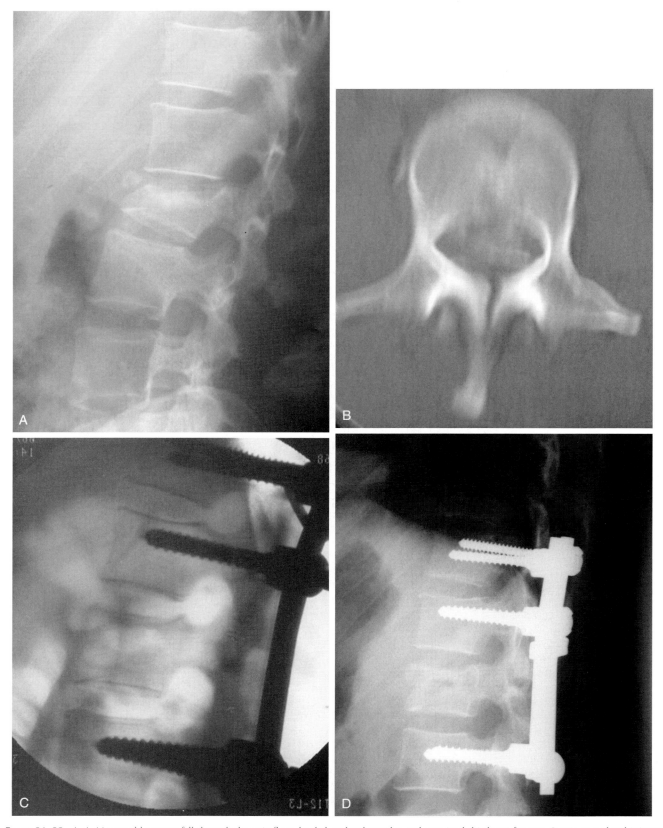

FIGURE 31–22. *A,* A 44-year-old woman fell through the attic floor, landed on her buttocks, and sustained this burst fracture. It was an isolated injury; however, the patient had loss of movement and sensation in the lower extremities for approximately 10 minutes after the fall. By the time that she was seen at the trauma center, she had recovered all neurologic function. Computed tomography *(B)* showed greater than 50% canal compromise, and she had approximately 30° of kyphosis. After discussion of the alternatives, she underwent reduction and fixation with two screws above and one below. Intraoperative images *(C)* showed complete reduction of the deformity. Six months postoperatively, she had lost slight correction of height *(D)* but achieved solid painless arthrodesis.

inferolateral edge of the facet, as suggested by Roy-Camille and associates[128] (Fig. 31–25B). Similarly, care must be taken to determine the proper angle of entry into the body. The orientation of the screws at each level is affected by several factors, including the positioning of the patient on the operating table, the amount of kyphotic deformity of the fracture, and the shape of the vertebra. In addition, distortion of the anatomy at the fractured apical level can make accurate placement difficult. Because laminectomy or laminotomy is frequently necessary, direct palpation of the pedicle might be possible and can be helpful in placement.

Beginning at the most proximal level, the facet joint is meticulously avoided and entry made through the posterior cortex with a 3-mm oval bur at the inferolateral corner of the pedicle. Such entry requires that the superior screw be angled approximately 15° superiorly toward the end-plate and 10° medially to have it enter through the pedicle. Although most surgeons probe the pedicle when placing pedicle screws during elective fusions, that technique may require significant force in a young individual with hard bone and an unstable spine. The pedicle can also be drilled with a 2- or 3.2-mm bit until the surgeon has ascertained that the pedicle has been entered. This technique is especially useful when attempting to place a screw in a fractured vertebra.

A 2.0-mm drill bit or Kirschner wire is then inserted, with care taken to not place it deeper than the depth of the pedicle. It should not be inserted into the body so that localizing radiographs or fluoroscopy can determine the site of entry accurately. Two drill bits at the same level can be reversed if AP and lateral radiographs are being used for localization, one with the point into the pedicle and one with the point out, so that the position of the two sides can be differentiated (see Fig. 31–25C). If image intensification is used, the image should be oriented parallel to the axis of each guide pin. The pin should appear in the inferolateral portion of the pedicle for the superior level and in the center of the pedicle for all other levels. The inferior level is at L5 for an L4 burst fracture and at S1 for an L5 burst fracture.

Screw placement at the L5 level is done in a fashion similar to that for the superior end of the construct, with several slight modifications. The position of the pedicle is determined in the same manner, although the starting hole for the screw is begun in the center of the pedicle with a high-speed bur to remove the inferior portion of the superior facet of L5. The angle of placement is inward approximately 10° and inferior approximately 15° (parallel to the superior L5 end-plate as the patient is positioned on the table) (see Fig. 31–25D).

If the inferior screw is to be placed into the sacrum, two options are available. For placement of a screw into the sacral ala, visualization of several landmarks is necessary. The capsule is removed from the L5–S1 facet, and the inferior edge of the first dorsal foramen is exposed. At a point midway between the facet and the first dorsal foramen, a slight indentation or "dimple" can be found and is the starting point for insertion of the screw. A 2.0-mm drill bit is placed into the indentation and aligned against the inferior edge of the L5 spinous process (if it exists). Such positioning should orient the drill with 35° of lateral tilt and 25° of inferior tilt (see Fig. 31–25E). The posterior cortex of the sacrum is then drilled in that orientation. The

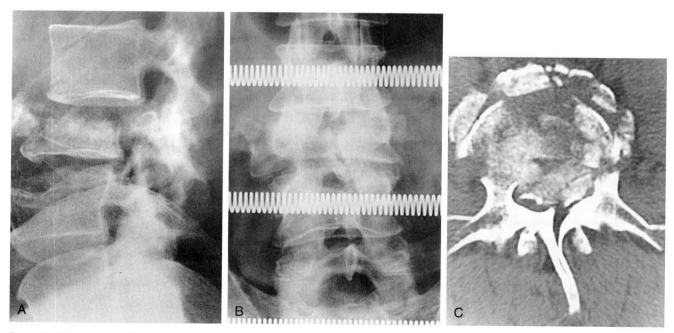

FIGURE 31–23. A 63-year-old man sustained a burst fracture of L3. *A,* A lateral preoperative radiograph demonstrates severe destruction and axial compression of the L3 body. The fracture demonstrates slight posterior translation but little angulation. *B,* An anteroposterior radiograph demonstrates severe comminution of the vertebral body with spreading of the pedicles and posterior element fractures. *C,* Computed tomography of the affected level demonstrates the critical radiologic features. Complete comminution of the entire vertebral body is apparent, as well as significant retropulsion of bone into the canal with nearly complete occlusion of the canal and comminution of the pedicles. Pressure applied to these pedicles would only drive the pedicles into the severely comminuted body and would not cause resultant lordosis and ligamentotaxis.

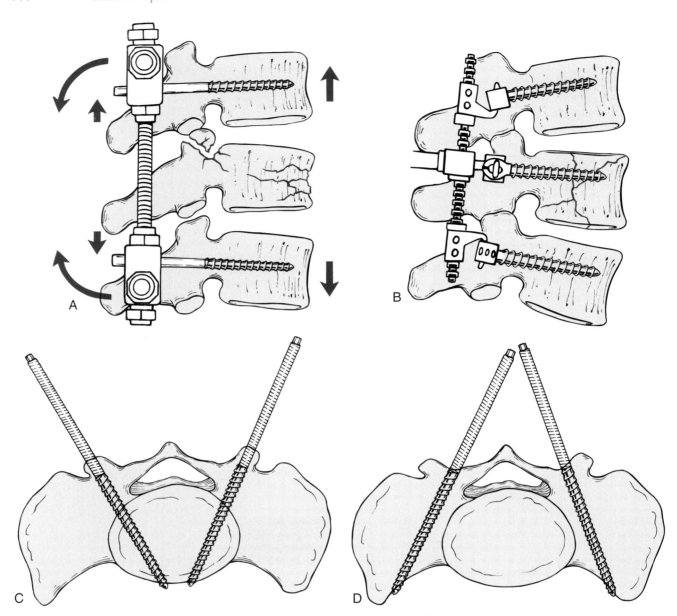

FIGURE 31–24. Multiple approaches to pedicle screw fixation of lumbar fractures may be used. The first variation is the number of points of fixation of the spine. *A,* Most spinal fixators rely on one point of fixation above and one point of fixation below the level of the fracture and achieve reduction by angulation of the vertebral bodies through the screw fixation points. *B,* Most plate systems, as well as rod-screw systems, have fixation at the level above the fracture, at the level below the fracture, and at the fracture level. The second variation is in the direction of sacral fixation. *C,* The fixation may be directed into the anterior portion of the S1 body, which is free of both vascular and neural structures. *D,* Alternatively, the fixation may be directed laterally out into the sacral alae and, if taken far enough, likewise lies in a zone free of both neural and vascular elements.

bit is advanced to the anterior cortex of the sacrum simply by pushing it through the soft cancellous bone until the anterior, dense cortical bone of the sacrum is encountered. The anterior cortex is not drilled at this point, but drill bits are placed as described previously, with one inverted, and their position is checked radiographically. On a true lateral view, the drill bit should be oriented parallel to or should slightly converge toward the superior end-plate of the sacrum, approximately 1 cm inferior to it. After checking the position, the hole is overdrilled to a size appropriate for the screw.

When drilling the anterior cortex, a hand drill should be used and the drill steadied with both hands to prevent plunging. Once the anterior cortex is felt to be engaged by

the drill bit, three quarters of an additional twist is necessary to penetrate the anterior cortex fully. A depth gauge is used to measure screw length, and care should be taken to medially orient the foot of the depth gauge so that the shortest possible length is used to engage the cortex (the ala slopes laterally, and therefore lateral measurements are always longer). If medial screw orientation into the vertebral body of S1 is necessary for the fixation device, the S1 pedicle must be located. An entrance hole is made at the base of the superior facet of S1, and the pedicle is probed and located in standard fashion. Because of the severe medial slope of the sacrum, 20° to 30° of medial and 25° of inferior orientation of the screw are necessary to attain adequate fixation in the sacral body.

If the pedicle screw system being used can accommodate fixation or requires fixation in the apical or fractured level, certain other factors must be considered. First, the configuration of the fractured body must be clearly delineated on the CT scan before attempting screw placement. The most common pattern for L4 and L5 burst fractures is that the superior portion of the body and the pedicle are comminuted but the inferior portion of the pedicle remains attached to the inferior portion of the vertebral body. This pattern can be accompanied by a sagittal split in the body so that the two halves of the vertebra are not attached. Most frequently, however, the area of best screw purchase is in the inferior portion of the body. Therefore, placement requires orientation of the drill bit in a much more inferiorly directed position than normal. In addition, if the two halves are split, a more directly anterior position (rather than medial orientation) might also be necessary for good purchase[30] (see Fig. 31–25F).

A common variation is that one pedicle and the lateral cortex of the body on that side are displaced significantly. It might not be possible to reduce this injury or place the final screw in that pedicle until vertebral height has been restored.

Finally, when placing the screws, other cracks and fissures in the body might be palpable as the vertebral body is probed. The surgeon should always be aware of the exact dimensions of that vertebral body and the depth of insertion of any instrument so that the anterior cortex of the body is not penetrated through a fracture line. Screw placement at the fracture level is accomplished in a manner similar to that at other vertebral levels, by opening the posterior cortex over the center of the pedicle with a 3-mm bur. This technique usually requires removal of the inferior portion of the superior facet and probing with a 3–0 curette before placement of a 2.0-mm drill bit. With all three levels prepared for screw insertion, devices requiring three points of pedicle fixation can be applied. Consideration of preparation of the spine for fusion is also necessary before final insertion of the hardware.

Assembly of the construct varies with the system. However, certain principles should be observed independent of the type of system and the number of screws inserted. First, it is critical that the kyphosis be corrected

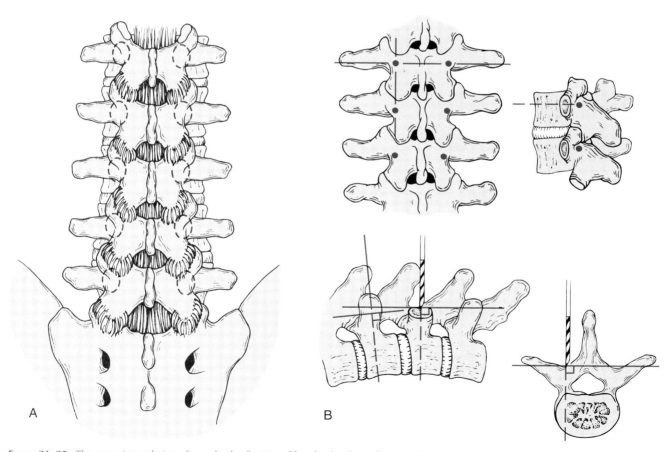

FIGURE 31–25. The operative technique for pedicular fixation of low lumbar burst fractures has many similarities from one system to the next. The technique shown emphasizes the critical features. When exposing the spine, care must be taken to not disrupt the interspinous ligament or the facet capsules proximal to the level of instrumentation. In exposing the transverse process opposite the superior pedicle, it is critical that the facet capsule not be disrupted. In view of the location of the pedicle and its proximity to the capsule (A), great care should be taken in this dissection. Screw position can be determined by a number of different techniques. The technique of Roy-Camille (B) positions the entry point at the intersection of a line through the transverse processes and a line through the inferolateral edge of the facet joint. Entry into the pedicle can be facilitated by using a 3-mm oval bur to remove the cortical bone at the location of the suggested entry point. A small probe, sound, or curette can be used to easily traverse the cancellous bone of the pedicle. This technique prevents inadvertent perforation of the pedicle walls.

Illustration continued on following page

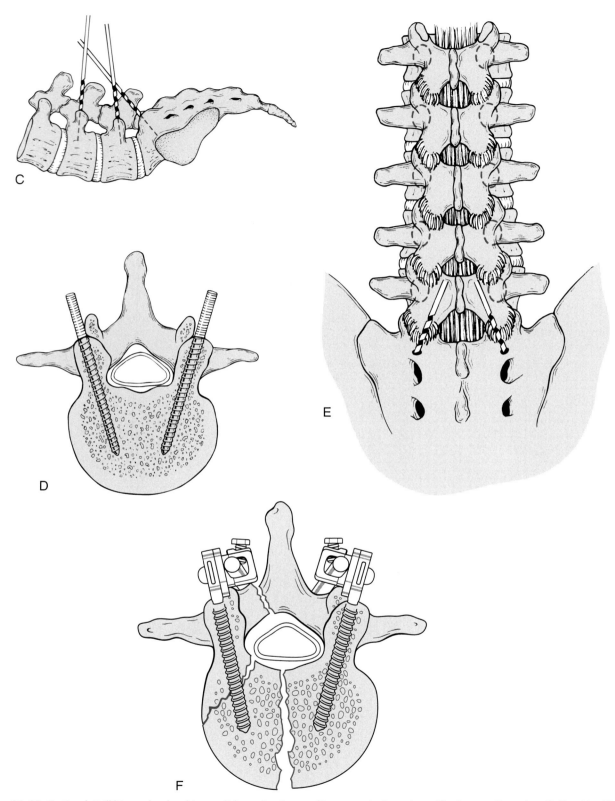

Figure 31–25 *Continued.* Drill bits can be placed into pedicles so that the use of intraoperative image intensification or radiographs will allow identification of the position of the drill bits within the pedicles (*C*). The orientation of the drill bits within the vertebral bodies changes with the level. In view of the angle of the side wall of L5, the screws should be oriented approximately 10° medially and 15° caudally to accommodate the lordosis of L5 (*D*). Orientation within the sacrum, as previously described, can be either medially into the body or laterally out into the sacral ala. Lateral orientation requires a 35° lateral tilt and a 25° inferior tilt (*E*).

For a pedicle screw system requiring screw fixation into the apical fractured level, a number of specific considerations are necessary. The configuration of the fracture body must be clearly understood before attempting screw placement. If the body is split sagittally, the two halves may be oriented in different directions. Therefore (*F*), one side may require vertical placement of the screw, whereas the other side, because of orientation, may require slight angulation medially. In addition, the screw may traverse a fracture within the body. The surgeon should feel the fracture site as the screws are placed. A transverse connector is recommended to increase the rigidity of the construct.

before applying distraction. When the fractured level is not instrumented, a straight or slightly contoured rod is inserted into the proximal screw or screws on both sides simultaneously. The rods are locked into the screw or screws in the correct orientation, and then by applying force to both rods either with a rod pusher or by using the reduction devices available with the system, the rods are reduced progressively down into the distal screw heads and preliminarily locked into position. If additional correction of kyphosis is necessary, the rods can be contoured with in situ bending irons. Once correction of the kyphosis has been achieved, the rod is loosened at one end and distraction applied until the interspinous ligament is appropriately tensioned, and then the quality of reduction is checked with image intensification. Additional distraction can be gradually applied while watching for restoration of body height of the fractured level.

If a screw is placed in the fractured vertebral level, the method of reduction can be slightly altered. For the Modular system, the central screw has a connector attached to it. Thus, after placing a straight rod and tightening it into the proximal and distal screws, the connector is lengthened to restore lordosis. Other systems also have an ability to apply an anteriorly directed force through the middle screw to achieve reduction. In rod systems without the ability to gradually achieve reduction with the system in place, the rod can be precontoured to the appropriate lordosis and then, for smaller degrees of deformity, either rotated into position similar to correction of scoliosis or attached to the middle and distal screws and reduced into the proximal screw. The reduction process is done in this sequence because most deformity exists at the upper end of the fractured level and the disc space above. Correction of height is done by keeping the middle screw tight and first loosening the distal screw to allow distraction to be applied across the normal disc space so that it is comparable to the one below. That screw is tightened, and then the proximal screw is loosened and distraction applied across the injured level until it is restored to normal.

In most systems it is necessary to thoroughly decorticate the transverse processes and lateral sides of the facets before assembling the construct. Epinephrine-soaked sponges can be used to diminish bleeding. If laminectomy is required, usually only one side of the hardware is assembled, that on the side opposite the surgeon. Partial reduction of the deformity is preferable before laminectomy both to achieve some fracture stability and to attain some fracture reduction if repair of a traumatic dural laceration or removal of a bony fragment is thought necessary. After completing the decompression or repair of the dural laceration, the second side of the construct is placed. The reduction is checked by either radiographic or image intensification; at least one cross lock should be placed, and the bone graft is harvested and placed in the decorticated lateral gutters.

Postoperatively, the patient is placed in a regular bed, and either a total-contact or a thoracolumbosacral orthosis, depending on the level of fracture, is applied on approximately the third postoperative day. If a thoracolumbosacral orthosis is used for an L5 fracture or for fixation extending to the sacrum, the leg extension is removed at 3

months and the patient is kept in the orthosis for an additional 3 months.

The three-screw technique is applicable to L4 and L5 burst fractures in which the body-pedicle junction is intact and to some L3 fractures. It relies on three-point fixation for applying slight distraction and lordosis to maintain sagittal alignment. This technique can also be used in patients with burst fractures and comminution of the pedicles at L3, as well as at L4 and L5. Difficulty might be encountered with severe comminution of the body or in obtaining solid screw fixation. By using the curette, the pedicle finder, and the 2.0-mm drill bit to feel through the pedicle and the body, however, it is possible to obtain reasonable fixation in most fractures. Small laminotomies at the apical level can aid in determining the orientation of the pedicle when fractured and in allowing solid fixation. Because the major force is a lordotic force at the apical level, satisfactory fixation in the pedicle and in some pieces of the body is all that is necessary to maintain three-point fixation, which achieves the reduction and rigid fixation. For most fractures at L2 and some at L3, fixation can be augmented by an additional level of purchase proximally or even, if necessary, an additional level distally with skipping of the fractured level.

Alternative Techniques

Various other techniques have their own advantages and disadvantages. They have been mainly used for the treatment of thoracic and thoracolumbar injuries, with a smaller percentage used for injuries to the upper lumbar area (these were simply included in the overall series). Their applicability is limited when considered for low lumbar (L4 and L5) injuries alone.

ROD-BASED INSTRUMENTATION

The first group involves rod-hook instrumentation, which as mentioned previously, has little applicability in the lumbar spine. Straight Harrington distraction rods provide only adjustable distraction for injuries resulting from flexion and compression. They have a number of disadvantages for use in the lumbar spine. First, they fail to provide the necessary three-point fixation and lordosis or any rotational control.[102, 108, 113, 120, 140, 148] They require long lever arms to achieve any reduction, and such length is contraindicated in the lumbar spine. In addition, junctional kyphosis can occur at the proximal end of the instrumented segment as a result of the forces applied to that hook-lamina junction. Because nothing is available to maintain the span of lumbar lordosis and the distance between the posterior elements and the rod, the fracture generally settles into kyphosis when the patient stands. In the lumbar spine, in addition, such instrumentation is complicated by frequent hook dislodgment. The use of sublaminar wires increases the stability, but with a straight rod, it aggravates the loss of lumbar lordosis and contributes to residual kyphosis.[51, 64, 112, 144] The length of the instrumented segment has been believed to be a disadvantage of this technique, although the concept of rod long–fuse short[2, 33] has been used to compensate for that deficiency.

Contoured rods provide distraction and three-point loading, but they also require accurate contouring, which might require repeated removal and recontouring to achieve optimal reduction. Engagement of the rod in the distal hook is often difficult because of the innate instability of the contoured rod, which has a tendency to rotate to the least stressed position. After assembly of a contoured rod construct, a significant rotational force is applied to the hook-lamina interface, thus increasing the chance of failure at that location. In addition, in areas with comminution of the apical posterior elements or in which laminectomy is required, no site is available for three-point contact of the central portion of the contour. Hook-rod techniques have limited applicability in lumbar fractures because of the dangers and difficulties of hook purchase at the L5 and S1 levels, the necessary end vertebrae for many lumbar rod constructs. The Jacobs rod[71] can also be contoured to use in these situations, and its application results in additional stability because of the clamping hooks and rotational control.

With any of the multiple hook-rod systems, using only hooks and standard construct length (two levels below and two or three levels above) has the same disadvantages of distal hook placement and long length in the lumbar spine. With multiple hook purchase sites, rigid fixation with maintenance of lumbar contours can be achieved, but difficulty has been encountered in shortening the construct. Systems with shorter constructs (one below and two above) have the disadvantage of inadequate reduction and laminar fracture and must be supplemented with an anterior procedure to ensure reliability and short length. Preliminary data suggest that the combination of pedicle screws and hooks with this system might be an effective solution to ensure short length of fixation and reliability.

All these previously mentioned rod-hook systems generally require a minimum of two levels below the fracture and two levels above the fracture, for a total of five instrumented levels and four interspaces. With laminar comminution, it can be extended to six or seven instrumented levels, but this option is undesirable in the lumbar spine, where the effort to preserve unaffected motion segments is critical.

SPINAL PLATES

Beginning with the work of Louis[93] and that of Roy-Camille and associates,[128] systems of spinal plates fixed with pedicle screws have been used for fractures. These systems have subsequently been modified by Steffee and colleagues[141] and by Luque. Even currently, Louis plates[92] are being advocated for use in the stabilization of spinal trauma. The strength of these plates lies in the fact that they can achieve rigid fixation of the spine with limited length of instrumentation. Roy-Camille plates for the lumbar spine allow two pedicle screws to be placed at each level in the large pedicles of the low lumbar spine. Similarly, they allow instrumentation at the apical level. Their shortcoming is that they rely on postural reduction for achieving reduction. They essentially plate the fracture in situ rather than applying pedicle screws in optimal position and then achieving reduction. In injuries with

severe malalignment or rotational instability, difficulty might be encountered in placing adjacent levels so that the screws line up with the plate at all levels. The plates are best restricted to low lumbar fractures, although they have been used by many for the treatment of upper lumbar and thoracolumbar spine fractures. The risk of missing the pedicle during insertion of the screw, however, increases as the pedicle diameter becomes smaller and as the thoracolumbar junction is approached; hence the value in comparison with that of rod fixation decreases. Plate systems such as the Steffee (VSP)[4, 5, 39, 96, 149] have been used for both thoracolumbar and lumbar fractures. However, significant loss of correction has been identified in patients with marked body comminution. Better results are achieved in low lumbar fractures without significant deformity or by augmenting the anterior column with a strut graft. Plate systems allow direct decompression, stabilization, and fusion in the absence of severe deformity.

ANTERIOR DECOMPRESSION AND FIXATION

Anterior surgical techniques are most beneficial for late direct decompression and stabilization of low lumbar fractures. Fractures in the lumbar spine from L2 to L5 can be visualized through a retroperitoneal approach, which is relatively straightforward. The technique allows excellent exposure to the vertebral bodies and the certainty of complete anterior decompression. In the acute trauma setting, the role of anterior surgery in the lumbar spine is somewhat less clear. The risks and complexity of direct anterior decompression and stabilization need to be balanced against the relative risks of the posterior surgery. In the lumbar spine, it has been demonstrated that the use of an anterior strut graft alone to reconstruct the spine is inadequate and results in anterior compression of the graft and kyphotic deformities. This complication can be avoided by applying posterior stabilization at the same sitting or by the use of some adjunctive anterior procedure. Use of the Kaneda device[73] or anterior plating[6, 52, 69] for neutralization can augment the results and achieve more rigid fixation, and these measures are adequate for long-term stabilization. Care must be taken that the devices do not protrude against the aorta, or vascular complications can arise.[15] The technique of retroperitoneal dissection and direct anterior decompression has been described in Chapter 30; it is essentially the same for the low lumbar spine. Dissection of L4 and especially L5 requires extreme care in handling the iliac vein.

FLEXION-DISTRACTION INJURIES

The two most common types of flexion-distraction injuries are Chance fractures (and related variants) and bilateral facet dislocation. As previously noted, the relative incidence of these two types of injury is reversed in the lumbar spine in comparison with the thoracolumbar junction. Flexion-distraction fractures, as classified by Gumley and associates[58] and by Gertzbein and Court-Brown,[55] are not generally amenable to any distraction techniques for stabilization. Fractures that traverse the spinous process, pedicle, and body can often be reduced in a hyperexten-

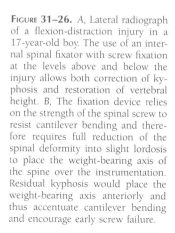
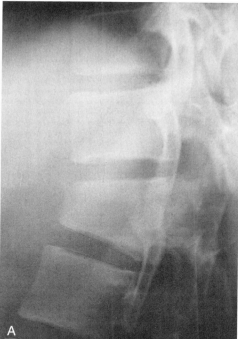
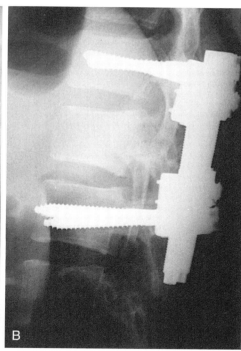

FIGURE 31–26. *A,* Lateral radiograph of a flexion-distraction injury in a 17-year-old boy. The use of an internal spinal fixator with screw fixation at the levels above and below the injury allows both correction of kyphosis and restoration of vertebral height. *B,* The fixation device relies on the strength of the spinal screw to resist cantilever bending and therefore requires full reduction of the spinal deformity into slight lordosis to place the weight-bearing axis of the spine over the instrumentation. Residual kyphosis would place the weight-bearing axis anteriorly and thus accentuate cantilever bending and encourage early screw failure.

sion cast and heal predictably. Those that cannot be reduced, however, and that will result in significant residual lumbar kyphosis should undergo surgical reduction and stabilization. In addition, fractures that traverse the posterior ligamentous complex, pedicle, and body commonly result in ligamentous instability after fracture healing and should undergo stabilization and fusion initially for an optimal result. Both these injury types can be treated with a posterior compression construct because of the absence of posterior wall comminution and disc involvement. Depending on the involvement of the posterior elements, the compression instrumentation requires two levels (one interspace) or three levels (two interspaces) (Fig. 31–26). The technique used can involve a rod-hook system, such as Harrington compression or Cotrel-Dubousset, TSRH, or most commonly a pedicle screw system. When the fracture line traverses the interspinous ligament and the posterior elements are left intact, the injury can be stabilized with a single-level construct. When pedicle fixation is considered, purchase in the fractured pedicle and body must be carefully assessed if two-level fixation is chosen (Fig. 31–27).

The most common flexion-distraction injury in the thoracolumbar spine is bilateral facet dislocation. This injury is distinctly rare in the lumbar spine but requires special consideration. Such injuries can result in severe posterior ligament and disc disruption. Patients with lumbar spine and lumbosacral dislocations tend to have incomplete neural injuries and thus increased potential for recovery. A tendency to consider the use of a one-level compression construct to save levels in the lumbar spine should be discouraged. An L2–L3 bilateral facet dislocation should therefore be directly reduced, and a one-level neutralization construct with pedicle fixation used to limit

the length of fixation. Because the disc disruption is so significant with this injury, if a single-level compression construct is used, extruded disc material might actually cause significant neural compression and additional deficit, either centrally or at either root.

Bilateral facet dislocations in the upper lumbar spine can also be treated satisfactorily with a one- or two-level pedicle screw construct. This technique is extremely straightforward because the posterior elements and posterior wall of both vertebral bodies are intact. Once the facets have been reduced, screws are placed in the pedicles of the level above and below the dislocation (assuming that no body fractures are present) and connected by a straight rod. Lordosis is achieved first and then just enough distraction applied to place the vertebral levels in normal orientation and the disc at normal height. Compression should not be used. Care should be taken during reduction of the bilateral facet dislocation so that the facets are not damaged, because they contribute significantly to the stability of the construct. Operative reduction of dislocated facets can be achieved with the following method: After complete delineation of the dislocated facets by meticulous dissection, the disrupted facet capsules and ligamentum flavum are resected. A laminar spreader is placed between the two spinous processes and gentle distraction applied until the tips of the facets are unlocked (Fig. 31–28A). The laminar spreader is twisted slightly to reduce the facet and then released to allow the facets to be reduced into normal position. An interspinous wire (18 gauge) is placed around the two spinous processes to complete the reduction (see Fig. 31–28B). The spine is now reduced and stabilized, and a short rod-sleeve technique or pedicle screw construct can be applied to complete the construct. At the end of the procedure, the interspinous wire can be left in place or removed. A multiple hook/rod construct can also be used if length is not a primary concern (upper lumbar spine).

Other techniques that can maintain the reduction with a short fixation length and without the use of compression can also be effective. In the low lumbar spine, where conservation of levels is important and a one-level construct is considered, prophylactic discectomy should be performed before a single-level compression construct. This procedure removes damaged disc material, prevents extrusion, and allows the use of a single-level compression construct. Specifically, an L4–L5 facet dislocation can be stabilized with a single-level L4–L5 compression construct and the proximal and distal levels left open.

SHEAR INJURIES AND COMPLEX DEFORMITIES

The optimal stabilization construct for shear injuries and complex deformities generally involves posterior stabilization, which with an operative plan allows stabilization of the various deforming forces. Each one needs to be individualized for the particular situation. Segmental

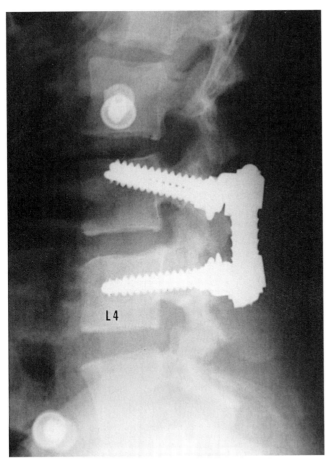

FIGURE 31–27. A 17-year-old girl sustained a Chance fracture of L4 and had flexion instability after nonoperative treatment. A posterior compression construct was able to reduce the kyphosis and eliminate the instability. One-level compression instrumentation can be used acutely in flexion-distraction injuries with posterior instability, but the purchase in the fractured body must be carefully assessed if a two-level/one-interspace construct is chosen.

fixation is often necessary to control the abnormal forces, especially in patients with stiff spines (see Figs. 31–17 and 31–18). Other constructs[20] have been used with success; however, the more points of fixation, the greater the degree of stability that can be achieved with these injuries.

Complications of Surgical Treatment

NEUROLOGIC DETERIORATION

Neurologic deterioration can occur intraoperatively and postoperatively. It has been demonstrated that a patient's lumbar spine is not well immobilized on a Stryker frame. As the patient rolls from a prone to a supine position, an unstable burst fracture can shift significantly, which could result in increased neurologic damage. Long-term immobilization on a logrolling frame can also cause shifting of fragments and potential neural damage. This situation is one indication for early surgical intervention. Intraoperative neurologic deterioration can be caused by applying distraction over a kyphotic segment of the lumbar spine, thus stretching the already tight neural elements over a prominent area. Reduction of kyphosis should be accomplished before any distraction maneuver. In addition, passing sublaminar wires or any fixation device in the canal at the apical level of the kyphosis and deformity can involve the risk of increased neurologic deficit secondary to placing objects in an already tight canal. Hook placement at L5 and S1 can also result in neurologic deficit because the very small canal and the severely lordotic lumbosacral junction can place the shoe of the hook in a position to compress the dural sac. Postoperative neurologic complications can be caused by dislodgment of anterior grafts or by recurrence of deformity. Placement of pedicle screws may be associated with either root deficit or more severe deficits, depending on the degree of error in placement (Fig. 31–29).

NONUNION

Nonunion of lumbar spine fractures is a frequent complication that has been reported in as many as 40% of fractures at the lumbosacral junction. More rigid fixation techniques with segmental fixation, as well as meticulous fusion techniques, are required to prevent this complication. Care must be taken to extend bone graft proximally above the upper hook in a rod construct to the transverse process on that side to achieve solid arthrodesis. In addition, with bulky posterior hardware, care must be taken that the device does not obscure pertinent areas for bony fusion.

LOSS OF CORRECTION

Most reports on spinal injury have noted loss of correction, as well as residual kyphosis. This complication is related to the inability of the fixation system selected to achieve rigid fixation that does not change with the patient's position. Proper selection of hardware and meticulous application with concern for counteracting deforming forces can minimize loss of correction.

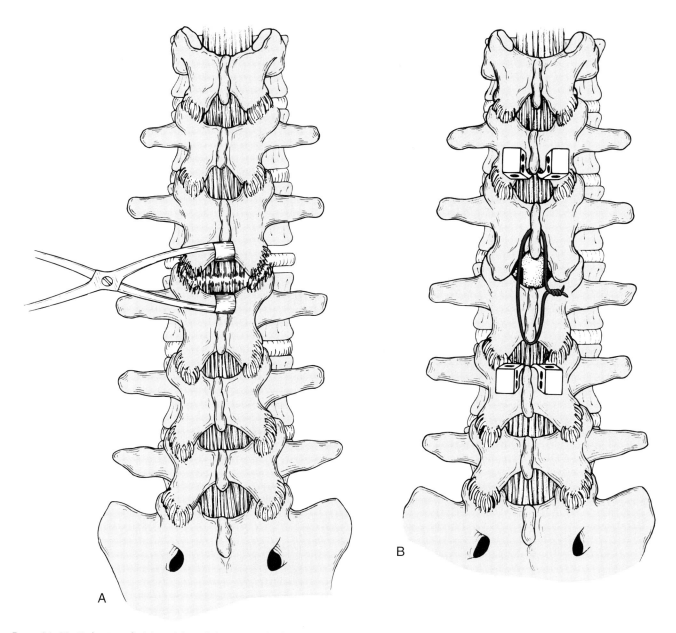

FIGURE 31–28. Reduction of a bilateral facet dislocation in the lumbar spine should be able to be accomplished in a controlled fashion with preservation of the facets to allow reestablishment of stability. Dissection of the soft tissues is accomplished, and the facet dislocations are identified. The ruptured ligamentum flavum is removed, as are the disrupted facet capsules. Cartilage is removed from the superior facet of the lower level under direct vision. A laminar spreader is then placed between the two spinous processes and gently manipulated until the facets are distracted. When the tips of the facets are disengaged, the laminar spreader is tipped to push the inferior facet anteriorly and pull the superior facets posteriorly. The distraction on the laminar spreader is then released to allow the facets to engage in a normal position. *A,* An interspinous wire is placed across the involved level and tightened to complete the reduction and reestablish stability. A short rod-sleeve construct can then be applied. *B,* The slight distraction applied by the rod-sleeve construct does not cause redislocation because the primary force is lordosis, which counteracts the flexion moment of the original injury.

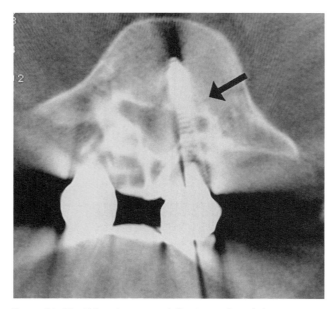

FIGURE 31–29. Although segmental fixation with pedicle screws can shorten the construct and more rigidly fix the lumbar lordosis, the surgical technique is more exacting. Especially in a traumatized spine, where normal landmarks may be obscured, misplacement of screws *(arrow)* is a potential complication.

SUMMARY

Treatment of lumbar fractures requires an understanding of the mechanics and normal functioning of the lumbar spine. Hardware selection depends on the goals to be achieved, the time to surgery, and the types of instabilities encountered. Appropriate consideration of the treatment goals for an individual patient and the injury leads to optimal results. The surgeon's selection of treatment should not be based on knowledge of a single technique, but rather on knowledge of the relative advantages and disadvantages of various nonoperative and operative procedures for the treatment of lumbar spine fractures.

REFERENCES

1. Akbarnia, B.A.; Moskowicz, A.; Merenda, J.T.; et al. Surgical treatment of thoracic spine fractures with Cotrel-Dubousset instrumentation. Poster exhibit presented at the Scoliosis Research Society, Amsterdam, September 1989.
2. Akbarnia, B.A.; Crandall, D.G.; Burkus, K.; et al. Use of long rods and a short arthrodesis for burst fractures of the thoracolumbar spine. J Bone Joint Surg Am 76:1629–1635, 1994.
3. Albert, T.J.; Levine, M.J.; An, H.S. Concomitant noncontiguous thoracolumbar and sacral fractures. Spine 18:1285–1291, 1994.
4. An, H.S.; Vaccaro, A.; Cotler, J.M.; et al. Low lumbar burst fractures. Comparison among body cast, Harrington rod, Luque rod, and Steffee plate. Spine 16(Suppl):440–444, 1991.
5. An, H.S.; Simpson, J.M.; Ebraheim, N.A.; et al. Low lumbar burst fractures: Comparison between conservative and surgical treatments. Orthopedics 15:367–373, 1992.
6. An, H.S.; Tae-Hong, L.; Jae-Won, Y.; et al; Biomechanical evaluation of anterior thoracolumbar spinal instrumentation. Spine 20:1979–1983, 1995.
7. Anderson, P.A.; Rivara, F.P.; Maier, R.V.; et al. The epidemiology of seatbelt-associated injuries. J Trauma 31:60–67, 1991.
8. Andreychik, D.; Alander, D.; Senica, K.; Stauffer, S. Burst fractures of the 2nd through the 5th lumbar vertebrae. J Bone Joint Surg Am 78:1156–1166, 1996.
9. Argenson, C.; Lovet, J.; de Peretti, F.; et al. Treatment of spinal fractures with Cotrel-Dubousset instrumentation. Results of the first 85 cases. Poster exhibit presented at the Scoliosis Research Society, Amsterdam, September 1989.
10. Asher, M.; Strippgen, W. Anthropometric studies of the human sacrum relating to dorsal transsacral implant design and development. Clin Orthop 203:58–62, 1986.
11. Bedbrook, G.M. Treatment of thoracolumbar dislocation and fractures with paraplegia. Clin Orthop 112:27–43, 1975.
12. Benson, D.R.; Burkus, J.K.; Montesano, P.X.; et al. Unstable thoracolumbar and lumbar burst fractures treated with an AO Fixateur Interne. J Spinal Disord 5:335–343, 1992.
13. Benzel, E.C.; Ball, P.A. Management of low lumbar fractures by dorsal decompression, fusion, and lumbosacral laminar distraction fixation. J Neurosurg 92(Suppl):142–148, 2000.
14. Boucher, M.; Bhandari, M.; Kwok, D.; Health related quality of life after short segment instrumentation of lumbar burst fractures. J Spinal Disord 14:417–426, 2001.
15. Brown, L.P.; Bridwell, K.H.; Holt, R.T.; et al. Aortic erosions and lacerations associated with the Dunn anterior spinal instrumentation. Orthop Trans 10:16, 1986.
16. Bucholz, R.W.; Gill, K. Classification of injuries to the thoracolumbar spine. Orthop Clin North Am 17:67–73, 1986.
17. Cain, J.E.; DeJong, J.T.; Dinenberg, A.S.; et al. Pathomechanical analysis of thoracolumbar burst fracture reduction. Spine 18:1647–1654, 1993.
18. Carl, A.L.; Tromanhauser, S.C.; Roger, D.J. Pedicle screw instrumentation for thoracolumbar burst fractures and fracture-dislocations. Spine 17(Suppl):317–324, 1992.
19. Chakera, T.M.H.; Bedbrook, G.; Bradley, C.M. Spontaneous resolution of spinal canal deformity after burst-dispersion fracture. AJNR Am J Neuroradiol 9:779–785, 1988.
20. Chaloupka, R. Complete rational burst fracture of the third lumbar vertebra managed by posterior surgery. Spine 24:302–305, 1999.
21. Chan, D.P.K.; Seng, N.K.; Kaan, K.T. Nonoperative treatment in burst fractures of the lumbar spine (L2-L5) without neurologic deficits. Spine 18:320–325, 1993.
22. Chance, G.Q. Note on a type of flexion fracture of the spine. Br J Radiol 21:452–453, 1948.
23. Chapman, J.R.; Anderson, P.A. Thoracolumbar spine fractures with neurologic deficit. Orthop Clin North Am 25:595–612, 1994.
24. Clohisy, J.C.; Akbarnia, B.A.; Bucholz, R.D.; et al. Neurologic recovery associated with anterior decompression of spine fractures at the thoracolumbar junction (T12-L1). Spine 17(Suppl):325–330, 1992.
25. Comissa, F.P.; Eismont, F.J.; Green, B.H. Dural laceration occurring with burst fractures and associated laminar fractures. J Bone Joint Surg Am 71:1044–1052, 1989.
26. Court-Brown, C.M.; Gertzbein, S.D. The management of burst fractures of the fifth lumbar vertebra. Spine 12:308–312, 1987.
27. Crutcher, J.P.; Anderson, P.A.; King, H.A.; et al. Indirect spinal canal decompression in patients with thoracolumbar burst fractures treated by posterior distraction rods. J Spinal Disord 4:39–48, 1991.
28. Dai, L.Y. Remodeling of the spinal canal after thoracolumbar burst fractures. Clin Orthop 382:119–123, 2001.
29. Davis, A.A.; Carragee, E.J. Bilateral facet dislocation at the lumbosacral joint. Spine 18:2540–2544, 1993.
30. De Boeck, H.; Opdecam, P. Split coronal fractures of the lumbar spine. Treatment by posterior internal fixation and transpedicular bone grafting. Int Orthop 23(2):87–90, 1999.
31. Dehner, J.R. Seatbelt injuries of the spine and abdomen. AJR Am J Roentgenol 111:833–843, 1971.
32. De Klerk, L.W.L.; Fontijne, W.P.J.; Stijnen, T.; et al. Spontaneous remodeling of the spinal canal after conservative management of the thoracolumbar burst fractures. Spine 23:1057–1060, 1998.
33. Dekutoski, M.B.; Conlan, S.; Salciccioli, G.G. Spinal mobility and deformity after Harrington rod stabilization and limited arthrodesis of thoracolumbar fractures. J Bone Joint Surg Am 75:168–176, 1993.
34. Denis, F. The three-column spine and its significance in the classification of acute thoracolumbar spinal injuries. Spine 8:817–831, 1983.
35. Denis, F. Spinal instability as defined by the three-column spine concept in acute spinal trauma. Clin Orthop 189:65–76, 1984.

36. Denis, F.; Burkus, J.K. Diagnosis and treatment of cauda equina entrapment in the vertebral lamina fracture of lumbar burst fractures. Spine 16(Suppl):433–439, 1991.

37. Dick, W. The "Fixateur Interne" as a versatile implant for spine surgery. Spine 12:882–900, 1987.

38. Doerr, T.E.; Montesano, P.X.; Burkus, J.K.; et al. Spinal canal decompression in traumatic thoracolumbar burst fractures: Posterior distraction rods versus transpedicular screw fixation. J Orthop Trauma 5:403–411, 1991.

39. Ebelke, D.K.; Asher, M.A.; Neff, J.R.; et al. Survivorship analysis of VSP spine instrumentation in the treatment of thoracolumbar and lumbar burst fractures. Spine 16(Suppl):428–432, 1991.

40. Edwards, C.C.; Levine, A.M. Early rod sleeve stabilization of the injured thoracic and lumbar spine. Orthop Clin North Am 17:121–145, 1986.

41. Elliot, H.C. Cross-sectional diameters and areas of the human spinal cord. Anat Rec 93:287–293, 1945.

42. Epstein, N.E.; Epstein, J.A. Limbus lumbar vertebral fractures in 27 adolescents and adults. Spine 16:962–966, 1991.

43. Esses, S.I.; Botsford, D.J.; Wright, T.; et al. Operative treatment of spinal fractures with the AO internal fixator. Spine 16(Suppl):146–150, 1991.

44. Ferguson, R.L.; Allen, B.L., Jr. A mechanistic classification of thoracolumbar spine fractures. Clin Orthop 189:77–88, 1984.

45. Fidler, M.W.; Plasmas, C.M.T. The effects of five types of support on the segmental mobility of the lumbosacral spine. J Bone Joint Surg Am 65:943–947, 1983.

46. Finn, C.A.; Stauffer, E.S. Burst fracture of the fifth lumbar vertebra. J Bone Joint Surg Am 74:398–403, 1992.

47. Fletcher, B.D.; Brogdon, B.G. Seatbelt fractures of the spine and sternum. JAMA 200:167–168, 1967.

48. Frankel, H.L. The value of postural reduction in the initial management of closed injuries of the spine with paraplegia and tetraplegia. Paraplegia 7:179–192, 1969.

49. Frederickson, B.E.; Yuan, H.A.; Miller, H. Burst fractures of the fifth lumbar vertebra. J Bone Joint Surg Am 64:1088–1094, 1982.

50. Frederickson, B.E.; Edwards, W.T.; Rauschning, W.; et al. Vertebral burst fractures: An experimental, morphologic, and radiographic study. Spine 17:1012–1021, 1992.

51. Gaines, R.W.; Breedlove, R.; Munson, G. Stabilization of thoracic and thoracolumbar fracture dislocations with Harrington rods and sublaminar wires. Clin Orthop 189:195–203, 1984.

52. Gardner, V.O.; Thalgott, J.S.; White, J.I. The contoured anterior spinal plate system (CASP). Indications, techniques, and results. Spine 19:550–555, 1994.

53. Garrett, J.W.; Braunstein, P.W. Seatbelt syndrome. J Trauma 2:220–237, 1962.

54. Gellad, F.E.; Levine, A.M.; Joslyn, J.N.; et al. Pure thoracolumbar facet dislocation: Clinical features and CT appearance. Radiology 161:505–508, 1986.

55. Gertzbein, S.D.; Court-Brown, C.M. Flexion-distraction injuries of the lumbar spine: Mechanisms of injury and classification. Clin Orthop 227:52–60, 1988.

56. Graziano, G.P. Cotrel-Dubousset hook and screw combination for spine fractures. J Spinal Disord 6:380–385, 1993.

57. Greenbaum, E.; Harris, L.; Halloran, W.X. Flexion fracture of the lumbar spine due to lap-type seatbelts. Cal Med 113:74–76, 1970.

58. Gumley, G.; Taylor, T.K.; Ryan, M.D. Distraction fractures of the lumbar spine. J Bone Joint Surg Br 64:520–525, 1982.

59. Gurwitz, G.S.; Dawson, J.M.; McNamera, M.J.; et al. Biomechanical analysis of three surgical approaches for lumbar burst fractures using short-segment instrumentation. Spine 18:977–982, 1993.

60. Haddad, G.H.; Zickel, R.E. Intestinal perforation and fracture of the lumbar spine caused by lap-type seatbelt. N Y J Med 67:930–932, 1967.

61. Handel, S.F.; Twiford, T.W., Jr.; Reigel, D.H.; et al. Posterior lumbar apophyseal fractures. Radiology 13:629–633, 1979.

62. Hardaker, W.T.; Cook, W.A.; Freidman, A.H.; et al. Bilateral transpedicular decompression and Harrington rod stabilization in the management of severe thoracolumbar burst fractures. Spine 17:162–171, 1992.

63. Harrington, R.M.; Budorick, T.; Hoyt, J.; et al. Biomechanics of indirect reduction of bone retropulsed into the spinal canal in vertebral fracture. Spine 18:692–699, 1993.

64. Herring, J.A.; Wenger, D.R. Segmental spinal instrumentation: A preliminary report of 40 consecutive cases. Spine 7:285–298, 1983.

65. Holdsworth, F.W. Fractures, dislocations and fracture-dislocations of the spine. J Bone Joint Surg Am 52:1534–1551, 1970.

66. Holdsworth, F.W.; Hardy, A. Early treatment of paraplegia from fractures of the thoracolumbar spine. J Bone Joint Surg Br 35:540–550, 1953.

67. Howland, W.J.; Curry, J.L.; Buffington, C.B. Fulcrum fractures of the lumbar spine. JAMA 193:240–241, 1965.

68. Hu, S.S.; Capen, D.A.; Rimolda, R.L.; et al. The effect of surgical decompression on neurologic outcome after lumbar fractures. Clin Orthop 288:166–173, 1993.

69. Huang, T.J.; Chen, J.Y.; Shih, H.N. et al. Surgical indications in low lumbar burst fractures: Experience with anterior locking plate system and the reduction-fixation system. J Trauma 39:910–914, 1995.

70. Huelke, D.F.; Kaufer, H. Vertebral column injuries and seatbelts. J Trauma 15:304–318, 1975.

71. Jacobs, R.R.; Casey, M.P. Surgical management of thoracolumbar spinal injuries: General principles and controversial considerations. Clin Orthop 189:22–35, 1984.

72. Jeanneret, B.; Ho, P.K.; Magerl, F. Burst-shear flexion-distraction injuries of the lumbar spine. J Spinal Disord 6:473–481, 1993.

73. Kaneda, K.; Abumi, K.; Fijiya, M. Burst fractures with neurologic deficits of the thoracolumbar-lumbar spine: Results of anterior decompression with anterior instrumentation. Spine 9:788–795, 1984.

74. Knight, R.Q.; Stornelli, D.P.; Chan, D.P.K.; et al. Comparison of operative versus nonoperative treatment of lumbar burst fractures. Clin Orthop 293:112–121, 1993.

75. Kostiuk, J.P.; Munting, E.; Valdevit, A. Biomechanical analysis of screw load sharing in pedicle fixation of the lumbar spine. J Spinal Disord 7:394–401, 1994.

76. Krag, M.H.; Beynnon, B.D.; Pope, M.H.; et al. An internal fixator for posterior application to short segments of the thoracic, lumbar or lumbosacral spine: Design and testing. Clin Orthop 203:75–88, 1986.

77. Krag, M.H.; Weaver, D.L.; Beynnon, B.D.; Haugh, B.D. Morphometry of the thoracic and lumbar spine related to transpedicular screw placement for surgical spinal fixation. Spine 13:27–32, 1988.

78. Kreitz, B.G.; Cote, P.; Cassidy, J.D. L5 vertebral compression fracture: A series of five cases. J Manipulative Physiol Ther 18(2):91–97, 1995.

79. Krompinger, W.J.; Frederickson, B.E.; Mino, D.E.; Yuan, H.A. Conservative management of fractures of the thoracic and lumbar spine. Clin Orthop 17:161–170, 1986.

80. Lagrone, M.O.; Bradford, D.S.; Moe, J.H.; et al. Treatment of symptomatic flatback after spinal fusion. J Bone Joint Surg Am 70:569–580, 1988.

81. Lemons, V.R.; Wagner, F.C.; Montesane, P.X. Management of thoracolumbar fractures with accompanying neurological injury. Neurosurgery 30:667–671, 1992.

82. Levine, A.M.; Edwards, C.C. Lumbar spine trauma. In: Camins, M.; O'Leary, P., eds. The Lumbar Spine. New York, Raven, 1987, pp. 185–212.

83. Levine, A.M.; Edwards, C.C.; Gellad, F. Indirect decompression of the spinal canal in the thoracolumbar spine. American Spinal Injury Association, Abstracts Digest, March 20–22, 1987, pp. 16–18.

84. Levine, A.M.; Edwards, C.C. Low lumbar burst fractures. Reduction and stabilization using the modular spine fixation system. Orthopedics 11:1427–1432, 1988.

85. Levine, A.M.; Bosse, M.; Edwards, C.C. Bilateral facet dislocations in the thoracolumbar spine. Spine 13:630–640, 1988.

86. Levine, A.M. The surgical treatment of low lumbar fractures. Semin Spine Surg 2:41–53, 1990.

87. Levine, A.M. Dural lacerations in low lumbar burst fractures. Paper presented at the American Academy of Orthopaedic Surgeons meeting, Washington, D.C., February 1992.

88. Levine, A.M. The long term follow-up of patients with L4 and L5 burst fractures treated with surgical stabilization. Submitted for publication.

89. Lewis, J.; McKibbin, B. The treatment of unstable fracture-dislocations of the thoracolumbar spine accompanied by paraplegia. J Bone Joint Surg Br 56:603–612, 1974.

90. Lindahl, S.; Willen, J.; Nordwall, A.; et al. The crush-cleavage fracture: A "new" thoracolumbar unstable fracture. Spine 8:559–569, 1983.

91. Lindsey, R.W.; Dick, W. The Fixateur Interne in the reduction and stabilization of thoracolumbar spine fractures in patients with neurologic deficit. Spine 16(Suppl):140–145, 1991.

92. Louis, C.A.; Gauthier, V.Y.; Louis, R.P. Posterior approach with Louis plates for fractures of the thoracolumbar and lumbar spine with and without neurologic deficits. Spine 23:2030–2040, 1998.

93. Louis, R. Fusion of the lumbar and sacral spine by internal fixation with screw plates. Clin Orthop 203:18–33, 1986.

94. Magerl, F.P. External skeletal fixation of the lower thoracic and lumbar spine. In: Uhthoff, H.K., ed. Current Concepts of External Fixation of Fractures. New York, Springer-Verlag, 1982, pp. 353–366.

95. Magerl, F.P. Stabilization of the lower thoracic and lumbar spine with external skeletal fixation. Clin Orthop 189:125–141, 1984.

96. Maiman, D.J.; Pintar, F.; Yoganandan, N.; et al. Effects of anterior vertebral grafting on the traumatized lumbar spine after pedicle screw-plate fixation. Spine 18:2423–2430, 1993.

97. Mann, K.A.; Found, E.M.; Yuan, H.A.; et al. Biomechanical evaluation of the effectiveness of anterior spinal fixation systems. Orthop Trans 11:378, 1987.

98. Markel, D.C.; Graziano, G.P. A comparison study of treatment of thoracolumbar fractures using the Ace posterior segmental fixator and Cotrel-Dubousset instrumentation. Orthopedics 18:679–686, 1995.

99. Marsh, H.O.; Bailey, D. Chance fractures caused by seatbelts: Presentation of three cases. J Kans Med Soc 71:361–365, 1970.

100. Marshall, D.; Johnell, O.; Wedel, H. Meta-analysis of how well measures of bone mineral density predict occurrences of osteoporotic fractures. BMJ 312:1254–1259, 1996.

101. McAfee, P.C.; Yuan, H.A.; Frederickson, B.E.; et al. The value of computed tomography in thoracolumbar fractures. An analysis of one hundred consecutive cases and a new classification. J Bone Joint Surg Am 65:461–473, 1983.

102. McAfee, P.C.; Werner, F.W.; Glisson, R.R. A biomechanical analysis of spinal instrumentation systems in thoracolumbar fractures. Spine 10:204–217, 1985.

103. McAfee, P.C.; Bohlman, H.H.; Yuan, H.A. Anterior decompression of traumatic thoracolumbar fractures with incomplete neurologic deficit using a retroperitoneal approach. J Bone Joint Surg Am 67:89–104, 1985.

104. McLain, R.F.; Sparling, E.; Benson, D.R. Early failure of short-segment pedicle instrumentation for thoracolumbar fractures. J Bone Joint Surg Am 75:162–167, 1993.

105. Melton, L.J. III; Lane, A.W.; Cooper, C.; et al. Prevalence and incidence of vertebral deformities. Osteoporos Int 3:113–119, 1993.

106. Micheli, L.J. Low back pain in the adolescent: Differential diagnosis. Am J Sports Med 7:362–364, 1979.

107. Mick, C.A.; Carl, A.; Sachs, B.; et al. Burst fractures of the fifth lumbar vertebra. Spine 18:1878–1884, 1993.

108. Mino, D.E.; Stauffer, E.S.; Davis, P.K.; et al. Torsional loading of Harrington distraction rod instrumentation compared to segmental sublaminar and spinous process supplementation. Orthop Trans 9:119, 1985.

109. Mirkovic, S.; Abitbol, J.J.; Steinman, J.; et al. Anatomic consideration for sacral screw placement. Spine 16(Suppl):289–294, 1991.

110. Miyakoshi, N.; Abe, E.; Shimada, Y.; et al. Anterior decompression with single segmental spinal interbody fusion for lumbar burst fractures. Spine 24:67–73, 1999.

111. Mumford, J.; Weinstein, J.N.; Spratt, K.F.; et al. Thoracolumbar burst fractures. Spine 18:955–970, 1993.

112. Munson, G.; Satterlee, C.; Hammond, S.; et al. Experimental evaluation of Harrington rod fixation supplemented with sublaminar wires in stabilizing thoracolumbar fracture dislocations. Clin Orthop 189:97–102, 1984.

113. Nagel, D.A.; Koogle, T.A.; Piziale, R.C.; et al. Stability of the upper lumbar spine following progressive disruptions and the application of individual internal and external fixation devices. J Bone Joint Surg Am 63:62–70, 1981.

114. Neumann, A.; Nordwall, A.; Osvalder, A.L. Traumatic instability of the lumbar spine. Spine 20:1111–1121, 1995.

115. Nevitt, M.C.; Ross, P.D.; Palermo, L.; et al. Association of prevalent vertebral fractures, bone density, and alendronate treatment with incident vertebral fractures: Effect of number and spinal location of fractures. Bone 25:613–619, 1999.

116. Norton, P.L.; Brown, T. The immobilizing efficiency of back braces. J Bone Joint Surg Am 39:111–131, 1957.

117. O'Callaghan, J.P.; Ullrich, C.G.; Yuan, H.A.; et al. CT of facet distraction in flexion injuries of the thoracolumbar spine: The "naked" facet. AJNR Am J Neuroradiol 1:97–102, 1980.

118. Olerud, S.; Karlstrom, G.; Sjostrom, L. Transpedicular fixation of thoracolumbar vertebral fractures. Clin Orthop 227:44–51, 1988.

119. Olinger A.; Hildebrant, U.; Mutshler, W.; Menger, M.D. First clinical experience with an endoscopic retroperitoneal approach for anterior fusion of lumbar spine fractures from levels T12 to L5. Surg Endosc 13:1215–1219, 1999.

120. Panjabi, M.M.; Abumi, K.; Duranceau, J.S. Three-dimensional stability of thoracolumbar fractures stabilized with eight different instrumentations. Trans Orthop Res Soc 12:458, 1987.

121. Panjabi, M.M.; Oda, T.; Wang, J.-L. The effects of pedicle screw adjustments on neural spaces in burst fracture surgery. Spine 25:1637–1643, 2000.

122. Parker, J.W.; Lane, J.R.; Karaikovic, E.E.; Gains, R.W. Injuries of the thoracolumbar spine associated with restraint use in head-on motor vehicle accidents. J Spinal Disord 13:297–304, 2000.

123. Rauschning, W. Correlative multiplanar computed tomographic anatomy of the normal spine. In: Post, J.D., ed. Computed Tomography of the Spine. Baltimore, Williams & Wilkins, 1984, pp. 20–67.

124. Rechtine, G.R. 2nd.; Cahill, D.; Chrin, A.M. Treatment of thoracolumbar trauma: Comparison of complications of operative versus nonoperative treatment. J Spinal Disord 12:406–409, 1999.

125. Rennie, W.; Mitchell, N. Flexion distraction fractures of the thoracolumbar spine. J Bone Joint Surg Am 55:386–390, 1973.

126. Ritchie, W.P., Jr.; Ersek, R.A.; Bunch, W.L.; et al. Combined visceral and vertebral injuries from lap-type seatbelts. Surg Gynecol Obstet 131:431–435, 1970.

127. Rogers, I.F. The roentgenographic appearance of transverse or Chance fractures of the spine: The seatbelt fracture. AJR Am J Roentgenol 111:844–849, 1971.

128. Roy-Camille, R.; Saillant, G.; Mazel, C. Plating of thoracic, thoracolumbar and lumbar injuries with pedicle plates. Orthop Clin North Am 17:147–159, 1986.

129. Saillant, G. Etude anatomique des pedicles, vertebreau, application chirurgicales. Rev Chir Orthop Traumatol 62:151–160, 1976.

130. Sasso, R.C.; Cotler, H.B.; Reuben, J.D. Posterior fixation of thoracic and lumbar spine fractures using DC plates and pedicle screws. Spine 16(Suppl):134–139, 1991.

131. Scoles, P.V.; Linton, A.E.; Latimer, B.; et al. Vertebral body and posterior element morphology: The normal spine in middle life. Spine 13:1082–1086, 1988.

132. Seybold, E.A.; Sweeny, C.A.; Fredrickson, B.E.; et al. Functional outcome of low lumbar burst fractures: A multicenter review of operative and nonoperative treatment of L3-L5. Spine 24:2154–2161, 1999.

133. Shen, W.J.; Liu, T.J.; Shen, Y.S. Nonoperative treatment versus posterior fixation for thoracolumbar junction burst fractures without neurologic deficit. Spine 26:1038–1045, 2001.

134. Shiba, K.; Katsuki, M.; Ueta, T.; et al. Transpedicular fixation with Zielke instrumentation in the treatment of thoracolumbar and lumbar injuries. Spine 19:1940–1949, 1994.

135. Shuman, W.P.; Rogers, J.V.; Sickler, M.E.; et al. Thoracolumbar burst fractures: CT dimensions of the spinal canal relative to postsurgical improvement. AJR Am J Roentgenol 145:337–341, 1985.

136. Sjostrom, L.; Jacobsson, O.; Karlstrom, G.; et al. Spinal canal remodeling after stabilization of thoracolumbar burst fractures. Eur Spine J 3:312–317, 1994.

137. Slosar, P.J.; Patwardhan, A.G.; Lorenz, M.; et al. Instability of the lumbar burst fracture and limitations of transpedicular instrumentation. Spine 20:1452–1461, 1995.

138. Smith, W.S.; Kaufer, H. Patterns and mechanisms of lumbar injuries associated with seatbelts. J Bone Joint Surg Am 51:239–254, 1969.

139. Stagnara, P.; De Mauroy, J.C.; Dran, G.; et al. Reciprocal angulation of vertebral bodies in a sagittal plane: Approach to references for the evaluation of kyphosis and lordosis. Spine 7:335–342, 1982.

140. Stauffer, E.S.; Neil, J.L. Biomechanical analysis of structural stability of internal fixation in fractures of the thoracolumbar spine. Clin Orthop 112:159–164, 1975.
141. Steffee, A.D.; Biscup, R.S.; Sitkowski, D.J. Segmental spine plates with pedicle screw fixation. Clin Orthop 203:45–53, 1986.
142. Stephens, G.C.; Devito, D.P.; McNamara, M.J. Segmental fixation of lumbar burst fractures with Cotrel-Dubousset instrumentation. J Spinal Disord 5:344–348, 1992.
143. Stromsoe, K.; Hem, E.S.; Auanan, E. Unstable vertebral fractures in the lower third of the spine treated with closed reduction and transpedicular posterior fixation: A retrospective analysis of 82 fractures in 78 patients. Eur Spine J 6:239–244, 1997.
144. Sullivan, J.A. Sublaminar wiring of Harrington distraction rods for unstable thoracolumbar spine fractures. Clin Orthop 189:178–185, 1984.
145. Takata, K.; Shum-Ichi, I.; Kazuhisa, T. Fracture of the posterior margin of a lumbar vertebral body. J Bone Joint Surg Am 70:589–594, 1988.
146. Viale, G.L.; Silvestro, C.; Francaviglia, N.; et al. Transpedicular decompression and stabilization of burst fractures of the lumbar spine. Surg Neurol 40:104, 1993.
147. Vornanen, M.J.; Bostman, O.M.; Myllynen, P.J. Reduction of bone retropulsed into the spinal canal in thoracolumbar vertebral body compression burst fractures. Spine 20:1699–1703, 1995.
148. Ward, J.J.; Nasca, R.J.; Lemons, J.E.; et al. Cyclic tortional testing of Harrington and Luque spinal implants. Orthop Trans 9:118, 1985.
149. Weyns, F; Rommens, P.M.; Van Calenbergh, F.; et al. Neurological outcome after surgery for thoracolumbar fractures. A retrospective study of 93 consecutive cases, treated with dorsal instrumentation. Eur Spine J 3:276–281, 1994.
150. White, A.A.; Panjabi, M.M. The basic kinematics of the spine: A review of past and current knowledge. Spine 3:12–20, 1978.
151. White, A.A.; Panjabi, M.M. Clinical Biomechanics of the Spine. Philadelphia, J.B. Lippincott, 1978.
152. Whitesides, T.E. Traumatic kyphosis of the thoracolumbar spine. Clin Orthop 128:79–92, 1977.
153. Wildburger, R.; Mahring, M.; Paszicsnyek, T.; et al. Dorsal stabilization of thoracolumbar spinal instability. Comparison of three different implantation systems. Arch Orthop Trauma Surg 113:244–247, 1994.
154. Willen, J.; Lindahl, S.; Irstam, I.; et al. Unstable thoracolumbar fractures: A study by CT and conventional roentgenology of the reduction effect of Harrington instrumentation. Spine 9:214–219, 1984.
155. Winter, R.B. Congenital Deformities of the Spine. New York, Thieme-Stratton, 1983.
156. Yuan, H.A.; Garfin, S.R.; Dickman, C.A.; et al. A Historical cohort study of pedicle screw fixation in thoracic, lumbar, and sacral spinal fusions. Spine 19(Suppl):2279–2296, 1994.
157. Zindrick, M.R.; Wiltsie, L.L.; Doornik, A.; et al. Analysis of the morphometric characteristics of the thoracic and lumbar pedicles. Spine 12:160–166, 1987.
158. Zou, D.; Yoo, J.U.; Edwards, T.; et al. Mechanics of anatomic reduction of thoracolumbar burst fractures. Spine 18:195–203, 1993.

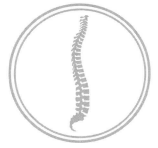

CHAPTER 32

Gunshot Wounds of the Spine

Frank J. Eismont, M.D.
Sebastian Lattuga, M.D.

The epidemiology of gunshot wounds of the spine, wound ballistics, and patient evaluation and treatment are critical factors in understanding an increasingly more prevalent type of spinal injury. Other penetrating injuries of the spine also have the potential for structural and cord injury. The incidence and severity of gunshot wounds of the spine will probably continue to increase in the civilian population in the future, and although some of the details may change, the principles of evaluation and treatment will remain the same.

DEMOGRAPHICS AND EPIDEMIOLOGY

In 1993, the Major Trauma Outcome Study[5] published information regarding the severity and outcome of 114,510 trauma patients in the United States and Canada from 1982 through 1989. The overall incidence of spinal cord injury was 2.6%, and 13.6% of the spinal cord injuries were caused by gunshot wounds. The study found that 79% of the victims were male and 21% were female; this same distribution was seen for spinal cord injury cases in general and for penetrating wounds of the spine. The average age of the patients was 33.5 years. In another study,[80] only 9% of penetrating wounds of the spine were classified as job-related injuries (presumably occurring to security guards, policeman, workers shot during robberies, and others). One study demonstrated that the likelihood of spinal cord injury from a gunshot wound was higher among those who had had previous gunshot wounds (30%) or who had prior involvement in the criminal justice system (52%).[53] Unlike sports injuries, which peak nationwide during the summer months, the incidence of penetrating wounds of the spine remained the same throughout the year, and 40% of them occurred on a Saturday or Sunday. Approximately 47% of all persons with spinal cord injuries are paraplegics, and 53% are quadriplegics. Sixty percent of all thoracic and lumbar cord injuries are complete lesions, as are 48% of the cervical injuries. For penetrating wounds of the spine, however, a significantly greater proportion are complete, and there is a much greater shift toward thoracic spinal injuries as compared with injuries of the neck or lumbar spine (Fig. 32–1).

Using these older data, it appears that approximately 1400 new spinal cord injuries occur each year as a result of gunshot wounds of the spine. However, in many areas of the United States, the number of spinal cord injuries caused by gunshot wounds of the spine doubled during the 10-year period from 1981 through 1991,[7] and this estimate therefore may be an optimistically low number. The data from the Regional Spinal Cord Injury Center of the Delaware Valley suggest a similar trend.[16] Even more difficult to estimate is the number of patients with more minor gunshot injuries to the spine (i.e., those that cause no paralysis), because nationwide numbers are not available for this type of injury. Based on what is seen at our own medical center and spinal cord injury unit, the number of gunshot wounds of the spine without paralysis is similar to the number with associated paralysis. To add perspective, in 1989, it was estimated that 48,700 people would be killed in motor vehicle accidents in the United States and that slightly more than 30,000 civilians would be killed with firearms.[46] Five times as many people are wounded as are killed by gunshots.

WOUND BALLISTICS

The term *ballistics* is defined in *Webster's New Universal Dictionary*, second edition, as "the modern science dealing with the motion and impact of projectiles, especially those discharged from firearms." In a medical sense, the term is defined as "the study of effects on the body produced by penetrating projectiles."[13] To understand the basic con-

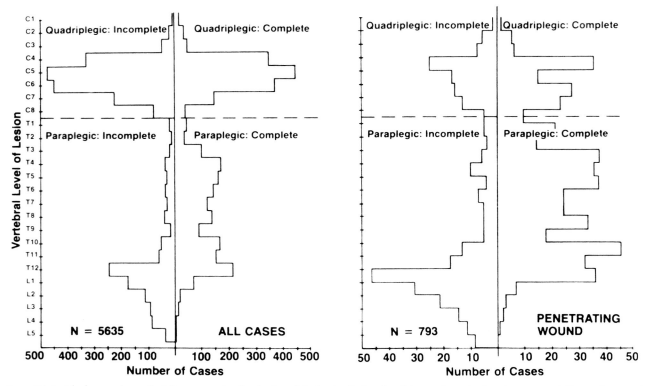

FIGURE 32–1. The bar graphs on the *left* represent the distribution of the levels of injury for all incomplete spinal cord injuries and all complete spinal cord injuries. The bar graph on the *right* shows the distribution for the penetrating wounds of the spine. A higher percentage of the penetrating wounds are complete injuries, and a proportionately higher number of thoracic injuries can be seen. (From Young, J.A.; Burns, P.E.; Bowen, A.M.; et al. Spinal Cord Injury Statistics: Experience of the Regional Spinal Cord Injury Systems. Phoenix, AZ, Good Samaritan Medical Center, 1982.)

cepts of ballistics, it is important to define some relevant terms:

Mass   The weight of the bullet is usually measured in grams. Most are in the range of 2 to 10 g.

Velocity   The velocity of the bullet can be given in feet per second or in meters per second. A .45 automatic handgun has a velocity of 869 ft/sec (265 m/sec); a .357 magnum has a velocity of 1393 ft/sec (425 m/sec); and an AK47 has a velocity of 2340 ft/sec (713 m/sec).

Fragmentation   This term indicates the extent to which a bullet disintegrates into multiple pieces as it courses through tissue. It is often described by comparing the largest final bullet fragment with the original weight of the bullet. This is one of the most important factors affecting the extent of final tissue injury.

Permanent cavity   This term refers to the permanent crush of tissue that results from passage of the bullet through the tissue.

Temporary cavity   This is the tissue stretch caused by passage of the bullet through the tissue. Elastic tissues such as muscle are relatively resistant to damage from this type of stretching, whereas more solid tissue is damaged more significantly under the same circumstances.

To better understand the mechanism of tissue injury with gunshot wounds, it is helpful to study the courses of bullets in tissue or gelatin tissue simulants.[14, 15] Several such models are shown in Figures 32–2 through 32–4. The cross-sectional area of the permanent cavity varies widely despite similarities in missile velocities. The tissue effects of bullet fragmentation and yaw (i.e., end-over-end rotation of the bullet) can be appreciated in these illustrations.

In a review of common misconceptions about wound ballistics, Fackler[13] makes the transition from the mechanical science of projectiles to the clinical art of patient care. Among the major misconceptions, he lists an overemphasis on bullet velocity and an exaggeration of tissue damage resulting from the effects of the temporary cavity. He also states that many of the positive effects of the administration of systemic antibiotics have been incorrectly attributed to the surgical débridement of tissue. He points out that the incidence of clostridial myositis decreased from 5% in World War I to 0.08% in the Korean War, even though débridement techniques remained relatively unchanged. This improvement can be more appropriately attributed to the increasing use of antibiotics on the battlefield. Fackler emphasizes that appropriate patient treatment can best be determined by evaluating the patient clinically with a hands-on physical examination and by standard roentgenography, looking for evidence of bullet fragmentation.

Composition of Bullets

The bullet projectile is usually composed of lead, but a portion of it may be copper or brass. A systemic toxicity may be caused by lead that leaches out of the bullet. This situation has been well described for bullets bathed in

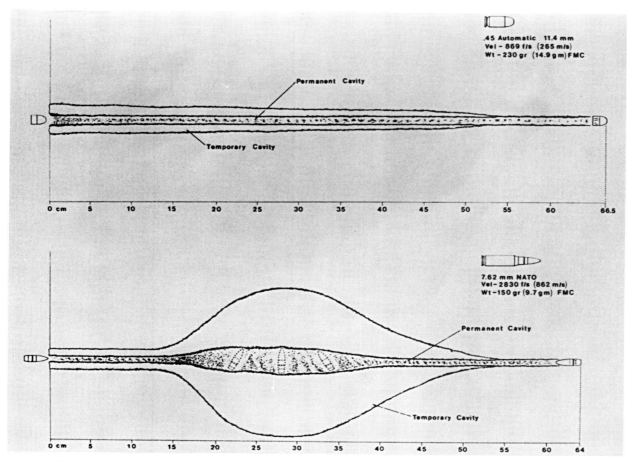

FIGURE 32–2. Injury profile after discharging weapons through a gelatin medium. For the first 15 cm of travel through tissue, the injury patterns are extremely similar despite a significant difference in bullet velocity. It is not until the bullet yaws that the permanent cavity becomes significantly larger for the rifle injury than for the handgun injury. (From Fackler, M.L.; et al. J Trauma 28[Suppl 1]:S21–S29, 1988.)

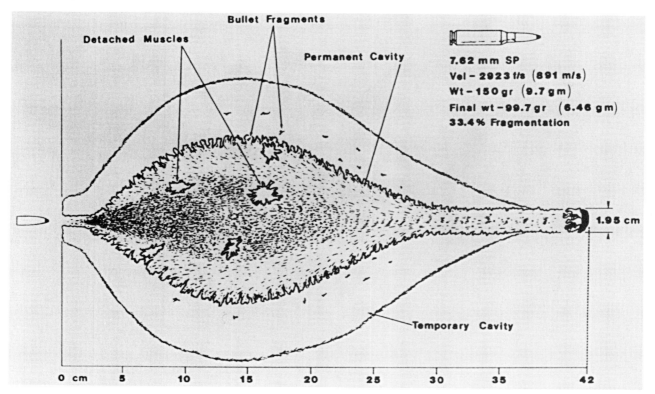

FIGURE 32–3. This wound profile is from the same rifle as that in the lower graph in Figure 32–2. The permanent cavity is significantly larger in this case because of the use of a soft-point bullet, which leads to significant bullet fragmentation. (From Fackler, M.L.; et al. J Trauma 28[Suppl 1]:S21–S29, 1988.)

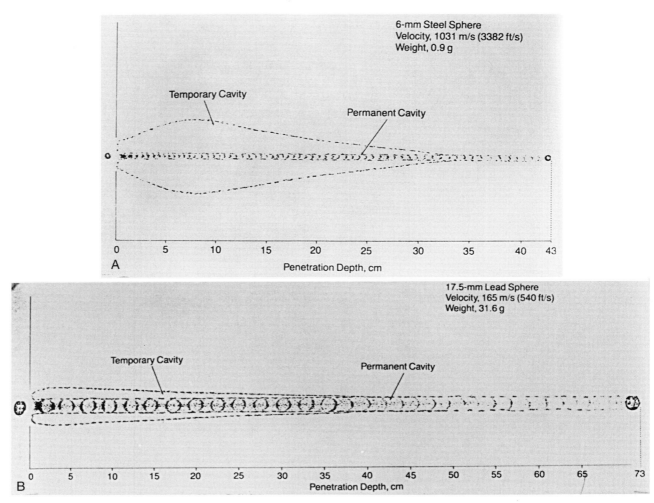

Figure 32–4. Wound profiles were obtained using a small sphere at a high velocity (*A*) to compare the injury with that of a large sphere at a slower velocity (*B*). The kinetic energy ($E = \frac{1}{2}mv^2$) is the same in each of these two examples. However, the larger sphere penetrated 30 cm deeper and produced a permanent cavity more than 50 times the volume of that produced by the smaller sphere. (From Fackler, M.L. JAMA 259:2730–2736, 1988. Copyright 1988, American Medical Association.)

synovial joint fluid[43, 71, 76] and lodged in the intervertebral disc space.[23] The exact incidence of this complication with gunshot wounds of the spine is unknown, but it is thought to be uncommon. If leaching is suspected, serum lead measurements can be obtained; if they are significantly elevated, bone marrow aspiration may be required to assess hematopoietic toxicity. If lead toxicity can be proved, surgical excision of the bullet is indicated.

The toxicity of lead, copper, and brass on a more local level has been investigated in brain tissue.[9, 64, 65] In the monkey brain, copper causes a severe necrotic local reaction, but the reaction is minimal with lead or with nickel-coated pellets. Although these other metal pellets remain where placed, the necrotic reaction can be severe enough to allow significant migration of the copper-coated pellet through the brain.[65] This is also seen when a copper powder is sprayed on monkey brain, causing a severe necrotizing foreign body reaction and death of the animal.[9]

The effect of metallic fragments on the spinal cord has been studied in rabbits,[72] using aluminum, lead, and copper fragments with one half of the fragments placed extradurally and one half placed intradurally. As expected, the extradural fragments had no effect on the neural tissue. Of the intradural fragments, the aluminum had no effect on the normal tissue, the lead caused mild to moderate neural tissue destruction, and the copper caused marked neural tissue damage (Figs. 32–5 to 32–7). Based on this study, we recommend that copper-jacketed bullets be removed from the spinal canal regardless of other considerations to avoid the local toxicity effects on the neural tissue. Most often, however, it is not known whether the bullet in the patient is copper jacketed.

The presence of wadding in the back of a shotgun cartridge must be appreciated for clinical reasons. The shotgun pellets are easily seen on plain films, but the wadding is not apparent. The shotgun wadding often acts as a significant foreign body unless it is removed. If a patient is shot with a shotgun at the close range of 6 m or less, the material should be sought within the wounds (Fig. 32–8).[4, 47]

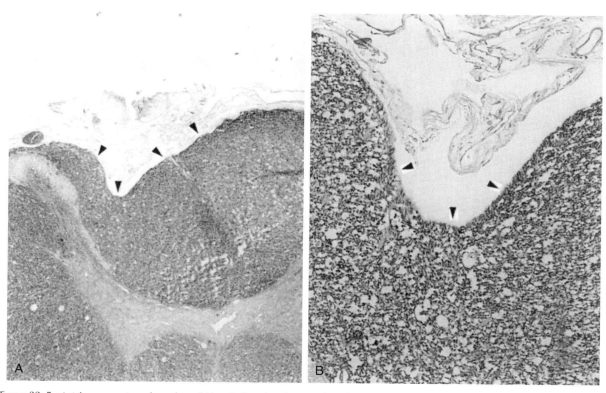

FIGURE 32–5. Axial cross sections through a rabbit spinal cord with an implanted intradural aluminum fragment. *A,* Some indentation of the spinal cord has occurred *(arrowheads)* (Solochrome Cyanine R, ×5). *B,* The underlying spinal cord tissue has minimal or no gliosis. The surrounding connective tissue matrix remains well organized (Solochrome Cyanine R, ×20). (From Tindel, N.L.; et al. J Bone Joint Surg Am 83:884–890, 2001.)

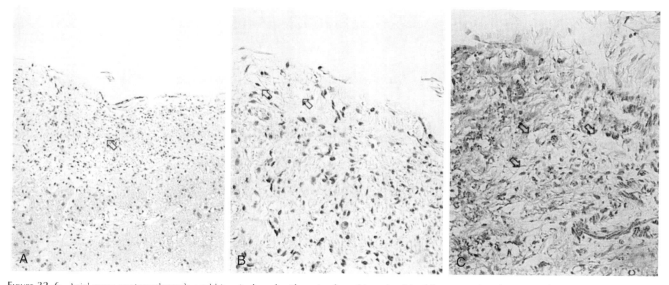

FIGURE 32–6. Axial cross sections through a rabbit spinal cord with an implanted intradural lead fragment. *A,* Indentation of the dorsal column with a small area of gliosis adjacent to the area of depression *(arrow)* (H&E, ×20). *B,* Areas of gliosis and breakdown of the supporting matrix *(arrows)* (H&E, ×40). *C,* Loss of axonal elements with disorganization of the surrounding connective tissue adjacent to the area of fragment implantation *(arrows)* (Solochrome Cyanine R, ×40). (From Tindel, N.L.; et al. J Bone Joint Surg Am 83:884–890, 2001.)

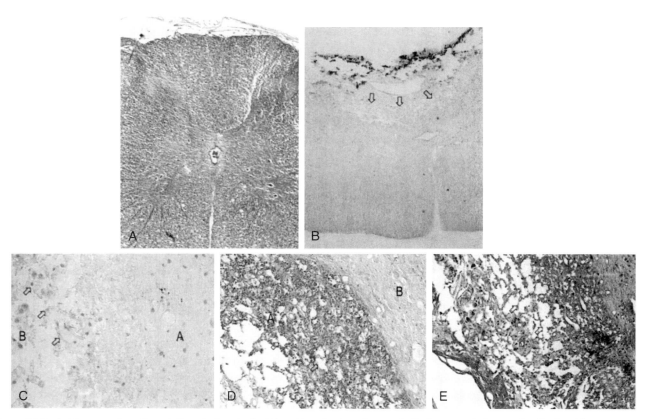

FIGURE 32–7. Axial cross sections through the spinal cords of rabbits with an implanted copper bullet fragment. *A,* An extradurally placed fragment caused no deformation or injury to the underlying spinal cord (trichome, ×5). *B,* Indentation and injury occurred to the underlying spinal cord tissue from an intradurally placed copper fragment *(arrows)* (×5). *C,* Destruction of the spinal cord parenchyma *(arrows).* The damage is confined to the white matter *(A);* the gray matter *(B)* is preserved (H&E, ×40). *D,* Vacuolization of the adjacent spinal cord tissue *(arrows)* with damage localized to the white matter *(A);* there is no damage in the gray matter *(B)* (Solochrome Cyanine R, ×40). *E,* Disruption of the connective-tissue matrix adjacent to the site of implantation of the bullet fragment *(arrows)* (trichrome, ×40). (From Tindel, N.L.; et al. J Bone Joint Surg Am 83:884–890, 2001.)

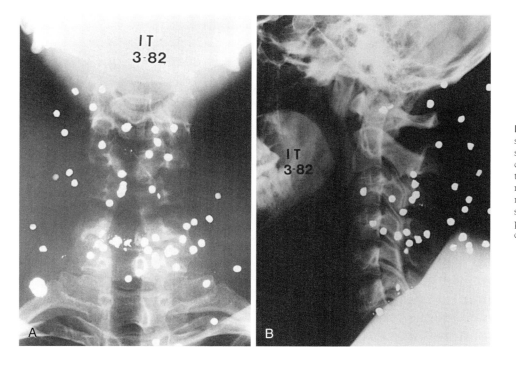

FIGURE 32–8. *A, B,* This patient was shot in the back of his neck with a shotgun using pellets. He was a complete quadriplegic as a result of this injury. Removal of the pellets is not indicated, but surgical débridement and especially removal of the shotgun wadding are necessary to prevent infection, because this was a close-range injury.

Pathology of Spinal Gunshot Wounds

Pathologic specimens were collected and described after World War I. The War Office Collection of 50 specimens has been described in the literature.[34] They show considerable variation, from relatively mild bone or ligament injuries to severe disruptions of the spinal column. The spinal cord often was intact, even though the patient sustained a complete spinal cord injury, presumably as a result of contusion of the spinal cord. With gunshot injuries to the posterior arch or pedicles, it was common to have associated secondary fractures of the vertebral body. If the vertebral body was the primary site of injury, there was seldom secondary injury to the posterior elements. The reason for this contrast was presumably that the vertebral body is composed primarily of cancellous bone, which is more easily deformed and hence transmits less energy to adjacent structures.

Klemperer and colleagues[37] investigated the pathology of indirect injuries to the spinal cord in animal models. They produced gunshot injuries to the posterior spinous processes or interspinous ligaments in anesthetized animals and found great variation among species in the presence and degree of spinal cord injury. The differences most likely correlated with the size of the spinal canal in relation to the size of the spinal cord. In animals with extremely small canals, the incidence of spinal cord injury was very high. The pathologic sections of the spinal cord varied as would be expected, but even in animals that had not sustained paralysis, there were often significant pathologic changes within the spinal cord.

PATIENT EVALUATION

The evaluation of patients with gunshot wounds of the spine should include the same detailed history, physical examination, and radiographic evaluation as would be performed for patients with other suspected spinal injuries. Attention is first given to the ABCs of emergency treatment protocols.

The history should include a general description of the weapon (e.g., handgun, rifle, assault weapon). Typically, this information is unavailable, but it can be helpful if known. The patient should be questioned about the presence of paralysis or paresthesias immediately after the injury. If the patient had an episode of transient paralysis, a more detailed neurologic follow-up is indicated.

The importance of the physical examination cannot be overemphasized. It should include examination of the entrance and exit wounds and palpation of the tissue to assess the presence of crepitation and the general turgor of the tissue. A very large exit wound with crepitus and increased tissue turgor is consistent with wounds that have a large permanent cavity and may very well have significant tissue necrosis.[13]

The physical examination should also include a detailed neurologic examination, as outlined in Chapter 25. The presence of paralysis or abnormal reflexes should be documented.

Radiographic evaluation of the patient is extremely important. Attention should be paid to the fracture type and the degree of bone comminution. The radiograph should be scrutinized to determine whether the bullet has remained in the torso and to assess the extent of bullet fragmentation. With increased bone comminution and increased bullet fragmentation, the wound is more likely to have a significant permanent cavity. If this is the case, the wound may be one of the few that require significant débridement.[13]

A computed tomography (CT) scan may help to further assess the extent of the spinal injury and the degree of spinal canal encroachment by bone or bullet fragments. The stability of the spine also can be better assessed with the help of a CT scan; this is addressed later in the section on Spinal Stability.

Magnetic resonance (MR) scans are not routinely performed on patients with gunshot wounds to the spine. There is, however, a report of 19 patients with gunshot wounds of the spine being studied with MR.[17] Six were studied within 3 weeks of injury, and the remaining 13 were studied 1 month to 6 years after injury. Ten had bullet fragments within the spinal canal. No patient reported untoward effects of the MR scan. The scans showed only mild artefact. The results of the MR scans led to surgical treatment for 3 of the 19 patients. The treating physician must understand that, if the projectile is ferromagnetic, there may be further local tissue damage. The same information may perhaps be obtained more safely with a postmyelogram CT scan of the spine in patients requiring imaging of the neural axis after a gunshot wound to the spine.

The general surgical team helping to assess the patient may recommend other studies (e.g., barium swallow, MR angiography, arteriography, intravenous pyelography) to evaluate the extent of soft tissue injuries to structures adjacent to the spine.[2]

TREATMENT OF GUNSHOT WOUNDS OF THE SPINE

Wound Care

Local wound care should be administered in the emergency department or in the formal operating room. The latter setting would be more appropriate for injuries that involve large exit wounds and those that by the physical and imaging findings may be associated with large permanent cavities. Although this type of wound is uncommon in civilian practice, such cases may be encountered.

Because of the proximity of the esophagus, the major blood vessels,[18, 21] and the larynx and trachea, general surgeons traditionally have strongly advised operative exploration of wounds of the neck, including all neck-penetrating wounds.[21, 60] Current recommendations more often advocate that the wounds should be explored only in patients with specific warning signs of serious injury and that those without such signs should be observed.[48, 50, 63] The same is true for penetrating injuries of the chest and abdomen.[2] The availability of emergency arteriography coupled with the use of intravascular hemostatic coils has also changed the indications for emergency exploratory surgery. Many cases that previously required surgery to achieve hemostasis can now be managed with minimally invasive techniques (Fig. 32–9).

Wound cultures should always be taken from the bullet tract. If the wound has been contaminated by passage of the bullet through the pharynx,[61, 62] esophagus, or colon,[58] or if contamination of the wound occurred after injury, it is even more essential that appropriate cultures be taken. For routine, uncontaminated spinal injuries, we recommend 3 days of treatment with parenteral antibiotics such as a second-generation cephalosporin at maximal intravenous dosage.[26] For contaminated wounds, such as a transcolonic gunshot wound of the spine, a 7- to 14-day antibiotic regimen is recommended (see the Associated Injuries section).[35, 39, 45, 58]

Spinal Stability: Assessment and Treatment

Most civilian gunshot injuries of the spine are stable.[30, 70, 79] In the cervical spine, 36% of the weight of the head is normally supported through the anterior vertebral bodies and discs, and 32% is supported through each of the two posterolateral columns (i.e., facet joints and lateral masses).[51] If none of these three columns is compromised, immobilization is not recommended.

If one of the columns is disrupted, a rigid cervical collar is recommended. If two or all of the three columns are disrupted, halo vest immobilization is recommended. In a review of 36 gunshot wounds of the spine,[30] 12 patients had cervical spinal injuries, and 4 were unstable, requiring a halo vest and then a rigid brace.

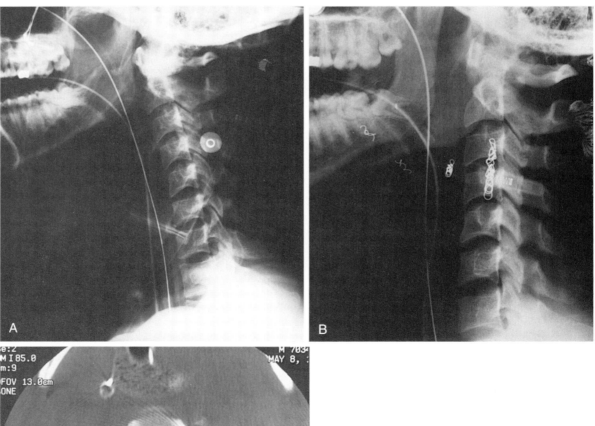

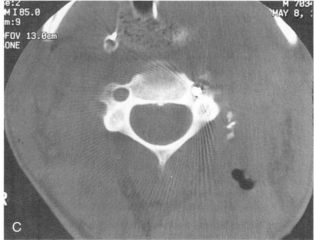

FIGURE 32–9. Lateral radiograph after a gunshot wound to the neck at the level of C3–C4. *A,* The patient's primary problem was significant bleeding. Angiography revealed an injury to the left vertebral artery. *B,* This lateral radiograph was taken after insertion of a hemostatic coil into the left vertebral artery, which achieved complete hemostasis. *C,* The computed tomography scan shows the location of the hemostatic coil within the left vertebral artery.

In the thoracic and lumbar spine, the three-column concept of Denis[11] can be applied, but the mechanism of destruction is considerably different from that seen in the closed injuries for which this classification was designed. If destruction is limited to one of the three columns, no particular immobilization is needed; if two or three columns are compromised by the gunshot wound, a thoracolumbosacral orthosis (TLSO brace) should be worn whenever the patient is out of bed. In the same review[30] of the 24 patients with thoracic and lumbar injuries, only 1 was unstable and was successfully treated in a brace. None required surgery for instability.

In contrast to closed spinal injuries, gunshot wounds of the spine rarely require operation for purposes of establishing stability. Immobilization for these injuries in any part of the spine usually lasts for 6 to 8 weeks. After that time, flexion and extension radiographs of the affected region are obtained to establish whether the spine has adequately healed and is stable.

The most unstable injuries are seen in small children, in whom the size of the vertebra is relatively small compared with the size and kinetic energy of the bullet. Other factors predisposing to a significant instability of the spine are injuries with severe bone comminution and bullet fragmentation and the effects of a previous laminectomy.[70] Even if the instability is significant, surgical treatment is seldom indicated. The temporary use of skull tong traction for severe instability of compound cervical spinal injuries or Roto Rest bed treatment for severe thoracic or lumbar compound injuries may be indicated for 2 to 3 weeks to allow early healing before routine mobilization with the braces described previously.

Associated Injuries

It is important to consider associated viscus injuries in patients with gunshot wounds of the spine. If the bullet first penetrated the pharynx,[61, 62] the esophagus, or the colon[58] before entering the spine, extra precautions should be taken to prevent spinal infection. This is essential only when the bullet has first penetrated the viscus and then penetrated the spine, and it does not seem to be important if the bullet first traversed the spine and then perforated the viscus. The general surgical team performs emergency surgery to repair the viscus,[2] places adequate drains, and recommends broad-spectrum antibiotics to cover organisms normally found in the viscus. This is less important for injuries of the stomach, duodenum, and small intestine, which normally have sterile contents, although spinal sepsis has been reported with gunshot wounds to these segments of the gastrointestinal tract.[25] In contrast to recommendations in the mid-1980s promoting radical spinal débridement,[59] the best results have been reported by Roffi and co-workers,[58] who recommended minimal or no spinal débridement and protection with 1 to 2 weeks of treatment with parenteral antibiotics. The broad-spectrum antibiotics should be directed at the bacteria normally associated with injury of the particular viscus. If the viscus repair has complications, the duration of antibiotic coverage may have to be extended. With this treatment protocol, the incidence of spinal infection has been

dramatically decreased and is now in the range of 5% to 15% for these severe injuries involving the pharynx, esophagus, or colon.

Treatment of transperitoneal colon injuries with a 2-day course of antibiotics plus irrigation of the missile tract at surgery has been recommended.[35] However, considering the findings of Roffi and co-workers and the small number of patients with colon injuries in this reported series, we recommend the longer course of antibiotics (1 to 2 weeks).

Bullet in the Disc Space

Three considerations influence whether surgery is indicated when the bullet is located in the disc space. The first consideration is whether the patient is likely to develop lead poisoning. There is good evidence to suggest that when a lead bullet is bathed in synovial fluid, the lead is leached out and can cause lead poisoning.[43, 71, 76] One article suggests that this may also be the case with a lead bullet located within the disc space,[23] and we have had a similar case at our institution. Because the literature does not reveal what percentage of patients with bullets in the disc space go on to develop lead poisoning, we are unable to make a sound recommendation about whether surgery should routinely be carried out. An alternative to routine surgical removal would be to obtain serum lead measurements in patients who are suspected of having signs of lead toxicity; if there is a rise of the serum lead to an abnormal level, the bullet should be removed.

The second consideration regarding surgery is whether there is mechanical disruption of the motion segment caused by the bullet within the disc space. Medical experience for this problem is also anecdotal. The patient can be monitored clinically, and if new symptoms of a mechanical problem develop (e.g., worsening of a local pain when upright and active and a decrease in pain with recumbency), consideration can be given to removal of the bullet with or without local fusion.

The third consideration is whether there has been disc extrusion as a result of the gunshot wound. If a disc extrusion has occurred and is causing significant neural compression that is symptomatic, surgery is indicated for removal of the disc fragments to achieve neural decompression. This condition is extremely uncommon, but it has been reported in the literature.[57]

Bullet in the Spinal Canal

Many articles have been written concerning removal of bullets from the spinal canal,[10, 28, 31, 40, 52, 66, 67, 70, 77] but this problem was not reviewed in a scientific fashion until recently. For conclusions to be valid, there must be two groups with equivalent pathologic conditions, with one group undergoing bullet removal and the other group having bullets left in place. It is also important for the study to be done on a prospective basis with adequate documentation of neurologic information and quantitative assessment of pain and other symptoms. Such a review was performed by Waters and Adkins.[73] They reviewed 90 patients, 32 with bullet removals and 58 with bullets left in place. They were able to conclude that, at the levels of T12 through L5, there was statistically significant neurologic motor improvement with removal of the bullet from the spinal canal (Fig. 32–10). However, there was no difference in improvement in the two groups with regard to sensation or pain experienced by the patients. In the thoracic spine (T1 through T11), there was no statistical

difference in the two groups for complete or incomplete injuries. Similarly, there was no difference with bullet removal in the cervical spine, although the number of patients with injuries in the cervical spine was too small to draw statistical conclusions.

Adding our own subjective opinion to these data, we recommend that patients with cervical injuries undergo

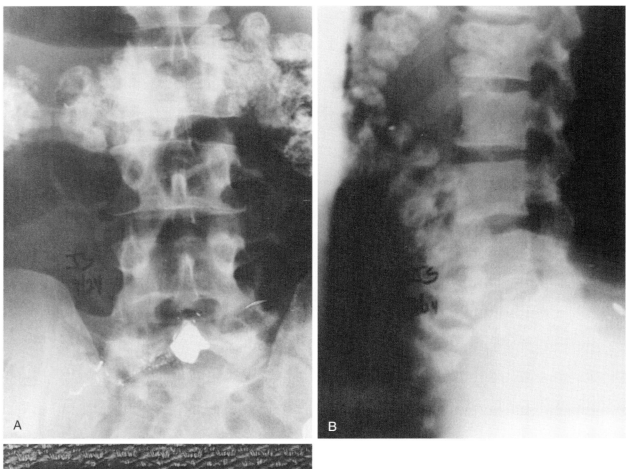

FIGURE 32–10. *A–C,* This young man was shot through his flank, with the bullet lodging within the spinal canal at the L5–S1 level. He had normal motor function in his legs but some dysesthesia in the S1 nerve root distribution, and there was some urinary dysfunction with elevated postvoid residuals. He was taken to surgery 8 days after his injury, and the bullet was easily removed. A small dural laceration was repaired. The patient had return of normal urologic function.

bullet removal, because this procedure significantly decreases the degree of spinal cord compression.[6] We recommend this approach even in complete injuries, with the expectation not of cord return but of nerve root improvement at the adjacent level over time. The rationale is the same as for closed spinal cord injuries of the cervical spine that have significant residual neural compression by bone or disc fragments and can improve after elective decompression.[1, 3]

It is generally agreed that surgery is indicated for patients with bullets within the spinal canal who are experiencing neurologic deterioration. We emphasize, however, that surgery should be performed only in patients with documented compression of the neural elements by bone, disc, bullet, or hematoma. Such deterioration is extremely uncommon but is occasionally seen (Fig. 32–11). In contrast, there can be neurologic deterioration on the basis of ascending spinal cord necrosis with no residual neural compression, and this particular pathology cannot be helped and may be worsened with surgery.

After the decision has been made to perform surgery to remove the bullet from the spinal canal, a scout radiograph should be taken in the operating room before the incision is made. The bullet can occasionally migrate within the spinal canal, depending on the position of the patient,[24, 33, 42, 54, 78] especially in patients with large spinal canals and relatively small bullets.

We usually recommend that surgery for removal of bullets from the spinal canal be performed 7 to 10 days after the injury, because at that time, cerebrospinal fluid (CSF) leakage, dural repair, and other problems are simplified considerably (Fig. 32–12). This approach does not apply if there is significant neurologic deterioration; such patients should be treated with immediate surgery, as described previously.

Rate of Neurologic Recovery

Most spinal cord injuries improve to some extent over time. Complete spinal cord injuries usually have root improvement at one or two levels, and incomplete injuries have a chance for dramatic improvement in spinal cord function and local root function. An early review of closed and open spinal cord injuries at the University of Miami showed statistically significant neurologic improvement at the 6-month follow-up in patients with complete or incomplete open spinal cord injuries (most of which were caused by gunshot wounds), but the improvements started slightly later than in those with closed injuries (Fig. 32–13).[22]

COMPLICATIONS OF GUNSHOT WOUNDS TO THE SPINE

Neurologic Injury

The use of steroids is contraindicated in the treatment of patients with spinal cord injury from gunshot wounds. In a retrospective review[26, 27] of patients treated with methylprednisolone or dexamethasone compared with those treated without steroids, the investigators found a higher incidence of complications but no difference in neurologic function using the American Spinal Injury Association (ASIA) motor score or Frankel grades. Infections were increased in the combined group receiving steroids as compared with those not receiving steroids (6.6% compared with 2.6%), but this finding was not statistically significant ($P = .23$). Gastrointestinal complications were increased in the dexamethasone group ($P = .021$), and pancreatitis was more frequent in the methylprednisolone group ($P = .040$). A second retrospective review similarly did not show any difference between those treated with or without steroids in neurologic function using Frankel scores.[44] This study, however, did not find a statistically significant difference in complications between the two groups.

The clinical outcome of paralysis resulting from gunshot wounds to the spine has been well studied and reported by Waters and associates.[74] Motor and sensory evaluations were performed on patients with neurologic injuries resulting from gunshot wounds. The study found that 57% of the injuries were complete and 43% were incomplete. At the 1-year follow-up examination, 67% of patients with complete lesions and 64% of those with incomplete lesions had no improvement in the neurologic level of injury (i.e., the most caudal intact motor and sensory level did not change). Overall, however, the patients had a statistically significant improvement in the ASIA motor index score at 1 year after injury ($P < .0001$), and more improvement was seen with incomplete injuries than with complete injuries.

Late neurologic deterioration in patients with an existing neurologic deficit caused by a gunshot wound to the spine has been reported by Gellad and colleagues.[19] Eleven such patients were prospectively evaluated clinically, radiologically, and surgically. The study found a syringomyelic cavity in seven patients, an arachnoid cyst in three, and osteomyelitis in one. The results of this study emphasize the need for immediate evaluation of patients who have sustained a gunshot wound to the spine and have further deterioration imposed on an initial deficit.

Late neurologic deterioration in patients who were initially intact is uncommon, but it has occurred even many years after a gunshot wound of the spine.[8, 32, 33, 38, 69] Instances of bullet migration within the spinal canal and the subsequent development of a neurologic deficit have been reported.[33] There are also cases of late development of spinal stenosis[32, 69] or cauda equina syndrome.[8] Late deterioration can be caused by an intraspinal bullet fragment causing local spinal canal narrowing[32, 69] or a combination of neural compression and local neurotoxic effects resulting from the type of metal in the bullet fragment.[38, 69, 72] These problems of late neurologic deterioration can often be successfully treated surgically. Although the algorithm for treatment of neurologic deficits associated with gunshot wounds to the spine has already been described, these cases suggest a cautious approach to the management of patients with retained bullets in the spinal canal.

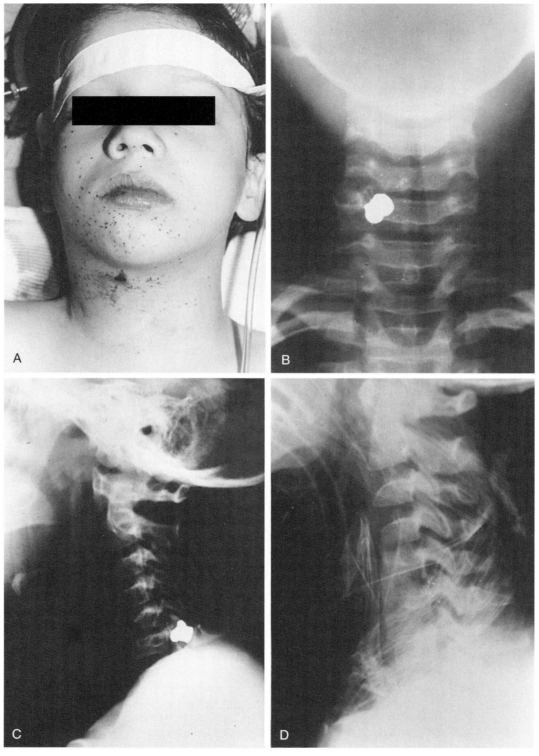

Figure 32–11. *A–D,* This young boy was accidentally shot in his neck and had progressive quadriparesis. Twenty-four hours after the injury, he had lost all motor function in his legs. Plain radiographs revealed that the bullet was filling the right side of the spinal canal. He was taken to surgery emergently, and an anterior cervical procedure was performed. His trachea and esophagus were found to be intact. A corpectomy of C5 and C6 was performed to remove the bullet. An anterior cervical fusion was then performed using autologous iliac crest bone graft. The patient regained ambulation, and his only residual weakness involved his arms.

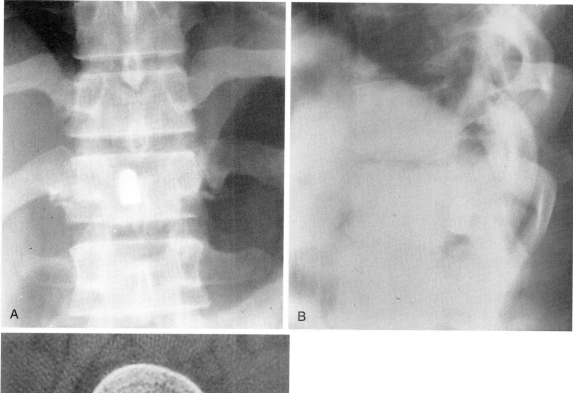

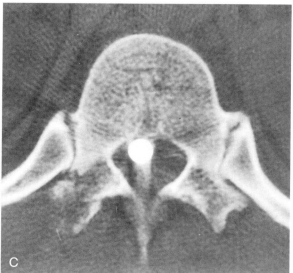

FIGURE 32–12. *A–C*, This patient presented to the emergency room with a complete paraplegia, including no bowel or bladder function and no motor or sensory function below L1. His neurologic condition was unchanged for 1 week. He was taken to surgery to remove the bullet, which was located within the dura. The goal of surgery was not to improve the function of the conus medullaris, but rather to maximize the chance for improvement of the L1–L4 nerve rootlets traveling past this level of injury.

Pain with Associated Spinal Cord Injury

Chronic dysesthetic pains have been reported as a complication of gunshot injuries to the spinal cord.[19] Most commonly, this is described as a searing, burning type of pain that radiates into the paralyzed extremities.

These pains often persist and may be completely disabling. They may often be helped with the use of gabapentin (Neurontin). Amitriptyline (Elavil) has been helpful in patients with burning diabetic neuropathic pain and postherpetic neuralgia,[41, 55, 75] and it seems to help patients with dysesthetic spinal cord injury pain. If none of the medications helps, a course of carbamazepine (Tegretol) may be tried.

Prevention or minimization of future pain is often cited as an indication for removal of bullet fragments in patients who have had a spinal cord injury (Fig. 32–14). Although patients who have sustained a spinal cord injury from a gunshot wound have an increased incidence of pain compared with patients with closed spinal cord injuries, studies show that surgical removal of the bullet is not helpful in reducing pain early after the injury or at 1 year.[56, 73] If surgery is contemplated for the different pain associated with gunshot wounds to the spine, then the dorsal root entry zone (DREZ) lesioning procedure with intraoperative assessment can offer some patients significant pain relief.[49, 68] This technique is best used in patients without distal motor function, because there is always a risk of increasing the distal neurologic deficit with this procedure.

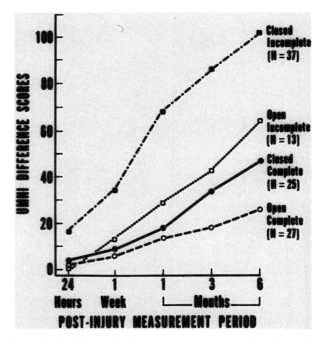

FIGURE 32–13. The graph shows that penetrating injuries of the spine have a worse prognosis for recovery than closed injuries. This is true for complete and incomplete injuries. (From Green, B.A.; et al. Comparison of open versus closed spinal cord injuries during the first year post injury. Paper presented at the Annual Meeting of the American Spinal Injury Association, New Orleans, 1981.)

Cerebrospinal Fluid Fistulas

CSF fistulas have been described after gunshot wounds to the spine. The fistulas can connect with skin or with other body cavities. Occasionally, they are seen as a direct result of a gunshot wound to the spine,[73] but they occur most commonly after acute surgical treatment with laminectomy (Fig. 32–15). Stauffer and co-workers[70] described their experience with 185 patients and observed that CSF cutaneous fistulas did not occur in patients who had not had laminectomies. In those treated with laminectomy, spinal débridement, and bullet removal, the incidence was 6%.

The fact that most CSF cutaneous fistulas occur after acute surgical treatment is another reason to delay removal of the bullet for 7 to 10 days, except when emergency surgical decompression is needed, as described in the preceding section. When surgery is performed to remove the bullet, meticulous dural repair and closure of the paraspinous muscles, deep fascia, and skin are necessary to minimize the chance of postoperative fistula.[12] At the time of repair of the dura, the seal should be checked with a Valsalva maneuver to make certain that it is watertight. If a watertight seal cannot be achieved, a lumbar subarachnoid drain (Fig. 32–16) should be placed to divert spinal fluid, promote proper healing, and prevent such problems as CSF cutaneous fistulas and subsequent meningitis.[36]

Subarachnoid pleural fistula is a relatively uncommon complication of gunshot wounds to the spine, and the diagnosis and treatment of this problem may be difficult. Often, the fistula is not clinically apparent immediately after the injury but is discovered later in the course of the hospitalization as a pleural effusion or with the development of postural headaches. Radionuclide scanning can be an effective method for localization of the fistula.[19] Delayed images are obtained after introduction of the radionuclide into the subarachnoid space through a lumbar puncture. The CT myelogram is also an effective means for detecting the fistula, although it may not be as sensitive. We recommend use of a lumbar subarachnoid drain as the first line of treatment for acute or semiacute injuries with a CSF pleural fistula. Conservative treatment

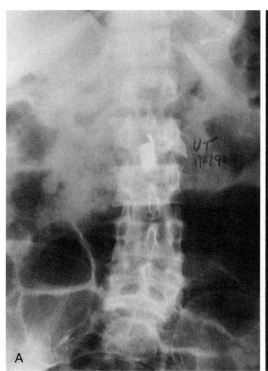

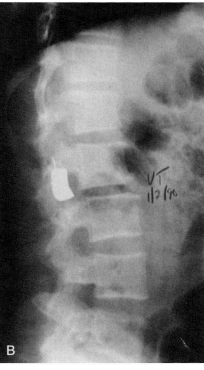

FIGURE 32–14. *A, B,* This patient had incomplete paraplegia caused by a gunshot wound of his spine. He had some function in almost every muscle group below this level of injury, but his main problem was severe pain radiating into his extremities. He had failed medical treatment using amitriptyline and allowing time to pass. After removal of the bullet, the patient had significant pain improvement. Unfortunately, this type of positive response with relief of the pain cannot be predicted with bullet removal.

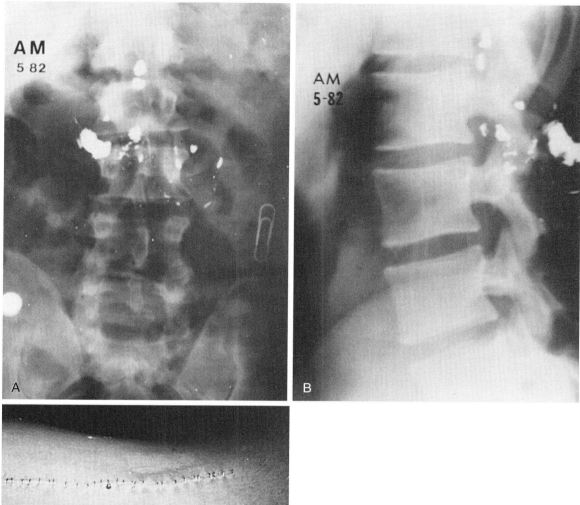

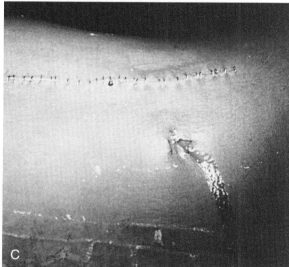

FIGURE 32–15. *A–C,* This patient was shot in the back, with the onset of a complete paraplegia at the L1 level. He was taken immediately to surgery, and a laminectomy was performed. Postoperatively, the patient developed a cerebrospinal fluid (CSF) cutaneous fistula through the site of the bullet wound. It is now appreciated that this type of surgery is unproductive, because there is no major bullet fragment within the spinal canal. The chance of developing the CSF cutaneous fistula was also heightened by performing the surgery immediately. Treatment requires placement of a subarachnoid CSF shunt and revision surgery to treat the CSF cutaneous fistula, the postoperative infection, and the secondary meningitis.

has not been effective with an established fistula, and surgical repair of the dural tear has been the only successful form of treatment.

Spinal Infections

Spinal infections occur infrequently after gunshot wounds to the spine. Most of those that do occur follow injuries to the pharynx,[61, 62] esophagus, or colon.[58] They seldom occur after injury to any other organs, including the stomach or small bowel. The preceding sections described treatment methods to minimize this complication, includ-

ing routine use of antibiotics for 72 hours after injury and for 7 to 14 days after associated injury of a contaminated viscus.[58, 61, 62]

The other common source of infection after gunshot wounds of the spine is iatrogenic infection after surgery. Stauffer and co-workers,[70] in their review of patients treated with laminectomy for bullet removal, found that 4% developed postoperative wound infections. These infections can be treated like any postoperative infection of the spine.[20]

Significant fistula formation may be seen in patients with spinal infections (Fig. 32–17). In patients with a contaminated viscus injury, there may be a fistula from the

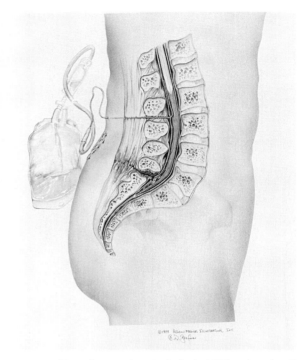

FIGURE 32–16. Use of a cerebrospinal fluid (CSF) subarachnoid-cutaneous shunt allows decompression of the dura and allows the original CSF cutaneous fistula to heal. (From Kitchell, S.; et al. J Bone Joint Surg Am 71:984–989, 1989.)

viscus to the spine. In these cases, it is not possible to resolve the infection without adequate correction of the pharyngeal, esophageal, or bowel fistula. This may require tactics such as diversionary drainage and prolonged hyperalimentation. Some patients have a cutaneous fistula

leading down to a vertebral osteomyelitis or disc space infection, but it is much more common for this to occur in patients with a viscus fistula.

The indications for surgical treatment of patients with spinal infections after gunshot wounds of the spine are the same as for any patient with a spinal infection. They include progressive paralysis associated with the infection, progressive deformity, lack of a known organism, suspected foreign body associated with the infection, and failure of conservative treatment. In most cases, the spinal infection is not identified until several weeks after the injury, and at that time, we normally recommend a CT-guided needle biopsy of the spine, followed by a 6-week course with maximal-dose parenteral antibiotics. Open surgery is reserved for the cases described previously.

OTHER PENETRATING INJURIES OF THE SPINE

Impalement Injuries

Impalement injuries of the spine are uncommon. The trauma is usually massive, and there is usually more gross wound contamination than in other injuries to the spine.[29] Patients with impalement injuries of the spine should be taken to surgery for spinal débridement. Cultures for aerobes, anaerobes, and fungi should carefully be obtained. Unlike the relatively clean gunshot wounds described previously, these injuries require a minimum of 3 weeks of parenteral treatment with broad-spectrum antibiotics designed to cover each of the organisms found during the original débridement. It is also extremely

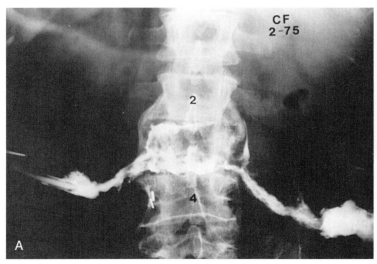

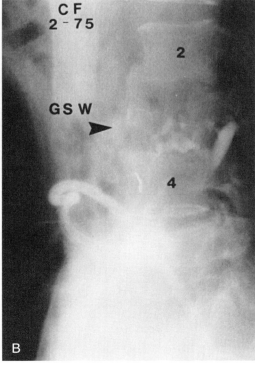

FIGURE 32–17. A, B, This patient had sustained a gunshot wound (GSW) with a perforation of his colon and with the bullet traversing the L3 vertebral body. He developed a chronic vertebral osteomyelitis with a sinus draining through each flank. The sinogram reveals the significant vertebral destruction. Treatment for this problem requires assessment of the gastrointestinal tract to be certain there is no remaining bowel fistula. This should then be followed by a vigorous spine débridement, packing the cavity with cancellous bone or viable soft tissue, and a protracted course of antibiotics.

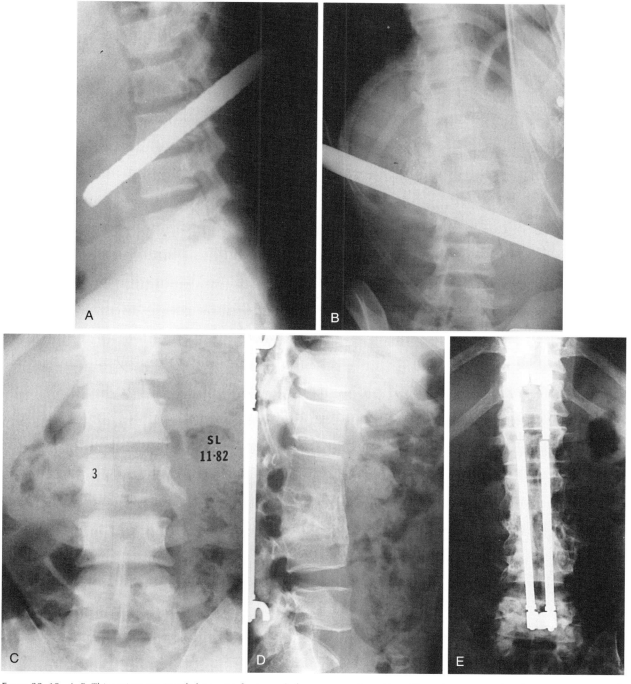

FIGURE 32–18. *A, B,* This patient was impaled on a reinforcing rod after a motorcycle accident. The rod was removed in the operating room with the use of anterior and posterior exposure of the spine. A spinal sample was cultured to identify pathogens, and the spine was vigorously débrided at the time of his initial emergency surgery. *C,* Despite coverage with 3 weeks of broad-spectrum antibiotics, the patient developed a persistent vertebral osteomyelitis with pain and continued vertebral destruction. Six weeks after his injury, he was returned to surgery for a simultaneous anterior and posterior débridement, fusion, and stabilization. Pieces of clothing were found within the vertebral body, and culture samples taken at surgery revealed standard pyogenic organisms and a fungus infection. *D, E,* Radiographs taken 10 years after the injury reveal complete resolution of the infection. Broken rods and a flat back deformity can be identified, but the patient is asymptomatic and is able to participate in full wheelchair activities with no pain.

important to rule out significant foreign bodies (e.g., pieces of clothing), which can be driven into the spine at the time of the injury (Fig. 32–18).

Patients who have sustained an impalement injury of the spine often have recurrent spinal infections and spontaneous drainage from sinus tracts. Successful treatment usually requires sinograms to define the course of the sinus and CT scans immediately after the sinogram to define the bone or disc pathology, followed by surgery to débride the spinal source of infection and excise the chronic sinus tract. Injection of methylene blue into the sinus tract helps to identify the tissue that needs to be excised (Fig. 32–19). However, this dye should never be used if there is a possibility of a dural cutaneous fistula, because intrathecal injection of methylene blue is fatal.

Stabbing Injuries

Stabbing injuries of the spine are seen much less often than gunshot wounds of the spine in the United States, but in some countries, they are the most common type of penetrating injury of the spine. Radiographs should be taken immediately to ensure that no foreign body remains. These foreign bodies are not sterile and can be the source of a persistent late infection; if found, they should be removed surgically (Fig. 32–20). Stab wounds are often associated with the Brown-Séquard type of paralysis and have the best prognosis of the incomplete spinal injuries. The general prognosis is significantly better than for patients with gunshot wounds of the spine with the same extent of incomplete paralysis.

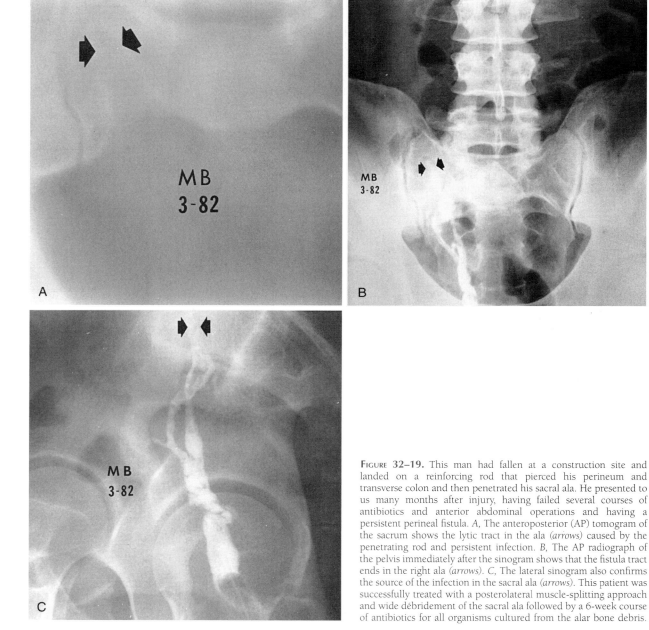

Figure 32–19. This man had fallen at a construction site and landed on a reinforcing rod that pierced his perineum and transverse colon and then penetrated his sacral ala. He presented to us many months after injury, having failed several courses of antibiotics and anterior abdominal operations and having a persistent perineal fistula. *A,* The anteroposterior (AP) tomogram of the sacrum shows the lytic tract in the ala (*arrows*) caused by the penetrating rod and persistent infection. *B,* The AP radiograph of the pelvis immediately after the sinogram shows that the fistula tract ends in the right ala (*arrows*). *C,* The lateral sinogram also confirms the source of the infection in the sacral ala (*arrows*). This patient was successfully treated with a posterolateral muscle-splitting approach and wide débridement of the sacral ala followed by a 6-week course of antibiotics for all organisms cultured from the alar bone debris.

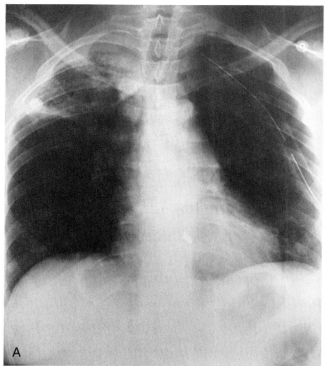

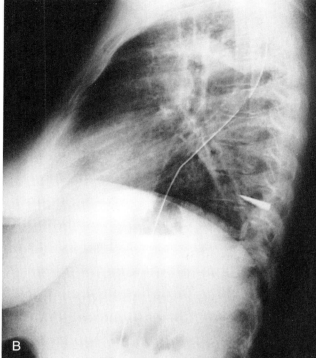

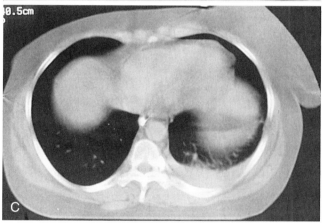

FIGURE 32-20. This patient presented to the emergency room after being stabbed with scissors. After emergency treatment for a pneumothorax, anteroposterior (A) and lateral (B) chest radiographs reveal a metallic foreign body adjacent to the thoracic spine. The computed tomography scan (C) verifies the location of the foreign body. The patient was taken to surgery for removal of the foreign body to minimize the chance of developing a persistent infection.

SUMMARY

The rising incidence of spinal cord injuries is caused by gunshot wounds of the spine, and physicians must become familiar with the evaluation and treatment of these patients. The importance of a good history, physical examination, and radiographic evaluation is emphasized. Most gunshot wounds of the spine can be treated nonoperatively, but it is important not to miss the rare injury that behaves clinically more like a typical war injury.

REFERENCES

1. Anderson, P.; Bohlman, H.H. Anterior decompression and arthrodesis of the cervical spine: Long term motor improvement. Part II: Improvement in complete traumatic quadriplegia. J Bone Joint Surg Am 74:683–692, 1992.
2. Bishop, M.; Shoemaker, W.C.; Avakian, S.; et al. Evaluation of a comprehensive algorithm for blunt and penetrating thoracic and abdominal trauma. Am Surg 57:737–746, 1991.
3. Bohlman, H.H.; Anderson, P. Anterior decompression and arthrodesis of the cervical spine: Long term motor improvement. Part I: Improvement in incomplete traumatic quadriparesis. J Bone Joint Surg Am 74:671–682, 1992.
4. Breitenecker, R. Shotgun wound patterns. Am J Clin Pathol 52:250–269, 1969.
5. Burney, R.E.; Maio, R.F.; Maynard, F.; Karunas, R. Incidence, characteristics, and outcome of spinal cord injury at trauma centers in North America. Arch Surg 128:596–599, 1993.
6. Cammisa, F.P.; Eismont, F.J.; Tolli, T. Penetrating injuries of the cervical spine. In: Camins, M.B.; O'Leary, P.F., eds. Disorders of the Cervical Spine. Baltimore, Williams & Wilkins, 1992, pp. 317–322.
7. Capen, D. Etiology of spinal cord injuries: Significant changes over ten years. Paper presented at the Annual Meeting of the American Academy of Orthopaedic Surgeons, San Francisco, February, 1993.
8. Conway, J.E.; Crofford, T.W.; Terry, A.F.; Protzman, R.R. Cauda equina syndrome occurring nine years after a gunshot injury to the spine. J Bone Joint Surg Am 75:760–763, 1993.
9. Cushid, J.G.; Kopeloff, L.M. Eleptogenic effects of metal powder implants in the motor cortex in monkeys. Int J Neuropsychiatry 3:24–28, 1968.

10. Cybulski, G.R.; Stone, J.L.; Kant, R. Outcome of laminectomy for civilian gunshot injuries of the terminal spinal cord and cauda equina: Review of 88 cases. Neurosurgery 24:392–397, 1989.

11. Denis, F. The three column spine and its significance in the classification of acute thoracolumbar spinal injuries. Spine 8:817–831, 1983.

12. Eismont, F.J.; Wiesel, S.W.; Rothman, R.H. Treatment of dural tears associated with spinal surgery. J Bone Joint Surg Am 63:1132–1136, 1981.

13. Fackler, M.L. Wound ballistics: A review of common misconceptions. JAMA 259:2730–2736, 1988.

14. Fackler, M.L.; Bellamy, R.F.; Malinowski, J.A. The wound profile: Illustration of the missile tissue interaction. J Trauma 28 (Suppl 1):S21–S29, 1988.

15. Fackler, M.L.; Malinowski, J.A. The wound profile: A visual method for quantifying gunshot wound components. J Trauma 25:522–529, 1985.

16. Farmer, J.C.; Vaccaro, A.R.; Balderston, R.A.; et al. The changing nature of admissions to a spinal cord injury center: Violence on the rise. J Spinal Disord 11:400–402, 1998.

17. Finitais, S.N.; Falcone, S.; Green, B.A. MR of the spine in the presence of metallic bullet fragments: Is the benefit worth the risk? Letter. Am J Neuroradiol 20:354–356, 1999.

18. Fitzgerald, L.F.; Simpson, R.K.; Trask, T. Locked-in syndrome resulting from cervical spine gunshot wound. J Trauma 42:147–149, 1997.

19. Gellad, F.E.; Paul, K.S.; Geisler, F.H. Early sequelae of gunshot wounds to the spine: Radiologic diagnosis. Radiology 167:523–526, 1983.

20. Gepstein, R.; Eismont, F.J. Postoperative spine infections. In: Garfin, S.R., ed. Complications of Spine Surgery. Baltimore, Williams & Wilkins, 1989, pp. 302–322.

21. Golueke, P.; Sclafani, S.; Phillips, T.; et al. Vertebral artery injury—Diagnosis and management. J Trauma 27:856–865, 1987.

22. Green, B.A.; Eismont, F.J.; Klose, K.J.; Goldberg, M.L. A comparison of open versus closed spinal cord injuries during the first year post injury. Paper presented at the Annual Meeting of the American Spinal Injury Association, New Orleans, 1981.

23. Grogan, D.P.; Bucholz, R.W. Acute lead intoxication from a bullet in an intervertebral disc space. J Bone Joint Surg Am 63:1180–1182, 1981.

24. Gupta, S.; Senger, R.L. Wandering intraspinal bullet. Br J Neurosurg 13:606–607, 1999.

25. Hales, D.D.; Duffy, K.; Dawson, E.G.; Delamarter, R. Lumbar osteomyelitis and epidural and paraspinous abscesses. Spine 16:380–383, 1991.

26. Heary, R.F.; Vaccaro, A.R.; Mesa, J.J.; Balderston, R.A. Thoracolumbar infections in penetrating injuries to the spine. Orthop Clin North Am 27:69–81, 1996.

27. Heary, R.F.; Vaccaro, A.R.; Mesa, J.J.; et al. Steroids and gunshot wounds to the spine. Neurosurgery 41:576–583, 1997.

28. Heiden, J.S.; Weiss, M.H.; Rosenberg, A.W.; et al. Penetrating gunshot wounds of the cervical spine in civilians: Review of 38 cases. J Neurosurg 42:575–579, 1975.

29. Horowitz, M.D.; Dove, D.B.; Eismont, F.J.; Green, B.A. Impalement injuries. J Trauma 25:914–916, 1985.

30. Isiklar, U.; Lindsey, R.W. Low-velocity civilian gunshot wounds of the spine. Orthopaedics 20:967–972, 1997.

31. Jacobson, S.A.; Bors, E. Spinal cord injury in Vietnamese combat. Paraplegia 7:263–281, 1969.

32. Jeffery, J.A.; Borgstein, R. Case report of a retained bullet in the lumbar spinal canal with preservation of cauda equina function. Injury 29:724–726, 1998.

33. Karim, N.O.; Nabors, M.W.; Golocovsky, M.; Cooney, F.D. Spontaneous migration of a bullet in the spinal subarachnoid space causing delayed radicular symptoms. Neurosurgery 18:97–100, 1986.

34. Keith, A.; Hall, M.E. Specimens of gunshot injuries of the face and spine, contained in the Army medical collection now on exhibition in the Museum of Royal College of Surgeons of England. Br J Surg 7:55–71, 1919–1920.

35. Kihtir, T.; Ivatury, R.R.; Simon, R.; Stahl, W.M. Management of transperitoneal gunshot wounds of the spine. J Trauma 31:1579–1583, 1991.

36. Kitchell, S.; Eismont, F.J.; Green, B.A. Closed subarachnoid drainage for management of cerebrospinal fluid leakage after an operation on the spine. J Bone Joint Surg Am 71:984–989, 1989.

37. Klemperer, W.W.; Fulton, J.F.; Lamport, H.; Schorr, M.G. Indirect spinal cord injuries due to gunshot wounds of the spinal column in animal and man. Mil Surgeon 114:263–265, 1954.

38. Kuijlan, J.M. Herpers, M.J.; Beuls, E.A. Neurogenic claudication: A delayed complication of a retained bullet. Spine 22:910–914, 1997.

39. Kumar, A.; Wood, G.W., II; Whittle, A.P. Low-velocity gunshot injuries of the spine with abdominal viscus trauma. J Orthop Trauma 12:514–517, 1998.

40. Kupcha, P.C.; An, H.S.; Cotler, J.M. Gunshot wounds to the cervical spine. Spine 15:1058–1063, 1990.

41. Kvinesdal, B.; Molin, J.; Frolund, A.; Gram, L.F. Imipramine treatment of painful diabetic neuropathy. JAMA 251:1727–1730, 1984.

42. Ledgerwood, A.M. The wandering bullet. Surg Clin North Am 57:97–109, 1977.

43. Leonard, M.H. The solution of lead by synovial fluid. Clin Orthop 64:255–261, 1969.

44. Levy, M.L.; Gans, W.; Wijesinghe, H.S.; et al. Use of methylprednisolone as an adjunct in the management of patients with penetrating spinal cord injury: Outcome analysis. Neurosurgery 39:1141–1148, 1996.

45. Lin, S.S.; Vaccaro, A.R.; Reich, S.M.; et al. Low-velocity gunshot wounds to the spine with an associated transperitoneal injury. J Spinal Disord 8:136–144, 1995.

46. Magnuson, E.; Leviton, J.; Riley, M. Seven deadly days. Time 134:30–61, July 17, 1989.

47. May, M.; West, J.W.; Heeneman, H.; et al. Shotgun wounds to the head and neck. Arch Otolaryngol 98:373–376, 1973.

48. Menawat, S.S.; Dennis, J.W.; Laneve, L.M; Frykberg, E.R. Are arteriograms necessary in penetrating zone II neck injuries? J Vasc Surg 16:307, 1992.

49. Nashold, B.S.; Ostdahl, R.H. Dorsal root entry zone lesions for pain relief. J Neurosurg 51:59–69, 1979.

50. Ordog, G.J.; Albin, D.; Wasserberger, J.; et al. 110 bullet wounds to the neck. J Trauma 25:238–246, 1985.

51. Pal, G.P.; Sherk, H.H. The vertical stability of the cervical spine. Spine 13:447–449, 1988.

52. Pool, J.L. Gunshot wounds of the spine: Observations from an evacuation hospital. Surg Gynecol Obstet 81:617–622, 1945.

53. Ragucci, M.V.; Gittler, M.M.; Balfanz-Vertiz, K.; Hunter, A. Societal risk factors associated with spinal cord injury secondary to gunshot wound. Arch Phys Med Rehabil 82:1720–1723, 2001.

54. Rajan, D.K.; Alcantara, A.L.; Michael, D.B. Where's the bullet? A migration in two acts. J Trauma 43:716–718, 1997.

55. Richards, J.S. Pain secondary to gunshot wounds during the initial rehabilitation process in spinal cord injury patients. J Rehabil Res Dev 25(Suppl):75, 1989.

56. Richards, J.S.; Stover, S.L., Jaworski, T. Effect of bullet removal on subsequent pain in persons with spinal cord injury secondary to gunshot wound. J Neurosurg 73:401–404, 1990.

57. Robertson, D.P.; Simpson, R.K; Narayan, R.K. Lumbar disc herniation from a gunshot wound to the spine. Spine 16:994–995, 1991.

58. Roffi, R.P.; Waters, R.L; Adkins, R.H. Gunshot wounds to the spine associated with a perforated viscus. Spine 14:808–811, 1989.

59. Romanick, P.C.; Smith, T.K.; Kopaniky, D.R.; Oldfield, D. Infection about the spine associated with low velocity missile injury to the abdomen. J Bone Joint Surg Am 67:1195–1201, 1985.

60. Saletta, J.D.; Lowe, R.J.; Lim, L.T.; et al. Penetrating trauma of the neck. J Trauma 16:579–587, 1976.

61. Schaeffer, S.D.; Bucholz, R.W.; Jones, R.E.; et al. Treatment of transpharyngeal missile wounds to the cervical spine. Laryngoscope 19:146–148, 1981.

62. Schaeffer, S.E.; Bucholz, R.W.; Jones, R.E.; Carder, H.M. The management of transpharyngeal gunshot wounds to the cervical spine. Surg Gynecol Obstet 152:27–29, 1981.

63. Sheely, C.H.; Mattox, K.L.; Reul, G.J.; et al. Current concepts in the management of penetrating neck trauma. J Trauma 15:895–900, 1975.

64. Sherman, I.J. Brass foreign body in the brain stem. J Neurosurg 17:483–485, 1960.

65. Sights, W.P.; Bye, R.J. The fate of retained intracerebral shotgun pellets. J Neurosurg 33:646–653, 1970.

66. Simpson, R.L.; Venger, B.H.; Narayan, R.K. Penetrating spinal cord injury in a civilian population: A retrospective analysis. Surg Forum 37:494–496, 1986.

67. Simpson, R.K.; Venger, B.H.; Narayan, R.K. Treatment of acute penetrating injuries to the spine: A retrospective analysis. J Trauma 29:42–45, 1989.

68. Spaic, M.; Petkovic, S.; Tadio, R.; Minic, L. DREZ surgery on conus medullaris (after failed implantation of vascular omental graft) for treating chronic pain due to spine (gunshot) injuries. Acta Neurochir 141:1309–1312, 1999.

69. Staniforth, P.; Watt, I. Extradural "plumboma": A rare cause of acquired spinal stenosis. Br J Radiol 55:772–774, 1982.

70. Stauffer, E.S.; Wood, W.; Kelly, E.G. Gunshot wounds of the spine: The effects of laminectomy. J Bone Joint Surg Am 61:389–392, 1979.

71. Switz, D.M.; Deyarle, W.M. Bullets, joints and lead intoxication. Arch Intern Med 136:939–941, 1976.

72. Tindel, N.L.; Marcillo, A.E.; Tay, B.K.-B.; et al. The effect of surgically implanted bullet fragments on the spinal cord in a rabbit model. J Bone Joint Surg Am 83:884–890, 2001.

73. Waters, R.L.; Adkins, R.H. The effects of removal of bullet fragments retained in the spinal canal. Spine 168:934–939, 1991.

74. Waters, R.L.; Adkins, R.H.; Yakura, J.; Sie, I. Profiles of spinal cord injury and recovery after gunshot injury. Clin Orthop 267:14–21, 1991.

75. Watson, C.P.; Evans, R.J.; Reed, K.; et al. Amitriptyline versus placebo in postherpetic neuralgia. Neurology 32:671–673, 1982.

76. Windler, E.F.; Smith, R.B.; Bryan, W.J.; et al. Lead intoxication and traumatic arthritis of the hip secondary to retained bullet fragment. J Bone Joint Surg Am 60:254–255, 1978.

77. Yashon, D.; Jane, J.A.; White, R.J. Prognosis and management of spinal cord and cauda equina bullet injuries in sixty-five civilians. J Neurosurg 32:163–170, 1970.

78. Yip, L.; Sweeny, P.J.; McCarroll, K.A. Spontaneous migration of an intraspinal bullet following a gunshot wound. Am J Emerg Med 8:569–570, 1990.

79. Yoshida, G.M.; Garland, C.; Waters, R.L. Gunshot wounds to the spine. Orthop Clin North Am 26:109–116, 1995.

80. Young, J.A.; Burns, P.E.; Bowen, A.M.; et al. Spinal Cord Injury Statistics: Experience of the Regional Spinal Cord Injury Systems. Phoenix, AZ, Good Samaritan Medical Center, 1982.

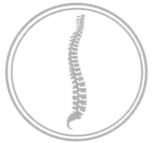

C H A P T E R 33

Fractures in the Stiff and Osteoporotic Spine

Oren G. Blam, M.D.
Jerome M. Cotler, M.D.

The structural integrity of the spine is a result of bony resistance to failure and of stability afforded by surrounding soft tissues. Disorders that affect these characteristics may produce a stiff and brittle spinal column predisposed to pathologic fracture, in the first instance by causing a thinning of the bone and in the second by reducing the energy-dissipating capacity of paraspinal ligaments and discs. Postmenopausal and advanced-age osteoporosis, ankylosing spondylitis, diffuse idiopathic skeletal hyperostosis, and other related conditions may predispose the spine to low-energy fracture and result in characteristic injury patterns. These injuries can be difficult to recognize because of the often subacute or chronic nature of neck or back pain in patients with these conditions. The radiographic appearance of the underlying disease state can complicate interpretation of fracture versus chronic changes after trivial trauma. Nevertheless, patients with these injuries are important to recognize because they may be at heightened risk for post-traumatic deformity and for neurologic deterioration, especially after a delay in diagnosis.

OSTEOPOROTIC SPINAL FRACTURES

Osteoporosis is becoming a more common cause of pathologic spinal fracture as population demographics reveal an increasing proportion of people older than age 65. The lifetime risk of a symptomatic vertebral osteoporotic fracture has been reported as 16% for women and 5% for men, with higher frequencies estimated when including asymptomatic fractures. Reported prevalences range from 10% in middle-aged women to 63% in elderly women.[28]

Osteoporosis is the progressive loss of bone content in the axial and appendicular skeleton, defined as a bone mineral density of less than 2.5 standard deviations below the mean for young, healthy people. Postmenopausal, or type I, osteoporosis results from altered bone turnover caused by decreasing circulating estrogen levels. Osteoclastic function increases out of proportion to osteoblastic function. Trabecular bone is affected more than cortical bone because of the greater surface area trabeculae present to osteoclasts for bone degradation. Postmenopausal women (usually older than age 50) are at risk, with higher incidences found for smokers, whites and Asians, women with short or thin builds, those with early menopause, and those with a positive family history of osteoporosis. Advanced-age, or type II, osteoporosis occurs equally in men and women older than age 70 and is caused by decreased osteoblastic bone formation, affecting cortical and trabecular bone equally.

In the osteoporotic spine, the vertebral body contains bone voids that can collapse, leading to end-plate scalloping, vertebral wedging, and kyphotic deformity. The cortical shell of the vertebral body contributes only 10% of compressive strength of the centrum,[36] and compressive strength of trabecular bone is related to the square of its apparent density.[32] Loss of trabecular bone can therefore have a profound effect on compressive strength of the vertebral body.

Prevention methods may prove to be most important in managing osteoporotic spinal fracture. Sufficient dietary calcium intake during the first 25 years of life may be most important because peak lifetime bone mass begins to decline afterward. Further adequate dietary intake of calcium and vitamin D during adulthood may slow this progressive decline; it is recommended that adults ingest 1500 mg of calcium and 800 international units of vitamin D each day.[25] People at risk for osteoporosis may be evaluated with bone density tests, the most accurate of which is dual-emission x-ray absorptiometry (DEXA). Medical management of osteoporosis includes dietary supplementation of calcium and vitamin D; antiresorptive agents such as estrogen, calcitonin, and bisphosphonates; and bone-stimulating agents such as fluoride. Teaching fall avoidance, proper lifting techniques, and overall body conditioning exercises also is important.[25]

The upper thoracic spine is the most common site for

osteoporotic spinal fracture. No antecedent history of trauma may be present, although back pain with tenderness over the spine usually occurs. Radicular pain or neurologic deficit may occur acutely. Late development of radicular symptoms or neurologic deterioration weeks after the initiation of spinal pain may also occur because of progressive vertebral collapse with ensuing nerve root impingement or even spinal cord compression. Cord compression is uncommon and usually self-limited.[26]

Osteoporotic fractures are usually caused by compression forces. Loss of anterior vertebral body height with wedging and kyphotic deformity occurs. Alternatively, the fractured osteoporotic vertebral body may fail at superior and inferior end-plates, resulting in a shortened but trapezoidal shape. Although a low-energy injury, the fracture may rarely propagate through the middle column, resulting in a burst-type fracture pattern (Fig. 33–1).

Plain radiography can delineate the fracture, but posterior cortical involvement with canal encroachment can be better visualized with computed tomography (CT). Radiographic and CT evidence of old, nonacute fractures includes bony sclerosis, rounded edges of the fracture fragments, and bony cyst formation. If the age of the fracture remains indeterminate, a bone scan may be

necessary to decide whether treatment is needed. A positive bone scan represents the presence of attempts at bone healing and may last 18 or more months. Magnetic resonance imaging (MRI) can be useful in the presence of neurologic deficit. It is, however, not definitive for differentiating between low-energy compression fractures in osteopenic bone and pathologic fractures caused by metastatic disease, except when a soft tissue mass is present in combination with the metastasis.

A short course of analgesia is the mainstay of treatment. Hospital admission is most commonly necessary for older individuals who present to the emergency department with the acute incidence of a low-energy compression fracture. Especially at the thoracolumbar junction or in the lumbar spine, there may be sufficient retroperitoneal bleeding from the fracture that causes an ileus and subsequent dehydration. It may be difficult to regulate pain medication in the elderly person with multiple co-morbidities in the acute emergency department setting. Long-acting and potent narcotics should be avoided, because side effects may be more common and less well tolerated in the elderly. Bracing can be useful for pain control if tolerated by the patient. Further immobilization with bedrest can lead to worsened osteopenia and pulmonary complications and should be avoided. Treatment of acute fractures should include institution of prophylactic medical measures to minimize further bone loss.

Surgical management of these fractures is uncommon, especially because it is often fraught with complications. Indications for surgery include persistent or progressive neurologic deficit, progressive deformity, and intractable pain. Surgical fixation in the osteoporotic spine is complicated by poor bone stock; the use of bone cement to augment screw purchase may be considered, although some argument exists about whether U.S. Food and Drug Administration (FDA) approval is available for polymethyl methacrylate in this circumstance. Segmental instrumentation further decreases the forces at any one level; sublaminar wires have been used in this way to maximize the area of fixation to the spine.[19] The greatest care must be used to prevent a "cheese slicer" effect of the wire on the porotic lamina. Laminar hooks alone are associated with increased pull-out and laminar fracture rates in the osteoporotic spine. Pedicle screws confer the most rigid fixation in the spine. Because the pedicle cortex is thinned in osteoporosis, pedicle screw purchase is enhanced by using the maximal screw diameter possible without breech.[5] If necessary, pedicle screws may be supplemented by hooks at the same or adjacent levels; this provides a construct with the highest pull-out strength.[17] However, the surgeon must consider the problem of subsequent transitional disease at a relatively early stage with this rigid fixation.

Vertebroplasty or vertebral compression fracture injection with polymethyl methacrylate is emerging as a nonoperative technique for pain management in selected patients. Such augmentation of a fractured osteoporotic vertebral body, a technique known as vertebroplasty (Fig. 33–2), may reduce flexion-extension and lateral loading compliance by more than 20%, yielding a stiffer vertebral body with greater compressive strength.[41] Clarification

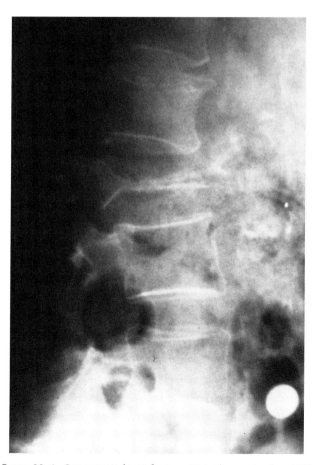

FIGURE 33–1. Osteoporotic burst fracture. Note the greater than 50% collapse of anterior vertebral body height and the involvement of the posterior cortex of the vertebral body.

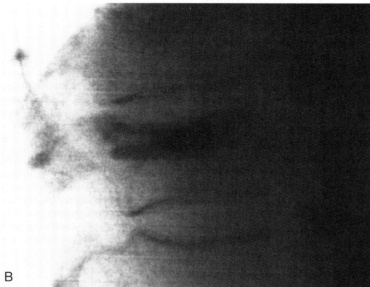

FIGURE 33–2. Vertebroplasty. *A,* A trephine is inserted trans-pedicularly into the posterior aspect of the fractured vertebral body. *B,* Cement injection fills the fractured vertebra, with the intent of conferring immediate stability to the fracture.

should be obtained from the FDA before embarking on this procedure. Success rates higher than 90% have been reported with short-term follow-up.[2] Pain may be reduced because of stabilization of microfractures in the vertebral body, because of load sharing by the cement, or because of cauterization of local nociceptive nerve endings.[41] The condition of the posterior cortex of the vertebral body must be ensured before vertebroplasty; bone cement extravasation into the spinal canal can be disastrous. Injection alone cannot reduce kyphotic angulation of a vertebral compression fracture. To address this problem, another procedure is being investigated. In kyphoplasty, percutaneous delivery of a balloon to the fracture site to lift a collapsed vertebra into reduction is followed by verte-broplasty. Use of a nonthermally curing, biodegradable, injectable substance, such as calcium phosphate, for vertebral augmentation instead of polymethyl methacryl-ate is an area of active research.[1]

ANKYLOSING SPONDYLITIS

A rheumatologic disorder belonging to the family of seronegative spondyloarthropathies, ankylosing spondyli-tis is an inflammatory disease that leads to bilateral sacroiliitis and cephalad-progressing spinal ankylosis. There may be variable expression of extraspinal manifes-tations, including iridocyclitis, urethritis, aortitis, pulmo-nary apical fibrosis, aortic valve insufficiency, cardiac conduction defects, and multiple arthralgias, especially in the hips and shoulders. The condition, also called Marie-Strümpell disease, occurs in less than 2% of people in the general population. There is a familial predilection with a strong inheritance association with the presence of the HLA-B27 histocompatibility antigen in about 90% of patients. Ankylosing spondylitis has been reported in men more than twice as frequently as in women, but it may be underreported in women because of a milder and slower progression of disease.[9]

Patients typically develop low back pain initially in the third and fourth decades. Anti-inflammatory medication may provide some symptomatic relief, but in patients with full expression of the disease, inexorable spinal fusion progresses through the years from a caudal to cephalad direction. The enthesopathy causes calcification of the anulus fibrosus, anterior longitudinal ligament, posterior longitudinal ligament, ligamentum flavum, and interspinous ligament, creating a squaring appearance of the vertebral bodies on plain radiographic imaging. Bone deposition progresses such that flowing syndesmophytes eventually link adjacent vertebral bodies and finally create the radiographic abnormality known as the bamboo spine (Fig. 33–3A).

In addition to pain management, proper conservative care in the early stages of this disease includes counseling on posture, avoiding pillows beneath the head or legs during sleep, and avoiding periods of lying totally flat in bed. Ankylosis of the flexed cervical and lumbar spine with loss of lordosis may lead to chin-on-chest and forward-bending fixed deformities with severe functional disability, such as an inability to observe traffic lights or difficulty opening the mouth, leading to nutritional depletion.

Rib articulations with the thoracic spine and sternum also become involved in ankylosing spondylitis. Fusion of these joints leads to decreased chest wall expansion during inspiration, and restrictive lung disease can ensue in severe cases. Limited chest wall expansion during maximal inspiration is the most specific diagnostic measure for ankylosing spondylitis. Pulmonary complications are common after operative and nonoperative management of spinal fracture in these patients.[11, 20, 35, 37, 38, 40]

Despite increased bony deposition in the soft tissues about the spine, vertebral bone density decreases, with measurable osteopenia throughout the spine even in the early stages.[30] This secondary form of osteoporosis may be a result of increased vascularity concordant with the inflammatory process. The surgeon must not be confused by the fact that the process occasionally may extend partially up the spine from the sacroiliac joints and stop or, uncommonly, manifest with skip areas of ankylosis in the spine.

Ankylosis often extends through the subaxial cervical spine, but the atlantoaxial and occipitocervical articulations may retain movement. Because these articulations may be the only mobile spinal joints in patients with extensive disease, they may experience increased shear forces. They may further be subject to chronic synovitis due to the underlying disease, becoming hypermobile and unstable. Traumatic atlantoaxial dislocation or occipitocervical dissociation, occasionally with associated odontoid fracture, is more common in these patients.[3, 23, 33, 40]

Patients with ankylosing spondylitis are predisposed to traumatic spinal fracture because of the increased stiffness and the decreased bone density of the spine. Long segments of fused vertebral levels lack discal and ligamentous energy-absorbing capability. Instead, applied traumatic moments have longer lever arms to act on the fused spine. The thinned bone has lower resistance to failure.

Low-energy injury may lead to fracture in this scenario, even with only physiologic loading.

Traumatic spinal injury in ankylosing spondylitis is often from a hyperextension mechanism and most often involves the cervical spine (see Fig. 33–3B), although the mechanism may carry through to the thoracic and lumbar areas as well.[20, 38, 40] Neurologic deficit is common, and mortality rates may be as high as 50%.*

Plain radiographic evaluation of the ankylosed spine after trauma is difficult because bony sclerosis from healing stress fractures and abundant bony syndesmophytes can obscure minimally displaced fractures.[20] Increased suspicion for occult fracture must be maintained in the patient with ankylosing spondylitis who sustains trauma, because delayed diagnosis may lead to progressive spinal deformity and neurologic deficit.[13, 14] Tomography[20] and CT evaluation are useful,[38] and sagittal and coronal CT reconstructions can help avoid missing a transverse plane fracture. Triple-phase bone scanning may help localize an occult fracture. MRI may be the most sensitive method for evaluating traumatic injury in the ankylosed spine, with intramedullary edema and surrounding hematoma being indicators of acute fracture.[14, 21]

Fractures are often transdiscal, with or without vertebral body involvement, and associated posterior element fracture is common.[25] The injury pattern of the long, fused spinal column mimics that in a long bone in which a transverse fracture occurs across its entire diameter; in the spine, the fracture occurs across the anterior, middle, and posterior columns.

Immobilization of the spine-injured patient with ankylosing spondylitis differs from the norm in that significant axial traction and straightened positioning should be avoided in favor of the preinjury position. These patients should be immobilized in the position of their chronic deformity with minimal change enacted. Iatrogenic displacement of a minimally displaced fracture can lead to spinal cord injury with paraplegia or quadriplegia if a chronically kyphotic cervical spine is forcibly altered into extension.[15, 25, 40] Disimpaction of these fractures may further lead to motion at the fracture site and epidural hematoma formation, a complication indigenous to this disease. Halo management of minimally displaced fractures must therefore preserve the pretrauma deformity. Custom-fit halo vests are often required. Nursing care may be complicated by chin-on-chest deformity, but pulmonary toilet remains critical in these patients, who may have preexisting pulmonary compromise.

Nonoperative management of fractures in patients with ankylosing spondylitis has been attempted for some nondisplaced fractures with no neurologic deficit. Prolonged bedrest with minimal traction, hard collar, or halo vest immobilization has been advocated for nondisplaced fractures.[16, 20, 35, 40] Nevertheless, nonunion and neurologic deterioration have been observed with the use of such conservative measures in some of these patients.[6, 11, 15, 35, 40] Cervical spinal fractures in ankylosing spondylitis often involve anterior and posterior column injuries, making the injury unstable and predisposing nonoperative treatment to failure. Operative management

---

*See references 6, 11, 13, 16, 20, 24, 35, 37, 38, 40.

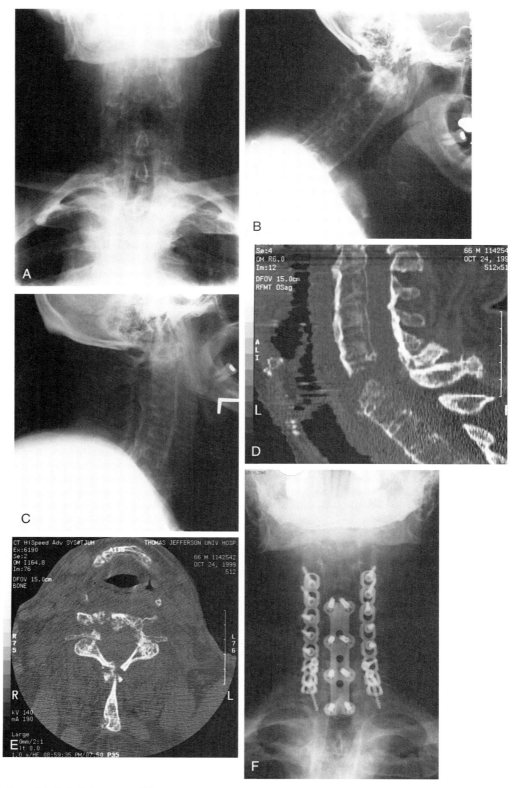

Figure 33–3. Ankylosing spondylitis. *A, B,* Anteroposterior (AP) and lateral radiographs of the cervical spine reveal the flowing syndesmophytes and bony ankylosis of severe ankylosing spondylitis in this 68-year-old man. *C,* On the lateral cervical spine radiograph of the same patient 1 month later after a fall from a standing height, notice the shear fracture through the C6 vertebral body. *D, E,* Sagittal and axial computed tomography cuts reveal a transosseous fracture pattern involving all three columns, as well as an acute kyphotic angulation of the spine with retrolisthesis. Because of three-column involvement and concerns about screw purchase in osteoporotic bone, anterior and posterior cervical fusions with instrumentation and autologous bone graft were performed, and an adjunctive halo was used in the postoperative period. *F, G,* AP and lateral postoperative radiographs reveal a reduced fracture with lateral mass screws and plates posteriorly and an anterior plate and vertebral body screws.

may therefore be preferred in many cases of spinal fracture in the setting of ankylosing spondylitis, especially in the presence of wide fracture displacement, progressive neurologic deficit, a large epidural hematoma, or severe deformity that could complicate pulmonary rehabilitation and make difficult the fitting of external bracing.

Posterior approaches are often preferred in the thoracic spine because of coexisting pulmonary compromise from restrictive lung disease and in the cervical spine because anterior exposure may be difficult as a result of exaggerated cervicothoracic kyphosis.[37] The posterior approach also allows greater exposure for longer segmental fusions. Inclusion of more points of fixation to the spine is important to decrease the stress at any one vertebral level in an already osteoporotic spine.[37] If an anterior procedure is desired because of a need for anterior decompression, a posterior fusion is usually added because of the tenuous fixation achievable in the osteoporotic vertebral bodies anteriorly (see Fig. 33–3D). Extreme care must be used with intraoperative positioning to prevent exaggeration of correction; intraoperative neurophysiologic monitoring is often helpful in these situations.

Hook placement in posterior thoracic fusions is difficult because of ossification of the ligamentum flavum. Transverse process hooks, pedicle screws, and spinous process wires may be easier forms of instrumentation in this setting, although the latter instrument is much weaker and less secure. Similarly, sublaminar wires in the cervical spine would require excision of the calcified ligamentum; instead, lateral mass plates, pedicle screws, and interspinous wires are options.

Epidural hematoma formation is more common after trauma in patients with ankylosing spondylitis and has been reported in 20% of these injuries.[20, 38] An epidural hematoma must be suspected when neurologic deterioration occurs, especially when such deterioration follows an initial deficit-free period. Spinal cord compression from an epidural hematoma may rarely be

further exacerbated by traumatic disc herniation in these patients.[35]

A different but related condition first described in 1987, the syndrome of synovitis, acne pustulosis, and hyperostosis osteitis (SAPHO), represents another condition that may lead to spinal ankylosis. With SAPHO syndrome, syndesmophytes link adjacent vertebrae, forming long columns predisposed to fracture. Sacroiliitis may be present as well. Although similar to spondyloarthropathy in these ways, the spinal ankylosis in SAPHO syndrome does not extend from the sacrum cephalad and does not have similar extraspinal manifestations. There is no association with HLA-B27 antigenicity. Associated findings instead include arthro-osteitis of the sternoclavicular and costosternal joints and skin manifestations of palmoplantar pustulosis, psoriasis, and severe acne.[10] Cervical spinal fracture has been reported with a hyperextension injury pattern similar to that seen in ankylosing spondylitis. Nonoperative treatment for nondisplaced fracture has been successful.[10]

DIFFUSE IDIOPATHIC SKELETAL HYPEROSTOSIS

Another disorder of idiopathic spinal ankylosis is diffuse idiopathic skeletal hyperostosis (DISH). With a slightly higher incidence in men than women, DISH occurs in people older than 50 years, with a prevalence approaching 10% to 20%.[4, 39] Unlike degenerative spondylosis with arthrosis of the facet and uncovertebral joints, which can lead to significant osteophyte growth but rarely intervertebral fusion, DISH results in an anterolateral fusion mass across many levels.[12] Also known as ankylosing hyperostosis or Forestier disease, DISH is diagnosed when there is anterolateral intervertebral fusion extending across at least four adjacent levels, preservation of disc height without significant disc disease, and absence of sacroiliac joint or apophyseal joint degeneration and fusion (Fig. 33–4A).[39]

Patients with DISH exhibit less spinal osteoporosis compared with ankylosing spondylitis, and peripheral skeletal involvement is usually absent in DISH.[29] Patients usually have some mild, chronic middle and lower back pain symptoms, with a mild decrease in flexion and extension; marked deformity as in ankylosing spondylitis does not typically occur. There may be skip areas in the fusion mass of DISH, unlike ankylosing spondylitis.

Although spinal ankylosis in DISH does not necessarily extend from the sacrum up through the cervical spine, as in severe cases of ankylosing spondylitis, long segmental vertebral fusions do create stiff areas with long lever arms through which destructive forces may act. These areas may be susceptible to low-energy hyperextension injury, resulting in three-column injury.[3, 18] The posterior element fracture and anterior spinal widening pattern characteristic of distraction-extension injuries may therefore occur after trauma in patients with DISH (see Fig. 33–4B).[7, 18, 22, 27]

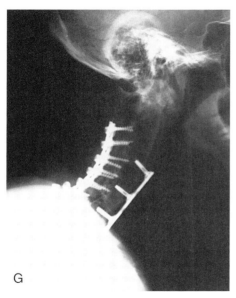

G

FIGURE 33-3 *Continued.*

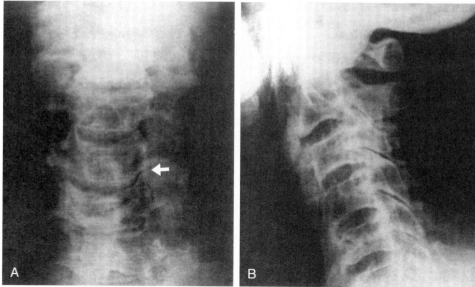

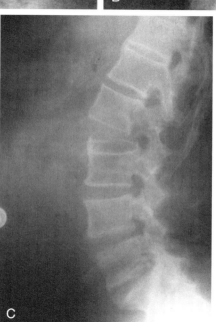

FIGURE 33–4. Diffuse idiopathic skeletal hyperostosis. A, B, Anteroposterior and lateral cervical spine radiographs of a patient with diffuse idiopathic skeletal hyperostosis (DISH). There is an anterolateral fusion mass from C2 to C5, but the facet joints, uncovertebral joints (white arrow), disc spaces, interspinous process ligaments, and ligamentum flavum are uninvolved. C, Lateral radiograph of the lumbar spine in a different patient after a car accident reveals a distraction extension injury at the L2–L3 level, immediately below a long segment of DISH in the thoracolumbar spine. (A, From Meyer, P.R., Jr. Clin Orthop 359:49–57, 1999.)

As in ankylosing spondylitis, the risk for neurologic deficit and post-traumatic mortality is high.[3, 18, 22, 29, 31] Delay in diagnosis may contribute to the development of secondary neurologic deterioration.[8, 18]

The hyperextension injury in the setting of DISH more often involves fracture through the vertebral body; hyperextension injuries in ankylosing spondylitis more often are transdiscal in nature. Plain radiographs, CT imaging, and MRI may be useful in delineating the injury.[7, 27] Management of hyperextension fractures associated with DISH follows principles similar to those for management of ankylosing spondylitis–associated fractures. Segmental fixation is useful to avoid overdistraction of the anteriorly deficient spinal column and to stabilize the posterior column.[7, 34] Usually, the bone quality in DISH is far better

than in ankylosing spondylitis and, as a result, is much more tolerant and responsive to alternative forms of fixation.

REFERENCES

1. Bai B; Jazrawi, L.M.; Kummer, F.J.; Spivak, J.M. The use of an injectable, biodegradable calcium phosphate bone substitute for the prophylactic augmentation of osteoporotic vertebrae and the management of vertebral compression fractures. Spine 24:1521–1526, 1999.
2. Barr, J.D.; Barr, M.S.; Lemley, T.J.; McCann, R.M. Percutaneous vertebroplasty for pain relief and spinal stabilization. Spine 25:923–928, 2000.
3. Bernini, P.M.; Floman, Y.; Marvel, J.P., Jr.; Rothman, R.H. Multiple thoracic spine fractures complicating ankylosing hyperostosis of the spine. J Trauma 21:811–814, 1981.

4. Bloom, R.A. The prevalence of ankylosing hyperostosis in a Jerusalem population—With a description of a method of grading the extent of disease. Scand J Rheumatol 13:181–189, 1984.
5. Brantley, A.G.V.; Mayfield, J.K.; Clark, K.R. The effects of pedicle screw fit: An in vitro study. Spine 19:1752–1758, 1994.
6. Broom, M.J.; Raycroft, J.F. Complications of fractures of the cervical spine in ankylosing spondylitis. Spine 13:763–766, 1998.
7. Burkus, J.K.; Denis, F. Hyperextension injuries of the thoracic spine in diffuse idiopathic skeletal hyperostosis: Report of 4 cases. J Bone Joint Surg Am 76:237–243, 1994.
8. Colterjohn, N.R.; Bednar, D.A. Identifiable risk factors for secondary neurologic deterioration in the cervical spine-injured patient. Spine 20:2293–2297, 1995.
9. Cooper, C.; Carbone, C.; Michet, C.J.; et al. Fracture risk in patients with ankylosing spondylitis: A population-based study. J Rheumatol 21:1877–1882, 1994.
10. Deltombe, T.; Nisolle, J.F.; Boutsen, Y.; et al. Cervical spinal cord injury in SAPHO syndrome. Spinal Cord 37:301–304, 1999.
11. Detwiler, K.N.; Loftus, C.M.; Godersky, J.C.; Menezes, A.H. Management of cervical spine injuries in patients with ankylosing spondylitis. J Neurosurg 72:210–215, 1990.
12. Fardon, D.F. Odontoid fracture complicating ankylosing hyperostosis of the spine. Spine 3:108–112, 1978.
13. Farmer, J.; Vaccaro, A.; Albert, T.J.; et al. Neurologic deterioration after cervical spinal cord injury. J Spinal Disord 11:192–196, 1998.
14. Finkelstein, J.A.; Chapman, J.R.; Mirza, S. Occult vertebral fractures in ankylosing spondylitis. Spinal Cord 37:444–447, 1999.
15. Fox, M.W.; Onofrio, B.N. Neurological complications of ankylosing spondylitis. J Neurosurg 78:871–878, 1993.
16. Graham, B.; Van Peteghem, P.K. Fractures of the spine in ankylosing spondylitis: Diagnosis, treatment, and complications. Spine 14:803–807, 1989.
17. Hasegawa, K.; Takahashi, H.E.; Uchiyama, S. An experimental study of a combination method using a pedicle screw and laminar hook for the osteoporotic spine. Spine 22:958–963, 1997.
18. Hendrix, R.W.; Melany, M.; Miller, F.; Rodgers, L.F. Fracture of the spine in patients with ankylosis due to diffuse idiopathic skeletal hyperostosis: Clinical and imaging findings. AJR Am J Roentgenol 162:899–904, 1994.
19. Hu, S.S. Internal fixation in the osteoporotic spine. Spine 22:43S–85S, 1997.
20. Hunter, T.; Dubo, H. Spinal fractures complicating ankylosing spondylitis: A long-term follow-up study. Arthritis Rheum 26:751–759, 1983.
21. Iplikcioglu, A.C. Magnetic resonance imaging in cervical trauma associated with ankylosing spondylitis: Report of two cases. J Trauma 36:412–413, 1994.
22. Israel, Z.; Mosheiff, R.; Gross, E.; et al. Hyperextension fracture-dislocation of the thoracic spine with paraplegia in a patient with diffuse idiopathic skeletal hyperostosis. J Spinal Disord 7:455–457, 1994.
23. Kaplan, S.L.; Tun, G.C.; Sarkarati, M. Odontoid fracture complicating ankylosing spondylitis: A case report and review of the literature. Spine 15:607–610, 1990.
24. Karasick, D.; Schweitzer, M.E.; Abidi, N.A.; Cotler, J.M. Fractures of the vertebra with spinal cord injuries in patients with ankylosing spondylitis. AJR Am J Roentgenol 165:1205–1208, 1995.
25. Lane, J.M. Osteoporosis: Medical prevention and treatment. Spine 22:32S–37S, 1997.
26. Lee, Y.L.; Yip, K.M. The osteoporotic spine. Clin Orthop 323:91–97, 1996.
27. Leltir, P.X.; Saulet, A.; LeGars, L.; et al. Hyperextension vertebral body fractures in diffuse idiopathic skeletal hyperostosis: A case of intravertebral fluidlike collections on MR imaging. AJR Am J Roentgenol 173:1679–1683, 1999.
28. Melton, L.J., III. Epidemiology of spinal osteoporosis. Spine 22:2S–11S, 1997.
29. Meyer, P.R., Jr. Diffuse idiopathic skeletal hyperostosis in the cervical spine. Clin Orthop 359:49–57, 1999.
30. Mitra, D.; Elvins, D.M.; Speden, D.J.; Collins, A.J. The prevalence of vertebral fractures in mild ankylosing spondylitis and their relationship to bone mineral density. Rheumatology 39:85–89, 2000.
31. Mody, G.M.; Charles, R.W.; Ranchord, H.A.; Rubin, D.L. Cervical spine fracture in diffuse idiopathic skeletal hyperostosis. J Rheumatol 15:129–131, 1991.
32. Myers, E.R.; Wilson, S.E. Biomechanics of osteoporosis and vertebral fracture. Spine 22:25S–31S, 1997.
33. Ozgocmen, S.; Ardicoglu, O. Odontoid fracture complicating ankylosing spondylitis. Spinal Cord 38:117–119, 2000.
34. Paley, D.; Schwartz, M.; Cooper, P.; et al. Fractures of the spine in diffuse idiopathic skeletal hyperostosis. Clin Orthop 267:22–32, 1991.
35. Rowed, D.W. Management of cervical spinal cord injury in ankylosing spondylitis: The intervertebral disk as a cause of cord compression. J Neurosurg 77:241–246, 1992.
36. Silva, M.J.; Keaveny, T.M.; Hayes, W.C. Load sharing between the shell and centrum in the lumbar vertebral body. Spine 22:140–150, 1997.
37. Taggard, D.A.; Traynelis, V.C. Management of cervical spine fractures in ankylosing spondylitis with posterior fixation. Spine 25:2035–2039, 2000.
38. Tico, N.; Ramon, S.; Garcia-Ortun, F.; et al. Traumatic spinal cord injury complicating ankylosing spondylitis. Spinal Cord 36:349–352, 1998.
39. Utsinger, P.D. Diffuse idiopathic skeletal hyperostosis. Clin Rheum Dis 11:325–351, 1985.
40. Weinstein, P.R.; Karpman, R.R.; Gall, E.P.; Pitt, M. Spinal cord injury, spinal fracture, and spinal stenosis in ankylosing spondylitis. J Neurosurg 57:609–616, 1982.
41. Wilson, D.R.; Myers, E.R.; Mathis, J.M.; et al. Effect of augmentation on the mechanics of vertebral wedge fractures. Spine 25:158–165, 2000.

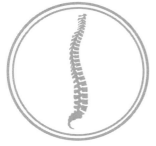

CHAPTER 34

Complications in the Treatment of Spinal Trauma

David J. Jacofsky, M.D.
Bradford L. Currier, M.D.
Choll W. Kim, M.D., Ph.D.
Michael J. Yaszemski, M.D., Ph.D.

Treatment of spinal trauma has been described as early as the Hippocratic era. His famous extension bench, known as "Scamnum" when popularized by Celsius, was used frequently for realignment of a fractured or deformed spine. In ancient and medieval times, forceful and brisk maneuvers accompanied by immobilization were the mainstay of spinal trauma treatment. A patient would often lie prone while attendants would pull on his ankles and axillae and a "physician" would sit or press on prominences such as a gibbus or palpable fracture deformity.

As recently as the late 1800s, Jean-Francis Calot and his contemporaries manipulated spinal deformities with their fists. In 1917, Hartmann (at the Accident Hospital for coal miners in Upper Silesia) treated a patient with a fracture-dislocation of the thoracolumbar junction by having two assistants suspend the patient by the armpits and pelvis while he performed reduction by forceful manipulation from below with his fists. Later, through the first 4 decades of the 20th century, methods of postural reduction by hyperextension were introduced. Davis, Rogers, and Bohlman were champions of such methods through the use of slings, frames, or similar devices.[37]

As one might imagine, such treatment led to unacceptably high rates of complications, including soft tissue breakdown, neurologic compromise, malunion, instability, and pulmonary compromise. Treatment of spinal trauma has changed significantly over the last 2 decades. However, despite better imaging, better understanding, better access to treatment, and the availability of internal fixation, challenging complications continue to exist today.

COMPLICATIONS OF NONOPERATIVE TREATMENT

Halo Vest Immobilization

Indications for use of the halo vest have evolved greatly since its description by Perry and Nickel in 1953. Initially

described for postoperative immobilization of patients who had undergone cervical fusion for neck paralysis from poliomyelitis, Thompson and Freeman extended its use to the treatment of fractures. Complications of halo vest immobilization can be divided into those related to application of the device and those related to its use. Traditionally, the use of plaster-molded vests carried a risk of cast syndrome, pressure sores, and respiratory problems in patients with limited respiratory reserves. Prefabricated padded plastic vests have helped decrease the incidence of these complications, but at the expense of decreased rigidity and increased cost. However, patient compliance has improved and the incidence of pin loosening has decreased with these lightweight prefabricated vests.

The pins themselves pose problems as well. Pin site infection is not uncommon but may be minimized with daily pin site care, including twice-daily application of a dilute hydrogen peroxide solution (50% in water). The reported incidence of pin site infection is approximately 30%.[51] Oral antibiotics are usually effective, but if a pin is loose and infected, a new pin should be placed in a nearby hole in the halo ring. If the pins are incorrectly placed cephalad to the equator of the skull, halo slippage may occur (Fig. 34-1). The pins should be torqued to 8 in-lb in adults and 6 in-lb or less in children. In patients with osteoporosis or when the pins are inadvertently placed in the temporal areas, the skull can be perforated. Dural penetration has been reported.[46]

No orthosis can apply predictable and continuous traction to the cervical spine when the patient is not supine. When the patient is sitting or standing, a previously distracted cervical spine can become compressed by the force of gravity on the head and halo vest construct (Fig. 34-2). Such compression can lead to loss of reduction and possibly a new neurologic deficit. Likewise, rotational forces are poorly constrained by a halo vest orthosis. Treatment of a unilateral facet dislocation, for example, may lead to persistent root compression and failure of therapy. Whitehill and colleagues[78] described five cases of loss of reduction in patients with facet dislocations immobilized in a halo vest. Glaser and associates[32] and Bucholz and Cheung[10] documented loss of reduction in 10% of all patients and in 37% of patients with facet subluxation and dislocation.

Anderson and co-workers[1] evaluated upright and supine lateral radiographs after halo immobilization in 42 patients with 45 noncontiguous levels of cervical spine injury. At noninjured levels, an average of 3.9° of angular change was found between adjacent levels from the occiput to C6. The greatest motion occurred more proximally (8.0° between the occiput and C1). No significant translation was seen at the noninjured levels. At the injured level, sagittal-plane angulation averaged 7.0° and the average translation was 1.7 mm. Significant fracture site motion was defined as greater than 3° of sagittal angulation or more than 1 mm of translation and occurred in 78% of the 45 injured levels. Three patients experienced loss of reduction that required reapplication of traction after vest removal. Asymptomatic malunion developed in 11 patients. One may postulate that it is this motion that contributes to such a high degree of nonunion in type II odontoid fractures treated in a halo vest.

Residual kyphosis of a post-traumatic cervical spine can lead to a multitude of complications. Neural impairment can occur from compression of the spinal cord as it drapes over the apex of the deformity (Fig. 34–3). Late neck pain may be seen as a result of the modified mechanics of the paraspinous musculature that occurs when the lever arm of the muscles is altered by the deformity. Additionally, facet degeneration of adjacent segments can ensue from hyperextension of adjacent vertebral levels in an attempt to compensate for the loss of cervical lordosis in a kyphotic cervical spine.[51]

In properly chosen patients, halo immobilization is an excellent treatment option that is associated with frequent, but usually minor complications. However, nonunion and malunion can occur and should obviously be considered

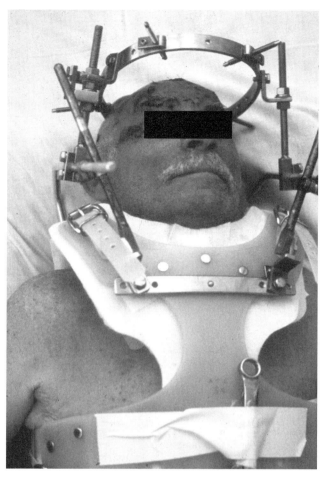

FIGURE 34–1. Failed halo pin sites. At follow-up, the halo pins of this gentleman had dislodged, and the vest and headpiece migrated proximally. His halo was removed and he was treated in a cervical collar for the remainder of treatment.

FIGURE 34–2. Poor axial immobilization by halo. Immobilization in the axial plane is difficult with all external fixation systems, including the halo. In this patient with a fracture through a severely ankylosed cervical spine, the fracture is gapped open when supine (A) but compressed when upright (B).

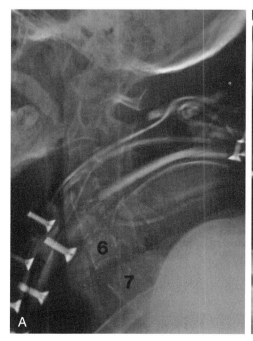

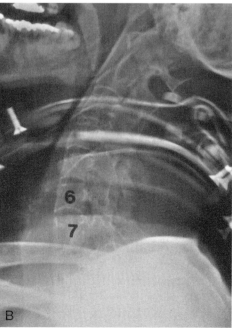

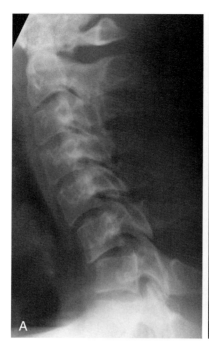
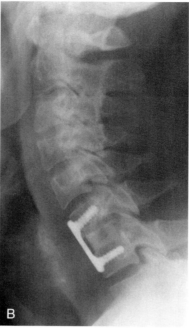

FIGURE 34–3. Failed external immobilization for cervical facet fractures. This patient was evaluated 1½ years after nonoperative treatment of an initially nondisplaced C6 lateral mass fracture. He complained of neck pain and paresthesia down the lateral aspect of his arm. *A,* Flexion radiographs showed subluxation and kyphosis. *B,* Treatment included anterior cervical discectomy and fusion. Preoperative planning, however, included the possible need for circumferential fusion.

markers of treatment failure. In patients with nonflexion injuries, the success rate of halo treatment approaches that of surgical fusion (87% vs. 95%).[65] However, in the group of patients with posterior ligamentous injury, the failure rate increases to as high as 46%.[11, 65]

Operative versus Nonoperative Treatment

In the age of modern medicine and modern implants, most clinicians intuitively believe that the risk of morbidity in patients with unstable spine fractures is higher in the nonoperative than the operative group. In the perioperative period, the risk of acute complications is no different. Rechtine and colleagues[61] examined 235 patients with unstable thoracolumbar spine fractures who were given a choice of undergoing operative or nonoperative treatment. The groups were statistically similar in all respects. Although the length of stay in the hospital was 24 days greater in the nonoperative group, the incidence of complications (with the obvious exception of wound infection) was similar for decubitus ulcers, pneumonia, deep vein thrombosis, pulmonary embolism, and death. Polytrauma was a risk factor for increased complications, and the primary predictor of sacral decubitus ulcers was time on a spine board. Curry and Casady[16] showed that a patient with spinal cord injury who is on a board for more than 8 hours is practically ensured of sacral skin breakdown. Admittedly, these studies have some inherent selection bias and are retrospective. However, it helps to show that aggressive nonoperative therapy can be as successful as operative management for properly chosen patients, and additionally it does not have the inherent risk of wound infection and iatrogenic injury.

COMPLICATIONS OF OPERATIVE TREATMENT

Patient Positioning

The potential for complications begins as early as or perhaps even before patient positioning on the operating table. Care must be taken to ensure that the airway is protected when the patient is transferred from a bed to the operating table, especially if the patient is also being turned from a supine to a prone position. In the prone position, the face must be padded evenly to avoid pressure ulceration. Prefabricated foam pads with holes for airway access are available and effective. Support devices with mirrored bases allow visual inspection of the facial structures throughout the operation. Direct pressure on the eye must be specifically avoided to prevent catastrophic retinal artery occlusion and loss of vision.[55, 83] Direct pressure applied to the scalp has been associated with alopecia, which is usually reversible but is occasionally permanent. Slight rotation of the patient's head throughout the procedure, if not clinically contraindicated, helps prevent such complications.

Meticulous padding of vulnerable areas, such as the elbows and knees, should help prevent neuropraxia or more serious nerve injuries to the ulnar and common peroneal nerves. The lateral femoral cutaneous nerves are easily injured by undue pressure at the proximal aspect of the thighs. The brachial plexus is at risk if the lateral decubitus or prone position is used. An axillary roll placed 5 to 10 cm distal to the axilla and avoidance of excessive abduction and forward flexion of the arm will help reduce the incidence of brachial plexopathy.

Venous return must be considered during patient

positioning as well. The abdomen and chest should remain free of pressure to prevent vena cava obstruction. Low venous return can lead to loss of cardiac preload and subsequent hypotension. Obstruction of caval flow can produce increased venous pressure around the sinusoids of the spine and thereby cause unnecessary and often significant increases in blood loss. The knee-chest position has been associated with reports of lower extremity compartment syndrome requiring fasciotomy.[3] In the dependent position with the hips and knees flexed, venous pooling occurs. Awareness of this potential postoperative complication is required for quick recognition should it occur.

Postoperative Deformity

Fixation failure, loss of reduction, and subsequent deformity are complications of spinal surgery for trauma. Flat back syndrome is due to loss of the normal lumbar lordosis. It is frequently the result of distraction instrumentation that ends caudally below L3 (Fig. 34–4). Although solid arthrodesis may be achieved, the flat back deformity can be problematic.[19, 48] Muscular strain and chronic pain are often reported as patients attempt to maintain their lordosis. Additionally, compensatory hyperlordosis above and below the fusion levels often causes degenerative spondylosis and stenosis. Avoidance of overdistraction and the use of appropriately contoured segmental fixation help prevent this complication. Flattening the lumbar lordosis facilitates decompression procedures by increasing the interlaminar distance, but if fusion is contemplated, lumbar lordosis must be maintained. Lumbar lordosis is increased by extension of the hips and decreased by hip flexion, as occurs when patients are placed in the knee-chest position or positioned on a four-post frame. Although hyperlordosis is much less common, it can lead to complications as well. Iatrogenic foraminal stenosis and nerve root impingement can occur secondary to excessive lordosis.[71]

The best treatment of iatrogenic deformity is avoidance, but if diagnosed early, it can be treated by realignment. Delay in diagnosis or treatment ultimately results in a more extensive procedure. Additionally, a patient who complains of pain in the presence of late iatrogenic deformity

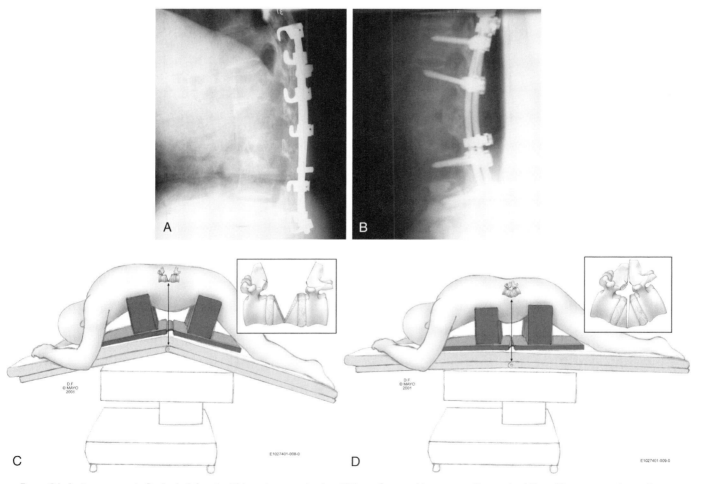

FIGURE 34–4. Post-traumatic flat back deformity. This patient sustained an L3 burst fracture 11 years ago. Progressive bilateral lower extremity weakness, right leg pain, and early fatigue prompted the current medical evaluation. Standing radiographs show significant sagittal imbalance and loss of lumbar lordosis (*A*). Treatment included anterior discectomy and interbody fusion, followed by removal of previous instrumentation, pedicle subtraction osteotomy, and instrumented fusion (*B*). Pedicle subtraction osteotomy is facilitated by the use of a hinged four-post frame (*C*), which allows gentle and gradual reduction of the osteotomy site (*D*). The *inset* shows the extent of bone resection for a pedicle subtraction osteotomy, which produces approximately 30° to 35° of correction.

can be a diagnostic problem because it may be difficult to know whether it is the malalignment that is responsible for the patient's symptoms.

Instrumentation Failure

Loss of stabilization may result from error in surgical technique, improper preoperative planning, or poor implant selection. Systems using rods and hooks may fail from hook pull-out, hook-rod disengagement, or rod fracture. Hook pull-out may be due to improper placement or osseous fracture. Lamina fracture may be associated with aggressive laminotomy, osteoporotic bone, or overdistraction (Fig. 34–5). Hook dislodgment is the most commonly reported complication of posterior Harrington rod instrumentation after spinal trauma.[7, 13, 25, 28, 31] Edwards and colleagues[24] noted four factors that account for hook dislodgment: rigidity of fixation, the anatomic level, hook design, and rod clearance. The rate of hook dislodgment depends on the spinal level, with the rate varying from 5% at L4 to 20% at S1.[31, 76] In older, semirigid Harrington models, rod clearance greater than 1 cm was needed to prevent rod-hook disengagement during flexion and rotation. The advent of segmental multihook fixation has decreased the incidence of hook failure. However, care must be taken to fully tighten the hooks on the rod to prevent motion at this interface.

The advent of pedicle screw fixation has expanded the armamentarium of the spine surgeon for treating trauma. Though largely avoidable, the potential complications associated with pedicle screw use can be significant. A short screw or a screw placed laterally has suboptimal fixation, whereas a medially placed screw may violate the canal and cause a dural tear or neurologic injury. A screw that is excessively long may violate the anterior aspect of the vertebral body and can cause potentially life-threatening perforation of the great vessels (Fig. 34–6). Pedicle screws can fracture the pedicle on insertion and can potentially loosen, break, or pull out. Although a larger-diameter screw has greater biomechanical pull-out strength, judgment is needed to avoid pedicle blow-out.[82, 88] In a large series of 4790 pedicle screws in 875 patients, Lonstein and co-workers[52] showed that in experienced hands, the rate of complications is quite low. In their series, reoperation was necessary for 11 screws (0.2%) because of nerve root irritation, and 25 (0.5%) screws were fractured at follow-up. More unusual complications of pedicle screw fixation have been reported as well. Some surgeons insert markers or Kirschner wires into the pedicle holes to check position with a radiograph or image intensifier before screw placement. At least one case of fatal cardiac tamponade from myocardial violation with a Kirschner wire has been reported. Fluoroscopy was used to confirm the position of the wire, and no evidence of complications was noted during the procedure itself.[38]

For many years, some surgeons have used translaminar or facet screws to facilitate fusion.[45, 53] Although violation of the canal or nerve root is possible, the reported rate of complications is low. The screws should be placed only after decortication and cancellous packing of the facets have been performed to maximize fusion rates and avoid screw notching.

Late Deformity

Late and progressive deformity and chronic pain as a result of spinal trauma can lead to significant disability. Although these sequelae can occur despite proper management, each injury pattern and each patient must be considered individually to minimize complications. Patient age, lifestyle, and preexisting deformity may all play a role, but the initial stability of the injury and its initial management are probably paramount in predicting future decompensation and deformity.[54]

The thoracolumbar junction is the most common site for acute fractures and the development of late post-traumatic deformity. The abrupt change between the more mobile lumbar spine and the more rigid thoracic spine with its stabilizing ribs and sternum places the thoracolumbar junction at high risk for decompensation. However, no area of the spine is immune to deformity, and decompensation is not limited to the sagittal plane; a complex three-dimensional deformity may be located anywhere from the occiput to the sacrum.

The most important aspect of managing spinal deformity is prevention, and to avert the development of such deformity, the initial injury must be well understood. Osseous destruction is only part of the equation; ligamentous injury and disc disruption must be evaluated as well. Andreychik and associates[2] attributed an increase in postoperative kyphosis without an increase in vertebral body compression to structural failure of adjacent disc spaces resulting from the initial injury. Because fractures extending into the disc space may not be appreciated on routine supine radiographs, physiologic loading may be required to fully assess stability. Missed posterior ligamentous injury can cause subsequent progressive deformity. Burst fractures, for example, typically settle less than 10° before the kyphotic deformity is checkreined by the posterior ligamentous structures. However, if these structures are disrupted, severe deformity can ensue.

Most clinicians agree that the goal of treatment is to restore normal alignment to an unstable spine for a period sufficient to allow healing through either spontaneous bony healing or surgical arthrodesis. Bedrest, casting, and bracing have all proved effective in the treatment of spine fractures in the proper injury and proper patient groups. If the injury, the patient's compliance, and the potential for healing permit the use of nonoperative management, close follow-up is critical. Clinical evaluation and serial standing radiographs should be carried out early should a deformity begin to develop.

The deleterious effects of laminectomy alone for neural decompression in the presence of spinal trauma are well documented (Fig. 34–7). Complete spondyloptosis and severe deformity have been reported.[79] Malcolm and co-workers[54] reported on 48 patients with post-traumatic kyphosis. Half of these patients had an isolated laminectomy at the time of injury, and detrimental effects were seen at all levels of the spine. In the thoracic spine, the kyphotic deformity was 15° greater in the group that underwent

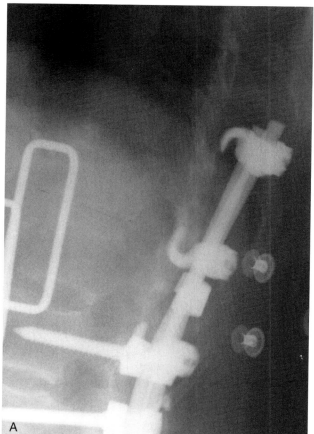

A

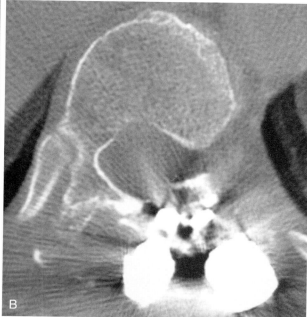

B

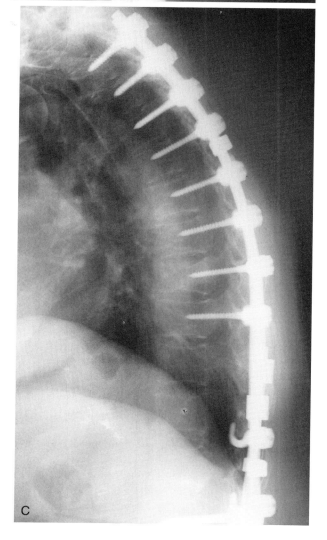

C

Figure 34–5. Hook failure. This patient has significant osteoporosis contributing to fractures of the lamina at the site of the proximal (T10) hooks as shown on a lateral radiograph (A) and computed tomographic scan (B). Treatment included proximal extension of the fusion with pedicle screw instrumentation (C).

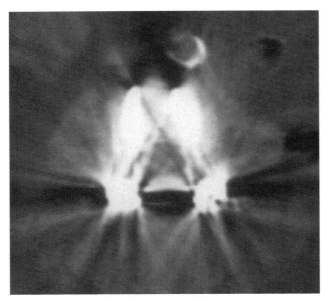

FIGURE 34–6. Pedicle screw malposition. Pedicle screws that are too long may penetrate the anterior cortex of the vertebral body and place the great vessels at risk, as seen on this computed tomographic scan.

decompression with laminectomy. At the thoracolumbar junction, the deformity was 13° more severe, and in the lumbar spine, the difference in kyphosis was 35° for those who had undergone laminectomy and 24° for those who did not.

Technical errors can precipitate deformity even in the face of posterior instrumentation. A fusion that is too short and does not span the zone of injury is more likely to lead to a junctional deformity, especially if the arthrodesis ends at the cervicothoracic or thoracolumbar junction or at the apex of the thoracic kyphosis (Fig. 34–8). Additionally, a short fusion that spans the defect but is placed posterior to destroyed anterior elements is more likely to fail unless the anterior column is restored (Fig. 34–9). Parker and others have developed and validated a classification scheme to help determine when an anterior strut graft is required to supplement a short posterior construct for thoracolumbar fractures.[60]

Clinical Features of Late Deformity. Symptoms attributable to deformity may be insidious in onset and may follow a painless period of indeterminate length. As many as 70% to 90% of patients experience some chronic pain at the region of the fracture regardless of the type of treatment or the degree of deformity.[18, 43, 59, 86] As many as 20% may be permanently disabled, and 40% report functional limitations. Debilitating pain is often the initial symptom and is the most common cause of reconstructive surgery for post-traumatic deformity. Though challenging, the clinician must try to isolate the cause of the patient's symptoms. Instability or nonunion is more amenable to surgical intervention than is mechanical back pain. "Mechanical back pain" in this setting is an activity-related pain that may be muscular, discogenic, or arthritic in nature. Alternatively, it may be due to stress fractures of adjacent vertebrae secondary to excessive loads caused by the deformity.

No consensus has been reached on the specific severity

of kyphosis that leads to pain and symptoms. Farcy and co-workers[26] showed that at the thoracolumbar junction, a threshold of 25° is tolerated before symptoms are likely to occur. The lumbar spine tolerated only 15° of deformity. However, Andreychik and co-workers[2] did not find any correlation between symptoms and the degree of deformity in their series of 55 burst fractures of the lumbar spine. Most authors, however, agree that more sedentary patients tolerate a greater degree of deformity than do active laborers or athletes, which is not surprising when one considers the muscular work involved in maintaining posture in the presence of deformity.

In a paraplegic patient, poor sitting balance because of progression of deformity may be of more concern than pain. Altered sitting balance can lead to soft tissue complications at the gibbus and in the buttock region. It can also impair the ability to power a wheelchair with the upper part of the body and arms. Additionally, subtle deformity may rapidly overcome the ability of weakened paraspinal muscles in patients with higher neurologic compromise.

Finally, some patients may be seen primarily with a progressive neurologic deficit. Malcolm and coauthors reported that approximately 27% of patients had a progressive neurologic deficit.[54] The neurologic deficit is a function of the degree of deformity and the amount of canal compromise secondary to retropulsed bone within the canal. Fidler[27] showed that typically bone fragments in the canal are resorbed over time but that severe angular deformity and abnormal transmission of stress may alter this remodeling process. Additionally, hypertrophic remodeling from segmental instability and perhaps the development of a post-traumatic syrinx can increase the stenosis of a given level. The deformity of the spine may be quite complex and must be appreciated in three dimensions. Full-length standing (or sitting) radiographs should be obtained. In addition, bending films can be used to assess flexibility. If pseudarthrosis is suspected, flexion and extension views may assist in the diagnosis of segmental instability. If the levels adjacent to the deformity are not flexible enough to compensate for kyphosis, a crouched gait may develop and lead to flexion contractures of the hips. These flexion deformities of the lower extremities should be addressed before correction of the spinal deformity.

Classification of Late Deformity. In 1993, Denis and Burkus proposed three types of post-traumatic deformity.[19] Each type includes three subtypes. This classification helps in planning the surgical approach and instrumentation, but it does not distinguish deformities on the basis of their relative magnitudes (Table 34–1).

Surgical Management of Late Deformity. Surgical indications for correction of deformity include incapacitating pain, progressive deformity, new or progressive neurologic deficit, or failure of a significant neurologic deficit to improve in the face of residual deformity and neural compression. Because the risks of extensive surgical interventions are significant, one should consider cosmetic deformity alone a relative indication for surgical intervention.

For Denis and Burkus type IA deformities of less than 15° that meet the criteria for surgical intervention, posterior spinal fusion is indicated. If the overall sagittal balance of the spine is acceptable and the patient's symptoms are

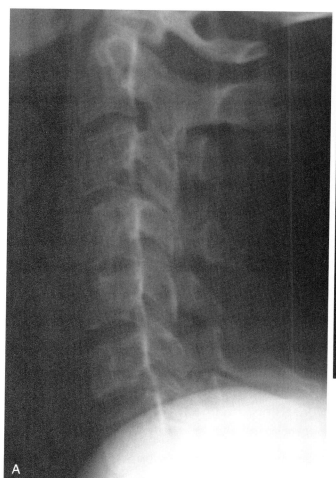

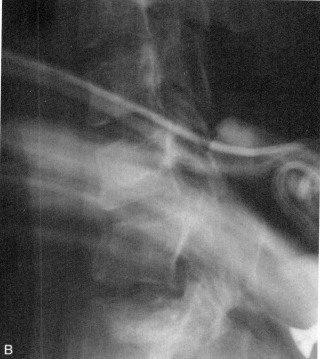

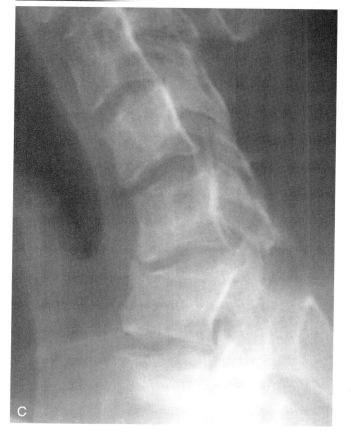

FIGURE 34–7. Postlaminectomy cervical kyphosis. *A,* This patient sustained posterior element fractures of the lower cervical spine and had an incomplete spinal cord injury. Advanced imaging studies showed canal compromise from the posterior element fractures. He was treated with laminectomy of C5 and C6 and halo immobilization. *B, C,* Serial radiographs showed gradual loss of reduction, with the development of kyphosis. The patient was eventually treated with corpectomy and fusion.

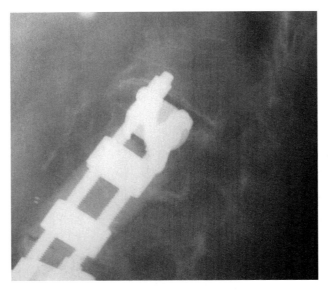

FIGURE 34–8. Junctional kyphosis after an L2 burst fracture treated with anterior L1–L3 instrumented fusion. Kyphosis developed at the thoracolumbar junction from an osteoporotic compression fracture adjacent to the fused segment.

located at the apex of the deformity, a short fusion with instrumentation will probably suffice, especially if pseudarthrosis or limited segmental instability is the source of the pain. As the magnitude of the deformity increases, an anterior procedure preceding the posterior fusion assists in correction of the deformity. However, Edwards and Rhyne[23] demonstrated that late correction of up to 30° of kyphosis is feasible through a posterior approach in the absence of an anterior bony bridge. These authors apply three-point loading through posterior constructs to cause viscoelastic relaxation of the anterior scar and ligaments. An osseous bridge anteriorly would require a limited anterior release before correction posteriorly. In the thoracic spine, assuming that infection has been eliminated from the differential diagnosis, a posterior compression construct will usually be adequate to repair a pseudarthrosis. In the presence of neurologic compromise (type IC), it may be possible to decompress the neural elements by correcting the deformity from a posterior approach if the deformity and compression are mild. This approach requires a longer construct with multiple attachment sites. However, compression from larger deformities or retropulsed bone in the canal mandates anterior decompression before a posterior approach.

Regardless of the approach, the goal is restoration of 40° or less of kyphosis from T2 through T12, which may necessitate the use of a longer posterior construct in patients with type IB deformities. If correction of kyphosis cannot be fully achieved through combined anterior and posterior approaches, wedge-type osteotomies, such as an eggshell or pedicle subtraction osteotomy, may be performed (typically in the lumbar spine below the level of the conus medullaris). Ending a fusion at a level of disc disease or instability should be avoided during the selection of fusion levels.

The thoracolumbar junction deserves special attention. Small deformities (e.g., less than 20°) with no

neurologic deficit (type IIA) can be treated with a short posterior construct that preserves lumbar motion segments. In type IIB deformities with associated hyperkyphosis of the thoracic spine, the construct must be extended and may require either a limited anterior release for a flexible deformity or a more extensive release if the upper thoracic deformity is fixed. Type IIC deformities with neurologic deficit and canal compromise of more than 25% require anterior decompression. Occasionally, short-segment decompression with a strut graft and anterior instrumentation may obviate the need for a posterior construct, but any residual posterior instability or the absence of a stable anterior reconstruction would mandate a staged procedure. The use of an anterior strut, however, may allow one to preserve lower lumbar motion segments.

McBride and Bradford[58] reported on their series of six patients with a mean thoracolumbar junctional kyphosis of 38° and a range of 20° to 83°. Five of the six had a neurologic deficit, and all had canal encroachment of 25% to 57%. All patients were treated by transthoracic vertebrectomy and an allograft strut augmented with a vascularized pedicle 10th rib graft. The mean correction was 26°, or 68%. All neurologically incomplete patients improved, and although one patient required revision for graft displacement, no pseudarthroses were reported. The authors note that such treatment requires a competent posterior osteoligamentous complex or the addition of either solid anterior instrumentation or a staged posterior construct.

In the lumbar spine, true kyphosis is rarely seen. Rather, kyphosis typically refers to the loss of lordosis, also called flat back deformity or hypolordosis. The first report of osteotomy of the spine for kyphosis was made by Smith-Petersen and colleagues.[71] Distraction and deformity of neural and vascular structures and subsequent complications led to investigation of alternative corrective procedures.

The method preferred today is an eggshell osteotomy, also called a pedicle subtraction osteotomy. This technique shortens rather than lengthens the vertebral column.[49, 73, 75] This osteotomy involves transpedicular fixation above and below the level to be osteotomized, usually at the apex of the deformity, and correction of the deformity through removal of cancellous bone from the vertebral body. Asymmetric decancellation can correct both coronal and sagittal deformities. Up to 50° of sagittal correction and 40° of coronal correction can be achieved. The osteotomy is started only after instrumentation is completed because the blood loss from the procedure can be severe and may necessitate expeditious closure of the bony osteotomy site. The osteotomy is closed by extension bending at the decancellation site, which is accomplished by extending the table. Reduction can be facilitated by positioning the patient on a hinged frame so that the table can be extended to help close the osteotomy (see Fig. 34–4). Adjacent nerve roots above and below the osteotomy then share a common foramen created by removal of the pedicle. Meticulous care must be used to avoid entrapment of nerve roots or dura. This procedure should be effective for most type III deformities.[62]

In the cervical spine, Vaccaro and colleagues[74] showed that long anterior reconstructions with static plates have an

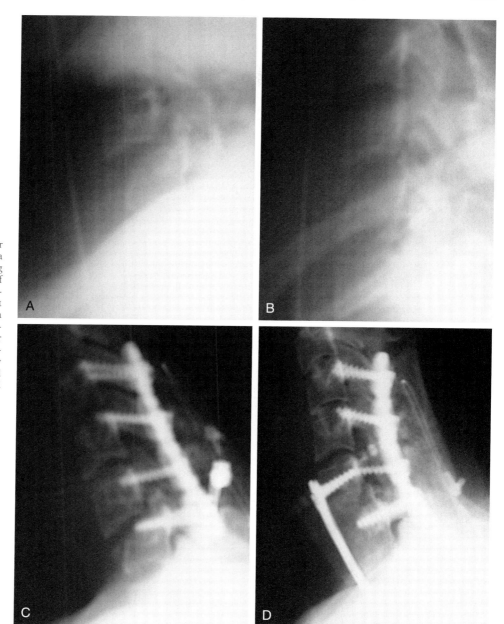

FIGURE 34–9. Failure of the anterior column. *A,* This patient suffered a C6–C7 fracture-dislocation resulting in damage to the superior end-plate of C7. *B,* Reduction was readily accomplished with traction. *C,* An attempt at posterior fusion with instrumentation and halo immobilization was inadequate because of a lack of anterior column support. *D,* Subsequent treatment with anterior C6 corpectomy and instrumented fusion restored proper alignment and resulted in solid fusion.

unacceptably high failure rate. In a retrospective, multi-center study examining the use of an anterior cervical locking plate and strut graft for a three-level corpectomy, the failure rate was 50% when a posterior construct was not used, as opposed to a 9% rate of graft or plate dislodgment when a two-level corpectomy was fused in a similar fashion. A higher incidence of graft failure was seen with increased age, failure to lock the screws into the plate, and the use of a peg-in-hole bone graft construct. The type of postoperative immobilization and violation of end-plates with screws had no statistically significant effect on failure rates. However, no comparison was made between traumatic and nontraumatic etiologies, and therefore it is unclear whether subclinical posterior ligamentous injury may increase the risk of failure.

McAfee and Bohlman[57] reviewed the results of 15 patients with multiple-level cervical corpectomies and an

TABLE 34–1 ....

Classification of Late Deformity

Type	Level	Neurologic Deficit	Distant Kyphotic Deformity
IA	Cephalad to T11	No	No
IB	Cephalad to T11	No	Yes
IC	Cephalad to T11	Yes	Yes
IIA	T12–L1	No	No
IIB	T12–L1	No	Yes
IIC	T12–L1	Yes	Yes
IIIA	L2–L4	No	No
IIIB	L2–L4	No	Yes
IIIC	L2–L4	Yes	Yes

Source: Denis, F.; Burkus, J.K. Semin Spine Surg 5:187–198, 1993.

anterior-posterior cervical fusion with instrumentation. No patient in their series had dislodgment of either the instrumentation or graft material. It seems logical that a posterior tension band construct would help decrease the bending moment experienced by the anterior plate and strut graft, but further study into such biomechanics is still needed before recommendations regarding the best construct can be made.

Adjacent-Segment Disease

Adjacent-segment disease should be a concern for all surgeons who perform spinal fusions. Many reports have highlighted the accelerated degeneration that occurs above and below the level of a rigid fusion.[42, 47] Additionally, it seems that instrumented fusions are even more prone to this phenomenon than are fusions without instrumentation. The etiology of this disease is still somewhat unclear, but it may be due to direct impingement of instrumentation on the facet joints. Some believe that denervation of the surrounding tissues, especially the facet capsule if injured, leads to neuropathic destruction of the facet. One can minimize this degeneration by protection of the facet capsule in joints outside the region of the fusion and by

attempting to never terminate a fusion in a region of stenosis, spondylolisthesis, posterior column deficiency, or an abnormal disc. This type of preoperative planning, however, is less feasible in the setting of trauma than in the setting of elective fusion for degenerative disease. Extending a fusion to a "normal" level may decrease the incidence of one complication in exchange for a further decrease in mobility of the spine.

Several studies have reported stress fractures of the pelvis in patients with long lumbosacral fusions.[36, 84] This phenomenon is most likely to occur in older osteoporotic women. The fracture typically occurs on the side from which bone graft is harvested and is probably due to a stress riser created in the ilium at graft acquisition (Fig. 34–10). Symptoms of stress fractures are usually seen in the first few months after surgery, and protected weight bearing is generally adequate for resolution of the symptoms.

Pseudarthrosis

Pseudarthrosis is a complication of both instrumented and noninstrumented fusions and refers to failure of arthrodesis after an attempt at bony fusion. Rates of

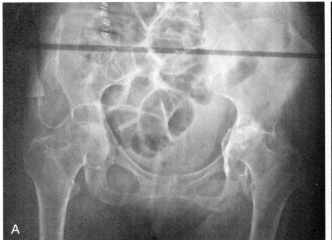

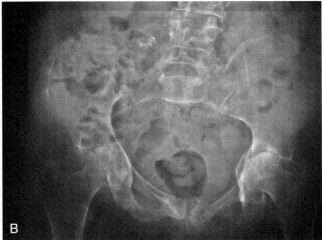

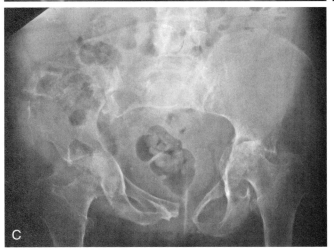

FIGURE 34–10. Pelvic fracture during iliac crest bone graft harvesting. In the setting of osteoporosis, aggressive bone graft harvesting may lead to fracture of the ilium. *A,* This 72-year-old woman with rheumatoid arthritis underwent bone graft harvest from the iliac crest. *B,* Pain developed in her hip area. Radiographs revealed a fracture at the bone graft site (*C*) with subsequent pelvic instability.

pseudarthrosis after posterior spinal fusion vary widely in the literature, from as low as 0% to as high as 30%.[4, 77] The major sequela of pseudarthrosis is pain, but the diagnosis of pseudarthrosis can be challenging in a patient with pain after fusion. Instrumentation often obscures radiographic evaluation, and back pain may be a mechanical phenomenon in a patient with a solid fusion. Implant failure is a strong indicator of fusion failure, and radiolucency about the fixation (e.g., pedicle screws) can support this diagnosis as well. Most orthopaedic surgeons agree that a change of more than 5° at a single functional spinal unit on flexion-extension radiographs is worrisome for pseudarthrosis.

The rate of pseudarthrosis increases with the number of levels being fused.[12] Additionally, advanced age, malnutrition, obesity, and the use of nonsteroidal anti-inflammatory medications have been associated with decreased rates of fusion. Brown and associates[9] showed that tobacco smoking decreases rates of fusion. In a comparison of patients undergoing lumbar laminectomy and fusion, pseudarthrosis developed in 40% of smokers, whereas nonunion developed in only 8% of nonsmokers. Recently, Glassman and colleagues showed that if patients stop smoking for at least 6 months after lumbar fusion surgery, the rate of nonunion is comparable to that of nonsmokers.[33] For smokers who did not stop smoking, the nonunion rate was 26.5%, whereas nonsmokers had a nonunion rate of 14.2%.[33] Similarly, Rogozinski and co-workers[66] looked at fusion rates in nonsmokers, preoperative smokers, and postoperative smokers. Although the fusion rate in the postoperative smoker group was less than 60%, the study indicated that nonsmokers and preoperative smokers had nearly the same rate of fusion. The negative impact of tobacco smoking on spinal arthrodesis has also been shown in the cervical spine.[39] In the setting of trauma, it is impossible to ask patients to stop smoking before surgery, but cessation of smoking after arthrodesis seems to confer a benefit. Autograft in some studies has also been shown to be superior to allograft as fusion material.[1] However, although autograft is generally incorporated more quickly, the rate of successful fusion is no different with the use of allograft in single-level anterior fusions in the cervical spine.[87]

The incidence of pseudarthrosis in the setting of trauma seems to be lower than that in the setting of degenerative disease or deformity. In 1979, Bohlman[8] reported on a large series of cervical spine fractures treated operatively without a single pseudarthrosis. Flesch and associates[28] reported only 1 nonunion in 40 patients with thoracolumbar spine fractures treated with Harrington instrumentation and fusion. Edwards and Levine[22] reported a 2% pseudarthrosis rate in 200 injuries of the thoracolumbar spine; the rate was almost four times higher at the lumbosacral junction. They noted that many of these pseudarthroses were due to technical error. Fusion rates can be enhanced with meticulous decortication of the transverse processes while trying to avoid fracture of these processes. Copious application of autograft and placement of graft beneath the posterior implants are recommended. Many spine surgeons favor the use of a gouge over the use of a bur for decortication because of the belief that thermal necrosis of bone occurs with bur decortication.

VASCULAR AND SOFT TISSUE COMPLICATIONS

Cervical Spine

Injuries to the vascular and soft tissues in the cervical spine usually occur during operative treatment of an injury. However, injuries to these structures as a direct result of trauma can occur as well. The common carotid artery and the contents of the carotid sheath are at risk during anterior exposure of the cervical spine. Blunt finger dissection and repeated, but gentle, palpation of the carotid artery to assess its location help decrease the likelihood of injury. Likewise, palpation of the nasogastric tube can identify the location of the esophagus. Mobilization of the longus colli muscles off the anterolateral vertebral bodies before placement of deep retractors also helps minimize vessel damage. Checking the temporal artery pulse of the patient during the procedure helps to assess whether excessive retraction is causing occlusion of the carotid artery. Carotid artery laceration, division, and thrombosis have been reported during anterior spinal fusion.[40] Some approaches to the cervical spine risk injury to either the internal or external jugular vein. Although in most circumstances these vessels can be ligated unilaterally with little clinical consequence, venous injury can lead to air embolism, which may cause pulmonary compromise, blindness, or death.

The vertebral artery is at risk from both anterior and posterior approaches to the cervical spine, especially in C1–C2 transarticular arthrodesis. In a review by Golfinos and colleagues[35] of 1215 cases, these injuries occurred in 1 case from retraction of soft tissues, in 1 case during screw tapping, and in 2 cases from lateral decompression. Most authors agree that the vertebral artery should not be repaired, but rather packed with thrombin-soaked absorbable gelatin sponges to achieve hemostasis through tamponade. When transarticular screw fixation is used, the contralateral side should not be instrumented if vertebral artery injury is suspected.

In the rare case in which ligation is required for hemostasis, intraoperative angiography may be performed to assess the ability of the patient to tolerate such a procedure. However, in these cases, such studies are probably impractical, and furthermore, some evidence indicates that sacrifice of one vertebral artery will not lead to permanent neurologic sequelae in most patients.[68] The ability of a patient to tolerate unilateral vertebral artery ablation is supported by a study of nine patients with traumatic occlusion of the vessel. In two of the nine, neurologic sequelae developed, but the findings were transient. However, Smith and associates[70] reported that in three of seven cases of vertebral artery ligation, symptomatic vertebrobasilar symptoms such as syncope, nystagmus, dizziness, and Wallenberg's syndrome developed. They supported repair of an injured vertebral artery whenever possible. As the use of lateral mass screw fixation expands, the number of vertebral artery injuries may increase. This complication from the placement of screws into the transverse foramen is best prevented by a knowledge of anatomy and bony landmarks.

Esophageal perforation after anterior spinal trauma or surgery is uncommon, but well recognized. The largest series of esophageal perforations to date was reported by Gaudinez and coauthors[30] from The Rocky Mountain Regional Spinal Injury Center. Over a 25-year period, 44 patients with esophageal perforation were treated at that institution. Although most pharyngoesophageal perforations occur in the early postoperative period, delayed perforations in patients who had fully convalesced from the acute postoperative period have been reported.[44] The most frequently occurring symptoms are neck and throat pain, odynophagia, dysphagia, hoarseness, and aspiration. In the series by Gaudinez and colleagues,[30] cervical osteomyelitis or cervical abscess developed in half the patients. Clinical findings may include fever, cervical tenderness and induration, weight loss, tachycardia, crepitus from emphysema, and hematemesis. Though far less common, expectoration of necrotic bone has been reported as well. A high index of suspicion is required because diagnostic imaging often yields negative results. In addition, they showed that 22.7% of patients had false-negative results from imaging studies. Endoscopy was 63.6% sensitive for definitive diagnosis in the 40 patients who underwent the procedure.[30]

Though not specifically mentioned in the aforementioned series, a combination of direct visualization and a swallow study is regarded by most to have the highest diagnostic yield. Management of esophageal perforation is variable. Conservative management includes observation, intravenous nutrition, a feeding tube or gastrostomy, appropriate antibiotic coverage, and aspiration precautions. These techniques may be effective for small, uncomplicated perforations. However, the literature suggests high morbidity and mortality with nonsurgical management of all but the smallest of perforations, especially with tears of the lower part of the esophagus. Consultation with a thoracic or esophageal surgical specialist is recommended in all cases. Prompt recognition of symptoms and pathology is paramount because a delay in diagnosis can lead to death. The esophagus should be examined carefully after any anterior cervical spinal operation, and any esophageal injury noted in the operative suite should be aggressively addressed with repair by an experienced surgeon. The repair can be augmented, when necessary, with a muscle flap, such as a proximally based medial pectoralis major rotational flap.

Thoracolumbar Spine

Anterior thoracolumbar surgery has a multitude of potential complications, including pneumothorax, hemothorax, and chylothorax. Massive hemothorax may occur from profuse vertebral body bleeding and can cause hemodynamic instability. It may require surgical tamponade of venous sinuses in the vertebral body with bone wax or ligation of bleeding segmental arteries.[60] Hemorrhage from a thoracic fracture causing persistent hemothorax has been reported in a patient with a complete neurologic injury induced by the fracture.[17] After more than 7 days of recurrent hemothorax, the patient underwent operative reduction and stabilization of the fracture, which led to the cessation of bleeding. This scenario defines an additional indication for early fixation of a high-energy thoracic vertebral fracture in patients with complete neurologic compromise.

The presence of a thoracic fracture should also alert the physician to the possibility of thoracic duct injury. The incidence of chylothorax in association with rib and thoracic fractures is increasing because of escalating numbers of vehicular accidents and nonpenetrating trauma. At least 13 patients with chylothorax secondary to thoracic fractures have been reported, and at least 2 of them died of the sequelae of the chylothorax itself, 1 from tension chylothorax.[85] Although most cases of traumatic chylothorax can be managed nonoperatively, the need for surgical intervention in the subset of patients with associated thoracic fractures is higher and approaches 50%.

Delayed appearance of a patient with chylothorax is a result of the formation of a mediastinal chyloma, which then ruptures into a pleural cavity, usually 7 to 10 days after the injury. Once suspected, diagnostic thoracentesis and tube thoracostomy should be undertaken. Oral intake should be discontinued because even low-fat, clear liquids markedly increase chyle flow.[34] Traditionally, continued chylous chest drainage despite 6 weeks of nonoperative therapy is an indication for surgical intervention. However, more recently, some authors have become more aggressive in preventing ongoing protein and lymphocyte losses and thereby minimizing the risk of infection. Some authors now recommend surgery if nonoperative management is unsuccessful after 2 weeks.[69] Most agree that a more aggressive approach is preferred in a patient with concomitant spinal fractures because of the high immunologic and nutritional cost of prolonged chest tube drainage.[69] Rare reports of iatrogenic chyle leaks after anterior thoracolumbar surgery have appeared. Most, however, agree that microlymphatic disruption is inevitable, and it seems likely that clinically insignificant chyle leaks are undiagnosed and heal spontaneously.

Diaphragmatic rupture or herniation may occur after thoracolumbar exposure or after the crus of the diaphragm is taken down and repaired to improve exposure at the thoracolumbar region. The ureters and great vessels are at risk during retroperitoneal dissection, especially in the revision setting. Consideration should be given to preoperative ureteral stenting in these revision procedures. Injury to the sympathetic plexus overlying the anterior aspect of the lower lumbar and upper sacral vertebrae may cause retrograde ejaculation.

Traditionally, much attention has been paid to the segmental blood supply of the thoracic cord. Specifically, the artery of Adamkiewicz is considered to be vital to cord perfusion. The transthoracic approach to the spine usually requires mobilization of the segmental vessels over a multitude of levels. Dwyer and Schafer,[21] however, have shown that ligation of multiple ipsilateral segmental arteries can be performed without neurologic compromise. DiChiro and colleagues[20] demonstrated in monkeys that even the arteria magna could be ligated without sequelae. However, if both this vessel and the anterior spinal artery were disrupted, paraplegia resulted. Much of the work and the case reports of neurologic compromise in the face of segmental artery disruption have been related to surgical treatment of deformity. The effect of deformity, especially if congenital, on the blood supply to the cord is unclear. In a polytrauma patient, cross-clamping of the aorta results in disruption of the segmental blood flow to the cord bilaterally, which may result in paralysis. Trauma to the cord and associated edema may make the spinal cord far more sensitive to the effects of mild ischemia.

The anterior approach to the lumbar spine for the operative treatment of spinal trauma is usually performed through the retroperitoneal or, less commonly, the transperitoneal approach. If the pathologic condition does not dictate the side, most surgeons prefer the left because the aorta is more forgiving and easier to mobilize than the vena cava. The left common iliac vein is the vessel most at risk during left-sided retroperitoneal and transperitoneal exposures. Regardless of the approach, instrumentation should be placed on the lateral side of the vertebral body and not in contact with the great vessels.

Vascular complications during posterior lumbar spine surgery are usually secondary to discectomy. Vascular injury during discectomy is most common at the L4–L5 level. Freeman[29] showed that the pituitary rongeur is the most frequent culprit. In the setting of trauma, one must be keenly aware of any disruption of the anterior longitudinal ligament. Incompetence of this ligament makes perforation of the great vessels more difficult to avoid. Unless acute hypotension occurs intraoperatively, these injures may initially go unnoticed. Late abdominal rigidity, abdominal pain, tachycardia, and anemia should alert the physician to this complication, which may be avoided by limiting the depth of insertion of the pituitary rongeur during discectomy.

The lateral extracavitary approach to the thoracolumbar spine deserves special mention. This approach, which is used to replace a two-incision front-back procedure, allows ventral decompression and dorsal fixation. The technique is technically demanding. Resnick and Benzel[63] reported a 55% incidence of morbidity in a series of 33 patients with acute fractures. The most common complication was hemothorax or effusion requiring tube thoracostomy, followed by pneumonia, which occurred in seven patients. Other authors have noted pseudohernias caused by sacrifice of the intercostal nerves. Although the morbidity associated with this procedure may be high, its risks should be weighed against the combined risk of a two-stage procedure.

Postoperative Infection

Postoperative infections may result from inoculation during the index procedure or from hematogenous seeding. The postoperative infection rate in the spine is 2% to 3%. Simple lumbar discectomy has less than a 1% infection rate, whereas combined fusion and instrumentation are associated with rates between 4% and 8%. Risk factors include increased age, obesity, diabetes, smoking, immunosuppression, duration of preoperative hospitalization, spinal dysraphism, myelodysplasia, revision surgery, operative time, and the use of instrumentation, bone graft, or methyl methacrylate.[14, 15, 41, 50, 56, 67, 72, 81]

The use of perioperative prophylaxis to prevent infec-

tion is widespread. Patients with instrumented fusions have a decreased infection rate with the use of prophylaxis when compared with those undergoing surgery without prophylaxis. Commonly, the antibiotic is administered before the incision and for 24 hours postoperatively, although some surgeons prefer to administer antibiotics until suction drains or catheters are removed. The choice of antibiotic is guided by consideration of multiple factors, including host immunocompetence, the bacterial flora common in the region, the type of procedure, cost, and the side effect profile. Most commonly, a cephalosporin is used. Because of increasing concern regarding the development of bacterial resistance, drugs such as vancomycin should be discouraged for prophylaxis and reserved only for patients at increased risk of methicillin-resistant staphylococcal infections. Such patients include those with lymphopenia, recent or current hospitalization, postoperative wound drainage, and alcohol abuse.

Once the diagnosis of postoperative infection is made clinically, early surgical intervention is necessary because medical management is likely to fail. Débridement should proceed in a systematic fashion. Each layer is débrided and cultured before advancing deeper with the dissection. If gross deep drainage or purulence is encountered with subfascial aspiration, deep débridement is performed.

Although solidly fixed instrumentation is typically left in place in the early postoperative period, all other foreign bodies such as bone wax and Gelfoam must be removed. Any hematoma should be thoroughly evacuated. Many authors retain bone grafts, especially if they are adherent. Others recommend removal of loose grafts and washing before replacement. If the graft is grossly purulent or necrotic, it should be discarded and another bone grafting procedure performed at a later débridement when the local infection is controlled. Hemostasis must be meticulous to prevent re-formation of a hematoma seeded with bacteria. Dead space must be obliterated, and the use of a rotation flap should be considered for dead space management. Primary wound closure over drains, often with retention sutures to prevent dehiscence, is favored when possible. Depending on the amount of devitalized tissue, routine serial débridement is often required. Simple wound infections may be packed open and allowed to close by secondary intention. More complex wound infections may require musculocutaneous flaps.

Postoperatively, antibiotic therapy is required for at least 10 to 14 days for straightforward soft tissue wound infections. Six weeks of parenteral antibiotic treatment is preferred in cases of bone involvement, deep infection, or retained foreign bodies (e.g., metal or graft).

In all cases, nutritional assessment and repletion are of paramount importance. Up to 35% of hospitalized patients have evidence of protein-calorie malnutrition. Weight loss of more than 10%, a serum transferrin level less than 1.5 g/L, anergy, a serum albumin concentration less than 3 g/dL, or a total lymphocyte count less than 1200 should raise suspicion of malnutrition. Protein-calorie malnutrition causes decreased cardiac output and peripheral oxygen tension as well as impaired pulmonary defenses, wound healing, and cell-mediated immune defenses. In addition to the treatment of malnutrition, its prevention must be considered in all hospitalized patients, especially those with increased metabolic demands because of fever, trauma, or surgery.

Metabolic Changes

As a result of inactivity and changes in body composition, most patients with chronic spinal cord injury undergo important metabolic changes. Glucose intolerance occurs more frequently in these patients than in the general population. Baumann and Spungen[5, 6] performed a 75-g oral glucose tolerance test on 100 veterans (50 with paraplegia and 50 with quadriplegia) and 50 able-bodied veteran controls. In the spinal cord–injured group, 22% of the subjects were diabetic by criteria established by the World Health Organization as compared with 6% in the control group. Normal oral glucose tolerance was noted in 82% of the controls, 50% of the paraplegics, and 38% of the quadriplegics. Insulin levels were lower in controls, thus indicating insulin resistance in the spinal cord–injured patients. This hyperinsulinemia may well play a role in the increased concentration of triglycerides and the decreased concentration of high-density lipoprotein cholesterol in spinal cord–injured patients. All these changes, coupled with inactivity, play a role in the high incidence of atherosclerosis seen in this group.

Spinal cord injury leads to unloading of the skeleton, and hypercalcemia and hypercalciuria ensue quickly. Restriction of dietary calcium does not treat the cause of the derangement, which is initially due to increased osteoclastic activity within the first 3 to 5 days and later involves a lifetime of decreased osteoblastic activity. Osteoporosis may lead to insufficiency or traumatic fractures, but these fractures may be markedly underdiagnosed and manifested as little more than swelling. Hypercalciuria may result in early nephrolithiasis and the recommendation that dietary calcium be forever avoided. However, such restriction often leads to deficiency and worsening of osteoporosis later in life, after the acute period of marked bone loss subsides, usually within 14 months.[64] Although their role still remains to be defined, bisphosphonates may be the best agent for management of this condition.[5, 64]

Some evidence supports the depression of endogenous anabolic hormones in spinal cord–injured patients. Decreased levels of serum testosterone, growth hormone, and insulin-like growth factor type I may exacerbate the body composition changes seen in these patients. In addition, exercise tolerance and strength may be decreased. Thyroid dysfunction is seen as well. Depressed levels of triiodothyronine (T_3) and reverse T_3 have been demonstrated, and this effect may also contribute to fatigue and an increase in adiposity. However, some believe that it is due to associated illness and metabolic derangement, and as such, the use of replacement therapy for this type of "deficiency" in the presence of normal thyroid tissue is controversial.

Although the medical management of each of these metabolic derangements is beyond the scope of this chapter, the orthopaedic surgeon must be cognizant that such medical issues exist and must use an appropriate team to minimize the late sequelae of these abnormalities. Amelioration of these abnormalities promises to improve the longevity and quality of life of persons with spinal cord injury.

Dural Tear

It is difficult, if not impossible, to know the true incidence of dural tears as a result of trauma. In patients with high-energy injuries and complete paraplegia of the thoracic spine, actual severance of the cord and dural sac is possible. Likewise, a gunshot wound to the spine may cause disruption of the dura. Iatrogenic dural tears also occur, especially during attempted posterolateral decompression. Cerebrospinal fluid (CSF) leaks may lead to positional headache, wound complications, meningitis, arachnoiditis, and pseudomeningocele.

The diagnosis of iatrogenic CSF leakage is fairly straightforward. Obvious egress of fluid from a visible tear in the dura is diagnostic. As the thecal sac decompresses because of a leak, the local pressure about the epidural veins decreases, and an increase in venous bleeding from the epidural space may be the first indication of a dural tear. Additionally, when the dural sac is decompressed, especially when reducing a kyphotic deformity, leakage may occur from a tear. Postoperatively, one must be alert for signs of clear drainage from the wound or the presence of a subcutaneous fluid collection. Severe headache exacerbated by an upright posture may be noted. Large volumes of fluid may be seen inasmuch as the choroid plexus produces over 20 mL of CSF hourly. If it is unclear whether the fluid is CSF, testing for β_2-transferrin can be useful. A pseudomeningocele may develop if a dural tear occurs and is not repaired in watertight fashion. It may occur days to months postoperatively.

Dural tears may be classified as dorsal, lateral, or ventral. Although the best treatment is prevention, most tears can be repaired primarily if they do occur. However, massive defects may be irreparable. The first step in repair is complete exposure of the dural rent. Magnification and adequate lighting are required. Dural elements must be returned to their intrathecal location and should not be incorporated into the repair inadvertently. The goal is a watertight repair that is free of tension. Usually, this objective can be accomplished with 6–0 polypropylene (Prolene) suture placed in a running locking stitch. The recommended location of the suture is 2 mm from the dural edge with 3 mm between sutures. A Valsalva maneuver may be simulated by the anesthesiologist after repair to assess for residual leak. If leakage occurs after repair, augmentation with additional suture, gelatin sponge, autogenous fat, or fibrin glue is required. More complex tears may require grafting with fascia lata or with commercially available dural patches. Meticulous watertight fascial closure is as important as the dural repair itself because the fascial barrier is relied on to prevent durocutaneous fistulas. Most surgeons avoid the use of intramuscular drains in the presence of a dural tear because negative pressure may encourage a persistent leak.

During a posterior approach, most posterior and lateral dural tears can be exposed directly. Below the level of the conus, an anterior tear may be approached through a posterior durotomy and gentle retraction of nerve roots to allow access to the anterior aspect of the dural tube. However, anterior tears during posterior exposure at cord levels may need to be treated indirectly.

Indirect repair is most commonly performed with fibrin glue, which is formed by mixing thrombin and cryoprecipitate that has been screened for human immunodeficiency and hepatitis virus. It forms a biologic glue with biomechanical "patchlike" properties, and it can seal tears that cannot be fully exposed for repair or it can be used to augment tenuous repairs. Cooling the individual components before mixing may improve the biomechanical strength of the product.[80] In addition to repair, diversion of CSF through a subarachnoid drain for 4 to 5 days may allow the dura, fascia, and surgical incision to heal.

SUMMARY

The complications of spinal trauma are numerous and challenging. They may occur as a direct result of the injury, because of a lack of appreciation of the injury and subsequent improper treatment, or as a result of the inherent risk of the treatment itself. Successful treatment of these complications relies on prompt recognition. Complications that occur as a result of spinal trauma are often related to immobilization. Prolonged bedrest leads to deconditioning, poor pulmonary function, and decubitus ulcers. Vigilance must be paid to these mundane, but clinically important issues, and proper understanding of the injury pattern provides another avenue by which to avoid complications. Spinal stability must be scrutinized with an eye toward potential deformity. Whether external or internal immobilization is used, all fractures should be monitored closely so that loss of reduction can be discovered early and treated expeditiously. Inadequate fixation techniques, neglecting to support the anterior column, and failing to restore normal alignment are the causes of most iatrogenic deformities. Meticulous attention to detail during all phases of treatment, combined with attentive medical care, will prevent most of the complications associated with spinal trauma.

REFERENCES

1. Anderson, P.A.; Budorick, T.E.; Easton, K.B.; et al. Failure of halo vest to prevent in vivo motion in patients with injured cervical spines. Spine 16(Suppl):501–505, 1991.
2. Andreychik, D.A.; Alander, D.H.; Senica, K.M.; Stauffer, E.S. Burst fractures of the second through fifth lumbar vertebrae. Clinical and radiographic results. J Bone Joint Surg Am 78:1156–1166, 1996.
3. Aschoff, A.; Steiner-Milz, H.; Steiner, H.H. Lower limb compartment syndrome following lumbar discectomy in the knee-chest position. Neurosurg Rev 13:155–159, 1990.
4. Axelsson, P.; Johnsson, R.; Stromqvist, B.; et al. Posterolateral lumbar fusion. Outcome of 71 consecutive operations after 4 (2–7) years. Acta Orthop Scand 65:309–314, 1994.
5. Bauman, W.A.; Spungen, A.M. Disorders of carbohydrate and lipid metabolism in veterans with paraplegia or quadriplegia: A model of premature aging. Metabolism 43:749–756, 1994.
6. Bauman, W.A.; Spungen, A.M. Metabolic changes in persons after spinal cord injury. Phys Med Rehabil Clin N Am 11:109–140, 2000.
7. Benzel, E.C.; Kesterson, L.; Marchand, E.P. Texas Scottish Rite Hospital rod instrumentation for thoracic and lumbar spine trauma. J Neurosurg 75:382–387, 1991.
8. Bohlman, H.H. Acute fractures and dislocations of the cervical spine. An analysis of three hundred hospitalized patients and review of the literature. J Bone Joint Surg Am 61:1119–1142, 1979.
9. Brown, C.W.; Orme, T.J.; Richardson, H.D. The rate of pseudarthrosis (surgical nonunion) in patients who are smokers and patients who are nonsmokers: A comparison study. Spine 11:942–943, 1986.
10. Bucholz, R.D.; Cheung, K.C. Halo vest versus spinal fusion for cervical injury: Evidence from an outcome study. J Neurosurg 70:884–892, 1989.
11. Chan, R.C.; Schweigel, J.F.; Thompson, G.B. Halo-thoracic brace immobilization in 188 patients with acute cervical spine injuries. J Neurosurg 58:508–515, 1983.
12. Cleveland, M.; Bosworth, D.; Thompson, F. Pseudarthrosis in the lumbosacral spine. J Bone Joint Surg Am 30:302–312, 1948.
13. Cotler, J.M.; Vernace, J.V.; Michalski, J.A. The use of Harrington rods in thoracolumbar fractures. Orthop Clin North Am 17:87–103, 1986.
14. Currier, B. Spinal infections. In: An, H., ed. Principles and Techniques of Spine Surgery. Baltimore, Williams & Wilkins, 1998, pp. 567–603.
15. Currier, B.; Heller, J.; Eismont, F.J. Spinal infections. In: Clark, C., ed. The Cervical Spine. Philadelphia, Lippincott-Raven, 1998, pp. 659–690.
16. Curry, K.; Casady, L. The relationship between extended periods of immobility and decubitus ulcer formation in the acutely spinal cord–injured individual. J Neurosci Nurs 24:185–189, 1992.
17. Dalvie, S.S.; Burwell, M.; Noordeen, M.H. Haemothorax and thoracic spinal fracture. A case for early stabilization. Injury 31:269–270, 2000.
18. Denis, F. The three column spine and its significance in the classification of acute thoracolumbar spinal injuries. Spine 8:817–831, 1983.
19. Denis, F.; Burkus, J.K. Classification and treatment of posttraumatic kyphosis in the thoracic and lumbar spine. Semin Spine Surg 5:187–198, 1993.
20. DiChiro, G.; Fried, L.C.; Doppman, J. Experimental spinal cord angiography. Br J Radiol 43:19–30, 1970.
21. Dwyer, A.F.; Schafer, M.F. Anterior approach to scoliosis. Results of treatment in fifty-one cases. J Bone Joint Surg Br 56:218–224, 1974.
22. Edwards, C.; Levine, A. Complications associated with posterior instrumentation in the treatment of thoracic and lumbar injuries. In: Garfin, S., ed. Complications of Spine Surgery. Baltimore, Williams & Wilkins, 1989.
23. Edwards, C.; Rhyne, A.L. Late treatments of posttraumatic kyphosis. Semin Spine Surg 2:63–69, 1990.
24. Edwards, C.; York, J.E.; Levine, A.; et al. Determinants of spinal dislodgement. Orthop Trans 10:8, 1986.
25. Edwards, C.C.; Levine, A.M. Early rod-sleeve stabilization of the injured thoracic and lumbar spine. Orthop Clin North Am 17:121–145, 1986.
26. Farcy, J.P.; Weidenbaum, M.; Glassman, S.D. Sagittal index in management of thoracolumbar burst fractures. Spine 15:958–965, 1990.
27. Fidler, M.W. Remodelling of the spinal canal after burst fracture. A prospective study of two cases. J Bone Joint Surg Br 70:730–732, 1988.
28. Flesch, J.R.; Leider, L.L.; Erickson, D.L.; et al. Harrington instrumentation and spine fusion for unstable fractures and fracture-dislocations of the thoracic and lumbar spine. J Bone Joint Surg Am 59:143–153, 1977.
29. Freeman, D. Major vascular complications of lumbar disk surgery. West J Surg Gynecol Obstet 69:175–177, 1961.
30. Gaudinez, R.F.; English, G.M.; Gebhard, J.S.; et al. Esophageal perforations after anterior cervical surgery. J Spinal Disord 13:77–84, 2000.
31. Gertzbein, S.D.; Macmichael, D.; Tile, M. Harrington instrumentation as a method of fixation in fractures of the spine. J Bone Joint Surg Br 64:526–529, 1982.
32. Glaser, J.A.; Whitehill, R.; Stamp, W.G.; Jane, J.A. Complications associated with the halo-vest. A review of 245 cases. J Neurosurg 65:762–769, 1986.
33. Glassman, S.D.; Anagnost, S.C.; Parker, A.; et al. The effect of cigarette smoking and smoking cessation on spinal fusion. Spine 25:2608–2615, 2000.
34. Goins, W.; Rodriguez, A. Traumatic chylothorax. In: Turney, S.; Rodriguez, A.; Cowley, R., eds. Management of Cardiothoracic Trauma. Baltimore, Williams & Wilkins, 1990.

35. Golfinos, J.G.; Dickman, C.A.; Zabramski, J.M.; et al. Repair of vertebral artery injury during anterior cervical decompression. Spine 19:2552–2556, 1994.

36. Grimm, J.; Jackson, R. Stress fracture of the pelvis: A complication following instrumented lumbar fusion. Paper presented at the 27th Annual Meeting of the Scoliosis Research Society, Kansas City, Missouri, 1992.

37. Guttmann, L. Spinal deformities in traumatic paraplegics and tetraplegics following surgical procedures. Paraplegia 7:38–58, 1969.

38. Heini, P.; Scholl, E.; Wyler, D.; Eggli, S. Fatal cardiac tamponade associated with posterior spinal instrumentation. A case report. Spine 23:2226–2230, 1998.

39. Hilibrand, A.S.; Fye, M.A.; Emery, S.E.; et al. Impact of smoking on the outcome of anterior cervical arthrodesis with interbody or strut-grafting. J Bone Joint Surg Am 83:668–673, 2001.

40. Hohf, R.P. Arterial injuries occurring during orthopaedic operations. Clin Orthop 28:21–37, 1963.

41. Horwitz, N.H.; Curtin, J.A. Prophylactic antibiotics and wound infections following laminectomy for lumber disc herniation. J Neurosurg 43:727–731, 1975.

42. Hsu, K.; Zucherman, J. The long term effect of lumbar spinal fusion: Deterioration of adjacent motion segments. In: Yonenobu, K.; Ono, K.; Takemitsu, Y., eds. Lumbar Fusion and Stabilization. Berlin, Springer-Verlag, 1993, pp. 54–64.

43. Jodoin, A.; Dupuis, P.; Fraser, M.; Beaumont, P. Unstable fractures of the thoracolumbar spine: A 10-year experience at Sacre-Coeur Hospital. J Trauma 25:197–202, 1985.

44. Kelly, M.F.; Spiegel, J.; Rizzo, K.A.; Zwillenberg, D. Delayed pharyngoesophageal perforation: A complication of anterior spine surgery. Ann Otol Rhinol Laryngol 100:201–205, 1991.

45. King, D. Internal fixation for lumbosacral fusions. J Bone Joint Surg Am 30:560–565, 1948.

46. Kostuik, J.P. Indications for the use of the halo immobilization. Clin Orthop 154:46–50, 1981.

47. Krag, M. Biomechanics of transpedicle spinal fixation. In: Weinstein, J.; Weisel, S., eds. The Lumbar Spine. Philadelphia, W.B. Saunders, 1990.

48. Lagrone, M.O.; Bradford, D.S.; Moe, J.H.; et al. Treatment of symptomatic flatback after spinal fusion. J Bone Joint Surg Am 70:569–580, 1988.

49. Lehmer, S.M.; Keppler, L.; Biscup, R.S.; et al. Posterior transvertebral osteotomy for adult thoracolumbar kyphosis. Spine 19:2060–2067, 1994.

50. Levi, A.D.; Dickman, C.A.; Sonntag, V.K. Management of postoperative infections after spinal instrumentation. J Neurosurg 86:975–980, 1997.

51. Levine, A.M.; Edwards, C.C. Complications in the treatment of acute spinal injury. Orthop Clin North Am 17:183–203, 1986.

52. Lonstein, J.E.; Denis, F.; Perra, J.H.; et al. Complications associated with pedicle screws. J Bone Joint Surg Am 81:1519–1528, 1999.

53. Magerl, F.P. Stabilization of the lower thoracic and lumbar spine with external skeletal fixation. Clin Orthop 189:125–141, 1984.

54. Malcolm, B.W.; Bradford, D.S.; Winter, R.B.; Chou, S.N. Posttraumatic kyphosis. A review of forty-eight surgically treated patients. J Bone Joint Surg Am 63:891–899, 1981.

55. Manfredini, M.; Ferrante, R.; Gildone, A.; Massari, L. Unilateral blindness as a complication of intraoperative positioning for cervical spinal surgery. J Spinal Disord 13:271–272, 2000.

56. Massie, J.B.; Heller, J.G.; Abitbol, J.J.; et al. Postoperative posterior spinal wound infections. Clin Orthop 284:99–108, 1992.

57. McAfee, P.C.; Bohlman, H.H. One-stage anterior cervical decompression and posterior stabilization with circumferential arthrodesis. A study of twenty-four patients who had a traumatic or a neoplastic lesion. J Bone Joint Surg Am 71:78–88, 1989.

58. McBride, G.G.; Bradford, D.S. Vertebral body replacement with femoral neck allograft and vascularized rib strut graft. A technique for treating post-traumatic kyphosis with neurologic deficit. Spine 8:406–415, 1983.

59. Nicoll, E. Fractures of the dorso-lumbar spine. J Bone Joint Surg Am 31:376–394, 1949.

60. Parker, J.W.; Lane, J.R.; Karaikovic, E.E.; Gaines, R.W. Successful short-segment instrumentation and fusion for thoracolumbar spine fractures: A consecutive 4½-year series. Spine 25:1157–1170, 2000.

61. Rechtine, G.R., 2nd; Cahill, D.; Chrin, A.M. Treatment of thoracolumbar trauma: Comparison of complications of operative versus nonoperative treatment. J Spinal Disord 12:406–409, 1999.

62. Reeg, S.; Boachie-Adjei, O. Management of late deformity after spine trauma. In: Capen, D.; Haye, W., eds. Comprehensive Management of Spine Trauma. St. Louis, C.V. Mosby, 1998.

63. Resnick, D.K.; Benzel, E.C. Lateral extracavitary approach for thoracic and thoracolumbar spine trauma: Operative complications. Neurosurgery 43:796–802, 1998.

64. Roberts, D.; Lee, W.; Cuneo, R.C.; et al. Longitudinal study of bone turnover after acute spinal cord injury. J Clin Endocrinol Metab 83:415–422, 1998.

65. Rockswold, G.L.; Bergman, T.A.; Ford, S.E. Halo immobilization and surgical fusion: Relative indications and effectiveness in the treatment of 140 cervical spine injuries. J Trauma 30:893–898, 1990.

66. Rogozinski, C.; Rogozinksi, A.; Weiss, H. Effect of cigarette smoking on instrumented lumbosacral fusion. Paper presented at the Annual Meeting of the American Academy of Orthopaedic Surgeons, Orlando, Florida, 1996.

67. Schulitz, K.P.; Assheuer, J. Discitis after procedures on the intervertebral disc. Spine 19:1172–1177, 1994.

68. Sen, C.; Eisenberg, M.; Casden, A.M.; et al. Management of the vertebral artery in excision of extradural tumors of the cervical spine. Neurosurgery 36:106–115, 1995.

69. Silen, M.L.; Weber, T.R. Management of thoracic duct injury associated with fracture-dislocation of the spine following blunt trauma. J Trauma 39:1185–1187, 1995.

70. Smith, M.D.; Emery, S.E.; Dudley, A.; et al. Vertebral artery injury during anterior decompression of the cervical spine. A retrospective review of ten patients. J Bone Joint Surg Br 75:410–415, 1993.

71. Smith-Petersen, M.N.; Larson, C.B.; Aufranc, O.E. Osteotomy of the spine for correction of flexion deformity in rheumatoid arthritis. Clin Orthop 66:6–9, 1969.

72. Stambough, J.L.; Beringer, D. Postoperative wound infections complicating adult spine surgery. J Spinal Disord 5:277–285, 1992.

73. Thiranont, N.; Netrawichien, P. Transpedicular decancellation closed wedge vertebral osteotomy for treatment of fixed flexion deformity of spine in ankylosing spondylitis. Spine 18:2517–2522, 1993.

74. Vaccaro, A.R.; Falatyn, S.P.; Scuderi, G.J.; et al. Early failure of long segment anterior cervical plate fixation. J Spinal Disord 11:410–415, 1998.

75. Weatherley, C.; Jaffray, D.; Terry, A. Vascular complications associated with osteotomy in ankylosing spondylitis: A report of two cases. Spine 13:43–46, 1988.

76. Weber, S.C.; Benson, D. A comparison of segmental fixation and Harrington instrumentation in the management of unstable thoracolumbar spine fractures. Orthop Trans 9:36, 1985.

77. West, J.L., 3rd; Ogilvie, J.W.; Bradford, D.S. Complications of the variable screw plate pedicle screw fixation. Spine 16:576–579, 1991.

78. Whitehill, R.; Richman, J.A.; Glaser, J.A. Failure of immobilization of the cervical spine by the halo vest. A report of five cases. J Bone Joint Surg Am 68:326–332, 1986.

79. Whitesides, T.E., Jr. Traumatic kyphosis of the thoracolumbar spine. Clin Orthop 128:78–92, 1977.

80. Wiegand, D.A.; Hartel, M.I.; Quander, T.; et al. Assessment of cryoprecipitate-thrombin solution for dural repair. Head Neck 16:569–573, 1994.

81. Wimmer, C.; Gluch, H.; Franzreb, M.; Ogon, M. Predisposing factors for infection in spine surgery: A survey of 850 spinal procedures. J Spinal Disord 11:124–128, 1998.

82. Wittenberg, R.H.; Lee, K.S.; Shea, M.; et al. Effect of screw diameter, insertion technique, and bone cement augmentation of pedicular screw fixation strength. Clin Orthop 296:278–287, 1993.

83. Wolfe, S.W.; Lospinuso, M.F.; Burke, S.W. Unilateral blindness as a complication of patient positioning for spinal surgery. A case report. Spine 17:600–605, 1992.

84. Wood, K.B.; Geissele, A.E.; Ogilvie, J.W. Pelvic fractures after long lumbosacral spine fusions. Spine 21:1357–1362, 1996.

85. Wright, P.; Gardner, A. Traumatic chylothorax: A case after dislocation of the thoracic spine. J Bone Joint Surg Br 34:64, 1952.

86. Young, M.H. Long-term consequences of stable fractures of the thoracic and lumbar vertebral bodies. J Bone Joint Surg Br 55:295–300, 1973.

87. Zdeblick, T.A.; Ducker, T.B. The use of freeze-dried allograft bone for anterior cervical fusions. Spine 16:726–729, 1991.

88. Zindrick, M.R.; Wiltse, L.L.; Widell, E.H.; et al. A biomechanical study of intrapeduncular screw fixation in the lumbosacral spine. Clin Orthop 203:99–112, 1986.

SECTION III

Pelvis

SECTION EDITOR

Alan M. Levine, M.D.

CHAPTER 35

Fractures of the Sacrum

Alan M. Levine, M.D.

Treatment of injuries to the sacrum requires consideration of a number of additional factors beyond those relevant to injuries of the thoracic and thoracolumbar spine. These factors are related to the anatomic complexity of the sacrum, difficulty with fixation to the sacrum, and the relatively large forces necessary to achieve and maintain reduction and increased normal mobility of the lumbosacral junction. Additionally, sacral fractures encompass a wide variety of entities that range in severity from a simple buckle fracture of the sacral ala to a severely comminuted fracture associated with major injury to the pelvis. The spectrum is also broad when the causes of the injury are considered along with the epidemiology of the affected individuals. These fractures may be the result of high-energy trauma such as motor vehicle and motorcycle accidents or suicide attempts involving younger individuals, as well as insufficiency fractures and low-energy falls involving older persons.

Throughout the 1970s and 1980s, the lack of satisfactory techniques for reduction and stabilization of injuries in the sacrum frequently resulted in less than optimal treatment results and led some authors to espouse nonoperative techniques as a better alternative.[14, 25, 27] Occasional reports, however, suggested that an operative approach yielded better anatomic results and perhaps even better functional outcomes.[44, 68] Even with the more widely accepted use of pedicle screw fixation in the lumbar spine and various methods of sacral fixation in North America, some early, poorly conceptualized operative approaches to fractures in this region also led to early failure.[4, 5, 40, 77] These results caused some surgeons to accept chronic pain and the failure to return to preinjury occupation as the norm in this very young group of patients.

The lumbosacral junction in particular must resist a number of large forces, but it must also permit a significant amount of motion. It has therefore been difficult to obtain anatomic reduction and reconstruction of the lumbar spine and sacrum until the most recent advances in instrumentation. This difficulty has led many authors to suggest either limited procedures and goals or "benign neglect" as the

methods of treatment of sacral injuries. In addition, in the sacrum, failure to recognize the nature of the injuries and their severity has resulted in a lack of organized treatment schemes. The normal kyphotic sagittal configuration of the sacrum and the many overlying structures have made imaging difficult, even with the use of standard two-dimensional computed tomography (CT). Fixation to the bone of the sacrum has been even more problematic. These numerous features and problems distinguish fractures of the sacrum from the more abundant and common fractures at the thoracolumbar junction.

More accurate diagnostic imaging studies, as well as advances in instrumentation techniques, should now allow us to treat sacral injuries with the same degree of accuracy and competence as more proximal spinal injuries. To this end, however, we must have a clear understanding of the anatomic and functional differences that distinguish the sacrum from the remainder of the more proximal areas of the spine.

Treatment goals for spine trauma in general are (1) anatomic reduction of the injury, (2) rigid fixation of the fracture, and when necessary, (3) decompression of the neural elements. For treatment of the sacral spine, we must add the considerations of (4) maintenance of sagittal alignment and (5) prevention of frequent complications (e.g., loss of sacral fixation, failure to attain decompression and reduction, and pseudarthrosis). As the characteristics of the sacrum are reviewed, it will become evident that techniques that were discussed in the previous section for the treatment of cervical, thoracic, thoracolumbar, and lumbar spine injuries are not applicable to the treatment of sacral injuries.

ETIOLOGY AND EPIDEMIOLOGY

Sacral fractures can be subdivided into several major categories based on etiology. The most common etiology of sacral fractures is high-energy trauma resulting in major pelvic disruption, which has a high incidence of associated sacral fractures. Pohlemann and associates[62] found that 28% of patients with pelvic ring injuries had sacral fractures (377 sacral fractures/1350 pelvic fractures), and Denis and colleagues reported a 30% incidence (236 sacral/776 pelvic).[18] Most of these fractures are vertical in orientation and may be either unilateral or bilateral; in addition, they may occasionally have a transverse component. Isolated sacral fractures are much more uncommon and represent approximately 5% to 10% of all traumatic injuries that occur as a result of high-energy accidents. Most of the isolated fractures are transverse and result from direct trauma such as a fall from a height.[74] The final type of sacral fracture is an insufficiency fracture, which occurs either spontaneously or after a trivial episode of trauma.[72] Most patients in whom insufficiency fractures of the sacrum develop have predisposing factors such as osteopenia, chronic steroid use, or pelvic irradiation.[52, 72] The actual incidence of this type of fracture is unknown because recognition and diagnosis have not been frequently emphasized. Although more than 500 cases have been reported in the literature,[24, 38] the incidence is considerably higher because insufficiency fractures are an unrecognized cause of back pain in elderly female patients.[15, 33]

ANATOMIC FEATURES

The sacrum forms both the terminal portion of the spine and the central portion of the pelvis. Its five fused vertebrae give rise to an overall kyphotic sagittal alignment that influences the alignment of the mobile spine above it. The normal kyphosis of the thoracic spine falls within a range of 15° to 49°,[86] whereas normal lumbar lordosis is generally thought to be less than 60°. These values are in part determined by the slope of the sacral base, which averages approximately 45° from the horizontal. This angle is critical in determining the amount of shear force[76] to which the lumbosacral junction is subjected. Anatomic differences in the structure of the lumbar vertebrae and sacrum influence therapeutic decisions and make attachment of fixation devices necessarily different from that for proximal levels in the thoracic and lumbar spine.

The sacroiliac joint, which joins the sacrum to the rest of the pelvis, includes the lateral portions of S1, S2, and part of S3, with the more caudal portions of the sacrum remaining free. The stability of the sacroiliac joint is maintained by strong ligamentous attachments such as the anterior and posterior sacroiliac ligaments, the sacrotuberous ligaments, and the sacrotransverse ligaments. The strength of this ligamentous complex helps determine the location of fractures of the sacrum, with transverse fractures commonly occurring at the midportion of S3 at the end of the sacroiliac attachment. Similarly, vertical fractures occur through the ala rather than through the joint as a result of the strength of the sacroiliac joint in resisting disruption.

With caudal descent in the lumbar spine, the overall dimensions of the canal enlarge, whereas the area occupied by the neural elements decreases. The cord in the thoracic region measures approximately 86.5 mm^2 and is housed within a canal that is generally 17.2 × 16.8 mm^2. Thus, in the thoracic region, the cord occupies about 50% of the canal area. In the thoracolumbar region, the conus broadens, as does the canal. The spinal cord usually terminates at approximately L1. In the lumbar region, the canal is typically large (23.4 × 17.4 mm^2).[21, 64] Here, the roots of the cauda equina are the only contents. In the sacrum, however, the diameter of the canal again begins to narrow and flatten. In addition, with the normal, slightly kyphotic angle at the midpoint of the sacrum (S2–S3), the roots are tethered in a relatively fixed location. This tethering of the roots allows less flexibility in placing any fixation devices within the canal in the sacrum. The sacral roots are responsible for urinary continence, micturition, fecal continence, defecation, and sexual function. After emanating from the conus medullaris, the sacral roots traverse the canal of the lumbar spine in a relatively posterior location and exit through the ventral and dorsal foramina. Fractures through the sacral ala can also result in an L5 root injury as demonstrated by Denis and associates.[18] This root exits the foramen and traverses over the top of the sacral ala such that displacement of the alar fracture can cause injury to the root. Denis and co-workers also evaluated the frequency of injury to individual sacral roots and found that root injury at the ventral foramen was less likely at S3 and S4 than at S1 and S2 because of a significant difference in the root-to-foramen ratio in the two areas. Because innervation of bowel and bladder function is by bilateral sacral roots, injury to one side does not disrupt sphincter function whereas bilateral injury does.[34]

With the increasing emphasis on innovative methods of fixation for injuries in the low lumbar spine and sacrum, an understanding of the pertinent anatomic dimensions takes on new significance. Previously, with hook fixation or sublaminar wiring to the posterior elements, the only important consideration was the posterior topographic anatomy. However, the dimensions, position, and orientation of the pedicles, as well as the shape of the vertebral body, are likewise critical. The initial anatomic description of pedicle morphology with respect to pedicle screw fixation was presented by Saillant[70] in 1976 and confirmed by two later studies from North America.[41, 87] The critical features are the sagittal and transverse width of the pedicles, pedicle length, pedicle angle, and chord length (depth to the anterior cortex along a fixed orientation). Understanding the three-dimensional anatomy of the various sacral levels, as well as the position of the neurovascular structures applied to the anterior surface of the sacrum, is critical to the conceptualization of adequate and safe fixation to the sacrum.

The anatomic constraints of the sacrum are quite severe, with its overall sagittal contour being gradually kyphotic at about 25° with the apex at S3. The sacral laminae are extremely thin and might be absent in some areas. At their maximal thickness, the sacral alae are between 40 and 45 mm. The area of maximal bone thickness is in the vestigial pedicle of each sacral segment, and this area rapidly decreases in size with progression to the distal segments. At S3 or S4, the maximal thickness may only be 20 mm. The anatomic structures that may be encountered at the level of the S1 body are the internal iliac vein, the lumbosacral plexus, and the sacroiliac joint. A safe zone about 2 cm wide and bordered by the sacral promontory medially and the iliac vein laterally is present and invariably entered with orientation of a screw along the S1 pedicle.[50] Screws can be directed only medially at the S1 level because the critical neurovascular structures will then lie lateral to the sacral promontory. Screws placed laterally at either 30° or 45° are aimed at a smaller lateral safe zone. The more lateral orientation provides for a longer screw length of 44 mm.[50] The S1 level is the only segment that will allow simultaneous screw placement in the lateral and medial directions. Screw placement should be bicortical for maximal purchase. At the S2 level, the only vulnerable structure is the sigmoid colon on the left side. Penetration through the cortex by more than 1 cm is usually necessary for injury. At the S2 level, the thickness of the sacral bone has decreased significantly compared with that at the S1 level, and thus, the holding power of the bone in an axis parallel to placement of S1 would be significantly less. To compensate for these deficiencies, orientation of fixation devices proximally and laterally will significantly increase the length of screw purchase and therefore pull-out strength. Variations in the amount of cancellous and cortical bone mass in different regions of the sacrum significantly affect fixation possibilities and the risks associated with fixation. Because of increased bone mass, sacrum fixation is more secure in the ala or vertebral bodies than in the very thin posterior laminar structures.

Anatomic considerations are different for vertical sacral alar fractures that require fixation. Iliosacral fixation is dependent on visualizing the anterior border of the ala on the inlet view, which can be difficult. As a result of the concavity of the ala, it is easy to misdirect screws anterior to the ala and jeopardize neurovascular structures. The starting point for percutaneous iliosacral screws is based on landmarks on the lateral aspect of the ilium. Preoperative planning based on CT allows accurate assessment of the anatomic relationships. The use of image intensification for screw guidance requires accurate identification of the anterior and superior aspects of the sacrum to avoid exiting the ala anteriorly and then reentering it more medially. As a result of the contour of the body, passage of screws is safer at S1 than at S2, and use of S2 should be reserved only for patients with severe comminution of the S1 ala.

SACRAL INJURY PATTERNS

Facet Fractures and Dislocations

Facet injuries to the lumbar spine occur infrequently. Levine and colleagues noted that bilateral facet dislocations below L1–L2 represent only 10% of the total cases,[45] and those at the lumbosacral junction are even less common. The important feature of this type of flexion-distraction injury is that it is mainly a soft tissue injury that results in complete disruption of the posterior ligamentous complex, as well as the intravertebral disc. The bony architecture of the facets may remain intact in many cases, but they are totally juxtaposed and dislocated. The minor compression of the anterior portion of the inferior body is merely a result of the severe ligamentous injury and does not contribute to the overall instability of the injury. The

posterior walls of the vertebral bodies remain intact, and canal compromise results from translation of one intact vertebral ring in relation to the adjacent ring. This injury must be differentiated from a facet fracture, which is a different injury mechanically and consists of comminution of the facets and sometimes also the laminae, pars interarticularis, and vertebral body.

The severe translation observed with facet dislocations may lead to partial or complete cauda equine syndrome. This severe translation is a result of posterior ligamentous disruption combined with severe disc disruption. Denis[17] suggested that complete posterior disruption is insufficient to account for the degree of flexion instability seen in this injury. Only incompetence of the posterior longitudinal ligament, anulus fibrosus, and disc could produce such a degree of translational instability. The anterior longitudinal ligament is often stripped from the anterior portion of the inferior body but remains intact. A number of authors[37, 46, 48, 84] have suggested that this might be a flexion-distraction injury with the axis of rotation posterior to the anterior longitudinal ligament.

Radiographs of facet fractures and dislocations at the lumbosacral junction are usually diagnostic. They demonstrate an intact posterior wall at L5 with significant translation, lesser degrees of anterior compression, and loss of disc height (Fig. 35–1). Anteroposterior (AP) radiographs of the lumbar spine often reveal dislocation of the facets. CT confirms the pathology and demonstrates an empty facet sign,[56] as well as the severity of canal compromise on sagittal reconstructions.[29]

Although unilateral facet dislocations and fracture-dislocations are rare in the thoracic or lumbar spine, unilateral facet injuries have been reported to occur to a disproportionate degree at the lumbosacral junction.[11, 13, 16, 19, 36, 42, 53, 71, 88] For unilateral facet dislocations to occur, a combination of flexion-rotation and distraction is required. Facet fracture-dislocations can occur when the extent of distraction is not sufficient to allow the inferior facet to clear the superior facet. An element of shear is present in both unilateral and bilateral facet fracture-dislocations. It is of note that in the more recent literature, a number of case reports have documented the combination of a unilateral lumbosacral facet dislocation and an associated sacral fracture.[13, 20, 35, 81] Recognition of these unusual high-energy injuries is predominantly due to improved imaging of the sacrum. The combination of a facet dislocation and a sacral fracture, especially if comminuted, can complicate fixation at the lumbosacral junction. The implications for postreduction stability are significantly different for a true facet dislocation (intact facets) and a fracture-dislocation. Unilateral dislocations or fracture-dislocations differ from bilateral dislocations in that on the AP view, a significant rotatory component can be seen in the former. In addition, in unilateral dislocations and fracture-dislocations, avulsion of the transverse processes may be seen.

Sacral Fractures

Until recently, fractures of the sacrum were combined with fractures of the pelvis,[28] although they were first men-

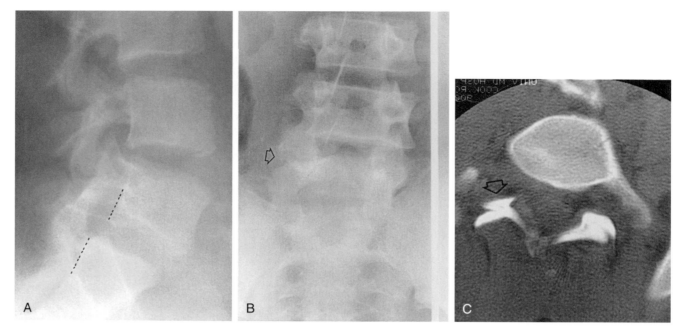

Figure 35-1. Unilateral facet dislocations in the lumbar spine are exceedingly rare and have a rotational abnormality that is often diagnostic. *A*, On a lateral radiograph, rotational malalignment is indicated by the step-off between the posterior walls of L5 and S1 (*dotted lines*). *B*, Anteroposterior radiograph demonstrating asymmetry of the disc space, as well as a suggestion of widening of the facet at L5 and S1 (*arrow*). *C*, Computed tomographic scan demonstrating a dislocated facet with the inferior articular process of L5 lying anterior to the superior articular process of S1 (*arrow*). (*A–C*, From Kramer, K.M.; Levine, A.M. J Bone Joint Surg Am 71:1258–1261, 1989.)

tioned by Malgaine in 1847. Bonin[7] was one of the first to attempt to characterize these injuries. He identified six different types of sacral fracture from a review of 44 pelvic injuries, 45% of which were also associated with sacral fractures. He also provided a discussion of the mechanisms of injury, as well as the occurrence of neurologic deficit. Although a number of reports have been published,[9, 10, 22, 23, 26, 49, 63, 85] less than 5% of all sacral fractures occur as isolated injuries. As mentioned previously, in addition to the association with pelvic fractures, the combination of lumbosacral dislocation with facet injury and sacral fracture is a relatively common pattern.[13, 35, 81] Similarly, a more recent study[3] identified 17 patients with concomitant noncontiguous thoracolumbar and sacral fractures. The implications are significant in that five of the sacral fractures were missed initially, thus resulting in the possibility of continued or additional injury to the distal roots. Two reports[18, 73] attempted to classify sacral fractures by manageable criteria so that they could be correlated with the fracture pattern, neurologic deficit, and treatment options. Sacral fractures can be caused by direct trauma to the sacrum, but most result from indirect forces acting on the pelvis or lumbar spine.

Sacral fractures are usually classified according to the direction of the fracture line; thus, fractures can be vertical, transverse, or oblique (Fig. 35–2). Most sacral injuries, however, are vertical. After reviewing the literature and their own series, these fractures were classified in a useful fashion by Schmidek and colleagues[73] into indirect and direct patterns. Indirect patterns of vertical fractures include (1) lateral mass fracture, (2) juxta-articular fracture, (3) cleaving fracture, and (4) avulsion fracture (Fig. 35–3). In addition, they included high transverse as

the final type of indirect mechanism and considered gunshot wounds and low transverse fractures to be direct mechanisms of injury. Sabiston and Wing suggested a simpler three-part classification[69] (Figure 35–4).

Denis and associates[18] classified 236 sacral fractures into zones based on both clinical and anatomic cadaveric studies of the sacrum. The three zones that they thought had clinical significance were zone 1, which was the sacral ala up to the lateral border of the neural foramen; zone 2, which was the neural foramen; and zone 3, which included the central portion of the sacrum and the canal (Fig. 35–5). In this series, 118 patients had fractures in zone 1, 5.9% of whom had neurologic deficits. These injuries were frequently fractures caused by lateral compression of the pelvis, vertical shear fractures, or sacrotuberous avulsions.[18] The next group was zone 2, or foraminal fractures. These fractures involved one or more foramina, and the fracture line exited through the sacral canal without involvement of the central neural canal. This type of fracture was found in 81 of 236 patients, and 28.4% of these patients had some neurologic findings. Zone 2 injuries often resulted from vertical shear fractures. The final group of patients had zone 3, or central sacral canal involvement. These injuries were seen less frequently, in only 21 of 236 patients, but had a high rate of neurologic deficit (56.7%). This group included some patients who had a transverse component of the fracture.

Oblique fractures most often combine some element of a transverse fracture with that of a vertical fracture. In addition, an oblique fracture is the type that may involve both the sacrum and the lumbosacral junction. Thus, an oblique component ends proximally in a fracture at the base of the S1 facet or goes directly through the facet joint.

As a result, the level and complexity of the instability are increased.

Transverse fractures of the sacrum occur less frequently than vertical fractures[7, 25, 68] and account for approximately 4.5% to 10% of each series. They most commonly result from high-energy injuries, such as falling from a height onto the lower extremities. As characterized by Roy-Camille and co-workers[68] from their own series of 13 patients and extensive cadaveric studies, these fractures are generally high transverse fractures (S1 or S2) with anterior bending (kyphosis) between the superior and the inferior fragments and verticalization of the distal fragment. They are frequently associated with bilateral alar fractures and fractures of the L5 transverse process. Displacement and tilting of the fragments can be related to the relative flexion or extension of the hips at the moment of impact. Direct blows to the sacrum can result in low transverse fractures (S3 or S4) by levering on the distal segments below the point of fixation by the sacroiliac joints. Three distinct types of fractures were identified. Type I was a flexion injury without significant deformity, type II was a flexion injury with posterior displacement of the cephalad frag-

ment, and type III was caused by extension with anterior displacement of the cephalad fragment. Depending on displacement, these transverse fractures can be associated with rectal perforation or cerebrospinal fluid leakage. They are frequently associated with neurologic deficits, including bowel and bladder dysfunction and perineal numbness. No motor weakness is usually detected. These fractures are, therefore, the most easily missed and have the gravest implications for significant neurologic deficit. Generally found in the S2–S3 region, they may be responsible for complete loss of bowel and bladder function. The diagnosis is usually very difficult on plain radiographs and may also be missed on CT because the fracture is parallel to the axial cuts and thus may not be well visualized even with two-dimensional reconstruction. Interestingly, the most predictable method of visualization for this particular type of sacral fracture seems to be magnetic resonance imaging (MRI) (see Fig. 35–6).

Recognition plus description of the patterns observed in sacral insufficiency fractures is a relatively recent occurrence that is in large part due to the use of MRI. Because the fractures are visualized infrequently on plain

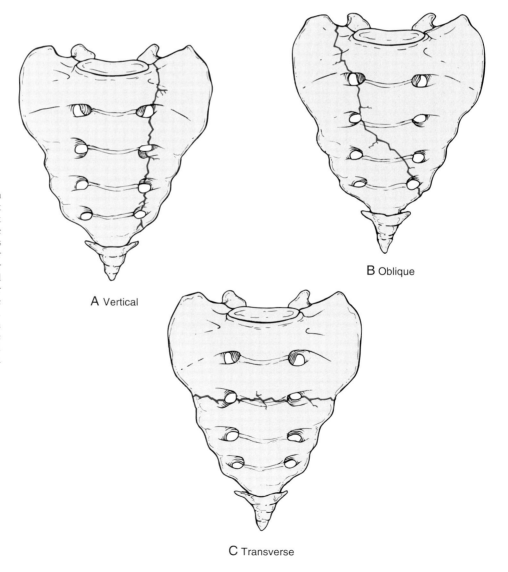

FIGURE 35–2. Fractures of the sacrum can be classified in a number of different ways. One of the most common is that of the direction of the fracture line within the sacrum. Therefore, fractures can be vertical (A), oblique (B), or transverse (C). These fractures can occur at any level in the sacrum. Vertical fractures may occur in the alae or through the foramina. Similarly, oblique fractures may occur at any location. Transverse fractures are less common and are found more frequently at the apex of the sacral kyphosis between S2 and S3, but they may also occur as a high transverse fracture at S1 or S2.

A Vertical

B Oblique

C Transverse

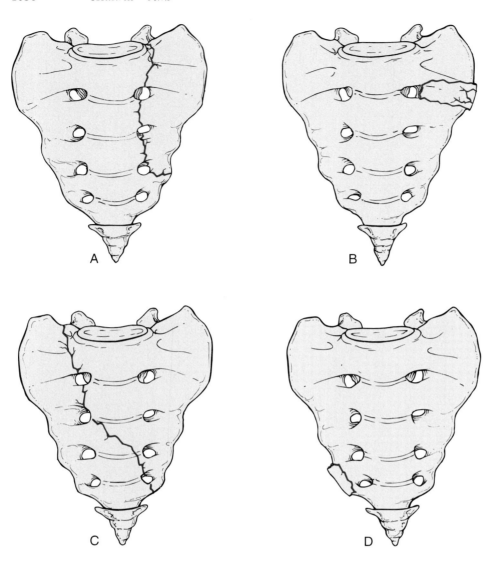

FIGURE 35–3. Schmidek and colleagues classified vertical fractures into four fracture patterns, including lateral mass fractures *(A)*, juxta-articular fractures *(B)*, cleaving fractures *(C)*, and avulsion fractures *(D)*. *(A–D,* Redrawn from Schmidek, H.H.; et al. Neurosurgery 15:735–746, 1984.)

radiographs, the observer must often depend on areas of edema and compaction observed on MRI to find all the fracture lines. A number of different patterns are seen, including a single vertical line parallel to the sacroiliac joint,[12, 32] but the most commonly described pattern is the "H" or "Honda" sign.[8, 58] Peh and coauthors[58] described a series of 21 patients with insufficiency fractures of the sacrum, 9 of whom had the "H" configuration. Four patients had high bilateral sacral fractures without the bar, and four had unilateral sacral ala fractures. Two had bilateral fractures with a partial transverse element, and one each had a unilateral ala fracture with a transverse component. The final patient had only a transverse component. Classification of these injuries may require a combination of bone scintigraphy, CT, and MRI.

EVALUATION

After resuscitation and general evaluation of a trauma victim, it is very important to ascertain the details of the accident from either the patient or the rescue personnel. High-energy decelerating injuries such as falls from a height or ejection from a motor vehicle or motorcycle have the potential for either a pelvic ring fracture combined with a sacral injury or an isolated sacral fracture. Physical examination should include palpation of the entire spinal column, pelvis, and sacrum, as well as visual inspection for ecchymosis or bruising. As part of the routine physical examination, the perineum and especially the anus should be assessed for normal sensation and tone. In patients with significant trauma to the urethra or the rectum, rectal perforation may be present. Rectal perforation may also occur in association with a transverse fracture of the sacrum without any other injury to the pelvis, depending on the direction of displacement of the sacral fracture.

Assessment of an elderly patient with low back or sacral pain should also include a very careful evaluation of the sacral region. A clinical history of previous irradiation, significant osteopenia resulting from a drug effect, or senile osteoporosis should also be elicited.[15, 33, 52, 82] Neurologic complications of insufficiency fractures are rare,[38] but a careful history of bowel and bladder function should be obtained. Such a history may be confusing, especially if the patient has been taking narcotics for the pain and now has constipation secondary to the pain medication obscuring changes in bowel function. In view of the low yield of plain radiographs in these patients, a technetium-labeled bone scan should be performed early in the course of the patient's symptoms.

Neurologic Deficit

Sacral injuries may be associated with neurologic deficit, depending on the type of injury and the direction of the fracture line. Patients with vertical fractures involving the sacral roots on just one side can have normal bowel and bladder function and only subtle sensory deficits, unless the S1 root is involved. Transverse fractures of the sacrum with translation, however, are accompanied by neurologic deficit in almost all patients. Zone 1 vertical alar fractures are associated with neurologic deficit in 5.9% of patients, and the deficit usually involves only the sciatic nerve or the L5 root and is generally minor. Zone 2 sacral fractures are associated with neurologic deficit in approximately 28.4%

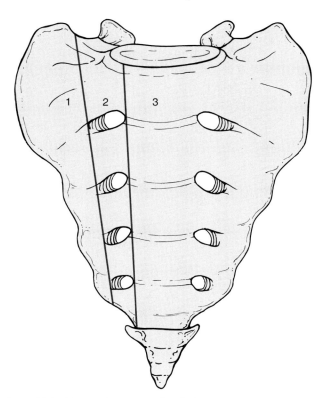

FIGURE 35–5. Denis and associates classified 236 fractures of the sacrum into zones. Zone 1 was the region of the ala, and fractures in this area occurred in 118 patients, 5.9% of whom had neurologic deficits. Zone 2 was the foraminal region, where the fracture line involved one or more foramina and exited without involvement of the central neural canal. This group comprised 81 patients, 28.4% of whom had neurologic findings. The final group of patients had zone 3 injuries, or central canal involvement. This pattern was seen in only 21 patients, but they had an extremely high rate of neurologic deficit (56.7%). (Redrawn from Denis, F.; et al. Clin Orthop 227:67–81, 1988.)

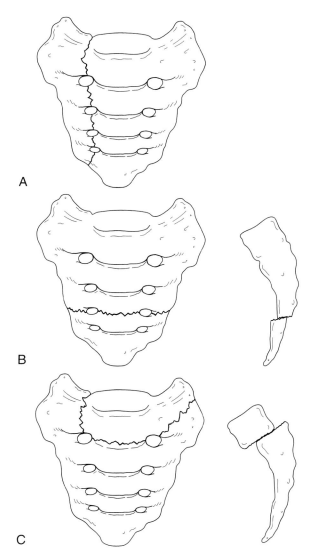

FIGURE 35–4. Sabiston and Wing's classification of sacral fractures had three main types. Type A included vertical fractures, type B consisted of transverse fractures below the level of the sacroiliac joint, and type C fractures were transverse at the level of the sacroiliac joint with vertical components. (Redrawn from Sabiston, C.P.; Wing, P.C. J Trauma 26:1113–1115, 1986.)

of patients, a small proportion of whom have bowel and bladder involvement. The remainder have sciatica associated with L5, S1, or S2. The L5 root can be associated with a displaced vertical shear fracture and fracture of the transverse process of L5, a combination that has been termed the *traumatic far-out syndrome*.[18] This injury is most frequently associated with footdrop. Zone 3 fractures involve the central sacral canal and are associated with neurologic deficit in at least 50% of patients. Most of these patients have bowel, bladder, and sexual dysfunction. The remainder of patients with injury at this level have L5 or S1 findings. With neurologic injury from S2 to S5, impairment of bowel and bladder function can occur, but patients might not have functional incontinence with preservation of at least one of the two S2 and S3 roots. Bilateral root disruption invariably leads to severe deficits.

Cystometry performed in conjunction with sphincter electromyography can be useful in correlating findings from clinical examination. With all sacral fractures, however, a complete investigation should be carried out because it is often difficult to ascertain whether the root involvement is a result of the pelvic fracture or the associated sacral fracture.

Neurologic complications of insufficiency fractures are exceedingly rare. In the few reported cases, the onset of neurologic deficit was delayed in relation to the onset of fracture symptoms.[38, 60] Urinary retention, as well as numbing and tingling of the feet, has been reported. The mechanism of onset of neurologic symptoms associated with this entity is unclear in that the onset is not always associated with displacement. Surgery is not generally required because resolution of the neurologic symptoms seems to occur spontaneously with resolution of the back symptoms. However, MRI is recommended for patients who do have a deficit; surgery for decompression is reserved for those with severe compression and displacement; and nonoperative treatment is given to the majority.[38]

Radiologic Evaluation

Radiographic diagnosis of sacral injuries is in general quite difficult. Plain AP and even lateral radiographs of either the pelvis or sacrum are often not helpful in visualizing fractures of the sacrum. Detail is often overlaid by soft tissue shadows and bowel gas, and in addition, the lumbar lordosis and kyphotic sagittal contour of the sacrum make the fracture lines oblique to the plane of the radiograph (Fig. 35–6). The Ferguson view is the best view of the upper portion of the sacrum and can demonstrate foraminal involvement. Lateral radiographs can help

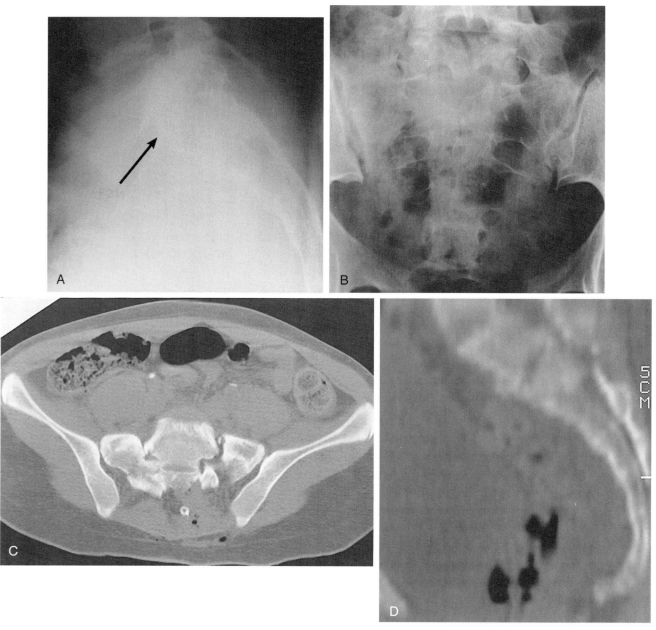

Figure 35–6. A 19-year-old woman was involved in a motor vehicle accident and sustained a transverse sacral fracture. The fracture was not visualized well on either the initial lateral (A) or the initial anteroposterior (AP) (B) radiographs and was thus not recognized at first. The lateral x-ray only shows a slight break in the round sagittal contour (arrow). On the AP view only the vertical component of the fracture is visible. Although the patient had loss of both bowel and bladder function, this also was not initially appreciated. When the neural deficit was recognized, a CT scan was obtained. C, The axial view shows only the vertical component of the fracture, not the transverse. D, Midsagittal reconstruction does not demonstrate clearly the configuration of the fracture.

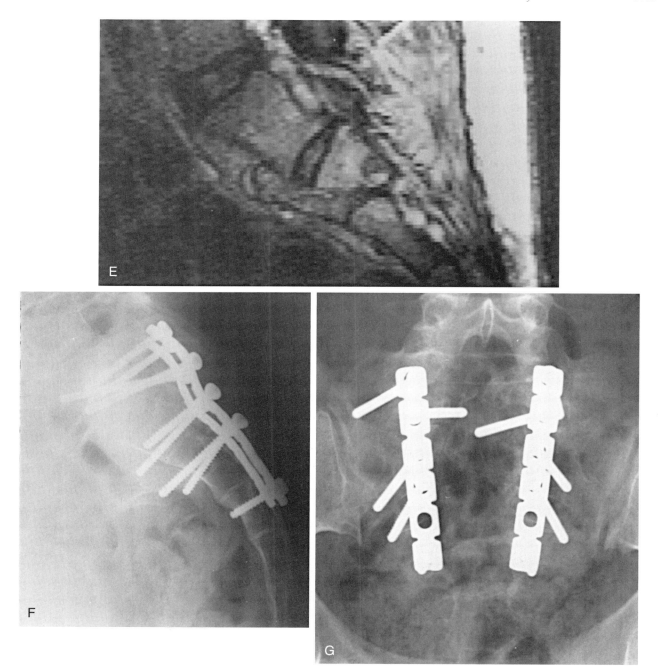

FIGURE **35-6** *Continued. E,*The MRI, however, showed an angulated fracture in the S2 region. The fracture was in kyphosis with the superior fragment displaced posterior to the inferior fragment. The patient underwent operative reduction and decompression with plate fixation as shown on lateral (*F*) and AP (*G*) views. The double screw fixation in S1 stabilized the proximal fragment, with the cephalad screw directed medially and the next screw directed laterally. The patient regained bowel and partial bladder function and return of perineal sensation.

diagnose transverse fractures of the sacrum. Denis and co-workers reported that up to 50% of patients in their series who were neurologically intact had a delay in diagnosis of the sacral fracture. Such delay still occasionally occurs even in patients with neurologic deficit. Plain radiographs show only 30% of sacral fractures in most series. Even with careful retrospective study, only another 35% of these injuries can be detected. Thus, clinical suspicion coupled with the mechanism of injury should trigger the use of ancillary studies for both acute traumatic injury and insufficiency fractures. CT has become the standard for evaluation of both pelvic and sacral frac-

tures[18, 39, 82] (Fig. 35–7). It provides better visualization of especially difficult fractures lateral to the sacral ala.[51] Transverse sacral fractures are difficult to delineate because they are parallel to the coronal plane of the primary CT scan and require sagittal reconstruction for demonstration. In addition, MRI can be helpful in delineating both the areas of neural compression in the sacrum and displacement of the fracture fragments. Whereas myelography was used previously to evaluate patients with neurologic deficit, MRI is now the study of choice for acute sacral injuries with deficit. MRI not only assesses the area of compression but also gives clear images of the displacement because the information is gathered primarily in both the axial and sagittal planes without reformatting (see Fig. 35–6).

Evaluation of an elderly patient with a suspected insufficiency fracture of the sacrum is more complicated. In this instance, the use of plain radiographs is generally unrewarding but should not be overlooked because they are helpful in ruling out other lumbosacral pathology. A technetium bone scan is the initial study and can be of help in these patients (Fig. 35–8). It will generally show activity in one of the patterns previously described, soon after the onset of symptoms.[31, 33, 52, 58] Standard imaging for a bone scan is an anterior and posterior projection, with the posterior view being more effective in demonstrating activity in these fractures. However, activity in the sacrum can sometimes be obscured by residual activity in the bladder, so an outlet view can be helpful in those circumstances. Although a bone scan is highly sensitive, it is not specific, and accurate confirmation of the fracture along with delineation of the pattern is more optimally achieved with CT. Proper alignment of the gantry and thin cuts (2 mm) allowing for reconstruction are critical to obtain the maximal amount of data from the study. Routine CT of the pelvis does not permit diagnostic resolution of this problem. Vertical fractures are viewed as a combination of the fracture line and sclerosis. The transverse component, when it exists, is best seen on a reconstruction. Additionally, other helpful changes are evident on CT besides the fracture lines and sclerosis in older fractures. A vacuum phenomenon can sometimes be appreciated both within the sacroiliac joint and within the fracture site (intraosseous).[59, 75] MRI can be used either as a screening tool in a symptomatic patient or to define the fracture. It is often helpful in a patient with previous irradiation to help rule out recurrence. MRI can both visualize and define the fracture with a single study. The fracture lines are defined as bands of decreased signal intensity on T1-weighted images, whereas on T2-weighted and STIR (short tau inversion recovery) images, the lines can be seen as areas of edema around the ala or body of the sacrum. Some authors believe that MRI is sensitive but nonspecific and suggest confirmation with CT, but recently it has been shown that the finding of fluid within the fracture seems to be helpful in confirming the diagnosis.[60]

MANAGEMENT

Indications

Various systems have been devised in an attempt to classify spinal injuries according to both mechanism and degree of instability. In addition, a number of definitions have been proposed—for example, stable versus unstable. A generic definition of spinal stability includes fracture patterns that are not likely to change position with physiologic loads and will therefore not cause additional neurologic deficit or increasing deformity. Although many systems that are applicable to lumbar spine injuries have been proposed, no pragmatic system has been devised that clearly groups the injuries so that treatment approaches can be differentiated. In general terms, surgical indications for sacral injuries are the following: (1) the presence of detectable motion at the fracture site that cannot be controlled by nonoperative methods (instability), (2) neurologic deficit, or (3) severe disruption of axial or sagittal spinal alignment. With a large canal-to–neural element ratio, significant translation or angulation must take place to cause a neural injury.

Because vertical sacral fractures usually occur in combination with other pelvic ring fractures, considerations of instability and treatment are discussed with the remainder of pelvic fractures. Transverse fractures of the sacrum are generally of two types. A greenstick type, which increases sacral kyphosis without translational deformity, is generally stable (Fig. 35–9). Proximal transverse fractures of the sacrum with neurologic deficit are often accompanied by gross translational instability for which no nonoperative solution is available.

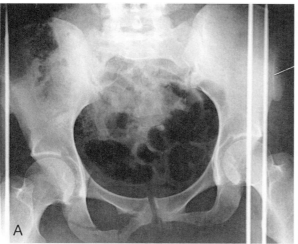 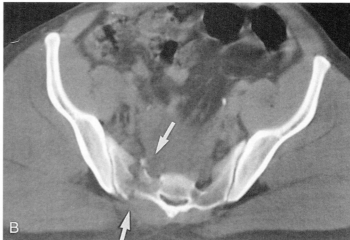

FIGURE 35–7. A 24-year-old woman sustained pelvic trauma in a motor vehicle accident. *A,* An anteroposterior radiograph of her pelvis demonstrates a fracture of her right pubis and ischium with an indistinct fracture through the sacrum. *B,* Computed tomography clearly shows the fracture line (*arrows*) traversing the neural foramina; thus, it is classified as a zone 2 fracture. This patient had radicular deficits in the S2 and S3 distributions.

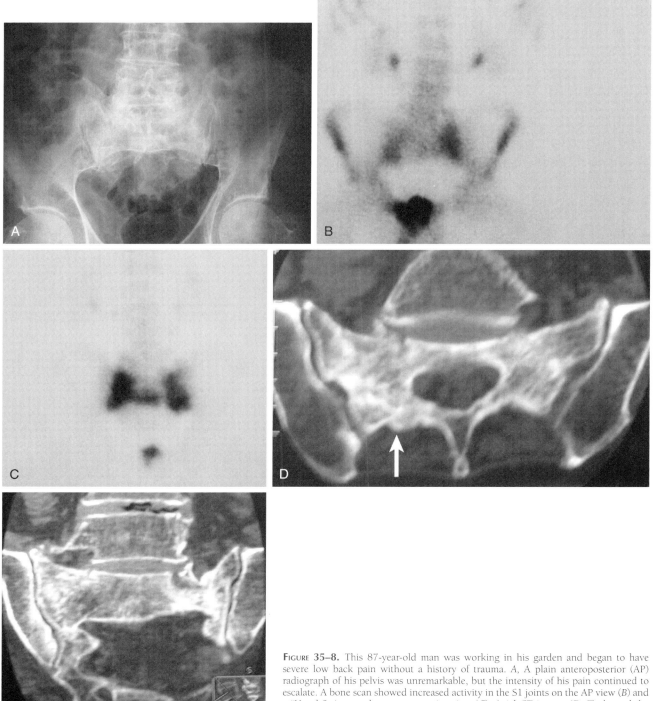

FIGURE 35–8. This 87-year-old man was working in his garden and began to have severe low back pain without a history of trauma. *A*, A plain anteroposterior (AP) radiograph of his pelvis was unremarkable, but the intensity of his pain continued to escalate. A bone scan showed increased activity in the S1 joints on the AP view (*B*) and a "Honda" sign on the posteroanterior view (*C*). Axial CT images (*D, E*) showed the fracture line (*D, arrow*) with coronal reconstruction (*E*) most effectively demonstrating the fracture pattern. MRI also helped to define the problem.

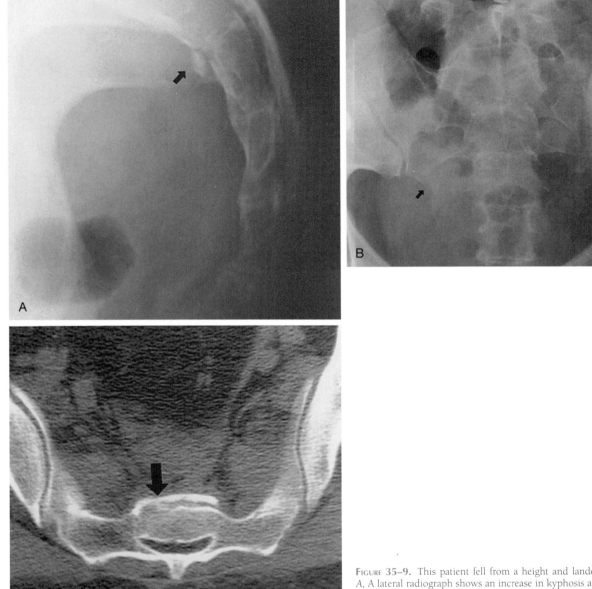

Figure 35–9. This patient fell from a height and landed on his buttocks. *A,* A lateral radiograph shows an increase in kyphosis and comminution of the anterior cortex (*arrow*). *B,* On an anteroposterior view, the fracture line was seen to occur at the level of the termination of the sacroiliac joint and its attachment to the sacrum (*arrows*). *C,* A computed tomographic scan shows minimal comminution with fracturing of only the anterior cortex (*arrow*).

The second criterion that constitutes an indication for treatment is neurologic deficit. Considerable controversy has arisen concerning the benefits of operative treatment of spinal injury with respect to neurologic recovery for cord-level injuries. In the small group of patients with high transverse sacral fractures, kyphosis, and neurologic deficit, reduction of deformity, laminectomy, and decompression of the involved roots are indicated and often provide return of neural function,[25, 68] although one very small series (four patients) suggests that an unspecified group can regain some function with nonoperative treatment.[61] Other neurologic injuries that accompany fractures of the sacrum are less likely to respond to direct operative intervention. A significant portion of these injuries are root avulsions, and the remainder are neurapraxias, which frequently respond to conservative treatment.

The next indication for treatment is severe sagittal- or coronal-plane deformity. Most fractures of the sacrum result in kyphotic deformities and may be accompanied by translational and rotational abnormalities. Because maintenance of normal sagittal alignment is critical for the normal weight-bearing axis of the body and therefore for optimal function of the paraspinous musculature, restoration to normal is a criterion for treatment of many fractures in the spine but to date has not been applied to the sacrum. However, this statement has not been fully verified because most of these injuries occur in relatively young individuals and the follow-up in most operative and nonoperative series is still relatively short. In the absence of neurologic deficit, clinically stable fractures that do not have significant associated kyphosis can be optimally treated nonoperatively.

Thus, in summary, fractures and dislocations involving the lumbosacral junction that result in neurologic deficit, instability, or deformity need to have operative treatment. This group includes oblique sacral fractures that destroy the stability of the lumbosacral articulation on either side. Reestablishment of pelvic stability when the sacral fracture is combined with a more significant pelvic injury is a critical goal of treatment and can be accomplished either operatively or nonoperatively. Finally, transverse sacral fractures that are either traumatic or insufficiency in type and cause marked root compression and deficit, especially with severe fracture site angulation or translation, also require surgical intervention. The paramount consideration for operative versus nonoperative treatment of traumatic sacral injuries is the presence or absence and the type of neurologic deficit. Patients with vertical fractures or some patients with oblique fractures who have an isolated root deficit are treated on the basis of the instability of the injury and not the deficit. Transverse fractures or some oblique fractures with loss of bowel and bladder function are treated with an attempt to recover these functions. Although nonoperative treatment can be considered in the latter circumstance,[61] other studies have suggested that decompression either indirectly by realignment or directly by removing the compression fragment yields better results. Gibbons and colleagues,[30] in a series of 23 patients with neurologic deficits from sacral fractures, showed that 88%

regained some function with operative treatment whereas only 20% regained any function with nonoperative treatment.

Treatment Options

A number of treatment measures can be used for the management of sacral fractures and generally involve either nonoperative or operative treatment. Nonoperative treatment consists mainly of bedrest or postural reduction, or both, in combination with external immobilization by a cast or orthosis. With the possible exception of pelvic and sacral fractures, the role of traction or external fixation is limited. Operative intervention can involve various procedures, including reduction, stabilization, and fusion of spinal fractures from a posterior approach,[1] with or without indirect or direct decompression of neural elements from a posterior or posterolateral approach.[2]

Patients with intact neurologic function and minimally displaced or angulated fractures (zone 1 or 2 in combination with a stable pelvic fracture) may require only a short period of bedrest followed by early mobilization with or without an orthosis (see Fig. 35–7). Weight bearing is progressively increased, depending on the fracture pattern and displacement. Occasionally, an external fixator is necessary for the anterior portion of the ring, whereas the interdigitation of the fragments may provide sufficient stability posteriorly.

Most insufficiency fractures of the sacrum can be treated nonoperatively, even those accompanied by neurologic deficit (see Fig. 35–8). The necessity of using bedrest as the initial portion of the treatment has, however, been a matter of debate. In fact, the use of bedrest initially does not preclude the subsequent development of a neurologic deficit.[38] However, many reports have advocated the use of bedrest[31, 38, 54, 57, 58, 83] despite the many complications associated with a period of bedrest in the elderly, including increased osteopenia, deep venous thrombosis, decreased muscle strength, and cardiac, gastrointestinal, and genitourinary complications.[6] Currently, however, no evidence is available in the literature to advocate one methodology over another. No published series has suggested that patients managed with bedrest have an unacceptable rate of complications; in addition, however, no evidence has indicated that the time to healing and relief of symptoms is shorter when an initial period of bedrest is used before progressive ambulation is initiated. Most studies demonstrate a prolonged period of symptoms lasting at least 3 months and often as long as 9 months before complete relief of symptoms and return to full function.[15, 31, 33, 58] Those with a previous history of irradiation may require an even longer period before resolution of symptoms, in some cases up to and exceeding 1 year.[52] Few reported patients had adverse outcomes; however, the duration of disability and symptoms was prolonged. Even those with neurologic symptoms who were treated nonoperatively had reasonable functional outcomes.[38]

For vertically unstable fractures in zone 1, the displacement should be initially reduced with the use of skeletal traction, followed by anterior or posterior fixation (or a combination of both). Fixation can be achieved with the use of anterior plating of the symphysis and posterior techniques such as posterior iliosacral plating, sacral bars, and tension band plates across the ilium. More recently, the use of iliosacral screws placed percutaneously has allowed stable fixation with less extensive surgery.[55, 65, 66, 79, 80] The method for that technique is well described in Chapter 36 and will not be repeated here. Satisfactory outcomes are dependent on achieving reduction of the sacral fracture before initiating the procedure and on obtaining adequate visualization of the sacrum with image intensification to ascertain that the screws remain within the sacrum.[65, 66]

For patients with either isolated transverse or oblique fractures with or without involvement of the L5/S1 articulation, either bilateral plating[43, 68] or other techniques[78] can be considered. These measures should not be considered for minimally displaced fractures.

Surgical Techniques for Specific Types of Injuries

FIXATION DEVICES

Beginning with the work of Louis[47] and Roy-Camille and associates,[67] systems of spinal plates fixed with pedicle screws have been used for fractures. Their use is most appropriate for fixation of both the lumbosacral junction and the sacrum. Especially for the sacrum, they not only provide a mode of fixation for sequential screws but, by proper bending of the plating, can also control displacement and angulation. The strength of these plates lies in the fact that they can achieve rigid fixation of the spine with limited length of instrumentation. Roy-Camille plates for the lumbar spine allow two pedicle screws to be placed at each level, which is especially important at S1. For localized fixation only at the lumbosacral junction, the use of a screw/rod construct is optimal. Screws are placed into the pedicle of L5, and after reduction of the dislocation or fracture-dislocation, the rods can be attached to screws directed either medially in S1 or laterally into the ala. Their utility is somewhat diminished if fixation needs to be carried to S2 to stabilize an oblique fracture line because the construct has a higher profile and somewhat less versatility than plate fixation on the sacrum proper.

LUMBOSACRAL FACET INJURIES AND DISLOCATIONS

The patient should be placed in the prone position with the table flexed at the level of the hips to allow easy reduction of the dislocation. After the dislocation is reduced, the table is extended to lock the reduction before beginning stabilization. A posterior incision is made from the midportion of the spinous process of L4 down to the level of S2. Care is taken during dissection to avoid disruption of the L4/L5 interspinous ligament or the facet capsules of the same level. Careful dissection of the L5/S1

facets is performed to ascertain whether any fracture lines have occurred through the articular processes or through the base of the S1 articular process and obliquely into the sacrum. If no fracture lines are present, reduction can be accomplished by applying distraction through towel clips placed on the spinous processes of L5 and S1 to disengage them (see Fig. 35–1). If reduction cannot be readily accomplished, additional flex is added to the table. Once the articular processes are disengaged, those of L5 are pulled posteriorly and inferiorly to lock them into the appropriate position. Usually, they do not completely engage until the table is switched from flexion to slight extension. It is inadvisable to resect the tips of the articular processes to perform the reduction maneuver because such resection compromises the stability of the final reduction. If it is difficult to achieve complete reduction or hold it because the spinous processes tend to spread apart, an interspinous wire can be placed temporarily to maintain the reduction until the final instrumentation is placed. Care should be taken to not attempt to compress the interspace with either the wire or the final construct because of the potential for compression of the disc, which can result in nerve root impingement. After reduction is achieved, the posterior aspect of the disc should be palpated to ensure that disc herniation and root impingement have not occurred. If such is the case, discectomy should be performed at this point after the initial reduction.

After the interspace is checked, pedicle screws should then be placed in routine fashion in L5 and S1. Medial placement of the screws at S1 is somewhat easier with this injury, and the final position of the hardware should be in only slight compression, just enough to maintain the reduction. Fusion is done with iliac crest graft. In patients with fractures through the tips of the articular processes, the fragments should be removed before attempting to achieve the reduction. The final reduction may not be as rotationally stable and may require wire fixation before placing the final construct. If a fracture line goes through the base of an articular process and then obliquely into the sacrum, the articular processes of that side may not have even been juxtaposed by the translation achieved by displacement. Therefore, reduction may be accomplished on the affected side simply by translating the fractured fragment posteriorly. This technique does not allow for stable reduction before the application of instrumentation. In this instance, a plate construct should be used as described later, with one screw in L5 and two in S1 and the plate extended as far distally as necessary to fully stabilize the oblique nature of the fragment.

SACRAL FRACTURES

Surgical treatment of sacral injuries has only recently been shown to provide significant benefit to the patient. Previously, surgical treatment was usually restricted to sacral laminectomies and decompression. Only rarely was an indication for reduction of any sacral deformities noted because no adequate methods of sacral stabilization existed. However, more recently it has been appreciated

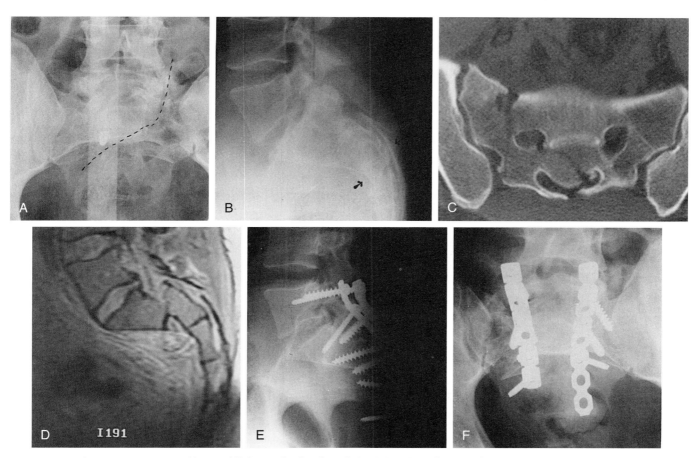

Figure 35–10. The patient, a 30-year-old man, fell from a height of 35 ft, landed on both feet, and fell backward onto his buttocks; he sustained multiple injuries to both feet and an oblique sacral fracture with a complete neural injury at the S2 level. *A,* An anteroposterior radiograph did not clearly demonstrate the oblique nature of the fracture line *(dashed line)* with extension into the L5–S1 articulation on one side. *B,* A lateral view shows the increase in kyphosis apparent at the fracture site *(arrow).* *C,* An axial computed tomographic scan clearly shows the oblique nature of the fracture line as it courses through the floor of the canal into the neural foramen and the ventral surface of the sacrum. *D,* The nature of the displacement is better seen on magnetic resonance imaging, with the proximal fragment displaced anteriorly and the distal fragment posteriorly. The fracture traversed the base of the S1 facet on the right and therefore required plating to the L5 pedicle *(E, F)* to achieve reduction and stabilization.

that transverse fractures with severe kyphosis might be improved by manipulation and stabilization to prevent skin compromise in thin individuals and afford decompression to compromised sacral roots. Vigorous manipulation of the fragments can carry the risk of rectal perforation and should be considered with great caution.

Patients with transverse fractures of the sacrum and neurologic deficit undeniably benefit from surgical decompression and stabilization.[3, 68, 78] Compression of the sacral roots may be due to combined causes. Most transverse fractures angulate into increased kyphosis and may indeed translate (Fig. 35–10). Thus, the sacral roots may be tented over the exaggerated kyphosis. Certainly, sacral laminectomy fails to decompress the roots because the kyphosis still remains. In addition, if decompression is achieved by removing or tamping the apex of the kyphosis down without stabilization, the impingement can recur with additional translation (see Fig. 35–10). Thus, in that instance, reduction of the distal fragment to

the proximal fragment is accomplished, followed by plate stabilization and subsequent removal of any unreduced fragments. If the fracture is more impacted and comminuted and not as angulated, compression of the roots is generally due to retropulsion of fragments into the canal. In that instance, reduction is not necessary because the impacted fragments should not be disturbed. Stabilization in situ should be performed and decompression then accomplished.

The technique for reduction and stabilization of an angulated transverse fracture of the sacrum is reasonably straightforward (Fig. 35–11). Most transverse fractures occur between S1 and S3. A radiolucent operating table is necessary for screw placement. For a transverse fracture or even one with an oblique component, the patient is placed on the operating table in the prone position with the hips and knees slightly flexed. A longitudinal incision is used for exposure from the L5 spinous process (sparing the L5–S1 facet capsule) to the S4 level if there is no

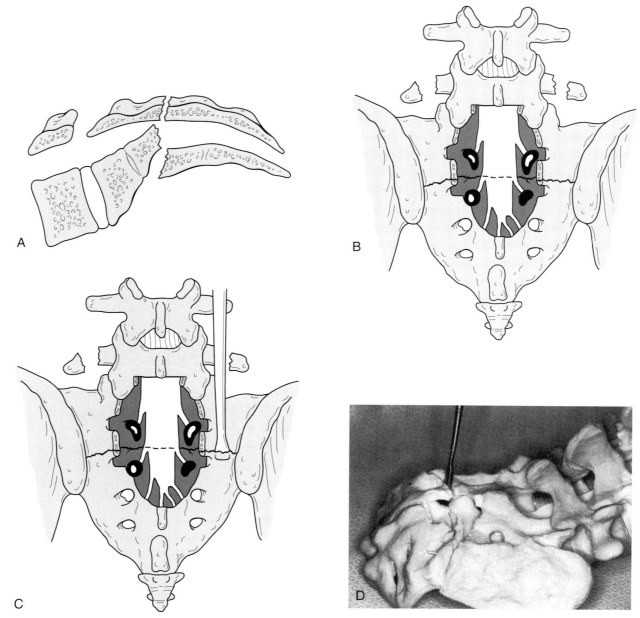

Figure 35–11. Technique of reduction and plate fixation of transverse sacral fractures. A transverse fracture line in the sacrum usually occurs at the region of the second or third dorsal foramen. *A,* A lateral view of the model demonstrates kyphosis of the fracture, as well as translational deformity. Most transverse sacral fractures occur in the most kyphotic area of the sacrum, S2–S3. After an appropriate workup to delineate the direction of the fracture and the area of maximal sacral root compression, the patient is placed in the prone position with the hips flexed 45°. The incision runs from the inferior tip of the L4 spinous process to the region of S4. Although the sacrum is approached through a midline incision and the posterior aspect is stripped subperiosteally, exposure is often insufficient. Detaching the inferior-most attachment of the paraspinal musculature from the sacrum at S3–S4 can broaden the exposure. *B,* The first step in reduction is to expose the complete fracture line and then perform a laminectomy approximately 2.5 cm in length and centered on the fracture line to clearly visualize the neural elements. It should be carried far enough laterally to extend out into the dorsal foramen. *C,* After the nerve roots are clearly delineated, the fracture line is opened on both sides of the sacrum, first with a small curette and then with a small Cobb elevator inserted gently in each side to pry apart the impacted fracture. By using the elevators to gently lever the fracture, the kyphosis and translation can be at least partially reduced (*D*).

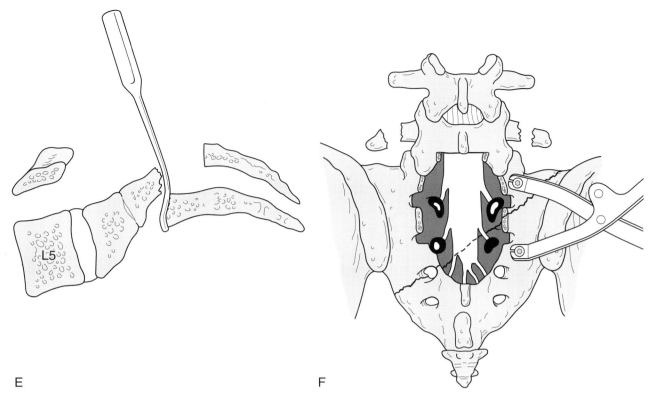

E   F

FIGURE **35–11** *Continued.* If the proximal fragment is posteriorly displaced *(E)*, the instrument should be placed under the ventral surface of the distal fragment. Separation of the fracture fragments and at least partial reduction are critical before plate fixation is begun. A 3.5- or 4.5-mm pelvic reconstruction plate is selected on the basis of hole spacing and the size of the sacrum. If anatomic positioning is achieved manually, the plate is contoured to directly match the contour of the posterior aspect of the sacrum; if the position is less than anatomic, the plate is slightly undercontoured. If the fracture is more oblique and shortened, a temporary screw can be placed in both the proximal and distal fragments and a distraction tool applied to achieve length while the final plate is being positioned. *F,* With the exception of the S1 segment, plate placement and screw starting points lie on a line along the dorsal foramen with the screw directed laterally into the residual pedicle. Two screws are placed at S1, the more proximal screw directed laterally from the dimple at the base of the S1 facet.

Illustration continued on following page

involvement of the L5–S1 facet on either side. If the fracture is more oblique, exposure to the L4 level is necessary to include the L5 pedicle in the instrumentation. Removing the distal attachment of the paraspinous musculature subperiosteally from the posterior aspect of the sacrum at its terminal position at S3 to S4 can facilitate exposure of the posterior aspect of the sacrum.

A sacral laminectomy is performed from S1 to S4 to expose the sacral roots (see Fig. 35–11), with dissection continued laterally to fully delineate the transverse fracture. The laminectomy is initiated at the proximal end of the sacrum, where the canal is larger, and directed distally until the fracture line is encountered. The decompression is extended laterally to identify the takeoff of the ventral roots and the bone of the vestigial pedicles. Although complete decompression is not necessary at this point, the fracture line may be entered with a curette laterally and the sacral canal partially undercut to remove the bone at the apical point of the kyphosis and prevent impingement of the roots after reduction (see Fig. 35–11). The fracture is disimpacted by opening the fracture line with Cobb elevators gently placed on both sides of the fracture or by using a distraction device temporarily placed proximal

and distal to the fracture to distract it. If the proximal fragment lies posteriorly, the Cobb elevator can be gently placed within the fracture lines laterally anterior to the ventral surface of the distal fragment to lever it posteriorly and correct the kyphosis. If the fracture is easily reduced by levering it with the Cobb elevators, the spine is prepared for fixation. In cases in which the fracture line passes through the canal at an oblique angle (20° to 40°), the sacrum may become foreshortened by sliding obliquely. Length can be regained by using a pelvic reduction clamp placed on two unicortical screws.

If the fracture does not involve the L5–S1 articulation, screw placement is begun in the area of the pedicles at each level from S1 to S4. The most proximal screw at the medial border of the S1 facet is directed 30° medially into the body of S1. The next screw just proximal to the first dorsal foramen is directed laterally at about 40° into the sacral ala. This technique allows two screws to be placed in S1, and a screw is then placed in each subsequent pedicle running parallel to the sacroiliac joint. At a point midway between each dorsal foramen and in a line just medial to the level of the foramen, a 2-mm drill bit is angled laterally between 30° and 45°, and a hole is drilled through both cortices. Each hole is depth gauged and tapped for the use of a cancellous screw. A malleable titanium or stainless steel plate (pelvic reconstruction plate) of correct length (about 40 mm in S1 and decreasing sequentially to 20 mm at S4) is then selected and its holes spaced to accommodate the predrilled holes when the sacral fracture is in the reduced position.

The fracture is reduced by gentle leverage with the Cobb elevators, and both plates are placed simultaneously. *Care should be taken to not use the plates to achieve fracture reduction!!* All screws are placed on both sides and tightened down sequentially (see Fig. 35–11). In patients with comminution, screws may be placed in the sacroiliac joint and posterior of the ilium or extended up to the L5 pedicle for more proximal involvement or for involvement of the L5–S1 articulation. At this point, if compression of the ventral surface of the roots is still occurring after reduction of the angular deformity, excavation lateral to the canal at the level of the fracture should be performed. Such excavation allows the bone to be removed with a pituitary rongeur from under the canal. The bone should not be tamped down but, instead, removed to ascertain that the decompression is complete. Bone grafting of the

fracture is not necessary in the body of the sacrum; however, if the construct is extended to L5, routine posterolateral graft application is indicated. The paraspinous musculature is then reapproximated over a drain. The patient is immobilized in a lumbosacral orthosis with the leg included for 3 months. Recovery of bowel and bladder function may be slow and take up to 12 to 18 months.

COMPLICATIONS

Few complications specific to these injuries are encountered. However, failure of recognition is the most common problem in both insufficiency fractures and traumatic injuries. In an elderly patient with an insidious onset of back pain and disability, the use of a bone scan or MRI will usually lead to the diagnosis. In a patient with acute trauma, careful evaluation of sphincter function is critical along with MRI if the neurologic assessment is not consistent in a patient with a history conducive to such an injury.

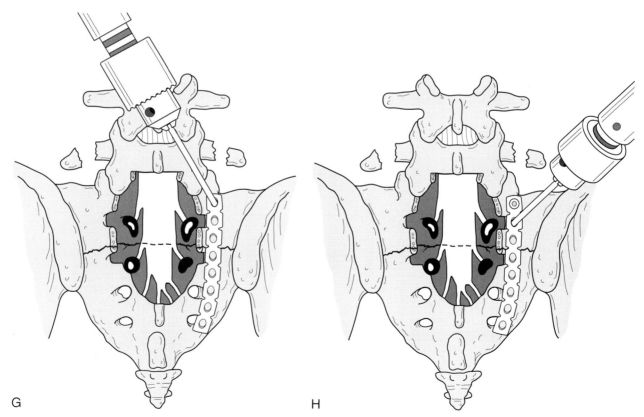

G   **H**

FIGURE 35–11 *Continued. G,* A bicortical hole is drilled and tapped, and then the screw inserted. *H,* The second screw in S1 is inserted and directed medially into the body. The screw hole is likewise tapped and the screw inserted either to the full depth of the body or bicortically.

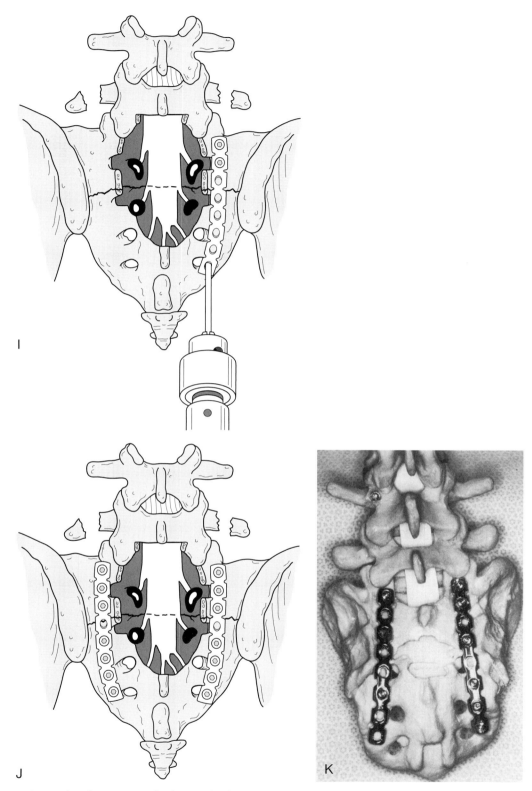

FIGURE 35–11 *Continued. I,* The starting site for the most distal screw is selected. A minimum of two and preferably three points of fixation need to be present distal to the fracture line. These screws are angled obliquely parallel to the sacroiliac joint for maximal length and fixation. An attempt should be made to place pairs of adjacent screws so that they converge in the caudocephalad direction for maximal pull-out strength. The distal-most screws rarely exceed 20 mm, whereas the more proximal screws average between 35 and 45 mm. The screw is tightened into position but is not used to achieve fracture reduction. If the reduction is not complete and the plate is completely in contact with the posterior aspect of the sacrum, further manual reduction is done before final tightening of all screws. Screws are then placed in every hole that does not fall directly over a dorsal foramen (*J*). The contralateral side is plated in a similar fashion (*K*).

SUMMARY
....

Recognition of the importance of sacral fractures both in patients with pelvic injuries and in patients with isolated traumatic fractures or insufficiency fractures is a relatively late occurrence. With increased awareness has come improved recognition of the natural history and the development of improved treatment methodologies.

REFERENCES

1. Akbarnia, B.A.; Moskowicz, A.; Merenda, J.T.; et al. Surgical Treatment of Thoracic Spine Fractures with Cotrel-Dubousset Instrumentation. Poster exhibit presented at the Scoliosis Research Society, Amsterdam, September 1989.
2. Akbarnia, B.A.; Crandall, D.G; Burkus, K; et al. Use of long rods and a short arthrodesis for burst fractures of the thoracolumbar spine. J Bone Joint Surg Am 76:1629–1635, 1994.
3. Albert, T.J.; Levine, M.J.; An, H.S. Concomitant noncontiguous thoracolumbar and sacral fractures. Spine 18:1285–1291, 1994.
4. An, H.S.; Vaccaro, A.; Cotler, J.M.; et al. Low lumbar burst fractures. Comparison among body cast, Harrington rod, Luque rod, and Steffee plate. Spine 16(Suppl):440–444, 1991.
5. An, H.S.; Simpson, J.M.; Ebraheim, N.A.; et al. Low lumbar burst fractures: Comparison between conservative and surgical treatments. Orthopedics 15:367–373, 1992.
6. Babayev, M.; Lachmann, E.; Nagler, W. The controversy surrounding sacral insufficiency fractures: To ambulate or not to ambulate? Am J Phys Med Rehabil 79:404–409, 2000.
7. Bonin, J.G. Sacral fractures and injuries to the cauda equina. J Bone Joint Surg Br 27:113–127, 1945.
8. Brahme, S.K.; Cervilla, V.; Vint, V.; et al. Magnetic resonance appearance of sacral insufficiency fractures. Skeletal Radiol 19:489–493, 1990.
9. Bucknill, T.M.; Blackburn, J.S. Fracture dislocations of the sacrum. Report of three cases. J Bone Joint Surg Br 58:467–470, 1976.
10. Byrnes, D.P; Russo, G.L.; Ducker, T.B.; Cowley, R.A. Sacral fractures and neurologic damage: Report of two cases. J Neurosurg 47:459–462, 1977.
11. Carl, A.L.; Blair, B. Unilateral lumbosacral facet fracture dislocation. Spine 16:218–221, 1991.
12. Chen, C.K.; Liang, H.L.; Lui P.H.; et al. Imaging diagnosis of insufficiency fracture of the sacrum. Chin Med J 62:591–597, 1999.
13. Connolly, P.J.; Esses, S.I.; Heggeness, M.H. Unilateral facet dislocation of the lumbosacral junction. Spine 17:1244–1248, 1992.
14. Court-Brown, C.M.; Gertzbein, S.D. The management of burst fractures of the fifth lumbar vertebra. Spine 12:308–312, 1987.
15. Dasgupta, B.; Shah, N.; Brown, H.; et al. Sacral inefficiency fractures: An unsuspected cause of low back pain. Br J Rheumatol 37:789–793, 1998.
16. De Das, S.; McCreath, S.W. Lumbosacral fracture dislocations: A report of four cases. J Bone Joint Surg Br 63:58–60, 1981.
17. Denis, F. The three column spine and its significance in the classification of acute thoracolumbar spinal injuries. Spine 8:817–831, 1983.
18. Denis, F; Davis, S.; Comfort, T. Sacral fractures; An important problem. Retrospective analysis of 236 cases. Clin Orthop 227:67–81, 1988.
19. Dewey, P.; Browne, P.S.H. Fracture and dislocation of the lumbosacral spine with cauda equina lesion. J Bone Joint Surg Br 50:635–638, 1968.
20. Ebraheim, N.A.; Savolaine, E.R.; Shapiro, P.; et al. Unilateral lumbosacral facet joint dislocation associated with vertical shear sacral fracture. Case report. J Orthop Trauma 5:498–503, 1991.
21. Elliot, H.C. Cross sectional diameters and areas of human spinal cord. Anat Rec 93:287–293, 1945.
22. Fardon, D.F. Displaced fracture of the lumbosacral spine with delayed cauda equina deficit. Clin Orthop 120:155–158, 1976.
23. Fardon, D.F. Displaced transverse fracture of the sacrum with nerve root injury: Report of case with successful operative management. J Trauma 19:119–122, 1979.
24. Finiels, H.; Finiels, P.J.; Jacquot, J.M.; Strubel, D. Fractures du sacrum par insuffisance osseuse meta-analysis de 508 cas. Presse Med 26:1568–1573, 1997.
25. Fountain, S.S.; Hamilton, R.D.; Jameson, R.M. Transverse fractures of the sacrum. A report of six cases. J Bone Joint Surg Am 59:486–489, 1977.
26. Frederickson, B.E.; Yuan, H.A.; Miller, H.E. Treatment of painful longstanding displaced fracture dislocations of the sacrum. A case report. Clin Orthop 166:93–95, 1982.
27. Frederickson, B.E.; Yuan, H.A.; Miller, H.E. Burst fractures of the fifth lumbar vertebra. J Bone Joint Surg Am 64:1088–1094, 1982.
28. Furey, W.W. Fractures of the pelvis with special reference to associated fractures of the sacrum. J Bone Joint Surg 47:89–96, 1942.
29. Gellad, F.E.; Levine, A.M.; Joslyn, J.N.; et al. Pure thoracolumbar facet dislocation: Clinical features and CT appearance. Radiology 161:505–508, 1986.
30. Gibbons, K.J.; Soloniuk, D.S.; Razack, N. Neurologic injury and patterns of sacral fractures. J Neurosurg 72:889–893, 1991.
31. Gotis-Graham, I.; McGuigan, L.; Diamond, T.; et al. Sacral insufficiency fractures in the elderly. J Bone Joint Surg Br 76:882–886, 1994.
32. Grangier, C.; Garcia, J.; Howarth, N.R.; et al. Role of MRI in the diagnosis of insufficiency fractures of the sacrum and acetabular roof. Skeletal Radiol 26:517–524, 1997.
33. Grasland, A.; Pouchot, J.; Mathieu, A.; et al. Sacral insufficiency fractures: An easily overlooked cause of back pain in elderly women. Arch Intern Med 156:668–674, 1996.
34. Guterberg, B. Effects of major resection of the sacrum. Acta Orthop Scand 162(Suppl):1–18, 1976.
35. Hanely, E.N.; Know, B.D.; Moossy, J.J. Traumatic lumbopelvic spondyloptosis. J Bone Joint Surg Am 75:1695–1698, 1993.
36. Herron, L.D.; Williams, R.C. Fracture dislocation of the lumbosacral spine: Report of a case and review of the literature. Clin Orthop 186:205–211, 1984.
37. Holdsworth, F.W.; Hardy, A. Early treatment of paraplegia from fractures of the thoracolumbar spine. J Bone Joint Surg Br 35:540–550, 1953.
38. Jacquot, J.M.; Finiels, H.; Fardjad, S.; et al. Neurologic complications in insufficiency fractures of the sacrum. Rev Rhum Engl Ed 66:109–114, 1999.
39. Kaehr, D.M; Anderson, P.A.; Mayo, K.; et al. Classification of sacral features based on CT imaging. J Orthop Trauma 3:163, 1989.
40. Knight, R.Q.; Stornelli, D.P; Chan, D.P.K.; et al. Comparison of operative versus nonoperative treatment of lumbar burst fractures. Clin Orthop 293:112–121, 1993.
41. Krag, M.H.; Weaver, D.L.; Beynnon, B.D.; Haugh, B.D. Morphometry of the thoracic and lumbar spine related to the transpedicular screw placement for surgical spinal fixation. Spine 13:27–32, 1988.
42. Kramer, K; Levine, A.M. Unilateral facet dislocation of the lumbosacral junction. J Bone Joint Surg Am 71:1258–1261, 1989.
43. Levine, A.M. Fixation of fractures of the sacrum. Operative Techn Orthop 7:221–231, 1997.
44. Levine, A.M.; Edwards, C.C. Low lumbar burst fractures. Reduction and stabilization using the modular spine fixation system. Orthopedics 11:1427–1432, 1988.
45. Levine, A.M.; Bosse, M.; Edwards, C.C. Bilateral facet dislocations in the thoracolumbar spine. Spine 13:630–640, 1988.
46. Lewis, J.; McKibbin, B. The treatment of unstable fracture-dislocations of the thoracolumbar spine accompanied by paraplegia. J Bone Joint Surg Br 56:603–612, 1974.
47. Louis, R. Fusion of the lumbar and sacral spine by internal fixation with screw plates. Clin Orthop 203:18–33, 1986.
48. McAfee, P.C.; Yuan, H.A.; Frederickson, B.E.; et al. The value of computed tomography in thoracolumbar fractures. An analysis of one hundred consecutive cases and a new classification. J Bone Joint Surg Am 65:461–473, 1983.
49. Meyer, T.L.; Wilkberger, G. Displaced sacral fractures. Am J Orthop 4:187, 1962.
50. Mirkovic, M.A.; Abitbol, J.J; Steinman, J.; et al. Anatomic consideration for sacral screw placement. Spine 16(Suppl):289–294, 1991.
51. Montana, M.A.; Richardson, M.L.; Kilcoyne, R.F; et al. CT of sacral injury. Radiology 161:499–503, 1986.
52. Moreno, A.; Clemente, J.; Crespo C.; et al. Pelvic insufficiency fractures in patients with pelvic irradiation. Int J Radiat Oncol Biol Phys 44:60–66, 1999.

53. Morris, B.D. Unilateral dislocation of a lumbosacral facet. A case report. J Bone Joint Surg Am 63:164–165, 1981.

54. Newhouse, K.E.; Elkhoury, G.; Buckwalter, J. Occult sacral fractures in osteopenic patients. J Bone Joint Surg Am 74:1472–1477, 1992.

55. Nork, S.E.; Jones, C.B; Harding, S.P.; et al. Percutaneous stabilization of U-shaped sacral fractures using iliosacral screws: Technique and early results. J Orthop Trauma 15:238–246, 2001.

56. O'Callaghan, J.P.; Ulrich, C.G.; Yuan, H.A.; et al. CT of facet distraction in flexion injuries of the thoracolumbar spine: The "naked" facet. AJNR Am J Neuroradiol 1:97–102, 1980.

57. Peh, W.C.G.; Ho, W.Y. Insufficiency fractures of the sacrum and os pubis. Br J Hosp Med 54:15–19, 1995.

58. Peh, W.C.G.; Khong, P.L.; Ho, W.Y.; et al. Sacral insufficiency fractures: Spectrum of radiological features. Clin Imaging 19:92–101, 1995.

59. Peh, W.C.G.; Ooi, G.C. Vacuum phenomena in the sacroiliac joints and in association with sacral insufficiency fractures. Spine 22:2005–2008, 1997.

60. Peh, W.C.G. Intrafracture fluid: A new diagnostic sign of insufficiency fractures of the sacrum and ilium. Br J Radiol 73:895–898, 2000.

61. Phelan, S.T.; Jones, D.A.; Bishay, M. Conservative management of transverse fractures of the sacrum with neurological features. J Bone Joint Surg Br 73:969–971, 1991.

62. Pohlemann, T.; Gansslen, A.; Tscherne, H. [The problem of sacral fractures. Clinical analysis of 377 cases] [German]. Orthopade 21:400–412, 1992.

63. Purser, D.W. Displaced fracture of the sacrum. Report of a case. J Bone Joint Surg Br 51:346–347, 1969.

64. Rauschning, W. Correlative multi-planar computed tomographic anatomy of the normal spine. In: Post, J.D., ed. Computed Tomography of the Spine. Baltimore, Williams & Wilkins, 1984, pp. 20–67.

65. Routt, M.L.C.; Simonian, P.T. Closed reduction and percutaneous skeletal fixation of sacral fractures. Clin Orthop 329:121–128, 1996.

66. Routt, M.L.C.; Simonian, P.T.; Agnew, S.G.; Mann, F.A. Radiographic recognition of the sacral alar slope for optimal placement of iliosacral screws: A cadaveric and clinical study. J Orthop Trauma 10:171–177, 1996.

67. Roy-Camille, R.; Salliant, G.; Mazel, C. Plating of thoracic, thoracolumbar and lumbar injuries with pedicle plates. Orthop Clin North Am 17:147–159, 1986.

68. Roy-Camille, R.; Saillant, G.; Gagna, G.; et al. Transverse fracture of the upper sacrum: Suicidal jumper's fracture. Spine 10:838–845, 1985.

69. Sabiston, C.P.; Wing, P.C. Classification and neurologic implications. J Trauma 26:1113–1115, 1986.

70. Saillant, G. Etude anatomique des pedicles, vertebreau, application chirurgicales. Rev Chir Orthop Traumatol 62:582–586, 1995.

71. Samberg, L.C. Fracture dislocation of the lumbosacral spine: A case report. J Bone Joint Surg Am 57:1007–1008, 1975.

72. Saraux, A.; Valls, I.; Guedes, C.; et al. Insufficiency fractures of the sacrum in elderly subjects. Rev Rhum Engl Ed 62:582–586, 1995.

73. Schmidek, H.H.; Smith, D.A.; Kristiansen, T.K. Sacral fractures. Neurosurgery 15:735–746, 1984.

74. Singh, H.; Rao, V.S.; Mangla, R.; Laheri, V.J. Traumatic transverse fracture of sacrum with cauda equina injury: A case report and review of literature. J Postgrad Med Vol 44:14–15, 1998.

75. Stabler, A.; Steiner, W.; Kohz, P.; et al. Time-dependent changes of insufficiency fractures of the sacrum: Intraosseous vacuum phenomenon as an early sign. Eur Radiol 6:655–657, 1996.

76. Stagnara, P.; De Mauroy, J.C.; Dran, G.; et al. Reciprocal angulation of vertebral bodies in a sagittal plane: Approach to references for the evaluation of kyphosis and lordosis. Spine 7:335–342, 1982.

77. Stephens, G.C.; Devito, D.P.; McNamara, M.J. Segmental fixation of lumbar burst fractures with Cotrel-Dubousset instrumentation. J Spinal Disord 5:344–348, 1992.

78. Strange-Vognsen, H.H.; Kiar, T.; Tondevoid, E. The Cotrel-Dubousset instrumentation for unstable sacral fractures. Acta Orthop Scand 65:219–220, 1994.

79. Taguchi, T.; Kawai, S.; Kaneko, K.; Yugue, D. Operative management of displaced fractures of the sacrum. J Orthop Sci 4:347–352, 1999.

80. Templeman, D.; Goulet, J.; Duwelius, P.J.; et al. Internal fixation of displaced fractures of the sacrum. Clin Orthop 329:180–185, 1996.

81. Van Savage, J.G.; Dahners, L.E.; Renner, J.B.; et al. Fracture dislocation of the lumbosacral spine: Case report and review of the literature. J Trauma 33:779–784, 1992.

82. Verhaegen, M.J.A.; Sauter, A.J.M. Insufficiency fractures, an often unrecognized diagnosis. Arch Orthop Trauma Surg 119:115–116, 1999.

83. Weber, M.; Hasier, P.; Gerber, H. Insufficiency fractures of the sacrum: Twenty cases and review of the literature. Spine 18:2507–2512, 1993.

84. Whitesides, T.E. Traumatic kyphosis of the thoracolumbar spine. Clin Orthop 128:79–92, 1977.

85. Wiesel, S.W.; Zeide, M.S.; Terry, R.L. Longitudinal fractures of the sacrum: Case report. J Trauma 19:70–71, 1979.

86. Winter, R.B. Congenital Deformities of the Spine. New York, Thieme-Stratton, 1983.

87. Zindrick, M.R.; Wiltsie, L.L.; Doornik, A.; et al. Analysis of the morphometric characteristics of the thoracic and lumbar pedicles. Spine 12:160–166, 1987.

88. Zoltan, J.D.; Giluls, L.A.; Murphy, W.A. Unilateral facet dislocation between the fifth lumbar and first sacral vertebrae. J Bone Joint Surg Am 61:767–769, 1979.

CHAPTER 36

Pelvic Ring Disruptions

James F. Kellam, M.D., F.R.C.S.(C.)
Keith Mayo, M.D.

The pelvis is the key link between the axial skeleton and the major weight-bearing locomotive structures, the lower extremities. The forces resulting from activities such as sitting and ambulating are transferred through its bony structure to the spine. Major structures of the vascular, neurologic, genitourinary, and gastrointestinal systems pass through or across its ring. Because the extensive disruption that results from significant injuries to this ring has important consequences for these associated structures, the potential for death and disability is high. Orthopaedic surgeons treating any multiply injured patient must understand and be prepared to deal with the consequences of major pelvic disruption.*

In addition, even after treatment of the pelvic injury, residual deformity can create significant problems in functional recovery.[44, 60] Pain has been reported as a common problem after major pelvic disruptions. Holds-worth[46] reported that 15 of 27 patients with sacroiliac joint dislocations were unable to return to work. His study concluded that displacement of the sacroiliac joint was a significant cause of this disability. Peltier[81] emphasized the posterior weight-bearing capacity of the sacroiliac area and its importance in mortality and morbidity from multiple injuries. Raf,[87] Dunn and Morris,[24] and Huittinen and Slatis[47] have all confirmed that displacement through the weight-bearing arch of the pelvis, particularly if the sacroiliac joint is involved, can lead to long-term problems of pain and inability to pursue a functional lifestyle.

A review by Tile[112] showed a significant difference between fractures that were classified as stable and those that were classified as unstable. The unstable group had a significant increase over the stable group in the incidence of pain in the posterior sacroiliac region. Leg length discrepancy indicating a malunion was significantly higher in the unstable group. Even nonunion of the pelvis was a problem, particularly in injuries that involved the sacroiliac joint. Patients in the series who had open anatomic

reduction and stabilization of the pelvic ring appeared to do better. This subdivision of pelvic fractures into two groups—stable and unstable—seems to be validated by other studies.[11, 20, 28] Stable fractures usually do well and cause minimal disability. Patients with unstable fractures have more significant problems, such as a higher mortality rate[9, 21, 30, 66] and a higher rate of dysfunction secondary to pain, malunion, and occasionally, nonunion.[43, 45] To minimize these problems, treatment of pelvic injuries should be based on an understanding of the anatomy and biomechanics of the pelvis, with particular regard to stability. These principles are applied by using a functional description of the injury so that the right treatment is used for the right injury. The goal is to restore the displaced pelvic ring to as close an anatomic position as possible with the minimum of complications.

ANATOMY

The pelvis is a ring structure made up of three bones: the sacrum and two innominate bones. The innominate bone is formed from the fusion of three ossification centers: the ilium, the ischium, and the pubis (Fig. 36–1). These three centers coalesce at the triradiate cartilage of the acetabulum and, when fused, form the complete innominate bone. The innominate bones join the sacrum posteriorly at the two sacroiliac joints. Anteriorly, they are joined to one another at the pubic symphysis.

The three bones and three joints composing the pelvic ring have no inherent stability without vital ligamentous structures.[106] The strongest and most important ligamentous structures occur in the posterior aspect of the pelvis. These ligaments connect the sacrum to the innominate bones. The stability provided by the posterior ligaments must withstand the forces of weight bearing transmitted across the sacroiliac joints from the lower extremities to the spine. The symphysis acts as a strut during weight bearing to maintain the structure of the pelvic ring. The posterior

*See references 7, 21, 30, 35, 39, 60, 68, 71, 73, 76, 85, 86, 89, 90, 92, 104, 105.

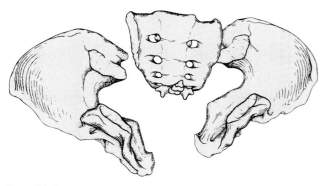

FIGURE 36–1. The bony architecture of the pelvis consists of the sacrum and the two innominate bones. Without their ligamentous attachments, these bones provide no inherent stability.

sacroiliac ligaments are divided into two components: short and long. The short posterior ligaments are oblique and run from the posterior ridge of the sacrum to the posterior superior and posterior inferior spines of the ilium. The long posterior ligaments are longitudinal fibers that run from the lateral aspect of the sacrum to the posterior superior iliac spines and merge with the sacrotuberous ligament. The long ligaments cover the short ligaments.

Anteriorly, the sacroiliac joint is covered by a flat, strong ligamentous structure that runs from the ilium to the sacrum. This structure provides some stability, but less than that provided by the posterior ligaments (Fig. 36–2).

The sacroiliac joint is made up of two parts. The inferior portion consists of the articular surface of the joint; the upper, more dorsal portion, between the posterior tuberosity of the ilium and the sacrum, contains the fibrous or ligamentous parts of the joint (interosseous ligaments). The anterior portion of this synovial joint is covered with articular cartilage on the sacral side and fibrocartilage on the iliac side. The joint itself has a small ridge on the sacral

side that provides minimal stability. In the upright position, the weight of the body pushes the sacrum down between the iliac wings and causes approximately 5° dorsoventral rotation.[79] The innominate bones move backward and downward as the pubic rami swing upward.[60] Precise reduction and reestablishment of the morphology of the sacroiliac joint may not be as important as for an extremity joint because tight contact between the articular surfaces never occurs in normal function[119] (Fig. 36–3).

The symphysis pubis consists of two opposed surfaces of hyaline cartilage. These surfaces are covered with fibrocartilage and surrounded by a thick band of fibrous tissue. The symphysis is reinforced inferiorly by muscle insertions and the arcuate ligament. The thickest portion of this fibrous joint is usually superior and anterior.

In addition to the interosseous ligaments that span these joints, connecting ligaments join various portions of the pelvic ring. The sacrotuberous ligament is a strong band running from the posterolateral aspect of the sacrum and the dorsal aspect of the posterior iliac spine to the ischial tuberosity. Its medial border thickens to form a falciform tendon that blends with the obturator membrane at the ischial tuberosity. It also merges into the posterior origin of the gluteus maximus. This ligament, in association with its ipsilateral posterior sacroiliac ligaments, is especially important in maintaining vertical stability of the pelvis.

The sacrospinous ligament is triangular. It runs from the lateral margins of the sacrum and coccyx and the sacrotuberous ligament to insert on the ischial spine. It divides the posterior column of the pelvis into the greater and lesser sciatic notches. The sacrospinous ligament may be important in maintaining rotational control of the pelvis if the posterior sacroiliac ligaments are intact (see Fig. 36–2).

Several ligaments run from the spine to the pelvis. The iliolumbar ligaments secure the pelvis to the lumbar spine. They originate from the L4 and L5 transverse processes and insert on the posterior iliac crest. The lumbosacral

FIGURE 36–2. Ligamentous complexes of the pelvis. *A,* Posteriorly, the major ligaments noted in the region of the sacroiliac joint are the posterior sacroiliac ligaments, both long and short. These structures blend with the sacrospinous and the sacrotuberous ligaments. *B,* In cross section, the orientation of the very thick posterior interosseous sacroiliac ligaments can be noted.

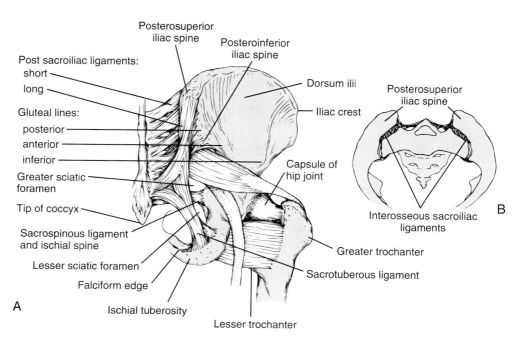

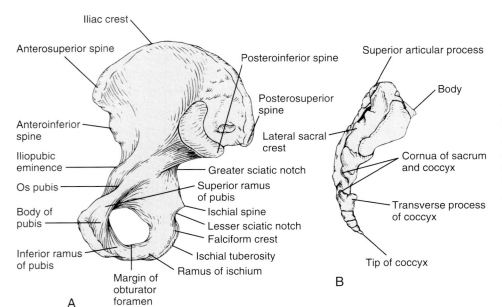

Iliac crest

Anterosuperior spine

Posteroinferior spine

Posterosuperior spine

Anteroinferior spine

Lateral sacral crest

Iliopubic eminence

Greater sciatic notch

Os pubis

Superior ramus of pubis

Body of pubis

Ischial spine

Lesser sciatic notch

Falciform crest

Inferior ramus of pubis

Ischial tuberosity

Ramus of ischium

Margin of obturator foramen

A

Superior articular process

Body

Cornua of sacrum and coccyx

Transverse process of coccyx

Tip of coccyx

B

FIGURE 36–3. The sacroiliac joint. *A,* Iliac side of the sacroiliac joint, as well as the remainder of the innominate bone and the important bony landmarks. *B,* Sacral side. The two portions of the sacroiliac joint can best be appreciated on these views. The articular surface of the sacroiliac joint on the sacrum has a ridge and is covered by articular cartilage. The posterior portion is filled with ligamentous structures.

ligaments run from the transverse process of L5 to the ala of the sacrum. They form a strong ridge anteriorly and abut the L5 root.

If its ligamentous structures are intact, the pelvis is a stable ring. The posterior sacroiliac ligaments consist of the lumbosacral and iliolumbar ligaments, and they form a posterior tension band for the pelvis. The transversely placed ligaments, including the short posterior sacroiliac and the anterior sacroiliac along with the iliolumbar and sacrospinous ligaments, resist rotational forces. The vertically placed ligaments, including the long posterior sacroiliac, sacrotuberous, and lateral lumbosacral ligaments, may resist vertical shear or vertical migration. Holographic analysis of pelvic stability has shown that removal of the sacrotuberous or sacrospinous ligaments, or both, has no effect on patterns of pelvic deformation. However, if the sacroiliac interosseous ligaments are excised, the sacrum becomes wedged deeply into the pelvis on erect loading.[119] These ligaments must act in unison to maintain pelvic stability.

The intact pelvis forms two major anatomic areas. The false pelvis and the true pelvis are divided by the pelvic brim, or the iliopectineal line, which runs from the sacral promontory along the junction between the ilium and the ischium onto the pubic ramus. No major muscular structures cross the pelvic brim. Above the brim, the false pelvis (greater pelvis) is contained by the sacral ala and the iliac wings. It forms part of the abdominal cavity. The inner false pelvic surface is covered by the iliopsoas muscle. The true pelvis (lesser pelvis) is below the brim, and its lateral wall consists of the pubis, ischium, and a small triangular portion of the ilium. It includes the obturator foramen, which is covered by muscles and membrane and opens superiorly and medially for passage of the obturator nerve and vessels. The obturator internus takes its origin from the membrane and curves out through the lesser sciatic notch to attach to the proximal end of the femur. The obturator internus tendon is an important structure

because it serves as a guide to access the posterior column (Fig. 36–4). The piriformis originates from the lateral aspect of the sacrum and is key to understanding the sciatic nerve. Commonly, the sciatic nerve leaves the pelvis beneath the piriformis and enters the greater sciatic notch. Occasionally, the peroneal division leaves through or above the piriformis (Fig. 36–5). The floor of the true pelvis consists of the coccyx, the coccygeal and levator ani muscles, and the urethra, rectum, and vagina, which pass through them.

The lumbosacral coccygeal plexus is made up of the anterior rami of T12 through S4, the most important of which are the L4 to S1 roots. The lumbar roots L4 and L5 enter the true pelvis from the false pelvis, whereas the sacral roots are part of the true pelvis. The L4 root runs between the L5 nerve and the sacroiliac joint and merges with L5 to form the lumbosacral trunk at the sacral promontory (12 mm from the joint line). The L5 root is 2 cm away from the sacroiliac joint as it exits the intervertebral foramen.[3] The sacral roots pass through the sacral foramen and join the plexus. Numerous branches extend to the major muscles within the pelvis. The superior gluteal and inferior gluteal nerves leave ventral to the piriformis and exit the pelvis through the greater sciatic notch.

Major blood vessels lie on the inner wall of the pelvis. The median sacral artery is situated on the anterior aspect of the midline of the sacrum. The superior rectal artery is a major branch lying midline and posterior. The common iliac divides and gives off the internal iliac, which runs over the pelvic brim. A branch of the internal iliac, the superior gluteal artery, crosses over the anteroinferior portion of the sacroiliac joint to exit the greater sciatic notch. As it sweeps around the notch, it lies directly on bone. The external iliac artery exits the pelvis anteriorly over the pelvic brim (pubic ramus). These arteries and associated veins can all be injured during pelvic disruption (Fig. 36–6).

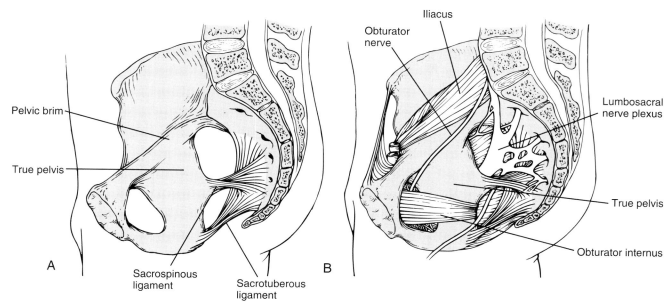

FIGURE 36–4. Internal aspect of the pelvis. *A,* The inner aspect of the pelvis consists of the true pelvis, which is below the pelvic brim or iliopectineal line, and the false pelvis above it. The sacrotuberous and sacrospinous ligaments are attached to their appropriate structures and form the basis of the pelvic floor. *B,* The major structures in the inner aspect of the pelvis are the lumbosacral plexus, which originates from the L5 and the sacral roots and leaves the pelvis through the greater sciatic notch as the sciatic nerve, and the superior gluteal artery. The obturator internus originates from the obturator membrane and loops out through the lesser sciatic notch. Note that no muscles cross the pelvic brim.

The major components of the genitourinary system involved in pelvic trauma are the bladder and urethra. The bladder is situated superior to the pelvic floor (i.e., coccygeal and levator ani muscles). These muscles arise in continuity from the ischial spines, obturator membrane, and pubis and insert into the coccyx and anal coccygeal raphe. They form a musculature diaphragm with a gap anteriorly through which pass the urethra, vagina, rectum,

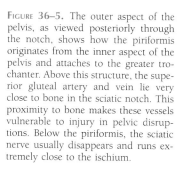

FIGURE 36–5. The outer aspect of the pelvis, as viewed posteriorly through the notch, shows how the piriformis originates from the inner aspect of the pelvis and attaches to the greater trochanter. Above this structure, the superior gluteal artery and vein lie very close to bone in the sciatic notch. This proximity to bone makes these vessels vulnerable to injury in pelvic disruptions. Below the piriformis, the sciatic nerve usually disappears and runs extremely close to the ischium.

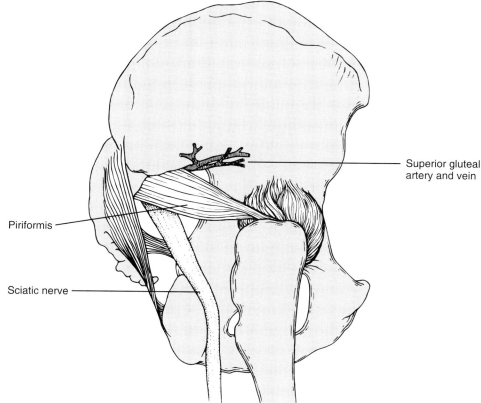

and support ligaments. The fascia of the pelvic floor is loose and mobile. In males, the prostate lies between the bladder and pelvic floor and is invested by a dense fascial membrane. The urethra passes through the prostate and exits below the pelvic floor. Associated with passage of the urethra through the urogenital diaphragm are pudendal arteries and veins, the pudendal nerve (S2–S4), and the autonomic nerves of the pelvis (S2–S4), which are all responsible for the erectile mechanism in males. The junction between the prostate and the pelvic floor is strong, as is the membranous urethra. The weak link in this area is the urethra below the pelvic diaphragm in its bulbous portion. Colapinto has shown that when the bladder is pulled forcefully, the urethra ruptures in its bulbous portion, which is the most common site of urethral rupture below the pelvic floor.[14] Occasionally, the membranous portion of the urethra ruptures at the upper surface of the pelvic floor. In females, the urethral injury is near the bladder neck. Urinary continence is dependent on the external (striated muscle) sphincter at the membranous urethra (midurethra in females) and the bladder neck (smooth muscle) in both males and females.

An understanding of pelvic anatomy will help orthopaedic surgeons maintain a high degree of suspicion for recognizing retroperitoneal bleeding, as well as injuries involving the genitourinary or gastrointestinal systems.

PELVIC STABILITY

A stable pelvic injury can be defined as one that can withstand normal physiologic forces without abnormal deformation. Tile and Hearn,[113] using a physiologic mechanical testing system, showed that with sitting or standing, the symphysis is in tension and the posterior complex is compressed. In single stance, the symphysis is compressed and the posterior complex is distracted. For this action to occur, the pelvic ring must maintain its anatomic integrity through its ligamentous and bony components.[113]

Sequential sectioning of the ligaments of the pelvis can help define the relative value of individual components of the entire spectrum of pelvic stability.[113] If only the symphysis is sectioned, mechanical testing of the pelvis reveals a symphyseal diastasis no greater than 2.5 cm. Further opening is inhibited by the sacrospinous and anterior sacroiliac ligaments. If the symphysis and anterior sacroiliac ligaments are sectioned, more than 2.5 cm of external rotation (diastasis) is noted (Fig. 36–7). Abutment of the posterior iliac spines against the sacrum stops the pelvis from any further rotation. These investigators noted that absolute vertical instability or posterior displacement did not occur because the posterior longitudinal ligaments and sacrotuberous ligaments remained intact. Ghanayem and colleagues have demonstrated the secondary effect of the abdominal muscles on maintaining rotational stability.[38] In this situation, the pelvis is rotationally unstable but vertically stable and can therefore be restored to its anatomic integrity by use of the intact posterior osseous ligamentous hinge.

With sectioning of the symphysis, sacrospinous, sacrotuberous, and posterior sacroiliac ligaments, the pelvis becomes vertically, posteriorly, and rotationally unstable (Fig. 36–8). However, if the symphysis remains intact while the posterior ligaments are sectioned, little posterior instability occurs because the posterior bony complex is compressed.[113] It must be kept in mind that some bone injuries produce instability equivalent to that caused by disruption of the posterior ligaments. Fractures through the iliac wing bypass the ligamentous structures and,

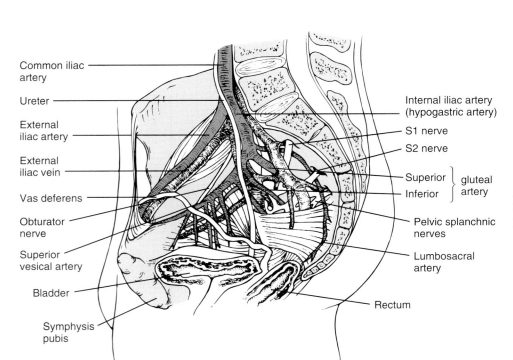

Common iliac artery
Ureter
External iliac artery
External iliac vein
Vas deferens
Obturator nerve
Superior vesical artery
Bladder
Symphysis pubis

Internal iliac artery (hypogastric artery)
S1 nerve
S2 nerve
Superior ⎫ gluteal
Inferior ⎭ artery
Pelvic splanchnic nerves
Lumbosacral artery
Rectum

FIGURE 36–6. Internal aspect of the pelvis showing the great vessels and the lumbosacral plexus, as well as the pelvic floor, bladder, and rectum.

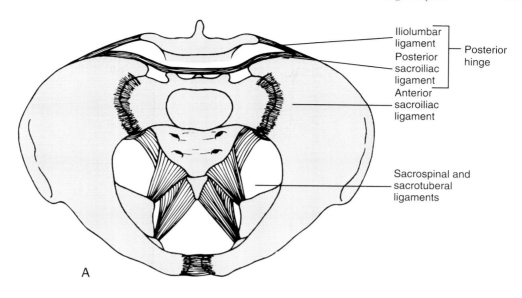

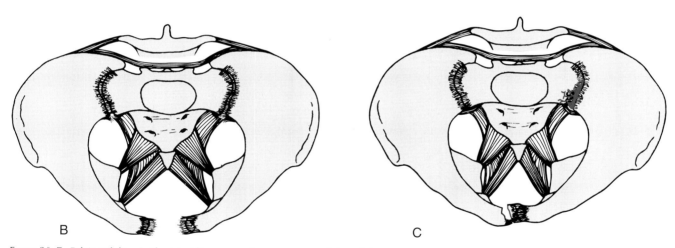

FIGURE 36–7. Pelvic stability. *A,* The intact ligamentous bony structures of the pelvis maintain its integrity with regard to stability. The posterior hinge, which consists of the posterior sacroiliac ligaments and the iliolumbar ligaments, is imperative for maintaining vertical stability. The sacrospinous ligament prevents rotation, and the sacrotuberous ligament prevents vertical migration. As long as those ligaments, the anterior sacroiliac ligament, and the symphysis are intact, the pelvis will remain stable. If, however, the anterior symphysis is separated or the sacrum is crushed posteriorly, as seen in *B* and *C,* the posterior hinge remains intact and the pelvis is usually stable vertically. The sacrospinous ligaments are intact, and rotatory abnormalities are thus prevented.

hence, are unstable unless they are impacted. A shear fracture, the result of violent force perpendicular to the bony trabeculae of the posterior ring, and fracture-dislocation of the sacroiliac joint are other injuries that can produce equivalent degrees of instability (Fig. 36–9).

PATHOMECHANICS AND MECHANISMS OF PELVIC DISRUPTION

Anteroposterior Force Pattern

Pelvic disruptions can be caused by four different force patterns. The first is the anteroposterior (AP) force pattern, which causes external rotation of the hemipelvis. As a result of a posteriorly directed force, the pelvis springs open and hinges on the intact posterior ligaments. This force ruptures the pelvic floor and anterior sacroiliac ligaments. No vertical instability occurs because the posterior ligamentous complex is intact.

Lateral Compression Force Pattern

The most common force pattern of pelvic fractures is lateral compression. The lateral compression force is commonly directed to the outer aspect of the iliac wing or pelvis and usually is parallel to the trabeculae of the sacrum. This injury creates compression or impaction of the cancellous bone of the sacrum. Depending on the area

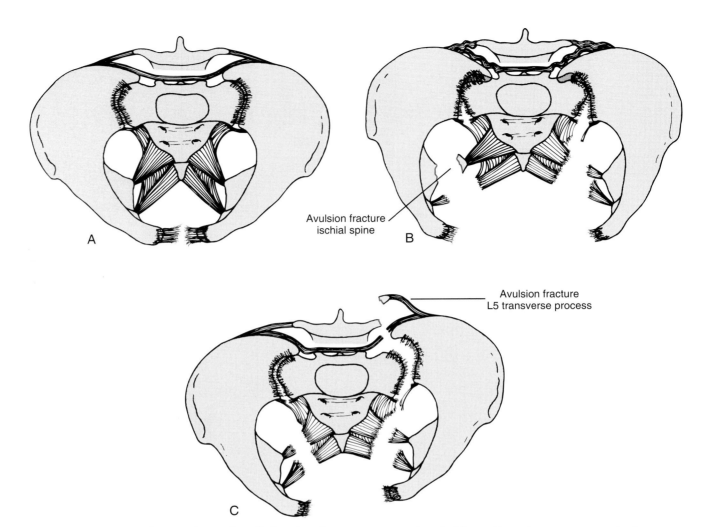

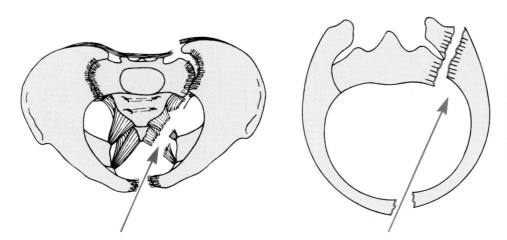

FIGURE 36–8. *A,* Division of the symphysis pubis will allow the pelvis to open to approximately 2.5 cm with no damage to any posterior ligamentous structures. *B,* Division of the anterior sacroiliac and sacrospinous ligaments, either by direct division of their fibers *(right)* or by avulsion of the tip of the ischial spine *(left),* will allow the pelvis to rotate externally until the posterior superior iliac spines abut the sacrum. Note, however, that the posterior ligamentous structures (e.g., the posterior sacroiliac and iliolumbar ligaments) remain intact. Therefore, no displacement in the vertical plane is possible. *C,* Division of the posterior tension band ligaments, that is, the posterior sacroiliac, as well as the iliolumbar, depicted here on the *left side,* plus avulsion of the transverse process of L5 will cause complete instability of the hemipelvis. Note that posterior displacement is now possible.

FIGURE 36–9. A shearing force *(arrows)* crosses perpendicular to the main trabecular pattern of the posterior pelvic complex in the vertical plane. These forces cause marked displacement of bone and gross disruption of soft tissues and result in major pelvic instability.

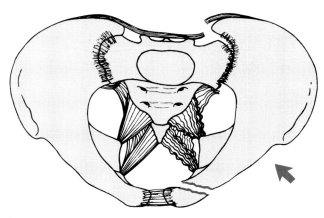

FIGURE 36–10. Lateral compression—unstable. In this mechanism, the force (*arrow*) is directed over the anterior aspect of the hemipelvis. The hemipelvis pivots around the anterior portion of the sacroiliac joint, thus compressing the sacrum or fracturing through the ilium (or both). Posteriorly, the posterior interosseous hinge is now disrupted and the pelvis is unstable in internal rotation. It may exhibit some degree of vertical instability. Vertical instability is limited by the intact sacrotuberous ligaments.

of impaction and the magnitude of this force, different lateral compression injuries are seen. If force is applied to the posterior aspect of the pelvis, a lateral compression impaction fracture into the sacrum results. It causes minimal soft tissue disruption because the posterior ligamentous structures relax as the hemipelvis is driven inward. Because the force of injury is essentially parallel to the ligament fibers and trabeculae of the bone, it produces a very stable fracture configuration.

In the second type of lateral compression, the force is directed over the anterior half of the iliac wing. This force tends to rotate the hemipelvis inward, with the pivot point being the anterior sacroiliac joint or anterior ala. Consequently, the anterior portion of the sacrum is crushed, and disruption of the posterior sacroiliac ligament complex follows.[21, 124] This injury becomes more unstable as disruption of the posterior osseous ligamentous structures increases. However, the sacrospinous and sacrotuberous ligaments are intact, and most important, the pelvic floor remains intact, thereby limiting translational instability (Fig. 36–10). This force can continue to push the hemipelvis across to the opposite side and compel the contralateral hemipelvis to externally rotate. This action produces a lateral compression injury on the side where the force has been applied and an external rotation injury on the contralateral side, with disruption of the anterior fibers of the sacroiliac joint.[124] The resulting anterior pelvic lesions may be any combination of ramus fractures or fracture-dislocations through the symphysis. Finally, a force applied over the greater trochanteric region also produces a lateral compression injury, usually associated with a transverse acetabular fracture.

External Rotation-Abduction Force Pattern

The third force, a common one in motorcycle accidents, is an external rotation-abduction force, which is usually

applied through the femoral shafts and hips. The leg is caught and externally rotated and abducted, a mechanism that tends to tear the hemipelvis from the sacrum. In analyzing postmortem specimens from motor vehicle accidents, Bucholz[11] has demonstrated that significant disruption of the posterior structures can occur and lead to an unstable injury through the sacroiliac area. He has confirmed pathologically that unstable AP compression injuries involve complete disruption of the posterior supporting ligamentous structures.

Shear Force Pattern

Shear fractures are the result of high-energy forces usually applied perpendicular to the bony trabeculae; these forces lead to an unstable vertical fracture with a variable degree of translational instability. Avulsion injuries through the pelvic ligamentous attachments and the lumbar transverse processes may occur with this mechanism of disruption. If this injury disrupts the sacrospinous and the sacrotuberous ligaments, the involved hemipelvis becomes vertically unstable.

The exact fracture pattern depends on both the amount of force applied and the bone strength in relation to the ligamentous structures. In an osteoporotic or elderly individual, bone strength is proportionately less than ligamentous strength and the bone, therefore, fails first. Conversely, in a young person, in whom bone strength is relatively greater, ligamentous disruptions usually occur primarily.

In conclusion, pelvic ring fractures occur when the pelvis is disrupted anteriorly and posteriorly.[40] The mechanism of injury should be determined from the clinical history and fracture pattern, and then stability must be assessed. Classifications and diagnostic tests are aimed at categorization of the stability to allow logical treatment decisions to be made.

CLASSIFICATION OF PELVIC DISRUPTIONS

Anatomic Classifications

Several anatomic classifications have been proposed. Letournel and Judet[58] suggested a classification based on the site of injury (Fig. 36–11). Bucholz[11] proposed a pathologic classification based on autopsy studies. Five sites of injury were characterized: (1) anterior vertical fractures dividing the obturator ring or adjacent bodies of the pubis, (2) transiliac fractures extending from the crest of the greater sciatic notch, (3) transsacral fractures either outside or inside the foramina, (4) pure separation of the symphysis, and (5) pure disruption of the sacroiliac joint.

Mechanism-of-Injury Classification (Young and Burgess)

A classification by Young and Burgess[124] based on the mechanism of injury alerts the surgeon to potential resuscitation problems associated with pelvic fractures. The classification has three major components. The first is an AP compression injury,[124] which is divided into three types. Type I, characterized by less than 2.5 cm of diastasis, consists of vertical fractures of one or both pubic rami or disruption of the symphysis. Because no posterior injury of significance occurs, problems with resuscitation are minimal. An AP compression type II injury has greater than 2.5 cm of symphyseal diastasis with opening of the sacroiliac joints, but vertical stability is maintained. An AP compression type III injury is a complete disruption anteriorly and posteriorly, with significant posterior diastasis and displacement of vertical pubic ramus fractures. This fracture is essentially completely unstable with significant associated injuries.

The second component in the Young and Burgess classification is a lateral compression injury.[124] A lateral compression type I injury results from a posteriorly applied force that causes sacral impaction. It is stable. Patients with these injuries usually have minimal problems with resuscitation. A lateral compression type II injury follows an anteriorly directed force with resultant disruption of the posterior osseous/ligamentous structures but maintenance of vertical stability. It may be associated with an anterior sacral crush injury. These two injuries are often coupled with head injuries and intra-abdominal trauma. A lateral compression type III injury results from a laterally directed force that has continued to cross the pelvis to produce an external rotation injury to the contralateral hemipelvis, similar to the isolated injuries caused by the patient being crushed or rolled over. This injury component is isolated to the pelvis and has a minimum of significant associated injuries.

The final component is a vertically unstable or shear injury and a combined mechanism injury leading to unstable fracture patterns with significant retroperitoneal hemorrhage and major associated injuries[21, 124] (Fig. 36–12).

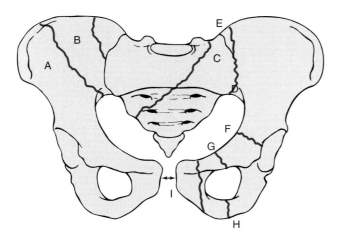

FIGURE 36–11. The Letournel and Judet classification of pelvic fractures is anatomic. A, Iliac wing fractures; B, ilium fractures with extension to the sacroiliac joint; C, transsacral fractures; D, unilateral sacral fractures; E, sacroiliac joint fracture-dislocation; F, acetabular fractures; G, pubic ramus fractures; H, ischial fractures; I, pubic symphysis separation. It should be remembered that combinations of all of these injuries could occur.

The Young and Burgess classification was developed to enable trauma surgeons to more adequately predict associated major injuries within the pelvis and abdomen and to allow resuscitative therapy to be carried out in a more logical and predictive fashion. AP injuries are associated with an increased incidence of pelvic vascular injuries and therefore an increased incidence of shock, sepsis, adult respiratory distress syndrome, and death. Lateral compression injuries carry a high incidence of associated brain and visceral injuries but a lesser incidence of pelvic vascular injuries and associated complications. Death caused by an AP injury is related to the combined effect of blood loss from pelvic vascular and visceral injuries, whereas death caused by a lateral compression injury is usually related to associated brain or severe intra-abdominal injury (or both). Vertical shear injuries tend to follow a pattern similar to that of lateral compression injuries with regard to associated injuries, pelvic vascular injuries, and death.[21]

The causes of each particular injury pattern are typically different. AP injuries usually occur in pedestrians and motorcyclists. Lateral compression injuries more commonly result from motor vehicle collisions and vertical shear injuries from falls.

Therefore, with knowledge of the mechanism of injury and review of the initial AP radiographs, a logical approach to resuscitation and appropriate surgical decisions can be made regarding the cause and surgical management of hypovolemic shock.[20, 21, 28]

Comprehensive Pelvic Disruption Classification (Modified after Tile)

This classification combines both the mechanism of injury and the degree of pelvic stability and can be used as an aid in determining the prognosis and treatment options[43, 112] (Fig. 36–13). Determination of pelvic stability with regard to rotation, vertical and posterior displacement, the history and mechanism of injury, and assessment of soft tissue injuries allows a complete classification to be made (Table 36–1).

Type A injuries preserve the bony and ligamentous integrity of the posterior complex of the pelvis and the pelvic floor. A type A1 injury consists of avulsion of the pelvic apophyses by a sudden muscular pull; these injuries are never unstable and usually require only symptomatic care. Type A2 injuries represent isolated iliac wing fractures. Because they have not violated the anterior or posterior osseous ligamentous hinge, they remain completely stable. This group also includes undisplaced low-energy pelvic ring injuries, which are usually seen in osteoporotic bone (Fig. 36–14). A type A3 injury consists of fractures of the sacrum and coccyx that do not involve a pelvic ring injury (below S2). As has been shown by Denis[22] and Kaehr[48] and their colleagues, appropriate assessment of these sacral fractures may be necessary to determine the extent of neurologic compromise and whether decompression is required. If the sacral fracture extends into the S1 and S2 vertebrae and is associated with an anterior injury, it is classified more appropriately as a pelvic ring disruption.

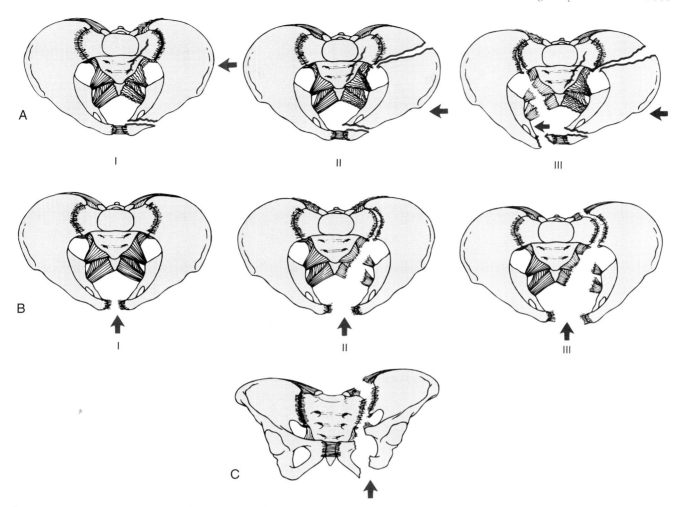

Figure 36–12. Young and Burgess classification. *A,* Lateral compression force. Type I: a posteriorly directed force causing a sacral crushing injury and horizontal pubic ramus fractures ipsilaterally. This injury is stable. Type II: a more anteriorly directed force causing horizontal pubic ramus fractures with an anterior sacral crushing injury and either disruption of the posterior sacroiliac joints or fractures through the iliac wing. This injury is ipsilateral. Type III: an anteriorly directed force that is continued and leads to a type I or type II ipsilateral fracture with an external rotation component to the contralateral side; the sacroiliac joint is opened posteriorly, and the sacrotuberous and spinous ligaments are disrupted. *B,* Anteroposterior (AP) compression fractures. Type I: an AP-directed force opening the pelvis but with the posterior ligamentous structures intact. This injury is stable. Type II: continuation of a type I fracture with disruption of the sacrospinous and potentially the sacrotuberous ligaments and an anterior sacroiliac joint opening. This fracture is rotationally unstable. Type III: a completely unstable or a vertical instability pattern with complete disruption of all ligamentous supporting structures. *C,* A vertically directed force or forces at right angles to the supporting structures of the pelvis leading to vertical fractures in the rami and disruption of all the ligamentous structures. This injury is equivalent to an AP type III or a completely unstable and rotationally unstable fracture. (*A–C,* Redrawn from Young, J.W.R.; Burgess, A.R. Radiologic Management of Pelvic Ring Fractures. Baltimore, Munich, Urban & Schwarzenberg, 1987.)

Type B fractures are incomplete disruptions of the posterior arch that allow rotation of the hemipelvis (see Fig. 36–13). A B1 injury is a unilateral external rotation or anterior compression (open-book) injury (Fig. 36–15*A*). A variable degree of widening of the sacroiliac joint may be present (see Fig. 36–15*B*). A type B3.1 injury is a bilateral external rotation injury with greater than 2.5 cm of symphyseal displacement. This injury is unstable in external rotation. The sacrotuberous ligament remains intact, as do most of the posterior ligaments, and no vertical instability occurs. If vertical instability is present, the injury is classified as a type C injury (see Fig. 36–15*C*).

Type B2 injuries are produced by lateral compression or internal rotation and are vertically stable (see Fig. 36–13*B*). A type B2.1 injury represents an anterior crush or

compression fracture of the sacrum associated with fractures of the pubic rami. This injury is usually caused by a force directed over the posterior iliac wing; the force produces a sacral impaction injury and spares the ligaments (Fig. 36–16). Unusual anterior arch injuries are a locked symphysis and a tilt fracture. A locked symphysis injury disrupts the symphysis rather than fracturing the rami as it drives one side of the symphysis behind the other (Fig. 36–17*B*). A tilt fracture is an unusual variant of a lateral compression injury in which the superior pubic ramus is fractured near the iliopectineal eminence and through the ischial ramus; the fragment tilts inferiorly and anteriorly into the perineum and dislocates the symphysis. This injury is seen more commonly in females than males. The major problem with this fracture is its position within the perineum, especially in females, where the pubic

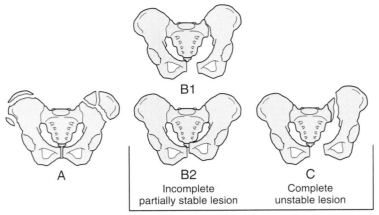

FIGURE 36–13. Modified Tile AO Müller classification. Pelvic ring injuries may be classified as stable or unstable depending on the integrity of the posterior arch. Stable lesions have an intact posterior arch (*A*), whereas unstable lesions can be divided into incompletely or rotationally unstable injuries with partial integrity of the arch or floor (*B1, B2*) or completely unstable injuries with no part of the floor or posterior arch intact (*C*). (*A–C*, Redrawn from Müller, E., ed. Comprehensive Classification of Pelvis and Acetabulum Fractures. Bern, Switzerland, Maurice E. Müller Foundation, 1995.)

ramus protrudes into the vagina and results in dyspareunia (see Fig. 36–17*C*).

A B2.2 injury is produced by a lateral compression force and involves a partial fracture/subluxation of the sacroiliac joint (see Fig. 36–16) associated with contralateral anterior ramus fractures (Fig. 36–18*A*), with four ramus fractures

---

TABLE 36–1 ....

Classification of Pelvic Ring Disruptions

TYPE A—STABLE, POSTERIOR ARCH INTACT

A1—Posterior arch intact, fracture of innominate bone (avulsion)
    A1.1—Iliac spine
    A1.2—Iliac crest
    A1.3—Ischial tuberosity
A2—Posterior arch intact, fracture of innominate bone (direct blow)
    A2.1—Iliac wing fractures
    A2.2—Unilateral fracture of anterior arch
    A2.3—Bifocal fracture of anterior arch
A3—Posterior arch intact, transverse fracture of sacrum caudal to S2
    A3.1—Sacrococcygeal dislocation
    A3.2—Sacrum undisplaced
    A3.3—Sacrum displaced

TYPE B—INCOMPLETE DISRUPTION OF POSTERIOR ARCH, PARTIALLY STABLE, ROTATION

B1—External rotation instability, open-book injury, unilateral
    B1.1—Sacroiliac joint, anterior disruption
    B1.2—Sacral fracture
B2—Incomplete disruption of posterior arch, unilateral, internal rotation (lateral compression)
    B2.1—Anterior compression fracture, sacrum
    B2.2—Partial sacroiliac joint fracture, subluxation
    B2.3—Incomplete posterior iliac fracture
B3—Incomplete disruption of posterior arch, bilateral
    B3.1—Bilateral open book
    B3.2—Open book, lateral compression
    B3.3—Bilateral lateral compression

TYPE C—COMPLETE DISRUPTION OF POSTERIOR ARCH, UNSTABLE

C1—Complete disruption of posterior arch, unilateral
    C1.1—Fracture through ilium
    C1.2—Sacroiliac dislocation and/or fracture-dislocation
    C1.3—Sacral fracture
C2—Bilateral injury, one side rotationally unstable, one side vertically unstable
C3—Bilateral injury, both sides completely unstable

....

at the front (see Fig. 36–18*B*), or with two ramus injuries and a fracture-dislocation through the symphysis (see Fig 36–18*C*). These vertically stable injuries are the equivalent of the Young and Burgess lateral compression type 2 injuries. Because the force of injury is applied in an oblique fashion across the pelvis, the involved portion of the pelvis acts like a bucket handle; as it is internally rotated, it tends to migrate superiorly, thereby leading to a leg length discrepancy and internal rotation deformity. The other (type B3) lesions are caused by combinations of anterior and external rotation (Fig. 36–19).

A type C injury is vertically, posteriorly, and rotationally unstable (see Fig. 36–13*C*). In severe C1 injuries, all posterior structures are disrupted, including the sacrotuberous and sacrospinous ligaments. Further subdivision is based on the nature of the posterior lesion. C1.1 is an iliac fracture, C1.2 is a sacroiliac dislocation or fracture-dislocation, and C1.3 is a fracture through the sacrum (Fig. 36–20). C2 injuries are bilateral disruptions in which one side is rotationally unstable (B types) and the other side is completely unstable (C types). C3 injuries represent bilateral, completely unstable disruptions (Fig. 36–21).

ASSESSMENT OF PELVIC DISRUPTION

Acute Management

The prehospital phase starts with paramedics taught to recognize the potential for an unstable pelvic ring injury from the history, characteristics of the crash, and physical examination. Lower limb deformity without a long bone fracture and a mobile pelvic injury confirmed by manual compression of the pelvis are clues to a pelvic injury. If such injury is present in the prehospital situation, application of a stabilization splint such as a pneumatic antishock garment (PASG), vacuum splint, or the newer pelvic stabilization belts may be lifesaving.[31]

Emergency and trauma unit assessment of the patient must include evaluation of the immediate life-threatening problems associated with pelvic fractures (Fig. 36–22). A

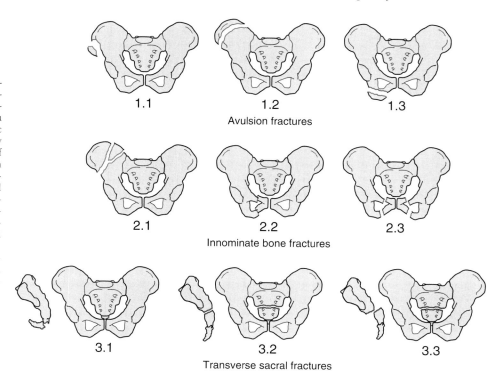

FIGURE 36–14. Modified Tile AO Müller classification. Type A: stable posterior arch with intact pelvic ring injuries. Group 1 represents avulsion fractures of the iliac spine (A1.1), iliac crest (A1.2), and ischial tuberosity (A1.3). Group 2 represents fractures of the innominate bone or injuries from direct blows: iliac wing (A2.1), unilateral anterior arch (A2.2), and bifocal anterior arch (A2.3). Group 3 represents transverse fractures of the sacrum caudal to S2: sacrococcygeal dislocation (A3.1), sacrum undisplaced (A3.2), and sacrum displaced (A3.3). (Redrawn from Müller, E., ed. Comprehensive Classification of Pelvis and Acetabulum Fractures. Bern, Switzerland, Maurice E. Müller Foundation, 1995.)

pelvic fracture is considered a signpost leading to other associated life-threatening injuries,[20, 21, 30, 66] including major head, chest, and abdominal injuries and, most important, retroperitoneal vascular injuries caused by the pelvic fracture.[9, 30, 35, 66, 78] A history of the injury may also give a clue regarding the energy absorbed. A low-energy pelvic injury is produced by a fall from a low height (<1 m), such as occurs with tripping, and is often seen in elderly, osteoporotic patients. High-energy injuries are usually caused by motor vehicle or motorcycle collisions or by falls from heights (>1 m).

Low-energy injuries may be isolated, but high-energy injuries can be associated with other significant problems, including hemorrhage in 75% of patients,[66] urogenital injuries in 12%, and lumbosacral plexus injuries in about 8%.[14, 66, 80] The likelihood of aortic rupture is eight times greater in high-energy pelvic fractures than in blunt trauma injury overall.[74, 78] The mortality rate in the high-energy group is about 15% to 25%.[21, 66] Sixty percent to 80% of patients with a high-energy pelvic fracture have other associated musculoskeletal injuries.[66] Consequently, a planned method of simultaneous assessment and treatment of this acute injury is required. Such management is best handled by an interdisciplinary team that includes a general surgeon, an emergency department physician, an anesthesiologist, and an orthopaedic surgeon. Standardized resuscitation priorities must be established to ensure that the patient is stabilized. Priority should be given to the treatment of airway, breathing, and circulatory problems. It is important that the orthopaedic surgeon be involved in the primary resuscitation and care of these patients to provide input to the group on the severity and stability of the pelvic fracture, which can assist in decision making. Second, it is important that the pelvis

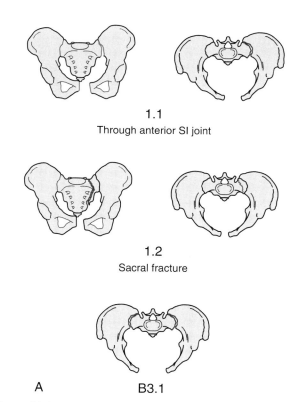

FIGURE 36–15. Modified Tile AO Müller classification. *A*, Type B: incomplete disruptions (external rotation). Injuries that disrupt the symphysis will also disrupt the anterior sacroiliac (SI) joint unilaterally (B1.1) or cause a fracture through the sacrum (B1.2). Bilateral disruptions of the SI joint from an external rotation force are classified in a separate group (B3.1) and then further subdivided according to SI joint or sacral involvement. These radiographs show external rotation of an unstable fracture classified by the Tile method as a B1 fracture.

Illustration continued on following page

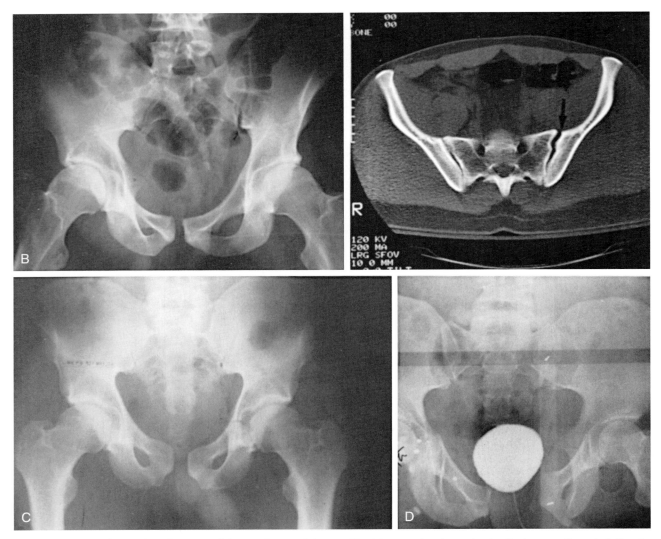

Figure 36–15 *Continued. B,* Unilateral opening of the symphysis and SI joint. This injury can be adequately visualized on a radiograph *(left)* and computed tomography (CT) scan *(right)* of the pelvis. *C,* Anteroposterior radiograph showing a bilateral open-book injury of the pelvic ring. Displacement is less than 2.5 cm. This injury is stable and usually handled quite adequately by symptomatic treatment. *D,* Radiograph showing bilateral opening of the SI joints associated with wide diastasis of the pubic rami. In this interesting variant of the fracture, the pubic rami are also fractured. This injury resulted from a direct blow posteriorly over the sacrum; the patient was thrown into a wall and at that time probably fractured his pubic rami as they externally rotated. (*A,* Redrawn from Müller, E., ed. Comprehensive Classification of Pelvis and Acetabulum Fractures. Bern, Switzerland, Maurice E. Müller Foundation, 1995.)

be thoroughly assessed acutely so that any evidence of instability can be documented and appropriate treatment planned and instituted early rather than late.

Once the airway and breathing are stabilized, care of the circulatory system (i.e., for hypovolemic shock) is mandatory. Most important is determination and control of the site of hemorrhage. Establishment of a minimum of two 14- to 16-gauge intravenous cannulas in the upper extremity is important. The use of lower extremity intravenous access in pelvic injuries may not be an efficient method of providing fluid because of significant pelvic vein disruption. An appropriate volume of fluid resuscitation must be given, as determined by ascertaining the degree of blood loss based on the patient's clinical condition[4, 5] (Table 36–2). The replacement volume can be estimated from the principle that 3 mL of crystalloid must be given for each 1 mL of blood lost. A minimum of

2 L of crystalloid solution is given over a 20-minute period. If a good response is obtained, the crystalloid infusion can be maintained until type-specific, fully matched blood is available. However, in patients with a transient response or no response, a further 2 L of crystalloid is infused, and then type-specific or uncross-matched universal-donor (group O negative) blood is given immediately. These latter two responses indicate ongoing blood loss, and bleeding control is urgently required. These patients require massive amounts of fluid; consequently, it should be assumed that they would have a dilutional coagulopathy. Platelets and fresh frozen plasma should be ordered initially. As a rule of thumb, 2 to 3 U of fresh frozen plasma and 7 to 8 U of platelets will be required for every 5 L of volume replacement.

Appropriate monitoring of the patient's response to ongoing resuscitation is mandatory. Perfusion pressure can

TABLE 36–2 ....

Estimated Fluid and Blood Loss Based on the Patient's Initial Clinical Findings*

	Class I	Class II	Class III	Class IV
Blood loss (mL)	Up to 750	750–1500	1500–2000	>2000
Blood loss (% of blood volume)	Up to 15	15–30	30–40	>40
Pulse rate	<100	>100	>120	>140
Blood pressure	Normal	Normal	Decreased	Decreased
Pulse pressure (mm Hg)	Normal or increased	Decreased	Decreased	Decreased
Respiratory rate	14–20	20–30	30–40	>35
Urine output (mL/hr)	>30	20–30	5–15	Negligible
Central nervous system and mental status	Slightly anxious	Mildly anxious	Anxious, confused	Confused, lethargic
Fluid replacement (3:1 rule)†	Crystalloid	Crystalloid	Crystalloid and blood	Crystalloid and blood

....

*For a 70-kg man.

†The "three-for-one" rule is derived from the empirical observation that most patients in hemorrhagic shock require as much as 300 mL of electrolyte solution for each 100 mL of blood loss. Applied blindly, these guidelines can result in excessive or inadequate fluid administration. For example, a patient with a crush injury to the extremity may have hypotension out of proportion to blood loss and require fluids in excess of the 3:1 guidelines. In contrast, a patient whose ongoing blood loss is being replaced by blood transfusion requires less than 3:1 fluids. The use of bolus therapy with careful monitoring of the patient's response can moderate these extremes.

Source: American College of Surgeons. *Advanced Trauma Life Support Instructor's Manual.* Chicago, American College of Surgeons, 1989, 1993.

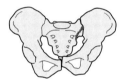

2.1
Anterior sacral compression injury

2.2
Partial fracture subluxation of sacroiliac joint

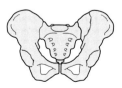

2.3
Incomplete posterior iliac fracture

FIGURE 36–16. Modified Tile AO Müller classification. Type B: incomplete disruptions (internal rotation). Internally directed or lateral compression forces cause anterior sacral compression injuries (B2.1), partial fracture-subluxations of the sacroiliac joint (B2.2), and incomplete posterior iliac wing fractures (B2.3). (Redrawn from Müller, E., ed. Comprehensive Classification of Pelvis and Acetabulum Fractures. Bern, Switzerland, Maurice E. Müller Foundation, 1995.)

be assessed by clinical signs of capillary refill, pulse volume, color, and temperature. More specific monitoring methods require a urinary catheter to assess urinary output (20 mL/hr) and an arterial line for direct arterial pressure measurements and determination of mean arterial pressure. Volume status can easily be assessed by these methods and can be confirmed by central venous pressure measurements.

Monitoring of core body temperature is mandatory if major fluid replacement is continued. Blood and crystalloid are usually at room temperature or may even be cooler. The use of large volumes during resuscitation cools the patient even further and thereby adds to the effect of hypovolemic shock and exposure in the field. Warming of intravenous fluid and blood is necessary to keep the core temperature at least in the range of 32°C to 35°C. A normal temperature of 37°C is preferred. Lower temperatures lead to coagulation problems, ventricular fibrillation, higher surgical infection rates, and acid-base disturbances.

A gastric tube should be inserted, but with the nasal route avoided if cribriform plate fractures are suspected. Catheterization of the bladder is used to decompress it before the minilaparotomy. Before catheterization in a male, assessment for evidence of blood at the urethral meatus, examination for scrotal hematomas, and evaluation of the prostate to make sure that it is palpable and in the appropriate position are mandatory. In females, a vaginal examination as well as inspection of the urethral meatus is performed. If any evidence of pelvic instability is noted in addition to any of the preceding findings, urinary catheterization should not be undertaken because of potential urethral injuries. Lowe and associates reported that 57% of men with urologic injury secondary to a pelvic fracture had none of the classic signs.[59] Urethrography is performed after the patient is hemodynamically normal.

Physical signs of pelvic instability include deformity of a lower extremity without a long bone fracture, usually an ipsilateral leg length discrepancy involving shortening or

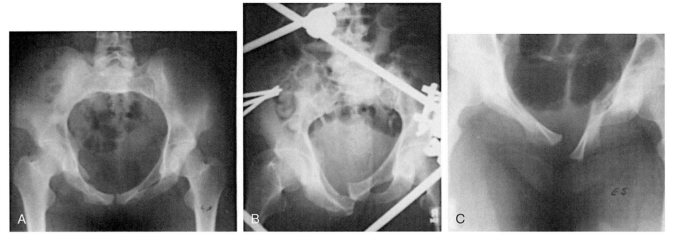

FIGURE 36–17. Modified Tile AO Müller classification. Injuries to the pelvic ring caused by internal rotation forces lead to vertically stable injuries classified as B2.1 fractures. *A*, Anteroposterior pelvic radiograph showing ipsilateral pubic ramus and ischial ramus fractures with minor crushing of the posterior of the sacrum. This fracture is slightly displaced in internal rotation, and some displacement is seen through the pubic rami but minimal displacement, if any, posteriorly. This type of injury is a stable fracture vertically but a potentially unstable rotational injury. *B*, Another of the internally rotated ipsilateral group, a locked symphysis. This radiograph demonstrates a locked symphyseal injury with one pubic body displaced behind the other. *C*, An unusual variant of a lateral compression injury—a tilt fracture. Notice how the superior pubic body has dislocated from the symphysis and been turned down into the perineum.

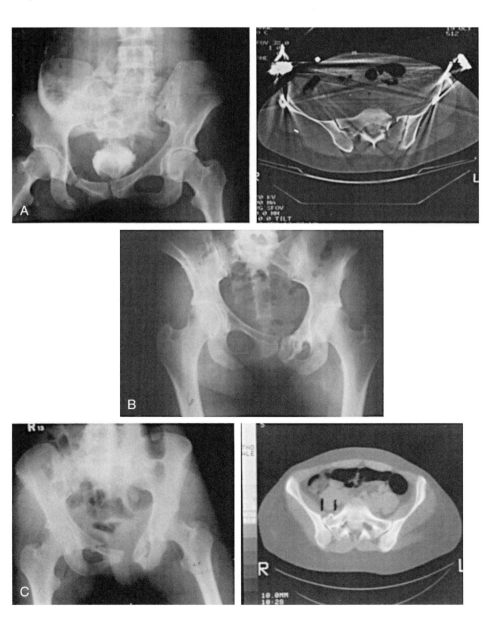

FIGURE 36–18. Severe variant of an internally rotated, unstable fracture—a contralateral type or bucket-handle type (B2.2). *A*, An internal rotation force crushed the sacrum as well as produced a fracture through the four rami anteriorly. Note how the computed tomographic (CT) scan of the hemipelvis on the right side demonstrates an internal rotation deformity of almost 45°. *B*, An anteroposterior radiograph of the pelvis again demonstrates a different contralateral injury, with an injury posteriorly on one side and ramus fractures on the opposite side. Also note the internal rotation deformity of the pelvis, as well as elevation of the hip on one side. This variant is not true vertical instability but is a rotational phenomenon. *C*, Final variety of a contralateral injury. In this injury, the anterior component is a fracture through the pubic rami, on either one or both sides, with dislocation or fracture-dislocation of the symphysis. Again, the hemipelvis has been rotated internally. Note on the CT scan (right) how the sacral injury is a crushing injury on the right posterior aspect. The sacrum has been driven in and has crushed cancellous bone, and it is thus relatively stable posteriorly.

3.2   3.3

FIGURE 36–19. Modified Tile AO Müller classification. Type B3: incomplete disruption (bilateral). Bilateral incomplete disruptions are represented by bilateral open-book injuries (see Fig. 36–15A, B3.1) and combination injuries consisting of open-book and internal rotation (B3.2) and bilateral internal rotation injuries (B3.3). (Redrawn from Müller, E., ed. Comprehensive Classification of Pelvis and Acetabulum Fractures. Bern, Switzerland, Maurice E. Müller Foundation, 1995.)

internal/external rotation (or both), depending on the injury. Massive flank or buttock contusions and swelling with hemorrhage are indicative of massive bleeding. Visual inspection of the posterior part of the pelvis is done when the patient is logrolled for examination of the back. Palpation of the posterior aspect of the pelvis may reveal a large hematoma, a gap through the disrupted fracture area, or dislocation of the sacroiliac joint. Similarly, palpation of the symphysis may lead to recognition of a gap. Signs of potential instability include an open pelvic fracture, scrotal hematomas, and neurologic injuries to the lumbosacral plexus.

Evaluation of the spine with lateral radiographs is mandatory to exclude the presence of any fractures. In 85% of cases, these films can rule out any significant injury that may cause further neurologic deterioration. A chest radiograph is also helpful to determine the width of the mediastinum or the occurrence of a pulmonary contusion. An AP radiograph of the pelvis is mandatory in all patients who have a depressed level of consciousness, who fail to respond to fluids when no intra-abdominal source of bleeding is noted, or who complain of pain or tenderness on examination of the pelvis.[53]

Once the patient is assessed and stabilization is started, the surgeon must be prepared to act efficiently if ongoing pelvic bleeding is observed.[30, 35, 66, 71, 116] The usual cause of ongoing pelvic bleeding is disruption of the posterior pelvic venous plexus. Bleeding of a large vessel such as the common, external, or internal iliac may also cause such bleeding. Injury to large vessels usually is associated with rapid, massive bleeding and loss of the distal pulse. The severity of the hemorrhage determines the appropriate management path. The five areas of potential hemorrhage are external, thoracic, intraperitoneal, retroperitoneal, and extremity fractures. A standardized protocol involving the orthopaedic surgeon and trauma surgeon is necessary to distinguish an intraperitoneal from a retroperitoneal source of hemorrhage. In an acutely injured patient, abdominal examination is unreliable. Therefore, rapid determination of the presence of intra-abdominal blood by supraumbilical diagnostic peritoneal lavage, ultrasonography, or computed tomography (CT) is mandatory.[73] Infraumbilical minilaparotomy is fraught with problems because the pelvic hematoma may track up through the anterior fascial planes and contaminate the specimen.

The major aim of the orthopaedic surgeon in controlling pelvic bleeding is stabilization of the unstable pelvic injury.[19, 35, 49, 66, 71, 73] Stabilization of the pelvic

injury prevents an increase in retroperitoneal volume, and therefore, decreases blood loss as tamponade of the bleeding vessels occurs.

Stabilization of a disrupted pelvis can be handled in several ways. The oldest is the application of a PASG.[35] This inflatable garment is placed over the lower extremities and around the abdomen and inflated until blood pressure is stabilized. The garment works by increasing peripheral vascular resistance. However, in this situation, the abdominal component of the trousers acts as a pneumatic splint and decreases continued motion of the pelvic fracture. This decrease in motion prevents any further disruption of the pelvic veins or the clots that have formed. At present, PASGs are recommended for the immediate stabilization of massive pelvic bleeding in the emergency department or for transport of the patient to a definitive care facility.[4] Once the garment is applied in the emergency situation, it should not be removed until the patient is receiving fluids in the operating room so that the bleeding can be controlled surgically. A PASG should not be used on a long-term basis unless the leg and abdominal components are alternately deflated every 2 hours to allow perfusion of the muscle compartments and skin.[35] Long-term use of these garments in hypotensive patients has led to the development of compartment syndromes and subsequent amputations.[65]

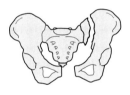

1.1
Through iliac wing

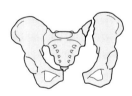

1.2
Through sacroiliac joint

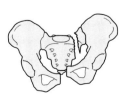

1.3
Through sacrum

FIGURE 36–20. Modified Tile AO Müller classification. Type C: complete disruptions. Complete disruptions can be unilateral or bilateral. Unilateral disruptions occur through the iliac wing (C1.1), through the sacroiliac joint (C1.2), and through the sacrum (C1.3). Bilateral injuries are combinations of incomplete, complete, and totally complete injuries and are not shown in this figure. (Redrawn from Müller, E., ed. Comprehensive Classification of Pelvis and Acetabulum Fractures. Bern, Switzerland, Maurice E. Müller Foundation, 1995.)

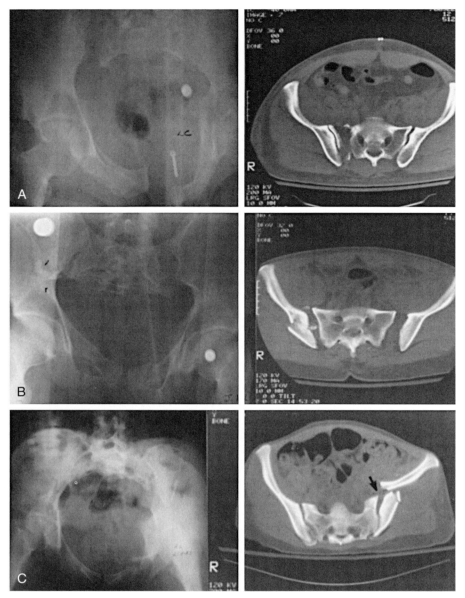

FIGURE 36–21. Type C injuries representing complete instability both vertically and rotationally. The injuries can occur through the sacrum, sacroiliac joint, or iliac wing. *A,* Inlet view *(left)* and computed tomography (CT) scan *(right)* of the pelvis. The inlet view demonstrates diastasis of the symphysis and a large gap through the sacrum anteriorly and posteriorly. Note how the hemipelvis has been displaced posteriorly in this view. The CT scan confirms the wide gap in the sacrum. This injury is an extra-articular sacral fracture and is unstable. Also note the slight widening on the left side of the sacroiliac joint. This widening may have been caused by an anteriorly or posteriorly directed force as the final stage in an open-book or externally rotated injury. *B,* An anteroposterior (AP) radiograph of the pelvis *(left)* demonstrates two injuries: dislocation through the sacroiliac joint and a fracture-dislocation involving the iliac wing and sacrum on the right side. The double density marked by the *arrow* shows where the iliac fracture has occurred. Also note the widening of the sacroiliac joint on the right side as well as the left. On the left side note the marked displacement of the hemipelvis. A CT scan *(right)* confirms the findings on the AP radiograph. A pure sacroiliac joint dislocation has occurred on the left side and a fracture-dislocation through the sacroiliac joint on the right side. *C,* Inlet view *(left)* of the pelvis demonstrating a fracture through the iliac wing. This view also shows some widening of the sacroiliac joint, but a CT scan *(right)* shows that most of this injury is through the iliac wing. The *arrow* indicates the anterior opening of the joint, but note that an opening does not appear to be present posteriorly and most of the structures are intact, thus giving stability. The instability in this fracture will occur through the iliac wing because the injury has bypassed the posterior interosseous ligamentous structures.

Other straightforward techniques can be used to control pelvic hemorrhage until the patient can be transferred to definitive care. The use of skeletal traction applied through the injured leg is effective in controlling venous bleeding. A traction pin is inserted into either the supracondylar region of the femur or the tibial tubercle, and 25 to 35 lb of traction is applied. This technique pulls the displaced hemipelvis into a more anatomic position and stabilizes it so that the tamponade is more effective. Internal rotation of the lower extremities closes an anterior pelvic diastasis, particularly if the posterior ligamentous structures still have some continuity. This position can be maintained by tying the internally rotated legs together. Finally, any encircling device such as a sheet wrapped around the pelvis or a wide belt can be used to close the anterior diastasis until more definitive management can be undertaken. A "beanbag" positioning device or vacuum body splint is effective. It be can be applied to the flanks of the patient to maintain access to the abdomen and groin. It is also useful as a splint for lower extremity injuries. Because it conforms to the patient, it provides a safe total-body splint to stabilize the spine and allow easy transport.[31]

A more efficient method of emergency pelvic stabilization is the application of specialized pelvic clamps.[12, 36] These clamps can be applied by a trained physician in the emergency department. A pelvic C-clamp[36] is applied to the posterior of the pelvis at the level of the sacroiliac joints. A pelvic stabilizer is applied to either the posterior or the anterior of the pelvis in the cancellous bone above the acetabulum.[7, 9] Control of massive venous bleeding is an indication for the use of these devices.

The standard method of controlling the hemipelvis is the application of an anterior external fixation frame.[50, 88, 90] The frame should be used in conjunction with traction on the involved leg to control vertical instability. Application of the frame requires operative

intervention, and it must be applied as quickly as possible (within 20 to 30 minutes). A hemodynamically stable patient does not require temporary stabilization unless it is thought that motion of the pelvic fracture may lead to recurrence of the hemorrhage.

The timing of placement of acute pelvic stabilization devices should be a decision made in consultation with the general surgeon or the physician in charge of the resuscitation.[72] Before placement of the fixator, the pelvic AP radiograph should be assessed. This radiograph reveals several clues regarding the exact nature of the injury and the potential for ongoing bleeding. A lateral compression injury usually has a horizontal or buckle-type fracture across the rami with evidence of an anterior sacral crushing injury if one looks along the arcuate line between the sacral promontory and the iliopectineal line. A line drawn vertically through the midline of the sacrum can also reveal a significant shift of the pelvis such as might occur in a lateral compression type 3 injury[124] (Fig. 36–23). An injury to the quadrilateral plate or a transverse acetabular fracture also indicates a lateral injury. An AP injury is usually recognized by the presence of vertical fractures through the rami that tend to be separated but

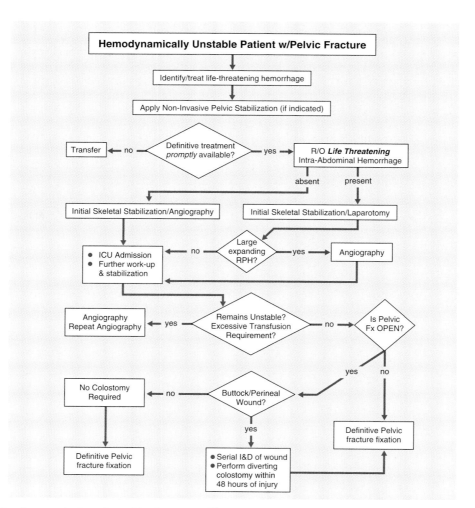

FIGURE 36–22. Algorithm for resuscitation after pelvic disruption. *Abbreviations:* C spine, cervical spine; ER, emergency room; Fx, fracture; IVs, intravenous lines; OR, operating room; PASG, pneumatic antishock garment; RPH, retroperitoneal hematoma; R/O, rule out.

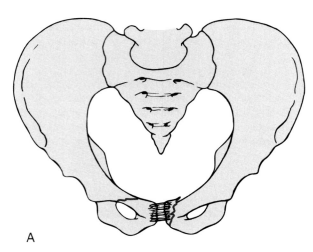

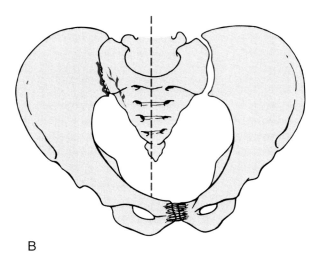

A

B

Figure 36–23. Emergency assessment of an anteroposterior pelvic radiograph. *A,* Lateral compression injuries that are stable are usually associated with horizontal fractures of the right superior pubic ramus or overlapped or compacted fractures, as seen in this figure. *B,* Combination lateral compression external rotation injury with translation of the hemipelvis past the midline, which is represented by the *dotted line.* Also seen is the opening of the sacroiliac joint. This fracture is more complex than that shown in *A* and may present an increased risk of hemorrhage. (*A, B,* Redrawn from Young, J.W.R.; Burgess, A.R. Radiologic Management of Pelvic Ring Fractures. Baltimore, Munich, Urban & Schwarzenberg, 1987.)

not vertically displaced. Fractures along the iliac wing or through the posterior acetabular region also indicate an AP compression injury. Posterior displacement of the hemipelvis can be inferred with the use of the second sacral arcuate line[124] (Fig. 36–24). Vertical displacement can be recognized by displacement greater than 1 cm through the posterior sacroiliac joint, by gaps occurring in the sacrum, by the impression that the pelvis itself has widened, or by an avulsion fracture through the sacrum. It should be remembered that lateral compression fractures are usually associated with major intra-abdominal and head injuries, as are vertical shear injuries. However, unstable AP compression injuries and completely unstable injuries

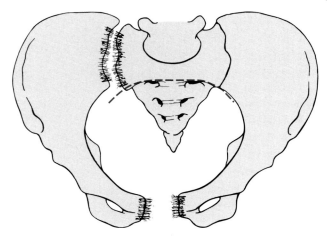

Figure 36–24. Assessment of posterior displacement and anteroposterior compression injuries. The *dashed line* represents a second sacral arcuate line drawn through the second sacral foramen. It should line up with the iliopectineal line, but on the right side it does not, thus demonstrating that the hemipelvis is displaced posteriorly as well as externally.

have a far greater incidence of retroperitoneal hemorrhage than intra-abdominal bleeding.

Decision making can be guided by the patient's response to resuscitation.[41] In the case of a negative test for intra-abdominal blood in a patient with ongoing hypovolemic shock (transient responder to fluid) and major pelvic disruption, it is mandatory that angiography be performed before the external fixator is applied. Angiography will demonstrate the site of bleeding and help determine the type of therapeutic embolization necessary. If the diagnostic peritoneal results are grossly positive (free flow of blood through the peritoneal catheter) and the patient responds only transiently, laparotomy is required to assess the intra-abdominal injury. After treatment of the intra-abdominal cause of bleeding, ongoing hemorrhage should resolve with retroperitoneal packing of the pelvis and the application of an external fixator. Attempts at pelvic packing will be of no value, however, unless the pelvis is immobilized. If the findings on peritoneal lavage are positive (i.e., >100,000 red blood cells per cubic millimeter) and the patient is hemodynamically stable, the frame should be applied before laparotomy. The laparotomy can subsequently be performed and the intra-abdominal bleeding controlled. If bleeding continues, a dilutional coagulopathy must be ruled out or treated; if indicated, angiography can then be performed.

A patient who fails to respond to appropriate fluid resuscitation and has a negative test for intra-abdominal blood is, by definition, bleeding from a large-caliber vessel. The patient then requires angiography to determine the source and whether embolization can be used to stop the bleeding, which depends on the caliber of the bleeding vessel. Temporary balloon occlusion of large-caliber arteries may be lifesaving until definitive control can be achieved by surgery. If possible, a pelvic stabilization device should be applied before angiography.

With a positive test for intra-abdominal blood in a patient who fails to respond, celiotomy is indicated, as well as the use of a pelvic stabilization device. If during celiotomy the retroperitoneal hematoma is expanding, packing of the presacral area and posterior aspect of the symphysis is carried out. For this technique to be effective, it is necessary to achieve reduction, which can be obtained by traction and manipulation of the pelvis by the C-clamp or fixator, guided by finger palpation or visualization through the transperitoneal approach.[84] If the patient remains hypotensive despite these methods, angiography must be performed immediately. Any clotted vessel seen during angiography should be treated by embolization to prevent delayed hemorrhage if the clot is dislodged or reabsorbed. In open pelvic fractures that are hemorrhaging through an open wound, packing of the area is mandatory to control the bleeding at the same time as the pelvis is acutely stabilized by the application of an external stabilization device.

Diagnostic and therapeutic angiography in patients with pelvic hemorrhage is difficult even in experienced hands. Selective embolization is most effective in controlling bleeding from small-diameter vessels (i.e., 3 mm or less). Angiography may assist in localizing large-vessel bleeding, but only if time and hemodynamic stability permit.[101] Compromising delays in resuscitation and treatment can occur if the angiography response time is slow or the angiographer is inexperienced. Arteriographic embolization is 100% successful in stopping bleeding and saving lives if done within 3 hours of injury.[1] The radiology department must have the necessary equipment available to administer lifesaving procedures in the event of cardiopulmonary collapse when performing embolization in these high-risk patients.[52] If the patient is stabilized and able to undergo a CT scan, it should be contrast enhanced. A patient with a positive contrast extravasation sign on a contrast-enhanced CT scan has a 40:1 likelihood of significant arterial bleeding requiring embolization.[110] Therefore, any patient who has a potential for arterial bleeding or is a transient responder must have a contrasted-enhanced CT scan early in care to document the potential for arterial bleeding. Such imaging may allow earlier control of the bleeding site.

After the patient has been stabilized, further assessment of the other intraperitoneal pelvic structures must be carried out. If any indication of an unstable fracture is noted, urethrography should be performed in male patients.[14, 71] This technique is accomplished by inserting a small catheter into the urethral meatus, inflating the balloon, and injecting approximately 25 to 30 mL of a radiopaque dye to outline the urethra. If no leak is evident, a catheter is inserted. It is best to do the radiograph of the pelvis in an oblique plane (e.g., as in a Judet view of the full pelvis) to put the urethra into full relief. However, in most situations, this view is difficult to obtain, and a standard AP radiograph is satisfactory. After urethrography, a cystogram should be obtained by filling the bladder with 400 mL of dye and taking a radiograph. After evacuation of the dye, a postvoid view is taken to determine any occult extraperitoneal bladder rupture. If these investigations do not reveal a cause of the hematuria, an intravenous pyelogram should

be obtained. In female patients, urethrography is rarely helpful and usually omitted. A thorough physical examination, including a vaginal examination, is performed before the catheter is placed, and even then a vaginal injury may be missed in up to 50% of cases.[83]

A thorough neurologic examination is always required to evaluate injuries to the lumbosacral plexus. Therapeutic decision making and the medicolegal environment necessitate a baseline examination.[30, 118]

An open pelvic fracture further complicates assessment and diagnosis.[83, 88, 89] The wound must be adequately evaluated. Wounds occurring in the anterior aspect of the pelvis or over the flank are relatively clean and can be treated like most open fractures. However, wounds that occur in the buttock and groin regions and any wound in the perineal region require exact assessment. Because they are usually contaminated by the contents of the rectum, any wounds that involve the rectum or the perineal or buttock regions must be débrided and an external fixation device applied. Performance of a colostomy to divert the fecal stream should be given serious consideration for this group of open pelvic fractures. Other fractures that do not involve these areas but are clean can be débrided, and then appropriate fixation can be instituted.

Occasionally, in a hemodynamically stable patient, external fixators are applied in the acute phase to facilitate care.[112, 113] The frame adequately stabilizes the pelvic disruption to allow patient mobility and nursing care.[90]

Definitive Management

After stabilization of an acutely injured patient, the pelvic injury must be reassessed to determine definitive management. Appropriate evaluation is necessary to decide whether the injury requires operative intervention to decrease the chance of late pain, malunion, and nonunion.[44, 46, 73, 84, 91, 104, 112] This assessment must include a determination of pelvic stability, the fracture pattern, and location, with emphasis on determining sacroiliac joint involvement and nerve injury, as well as an evaluation of the soft tissue components of the injury.

HISTORY

Assessment of the mechanism and the type of force that was applied to create the injury should be carried out. Direct crushing injuries cause serious soft tissue disruption, which leads to wound-healing problems. Indirectly applied force usually spares the soft tissue and does not lead to wound problems. Knowledge of the age and occupation of the patient and, most important, the patient's expectations is necessary if the surgeon and the patient are to have a common treatment goal.

PHYSICAL EXAMINATION

Appropriate measurement of leg length discrepancies and evaluation of internal and external rotational abnormalities and open wounds are important. Of equal importance is the evaluation of soft tissue injuries (e.g., contusions, hemorrhage, and hematomas). After inspection, palpation of the areas of injury should be carried out to determine soft tissue disruption, bony gaps, and hematomas. Thorough assessment of soft tissues in the preoperative period helps prevent wound slough from the injudicious placement of incisions.

Rotational instability can be assessed by pushing on the anterior superior iliac wings both internally and externally to determine whether the pelvis opens and closes. Push-pull evaluation of the leg can be used to detect any vertical migration of the pelvis. Confirmation can be obtained with radiographs or image intensification. This assessment is best done when the patient is initially examined; however, if the stability of the pelvis is at all in doubt, examination under anesthesia is mandatory.[49]

Radiographic Assessment

Before definitive treatment decisions are made, a complete radiographic assessment of the pelvis should be done, including AP, inlet, and outlet views and a CT scan. It is important to remember that the pelvis, in the supine position, lies 45° to 60° oblique to the long axis of the skeleton. Consequently, an AP radiograph is essentially an oblique radiograph of the pelvis. To appropriately determine displacement, it is mandatory to evaluate two radiographs taken at right angles, which has led to development of the inlet and outlet views by Pennal and Sutherland.[28, 82]

ANTEROPOSTERIOR RADIOGRAPH

The AP radiograph (Fig. 36–25) is very useful in providing an overview of the pelvic injury. Assessment of anterior ring lesions with regard to pubic ramus fractures and symphysis displacement is important. The sacroiliac joint, sacral and iliac fractures, and avulsion of the sacral spines, lateral margin of the sacrum, and L5 transverse process are seen in this view. Use of the sacral promontory and sacral

arcuate lines, along with a vertical line through the midline of the sacrum, is important to determine displacement. Leg length discrepancies can be noted by the level of the hip joints.

INLET RADIOGRAPH

The inlet view (Fig. 36–26) is taken with the patient in the supine position. The tube is directed from the head toward the feet at 60°.[82] It is therefore perpendicular to the pelvic brim, and the radiographic view is a true inlet picture of the pelvis. On this view can be seen the pelvic brim, including the iliopectineal line, the pubic rami, the sacroiliac joints, and the ala and body of the sacrum, as well as the posterior tubercles. This view is useful for determining posterior displacement of the sacroiliac joint, sacrum, or iliac wing; internal rotation deformities of the ilium; and sacral impaction injuries. Inspection of the sacral ala, particularly along the arcuate line, demonstrates sacral crush injuries as a buckling through this line or a shortening of the sacrum on one side in comparison to the other. Ischial spine avulsions can also be seen on this view.

OUTLET RADIOGRAPH

The outlet view (Fig. 36–27) is taken with the tube directed 45° to the long axis of the patient, but at the foot of the patient.[82] The tube is directed toward the head. This radiograph is very useful for determining superior rotation of the hemipelvis, which is seen in the bucket-handle type of injury. Displacement or leg length discrepancy is determined from the level of the hip joints. Vertical migration can also be determined, and fractures through or near the sacral foramina are easily seen.

Computed Tomography

The use of CT has revolutionized assessment of the posterior osseous ligamentous structures of the pelvis. It

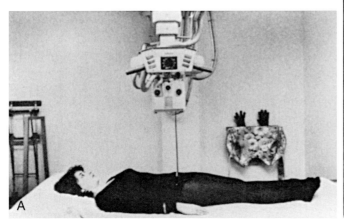
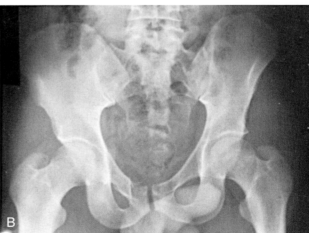

FIGURE 36–25. *A,* For the anteroposterior (AP) projection, the beam is directed perpendicular to the midpelvis and the radiologic plate. *B,* Radiographic appearance of the pelvis in the AP plane.

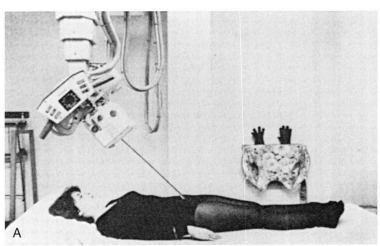

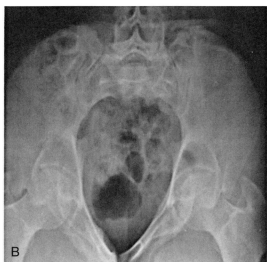

FIGURE 36–26. *A,* For the inlet projection, the beam is directed from the head to the midpelvis at an angle of 60° to the plate. *B,* Radiographic appearance in the inlet projection.

is mandatory for determining the exact nature of a posterior injury (Fig. 36–28*A*). It reveals whether an injury through the sacrum is a crushing injury or a shearing injury with a large gap. Sacroiliac joint displacement is valuable in determining the stability of this posterior injury. Anterior opening of the joint with a closed posterior portion represents a rotationally unstable injury with intact posterior ligaments (type B). If the joint is open throughout its course, the posterior ligaments are disrupted and the injury is translationally unstable (type C). CT is also helpful in defining acetabular injuries. Many pubic ramus fractures that occur near the base of the anterior column enter the acetabulum, and appropriate assessment of these injuries is necessary. Advances in technology have shown that three-dimensional reconstructions of CT scans may

provide a more useful evaluation of the overall displacement of a pelvic fracture (see Fig. 36–28*B*). Close scrutiny of the upper sacral vertebral bodies and lumbosacral junction must be done to assess the anatomic abnormalities in preparation for posterior stabilization and treatment of L5–S1 facet joint injuries.

Examination under Anesthesia

If after all these investigations the true instability pattern of the pelvis is unclear, the physician should not hesitate to examine the patient under anesthesia within the first 5 to 7 days after injury because the results may dictate major changes in the management of these patients.

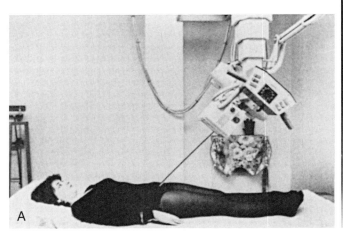

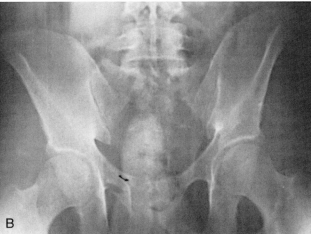

FIGURE 36–27. *A,* For the outlet projection, the beam is directed from the foot to the symphysis at an angle of 40° to the plate. *B,* Radiographic appearance in the outlet projection.

DECISION MAKING

After a full assessment of the pelvic injury is complete, a decision can be made regarding appropriate treatment[17] (Fig. 36–29). The first component to be considered is instability. Fractures that are stable include AP compression injuries with less than 2.5 cm of displacement (type B1.1) and lateral compression injuries with sacral impaction (type B2.1).

Instability with symphysis disruption[106, 113] of more than 2.5 cm is an indication for operative stabilization. Fractures and dislocations through the sacroiliac joint have a high incidence of sequelae such as long-term pain, discomfort, and nonunion.[43, 44, 46, 49, 55, 93, 102, 105] To avoid these problems, operative stabilization of the pelvis is commonly indicated to ensure reduction and stability. Extra-articular sacroiliac joint fractures occurring through the iliac wing (C1.1) or sacrum in patients with isolated injuries can usually be managed by appropriate closed reduction and traction and the application of an external fixator to control the rotatory abnormality[50, 51] (Table 36–3). If closed reduction is unsuccessful, operative care is recommended. If associated injuries are present that require mobilization of the patient or if the patient wishes to accept the risks of operative treatment, surgical intervention can be carried out.

Significant displacement is defined as the following:

1. Leg length discrepancy of more than 1 to 1.5 cm.
2. Significant internal rotation abnormality with no external rotation of the lower extremity past neutral. Similarly, the lack of internal rotation in an external rotation–type fracture is significant.

Obviously, a tilt fracture leads to a significant deformity, particularly in females, who may be subject to dyspareunia because of a displaced fragment near the vagina. If a stable fracture is significantly displaced, intervention may be required.

Treatment of associated injuries, particularly injuries to the acetabulum or long bones of the lower extremity, must also be considered when planning operative procedures. A femoral shaft fracture associated with a major pelvic disruption treated by traction may lead to significant knee stiffness. This combination of a pelvic fracture and an ipsilateral femur fracture leads to a higher mortality rate than either injury does alone. The presence of multiple lower limb long bone fractures associated with an acetabular fracture is usually an indication for surgery to maximize functional rehabilitation.

REDUCTION AND FIXATION TECHNIQUES

Biomechanics of Pelvic Fixation

To make logical decisions regarding the stabilization of pelvic disruptions, knowledge of the mechanical stability

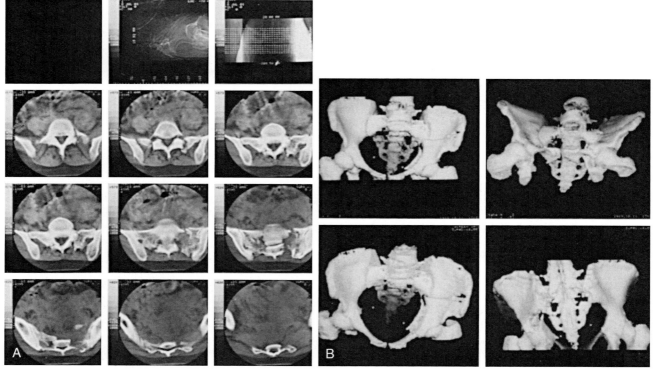

FIGURE 36–28. The use of computed tomography (CT) for evaluation of the posterior structures of the pelvis is imperative. *A,* This series of CT scans demonstrates a shear fracture through the sacrum that is disrupting the bone and causing a large gap. Also note some fracturing in the posterior elements on the opposite side. CT can also be used for evaluating anterior lesions, particularly in the acetabulum and in iliac wing fractures. *B,* New advances in computer technology now allow three-dimensional reconstruction. The three-dimensional reconstruction of this pelvis demonstrates how well it will aid in determining the complete injury.

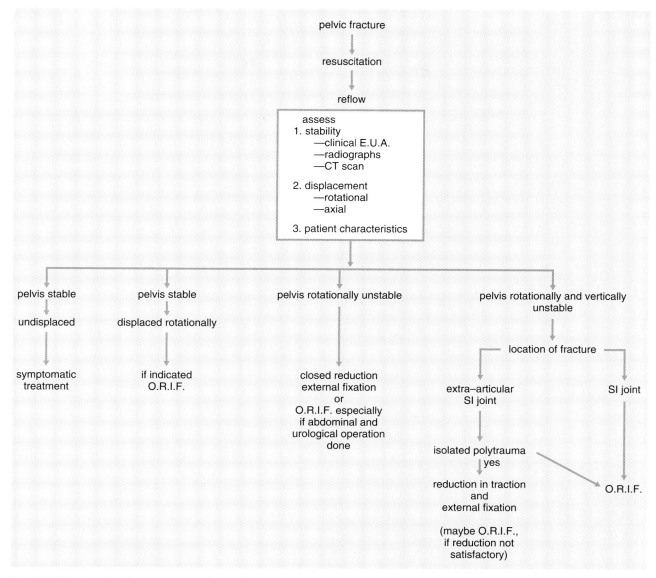

FIGURE **36–29.** Algorithm for management of pelvic fractures. *Abbreviations:* E.U.A., examination under anesthesia; O.R.I.F., open reduction and internal fixation; SI, sacroiliac.

of different internal and external techniques is necessary. A mechanical study showed that in bilateral unstable posterior injuries, the anterior external fixator frame does not afford enough stabilization to allow weight bearing.[113] Mears and Rubash[68] attempted to improve the mechanical stability of external fixation by using pelvic transfixation pins, but this technique led to insertional difficulties and problems with nursing care. By adding another cluster of pins to the anterior inferior spine region, Mears and Rubash achieved increased stability.[68] McBroom and Tile[62] suspended a pelvis from the sacrum, which allowed full triplanar motion and showed that all existing external frames would stabilize the pelvic ring sufficiently to allow mobilization of the patient if the posterior osseous ligamentous hinge remained intact. With disruption of this posterior hinge, unstable pelvic disruptions could not be stabilized with any of the existing external frames. The

best external frame design was a rectangular construct mounted on two to three 5-mm pins spaced 1 cm apart and inserted into the iliac crest.[62]

Using a similar model, McBroom and Tile showed that internal fixation could significantly increase the force resisted by the pelvic ring when compared with external fixation.[62] In stable injuries, failure was ultimately caused

TABLE 36–3
Indications for External Fixation

Resuscitation
Rotationally unstable fractures
    Open-book fracture
    Bucket-handle fracture
Adjunct to traction in unstable fractures (type C)

by screw pull-out; therefore, in stable open-book fractures, anterior fixation allowed early mobilization. However, in an unstable injury with a disrupted posterior hinge, anterior symphysis plates did not stabilize the pelvic ring. A moderate increase in stability could be achieved by anterior symphysis plating and a trapezoidal external frame. However, the only direct method of stabilizing this unstable pelvic ring injury was by posterior and anterior fixation. The strongest available fixation was achieved by two plates at right angles across the symphysis along with posterior screw fixation or transiliac bar fixation. From mechanical studies, it is recommended that for iliac wing fractures, open reduction and stable internal fixation with interfragmental compression and neutralization plates be performed. For unilateral sacroiliac dislocation, direct fixation across the joint with cancellous screws or anterior sacroiliac fixation with plates failed at similar loads.[109] Tile and Hearn showed that iliosacral lag screws have the best pull-out strength if they have a 32-mm thread length and are positioned in the sacral body.[113] For unilateral sacral fractures, two transiliac bars should provide adequate fixation. Posterior iliosacral screws that have purchase in the sacral body (S1) provide a suitable technique, but insertion may be complicated by neurologic or vascular injury. Pohlemann and colleagues[84] achieved sacral fixation with 3.5-mm plates. They tested osteosynthesis with the plate versus sacral rods and an internal spinal fixator. The results showed that plates failed at 74%

of body weight and sacral rods failed at 85% of body weight. Albert and Miller[2] described the use of a 4.5-mm reconstruction plate fixed to the posterior tubercles and iliac wings. Mechanical testing showed that this construct failed at an average of 1000 N. Although these results are the best reported, they were done in plastic bone.[50] If the anterior injury is easily amenable to surgery, plate fixation of the symphysis is the best treatment. If it is not amenable to surgery and the anterior injury remains displaced and unstable, external fixation to control the anterior injury may be helpful. In bilateral posterior unstable disruptions, fixation of the displaced portion of the pelvis to the sacral body is necessary and can be accomplished only through posterior screw fixation (Fig. 36–30).

The results of all mechanical studies are routinely reported in newtons. A newton is equal to 0.22 lb of force. Failure of posterior sacroiliac joint plating at 387 N is equal to failure at 85.14 lb of force, which is much less than the body weight of an average adult. Caution must be exercised in the postoperative period to not overly stress the internal fixation construct by weight bearing or an upright position.

Symphyseal Reduction and Stabilization

Disruption of the symphysis is related to an AP or external rotation injury to the pelvis. Consequently, the principle of

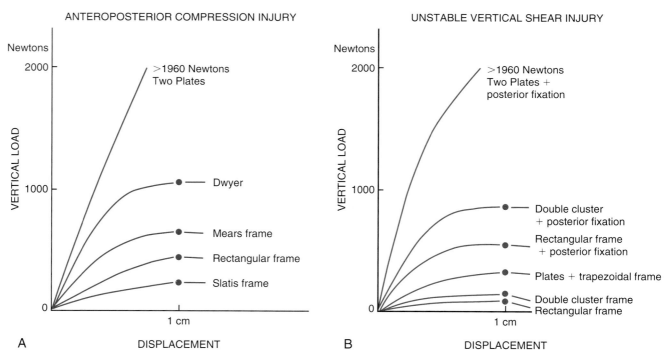

FIGURE 36–30. A, Results of mechanical testing on a vertically stable open-book injury produced by division of the symphysis pubis and the anterior sacroiliac ligaments. External frames gave adequate fixation for this type of injury, but two plates across the symphysis provided better stability. B, Results of fixation of an unstable vertical shear injury produced in the laboratory by division of the symphysis pubis, fracture of the ilium posteriorly, and division of the pelvic floor ligaments. All forms of anterior fixation failed under a 20-kg load (1 kg = 10 N); posterior internal fixation proved to be far superior. Internal stabilization of the unstable posterior injury and the symphysis pubis produced excellent stability of the pelvic ring. (A, B, Modified from Tile, M., ed. Fractures of the Pelvis and Acetabulum, 2nd ed. Baltimore, Williams & Wilkins, 1984.)

reduction is to close the pelvic ring by internal rotation, which can be accomplished by closed manual pressure over the anterior superior iliac spines. However, this technique is relatively inefficient and is supplemented by internal rotation of the femurs by an assistant. Closed reduction can be accomplished through internal rotation of the femurs and their attachment to the hemipelvis. If the reduction is unacceptable, the patient is turned onto the uninvolved side so that gravity will assist in reduction of the upper portion of the hemipelvis. With these closed reductions, stabilization of the symphysis is external.

APPLICATION OF EXTERNAL FIXATION TO THE PELVIS

The external fixator is a mainstay in the treatment of pelvic disruptions. Orthopaedic surgeons should become comfortable with and competent in efficient application of an external frame.[123] During the resuscitation phase, this device may have to be applied quickly, in as little as 20 to 30 minutes.

Important principles are the use of 5-mm pins with the threads buried into the thick anterior half of the iliac wing. These pins should be placed a minimum of 1 cm apart to increase their stability. It is mandatory to place two pins per side, but it may be advantageous to insert three in case one pin is not completely placed within the iliac crest. The standard rectangular frame is probably all that is needed in most situations. Rarely, a more rigid, multiplanar frame is required.[68] With a small iliac crest or a fracture that may extend into the iliac crest, application of pins in the anterior inferior spine region of the pelvis may be necessary.

Application of the frame requires consideration of the deformity and subsequent reduction technique. If the hemipelvis has migrated vertically, the first reduction maneuver is traction through a distal femoral or proximal tibial traction pin and the application of 25 to 30 lb of traction. If traction greater than 30 lb is necessary, the pin must be placed into the distal part of the femur. Because the displacement is usually posterosuperior, it is helpful to apply traction in an anteriorly directed fashion with the hip in about 45° to 90° of flexion. It is usually necessary to maintain this traction for 4 to 6 weeks to preserve vertical stability if posterior internal fixation is not used.

With the posterior deformity corrected, stab incisions for the pins must be placed through the skin in a rotationally reduced position. If a percutaneous method is to be used, it is advantageous to use transverse incisions angled across the iliac crest at 90° and directed toward the umbilicus. The most anterior pin is positioned 2 cm dorsal to the anterior superior iliac spine to avoid the lateral femoral cutaneous nerve. However, if a later iliac crest incision is planned, standard stab wounds parallel to the crest are preferred to avoid compromise of the incision by these wounds. The advantages of angled stab incisions are that they avoid long wounds that can decompress extraperitoneal hematomas and they are in the direction of any correction of displacement of the hemipelvis.

Regardless of whether a percutaneous closed or an open method is used, it is imperative to understand the anatomy of the iliac wing. The opening of the iliac wing is angled 45° oblique to the operating table or the floor, and the lateromedial flare of the wings is also 45°. The iliac crest has a lateral overhang. A model pelvis in the operating room helps the surgeon determine the exact pin orientation. A small guide such as a spinal needle can be placed along the iliac crest to act as a directional finder for the drill and the pin. Image intensification oriented in the plane of the crest helps guide pin placement. When placing the pins, it is important to start the pin just medial to the midline of the iliac crest. The pin should then be directed along the angle of the iliac crest. Drilling of the pins perpendicular to the long axis of the patient or to the floor will result in passage of the pins through the iliac crest and out its lateral aspect (Fig. 36–31).

After the crest is identified, a drill bit is directed in the appropriate orientation as determined by the guide. A drill hole that just perforates the iliac crest is made. The pin is inserted into the drill hole and seated with several gentle blows of a hammer. The size of the drill hole is determined by the system in use. Normally, for 5-mm pins, a 3.2- to 3.5-mm drill bit is required. Once the pin has been seated in the predrilled hole, it is gently turned by hand and allowed to seek its way between the inner and outer cortical tables of the hemipelvis while being directed toward the greater trochanter (Fig. 36–32). The complete threads of the pin should be buried within the iliac bone. Once the pins have been placed into both hemipelves, they can be used cautiously as a handle to assist in reduction of the hemipelvis. If the patient's condition permits, pin placement must be checked before leaving the operating room. The outlet view reveals whether the pin is out of the crest. The obturator oblique view is tangential to the crest and shows whether the pins are between the two tables. A combination of both views will provide excellent visualization of the iliac crest to guide insertion.

After pin placement and verification, the frame can be constructed. Several basic principles should be observed. With a simple rectangular frame, the two crossbars should be joined together with bars or 6-mm Steinmann pins. With this connected double bar across the front, rotational control is enhanced. Care must be taken to apply the frame so that sufficient clearance is present in the abdominal region to allow for postoperative distention. If the frame does not allow enough clearance, it should be revised.

Once the frame has been applied, an image intensifier is brought into position with the patient on a radiolucent table. Closed reduction is carried out by methods described previously. Reduction can be confirmed on the AP, inlet, and outlet views by rotating the image intensifier either 45° to the head or 45° to the feet. After anatomic reduction is obtained (i.e., with the symphysis closed as much as possible and no superior rotation through the symphysis), the frame is tightened.

If a triangular and more complex frame is required (i.e., pins into the iliac crest and the region of the anterior inferior iliac spine), the lower pins are inserted through an

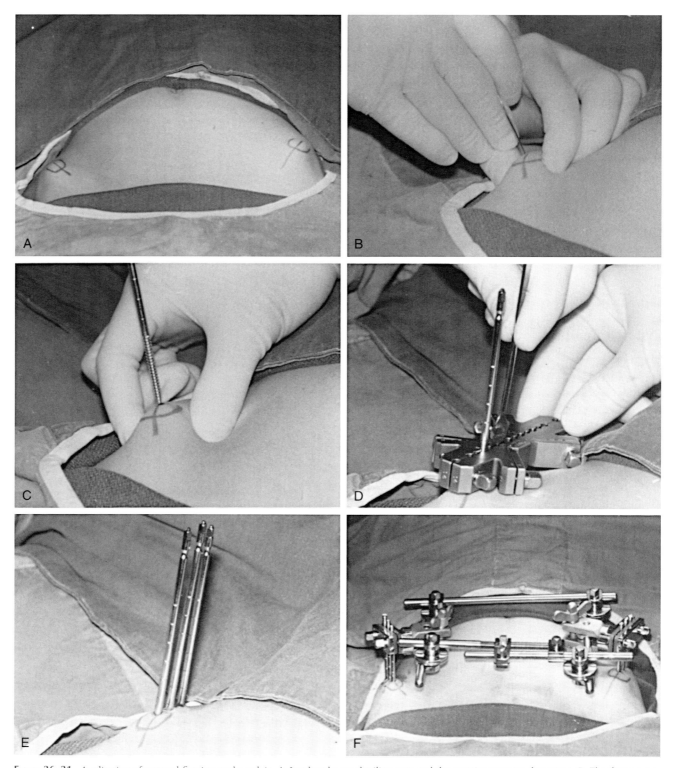

FIGURE 36–31. Application of external fixation to the pelvis. A, Landmarks are the iliac crest and the anterior superior iliac spine. B, The iliac wing is palpated to determine its orientation. It may also be determined by the use of an open technique or by spinal needles to outline both the inner and the outer aspects of the pelvis. C, Appropriate orientation of the iliac wing; note the pin orientation on an angle to the body. D, After insertion of the first pin, the second and third pins are inserted freehand or with a guide device. E, The pins in place match the orientation of the iliac wing. F, The final frame.

incision made between the anterior superior and anterior inferior spines to expose the interspinous bone. Care must be taken to protect the lateral cutaneous nerve to the thigh. The origins of the sartorius and rectus femoris between the spines are removed. Pins are then placed in a similar manner through the anterior inferior spine into the thick bone above the acetabulum. This technique is best done under image intensification to avoid entering the hip joint

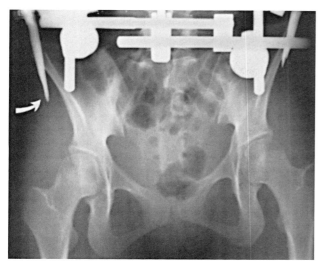

FIGURE 36–32. Improper pin position. It can be seen from the pelvic radiograph that the pins have gone through the iliac wing and out the lateral aspect (*arrow*). Note that the orientation of these pins is far too perpendicular and, therefore, the direction of the iliac wing has been forgotten. These pins are inadequate for long-term use and would have to be replaced.

(Fig. 36–33). Potential problems with this approach are the loss of tamponade as a result of stripping of tissue from the inner pelvic wall, exposure of the anterior aspect of the pelvis, and penetration of the hip joint.

With two pins in the anterior inferior spine region and two in the iliac crest, the pin clusters are developed by using pin-to-bar clamps and a bar. The two pin clusters are connected by separate bars to form a triangle. The two triangular portions are then joined across the patient's abdomen to complete the frame (Fig. 36–34). A simpler

frame construct uses one pin in each anterior inferior spine with a rectangular frame. This frame must allow at least 90° of hip flexion so that the patient can sit.

Open Reduction of Symphyseal Disruptions

If open reduction–internal fixation of a symphyseal disruption is necessary, a decision whether to use one or two plates must be made. If the posterior osseous ligament hinge is intact (a stable AP compression injury), the use of a single plate placed on the superior aspect of the pubic bodies and crossing the symphysis is adequate.[49, 54, 107, 108] If the posterior osseous ligamentous hinge is disrupted and will not be stabilized internally, the use of a second plate (four holes or more) placed on the anterior pubic bodies is recommended. However, if posterior stabilization will be carried out, single-plate fixation is satisfactory. A two-hole or greater, 3.5- or 4.5-mm plate is used to provide suitable stability. The symphysis cycles in tension and compression, depending on the patient's position, and a four-hole or larger plate will limit this motion and thereby potentially lead to breakage of the plate. A two-hole plate allows such motion to occur, although failure of implant fixation may result from screw loosening. Determination of plate size should be based on the plate that best fits the pubic bodies.[54]

OPEN REDUCTION AND INTERNAL FIXATION OF THE SYMPHYSIS: TECHNIQUE

A Foley catheter is inserted for bladder decompression.[49, 54] It may be instilled with fluid intraoperatively to identify the bladder. The standard approach to the

FIGURE 36–33. Technique of insertion of the double-cluster external fixator. The iliac crest is exposed as shown in *A* from the anterior inferior iliac spine to a point 4 cm posterior to the anterior superior iliac spine. The 5-mm pelvic pins are inserted under direct vision, as indicated, and the double frame is assembled. This exposure may be avoided by the use of image intensification to guide percutaneous insertion of the pins (*A*, Redrawn from Mears, D.C. External Skeletal Fixation. Baltimore, Williams & Wilkins, 1983.)

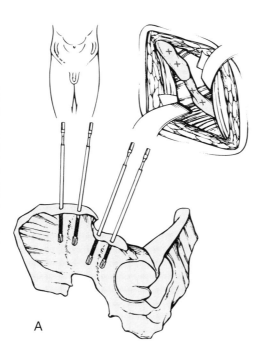

A

B

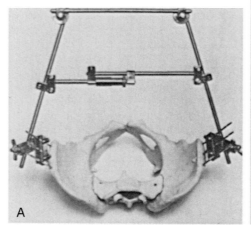

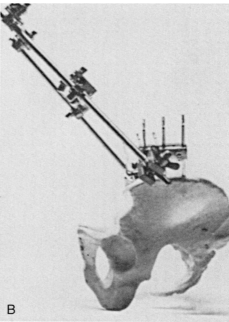

FIGURE **36–34.** Types of external frames. *A, B,* Trapezoidal (Slatis) frame, which was proposed to be able to control posterior instability. It is a good frame for stabilization of the pelvis because it allows the arms to be moved in an outward direction away from the abdomen for work on the abdomen. *C,* Double-cluster frame of Mears.

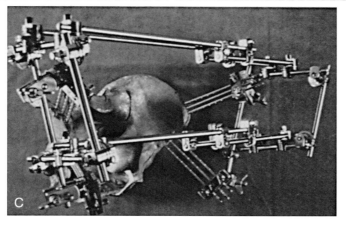

symphysis is through the Pfannenstiel incision, which is usually located approximately 2 cm above the symphysis. The incision should extend from one external inguinal ring to the other. After the skin and subcutaneous tissues have been incised, the fascia over the rectus abdominis muscles and the external oblique muscle is identified. In males, the spermatic cord should be protected to prevent iatrogenic injury. In most cases of symphyseal disruption, the rectus abdominis is traumatically disrupted from one or both pubic bodies. Consequently, the exposure can be carried out very easily. However, if the rectus abdominis has not been torn off its insertion, the insertion of this muscle onto the pubic bodies must be elevated to access the symphysis.

The inferior 8 to 10 cm of the linea alba is split down to the symphysis. The insertion of the recti onto the pubic bodies can be elevated to reveal the anterior aspect of the pubis and the medial aspect of the obturator foramen. Posteriorly, the space of Retzius is opened, with care taken to not damage the bladder. By remaining on the pubic bodies, the exposure can be extended laterally to expose the superior pubic rami to the iliopectineal eminence. This approach may be done through a midline abdominal

incision. Beware that the standard midline laparotomy incision does not extend the incision distally enough to expose the symphysis. An orthopaedic surgeon must be present if the trauma surgeon is making the incision so that the appropriate length is achieved (Fig 36–35).

Once the exposure has been completed, a pelvic reduction clamp can be applied to the anterior body of the symphysis through appropriate screw fixation, or pointed reduction clamps can be placed through the obturator foramen anteriorly, and then reduction can be accomplished. If the reduction has any rotational component or displacement at the symphysis, a second clamp can be applied anteriorly or superiorly to control this aspect of the displacement (Fig. 36–36). The appropriate plate is contoured and applied to the superior aspect of the pubic bodies. Palpation of the posterior aspect of the pubic body determines the orientation of the drill so that the screw can be placed through the full length of the pubic body. Usually, a 40- to 50-mm screw can be placed into the body of the pubis. If a second plate is required, it can be contoured along the anterior aspect of the pubic bodies and the screws placed in an anterior-to-posterior direction

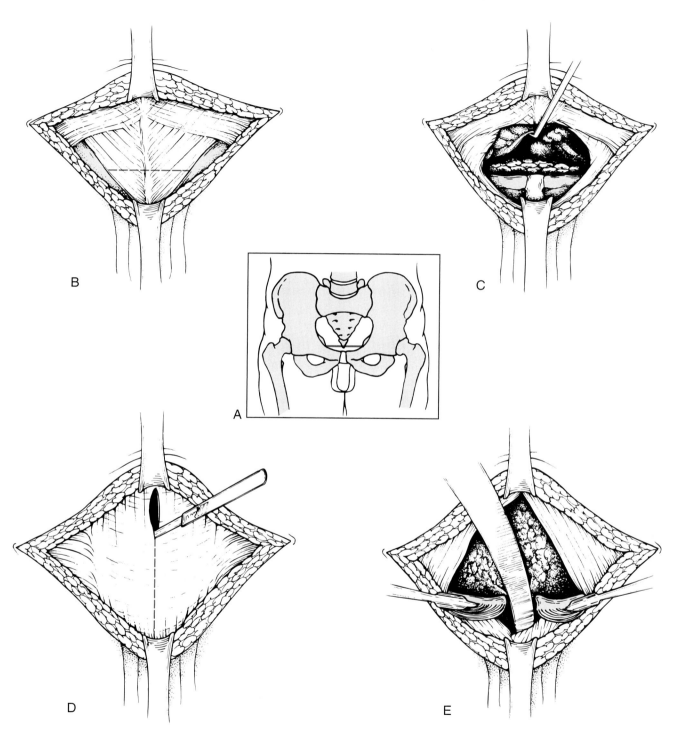

FIGURE 36–35. Exposure of the symphysis and pubic body. *A,* A Pfannenstiel transverse skin incision made approximately 1 to 2 cm above the palpable symphysis and pubic body. This incision usually extends from one external ring to the other external ring. *B,* After subcutaneous dissection, the rectus sheath is identified from its outer borders. Note the spermatic cord. Care should be taken to avoid it, and retraction can be carried out once it is mobilized laterally. The rectus sheath is then divided just above the symphysis while making sure that a cuff of tissue is left anteriorly to attach it. *C,* Exposure is completed by subperiosteally taking away the prebladder fat. *D,* An alternative method whereby the linea alba is split along its fibers down to the rectus and then pulled back to the obturator foramen with the use of a Hohmann retractor. *E,* This method allows exposure of the symphysis but maintains some attachments of the rectus to the pubic body.

between the superiorly placed plate screws. These screws must not be left long to avoid erosion into the bladder. After fixation has been achieved, the incisions are closed while making sure that the rectus abdominis is well apposed to its insertion, which may require complete muscle relaxation as well as flexing of the table so that the muscles are brought together to facilitate reattachment. The external oblique aponeurosis must be repaired, and if the external ring has been entered, care must be taken to repair it anatomically so that an inguinal hernia does not develop.

If a pubic ramus fracture requires exposure, it can be done by extending the surgical exposure along the pubic ramus. The reduction can be accomplished, and stabilization of the symphysis will usually control displacement of the pubic ramus. If the displacement is within the first 4 cm lateral to the body of the pubis, the plate may be extended out onto this area to achieve plate fixation. If an extensile approach is required for reduction and stabilization of a pubic ramus fracture, particularly at the root of the acetabulum, it is accomplished with an ilioinguinal anterior approach, as described by Letournel.[58, 121] This approach allows adequate exposure of the whole anterior aspect of the pelvis and appropriate plate fixation with a well-contoured 3.5-mm reconstruction plate (Figs. 36–37 and 36–38). An alternative approach is the modified Stoppa approach to the inner aspect of the pelvis.[15, 45] With the patient in the spine position and the involved extremity draped free, a transverse incision is made 2 cm above the symphysis similar to the Pfannenstiel incision. The recti are split along the linea alba and sharply elevated from the pubic body and rami. The rectus and neurovascular structures are retracted laterally and anteriorly. With the surgeon standing on the opposite side of the table from the fracture, the vascular anastomoses between the inferior epigastrics and the obturator vessels are ligated. Before elevation of the posterior iliacus, the iliolumbar artery is ligated. Full access is achieved by dividing the iliopectineal fascia superiorly and the obturator fascia inferiorly. This exposure will allow access to the sacroiliac joint by retracting the psoas and iliac vessels. Flexion of the ipsilateral leg facilitates the exposure by relaxing the psoas. The obturator nerve and vessel must be protected throughout this approach.

The standard fixation is plate osteosynthesis. Screws inserted at or lateral to the iliopectineal eminence will be in the hip joint. Retrograde intramedullary screw fixation of ramus fractures has been developed by Routt.[98, 108]

Sacroiliac Joint Reduction and Fixation

Dislocations or fracture-dislocations through the sacroiliac joint can be reduced and stabilized either anteriorly or posteriorly.[49, 61, 64, 99, 109] Advantages of the anterior approach include better visualization of the sacroiliac joint, which allows reduction under direct visualization.[109] It is also easier to denude the articular cartilage of the sacroiliac joint to facilitate the insertion of a bone graft for potential fusion of this joint.[49, 109] The disadvantage of this approach is the close relationship of the L4, L5, and lumbosacral trunk to the sacroiliac joint. The L4 nerve root runs between the L5 root and the sacroiliac joint and merges with the L5 root to form the lumbosacral trunk an average of 11.49 mm from the joint line at the level of the sacral promontory. It is at risk for a traction palsy if adequate exposure is not obtained and excessive retraction is necessary.[3, 47]

Advantages of the posterior approach are simplicity in exposing the iliac wing and sacroiliac joint and the ability

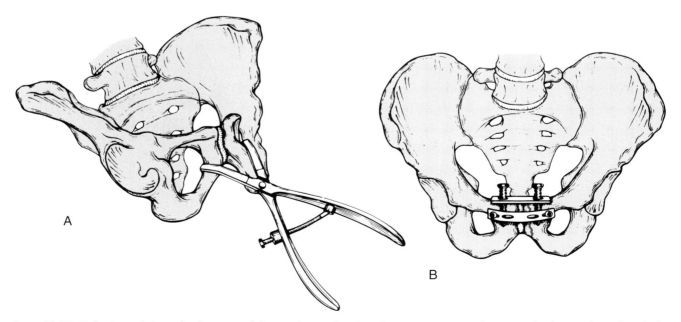

A

B

FIGURE 36–36. Reduction techniques for disruption of the symphysis pubis. A, Reduction using a pointed or serrated reduction clamp through the obturator foramen to hold the pelvis together. B, Use of pelvic reduction clamps applied to the anterior aspect of the pubic body on both sides of the symphysis and then closing the symphysis. This technique gives better control and allows for more rotational correction through the clamps themselves. (A, B, Redrawn from Schatzker, J.; Tile, M. Rationale of Operative Fracture Care. New York, Springer-Verlag, 1987, p. 165.)

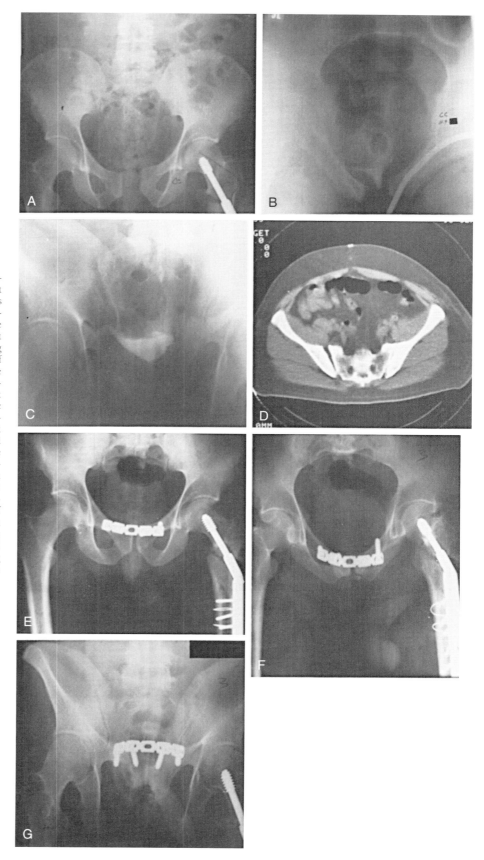

FIGURE 36–37. Series of radiographs demonstrating an open-book (B1.3) injury that is unstable in external rotation and requires fixation. *A,* Anteroposterior pelvic radiograph demonstrating the diastasis of the symphysis, which is unilateral on the left side. *B,* Inlet view confirming the opening of the symphysis, as well as the opening of the sacroiliac joint. *C,* Outlet view of the pelvis showing the diastasis of the symphysis, well as widening of the sacroiliac joint on the left side. *D,* Computed tomographic scan confirming the opening of the sacroiliac joint on the left side. Note that posterior subluxation has not occurred and that the posterior structures appear to be intact because of the absence of displacement in this area. It appears that the right hemipelvis has been hinged posteriorly. Note the normal right side. *E,* Postoperative radiograph showing plate fixation of the symphysis. A five-hole plate has been used. This injury could also have been treated with a two-hole plate. Inlet (*F*) and outlet (*G*) views of the pelvis during anatomic reduction and closure of the symphysis and sacroiliac joint.

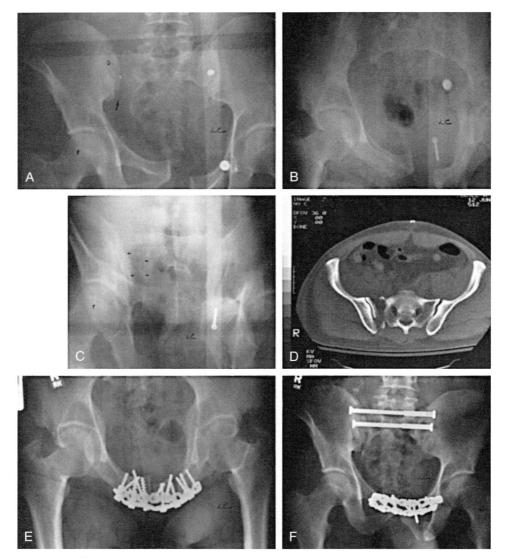

Figure 36–38. Example of anterior fixation showing the use of double plating of the symphysis in unstable fractures in which posterior fixation may be contraindicated either because of poor posterior soft tissue or because of the patient's condition. *A,* Anteroposterior radiograph of the pelvis of a man who was crushed between two pieces of heavy equipment. Note the diastasis of the symphysis with an associated fracture posteriorly *(closed arrow)*. Also note a component of the sacrum left attached to the iliac wing *(open arrow)*. *B,* Inlet view again showing the diastasis of the symphysis with a wide posterior gap and posterior displacement. *C,* Outlet view again showing the large gap and superior vertical migration of the hemipelvis on the right side *(arrows)*. *D,* Computed tomographic scan confirming a shear fracture through the sacrum with the sacral side of the sacroiliac joint left intact. Note the widening of this injury and avulsion of the posterior tubercle indicative of complete disruption of the posterior ligaments. *E,* At the time of laparotomy, immediate internal fixation of the symphysis was performed. Because of this man's condition, potential problems with returning to the operating room to stabilize the posterior injury were considered remote. Consequently, a double plate was applied across the anterior of the ring and supplemented by external fixation. *F,* This man did improve, and posterior transiliac bar fixation was used to close the sacral fracture and stabilize it. It should be noted that this is the only time that double-plate fixation of the symphysis should be used for unstable posterior injuries when the potential for nonoperative treatment exists.

to reduce either sacral or sacroiliac fractures and fracture-dislocations.[64] The major disadvantage of this approach is that the patient must be turned prone or lateral, which may be difficult in a multiply injured patient. Because the screws can be placed into either the sacral ala or the body, precise reduction of the fracture and image intensification are required so that exact placement of the screws can be observed. Damage to the anterior vascular structures in front of the sacrum or to the cauda equina by inadvertent perforation with the screws must also be avoided. Posterior soft tissue crush injuries or significant skin loss may also cause problems.[49]

Both techniques carry a risk for significant complications, of which the surgeon must be well aware, but no definite proof has been presented that either approach is better. As long as appropriate precautions are taken, both approaches provide adequate reduction and stabilization of fractures or fracture-dislocations of the sacroiliac joint.

The decision regarding which approach to use is determined by the characteristics of the soft tissue injury and the fracture. The anterior approach is indicated for sacroiliac joint dislocations and fracture-dislocations involving the ilium, for iliac wing fractures, and for associated anterior pelvic fractures that require fixation.

The anterior approach is not indicated for sacral fractures or when the risk of infection from an external fixator pin, colostomy, suprapubic catheter, or overhanging abdominal pannus is high. The posterior approach is indicated for sacral fractures, fracture-dislocations involving the sacroiliac joint, and fractures of either the ilium or sacrum and the iliac wing. Contraindications to a posterior approach are crush or degloving injuries to the posterior skin or wounds that communicate with the perineum and ischiorectal area.

For all internal fixations of the pelvis, the use of an image intensifier and a radiolucent operating table is mandatory. The C-arm is necessary to confirm reduction and screw placement. Familiarity with the three pelvic radiographic views is necessary. Patient size, bowel gas, and radiographic dye may hinder the ability to obtain quality radiographs and force a change in treatment or radiographic technique.

ANTERIOR APPROACH TO THE SACROILIAC JOINT: EXPOSURE AND REDUCTION

The patient is placed in the supine position on a radiolucent table. A small radiolucent roll is placed just lateral to the midline on the involved side to elevate the involved hemipelvis for easier manipulation[109] (Fig. 36–39). The involved leg is draped free so that it is available to assist in the reduction. This approach can also be performed with the patient in the lateral decubitus position. The incision starts approximately 6 cm behind the highest point of the iliac crest and is carried forward to just past the anterior superior iliac spine. Posteriorly, the muscles of the lateral abdominal wall are split in the direction of their fibers to expose the posterior half of the iliac crest. The iliac fascia and the insertions of the external muscles of the abdomen onto the iliac crest are incised, and the iliacus muscle is then stripped off the internal iliac wing. The lateral femoral cutaneous nerve is located just medial to the anterior superior spine and must be protected in this approach. At this point, with flexion and internal rotation of the hip to relax the psoas and iliacus, careful dissection along the iliac wing will bring the sacroiliac joint into view. Because the iliac wing usually displaces posteriorly, the sacrum is generally found anterior to the iliac wing. Care should be taken to avoid going through the iliacus onto the sacrum and damaging the L5 root. By following the displaced iliac wing, the articular cartilage of the sacroiliac joint can be identified, and by moving both superiorly and posteriorly, the sacral ala can be identified. Subperiosteal dissection is then carried along the ala. Care should be taken to gently retract the soft tissues medially, including the L4 and L5 roots. The L5 root normally lies 2 to 3 cm medial to the S1 joint in a small groove and then goes over the anterior aspect of the sacrum to drop into the pelvis. After the superior aspect of the sacral ala has been identified, dissection continues along the anterior aspect of the ala and the pelvic brim down inside the true pelvis to identify the notch. The surgeon must take care that the dissection remains subperiosteal and avoid injury to the superior gluteal artery. If bleeding does occur, packing of the area can usually control it. After the dislocation or fracture-

dislocation has been identified, the sacroiliac joint is denuded of cartilage on its sacral side and the subchondral plate roughened if fusion of the joint is desired. A small bone graft can be taken from the anterior iliac crest. The fracture or dislocation is then reduced.

Reduction is best accomplished by placing bone-holding forceps on the iliac wing through the interval between the anterior superior and anterior inferior iliac spines to grasp the hemipelvis and pull it forward. The use of 5-mm Schanz pins in the iliac crest is helpful to obtain the correct rotational position of the hemipelvis. By pulling the pelvis forward with the bone-holding clamp and rotating it with the Schanz pins, reduction is obtained at the level of the sacroiliac joint (Fig. 36–40). By using an asymmetric pelvic reduction clamp, the sacroiliac joint can be reduced and stabilized provisionally. One arm of the clamp is placed on the posterior aspect of the iliac crest and the other on the anterior aspect of the sacral ala. The direction of force is such that the joint will be pushed anteriorly and closed down posteriorly. With a fracture through the iliac wing, this maneuver helps reduce the dislocation. Reduction may also be accomplished by placing one screw into the sacral ala and one into the iliac wing and then applying the pelvic reduction clamps. Provisional stabilization is achieved by placing a 3.2-mm Steinmann pin percutaneously through the iliac wing into the ala. Before reduction, this pin may be inserted through the ilium into the iliac side of the sacroiliac joint so that its position is confirmed under direct vision. A staple across the sacroiliac joint may also be used as a temporary stabilization device.[57]

A 3.5- or 4.5-mm three- or four-hole reconstruction plate is then contoured. One screw is placed into the sacral ala and directed parallel to the sacroiliac joint. The direction of the screw can be determined by placing a 1.6-mm Kirschner wire (K-wire) in the joint at the time of reduction. These screws are usually 30 to 40 mm long. The plate is attached to the iliac wing by fully threaded cancellous screws, which usually traverse the length of the posterior tubercle. The pelvic reduction clamp can then be removed and replaced by a second plate. Specialized plates have been developed for sacroiliac joint stabilization, but they do not allow incorporation of iliac wing fracture fixation.[109] At times, a small ridge may overgrow the sacroiliac joint on either the iliac or the sacral side. This ridge may make reduction and plate fixation difficult and can be removed. A final way of stabilizing the joint once reduction is achieved is by insertion of a percutaneous cancellous screw into the sacral body and neutralization with a three- or four-hole 3.5- or 4.5-mm anterior sacroiliac plate. After image intensification or plain radiographs confirm reduction, the wound is closed in the appropriate fashion (Figs. 36–41 and 36–42).

POSTERIOR APPROACH TO THE SACROILIAC JOINT: EXPOSURE AND REDUCTION

For a posterior approach to the sacroiliac joint, the patient must be placed either prone on bolsters or in the lateral decubitus position with the involved side up[64, 100] (Fig. 36–43). This approach is similar to that used for the insertion of transiliac bars. It is also wise to drape the

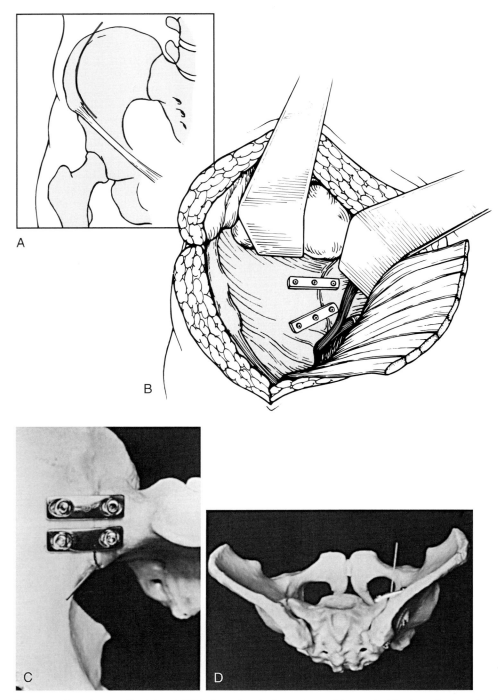

FIGURE 36–39. Anterior approach to the sacroiliac joint. A, With the patient in the supine position, an incision is made along the iliac crest, starting at the anterior superior iliac spine and extending back past the posterior tubercle and into the external oblique musculature. B, With dissection along the iliac wing, the iliopsoas muscle is reflected medially. Note the orientation of the L5 root and its relationship to the sacroiliac joint. Full exposure reveals the iliac wing, as well as the sacrum and the sacroiliac joint. It can be appreciated that fractures through the iliac wing and into the sacroiliac joint can be treated with this exposure. C, Two-plate fixation of the sacroiliac joint. One screw is placed in the sacrum, and one or two screws, depending on the size of the patient, are placed on the iliac side. A wire is inserted in the sacroiliac joint to show the orientation of the joint so that screws can be placed parallel to it. D, The orientation of the plate and screws, as well as the sacroiliac joint, can be seen. It is possible to lag the posterior tubercle of the iliac wing into the sacroiliac joint through the sacral screws.

involved leg free to facilitate the reduction through manipulation of this extremity.

To commence, a longitudinal incision is made just adjacent to the posterior superior iliac spine, either medial or lateral, depending on whether the ilium or the sacrum is to be exposed. The incision is extended from just above the upper margin of the iliac crest to 4 to 6 cm below the projected area of the posterior aspect of the sacral notch. The gluteal musculature as it inserts onto the posterior spine is then elevated sharply and, with subperiosteal dissection, is lifted off the outer aspect of the posterior wing of the ilium. Fractures in the iliac wing can easily be identified. The sacral notch is exposed by sharp reflection of the insertion of the gluteus maximus fibers from the lumbodorsal fascia, the erector spinae, and the multifidus muscles. After the sacral notch is identified, the fascial origin of the piriformis must be taken down. Care must be taken to avoid damage to the superior gluteal artery. Once the piriformis has been released, it is relatively easy to identify the dislocation of the sacroiliac joint. With the use of a lamina spreader, the joint or fracture may be distracted and débrided. On completion of débridement of the joint or fracture, reduction is accomplished with the use of pointed reduction clamps, a femoral distractor, and pelvic reduction forceps. Palpation with the surgeon's finger through the notch and along the anterior aspect of the sacroiliac joint allows appreciation of the reduction anteriorly. Palpation along the superior border of the sacral

ala and the iliac crest can also be carried out. Confirmation of the reduction by radiographs or image intensification is necessary (Fig. 36–44). The reduction can then be maintained with the use of a clamp from the sacrum and a small unicortical drill hole into the posterior spine. It may also be maintained by placing a K-wire under image intensification into the sacral ala. If an iliac wing fracture is present, anatomic reduction of the fracture with interfragmental compression and plate fixation usually allows anatomic reduction of the sacroiliac joint or at least facilitates it.

After the fracture has been reduced, iliosacral screw fixation must be undertaken. As an open procedure, the guide wire or drill starts on the outer aspects of the iliac crest and is kept cephalad to the dorsal S1 foramen and approximately 2.5 cm dorsal to a line from the

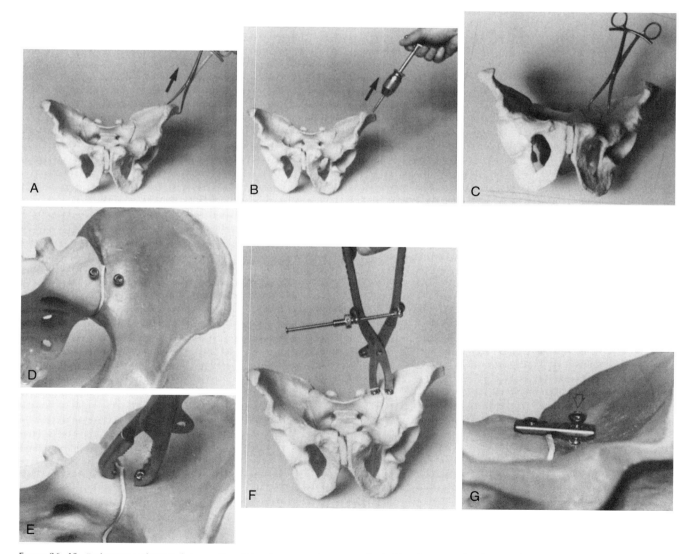

FIGURE 36–40. Reduction technique for sacroiliac dislocation—anterior approach. *A,* Use of a pointed reduction clamp to apply traction and control rotation. *B,* A Schanz screw in the iliac crest to apply traction, produce translation, and control rotation. *C,* A pointed reduction clamp may be used to maintain reduction through a previously drilled hole in the sacrum and the iliac wing, or a large asymmetric pointed clamp may be placed onto the anterior aspect of the sacrum, just medial to the sacroiliac joint, and then passed over the posterior aspect of the iliac crest (not shown). *D,* Preinsertion of two screws on either side of the sacral iliac joint. The reduction may be performed with a Farabeuf clamp. *E, F,* Pelvic reduction clamp. *G,* Reduction may also be achieved indirectly by using a plate attached to the sacrum with one screw and, subsequently, using a second screw to pull the pelvis up and in. The flat plate is inserted into the sacrum and fixed. A gap is left under the sacroiliac joint but will be reduced when the iliac screw (*arrow*) is tightened. (*A–G,* From Tile, M., ed. Fractures of the Pelvis and Acetabulum, 2nd ed. Baltimore, Williams & Wilkins, 1995.)

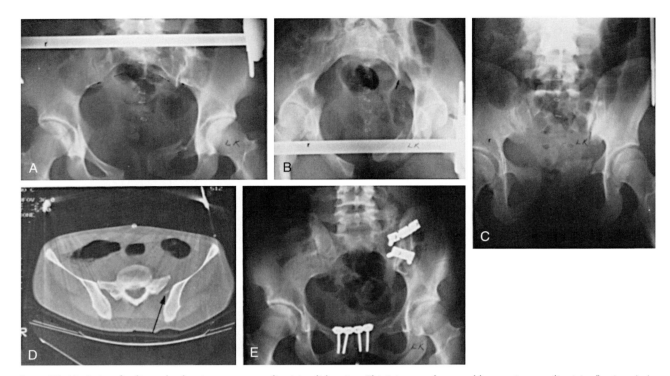

Figure 36–41. Series of radiographs showing a pure sacroiliac joint dislocation. This injury can be treated by anterior sacroiliac joint fixation. *A,* An anteroposterior view of this pelvis shows that the sacroiliac joint has narrowed on the left side. The anterior lesion is a symphysis diastasis with a fracture through the pubic and ischial rami. *B,* Inlet view. Note the posterior displacement of the sacroiliac joint *(arrow).* Provisional stabilization was accomplished with an external fixator. *C,* Note the continuing wide diastasis anteriorly, indicative of malrotation. Also note the vertical orientation of the external fixation pin on the left side as it perforates both the inner and the outer cortices of the iliac wing; it does not obtain good purchase because it was drilled in the wrong direction. *D,* Pure sacroiliac joint dislocation. Note the *arrow* pointing to a small piece of bone in the joint. At the time of surgery, this dislocation represented complete avulsion of the articular cartilage of the sacroiliac joint. It was removed as a complete shell with a minor amount of bone in place. *E,* In a Pfannenstiel approach, the symphysis was first reduced and plated. It was not necessary at this time to deal with the pubic rami fractures because they had soft tissue attachments and appeared to be adequately reduced at the time of symphyseal fixation. Through an anterior approach, two plates were placed across the sacroiliac joint to stabilize the reduction. Because the articular cartilage was avulsed, further denuding of cartilage was not necessary, and primary fusion was probable. Note the position of the plates on the sacrum (i.e., approximately 1 to 2 cm inside the joint). The screws are directed posteriorly. Plates on the iliac side tend to diverge, so good bone purchase can be obtained with screw fixation.

posterior superior to the posterior inferior spine (crista glutea) and 2.5 cm above the greater sciatic notch.[75] The use of a specific point on the iliac wing demands that the sacroiliac joint be anatomically reduced or any implants started in this position will be malpositioned in the sacrum (Fig. 36–45). With an anatomic reduction, the fixation may be started in this position and placed into the sacral ala. AP and inlet views determine the AP position of the screw, the outlet view is used to determine the superoinferior position of the screw, and guide wire or drill bit placement is confirmed to be aimed into the sacral body (see Fig. 36–44). At the time of drilling, it is very important to gently advance the drill in steps to ensure that the drill bit remains in bone. Three cortical barriers should be crossed (i.e., the outer iliac wing, the iliac side of the sacroiliac joint, and the sacroiliac joint subchondral bone). If a fourth cortical barrier is encountered, the drill bit is about to leave the sacrum, with potential danger either to the cauda equina or to the anteriorly placed neurologic and vascular structures. If the position of the drill or guide wire is not correct, it is withdrawn completely and redirected. A small two- or three-hole plate can be applied to the outer aspect of the iliac wing, or a washer can be used to prevent penetration of the screws. In sacroiliac

dislocations, cancellous screws with a 32-mm thread length and a 6.5- or 7.3-mm diameter are normally used (Fig. 36–46). However, the surgeon should make sure that the threads cross into the sacral ala and are not in the sacroiliac joint and blocking interfragmental compression of the reduction. Mechanically, a screw with a 16-mm thread length may be stronger than a screw with a 32-mm thread length because the junction of the screw shaft and threads is further from the potentially mobile fracture site. Although screw position can be evaluated by direct visualization posteriorly and by palpation of the ala superiorly and anteriorly, it is mandatory that C-arm fluoroscopy be used to confirm its safe position.

A similar approach using the lateral position can combine both anterior and posterior exposures of the sacroiliac joint. By placing the patient in the lateral decubitus position and carrying the incision along the iliac crest to the posterior tubercle and then down as described previously, the surgeon can peel off the gluteal mass from the outer aspect of the pelvic ring. Then, by moving inside the posterior tubercle, the surgeon can identify the sacral ala and the sacroiliac joint by detaching the abdominal musculature and iliacus from their attachments to the inner aspect of the iliac crest. Reduction can be accomplished under direct vision, and screws can be seen entering through the sacroiliac joint into the ala. This approach is probably best used for very difficult fractures or late fractures that require greater mobilization for reduction.

PERCUTANEOUS ILIOSACRAL SCREW FIXATION UNDER FLUOROSCOPIC CONTROL

Because of the potential for severe soft tissue complications with an open posterior exposure, the concept of limiting the amount of surgical dissection for reduction and fixation has become popular. This practice has led to the development of percutaneous techniques for posterior pelvic stabilization.[25, 64, 94, 99, 111] It is a technique that is suitable for stabilization of sacroiliac joint dislocations and sacral fractures. To use this method, the fracture must be reduced and the surgeon must understand the radio-

graphic anatomy of the sacrum, posterior iliac wing, and related soft tissues.

Screw placement is critical to achieve maximal stability and avoid complications. The screw must start on the outer aspect of the iliac wing, cross the sacroiliac joint, follow the S1 pedicle mass into the body of S1, and remain completely in bone. Safe placement demands thorough understanding of sacral radiographic anatomy because this technique is performed completely percutaneously, with no options to guide or confirm screw placement by palpation or visualization. The S1 pedicle is bordered inferiorly by the S1 root canal and foramen. The pedicle is approximately 28 mm (width) by 28 mm (height) in cross section. The superior surface slopes downward in a posterior-to-anterior direction at an angle of 45°, with a gutter for the L5 root located 2 cm medial to the sacroiliac joint.[77] The internal iliac artery lies anterior to the ala and gives off its largest branch, the superior gluteal artery,

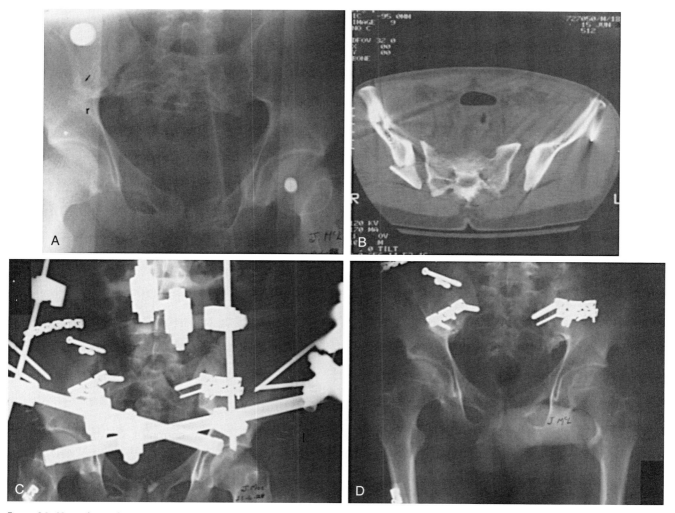

FIGURE 36–42. Radiographs representing a bilateral, posteriorly unstable injury. *A*, Anteroposterior (AP) radiograph demonstrating a dislocation of the sacroiliac joint on the left side. On the right side is a fracture-dislocation of the sacroiliac joint. The *arrow* shows the double density where the fracture line has overlapped. *B*, CT scan confirming the bilateral fractures and showing the fracture-dislocation on the right and the dislocation on the left. *C*, AP radiograph showing the bilateral anterior approaches to the sacroiliac joint. By using plate fixation to reduce the iliac wing fracture, as well as lag screw fixation into the posterior tubercle, the iliac wing was reduced and stabilized. A plate on the anterior portion stabilized the sacroiliac joint component. The anterior lesions were stabilized with the use of an external fixator to maintain the reduction obtained. *D*, Final result at approximately 8 months after the injury. Note how the fractures have united. It appears that the sacroiliac has fused on the left side as well as on the right.

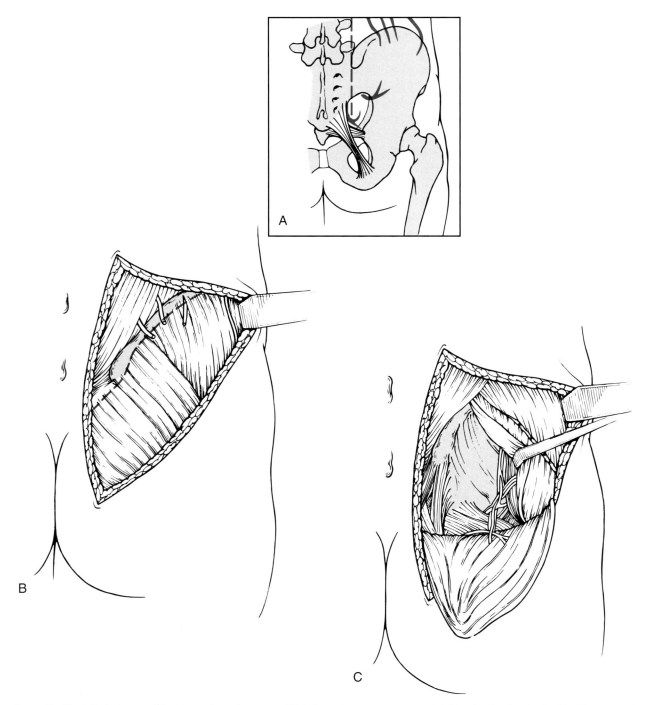

Figure 36–43. *A,* Posterior sacroiliac joint and sacral exposure. With the patient prone, exposure is initiated with a longitudinal incision centered over the posterior tubercle. This incision must be extended distally to traverse the origin of the piriformis or the area of the greater sciatic notch. *B,* The incision is carried down onto the posterior tubercle. The gluteus maximus is then reflected off the iliac crest posterior spine and its attachment to the spinal muscles. *C,* With the gluteus maximus muscle reflected laterally and inferiorly, the origin of the piriformis can be noted in the depth along the greater sciatic notch and must be detached. Detachment of the origin of the piriformis allows access to the posterior iliac crest, and if the dissection is carried medially, the sacrum may be exposed posteriorly for sacral reductions. Beware of the superior gluteal artery and its branches at the greater sciatic notch above the piriformis. With the piriformis detached from the notch, access to the inner aspect of the pelvis is obtained.

anterior to the sacroiliac joint.[96] These three structures are at risk of injury if the drill bit, guide wire, or screw penetrates through the ala. The body of the sacrum joins both alae through the pedicles and is surrounded by the cauda equina posteriorly, the pelvic viscera anteriorly, the

L5–S1 intervertebral disc superiorly, and the fused S1–S2 disc space inferiorly. The S1 body has an anteriorly protruding bony prominence, the sacral promontory, that is anterior to the sacral ala (Fig. 36–47). Screws aimed toward the promontory will not traverse the bony sacral

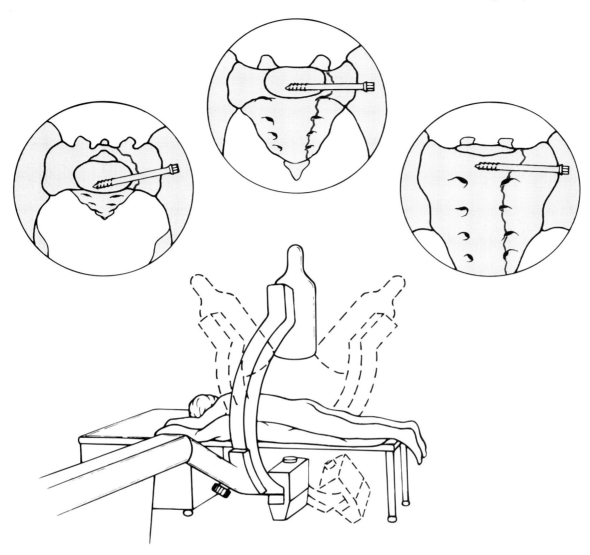

FIGURE 36–44. To make sure that the screw fixation into the sacrum or sacral ala is placed safely, the use of image intensification is mandatory. On a radiolucent table, an image intensifier is brought in so that anteroposterior 40° caudal and 40° cephalad views can be obtained. The screws can then be directed under direct radiographic control into the sacral ala and body superior to the S1 foramen and thereby avoid the cauda.

FIGURE 36–45. Starting position for posterior screw fixation of pelvic disruptions. *A,* The proper starting position is approximately 15 mm from the elevated attachment of the gluteus maximus muscles on a line drawn from the top of the greater sciatic notch on the iliac crest. *B,* Another similar location, found by starting approximately 2.5 cm (2 to 3 fingerbreadths) lateral to the posterior superior iliac spine and 2 fingerbreadths cranial to the greater sciatic notch. Both these starting positions require anatomic reduction of the disruption.

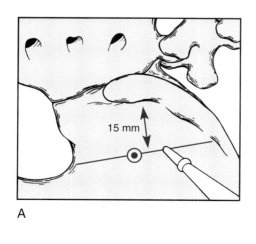

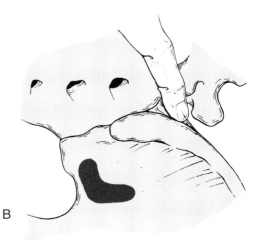

pedicular canal and may cause injury to the neurovascular structures that lie anterior to the pedicle/ala (Fig. 36–48). More than half of the S1 root canal is filled by the S1 nerve root. It runs inferiorly and laterally to the anterior S1 foramen. Because of this inferior, sloping course, the posterior half of the body of S1 is not available for screw placement because the screw could traverse the S1 root canal. Only the middle portion of the S1 body is therefore left for screw placement near the upper S1 end-plate. For safe placement of the screws, only the sacral landmarks should be used; the iliac landmarks are important to confirm reduction. The sacral landmarks are identified by using four fluoroscopic views of the pelvis—the AP, the inlet and outlet (tangential), and the lateral sacral views[93, 94, 96, 111] (Fig. 36–49).

Indications

This technique is indicated if the following criteria are met:

1. It can be performed within 5 days of injury.
2. Preoperatively, the pelvis has been placed in traction to correct displacement.

Severe soft tissue injury, bowel injury, or a combination of both these injuries is a good indication because this technique avoids large exposure and the risk of infection. It is useful for sacroiliac dislocations, fracture-dislocations, and sacral fractures.

Contraindications

This technique is contraindicated if the following are present:

1. Failure to reduce the fracture by closed means.
2. Failure to visualize the posterior and lateral sacral structures with a C-arm.
3. The presence of sacral dysmorphism[95, 96] (transitional vertebra), which occurs in 30% to 40% of people. Sacral dysmorphism is recognized by

   • The upper part of the sacrum and iliac crests co-linear on the outlet view.
   • A residual disc between S1 and S2 on the outlet view.
   • Alar mammillary processes.
   • An abnormal upper sacral ala.
   • Iliac cortical density not co-planar with the alar slope.
4. Osteoporosis.

Technique

The percutaneous method is usually done with the patient in the supine position because of the ease of reduction and because simultaneous anterior fixation can be achieved without changing the patient's position. Prone positioning is necessary if open reduction of the sacrum is planned. It may also be the surgeon's preference. The patient is placed supine on a radiolucent table and positioned to allow the C-arm full rotation so that inlet and outlet views can be obtained. A soft radiolucent support is placed under the

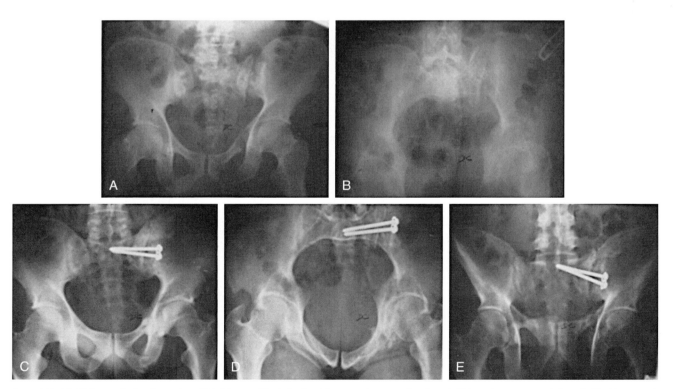

FIGURE 36–46. This man had a disruption of his left sacroiliac joint fixed by posterior screw fixation. *A,* This patient was struck from behind by a truck and suffered a displaced fracture through the sacroiliac joint and pubic rami anteriorly. *B,* Inlet view confirming posterior displacement at the sacroiliac joint on the left side. *C,* Anteroposterior view demonstrating posterior screw fixation of the pelvis. Note how the screws have been placed across and into the body of the sacrum. Such placement is necessary for sacral fractures, but it also gains good purchase in sacroiliac joint dislocations. The screws are above the first sacral foramen. *D,* Good screw placement is noted on the inlet view, which shows that reduction has been achieved and adequate fixation has occurred with screws in the ala and body of the sacrum. *E,* Outlet view again confirming proper position of the screws.

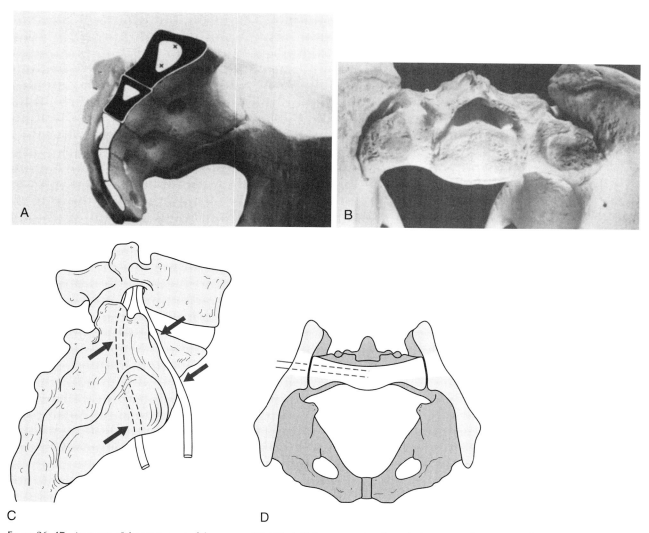

FIGURE 36–47. Anatomy of the upper part of the sacrum (S1–S2). *A,* This cross section through the sacrum demonstrates the promontory of S1 and the concavity of the sacral ala. Safe placement of screws is marked by the *white area. B,* From above the promontory the concavity of the ala can again be appreciated, as can the location of the posterior sacral wall. *C,* This diagram represents the course of the L5 root (*arrow*) going over the gutter of the sacral ala and descending in front of the sacroiliac joint and the course of the S1 root in a medial-to-lateral direction. One can see where the safe position is for screw placement. *D,* This diagram shows the area that must be taken into account for placement of a percutaneous screw from outside the iliac wing into the body of the sacrum. (*A, B, D,* From Tile, M., ed. Fractures of the Acetabulum and Pelvis, 2nd ed. Baltimore, Williams & Wilkins, 1995. *C,* Redrawn from Routt, M.L.C., Jr.; et al. J Orthop Trauma 10:173, 1996.)

patient's lumbosacral spine to elevate the buttocks off the table and ensure that the lateral aspect of the flank is accessible so that the starting point for the screw is not compromised. The C-arm is used to visualize the lateral aspect of the sacrum. Ensuring that the radiographic images of the femoral heads and greater sciatic notches are superimposed checks this position. The body of S1 is centered in the fluoroscope's screen. The AP view is now obtained by rotating the C-arm. To obtain the inlet view, the C-arm is then tilted so that the anterior cortex of S1 overlaps that of S2. If such visualization is not done, the concavity of the sacrum will not be appreciated and the screw may exit anteriorly. However, the posterior cortex of S1 is best seen if the anterior cortex of S1 is over the coccyx. This projection is needed to ensure that the screw does not exit posteriorly. The outlet view is obtained by rotating the C-arm 90° so that the pubic tubercles lie just

inferior to the S1 foramen and the symphysis overlies the midline of the sacrum.[64]

After complete radiographic visualization has been obtained, fracture reduction can be undertaken after induction of muscle-relaxing anesthesia. Closed reduction is usually possible within 2 to 5 days of the injury. Closed reduction requires knowledge of the displacement of the fracture. A completely unstable hemipelvis is displaced vertically and posteriorly and is externally rotated. However, depending on the mechanism of injury, the displacements may differ, so review of the history and radiographic studies is mandatory before reduction is attempted. The patient is prepared from the costal margins to the knees on both sides and down to the table on the involved side. The involved leg is prepared and draped free to allow manipulation. The first displacement to be corrected is the axial malposition, which is accomplished by longitudinal skeletal traction through a traction pin inserted in the distal end of the femur. If the fracture is posteriorly displaced, the traction is directed upward to correct it. Rotational displacement is corrected by placing one or two Schanz screws into the involved iliac crest and using them to manipulate the hemipelvis into place. The external fixator can be used to reduce this component as well. Posterior translational displacement is reduced by closing this gap with a ball-spiked pusher. These reduction maneuvers may require one or two assistants. Once the reduction is achieved, it is confirmed by C-arm visualization with the three views of the hemipelvis. Provisional fixation is possible with a K-wire inserted into the ala or use of the pelvic resuscitation C-clamp.

The superficial skin location for screw insertion is 2 cm posterior to the intersection of a line from the femoral shaft and a line dropped from the anterior superior iliac spine. The guide wire or drill bit is placed through a stab wound down to the posterolateral aspect of the ilium. The AP view shows that this device is aimed into the S1 body and perpendicular to the sacroiliac joint. At this point, the C-arm is used to visualize the lateral part of the sacrum. The position of the drill bit or guide wire is confirmed to be in the middle of the S1 body. It is important to make sure that the screw is placed so that it is below the cortical projection of the sacral ala, which is seen only on the lateral view.[94, 96, 111] If the position is correct, the drill bit or guide wire is advanced toward the body of S1. It is

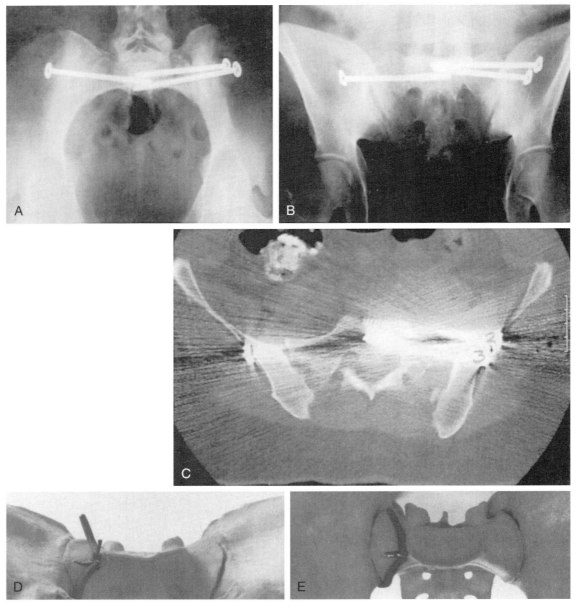

FIGURE 36–48. Penetration of the ala with screw placement. Inlet (*A*) and outlet (*B*) views of the pelvis show that the screw appears to be intraosseous. *C*, A postoperative computed tomographic scan shows that the anterior cephalad screw is extraosseous. The patient's left L5 nerve root was injured. *D, E,* A plastic model shows how this injury can occur. (*A–C,* From Routt, M.L.C., Jr.; et al. J Orthop Trauma 10:175, 1996. *D, E,* From Tile, M., ed. Fractures of the Acetabulum and Pelvis, 2nd ed. Baltimore, Williams & Wilkins, 1995.)

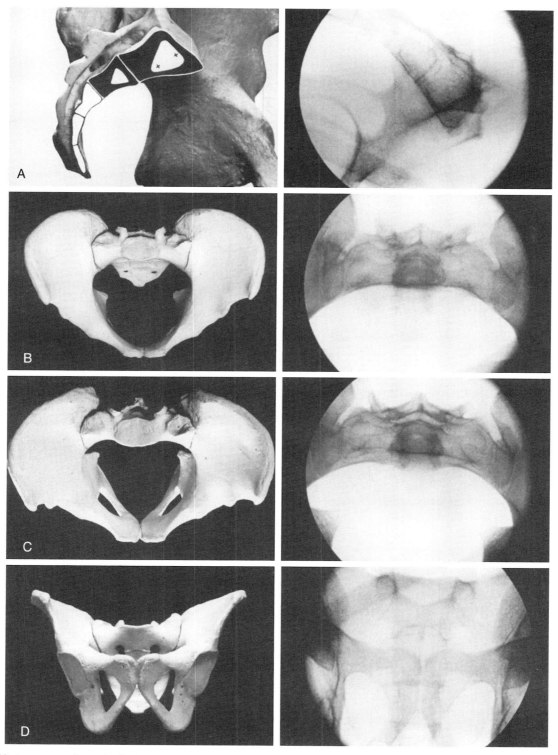

FIGURE 36–49. Important radiographic landmarks for the insertion of percutaneous iliosacral screws. *A,* Cross section of the pelvis showing the sacral promontory and important aspects as visualized on a lateral sacral radiograph. The sacral promontory and the alar slope should be recognized in these views. *B,* Inlet view of the pelvis showing both the bony pelvis and the radiographic appearance of the anterior cortex of S1 and S2 superimposed. *C,* Inlet view of the bony pelvis and radiographic image showing that increasing the angle on the C-arm allows the anterior cortex of S2 to be visualized, but the posterior cortex of the sacral spinal canal is now seen. *D,* Outlet pelvic view and radiographic image showing the pubic tubercles just below the S1 foramen. (*A–D,* From Tile, M., ed. Fractures of the Acetabulum and Pelvis, 2nd ed. Baltimore, Williams & Wilkins, 1995.)

useful to halt insertion of the pin when the tip reaches the superior aspect of the lateral border of the first sacral foramen on the outlet view. A true lateral view of the sacrum is obtained again to confirm that the tip of the pin is in the alar safe zone (pedicle). The progress of the drilling is watched on the three pelvic views. The drill bit or guide wire perforates three cortical barriers (outer part of the ilium, inner iliac side of the sacroiliac joint, and sacral side of the sacroiliac joint). If a fourth cortical barrier is encountered, insertion is stopped and the drill bit or guide wire is realigned because it is potentially about to leave the safe channel and injure a major structure. Any misdirected drill bits or guide wires must be completely removed and restarted to create a new tract. Once the position of the drill bit or guide wire is confirmed, the screw is inserted. A lag screw is used to fix a sacroiliac dislocation so that any residual gap can be closed. In foraminal or body fractures of the sacrum, a fully threaded large-fragment screw can be used as a position screw to maintain the reduction but not overly reduce or compress the fracture for fear of injuring a nerve root. Screw head position is confirmed by over-rotating the anteroposteriorly positioned C-arm 20° to 30° toward the involved side. This view shows the outer cortex of the ilium so that the position of the screw head is confirmed to abut the cortex. Medial placement past midline is difficult because of superimposition of the opposite-side alar cortical slope. Care must be taken if the screw is inserted past the midline to avoid the risk of perforation of the anterior sacral surface. This procedure can be done with the patient in the prone or lateral position. It is imperative that this technique not be attempted if the pelvic bony landmarks cannot be visualized radiographically. If these problems occur, the percutaneous technique must be aborted (Fig. 36–50).

OPEN REDUCTION AND INTERNAL FIXATION OF UNSTABLE SACRAL FRACTURES

Fractures through the sacrum are probably the most difficult to reduce and stabilize.[47, 112] Open reduction of these fractures is usually handled posteriorly, and consequently, a good evaluation of the posterior soft tissues must be carried out. These unstable fractures must not be fixed by open techniques until the skin and soft tissues are able to tolerate surgery. If possible, closed reduction should be performed and may allow the use of a percutaneous fixation technique. The patient is then placed in the prone position, on bolsters, to allow the abdominal contents to be free and facilitate reduction. Three basic methods of stabilization can be used. The first is the posterior iliosacral screw fixation method described previously. The screw fixation must enter the sacral body. The principle to remember is that if a lag screw technique is selected, the threads must not cross the fracture if compression is to be effective. If nerve root impingement is a possibility, a fully threaded position screw must be used to maintain the reduction. The approach to this area is no different from that described previously for posterior screw fixation of the sacroiliac joint. However, the surgeon may move the incision medially to identify the fracture and use it as a guide for the reduction. The fracture can be opened with

a laminar spreader and the sacral roots visualized and decompressed if necessary. A femoral distractor applied to both posterior tubercles is very helpful in controlling and maintaining the reduction.[63] Reduction is usually accomplished by traction to reduce vertical displacement and by direct manipulation with reduction clamps to correct anterior, posterior, and rotational displacement. The reduction is done by manually lifting and rotating the distractor to correct the AP and vertical displacement. Fine adjustments are made with the pointed reduction forceps and held in place for provisional fixation.[63, 83]

The second method of fixation indicated for a unilateral sacral fracture is the transiliac bar technique. This technique requires that one side of the pelvic ring be stable and that an intact posterior tubercle be present on both sides. The fracture is reduced and provisionally held by clamps. Transiliac bars, which are at least 6-mm fully threaded rods, are inserted from the outer aspect of the ipsilateral posterior tubercle to the contralateral tubercle. The first bar should be inserted at the level of the L5–S1 disc space from one tubercle to the other. It is passed posterior to the sacral lamina, not through the sacrum or under the lamina. To do so, a second incision is required on the opposite side. This incision can be small and used only to apply the washer and nuts. The bar is then suitably stabilized with a washer and two nuts at both ends of the rod. A second rod is placed in a similar fashion approximately 3 to 6 cm below the superior rod (S1–S2 interspace) and parallel to it. Nuts are placed on the screws and tightened, with compression applied to the sacral fracture line. They usually slide because the bone has enough "give," and the threads are shallow enough that they cannot achieve bony purchase (Fig. 36–51). This technique produces a lag effect across the fracture. Overcompression of the fracture at the sacrum, particularly if it involves the foramen, should be avoided to prevent impingement of the sacral nerve roots. Once the rods have been fixed, the double nuts are tightened against themselves and crimped to prevent them from backing off. The rods are then cut flush against the nuts, and the incisions are closed in layers. This method has provided suitable fixation for stabilization of unilateral sacral disruptions (Fig. 36–52). If bilateral unstable sacral disruptions are present, this technique is useful to handle one side, but one of the unstable disruptions must be fixed to the sacrum to provide suitable stability for this system to obtain purchase.

The third method of fixation is the use of plate fixation posteriorly. Through similar incisions on both sides, the posterior muscles can be elevated from the iliac wing, with their attachment to the gluteal muscles left intact. After these muscles have been incised at the level of the posterior aspect of the sacrum, subperiosteal dissection can be carried down to peel back the gluteal muscles attached to the posterior tubercle. A tunnel is then made under the tissues and muscles lying over the sacrum at the level of the S3 foramina. The spinous processes are removed. A plate specially designed by Mears and co-workers[11, 67] (the double cobra plate) or 3.5- or 4.5-mm reconstruction plates that can be contoured to come across the posterior aspect of the sacrum and down both iliac wings are fixed to the iliac crest. However, screws are not

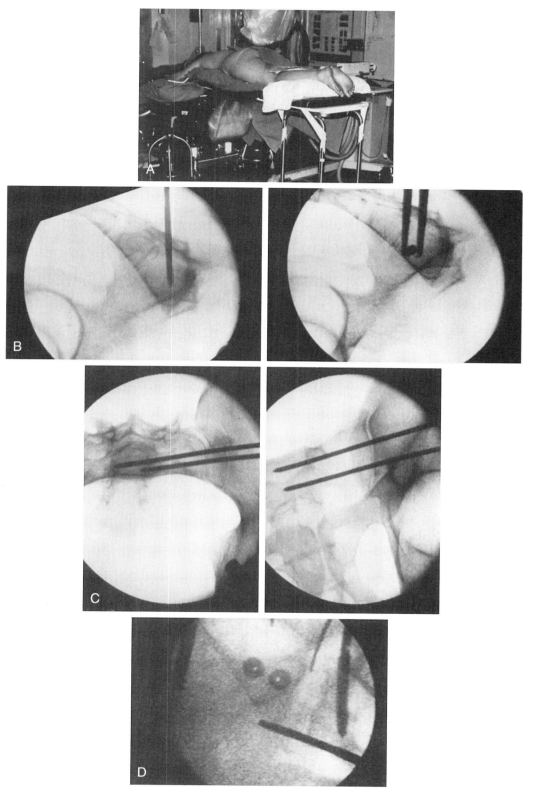

FIGURE 36–50. Technique for insertion of percutaneous iliosacral screws. *A,* The prone position on a radiolucent table. Similarly, screw insertion may be accomplished with the patient in a supine position with access by the C-arm for all three views. *B,* Alignment of the guide wire or drill for placing a screw into the sacrum. Note that the alignment is behind the S2 cortex in the central portion of the body to avoid the pedicles and the promontory and is below the alar slope line. *C,* Inlet view with S1 and S2 superimposed to show the position of the guide pins in place and avoid penetration of the ala and the posterior cortex of the sacrum. The outlet view confirms the appropriate position in the S1 body to avoid the S1 foramen. *D,* Final placement of screws in the safe zone of the sacrum. (*A–D,* From Tile, M., ed. Fractures of the Acetabulum and Pelvis, 2nd ed. Baltimore, Williams & Wilkins, 1995.)

inserted into the sacrum. One screw should be placed down the posterior tubercles along the iliac wing to acquire good fixation. By overcontouring the plate slightly and with fixation through the posterior tubercles, the iliac wing components of the plate are made to compress the sacral fracture. Albert and Miller[2] described a similar technique, but they undercut the inferior aspects of the posterior tubercles to allow the plate to be buried beneath the posterior spines to avoid any prominence of the fixation (see Fig. 36–51A and B).

Pohlemann and colleagues described an additional plate technique that allows direct plate fixation of the sacrum with small fragment plates.[84] The operative approach is through a single dorsal incision with the patient in a prone position. The important landmarks for the skin incision are the L4 and L5 spinous processes, the posterior iliac crests, and the upper gluteal cleft. Unilateral sacral fractures are approached through an incision midway between the sacral spines and the posterior iliac crest on the involved side. For bilateral sacral ala exposure, an incision slightly lateral to the sacral spines is used. Deep exposure of unilateral fractures is achieved by incising the lumbodorsal fascia close to the sacral spines and elevating the muscle from the sacrum. If a more extensile approach is needed, the complete erector spinae can be elevated by detaching its distal and lateral attachments to the sacrum

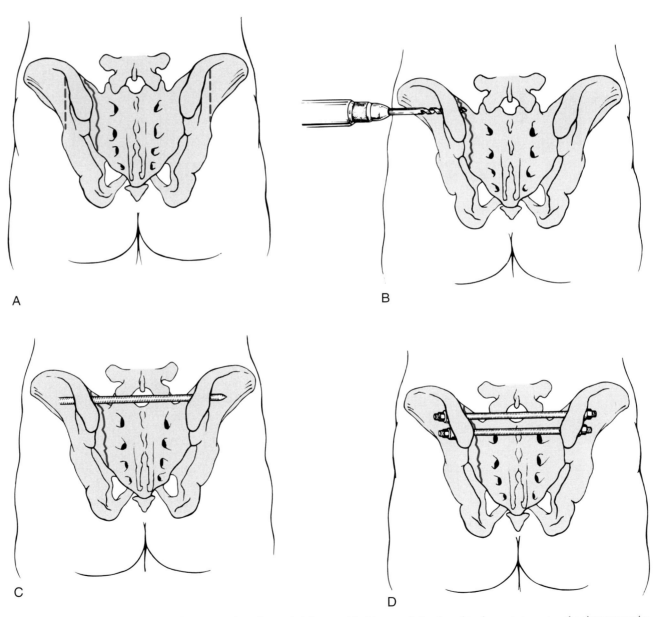

A

B

C

D

FIGURE 36–51. Transiliac bar posterior fixation. A, Through two slightly curved incisions made just lateral to the posterior spine, the gluteus muscles can be reflected laterally and the sacral fracture exposed. Reduction is then accomplished. B, After a 6.4-mm drill bit is used to provide a gliding hole, a drill hole is placed through the posterior iliac spine or crest; a long drill bit can then make a hole in the opposite crest. The drill and rods are kept superior to the sacrum. C, After predrilling, the sacral rod is placed through the holes to stabilize the pelvis. D, Washers and nuts are then applied and tightened while watching the fracture so that overcompression does not occur.

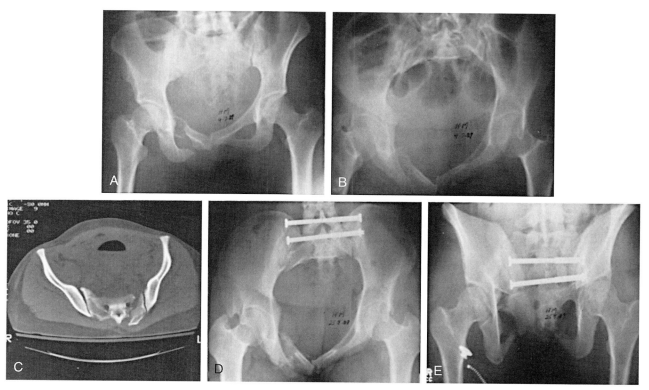

FIGURE 36–52. *A,* Radiographs demonstrating a sacral fracture that is unstable. Note that on the anteroposterior radiograph, the left posterior aspect of the hemipelvis appears to be disrupted. Some translation and shortening of the hemipelvis, as well as rotation, appear to be present. *B,* In this view, disruption of the sacrum can be noted on the posterior aspect. Posterior displacement as well as rotation can be appreciated. *C,* Computed tomographic scan confirming the gap or shearing injury through the posterior aspect of the pelvis. Note how this fracture has been displaced posteriorly with a large bony fragment. *D, E,* Transiliac rod fixation. A reasonable reduction has been performed posteriorly, although slight compression and medial translation of the pelvis have occurred. Because this injury is extra-articular, it is probably not significant. The outlet view shows reasonable reduction and good fixation.

and posterior iliac crest. For bilateral exposure, the unilateral approach can be performed on both sides. Reduction is accomplished as described previously (Fig. 36–53). Screws placed laterally into the ala and medially into the sacral bone between the posterior foramina attach the posterior sacral plates as close to the sacroiliac joint as allowed by the attachments of the iliosacral ligaments. The lateral alar screws are safely placed if their orientation is parallel to the plane of the sacroiliac joint, as identified by a K-wire placed into the joint posteriorly. Plunging with the drill bit is dangerous because of the anteriorly placed internal iliac vessels and lumbosacral trunk. The S1 alar screw must not exit the superior surface of the ala. Palpation of this surface is possible between the L5 transverse process and the sacrum. The medial screw at S1 is placed directly inferior to the distal border of the L5–S1 facet. Enough room is available to insert two 3.5-mm screws. The screw is oriented in the sagittal plane and parallel to the cranial sacral lamina for lateral fractures. For transforaminal fractures, the screw is angulated 20° laterally in the horizontal plane and parallel to the cranial sacral lamina in the sagittal and frontal planes. It is aimed at the sacral promontory, so it has an average length of 50 to 80 mm. For S2–S4 medial screws, the entry point is along an imaginary vertical line through the foramina and in the midpoint between them. The direction of placement is perpendicular to the posterior sacral lamina. A more

medial direction would be dangerous because the screw would enter the central canal. The implants used are standard small-fragment plates that are cut to fit. Each fracture line must be crossed by at least two plates, preferably at S1, S3, or S4. For transalar fractures, H-plates are used at the S1 and lower levels. If the fragmentation extends too far laterally for secure screw placement, the plate must extend onto the ilium. If a medial screw cannot be inserted, a dynamic compression plate must cross the midline to the opposite ala. Transforaminal fractures are stabilized in a similar manner. Two dynamic compression plates parallel to each other at S1 and S3 stabilize bilateral (zone 3) fractures. These plates cross the midline and are fixed to the alar region. Supplemental thinner plates such as H-plates or one-third tubular plates may be added, depending on the fracture pattern. After posterior fixation, anterior pelvic stabilization is necessary to supplement this tension band–type fixation. Such stabilization may be accomplished by symphyseal plating or anterior external fixation based on the anterior injury.

Another technique of sacral fracture fixation is the use of a transiliac 4.5-mm reconstruction plate.[2] The patient is in the prone position and three posterior incisions are made, a midline incision that dissects down to the spinous processes of S1 and S2 and two lateral incisions that begin at the posterior superior iliac spine and are directed obliquely in an inferolateral direction. The muscle and

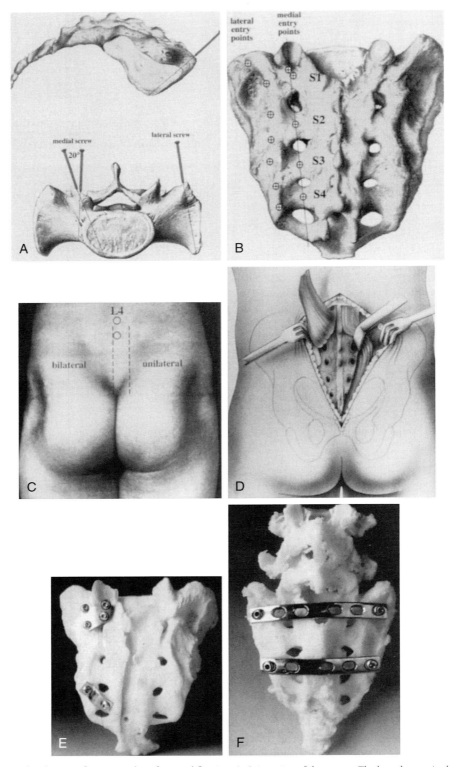

FIGURE 36–53. Placement and technique of inserting plates for sacral fixation. *A,* Orientation of the screws. The lateral screw is always parallel to the plane of the sacroiliac joint, and the medial screw is perpendicular to the dorsal sacral lamina. At S1, two orientations are possible. *B,* Placement of screws from the posterior aspect of the sacrum. *C,* Landmarks for the skin incision with the patient prone. *D,* Deep exposure showing the lumbar sacral fascia incised and the erector spinae completely elevated from the sacrum for an extensile approach. Small plates were used for fixation of transforaminal fractures *(E)* and plates spanning from one ala to the other for fixation of bilateral fractures *(F).* (*A–F,* From Pohlemann, T.; Tscherne, H. Techn Orthop 9:315, 1994.)

fascia are then split to expose the iliac wing. With a 4.5-mm drill bit, two holes are placed 0.5 cm apart, 1 cm lateral to the posterior superior iliac spine. A 4.5-mm reconstruction plate (with 10 to 11 holes) preoperatively templated is then chiseled through the iliac spine across the dorsum of the sacrum to the opposite side. The direction of the plate can be controlled through the midline incision. Similar holes are placed on the opposite posterior superior iliac spine. The ends of the plates are then contoured with an impactor and fixed to the iliac wing with 6.5-mm cancellous screws (Fig. 36–54).

FIXATION OF THE ILIAC WING

Occasionally, a markedly displaced iliac wing fracture requires internal fixation, which can usually be accomplished through an anterior approach, as has been described for fixation of the sacroiliac joint. Fixation is achieved by interfragmental compression and the application of neutralization plates. Normally, on the inner wall of the pelvis, the application of a plate should be just under the crest, where the bone is good and thick, and along the sciatic buttress. The use of a plate in the midportion of the iliac wing is unsuitable because the bone is very thin in this area. If it is necessary for a plate to span this area, a longer plate is required to get more screw fixation and better stabilization. If a posterior approach is used, similar plates should be placed in the area of the thickest bone, which is usually along the sciatic buttress and just below the iliac crest. Thick bone is also present posteriorly, where the tubercle is available for plate fixation.

POSTOPERATIVE PLAN

The postoperative plan for these patients is ideally one of early mobilization. However, such mobilization must be tempered by the ability to achieve stable fixation of the fracture and the quality of bone. If bone quality is good and if suitable, stable fixation is achieved in a rotationally unstable injury, the patient can be mobilized within 3 to 5 days on crutches, with full weight bearing on the uninvolved side. Partial weight bearing can be allowed between 3 and 6 weeks, with progression to full weight bearing by 6 weeks and off all aids by 3 months.

However, for completely unstable fractures with stable fixation, the patient should be mobilized from bed to a chair 5 to 10 days after surgery. Early weight bearing should be avoided until fracture healing is observed, and it may be necessary to avoid weight bearing for up to 3 months. If the fixation is unstable because of fracture patterns or if good anterior fixation cannot be achieved but the patient is not multiply injured, the use of postoperative traction to protect the fixation for 4 to 6 weeks should be considered. Traction maintains length and takes some of

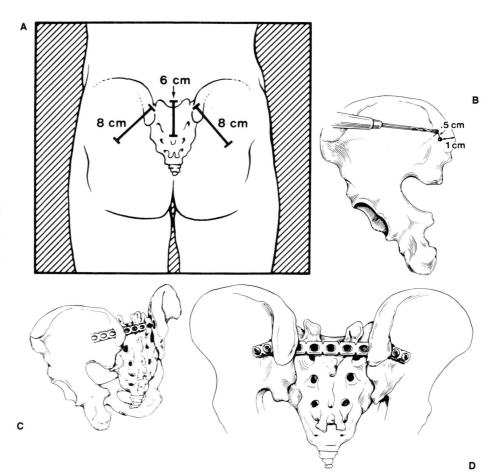

FIGURE 36–54. Technique of transiliac plate fixation for sacral fractures. *A,* Skin incisions. *B,* Placement of drill holes for insertion of the plate. *C,* Direction of plate insertion. *D,* Final configuration. (*A–D,* From Albert, M.J.; et al. J Orthop Trauma 7:228, 1993.)

the force off the fixation, thereby decreasing the possibility of fixation failure. However, this technique is useful only for an isolated pelvic fracture, which is uncommon. The use of external fixation as a supplement to internal fixation allows the patient to be in the upright position in bed or on a chair.

Radiographic follow-up is usually done in the early postoperative phase before hospital discharge, at 6 weeks, and at 3 months. At 3 months, the healing is usually satisfactory to allow full weight bearing, and no further radiographs are necessary for 1 year. After this interval, radiographs are necessary only if indicated by patient complaints.

Generally, removal of pelvic internal fixation is not done. The only fixation that usually causes problems is that placed just below or on the iliac crest or on the symphysis. Such fixation may require removal if it causes symptoms; however, extensive exposure is required for this type of procedure.

GENITOURINARY INJURIES

Management of genitourinary injuries requires a team approach. The urologist and orthopaedic surgeon need to have a protocol to handle these injuries effectively. Extraperitoneal bladder ruptures are usually managed nonoperatively unless the pelvic ring injury will require operative intervention. In this case, open bladder repair is recommended to prevent infection of the fixation or persistent fistula formation. This repair is usually performed as early as the patient is stable and is combined with pelvic fracture osteosynthesis.

Treatment of urethral rupture is more controversial. Three options exist: immediate exploration and realignment over a catheter, primary urethroplasty, and suprapubic cystostomy drainage with delayed urethroplasty. Timing is dictated by the magnitude of the injury and complicating injuries to adjacent structures. The most important factor appears to be related to avoiding further surgical damage to the pelvic floor to keep the incidence of stricture and impotence low. Recent indirect open realignment procedures have been effective in early care with limited complications.[56, 97]

In women, urinary complaints were more frequent in patients with residual pelvic displacement (≥5 mm), as was dyspareunia. Other than a higher incidence of cesarean section in displaced pelvic fractures (≥5 mm), no difference in miscarriage or infertility was noted.[18]

OPEN PELVIC FRACTURES

An open pelvic fracture is defined as any fracture of the pelvic ring in which the fracture site is or has the potential for bacterial contamination as a consequence of the injury. This concept includes a fracture site open to the external environment, as well as a fracture site communicating with a vaginal or rectal laceration. For this injury to occur, a massive amount of energy must be transferred to the pelvis. This type of injury pattern leads to significant bony disruption and, more importantly, to severe soft tissue disruption and resultant disabilities and infection.[8] Raffe and Christensen[88] described 26 patients with open pelvic fractures. Disruption of the genitourinary system occurred in 12 and disruption of the gastrointestinal system in 7. Perry[83] and Richardson and associates[89] have emphasized the potential for major vessel disruption and resultant fatal hemorrhage as one of the most important early complications of this injury.

Assessment

Assessment of a patient with an open pelvic fracture must be meticulous. The best method of determining the extent of soft tissue damage is to describe the exact injury. Anteriorly or laterally directed wounds in the flank usually occur through muscle and do not involve rectal or genitourinary contamination. Wounds that occur in the perineum with extension into the rectum posteriorly and wounds that extend into the rectal or genitourinary region are contaminated by a rectal tear or have the potential for contamination at a later date.[27] Faringer and colleagues[32] attempted to delineate the location of the wound by dividing the pelvic region and upper part of the thighs into three distinct zones. Zone 1 is the perineum and extends from the lower anterior abdominal wall to posteriorly over the sacrum. Zone 2 is the medial aspect of the thigh from the anterior midline to the posterior midline. Zone 3 is the flank and posterolateral region of the buttock. A urethrogram and a cystogram reveal the genitourinary involvement. Rectal and vaginal examinations are mandatory in all patients with pelvic fractures. The presence of blood on either examination is an indication for visual inspection of that orifice to rule out an open injury.[76] Evaluation of neurologic status must also be undertaken immediately to determine which structures are not functioning.[122] Finally, contamination of the wound from both external and internal (intestinal) sources must be determined. After evaluation of the soft tissue injuries, appropriate radiographic evaluation of the pelvic fracture must be undertaken.

Management

Management of these patients must be organized and meticulous because they can die early of hemorrhage. Rapid resuscitation with universal-donor blood and prompt noninvasive pelvic immobilization, such as with PASG trousers, in association with packing of the open wound, will help control major vessel bleeding.[1, 19] These injuries represent internal traumatic hemipelvectomies and, in fact, conversion to an actual hemipelvectomy may be lifesaving in some patients. Once hemodynamic stabilization has occurred, appropriate débridement of the wounds is necessary. This procedure may involve consultation with general surgeons, urologists, and gynecologists so that the wounds can be explored adequately. If any wound enters the perineum (zone 1), especially if it has rectal involvement, a defunctioning colostomy must be performed.[32] This intervention should probably be a loop colostomy placed in the area of the transverse colon so that it is well out of the way of any surgical access to the pelvis. Distal colonic washout should be undertaken so that the colon, from the colostomy site through to the rectum, is immediately cleansed (i.e., débrided). Broad-spectrum antibiotics, in particular those necessary to handle bowel contamination, should be started immediately and used prophylactically for 24 to 48 hours.

One very serious injury that occurs to the soft tissues is shearing and avulsion of the skin and subcutaneous tissue from the underlying muscle. In a sense, the skin has become devascularized by the loss of its blood supply from the vessels from the underlying muscle. In these situations, a decision must be made regarding the extent of débridement required. These avulsions can be massive, and determination of their extent is usually guided by an evaluation of the skin and subcutaneous bleeding. All tissue that is dead and thought to be potentially nonviable must be removed. If débridement is inadequate and a large quantity of devitalized soft tissue remains, sepsis may result and compromise the patient's outcome. If the exact amount and extent of devitalized tissue are not initially evident, repetitive débridement is mandatory.

In fractures with significant contamination involving the perineum or rectum and in situations in which it is impossible to obtain a clean surgical wound, external fixation should be used. Such fixation provides a relatively stable pelvic ring so that the patient can be mobilized and repeated débridement can be performed. After the soft tissues have demonstrated viability and healing is progressing, definitive stabilization can then be carried out.

If the wound does not involve the perineum and is not significantly contaminated and if a clean surgical wound can be achieved, the use of primary internal fixation to stabilize the fracture is possible; often, the open wound may allow reasonable access to these areas. This technique can also be supplemented by external fixation. The use of minimal lag screw fixation along with external fixation may be the best method to obtain stability with this injury.

If the urethra or bladder is involved and the abdomen has been opened, stabilization of the anterior injury can be done by internal fixation if the fracture pattern is amenable.

In females with an open fracture into the vagina, débridement of the open fracture, usually through the vagina, is all that is required. If the vaginal laceration is clean, it can be closed primarily. Any potentially contaminated vaginal wound should be left open to heal secondarily. Stabilization of the pelvis in the acute phase is best accomplished by external fixation.

Follow-up Care

After the patient is hemodynamically stable and the pelvis has been stabilized, definitive fracture care can be undertaken. Further soft tissue treatment can be carried out, such as repair of the genitourinary system, and the colostomy can be closed at 6 to 12 weeks, after the soft tissue and rectal injuries have healed.

With aggressive care of patients with pelvic fractures,

the nominal mortality rate of up to 50% can be reduced to 20%, a rate associated with a completely unstable pelvic ring injury (type C).[8] Richardson and associates[89] showed that with very aggressive surgical intervention, early colostomy, and extensive débridement, the treatment results of open pelvic fracture could be markedly improved.

COMPLICATIONS

Because of the systemic nature of the injury and the wide spectrum of methods of treatment required, complications of pelvic fractures are often frequent and severe. The polytrauma setting and the systemic nature of the injury make the patient susceptible to the development of adult respiratory distress syndrome, thromboembolic disease, pneumonia, and multiple organ failure.

Early Complications

INFECTION

Postoperative infection can occur after either external or internal fixation. Infection with the use of external fixation devices usually occurs around the pin tracts. Pin tract infection can generally be managed adequately by appropriate release of the skin about the pins and changing dressings as required to maintain drainage from the pin tracts. Antibiotic coverage should be used if cultures are positive. Pin tract loosening is a potential problem when infection is present. The clamps around the pins must be released and the pins checked for stability within the bone. If a pin is loose, it is usually very difficult to reinsert because of the localized infection. Consequently, the fixator may have to be removed, or alternative placement of the pins may be necessary. If the fixator has been placed in the standard iliac crest position, it is usually safe to place these new pins between the anterior superior and anterior inferior iliac spines. Most pin tract infections resolve with removal of the pins and débridement of the pin tract itself.

Postoperative infections after internal fixation usually occur secondary to significant soft tissue integrity or healing problems. These complications are common after a posterior approach in which an incision has been made through devitalized and nonviable skin and muscle. Very careful evaluation of the soft tissue injury must be undertaken. Even if this problem occurs anteriorly, the approach must be altered to operate and stabilize through viable soft tissue.[49]

If a postoperative infection does develop around the fixation, the same treatment principles apply as for acute postoperative infections after internal fixation. Incision and drainage plus débridement must begin early. The wound should be left open and the fixation evaluated for stability. If it is solidly fixed to bone, it can be left in place. If it is loose and not maintaining stability, it must be removed and supplemented or changed to an alternative. Pelvic osteomyelitis is a rare but disastrous complication. Repetitive débridement is the only treatment method. It may be necessary to excise major portions of the iliac crest to control the osteomyelitis.

LOSS OF FIXATION

Loss of fixation often occurs when the expected degree of healing cannot be achieved during the early phase of pelvic fixation. Honest assessment of the stability of the fixation must be made at the end of any surgical intervention. The use of external fixation or traction to supplement internal fixation must always be considered. If the adequacy of the fixation is uncertain, it is better to maintain the patient on bedrest with external fixation or traction and to delay mobilization until internal bone union has occurred. Early mobilization with loss of reduction and fixation may compromise the end result. Failure to attain reduction will probably not cause significant problems unless the sacroiliac joint is involved. Therefore, all attempts to achieve anatomic reduction of the sacroiliac joint should be instituted. This necessity for anatomic reduction has led to the development of a technique for primary fusion of the sacroiliac joint to avoid any minor incongruencies in this area that may lead to long-term discomfort and pain.[109] Routt and co-workers[93] reported the complications associated with the percutaneous technique of insertion of an iliosacral lag screw. They evaluated 244 screws in 159 patients. Malreduction was noted in 19 of 159 patients. An inability to adequately image the posterior of the pelvis occurred in 18 patients because of obesity or residual intestinal contrast. Five screws were malpositioned because of failure to understand the value of the lateral sacral view. Fixation failure occurred in 7 patients.

NEUROLOGIC INJURY

Permanent nerve damage is a common disability after pelvic disruption, with an incidence of about 10% to 15% overall.[122] In unstable, double vertical-type fractures, the incidence rises to 46%. Huittinen and Slatis,[47] in their series of 85 patients, reported that a significant number had L5 or S1 root involvement. These appeared to be traction injuries, but anatomic studies suggested that root avulsions may actually occur. Recent interest has led to the development of a classification of sacral fractures[22] that may lead to a better understanding of the injury patterns and the injury site. Fractures through or medial to the foramina are associated with a high incidence of neurologic injury, as are transverse fractures of the sacrum with a kyphotic deformity. Reduction and stabilization of these pelvic injuries may improve recovery. Decompression of any sacral transverse fracture with a kyphotic deformity or any burst fracture of the sacrum that appears to compromise the root posteriorly may be of some value (see Chapter 35). However, the long-term results are disheartening.

Causalgia resulting from injuries to the L5 or S1 root (or both) or to the sciatic nerve can be particularly difficult to manage, both acutely and on a long-term basis, because of an inability to control pain. The use of specific medications has not been a great help. However, it appears that early intervention with a lumbar sympathetic block to break the pain cycle may be of some value. Consultation with pain management physicians should be carried out to determine an approach to alleviate some of the long-term disability. Lumbar sympathetic blocks may also help control chronic causalgia pain. If these blocks are effective, phenol or surgical obliteration of the sympathetic plexus may help.

Iatrogenic nerve injury secondary to operative treatment may occur. Attempts to modify its incidence by nerve-monitoring techniques have not reliably decreased its incidence.[42] The use of electromyographic monitoring techniques might be beneficial.[70, 120]

Neurologic damage should be managed with an appropriate splint or brace, and surgical intervention should be carried out if indicated. Repair or decompression of the sciatic nerve has not to date been done with great success. Repair of the femoral nerve, which has a shorter travel route than the sciatic nerve, may be indicated if the nerve has been lacerated.

THROMBOEMBOLISM

Thromboembolic complications may occur more commonly in patients with a major pelvic disruption, especially those with associated lower extremity fractures.[10, 13, 29, 37] Screening has not been successful in determining the at-risk group because most clots are located in the internal pelvic venous plexus, which is not amenable to standard screening methods. At the present time, it is suggested that some method of prophylaxis based on the patient's overall clinical situation be considered. Many different protocols are used, but none has proved more effective than another or even better than no prophylaxis in the prevention of fatal pulmonary emboli.[6, 33, 34, 117]

Late Complications

PAIN

Pain can develop from malunion, nonunion, or osteoarthritis of the sacroiliac joint. Some patients, despite having had anatomic reduction and adequate fracture union (or a fused sacroiliac joint), continue to complain of discomfort and pain. The pain is usually localized to the area of the sacroiliac joint. Evaluation of the lower lumbar spine must be carried out, initially and late, to ensure that no occult fractures are present in this area. Other causes of this pain include significant soft tissue injury, particularly to the muscles and neurologic structures.

MALUNION

The incidence of a symptomatic deformity is about 5% in all major pelvic disruptions treated nonoperatively. Deformity can be avoided with appropriate assessment and recognition of pelvic displacement and the potential problems of pelvic instability. The major problem appears to occur with malunion in the region of the sacroiliac joint. These malunions cause leg length discrepancies, but unless the malunion occurs through the sacroiliac joint, pain is unlikely. However, leg length discrepancies with displacement of one hemipelvis more than 1 cm may lead to sitting problems. Patients usually experience pain in the sacroiliac joint or over the ischial tuberosities because these structures are at an unequal level and, therefore, subjected to excessive pressure. Occasionally, severely displaced lateral compression fractures (type B2) can result in an internal rotational deformity that leads to pelvic obliquity and leg length discrepancies. Patients present with pain, deformity, leg length discrepancy, and gait abnormalities. Careful evaluation of the patient's functional and physical disability is mandatory, and the need for surgical treatment must be determined. Leg length discrepancy without pelvic symptoms can be handled by standard surgical techniques for limb equalization. However, if pelvic symptoms exist, especially pain or sitting problems, direct osteotomy of the malunion site is required. A malreduction of the sacroiliac joint that causes pain is usually treated by sacroiliac fusion.

NONUNION

Nonunion is an uncommon but well-recognized complication of vertically unstable pelvic disruptions. Pelvic pain and instability are the most common initial symptoms. Lateral compression injuries may lead to anterior ramus nonunion, which is usually relatively asymptomatic. Complete evaluation of the patient's symptoms and bony pelvic abnormalities is mandatory. The principles of surgical treatment are stable pelvic ring fixation and bone grafting of the nonunion. Most cases require stable fixation both anteriorly and posteriorly, accompanied by osteotomy or takedown of the nonunion to allow correction of any significant malposition.[26]

RESULTS

Although the techniques of internal fixation of a disrupted pelvis are being refined, little proof has been presented that these techniques provide the patient any better result than closed reduction and stabilization by traction or external fixation. Reimer and colleagues[69, 90] showed that the functional outcome in unstable pelvic disruptions treated by closed reduction and external fixation, as measured by the SF36, is no different from the result achieved with a stable pelvic ring fracture. This result was again demonstrated by Nepola and co-workers, who showed that functional outcomes using validated scores did not differ when related to residual vertical displacement.[75] Scheid and co-workers,[103, 104] in a review of unstable pelvic ring injuries treated by internal fixation, found that 52% of patients experienced pain and a change in lifestyle. This percentage was similar to that reported by Kellam and associates[51] for a similar group of patients from the same institution with the same surgeons. These results were correlated with the location of the fracture, with sacral fractures and pure sacroiliac dislocation having the worst results. Dujardin and colleagues reviewed two consecutive cohorts of patients with unstable pelvic ring injuries by using anatomic measures and the validated pelvic outcome score of Majeed.[23] One group was treated by external fixation and the other by internal fixation based on protocol. The overall functional result depended

on the location of the posterior lesion and the ability to reduce it anatomically. Pure sacroiliac joint dislocations fared poorly if anatomic reduction was not achieved. Fractures of the iliac wing or associated fracture-dislocations of the wing and sacroiliac joint did very well because they were easily reduced and stabilized. Sacral fractures did poorly despite good reduction because functional outcome was related to the associated nerve injury. Cole and associates[16] and Tornetta and Matta[115] have also shown that although anatomic reduction plus stable internal fixation is possible in completely unstable pelvic ring injuries and leads to excellent anatomic results, the final functional outcome is usually determined by the associated soft tissue injury or other nonorthopaedic traumatic injuries. In the rotationally unstable group, the results of internal fixation are much better, with up to 96% of patients having no pain on strenuous exercise.[114] There is probably little disagreement that patients with unreduced sacroiliac joint injuries do not do well unless the injuries are reduced and stabilized, but it cannot be guaranteed that this result is as consistent as the results of operative treatment of sacroiliac joint fracture-dislocation or iliac wing fractures. Until a randomized prospective trial is conducted to determine which method of treatment of a sacral fracture, fracture-dislocation of the sacroiliac joint, and fracture of the iliac wing (crescent) is most effective, surgeons must treat the patient's injury with prompt recognition of any problems, reduction of the displacement, and stabilization. If such treatment is not possible, referral to appropriate care is mandatory.

SUMMARY

Treatment of pelvic ring injuries requires an in-depth understanding of the anatomy of the pelvis and the mechanisms of injury. With this understanding and precise clinical and radiographic evaluation of the injury, appropriate management can be chosen. A determination of pelvic stability is imperative; along with assessment of displacement, pelvic stability guides the surgeon in deciding the best form of treatment. Although surgical intervention to stabilize unstable fractures is usually the best method of achieving an intact pelvic ring and ensuring a good result, not all pelvic ring disruptions require stabilization. The complications of management of these injuries are formidable, but they can be lessened by appropriate evaluation.

REFERENCES

1. Agolini, S.F.; Shah, K.; Gaffe J.; et al. Arterial immobilization is a rapid and effective technique for controlling pelvic fracture hemorrhage. J Orthop Trauma 43:395–399, 1997.
2. Albert, M.J.; Miller, M.E.; MacNaughton, M.; Hutton, W.C. Posterior pelvic fixation using a transiliac 4.5 mm reconstruction plate: A clinical and biomechanical study. J Orthop Trauma 7:226–232, 1993.
3. Altoona, D.; Tekdemir, I.; Ates, Y.; Elhan, A. Anatomy of the anterior sacroiliac joint with reference to lumbosacral nerves. Clin Orthop 376:236–241, 2000.
4. American College of Surgeons. Advanced Trauma Life Support Manual. Chicago, American College of Surgeons, 1989.

5. Anglen, J.O.; DiPasquale, T. The reliability of detecting screw penetration of the acetabulum by intraoperative auscultation. J Orthop Trauma 8:404–408, 1994.

6. Asprinio, D.E.; Helfet, D.L.; Tile, M. Complications. In: Tile, M., ed. Fractures of the Pelvis and Acetabulum. Baltimore, Williams & Wilkins, 1984, pp. 243–245.

7. Bone, L.B.; McNamara, K.; Shine, B.; Border, J. Mortality in multiple trauma patients with fractures. J Trauma 37:262–264, 1994.

8. Brennerman, F.D.; Katyal, D.; Boulanger, B.R.; et al. Long-term outcomes in open pelvic fractures. J Trauma 42:773–777, 1997.

9. Brown, J.J.; Greene, F.L.; McMillin, R.D. Vascular injuries associated with pelvic fractures. Am Surg 50:150–154, 1984.

10. Browner, B.D., ed. Internal fixation of pelvic ring disruptions. Techn Orthop, Vol. 9, 1994.

11. Bucholz, R.W. The pathological anatomy of the Malgaigne fracture dislocation of the pelvis. J Bone Joint Surg Am 63:400–404, 1981.

12. Buckle, R.; Browner, B.D.; Morandi, M. A new external fixation device for emergent reduction and stabilization of displaced pelvic fractures associated with massive hemorrhage. J Orthop Trauma 7:177–178, 1993.

13. Buerger, P.M.; Peoples, J.B.; Lemmon, G.W.; McCarthy, M.C. Risk of pulmonary emboli in patients with pelvic fractures. Am Surg 59:505–508, 1993.

14. Colapinto, V. Trauma to the pelvis: Urethral injury. Clin Orthop 151:46–55, 1980.

15. Cole, J.D.; Bolhofner, B.R. Acetabular fracture fixation via a modified Stoppa limited intrapelvic approach. Clin Orthop 305:112–123, 1994.

16. Cole, J.D.; Blum, D.A.; Ansel, L.J. Outcome after fixation of unstable posterior ring injuries. Clin Orthop 329:160–179, 1996.

17. Connolly, J.F. Closed treatment of pelvic and lower extremity fractures. Clin Orthop 240:115–128, 1989.

18. Copeland, C.E.; Bosse, M.J.; McCarthy, M.L.; et al. Effect of trauma and pelvic fracture on female genitourinary, sexual and reproductive function. J Trauma 11(2):73–81, 1997.

19. Cotler, H.B.; LaMont, J.G.; Hansen, S.T. Immediate spica cast for pelvic fractures. J Orthop Trauma 2:222–228, 1988.

20. Cryer, H.M.; Miller, F.B.; Evers, M.; et al. Pelvic fracture classification: Correlation with hemorrhage. J Orthop Trauma 28:973–980, 1988.

21. Delal, S.; Burgess, A.; Young, J.; et al. Pelvic fractures: Classification by force vector in relationship to associated injuries. Paper presented at an Orthopaedic Trauma Association Meeting, Dallas, October 27–28, 1988.

22. Denis, F.; Davis, S.; Comfort, T. Sacral fractures: An important problem. Clin Orthop 227:67–81, 1988.

23. Dujardin, F.H.; Hossenbaccus, M.; Duparc, F.; et al. Long-term functional prognosis of posterior injuries in high-energy pelvic disruptions. J Trauma 12(3):145–150, discussion 150–151, 1998.

24. Dunn, A.W.; Morris, H.D. Fractures and dislocations of the pelvis. J Bone Joint Surg Am 50:1639–1648, 1968.

25. Duwelius, P.J.; Van Allen, M.; Bray, T.J.; Nelson, D. Computed tomography guided fixation of unstable posterior pelvic ring disruptions. J Orthop Trauma 6:420–426, 1992.

26. Ebraheim, N.A.; Biyani, A.; Wong, F. Nonunion of pelvic fractures. J Trauma 44(1):202–204, 1998.

27. Ebraheim, N.A.; Savolainen, E.R.; Rusin, J.R.; et al. Occult rectal perforation in a major pelvic fracture. J Orthop Trauma 2:340–343, 1988.

28. Edeiken-Monroe, B.S.; Browner, B.D.; Jackson, H. The role of standard roentgenograms in the evaluation of instability of pelvic ring disruption. Clin Orthop 240:63–76, 1989.

29. Ellison, M.; Timberlake, G.A.; Kerstein, M.D. Impotence following pelvic fracture. J Orthop Trauma 28:695–696, 1988.

30. Evers, M.B.; Cryer, H.M.; Miller, F.B. Pelvic fracture hemorrhage. Arch Surg 124:422–424, 1989.

31. Falcone, R.E., Thomas, B.W. "Bean bag" pelvic stabilization. Ann Emerg Med 28:458, 1996.

32. Faringer, P.D.; Mullins, R.J.; Feliciano, P.D.; et al. Selective fecal diversion in complex open pelvic fractures from blunt trauma. Arch Surg 129:958–964, 1994.

33. Fisher, C.G.; Blachut, P.A.; Salvian, A.J.; et al. Effectiveness of pneumatic leg compression devices for the prevention of thromboembolic disease in orthopaedic trauma patients: A prospective, randomized study of compression alone versus no prophylaxis. J Orthop Trauma 9:1–7, 1995.

34. Fishmann, A.J.; Greeno, R.A.; Brooks, L.R.; Matta, J.M. Prevention of deep vein thrombosis and pulmonary embolism in acetabular and pelvic fracture surgery. Clin Orthop 305:133–137, 1994.

35. Flint, L.M.; Brown, A.; Richardson, J.D. Definitive control of bleeding from severe pelvic fractures. Ann Surg 189:709–716, 1979.

36. Ganz, R.; Krushell, R.J.; Jakob, R.P.; Kuffer, J. The antishock pelvic clamp. Clin Orthop 267:71–78, 1991.

37. Geertz, W.H.; Code, K.I.; Jay, R.M.; et al. A prospective study of venous thromboembolism after major trauma. N Engl J Med 331:1601–1606, 1994.

38. Ghanayem, A.J.; Wilbur, J.H.; Leiberman, J.M.; Mogta, A.O. The effect of laparotomy and external fixator stabilization on pelvic volume in an unstable pelvic ring injury. J Trauma 38:396–401, 1995.

39. Gilliland, M.D.; Ward, R.E.; Barton, R.M.; et al. Factors affecting mortality in pelvic fractures. J Orthop Trauma 22:691–693, 1982.

40. Gokcen, E.C.; Burgess, A.R.; Siegel, J.H.; et al. Pelvic fracture mechanism of injury in vehicular trauma patients. J Trauma 36:789–796, 1994.

41. Gruen, G.S.; Leit, M.E.; Gruen, R.J.; Peitzman, A.B. The acute management of hemodynamically unstable multiple trauma patients with pelvic ring fractures. J Trauma 36:706–713, 1994.

42. Helfet, D.L.; Koval, K.J.; Hissa, E.A.; et al. Intraoperative somatosensory evoked potential monitoring during acute pelvic fracture surgery. J Orthop Trauma 9:28–34, 1995.

43. Helfet, D.L. Pelvic ring, the three "types." In: Müller, M.E., ed. Comprehensive Classification of Pelvis and Acetabulum Fractures. Bern, Switzerland, Maurice E. Müller Foundation, 1995, p. 61.

44. Henderson, R.C. The long-term results of nonoperatively treated major pelvic disruptions. J Orthop Trauma 3:41–47, 1988.

45. Hirvensalo, E.; Lindahl, J.; Bostman, O. A new approach to the internal fixation of unstable pelvic fractures. Clin Orthop 297:28–32, 1993.

46. Holdsworth, F.W. Dislocation and fracture dislocation of the pelvis. J Bone Joint Surg Br 30:461–466, 1948.

47. Huittinen, V.M.; Slatis, P. Fractures of the pelvis, trauma mechanism, types of injury and principles of treatment. Acta Chir Scand 138:563–569, 1972.

48. Kaehr, D.; Anderson, P.; Mayo, K.; et al. Classification of sacral fractures based on CT imaging. Paper presented at an Orthopaedic Trauma Association Meeting, Dallas, October 27–28, 1988.

49. Kellam, J.F.; McMurtry, R.Y.; Tile, M. The unstable pelvic fracture. Orthop Clin North Am 18:25–41, 1987.

50. Kellam, J.F. The role of external fixation in pelvic disruptions. Clin Orthop 241:66–82, 1989.

51. Kellam, J.F.; Boyer, M.; Dean, R.; Tile, M. Results of external fixation of the pelvis. Paper presented at the 12th International Congress on Hoffman External Fixation, Garmisch Partenkirchen Murnau, Bavaria, West Germany, October 9–10, 1986.

52. Kiting, J.F.; Wearier, J.; Blackout, P.; et al. Early fixation of the vertically unstable pelvis: The role of iliosacral screw fixation in the management of the vertically unstable pelvis. J Trauma 13:107–113, 1999.

53. Koury, H.I.; Peschiera, J.L.; Welling, R.E. Selective use of pelvic roentgenograms in blunt trauma patients. J Trauma 34:236–237, 1993.

54. Lange, R.H.; Hansen, S. Pelvic ring disruptions with symphysis pubis diastasis. Indications, techniques and application of anterior internal fixation. Clin Orthop 201:130–137, 1985.

55. Latenser, B.A.; Gentilello, L.M.; Tarver, A.A.; et al. Improved outcome with early fixation of skeletally unstable pelvic fractures. J Trauma 31:28–31, 1991.

56. Lee, J.; Abrahamson, B.S.; Harrington, T.G.; et al. Urologic complications of diastasis of the pubic symphysis: A trauma case report and review of world literature. J Trauma 48:133–136, 2000.

57. Leighton, R.K.; Waddell, J.P. Techniques for reduction and posterior fixation through the anterior approach. Clin Orthop 329:115–120, 1996.

58. Letournel, E. Acetabular fractures: Classification and management. Clin Orthop 151:81–106, 1980.

59. Lowe, M.A.; Mason, J.T.; Luna G.K.; et al. Risk factors for urethral injuries in men with traumatic pelvic fractures. J Urol 140:506–507, 1988.

60. MacKenzie, E.J.; Cushing, B.M.; Jurkovich, G.J.; et al. Physical impairment and functional outcomes six months after severe lower extremity fractures. J Trauma 34:528–539, 1993.

61. Matta, J.M.; Saucedo, T. Internal fixation of pelvic ring fractures. Clin Orthop 242:83–97, 1989.

62. McBroom, R.; Tile, M. Disruptions of the pelvic ring. Presented at the Canadian Orthopaedic Research Society Convention. Kingston, Ontario, Canada. June, 1982.

63. McCoy, G.F.; Johnstone, R.A.; Kenwright, K. Biomechanical aspects of pelvic and hip injuries in road traffic accidents. J Orthop Trauma 3:118–123, 1989.

64. McLaren, A. Internal fixation in fractures of the pelvis and acetabulum. In: Tile, M., ed. Fractures of the Pelvis and Acetabulum, 2nd ed. Baltimore, Williams & Wilkins, 1995, pp. 183–189.

65. McLellan, B.A.; Phillips, J.P.; Hunter, G.A.; et al. Bilateral lower extremity amputations after prolonged application of the PASG. A case report. J Surg 30:55–56, 1987.

66. McMurtry, R.Y.; Walton, D.; Dickinson, D.; et al. Pelvic disruption in the polytraumatized patient. A management protocol. Clin Orthop 151:22–30, 1980.

67. Mears, D.C.; Capito, C.P.; Deleeuw, H. Posterior pelvic disruptions managed by the use of the double cobra plate. Instr Course Lect 37:143–150, 1988.

68. Mears, D.C.; Rubash, H.E. Pelvic and Acetabular Fractures. Thorofare, NJ, Slack, 1986.

69. Miranda, M.A.; Riemer, B.L.; Butterfield, S.L.; Burke, C.J. Pelvic ring injuries: A long-term functional outcome study. Clin Orthop 329:152–159, 1996.

70. Moed, B.R.; Hartman, M.J.; Ahmad, B.K.; et al. Evaluation of intraoperative nerve monitoring during insertion of an iliosacral implant in an animal model. J Bone Joint Surg Am 81:1529–1537, 1999.

71. Moreno, C.; Moore, E.E.; Rosenberger, A.; Cleveland, H.C. Hemorrhage associated with major pelvic fracture: A multispecialty challenge. J Trauma 26:987–994, 1986.

72. Murr, P.C.; Moore, E.E.; Lipscomb, R.; Johnston, R.M. Abdominal trauma associated with pelvic fracture. J Trauma 20:919–923, 1980.

73. Nallathambi, M.N.; Ferreiro, J.; Ivatury, R.R.; et al. The use of peritoneal lavage and urological studies in major fractures of the pelvis—A reassessment. Br J Accident Surg 18:379–383, 1987.

74. Nelson, D.W.; Duwelius, P.J. CT-guided fixation of sacral fractures and sacroiliac joint disruptions. Radiology 180:527–532, 1991.

75. Nepola, J.V.; Trenhaile, S.W.; Miranda, M.A.; et al. Vertical shear injuries: Is there a relationship between residual displacement and functional outcome? J Trauma 46:1024–1030, 1999.

76. Niemi, T.A.; Norton, L.W. Vaginal injuries in patients with pelvic fractures. J Trauma 25:547–551, 1985.

77. Noojin, F.K.; Malkani, A.L.; Haikal, L.; et al. Cross-sectional geometry of the sacral ala for safe insertion of iliosacral lag screws: A computed tomography model. J Trauma 14:31–35, 2000.

78. Ochsner, M.G.; Hoffman, A.P.; DiPasquale, D.; et al. Associated aortic rupture pelvic fracture: An alert for orthopedic and general surgeons. J Trauma 33:429–434, 1992.

79. Oonishi, H.; Isha, H.; Hasegawa, T. Mechanical analysis of the human pelvis and its application to the artificial hip joint by means of the three-dimensional finite element method. J Biomech 16:427–444, 1983.

80. Pattimore, D.; Thomas, P.; Dave, S.H. Torso injury patterns and mechanisms in car crashes: An additional diagnostic tool. Injury 23:123–126, 1992.

81. Peltier, L.F. Complications associated with fractures of the pelvis. J Bone Joint Surg Am 47:1060–1069, 1965.

82. Pennal, G.F.; Sutherland, G.O. Fractures of the Pelvis. Motion picture. Chicago, American Academy of Orthopaedic Surgeons Film Library, 1961.

83. Perry, J.F. Pelvic open fractures. Clin Orthop 151:41–45, 1980.

84. Pohlemann, T.; Bosch, U.; Gansslen, A.; Tscherne, H. The Hannover experience in management of pelvic fractures. Clin Orthop 305:69–80, 1994.

85. Poole, G.V.; Ward, E.F. Causes of mortality in patients with pelvic fractures. Orthopedics 17:691–696, 1994.

86. Poole, G.V.; Ward, E.F.; Muakkassa, F.F.; et al. Pelvic fracture from major blunt trauma. Ann Surg 213:532–539, 1991.

87. Raf, L. Double vertical fractures of the pelvis. Acta Chir Scand 131:298–305, 1966.

88. Raffe, J.; Christensen, M. Compound fractures of the pelvis. Am J Surg 132:282–286, 1976.

89. Richardson, J.D.; Harty, J.; Amin, M. Open pelvic fractures. J Trauma 22:533–538, 1982.

90. Riemer, B.L.; Butterfield, S.L.; Diamond, D.L.; et al. Acute mortality associated with injuries to the pelvic ring: The role of early patient mobilization and external fixation. J Trauma 35:671–677, 1993.

91. Robinson, D.; Hendel, D.; Halperin, N. An overlapping pubic dislocation treated by closed reduction: Case report and review of the literature. J Trauma 29:883–885, 1989.

92. Rothenberg, D.A.; Fischer, R.P.; Strate, R.G. The mortality associated with pelvic fractures. Surgery 84:356–361, 1978.

93. Routt, M.L.C.; Kregor, P.J.; Mayo, K. Early results of percutaneous iliosacral screws placed with the patient in the supine position. J Orthop Trauma 9:207–214, 1995.

94. Routt, M.L.C.; Meier, M.C.; Kregor, P.J. Percutaneous iliosacral screws with the patient supine technique. Op Techn Orthop 3:35–45, 1993.

95. Routt, M.L.; Nork, S.E.; Mills, W.J. Percutaneous fixation of pelvic ring disruptions. Clin Orthop 375:15–29, 2000.

96. Routt, M.L.C.; Simonian, P.T.; Agnew, S.G.; Mann, F.A. Radiographic recognition of the sacral alar slope for optimal placement of iliosacral screws: A cadaveric and clinical study. J Orthop Trauma 10:171–177, 1996.

97. Routt, M.L.; Simonian, P.T.; Defalco, A.J.; et al. Internal fixation in pelvic fractures and primary repairs of associated genitourinary disruptions: A team approach. J Trauma 40:784–790, 1996.

98. Routt, M.L.C.; Simonian, P.T.; Grujic, L. The retrograde medullary superior pubic ramus screw for the treatment of anterior pelvic ring disruptions: A new technique. J Orthop Trauma 9:35–44, 1995.

99. Routt, M.L.C.; Simonian, P.T.; Inaba, J. Iliosacral screw fixation of the disrupted sacroiliac joint. Techn Orthop 9:300–314, 1994.

100. Ruedi, T.; von Hochstetter, A.H.C.; Schlumpf, R. Surgical Approaches for Internal Fixation. Berlin, Springer-Verlag, 1984, pp. 77–83.

101. Saibel, E.A.; Maggisano, R.; Witchell, S.S. Angiography in the diagnosis and treatment of trauma. J Can Assoc Radiogr 34:218–227, 1983.

102. Schatzker, J.; Tile, M. Rationale of Operative Fracture Care. New York, Springer-Verlag, 1987, p. 165.

103. Scheid, D.K. Internal fixation. In: Tile, M., ed. Fractures of the Pelvis and Acetabulum, 2nd ed. Baltimore, Williams & Wilkins, 1995, p. 197.

104. Scheid, D.K.; Kellam, J.F.; Tile, M. Open reduction and internal fixation of pelvic ring fractures. J Orthop Trauma 5:226, 1991.

105. Semba, R.T.; Yasukawa, K.; Gustilo, R.B. Critical analysis of results of 53 Malgaigne fractures of the pelvis. J Trauma 23:535–537, 1983.

106. Simonian, P.T.; Routt, M.L.C.; Harrington, R.M.; et al. Biomechanical simulation of the anteroposterior compression injury of the pelvis. Clin Orthop 309:245–256, 1994.

107. Simonian, P.T.; Routt, M.L.C.; Harrington, R.M.; Tencer, A.F. Box plate fixation of the symphysis pubis: Biomechanical evaluation of a new technique. J Orthop Trauma 8:483–489, 1994.

108. Simonian, P.T.; Routt, M.L.C.; Harrington, R.M.; Tencer, A.F. Internal fixation of the unstable anterior pelvic ring: A biomechanical comparison of standard plating techniques and the retrograde medullary superior pubic ramus screw. J Orthop Trauma 8:476–482, 1994.

109. Simpson, L.A.; Waddell, J.P.; Leighton, R.K.; et al. Anterior approach and stabilization of the disrupted sacroiliac joint. J Trauma 27:1332–1339, 1987.

110. Stephen, D.J.; Kreder, H.J.; Day, A.C.; et al. Early detection of arterial bleeding in acute pelvic trauma. J Trauma 47:638–642, 1999.

111. Tile, M. Internal fixation. In: Tile, M., ed. Fractures of the Pelvis and Acetabulum, 2nd ed. Baltimore, Williams & Wilkins, 1995, pp. 189–193.

112. Tile, M. Pelvic ring fractures. Should they be fixed? J Bone Joint Surg Br 70:1–12, 1988.

113. Tile, M.; Hearn, T. Biomechanics. In: Tile, M., ed. Fractures of the Pelvis and Acetabulum, 2nd ed. Baltimore, Williams & Wilkins, 1995, pp. 22–36.

114. Tornetta, P.; Dickson, K.; Matta, J.M. Outcome of rotationally unstable pelvic ring injuries treated operatively. Clin Orthop 329:147–151, 1996.

115. Tornetta, P.; Matta, J.M. Outcome of operatively treated unstable posterior pelvic ring disruptions. Clin Orthop 329:186–193, 1996.

116. Trunkey, D.D.; Chapman, M.W.; Lim, R.C. Management of pelvic fractures and blunt traumatic injury. J Trauma 14:912–923, 1974.

117. Velmahos, G.C.; Kern, J.; Chan, L.S.; et al. Prevention of venous thromboembolism after injury: An evidence-based report—Part I: Analysis of risk factors and evaluation of the role of vena caval filters. J Trauma 49:132–139, 2000.

118. Vrahas, M.; Gordon, R.G.; Mears, D.C.; et al. Intraoperative somatosensory evoked potential monitoring of pelvic and acetabular fractures. J Orthop Trauma 6:50–58, 1992.

119. Vukicevic, S.; Marusic, A.; Stavljenic, A.; et al. Holographic analysis of the human pelvis. Spine 16:209–214, 1991.

120. Webb, L.X.; de Araujo, W.; Donofrio, P.; et al. Electromyography monitoring for percutaneous placement of iliosacral screw. J Trauma 14:245–254, 2000.

121. Weber, T.G.; Mast, J.W. The extended ilioinguinal approach for specific both column fractures. Clin Orthop 305:106–111, 1994.

122. Weis, E.B. Subtle neurological injuries in pelvic fractures. J Trauma 24:983–985, 1984.

123. Wild, J.J.; Hanson, G.W.; Tullos, H.S. Unstable fractures of the pelvis treated by external fixation. J Bone Joint Surg Am 64:1010–1020, 1982.

124. Young, J.W.R.; Burgess, A.R. Radiological Management of Pelvic Ring Fractures. Baltimore, Urban & Schwarzenberg, 1987, pp. 22, 27, 41, 55.

CHAPTER 37

Surgical Treatment of Acetabular Fractures

Joel M. Matta, M.D.

BASIC CONSIDERATIONS

Fractures of the acetabulum occur primarily in young adult patients as the result of high-energy trauma.[20] The displacement of fracture fragments of the acetabulum creates an incongruity between the cartilage of the femoral head and acetabulum. In effect, the contact area between the femoral head and acetabulum is markedly decreased. If the acetabular fracture is allowed to heal in the displaced position, weight-bearing forces applied to the small remaining area of contact can lead to rapid breakdown of the articulator cartilage and result in post-traumatic arthritis. Severe incongruity can cause wear of the femoral head, which is often misdiagnosed as avascular necrosis. Surgical treatment of the acetabular fracture should accurately restore the normal shape of the acetabulum, normal topography of the contact area, and normal pressure distribution within the joint.[2, 3, 6, 10, 12, 16, 28, 50]

Bony Anatomy

The acetabulum is formed as a portion of the innominate bone. It ties at the point where the ilium, ischium, and pubis are joined by the triradiate cartilage, which later fuses to form the innominate bone. It is useful for the surgeon to divide the acetabulum and innominate bone into anterior and posterior columns. The anterior column comprises the anterior border of the iliac wing, the entire pelvic brim, the anterior wall of the acetabulum, and the superior pubic ramus. The posterior column comprises the ischial portion of the bone, including the greater and lesser sciatic notch, the posterior wall of the acetabulum, and the ischial tuberosity (Fig. 37–1). The surgeon must be familiar with the anatomy and various bony landmarks and contours of the innominate bone.

Radiographic Diagnosis

The initial diagnosis of an acetabular fracture is made from an anteroposterior (AP) view of the pelvis.[44] After this, 45° oblique views of the pelvis should be obtained for all patients with an acetabular fracture.[5] After examination of the plain films, a computed tomography (CT) scan should be obtained to provide additional information about the fracture configuration and answer any questions that might remain after examining the plain films. Three-dimensional reconstruction of the CT scan (3-D CT) can also be useful for understanding the fracture configuration and displacement.[1, 16]

Interpretation of the plain films is based on understanding the normal radiographic lines of the acetabulum and what each line represents. Disruption of any of the normal lines of the acetabulum represents a fracture involving that portion of the bone.[24, 43]

On the AP view, the iliopectineal line roughly follows the pelvic brim and represents involvement of the anterior column. The ilioischial line is formed by the tangency of the x-ray beam to the posterior portion of the quadrilateral surface and is therefore a radiographic landmark of the posterior column (Fig. 37–2).

The 45° obturator oblique view is taken with the fractured acetabulum rotated toward the x-ray tube. It shows the obturator foramen in its largest dimension and profiles the anterior column and posterior rim of the acetabulum.

The iliac oblique view is taken with the fractured acetabulum rotated away from the x-ray tube. It shows the iliac wing in its largest dimension and profiles the greater and lesser sciatic notches and the anterior rim of the acetabulum.

Most fractures can be properly classified from plain radiographs alone. They are usually best for assessing the congruence between the femoral head and roof of the acetabulum.

The CT scan is advantageous for assessing fracture lines

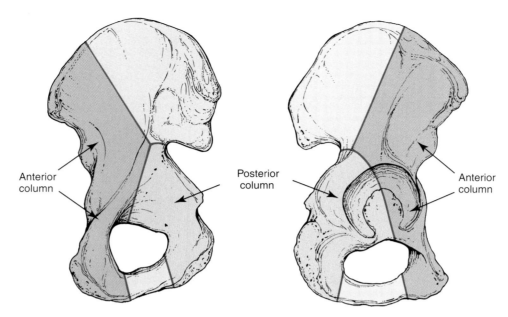

FIGURE 37–1. The extent of the anterior and posterior columns on the inner and outer aspects of the bone.

in several areas.[15] It provides an excellent picture of sacral fractures. It shows minimally displaced fractures of the iliac wing that are often missed on plain films and shows fractures through the quadrilateral surface that may be invisible on plain films. It often best demonstrates the degree of gap in a fracture through the roof of the acetabulum, although it does not reveal a vertical step at the fracture line through the roof or demonstrate congruity between the femoral head and roof. The CT scan can miss fracture lines that lie in a transverse plane and therefore most surgeons rely primarily on plane films to visualize those fractures.

Free fragments of bone that are lodged between the femoral head and walls of the acetabulum are often best seen on the CT scan, but the CT scan may not adequately demonstrate an incarcerated fragment of bone located between the top of the femoral head and the roof of the acetabulum.

A 3-D CT scan can provide a good overall picture of the fracture configuration, particularly in widely displaced fractures.[4] The 3-D scan, however, lacks fine detail, and fracture lines displaced less than 3 mm may not be represented. Assessment is aided by the computer removing the femoral head from the picture.

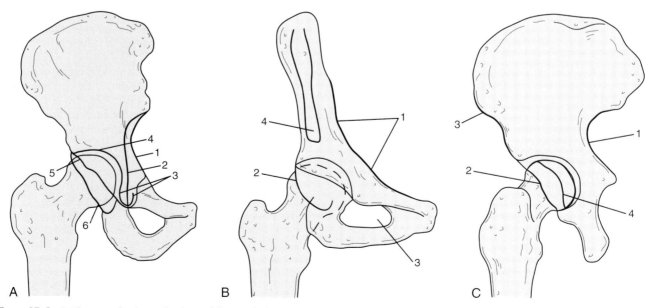

FIGURE 37–2. *A,* The normal radiographic lines of the acetabulum as they appear in the anteroposterior (AP) radiographic view. 1, The iliopectineal line; 2, ilioischial line; 3, roentgenographic U, or teardrop; 4, roof; 5, anterior rim; 6, posterior rim. *B,* The normal radiographic landmarks of the obturator oblique view. 1, The iliopectineal line; 2, posterior rim; 3, obturator ring; 4, anterior superior iliac spine. *C,* The normal radiographic landmarks of the iliac oblique view. 1, Posterior border of innominate bone; 2, anterior rim; 3, anterior border of iliac wing; 4, posterior rim. (*A–C,* Redrawn from Judet, R.; et al. J Bone Joint Surg Am 46:1615–1646, 1964.)

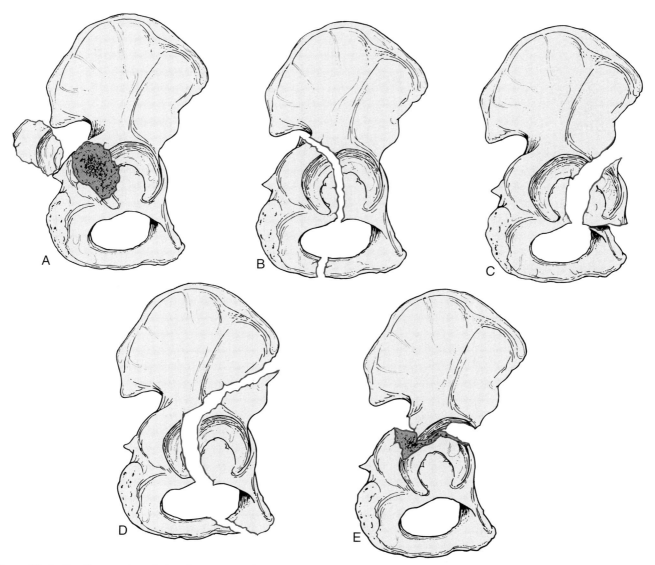

FIGURE 37–3. Classification of acetabulum fractures according to Letournel. *A,* Posterior wall fracture. *B,* Posterior column fracture. *C,* Anterior wall fracture. *D,* Anterior column fracture. *E,* Transverse fracture.
Illustration continued on following page

Classification

An anatomic classification of acetabular fractures was published by Judet and colleagues in 1964 and has been altered slightly by Letournel since then.[21, 54] Letournel's classification is the most useful for surgeons.[26, 54] A thorough knowledge of all fracture types is essential to decision making in surgical management and for understanding the technical aspects of the surgery.

Fractures of the acetabulum are divided into five simple fracture types and five associated fracture types, which are formed by combinations of the simple fracture types.[48, 49, 55] The simple fracture types are posterior wall, posterior column, anterior wall, anterior column, and transverse fractures. The five associated fracture types are associated posterior and posterior wall, associated transverse and posterior wall, T-shaped, associated anterior column and posterior hemitransverse, and both-column fractures (Fig. 37–3).

Fractures of the posterior wall typically involve the posterior rim of the acetabulum, a portion of the retroacetabular surface, and a variable segment of the articular cartilage. A common finding is impaction of the articular cartilage, which should be diagnosed preoperatively on the basis of plain films or a CT scan. Extended posterior wall fractures can involve the entire retroacetabular surface and include a portion of the greater or lesser sciatic notch, the ischial tuberosity, or both areas. The ilioischial line remains intact on the AP view.

Posterior column fractures include only the ischial portion of the bone. The entire retroacetabular surface is displaced with the posterior column. As the vertical line separating the anterior from the posterior column traverses inferiorly, it most commonly enters the obturator foramen. There is an associated fracture of the inferior pubic ramus. Sometimes, the fracture line traverses just posterior to the obturator foramen, splitting the ischial tuberosity. On the AP view, the ilioischial line is displaced.

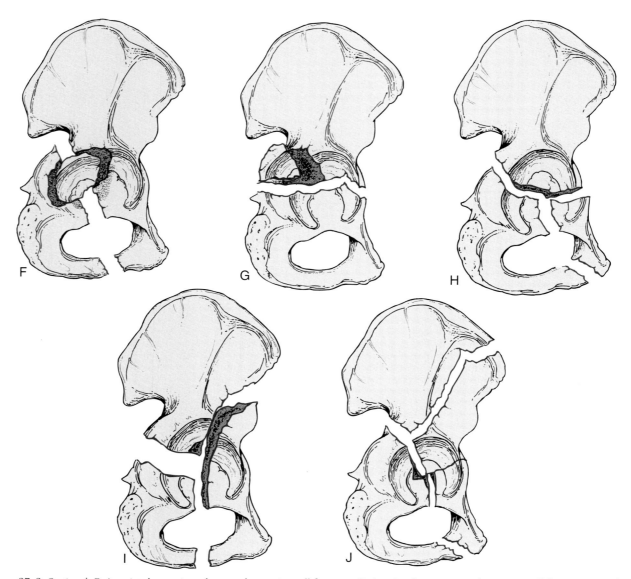

Figure 37-3 *Continued. F*, Associated posterior column and posterior wall fractures. *G*, Associated transverse and posterior wall fractures. *H*, T-shaped fracture. *I*, Associated anterior and posterior hemitransverse fractures. *J*, Both-column fracture.

Fractures of the anterior wall involve the central portion of the anterior column. The inferior pubic ramus is not fractured. The pelvic brim is displaced in its midportion, and the AP radiograph shows a displacement of the iliopectineal line.

Anterior column fractures can occur anywhere from a very low to a very high level. Low fractures involve only the superior ramus and pubic portion of the acetabulum. High fractures can involve the entire anterior border of the innominate bone. The pelvic brim and iliopectineal line are displaced.

Transverse fractures divide the innominate bone into two portions. A horizontally oriented fracture line can cross the acetabulum at various levels. The innominate bone is then divided into a superior part composed of the iliac wing and a portion of the roof of the acetabulum. The lower part of the bone, the ischiopubic segment, is composed of an intact obturator foramen with the anterior and posterior walls of the acetabulum.[5]

The association of a posterior column and posterior wall fracture divides the posterior column into a larger posterior column segment and an associated smaller posterior wall segment. The association of the transverse plus posterior wall fracture combines a normal transverse configuration with one or more separate posterior wall fragments. The **T** fracture is similar to the transverse fracture, except for the addition of a vertical split along the quadrilateral surface and acetabular fossa, which divides the anterior from the posterior column. An associated fracture of the inferior pubic ramus exists. The anterior plus posterior hemitransverse fracture combines an anterior wall or anterior column fracture with a horizontal transverse component, which traverses the posterior column at a low level and crosses the posterior border of the bone near the ischial spine. The anterior component is typically at a higher level and is more displaced than the posterior component.

Both-column fractures form a distinct category because all articular segments are detached from the intact portion of the ilium, which remains attached to the sacrum. The area of intact ilium depends on the course of the anterior column fracture. The least iliac involvement is present when the anterior column fracture reaches the anterior border of the bone at the interspinous notch (between the anterior superior and anterior inferior iliac spines). In most cases, the anterior column fracture reaches the iliac crest. The greatest iliac involvement occurs when fracture lines of the anterior or posterior column cross the sacroiliac joint.

The surgeon should realize that transverse, associated transverse plus posterior wall, T-shaped, and anterior plus posterior hemi-transverse fractures show involvement of the anterior plus the posterior column of the acetabulum but are not both-column fractures. In these four fracture types, a portion of the articular surface remains in its normal position, attached to the intact portion of the ilium. The both-column fracture is therefore unique, with its division of all segments of articular cartilage from the ilium.

Indications for Operative Treatment

Operative treatment is indicated for most displaced acetabular fractures to allow early ambulatory function and to decrease the chance of post-traumatic arthritis. Nonoperative treatment, however, can still be successful for a minority of displaced acetabular fractures.

Indications for nonoperative treatment are based on the analysis of the fracture configuration. The decision about whether to operate is based on the initial series of plane films and CT scans. Attempts at closed reduction by manipulation under anesthesia or skeletal traction are not applicable for assessing the indication for surgical treatment. If the surgeon concludes from the initial radiographs that an accurate reduction of the articular surface is necessary to ensure a good prognosis, operation is indicated. Nonoperative treatment is reserved for patients in whom a tolerable incongruity is present and also for those with contraindications to surgery. Contraindications include local or systemic infection and severe osteoporosis, although many elderly patients, even with some degree of osteoporosis, can benefit from surgery. Satisfactory bone stock can be found for fixation, particularly along the pelvic brim and greater sciatic notch. Relative contraindications include age, associated medical conditions, and associated soft tissue and visceral injuries.

Displaced fractures that should be considered for nonoperative treatment are usually in one of two categories:

1. A large portion of the acetabulum remains intact, and the femoral head remains congruous with this portion of the acetabulum.
2. A secondary congruence exists after only moderate displacement of a both-column fracture.

The first situation, in which a large portion of the acetabulum remains intact, can occur with any of several different fracture types. In the case of posterior wall fractures, only a small portion of the posterior wall may be displaced. If the CT scan shows less than 50% of the width of the posterior articular cartilage displaced on

the CT cut that shows maximal involvement, nonoperative treatment may be considered. The cranial-caudad location of the fracture also should be considered. A small fragment displaced at the level of the roof may be more important to reduce than a larger one near the inferior portion of the posterior articular surface. Some authorities have advocated a test for stability of the hip against posterior dislocation with the patient under anesthesia. I, however, have never based my indication on the results of manipulation and am not aware of follow-up data to support its use. In practice, therefore, surgery is appropriate for most posterior wall fractures.

Many low anterior column fractures that involve only the pubic portion of the acetabulum can be treated by nonoperative means. A minority of low, T-shaped or transverse fractures can be treated nonoperatively.

In assessing the size of the intact portion of acetabulum, it is useful to perform roof arc measurements.[30, 31, 33] These are made on the AP, obturator, and iliac oblique radiographic views. A vertical line is drawn to the geometric center of the acetabulum. Another line is drawn through the point where the fracture line intersects the acetabulum and again to the geometric center of the acetabulum. The angle drawn in this way represents the medial, anterior, or posterior roof arc as seen on the AP, obturator oblique, or iliac oblique view, respectively. If nonoperative treatment is to be considered, all roof arc measurements should be more than 45°, and the head should remain congruous with the roof of the acetabulum with the patient out of traction.

The CT subchondral arc technique of Olson and colleagues[48] appears to be most effective for evaluating the superior acetabulum. Demonstration of no involvement of the upper 10 mm of the acetabulum by CT corresponds to an intact 45° roof arc on the three plain film views.

The roof arc and CT subchondral arc were initially devised as study techniques. Rowe and Lowell[31] described the "intact weight-bearing dome" as an indication for nonoperative treatment but did not precisely describe the portion of the acetabulum they were referring to or how to evaluate it radiographically. This area is still incompletely studied, although an intact 45° anterior roof arc or CT subchondral arc is reliable for predicting a good outcome for displaced, low anterior column fractures. This knowledge is useful for assessing when an operation is not needed or for planning the extent of surgery that must be performed. For some operations, reduction and fixation of the lower portion (i.e., below the 10-mm CT cut) of the anterior column can be deferred if it would require increased operative exposure or prolonged time. For an intact medial or posterior 45° arc or CT arc, nonoperative treatment may not be indicated.

The second category of fractures (i.e., both-column fractures with secondary congruence) presents a unique situation. Because both-column fractures detach all articular segments from the intact ilium, even though displacement of the fracture has occurred, the fracture fragments can remain congruously grouped around the femoral head despite medial and proximal displacement of the femoral head and some rotational displacement of the fragments.[6, 26, 30, 34, 50] This congruence can be assessed on the three plain film views and the CT scan. Perfect secondary congruence may be theoretical, and most actual situations may show some lack of congruence between the head and the walls of the acetabulum, although instances of long-term good function and freedom from arthritis have been observed. Predicting a good outcome, however, is less reliable than a perfect reduction, and surgery is recommended in most cases.

The goal of nonoperative treatment is prevention of the displacement from worsening. Skeletal traction through a proximal tibia pin is often used. Neufeld roller traction is a useful form of treatment that allows motion of the hip and knee while the patient is in traction.[38] The amount of traction should not be so great that it distracts the femoral head from the acetabulum. Lateral skeletal traction through the greater trochanter is not beneficial in achieving a reduction and can even cause severe problems, such as infection of the greater trochanter or soft tissues lateral to the hip joint. Traction through the greater trochanter must not be used if surgical treatment is being considered.

Surgery is usually undertaken 2 to 3 days after the injury, when the initial bleeding from the fracture and intrapelvic vessels has subsided. Ideally, the operation should be performed before 10 days so that the fracture fragments remain mobile. Three weeks after injury, a bony callus is usually present, which makes reduction of the fracture more difficult.

A final and important consideration regarding the indication for surgery is the capability of the surgeon and the environment in which he or she operates. As with other forms of fracture surgery, the best and worst results follow surgery. If the surgeon is not confident that he or she can achieve and maintain an anatomic or near anatomic reduction with a low chance of complication, the value of surgery is questionable, and it may actually do harm.

Choice of Surgical Approach

No one surgical incision is ideal for all fractures of the acetabulum. After radiographic analysis and classification of the fracture, the surgeon should be able to draw the fracture configuration on a model or a drawing of the innominate bone. Preoperative considerations should include an understanding of the fracture configuration on the outside and inside of the bone and of the orientation of the fracture planes as they traverse the inner aspect of the bone. From this information and from knowledge of the benefits and limitations of each surgical approach, the appropriate surgical procedure can be chosen.

The Kocher-Langenbeck, ilioinguinal, and extended iliofemoral approaches are the most commonly used. Alternatively, the triradiate approach gives an exposure roughly comparable to that of the extended iliofemoral but has a few limitations. All surgical approaches provide some access to the anterior and posterior columns, but each has advantages and disadvantages.

The Kocher-Langenbeck approach provides the best access to the posterior column. The ilioinguinal approach gives the best access to the anterior column and the inner aspect of the innominate bone. The extended iliofemoral approach gives the best simultaneous access to the two columns. The surgical approach should be chosen with the expectation that the entire reduction and fixation can be done through that single approach. Combined approaches performed concurrently or successively are less desirable than the single approach. The patient is generally positioned appropriately for the single approach: prone for the Kocher-Langenbeck, supine for the ilioinguinal, or lateral for the extended iliofemoral. Although the extended iliofemoral provides the most commanding access to the bone, it has the longest period of postoperative recovery and the highest incidence of ectopic bone formation. It is therefore preferable to choose the ilioinguinal or Kocher-Langenbeck approach if the reduction is judged to be feasible through either of these approaches.

Types of Surgical Approaches

KOCHER-LANGENBECK APPROACH

The patient is usually positioned in a prone position on the fracture table. The incision starts lateral to the posterior superior iliac spine, proceeds to the greater trochanter, and then continues along the axis of the femur to almost the midpoint of the thigh (Fig. 37–4A). The gluteal fascia is split in line with the fibers of the gluteus maximus. The fascia lata is split in line with the axis of the femur. After posterior reflection of the gluteus maximus, the sciatic nerve is identified on the posterior surface of the quadratus femoris and followed proximally until it disappears beneath the piriformis (see Fig. 37–4B). The tendons of the piriformis and obturator internus are transected at their trochanteric insertion and retracted posteriorly, exposing the greater and lesser sciatic notch.

Subperiosteal elevation exposes the inferior aspect of the iliac wing. The capsule can be opened along its rim and the femoral head distracted to expose the internal aspect of the joint (see Fig. 37–4C). A trochanteric osteotomy can help in further visualization of the inferior iliac wing and the interior of the joint. Alternatively, the tendon of the gluteus medius can be partially transected. The gluteus maximus tendon is transected at its femoral insertion.

At completion of the procedure, the detached tendons are reattached to the femur at their normal points of insertion. Hemovac drains are usually placed, with one in the greater sciatic notch and the other in the external iliac fossa. An important access with this approach is to the quadrilateral surface through the greater sciatic notch. Fracture lines traversing the quadrilateral surface and pelvic brim can be palpated through the sciatic notch and the reduction thereby assessed.

ILIOINGUINAL APPROACH

The patient is normally placed in the supine position on a fracture table. It is useful to have lateral traction through the greater trochanter available, if needed, intraoperatively. The incision starts at the midline 2 fingerbreadths above the symphysis pubis, proceeds to the anterior superior spine, and then continues posteriorly along the line of the iliac crest about two thirds of the way around the iliac crest (Fig. 37–5A). The periosteum is sharply

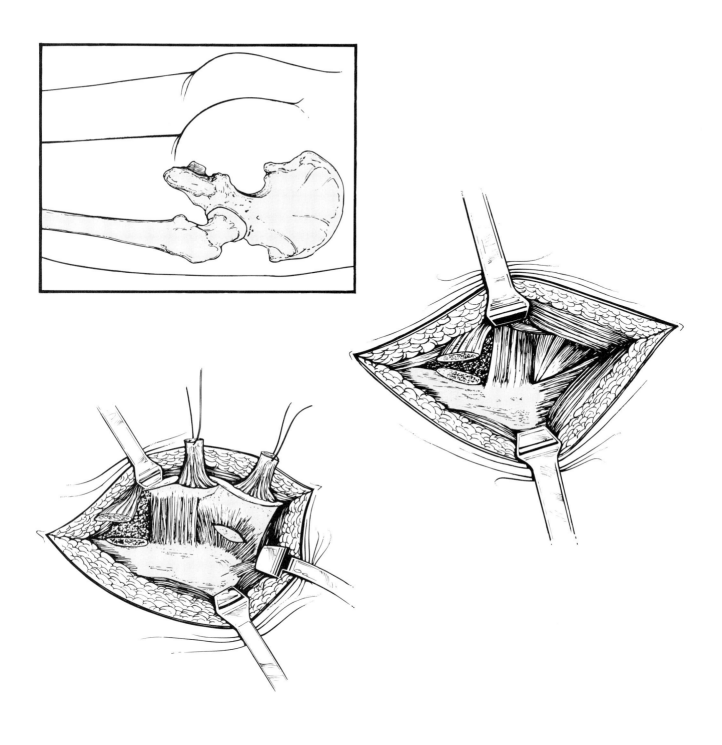

incised along the iliac crest. The attachment of the abdominals and iliacus is mobilized from the crest and internal iliac fossa. Elevation of the iliacus from the internal iliac fossa exposes the anterior sacroiliac joint and pelvic brim. The aponeurosis of the external obliquus is incised in line with the skin incision. This layer is reflected distally, unroofing the inguinal canal. The spermatic cord is isolated with a finger, and a rubber drain is placed around the spermatic cord for retraction (see Fig. 37–5B).

An incision is carefully made along the inguinal ligament from its medial attachment to the pubis to the anterior superior spine. Approximately 1 mm of the ligament is split away from its main portion, releasing the transversalis fascia from the ligament medially and freeing the common origin of the internal oblique and transversus abdominis from the lateral portion of the ligament. The conjoined tendon and tendon of the rectus abdominis are often transected in the medial portion of the incision. This incision along the inguinal ligament provides access to the retropubic space of Retzius medi-

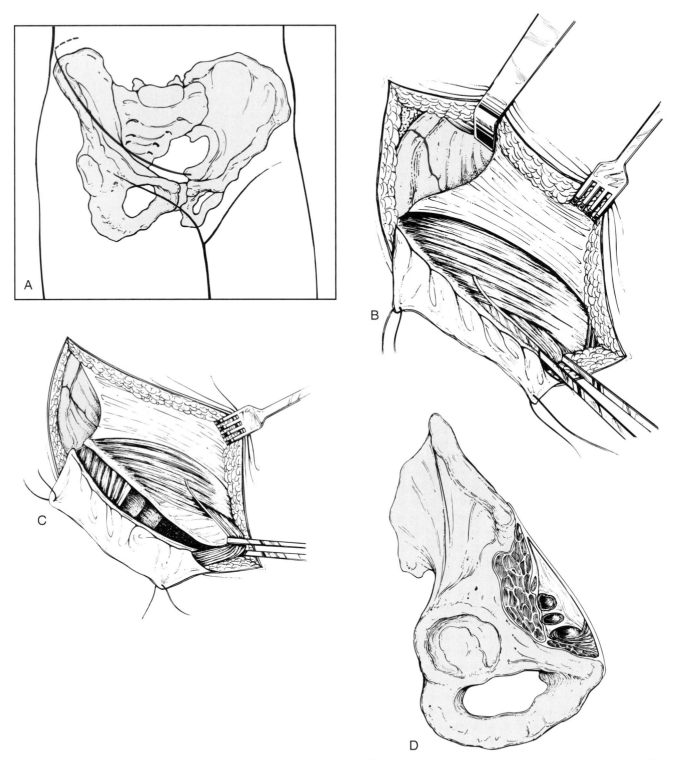

FIGURE 37–5. The ilioinguinal approach. *A*, The skin incision. *B*, The internal iliac fossa has been exposed and the inguinal canal has been unroofed by distal reflection of the external oblique aponeurosis. *C*, An incision along the inguinal ligament detaches the abdominal muscles and transversalis fascia, giving access to the psoas sheath, the iliopectineal fascia, the external aspect of the femoral vessels, and the retropubic space of Retzius. *D*, An oblique section through the lacuna musculorum and lacuna vascularum at the level of the inguinal ligament.

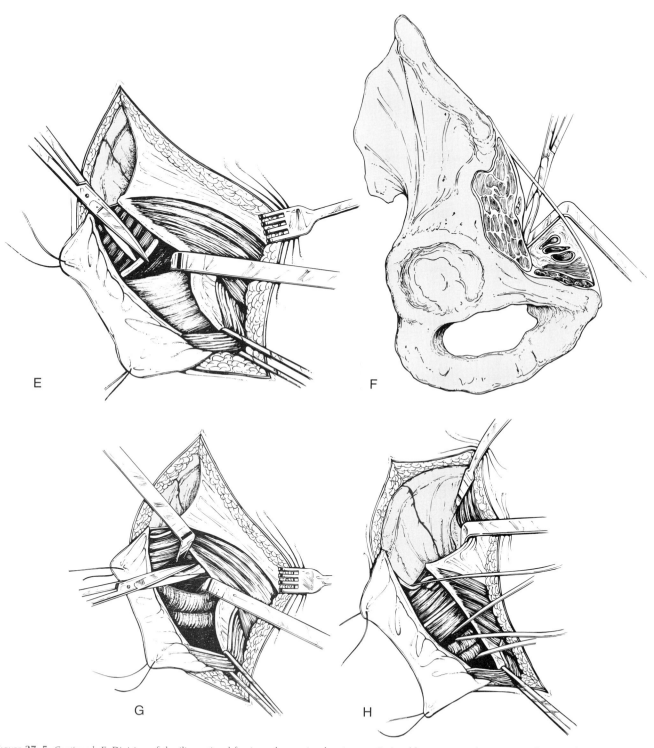

Figure 37–5 *Continued. E,* Division of the iliopectineal fascia to the pectineal eminence. *F,* An oblique section demonstrates division of the iliopectineal fascia. *G,* Proximal division of the iliopectineal fascia from the pelvic brim allows access to the true pelvis. *H,* The first window of the ilioinguinal approach gives access to the internal iliac fossa, the anterior sacroiliac joint, and the upper portion of the anterior column.

Illustration continued on following page

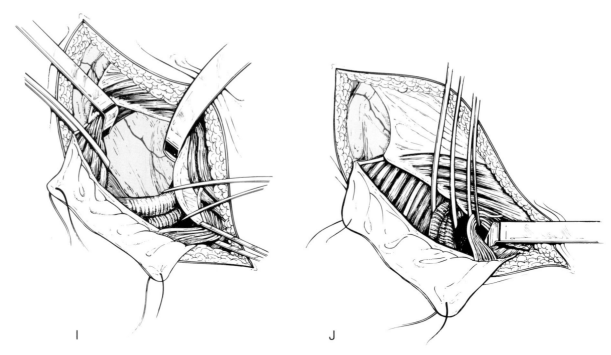

I   J

Figure 37–5 *Continued. I*, The second window of the ilioinguinal approach gives access to the pelvic brim from the anterior sacroiliac joint to the lateral extremity of the superior pubic ramus. The quadrilateral surface and posterior column are accessible beyond the pelvic brim. *J*, Access to the symphysis pubis and retropubic space of Retzius, medial to the spermatic cord and femoral vessels. (*I–J*, Redrawn from Matta, J.M. Surgical Approaches to Fractures of the Acetabulum and Pelvis. Los Angeles, J.M. Matta Publisher, 1986.)

ally, the external aspect of the iliac vessels, and the psoas sheath.

The lateral cutaneous nerve of the thigh and the femoral nerve are found within the psoas sheath (see Fig. 37–5C). A periosteal elevator is used along the pelvic brim, superior ramus, and quadrilateral surface to obtain a better view of the bone.

The obturator nerve and artery are visualized medial or lateral to the vessels as they enter the obturator foramen. The surgeon should check for an anomalous origin of the obturator artery from the external iliac system. If present, it should be clamped, transected, and ligated so that it does not tear during the procedure and cause bleeding, which is difficult to control.

The interior of the joint can be approached and visualized by distraction of the fracture lines, but the interior of the joint is not visible after reduction of the fracture. The entire anterior column is exposed through the ilioinguinal approach (see Fig.37–5H). Limited but useful access to the posterior column can be obtained by manipulating the quadrilateral surface through the second window of the ilioinguinal approach (see Fig. 37–5I). Rubber drains are also placed around the iliopsoas and femoral nerves and around the external iliac vessels with their lymphatics to manipulate and retract them for the reduction and internal fixation (see Fig. 37–5J). It is often necessary to release the inguinal ligament and sartorius origin from the anterosuperior spine and to elevate the tensor fascia lata origin from the outer aspect of the bone to place reduction forceps across the anterior border of the bone.

At the completion of the procedure, Hemovac drains are placed in the retropubic space along the quadrilateral surface and in the internal iliac fossa. The iliopectineal fascia is not repaired, but all other structures are repaired anatomically.

MODIFIED STOPPA ANTERIOR APPROACH

Cole and Bolhofner[7] described the use of the modified Stoppa anterior approach to access the medial wall of the acetabulum, quadrilateral surface, and sacroiliac joint. The patient is positioned supine on the table, and a horizontal incision is made 2 cm above the symphysis pubis, extending from external ring to external ring. The rectus abdominis muscle is then split vertically and incised sharply from its insertion on the pubic surface bilaterally. The bladder is protected. Anastomotic vascular connections between the inferior epigastric and obturator vessels and between the external iliac and bladder, as well as nutrient vessels to the pelvis, must be identified and clipped. The surgical approach passes under the external iliac vessels and femoral nerve. Full access to the inner pelvic surface is achieved by sharply dividing and elevating the iliopectineal fascia along the pelvic rim. While flexing the ipsilateral hip to relax the iliopsoas muscle, it can be elevated from the internal iliac fossa to enhance the superior exposure. Multiple retractors, including Hohmann and malleable devices and abdominal retractors such as those designed by Deaver and Harrington, are held by an assistant standing on the side of the pelvic injury. The operating surgeon stands on the side opposite the injury to gain the best view of the fracture. Reduction is achieved with direct pressure on the pelvic surface with the ball-spike pusher, a bone hook through the sciatic notch, Schantz screws in the pelvic rim and greater trochanter, and reduction forceps. Fixation is achieved with reconstruction plates and 3.5-mm screws inserted just below the pelvic brim on the medial surface. By avoiding dissection of the gluteal muscles, the modified Stoppa approach achieves a low incidence of heterotopic bone formation, similar to the ilioinguinal approach. Wound closure, which includes reattachment of the rectus abdominis, is simplified because of the size and location of the incision.

EXTENDED ILIOFEMORAL APPROACH

The extended iliofemoral approach was developed by Emile Letournel as a simultaneous approach to the two columns of the acetabulum.[23, 25, 26, 54] It can be regarded as the lateral approach to the innominate bone that primarily exposes the external aspect of the bone. The internal iliac fossa, however, can also be exposed, and circumferential access to the bone can be obtained by palpating the quadrilateral surface from the pelvic rim to the greater sciatic notch.

The patient is usually placed in the lateral position on the fracture table. The knee is kept in at least 60° of flexion to relax the sciatic nerve. The incision starts at the posterosuperior iliac spine, follows the iliac crest to the anterosuperior spine, and then turns slightly laterally to parallel the femur on the anterolateral aspect of the thigh (Fig. 37–6A).

The periosteum is sharply incised along the iliac crest, and the gluteal muscles are reflected from the lateral aspect of the iliac wing. The fascia lata is incised over the tensor fascia lata muscle. The incision is usually carried distally enough so that the distal extent of the tensor fascia lata muscle can be located. The tensor fascia lata muscle is retracted posteriorly, exposing a fascia layer that separates it from the rectus femoris. This fascial layer is opened. Another fascial layer separating the rectus femoris from the vastus lateralis is split longitudinally, and the lateral femoral circumflex vessels are found immediately beneath this fascial layer.

The lateral femoral circumflex vessels are clamped, transected, and ligated. The strong aponeurotic fibers that traverse the anterior aspect of the femur must also be transected to provide access to the trochanter. The tendon of the gluteus minimus is identified at its anterior insertion on the trochanter. It is transected in its midportion and tagged with suture. The tendon is then also released from its attachment to the anterior and superior hip capsule. The gluteus medius tendon is identified as a broad band over the external aspect of the greater trochanter. It is transected in its midsubstance and tagged with multiple sutures (see Fig. 37–6C). Although the medius tenotomy has been used for most of my cases, I now prefer to osteotomize the greater trochanter with a thin oscillating saw after sectioning the minimus tendon to mobilize the medius. An osteotomy should not go medial to the posterior ridge of the greater trochanter, or it may damage the femoral head vascularity.

The piriformis and obturator internus tendons are identified at their insertion on the proximal femur. These are transected and tagged with suture. As they are retracted

posteriorly, the greater and lesser sciatic notches are exposed, as are the ischial spine and ischial tuberosity. The reflected tendon of the rectus femoris is identified and is usually excised. An incision along the rim of the acetabulum provides access to the interior of the joint as the femoral head is distracted from the joint (see Fig. 37–6D). Access to the internal iliac fossa and anterior column is made possible by detachment of the sartorius and rectus femoris origins from the anterior border of the bone and by elevation of the iliacus from the distal portion of the internal iliac fossa. If the iliac crest is not involved by the fracture (e.g., transverse or T shaped), the surgeon can alternatively osteotomize the anterior superior iliac spine for muscle detachment and exposure. The upper portion of the anterior column is accessible, but the anterior column is not accessible distal to the pectineal eminence (see Fig. 37–6E).

In the case of a both-column fracture with an anterior column fracture traversing the anterior portion of the iliac wing to the iliac crest, it is possible to devascularize the anterior column by removing all muscle attachments from the outer and inner aspects of this bone segment. As with other types of fracture surgery, soft tissue pedicles should be left attached to all bony fragments to prevent loss of vascularity.

At completion of the procedure, Hemovac drains are usually placed along the external aspect of the bone and into the greater sciatic notch. The internal iliac fossa should also be drained if it has been exposed. The origins of the sartorius and rectus femoris are reattached to the anterior border of the bone with suture placed through drill holes (or an osteotomy repaired with 3.5-mm screws). The tendons of the piriformis, obturator internus, gluteus medius, and gluteus minimus are reattached to their anatomic positions on the femur with multiple sutures (or the trochanter and medius origin fixed with 3.5-mm screws). The fascia lata is reattached to the abdominal fascia along the iliac crest, and the fascia lata is closed over the thigh. During the suture of the fascia lata to the abdominals, the hip should be placed in abduction to facilitate the repair, which necessitates removal of the leg from its Judet table attachment. In addition to the interrupted sutures, a second continuous suture reinforces the repair from posterior to the gluteus medius tubercle to distal to the anterior superior spine. Before surgery, the femur has often been displaced to an intrapelvic position, and returning it to its normal, more lateral position creates initial tension on the abductor repair, which is lessened when the limb is abducted. This abducted position should be maintained as patients are returned to their beds from the table, and an abductor pillow is secured between the legs for the first 5 days.

Care must be taken throughout the procedure to avoid undue injury to the large muscle flap or to the superior gluteal vessels that vascularize it. The muscle should also be prevented from becoming desiccated by applying irrigant and irrigant-soaked sponges.

TRIRADIATE APPROACH

The triradiate approach offers an alternative exposure to the external aspect of the innominate bone.[40] It provides

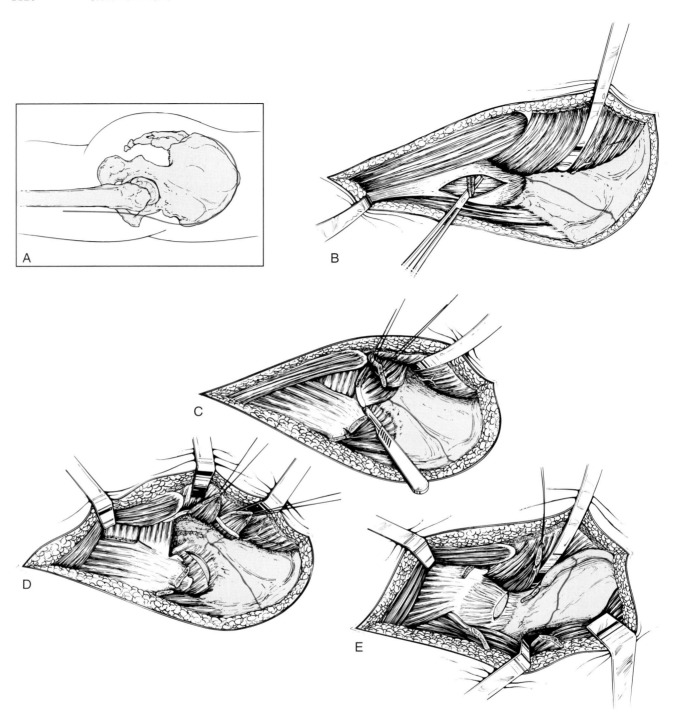

FIGURE 37–6. The extended iliofemoral approach. *A*, The skin incision. *B*, The gluteal muscle has been elevated from the wing. The lateral femoral circumflex vessels will be transected and ligated. *C*, The tendons of the gluteus minimus and medius are transected in midsubstance at their trochanteric insertions. *D*, The completed exposure of the external aspect of the bone with a capsulotomy along the acetabular rim. *E*, The completed exposure of the internal aspect of the bone. (*C–E*, Redrawn from Matta, J.M. Surgical Approaches to Fractures of the Acetabulum and Pelvis. Los Angeles, J.M. Matta Publisher, 1986.)

almost the same exposure to the bone as the extended iliofemoral approach, but the exposure to the posterior part of the ilium is not as good. The incision starts as with the Kocher-Langenbeck approach, dissecting between the fibers of the gluteus maximus and splitting the fascia lata. An anterior limb of the incision is then incised from the

anterosuperior greater spine to the trochanter (Fig. 37–7A). The fascia lata is reflected off the external aspect of the tensor fascia lata muscle. The greater trochanter is osteotomized, and the abductor insertion, along with the tensor fascia lata muscle, is retracted proximally. Further exposure to the iliac wing can be obtained by release of the fascia lata from the iliac crest, as with the extended iliofemoral approach (see Fig. 37–7*B*). A medial limb of the incision can also be extended across the lower abdomen to obtain some exposure to the inner aspect of the bone.

COMBINED APPROACHES

The high incidence of heterotopic bone formation and other complications that have been associated with the use of extensile approaches by some surgeons has led them to adopt combined approaches. Simultaneous anterior and posterior approaches are performed to afford adequate access to the external and internal surfaces of the pelvis. Anteriorly, the approaches used include the Smith-Petersen iliofemoral, ilioinguinal, and Stoppa. Posteriorly,

the Kocher-Langenbeck is generally chosen. The combined approach is used in lieu of an extensile approach to access both columns. The patient is positioned in a so-called floppy lateral position so that access can be increased at will to the anterior and posterior approaches. With the combined approaches of a significant operation, it is thought that complications are reduced by limiting the dramatic muscle stripping that is employed in the extensile approaches.

Table and Positioning

One of the main differences in technique between surgeons is to operate with or without the Judet (or other) fracture

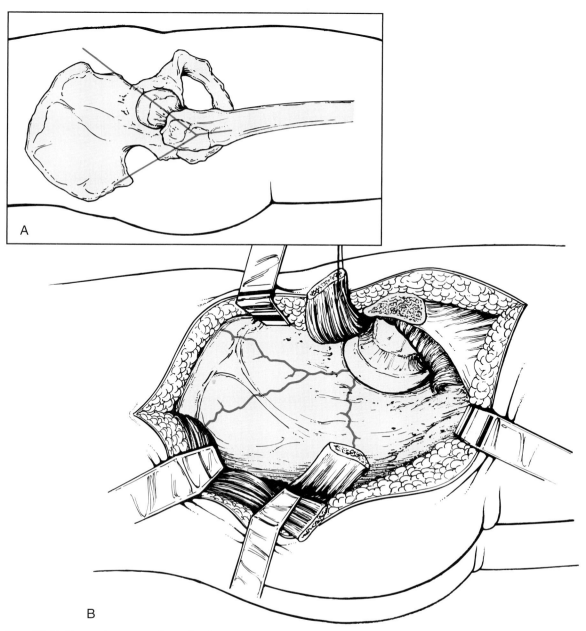

FIGURE 37–7. The triradiate approach. *A*, The skin incision. *B*, The completed exposure of the external aspect of the bone.

table. The Judet table maximizes the capabilities of each surgical approach. This is particularly important with the Kocher-Langenbeck and ilioinguinal approaches to avoid the extended iliofemoral or two approaches when possible. Using the Judet table, the patient is positioned specifically for the approach to be performed: prone for Kocher-Langenbeck, supine for ilioinguinal, or lateral for an extended iliofemoral approach. When the extended ilio-femoral approach is chosen, the Judet table aids reduction and visualization of the articular surface.

Other surgeons use a standard table and place the patient in a floppy lateral position. The advantage of this is the ability to go to a second approach if desired. From this position, they most often begin with the Kocher-Langenbeck approach and drape the patient to allow a subsequent ilioinguinal procedure to be performed simul-taneously if the need arises. This position also allows extension of the Kocher-Langenbeck to the triradiate ap-proach. The disadvantage of the floppy lateral position on a standard table is that the surgeon impairs his or her capabilities to reduce the fracture through the initial Kocher-Langenbeck approach. If a subsequent ilioinguinal approach is performed, the surgeon also works at a disadvantage.

In effect, choosing the floppy lateral position for the purpose of allowing two approaches makes the possibility of requiring two approaches more likely. If care is taken in the choice of approach and the patient is positioned appropriately on the Judet table, the frequency of an unexpected second approach is about 2%.

Preparing and Draping for Surgery

Preparing and draping the patient for surgery may seem an elementary and mundane subject to the accomplished fracture surgeon, but a significant portion of the success in controlling and decreasing the infection rate can be attributed to this discipline. Because infection can almost be as devastating as death or amputation in importance as a complication, the surgeon must carefully supervise this routine.

Before positioning the patient, the physician begins with an examination of all areas of the skin. Because of pain and difficulty in dealing with other injuries, the trauma patient may have skin areas that have been incompletely cleaned and evaluated. If the skin has not been properly cleaned before surgery, it should be done in the operating room before positioning, preparing, and draping, paying partic-ular attention to the gluteal crease and perineum. Draping out dirty areas is not sufficient. Examination in the operating room may also disclose skin damage or subcuta-neous hematoma sufficient to require débridement and postponement of surgery.

After patient positioning, adhesive plastic drapes are applied to the borders of the area to be prepared, and their adhesive is enhanced with tincture of benzoin applied to the skin. When possible, these border drapes should be placed a minimum of 8 to 10 cm from the planned incision. Subsequent drapes are attached to the skin with staples along their edges and should not narrow this 8- to 10-cm margin of exposed skin. The border drapes, staples,

and adhesive vinyl skin covering applied subsequently should maintain the drapes attached to the skin to lessen the chance of contamination from the anus and perineum. Before applying the final adhesive Betadine-impregnated vinyl skin covering, the skin should be wiped with alcohol and then dried to enhance adhesion. The skin surface is usually folded and convoluted, and it is best to not apply the vinyl skin drape under tension, because a skin drape under tension usually becomes detached from concave areas of the skin surface. The final appearance of the skin drape therefore includes wrinkles and folds, but it is less likely to detach. Air pockets are punctured and pressed down. Attempting to "walk" air bubbles to the side is not done because it damages drape adhesion.

Increased skin area is exposed by a fracture table because the pelvis is supported by a narrow sacral support rather than the broad flat top of a standard table. This larger area of exposed skin makes it easier to maintain an adequate margin between border drapes and the wound and lessens the chance of "looking at the table" during surgery. A stable pelvis position in relation to the table rather than a floppy one also enhances drape security.

Techniques of Reduction and Internal Fixation

After the preoperative radiographic evaluation and decision-making process have been completed, reduction of the fracture remains the primary problem facing the surgeon. The goal of surgery is an anatomic reduction of the innominate bone and acetabulum. Displacements greater than 1 mm correlate with an impaired prognosis. Even after determining the precise fracture configuration and performing the appropriate surgical approach, reduc-tion of an acetabular fracture can be an extremely challeng-ing problem, even with appropriate instrumentation.

The technique of reduction is always individualized to the fracture type. It often varies, even for a specific fracture type, and frequently depends on the exact configuration of the individual fracture.[32]

A fracture table, particularly the Judet fracture table, aids in the reduction of the fracture and helps to maximize the possibilities of what can be done through each surgical approach. The fracture table does not complete the fracture reduction but does distract the femoral head from its usual centrally displaced position to allow reduction of the acetabulum and, with the Kocher-Langenbeck or extended iliofemoral approach, allows visualization of the interior of the joint. With the Judet fracture table, the patient and extremity can be tilted for better visualization. Its use also facilitates easy repositioning of the limb during surgery as the limb remains in traction. An alternative to the fracture table is the ASIF femoral distractor, which can be placed between the ilium and proximal femur to apply distraction across the hip joint. Although it can be effective, the direction of pull is sometimes not ideal, and the femoral distractor is another instrument that can impede access to the wound.

Various reduction forceps are useful for reducing acetab-ular fractures. Several types can grasp heads of screws.

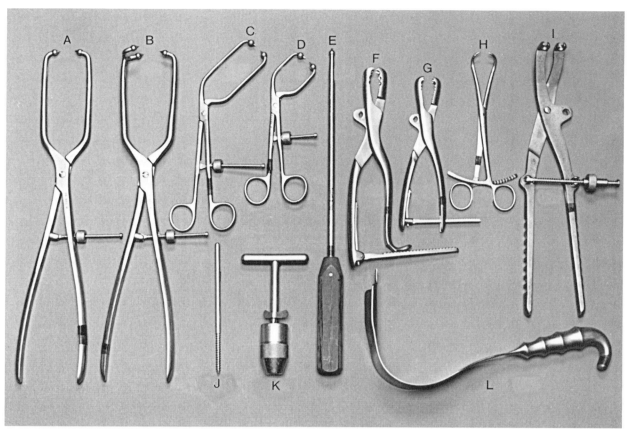

FIGURE 37–8. Instruments for open reduction of acetabulum fractures. *A–D* and *H*, Variously shaped pointed reduction forceps to accommodate the different contours of the innominate bone. *E*, The ball-spike instrument for pushing fragments. *F* and *G*, Farabeuf reduction forceps for direct application to the bone and for grasping the heads of 4.5- and 3.5-mm screws. *I*, Pelvic reduction forceps for application to 4.5-mm screws. *J* and *K*, Six-millimeter Schanz screw and T-handled chuck for insertion and manipulation. *L*, Sciatic nerve retractor.

These include Farabeuf clamps, adapted to grasp 3.5- or 4.5-mm diameter screws, and pelvic reduction forceps available from several manufacturers. Pointed reduction forceps are helpful, as is a ball-spiked instrument that can be used for pushing fracture fragments. A femoral head corkscrew or 6-mm Schanz screw can be inserted into the bone to control rotational displacement (Fig. 37–8).

The reduction and fixation usually proceed in a stepwise fashion, with reduction followed by fixation of individual fragments and then building on the assembled parts[59] (Figs. 37–9 to 37–26). Initial lag screw fixation[47, 51] usually allows removal of the reduction forceps, followed by more definitive plate fixation (Fig. 37–27). K-wires do not always provide adequate stability for temporarily securing a reduction. The reduction is assessed by visualization of the fracture lines and by palpation of fracture lines that cannot be observed directly. It is usually preferable to visualize the final reduction on the articular surface, although the surgical approach sometimes may not allow this. The final articular reduction is often inferred to be correct by reduction of the fracture lines on the extra-articular cortex of the innominate bone.

It is usually helpful to include extra-articular fragments in the reduction and fixation; they are commonly found along the pelvic brim, sciatic notch, or iliac crest. These small fragments are often essential for the reduction of the

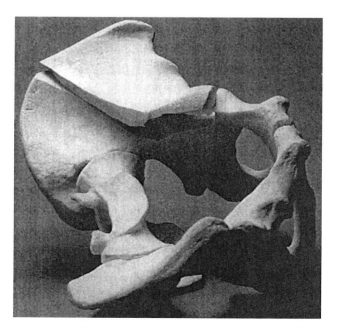

FIGURE 37–9. Model showing an anterior column fracture. (From Tornetta, P., III; Riina, J. Oper Tech Orthop 7:184–195, 1997.)

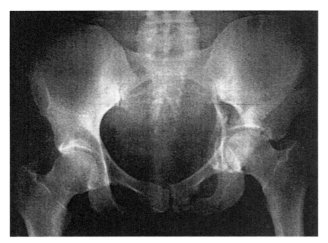

FIGURE 37-10. Anterior-posterior radiograph of a 32-year-old woman with a both-column fracture. The femoral head is medialized because of the muscle forces across the hip. (From Tornetta, P., III; Riina, J. Oper Tech Orthop 7:184–195, 1997.)

larger articular fragments and aid in providing final stability. In reducing the initial fragments, it is important to obtain accurate reduction of even the extra-articular fragments, because any errors in reduction are compounded as additional fracture fragments are added.

Reduction and fixation are carried out most effectively when the surgeon plans several steps ahead. Clamps must be placed so they are effective in reduction and allow access to the bone for screw and, sometimes, for plate fixation before clamp removal. Screws must be placed in an effective position and placed so their heads do not interfere with a subsequent plate. Sometimes, reduction of the wrong fragment first blocks reduction of a subsequent fragment. The surgeon should have a fairly good picture of the entire process and the desired final construct before starting the first step.

A few tips are valuable. Although great force sometimes is needed for reduction, it is usually best carried out with a finesse that avoids damage to the bone and increasing difficulties. What seems initially to be an uncorrectable displacement sometimes can be corrected easily when the

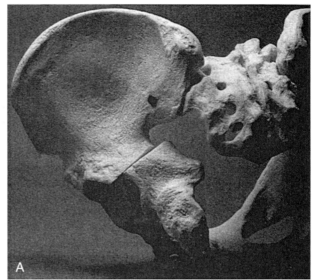

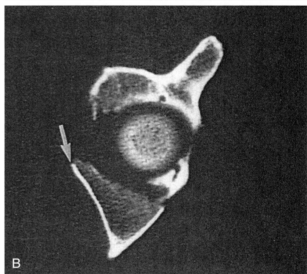

FIGURE 37-12. A, Model viewed from behind shows the typical medial displacement of the posterior column after anterior fixation. B, Computed tomography shows the internal rotation of the posterior column (arrow). (From Tornetta, P., III; Riina, J. Oper Tech Orthop 7:184–195, 1997.)

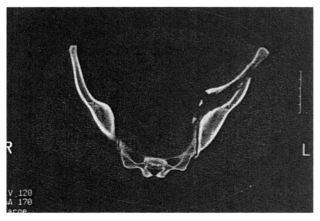

FIGURE 37-11. Computed tomographic scan of an anterior column fracture shows the external rotation of the displaced fragment. (From Tornetta, P., III; Riina, J. Oper Tech Orthop 7:184–195, 1997.)

proper instrument and direction of force are used. Fixation needs to be stable, but the surgeon should not overdo it. Precise placement of fixation is more important and effective than quantity. Many plates are applied with one or more screw holes left empty. The final stability of the construct depends on both reduction and fixation. An imperfect reduction is less stable and its fixation more likely to fail. When possible, the surgeon should strive for a perfect reduction. This process may take an extra hour, but it can affect the rest of the patient's life.

Percutaneous Fixation

There has been increased discussion in the literature about percutaneous fixation of acetabular fractures.[29] This method has been proposed and used for several
Text continued on page 1133

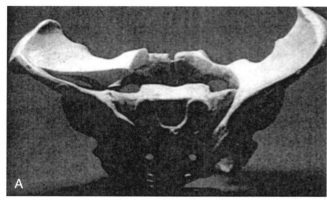

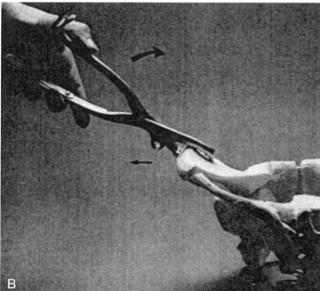

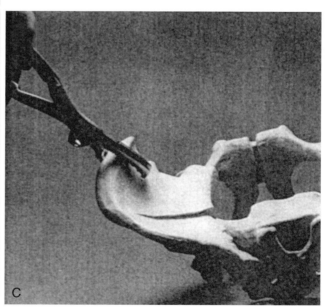

FIGURE 37–13. *A,* View of an anterior column fracture with the typical external rotation deformity. A Farabauf clamp is placed on the iliac wing. *B* and *C,* By pulling the clamp laterally and internally rotating *(arrows)* it, most of the reduction is possible. (From Tornetta, P., III; Riina, J. Oper Tech Orthop 7:184–195, 1997.)

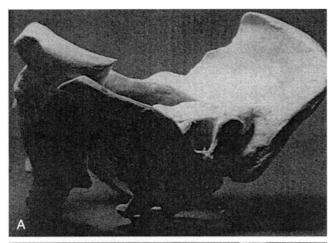

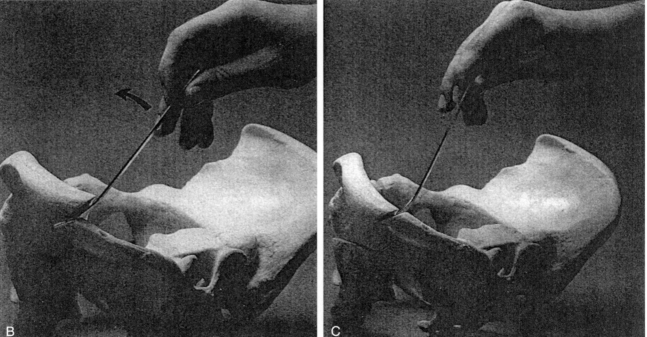

FIGURE 37–14. *A*, Model shows overlap of the displaced anterior column on the intact ilium. *B* and *C*, A mini-Hohmann or curved osteotome can be used as a pry bar to reduce this displacement. (From Tornetta, P., III; Riina, J. Oper Tech Orthop 7:184–195, 1997.)

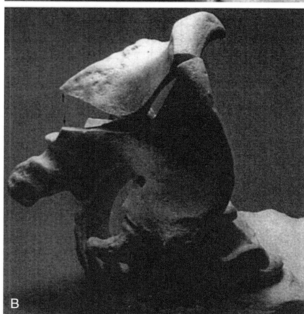

FIGURE 37–15. *A*, A model of an anterior column fracture viewed from the inside of the pelvis reveals only slight displacement at the lateral edge of the iliac wing (*arrowhead*). *B*, This small amount of rotational deformity found at the wing may translate into a large displacement at the articular surface. (From Tornetta, P., III; Riina, J. Oper Tech Orthop 7:184–195, 1997.)

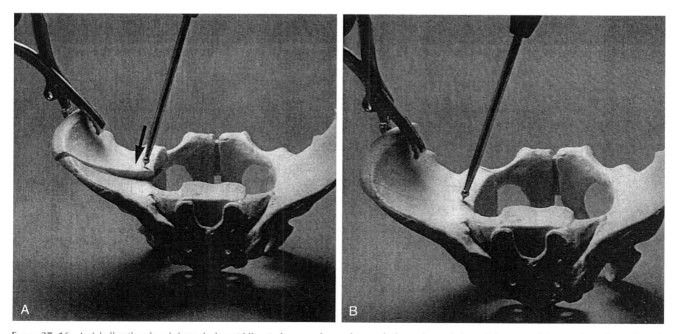

FIGURE 37–16. *A*, A ball spike placed through the middle window may be used to push down the cephalomedial corner of the anterior column (*arrow*). *B*, This action reduces the fracture. (From Tornetta, P., III; Riina, J. Oper Tech Orthop 7:184–195, 1997.)

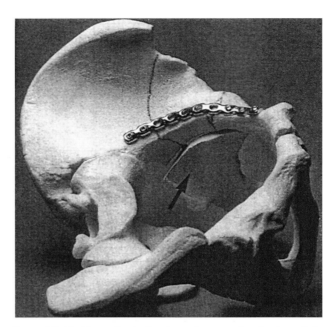

FIGURE 37–17. Model shows bone tenaculum holding the iliac wing reduction. With a Farabauf clamp on the wing, a ball-spike instrument can be used to push the inferior aspect of the fracture into its anatomic position. The use of multiple clamps is often required for the reduction of the anterior column. (From Tornetta, P., III; Riina, J. Oper Tech Orthop 7:184–195, 1997.)

FIGURE 37–18. View of a both-column fracture after fixation of the anterior column. The posterior column is displaced medially and posteriorly and is internally rotated. The quadrilateral surface (arrow) is used for placement of clamps. (From Tornetta, P., III; Riina, J. Oper Tech Orthop 7:184–195, 1997.)

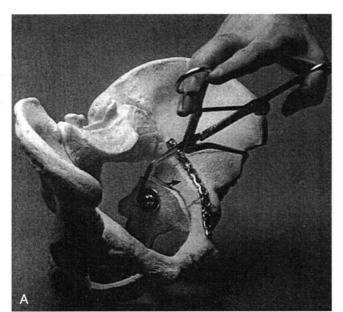

FIGURE 37–19. A, B, A Matta clamp placed from the anterior inferior iliac spine to the quadrilateral surface effects a lateral reduction force on the posterior column, pictured here with a spiked disc to disperse the force of the clamp. C, A Mayo offset clamp can be used in the same fashion to reduce the posterior column. (From Tornetta, P., III; Riina, J. Oper Tech Orthop 7:184–195, 1997.)

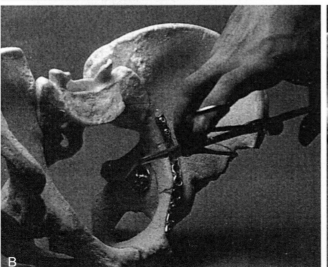

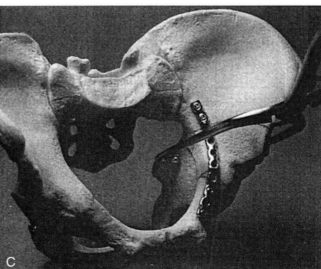

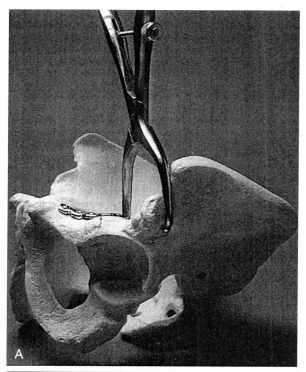

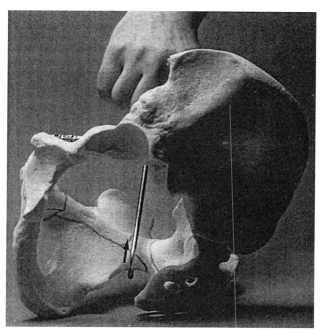

Figure 37–21. A bone hook placed in the sciatic notch can pull the posterior column anteriorly *(arrow)*. (From Tornetta, P., III; Riina, J. Oper Tech Orthop 7:184–195, 1997.)

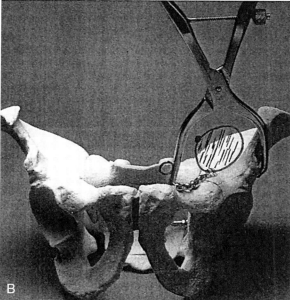

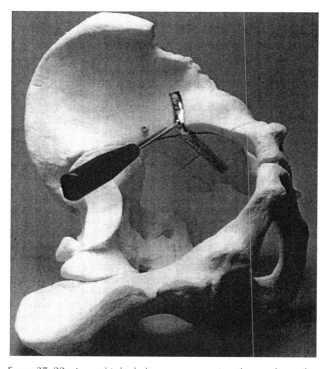

Figure 37–20. *A,* Lateral view of the pelvis shows the position of the Mayo clamp on the outside of the innominate bone. *B,* A view of the pelvis from below shows the location of the psoas and femoral nerve (between the arms of the clamp) and the external iliac vessels (medial to the clamp). Clamps in these positions place tension on the vessels by displacing them medially. A pulse should always be closely observed when these reduction clamps are used. (From Tornetta, P., III; Riina, J. Oper Tech Orthop 7:184–195, 1997.)

Figure 37–22. A one-third tubular or reconstruction plate can be used to reduce and hold the quadrilateral surface when it is comminuted. This is usually placed under the anterior column plate. (From Tornetta, P., III; Riina, J. Oper Tech Orthop 7:184–195, 1997.)

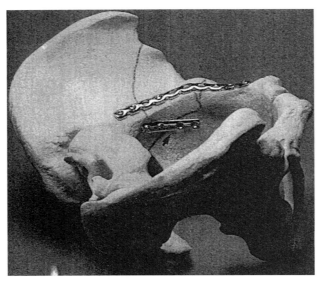

FIGURE 37–23. A push plate placed through the medial window or a modified Stoppa approach can be used to reduce and support the medial displacement of the posterior column *(arrow)*. (From Tornetta, P., III; Riina, J. Oper Tech Orthop 7:184–195, 1997.)

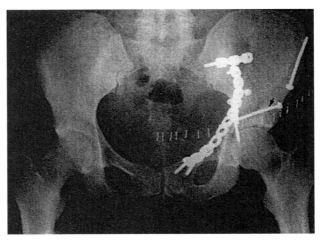

FIGURE 37–25. Postoperative anteroposterior radiograph of the patient shown in Figure 37–10. An *arrow* identifies the percutaneously placed lag screw from the retroacetabular surface to the quadrilateral surface. The sacroiliac joint was also fixed because of posterior instability. (From Tornetta, P., III; Riina, J. Oper Tech Orthop 7:184–195, 1997.)

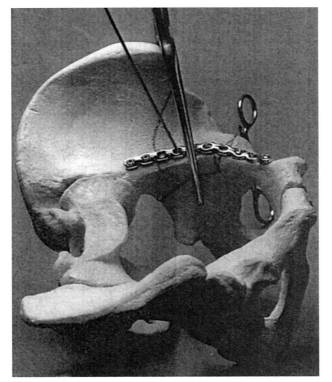

FIGURE 37–24. The long 2.5-mm oscillating drill bit is pictured going through the anterior column plate into the posterior column to maintain the reduction gained using the Mayo clamp. This screw is placed parallel to the quadrilateral surface. (From Tornetta, P., III; Riina, J. Oper Tech Orthop 7:184–195, 1997.)

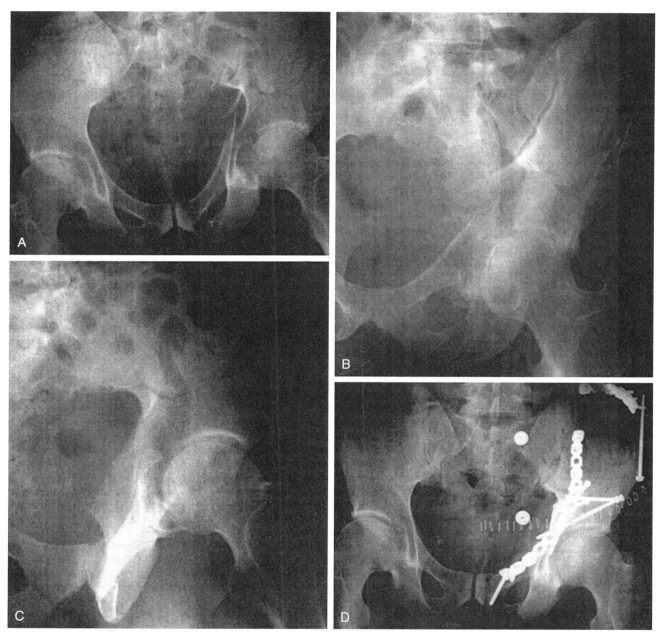

FIGURE 37–26. Preoperative anteroposterior (*A*), obturator oblique (*B*), and iliac oblique (*C*) views of a 23-year-old man with a both-column fracture.
Illustration continued on following page

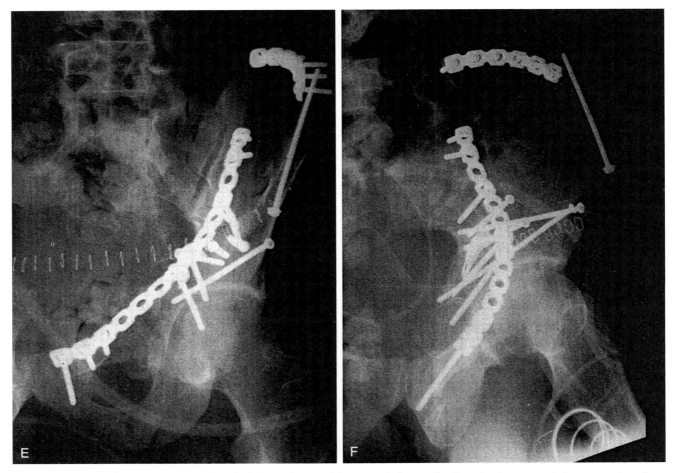

Figure 37–26 *Continued.* Postoperative views (*D* and *E*) show reduction of the joint with the use of an iliac wing lag screw and plate, an anterior column plate, posterior column lag screws placed from the pelvic brim through the plate and percutaneously from the retroacetabular surface, and a posterior column push plate, which is seen best on the iliac oblique view (*F*). (From Tornetta, P., III; Riina, J. Oper Tech Orthop 7:184–195, 1997.)

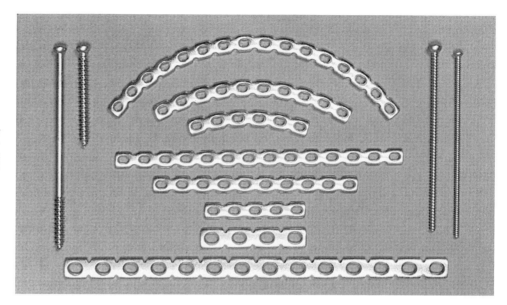

FIGURE 37-27. Plates and screws for internal fixation of acetabulum fractures include curved and straight plates accepting screws 3.5, 4.5, and 6.5 mm in diameter.

indications: nondisplaced fractures, fractures in elderly patients, and when the chosen surgical approach does not allow access for a desired screw.

Although it is possible to place fixation percutaneously, the indications remain controversial. Would nondisplaced fractures have a different prognosis if they were not fixed? Most authorities would say no. Does this benefit elderly patients? This outcome has not been demonstrated. The question for most elderly patients is not whether they can undergo an open procedure, but whether an adequate reduction and fixation can be obtained. Percutaneous fixation cannot enhance reduction and can be expected to impair it. Fixation is less effective when reduction is not obtained and fixation is achieved with screws alone.

Percutaneous fixation may be considered when the surgical approach does not allow access for a desired screw. The most common situation encountered is soft tissue restriction of the drill and screw direction. In these cases, the point for screw insertion usually is seen in the wound, whereas the drill and screw enter through a small, separate insertion wound. This is useful sometimes when a screw is placed to the anterior column while operating through the Kocher-Langenbeck approach.

Percutaneous techniques do not address the most important problems of reduction and fixation that remain to be solved in acetabular fracture surgery.

SURGICAL TREATMENT OF INDIVIDUAL FRACTURE TYPES

Posterior Wall Fracture

The posterior wall fracture is the most common acetabular fracture. It is usually the most straightforward to treat surgically. The surgeon should be aware, however, that these fractures can be demanding in their reduction and fixation and that treatment can be unsuccessful if errors are made during surgery.[8, 18]

Most posterior wall fractures that leave a portion of the retroacetabular surface intact can be effectively operated on with the patient in the lateral position on the standard operating table. A Kocher-Langenbeck approach is used. The hip is usually dislocated posteriorly during surgery to remove incarcerated fragments and to excise the torn ligamentum teres. After congruous reduction of the hip, the posterior wall fragments are repositioned using the femoral head as a mold for the reduction. Impaction of the articular surface must be recognized preoperatively and always corrected during surgery. If there is a bone defect after elevation of the impaction, it should be buttressed using an autogenous cancellous graft. Free fragments that include only cartilage and a segment of underlying cancellous bone are commonly found. The fragments should be reduced into their anatomic position and, if not directly fixed, should be held in place by the overlying posterior wall fragments that include a portion of the retroacetabular surface. Small fragments are eventually discarded, but an effort should be made to save and reduce all fragments, because discarding fragments can lead to defects in the posterior wall that may lead to an instability of the hip and redislocation.

After reduction, the fragments are fixed with one or two lag screws, followed by fixation with a plate placed from the superior pole of the ischium to the inferior iliac wing. The plate should be curved so that it roughly parallels the rim of the acetabulum (Fig. 37-28). It is easy for screws inserted into the retroacetabular surface to enter the joint. The screws are normally directed away from the joint, oblique to the retroacetabular surface.

Extended posterior wall fractures that displace the entire retroacetabular surface and involve the greater or lesser sciatic notch (or both) are usually best operated on with prone positioning of the patient on the Judet table. This arrangement provides for better control of the femoral

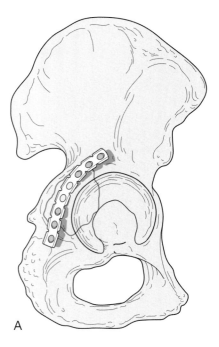
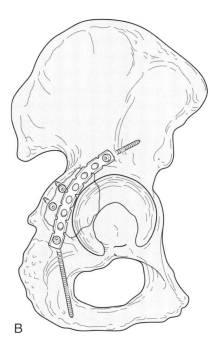

A

B

FIGURE 37–28. Application of a posterior wall buttress plate. *A,* The posterior wall fragment is reduced and held with provisional inter-fragmentary screws. A posterior buttress plate is applied. The plate should be slightly undercontoured so that the plate produces a buttress effect, applying a force to the posterior wall perpendicular to the undersurface of the plate. *B,* The inferior screw of the posterior plate can often be placed into the ischium. This provides excellent fixation to the inferior aspect of the plate. The posterior plate should be curved around the acetabular rim, avoiding excessive dissection along the superior iliac wing. Ideally, two screws should be used above and below the fracture. Interfragmentary screws can also be applied through the plate.

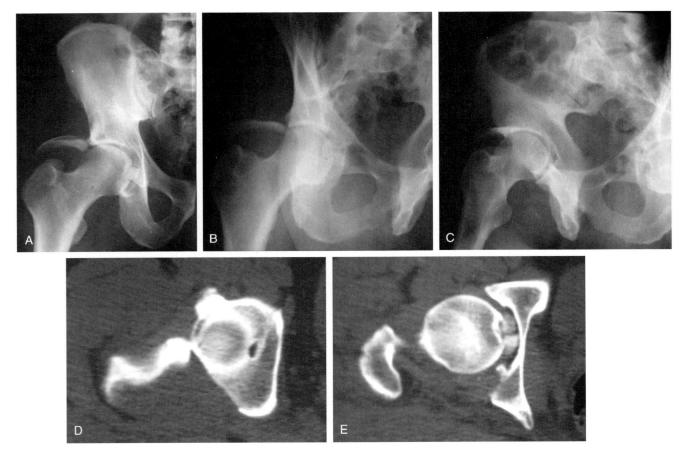

FIGURE 37–29. *A,* Anteroposterior (AP) view of the right hip and innominate bone of a 42-year-old man with a fracture of the posterior wall of the acetabulum. Seen are the displaced posterior wall fragment, the defect in the line of the posterior rim, an incarcerated fragment medial to the head, and slight lateral displacement of the head. *B,* Obturator oblique view. *C,* Iliac oblique view. *D,* Computed tomographic (CT) scan just distal to the roof, demonstrating the posterior wall fracture fragment. *E,* CT scan through the midportion of the joint, demonstrating the posterior wall defect and incarcerated segments of the posterior wall medial to the femoral head.

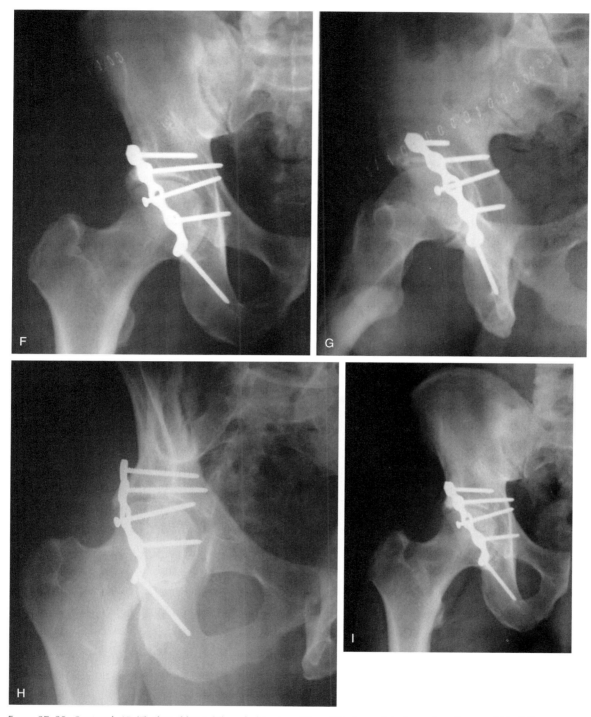

FIGURE 37–29 *Continued.* AP (*F*), iliac oblique (*G*), and obturator oblique (*H*) views of the innominate bone and hip following open reduction and internal fixation of the fracture performed through the Kocher-Langenbeck approach with the patient in the prone position on the Judet table. The incarcerated fragments have been removed from the joint and incorporated into the posterior wall reduction and fixation. A curved pelvic plate of 88-mm radius is used for fixation, as well as one 3.5-mm diameter screw outside the plate and four through the plate. Note that the curved plate parallels the posterior rim of the acetabulum and does not diverge from the acetabular rim proximally. *I,* AP radiograph of innominate bone and hip 2 years following the injury demonstrates no arthritic changes. The patient's hip function was rated excellent.

head reduction and easier access to the greater and lesser sciatic notches. In this case, the hip is not re-dislocated posteriorly, but distraction of the femoral head from the acetabulum provides for removal of free fragments (Fig. 37–29).

Posterior Column Fractures

Posterior column fractures are normally operated on with the patient in the prone position on the Judet table. Using the Kocher-Langenbeck approach, the fracture lines are distracted initially using a lamina spreader or the AO/ASIF femoral distractor. Blood clot and granulation tissue are thoroughly removed from the fracture lines, as are any free bone fragments that may impede reduction. The displacement is usually corrected by the two-screw technique. The position each screw is placed in before attempting reduction greatly influences the success of this procedure.

The posterior column usually rotates along its longitudinal axis as it displaces. This rotation must always be corrected, usually by a rotational lever placed into the ischial tuberosity. This device can be a femoral head corkscrew or a Schanz screw.

The reduction is assessed by visualizing the retroacetabular surface and the cartilage of the joint by distraction of the femur and by palpating the quadrilateral surface through the greater sciatic notch. Palpation of the quadrilateral surface is particularly useful for assessing rotational deformities of the posterior column. Initial fixation is usually achieved with a lag screw that is placed from posterior to anterior and followed by placement of a curved plate on the retroacetabular surface.

Transverse Fractures

For reduction of transverse fractures, the patient usually is positioned prone on the Judet table, and the Kocher-Langenbeck approach is used. The reduction technique is similar to that used for the posterior column fracture. Typically, the two-screw technique is used to control displacement, and a rotational lever is placed into the ischial tuberosity. As the rotational lever is being applied, the entire ischiopubic segment is rotated rather than the posterior column alone. Reduction of the anterior portion of the transverse fracture is assessed by palpation of the quadrilateral surface and pelvic brim through the greater sciatic notch. Initial fixation is achieved with a lag screw inserted into the retroacetabular surface and directed

toward the anterior column. The lag screw crosses the transverse fracture from a proximal to distal direction, and a plate is then placed along the retroacetabular surface to complete the fixation.[14]

A few transverse fractures are best treated through the ilioinguinal approach, with the patient in the supine position on the Judet table. The ilioinguinal approach can be used for relatively high anterior and low posterior transverse fractures and for those that are more displaced along the anterior articular surface. The reduction is usually obtained by a Farabeuf clamp applied to two screws along the pelvic brim or with pointed reduction forceps applied along the internal aspect of the bone. Fixation is attained with a curved plate along the pelvic brim.

Associated Transverse and Posterior Wall Fractures

Most associated transverse and posterior wall fractures can be operated on through the Kocher-Langenbeck approach, with prone positioning of the patient on the Judet table. The femoral head is initially distracted, and incarcerated fragments are removed. Reduction of the transverse fracture is carried out first, using the standard technique and fixation with a lag screw. Sometimes, it is not possible to obtain initial fixation with a lag screw, and the first fixation should then be done with a plate along the greater sciatic notch. After fixation of the transverse fracture, the reduction clamps are removed from the wound, and the posterior wall fracture is reduced and initially fixed with lag screws. A curved plate, applied from the ischial tuberosity to the inferior ilium, bridges the transverse and the posterior wall fracture (Fig. 37–30).

Some associated transverse plus posterior wall fractures offer unusual difficulties, such as a transverse fracture associated with an extended posterior wall fracture. In this

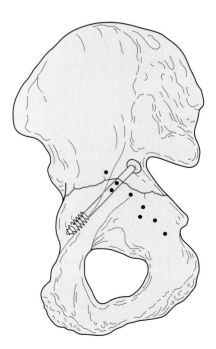
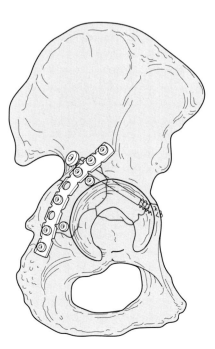

FIGURE 37–30. Internal fixation of a transverse plus a posterior wall fracture as performed through the Kocher-Langenbeck approach.

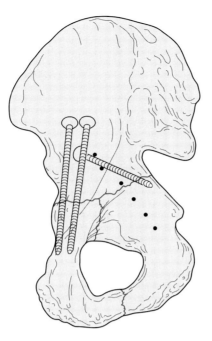
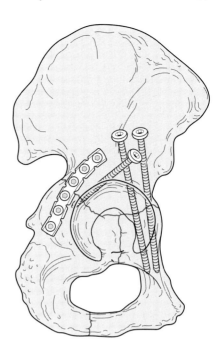

FIGURE 37–31. Internal fixation of a T-shaped fracture performed through the extended iliofemoral approach.

case, the extended iliofemoral or triradiate approach would be the best choice.

T-Shaped Fractures

Many **T** fractures can be operated on through the Kocher-Langenbeck approach, with prone positioning of the patient on the Judet table.[55] The fracture of the anterior column can be visualized on the acetabular articular surface after distraction of the posterior column fracture line. The anterior column can be reduced with a bone hook or pointed reduction forceps, followed by fixation with lag screws placed from a posterior to anterior direction. The posterior column is reduced and fixed in the usual fashion. If the surgeon finds it impossible to reduce the anterior column through the Kocher-Langenbeck approach, the posterior column is fixed, and the patient is turned supine for a subsequent ilioinguinal approach. If staged approaches are to be used, great care must be taken not to place screws into the posterior column, which would block subsequent reduction of the anterior column. If there is doubt about whether the reduction can be performed through the Kocher-Langenbeck approach, the extended iliofemoral approach can be chosen initially (Fig. 37–31). Another satisfactory option is the triradiate approach. The surgeon can start with the Kocher-Langenbeck approach and proceed to the anterior limb of the triradiate approach, as indicated.

Anterior Wall Fractures

Anterior wall fractures are operated on through the ilioinguinal approach, with supine positioning of the patient on the Judet table. Traction removes the femoral head from the centrally displaced position. Reduction is performed with pressure applied by means of the ball-spike instrument and

with the pointed reduction forceps. Fixation is accomplished with a curved plate placed along the pelvic brim from the superior pubic ramus to the internal iliac fossa. Because screws are placed along the brim, the acetabulum can be entered easily. The screws should be placed close to the pelvic brim and parallel to the quadrilateral surface. In the area of the pectineal eminence, usually only a short screw (approximately 12 or 14 mm long) is placed to avoid entering the joint (Fig. 37–32). After fixation, the reduction can be checked using an image intensifier, which additionally confirms that screws are clear of the joint.

Anterior Column Fractures

Anterior column fractures are operated on through the ilioinguinal approach, with supine positioning of the patient on the Judet table. The anterior wall or column is reduced and fixed in the normal manner, but care is taken to prevent screws from crossing the posterior column fracture line.[9] The posterior column is reduced through the second window of the ilioinguinal approach by pressure applied to the quadrilateral surface or by pointed reduction forceps applied to the quadrilateral surface. The posterior column is then internally fixed with long lag screws placed from the pelvic brim and directed parallel to the quadrilateral surface, roughly in the direction of the ischial spine and lesser sciatic notch.

Both-Column Fractures

Most both-column fractures can be reduced and fixed through the ilioinguinal approach, but approximately one third require the extended iliofemoral approach. The ilioinguinal approach is preferable, when possible, because it leaves a more cosmetically pleasing scar; involves minimal stripping of the outer aspect of the bone, which

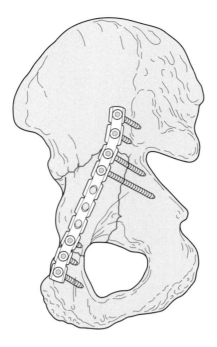

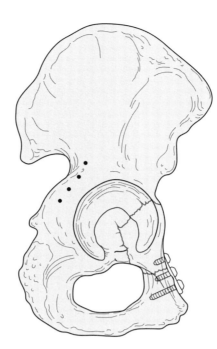

FIGURE 37–32. Internal fixation of an anterior wall fracture performed through the ilioinguinal approach.

leads to a quick postoperative recovery, and results in almost no ectopic bone formation. Fractures requiring the extended iliofemoral approach are those that have displaced fracture lines crossing the sacroiliac joint and those with complex involvement of the posterior column.

When the ilioinguinal approach is chosen, the anterior column is reduced and internally fixed first. An anterior column fracture usually extends to the crest of the ilium and is reduced and fixed as is normally done for a high anterior column fracture (Fig. 37–33). If a plate is used along the pelvic brim, many screw holes are initially left open so that the screws do not enter the posterior column fracture site. The posterior column segment is then reduced through the second window of the ilioinguinal approach by pressure on the quadrilateral surface and with pointed reduction forceps placed from the pelvic brim or from the outer aspect of the anterior column to the quadrilateral surface (Fig. 37–34). The reduction is assessed by visualizing and palpating the quadrilateral surface and by palpating the greater sciatic notch. Fixation is performed with lag screws from the pelvic brim placed into the posterior column (Fig. 37–35). The image intensifier is useful at the completion of surgery to confirm the reduction and to ensure that all screws are clear of the joint.

When the extended iliofemoral approach is chosen, the patient is positioned in the lateral position on the Judet table. The anterior column is usually reduced and fixed to the intact portion of the ilium before the posterior column. If the posterior column segment is large and especially if the displaced posterior column segments involve a portion of the sacroiliac joint, it may be best to proceed with reduction and fixation of the posterior column first, followed by the anterior column reduction and fixation. Reduction techniques include the two-screw technique, the use of pointed reduction forceps, and careful control of rotation of the two columns of the acetabulum using

standard techniques (Figs. 37–36 to 37–38). Generally, the extended iliofemoral approach provides the most commanding access to both-column fractures and provides the easiest assessment of reduction through wide visualization of the bone and by visualization of the articular surface (Fig. 37–39). As surgeons gain experience with the ilioinguinal approach, they realize that it is effective and provides significant advantages for the patient (Fig. 37–40).

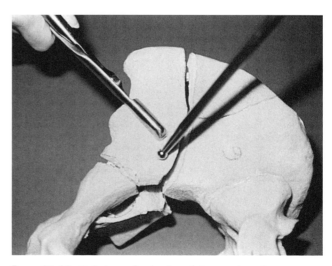

FIGURE 37–33. Technique of reduction of the anterior column component of a both-column fracture through the ilioinguinal approach. The Farabeuf clamp is applied along the anterior border of the bone to control rotation of the anterior column. The ball spike is applied for pressure along the pelvic brim. The same technique can be used for reduction with an isolated anterior column fracture or an anterior column and posterior hemitransverse fracture.

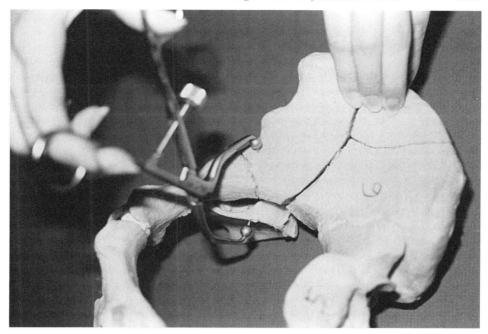

FIGURE 37–34. Technique of reduction of the posterior column through the ilioinguinal approach. An angled-jaw, pointed reduction forceps is applied from the anterior to the posterior column, across the pelvic brim.

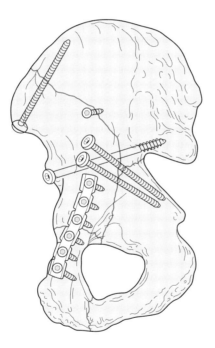

FIGURE 37–35. Internal fixation of a fracture of both columns performed through the ilioinguinal approach.

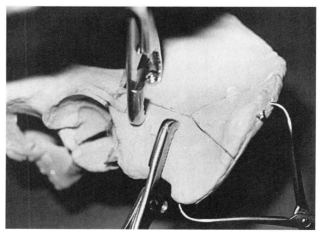

FIGURE 37–36. Technique of reduction of the anterior column performed through the extended iliofemoral approach. A Farabeuf clamp grasps two screw heads just above the level of the greater sciatic notch. A second Farabeuf clamp grasps the anterior border of the bone and controls anterior column rotation. A pointed reduction forceps is applied to the iliac crest.

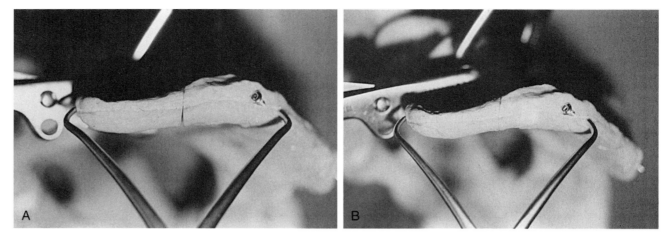

FIGURE 37–37. Assessment of rotation of the anterior column at the iliac crest. *A*, Residual rotation is evidenced by medial gaping of the fracture line. *B*, The reduction is correct.

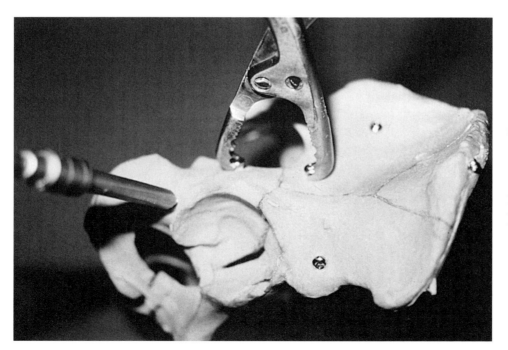

FIGURE 37–38. Reduction technique for the posterior column segment of a fracture of both columns performed through the extended iliofemoral approach. A Farabeuf clamp grasps screw heads on either side of the fracture. A screw has been inserted into the ischium for rotational control.

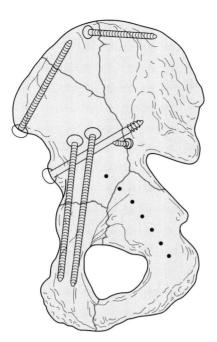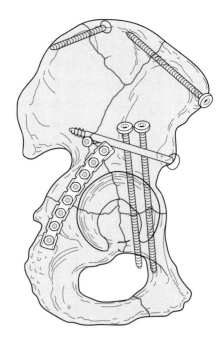

FIGURE 37–39. Internal fixation of a fracture of both columns performed through the extended iliofemoral approach.

Avoiding Intra-articular Screws

A screw placed and left protruding into the joint typically destroys the articular surface. The surgeon's knowledge of the anatomy of the innominate bone and his perception of screw length and direction are the primary factors in preventing this complication. Intra-articular visualization and radiographs are also useful. The surgeon must be satisfied before the patient leaves the operating room, and certainly before the patient leaves the hospital, that all screws are outside the joint. Screws that traverse the acetabular fossa medial to and not in contact with the head may sometimes be safe, but generally these screws should not be left in place. When a screw is in doubt and beyond vision, radiographs are necessary. In almost all cases, fluoroscopy and, sometimes, plain films are the most useful modalities. The CT scan is often confusing and useful only in exceptional cases of other implants blocking a plain film or fluoroscopy view. The fluoroscope is most useful because it can be manipulated into an infinite number of obliquities in an attempt to find one view that shows the screw to be outside the joint. If this view cannot be found, the screw must be removed.

POSTOPERATIVE CARE

The patient is placed on bedrest initially, although allowed to ambulate with external support when symptoms allow. However, for the extended iliofemoral approach, 5 days of absolute bedrest after surgery is preferable to allow for edema to subside and initial wound healing to occur before starting ambulation. Passive motion of the hip and extremity can be instituted by a physical therapist or by the continuous passive motion machine. By 2 days postoperatively, pain has usually subsided enough so that the patient can start gait training. Fifteen kilograms of weight bearing

is allowed. The patient is encouraged to ambulate with a step-through gait and a heel-toe walking motion, using crutches or a walker. The patient is instructed in active flexion, abduction, and extension exercises to be performed at the hip while standing. For the extended iliofemoral approach, however, active abduction and passive adduction are not allowed during the first 3 weeks. Limitation of weight bearing is continued for 8 weeks postoperatively, at which time the patient is allowed to bear weight to tolerance and to use external support only as needed. If the fracture has been reduced accurately and ectopic bone does not develop, the range of motion can be expected to return to 90% of normal without difficulty. Physical therapy is therefore directed primarily toward regaining muscle strength at the hip, particularly abductor muscle strength.

An AP radiograph of the pelvis is usually obtained at the completion of the operation for preliminary confirmation of the reduction.[57, 58] When patients are more comfortable, they are sent to the radiology department for AP and 45° oblique views of the pelvis. After gait training and before discharge, another AP pelvic radiograph is generally obtained to confirm that loss of reduction has not occurred during ambulation. A single AP pelvic radiograph is obtained at each follow-up examination.

COMPLICATIONS

The most common serious complications after operative treatment of an acetabular fracture include operative wound infection, iatrogenic nerve palsy, periarticular ectopic bone formation, and thromboembolic complications.[45, 53, 56] Post-traumatic arthritis is the most common late complication.[37]

If the patient's general condition is good and no associated injuries exist, the risk of infection should not be

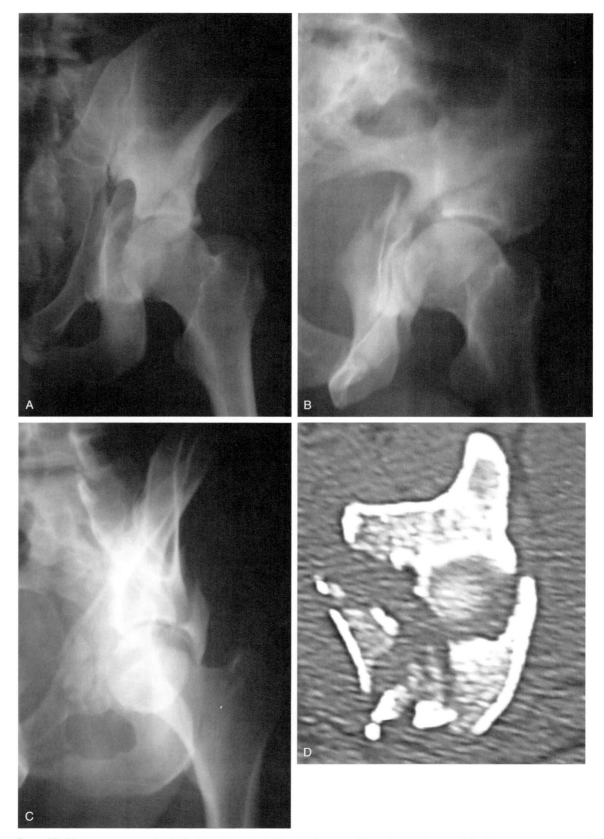

FIGURE 37–40. Anteroposterior (AP) (*A*), iliac oblique (IO) (*B*), and obturator oblique (OO) (*C*) views of the left innominate bone and hip in a 38-year-old man, demonstrating an acute both-column fracture of the left acetabulum. All of the normal radiographic landmarks of the acetabulum are disrupted, and the roof is not in its normal position. *C,* The OO view demonstrates a separate segment of the posterior wall. *D,* A computed tomographic (CT) cut just distal to the roof demonstrates all of the major fracture segments: the anterior column, the posterior column seen only as a segment of the quadrilateral surface, the intact ileum seen only as a small triangular posterior segment, and the pelvis posterior wall with its articulator surface.

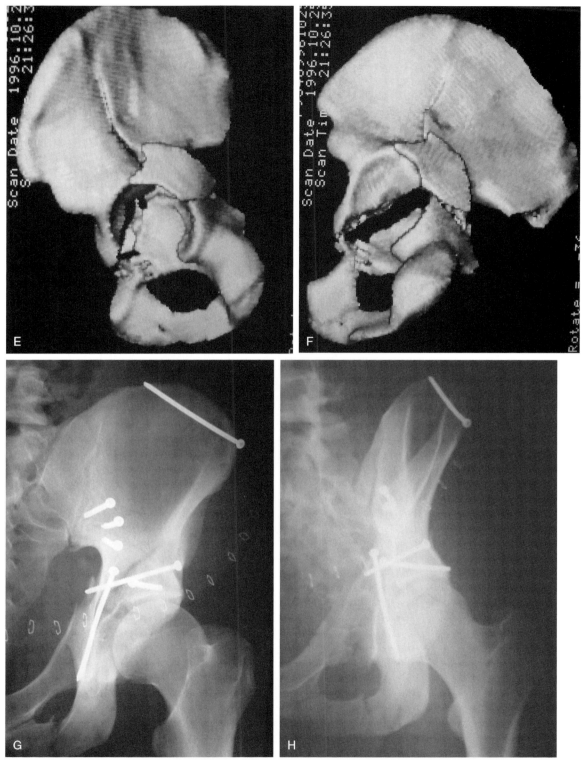

FIGURE 37–40 *Continued. E, F,* Two three-dimensional reconstructions of the CT scan show the outer aspect of the innominate bone and the interior of the joint. The displacement along the rim of the acetabulum is not great, and this indicates that the acetabular labrum and capsule probably remain attached to all of the articular segments along the acetabular rim. These soft tissue attachments are an essential aid to reduction of the acetabulum if the ilioinguinal approach is chosen. *G,* AP view following open reduction and internal fixation of the fracture through the ilioinguinal approach performed with the patient supine on the Judet table. Following reduction, the posterior column is fixed with two screws. One is seen to be relatively horizontal and traverses from the outer aspect of the anterior column near the pelvic brim and parallels the quadrilateral surface just posterior and medial to the joint and exits the posterior border of the bone distal to the ischial spine. I prefer this type of posterior column fixation to a quadrilateral surface plate. *H,* The OO view demonstrates the reduction of the posterior wall, as well as the screw from the inner aspect of the anterior column to the retroacetabular surface that fixes it. The reduction of the posterior column was performed by limiting exposure to the outer aspect of the bone and placing a pointed clamp around the anterior border of the bone.

Illustration continued on following page

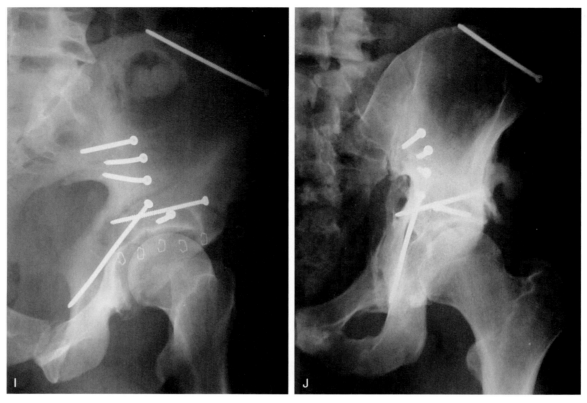

FIGURE 37–40 *Continued. I,* The IO view demonstrates the reduction and also the position of the long screw that fixes the posterior column and exits the bone distal to the ischial spine. *J,* AP radiograph 2 years after the injury demonstrates no arthritic changes and some heterotopic bone distant from the joint. The clinical result was rated excellent.

higher than for other types of hip surgery. Unfortunately, most patients with acetabular fractures have associated injuries. These can include injuries of the abdominal or pelvic viscera or of the extremities. A bladder rupture or a bowel, rectal, or vaginal injury can increase the chance of operative wound infection and can influence the indications for operation. Open fractures of the ipsilateral lower extremity can also increase the risk for wound infection in the acetabular fracture.

A relatively common problem associated with acetabular fracture is local soft tissue injury, including local wounds, abrasions, and a closed, degloving injury. With the closed, degloving injury, the subcutaneous tissue is torn away from the underlying fascia, and a significant cavity results that contains hematoma and liquefied fat between the subcutaneous tissue and deep fascia. This condition results from the blunt trauma that caused the acetabular fracture. When this lesion exists over the greater trochanter, it is known as a Morel-Lavale lesion.[13] These areas must be drained and débrided before or during surgery to decrease the chance of infection. After drainage and débridement, it is advisable to leave this area open through the surgical incision or a separate incision. Dressing changes and wound packing are sometimes necessary over a prolonged period, until the wound has closed secondarily. Primary excision of the necrotic fat and closure over drainage tubes has not been routinely successful.

Wound infection remains a danger, even without associated injuries. There is an increased risk of postoperative

hematoma formation in the large wounds that are necessary for acetabular surgery. Liberal use of suction drains is advised. Hemostasis at the time of wound closure is always desirable. During the procedure, the large areas of exposed soft tissue should be kept moist and be irrigated frequently with antibiotic solution. Moist sponges placed over exposed soft tissue help to prevent desiccation. The surgeon should always strive to preserve soft tissue pedicles to all bone fragments to maintain vascularity of the bone. If a fragment is devascularized, it usually revascularizes rapidly if no infection develops. In the presence of infection, however, bacteria rapidly colonize an avascular fragment, and it usually needs to be débrided and excised. Some bloody drainage can seep from the wound for the first 1 to 2 days after surgery, although the seepage should subside rapidly. It is not uncommon for a clear, yellow, serous drainage to continue for as long as 10 days after surgery without infection being present. If the wound has been benign for a number of days, however, and bloody or cloudy yellowish drainage then occurs, the patient should be returned to the operating room immediately for irrigation and débridement of the wound. If a wound hematoma exists, the amount of hematoma is usually much greater than initially suspected by inspecting the wound, and surgical drainage is indicated.

If infection is suspected, the surgeon should not wait for definitive results of the wound culture but should proceed with reopening the wound on the clinical basis alone. If it is later found that no infection existed, little harm has been done, and an infection possibly has been prevented. If an infection existed at the time of the earliest clinical suspicion, the surgeon has acted properly by treating the infection expeditiously.

After evacuation of a wound hematoma, the wound is usually closed over suction drainage. In the case of débridement for infection, all implants that are stable and aid in the fixation are left in place. Avascular and infected bone fragments must be removed. If the diagnosis of infection is made early, before abscess formation, the wound can be closed over suction drainage tubes and appropriate antibiotic therapy instituted. If infection is not diagnosed quickly and a significant abscess has developed, it may be necessary to leave a portion of the wound open, with later débridement and closure over drainage tubes. In severe cases, it may be necessary to allow the wound to granulate secondarily.

If the infection is extra-articular, it can probably be controlled successfully, and the functional result will not be impaired. In the case of an intra-articular infection, the cartilage of the joint is almost invariably destroyed, and hip function is significantly impaired.

Iatrogenic nerve palsy is caused almost exclusively by vigorous or prolonged retraction of the sciatic nerve. This occurs primarily with the Kocher-Langenbeck approach and mainly involves the peroneal branch of the sciatic nerve. There is also a small chance of a stretch injury to the sciatic nerve with the extended iliofemoral approach and a slight possibility of injuring the femoral nerve by stretch injury during the ilioinguinal approach, but this result is unusual. The surgeon must constantly monitor the force and duration of pull that the surgical assistants place on the sciatic nerve.[17, 42] It is helpful to keep the patient's knee flexed at least 60° and the hip extended when the Kocher-Langenbeck or extended iliofemoral approach is used. If a nerve palsy develops, it is best treated with an ankle-foot orthosis. There is some chance for recovery of the sciatic nerve for up to 3 years after injury. Tendon transfer procedures to correct a footdrop should not be performed during these initial 3 years.

Ectopic bone formation occurs almost exclusively with the lateral exposure of the innominate bone.[35] The incidence of significant ectopic bone formation is highest with the extended iliofemoral approach, followed by the Kocher-Langenbeck approach; it is almost nonexistent with the ilioinguinal or modified Stoppa approach. Part of the prevention of ectopic bone formation should be directed toward choosing the ilioinguinal or modified Stoppa approach when possible and limiting muscle trauma during surgery by careful handling of soft tissue. Indomethacin, given in a dose of 25 mg three times daily perioperatively and for several weeks after surgery, has been reported to decrease the incidence of ectopic bone, but at least in one series this was not confirmed. Postoperative irradiation has been shown to be effective in decreasing the incidence of ectopic bone formation, but the long-term carcinogenic effects are unknown.[1, 19, 46] A prospective, randomized study comparing indomethacin with localized irradiation after surgical treatment of acetabular fractures found that both provided equally effective prophylaxis for heterotopic bone formation.[3] The sample size may not have been large enough, however, to reach a definitive conclusion on this issue. Ectopic bone formation is influenced by the surgical approach and probably by the initial muscle trauma suffered by the patient and other associated injuries. The combination of the two creates an inflammatory response that triggers the formation of bone.

Many patients show a significant amount of ectopic bone on radiography, but muscle function and range of motion are satisfactory. In other patients, rotation and abduction are limited, but if patients can fully extend the hip to the neutral position and have satisfactory flexion of at least 90°, they may be happy with the result and have no desire for further surgery to excise the bone.

When possible, surgery for excision of ectopic bone should be delayed for 15 to 18 months after injury. If it is performed at this time, there is usually no problem with recurrence, and motion can be expected to return to more than 80% of normal, assuming no arthritis exists. A few patients show a spontaneous regression of ectopic bone over several years. If the indications for excision of the bone are equivocal, it may be best to wait, with the hope of some spontaneous regression of the ectopic bone and improvement of motion.

There is significant potential for deep venous thrombosis and pulmonary embolism with fractures of the acetabulum.[45, 53, 56] Routine use of Doppler ultrasound evaluation of the lower extremity veins before surgery plus prophylaxis will reduce the incidence of embolism-induced deaths. If a thrombosis is found and thought to be recently formed, it may resolve over a 5-day trial of therapeutic-level heparin (assuming surgery is not urgent). If the clot does not resolve or heparin therapy is deferred, an inferior vena cava filter should be placed before surgery. Contrast-enhanced magnetic resonance imaging (MRI) has been reported to be more sensitive in detecting lower extremity and particularly pelvic thrombi. However, it adds expense and difficulty to the evaluation, and the current protocol has not been associated with death from pulmonary embolus. Use of MRI has resulted in up to 30% of patients receiving inferior vena cava filters, compared with less than 5% in my own series. Below-knee pneumatic compression boots on both lower extremities from the time of admission are also applied until the patient is fully ambulatory. Warfarin is started at 48 hours after surgery, and the patient is discharged to his or her home with warfarin anticoagulation for 6 weeks after surgery. The level of anticoagulation with warfarin is maintained at about 1.5 times normal. Although the potential for thromboembolic complications is always present, the surgeon must be cautious about too much anticoagulation, because a large wound hematoma can have a devastating effect on the patient if a deep infection occurs in the hip.[45, 56] An adjunct team of medical specialists for managing this protocol is very beneficial for the patient.

TREATMENT OF COMPLEX RECONSTRUCTIVE PROBLEMS

Three weeks after injury, bony callus is present in the fracture lines, making operation more difficult and possibly changing the operative indications. In a young adult patient with a clearly bad prognosis, the surgeon should usually proceed with surgery as long as the femoral head is in good condition and has not been damaged by wear. For the older patient, particularly if the prognosis for nonoperative treatment is not obviously bad, the surgeon can consider nonoperative therapy. For a posterior wall or posterior column fracture, the old fracture can be approached as usual through the Kocher-Langenbeck approach. For an anterior wall or anterior column fracture, the approach remains the ilioinguinal. For all other fracture types, the extended iliofemoral approach is necessary, with the possibility for circumferential access to the bone. Maximum access to the bone is necessary for excision of callus or osteotomy and for intra-articular visualization of the reduction. It may also be necessary to osteotomize the superior or inferior pubic ramus to gain mobility of the acetabular fracture. Operation of old acetabular fractures is technically demanding and should probably be undertaken only by surgeons with extensive experience in the operation of acute fractures.

Total Hip Replacement after Acetabular Fracture

A total hip replacement (THR) may be indicated after acetabular fracture following a bad result caused by arthritic wear or osteonecrosis of the femoral head.[20] For patients with a gradual onset of arthritis, the indication for surgery is typically pain. If the patient, however, shows ongoing wear of the femoral head or acetabulum, THR surgery should not be delayed, because acetabular bone stock is being lost, as is the available femoral head graft[2] (Fig. 37–41).

The surgical approach used for an initial fixation may influence the choice of approach for THR but typically does not determine it. Most surgeons use the Kocher-Langenbeck approach for THR, and it can be used after a previous Kocher-Langenbeck, ilioinguinal, or extended iliofemoral approach for fracture fixation. However, previous plates and screws can sometimes be removed through a separate approach. Although the THR may be straightforward, the greatest problems involve cases with bony defects or deformities.

The most common bony defect involves the posterior wall. On first exposing the joint, the extent of the defect may not be apparent, but thorough débridement of all nonhealed or necrotic posterior wall fragments must be carried out. The femoral head and neck are used as a graft against the intact viable bone to substitute for the posterior wall. The block graft is contoured and fixed with a plate, as is done in treating a posterior wall fracture. Nonunions of a transverse fracture or one or both columns of the acetabulum must be internally fixed, and it is often best to consider a two-stage procedure, with implantation of the femoral portion of the THR carried out only after the bone and graft have healed around the prosthetic acetabulum (about 3 months).[12]

Severe malunions of the innominate bone should be corrected at the time of surgery, rather than attempting a THR in the presence of such a deformity. This step is particularly important in young people undergoing THR who may have one or more revision surgeries during their lifetimes. Depending on the severity of the problem, this may be performed as a two-stage or one-stage procedure.

Many patients have an increased tendency for postoperative dislocation because of partially compromised soft tissues and, in some cases, a recurrent dislocation. THR components more resistant to dislocation (i.e., increased offset neck, large head, and hooded acetabular liner) should often be considered.

Hip arthrodesis is also a consideration for treatment of a poor result after acetabular fracture. Possible indications are very young age, associated bone loss, and infection. The Smith-Peterson exposure, with the patient supine and an anterior plate from the pelvis to the femur, is a preferable approach.

Primary Total Hip Replacement for Acute Fracture

The indication for a primary THR as a treatment for an acute acetabular fracture, is unusual but sometimes necessary in elderly patients.[2, 39, 41] For cases of impaction of the acetabulum or femoral head (or both) in the elderly with impaired bone stock, THR may be combined with open reduction and internal fixation (ORIF) of the fracture. Placing a THR requires a stable and reduced acetabulum. A porous-coated acetabular shell with screws placed through the holes cannot be considered adequate fixation of an acetabular fracture. Because of comminution, osteoporosis, or both conditions in elderly patients, the fracture sometimes may be judged to be impossible to reconstruct. The judgment that the surgeon will probably not have success by ORIF alone does not necessarily mean that the fracture can be treated successfully by THR. A successful ORIF is necessary before acetabular shell placement.

The most common indication for primary THR is an anterior column or associated anterior plus posterior hemi-transverse fracture in an elderly patient, although most of these elderly patients are treated by ORIF alone. These are common fracture types for a slip and fall injury in the elderly population. When the prognosis is doubtful for return of hip function by ORIF alone or conservative care, THR plus ORIF can be considered. In these cases, the patient should be placed in the supine position on the Judet table and the site exposed through the Smith-Peterson approach. Exposure of the internal iliac fossa and pelvic brim is used to reduce and fix the anterior column fracture.[12] The quadrilateral surface often is reached by palpation or by clamps. The femoral neck is osteotomized and the head removed before final fracture fixation. The acetabular shell is placed into the fixed acetabulum, often over bone from the head used as morselized graft.[20]

Treatment of acetabular fractures has been enhanced by ORIF techniques that can restore the anatomy of the innominate bone and the congruency of the articular surfaces.[52] These procedures, however, remain technically demanding and are potentially dangerous to the patient.[36]

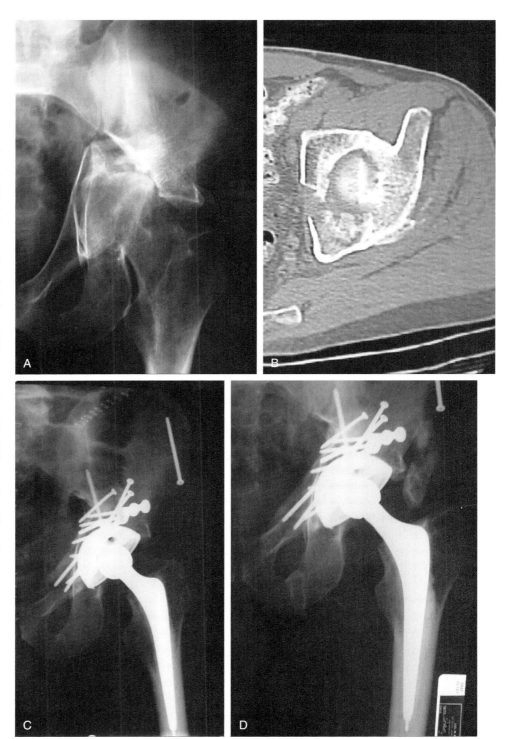

FIGURE 37–41. A, Anteroposterior (AP) hip radiograph of a 32-year-old man 1 year after nonoperative treatment of a T-shaped fracture of the left acetabulum. The patient had a painful hip and impaired ambulatory capabilities. The radiograph demonstrates a malunion of the acetabulum and wear of the femoral head. B, Computed tomographic scan at the level of the superior femoral head demonstrates union of the transverse component of the fracture. C, Postoperative AP hip radiograph shows the results following osteotomy and reduction of the malunion and total hip arthroplasty performed during the same procedure through the extended iliofemoral approach. Osteotomy of the femoral neck and removal of the head and neck from the wound allows access to the posterior column without the normal tenotomy of the gluteus medius and minimus. Although an acetabular prosthesis could have been placed in a medial position without altering the malunion, I prefer to correct such a severe malunion in a young adult. A young person can expect future revision surgery and progressively decreasing bone stock. The bone stock problem would be increased if the malunion were left uncorrected. D, AP hip radiograph 2 years after the surgery demonstrates a healed osteotomy, stable components, and an area of heterotopic bone. Functional recovery was satisfactory, and motion was not impaired.

Although the results of treatment have undoubtedly been improved by newer techniques, surgeons must always keep their own experience and abilities in mind and consider the potential risks to the patient.

REFERENCES

1. Anglen, J.O.; Moore, K.D. Prevention of heterotopic bone formation after acetabular fracture fixation by single-dose radiation therapy: A preliminary report. J Orthop Trauma 10:258–263, 1996.
2. Berry, D.J. Total hip arthroplasty following acetabular fracture. Orthopedics 22:837–839, 1999.
3. Burd, T.A.; Lowry, K.J.; Anglen, J.O. Indomethacin compared with localized irradiation for the prevention of heterotopic ossification following surgical treatment of acetabular fractures. J Bone Joint Surg Am 83:1783–1788, 2001.
4. Burk, D.L, Jr.; Mears, D.C.; Kennedy, W.H.; et al. Three-dimensional computed tomography of acetabular fractures. Radiology 155:183–185, 1985.
5. Chang, J.K.; Gill, S.S.; Zura, R.D.; et al. Comparative strength of three methods of fixation of transverse acetabular fractures. Clin Orthop 392:433–441, 2001.
6. Chen, C.M.; Chiu, F.Y.; Chuang, T.Y.; Lo, W.H. Treatment of acetabular fractures: 10-year experience. Chung Hua I Hseuh Tsa Chih 63:384–390, 2000.
7. Cole, J.D.; Bolhofner, B.R. Acetabular fracture fixation via a modified Stoppa limited intrapelvic approach. Description of operative technique and preliminary treatment results. Clin Orthop Rel Res 305:112–123, 1994.
8. Deo, S.D.; Tavares, S.P.; Pandey, R.K.; et al. Operative management of acetabular fractures in Oxford. Injury 32:581–586, 2001.
9. Ebraheim, N.A.; Xu, R.; Biyani, A.; Benedetti, J.A. Anatomic basis of lag screw placement in the anterior column of the acetabulum. Clin Orthop Rel Res 339:200–205, 1997.
10. Epstein, H.C. Open management of fractures of the acetabulum. In: The Hip: Proceedings of the Seventh Open Scientific Meeting of the Hip Society. St. Louis, C.V. Mosby, 1979, pp. 17–41.
11. Epstein, H.C. Traumatic Dislocations of the Hip. Baltimore, Williams & Wilkins, 1980.
12. Hak, D.J.; Hamel, A.J.; Bay, B.K.; et al. Consequences of transverse acetabular fracture malreduction on load transmission across the hip joint. J Orthop Trauma 12:90–100, 1998.
13. Hak, D.J.; Olson, S.A.; Matta, J.M. Diagnosis and management of closed internal degloving injuries associated with pelvic and acetabular fractures: The Morel-Lavale lesion. J Trauma 42:1046–1051, 1997.
14. Hardy, S.L. Femoral nerve palsy associated with an associated posterior wall transverse acetabular fracture. J Orthop Trauma 11:40–42, 1997.
15. Harley, J.; Mack, L; Winquist, R. CT of acetabular fractures. AJR Am J Roentgenol 138:413–417, 1982.
16. Haveri, M.; Junila, J.; Suramo, I.; Lahde, S. Multiplanar and 3D CT of acetabular fractures. Acta Radiol 39:257–264, 1998.
17. Helfet, D.L.; Malkani, A.L.; Heise, C.; et al. Intraoperative monitoring of motor pathways during operative fixation of acute acetabular fractures. J Orthop Trauma 11:2–6, 1997.
18. Hull, J.B.; Raza, S.A.; Stockley, I.; Elson, R.A. Surgical management of fractures of the acetabulum: The Sheffield experience 1976–1994. Injury 28:35–40, 1997.
19. Johnson, E.E.; Kay, R.M.; Dorey, F.J. Heterotropic ossification prophylaxis following operative treatment of acetabular fractures. Clin Orthop 305:88–95, 1994.
20. Jimenez, M.L.; Tile, M.; Schenk, R.S. Total hip replacement after acetabular fracture. Orthop Clin North Am 28:435–446, 1997.
21. Judet, R.; Judet, J.; Letournel, E. Fractures of the acetabulum. Classification and surgical approaches for open reduction. J Bone Joint Surg Am 46:1615–1638, 1964.
22. Knight, R.A.; Smith, H. Central fractures of the acetabulum. J Bone Joint Surg Am 40:1–16, 1958.
23. Letournel, E. Les fractures du cotyle. Etude d'une série de 75 cas. Medical thesis. Paris, Arnette, 1961.
24. Letournel, E. Les fractures du cotyle. Etude d'une série de 75 cas. J Chir 82:47–87, 1961.
25. Letournel, E. The results of acetabular fractures treated surgically. Twenty-one years' experience. In: The Hip: Proceedings of the Seventh Open Scientific Meeting of The Hip Society. St. Louis, C.V. Mosby, 1979, pp. 42–85.
26. Letournel, E. Fractures of the Acetabulum. New York, Springer-Verlag, 1981.
27. Levine, M.A. A treatment of central fractures of the acetabulum. J Bone Joint Surg Am 25:902–906, 1943.
28. Matta JM. Fractures of the acetabulum: Accuracy of the reduction and clinical results in patients managed operatively within three weeks after the injury. J Bone Joint Surg Am 78:1632–1645, 1996.
29. Matta, J.M. Percutaneous fixation of acetabular fractures. J Orthop Trauma 12:370, 1998.
30. Matta, J. Operative indications and choice of surgical approach for fractures of the acetabulum. Tech Orthop 1:13–22, 1986.
31. Matta, J.; Anderson, L.; Epstein, H.; Hendrick, P. Fractures of the acetabulum: A retrospective analysis. Clin Orthop 205:230–240, 1986.
32. Matta, J.; Letournel, E.; Browner, B. Surgical management of acetabular fractures. Instr Course Lect 35:382–397, 1986.
33. Matta, J.; Mehne, D.; Roffi, R. Fractures of the acetabulum: Early results of a prospective study. Clin Orthop 205:241–250, 1986.
34. Matta, J.M.; Merritt, P.O. Displaced acetabular fractures. Clin Orthop 230:83–97, 1988.
35. Matta, J.M.; Siebenrock, K.A. Does indomethacin reduce heterotopic bone formation after operations for acetabular fractures? A prospective randomized study. J Bone Joint Surg Br 79:959–963, 1997.
36. Malkani, A.L.; Voor, M.J.; Rennirt, G.; et al. Increased peak contact stress after incongruent reduction of transverse acetabular fractures: A cadaveric model. 51:704–709, 2001.
37. Marti, R.K.; Chaldecott, L.R.; Kloen, P. Intertrochanteric osteotomy for posttraumatic arthritis after acetabular fractures. J Orthop Trauma 15:384–393, 2001.
38. Mays, J.; Neufeld, A.J. Skeletal traction methods. Clin Orthop 102:144–151, 1974.
39. Mears, D.C. Surgical treatment of acetabular fractures in elderly patients with osteoporotic bone. J Am Acad Orthop Surgeons 7:128–141, 1999.
40. Mears, D.C.; Rubash, H. Pelvic and Acetabular Fractures. Thorofare, NJ, Slack, 1986.
41. Mears, D.C.; Shirhama, M. Stabilization of an acetabular fracture with cables for acute total hip arthroplasty. J Arthroplasty 13:104–107, 1998.
42. Middlebrooks, E.S.; Sims, S.H.; Kellam, J.F.; Bosse, M.J. Incidence of sciatic nerve injury in operatively treated acetabular fractures without somatosensory evoked potential monitoring. J Orthop Trauma 11:327–329, 1997.
43. Moed, B.R.; Smith, S.T. Three-view radiographic assessment of heterotopic ossification after acetabular fracture surgery. J Orthop Trauma 10:93–98, 1996.
44. Montgomery, K.D.; Potter, H.G.; Helfet, D.L. Magnetic Resonance venography to evaluate the deep venous system of the pelvis in patients who have an acetabular fracture. J Bone Joint Surg Am 77:1639–1649, 1995.
45. Montgomery, K.D.; Potter, H.G.; Helfet, D.L. The detection and management of proximal deep venous thrombosis in patients with acute acetabular fractures: A follow-up report. J Orthop Trauma 11:330–336, 1997.
46. Moore, K.D.; Goss, K.; Anglen, J.O. Indomethacin versus radiation therapy for prophylaxis against heterotropic ossification in acetabular fractures: A randomized, prospective study. J Bone Joint Surg Br 80:259–263, 1998.
47. Muller, M.E.; Allgoer, M. Manual of Internal Fixation. New York, Springer-Verlag, 1979.
48. Olson, S.A.; Bay, B.K.; Chapman, M.W.; Sharkey, N.A. Biomechanical consequences of fracture and repair of the posterior wall of the acetabulum. J Bone Joint Surg Am 77:1184–1192, 1995.
49. Olson, S.A.; Bay, B.K.; Pollak, A.N.; et al. The effect of variable size posterior wall acetabular fractures on contact characteristics of the hip joint. J Orthop Trauma 10:395–402, 1996.
50. Oransky, M.; Sanguinetti, C. Surgical treatment of displaced acetabular fractures: Results of 50 consecutive cases. J Orthop Trauma 7:28–32, 1993.
51. Parker, P.J.; Copeland, C. Percutaneous fluoroscopic screw fixation of acetabular fractures. Injury 28:597–600, 1997.

52. Plaiser, B.R.; Meldon, S.W.; Super, D.M.; Malangoni, M.A. Improved outcome after early fixation of acetabular fractures. Injury 31:81–84, 2000.

53. Russell, G.V., Jr.; Norsk, S.E.; Chip Routt, M.L., Jr. Perioperative complications associated with operative treatment of acetabular fractures. J Trauma 51:1098–1103, 2001.

54. Saterbak, A.M.; Marsh, J.L.; Turbett, T.; Brandser, E. Acetabular fractures classification of Letournel and Judet—A systematic approach. Iowa Orthop J 15:184–196, 1995.

55. Simonian, P.T.; Routt ML; Harrington, R.M.; Tencer, A.F. The acetabular T-type fracture. A biomechanical evaluation of internal fixation. Clin Orthop Rel Res 314:234–240, 1995.

56. Stannard, J.P.; Riley, R.S.; McClenney, M.D.; et al. Medical prophylaxis against deep-vein thrombosis after pelvic and acetabular fractures. J Bone Joint Surg Am 83:1047–1051, 2001.

57. Starr, A.J.; Jones, A.L.; Reinert, C.M.; Borer, D.S. Preliminary results and complications following limited open reduction and percutaneous screw fixation of displaced fractures of the acetabulum. Injury 32(Suppl 1):SA45–50, 2001.

58. Tile, M. Fractures of the Pelvis and Acetabulum. Baltimore, Williams & Wilkins, 1984.

59. Tornetta, P., III; Riina, J. Acetabular reduction techniques via the anterior approach. Oper Tech Orthop 7:185–195, 1997.

INDEX

••

Note: Page numbers followed by f indicate figures; page numbers followed by t indicate tables.